Tax Formula for Corporate Taxp

Income *(from whatever source)*	
Less: Exclusions from gross income	
Gross Income	$ xxx,xxx
Less: Deductions	− xx,xxx
Taxable Income	$ xxx,xxx
Applicable tax rates	× xx%
Gross Tax	$ xx,xxx
Less: Tax credits and prepayments	− x,xxx
Tax Due *(or refund)*	$ xx,xxx

STUDENTS – GET STUDY HELP NOW FOR YOUR TAX COURSE

Do you need more help studying for your taxation class?
Order the Study Guide to this textbook and get up-to-date help fast!

- **Study Highlights** – an outline of key topics for each chapter.
- **Key Terms** used in the chapter.
- **Self-Quizzing** with helpful, annotated answers.

Check with your bookstore. Ask for ISBN 978-1-133-49551-2.

Or Order Online Now. Go to **www.cengagebrain.com**. Select your text from the titles listed. At the Student Resources page for your text, select Book Supplements. Click on the link for Study Guide and add it to the shopping cart.

Test Drive the Study Guide with Free Sample Chapter. Go to **www.cengagebrain.com**, select your text from the titles listed, go to the Student Resources page, and click on the Sample Study Guide Chapter link to download a chapter.

GET EVEN MORE HELP – *ASK YOUR INSTRUCTOR* ABOUT ASSIGNING THESE PRACTICE SETS

- *For Individual Taxation:*
  Practice Sets for South-Western Federal Taxation: Individual Income Taxes, 2013 Edition. These practice sets, by Raymond Wacker (Southern Illinois University), are comprehensive and designed to be completed near the end of the course using tax preparation software such as H&R BLOCK At Home™. ISBN: 978-1-133-18914-5
- *For Corporations, S Corporations, and Partnerships:*
  Practice Sets for South-Western Federal Taxation: Corporations, Partnerships, Estates & Trusts, 2013 Edition. These practice sets, by Don Trippeer (SUNY College at Oneonta), allow you to put your corporations and partnerships knowledge to use, ensuring proper understanding of concepts and procedures using H&R BLOCK At Home™ or other tax preparation software. ISBN: 978-1-133-49555-0

Practice sets work with the latest tax forms and are available for purchase online by visiting
www.cengagebrain.com

Check with your instructor before buying practice sets. Solutions are available to instructors only in a separate volume.

ISBN-13: 978-1-133-93492-9 • ISBN-10: 1-133-93492-7

With your purchase of this new **Cengage Learning** Taxation textbook, you have 6-month access to select **CPAexcel** content, *the best CPA review course for busy students!* With CPA exam content matched to your taxation course, you will have access to:

- Online exam preparation activities that may be accessed anytime and anywhere.
- Over 800 past exam questions and proficiency questions.
- Exam-identical simulations and comprehensive diagnostics.

To register, visit **www.cengage.com/login**

Please register with the following access code:

Access Code:

By purchasing this New Edition, you qualify to receive 20% off the purchase price of CPAexcel review courses!

Don't Throw This Away!

For technical support, please visit **www.cengage.com/support**

ISBN-13: 978-1-133-49560-4 • ISBN-10: 1-133-49560-5

SOUTH-WESTERN
FEDERAL TAXATION

CORPORATIONS, PARTNERSHIPS, ESTATES & TRUSTS

2013

General Editors

William H. Hoffman, Jr.
J.D., Ph.D., CPA

James E. Smith
Ph.D., CPA

William A. Raabe
Ph.D., CPA

David M. Maloney
Ph.D., CPA

Contributing Authors

James H. Boyd
Ph.D., CPA
Arizona State University

D. Larry Crumbley
Ph.D., CPA
Louisiana State University

Jon S. Davis
Ph.D., CPA
University of Wisconsin–Madison

Steven C. Dilley
J.D., Ph.D., CPA
Michigan State University

William H. Hoffman, Jr.
J.D., Ph.D., CPA
University of Houston

David M. Maloney
Ph.D., CPA
University of Virginia

Mark B. Persellin
Ph.D., CPA, CFP®
St. Mary's University

William A. Raabe
Ph.D., CPA
The Ohio State University

Boyd C. Randall
J.D., Ph.D.
Brigham Young University

Debra L. Sanders
Ph.D., CPA
Washington State University, Vancouver

W. Eugene Seago
J.D., Ph.D., CPA
Virginia Polytechnic Institute and State University

James E. Smith
Ph.D., CPA
College of William and Mary

Australia • Brazil • Japan • Korea • Mexico • Singapore • Spain • United Kingdom • United States

South-Western Federal Taxation: Corporations, Partnerships, Estates & Trusts, 2013 Edition

William H. Hoffman, Jr., William A. Raabe, James E. Smith, David M. Maloney

Vice President of Editorial, Business: Jack W. Calhoun

Editor-in-Chief: Rob Dewey

Executive Editor: Mike Schenk

Senior Developmental Editor: Craig Avery

Editorial Assistant: Ann Loch

Associate Marketing Manager: Heather Mooney

Senior Content Project Manager: Colleen A. Farmer

Media Editor: Chris Valentine

Manufacturing Planner: Doug Wilke

Marketing Communications Manager: Libby Shipp

Production Service: Cenveo Publisher Services

Senior Art Director: Michelle Kunkler

Internal and Cover Designer: Kim Torbeck/Imbue Design

Cover Image: © Dennis Flaherty/Getty Images, Inc.

Rights Acquisitions Director (Text and Photo): Audrey Pettengill

Student Edition ISBN 13: 978-1-133-49549-9
Student Edition ISBN 10: 1-133-49549-4
Student Edition with CD ISBN 13: 978-1-133-49550-5
Student Edition with CD ISBN 10: 1-133-49550-8

ISSN: 0270-5265
2013 Annual Edition

South-Western
5191 Natorp Boulevard
Mason, OH 45040
USA

Cengage Learning products are represented in Canada by Nelson Education, Ltd.

For your course and learning solutions, visit **www.cengage.com**
Purchase any of our products at your local college store or at our preferred online store **www.cengagebrain.com**

Printed in the United States of America
1 2 3 4 5 6 7 16 15 14 13 12

Preface

To The Student

The Leadership You Trust.
The Innovation You Expect.
The Knowledge You Will Need.

South-Western Federal Taxation is the most trusted and best-selling series in college taxation. We are focused exclusively on providing the most useful, comprehensive, and up-to-date tax texts, online study aids, tax preparation tools, and printed study guides to help you succeed in your tax courses and beyond.

Studying Is Easier with the Right Tools. ***Corporations, Partnerships, Estates & Trusts, 2013 Edition*** provides a dynamic learning experience inside and outside of the classroom. Built with resources and tools that students have identified as the most important, our complete study system provides options for the way you learn.

Here's how ***Corporations, Partnerships, Estates & Trusts, 2013 Edition*** is designed to help you learn!

Practical Tax Scenarios at the Start of Every Chapter…

The Big Picture: Tax Solutions for the Real World. Taxation comes alive at the start of each chapter. **The Big Picture** is a glimpse into the lives, families, careers, and tax situations of typical filers. Each **Big Picture** case asks you to apply what you will learn in the upcoming chapter to develop the best tax solution to these real-life dilemmas.

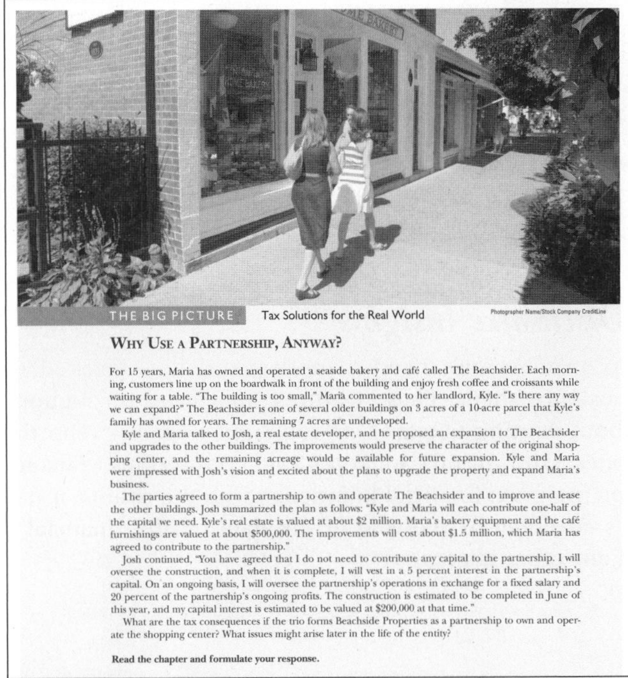

THE BIG PICTURE Tax Solutions for the Real World

Photographer Name/Stock Company CreditLine

Why Use a Partnership, Anyway?

For 15 years, Maria has owned and operated a seaside bakery and café called The Beachsider. Each morning, customers line up on the boardwalk in front of the building and enjoy fresh coffee and croissants while waiting for a table. "The building is too small," Maria commented to her landlord, Kyle. "Is there any way we can expand?" The Beachsider is one of several older buildings on 3 acres of a 10-acre parcel that Kyle's family has owned for years. The remaining 7 acres are undeveloped.

Kyle and Maria talked to Josh, a real estate developer, and he proposed an expansion to The Beachsider and upgrades to the other buildings. The improvements would preserve the character of the original shopping center, and the remaining acreage would be available for future expansion. Kyle and Maria were impressed with Josh's vision and excited about the plans to upgrade the property and expand Maria's business.

The parties agreed to form a partnership to own and operate The Beachsider and to improve and lease the other buildings. Josh summarized the plan as follows: "Kyle and Maria will each contribute one-half of the capital we need. Kyle's real estate is valued at about $2 million. Maria's bakery equipment and the café furnishings are valued at about $500,000. The improvements will cost about $1.5 million, which Maria has agreed to contribute to the partnership."

Josh continued, "You have agreed that I do not need to contribute any capital to the partnership. I will oversee the construction, and when it is complete, I will vest in a 5 percent interest in the partnership's capital. On an ongoing basis, I will oversee the partnership's operations in exchange for a fixed salary and 20 percent of the partnership's ongoing profits. The construction is estimated to be completed in June of this year, and my capital interest is estimated to be valued at $200,000 at that time."

What are the tax consequences if the trio forms Beachside Properties as a partnership to own and operate the shopping center? What issues might arise later in the life of the entity?

Read the chapter and formulate your response.

... Big Picture Examples to Help you Follow Clients Through the Chapter ...

Among the many examples in every chapter are an average of over four examples per chapter based on the **Big Picture** tax situation that opens the text. That means less confusion understanding new topics, a more consistent application of data for you to learn, and practical tax stories that span the whole chapter.

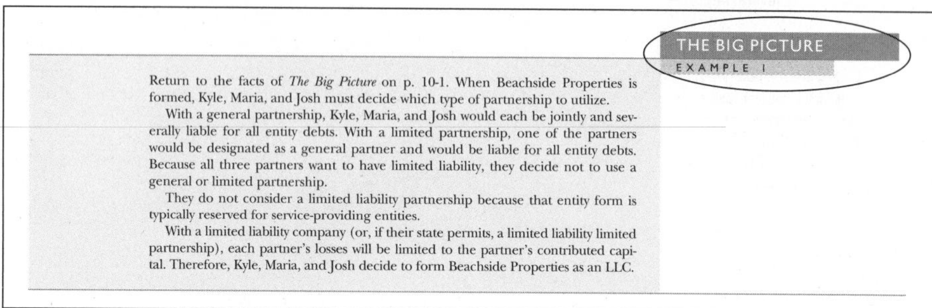

THE BIG PICTURE
EXAMPLE 1

Return to the facts of *The Big Picture* on p. 10-1. When Beachside Properties is formed, Kyle, Maria, and Josh must decide which type of partnership to utilize.

With a general partnership, Kyle, Maria, and Josh would each be jointly and severally liable for all entity debts. With a limited partnership, one of the partners would be designated as a general partner and would be liable for all entity debts. Because all three partners want to have limited liability, they decide not to use a general or limited partnership.

They do not consider a limited liability partnership because that entity form is typically reserved for service-providing entities.

With a limited liability company (or, if their state permits, a limited liability limited partnership), each partner's losses will be limited to the partner's contributed capital. Therefore, Kyle, Maria, and Josh decide to form Beachside Properties as an LLC.

...And Practical Conclusions to Those Tax Scenarios

Refocus on the Big Picture. Returning to the client situations introduced in the chapter-opening **Big Picture**, these end-of-chapter summaries and tax planning scenarios apply concepts and topics from the chapter in a reasonable and professional solution. A **What If?** section then demonstrates how tax treatments might change as a result of potential changes in the filer's situation—making **What If?** a valuable consideration in tax planning.

What If? adds realistic options that will spur you to think about how changes in taxpayers' situations affect how they would file their returns.

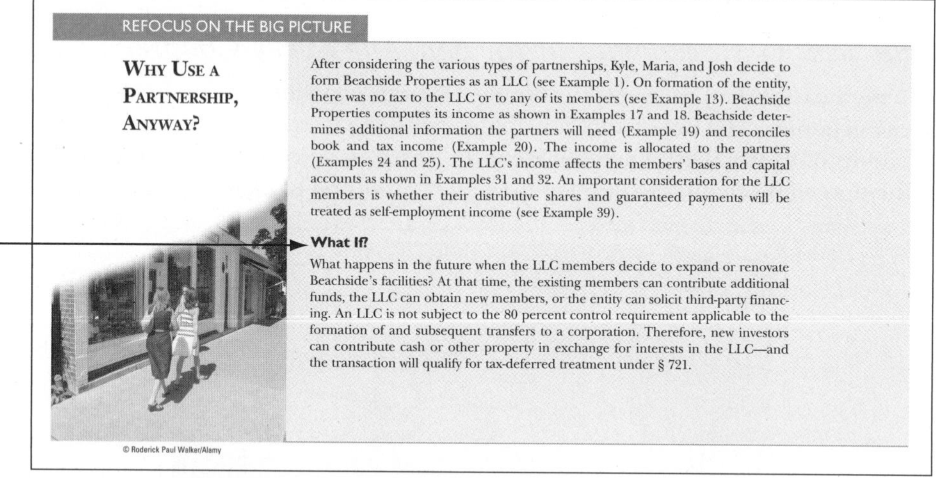

REFOCUS ON THE BIG PICTURE

WHY USE A PARTNERSHIP, ANYWAY?

After considering the various types of partnerships, Kyle, Maria, and Josh decide to form Beachside Properties as an LLC (see Example 1). On formation of the entity, there was no tax to the LLC or to any of its members (see Example 13). Beachside Properties computes its income as shown in Examples 17 and 18. Beachside determines additional information the partners will need (Example 19) and reconciles book and tax income (Example 20). The income is allocated to the partners (Examples 24 and 25). The LLC's income affects the members' bases and capital accounts as shown in Examples 31 and 32. An important consideration for the LLC members is whether their distributive shares and guaranteed payments will be treated as self-employment income (see Example 39).

What If?

What happens in the future when the LLC members decide to expand or renovate Beachside's facilities? At that time, the existing members can contribute additional funds, the LLC can obtain new members, or the entity can solicit third-party financing. An LLC is not subject to the 80 percent control requirement applicable to the formation of and subsequent transfers to a corporation. Therefore, new investors can contribute cash or other property in exchange for interests in the LLC—and the transaction will qualify for tax-deferred treatment under § 721.

© Roderick Paul Walker/Alamy

Financial Disclosure Insights

Increasingly, tax professionals need to understand how taxes affect the income statement and balance sheet. These features, appearing throughout the text, use current data about existing taxpayers to highlight book-tax reporting differences, effective tax rates, and trends in reporting conventions. **Financial Disclosure Insights** help you integrate financial knowledge with the results of state and Federal tax law. **SWFT's coverage of the role of tax data on the financial statements far exceeds that of any other tax text.**

FINANCIAL DISCLOSURE INSIGHTS **The Alternative Minimum Tax as Prepayment**

Tax professionals often describe the alternative minimum tax (AMT) as a "mere prepayment device," in that by applying the minimum tax credit, the entity recovers its payment for the AMT in a later tax year when it returns to regular tax status. Critics observe that this statement is misleading for several important reasons.

- Due to the makeup of their assets or income sources, many businesses are subject to the AMT every year. Thus, the minimum tax credit never will be available as there will not be another regular tax year in the foreseeable future.
- Any prepayment of tax reduces the present value of the credit that is claimed in a future tax year. Consequently, the AMT generates a permanent loss of funds to the taxpayer. For example, if the after-tax rate of return for the entity is 6 percent, a $1 million minimum tax credit that is claimed five years after the AMT is paid is worth only about $750,000 (Tables 7.1 and 7.2 in Chapter 7 can be used to make these analyses).

If the minimum tax credit is to be claimed in future years, a deferred tax asset is created on the taxpayer's GAAP balance sheet. This deferred tax asset might also address the basis differences for assets that are depreciated under MACRS for regular tax purposes and ADS in computing the AMT. In a recent year, the trucking firm Ryder Systems reported a deferred tax asset of approximately $10 million relating to the application of the AMT for the year. For the prior year, the Ryder deferred tax asset for the AMT had been approximately $12.5 million; so one can infer that some of the minimum tax credit had been claimed at least for that tax year.

Examples and Learning Objectives to Help You Study and Excel at Homework

Examples You'll Use in Every Chapter. An **average of 38 examples in each chapter** use realistic situations to illustrate the complexities of the tax law and demonstrate concepts.

EXAMPLE 2

Carla makes a gift to Antonio of shares of stock in Green Corporation. The transactions involving this stock that occurred closest to the date of the gift took place two trading days before the date of the gift at a mean selling price of $10 and three trading days after the gift at a mean selling price of $15. The $12 fair market value of each share of Green stock is determined as follows.

$$\frac{(3 \times \$10) + (2 \times \$15)}{5} = \$12$$

■

Homework Linked to Chapter Learning Objectives. Students tell us that for maximum learning value, homework assignments should refer back to specific chapter topics and sections. Each end-of-chapter Question and Problem is labeled with the Learning Objective(s) that appear beside key topics in the text margins. **It is easier to go back to the section of the text where the concept in the homework item is covered—saving you time, better organizing your study, and increasing your confidence in earning a better grade.**

8. **LO.2, 8, 13** Orange, LLC, was formed when Green, Inc., contributed $400,000 of cash and Rose contributed nondepreciable assets valued at $200,000 with a basis of $10,000. In addition, Rose will perform significant management services for the LLC. For most items, the members intend to allocate profits, losses, and liquidating distributions equally. How can (or must) special allocations be used to compensate the members for the differences between the bases and values of contributed property and time devoted to LLC activities?

Online Resources and Study Tools

NEW CengageNOW™ is a powerful online homework tool that improves students' learning experience and helps you gain better understanding of tax concepts as you work the assignments. All end-of-chapter homework is included, expanded, and enhanced to follow the workflow a professional would follow to solve various client scenarios. CengageNOW provides enhanced feedback and a step-through approach to improve your homework performance!

Aplia™ is an online interactive homework solution that improves learning by increasing student effort and engagement. Aplia for tax ensures that you stay on top of your coursework with regularly scheduled homework assignments. The Aplia assignments are derived from select end-of-chapter problems from the textbook, allowing you to apply what you learn. To explore the benefits Aplia offers, ask your instructor or visit **www.aplia.com/tax**.

THOMSON REUTERS
CHECKPOINT®

Checkpoint® Student Edition

Checkpoint® Student Edition from Thomson Reuters comes with every new copy of this textbook to help you succeed in the tax research portion of your studies.*

3 Simple Ways Checkpoint® Helps You Make Sense of All Those Taxes:

- Intuitive web-based design makes it fast and simple to find what you need.
- A comprehensive collection of primary tax law, cases, and rulings along with analytical insight you simply can't find anywhere else.
- Checkpoint® has built-in productivity tools such as calculators to make research more efficient—a resource more tax pros use than any other.

CPAexcel™ CPA EXAM REVIEW

Passing the Uniform CPA Examination can be your key to career success. With your purchase of a new copy of ***Corporations, Partnerships, Estates & Trusts****, you have a 6-month access to CPAexcel content, the best CPA review course for busy students! **With CPA exam content matched to your taxation course**, you will have access to:

- Online exam review that may be accessed anytime, anywhere.
- Over 800 past exam and proficiency questions.
- Exam-identical simulations and comprehensive diagnostics.

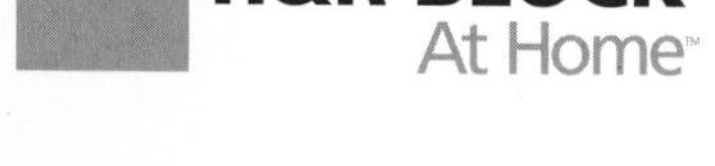

H&R Block At Home™

More than software: Put the experience of H&R Block tax professionals on your side.

- A step-by-step interview guides you through a customized process.
- Accurate calculations and 100% satisfaction—guaranteed.
- Worry-free Audit Support™ and tax advice from an H&R Block tax professional.

H&R Block At Home™ is offered with each new copy of **South-Western Federal Taxation**—at no additional cost to students!

CENGAGE**brain**.com

Online Student Resources

Go to **www.cengagebrain.com** for free resources to help you study as well as the opportunity to purchase additional study aids. These valuable free study resources will help you earn a better grade:

- **Interactive quizzes** are short and auto-graded to help you brush up on important chapter topics.
- **Flashcards** use chapter terms and definitions to aid you in learning tax terminology for each chapter.
- **Online glossary** for each chapter provides terms and definitions from the text in alphabetical order for easy reference.
- **Learning objectives** can be downloaded for each chapter to help keep you on track.
- **Tax Tips for the Recent Graduate** introduce the college graduate to some common tax considerations that could be beneficial in reducing the dreaded "tax bite."
- **Tax Updates** provide the most recent tax information and major changes to the tax law.
- **Tax tables** used in the textbook are downloadable for reference.

*Not available with the Professional Editions of *South-Western Federal Taxation.*

Additional Student Resources

Study Guide, ISBN 978-1-133-49551-2

Do you need more help studying for your taxation class? Order the study guide to receive:

- **Study Highlights**—an outline of key topics for each chapter.
- **Key Terms** used in the chapter.
- **Self-Quizzing** with helpful, annotated answers that are keyed to pages in the 2013 Edition.

Check with your bookstore or order on **CengageBrain.com**.

Corporations, S Corporations, and Partnerships Practice Sets, ISBN 978-1-133-49555-0
Ask your instructor about assigning these practice sets.

Written specifically for ***Corporations, Partnerships, Estates & Trusts, 2013 Edition***, these practice sets are comprehensive and designed to be completed near the end of the course using tax preparation software such as H&R Block at Home™.

Check with your instructor before ordering practice sets. Solutions are available to instructors only.

For over 35 years, the **South-Western Federal Taxation** Series has guided more than 1.5 million students through the ever-changing field of Federal taxation.

With our promise of leadership, innovation, and the knowledge you need, we are committed to your success both now and in the future.

About the Editors

William H. Hoffman Jr. earned B.A. and J.D. degrees from the University of Michigan and M.B.A. and Ph.D. degrees from The University of Texas. He is a licensed CPA and attorney in Texas. His teaching experience includes The University of Texas (1957–1961), Louisiana State University (1961–1967), and the University of Houston (1967–1999). Professor Hoffman has addressed many tax institutes and conferences and has published extensively in academic and professional journals. His articles appear in *The Journal of Taxation, The Tax Adviser, Taxes—The Tax Magazine, The Journal of Accountancy, The Accounting Review,* and *Taxation for Accountants.*

William A. Raabe teaches tax courses in the Fisher College of Business at The Ohio State University. A graduate of Carroll University (Wisconsin) and the University of Illinois, Dr. Raabe's teaching and research interests include international and multistate taxation, technology in tax education, personal financial planning, and the economic impact of sports teams and fine arts groups. Professor Raabe also writes *Federal Tax Research* and the PricewaterhouseCoopers Tax Case Studies. He has written extensively about book-tax differences in financial reporting, including a book about the corporate Schedule M–3 and articles and cases addressing FIN 48 issues. Dr. Raabe has been a visiting tax faculty member for a number of public accounting firms, bar associations, and CPA societies. He has received numerous teaching awards, including the Accounting Educator of the Year award from the Wisconsin Institute of CPAs. He has been the faculty adviser for student teams in the Deloitte Tax Case Competition (national finalists at three different schools) and the PricewaterhouseCoopers Extreme Tax policy competition (national finalist). For more information about Dr. Raabe, visit **http://fisher.osu.edu/~raabe_12** and at BillRaabeTax on YouTube and Twitter.

James E. Smith is the John S. Quinn Professor of Accounting at the College of William and Mary. He has been a member of the Accounting Faculty for over 30 years. He received his Ph.D. degree from the University of Arizona. Professor Smith has served as a discussion leader for Continuing Professional Education programs for the AICPA, Federal Tax Workshops, and various state CPA societies. He has conducted programs in more than 40 states for approximately 25,000 CPAs. He has been the recipient of the AICPA's Outstanding Discussion Leader Award and the American Taxation Association/Arthur Andersen Teaching Innovation Award. Among his other awards are the Virginia Society of CPAs' Outstanding Accounting Educator Award and the James Madison University's Outstanding Accounting Educator Award. He was the President of the Administrators of Accounting Programs Group (AAPG) in 1991–1992. He was the faculty adviser for the William and Mary teams that received first place in the Andersen Tax Challenge in 1994, 1995, 1997, 2000, and 2001 and in the Deloitte Tax Case Study Competition in 2002, 2004, 2005, 2006, 2008, and 2011.

David M. Maloney, Ph.D., CPA, is the Carman G. Blough Professor of Accounting at the University of Virginia's McIntire School of Commerce. He completed his undergraduate work at the University of Richmond and his graduate work at the University of Illinois at Urbana-Champaign. Since joining the Virginia faculty in January 1984, Professor Maloney has taught Federal taxation in the graduate and undergraduate programs and has received major research grants from the Ernst & Young and KPMG Foundations. In addition, his work has been published in numerous professional journals, including *Journal of Taxation, The Tax Adviser, Tax Notes, Corporate Taxation, Accounting Horizons, Journal of Taxation of Investments,* and *Journal of Accountancy.* He is a member of several professional organizations, including the American Accounting Association and the American Taxation Association.

Brief Contents

© Pali Rao, iStockphoto

Part 1: Introduction

Part 2: Corporations

Part 3: Flow-Through Entities

Part 4: Advanced Tax Practice Considerations

Part 5: Family Tax Planning

Contents

Part 1: Introduction

Part 2: Corporations

Part 3: Flow-Through Entities

part 1

INTRODUCTION

CHAPTER 1 Understanding and Working with the Federal Tax Law

The Federal law is an unbelievably complex set of rules. In working with these rules, however, it is helpful to understand why they came about. Also necessary is the ability to locate the sources of these rules. Part 1, therefore, is devoted to the "whys" of the tax law and the applications of the tax research process.

CHAPTER

1 Understanding and Working with the Federal Tax Law

LEARNING OBJECTIVES: *After completing Chapter 1, you should be able to:*

LO.1 Stress the importance of revenue needs as an objective of Federal tax law.

LO.2 Demonstrate the influence of economic, social, equity, and political considerations on the development of the tax law.

LO.3 Illustrate how the IRS, as the protector of the revenue, has affected tax law.

LO.4 Recognize the role of the courts in interpreting and shaping tax law.

LO.5 Identify tax law sources—statutory, administrative, and judicial.

LO.6 List and assess tax law sources.

LO.7 Demonstrate tax research.

LO.8 Assess the validity and weight of tax law sources.

LO.9 Describe various tax planning procedures.

LO.10 Explain the role of taxation on the CPA examination.

CHAPTER OUTLINE

1.1 The Whys of the Tax Law

The Federal tax law is a mixture of statutory provisions, administrative pronouncements, and court decisions. Anyone who has attempted to work with this body of knowledge is familiar with its complexity. Commenting on his 48-page tax return, author James Michener said, "It is unimaginable in that I graduated from one of America's better colleges, yet I am totally incapable of understanding tax returns." For the person who has to wade through rule upon rule to find the solution to a tax problem, it may be of some consolation to know that the law's complexity can be explained. There is a reason for the formulation of every rule. Knowing these reasons, therefore, is a considerable step toward understanding the Federal tax law.

The major objective of the Federal tax law is the raising of revenue. Despite the importance of the fiscal needs of the government, however, other considerations explain certain portions of the law. In particular, economic, social, equity, and political factors play a significant role. Added to these factors is the marked impact the Internal Revenue Service (IRS) and the courts have had and will continue to have on the evolution of Federal tax law. These matters are treated in the first part of this chapter. Wherever appropriate, the discussion is related to subjects covered later in the text.

Revenue Needs

LO.1

Stress the importance of revenue needs as an objective of Federal tax law.

The foundation of any tax system has to be the raising of revenue to absorb the cost of government operations. Ideally, annual outlays should not exceed anticipated revenues. This situation leads to a balanced budget with no deficit. Many states have achieved this objective by passing laws or constitutional amendments precluding deficit spending. Unfortunately, the Federal government has no such prohibition, and the national debt is heading off the charts, reaching more than $14.7 trillion, or more than $47,000 per citizen, in early September 2011. According to the U.S. National Debt Clock, the U.S. total debt is $55 trillion.

When enacting tax legislation, Congress is often guided by the concept of **revenue neutrality** so that any changes neither increase nor decrease the net revenues raised under the prior rules. Revenue neutrality does not mean that any one taxpayer's tax liability remains the same. Because this liability depends upon the circumstances involved, one taxpayer's increased tax liability could be another's tax saving. Revenue-neutral tax reform does not reduce deficits, but at least it does not aggravate the problem.

Economic Considerations

LO.2

Demonstrate the influence of economic, social, equity, and political considerations on the development of the tax law.

Using the tax system to attempt to accomplish economic objectives has become increasingly popular in recent years. Generally, this process involves amending the Internal Revenue Code[1] through tax legislation and emphasizes measures designed to help control the economy or encourage certain activities and businesses.

Control of the Economy

Congress has made use of depreciation write-offs as a means of controlling the economy. Theoretically, shorter asset lives and accelerated methods should encourage additional investments in depreciable property acquired for business use. Conversely, longer class lives and the required use of the straight-line method of depreciation dampen the tax incentive for capital outlays.

Another approach that utilizes depreciation as a means of controlling capital investment is the amount of write-off allowed upon the acquisition of assets. This approach is followed by the § 179 election to immediately expense assets up to a

[1]The Internal Revenue Code is a compilation of Federal tax legislation that appears in Title 26 of the U.S. Code.

TAX IN THE NEWS Stimulating the Economy

During the current economic downturn, there has been considerable discussion about what the government should do. There are two primary ways to stabilize an economy through government policy: fiscal policy and monetary policy. Fiscal policy involves spending and taxation.

There are two forms of fiscal policy: discretionary and automatic. President Obama's stimulus package, which provided various tax cuts and incentives and increased government spending by statute, also thereby increasing government deficits, is an example of discretionary fiscal policy. Income tax is an example of an automatic fiscal stabilizer—it is automatic because as incomes decline during a recession, taxes owed also decline. In general, in recent years, changes in the Internal Revenue Code have become less important than government spending programs as a way to stimulate the economy.

Source: Adapted from Yair Listokin, "Stabilizing the Economy through the Income Tax Code," *Tax Notes*, June 29, 2009, pp. 1575–1577.

certain amount. It also was the approach used by Congress in various provisions that permitted up to 50 percent additional first-year depreciation.

A change in the tax rate structure has a more immediate impact on the economy. When tax rates are lowered, taxpayers are able to obtain additional spendable funds. In the interest of revenue neutrality, however, rate decreases may be accompanied by a reduction or elimination of deductions or credits. Thus, lower rates do not always mean lower taxes.

Encouragement of Certain Activities

Without passing judgment on the wisdom of any such choices, it is quite clear that the tax law does encourage certain types of economic activity or segments of the economy. For example, the desire to foster technological progress helps explain the favorable treatment accorded to research and development expenditures. Under the tax law, such expenditures can be deducted in the year incurred or, alternatively, capitalized and amortized over a period of 60 months or more. In terms of timing the tax saving, such options usually are preferable to a capitalization of the cost with a write-off over the estimated useful life of the asset created.[2]

The encouragement of technological progress also can explain why the tax law places the inventor in a special position. Besides the fact that patents can qualify as capital assets, under certain conditions, their disposition automatically carries long-term capital gain treatment.[3]

Are ecological considerations a desirable objective? If they are, it explains why the tax law permits a 60-month amortization period for costs incurred in the installation of pollution control facilities.

With a view toward conserving and developing national energy resources, in 2005 and 2008, Congress enacted legislation that provides tax incentives to encourage certain activities. Not only are various tax credits made available for home energy conservation expenditures but favorable tax treatment is extended to the purchase of "clean fuel" vehicles. Further, the law provides significant tax incentives to encourage the development of more efficient and reliable energy infrastructure (i.e., power grids).

Does stimulating the development and rehabilitation of low-income rental housing benefit the economy? The tax law definitely favors these activities by allowing generous tax credits to taxpayers incurring such costs.

Is saving desirable for the economy? Saving leads to capital formation and thus makes funds available to finance home construction and industrial expansion. The tax law provides incentives to encourage saving by giving private retirement plans

[2]If the asset developed has no estimated useful life, no write-off would be available without the two options allowed by the tax law.

[3]A long-term capital gain has a favorable tax advantage for individuals.

preferential treatment. Not only are contributions to Keogh (H.R. 10) plans and certain Individual Retirement Accounts (IRAs) deductible, but income from such contributions accumulates on a tax-free basis. As noted in a following section, the encouragement of private-sector pension plans can be justified under social considerations as well.

Encouragement of Certain Industries

Who can question the proposition that a sound agricultural base is necessary for a well-balanced national economy? Undoubtedly, this belief can explain why farmers are accorded special treatment under the Federal tax system. Among the benefits are the election to expense rather than capitalize certain expenditures for soil and water conservation and fertilizers and the election to defer the recognition of gain on the receipt of crop insurance proceeds.

The tax law favors the development of natural resources by permitting the use of percentage depletion on the extraction and sale of oil and gas and specified mineral deposits and a write-off (rather than a capitalization) of certain exploration costs. The railroad and banking industries also receive special tax treatment. All of these provisions can be explained, in whole or in part, by economic considerations.

A well-balanced economy also should include a vigorous and dynamic manufacturing industry. To encourage this sector, Congress has enacted a tax incentive based on profits from manufacturing. Known as the domestic production activities deduction, the benefit is structured in such a manner as to stimulate the creation of jobs.

Encouragement of Small Business

At least in the United States, a consensus exists that what is good for small business is good for the economy as a whole. This assumption has led to a definite bias in the tax law favoring small business.

In the corporate tax area, several provisions can be explained by the desire to benefit small business. One provision enables a shareholder in a small business corporation to obtain an ordinary deduction for any loss recognized on a stock investment. Normally, such a loss would receive the less attractive capital loss treatment. The point of this favoritism is to encourage additional equity investments in small business corporations.[4] Another provision permits the shareholders of a small business corporation to make a special election that generally will avoid the imposition of the corporate income tax.[5] Furthermore, such an election enables the corporation to pass through to its shareholders any of its operating losses.[6]

The tax rates applicable to corporations tend to favor small business in that size is relative to the amount of taxable income generated in any one year. Because a corporate tax rate of 34 percent applies only to taxable income in excess of $75,000, corporations that stay within this limit are subject to lower average tax rates.

EXAMPLE 1

For calendar year 2012, Brown Corporation has taxable income of $75,000 and Red Corporation has taxable income of $100,000. Based on this information, the corporate income tax is $13,750 for Brown Corporation and $22,250 for Red Corporation (see Chapter 2). Brown Corporation is subject to an average tax rate of 18.33% ($13,750/$75,000), while Red Corporation is subject to an average rate of 22.25% ($22,250/$100,000). ■

If a corporation has taxable income in excess of $100,000, the benefits of the lower brackets are phased out until all income is taxed at the maximum rate of 34 percent. Once taxable income reaches $10 million, the rate becomes 35 percent.

[4] Known as Section 1244 stock, this subject is covered in Chapter 4.

[5] Known as the S corporation election, the subject is discussed extensively in Chapter 12.

[6] In general, an operating loss can benefit only the corporation incurring the loss through a carryback or carryover to profitable years. Consequently, the shareholders of the corporation usually cannot take advantage of any such loss.

TAX IN THE NEWS Did Rome Fall because of Taxation?

Some scholars believe that crippling taxation contributed to the fall of the Roman Empire. In 1966, classicist M. I. Finley said that "the army could not be enlarged because the land could not stand further depletion of manpower; the situation of the land had deteriorated because taxes were too high."

The real problem, however, may have been tax evasion. Large landowners evaded their taxes through a variety of legal and illegal means. Bribery was used to obtain low assessments, and the large landowners would stall the tax collectors and use their influence to obtain amnesties. As the U.S. tax system becomes more progressive, with taxes being paid mostly by the wealthy, will taxation—and tax evasion—lead to the fall of the United States?

Source: Adapted from Charles Adams, *Fight, Flight, Fraud: The Story of Taxation* (Buffalo: Euro-Dutch Publishers, 1982), p. 95.

One of the justifications for the enactment of the tax law governing corporate reorganizations (see Chapter 7) was the economic benefit it would provide for small businesses. By allowing corporations to combine without adverse tax consequences, small corporations would be in a position to compete more effectively with larger concerns.

Social Considerations

Some of the tax laws, especially those related to the Federal income tax of individuals, can be explained by social considerations. Rather than using loans, grants, and other programs to reach desired goals, Congress often uses the Tax Code to provide incentives and benefits (e.g., the higher education incentives). Following are some notable examples:

- The refundable earned income tax credit. As Congress has deemed it socially desirable to reduce the number of people on the welfare rolls and to cut funding for welfare programs, this credit has come to replace some welfare programs.
- The nontaxability of certain benefits provided to employees through accident and health plans financed by employers. It is socially desirable to encourage such plans because they provide medical benefits in the event of an employee's illness or injury.
- The nontaxability to the employee of some of the premiums paid by an employer for group term insurance covering the life of the employee. These arrangements can be justified in that they provide funds to help the family unit adjust to the loss of wages caused by the employee's death.
- The tax treatment to the employee of contributions made by an employer to qualified pension or profit sharing plans. The contribution and any income it earns are not taxed to the employee until the funds are distributed. Private retirement plans are encouraged because they supplement the subsistence income level the employee would otherwise have under the Social Security system.[7]
- The deduction allowed for contributions to qualified charitable organizations. The deduction attempts to shift some of the financial and administrative burden of socially desirable programs from the public (the government) to the private (the citizens) sector.
- Various tax credits, deductions, and exclusions that are designed to encourage taxpayers to obtain additional education (e.g., American Opportunity tax

[7]The same rationale explains the availability of similar arrangements for self-employed persons (the H.R. 10 or Keogh plan).

credit, lifetime learning credit, and the Coverdell Education Savings Account).[8]

- The credit allowed for amounts spent to furnish care for certain minor or disabled dependents to enable the taxpayer to seek or maintain gainful employment. Who could deny the social desirability of encouraging taxpayers to provide care for their children while they work?
- The disallowance of a tax deduction for certain expenditures that are deemed to be contrary to public policy. This disallowance extends to such items as fines, penalties, illegal kickbacks, and bribes to government officials. Public policy considerations also have been used to disallow gambling losses in excess of gambling gains and political campaign expenditures in excess of campaign contributions. Social considerations dictate that the tax law should not encourage these activities by permitting a deduction.
- The adoption tax credit to cover some (or all) of the expenses incurred by individuals who adopt or attempt to adopt a child.

Many other examples could be included, but the conclusion would be unchanged: social considerations do explain a significant part of the Federal tax law.

Equity Considerations

The concept of equity is relative. Reasonable persons can, and often do, disagree about what is fair or unfair. In the tax area, moreover, equity is generally tied to a particular taxpayer's personal situation. To illustrate, Ms. Jones may have difficulty understanding why none of the rent she pays on her apartment is deductible, while her brother, Mr. Jones, is able to deduct a large portion of the monthly payments he makes on his personal residence in the form of interest and taxes.[9]

In the same vein, compare the tax treatment of a corporation with that of a partnership. Two businesses may be equal in size, similarly situated, and competitors in the production of goods or services, but they are not comparably treated under the tax law. The corporation is subject to a separate Federal income tax; the partnership is not. Whether the differences in tax treatment can be logically justified in terms of equity is beside the point. The tax law can and does make a distinction between these business forms.

Equity, then, is not what appears fair or unfair to any one taxpayer or group of taxpayers. It is, instead, what the tax law recognizes. Some recognition of equity does exist, however, and explains part of the law. The concept of equity appears in tax provisions that alleviate the effect of multiple taxation and postpone the recognition of gain when the taxpayer lacks the ability or wherewithal to pay the tax. Equity also helps mitigate the effect of the application of the annual accounting period concept and helps taxpayers cope with the eroding result of inflation.

Alleviating the Effect of Multiple Taxation

The same income earned by a taxpayer may be subject to taxes imposed by different taxing authorities. If, for example, the taxpayer is a resident of New York City, income might generate Federal, New York State, and New York City income taxes. To compensate for this inequity, the Federal tax law allows a taxpayer to claim a deduction for state and local income taxes. The deduction, however, does not neutralize the effect of multiple taxation because the benefit derived depends on the taxpayer's Federal income tax rate.[10]

---

[8] These provisions also can be justified under the category of economic considerations. No one can take issue with the conclusion that a better educated workforce carries a positive economic impact.

[9] The encouragement of home ownership can be justified on both economic and social grounds. In this regard, it is interesting to note that some state income tax laws allow a form of relief (e.g., tax credit) to the taxpayer who rents his or her personal residence.

[10] A tax credit rather than a deduction would eliminate the effects of multiple taxation on the same income.

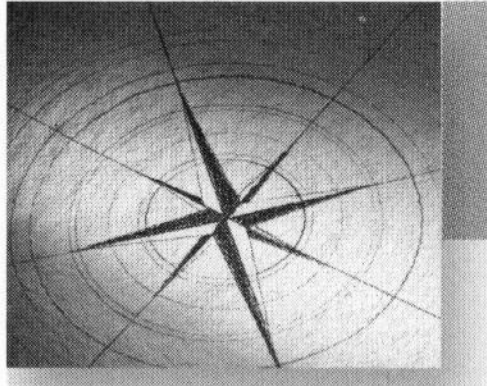

ETHICS & EQUITY Treating Everyone the Same

The justification for allowing a Federal income tax deduction for state and local income taxes paid is to mitigate the effect of having the same income be taxed twice. But what if instead of imposing an income tax a state derives comparable amounts of revenue from a general sales tax? Is it fair to deny a deduction to taxpayers in that state just because the tax the state levies is imposed on sales rather than income?

Congress, in the American Jobs Creation Act of 2004, resolved this purported inequity by allowing a Federal income tax deduction for state and local general sales taxes. However, a taxpayer who is subject to both state income and sales taxes must make a choice. One or the other, but not both, can be claimed as a deduction.

Comment on the equity of a tax system that requires this choice.

© LdF, iStockphoto

Equity considerations can explain the Federal tax treatment of certain income from foreign sources. Because double taxation results when the same income is subject to both foreign and U.S. income taxes, the tax law permits the taxpayer to choose either a credit or a deduction for the foreign taxes paid.

The imposition of a separate income tax on corporations leads to multiple taxation of the same income.

EXAMPLE 2

During the current year, Gray Corporation has net income of $100,000, of which $5,000 was received as dividends from stock it owns in IBM Corporation. Assume that Gray Corporation distributes the after-tax income to its shareholders (all individuals). At a minimum, the distribution received by the shareholders will be subject to two income taxes: the corporate income tax when the income is earned by Gray Corporation and the individual income tax when the balance is distributed to the shareholders as a dividend. The $5,000 that Gray receives from IBM Corporation fares even worse. Because it is paid from income earned by IBM, it has been subjected to a third income tax (the corporate income tax imposed on IBM).[11] ■

For corporate shareholders, for whom triple taxation is possible, the law provides a deduction for dividends received from certain domestic corporations. The deduction, usually 70 percent of the dividends, would be allowed to Gray Corporation for the $5,000 it received from IBM Corporation (see the discussion in Chapter 2). For the individual shareholder, legislation has reduced the tax on qualified dividends to 15 percent (0 percent for lower-bracket shareholders). By allowing a preferential lower tax rate, the approach is to *mitigate* (not *eliminate*) the effect of multiple taxation (see the discussion in Chapter 5).

In the area of the Federal estate tax, several provisions reflect attempts to mitigate the effect of multiple taxation. Some degree of equity is achieved, for example, by allowing a limited credit against the estate tax for foreign death taxes imposed on the same transfer. Other estate tax credits are available and can be explained on the same grounds.[12]

The Wherewithal to Pay Concept

The **wherewithal to pay** concept recognizes the inequity of taxing a transaction when the taxpayer lacks the means with which to pay the tax. It is particularly suited to situations when the taxpayer's economic position has not changed significantly as a result of a transaction.

---

[11]This result materializes because under the tax law, a corporation is not allowed a deduction for the dividend distributions it makes.

[12]See Chapter 18.

EXAMPLE 3

White Corporation holds unimproved land as an investment. The land has a basis to White of $60,000 and a fair market value of $100,000. The land is exchanged for a building (worth $100,000) that White will use in its business.[13] ■

EXAMPLE 4

White Corporation owns a warehouse that it uses in its business. At a time when the warehouse has an adjusted basis of $60,000, it is destroyed by fire. White collects the insurance proceeds of $100,000, and within two years of the end of the year in which the fire occurred, White uses all of the proceeds to purchase a new warehouse.[14] ■

EXAMPLE 5

Tom, a sole proprietor, decides to incorporate his business. In exchange for the business's assets (adjusted basis of $60,000 and a fair market value of $100,000), Tom receives all of the stock of Azure Corporation, a newly created corporation.[15] The Azure stock is worth $100,000. ■

EXAMPLE 6

Rose, Sam, and Tom want to develop unimproved land owned by Tom. The land has a basis to Tom of $60,000 and a fair market value of $100,000. The RST Partnership is formed with the following investments: land worth $100,000 transferred by Tom, $100,000 cash by Rose, and $100,000 cash by Sam. Each party receives a one-third interest in the RST Partnership.[16] ■

EXAMPLE 7

Amber Corporation and Crimson Corporation decide to consolidate to form Aqua Corporation.[17] Pursuant to the plan of reorganization, Tera exchanges her stock in Amber Corporation (basis of $60,000 and fair market value of $100,000) for stock in Aqua Corporation worth $100,000. ■

In all of the preceding examples, White Corporation, Tom, or Tera had a realized gain of $40,000 [$100,000 (fair market value of the property received) − $60,000 (basis of the property given up)].[18] It seems inequitable to force the taxpayer to recognize any of this gain for two reasons. First, without disposing of the property or interest acquired, the taxpayer would be hard-pressed to pay the tax.[19] Second, the taxpayer's economic situation has not changed significantly. To illustrate by referring to Example 5, can it be said that Tom's position as sole shareholder of Azure Corporation is much different from his prior status as owner of a sole proprietorship?

Several warnings are in order concerning the application of the wherewithal to pay concept. Recognized gain is merely postponed and not necessarily avoided. Because of the basis carryover to the new property or interest acquired in these nontaxable transactions, the gain element is still present and might be recognized upon a subsequent taxable disposition. Referring to Example 5, suppose Tom later sold the stock in Azure Corporation for $100,000. Tom's basis in the stock is $60,000 (the same basis as in the assets transferred), and the sale results in a recognized gain of $40,000. Also, many of the provisions previously illustrated prevent the recognition of realized losses. Because such provisions are automatic in application (not elective with the taxpayer), they could operate to the detriment of a taxpayer who wants to obtain a deduction for a loss. The notable exception involves

[13]The nontaxability of like-kind exchanges applies to the exchange of property held for investment or used in a trade or business for property to be similarly held or used.

[14]The nontaxability of gains realized from involuntary conversions applies when the proceeds received by the taxpayer are reinvested within a prescribed period of time in property similar or related in service or use to that converted. Involuntary conversions take place as a result of casualty losses, theft losses, and condemnations by a public authority.

[15]Transfers of property to controlled corporations are discussed in Chapter 4.

[16]The formation of a partnership is discussed in Chapter 10.

[17]Corporate reorganizations are discussed in Chapter 7.

[18]Realized gain can be likened to economic gain. However, the Federal income tax is imposed only on that portion of realized gain considered to be recognized under the law. Generally, recognized (or taxable) gain can never exceed realized gain.

[19]If the taxpayer ends up with other property (boot) as part of the transfer, gain may be recognized to this extent. The presence of boot, however, helps solve the wherewithal to pay problem because it provides property (other than the property or interest central to the transaction) with which to pay the tax.

involuntary conversions (Example 4). Here nonrecognition treatment is elective with the taxpayer and also will not apply to a realized loss if it is otherwise deductible.

The wherewithal to pay concept has definitely served as a guideline in shaping part of the tax law. Nevertheless, it is not a hard-and-fast principle that is followed in every case. Only when the tax law specifically provides for no tax consequences will this result materialize.

EXAMPLE 8

Mary Jo exchanges stock in Green Corporation (basis of $60,000 and fair market value of $100,000) for stock in Purple Corporation (fair market value of $100,000). The exchange is not pursuant to a reorganization. Under these circumstances, Mary Jo's realized gain of $40,000 is recognized for Federal income tax purposes.[20] ■

The result reached in Example 8 seems harsh in that the exchange does not place Mary Jo in a position to pay the tax on the $40,000 gain. How can this result be reconciled with that reached in Example 7 when the exchange was nontaxable? In other words, why does the tax law apply the wherewithal to pay concept to the exchange of stock pursuant to a corporate reorganization (Example 7) but not to certain other stock exchanges (Example 8)?

Recall that the wherewithal to pay concept is particularly suited to situations in which the taxpayer's economic position has not changed significantly as a result of a transaction. In Example 7, Tera's stock investment in Amber Corporation really continues in the form of the Aqua Corporation stock because Aqua was formed through a consolidation of Amber and Crimson Corporations.[21] In Example 8, however, the investment has not continued. Here Mary Jo's ownership in Green Corporation has ceased, and an investment in an entirely different corporation has been substituted.

Mitigating the Effect of the Annual Accounting Period Concept

For purposes of effective administration of the tax law, all taxpayers must report to and settle with the Federal government at periodic intervals. Otherwise, taxpayers would remain uncertain as to their tax liabilities, and the government would have difficulty judging revenues and budgeting expenditures. The period selected for final settlement of most tax liabilities is one year. At the close of each year, a taxpayer's position becomes complete for that particular year. Referred to as the annual accounting period concept, the effect is to divide each taxpayer's life into equal annual intervals for tax purposes.

The finality of the annual accounting period concept can lead to dissimilar tax treatment for taxpayers who are, from a long-range standpoint, in the same economic position.

EXAMPLE 9

Rena and Samuel are both sole proprietors and have experienced the following results during the past three years:

	Profit (or Loss)	
Year	**Rena**	**Samuel**
2010	$50,000	$150,000
2011	60,000	60,000
2012	60,000	(40,000)

Although Rena and Samuel have the same profit of $170,000 over the period 2010–2012, the finality of the annual accounting period concept places Samuel at a definite disadvantage for tax purposes. The net operating loss procedure offers Samuel some relief by allowing him to apply some or all of his 2012 loss to the earliest profitable years (in this

[20] The exchange of stock does not qualify for nontaxable treatment as a like-kind exchange (refer to Example 3).

[21] This continuation is known as the continuity of interest concept, which forms the foundation for all nontaxable corporate reorganizations. The concept is discussed at length in Chapter 7.

case, 2010). Thus, Samuel, with a net operating loss carryback, is placed in a position to obtain a refund for some of the taxes he paid on the $150,000 profit reported for 2010. ■

The same reasoning used to support the deduction of net operating losses can be applied to explain the special treatment that excess capital losses and excess charitable contributions receive. Carryback and carryover procedures help mitigate the effect of limiting a loss or a deduction to the accounting period in which it is realized. With such procedures, a taxpayer may be able to salvage a loss or a deduction that might otherwise be wasted.

The installment method of recognizing gain on the sale of property allows a taxpayer to spread tax consequences over the payout period.[22] The harsh effect of taxing all of the gain in the year of sale is avoided. The installment method also can be explained by the wherewithal to pay concept because recognition of gain is tied to the collection of the installment notes received from the sale of the property. Tax consequences tend to correspond to the seller's ability to pay the tax.

EXAMPLE 10

In 2010, Tim sold unimproved real estate (cost of $40,000) for $100,000. Under the terms of the sale, Tim receives two notes from the purchaser, each for $50,000 (plus interest). One note is payable in 2011; the other, in 2012. Without the installment method, Tim would have to recognize and pay a tax on the gain of $60,000 for the year of the sale (2010). This result is harsh because none of the sale proceeds will be received until 2011 and 2012. With the installment method, and presuming the notes are paid when each comes due, Tim recognizes half of the gain ($30,000) in 2011 and the remaining half in 2012. ■

The annual accounting period concept has been modified to apply to situations in which taxpayers may have difficulty accurately assessing their tax positions by year-end. In many such cases, the law permits taxpayers to treat transactions taking place in the next year as having occurred in the prior year.

EXAMPLE 11

Monica, a calendar year taxpayer, is a participant in an H.R. 10 (Keogh) retirement plan (see Appendix C for a definition of a Keogh plan). Under the plan, Monica contributes 20% of her net self-employment income, such amount being deductible for Federal income tax purposes. On April 9, 2012, Monica determines that her net self-employment income for calendar year 2011 was $80,000. Consequently, she contributes $16,000 (20% × $80,000) to the plan. Even though the $16,000 contribution was made in 2012, the law permits Monica to claim it as a deduction for tax year 2011. Requiring Monica to make the contribution by December 31, 2011, to obtain the deduction for that year would force her to arrive at an accurate determination of net self-employment income long before her income tax return must be prepared and filed. ■

Similar exceptions to the annual accounting period concept cover certain charitable contributions by accrual basis corporations (Chapter 2) and the dividend distributions by S corporations (Chapter 12).

Coping with Inflation

During periods of inflation, bracket creep has plagued the working person. Because of the progressive nature of the income tax, any wage adjustment to compensate for inflation can increase the income tax bracket of the recipient. The overall impact is an erosion of purchasing power. Congress recognized this problem and began to adjust various income tax components (the **indexation** procedure) in 1985 based upon the rise in the consumer price index over the prior year. For example, due to the inflation factor, the amount of a personal and dependency exemption has been

[22]Under the installment method, each payment received by the seller represents a return of basis (the nontaxable portion) and profit from the sale (the taxable portion).

increased over the years. Indexation also applies to dollar amounts of other components, including the tax brackets and the standard deduction.

Political Considerations

A large segment of the Federal tax law is made up of statutory provisions. Because these statutes are enacted by Congress, is it any surprise that political considerations influence tax law? For purposes of discussion, the effect of political considerations on the tax law is divided into the following topics: special interest legislation, political expediency, and state and local influences.

Special Interest Legislation

Unquestionably, certain provisions of the tax law can be explained largely by looking to the political influence some pressure groups have exerted on Congress. For example, is there any other reason why prepaid subscription and dues income is not taxed until earned while prepaid rents are taxed to the landlord in the year received? These exceptions came about because certain organizations (e.g., the American Automobile Association) convinced Congress that special tax treatment was needed to cover income received from multiyear dues and subscriptions.

Special interest legislation is not necessarily to be condemned if it can be justified on economic or social grounds. At any rate, it is an inevitable product of our political system.

Political Expediency

Various tax reform proposals rise and fall in favor depending upon the shifting moods of the American public. That Congress is sensitive to popular feeling is an accepted fact. Therefore, certain provisions of the tax law can be explained on the basis of the political climate at the time of enactment. Once the general public became aware that certain large and profitable corporations were able to avoid the corporate income tax, Congress responded with an alternative minimum tax. Since a portion of a corporation's adjusted current earnings has been made a tax preference item, many large corporations no longer escape taxation (see Chapter 3).

Measures that deter more affluent taxpayers from obtaining so-called preferential tax treatment have always had popular appeal and, consequently, the support of Congress. Provisions such as the alternative minimum tax, the imputed interest rules, and the limitation on the deductibility of interest on investment indebtedness can be explained on this basis. In the same vein are the provisions imposing penalty taxes on corporations that unreasonably accumulate earnings or are classified as personal holding companies (see Chapter 3).

The provisions raising income tax rates on more affluent taxpayers and increasing the amount of the earned income credit are also at least partially attributable to political expediency.

State and Local Influences

Political considerations have played a major role in the exclusion from gross income of interest received on state and local obligations. In view of the furor that state and local political figures have raised every time repeal of this tax provision has been proposed, one might well regard it as sacred.

Somewhat less apparent has been the influence state law has had in shaping our present Federal tax law. Of prime importance in this regard has been the effect of the community property system employed in some states.[23] At one time, the tax

[23]The states with community property systems are Louisiana, Texas, New Mexico, Arizona, California, Washington, Idaho, Nevada, Wisconsin, and (if elected by the spouses) Alaska. The rest of the states are classified as common law jurisdictions. The difference between common law and community property systems centers around the property rights possessed by married persons. In a common law system, each spouse owns whatever he or she earns. Under a community property system, one-half of the earnings of each spouse is considered owned by the other spouse. Assume, for example, that Harold and Ruth are husband and wife and that their only income is the $80,000 annual salary Harold receives. If they live in New York (a common law state), the $80,000 salary belongs to Harold. If, however, they live in Texas (a community property state), the $80,000 salary is divided equally, in terms of ownership, between Harold and Ruth.

position of the residents of these states was so advantageous that many common law states actually adopted community property systems.[24] The political pressure placed on Congress to correct the disparity in tax treatment was considerable. To a large extent, this was accomplished in the Revenue Act of 1948, which extended many of the community property tax advantages to residents of common law jurisdictions.[25] Thus, common law states avoided the trauma of discarding the time-honored legal system familiar to everyone. The impact of community property law on the Federal estate and gift taxes is further explored in Chapters 18 and 19.

Influence of the Internal Revenue Service

LO.3

Illustrate how the IRS, as the protector of the revenue, has affected tax law.

The IRS has been influential in many areas beyond its role in issuing administrative pronouncements. In its capacity as the protector of the national revenue, the IRS has been instrumental in securing the passage of much legislation designed to curtail the most flagrant tax avoidance practices (closing tax loopholes). In its capacity as the administrator of the tax laws, the IRS has sought and obtained legislation to make its job easier (administrative feasibility).

The IRS as Protector of the Revenue

Innumerable examples can be given of provisions in the tax law that have stemmed from the direct efforts of the IRS to prevent taxpayers from exploiting a loophole. Working within the letter of existing law, ingenious taxpayers and their advisers devise techniques that accomplish indirectly what cannot be accomplished directly. As a consequence, legislation is enacted to close the loophole that taxpayers have located and exploited. The following examples can be explained in this fashion and are discussed in more detail in the chapters to follow:

- The use of a fiscal year by personal service corporations, partnerships, S corporations, and trusts to defer income recognition to the owners (see Chapters 2, 10, 12, and 20).
- The use of the cash basis method of accounting by certain large corporations (see Chapter 2).
- The deduction of passive investment losses and expenses against other income (see Chapters 2 and 10).
- The shifting of income to lower-bracket taxpayers through the use of reversionary trusts (see Chapter 20).

In addition, the IRS has secured from Congress legislation of a more general nature that enables it to make adjustments based upon the substance rather than the formal construction of what a taxpayer has done. One provision, for example, authorizes the IRS to establish guidelines on the thin capitalization issue. This question involves when corporate debt will be recognized as debt for tax purposes and when it will be reclassified as equity or stock (see the discussion of thin capitalization in Chapter 4). Another provision permits the IRS to make adjustments to a taxpayer's method of accounting when the method used by the taxpayer does not clearly reflect income. The IRS has also been granted the authority to allocate income and deductions among businesses owned or controlled by the same interests when the allocation is necessary to prevent the evasion of taxes or to reflect the income of each business clearly.

EXAMPLE 12

Gold Corporation and Silver Corporation are brother-sister corporations (the stock of each is owned by the same shareholders), and both use the calendar year for tax purposes. For the current tax year, each has taxable income as follows: $335,000 for Gold

[24] Such states included Michigan, Oklahoma, and Pennsylvania.

[25] The major advantage extended was the provision allowing married taxpayers to file joint returns and compute the tax liability as if each spouse had earned one-half of the income. This result is automatic in a community property state because half of the income earned by one spouse belongs to the other spouse. The income-splitting benefits of a joint return are now incorporated as part of the tax rates applicable to married taxpayers.

Corporation and $50,000 for Silver Corporation. Not included in Gold Corporation's taxable income, however, is $10,000 of rent income usually charged Silver Corporation for the use of some property owned by Gold. Since the parties have not clearly reflected the taxable income of each business, the IRS can allocate $10,000 of rent income to Gold Corporation. After the allocation, Gold Corporation has taxable income of $345,000 and Silver Corporation has taxable income of $40,000.[26] ■

Also of a general nature is the authority Congress has given the IRS to prevent taxpayers from acquiring corporations to obtain a tax advantage when the principal purpose of the acquisition is the evasion or avoidance of the Federal income tax. The provision of the tax law that provides this authority is discussed briefly in Chapter 7.

Administrative Feasibility

Some of the tax law is justified on the grounds that it simplifies the task of the IRS in collecting the revenue and administering the law. With regard to collecting the revenue, the IRS long ago realized the importance of placing taxpayers on a pay-as-you-go basis. Elaborate withholding procedures apply to wages, while the tax on other types of income may have to be paid at periodic intervals throughout the year. The IRS has been instrumental in convincing the courts that accrual basis taxpayers should pay taxes on prepaid income in the year received and not when earned. This approach may be contrary to generally accepted accounting principles, but it is consistent with the wherewithal to pay concept.

Of considerable aid to the IRS in collecting revenue are the numerous provisions that impose interest and penalties on taxpayers for noncompliance with the tax law. These provisions include penalties for failure to pay a tax or to file a return that is due and the negligence penalty for intentional disregard of rules and regulations. Various penalties for civil and criminal fraud also serve as deterrents to taxpayer noncompliance. This aspect of the tax law is discussed in Chapter 17.

One of the keys to the effective administration of our tax system is the audit process conducted by the IRS. To carry out this function, the IRS is aided by provisions that reduce the chance of taxpayer error or manipulation and therefore simplify the audit effort that is necessary. An increase in the amount of the standard deduction reduces the number of individual taxpayers who will be in a position to claim itemized deductions. With fewer deductions to check, the audit function is simplified.[27] The same objective can be used to explain the $13,000 annual gift tax exclusion (see Chapter 18). This provision decreases the number of tax returns that must be filed (as well as reduces the taxes paid) and thereby saves audit effort.[28]

LO.4

Recognize the role of the courts in interpreting and shaping tax law.

Influence of the Courts

In addition to interpreting statutory provisions and the administrative pronouncements issued by the IRS, the Federal courts have influenced tax law in two other respects.[29] First, the courts have formulated certain judicial concepts that serve as guides in the application of various tax provisions. Second, certain key decisions have led to changes in the Internal Revenue Code. Understanding this influence helps explain some of our tax laws.

[26]By shifting $10,000 of income to Gold Corporation (which is in the 34% bracket), the IRS gains $3,400 in taxes. Allowing the $10,000 deduction to Silver Corporation (which is in the 15% bracket) costs the IRS only $1,500. See Chapter 2 for further discussion of the income tax rates applicable to corporations.

[27]The IRS gave the same justification when it proposed to Congress the $100 per event limitation on personal casualty and theft losses. Imposition of the limitation eliminated many casualty and theft loss deductions and, as a consequence, saved the IRS considerable audit time. Also, an additional limitation equal to 10% of adjusted gross income applies to the total of nonbusiness losses after reduction by the floor of $100 for each loss.

[28]Particularly in the case of nominal gifts among family members, taxpayer compliance in reporting and paying a tax on such transfers would be questionable. The absence of the $13,000 gift tax exclusion would create a serious enforcement problem for the IRS.

[29]A great deal of case law is devoted to ascertaining congressional intent. The courts, in effect, ask: What did Congress have in mind when it enacted a particular tax provision?

Judicial Concepts Relating to Tax Law

Although ranking the tax concepts developed by the courts in order of importance is difficult, the concept of substance over form would almost certainly be near the top of any list. Variously described as the "telescoping" or "collapsing" process or the "step transaction approach," it involves determining the true substance of what occurred. In a transaction involving many steps, any one step may be collapsed (or disregarded) to arrive directly at the result reached.

EXAMPLE 13

In 2012, Mrs. Greer, a widow, wants to give $26,000 to Jean without incurring any gift tax liability.[30] She knows that the law permits her to give up to $13,000 each year per person without any tax consequences (the annual exclusion). With this in mind, the following steps are taken: a gift by Mrs. Greer to Jean of $13,000 (nontaxable because of the $13,000 annual exclusion), a gift by Mrs. Greer to Ben of $13,000 (also nontaxable), and a gift by Ben to Jean of $13,000 (nontaxable because of Ben's annual exclusion). Considering only the form of what Mrs. Greer and Ben have done, all appears well from a tax standpoint. In substance, however, what has happened? By collapsing the steps involving Ben, it is apparent that Mrs. Greer has made a gift of $26,000 to Jean and therefore has not avoided the Federal gift tax. ■

The substance over form concept plays an important role in transactions involving corporations.

Another leading tax concept developed by the courts deals with the interpretation of statutory tax provisions that operate to benefit taxpayers. The courts have established the rule that these relief provisions are to be narrowly construed against taxpayers if there is any doubt about their application. Suppose, for example, that Beige Corporation wants to be treated as an S corporation (see Chapter 12) but has not satisfied the statutory requirements for making the required election. Because S corporation status is a relief provision favoring taxpayers, chances are the courts will deny Beige Corporation this treatment.

Important in the area of corporate-shareholder dealings (see the discussion of constructive dividends in Chapter 5) and in the resolution of valuation problems for estate and gift tax purposes (see Chapters 18 and 19) is the **arm's length concept**. Particularly in dealings between related parties, transactions can be tested by questioning whether the taxpayers acted in an "arm's length" manner. The question to be asked is: Would unrelated parties have handled the transaction in the same way?

EXAMPLE 14

The sole shareholder of a corporation leases property to the corporation for a monthly rental of $50,000. To test whether the corporation should be allowed a rent deduction for this amount, the IRS and the courts will apply the arm's length concept. Would the corporation have paid $50,000 a month in rent if the same property had been leased from an unrelated party (rather than from the sole shareholder)? ■

The **continuity of interest concept** originated with the courts but has, in many situations, been incorporated into statutory provisions of the tax law. Primarily concerned with business readjustments, the concept permits tax-free treatment only if the taxpayer retains a substantial continuing interest in the property transferred to the new business. Due to the continuing interest retained, the transfer should not have tax consequences because the position of the taxpayer has not changed. This concept applies to transfers to controlled corporations (Chapter 4), corporate reorganizations (Chapter 7), and transfers to partnerships (Chapter 10). The

[30]The example assumes that Mrs. Greer has exhausted her unified tax credit. See Chapter 18.

continuity of interest concept helps explain the results reached in Examples 5 through 7 of this chapter. This concept is further discussed in Chapter 7.

Also developed by the courts, the **business purpose concept** principally applies to transactions involving corporations. Under this concept, some sound business reason that motivates the transaction must be present for the prescribed tax treatment to result. The avoidance of taxation is not considered a sound business purpose.

EXAMPLE 15

Beth and Charles are equal shareholders in Brown Corporation. They have recently disagreed about the company's operations and are at an impasse about the future of Brown Corporation. This shareholder disagreement on corporate policy constitutes a sound business purpose and would justify a division of Brown Corporation that will permit Beth and Charles to go their separate ways. Whether the division of Brown would be nontaxable to the parties depends on their compliance with the statutory provisions dealing with corporate reorganizations. The point is, however, that compliance with statutory provisions would not be enough to ensure nontaxability without a business purpose for the transaction. ■

The business purpose concept is discussed further in Chapter 7.

Judicial Influence on Statutory Provisions

Some court decisions have been of such consequence that Congress has incorporated them into statutory tax law. An illustration of this influence appears in Example 16.

EXAMPLE 16

In 1983, Brad claimed a capital loss of $100,000 for Tan Corporation stock that had become worthless during the year. In the absence of any offsetting gains, the capital loss deduction produced no income tax savings for Brad either in 1983 or in future years. In 1986, Brad institutes a lawsuit against the former officers of Tan Corporation for their misconduct that resulted in the corporation's failure and thereby led to Brad's $100,000 loss. In settlement of the suit, the officers pay $50,000 to Brad. The IRS argued that the full $50,000 should be taxed as gain to Brad. The Tan stock was written off in 1983 and had a zero basis for tax purposes. The $50,000 recovery that Brad received on the stock was, therefore, all gain. The IRS's position was logical but not equitable. The court stated that Brad should not be taxed on the recovery of an amount previously deducted unless the deduction produced a tax savings. Because the $100,000 capital loss deduction in 1983 produced no tax benefit, none of the $50,000 received in 1986 results in gain. ■

The decision reached by the courts in Example 16, known as the **tax benefit rule**, is part of the statutory tax law.

Court decisions sometimes create uncertainty about the tax law. Such decisions may reach the right result but do not produce the guidelines necessary to enable taxpayers to comply. In many situations, Congress may be compelled to add certainty to the law by enacting statutory provisions specifying when a particular tax consequence will or will not materialize. The following are examples of this type of judicial "cause" and the statutory "effect":

- When a stock redemption will be treated as an exchange or as a dividend (see Chapter 6).
- What basis a parent corporation will have in the assets received from a subsidiary that is liquidated shortly after its acquisition (see Chapter 6).

Some of the statutory provisions can be explained by a negative reaction by Congress to a particular court decision. One decision, for example, held that the transfer of a liability to a controlled corporation should be treated as boot received by the transferor (see Chapter 4). Congress apparently disagreed with this treatment and promptly enacted legislation to change the result.

1.2 Summary

In addition to its revenue-raising objective, the Federal tax law has developed in response to several other factors:

- *Economic considerations.* Here the emphasis is on tax provisions that help regulate the economy and encourage certain activities and types of businesses.
- *Social considerations.* Some tax provisions are designed to encourage or discourage certain socially desirable or undesirable practices.
- *Equity considerations.* Of principal concern in this area are tax provisions that alleviate the effect of multiple taxation, recognize the wherewithal to pay concept, mitigate the effect of the annual accounting period concept, and recognize the eroding effect of inflation.
- *Political considerations.* Of significance in this regard are tax provisions that represent special interest legislation, reflect political expediency, and illustrate the effect of state law.
- *Influence of the IRS.* Many tax provisions are intended to aid the IRS in collecting revenue and administering the tax law.
- *Influence of the courts.* Court decisions have established a body of judicial concepts relating to tax law and have, on occasion, led Congress to enact statutory provisions that either clarify or negate their effect.

These factors explain various tax provisions and thereby help in understanding why the tax law developed to its present state. The next step involves learning to work with the tax law.

1.3 Reconciling Accounting Concepts

The vast majority of an entity's business transactions receive the same treatment for financial accounting purposes as they do under Federal and state tax law. But "book-tax differences" exist. When variances between **Generally Accepted Accounting Principles (GAAP)** or **International Financial Reporting Standards (IFRS)** and tax rules do arise, these are highlighted and discussed in a special feature titled *Financial Disclosure Insights.*

1.4 Working with the Tax Law—Tax Sources

Understanding taxation requires a mastery of the sources of tax law. These sources include not only the legislative provisions in the Internal Revenue Code but also congressional Committee Reports, Regulations, Treasury Department pronouncements, and court decisions. Thus, the primary sources of tax information are the pronouncements of the three branches of government: legislative, executive, and judicial.

The law is of little significance, however, until it is applied to a set of facts and circumstances. A tax researcher not only must be able to read and interpret the sources of the law but also must understand the relative weight of authority within the rules of law. Learning to work with the tax law involves three basic steps:

1. Familiarity with the sources of the law.
2. Application of research techniques.
3. Effective use of planning procedures.

The remainder of this chapter introduces the sources of tax law and explains how the law is applied to problems and conditions of individual and business transactions. Statutory, administrative, and judicial sources of the tax law are considered first.

TAX IN THE NEWS **Fink Fee Results in $4.5 Million Payoff**

Since 2007, the IRS has had a whistle-blower award that mandates an award of 15 to 30 percent of the amount recouped. Senator Charles Grassley said, "It ought to encourage a lot of people to squeal."

An accountant's tip gave the IRS $20 million in taxes and interest from a financial services firm. The accountant received a $4.5 million reward minus, of course, a 28 percent tax hit. The accountant's lawyer got a sizable chunk also.

Source: Adapted from "IRS Awards $4.5M to Whistleblower," FoxNews.com, April 8, 2011, **www.foxnews.com/politics/2011/04/08/irs-awards-45m-whistleblower.**

LO.5

Identify tax law sources—statutory, administrative, and judicial.

Statutory Sources of the Tax Law

Origin of the Internal Revenue Code

Before 1939, the statutory provisions relating to taxation were contained in the individual revenue acts enacted by Congress. The inconvenience and confusion that resulted from dealing with many separate acts led Congress to codify all of the Federal tax laws. Known as the Internal Revenue Code of 1939, the codification arranged all Federal tax provisions in a logical sequence and placed them in a separate part of the Federal statutes. A further rearrangement took place in 1954 and resulted in the Internal Revenue Code of 1954.

Perhaps to emphasize the magnitude of the changes made by the Tax Reform Act (TRA) of 1986, Congress redesignated the Internal Revenue Code of 1954 as the Internal Revenue Code of 1986. This change is somewhat deceiving because the tax law was not recodified in 1986, as it had been in 1954. TRA of 1986 merely amended, deleted, or added provisions to the Internal Revenue Code of 1954. For example, before TRA of 1986, § 336 provided the general rule that no gain or loss would be recognized by a corporation when it distributed assets in kind to its shareholders in complete liquidation. After the effective date of TRA of 1986, § 336 provides that gain or loss will be recognized upon the same distributions (see Chapter 6).

The following observations will help clarify the significance of the three Codes:

- Neither the 1939, the 1954, nor the 1986 Code changed all of the tax law existing on the date of enactment. Much of the 1939 Code, for example, was incorporated into the 1954 Code. The same can be said for the transition from the 1954 to the 1986 Code. This point is important in assessing judicial and administrative decisions interpreting provisions under prior Codes. For example, a decision interpreting § 61 of the Internal Revenue Code of 1954 will have continuing validity because this provision carried over unchanged to the Internal Revenue Code of 1986.
- Statutory amendments to the tax law are integrated into the existing Code. Thus, the tax provisions of the Tax Relief Act of 2010 became part of the Internal Revenue Code of 1986.

Do not conclude, however, that the codification and recodification process has made the Internal Revenue Code a simplistic body of laws. To a large extent, the complexity of our current Code can be attributed to its growth.

The Legislative Process

Federal tax legislation generally originates in the House of Representatives, where it is first considered by the House Ways and Means Committee. Tax bills originate in the Senate when they are attached as riders to other legislative proposals.[31] If acceptable to the House Ways and Means Committee, the proposed bill is referred

[31]The Tax Equity and Fiscal Responsibility Act of 1982 originated in the Senate; its constitutionality was unsuccessfully challenged in the courts. The Senate version of the Deficit Reduction Act of 1984 was attached as an amendment to the Federal Boat Safety Act.

to the entire House of Representatives for approval or disapproval. Approved bills are sent to the Senate, where they are referred to the Senate Finance Committee for further consideration.

In the next step, the bill is referred from the Senate Finance Committee to the whole Senate. Assuming no disagreement between the House and the Senate, a bill passed by the Senate is referred to the President for approval or veto. If the bill is approved or if the President's veto is overridden by a two-thirds vote, the bill becomes law and part of the Internal Revenue Code.

When the Senate version of the bill differs from that passed by the House, the Joint Conference Committee resolves these differences. The Joint Conference Committee includes members of the House Ways and Means Committee and the Senate Finance Committee.

Referrals from the House Ways and Means Committee, the Senate Finance Committee, and the Joint Conference Committee are usually accompanied by Committee Reports. These Committee Reports often explain the provisions of the proposed legislation and are therefore a valuable source in ascertaining the *intent* of Congress. What Congress has in mind when it considers and enacts tax legislation is, of course, the key to interpreting that legislation. Because Regulations normally are not issued immediately after a statute is enacted, taxpayers often look to Committee Reports to ascertain congressional intent.

The typical legislative process dealing with tax bills can be summarized as follows:

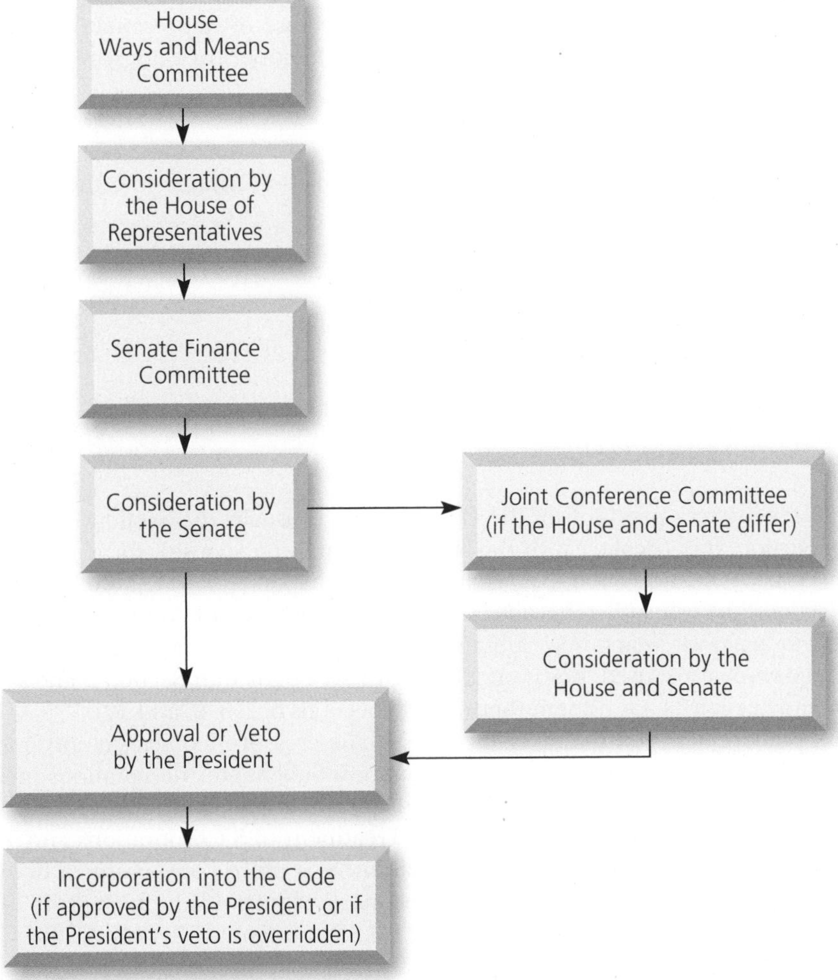

The role of the Joint Conference Committee indicates the importance of compromise in the legislative process. The practical effect of the compromise process can be illustrated by reviewing what happened in the Hiring Incentives to Restore Employment Act of 2010 regarding a new credit.

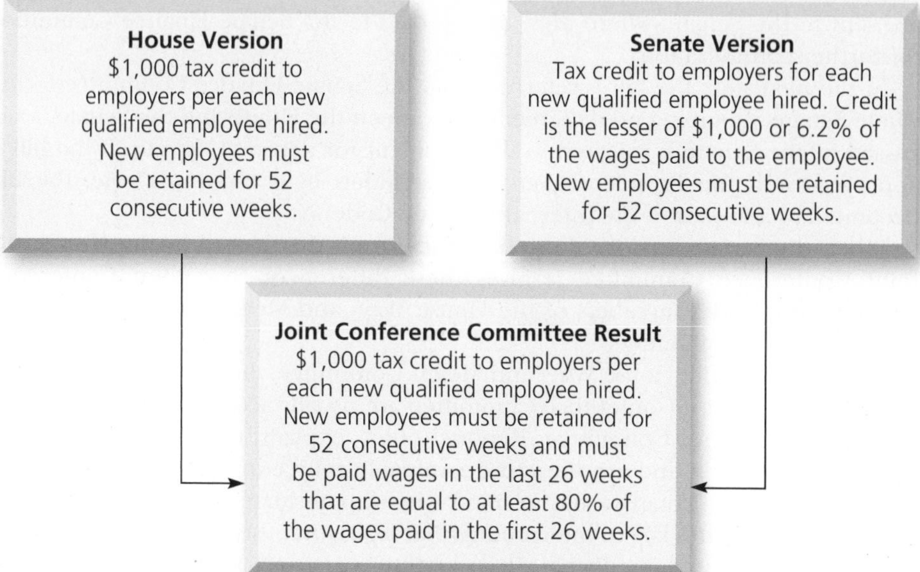

Some tax provisions are commonly referred to by the number the bill received in the House when first proposed or by the name of the member of Congress sponsoring the legislation. For example, the Self-Employed Individuals Tax Retirement Act of 1962 is popularly known as H.R. 10 (the House of Representatives Bill No. 10) or as the Keogh Act (Keogh being one of the members of Congress sponsoring the bill).

Arrangement of the Code

In working with the Code, it helps to understand the format. Note the following partial table of contents:

Subtitle A. Income Taxes
Chapter 1. Normal Taxes and Surtaxes
Subchapter A. Determination of Tax Liability
Part I. Tax on Individuals
Sections 1–5
Part II. Tax on Corporations
Sections 11–12

* * *

In referring to a provision of the Code, the *key* is usually the Section number. In citing Section 2(a) (dealing with the status of a surviving spouse), for example, it is unnecessary to include Subtitle A, Chapter 1, Subchapter A, Part I. Merely mentioning Section 2(a) will suffice because the Section numbers run consecutively and do not begin again with each new Subtitle, Chapter, Subchapter, or Part. Not all Code Section numbers are used, however. Note that Part I ends with Section 5 and Part II starts with Section 11 (at present there are no Sections 6, 7, 8, 9, and 10).[32]

Tax practitioners commonly refer to a specific area of income taxation by Subchapter designation. Some of the more common Subchapter designations include Subchapter C (Corporate Distributions and Adjustments), Subchapter K (Partners and Partnerships), and Subchapter S (Tax Treatment of S Corporations and Their Shareholders). Particularly in the last situation, it is more convenient to describe the subject of the applicable Code provisions (Sections 1361 through 1379) as S corporation status rather than as the "Tax Treatment of S Corporations and Their Shareholders."

[32]When the 1954 Code was drafted, Section numbers were intentionally omitted. This omission provided flexibility to incorporate later changes into the Code without disrupting its organization. When Congress does not leave enough space, subsequent Code Sections are given A, B, C, etc., designations. A good example is the treatment of §§ 280A through 280H.

Citing the Code

Code Sections often are broken down into subparts.[33] Section 2(a)(1)(A) serves as an example.

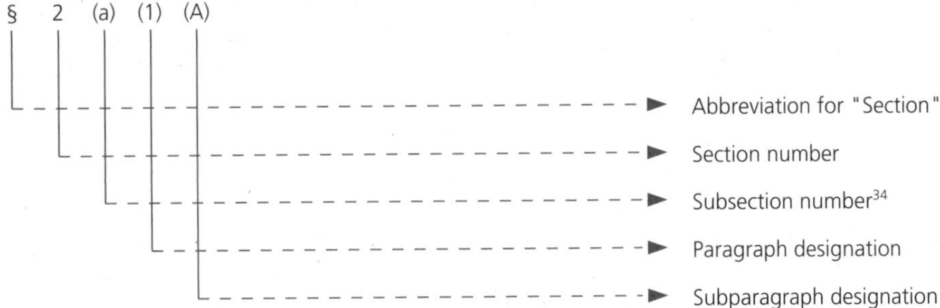
§ 2 (a) (1) (A)
Abbreviation for "Section"
Section number
Subsection number[34]
Paragraph designation
Subparagraph designation

Broken down as to content, § 2(a)(1)(A) becomes:

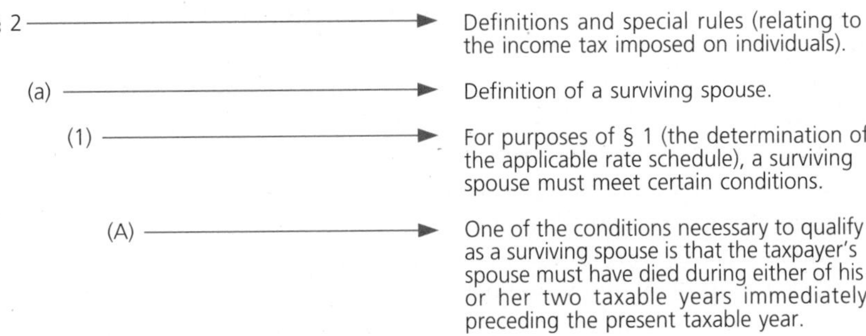
§ 2
Definitions and special rules (relating to the income tax imposed on individuals).
(a)
Definition of a surviving spouse.
(1)
For purposes of § 1 (the determination of the applicable rate schedule), a surviving spouse must meet certain conditions.
(A)
One of the conditions necessary to qualify as a surviving spouse is that the taxpayer's spouse must have died during either of his or her two taxable years immediately preceding the present taxable year.

Throughout this text, references to Code Sections are in the form just given. The symbols "§" and "§§" are used in place of "Section" and "Sections." Unless otherwise stated, all Code references are to the Internal Revenue Code of 1986. The format followed in the remainder of the text is summarized as follows:

Complete Reference	Text Reference
Section 2(a)(1)(A) of the Internal Revenue Code of 1986	§ 2(a)(1)(A)
Sections 1 and 2 of the Internal Revenue Code of 1986	§§ 1 and 2
Section 2 of the Internal Revenue Code of 1954	§ 2 of the Internal Revenue Code of 1954
Section 12(d) of the Internal Revenue Code of 1939[35]	§ 12(d) of the Internal Revenue Code of 1939

Administrative Sources of the Tax Law

The administrative sources of the Federal tax law can be grouped as follows: Treasury Department Regulations, Revenue Rulings and Procedures, and various other administrative pronouncements. All are issued by either the U.S. Treasury Department or the IRS. The role played by the IRS in this process is considered in greater depth in Chapter 17.

Treasury Department Regulations

Regulations are issued by the U.S. Treasury Department under authority granted by Congress. Interpretative by nature, they provide taxpayers with considerable guidance

[33] Some Code Sections do not have subparts. See, for example, § 482.

[34] Some Code Sections omit the subsection designation and use, instead, the paragraph designation as the first subpart. See, for example, §§ 212(1) and 1222(1).

[35] Section 12(d) of the Internal Revenue Code of 1939 is the predecessor to § 2 of the Internal Revenue Code of 1954. Keep in mind that the 1954 Code superseded the 1939 Code.

on the meaning and application of the Code. Although not issued by Congress, Regulations do carry considerable weight. They are an important factor to consider in complying with the tax law. Anyone taking a position contrary to a finalized Regulation must disclose that fact on Form 8275 or Form 8275–R to avoid costly penalties.

Because Regulations interpret the Code, they are arranged in the same sequence. Regulations are, however, prefixed by a number that indicates the type of tax or administrative, procedural, or definitional matter to which they relate. For example, the prefix 1 designates the Regulations under the income tax law. Thus, the Regulations under Code § 2 would be cited as Reg. § 1.2, with subparts added for further identification. The numbering of these subparts often has no correlation with the Code subsections. The prefix 20 designates estate tax Regulations; 25 covers gift tax Regulations; 31 relates to employment taxes; and 301 refers to Regulations dealing with procedure and administration. This listing is not all-inclusive.

New Regulations and changes in existing Regulations usually are issued in proposed form before they are finalized. The time interval between the proposal of a Regulation and its finalization permits taxpayers and other interested parties to comment on the propriety of the proposal. **Proposed Regulations** under Code § 2, for example, would be cited as Prop.Reg. § 1.2.

Sometimes the Treasury Department issues **Temporary Regulations** relating to elections and other matters where immediate guidance is critical. Temporary Regulations often are needed for recent legislation that takes effect immediately. Temporary Regulations have the same authoritative value as final Regulations and may be cited as precedent for three years. Temporary Regulations also are issued as Proposed Regulations and automatically expire within three years after the date of issuance. Temporary Regulations and the simultaneously issued Proposed Regulations carry more weight than traditional Proposed Regulations. An example of a Temporary Regulation is Temp. Reg. § 51.1T, which provides guidance on ACA branded prescription drug fees.

Proposed, final, and Temporary Regulations are published in the *Federal Register* (now online) and are reproduced in major tax services. Final Regulations are issued as Treasury Decisions (TDs).

Revenue Rulings and Revenue Procedures

Revenue Rulings are official pronouncements of the National Office of the IRS. Like Regulations, Revenue Rulings are designed to provide interpretation of the tax law. However, they do not carry the same legal force and effect as Regulations and usually deal with more restricted problems.

A Revenue Ruling often results from a specific taxpayer's request for a letter ruling (as discussed below). If the IRS believes that a taxpayer's request for a letter ruling deserves official publication due to its widespread impact, the holding will be converted into a Revenue Ruling. In making this conversion, names, identifying facts, and money amounts are changed to disguise the identity of the requesting taxpayer. The IRS then issues what would have been a letter ruling as a Revenue Ruling.

Revenue Procedures are issued in the same manner as Revenue Rulings, but deal with the internal management practices and procedures of the IRS. Familiarity with these procedures increases taxpayer compliance and helps make the administration of the tax laws more efficient. Revenue Procedures often involve mechanical rules, but sometimes substantive positions are embedded in them as well. Revenue Rulings and Revenue Procedures serve an important function in that they provide guidance to both IRS personnel and taxpayers in handling routine tax matters.

Both Revenue Rulings and Revenue Procedures are published weekly by the U.S. Government in the *Internal Revenue Bulletin* (I.R.B.). Semiannually, the bulletins for a six-month period are gathered together and published in a bound volume called the *Cumulative Bulletin* (C.B.).[36] The proper form for citing Rulings and

[36]Generally, only two volumes of the *Cumulative Bulletin* are published each year. The I.R.B.'s are available at **www.irs.gov**. Another excellent online source for finding the I.R.B.'s is Tax Almanac (**www.taxalmanac.org**).

Procedures depends on whether the item has been published in the *Cumulative Bulletin* or is available in I.R.B. form. Consider, for example, the following transition:

Temporary Citation	Rev.Rul. 2008–38, I.R.B. No. 31, 249. *Explanation:* Revenue Ruling Number 38, appearing on page 249 of the 31st weekly issue of the *Internal Revenue Bulletin* for 2008.
Permanent Citation	Rev.Rul. 2008–38, 2008–2 C.B. 249. *Explanation:* Revenue Ruling Number 38, appearing on page 249 of volume 2 of the *Cumulative Bulletin* for 2008.

Note that the page reference of 249 is the same for both the I.R.B. (temporary) and the C.B. (permanent) versions of the Ruling. The IRS numbers the pages of the I.R.B.'s consecutively for each six-month period to facilitate their conversion to C.B. form.

Because of the 1999 change making the I.R.B. and C.B. page numbers the same, there is little difference between the temporary and permanent citations. Thus, there is little incentive for the Government Printing Office to stay current on the C.B.s.

Revenue Procedures are cited in the same manner, except that "Rev.Proc." is substituted for "Rev.Rul." Procedures, like Rulings, are published in the *Internal Revenue Bulletin* (the temporary source) and later transferred to the *Cumulative Bulletin* (the permanent source).

Other Administrative Pronouncements

Treasury Decisions (TDs) are issued by the Treasury Department to promulgate new Regulations, to amend or otherwise change existing Regulations, or to announce the position of the Government on selected court decisions. Like Revenue Rulings and Revenue Procedures, TDs are published in the *Internal Revenue Bulletin* and subsequently transferred to the *Cumulative Bulletin.*

Technical Information Releases (TIRs) are usually issued to announce the publication of various IRS pronouncements (e.g., Revenue Rulings, Revenue Procedures).

Letter rulings are issued for a fee by the National Office of the IRS upon a taxpayer's request and describe how the IRS will treat a proposed transaction for tax purposes. In general, they apply only to the taxpayer who asks for and obtains the ruling, but post-1984 rulings may be substantial authority for purposes of avoiding the accuracy-related penalties.[37] Although this procedure may sound like the only real way to carry out effective tax planning, the IRS limits the issuance of letter rulings to restricted, preannounced areas of taxation. Thus, a ruling may not be obtained on many of the problems that are particularly troublesome for taxpayers.[38] For example, the IRS will not issue a ruling as to whether compensation paid to shareholder-employees is reasonable (see Chapter 5) or whether § 269 applies (the acquisition of a corporation to evade or avoid income tax [see Chapter 7]). The main reason the IRS will not rule on such matters is that they involve fact-oriented situations.

The IRS must make letter rulings available for public inspection after identifying details are deleted. Published digests of private letter rulings can be found in *Private Letter Rulings* (published by Research Institute of America), BNA *Daily Tax Reports*, and Tax Analysts *Tax Notes.* In addition, computerized databases of letter rulings are available through several private publishers.

Around 2,000 letter rulings are issued annually. In contrast, Revenue Rulings have declined from a high of 128 in 2003 to 40 in 2009.

The National Office of the IRS releases technical advice memoranda (TAMs) weekly. TAMs resemble letter rulings in that they give the IRS's determination of an issue. Letter rulings, however, are responses to requests by taxpayers, whereas TAMs are issued by the National Office of the IRS in response to questions raised by taxpayers or IRS field personnel during audits. TAMs deal with completed

[37]Notice 90–20, 1990–1 C.B. 328, part V (A).

[38]Rev.Proc. 2012–3, I.R.B. No. 1, 114, contains a list of areas in which the IRS will not issue advance rulings. From time to time, subsequent Revenue Procedures are issued that modify or amplify Rev.Proc. 2012–3.

rather than proposed transactions and are often requested for questions relating to exempt organizations and employee plans. Post-1984 TAMs may be substantial authority for purposes of the accuracy-related penalties. See Chapter 17 for a discussion of these penalties.

Both letter rulings and TAMs are issued with multidigit file numbers. Consider, for example, Ltr.Rul. 201125030, which provides information about bonus depreciation. Broken down by digits, the file number reveals the following information:

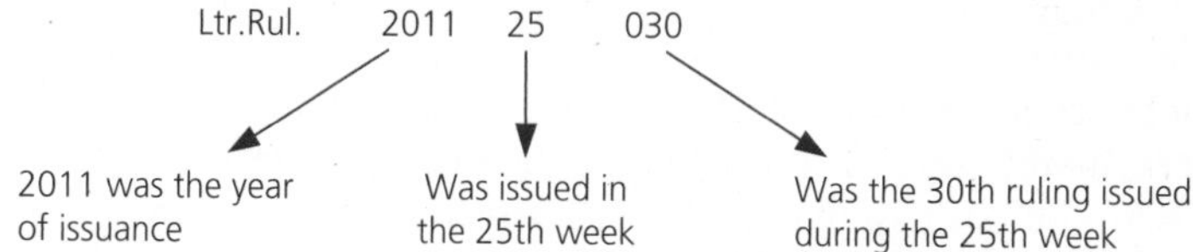

Letter rulings and TAMs issued before 2000 are often cited with only two-digit years (e.g., Ltr.Rul. 9933108).

Like letter rulings, **determination letters** are issued at the request of taxpayers and provide guidance concerning the application of the tax law. They differ from individual rulings in that the issuing source is the Area Director rather than the National Office of the IRS. Also, determination letters usually involve completed (as opposed to proposed) transactions. Determination letters are not published and are made known only to the party making the request.

The following examples illustrate the distinction between individual rulings and determination letters:

EXAMPLE 17

The shareholders of Black Corporation and White Corporation want assurance that the consolidation of the corporations into Gray Corporation will be a nontaxable reorganization (see Chapter 7). The proper approach is to request from the National Office of the IRS an individual ruling concerning the income tax effect of the proposed transaction. ■

EXAMPLE 18

Gilbert operates a barbershop in which he employs eight barbers. To comply with the rules governing income tax and payroll tax withholdings, Gilbert wants to know whether the barbers working for him are employees or independent contractors. The proper procedure is to request a determination letter on the status of the barbers from the Area Director in Holtsville, New York, or Newport, Vermont, depending on the location of the requesting firm. ■

Judicial Sources of the Tax Law

The Judicial Process in General

After a taxpayer has exhausted some or all of the remedies available within the IRS (no satisfactory settlement has been reached at the agent or at the conference level discussed in Chapter 17), the dispute can be taken to the Federal courts. The dispute is first considered by a court of original jurisdiction (known as a trial court) with any appeal (either by the taxpayer or the IRS) taken to the appropriate appellate court. In most situations, the taxpayer has a choice of any of four trial courts: a Federal District Court, the U.S. Court of Federal Claims, the Tax Court, or the Small Cases Division of the Tax Court. The trial and appellate court system for Federal tax litigation is illustrated in Figure 1.1.

The broken line between the Tax Court and the Small Cases Division indicates that there is no appeal from the Small Cases Division. Currently, the jurisdiction of the Small Cases Division of the Tax Court is limited to $50,000 or less. The proceedings of the Small Cases Division are informal, and its decisions are not precedents for any other court decision and are not reviewable by any higher court. Proceedings can be more timely and less expensive in the Small Cases Division. Some of these cases can now be found on the U.S. Tax Court Internet site.

FIGURE 1.1 **Federal Judicial Tax Process**

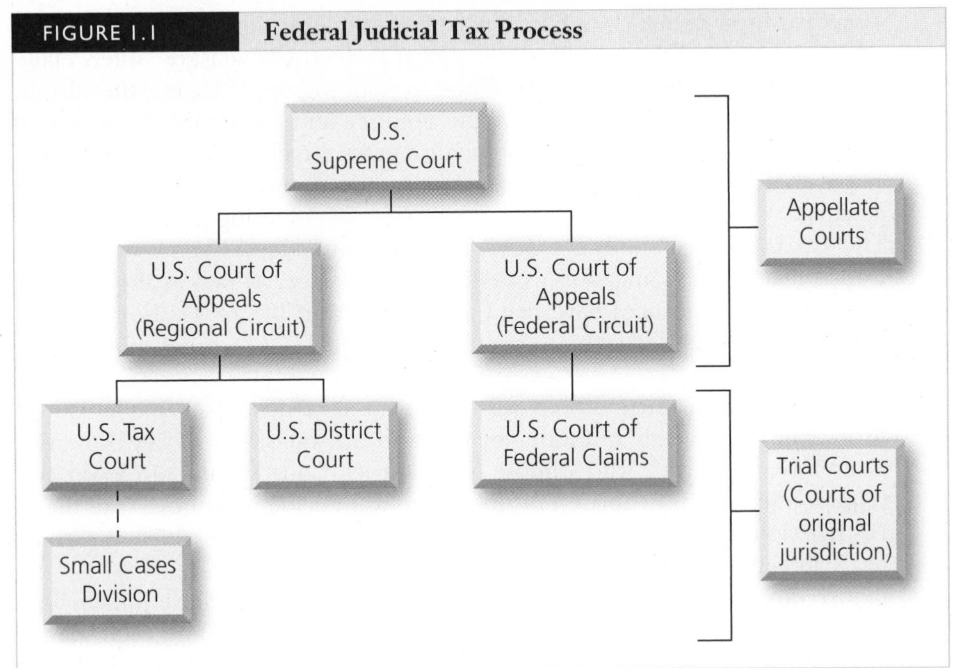

American law, following English law, is frequently *made* by judicial decisions. Under the doctrine of *stare decisis*, each case (except in the Small Cases Division) has precedential value for future cases with the same controlling set of facts.

Judges are not required to follow judicial precedent beyond their own jurisdiction. For example, the decisions of an appellate court are binding only on the trial courts within its jurisdiction and not on other trial courts. Different appellate courts may reach different opinions about the same issue. Further, the doctrine of precedential authority requires a court to follow prior cases only when the issues and material facts of the current case are essentially the same as those involved in the prior decisions.

Most Federal and state appellate court decisions and some decisions of trial courts are published. Published court decisions are organized by jurisdiction (Federal or state) and level of court (appellate or trial).

Trial Courts

The differences between the various trial courts (courts of original jurisdiction) can be summarized as follows:

- There is only one Court of Federal Claims and only one Tax Court, but there are many Federal District Courts. The taxpayer does not select the District Court that will hear the dispute, but must sue in the one that has jurisdiction.
- The U.S. Court of Federal Claims has jurisdiction over any claim against the United States that is based on the Constitution, any Act of Congress, or any regulation of an executive department.
- Each of the 94 District Courts has only one judge, the Court of Federal Claims has 16 judges, and the Tax Court has 19 regular judges. In the case of the Tax Court, the whole court will review a case (the case is sent to court conference) only when more important or novel tax issues are involved. Many cases will be heard and decided by one of the 19 regular judges. If a case is reviewed by the full Tax Court, such an *en banc* decision has compelling authority.
- The Court of Federal Claims meets most often in Washington, D.C., while a District Court meets at a prescribed seat for the particular district. Because each state has at least one District Court and many of the populous states have

more, the inconvenience and expense of traveling for the taxpayer and counsel (present with many suits in the Court of Federal Claims) are largely eliminated. The Tax Court is officially based in Washington, D.C., but the various judges travel to different parts of the country and hear cases at predetermined locations and dates. This procedure eases the distance problem for the taxpayer, but it can mean a delay before the case comes to trial and is decided.

- The Tax Court hears only tax cases; the Court of Federal Claims and District Courts hear nontax litigation as well. This difference, as well as the fact that many Tax Court justices have been appointed from IRS or Treasury Department positions, has led some to conclude that the Tax Court has more expertise in tax matters.
- The only court in which a taxpayer can obtain a jury trial is a District Court. Juries can decide only questions of fact and not questions of law, however. Therefore, taxpayers who choose the District Court route often do not request a jury trial. In this event, the judge will decide all issues. Note that a District Court decision is controlling only in the district in which the court has jurisdiction.
- Before the Court of Federal Claims or a District Court can have jurisdiction, the taxpayer must pay the tax deficiency assessed by the IRS and then sue for a refund. If the taxpayer wins (assuming no successful appeal by the IRS), the tax paid plus appropriate interest will be recovered. Jurisdiction in the Tax Court, however, is usually obtained without first paying the assessed tax deficiency. In the event the taxpayer loses in the Tax Court (and no appeal is taken or any appeal is unsuccessful), the deficiency must be paid with accrued interest.
- Appeals from a District Court or a Tax Court decision are to the appropriate U.S. Court of Appeals. Appeals from the Court of Federal Claims go to the Court of Appeals for the Federal Circuit.
- Special trial judges hear small tax cases and write summary opinions. The IRS's deficiency recovery rate is higher here than in regular Tax Court decisions. Beginning in 2001, these summary opinions are posted on the U.S. Tax Court's Internet site; regular decisions have been posted there since 1995.
- Because there are "gray areas" in the tax laws, courts may disagree as to the proper tax treatment of a dispute. With these splits in judicial authority, a taxpayer may have some flexibility to "forum shop"—choose the most favorable route to bring a lawsuit.

Some of the characteristics of the judicial system just described are summarized in Concept Summary 1.1.

Appellate Courts

An appeal from a trial court goes to the U.S. Court of Appeals of appropriate jurisdiction. Generally, a three-judge panel hears a Court of Appeals case, but occasionally the *full* court will decide more controversial conflicts. A jury trial is not available.

Figure 1.2 shows the geographic area within the jurisdiction of each Federal Court of Appeals.

If the IRS loses at the trial court level (District Court, Tax Court, or Court of Federal Claims), it need not (and frequently does not) appeal. The fact that an appeal is not made, however, does not indicate that the IRS agrees with the result and will not litigate similar issues in the future.

The IRS may decide not to appeal for a number of reasons. First, the current litigation load may be heavy. As a consequence, the IRS may decide that available personnel should be assigned to other more important cases. Second, the IRS may determine that this is not a good case to appeal. For example, the taxpayer may be in a sympathetic position or the facts may be particularly strong in his or her favor.

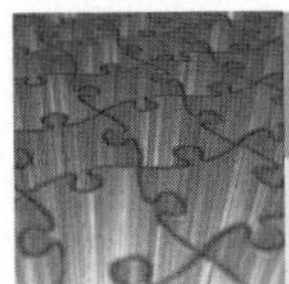

CONCEPT SUMMARY 1.1

Federal Judicial System

Issue	U.S. Tax Court	U.S. District Court	U.S. Court of Federal Claims
Number of judges per court	19*	1	16
Payment of deficiency before trial	No	Yes	Yes
Jury trial available	No	Yes	No
Types of disputes	Tax cases only	Most criminal/civil cases	Claims against the United States
Jurisdiction	Nationwide	Location of taxpayer	Nationwide
Appeal route	U.S. Court of Appeals	U.S. Court of Appeals	U.S. Court of Appeals for the Federal Circuit

*There are also 14 special trial judges and 9 senior judges.

In such event, the IRS may wait to test the legal issues involved with a taxpayer who has a much weaker case. Third, if the appeal is from a District Court or the Tax Court, the Court of Appeals of jurisdiction could have some bearing on whether the IRS decides to pursue an appeal. Based on past experience and precedent, the IRS may conclude that the chance for success on a particular issue might be more promising in another Court of Appeals. The IRS will wait for a similar case to arise in a different jurisdiction.

District Courts, the Tax Court, and the Court of Federal Claims must abide by the precedents set by the Court of Appeals of jurisdiction. A particular Court of Appeals need not follow the decisions of another Court of Appeals. All courts, however, must follow the decisions of the U.S. Supreme Court.

The role of appellate courts is limited to a review of the trial record compiled by the trial courts. Thus, the appellate process usually involves a determination of whether the trial court applied the proper law in arriving at its decision. Usually, an appellate court will not dispute a lower court's fact-finding determination.

An appeal can have any of a number of possible outcomes. The appellate court may approve (affirm) or disapprove (reverse) the lower court's finding, and it also may send the case back for further consideration (remand). When many issues are involved, it is not unusual to encounter a mixed result. Thus, the lower court may be affirmed (*aff'd*) on Issue A and reversed (*rev'd*) on Issue B, while Issue C is remanded (*rem'd*) for additional fact finding.

When more than one judge is involved in the decision-making process, disagreement is not uncommon. In addition to the majority view, one or more judges may concur (agree with the result reached but not with some or all of the reasoning) or dissent (disagree with the result). In any one case, the majority view controls. But concurring and dissenting views can have influence on other courts or, at some subsequent date when the composition of the court has changed, even on the same court.

Appealing from the Tax Court The Tax Court is a national court, meaning that it hears and decides cases from all parts of the country. For many years, the Tax Court followed a policy of deciding cases based on what it thought the result should be, even when its decision might be appealed to a Court of Appeals that had previously decided a similar case differently.

Some years ago this policy was changed. Now the Tax Court will still decide a case as it believes the law should be applied *only* if the Court of Appeals of appropriate jurisdiction has not yet ruled on the issue or has previously decided a similar case in accordance with the Tax Court's decision. If the Court of Appeals of

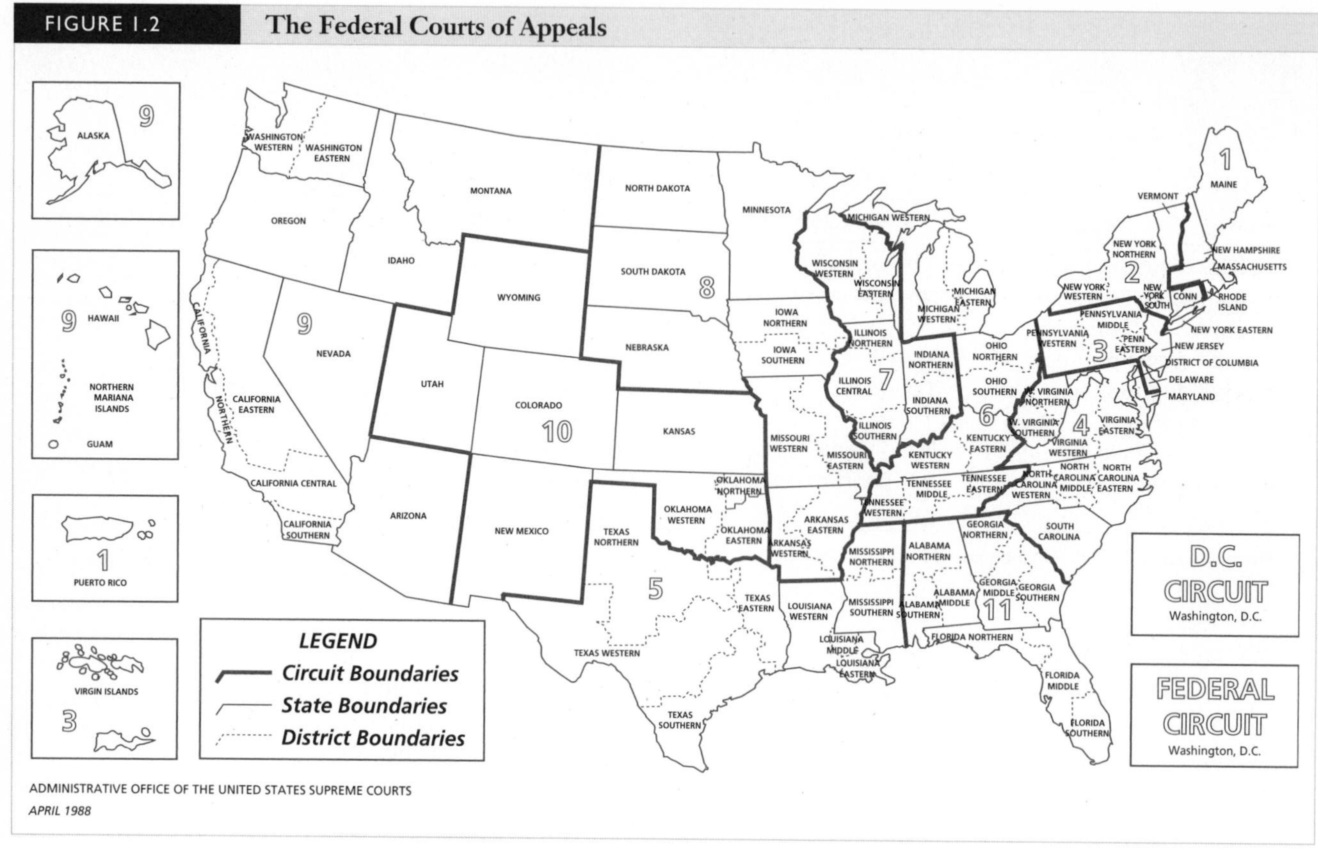

FIGURE 1.2 The Federal Courts of Appeals

appropriate jurisdiction has previously held squarely on point otherwise, the Tax Court will conform even though it disagrees with the holding.[39] This policy is known as the *Golsen* rule.

EXAMPLE 19

Gene lives in Texas and sues in the Tax Court on Issue A. The Fifth Circuit Court of Appeals, the appellate court of appropriate jurisdiction, has already decided, in a case involving similar facts but a different taxpayer, that Issue A should be resolved against the IRS. Although the Tax Court believes that the Fifth Circuit Court of Appeals is wrong, under the *Golsen* rule, it will render judgment for Gene. Shortly thereafter, Beth, a resident of New York, in a comparable case, sues in the Tax Court on Issue A. Assume that the Second Circuit Court of Appeals, the appellate court of appropriate jurisdiction, has never expressed itself on Issue A. Presuming that the Tax Court has not reconsidered its position on Issue A, it will decide against Beth. Thus, it is entirely possible for two taxpayers suing in the same court to end up with opposite results merely because they live in different parts of the country. ■

Appeal to the U.S. Supreme Court Appeal to the U.S. Supreme Court is by Writ of **Certiorari**. If the Court agrees to hear the case, it will grant the Writ (*cert. granted*). Most often it will deny jurisdiction (*cert. denied*). For whatever reason or reasons, the Supreme Court rarely hears tax cases. The Court usually grants certiorari when it must resolve a conflict among the Courts of Appeals (e.g., two or more appellate courts have assumed opposing positions on a particular issue) or when the tax issue is extremely important. The granting of a Writ of Certiorari indicates that at least four members of the Supreme Court believe that the issue is of sufficient importance to be heard by the full Court.

[39] *Jack E. Golsen*, 54 T.C. 742 (1970); see also *John A. Lardas*, 99 T.C. 490 (1992).

Judicial Citations

Having briefly described the judicial process, it is appropriate to consider the more practical problem of the relationship of case law to tax research. As previously noted, court decisions are an important source of tax law. Therefore, the ability to cite a case and to locate it is a must in working with the tax law. The usual pattern for a judicial citation is as follows: case name, volume number, reporter series, page or paragraph number, and court (where necessary).

Judicial Citations—The U.S. Tax Court A good starting point is the U.S. Tax Court. The Tax Court issues three types of decisions: Regular decisions, Memorandum decisions, and summary opinions. They differ in both substance and form. In terms of substance, Memorandum decisions deal with situations necessitating only the application of already established principles of law. Regular decisions involve novel issues not previously resolved by the Tax Court. In actual practice, this distinction is not always preserved. Not infrequently, Memorandum decisions will be encountered that appear to warrant Regular status and vice versa. At any rate, do not conclude that Memorandum decisions possess no value as precedents. Both Memorandum and Regular decisions represent the position of the Tax Court and, as such, can be relied upon. Summary opinions, on the other hand, are issued in small tax cases and may not be used as precedent in any other case.

Regular decisions are published by the U.S. Government in a series called *Tax Court of the United States Reports* (T.C.). Each volume of these reports covers a six-month period (January 1 through June 30 and July 1 through December 31) and is given a succeeding volume number. But there is usually a time lag between the date a decision is rendered and the date it appears in bound form. A temporary citation may be necessary to help the researcher locate a recent Regular decision. Consider, for example, the temporary and permanent citations for *Michael C. Winter*, a decision filed on August 25, 2010:

Temporary Citation	*Michael C. Winter*, 135 T.C. ___, No. 12 (2010). *Explanation:* Page number left blank because not yet known.
Permanent Citation	*Michael C. Winter*, 135 T.C. 238 (2010). *Explanation:* Page number now available.

Both citations tell us that the case ultimately will appear in Volume 135 of the *Tax Court of the United States Reports*. But until this volume is bound and made available to the general public, the page number must be left blank. Instead, the temporary citation identifies the case as being the 12th Regular decision issued by the Tax Court since Volume 134 ended. With this information, the decision can be easily located in either of the special Tax Court services published by Commerce Clearing House (CCH) and by Research Institute of America (RIA—formerly by Prentice Hall [PH]). Once Volume 135 is released, the permanent citation can be substituted and the number of the case dropped. Starting in 1995, both Regular and Memorandum decisions are issued on the U.S. Tax Court website (**www.ustaxcourt.gov**).

Before 1943, the Tax Court was called the Board of Tax Appeals and its decisions were published as the *United States Board of Tax Appeals Reports* (B.T.A.). These 47 volumes cover the period from 1924 to 1942. For example, the citation *Karl Pauli*, 11 B.T.A. 784 (1928) refers to the 11th volume of the *Board of Tax Appeals Reports*, page 784, issued in 1928.

Memorandum decisions are published by CCH and by RIA. Consider for example, the three different ways *Nick R. Hughes* can be cited:

Nick R. Hughes, T.C.Memo. 2009–94
The 94th Memorandum decision issued by the Tax Court in 2009.

Nick R. Hughes, 97 TCM 1488
Page 1488 of Vol. 97 of the CCH *Tax Court Memorandum Decisions.*

Nick R. Hughes, 2009 RIA T.C. Memo. ¶2009,094
Paragraph 2009,094 of the RIA *T.C. Memorandum Decisions.*

Note that the third citation contains the same information as the first. Thus, ¶2009,094 indicates the following information about the case: year 2009, 94th T.C. Memo. decision. Before the Prentice Hall Service division was incorporated into the Research Institute of America, "PH" was used in the third citation instead of "RIA."[40]

Summary opinions may not be treated as precedent, but they are cited as in the following example for *Christopher P. Johnson*, filed on August 15, 2011:

Christopher P. Johnson, T.C. Summary Opinion 2011–100.

Starting in 2001, summary opinions are reported on the U.S. Tax Court website.

Judicial Citations—The U.S. District Courts, Claims Court, and Courts of Appeals District Court, Claims Court (now Court of Federal Claims), Court of Appeals, and Supreme Court decisions dealing with Federal tax matters are reported in both the CCH *U.S. Tax Cases* (USTC) and the RIA *American Federal Tax Reports* (AFTR) series.

Federal District Court decisions, dealing with *both* tax and nontax issues, are also published by West (owned by Thomson Reuters) in its *Federal Supplement* (F.Supp.) series. The following examples illustrate how a District Court case can be cited in three different forms:

Turner v. U.S., 2004–1 USTC ¶60,478 (D.Ct. Tex., 2004).
Explanation: Reported in the first volume of the *U.S. Tax Cases* published by Commerce Clearing House for calendar year 2004 (2004–1) and located at paragraph 60,478 (¶ 60,478).

Turner v. U.S., 93 AFTR 2d 2004–686 (D.Ct. Tex., 2004).
Explanation: Reported in the 93rd volume of the second series of the *American Federal Tax Reports* (AFTR 2d) published by RIA and beginning on page 686.

Turner v. U.S., 306 F.Supp.2d 668 (D.Ct. Tex., 2004).
Explanation: Reported in the 306th volume of the second series of the *Federal Supplement* (F.Supp.2d) published by West and beginning on page 668.

In all of the preceding citations, note that the name of the case is the same (Turner being the taxpayer), as is the reference to the Federal District Court of Texas (D.Ct. Tex.) and the year the decision was rendered (2004).[41]

Beginning in October 1982, decisions of the Claims Court are reported by West in a series designated *Federal Claims Reporter.* Thus, the Claims Court decision in *Recchie v. U.S.* appears as follows:

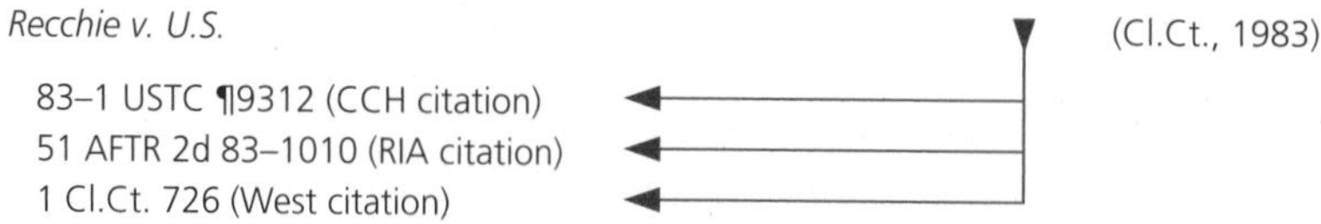

Beginning on October 30, 1992, the Claims Court underwent a further name change. The new designation, U.S. Court of Federal Claims, began with Volume 27 of the former Cl.Ct. (West citation), now abbreviated as Fed.Cl.

[40]In this text, the Research Institute of America (RIA) citation for Memorandum decisions of the U.S. Tax Court is omitted. Thus, *Nick R. Hughes* will be cited as 97 TCM 1488, T.C.Memo. 2009–94.

[41]In the text, the case will be cited in the following form: *Turner v. U.S.*, 2004–1 USTC ¶60,478, 93 AFTR 2d 2004–686, 306 F.Supp.2d 668 (D.Ct. Tex., 2004).

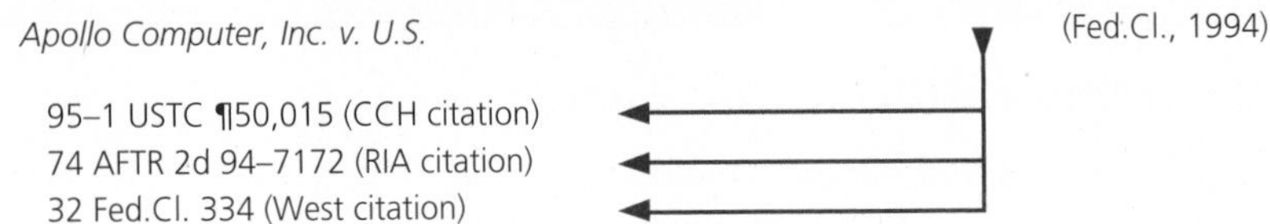

Decisions of the Courts of Appeals are published in a West reporter designated as the *Federal Third* (F.3d) series, which began in October 1993, at the conclusion of the *Federal Second* (F.2d) series. Illustrations of the different forms follow:

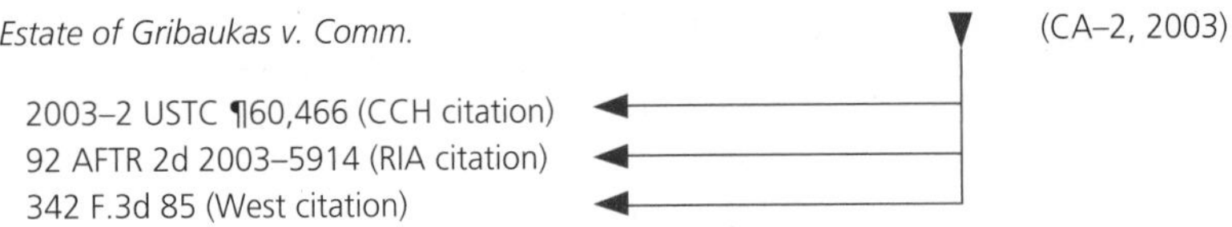

Note that *Estate of Gribaukas v. Comm.* is a decision rendered by the Second Circuit Court of Appeals in 2003 (CA–2, 2003).

If the IRS loses in a decision, it may indicate whether it agrees or disagrees with the results reached by the court by publishing an **acquiescence** ("A" or "*Acq.*") or **nonacquiescence** ("NA" or "*Nonacq.*"), respectively. The acquiescence or nonacquiescence is published in the *Internal Revenue Bulletin* and the *Cumulative Bulletin* as an *Action on Decision.* The IRS can retroactively revoke an acquiescence or nonacquiescence. Originally, acquiescences and nonacquiescences were published only for Regular U.S. Tax Court decisions, but since 1991, the IRS has expanded its acquiescence program to include other civil tax cases where guidance is helpful.

Judicial Citations—The U.S. Supreme Court Like all other Federal tax cases (except those rendered by the U.S. Tax Court), Supreme Court decisions are published by Commerce Clearing House in the USTCs and by Research Institute of America in the AFTRs. The U.S. Government Printing Office also publishes these decisions in the *United States Supreme Court Reports* (U.S.) as does West in its *Supreme Court Reporter* (S.Ct.) and the Lawyer's Co-operative Publishing Company in its *United States Reports, Lawyer's Edition* (L.Ed.). The following illustrates the different ways the same decision can be cited:

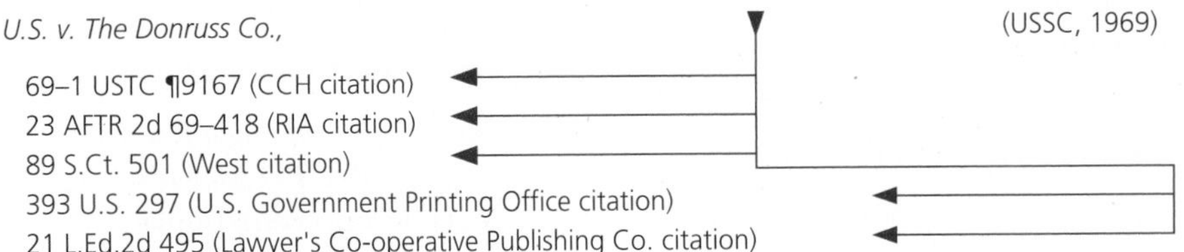

The parenthetical reference (USSC, 1969) identifies the decision as having been rendered by the U.S. Supreme Court in 1969. The citations given in this text for Supreme Court decisions will be limited to the CCH (USTC), the RIA (AFTR), and the West (S.Ct.) versions.

Other Sources of the Tax Law

Other sources of the tax law include tax treaties and tax periodicals.

Effect of Treaties

The United States signs certain tax treaties (sometimes called tax conventions) with foreign countries to render mutual assistance in tax enforcement and to avoid double taxation. The Technical and Miscellaneous Revenue Act of 1988 provided that neither a tax law nor a tax treaty takes general precedence. Thus, when there is a direct conflict between a treaty and the Code, the most recent item takes precedence. More than 34 Sections of the Code contain direct references to treaties [e.g., § 245(a)(10)].

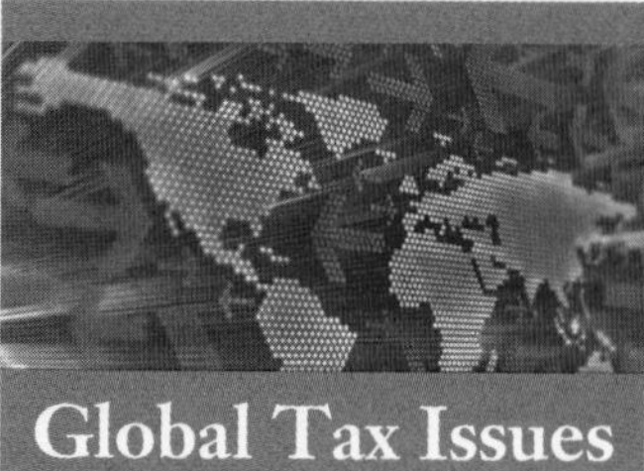

© Andrey Prokhorov, iStockphoto

Rolling Stones Gather Little Taxes

The Rolling Stones—Sir Mick Jagger, Charlie Watts, and Keith Richards—paid tax of only 1.6 percent on their earnings of approximately $455 million over the past 20 years. Not only did they use offshore trusts and companies to obtain tax breaks, but more importantly, they became tax exiles from Great Britain, moving to the Netherlands in 1972. There is no direct tax on royalties under Dutch law. Sir Mick Jagger's fortune is estimated to be approximately $385 million. International tax planning does help a poor soul.

Tax Periodicals

The use of tax periodicals can often shorten the research time needed to resolve a tax problem. If the article is relevant to the issue at hand, it may provide the references needed to locate the primary sources of the tax that apply (e.g., citations to judicial decisions, Regulations, and other IRS pronouncements). Thus, the researcher obtains a "running start" in arriving at a solution to the problem.

Among the many indexes available for locating tax articles are *Federal Tax Articles* (published by CCH) and *Index to Federal Tax Articles* (published by Warren, Gorham, and Lamont). These indexes are updated periodically but are available only in print form.

Following are some of the more useful tax periodicals with their online addresses (usually preceded by **http://**):

Journal of Taxation
Journal of International Taxation
Practical Tax Strategies
Estate Planning
Corporate Taxation
Business Entities
ria.thomsonreuters.com/journals

The Tax Executive
www.tei.org

The Tax Adviser
www.aicpa.org/pubs/taxadv

Journal of the American Taxation Association
aaahq.org/ata/_atamenu/atapubjata.html

The ATA Journal of Legal Tax Research
aaahq.org/ata/_atamenu/atapubjltr.html

Oil, Gas & Energy Quarterly
www.bus.lsu.edu/accounting/faculty/lcrumbley/oilgas.html

Trusts and Estates
trustsandestates.com

Journal of Passthrough Entities
TAXES—The Tax Magazine
tax.cchgroup.com/books

Tax Notes
www.taxanalysts.com

1.5 Working With the Tax Law—Locating and Using Tax Sources

LO.6

List and assess tax law sources.

Tax law consists of a body of legislative (e.g., Code Sections and tax treaties), administrative (e.g., Regulations and Rulings), and judicial (e.g., court cases) pronouncements. Working with the tax law, moreover, requires being able to locate and effectively use these sources. A key consideration is the time required to carry out this search and find activity.

FINANCIAL DISCLOSURE INSIGHTS Where Does GAAP Come From?

As this chapter has explained, the tax law has many sources, including Congress and the legislators of other countries, the courts, and the IRS. Similarly, accounting principles also have many sources. In reconciling the tax and financial accounting reporting of a transaction, the tax professional may need to know the hierarchy of authority of accounting principles so that the proper level of importance can be assigned to a specific GAAP document. The diagram shown below presents the sources of GAAP, listed in general order of authority, from highest to lowest.

Professional research is conducted to find and analyze the sources of accounting reporting standards in much the same way tax professionals conduct research into open tax questions. In fact, many of the publishers that provide tax research materials also can be used to find GAAP and IFRS documents. These include the Research Institute of America (RIA) and Commerce Clearing House (CCH). The Financial Accounting Standards Board (FASB) also makes its standards and interpretations available by subscription.

Highest Authority

- Financial Accounting Standards and Interpretations of the FASB.
- Pronouncements of bodies that preceded the FASB, such as the Accounting Principles Board (APB).

- FASB Technical Bulletins.
- Audit and Accounting Guides, prepared by the American Institute of CPAs (AICPA) and cleared by the FASB.
- Practice Bulletins, prepared by the AICPA and cleared by the FASB.

- Interpretation Guides of the FASB Staff.
- Accounting Interpretations of the AICPA.
- IASB Accounting Standards
- FASB Concepts Standards.
- Widely accepted accounting practices, professional journals, accounting textbooks, and treatises.

Unless the problem is simple (e.g., the Code Section is known and there is a Regulation on point), the research process will begin with a tax service.

Commercial Tax Services

Due to various changes, categorizing tax services has become an almost impossible task. The old classification of *annotated* (i.e., organized by Internal Revenue Code) or *topical* (i.e., organized by major topics) is no longer appropriate for many services as their format has been modified. Often the change is due to the acquisition of a competing service. For example, the *United States Tax Reporter* (annotated) now has a version containing the *Federal Tax Coordinator 2d* (topical).

In addition, services can no longer be distinguished based on whether they are available in hard copy or online versions. *Tax Management Portfolios*, for example, was previously solely a print publication. Now, like most other services, it is also accessible online.

The list of publishers producing the tax services has also changed. Not only have ownership changes occurred (e.g., Research Institute of America [RIA] now owns Prentice Hall [PH]), but new players have arrived. LexisNexis, for example, through *Tax Center*, now offers primary tax services such as the Code and Regulations as well as material obtained from the Matthew Bender and Kleinrock services. Due to the common ownership by Thomson Reuters, Westlaw offers the RIA products as well as the Mertens service.

Like automobiles, many new services are available in standard models or with extra features depending on the practitioner's needs and financial resources. Thus, a practitioner with minimal tax research needs can select an abbreviated version of the regular ("standard") service (e.g., CCH and its two-volume *Federal Tax Guide*), while another chooses a product with "extras" (e.g., CCH and its *Federal Excise Tax Reporter*).

A partial list of the available commercial services includes the following:

- *Standard Federal Tax Reporter*, Commerce Clearing House.
- *Tax Research NetWork*, Commerce Clearing House Internet service.
- *United States Tax Reporter*, Research Institute of America.
- *RIA Checkpoint*, Research Institute of America. This is the online version of *United States Tax Reporter* and may also include the *Federal Tax Coordinator*.
- ATX/Kleinrock *Tax Expert*, CCH/Wolters Kluwer Business Services.
- *Tax Management Portfolios*, Bureau of National Affairs.
- *Mertens Law of Federal Income Taxation*, West Group.
- Westlaw services—compilations include access to *Tax Management Portfolios*, *Federal Tax Coordinator 2d*, and *Mertens*.
- *Tax Center*, LexisNexis compilation of primary sources and various materials taken from CCH, Matthew Bender, Kleinrock, and Bureau of National Affairs.
- *Federal Research Library*, Tax Analysts (a nonprofit organization) databases dealing with explanations and commentaries on primary source materials.

Using Online Services

Instructions on how to use a tax service are not particularly worthwhile unless a specific service is involved. Even then, instructions need to be followed by hands-on experience. Following certain procedures, however, can simplify the process of using an online version of a tax service. Because a practitioner's time is valuable and various research services base usage charges on time spent, time is of the essence.

Given this emphasis on time, every shortcut helps. Some suggestions (most of which are familiar to any user of the Internet) follow.[42]

- Take care in choosing keywords for the search. Words with a broad usage, such as *income*, are worthless when standing alone. If the researcher is interested in qualified dividend income, even *dividend income* is too broad as it will call up a variety of subjects such as stock dividends, constructive dividends, and liquidating dividends. By using *qualified dividend income* at the outset, the search is considerably narrowed. In RIA *Checkpoint*, for example, these two modifications narrowed the search from 10,000 items to 3,824 and finally to 884. Obviously, further contraction will be needed, but at least the researcher is starting with a considerably narrower field.
- Take advantage of *connectors* to place parameters on the search and further restrict the output. Although each service has its own set of connectors, many are common as to usage. Thus, enclosing words in quotation marks (e.g., "personal service corporation") means "exact phrase" in both RIA *Checkpoint* and CCH *NetWork*.
- Be selective in choosing a database. For example, if the research project will not involve case law, there is no point in including judicial decisions in the search database. Doing so just adds to the output and will necessitate further screening through a search modification.
- Although the keyword approach is most frequently used, consider using the table of contents or index or searching by citation. The first two of these methods are the usual approach with print versions of a tax service. Citations may be used to search for statutory (e.g., Code Section), administrative (e.g., Rev.Rul.),

[42]For a more complete discussion of the use of RIA *Checkpoint* and CCH *Tax Research NetWork*, as well as Internet research in taxation in general, see William A. Raabe, Gerald E. Whittenburg, and Debra L. Sanders, *Federal Tax Research*, 9th ed. (Cincinnati, OH: South-Western Cengage Learning, 2011), Chapters 6 and 7.

EXHIBIT 1.1 **The IRS's Home Page**

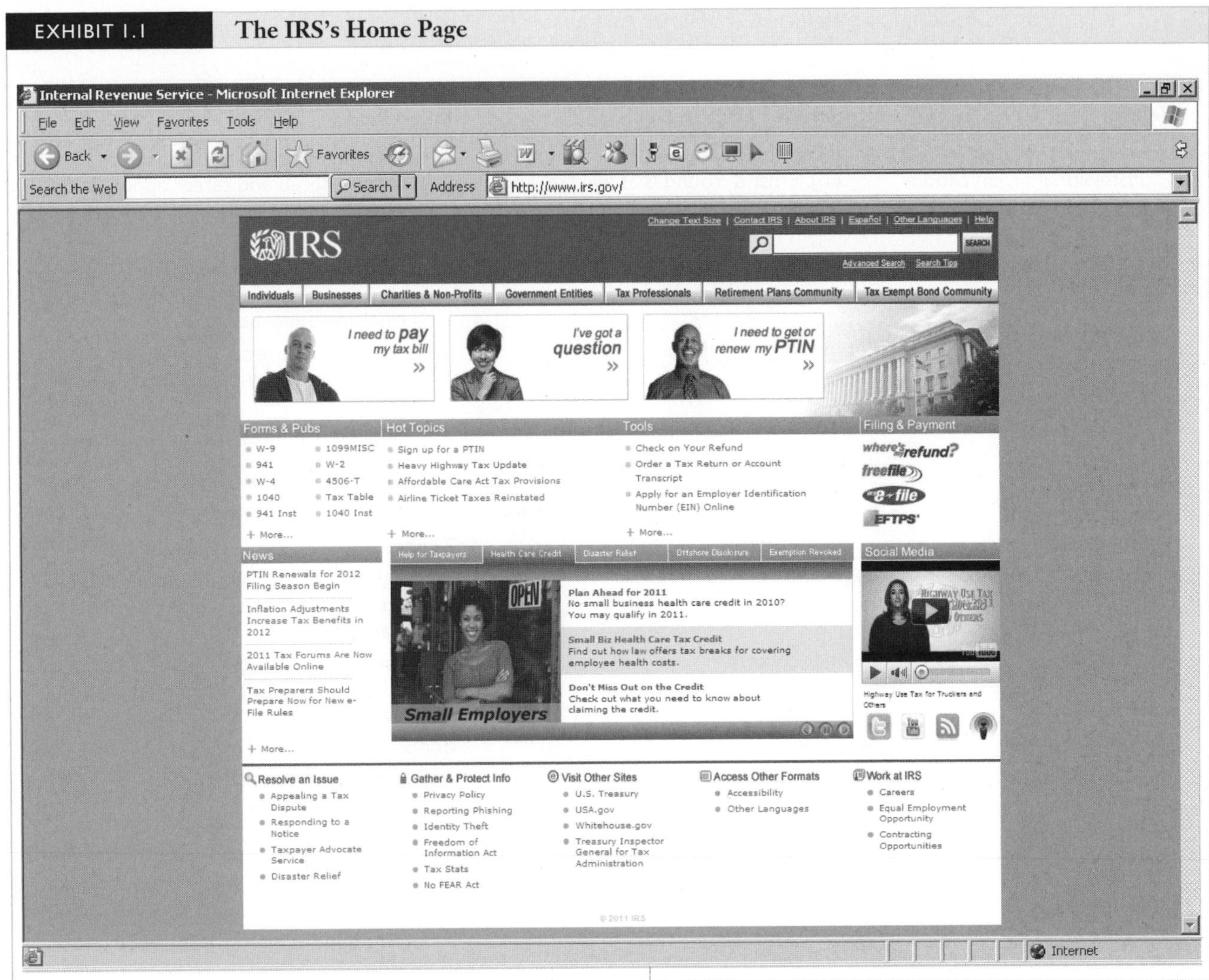

or judicial (e.g., Tax Court) sources depending on the service. When a judicial citation is wanted and only the taxpayer's last name is known, however, problems can arise. For example, how many responses would a taxpayer named Smith yield? Likewise, before a Code Section is used, consider its scope. How many items would § 162 retrieve? Nevertheless, the use of content, index, or citation can be a valuable time-saver under the right circumstances.

Noncommercial Online Sources

The Internet provides a wealth of tax information in several popular forms, sometimes at no direct cost to the researcher. Using so-called browser software that often is distributed with new computer systems and their communication devices, the tax professional can access information provided around the world that can aid the research process.

- *Home pages (sites) on the Web* are provided by accounting and consulting firms, publishers, tax academics and libraries, and governmental bodies as a means of making information widely available or of soliciting subscriptions or consulting engagements. The best sites offer links to other sites and direct contact to the site providers. One of the best sites available to the tax practitioner is the Internal Revenue Service's home page, illustrated in Exhibit 1.1. This site offers downloadable forms and instructions, "plain English" versions of Regulations, and news update items. Exhibit 1.2 lists some of the websites that

EXHIBIT 1.2 **Tax-Related Websites**

Website	WWW Address at Press Date (Usually preceded by http://www.)	Description
Accounting firms and professional organizations	For instance, the AICPA's page is at **aicpa .org**, Ernst & Young is at **ey.com**, and KPMG is at **kpmg.com**	Tax planning newsletters, descriptions of services offered and career opportunities, and exchange of data with clients and subscribers
Cengage Learning South-Western	**cengagebrain.com**	Informational updates, newsletters, support materials for students and adopters, and continuing education
Commercial tax publishers	For instance, **tax.com** and **cch.com**	Information about products and services available for subscription and newsletter excerpts
Court opinions	The site at **lexisone.com/lx1/caselaw/ freecaselaw** covers some state, Federal circuit (last 10 years), and Supreme Court (all years) decisions but not Tax Court	A synopsis of result reached by the court
Federal Register	**gpoaccess.gov/fr**	Releases from the IRS (e.g., Regulations)
Internal Revenue Service	**irs.gov**	News releases, downloadable forms and instructions, tables, Circular 230, and e-mail
Tax Analysts	**taxanalysts.com**	Policy-oriented readings on the tax law and proposals to change it and moderated bulletins on various tax subjects
Tax Foundation	**taxfoundation.org**	Nonprofit educational organization that promotes sound tax policy and measures tax burdens
Tax laws online	Regulations are at **law.cornell.edu/cfr** and the Code is at **uscode.house.gov/ search/criteria.shtml**	
Tax Sites Directory	**taxsites.com**	References and links to tax sites on the Internet, including state and Federal tax sites, academic and professional pages, tax forms, and software
U.S. Tax Court decisions	**ustaxcourt.gov**	Recent U.S. Tax Court decisions

Caution: Addresses change frequently.

may be most useful to tax researchers and the Internet addresses as of press date. Particularly useful is the directory at **http://taxsites.com**, which provides links to accounting and tax sources (includes international as well as payroll).

- *Newsgroups* provide a means by which information related to the tax law can be exchanged among taxpayers, tax professionals, and others who subscribe to the group's services. Newsgroup members can read the exchanges among other members and offer replies and suggestions to inquiries as desired. Discussions address the interpretation and application of existing law, analysis of proposals and new pronouncements, and reviews of tax software.

1.6 Working with the Tax Law—Tax Research

LO.7

Demonstrate tax research.

Tax research is the method used to determine the best available solution to a situation that possesses tax consequences. In other words, it is the process of finding a

FIGURE 1.3 **Tax Research Process**

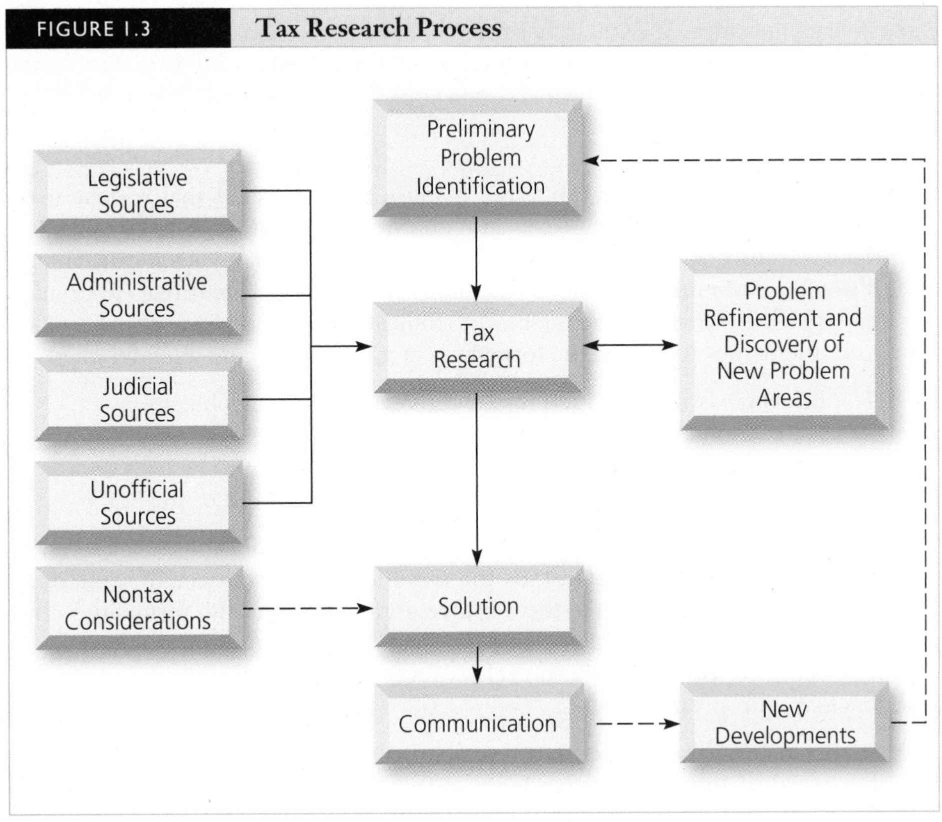

competent and professional conclusion to a tax problem. The problem may originate from either completed or proposed transactions. In the case of a completed transaction, the objective of the research is to determine the tax result of what has already taken place. For example, is the expenditure incurred by the taxpayer deductible or not deductible for tax purposes? When dealing with proposed transactions, the tax research process is concerned with the determination of possible alternative tax consequences. To the extent that tax research leads to a choice of alternatives or otherwise influences the future actions of the taxpayer, it becomes the key to effective tax planning.

Tax research involves the following procedures:

- Identifying and refining the problem.
- Locating the appropriate tax law sources.
- Assessing the validity of the tax law sources.
- Arriving at the solution or at alternative solutions while giving due consideration to nontax factors.
- Effectively communicating the solution to the taxpayer or the taxpayer's representative.
- Following up on the solution (where appropriate) in light of new developments.

This process is depicted schematically in Figure 1.3. The broken lines indicate steps of particular interest when tax research is directed toward proposed rather than completed transactions.

Identifying the Problem

Problem identification starts with a compilation of the relevant facts involved. In this regard, *all* of the facts that might have a bearing on the problem must be gathered as any omission could modify the solution reached. To illustrate, consider what appears to be a very simple problem.

EXAMPLE 20

Dana Pehrson advances $92,000 to her nephew in 2005 to enable him to attend a private college. Seven years later she claims a bad debt deduction for $77,000 that the nephew has not repaid. The problem: Is Dana entitled to a bad debt deduction? ■

Refining the Problem

Before a bad debt deduction can arise, it must be established that a debt really existed. In a related-party setting (e.g., aunt and nephew), the IRS may contend that the original advance was not a loan but was, in reality, a gift. Of key significance in this regard would be whether the lender (the aunt) had an honest and real expectation of payment by the borrower (the nephew).[43] Indicative of this repayment expectation is whether the parties preserved the formalities of a loan, including the following:

- The borrower issued a written instrument evidencing the obligation.
- The loan arrangement provided for interest.
- The note specified a set due date.
- Collateral was available to the lender in the event of default by the borrower.[44]

The presence of some or all of these formalities does not, however, guarantee that a bona fide loan will be found. By the same token, the absence of some or all of the formalities does not make the advance a gift. Applying the formalities criteria to Example 20 is not possible because key facts (e.g., the presence or absence of a written note) are not given. Nevertheless, several inferences might be made that lead to a loan interpretation:

- It appears that the nephew has repaid at least $15,000 of the $92,000 that he borrowed. If the parties intended a gift of the full amount of the loan, why was partial repayment made?
- Although one would not expect a nephew on his way to college to have assets to serve as collateral for a loan, the fact that he was obtaining additional education could reinforce any expectation of repayment. In most situations, a person with a college education will possess a higher earning potential than one without such education. This education would improve the nephew's financial ability to repay the loan.

Further Refinement of the Problem

It may be impossible to determine with any degree of certainty whether the advance constitutes a loan or a gift. In either event, however, the tax consequences of each possibility must be ascertained.

If the advance is determined to be a gift, it is subject to the Federal gift tax.[45] Whether a gift tax results depends upon how much of the unified tax credit the aunt has available to absorb the gift tax on $81,000 [$92,000 (total gift) − $11,000 (annual exclusion in 2005)].[46] Whether the transfer results in a gift tax or not, it must be reported on Form 709 (United States Gift Tax Return) since the amount of the gift exceeds the annual exclusion.

Even if it is assumed that Dana made a gift to her nephew in 2005, does not the intervention of seven years preclude the IRS from assessing any gift tax that might be due as a result of the transfer?[47] Further research indicates that the statute of limitations on assessments does not begin to run when a tax return is not filed.[48]

[43] *William F. Mercil*, 24 T.C. 1150 (1955), and *Evans Clark*, 18 T.C. 780 (1952), *aff'd* 53–2 USTC ¶9452, 44 AFTR 70, 205 F.2d 353 (CA–2, 1953).

[44] *Arthur T. Davidson*, 37 TCM 725, T.C.Memo. 1978–167.

[45] The transfer does not come within the unlimited gift tax exclusion of § 2503(e)(2)(A) because the aunt did not pay the amount directly to an educational institution. Besides, the exclusion covers only tuition payments and not other costs attendant on going to college (e.g., room and board).

[46] The tax, in turn, depends upon the amount of taxable gifts the aunt has made in the past. For a discussion of the mechanics of the Federal gift tax, see Chapter 18.

[47] Throughout the discussion of Example 20, the assumption has been made that if a gift occurred, it took place in 2005. That assumption need not be the case. Depending upon the aunt's intent, she could have decided to make a gift of the unpaid balance anytime after the loan was made (e.g., 2006 or 2007).

[48] See § 6501(c)(3) and the discussion of the statute of limitations in Chapter 17.

To complete the picture, what are the tax consequences if the advance is treated as a loan? Aside from the bad debt deduction aspects (covered later in the chapter), the tax law provides more immediate tax ramifications:[49]

- If interest is not provided for, it is imputed with the following effect:
  a. The lender (the aunt) must recognize interest income as to the imputed value.
  b. Because the lender has not received the interest, she is deemed to have made a gift of the interest to the borrower.
  c. The borrower (nephew) may be entitled to deduct (as an itemized expense) in some tax years a portion of the amount of interest deemed paid to the lender (aunt).
- If interest is provided for but the rate is lower than market (as determined by the yield on certain U.S. government securities), the differential is treated as noted above.
- For gift loans of $100,000 or less, the imputed element cannot exceed the net investment income of the borrower.

Locating the Appropriate Tax Law Sources

Once the problem is clearly defined, what is the next step? Although the next step is a matter of individual judgment, most tax research begins with the index volume of a hard copy tax service or a keyword search on an online tax service (see the earlier discussion). If the problem is not complex, the researcher may bypass the tax service and turn directly to the Internal Revenue Code and the Treasury Regulations. For the beginner, this procedure saves time and will solve many of the more basic problems. If the researcher does not have a personal copy of the Code or Regulations, resorting to the appropriate volume(s) of a tax service may be necessary. Several of the major tax services publish paperback editions of the Code and Treasury Regulations that can be purchased at modest prices. These editions are usually revised twice each year.

Assessing the Validity of Tax Law Sources

LO.8

Assess the validity and weight of tax law sources.

After a source has been located, the next step is to assess the source in light of the problem at hand. Proper assessment involves careful interpretation of the tax law and consideration of the law's relevance and validity.

Interpreting the Internal Revenue Code

The language of the Code often is extremely difficult to comprehend. For example, a former subsection [§ 341(e)] relating to collapsible corporations contained *one* sentence of more than 450 words (twice as many as in the Gettysburg Address). Within this same subsection was another sentence of 300 words.

The Code must be read carefully for restrictive language such as "*at least* 80 percent" and "*more than* 80 percent" or "*less than* 50 percent" and "*exceeds* 50 percent." It also makes a great deal of difference, for example, whether two or more clauses are connected by *or* or by *and.*

If an answer is not in the Code, it may be necessary to resort to the Regulations and judicial decisions. In 1969, Congress directed the Treasury Department to promulgate Regulations under § 385 to distinguish corporate debt from corporate equity. As of yet, there are no Regulations under § 385. The researcher, therefore, must resort to past judicial decisions for a definition of debt.

Sometimes the Code directs the researcher elsewhere for the answer. For example, § 162(c) refers to the Foreign Corrupt Practices Act for purposes of determining when payments to foreign officials are deductible.

Cross-referencing between Code Sections is often poor or nonexistent. Code Sections are enacted at different times by Congresses that are operating under stringent deadlines. Consequently, a certain lack of integration within the Code is frequently apparent.

---

[49] § 7872.

Definitions vary from one Code Section to another. For example, § 267 disallows losses between related parties and includes brothers and sisters in the definition of related parties. Not so with § 318, which deals with the definition of related parties as to certain stock redemptions.

Assessing the Validity of a Treasury Regulation

Treasury Regulations are often said to have the force and effect of law. This statement is certainly true for most Regulations, but some judicial decisions have held a Regulation or a portion thereof invalid. Usually, this is done on the grounds that the Regulation is contrary to the intent of Congress.

Keep the following observations in mind when assessing the validity of a Regulation:

- In a challenge, the burden of proof is on the taxpayer to show that the Regulation is wrong. However, a court may invalidate a Regulation that varies from the language of the statute and has no support in the Committee Reports.
- If the taxpayer loses the challenge, the negligence penalty may be imposed. This accuracy-related provision deals with the "intentional disregard of rules and regulations" on the part of the taxpayer and is explained further in Chapter 17.
- Some Regulations merely reprint or rephrase what Congress has stated in its Committee Reports issued in connection with the enactment of tax legislation. Such Regulations are "hard and solid" and almost impossible to overturn because they clearly reflect the intent of Congress.
- In some Code Sections, Congress has given to the "Secretary or his delegate" the authority to prescribe Regulations to carry out the details of administration or to otherwise complete the operating rules. Under such circumstances, it could almost be said that Congress is delegating its legislative powers to the Treasury Department. The Congressional Research Service found that Congress delegated regulatory authority to the Treasury on more than 240 occasions from 1992 through 2000, an average of more than 26 delegations per year. Regulations issued pursuant to this type of authority truly possess the force and effect of law and are often called "legislative" Regulations. They are to be distinguished from "interpretative" Regulations, which purport to explain the meaning of a particular Code Section. Examples of legislative Regulations are those dealing with consolidated returns issued under §§ 1501 through 1505. As a further example, note the authority granted to the Treasury Department by § 385 to issue Regulations setting forth guidelines on when corporate debt can be reclassified as equity (see Chapter 4).

Assessing the Validity of Other Administrative Sources of the Tax Law

Revenue Rulings issued by the IRS carry less weight than Treasury Department Regulations. Rulings are important, however, in that they reflect the position of the IRS on tax matters. In any dispute with the IRS on the interpretation of tax law, taxpayers should expect agents to follow the results reached in any applicable rulings.

Actions on Decisions further tell the taxpayer the IRS's reaction to certain court decisions. Recall that the IRS follows a practice of either acquiescing (agreeing) or nonacquiescing (not agreeing) with court decisions where guidance may be helpful. This practice does not mean that a particular decision has no value if the IRS has nonacquiesced in the result. It does, however, indicate that the IRS will continue to litigate the issue involved.

The validity of individual letter rulings issued by the IRS is discussed in Chapter 17.

Assessing the Validity of Judicial Sources of the Tax Law

The judicial process as it relates to the formulation of tax law has been described. How much reliance can be placed on a particular decision depends upon the following variables:

- The level of the court. A decision rendered by a trial court (e.g., a Federal District Court) carries less weight than one issued by an appellate court (e.g., the Fifth Circuit Court of Appeals). Unless Congress changes the Code, decisions by the U.S. Supreme Court represent the last word on any tax issue.

- The legal residence of the taxpayer. If, for example, a taxpayer lives in Texas, a decision of the Fifth Circuit Court of Appeals means more than one rendered by the Second Circuit Court of Appeals. This is true because any appeal from a U.S. District Court or the U.S. Tax Court would be to the Fifth Circuit Court of Appeals, not to the Second Circuit Court of Appeals.
- Whether the decision represents the weight of authority on the issue. In other words, is it supported by the results reached by other courts?
- The outcome or status of the decision on appeal. For example, was the decision appealed and, if so, with what result?

In connection with the last two variables, the use of a manual citator or a computer search is invaluable to tax research. A citator provides the history of a case, including the authority relied on (e.g., other judicial decisions) in reaching the result. Reviewing the references listed in the citator discloses whether the decision was appealed and, if so, with what result (e.g., affirmed, reversed, or remanded). It also reveals other cases with the same or similar issues and explains how they were decided. Thus, a citator reflects on the validity of a case and may lead to other relevant judicial material.[50]

Assessing the Validity of Other Sources

Primary sources of tax law include the Constitution, legislative history materials, statutes, treaties, Treasury Regulations, IRS pronouncements, and judicial decisions. The IRS regards only primary sources as substantial authority. However, reference to secondary materials such as legal periodicals, treatises, legal opinions, general counsel memoranda, technical advice memoranda, and written determinations can be useful. In general, secondary sources are not authority.

Although the statement that the IRS regards only primary sources as substantial authority is generally true, there is one exception. For purposes of the accuracy-related penalty in § 6662, the IRS has expanded the list of substantial authority to include a number of secondary materials (e.g., letter rulings, general counsel and technical advice memoranda, and the "Blue Book").[51] The "Blue Book" is the general explanation of tax legislation prepared by the Joint Committee on Taxation of the U.S. Congress.

As under former § 6661, "authority" does not include conclusions reached in treatises, legal periodicals, and opinions rendered by tax professionals.

Arriving at the Solution or at Alternative Solutions

Returning to Example 20, assume that the parties decide that the loan approach can be justified from the factual situation involved. Does this assumption lead to a bad debt deduction for the aunt? Before this question can be resolved, the loan needs to be classified as either a business or nonbusiness debt. One of the reasons the classification is important is that a nonbusiness bad debt cannot be deducted until it becomes entirely worthless. Unlike a business debt, no deduction for partial worthlessness is allowed.[52]

It is very likely that the loan the aunt made in 2005 falls into the nonbusiness category. Unless exceptional circumstances exist (e.g., the lender was in the trade or business of lending money), loans in a related-party setting are treated as nonbusiness. The probability is high that the aunt would be relegated to nonbusiness bad debt status.

The aunt has the burden of proving that the remaining unpaid balance of $77,000 is *entirely* worthless.[53] In this connection, what collection effort, if any, has the aunt made? But would any such collection effort be fruitless? Perhaps the nephew is insolvent, ill or unemployed, or has departed for parts unknown.

Even if the debt is entirely worthless, one further issue remains to be resolved. In what year did the worthlessness occur? It could be, for example, that worthlessness took place in a year before it was claimed.[54]

---

[50]The major manual citators are published by Commerce Clearing House; RIA; and Shepard's Citations, Inc. The CCH and RIA versions are available online through the CCH *Network* service and RIA's *Checkpoint*, respectively. Shepard's Internet version is part of LexisNexis.

[51]Notice 90–20, 1990–1 C.B. 328, part V (A).

[52]See § 166 and the discussion of investor losses in Chapter 4.

[53]Compare *John K. Sexton*, 48 TCM 512, T.C.Memo. 1984–360, with *Stewart T. Oatman*, 45 TCM 214, T.C.Memo. 1982–684.

[54]*Ruth Wertheim Smith*, 34 TCM 1474, T.C.Memo. 1975–339.

FIGURE 1.4 Client Letter

Hoffman, Raabe, Smith, & Maloney, CPAs
5191 Natorp Boulevard
Mason, OH 45040

August 25, 2012

Dana Pehrson
111 Avenue G
Lakeway, OH 45232

Dear Ms. Pehrson:

This letter is in response to your question with respect to your $92,000 advance to your nephew in 2005. I need the following additional information:

1. Is there a written instrument evidencing this obligation, and is an interest rate specified?
2. When and how much has your nephew paid on the loan?
3. What factors exist to indicate whether the remaining debt will be repaid (for example, does he live within his means)?
4. Does he have a job?
5. Does he owe money to other people?
6. What is his credit rating?
7. How much credit card debt does he have?
8. What collection efforts, if any, have you made to collect the remaining $77,000?

Any other information or material you can provide would be greatly appreciated.

Sincerely,

James Hicks, CPA
Partner

A clear-cut answer may not be possible as to a bad debt deduction for the aunt in year 2012 (seven years after the advance was made). This uncertainty does not detract from the value of the research. Often a guarded judgment is the best possible solution to a tax problem.

Communicating Tax Research

Once the problem has been researched adequately, a memo, letter, or spoken presentation setting forth the result may be required. The form such a communication takes could depend on a number of considerations. For example, is any particular procedure or format for communicating tax research recommended by either an employer or an instructor? Are the research results to be given directly to the client, or will they first pass to the preparer's employer? If an oral presentation is required, who will be the audience? How long should you talk?[55] Whatever form it takes, a good tax research communication should contain the following elements:

- A clear statement of the issue.
- In more complex situations, a short review of the factual pattern that raises the issue.
- A review of the pertinent tax law sources (e.g., Code, Regulations, rulings, and judicial authority).
- Any assumptions made in arriving at the solution.
- The solution recommended and the logic or reasoning in its support.
- The references consulted in the research process.

Figures 1.4, 1.5, and 1.6 present a sample client letter and memoranda for the tax files.

[55]For more on crafting oral presentations, see W. A. Raabe and G. E. Whittenburg, "Talking Tax: How to Make a Tax Presentation," *Tax Adviser*, March 1997, pp. 179–182.

FIGURE 1.5 **Tax File Memorandum**

August 18, 2012

TAX FILE MEMORANDUM

FROM: James Hicks

SUBJECT: Dana Pehrson
Engagement Issues

Today I talked to Dana Pehrson with regard to her letter of August 14, 2012.

Dana Pehrson advanced $92,000 to her nephew in 2005 to enable him to attend a private college. Seven years later she claims a bad debt deduction for $77,000 that the nephew has not repaid.

ISSUE: Is Dana entitled to a bad debt deduction?

FIGURE 1.6 **Tax File Memorandum**

August 26, 2012

TAX FILE MEMORANDUM

FROM: James Hicks

SUBJECT: Dana Pehrson

Tentative Conclusions

The initial advance could have been a gift rather than a loan and possibly subject to the gift tax. In any case, if the advance was a gift, it should have been reported on Form 709. Further, the statute of limitations does not begin to run when a tax return is not filed.

If the advance is treated as a loan, the probability is high that the aunt would receive nonbusiness bad debt status. This classification means that Ms. Pehrson has the burden of proving that the $77,000 unpaid balance is entirely worthless.

1.7 Working with the Tax Law—Tax Planning

LO.9

Describe various tax planning procedures.

Tax research and tax planning are inseparable. The main purpose of effective tax planning is to reduce the taxpayer's total tax bill. This reduction does not mean that the course of action selected must produce the lowest possible tax under the circumstances. The minimization of tax payments must be considered in the context of the legitimate business goals of the taxpayer.

Nontax Considerations

There is a danger that tax motivations may take on a significance that does not conform to the true values involved. In other words, tax considerations can operate to impair the exercise of sound business judgment. Thus, the tax planning process can lead to ends that are socially and economically objectionable. Unfortunately, a tendency exists for planning to move toward the opposing extremes of either not enough or too much emphasis on tax considerations. The happy medium is a balance that recognizes the significance of taxes, but not beyond the point at which planning detracts from the exercise of good business judgment.

The remark is often made that a good rule to follow is to refrain from pursuing any course of action that would not be followed were it not for certain tax considerations. This statement is not entirely correct, but it does illustrate the desirability of preventing business logic from being "sacrificed at the altar of tax planning."

TAX IN THE NEWS Tax Avoidance and Tax Evasion

There is a fine line between legal tax planning and illegal tax planning—**tax avoidance** versus **tax evasion**. Although both aim to eliminate or reduce taxes, tax evasion implies the use of subterfuge and fraud as a means to this end. The IRS believes that through tax evasion, taxpayers shortchanged the government by a staggering $345 billion in a recent year. This gross tax gap is the annual difference between Federal taxes owed and those timely paid.

Tax avoidance, however, is merely tax minimization through legal techniques. In this sense, tax avoidance becomes the proper objective of all tax planning. Perhaps because common goals are involved, popular usage has blurred the distinction between tax avoidance and tax evasion. Consequently, the association of the two concepts has kept some taxpayers from properly taking advantage of planning possibilities. The now-classic words of Judge Learned Hand in *Commissioner v. Newman** reflect the true values a taxpayer should have:

> Over and over again courts have said that there is nothing sinister in so arranging one's affairs as to keep taxes as low as possible. Everybody does so, rich or poor; and all do right, for nobody owes any public duty to pay more than the law demands: taxes are enforced extractions, not voluntary contributions. To demand more in the name of morals is mere cant.

*47-1 USTC ¶9175, 35 AFTR 857, 159 F.2d 848 (CA-2, 1947).

Components of Tax Planning

Popular perception of tax planning often is restricted to the adage "defer income and accelerate deductions." Although this timing approach does hold true and is important, meaningful tax planning involves considerably more.

Preferable to deferring income is complete *avoidance.* Consider, for example, the corporate employee who chooses nontaxable fringe benefits over a fully taxable future pay increase.[56] Complete avoidance of gain recognition also occurs when the owner of appreciated property transfers it by death. Presuming a step-up in basis occurs, the built-in appreciation forever escapes the income tax.[57]

If the recognition of income cannot be avoided, its deferral will postpone income tax consequences. A tax paid in the future costs less than a tax paid today because of the time value of money. *Deferral* of income can take many forms. Besides like-kind exchanges and involuntary conversions, most retirement plans put off income tax consequences until the payout period. Deferral of gain recognition also can occur when appreciated property is transferred to a newly formed corporation or partnership.[58]

A corollary to the deferral of income is the acceleration of deductions. For example, an accrual basis, calendar year corporation wants an additional charitable deduction for 2012 but has a cash-flow problem. If the corporation authorizes the contribution in 2012 and pays it on or before March 15, 2013, the deduction can be claimed for 2012.[59] Taxes can be saved by *shifting* income to lower-bracket taxpayers. Gifts of appreciated property to lower-bracket family members can reduce the applicable capital gain rate on a later sale by 15 percentage points (from 15 percent to 0 percent).[60]

If income cannot be avoided, deferred, or shifted, the nature of the gain can be *converted.* By changing the classification of property, income taxes can be reduced. Thus, the taxpayer who transfers appreciated inventory to a controlled corporation has converted ordinary income property to a capital asset. When the stock is later sold, preferential capital gain rates apply.[61]

The conversion approach also can work in tax planning for losses. Properly structured, a loan to a corporation that becomes worthless can be an ordinary loss rather than the less desirable capital loss. Likewise, planning with § 1244 permits

[56] See Example 10 in Chapter 13.
[57] See Example 19 in Chapter 19.
[58] See Example 1 in Chapter 4 and Example 4 in Chapter 10.
[59] See Example 17 in Chapter 2.
[60] See Example 32 in Chapter 19.
[61] See Concept Summary 13.1 in Chapter 13.

an investor in qualified small business stock to convert what would be a capital loss into an ordinary loss.[62]

Effective tax planning requires that careful consideration be given to the *choice of entity* used for conducting a business. The corporate form results in double taxation but permits shareholder-employees to be covered by fringe benefit programs. Partnerships and S corporations allow a pass-through of losses and other tax attributes, but transferring ownership interests as gifts to family members may be difficult.[63]

Although the substance of a transaction rather than its form generally controls, this rule is not always the case with tax planning. *Preserving formalities* often is crucial to the result. Is an advance to a corporation a loan or a contribution to capital? The answer may well depend on the existence of a note. Along with preserving formalities, the taxpayer should keep records that support a transaction. Returning to the issue of loan versus contribution to capital, how is the advance listed on the books of the borrower? What do the corporate minutes say about the advance?

Finally, effective tax planning requires *consistency* on the part of taxpayers. A shareholder who treats a corporate distribution as a return of capital cannot later avoid a stock basis adjustment by contending that the distribution was really a dividend.

In summary, the key components of tax planning include the following:

- *Avoid* the recognition of income (usually by resorting to a nontaxable source or nontaxable event).
- *Defer* the recognition of income (or accelerate deductions).
- *Convert* the classification of income (or deductions) to a more advantageous form (e.g., ordinary income into capital gain).
- *Choose* the business *entity* with the desired tax attributes.
- Preserve *formalities* by generating and maintaining supporting documentation.
- Act in a manner *consistent* with the intended objective.

Tax Planning—A Practical Application

Returning to the facts in Example 20, what should be done to help protect the aunt's bad debt deduction?

- All formalities of a loan should be present (e.g., written instrument and definite and realistic due date).
- Upon default, the lender (aunt) should make a reasonable effort to collect from the borrower (nephew). If not, the aunt should be in a position to explain why any such effort would be to no avail.
- If interest is provided for, it should be paid.
- Any interest paid (or imputed under § 7872) should be recognized as income by the aunt.
- Because of the annual exclusion of $11,000 in 2005 (now $13,000), it appears doubtful that actual (or imputed) interest would necessitate the filing of a Federal gift tax return by the aunt. But should one be due, it should be filed.
- If § 7872 applies (not enough or no interest is provided for), the nephew should keep track of his net investment income. This record keeping is important because the income the aunt must recognize may be limited by this amount.

In terms of the components of tax planning (see prior discussion beginning on p. 1-42), what do these suggestions entail? Note the emphasis on the formalities—written instrument and definite and realistic due date. Also, much is done to provide the needed documentation—gift tax returns, if necessary, are filed, and the nephew keeps track of his investment income. Most important, however, is that the aunt will have been *consistent* in her actions—recognizing actual (or imputed) interest income and making a reasonable effort to collect on the loan.

[62]See Examples 30 and 31 in Chapter 4.

[63]See Examples 46 and 47 in Chapter 11 and Example 43 in Chapter 12

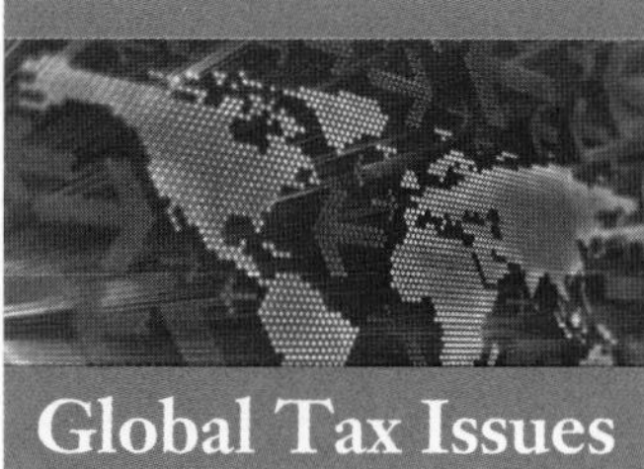

© Andrey Prokhorov, iStockphoto

Australia Holds Crocodile Dundee Hostage for Tax Sham

Actor Paul Hogan, star of the *Crocodile Dundee* movies, went to Australia to attend his 101-year-old mother's funeral. While he was there, the Australian Taxation Office served him with a departure-prohibition order that stranded him Down Under.

The Australian Taxation Office accused Hogan of misrepresenting his tax residency status to the United States and Australia between 2002 and 2005 to dodge taxes. The result was a $34 million tax deficiency.

The Golden Globe–winning actor and his tax adviser, Tony Stewart, allegedly engaged in a "scheme or conspiracy" to allow money to be paid to Hogan when he "was not a tax resident of any country and therefore the payment was free of tax." So an actor may avoid the strong jaws of a crocodile, but cannot escape the strong arms of international tax laws. Does Hogan owe the U.S. government any taxes?

The five-year investigation of Hogan was stopped in November 2009, and the actor is suing the Australian government for $80 million for damaging his reputation. The government spent $10 million pursuing him for alleged tax evasion.

Source: Adapted from "Stranded Actor Paul Hogan in Australia Tax Deal," Yahoo! News, September 3, 2010; D. Snow and E. Sexton, "Crime Body Suspects Hogan of Travel Sham," **www.theage.com.au**, August 22, 2008; Chis Seage, "Who's Who to Be Summoned in Hogan's Lawsuit." Crikey, January 19, 2011, **www.crikey.com.au/2011/01/19/who%e2%80%99s-who-to-be-summonsed-in-hoges-lawsuit**.

Throughout this text, each chapter concludes with observations on Tax Planning. Such observations are not all-inclusive but are intended to illustrate some of the ways in which the material in the chapter can be effectively used to minimize taxes.

Follow-Up Procedures

Tax planning usually involves a proposed (as opposed to a completed) transaction and is based upon the continuing validity of the advice resulting from tax research. A change in the tax law (legislative, administrative, or judicial) could alter the original conclusion. Additional research may be necessary to test the solution in light of current developments.

Under what circumstances does a tax practitioner have an obligation to inform a client as to changes in the tax law? The legal and ethical aspects of this question are discussed in Chapter 17.

1.8 Taxation on the CPA Examination

LO.10

Explain the role of taxation on the CPA examination.

The CPA examination has changed from a paper-and-pencil exam to a computer-based exam with increased emphasis on information technology and general business knowledge. The 14-hour exam has four sections, and taxation is included in the 3-hour Regulation section.

As of January 1, 2011, the CPA examination has been reorganized, with all written communication tasks now concentrated in the Business Environment & Concepts section. Shorter simulations are replacing the longer simulations.

Each exam section includes multiple-choice questions, and the Regulation section and two other sections also have short task-based simulation (TBS) questions. The Regulation section is 60 percent Taxation and 40 percent Law & Professional Responsibilities (all areas other than Business Structure). The Regulation section has a new format:

- Three multiple-choice question (MCQ) testlets consisting of 72 questions.
- One testlet containing six short, task-based simulations with the research question in a new format.

A candidate may review and change answers within each testlet but cannot go back after exiting a testlet. Candidates take different but equivalent exams.

Simulations are small case studies designed to test a candidate's tax knowledge and skills using real-life work-related situations. Simulations include a four-function pop-up calculator, a blank spreadsheet with some elementary functionality, and authoritative literature appropriate to the subject matter. The taxation database includes authoritative excerpts (e.g., Internal Revenue Code and Regulations, IRS publications, and Federal tax forms) that are necessary to complete the tax case study simulations. Examples of the simulations follow.

EXAMPLE 21

The *tax citation type* simulation requires the candidate to research the Internal Revenue Code and enter a Code Section and subsection. For example, Amber Company is considering using the simplified dollar-value method of pricing its inventory for purposes of the LIFO method that is available to certain small businesses. What Code Section is the relevant authority in the Internal Revenue Code to which you should turn to determine whether the taxpayer is eligible to use this method? To be successful, the candidate needs to find § 474. ■

EXAMPLE 22

A *tax form completion* simulation requires the candidate to fill out a portion of a tax form. For example, Blue Company is a limited liability company (LLC) for tax purposes. Complete the income section of the 2011 IRS Form 1065 for Blue Company using the values found and calculated on previous tabs along with the following data:

Ordinary income from other partnerships	$ 5,200
Net gain (loss) from Form 4797	2,400
Management fee income	12,000

The candidate is provided with page 1 of Form 1065 on which to record the appropriate amounts. Any field that requires an entry is a shaded rectangular cell. Some white rectangular cells automatically calculate based on the entries in the shaded cell. ■

Candidates can learn more about the CPA examination at **www.cpa-exam.org**. This online tutorial site's topics include the following:

- Common tools.
- Navigation.
- Forms completion.
- Numeric entry.
- Research questions.
- Authoritative literature search.
- Written communication.

The common tools are a calculator, a spreadsheet, reminder flags, and an examination clock. A 30- to 60-minute sample examination will familiarize a candidate with the type of questions on the exam.

KEY TERMS

Acquiescence, 1-29
Arm's length concept, 1-13
Business purpose concept, 1-14
Certiorari, 1-26
Continuity of interest concept, 1-13
Determination letters, 1-22
Generally Accepted Accounting Principles (GAAP), 1-15
Indexation, 1-9
International Financial Reporting Standards (IFRS), 1-15
Letter rulings, 1-21
Nonacquiescence, 1-29
Proposed Regulations, 1-20
Revenue neutrality, 1-1
Revenue Procedures, 1-20
Revenue Rulings, 1-20
Tax avoidence, 1-42
Tax benefit rule, 1-14
Tax evasion, 1-42
Temporary Regulations, 1-20
Wherewithal to pay, 1-6

DISCUSSION QUESTIONS

1. **LO.1** What is meant by *revenue neutrality?*
2. **LO.2** In terms of asset acquisitions, what tax provisions can Congress use to control the economy?
3. **LO.2** List some tax provisions that encourage particular industries.
4. **LO.2** What economic objective is encouraged by favorable tax treatment of research and development expenditures?
5. **LO.2** List three tax provisions that can be justified by social considerations.
6. **LO.2** What purpose is served by the nontaxability to an employee of some of the premiums paid by an employer for group term life insurance covering the life of the employee?
7. **LO.2** What is the justification for the tax treatment to an employee of contributions made by an employer to qualified pension plans?
8. **LO.2** The concept of equity is relative. Explain.
9. **LO.2** Give an example where the concept of equity may explain a provision in the tax law.
10. **LO.2** Does a deduction for New York state and local taxes on the Federal income tax return neutralize the effect of multiple taxation? Explain.
11. **LO.2** What is the justification for the Federal tax treatment of certain income from foreign sources?
12. **LO.2** If a person is subject to both a sales tax and state income tax, what are his or her choices for Federal income tax purposes?

Issue ID

13. **LO.2** A provision of the Code allows a taxpayer a deduction for Federal income tax purposes for state and local income taxes paid. Does this provision eliminate the effect of multiple taxation of the same income? Why or why not? In this connection, consider the following:
    a. Taxpayer, an individual, has itemized deductions that are less than the standard deduction.
    b. Taxpayer is in the 10% tax bracket for Federal income tax purposes. The 33% tax bracket.
14. **LO.2** Heather and her partners operate a profitable partnership. Because the business is expanding, the partners would like to transfer it to a newly created corporation. Heather is concerned, however, over the possible tax consequences that would result from incorporating. Please comment.

Issue ID

15. **LO.2** Assume the same facts as in Question 14. Heather is also worried that once the partnership incorporates, the business will be subject to the Federal corporate income tax. What suggestions do you have?
16. **LO.2** Give some examples of the wherewithal to pay concept.
17. **LO.2** Can recognized gain exceed the realized gain? Explain.
18. **LO.2** In a like-kind exchange, recognized gain is postponed and not avoided. Explain.
19. **LO.2** Under the annual accounting period concept, what time period is normally selected for final settlement of most tax liabilities?
20. **LO.2** How does the installment method overcome the harsh treatment of the annual accounting treatment concept?
21. **LO.2** Why is there a grace period for contributions to a Keogh retirement plan?
22. **LO.2** What is "bracket creep"?
23. **LO.2** List the community property states.
24. **LO.2** Contrast the tax treatment between a community property state and a common law state.

25. **LO.2** List some tax provisions used to deter affluent taxpayers from obtaining preferential tax treatment.

26. **LO.3** How does the $13,000 annual gift tax exclusion help the IRS?

27. **LO.4** Explain the continuity of interest concept.

28. **LO.3** Yellow Corporation lends $235,000 to Red Corporation with no provision for interest. Yellow Corporation and Red Corporation are owned by the same shareholders. How might the IRS restructure this transaction with adverse tax consequences? **Issue ID**

29. **LO.5** Did Congress recodify the Internal Revenue Code in 1986? Explain.

30. **LO.5** Federal tax legislation generally originates in the Senate Finance Committee. Comment on the validity of this statement.

31. **LO.5** If a tax bill is vetoed by the President, the provisions cannot become law. Evaluate this statement.

32. **LO.5** In what subtitle are the Internal Revenue Code Sections located?

33. **LO.5** Determine the subparts of § 1411(a)(2)(A).

34. **LO.5** Is § 1221(1) a proper Code Section citation? Why or why not?

35. **LO.5** Why are certain Code Section numbers missing from the Internal Revenue Code (e.g., §§ 6, 7, 8, 9, 10)?

36. **LO.6** Where can a researcher find newly issued Proposed, final, and Temporary Regulations?

37. **LO.6** Interpret each of the following citations:
    a. Temp.Reg. § 1.428–7T(b)(4).
    b. Rev.Rul. 60–11, 1960–1 C.B. 174.
    c. TAM 8837003.

38. **LO.5** Sammy Young calls you requesting an explanation of the fact-finding determination of a Federal Court of Appeals. Prepare a letter to be sent to Sammy answering this query. His address is 1072 Richmond Lane, Acton, MA 01720. **Communications**

39. **LO.5** Cody Pappas calls you with respect to a tax issue. He has found a tax case in the U.S. District Court of South Carolina that is in favor of his position. The IRS lost and did not appeal the case. Over the phone, you explain to Cody the significance of the failure to appeal. Prepare a tax file memorandum outlining your remarks to Cody. **Communications**

40. **LO.5, 8** In assessing the validity of a court decision, discuss the significance of the following:
    a. The decision was rendered by the U.S. District Court of Wyoming. Taxpayer lives in Wyoming.
    b. The decision was rendered by the U.S. Court of Federal Claims. Taxpayer lives in Wyoming.
    c. The decision was rendered by the Second Circuit Court of Appeals. Taxpayer lives in California.
    d. The decision was rendered by the U.S. Supreme Court.
    e. The decision was rendered by the U.S. Tax Court. The IRS has acquiesced in the result.
    f. Same as (e) except that the IRS has issued a nonacquiescence as to the result.

41. **LO.5** Referring to the citations only, determine which court issued these decisions.
    a. *U.S. v. Gilmore*, 372 U.S. 39 (1963).
    b. *Pope v. USPS*, 114 F.3d 1144 (CA–DC, 1997).
    c. *Claymont Investment, Inc.*, T.C. Memo. 2005–254.
    d. *Zaninovich v. U.S.*, 616 F.2d 429 (CA–9, 1980).
    e. *David E. Watson PC*, 714 F. Supp. 2d. 954 (D.Ct. Iowa, 2010).
    f. Ltr.Rul. 200905001.

42. **LO.6** Jack Rogers needs to learn quickly about partial liquidations. How should Jack approach his research? **Decision Making**

43. **LO.8** Determine whether the following items are primary sources or secondary sources for the purpose of substantial authority.
   a. Revenue Ruling.
   b. Article written by a judge in *Tax Notes.*
   c. U.S. Tax Court decision.
   d. The "Blue Book."
   e. A general counsel memorandum.

44. **LO.9** What are the key components of effective tax planning?

PROBLEMS

45. **LO.4** Thelma owns some real estate (basis of $120,000 and fair market value of $65,000) that she would like to sell to her son, Sandy, for $65,000. Thelma is aware, however, that losses on sales between certain related parties are disallowed for Federal income tax purposes [§ 267(a)(1)]. Thelma therefore sells the property to Paul (an unrelated party) for $65,000. The next day Paul sells the property to Sandy for the same amount. Is Thelma's realized loss of $55,000 deductible? Explain.

46. **LO.2** Bart exchanges some real estate (basis of $800,000 and fair market value of $1 million) for other real estate owned by Roland (basis of $1.2 million and fair market value of $900,000) and $100,000 in cash. The real estate involved is unimproved and is held by Bart and Roland, before and after the exchange, as investment property.
   a. What is Bart's realized gain on the exchange? Recognized gain?
   b. What is Roland's realized loss? Recognized loss?
   c. Support your results to (a) and (b) under the wherewithal to pay concept as applied to like-kind exchanges (§ 1031).

47. **LO.2, 3** Using the legend provided, classify the overall objective of the particular tax provision.

Legend	
CE = Control of the economy	W = Wherewithal to pay concept
EA = Encouragement of certain activities	AF = Administrative feasibility
EI = Encouragement of certain industries	ESB = Encouragement of small business
SC = Social considerations	

   a. Like-kind exchange treatment.
   b. An increase in the individual tax rate.
   c. The S corporation election.
   d. Adoption expense credit.
   e. Percentage depletion.
   f. Unified estate tax credit.
   g. Charitable contribution deduction.

48. **LO.2** Determine whether the following states are community property or common law states:
   a. Texas.
   b. Georgia.
   c. New Mexico.
   d. New York.
   e. Alaska.
   f. Nevada.

49. **LO.4** Roy sells property (basis of $30,000) to Beige Corporation for $60,000. Based on the following conditions, how could the IRS challenge this transaction?
   a. Roy is the sole shareholder of Beige Corporation.
   b. Roy is the son of the sole shareholder of Beige Corporation.
   c. Roy is neither a shareholder in Beige Corporation nor related to any of Beige's shareholders.

50. **LO.5** Answer the following questions:
    a. What are letter rulings?
    b. What are technical advice memoranda (TAMs)?

51. **LO.5** Explain what is meant by the following citations:
    a. Rev.Proc. 2001–10, 2001–1 C.B. 272.
    b. Rev.Rul. 93–86, 1993–2 C.B. 71.
    c. Notice 2001–76, 2001–2 C.B. 613.

52. **LO.6** Using the legend provided, classify each of the following citations as to the location. A citation may have more than one answer.

Legend	
IRC = Internal Revenue Code	FR = *Federal Register*
IRB = *Internal Revenue Bulletin*	NA = Not applicable
CB = *Cumulative Bulletin*	

    a. Rev.Rul. 93–86, 1993–2 C.B. 71.
    b. § 351.
    c. *Jack E. Golsen*, 54 T.C. 742 (1970).
    d. TD 9229.
    e. Reg. § 1.401–1(b).
    f. Ltr.Rul. 9015014.
    g. Temp.Reg. § 1.444–2T.

53. **LO.5** To which U.S. Court of Appeals would a person living in each of the following states appeal from the U.S. Tax Court?
    a. Louisiana.
    b. Utah.
    c. Alabama.
    d. Idaho.
    e. Vermont.

54. **LO.5** Using the legend provided, classify each of the following citations as to the court:

Legend	
T = U.S. Tax Court	D = U.S. District Court
C = U.S. Court of Federal Claims	A = U.S. Court of Appeals
U = U.S. Supreme Court	N = None of the above

    a. 2003–102, 2003–2 C.B. 559.
    b. 330 F.Supp. 2d 122 (D.Ct. Conn., 2004).
    c. 81 T.C. 782 (1983).
    d. 3 B.T.A. 1042 (1926).
    e. T.C.Memo 2001–144.
    f. 597 F.2d 760 (Ct.Cl., 1979).
    g. 281 U.S. 115 (1930).
    h. 753 F.2d 1490 (CA–9, 1985).

55. **LO.6** Locate the following tax services in your library and indicate the name of the publisher:
    a. *United States Tax Reporter.*
    b. *Standard Federal Tax Reporter.*
    c. *Federal Tax Coordinator 2d.*
    d. *Mertens Law of Federal Income Taxation.*
    e. *Tax Management Portfolios.*
    f. *CCH's Tax Research Consultant.*

56. **LO.5, 8** Using the legend provided, classify each of the following tax sources:

Legend	
P = Primary tax source	B = Both
S = Secondary tax source	N = Neither

a. Sixteenth Amendment to the Constitution.
b. Tax treaty between the United States and Russia.
c. Temporary Regulations.
d. Revenue Ruling.
e. General counsel memoranda (1988).
f. Tax Court Memorandum decision.
g. *Journal of Taxation* article.
h. Legislative Regulations.
i. Letter ruling (before 1985).
j. District Court decision.
k. Small Cases Division of U.S. Tax Court decision.
l. House Ways and Means Committee Report.
m. Technical advice memorandum (1991).
n. Proposed Regulations.

57. **LO.5** Interpret each of the following citations:
a. 54 T.C. 1514 (1970).
b. 408 F.2d 1117 (CA–2, 1969).
c. 69–1 USTC ¶ 9319 (CA–2, 1969).
d. 23 AFTR 2d 69–1090 (CA–2, 1969).
e. 293 F.Supp. 1129 (D.Ct. Miss., 1967).
f. 67–1 USTC ¶ 9253 (D.Ct. Miss., 1967).
g. 19 AFTR 2d 647 (D.Ct. Miss., 1967).
h. 56 S.Ct. 289 (USSC, 1935).
i. 36–1 USTC ¶ 9020 (USSC, 1935).
j. 16 AFTR 1274 (USSC, 1935).
k. 422 F.2d 1336 (Ct.Cl., 1970).

RESEARCH PROBLEMS

THOMSON REUTERS
CHECKPOINT®

Note: Solutions to Research Problems can be prepared by using the **Checkpoint® Student Edition** online research product, which is available to accompany this text. It is also possible to prepare solutions to the Research Problems by using tax research materials found in a standard tax library.

Research Problem 1. Is the two-year statute of limitations for the innocent spouse provision contained in Reg.Sec. 1.6015–5(b)(1) valid? Why or why not?

Research Problem 2. Find the *SOI Bulletin*, Summer 2010.
a. For tax year 2008, how many individuals reported nonfarm sole proprietorship activity?
b. Which sector had the largest profit?
c. What percentage of all U.S. corporate income tax returns did foreign-controlled domestic corporations account for in 2007?

Research Problem 3. Are Technical Expedited Advice Memoranda (TEAMs) still being issued?

Research Problem 4. The TV show TMZ spoke with Larry Edema from Michigan, who was selected to be in the audience for Oprah's big giveaway: a free trip to Australia. Supposedly, Winfrey had a certified public accountant on hand to address the tax issue right after the taping. Edema said that the CPA assured the group that all taxes associated with the trip would be "handled by the Oprah show"; so the trip would truly be 100% free. The CPA also explained that Oprah would cover all sightseeing costs and travel-related expenses, including passport costs for people who could not afford them. It was a big change from Oprah's 2004 controversy when she famously gave away brand-new cars but saddled audience members with as much as $7,000 in income taxes.

Discuss any tax aspects or problems with this statement.

Internet Activity

Use the tax resources of the Internet to address the following questions. Do not restrict your search to the Web, but include a review of newsgroups and general reference materials, practitioner sites and resources, primary sources of the tax law, chat rooms and discussion groups, and other opportunities.

Research Problem 5. Go to each of the following Internet locations:

a. Several primary sources of the tax law, including the U.S. Supreme Court, a Court of Appeals, the Internal Revenue Service, the U.S. Tax Court, and final Regulations.
b. Sources of proposed Federal tax legislation.
c. A collection of tax rules for your state.

Research Problem 6. Using the Internet, obtain definitions of these terms:

a. Rule 155.
b. *En banc.*
c. *Pro se.*
d. Dicta.
e. Parallel cite.
f. Sunset provisions.
g. Work product.

part 2

CORPORATIONS

Corporations are separate entities for Federal income tax purposes. Subchapter C of the Code is devoted to the tax treatment of regular corporations. Part 2 deals mainly with the operating rules contained in Subchapter C that apply to regular corporations and with the effects of various capital transactions on the C corporation and its shareholders. Part 2 also sets forth the special rules that apply when a U.S. corporation (or an affiliated entity) does business in a foreign setting.

CHAPTER

2 Corporations: Introduction and Operating Rules

LEARNING OBJECTIVES: *After completing Chapter 2, you should be able to:*

LO.1 Summarize the tax treatment of various forms of conducting a business.

LO.2 Compare the taxation of individuals and corporations.

LO.3 List and apply the tax rules unique to corporations.

LO.4 Compute the corporate income tax.

LO.5 Explain the rules unique to computing the tax of related corporations.

LO.6 Describe and illustrate the reporting process for corporations.

LO.7 Evaluate corporations as an entity form for conducting a business.

CHAPTER OUTLINE

THE BIG PICTURE Tax Solutions for the Real World

© Ryan McVay/Photodisc/Getty Images

A Half-Baked Idea?

Samantha Johnson owns Skylark Bakery. Currently, the bakery is operated as a sole proprietorship and generates an annual operating profit of $100,000. In addition, the bakery earns annual dividends of $5,000 from investing excess working capital in the stock of publicly traded corporations. These stock investments typically are held for a minimum of three to four months before funds are required for the business. As a result of income from other business ventures and investments, Samantha is in the 35 percent marginal tax rate bracket irrespective of the bakery. In the past, Samantha has withdrawn $50,000 annually from the bakery, which she regards as reasonable payment for her services.

Samantha has asked you about the tax consequences of conducting the business as a regular (C) corporation. Based on the given information, what would be the annual income tax savings (or cost) of operating the bakery as a corporation? For purposes of this analysis, use the 2012 tax rates and ignore any employment tax or state tax considerations.

Read the chapter and formulate your response.

2.1 Tax Treatment of Various Business Forms

LO.1

Summarize the tax treatment of various forms of conducting a business.

Business operations can be conducted in a number of different forms. Among the various possibilities are the following:

- Sole proprietorships.
- Partnerships.
- Trusts and estates.
- S corporations (also called Subchapter S corporations).
- Regular corporations (also called Subchapter C or C corporations).
- Limited liability companies.

For Federal income tax purposes, the distinctions among these forms of business organization are very important. The following discussion of the tax treatment of sole proprietorships, partnerships, and regular corporations highlights these distinctions. Limited liability companies, which are taxed as one of the three preceding entity forms, are also discussed. Trusts and estates are covered in Chapter 20, and S corporations are discussed in Chapter 12.

Sole Proprietorships

A sole proprietorship is not a taxable entity separate from the individual who owns the proprietorship. The owner of a sole proprietorship reports all business income and expenses of the proprietorship on Schedule C of Form 1040. The net profit or loss from the proprietorship is then transferred from Schedule C to Form 1040, which is used by the taxpayer to report taxable income. The proprietor reports all of the net profit from the business, regardless of the amount actually withdrawn during the year.

Income and expenses of the proprietorship retain their character when reported by the proprietor. For example, ordinary income of the proprietorship is treated as ordinary income when reported by the proprietor, and capital gain is treated as capital gain.

THE BIG PICTURE

EXAMPLE 1

Return to the facts of *The Big Picture* on p. 2-1. Samantha, the sole proprietor of Skylark Bakery, reports the $100,000 operating profit from the business on Schedule C of her individual tax return. Even though she withdrew only $50,000, Samantha reports all of the $100,000 operating profit from the business on Form 1040, where she computes taxable income for the year. She also reports dividend income of $5,000 on Schedule B of Form 1040.

Partnerships

Partnerships are not subject to a Federal income tax. However, a partnership is required to file Form 1065, which reports the results of the partnership's business activities. Most income and expense items are aggregated in computing the ordinary business income (loss) of the partnership on Form 1065. Any income and expense items that are not aggregated in computing the partnership's ordinary business income (loss) are reported separately to the partners. Some examples of separately reported income items are interest income, dividend income, and long-term capital gain. Examples of separately reported expenses include charitable contributions and expenses related to investment income. Partnership reporting is discussed in detail in Chapter 10.

The partnership ordinary business income (loss) and the separately reported items are allocated to the partners according to the partnership's profit and loss sharing agreement. Each partner receives a Schedule K–1 that reports the partner's share of the partnership ordinary business income (loss) and separately reported income and expense items. Each partner reports these items on his or her own tax return.

EXAMPLE 2

Jim and Bob are equal partners in Canary Enterprises, a calendar year partnership. During the year, Canary Enterprises had $500,000 gross income and $350,000 operating expenses. In addition, the partnership sold land that had been held for investment purposes for a long-term capital gain of $60,000. During the year, Jim withdrew $40,000 from the partnership, and Bob withdrew $45,000. The partnership's Form 1065 reports ordinary business income of $150,000 ($500,000 income − $350,000 expenses). The partnership also reports the $60,000 long-term capital gain as a separately stated item on Form 1065. Jim and Bob each receive a Schedule K–1 reporting ordinary business income of $75,000 and separately stated long-term capital gain of $30,000. Each partner reports ordinary business income of $75,000 and long-term capital gain of $30,000 on his own return. ■

Corporations

Corporations are governed by Subchapter C or Subchapter S of the Internal Revenue Code. Those governed by Subchapter C are referred to as **C corporations** or **regular corporations**. Corporations governed by Subchapter S are referred to as **S corporations**.

S corporations, which generally do not pay Federal income tax, are similar to partnerships in that ordinary business income (loss) flows through to the shareholders to be reported on their separate returns. Also like partnerships, S corporations do not aggregate all income and expense items in computing ordinary business income (loss). Certain items flow through to the shareholders and retain their separate character when reported on the shareholders' returns. The S corporation ordinary business income (loss) and the separately reported items are allocated to the shareholders according to their stock ownership interests. See Chapter 12 for detailed coverage of S corporations.

Unlike proprietorships, partnerships, and S corporations, C corporations are subject to an entity-level Federal income tax. This results in what is known as a *double taxation* effect. A C corporation reports its income and expenses on Form 1120. The corporation computes tax on the taxable income reported on the Form 1120 using the rate schedule applicable to corporations (see Exhibit 2.1 later in this section). When a corporation distributes its income, the corporation's shareholders report dividend income on their own tax returns. Thus, income that has already been taxed at the corporate level is also taxed at the shareholder level. The effects of double taxation are illustrated in Examples 3 and 4.

EXAMPLE 3

Lavender Corporation has taxable income of $100,000 in 2012. It pays corporate tax of $22,250 (refer to Exhibit 2.1 on p. 2-5). This leaves $77,750, all of which is distributed as a dividend to Mike, a 43-year-old single individual and the corporation's sole shareholder. Mike has no income sources other than Lavender Corporation. Mike has taxable income of $68,000 ($77,750 − $5,950 standard deduction − $3,800 personal exemption). He pays tax at the preferential rate applicable to dividends received by individuals. His tax is $4,898 [($35,350 × 0%) + ($32,650 × 15%)]. The combined tax on the corporation's net profit is $27,148 ($22,250 paid by the corporation + $4,898 paid by the shareholder). ■

EXAMPLE 4

Assume the same facts as in Example 3, except that the business is organized as a sole proprietorship. Mike reports the $100,000 profit from the business on his tax return. He has taxable income of $90,250 ($100,000 − $5,950 standard deduction − $3,800 personal exemption) and pays tax of $18,731. Therefore, operating the business as a sole proprietorship results in a tax *savings* of $8,417 in 2012 ($27,148 from Example 3 − $18,731). ■

In many cases, the tax burden will be greater if the business is operated as a corporation (as in Example 3), but sometimes operating as a corporation can result in tax savings, as illustrated in Examples 5 and 6.

EXAMPLE 5

In 2012, Tan Corporation files Form 1120 reporting taxable income of $100,000. The corporation pays tax of $22,250 and distributes the remaining $77,750 as a dividend to Carla, the sole shareholder of the corporation. Carla has income from other sources and is in the top individual tax bracket of 35% in 2012. As a result, she pays tax of $11,663 ($77,750 × 15% rate on dividends) on the distribution. The combined tax on the corporation's earnings is $33,913 ($22,250 paid by the corporation + $11,663 paid by the shareholder). ■

EXAMPLE 6

Assume the same facts as in Example 5, except that the business is a sole proprietorship. Carla reports the $100,000 profit from the business on her tax return and pays tax of $35,000 ($100,000 × 35% marginal rate). Therefore, operating the business as a sole proprietorship results in a tax *cost* of $1,087 in 2012 ($35,000 – $33,913 tax from Example 5). ■

The conclusions reached in these examples cannot be extended to all decisions about a form of business organization, as each specific set of facts and circumstances requires a thorough analysis of the tax factors. Further, the effect of other taxes (e.g., payroll and self-employment taxes and state income and franchise taxes) must be considered in such an analysis.

Taxation of Dividends

As noted earlier, the income of a C corporation is subject to double taxation—once at the corporate level when it is earned and again at the shareholder level when it is distributed as dividends. Double taxation stems, in part, from the fact that dividend distributions are not deductible by the corporation. Shareholders of closely held corporations frequently attempt to circumvent this disallowance by disguising a dividend distribution as some other purported transaction. One of the more common ways of disguising dividend distributions is to pay excessive compensation to shareholder-employees of a closely held corporation. The IRS scrutinizes compensation and other economic transactions (e.g., loans, leases, and sales) between shareholders and closely held corporations to ensure that payments are reasonable in amount. (See Chapter 5 for more discussion on constructive dividends.)

Double taxation also stems from the fact that dividend distributions are taxable to the shareholders. Historically, dividend income has been taxed at the same rates as ordinary income. However, to alleviate some of the double taxation effect, Congress reduced the tax rate applicable to dividend income of individuals for years after 2002. Qualified dividend income is currently taxed at the same preferential rate as long-term capital gains—15 percent (0 percent for taxpayers in the bottom two tax brackets). The preferential rate on dividend income is set to expire for years after 2012.

Comparison of Corporations and Other Forms of Doing Business

Chapter 13 presents a detailed comparison of sole proprietorships, partnerships, S corporations, and C corporations as forms of doing business. However, it is appropriate at this point to consider some of the tax and nontax factors that favor corporations over proprietorships.

Consideration of tax factors requires an examination of the corporate rate structure. The income tax rate schedule applicable to corporations is reproduced in Exhibit 2.1. As this schedule shows, the marginal rates for corporations range from 15 percent to 39 percent. In comparison, the marginal rates for individuals range from 10 percent to 35 percent. The corporate form of doing business presents tax savings opportunities when the applicable corporate marginal rate is lower than the applicable individual marginal rate.

EXHIBIT 2.1 **Corporate Income Tax Rates**

Taxable Income		Tax Is:	
Over—	**But Not Over—**		**Of the Amount Over—**
$ 0	$ 50,000	15%	$ 0
50,000	75,000	$ 7,500 + 25%	50,000
75,000	100,000	13,750 + 34%	75,000
100,000	335,000	22,250 + 39%	100,000
335,000	10,000,000	113,900 + 34%	335,000
10,000,000	15,000,000	3,400,000 + 35%	10,000,000
15,000,000	18,333,333	5,150,000 + 38%	15,000,000
18,333,333	—	35%	0

EXAMPLE 7

Susanna, an individual taxpayer in the 35% marginal tax rate bracket, can generate $100,000 of additional taxable income in the current year. If the income is taxed to Susanna, the associated tax is $35,000 ($100,000 × 35%). If, however, Susanna is able to shift the income to a newly created corporation, the corporate tax is $22,250 (see Exhibit 2.1). Thus, by taking advantage of the lower corporate marginal tax rates, a tax *savings* of $12,750 ($35,000 − $22,250) is achieved. ■

Any attempt to arbitrage the difference between the corporate and individual marginal tax rates also must consider the double taxation effect. When the preferential rate for dividend income is considered, however, tax savings opportunities still exist.

EXAMPLE 8

Assume in Example 7 that the corporation distributes all of its after-tax earnings to Susanna as a dividend. The dividend results in tax of $11,663 [($100,000 − $22,250) × 15%] to Susanna. Thus, even when the double taxation effect is considered, the combined tax burden of $33,913 ($22,250 paid by the corporation + $11,663 paid by the shareholder) represents a tax *savings* of $1,087 when compared to the $35,000 of tax that results when the $100,000 of income is subject to Susanna's 35% marginal rate. ■

Examples 7 and 8 ignore other tax issues that also must be considered in selecting the proper form of doing business, but they illustrate the tax savings that can be achieved by taking advantage of rate differentials. Some of the other tax considerations that could affect the selection of a business form include the character of business income, the expectation of business losses, payroll taxes, and state taxes.

All income and expense items of a proprietorship retain their character when reported on the proprietor's tax return. In the case of a partnership or an S corporation, separately reported items (e.g., charitable contributions and long-term capital gains) retain their character when passed through to the partners or shareholders, respectively. However, the tax attributes of income and expense items of a C corporation do not pass through the corporate entity to the shareholders. As a result, if the business is expected to generate tax-favored income (e.g., tax-exempt income or long-term capital gains), one of the other (non-C corporation) forms of business may be desirable.

Losses of a C corporation are treated differently than losses of a proprietorship, a partnership, or an S corporation. A loss incurred by a proprietorship may be deductible by the owner, because all income and expense items are reported by the proprietor. Partnership losses are passed through the partnership entity and may be deductible by the partners, and S corporation losses are passed through to the shareholders. C corporation losses, however, have no effect on the taxable income of the shareholders. Therefore, one of the non-C corporation forms of business may be desirable if business losses are anticipated.

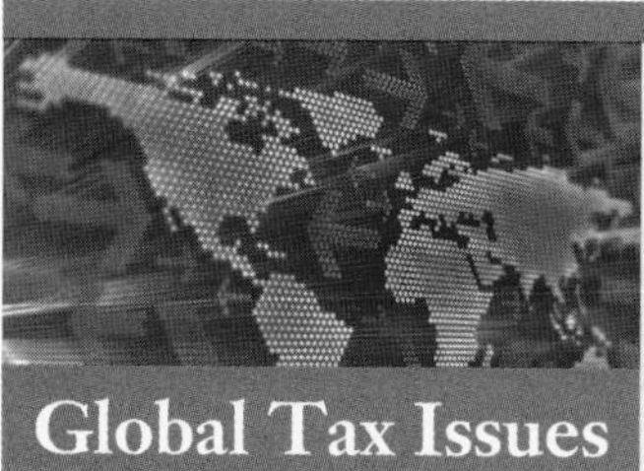

© Andrey Prokhorov, iStockphoto

U.S. Corporate Tax Rate and Global Competitiveness

According to the Organization for Economic Cooperation and Development (OECD), the U.S. combined Federal and state corporate income tax rate of 39.2% is the second highest among member states. Only Japan (39.5%) has a higher combined corporate tax rate than the United States, and Japan's new prime minister has vowed to reduce his country's corporate tax burden. The effective tax rate that most corporations pay in the United States is substantially less than the top statutory rate, however, as taxpayers reduce their exposure to the corporate tax through the use of exclusions, deductions, credits, and deferral provisions. Still, the relatively high corporate tax rate puts the United States at a competitive disadvantage in attracting capital investment, and it encourages U.S. corporations to utilize foreign entities to shelter income from U.S. taxation.

Source: www.oecd.org/ctp/taxdatabase.

EXAMPLE 9

Franco plans to start a business this year. He expects that the business will incur operating losses for the first three years and then become highly profitable. Franco decides to operate as an S corporation during the loss period, because the losses will flow through and be deductible on his personal return. When the business becomes profitable, he intends to switch to C corporation status. ■

Employment taxes must be factored into any analysis of a business form. The net income of a proprietorship is subject to the self-employment tax, as are some partnership allocations of income to partners. In the alternative, wages paid to a shareholder-employee of a corporation (C or S) are subject to payroll taxes. The combined corporation-employee payroll tax burden should be compared with the self-employment tax associated with the proprietorship and partnership forms of business. This analysis should include the benefit of the deduction available to a corporation for payroll taxes paid, as well as the deduction available to an individual for part of the self-employment taxes paid.

State taxation also must be considered in the selection of a business form. At the entity level, state corporate income taxes and/or franchise taxes are applicable for businesses formed as corporations. Although no entity-level Federal income tax is typically assessed on S corporations, limited liability companies (LLCs), or partnerships, a few states impose a corporate income tax or franchise tax on such business forms. Consideration of state taxation when selecting a business form is particularly relevant for businesses that operate in more than one state. (See Chapter 16 for a discussion of the taxation of multistate corporations.) At the owner level, the income of sole proprietorships, S corporations, and partnerships (including most LLCs) is subject to state individual income taxation. Similarly, dividend income from corporate distributions is subject to state income taxation and without any rate preference for such income.

Nontax Considerations

Nontax considerations will sometimes override tax considerations and lead to the conclusion that a business should be operated as a corporation. The following are some of the more important nontax considerations:

- Sole proprietors and general partners in partnerships face the danger of *unlimited liability*. That is, creditors of the business may file claims not only against the assets of the business but also against the personal assets of proprietors or general partners. State corporate law protects shareholders from claims against their personal assets for corporate debts.

- The corporate form of business can provide a vehicle for raising large amounts of capital through widespread stock ownership. Most major businesses in the United States are operated as corporations.
- Shares of stock in a corporation are freely transferable, whereas a partner's sale of his or her partnership interest is subject to approval by the other partners.
- Shareholders may come and go, but a corporation can continue to exist. Death or withdrawal of a partner, on the other hand, may terminate the existing partnership and cause financial difficulties that result in dissolution of the entity. This *continuity of life* is a distinct advantage of the corporate form of doing business.
- Corporations have *centralized management*. All management responsibility is assigned to a board of directors, who appoint officers to carry out the corporation's business. Partnerships, by contrast, may have decentralized management, in which every partner has a right to participate in the organization's business decisions. **Limited partnerships**, though, may have centralized management. Centralized management is essential for the smooth operation of a widely held business.

Limited Liability Companies

The **limited liability company (LLC)** has proliferated greatly in recent years, particularly since 1988 when the IRS first ruled that it would treat qualifying LLCs as partnerships for tax purposes. All 50 states and the District of Columbia have passed laws that allow LLCs, and thousands of companies have chosen LLC status. As with a corporation, operating as an LLC allows its owners ("members") to avoid unlimited liability, which is a primary *nontax* consideration in choosing the form of business organization. The tax advantage of LLCs is that qualifying businesses may be treated as proprietorships or partnerships for tax purposes, thereby avoiding the problem of double taxation associated with regular corporations.

Some states allow an LLC to have centralized management, but not continuity of life or free transferability of interests. Other states allow LLCs to adopt any or all of the corporate characteristics of centralized management, continuity of life, and free transferability of interests. The comparison of business entities in Chapter 13 includes a discussion of LLCs.

Entity Classification

Can an organization not qualifying as a corporation under state law still be treated as such for Federal income tax purposes? The tax law defines a corporation as including "associations, joint stock companies, and insurance companies."[1] Unfortunately, the Code contains no definition of what constitutes an *association*, and the issue became the subject of frequent litigation.

It was finally determined that an entity would be treated as a corporation if it had a majority of characteristics common to corporations. For this purpose, relevant characteristics are:

- Continuity of life.
- Centralized management.
- Limited liability.
- Free transferability of interests.

These criteria did not resolve all of the problems that continued to arise over corporate classification. When a new type of business entity—the limited liability company—was developed, the IRS was deluged with inquiries regarding its tax status. As LLCs became increasingly popular with professional groups, all states enacted statutes allowing some form of this entity. Invariably, the statutes permitted

[1]§ 7701(a)(3).

the corporate characteristic of limited liability and, often, that of centralized management. Because continuity of life and free transferability of interests are absent, partnership classification was hoped for. This treatment avoided the double taxation inherent in the corporate form.

In 1996, the IRS eased the entity classification problem by issuing the **check-the-box Regulations.**[2] The Regulations enable taxpayers to choose the tax status of a business entity without regard to its corporate (or noncorporate) characteristics. These rules simplified tax administration considerably and eliminated much of the litigation that arose with regard to the association (i.e., corporation) status.

Under the check-the-box rules, entities with more than one owner can elect to be classified as either a partnership or a corporation. An entity with only one owner can elect to be classified as a sole proprietorship or as a corporation. Eligible entities make the election as to tax status by filing Form 8832 (Entity Classification Election). In the event of default (i.e., no election is made), multi-owner entities are classified as partnerships and single-person businesses as sole proprietorships.

The election is not available to entities that are actually incorporated under state law or to entities that are required to be taxed as corporations under Federal law (e.g., certain publicly traded partnerships). Otherwise, LLCs are not treated as being incorporated under state law. Although LLCs are generally disregarded entities for income tax purposes, they are obligated to report and pay employment and excise taxes.

2.2 An Introduction to the Income Taxation of Corporations

LO.2

Compare the taxation of individuals and corporations.

An Overview of Corporate versus Individual Income Tax Treatment

When examining how corporations are treated under the Federal income tax, a useful approach is to compare their treatment with that applicable to individual taxpayers. The tax formula for computing the Federal income tax for a corporation is compared with that of an individual taxpayer in Figure 2.1, and the following discussion highlights similarities and differences between the two formulas.

Similarities

Gross income of a corporation is determined in much the same manner as it is for individuals. Thus, gross income includes compensation for services rendered, income derived from a business, gains from dealings in property, interest, rents, royalties, and dividends—to name only a few items. Both individuals and corporations are entitled to exclusions from gross income. However, corporate taxpayers are allowed fewer exclusions. Interest on municipal bonds and life insurance proceeds are two exclusions that are applicable to both individual and corporate taxpayers.

Gains and losses from property transactions are handled similarly. For example, whether a gain or loss is capital or ordinary depends upon the nature of the asset in the hands of the taxpayer making the taxable disposition. In defining what is not a capital asset, § 1221 makes no distinction between corporate and noncorporate taxpayers.

In the area of nontaxable exchanges, corporations are like individuals in that they do not recognize gain or loss on a like-kind exchange and may defer recognized gain on an involuntary conversion of property. The exclusion of gain from the sale of a personal residence does not apply to corporations. The disallowance of losses on sales of property to related parties and on wash sales of securities applies equally to individual and corporate taxpayers.

[2] Reg. §§ 301.7701–1 through –4, and –7.

FIGURE 2.1 **Tax Formulas**

Corporations	Individuals
Income (broadly conceived)	Income (broadly conceived)
(Exclusions)	(Exclusions)
Gross income	Gross income
(Deductions except for NOL and DRD)*	(Deductions for AGI)**
Taxable income before NOL and DRD	Adjusted gross income
(Net operating loss deduction)	(Greater of itemized or standard deductions)
(Dividends received deduction)	(Personal and dependency exemptions)
Taxable income	Taxable income
Tax on taxable income	Tax on taxable income
(Tax credits)	(Tax credits)
Tax due (or refund)	Tax due (or refund)

*NOL = net operating loss; DRD = dividends received deduction.
**AGI = adjusted gross income.

The business deductions of corporations also parallel those available to individuals. Deductions are allowed for all ordinary and necessary expenses paid or incurred in carrying on a trade or business. Specific provision is made for the deductibility of interest, certain taxes, losses, bad debts, accelerated cost recovery, charitable contributions, net operating losses, research and experimental expenditures, and other less common deductions. There is no distinction between business and nonbusiness interest or business and nonbusiness bad debts for corporations. Thus, these amounts are deductible in full as ordinary deductions by corporations. Like individuals, corporations are not allowed a deduction for interest paid or incurred on amounts borrowed to purchase or carry tax-exempt securities. The same holds true for expenses contrary to public policy and certain accrued expenses between related parties.

Some of the tax credits available to individuals, such as the foreign tax credit, can also be claimed by corporations. Not available to corporations are certain credits that are personal in nature, such as the child tax credit, the credit for elderly or disabled taxpayers, and the earned income credit.

Dissimilarities

The income taxation of corporations and individuals also differs significantly. As noted earlier, different tax rates apply to corporations and to individuals. Corporate tax rates are discussed in more detail later in the chapter (see Examples 30 and 31).

All allowable corporate deductions are treated as business deductions. Thus, the determination of adjusted gross income (AGI), so essential for individual taxpayers, has no relevance to corporations. Taxable income is computed simply by subtracting from gross income all allowable deductions. Itemized deductions, the standard deduction, and the deduction for personal and dependency exemptions do not apply to corporations. The $100 floor and 10 percent-of-AGI limitations on the deductible portion of personal casualty and theft losses applicable to individuals do not apply to corporations.

Specific Provisions Compared

A comparison of the income taxation of individuals and corporations appears in Concept Summary 2.1 located at the end of this chapter. In making this comparison, the following areas warrant special discussion:

- Accounting periods and methods.
- Capital gains and losses.

- Recapture of depreciation.
- Passive losses.
- Charitable contributions.
- Domestic production activities deduction.
- Net operating losses.
- Special deductions available only to corporations.

Accounting Periods and Methods

Accounting Periods

Corporations generally have the same choices of accounting periods as do individual taxpayers. Like an individual, a corporation may choose a calendar year or a fiscal year for reporting purposes. Corporations usually can have different tax years from those of their shareholders. Also, newly formed corporations (as new taxpayers) usually have a choice of any approved accounting period without having to obtain the consent of the IRS. **Personal service corporations (PSCs)** and S corporations, however, are subject to severe restrictions in the use of a fiscal year. The rules applicable to S corporations are discussed in Chapter 12.

A PSC has as its principal activity the performance of personal services, and such services are substantially performed by shareholder-employees. The performance of services must be in the fields of health, law, engineering, architecture, accounting, actuarial science, performing arts, or consulting.[3] To limit the deferral of income possible when a PSC has a tax year different from that of its calendar year shareholder-employees, a PSC must generally use a calendar year.[4] However, a PSC can *elect* a fiscal year under any of the following conditions:

- A business purpose for the year can be demonstrated.
- The PSC year results in a deferral of not more than three months' income. An election under § 444 is required, and the PSC will be subject to the deduction limitations of § 280H. Under the latter provision, a PSC's deduction for shareholder-employee salaries will be limited if payment of those salaries is disproportionately postponed beyond December 31 (see Example 11).
- The PSC retained the same year that was used for its fiscal year ending 1987, provided an election was made under § 444 and subject to the deduction limitations of § 280H.

EXAMPLE 10

Valdez & Vance is a professional association of public accountants that receives over 40% of its gross receipts in March and April of each year from the preparation of tax returns. Valdez & Vance may be able to qualify for a May 1 to April 30 fiscal year. Under these circumstances, the IRS might permit Valdez & Vance to use the fiscal year chosen because it reflects a natural business cycle (the end of the tax season). Valdez & Vance has a business purpose for using a fiscal year.

EXAMPLE 11

Beige Corporation, a PSC, has made an election under § 444 to use a fiscal year ending September 30. For its fiscal year ending September 30, 2012, Beige paid Burke, its sole shareholder, $120,000 in salary. Under § 280H, Burke must receive at least $30,000 [(3 months ÷ 12 months) × $120,000] as salary during the period October 1 through December 31, 2012. ■

Accounting Methods

As a general rule, the cash method of accounting is unavailable to corporations.[5] However, several important exceptions apply in the case of the following types of corporations:

[3] § 448(d)(2)(A).

[4] § 441(i).

[5] § 448.

- S corporations.
- Corporations engaged in the trade or business of farming and timber.
- Qualified PSCs.
- Corporations with average annual gross receipts of $5 million or less for the most recent three-year period.

Most individuals and corporations that maintain inventory for sale to customers are required to use the accrual method of accounting for determining sales and cost of goods sold. However, as a matter of administrative convenience, the IRS will permit any entity with average annual gross receipts of not more than $1 million for the most recent three-year period to use the cash method. This applies even if the taxpayer is buying and selling inventory. Also as a matter of administrative convenience, the IRS will permit certain entities with average annual gross receipts greater than $1 million but not more than $10 million for the most recent three-year period to use the cash method.[6]

A corporation that uses the accrual method of accounting must observe a special rule in dealing with cash basis related parties. If the corporation has an accrual outstanding at the end of any taxable year with respect to such a related party, it cannot claim a deduction until the recipient reports the amount as income.[7] This rule is most often encountered when a corporation deals with an individual who owns (directly or indirectly) more than 50 percent of the corporation's stock.

THE BIG PICTURE

EXAMPLE 12

Return to the facts of *The Big Picture* on p. 2-1. Assume that Samantha incorporates her business as Skylark Bakery, Inc., a calendar year, accrual method C corporation. Samantha, a cash method taxpayer, owns 100% of the corporation's stock at the end of 2012. On December 31, 2012, Skylark Bakery has accrued a $10,000 bonus to Samantha. Samantha receives the bonus in 2013 and reports it on her 2013 tax return. Skylark Bakery cannot claim a deduction for the $10,000 until 2013.

Capital Gains and Losses

Capital gains and losses result from the taxable sales or exchanges of capital assets.[8] Whether these gains and losses are long-term or short-term depends upon the holding period of the assets sold or exchanged. Each year, a taxpayer's short-term gains and losses are combined, and long-term gains and losses are combined. The result is a net short-term capital gain or loss and a net long-term capital gain or loss. If gains *and* losses result (e.g., net short-term capital gain and net long-term capital loss), such amounts are further netted against each other. If instead the results are *all* gains or *all* losses (e.g., net short-term capital loss and net long-term capital loss), no further combination is necessary.

Capital Gains

Individuals generally pay a preferential tax rate of 15 percent on net capital gains (i.e., excess of net long-term capital gain over net short-term capital loss).[9] Corporations, however, receive no favorable tax rate on long-term capital gains, and such income is taxed at the normal corporate tax rates.

Capital Losses

Net capital losses of corporate and individual taxpayers receive different income tax treatment. Generally, individual taxpayers can deduct up to $3,000 of such net

[6]Rev.Proc. 2001–10, 2001–1 C.B. 272, and Rev.Proc. 2002–28, 2002–1 C.B. 815.

[7]§ 267(a)(2).

[8]See Chapter 16 of *South-Western Federal Taxation: Individual Income Taxes* (2013 Edition) for a detailed discussion of capital gains and losses.

[9]A 0% rate applies to individual taxpayers in the 10% and 15% brackets.

losses against other income. Any remaining capital losses can be carried forward to future years until absorbed by capital gains or by the $3,000 deduction.[10] Loss carryovers retain their identity as either long term or short term.

EXAMPLE 13

Robin, an individual, incurs a net long-term capital loss of $7,500 for calendar year 2012. Assuming adequate taxable income, Robin may deduct $3,000 of this loss on his 2012 return. The remaining $4,500 ($7,500 − $3,000) of the loss is carried to 2013 and years thereafter until completely deducted. The $4,500 will be carried forward as a long-term capital loss. ■

Unlike individuals, corporate taxpayers are not permitted to claim any net capital losses as a deduction against ordinary income. Capital losses, therefore, can be used only as an offset against capital gains. Corporations, however, carry back net capital losses to three preceding years, applying them first to the earliest year in point of time. Carryforwards are allowed for a period of five years from the year of the loss. When carried back or forward, a long-term capital loss is treated as a short-term capital loss.

EXAMPLE 14

Assume the same facts as in Example 13, except that Robin is a corporation. None of the $7,500 long-term capital loss incurred in 2012 can be deducted in that year. Robin Corporation may, however, carry back the loss to 2009, 2010, and 2011 (in this order) and offset it against any capital gains recognized in these years. If the carryback does not exhaust the loss, it may be carried forward to 2013, 2014, 2015, 2016, and 2017 (in this order). The long-term capital loss is treated as short term in any carryover year. ■

Recapture of Depreciation

In general, the recapture rules under §§ 1245 and 1250 are equally applicable to both individual and corporate taxpayers. However, corporations may have more depreciation recapture (ordinary income) on the disposition of § 1250 property than individuals. Under § 291, a corporation will have additional ordinary income equal to 20 percent of the excess of the amount of depreciation recapture that would arise if the property was § 1245 property over the amount of depreciation recapture computed under § 1250 (without regard to § 291). As a result, the § 1231 portion of the corporation's gain on the disposition is correspondingly reduced by the additional recapture.

Under § 1250, recapture is limited to the excess of accelerated depreciation over straight-line depreciation. In general, only straight-line depreciation is allowed for real property placed in service after 1986; thus, there will usually be no depreciation recapture on the disposition of § 1250 property (without regard to § 291). In contrast, all depreciation taken on § 1245 property is subject to recapture under that provision.

EXAMPLE 15

Red Corporation purchases nonresidential real property on May 2, 1997, for $800,000. Straight-line depreciation is taken in the amount of $316,239 before the property is sold on October 8, 2012, for $1.2 million.

First, determine the recognized gain:

Sales price		$1,200,000
Less: Adjusted basis—		
Cost of property	$ 800,000	
Less: Cost recovery	(316,239)	(483,761)
Recognized gain		$ 716,239

[10] § 1212.

Second, determine the § 1245 recapture potential. This is the lesser of $716,239 (recognized gain) or $316,239 (cost recovery claimed).

Third, determine the normal § 1250 recapture amount:

Cost recovery taken	$ 316,239
Less: Straight-line cost recovery	(316,239)
§ 1250 ordinary income	$ –0–

Fourth, because the taxpayer is a corporation, determine the additional § 291 amount:

§ 1245 recapture potential	$ 316,239
Less: § 1250 recapture amount	(–0–)
Excess § 1245 recapture potential	$ 316,239
Apply § 291 percentage	× 20%
Additional ordinary income under § 291	$ 63,248

Red Corporation's recognized gain of $716,239 is accounted for as follows:

Ordinary income under § 1250	$ –0–
Ordinary income under § 291	63,248
§ 1231 gain	652,991
Total recognized gain	$ 716,239

■

Passive Losses

The **passive loss** rules apply to individual taxpayers and to closely held C corporations and personal service corporations (PSCs).[11] For S corporations and partnerships, passive income or loss flows through to the owners, and the passive loss rules are applied at the owner level. The passive loss rules are applied to closely held C corporations and to PSCs to prevent taxpayers from incorporating to avoid the passive loss limitation.

A corporation is closely held if, at any time during the last half of the taxable year, more than 50 percent of the value of the corporation's outstanding stock is owned, directly or indirectly, by or for not more than five individuals. A corporation is classified as a PSC if it meets the following requirements:

- The principal activity of the corporation is the performance of personal services.
- The services are substantially performed by shareholder-employees.
- More than 10 percent of the stock (in value) is held by shareholder-employees. *Any* stock held by an employee on *any* one day causes the employee to be a shareholder-employee.

The general passive loss rules apply to PSCs. Passive losses cannot be offset against either active income or portfolio income. The application of the passive loss rules is not as harsh for closely held C corporations. They may offset passive losses against active income, but not against portfolio income.

EXAMPLE 16

Brown, a closely held C corporation that is not a PSC, has $300,000 of passive losses from a rental activity, $200,000 of active business income, and $100,000 of portfolio income. The corporation may offset $200,000 of the $300,000 passive loss against the $200,000 active business income, but may not offset the remainder against the $100,000 of portfolio income. If Brown is a PSC, then none of the $300,000 of passive losses is deductible in the current year. ■

[11]§ 469(a). For definitions, see § 469(j)(1) (closely held) and § 469(j)(2) (PSC).

Subject to certain exceptions, individual taxpayers are not allowed to offset passive losses against *either* active or portfolio income.

Charitable Contributions

Both corporate and individual taxpayers may deduct charitable contributions if the recipient is a qualified charitable organization. Generally, a deduction will be allowed only for the year in which the payment is made. However, an important exception is made for *accrual basis corporations.* They may claim the deduction in the year preceding payment if two requirements are met. First, the contribution must be authorized by the board of directors by the end of that year. Second, it must be paid on or before the fifteenth day of the third month of the next year.

EXAMPLE 17

On December 28, 2012, Blue Company, a calendar year, accrual basis taxpayer, authorizes a $5,000 donation to the Atlanta Symphony Association (a qualified charitable organization). The donation is made on March 12, 2013. If Blue Company is a partnership, the contribution can be deducted only in 2013.[12] However, if Blue Company is a corporation and the December 28, 2012 authorization was made by its board of directors, Blue may claim the $5,000 donation as a deduction for calendar year 2012. ■

Property Contributions

Generally, a charitable contribution of property results in a deduction equal to the property's fair market value at the date of the gift. As a result of this rule, a contribution of loss property (fair market value less than basis) should be avoided as the loss inherent in the property (i.e., the excess of basis over fair market value) would never be recognized. A sale of the property to recognize the loss, followed by a charitable contribution of the sale proceeds, would produce a more favorable tax result.

EXAMPLE 18

Heron Corporation owns inventory with a basis of $10,000 and a fair market value of $8,000. A charitable contribution of the inventory results in a deductible amount of $8,000, the inventory's fair market value. However, a sale of the inventory, for a recognized loss of $2,000 ($8,000 amount realized – $10,000 basis), and donation of the sale proceeds, for a charitable deduction of $8,000, results in a deductible amount of $10,000. ■

Fair market value also is the valuation amount for most charitable contributions of capital gain property. *Capital gain property* is property that, if sold, would result in long-term capital gain or § 1231 gain for the taxpayer.

EXAMPLE 19

During the current year, Mallard Corporation donates a parcel of land (a capital asset) to Oakland Community College. Mallard acquired the land in 1988 for $60,000, and the fair market value on the date of the contribution is $100,000. The corporation's charitable contribution deduction (subject to a percentage limitation discussed later) is measured by the asset's fair market value of $100,000, even though the $40,000 appreciation on the land has never been included in income. ■

In two situations, a charitable contribution of capital gain property is measured by the basis of the property, rather than fair market value. If the corporation contributes *tangible personal property* and the charitable organization puts the property to an unrelated use, the appreciation on the property is not deductible. Unrelated use is defined as use that is not related to the purpose or function that qualifies the organization for exempt status.

[12]Each calendar year partner will report an allocable portion of the charitable contribution deduction as of December 31, 2013 (the end of the partnership's tax year). See Chapter 10.

EXAMPLE 20

White Corporation donates a painting worth $200,000 to Western States Art Museum (a qualified organization), which exhibits the painting. White had acquired the painting in 1980 for $90,000. Because the museum put the painting to a related use, White is allowed to deduct $200,000, the fair market value of the painting. ■

EXAMPLE 21

Assume the same facts as in the previous example, except that White Corporation donates the painting to the American Cancer Society, which sells the painting and deposits the $200,000 proceeds in the organization's general fund. White's deduction is limited to the $90,000 basis because it contributed tangible personal property that was put to an unrelated use by the charitable organization. ■

The deduction for charitable contributions of capital gain property to certain private nonoperating foundations is also limited to the basis of the property.

As a general rule, the deduction for a contribution of ordinary income property is limited to the *basis* of the property. *Ordinary income property* is property that, if sold, would result in ordinary income for the taxpayer. Examples of ordinary income property include inventory and capital assets that have not been held more than 12 months. In addition, § 1231 property (depreciable property used in a trade or business) is treated as ordinary income property to the extent of any depreciation recaptured under § 1245 or § 1250 (as adjusted under § 291). On certain contributions of inventory by *corporations*, however, the amount of the deduction is equal to the lesser of (1) the sum of the property's basis plus 50 percent of the appreciation on the property or (2) twice the property's basis. The following contributions of inventory qualify for this increased contribution amount.

- A contribution of property to a charitable organization for use that is related to the organization's exempt function and such use is solely for the care of the ill, needy, or infants. (Individual taxpayers also qualify for this exception if the property is "wholesome food.")
- A contribution of books to a public school (K through 12) that uses the books in its educational programs.
- A contribution of tangible personal research property constructed by the corporation to a qualified educational or scientific organization that uses the property for research or experimentation, or research training. (The property must be contributed within two years from the date of its construction by the donor, and its original use must begin with the donee.)
- A contribution of computer equipment and software to a qualified educational organization or public library that uses the property for educational purposes. (This provision is not limited to property held as inventory. However, the property must be contributed within three years from the date of its acquisition or construction by the donor, and its original use must begin with the donor or donee.)[13]

EXAMPLE 22

Lark Corporation, a clothing retailer, donates children's clothing to the Salvation Army to be used to attire homeless children. Lark's basis in the clothes is $2,000, and the fair market value is $3,000. Lark's deduction is $2,500 [$2,000 basis + 50%($3,000 − $2,000)]. If, instead, the fair market value is $7,000, Lark's deduction is $4,000 (2 × $2,000 basis). ■

[13]These conditions are set forth in §§ 170(e)(3), (4), and (6). At the time of this writing, the enhanced deduction associated with the contribution of food, book, and computer equipment inventory is available only for contributions made by December 31, 2011. However, the general consensus is that Congress will extend some or all of these provisions.

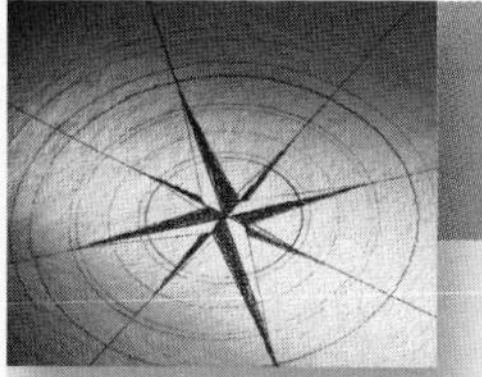

ETHICS & EQUITY Art Is in the Eye of the Beholder!

Snipe Corporation, your client, donated a painting to the Lexington Museum of Art. The painting, which had been displayed in the corporate offices for several years, had a fair market value of $150,000 at the time of the donation (basis of $60,000). Snipe deducted a charitable contribution of $150,000 for the gift. You have learned that the museum, also a client of yours, did not display the painting because it did not fit well with the museum's collection. Instead, the museum sold the painting for $150,000 and placed the funds in its operating budget. What action, if any, should you take?

Limitations Imposed on Charitable Contribution Deductions

Like individuals, corporations are subject to percentage limits on the charitable contribution deduction.[14] For any tax year, a corporate taxpayer's contribution deduction is limited to 10 percent of taxable income. For this purpose, taxable income is computed without regard to the charitable contribution deduction, any net operating loss carryback or capital loss carryback, dividends received deduction, and domestic production activities deduction. Any contributions in excess of the 10 percent limitation may be carried forward to the five succeeding tax years. Any carryforward must be added to subsequent contributions and will be subject to the 10 percent limitation. In applying this limitation, the current year's contributions must be deducted first, with carryover amounts from previous years deducted in order of time.[15]

EXAMPLE 23

During 2012, Orange Corporation (a calendar year taxpayer) had the following income and expenses:

Income from operations	$140,000
Expenses from operations	110,000
Dividends received	10,000
Charitable contributions made in May 2012	6,000

For purposes of the 10% limitation *only*, Orange Corporation's taxable income is $40,000 ($140,000 − $110,000 + $10,000). Consequently, the allowable charitable deduction for 2012 is $4,000 (10% × $40,000). The $2,000 unused portion of the contribution can be carried forward to 2013, 2014, 2015, 2016, and 2017 (in that order) until exhausted. ■

EXAMPLE 24

Assume the same facts as in Example 23. In 2013, Orange Corporation has taxable income (for purposes of the 10% limitation) of $50,000 and makes a charitable contribution of $4,500. The maximum deduction allowed for 2013 is $5,000 (10% × $50,000). The first $4,500 of the allowed deduction must be allocated to the contribution made in 2013, and the $500 balance is carried over from 2012. The remaining $1,500 of the 2012 contribution may be carried over to 2014, etc. ■

Domestic Production Activities Deduction

One important purpose of the American Jobs Creation Act of 2004 was to replace certain tax provisions that our world trading partners regarded as allowing unfair advantage to U.S. exports. Among other changes, the Act created a deduction based on the income from manufacturing activities (designated as *domestic production activities*). For 2012, the **domestic production activities deduction (DPAD)** is 9 percent of the lower of:

[14] The percentage limitations applicable to individuals and corporations are set forth in § 170(b).

[15] The carryover rules relating to all taxpayers are in § 170(d).

- Qualified production activities income, or
- Taxable income (computed without regard to the DPAD).[16]

For individuals, adjusted gross income is substituted for "taxable income." The DPAD cannot exceed 50 percent of an employer's W–2 wages related to qualified production activities income.

EXAMPLE 25

Elk Corporation, a calendar year taxpayer, manufactures golf equipment. For 2012, Elk had taxable income of $360,000 (before considering the DPAD) and qualified production activities income of $380,000. Elk's deduction is $32,400 [9% × $360,000 (the lesser of $380,000 or $360,000)]. Elk's W–2 wages related to qualified production activities income were $70,000, so the W–2 wage limitation ($70,000 × 50% = $35,000) does not apply. ■

See Chapter 3 for a detailed discussion of the domestic production activities deduction.

Net Operating Losses

Like the net operating loss (NOL) of an individual, the NOL of a corporation may be carried back 2 years and forward 20 to offset taxable income for those years. Similarly, corporations also may elect to forgo the carryback period and just carry forward an NOL. Unlike individual taxpayers, however, a corporation does not adjust its tax loss for the year for capital losses, because a corporation is not permitted a deduction for net capital losses. Nor does a corporation make adjustments for any nonbusiness deductions as individual taxpayers do. Further, a corporation is allowed to include the dividends received deduction (discussed below) in computing its NOL.[17]

EXAMPLE 26

In 2012, Green Corporation has gross income (including dividends) of $200,000 and deductions of $300,000 excluding the dividends received deduction. Green Corporation had received $100,000 of dividends from Fox, Inc., in which Green holds a 5% stock interest. Green has an NOL computed as follows:

Gross income (including dividends)		$200,000
Less:		
Business deductions	$300,000	
Dividends received deduction (70% of $100,000)	70,000	(370,000)
Taxable income (or loss)		($170,000)

The NOL is carried back two years to 2010. (Green Corporation may forgo the carryback option and elect instead to carry forward the loss.) Assume that Green had taxable income of $40,000 in 2010. The carryover to 2011 is computed as follows:

Taxable income for 2010	$ 40,000
Less: NOL carryback	(170,000)
Taxable income for 2010 after NOL carryback (carryover to 2011)	($130,000)

■

Deductions Available Only to Corporations

LO.3

List and apply the tax rules unique to corporations.

Dividends Received Deduction

The purpose of the **dividends received deduction** is to mitigate multiple taxation of corporate income. Without the deduction, income paid to a corporation in the form of a dividend would be taxed to the recipient corporation with no corresponding deduction to the distributing corporation. Later, when the recipient corporation paid the income to its shareholders, the income would again be subject to taxation with no corresponding deduction to the corporation. The dividends

[16] § 199.

[17] The modifications required to arrive at the amount of NOL that can be carried back or forward are in § 172(d).

received deduction alleviates this inequity by causing only some or none of the dividend income to be taxable to the recipient corporation.

As the following table illustrates, the amount of the dividends received deduction depends upon the percentage of ownership (voting power and value) the recipient corporate shareholder holds in a *domestic corporation* making the dividend distribution.[18]

Percentage of Ownership by Corporate Shareholder	Deduction Percentage
Less than 20%	70%
20% or more (but less than 80%)	80%
80% or more*	100%

*The payor corporation must be a member of an affiliated group with the recipient corporation.

The dividends received deduction is limited to a percentage of the taxable income of a corporation. For this purpose, taxable income is computed without regard to the NOL deduction, the domestic production activities deduction, the dividends received deduction, and any capital loss carryback to the current tax year. The percentage of taxable income limitation corresponds to the deduction percentage. Thus, if a corporate shareholder owns less than 20 percent of the stock in the distributing corporation, the dividends received deduction is limited to 70 percent of taxable income. However, the taxable income limitation does not apply if the corporation has an NOL for the current taxable year.[19]

The following steps are useful in applying these rules.

1. Multiply the dividends received by the deduction percentage.
2. Multiply the taxable income by the deduction percentage.
3. The deduction is limited to the lesser of step 1 or step 2, unless deducting the amount derived in step 1 results in an NOL. If so, the amount derived in step 1 should be used. This is referred to as the NOL rule.

EXAMPLE 27

Red, White, and Blue Corporations, three unrelated calendar year corporations, have the following information for the year:

	Red Corporation	White Corporation	Blue Corporation
Gross income from operations	$ 400,000	$ 320,000	$ 260,000
Expenses from operations	(340,000)	(340,000)	(340,000)
Dividends received from domestic corporations (less than 20% ownership)	200,000	200,000	200,000
Taxable income before the dividends received deduction	$ 260,000	$ 180,000	$ 120,000

In determining the dividends received deduction, use the three-step procedure described above:

	Red	White	Blue
Step 1 (70% × $200,000)	$140,000	$140,000	$140,000
Step 2			
70% × $260,000 (taxable income)	$182,000		
70% × $180,000 (taxable income)		$126,000	
70% × $120,000 (taxable income)			$ 84,000
Step 3			
Lesser of step 1 or step 2	$140,000	$126,000	
Deduction results in an NOL			$140,000

■

[18] § 243(a). Dividends from foreign corporations generally do not qualify for a dividends received deduction. But see § 245.

[19] Further, the limitation does not apply in the case of the 100% deduction available to members of an affiliated group. § 246(b).

TAX IN THE NEWS The President's Economic Recovery Advisory Board Offers Options for Corporate Tax Reform

In February 2009, President Obama established the President's Economic Recovery Advisory Board (PERAB). Chaired by Paul Volcker (former chair of the Federal Reserve), PERAB was charged, in part, with providing the President with options for reforming the corporate tax system. On August 27, 2010, PERAB released "The Report on Tax Reform Options: Simplification, Compliance, and Corporate Taxation." With a view toward reducing economic distortions associated with the current corporate tax system, PERAB's emphasis was on a broader corporate tax base and a lower corporate tax rate. The report offers several options for corporate tax reform, including the following:

- Reduce the corporate tax rate.
- Allow immediate expensing of new investments in business assets.
- Limit deductibility of interest expense.
- Impose the corporate tax on unincorporated businesses possessing certain corporate characteristics.
- Eliminate or reduce certain tax benefits (e.g., the domestic production activities deduction).

PERAB's report could serve as a blueprint for any future attempts at comprehensive corporate tax reform.

White Corporation is subject to the 70 percent of taxable income limitation. It does not qualify for NOL rule treatment because subtracting $140,000 (step 1) from $180,000 (taxable income before the DRD) does not yield a negative figure. Blue Corporation does qualify for NOL rule treatment because subtracting $140,000 (step 1) from $120,000 (taxable income before the DRD) yields a negative figure. In summary, each corporation has a dividends received deduction for the year as follows: $140,000 for Red Corporation, $126,000 for White Corporation, and $140,000 for Blue Corporation.

No dividends received deduction is allowed unless the corporation has held the stock for more than 45 days.[20] This restriction was enacted to close a tax loophole involving dividends on stock that is held only transitorily. When stock is purchased shortly before a dividend record date and soon thereafter sold ex-dividend, a capital loss corresponding to the amount of the dividend often results (ignoring other market valuation changes). If the dividends received deduction was allowed in such cases, the capital loss resulting from the stock sale would exceed the taxable portion of the related dividend income.

EXAMPLE 28

On October 1, 2012, Pink Corporation (5 million shares outstanding) declares a $1 per share dividend for shareholders of record as of November 1, 2012, and payable on December 1, 2012. Black Corporation purchases 10,000 shares of Pink stock on October 29, 2012, for $25,000, and sells those 10,000 shares ex-dividend on November 5, 2012, for $15,000. (It is assumed that there is no fluctuation in the market price of the Pink stock other than the dividend element.) The sale results in a short-term capital loss of $10,000 ($15,000 amount realized − $25,000 basis). On December 1, Black receives a $10,000 dividend from Pink. Without the holding period restriction, Black Corporation would recognize a $10,000 deduction (subject to the capital loss limitation) but only $3,000 of income [$10,000 dividend – $7,000 dividends received deduction ($10,000 × 70%)], or a $7,000 net loss. However, because Black did not hold the Pink stock for more than 45 days, no dividends received deduction is allowed. ■

Another restriction applies to the dividends received deduction when the underlying stock is debt financed. Like the holding period restriction, this provision also was enacted to close a tax loophole. A corporation that finances the purchase of dividend-paying stock receives an interest expense deduction from such financing,

[20]The stock must be held more than 45 days during the 91-day period beginning on the date that is 45 days before the ex-dividend date (or in the case of preferred stock, more than 90 days during the 181-day period beginning on the date that is 90 days before the ex-dividend date). § 246(c).

but would report only a small amount of the related income if the dividends received deduction was allowed unabated. In general, the debt-financed stock restriction reduces the dividends received deduction with respect to any dividend-paying stock by the percentage of the investment in the stock that is debt financed.[21] For instance, if a stock purchase is financed 50 percent by debt, the dividends received deduction for dividends on such stock is reduced by 50 percent. However, the reduction in the dividends received deduction cannot exceed the amount of the interest deduction allocable to the dividend.

Organizational Expenditures Deduction

Expenses incurred in connection with the organization of a corporation normally are chargeable to a capital account. That they benefit the corporation during its existence seems clear. But how can they be amortized when most corporations possess unlimited life? The lack of a determinable and limited estimated useful life would therefore preclude any tax write-off. Section 248 was enacted to solve this problem.

Under § 248, a corporation may elect to amortize **organizational expenditures** over the 180-month period beginning with the month in which the corporation begins business.[22] Organizational expenditures include the following:

- Legal services incident to organization (e.g., drafting the corporate charter, bylaws, minutes of organizational meetings, and terms of original stock certificates).
- Necessary accounting services.
- Expenses of temporary directors and of organizational meetings of directors or shareholders.
- Fees paid to the state of incorporation.

Expenditures that *do not qualify* as organizational expenditures include those connected with issuing or selling shares of stock or other securities (e.g., commissions, professional fees, and printing costs) or with the transfer of assets to a corporation. These expenditures reduce the amount of capital raised and are not deductible at all.

The first $5,000 of organizational costs can be immediately expensed, with any remaining amount of organizational costs amortized over a 180-month period. However, this $5,000 expensing amount is phased out on a dollar-for-dollar basis when these costs exceed $50,000. For example, a corporation with $52,000 of organizational costs would expense $3,000 [$5,000 − ($52,000 − $50,000)] of this amount and amortize the $49,000 balance ($52,000 − $3,000) over 180 months.

To qualify for the election, the expenditure must be *incurred* before the end of the taxable year in which the corporation begins business. In this regard, the corporation's method of accounting is of no consequence. Thus, an expense incurred by a cash basis corporation in its first tax year qualifies even though the expense is not paid until a subsequent year.

A corporation is deemed to have made the election to amortize organizational expenditures for the taxable year in which it begins business. No separate statement or specific identification of the deducted amount as organizational expenditures is required. A corporation can elect to forgo the deemed election by clearly electing to capitalize organizational expenditures on a timely filed return for its first taxable year. In that case, the capitalized amount will be deductible by the corporation at such time as it ceases to do business and liquidates.

EXAMPLE 29

Black Corporation, an accrual basis taxpayer, was formed and began operations on April 1, 2012. The following expenses were incurred during its first year of operations (April 1–December 31, 2012):

[21] § 246A.

[22] The month in which a corporation begins business may not be immediately apparent. Ordinarily, a corporation begins business when it starts the business operations for which it was organized. Reg. § 1.248–1(d). For a similar problem in the Subchapter S area, see Chapter 12.

Expenses of temporary directors and of organizational meetings	$15,500
Fee paid to the state of incorporation	2,000
Accounting services incident to organization	18,000
Legal services for drafting the corporate charter and bylaws	32,000
Expenses incident to the printing and sale of stock certificates	48,000

Black Corporation elects to amortize organizational costs under § 248. Because of the dollar cap (i.e., dollar-for-dollar reduction for amounts in excess of $50,000), no immediate expensing under the $5,000 rule is available. The monthly amortization is $375 [($15,500 + $2,000 + $18,000 + $32,000) ÷ 180 months], and $3,375 ($375 × 9 months) is deductible for tax year 2012. Note that the $48,000 of expenses incident to the printing and sale of stock certificates does not qualify for the election. These expenses cannot be deducted at all but reduce the amount of the capital realized from the sale of stock. ■

Organizational expenditures are distinguished from *startup expenditures.*[23] Startup expenditures include various investigation expenses involved in entering a new business, whether incurred by a corporate or an individual taxpayer. Startup expenses also include operating expenses such as rent and payroll that are incurred by a corporation before it actually begins to produce any gross income. At the election of the taxpayer, such expenditures (e.g., travel, market surveys, financial audits, and legal fees) are deductible in the same manner as organizational expenditures. Thus, up to $5,000 can be immediately expensed (subject to the phaseout) and any remaining amounts amortized over a period of 180 months. The same rules that apply to the deemed election (and election to forgo the deemed election) for organizational expenditures also apply to startup expenditures.

2.3 Determining the Corporate Income Tax Liability

LO.4

Compute the corporate income tax.

Corporate Income Tax Rates

Corporate income tax rates have fluctuated widely over the years, with the current rate structure reflecting a significant reduction that occurred in the Tax Reform Act of 1986. Refer to Exhibit 2.1 for a schedule of current corporate income tax rates. Unlike the individual income tax rate brackets, the corporate income tax rate brackets are *not* indexed for inflation.

THE BIG PICTURE

EXAMPLE 30

Return to the facts of *The Big Picture* on p. 2-1. Assume that Samantha incorporates her business as Skylark Bakery, Inc., a calendar year C corporation. The corporation pays Samantha a salary of $50,000 for the current year. For 2012, Skylark Bakery has taxable income of $51,500 [$100,000 operating profit + $5,000 dividends − $50,000 salary expense − $3,500 dividends received deduction ($5,000 × 70%)]. Its income tax liability is $7,875, determined as follows:

Tax on $50,000 at 15%	$7,500
Tax on $1,500 at 25%	375
Tax liability	$7,875

[23] § 195.

TAX IN THE NEWS Not All Corporations Are Created Equal

Critics of the U.S. corporate income tax argue that the statutory tax rates are too high, relative to those imposed by other industrialized countries. Consequently, domestic corporations are at a competitive disadvantage in the world marketplace. The U.S. corporate tax rates often are cited as the major force behind the shift of businesses and profits overseas. Recently, there has been a sharp increase in the call for corporate tax reform that would have at its centerpiece a significant reduction in the tax rates. However, given the current environment of Federal budget deficits, any corporate tax reform likely would have to be revenue-neutral to pass Congress. Thus, any reduction in the tax rates would have to be accompanied with a reduction of corporate tax breaks (e.g., deductions, credits, and accounting methods). Complicating the process is the fact that not all corporations are treated equally under the current system and that, inevitably, many corporations would see an increased tax burden as a result of corporate tax reform. Corporations projected as "losers" in any tax reform proposal can be expected to lobby against such legislation. As an example of the varied tax burdens borne by U.S. corporations under the current tax system, consider the effective tax rates assessed on the following select industries:

Industry	Effective U.S. Corporate Tax Rate
Heavy construction	33.76%
Cable TV	21.86%
Hotel/Gaming	13.01%
Pharmaceutical	5.94%

Source: Adapted from David Wessell, "Shifting Options on Corporate Tax Rates," *Wall Street Journal*, December 30, 2010, p. A2.

For taxable income in excess of $100,000 for any tax year, the amount of the tax is increased by the lesser of (1) 5 percent of the excess or (2) $11,750. In effect, the additional tax means a 39 percent rate for every dollar of taxable income from $100,000 to $335,000.

EXAMPLE 31

Silver Corporation, a calendar year taxpayer, has taxable income of $335,000 for 2012. Its income tax liability is $113,900, determined as follows:

Tax on $100,000	$ 22,250
Tax on $235,000 × 39%	91,650
Tax liability	$113,900

Note that the tax liability of $113,900 is 34% of $335,000. Thus, due to the 39% rate (34% normal rate + 5% additional tax on taxable income between $100,000 and $335,000), the benefit of the lower rates on the first $75,000 of taxable income completely phases out at $335,000. The tax rate drops back to 34% on taxable income between $335,000 and $10 million. ■

Under § 11(b)(2), personal service corporations are taxed at a flat 35 percent rate on all taxable income. Thus, PSCs do not enjoy the tax savings of the 15 to 34 percent brackets applicable to other corporations. For this purpose, a PSC is a corporation that is substantially employee owned. Also, it must engage in one of the following activities: health, law, engineering, architecture, accounting, actuarial science, performing arts, or consulting.

Alternative Minimum Tax

Corporations are subject to an alternative minimum tax (AMT) that is similar to the AMT applicable to individuals, both in objective and in application.[24] The AMT for corporations, as for individuals, involves a broader tax base than does the

[24]Small corporations are not subject to the alternative minimum tax.

regular tax. Like an individual, a corporation is required to apply a minimum tax rate to the expanded base and pay an AMT equal to the difference between the tentative AMT and the regular tax. Many of the adjustments and tax preference items necessary to arrive at alternative minimum taxable income (AMTI) are the same for individuals and corporations. The AMT rate and exemption amount for corporations are different from those applicable to individuals, however. Computation of the AMT for corporations is discussed in Chapter 3.

Tax Liability of Related Corporations

LO.5

Explain the rules unique to computing the tax of related corporations.

Members of a controlled group of corporations (**related corporations**) are subject to special rules for computing the income tax, the accumulated earnings credit, and the AMT exemption.[25] If these restrictions did not exist, the shareholders of a corporation could gain significant tax advantages by splitting a single corporation into *multiple* corporations. The next two examples illustrate the potential *income tax* advantage of multiple corporations.

EXAMPLE 32

Gray Corporation annually yields taxable income of $300,000. The corporate tax on $300,000 is $100,250, computed as follows:

Tax on $100,000	$ 22,250
Tax on $200,000 × 39%	78,000
Tax liability	$100,250

■

EXAMPLE 33

Assume that Gray Corporation in the previous example is divided equally into four corporations. Each corporation would have taxable income of $75,000, and the tax for each (absent the special provisions for related corporations) would be computed as follows:

Tax on $50,000	$ 7,500
Tax on $25,000 × 25%	6,250
Tax liability	$13,750

The total liability for the four corporations would be $55,000 ($13,750 × 4). The savings would be $45,250 ($100,250 − $55,000). ■

A comparison of Examples 32 and 33 reveals that the income tax savings that could be achieved by using multiple corporations result from having more of the total taxable income taxed at lower rates. To close this loophole, the law limits a controlled group's taxable income in the tax brackets below 35 percent to the amount the corporations in the group would have if they were one corporation. Thus, in Example 33, under the controlled corporation rules, only $12,500 (one-fourth of the first $50,000 of taxable income) for each of the four related corporations would be taxed at the 15 percent rate. The 25 percent rate would apply to the next $6,250 (one-fourth of the next $25,000) of taxable income of each corporation. This equal allocation of the $50,000 and $25,000 amounts is required unless all members of the controlled group consent to an apportionment plan providing for an unequal allocation. Controlled groups include parent-subsidiary groups, brother-sister groups, combined groups, and certain insurance companies.

Similar limitations apply to controlled groups with respect to the $250,000 accumulated earnings credit and the $40,000 AMT exemption amount. Both the accumulated earnings tax and the AMT are discussed in Chapter 3. Controlled groups are discussed in detail in Chapter 8.

[25] § 1561(a).

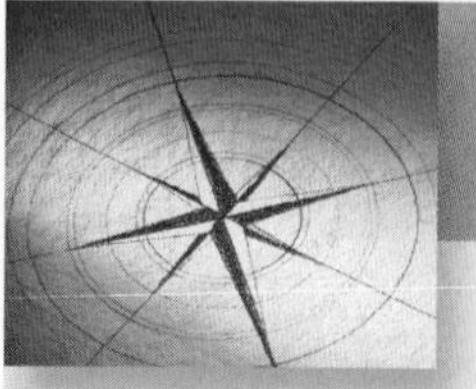

ETHICS & EQUITY A Long Lost Relative?

Brenda Gathers, the president and majority shareholder of both Pelican Corporation and Seagull Corporation, has contracted you to prepare the 2012 tax returns for the two corporations. All prior years' tax returns for the corporations had been prepared by the bookkeepers for each of the corporations. You learn that the bookkeepers have little tax knowledge. What are the tax issues, and what action, if any, should you take?

2.4 Procedural Matters

LO.6

Describe and illustrate the reporting process for corporations.

Filing Requirements for Corporations

A corporation must file a Federal income tax return whether or not it has taxable income.[26] A corporation that was not in existence throughout an entire annual accounting period is required to file a return for the portion of the year during which it was in existence. In addition, a corporation must file a return even though it has ceased to do business if it has valuable claims for which it will bring suit. A corporation is relieved of filing income tax returns only when it ceases to do business and retains no assets.

The corporate return is filed on Form 1120. Corporations electing under Subchapter S (see Chapter 12) file on Form 1120S. Forms 1120 and 1120S are reproduced in Appendix B. Corporations with assets of $10 million or more generally are required to file returns electronically.

The return must be filed on or before the fifteenth day of the third month following the close of a corporation's tax year. As noted previously, a regular corporation, other than a PSC, can use either a calendar year or a fiscal year to report its taxable income. The tax year of the shareholders has no effect on the corporation's tax year.

Corporations can receive an automatic extension of six months for filing the corporate return by filing Form 7004 by the due date for the return. However, the IRS may terminate the extension by mailing a 10-day notice to the corporation. A Form 7004 must be accompanied by the corporation's estimated tax liability.[27]

Estimated Tax Payments

A corporation must make payments of estimated tax unless its tax liability can reasonably be expected to be less than $500. The required annual payment (which includes any estimated AMT liability) is the *lesser* of (1) 100 percent of the corporation's tax for the current year or (2) 100 percent of the tax for the preceding year (if that was a 12-month tax year and the return filed showed a tax liability).[28] Estimated payments can be made in four installments due on or before the fifteenth day of the fourth month, the sixth month, the ninth month, and the twelfth month of the corporate taxable year. The full amount of the unpaid tax is due on the due date of the return. For a calendar year corporation, the payment dates are as follows:

April 15
June 15
September 15
December 15

A corporation failing to pay its required estimated tax payments will be subjected to a nondeductible penalty on the amount by which the installments are less than

[26] § 6012(a)(2).
[27] Reg. § 1.6081–3.
[28] §§ 6655(d) and (e).

the tax due. However, the underpayment penalty will not be imposed if the estimated payments are timely and are equal to the tax liability of the corporation for the prior year or equal to the tax due computed on an annualized basis. If the annualized method is used for one installment and the corporation does not use this method for a subsequent installment, any shortfall from using the annualized method for a prior payment(s) must be made up in the subsequent installment payment. The penalty is imposed on each installment; that is, a corporation must pay one-fourth of its required annual payment by the due date of each installment.

A *large* corporation cannot base its installment payments on its previous year's tax liability except for its first installment payment. A corporation is considered large if it had taxable income of $1 million or more in any of its three preceding years.

EXAMPLE 34

Condor Corporation, a calendar year C corporation, has taxable income of $1.5 million and $2 million for 2011 and 2012, respectively. The required 2012 estimated tax installment payments for Condor, a "large corporation," are computed as follows:

Payment	Amount
April 15, 2012	$127,500*
June 15, 2012	212,500**
September 15, 2012	170,000
December 15, 2012	170,000
Total	$680,000

* Based on preceding year's tax, for first installment only:
[$1.5 million taxable income × 34%
(see Exhibit 2.1)] = $510,000 ÷ 4 = $127,500.

** Based on current year's tax, for remaining installments:
[$2 million taxable income × 34% (see Exhibit 2.1)] = $680,000 ÷ 4 = $170,000.
Second installment must include shortfall from first installment:
[$170,000 + ($170,000 − $127,500)] = $212,500.

Schedule M–1—Reconciliation of Taxable Income and Financial Net Income

Schedule M–1 of Form 1120 is used to *reconcile* net income as computed for financial accounting purposes with taxable income reported on the corporation's income tax return (commonly referred to as book-tax differences). Schedule M–1 is required of corporations with less than $10 million of total assets.

The starting point on Schedule M–1 is net income (loss) per books. Additions and subtractions are entered for items that affect financial accounting net income and taxable income differently. The following items are entered as additions (see lines 2 through 5 of Schedule M–1):

- Federal income tax per books (deducted in computing net income per books but not deductible in computing taxable income).
- The excess of capital losses over capital gains (deducted for financial accounting purposes but not deductible by corporations for income tax purposes).
- Income that is reported in the current year for tax purposes but is not reported in computing net income per books (e.g., prepaid income).
- Various expenses that are deducted in computing net income per books but are not allowed in computing taxable income (e.g., charitable contributions in excess of the 10 percent ceiling applicable to corporations).

The following subtractions are entered on lines 7 and 8 of Schedule M–1:

- Income reported for financial accounting purposes but not included in taxable income (e.g., tax-exempt interest).
- Deductions taken on the tax return but not expensed in computing net income per books (e.g., domestic production activities deduction).

The result is taxable income (before the NOL deduction and the dividends received deduction).

EXAMPLE 35

During the current year, Tern Corporation had the following transactions:

Net income per books (after tax)	$92,400
Taxable income	50,000
Federal income tax per books (15% × $50,000)	7,500
Interest income from tax-exempt bonds	5,000
Interest paid on loan, the proceeds of which were used to purchase the tax-exempt bonds	500
Life insurance proceeds received as a result of the death of a key employee	50,000
Premiums paid on key employee life insurance policy	2,600
Excess of capital losses over capital gains	2,000

For book and tax purposes, Tern Corporation determines depreciation under the straight-line method. Tern's Schedule M–1 for the current year is as follows:

Schedule M-1 **Reconciliation of Income (Loss) per Books With Income per Return**
Note: Schedule M-3 required instead of Schedule M-1 if total assets are $10 million or more—see instructions

1	Net income (loss) per books	92,400	7	Income recorded on books this year not included on this return (itemize): Tax-exempt interest $ 5,000 Life insurance proceeds 50,000	55,000
2	Federal income tax per books	7,500			
3	Excess of capital losses over capital gains	2,000			
4	Income subject to tax not recorded on books this year (itemize):		8	Deductions on this return not charged against book income this year (itemize):	
5	Expenses recorded on books this year not deducted on this return (itemize):		a	Depreciation $	
a	Depreciation $		b	Charitable contributions $	
b	Charitable contributions $				
c	Travel and entertainment $ Prem.–life ins. $2,600; Int.– state bonds $500	3,100	9	Add lines 7 and 8	55,000
6	Add lines 1 through 5	105,000	10	Income (page 1, line 28)—line 6 less line 9	50,000

Schedule M–2 reconciles unappropriated retained earnings at the beginning of the year with unappropriated retained earnings at year-end. Beginning balance plus net income per books, as entered on line 1 of Schedule M–1, less dividend distributions during the year equals ending retained earnings. Other sources of increases or decreases in retained earnings are also listed on Schedule M–2.

EXAMPLE 36

Assume the same facts as in Example 35. Tern Corporation's beginning balance in unappropriated retained earnings is $125,000. During the year, Tern distributed a cash dividend of $30,000 to its shareholders. Based on these further assumptions, Tern's Schedule M–2 for the current year is as follows:

Schedule M-2 **Analysis of Unappropriated Retained Earnings per Books (Line 25, Schedule L)**

1	Balance at beginning of year	125,000	5	Distributions: a Cash	30,000
2	Net income (loss) per books	92,400		b Stock	
3	Other increases (itemize):			c Property	
			6	Other decreases (itemize):	
			7	Add lines 5 and 6	30,000
4	Add lines 1, 2, and 3	217,400	8	Balance at end of year (line 4 less line 7)	187,400

Form **1120**

Corporations with less than $250,000 of gross receipts and less than $250,000 in assets do not have to complete Schedule L (balance sheet) and Schedules M–1 and M–2 of Form 1120. Similar rules apply to Form 1120S. These rules are intended to ease the compliance burden on small business.

Schedule M–3—Net Income (Loss) Reconciliation for Corporations with Total Assets of $10 Million or More

Corporate taxpayers with total assets of $10 million or more are required to report much greater detail relative to differences between income (loss) reported for financial purposes and income (loss) reported for tax purposes. This expanded reconciliation of book and taxable income (loss) is reported on **Schedule M–3.**

FINANCIAL DISCLOSURE INSIGHTS Processing the Corporate Income Tax Return

Seldom is a Form 1120 prepared by itself. In almost every case, the taxpayer and its tax advisers start with the financial accounting records; then they modify book income directly with the book-tax differences that are known by the financial accountants and independent auditors. The tax professionals take these computations, adjust them for tax law changes, and clarify items that require detailed tax research. As the figure illustrates, taxable income for the Form 1120 results from this process.

Notice that this process mirrors that of the preparation of Schedule M–1 or M–3. In preparing these schedules, book income is modified to account for various temporary and permanent book-tax differences as specified by the layout of the forms, resulting in the taxable income amount that is used on page 1 of Form 1120. Some tax professionals maintain that, given the detail required to complete Schedule M–3, the traditional structure of Form 1120 is redundant for large entities. In this regard, page 1 of Form 1120 could be eliminated—taxable income could be computed using Schedule M–3 alone.

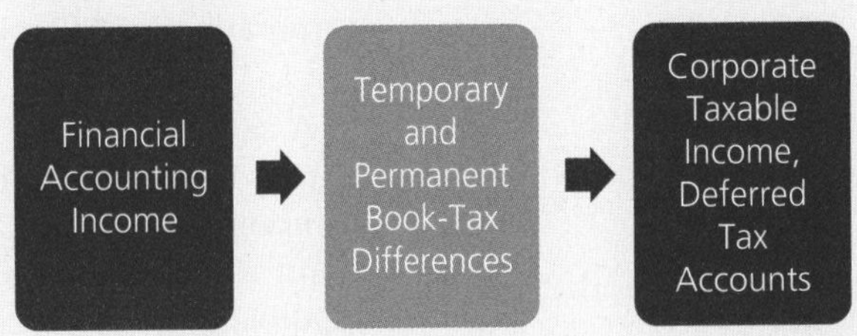

Corporations that are not required to file Schedule M–3 may do so voluntarily. Any corporation that files Schedule M–3 is not allowed to file Schedule M–1. Comparison of Schedule M–3 with Schedule M–1 (illustrated in Example 35) reveals the significantly greater disclosure requirements. Schedule M–3 is reproduced in Appendix B of this text.

Schedule M–3 is a response, at least in part, to financial reporting scandals such as Enron and WorldCom. One objective of Schedule M–3 is to create greater transparency between corporate financial statements and tax returns. Another objective is to identify corporations that engage in aggressive tax practices by requiring that transactions that create book/tax differences be disclosed on corporate tax returns. The increase in transparency and disclosure comes at a cost, however, as the IRS estimates that, on average, almost 89 hours are needed to comply with the requirements of Schedule M–3, and many tax professionals believe that estimate is too low.

Total assets for purposes of the $10 million test and the income and expense amounts required by Schedule M–3 are determined from the taxpayer's financial reports. If the taxpayer files Form 10–K with the Securities and Exchange Commission (SEC), that statement is used. If no 10–K is filed, information from another financial source is used, in the following order: certified financial statements, prepared income statements, or the taxpayer's books and records.

Part I—Financial Information and Net Income (Loss) Reconciliation

Part I requires the following financial information about the corporation:

- The source of the financial net income (loss) amount used in the reconciliation—SEC Form 10–K, audited financial statements, prepared financial statements, or the corporation's books and records.
- Any restatements of the corporation's income statement for the filing period, as well as any restatements for the past five filing periods.
- Any required adjustments to the net income (loss) amount referred to above (see Part I, lines 5 through 10).

The adjusted net income (loss) amount must be reconciled with the amount of taxable income reported on the corporation's Form 1120.

Because of Schedule M–3's complexity, the coverage in this chapter will be limited to some of the more important concepts underlying the schedule. A series of examples adapted from the instructions for Schedule M–3 will be used to illustrate these concepts.

EXAMPLE 37

Southwest Sportsman's Corporation (SSC) sells hunting and fishing equipment to sportsmen. SSC has several stores in Texas, New Mexico, and Arizona. It also has a subsidiary in Mexico, which is organized as a Mexican corporation. SSC, which does not file a Form 10–K with the SEC, reports income from its Mexican subsidiary on its audited financial statements, which show net income of $45 million in 2012. The Mexican corporation, which is not consolidated by SSC for tax purposes and is therefore not an includible corporation, had net income of $7 million. SSC must enter $7 million on Part I, line 5a of Schedule M–3, resulting in net income per income statement of includible corporations of $38 million. ■

A situation similar to that described in Example 37 could result in additional entries in Part I of Schedule M–3. For example, if SSC engaged in transactions with its nonincludible Mexican subsidiary, an entry would be required on line 8 (adjustment to eliminations of transactions between includible corporations and nonincludible entities).

Part II—Reconciliation of Net Income (Loss) per Income Statement of Includible Corporations with Taxable Income per Return

Part II reconciles income and loss items of includible corporations, while Part III reconciles expenses and deductions. As indicated in Example 37, corporations included in a financial reporting group may differ from corporations in a tax reporting group. Corporations may also be partners in a partnership, which is a flow-through entity. The following example illustrates the adjustments that are required in this situation.

EXAMPLE 38

Southwest Sportsman's Corporation also owns an interest in a U.S. partnership, Southwest Hunting Lodges (SHL). On its audited financial statements, SSC reported net income of $10 million as its distributive share from SHL. SSC's Schedule K–1 from SHL reports the following amounts:

Ordinary income	$5,000,000
Long-term capital gain	7,000,000
Charitable contributions	4,000,000
Section 179 expense	100,000

To adjust for the flow-through items from the partnership, SSC must report these items on Schedule M–3, Part II, line 9 [Income (loss) from U.S. partnerships]. The corporation reports $10 million (book income) on line 9, column (a). SSC reports income per tax return of $7.9 million ($5,000,000 + $7,000,000 − $4,000,000 − $100,000) in column (d) of line 9 and a permanent difference of $2.1 million in column (c). ■

Part III—Reconciliation of Expense/Deduction Items

Part III lists 36 reconciling items relating to expenses and deductions. For these items, taxpayers must reconcile differences between income statement amounts (column a) and tax return amounts (column d), then classify these differences as temporary (column b) or permanent (column c) differences. The totals of the reconciling items from Part III are transferred to Part II, line 27, and are included with other items required to reconcile financial statement net income (loss) to tax return net income (loss).

EXAMPLE 39

Southwest Sportsman's Corporation acquired intellectual property in 2012 and deducted amortization of $20,000 on its financial statements, which were prepared according to GAAP. For Federal income tax purposes, SSC deducted $30,000. The corporation must report the amortization on line 28, Part III as follows: $20,000 book amortization in column (a), $10,000 temporary difference in column (b), and $30,000 tax return amortization in column (d). ■

EXAMPLE 40

In January 2012, Southwest Sportsman's Corporation established an allowance for uncollectible accounts (bad debt reserve) of $35,000 on its books and increased the allowance by $65,000 during the year. As a result of a client's bankruptcy, SSC decreased the allowance by $25,000 in November 2012. The corporation deducted the $100,000 of increases to the allowance on its 2012 income statement but was not allowed to deduct that amount on its tax return. On its 2012 tax return, the corporation was allowed to deduct the $25,000 actual loss sustained because of its client's bankruptcy. These amounts must be reported on line 32, Part III as follows: $100,000 book bad debt expense in column (a), $75,000 temporary difference in column (b), and $25,000 tax return bad debt expense in column (d). ■

Example 39 illustrates the Schedule M–3 reporting when book expenses are less than tax return deductions. Example 40 illustrates reporting procedures when book expenses are greater than tax return deductions. Both examples illustrate the reporting of temporary differences. The amounts from both examples are included in the totals derived in Part III and are carried to Part II, line 27. The reconciliation of book income and taxable income occurs in lines 26 through 30. The reconciled amount on Part II, line 30, column (a) must be equal to the net income per income statement of includible corporations on Part I, line 11. The reconciled amount on Part II, line 30, column (d) must be equal to the taxable income reported on Form 1120.

Effect of Taxes on the Financial Statements

Because differences exist between taxable income and net income per books, what effect do these differences have on an entity's financial statements? How are income tax accruals arrived at and reported for accounting purposes? What other types of disclosures regarding present and potential tax liabilities are required to satisfy accounting standards? These and other questions are answered and discussed at length in Chapter 14.

Beginning with 2010 tax returns, a corporation with total assets of $100 million or more must file new Schedule UTP (Uncertain Tax Position Statement) with its Form 1120. A lower filing requirement of $10 million or more of assets will be fully phased in for 2014 returns. In general, a corporation is required to report tax positions taken on a current or prior year's Federal income tax return and for which the corporation recorded a reserve for Federal income tax in its audited financial statements (or for which no reserve was recorded because of an expectation to litigate). Financial reporting of tax positions is discussed in Chapter 14.

Form 1120 Illustrated

To provide an example on the use of the corporate income tax return, a Form 1120, which follows, has been completed for Swift Corporation. Due to the $10 million test, Swift Corporation does not require the use of Schedule M–3.

Swift Corporation was formed on January 10, 1985, by James Brown and Martha Swift to sell men's clothing. Pertinent information regarding Swift is summarized as follows:

- The business address is 6210 Norman Street, Buffalo, TX 75831.
- The employer identification number is 11–1111111; the principal business activity code is 448110.

- James Brown and Martha Swift each own one-half of the outstanding common stock; no other class of stock is authorized. James Brown is president of the company, and Martha Swift is secretary-treasurer. Both are full-time employees of the corporation, and each receives a salary of $70,000. James's Social Security number is 123-45-6789; Martha's Social Security number is 987-65-4321.
- The corporation uses the accrual method of accounting and reports on a calendar basis. The specific chargeoff method is used in handling bad debt losses, and inventories are determined using the lower of cost or market method. For book and tax purposes, the straight-line method of depreciation is used.
- During 2011, the corporation distributed a cash dividend of $35,000. Selected portions of Swift's profit and loss statement reflect the following debits and credits:

Account		Debit	Credit
Gross sales			$1,040,000
Sales returns and allowances		$ 50,000	
Purchases		506,000	
Dividends received from stock investments in less-than-20%-owned U.S. corporations			60,000
Interest income			
State bonds	$ 9,000		
Certificates of deposit	11,000		20,000
Premiums on term life insurance policies on the lives of James Brown and Martha Swift; Swift Corporation is the designated beneficiary		8,000	
Salaries—officers		140,000	
Salaries—clerical and sales		100,000	
Taxes (state, local, and payroll)		35,000	
Repairs		20,000	
Interest expense			
Loan to purchase state bonds	$ 4,000		
Other business loans	10,000	14,000	
Advertising		8,000	
Rental expense		24,000	
Depreciation		16,000	
Other deductions		21,000	

A comparative balance sheet for Swift Corporation reveals the following information:

Assets	January 1, 2011	December 31, 2011
Cash	$ 240,000	$ 163,850
Trade notes and accounts receivable	104,200	142,300
Inventories	300,000	356,000
Federal bonds	50,000	50,000
State bonds	100,000	100,000
Prepaid Federal tax	—	1,700
Stock investment	300,000	400,000
Buildings and other depreciable assets	120,000	120,000
Accumulated depreciation	(44,400)	(60,400)
Land	10,000	10,000
Other assets	1,800	1,000
Total assets	$1,181,600	$1,284,450

Liabilities and Equity	January 1, 2011	December 31, 2011
Accounts payable	$ 150,000	$ 125,000
Other current liabilities	40,150	33,300
Mortgages	105,000	100,000
Capital stock	250,000	250,000
Retained earnings	636,450	776,150
Total liabilities and equity	$1,181,600	$1,284,450

Net income per books (before any income tax accrual) is $234,000. During 2011, Swift Corporation made estimated tax payments to the IRS of $61,000. Swift Corporation's Form 1120 for 2011 is reproduced on the following pages.

Although most of the entries on Form 1120 for Swift Corporation are self-explanatory, the following comments may be helpful:

- To arrive at the cost of goods sold amount (line 2 on page 1), Form 1125–A must be completed.
- Reporting of dividends requires the completion of Schedule C (page 2). Gross dividends are shown on line 4 (page 1), and the dividends received deduction appears on line 29b (page 1). Separating the dividend from the deduction facilitates the application of the taxable income limitation (which did not apply in Swift's case).
- Income tax liability is $59,300, computed as follows:

Tax on $100,000	$22,250
Tax on $95,000 at 39%	37,050
	$59,300

  The result is transferred to line 2 of Schedule J and ultimately is listed on line 31 (page 1). Because the estimated tax payment of $61,000 is more than the tax liability of $59,300, Swift will receive a tax refund of $1,700.
- Schedule K, line 4b, requires a Schedule G to be completed, but the schedule is not shown in the illustrated example.
- In completing Schedule M–1 (page 5), the net income per books (line 1) is net of the Federal income tax ($234,000 – $59,300). The left side of Schedule M–1 (lines 2–5) represents positive adjustments to net income per books. After the negative adjustments are made (line 9), the result is taxable income before NOLs and special deductions (line 28, page 1).
- In completing Schedule M–2 (page 5), the beginning retained earnings figure of $636,450 is added to the net income per books as entered on Schedule M–1 (line 1). The dividends distributed in the amount of $35,000 are entered on line 5 and subtracted to arrive at the ending balance in unappropriated retained earnings of $776,150.
- Because this example lacks certain details, supporting schedules that would be attached to Form 1120 have not been included. For example, a Form 4562 would be included to verify the depreciation deduction (line 20, page 1), and other deductions (line 26, page 1) would be supported by a schedule.

Consolidated Returns

Corporations that are members of a parent-subsidiary affiliated group may be able to file a consolidated income tax return for a taxable year. Consolidated returns are discussed in Chapter 8.

Form **1120**
Department of the Treasury
Internal Revenue Service

U.S. Corporation Income Tax Return

For calendar year 2011 or tax year beginning ________, 2011, ending ________, 20 __

▶ See separate instructions.

OMB No. 1545-0123

2011

A Check if:
1a Consolidated return (attach Form 851) ☐
b Life/nonlife consolidated return ☐
2 Personal holding co. (attach Sch. PH) ☐
3 Personal service corp. (see instructions) ☐
4 Schedule M-3 attached ☐

TYPE OR PRINT

Name: *Swift Corporation*
Number, street, and room or suite no. If a P.O. box, see instructions.: *6210 Norman Street*
City or town, state, and ZIP code: *Buffalo, TX 75831*

B Employer identification number: *11–1111111*
C Date incorporated: *1-10-85*
D Total assets (see instructions): $ *1,284,450 | 00*

E Check if: (1) ☐ Initial return (2) ☐ Final return (3) ☐ Name change (4) ☐ Address change

Income	1a	Merchant card and third-party payments. For 2011, enter -0-	1a			
	b	Gross receipts or sales not reported on line 1a (see instructions)	1b	*1,040,000 00*		
	c	Total. Add lines 1a and 1b	1c	*1,040,000 00*		
	d	Returns and allowances plus any other adjustments (see instructions)	1d	*50,000 00*		
	e	Subtract line 1d from line 1c			1e	*990,000 00*
	2	Cost of goods sold from Form 1125-A, line 8 (attach Form 1125-A)			2	*450,000 00*
	3	Gross profit. Subtract line 2 from line 1e			3	*540,000 00*
	4	Dividends (Schedule C, line 19)			4	*60,000 00*
	5	Interest			5	*11,000 00*
	6	Gross rents			6	
	7	Gross royalties			7	
	8	Capital gain net income (attach Schedule D (Form 1120))			8	
	9	Net gain or (loss) from Form 4797, Part II, line 17 (attach Form 4797)			9	
	10	Other income (see instructions—attach schedule)			10	
	11	**Total income.** Add lines 3 through 10 ▶			11	*611,000 00*
Deductions (See instructions for limitations on deductions.)	12	Compensation of officers from Form 1125-E, line 4 (attach Form 1125-E) ▶			12	*140,000 00*
	13	Salaries and wages (less employment credits)			13	*100,000 00*
	14	Repairs and maintenance			14	*20,000 00*
	15	Bad debts			15	
	16	Rents			16	*24,000 00*
	17	Taxes and licenses			17	*35,000 00*
	18	Interest			18	*10,000 00*
	19	Charitable contributions			19	
	20	Depreciation from Form 4562 not claimed on Form 1125-A or elsewhere on return (attach Form 4562)			20	*16,000 00*
	21	Depletion			21	
	22	Advertising			22	*8,000 00*
	23	Pension, profit-sharing, etc., plans			23	
	24	Employee benefit programs			24	
	25	Domestic production activities deduction (attach Form 8903)			25	
	26	Other deductions (attach schedule)			26	*21,000 00*
	27	**Total deductions.** Add lines 12 through 26 ▶			27	*374,000 00*
	28	Taxable income before net operating loss deduction and special deductions. Subtract line 27 from line 11.			28	*237,000 00*
	29a	Net operating loss deduction (see instructions)	29a			
	b	Special deductions (Schedule C, line 20)	29b	*42,000 00*		
	c	Add lines 29a and 29b			29c	*42,000 00*
Tax, Refundable Credits, and Payments	30	**Taxable income.** Subtract line 29c from line 28 (see instructions)			30	*195,000 00*
	31	Total tax (Schedule J, Part I, line 11)			31	*59,300 00*
	32	Total payments and refundable credits (Schedule J, Part II, line 21)			32	*61,000 00*
	33	Estimated tax penalty (see instructions). Check if Form 2220 is attached ▶ ☐			33	
	34	**Amount owed.** If line 32 is smaller than the total of lines 31 and 33, enter amount owed			34	
	35	**Overpayment.** If line 32 is larger than the total of lines 31 and 33, enter amount overpaid			35	*1,700 00*
	36	Enter amount from line 35 you want: **Credited to 2012 estimated tax ▶**		**Refunded ▶**	36	*1,700 00*

Sign Here

Under penalties of perjury, I declare that I have examined this return, including accompanying schedules and statements, and to the best of my knowledge and belief, it is true, correct, and complete. Declaration of preparer (other than taxpayer) is based on all information of which preparer has any knowledge.

▶ Signature of officer | Date | ▶ Title

May the IRS discuss this return with the preparer shown below (see instructions)? ☐ **Yes** ☐ **No**

Paid Preparer Use Only

Print/Type preparer's name	Preparer's signature	Date	Check ☐ if self-employed	PTIN
Firm's name ▶			Firm's EIN ▶	
Firm's address ▶			Phone no.	

For Paperwork Reduction Act Notice, see separate instructions. Cat. No. 11450Q Form **1120** (2011)

Form 1120 (2011) Page **2**

Schedule C **Dividends and Special Deductions** (see instructions)	**(a)** Dividends received	**(b)** %	**(c)** Special deductions **(a)** × **(b)**
1 Dividends from less-than-20%-owned domestic corporations (other than debt-financed stock)	60,000	70	42,000
2 Dividends from 20%-or-more-owned domestic corporations (other than debt-financed stock)		80	
3 Dividends on debt-financed stock of domestic and foreign corporations		see instructions	
4 Dividends on certain preferred stock of less-than-20%-owned public utilities		42	
5 Dividends on certain preferred stock of 20%-or-more-owned public utilities		48	
6 Dividends from less-than-20%-owned foreign corporations and certain FSCs		70	
7 Dividends from 20%-or-more-owned foreign corporations and certain FSCs		80	
8 Dividends from wholly owned foreign subsidiaries		100	
9 **Total.** Add lines 1 through 8. See instructions for limitation			42,000
10 Dividends from domestic corporations received by a small business investment company operating under the Small Business Investment Act of 1958		100	
11 Dividends from affiliated group members		100	
12 Dividends from certain FSCs		100	
13 Dividends from foreign corporations not included on lines 3, 6, 7, 8, 11, or 12			
14 Income from controlled foreign corporations under subpart F (attach Form(s) 5471)			
15 Foreign dividend gross-up			
16 IC-DISC and former DISC dividends not included on lines 1, 2, or 3			
17 Other dividends			
18 Deduction for dividends paid on certain preferred stock of public utilities			
19 **Total dividends.** Add lines 1 through 17. Enter here and on page 1, line 4 ▶	60,000		
20 **Total special deductions.** Add lines 9, 10, 11, 12, and 18. Enter here and on page 1, line 29b ▶			42,000

Form **1120** (2011)

Form 1120 (2011) Page **3**

Schedule J Tax Computation and Payment (see instructions)

Part I–Tax Computation

1	Check if the corporation is a member of a controlled group (attach Schedule O (Form 1120)) ▶ ☐					
2	Income tax. Check if a qualified personal service corporation (see instructions) ▶ ☐			2	59,300	00
3	Alternative minimum tax (attach Form 4626)			3		
4	Add lines 2 and 3			4	59,300	00
5a	Foreign tax credit (attach Form 1118)	5a				
b	Credit from Form 8834, line 30 (attach Form 8834)	5b				
c	General business credit (attach Form 3800)	5c				
d	Credit for prior year minimum tax (attach Form 8827)	5d				
e	Bond credits from Form 8912	5e				
6	**Total credits.** Add lines 5a through 5e			6		
7	Subtract line 6 from line 4			7	59,300	00
8	Personal holding company tax (attach Schedule PH (Form 1120))			8		
9a	Recapture of investment credit (attach Form 4255)	9a				
b	Recapture of low-income housing credit (attach Form 8611)	9b				
c	Interest due under the look-back method—completed long-term contracts (attach Form 8697)	9c				
d	Interest due under the look-back method—income forecast method (attach Form 8866)	9d				
e	Alternative tax on qualifying shipping activities (attach Form 8902)	9e				
f	Other (see instructions—attach schedule)	9f				
10	**Total.** Add lines 9a through 9f			10		
11	**Total tax.** Add lines 7, 8, and 10. Enter here and on page 1, line 31			11	59,300	00

Part II–Payments and Refundable Credits

12	2010 overpayment credited to 2011			12		
13	2011 estimated tax payments			13	61,000	00
14	2011 refund applied for on Form 4466			14	(	)
15	Combine lines 12, 13, and 14			15	61,000	00
16	Tax deposited with Form 7004			16		
17	Withholding (see instructions)			17		
18	**Total payments.** Add lines 15, 16, and 17			18	61,000	00
19	Refundable credits from:					
a	Form 2439	19a				
b	Form 4136	19b				
c	Form 3800, line 17c and Form 8827, line 8c	19c				
d	Other (attach schedule—see instructions)	19d				
20	**Total credits.** Add lines 19a through 19d			20		
21	**Total payments and credits.** Add lines 18 and 20. Enter here and on page 1, line 32			21	61,000	00

Schedule K Other Information (see instructions)

		Yes	No
1	Check accounting method: a ☐ Cash b ☒ Accrual c ☐ Other (specify) ▶		
2	See the instructions and enter the:		
a	Business activity code no. ▶ *448110*		
b	Business activity ▶ *Retail sales*		
c	Product or service ▶ *Men's clothing*		
3	Is the corporation a subsidiary in an affiliated group or a parent-subsidiary controlled group? If "Yes," enter name and EIN of the parent corporation ▶		X
4	At the end of the tax year:		
a	Did any foreign or domestic corporation, partnership (including any entity treated as a partnership), trust, or tax-exempt organization own directly 20% or more, or own, directly or indirectly, 50% or more of the total voting power of all classes of the corporation's stock entitled to vote? If "Yes," complete Part I of Schedule G (Form 1120) (attach Schedule G)		X
b	Did any individual or estate own directly 20% or more, or own, directly or indirectly, 50% or more of the total voting power of all classes of the corporation's stock entitled to vote? If "Yes," complete Part II of Schedule G (Form 1120) (attach Schedule G)	X	

Form **1120** (2011)

Form 1120 (2011) Page **4**

Schedule K **Other Information** *continued* (see instructions)

		Yes	No
5	At the end of the tax year, did the corporation:		
a	Own directly 20% or more, or own, directly or indirectly, 50% or more of the total voting power of all classes of stock entitled to vote of any foreign or domestic corporation not included on **Form 851,** Affiliations Schedule? For rules of constructive ownership, see instructions. If "Yes," complete (i) through (iv) below.		*X*

(i) Name of Corporation	**(ii)** Employer Identification Number (if any)	**(iii)** Country of Incorporation	**(iv)** Percentage Owned in Voting Stock

		Yes	No
b	Own directly an interest of 20% or more, or own, directly or indirectly, an interest of 50% or more in any foreign or domestic partnership (including an entity treated as a partnership) or in the beneficial interest of a trust? For rules of constructive ownership, see instructions. If "Yes," complete (i) through (iv) below.		*X*

(i) Name of Entity	**(ii)** Employer Identification Number (if any)	**(iii)** Country of Organization	**(iv)** Maximum Percentage Owned in Profit, Loss, or Capital

		Yes	No
6	During this tax year, did the corporation pay dividends (other than stock dividends and distributions in exchange for stock) in excess of the corporation's current and accumulated earnings and profits? (See sections 301 and 316.)		*X*
	If "Yes," file **Form 5452,** Corporate Report of Nondividend Distributions. If this is a consolidated return, answer here for the parent corporation and on Form 851 for each subsidiary.		
7	At any time during the tax year, did one foreign person own, directly or indirectly, at least 25% of **(a)** the total voting power of all classes of the corporation's stock entitled to vote or **(b)** the total value of all classes of the corporation's stock?		*X*
	For rules of attribution, see section 318. If "Yes," enter: **(i)** Percentage owned ▶ ______ and **(ii)** Owner's country ▶ ______		
	(c) The corporation may have to file **Form 5472,** Information Return of a 25% Foreign-Owned U.S. Corporation or a Foreign Corporation Engaged in a U.S. Trade or Business. Enter the number of Forms 5472 attached ▶ ______		
8	Check this box if the corporation issued publicly offered debt instruments with original issue discount . . . . ▶ ☐		
	If checked, the corporation may have to file **Form 8281,** Information Return for Publicly Offered Original Issue Discount Instruments.		
9	Enter the amount of tax-exempt interest received or accrued during the tax year ▶ $ *9,000*		
10	Enter the number of shareholders at the end of the tax year (if 100 or fewer) ▶ *2*		
11	If the corporation has an NOL for the tax year and is electing to forego the carryback period, check here . . . . . . ▶ ☐		
	If the corporation is filing a consolidated return, the statement required by Regulations section 1.1502-21(b)(3) must be attached or the election will not be valid.		
12	Enter the available NOL carryover from prior tax years (do not reduce it by any deduction on line 29a.) ▶ $ ______		
13	Are the corporation's total receipts (line 1c plus lines 4 through 10 on page 1) for the tax year **and** its total assets at the end of the tax year less than $250,000?		*X*
	If "Yes," the corporation is not required to complete Schedules L, M-1, and M-2 on page 5. Instead, enter the total amount of cash distributions and the book value of property distributions (other than cash) made during the tax year. ▶ $ ______		
14	Is the corporation required to file Schedule UTP (Form 1120), Uncertain Tax Position Statement (see instructions)?		*X*
	If "Yes," complete and attach Schedule UTP.		
15a	Did the corporation make any payments in 2011 that would require it to file Form(s) 1099 (see instructions)?		*X*
b	If "Yes," did or will the corporation file all required Forms 1099?		

Form **1120** (2011)

Form 1120 (2011) Page 5

Schedule L Balance Sheets per Books

Assets	Beginning of tax year (a)	(b)	End of tax year (c)	(d)
1 Cash		240,000		163,850
2a Trade notes and accounts receivable	104,200		142,300	
b Less allowance for bad debts	( )	104,200	( )	142,300
3 Inventories		300,000		356,000
4 U.S. government obligations		50,000		50,000
5 Tax-exempt securities (see instructions)		100,000		100,000
6 Other current assets (attach schedule)				1,700
7 Loans to shareholders				
8 Mortgage and real estate loans				
9 Other investments (attach schedule)		300,000		400,000
10a Buildings and other depreciable assets	120,000		120,000	
b Less accumulated depreciation	(44,400)	75,600	(60,400)	59,600
11a Depletable assets				
b Less accumulated depletion	( )		( )	
12 Land (net of any amortization)		10,000		10,000
13a Intangible assets (amortizable only)				
b Less accumulated amortization	( )		( )	
14 Other assets (attach schedule)		1,800		1,000
15 Total assets		1,181,600		1,284,450
Liabilities and Shareholders' Equity				
16 Accounts payable		150,000		125,000
17 Mortgages, notes, bonds payable in less than 1 year				
18 Other current liabilities (attach schedule)		40,150		33,300
19 Loans from shareholders				
20 Mortgages, notes, bonds payable in 1 year or more		105,000		100,000
21 Other liabilities (attach schedule)				
22 Capital stock: a Preferred stock				
b Common stock	250,000	250,000	250,000	250,000
23 Additional paid-in capital				
24 Retained earnings—Appropriated (attach schedule)				
25 Retained earnings—Unappropriated		636,450		776,150
26 Adjustments to shareholders' equity (attach schedule)				
27 Less cost of treasury stock		( )		( )
28 Total liabilities and shareholders' equity		1,181,600		1,284,450

Schedule M-1 Reconciliation of Income (Loss) per Books With Income per Return

Note: Schedule M-3 required instead of Schedule M-1 if total assets are $10 million or more—see instructions

1 Net income (loss) per books	174,700		7 Income recorded on books this year not included on this return (itemize): Tax-exempt interest $ 9,000	9,000
2 Federal income tax per books	59,300			
3 Excess of capital losses over capital gains				
4 Income subject to tax not recorded on books this year (itemize):			8 Deductions on this return not charged against book income this year (itemize):	
5 Expenses recorded on books this year not deducted on this return (itemize):			a Depreciation $	
a Depreciation $			b Charitable contributions $	
b Charitable contributions $				
c Travel and entertainment $				
Prem.– life ins. $8,000; Int.– state bonds $4,000	12,000		9 Add lines 7 and 8	9,000
6 Add lines 1 through 5	246,000		10 Income (page 1, line 28)—line 6 less line 9	237,000

Schedule M-2 Analysis of Unappropriated Retained Earnings per Books (Line 25, Schedule L)

1 Balance at beginning of year	636,450	5 Distributions: a Cash	35,000
2 Net income (loss) per books	174,700	b Stock	
3 Other increases (itemize):		c Property	
		6 Other decreases (itemize):	
		7 Add lines 5 and 6	35,000
4 Add lines 1, 2, and 3	811,150	8 Balance at end of year (line 4 less line 7)	776,150

Form **1120** (2011)

Form **1125-A** (December 2011) Department of the Treasury Internal Revenue Service

Cost of Goods Sold

▶ **Attach to Form 1120, 1120-C, 1120-F, 1120S, 1065, and 1065-B.**

OMB No. 1545-2225

Name		Employer identification number
Swift Corporation		*11-1111111*
1 Inventory at beginning of year	1	*300,000*
2 Purchases	2	*506,000*
3 Cost of labor	3	
4 Additional section 263A costs (attach schedule)	4	
5 Other costs (attach schedule)	5	
6 **Total.** Add lines 1 through 5	6	*806,000*
7 Inventory at end of year	7	*356,000*
8 **Cost of goods sold.** Subtract line 7 from line 6. Enter here and on Form 1120, page 1, line 2 or the appropriate line of your tax return (see instructions)	8	*450,000*

9a Check all methods used for valuing closing inventory:
(i) ☐ Cost
(ii) ☑ Lower of cost or market
(iii) ☐ Other (Specify method used and attach explanation.) ▶ ____

b Check if there was a writedown of subnormal goods ▶ ☐

c Check if the LIFO inventory method was adopted this tax year for any goods (if checked, attach Form 970) ▶ ☐

d If the LIFO inventory method was used for this tax year, enter amount of closing inventory computed under LIFO 9d ____

e If property is produced or acquired for resale, do the rules of section 263A apply to the corporation? ☐ Yes ☑ No

f Was there any change in determining quantities, cost, or valuations between opening and closing inventory? If "Yes," attach explanation ☐ Yes ☑ No

Section references are to the Internal Revenue Code unless otherwise noted.

General Instructions

Future Developments. The IRS has created a page on IRS.gov for information about Form 1125-A and its instructions at *www.irs.gov/form1125a*. Information about any future developments affecting Form 1125-A (such as legislation enacted after we release it) will be posted on that page.

Purpose of Form

Use Form 1125-A to calculate and deduct cost of goods sold for certain entities.

Who Must File

Filers of Form 1120, 1120-C, 1120-F, 1120S, 1065, or 1065-B, must complete and attach Form 1125-A if the applicable entity reports a deduction for cost of goods sold.

Inventories

Generally, inventories are required at the beginning and end of each tax year if the production, purchase, or sale of merchandise is an income-producing factor. See Regulations section 1.471-1. If inventories are required, you generally must use an accrual method of accounting for sales and purchases of inventory items.

Exception for certain taxpayers. If you are a qualifying taxpayer or a qualifying small business taxpayer (defined below), you can adopt or change your accounting method to account for inventoriable items in the same manner as materials and supplies that are not incidental.

Under this accounting method inventory costs for raw materials purchased for use in producing finished goods and merchandise purchased for resale are deductible in the year the finished goods or merchandise are sold (but not before the year you paid for the raw materials or merchandise, if you are also using the cash method). For additional guidance on this method of accounting, see Pub. 538, Accounting Periods and Methods. For guidance on adopting or changing to this method of accounting, see Form 3115, Application for Change in Accounting Method, and its instructions

If you account for inventoriable items in the same manner as materials and supplies that are not incidental, you can currently deduct expenditures for direct labor and all indirect costs that would otherwise be included in inventory costs.

Qualifying taxpayer. A qualifying taxpayer is a taxpayer that, (a) for each prior tax year ending after December 16, 1998, has average annual gross receipts of $1 million or less for the 3 prior tax years and (b) its business is not a tax shelter (as defined in section 448(d)(3)). See Rev. Proc. 2001-10, 2001-2 I.R.B. 272.

Qualifying small business taxpayer. A qualifying small business taxpayer is a taxpayer that, (a) for each prior tax year ending on or after December 31, 2000, has average annual gross receipts of $10 million or less for the 3 prior tax years, (b) whose principal business activity is not an ineligible activity, and (c) whose business is not a tax shelter (as defined in section 448 (d)(3)). See Rev. Proc. 2002-28, 2002-18, I. R.B. 815.

Uniform capitalization rules. The uniform capitalization rules of section 263A generally require you to capitalize, or include in inventory, certain costs incurred in connection with the following.

- The production of real property and tangible personal property held in inventory or held for sale in the ordinary course of business.
- Real property or personal property (tangible and intangible) acquired for resale.
- The production of real property and tangible personal property by a corporation for use in its trade or business or in an activity engaged in for property.

See the discussion on section 263A uniform capitalization rules in the instructions for your tax return before completing Form 1125-A. Also see Regulations sections 1.263A-1 through 1.263A-3. See Regulations section 1.263A-4 for rules for property produced in a farming business.

For Paperwork Reduction Act Notice, see instructions. Cat. No. 55988R Form **1125-A** (12-2011)

2.5 Tax Planning

LO.7

Evaluate corporations as an entity form for conducting a business.

Corporate versus Noncorporate Forms of Business Organization

The decision to use the corporate form in conducting a trade or business must be weighed carefully. Besides the nontax considerations of the corporate form (limited liability, continuity of life, free transferability of interests, and centralized management), tax ramifications will play an important role in any such decision. Close attention should be paid to the following:

1. Operating as a regular corporate entity (C corporation) results in the imposition of the corporate income tax. Corporate taxable income will be taxed twice—once as earned by the corporation and again when distributed to the shareholders. Because dividends are not deductible, a closely held corporation may have a strong incentive to structure corporate distributions in a deductible form. Before legislation in 2003 lowered the rate on qualified dividends to 15 percent, shareholders had a tax incentive to bail out profits in the form of salaries, interest, or rent.[29] With the 15 percent rate on qualified dividends, shareholders may save taxes by having the corporation pay dividends rather than salaries, rent, or interest, which could be taxed at an individual marginal rate as high as 35 percent. The decision should be made only after comparing the tax cost of the two alternatives. The window of opportunity for reaping the benefit of the preferential tax rate on dividend income is set to close by 2013, however, and this must be considered in the analysis.
2. The differences in Federal tax brackets between an individual and a corporation may not be substantial. Furthermore, several state and local governments impose higher taxes on corporations than on individuals. In these jurisdictions, the combined Federal, state, and local tax rates on the two types of taxpayers are practically identical. Consequently, the tax ramifications of incorporating can be determined *only* on a case-by-case basis.
3. Corporate-source income loses its identity as it passes through the corporation to the shareholders. Thus, items that normally receive preferential tax treatment (e.g., interest on municipal bonds) are not taxed as such to the shareholders.
4. As noted in Chapter 5, it may be difficult for shareholders to recover some or all of their investment in the corporation without an ordinary income result. Most corporate distributions are treated as dividends to the extent of the corporation's earnings and profits. However, with the 15 percent rate on qualified dividends, dividends are taxed at the same rate as net capital gains.
5. Corporate losses cannot be passed through to the shareholders.[30]
6. The liquidation of a corporation will normally generate tax consequences to both the corporation and its shareholders (see Chapter 6).
7. The corporate form provides shareholders with the opportunity to be treated as employees for tax purposes if the shareholders render services to the corporation. Such status makes a number of attractive tax-sheltered fringe benefits available. They include, but are not limited to, group term life insurance and excludible meals and lodging. One of the most attractive benefits of incorporation is the ability of the business to provide accident and health insurance to its employees, including shareholder-employees. Such benefits are not included in the employee's gross income. Similar rules apply to other

[29] Such procedures lead to a multitude of problems, one of which, the reclassification of debt as equity, is discussed in Chapter 4. The problems of unreasonable salaries and rents are covered in Chapter 5 in the discussion of constructive dividends.

[30] Points 1, 2, and 5 could be resolved through a Subchapter S election (see Chapter 12), assuming that the corporation qualifies for such an election. In part, the same can be said for point 3.

FINANCIAL DISCLOSURE INSIGHTS Deferred Taxes on the Balance Sheet

A business entity that follows GAAP, whether it is incorporated or not, typically records deferred tax assets and liabilities on its Statement of Financial Position (the "balance sheet"). These differences between the entity's total tax expense and its current tax expense can represent sizable amounts on the balance sheet. Because certain transactions result in deferred tax assets and others in deferred tax liabilities, many balance sheets include dollar amounts for both accounts, as indicated by the following estimates from recent financial reports.

	Deferred Tax Liabilities ($000)	Deferred Tax Assets ($000)
General Electric	34,200	22,000
ExxonMobil	30,200	11,200
Berkshire Hathaway	22,500	4,300
Ford Motor	14,500	15,000

As deferred tax amounts "reverse" themselves into the Statement of Earnings and Comprehensive Income (the "income statement"), shareholders and investment analysts must determine whether and how the tax deferrals indicate the current and future profitability of the entity. This becomes especially difficult when any of the following occur:

- The taxpayer wins or loses an audit or other appeal with a taxing jurisdiction, creating an unusual amount due or refund.
- Tax rates change, and the amounts of the tax deferrals change accordingly.
- A multinational entity deals with countries outside the United States that apply a different mix of taxes and rates.

Much of the public information regarding tax deferrals is found in the footnotes to the entity's financial statements, but these data can be difficult to interpret for large businesses with complex legal structures.

medical costs paid by the employer. These benefits are not available to partners, sole proprietors, and more-than-2 percent shareholder-employees of S corporations.

Operating the Corporation

Tax planning to reduce corporate income taxes should occur before the end of the tax year. Effective planning can cause income to be shifted to the next tax year and can produce large deductions by incurring expenses before year-end. Particular attention should be focused on the following.

Charitable Contributions

Recall that accrual basis corporations may claim a deduction for charitable contributions in the year preceding payment. The contribution must be authorized by the board of directors by the end of the tax year and paid on or before the fifteenth day of the third month of the following year. It might be useful to authorize a contribution even though it may not ultimately be made. A deduction cannot be thrown back to the previous year (even if paid within the two and one-half months) if it has not been authorized.

The enhanced deduction amount for contributions of qualified inventory can produce significant tax savings. Gifts of inventory should be designed to take advantage of this provision whenever feasible. Effort should be taken to properly document the type of inventory donated and each recipient charitable organization, as the statutory provisions that allow for an enhanced deduction have very specific requirements for qualification. Further, a corporation's cost of goods sold must be reduced to reflect any charitable contribution of inventory.

The five-year carryover period for excess charitable contributions, coupled with the requirement that a current year's contribution be applied against the 10 percent-of-taxable-income limitation before the utilization of any carryover amount, may require some tax planning. Under these rules, a charitable contribution in the current year could preclude any deduction for an amount in its fifth year of the carryover period. For a corporation with an annual gift-giving plan, this dilemma may require the deferral of a current year's contribution to obtain a deduction for the expiring carryover amount.

Timing of Capital Gains and Losses

A corporation should consider offsetting profits on the sale of capital assets by selling some of the depreciated securities in the corporate portfolio. In addition, any already realized capital losses should be carefully monitored. Recall that corporate taxpayers are not permitted to claim any net capital losses as deductions against ordinary income. Capital losses can be used only as an offset against capital gains. Further, net capital losses can only be carried back three years and forward five. Gains from the sales of capital assets should be timed to offset any capital losses. The expiration of the carryover period for any net capital losses should be watched carefully so that sales of appreciated capital assets occur before that date.

Net Operating Losses

In some situations, electing to forgo an NOL carryback and utilizing the carryforward option may generate greater tax savings.

EXAMPLE 41

Ruby Corporation incurred a $50,000 NOL in 2012. Ruby, which was in the 15% bracket in 2010 and 2011, has developed a new product that management predicts will push the corporation into the 34% bracket in 2013. If Ruby carries the NOL back, the tax savings will be $7,500 ($50,000 × 15%). However, if Ruby elects to carry the NOL forward, assuming that management's prediction is accurate, the tax savings will be $17,000 ($50,000 × 34%). ■

When deciding whether to forgo the carryback option, several factors should be considered. First, the time value of the tax refund that is lost by not using the carryback procedure should be calculated. Second, the election to forgo an NOL carryback is irrevocable. Thus, one cannot later choose to change if the predicted high profits do not materialize. Third, consider the future increases (or decreases) in corporate income tax rates that can reasonably be anticipated. This last consideration is the most difficult to work with. Although corporate tax rates have remained relatively stable in recent years, taxpayers have little assurance that future rates will remain constant.

Dividends Received Deduction

In those cases where the taxable income limitation is applicable to a corporation's dividends received deduction, consideration should be given to the proper timing of income and deductions so as to bring the NOL rule into play. The NOL rule, the exception to the taxable income limitation, can result in a significant increase in the amount of a corporation's dividends received deduction.

EXAMPLE 42

Pearl Corporation, a calendar year C corporation, has the following information for the year:

Gross income from operations	$ 200,000
Expenses from operations	(225,000)
Dividends received from domestic corporations (less than 20% ownership)	100,000
Taxable income before dividends received deduction	$ 75,000

Pearl's dividends received deduction is $52,500 [70% × $75,000 (taxable income limitation)]. If, however, Pearl incurs additional expenses of $5,001 (or defers $5,001 of income), then the NOL rule applies and Pearl's dividends received deduction is $70,000 [70% × $100,000 (dividends received)]. ■

The other two limitations applicable to the dividends received deduction can be avoided with some basic planning tenets. First, the holding period requirement is satisfied by holding stock for at least 46 days. Second, the debt-financed stock restriction is avoided if indebtedness is not directly attributable to an investment in stock. Clearly, indebtedness incurred specifically to acquire stock should be avoided. However, the use of stock as security for a loan should also be avoided, as the debt-financed restriction can apply in such cases.

Organizational Expenditures

To qualify for the 180-month amortization procedure of § 248, only organizational expenditures incurred in the first taxable year of the corporation can be considered. This rule could prove to be an unfortunate trap for corporations formed late in the year.

EXAMPLE 43

Thrush Corporation is formed in December 2012. Qualified organizational expenditures are incurred as follows: $62,000 in December 2012 and $30,000 in January 2013. If Thrush uses the calendar year for tax purposes, only $62,000 of the organizational expenditures can be written off over a period of 180 months. ■

The solution to the problem posed by Example 43 is for Thrush Corporation to adopt a fiscal year that ends on or beyond January 31. All organizational expenditures will then have been incurred before the close of the first taxable year.

Shareholder-Employee Payment of Corporate Expenses

In a closely held corporate setting, shareholder-employees often pay corporate expenses (e.g., travel and entertainment) for which they are not reimbursed by the corporation. The IRS often disallows the deduction of these expenses by the shareholder-employee because the payments are voluntary on his or her part. If the deduction is more beneficial at the shareholder-employee level, a corporate policy against reimbursement of such expenses should be established. Proper planning in this regard would be to decide before the beginning of each tax year where the deduction would do the most good. Corporate policy on reimbursement of such expenses could be modified on a year-to-year basis depending upon the circumstances.

In deciding whether corporate expenses should be kept at the corporate level or shifted to the shareholder-employee, the treatment of unreimbursed employee expenses must be considered. First, because employee expenses are itemized deductions, they will be of no benefit to the taxpayer who chooses the standard deduction option. Second, these expenses will be subject to the 2 percent-of-AGI floor. No such limitation will be imposed if the corporation claims the expenses.

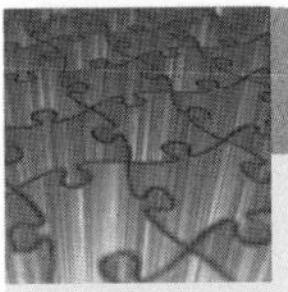

CONCEPT SUMMARY 2.1

Income Taxation of Individuals and Corporations Compared

	Individuals	Corporations
Computation of gross income	§ 61.	§ 61.
Computation of taxable income	§§ 62, 63(b) through (h).	§ 63(a). Concept of AGI has no relevance.
Deductions	Trade or business (§ 162); nonbusiness (§ 212); some personal and employee expenses (generally deductible as itemized deductions).	Trade or business (§ 162).

Income Taxation of Individuals and Corporations Compared—Continued

	Individuals	Corporations
Charitable contributions	Limited in any tax year to 50% of AGI; 30% for capital gain property unless election is made to reduce fair market value of gift.	Limited in any tax year to 10% of taxable income computed without regard to the charitable contribution deduction, NOL carryback, capital loss carryback, dividends received deduction, and domestic production activities deduction.
	Excess charitable contributions carried over for five years.	Same as for individuals.
	Amount of contribution is the fair market value of capital gain property; ordinary income property is limited to adjusted basis; capital gain property is treated as ordinary income property if certain tangible personalty is donated to a nonuse charity or a private nonoperating foundation is the donee.	Same as for individuals, but exceptions allowed for certain inventory and for scientific property where one-half of the appreciation is allowed as a deduction.
	Time of deduction—year in which payment is made.	Time of deduction—year in which payment is made unless accrual basis taxpayer. Accrual basis corporation can take deduction in year preceding payment if contribution was authorized by board of directors by end of year and contribution is paid by fifteenth day of third month of following year.
Casualty losses	$100 floor on personal casualty and theft losses; personal casualty losses deductible only to extent losses exceed 10% of AGI.	Deductible in full.
Net operating loss	Adjusted for several items, including nonbusiness deductions over nonbusiness income and personal exemptions.	Generally no adjustments.
	Carryback period is 2 years, while carryforward period is 20 years.	Same as for individuals.
Dividends received deduction	None.	70%, 80%, or 100% of dividends received depending on percentage of ownership by corporate shareholder.
Net capital gains	Taxed in full. Tax rate generally cannot exceed 15% on net long-term capital gains.	Taxed in full.
Capital losses	Only $3,000 of capital loss per year can offset ordinary income; unused loss is carried forward indefinitely to offset capital gains or ordinary income up to $3,000; short-term and long-term carryovers retain their character.	Can offset only capital gains; unused loss is carried back three years and forward five; carryovers and carrybacks are characterized as short-term losses.
Passive losses	In general, passive losses cannot offset either active income or portfolio income.	Passive loss rules apply to closely held C corporations and personal service corporations.
		For personal service corporations, passive losses cannot offset either active income or portfolio income.
		For closely held C corporations, passive losses may offset active income but not portfolio income.
Domestic production activities deduction	Based on 9% of the lesser of qualified production activities income (QPAI) *or* modified AGI.	Based on 9% of the lesser of qualified production activities income (QPAI) *or* taxable income.

Income Taxation of Individuals and Corporations Compared—Continued

	Individuals	Corporations
Tax rates	Progressive with six rates (10%, 15%, 25%, 28%, 33%, and 35%).	Progressive with four rates (15%, 25%, 34%, and 35%). Two lowest brackets phased out between $100,000 and $335,000 of taxable income, and additional tax imposed between $15,000,000 and $18,333,333 of taxable income.
Alternative minimum tax	Applied at a graduated rate schedule of 26% and 28%. Exemption allowed depending on filing status (e.g., $74,450 in 2011 for married filing jointly); phaseout begins when AMTI reaches a certain amount (e.g., $150,000 for married filing jointly).	Applied at a 20% rate on AMTI less exemption; $40,000 exemption allowed but phaseout begins when AMTI reaches $150,000; adjustments and tax preference items are similar to those applicable to individuals but also include 75% adjusted current earnings. Small corporations (gross receipts of $5 million or less) are not subject to AMT.

REFOCUS ON THE BIG PICTURE

COOKED TO PERFECTION

Conducting Skylark Bakery as a corporation would save Samantha $10,375 in income taxes annually, computed as follows:

Bakery Operated as Sole Proprietorship

Operating profit of $100,000:	
Tax on $100,000 @ 35%	$35,000
Dividends of $5,000:	
Tax on $5,000 @ 15%	750
Withdrawals of $50,000:	
No tax	-0-
Total income tax when operated as sole proprietorship	$35,750

Bakery Operated as Regular Corporation

Corporate taxable income of $51,500* (see below):	
Tax on $50,000 @ 15%	$ 7,500
Tax on $1,500 @ 25%	375
Total corporate income tax	$ 7,875
Samantha's salary of $50,000:	
Tax on $50,000 @ 35%	17,500
Total income tax when operated as C corporation	$25,375

*Computation of corporate taxable income:

Operating profit	$100,000
Dividends	5,000
Less: Salary to Samantha	(50,000)
Dividends received deduction (70%)	(3,500)
Taxable income	$ 51,500

© Ryan McVay/Photodisc/Getty Images

CONTINUED

The example illustrates the tax savings available when a high-income individual taxpayer takes advantage of the lower marginal tax rates of corporations. However, other issues, such as employment tax considerations and the planned expiration of the preferential tax rate on dividend income, also should be considered. Further, other potential entity options, such as the LLC and S corporation, also should be evaluated.

What If?

What if the bakery in the first year it becomes a corporation generates a $10,000 short-term capital loss (STCL) on the disposition of some of its stock investments? Regular corporations can only deduct capital losses against capital gains; thus, the $10,000 STCL would not be deductible currently by the corporation and, instead, would be carried forward for up to five years. If the bakery is operated as a sole proprietorship, Samantha would report the capital loss on her individual return. She could use the $10,000 STCL to offset any capital gains she may have and deduct up to $3,000 of the loss against ordinary income.

KEY TERMS

C corporations, 2-3
Check-the-box Regulations, 2-8
Dividends received deduction, 2-17
Domestic production activities deduction (DPAD), 2-16
Limited liability company (LLC), 2-7
Limited partnerships, 2-7
Organizational expenditures, 2-20
Passive loss, 2-13
Personal service corporations (PSCs), 2-10
Regular corporations, 2-3
Related corporations, 2-23
S corporations, 2-3
Schedule M–1, 2-25
Schedule M–3, 2-26

DISCUSSION QUESTIONS

1. **LO.1** Jennifer and Jamie are starting a business and have asked you for advice about whether they should form a partnership, a corporation, or some other type of entity. Prepare a list of questions you would ask in helping them decide which type of entity they should choose. Explain your reasons for asking each of the questions.

2. **LO.1** Barbara owns 40% of the stock of Cassowary Corporation (a C corporation) and 40% of the stock of Emu Corporation (an S corporation). During 2012, each corporation has operating income of $120,000 and tax-exempt interest income of $8,000. Neither corporation pays any dividends during the year. Discuss how this information will be reported by the corporations and Barbara for 2012.

Decision Making

3. **LO.1, 7** Art, an executive with Azure Corporation, plans to start a part-time business selling products on the Internet. He will devote about 15 hours each week to running the business. Art's salary from Azure places him in the 35% tax bracket. He projects substantial losses from the new business in each of the first three years and expects sizable profits thereafter. Art plans to leave the profits in the business for several years, sell the business, and retire. Would you advise Art to incorporate the business or operate it as a sole proprietorship? Why?

4. **LO.1, 2** In 2012, Plover Corporation, a C corporation with four equal shareholders, had an operating loss of $80,000 and a long-term capital gain of $20,000. Also in 2012, Vireo Partnership, with four equal partners, had an operating loss of $80,000 and a long-term capital gain of $20,000. Plover did not pay any dividends, and Vireo's partners did not make any withdrawals. Contrast the tax treatment of the entities and their owners.

5. **LO.1, 2** Samantha is the sole owner of Blue Company. In 2012, Blue had operating income of $200,000, a short-term capital loss of $10,000, and tax-exempt interest income of $3,000. Samantha withdrew $50,000 of profit from Blue. How should Samantha report this information on her individual tax return for 2012 if Blue Company is:
   a. An LLC?
   b. An S corporation?
   c. A C corporation?

6. **LO.1, 7** Shareholders of closely held corporations frequently engage in dealings with such corporations. These dealings provide an opportunity to extract earnings out of a corporate entity in some form other than a nondeductible dividend distribution. Provide several examples of shareholder-corporation transactions, and for each example, briefly note the requirement that would need to be satisfied to avoid recharacterization by the IRS as a disguised dividend distribution. **Issue ID**

7. **LO.1** Contrast the marginal tax rates of C corporations with those of individuals.

8. **LO.1** Briefly describe how LLCs are treated for Federal income tax purposes.

9. **LO.1** In the current year, Juanita and Joseph form a two-member LLC and do not file Form 8832 (Entity Classification Election). As a result, the LLC will be treated as a partnership for Federal tax purposes. Assess the validity of this statement.

10. **LO.2** A corporate taxpayer may select either a calendar year or a fiscal year for its reporting period. Assess the validity of this statement.

11. **LO.2** Ann is the sole shareholder of Salmon Corporation, a newly formed C corporation. Fran is the sole shareholder of Scarlet Corporation, a newly formed C corporation that is a personal service corporation. Both Ann and Fran plan to have their corporations elect a March 31 fiscal year-end. Will the IRS treat both corporations alike with respect to the fiscal year election? Why or why not?

12. **LO.2** Which of the following C corporations will be allowed to use the cash method of accounting for 2012? Explain your answers.
    a. Jade Corporation, which had gross receipts of $5.3 million in 2009, $4.1 million in 2010, and $5 million in 2011.
    b. Lime Corporation, a personal service corporation, which had gross receipts of $5.8 million in 2009, $5.2 million in 2010, and $4.4 million in 2011.

13. **LO.2** Wang, a cash basis taxpayer, owns 65% of the stock of Pink, Inc., a calendar year, accrual basis C corporation. On January 2, 2012, Wang loaned Pink a substantial amount of money. On December 31, 2012, Pink, Inc., accrued $35,000 of interest expense on the loan but does not pay the interest to Wang until February 1, 2013. In which year can Pink deduct the interest? When must Wang report the interest income?

14. **LO.2** In 2012, Jeanette, an individual in the 35% marginal tax bracket, recognized a $50,000 long-term capital gain. Also in 2012, Parrot Corporation, a C corporation in the 35% marginal tax bracket, recognized a $50,000 long-term capital gain. Neither taxpayer had any other property transactions in the year. What tax rates are applicable to these capital gains?

15. **LO.2** John (a sole proprietor) and Eagle Corporation (a C corporation) each recognize a short-term capital gain of $6,000 and a long-term capital loss of $8,000 on the sale of capital assets. Neither taxpayer had any other property transactions during the year. Describe the tax consequences of these gains and losses for John and for Eagle.

16. **LO.2** A taxpayer sells a warehouse for a recognized gain. Depreciation had been properly claimed on the property, based on the straight-line method over a 39-year recovery period. Will the same amount of depreciation recapture result whether the taxpayer is an individual or a C corporation? Explain.

17. **LO.2** Osprey Corporation, a closely held corporation, has $75,000 of active income, $25,000 of portfolio income, and a $60,000 loss from a passive activity.
    a. How much of the passive loss can Osprey deduct in the current year if it is a PSC?
    b. If it is not a PSC?

18. **LO.2** Hummingbird Corporation, a closely held corporation that is not a PSC, has $40,000 of active income, $15,000 of portfolio income, and a $45,000 loss from a passive activity. What is Hummingbird's taxable income for the year?

19. **LO.2** On December 20, 2012, the directors of Partridge Corporation, an accrual basis calendar year taxpayer, authorized a cash contribution of $25,000 to the American Cancer Association. The payment is made on February 14, 2013. Can Partridge deduct the charitable contribution in 2012? Explain.

20. **LO.2** Briefly describe how the amount of a charitable contribution of property by a C corporation is determined.

Issue ID

21. **LO.2, 7** The board of directors of Orange Corporation, a calendar year taxpayer, is holding its year-end meeting on December 28, 2012. One topic on the board's agenda is the approval of a $25,000 gift to a qualified charitable organization. Orange has a $20,000 charitable contribution carryover to 2012 from a prior year. Identify the tax issues the board should consider regarding the proposed contribution.

22. **LO.2** For 2012, the domestic production activities deduction for a C corporation is 9% of the taxpayer's qualified production activities income. Assess the validity of this statement.

Issue ID

23. **LO.2, 3, 7** Gold Corporation, a calendar year C corporation, was formed in 2006 and has been profitable until the current year. In 2012, Gold incurs a net operating loss. Identify the issues that Gold Corporation should consider regarding its NOL carryback and carryover options.

24. **LO.1, 3** Marmot Corporation pays a dividend of $250,000 in 2012. Otter Corporation, which is in the 35% marginal bracket, owns 15% of Marmot's stock. Gerald, an individual taxpayer in the 35% marginal bracket, also owns 15% of Marmot's stock. Compare and contrast the treatment of the dividend by Otter Corporation and Gerald.

25. **LO.3** Mauve Corporation (a C corporation) owns 85% of the stock of Lavender Corporation (a C corporation), which pays Mauve a substantial dividend each year. Mauve Corporation plans on selling half of its stock in Lavender Corporation. How will this stock disposition affect the amount of Mauve's dividends received deduction?

26. **LO.3** Describe the holding period requirement of the dividends received deduction.

27. **LO.3** Determine whether the following expenditures by Cuckoo Corporation are organizational expenditures, startup expenditures, or neither.
    a. Legal expenses incurred for drafting the corporate charter and bylaws.
    b. Expenses incurred in printing stock certificates.
    c. Expenses of temporary board of directors' organizational meetings.
    d. Employee salaries incurred during the training period before opening for business.
    e. State incorporation fee.

28. **LO.4** The highest marginal tax rate for a C corporation is 35%. Assess the validity of this statement.

29. **LO.5** Omar is the sole shareholder of Plum Corporation, which has annual taxable income of approximately $200,000. Omar formed a new solely owned corporation, Ivory Corporation, and had Plum Corporation transfer one-half of its assets to Ivory Corporation. Because this results in each of the two corporations having approximately $100,000 of taxable income each year, Omar believes it will reduce overall corporate income taxes. Will Omar's plan work? Discuss.

30. **LO.6** When are C corporations required to make estimated tax payments? How are these payments calculated?

31. **LO.6** Schedule M–1 of Form 1120 is used to reconcile financial net income with taxable income reported on the corporation's income tax return as follows: net income per books + additions − subtractions = taxable income. Classify the following items as additions or subtractions in the Schedule M–1 reconciliation.
    a. Nondeductible portion of meals and entertainment.
    b. Tax depreciation in excess of book depreciation.
    c. Federal income tax per books.

d. Capital loss in excess of capital gain.
e. Charitable contributions in excess of taxable income limitation.
f. Tax-exempt interest income.
g. Domestic production activities deduction.

32. **LO.6** In 2012, Woodpecker, Inc., a C corporation with $8.5 million in assets, deducted amortization of $40,000 on its financial statements and $55,000 on its Federal tax return. Is Woodpecker required to file Schedule M–3? If a Schedule M–3 is filed by Woodpecker, how is the difference in amortization amounts treated on that schedule?

PROBLEMS

33. **LO.1** In 2012, Osprey Company had operating income of $320,000, operating expenses of $270,000, and a long-term capital gain of $20,000. How does Juanita, the sole owner of Osprey Company, report this information on her individual tax return under the following assumptions?
    a. Osprey Company is a proprietorship, and Juanita did not make any withdrawals from the business during the year.
    b. Osprey Company is a C corporation and pays no dividends during the year.

34. **LO.1** Ellie and Linda are equal owners in Otter Enterprises, a calendar year business. During the year, Otter Enterprises has $320,000 of gross income and $210,000 of operating expenses. In addition, Otter has a short-term capital loss of $15,000 and makes distributions to Ellie and Linda of $25,000 each. Discuss the impact of this information on the taxable income of Otter, Ellie, and Linda if Otter is:
    a. A partnership.
    b. An S corporation.
    c. A C corporation.

35. **LO.1, 2** In the current year, Azure Company has $350,000 of net operating income before deducting any compensation or other payment to its sole owner, Sasha. In addition, Azure has interest on municipal bonds of $25,000. Sasha has significant income from other sources and is in the 35% marginal tax bracket. Based on this information, determine the income tax consequences to Azure Company and to Sasha during the year for each of the following independent situations.
    a. Azure is a C corporation and pays no dividends or salary to Sasha.
    b. Azure is a C corporation and distributes $75,000 of dividends to Sasha.
    c. Azure is a C corporation and pays $75,000 of salary to Sasha.
    d. Azure is a sole proprietorship, and Sasha withdraws $0.
    e. Azure is a sole proprietorship, and Sasha withdraws $75,000.

36. **LO.1, 2** Charlene owns 100% of Taupe Corporation, which had net operating income of $420,000 and long-term capital gain of $30,000 in 2012. Charlene has sufficient income from other sources to be in the 35% marginal tax bracket without regard to the results of Taupe Corporation. The corporation makes no distributions to Charlene during the year. Explain the tax treatment if Taupe Corporation is:
    a. An S corporation.
    b. A C corporation.

37. **LO.1** Purple Company has $200,000 in net income for 2012 before deducting any compensation or other payment to its sole owner, Kirsten. Kirsten is single and has no dependents. She claims the $5,950 standard deduction, and her personal exemption is $3,800 for 2012. Purple Company is Kirsten's only source of income. Ignoring any employment tax considerations, compute Kirsten's after-tax income if:
    a. Purple Company is a proprietorship and Kirsten withdraws $50,000 from the business during the year.
    b. Purple Company is a C corporation and the corporation pays out all of its after-tax income as a dividend to Kirsten.
    c. Purple Company is a C corporation and the corporation pays Kirsten a salary of $138,750.

38. **LO.2** In 2012, Wilson Enterprises, a calendar year taxpayer, suffers a casualty loss of $90,000. How much of the casualty loss will be deductible by Wilson under the following circumstances?
    a. Wilson is an individual proprietor and has AGI of $225,000. The casualty loss was a personal loss, and the insurance recovered was $50,000.
    b. Wilson is a corporation, and the insurance recovered was $50,000.

Decision Making
Communications

39. **LO.1, 4, 7** Benton Company (BC) has one owner, who is in the 35% Federal income tax bracket. BC's gross income is $295,000, and its ordinary trade or business deductions are $135,000. Compute the tax liability on BC's income for 2012 under the following assumptions:
    a. BC is operated as a proprietorship, and the owner withdraws $70,000 for personal use.
    b. BC is operated as a corporation, pays out $70,000 as salary, and pays no dividends to its shareholder.
    c. BC is operated as a corporation and pays out no salary or dividends to its shareholder.
    d. BC is operated as a corporation, pays out $70,000 as salary, and pays out the remainder of its earnings as dividends.
    e. Assume that Robert Benton of 1121 Monroe Street, Ironton, OH 45638 is the owner of BC, which was operated as a proprietorship in 2012. Robert is thinking about incorporating the business in 2013 and asks your advice. He expects about the same amounts of income and expenses in 2013 and plans to take $70,000 per year out of the company whether he incorporates or not. Write a letter to Robert [based on your analysis in (a) and (b)] containing your recommendations.

40. **LO.2, 4** Juan, an attorney, is the sole shareholder of Carmine Corporation, a C corporation and professional association. The corporation paid Juan a salary of $336,000 during its fiscal year ending September 30, 2012.
    a. How much salary must Carmine pay Juan during the period October 1 through December 31, 2012, to permit the corporation to continue to use its fiscal year without negative tax effects?
    b. Carmine Corporation had taxable income of $95,000 for the year ending September 30, 2012. Compute the corporation's income tax liability for the year.

41. **LO.2** Broadbill Corporation, a calendar year C corporation, has two unrelated cash method shareholders: Marcia owns 51% of the stock, and Zack owns the remaining 49%. Each shareholder is employed by the corporation at an annual salary of $240,000. During 2012, Broadbill paid each shareholder-employee $220,000 of his or her annual salary, with the remaining $20,000 paid in January 2013. How much of the 2012 salaries for Marcia and Zack is deductible by Broadbill in 2012 if the corporation is:
    a. A cash method taxpayer?
    b. An accrual method taxpayer?

42. **LO.2, 4** Ramona owns 100% of Violet Company. In 2012, Violet recognizes a long-term capital gain of $85,000 and no other income (or loss). Ramona is in the 35% tax bracket and has no recognized capital gains (or losses) before considering her ownership interest in Violet. How much income tax results from the $85,000 long-term capital gain if Violet is:
    a. A C corporation?
    b. A proprietorship?

43. **LO.2** In the current year, Sandpiper Corporation (a C corporation) had operating income of $215,000 and operating expenses of $155,000. In addition, Sandpiper had a long-term capital gain of $12,000 and a short-term capital loss of $27,000.
    a. Compute Sandpiper's taxable income and tax for the year.
    b. Assume the same facts except that Sandpiper's long-term capital gain was $35,000. Compute Sandpiper's taxable income and tax for the year.

44. **LO.2** In 2012, Bronze Company had operating profit of $75,000 ($125,000 operating income − $50,000 operating expenses). In addition, Bronze had a short-term capital gain of $16,000 and a long-term capital loss of $31,000. How much of the long-term

capital loss may be deducted in 2012, and how much is carried back or forward under the following circumstances?

a. Bronze Company is a proprietorship owned by Kenneth, and he had no other property transactions in 2012.
b. Bronze Company is a C corporation.

45. **LO.2** During 2012, Gorilla Corporation has net short-term capital gains of $70,000, net long-term capital losses of $195,000, and taxable income from other sources of $620,000. Prior years' transactions included the following:

2008 net short-term capital gains	$30,000
2009 net long-term capital gains	55,000
2010 net short-term capital gains	15,000
2011 net long-term capital gains	40,000

a. How are the capital gains and losses treated on Gorilla's 2012 tax return?
b. Determine the amount of the 2012 capital loss that is carried back to each of the previous years.
c. Compute the amount of capital loss carryover, if any, and indicate the years to which the loss may be carried.
d. If Gorilla is a sole proprietorship, rather than a corporation, how would the owner report these transactions on her 2012 tax return?

46. **LO.2** Heron Company purchases commercial realty on November 13, 1994, for $650,000. Straight-line depreciation of $287,492 is claimed before the property is sold on February 22, 2012, for $850,000. What are the tax consequences of the sale of realty if Heron is:

a. A C corporation?
b. A sole proprietorship?

47. **LO.2** In 2012, Condor Corporation, a closely held C corporation that is not a PSC, has $225,000 of active business income, $35,000 of portfolio income, and a $300,000 passive loss from a rental activity. How much of the passive loss can Condor deduct in 2012? Would your answer differ if Condor were a PSC? Explain.

48. **LO.2** Aquamarine Corporation, a calendar year C corporation, makes the following donations to qualified charitable organizations during the current year:

	Adjusted Basis	Fair Market Value
Painting held four years as an investment, to a church, which sold it immediately	$15,000	$25,000
Apple stock held two years as an investment, to United Way, which sold it immediately	40,000	90,000
Canned groceries held one month as inventory, to Catholic Meals for the Poor	10,000	17,000

Determine the amount of Aquamarine Corporation's charitable deduction for the current year. (Ignore the taxable income limitation.)

49. **LO.2, 7** Joseph Thompson is president and sole shareholder of Jay Corporation. In December 2012, Joe asks your advice regarding a charitable contribution he plans to have the corporation make to the University of Maine, a qualified public charity. Joe is considering the following alternatives as charitable contributions in December 2012:

Decision Making

Communications

	Fair Market Value
(1) Cash donation	$200,000
(2) Unimproved land held for six years ($310,000 basis)	200,000
(3) Maize Corporation stock held for eight years ($120,000 basis)	200,000
(4) Brown Corporation stock held for nine months ($70,000 basis)	200,000

Joe has asked you to help him decide which of these potential contributions will be most advantageous taxwise. Jay's taxable income is $3.5 million before considering the contribution. Rank the four alternatives and write a letter to Joe communicating your advice. The corporation's address is 1442 Main Street, Freeport, ME 04032.

Decision Making

50. **LO.2, 7** In 2012, Gray Corporation, a calendar year C corporation, has a $75,000 charitable contribution carryover from a gift made in 2007. Gray is contemplating a gift of land to a qualified charity in either 2012 or 2013. Gray purchased the land as an investment five years ago for $100,000 (current fair market value is $250,000). Before considering any charitable deduction, Gray projects taxable income of $1 million for 2012 and $1.2 million for 2013. Should Gray make the gift of the land to charity in 2012 or in 2013? Provide support for your answer.

Decision Making

Communications

51. **LO.2, 7** Dan Simms is the president and sole shareholder of Simms Corporation, 1121 Madison Street, Seattle, WA 98121. Dan plans for the corporation to make a charitable contribution to the University of Washington, a qualified public charity. He will have the corporation donate Jaybird Corporation stock, held for five years, with a basis of $11,000 and a fair market value of $25,000. Dan projects a $310,000 net profit for Simms Corporation in 2012 and a $100,000 net profit in 2013. Dan calls you on December 13, 2012, and asks whether he should make the contribution in 2012 or 2013. Write a letter advising Dan about the timing of the contribution.

52. **LO.2** White Corporation, a calendar year C corporation, manufactures plumbing fixtures. For 2012, White has taxable income [before the domestic production activities deduction (DPAD)] of $900,000, qualified production activities income (QPAI) of $1.2 million, and W–2 wages attributable to QPAI of $200,000.
    a. How much is White Corporation's DPAD for 2012?
    b. Assume instead that W–2 wages attributable to QPAI are $150,000. How much is White's DPAD for 2012?

53. **LO.2, 3** During the current year, Swallow Corporation, a calendar year C corporation, has the following transactions:

Income from operations	$660,000
Expenses from operations	720,000
Dividends received from Brown Corporation	240,000

    a. Swallow Corporation owns 12% of Brown Corporation's stock. How much is Swallow's taxable income or NOL for the year?
    b. Assume instead that Swallow Corporation owns 26% of Brown Corporation's stock. How much is Swallow's taxable income or NOL for the year?

54. **LO.3** In each of the following independent situations, determine the dividends received deduction. Assume that none of the corporate shareholders owns 20% or more of the stock in the corporations paying the dividends.

	Green Corporation	Orange Corporation	Yellow Corporation
Income from operations	$ 700,000	$ 700,000	$ 700,000
Expenses from operation	(650,000)	(750,000)	(850,000)
Qualifying dividends	200,000	200,000	200,000

55. **LO.3** Gull Corporation, a cash method, calendar year C corporation, was formed and began business on July 1, 2012. Gull incurred the following expenses during its first year of operations (July 1, 2012–December 31, 2012):

Expenses of temporary directors and organizational meetings	$17,000
Fee paid to state of incorporation	2,500
Expenses for printing and sale of stock certificates	8,000
Legal services for drafting the corporate charter and bylaws (not paid until January 2013)	25,000

    a. Assuming that Gull Corporation elects under § 248 to expense and amortize organizational expenditures, what amount may be deducted in 2012?

b. Assume the same facts as above, except that the amount paid for the legal services was $35,000 (instead of $25,000). What amount may be deducted as organizational expenditures in 2012?

56. **LO.3** Egret Corporation, a calendar year C corporation, was formed on March 7, 2012, and opened for business on July 1, 2012. After its formation but prior to opening for business, Egret incurred the following expenditures:

Accounting	$ 7,000
Advertising	14,500
Employee payroll	11,000
Rent	8,000
Utilities	1,000

What is the maximum amount of these expenditures that Egret can deduct in 2012?

57. **LO.4** In each of the following independent situations, determine the corporation's income tax liability. Assume that all corporations use a calendar year for tax purposes and that the tax year involved is 2012.

	Taxable Income
Purple Corporation	$ 45,000
Azul Corporation	310,000
Pink Corporation	2,350,000
Turquoise Corporation	21,000,000
Teal Corporation (a personal service corporation)	80,000

58. **LO.5** Red Corporation and White Corporation, both calendar year C corporations, are members of a controlled group of corporations. For 2012, Red has taxable income of $130,000, and White has taxable income of $200,000. Assuming that the controlled group does not make an election regarding the apportionment of the marginal tax brackets, what is the income tax liability for each of the corporations?

59. **LO.6** Grouse Corporation, a calendar year C corporation, had taxable income of $1.4 million, $1.2 million, and $700,000 for 2009, 2010, and 2011, respectively. Grouse has taxable income of $1.6 million for 2012. What are Grouse Corporation's minimum required estimated tax payments for 2012?

60. **LO.6** Eagle Corporation, a calendar year and accrual method taxpayer, provides the following information and asks you to prepare Schedule M–1 for 2012:

Net income per books (after-tax)	$386,250
Federal income tax per books	30,050
Tax-exempt interest income	5,000
Life insurance proceeds received as a result of death of corporate president	300,000
Nondeductible penalties	2,500
Interest on loan to purchase tax-exempt bonds	1,700
Excess of capital loss over capital gains	5,300
Premiums paid on life insurance policy on life of Eagle's president	4,200
Domestic production activities deduction	2,000
Excess of tax depreciation over book depreciation	3,000

61. **LO.6** The following information for 2012 relates to Sparrow Corporation, a calendar year, accrual method taxpayer.

Net income per books (after-tax)	$174,100
Federal income tax per books	86,600
Tax-exempt interest income	4,500
MACRS depreciation in excess of straight-line depreciation used for financial purposes	7,200

Excess of capital loss over capital gains	$ 9,400
Nondeductible meals and entertainment	5,500
Interest on loan to purchase tax-exempt bonds	1,100

Based on the above information, use Schedule M–1 of Form 1120, which is available on the IRS website, to determine Sparrow's taxable income for 2012.

62. **LO.6** Swan Corporation, a calendar year C corporation, had the following information for 2012:

Net income per books (after-tax)	$174,700
Taxable income	195,000
Federal income tax per books	59,300
Cash dividend distributions	35,000
Unappropriated retained earnings, as of January 1, 2012	636,450

Based on the above information, use Schedule M–2 of Form 1120 (see Example 36 in the text) to determine Swan's unappropriated retained earnings balance as of December 31, 2012.

63. **LO.6** In the current year, Pelican, Inc., incurs $10,000 of meals and entertainment expenses that it deducts in computing net income per the corporation's financial statements. All of the meals and entertainment expenditures are subject to the 50% cutback rule applicable to such expenditures. How is this information reported on Schedule M–3?

64. **LO.6** In the current year, Pelican, Inc., incurs $50,000 of nondeductible fines and penalties. Its depreciation expense is $245,000 for financial statement purposes and $310,000 for tax purposes. How is this information reported on Schedule M–3?

65. **LO.6** In January 2012, Pelican, Inc., established an allowance for uncollectible accounts (bad debt reserve) of $70,000 on its books and increased the allowance by $120,000 during the year. As a result of a client's bankruptcy, Pelican, Inc., decreased the allowance by $60,000 in November 2012. Pelican, Inc., deducted the $190,000 of increases to the allowance on its 2012 income statement but was not allowed to deduct that amount on its tax return. On its 2012 tax return, the corporation was allowed to deduct the $60,000 actual loss sustained because of its client's bankruptcy. On its financial statements, Pelican, Inc., treated the $190,000 increase in the bad debt reserve as an expense that gave rise to a temporary difference. On its 2012 tax return, Pelican, Inc., took a $60,000 deduction for bad debt expense. How is this information reported on Schedule M–3?

Issue ID

66. **LO.2, 3, 7** In January, Don and Steve each invested $100,000 cash to form a corporation to conduct business as a retail golf equipment store. On January 5, they paid Bill, an attorney, to draft the corporate charter, file the necessary forms with the state, and write the bylaws. They leased a store building and began to acquire inventory, furniture, display equipment, and office equipment in February. They hired a sales staff and clerical personnel in March and conducted training sessions during the month. They had a successful opening on April 1, and sales increased steadily throughout the summer. The weather turned cold in October, and all local golf courses closed by October 15, which resulted in a drastic decline in sales. Don and Steve expect business to be very good during the Christmas season and then to taper off significantly from January 1 through the end of February. The corporation accrued bonuses to Don and Steve on December 31, payable on April 15 of the following year. The corporation made timely estimated tax payments throughout the year. The corporation hired a bookkeeper in February, but he does not know much about taxation. Don and Steve have retained you as a tax consultant and have asked you to identify the tax issues they should consider.

TAX RETURN PROBLEMS

1. On November 1, 2005, Janet Morton and Kim Wong formed Pet Kingdom, Inc., to sell pets and pet supplies. Pertinent information regarding Pet Kingdom is summarized as follows:
   - Pet Kingdom's business address is 1010 Northwest Parkway, Dallas, TX 75225; its telephone number is (214) 555-2211; and its e-mail address is petkingdom@pki.com.
   - The employer identification number is 11-1111111, and the principal business activity code is 453910.

- Janet and Kim each own 50% of the common stock; Janet is president and Kim is vice president of the company. No other class of stock is authorized.
- Both Janet and Kim are full-time employees of Pet Kingdom. Janet's Social Security number is 123–45–6789, and Kim's Social Security number is 987–65–4321.
- Pet Kingdom is an accrual method, calendar year taxpayer. Inventories are determined using FIFO and the lower of cost or market method. Pet Kingdom uses the straight-line method of depreciation for book purposes and accelerated depreciation (MACRS) for tax purposes.
- During 2011, the corporation distributed cash dividends of $300,000.

Pet Kingdom's financial statements for 2011 are shown below.

Income Statement

Income			
Gross sales			$ 6,900,000
Sales returns and allowances			(240,000)
Net sales			$ 6,660,000
Cost of goods sold			(2,760,000)
Gross profit			$ 3,900,000
Dividends received from stock investments in less-than-20%-owned U.S. corporations			52,500
Interest income:			
State bonds	$ 18,000		
Certificates of deposit	24,000		42,000
Total income			$ 3,994,500
Expenses			
Salaries—officers			
Janet Morton	$315,000		
Kim Wong	315,000	$630,000	
Salaries—clerical and sales		870,000	
Taxes (state, local, and payroll)		285,000	
Repairs and maintenance		168,000	
Interest expense:			
Loan to purchase state bonds	$ 10,500		
Other business loans	261,000	271,500	
Advertising		69,000	
Rental expense		129,000	
Depreciation*		120,000	
Charitable contributions		45,000	
Employee benefit programs		72,000	
Premiums on term life insurance policies on lives of Janet and Kim; Pet Kingdom is the designated beneficiary		48,000	
Total expenses			(2,707,500)
Net income before taxes			$ 1,287,000
Federal income tax			(423,555)
Net income per books			$ 863,445

*Depreciation for tax purposes is $165,000. You are not provided enough detailed data to complete a Form 4562 (depreciation). If you solve this problem using H&R BLOCK At Home, enter the amount of depreciation on line 20 of Form 1120.

Balance Sheet

Assets	January 1, 2011	December 31, 2011
Cash	$ 1,056,000	$ 748,000
Trade notes and accounts receivable	1,815,000	2,021,000
Inventories	3,300,000	3,636,000
Stock investment	990,000	990,000
State bonds	330,000	330,000
Certificates of deposit	385,000	385,000
Prepaid Federal tax	—	4,445
Buildings and other depreciable assets	4,805,000	4,805,000
Accumulated depreciation	(727,000)	(847,000)
Land	715,000	715,000
Other assets	123,000	113,000
Total assets	$12,792,000	$12,900,445

Liabilities and Equity	January 1, 2011	December 31, 2011
Accounts payable	$ 2,035,000	$ 1,837,000
Other current liabilities	213,000	184,000
Mortgages	4,550,000	4,322,000
Capital stock	3,000,000	3,000,000
Retained earnings	2,994,000	3,557,445
Total liabilities and equity	$12,792,000	$12,900,445

During 2011, Pet Kingdom made estimated tax payments of $107,000 each quarter to the IRS. Prepare a Form 1120 for Pet Kingdom for tax year 2011. Suggested software: H&R BLOCK At Home.

2. Belinda Jackson and Ahmad Sharma each own 50% of the common stock of By the Numbers, Inc. (BNI). No other class of stock is authorized. On August 8, 2005, they formed BNI to provide actuarial services. Pertinent information regarding BNI is summarized as follows:

- BNI's business address is 1001 N. Main Street, Los Angeles, CA 90012; its telephone number is (562) 541-1122; and its e-mail address is BNI@BNI.com.
- The employer identification number is 11–1111111, and the principal business activity code is 541990.
- Belinda is president of the company, and Ahmad is vice president.
- Belinda and Ahmad are the only full-time actuaries employed by BNI, and they perform all of the professional actuarial services of the corporation. Belinda's Social Security number is 123–45–6789, and Ahmad's Social Security number is 987–65–4321.
- BNI is a cash method, calendar year taxpayer. BNI uses the straight-line method of depreciation for both book and tax purposes. The corporation does not maintain any inventory.
- During 2011, the corporation distributed cash dividends of $20,000.

BNI's financial statements for 2011 follow.

Income Statement

Income	
Professional fees	$ 530,000
Interest income (state bonds)	3,000
Total income	$ 533,000

Expenses			
Salaries—officers:			
Belinda Jackson	$125,000		
Ahmed Sharma	125,000	$250,000	
Salaries—clerical		55,000	
Taxes:			
Property	$ 21,500		
Payroll	20,020		
State income	2,250		
Other miscellaneous	1,700	45,470	
Repairs and maintenance		9,500	
Meals and entertainment		7,600	
Travel		6,300	
Charitable contributions		1,000	
Interest expense on business loans		12,800	
Advertising		19,300	
Rental expense		4,100	
Depreciation*		22,400	
Contributions to pension plans		25,000	
Employee benefit programs		16,900	
Accounting services		7,300	
Dues and subscriptions		4,900	
Insurance		15,000	
Legal and professional services		12,500	
Miscellaneous expenses		3,000	
Telephone		2,400	
Total expenses			(520,470)
Net income before taxes			$ 12,530
Federal income tax			(4,666)
Net income per books			$ 7,864

*You are not provided enough detailed data to complete a Form 4562 (depreciation). If you solve this problem using H&R BLOCK At Home, enter the amount of depreciation on line 20 of Form 1120.

Balance Sheet

Assets	**January 1, 2011**	**December 31, 2011**
Cash	$ 23,220	$ 26,300
Trade notes and accounts receivable	35,850	32,100
State bonds	75,000	75,000
Buildings and other depreciable assets	295,600	311,700
Accumulated depreciation	(63,500)	(85,900)
Land	35,000	35,000
Other assets	2,980	2,110
Total assets	$404,150	$396,310

Liabilities and Equity	January 1, 2011	December 31, 2011
Accounts payable	$ 34,800	$ 35,596
Other current liabilities	9,350	18,250
Mortgages	114,000	108,600
Capital stock	200,000	200,000
Retained earnings	46,000	33,864
Total liabilities and equity	$404,150	$396,310

During 2011, BNI made estimated tax payments of $1,250 each quarter to the IRS. Prepare a Form 1120 for BNI for tax year 2011. Suggested software: H&R BLOCK At Home.

RESEARCH PROBLEMS

THOMSON REUTERS
CHECKPOINT®

Note: Solutions to Research Problems can be prepared by using the **Checkpoint® Student Edition** online research product, which is available to accompany this text. It is also possible to prepare solutions to the Research Problems by using tax research materials found in a standard tax library.

Research Problem 1. A personal service corporation (PSC) generally is limited to the calendar year for reporting purposes. One exception to this rule is when the PSC can demonstrate a business purpose for a fiscal year-end. Discuss the business purpose exception, including examples of when the standard is and is not satisfied. Support your research with proper citations of tax authority.

Partial list of research aids:
§ 441(i).
Reg. § 1.441–3.

Communications

Research Problem 2. A new client, Southwest Grocers, is a calendar year C corporation that owns and operates a chain of grocery stores. Southwest Grocers is interested in donating food inventory to one or more charitable organizations. In some cases, the donated items would consist of dented canned food and fungible food items (e.g., baked goods) nearing their freshness expiration dates. Inedible food or food past its expiration date would not be included in any donation. Prepare an outline detailing the information you would provide to Southwest Grocers regarding charitable contributions of food inventory. Make sure you include support for the content of your outline.

Communications

Research Problem 3. Tern Corporation, a calendar year C corporation, is solely owned by Jessica Ramirez. Tern's only business since its incorporation in 2009 has been land surveying services. In Tern's state of incorporation, land surveying can be performed only by a licensed surveyor. Jessica, Tern's only employee, is a licensed surveyor but is not a licensed engineer. Upon audit of Tern's 2009 and 2010 tax returns, the IRS assessed tax deficiencies stemming from its conclusion that the corporation was a personal service corporation subject to the flat tax rate of 35%. Jessica believes that the IRS's determination is incorrect, and she has asked you for advice on how to proceed. Evaluate the IRS's position regarding the treatment of Tern Corporation as a personal service corporation, and prepare a memo for the client files describing the results of your research.

Internet Activity

Use the tax resources of the Internet to address the following questions. Do not restrict your search to the Web, but include a review of newsgroups and general reference materials, practitioner sites and resources, primary sources of the tax law, chat rooms and discussion groups, and other opportunities.

Communications

Research Problem 4. Some states assess a corporate income tax or franchise tax on entities formed as S corporations, LLCs, and/or partnerships. To compare the overall tax burdens associated with the various entity forms, consideration must be given to state taxation of the entities and their owners. Using only the Internet for your research, prepare an outline describing state tax ramifications of the various business forms. Your outline should include as examples the tax policies of several specific states.

Research Problem 5. A significant percentage of U.S. corporations are closely held corporations, with the stock of such corporations often owned predominately or exclusively by family members. Using the Internet as your sole research source, prepare an outline describing the tax implications and planning opportunities unique to family-owned, closely held corporations.

Communications

Research Problem 6. Download Schedule M–3 and the accompanying instructions from the IRS website. The instructions provide several examples of adjustments that are reported on Schedule M–3. Select three of these examples, and make the required entries on the appropriate parts and lines of Schedule M–3.

CHAPTER

3 Corporations: Special Situations

LEARNING OBJECTIVES: *After completing Chapter 3, you should be able to:*

LO.1 Explain the reasons for the domestic production activities deduction (DPAD).

LO.2 Identify the components of the domestic production activities deduction (DPAD).

LO.3 Recognize and work with the different types of domestic production gross receipts (DPGR).

LO.4 Illustrate the necessary adjustments to DPGR to arrive at qualified production activities income (QPAI).

LO.5 List the collateral problems associated with the domestic production activities deduction (DPAD).

LO.6 Explain the reason for the alternative minimum tax.

LO.7 Calculate the alternative minimum tax applicable to corporations.

LO.8 Review and illustrate the function of adjusted current earnings (ACE).

LO.9 Evaluate the current status of the penalty taxes on corporate accumulations.

LO.10 Demonstrate the operation of the accumulated earnings and personal holding company taxes.

LO.11 Apply various tax planning procedures to maximize the domestic production activities deduction (DPAD) and to minimize the imposition of the AMT.

CHAPTER OUTLINE

THE BIG PICTURE Tax Solutions for the Real World

© Leonid Shcheglov/Shutterstock.com

DEALING WITH THE DPAD AND THE AMT

Determining DPGR for the Domestic Production Activities Deduction

Mocha, Inc., produces ice cream at various manufacturing facilities throughout the South and sells it to food stores and restaurants. Mocha also operates snack shops next to its facilities where it sells ice cream, coffee, and other snacks to the general public.

Mocha has gross receipts of $42 million from the wholesale sale of its ice cream and $5 million from the operation of the snack shops. What receipts are considered to be domestic production gross receipts (DPGR) for the domestic production activities deduction (DPAD)? What planning tip might you give to Mocha?

Read the chapter and formulate your response.

Who Pays the AMT?

Carmine Corporation and Taupe Corporation are calendar year C corporations, not related to each other, formed on January 1, 2010. Their gross receipts for the first three years of operations are as follows:

Calendar Year	Carmine Corporation	Taupe Corporation
2010	$ 4 million	$6 million
2011	8 million	4 million
2012	10 million	7 million

Which corporation, if either, is exempt from the application of the AMT and for which years (i.e., 2010–2011)?

Read the chapter and formulate your response.

3 Introduction

When a business is operated as a C corporation, situations are encountered that require the application of specialized tax rules. This chapter discusses these situations, which involve the following provisions of the tax law:

- The domestic production activities deduction (DPAD) of § 199.
- The alternative minimum tax (AMT) of § 55.
- The penalty taxes of § 531 and § 541.

The DPAD (also known as the "manufacturers' deduction") is not limited to C corporations and is available to other types of entities as well. Nevertheless, the DPAD is more apt to be found among corporations (either C or S types) than among individuals. The reason is that manufacturing activities require capital, which is easily raised through the use of a corporate entity. Moreover, the DPAD presents unique problems for C corporations, particularly when extended affiliated group members are involved.

Like the DPAD, the AMT is not limited to C corporations and applies to other types of entities as well. Fewer corporations may be subject to the AMT than to the DPAD due to the exemption for small corporations. An ACE adjustment relates only to certain corporations and is not required of other taxpayers.

The penalty taxes of § 531 and § 541 are unique to C corporations. The taxes are characteristically imposed on closely held corporations that accumulate profits to avoid dividend distributions. Because dividends may be taxed as ordinary income after 2012, steps should be taken to avoid these penalty taxes. Awareness of the potential danger is necessary to preclude a punitive tax. This awareness is particularly needed with the tax on personal holding companies (i.e., § 541) because its imposition is not dependent on the existence of a tax avoidance motive.

3.1 Domestic Production Activities Deduction

LO.1

Explain the reasons for the domestic production activities deduction (DPAD).

The **domestic production activities deduction (DPAD)** is a special deduction that is available for organizations with domestic production activities, including those in manufacturing, film production, construction, print media, engineering, and power generation. The deduction, which was fully phased in at 9 percent by 2010, reduces the corporate tax rates by about 3 percentage points.

There is an important limitation on the amount of the deduction. The DPAD cannot exceed 50 percent of the **W–2 wages** paid by the taxpayer during the tax year. The purpose of this limitation is to preserve U.S. manufacturing jobs and discourage their outsourcing.

The deduction is available to a variety of taxpayers, including individuals, partnerships, S corporations, cooperatives, estates, and trusts. For a pass-through entity (e.g., partnerships and S corporations), the deduction flows through to the individual owners. In the case of a sole proprietor, a deduction *for* adjusted gross income (AGI) results and is claimed on Form 1040, line 35, page 1. A Form 8903 must be attached to support the deduction. The Joint Committee on Taxation estimates that about 25 percent of the total benefit will accrue to 45,000 S corporations, 15,000 partnerships, and 50,000 sole proprietorships. Table 3.1 reflects the present savings that this provision will offer for C corporations.

EXAMPLE 1

The DPAD applies to more companies than just the typical manufacturer. The tax benefit is available to farmers, fishermen, miners, and the construction industry. Businesses involved in painting, drywalling, and landscaping qualify. Engineering and architectural firms qualify as long as their services relate to construction, even if no actual

TABLE 3.1 **Maximum DPAD Savings for C Corporations (Years after 2009)**

Taxable Income Range	Marginal Tax Rate*	Maximum Tax Savings**
$1–$50,000	15%	$675
$50,001–$75,000	25%	$1,688
$75,001–$100,000	35%	$3,150
$100,001–$335,000	39%	$11,758
$335,001–$10,000,000	34%	$306,000
$10,000,001–$15,000,000	35%	$472,500
$15,000,001–$18,333,333	35%	$577,500
>$18,333,333	35%	>$577,500

*Assumptions: Corporate tax rates remain the same for 2012 as in 2009, and the § 199 deduction does not reduce taxable income sufficiently to reduce the marginal tax rate.
**Taxable income × 0.09 × marginal tax rate.

Source: Adapted from S. C. Dilley and Fred Jacobs, "The Qualified Production Activities Deduction: Some Planning Tools," *Tax Notes*, July 4, 2005, p. 95.

construction takes place. Businesses conducting feasibility and environmental impact studies also qualify for the deduction. ■

The DPAD is designed to provide a tax benefit in a somewhat unique manner. Unlike other deductions, the DPAD does not result from a direct expenditure or other outlay. Instead, it is a deduction based on the net income earned from a specified source. A manufacturing concern, therefore, will determine its DPAD on the profit from the sale of the item produced, not on the cost of production. Thus, the DPAD is a deduction based on income.

Because the DPAD requires no additional outlay, the overall tax effect is similar to that of a rate reduction or a tax credit. The DPAD should not directly reduce earnings and profits, and FASB requires this benefit to be reported as a special charge (e.g., similar to a tax credit).[1]

The DPAD rules introduce a number of terms and related acronyms. To help clarify the discussion that follows, Exhibit 3.1 lists some of the more common acronyms found in § 199.

Components of the Deduction

LO.2

Identify the components of the domestic production activities deduction (DPAD).

The domestic production activities deduction (DPAD) is based on the following formula after 2009.[2]

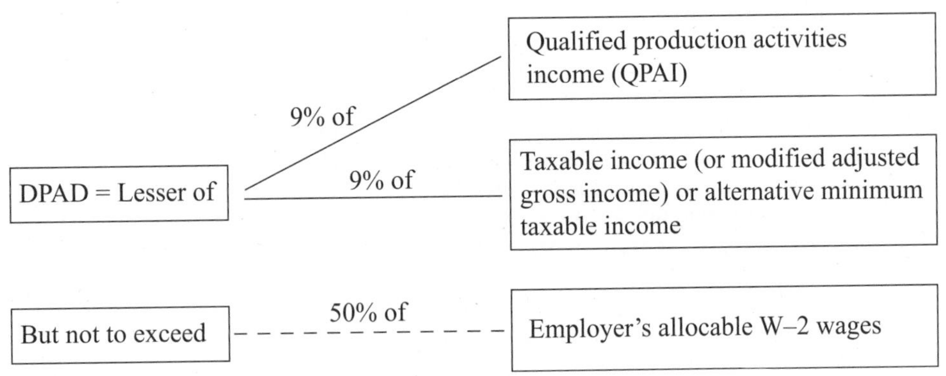

[1] FASB Staff Position No. FAS 109-1. **http://72.3.243.42/pdf/fsp_fas109-1.pdf**.

[2] A 6% rate applied to 2008–2009.

EXHIBIT 3.1	Some Common § 199 Acronyms
CGS	= cost of goods sold
DPAD	= domestic production activities deduction
DPGR	= domestic production gross receipts
EAG	= expanded affiliated group
MPGE	= manufactured, produced, grown, or extracted
QPAI	= qualified production activities income
QPP	= qualified production property
TPP	= tangible personal property

Taxable income is determined without regard to the DPAD. In the case of an individual (a sole proprietor or an owner of a flow-through entity), modified AGI is substituted for taxable income.[3]

The taxable income limitation is determined after the application of any net operating loss (NOL) deduction for the tax year. Thus, a company with an NOL carryforward for a tax year is ineligible for the DPAD if such carryforward eliminates current taxable income. Further, a taxpayer may lose part or all of the DPAD benefit if there is an NOL carryback for that year. As taxable income is reduced by the NOL carryback, there is a corresponding reduction in the DPAD. If **qualified production activities income (QPAI)** cannot be used in a particular year due to the taxable income limitation (see the formula on the previous page), it is lost forever.

EXAMPLE 2

Opal, Inc., manufactures and sells costume jewelry. It also sells costume jewelry purchased from other manufacturers. During 2012, Opal had a *profit* of $200,000 (QPAI) from the sale of its own manufactured jewelry and a *loss* of $50,000 from the sale of the purchased jewelry. Based on this information, Opal's QPAI is $200,000 and its taxable income (TI) is $150,000 ($200,000 − $50,000). Opal's DPAD becomes $13,500 [9% of the lesser of $200,000 (QPAI) or $150,000 (TI)]. ■

EXAMPLE 3

Assume the same facts as in Example 2, except that Opal also has an NOL carryover of $300,000 from 2011. As taxable income for 2012 is zero ($200,000 − $50,000 − $300,000), there is no DPAD. ■

The DPAD is further limited by 50 percent of the W–2 wages paid by the taxpayer that are allocable to domestic production gross receipts (DPGR), including the sum of the aggregate amount of wages and elective deferrals, required to be included on the W–2 wage statement for the employees during the employer's taxable year. Thus, the lower a taxpayer's W–2 wages, the less the potential deduction. If an employer has employees whose activities are applicable to providing services or other activities that do not create DPGR or QPAI, such W–2 wages are not included in the favorable category.[4]

EXAMPLE 4

In 2012, Red, Inc., has QPAI of $2 million and taxable income of $2.1 million. Because Red outsources much of its work to independent contractors, its W–2 wage base that relates entirely to domestic production activities is $80,000. Although Red's DPAD normally would be $180,000 [9% of the lesser of $2 million (QPAI) or $2.1 million (TI)], it is limited to $40,000 [50% of $80,000 (W–2 wages)]. ■

[3] § 199(d)(2). Modified AGI means AGI without any DPAD allowance and determined in accordance with the instructions to Form 8903.

[4] §§ 199(b)(2)(B) and (C); Reg. § 1.199–2T. W–2 wages do not include any amount that is not properly included in a return filed with the Social Security Administration on or before the sixtieth day after the due date (including extensions) for such return.

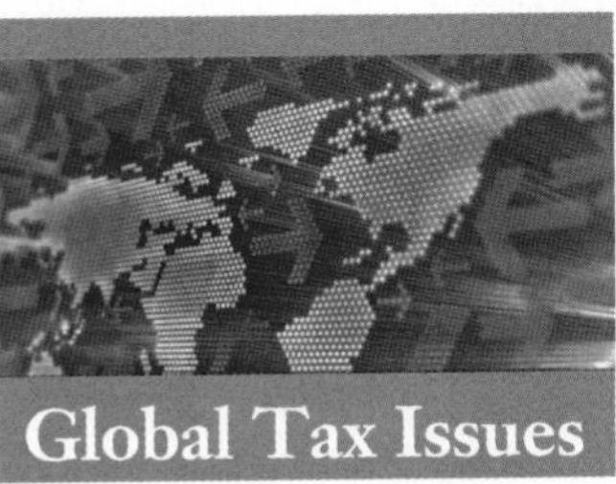

Congress Works in Strange Ways

To improve the balance of trade and mitigate the effect of its relatively high corporate tax rates, the United States has had a number of export incentives—the last of which was the extraterritorial income (ETI) regime. The ETI regime provided the benefit of an exclusion from income for certain foreign sales. Consequently, it is not surprising that the World Trade Organization found the ETI provisions to be an illegal export subsidy.

The American Jobs Creation Act of 2004 repealed the ETI exclusion but did not replace it with a comparable tax benefit for U.S. exporters. Instead, a new broad-based "domestic production activities deduction" for U.S. manufacturers was enacted.* Certain domestic producers can claim a deduction equal to 9 percent of qualified production activities income subject to several limitations. To curtail revenue loss, the deduction was phased in as follows: 3 percent for tax years beginning in 2005 or 2006, 6 percent for tax years beginning in 2007 to 2009, and 9 percent for tax years thereafter.**

The domestic production activities deduction, as a replacement for ETI, no longer presents an "international tax" issue—the deduction does not require exporting or any other activity outside the United States. Also, the deduction is not limited to the taxpayers that benefited from the ETI provisions and provides benefits to more businesses than just those considered manufacturers. Thus, Congress tried to solve an international export subsidy and ended up encouraging domestic manufacturing.

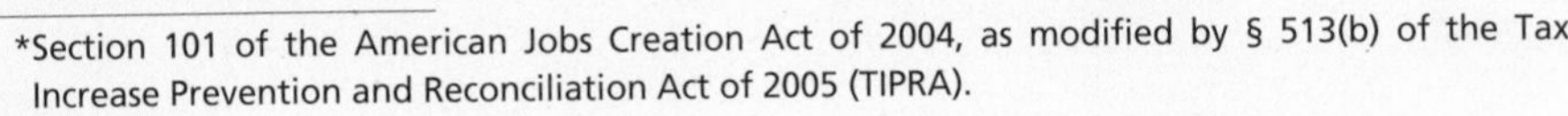

*Section 101 of the American Jobs Creation Act of 2004, as modified by § 513(b) of the Tax Increase Prevention and Reconciliation Act of 2005 (TIPRA).

**§ 199(a)(2).

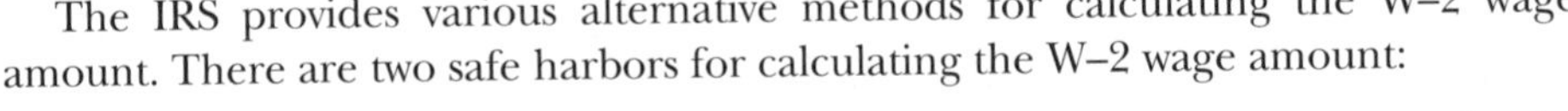

The IRS provides various alternative methods for calculating the W–2 wage amount. There are two safe harbors for calculating the W–2 wage amount:

1. With a wage-expense method, the employer multiplies the W–2 wages by the ratio of the wage expenses used to determine QPAI to the total wage expenses used to determine taxable income for the tax year.
2. Under a small business simplified overall method, W–2 wages are charged against DPGR in the same proportion as DPGR bears to total gross receipts.

Presuming that the taxable income and W–2 wage limitations are not applicable, the DPAD is a percentage of qualified production activities income (QPAI). QPAI is the excess of **domestic production gross receipts (DPGR)** over the sum of cost of goods sold (CGS) and other deductions and a ratable portion of deductions not directly allocable to such receipts.[5]

ETHICS & EQUITY A Proper Allocation for W–2 Wages Purposes?

Egret, a closely held C corporation, owns and operates a factory and a repair shop in southwest Texas. At its factory, it manufactures components for RVs, while at the repair shop, it repairs RVs of those traveling south for the winter (i.e., snowbirds). Egret's labor force consists of independent contractors, workers *with* Social Security numbers (i.e., W–2 wage earners), and those who have "lost" their Social Security numbers. In arriving at the QPAI for the manufacturing activity, Egret reduces the DPGR only by the W–2 wages. All other wage and labor payments are assigned to the repair activity (i.e., non-DPGR). Egret claims a DPAD based on QPAI from the manufacturing operation. Comment on the propriety of Egret's actions.

[5] § 199(c); Notice 2004–14, 2005–1 C.B. 498.

FIGURE 3.1 Scheme of the § 199 Domestic Production Activities Deduction (DPAD)

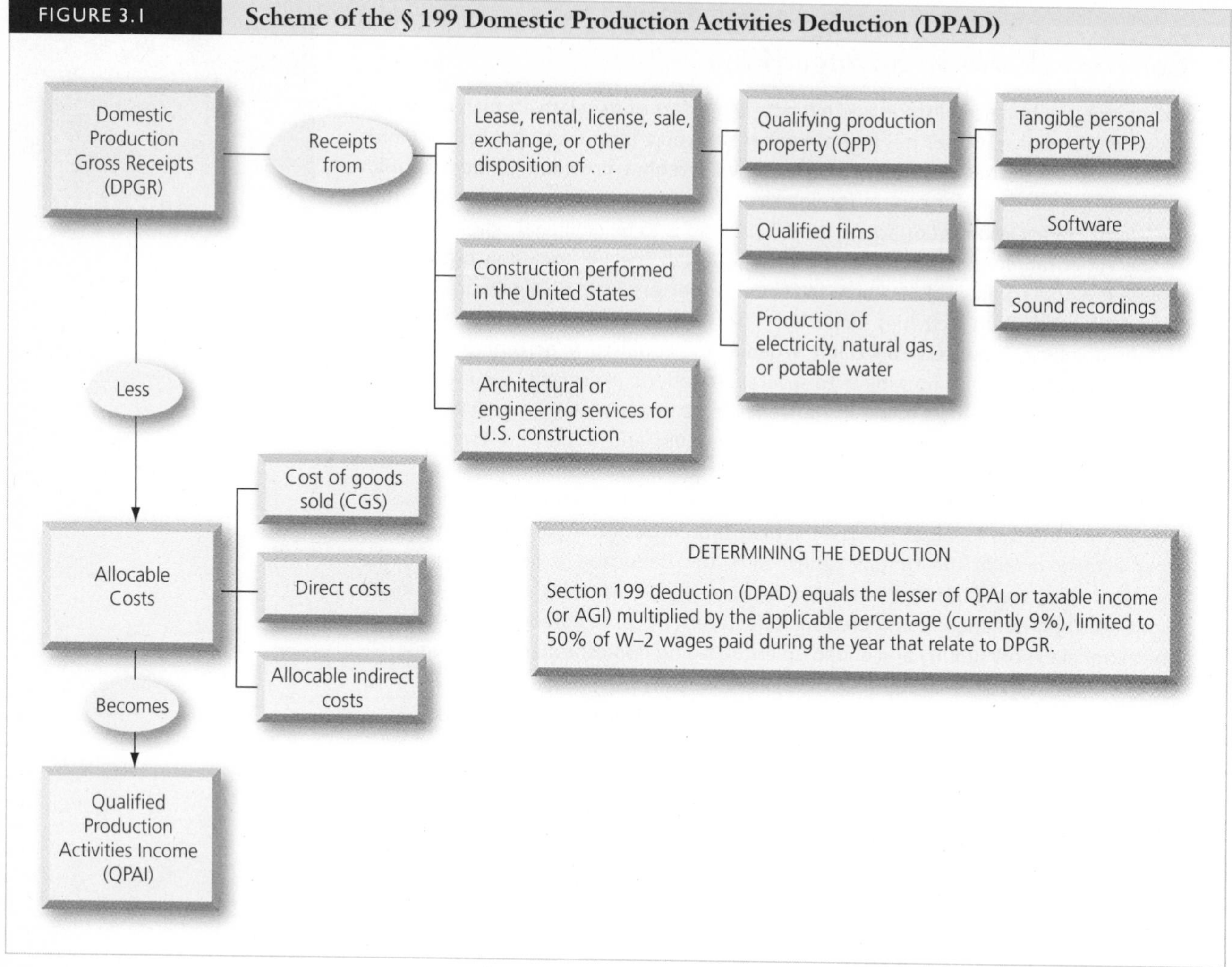

LO.3

Recognize and work with the different types of domestic production gross receipts (DPGR).

Domestic Production Gross Receipts

These five specific categories of DPGR qualify for the DPAD:

- Lease, rental, license, sale, exchange, or other disposition of qualified production property (QPP) that was manufactured, produced, grown, or extracted (MPGE) in the United States.
- Qualified films largely created in the United States.
- Production of electricity, natural gas, or potable water.
- Construction (but not self-construction) performed in the United States.
- Engineering and architectural services for domestic construction.

The operation of these categories is illustrated in Figure 3.1. In general, DPGR does not include any gross receipts derived from property leased, licensed, or rented for use by a related person.

The sale of food and beverages prepared by a taxpayer at a retail establishment and the transmission or distribution of electricity, natural gas, or potable water are specifically excluded from the definition of DPGR.

Gross Receipts That Qualify

In many cases, a taxpayer must determine the portion of its total gross receipts that is DPGR. For example, suppose a taxpayer produces a product in the United States

(QPP) includes tangible personal property (TPP), computer software, and sound recordings (see Figure 3.1). Local law is not controlling for purposes of determining whether property is considered tangible personal property. Tangible personal property does not include land; buildings; structural components of buildings; or intangible property such as patents, copyrights, and subscription lists. Tangible personal property does include items such as automobiles, books, food, clothing, display racks and shelves, and grocery counters.

Machinery and equipment that are not inherently permanent structures are also tangible personal property. An inherently permanent structural component of a building is real property. Real property also includes swimming pools, paved parking lots, water systems, railroad spurs, communication facilities, sewers, sidewalks, walls, doors, plumbing, pipes and ducts, elevators and escalators, central air-conditioning and heating systems, oil and gas wells, cable, wiring, and inherently permanent oil and gas platforms.[9]

To qualify as DPGR, QPP must be manufactured, produced, grown, or extracted (MPGE) *in whole or in significant part* in the United States. Included in this MPGE definition is the making of QPP out of salvage, scrap, or junk materials or by the use of new or raw materials. "Making" can involve processing, manipulating, refining, or changing the form of an article or combining or assembling two or more articles. Cultivating soil, raising livestock, fishing, and mining minerals fall under MPGE.

The "in whole or in significant part" requirement is satisfied if the employer's MPGE activity is substantial in nature. The substantial in nature requirement is relevant in deciding whether the MPGE activity (already determined to have occurred) was performed in whole or in significant part by the taxpayer in the United States. The requirement is applied by taking into account all of the facts and circumstances. This substantial in nature test is a facts and circumstances test, and a taxpayer cannot use the analogous authorities under the Subpart F Regulations (dealing with controlled foreign corporations—see Chapter 9) in applying this standard. There is a safe harbor if an employer incurs conversion costs (direct labor and related factory burden) related to MPGE of the property in the United States and the costs account for 20 percent or more of the property's cost of goods sold.[10]

EXAMPLE 9

Ecru, Inc., pays $75 to purchase a small motor and other parts and materials from related suppliers in Mexico. Ecru incurs $25 in labor costs at its factory in the United States to fabricate a plastic tank body from the materials and to assemble a toy tank. The company also incurs packaging, selling, and other costs of $2 and sells the toy tank for $112.

The toy tank will be treated as manufactured by the employer "in significant part" because Ecru's labor costs are substantial—they are more than 20% of the taxpayer's total cost for the toy tank [$25/($25 + $75) = 25%]. As a result, Ecru's DPGR is $112, and the full $10 in profit ($112 − $75 − $25 − $2) is QPAI. ■

EXAMPLE 10

Assume the same facts as in Example 9, except that Ecru incurred only $15 (instead of $25) in labor costs. Now the "significant part" requirement is not met because Ecru's MPGE activity is not substantial under the safe-harbor provision: 16.7% [$15/($15 + $75)] is less than 20%. Therefore, none of the profit is DPGR, and there is no producers' deduction (DPAD). ■

Only one producer may claim the DPAD. The taxpayer that has the benefits and burdens of ownership under the Federal income tax system during the period the qualifying activity occurs may claim the deduction.

[9] Reg. § 1.48–1(c); Notice 2005–14, § 3.04(11)(c).

[10] Reg. § 1.199–3(g)(3).

EXAMPLE 11

Crimson, Inc., enters into an agreement to have an unrelated supplier, Gray, Inc., manufacture items for Crimson. Only one of the taxpayers is treated as having MPGE the items for purposes of the DPAD. Crimson may obtain the deduction only if it bears the benefits and burdens of ownership.[11] ■

Barring a special agreement establishing ownership, the result in Example 11 will usually favor Gray, Inc. Most often, the party providing the manufacturing facility will have title to the goods being manufactured. In many situations, moreover, title may change as a product moves through the manufacturing process.

EXAMPLE 12

Crimson manufactures and sells lawn mowers. The lawn mowers are powered by motors that Crimson purchases from Gray, an unrelated domestic producer. Assuming no arrangement to the contrary, Gray has DPGR from the sale of the motors, while Crimson has DPGR from the sale of the lawn mowers. Gray has title to the motors while they are being manufactured, and Crimson owns the rest of the mower it produces. Crimson will not have a double DPAD because it will have to deduct what it paid for the motors (part of cost of goods sold) in arriving at QPAI (see Figure 3.1). ■

Qualified Films

A qualified film includes any motion picture film or videotape, as well as live or delayed television programming, if not less than 50 percent of the total compensation relating to the production of the property is compensation for services performed in the United States by actors, production personnel, directors, and producers. A taxpayer that MPGE a qualified film may treat the tangible medium to which the qualified film is affixed (e.g., DVD and Blu-ray Disc) as part of the qualified film, even if the taxpayer purchased the tangible medium. A taxpayer may subcontract the affixing of the film onto a tangible medium. Ticket sales for viewing qualified films do not constitute DPGR. Merely writing a screenplay or other similar material does not result in qualified gross receipts.

EXAMPLE 13

Maize, Inc., produces a qualified film and contracts with Magenta, Inc., an unrelated party, to duplicate the film onto DVDs. Magenta manufactures blank DVDs and duplicates Maize's film onto the DVDs in the United States. It sells the DVDs with the qualified film to Maize, which then sells them to customers. Magenta's gross receipts from manufacturing the DVDs and duplicating the film onto the DVDs are DPGR (assuming that all of the other requirements are met). Maize's gross receipts from the sale of the DVDs to customers are DPGR (assuming that all of the other requirements are met). ■

Construction Projects

The DPAD is available to a taxpayer who is involved in the trade or business of construction and performs a qualifying construction activity with respect to U.S. real property. The deduction is not available for taxpayers who self-construct real property. The term *construction* includes most activities that are typically performed in connection with the erection or substantial renovation of real property.

Real property includes residential and commercial buildings (including structural components), inherently permanent structures (but not machinery), and inherently permanent land improvements and infrastructure. Appliances, furniture, and fixtures sold as part of a construction site are not considered to be real property. If, however, more than 95 percent of the total gross receipts derived by a taxpayer from a construction project are attributable to real property, the total gross receipts are DPGR from construction.

Tangential services such as the hauling of trash and debris and the delivery of materials are excluded from DPGR, unless the taxpayer is performing such services

[11]There is much dissatisfaction with this "one owner" rule as to contract manufacturing, which often takes place on a consignment basis.

in connection with a construction project. Also, proceeds attributable to the disposition of land are not considered gross receipts derived from construction. Further, DPGR does not include gross receipts from the lease or rental of constructed real property.

With respect to land, there is a safe harbor for allocating gross receipts between the proceeds from the sale, exchange, or other disposition of real property constructed by the taxpayer, which qualify for DPGR, and the gross receipts attributable to the sale, exchange, or other disposition of land, which do not qualify. The taxpayer is able to reduce its DPGR costs by certain land costs plus a percentage based on the number of months that lapse between the date the taxpayer acquires the land and the date the taxpayer sells each item of rental property on the land (e.g., 5 percent for land held not more than 60 months).[12]

Gross receipts attributable to the sale or other disposition of land, (including zoning, planning, and entitlement costs) are considered gross receipts attributable to the land, and not to a qualifying construction activity, and therefore are non-DPGR. Costs incurred for cleaning, grading, and demolition in connection with a construction project are now construction activities under the Final Regulations. Any income stream (e.g., rent) from renting apartments in a building prior to its sale is not DPGR.

EXAMPLE 14

Gold Construction Company purchases five residential lots in a new subdivision for $500,000. On these lots, it builds five residences that it sells for $4 million. Because the proceeds attributable to the sale of the land cannot qualify, Gold has DPGR of only $3.5 million ($4,000,000 – $500,000). ■

EXAMPLE 15

A business owner (not engaged in construction activities) retains a general contractor to oversee a substantial renovation of a building, and the general contractor hires a subcontractor to install an electrical system as part of the substantial renovation. Here, both the amount the general contractor receives from the building owner and the amount the subcontractor receives from the general contractor qualify as DPGR from construction. However, the amount the building owner receives from the sale upon the disposition of the building does not qualify as DPGR because the owner was not involved in qualified construction activity with respect to the building.[13] ■

Construction activities need not satisfy the legal title restrictions that are applicable under the QPP rules to the manufacture of tangible personal property (see the discussion in connection with Examples 11 and 12). In Example 15, for instance, note that neither the general contractor nor the subcontractor owned the building they were working on, yet their income qualified for DPGR treatment.

Substantial renovation refers to the renovation of a major component or substantial structural part of real property that materially increases the value of the property, substantially prolongs the useful life of the property, or adapts the property to a new or different use. Thus, cosmetic changes such as painting and replacing shingles would not qualify.

Production of Electricity, Natural Gas, and Potable Water

DPGR includes gross receipts derived from any lease, rental, license, sale, exchange, or other disposition of electricity, natural gas, or potable water produced in the United States (see Figure 3.1). It does not include those receipts derived from the transmission or distribution of these items to final customers. An integrated taxpayer that carries out all of these functions must allocate the gross receipts among production, transmission, and delivery.

[12]Reg. § 1.199–3(m)(6)(iv)(A). The percentage is 10% for land held more than 60 months but not more than 120 months; it is 15% for land held more than 120 months but not more than 180 months. Land held more than 180 months is not eligible.

[13]Reg. § 1.199–3(m).

TAX IN THE NEWS Are Your Profits Too High?

Some members of Congress were disturbed by the record profits reported by some of the major oil companies in recent years. Two of the more favorable tax-saving provisions for oil and gas companies are the DPAD and FIFO. Although proposals were advanced that would have imposed a special excess profits tax on such earnings, Congress settled on a less direct approach. Under the Emergency Economic Stabilization Act of 2008, oil and gas companies are denied the increase to 9 percent of QPAI for purposes of the DPAD. In other words, the allowance is frozen at 6 percent for all taxpayers with QPAI that is oil- and gas-related.

EXAMPLE 16

PowerCo generates electricity that it sells to TransmissionCo. TransmissionCo sells the electricity to ElectricCo, which, in turn, retails it to user-customers. Only PowerCo's gross receipts qualify as DPGR. ■

EXAMPLE 17

Assume the same facts as in Example 16, except that PowerCo is an integrated producer that generates electricity and delivers it to end users. The gross receipts attributable to the transmission of electricity from the generating facility to a point of local distribution and any gross receipts attributable to the distribution of electricity to final customers are not qualified DPGR. ■

The term *natural gas* includes only natural gas extracted from a natural deposit, not methane gas extracted from a landfill. Natural gas production includes all activities involved in extracting natural gas from the ground and processing the gas into pipeline-quality gas. Gross receipts from the transmission of pipeline-quality gas from a natural gas field or plant to a local distribution company are not DPGR. Further, gross receipts from the transmission from the local gas distribution company to local customers do not qualify.

Production activities with respect to potable water include the acquisition, collection, and storage of untreated water; transportation of such water to a water treatment facility; and treatment of untreated water at such a facility. Potable water refers to unbottled drinking water. DPGR does not include gross receipts derived from the storage of potable water (after completion of treatment) or the delivery of potable water to customers. The IRS believes this provision applies to water utilities and not to taxpayers engaged in the trade or business of producing bottled water. Thus, bottled water companies are to be treated as the producers of tangible personal property.

LO.4

Illustrate the necessary adjustments to DPGR to arrive at qualified production activities income (QPAI).

Adjustments in Arriving at QPAI

Once DPGR is determined, certain adjustments must be made to arrive at qualified production activities income (QPAI). Recall that it is usually 9 percent of QPAI that yields the DPAD. The adjustments that are necessary are listed in Figure 3.1 and include the following:

1. Cost of goods sold (CGS).
2. Direct costs.
3. Allocable indirect costs.

CGS is equal to beginning inventory plus purchases and production costs and less ending inventory. If a taxpayer can identify from its books and records the CGS allocable to DPGR, that amount is allocable to DPGR. If identification is not possible, a taxpayer must use a reasonable method, but it may not use a different allocation method than it used to allocate gross receipts between DPGR and non-DPGR. Reasonable methods may include those based on gross receipts, number of units sold, number of units produced, or total production costs.

TAX IN THE NEWS States Are Decoupling from the DPAD

Most states impose an income tax on corporations. Unless otherwise provided, these state income taxes generally use as a tax base the taxable income as determined for Federal income tax purposes. Thus, a DPAD claimed on Form 1120 reduces not only Federal income taxes but also state income taxes.

With many states facing budget shortfalls and with the DPAD percentage now at 9 percent, more than 20 states have eliminated the deduction. In decoupling from the DPAD, these states require that any DPAD be added back to taxable income for state income tax purposes. Thus, the DPAD is allowed for Federal, but not state, income tax purposes.

Unless economic conditions substantially improve, the number of states decoupling from the DPAD probably will increase. One report indicates that 27 states can reduce revenue losses by decoupling from § 199.

Source: Jason Levitis, Nicholas Johnson, and Katherine Lira, "States Can Opt Out of the Costly and Ineffective Domestic Production Deduction Corporate Tax Break," Center on Budget and Policy Priorities, July 29, 2009.

The second category of expenses (direct costs) includes selling and marketing expenses. The third category (allocable indirect costs) is further removed and includes, for example, general and administrative expenses attributable to the selling and marketing expenses.

The second and third categories of expenses (i.e., direct allocable and indirect allocable) may be allocated by one of three methods:

- The *§ 861 Regulation method* may be used by *all* taxpayers but *must* be used by those taxpayers with average annual gross receipts of more than $100 million. Essentially, certain deductions incurred by a U.S. taxpayer must be allocated to various classes of gross income and apportioned between foreign sources and domestic sources. Although time-consuming, the § 861 Regulation method is most accurate. Unfortunately, for those concerns without international operations, the use of this method will necessitate a resort to unfamiliar rules. The mechanics of the § 861 Regulations are explained and illustrated in Chapter 9 under the heading Allocation and Apportionment of Deductions.
- For employers with average annual gross receipts of $100 million or less or total assets at the end of the taxable year of $10 million or less, a *simplified deduction method* based on relative gross receipts is available. The deductions are apportioned to DPGR in the same proportion as DPGR bears to total gross receipts.
- For taxpayers that have average gross receipts of $5 million or less or are eligible to use the cash method, a *small business simplified overall method* is available. This method is the same as the previous method except that it can also be used to arrive at CGS.

EXAMPLE 18

Brown, Inc., a qualifying small taxpayer,[14] has total gross receipts of $4.3 million; DPGR of $3.1 million; CGS of $1.3 million; and advertising, selling, and administrative expenses of $500,000. Under the small business simplified overall method, CGS and deductions are apportioned to DPGR in the same proportion DPGR bears to total gross receipts.

Thus, Brown's QPAI is computed as follows:

DPGR	$3,100,000
Less allowable CGS:	
[($3.1 million/$4.3 million) × $1.3 million]	(937,209)
Less allocable expenses:	
[($3.1 million/$4.3 million) × $500,000]	(360,465)
QPAI	$1,802,326

[14]As defined in Reg. § 1.199–4(f)(2).

Presuming that the taxable income and W–2 wage limitations do not intervene, Brown's DPAD for 2012 is $162,209 (9% × $1,802,326). ■

To determine whether one of the simplified methods may be used, the average annual gross receipts must be determined at the expanded affiliated group level (discussed later). Also, a member of the expanded affiliated group that qualifies to use one of the simplified methods may do so only if all members of the group elect to use that method.

LO.5

List the collateral problems associated with the domestic production activities deduction (DPAD).

Collateral Problems

Disallowed Production Activities—Preparation of Food and Beverages

DPGR does not include gross receipts from the sale of food and beverages prepared by a taxpayer at a retail establishment.[15] A retail establishment includes real property leased, occupied, or otherwise used by a taxpayer in its trade or business of selling food or beverages to the public and at which the taxpayer makes retail sales. A facility is not a retail establishment if the employer uses the facility only to prepare food or beverages for wholesale sale. There is a 5 percent *de minimis* safe harbor.

EXAMPLE 19

Silver Company buys coffee beans that it roasts and packages at a special facility. The company sells the roasted coffee through a variety of unrelated third-party vendors as well as at its own retail establishments. These receipts are qualified DPGR.

At Silver's retail establishments, it prepares and sells brewed coffee and food. These receipts are not DPGR. Nevertheless, part of the receipts from the sale of the brewed coffee may be allocated to DPGR to the extent of the value of the roasted beans used to brew the coffee. The amount to be allocated is determined by the price Silver receives from the sale of the roasted beans. ■

THE BIG PICTURE

EXAMPLE 20

Return to the facts of *The Big Picture* on p. 3-1. Suppose Mocha has $42 million from the wholesale sale of its ice cream and only $2 million from the operation of the snack shops next to its facilities where it sells ice cream to the general public. The full $44 million is DPGR because the $2 million falls under the *de minimis* safe-harbor exception [$2 million is less than 5% of $44 million ($42 million + $2 million)].

The prohibition against the retail sale of prepared food cannot be avoided by restricting sales to take-out orders. The prohibition does not, however, apply to the sale of prepared meals to others for resale.

EXAMPLE 21

Beige Brothers operates a food service business that prepares meals. Some of the meals are served to diners at a café it owns adjacent to the plant, some are sold to customers on a take-out basis, and some are frozen and sold to supermarkets for resale. Only the proceeds from the latter operation will qualify as DPGR. ■

The prepared food restrictions may have been motivated by the trauma experienced by Canada before it rescinded its producers' deduction—see the discussion in the "Global Tax Issues" earlier in this chapter. As a result, the broiling and assembly of hamburgers and salads by Burger King will not qualify under the U.S. version of the producers' deduction.

Expanded Affiliated Group Rules

Special rules apply to corporations that are members of an **expanded affiliated group (EAG)**. An EAG is an affiliated group as defined for purposes of the

[15] § 199(c)(4)(B)(i).

consolidated return rules, except that the stock ownership requirement is reduced to more than 50 percent (from 80 percent) and insurance companies and possession credit corporations are not excluded from the group.[16]

In the case of corporations that are members of an EAG, the DPAD is determined by treating the group as a single taxpayer. In effect, therefore, each member of the group is treated as being engaged in the same activities as every other member. The deduction is then allocated among the members in proportion to each member's respective amount of QPAI.

EXAMPLE 22

Red Corporation and Blue Corporation are members of an EAG but do not file a consolidated return. Red manufactures a machine at a cost of $3,000, which it then sells to Blue for $5,000. Blue incurs additional costs of $1,000 on marketing, then sells the machine to an unrelated customer for $7,000. QPAI is $3,000 ($7,000 − $3,000 − $1,000) even though Blue did not perform any manufacturing. Note that this is the same result that would be reached if Blue had not been involved and Red had conducted its own marketing function. ■

EXAMPLE 23

Assume the same facts as in Example 22, except that the parties are not related. Under these circumstances, Red Corporation has QPAI of $2,000 ($5,000 − $3,000), and Blue Corporation has none. Blue's activities when considered alone are not QPAI because they involve marketing and not production. ■

If all of the members of an EAG are members of the same consolidated group, the consolidated group's DPAD is calculated based on the group's consolidated taxable income or loss, and not the separate taxable income or loss of its members. The DPAD of a consolidated group must be allocated to the group's members in proportion to each member's QPAI (if any), regardless of whether the member has separate taxable income or loss for the tax year and whether the member has W–2 wages for the tax year.

Pass-Through Entities Provisions

In the case of pass-through entities (i.e., partnerships, S corporations, trusts, and estates), special rules apply for handling DPADs. Because the deduction is determined at the owner level, each partner or shareholder must make the computation separately.[17] Consequently, the entity allocates to each owner his or her share of QPAI. The QPAI allocated is then combined with the domestic production activities the owner may have from other sources (e.g., a partner also conducts a manufacturing activity of his or her own).

In working with the wage limitation in a pass-through setting, an allocable portion of W–2 wages of the pass-through entity is passed through to the owner, but only those wages properly allocable to DPGR. The partner or shareholder, however, may add any wages separately paid to the amount allocated from the entity. In the case of a partnership, guaranteed payments are not regarded as W–2 wages. Also, if QPAI (computed taking into account only partnership items allocated to the partner for the tax year) is not greater than zero, a partner cannot use any partnership W–2 wages in calculating the DPAD.[18] The wage limitation applies to non-grantor trusts and estates in the same way it applies to partnerships and S corporations.

Generally, the DPAD is determined at the owner level in a pass-through entity situation. In some instances, however, the pass-through of the data needed to make this determination can be cumbersome and burdensome. To simplify matters, therefore, the IRS allows eligible partnerships and S corporations to calculate QPAI and W–2 wages for some or all of the owners at the entity level.[19]

The DPAD has no effect on an S shareholder's stock basis because the deduction is not listed in § 1367(a). Further, an S corporation or partnership that is a qualified small taxpayer may use the small business simplified overall method to

[16] § 199(d)(4).

[17] § 199(d)(1)(A).

[18] Reg. § 1.199–9(b)(3).

[19] Rev.Proc. 2007–34, 2007–1 C.B. 1345.

apportion cost of goods sold and deductions between DPGR and non-DPGR at the entity level. Also, the IRS may permit a partnership or an S corporation to calculate a shareholder's share of QPAI at the entity level, which is then combined with the shareholder's QPAI.[20] The owner is not allowed to use another cost allocation method to reallocate the costs of the pass-through entity regardless of the method used by the owner to allocate or apportion costs.

The pass-through information is reported by the entity on its Schedule K–1 of Form 1065 (partnership) or Form 1120S (S corporation). Owners include their share of QPAI and W–2 wages on Lines 7 and 17 of Form 8903 (Domestic Production Activities Deduction).

When an entity uses a different tax year than its owners, the pass-through of DPAD attributes may be delayed. As § 199 took effect for tax years beginning after December 31, 2004, coverage for a fiscal year entity could begin only in 2005.

EXAMPLE 24

John, a calendar year taxpayer, is a partner in Crimson Partnership, which uses a July 1–June 30 fiscal year. John will not be able to pick up any of the partnership's 2011–2012 QPAI until his 2012 individual return (the June 30, 2012 pass-through on Crimson's 2011–2012 fiscal year), which he will file in 2013. ■

Coordination with the AMT

The DPAD is allowed for purposes of the alternative minimum tax (AMT), except that after 2009, the deduction is equal to 9 percent of the smaller of (1) QPAI or (2) alternative minimum taxable income (without considering the DPAD) for the tax year. In the case of an individual, modified AGI (ignoring the DPAD) is substituted for AMTI.[21]

3.2 Alternative Minimum Tax

LO.6

Explain the reason for the alternative minimum tax.

The perception that many large corporations were not paying their fair share of Federal income tax was especially widespread in the early 1980s. A study released in 1986 reported that 130 of the 250 largest corporations in the United States paid zero or less in Federal taxes in at least one year between 1981 and 1985 (e.g., Reynolds Metals, General Dynamics, Georgia Pacific, and Texas Commerce Bankshares).

Political pressure subsequently led to the adoption of an alternative minimum tax to ensure that corporations with substantial economic income pay a minimum amount of Federal taxes. Corporations are now less able to use exclusions, deductions, and credits available under the law to pay no taxes. A separate tax system with a quasi-flat tax rate is applied each year to a corporation's economic income. If the tentative alternative minimum tax is greater than the regular corporate income tax under § 11, then the corporation must pay the regular tax plus this excess, the **alternative minimum tax (AMT)**.

In general, a corporation is likely to pay an AMT for one or more of three reasons:

- A high level of investment in assets such as equipment and structures.
- Low taxable income due to a cyclical downturn, strong international competition, a low-margin industry, or other factors.
- Investment at low real interest rates, which increases the company's deductions for depreciation relative to those for interest payments.

The 20 percent AMT applicable to many regular corporations is similar to the AMT applicable to individuals.[22] Many of the adjustments and tax preference items necessary to arrive at **alternative minimum taxable income (AMTI)** are the same. The rates and exemptions are different, but the objective is identical—to force

[20] Reg. §§ 1.199–9(b)(1)(ii) and 1.199–9(c)(1)(ii).

[21] § 199(d)(6).

[22] The AMT provisions for both corporate and noncorporate taxpayers are contained in §§ 55 through 59. The individual AMT rates are 26%/28%.

FIGURE 3.2 **AMT Formula for Corporations**

Regular taxable income before NOL deduction		
Plus/minus:		AMT adjustments (except ACE adjustment)
Plus:		Tax preferences
	Equals:	AMTI before AMT NOL deduction and ACE adjustment
Plus/minus:		ACE adjustment
	Equals:	AMTI before AMT NOL deduction
Minus:		AMT NOL deduction (limited to 90%)
	Equals:	Alternative minimum taxable income (AMTI)
Minus:		Exemption
	Equals:	Tentative minimum tax base
Times:		20% rate
	Equals:	Tentative minimum tax before AMT foreign tax credit
Minus:		AMT foreign tax credit
	Equals:	Tentative minimum tax
Minus:		Regular tax liability before credits minus regular foreign tax credit
	Equals:	Alternative minimum tax (AMT)

taxpayers that are more profitable than their taxable income reflects to pay additional income taxes.

As the AMT is in addition to the regular corporate tax, it is computed somewhat differently. Separate and independent calculations of the amount and character of all items affecting the computation of the AMT are required. The Code itself mandates the treatment of many items affecting the computation of the AMT. Regulations provide broad rules governing the treatment of other items for AMT purposes. However, the Code and Regulations do not provide guidance for many items.

The formula for determining the AMT liability of corporate taxpayers appears in Figure 3.2 and follows the format of Form 4626 (Alternative Minimum Tax—Corporations).

Small Corporation Exemption

For tax years beginning after December 31, 1997, many smaller corporations are not subject to the AMT. Certain corporations that meet several gross receipts tests are exempted from the AMT as long as they remain "small corporations." A corporation initially qualifies as a small corporation in its first tax year in existence regardless of its gross receipts. After the initial year, the exemption applies if these two requirements are met:

- The corporation must have been qualified as a small corporation exempt from the AMT for all prior years beginning after 1997.
- Average annual gross receipts for the three-year tax period (or portion thereof during which the corporation was in existence) ending before its tax year beginning in 2012 did not exceed $7.5 million ($5 million if the corporation has only one prior year).

Thus, the $5 million rule only applies in testing for the second year of a new corporation's life. So if a corporation had gross receipts of $5 million or less its first year, the second year is exempt.[23]

[23] § 55(e).

TAX IN THE NEWS Ineffective Corporate Alternative Minimum Tax

In 2010, General Electric paid little or no taxes on about $5.1 billion of income. How did it avoid the AMT? Bill Egnor says that companies such as GE and Bank of America avoid the AMT by moving their profits offshore. They do not pay taxes on these funds until the funds are repatriated. Yet our tax laws give the companies a credit against the AMT for taxes they pay the foreign countries. Thus, the foreign taxes benefit foreign countries, and our present tax laws permit the companies' write-off against their U.S. income.

Source: Adapted from Bill Egnor, "Time to Fix the Corporate Alternative Minimum Tax," My FDL, March 28, 2011, **http://my.firedoglake.com/somethingthedogsaid/2011/03/28/time-to-fix-the-corporate-alternative-minimum-tax/**.

THE BIG PICTURE

EXAMPLE 25

Return to the facts of *The Big Picture* on p. 3-1. Both Carmine and Taupe are safe for 2010 because the first-year rule applies (gross receipts are irrelevant). In the second year (2011), Carmine is safe as a result of the $5 million exemption, but Taupe fails the $5 million test because of $6 million gross receipts in the first year (2010). For 2012, Carmine still is safe because the $6 million average [($4 million + $8 million)/2] is under $7.5 million. Taupe, of course, will never qualify for the small corporation exemption again after failing in 2011.

A corporation that passes the $5 million average gross receipts test in the second year will continue to be treated as a small corporation as long as its *average* gross receipts for the three-year period preceding the taxable year do not exceed $7.5 million. For both the $7.5 million and the $5 million test, certain aggregating rules apply to related taxpayers. Once a corporation loses its small corporation protection, the corporation is liable for the AMT for that year and future years. However, many of the AMT and adjusted current earnings adjustments are modified so that they pertain only to transactions and investments that were entered into *after* the corporation loses its small corporation status (e.g., property placed into service in or after the change year).

These calculations are based on gross receipts and not gross income or net income. Gross receipts is determined by using a corporation's tax accounting method and includes total sales (net of returns and allowances), amounts received for services, and income from investments and other sources. Once a company fails the small corporation exemption, the meager $40,000 statutory exemption is available. A corporation is treated as a small business corporation in its first tax year regardless of its gross receipts for the year.

THE BIG PICTURE

EXAMPLE 26

Refer to the facts of *The Big Picture* on p. 3-1. Carmine Corporation has gross receipts of $4 million in 2010, $8 million in 2011, and $10 million in 2012. What amount of gross receipts for 2013 would eliminate Carmine from the small corporation exemption in 2014?

If Carmine Corporation has more than $4.5 million of gross receipts in 2013, the company could not be a small corporation in 2014 [($8 million + $10 million + $4.5 million)/3 = $7.5 million].

AMT Adjustments

LO.7

Calculate the alternative minimum tax applicable to corporations.

As Figure 3.2 indicates, the starting point for computing AMTI is the taxable income of the corporation before any NOL deduction. Certain adjustments must be made to this amount. Unlike tax preference items, which are always additions, **AMT adjustments** may either increase or decrease taxable income. For example, the deduction for domestic manufacturing activities (DPAD) is available for purposes of computing minimum taxable income (as well as adjusted current earnings). However, the deduction is limited to the smaller of the qualified production income as determined for the § 11 tax (the regular corporate income tax) or the AMTI without regard to the manufacturing deduction.

The positive adjustments arise as a result of timing differences and are added back to the taxable income in computing AMTI. Because most adjustments only defer taxes, a corporation may recoup AMT paid on these adjustments when the deferral of regular tax created by the adjustment is reversed and the regular tax is due. Once AMT adjustments reverse themselves, they are deducted from taxable income to arrive at AMTI. This mechanism is called the *netting process.*

Although NOLs are separately stated in Figure 3.2, they are actually negative adjustments. They are separately stated in Figure 3.2 and on Form 4626 because they may not exceed 90 percent of AMTI. Thus, such adjustments cannot be determined until all other adjustments and tax preference items are considered.

Other adjustments to regular taxable income include the following:

- A portion of depreciation on property placed in service after 1986. Depreciation allowances for purposes of the AMT are generally much less favorable than for the regular corporate income tax. For property placed into service after 1998, this adjustment applies only to MACRS 3-, 5-, 7-, and 10-year property that is depreciated using the 200 percent declining-balance method. The adjustment is the difference between the depreciation claimed for regular tax purposes and the depreciation using the 150 percent declining-balance method over the property's shorter regular MACRS recovery period.

EXAMPLE 27

Purple Corporation placed an asset costing $10,000 in service on March 15, 2011. Based upon a three-year recovery class life, this personalty has the following effect upon AMTI:

Year	Tax Deduction 200%	AMT Deduction 150%	Increase or (Decrease) AMT Adjustment
2011	$3,333	$2,500	$ 833
2012	4,445	3,750	695
2013	1,481	2,500	(1,019)
2014	741	1,250	(509)

■

- Because different depreciation methods may be used for AMT and regular tax purposes, the adjusted bases for these depreciable assets are affected. When the bases are different and the asset is disposed of, a basis adjustment is necessary to reflect the difference in the AMT gain or loss *and* the regular tax gain or loss.

EXAMPLE 28

Assume the same facts as in Example 27, except that the asset is sold at the end of the second year for $4,000. For regular tax purposes, the basis is $2,222 ($10,000 – $3,333 – $4,445), and the basis for AMT purposes is $3,750 ($10,000 – $2,500 – $3,750). Thus, the regular tax gain is $1,778 ($4,000 – $2,222), and the AMT gain is $250 ($4,000 – $3,750). Consequently, a $1,528 negative basis adjustment is required when computing AMT ($250 – $1,778). ■

- Passive activity losses of certain closely held corporations and personal service corporations.

- The excess of mining exploration and development costs deducted over what would have resulted if the costs had been capitalized and written off over 10 years.
- The difference between completed contract and percentage of completion reporting on long-term construction contracts, for some contracts reported under the completed contract method.
- Amortization claimed on certified pollution control facilities.
- The difference between installment and total gain, for dealers using the installment method to account for sales. The installment method is not allowed for AMTI purposes.
- A portion of the difference between adjusted current earnings (ACE) and unadjusted AMTI (post-1989)—see below.

Tax Preferences

AMTI includes designated **tax preference items**. In many cases, this inclusion has the effect of subjecting nontaxable income to the AMT. Some of the most common tax preferences include the following:

- Accelerated depreciation on real property in excess of straight-line (placed in service before 1987).
- Tax-exempt interest on state and local bonds where the generated funds are not used for an essential function of the government (but not for bonds issued in 2009 and 2010).
- Percentage depletion claimed in excess of the adjusted basis of property.
- For integrated oil companies (ExxonMobil, Chevron), the excess of intangible drilling costs over 10-year amortization if in excess of 65 percent of net oil and gas income. This item is not a tax preference for independent oil and gas producers and royalty owners.

Computing Alternative Minimum Taxable Income

The various modifications needed to arrive at the AMTI of a corporation are set forth in Concept Summary 3.1. The Concept Summary shows the effect of the different adjustments and preferences as applied to the taxable income of a C corporation. Some of the items included in the Concept Summary are not discussed in the text. Refer to the instructions to Form 4626 for further coverage of these items.

The following example illustrates the effect of tax preferences and adjustments in arriving at AMTI.

EXAMPLE 29

For 2012, Tan Corporation (a calendar year, integrated oil company) had the following transactions:

Taxable income	$6,000,000
Mining exploration costs	500,000
Percentage depletion claimed (the property has a zero adjusted basis)	700,000
Donation of land held since 1980 as an investment (basis of $400,000 and fair market value of $500,000) to a qualified charity	500,000
Excess intangible drilling costs	300,000

Tan Corporation's AMTI for 2012 is determined as follows:

Taxable income		$6,000,000
Adjustments:		
Excess mining exploration costs [$500,000 (amount expensed) − $50,000 (amount allowed over a 10-year amortization period)]		450,000
Tax preferences:		
Excess depletion	$700,000	
Excess intangible drilling costs	300,000	1,000,000
AMTI		$7,450,000

■

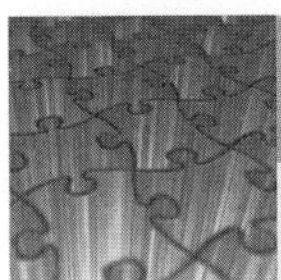

CONCEPT SUMMARY 3.1

AMT Adjustments and Preferences for Corporations

Adjustments	Positive	Negative	Either[1]
Depreciation of post-1986 real property			X
Depreciation of post-1986 personal property			X
Pollution control facilities			X
Mining exploration and development costs			X
Circulation expenditures[2]			X
Completed contract method			X
Adjusted gain or loss			X
Passive activity losses[2,3]			X
Alternative minimum tax NOL deduction		X	
Loss limitation			X
Nondealer installment sales			X
Adjusted current earnings adjustment			X
Domestic production activities deduction			X
Preferences			
Percentage depletion in excess of adjusted basis	X		
Accelerated depreciation on pre-1987 real property	X		
Intangible drilling costs[4]	X		
Private activity bond interest income[5]	X		

[1] Timing difference.
[2] Personal service corporations.
[3] Closely held corporations.
[4] Integrated oil companies only.
[5] Not for bonds issued in 2009 and 2010.

Adjusted Current Earnings (ACE)

LO.8

Review and illustrate the function of adjusted current earnings (ACE).

The purpose of **adjusted current earnings (ACE)** is to ensure that the mismatching of earnings and profits (E & P) and taxable income will not produce inequitable results. The calculation of ACE is similar to the calculation of E & P (which is similar to the economic concept of income). S corporations, real estate investment trusts, regulated investment companies, and real estate mortgage investment conduits are not subject to the ACE provisions.

The ACE adjustment is tax-based and can be a negative amount. AMTI is increased by 75 percent of the excess of ACE over unadjusted AMTI. Or AMTI is reduced by 75 percent of the excess of unadjusted AMTI over ACE. This negative adjustment is limited to the aggregate of the positive adjustments under ACE for prior years reduced by the previously claimed negative adjustments (see Figure 3.3). Thus, the ordering of the timing differences is crucial because any unused negative adjustment is lost forever. Unadjusted AMTI is AMTI without the ACE adjustment or the AMT NOL.

EXAMPLE 30

A calendar year corporation has the following data:

	2011	2012	2013
Unadjusted AMTI	$6,000,000	$6,000,000	$6,100,000
Adjusted current earnings	7,000,000	6,000,000	5,000,000

In 2011, because ACE exceeds unadjusted AMTI by $1 million, $750,000 (75% × $1,000,000) is included as a positive adjustment to AMTI. No adjustment is necessary for 2012. Unadjusted AMTI exceeds ACE by $1.1 million in 2013, so there is a potential

FIGURE 3.3 **Determining the ACE Adjustment**

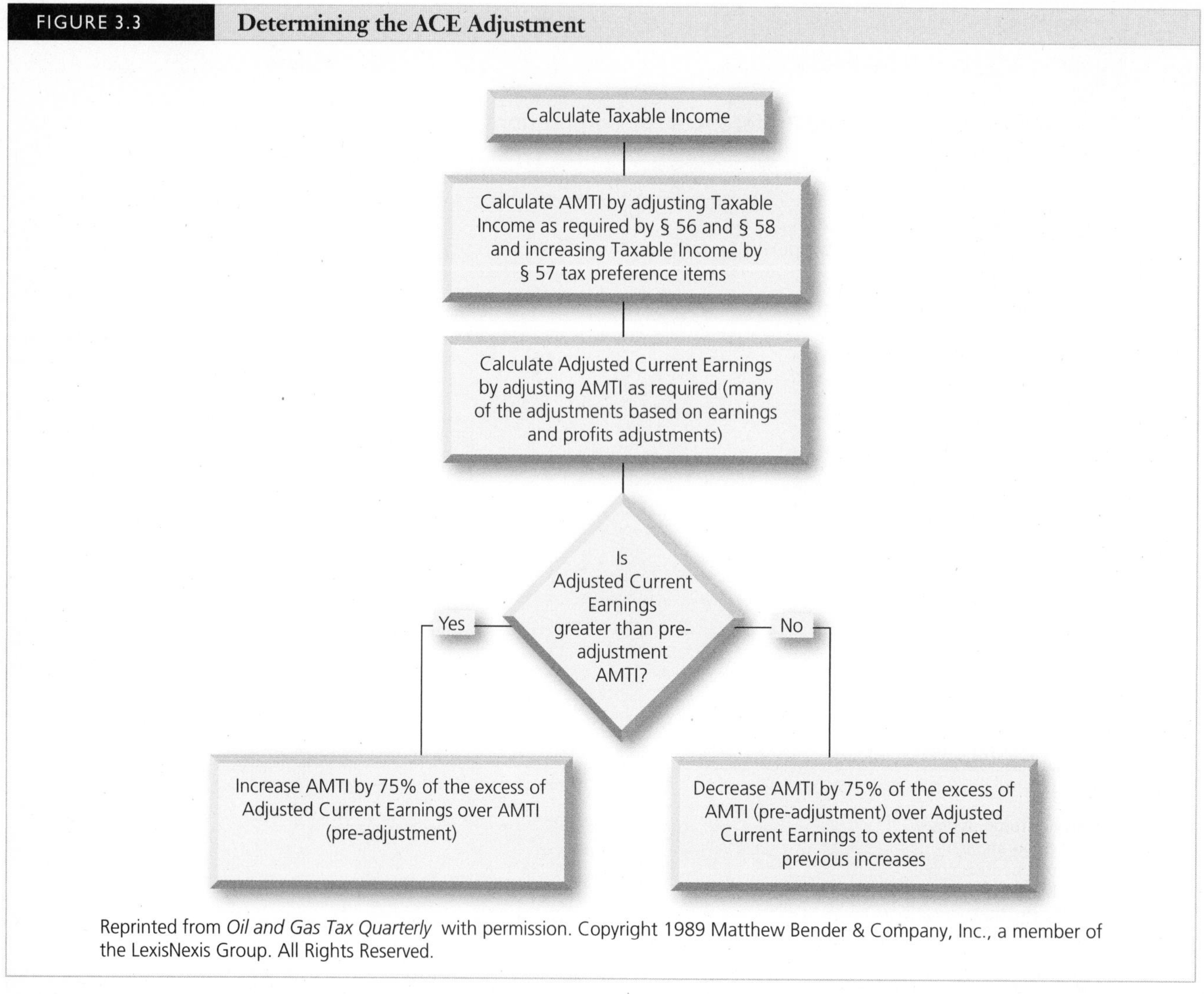
Calculate Taxable Income
Calculate AMTI by adjusting Taxable Income as required by § 56 and § 58 and increasing Taxable Income by § 57 tax preference items
Calculate Adjusted Current Earnings by adjusting AMTI as required (many of the adjustments based on earnings and profits adjustments)
Is Adjusted Current Earnings greater than pre-adjustment AMTI?
Yes
No
Increase AMTI by 75% of the excess of Adjusted Current Earnings over AMTI (pre-adjustment)
Decrease AMTI by 75% of the excess of AMTI (pre-adjustment) over Adjusted Current Earnings to extent of net previous increases

negative adjustment to AMTI of $825,000. Because the total increases to AMTI for prior years equal $750,000 (and there are no negative adjustments), only $750,000 of the potential negative adjustment will reduce AMTI for 2013. Further, $75,000 of the negative amount is lost forever ($825,000 − $750,000). Prior book income adjustments are ignored for limitation purposes. ■

ACE should not be confused with current E & P. Many items are treated in the same manner, but certain items that are deductible in computing E & P (but are not deductible in calculating taxable income) generally are not deductible in computing ACE (e.g., Federal income taxes). Concept Summary 3.2 shows the impact of various transactions on ACE, while the rules relating to E & P and its determination are discussed at length in Chapter 5.

The starting point for computing ACE is unadjusted AMTI (as specially computed for purposes of computing ACE). This specially computed AMTI is the corporation's regular taxable income after all of the normal AMT adjustments other than the ACE adjustment and the AMT NOL adjustment and after tax preferences.[24] Essentially, a corporation must keep at least three sets of books to calculate its Federal tax burden: one for the regular tax, a second for the AMTI, and a third for the ACE adjustments. The resulting figure is adjusted for the following items to determine ACE:

- *Exclusion items.* These are income items (net of related expenses) that will never be included in regular taxable income or AMTI (except on liquidation or disposal of a business). In essence, items that are permanently excluded

[24]The tax rules pertaining to the ACE adjustment are contained in § 56(g).

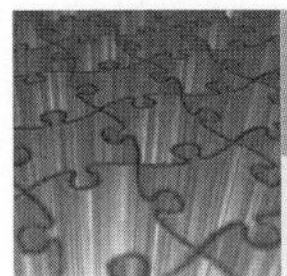

CONCEPT SUMMARY 3.2

Impact of Various Transactions on ACE

	Effect on Unadjusted AMTI in Arriving at ACE
Tax-exempt income (net of expenses)	Add
Federal income tax	No effect
Dividends received deduction (80% and 100% rules)	No effect
Dividends received deduction (70% rule)	Add
Exemption amount of $40,000	No effect
Excess charitable contribution	No effect
Excess capital losses	No effect
Disallowed travel and entertainment expenses	No effect
Penalties and fines	No effect
Intangible drilling costs deducted currently	Add
Deferred gain on installment sales	Add
Realized (not recognized) gain (e.g., involuntary conversion and like-kind exchanges)	No effect
Loss on sale between related parties	No effect
Key employee insurance proceeds	Add
Premiums paid on key employee insurance	Subtract
Net buildup on life insurance policy	Add

from unadjusted AMTI are therefore included in ACE (e.g., life insurance proceeds, interest on tax-exempt bonds, and tax benefit rule exclusions).

- *Disallowed items.* Because the starting point for ACE is AMTI before the NOL, no adjustment is necessary for the NOL. A deduction *is not allowed* for the dividends received deduction of 70 percent (less than 20 percent ownership). But a deduction *is allowed* for the dividends received deduction of 80 percent (20 percent but less than 80 percent ownership) and 100 percent (80 percent or more ownership).
- *Other adjustments.* Adjustments for the following items are necessary: intangible drilling costs, circulation expenditures, organization expense amortization, and installment sales deferrals.
- *Both AMTI and ACE.* Certain deductible items do not reduce ACE: excess charitable contributions, excess capital losses, disallowed travel and entertainment expenses, penalties, fines, bribes, and golden parachute payments.
- *Lessee improvements.* The value of improvements made by a lessee to a lessor's property that is excluded from the lessor's income is excluded from both unadjusted AMTI and ACE.
- *LIFO recapture adjustments.* An increase or a decrease in the LIFO recapture amount will result in a corresponding increase or decrease in ACE.

EXAMPLE 31

Crimson Corporation makes the ACE adjustment calculation as follows:

AMTI		$5,780,000
Plus:		
Municipal bond interest	$210,000	
Installment gain	140,000	
70% dividends received deduction	300,000	
Income element in cash surrender life insurance	60,000	
Organization expense amortization	70,000	780,000
		$6,560,000

FINANCIAL DISCLOSURE INSIGHTS The Alternative Minimum Tax as Prepayment

Tax professionals often describe the alternative minimum tax (AMT) as a "mere prepayment device," in that by applying the minimum tax credit, the entity recovers its payment for the AMT in a later tax year when it returns to regular tax status. Critics observe that this statement is misleading for several important reasons.

- Due to the makeup of their assets or income sources, many businesses are subject to the AMT every year. Thus, the minimum tax credit never will be available as there will not be another regular tax year in the foreseeable future.
- Any prepayment of tax reduces the present value of the credit that is claimed in a future tax year. Consequently, the AMT generates a permanent loss of funds to the taxpayer. For example, if the after-tax rate of return for the entity is 6 percent, a $1 million minimum tax credit that is claimed five years after the AMT is paid is worth only about $750,000 (Tables 7.1 and 7.2 in Chapter 7 can be used to make these analyses).

If the minimum tax credit is to be claimed in future years, a deferred tax asset is created on the taxpayer's GAAP balance sheet. This deferred tax asset might also address the basis differences for assets that are depreciated under MACRS for regular tax purposes and ADS in computing the AMT. In a recent year, the trucking firm Ryder Systems reported a deferred tax asset of approximately $10 million relating to the application of the AMT for the year. For the prior year, the Ryder deferred tax asset for the AMT had been approximately $12.5 million; so one can infer that some of the minimum tax credit had been claimed at least for that tax year.

Less:		
Decreases in LIFO recapture amount	$230,000	
Life insurance premiums paid on key employee policy	10,000	240,000
Adjusted current earnings		$6,320,000
AMTI		−5,780,000
Difference		$ 540,000
Times		.75
ACE adjustment (positive)		$ 405,000

■

Exemption

The AMT is 20 percent of AMTI that exceeds the exemption amount. The exemption amount for a corporation is $40,000 reduced by 25 percent of the amount by which AMTI exceeds $150,000.[25]

EXAMPLE 32

Beige Corporation has lost its small corporation status and has AMTI of $180,000. Because the exemption amount is reduced by $7,500 [25% × ($180,000 − $150,000)], the amount remaining is $32,500 ($40,000 − $7,500). Thus, Beige Corporation's alternative minimum tax base (refer to Figure 3.2) is $147,500 ($180,000 − $32,500). ■

Note that the exemption phases out entirely when AMTI reaches $310,000. With the $7.5 million and $5 million small corporation exceptions, this exemption is less important to profitable corporations.

Minimum Tax Credit

The AMT is a separate tax system that is computed side by side with the regular tax. Along with the "netting concept," a **minimum tax credit** is available to eliminate the possibility of double taxation.[26] Essentially, the AMT paid in one tax year may be carried forward indefinitely and used as a credit against the corporation's future *regular* tax liability that exceeds its tentative minimum tax. The minimum tax credit may not be carried back and may not be offset against any future *minimum* tax liability. The credit can be used to reduce regular tax liability in future years (but not below the tentative AMT).

[25] § 55(d)(2).

[26] § 53.

Unfortunately, the law does not cover the reverse situation (a preference item generates a regular tax in one year and results in an AMT in a later year). An example could be unearned income that is taxed in the year of receipt but is not recognized for book income purposes until the year earned. Consequently, it is entirely possible that the same income could be taxed twice.

EXAMPLE 33

Returning to the facts of Example 29, Tan Corporation's AMTI exceeds $310,000, so there is no exemption amount. The tentative minimum tax is $1,490,000 (20% of $7,450,000). Assuming that the regular tax liability in 2012 is $1,400,000, the AMT liability is $90,000 ($1,490,000 − $1,400,000). The amount of the minimum tax credit carryover is $90,000, which is all of the current year's AMT. ■

Because the tentative minimum tax of a small corporation will be zero, a small corporation with unused minimum tax credits after 1997 may use them up to the amount of the corporation's regular tax liability (after other credits) *less* 25 percent of the excess, if any, of the regular tax liability over $25,000. This will accelerate a small corporation's ability to use any available tax credits.

EXAMPLE 34

Purple Corporation, a small company, has a significant amount of minimum tax credits, but no AMT liability in 2012. The corporation's regular tax liability (less other credits) for 2012 is $75,000. Purple's allowable minimum tax credit for 2012 is limited to $62,500 [$75,000 − .25 ($75,000 − $25,000)]. ■

Other Aspects of the AMT

In addition to paying their regular tax liability, corporations have to make estimated tax payments of the AMT liability. Even corporations that prepare quarterly financial statements may find that this requirement adds to compliance costs. Unfortunately, the estimated tax payment dates will not coincide with the dates of the financial statements. Accordingly, estimating book income accurately for AMT purposes from the information usually available may be difficult.

Form 4626 Illustrated

Form 4626 is used to compute the alternative minimum tax for a corporation that is not exempt from the AMT. For an affiliated group filing a consolidated tax return, the AMT must be computed on a consolidated basis.

A corporation must file Form 4626 if any of the following apply:

- The corporation is not a "small corporation" exempt from the AMT.
- The corporation's taxable income or loss before the NOL deduction plus its adjustments and preferences totals more than $40,000 or, if smaller, its allowable exemption amount.
- The corporation claims any general business credit, any qualified electric vehicle passive activity credit from prior years, or the credit for prior year minimum tax.

EXAMPLE 35

The following facts apply to a calendar year corporation in 2011 that is not a small corporation:

Taxable income before NOL	$3,417,640
Domestic production activities deduction	(18,222)
Tax-exempt interest from specified private activity bonds	11,021
Adjusted loss	(33,014)
Amortization of mining exploration and development costs	(19,421)
Amortization of certified pollution control facilities	53,013
Depreciation of post-1986 property	476,557
ACE from line 10 of worksheet	5,100,460
Line 4d	244,225

Review Form 4626 on the next page to see how the corporation arrived at no AMT. ■

Form **4626**

Department of the Treasury
Internal Revenue Service

Alternative Minimum Tax—Corporations

▶ See separate instructions.
▶ Attach to the corporation's tax return.

OMB No. 1545-0175

2011

Name | Employer identification number

Note: *See the instructions to find out if the corporation is a small corporation exempt from the alternative minimum tax (AMT) under section 55(e).*

1	Taxable income or (loss) before net operating loss deduction			1	3,417,640
2	**Adjustments and preferences:**				
a	Depreciation of post-1986 property			2a	476,557
b	Amortization of certified pollution control facilities			2b	53,013
c	Amortization of mining exploration and development costs			2c	(19,421)
d	Amortization of circulation expenditures (personal holding companies only)			2d	
e	Adjusted gain or loss			2e	(33,014)
f	Long-term contracts			2f	
g	Merchant marine capital construction funds			2g	
h	Section 833(b) deduction (Blue Cross, Blue Shield, and similar type organizations only)			2h	
i	Tax shelter farm activities (personal service corporations only)			2i	
j	Passive activities (closely held corporations and personal service corporations only)			2j	
k	Loss limitations			2k	
l	Depletion			2l	
m	Tax-exempt interest income from specified private activity bonds			2m	11,021
n	Intangible drilling costs			2n	
o	Other adjustments and preferences			2o	(18,222)
3	Pre-adjustment alternative minimum taxable income (AMTI). Combine lines 1 through 2o			3	3,887,574
4	**Adjusted current earnings (ACE) adjustment:**				
a	ACE from line 10 of the ACE worksheet in the instructions	4a	5,100,460		
b	Subtract line 3 from line 4a. If line 3 exceeds line 4a, enter the difference as a negative amount (see instructions)	4b	1,212,886		
c	Multiply line 4b by 75% (.75). Enter the result as a positive amount	4c	909,664		
d	Enter the excess, if any, of the corporation's total increases in AMTI from prior year ACE adjustments over its total reductions in AMTI from prior year ACE adjustments (see instructions). **Note:** *You* ***must*** *enter an amount on line 4d (even if line 4b is positive).*	4d	244,225		
e	ACE adjustment. • If line 4b is zero or more, enter the amount from line 4c • If line 4b is less than zero, enter the **smaller** of line 4c or line 4d as a negative amount			4e	909,664
5	Combine lines 3 and 4e. If zero or less, stop here; the corporation does not owe any AMT			5	4,797,238
6	Alternative tax net operating loss deduction (see instructions)			6	0
7	**Alternative minimum taxable income.** Subtract line 6 from line 5. If the corporation held a residual interest in a REMIC, see instructions			7	
8	**Exemption phase-out** (if line 7 is $310,000 or more, skip lines 8a and 8b and enter -0- on line 8c):				
a	Subtract $150,000 from line 7 (if completing this line for a member of a controlled group, see instructions). If zero or less, enter -0-	8a			
b	Multiply line 8a by 25% (.25)	8b			
c	Exemption. Subtract line 8b from $40,000 (if completing this line for a member of a controlled group, see instructions). If zero or less, enter -0-			8c	0
9	Subtract line 8c from line 7. If zero or less, enter -0-			9	4,797,238
10	Multiply line 9 by 20% (.20)			10	959,448
11	Alternative minimum tax foreign tax credit (AMTFTC) (see instructions)			11	-
12	Tentative minimum tax. Subtract line 11 from line 10			12	959,448
13	Regular tax liability before applying all credits except the foreign tax credit			13	1,161,997
14	**Alternative minimum tax.** Subtract line 13 from line 12. If zero or less, enter -0-. Enter here and on Form 1120, Schedule J, line 3, or the appropriate line of the corporation's income tax return			14	0

For Paperwork Reduction Act Notice, see the instructions. Cat. No. 12955I Form **4626** (2011)

3.3 Penalty Taxes on Corporate Accumulations

LO.9

Evaluate the current status of the penalty taxes on corporate accumulations.

When dividends were taxed as ordinary income, avoiding corporate distributions often proved desirable. In closely held settings where a few high-bracket shareholders controlled corporate policy, the following approach would be taken:

- Accumulate earnings within the corporation. Distribute dividends, if at all, only when the shareholders are in a favorable tax position (e.g., are in low brackets or have offsetting losses).
- The accumulations will cause the stock to appreciate in value.
- The shareholders ultimately can recognize this appreciation in value at favorable capital gain rates by selling the stock. Or if the stock is transferred by death, no gain is ever recognized due to the step-up in basis under § 1014 (see Chapter 19).

Consequently, by not paying dividends, a tax rate of 15 percent (i.e., maximum rate on capital gains) has been substituted for 35 percent (i.e., maximum rate on ordinary income). Equally beneficial, recognition of gain has been deferred (to the date of sale) or completely avoided (transfer by death).

Due to the tax avoidance that was occurring through corporate accumulations, the penalty taxes of § 531 (**accumulated earnings tax**) and § 541 (**personal holding company tax**) were enacted. These provisions imposed a penalty tax equal to the highest rate applicable to individuals on corporations used to avoid taxes on shareholders. Prior to the Jobs and Growth Tax Relief Reconciliation Act (JGTRRA) of 2003, the penalty tax rate was 39.6 percent. The penalty tax was imposed in addition to the regular corporate income tax of § 11.

JGTRRA of 2003 temporarily reduced the motivation to accumulate at the corporate level with two changes. First, dividends are no longer taxed as ordinary income but are subject to a top rate of 15 percent (before 2013). Second, the penalty tax rate under § 531 and § 541 was reduced to 15 percent (before 2013).

Beginning in 2013, however, dividends may be taxed at the highest individual tax rate (39.6 percent), which increases the motivation to accumulate earnings. Likewise, beginning in 2013, both of the penalty tax rates become the highest individual tax rate (e.g., 39.6 percent), causing both taxes to again be punitive. For example, a personal holding company with $2.2 million undistributed after-tax income would owe $871,200 of personal holding company tax in 2013 ($2,200,000 × 39.6%), above and beyond corporate income taxes.

Accumulated Earnings Tax (§§ 531–537)

LO.10

Demonstrate the operation of the accumulated earnings and personal holding company taxes.

The § 531 tax of 15 percent (before 2013) is imposed on **accumulated taxable income (ATI)**, determined as follows:[27]

$$\text{ATI} = \text{Taxable income} \pm \text{Adjustments} - \text{Dividends paid} \\ - \text{Accumulated earnings credit}$$

Taxable income is determined in the same manner as in the case of the regular corporate income tax. The adjustments to taxable income generally pertain to a corporation's ability to pay a dividend. Thus, deductions include the corporate income tax, excess charitable contributions, and long-term capital gains (net of tax), while additions include the NOL and dividends received deductions.

The **accumulated earnings credit** is the greater of the minimum credit of $250,000 ($150,000 for personal service corporations) or the current E & P for the year needed to meet the **reasonable needs of the business**. In determining the minimum

[27] § 535.

credit or the current E & P required to meet the reasonable needs of the business, the balance of past (i.e., accumulated) E & P must be considered. This balance, once it reaches $250,000, also eliminates the use of the minimum credit.

EXAMPLE 36

Hazel, a calendar year C corporation, has accumulated E & P of $3.1 million as of January 1, 2012. Its current E & P for 2012 is $500,000, and it has reasonable business needs of $3.5 million. Hazel Corporation's accumulated earnings credit is $400,000 [$3.5 million (reasonable needs) – $3.1 million (accumulated E & P)]. Presuming that Hazel Corporation's current E & P is the same as taxable income as adjusted (see preceding formula), its ATI for 2012 is $100,000 [$500,000 (taxable income as adjusted) – $400,000 (accumulated earnings credit)]. ■

EXAMPLE 37

Assume the same facts as in Example 36, except that Hazel Corporation distributes a cash dividend of $100,000 to its shareholders during 2012. Hazel's ATI for 2012 now becomes $0 [$500,000 (taxable income as adjusted) – $400,000 (accumulated earnings credit) – $100,000 (dividends paid)]. ■

In most cases, ATI and vulnerability to the § 531 penalty tax are avoided by resorting to the accumulated earnings credit. Hence, it is important to recognize what constitutes the reasonable needs of the business. These include expansion of the business, replacement of plant and equipment, working capital needs, product liability losses, debt retirement, self-insurance, and loans to suppliers and customers.[28] Reasonable needs do not include loans to shareholders, investments in unrelated properties or businesses, and unrealistic hazards and contingencies.[29] Finally, if the accumulated earnings credit does not suffice, dividend payments will reduce or eliminate ATI (see Example 37 above).

Personal Holding Company Tax (§§ 541–547)

Often referred to as the tax on "incorporated pocketbooks," the § 541 tax is aimed at the use of the corporate form to shelter investment income. As was true of the § 531 tax, the assumption is that the income will be taxed, if at all,[30] at a lower rate in the hands of a corporate investor than in the case of an individual.

Before the § 541 tax can apply, the corporation must be a personal holding company (PHC). To be a PHC, both the stock ownership and the gross income tests must be satisfied.[31] Under the stock ownership test, more than 50 percent of the value of the outstanding stock must be owned by five or fewer individuals at any time during the last half of the taxable year. Under the gross income test, 60 percent or more of gross income (as adjusted) must consist of personal holding company income (PHCI).

Under the stock ownership test, constructive ownership is taken into account to cover indirect interests. Broad stock attribution rules apply for both family and entity ownership.[32] Closely held family corporations will find the stock ownership test difficult to avoid.

Regarding the gross income test, gross income is adjusted by subtracting capital and § 1231 gains and certain other expenses.[33] PHCI consists of passive types of income such as dividends, interest, rents, and royalties. Rents *or* royalties may be excluded if they are significant in amount (i.e., comprise more than 50 percent of the adjusted gross income). In limited situations, income from personal service contracts performed by a shareholder-employee may be PHCI.[34]

If the PHC definition is satisfied, the penalty tax of 15 percent (before 2013) is imposed on **undistributed PHCI**.[35] Undistributed PHCI is taxable income plus or

[28] § 537 and Reg. § 1.537–1.

[29] Reg. § 1.537–2(c).

[30] Although capital gains are subject to the corporate income tax, they are not taxed under either the § 531 or § 541 penalty taxes.

[31] § 542(a).

[32] § 544.

[33] As prescribed by § 543(b)(2).

[34] § 543(a).

[35] § 541.

minus various adjustments and less the dividends paid deduction.[36] The adjustments are similar to those made in arriving at ATI (for purposes of the § 531 tax) and largely reflect the corporation's financial capacity to pay dividends. Thus, the dividends received and NOL deductions are added back, and the corporate income tax, excess charitable contributions (i.e., in excess of the 10 percent limitation), and long-term capital gain (net of tax) are subtracted.

Note that taxable dividend payments *reduce* both ATI and undistributed PHCI. As these are the bases on which the § 531 tax or the § 541 tax is imposed, either tax can be completely avoided by paying sufficient dividends. This escape hatch is consistent with the reason for these penalty taxes—to punish the use of corporations that improperly accumulate surplus (by not paying dividends).

Both the § 531 tax and the § 541 tax cannot be imposed in the same situation. If a corporation could be subject to both taxes, the § 541 tax predominates.[37] A corporation that qualifies as a PHC is required to attach a Schedule PH calculating the PHC tax to its annual Form 1120.

3.4 Tax Planning

LO.11

Apply various tax planning procedures to maximize the domestic production activities deduction (DPAD) and to minimize the imposition of the AMT.

Domestic Production Activities Deduction

In most states, one problem to be faced with the producers' deduction is its status under local law. Even in those states that do not impose an income tax on individuals, an income tax on corporations may exist. Also, the franchise tax levied on corporations may possess some of the characteristics of an income tax. Do these state taxes allow the DPAD? As described in the "Tax in the News" earlier in this chapter, many states are decoupling from the Federal rules and are not permitting the deduction for state income tax purposes—a trend that has become more pronounced since the DPAD rate increased to 9 percent in 2010. Any decoupling from the DPAD adds to the discrepancy that exists between the Federal and state tax treatment of income and deductions. For taxpayers with multistate operations, however, it could mean a shifting of some operations to the more tax-friendly jurisdictions (see Tax Planning in Chapter 16).

The DPAD will compel taxpayers to use extreme care in structuring business transactions. As an illustration, how should the cost of embedded services be treated? Should the cost of a warranty be included as part of the price of the product, or should it be accounted for separately? The answer may depend on what the taxpayer does in the normal course of business. If the warranty is not separately bargained for and is customarily included in the price of the product, then the embedded service qualifies for the DPAD and requires no unbundling (i.e., separation). Also, the *de minimis* rule can avoid the embedded service hurdle if properly used (see Example 8 in this chapter).

When contract manufacturing is involved, the key to the availability of the DPAD depends on the incidents of ownership. Here, advance planning becomes crucial. The parties should decide beforehand who is to receive the deduction. Legal title to the property being produced should then be placed in conformance with this decision (see Examples 11 and 12 in this chapter). But see the discussion of the W–2 wage hurdle in the *Tax in the News* on p. 3-30.

If the production process includes offshore activity, recall that § 199 requires that a "significant part" be performed in the United States. According to the IRS, *significant* means "substantial," and this condition can be satisfied by meeting a 20 percent safe-harbor rule (see Examples 9 and 10 in this chapter). In cases where compliance with this safe-harbor rule is questionable, a ready solution would be to shift some of the offshore production to the United States.

---

[36] § 545.

[37] § 532(b)(1).

TAX IN THE NEWS W–2 Limitations May Restrict Manufacturers' Deduction

Because only one party may claim the DPAD with respect to the same function performed, taxpayers must maintain the benefits and burdens of ownership while the qualified production activity takes place. But these taxpayers must incur their own W–2 wages in performing the qualified production activities. For certain industries, these overlapping requirements could jeopardize the deduction. For example, if a contract manufacturer's labor and overhead are attributed to a contractor with the ownership of the property, there may be no attribution regarding W–2 wages paid by the contract manufacturer. Furthermore, even if a contract manufacturer retains ownership, the deduction is lost if the taxpayer has no common law employees engaged in the qualified production activities.

Particularly with a DPAD rate of 9 percent of QPAI, many shareholders of C corporations may prefer a pass-through of the deduction. In such cases, making an S election becomes a viable course of action.

Pass-through entities should consider these approaches:

- An S corporation or a partnership that is a qualified small taxpayer may use the small business simplified method to apportion CGS and deductions between DPGR and non-DPGR at the entity level.
- The IRS permits a partnership or an S corporation to calculate the pass-through portions of QPAI at the entity level, which then can be combined with the owner's QPAI.

To avoid the W–2 wage limitation imposed on the DPAD, the following observations should be considered:

- For sole proprietors, the self-employment tax does not qualify. In some cases, family members may need to be placed on the payroll to meet the W–2 wage limitation.
- Wages paid and not reported cannot be counted.
- Amounts paid to independent contractors do not qualify.
- Guaranteed payments made to a partner do not qualify.
- Taxpayers that have both qualifying and nonqualifying sales must keep careful records to allocate their W–2 wages.
- A taxpayer's payments to employees for domestic services in a private home are not included in W–2 wages for purposes of the DPAD.
- An individual filing as part of a joint return may take into account wages paid to employees of his or her spouse, provided the wages are paid in a trade or business (and other requirements are met). This is not true if a taxpayer and spouse file separate returns.

If the taxpayer wants to avoid the allocation and apportionment procedures prescribed by the IRS, complete accounting records that identify the relevant receipts and expenses are essential. For example, the records should reflect what portion of gross receipts qualifies as DPGR and what part does not. In arriving at QPAI, what expenses (including CGS) should be allocated to DPGR and which should not? When based on specific identification, the results reached by a taxpayer should weather any IRS challenge. This type of sophisticated accounting system, however, will generate considerable compliance costs for many taxpayers.

Alternative Minimum Tax

Planning for the AMT is complicated by the fact that many of the procedures recommended run counter to what is done to reduce the regular corporate income tax. Further, the AMT has the perverse effect of increasing a company's effective tax rate during economic slowdowns.

Avoiding Preferences and Adjustments

Investments in state and local bonds are attractive for income tax purposes because the interest is not included in gross income. Some of these bonds are issued to generate funds that are not used for an essential function of the government. The interest on such bonds could be a tax preference item and could lead to the imposition of the AMT. When the AMT applies, an investment in regular tax-exempt bonds or even fully taxed private-sector bonds might yield a higher after-tax rate of return.

For a corporation anticipating AMT problems, capitalizing rather than expensing certain costs can avoid generating preferences and adjustments. The decision should be based on the present discounted value of after-tax cash flows under the available alternatives. Costs that may be capitalized and amortized, rather than expensed, include circulation expenditures, mining exploration and development costs, and research and experimentation expenditures.

Controlling the Timing of Preferences and Adjustments

In many situations, smaller corporations may be able to avoid the AMT by making use of the exemption. To maximize the exemption, taxpayers should attempt to avoid bunching positive adjustments and tax preferences in any one year. When the expenditure is largely within the control of the taxpayer, timing to avoid bunching is more easily accomplished.

Optimum Use of the AMT and Regular Corporate Income Tax Rate Difference

A corporation that cannot avoid the AMT in a particular year can often save taxes by taking advantage of the difference between the AMT and the regular tax rates. In general, a corporation that expects to be subject to the AMT should accelerate income and defer deductions for the remainder of the year. Because the difference between the regular tax and the AMT may be as much as 14 or 15 percentage points, this strategy results in the income being taxed at less than it would be if reported in the next year. There is always the risk that the regular corporate rates may increase in future years. If the same corporation expects to be subject to the AMT for the next year (or years), this technique must be reversed. The corporation should defer income and accelerate deductions. The strategy delays the date the corporation has to pay the tax.

EXAMPLE 38

Falcon Corporation expects to be in the 34% tax bracket in 2013 but is subject to the AMT in 2012. In late 2012, Falcon is contemplating selling a tract of unimproved land (basis of $200,000 and fair market value of $1 million). Under these circumstances, it is preferable to sell the land in 2012. The gain of $800,000 ($1,000,000 − $200,000) generates a tax of $160,000 [$800,000 (recognized gain) × 20% (AMT rate)]. However, if the land is sold in 2013, the resulting tax is $272,000 [$800,000 (recognized gain) × 34% (regular corporate income tax rate)]. A savings of $112,000 ($272,000 − $160,000) materializes by making the sale in 2012. ■

The S Corporation Option

Corporations that make the S election will not be subject to the corporate AMT. As noted in Chapter 12, however, various AMT adjustments and preferences pass through to the individual shareholders. But one troublesome adjustment, the one involving the ACE adjustment, is eliminated because it does not apply to individual taxpayers. Similarly, the accumulated earnings and personal holding company taxes cannot be imposed on an S corporation.

REFOCUS ON THE BIG PICTURE

DEALING WITH THE DPAD AND THE AMT

Determining DPGR for the DPAD

The $42 million gross receipts from the wholesale sale of Mocha's ice cream are considered DPGR. However, the *de minimis* safe-harbor 5 percent exception does not apply to include the gross receipts from the sale of the ice cream and coffee at the snack shops ($5 million divided by $47 million = 10.6%). The sales from the snack shops could qualify as DPGR if Mocha were to restrict sales somewhat to take advantage of the 5 percent *de minimis* exception. For example, keeping snack sales at around $2.2 million would satisfy the 5 percent exception. Thus, Mocha will have to decide whether the 9 percent DPAD is worth forgoing the profit on the snack sales. Keep in mind that the DPAD is allowed for the AMT.

Who Pays the AMT?

Referring back to the facts of *The Big Picture* on p. 3-1, there was poor planning or a lack of planning on the part of Taupe Corporation. As a new corporation, Taupe should have shifted at least $1 million of the $6 million in gross receipts from 2010 to 2011. If this shifting had been done, Taupe would have fallen under the small business exception through 2012.

KEY TERMS

Accumulated earnings credit, 3-27
Accumulated earnings tax, 3-27
Accumulated taxable income (ATI), 3-27
Adjusted current earnings (ACE), 3-21
Alternative minimum tax (AMT), 3-16
Alternative minimum taxable income (AMTI), 3-16
AMT adjustments, 3-19
Domestic production activities deduction (DPAD), 3-2
Domestic production gross receipts (DPGR), 3-5
Expanded affiliated group (EAG), 3-14
Minimum tax credit, 3-24
Personal holding company tax, 3-27
Qualified production activities income (QPAI), 3-4
Reasonable needs of the business, 3-27
Tax preference items, 3-20
Undistributed PHCI, 3-28
W–2 wages, 3-2

DISCUSSION QUESTIONS

1. **LO.1** Indicate how a flow-through entity (e.g., sole proprietor) handles the DPAD.
2. **LO.1** What impact can W–2 wages have on the amount of the DPAD?
3. **LO.1, 2, 3, 4, 5** Explain the relationship between the following items:
   a. DPAD and W–2 wages.
   b. DPAD and QPAI.
   c. DPAD and TI.
   d. DPGR and QPAI.
   e. DPAD and AMT.
   f. EAG and DPAD.
4. **LO.1** How is the maximum DPAD savings for a C corporation calculated?
5. **LO.1** How is the DPAD treated for financial statement purposes?

6. **LO.1, 2** How do NOLs affect the taxable income limitation for DPAD purposes?
7. **LO.1, 2** Do all W–2 wages have an impact on the DPAD? Explain.
8. **LO.1, 2** What are the two safe harbors for calculating the W–2 wage amounts?
9. **LO.1, 2** Define *qualified production activities income.*
10. **LO.3** List the five categories of DPGR that qualify for the DPAD.
11. **LO.3, 11** Only one producer may claim the DPAD. Explain.
    a. Why is this rule important in the area of contract manufacturing?
    b. Does the rule present any planning opportunities? If so, describe them.
12. **LO.4** Once DPGR is determined, what adjustments are necessary to arrive at QPAI?
13. **LO.3, 5** Erica operates a chain of Tex-Mex fast-food outlets. She also wholesales frozen prepared meals to grocery stores.
    a. Can Erica claim a DPAD? Explain.
    b. Would it matter if all of the fast-food sales are on a take-out basis as the retail outlets have no dining facilities? Explain.
14. **LO.3, 5** MASH, Inc., produces two live television programs and licenses the first program to Clear, Inc., a television station. MASH licenses the second television program to Zebra's television station, which broadcasts the program on its channel. Both programs contain product placements and advertising for which MASH receives compensation. MASH and Clear are unrelated parties and are not members of an EAG. Discuss the DPGR tax result. **Issue ID**
15. **LO.2, 5** Justin and Kathleen are equal partners in Blue Partnership. For the year, they receive a pass-through of the same amount of QPAI and W–2 wages from Blue. Justin, however, is able to claim a larger DPAD on his income tax return than Kathleen. Why? **Issue ID**
16. **LO.5** Is the DPAD available for purposes of the alternative minimum tax (AMT)? Explain.
17. **LO.6** If the AMT is greater than the regular corporate tax, the corporation must pay the greater AMT. Discuss.
18. **LO.6** What is the small corporation exemption from the AMT? When is it available and not available?
19. **LO.6, 7** Because tax preference items are merely timing differences, they may be positive or negative. Assess the validity of this statement.
20. **LO.7** Percentage depletion claimed by a taxpayer is a tax preference item. Assess the validity of this statement.
21. **LO.6, 7** In arriving at AMTI, why are NOLs stated separately instead of being included with other adjustments?
22. **LO.7, 8** Using the legend provided, classify the impact that each of the following items has on unadjusted AMTI in arriving at ACE:

Legend
I = Increase in AMTI
D = Decrease in AMTI
E = Either an increase or a decrease in AMTI
N = No impact

    a. Currently deducted intangible drilling costs.
    b. Loss on sale of a piece of equipment to a related party.
    c. Purchase of raw materials.
    d. Nondeductible transportation fines.
    e. Dividends received deduction for a 15%-owned business.

f. Proceeds from a key employee insurance policy.
g. Tax-exempt interest.

23. **LO.6, 7, 8** Using the legend provided, classify the impact that each of the following items has when starting with regular taxable income or loss and then computing AMTI. Ignore the ACE adjustment.

Legend
I = Increase from taxable income
D = Decrease from taxable income
E = Either an increase or a decrease in taxable income
N = No change to taxable income

a. Amortization claimed on certified pollution control facilities.
b. Adjusted current earnings (ACE) adjustment.
c. AMT net operating loss deduction.
d. Excess mining exploration and development costs.
e. Statutory AMT exemption.
f. Accelerated depreciation on post-1986 property acquisitions.
g. Tax-exempt interest on private activity municipal bonds.
h. LIFO inventory recapture amount.
i. Excess percentage depletion of an integrated oil company.

Communications

24. **LO.8** Alice Tiras, an auditor on your staff, calls you to ask what impact current E & P has on ACE. She wants to know if ACE is the same as current E & P. Prepare a tax file memo indicating what you told Ms. Tiras.

25. **LO.8** What is the effect of the following on unadjusted AMTI in arriving at ACE?
a. Proceeds from life insurance on key employee.
b. Tax-exempt income (net of expenses).
c. Exemption amount of $40,000.
d. IDC deducted currently.
e. Excess capital loss.
f. Deferred gain on installment sales.
g. Excess charitable contributions.
h. Premiums paid on key employee insurance policy.

26. **LO.8** Which of the following credits may be used to offset the AMT?
a. General business credit.
b. Federal solar credit.
c. Foreign tax credit.
d. Qualified electric vehicle.

27. **LO.8** When must a corporation file Form 4626?

28. **LO.10** In making the "adjustments" necessary to arrive at accumulated taxable income, which of the following items should be added (+), should be subtracted (−), or have no effect (*NE*) on taxable income?
a. Corporate income tax incurred and paid.
b. A nontaxable stock dividend distributed by the corporation to its shareholders.
c. Charitable contributions paid in the amount of 10% of taxable income.
d. The dividends received deduction.
e. Deduction of an NOL carried over from a prior year.

29. **LO.10** ATI = Taxable income ± Adjustments + Dividends received − Accumulated earnings credit. Comment on the validity of this formula.

Communications

30. **LO.6, 7, 8, 11** A regular corporation anticipates AMT problems next year. Prepare PowerPoint slides for a technical presentation to the audit staff pointing out some strategies available to avoid or minimize the AMT.

31. **LO.10** Ashley McQuiston calls to ask you what impact future tax rates on dividends and capital gains will have on his closely held corporation. He is worried about the accumulated earnings tax. What will you tell him?

PROBLEMS

32. **LO.1** Tiger, Inc., has $13 million of taxable income. What is the tax savings from Tiger's maximum DPAD in 2012?

33. **LO.2** In each of the following *independent* situations, determine the DPAD for 2012 for the corporation involved.

	Taxpayer	QPAI	TI	W–2 Wages
a.	White	$800,000	$600,000	$120,000
b.	Red	400,000	500,000	20,000
c.	Black	900,000	900,000*	300,000
d.	Purple	700,000	900,000	200,000
e.	Orange	900,000	900,000	200,000**

*Does not include a $100,000 NOL carryover from the previous year.
**Only $60,000 relates directly to manufacturing activities.

34. **LO.3** Tern Corporation produces and sells refrigerators for outdoor use (e.g., patios, porches, and verandas). Its major manufacturing facility is in Georgia, but it also has a smaller plant in Nicaragua. Gross receipts for the current year are derived as follows: $8.2 million from Georgia and $1 million from Nicaragua.
    a. What is Tern's DPGR for the current year?
    b. What if the gross receipts from the Nicaragua plant are only $400,000 (not $1 million)?

35. **LO.3** Cowbird, Inc., refines and sells gasoline in the United States. Of the gasoline it sells, about 4% is refined in Louisiana and the remaining 96% is purchased from a non-related source in the Middle East. Suppose that currently the benefits of § 199 to Cowbird are so minimal that the tax savings are not worth the costs of compliance. Is there anything that Cowbird can do? Explain.

36. **LO.3** Hope Corporation manufactures and sells climate-controlled wine cabinets. Its most popular model sells for $3,000 and comes with a basic 90-day warranty. For an extra $150, this warranty is extended to 3 years, and for $300, the warranty is extended to 10 years.
    a. If a customer buys a wine cabinet with the basic warranty, how much of the $3,000 paid represents DPGR to Hope?
    b. Assume that a customer pays $3,150 to include the extended 3-year warranty. How much of this amount is DPGR?
    c. Assume that $3,300 is paid to include the extended 10-year warranty. How much is DPGR?
    d. Could the sales agreement be modified so as to increase the amount qualifying as DPGR? Explain.

37. **LO.3, 4** Stilt Corporation sells portable water filtration systems by means of the Internet and direct mail orders. Most of the components are purchased from foreign suppliers at a cost of $1,600. Stilt supplies the remaining components and assembles the final product at a cost of $400. Stilt's marketing, packaging, and shipping expenses total $50 per unit. Each unit is sold for $2,800.
    a. What is Stilt's DPGR per unit?
    b. Its QPAI?

38. **LO.3, 4** Assume the same facts as in Problem 37, except that Stilt incurred only $340 (not $400) in production costs.
    a. What is Stilt's DPGR per unit? Its QPAI?
    b. How could this result have been avoided?

39. **LO.3** Don is the owner of a large apartment complex that was built 30 years ago. As the complex is in serious need of renovation, Don pays Cardinal Construction Corporation $2.8 million to do the work. Don also pays an architect $400,000 to draw up plans for the project. Because the rewiring requirements are so extensive, Cardinal pays Dove

Issue ID

Electric Company $500,000 to handle this part of the renovation. At all times, title to the apartment complex remains with Don. Who has DPGR and in what amount?

40. **LO.2, 3, 4** Danping Corporation, a calendar year taxpayer, sells lawn furniture through big box stores. It manufactures some of the furniture and imports some from unrelated foreign producers. For tax year 2012, Danping's records reveal the following information:

	Furniture Sold	
	Manufactured	**Imported**
Gross receipts	$2,600,000	$1,600,000
CGS	1,100,000	850,000

Danping also has selling and marketing expenses of $700,000 and administrative expenses of $300,000. Under the simplified deduction method, what is Danping's:
a. DPGR?
b. QPAI?
c. DPAD?

41. **LO.2, 3, 4** Assume the same facts as in Problem 40, except that Danping's records do not identify its CGS (as between manufactured and imported furniture) but reflect an unallocated amount of $1,950,000. Further assume that Danping is qualified to (and does) use the small business simplified method of allocating CGS and other expenses. What is Danping's:
a. QPAI?
b. DPAD?

42. **LO.5** Parson, Inc., a calendar year taxpayer, manufactures ice cream that it wholesales to grocery stores and other food outlets. The company also operates an ice cream shop near its factory, where it sells directly to the general public. For tax years 2011 and 2012, gross receipts are as follows:

	Gross Receipts	
	Wholesale	**Snack Shop**
2011	$4,000,000	$220,000
2012	5,000,000	260,000

What is Parson's DPGR for:
a. 2011?
b. 2012?

43. **LO.2, 3, 4, 5** Lee Corporation manufactures a treadmill at a cost of $1,600 and sells the machine to Crimson, Inc., for $2,400 in 2012. Crimson incurs TV advertising expenses of $600 and sells the machines by phone orders for $3,200. If Lee and Crimson are not related parties, determine their:
a. DPGR.
b. QPAI.
c. DPAD.

44. **LO.2, 3, 4, 5** Assume the same facts as in Problem 43, except that Lee Corporation and Crimson, Inc., are members of an EAG. Determine their:
a. DPGR.
b. QPAI.
c. DPAD.

45. **LO.1, 2, 5** The Ryan LLC has two equal members in the 35% marginal tax bracket. If the LLC has QPAI of $13 million in 2011 and $11 million in 2012, what would be the maximum tax savings for this LLC and its members?

46. **LO.6** Vorhies, Inc., a calendar year corporation that was created in January 2008, has gross receipts as follows:

Year	Gross Receipts
2008	$3,250,000
2009	3,700,000
2010	4,950,000
2011	7,800,000
2012	9,200,000

a. Does Vorhies, Inc., qualify for the small corporation exemption for each year? Explain.
b. If Vorhies's gross receipts fall to $8.6 million for 2013, would Vorhies qualify for the small corporation exemption in 2014? Explain.

47. **LO.6, 7** For 2012, Apple Corporation (a calendar year integrated oil company) had the following transactions:

Taxable income	$4,000,000
Regular tax depreciation on realty in excess of ADS (placed in service in 1989)	1,700,000
Excess intangible drilling costs	500,000
Percentage depletion in excess of the property's adjusted basis	700,000

Assume no ACE adjustment.
a. Determine Apple Corporation's AMTI for 2012.
b. Determine the tentative minimum tax base (refer to Figure 3.2).
c. Determine the tentative minimum tax.
d. What is the amount of any AMT?

48. **LO.6, 7** For 2012, Gold Corporation (a calendar year business) had the following transactions:

Taxable income	$4,200,000
Accelerated depreciation on pre-1987 real property (in excess of straight-line depreciation)	1,500,500
Excess intangible drilling costs	575,250
AMT NOL deduction	989,570

Assume no ACE adjustment.
a. Determine Gold Corporation's AMTI for 2012.
b. Determine the tentative minimum tax base (refer to Figure 3.2).
c. Determine the tentative minimum tax.
d. What is the amount of the AMT, if any?

49. **LO.6, 7** For 2012, Silver Corporation (a calendar year business) incurred the following transactions:

Taxable income	$3,950,000
Accelerated depreciation on pre-1987 real property (in excess of straight-line depreciation)	1,240,000
Excess intangible drilling cost	475,000
AMT NOL deduction	790,000
ACE adjustment (positive)	1,500,000

a. Determine Silver Corporation's AMTI for 2012.
b. Determine the tentative minimum tax base (refer to Figure 3.2).
c. Determine the tentative minimum tax.
d. What is the amount of any AMT?

50. **LO.8** Brown Corporation, a calendar year taxpayer, began operations in 2009. It reports the following pre-adjusted AMTI and ACE for 2009 through 2012:

	Pre-adjusted AMTI	ACE
2009	$80,000,000	$70,000,000
2010	60,000,000	90,000,000
2011	50,000,000	40,000,000
2012	55,000,000	20,000,000

Calculate Brown's positive and negative adjustments, if any, for ACE.

51. **LO.8** Based upon the following facts of Fred, Inc., calculate adjusted current earnings (ACE):

Alternative minimum taxable income (AMTI)	$7,220,000
Municipal bond interest	630,000
Expenses related to municipal bonds	61,000
Key employee life insurance proceeds in excess of cash surrender value	2,000,000
Increase in LIFO recapture amount	170,000
Organization expense amortization	200,000
Cost of goods sold	4,922,000
Advertising expenses	631,000
Loss between related parties	230,000
Life insurance premiums paid on key person policy	310,000
Administrative expenses	521,014

52. **LO.6, 7** In each of the following independent situations, determine the tentative minimum tax (assume that the companies are not in small corporation status):

	AMTI (before the Exemption Amount)
Brant Corporation	$170,000
Tern Corporation	190,000
Snipe Corporation	325,000

53. **LO.8** A manufacturing company has the following items related to AMT:

Alternative minimum taxable base	$98,502,900
Regular tax	11,202,098
Foreign AMT tax credit	1,400,000
Negative ACE adjustment from a prior year	760,000

Calculate the company's AMT, if any.

54. **LO.10** In each of the following *independent* situations relating to the penalty tax under § 531, determine the dividend the corporation would have to pay to make its ATI (accumulated taxable income) be $0.

Corporation	Beginning Balance in Accumulated E & P	Taxable Income (as Adjusted)	Reasonable Needs of the Business
a. Apt	$2,000,000	$200,000	$2,100,000
b. Bud	2,900,000	300,000	3,000,000
c. Chen	3,000,000	300,000	3,500,000
d. Don	6,000,000	400,000	6,000,000

55. **LO.10** Your client is facing a possible personal holding company tax or accumulated earnings tax in 2012. Advise the client as to the total tax due and what the effective tax rate will be for this manufacturing company based on these facts:

Taxable income	$520,000
Dividends received deduction	52,000
Accumulated earnings credit	24,300
Dividends paid	71,000
Federal income taxes	170,840
Cost of Goods Sold	146,500
Excess charitable contributions	22,800

RESEARCH PROBLEMS

Note: Solutions to Research Problems can be prepared by using the **Checkpoint® Student Edition** online research product, which is available to accompany this text. It is also possible to prepare solutions to the Research Problems by using tax research materials found in a standard tax library.

THOMSON REUTERS CHECKPOINT®

Research Problem 1. An engineering and heavy construction contractor, P, repairs and renovates streets, bridges, airport runways, and other real property that have fallen into disrepair or have been damaged by casualties. If a contractor does not build an entire building, is a DPAD available? Would the receipts be considered DPGR? Explain.

Research Problem 2. Two members of an expanded affiliated group (EAG), which do not file a consolidated Federal tax return, have positive QPAI. Dane, Inc., has taxable income, but Sloane, Inc., has a $230,000 net operating loss that offsets Dane's taxable income (and reduces any DPAD). However, the NOL could be carried back or forward to another tax year and reduce the EAG member's QPAI again, thus reducing the EAG's taxable income a second time. Advise the CFO of Dane as to this problem.

Research Problem 3. How does the IRS suggest that corporate taxpayers apportion prior period compensation expenses that are not part of cost of goods sold? See Industry Director Directive (LMSB 04-0209-004), March 2009.

Communications

Research Problem 4. Owl, Inc., was owned entirely by Jeri Bell and Jerry Gore, each owning 620,000 of the 1,240,000 shares of common stock outstanding. On January 1, 2012, Owl established an employee stock ownership plan (ESOP) that later received a favorable determination letter from the IRS.

On February 1, 2012, Bell and Gore each sold 500,000 of their shares to the ESOP, each receiving $2.5 million. To facilitate the transaction, the ESOP borrowed $5 million from a local bank; the loan was guaranteed by Owl. During the year, Owl paid $1.4 million in cash dividends to the ESOP with respect to its stock. The ESOP transferred the cash to the bank as payment of principal and interest under the note.

Jeri Bell calls you and asks if Owl may claim a deduction under § 404(k) for the $1.4 million cash dividends. Does Owl have to include the dividends in its computation of ACE, thus avoiding any AMT? Write a memo for the tax files in response to Ms. Bell.

Research Problem 5. The excess of the depletion deduction allowable under § 611 over the "adjusted basis of the property" at the end of the tax year (determined without regard to the depletion deduction for the tax year) is an item of tax preference.

a. Should a taxpayer include in the basis of a § 614 property any unamortized basis under § 56(a)(2)? Explain.

b. Should the basis used for this purpose be the property's AMT basis or its regular income tax basis?

© Alex Slobodkin, iStockphoto

Use the tax resources of the Internet to address the following questions. Do not restrict your search to the Web, but include a review of newsgroups and general reference materials, practitioner sites and resources, primary sources of the tax law, chat rooms and discussion groups, and other opportunities.

Communications

Research Problem 6. Prepare a report for a client as to the current administration's position on the retention of § 199.

Research Problem 7. In 2013, dividends become taxable as ordinary income, and the accumulated earnings and personal holding company rates move to 39.6%. What impact will these changes have on closely held corporations?

WWW **For the latest in changes to tax legislation, visit www.cengagebrain.com**

CHAPTER

4 Corporations: Organization and Capital Structure

LEARNING OBJECTIVES: *After completing Chapter 4, you should be able to:*

LO.1 Identify the tax consequences of incorporating a business.

LO.2 Describe the special rules that apply when liabilities are assumed by a corporation.

LO.3 Recognize the basis issues relevant to the shareholder and the corporation.

LO.4 Explain the tax aspects of the capital structure of a corporation.

LO.5 Recognize the tax differences between debt and equity investments.

LO.6 Handle the tax treatment of shareholder debt and stock losses.

LO.7 Identify tax planning opportunities associated with organizing and financing a corporation.

CHAPTER OUTLINE

THE BIG PICTURE Tax Solutions for the Real World

© John Lund/Marc Romane/Blend Images/SuperStock

Tax Issues Associated with Growing into the Corporate Form

Emily has operated her business as a sole proprietorship since it was formed 10 years ago. Now, however, she has decided to incorporate the business as Garden, Inc., because the corporate form offers several important nontax advantages (e.g., limited liability). Also, the incorporation would enable her husband, David, to become a part owner in the business. Emily expects to transfer her business assets in exchange for Garden stock, while David will provide services for his equity interest. Emily's sole proprietorship assets available for transfer to the new corporation are as follows:

	Adjusted Basis	Fair Market Value
Accounts receivable	$ -0-	$ 25,000
Building	50,000	200,000
Other assets	150,000	275,000
	$200,000	$500,000

Aware of the problem of double taxation associated with operating as a regular corporation, Emily is considering receiving some corporate debt at the time of incorporation. The interest expense on the debt will then provide a deduction for Garden, Inc. Emily's main concern, however, is that the incorporation will be a taxable transaction. Can her fears be allayed?

Read the chapter and formulate your response.

4 Introduction

Chapters 2 and 3 dealt with four principal areas fundamental to working with corporations: (1) determination of whether an entity is a corporation for Federal income tax purposes, (2) tax rules applicable to the day-to-day operation of a corporation, (3) filing and reporting procedures, and (4) special situations involving corporations.

Chapter 4 addresses more sophisticated issues involving corporations:

- The tax consequences to the shareholders and the corporation upon the organization of and original transfer of property to the corporation.
- The tax result that ensues when shareholders make transfers of property to a corporation after organization.
- The capital structure of a corporation, including equity and debt financing.
- The tax treatment of investor losses.

4.1 Organization of and Transfers to Controlled Corporations

LO.1

Identify the tax consequences of incorporating a business.

In General

Property transactions normally produce tax consequences if a gain or loss is realized. As a result, unless an exception in the Code applies, a transfer of property to a corporation in exchange for stock constitutes a taxable sale or exchange of property. The amount of gain or loss is measured by the difference between the value of the stock received and the tax basis of the property transferred.

When a taxpayer's economic status has not changed and the wherewithal to pay is lacking, however, the Code provides special exceptions to the requirement that realized gain or loss be recognized. One such exception pertains to like-kind exchanges. When a taxpayer exchanges property for other property of a like kind, § 1031 provides that gain (or loss) on the exchange is not recognized because a substantive change in the taxpayer's investment has not occurred. Section 1031 is merely a deferral mechanism and does not authorize the permanent nonrecognition of gain or loss. The deferral mechanism is accomplished by calculating a substituted basis for the like-kind property received. With this substituted basis, the realized gain or loss associated with the property given up is ultimately recognized when the property received in the exchange is sold.

Another exception to the general rule deals with transfers to controlled corporations. Section 351 provides that gain or loss is not recognized upon the transfer of property to a corporation when certain conditions are met. This provision reflects the principle that gain should not be recognized when a taxpayer's investment has not substantively changed. For example, when a business is incorporated, the owner's economic status remains the same; only the *form* of the investment has changed. The investment in the business assets carries over to the investment in corporate stock. Further, if only stock in the corporation is received, the taxpayer is hardly in a position to pay a tax on any realized gain. Thus, this approach also is justified under the wherewithal to pay concept discussed in Chapter 1. As noted later, however, if the taxpayer receives property other than stock (i.e., cash or other "boot") from the corporation, realized gain is recognized.

Finally, § 351 exists because Congress believes that tax rules should not impede the exercise of sound business judgment (e.g., choice of the corporate form of doing business). For example, a taxpayer would think twice about forming a corporation if gain recognition (and the payment of a tax) would always be a consequence.

Therefore, the same principles govern the nonrecognition of gain or loss under § 1031 and § 351. With both provisions, gain or loss is postponed until a substantive change in the taxpayer's investment occurs (e.g., a sale to outsiders).

Choice of Organizational Form When Operating Overseas

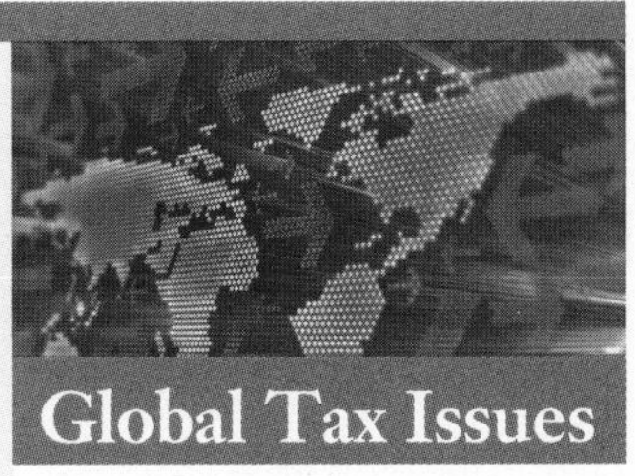

© Andrey Prokhorov, iStockphoto

When the management of a corporation decides to expand its business by establishing a presence in a foreign market, the new business venture may take one of several organizational forms. As each form comes with its respective advantages and disadvantages, making the best choice can be difficult.

One common approach is to conduct the foreign activity as a *branch* operation of the U.S. corporation. The foreign branch is not a separate legal entity, but a division of the U.S. corporation established overseas. As a result, any gains and losses produced by the foreign unit are included in the corporation's overall financial results.

Another possibility is to organize the foreign operations as a *subsidiary* of the U.S. parent corporation. If this route is chosen, the subsidiary may be either a *domestic* subsidiary (i.e., organized in the United States) or a *foreign* subsidiary (organized under the laws of a foreign country).

One fundamental tax difference between these two approaches is that the gains and losses of a domestic subsidiary may be consolidated with the operations of the U.S. parent, while the operations of a foreign subsidiary cannot. Thus, the use of a domestic subsidiary to conduct foreign operations generally yields the same final result as the use of a branch. With both approaches, the financial statements of the U.S. parent reflect the results of its worldwide operations.

EXAMPLE 1

Ron is considering incorporating his sole proprietorship to obtain the limited liability of the corporate form. Ron realizes that if he incorporates, he will be personally liable only for the debts of the business that he has guaranteed. If Ron incorporates his business, the following assets will be transferred to the corporation:

	Tax Basis	Fair Market Value
Cash	$ 10,000	$ 10,000
Furniture and fixtures	20,000	60,000
Land and building	240,000	300,000
	$270,000	$370,000

In this change of business form, Ron will receive the corporation's stock worth $370,000 in exchange for the assets he transfers. Without the nonrecognition provisions of § 351, Ron would recognize a taxable gain of $100,000 on the transfer ($370,000 value of the stock received − $270,000 basis of the assets transferred). Under § 351, however, Ron does not recognize any gain because his economic status has not really changed. Ron's investment in the assets of his sole proprietorship is now represented by his ownership of stock in the corporation. Thus, § 351 provides for tax neutrality on the incorporation decision. ■

In a like-kind exchange, the recognition of gain is avoided only to the extent the taxpayer receives like-kind property. However, the taxpayer must recognize some or all of the realized gain when receiving "boot" (i.e., property of an unlike kind, such as cash). For example, if a taxpayer exchanges a truck used in a business for another truck to be used in the business and also receives cash, the taxpayer has the wherewithal to pay an income tax on the cash involved. Further, the taxpayer's economic status has changed to the extent that cash is received. Thus, realized gain on the exchange is recognized to the extent of the cash received. In like manner, if a taxpayer transfers property to a corporation and receives cash or property other than stock, gain (but not loss) is recognized to the extent of the lesser of the gain realized or the boot received (i.e., the amount of cash and the fair market value of other property received). Any gain recognized is classified (e.g., ordinary, capital) according to the type of assets transferred.[1] As discussed later, the nonrecognition of gain or loss is accompanied by a substituted basis in the shareholder's stock.[2]

EXAMPLE 2

Amanda and Calvin form Quail Corporation. Amanda transfers property with an adjusted basis of $30,000, fair market value of $60,000, for 50% of the stock, worth $60,000. Calvin transfers property with an adjusted basis of $70,000, fair market value of $60,000, for the remaining 50% of the stock. The transfers qualify under § 351. Amanda has an unrecognized gain of $30,000, and Calvin has an unrecognized loss of $10,000. Both have a substituted basis in the stock in Quail Corporation. Amanda has a basis of $30,000 in her stock, and Calvin has a basis of $70,000 in his stock. Therefore, if either Amanda or Calvin later disposes of the Quail stock in a taxable transaction (e.g., a sale), this deferred gain/loss will then be fully recognized—a $30,000 gain to Amanda and a $10,000 loss to Calvin. ■

Section 351 is *mandatory* if a transaction satisfies the provision's requirements. The three requirements for nonrecognition of gain or loss under § 351 are that (1) *property* is transferred (2) in exchange for *stock* and (3) the property transferors are in *control* of the corporation after the exchange. Therefore, if recognition of gain or loss is *desired*, the taxpayer must plan to fail to meet at least one of these requirements.

Property Defined

Questions have arisen concerning what constitutes **property** for purposes of § 351. In general, the definition of property is comprehensive. For example, along with plant and equipment, unrealized receivables of a cash basis taxpayer and installment obligations are considered property.[3] Although the disposition of an installment note receivable normally triggers deferred gain, its transfer under § 351 is not treated as a disposition. Thus, gain is not recognized to the transferor. Secret processes and formulas as well as secret information in the general nature of a patentable invention also qualify as property under § 351.[4]

However, the Code specifically excludes services rendered from the definition of property. Services are not considered to be property under § 351 for a critical reason. A taxpayer must report as income the fair market value of any consideration received as compensation for services rendered.[5] Consequently, when a taxpayer receives stock in a corporation as consideration for rendering services to the corporation, taxable income results. In this case, the amount of income recognized by the taxpayer is equal to the fair market value of the stock received. The taxpayer's basis in the stock received is its fair market value.

EXAMPLE 3

Ann and Bob form Olive Corporation with the transfer of the following consideration:

	Consideration Transferred		
	Basis to Transferor	**Fair Market Value**	**Number of Shares Issued**
From Ann:			
Personal services rendered to Olive Corporation	$ -0-	$20,000	200
From Bob:			
Installment obligation	5,000	40,000	
Inventory	10,000	30,000	800
Secret process	-0-	10,000	

[1] § 351(b) and Rev.Rul. 68–55, 1968–1 C.B. 140.

[2] § 358(a). See the discussion preceding Example 20.

[3] *Hempt Brothers, Inc. v. U.S.*, 74–1 USTC ¶9188, 33 AFTR 2d 74–570, 490 F.2d 1172 (CA–3, 1974), and Reg. § 1.453–9(c)(2).

[4] Rev.Rul. 64–56, 1964–1 C.B. 133; Rev.Rul. 71–564, 1971–2 C.B. 179.

[5] §§ 61 and 83.

The value of each share in Olive Corporation is $100.[6] Ann has income of $20,000 on the transfer because services do not qualify as "property." She has a basis of $20,000 in her 200 shares of Olive (i.e., Ann is treated as having bought some of the Olive stock by rendering services). Bob has no recognized gain on the receipt of stock because all of the consideration he transfers to Olive qualifies as "property" and he has "control" of Olive after the transfer; see the discussion concerning control that follows. Bob has a substituted basis of $15,000 in the Olive stock. ■

Stock Transferred

Nonrecognition of gain occurs only when the shareholder receives stock. Stock includes common and most preferred. However, it does not include "nonqualified preferred stock," which possesses many of the attributes of debt. In addition, the Regulations state that the term *stock* does not include stock rights and stock warrants. Otherwise, the term *stock* generally needs no clarification.[7]

Thus, any corporate debt or **securities** (e.g., long-term debt such as bonds) received are treated as boot because they do not qualify as stock. Therefore, the receipt of debt in exchange for the transfer of appreciated property to a controlled corporation causes recognition of gain.

THE BIG PICTURE

EXAMPLE 4

Return to the facts of *The Big Picture* on p. 4-1. Assume that the proposed transaction qualifies under § 351 (i.e., the transfer of *property* in exchange for *stock* meets the *control* test), but Emily decides to receive some corporate debt along with the stock. If she receives Garden stock worth $450,000 and Garden debt of $50,000 in exchange for the property transferred, Emily realizes gain of $300,000 [$500,000 (value of consideration received) – $200,000 (basis in the transferred property)]. However, because the transaction qualifies under § 351, only $50,000 of gain is recognized—the $50,000 of Garden debt is treated as boot. The remaining realized gain of $250,000 is deferred.

Control of the Corporation

For the transaction to qualify as nontaxable under § 351, the property transferors must be in **control** of the corporation immediately after the exchange. Control means that the person or persons transferring the property must have at least an 80 percent stock ownership in the corporation. More specifically, the property transferors must own stock possessing at least 80 percent of the total combined *voting power* of all classes of stock entitled to vote *and* at least 80 percent of the total *number of shares* of all other classes of stock.[8]

Control Immediately after the Transfer

Immediately after the exchange, the property transferors must control the corporation. Control can apply to a single person or to several taxpayers if they are all parties to an integrated transaction. When more than one person is involved, the exchange does not necessarily require simultaneous exchanges by those persons. However, the rights of those transferring property to the corporation must be previously set out and determined. Also, the agreement to transfer property should be

[6]The value of closely held stock normally is presumed to be equal to the value of the property transferred.

[7]§ 351(g). Examples of nonqualified preferred stock include preferred stock that is redeemable within 20 years of issuance and whose dividend rate is based on factors other than corporate performance. Therefore, gain is recognized up to the fair market value of the nonqualified preferred stock received. Loss may be recognized when the transferor receives *only* nonqualified preferred stock (or nonqualified preferred stock and other boot) in exchange for property. See also Reg. § 1.351–1 (a)(1)(ii).

[8]§ 368(c). Nonqualified preferred stock is treated as stock, not boot, for purposes of this control test.

executed "with an expedition consistent with orderly procedure."[9] Therefore, if two or more persons transfer property to a corporation for stock and want to defer gain, it is helpful if the transfers occur close together in time and are made in accordance with an agreement among the parties.

EXAMPLE 5

Jack exchanges property, basis of $60,000 and fair market value of $100,000, for 70% of the stock of Gray Corporation. The other 30% of the stock is owned by Jane, who acquired it several years ago. The fair market value of Jack's stock is $100,000. Jack recognizes a taxable gain of $40,000 on the transfer because he does not have control of the corporation after his transfer and his transaction cannot be integrated with Jane's for purposes of the control requirement. ■

EXAMPLE 6

Rebecca, Daryl, and Paige incorporate their businesses by forming Green Corporation. Rebecca exchanges her property for 300 shares in Green on January 6, 2012. Daryl exchanges his property for 400 shares of Green Corporation stock on January 13, 2012, and Paige exchanges her property for 300 shares in Green on March 5, 2012. Because the three exchanges are part of a prearranged plan and the control test is met, the nonrecognition provisions of § 351 apply to all of the exchanges. ■

Stock need not be issued to the property transferors in the same proportion as the relative value of the property transferred by each. However, when stock received is not proportionate to the value of the property transferred, the actual effect of the transactions must be properly characterized. For example, in such situations, one transferor may actually be making a gift of valuable consideration to another transferor.

EXAMPLE 7

Ron and Shelia, father and daughter, form Oak Corporation. Ron transfers property worth $50,000 in exchange for 100 shares of stock, while Shelia transfers property worth $50,000 for 400 shares of stock. The transfers qualify under § 351 because Ron and Shelia have control of the Oak stock immediately after the transfers of property. However, the implicit gift by Ron to Shelia must be recognized and appropriately characterized. As such, the value of the gift might be subject to the gift tax (see Chapter 18). ■

ETHICS & EQUITY A Professional-Free Incorporation

Allen and Beth agree to form Jay Corporation. Allen, who has a reputation for being extremely frugal, decides to follow instructions for incorporating a business that he has found on a free Internet site. Based on his plan, Allen transfers appreciated property to Jay Corporation in exchange for 75 percent of its stock. Beth agrees to provide services to the business for 25 percent of the stock.

Several months later Allen learns that he has made a terrible blunder. To avoid paying tax on the transfer of his appreciated property, he should have received 80 percent, not 75 percent, of the stock. To correct the problem, Allen persuades Beth to transfer to him 5 percent of the corporation's stock. In return, Allen will give Beth some antiques he has collected. Allen tells Beth that this is a better deal for her because now she will have to report the value of only 20 percent of the corporation's stock as income (instead of 25 percent). Further, she receives the antiques as a tax-free gift.

How do you react to Allen's actions?

Once control has been achieved, it is not necessarily lost if, shortly after the transaction, stock received by shareholders is sold or given to persons who are not parties to the exchange. However, a different result might materialize if a *plan* for the ultimate disposition of the stock existed *before* the exchange.[10]

[9] Reg. § 1.351–1(a)(1).

[10] *Wilgard Realty Co. v. Comm.*, 42–1 USTC ¶9452, 29 AFTR 325, 127 F.2d 514 (CA–2, 1942).

EXAMPLE 8

Naomi and Eric form Eagle Corporation. They transfer appreciated property to the corporation with each receiving 50 shares of the stock. Shortly after the formation, Naomi gives 25 shares to her son. Because Naomi was not committed to make the gift, she is considered to own her original shares of Eagle Corporation stock and, along with Eric, to control Eagle "immediately after the exchange." Therefore, the requirements of § 351 are met, and neither Naomi nor Eric is taxed on the exchange. Alternatively, had Naomi immediately given 25 shares to a business associate pursuant to a plan to satisfy an outstanding obligation, the formation of Eagle would have been taxable to Naomi and Eric because of their lack of control (i.e., Naomi and Eric, the property transferors, would have owned only 75% of the stock). ■

Transfers for Property and Services

Nonrecognition treatment for the property transferors may be lost if "too much" stock is transferred to persons who did not contribute property.

THE BIG PICTURE

EXAMPLE 9

Return to the facts of *The Big Picture* on p. 4-1. Assume that Emily transfers her $500,000 of property to Garden, Inc., and receives 50% of its stock. David receives the other 50% of the stock for services rendered (worth $500,000). Both Emily and David have tax consequences from the transfers. David has ordinary income of $500,000 because he does not exchange property for stock. Emily has a taxable gain of $300,000 [$500,000 (fair market value of the stock in Garden) − $200,000 (basis in the transferred property)]. As the sole transferor of property, she receives only 50% of Garden's stock.

A person who receives stock in exchange for services and for property transferred may be treated as a member of the transferring group for purposes of the control test. When this is the case, the person is taxed on the value of the stock issued for services but not on the stock issued for property, assuming the property transferors control the corporation. In this case, all stock received by the person transferring both property and services is counted in determining whether the transferors acquired control of the corporation.[11]

THE BIG PICTURE

EXAMPLE 10

Assume the same facts as in Example 9 except that David transfers property worth $400,000 (basis of $130,000) in addition to services rendered to Garden, Inc. (valued at $100,000). Now David becomes a part of the control group. Emily and David, as property transferors, together receive 100% of the corporation's stock. Consequently, § 351 is applicable to the exchanges. As a result, Emily has no recognized gain. David does not recognize gain on the transfer of the property, but he recognizes ordinary income to the extent of the value of the shares issued for services rendered. Thus, David recognizes $100,000 of ordinary income currently.

Transfers for Services and Nominal Property

To be a member of the group and to aid in qualifying all transferors under the 80 percent control test, the person contributing services must transfer property having more than a "relatively small value" compared to the services performed. The Regulations provide that stock issued for property whose value is relatively small compared to the value of the stock already owned (or to be received for services

[11]Reg. § 1.351–1(a)(2), Ex. 3.

rendered) will not be treated as issued in return for property. This will be the result when the primary purpose of the transfer is to qualify the transaction under § 351 for concurrent transferors.[12]

EXAMPLE 11

Rosalyn and Mark transfer property to Redbird Corporation, each in exchange for one-third of the stock. Reed receives the other one-third of the stock for services rendered. The transaction does not qualify under § 351 because Reed is not a member of the group transferring property and Rosalyn and Mark, as the sole property transferors, together receive only 66⅔% of the stock. As a result, the post-transfer control requirement is not met.

Assume instead that Reed also transfers a substantial amount of property. Then he is a member of the group, and the transaction qualifies under § 351. Reed is taxed on the value of the stock issued for services, but the remainder of the transaction does not trigger gain or loss recognition. However, if the property transferred by Reed is of relatively small value in comparison to the stock he receives for his services and the primary purpose for transferring the property is to cause the transaction to be tax-free for Rosalyn and Mark, the exchange does not qualify under § 351 for any of the taxpayers. ■

Exactly when a taxpayer who renders services and transfers property is included in the control group is often subject to question. However, the IRS has stated that such a transferor can be included in the control group if the value of the property transferred is at least 10 percent of the value of the services provided.[13] If the value of the property transferred is less than this amount, the IRS will not issue an advance ruling that the exchange meets the requirements of § 351.

EXAMPLE 12

Sara and Rick form Grouse Corporation. Sara transfers land (worth $100,000, basis of $20,000) for 50% of the stock in Grouse. Rick transfers equipment (worth $50,000, adjusted basis of $10,000) and provides services worth $50,000 for 50% of the stock. Because the value of the property Rick transfers is not small relative to the value of the services he renders, his stock in Grouse Corporation is counted in determining control for purposes of § 351; thus, the transferors own 100% of the stock in Grouse. In addition, all of Rick's stock, not just the shares received for the equipment, is counted in determining control. As a result, Sara does not recognize gain on the transfer of the land. Rick, however, must recognize income of $50,000 on the transfer of services. Even though the transfer of the equipment qualifies under § 351, his transfer of services for stock does not.

Alternatively, had the value of Rick's property been small relative to the value of his services, the transaction would be fully taxable to both Sara and Rick. In that situation, Sara, the sole property transferor, would not have at least 80% control of Grouse Corporation following the transfer. As a result, she would fully recognize her realized gain. Further, because Rick would not be treated as having transferred property, the § 351 deferral would not be available to him either. ■

Transfers to Existing Corporations

Once a corporation is in operation, § 351 also applies to any later transfers of property for stock by either new or existing shareholders.

EXAMPLE 13

Tyrone and Seth formed Blue Corporation three years ago. Both Tyrone and Seth transferred appreciated property to Blue in exchange for 50 shares each in the corporation. The original transfers qualified under § 351, and neither Tyrone nor Seth was taxed on the exchange. In the current year, Tyrone transfers property (worth $90,000, adjusted basis of $5,000) for 50 additional Blue shares. Tyrone has a taxable gain of

[12] Reg. § 1.351–1(a)(1)(ii).

[13] Rev.Proc. 77–37, 1977–2 C.B. 568.

$85,000 on the transfer. The exchange does not qualify under § 351 because Tyrone does not have 80% control of Blue Corporation immediately after the transfer—he owns 100 shares of the 150 shares outstanding, or a 66⅔% interest. ■

See the Tax Planning portion of this chapter for additional discussion of this issue.

Assumption of Liabilities—§ 357

LO.2

Describe the special rules that apply when liabilities are assumed by a corporation.

Without a provision to the contrary, the transfer of mortgaged property to a controlled corporation could trigger gain to the property transferor if the corporation took over the mortgage. This would be consistent with the treatment given in like-kind exchanges under § 1031. Generally, when liabilities are assumed by another party, the party who is relieved of the debt is treated as having received cash or boot. Section 357(a) provides, however, that when the acquiring corporation assumes a liability in a § 351 transaction, the liability is not treated as boot received for gain recognition purposes. Nevertheless, liabilities assumed by the transferee corporation are treated as boot in determining the basis of the stock received by the shareholder. As a result, the basis of the stock received is reduced by the amount of the liabilities assumed by the corporation. See the more complete discussion of basis computations later.

THE BIG PICTURE

EXAMPLE 14

Return to the facts of *The Big Picture* on p. 4-1. Assume that you learn that Emily's husband, David, becomes disinterested in becoming a stockholder in Garden, Inc., and that Emily's building is subject to a liability of $35,000 that Garden assumes. Consequently, Emily receives 100% of the Garden stock and is relieved of the $35,000 liability in exchange for property with an adjusted basis of $200,000 and fair market value of $500,000. The exchange is tax-free under § 351 because the release of a liability is not treated as boot under § 357(a). However, the basis to Emily of the Garden stock is $165,000 [$200,000 (basis of property transferred) − $35,000 (amount of the liability assumed by Garden)].

The general rule of § 357(a) has two exceptions: (1) § 357(b) provides that if the principal purpose of the assumption of the liabilities is to avoid tax *or* if there is no bona fide business purpose behind the exchange, the liabilities are treated as boot; (2) § 357(c) provides that if the sum of the liabilities exceeds the adjusted basis of the properties transferred, the excess is taxable gain.

Exception (1): Tax Avoidance or No Bona Fide Business Purpose

Unless liabilities are incurred shortly before incorporation, § 357(b) generally poses few problems. A tax avoidance purpose for transferring liabilities to a controlled corporation normally is not a concern in view of the basis adjustment as noted above. Because the liabilities transferred reduce the basis of the stock received, any realized gain merely is deferred and not completely eliminated. Any postponed gain is recognized when and if the stock is disposed of in a taxable sale or exchange.

Satisfying the bona fide business purpose requirement is not difficult if the liabilities were incurred in connection with the transferor's normal course of conducting a trade or business. But this requirement can cause difficulty if the liability is taken out shortly before the property is transferred and the proceeds are utilized for personal purposes.[14] This type of situation is analogous to a cash distribution by the corporation to the shareholder, which is taxed as boot.

[14]See, for example, *Campbell, Jr. v. Wheeler*, 65–1 USTC ¶9294, 15 AFTR 2d 578, 342 F.2d 837 (CA-5, 1965).

EXAMPLE 15

Dan transfers real estate (basis of $40,000 and fair market value of $90,000) to a controlled corporation in return for stock in the corporation. However, shortly before the transfer, Dan mortgages the real estate and uses the $20,000 proceeds to meet personal obligations. Thus, along with the real estate, the mortgage is transferred to the corporation. In this case, the assumption of the mortgage lacks a bona fide business purpose. Consequently, the release of the liability is treated as boot received, and Dan has a taxable gain on the transfer of $20,000.[15]

Amount realized:	
Stock	$ 70,000
Release of liability—treated as boot	20,000
Total amount realized	$ 90,000
Less: Basis of real estate	(40,000)
Realized gain	$ 50,000
Recognized gain	$ 20,000

■

The effect of the application of § 357(b) is to taint *all* liabilities transferred even if some are supported by a bona fide business purpose.

EXAMPLE 16

Tim, an accrual basis taxpayer, incorporates his sole proprietorship. Among the liabilities transferred to the new corporation are trade accounts payable of $100,000 and a credit card bill of $5,000. Tim had used the credit card to purchase an anniversary gift for his wife. Under these circumstances, *all* of the $105,000 liabilities are treated as boot and trigger the recognition of gain to the extent gain is realized. ■

Exception (2): Liabilities in Excess of Basis

The second exception, § 357(c), provides that if the amount of the liabilities assumed exceeds the total of the adjusted bases of the properties transferred, the excess is taxable gain. Without this provision, when **liabilities exceed the basis** in property exchanged, a taxpayer would have a negative basis in the stock received in the controlled corporation.[16] Section 357(c) precludes the negative basis possibility by treating the excess over basis as gain to the transferor.

EXAMPLE 17

Andre transfers land and equipment with adjusted bases of $35,000 and $5,000, respectively, to a newly formed corporation in exchange for 100% of the stock. The corporation assumes the liability on the transferred land in the amount of $50,000. Without § 357(c), Andre's basis in the stock of the new corporation would be a negative $10,000 [$40,000 (bases of properties transferred) + $0 (gain recognized) − $0 (boot received) − $50,000 (liability assumed)]. Section 357(c), however, requires Andre to recognize a gain of $10,000 ($50,000 liability assumed − $40,000 bases of assets transferred). As a result, the stock has a zero basis in Andre's hands, determined as follows:

Bases in the properties transferred ($35,000 + $5,000)	$ 40,000
Plus: Gain recognized	10,000
Less: Boot received	–0–
Less: Liability assumed	(50,000)
Basis in the stock received	$ –0–

Thus, Andre recognizes $10,000 of gain, and a negative stock basis is avoided. ■

The definition of liabilities under § 357(c) excludes obligations that would have been deductible to the transferor had those obligations been paid before the transfer. Therefore, accounts payable of a cash basis taxpayer are not considered

15 § 351(b).

16 *Jack L. Easson*, 33 T.C. 963 (1960), *rev'd* in 61–2 USTC ¶9654, 8 AFTR 2d 5448, 294 F.2d 653 (CA–9, 1961).

liabilities for purposes of § 357(c). In addition, they are not considered in the computation of the shareholder's stock basis.

EXAMPLE 18

Tina, a cash basis taxpayer, incorporates her sole proprietorship. In return for all of the stock of the new corporation, she transfers the following items:

	Adjusted Basis	Fair Market Value
Cash	$10,000	$10,000
Unrealized accounts receivable (amounts due to Tina but not yet received by her)	–0–	40,000
Trade accounts payable	–0–	30,000
Note payable	5,000	5,000

Because the unrealized accounts receivable and trade accounts payable have a zero basis under the cash method of accounting, no income is recognized until the receivables are collected and no deduction materializes until the payables are satisfied. The note payable has a basis because it was issued for consideration received.

In this situation, the trade accounts payable are disregarded for gain recognition purposes and in determining Tina's stock basis. Thus, for purposes of § 357(c), because the balance of the note payable does not exceed the basis of the assets transferred, Tina does not have a problem of liabilities in excess of basis (i.e., the note payable of $5,000 does not exceed the aggregate basis in the cash and accounts receivable of $10,000). ■

Conceivably, a situation could arise where both §§ 357(b) and (c) apply in the same transfer. In such a situation, § 357(b) predominates.[17] This could be significant because § 357(b) does not create gain on the transfer, as does § 357(c), but merely converts the liability to boot. Thus, the realized gain limitation continues to apply to § 357(b) transactions.

EXAMPLE 19

Chris forms Robin Corporation by transferring land with a basis of $100,000, fair market value of $1 million. The land is subject to a mortgage of $300,000. One month prior to incorporating Robin, Chris borrows $200,000 for personal purposes and gives the lender a second mortgage on the land. Therefore, on the incorporation, Robin issues stock worth $500,000 to Chris and assumes the two mortgages on the land. Section 357(c) seems to apply to the transfer, given that the mortgages on the property ($500,000) exceed the basis of the property ($100,000). Thus, Chris would have a gain of $400,000 under § 357(c). Section 357(b), however, also applies to the transfer because Chris borrowed $200,000 just prior to the transfer and used the loan proceeds for personal purposes. Thus, under § 357(b), Chris has boot of $500,000 in the amount of the liabilities. Note that *all* of the liabilities are treated as boot, not just the tainted $200,000 liability. Consequently, he has realized gain of $900,000 [$1,000,000 (stock of $500,000 and assumption of liabilities of $500,000) – $100,000 (basis in the land)], and gain is recognized to the extent of the boot received of $500,000. Unfortunately for Chris, the relatively more onerous rule of § 357(b) predominates over § 357(c). ■

Basis Determination and Related Issues

LO.3

Recognize the basis issues relevant to the shareholder and the corporation.

Recall that § 351(a) postpones gain or loss until the transferor-shareholder disposes of the stock in a taxable transaction. The postponement of shareholder gain or loss has a corollary effect on the basis of the stock received by the shareholder and the basis of the property received by the corporation. This procedure ensures that any gain or loss postponed under § 351 ultimately will be recognized when the affected asset is disposed of in a taxable transaction.

[17] § 357(c)(2)(A).

FIGURE 4.1	Shareholder's Basis of Stock Received in Exchange for Property
Adjusted basis of property transferred	$xx,xxx
Plus: Gain recognized	xxx
Minus: Boot received (including any liabilities transferred)	(xxx)
Minus: Adjustment for loss property (if elected)	(xxx)
Equals: Basis of stock received	$xx,xxx

Basis of Stock to Shareholder

For a taxpayer transferring property to a corporation in a § 351 transaction, the *stock* received in the transaction is given a substituted basis. Essentially, the stock's basis is the same as the basis the taxpayer had in the property transferred, increased by any gain recognized on the exchange of property and decreased by boot received. Recall that for basis purposes, boot received includes liabilities transferred by the shareholder to the corporation. Also note that if the shareholder receives *other property* (i.e., boot) along with the stock, it takes a basis equal to its fair market value.[18] In Figure 4.1, the reference to gain recognized does not consider any income resulting from the performance of personal services. (Recall from earlier discussions that the basis of stock received for services rendered equals its fair market value.) See the discussion that follows relating to an elective stock basis reduction that may be made when a shareholder contributes property with a net built-in loss.

Basis of Property to Corporation

The basis of *property* received by the corporation generally is determined under a carryover basis rule. This rule provides that the property's basis to the corporation is equal to the basis in the hands of the transferor increased by the amount of any gain recognized on the transfer by the transferor-shareholder.[19]

These basis rules are illustrated in Examples 20 and 21.

EXAMPLE 20

Kesha and Ned form Brown Corporation. Kesha transfers land (basis of $30,000 and fair market value of $70,000); Ned invests cash ($60,000). They each receive 50 shares in Brown Corporation, worth $60,000, but Kesha also receives $10,000 in cash from Brown. The transfers of property, the realized and recognized gain on the transfers, and the basis of the stock in Brown Corporation to Kesha and Ned are as follows:

	A	B	C	D	E	F
	Basis of Property Transferred	FMV of Stock Received	Boot Received	Realized Gain (B + C − A)	Recognized Gain (Lesser of C or D)	Basis of Stock in Brown (A − C + E)
From Kesha:						
Land	$30,000	$60,000	$10,000	$40,000	$10,000	$30,000
From Ned:						
Cash	60,000	60,000	–0–	–0–	–0–	60,000

Brown Corporation has a basis of $40,000 in the land (Kesha's basis of $30,000 plus her recognized gain of $10,000). ■

[18] § 358(a).

[19] § 362(a).

FIGURE 4.2 Corporation's Basis in Property Received

Adjusted basis of property transferred	$xx,xxx
Plus: Gain recognized by transferor-shareholder	xxx
Minus: Adjustment for loss property (if required)	(xxx)
Equals: Basis of property to corporation	$xx,xxx

EXAMPLE 21

Assume the same facts as in Example 20 except that Kesha's basis in the land is $68,000 (instead of $30,000). Because recognized gain cannot exceed realized gain, the transfer generates only $2,000 of gain to Kesha. The realized and recognized gain and the basis of the stock in Brown Corporation to Kesha are as follows:

	A	B	C	D	E	F
	Basis of Property Transferred	FMV of Stock Received	Boot Received	Realized Gain (B + C − A)	Recognized Gain (Lesser of C or D)	Basis of Stock in Brown (A − C + E)
Land	$68,000	$60,000	$10,000	$2,000	$2,000	$60,000

Brown's basis in the land is $70,000 ($68,000 basis to Kesha + $2,000 gain recognized by Kesha). ■

Figure 4.2 summarizes the basis calculation for property received by a corporation. Concept Summary 4.1 shows the shareholder and corporate consequences of a transfer of property to a corporation for stock, with and without the application of § 351. The facts applicable to shareholder Kesha's transfer in Example 20 are used to illustrate the differences between the transaction being tax-deferred and taxable.

Basis Adjustment for Loss Property

As noted above, when a corporation receives property in a § 351 transaction, the basis for that property is carried over from the shareholder. As a result, the corporation's basis for the property has no correlation to its fair market value. However, in certain situations when **built-in loss property** is contributed to a corporation, its aggregate basis in the property may have to be stepped down so that the basis does not exceed the fair market value of the property transferred. This basis adjustment is necessary to prevent the parties from obtaining a double benefit from the losses involved.

The anti-loss duplication rule applies when the aggregate basis of the assets transferred by a shareholder exceeds their fair market value. When this built-in loss situation exists, the basis in the loss properties is stepped down. The step-down in basis is allocated proportionately among the assets with the built-in loss.[20]

EXAMPLE 22

In a transaction qualifying under § 351, Charles transfers the following assets to Gold Corporation in exchange for all of its stock:

	Tax Basis	Fair Market Value	Built-in Gain/(Loss)
Equipment	$100,000	$ 90,000	($10,000)
Land	200,000	230,000	30,000
Building	150,000	100,000	(50,000)
	$450,000	$420,000	($30,000)

[20] § 362(e)(2). This adjustment is determined separately with respect to each property transferor. This adjustment also is required in the case of a contribution to capital by a shareholder.

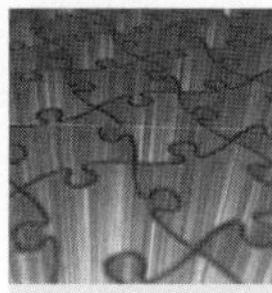

CONCEPT SUMMARY 4.1

Tax Consequences to the Shareholders and Corporation: With and Without the Application of § 351 (Based on the Facts of Example 20)

	With § 351			Without § 351		
Shareholder	**Gain/Loss Recognized**	**Stock Basis**	**Other Property Basis**	**Gain/Loss Recognized**	**Stock Basis**	**Other Property Basis**
Kesha	Realized gain recognized to extent of boot received; loss not recognized.	Substituted (see Figure 4.1).	FMV	All realized gain or loss recognized.	FMV	FMV
	$10,000	$30,000	$10,000	$40,000	$60,000	$10,000

	With § 351		Without § 351	
Corporation	**Gain/Loss Recognized**	**Property Basis**	**Gain/Loss Recognized**	**Property Basis**
Brown	No gain or loss recognized on the transfer of corporate stock for property.	Carryover (see Figure 4.2).	No gain or loss recognized on the transfer of corporate stock for property.	FMV
	$0	$40,000	$0	$70,000

Note that the benefit to Kesha of deferring $30,000 of gain under § 351 comes with a cost: her stock basis is $30,000 (rather than $60,000), and the corporation's basis in the property received is $40,000 (rather than $70,000).

Charles's stock basis is $450,000 [$450,000 (basis of the property transferred) + $0 (gain recognized) − $0 (boot received)]. However, Gold's basis for the loss assets transferred must be reduced by the amount of the net built-in loss ($30,000) in proportion to each asset's share of the loss.

	Unadjusted Tax Basis	Adjustment	Adjusted Tax Basis
Equipment	$100,000	($ 5,000)*	$ 95,000
Land	200,000		200,000
Building	150,000	(25,000)**	125,000
	$450,000	($30,000)	$420,000

* $\frac{\text{\$10,000 (loss attributable to equipment)}}{\text{\$60,000 (\textit{total} built-in loss)}} \times \text{\$30,000 (\textit{net} built-in loss)}$
= $5,000 (adjustment to basis in equipment).

** $\frac{\text{\$50,000 (loss attributable to building)}}{\text{\$60,000 (\textit{total} built-in loss)}} \times \text{\$30,000 (\textit{net} built-in loss)}$
= $25,000 (adjustment to basis in building). ■

Note the end result of Example 22:

- Charles still has a built-in loss in his stock basis. Thus, if he sells the Gold Corporation stock, he will recognize a loss of $30,000 [$420,000 (selling price based on presumed value of the stock) − $450,000 (basis in the stock)].
- Gold Corporation can no longer recognize any loss on the sale of *all* of its assets [$420,000 (selling price based on value of assets) − $420,000 (adjusted basis in assets) = $0 (gain or loss)].

In the event a corporation is subject to the built-in loss adjustment, an alternative approach is available. If both the shareholder and the corporation elect, the basis reduction can be made to the shareholder's stock rather than to the corporation's property.

EXAMPLE 23

Assume the same facts as in the previous example. If Charles and Gold elect, Charles can reduce his stock basis to $420,000 ($450,000 – $30,000). As a result, Gold's aggregate basis in the assets it receives is $450,000. If Charles has no intention of selling his stock, this election could be desirable as it benefits Gold by giving the corporation a higher depreciable basis in the equipment and building. ■

Note the end result of Example 23:

- Charles has no built-in loss. Thus, if he sells the Gold Corporation stock, he will recognize no gain or loss [$420,000 (presumed value of the stock) – $420,000 (basis in the stock)].
- Gold Corporation has a built-in loss. Thus, if it sells *all* of its assets [$420,000 (selling price based on value of assets) – $450,000 (basis in assets)], it recognizes a loss of $30,000.

Consequently, the built-in loss adjustment places the loss with either the shareholder or the corporation but not both (compare Examples 22 and 23).

Stock Issued for Services Rendered

A transfer of stock for services is not a taxable transaction to a corporation.[21] But another issue arises: Can a corporation deduct as a business expense the fair market value of the stock it issues in consideration of services? Yes, unless the services are such that the payment is characterized as a capital expenditure.[22]

THE BIG PICTURE

EXAMPLE 24

Return to the facts of *The Big Picture* on p. 4-1. Emily transfers her $500,000 of property to Garden, Inc., and receives 50% of the stock. In addition, assume that David transfers property worth $400,000 (basis of $130,000) and agrees to serve as manager of the corporation for one year (services worth $100,000) for 50% of the stock. Emily's and David's transfers qualify under § 351. Neither Emily nor David is taxed on the transfer of his or her property. However, David has income of $100,000, the value of the stock received for the services he will render to Garden, Inc. Garden has a basis of $130,000 in the property it acquired from David, and it may claim a compensation expense deduction under § 162 for $100,000. David's stock basis is $230,000 [$130,000 (basis of property transferred) + $100,000 (income recognized for services rendered)].

THE BIG PICTURE

EXAMPLE 25

Assume the same facts as in Example 24 except that David provides legal services (instead of management services) in organizing the corporation. The value of David's legal services is $100,000. David has no gain on the transfer of the property but has income of $100,000 for the value of the stock received for the services rendered. Garden, Inc., has a basis of $130,000 in the property it acquired from David and must capitalize the $100,000 as an organizational expenditure. David's stock basis is $230,000 [$130,000 (basis of property transferred) + $100,000 (income recognized for services rendered)].

[21]Reg. § 1.1032–1(a).

[22]Rev.Rul. 62–217, 1962–2 C.B. 59, modified by Rev.Rul. 74–503, 1974–2 C.B. 117.

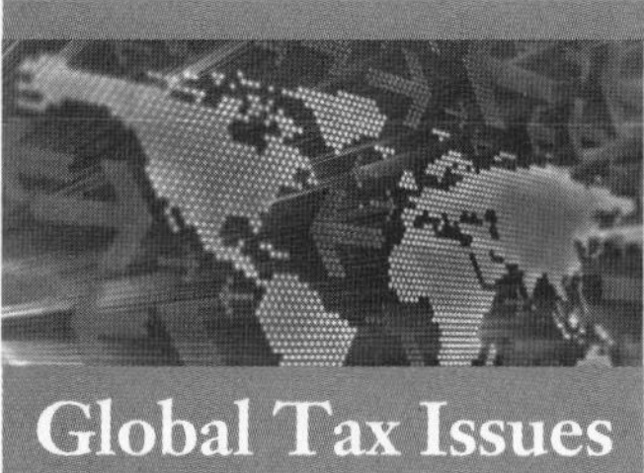

© Andrey Prokhorov, iStockphoto

Does § 351 Cover the Incorporation of a Foreign Business?

When a taxpayer wants to incorporate a business overseas by moving assets across U.S. borders, the deferral mechanism of § 351 applies in certain situations, but not in others. In general, § 351 is available to defer gain recognition when starting up a new corporation outside the United States unless so-called tainted assets are involved. Under § 367, tainted assets, which include assets such as inventory and accounts receivable, are treated as having been sold by the taxpayer prior to the corporate formation; therefore, their transfer results in the current recognition of gain. The presence of tainted assets triggers gain because Congress does not want taxpayers to be able to shift the gain outside the U.S. jurisdiction. The gain recognized is ordinary or capital depending on the nature of the asset involved.

Holding Period for Shareholder and Transferee Corporation

In a § 351 transfer, the shareholder's holding period for stock received in exchange for a capital asset or § 1231 property includes the holding period of the property transferred to the corporation. That is, the holding period of the property is "tacked on" to the holding period of the stock. The holding period for stock received for any other property (e.g., inventory) begins on the day after the exchange. The corporation's holding period for property acquired in a § 351 transfer is the holding period of the transferor-shareholder regardless of the character of the property in the transferor's hands.[23]

Recapture Considerations

In a § 351 transfer where no gain is recognized, the depreciation recapture rules do not apply.[24] However, any recapture potential associated with the property carries over to the corporation as it steps into the shoes of the transferor-shareholder for purposes of basis determination.

EXAMPLE 26

Paul transfers equipment (adjusted basis of $30,000, original cost of $120,000, and fair market value of $100,000) to a controlled corporation in return for stock. If Paul had sold the equipment, it would have yielded a gain of $70,000, all of which would have been recaptured as ordinary income under § 1245. Because the transfer comes within § 351, Paul has no recognized gain and no depreciation to recapture. However, if the corporation later disposes of the equipment in a taxable transaction, it must take into account the § 1245 recapture potential originating with Paul. ■

4.2 Capital Structure of a Corporation

LO.4

Explain the tax aspects of the capital structure of a corporation.

Capital Contributions

When a corporation receives money or property in exchange for capital stock (including treasury stock), neither gain nor loss is recognized by the corporation.[25] Nor does a corporation's gross income include shareholders' contributions of money or property to the capital of the corporation. Moreover, additional money or property received from shareholders through voluntary pro rata transfers also is not income to the corporation. This is the case even though there is no increase in

[23] §§ 1223(1) and (2).

[24] §§ 1245(b)(3) and 1250(d)(3).

[25] § 1032.

TAX IN THE NEWS Local and State Governments Pay to Attract New Business—But Expect Results

As a business seeks to grow and strategies shift, managers must be on the lookout for locations that will best suit their needs. Among the factors that can make a critical difference in an expansion or relocation decision is the availability of tax incentives offered by state and local governments as inducements.

But what happens when companies that have accepted these relocation incentives fail to produce? In some cases, the companies are being asked to return portions of the tax grants and incentives previously awarded. Massachusetts, Ohio, and New Mexico are among a number of states that are watching previous grant recipients for "nonperformance." These states are "clawing back" grants awarded for lack of performance.

Source: Adapted from Jennifer Levitz, "States to Business: Give Our Cash Back," *Wall Street Journal*, April 22, 2011, pp. A1 and A10.

the outstanding shares of stock of the corporation. The contributions represent an additional price paid for the shares held by the shareholders and are treated as additions to the operating capital of the corporation.[26]

Contributions by nonshareholders, such as land contributed to a corporation by a civic group or a governmental group to induce the corporation to locate in a particular community, are also excluded from the gross income of a corporation.[27] However, if the property is transferred to a corporation by a nonshareholder in exchange for goods or services, the corporation must recognize income.[28]

EXAMPLE 27

A cable television company charges its customers an initial fee to hook up to a new cable system installed in the area. These payments are used to finance the total cost of constructing the cable facilities. In addition, the customers will make monthly payments for the cable service. The initial payments are used for capital expenditures, but they represent payments for services to be rendered by the cable company. As such, they are taxable income to the cable company and not contributions to capital by nonshareholders. ■

The basis of property received by a corporation from a shareholder as a **capital contribution** is equal to the basis of the property in the hands of the shareholder, although the basis is subject to a downward adjustment when loss property is contributed. The basis of property transferred to a corporation by a nonshareholder as a contribution to capital is zero.

If a corporation receives *money* as a contribution to capital from a nonshareholder, a special rule applies. The basis of any property acquired with the money during a 12-month period beginning on the day the contribution was received is reduced by the amount of the contribution. The excess of money received over the cost of new property reduces the basis of other property held by the corporation and is applied in the following order:

- Depreciable property.
- Property subject to amortization.
- Property subject to depletion.
- All other remaining properties.

The basis of property within each category is reduced in proportion to the relative bases of the properties.[29]

[26] § 118 and Reg. § 1.118–1.

[27] See *Edwards v. Cuba Railroad Co.*, 1 USTC ¶139, 5 AFTR 5398, 45 S.Ct. 614 (USSC, 1925).

[28] Reg. § 1.118–1. See also *Teleservice Co. of Wyoming Valley*, 27 T.C. 722 (1957), *aff'd* in 58–1 USTC ¶9383, 1 AFTR 2d 1249, 254 F.2d 105 (CA–3, 1958), *cert. den.* 78 S.Ct. 1360 (USSC, 1958).

[29] § 362(a) and Reg. § 1.362–2(b).

EXAMPLE 28

A city donates land worth $400,000 to Teal Corporation as an inducement for Teal to locate in the city. The receipt of the land produces no taxable income to Teal, and the land's basis to the corporation is zero. If, in addition, the city gives the corporation $100,000 in cash, the money is not taxable income to the corporation. However, if the corporation purchases property with the $100,000 cash within the next 12 months, the basis of the acquired property is reduced by $100,000. Any excess cash retained by Teal is handled according to the ordering rules noted previously. ■

LO.5

Recognize the tax differences between debt and equity investments.

Debt in the Capital Structure

Advantages of Debt

Significant tax differences exist between debt and equity in the capital structure. The advantages of issuing long-term debt instead of stock are numerous. Interest on debt is deductible by the corporation, while dividend payments are not. Further, loan repayments are not taxable to investors unless the repayments exceed basis. A shareholder's receipt of property from a corporation, however, cannot be tax-free as long as the corporation has earnings and profits (see Chapter 5). Such distributions will be taxed as dividends to the extent of earnings and profits of the distributing corporation.

Currently, another distinction between debt and equity relates to the taxation of dividend and interest income. Dividend income on equity holdings is taxed to individual investors at low capital gains rates, while interest income on debt is taxed at higher ordinary income rates.

EXAMPLE 29

Wade transfers cash of $100,000 to a newly formed corporation for 100% of the stock. In its initial year, the corporation has net income of $40,000. The income is credited to the earnings and profits account of the corporation. If the corporation distributes $9,500 to Wade, the distribution is a taxable dividend to Wade with no corresponding deduction to the corporation. Assume, instead, that Wade transfers to the corporation cash of $50,000 for stock and cash of $50,000 for a note of the same amount. The note is payable in equal annual installments of $5,000 and bears interest at the rate of 9%. At the end of the year, the corporation pays Wade interest of $4,500 ($50,000 × 9%) and a note repayment of $5,000. The interest payment is deductible to the corporation and taxable to Wade. The $5,000 principal repayment on the note is neither deducted by the corporation nor taxed to Wade. The after-tax impact to Wade and the corporation under each alternative is illustrated below.

	If the Distribution Is	
	$9,500 Dividend	**$5,000 Note Repayment and $4,500 Interest**
*After-tax benefit to Wade**		
[$9,500 × (1 − 15%)]	$8,075	
{$5,000 + [$4,500 × (1 − 35%)]}		$7,925
*After-tax cost to corporation***		
No deduction to corporation	9,500	
{$5,000 + [$4,500 × (1 − 35%)]}		7,925

*Assumes that Wade's dividend income is taxed at the 15% capital gains rate and that his interest income is taxed at the 35% ordinary income rate.
**Assumes that the corporation is in the 35% marginal tax bracket. ■

Reclassification of Debt as Equity (Thin Capitalization Problem)

In situations where the corporation is said to be thinly capitalized, the IRS contends that debt is an equity interest and denies the corporation the tax advantages of debt financing. If the debt instrument has too many features of stock, it may be treated for tax purposes as stock. In that case, the principal and interest payments are considered dividends. In the current environment, however, the IRS may be less inclined to raise the thin capitalization issue because the conversion of interest income to dividend income would produce a tax benefit to individual investors.

Section 385 lists several factors that *may* be used to determine whether a debtor-creditor relationship or a shareholder-corporation relationship exists. The section authorizes the Treasury to prescribe Regulations that provide more definitive guidelines. To date, the Treasury has not drafted acceptable Regulations. Consequently, taxpayers must rely on judicial decisions to determine whether a true debtor-creditor relationship exists.

For the most part, the principles used to classify debt as equity developed in connection with closely held corporations. Here the holders of the debt are also shareholders. Consequently, the rules have often proved inadequate for dealing with such problems in large, publicly traded corporations.

Together, Congress, through § 385, and the courts have identified the following factors to be considered in resolving the **thin capitalization** issue:

- Whether the debt instrument is in proper form. An open account advance is more easily characterized as a contribution to capital than a loan evidenced by a properly written note.[30]
- Whether the debt instrument bears a reasonable rate of interest and has a definite maturity date. When a shareholder advance does not provide for interest, the return expected may appear to be a share of the profits or an increase in the value of the shares.[31] Likewise, a lender unrelated to the corporation will usually be unwilling to commit funds to the corporation without a definite due date.
- Whether the debt is paid on a timely basis. A lender's failure to insist upon timely repayment or satisfactory renegotiation indicates that the return sought does not depend upon interest income and the repayment of principal.
- Whether payment is contingent upon earnings. A lender ordinarily will not advance funds that are likely to be repaid only if the venture is successful.
- Whether the debt is subordinated to other liabilities. Subordination tends to eliminate a significant characteristic of the creditor-debtor relationship. Creditors should have the right to share with other general creditors in the event of the corporation's dissolution or liquidation. Subordination also destroys another basic attribute of creditor status—the power to demand payment at a fixed maturity date.[32]
- Whether holdings of debt and stock are proportionate (e.g., each shareholder owns the same percentage of debt as stock). When debt and equity obligations are held in the same proportion, shareholders are, apart from tax considerations, indifferent as to whether corporate distributions are in the form of interest or dividends.
- Whether funds loaned to the corporation are used to finance initial operations or capital asset acquisitions. Funds used to finance initial operations or to acquire capital assets the corporation needs are generally obtained through equity investments.
- Whether the corporation has a high ratio of shareholder debt to shareholder equity. Thin capitalization occurs when shareholder debt is high relative to shareholder equity. This indicates that the corporation lacks reserves to pay interest and principal on debt when corporate income is insufficient to meet current needs.[33] In determining a corporation's debt-equity ratio, courts look at the relation of the debt both to the book value of the corporation's assets and to their actual fair market value.[34]

[30]*Estate of Mixon, Jr. v. U.S.*, 72–2 USTC ¶9537, 30 AFTR 2d 72–5094, 464 F.2d 394 (CA–5, 1972).

[31]*Slappey Drive Industrial Park v. U.S.*, 77–2 USTC ¶9696, 40 AFTR 2d 77–5940, 561 F.2d 572 (CA–5, 1977).

[32]*Fin Hay Realty Co. v. U.S.*, 68–2 USTC ¶9438, 22 AFTR 2d 5004, 398 F.2d 694 (CA–3, 1968).

[33]A court held that a debt-equity ratio of approximately 14.6:1 was not excessive. See *Tomlinson v. 1661 Corp.*, 67–1 USTC ¶9438, 19 AFTR 2d 1413, 377 F.2d 291 (CA–5, 1967). A 26:1 ratio was found acceptable in *Delta Plastics, Inc.*, 85 TCM 940, T.C.Memo. 2003–54.

[34]In *Bauer v. Comm.*, 84–2 USTC ¶9996, 55 AFTR 2d 85–433, 748 F.2d 1365 (CA–9, 1984), a debt-equity ratio of 92:1 resulted when book value was used. But the ratio ranged from 2:1 to 8:1 when equity included both paid-in capital and accumulated earnings.

Under § 385, the IRS also has the authority to classify an instrument either as *wholly* debt or equity or as *part* debt and *part* equity. This flexible approach is important because some instruments cannot readily be classified either wholly as stock or wholly as debt. It may also provide an avenue for the IRS to address problems in publicly traded corporations.

4.3 Investor Losses

LO.6

Handle the tax treatment of shareholder debt and stock losses.

The difference between equity and debt financing involves a consideration of the tax treatment of worthless stock and securities versus that applicable to bad debts.

Stock and Security Losses

If stocks and bonds are capital assets in their owner's hands, losses from their worthlessness are governed by § 165(g)(1). Under this provision, a capital loss materializes as of the last day of the taxable year in which the stocks or bonds become worthless. No deduction is allowed for a mere decline in value. The burden of proving complete worthlessness is on the taxpayer claiming the loss. One way to recognize partial worthlessness is to dispose of the stocks or bonds in a taxable sale or exchange.[35] But even then, the **investor loss** is disallowed if the sale or exchange is to a related party as defined under § 267(b) (e.g., parents and children are related, but aunts, uncles, and cousins are not considered related).

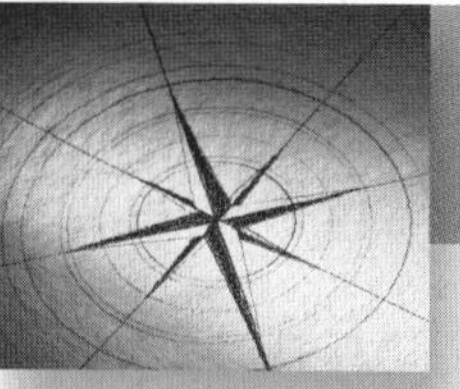

ETHICS & EQUITY Can a Loss Produce a Double Benefit?

In late 2001, Sally invested $100,000 in TechCo, a startup high-tech venture. Although she had great expectations of financial gain, TechCo's efforts were not well received in the market, and the value of its stock plummeted. Four years ago when TechCo declared bankruptcy, Sally wrote off her $100,000 stock investment as worthless securities.

To Sally's surprise, this year she receives $40,000 from the bankruptcy trustee as a final settlement for her TechCo stock. Sally now realizes that she probably should not have claimed the loss four years ago because the stock was not *completely* worthless. However, as the statute of limitations has passed, she does not plan to amend her tax return from four years ago. She also decides that the $40,000 is not income but is merely a recovery of some of her original investment. How do you react to Sally's plans?

When the stocks or bonds are not capital assets, worthlessness yields an ordinary loss.[36] For example, if the stocks or bonds are held by a broker for resale to customers in the normal course of business, they are not capital assets. Usually, however, stocks and bonds are held as investments and, as a result, are capital assets.

Under certain circumstances involving stocks and bonds of affiliated corporations, an ordinary loss is allowed upon worthlessness.[37] A corporation is an affiliate of another corporation if the corporate shareholder owns at least 80 percent of the voting power of all classes of stock entitled to vote and 80 percent of each class of nonvoting stock. Further, to be considered affiliated, the corporation must have derived more than 90 percent of its aggregate gross receipts for all taxable years from sources other than passive income. Passive income for this purpose includes items such as rents, royalties, dividends, and interest.

[35] Reg. § 1.165–4(a).

[36] § 165(a) and Reg. § 1.165–5(b).

[37] § 165(g)(3).

TAX IN THE NEWS **Losses Arising from Stock Market Investments: Capital Losses or Theft Losses?**

Losses incurred by individuals from poor-performing stocks and securities, whether from actual sales or due to worthlessness, receive capital loss treatment. Thus, the losses can offset any capital gains, and if a net loss results, a deduction of up to $3,000 may be taken for the year. If the net loss exceeds $3,000, the excess may be carried over to future years. However, many years may have to pass before a large net capital loss is fully deductible.

As an alternative, if the loss on the security is due to theft, it is not subject to the capital loss limitation. Instead, the theft loss is ordinary and could totally wipe out a taxpayer's income, and in some cases, it could be carried back or forward as a net operating loss deduction. Among the taxpayers who can utilize theft loss treatment are the unfortunate investors who lost billions of dollars in the well-publicized Madoff scam. Revenue Ruling 2009–9 (2009-1 C.B. 735) provides theft loss treatment for investors who paid money to investment advisers such as Bernard Madoff who later were discovered to have used the funds in a Ponzi-style scheme. Further, because the taxpayers originally engaged in such "investments" with an expectation of generating profits, the deductions *are not* subject to the restrictions applicable to personal casualty and theft loss (e.g., the 10 percent-of-AGI floor). Thus, these unhappy fraud victims may find some solace in the favorable tax treatment that provides an immediate and full deduction for the losses sustained.

Business versus Nonbusiness Bad Debts

In addition to worthlessness of stocks and bonds, the financial demise of a corporation can result in bad debt deductions to those who have extended credit to the corporation. These deductions can be either business bad debts or **nonbusiness bad debts**. The distinction between the two types of deductions is important for tax purposes in the following respects:

- Business bad debts are deducted as ordinary losses, while nonbusiness bad debts are treated as short-term capital losses.[38] A business bad debt can generate a net operating loss, but a nonbusiness bad debt cannot.[39]
- A deduction is allowed for the partial worthlessness of a business debt, but nonbusiness debts can be written off only when they become entirely worthless.[40]
- Nonbusiness bad debt treatment is limited to noncorporate taxpayers. However, all of the bad debts of a corporation qualify as business bad debts.[41]

When is a debt business or nonbusiness? Unfortunately, because the Code sheds little light on the matter, the distinction has been left to the courts.[42] In a leading decision, the Supreme Court somewhat clarified the picture when it held that if individual shareholders lend money to a corporation in their capacity as investors, any resulting bad debt is classified as nonbusiness.[43] Nevertheless, the Court did not preclude the possibility of a shareholder-creditor incurring a business bad debt.

If a loan is made in some capacity that qualifies as a trade or business, nonbusiness bad debt treatment is avoided. For example, if an employee who is also a shareholder makes a loan to preserve employment status, the loan qualifies for business bad debt treatment.[44] Shareholders also receive business bad debt treatment if they are in the trade or business of lending money or of buying, promoting, and selling corporations. If the shareholder has multiple motives for making the loan, according to the Supreme Court, the "dominant" or "primary" motive for making the loan controls the classification of the loss.[45]

[38]Compare § 166(a) with § 166(d)(1)(B).

[39]Note the modification required by § 172(d)(2).

[40]Compare § 166(a)(2) with § 166(d)(1)(A).

[41]§ 166(d)(1).

[42]For definitional purposes, § 166(d)(2) is almost as worthless as the debt it purports to describe.

[43]*Whipple v. Comm.*, 63–1 USTC ¶9466, 11 AFTR 2d 1454, 83 S.Ct. 1168 (USSC, 1963).

[44]*Trent v. Comm.*, 61–2 USTC ¶9506, 7 AFTR 2d 1599, 291 F.2d 669 (CA–2, 1961).

[45]*U.S. v. Generes*, 72–1 USTC ¶9259, 29 AFTR 2d 72–609, 92 S.Ct. 827 (USSC, 1972).

EXAMPLE 30

Norman owns 48% of the stock of Lark Corporation, which he acquired several years ago at a cost of $600,000. Norman is also employed by the corporation at an annual salary of $240,000. At a time when Lark Corporation is experiencing financial problems, Norman lends it $300,000. Subsequently, the corporation becomes bankrupt, and both Norman's stock investment and his loan become worthless. ■

Norman's stock investment is treated as a long-term capital loss (assuming § 1244 does not apply, as discussed below). But how is the bad debt classified? If Norman can prove that his dominant or primary reason for making the loan was to protect his salary, a business bad debt deduction results. If not, it is assumed that Norman was trying to protect his stock investment, and nonbusiness bad debt treatment results. Factors to be considered in resolving this matter include the following:

- A comparison of the amount of the stock investment with the trade or business benefit derived. In Example 30, the stock investment of $600,000 is compared with the annual salary of $240,000. In this regard, the salary should be considered as a recurring item and not viewed in isolation. A salary of $240,000 each year means a great deal to a person who has no other means of support and may have difficulty obtaining similar employment elsewhere.
- A comparison of the amount of the loan with the stock investment and the trade or business benefit derived.
- The percentage of ownership held by the shareholder. A minority shareholder, for example, is under more compulsion to lend the corporation money to protect a job than a person who is in control of corporate policy.

In summary, without additional facts, it is impossible to conclude whether Norman in Example 30 suffered a business or nonbusiness bad debt. Even with such facts, the guidelines are vague. Recall that a taxpayer's intent or motivation is at issue. For this reason, the problem is frequently the subject of litigation.[46]

Section 1244 Stock

In an exception to the capital treatment that generally results, § 1244 permits ordinary loss treatment for losses on the sale or worthlessness of stock of so-called small business corporations. By placing shareholders on a more nearly equal basis with proprietors and partners in terms of the tax treatment of losses, the provision encourages investment of capital in small corporations. Gain on the sale of § 1244 stock remains capital. Consequently, the shareholder has nothing to lose and everything to gain by complying with § 1244.

Qualification for § 1244

The ordinary loss treatment for **§ 1244 stock** applies to the first $1 million of capitalized value of the corporation's stock. If more than $1 million of the corporation's stock is issued, the entity designates which of the shares qualify for § 1244 treatment.[47] In measuring the capitalization of the newly issued stock, property received in exchange for stock is valued at its adjusted basis, reduced by any liabilities assumed by the corporation or to which the property is subject. The fair market value of the property is not considered. The $1 million limitation is determined on the date the stock is issued. Consequently, even though a corporation fails to meet these requirements when the stock is disposed of later by the shareholder, the stock can still qualify as § 1244 stock if the requirements were met on the date the stock was issued.

Mechanics of the Loss Deduction

The amount of ordinary loss deductible in any one year from the disposition of § 1244 stock is limited to $50,000 (or $100,000 for spouses filing a joint return).

[46]See, for example, *Kelson v. U.S.*, 74–2 USTC ¶9714, 34 AFTR 2d 74–6007, 503 F.2d 1291 (CA–10, 1974) and *Kenneth W. Graves*, 87 TCM 1409, T.C. Memo. 2004–140.

[47]Reg. § 1.1244(c)–2(b)(2).

If the amount of the loss sustained in the taxable year exceeds these amounts, the remainder is considered a capital loss.

EXAMPLE 31

Harvey acquires § 1244 stock at a cost of $100,000. He sells the stock for $10,000 in the current year. He has an ordinary loss of $50,000 and a capital loss of $40,000. Alternatively, on a joint return, the entire $90,000 loss is ordinary. ■

Only the original holder of § 1244 stock, whether an individual or a partnership, qualifies for ordinary loss treatment. If the stock is sold or donated, it loses its § 1244 status.

Special treatment applies if § 1244 stock is issued by a corporation in exchange for property that has an adjusted basis above its fair market value immediately before the exchange. For purposes of determining ordinary loss upon a subsequent sale, the stock basis is reduced to the fair market value of the property on the date of the exchange.

EXAMPLE 32

Dana transfers property with a basis of $10,000 and a fair market value of $5,000 to a corporation in exchange for shares of § 1244 stock. Assuming that the transfer qualifies under § 351, the basis of the stock under the general rule is $10,000, the same as Dana's basis in the property. However, for purposes of § 1244 and measuring the amount of ordinary loss, the stock basis is only $5,000. If the stock is later sold for $3,000, the total loss sustained is $7,000 ($3,000 − $10,000); however, only $2,000 of the loss is ordinary ($3,000 − $5,000). The remaining portion of the loss, $5,000, is a capital loss. ■

Recall the advantages of issuing some debt to shareholders in exchange for cash contributions to a corporation. A disadvantage of issuing debt is that it does not qualify under § 1244. Should the debt become worthless, the taxpayer generally has a short-term capital loss rather than the ordinary loss for § 1244 stock.

4.4 GAIN FROM QUALIFIED SMALL BUSINESS STOCK

Shareholders are given special tax relief for gains recognized on the sale or exchange of stock acquired in a **qualified small business corporation**. The holder of **qualified small business stock** may exclude 50 percent of any gain from the sale or exchange of such stock. However, under the American Recovery and Reinvestment Tax Act of 2009, the exclusion increases to 75 percent for qualified small business stock acquired after February 17, 2009, and from legislation in 2010, the exclusion increases to 100 percent for qualified stock acquired after September 27, 2010, and before 2012.[48] To qualify for the exclusion, the taxpayer must have held the stock for more than five years and must have acquired the stock as part of an original issue.[49] Only noncorporate shareholders qualify for the exclusion.

A qualified small business corporation is a C corporation whose aggregate gross assets did not exceed $50 million on the date the stock was issued.[50] The corporation must be actively involved in a trade or business. This means that at least 80 percent of the corporation's assets must be used in the active conduct of one or more qualified trades or businesses.

[48] § 1202. The Obama administration's proposed 2012 budget calls for the full exclusion of gain to be made permanent. At the time of this writing, the proposal is still pending. The 0% and 15% capital gains rates do not apply. Thus, the maximum effective tax rate on the sale of qualified small business stock is 14% (28% × 50%), 7% (28% × 25%), or 0% (28% × 0%).

[49] The stock must have been issued after August 10, 1993, which is the effective date of § 1202 as originally enacted.

[50] § 1202(d). Its aggregate assets may not exceed this amount at any time between August 10, 1993, and the date the stock was issued.

TAX IN THE NEWS Making the Most of a Window of Opportunity

In general, all gain realized from property transactions is recognized when the transaction occurs. Nonetheless, in certain cases, the *timing* of gain recognition may be delayed—recall that § 351 allows for the *deferral* of gain. However, it is extremely rare under Federal tax law for realized gain to be permanently excluded from taxation. With qualified small business stock, an opportunity is available to *completely and forever* avoid income tax on gain realized.

Under existing law, this window of opportunity for *complete* avoidance closed at the end of 2011 and reverted to a 50 percent exclusion. However, the Obama administration favors making the 100 percent exclusion provision permanent in the hopes that it will stimulate new investments in small business and contribute to a stronger economy. Nonetheless, only with the passage of time will taxpayers know how Congress reacts to the President's proposal.

A shareholder can apply the exclusion to the greater of (1) $10 million or (2) 10 times the shareholder's aggregate adjusted basis in the qualified stock disposed of during a taxable year.[51]

4.5 Tax Planning

LO.7

Identify tax planning opportunities associated with organizing and financing a corporation.

Working with § 351

Effective tax planning with transfers of property to corporations requires a clear understanding of § 351 and its related Code provisions. The most important question in planning is simply this: Does the desired tax result come from complying with § 351 or from avoiding it?

Utilizing § 351

If the tax-free treatment of § 351 is desired, ensure that the parties transferring property (which includes cash) receive control of the corporation. Simultaneous transfers are not necessary, but a long period of time between transfers could be disastrous if the transfers are not properly documented as part of a single plan. The parties should document and preserve evidence of their intentions. Also, it is helpful to have some reasonable explanation for any delay in the transfers.

To meet the requirements of § 351, mere momentary control on the part of the transferor may not suffice if loss of control is compelled by a prearranged agreement.[52]

EXAMPLE 33

For many years, Paula operated a business as a sole proprietor employing Brooke as manager. To dissuade Brooke from quitting and going out on her own, Paula promised her a 30% interest in the business. To fulfill this promise, Paula transfers the business to newly formed Green Corporation in return for all of its stock. Immediately thereafter, Paula transfers 30% of the stock to Brooke. Section 351 probably does not apply to Paula's transfer to Green Corporation because it appears that Paula was under an obligation to relinquish control. If this preexisting obligation exists, § 351 will not be available to Paula because, as the sole property transferor, she does not have control of Green Corporation. However, if there is no obligation and the loss of control was voluntary on Paula's part, momentary control would suffice.[53] ■

[51] § 1202(b). The amount is $5 million for married taxpayers filing separately.

[52] Rev.Rul. 54–96, 1954–1 C.B. 111.

[53] Compare *Fahs v. Florida Machine and Foundry Co.*, 48–2 USTC ¶9329, 36 AFTR 1161, 168 F.2d 957 (CA–5, 1948), with *John C. O'Connor*, 16 TCM 213, T.C.Memo. 1957–50, *aff'd* in 58–2 USTC ¶9913, 2 AFTR 2d 6011, 260 F.2d 358 (CA–6, 1958).

Make sure that later transfers of property to an existing corporation satisfy the control requirement if recognition of gain is to be avoided. In this connection, another transferor's interest cannot be counted if the value of stock received is relatively small compared with the value of stock already owned and the primary purpose of the transfer is to qualify other transferors for § 351 treatment.[54]

Avoiding § 351

Because § 351 provides for the nonrecognition of gain on transfers to controlled corporations, it is often regarded as a favorable relief provision. In some situations, however, avoiding § 351 may produce a more advantageous tax result. The transferors might prefer to recognize gain on the transfer of property if they cannot be particularly harmed by the gain. For example, they may be in low tax brackets, or the gain may be a capital gain from which substantial capital losses can be offset. The corporation will then have a stepped-up basis in the transferred property.

A transferor might also prefer to avoid § 351 to allow for immediate recognition of a loss. Recall that § 351 provides for the nonrecognition of both gains and losses. A transferor who wants to recognize loss has several alternatives:

- Sell the property to the corporation for its stock. The IRS could attempt to collapse the "sale," however, by taking the approach that the transfer really falls under § 351.[55] If the sale is disregarded, the transferor ends up with a realized but unrecognized loss.
- Sell the property to the corporation for other property or boot. Because the transferor receives no stock, § 351 is inapplicable.
- Transfer the property to the corporation in return for securities or nonqualified preferred stock. Recall that § 351 does not apply to a transferor who receives securities or nonqualified preferred stock. In both this and the previous alternatives, watch for the possible disallowance of the loss under the related-party rules.

Suppose the loss property is to be transferred to the corporation and no loss is recognized by the transferor due to § 351. This could present an interesting problem in terms of assessing the economic realities involved.

EXAMPLE 34

Iris and Lamont form Wren Corporation with the following investments: property by Iris (basis of $40,000 and fair market value of $50,000) and property by Lamont (basis of $60,000 and fair market value of $50,000). Each receives 50% of the Wren stock. Has Lamont acted wisely in settling for only 50% of the stock? At first, it would appear so because Iris and Lamont each invested property of the same value ($50,000). But what about tax considerations? By applying the general carryover basis rules, the corporation now has a basis of $40,000 in Iris's property and $60,000 in Lamont's property. In essence, Iris has shifted a possible $10,000 gain to the corporation while Lamont has transferred a $10,000 potential loss. Thus, an equitable allocation of the Wren stock would call for Lamont to receive a greater percentage interest than Iris would receive. This issue is further complicated by the special basis adjustment required when a shareholder such as Lamont contributes property with a built-in loss to a corporation. In this situation, if Wren is to take a carryover basis in Lamont's property, Lamont must reduce his stock basis by the $10,000 built-in loss. This reduced stock basis, of course, could lead to a greater tax burden on Lamont when he sells the Wren stock. This may suggest additional support for Lamont having a greater percentage interest than Iris has. ■

[54] Reg. § 1.351–1(a)(1)(ii).

[55] *U.S. v. Hertwig*, 68–2 USTC ¶9495, 22 AFTR 2d 5249, 398 F.2d 452 (CA–5, 1968).

Selecting Assets to Transfer

When a business is incorporated, the organizers must determine which assets and liabilities should be transferred to the corporation. A transfer of assets that produce passive income (rents, royalties, dividends, and interest) can cause the corporation to be a personal holding company in a tax year when operating income is low. Thus, the corporation could be subject to the personal holding company penalty tax (see the discussion in Chapter 3) in addition to the regular income tax.

Leasing property to the corporation may be a more attractive alternative than transferring ownership. Leasing provides the taxpayer with the opportunity to withdraw money from the corporation in a deductible form without the payment being characterized as a nondeductible dividend. If the property is given to a family member in a lower tax bracket, the lease income can be shifted as well. If the depreciation and other deductions available in connection with the property are larger than the lease income, the taxpayer would retain the property until the income exceeds the deductions.

When an existing cash basis business is incorporated, an important issue to consider is whether the business's accounts receivable and accounts payable will be transferred to the new corporation or be retained by the owner of the unincorporated business. Depending on the approach taken, either the new corporation or the owner of the old unincorporated business will recognize the income associated with the cash basis receivables when they are collected. The cash basis accounts payable raise the corresponding issue of who will claim the deduction.

THE BIG PICTURE

EXAMPLE 35

Return to the facts of *The Big Picture* on p. 4-1. If Emily decides to retain the $25,000 of cash basis accounts receivable rather than transfer them to the newly formed Garden, Inc., she will recognize $25,000 of ordinary income upon their collection. Alternatively, if the receivables are transferred to Garden as the facts suggest, the corporation will recognize the ordinary income. However, a subsequent corporate distribution to Emily of the cash collected could be subject to double taxation as a dividend (see Chapter 5 for further discussion). Given the alternatives available, Emily needs to evaluate which approach is better for the parties involved.

Another way to shift income to other taxpayers is by the use of corporate debt. Shareholder debt in a corporation can be given to family members in a lower tax bracket. This technique also causes income to be shifted without a loss of control by the corporation.

Debt in the Capital Structure

The advantages and disadvantages of debt as opposed to equity have previously been noted. To increase debt without incurring the thin capitalization problem, consider the following:

- Preserve the formalities of the debt. This includes providing for written instruments, realistic interest rates, and specified due dates.
- If possible, have the corporation repay the debt when it comes due. If this is not possible, have the parties renegotiate the arrangement. Try to proceed as a nonshareholder creditor would. It is not unusual, for example, for bondholders of publicly held corporations to extend due dates when default occurs. The alternative is to foreclose and perhaps seriously impair the amount the creditors will recover.
- Avoid provisions in the debt instrument that make the debt convertible to equity in the event of default. These provisions are standard practice when nonshareholder creditors are involved. They serve no purpose if the shareholders are also the creditors and hold debt in proportion to ownership shares.

EXAMPLE 36

Gail, Cliff, and Ruth are equal shareholders in Magenta Corporation. Each transfers cash of $100,000 to Magenta in return for its bonds. The bond agreement provides that the holders will receive additional voting rights in the event Magenta Corporation defaults on its bonds. The voting rights provision is worthless and merely raises the issue of thin capitalization. Gail, Cliff, and Ruth already control Magenta Corporation, so what purpose is served by increasing their voting rights? The parties probably used a boilerplate bond agreement that was designed for third-party lenders (e.g., banks and other financial institutions). ■

- Pro rata holding of debt is difficult to avoid. For example, if each of the shareholders owns one-third of the stock, each will want one-third of the debt. Nevertheless, some variation is possible.

EXAMPLE 37

Assume the same facts as Example 36 except that only Gail and Cliff acquire the bonds. Ruth leases property to Magenta Corporation at an annual rent that approximates the yield on the bonds. Presuming the rent passes the arm's length test (i.e., what unrelated parties would charge), all parties reach the desired result. Gail and Cliff withdraw corporate profits in the form of interest income, and Ruth is provided for with rent income. Magenta Corporation can deduct both the interest and the rent payments. ■

- Try to keep the debt-equity ratio within reasonable proportions. A problem frequently arises when the parties form the corporation. Often the amount invested in capital stock is the minimum required by state law. For example, if the state of incorporation permits a minimum of $1,000, limiting the investment to this amount does not provide much safety for later debt financing by the shareholders.
- Stressing the fair market value of the assets rather than their tax basis to the corporation can be helpful in preparing to defend debt-equity ratios.

EXAMPLE 38

Emily, Josh, and Miles form Black Corporation with the following capital investments: cash of $200,000 from Emily; land worth $200,000 (basis of $20,000) from Josh; and a patent worth $200,000 (basis of $0) from Miles. To state that the equity of Black Corporation is $220,000 (the tax basis to the corporation) does not reflect reality. The equity account is more properly stated at $600,000 ($200,000 + $200,000 + $200,000). ■

- The nature of the business can have an effect on what is an acceptable debt-equity ratio. Capital-intensive industries (e.g., manufacturing and transportation) characteristically rely heavily on debt financing. Consequently, larger debt should be tolerated.

What if a corporation's efforts to avoid the thin capitalization problem fail and the IRS raises the issue on audit? What steps should the shareholders take? They should hedge their position by filing a protective claim for refund, claiming dividend treatment on the previously reported interest income. In such an event, ordinary income would be converted to preferential dividend income treatment. Otherwise, the IRS could ultimately invoke the statute of limitations and achieve the best of all possible worlds—the shareholders would have been taxed on the interest income at the ordinary income rates while the corporation would receive no deduction for what is now reclassified as a dividend. By filing the claim for refund, the shareholders have kept the statute of limitations from running until the thin capitalization issue is resolved at the corporate level.

Investor Losses

Be aware of the danger of losing § 1244 attributes. Only the original holder of § 1244 stock is entitled to ordinary loss treatment. If after a corporation is formed the owner transfers shares of stock to family members to shift income within the family group, the benefits of § 1244 are lost.

EXAMPLE 39

Norm incorporates his business by transferring property with a basis of $100,000 for 100 shares of stock. The stock qualifies as § 1244 stock. Norm later gives 50 shares each to his children, Susan and Paul. Eventually, the business fails, and the shares of stock become worthless. If Norm had retained the stock, he would have had an ordinary loss deduction of $100,000 (assuming that he filed a joint return). Susan and Paul, however, have a capital loss of $50,000 each because the § 1244 attributes are lost as a result of the gift (i.e., neither Susan nor Paul was an original holder of the stock). ■

REFOCUS ON THE BIG PICTURE

Tax Issues Can Be Neutralized When Growing into the Corporate Form

Emily, the sole property transferor, must acquire at least 80 percent of the stock issued by Garden, Inc., for the transaction to receive tax-deferred treatment under § 351. Otherwise, a tremendous amount of gain (up to $300,000) will be recognized. As a corollary, David must not receive more than 20 percent of Garden's stock in exchange for his services (see Example 9). However, even if § 351 is available, any debt issued by the corporation will be treated as boot and will trigger gain recognition to Emily (see Example 4). Therefore, she must evaluate the cost of recognizing gain now versus the benefit of Garden obtaining an interest deduction later.

What If?

Can the § 351 transaction be modified to further reduce personal and business tax costs, both at the time of formation and in future years? Several strategies may be worth considering.

- Instead of having Garden issue debt on formation, Emily might withhold certain assets. If the building is not transferred, for example, it can be leased to the corporation. The resulting rent payment would mitigate the double tax problem by producing a tax deduction for Garden.
- An additional benefit results if Emily does not transfer the cash basis receivables to Garden. This approach avoids a tax at the corporate level and a further tax when the receipts are distributed to Emily in the form of a dividend. If the receivables are withheld, their collection is taxed only to Emily (see Example 35).
- No mention is made as to the existence (or nonexistence) of any accounts payable outstanding at the time of corporate formation. If they do exist, which is likely, it might be wise for Emily to transfer them to Garden. The subsequent corporate payment of the liability produces a corporate deduction that will reduce any corporate tax.

Double taxation can be mitigated in certain situations with a modest amount of foresight!

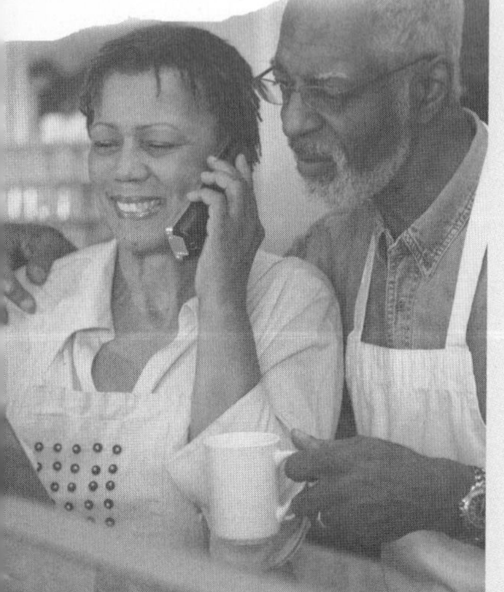

KEY TERMS

Built-in loss property, 4-13
Capital contribution, 4-17
Control, 4-5
Investor loss, 4-20
Liabilities in excess of basis, 4-10
Nonbusiness bad debts, 4-21
Property, 4-4
Qualified small business corporation, 4-23
Qualified small business stock, 4-23
Section 1244 stock, 4-22
Securities, 4-5
Thin capitalization, 4-19

DISCUSSION QUESTIONS

1. **LO.1** In terms of justification and effect, § 351 (transfer to a controlled corporation) and § 1031 (like-kind exchange) are much alike. Explain.

2. **LO.1** Under what circumstances will gain and/or loss be recognized on a § 351 transfer?

3. **LO.1** What does "property" include for purposes of § 351?

4. **LO.1** Does "stock" include stock rights and stock warrants under § 351? Does it include preferred stock?

5. **LO.1** Does the receipt of a 10-year note in exchange for the transfer of appreciated property to a controlled corporation cause recognition of gain? Explain.

6. **LO.1** What is the control requirement of § 351? Describe the effect of the following in satisfying this requirement:
   a. A shareholder renders only services to the corporation for stock.
   b. A shareholder renders services and transfers property to the corporation for stock.
   c. A shareholder has only momentary control after the transfer.
   d. A long period of time elapses between the transfers of property by different shareholders.

7. **LO.1** Nancy and her daughter, Kathleen, have been working together in a cattery called "The Perfect Cat." Nancy formed the business in 1997 as a sole proprietorship, and it has been very successful. Assets have a fair market value of $450,000 and a basis of $180,000. On the advice of their tax accountant, Nancy decides to incorporate "The Perfect Cat." Because of Kathleen's participation, Nancy would like her to receive shares in the corporation. What are the relevant tax issues?

Issue ID

8. **LO.1, 2, 7** Four friends plan to form a corporation for purposes of constructing a shopping center. Charlie will be contributing the land for the project and wants more security than shareholder status provides. He is contemplating two possibilities: receive corporate bonds for his land or take out a mortgage on the land before transferring it to the corporation. Comment on the choices Charlie is considering. What alternatives can you suggest?

Issue ID
Decision Making

9. **LO.1** Bruce and Joyce form Warbler Corporation by transferring appreciated property in exchange for 50 shares each of Warbler stock. If Bruce donates his shares to a qualified charity immediately after the exchange, does this make the incorporation taxable? Explain.

10. **LO.1** Should a transferor who receives stock for both property and services be included in the control group in determining whether an exchange meets the requirement of § 351? Explain.

11. **LO.1** At a point when Robin Corporation has been in existence for six years, shareholder Ted transfers real estate (adjusted basis of $20,000 and fair market value of $100,000) to the corporation for additional stock. At the same time, Peggy, the other shareholder, acquires one share of stock for cash. After the two transfers, the percentages of stock ownership are as follows: 79% by Ted and 21% by Peggy.
    a. What were the parties trying to accomplish?
    b. Will it work? Explain.

Issue ID

12. **LO.2** How does the transfer of mortgaged property to a controlled corporation affect the transferor-shareholder's basis in stock received? Assume that no gain is recognized on the transfer.

13. **LO.2** Before incorporating her apartment rental business, Libbie takes out second mortgages on several of the units. She uses the mortgage proceeds to make capital improvements to the units. Along with all of the rental units, Libbie transfers the mortgages to the newly formed corporation in return for all of its stock. Discuss the tax consequences of these procedures.

14. **LO.2** If both § 357(b) and § 357(c) apply to a transfer of property to a corporation under § 351, which provision takes precedence?

15. **LO.3** Discuss how each of the following affects the calculation of the basis of stock received by a shareholder in a § 351 transfer:
    a. The transfer of a liability to the corporation along with property.
    b. Property that has been transferred has built-in losses.
    c. The basis in the property transferred to the corporation.
    d. The receipt of "other property" (i.e., boot) in addition to stock.

16. **LO.3** Identify a situation when a corporation can deduct the value of the stock it issues for the rendition of services. Identify a situation when a deduction is not available.

17. **LO.3** In a § 351 transfer, Jorge transfers appreciated property to Bluebird Corporation in exchange for Bluebird stock.
    a. What is Bluebird's holding period for the property it received from Jorge?
    b. What is Jorge's holding period for the Bluebird stock?

18. **LO.4** A corporation acquires property as a contribution to capital from a shareholder and from a nonshareholder. Are the rules pertaining to the property's basis the same? Explain.

19. **LO.5** In structuring the capitalization of a corporation, what are the advantages and disadvantages of utilizing debt rather than equity?

20. **LO.5** In determining whether debt of a corporation should be reclassified as stock, comment on the relevance of the following:
    a. The loan is on open account.
    b. The loan is payable on demand.
    c. The corporation does not make timely repayments.
    d. Payments are contingent on earnings.
    e. The loans are in the same proportion as the shareholdings, and the corporation uses the funds to purchase a new building.
    f. The corporation's debt-equity ratio is 5:1.

21. **LO.6** Assuming that § 1244 does not apply, what is the tax treatment of stock that has become worthless?

22. **LO.6** Under what circumstances, if any, may a shareholder deduct a business bad debt on a loan made to the corporation?

Decision Making

23. **LO.6** Four years ago Nelson purchased stock in Black Corporation for $37,000. The stock has a current value of $5,000. Nelson needs to decide which of the following alternatives to pursue. Determine the tax effect of each.
    a. Without selling the stock, Nelson deducts $32,000 for the partial worthlessness of the Black Corporation investment.
    b. Nelson sells the stock to his aunt for $5,000 and deducts a $32,000 long-term capital loss.
    c. Nelson sells the stock to a third party and deducts an ordinary loss.
    d. Nelson sells the stock to his mother for $5,000 and deducts a $32,000 long-term capital loss.
    e. Nelson sells the stock to a third party and deducts a $32,000 long-term capital loss.

Issue ID

24. **LO.1, 7** Keith's sole proprietorship holds assets that, if sold, would yield a gain of $100,000. It also owns assets that would yield a loss of $30,000. Keith incorporates his business using only the gain assets. Two days later Keith sells the loss assets to the newly formed corporation. What is Keith trying to accomplish? Will he be successful? Explain.

Issue ID

25. **LO.7** Sarah incorporates her small business but does not transfer the machinery and equipment the business uses to the corporation. Subsequently, the machinery and equipment are leased to the corporation for an annual rent. What tax reasons might Sarah have for not transferring the machinery and equipment to the corporation when the business was incorporated?

PROBLEMS

26. **LO.1, 3** Elizabeth, Rod, June, and Whit form Zelcova Corporation with the following consideration:

	Consideration Transferred		
	Basis to Transferor	**Fair Market Value**	**Number of Shares Issued**
From Elizabeth—			
Personal services rendered to Zelcova Corporation	$ -0-	$ 30,000	30
From Rod—			
Equipment	345,000	300,000	300
From June—			
Unrealized accounts receivable	-0-	150,000	130*
From Whit—			
Land and building	210,000	450,000	
Mortgage on land and building	300,000	300,000	150

*June receives $20,000 in cash in addition to the 130 shares.

Zelcova Corporation assumes the mortgage transferred by Whit. The value of each share of Zelcova stock is $1,000. As to these transactions, provide the following information:

a. Elizabeth's recognized gain, income, or loss. Identify the nature of any such gain, income, or loss.
b. Elizabeth's basis in the Zelcova stock.
c. Rod's recognized gain or loss. Identify the nature of any such gain or loss.
d. Rod's basis in the Zelcova stock. What election may Rod consider making as to his stock basis because the property he contributes to Zelcova has a built-in loss?
e. Zelcova Corporation's basis in the equipment. What is the impact to Zelcova if Rod makes the election noted in part (d) above?
f. June's recognized gain or loss. Identify the nature of any such gain or loss.
g. June's basis in the Zelcova stock.
h. Zelcova Corporation's basis in the unrealized receivables.
i. Whit's recognized gain or loss. Identify the nature of any such gain or loss.
j. Whit's basis in the Zelcova stock.
k. Zelcova Corporation's basis in the land and building.

27. **LO.1, 3** Ron and Gail form Maple Corporation with the following consideration:

	Consideration Transferred		
	Basis to Transferor	**Fair Market Value**	**Number of Shares Issued**
From Ron—			
Cash	$ 50,000	$ 50,000	
Installment obligation	140,000	250,000	30
From Gail—			
Cash	150,000	150,000	
Equipment	125,000	250,000	
Patent	10,000	300,000	70

The installment obligation has a face amount of $250,000 and was acquired last year from the sale of land held for investment purposes (adjusted basis of $140,000). As to these transactions, provide the following information:

a. Ron's recognized gain or loss.
b. Ron's basis in the Maple Corporation stock.
c. Maple Corporation's basis in the installment obligation.

d. Gail's recognized gain or loss.
e. Gail's basis in the Maple Corporation stock.
f. Maple Corporation's basis in the equipment and the patent.
g. How would your answers to the preceding questions change if Ron received common stock and Gail received preferred stock?
h. How would your answers change if Gail was a partnership?

Decision Making

28. **LO.1, 7** Jane, Jon, and Clyde incorporate their respective businesses and form Starling Corporation. On March 1 of the current year, Jane exchanges her property (basis of $50,000 and value of $150,000) for 150 shares in Starling Corporation. On April 15, Jon exchanges his property (basis of $70,000 and value of $500,000) for 500 shares in Starling. On May 10, Clyde transfers his property (basis of $90,000 and value of $350,000) for 350 shares in Starling.
   a. If the three exchanges are part of a prearranged plan, what gain will each of the parties recognize on the exchanges?
   b. Assume that Jane and Jon exchanged their property for stock four years ago, while Clyde transfers his property for 350 shares in the current year. Clyde's transfer is not part of a prearranged plan with Jane and Jon to incorporate their businesses. What gain will Clyde recognize on the transfer?
   c. Returning to the original facts, if the property that Clyde contributes has a basis of $490,000 (instead of $90,000), how might the parties otherwise structure the transaction?

Communications

29. **LO.1** Michael Robertson (1635 Maple Street, Syracuse, NY 13201) exchanges property (basis of $200,000 and fair market value of $850,000) for 75% of the stock of Red Corporation. The other 25% is owned by Sarah Mitchell, who acquired her stock several years ago. You represent Michael, who asks whether he must report gain on the transfer. Prepare a letter to Michael and a memorandum for the tax files documenting your response.

30. **LO.1** Dan and Patricia form Crane Corporation. Dan transfers land (worth $200,000, basis of $60,000) for 50% of the stock in Crane. Patricia transfers machinery (worth $150,000, adjusted basis of $30,000) and provides services worth $50,000 for 50% of the stock.
   a. Will the transfers qualify under § 351? Explain.
   b. What are the tax consequences to Dan and Patricia?
   c. What is Crane Corporation's basis in the land and the machinery?

31. **LO.1** Juan organized Teal Corporation 10 years ago. He contributed property worth $1 million (basis of $200,000) for 2,000 shares of stock in Teal (representing 100% ownership). Juan later gave each of his children, Julie and Rachel, 500 shares of the stock. In the current year, Juan transfers property worth $400,000 (basis of $150,000) to Teal for 500 more of its shares. What gain, if any, will Juan recognize on the transfer?

32. **LO.1, 3** Ann and Bob form Robin Corporation. Ann transfers property worth $420,000 (basis of $150,000) for 70 shares in Robin Corporation. Bob receives 30 shares for property worth $165,000 (basis of $30,000) and for legal services (worth $15,000) in organizing the corporation.
   a. What gain or income, if any, will the parties recognize on the transfer?
   b. What basis do Ann and Bob have in the stock in Robin Corporation?
   c. What is Robin Corporation's basis in the property and services it received from Ann and Bob?

33. **LO.1, 3** Assume in Problem 32 that the property Bob transfers to Robin Corporation is worth $15,000 (basis of $3,000) and that his services in organizing the corporation are worth $165,000. What are the tax consequences to Ann, Bob, and Robin Corporation?

34. **LO.3** Kim is an employee of Azure Corporation. In the current year, she receives a salary of $30,000 and is given 10 shares of Azure stock for services she renders to the corporation. The shares in Azure Corporation are worth $1,000 each. For tax purposes, how will Kim treat the receipt of the 10 shares? What is Azure Corporation's total compensation deduction for Kim's services?

Decision Making

35. **LO.1, 7** Rhonda Johnson owns 50% of the stock of Peach Corporation. She and the other 50% shareholder, Rachel Powell, have decided that additional contributions of

capital are needed if Peach is to remain successful in its competitive industry. The two shareholders have agreed that Rhonda will contribute assets having a value of $200,000 (adjusted basis of $15,000) in exchange for additional shares of stock. After the transaction, Rhonda will hold 75% of Peach Corporation and Rachel's interest will fall to 25%.

a. What gain is realized on the transaction? How much of the gain will be recognized?
b. Rhonda is not satisfied with the transaction as proposed. How would the consequences change if Rachel agrees to transfer $1,000 of cash in exchange for additional stock? In this case, Rhonda will own slightly less than 75% of Peach and Rachel's interest will be slightly more than 25%.
c. If Rhonda still is not satisfied with the result, what should be done to avoid any gain recognition?

36. **LO.1, 2, 3** Adam transfers property with an adjusted basis of $50,000 (fair market value of $400,000) to Swift Corporation for 90% of the stock. The property is subject to a liability of $60,000, which Swift assumes.
    a. What is the basis of the Swift stock to Adam?
    b. What is the basis of the property to Swift Corporation?

37. **LO.1, 2, 3** Four years ago Gene exchanged commercial real estate worth $1.5 million (basis of $300,000) and subject to a mortgage of $200,000 for land worth $1.15 million, subject to a mortgage of $150,000, and cash of $300,000. In the current year, Gene transfers the land he received in the exchange to newly formed Bronze Corporation for all of its stock. Bronze Corporation assumes the original mortgage on the land, current face amount of $100,000, and a second mortgage, face amount of $20,000. Gene had placed the second mortgage on the land to secure the purchase of some equipment that he used in this business. What are the tax issues?

Issue ID

38. **LO.1, 2, 3** David organizes White Corporation with a transfer of land (basis of $200,000, fair market value of $600,000) that is subject to a mortgage of $150,000. A month before the incorporation, David borrowed $100,000 for personal purposes and gave the bank a lien on the land. White Corporation issues stock worth $350,000 to David and assumes the mortgage of $150,000 and the personal loan of $100,000. What are the tax consequences of the incorporation to David and to White Corporation?

39. **LO.1, 3** Michael transfers the following assets to Peach Corporation in exchange for all of its stock. (Assume that neither Michael nor Peach plans to make any special tax elections at the time of incorporation.)

Decision Making

Assets	Michael's Adjusted Basis	Fair Market Value
Inventory	$ 85,000	$100,000
Equipment	160,000	120,000
Trucks	150,000	130,000

a. What is Michael's recognized gain or loss?
b. What is Michael's basis in the stock?
c. What is Peach's basis in the inventory, equipment, and trucks?
d. If Michael has no intentions of selling his Peach stock for at least 15 years, what action would you recommend that Michael and Peach Corporation consider? How does this change the previous answers?

40. **LO.1, 2, 3** Fay, a sole proprietor, is engaged in a cash basis service business. In the current year, she incorporates the business to form Robin Corporation. She transfers assets with a basis of $400,000 (fair market value of $1.2 million), a bank loan of $360,000 (which Robin assumes), and $80,000 in trade payables in return for all of Robin's stock. What are the tax consequences of the incorporation of the business?

41. **LO.1, 3** Alice and Jane form Osprey Corporation. Alice transfers property, basis of $25,000 and value of $200,000, for 50 shares in Osprey Corporation. Jane transfers property, basis of $50,000 and value of $165,000, and agrees to serve as manager of Osprey for one year; in return, Jane receives 50 shares in Osprey. The value of Jane's services to Osprey is $35,000.

a. What gain or income do Alice and Jane recognize on the exchange?
b. What is Osprey Corporation's basis in the property transferred by Alice and Jane? How does Osprey treat the value of the services that Jane renders?

42. **LO.1, 3** Assume in Problem 41 that Jane receives the 50 shares of Osprey Corporation stock in consideration for the appreciated property and for the provision of accounting services in organizing the corporation. The value of Jane's services is $35,000.
   a. What gain or income does Jane recognize?
   b. What is Osprey Corporation's basis in the property transferred by Jane? How does Osprey treat the value of the services that Jane renders?

43. **LO.1, 3** On January 6, 2012, Donna transferred machinery worth $100,000 (basis of $30,000) to a controlled corporation, Jay, in a transfer that qualified under § 351. Donna had deducted depreciation on the machinery in the amount of $80,000 when she held the machinery for use in her proprietorship. On November 16, 2012, Jay Corporation sells the machinery for $95,000. What are the tax consequences to Donna and to Jay Corporation on the sale of the machinery?

44. **LO.4** Red Corporation wants to set up a manufacturing facility in a midwestern state. After considerable negotiations with a small town in Ohio, Red accepts the following offer: land (fair market value of $3 million) and cash of $1 million.
   a. How much gain or income, if any, must Red Corporation recognize?
   b. What basis will Red Corporation have in the land?
   c. Within one year of the contribution, Red constructs a building for $800,000 and purchases inventory for $200,000. What basis will Red Corporation have in each of those assets?

Communications

45. **LO.5, 6** Emily Patrick (36 Paradise Road, Northampton, MA 01060) formed Teal Corporation a number of years ago with an investment of $200,000 cash, for which she received $20,000 in stock and $180,000 in bonds bearing interest of 8% and maturing in nine years. Several years later Emily lent the corporation an additional $50,000 on open account. In the current year, Teal Corporation becomes insolvent and is declared bankrupt. During the corporation's existence, Emily was paid an annual salary of $60,000. Write a letter to Emily in which you explain how she would treat her losses for tax purposes.

Communications

46. **LO.5, 6** Stock in Jaybird Corporation (555 Industry Lane, Pueblo, CO 81001) is held equally by Vera, Wade, and Wes. Jaybird seeks additional capital in the amount of $900,000 to construct a building. Vera, Wade, and Wes each propose to lend Jaybird Corporation $300,000, taking from Jaybird a $300,000 four-year note with interest payable annually at two points below the prime rate. Jaybird Corporation has current taxable income of $2 million. You represent Jaybird Corporation. Jaybird's president, Steve Ferguson, asks you how the payments on the notes might be treated for tax purposes. Prepare a letter to Ferguson and a memo for your tax files where you document your conclusions.

47. **LO.6** Sam, a single taxpayer, acquired stock in a corporation that qualified as a small business corporation under § 1244 at a cost of $100,000 three years ago. He sells the stock for $10,000 in the current tax year.
   a. How will the loss be treated for tax purposes?
   b. Assume instead that Sam sold the stock to his sister, Kara, a few months after it was acquired for $100,000 (its fair market value). If Kara sells the stock for $60,000 in the current year, how should she treat the loss for tax purposes?

Communications

48. **LO.6** Three years ago and at a cost of $40,000, Paul Sanders acquired stock in a corporation that qualified as a small business corporation under § 1244. A few months after he acquired the stock, when it was still worth $40,000, he gave it to his brother, Mike Sanders. Mike, who is married and files a joint return, sells the stock for $25,000 in the current tax year. Mike asks you, his tax adviser, how the sale will be treated for tax purposes. Prepare a letter to your client and a memo for the file. Mike's address is 10 Hunt Wood Drive, Hadley, PA 16130.

49. **LO.6** Susan transfers property (basis of $50,000 and fair market value of $25,000) to Thrush Corporation in exchange for shares of § 1244 stock. (Assume that the transfer qualifies under § 351.)

a. What is the basis of the stock to Susan? (Susan and Thrush do not make an election to reduce her stock basis.)
b. What is the basis of the stock to Susan for purposes of § 1244?
c. If Susan sells the stock for $20,000 two years later, how will the loss be treated for tax purposes?

50. **LO.5, 7** Frank, Cora, and Mitch are equal shareholders in Purple Corporation. The corporation's assets have a tax basis of $50,000 and a fair market value of $600,000. In the current year, Frank and Cora each loan Purple Corporation $150,000. The notes to Frank and Cora bear interest of 8% per annum. Mitch leases equipment to Purple Corporation for an annual rental of $12,000. Discuss whether the shareholder loans from Frank and Cora might be reclassified as equity. Consider in your discussion whether Purple Corporation has an acceptable debt-equity ratio.

Decision Making

RESEARCH PROBLEMS

THOMSON REUTERS
CHECKPOINT®

Note: Solutions to Research Problems can be prepared by using the **Checkpoint® Student Edition** online research product, which is available to accompany this text. It is also possible to prepare solutions to the Research Problems by using tax research materials found in a standard tax library.

Decision Making
Communications

Research Problem 1. Lynn Jones, Shawn, Walt, and Donna are trying to decide whether they should organize a corporation and transfer their shares of stock in several corporations to this new corporation. All of their shares are listed on the New York Stock Exchange and are readily marketable. Lynn would transfer shares in Brown Corporation; Shawn would transfer stock in Rust Corporation; Walt would transfer stock in White Corporation; and Donna would transfer stock in several corporations. The stock would be held by the newly formed corporation for investment purposes. Lynn asks you, her tax adviser, whether she would have gain on the transfer of her substantially appreciated shares in Brown Corporation if she transfers the shares to a newly formed corporation. She also asks whether there will be tax consequences if she, Shawn, Walt, and Donna form a partnership, rather than a corporation, to which they would transfer their readily marketable stock. Your input will be critical as they make their decision. Prepare a letter to the client, Lynn Jones, and a memo for the firm's files. Lynn's address is 1540 Maxwell Avenue, Highland, KY 41099.

Research Problem 2. Joel has operated his business as a sole proprietorship for many years but has decided to incorporate the business to limit his exposure to personal liability. The balance sheet of his business is as follows:

	Adjusted Basis	Fair Market Value
Assets:		
Cash	$ 50,000	$ 50,000
Accounts receivable	40,000	40,000
Inventory	30,000	60,000
Fixed assets	10,000	200,000
	$130,000	$ 350,000
Liabilities:		
Trade accounts payable	$ 25,000	$ 25,000
Notes payable	175,000	175,000
Owner's equity	(70,000)	150,000
	$130,000	$ 350,000

One problem with this plan is that the liabilities of Joel's sole proprietorship exceed the basis of the assets to be transferred to the corporation by $70,000 ($200,000 – $130,000). Therefore, Joel would be required to recognize a gain of $70,000. He is not pleased with this result and asks you about the effect of drawing up a $70,000 note that he would transfer to the corporation. Would the note, which promises a future payment to the corporation of $70,000, enable Joel to avoid recognition of the gain? Explain.

Partial list of research aids:
§ 357(c).

Research Problem 3. Tim is a real estate broker who specializes in commercial real estate. Although he usually buys and sells on behalf of others, he also maintains a portfolio of property of his own. He holds this property, mainly unimproved land, either as an investment or for sale to others.

In early 2011, Irene and Al contact Tim regarding a tract of land located just outside the city limits. Tim bought the property, which is known as the Moore farm, several years ago for $600,000. At that time, no one knew that it was located on a geological fault line. Irene, a well-known architect, and Al, a building contractor, want Tim to join them in developing the property for residential use. They are aware of the fault line but believe that they can circumvent the problem by using newly developed design and construction technology. Because of the geological flaw, however, they regard the Moore farm as being worth only $450,000. Their intent is to organize a corporation to build the housing project, and each party will receive stock commensurate to the property or services contributed.

After consulting his tax adviser, Tim agrees to join the venture if certain modifications to the proposed arrangement are made. The transfer of the land would be structured as a sale to the corporation. Instead of receiving stock, Tim would receive a note from the corporation. The note would be interest-bearing and be due in five years. The maturity value of the note would be $450,000—the amount that even Tim concedes is the fair market value of the Moore farm.

What income tax consequences ensue from Tim's suggested approach? Compare this result with what would happen if Tim merely transferred the Moore farm in return for stock in the new corporation.

Research Problem 4. Sarah is the sole owner of Bluegrass Corporation. The basis and value of her stock investment in Bluegrass are approximately $100,000. In addition, she manages Bluegrass's operations on a full-time basis and pays herself an annual salary of $40,000. Because of a recent downturn in business, she needs to put an additional $80,000 into her corporation to help meet short-term cash-flow needs (e.g., inventory costs, salaries, and administrative expenses). Sarah believes that the $80,000 transfer can be structured in one of three ways: as a capital contribution, as a loan made to protect her stock investment, or as a loan intended to protect her job. From a tax perspective, which alternative would be preferable in the event that Bluegrass's economic slide worsens and bankruptcy results? Explain your answer.

Partial list of research aids:
Kenneth W. Graves, 87 TCM 1409, T.C.Memo. 2004–140.

Internet Activity

Use the tax resources of the Internet to address the following questions. Do not restrict your search to the Web, but include a review of newsgroups and general reference materials, practitioner sites and resources, primary sources of the tax law, chat rooms and discussion groups, and other opportunities.

Research Problem 5. Identify two publicly traded corporations that have issued more than one class of stock to their shareholders. Was the issuance of the additional classes of stock part of the original incorporation, or did it occur later? Determine the rationale for the corporations' actions.

Research Problem 6. Have the provisions of § 1202, which relate to qualified small business stock, been widely used since their enactment? What leads you to this conclusion? What rationale did Congress provide as a justification for the provision's enactment? What justification was offered for increasing the exclusion percentage in 2009 and 2010? Evaluate recent Obama administration budget proposals that would make the 100 percent exclusion permanent.

Communications

Research Problem 7. Owners and financiers of businesses often have reasons to structure their investments as either debt or equity. Locate the July 11, 2011, report prepared by the Staff of the Joint Committee on Taxation that contains a discussion of the taxation of business debt. Summarize for your professor its conclusion on the (1) tax incentives for debt, (2) tax incentives for equity, and (3) incentives to create hybrid instruments.

CHAPTER

5

Corporations: Earnings & Profits and Dividend Distributions

LEARNING OBJECTIVES: *After completing Chapter 5, you should be able to:*

LO.1 Explain the role that earnings and profits play in determining the tax treatment of distributions.

LO.2 Compute a corporation's earnings and profits.

LO.3 Determine taxable dividends paid during the year by correctly allocating current and accumulated E & P to corporate distributions.

LO.4 Describe the tax treatment of dividends for individual shareholders.

LO.5 Evaluate the tax impact of property dividends by computing the shareholder's dividend income, basis in the property received, and the effect on the distributing corporation's E & P and taxable income.

LO.6 Recognize situations when constructive dividends exist and compute the tax resulting from such dividends.

LO.7 Compute the tax arising from receipt of stock dividends and stock rights and the shareholder's basis in the stock and stock rights received.

LO.8 Structure corporate distributions in a manner that minimizes the tax consequences to the parties involved.

CHAPTER OUTLINE

THE BIG PICTURE Tax Solutions for the Real World

© Alexander Raths/Shutterstock.com

TAXING CORPORATE DISTRIBUTIONS

Lime Corporation, an ice cream manufacturer, has had a very profitable year. To share its profits with its two shareholders, Orange Corporation and Gustavo, it distributes cash of $200,000 to Orange and real estate worth $300,000 (adjusted basis of $20,000) to Gustavo. The real estate is subject to a mortgage of $100,000, which Gustavo assumes. The distribution is made on December 31, Lime's year-end.

Lime Corporation has had both good and bad years in the past. More often than not, however, it has lost money. Despite this year's banner profits, the GAAP-based balance sheet for Lime indicates a year-end deficit in retained earnings. Consequently, the distribution of cash and land is treated as a liquidating distribution for financial reporting purposes, resulting in a reduction of Lime's paid-in capital account.

The tax consequences of the distributions to the corporation and its shareholders depend on a variety of factors that are not directly related to the financial reporting treatment. Identify these factors and explain the tax effects of the distributions to both Lime Corporation and its two shareholders.

Read the chapter and formulate your response.

5 INTRODUCTION

Chapter 4 examined the tax consequences of corporate formation. In Chapters 5 and 6, the focus shifts to the tax treatment of corporate distributions, a topic that plays a leading role in tax planning. The importance of corporate distributions derives from the variety of tax treatments that may apply. From the shareholder's perspective, distributions received from the corporation may be treated as ordinary income, preferentially taxed dividend income, capital gain, or a nontaxable recovery of capital. From the corporation's perspective, distributions made to shareholders are generally not deductible. However, a corporation may recognize losses in liquidating distributions (see Chapter 6), and gains may be recognized at the corporate level on distributions of appreciated property. In the most common scenario, a distribution triggers dividend income to the shareholder and provides no deduction to the paying corporation, resulting in a double tax (at both the corporate and the shareholder level). This double tax may be mitigated by a variety of factors including the corporate dividends received deduction and preferential tax rates on qualified dividends paid to individuals.

As will become apparent in the subsequent discussion, the tax treatment of corporate distributions can be affected by a number of considerations:

- The availability of earnings to be distributed.
- The basis of the shareholder's stock.
- The character of the property being distributed.
- Whether the shareholder gives up ownership in return for the distribution.
- Whether the distribution is liquidating or nonliquidating.
- Whether the distribution is a "qualified dividend."
- Whether the shareholder is an individual or another kind of taxpaying entity.

This chapter discusses the tax rules related to nonliquidating distributions of cash and property. Distributions of stock and stock rights are also addressed. Chapter 6 extends the discussion to the tax treatment of stock redemptions and corporate liquidations.

5.1 CORPORATE DISTRIBUTIONS—OVERVIEW

LO.1

Explain the role that earnings and profits play in determining the tax treatment of distributions.

To the extent that a distribution is made from corporate earnings and profits (E & P), the shareholder is deemed to receive a dividend, taxed as ordinary income or as preferentially taxed dividend income.[1] Generally, corporate distributions are presumed to be paid out of E & P (defined later in this chapter) and are treated as dividends *unless* the parties to the transaction can show otherwise. Distributions not treated as dividends (because of insufficient E & P) are nontaxable to the extent of the shareholder's stock basis, which is reduced accordingly. The excess of the distribution over the shareholder's basis is treated as a gain from sale or exchange of the stock.[2]

EXAMPLE 1

At the beginning of the year, Amber Corporation (a calendar year taxpayer) has E & P of $15,000. The corporation generates no additional E & P during the year. On July 1, the corporation distributes $20,000 to its sole shareholder, Bonnie, whose stock basis is $4,000. In this situation, Bonnie recognizes dividend income of $15,000 (the amount of E & P distributed). In addition, she reduces her stock basis from $4,000 to zero, and she recognizes a taxable gain of $1,000 (the excess of the distribution over the stock basis). ■

5.2 EARNINGS AND PROFITS (E & P)—§ 312

LO.2

Compute a corporation's earnings and profits.

The notion of **earnings and profits (E & P)** is similar in many respects to the accounting concept of retained earnings. Both are measures of the firm's accumulated capital (E & P includes both the accumulated E & P of the corporation since February 28,

[1] §§ 301(c)(1), 316, and 1(h)(11).

[2] §§ 301(c)(2) and (3).

1913, and the current year's E & P). A difference exists, however, in the way these figures are calculated. The computation of retained earnings is based on financial accounting rules, while E & P is determined using rules specified in the tax law.

E & P fixes the upper limit on the amount of dividend income that shareholders must recognize as a result of a distribution by the corporation. In this sense, E & P represents the corporation's economic ability to pay a dividend without impairing its capital. Thus, the effect of a specific transaction on E & P can often be determined by assessing whether the transaction increases or decreases the corporation's capacity to pay a dividend.

Computation of E & P

The Code does not explicitly define the term *earnings and profits.* Instead, a series of adjustments to taxable income are identified to provide a measure of the corporation's economic income. Both cash basis and accrual basis corporations use the same approach when determining E & P.[3]

Additions to Taxable Income

To determine current E & P, it is necessary to add *all* previously excluded income items back to taxable income. Included among these positive adjustments are interest on municipal bonds, excluded life insurance proceeds (in excess of cash surrender value), and Federal income tax refunds from tax paid in prior years.

EXAMPLE 2

A corporation collects $100,000 on a key employee life insurance policy (the corporation is the owner and beneficiary of the policy). At the time the policy matured on the death of the insured employee, it possessed a cash surrender value of $30,000. None of the $100,000 is included in the corporation's taxable income, but $70,000 is added to taxable income when computing current E & P. The distribution of the $30,000 cash surrender value does not increase E & P because it does not reflect an increase in the corporation's dividend-paying capacity. Instead, it represents a shift in the corporation's assets from life insurance to cash. ■

In addition to excluded income items, the dividends received deduction and the domestic production activities deduction are added back to taxable income to determine E & P. Neither of these deductions decreases the corporation's assets. Instead, they are partial exclusions for specific types of income (dividend income and income from domestic production activities). Because they do not impair the corporation's ability to pay dividends, they do not reduce E & P.

Subtractions from Taxable Income

When calculating E & P, it is also necessary to subtract certain nondeductible expenses from taxable income. These negative adjustments include the nondeductible portion of meal and entertainment expenses, related-party losses, expenses incurred to produce tax-exempt income, Federal income taxes paid, nondeductible key employee life insurance premiums (net of increases in cash surrender value), nondeductible fines, penalties, and lobbying expenses.

EXAMPLE 3

A corporation sells property with a basis of $10,000 to its sole shareholder for $8,000. Because of § 267 (disallowance of losses on sales between related parties), the $2,000 loss cannot be deducted when calculating the corporation's taxable income. However, because the overall economic effect of the transaction is a decrease in the corporation's assets by $2,000, the loss reduces the current E & P for the year of sale. ■

[3] Section 312 describes many of the adjustments to taxable income necessary to determine E & P. Regulation § 1.312–6 addresses the effect of accounting methods on E & P.

EXAMPLE 4

A corporation pays a $10,000 premium on a key employee life insurance policy covering the life of its president. As a result of the payment, the cash surrender value of the policy is increased by $7,000. Although none of the $10,000 premium is deductible for tax purposes, current E & P is reduced by $3,000. The $7,000 increase in cash surrender value is not subtracted because it does not represent a decrease in the corporation's ability to pay a dividend. Instead, it represents a shift in the corporation's assets, from cash to life insurance. ■

Timing Adjustments

Some E & P adjustments shift the effect of a transaction from the year of its inclusion in or deduction from taxable income to the year in which it has an economic effect on the corporation. Charitable contributions, net operating losses, and capital losses all necessitate this kind of adjustment.

EXAMPLE 5

During 2012, a corporation makes charitable contributions, $12,000 of which cannot be deducted when calculating the taxable income for the year because of the 10% taxable income limitation. Consequently, the $12,000 is carried forward to 2013 and fully deducted in that year. The excess charitable contribution reduces the corporation's current E & P for 2012 by $12,000 and increases its current E & P for 2013 (when the deduction is allowed) by the same amount. The increase in E & P in 2013 is necessary because the charitable contribution carryover reduces the taxable income for that year (the starting point for computing E & P) but already has been taken into account in determining the E & P for 2012. ■

Gains and losses from property transactions generally affect the determination of E & P only to the extent they are recognized for tax purposes. Thus, gains and losses deferred under the like-kind exchange provision and deferred involuntary conversion gains do not affect E & P until recognized. Accordingly, no timing adjustment is required for these items.

Accounting Method Adjustments

In addition to the above adjustments, accounting methods used for determining E & P are generally more conservative than those allowed for calculating taxable income. For example, the installment method is not permitted for E & P purposes.[4] Thus, an adjustment is required for the deferred gain from property sales made during the year under the installment method. All principal payments are treated as having been received in the year of sale.

EXAMPLE 6

In 2012, Cardinal Corporation, a calendar year taxpayer, sells unimproved real estate with a basis of $20,000 for $100,000. Under the terms of the sale, Cardinal will receive two annual payments of $50,000 beginning in 2013, each with interest of 9%. Cardinal Corporation does not elect out of the installment method. Because Cardinal's taxable income for 2012 will not reflect any of the gain from the sale, the corporation must make an $80,000 positive adjustment for 2012 (the deferred gain from the sale). Similarly, $40,000 negative adjustments will be required in 2013 and 2014 when the deferred gain is recognized under the installment method. ■

The alternative depreciation system (ADS) must be used for purposes of computing E & P.[5] This method requires straight-line depreciation over a recovery period equal to the Asset Depreciation Range (ADR) midpoint life.[6] Also, ADS prohibits additional first-year depreciation.[7] If MACRS cost recovery is used for income tax purposes, a positive or negative adjustment equal to the difference between MACRS and ADS must be made each year. Likewise, when assets are disposed of, an additional adjustment to taxable income is required to allow for the difference in gain or loss caused by the gap

[4]§ 312(n)(5).

[5]§ 312(k)(3)(A).

[6]See § 168(g)(2). The ADR midpoint lives for most assets are set out in Rev.Proc. 87–56, 1987–2 C.B. 674. The recovery period is 5 years for automobiles and light-duty trucks and 40 years for real property. For assets with no class life, the recovery period is 12 years.

[7]§ 168(k)(2). A special additional first-year cost recovery allowance was allowed for certain property placed in service prior to 2005. In addition, it is available for certain assets placed in service from 2008 through 2012.

between income tax basis and E & P basis.[8] The adjustments arising from depreciation are illustrated in the following example.

EXAMPLE 7

On January 2, 2010, White Corporation paid $30,000 to purchase equipment with an ADR midpoint life of 10 years and a MACRS class life of 7 years. The equipment was depreciated under MACRS. The asset was sold on July 2, 2012, for $27,000. For purposes of determining taxable income and E & P, cost recovery claimed on the equipment is summarized below. Assume that White elected not to claim § 179 expense or additional first-year depreciation on the property.

Year	Cost Recovery Computation	MACRS	ADS	Adjustment Amount
2010	$30,000 × 14.29%	$ 4,287		
	$30,000 ÷ 10-year ADR recovery period × ½ (half-year for first year of service)		$1,500	$2,787
2011	$30,000 × 24.49%	7,347		
	$30,000 ÷ 10-year ADR recovery period		3,000	4,347
2012	$30,000 × 17.49% × ½ (half-year for year of disposal)	2,624		
	$30,000 ÷ 10-year ADR recovery period × ½ (half-year for year of disposal)		1,500	1,124
Total cost recovery		$14,258	$6,000	$8,258

Each year, White Corporation will increase taxable income by the adjustment amount indicated above to determine E & P. In addition, when computing E & P for 2012, White will reduce taxable income by $8,258 to account for the excess gain recognized for income tax purposes, as shown below.

	Income Tax	E & P
Amount realized	$ 27,000	$ 27,000
Adjusted basis for income tax ($30,000 cost − $14,258 MACRS)	(15,742)	
Adjusted basis for E & P ($30,000 cost − $6,000 ADS)		(24,000)
Gain on sale	$ 11,258	$ 3,000
Adjustment amount ($3,000 − $11,258)	($ 8,258)	

■

In addition to more conservative depreciation methods, the E & P rules impose limitations on the deductibility of § 179 expense. In particular, this expense must be deducted over a period of five years.[9] Thus, in any year that § 179 is elected, 80 percent of the resulting expense must be added back to taxable income to determine current E & P. In each of the following four years, a negative adjustment equal to 20 percent of the § 179 expense must be made.

The E & P rules also require specific accounting methods in various situations, making adjustments necessary when certain methods are used for income tax purposes. For example, E & P requires cost depletion rather than percentage depletion. When accounting for long-term contracts, E & P rules specify the percentage of completion method rather than the completed contract method.[10] As the E & P determination does not allow for the amortization of organizational expenses, any such expense deducted when computing taxable income must be added back to determine E & P.[11] To account for income deferral under the LIFO inventory method, the E & P computation requires an adjustment for changes in the LIFO recapture amount (the excess of FIFO over LIFO inventory value) during the year. Increases in LIFO recapture are added to taxable income, and decreases are

[8] § 312(f)(1).
[9] § 312(k)(3)(B).
[10] § 312(n)(6).
[11] § 312(n)(3).

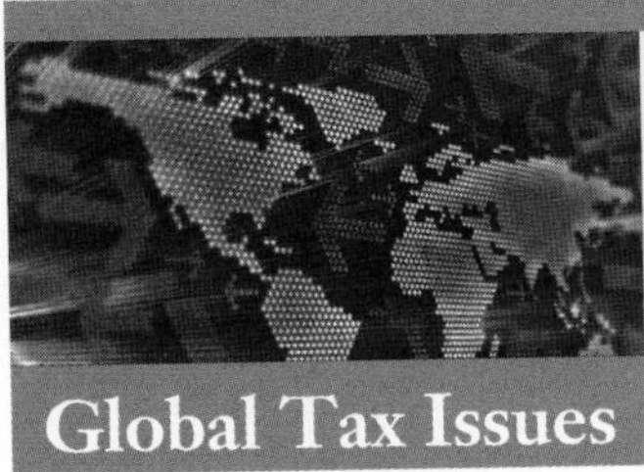

© Andrey Prokhorov, iStockphoto

E & P in Controlled Foreign Corporations

U.S. multinational companies often conduct business overseas using foreign subsidiaries known as "controlled foreign corporations," or CFCs. This organizational structure would seem to be ideal for income tax avoidance if the CFC is incorporated in a low-tax jurisdiction (a tax haven country). In the absence of any rules to the contrary, the higher U.S. tax on foreign earnings could be deferred until the earnings are repatriated to the United States through dividends paid to the U.S. parent.

To prevent this deferral, the tax law compels a U.S. parent corporation to recognize some of the unrepatriated earnings of the CFC as income. The foreign corporation's E & P is used to determine the amount of income that is recognized annually by the U.S. parent corporation. Determining the CFC's E & P is no easy task. Foreign corporations (including CFCs) typically compute their book income using foreign generally accepted accounting principles (GAAP). Because the starting point for computing E & P for foreign corporations is U.S. GAAP book income rather than taxable income, an extra layer of complexity is introduced. First, the foreign company's book income must be converted to a U.S. GAAP basis, and then a series of adjustments must be made (similar to the adjustments reflected in Concept Summary 5.1) to U.S. book income to determine E & P.

subtracted.[12] E & P rules also specify that intangible drilling costs and mine exploration and development costs be amortized over a period of 60 months and 120 months, respectively. For income tax purposes, however, these costs can be deducted in the current year.[13]

Summary of E & P Adjustments

E & P serves as a measure of a corporation's earnings that are available for distribution as taxable dividends to the shareholders. Current E & P is determined by making a series of adjustments to the corporation's taxable income that are outlined in Concept Summary 5.1. Other items that affect E & P, such as property dividends, are covered later in the chapter. The effect of stock redemptions on E & P is covered in Chapter 6.

Current versus Accumulated E & P

Accumulated E & P is the total of all previous years' current E & P (since February 28, 1913) reduced by distributions made from E & P in previous years. It is important to distinguish between **current E & P** and **accumulated E & P** because the taxability of corporate distributions depends on how these two accounts are allocated to each distribution made during the year. A complex set of rules governs the allocation process.[14] These rules are described in the following section and summarized in Concept Summary 5.2.

Allocating E & P to Distributions

LO.3

Determine taxable dividends paid during the year by correctly allocating current and accumulated E & P to corporate distributions.

When a positive balance exists in both the current and the accumulated E & P accounts, corporate distributions are deemed to be made first from current E & P and then from accumulated E & P. When distributions exceed the amount of current E & P, it becomes necessary to allocate current and accumulated E & P to each distribution made during the year. Current E & P is applied first on a pro rata basis (using dollar amounts) to each distribution. Then accumulated E & P is applied in chronological order, beginning with the earliest distribution. As seen in the following example, this allocation is important if any shareholder sells stock during the year.

[12] § 312(n)(4).

[13] § 312(n)(2).

[14] Regulations relating to the source of a distribution are at Reg. § 1.316–2.

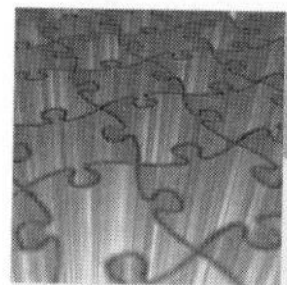

CONCEPT SUMMARY 5.1

E & P Adjustments

Nature of the Transaction	Adjustment to Taxable Income to Determine Current E & P	
	Addition	**Subtraction**
Tax-exempt income	X	
Dividends received deduction	X	
Domestic production activities deduction	X	
Collection of proceeds from insurance policy on life of corporate officer (in excess of cash surrender value)	X	
Deferred gain on installment sale (all gain is added to E & P in year of sale)	X	
Future recognition of installment sale gross profit		X
Excess charitable contribution (over 10% limitation) and excess capital loss in year incurred		X
Deduction of charitable contribution, NOL, or capital loss carryovers in succeeding taxable year (increase E & P because deduction reduces taxable income while E & P was reduced in a prior year)	X	
Federal income taxes paid		X
Federal income tax refund	X	
Loss on sale between related parties		X
Nondeductible fines, penalties, and lobbying expenses		X
Nondeductible meal and entertainment expenses		X
Payment of premiums on insurance policy on life of corporate officer (in excess of increase in cash surrender value of policy)		X
Realized gain (not recognized) on an involuntary conversion	No effect	
Realized gain or loss (not recognized) on a like-kind exchange	No effect	
Excess percentage depletion (only cost depletion can reduce E & P)	X	
Accelerated depreciation (E & P is reduced only by straight-line, units-of-production, or machine hours depreciation)	X	X
Additional first-year depreciation	X	
Section 179 expense in year elected (80%)	X	
Section 179 expense in four years following election (20% each year)		X
Increase (decrease) in LIFO recapture amount	X	(X)
Intangible drilling costs deducted currently (reduce E & P in future years by amortizing costs over 60 months)	X	
Mine exploration and development costs (reduce E & P in future years by amortizing costs over 120 months)	X	

EXAMPLE 8

On January 1 of the current year, Black Corporation has accumulated E & P of $10,000. Current E & P for the year amounts to $30,000. Megan and Matt are sole *equal* shareholders of Black from January 1 to July 31. On August 1, Megan sells all of her stock to Helen. Black makes two distributions to shareholders during the year: $40,000 to Megan and Matt ($20,000 to each) on July 1 and $40,000 to Matt and Helen ($20,000 to each) on December 1. Current and accumulated E & P are applied to the two distributions as follows:

	Source of Distribution		
	Current E & P	Accumulated E & P	Return of Capital
July 1 distribution ($40,000)	$15,000	$10,000	$15,000
December 1 distribution ($40,000)	15,000	—	25,000

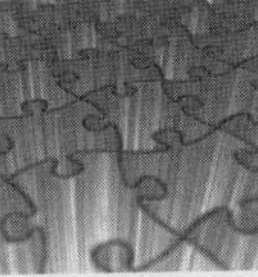

CONCEPT SUMMARY 5.2

Allocating E & P to Distributions

1. Current E & P is applied first to distributions on a pro rata basis; then accumulated E & P is applied (as necessary) in chronological order beginning with the earliest distribution. See Example 8.
2. Until the parties can show otherwise, it is presumed that current E & P covers all distributions. See Example 9.
3. When a deficit exists in accumulated E & P and a positive balance exists in current E & P, distributions are regarded as dividends to the extent of current E & P. See Example 10.
4. When a deficit exists in current E & P and a positive balance exists in accumulated E & P, the two accounts are netted at the date of distribution. If the resulting balance is zero or a deficit, the distribution is treated as a return of capital, first reducing the basis of the stock to zero, then generating taxable gain. If a positive balance results, the distribution is a dividend to the extent of the balance. Any loss in current E & P is deemed to accrue ratably throughout the year unless the corporation can show otherwise. See Example 11.

Because 50% of the total distributions are made on July 1 and December 1, respectively, one-half of current E & P is applied to each of the two distributions. Accumulated E & P is applied in chronological order, so the entire amount attaches to the July 1 distribution. The tax consequences to the shareholders are presented below.

	Shareholder		
	Megan	Matt	Helen
July distribution ($40,000)			
Dividend income—			
From current E & P ($15,000)	$ 7,500	$ 7,500	$ –0–
From accumulated E & P ($10,000)	5,000	5,000	–0–
Return of capital ($15,000)	7,500	7,500	–0–
December distribution ($40,000)			
Dividend income—			
From current E & P ($15,000)	–0–	7,500	7,500
From accumulated E & P ($0)	–0–	–0–	–0–
Return of capital ($25,000)	–0–	12,500	12,500
Total dividend income	$12,500	$20,000	$ 7,500
Nontaxable return of capital (assuming sufficient basis in the stock investment)	$ 7,500	$20,000	$12,500

Because the balance in the accumulated E & P account is exhausted when it is applied to the July 1 distribution, Megan has more dividend income than Helen, even though both receive equal distributions during the year. In addition, each shareholder's basis is reduced by the nontaxable return of capital; any excess over basis results in taxable gain. ■

When the tax years of the corporation and its shareholders are not the same, it may be impossible to determine the amount of current E & P on a timely basis. For example, if shareholders use a calendar year and the corporation uses a fiscal year, then current E & P may not be ascertainable until after the shareholders' returns have been filed. To address this timing issue, the allocation rules presume that current E & P is sufficient to cover every distribution made during the year until the parties can show otherwise.

EXAMPLE 9

Green Corporation uses a June 30 fiscal year for tax purposes. Carol, Green's only shareholder, uses a calendar year. On July 1, 2012, Green Corporation has a zero balance in its accumulated E & P account. For fiscal year 2012–2013, the corporation suffers a $5,000 deficit in current E & P. On August 1, 2012, Green distributed $10,000 to Carol. The distribution is dividend income to Carol and is reported when she files her income tax return for the 2012 calendar year on or before April 15, 2013. Because Carol cannot prove until June 30, 2013, that the corporation has a deficit for the 2012–2013 fiscal year, she must assume that the $10,000 distribution is fully covered by current E & P. When Carol learns of the deficit, she can file an amended return for 2012 showing the $10,000 as a return of capital. ■

Additional difficulties arise when either the current or the accumulated E & P account has a deficit balance. In particular, when current E & P is positive and accumulated E & P has a deficit balance, accumulated E & P is *not* netted against current E & P. Instead, the distribution is deemed to be a taxable dividend to the extent of the positive current E & P balance.

THE BIG PICTURE

EXAMPLE 10

Return to the facts of *The Big Picture* on p. 5-1. Recall that Lime Corporation had a deficit in GAAP-based retained earnings at the start of the year and banner profits during the year. Assume that these financial results translate into an $800,000 deficit in accumulated E & P at the start of the year and current E & P of $600,000. In this case, current E & P would exceed the $500,000 of cash and property distributed to the shareholders. The distributions are treated as taxable dividends; they are deemed to be paid from current E & P even though Lime still has a deficit in accumulated E & P at the end of the year.

In contrast to the previous rule, when a deficit exists in current E & P and a positive balance exists in accumulated E & P, the accounts are netted at the date of distribution. If the resulting balance is zero or negative, the distribution is a return of capital. If a positive balance results, the distribution is a dividend to the extent of the balance. Any loss in current E & P is deemed to accrue ratably throughout the year unless the parties can show otherwise.

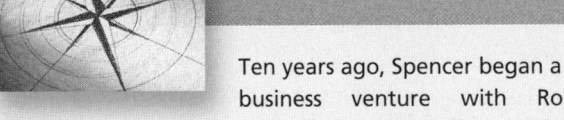

ETHICS & EQUITY Shifting E & P

Ten years ago, Spencer began a new business venture with Robert. Spencer owns 70 percent of the outstanding stock, and Robert owns 30 percent. The business has had some difficult times, but current prospects are favorable.

On November 15, Robert decides that he wants to quit the venture at the beginning of the following year and is planning to sell all of his stock to Spencer's sister, Heidi. He would sell immediately, but he wants to wait until after the company pays out the current-year shareholder distribution of about $250,000. Heidi has been a longtime employee of the business and has expressed an interest in becoming more involved. Spencer is looking forward to working with his sister, but he now faces a terrible dilemma.

The corporation has a $700,000 deficit in accumulated E & P and only about $40,000 of current E & P to date. Within the next two months, however, Spencer expects to sign a major deal with a large client. If Spencer signs the contract before the end of the year, the corporation will have a $600,000 increase in current E & P, thereby causing the forthcoming dividend to be fully taxable to Robert. As a result, most of next year's distribution would be treated as a tax-free return of capital for Heidi. Alternatively, if Spencer waits until January, both he and Robert will receive a nontaxable distribution this year. However, next year's annual distribution will be taxable as a dividend to his sister. What should Spencer do?

EXAMPLE 11

At the beginning of the current year, Gray Corporation (a calendar year taxpayer) has accumulated E & P of $10,000. During the year, the corporation incurs a $15,000 deficit in current E & P that accrues ratably. On July 1, Gray Corporation distributes $6,000 in cash to Hal, its sole shareholder. To determine how much of the $6,000 cash distribution represents dividend income to Hal, the balances of both accumulated and current E & P as of July 1 are determined and netted. This is necessary because of the deficit in current E & P.

	Source of Distribution	
	Current E & P	Accumulated E & P
January 1		$10,000
July 1 (½ of $15,000 net loss)	($7,500)	2,500
July 1 distribution of $6,000:		
Dividend income: $2,500		
Return of capital: $3,500		

The balance in E & P just before the July 1 distribution is $2,500. Thus, of the $6,000 distribution, $2,500 is taxed as a dividend, and $3,500 represents a return of capital. ■

5.3 Dividends

LO.4

Describe the tax treatment of dividends for individual shareholders.

As noted earlier, distributions by a corporation from its E & P are treated as dividends. The tax treatment of dividends varies, depending on whether the shareholder receiving them is a corporation or another kind of taxpaying entity. All corporations treat dividends as ordinary income and are permitted a dividends received deduction (see Chapter 2). Through 2012, qualified dividend income earned by individuals is taxed at reduced tax rates. Beginning in 2013, dividends will be taxed as ordinary income for individuals if Congress does not act to extend the reduced tax rate.

Rationale for Reduced Tax Rates on Dividends

The double tax on corporate income has always been controversial. Arguably, taxing dividends twice creates several undesirable economic distortions, including:

- An incentive to invest in noncorporate rather than corporate entities.
- An incentive for corporations to finance operations with debt rather than with equity because interest payments are deductible. Notably, this behavior increases the vulnerability of corporations in economic downturns because of higher leverage.
- An incentive for corporations to retain earnings and structure distributions of profits to avoid the double tax.

Collectively, these distortions raise the cost of capital for corporate investments. Estimates are that eliminating the double tax would increase capital stock in the corporate sector by as much as $500 billion.[15] In addition, some argue that elimination of the double tax would make the United States more competitive globally. Bear in mind that a majority of our trading partners assess only one tax on corporate income.

While many support a reduced or no tax rate on dividends, others contend that the double tax should remain in place because of the concentration of economic power held by publicly traded corporations. Furthermore, many of the distortions noted above can be avoided through the use of deductible payments by C corporations and by utilizing other forms of doing business (e.g., partnerships, limited

[15]Integration of Individual and Corporate Tax Systems, Report of the Department of the Treasury (January 1992).

Corporate Integration

From an international perspective, the double taxation of dividends is unusual. Most countries have adopted a policy of corporate integration, which imposes a single tax on corporate profits. Corporate integration takes several forms. One popular approach is to impose a tax at the corporate level, but allow shareholders to claim a credit for corporate-level taxes paid when dividends are received. A second alternative is to allow a corporate-level deduction for dividends paid to shareholders. A third approach is to allow shareholders to exclude corporate dividends from income. A fourth alternative suggested in the past by the U.S. Treasury is the "comprehensive business income tax," which excludes both dividend and interest income while disallowing deductions for interest expense.

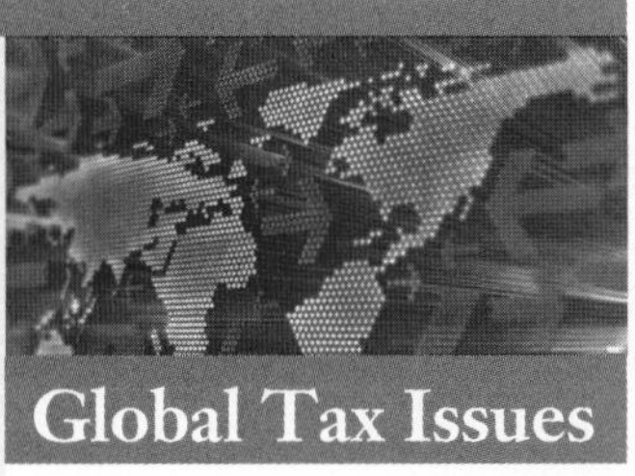

liability companies, and Subchapter S corporations). Those favoring retention of the double tax also note that the benefits of reduced tax rates on dividends flow disproportionately to the wealthy.[16]

The United States continues to struggle to find the appropriate course to follow on the taxation of dividends. The reduced tax rate on **qualified dividends** for individuals applicable through 2012 reflects a compromise between the complete elimination of tax on dividends and the treatment of dividends as ordinary income. At this time, the tax treatment of dividends is uncertain. Congress may act to extend the current reduced rates on qualified dividends for individuals. If new legislation is not enacted, however, beginning in 2013, qualified dividends will once again be taxed as ordinary income.

Qualified Dividends

Qualified Dividends—Application and Effect

Under current law, dividends that meet certain requirements are subject to a 15 percent tax rate for most individual taxpayers from 2003 through 2012. Individuals in the 10 or 15 percent rate brackets were subject to a 5 percent rate on dividends paid from 2003 through 2007. Beginning in 2008, dividends are exempt from tax for these lower-income taxpayers.[17]

Qualified Dividends—Requirements

To be taxed at the lower rates, dividends must be paid by either domestic or certain qualified foreign corporations. Qualified foreign corporations include those traded on a U.S. stock exchange or any corporation located in a country that (1) has a comprehensive income tax treaty with the United States, (2) has an information-sharing agreement with the United States, and (3) is approved by the Treasury.[18]

Two other requirements must be met for dividends to qualify for the favorable rates. First, dividends paid to shareholders who hold both long and short positions in the stock do not qualify. Second, the stock on which the dividend is paid must be held for more than 60 days during the 121-day period beginning 60 days before the ex-dividend date.[19] To allow for settlement delays, the ex-dividend date is typically two days before the date of record on a dividend. This holding period rule parallels the rule applied to corporations that claim the dividends received deduction.[20]

[16]The Urban Institute–Brookings Institution Tax Policy Center estimates that more than one-half—53%—of the benefits from the reduced tax rate on dividends go to the 0.2% of households with incomes over $1 million.

[17]See §§ 1(h)(1) and (11).

[18]In Notice 2006–101, 2006–2 C.B. 930, the Treasury identified 55 qualifying countries (among those included in the list are the members of the European Union, the Russian Federation, Canada, and Mexico). Nonqualifying countries not on the list include most of the former Soviet republics (except Kazakhstan), Bermuda, and the Netherlands Antilles.

[19]§ 1(h)(11)(B)(iii)(I).

[20]See § 246(c) and Chapter 2.

EXAMPLE 12

In June of the current year, Green Corporation announces that a dividend of $1.50 will be paid on each share of its common stock to shareholders of record on July 15. Amy and Corey, two unrelated shareholders, own 1,000 shares of the stock on the record date (July 15). Consequently, each receives $1,500 (1,000 shares × $1.50). Assume that Amy purchased her stock on January 15 of this year, while Corey purchased her stock on July 1. Both shareholders sell their stock on July 20. To qualify for the lower dividend rate, stock must be held for more than 60 days during the 121-day period beginning 60 days prior to July 13 (the ex-dividend date). The $1,500 Amy receives is subject to preferential 15%/0% treatment. The $1,500 Corey receives, however, is not. Corey did not meet the 60-day holding requirement, so her dividend will be taxed as ordinary income. ■

Qualified dividends are not considered investment income for purposes of determining the investment interest expense deduction. Taxpayers can, however, elect to treat qualified dividends as ordinary income (taxed at regular rates) and include them in investment interest income. Thus, taxpayers subject to an investment interest expense limitation must evaluate the relative benefits of taxing qualified dividends at low rates versus using the dividends as investment income to increase the amount of deductible investment interest expense.

ETHICS & EQUITY Is the Double Tax on Dividends Fair?

As noted in this chapter, the double tax on dividends remains controversial. The tax rate on qualified dividends has, in the past, been as high as 70 percent, and it is possible that the current 15 percent tax rate will be increased when it expires at the end of 2012. Yet, in most countries throughout the world, there is no double tax on dividend income. Many arguments for and against the double tax have been made, usually reflecting the vested interests of the individuals or organizations involved. Arguments supporting repeal of the double tax focus on capital formation and economic stimulus, while those against repeal are based on equity. What do *you* believe? Is the double tax imposed on dividends fair? Why or why not?

LO.5

Evaluate the tax impact of property dividends by computing the shareholder's dividend income, basis in the property received, and the effect on the distributing corporation's E & P and taxable income.

Property Dividends

Although most corporate distributions are cash, a corporation may distribute a **property dividend** for various reasons. The shareholders could want a particular property that is held by the corporation. Similarly, a corporation with low cash reserves may still want to distribute a dividend to its shareholders.

Property distributions have the same impact as distributions of cash except for effects attributable to any difference between the basis and the fair market value of the distributed property. In most situations, distributed property is appreciated, so its sale would result in a gain to the corporation. Distributions of property with a basis that differs from fair market value raise several tax questions.

- For the shareholder:
  - What is the amount of the distribution?
  - What is the basis of the property in the shareholder's hands?
- For the corporation:
  - Is a gain or loss recognized as a result of the distribution?
  - What is the effect of the distribution on E & P?

Property Dividends—Effect on the Shareholder

When a corporation distributes property rather than cash to a shareholder, the amount distributed is measured by the fair market value of the property on the date of distribution.[21] As with a cash distribution, the portion of a property

[21]Section 301 describes the tax treatment of corporate distributions to shareholders.

TAX IN THE NEWS Higher Taxes on Dividends Don't Mean Lower Dividends

The potential expiration of the reduced tax rate on dividends in 2013 is not likely to have much impact on corporations' dividend policies. The sensitivity of some companies to how the market may react to dividend cuts will likely deter them from reducing their dividends. In addition, shareholders who are not subject to individual tax rates, such as pension funds and foreign investors, own a large portion of U.S. equities. Reuvan Avi-Yonah, a professor at the University of Michigan Law School, suggests that during the last decade, companies pandered to foreign hedge fund shareholders by favoring stock redemptions over dividends as a means of paying assets to shareholders. As a result, he argues, the tax cut was not effective in encouraging companies to pay out dividends.

Other research by three accounting professors (Doug Shackelford, Jennifer Blouin, and Jana Raedy) found that the dividend tax cut did lead to larger dividend payouts by firms. However, the effect was greatest when corporate officers and directors held large interests in the company. This suggests that the increased dividend payouts in these companies was motivated by the self-interested behavior of those who set dividend policies. Even if the tax cuts spurred dividend payments by corporations, most academics agree that the effect was not as large as anticipated.

Source: Martin Vaughan, "Higher Taxes May Not Push Firms to Cut Dividends," *Wall Street Journal,* August 30, 2010.

distribution covered by existing E & P is a dividend, and any excess is treated as a return of capital. If the fair market value of the property distributed exceeds the corporation's E & P and the shareholder's basis in the stock investment, a capital gain usually results.

The amount distributed is reduced by any liabilities to which the distributed property is subject immediately before and immediately after the distribution and by any liabilities of the corporation assumed by the shareholder. The basis of the distributed property for the shareholder is the fair market value of the property on the date of the distribution.

THE BIG PICTURE

EXAMPLE 13

Return to the facts of *The Big Picture* on p. 5-1. Lime Corporation distributed property with a $300,000 fair market value and $20,000 adjusted basis to one of its shareholders, Gustavo. The property was subject to a $100,000 mortgage, which Gustavo assumed. As a result, Gustavo has a taxable dividend of $200,000 [$300,000 (fair market value) – $100,000 (liability)]. The basis of the property to Gustavo is $300,000.

EXAMPLE 14

Red Corporation owns 10% of Tan Corporation. Tan has ample E & P to cover any distributions made during the year. One distribution made to Red Corporation consists of a vacant lot with an adjusted basis of $75,000 and a fair market value of $50,000. Red has a taxable dividend of $50,000, and its basis in the lot becomes $50,000. ■

Distributing property that has depreciated in value as a property dividend may reflect poor planning. Note what happens in Example 14. Basis of $25,000 disappears due to the loss (adjusted basis of $75,000, fair market value of $50,000). As an alternative, Tan Corporation could sell the lot and use the loss to reduce its taxes. Then Tan could distribute the $50,000 of proceeds to shareholders.

Property Dividends—Effect on the Corporation

All distributions of appreciated property generate gain to the distributing corporation.[22] In effect, a corporation that distributes gain property is treated as if

[22]Section 311 describes how corporations are taxed on distributions.

TAX IN THE NEWS The Case of the Disappearing Dividend Tax

During the last few years, U.S. banks and offshore hedge funds have developed a novel technique for avoiding the tax on dividends entirely. The strategy involves the use of financial derivatives. A simple version of the strategy is called a dividend swap. In the swap, a U.S. bank buys a block of stock from an offshore hedge fund. The bank and the hedge fund also enter into a derivatives contract. The contract requires the bank to make payments to the hedge fund equal to the total return on the stock (both increases in fair market value and dividends) for a designated time period. These payments equal the income and gain the stock would have provided to the hedge fund if it had continued to own the stock. In exchange for these payments, the hedge fund agrees to pay the bank an amount based on some benchmark interest rate. The hedge fund also agrees that it will pay the bank an amount equal to the loss if the fair market value of the stock declines.

After purchasing the stock from the hedge fund, the bank receives taxable dividend income. For tax purposes, however, the dividend income is completely offset by the expense of payments made to the hedge fund under the derivatives contract. In return, the bank receives compensation from the hedge fund equal to a benchmark interest rate. The overseas hedge fund no longer receives taxable dividend income, and the swap payments received are not subject to U.S. taxation. As a result, taxable dividend income is converted to tax-free income.

Some experts estimate that the strategy has allowed hedge funds to avoid paying more than $1 billion a year in taxes on U.S. dividends. Recent legislation (the Foreign Account Tax Compliance Act of 2009) attacks this approach to avoiding taxes on dividends by treating payments made to the hedge fund as taxable equivalents to dividends.

Source: Kevin E. Packman and Mauricio D. Rivero, "The Foreign Account Tax Compliance Act: Taxpayers Face More Disclosures and Potential Penalties," *Journal of Accountancy*, August 2010.

it had sold the property to the shareholder for its fair market value. However, the distributing corporation does *not* recognize loss on distributions of property.

THE BIG PICTURE

EXAMPLE 15

Return to the facts of *The Big Picture* on p. 5-1. Lime Corporation distributed property with a fair market value of $300,000 and an adjusted basis of $20,000 to Gustavo, one of its shareholders. As a result, Lime recognizes a $280,000 gain on the distribution.

EXAMPLE 16

A corporation distributes land with a basis of $30,000 and a fair market value of $10,000. The corporation does not recognize a loss on the distribution. ■

If the distributed property is subject to a liability in excess of basis or the shareholder assumes such a liability, a special rule applies. For purposes of determining gain on the distribution, the fair market value of the property is treated as not being less than the amount of the liability.[23]

EXAMPLE 17

Assume that the land in Example 16 is subject to a liability of $35,000. The corporation recognizes gain of $5,000 on the distribution. ■

Corporate distributions reduce E & P by the amount of money distributed or by the greater of the fair market value or the adjusted basis of property distributed, less the amount of any liability on the property.[24] E & P is increased by gain recognized on appreciated property distributed as a property dividend.

[23] § 311(b)(2).

[24] §§ 312(a), (b), and (c).

EXAMPLE 18

Crimson Corporation distributes property (basis of $10,000 and fair market value of $20,000) to Brenda, its shareholder. Crimson Corporation recognizes a gain of $10,000. Crimson's E & P is increased by the $10,000 gain and decreased by the $20,000 fair market value of the distribution. Brenda has dividend income of $20,000 (presuming sufficient E & P). ■

EXAMPLE 19

Assume the same facts as in Example 18, except that the adjusted basis of the property in the hands of Crimson Corporation is $25,000. Because loss is not recognized and the adjusted basis is greater than fair market value, E & P is reduced by $25,000. Brenda reports dividend income of $20,000. ■

EXAMPLE 20

Assume the same facts as in Example 19, except that the property is subject to a liability of $6,000. E & P is now reduced by $19,000 [$25,000 (adjusted basis) – $6,000 (liability)]. Brenda has a dividend of $14,000 [$20,000 (amount of the distribution) – $6,000 (liability)], and her basis in the property is $20,000. ■

Under no circumstances can a distribution, whether cash or property, either generate a deficit in E & P or add to a deficit in E & P. Deficits can arise only through corporate losses.

EXAMPLE 21

Teal Corporation has accumulated E & P of $10,000 at the beginning of the current tax year. During the year, it has current E & P of $15,000. At the end of the year, it distributes cash of $30,000 to its sole shareholder, Walter. Teal's E & P at the end of the year is zero. The accumulated E & P of $10,000 is increased by current E & P of $15,000 and reduced $25,000 by the dividend distribution. The remaining $5,000 of the distribution to Walter does not reduce E & P because a distribution cannot generate a deficit in E & P. ■

Constructive Dividends

LO.6

Recognize situations when constructive dividends exist and compute the tax resulting from such dividends.

Any measurable economic benefit conveyed by a corporation to its shareholders can be treated as a dividend for Federal income tax purposes even though it is not formally declared or designated as a dividend. Also, it need not be issued pro rata to all shareholders[25] or satisfy the legal requirements of a dividend. Such a benefit, often described as a **constructive dividend**, is distinguishable from actual corporate distributions of cash and property in form only.

For tax purposes, constructive distributions are treated the same as actual distributions.[26] Thus, corporate shareholders are entitled to the dividends received deduction (see Chapter 2), and other shareholders receive preferential tax rates (0 or 15 percent) through 2012 on qualified constructive dividends. The constructive distribution is taxable as a dividend only to the extent of the corporation's current and accumulated E & P. The burden of proving that the distribution constitutes a return of capital because of inadequate E & P rests with the taxpayer.[27]

Constructive dividend situations usually arise in closely held corporations. Here, the dealings between the parties are less structured, and frequently, formalities are not preserved. The constructive dividend serves as a substitute for actual distributions and is usually intended to accomplish some tax objective not available through the use of direct dividends. The shareholders may be attempting to distribute corporate profits in a form deductible to the corporation.[28] Alternatively, the shareholders may be seeking benefits for themselves while avoiding the recognition of income. Although some constructive dividends are disguised dividends, not all are deliberate attempts to avoid actual and formal dividends; many are inadvertent.

[25]See *Lengsfield v. Comm.*, 57–1 USTC ¶9437, 50 AFTR 1683, 241 F.2d 508 (CA–5, 1957).

[26]*Simon v. Comm.*, 57–2 USTC ¶9989, 52 AFTR 698, 248 F.2d 869 (CA–8, 1957).

[27]*DiZenzo v. Comm.*, 65–2 USTC ¶9518, 16 AFTR 2d 5107, 348 F.2d 122 (CA–2, 1965).

[28]Recall that dividend distributions do not provide the distributing corporation with an income tax deduction, although they do reduce E & P.

Thus, an awareness of the various constructive dividend situations is essential to protect the parties from unanticipated, undesirable tax consequences. The most frequently encountered types of constructive dividends are summarized below.

Shareholder Use of Corporate-Owned Property

A constructive dividend can occur when a shareholder uses corporation property for personal purposes at no cost. Personal use of corporate-owned automobiles, airplanes, yachts, fishing camps, hunting lodges, and other entertainment facilities is commonplace in some closely held corporations. In these situations, the shareholder has dividend income equal to the fair rental value of the property for the period of its personal use.[29]

Bargain Sale of Corporate Property to a Shareholder

Shareholders often purchase property from a corporation at a cost below the fair market value. These bargain sales produce dividend income equal to the difference between the property's fair market value on the date of sale and the amount the shareholder paid for the property.[30] These situations might be avoided by appraising the property on or about the date of the sale. The appraised value should become the price paid by the shareholder.

Bargain Rental of Corporate Property

A bargain rental of corporate property by a shareholder also produces dividend income. Here the measure of the constructive dividend is the excess of the property's fair rental value over the rent actually paid. Again, appraisal data should be used to avoid any questionable situations.

Payments for the Benefit of a Shareholder

If a corporation pays an obligation of a shareholder, the payment is treated as a constructive dividend. The obligation in question need not be legally binding on the shareholder; it may, in fact, be a moral obligation.[31] Forgiveness of shareholder indebtedness by the corporation creates an identical problem.[32] Also, excessive rentals paid by a corporation for the use of shareholder property are treated as constructive dividends.

Unreasonable Compensation

A salary payment to a shareholder-employee that is deemed to be **unreasonable compensation** is frequently treated as a constructive dividend. As a consequence, it is not deductible by the corporation. In determining the reasonableness of salary payments, the following factors are considered:

- The employee's qualifications.
- A comparison of salaries with dividend distributions.
- The prevailing rates of compensation for comparable positions in comparable business concerns.
- The nature and scope of the employee's work.
- The size and complexity of the business.
- A comparison of salaries paid with both gross and net income.
- The taxpayer's salary policy toward all employees.
- For small corporations with a limited number of officers, the amount of compensation paid to the employee in question in previous years.
- Whether a reasonable shareholder would have agreed to the level of compensation paid.[33]

[29] See *Daniel L. Reeves*, 94 TCM 287, T.C.Memo. 2007–273.

[30] Reg. § 1.301–1(j).

[31] *Montgomery Engineering Co. v. U.S.*, 64–2 USTC ¶9618, 13 AFTR 2d 1747, 230 F.Supp. 838 (D.Ct. N.J., 1964), *aff'd* in 65–1 USTC ¶9368, 15 AFTR 2d 746, 344 F.2d 996 (CA–3, 1965).

[32] Reg. § 1.301–1(m).

[33] All but the final factor in this list are identified in *Mayson Manufacturing Co. v. Comm.*, 49–2 USTC ¶9467, 38 AFTR 1028, 178 F.2d 115 (CA–6, 1949).

The last factor above, known as the "reasonable investor test," is a relatively new development in the law on reasonable compensation.[34] Its use by the courts has been inconsistent. In some cases, the Seventh Circuit Court of Appeals has relied solely on the reasonable investor test in determining reasonableness, whereas the Tenth Circuit Court of Appeals has largely ignored this factor. Other Federal circuits have used an approach that considers all of the factors in the list.[35]

Loans to Shareholders

Advances to shareholders that are not bona fide loans are constructive dividends. Whether an advance qualifies as a bona fide loan is a question of fact to be determined in light of the particular circumstances. Factors considered in determining whether the advance is a bona fide loan include the following:[36]

- Whether the advance is on open account or is evidenced by a written instrument.
- Whether the shareholder furnished collateral or other security for the advance.
- How long the advance has been outstanding.
- Whether any repayments have been made.
- The shareholder's ability to repay the advance.
- The shareholder's use of the funds (e.g., payment of routine bills versus nonrecurring, extraordinary expenses).
- The regularity of the advances.
- The dividend-paying history of the corporation.

Even when a corporation makes a bona fide loan to a shareholder, a constructive dividend may be triggered, equal to the amount of imputed (forgone) interest on the loan.[37] Imputed interest equals the amount by which the interest paid by the Federal government on new borrowings, compounded semiannually, exceeds the interest charged on the loan. When the imputed interest provision applies, the shareholder is deemed to have made an interest payment to the corporation equal to the amount of imputed interest and the corporation is deemed to have repaid the imputed interest to the shareholder through a constructive dividend. As a result, the corporation receives interest income and makes a nondeductible dividend payment, and the shareholder has taxable dividend income that might be offset with an interest deduction.

EXAMPLE 22

Mallard Corporation lends its principal shareholder, Henry, $100,000 on January 2 of the current year. The loan is interest-free and payable on demand. On December 31, the imputed interest rules are applied. Assuming that the Federal rate is 6%, compounded semiannually, the amount of imputed interest is $6,090. This amount is deemed paid by Henry to Mallard in the form of interest. Mallard is then deemed to return the amount to Henry as a constructive dividend. Thus, Henry has dividend income of $6,090, which might be offset with a deduction for the interest paid to Mallard. Mallard has interest income of $6,090 for the interest received, with no offsetting deduction for the dividend payment. ■

Loans to a Corporation by Shareholders

Shareholder loans to a corporation may be reclassified as equity because the debt has too many features of stock. Any interest and principal payments made by the corporation to the shareholder are then treated as constructive dividends. This

[34]For example, see *Alpha Medical, Inc. v. Comm.*, 99–1 USTC ¶50,461, 83 AFTR 2d 99–697, 172 F.3d 942 (CA–6, 1999).

[35]See *Vitamin Village, Inc.*, 94 TCM 277, T.C.Memo. 2007–272, for an example of a case that uses both the reasonable investor test and other factors.

[36]*Fin Hay Realty Co. v. U.S.*, 68–2 USTC ¶9438, 22 AFTR 2d 5004, 398 F.2d 694 (CA–3, 1968). But see *Nariman Teymourian*, 90 TCM 352, T.C.Memo. 2005–302, for an example of how good planning can avoid constructive dividends in the shareholder loan context.

[37]See § 7872.

topic was covered more thoroughly in the discussion of "thin capitalization" in Chapter 4.

Stock Dividends and Stock Rights

LO.7

Compute the tax arising from receipt of stock dividends and stock rights and the shareholder's basis in the stock and stock rights received.

Stock Dividends—§ 305

Historically, **stock dividends** were excluded from income on the theory that the ownership interest of the shareholder was unchanged as a result of the distribution.[38] Recognizing that some distributions of stock could affect ownership interests, the 1954 Code included a provision (§ 305) taxing stock dividends where (1) the stockholder could elect to receive either stock or property or (2) the stock dividends were in discharge of preference dividends. However, because this provision applied to a narrow range of transactions, corporations were able to develop an assortment of alternative methods that circumvented taxation and still affected shareholders' proportionate interests in the corporation.[39] In response, the scope of § 305 was expanded.

In its current state, the provisions of § 305 are based on the proportionate interest concept. As a general rule, stock dividends are excluded from income if they are pro rata distributions of stock or stock rights, paid on common stock. Listed below are five exceptions to this general rule. Each represents a disproportionate distribution situation in which the stock distribution may be taxed.

1. Distributions payable in either stock or property at the election of the shareholder.
2. Distributions of property to some shareholders with a corresponding increase in the proportionate interest of other shareholders in either assets or E & P of the distributing corporation.
3. Distributions of preferred stock to some common shareholders and of common stock to other common shareholders.
4. Distributions of stock to preferred shareholders. However, changes in the conversion ratio of convertible preferred stock to account for a stock dividend or stock split are not taxable in some circumstances.
5. Distributions of convertible preferred stock unless it can be shown that the distribution will not result in a disproportionate distribution.

Holders of convertible securities are considered shareholders. Thus, under the second exception above, when interest is paid on convertible debentures and stock dividends are paid on common stock, the stock dividends are taxable. This result is avoided if the conversion ratio or conversion price is adjusted to reflect the price of the stock dividend.[40]

If stock dividends are not taxable, the corporation's E & P is not reduced.[41] If the stock dividends are taxable, the distributing corporation treats the distribution in the same manner as any other taxable property dividend.

If a stock dividend is taxable, the shareholder's basis for the newly received shares is fair market value and the holding period starts on the date of receipt. If a stock dividend is not taxable, the basis of the stock on which the dividend is distributed is reallocated.[42] If the dividend shares are identical to these formerly held shares, basis for the old stock is reallocated by dividing the taxpayer's cost in the old stock by the total number of shares. If the dividend stock is not identical to the underlying shares (e.g., a stock dividend of preferred on common), basis is determined by allocating the basis of the formerly held shares between the old and new stock according to the fair market value of each. The holding period includes the holding period of the formerly held stock.[43]

[38]See *Eisner v. Macomber*, 1 USTC ¶32, 3 AFTR 3020, 40 S.Ct. 189 (USSC, 1920).

[39]See "Stock Dividends," Senate Report 91–552, 1969–3 C.B. 519.

[40]See Reg. § 1.305–3(d) for illustrations of how to compute required adjustments of conversion ratios or prices.

[41]§ 312(d)(1).

[42]§ 307(a).

[43]§ 1223(5).

TAX IN THE NEWS Repatriation Dividend Tax Holidays

As described in the "Global Tax Issues" feature earlier in this chapter, the tax law requires a U.S. parent corporation to recognize some of the unrepatriated earnings of a controlled foreign corporation (CFC) as income. The U.S. parent's basis in the CFC stock is increased by the amount of the taxed but unrepatriated earnings. Subsequently, when cash or property is actually paid to the U.S. parent (i.e., when taxed earnings are repatriated), no income results. Thus, the CFC rules preclude some deferral but do not lead to double taxation.

In an effort to boost the economy, in 2004, Congress introduced a temporary one-year tax holiday for CFCs. The provision allowed an 85 percent deduction for cash dividends paid from untaxed earnings by CFCs to U.S. corporate shareholders. For many corporations, this provision reduced the tax on repatriated foreign earnings from 35 percent to 5.25 percent. Studies recently completed by the National Bureau of Economic Research, the Congressional Research Service, and private groups have concluded that the legislation did not lead to increased investment or job growth in the United States.

Recently, bills were introduced in both the House and Senate to allow a second repatriation dividend tax holiday. Proponents for a second tax holiday on repatriation dividends argue that the holiday would enable corporations to bring large sums of cash back to the United States, thereby allowing them to create jobs and expand their domestic businesses. Opponents point to the failure of the 2004 tax holiday to create domestic investment and job growth. A recent report by the Senate Permanent Subcommittee on Investigations also casts a shadow on the tax holiday bills, suggesting that the bills might create an expectation that more holidays will be allowed in the future. If so, an incentive will exist for companies to shift profits offshore and then wait for the next tax holiday before bringing the money back to the United States. Thus, a new tax holiday might ultimately reduce domestic investment rather than enhance it.

Source: Adapted from Editorial, "No Holiday," *New York Times*, October 23, 2011, p. A22.

EXAMPLE 23

Gail bought 1,000 shares of common stock two years ago for $10,000. In the current tax year, Gail receives 10 shares of common stock as a nontaxable stock dividend. Gail's basis of $10,000 is divided by 1,010. Each share of stock has a basis of $9.90 instead of the pre-dividend $10 basis. ■

EXAMPLE 24

Assume that Gail received, instead, a nontaxable preferred stock dividend of 100 shares. The preferred stock has a fair market value of $1,000, and the common stock, on which the preferred is distributed, has a fair market value of $19,000. After the receipt of the stock dividend, the basis of the common stock is $9,500, and the basis of the preferred is $500, computed as follows:

Fair market value of common	$19,000
Fair market value of preferred	1,000
	$20,000
Basis of common: 19/20 × $10,000	$ 9,500
Basis of preferred: 1/20 × $10,000	$ 500

■

Stock Rights

The rules for determining taxability of **stock rights** are identical to those for determining taxability of stock dividends. If the rights are taxable, the recipient has income equal to the fair market value of the rights. The fair market value then becomes the shareholder-distributee's basis in the rights.[44] If the rights are exercised, the holding period for the new stock begins on the date the rights (whether taxable or nontaxable) are exercised. The basis of the new stock is the basis of the rights plus the amount of any other consideration given.

[44]Reg. § 1.305–1(b).

If stock rights are not taxable and the value of the rights is less than 15 percent of the value of the old stock, the basis of the rights is zero. However, the shareholder may elect to have some of the basis in the formerly held stock allocated to the rights.[45] The election is made by attaching a statement to the shareholder's return for the year in which the rights are received.[46] If the fair market value of the rights is 15 percent or more of the value of the old stock and the rights are exercised or sold, the shareholder *must* allocate some of the basis in the formerly held stock to the rights.

EXAMPLE 25

A corporation with common stock outstanding declares a nontaxable dividend payable in rights to subscribe to common stock. Each right entitles the holder to purchase one share of stock for $90. One right is issued for every two shares of stock owned. Fred owns 400 shares of stock purchased two years ago for $15,000. At the time of the distribution of the rights, the market value of the common stock is $100 per share, and the market value of the rights is $8 per right. Fred receives 200 rights. He exercises 100 rights and sells the remaining 100 rights three months later for $9 per right.

Fred need not allocate the cost of the original stock to the rights because the value of the rights is less than 15% of the value of the stock ($1,600 ÷ $40,000 = 4%). If Fred does not allocate his original stock basis to the rights, the tax consequences are as follows:

- Basis of the new stock is $9,000 [$90 (exercise price) × 100 (shares)]. The holding period of the new stock begins on the date the stock was purchased.
- Sale of the rights produces long-term capital gain of $900 [$9 (sales price) × 100 (rights)]. The holding period of the rights starts with the date the original 400 shares of stock were acquired.

If Fred elects to allocate basis to the rights, the tax consequences are as follows:

- Basis of the stock is $14,423 [$40,000 (value of stock) ÷ $41,600 (value of rights and stock) × $15,000 (cost of stock)].
- Basis of the rights is $577 [$1,600 (value of rights) ÷ $41,600 (value of rights and stock) × $15,000 (cost of stock)].
- When Fred exercises the rights, his basis for the new stock will be $9,288.50 [$9,000 (cost) + $288.50 (basis for 100 rights)].
- Sale of the rights would produce a long-term capital gain of $611.50 [$900 (sales price) − $288.50 (basis in the remaining 100 rights)]. ■

5.4 Tax Planning

LO.8

Structure corporate distributions in a manner that minimizes the tax consequences to the parties involved.

Corporate Distributions

The following points are especially important when planning for corporate distributions.

- Because E & P is the pool of funds from which dividends may be distributed, its periodic determination is essential to corporate planning. Thus, an E & P account should be established and maintained, particularly if the possibility exists that a corporate distribution might be a return of capital.
- Accumulated E & P is the sum of all past years' current E & P. Because there is no statute of limitations on the computation of E & P, the IRS can redetermine a corporation's current E & P for a tax year long since passed. Such a change affects accumulated E & P and has a direct impact on the taxability of current distributions to shareholders.
- Distributions can be planned to avoid or minimize dividend exposure.

[45] § 307(b)(1).

[46] Reg. § 1.307–2.

EXAMPLE 26

Flicker Corporation has accumulated E & P of $100,000 as of January 1 of the current year. During the year, it expects to have earnings from operations of $80,000 and to sell an asset for a loss of $100,000. Thus, it anticipates a current E & P deficit of $20,000. Flicker Corporation also expects to make a cash distribution of $60,000. The best approach is to recognize the loss as soon as possible and, immediately thereafter, make the cash distribution to the shareholders. Suppose these two steps take place on January 1. Because the current E & P has a deficit, the accumulated E & P account must be updated (refer to Example 11 in this chapter). Thus, at the time of the distribution, the combined E & P balance is zero [$100,000 (beginning balance in accumulated E & P) − $100,000 (existing deficit in current E & P)], and the $60,000 distribution to the shareholders constitutes a return of capital. Current deficits are deemed to accrue pro rata throughout the year unless the parties can prove otherwise; here, they can. ■

EXAMPLE 27

After several unprofitable years, Darter Corporation has a deficit in accumulated E & P of $100,000 as of January 1, 2012. Starting in 2012, Darter expects to generate annual E & P of $50,000 for the next four years and would like to distribute this amount to its shareholders. The corporation's cash position (for dividend purposes) will correspond to the current E & P generated. Consider the following two distribution schedules:

1. On December 31 of 2012, 2013, 2014, and 2015, Darter Corporation distributes cash of $50,000.
2. On December 31 of 2013 and 2015, Darter Corporation distributes cash of $100,000.

The two alternatives are illustrated below.

Year	Accumulated E & P (First of Year)	Current E & P	Distribution	Amount of Dividend
		Alternative 1		
2012	($100,000)	$50,000	$ 50,000	$50,000
2013	(100,000)	50,000	50,000	50,000
2014	(100,000)	50,000	50,000	50,000
2015	(100,000)	50,000	50,000	50,000
		Alternative 2		
2012	($100,000)	$50,000	$ –0–	$ –0–
2013	(50,000)	50,000	100,000	50,000
2014	(50,000)	50,000	–0–	–0–
2015	–0–	50,000	100,000	50,000

Alternative 1 produces $200,000 of dividend income because each $50,000 distribution is fully covered by current E & P. Alternative 2, however, produces only $100,000 of dividend income for the shareholders. The remaining $100,000 is a return of capital. Why? At the time Darter Corporation made its first distribution of $100,000 on December 31, 2013, it had a deficit of $50,000 in accumulated E & P (the original deficit of $100,000 is reduced by the $50,000 of current E & P from 2012). Consequently, the $100,000 distribution yields a $50,000 dividend (the current E & P for 2013), and $50,000 is treated as a return of capital. As of January 1, 2014, Darter's accumulated E & P now has a deficit balance of $50,000 because a distribution cannot increase a deficit in E & P. After adding the remaining $50,000 of current E & P from 2014, the balance on January 1, 2015, is zero. Thus, the second distribution of $100,000, made on December 31, 2015, also yields $50,000 of dividends (the current E & P for 2015) and a $50,000 return of capital. ■

Planning for Qualified Dividends

Retirement Plans

The reduced tax rates available to individual taxpayers on net capital gain and qualified dividend income reinforce the inadvisability of funding retirement accounts with stock. Because income in § 401(k) plans and IRAs is not taxed when earned, the benefits of the lower tax rates on these forms of income are lost. Instead, distributions from the plans are taxed at ordinary income tax rates.

Individual Alternative Minimum Tax

The lower rates on dividends and long-term capital gains through 2012 apply under both the regular income tax and the alternative minimum tax. This increases the exposure of many individuals to the alternative minimum tax, particularly those with significant income from dividends or long-term capital gain. As a result, individual taxpayers who pay the alternative minimum tax should reconsider their investment strategies to manage the mix of ordinary income, dividend income, and capital gain.

Closely Held Corporations

Closely held corporations have considerable discretion regarding their dividend policies. In the past, the double tax result provided strong motivation to avoid the payment of dividends. Instead, the incentive was to bail out corporate profits in a manner that provided tax benefits to the corporation. Hence, liberal use was made of compensation, loan, and lease arrangements because salaries, interest, and rent are deductible. Under current law, however, shareholders prefer dividends because salaries, interest, and rent are fully taxed while dividends receive preferential treatment. Thus, the question becomes this: *Should the corporation or the shareholders benefit?* In general, the best strategy considers the tax consequences to both parties.

EXAMPLE 28

Consider a corporation paying tax at the 34% rate and an individual shareholder in the 35% tax bracket. A deductible $10,000 payment to the shareholder will *save* the corporation $3,400 in tax, resulting in an after-tax cost of $6,600. The shareholder will pay $3,500 in tax, resulting in after-tax income of $6,500. This creates a joint tax burden of $100 ($3,500 tax paid by the shareholder − $3,400 tax saved by the corporation). If, instead, the corporation paid a $10,000 qualified dividend (subject to a 15% tax rate) to the shareholder, no tax savings would be realized by the corporation, resulting in an after-tax cost of $10,000. The shareholder would owe $1,500 in taxes, leaving $8,500 of income. Considering both the corporation and the shareholder, a dividend creates $1,400 more tax liability than a deductible payment, so the deductible payment is more tax-efficient. ■

In Example 28, when the deductible payment is made, the shareholder bears an increased tax burden of $2,000 ($3,500 tax due from the deductible payment − $1,500 tax due from the dividend) while the corporation saves $3,400 ($3,400 tax saved because of the deductible payment − $0 tax saved because of the dividend). Both parties could actually benefit if the corporation transfers part of its benefit to the shareholder through a larger deductible payment.

EXAMPLE 29

Assume the same facts as in Example 28, except that the corporation pays a $14,000 deductible payment. In this case, the corporation will save $4,760 ($14,000 × 34%) in tax, resulting in an after-tax cost of $9,240. From the corporation's perspective, this is preferable to a $10,000 dividend because it costs $760 less after tax ($10,000 dividend cost − $9,240 after-tax cost of a $14,000 deductible payment). The shareholder will pay taxes of $4,900 on the deductible payment, resulting in after-tax income of $9,100. The shareholder will also prefer this payment to a dividend because it generates $600 more after-tax income ($9,100 − $8,500 from a dividend). ■

Thus, if properly structured, deductible payments by the corporation to the shareholder still appear to be preferable to dividends in most situations (unless the corporation faces a low tax rate). The benefit of this strategy will be even greater if the shareholder is paying alternative minimum tax.

Constructive Dividends

Tax planning can be particularly effective in avoiding constructive dividend situations. Shareholders should try to structure their dealings with the corporation on an arm's length basis. For example, reasonable rent should be paid for the use of corporate property, and a fair price should be paid for its purchase. The parties should make every effort to support the amount involved with appraisal data or market information obtained from reliable sources at or near the time of the transaction. Dealings between shareholders and a closely held corporation should be as formal as possible. In the case of loans to shareholders, for example, the parties should provide for an adequate rate of interest and written evidence of the debt. Shareholders also should establish and follow a realistic repayment schedule.

If shareholders want to bail out corporate profits in a form deductible to the corporation, a balanced mix of the possible alternatives lessens the risk of constructive dividend treatment. Rent for the use of shareholder property, interest on amounts borrowed from shareholders, or salaries for services rendered by shareholders are all feasible substitutes for dividend distributions. Overdoing any one approach, however, may attract the attention of the IRS. Too much interest, for example, may mean that the corporation is thinly capitalized, and some of the debt may be reclassified as equity investment.

Much can be done to protect against the disallowance of unreasonable compensation. Example 30 is an illustration, all too common in a family corporation, of what *not* to do.

EXAMPLE 30

Bob Cole wholly owns Eagle Corporation. Corporate employees and annual salaries include Mrs. Cole ($120,000), Cole Jr. ($80,000), Bob Cole ($640,000), and Ed ($320,000). The operation of Eagle Corporation is shared about equally between Bob Cole and Ed, who is an unrelated party. Mrs. Cole performed significant services for Eagle during its formative years, but now merely attends the annual meeting of the board of directors. Cole Jr., Bob Cole's son, is a full-time student and occasionally signs papers for the corporation in his capacity as treasurer. Eagle Corporation has not distributed a dividend for 10 years although it has accumulated substantial E & P. Mrs. Cole, Cole Jr., and Bob Cole run the risk of a finding of unreasonable compensation, based on the following factors:

- Mrs. Cole's salary is vulnerable unless proof is available that some or all of her $120,000 annual salary is payment for services rendered to the corporation in prior years and that she was underpaid for those years.[47]
- Cole Jr.'s salary is also vulnerable; he does not appear to earn the $80,000 paid to him by the corporation. Neither Cole Jr. nor Mrs. Cole is a shareholder, but each one's relationship to Bob Cole is enough of a tie-in to raise the unreasonable compensation issue.
- Bob Cole's salary appears susceptible to challenge. Why is he receiving $320,000 more than Ed when it appears that they share equally in the operation of the corporation?
- The fact that Eagle Corporation has not distributed dividends over the past 10 years, even though it is capable of doing so, increases the likelihood of a constructive dividend. ■

What could have been done to improve the tax position of the parties in Example 30? Mrs. Cole and Cole Jr. are not entitled to a salary as neither seems to be performing any services for the corporation. Paying them a salary simply aggravates the problem. The IRS is more apt to consider *all* the family members' salaries excessive under the circumstances. Bob Cole should probably reduce his compensation to correspond with that paid to Ed. He can then attempt to distribute corporate earnings to himself in some other form.

[47]See, for example, *R.J. Nicoll Co.*, 59 T.C. 37 (1972).

Paying some dividends to Bob Cole would also help alleviate the problem raised in Example 30. The IRS has been successful in denying a deduction for salary paid to a shareholder-employee, even when the payment was reasonable, in a situation where the corporation had not distributed any dividends.[48] Most courts, however, have not denied deductions for compensation solely because a dividend was not paid. A better approach is to compare an employee's compensation with the level of compensation prevalent in the particular industry.

The corporation can provide *indirect* compensation to Bob Cole by paying expenses that benefit him personally, but are nevertheless deductible to the corporation. For example, premiums paid by the corporation for sickness, accident, and hospitalization insurance for Bob Cole are deductible to the corporation and nontaxable to him.[49] Any payments under the policy are not taxable to Bob Cole unless they exceed his medical expenses.[50] The corporation can also pay for travel and entertainment expenses incurred by Cole on behalf of the corporation. If these expenses are primarily for the benefit of the corporation, Bob Cole will not recognize any taxable income and the corporation will receive a deduction.[51]

When testing for reasonableness, the IRS looks at the total compensation package, including indirect compensation payments to a shareholder-employee. Thus, indirect payments must not be overlooked.

ETHICS & EQUITY Forgetting About the Past

Michael is the CEO and sole shareholder of Cormorant Corporation. Michael recently approached you, a tax adviser in private practice, about taking on Cormorant as a client.

In your initial interview with Michael, you learn that Cormorant claimed a $1 million deduction for his salary last year. In an audit last month, the IRS disallowed $800,000 of the salary deduction as unreasonable compensation. In the future, Cormorant fully intends to take the same salary deduction of $1 million for Michael, given his active role in the organization. In short, Cormorant believes that the salary is appropriate.

Should you accept Cormorant Corporation as a new client? If so, can you claim the same salary deduction of $1 million?

EXAMPLE 31

Cora, the president and sole shareholder of Willet Corporation, is paid an annual salary of $100,000 by the corporation. Cora would like to draw funds from the corporation, but is concerned that additional salary payments might cause the IRS to contend that her salary is unreasonable. Cora does not want Willet to pay any dividends. She also wants to donate $50,000 to her alma mater to establish scholarships for needy students. In this situation, Willet Corporation can make the contribution on Cora's behalf. The payment clearly benefits Cora, but she will not be taxed on the amount of the contribution,[52] and Willet can take a charitable contribution deduction for the payment. ■

EXAMPLE 32

Assume in Example 31 that Cora has made an individual pledge to the university to provide $50,000 for scholarships for needy students. Willet Corporation satisfies Cora's pledge by paying the $50,000 to the university, but she will be taxed on the amount.[53] In this context, the $50,000 payment to the university may be treated as *indirect* compensation to Cora. In determining whether Cora's salary is unreasonable, both the *direct* payment of $100,000 and the *indirect* $50,000 payment will be considered—a total compensation package of $150,000. ■

[48] *McCandless Tile Service v. U.S.*, 70–1 USTC ¶9284, 25 AFTR 2d 70–870, 422 F.2d 1336 (Ct.Cls., 1970). The court in *McCandless* concluded that a return on equity of 15% of net profits was reasonable.

[49] Reg. § 1.162–10.

[50] The medical reimbursement plan must meet certain nondiscrimination requirements of § 105(h)(2).

[51] Reg. § 1.62–2(c)(4).

[52] *Henry J. Knott*, 67 T.C. 681 (1977).

[53] *Schalk Chemical Co. v. Comm.*, 62–1 USTC ¶9496, 9 AFTR 2d 1579, 304 F.2d 48 (CA–9, 1962).

REFOCUS ON THE BIG PICTURE

TAXING CORPORATE DISTRIBUTIONS

A number of factors affect the tax treatment of Lime Corporation's distributions. The amount of current and accumulated E & P (which differ from the financial reporting concept of retained earnings) partially determines the tax effect on the shareholders. Given that Lime Corporation has had a highly profitable year, it is likely that there is sufficient current E & P to cover the distributions. If so, they are dividends to the shareholders rather than a return of capital. Orange Corporation receives $200,000 of dividend income that is mostly offset by the dividends received deduction. The amount of the offsetting deduction depends on the ownership percentage that Orange has in Lime. Gustavo has $200,000 of dividend income (i.e., $300,000 value of the land less the $100,000 mortgage). Assuming that Lime is a domestic corporation and that Gustavo has held his stock for the entire year, the land is a qualified dividend. As a result, the dividend is either tax-free (if Gustavo has a marginal rate of 10 or 15 percent) or subject to a 15 percent tax rate. Gustavo's basis in the land is its fair market value at distribution, or $300,000.

From Lime Corporation's perspective, the distribution of appreciated property creates a deemed gain. Thus, a $280,000 gain results ($300,000 fair market value of the land less its adjusted basis of $20,000). While the gain increases Lime's E & P, the distributions to the shareholders reduce it by $200,000 for the cash and $200,000 for the land ($300,000 fair market value reduced by the $100,000 mortgage).

What If?

What if current E & P is less than the cash and land distributed to the shareholders? Current E & P is applied pro rata to the cash and the land. Because the amounts received by the two shareholders are equal ($200,000 each), the current E & P applied is taxed as a dividend and is treated as described above. To the extent the distributions are not covered by current E & P, accumulated E & P is then applied in a pro rata fashion (because both distributions were made on December 31). However, Lime probably has a deficit in accumulated E & P. As a result, the remaining amounts distributed to the two shareholders are first a tax-free recovery of stock basis, and any excess is taxed as a sale of the stock (probably classified as capital gain).

KEY TERMS

Accumulated E & P, 5-6
Constructive dividend, 5-15
Current E & P, 5-6
Earnings and profits (E & P), 5-2
Property dividend, 5-12
Qualified dividends, 5-11
Stock dividends, 5-18
Stock rights, 5-19
Unreasonable compensation, 5-16

DISCUSSION QUESTIONS

1. **LO.2** What is meant by the term *earnings and profits*?
2. **LO.1** What factors affect the tax treatment of corporate distributions?

3. **LO.2** In determining Blue Corporation's current E & P for 2012, how should taxable income be adjusted as a result of the following transactions?
   a. A capital loss carryover from 2012, fully used in 2013.
   b. Nondeductible meal expenses in 2012.
   c. Interest on municipal bonds received in 2012.
   d. Nondeductible lobbying expenses in 2012.
   e. Loss on a sale between related parties in 2012.
   f. Federal income tax refund received in 2012.

4. **LO.5** Discuss the impact each of the following has on generating or adding to a deficit in E & P.
   a. The distribution of a property dividend, where the basis of the property exceeds its fair market value.
   b. An operating loss of the corporation.

5. **LO.2** In what ways does the computation of E & P require more conservative accounting than the computation of taxable income?

6. **LO.3** Describe the effect of a distribution in a year when the distributing corporation has:
   a. A deficit in accumulated E & P and a positive amount in current E & P.
   b. A positive amount in accumulated E & P and a deficit in current E & P.
   c. A deficit in both current and accumulated E & P.
   d. A positive amount in both current and accumulated E & P.

7. **LO.3** A calendar year corporation has substantial accumulated E & P, but it expects to incur a deficit in current E & P for the year due to significant losses in the last half of the year. A cash distribution to its shareholders on January 1 should result in a return of capital. Comment on the validity of this statement.

8. **LO.4** Discuss the rationale for the reduced tax rates on dividends paid to individuals.

Issue ID

9. **LO.1, 2, 3, 4, 5** Red Corporation distributes $500,000 in cash to each of its three shareholders: Jack, Susan, and Orange Corporation. What factors must be considered when determining how the distribution is treated for tax purposes by the shareholders?

Issue ID

10. **LO.5** Assume the same facts as in Question 9, except that property is distributed. What factors must be considered when determining how the distribution is treated for tax purposes by Red Corporation?

11. **LO.5** Ochre Corporation's board of directors decides to distribute property to its shareholders rather than pay a cash dividend. Why might Ochre's board make this decision?

Decision Making

12. **LO.5** Seagull Corporation owns three machines that it uses in its business. It no longer needs two of these machines and is considering distributing them to its two shareholders as a property dividend. All three machines have a fair market value of $40,000 each. The basis of each machine is as follows: Machine A, $47,000; Machine B, $40,000; and Machine C, $32,000. The corporation has asked you for advice. What do you recommend?

13. **LO.5** What is the effect on the corporation when it makes a property distribution?

Issue ID

14. **LO.5** Tangerine Corporation is considering a property distribution to its shareholders. If appreciated property is to be used, does it matter to Tangerine whether the property distributed is a long-term capital asset or depreciable property subject to recapture? Would your answer differ if the property distributed has a fair market value less than the adjusted basis? Explain.

15. **LO.6** To be treated as a dividend for tax purposes, must a corporation's distribution to its shareholders meet the legal requirements of a dividend, be formally declared, or be issued pro rata to all shareholders? Discuss.

Issue ID

16. **LO.6** Judy is the president and sole shareholder of Parakeet Corporation. She is paid an annual salary of $600,000, while her son, Mike, the company's chief financial officer, is paid a salary of $375,000. Mike works for Parakeet on a part-time basis and spends most of his time training for triathlons. Parakeet advances $80,000 to Judy as an interest-free loan. What are the tax issues?

17. **LO.6** Whether compensation paid to a corporate employee is reasonable is a question of fact to be determined from the surrounding circumstances. How would the resolution of this problem be affected by each of the following factors?
    a. The employee owns no stock but is the mother-in-law of the sole shareholder.
    b. The shareholder-employee does not have a college degree.
    c. The shareholder-employee works 40 hours per week for another unrelated employer.
    d. The shareholder-employee was underpaid for services during the formative period of the corporation.
    e. The corporation has never paid a dividend.
    f. Year-end bonuses are paid to all employees, but officer-shareholders receive disproportionately larger bonuses.

18. **LO.4, 8** Orange Corporation would like to transfer excess cash to its sole shareholder, Danielle, who is also an employee. Danielle is in the 28% tax bracket, and Orange is in the 34% bracket. Because Danielle's contribution to the business is substantial, Orange believes that a $50,000 bonus in the current year is reasonable compensation and should be deductible by the corporation. However, Orange is considering paying Danielle a $50,000 dividend because the tax rate on dividends is lower than the tax rate on compensation. Is Orange correct in believing that a dividend is the better choice? Why or why not? **Decision Making**

19. **LO.6, 8** Green Corporation has several employees. Their names and salaries are listed below.

Samantha	$600,000
Chris (Samantha's daughter)	100,000
Joey (Samantha's son)	100,000
Jack (an unrelated third party)	250,000

Chris and Joey are the only shareholders of Green Corporation. Samantha and Jack share equally in the management of the company's operations. Chris and Joey are both full-time college students at a university 200 miles away. Green has substantial E & P and has never distributed a dividend. Discuss problems related to Green's salary arrangement.

20. **LO.6, 8** Condor Corporation pays its president and sole shareholder, Katrina, an annual salary of $500,000. Katrina wants to avoid dividends because of the double tax result. However, she is concerned that if she were to receive any more salary, the IRS might treat it as unreasonable compensation and a constructive dividend. Instead, Katrina is thinking of having Condor contribute $150,000 to her favorite charity. Would there be a problem if Katrina makes a pledge for this amount and Condor pays it on her behalf? Explain.

21. **LO.7** Your client, Raptor Corporation, declares a dividend permitting its common shareholders to elect to receive 9 shares of cumulative preferred stock or 3 additional shares of Raptor common stock for every 10 shares of common stock held. Raptor has only common stock outstanding (fair market value of $45 per share). One shareholder elects to receive preferred stock, while the remaining shareholders choose the common stock. Raptor asks you whether the shareholders have any taxable income on the receipt of the stock. Prepare a letter to Raptor and a memo for the file regarding this matter. Raptor's address is 1812 S. Camino Seco, Tucson, AZ 85710. **Communications**

22. **LO.7** Describe the rationale underlying the tax treatment of stock distributions.

23. **LO.7** How are nontaxable and taxable stock rights handled for tax purposes?

PROBLEMS

24. **LO.1, 4** At the start of the current year, Indigo Corporation (a calendar year taxpayer) has accumulated E & P of $240,000. Indigo's current E & P is $160,000, and at the end of the year, it distributes $440,000 ($220,000 each) to its equal shareholders, Sarah and Mason. Their basis in the stock is $8,000 for Sarah and $32,000 for Mason. How is the distribution treated for tax purposes?

25. **LO.2** Capon Corporation, a calendar year taxpayer, receives dividend income of $600,000 from a corporation in which it holds a 12% interest. Capon also receives interest income of $90,000 from municipal bonds. (The municipality used the proceeds from the bond issue to construct a library.) Capon borrowed funds to purchase the municipal bonds and pays $50,000 of interest on the loan. Excluding these items, Capon's taxable income is $1.2 million.
    a. What is Capon Corporation's taxable income after these items are taken into account?
    b. What is Capon Corporation's accumulated E & P at the start of next year if its beginning balance this year is $400,000?

26. **LO.1, 2, 3** On September 30, Jade Corporation, a calendar year taxpayer, sold a parcel of land (basis of $300,000) for a $900,000 note. The note is payable in five installments, with the first payment due next year. Because Jade did not elect out of the installment method, none of the $600,000 gain is taxed this year.

    Jade Corporation had a $400,000 deficit in accumulated E & P at the beginning of the year. Before considering the effect of the land sale, Jade had a deficit in current E & P of $100,000.

    Robert, the sole shareholder of Jade, has a basis of $150,000 in his stock. If Jade distributes $950,000 to Robert on December 31, how much income must he report for tax purposes?

27. **LO.2** Sparrow Corporation (a calendar year, accrual basis taxpayer) had the following transactions in 2012, its second year of operation.

Taxable income	$330,000
Federal income tax liability paid	112,000
Tax-exempt interest income	5,000
Meals and entertainment expenses (total)	3,000
Premiums paid on key employee life insurance	3,500
Increase in cash surrender value attributable to life insurance premiums	700
Proceeds from key employee life insurance policy	130,000
Cash surrender value of life insurance policy at distribution	20,000
Excess of capital losses over capital gains	13,000
MACRS deduction	26,000
Straight-line depreciation using ADS lives	16,000
Section 179 expense elected during 2011	100,000
Dividends received from domestic corporations (less than 20% owned)	25,000

    Sparrow uses the LIFO inventory method, and its LIFO recapture amount increased by $10,000 during 2012. In addition, Sparrow sold property on installment during 2011. The property was sold for $40,000 and had an adjusted basis at sale of $32,000. During 2012, Sparrow received a $15,000 payment on the installment sale. Finally, assume that no additional first-year depreciation was claimed. Compute Sparrow's current E & P.

28. **LO.2** In each of the following independent situations, indicate the effect on taxable income and E & P, stating the amount of any increase (or decrease) as a result of the transaction. Assume that E & P has already been increased by taxable income.

	Transaction	Taxable Income Increase (Decrease)	E & P Increase (Decrease)
a.	Realized gain of $80,000 on involuntary conversion of building ($10,000 of gain is recognized).	______	______
b.	Mining exploration costs incurred on May 1 of the current year; $24,000 is deductible from current-year taxable income.	______	______
c.	Sale of equipment to unrelated third party for $240,000; basis is $120,000 (no election out of installment method; no payments are received in the current year).	______	______
d.	Dividends of $20,000 received from 5% owned corporation, together with dividends received deduction (assume that taxable income limit does not apply).	______	______
e.	Domestic production activities deduction of $45,000 claimed in current year.	______	______
f.	Section 179 expense deduction of $100,000 in current year.	______	______
g.	Impact of current-year § 179 expense deduction in succeeding year.	______	______
h.	MACRS depreciation of $80,000. ADS depreciation would have been $90,000.	______	______
i.	Federal income taxes of $80,000 paid in the current year.	______	______

29. **LO.2** Osprey Corporation, a calendar year taxpayer, made estimated tax payments of $12,000 for 2012 ($3,000 per quarter). Osprey filed its Federal income tax return for 2012 reflecting a tax liability of $5,000. Due to its overpayments, in 2013 Osprey received a $7,000 refund. What is the impact on Osprey's E & P of the payment of estimated taxes and the receipt of the Federal income tax refund?

30. **LO.1, 3** Lark Corporation is a calendar year taxpayer. At the beginning of the current year, Lark has accumulated E & P of $330,000. The corporation incurs a deficit in current E & P of $460,000 that accrues ratably throughout the year. On June 30, Lark distributes $200,000 to its sole shareholder, Adrienne. If Adrienne's stock has a basis of $40,000, how is she taxed on the distribution?

31. **LO.1, 3** At the beginning of the year, Teal Corporation had E & P of $225,000. On March 30, Teal sold an asset at a loss of $225,000. For the calendar year, Teal incurred a deficit in current E & P of $305,000, which includes the $225,000 loss on the sale of the asset. If Teal made a distribution of $50,000 to its sole shareholder on April 1, how will the shareholder be taxed?

32. **LO.1, 3** Cardinal Corporation (a calendar year taxpayer) had a deficit in accumulated E & P of $500,000 at the beginning of the current year. Its net profit for the period January 1 through July 30 was $600,000, but its E & P for the entire taxable year was only $80,000. If Cardinal made a distribution of $120,000 to its sole shareholder on August 1, how will the shareholder be taxed?

33. **LO.1, 3** Bunting Corporation and Jennifer each own 50% of Sparrow Corporation's common stock. On January 1, Sparrow has a deficit in accumulated E & P of $150,000.

Its current E & P is $65,000. During the year, Sparrow makes cash distributions of $30,000 each to Bunting and Jennifer.

a. How are the two shareholders taxed on the distribution?
b. What is Sparrow Corporation's accumulated E & P at the end of the year?

34. **LO.1, 3** Complete the following schedule for each case. Unless otherwise indicated, assume that the shareholders have ample basis in the stock investment.

	Accumulated E & P Beginning of Year	Current E & P	Cash Distributions (All on Last Day of Year)	Dividend Income	Return of Capital
a.	($200,000)	$ 70,000	$130,000	$______	$______
b.	150,000	(120,000)	210,000	______	______
c.	90,000	70,000	150,000	______	______
d.	120,000	(60,000)	130,000	______	______
e.	Same as (d), except that the distribution of $130,000 is made on June 30 and the corporation uses the calendar year for tax purposes.			______	______

35. **LO.1, 3** Mike, the sole shareholder of Daffodil Corporation, sold his Daffodil stock to Steve on July 30 for $200,000. Mike's basis in the stock was $150,000 at the beginning of the year. Daffodil had accumulated E & P of $110,000 on January 1 and current E & P of $170,000. During the year, Daffodil made the following distributions: $300,000 cash to Mike on July 1 and $100,000 cash to Steve on December 30. How will Mike and Steve be taxed on the distributions? How much gain will Mike recognize on the sale of his stock to Steve?

Decision Making

36. **LO.4** Sean, a shareholder of Crimson Corporation, is in the 35% tax bracket. This year, he receives a $7,000 qualified dividend from Crimson. Sean has investment interest expense of $16,000 and net investment income of $9,000 (not including the qualified dividend). Assume that Sean does not expect to have any investment income in the foreseeable future. Should Sean treat the distribution as a qualified dividend (subject to a 15% tax rate) or classify it as net investment income?

37. **LO.4** In November of the current year, Emerald Corporation declared a dividend of $2 per share (the shareholder record date is December 15). Assume that Emerald has sufficient current E & P to cover the dividend payment. If Judy purchases 500 shares of Emerald stock on December 5 and sells the stock on December 25, how is she taxed on the $1,000 dividend?

38. **LO.1, 5** Heather, an individual, owns all of the outstanding stock in Silver Corporation. Heather purchased her stock in Silver nine years ago, and her basis is $56,000. At the beginning of this year, the corporation has $76,000 of accumulated E & P and no current E & P (before considering the effect of the distributions). What are the tax consequences to Heather (amount and type of income and basis in property received) and Silver Corporation (gain or loss and effect on E & P) in each of the following situations?

a. Silver distributes land to Heather. The land was held as an investment and has a fair market value of $54,000 and an adjusted basis of $42,000.
b. Assume that Silver Corporation has no current or accumulated E & P prior to the distribution. How would your answer to (a) change?
c. Assume that the land distributed in (a) is subject to a $46,000 mortgage (which Heather assumes). How would your answer change?
d. Assume that the land has a fair market value of $54,000 and an adjusted basis of $62,000 on the date of the distribution. How would your answer to (a) change?
e. Instead of distributing land in (a), assume that Silver decides to distribute equipment used in its business. The equipment has a $14,000 market value, a $1,200 adjusted basis for income tax purposes, and a $5,200 adjusted basis for E & P purposes. When the equipment was purchased four years ago, its original fair market value was $18,000.

39. **LO.1, 5** Peach Corporation distributes property ($250,000 basis and $300,000 fair market value) to its sole shareholder, Karla. The property is subject to a liability of $400,000, which Karla assumes. Peach has E & P of $650,000 prior to the distribution.

a. What gain, if any, does Peach recognize on the distribution? What is Peach's accumulated E & P at the start of the following year?

b. What is the amount of Karla's dividend income on the distribution? What is her basis in the property received?

40. **LO.1, 5** Lime Corporation, with E & P of $500,000, distributes land (worth $300,000, adjusted basis of $350,000) to Harry, its sole shareholder. The land is subject to a liability of $120,000, which Harry assumes. What are the tax consequences to Lime and to Harry?

41. **LO.1, 3** At the beginning of the year, Penguin Corporation (a calendar year taxpayer) has accumulated E & P of $55,000. During the year, Penguin incurs a $36,000 loss from operations that accrues ratably. On October 1, Penguin distributes $40,000 in cash to Holly, its sole shareholder. How is Holly taxed on the distribution?

42. **LO.1, 5** Cornflower Corporation distributes equipment (adjusted basis of $70,000, fair market value of $55,000) to its shareholder, Roy. What are the tax consequences to Cornflower Corporation and to Roy?

43. **LO.1, 2, 3, 4, 5** Cerulean Corporation has two equal shareholders, Eloise and Olivia. Eloise acquired her Cerulean stock three years ago by transferring property worth $700,000, basis of $300,000, for 70 shares of the stock. Olivia acquired 70 shares in Cerulean Corporation two years ago by transferring property worth $660,000, basis of $110,000. Cerulean Corporation's accumulated E & P as of January 1 of the current year is $350,000. On March 1 of the current year, the corporation distributed to Eloise property worth $120,000, basis to Cerulean of $50,000. It distributed cash of $220,000 to Olivia. On July 1 of the current year, Olivia sold her stock to Magnus for $820,000. On December 1 of the current year, Cerulean distributed cash of $90,000 each to Magnus and Eloise. What are the tax issues?

Issue ID

44. **LO.1, 2, 5** Petrel Corporation has accumulated E & P of $85,000 at the beginning of the year. Its current-year taxable income is $320,000. On December 31, Petrel distributed business property (worth $140,000, adjusted basis of $290,000) to Juan, its sole shareholder. Juan assumes a $70,000 liability on the property. Included in the determination of Petrel's current taxable income is $16,000 of income recognized from an installment sale in a previous year. In addition, the corporation incurred a Federal income tax liability of $112,000, paid life insurance premiums of $4,500, and received term life insurance proceeds of $150,000 on the death of an officer.

Decision Making

a. What is Juan's gross income from the distribution?

b. What is the E & P of Petrel Corporation after the property distribution?

c. What is Juan's tax basis in the property received?

d. How would your answers to (a) and (b) change if Petrel had sold the property at its fair market value, used $70,000 of the proceeds to pay off the liability, and distributed the remaining cash and any tax savings to Juan?

45. **LO.5** Iris Corporation owns 30% of Fresia Corporation's stock. On November 15, Fresia Corporation, with current E & P of $320,000, distributes land (fair market value of $100,000; basis of $160,000) to Iris. The land is subject to a liability of $80,000, which Iris assumes.

a. How is Iris Corporation taxed on the distribution?

b. What is Fresia Corporation's E & P after the distribution?

46. **LO.6** Wren Corporation makes a loan evidenced by a written note to its sole shareholder, James. The loan is collateralized by James's cabin in the Lake Superior area, but the loan is interest-free. Discuss whether the advance is a bona fide loan. Will you need additional information to complete your analysis? If so, describe what information you will need.

47. **LO.6** Parrot Corporation is a closely held company with accumulated E & P of $300,000 and current E & P of $350,000. Tom and Jerry are brothers; each owns a 50% share in Parrot, and they share management responsibilities equally. What are the tax consequences of each of the following independent transactions involving Parrot, Tom, and Jerry? How does each transaction affect Parrot's E & P?

a. Parrot sells an office building (adjusted basis of $350,000; fair market value of $300,000) to Tom for $275,000.
b. Parrot lends Jerry $250,000 on March 31 of this year. The loan is evidenced by a note and is payable on demand. No interest is charged on the loan (the current applicable Federal interest rate is 7%).
c. Parrot owns an airplane that it leases to others for a specified rental rate. Tom and Jerry also use the airplane for personal use and pay no rent. During the year, Tom used the airplane for 120 hours, and Jerry used it for 160 hours. The rental value of the airplane is $350 per hour, and its maintenance costs average $80 per hour.
d. Tom leases equipment to Parrot for $20,000 per year. The same equipment can be leased from another company for $9,000 per year.

48. **LO.7** Katie purchased 5,000 shares of Grebe Corporation common stock six years ago for $80,000. In the current year, Katie received a preferred stock dividend of 400 shares, while the other holders of common stock received a common stock dividend. The preferred stock Katie received has a fair market value of $40,000, and her common stock has a fair market value of $120,000. Assume that Grebe has ample E & P to cover any distributions made during the year. What is Katie's basis in the preferred and common stock after the dividend is received? When does her holding period commence for the preferred stock?

Communications

49. **LO.7** Jacob Corcoran bought 10,000 shares of Grebe Corporation stock two years ago for $24,000. Last year, Jacob received a nontaxable stock dividend of 2,000 shares in Grebe Corporation. In the current tax year, Jacob sold all of the stock received as a dividend for $18,000. Prepare a letter to Jacob and a memo for the file describing the tax consequences of the stock sale. Jacob's address is 925 Arapahoe Street, Boulder, CO 80304.

50. **LO.7** Denim Corporation declares a nontaxable dividend payable in rights to subscribe to common stock. One right and $60 entitle the holder to subscribe to one share of stock. One right is issued for every two shares of stock owned. At the date of distribution of the rights, the market value of the stock is $110 per share, and the market value of the rights is $55 per right. Lauren owns 300 shares of stock that she purchased two years ago for $9,000. Lauren receives 150 rights, of which she exercises 105 to purchase 105 additional shares. She sells the remaining 45 rights for $2,475. What are the tax consequences of this transaction to Lauren?

Decision Making

51. **LO.4, 8** Kristen, the president and sole shareholder of Egret Corporation, has earned a salary bonus of $30,000 for the current year. Because of the lower tax rates on qualifying dividends, Kristen is considering substituting a dividend for the bonus. Assume that the tax rates are 28% for Kristen and 34% for Egret Corporation.
a. How much better off would Kristen be if she were paid a dividend rather than salary?
b. How much better off would Egret Corporation be if it paid Kristen a salary rather than a dividend?
c. If Egret Corporation pays Kristen a salary bonus of $40,000 instead of a $30,000 dividend, how would your answers to (a) and (b) change?
d. What should Kristen do?

Communications

52. **LO.1, 3, 8** Your client, Heron Corporation, has a deficit in accumulated E & P of $300,000. Starting this year, it expects to generate annual E & P of $150,000 for the next four years and would like to distribute this amount to its shareholders. How should Heron Corporation distribute the $600,000 over the four-year period to provide the least amount of dividend income to its shareholders (all individuals)? In a letter to your client, make appropriate suggestions on how this should be done. Also prepare a memo for your firm's file. Heron Corporation's address is 12 Nature Trail Way, Daytona Beach, FL 32114.

RESEARCH PROBLEMS

THOMSON REUTERS
CHECKPOINT®

Note: Solutions to Research Problems can be prepared by using the **Checkpoint® Student Edition** online research product, which is available to accompany this text. It is also possible to prepare solutions to the Research Problems by using tax research materials found in a standard tax library.

Communications

Research Problem 1. Kenny Merinoff and his son, John, own all outstanding stock of Flamingo Corporation. Both John and Kenny are officers in the corporation and, together with their uncle, Ira, comprise the entire board of directors. Flamingo uses the cash method of accounting and has a calendar year-end. In late 2006, the board of directors adopted the following legally enforceable resolution (agreed to in writing by each of the officers):

> Salary payments made to an officer of the corporation that shall be disallowed in whole or in part as a deductible expense for Federal income tax purposes shall be reimbursed by such officer to the corporation to the full extent of the disallowance. It shall be the duty of the board of directors to enforce payment of each such amount.

In 2010, Flamingo paid Kenny $800,000 in compensation. John received $650,000. On an audit in late 2011, the IRS found the compensation of both officers to be excessive. It disallowed deductions for $400,000 of the payment to Kenny and $350,000 of the payment to John. The IRS recharacterized the disallowed payments as constructive dividends. Complying with the resolution by the board of directors, both Kenny and John repaid the disallowed compensation to Flamingo Corporation in 2012. John and Kenny have asked you to determine how their repayments should be treated for tax purposes. John is still working as a highly compensated executive for Flamingo, while Kenny is retired and living off his savings. Prepare a memo for your firm's client files describing the results of your research.

Partial list of research aids:
§ 1341.
Vincent E. Oswald, 49 T.C. 645 (1968).

Communications

Research Problem 2. Oriole Corporation wholly owns Canary Corporation, which was formed six years ago with the transfer of several assets and a substantial amount of cash. Oriole's basis in the Canary stock is $11.5 million. Since it was formed, Canary has been a very successful manufacturing company and currently has accumulated E & P of $8 million. The company's principal assets are property, plant, and equipment (worth $11 million) and cash and marketable securities of $8.5 million, for a total fair market value of $19.5 million.

Oriole and Canary are members of an affiliated group and have made the election under § 243(b) to entitle Oriole to a 100% dividends received deduction. From a strategic perspective, Oriole is no longer interested in manufacturing and is considering a sale of Canary. In anticipation of a sale in the next year or two, the management of Oriole has contacted you for advice. If Canary is sold outright, Oriole will have a capital gain of $8 million ($19.5 million fair market value less a basis of $11.5 million). As an alternative, taxes on a future sale would be minimized if Canary first pays Oriole an $8 million dividend equal to its E & P. With the 100% dividends received deduction, the payment would be tax-free to Oriole. Subsequent to the dividend payment, Canary can be sold for its remaining value of $11.5 million ($11 million in property, plant, and equipment plus $500,000 in cash), resulting in no gain or loss to Oriole.

a. Prepare a letter to Louise Jones, the president of Oriole Corporation, describing the results of the proposed plan. Oriole's address is 974 State Street, La Crosse, WI 53786.
b. Prepare a memo for your firm's client files.

Partial list of research aids:
Waterman Steamship Corp. v. Comm., 70–2 USTC ¶9514, 26 AFTR 2d 70–5185, 430 F.2d 1185 (CA–5, 1970).

Research Problem 3. Your client, White Corporation, has done well since its formation 20 years ago. This year, it recognized a $50 million capital gain from the sale of a subsidiary. White's CEO has contacted you to discuss a proposed transaction to reduce the tax on the capital gain. Under the proposal, White will purchase all of the common stock in Purple Corporation for $200 million. Purple is a profitable corporation that has $63 million in cash and marketable securities, $137 million in operating assets, and approximately $280 million in E & P. After its acquisition, Purple will distribute $50 million in cash and marketable securities to White. Due to the 100% dividends received deduction, no taxable income results to White from the dividend. White will then resell Purple for $150 million. The subsequent sale of Purple generates a $50 million capital loss [$200 million (stock basis) – $150 million (sales price)]. The loss from the stock sale can then be used to offset the preexisting $50 million capital gain. Will the proposed plan work? Why or why not?

Partial list of research aids:
§ 1059.

Communications

Research Problem 4. Emerald Corporation is required to change its method of accounting for Federal income tax purposes. The change will require an adjustment to income to be made over three tax periods. Jonas, the sole shareholder of Emerald Corporation, wants to better understand the implications of this adjustment for E & P purposes, as he anticipates a distribution from Emerald in the current year. Prepare a memo for your firm's client files describing the results of your research.

Partial list of research aids:
§ 481(a).
Rev.Proc. 97–27, 1997–1 C.B. 680.

Internet Activity

Use the tax resources of the Internet to address the following questions. Do not restrict your search to the Web, but include a review of newsgroups and general reference materials, practitioner sites and resources, primary sources of the tax law, chat rooms and discussion groups, and other opportunities.

Research Problem 5. Just how common are dividend distributions? Are dividends concentrated in the companies traded on the New York Stock Exchange, or do closely held corporations pay dividends with the same frequency and at the same rates? Did dividends increase following the reduction in tax rates in 2003? Did dividends decrease during the financial downturn of 2008 and 2009? Financial institutions and observers are acutely interested in these issues. Search for comments on such questions at various commercial websites as well as one or two academic journals or newsgroups.

Research Problem 6. The law allowing a reduced tax rate on dividends (part of the "Bush tax cuts") was scheduled to expire at the end of 2010. During the year leading up to the scheduled expiration, there was considerable debate surrounding the desirability of extending the reduced rate beyond 2010. Search the Internet for arguments for and against extending the reduced rates on dividends for individuals. Summarize the arguments made on both sides. Which side do you agree with? Why?

Research Problem 7. Over the last few years, there have been several proposals to reform the Federal income tax. Use the Internet to ascertain how these proposals have addressed the tax treatment of corporate distributions.

CHAPTER

6 Corporations: Redemptions and Liquidations

LEARNING OBJECTIVES: *After completing Chapter 6, you should be able to:*

LO.1 Identify the stock redemptions that qualify for sale or exchange treatment.

LO.2 Determine the tax impact of stock redemptions on the distributing corporation.

LO.3 Recognize the restrictions on sale or exchange treatment for certain redemption-like transactions.

LO.4 Determine the tax consequences of complete liquidations for both the corporation and its shareholders.

LO.5 Determine the tax consequences of subsidiary liquidations for both the parent and the subsidiary corporations.

LO.6 Identify planning opportunities available to minimize the tax impact in stock redemptions and complete liquidations.

CHAPTER OUTLINE

THE BIG PICTURE Tax Solutions for the Real World

© STOCK4B Creative/Gett Images

Family Corporations and Stock Redemptions

Christina Flores formed Orange Corporation 15 years ago, and she continues to own all 10,000 shares of Orange stock outstanding (basis of $400,000). Christina has been employed full-time with Orange since its inception, handling all of the corporation's management and strategy decisions during that time. Christina receives an annual salary of $250,000 from Orange for this work. Within the next five to seven years, Christina would like to retire and transfer ownership in Orange to her two children, ages 24 and 22. The children have worked full-time with Orange over the last two years and have demonstrated both the capacity and the willingness to take over the business after their mother's retirement. Currently, the Orange stock is worth $6 million, and it is expected to be worth $8 million by the time of Christina's retirement. The stock represents approximately 80 percent of Christina's net worth. Orange Corporation (E & P of $2 million) generates strong positive cash flow, but a significant investment in property, plant, and equipment will be required over the next several years. The children are not expected to have the financial wherewithal to purchase the Orange stock from their mother at the time of her retirement, although Christina would be receptive to taking notes in exchange for her Orange stock.

How could a stock redemption be used to assist Christina in achieving her goal of transferring control of Orange to the children upon her retirement?

Read the chapter and formulate your response.

6 Introduction

When a shareholder sells stock to an unrelated third party, the transaction typically is treated as a sale or exchange whereby the amount realized is offset by the shareholder's stock basis and a capital gain (or loss) results. In such cases, the Code treats the proceeds as a return *of* the shareholder's investment.

THE BIG PICTURE

EXAMPLE 1

Return to the facts of *The Big Picture* on p. 6-1. Assume that Christina sells 2,000 shares of Orange Corporation stock to a third party for $1.2 million. If the transaction is treated as a sale or exchange (return *of* the owner's investment), Christina has a long-term capital gain of $1,120,000 [$1.2 million (amount realized) – $80,000 (stock basis)].

In a *stock redemption*, where a shareholder sells stock back to the issuing corporation, the transaction can have the *effect* of a dividend distribution rather than a sale or exchange. This is particularly the case when the stock of the corporation is closely held. For instance, consider a redemption of stock from a sole shareholder. In such a case, the shareholder's ownership interest remains unaffected by the stock redemption, as the shareholder continues to own 100 percent of the corporation's outstanding shares after the transaction. If such redemptions were granted sale or exchange treatment, dividend income could be avoided entirely by never formally distributing dividends and, instead, effecting stock redemptions whenever corporate funds were desired by shareholders. Nontaxable stock dividends could be used to replenish shares as needed.

The key distinction between a sale of stock to an unrelated third party and some stock redemptions is the effect of the transaction on the shareholder's ownership interest in the corporation. In a sale of stock to an unrelated third party, the shareholder's ownership interest in the corporation is diminished. In the case of many stock redemptions, however, there is little or no change to the shareholder's ownership interest. In general, if a shareholder's ownership interest is *not* diminished as a result of a stock redemption, the Code will treat the transaction as a dividend distribution (return *from* the shareholder's investment).

THE BIG PICTURE

EXAMPLE 2

Return to the facts of *The Big Picture* on p. 6-1. Assume that Orange Corporation redeems 2,000 of its shares from Christina for $1.2 million. If the transaction is treated as a dividend distribution (return *from* the owner's investment), Christina has $2 million of dividend income. After the redemption, Christina continues to own 100% of the Orange shares outstanding (8,000 shares ÷ 8,000 shares).

The Code does allow sale or exchange treatment for *certain* kinds of stock redemptions. In these transactions, as a general rule, the shareholder's ownership interest is diminished as a result of the redemption. In addition, a disposition of stock in a complete liquidation of a corporation generally produces sale or exchange treatment to the shareholder. This chapter examines the tax implications of corporate distributions that are stock redemptions and complete liquidations.

LO.1

Identify the stock redemptions that qualify for sale or exchange treatment.

6.1 Stock Redemptions—In General

Under § 317(b), a **stock redemption** occurs when a corporation acquires its stock from a shareholder in exchange for cash or other property. Although a sale of stock to an outsider invariably results in sale or exchange treatment, only a *qualifying* stock redemption is treated as a sale for tax purposes. Nonqualified stock redemptions are denied sale or exchange treatment because they are deemed to have the same effect as dividend distributions.

Stock redemptions occur for a variety of reasons. Publicly traded corporations often reacquire their shares with the goal of increasing shareholder value. For corporations where the stock is closely held, redemptions frequently occur to achieve shareholder objectives. For instance, a redemption might be used to acquire the stock of a deceased shareholder of a closely held corporation. Using corporate funds to purchase the stock from the decedent's estate relieves the remaining shareholders of the need to use their own money to acquire the stock. Stock redemptions also occur as a result of property settlements in divorce actions. When spouses jointly own 100 percent of a corporation's shares, a divorce decree may require that the stock interest of one spouse be bought out. A redemption of that spouse's shares relieves the other spouse from having to use his or her own funds for the transaction. Stock redemptions are also frequently incorporated into buy-sell agreements between shareholders so that corporate funds can be used to buy the stock of a shareholder terminating his or her ownership interest.

6.2 Stock Redemptions—Sale or Exchange Treatment

Noncorporate shareholders generally prefer to have a stock redemption treated as a sale or exchange rather than as a dividend distribution. For individual taxpayers, the maximum tax rate for long-term capital gains is currently 15 percent (0 percent for taxpayers in the 10 or 15 percent marginal tax bracket). The preference for qualifying stock redemption treatment is based on the fact that such transactions result in (1) the tax-free recovery of the redeemed stock's basis and (2) capital gains that can be offset by capital losses. In a nonqualified stock redemption, the *entire* distribution is taxed as dividend income (assuming adequate E & P), which, although generally taxed at the same rate as long-term capital gains, cannot be offset by capital losses.

EXAMPLE 3

Abby, an individual in the 35% tax bracket, acquired stock in Quail Corporation four years ago for $300,000. In the current year, Quail Corporation (E & P of $1 million) redeems her shares for $450,000. If the redemption qualifies for sale or exchange treatment, Abby will have a long-term capital gain of $150,000 [$450,000 (redemption amount) − $300,000 (basis)]. Her tax liability on the $150,000 gain will be $22,500 ($150,000 × 15%). If the stock redemption does not qualify as a sale or exchange, the entire distribution will be treated as a dividend, and her tax liability will be $67,500 ($450,000 × 15%). Thus, Abby will save $45,000 ($67,500 − $22,500) in income taxes if the transaction is a qualifying stock redemption. ■

EXAMPLE 4

Assume in Example 3 that Abby has a capital loss carryover of $100,000 in the current tax year. If the transaction is a qualifying stock redemption, Abby can offset the entire $100,000 capital loss carryover against her $150,000 long-term capital gain. As a result, only $50,000 of the gain will be taxed and her tax liability will be only $7,500 ($50,000 × 15%). On the other hand, if the transaction does not qualify for sale or exchange treatment, the entire $450,000 will be taxed as a dividend at 15%. In addition, assuming that she has no capital gains in the current year, Abby will be able to deduct only $3,000 of the $100,000 capital loss carryover to offset her ordinary income. ■

In contrast, however, *corporate* shareholders normally receive more favorable tax treatment from a dividend distribution than would result from a qualifying stock redemption. Corporate taxpayers typically report only a small portion of a dividend distribution as taxable income because of the dividends received deduction (see Chapter 2). Further, the preferential tax rate applicable to dividend and long-term

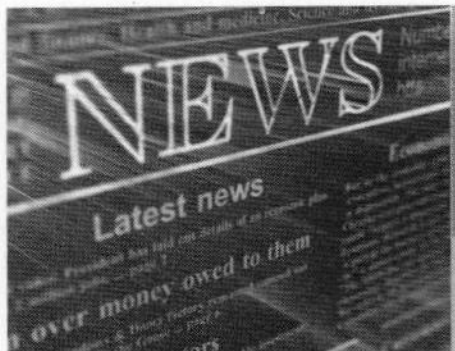

TAX IN THE NEWS **To Buy Back, or Not to Buy Back, That Is the Question**

In recent years, publicly traded corporations have amassed large cash balances. Reluctant to increase capital investment or hiring in the uncertain economy, many corporations have instead used some of their cash hoard to buy back stock. Most frequently, stock buyback programs are presented as an attempt to increase shareholder value. But not all corporations are in agreement that stock buyback programs are an efficient use of cash. Consider three major oil companies as an example. In a recent six-month period, ExxonMobil spent over $11 billion on stock buybacks, or 38 percent of its operating cash, and ConocoPhillips spent almost $5 billion on stock buybacks, or 57 percent of its operating cash. During that same period, however, Chevron spent less than $2 billion on stock buybacks, or 8.5 percent of its operating cash. Instead, Chevron embarked on a $26 billion capital expenditures program in an effort to increase its oil and gas production and reserves. Investors appear to favor Chevron's cash management approach, as its stock has appreciated more over the year than that of either ExxonMobil or ConocoPhillips.

Source: Adapted from Isabel Ordonez, "Chevron Bucks Buybacks: Oil Company Hoards Cash, Citing Shaky Economy and Capital Investment," *Wall Street Journal*, September 10, 2011, p. B3.

capital gain income is not available to corporations. Consequently, tax planning for stock redemptions must consider the different preferences of corporate and noncorporate shareholders.

EXAMPLE 5

Assume in Example 3 that Abby is a corporation, that the stock represents a 40% ownership interest in Quail Corporation, and that Abby has corporate taxable income of $850,000 before the redemption transaction. If the transaction is a qualifying stock redemption, Abby will have a long-term capital gain of $150,000 that will be subject to tax at 34%, or $51,000. On the other hand, if the $450,000 distribution is treated as a dividend, Abby will have a dividends received deduction of $360,000 ($450,000 × 80%); so only $90,000 of the payment will be taxed. Consequently, Abby's tax liability on the transaction will be only $30,600 ($90,000 × 34%). ■

When a qualifying stock redemption results in a *loss* to the shareholder rather than a gain, § 267 disallows loss recognition if the shareholder owns (directly or indirectly) more than 50 percent of the corporation's stock. A shareholder's basis in property received in a stock redemption, qualifying or nonqualified, generally will be the property's fair market value, determined as of the date of the redemption. Further, the holding period of the property begins on that date.

The Code establishes the criteria for determining whether a transaction is a qualifying stock redemption for tax purposes. The terminology in an agreement between the parties is not controlling, nor is state law. Section 302(b) provides four types of qualifying stock redemptions. In addition, certain distributions of property to an estate in exchange for a deceased shareholder's stock are treated as qualifying stock redemptions under § 303.

Historical Background and Overview

Under prior law, the *dividend equivalency rule* was used to determine which stock redemptions qualified for sale or exchange treatment. Under that rule, if the facts and circumstances of a redemption indicated that it was essentially equivalent to a dividend, the redemption did not qualify for sale or exchange treatment. Instead, the entire amount received by the shareholder was taxed as dividend income to the extent of the corporation's E & P.

The uncertainty and subjectivity surrounding the dividend equivalency rule led Congress to enact several objective tests for determining the status of a redemption. Currently, the following five types of stock redemptions qualify for sale or exchange treatment:

Foreign Shareholders Prefer Sale or Exchange Treatment in Stock Redemptions

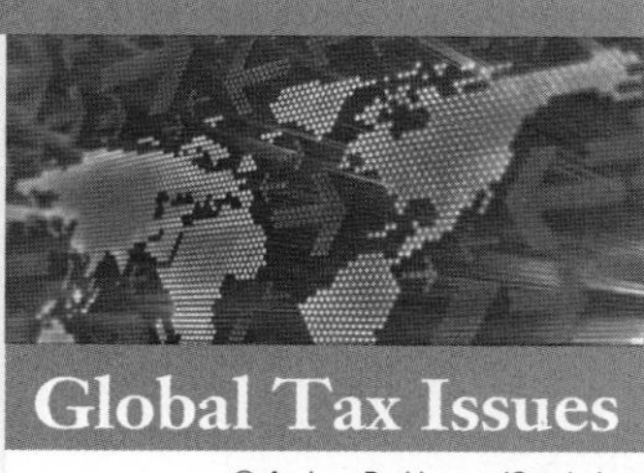

© Andrey Prokhorov, iStockphoto

As a general rule, foreign shareholders are subject to U.S. tax on dividend income from U.S. corporations but not on capital gains from the sale of U.S. stock. In some situations, a nonresident alien is taxed on a capital gain from the disposition of stock in a U.S. corporation, but only if the stock was effectively connected with the conduct of a U.S. trade or business of the individual. Foreign corporations are similarly taxed on gains from the sale of U.S. stock investments. Whether a stock redemption qualifies for sale or exchange treatment therefore takes on added significance for foreign shareholders. If one of the qualifying stock redemption rules can be satisfied, the foreign shareholder typically will avoid U.S. tax on the transaction. If, instead, dividend income is the result, a 30 percent withholding tax typically applies. For further details, see Chapter 9.

- Distributions not essentially equivalent to a dividend ("not essentially equivalent redemptions").
- Distributions substantially disproportionate in terms of shareholder effect ("disproportionate redemptions").
- Distributions in complete termination of a shareholder's interest ("complete termination redemptions").
- Distributions to noncorporate shareholders in partial liquidation of a corporation ("partial liquidations").
- Distributions to pay a shareholder's death taxes ("redemptions to pay death taxes").

Concept Summary 6.1 later in this chapter summarizes the requirements for each of the qualifying stock redemptions.

Stock Attribution Rules

To qualify for sale or exchange treatment, a stock redemption generally must result in a substantial reduction in the shareholder's ownership interest in the corporation. In the absence of this reduction in ownership interest, the redemption proceeds are taxed as dividend income. In determining whether a stock redemption has sufficiently reduced a shareholder's interest, the stock owned by certain related parties is attributed to the redeeming shareholder.[1] Thus, the stock **attribution** rules must be considered in applying the stock redemption provisions. Under these rules, related parties are defined to include the following family members: spouses, children, grandchildren, and parents. Attribution also takes place *from* and *to* partnerships, estates, trusts, and corporations (50 percent or more ownership required in the case of regular corporations). Exhibit 6.1 summarizes the stock attribution rules.

THE BIG PICTURE

EXAMPLE 6

Return to the facts of *The Big Picture* on p. 6-1. Assume instead that Christina owns only 80% of the stock in Orange Corporation, with the other 20% being held by her two children. For purposes of the stock attribution rules, Christina is treated as owning 100% of the stock in Orange Corporation. She owns 80% directly and, because of the family attribution rules, 20% indirectly through her children.

[1]§ 318.

EXHIBIT 6.1 **Stock Attribution Rules**

	Deemed or Constructive Ownership
• Family	An individual is deemed to own the stock owned by his or her spouse, children, grandchildren, and parents (not siblings or grandparents).
• Partnership	A partner is deemed to own the stock owned by a partnership to the extent of the partner's proportionate interest in the partnership.
	Stock owned by a partner is deemed to be owned in full by a partnership.
• Estate or trust	A beneficiary or an heir is deemed to own the stock owned by an estate or a trust to the extent of the beneficiary's or heir's proportionate interest in the estate or trust.
	Stock owned by a beneficiary or an heir is deemed to be owned in full by an estate or a trust.
• Corporation	Stock owned by a corporation is deemed to be owned proportionately by any shareholder owning 50% or more of the corporation's stock.
	Stock owned by a shareholder who owns 50% or more of a corporation is deemed to be owned in full by the corporation.

EXAMPLE 7

Chris owns 40% of the stock in Gray Corporation. The other 60% is owned by a partnership in which Chris has a 20% interest. Chris is deemed to own 52% of Gray Corporation: 40% directly and, because of the partnership interest, 12% indirectly (20% × 60%). ■

As discussed later, the *family* attribution rules (refer to Example 6) can be waived in the case of some complete termination redemptions. In addition, the stock attribution rules do not apply to partial liquidations or redemptions to pay death taxes.

Not Essentially Equivalent Redemptions

Under § 302(b)(1), a redemption qualifies for sale or exchange treatment if it is "not essentially equivalent to a dividend." This provision represents a continuation of the dividend equivalency rule applicable under prior law. The earlier redemption language was retained principally for redemptions of preferred stock because shareholders often have no control over when corporations call in such stock.[2] Like its predecessor, the **not essentially equivalent redemption** lacks an objective test. Instead, each case must be resolved on a facts and circumstances basis.[3]

Based upon the Supreme Court's decision in *U.S. v. Davis*,[4] a redemption will qualify as a not essentially equivalent redemption only when the shareholder's interest in the redeeming corporation has been meaningfully reduced. In determining whether the **meaningful reduction test** has been met, the stock attribution rules apply. A decrease in the redeeming shareholder's voting control appears to be the most significant indicator of a meaningful reduction,[5] but reductions in the rights of redeeming shareholders to share in corporate earnings or to receive corporate assets upon liquidation are also considered.[6] The meaningful reduction test is applied whether common stock or preferred stock is being redeemed.

[2]See S.Rept. No. 1622, 83d Cong., 2d Sess. 44 (1954).

[3]Reg. § 1.302–2(b)(1).

[4]70–1 USTC ¶9289, 25 AFTR 2d 70–827, 90 S.Ct. 1041 (USSC, 1970).

[5]See, for example, *Jack Paparo*, 71 T.C. 692 (1979).

[6]See, for example, *Grabowski Trust*, 58 T.C. 650 (1972).

EXAMPLE 8

Pat owns 58% of the common stock of Falcon Corporation. As a result of a redemption of some of his stock, Pat's ownership interest in Falcon is reduced to 51%. Because Pat continues to have dominant voting rights in Falcon after the redemption, the distribution is treated as essentially equivalent to a dividend. The entire amount of the distribution therefore is taxed as dividend income (assuming adequate E & P). ■

EXAMPLE 9

Maroon Corporation redeems 2% of its stock from Maria. Before the redemption, Maria owned 10% of Maroon Corporation. In this case, the redemption may qualify as a not essentially equivalent redemption. Maria experiences a reduction in her voting rights, her right to participate in current earnings and accumulated surplus, and her right to share in net assets upon liquidation. ■

When a redemption *fails* to satisfy any of the qualifying stock redemption rules, the basis of the redeemed shares does not disappear. Typically, the basis will attach to the basis of the redeeming shareholder's remaining shares in the corporation. If, however, the redeeming shareholder has terminated his or her direct stock ownership and the redemption is nonqualified due to the attribution rules, the basis of the redeemed shares will attach to the basis of the constructively owned stock.[7] In this manner, a nonqualified stock redemption can result in stock basis being shifted from one taxpayer (the redeeming shareholder) to another taxpayer (the shareholder related under the attribution rules).

EXAMPLE 10

Floyd and Fran, husband and wife, each own 50 shares in Grouse Corporation, representing 100% of the corporation's stock. All of the stock was purchased for $50,000. Both Floyd and Fran serve as directors of the corporation. The corporation redeems Floyd's 50 shares, but he continues to serve as a director of the corporation. The redemption is treated as a dividend distribution (assuming adequate E & P) because Floyd constructively owns Fran's stock, or 100% of the Grouse stock outstanding. Floyd's $25,000 basis in the 50 shares redeemed attaches to Fran's stock; thus, Fran now has a basis of $50,000 in the 50 shares she owns in Grouse. ■

Disproportionate Redemptions

A stock redemption qualifies for sale or exchange treatment under § 302(b)(2) as a **disproportionate redemption** if the following conditions are met:

- After the distribution, the shareholder owns *less than* 80 percent of the interest owned in the corporation before the redemption. For example, if a shareholder owns a 60 percent interest in a corporation that redeems part of the stock, the shareholder's ownership interest after the redemption must be less than 48 percent (80 percent of 60 percent).
- After the distribution, the shareholder owns *less than* 50 percent of the total combined voting power of all classes of stock entitled to vote.

In determining a shareholder's ownership interest before and after a redemption, the attribution rules apply.

EXAMPLE 11

Bob, Carl, and Dan, unrelated individuals, own 30 shares, 30 shares, and 40 shares, respectively, in Wren Corporation. Wren has 100 shares outstanding and E & P of $200,000. The corporation redeems 20 shares of Dan's stock for $30,000. Dan paid $200 a share for the stock two years ago. Dan's ownership in Wren Corporation before and after the redemption is as follows:

	Total Shares	Dan's Ownership	Ownership Percentage	80% of Original Ownership
Before redemption	100	40	40% (40 ÷ 100)	32% (80% × 40%)
After redemption	80	20	25% (20 ÷ 80)*	

*Note that the denominator of the fraction is reduced after the redemption (from 100 to 80).

[7]Reg. § 1.302–2(c). But see Prop.Reg. § 1.302–5.

Dan's 25% ownership after the redemption meets both tests of § 302(b)(2). It is less than 80% of his original ownership and less than 50% of the total voting power. The distribution therefore qualifies as a disproportionate redemption and receives sale or exchange treatment. As a result, Dan has a long-term capital gain of $26,000 [$30,000 − $4,000 (20 shares × $200)]. ■

EXAMPLE 12

Assume that Carl and Dan are father and son. The redemption described above would not qualify for sale or exchange treatment because of the effect of the attribution rules. Dan is deemed to own Carl's stock before and after the redemption. Dan's ownership in Wren Corporation before and after the redemption is as follows:

	Total Shares	Dan's Direct Ownership	Carl's Ownership	Dan's Direct and Indirect Ownership	Ownership Percentage	80% of Original Ownership
Before redemption	100	40	30	70	70% (70 ÷ 100)	56% (80% × 70%)
After redemption	80	20	30	50	62.5% (50 ÷ 80)	

Dan's direct and indirect ownership of 62.5% fails to meet either of the tests of § 302 (b) (2). After the redemption, Dan owns more than 80% of his original ownership and more than 50% of the voting stock. Thus, the redemption does not qualify for sale or exchange treatment and results in a dividend distribution of $30,000 to Dan. The basis in the 20 shares redeemed is added to Dan's basis in his remaining 20 shares. ■

A redemption that does not qualify as a disproportionate redemption may still qualify as a not essentially equivalent redemption if it meets the meaningful reduction test (see Example 9).

Complete Termination Redemptions

A redemption that terminates a shareholder's *entire* stock ownership in a corporation qualifies for sale or exchange treatment under § 302(b)(3). The attribution rules generally apply in determining whether the shareholder's stock ownership has been completely terminated. However, the *family* attribution rules do not apply to a **complete termination redemption** if the following conditions are met:

- The former shareholder has no interest, other than that of a creditor, in the corporation for at least 10 years after the redemption (including an interest as an officer, a director, or an employee).
- The former shareholder files an agreement to notify the IRS of any prohibited interest acquired within the 10-year postredemption period and to retain all necessary records pertaining to the redemption during this time period.

Acquisition of stock in the corporation by bequest or inheritance will not constitute a prohibited interest. The required agreement should be in the form of a separate statement signed by the former shareholder and attached to the return for the year in which the redemption occurs. The agreement should state that the former shareholder agrees to notify the IRS within 30 days of acquiring a prohibited interest in the corporation during the 10-year postredemption period.[8]

EXAMPLE 13

Kevin owns 50% of the stock in Green Corporation, while the remaining interest in Green is held as follows: 40% by Wilma (Kevin's wife) and 10% by Carmen (a key employee). Green redeems all of Kevin's stock for its fair market value. As a result, Wilma and Carmen are the only remaining shareholders, now owning 80% and 20%, respectively. If the requirements for the family attribution waiver are met, the transaction will qualify as a complete termination redemption and result in sale or exchange treatment. If the waiver requirements are not satisfied, Kevin will be deemed to own Wilma's (his wife's) stock and the entire distribution will be taxed as a dividend (assuming adequate E & P). ■

[8]Reg. § 1.302–4(a).

EXAMPLE 14

Assume in Example 13 that Kevin qualifies for the family attribution waiver for the redemption. In the year of the redemption, Kevin treats the transaction as a sale or exchange. However, if he purchases Carmen's stock seven years after the redemption, he has acquired a prohibited interest and the redemption distribution is reclassified as a dividend. Kevin will owe additional taxes due to this revised treatment. ■

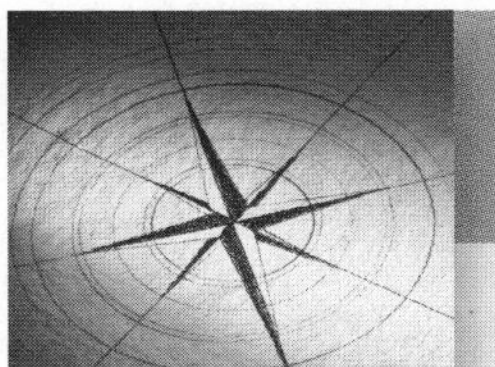

ETHICS & EQUITY Convertible Preferred Stock—Conversion or Redemption?

Four years ago, a corporation that does not sell its stock publicly sold some convertible preferred stock to a small investment group. At the option of the shareholders, the preferred stock can be converted into common stock at any time. The preferred stock also has a call feature, allowing the corporation to call (redeem) the stock at any time during the first five years after its issuance.

The corporation recently developed a successful invention that it has not yet publicly disclosed. The corporate board of directors expects that the corporation will experience significant earnings growth in the future as a result of the invention. The directors, all of whom own common stock in the corporation, would like to call the preferred stock so that those shares cannot be converted into common stock and otherwise participate in the corporation's future earnings growth. The call price set out in the preferred stock indenture provides a premium to the shareholders upon redemption. The directors vote to redeem all of the outstanding preferred stock and notify the preferred shareholders of the board's decision. Did the board of directors act ethically? Explain.

Partial Liquidations

Under § 302(b)(4), a *noncorporate* shareholder is allowed sale or exchange treatment for a distribution that qualifies as a **partial liquidation**. A partial liquidation is a distribution that (1) is *not essentially equivalent to a dividend* and (2) is both pursuant to a plan and made within the plan year or within the succeeding taxable year. A stock redemption pursuant to a partial liquidation may be pro rata with respect to the shareholders. In the case of a pro rata distribution, an actual surrender of stock is not required to qualify the transaction as a partial liquidation.[9]

In determining whether a distribution is not essentially equivalent to a dividend, the effect of the distribution on the *corporation* is examined.[10] Consequently, to qualify as a partial liquidation, the distribution must result in a *genuine contraction* of the business of the corporation.

EXAMPLE 15

Dove Corporation owned a building with seven floors. Part of the building was rented, and part was used directly in Dove's business. A fire destroyed the two top floors, and Dove received insurance proceeds in reimbursement for the damage sustained. For business reasons, Dove did not rebuild the two floors and, instead, chose to operate on a smaller scale than before the fire. Pursuant to a plan adopted in the current year, Dove uses the insurance proceeds to redeem some stock from its shareholders. The distribution is not essentially equivalent to a dividend and qualifies as a partial liquidation.[11] ■

Applying the genuine contraction of a corporate business concept has proved difficult due to the lack of objective tests. The IRS has ruled that neither the sale of investments nor the sale of excess inventory will satisfy the genuine contraction test.[12] To minimize uncertainty, the genuine contraction test should be relied upon only after obtaining a favorable ruling from the IRS.

[9] See *Fowler Hosiery Co. v. Comm.*, 62–1 USTC ¶9407, 9 AFTR 2d 1252, 301 F.2d 394 (CA–7, 1962); and Rev.Rul. 90–13, 1990–1 C.B. 65.

[10] § 302(e)(1)(A).

[11] See *Joseph W. Imler*, 11 T.C. 836 (1948), *acq.* 1949–1 C.B. 2; and Reg. § 1.346–1(a)(2).

[12] Rev.Rul. 60–322, 1960–2 C.B. 118.

THE BIG PICTURE

EXAMPLE 16

Return to the facts of *The Big Picture* on p. 6-1. Assume that Orange Corporation loses a major customer and that a severe drop in sales occurs. The corporation reduces its inventory investment and has $600,000 of excess cash on hand as a result. It distributes the excess cash to Christina in redemption of 10% of her stock. Because Christina's ownership interest in Orange remains unchanged (100%), the redemption does not qualify as a not essentially equivalent redemption, a disproportionate redemption, or a complete termination redemption. Further, the reduction in inventory does not qualify as a genuine contraction of Orange Corporation's business; thus, the distribution is not a partial liquidation. Therefore, the $600,000 is dividend income to Christina. The $40,000 basis in the stock redeemed (10% × $400,000) attaches to the basis of Christina's remaining shares of Orange.

A safe-harbor rule, the *termination of a business* test, will satisfy the not essentially equivalent to a dividend requirement. In contrast to the genuine contraction test, the termination of a business test does follow objective requirements. A distribution will qualify under the termination of a business test if the following conditions are met:

- The corporation has two or more qualified trades or businesses. A qualified trade or business is any trade or business that (1) has been actively conducted for the five-year period ending on the date of the distribution and (2) was not acquired in a taxable transaction during that five-year period.
- The distribution consists of the assets of a qualified trade or business or the proceeds from the sale of such assets.
- The corporation is actively engaged in the conduct of a qualified trade or business immediately after the distribution.

EXAMPLE 17

Loon Corporation, the owner and operator of a wholesale grocery business with a substantial amount of excess cash, purchased a freight-hauling concern. Six years later, Loon distributes the freight-hauling assets in kind on a pro rata basis to its shareholders. The distribution satisfies the termination of a business test. Loon had conducted both businesses for at least five years and continues to conduct the wholesale grocery business. Thus, for noncorporate shareholders, the distribution qualifies as a partial liquidation and is treated as a sale or exchange to the shareholders. For corporate shareholders of Loon, the distribution will be taxed as dividend income (assuming adequate E & P). ■

Redemptions to Pay Death Taxes

Section 303 provides sale or exchange treatment to a redemption of stock included in, and representing a substantial part of, a decedent's gross estate. The purpose of this provision is to provide an estate with liquidity to pay death-related expenses when a significant portion of the estate consists of stock in a closely held corporation. Often, such stock is not easily marketable, and a stock redemption represents the only viable option for its disposition. The redemption might not satisfy any of the other qualifying stock redemption provisions because of the attribution rules (e.g., attribution to estate from beneficiaries). A **redemption to pay death taxes** provides sale or exchange treatment without regard to the attribution rules, but the provision limits this treatment to the sum of the death taxes and funeral and administration expenses. A redemption in excess of these expenses may qualify for sale or exchange treatment under one of the § 302 provisions.

An estate's basis in property acquired from a decedent is generally the property's fair market value on the date of death.[13] Typically, there is little change in the fair market value of stock from the date of a decedent's death to the date of a

[13]If available and elected, an alternate valuation date would apply. § 1014(a).

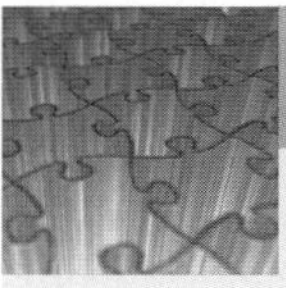

CONCEPT SUMMARY 6.1

Summary of the Qualifying Stock Redemption Rules

Type of Redemption	Requirements to Qualify
Not essentially equivalent to a dividend [§ 302(b)(1)]	Meaningful reduction in shareholder's voting interest. Reduction in shareholder's right to share in earnings or in assets upon liquidation also considered. Stock attribution rules apply.
Substantially disproportionate [§ 302(b)(2)]	Shareholder's interest in the corporation, after the redemption, must be less than 80% of interest before the redemption and less than 50% of total combined voting power of all classes of stock entitled to vote. Stock attribution rules apply.
Complete termination [§ 302(b)(3)]	Entire stock ownership terminated. In general, stock attribution rules apply. However, *family* attribution rules are waived when former shareholder has no interest, other than as a creditor, in the corporation for at least 10 years and files an agreement to notify IRS of any prohibited interest acquired during 10-year period. Shareholder must retain all necessary records during 10-year period.

Partial liquidation [§ 302(b)(4)]	Not essentially equivalent to a dividend.
	• Genuine contraction of corporation's business.
	• Termination of a business.
	  • Corporation has two or more qualified trades or businesses.
	  • Corporation terminates one qualified trade or business while continuing another qualified trade or business.
	Distribution may be in form of cash or property.
	Redemption may be pro rata.
	Stock attribution rules do not apply.

Redemption to pay death taxes [§ 303]	Value of stock of one corporation in gross estate exceeds 35% of value of adjusted gross estate. Stock of two or more corporations treated as stock of a single corporation in applying the 35% test if decedent held a 20% or more interest in the stock of the corporations. Redemption limited to sum of death taxes and funeral and administration expenses. Generally tax-free because tax basis of stock is FMV on date of decedent's death and value is unchanged at redemption. Stock attribution rules do not apply.

redemption to pay death taxes. When the redemption price in a redemption to pay death taxes is the same as the estate's basis in the stock, the estate will recognize no gain (or loss) on the transaction.

Section 303 applies only to a distribution made with respect to stock of a corporation that is included in the gross estate of a decedent and whose value *exceeds* 35 percent of the value of the adjusted gross estate. (For definitions of *gross estate* and *adjusted gross estate,* see the Glossary in Appendix C.)

EXAMPLE 18

Juan's adjusted gross estate is $7 million. The death taxes and funeral and administration expenses of the estate total $720,000. Included in the gross estate is stock of Yellow Corporation valued at $2.8 million. Juan had acquired the stock nine years ago at a cost of $300,000. Yellow redeems $720,000 of the stock from Juan's estate. Because the value of the Yellow stock in Juan's estate exceeds the 35% threshold ($2.8 million ÷ $7 million = 40%), the redemption qualifies under § 303 as a sale or exchange to

Juan's estate. Assuming that the value of the stock has remained unchanged since the date of Juan's death, there is no recognized gain (or loss) on the redemption [$720,000 (amount realized) − $720,000 (estate's stock basis)]. ■

In determining whether the value of stock of one corporation exceeds 35 percent of the value of the adjusted gross estate, the stock of two or more corporations in which the decedent held a 20 percent or more interest is treated as the stock of one corporation.[14] When this exception applies, the stock redeemed can be that of any of the 20 percent or more shareholder interests.

EXAMPLE 19

The adjusted gross estate of a decedent is $8 million. The gross estate includes stock of Owl and Robin Corporations valued at $1.6 million and $1.4 million, respectively. Unless the two corporations are treated as a single corporation for purposes of the 35% test, § 303 does not apply to a redemption of the stock of either corporation. If the decedent owned at least 20% of the stock of both Owl and Robin, § 303 can apply to a redemption of such stock. The 35% test is met when the stock of Owl and Robin is treated as that of a single corporation [($1.6 million + $1.4 million) ÷ $8 million = 37.5%]. The stock of Owl or Robin (or both) can be redeemed under § 303, to the extent of the sum of the death taxes and funeral and administration expenses. ■

6.3 Effect on the Corporation Redeeming Its Stock

LO.2

Determine the tax impact of stock redemptions on the distributing corporation.

Thus far, the discussion has focused on the tax consequences of stock redemptions to the *shareholder*. There are also several tax issues surrounding the redeeming *corporation* that must be addressed, including the recognition of gain or loss on property distributed pursuant to a redemption, the effect on a corporation's E & P from a distribution that is a qualifying stock redemption, and the deductibility of expenditures incurred in connection with a redemption. These issues are discussed in the following paragraphs.

Recognition of Gain or Loss

Distributions in redemption of stock, qualifying or not, are nonliquidating distributions. Section 311 provides that corporations recognize *gain* on all nonliquidating distributions of appreciated property as if the property had been sold for its fair market value. When distributed property is subject to a corporate liability, the fair market value of that property is treated as not being less than the amount of the liability.

Losses are not recognized on nonliquidating distributions of property. Therefore, a corporation should avoid distributing loss property (fair market value less than basis) as consideration in the redemption of a shareholder's stock. However, the corporation could sell the property in a taxable transaction in which it can recognize a loss and then distribute the proceeds.

EXAMPLE 20

To carry out a stock redemption, Blackbird Corporation distributes land (basis of $80,000, fair market value of $300,000) to a shareholder. Blackbird has a recognized gain of $220,000 ($300,000 − $80,000). If the land is subject to a liability of $330,000, Blackbird has a recognized gain of $250,000 ($330,000 − $80,000). If the value of the property distributed was less than its adjusted basis, the realized loss would not be recognized. ■

[14] § 303(b)(2)(B).

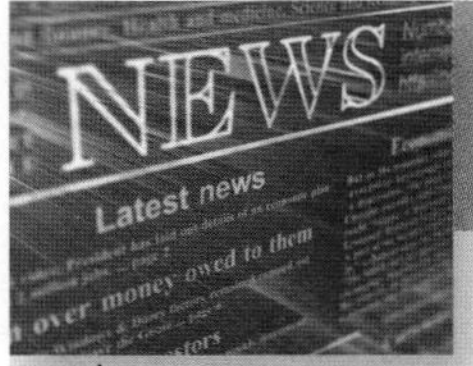

TAX IN THE NEWS **Redemption Forbearance Expenditures Are Deductible**

Section 162(k) denies a deduction for any expenditure incurred in connection with a stock redemption. The Tax Court recently addressed whether the § 162(k) disallowance applies to payments made to shareholders to forbear their right to have stock redeemed by the corporation [*Media Space Inc.*, 135 T.C. 424 (2010)]. In this case, preferred shareholders of the taxpayer had the right to have their stock redeemed by the entity beginning in 2003. At that time, however, the taxpayer's cash position was such that a stock redemption would have resulted in a going concern statement issued on its financial statements, which in turn would have endangered a refinancing that the taxpayer was negotiating with its banker. Instead, the taxpayer agreed to pay the shareholders "interest" on the redemption amounts in exchange for their agreement to forbear temporarily the redemption rights. The original forbearance agreement was for one year, but continued liquidity issues required six extensions of the agreement.

At issue in the case were the taxpayer's deductions related to the forbearance agreements for tax years 2004 ($874,955 as § 163 interest expense) and 2005 ($1,229,367 as § 162 trade or business expense). The Tax Court found that the forbearance payments were not deductible as interest because they did not relate to an existing indebtedness. However, the court ruled the payments deductible as § 162 trade or business expenditures (subject to § 263 capitalization for payments related to the second and later extensions). The Tax Court rejected the IRS's contention that the § 162(k) disallowance prohibited the deduction of the forbearance payments, holding that the forbearance agreement did not constitute a stock redemption.

Effect on Earnings and Profits

In a qualifying stock redemption, the E & P of the distributing corporation is reduced by an amount not in excess of the ratable share of the corporation's E & P attributable to the stock redeemed.[15]

EXAMPLE 21

Navy Corporation has 100 shares of stock outstanding. In a qualifying stock redemption, Navy distributes $200,000 in exchange for 30 of its shares. At the time of the redemption, Navy has paid-in capital of $120,000 and E & P of $450,000. The charge to E & P is limited to 30% of the corporation's E & P ($135,000), and the remainder of the redemption price ($65,000) is a reduction of the Navy paid-in capital account. If, instead, the 30 shares were redeemed for $80,000, the charge to E & P would be limited to $80,000, the amount paid by the corporation to carry out the stock redemption. ■

Redemption Expenditures

In redeeming its shares, a corporation may incur certain expenses such as accounting, brokerage, legal, and loan fees. Section 162(k) specifically denies a deduction for expenditures incurred in connection with a stock redemption. The disallowance does not apply to amounts otherwise deductible as interest under § 163, such as interest from debt-financed redemptions.

6.4 Stock Redemptions—Additional Limitations

LO.3

Recognize the restrictions on sale or exchange treatment for certain redemption-like transactions.

Stock redemptions that do not fall under any of the qualifying stock redemption provisions are treated as dividend distributions to the extent of the corporation's E & P. Resourceful taxpayers, however, devised ways to circumvent the redemption provisions. Two types of these transactions involved structuring what was, in effect, a stock redemption or a dividend distribution as a sale of the stock. The widespread

[15] § 312(n)(7).

use of these approaches to obtain sale or exchange treatment led to the enactment of § 306, dealing with preferred stock bailouts, and § 304, dealing with sales of stock to related corporations. These two loophole-closing provisions are explained next. Some corporate divisions resemble stock redemptions, and those distributions are also briefly discussed.

Preferred Stock Bailouts

When a corporation's stock is owned entirely (or predominantly) by a few family members and/or related entities, the attribution rules severely limit the opportunities for effecting a qualifying stock redemption. Nonetheless, clever taxpayers devised a scheme called the **preferred stock bailout** in an attempt to obtain the benefits of a qualifying stock redemption without the attendant limitations.[16] Under this scheme, a corporation issued a nontaxable (nonvoting) preferred stock dividend on common stock,[17] the shareholder assigned a portion of his or her basis in the common stock to the preferred stock,[18] and the preferred stock was sold to a third party. Because the disposition did not take the form of a stock redemption, the related limitations on sale or exchange treatment did not apply. As a result, the sale of the preferred stock was treated like any other capital asset disposition where the sales proceeds were offset by the stock's basis and the gain was taxed using the favorable capital gains rate. Unlike a sale of common shares, however, the sale of the preferred stock did not reduce the shareholder's ownership interest in the corporation.

The tax avoidance possibilities of the preferred stock bailout led to the enactment of § 306. In the case of a sale of *§ 306 stock* to a third party, the shareholder generally has ordinary income on the sale equal to the fair market value of the preferred stock on the date of the stock dividend.[19] The ordinary income is *treated* as a dividend for purposes of the 15 percent (or 0 percent) maximum tax rate on dividend income[20] but has no effect on the issuing corporation's E & P. No loss is recognized on the sale of the preferred stock;[21] instead, the unrecovered basis in the preferred stock sold is added to the basis of the shareholder's common stock.[22] If, instead of a sale to a third party, the issuing corporation redeems the preferred stock from the shareholder, the redemption proceeds constitute dividend income to the extent of the corporation's E & P (see Chapter 5).[23]

ETHICS & EQUITY A Good Preferred Stock Bailout?

Several individuals form a new corporation by transferring cash and patents in exchange for all of the corporation's common and preferred stock in a § 351 transaction. The individuals are convinced that the corporation's business, the manufacture and sale of products stemming from the patents, will be very profitable. The individuals intend to sell the preferred stock in a few years to unrelated third parties as a plan to bail out corporate earnings at capital gains rates. Because no E & P exists at the time the preferred stock is issued, the preferred stock does not constitute § 306 stock; thus, any gain on the sale of the stock will be taxed at the favorable long-term capital gains rate. Have the shareholders acted in an ethical manner? Explain.

[16] See, for example, *Chamberlin v. Comm.*, 53–2 USTC ¶9576, 44 AFTR 494, 207 F.2d 462 (CA–6, 1953), *cert. den.* 74 S.Ct. 516 (USSC, 1954).

[17] See § 305(a).

[18] See § 307(a).

[19] The ordinary income taint is limited to the stock's ratable share of the corporation's E & P at the date of the distribution. § 306(a)(1).

[20] § 306(a)(1)(D).

[21] § 306(a)(1)(C).

[22] Reg. § 1.306–1(b)(2), Example (2).

[23] See § 306(a)(2).

THE BIG PICTURE

EXAMPLE 22

Return to the facts of *The Big Picture* on p. 6-1. Assume that on January 3 of the current year, Orange Corporation (E & P of $2 million) declares and issues a nontaxable preferred stock dividend of 1,000 shares to Christina. After the stock dividend, the fair market value of one share of common is $540, and the fair market value of one share of preferred is $600. Two days later, Christina sells the 1,000 shares of preferred stock to Emily, an unrelated party, for $600,000. Section 306 produces the following results:

- After the distribution and before the sale, the preferred stock has a basis to Christina of $40,000 [($600,000 value of preferred ÷ $6 million value of preferred and common) × $400,000 (original basis of common stock)]. At this time, the common stock has a new basis of $360,000.
- The sale of the preferred stock generates $600,000 of ordinary income to Christina. This is the amount of dividend income Christina would have recognized had cash been distributed instead of preferred stock (i.e., the § 306 taint). The 15% maximum tax rate on dividend income is applicable to the $600,000.
- The $40,000 basis allocated to the preferred stock is added back to the basis of the common stock; thus, the common stock basis is increased back to $400,000.
- Orange Corporation's E & P is unaffected by either the stock dividend or its subsequent sale.

Section 306 stock is stock other than common that (1) is received as a nontaxable stock dividend, (2) is received tax-free in a corporate reorganization or separation to the extent that either the effect of the transaction was substantially the same as the receipt of a stock dividend or the stock was received in exchange for § 306 stock, or (3) has a basis determined by reference to the basis of § 306 stock (e.g., a gift of § 306 stock). (Corporate reorganizations are discussed in Chapter 7.) If a corporation has no E & P on the date of distribution of a nontaxable preferred stock dividend, the stock will not be § 306 stock.[24]

Redemptions through the Use of Related Corporations

A shareholder possessing a controlling interest (i.e., direct or indirect ownership of at least 50 percent)[25] in two or more corporations could, in the absence of any statutory limitation, obtain sale or exchange treatment by having one corporation purchase some of the shareholder's stock in a second related corporation. This result could occur even if the shareholder's ownership interest in the corporation whose stock is sold has not been substantively reduced. Section 304 closes this loophole by treating the sale of stock of one corporation to a related corporation as a stock redemption subject to the rules discussed earlier in this chapter. This provision applies to a transfer involving brother-sister corporations as well as to parent-subsidiary situations (see Chapters 2 and 8).

In general, § 304 requires a redemption through the use of related corporations to result in a reduction of ownership interest that would satisfy one of the qualifying stock redemptions of § 302 (e.g., disproportionate redemption) or § 303.[26] If the redemption does not qualify under those rules, the transaction is characterized as a dividend distribution.[27] When brother-sister corporations are involved, the shareholder increases the basis in the stock of the acquiring corporation by the basis of the stock surrendered in the transaction. Likewise, the acquiring corporation's basis in the stock acquired is equal to the basis the shareholder had in such shares.[28]

[24]§ 306(c).
[25]§ 304(c).
[26]See § 304(a)(1).
[27]The distribution is given dividend income treatment to the extent of the sum of E & P of the two related corporations. § 304(b)(2).
[28]Reg. § 1.304–2(a) and § 362(a).

Distribution of Stock and Securities of a Controlled Corporation

If one corporation controls another corporation, stock in the subsidiary corporation can be distributed to the shareholders of the parent corporation tax-free under § 355. When a subsidiary is newly formed to perfect a corporate division, this provision applies through the divisive corporate reorganization rules discussed in Chapter 7. When a subsidiary already exists, § 355 alone applies and the transaction can resemble a dividend, a stock redemption, or a complete liquidation. The rules surrounding these transactions are covered in detail in Chapter 7.

6.5 Liquidations—In General

LO.4

Determine the tax consequences of complete liquidations for both the corporation and its shareholders.

When a corporation makes a nonliquidating distribution (e.g., stock redemption), the entity typically will continue as a going concern. With a complete liquidation, however, corporate existence terminates, as does each shareholder's ownership interest. A complete liquidation, like a qualifying stock redemption, produces sale or exchange treatment to the *shareholder.* However, the tax effects of a liquidation to the *corporation* vary somewhat from those of a redemption. Sale or exchange treatment is the general rule for the liquidating corporation, although some losses are disallowed.

The Liquidation Process

A **corporate liquidation** exists when a corporation ceases to be a going concern. The corporation continues solely to wind up affairs, pay debts, and distribute any remaining assets to its shareholders. Legal dissolution under state law is not required for a liquidation to be complete for tax purposes. A liquidation can exist even if the corporation retains a nominal amount of assets to pay remaining debts and preserve legal status.[29]

Shareholders may decide to liquidate a corporation for one or more reasons, including the following:

- The corporate business has been unsuccessful.
- The shareholders want to acquire the corporation's assets.
- Another person or entity wants to purchase the corporation's assets. The purchaser may buy the shareholders' stock and then liquidate the corporation to acquire the assets. Alternatively, the purchaser may buy the assets directly from the corporation. After the assets are sold, the corporation distributes the sales proceeds to its shareholders and liquidates.

As one might expect, the different means used to liquidate a corporation produce varying tax results.

Liquidating and Nonliquidating Distributions Compared

As noted previously, a *nonliquidating* property distribution produces gain (but not loss) to the distributing corporation. For the shareholder, the receipt of cash or property produces dividend income to the extent of the corporation's E & P or, in the case of a qualifying stock redemption, results in sale or exchange treatment.

Similar to a qualifying stock redemption, a *liquidation* produces sale or exchange treatment for the shareholders. E & P has no impact on the gain or loss to be recognized by the shareholder in either type of distribution.[30] However, a liquidation produces different tax consequences to the distributing corporation. With certain exceptions, a liquidating corporation recognizes gain *and* loss upon the distribution of its assets.

[29] Reg. § 1.332–2(c).

[30] § 331.

TAX IN THE NEWS Closing a Chapter of a Good Book(store)

In 1971, two brothers, Tom and Louis Borders, opened a used bookstore in Ann Arbor, Michigan. By 2010, the Borders bookstore brand had expanded into a conglomerate (the Borders Group) that operated over 650 Borders and Waldenbooks bookstores and employed over 19,000 people. Unable to compete in the digital era, where more and more consumers buy (e.g., amazon.com) and read (e.g., e-readers) their books electronically, the Borders Group filed for bankruptcy in February 2011 and closed its stores for good in September 2011. As is common with liquidations of large concerns, third-party liquidators handled the actual disposition of Borders' remaining assets (e.g., book and music inventory, fixtures, furniture, and equipment). A consortium of liquidators won the liquidation rights with a bid that was expected to pay Borders' creditors a minimum of $252 million. To generate a profit for their work, the liquidators would need to sell Borders' assets for an amount that exceeded any guaranteed minimum payout to those creditors. This fact probably was not lost on customers who went to their neighborhood Borders during the liquidation sale in search of steep discounts on popular books and music.

EXAMPLE 23

Goose Corporation, with E & P of $40,000, makes a cash distribution of $50,000 to its sole shareholder. The shareholder's basis in the Goose stock is $20,000. If the distribution is not a qualifying stock redemption or in complete liquidation, the shareholder recognizes dividend income of $40,000 (the amount of Goose's E & P) and treats the remaining $10,000 of the distribution as a return of capital (i.e., stock basis is reduced to $10,000). If the distribution is a qualifying stock redemption or is pursuant to a complete liquidation, the shareholder has a capital gain of $30,000 ($50,000 distribution − $20,000 stock basis). In the case of these distributions, Goose's E & P is of no consequence to the shareholder's tax result. ■

In the event a corporate distribution results in a *loss* to the shareholder, another distinction exists between nonliquidating distributions and liquidations. Section 267 disallows recognition of losses between related parties in nonliquidating distributions but not in complete liquidations.

EXAMPLE 24

The stock of Tern Corporation is owned equally by three brothers, Rex, Sam, and Ted. When Ted's basis in his stock is $40,000, the corporation distributes $30,000 to him in cancellation of all of his shares. If the distribution is a qualifying stock redemption, the $10,000 realized loss is not recognized because Ted and Tern Corporation are related parties. Under § 267, Ted is deemed to own more than 50% in value of the corporation's outstanding stock. Ted's direct ownership is limited to $33\frac{1}{3}$%, but through his brothers, he owns indirectly another $66\frac{2}{3}$% for a total of 100%. On the other hand, if the distribution is pursuant to a complete liquidation, Ted's $10,000 realized loss is recognized. ■

The rules governing the basis of property received from a corporation are identical for both nonliquidating and liquidating distributions. Section 301(d) specifies that the basis of property received in a nonliquidating distribution is its fair market value on the date of distribution, while § 334(a) provides the same treatment for property received in a liquidating distribution.

In the following pages, the tax consequences of a complete liquidation are examined first from the view of the distributing corporation and then in terms of the shareholder. Because the tax rules differ when a subsidiary corporation is liquidated, the rules relating to the liquidation of a subsidiary corporation are discussed separately.

6.6 Liquidations—Effect on the Distributing Corporation

The General Rule

Section 336(a) provides that a corporation recognizes *gain or loss* on the distribution of property in a complete liquidation. The property is treated as if it were sold at its fair market value. This treatment is consistent with the notion of double taxation that is inherent in operating a business as a C corporation—once at the corporate level and again at the shareholder level.

As in the case of a nonliquidating distribution, when property distributed in a complete liquidation is subject to a liability of the liquidating corporation, the fair market value used to calculate gain or loss may not be less than the amount of the liability.

EXAMPLE 25

Pursuant to a complete liquidation, Warbler Corporation distributes to its shareholders land held as an investment (basis of $200,000, fair market value of $300,000). If no liability is involved, Warbler has a gain of $100,000 on the distribution ($300,000 − $200,000). Likewise, if the land is subject to a liability of $250,000, Warbler Corporation has a gain of $100,000. If, instead, the liability were $350,000, Warbler's gain on the distribution would be $150,000 ($350,000 − $200,000). ■

Liquidation expenses incurred by a corporation are deductible as trade or business expenses under § 162. Examples include accounting and legal costs of drafting and implementing a plan of liquidation and the cost of revoking the corporation's charter. However, expenditures incurred in the sale of property, such as brokerage commissions and legal costs incurred in title transfers, are treated as offsets against the selling price and reduce the amount realized on the disposition.

There are four exceptions to the general rule of gain and loss recognition by a liquidating corporation:

- *Losses* are not recognized on certain liquidating distributions to related-party shareholders.
- *Losses* are not recognized on certain sales and liquidating distributions of property that was contributed to the corporation with a built-in loss shortly before the adoption of a plan of liquidation.
- A subsidiary corporation does not recognize *gains or losses* on liquidating distributions to its parent corporation.
- A subsidiary corporation does not recognize *losses* on liquidating distributions to its minority shareholders.

The first two exceptions, referred to as the "antistuffing rules," are discussed in detail in the next section and are summarized in Concept Summary 6.2 at the end of the section. The last two exceptions, dealing with the liquidation of a subsidiary corporation, are discussed later in this chapter.

Antistuffing Rules

When property is transferred to a corporation in a § 351 transaction or as a contribution to capital, carryover and substituted basis rules generally apply (see Chapter 4). Generally, the transferee corporation takes a basis in the property equal to that of the transferor-shareholder, and the shareholder takes an equal basis in the stock received in the exchange (or adds such amount to existing stock basis in the case of a capital contribution). Without special limitations, a transfer of loss property (fair market value less than basis) in a carryover basis transaction would present opportunities for the duplication of losses.

THE BIG PICTURE

EXAMPLE 26

Return to the facts of *The Big Picture* on p. 6-1. Assume that Christina transfers property (basis of $100,000, fair market value of $55,000) to Orange Corporation in exchange for additional stock. The exchange qualifies under § 351. Absent any exceptions to the contrary, the general rule of carryover basis would apply and Orange would take a carryover basis of $100,000 in the property while Christina would take a $100,000 basis in the additional stock. A sale or liquidating distribution of the property by Orange Corporation would result in a $45,000 loss [$55,000 (fair market value of property) − $100,000 (property basis)]. Similarly, a sale by Christina of the stock acquired in the § 351 exchange would also result in a $45,000 loss [$55,000 (fair market value of stock) − $100,000 (stock basis)].

Congress addressed this loss duplication issue in the Tax Reform Act of 1986 by enacting two loss limitation ("antistuffing") rules under § 336(d) that apply to corporations upon liquidation. The effect of these rules is to disallow some or all of a loss realized by a corporation in liquidating distributions (and, in some cases, sales) of certain property.

The antistuffing rules limited the duplication of losses realized upon a corporation's liquidation, but loss trafficking was still possible if the corporation sold high-basis property in the normal course of business instead of upon or pursuant to liquidation. As a result, Congress revisited the loss duplication issue and, in 2004, enacted limitations to the general basis rules in § 351 and contribution to capital transactions. Unlike the antistuffing rules that disallow losses, the § 362(e)(2) rules require a corporation to step down the basis of property acquired in a § 351 or contribution to capital transaction by the amount of any net built-in loss embodied in such property. The basis step-down is required when a shareholder transfers properties having an aggregate basis in excess of their aggregate fair market value ("net built-in loss"), and it is allocated proportionately among the properties having built-in losses. Alternatively, the transferor-shareholder can elect to reduce his or her stock basis by the amount of net built-in loss. (See Chapter 4 for further discussion of the basis adjustment rules.) The antistuffing rules of § 336(d) continue to apply in the case of liquidating distributions (and certain sales) of loss property, but their bite has been lessened somewhat by the § 362(e)(2) basis step-down rules.

Related-Party Loss Limitation

Losses are disallowed on distributions to *related parties* in either of the following cases:

- The distribution is *not* pro rata, or
- The property distributed is disqualified property.[31]

A corporation and a shareholder are considered related if the shareholder owns (directly or indirectly) more than 50 percent in value of the corporation's outstanding stock.[32]

A *pro rata distribution* is a distribution where *each* shareholder receives his or her proportionate share of the corporate asset distributed. *Disqualified property* is property that is acquired by the liquidating corporation in a § 351 or contribution to capital transaction during the five-year period ending on the date of the distribution. The related-party loss limitation can apply even if the property was appreciated (fair market value greater than basis) when it was transferred to the corporation.

[31] § 336(d)(1).

[32] Section 267 provides the definition of a related party for purposes of this provision. The rules are similar to the stock attribution rules discussed earlier in this chapter; one exception, however, is that stock owned by a sibling is treated as owned by the taxpayer under § 267.

EXAMPLE 27

Bluebird Corporation stock is owned by Ana and Sanjay, who are unrelated. Ana owns 80% and Sanjay owns 20% of the stock in the corporation. Bluebird has the following assets (none of which were acquired in a § 351 or contribution to capital transaction) that are distributed in complete liquidation of the corporation:

	Adjusted Basis	Fair Market Value
Cash	$600,000	$600,000
Equipment	150,000	200,000
Building	400,000	200,000

Assume that Bluebird Corporation distributes the equipment to Sanjay and the cash and the building to Ana. Bluebird recognizes a gain of $50,000 on the distribution of the equipment. The loss of $200,000 on the building is disallowed because the property is distributed to a related party and the distribution is not pro rata (i.e., the building is not distributed 80% to Ana and 20% to Sanjay). ■

EXAMPLE 28

Assume in Example 27 that Bluebird Corporation distributes the cash and equipment to Ana and the building to Sanjay. Again, Bluebird recognizes the $50,000 gain on the equipment. However, it now recognizes the $200,000 loss on the building because the property is not distributed to a related party (i.e., Sanjay does not own more than 50% of the stock in Bluebird Corporation). ■

EXAMPLE 29

Wren Corporation's stock is held equally by three brothers. Four years before Wren's liquidation, the shareholders transfer jointly owned property (basis of $150,000, fair market value of $200,000) to the corporation in return for stock in a § 351 transaction. When the property is worth $100,000, it is transferred pro rata to the brothers in a liquidating distribution. Because each brother owns directly and indirectly more than 50% (i.e., 100% in this situation) of the stock and disqualified property is involved, none of the $50,000 realized loss [$100,000 (fair market value) − $150,000 (basis)] is recognized by Wren Corporation. ■

EXAMPLE 30

Assume in Example 29 that the property's fair market value is $100,000 at the time of the § 351 transfer and $75,000 at the time of the liquidating distribution to the brothers. As a result of the § 362(e)(2) basis step-down rules, Wren Corporation's basis in the property is $100,000 [$150,000 (basis to brothers) − $50,000 (net built-in loss of property transferred)]. In a liquidating distribution of the property to the brothers, Wren would realize a loss of $25,000 [$75,000 (fair market value of property at distribution) − $100,000 (Wren's stepped-down basis in property)]. Because this is a distribution of disqualified property to related parties, none of the $25,000 loss is recognized by Wren. ■

Built-in Loss Limitation

A second loss limitation applies to sales, exchanges, or distributions of built-in loss property (fair market value less than basis) that is transferred to a corporation shortly before the corporation is liquidated. The built-in loss limitation applies when the following conditions are met:

- The property was acquired by the corporation in a § 351 or contribution to capital transaction.
- Such acquisition was part of a plan whose principal purpose was to recognize a loss on that property by the liquidating corporation. A tax avoidance purpose is presumed in the case of transfers occurring within two years of the adoption of a plan of liquidation.

This disallowance rule applies only to the extent that a property's built-in loss at transfer is not eliminated by a stepped-down basis. Some built-in losses on property transfers will avoid the basis step-down either because built-in gain properties were also transferred by the shareholder (see Chapter 4, Example 22) or because the shareholder elected to step down the basis of his or her stock instead. Any loss attributable to a decline in a property's value after its transfer to the corporation is not subject to the built-in loss limitation.[33]

EXAMPLE 31

On January 4, 2012, Brown Corporation acquires two properties from a shareholder in a transaction that qualifies under § 351.

	Shareholder's Basis	Fair Market Value	Built-in Gain/(Loss)
Land	$100,000	$50,000	($50,000)
Securities	10,000	35,000	25,000
			($25,000)

The net built-in loss of $25,000 results in a stepped-down basis of $75,000 in the land for Brown Corporation [$100,000 (shareholder's basis) – $25,000 (step-down equal to net built-in loss)]. Brown adopts a plan of liquidation on July 9, 2012, and distributes the land to an unrelated shareholder on November 12, 2012, when the land is worth $30,000. Of the $45,000 loss realized [$30,000 (value of land on date of distribution) – $75,000 (basis in land)] by Brown on the distribution, $25,000 is disallowed by the built-in loss limitation [$50,000 (value of land when acquired by Brown) – $75,000 (stepped-down basis in land)], and $20,000 is recognized (equal to the decline in value occurring after acquisition by Brown). ■

The built-in loss limitation applies to a broader range of transactions than the related-party exception, which disallows losses only on certain distributions to related parties (i.e., more-than-50 percent shareholders). The built-in loss limitation can apply to distributions of property to any shareholder, including an unrelated party, and to a *sale or exchange* of property by a liquidating corporation. However, the limitation is narrower than the related-party exception in that it applies only to property that had a built-in loss upon its acquisition by the corporation and only as to the amount of the built-in loss (as adjusted by the basis step-down rules).

EXAMPLE 32

Assume in Example 31 that the land was worth $120,000 on the date Brown Corporation acquired the property. As there is no net built-in loss on the transfer, Brown will have a basis of $100,000 in the land. If the distribution is to an unrelated shareholder, Brown Corporation will recognize the entire $70,000 loss [$30,000 (fair market value on date of distribution) – $100,000 (basis)]. However, if the distribution is to a related party, Brown cannot recognize any of the loss under the related-party loss limitation because the property is disqualified property. When the distribution is to a related party, the loss is disallowed even though the entire decline in value occurred during the period the corporation held the property. ■

The built-in loss limitation will apply only in rare cases if the corporation has held the property more than two years prior to liquidation. The presumption of a tax avoidance purpose for property transferred to a corporation in the two years preceding the liquidation can be rebutted if there is a clear and substantial relationship between the contributed property and the (current or future) business of the corporation. When there was a business reason for the transfer, the built-in loss limitation will not apply.

EXAMPLE 33

Cardinal Corporation's stock is held by two unrelated individuals: 60% by Manuel and 40% by Jack. One year before Cardinal's liquidation, Manuel transfers land (basis of $150,000, fair market value of $100,000) and equipment (basis of $10,000, fair market value of $70,000)

[33] § 336(d)(2).

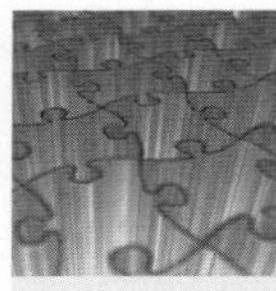

CONCEPT SUMMARY 6.2

Summary of Antistuffing Loss Disallowance Rules

Related-Party Loss Limitation

Distribution of loss property to a related party *and* distribution is not pro rata *or* property is disqualified property.

- Related party if shareholder owns directly or indirectly *more than* 50% in value of stock.
  - Section 267 attribution rules apply. Similar to § 318 attribution rules but includes stock owned by siblings.
- Distribution is pro rata if each shareholder receives proportional interest in property.
- Disqualified property is property acquired by corporation within five years of distribution date in a § 351 or contribution to capital transaction.

Limitation can apply even if a corporation acquired property by purchase or in a carryover basis transaction with no built-in loss (i.e., fair market greater than basis).

Limitation does not apply to *sales* of loss property.

Built-in Loss Limitation

Distribution, sale, or exchange of certain built-in loss property (fair market value less than basis).

- Property was acquired in a § 351 or contribution to capital transaction.
- Acquisition was part of a plan whose principal purpose was to recognize a loss on the property by the corporation upon liquidation.
  - Presumption of tax avoidance purpose if property was acquired within two years of the date of the plan of liquidation.
  - Clear and substantial business purpose for a transfer of property to a corporation can rebut the presumption.
  - Transfers occurring more than two years before liquidation are rarely subject to the loss limitation.

Loss limitation applies only to amount of the built-in loss at the time of transfer to a corporation (excess of corporation's basis in property over fair market value of property).

- Basis step-down rules will eliminate many built-in losses. However, loss limitation remains applicable where built-in loss is not entirely eliminated by basis step-down (i.e., built-in gain property transferred with built-in loss property) or where shareholder elected to step-down basis of stock.

to the corporation as a contribution to capital. As there is no net built-in loss on the transfer, Cardinal will have a basis of $150,000 in the land. There is no business reason for the transfer. In liquidation, Cardinal distributes the land (now worth $90,000) to Jack. Even though the distribution is to an unrelated party, the built-in loss of $50,000 is not recognized. However, Cardinal Corporation can recognize the loss of $10,000 ($90,000 − $100,000) that occurred while it held the land. If, instead, the land is distributed to Manuel, a related party, the entire $60,000 loss is disallowed under the related-party loss limitation. ■

EXAMPLE 34

Assume in Example 33 that the land and equipment are transferred to Cardinal Corporation because a bank required the additional capital investment as a condition to making a loan to the corporation. Because there is a business purpose for the transfer, all of the $60,000 loss is recognized if the land is distributed to Jack in liquidation. If, instead, the land is distributed to Manuel, a related party, the entire loss is still disallowed under the related-party loss limitation. ■

6.7 Liquidations—Effect on the Shareholder

The tax consequences to the shareholders of a corporation in the process of liquidation are governed either by the general rule of § 331 or by the exception of § 332 relating to the liquidation of a subsidiary.

The General Rule

In the case of a complete liquidation, § 331(a) provides for sale or exchange treatment for the shareholders. Thus, the difference between the fair market value of the assets received from the corporation and the adjusted basis of the stock surrendered is the gain or loss recognized by the shareholder. The fair market value of property received subject to a corporate liability is reduced by the amount of such liability. Typically, the stock is a capital asset in the hands of the shareholder, and capital gain or loss results. The burden of proof is on the taxpayer to furnish evidence as to the adjusted basis of the stock. In the absence of such evidence, the stock is deemed to have a zero basis, and the full amount of the liquidation proceeds equals the amount of the gain recognized.[34] The basis of property received in a liquidation is the property's fair market value on the date of distribution.[35]

To the extent that a corporation pays tax on the net amount of gain recognized as a result of its liquidation, the proceeds available to be distributed to the shareholders are likewise reduced. This reduction for the payment of taxes will reduce the amount realized by the shareholders, which will then reduce their gain (or increase the loss) recognized.

EXAMPLE 35

Purple Corporation's assets are valued at $2 million after payment of all corporate debts, except for $300,000 of taxes payable on net gains it recognized on the liquidation. Shawn, an individual and the sole shareholder of Purple, has a basis of $450,000 in his stock. Shawn has a gain recognized of $1,250,000 [$1.7 million amount realized ($2,000,000 – $300,000) – $450,000 basis] as a result of the liquidation. ■

Special Rule for Certain Installment Obligations

Corporations often sell assets pursuant to a plan of liquidation, and sometimes these sales are made on the installment basis. If the installment notes are then distributed in liquidation, the corporation recognizes gain (or loss) equal to the difference between the fair market value of the notes and the corporation's basis in the notes.[36] However, shareholders can use the installment method to defer to the point of collection the portion of their gain that is attributable to the notes. This treatment requires the shareholders to allocate their stock basis between the installment notes and the other assets received from the corporation.[37]

EXAMPLE 36

After a plan of complete liquidation has been adopted, Beige Corporation sells its only asset, unimproved land held as an investment. The land has appreciated in value and is sold to Jane (an unrelated party) for $100,000. Under the terms of the sale, Beige Corporation receives cash of $25,000 and Jane's notes for the balance of $75,000. The notes are payable over 10 years ($7,500 per year) and carry an appropriate rate of interest. Immediately after the sale, Beige Corporation distributes the cash and notes to Earl, the sole shareholder. Earl has an adjusted basis of $20,000 in the Beige stock, and the installment notes have a value equal to their face amount ($75,000). These transactions have the following tax results:

- Beige Corporation recognizes gain on the distribution of the installment notes, measured by the difference between the $75,000 fair market value and the basis Beige had in the notes.
- Earl may defer the gain on the receipt of the notes to the point of collection.
- Earl must allocate the adjusted basis in his stock ($20,000) between the cash and the installment notes as follows:

[34] *John Calderazzo*, 34 TCM 1, T.C.Memo. 1975–1.

[35] § 334(a).

[36] § 453B(a). Gain is not recognized in the distribution of installment notes by a subsidiary liquidating pursuant to § 332. See the discussion below and §§ 337(a) and 453B(d).

[37] § 453(h). Installment notes attributable to the sale of inventory qualify only if the inventory was sold in a bulk sale to one person.

$$\frac{\text{Cash}}{\text{Total receipts}} = \frac{\$25{,}000}{\$100{,}000} \times \$20{,}000 = \$5{,}000 \text{ basis allocated to the cash}$$

$$\frac{\text{Notes}}{\text{Total receipts}} = \frac{\$75{,}000}{\$100{,}000} \times \$20{,}000 = \$15{,}000 \text{ basis allocated to the notes}$$

- On the cash portion of the transaction, Earl must recognize $20,000 of gain [$25,000 (cash received) − $5,000 (basis allocated to the cash)] in the year of liquidation.
- Over the next 10 years, Earl must recognize a total gain of $60,000 on the collection of the notes, computed as follows:

  $75,000 (fair market value) – $15,000 (basis allocated to the notes)
  = $60,000 (gross profit)

- The gross profit percentage on the notes is 80%, computed as follows:

$$\frac{\$60{,}000 \text{ (gross profit)}}{\$75{,}000 \text{ (contract price)}} = 80\%$$

  Thus, Earl must report a gain of $6,000 [$7,500 (amount of note) × 80% (gross profit percentage)] on the collection of each note over the next 10 years.
- The interest element is accounted for separately. ■

6.8 Liquidations—Parent-Subsidiary Situations

LO.5

Determine the tax consequences of subsidiary liquidations for both the parent and the subsidiary corporations.

Section 332, an exception to the general rule of § 331, provides that a parent corporation does *not* recognize gain or loss on a liquidation of a subsidiary. In addition, the subsidiary corporation recognizes *neither gain nor loss* on distributions of property to its parent.[38]

The requirements for applying § 332 are as follows:

- The parent must own at least 80 percent of the voting stock of the subsidiary and at least 80 percent of the value of the subsidiary's stock.
- The subsidiary must distribute all of its property in complete cancellation of all of its stock within the taxable year or within three years from the close of the tax year in which the first distribution occurred.
- The subsidiary must be solvent.[39]

If these requirements are met, nonrecognition of gains and losses becomes mandatory. However, if the subsidiary is insolvent, the parent corporation will have an ordinary loss deduction under § 165(g).

When a series of distributions occurs in the liquidation of a subsidiary corporation, the parent corporation must own the required amount of stock (80 percent) on the date the plan of liquidation is adopted and at all times until all property has been distributed.[40] If the parent fails the control requirement at any time, the provisions for nonrecognition of gain or loss do not apply to any distribution.[41]

The parent-subsidiary rules are set out in Concept Summary 6.3.

Minority Shareholder Interests

In a § 332 parent-subsidiary liquidation, up to 20 percent of the subsidiary's stock can be owned by minority shareholders. In such liquidations, a distribution of property to a minority shareholder is treated in the same manner as a *nonliquidating* distribution. That is, the subsidiary corporation recognizes gain (but not loss) on the property distributed to the minority shareholder.[42]

[38] § 337(a). This is an exception to the general rule of § 336.

[39] § 332(b) and Reg. §§ 1.332–2(a) and (b).

[40] Establishing the date of the adoption of a plan of complete liquidation could be crucial in determining whether § 332 applies. See, for example, *George L. Riggs, Inc.*, 64 T.C. 474 (1975).

[41] § 332(b)(3) and Reg. § 1.332–2(a).

[42] §§ 336(a) and (d)(3).

Basis Rules for Liquidations of Foreign Subsidiaries

The basis of property acquired by a parent corporation in the liquidation of a subsidiary corporation is generally equal to the basis the subsidiary had in such property. However, legislation in 2004 modified the basis rules regarding property acquired by a U.S. parent in some § 332 liquidations of foreign subsidiaries. In general, if the aggregate basis in a foreign subsidiary's assets exceeds their aggregate fair market value, the U.S. parent will take a fair market value basis in the property acquired. The purpose of this amendment is to deny the importation of built-in losses (excess of basis over fair market value). [See §§ 334(b)(1)(B) and 362(e)(1)(B).]

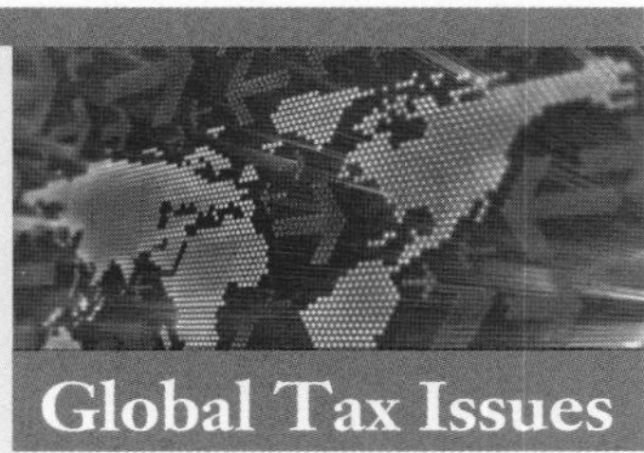

EXAMPLE 37

The stock of Tan Corporation is held as follows: 80% by Mustard Corporation and 20% by Arethia. Tan Corporation is liquidated on December 10, 2012, pursuant to a plan adopted on January 5, 2012. At the time of its liquidation, Tan Corporation has assets with a basis of $100,000 and fair market value of $500,000. Tan Corporation distributes the property pro rata to Mustard Corporation and to Arethia. Tan must recognize gain of $80,000 [($500,000 fair market value − $100,000 basis) × 20% minority interest]. Because the corporate tax due in this liquidation relates entirely to the minority shareholder distribution, that amount will most likely be deducted from the $100,000 distribution ($500,000 × 20%) going to Arethia. The remaining gain of $320,000 is not recognized because it is attributable to property being distributed to Mustard, the parent corporation. ■

A minority shareholder is subject to the general rule requiring the recognition of gain or loss in a liquidation. Accordingly, the difference between the fair market value of the assets received and the basis of the minority shareholder's stock is the amount of gain or loss recognized. Further, the basis of property received by the minority shareholder is the property's fair market value on the date of distribution.[43]

Indebtedness of the Subsidiary to the Parent

If a subsidiary transfers appreciated property to its parent to satisfy a debt, it must recognize gain on the transaction unless the subsidiary is liquidating and the conditions of § 332 (discussed above) apply. When § 332 applies, the subsidiary does not recognize gain or loss upon the transfer of properties to the parent in satisfaction of indebtedness.[44]

EXAMPLE 38

Eagle Corporation owes its parent, Finch Corporation, $20,000. It satisfies the obligation by transferring land (basis of $8,000, fair market value of $20,000) to Finch. Normally, Eagle would recognize a gain of $12,000 on the transaction. However, if the transfer is made pursuant to a liquidation under § 332, Eagle does not recognize a gain. ■

This nonrecognition provision does not apply to the parent corporation. The parent corporation recognizes gain or loss on the receipt of property in satisfaction of indebtedness, even if the property is received during liquidation of the subsidiary.

EXAMPLE 39

Pelican Corporation owns bonds (basis of $95,000) of its subsidiary, Crow Corporation, that were acquired at a discount. Upon liquidation of Crow pursuant to § 332, Pelican receives a distribution of $100,000, the face amount of the bonds. The transaction has no tax effect on Crow. However, Pelican Corporation recognizes gain of $5,000 [$100,000 (amount realized) − $95,000 (basis in bonds)]. ■

[43] § 334(a).

[44] § 337(b)(1).

Basis of Property Received by the Parent Corporation—The General Rule

Property received in the complete liquidation of a subsidiary has the same basis it had in the hands of the subsidiary.[45] Unless the parent corporation makes a § 338 election (discussed below), this carryover basis in the assets generally will differ significantly from the parent's basis in the stock of the subsidiary. Because the liquidation is a nontaxable exchange, the parent's gain or loss on the difference in basis is not recognized. Further, the parent's basis in the stock of the subsidiary disappears.

EXAMPLE 40

Lark Corporation has a basis of $200,000 in the stock of Heron Corporation, a subsidiary in which it owns 85% of all classes of stock. Lark purchased the Heron stock 10 years ago. In the current year, Lark liquidates Heron Corporation and acquires assets that are worth $800,000 and have a tax basis to Heron of $500,000. Lark Corporation takes a basis of $500,000 in the assets, with a potential gain upon their sale of $300,000. Lark's $200,000 basis in Heron's stock disappears. ■

EXAMPLE 41

Indigo Corporation has a basis of $600,000 in the stock of Kackie Corporation, a wholly owned subsidiary acquired 10 years ago. It liquidates Kackie Corporation and receives assets that are worth $400,000 and have a tax basis to Kackie of $300,000. Indigo Corporation takes a basis of $300,000 in the assets it acquires from Kackie. If Indigo sells the assets, it has a gain of $100,000 even though its basis in the Kackie stock was $600,000. Indigo's loss on its stock investment in Kackie will never be recognized. ■

In addition to the parent corporation taking the subsidiary's basis in its assets, the parent's holding period for the assets includes that of the subsidiary.[46] Further, the carryover rules of § 381 apply (see Chapter 7). Under that provision, the parent acquires other tax attributes of the subsidiary, including the subsidiary's net operating loss carryover, business credit carryover, capital loss carryover, and E & P.

Basis of Property Received by the Parent Corporation—§ 338 Election

Background

As discussed above, the liquidation of a subsidiary generally is a nontaxable transaction resulting in the nonrecognition of gain or loss for both the parent and the subsidiary corporations and the carryover of the subsidiary's asset bases (and other tax attributes). This treatment reflects the fact that such a liquidation often is merely a change in corporate structure and not a change in substance. This is particularly the case when the parent has owned the stock of the subsidiary since the subsidiary's inception. In such cases, the carried-over bases are comparable to what the parent would have in the subsidiary's assets if the parent, and not the subsidiary, had originally acquired the assets.

The carryover basis rule for § 332 liquidations can result in some inequities when the subsidiary has been in existence for some time prior to the parent's acquisition of the subsidiary's stock. The parent's basis in the stock of the subsidiary will reflect the fair market value of the subsidiary's assets (and goodwill) at the time of the stock purchase. As a result, the parent's basis in the stock of the subsidiary will usually be greater than the subsidiary's basis in its assets. Under the carryover basis rule, a liquidation of the subsidiary would result in the parent taking a basis in the subsidiary's assets that is less than the parent's basis in the stock of the

[45] § 334(b)(1) and Reg. § 1.334–1(b). But see § 334(b)(1)(B) (exception for property acquired in some liquidations of foreign subsidiaries).

[46] § 1223(2).

subsidiary. This is the case even if the parent acquired the subsidiary stock solely to obtain the subsidiary's assets.

If the parent could treat the purchase of the subsidiary stock as a purchase of its assets, the parent could take a basis in the assets equal to the acquisition cost of the stock. In most cases, this would mean a higher asset basis and, as a result, larger depreciation deductions and lower gains upon disposition for the parent. To obtain this stock-basis-for-asset-basis result, taxpayers successfully devised stock purchase/subsidiary liquidation transactions that fell outside the purview of § 332.[47] Congress codified this treatment by enacting § 338, which permits the purchase of a controlling interest of stock to be treated as a purchase of the subsidiary's assets.

Requirements for Application

A corporation (the "parent") may *elect* the provisions of § 338 if it acquires stock representing at least 80 percent of the voting power and at least 80 percent of the value of another corporation (the "subsidiary") within a 12-month period ("*qualified stock purchase*"). The stock must be acquired in a taxable transaction (i.e., § 351 and other nonrecognition provisions do not apply). An acquisition of stock by any member of an affiliated group that includes the parent corporation is considered to be an acquisition by the parent. The **§ 338 election** must be made by the fifteenth day of the ninth month beginning after the month in which a qualified stock purchase occurs. If made, the election is irrevocable.

Tax Consequences

Upon a § 338 election, the subsidiary is treated as having sold its assets on the qualified stock purchase date for a value that is determined with reference to the parent's basis in the subsidiary stock plus any liabilities of the subsidiary ("aggregate deemed sale price").[48] The subsidiary is then treated as a new corporation that purchased those assets for a similarly computed amount ("adjusted grossed-up basis") on the day following the qualified stock purchase date.[49] The deemed sale results in gain (or loss) recognition to the subsidiary, and the deemed purchase results in a stepped-up (or -down) basis for the subsidiary's assets.[50] The subsidiary may, but need not, be liquidated. If the subsidiary is liquidated, the parent will obtain a carryover of the stepped-up (or -down) basis of the subsidiary's assets.

A Comparison of the General Rule and the § 338 Election

Under the general rule of nonrecognition, the liquidation of a subsidiary is tax-free to both the subsidiary (except for any minority interest) and the parent corporation. Under § 338, the subsidiary recognizes gain (or loss) on the deemed disposition of its assets. A liquidation of the subsidiary remains tax-free to the parent. While a carryover basis rule applies in both cases, the subsidiary's assets generally will have a stepped-up basis as a result of the § 338 election and a liquidation of the subsidiary will result in a carryover of the stepped-up basis to the parent. Further, a liquidation of the subsidiary results in a carryover of its other tax attributes (e.g., E & P) to the parent regardless of whether a § 338 election is made. However, when the election is made, the subsidiary is treated as a new corporation as of the day following the qualified stock purchase date; as a result, any tax attributes acquired by the parent are likely to be nominal (or zero) in amount.

The holding period of the subsidiary's assets is determined with reference to the substance of the transaction. When the subsidiary is liquidated and there is no § 338 election, the subsidiary's historical holding period in its assets carries over to the parent. This is the typical carryover rule found in other nonrecognition

[47]See, for example, *U.S. v. M.O.J. Corp.*, 60–1 USTC ¶9209, 5 AFTR 2d 535, 274 F.2d 713 (CA–5, 1960). See also *Kimbell-Diamond Milling Co.*, 14 T.C. 74 (1950), *aff'd* 51–1 USTC ¶9201, 40 AFTR 328, 187 F.2d 718 (CA–5, 1951), *cert. den.* 72 S.Ct. 50 (USSC, 1951) (IRS argued stock-for-asset basis).

[48]See §§ 338(a)(1) and (b) and Reg. § 1.338–4.

[49]See §§ 338(a)(2) and (b) and Reg. § 1.338–5.

[50]For the rules governing the allocation of the purchase price to the assets, see § 338(b)(5) and Reg. § 1.338–6.

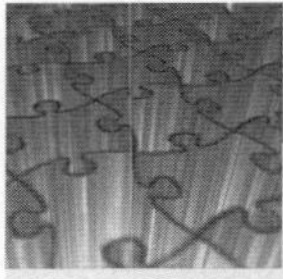

CONCEPT SUMMARY 6.3

Summary of Liquidation Rules

Effect on the Shareholder	Basis of Property Received	Effect on the Corporation
§ 331—The general rule provides for gain or loss treatment on the difference between the FMV of property received and the basis of the stock in the corporation. Gain allocable to installment notes received can be deferred to point of collection.	§ 334(a)—Basis of assets received by the shareholder will be the FMV on the date of distribution (except for installment obligations on which gain is deferred to the point of collection).	§ 336—Gain or loss is recognized for distributions in kind and for sales by the liquidating corporation. Losses are not recognized for distributions to related parties if the distribution is not pro rata or if disqualified property is distributed. Losses may be disallowed on sales and distributions of built-in loss property even if made to unrelated parties.
§ 332—In liquidation of a subsidiary, no gain or loss is recognized to the parent. Subsidiary must distribute all of its property within the taxable year or within three years from the close of the taxable year in which the first distribution occurs. Minority shareholders taxed under general rule of § 331.	§ 334(b)(1)—Property has the same basis as it had in the hands of the subsidiary. Parent's basis in the stock disappears. Carryover rules of § 381 apply. Minority shareholders get FMV basis under § 334(a).	§ 337—No gain or loss is recognized to the subsidiary on distributions to the parent. Gain (but not loss) is recognized on distributions to minority shareholders.
	§ 338—Subsidiary need not be liquidated. If subsidiary is liquidated, parent's basis is new stepped-up (or -down) basis. Parent's basis in the stock disappears. Carryover rules of § 381 apply, but such amounts are likely to be nominal.	§ 338—Gain or loss is recognized to the subsidiary. Subsidiary is treated as a new corporation, and its basis in assets is stepped up (or down) to reflect parent's basis in subsidiary stock plus subsidiary's liabilities. New basis is allocated among various asset classes.

provisions. A § 338 election, however, assumes a sale and repurchase of the subsidiary's assets. As a result of these deemed transactions, the holding period starts anew. If there is a § 338 election and the subsidiary is liquidated, the holding period of the property received by the parent begins on the date of the qualified stock purchase. On the other hand, if there is a § 338 election and the subsidiary is not liquidated, the holding period of the assets begins on the day after the qualified stock acquisition date. Figure 6.1 illustrates the consequences of a § 338 election to both the parent and subsidiary corporations.

6.9 Tax Planning

LO.6

Identify planning opportunities available to minimize the tax impact in stock redemptions and complete liquidations.

Stock Redemptions

Stock redemptions offer several possibilities for tax planning:

- The alternative to a qualifying stock redemption is dividend treatment. The 15 percent (0 percent for taxpayers in the 10 or 15 percent marginal tax bracket) preferential tax rate on dividend income reduces some of the adverse consequences of a nonqualified stock redemption. However, the dividend tax rate preference is scheduled to lapse after 2012. Qualifying a

FIGURE 6.1 Consequences of a Section 338 Election

Assume the following:

- Parent acquires 100% of subsidiary's stock for $750,000 on August 1, 2012.
- Subsidiary (E & P of $400,000) has only one asset, land (fair market value of $1 million, basis of $504,000), no liabilities, and no loss or tax credit carryovers. Subsidiary's tax rate is 34%.
- Parent files a timely § 338 election, and both aggregate deemed sale price (ADSP) and adjusted grossed-up basis (AGUB) are $876,727.

Subsidiary is liquidated

Consequences to Subsidary:

Deemed to have sold the land for ADSP of $876,727, which results in a recognized gain of $372,727 [$876,727 (ADSP) – $504,000 (basis)], and tax of $126,727 ($372,727 × 34%). The land's new basis is $876,727 (AGUB). No gain or loss recognized on distribution of land to parent.

Consequences to Parent:

No gain or loss recognized on receipt of land from subsidiary. Basis in land is $876,727; holding period for the land begins on August 1, 2012; and basis in subsidiary stock disappears. Acquires subsidiary's E & P, but that amount is $0 as a result of the § 338 election.

Subsidiary is *not* liquidated

Consequences to Subsidary:

Deemed to have sold the land for ADSP of $876,727, which results in a recognized gain of $372,727 [$876,727 (ADSP) – $504,000 (basis)], and tax of $126,727 ($372,727 × 34%). Treated as a new corporation (e.g., E & P of $0) as of August 2, 2012; land's new basis is $876,727 (AGUB); and holding period for the land begins on August 2, 2012.

Consequences to Parent:

No tax consequences. Basis in subsidiary stock remains unchanged at $750,000.

redemption for sale or exchange treatment takes on greater import if dividend income is taxed at ordinary income tax rates.

- A nonqualified redemption may be preferable to a redemption that produces sale or exchange treatment if the distributing corporation has little or no E & P or the distributee-shareholder is another corporation. In the latter situation, dividend treatment may be preferred due to the availability of the dividends received deduction.
- Stock redemptions are particularly well suited for purchasing the interest of a retiring or deceased shareholder. Rather than the remaining shareholders buying the stock of the retiring or deceased shareholder, corporate funds are used to redeem the stock from the retiring shareholder or from the decedent shareholder's estate. A corporate buy-sell agreement can be used to effect a redemption of a retiring or deceased shareholder's stock. The ability to use the corporation's funds to buy out a shareholder's interest is also advantageous in property settlements between divorcing taxpayers. The redeeming corporation need not finance the redemption entirely with cash, as it can issue its own notes as consideration in the transaction without adverse tax consequences to the shareholder.
- A third party who wants to purchase all of the stock of a corporation can utilize a stock redemption to finance some of the stock acquisition cost. This technique is referred to as a "bootstrap acquisition." The third party first purchases a small amount of stock from the shareholders. The corporation then redeems all of its outstanding stock except that of the third party. The third party becomes the sole shareholder of the corporation, but corporate funds finance most of the acquisition.

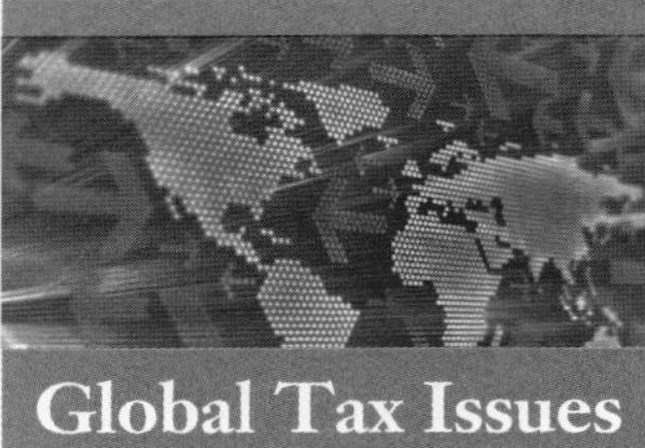

Exception to § 332 for Liquidations of U.S. Subsidiaries of Foreign Corporations

When a U.S. subsidiary is liquidated into a U.S. parent, gains (or losses) are not recognized immediately, but rather are deferred as a result of the carryover basis rule. Gains inherent in the transferred assets will be recognized upon their disposition by the parent. Foreign corporations generally are not subject to U.S. taxation, so the liquidation of a U.S. subsidiary into a foreign parent could avoid gain recognition entirely if § 332 were to apply unabated. Section 367(b) overrides § 332 when a U.S. subsidiary is liquidated into a foreign parent, however. Under § 367(b), the subsidiary will recognize gain on the transfer of certain "tainted" assets. Tainted assets include inventory, installment obligations, accounts receivable, and depreciable property (to the extent of depreciation recapture). For further details, see Chapter 9.

- A not essentially equivalent redemption provides minimal utility and generally should be relied upon only as a last resort. Instead, a redemption should be structured to satisfy the objective tests required of one of the other qualifying redemptions.
- The timing and sequence of a redemption should be considered carefully, as a series of redemptions may have the effect of a dividend distribution. The following example illustrates this point.

EXAMPLE 42

Sparrow Corporation's stock is held by three unrelated shareholders: Alma (60 shares), Antonio (20 shares), and Ali (20 shares). The corporation redeems 24 of Alma's shares. Shortly thereafter, it redeems 5 of Antonio's shares. Does Alma's redemption qualify as a disproportionate redemption? Taken in isolation, it satisfies the 80% and 50% tests. Yet, if the IRS takes into account the later redemption of Antonio's shares, Alma has not satisfied the 50% test; she still owns $^{36}/_{71}$ of the corporation after the two redemptions. A greater time lag between the redemptions places Alma in a better position to argue against collapsing the two redemptions as parts of one integrated plan. ■

- For a family corporation in which all of the shareholders are related to each other, the only hope of achieving sale or exchange treatment may lie in the use of a redemption that completely terminates a shareholder's interest or that follows a shareholder's death. In a complete termination redemption, it is important that the family stock attribution rules be avoided. Here, strict compliance with the requirements for the family attribution waiver (e.g., the withdrawing shareholder does not acquire a prohibited interest in the corporation within 10 years) is crucial.
- In a redemption to pay death taxes, the amount to be sheltered from dividend treatment is limited to the sum of death taxes and funeral and administration expenses. However, a redemption in excess of the limitation does not destroy the applicability of § 303. Further, if the transaction is structured properly, the excess amount can qualify for sale or exchange treatment under one of the other redemption rules.

Disposing of § 306 Stock

Distributing the preferred stock dividend at a time when the corporation has no E & P avoids the § 306 taint altogether. Otherwise, avoiding ordinary income on the disposition of § 306 stock is a difficult feat. Unless the corporation's E & P was nominal at the time of the stock dividend (in the case of a § 306 stock sale) or at the time of the redemption (in the case of a § 306 stock redemption), the disposition of § 306 stock typically produces only ordinary income. The 15 percent (or 0 percent) tax rate applicable to dividend income (through 2012) lessens the bite of such treatment. A gift of § 306 stock does not defeat the ordinary income taint, as the taint remains with the stock. However, if the donee is in the 10 or 15 percent marginal tax bracket, the tainted income at disposition would be taxed at the 0 percent tax rate applicable to dividends for the lowest-bracket taxpayers. In a charitable contribution of § 306 stock, the deduction is reduced under § 170(e) by the amount of the ordinary income taint.

A sale of § 306 stock in a transaction that terminates the shareholder's entire direct and indirect stock interest (common and preferred) in the corporation will avoid ordinary income treatment, as will a disposition in liquidation of the corporation. Similarly, a redemption of § 306 stock in a complete termination redemption or a partial liquidation avoids the ordinary income result. However, these exceptions are of limited use in the typical disposition of § 306 stock.

Corporate Liquidations

With the exception of parent-subsidiary liquidations, distributions in liquidation are taxed at both the corporate level and the shareholder level. When a corporation liquidates, it can, as a general rule, claim losses on assets that have depreciated in value. These assets should not be distributed in the form of a property dividend or stock redemption because losses are not recognized on nonliquidating distributions.

Shareholders faced with large prospective gains in a liquidation may consider shifting part or all of that gain to other taxpayers. One approach is to donate stock to charity. A charitable contribution of the stock produces a deduction equal to the stock's fair market value (see Chapter 2). Alternatively, the stock may be given to family members. If the family member is in the 10 or 15 percent marginal tax bracket, some or all of the gain on liquidation could be taxed at the 0 percent preferential rate on long-term capital gains. Whether these procedures will be successful in shifting the liquidation-related gain from the taxpayer depends on the timing of the transfer. If the donee of the stock is not in a position to prevent the liquidation of the corporation, the donor may be deemed to have made an anticipatory assignment of income. In such a case, the gain is still taxed to the donor. In addition, possible gift tax issues on the stock transfer must be considered (see Chapter 18). Advance planning of stock transfers, therefore, is crucial in arriving at the desired tax result.

The installment sale provisions provide some relief from the general rule that a shareholder recognizes all gain upon receiving a liquidating distribution. If the assets of the liquidating corporation are not to be distributed in kind, a sale of the assets in exchange for installment notes should be considered. Shareholders receiving the notes in a liquidation can then report their gain on the installment method as the notes are collected. Gain deferred under the installment method is subject to the tax rates applicable in each year of collection. Under current tax law, the preferential tax rate for long-term capital gains is scheduled to increase to 20 percent (from 15 percent) after 2012. Thus, the deferral of gain on installment obligations received in a liquidation must be weighed against the anticipated 5 percentage point increase in the applicable tax rate for gains deferred beyond 2012.

Parent-Subsidiary Liquidations

The nonrecognition provision applicable to the liquidation of a subsidiary, § 332, is not elective. Nevertheless, some flexibility may be available:

- Whether § 332 applies depends on the 80 percent stock ownership test. A parent corporation may be able to avoid § 332 by reducing its stock ownership in the subsidiary below this percentage to allow for recognition of a loss. On the other hand, the opposite approach may be desirable to avoid gain recognition. A corporate shareholder possessing less than the required 80 percent ownership may want to acquire additional stock to qualify for § 332 treatment.
- Once § 332 becomes effective, less latitude is allowed in determining the parent's basis in the subsidiary's assets. Generally, the subsidiary's existing basis in its assets carries over to the parent. If a timely § 338 election is made, the subsidiary's basis in its assets is stepped up to reflect, in part, the parent's basis in the subsidiary stock. If the subsidiary also is liquidated, the parent obtains assets with the stepped-up basis.

- An election to have the § 338 rules apply should be carefully weighed as the election can be detrimental. The income tax liability on the subsidiary's recognized gain that results from the deemed sale of its assets is the cost under § 338 for obtaining the stepped-up basis. As a result, a § 338 election may be a viable option only when the subsidiary possesses loss and/or credit carryovers that can be used to offset the associated tax.

Asset Purchase versus Stock Purchase

The acquisition of a corporation's assets generally takes one of two forms. In one form, the acquiring corporation purchases the stock of the target corporation, and then the target (subsidiary) is liquidated. In the other form, the acquiring corporation purchases the assets of the target corporation, and then the target distributes the proceeds to its shareholders in liquidation. Nontax considerations may affect the form of acquisition, with each form having both favorable and unfavorable aspects.

An asset purchase requires that title be transferred and that creditors be notified. Further, an asset purchase may not be feasible if valuable nontransferable trademarks, contracts, or licenses are involved. Alternatively, an asset purchase may be preferable to a stock purchase if the target's shareholders refuse to sell their stock. In addition, an asset purchase avoids the transfer of liabilities (including unknown liabilities) generally inherent in stock acquisitions. An asset purchase also has the advantage of allowing the purchaser to avoid the acquisition of unwanted assets, whereas a stock purchase would involve all of a target's assets.

REFOCUS ON THE BIG PICTURE

A Family Attribution Waiver Is a Valuable Tool in Succession Planning

With proper planning, a complete termination redemption could be utilized to achieve Christina's objectives. In the years remaining before her retirement, Christina should ensure that her children are actively involved in the management and strategy decisions of Orange Corporation. Also, an ownership interest in Orange should be shifted to each of the children so that they are in minority shareholder positions by the time Christina retires. The children could purchase Orange shares from Christina or newly issued shares from Orange. Alternatively, Christina could make annual gifts of Orange stock to the children. In addition to eliminating the need for the children to raise capital for a stock purchase, this alternative would produce favorable estate tax consequences. Upon Christina's retirement, Orange would redeem her remaining ownership interest, and the two children would be the sole shareholders of Orange Corporation. Assuming that Christina satisfies the requirements of the family attribution waiver, the transaction would qualify as a complete termination redemption. Orange Corporation could issue notes to finance the stock redemption, and Christina could use the installment method to report her gain. (The notes should specify a reasonable rate of interest.)

What If?

What if Christina passes away before her retirement date? A redemption to pay death taxes could be utilized to redeem Orange stock from Christina's estate, as it appears that the requirements of § 303 would be satisfied. However, a redemption would qualify under § 303 only to the extent of the estate's death taxes and funeral and administration expenses. A redemption of an amount greater than the sum of these expenditures probably would not satisfy any of the § 302 qualifying stock redemption provisions, as the children would be the primary or sole beneficiaries of Christina's estate. After the redemption to pay death taxes, the estate's remaining shares of Orange would be distributed to the children, and they would control 100 percent of the outstanding shares of the corporation.

KEY TERMS

Attribution, 6-5
Complete termination redemption, 6-8
Corporate liquidation, 6-16
Disproportionate redemption, 6-7
Meaningful reduction test, 6-6
Not essentially equivalent redemption, 6-6
Partial liquidation, 6-9
Preferred stock bailout, 6-14
Redemption to pay death taxes, 6-10
Section 338 election, 6-27
Stock redemption, 6-2

DISCUSSION QUESTIONS

1. **LO.1** Contrast the tax treatment of distributions that are a return *from* an investment with the treatment of those that are a return *of* an investment.

2. **LO.1** Why does the Code limit sale or exchange treatment on stock redemptions to qualifying stock redemptions?

3. **LO.1, 2, 6** Chao, Louis, and Mari, unrelated individuals, own all of the shares of Cerise Corporation. All three shareholders have been active in the management of Cerise since its inception. In the current year, Chao wants to retire and sell all of her shares in the corporation. What issues should be considered in determining whether Chao should sell her stock to one of the other shareholders, to Cerise Corporation, or to a third party? **Issue ID**

4. **LO.1** During the current year, Gnatcatcher, Inc., distributed $100,000 each to Brandi and Yuen in redemption of some of their Gnatcatcher stock. The two shareholders acquired their shares five years ago. Each shareholder is in the 28% tax bracket, and each had a $40,000 basis in her redeemed stock. Brandi incurred $9,000 of tax on her redemption, but Yuen incurred $15,000 on her redemption. Discuss the likely reason for the difference in tax liabilities arising from the stock redemptions.

5. **LO.1** Would a shareholder prefer a qualifying stock redemption or a nonqualified stock redemption? Why?

6. **LO.1** Rosalie owns 50% of the outstanding stock of Salmon Corporation. In a qualifying stock redemption, Salmon distributes $80,000 to Rosalie in exchange for one-half of her shares, which have a basis of $100,000. As a result of the redemption, Rosalie has a recognized loss of $20,000. Assess the validity of this statement.

7. **LO.1** A shareholder's basis in property received in a qualifying stock redemption is the property's fair market value on the date of the redemption, but a shareholder's basis in property received in a nonqualified stock redemption is the basis the distributing corporation had in such property. Comment on the validity of this statement.

8. **LO.1** Would qualifying stock redemption treatment be ensured if the distribution was treated as a sale or exchange of the stock under applicable state law? Explain.

9. **LO.1** How do the § 318 stock attribution rules apply to partnerships and their partners?

10. **LO.1** The stock attribution rules apply to all stock redemptions. Assess the validity of this statement.

11. **LO.1** Briefly discuss the requirements for a redemption to qualify as a not essentially equivalent redemption.

12. **LO.1** Explain the requirements for a disproportionate redemption.

13. **LO.1, 2** Tammy and Barry formed Pheasant Corporation several years ago in a transaction that qualified under § 351. Both shareholders serve as officers and on the board of directors of Pheasant. In the current year, Pheasant Corporation redeemed all of Barry's shares in the corporation with a property distribution. What are the tax issues for Barry and Pheasant? **Issue ID**

14. **LO.1, 6** Lauren owns 600 shares in Viridian Corporation. The remaining 400 shares of Viridian are owned by Lauren's son, Brett. Currently, Lauren is both President and Chair of the board of directors of Viridian Corporation. If Viridian redeems Lauren's 600 shares, can the redemption qualify for sale or exchange treatment? Explain.

15. **LO.1** The termination of a business test is a safe-harbor rule that satisfies the not essentially equivalent to a dividend requirement for a partial liquidation. Briefly outline the requirements for the termination of a business test.

Issue ID

16. **LO.1, 2** Brown Corporation operates several trades and businesses. In the current year, Brown discontinues the operation of one of its trades and businesses. Brown is considering distributing to its shareholders either the assets of the discontinued business or the proceeds from the sale of such assets. Considering both of these alternatives, what are the tax issues for Brown Corporation and its shareholders?

17. **LO.1** A redemption to pay death taxes usually results in little or no gain or loss being recognized by the estate. Evaluate this statement.

18. **LO.1, 2** Explain the requirements for a redemption to pay death taxes. What are the tax consequences of a redemption to pay death taxes for the shareholder and the corporation?

Issue ID

19. **LO.1, 2** Angie and her daughter, Ann, who are the only shareholders of Bluebird Corporation, each paid $100,000 four years ago for their shares in Bluebird. Angie also owns 20% of the stock in Redbird Corporation. The Redbird stock is worth $500,000, and Angie's basis in the stock is $50,000. Angie dies in 2012 leaving all of her property to her husband, Gary, but Ann wants to be the sole shareholder of Bluebird Corporation. Bluebird has assets worth $4 million (basis of $700,000) and E & P of $1 million. Angie's estate is worth approximately $6 million. Angie has made gifts during her lifetime to Ann. What are the tax issues for Angie's estate, Ann, and Bluebird?

Decision Making

20. **LO.2, 6** Indigo Corporation wants to transfer cash of $150,000 or property worth $150,000 to one of its shareholders, Linda, in a redemption transaction that will be treated as a qualifying stock redemption. If Indigo distributes property, the corporation will choose between two assets that are each worth $150,000 and are no longer needed in its business: Property A (basis of $75,000) and Property B (basis of $195,000). Indigo is indifferent as to the form of the distribution, but Linda prefers a cash distribution. Considering the tax consequences to Indigo on the distribution to redeem Linda's shares, what should Indigo distribute?

Issue ID

21. **LO.2** Kackie Corporation (E & P of $1 million) is currently in negotiations to redeem stock from one or more of its shareholders. The form (i.e., cash and/or property) and amount of the distribution(s) to the shareholder(s) are key points of the negotiations. What are the tax issues for Kackie Corporation?

22. **LO.2** Discuss the deductibility of expenditures, such as legal, accounting, transfer agent, brokerage, and appraisal fees, a corporation might incur in connection with a redemption of its stock.

23. **LO.3** In general, what are the tax consequences surrounding the sale of § 306 stock?

24. **LO.3** What issues arise when a shareholder sells shares owned in one corporation to another corporation in which he or she is a shareholder?

25. **LO.4** What are some reasons the shareholders of a corporation might want to liquidate the corporation?

26. **LO.4** Under what circumstances are losses disallowed to a corporation in liquidation?

27. **LO.1, 2, 4** One difference between the tax treatment of a liquidation and a qualifying stock redemption is the applicability of § 267. Explain this statement from the perspective of both the shareholder and the corporation.

28. **LO.4** For purposes of the related-party loss limitation within the context of a complete liquidation, what is the definition of *disqualified property*?

29. **LO.4** When properties transferred by a shareholder in a § 351 transaction have a net built-in loss (aggregate fair market value less than aggregate basis), the basis step-down

rule must be applied. Discuss the relevance of the built-in loss limitation given the enactment of the basis step-down rule.

30. **LO.4** Explain the tax consequences to a shareholder of a corporation in the process of liquidation under the general rule of § 331. May a shareholder use the installment method to report gain on a complete liquidation? Why or why not?

31. **LO.5** Discuss the tax consequences to the parent corporation in a § 332 liquidation of a subsidiary.

32. **LO.5** Does § 332 apply to the liquidation of an insolvent subsidiary? If not, then how does the parent corporation treat such a liquidation?

33. **LO.5** A subsidiary corporation is liquidated under § 332. Pursuant to its liquidation, the subsidiary transferred property to a minority shareholder. With respect to this distribution, what are the tax consequences to the subsidiary corporation and to the minority shareholder?

34. **LO.5** In the context of a § 332 liquidation, a subsidiary corporation distributes property to its parent corporation in satisfaction of indebtedness. Discuss the tax consequences of this distribution for the subsidiary and parent corporations.

35. **LO.5** What happens to a subsidiary's tax attributes (e.g., net operating loss, E & P, and capital loss carryover) upon a § 332 liquidation?

36. **LO.5** In general, what are the tax consequences of a § 338 election?

37. **LO.5** From the perspective of the parent corporation, contrast the tax consequences of a subsidiary liquidation under the general nonrecognition rules with a subsidiary liquidation that follows a § 338 election.

PROBLEMS

38. **LO.1, 2, 6** Teal Corporation, with E & P of $1.9 million, distributes property with a basis of $180,000 and a fair market value of $250,000 to Grace. She owns 28% of the outstanding Teal shares. **Decision Making**
    a. What are the tax consequences to Teal Corporation and to Grace if the distribution is a property dividend?
    b. What are the tax consequences in (a) if Grace is a corporation?
    c. What are the tax consequences to Teal Corporation and to Grace if the distribution is a qualifying stock redemption? Assume that half of Grace's stock is redeemed in the transaction. Her basis in the redeemed shares is $70,000.
    d. What are the tax consequences in (c) if Grace is a corporation?
    e. If the parties involved could choose from among the preceding options, which would they choose? Why?

39. **LO.1** Julio is in the 35% tax bracket. He acquired 2,000 shares of stock in Gray Corporation seven years ago at a cost of $200 per share. In the current year, Julio received a payment of $450,000 from Gray Corporation in exchange for 1,000 of his shares in Gray. Gray has E & P of $1 million. What tax liability would Julio incur on the $450,000 payment in each of the following situations? Assume that Julio has no capital losses.
    a. The payment qualifies for stock redemption (i.e., sale or exchange) treatment.
    b. The payment does not qualify for stock redemption (i.e., sale or exchange treatment is not applicable) treatment.

40. **LO.1** How would your answer to Problem 39 differ if Julio were a corporate shareholder (in the 34% tax bracket) rather than an individual shareholder and the stock ownership in Gray Corporation represented a 25% interest?

41. **LO.1** Assume in Problem 39 that Julio has a capital loss carryover of $50,000 in the current tax year. Julio has no other capital gain transactions during the year. What amount of the capital loss may Julio deduct in the current year in the following situations? **Decision Making**

a. The $450,000 payment from Gray Corporation is a qualifying stock redemption for tax purposes (i.e., receives sale or exchange treatment).
b. The $450,000 payment from Gray Corporation does not qualify as a stock redemption for tax purposes (i.e., does not receive sale or exchange treatment).
c. If Julio had the flexibility to structure the transaction as described in either (a) or (b), which form would he choose? Why?

42. **LO.1** How would your answer to parts (a) and (b) of Problem 41 differ if Julio were a corporate shareholder (in the 34% tax bracket) rather than an individual shareholder and the stock ownership in Gray Corporation represented a 25% interest?

43. **LO.1** Magpie Corporation has 3,000 shares of common stock outstanding. Josephina owns 800 shares, Josephina's daughter owns 500 shares, Josephina's brother owns 800 shares, Tern Corporation owns 600 shares, and Petrel Partnership owns 300 shares. Josephina owns 45% of the stock of Tern Corporation, and she owns a 60% interest in Petrel Partnership.
a. Applying the § 318 stock attribution rules, how many shares does Josephina own in Magpie Corporation?
b. Assume that Josephina owns 75% of the stock of Tern Corporation. How many shares does Josephina own, directly and indirectly, in Magpie Corporation?

44. **LO.1** Pedro owns 700 of the 1,000 shares outstanding of Indigo Corporation (E & P of $950,000). Pedro paid $170 per share for the stock 12 years ago. The remaining stock in Indigo is owned by unrelated individuals. What are the tax consequences to Pedro in the following independent situations?
a. Indigo redeems 350 shares of Pedro's stock for $175,000.
b. Indigo redeems 450 shares of Pedro's stock for $225,000.

Communications

45. **LO.1, 2** Stork Corporation (E & P of $850,000) has 1,000 shares of common stock outstanding. The shares are owned by the following individuals: Lana Johnson, 450 shares; Lori Johnson (Lana's sister), 450 shares; and Leo Johnson (Lana's son), 100 shares. Lana paid $200 per share for the Stork stock eight years ago. Lana is interested in reducing her stock ownership in Stork via a stock redemption for $1,000 per share, the fair market value of the stock. Stork Corporation would distribute cash for the entire redemption transaction. Lana has inquired as to the minimum number of shares she would have to redeem to obtain favorable long-term capital gain treatment and the overall tax consequences of such a redemption to both her and Stork Corporation. Prepare a letter to Lana (1000 Main Street, St. Paul, MN 55166) and a memo for the file in which you explain your conclusions.

46. **LO.1** Cyan Corporation (E & P of $700,000) has 4,000 shares of common stock outstanding. The shares are owned as follows: Angelica, 2,000 shares; Dean (Angelica's son), 1,500 shares; and Walter (Angelica's uncle), 500 shares. In the current year, Cyan redeems all of Angelica's shares. Determine whether the redemption can qualify for sale or exchange treatment under the complete termination redemption rules in each of the following independent circumstances.
a. Angelica remains as a director of Cyan Corporation.
b. Three years after the redemption, Angelica loans $100,000 to Cyan Corporation and receives in return a two-year note receivable.
c. Dean replaces Angelica as president of Cyan Corporation.
d. Six years after the redemption, Angelica receives 250 shares in Cyan as a gift from Walter.

47. **LO.1, 2** Robert and Lori (Robert's sister) own all of the stock in Swan Corporation (E & P of $700,000). Each owns 500 shares and has a basis of $25,000 in the shares. Robert wants to sell his stock for $400,000, the fair market value, but he will continue to be employed as an officer of Swan Corporation after the sale. Lori would like to purchase Robert's shares and, thus, become the sole shareholder in Swan, but Lori is short of funds. What are the tax consequences to Robert, Lori, and Swan Corporation under the following circumstances?
a. Swan Corporation distributes cash of $400,000 to Lori, and she uses the cash to purchase Robert's shares.
b. Swan Corporation redeems all of Robert's shares for $400,000.

48. **LO.1, 2** For the last eleven years, Lime Corporation has owned and operated four different trades or businesses. Lime also owns stock in several corporations that it purchased for investment purposes. The stock in Lime Corporation is held equally by Sultan, an individual, and by Turquoise Corporation. Both Sultan and Turquoise own 1,000 shares in Lime that were purchased nine years ago at a cost of $200 per share. Determine whether the following independent transactions qualify as partial liquidations under § 302(b)(4). In each transaction, determine the tax consequences to Lime Corporation, to Turquoise Corporation, and to Sultan.
    a. Lime Corporation sells one of its trades or businesses (basis of $500,000, fair market value of $700,000) and distributes the proceeds equally to Sultan and Turquoise Corporation in redemption of 250 shares from each shareholder. Lime Corporation has E & P of $2.1 million as of the date of the distribution.
    b. Lime Corporation distributes the stock (basis of $425,000, fair market value of $700,000) it holds in other corporations to Sultan and Turquoise Corporation equally in redemption of 250 shares from each shareholder. Lime Corporation has E & P of $2.1 million as of the date of the distribution.

49. **LO.1, 2** The gross estate of Tanya, decedent, includes stock of Finch Corporation (E & P of $2 million) valued at $1.4 million. At the time of her death in 2012, Tanya owned 40% of the Finch stock outstanding, and she had a basis of $220,000 in the stock. The death taxes and funeral and administration expenses related to Tanya's estate amount to $1.4 million, and the adjusted gross estate is $7 million. The remainder of the Finch stock is owned by shareholders unrelated to Tanya (or her estate). Tanya named her son, Taylor, as the sole heir of her estate. In the current year, Finch Corporation distributes $1.4 million to the estate in redemption of all of its stock in the corporation. What are the tax consequences of the redemption to Tanya's estate and to Finch Corporation?

50. **LO.1** The gross estate of Bridgett, decedent, includes stock of Crane Corporation (E & P of $1.3 million) and Eagle Corporation (E & P of $1 million) valued at $750,000 and $2 million, respectively. At the time of her death in 2012, Bridgett owned 26% of the Crane stock outstanding and 32% of the Eagle stock outstanding. Bridgett had a basis of $240,000 in the Crane stock and $165,000 in the Eagle stock. Bridgett's adjusted gross estate is $7.5 million, and the death taxes and funeral and administration expenses total $750,000. What are the tax consequences to Bridgett's estate if Crane Corporation redeems all of the Crane Corporation stock for $750,000?

51. **LO.1, 2** Broadbill Corporation (E & P of $650,000) has 1,000 shares of common stock outstanding. The shares are owned by the following individuals: Tammy, 300 shares; Yvette, 400 shares; and Jeremy, 300 shares. Each of the shareholders paid $50 per share for the Broadbill stock four years ago. In the current year, Broadbill Corporation distributes $75,000 to Tammy in redemption of 150 of her shares. Determine the tax consequences of the redemption to Tammy and to Broadbill under the following independent circumstances.
    a. Tammy and Jeremy are grandmother and grandson.
    b. The three shareholders are siblings.

52. **LO.2** Crane Corporation has 2,000 shares of stock outstanding. It redeems 500 shares for $370,000 when it has paid-in capital of $300,000 and E & P of $1.2 million. The redemption qualifies for sale or exchange treatment for the shareholder. Crane incurred $13,000 of accounting and legal fees in connection with the redemption transaction and $18,500 of interest expense on debt incurred to finance the redemption. What is the effect of the distribution on Crane Corporation's E & P? Also, what is the proper tax treatment of the redemption expenditures? Prepare a letter to the president of Crane Corporation (506 Wall Street, Winona, MN 55987) and a memo for the file in which you explain your conclusions. **Communications**

53. **LO.3** Ramon and Sophie are the sole shareholders of Gull Corporation. Ramon and Sophie each have a basis of $75,000 in their 500 shares of Gull common stock. When its E & P was $500,000, Gull Corporation issued a preferred stock dividend on the common shares of Ramon and Sophie, giving each 500 shares of preferred stock with a par value

of $200 per share. Fair market value of one share of common was $300, and fair market value of one share of preferred was $200.

a. What are the tax consequences of the distribution to Ramon and Sophie?
b. What are the tax consequences to Ramon if he later sells his preferred stock to Anthony for $100,000? Anthony is not related to Ramon.
c. What are the tax consequences if, instead of Ramon selling the preferred stock to Anthony, Gull Corporation redeems the stock from Ramon for $100,000? Assume that Gull's E & P at the time of the redemption is $550,000.

54. **LO.3** Martin owns 1,000 shares of stock in Black Corporation and 500 shares of stock in Blue Corporation, representing 100% ownership of Black and 50% ownership of Blue. Martin sells 200 Blue shares to Black Corporation for $300,000. Martin purchased the Blue stock four years ago at a cost of $600 per share. What are the tax consequences of the sale assuming that Black Corporation has E & P of $800,000 and Blue Corporation has E & P of $1 million?

55. **LO.1, 2, 4** Dove Corporation (E & P of $650,000) has 1,000 shares of stock outstanding. The shares are owned as follows: Julia, 600 shares; Maxine (Julia's daughter), 300 shares; and Janine (Julia's granddaughter), 100 shares. Dove Corporation owns land (basis of $470,000, fair market value of $330,000) that it purchased as an investment seven years ago. Dove distributes the land to Julia in exchange for all of her shares in the corporation. Julia had a basis of $350,000 in the shares. What are the tax consequences for both Dove Corporation and Julia if the distribution is:

a. A qualifying stock redemption?
b. A liquidating distribution?

56. **LO.4** Pursuant to a complete liquidation, Oriole Corporation distributes to its shareholders land held for three years as an investment (adjusted basis of $250,000, fair market value of $490,000). The land is subject to a liability of $520,000.

a. What are the tax consequences to Oriole Corporation on the distribution of the land?
b. If the land is, instead, subject to a liability of $400,000, what are the tax consequences to Oriole on the distribution?

57. **LO.4** Bronze Corporation's stock is held equally by three brothers: Mitchell, Alex, and Ron. Four years ago, the brothers transferred to Bronze Corporation land in which they had owned equal interests. The transfer of the land (basis of $260,000, fair market value of $300,000) qualified under § 351. Pursuant to a liquidation in the current year, Bronze distributed the land pro rata to the three brothers. The land had a fair market value of $215,000 on the date of the distribution. What amount of loss may Bronze Corporation recognize on the distribution of the land?

58. **LO.4** On April 21, 2011, Crow Corporation acquired land and equipment in a § 351 transaction. At that time, the land had a basis of $300,000 and a fair market value of $225,000, and the equipment had a basis of $20,000 and a fair market value of $100,000. The land and equipment were transferred to Crow Corporation for use as security for a loan the corporation was in the process of obtaining from a local bank. The bank required the additional capital investment as a condition for making the loan. Crow Corporation adopted a plan of liquidation on October 3, 2012. On December 4, 2012, Crow Corporation distributes the land to Ali, a 40% shareholder. On the date of the distribution, the land had a fair market value of only $150,000. What amount of loss may Crow Corporation recognize on the distribution of the land?

59. **LO.4** On March 4, 2011, a shareholder transferred land (basis of $650,000, fair market value of $575,000) to Roadrunner Corporation in a § 351 transaction. This was the only property transferred to Roadrunner at that time. On February 3, 2012, Roadrunner Corporation adopted a plan of liquidation. On May 16, 2012, Roadrunner distributed the land to Rhonda, a 15% shareholder. On the date of the distribution, the land had a fair market value of $400,000. Roadrunner Corporation never used the land for business purposes during the time it owned the property. What amount of loss may Roadrunner recognize on the distribution of the land?

Decision Making

60. **LO.4** Pink Corporation acquired land and securities in a § 351 tax-free exchange in 2011. On the date of the transfer, the land had a basis of $720,000 and a fair market value of $1 million, and the securities had a basis of $110,000 and a fair market value of

$250,000. Pink Corporation has two shareholders, Maria and Paul, unrelated individuals. Maria owns 85% of the stock in Pink Corporation, and Paul owns 15%. The corporation adopts a plan of liquidation in 2012. On this date, the value of the land has decreased to $500,000. What is the effect of each of the following on Pink Corporation? Which option should be selected?

a. Distribute all of the land to Maria.
b. Distribute all of the land to Paul.
c. Distribute 85% of the land to Maria and 15% to Paul.
d. Distribute 50% of the land to Maria and 50% to Paul.
e. Sell the land and distribute the proceeds of $500,000 proportionately to Maria and to Paul.

61. **LO.4** Assume in Problem 60 that the land had a fair market value of $630,000 on the date of its transfer to Pink Corporation. On the date of the liquidation, the land's fair market value has decreased to $500,000. How would your answer to Problem 60 change if: **Decision Making**

a. All of the land is distributed to Maria?
b. All of the land is distributed to Paul?
c. The land is distributed 85% to Maria and 15% to Paul?
d. The land is distributed 50% to Maria and 50% to Paul?
e. The land is sold and the proceeds of $500,000 are distributed proportionately to Maria and to Paul?

62. **LO.4** Pursuant to a complete liquidation in the current year, Scarlet Corporation distributes to Jake land (basis of $425,000, fair market value of $390,000) that was purchased three years ago and held as an investment. The land is subject to a liability of $250,000. Jake, who owned 35% of the Scarlet shares outstanding, had a basis of $60,000 in the stock. What are the tax consequences of the liquidating distribution to Scarlet Corporation and to Jake?

63. **LO.4** After a plan of complete liquidation has been adopted, Purple Corporation sells its only asset, land, to Rex (an unrelated party) for $500,000. Under the terms of the sale, Purple receives cash of $100,000 and Rex's note in the amount of $400,000. The note is payable over five years ($80,000 per year) and carries an appropriate rate of interest. Immediately after the sale, Purple distributes the cash and note to Helen, the sole shareholder of Purple Corporation. Helen has a basis of $50,000 in the Purple stock. What are the tax results to Helen if she wants to defer as much gain as possible on the transaction? Assume that the installment note possesses a value equal to its face amount.

64. **LO.4, 5** The stock of Magenta Corporation is owned by Fuchsia Corporation (90%) and Marta (10%). Magenta is liquidated in the current year, pursuant to a plan of liquidation adopted earlier in the year. In the liquidation, Magenta distributes various assets worth $1,620,000 (basis of $1,950,000) to Fuchsia (basis of $1.2 million in Magenta stock) and a parcel of land worth $180,000 (basis of $165,000) to Marta (basis of $35,000 in Magenta stock). Assuming that the § 338 election is not made, what are the tax consequences of the liquidation to Magenta, Fuchsia, and Marta?

65. **LO.4, 5** The stock in Ivory Corporation is owned by Gold Corporation (80%) and Imelda (20%). Gold Corporation purchased its shares in Ivory nine years ago at a cost of $650,000, and Imelda purchased her shares in Ivory four years ago at a cost of $175,000. Ivory Corporation has the following assets that are distributed in complete liquidation:

	Adjusted Basis	Fair Market Value
Cash	$600,000	$600,000
Inventory	80,000	200,000
Equipment	350,000	200,000

a. Assume that Ivory Corporation distributes the cash and inventory to Gold Corporation and the equipment to Imelda. What are the tax consequences of the distributions to Ivory Corporation, to Gold Corporation, and to Imelda?

b. Assume that Ivory Corporation distributes the cash and equipment to Gold Corporation and the inventory to Imelda. What are the tax consequences of the distributions to Ivory Corporation, to Gold Corporation, and to Imelda?

66. **LO.5** Orange Corporation purchased bonds (basis of $185,000) of its wholly owned subsidiary, Green Corporation, at a discount. Upon liquidation of Green pursuant to § 332, Orange receives payment in the form of land worth $200,000, the face amount of the bonds. Green had a basis of $220,000 in the land. What are the tax consequences of this land transfer to Green Corporation and to Orange Corporation?

67. **LO.5** At the time of its liquidation under § 332, Cardinal Corporation (E & P of $560,000) had the following assets and liabilities: cash ($175,000); marketable securities (fair market value of $230,000, basis of $250,000); unimproved land (fair market value of $600,000, basis of $300,000); unsecured note payable ($50,000); and mortgage on the unimproved land ($270,000). Cardinal also had a net operating loss carryover of $45,000. Wren Corporation acquired all of the stock of Cardinal seven years ago for $160,000.
   a. How much gain (or loss) will Cardinal Corporation recognize upon the liquidating distribution of its assets and liabilities to Wren Corporation?
   b. How much gain (or loss) will Wren Corporation recognize in the liquidation of Cardinal?
   c. What basis will Wren have in the marketable securities and unimproved land it receives in the liquidation?
   d. What happens to Cardinal's E & P and net operating loss carryover?

68. **LO.5** On July 21, 2011, Lilac Corporation purchased 25% of the Coffee Corporation stock outstanding. Lilac Corporation purchased an additional 40% of the stock in Coffee on March 23, 2012, and an additional 20% on May 2, 2012. On September 23, 2012, Lilac Corporation purchased the remaining 15% of Coffee Corporation stock outstanding. For purposes of the § 338 election, on what date does a qualified stock purchase occur? What is the due date for making the § 338 election?

RESEARCH PROBLEMS

THOMSON REUTERS
CHECKPOINT®

Note: Solutions to Research Problems can be prepared by using the **Checkpoint® Student Edition** online research product, which is available to accompany this text. It is also possible to prepare solutions to the Research Problems by using tax research materials found in a standard tax library.

Communications

Research Problem 1. Six years ago, Coastal Drillers, Inc., redeemed all of the stock owned directly by Jeremiah Cranston (6870 Vinton Court, Los Angeles, CA 90034). At the time of the redemption, Jeremiah and his immediate family members owned 100% of the stock of Coastal Drillers. Jeremiah satisfied all of the requirements of the family attribution waiver [under § 302(c)(2)]; thus, the transaction qualified as a complete termination redemption and resulted in a significant long-term capital gain. Coastal Drillers' E & P at the time of the transaction exceeded the redemption proceeds. Treatment of the redemption proceeds as a dividend would have resulted in a $200,000 greater tax liability for Jeremiah. In the current year, Coastal Drillers has offered Jeremiah a consulting engagement. The consulting engagement would be for a one-year term, but options to renew could extend the contract to a total of five years. Assuming that all options are exercised, Jeremiah would earn $150,000 under the contract. Based on the terms of the contract, Jeremiah would properly be classified as an independent contractor, not as an employee of Coastal Drillers. Jeremiah has contacted you regarding the effect, if any, of the proposed consulting engagement on the tax treatment of his earlier stock redemption. Prepare a letter to Jeremiah and a memo for the file documenting your conclusions.

Research Problem 2. Tammy Olsen has owned 100% of the common stock of Green Corporation (basis of $75,000) since the corporation's formation in 2003. In 2009, when Green had E & P of $320,000, the corporation distributed to Tammy a nontaxable dividend of 500 shares of preferred stock (value of $100,000 on date of distribution) on her common stock interest (value of $400,000 on date of distribution). In 2010, Tammy donated the 500 shares of preferred stock to her favorite charity, State University. Tammy deducted $100,000, the fair market value of the stock on the date of the gift, as a charitable contribution on her

2010 income tax return. Tammy's adjusted gross income for 2010 was $420,000. Six months after the contribution, Green Corporation redeemed the preferred stock from State University for $100,000. Upon audit of Tammy's 2010 return, the IRS disallowed the entire deduction for the gift to State University, asserting that the preferred stock was § 306 stock and that § 170(e)(1)(A) precluded a deduction for contributions of such stock. What is the proper tax treatment for Tammy's contribution of Green Corporation preferred stock?

Partial list of research aids:
Reg. § 1.170A–4(b)(1).
§ 306(b)(4).

Research Problem 3. Berta Jackson owns 100% of the common stock of Almond Corporation (E & P of $1.5 million), having purchased the stock 15 years ago. Berta is contemplating a gift of 45% of her shares in Almond (basis of $100,000, fair market value of $1 million) to a qualified charitable organization. Under Berta's plan, Almond would then redeem the charitable organization's shares in the corporation, and the charity would use the redemption proceeds to finance the construction of a soccer complex in a low-income neighborhood. Berta's objectives are to claim a charitable contribution deduction of $1 million for the gift of the Almond shares and retain sole ownership in Almond after the corporation's redemption of stock from the charitable organization. However, a CPA friend of Berta's has warned her to be careful to avoid the assignment of income doctrine. Uncertain as to the meaning of her friend's warning, Berta has asked you for advice as to how to proceed with her plan. What advice would you give Berta so that she can achieve her objectives?

Communications

Research Problem 4. Shelly Zumaya (2220 East Hennepin Avenue, Minneapolis, MN 55413) is the president and sole shareholder of Kiwi Corporation (stock basis of $400,000). Incorporated in 2002, Kiwi Corporation's sole business has consisted of the purchase and resale of used farming equipment. In December 2010, Kiwi transferred its entire inventory (basis of $1.2 million) to Shelly in a transaction described by the parties as a sale. According to Shelly and collaborated by the minutes of the board of directors, the inventory was sold to her for the sum of $2 million, the fair market value of the inventory. The terms of the sale provided that Shelly would pay Kiwi Corporation the $2 million at some future date. This debt obligation was not evidenced by a promissory note, and to date, Shelly has made no payments (principal or interest) on the obligation. The inventory transfer was not reported on Kiwi's 2010 tax return, either as a sale or a distribution. After the transfer of the inventory to Shelly, Kiwi Corporation had no remaining assets and ceased to conduct any business. Kiwi did not formally liquidate under state law. Upon an audit of Kiwi Corporation's 2010 tax return, the IRS asserted that the transfer of inventory constituted a liquidation of Kiwi and, as such, that the corporation recognized a gain on the liquidating distribution in the amount of $800,000 [$2 million (fair market value) – $1.2 million (inventory basis)]. Further, because Kiwi Corporation is devoid of assets, the IRS assessed the entire tax liability against Shelly, based on transferee liability. Finally, the IRS assessed a tax due from Shelly for her gain recognized in the purported liquidating distribution. Shelly has contacted you regarding the IRS's determination. Prepare a letter to Shelly Zumaya and a memo for the file, documenting your research.

Internet Activity

Use the tax resources of the Internet to address the following questions. Do not restrict your search to the Web, but include a review of newsgroups and general reference materials, practitioner sites and resources, primary sources of the tax law, chat rooms and discussion groups, and other opportunities.

Communications

Research Problem 5. Buy-sell agreements are frequently used to address the disposition of a retiring or deceased shareholder's stock in a closely held corporation. Using the Internet as your sole research source, prepare an outline on the planning opportunities and pitfalls of using a buy-sell agreement in conjunction with the qualifying stock redemption provisions.

Communications

Research Problem 6. The requirements for effectively liquidating a corporate entity under state law vary from state to state. Using the Internet as your sole research source, prepare an outline discussing how an entity incorporated in your home state is liquidated, including any reporting requirements associated with such liquidation.

CHAPTER

7 Corporations: Reorganizations

LEARNING OBJECTIVES: *After completing Chapter 7, you should be able to:*

LO.1 Identify the general requirements of corporate reorganizations.

LO.2 Determine the tax consequences of a corporate reorganization.

LO.3 Explain the statutory requirements for the different types of reorganizations.

LO.4 Delineate the judicial and administrative conditions for a nontaxable corporate reorganization.

LO.5 Apply the rules pertaining to the carryover of tax attributes in a corporate reorganization.

LO.6 Structure corporate reorganizations to obtain the desired tax consequences.

CHAPTER OUTLINE

THE BIG PICTURE Tax Solutions for the Real World

© Edward Rozzo/Corbis/Glow Images, Inc.

STRUCTURING ACQUISITIONS

Rock & Water Corporation (R&W) specializes in industrial park landscaping featuring rock walls, holding ponds, water fountains, and indigenous vegetation. One of R&W's central missions is to cause as little negative impact on the environment as possible. Until recently, R&W applied this policy only to its own work, but the new CEO, Tony Turner, wants to extend its corporate responsibility to its suppliers.

R&W uses several types of chemicals and fertilizers in its business and is aware that three of its suppliers do not use environmentally sound practices. Realizing that simply changing suppliers will not eliminate these polluting practices, R&W is considering acquiring these three suppliers. Using this strategy, R&W would control the production practices of these corporations.

R&W is unsure of how to structure these potential acquisitions of its suppliers and seeks your advice. R&W gives you the following information about these potential acquisitions:

- BrineCo is a profitable corporation that has been owned predominantly by the Adams family since its incorporation in 1950.
- AcidCo started in 1967. AcidCo has been having legal troubles and has continually been fined since more stringent EPA standards came into existence. Besides chemicals used by R&W, AcidCo produces acids for the mining industry.
- ChemCo is a new fertilizer producer with the technology to produce environmentally safe products. Its management is inexperienced, however, and the result has been inefficiencies in production and unintended harm to its surroundings. ChemCo has yet to show a profit.

How will you advise R&W to approach each of these acquisitions?

Read the chapter and formulate your response.

7 Introduction

One tenet of U.S. tax policy is to encourage business development. Accordingly, the tax laws allow entities to form without taxation, assuming that certain requirements are met. As an extension of this policy, corporate restructurings are also favored with tax-free treatment. Corporations may engage in a variety of acquisitions, combinations, consolidations, and divisions tax-free, as long as the "reorganization" requirements in the Code are met.

Because the dollar value of most reorganizations is substantial, the tax implications are significant; thus, the tax law often dictates the form of the restructuring. The taxable gain for shareholders is likely to be treated as either a dividend or a capital gain. For individual shareholders, both dividends and capital gains are subject to lower tax rates than apply to ordinary income. Corporate shareholders are allowed the dividends received deduction, if the gains are categorized as a dividend. However, because corporations receive no tax rate reduction for capital gains, corporate shareholders and the corporations involved in the restructuring would be taxed at their highest marginal rate on any gains classified as capital.

Careful planning can reduce or totally eliminate the tax possibilities for both the corporations and their shareholders. Consequently, when feasible, parties contemplating a corporate reorganization should apply for and obtain from the IRS a letter ruling determining the income tax effect of the transactions. Assuming that the parties proceed with the transactions as proposed in the ruling request, a favorable ruling provides, in effect, an insurance policy as to the tax treatment of the restructuring.[1]

Courts originally concluded that even minor changes in a corporation's structure would produce taxable gains for the shareholders involved.[2] Congress, however, determined that businesses should be allowed to make necessary capital adjustments without being subject to taxation.[3] The theory for nonrecognition in certain corporate reorganizations is similar to that underlying § 351 treatment and like-kind exchanges. As the Regulations state:

> the new property is substantially a continuation of the old investment ... and, in the case of reorganizations, ... the new enterprise, the new corporate structure, and the new property are substantially continuations of the old.[4]

7.1 Reorganizations—In General

LO.1

Identify the general requirements of corporate reorganizations.

Although the term **reorganization** is commonly associated with a corporation in financial difficulty, for tax purposes, the term refers to any corporate restructuring that may be tax-free under § 368. To qualify as a tax-free reorganization, a corporate restructuring must meet not only the specific requirements of § 368 but also several general requirements. These requirements include the following.

1. There must be a *plan of reorganization.*
2. The reorganization must meet the *continuity of interest* and the *continuity of business enterprise* tests provided in the Regulations.
3. The restructuring must meet the judicial doctrine of having a *sound business purpose.*
4. The court-imposed *step transaction* doctrine should not apply to the reorganization.

All of these concepts are discussed in this chapter. The initial and most important consideration, however, is whether the reorganization qualifies for nonrecognition status under § 368.

---

[1]To expedite the letter ruling process, the IRS attempts to issue rulings within 10 weeks from the date of request. Rev.Proc. 2005–68, 2005–2 C.B. 694.

[2]*U.S. v. Phellis,* 1 USTC ¶54, 3 AFTR 3123, 42 S.Ct. 63 (USSC, 1921).

[3]Reg. § 1.368–1(b). See S.Rept. No. 275, 67th Cong., 1st Sess. (1921), at 1939–1 C.B. 181.

[4]Reg. § 1.1002–1(c).

Summary of the Different Types of Reorganizations

Section 368(a) specifies seven corporate restructurings or *reorganizations* that will qualify as nontaxable exchanges. If the transaction fails to qualify as a reorganization, it will not receive the special tax-favored treatment. Therefore, a corporation considering a business reorganization must determine in advance if the proposed transaction specifically falls within one of these seven types.

The Code states, in § 368(a)(1), that the term *reorganization* applies to any of the following.

A. A statutory merger or consolidation.
B. The acquisition by a corporation of another using solely stock of each corporation (voting-stock-for-stock exchange).
C. The acquisition by a corporation of substantially all of the property of another corporation in exchange for voting stock (voting-stock-for-asset exchange).
D. The transfer of all or part of a corporation's assets to another corporation when the original corporation's shareholders are in control of the new corporation immediately after the transfer (divisive exchange, also known as a spin-off, split-off, or split-up).
E. A recapitalization.
F. A mere change in identity, form, or place of organization.
G. A transfer by a corporation of all or a part of its assets to another corporation in a bankruptcy or receivership proceeding.

These seven types of tax-free reorganizations typically are designated by their identifying letters: "Type A," "Type B," "Type C," etc. Each will be described in more detail later in the chapter.

Summary of Tax Consequences in a Tax-Free Reorganization

LO.2

Determine the tax consequences of a corporate reorganization.

The tax treatment for the parties involved in a tax-free reorganization almost exactly parallels the treatment under the like-kind exchange provisions of § 1031. In the simplest like-kind exchange, neither gain nor loss is recognized on the exchange of "like-kind" property. When "boot" (defined as non-like-kind property) is received, gain may be recognized. The four-column template of Concept Summary 7.1 computes the amount of gain recognized and the adjusted basis in the new asset received in the like-kind exchange.

Unfortunately, the like-kind exchange provisions do not apply to the exchange of stock or securities.[5] Therefore, the general rule is that when an investor exchanges stock in one corporation for stock in another, the exchange is a taxable transaction. If the transaction qualifies as a reorganization under § 368, however, the exchange receives tax-deferred treatment. Thus, a § 368 reorganization, in substance, is similar to a nontaxable exchange of like-kind property, and the four-column template of Concept Summary 7.1 is useful for reorganizations as well.

EXAMPLE 1

José holds 1,000 shares of Lotus stock that he purchased for $10,000 several years ago. In a merger of Lotus into Blossom, Inc., José exchanges his 1,000 Lotus shares for 1,000 Blossom shares. Both investments are valued at $18 per share. Thus, José's stock is valued at $18,000 ($18 per share × 1,000 shares). Assuming that this exchange qualifies for tax-free treatment under § 368, José's recognized gain and basis in his Blossom stock are computed as follows.

[5] § 1031(a)(2)(B).

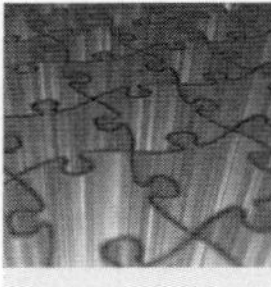

CONCEPT SUMMARY 7.1

Gain and Basis Rules for Nontaxable Exchanges

(1) Realized Gain/Loss	(2) Recognized Gain (Not Loss)	(3) Postponed Gain/Loss	(4) Basis of New Asset
Amount realized − Adjusted basis of asset(s) surrendered	Lesser of boot received or gain realized	Realized gain/loss (column 1) − Recognized gain (column 2)	FMV of asset (stock) received − Postponed gain (column 3) or + Postponed loss (column 3)
Realized gain/loss	Recognized gain	Postponed gain/loss	Adjusted basis in new asset (stock)

Realized Gain	Recognized Gain	Postponed Gain	Basis in Blossom Stock
$18,000	$-0-	$8,000	$18,000
−10,000			− 8,000
$ 8,000			$10,000

The exchange of José's stock has no tax consequences for Lotus or Blossom. ■

Gain or Loss

Corporations meeting the § 368 requirements do not recognize gain or loss on a restructuring. There are exceptions to the nonrecognition rule, however. If the acquiring corporation transfers property to the target corporation along with its stock and securities, gain, but not loss, may be recognized. When the target receives other property (called **boot**) in the restructuring and fails to distribute it, or distributes its own appreciated property to its shareholders, gain, but not loss, is recognized. **Other property** for restructurings is any asset other than stock or securities and, thus, is treated as boot.[6]

EXAMPLE 2

In a qualifying reorganization, Acquiring Corporation exchanges $800,000 of stock and land with a $200,000 fair market value and a $150,000 basis for all of Target Corporation's assets, which have a $1 million fair market value and a $600,000 basis. Due to the *other property* (land) it used in the transfer, Acquiring recognizes a $50,000 gain ($200,000 − $150,000) on the reorganization. If Target distributes the land to its shareholders, it does not recognize gain. If Target retains the land, however, it recognizes gain to the extent of the *other property* received, $200,000. ■

Generally, the shareholders of corporations involved in a tax-free reorganization do not recognize gain or loss when exchanging their stock unless they receive cash or other property in addition to stock. The cash or other property is considered boot, and the gain recognized by the stockholder is the lesser of the boot received or the realized gain. This is analogous to the treatment of boot in a like-kind exchange. The only instance when shareholders may recognize losses in reorganizations is when they receive solely boot and no stock.

[6] §§ 361(a) and (b).

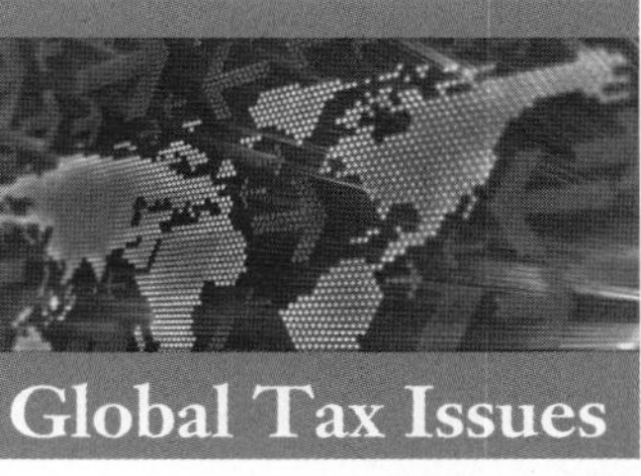

© Andrey Prokhorov, iStockphoto

Mining M&As Are Good as Gold

When the economy is weak, gold is strong. And when gold is strong, merger and acquisition (M&A) activity spikes in the mining industry. Currently, the gold mining industry is undergoing a remarkable consolidation. This is not surprising with gold prices increasing 400 percent in the past 10 years and rising 25 percent in the last year alone.

China, Australia, South Africa, the United States, Russia, and Peru are the world's largest gold producers. Together, they account for almost 50 percent of the global total. At one time, South Africa produced more than 50 percent of the total, and Africa continues to be a magnet for mining companies. A new area of interest is the Philippines.

One of the fuels for this M&A activity is the diminishing likelihood of discovering new gold deposits that are economically feasible. With the amount of gold on the planet finite and the demand for gold increasing, mining corporations are using M&A activities to add to their reserves. Using this method, a company can concentrate its capital on extracting from proven mines rather than on risky prospecting for new gold fields, which is becoming increasingly more expensive.

Sources: Liezel Hill, "African Barrick Looking in West, North-East Africa for Potential M&A," *miningweekly.com,* October 29, 2010; and Scott Wright (Zeal Intelligence, LLC), "Gold Mining M&A," October 29, 2010.

EXAMPLE 3

Kalla, the sole shareholder of Target Corporation in Example 2, has a $700,000 basis in her stock. She exchanges her Target stock for the $800,000 of Acquiring stock plus the land ($200,000) transferred by Acquiring to Target. Kalla has a $200,000 recognized gain due to receiving the land (boot). The computations are as follows.

Realized Gain	Recognized Gain	Postponed Gain	Basis in Acquiring Stock
$1,000,000*	$200,000	$100,000	$800,000
−700,000			−100,000
$ 300,000			$700,000

*$800,000 stock + $200,000 land. ■

Once the gain is recognized, its character must be determined. The following are the possibilities for gain characterization.

- Dividend to the extent of the shareholder's proportionate share of earnings and profits (E & P). The remaining gain is generally capital gain.
    - The distinction between dividends and long-term capital gain is important when the taxpayer has capital losses to offset or when the capital gain would be classified as short term and therefore not subject to the special tax rates.
- If the requirements of § 302(b) can be met, the transaction will qualify for stock redemption treatment (see Chapter 6).
    - Gains from qualifying stock redemptions are treated as capital gains.
    - In computing the shareholder's ownership reduction, shares actually received in the acquiring corporation are compared with the number of shares the shareholder would have received if solely the acquiring corporation's stock had been distributed in the reorganization.[7]

[7] *Comm. v. Clark,* 89–1 USTC ¶9230, 63 AFTR 2d 89–860, 109 S.Ct. 1455 (USSC, 1989), and Rev.Rul. 93–61, 1993–2 C.B. 118.

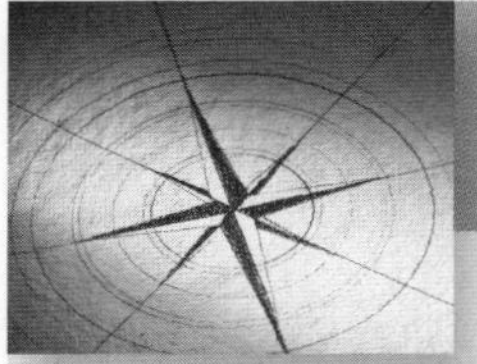

ETHICS & EQUITY A White Knight Turns Black

Retail Corporation is a small regional chain of upscale clothing stores. As business casual has become the accepted dress for professionals, Retail has become very profitable. Consequently, it has substantial liquid assets and few liabilities. Retail is so encouraged by its profitability that it is considering becoming a national chain.

Retail's success has not gone unnoticed in the marketplace. Mega Corporation, a privately owned conglomerate, makes an unsolicited tender offer for the Retail stock. In the past, Mega has made such offers for other small corporations with substantial liquid assets. Once it owns enough stock to take control of the board of directors, Mega forces the liquidation of the company to obtain its liquid assets. Therefore, Retail is very concerned about Mega's tender offer. To avoid being taken over by Mega, Retail negotiates with Cotton Corporation, one of its suppliers, for a merger of the two companies. Cotton is fully aware of the dangers faced by Retail as it was the target of an unsuccessful takeover by Mega in the past. It was rescued from the takeover by a similar "white knight" merger with one of its competitors.

Through an informer at Cotton, Mega discovers Retail's plan to foil its hostile takeover. To sabotage the Retail-Cotton merger, Mega offers Cotton an exclusive contract for producing its line of children's school clothes for Mega's national chain of discount department stores. The contract requires that Cotton not be affiliated with any other corporation in the retail clothing business. Cotton's directors believe this contract could boost profits by 20 percent. Therefore, the board votes to enter into the contract with Mega and abandon its merger negotiations with Retail. Retail ultimately is taken over by Mega and liquidated. All of its 1,000 employees lose their jobs. What ethical issues, if any, did Cotton's directors face in their dealings with Mega and Retail?

THE BIG PICTURE

EXAMPLE 4

Return to the facts of *The Big Picture* on p. 7-1. R&W proceeds with its acquisition of BrineCo. Sam acquired a 30% interest in BrineCo 15 years ago for $80,000. He exchanges his BrineCo stock for $25,000 cash and stock in R&W worth $125,000. At the time of the reorganization, BrineCo's E & P is $50,000. Sam has a $70,000 realized gain ($150,000 cash and stock received − $80,000 BrineCo stock basis) and a $25,000 recognized gain (cash boot received). The first $15,000 ($50,000 BrineCo E & P × 30%) is taxable as a dividend, and the remaining $10,000 is treated as capital gain. Both are taxed at special tax rates.

Suppose instead that Sam receives 10% of the R&W stock with a $100,000 fair market value and $50,000 cash. If Sam had received solely stock, he would have received 15% of the R&W stock. Because Sam owns less than 80% of the stock he would have owned if solely stock had been distributed (10% ÷ 15% is 67%) and less than 50% of R&W, he qualifies for sale or exchange treatment under § 302(b)(2). Therefore, Sam's $50,000 recognized gain is a long-term capital gain.

Debt security holders receive treatment similar to shareholders. They recognize gain only when the principal (face) amount of the securities received is greater than the principal (face) amount of the securities surrendered. If securities are received and none are relinquished, gain will be recognized.

The term **security** is not defined in the Code or the Regulations. Generally, however, debt instruments with terms longer than 10 years (e.g., bonds) are treated as securities, and those with terms of 5 years or less (e.g., notes) are not. An exception to this general rule occurs when the debt instrument issued by the acquiring corporation is exchanged for target securities having the same term and/or maturity date.[8]

[8]Rev.Rul. 2004–78, 2004–2 C.B. 108.

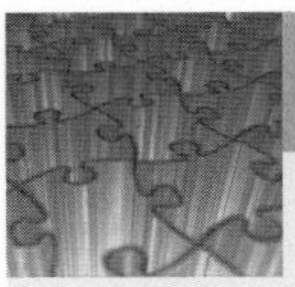

CONCEPT SUMMARY 7.2

Basis Rules for a Tax-Free Reorganization

Basis to Acquiring Corporation of Property Received	
Target's basis in property transferred	$xx,xxx
Plus: Gain recognized by target on the transaction	x,xxx
Equals: Basis of property to acquiring corporation	$xx,xxx

Basis to Target Shareholders of Stock and Securities Received	
Basis of stock and securities transferred	$xx,xxx
Plus: Gain and dividend income recognized	x,xxx
Minus: Money and fair market value of other property received	(x,xxx)
Equals: Basis of stock and securities received	$xx,xxx

EXAMPLE 5

Alejandra holds a debt instrument from Hibiscus Corporation. The debt's principal value is $10,000, and its maturity date is December 31, 2015. In connection with the merger of Hibiscus and Tea Corporation, Alejandra exchanges her Hibiscus debt for a $10,000 Tea note that matures on December 31, 2015. Even though these notes do not have a term remaining of more than five years, they qualify for tax-free reorganization treatment because they have the same term. ■

EXAMPLE 6

Assume the same facts as in Example 5, except that in exchange for her $10,000 debt instrument, Alejandra receives a note from Tea with a $15,000 principal value. Alejandra recognizes a $5,000 capital gain on the exchange. ■

Basis

The assets transferred from the target corporation to the acquiring corporation retain their basis. The acquiring corporation's carryover basis is increased by any gain recognized by the target corporation on the reorganization. Concept Summary 7.2 shows this computation.

EXAMPLE 7

Target exchanges its assets with a $5 million fair market value and a $3 million basis for $4.5 million of Acquiring stock and $500,000 of land. Target does not distribute the land to its shareholders. Target recognizes a $500,000 gain on the reorganization (due to the other property not being distributed). Acquiring's basis in the assets received from Target is $3.5 million [$3,000,000 (Target's basis) + $500,000 (Target's gain recognized)]. ■

The tax basis of the stock and securities received by a shareholder/bondholder pursuant to a tax-free reorganization generally is the same as the basis of those surrendered. This basis is decreased by the fair market value of boot received and increased by the gain and/or dividend income recognized on the transaction. Concept Summary 7.2 provides a summary of these calculations. Another way to compute the basis in the stock and securities received, using the Concept Summary 7.1 template, is to subtract the gain (or add the loss) postponed from the fair market value of the stock and securities received. This basis computation ensures that the postponed gain or loss will be recognized when the new stock or securities are disposed of in a taxable transaction.

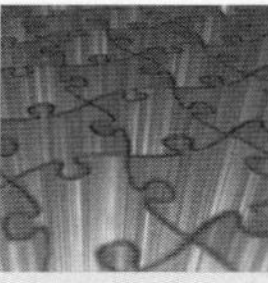

CONCEPT SUMMARY 7.3

Tax Consequences of Tax-Free Reorganizations

Treatment is similar to like-kind exchanges.

- No gain or loss is recognized by the acquiring or target corporation unless other property (i.e., boot) is transferred or received by any parties to the reorganization.
- Basis in the assets received by the acquiring corporation is generally carried over from the target corporation.
- The stock received by the target corporation's shareholders takes a substituted basis, derived from their target stock basis.
- Gain, but not loss, may be recognized when boot is transferred by the acquiring corporation.
- Gain, but not loss, may be recognized when the target corporation receives boot and does not distribute the boot to its shareholders.
- Gain, but not loss, may be recognized when target shareholders receive anything other than stock (i.e., boot) in exchange for their target stock.

EXAMPLE 8

Quinn exchanges all of his Target Corporation stock for Acquiring Corporation stock plus $3,000 cash. The exchange is pursuant to a tax-free reorganization. Quinn paid $10,000 for the Target stock two years ago. The Acquiring stock received by Quinn has a $12,000 fair market value. Quinn has a $5,000 realized gain, which is recognized to the extent of the boot received, $3,000. Quinn's basis in the Acquiring stock is $10,000. This can be computed as follows.

Realized Gain	Recognized Gain	Postponed Gain	Basis in Acquiring Stock
$15,000*	$3,000	$2,000	$12,000
−10,000			− 2,000
$ 5,000			$10,000

*$12,000 stock + $3,000 cash. ■

EXAMPLE 9

Assume the same facts as in Example 8, except that Quinn's Target stock basis was $16,000. Quinn realizes a $1,000 loss on the exchange, none of which is recognized. His basis in the Acquiring stock is $13,000, computed as follows.

Realized Gain	Recognized Loss	Postponed Loss	Basis in Acquiring Stock
$15,000*	$−0−	($1,000)	$12,000
−16,000			+ 1,000
($ 1,000)			$13,000

*$12,000 stock + $3,000 cash. ■

Concept Summary 7.3 reviews the tax consequences for tax-free reorganizations.

7.2 TYPES OF TAX-FREE REORGANIZATIONS

LO.3

Explain the statutory requirements for the different types of reorganizations.

Type A

"Type A" reorganizations can be classified as either mergers or consolidations. A **merger** is the union of two or more corporations, with one of the corporations retaining its corporate existence and absorbing the others. The other corporations cease to exist by operation of law. A **consolidation** occurs when a new corporation is created to take the place of two or more corporations. The "Type A" reorganizations are illustrated in Figure 7.1. To qualify as a "Type A" reorganization, mergers and consolidations must comply with the requirements of foreign, state, or Federal statutes.

EXAMPLE 10

Acquiring Corporation obtains all of the assets of Target Corporation, a French corporation, in exchange for 5,000 shares of Acquiring stock. Target is liquidated by distributing the Acquiring stock to its shareholders in exchange for their shares in Target. All French law requirements are met. This transaction qualifies as a "Type A" statutory merger. ■

THE BIG PICTURE

EXAMPLE 11

Return to the facts of *The Big Picture* on p. 7-1. The Rock & Water Corporation (R&W) formation occurred as follows. Roca and Agua Corporations were united under state law into the new R&W Corporation by transferring all of their assets to R&W in exchange for all of R&W's stock. By operation of state law, Roca and Agua liquidated by distributing R&W stock to their shareholders in exchange for the shareholders' stock in Roca and Agua. This "Type A" reorganization is a consolidation.

Advantages and Disadvantages

The "Type A" reorganization allows more flexibility than the other types of reorganizations.

- Unlike both "Type B" and "Type C" reorganizations, the acquiring stock transferred to the target need not be voting stock.
- The acquiring corporation can transfer money or other property to the target corporation without destroying tax-free treatment for the stock also exchanged.
    - Money or other property, however, constitutes boot and may cause gain recognition by the acquiring corporation, the target, and/or the target's shareholders.
- When consideration other than stock is given by the acquiring corporation, care must be taken not to run afoul of the continuity of interest test.
    - This test, promulgated by the courts and the Treasury, requires that the consideration given by the acquiring corporation be a substantial proprietary interest (i.e., at least 40 percent stock).[9]
- There is no requirement that "substantially all" of the target's assets be transferred to the acquiring corporation as in a "Type C" reorganization.
    - The target can sell or dispose of assets not desired by the acquiring corporation without affecting the tax-free nature of the restructuring.

A "Type A" is not without its disadvantages.

- Each corporation involved in the restructuring must obtain the approval of the majority of its shareholders.
- In almost every state, dissenting shareholders can require that their shares be appraised and purchased.
    - Meeting the demands of objecting shareholders can become so cumbersome and expensive that the parties may be forced to abandon the "Type A" reorganization.
- The acquiring corporation must assume *all* liabilities (including unknown and contingent liabilities) of the target corporation as a matter of state law.

[9]Temp.Reg. 1.368–1T(e)(2)(v), Ex.1; Notice 2010–25, 2010–14 I.R.B. 527.

FIGURE 7.1 "Type A" Reorganization

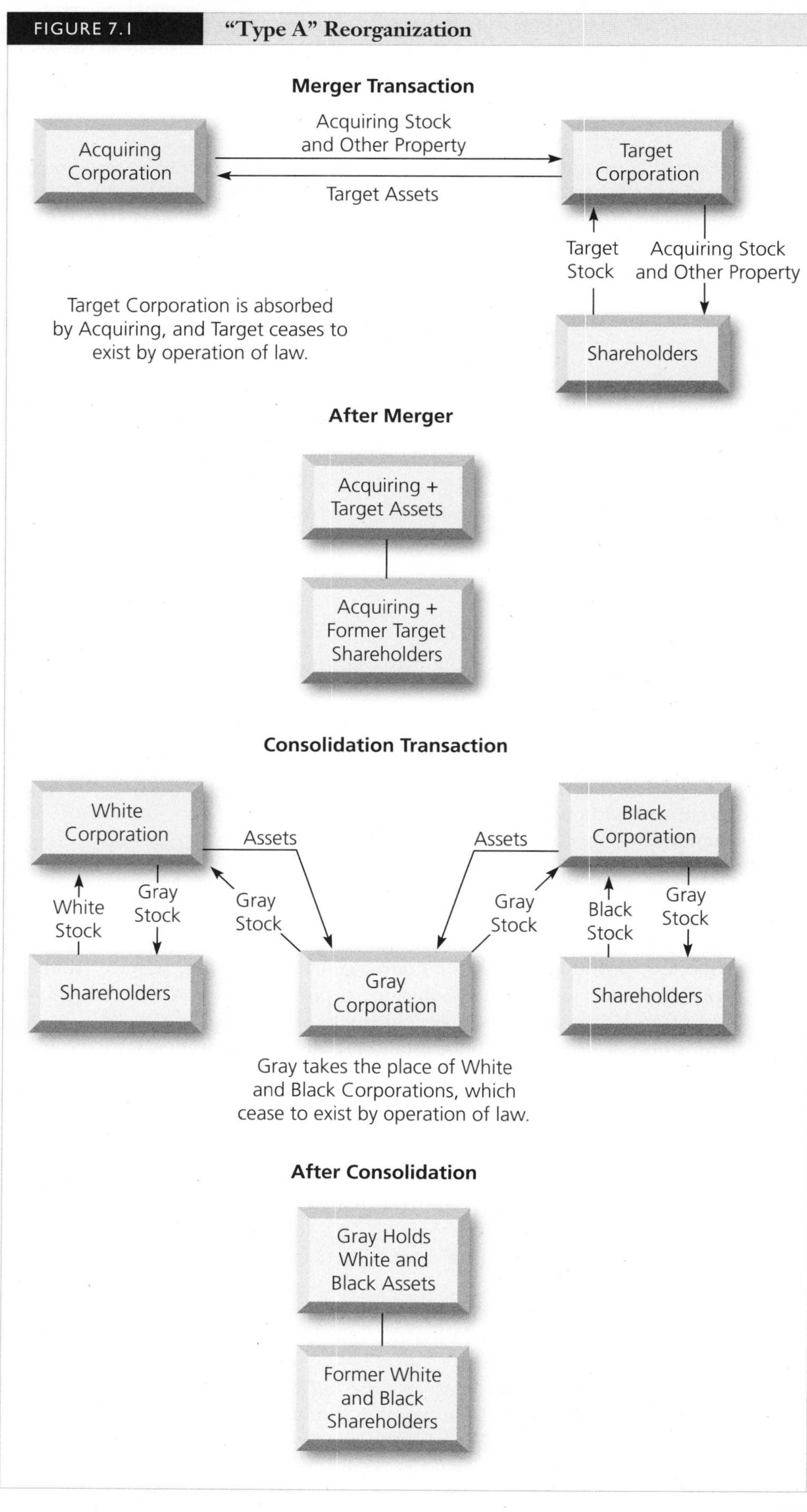

FIGURE 7.2 **"Type B" Reorganization**

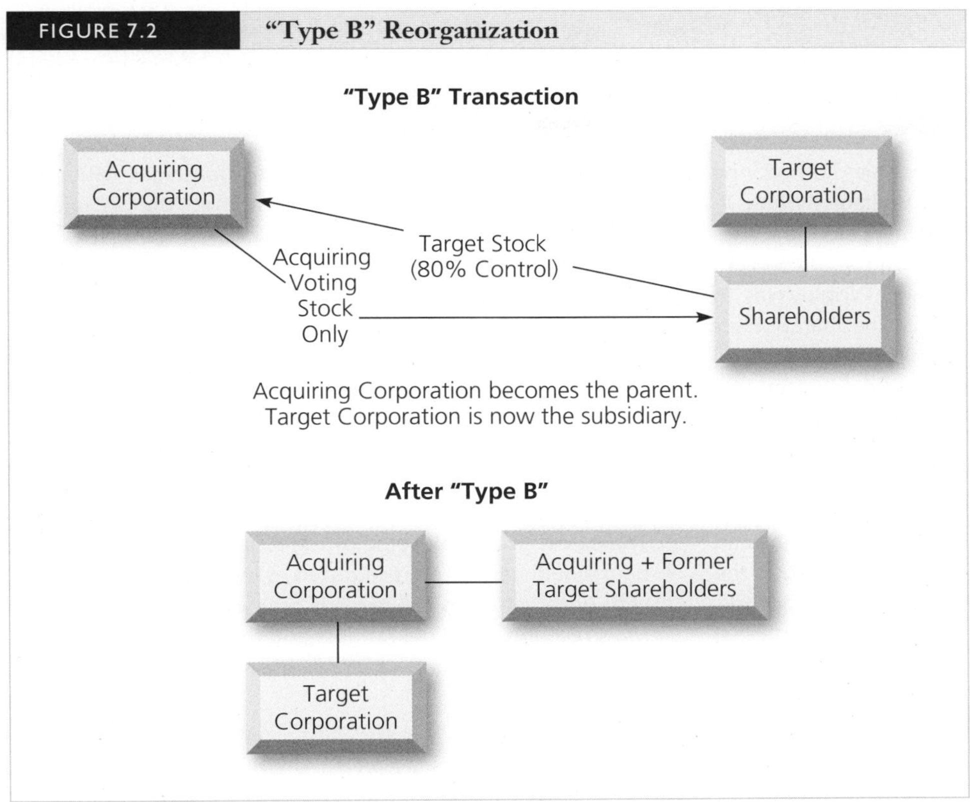

Type B

In a "Type B" reorganization, the acquiring corporation obtains "control" of the target corporation in an exchange involving solely stock. Both corporations survive, and a parent-subsidiary relationship is created. In simple terms, this transaction is an exchange of acquiring voting stock for target stock. Voting stock must be the *sole* consideration given by the acquiring corporation,[10] a requirement that is strictly construed.[11] The target's stock relinquished in the transaction may be common or preferred, voting or nonvoting.

Because the use of boot is precluded, gain is never recognized in a "Type B" reorganization. An exception to the solely voting stock requirement occurs when the target shareholders receive fractional shares of the acquiring corporation's stock. Cash rather than fractional shares of acquiring stock may be paid to the target shareholders.[12] The "Type B" reorganization is illustrated in Figure 7.2.

THE BIG PICTURE

EXAMPLE 12

Return to the facts of *The Big Picture* on p. 7-1. R&W Corporation proceeds with the acquisition of AcidCo. In the transaction between R&W and AcidCo shareholders, 20% of R&W voting stock is exchanged for 90% of all classes of stock in AcidCo. The exchange qualifies as a "Type B" reorganization. R&W becomes the parent of AcidCo.

[10]The exchange of the acquiring corporation's bonds for the target's bonds may be considered a separate and distinct transaction from a "Type B" reorganization according to Rev.Rul. 98–10, 1998–1 C.B. 643. Consequently, this exchange will not affect an otherwise qualifying "Type B" reorganization.

[11]*A. S. Heverly v. Comm.*, 80–1 USTC ¶9322, 45 AFTR 2d 80–1122, 621 F.2d 1227 (CA–3, 1980), and *E. S. Chapman v. Comm.*, 80–1 USTC ¶9330, 45 AFTR 2d 80–1290, 618 F.2d 856 (CA–1, 1980).

[12]Rev.Rul. 66–365, 1966–2 C.B. 116.

FINANCIAL DISCLOSURE INSIGHTS Creating the King of Sweets

When two of the largest candy companies united, the Sugar King was created. Publicly held William Wrigley Jr. Company became a subsidiary of privately held Mars, Inc., when Mars paid approximately $23 billion for 100 percent of the Wrigley stock. After the acquisition, Wrigley was no longer a listed company. Although all of the shareholders recognized gains on the sale of their Wrigley stock, neither Mars nor Wrigley had any gain or loss recognition. Because Wrigley continues to exist, there has been no change in the tax basis of its assets. Thus, Wrigley is essentially the same; it just has different shareholders.

The transaction was designed as a sale so that Mars could remain a privately held company. If Mars instead had used its voting stock to acquire the Wrigley stock, the deal would have qualified as a "Type B" voting stock-for-stock reorganization. The resulting organizational structure would have been the same as in the taxable transaction—a parent-subsidiary relationship. With a "Type B," the only difference is that the Wrigley shareholders would not have recognized any gain.

What is the financial accounting treatment for this transaction? Even though Wrigley is a subsidiary of Mars, the acquisition method of accounting treats this transaction as if Mars had purchased Wrigley's assets. Thus, every asset was stepped up or down to its fair value at the time of the transaction. If Mars paid more for the assets than their individual fair values, the excess created a goodwill asset. On the other hand, if Mars paid less than the fair value of the assets, Mars had a bargain purchase. The excess of the fair value of the assets over the amount paid would have been recognized as income! This result is very different from the tax outcome where Wrigley and Mars recognized no gain or loss and the basis in Wrigley's assets remains the same as before the restructuring.

Control Requirements

The "Type B" reorganization requires that the acquiring corporation be in "control" of the target corporation immediately after the reorganization. **Control** for this purpose requires owning at least 80 percent of all classes of the target corporation's stock. The 80 percent-control-after-reorganization requirement does not mean that all 80 percent must be "acquired" in the restructuring transaction. Stock previously purchased in separate transactions can be counted in determining the 80 percent ownership.[13] Further, the stock may be acquired from the shareholders directly or from the target corporation.

EXAMPLE 13

Acquiring Corporation purchased 30% of Target's stock for cash six years ago. It acquires another 55% in the current year by exchanging its voting stock with Target's shareholders. Thus, even though some of the Target shares were acquired with cash, the "Type B" requirements are satisfied through the current 55% exchange.

What if Acquiring Corporation purchased 30% of Target's stock for cash three months ago? Now the acquisition of the additional 55% of Target's stock for voting stock seems to be part of a two-step transaction. The acquisition of the remaining stock for voting stock is probably not tax-free due to the step transaction doctrine. ■

Disadvantages and Advantages

The solely voting stock consideration requirement is a substantial disadvantage of the "Type B" reorganization. Another disadvantage is that if the acquiring corporation does not obtain 100 percent control of the target corporation, problems may arise with the minority interest remaining in the target.

Nevertheless, the voting-stock-for-stock acquisition has the advantage of simplicity. Generally, the target corporation's shareholders act individually in transferring their stock to the acquiring corporation. Thus, the target corporation itself and the acquiring corporation's shareholders are not directly involved as long as the acquiring corporation has sufficient treasury or unissued shares to effect the transaction.

[13] Reg. § 1.368–2(c).

FIGURE 7.3 **"Type C" Reorganization**

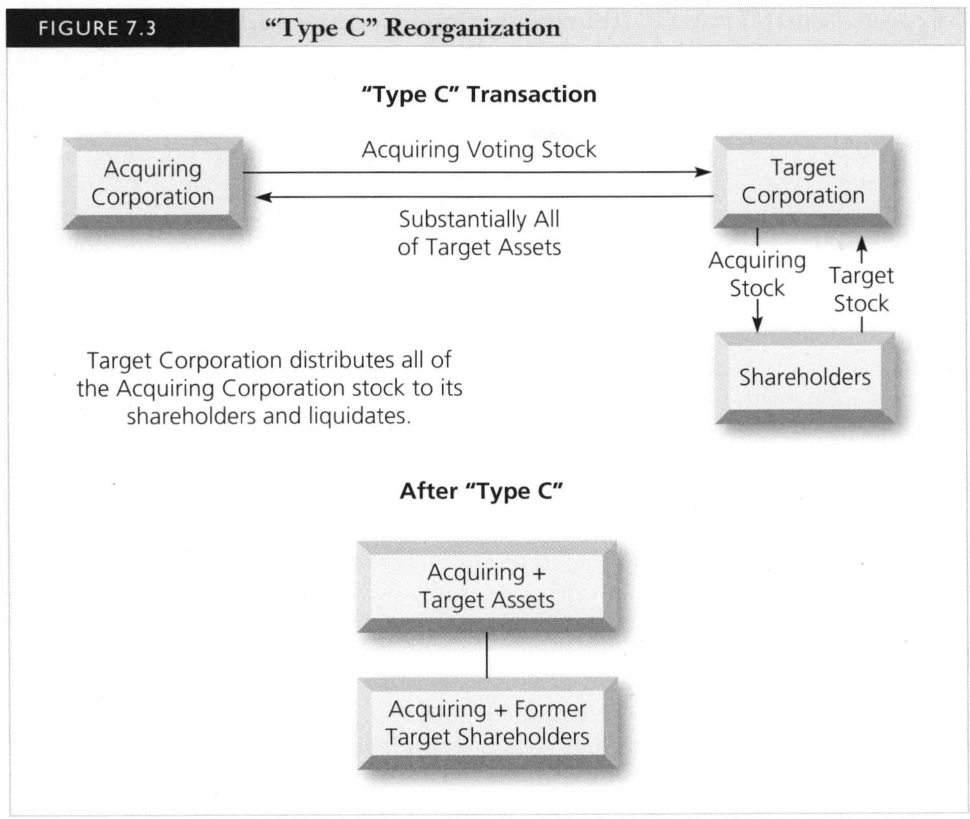

Type C

In the "Type C" reorganization, the acquiring corporation obtains substantially all of the target corporation's assets in exchange for acquiring voting stock and a limited amount of other property. The target corporation must distribute all assets received in the reorganization, as well as any of its own property retained. The target corporation then liquidates.[14] Thus, a "Type C" reorganization is essentially a voting-stock-for-assets exchange followed by liquidation of the target corporation. The exchange is a taxable transaction for the shareholders to the extent they receive assets other than acquiring corporation stock. The "Type C" reorganization is illustrated in Figure 7.3.

THE BIG PICTURE

EXAMPLE 14

Return to the facts of *The Big Picture* on p. 7-1. R&W Corporation proceeds with the acquisition of ChemCo. R&W transfers voting stock representing a 30% ownership interest to ChemCo for substantially all of ChemCo's assets. After the exchange, ChemCo's only assets are cash and R&W voting stock. ChemCo distributes the R&W stock and cash to its shareholders in exchange for their ChemCo stock. The exchange qualifies as a "Type C" reorganization if ChemCo liquidates after the distribution. The exchange is taxable to the shareholders to the extent of the cash they received.

[14]Distributions may be to creditors as well as to shareholders. § 368(a)(2)(G).

"Type A" and "Type C" Reorganizations Compared

The outcome of a "Type C" reorganization and a "Type A" merger are similar, as can be seen by comparing the diagrams for these reorganizations (Figure 7.3 versus Figure 7.1). However, their requirements differ. A "Type C" has more restrictions regarding the consideration that may be used by the acquiring corporation. Nevertheless, the "Type C" can be preferable to the "Type A," because in the "Type C," the acquiring corporation assumes only the target liabilities for which it negotiates. Normally, the acquiring corporation in a "Type C" is not liable for unknown or contingent liabilities of the target. Thus, when the target liquidates, the unknown liabilities become the responsibility of the former target shareholders, causing them additional risks.[15] Finally, in many states, the "Type C" restructuring only needs to be approved by a majority of the target shareholders. Thus, unlike in a "Type A" merger, the acquiring shareholders' vote of approval is not necessary.

Consideration in the "Type C" Reorganization

The acquiring corporation's consideration in a "Type C" reorganization normally consists of voting stock. However, there are exceptions to this rule. Cash and other property do not destroy a "Type C" reorganization if at least 80 percent of the fair market value of the target's gross property is obtained with voting stock.

Although the acquiring corporation has more freedom in the consideration given in a "Type C" than in a "Type B," this freedom is not without a cost. When the acquiring corporation gives solely voting stock for the target corporation's assets, the target corporation's liabilities assumed by the acquiring corporation are not considered other property (i.e., boot) in the exchange.[16] The transaction is a voting-stock-for-assets exchange, and the 80 percent-of-property requirement is met. However, liabilities assumed by the acquiring corporation *are* treated as other property if the target corporation receives any property other than voting stock in the reorganization.[17] Target liabilities assumed by the acquiring corporation are likely to exceed 20 percent of the fair market value of the target assets acquired and, consequently, destroy the "Type C" reorganization.

EXAMPLE 15

Target Corporation exchanges $850,000 assets and a $250,000 liability for Acquiring stock worth $600,000. Target distributes the stock to its shareholders and liquidates. The transaction qualifies as a "Type C" reorganization. The liability is not treated as *other property* received. Acquiring obtained 100% of Target's assets for voting stock. The liability assumed by Acquiring is disregarded as boot in this situation.

Suppose Target exchanged its $850,000 assets and $250,000 liability for Acquiring stock worth $590,000 and $10,000 in cash. The liability now is considered *other property* because Target also received cash. *Other property* amounts to $260,000, which exceeds 20% of the fair market value of Target's assets ($850,000 × 20% = $170,000). This transaction would not qualify as a "Type C" reorganization.

If Target pays its $250,000 liability and then transfers its $600,000 remaining assets to Acquiring for $550,000 of stock and $50,000 cash, the transaction will qualify as a "Type C" reorganization. No liabilities are assumed, and the *other property* transferred is less than 20% of the fair market value of the assets [$50,000 < (20% × $550,000)]. ■

The acquiring corporation's prior ownership of the target's stock will not prevent the transaction from meeting the "solely-for-voting-stock" requirement in a "Type C" reorganization. If the acquiring corporation purchased stock in the target corporation in an earlier unrelated transaction, the previously acquired stock will not be considered in determining whether 80 percent of the target's assets were obtained with the acquiring corporation's stock.[18]

[15]Byron F. Egan, "Acquisition Agreement Issues," 7th Annual Institute on Corporate, Securities, and Related Aspects of Mergers and Acquisitions, October 8, 2010.

[16]§ 368(a)(1)(C).

[17]§ 368(a)(2)(B).

[18]Reg. § 1.368–2(d).

EXAMPLE 16

Acquiring Corporation purchased 30% of Target Corporation's stock five years ago. In the current year, the fair market value of Target's assets is $1 million. Acquiring transfers $700,000 of its voting stock to Target in exchange for the 70% of Target's assets that Acquiring currently does not own. This qualifies as a "Type C" reorganization. The previous purchase of Target stock is not considered to be part of the reorganization transaction. Therefore, Acquiring is exchanging solely voting stock for 100% control over Target's assets. ■

Asset Transfers

The "Type C" reorganization requires that substantially all of the target corporation's assets be transferred to the acquiring corporation. However, there is no statutory definition of "substantially all." To receive a favorable IRS ruling, the target must transfer to the acquiring corporation at least 90 percent of its net asset value and 70 percent of its gross asset value.[19] Smaller percentages may qualify depending on the facts and circumstances of the reorganization.[20]

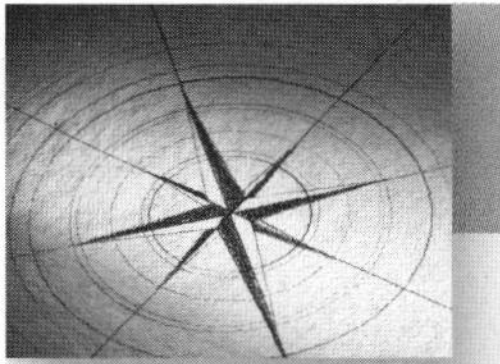

ETHICS & EQUITY Valuing Assets for D Reorganization

EarMed is a corporation that develops medications for ear infections. It has been very successful and is looking to expand its business. HearCo is a struggling corporation that has invented a hearing aid capable of being implanted in the ear for up to three years. EarMed has the management expertise needed by HearCo, and EarMed is sure it can generate substantial profits from producing and marketing this hearing aid. Because EarMed recently had its name tarnished by an FDA investigation of its inner ear canal medication, EarMed would like the merger to be structured as an acquisitive "Type D" reorganization.

As an associate for the tax consulting firm representing HearCo, you are documenting whether EarMed is transferring substantially all of its assets to HearCo. You find Revenue Procedure 86–42, which states that the IRS expects at least 90 percent of the asset's net FMV and 70 percent of the asset's gross FMV be transferred. You compute these requirements and determine that the assets being transferred by EarMed to HearCo are 95 percent of net FMV but only 40 percent of the gross FMV. You report this shortfall to your manager, who requests clarification from HearCo and EarMed on this issue.

HearCo supplies new documents to your firm two days later. In examining the new documents, you realize that EarMed merely has restated the FMV of the assets to be retained and transferred so that the transferred assets will almost meet the 70 percent of gross FMV requirement. The actual assets being transferred have not changed. When you inform your manager of this fact, the manager indicates that this is not an audit and that you can use the numbers provided by EarMed because HearCo has agreed to these values in reorganization negotiations.

HearCo needs this reorganization to stay afloat, and the manager explains that it is not your firm's job to second-guess HearCo's valuation of EarMed's assets being transferred. What should you do?

Type D

The first three types of tax-free corporate reorganizations are designed for corporate combinations. The "Type D" reorganization is different; it is generally used to effect a corporate division, called a "divisive" reorganization. However, the "Type D" can also be used to combine corporations—an "acquisitive" reorganization. In contrast with other restructurings, in the "Type D" reorganization, the entity transferring assets is considered the acquiring corporation, and the corporation receiving the property is the target.

---

[19] Rev.Proc. 77–37, 1977–2 C.B. 568, amplified by Rev.Proc. 86–42, 1986–2 C.B. 722.

[20] Where 70% of the assets were transferred and 30% were retained to discharge the target's liabilities prior to liquidation, the IRS found that substantially all of the assets were transferred. Rev.Rul. 57–518, 1957–2 C.B. 253.

FIGURE 7.4 Acquisitive "Type D" Reorganization

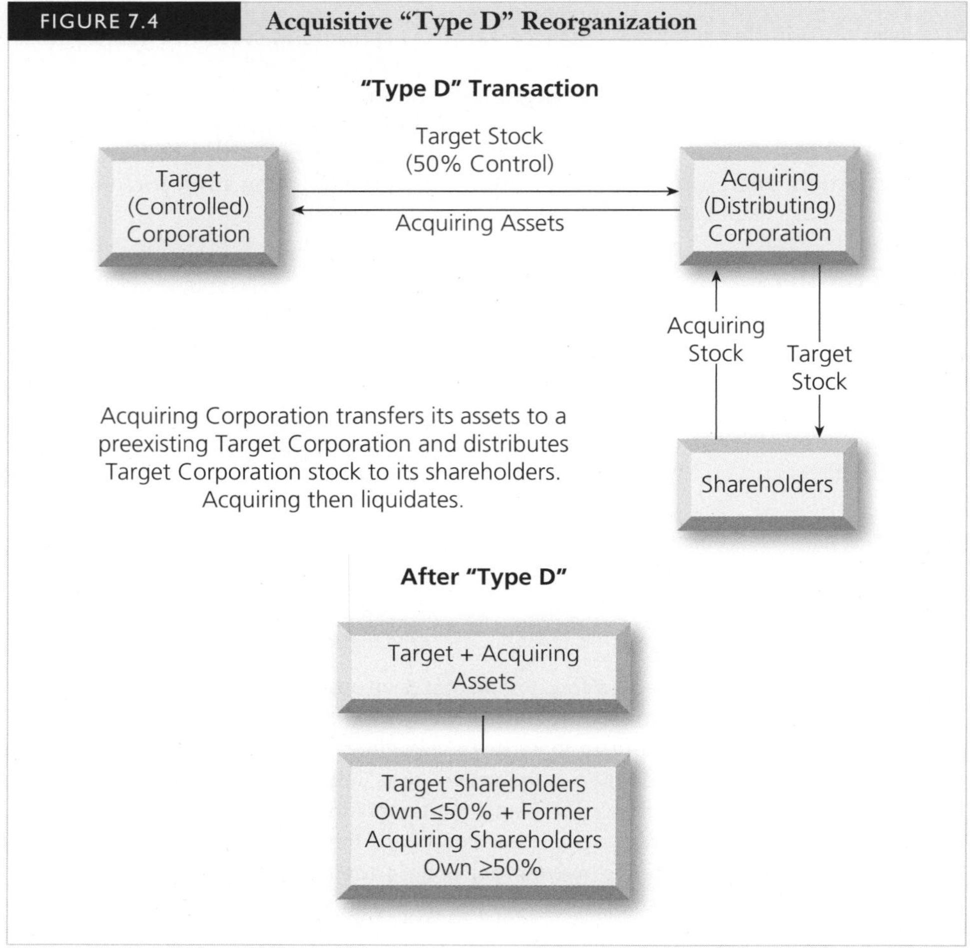

Acquisitive Type D Reorganization

If a combination meets the following requirements, it will be treated as a "Type D" reorganization.

- Substantially all of the acquiring corporation's property must be transferred to the target corporation. "Substantially all" means the same here as it does for a "Type C" reorganization.
- The acquiring corporation must be in control (at least 50 percent) of the target after the transaction.[21]
- Target stock received by the acquiring corporation, as well as any remaining assets of the acquiring corporation, must be distributed to its shareholders.
- The acquiring corporation must liquidate.

This type of transaction may also meet the "Type C" requirements (from the target's viewpoint). If the transaction can be classified as both a "Type C" and a "Type D" reorganization, it is treated as a "Type D" reorganization.[22] The "Type D" acquisitive reorganization is diagrammed in Figure 7.4. A comparison of Figure 7.4 with Figure 7.3 will illustrate how a "Type D" may also qualify as a "Type C" reorganization.

EXAMPLE 17

Acquiring Corporation wants to control Target Corporation ($300,000 value), but Target holds a nontransferable license. Thus, Target must be the surviving corporation.

[21]No attribution of ownership is used in determining whether there is 50% control. §§ 368(a)(2)(H) and 304(c).

[22]Reg. § 1.368–2(d)(3).

Acquiring transfers all of its assets valued at $700,000 to Target for 70% of Target's stock. Acquiring then distributes all of the Target stock to its shareholders in exchange for their Acquiring stock and liquidates. The transaction qualifies as a "Type D" reorganization. ■

Divisive Type D Reorganization

Rather than combining, shareholders may want to divide the corporation by distributing its assets among two or more corporations. This might occur for many reasons, including antitrust problems, differences of opinion among the shareholders, product liability concerns, increasing shareholder value, and family tax planning. The more typical divisive "Type D" reorganization allows shareholders to accomplish their goals without incurring a current tax liability. In a divisive reorganization, one or more new corporations are formed to receive part or all of the distributing corporation's assets. In exchange for its assets, the distributing corporation must receive stock.

The remaining requirements for divisive "Type D" reorganizations are as follows.

- The stock received by the distributing corporation must constitute control (80 percent) of the new corporation(s).
- The stock of the controlled corporation(s) must be transferred to the distributing corporation's shareholders.
- Both the assets transferred and the assets retained by the distributing corporation must represent active businesses that have been owned and conducted by the distributing corporation for at least five years before the transfer.
- The stock and securities transfers to the shareholders cannot be principally a device for distributing the earnings and profits of either the distributing corporation or the controlled corporation(s).[23]

EXAMPLE 18

Bell is a manufacturing corporation. It also owns investment securities. Bell transfers the investment securities to a newly formed corporation and distributes the stock of the new corporation to its shareholders. The transaction does not qualify as a "Type D" reorganization. Holding investment securities does not constitute a trade or business. The Bell shareholders are taxed on the stock they receive. ■

EXAMPLE 19

Jane and Ivan are the sole shareholders of WB Corporation. WB was organized 10 years ago and is actively engaged in manufacturing two products, widgets and bolts. Considerable friction has developed between Jane and Ivan, who now want to divide the business. Jane wants the assets used in manufacturing widgets, and Ivan wants to continue manufacturing bolts. The division of the business assets between the shareholders can be accomplished tax-free using one of the divisive "Type D" reorganizations. ■

EXAMPLE 20

Cube, Inc., has manufactured a single product at two plants for the past 10 years. It transfers one plant and related activities to a new corporation, Square, Inc. Cube then distributes the Square stock to its shareholders. Each plant's activities constitute a trade or business. The transaction qualifies as a "Type D" reorganization. ■

Spin-Offs, Split-Offs, and Split-Ups

There are three different types of divisive "Type D" reorganizations: spin-offs, split-offs, and split-ups.

- In a **spin-off**, a new corporation is formed to receive some of the distributing corporation's assets in exchange for the new corporation's stock.[24] The

[23] § 355(a)(1)(B) and Reg. § 1.355–2(b)(4).

[24] Alternatively, an existing corporation can be the target in a divisive "Type D" reorganization.

distributing corporation's shareholders receive the new corporation's stock without surrendering any of their distributing corporation stock. The shareholders' basis in their distributing corporation stock is allocated between the distributing corporation stock and the new stock, based on the relative fair market value of each.

- A **split-off** resembles a spin-off except that in a split-off, the shareholders surrender distributing corporation stock in exchange for stock in the new corporation. Stock basis is computed in the same manner as for a spin-off.
- In a **split-up**, two or more new corporations are formed to receive substantially all of the distributing corporation's assets. The stock of each new corporation is exchanged for the distributing corporation stock. The distributing corporation is then liquidated. The shareholders' basis in the relinquished distributing corporation stock carries over as the basis of stock in the new corporations.

The spin-off and split-off are illustrated in Figure 7.5, and the split-up is illustrated in Figure 7.6.

EXAMPLE 21

Shawnee purchased 10% (500 shares) of DistributingCo eight years ago for $60,000. Before the spin-off reorganization, DistributingCo's stock value was $900,000, and Shawnee's shares were valued at $90,000, or $180 per share ($90,000 ÷ 500 shares). DistributingCo spins off 30% of its business assets into NewCo (fair value $270,000) and distributes 10,000 shares of NewCo stock to its shareholders. Shawnee's 1,000 NewCo shares are worth $27,000. After the spin-off, the value of DistributingCo is reduced to $630,000; therefore, the value of Shawnee's stock in DistributingCo is $63,000. Shawnee's $60,000 beginning basis in DistributingCo is allocated to the two companies' stock as follows: $18,000 to NewCo stock [$60,000 × ($27,000/$90,000)] and $42,000 to DistributingCo stock [$60,000 × ($63,000/$90,000)]. ■

EXAMPLE 22

Assume the same facts as in Example 21, except that DistributingCo creates NewCo through a split-off. Shawnee is required to surrender 30% of her DistributingCo stock (150 shares) to receive the 1,000 NewCo shares. Shawnee's 350 DistributingCo shares (500 − 150) now have a value of $63,000 ($180 × 350), and her NewCo stock is worth $27,000 ($90,000 − $63,000). Shawnee's $60,000 beginning basis in DistributingCo is allocated to the two companies' stock as follows: $42,000 to the DistributingCo stock [$60,000 × ($63,000/$90,000)] and $18,000 to the 1,000 NewCo shares [$60,000 × ($27,000/$90,000)]. ■

THE BIG PICTURE

EXAMPLE 23

Return to the facts of *The Big Picture* on p. 7-1. R&W Corporation proceeds with its acquisition of AcidCo. Gail and Gary are equal shareholders of AcidCo, which was organized six years ago. To prepare for the restructuring transaction with R&W, AcidCo creates two new corporations to receive its business lines. AbraseCo will receive all of the assets related to the landscaping chemical business. These are the assets that R&W wants. The remaining mining acid assets are transferred to MineCo.

The AbraseCo and MineCo stock received in exchange for AcidCo's assets is transferred equally to Gary and Gail in exchange for all of their shares in AcidCo. Gail and Gary now are 100% owners of both AbraseCo and MineCo. Having no assets, AcidCo liquidates.

This transaction qualifies as a "Type D" split-up. Neither Gary nor Gail recognizes any gain or loss on the exchange. Gary and Gail take a basis in the AbraseCo and MineCo stock equal to their basis in their AcidCo stock. The allocation between AbraseCo and MineCo is performed in the manner utilized in Examples 21 and 22.

FIGURE 7.5 "Type D" Reorganizations: Spin-Off and Split-Off

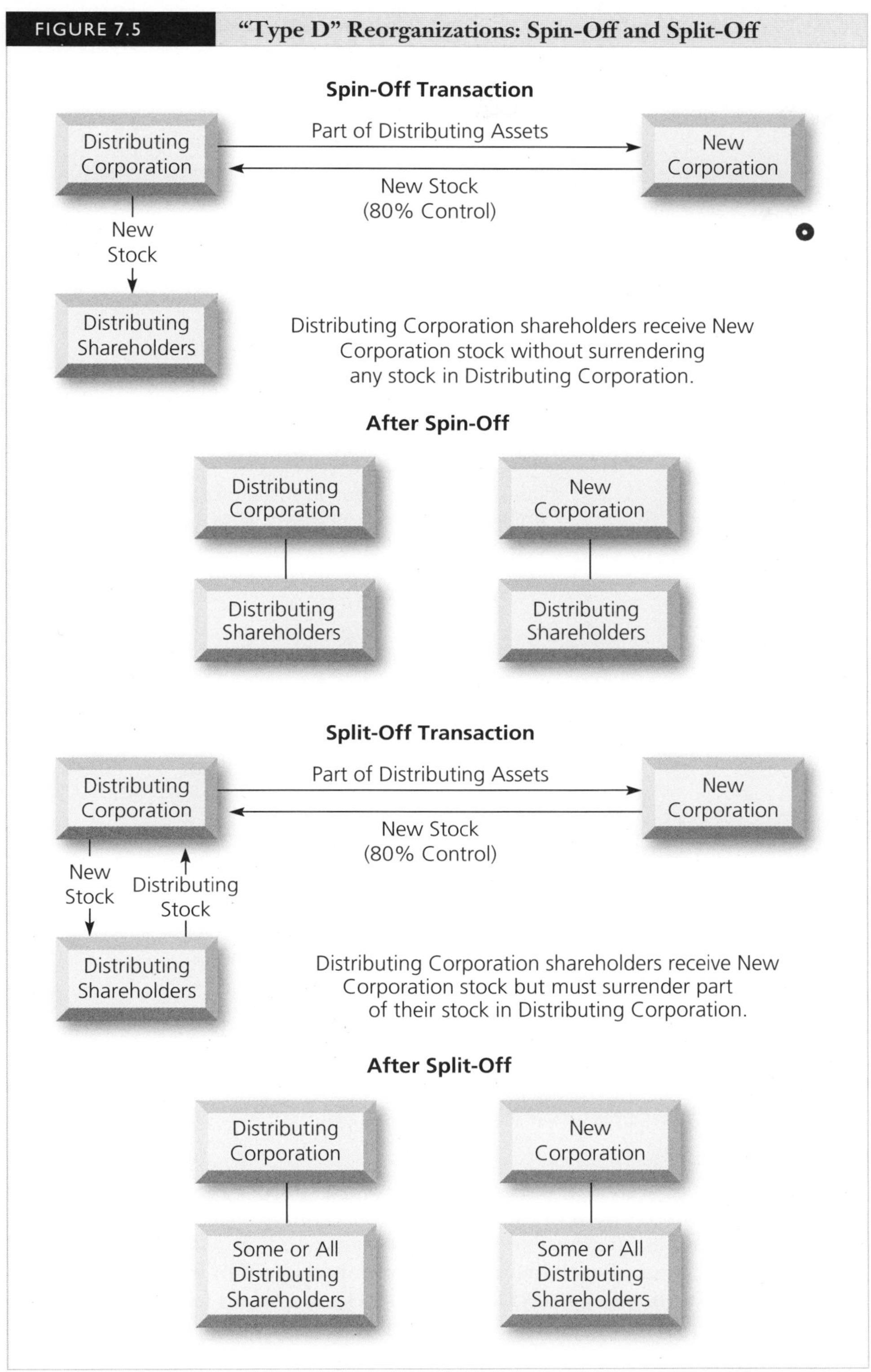

Type E

The "Type E" reorganization is a **recapitalization**—a major change in the character and amount of outstanding capital stock, securities, or paid-in capital of a corporation. The transaction is significant only for the stock- or bondholders who exchange their equity or securities. Because no property, stocks, or bonds are exchanged with another corporation, the "Type E" reorganization has no tax

FIGURE 7.6 "Type D" Reorganization: Split-Up

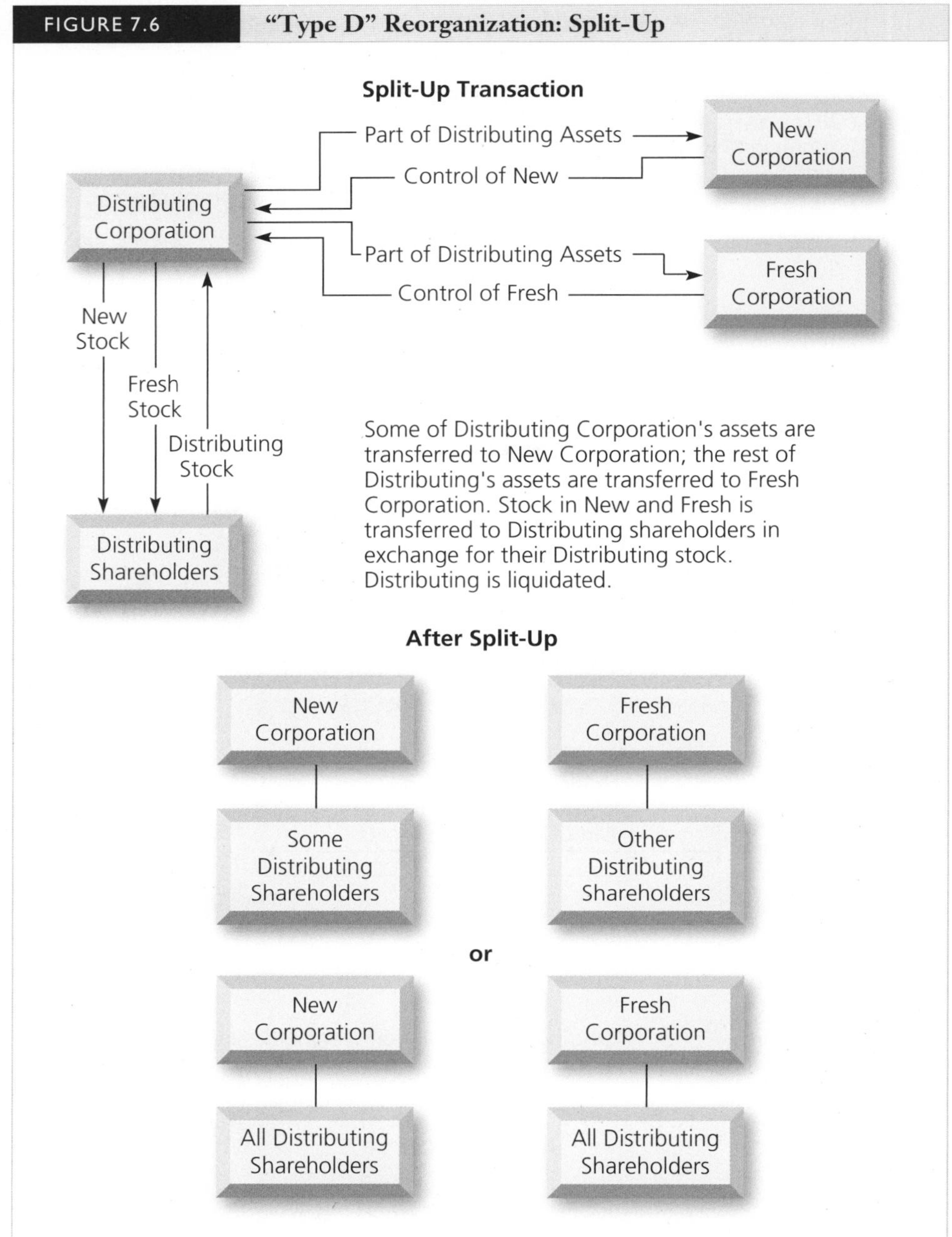

implications for the corporation involved. Further, transactions in a corporation's own stock or bonds are not taxable events to that corporation.[25]

The following types of exchanges qualify for nonrecognition treatment as "Type E" reorganizations: bonds for stock, stock for stock, and bonds for bonds. A corporation can exchange its common stock for preferred stock or its preferred stock for common stock tax-free. The exchange of bonds for other bonds is tax-free when the principal (face) amount of the debt received is not more than the surrendered debt's principal (face) amount.

EXAMPLE 24

All of Mesquite Corporation's bondholders exchange their $1,000, 3% interest-bearing bonds for $1,000, 4% interest-bearing bonds. This qualifies as a "Type E" reorganization because the surrendered bonds' face amount is equal to the face amount of the bonds received. ■

[25] Reg. §§ 1.1032–1(a) and (c).

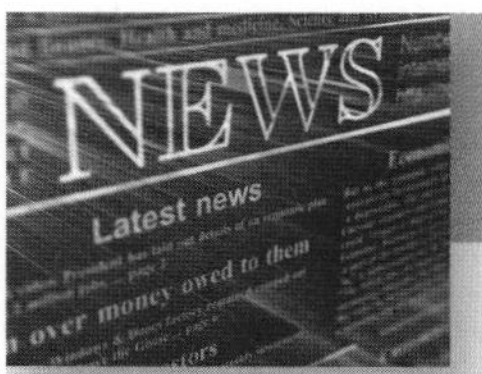

TAX IN THE NEWS NYSE Tries to Get a Bigger Board

The New York Stock Exchange, also known as the Big Board, began with fewer than 25 brokers on May 17, 1792, under a buttonwood tree on Wall Street. With the organization's first constitution, its name became the New York Stock & Exchange Board, and in 1863, the title was shortened to the New York Stock Exchange (NYSE).

Until going public in 2006, the NYSE was a private "members only" organization with 1,366 seats on the board. To work on the exchange, a member had to own one of the existing seats. In 2007, the NYSE merged with Euronext, and in 2008, the American Stock Exchange (AMEX) became part of the NYSE in an all-stock deal. Recently, Deutsche Börse was interested in combining with NYSE Euronext in an all-stock transaction that would have created a new entity incorporated in the Netherlands, resulting in the Deutche Börse shareholders owning 60 percent and NYSE Euronext owning 40 percent of the new entity. The stock division among the two exchanges' shareholders was based on the value of each entity. The exchanges were to retain their names in their home countries and would not have operated differently than they did before the merger.

Before the combination could occur, the transaction needed to be approved by the shareholders of both companies (which were obtained in July 2011), as well as more than 40 regulatory agencies worldwide. In August 2011, the proposed $16.6 billion merger received the blessing of the U.S. Committee on Foreign Investment in the United States (CFIUS). This government agency, led by the Treasury, considers whether mergers and acquisitions of U.S. companies with foreign entities raise national security concerns. Thus, this approval was an important step in combining the exchanges. However, the final approval of the merger by the European Union Competition Commission (EUCC) was not received. Without this approval, NYSE Euronext and Deutsche Börse had no option but mutually to terminate the merger they had been planning for over a year.

This merger was part of a recent movement among the world exchanges to consolidate for better competitive advantages through revenue synergies and cost savings. The rejection by the EUCC of this merger is likely to bring to an end any more exchange consolidations.

Sources: Adapted from Jacob Bunge, Harriet Torry, and Alexandra Edinger, "Exchange Merger Clears U.S. Hurdle," *New York Times*, August 23, 2011; NYSE Euronext website, **http://corporate.nyx.com/en**; and Jacob Bunge, "NYSE-Deutsche Börse Joins Dead-Deal List," *New York Times*, February 2, 2012.

THE BIG PICTURE

EXAMPLE 25

Return to the facts of *The Big Picture* on p. 7-1. BrineCo's stock is owned 80% by Gomez Adams and 20% by his children. Gomez wants to relinquish his corporate control to his children. He exchanges his common voting stock for nonvoting preferred stock. The exchange qualifies as a "Type E" reorganization. However, any difference in value between stock received and stock surrendered could be treated as compensation to Gomez or as a gift to Gomez's children.

EXAMPLE 26

Cedar Corporation exchanges each of its $1,000 bonds for 10 shares of common stock worth $100 per share. This qualifies as a "Type E" reorganization, and no gain is recognized because the bond value given up is equal to the stock value received ($1,000 = 10 × $100). ■

Type F

The "Type F" reorganization is "a mere change in identity, form, or place of organization . . . however effected."[26] Since "Type F" reorganizations involve only slight changes to a single operating corporation, the successor corporation is the same corporation as its predecessor. Consequently, the tax characteristics of the predecessor carry over to the successor. A "Type F" reorganization does not jeopardize

[26] § 368(a)(1)(F).

FINANCIAL DISCLOSURE INSIGHTS How Helpful Are Financial Statements in Predicting Bankruptcy?

With the world markets seeing bankruptcies on the rise, how useful are financial statements in predicting the future success or failure of a company? An analysis by professors and a student at Stanford Graduate School of Business indicates that using information from financial statements led to predicting over 90 percent of the companies that would file for bankruptcy over a 40-year period. The financial statement analysis used a number of financial ratios, such as return on assets, cash flow to total liabilities, and liabilities to total assets, as well as market-based variables. In fact, the ratios were helpful in flagging potential bankruptcy as much as five years in advance.

The work of the Financial Accounting Standards Board (FASB) and the Securities and Exchange Commission (SEC) to increase the usefulness of financial statement information has been a success. Fundamental analyses of financial statements are able to predict important future events such as bankruptcy of a corporation.

Source: Based on findings from William Beaver, Maureen McNichols, and Jung-Wu Rhie, "Have Financial Statements Become Less Informative? Evidence from the Ability of Financial Ratios to Predict Bankruptcy," *Review of Accounting Studies*, March 2005.

the status of § 1244 stock, nor will it terminate a valid S corporation election unless termination is desired. The IRS has ruled that if a restructuring could qualify as a "Type A," "Type C," or "Type D" as well as a "Type F" reorganization, the "Type F" treatment prevails.[27]

EXAMPLE 27

Conifer Corporation changes its name to Evergreen Corporation. This is a "Type F" reorganization. ■

EXAMPLE 28

Orchard Corporation is organized as a Subchapter S corporation. Its shareholders want to revoke its S election. Changing from an S corporation to a regular C corporation qualifies as a "Type F" reorganization. ■

Type G

Bankruptcy legislation introduced the "Type G" reorganization. In an acquisitive restructuring, substantially all of the debtor corporation's assets are transferred to an acquiring corporation in exchange for its stock and securities. This stock and these securities are distributed to the senior creditors in exchange for their claims against the debtor corporation. To qualify for "Type G" reorganization treatment, the debtor corporation must be insolvent before the reorganization and may be in Chapter 11 bankruptcy or a similar Federal or state court proceeding.

Like other reorganizations, the "Type G" must meet the sound business purpose, continuity of business, and continuity of interest requirements. However, the continuity of interest test is more lenient for "Type G" reorganizations. When a corporation is insolvent, the creditors become the true owners of the corporate assets.[28] Thus, rather than the shareholders, the creditors should be the ones with the continuing interest in the property of the insolvent corporation. The former shareholders need not receive stock in the acquiring corporation for the restructuring to qualify as a "Type G" reorganization.[29]

The acquiring corporation in a "Type G" reorganization must reduce the tax attributes carried over from the bankrupt corporation to the extent of the cancellation-of-debt-income (COD income) relief. The tax attributes reduced include the following.

[27] Rev.Rul. 57–276, 1957–1 C.B. 126.

[28] *Helvering v. Alabama Asphaltic Limestone Co.*, 42–1 USTC ¶9245, 28 AFTR 567,62 S.Ct. 540 (USSC, 1942).

[29] Private Letter Ruling 8909007; Reg. § 1.368–1(e)(8), Example 10.

- Net operating losses (NOLs).
- General business credits (GBCs).
- Minimum tax credits (MTCs).
- Capital loss carryovers.
- Basis in property.

These attributes are reduced in the order listed above; however, the acquiring corporation may elect to reduce the basis of depreciable property first.

EXAMPLE 29

Worthless Corporation files for Chapter 11 protection when its liabilities exceed its assets by $100,000 (COD income relief). Worthless has a $60,000 NOL carryover and a $30,000 capital loss carryover at the time of its restructuring. Through a "Type G" reorganization, NewStart, Inc., becomes the successor corporation to Worthless. NewStart must reduce the carryover attributes by $100,000. Consequently, NewStart has no NOL or capital loss carryovers from Worthless, and it must reduce the basis in the assets by $10,000 ($100,000 total carryovers reduction − $60,000 NOL − $30,000 capital losses = $10,000 basis reduction). ■

A summary of the advantages and disadvantages of the corporate reorganizations described in this chapter is found in Concept Summary 7.4.

7.3 Judicial Doctrines

LO.4

Delineate the judicial and administrative conditions for a nontaxable corporate reorganization.

Besides the statutory requirements for reorganizations, several judicially created doctrines have become basic requirements for tax-free treatment. These doctrines include the sound business purpose, continuity of interest, and continuity of business enterprise doctrines. The courts have also formulated the step transaction doctrine to determine the tax status of a reorganization that occurs through a series of related transactions. In addition, a reorganization plan that is consistent with one of the Code reorganizations is required.

Sound Business Purpose

Even if the statutory reorganization requirements are literally followed, a transaction will not be tax-free unless it exhibits a **business purpose**.[30] The business purpose requirement is meant to limit nonrecognition treatment to transactions that are motivated, at least in part, by valid corporate needs. The transaction must have economic consequences germane to the businesses that go beyond mere tax avoidance. Although tax avoidance is not, by itself, considered a business purpose, the absence of a tax avoidance motive does not establish that there was the requisite business purpose.[31]

Given that a business purpose is required for a tax-free treatment, whose business purpose must it be—the corporation's or the shareholders'? The Regulations indicate that the corporation's business purpose should be paramount. However, the courts have considered both corporate and shareholder purposes because it is sometimes impossible to distinguish between them.[32]

EXAMPLE 30

Joe owns 30% of IMS Corporation. The other 70% is owned equally by Greg and Wu. Joe has become very disagreeable toward Greg and Wu personally and toward the management of IMS. Consequently, IMS splits off an active business that it has operated for the last seven years. In exchange for all of Joe's IMS stock, Joe receives all of the split-off corporation's stock. Was the business purpose of the reorganization that of IMS, Greg and Wu, or both corporate and shareholder? ■

[30] Reg. §§ 1.368–1(c) and 1.355–2. See also *Gregory v. Helvering*, 35–1 USTC ¶9043, 14 AFTR 1191, 55 S.Ct. 266 (USSC, 1935). The doctrine as developed in the *Gregory* case became a precedent for all transactions that might be shams devised merely for tax avoidance purposes. It brought about the principle of substance over form. All business transactions must have a sound business purpose.

[31] Reg. § 1.355–2(b) and *Comm. v. Marne S. Wilson*, 66–1 USTC ¶9103, 16 AFTR 2d 6030, 353 F.2d 184 (CA–9, 1966).

[32] *Lewis Trustee v. Comm.*, 49–2 USTC ¶9377, 38 AFTR 377, 176 F.2d 646 (CA–1, 1949); *Estate of Parshelsky v. Comm.*, 62–1 USTC ¶9460, 9 AFTR 2d 1382, 303 F.2d 14 (CA–2, 1962).

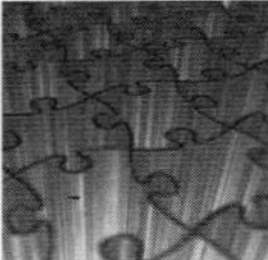

CONCEPT SUMMARY 7.4

Summary of Corporate Reorganization Advantages and Disadvantages

Reorganization	Type	Advantages	Disadvantages
A	Merger or consolidation	• No requirement that consideration be voting stock. As much as 60% of consideration can be cash and property without tax consequences for the stock received (cash and other property received *are* taxed).	• All liabilities of target corporation are assumed by acquiring corporation as a matter of law. • Acquiring approval of majority shareholders, dealing with dissenters' rights, and holding shareholder meetings, as required by foreign, state, or Federal law, may present problems.
B	Voting-stock-for-stock exchange	• Stock may be acquired from shareholders. • Procedures to effect reorganization are not complex.	• *Only* voting stock of acquiring corporation may be used. • Must have 80% control of a target corporation. • May have minority interest remaining in target corporation.
C	Stock-for-assets exchange	• Less complex than "Type A"; no foreign, state, or Federal law to follow. • Cash or property consideration for 20% or less of fair market value of property transferred is acceptable. • Acquiring corporation assumes only the target's liabilities that it chooses.	• *Substantially all* assets of target corporation must be transferred. • Liabilities count as *other property* for 20% rule if any consideration other than stock and liabilities is used. • The target corporation must distribute the stock, securities, and other properties it receives in the reorganization to its shareholders.
D	Corporate division: spin-off, split-off, split-up	• Permits corporate division without tax consequences if no *boot* is involved.	• Control requirements of 50% for an acquisitive reorganization and 80% for a divisive reorganization must be met.
	Acquisitive	• Allows smaller target corporation to retain its existence.	
E	Recapitalization	• Allows for major changes in corporate equity structure.	
F	Change in identity, form, or place of organization	• Survivor is treated as same entity as predecessor; thus, tax attributes of predecessor are retained.	
G	Court-approved reorganization of bankrupt corporation	• Creditors can exchange debts for stock tax-free. • State merger laws need not be followed.	• Planning for use is limited.

ETHICS & EQUITY The Damage from Structural Problems

Your firm is involved in structuring a reorganization for your client, Eagle Corporation. Your manager has mentioned several times that this reorganization is very important to Eagle as it provides a solution to Eagle's financial problems.

Quail Corporation, the other party to the reorganization, requests information about the structural stability of an apartment building, which is a significant part of the transaction. Jeanne Smith, Eagle's tax director, tells you that no structural problems with the building have been documented. After you give this information to Quail, you find out from a friend that the consensus in the construction community is that the building has substantial hidden structural damage. The steel used in the building was produced by a company whose products have caused structural instability in other buildings.

In your research, you have determined that this reorganization is a huge transaction for Quail and that if problems occur, Quail could face bankruptcy, not to mention the innocent renters who could be harmed. Quail's managers have said that they are impressed with your firm's integrity. After the merger, Quail will be looking for a new auditing firm, and based on their interactions with you, Quail would consider your firm. Your manager thinks this will be a good business opportunity once the transaction is completed and no conflict of interest remains.

What will you do with your information about the structural instability of the apartment building? Address how your actions will affect Eagle, Quail, your firm, and you.

Continuity of Interest

The **continuity of interest** requirement prevents transactions that appear to be sales from qualifying as nontaxable reorganizations. Therefore, the continuity of interest test provides that if the shareholders have substantially the same investment after the restructuring as before, the transaction may qualify as a nontaxable event. To qualify for tax-favored status, the target corporation shareholders must receive an equity interest in the acquiring corporation.[33]

The Regulations deem that the continuity of interest test is met when the target corporation shareholders receive acquiring corporation stock equal to at least 40 percent of their prior stock ownership in a merger with the target.[34] Not all target shareholders need to receive stock in the surviving corporation. The requirement is applied to the aggregate consideration given by the acquiring corporation.

EXAMPLE 31

Target Corporation merges into Acquiring Corporation pursuant to state statutes. Under the merger plan, Target's shareholders can elect to receive either cash or stock in Acquiring. The shareholders who hold 45% of Target's outstanding stock elect to receive cash; the remaining 55% of the shareholders elect to receive Acquiring stock. This plan satisfies the continuity of interest test. The shareholders receiving cash are taxed on the transaction. Those receiving stock are not taxed. ■

EXAMPLE 32

Juanita owns 100% of Target Corporation. Target merges into Acquiring Corporation. Juanita receives 1% of Acquiring's outstanding stock in exchange for all of her Target stock. The continuity of interest test is met; Juanita received only stock for her interest. ■

If the continuity of interest requirement is met at the time of the reorganization, a sale of stock to an unrelated party immediately before or after the restructuring will not destroy the continuity of interest. Unrelated parties here include

[33] *Pinellas Ice & Cold Storage v. Comm.*, 3 USTC ¶1023, 11 AFTR 1112, 53 S.Ct. 257 (USSC, 1933), and *LeTulle v. Scofield*, 40–1 USTC ¶9150, 23 AFTR 789, 60 S.Ct. 313 (USSC, 1940). In *LeTulle*, a corporation transferred all of its assets to another corporation for cash and bonds. The Court held that the transaction was not a tax-free reorganization if the transferor's only retained interest was that of a creditor. This concept is now in Reg. §§ 1.368–1(b) and (c).

[34] See footnote 9.

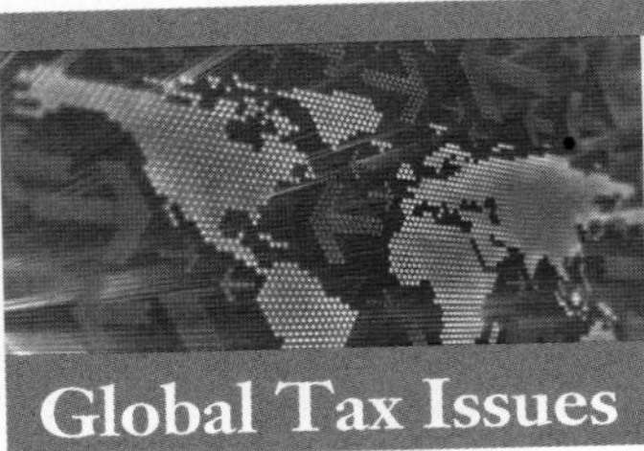

© Andrey Prokhorov, iStockphoto

Brewers Are Consolidating Globally

In 2000, one-third of global beer sales were divided among the top 10 brewers. Now, due to mergers and acquisitions (M&A), almost 50 percent of global beer sales by volume and 75 percent of the profits belong to four mega-beverage companies—Anheuser-Busch InBev, SABMiller, Heineken, and Carlsberg. The highlights of the big M&A activity in the brewing industry include:

- **2002:** South African Breweries (SAB) buys U.S. Miller Brewing from Philip Morris. Through this combination, SABMiller becomes the world's second-largest brewer after Anheuser-Busch.
- **2004:** Belgium's Interbrew (ranked third) merges with Brazil-based AmBev (ranked fifth) to create the world's largest brewer. Originally, the company was called InterbrewAmBev, but wisely it was renamed InBev.
- **2005:** The U.S. company Adolph Coors and Canadian Molson merge to create Molson Coors Brewing and become the world's fifth-largest brewer.
- **2008 (June):** SABMiller combines its U.S. breweries with the U.S. operations of Molson Coors to create MillerCoors. InBev makes an unsolicited offer for Anheuser-Busch, at the time the world's second-largest brewer. After much legal maneuvering, the two companies negotiate a friendly takeover that creates the world's largest brewer.
- **2010:** Heineken acquires Femsa, Latin America's largest brewer with labels such as Sol and Dos Equis. The deal boosts Heineken sales in Mexico. Heineken also becomes a top brewer in Brazil, the second-largest beer market behind the United States.
- **2011 (December):** SABMiller acquires Fosters for $10.1 billion. Fosters owns 7 of the top 10 beer brands in Australia and controls about 50% of its market. This acquisition will be the biggest ever for SABMiller.

Sources: Adapted from Theresa Howard, "Beer's Been Going Global for Years; Consolidation Has Long Been the Name of the Game," *USA TODAY*, July 14, 2008; "For Heineken, Femsa Deal Is a Beer Balancing Act," *New York Times*, January 12, 2010; and "SABMiller Gets Board OK to Buy Foster's," *Los Angeles Times*, September 22, 2011.

individuals, noncorporate entities, and corporations that are not part of either the acquirer's or the target's affiliated group.[35]

EXAMPLE 33

Pursuant to a preexisting contract, Juanita, in Example 32, sells all of her Acquiring Corporation stock to Ying for its value. This sale occurs one week after the reorganization. Because Ying is not considered a party related to Juanita, the sale to Ying does not affect the continuity of interest test. ■

Continuity of Business Enterprise

The **continuity of business enterprise** requirement ensures that tax-free reorganization treatment is limited to situations where there is a continuing interest in the target's business. Specifically, this test requires the acquiring corporation to either (1) continue the target corporation's historic business (**historic business test**) or (2) use a significant portion of the target corporation's assets in its business (**asset use test**). Continuing one of the target corporation's significant business lines satisfies the historic business test. Determining whether the acquiring corporation's use of the target's assets is "significant" is based on the relative importance of the assets to the target's former business or their net fair market value.[36] Thus, meeting the asset use test depends on facts and circumstances.

[35]Reg. § 1.368–1(e)(3).

[36]Reg. § 1.368–1(d).

FINANCIAL DISCLOSURE INSIGHTS Corporate Restructurings and the Effective Tax Rate

Book-tax differences often are created by corporate reorganizations falling under § 368. The tax-free nature of the § 368 reorganizations leads to temporary differences due to the timing of income/loss recognition—current for books and postponed for tax. The expenses incurred in corporate restructurings are capitalized for tax purposes but are allowed as expenses for financial accounting, thus resulting in permanent book-tax differences.

While acquisition and divestiture strategies are utilized to achieve corporate goals, the results of these restructurings influence the financial statements and ultimately the effective income tax rates. For example, Motorola's and Coca-Cola's effective tax rates were positively affected by the tax benefits accorded to the restructuring charges, whereas Cisco's realignments boosted its effective rate by over 2 percentage points in one year. This increase occurred because the foreign restructuring costs that Cisco incurred did not create tax deductions in the United States.

Ford took a bigger hit due to its restructuring. Over a three-year period, its effective tax rate increased by about 6 percentage points due to its capital transactions.

The continuity of interest and business doctrines apply to reorganizations that involve two or more corporations. In these situations, there can be a discontinuance because the transaction may be a sale rather than a corporate restructuring. When the reorganization involves only one corporation, the continuation of the interest or business is not a concern. Accordingly, these two doctrines do not apply to "Type E" and "Type F" reorganizations.

Step Transaction

The **step transaction** doctrine prevents taxpayers from engaging in a series of transactions for the purpose of obtaining tax benefits that would not be allowed if the transaction was accomplished in a single step. When the steps are so interdependent that the accomplishment of one step would be fruitless without the completion of the series of steps, the transactions may be collapsed into a single step.[37]

The step transaction doctrine presents problems for reorganizations when the acquiring corporation does not want all of the target's assets. For a "Type C" and acquisitive "Type D," the target (acquirer for "Type D") must transfer substantially all of its assets to the acquiring (target for "Type D") corporation. If the target corporation attempts to dispose of its unwanted assets before a reorganization, the step transaction doctrine could ruin the reorganization's tax-favored status. The acquiring corporation would have failed to obtain substantially all of the target corporation's assets. Without direct evidence to the contrary, the IRS generally views any transactions occurring within one year of a reorganization as part of the restructuring.[38]

7.4 Tax Attribute Carryovers

LO.5

Apply the rules pertaining to the carryover of tax attributes in a corporate reorganization.

Some target corporation tax attributes (loss carryovers, tax credits, and E & P deficits) are welcomed by the successor corporation. Others may prove less desirable (positive E & P and assumption of liabilities). The mandatory carryover rules should be carefully considered in every corporate acquisition; they may, in fact, determine the form of the transaction.

[37] *American Bantam Car Co.*, 11 T.C. 397 (1948), *aff'd* in 49–2 USTC ¶9471, 38 AFTR 820, 177 F.2d 513 (CA–3, 1949), *cert. den.* 70 S.Ct. 622 (USSC, 1950). If the steps have independent economic significance, the doctrine does not apply. See *Esmark, Inc.*, 90 T.C. 171 (1988) and Rev.Rul. 79–250, 1979–2 C.B. 156.

[38] Reg. § 1.368–2(c), but in Rev.Rul. 69–48, 1969–1 C.B. 106, the IRS applied the step transaction doctrine to transactions that were 22 months apart.

Assumption of Liabilities

Because a corporate reorganization must result in some continuation of the previous corporation's business activities, existing liabilities are rarely liquidated (a "Type G" reorganization is the exception). The acquiring corporation either assumes the target corporation's liabilities or takes the target's assets subject to their liabilities. These liabilities are generally not considered boot when determining gain recognition for the corporations involved in the restructuring. Liabilities are problematic only in the "Type C" reorganization, when the acquiring corporation transfers other property to the target as well as stock. In this situation, the liabilities are considered boot and, therefore, can cause a violation of the 80 percent-of-assets-for-voting-stock requirement.

Allowance of Carryovers

When a corporation acquires a target corporation's property, it also acquires the target's tax attributes. This occurs in the "Type A," "Type C," acquisitive "Type D," and "Type G" reorganizations. Section 381 determines which of the target corporation's tax benefits can be carried over to the successor. The "Type B," "Type E," and "Type F" reorganizations do not fall under the § 381 carryover rules because the original target corporation remains intact and retains its own tax attributes. In a "Type B" reorganization, the target corporation merely becomes a subsidiary of the acquiring corporation. The "Type E" and "Type F" reorganizations involve only the original corporation; thus, no assets or tax attributes are being acquired. A divisive "Type D" reorganization also is not subject to § 381. In a spin-off or split-off, the old distributing corporation retains its tax attributes, and the new corporation starts fresh with regard to its tax attributes (with the exception of E & P). In a split-up, on the other hand, the tax attributes of the distributing corporation disappear when it liquidates.

Net Operating Loss Carryovers

A target corporation's NOL is one of the beneficial tax attributes (and sometimes its most valuable asset) that may be carried forward to the acquiring corporation. Although the NOL cannot be carried back to a prior acquiring corporation tax year, it can be used prospectively. Thus, an NOL is a valuable target corporation asset to the acquirer, because it can offset future income of the combined successor corporation.

THE BIG PICTURE

EXAMPLE 34

Return to the facts of *The Big Picture* on p. 7-1. R&W Corporation proceeds with its acquisition of ChemCo. Prior to the merger, ChemCo accumulated a $3 million NOL. After the reorganization, R&W generates $5 million of taxable income. ChemCo's $3 million NOL carries over to offset the $5 million taxable income, reducing it to $2 million. R&W saves $1,020,000 in Federal income taxes by being able to utilize ChemCo's NOL carryover ($3 million NOL carryover × 34%). Thus, the $3 million NOL is a valuable asset that may be worth more than $1 million to R&W.

Ownership Changes

To curtail the tax benefits received from NOL carryovers, § 382 limits the yearly amount of NOL that may be utilized by the successor corporation. The **§ 382 limitation** applies when there is a more than 50-percentage-point ownership change (by value) for the common shareholders of the target (loss) corporation. An **ownership change** takes place on the day (*change date*) that either an *owner shift* or an *equity structure shift* occurs.

TAX IN THE NEWS Staple Financing in M & A Deals

In a case involving Barclays Bank and the Del Monte Corporation, shareholders received one of the largest settlements (almost $90 million) for challenging an acquisition transaction. The case raised conflict of interest concerns regarding Barclays providing advice to the seller (Del Monte) and staple financing to the buyers. Staple financing is a prearranged financing package that the investment banker advising the selling company "staples" to the acquisition information provided to potential buyers. The investment bank can earn as much or more in fees from the potential financing agreement with the buyer as it makes consulting for the seller. Accordingly, receiving fees from both the buyer and the seller can cause a conflict of interest for the investment banker. To which party does the bank owe its primary loyalty when the buyer and seller have diverging needs?

The advantage of staple financing is that potential buyers have a prearranged financing package without having to seek the financing on their own. This eliminates the risk of the acquisition failing because the buyer cannot arrange financing. The prearranged financing allows buyers to provide more timely bids, and the bidding for the firm may be more competitive; thus, the seller may receive a higher price.

Until the Del Monte case, this type of financing was fairly common. Now many investment bankers are declining requests to assist potential buyers when they are acting as the consultant for the seller. Those banks still offering staple financing have implemented stricter review processes and are offering the service only for closely held companies where there is no risk of public shareholder litigation.

Sources: Adapted from Jeffrey McCracken, Cristina Alesci, and Zachary R. Mider, "Barclays Leads LBO Financing Retreat After Del Monte Slap," *Bloomberg Businessweek*, September 14, 2011; and Gina Chon and Anupreeta Das, "Settlement Chills Use of M&A Tactic," *Wall Street Journal*, October 7, 2011.

- An **owner shift** is any change in the common stock ownership of shareholders owning at least 5 percent. Owner shifts can be caused by purchases, stock issuances, redemptions, recapitalizations, transfers to controlled corporations, and equity structure shifts.
- An **equity structure shift** occurs in tax-free reorganizations other than "Type F," divisive "Type D," or divisive "Type G" restructurings. The change date for determining the equity structure shift is the date when the reorganization is considered to have occurred.
- Although equity structure shifts and owner shifts are defined as separate ownership changes, the end result of an equity structure shift most likely is to create an owner shift. The tax treatment for both types of shifts is the same.

Whether an ownership change has occurred is determined by examining the common stock ownership during the testing period, generally the prior three years.[39] Shareholders owning less than a 5 percent interest during the testing period are aggregated and treated as one shareholder for determining an owner shift. Thus, transfers between shareholders who own less than 5 percent do not influence the percentage-point ownership change computation.

EXAMPLE 35

Target Corporation is merged into Acquiring Corporation in a "Type A" reorganization. At the time of the merger, Target had an NOL of $100,000. Pursuant to the merger, Target's shareholders, none of whom own a 5% interest, receive 40% of Acquiring's stock. An equity structure shift has taken place. Because all of Target's shareholders owned less than 5%, they are aggregated in determining the owner shift. As a group, these shareholders owned 100% of the loss corporation prior to the restructuring and only 40% of the successor corporation after the reorganization. A more than 50-percentage-point ownership change has occurred because of the equity structure shift. ■

[39]The testing period is the period following the most recent ownership change if that change occurred within the past three years. Further, the testing period cannot begin before the year in which the carryforward being tested occurs. See § 382(i).

When an ownership change occurs, the yearly NOL amount usable by the successor corporation is restricted. The limit is based on the fair market value of the loss corporation's stock (both common and preferred) multiplied by the **long-term tax-exempt rate** (the highest adjusted Federal long-term rate for the prior three-month period).[40] The stock received in a reorganization or the price paid for the loss corporation's stock generally indicates its fair market value.

Because the § 382 limitation is based on the loss corporation's value, there is an incentive to inflate its value prior to the ownership change. This could be accomplished through capital contributions. The so-called anti-stuffing rules prohibit this behavior by disregarding assets contributed in the two years prior to the change date.

EXAMPLE 36

Winner Corporation acquires Loser Corporation when Loser has a $250,000 NOL carryforward. Winner exchanges 30% of its stock valued at $600,000 for all of Loser's assets. The applicable long-term tax-exempt rate at the change date is 5%. Several months before the acquisition by Winner, Loser's shareholders contributed investment assets with a fair market value of $100,000, thus increasing Loser's value from $500,000 to $600,000. The § 382 limitation computation will not include the recent increase in Loser's fair market value. Consequently, the yearly § 382 limitation is $25,000 ($500,000 × 5%). ■

The objective of the § 382 limitation is to restrict NOL use to a hypothetical future income stream from the loss corporation. This future income stream is defined as the yield that would be received if the stock was sold and the proceeds were invested in long-term tax-exempt securities. Thus, the formula for computing the § 382 limitation is as follows.

Loss corporation's FMV on change date
× Federal long-term tax-exempt rate
= Yearly § 382 limitation

Section 382 does not disallow an NOL. It merely limits the amount of NOL carryover the successor corporation can utilize on an annual basis. In some cases, however, due to the § 382 limitation, the NOL may expire before it is utilized fully. Therefore, the § 382 limitation should be considered when determining the tax benefit an acquiring corporation receives from the target corporation's NOL. Because the NOL tax benefit may be the target's most valuable asset, a present value analysis is highly relevant for determining the amount the acquiring corporation is willing to exchange for the NOL asset. Tax benefits received in future years are not worth as much as tax benefits received currently. The farther in the future the NOL deduction is taken, the less it is worth today. At some point, depending on the discount factor used, the NOL postponed to distant future years may be almost worthless in present value dollar terms. Present value table excerpts are found in Tables 7.1 and 7.2 (located at the end of the chapter text).

EXAMPLE 37

MakingIt Corporation acquires WashedUp Corporation in a transaction that subjects WashedUp's $600,000 NOL to a $40,000 per year § 382 limitation. After the acquisition, there are 15 years remaining for deducting the NOL. Given that MakingIt uses a discount factor of 10% for evaluating the benefit of possible transactions, the present value of a $40,000 deduction every year for the next 15 years, assuming a corporate tax rate of 35%, is $106,484. Thus, MakingIt should not value the NOL for more than $106,484. This means that because of the time value of money, the NOL is worth much less than its face value! The present value of the NOL is computed as follows.

$40,000 × 35% tax rate = $14,000 tax saving per year × 7.606 (discount factor for present value of annuity for 15 years at a 10% discount rate) = $106,484 ■

[40]The determination of value occurs immediately *after* the ownership change in the case of redemptions or other contractions that are associated with the ownership change.

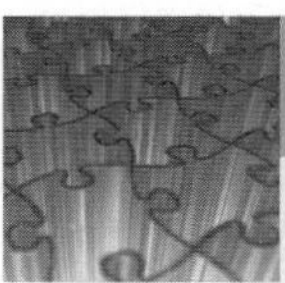

CONCEPT SUMMARY 7.5

Summary of Carryover Rules

Tax attributes that carry over from a loss corporation to the successor corporation:

1. Loss carryovers—subject to the § 382 limitation.
   A. Annual limitations on carryover use are evoked when there is an ownership change—a more than 50-percentage-point owner shift or an equity structure shift.
      - Owner shift is a change in the ownership of shareholders owning 5% or more of the corporate stock.
      - Equity shift occurs in tax-free reorganizations, other than a divisive "Type D" and "Type G" or a "Type F."

   B. Annual carryover usage cannot exceed the value of the old loss corporation on the change date (date of transfer) multiplied by the highest long-term tax-exempt Federal rate for the three calendar months prior to the structure change.

   C. Year of transfer. The loss claimed in the year of transfer is limited to the annual limitation multiplied by a percentage representing the remaining days in the year of transfer.

   D. Loss corporation carryovers are applied to the § 382 limitation in this order: built-in capital losses, capital loss carryovers, built-in ordinary losses, NOL carryovers, foreign tax credits, business credit carryovers, and minimum tax credit carryovers.
2. Earnings and profits.
   A. Positive E & P of an acquired corporation carries over.
   B. If either corporation has a deficit in E & P, the successor corporation will have two E & P accounts. One account contains the total positive accumulated E & P as of the date of the transfer. The other contains the total deficit as of the date of the transfer. Future positive E & P may offset the deficit E & P account.
3. Other tax attributes.
   A. Depreciation and cost recovery methods carry over.
   B. The installment method of reporting carries over.

EXAMPLE 38

Assume the same facts as Example 37 except that the § 382 yearly limitation is $120,000 rather than $40,000. Now the NOL can be fully deducted in 5 years rather than 15 years. Using the same discount factor (10%), the value of the NOL benefit to MakingIt increases to $159,222, computed as follows.

$120,000 × 35% tax rate = $42,000 tax savings per year × 3.791 (discount factor for present value of annuity for 5 years at a 10% discount rate) = $159,222 ■

If the successor corporation's current-year taxable income is insufficient to offset the authorized NOL deduction, the amount not utilized may be carried forward and added to the next year's § 382 limitation.

EXAMPLE 39

Profit Corporation acquires Loss Corporation and its $300,000 NOL in a transaction causing an equity structure shift. Loss's value on the change date is $500,000, and the applicable long-term tax-exempt rate is 5%. Therefore, the yearly § 382 limitation is $25,000 ($500,000 × 5%). During the current year, Profit/Loss successor corporation has $20,000 net income before the NOL deduction. The successor corporation may offset its taxable income by $20,000 of the NOL. Because the § 382 limit is $25,000, the NOL limit for next year will be $30,000 ($25,000 current + $5,000 prior year carryover) rather than $25,000. ■

A further limitation on the ability to utilize the NOL carryforward arises in the year the ownership change occurs (change year). The NOL amount available to the successor corporation in the change year is limited to the percentage of days remaining in the tax year after the change day. The § 382 yearly NOL limitation is multiplied by this percentage.

The formula for this computation is as follows.

Yearly § 382 limitation
× Number of days remaining in year/365 (366 in leap year)
= Initial year § 382 limitation

Finally, the NOL carryover is disallowed for future taxable years if the successor corporation fails to satisfy the continuity of the target's business enterprise requirement for at least two years following any ownership change.[41] The continuity of business enterprise test is the same as for tax-free reorganizations. That is, the target's historic business or asset use test must be met by the successor.

EXAMPLE 40

On December 1, Minus transfers all of its assets to Plus (a calendar year corporation) in exchange for 40% of Plus's stock. At the time of the merger, Minus is valued at $900,000 and has an NOL carryover of $200,000. The long-term tax-exempt rate is 5%. Because a more than 50-percentage-point ownership change has occurred for Minus's shareholders, the amount of NOL available for use in the merger year is $3,699 [$900,000 × 5% = $45,000 × (30/365)]. The NOL available to reduce the successor corporation's taxable income in the next year is $45,000. If Plus fails to continue Minus's historic business or use a significant portion of its assets for a two-year period, Plus cannot use any of Minus's NOL. ■

Earnings and Profits

The E & P of an acquired corporation carries over to a successor corporation.[42] Thus, the positive E & P of the acquiring and target corporations are added together and become the accumulated E & P for the successor corporation. However, a successor corporation is not permitted to apply the acquired corporation's E & P deficit against its own E & P.[43] Thus, the E & P of a deficit corporation is deemed to be received by the successor corporation as of the change date. A deficit may be used only to offset E & P accumulated by the successor corporation after the change date.[44]

Consequently, the successor corporation must maintain two separate E & P accounts after the change date: one account contains the successor's prior accumulated E & P as of the change date, and the other contains the deficit transferred from the target plus the E & P accumulated since the change date. The deficit in the post-transfer account may not be used to reduce accumulated E & P in the pre-transfer account.

EXAMPLE 41

Target Corporation is merged into Acquiring Corporation on December 31, 2012. On that date, the E & P balance for Target is a negative $75,000, and for Acquiring, it is a positive $400,000. In 2013, current E & P for Acquiring is $50,000. Acquiring now has two E & P balances: pre-2013 $400,000 and post-2012 negative $25,000 ($50,000 − $75,000).

	12/31/2012	E & P 2013	12/31/2013
Post-2012 E & P	($ 75,000)	$50,000	($ 25,000)
Pre-2013 E & P	400,000		400,000

■

In corporate "Type D" divisions, the E & P of the distributing corporation must be allocated among the newly created corporations and the distributing corporation based on the fair market value in each entity.[45]

[41] § 382(c)(1).

[42] *Comm. v. Sansome*, 3 USTC ¶978, 11 AFTR 854, 60 F.2d 931 (CA–2, 1931), *cert. den.* 53 S.Ct. 291 (USSC, 1932).

[43] *Comm. v. Phipps*, 49–1 USTC ¶9204, 37 AFTR 827, 69 S.Ct. 616 (USSC, 1949).

[44] § 381(c)(2) and Reg. § 1.381(c)(2)–1(a)(5).

[45] Reg. § 1.312–10.

FINANCIAL DISCLOSURE INSIGHTS Takeovers Gone Wrong

Not all corporate takeovers live up to their financial expectations or possibilities. Notorious examples such as the acquisition of Time Warner by AOL and of Snapple by Quaker Oats are still talked about long after the combined group failed and the target company was sold.

Corporate deals that fail to succeed have financial accounting results as well. AOL had high hopes when it acquired the social networking site Bebo, but visitors to Facebook and Twitter far exceeded those to Bebo; so AOL sold its subsidiary within about two years. Because a private equity group was the buyer, the precise sales price is not available, but industry estimates put it at less than $10 million, much less than AOL's initial acquisition price of $850 million.

A loss on subsidiary stock like the Bebo sale is claimed under GAAP rules, and the stock market rewarded AOL with a share price increase of more than 2 percent after the sale. But such a loss is not immediately deductible in full for Federal income taxes. This timing difference created a deferred tax asset for AOL of about $300 million.

Another GAAP result of the Bebo sale was a hit to AOL's intangible assets. AOL determined that it would test whether its goodwill had been impaired due to the unwise investment in Bebo. Often, corporate failures such as this mean that former employees receive severance packages. These benefits usually are treated using GAAP reserves, which would create another temporary book-tax difference for AOL.

EXAMPLE 42

Gaming Corporation distributes its computer gaming line of business to the newly created Compgame in a transaction qualifying as a "Type D" spin-off reorganization. Before the distribution, Gaming is worth $1 million and its E & P balance is $300,000. After the spin-off, Gaming's value is $600,000, and Compgame's value is $400,000. Compgame starts with an E & P balance of $120,000 ($300,000 × $400,000/$1,000,000), and Gaming retains an E & P balance of $180,000 ($300,000 − $120,000). ■

Other Carryovers

The capital losses and excess tax credits carried over to the successor corporation are also limited by § 382 if there is an ownership change for the loss corporation's shareholders.[46] The year-of-transfer limitations also apply to the use of capital losses and excess credits. When a corporation has several types of loss corporation carryovers, they are applied to the § 382 limitation in the following order.

1. Built-in capital losses.
2. Capital losses.
3. Built-in ordinary losses.
4. NOLs.
5. Foreign tax credits.
6. Business credits.
7. Minimum tax credits.[47]

Computing the amount of excess credits allowable in the current year is more complicated than determining the capital loss or NOL carryover, as the steps below indicate.

1. Calculate regular tax liability after allowable losses.
2. Compute regular tax liability as if the full § 382 limitation is deductible.
3. Subtract the tax liability in step 2 from the tax liability in step 1. The remainder is the § 382 limitation applicable to excess credits.

---

[46] § 383.

[47] Reg. § 1.383–1(d).

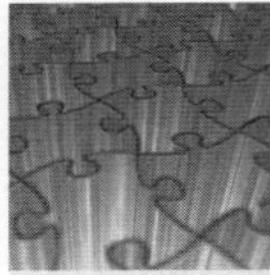

CONCEPT SUMMARY 7.6

Summary of Corporate Reorganization Requirements

Reorganization Type	Type of Consideration	Amount of Stock Ownership	Carryover of Tax Attributes	Treatment of E & P	Resulting Corporation(s)
"Type A" merger	Stock, cash, and property	At least 40% continuing interest by target shareholders	Yes	Combine if positive	Acquiring corporation continues, and target corporation ceases to exist.
"Type A" consolidation	Stock, cash, and property	At least 40% continuing interest by contributing corporations' shareholders	Yes	Combine if positive	New corporation continues, and contributing corporations cease to exist.
"Type B"	Solely voting stock	At least 80% control of target corporation	No, remain with target	Remains with target	Parent-subsidiary relationship
"Type C"	Voting stock and limited other cash and property	At least 80% of target corporation assets acquired with voting stock	Yes	Combine if positive	Acquiring corporation continues, and target corporation ceases to exist.
"Type D" acquisitive	Substantially all assets of distributing corporation	At least 50% control of target corporation	Yes	Combine if positive	Target corporation continues, and distributing corporation ceases to exist.
"Type D" divisive	Assets of distributing corporation	At least 80% control of target corporations	No	Allocate among entities	Distributing corporation and target corporations continue except for split-up; only target corporations continue.
"Type E"	Stock for stock Bonds for bonds Bonds for stock	N/A	Yes, same corporation	N/A	Original corporation continues.
"Type F"	N/A	N/A	Yes	Carries over	Old corporation continues as new corporation.
"Type G"	Stock	At least 40% continuing interest by creditors	Yes	N/A	Acquiring corporation continues, and debtor corporation ceases to exist.

THE BIG PICTURE

EXAMPLE 43

Return to the facts of *The Big Picture* on p. 7-1. R&W Corporation proceeds with the acquisition of ChemCo, causing an owner shift for the ChemCo shareholders. Assume that the § 382 limitation for the current year is $150,000. R&W Corporation's taxable income before considering carryovers is $400,000 ordinary income and $100,000 capital gain. The ChemCo carryovers include a $20,000 capital loss, a $60,000 NOL, and $30,000 of excess business credits. The capital loss is utilized first to offset the capital gain; then the NOL is used against the ordinary income. Taxable income becomes $420,000 [($100,000 − $20,000) + ($400,000 − $60,000)]. If the full § 382 limitation were utilized, taxable income would be $350,000 [($400,000 + $100,000) − $150,000]. The amount of excess business credit allowable in the current year would be $23,800, computed as follows.

Step 1. Regular tax liability ($420,000 × 34%)	$142,800
Step 2. Tax liability with full § 382 limitation ($350,000 × 34%)	119,000
Step 3. Subtract step 2 from step 1	$ 23,800

The benefit from all loss corporation carryovers taken in the current year cannot, in total, exceed the calculated yearly § 382 limitation. Nor can the loss carryovers exceed the year-of-transfer limitation.

Disallowance of Carryovers

Irrespective of the carryover rules, the IRS can utilize § 269 to disallow the carryover of tax benefits if a tax avoidance scheme is apparent. Such items are disallowed when a corporation acquires property of another corporation primarily to evade or avoid Federal income tax by securing the benefits that the acquiring corporation would not otherwise enjoy. Whether the principal purpose is tax evasion or avoidance is a question of fact. If the loss corporation's business is promptly discontinued after a corporate reorganization, the IRS may use § 269 to disallow the loss carryovers.

7.5 Tax Planning

LO.6

Structure corporate reorganizations to obtain the desired tax consequences.

Assessing the Possible Benefits of Restructuring Options

Reorganizations are valuable tools in corporate tax-free restructurings. However, it may not be possible to achieve the desired corporate structure by utilizing a single reorganization type. For this reason, reorganizations should not be seen as mutually exclusive transactions; they can be combined with other tax-favored transactions into a comprehensive plan. The tax law allows a series of tax-favored transactions to be recognized as legitimate separate steps when the statutory requirements for each are met. Thus, the step transaction doctrine can be beneficially applied to facilitate the tax treatment desired by the taxpayer.

EXAMPLE 44

Black Corporation operates two businesses, both of which have been in existence for five years. One business is a manufacturing operation; the other is a wholesale distributorship. White Corporation wants to acquire only the manufacturing business and refuses to acquire all of Black's assets. ■

What course of action might be advisable to transfer the manufacturing operation from Black to White with the least, if any, tax costs? Compare the following three possibilities.

1. Black Corporation transfers the manufacturing operation to White Corporation in return for 51 percent of White's stock.
2. Black Corporation forms Orange Corporation and transfers the manufacturing business to it in return for all of Orange's stock. The Orange stock is then distributed to Black's shareholders. This portion of the arrangement is a nontaxable spin-off. Orange now transfers the manufacturing operation to White Corporation in exchange for 51 percent of White's stock.
3. Rather than transferring the manufacturing business as described in possibility 2, Black transfers the wholesale distributorship. White exchanges some of its voting stock for the Black stock. Black is now a subsidiary of White.

Possibility 1 probably will not fit within the definition of a "Type C" reorganization because Black does not transfer substantially all of its assets in return for White stock. The manufacturing operation is transferred, but the wholesale distributorship is not. As a result, Black continues to exist. It cannot qualify as a "Type A" reorganization either because the target corporation must liquidate after the reorganization.

Possibility 2 is a spin-off of the assets *desired* by White, followed by a "Type C" reorganization between Orange and White. This approach is acceptable to the IRS even though White does not acquire "substantially all" of Black's assets. The transaction is treated as successfully creating a separate corporation (Orange) through a "Type D" reorganization. The "Type C" is considered to be only between White and Orange. Black is not a party to the latter reorganization.[48]

Possibility 3 follows a different approach. It starts with the spin-off of the *unwanted* assets and concludes with White obtaining the *wanted* assets by exchanging 51 percent of its stock for the Black stock. Taken by itself, this last step satisfies the voting-stock-for-stock requirement of a "Type B" reorganization. If, however, the step transaction doctrine is applied and the spin-off is disregarded, the Orange stock distributed to Black's shareholders might be considered as property *other than voting stock* in White. The IRS has not chosen to take this position and probably will recognize the nontaxability of a spin-off of *unwanted* assets followed by a "Type B" reorganization.[49]

EXAMPLE 45

Major and Minor are unrelated corporations in separate lines of business. For valid business purposes, Major would like to acquire Minor through a nontaxable transaction. Major will continue Minor's line of business after the reorganization and, in light of product liability issues, would like to keep the companies separate. However, there are substantial investment assets in Minor that Major would like to possess. How can Major acquire Minor's investments and still keep Minor as a separate entity? ■

Combining a corporate reorganization with a distribution allows Major to receive the investments and have Minor continue as a corporation. Major exchanges its voting stock for all of Minor's stock. This is accomplished either by a direct exchange with the Minor shareholders or by Minor recalling its stock and distributing the Major voting stock to its shareholders. Because Major exchanges only voting stock for Minor's stock, the transaction qualifies as a tax-deferred "Type B" reorganization. Minor is now a wholly owned subsidiary of Major. Minor then distributes the investment assets as a dividend to its parent, Major. This distribution qualifies for the 100 percent dividends received deduction. The IRS will not recast this as an acquisition of Minor's assets and stock for voting stock of Major.[50]

Carryover Considerations

Careful consideration of the restructuring alternative can help preserve desirable tax carryover attributes.

EXAMPLE 46

Acquiring Corporation wants to obtain the assets of Target Corporation. These assets have a $600,000 basis to Target and a $500,000 fair market value. Target has incurred

[48]Rev.Rul. 2003–79, I.R.B. 2003–29.
[49]Rev.Rul. 70–434, 1970–2 C.B. 83.
[50]Rev.Rul. 74–35, 1974–1 C.B. 85.

losses in its operations during the past several years and possesses a $250,000 NOL, with 15 years of carryover remaining. Acquiring plans to continue the business conducted by Target, hoping to do so on a profitable basis. ■

To accomplish the planned acquisition of Target's assets, Acquiring could consider the following alternatives.

1. Using cash and/or other property, Acquiring purchases the assets directly from Target. Following the purchase, Target liquidates and distributes the cash and/or property to its shareholders.
2. Acquiring purchases for cash and/or other property all of the stock in Target from its shareholders. Shortly thereafter, Acquiring liquidates Target.
3. Utilizing a "Type A" or "Type C" reorganization, Target merges into Acquiring. In exchange for their stock, Target's shareholders receive stock in Acquiring.

A satisfactory solution must center around the preservation of Target Corporation's favorable tax attributes—the high basis in the assets and the NOL carryover. Alternative 1 is highly unsatisfactory. It will not retain Target's favorable tax attributes. The purchase price (probably $500,000) becomes the basis of the assets in the hands of Acquiring Corporation. Further, any unused NOLs disappear upon Target's liquidation. Target has a realized loss of $100,000 [$600,000 (basis in the assets) − $500,000 (sale proceeds)] from the sale of its assets. Yet the realized loss may generate little, if any, tax savings to Target. In view of Target's unabsorbed NOL carryover, it appears doubtful that the company will generate much taxable income in the year of sale.

Alternative 2 appears to be a better solution but has a major risk. When a subsidiary is liquidated under § 332, the subsidiary's basis in its assets carries over to the acquiring corporation.[51] Therefore, Target's $600,000 basis in its assets becomes Acquiring's basis in the assets. What Acquiring paid for the Target stock becomes irrelevant. Target's NOLs also carry over to Acquiring. However, § 269 (disallowing any deduction or credit when the acquisition was made to evade or avoid income tax) could present a problem.[52]

Alternative 3, using a "Type A" or "Type C" reorganization, should accomplish the same tax result, but with less tax risk. Presuming that Acquiring can establish a business purpose for the "Type A" or "Type C" reorganization, § 269 can be avoided. The preservation of favorable tax attributes, such as the NOL carryover, should be considered when acquiring a small corporation.

How much should Acquiring offer for Target Corporation in Alternative 3? By preserving the NOL tax attribute, Acquiring is obtaining a value greater than the fair market value of the assets of $500,000. Assume the following facts.

- The Federal long-term interest rate is 5 percent.
- Acquiring uses a 6 percent discount factor for business decisions.
- Acquiring's marginal income tax rate is 35 percent for all years involved.

The § 382 limitation would allow Acquiring to utilize $25,000 of the NOL each year ($500,000 × 5%). Thus, it would take Acquiring 10 years to utilize the NOL ($250,000 ÷ $25,000). The net present value of the NOL to Acquiring is $64,400, computed as follows.

$25,000 × 35% = $8,750 tax benefit × 7.360 factor (10-year annuity at 6%)
= $64,400

Therefore, Acquiring should not pay more than $64,400 for the NOL.

EXAMPLE 47

Cardinal Corporation, worth $200,000, has a $150,000 NOL. The stock in Cardinal is owned by Kevin, 55%, and Fran, 45%. Kevin wants to sell his interest in Cardinal and retire. What happens to the NOL if Kevin sells his entire interest? There would be a more than 50-percentage-point change in the ownership of Cardinal Corporation. Therefore, the § 382 limitation would be $200,000 times the long-term tax-exempt rate. Assume that the rate is 4%. The loss of $150,000 is now limited to $8,000 annually. Can a sale be structured so that the NOL is not limited?

---

[51] § 334(b)(1).

[52] § 269(b) specifically applies to a liquidation within two years after an acquisition date.

An owner shift is calculated for the three-year testing period. Kevin could sell 35% of Cardinal stock in year 1, 5% in year 2, 5% in year 3, and 10% in year 4. None of the three-year testing periods has a more than 50-percentage-point change in the ownership of the corporation. Thus, there is no § 382 limitation. Cardinal can deduct the entire $150,000 NOL sooner rather than later. ■

REFOCUS ON THE BIG PICTURE

STRUCTURING ACQUISITIONS

Rock & Water Corporation (R&W) is unsure how to structure the potential acquisitions of its three suppliers. The first target is BrineCo, a profitable corporation that has been owned predominantly by the Adams family since its incorporation in 1950. In negotiations with BrineCo, R&W determines that it has virtually no debt because most of its assets date from its incorporation. Senior Adams family members are ready to retire, and the younger generation has no interest in the business. Consequently, all members would like some cash in the transaction. The "Type A" reorganization would be a good choice for this acquisition. R&W can exchange cash, preferred stock, and voting stock for only those assets it wants to acquire. Because BrineCo has few liabilities, acquiring all of them will not be an issue, nor will obtaining the approval of the BrineCo shareholders. The assets not transferred to R&W will be distributed to the Adams family, along with the stock and cash received from R&W in complete liquidation of BrineCo.

The next target, AcidCo, has been struggling financially and is having legal liability issues related to its failure to meet environmental standards. Because its landscaping chemical and mining acid lines of business are active and have been in existence for more than five years, AcidCo can, through a divisive "Type D" reorganization, spin off or split off its mining acid business and retain the landscaping chemical line. Once this is accomplished, R&W can acquire AcidCo stock from its shareholders by exchanging R&W voting stock in a "Type B" reorganization. This restructuring would protect R&W's assets from AcidCo's legal liability issues until R&W can clean up the environmental problems.

Finally, ChemCo has the technology to produce environmentally safe products, but its inexperienced management has resulted in it being unprofitable. R&W can use a "Type C" reorganization to acquire substantially all of ChemCo's assets and can select which liabilities it assumes. To avoid having the liability assumption treated as boot, R&W should use solely voting stock for the exchange. ChemCo must terminate after the reorganization. Given that ChemCo has NOL, capital loss, and business credit carryovers, R&W must meet the continuity of business enterprise requirement for at least two years. Most likely, the § 382 limitation will apply as ChemCo shareholders will experience an equity structure shift of greater than 50 percentage points; thus, the amount of carryover tax attributes that R&W may use in any one year will be limited. A net present value analysis should be performed to determine what R&W is willing to pay for ChemCo's tax attributes. Finally, R&W will need to keep two E & P accounts: one for its pre-reorganization E & P and another with ChemCo's negative E & P that will be offset by future profits of the combined company.

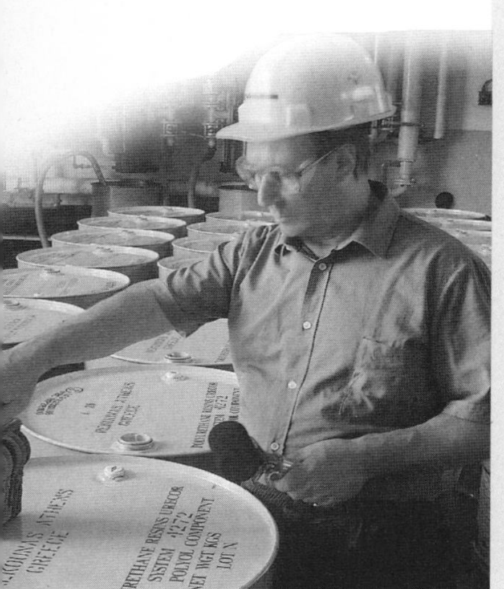

TABLE 7.1 Present Value of $1 per Period at i% for n Periods, PVIF(i, n)

Period	1%	2%	3%	4%	5%	6%	7%	8%	9%	10%	11%	12%	13%	14%	15%
1	0.990	0.980	0.971	0.962	0.952	0.943	0.935	0.926	0.917	0.909	0.901	0.893	0.885	0.877	0.870
2	0.980	0.961	0.943	0.925	0.907	0.890	0.873	0.857	0.842	0.826	0.812	0.797	0.783	0.769	0.756
3	0.971	0.942	0.915	0.889	0.864	0.840	0.816	0.794	0.772	0.751	0.731	0.712	0.693	0.675	0.658
4	0.961	0.924	0.888	0.855	0.823	0.792	0.763	0.735	0.708	0.683	0.659	0.636	0.613	0.592	0.572
5	0.951	0.906	0.863	0.822	0.784	0.747	0.713	0.681	0.650	0.621	0.593	0.567	0.543	0.519	0.497
6	0.942	0.888	0.837	0.790	0.746	0.705	0.666	0.630	0.596	0.564	0.535	0.507	0.480	0.456	0.432
7	0.933	0.871	0.813	0.760	0.711	0.665	0.623	0.583	0.547	0.513	0.482	0.452	0.425	0.400	0.376
8	0.923	0.853	0.789	0.731	0.677	0.627	0.582	0.540	0.502	0.467	0.434	0.404	0.376	0.351	0.327
9	0.914	0.837	0.766	0.703	0.645	0.592	0.544	0.500	0.460	0.424	0.391	0.361	0.333	0.308	0.284
10	0.905	0.820	0.744	0.676	0.614	0.558	0.508	0.463	0.422	0.386	0.352	0.322	0.295	0.270	0.247
11	0.896	0.804	0.722	0.650	0.585	0.527	0.475	0.429	0.388	0.350	0.317	0.287	0.261	0.237	0.215
12	0.887	0.788	0.701	0.625	0.557	0.497	0.444	0.397	0.356	0.319	0.286	0.257	0.231	0.208	0.187
13	0.879	0.773	0.681	0.601	0.530	0.469	0.415	0.368	0.326	0.290	0.258	0.229	0.204	0.182	0.163
14	0.870	0.758	0.661	0.577	0.505	0.442	0.388	0.340	0.299	0.263	0.232	0.205	0.181	0.160	0.141
15	0.861	0.743	0.642	0.555	0.481	0.417	0.362	0.315	0.275	0.239	0.209	0.183	0.160	0.140	0.123
16	0.853	0.728	0.623	0.534	0.458	0.394	0.339	0.292	0.252	0.218	0.188	0.163	0.141	0.123	0.107
17	0.844	0.714	0.605	0.513	0.436	0.371	0.317	0.270	0.231	0.198	0.170	0.146	0.125	0.108	0.093
18	0.836	0.700	0.587	0.494	0.416	0.350	0.296	0.250	0.212	0.180	0.153	0.130	0.111	0.095	0.081
19	0.828	0.686	0.570	0.475	0.396	0.331	0.277	0.232	0.194	0.164	0.138	0.116	0.098	0.083	0.070
20	0.820	0.673	0.554	0.456	0.377	0.312	0.258	0.215	0.178	0.149	0.124	0.104	0.087	0.073	0.061
25	0.780	0.610	0.478	0.375	0.295	0.233	0.184	0.146	0.116	0.092	0.074	0.059	0.047	0.038	0.030
30	0.742	0.552	0.412	0.308	0.231	0.174	0.131	0.099	0.075	0.057	0.044	0.033	0.026	0.020	0.015
35	0.706	0.500	0.355	0.253	0.181	0.130	0.094	0.068	0.049	0.036	0.026	0.019	0.014	0.010	0.008
40	0.672	0.453	0.307	0.208	0.142	0.097	0.067	0.046	0.032	0.022	0.015	0.011	0.008	0.005	0.004
50	0.608	0.372	0.228	0.141	0.087	0.054	0.034	0.021	0.013	0.009	0.005	0.003	0.002	0.001	0.001

TABLE 7.2 Present Value of an (Ordinary) Annuity of $1 per Period at i% for n Periods, PVIFA(i, n)

Period	1%	2%	3%	4%	5%	6%	7%	8%	9%	10%	11%	12%	13%	14%	15%
1	0.990	0.980	0.971	0.962	0.952	0.943	0.935	0.926	0.917	0.909	0.901	0.893	0.885	0.877	0.870
2	1.970	1.942	1.913	1.886	1.859	1.833	1.808	1.783	1.759	1.736	1.713	1.690	1.668	1.647	1.626
3	2.941	2.884	2.829	2.775	2.723	2.673	2.624	2.577	2.531	2.487	2.444	2.402	2.361	2.322	2.283
4	3.902	3.808	3.717	3.630	3.546	3.465	3.387	3.312	3.240	3.170	3.102	3.037	2.974	2.914	2.855
5	4.853	4.713	4.580	4.452	4.329	4.212	4.100	3.993	3.890	3.791	3.696	3.605	3.517	3.433	3.352
6	5.795	5.601	5.417	5.242	5.076	4.917	4.767	4.623	4.486	4.355	4.231	4.111	3.998	3.889	3.784
7	6.728	6.472	6.230	6.002	5.786	5.582	5.389	5.206	5.033	4.868	4.712	4.564	4.423	4.288	4.160
8	7.652	7.325	7.020	6.733	6.463	6.210	5.971	5.747	5.535	5.335	5.146	4.968	4.799	4.639	4.487
9	8.566	8.162	7.786	7.435	7.108	6.802	6.515	6.247	5.995	5.759	5.537	5.328	5.132	4.946	4.772
10	9.471	8.983	8.530	8.111	7.722	7.360	7.024	6.710	6.418	6.145	5.889	5.650	5.426	5.216	5.019
11	10.368	9.787	9.253	8.760	8.306	7.887	7.499	7.139	6.805	6.495	6.207	5.938	5.687	5.453	5.234
12	11.255	10.575	9.954	9.385	8.863	8.384	7.943	7.536	7.161	6.814	6.492	6.194	5.918	5.660	5.421
13	12.134	11.348	10.635	9.986	9.394	8.853	8.358	7.904	7.487	7.103	6.750	6.424	6.122	5.842	5.583
14	13.004	12.106	11.296	10.563	9.899	9.295	8.745	8.244	7.786	7.367	6.982	6.628	6.302	6.002	5.724
15	13.865	12.849	11.938	11.118	10.380	9.712	9.108	8.559	8.061	7.606	7.191	6.811	6.462	6.142	5.847
16	14.718	13.578	12.561	11.652	10.838	10.106	9.447	8.851	8.313	7.824	7.379	6.974	6.604	6.265	5.954
17	15.562	14.292	13.166	12.166	11.274	10.477	9.763	9.122	8.544	8.022	7.549	7.120	6.729	6.373	6.047
18	16.398	14.992	13.754	12.659	11.690	10.828	10.059	9.372	8.756	8.201	7.702	7.250	6.840	6.467	6.128
19	17.226	15.678	14.324	13.134	12.085	11.158	10.336	9.604	8.950	8.365	7.839	7.366	6.938	6.550	6.198
20	18.046	16.351	14.877	13.590	12.462	11.470	10.594	9.818	9.129	8.514	7.963	7.469	7.025	6.623	6.259
25	22.023	19.523	17.413	15.622	14.094	12.783	11.654	10.675	9.823	9.077	8.422	7.843	7.330	6.873	6.464
30	25.808	22.396	19.600	17.292	15.372	13.765	12.409	11.258	10.274	9.427	8.694	8.055	7.496	7.003	6.566
35	29.409	24.999	21.487	18.665	16.374	14.498	12.948	11.655	10.567	9.644	8.855	8.176	7.586	7.070	6.617
40	32.835	27.355	23.115	19.793	17.159	15.046	13.332	11.925	10.757	9.779	8.951	8.244	7.634	7.105	6.642
50	39.196	31.424	25.730	21.482	18.256	15.762	13.801	12.233	10.962	9.915	9.042	8.304	7.675	7.133	6.661

KEY TERMS

DISCUSSION QUESTIONS

1. **LO.1** Explain why it is wise to obtain a private letter ruling from the IRS when structuring a corporate reorganization.

2. **LO.1** Why do the tax laws often dictate the legal form of corporate reorganizations? Be specific.

3. **LO.1** Provide a description of the corporate reorganizations available under § 368(a)(1).

4. **LO.2** Summarize the tax consequences of a § 368 reorganization.

5. **LO.2** How is the four-column template in Concept Summary 7.1 used to determine a shareholder's basis in the new stock received in a corporate restructuring?

6. **LO.1, 2, 3** An acquiring corporation transfers property and stock to the target corporation in a reorganization and receives the target's assets in exchange. What are the relevant tax issues? **Issue ID**

7. **LO.3** How does a "Type A" reorganization differ from a "Type B" with regard to the consideration that is permissible in the restructuring?

8. **LO.3** Compare the relationship between the acquiring and target corporations immediately after a "Type B" and a "Type C" reorganization.

9. **LO.3** What is the difference in the treatment of liabilities between a "Type A" and a "Type C" reorganization?

10. **LO.3** A "Type C" reorganization requires that substantially all of the target's assets be transferred to the acquiring corporation. Explain what is meant by "substantially all" of the assets.

11. **LO.3** What is the difference between a split-up, a split-off, and a spin-off? How do these differ from an acquisitive "Type D" reorganization?

12. **LO.3** What types of transactions receive tax-free treatment in "Type E" reorganizations?

13. **LO.3** Why do "Type F" reorganizations not jeopardize the predecessor's tax characteristics, such as its § 1244 stock or other corporate attributes?

14. **LO.3** The acquiring corporation in a "Type G" reorganization must reduce the tax attributes carried over from the bankrupt corporation. To what extent must the attributes be reduced? In what order are they reduced?

15. **LO.3, 4, 5** Alpha Corporation is interested in acquiring Beta Corporation. Beta produces equipment for scuba diving, and Alpha manufactures parachutes for skydiving. Beta has had some setbacks on its investments and has a substantial capital loss carryforward. Conversely, Alpha's investments have increased in value and have considerable built-in gains. **Issue ID**

If a restructuring occurs, Alpha will exchange 20% of its stock and some liquid assets for most of Beta's assets. Alpha also would like to have Beta switch to producing air tanks to be used by the military in extremely high-altitude ejections from fighter planes.

As the tax manager for Alpha, what concerns do you have regarding this proposed transaction between Alpha and Beta?

16. **LO.4** Briefly describe the judicial doctrines of sound business purpose, continuity of business enterprise, and the step transaction doctrine.

17. **LO.3, 4** Alpha Corporation would like to acquire the rights to an electrical process owned by Beta Corporation. Beta cannot sell the process because the rights are not transferrable under the current contract.

    Beta suggests an acquisitive "Type D" reorganization instead. Thirty percent of the Alpha shareholders are not interested in being shareholders of Beta, so they dissent to the transaction. Alpha creates a new corporation, Nu, and transfers 30% of its assets to Nu. It exchanges the Nu stock for the dissenting shareholder's stock in Alpha and then proceeds with the acquisitive "Type D" reorganization.

    Explain whether the acquisition of Beta by Alpha will meet the statutory requirements of the "Type D" reorganization given the steps proposed in the transaction.

18. **LO.5** What types of reorganizations are subject to the § 381 limitation?

19. **LO.5** Explain why the assumption of the target's liabilities is problematic for certain reorganizations and not for others.

20. **LO.5** What are owner shifts and equity shifts? What is the difference in their ability to invoke the § 382 limitation?

21. **LO.5** Provide the formulas for the § 382 limitation and the restriction on the § 382 limitation in the year of the ownership change.

22. **LO.5** Why does the calculation of the § 382 limitation for business credits require calculations beyond what is necessary for NOLs?

23. **LO.5** Explain how the earnings and profits (E & P) of the acquired corporation are treated by the successor corporation when the E & P balance is positive. When the E & P balance is negative. How are earnings and profits treated in a divisive "Type D" reorganization?

24. **LO.5, 6** Alpha Corporation is considering acquiring Beta Corporation. Beta has a good product line and a fairly new production plant; however, it has made some unprofitable investments. Currently, Beta holds a five-year capital loss carryforward of $50,000. Alpha holds its own $20,000 capital loss carryover that will expire in two years. In its acquisition of Beta, what should Alpha consider when determining the fair market value of Beta's capital loss carryover?

25. **LO.5** Demonstrate how a 55 percent ownership interest can be sold over the shortest period of time without causing an owner shift in any one year.

PROBLEMS

Decision Making

26. **LO.3** Determine whether the following transactions are taxable. If a transaction is not taxable, indicate what type of reorganization is effected, if any.
    a. Alpha Corporation owns assets valued at $400,000 and liabilities of $100,000. Beta Corporation transfers $160,000 of its voting stock and $40,000 in cash for 75% of Alpha's assets and all of its liabilities. Alpha distributes its remaining assets and the Beta stock to its shareholders. Alpha then liquidates.
    b. Alpha Corporation owns assets valued at $300,000 with liabilities of $100,000, and Beta Corporation holds assets valued at $1 million with liabilities of $200,000. Alpha exchanges 80% of its voting stock for 100% of Beta's assets and liabilities. Beta distributes the Alpha stock to its shareholders. Beta then liquidates.
    c. Alpha Corporation obtained 200,000 shares of Beta Corporation's stock 10 years ago. In the current year, Alpha exchanges 40% of its stock for 500,000 of the remaining 600,000 shares of Beta stock. After the transaction, Alpha owns 700,000 of the 800,000 Beta shares outstanding.

d. Alpha Corporation has two divisions that have been in existence for seven years. The nail division has assets valued at $455,000 and liabilities of $75,000, whereas the hammer division has assets valued at $670,000 and liabilities of $50,000. Alhpa would like the two divisions to be separate corporations. It creates Beta Corporation and transfers all of the hammer division assets and liabilities in exchange for 100% of Beta's stock. Alpha then distributes the Beta stock to its shareholders.

e. Alpha Corporation owns assets valued at $750,000 with liabilities of $230,000, and Beta holds assets valued at $1.5 million with liabilities of $500,000. Beta transfers 33% of its stock for $700,000 of Alpha's assets and $200,000 of its liabilities. Alpha distributes the Beta stock and its remaining assets and liabilities to its shareholders in exchange for their stock in Alpha. Alpha then terminates.

f. Beta Corporation has not been able to pay its creditors in the last year. To avoid foreclosure, Beta transfers its assets valued at $650,000 and liabilities of $700,000 to a new corporation, Alpha, Inc., in accordance with a state court proceeding. The creditors receive shares of Alpha voting stock valued at $300,000 and cancel the outstanding debt. The former Beta shareholders receive the remaining shares in Alpha.

27. **LO.2** Cole acquired 55% of Dane Corporation for $400,000 eight years ago. In the current year, Dane merges with Great Corporation, and Cole receives 7.5% of Great's stock plus $300,000 in land. The Great stock received by Cole is valued at $900,000. At the time of the transaction, Dane's E & P is $450,000, and Great's E & P is $1.8 million. As an individual shareholder, how should Cole treat this transaction for tax purposes?

28. **LO.2** Tri Corporation and Angle Corporation are combining to form Triangle Corporation in a restructuring that qualifies as a "Type A" consolidation reorganization. Tyron, the sole shareholder of Tri, has a basis of $250,000 in his stock, which he purchased 10 years ago. Anna, the sole shareholder of Angle, also has a basis of $250,000 in her stock. She purchased the stock four months ago. Tri transfers all of its assets valued at $650,000 (adjusted basis of $280,000) and $250,000 in liabilities to Triangle for $50,000 in cash and $350,000 in Triangle stock.

    Angle transfers all of its assets valued at $250,000 (adjusted basis of $200,000) and $50,000 in liabilities to Triangle for $30,000 in cash and $170,000 in Triangle stock. Upon completion of the consolidation, the Triangle stock and cash are transferred to Tyron and Anna, and both Tri and Angle cease to exist by operation of law.

    Determine the gain or loss that Tri, Angle, Tyron, Anna, and Triangle recognize from the reorganization. What are Triangle's bases in the assets it receives and Tyron's and Anna's new bases in their Triangle stock?

29. **LO.2** Sahara Corporation acquires Oasis Corporation in a "Type A" reorganization by exchanging 35% of its stock for all of the Oasis assets (fair market value of $950,000), liabilities ($300,000), and accumulated E & P ($140,000). Rama, a 60% shareholder of Oasis, exchanges her interest in Oasis (basis of $225,000) for Sahara stock and $100,000 cash. What is the tax treatment of Rama's exchange of Oasis stock for Sahara stock and cash?

30. **LO.2, 3** Spinone Corporation directs its sole shareholder to exchange all of his common stock valued at $200,000 (basis of $50,000) for $100,000 of common stock, $80,000 of preferred stock, and $20,000 in cash. In addition, Spinone directs its sole bondholder to exchange her $150,000 of bonds paying 6.0% for $170,000 of bonds paying 5.3%. How are these transactions treated for tax purposes by the shareholder, the bondholder, and Spinone? **Decision Making**

31. **LO.2** Quail Corporation was created in 2000 through contributions from Kasha ($800,000) and Frank ($200,000). In a transaction qualifying as a reorganization, Quail exchanges all of its assets currently valued at $2 million (basis of $1.5 million) for Covey Corporation stock valued at $1.9 million plus $100,000 in Covey bonds. Quail distributes the Covey stock and bonds proportionately to Frank and Kasha in exchange for their stock in Quail. Quail's current and accumulated E & P before the reorganization amounts to $70,000.

    a. How do Kasha and Frank treat this transaction for tax purposes?
    b. How do Quail and Covey treat this transaction for tax purposes? What is Covey's basis in the assets it receives from Quail?

32. **LO.2** Jed acquired 25% of the stock of Alpha Corporation (basis of $100,000) 12 years ago, and the other 75% was purchased by Zia (basis of $510,000) three years ago. Jed also holds a 10-year, $150,000 Alpha bond paying 6% interest.

Alpha enters into a tax-free consolidation with Beta Corporation, in which Jed will receive an 8% interest in the new AlphaBeta Corporation (value $144,000) plus $36,000 and Zia will receive a 27% interest (value $486,000) plus $54,000 of land. Alpha's basis in the land is $35,000. Jed also will exchange his $150,000 Alpha bond for a 10-year, $155,000 AlphaBeta bond paying 5.8% interest.

Before the reorganization or distributions to its shareholders, Alpha's value is $720,000, and Beta's value is $1,170,000.

a. What are Jed's and Zia's bases in their new AlphaBeta stock?
b. What is the amount of gain (loss) recognized by Jed, Zia, Alpha, and Beta on the reorganization?
c. Diagram the consolidation of Alpha and Beta Corporation.

33. **LO.2, 3** Target Corporation holds assets with a fair market value of $4 million (adjusted basis of $2.2 million) and liabilities of $1.5 million. It transfers assets worth $3.7 million to Acquiring Corporation in a ''Type C'' reorganization, in exchange for Acquiring voting stock and the assumption of $1.4 million of Target's liabilities.

Target retained a building worth $300,000 (adjusted basis of $225,000). Target distributes the Acquiring voting stock and the building with its $100,000 mortgage to Wei, its sole shareholder, for all of her stock in Target. Wei's basis in her stock is $2.6 million.

a. Explain whether this transaction meets the requirements for a "Type C" reorganization.
b. What is the value of the stock transferred from Acquiring to Target?
c. What is the amount of gain (loss) recognized by Wei, Target, and Acquiring on the reorganization?
d. What is Wei's basis in the stock and building she received?

Decision Making

34. **LO.3** Determine whether the following transactions are taxable. If a transaction is not taxable, indicate what type of reorganization is effected, if any.

a. AlphaPsi Corporation owns two lines of business that it has conducted for the last eight years. For liability protection, AlphaPsi's shareholders decide that it would be best to separate into two corporations. The assets and liabilities of the garbage collection division are transferred to Alpha Corporation in exchange for all of its stock. The manufacturing division's assets and liabilities are exchanged for all of the stock of Psi Corporation. The Alpha and Psi stocks are distributed to the AlphaPsi shareholders in return for all of their AlphaPsi stock. Then AlphaPsi liquidates.
b. Alpha, Inc., owns assets valued at $1 million and liabilities of $450,000. Beta Corporation transfers $500,000 of its voting stock and $50,000 in cash for all of Alpha's assets. Beta assumes Alpha's liabilities. Alpha distributes the Beta stock and cash to its shareholders and then liquidates.
c. Alpha Corporation moves its headquarters and state of legal incorporation from Salem, Oregon, to Dover, Delaware. It also changes its name to Beta, Inc.
d. Beta Company holds assets valued at $850,000 and liabilities of $50,000. Alpha, Inc., transfers $790,000 of its voting and $10,000 of nonvoting common stock for all of Beta's common and preferred stock. Beta becomes a subsidiary of Alpha.
e. Alpha, Inc., owns assets valued at $600,000 and liabilities of $150,000. Beta Corporation exchanges $270,000 of its voting stock and investments worth $180,000 for all of Alpha's assets and liabilities. Alpha distributes the Beta stock to its shareholders for 60% of their stock and retains the investments.
f. Beta Company holds assets valued at $3 million and liabilities of $100,000. Nu Company transfers $2.85 million of its voting stock for 95% of Beta's assets. Beta distributes the Nu stock, the remaining assets, and the liabilities to its shareholders; it then liquidates.

Decision Making

35. **LO.3, 6** Several years ago, Apso, Inc., was organized with equal contributions from April, ShibCo, and Otter Corporation. Last year, April purchased additional Apso stock from Otter, such that her Apso ownership percentage now is 57%. Otter currently owns 10% of Apso, and ShibCo owns 33%. In the current year, ShibCo decides that it wants a controlling interest in Apso. April is willing to exchange her Apso stock for ShibCo stock. Otter does not want to be a shareholder of ShibCo. It prefers to remain a shareholder of Apso, but if there is no other solution, it will liquidate its interest. Apso

currently holds assets worth $12 million (basis of $6.5 million) and $2 million of liabilities. Explain whether ShibCo can accomplish the restructuring using a "Type B" or "Type C" reorganization.

36. **LO.3, 6** Birdie Corporation has obtained a patent on a revolutionary putter that is sure to be an instant success with serious golfers. Unfortunately, Birdie does not have the capital to market the new putter adequately. Therefore, it is considering joining forces with Bogie Corporation, a company with substantial liquid assets and experience in marketing golfing products. Although Bogie has had some unfavorable press lately that has tarnished its reputation, Birdie believes a union between the two would be beneficial to both corporations. **Communications**

Birdie's president, Xanna Jackson, requests your guidance as to what type of reorganization Birdie and Bogie should consider. She provides you with the following information.

Corporation	FMV of Assets	Adjusted Basis	Liabilities
Birdie	$200,000	$160,000	$150,000
Bogie	800,000	600,000	100,000

Write a letter to Ms. Jackson explaining the appropriateness of using a "Type A" consolidation, a "Type C" reorganization, or an acquisitive "Type D" reorganization. Birdie's address is 460 Lakeview Drive, Lake Oswego, OR 97034.

37. **LO.3, 6** Big Corporation currently owns 25% of Small, Inc. Big acquired this stock two years ago by exchanging $375,000 of its preferred stock with Allie, one of the original owners of Small. Big had tried to acquire the assets of Small, but management was not in favor of the acquisition. In the current year, Big enters into a transaction with Small shareholders in which it acquires $712,500 of Small's voting stock and $200,000 of preferred stock. Big now owns 95% of the Small common stock and 100% of its preferred stock. **Issue ID**
    a. Diagram the current year corporate reorganization.
    b. Identify the tax issues in the proposed transaction.

38. **LO.3, 6** Eta Corporation approaches Lily White, the CEO and sole shareholder of MuCo, regarding the acquisition of MuCo's cat toy division assets (worth $1.3 million). As selling the assets would create a $600,000 gain, ($1.3 million value – $700,000 basis), Lily declines the offer. **Communications**

Eta counters and suggests a "Type C" reorganization as a method of acquiring all of MuCo by exchanging its voting stock for all assets (now worth $1.5 million) and all liabilities ($650,000) of MuCo. The other division of MuCo, Cat Publications, is small, with assets worth $200,000 and liabilities of $150,000. Lily agrees to the reorganization if MuCo receives the net value of the Cat Publication division ($50,000) in cash, as Lily would like money as well as stock.

Lily requests your advice on whether the transaction can be structured as a ''Type C'' reorganization as it is currently described. If it cannot meet the "Type C" requirements, suggest an alternative plan that will allow the transaction to qualify as a "Type C" reorganization. MuCo's address is 3443 E. Riverbank Road, Walla Walla, WA 99362. Include your analysis in a letter to Ms. White.

39. **LO.3, 6** In 2000, Canine Corporation was organized to manufacture dog food with equal contributions from Jane, Claire, and Brian. In 2002, Canine opened retail pet stores in North Dakota. In 2004, Canine developed a line of healthy snacks for dogs. Each line of business has a net value of $1 million. In the current year, there have been substantial disagreements among the three shareholders as to Canine's future direction; consequently, the shareholders have decided to go their separate ways. Canine must cease to exist, as none of the shareholders wants the others to obtain the Canine name. **Decision Making**
    a. Develop a plan to divide Canine among the shareholders that meets their desires and creates the least amount of Federal income taxes.
    b. Diagram the corporate division.

40. **LO.3** Hefty Corporation would like to buy mineral leases owned by Tiny Corporation for $550,000. Tiny informs Hefty that these leases are not transferable under its current contract. Given that the leases are Tiny's only valuable asset, Hefty suggests a reorganization, with Tiny being the entity that survives.

Tiny has a basis in the leases of $100,000 and $25,000 of liabilities associated with the leases. Hefty's assets are valued at $3.6 million, and it holds $625,000 in liabilities.

a. How do Hefty and Tiny complete this reorganization with the least amount of taxes? Include in your discussion of the restructuring the value of the stock and assets transferred by each corporation and the resulting ownership by each former shareholder group.
b. Under what "type" of tax-free reorganization does this restructuring fall?
c. Diagram the restructuring transaction and indicate the corporate and shareholder relationships after the transaction.

Decision Making

41. **LO.2, 3** The Rho Corporation was incorporated in 2001 by Tyee and Danette. Tyee received 5,000 shares of common stock for his $100,000 contribution, and Danette received 10,000 shares of common stock for her $200,000 contribution. In 2005, both Tyee and Danette acquired $50,000 of Rho bonds paying 3% interest.

    In the current year, Rho's common stock is valued at $900,000. SheenCo would like to acquire a 25% interest in Rho by purchasing common stock from Rho. Tyee and Danette see this as a good time to restructure Rho's capital. They would like to own bonds paying 5% interest, and each would like to receive $120,000 of preferred stock in exchange for some of his or her common stock. What advice would you give to Rho?

Communications

42. **LO.3** Beach Corporation, a service business, is owned by 50 unrelated shareholders. It just lost a $1.5 million product liability lawsuit. Its assets currently have a value of $6 million, and its outstanding liabilities, including the payables from the lawsuit, total $4.6 million. As a result of the lawsuit, Beach's future revenue stream appears to be substantially impaired.

    Beach's president, Sandy Shores, asks your advice regarding the possibility of:

    - Restructuring Beach from a C corporation to an S corporation so that the losses will flow through to the owners.
    - Renaming the corporation Ocean.
    - Moving to a state that has a coastline and that recognizes S status.

    Write a letter to Sandy explaining her choices in restructuring Beach. Beach's address is 9180 Laurel Street, Florence, OR 97439.

43. **LO.3** TinCo has product liability problems and has filed for bankruptcy protection in the state court. Currently, its liabilities are $1 million, and its depreciable assets are valued at $550,000 (basis of $400,000). Through the "Type G" reorganization, a new entity, ZinCo, has been created to succeed TinCo. At the time of the restructuring, TinCo has an NOL carryforward of $200,000, general business credits of $50,000, and a capital loss carryforward of $100,000. Explain the tax consequences for TinCo and ZinCo if ZinCo elects to reduce the basis of the depreciable property first in the "Type G" reorganization.

Issue ID

44. **LO.3, 4** Joe, Greg, Lynn, and Shanna each own a 25% interest in Norwich Corporation, which manufactures shoe polish. Joe is irascible and often argues with the other three shareholders. They tend to give in to Joe because he is so persistent. Now Joe has caused Norwich to acquire a wine store by exchanging 30% of the Norwich stock for all of the assets ($300,000) of the wine store. The Norwich stock was distributed to the wine store's owner, and then the wine store entity liquidated. After Joe has run the wine business for a few months, the other shareholders vote to drop the wine business into a separate corporation, with Joe receiving all of the stock for his 25% interest in Norwich. Joe no longer will be a shareholder of Norwich. Identify the tax issues regarding these transactions.

Issue ID

45. **LO.2, 3, 4, 5, 6** Float Corporation is in the luxury yacht business and has been hit hard by the downturn in the economy. It has been barely breaking even, and its investments of its previous profits have substantial built-in capital losses. It has not sold these investment assets because it cannot utilize the resulting tax losses. Float's attorney suggests that it try to merge with a profitable company, specifically one with built-in capital gains. A profitable company would be willing to acquire Float just for its built-in capital losses.

    Float advertises for a merger partner, and Fierce, Inc., contacts Float. Fierce manufactures and installs home security systems. In the discussion, Float determines that Fierce could use a small fraction of Float's business assets and might consider developing security systems for yachts, but is not at all interested in manufacturing yachts. Most important, Fierce is very interested in acquiring Float's built-in capital losses.

Fierce offers 10% of its stock and $500,000 in exchange for all of Float's assets. Float can use the cash to buy the stock of the shareholders who oppose the merger. What tax issues should Fierce and Float consider before agreeing to this merger as structured?

46. **LO.5** Through a "Type B" reorganization, Golden Corporation acquired 90% of RetrieverCo stock by October 2 of the current tax year ending December 31. At the time the 90% was acquired, RetrieverCo was worth $800,000 and the Federal long-term tax-exempt rate was 3%. RetrieverCo holds capital loss carryovers of $50,000. If Golden reports taxable income of $300,000, which includes $30,000 of capital gains, how much of the RetrieverCo capital loss carryover may Golden use in the current year to offset its income?

47. **LO.5** Through an acquisitive "Type D" reorganization, Border, Inc., is merged into Collie Corporation on September 2 of the current calendar tax year. The Federal long-term tax-exempt rate for September 2 is 5%. Border shareholders receive 70% of the Collie stock in exchange for all of their Border shares. Border liquidates immediately after the exchange. At the time of the merger, Border was worth $1 million and held a $500,000 NOL.

    If Collie reports taxable income of $400,000 for the current year, how much of the Border NOL can be utilized in the current year? How much of the Border NOL may Collie utilize next year if its taxable income remains the same?

48. **LO.3, 5** Through a "Type C" reorganization, Springer Corporation was merged into Spaniel Corporation last year. Springer shareholders received 40% of the Spaniel stock in exchange for all of their Springer shares. Springer liquidated immediately after the exchange. At the time of the merger, Springer was worth $2 million and held a $500,000 NOL. If Spaniel reports taxable income of $800,000 for the current year, how much of the Springer NOL can be utilized by Spaniel? Assume that the applicable Federal long-term tax-exempt rate is 4%.

49. **LO.5** Five years ago, Jack purchased an Inu Corporation 15-year bond having a face value of $150,000 and paying 6% annual interest. In a "Type E" reorganization, Inu is going to exchange Jack's bond with 10 years remaining for a 5-year bond having a face value of $180,000 and paying 4% annual interest. Jack uses a 6% discount factor and is in the 25% tax bracket for all years. The capital gain rate is 15% for all years. Determine whether this is an equitable exchange for Jack. **Decision Making**

50. **LO.5** Global Corporation is negotiating a merger ("Type A" reorganization) with State Corporation, to be effective on December 31 of the current year. Global is a profitable corporation with $10 million in assets and taxable income of approximately $5 million, whereas State is struggling with built-up NOLs of $560,000 and net assets valued at $800,000. If Global's discount rate for investment decisions is 7%, what is the maximum value to Global of State's NOL? Assume that the Federal long-term tax-exempt rate is 5% for this merger.

51. **LO.5** Zeta Corporation is interested in acquiring Tau Corporation through a "Type A" reorganization on January 2 of the current year. Zeta is valued at $50 million and generates taxable income of $5 million per year, whereas Tau is valued at $7 million and holds a $1.47 million NOL with nine years remaining in its carryover period. If Zeta uses a 7% discount rate for its business investment decisions and the Federal long-term tax-exempt rate is 3%, what value should Zeta place on Tau's NOL? **Decision Making**

52. **LO.5** On December 31, 2011, Alpha Corporation, valued at $10 million, acquired BetaCo when BetaCo was valued at $5 million. BetaCo holds a capital loss carryforward of $220,000 and excess business credits of $435,000. At the end of 2012, Alpha reports taxable income before any carryovers of $750,000, consisting of $150,000 capital gains and $600,000 operating income. The applicable Federal long-term rate is 4%, and Alpha uses an 8% discount rate for its business decisions.
    a. How much of the BetaCo carryovers may Alpha utilize in 2012?
    b. Alpha expects to generate $600,000 of taxable operating income for 2013 and 2014. In 2015, it expects to record $700,000 taxable income, including $100,000 of capital gains. What is the value of the capital loss carryforward and excess business credits to Alpha after 2012?

53. **LO.5** Through a "Type A" reorganization, VizslaCo acquires 100% of Puli Corporation by exchanging 30% of its stock for all of Puli's assets and liabilities. The VizslaCo stock was exchanged for all of the stock of the Puli shareholders. Then Puli liquidated. The net value of Puli's assets at the time of the restructuring was $500,000, and the Federal long-term tax-exempt rate was 5%. Puli held business tax credit carryovers of $61,250. If VizslaCo is always in the 35% tax bracket, what is the value of these credits to VizslaCo assuming that it uses a discount rate of 8%?

54. **LO.5** Shepherd Corporation is considering acquiring RentCo by exchanging its stock (value of $10 per share) for RentCo's only asset, a tract of land (adjusted basis of $150,000 and no liability). The yearly net rent that RentCo receives on the land is $50,000. Shepherd anticipates that it will receive the same net rent for the land over the next 20 years. At the end of that time, it would sell the land for $400,000.

    What is the maximum number of shares that RentCo shareholders can expect Shepherd to offer for 100% of their RentCo stock? Assume that Shepard uses a 10% discount rate and is in the 34% tax bracket for all years. What type of reorganization is this contemplated transaction?

Decision Making

55. **LO.3** In 2001, Xio and Xandra each invest $300,000 to create Xava Corporation. Xava develops and manufactures rock climbing and bungee jumping equipment. The business has become very profitable (it now is valued at $3 million), and Xandra would like to benefit from this profitability by selling the business. Xio, however, wants to reinvest the profitability and expand the business into ice diving. Because they have different expectations, Xio and Xandra agree that the best solution is to divide up the company. Xandra will receive the bungee division; Xio, the rock climbing. After the reorganization, Xandra sells her stock in the bungee division for $1.5 million at the beginning of the current year. Xio retains her ownership of the rock climbing division.
    a. What type of reorganization would be used to divide Xava Corporation between Xio and Xandra?
    b. Xio sells the rock climbing stock for $2 million at the end of the six years. Using a 7% discount factor, determine whether Xandra or Xio made a better decision. Assume that the tax on capital gains remains at its current rate. (*Hint:* Determine the present value of the after-tax cash flow for Xio and Xandra on the sale of the stock.)

RESEARCH PROBLEMS

THOMSON REUTERS **CHECKPOINT**®

Note: Solutions to Research Problems can be prepared by using the **Checkpoint® Student Edition** online research product, which is available to accompany this text. It is also possible to prepare solutions to the Research Problems by using tax research materials found in a standard tax library.

Communications

Research Problem 1. Exterminator Corporation was a small, closely held business that provided pest control services to commercial businesses. Generally, Exterminator's clients purchased three- or six-month contracts, with full payment due when the contracts were signed. These payments were treated as liabilities and converted into income only when services were rendered. This is the customary industry standard and is accepted by the IRS as proper reporting.

A few years ago, a large national corporation, Terminator, Inc., moved into Exterminator's territory and undercut its prices. This substantially hurt its business, and Exterminator accumulated a $300,000 NOL. Realizing that the only way to survive was to merge with Terminator, the Exterminator shareholders in 2011 exchanged 100% of their stock for a 5% interest in Terminator, in a transaction qualifying as a "Type C" reorganization. At the time of the reorganization, Exterminator held assets valued at $600,000, services liabilities of $100,000, other liabilities of $50,000, and an adjusted basis in its assets of $150,000.

After the reorganization, Terminator provided services to Exterminator customers and converted the liabilities into income. Terminator treated the income as recognized built-in gains when computing the yearly § 382 limitation.

Upon audit, the IRS disallowed this treatment. The IRS did not question the timing of the income recognition, but it did inquire whether these prepaid pre-change amounts constituted built-in gains for § 382.

Prepare a memo for Terminator's tax file explaining whether the IRS is correct in disallowing the built-in gains treatment.

Research Problem 2. Pan, an S corporation, is in the home construction business and has sustained $500,000 in losses in excess of the shareholders' bases in their stock. Thus, these losses have been suspended and are not likely to be available to the shareholders in the near future. To finance its construction in the last couple of years, Pan has issued notes for $1 million, and it is currently in default on these notes. Pan sells its investment assets and accounts receivables. It uses the proceeds to partially pay the note holders.

Once Pan realizes that it is no longer a viable going concern, it files a petition for bankruptcy under Chapter 11 with the bankruptcy court. To rehabilitate its business, Pan is considering the following. It will create a new C corporation, called Clipper, into which Pan will merge. Thus, Clipper will be the surviving corporation. The note holders will receive 80% of the Clipper stock in exchange for relinquishing their rights to the outstanding principals on their notes. The other 20% of the stock will be exchanged with the former shareholders of Pan. Clipper will acquire 60% of the fair market value of Pan's gross assets and 100% of the fair market value of the operating assets held at the bankruptcy filing date. The operating assets are all of Pan's assets except those previously sold to pay the note holders. Following the merger, Clipper will continue in the home construction industry.

Will the merger, as described, meet the requirements of the "Type G" reorganization? Specifically, explain whether the proposed reorganization meets the requirement that substantially all of the assets of the old corporation have been transferred to the new corporation.

Research Problem 3. Marula Corporation was formed in 2000, with Adede contributing $34,000 of machinery, Buru contributing $33,000 cash, and Chipo contributing $33,000 of land. Marula has been a very successful firm and now is valued at $1 million. Based on the success of Marula, Adede, Buru, and Chipo join with Dube to create the Kudu Corporation this year. Adele, Buru, and Chipo each contribute $132,000 for 99% of the stock (33% each). Dube contributes $4,000 for 1% of the shares.

Through Dube's contacts, Kudu is able to obtain a very lucrative government contract. Unfortunately, Kudu does not have the facilities to service this contract. Marula easily could fulfill the government orders, but Dube had the contract written in such a manner that it is not transferable. Consequently, Marula transfers all of its assets to Kudu in exchange for $200,000 of cash and immediately liquidates. Will this restructuring qualify as a "Type D" reorganization even though no stock was transferred from Kudu to Marula's shareholders? What gain or loss do the Marula shareholders recognize on this transaction?

Communications

Research Problem 4. Pyramid Corporation wants to acquire one of Pharaoh, Inc.'s active lines of business that Pharaoh has run since its incorporation in 1952. In contemplation of the acquisition, Pharaoh creates TutCo by transferring the desired line of business to TutCo in exchange for all of its stock. This stock is distributed to part of the Pharaoh shareholders in exchange for their shares.

Meanwhile, Pyramid arranges financing to repurchase enough of its own stock to complete the acquisition of 85% of TutCo with voting stock. After the exchange of Pyramid stock for TutCo stock in December of the current year, TutCo is a subsidiary of Pyramid.

To orchestrate this acquisition, Pyramid, Pharaoh, and TutCo have incurred substantial legal fees, asset and stock valuation costs, state fees, and financing fees. Determine how the costs paid to facilitate the acquisition of TutCo are treated for Federal income tax purposes. Provide citations to primary tax sources in a research memo for the tax file.

Internet Activity

Use the tax resources of the Internet to address the following questions. Do not restrict your search to the Web, but include a review of newsgroups and general reference materials, practitioner sites and resources, primary sources of the tax law, chat rooms and discussion groups, and other opportunities.

Communications

Research Problem 5. State income tax law may include provisions for corporate reorganizations that differ from those of the Federal income tax rules. Find your state's statutes that indicate the treatment of reorganizations that are tax-deferred for Federal purposes. Provide a written summary of the provision(s) with citations in a memo for the tax research file.

Communications

Research Problem 6. Find a recent merger or acquisition in the mining industry. Prepare a written summary of the transaction, including the companies involved, and send your document to your professor.

Communications

Research Problem 7. Find a news article discussing a recent stock-for-stock corporate acquisition. Prepare a one-page summary of the reorganization, including the names of the companies and the value of the transaction. Send your report to your professor.

Communications

Research Problem 8. When corporations are contemplating reorganization transactions, it is suggested that they obtain a private letter ruling (PLR) from the IRS to ensure the treatment they desire. How does a taxpayer request a PLR? E-mail a one-page memo to your professor explaining the current procedures by which to request a PLR.

CHAPTER

8 Consolidated Tax Returns

LEARNING OBJECTIVES: *After completing Chapter 8, you should be able to:*

LO.1 Apply the fundamental concepts of consolidated tax returns.

LO.2 Identify the sources of the rules for consolidated taxable income.

LO.3 List the major advantages and disadvantages of filing consolidated tax returns.

LO.4 Identify the corporations that are eligible to file on a consolidated basis.

LO.5 Explain the compliance aspects of consolidated returns.

LO.6 Compute a parent's investment basis in a subsidiary.

LO.7 Account for intercompany transactions of a consolidated group.

LO.8 Identify limitations that restrict the use of losses and credits of group members derived in separate return years.

LO.9 Derive deductions and credits on a consolidated basis.

LO.10 Demonstrate tax planning opportunities available to consolidated groups.

CHAPTER OUTLINE

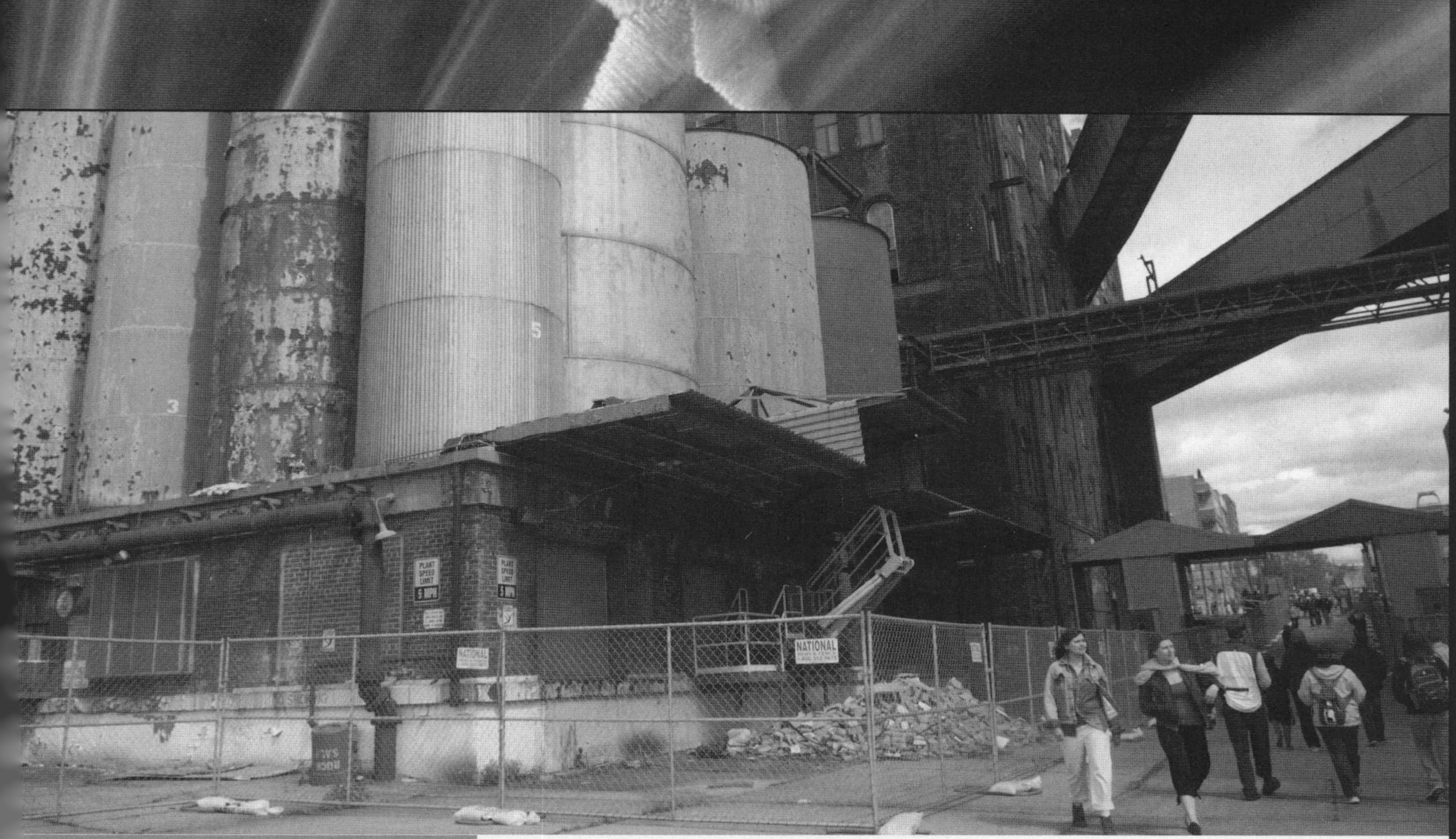

THE BIG PICTURE Tax Solutions for the Real World

© Frances Roberts/Alamy

A Corporation Contemplates a Merger

Alexander Corporation has had a long-term association with one of its suppliers, Hamilton Corporation. In the past, Hamilton was a highly profitable operation and was even able to make loans to Alexander to cover short-term working capital needs. Recently, however, Hamilton has been consistently late in meeting current obligations. Alexander has had to grant extensions of up to nine months on Hamilton's payables. Several vendors have even ceased doing business with Hamilton. Nevertheless, Alexander feels confident that Hamilton's fortunes will improve. If this financial turnaround occurs, Alexander will continue dealing with Hamilton in the same manner as in the past.

But Alexander's tax advisers have suggested another alternative. They say that Alexander should consider acquiring Hamilton in a merger or other takeover that qualifies as a tax-favored reorganization (see Chapter 7) to avoid any immediate Federal income tax liability. Hamilton's downturn has left it with sizable net operating losses that would be attractive to Alexander for use on future joint tax returns. Because Hamilton's name, reputation, and location still have value in the marketplace, it could continue as a separate division or subsidiary of Alexander. Furthermore, the takeover would give other businesses greater assurance of Hamilton's financial viability. Finally, there could be tax advantages to Alexander, the new parent of a two-corporation group.

Evaluate this and other viable alternatives for Alexander taking into account various possible outcomes (e.g., the success or failure of Hamilton's business).

Read the chapter and formulate your response.

8.1 Context of the Consolidated Return Rules

To this point, the discussion has centered on the computation of the tax liability of individual corporations under the regular tax calculation, along with specific penalty taxes and the alternative minimum tax. This is an appropriate approach to the study of corporate taxation, as more than 90 percent of the roughly 7 million U.S. corporations are closely held (i.e., either by a small group of operators/investors or by members of the same family).

Although some of these family businesses operate in a multiple-corporation environment, the vast majority of the assets held by businesses nationwide are owned by no more than 50,000 large corporate conglomerates. These corporations conduct the bulk of the country's "big business," and they account for over 95 percent of all net Federal corporate taxable income. In addition, these corporate groups face some special tax rules, which are the subject of this chapter.

Motivations to Consolidate

Corporate conglomerates are present in every aspect of life. The local dairy or bakery is likely to be owned by General Mills or General Foods. Oil and insurance companies own movie-making corporations. Professional sports teams are corporate cousins of the newspapers and television/radio stations that carry their games. The same corporate group that produces night-lights for a child's nursery may manufacture control equipment for bombers and other elements of the Defense Department's arsenal.

What brings together these sometimes strange corporate bedfellows? For the most part, nontax motivations provide the strongest incentives for multiple-corporation acquisitions and holdings. Among the many commonly encountered motivations are the following.

- A desire to isolate assets of other group members from the liabilities of specific operating divisions (e.g., to gain limited liability for a tobacco or asbestos company within an operating conglomerate).
- A need to carry out specific estate planning objectives (e.g., by transferring growth or high-risk assets to younger-generation shareholders).
- A preference to isolate the group's exposure to losses and liabilities incurred in joint ventures with "outside" entities (especially when such venturers are not based in the United States).
- A perception that separate divisions/group members will be worth more on the market if they maintain unique identities or otherwise avoid a commingling of assets and liabilities with other group members (e.g., where a trade name or patent is especially valuable or carries excessive goodwill in the marketplace).
- Conversely, an attempt to shield the identities of a subsidiary's true owners from the public where negative goodwill exists (e.g., with respect to the consequences of a nuclear or industrial accident, or the use of a long-held name of an oil or tobacco company).

LO.1

Apply the fundamental concepts of consolidated tax returns.

Although nontax concerns may be the primary reason for the creation of many conglomerates, tax incentives may also play a role. To a large extent, these incentives can be found in the rules that control the filing of **consolidated returns**. In general terms, the IRS allows certain corporate groups to be treated as a single entity for Federal income tax purposes. This enables the group to use available tax exemptions and brackets optimally among its members and to shelter the income of profitable members with the losses of other members. Thus, through the consolidated return rules, corporate taxpayers have an opportunity to manage the combined tax liability of the members of the group.

The consolidated return rules may be available to a taxpayer as a result of various business decisions.

TAX IN THE NEWS Do Conglomerates Create Conflicts of Interest?

The Internet may have brought dark days for the journalism profession, but the media still can perform a "watchdog" function that keeps governments and businesses under the microscope. Conglomerates that have communications subsidiaries often argue that it takes a lot of capital to staff news bureaus in Europe or to produce movies with expensive special effects. Thus, some of the most recognizable television networks and news organizations have been acquired by large corporations with multiple subsidiaries.

But can the disparate members of a conglomerate resist the temptation to act in concert for the good of the entire group? Charges of "soft reporting" among corporate cousins often arise when critical reporting seems lacking. Given that General Electric owns an interest in NBC Universal, will we ever see a *Dateline* segment about how GE may bend the rules to obtain Defense Department contracts? Can ABC online critics comment negatively on the 3-D version of *The Lion King*, a movie from Disney, its corporate parent?

- A consolidated return may result from a merger, an acquisition, or another corporate combination (discussed in Chapter 7).

EXAMPLE 1

When Dover Corporation acquires all of the stock of Edwards Corporation, a new corporate group, Dover and Edwards Corporation, is formed. The two group members can elect to file their tax return on a consolidated basis. ■

- A group of business taxpayers may be restructured to comply with changes in regulatory requirements, meet the demands of a competitive environment, or gain economies of scale and operate more efficiently in a larger arrangement. Consequently, an election to file a consolidated return becomes available.

EXAMPLE 2

External Corporation, a retailer, acquires Internal Corporation, a wholesaler, in an effort to control its flow of inventory in unstable economic times. The two group members can elect to file their tax returns on a consolidated basis. ■

- The taxpayers may be seeking to gain tax, financial reporting, and other financial advantages that are more readily available to corporate combinations.

EXAMPLE 3

Over the next three years, Mary Corporation will be selling a number of its business assets at a loss. If Norbert Corporation acquires all of Mary's stock and the group elects to file its tax returns on a consolidated basis, Norbert will be able to combine its gains from the sale of business property with Mary's losses in computing the group's consolidated § 1231 gain/loss for the year. ■

Source and Philosophy of Consolidated Return Rules

Some form of consolidated corporate tax return has been allowed for Federal purposes since World War I. At that time, the Treasury became suspicious that conglomerates were shifting taxable income to a number of smaller entities to avoid the high marginal rates of the excess profits tax that had been imposed to finance the war effort. Thus, the consolidated return rules may be seen as the earliest effort of the IRS to limit the tax benefits available to multiple corporations.

EXAMPLE 4

Assume that the marginal Federal income tax rate is 10% on the first $100,000 of taxable income and 15% on any taxable income in excess of $100,000. The additional 5 percentage points constitute a war profits tax, and the revenue raised is used for the war effort.

Further assume that the tax law includes no restrictions on the tax computations of related corporations. A corporation with annual taxable income of $1 million can eliminate its entire exposure to the war profits tax by splitting its business evenly among 10 separate corporations. ■

LO.2

Identify the sources of the rules for consolidated taxable income.

At various times, Congress has modified the pertinent Regulations and imposed a higher tax rate or surcharge on consolidated groups to increase the cost of making the consolidation election. During World War II, when it feared that "too much" income of profiteers was being sheltered in consolidated groups, Congress suspended the application of the rules for most taxpayers. On other occasions, including the present, complex limitations were placed on the use and timing of positive tax benefits, such as net operating loss (NOL) carryovers, that were acquired in a corporate consolidation. Congress imposed these limits to discourage profitable corporations from "trafficking" in businesses that had generated net losses.

Currently, Congress has delegated most of its legislative authority involving consolidated returns to the Treasury. As a result, the majority of the rules that affect consolidated groups are found in the Regulations. The Code provisions dealing with consolidated returns are strictly definitional in nature and broad in scope,[1] while the related Regulations dictate the computational and compliance requirements of the group.[2]

As discussed in Chapter 1, "legislative" Regulations of this sort carry the full force and effect of law. Challenges to the content of these Regulations seldom are supported by the courts. Consequently, taxpayers generally participate actively in the hearings process in an effort to have their interpretations included in the final Regulations.

The length and detail of these Regulations make the consolidated return rules among the most complex in the Federal income tax law. For the most part, the underlying objective of the rules remains one of organizational neutrality; that is, a group of closely related corporations should have neither a tax advantage nor a disadvantage relative to taxpayers who file separate corporate returns.

ETHICS & EQUITY Delegating Authority to the Nonelected

In no other area of the tax law has Congress given the Treasury such leeway in crafting both major principles and details as in the area of consolidated returns. Because Treasury staff members are not elected officials, this delegation of authority might appear to be a shirking of congressional duty and a dangerous assignment of legislative power to an isolated group of individuals.

To what extent should Congress delegate its powers over the country's largest businesses (not only the largest players in the global economy but also the largest contributors to campaign and reelection funds)? Can the delegation of congressional powers to Washington-based civil servants, who are virtually immune to the checks and balances of the election process, be healthy for all taxpayers?

You are a member of the House Ways and Means Committee, and your chances of reelection are jeopardized when you must take a position on a consolidated tax return issue: Taxes on old-line manufacturers would increase, while those on more environmentally friendly, high-tech industries would fall. Should you avoid the debate altogether by deferring the issue to the Regulations process?

[1] §§ 1501–1505.

[2] Reg. §§ 1.1501–1, 1.1502–0 through 1.1502–100, 1.1503–1 through 1.1503–2T, and 1.1504–1.

FINANCIAL DISCLOSURE INSIGHTS GAAP and Tax Treatment of Consolidations

Both U.S. financial accounting and tax rules use the term *consolidation*, but there is only a slight resemblance in the content of those rules. Here are some of the key similarities and differences between the book and tax treatment of conglomerates.

- GAAP consolidations for the most part are *mandatory* when specified ownership levels are met. Federal income tax consolidation is an *election* by the affiliates to join the parent's tax return.
- GAAP consolidations can include entities such as partnerships and non-U.S. entities. Federal income tax rules generally limit the consolidated return only to U.S. C corporations.
- Ownership levels required for a target to consolidate with a parent generally are 50 percent for GAAP and 80 percent for Federal income tax.
- Tax rules treat a merger or an acquisition of a target corporation by a parent as a like-kind exchange, assuming that the requirements of a § 368 reorganization are met (see Chapter 7). Under GAAP, the transaction usually is reported as a purchase of the target's identifiable assets and liabilities.
- After a takeover occurs, book cost amounts are assigned at fair market value and any excess purchase price is deemed to be goodwill. For Federal income tax purposes, if reorganization treatment is available, the target's basis in its assets carries over to the parent's accounts.
- Goodwill is treated differently under book and tax rules. Financial accounting goodwill cannot be amortized, but impairments to its value are reported as operating losses. Book income results if that impairment of the goodwill is reversed, fox example, because the value of the goodwill has increased. For Federal income tax purposes, purchased goodwill is amortized over 15 years.

On page 1 of the Form 1120 Schedule M-3, the consolidated group reconciles its GAAP income with the taxable income that is reported on the consolidated return. This entails, for instance, disregarding the operating results of non-U.S. corporations and of noncorporate entities.

8.2 Assessing Consolidated Return Status

LO.3

List the major advantages and disadvantages of filing consolidated tax returns.

As Concept Summary 8.1 illustrates, all of the members of a corporate group must meet three broad requirements to be eligible to elect and maintain the right to file a consolidated income tax return.

- The corporations must meet the statutory ownership requirements to be classified as an affiliated group.[3]
- The corporations must be eligible to make a consolidation election.[4]
- The group must meet various tax accounting and compliance requirements.[5]

Before making an election to file consolidated tax returns, related taxpayers must weigh the resulting tax advantages and disadvantages.

The potential advantages of filing consolidated returns are many.

- The operating and capital loss carryovers of one group member may be used to shelter the corresponding income of other group members.
- The taxation of all intercompany dividends may be eliminated.
- Recognition of income from certain intercompany transactions can be deferred.
- Certain deductions and credits may be optimized by using consolidated amounts in computing pertinent limitations (e.g., the deductions for charitable contributions and dividends received, and foreign tax credits).
- The tax basis of investments in the stock of subsidiaries is increased as the members contribute to consolidated taxable income.

[3]§§ 1504(a)(1) and (2).

[4]This is a negative definition, rooted in §§ 1504(b) through (f).

[5]See especially Reg. §§ 1.1502–75, –76, and –77.

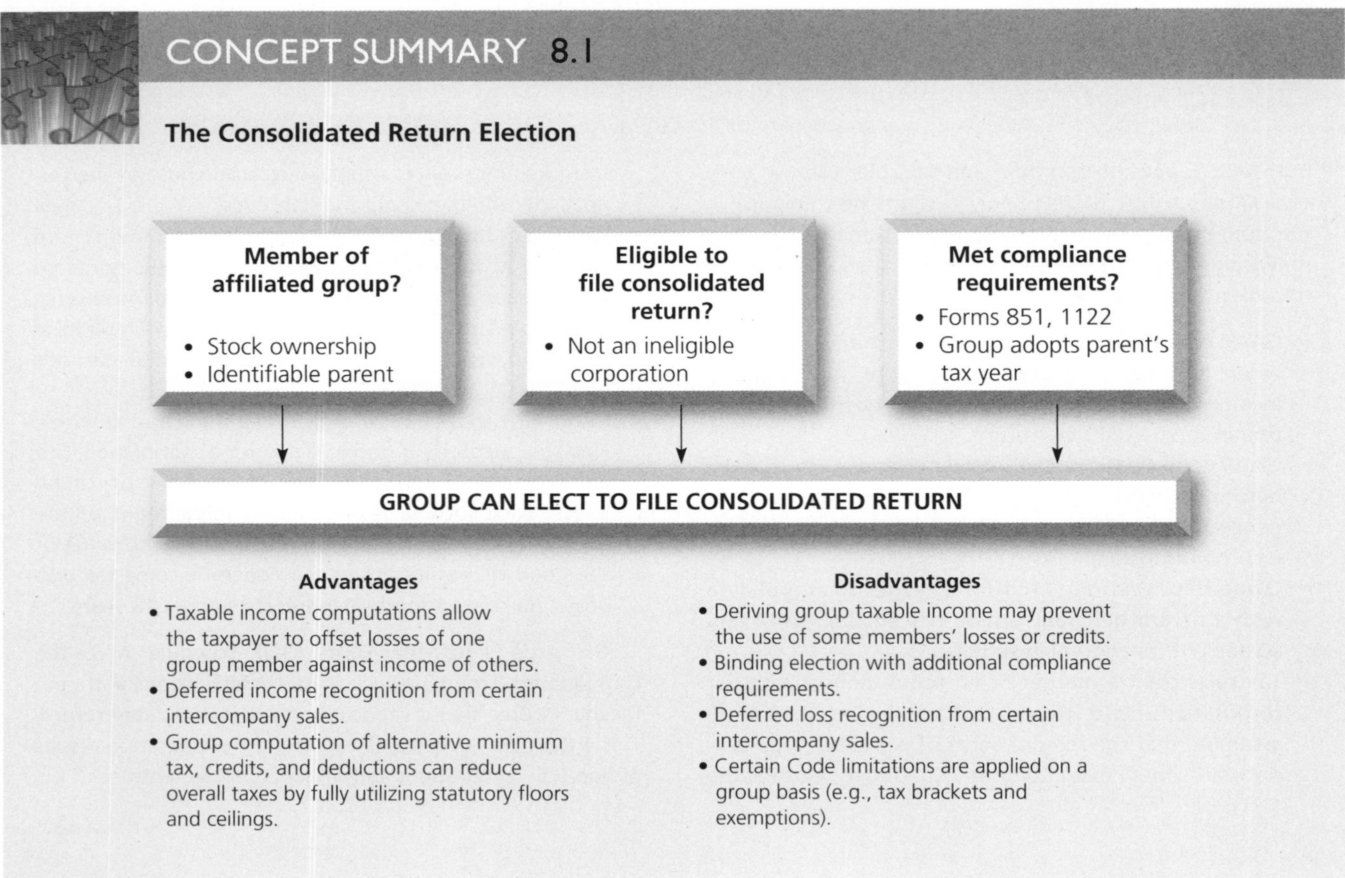

- The domestic production activities deduction of a group might be greater than the sum of the deductions for all of the affiliates, as the formula for determining the deduction permits various components to be aggregated.
- The alternative minimum tax (AMT) attributes of all group members can be used in deriving consolidated alternative minimum taxable income (AMTI). This can reduce the adjusted current earnings (ACE) adjustment and optimize other AMT preferences and adjustments.
- The shareholdings of all group members can be used in meeting other statutory requirements.[6]

Consolidated returns also have a number of potential disadvantages.

- The election is binding on all subsequent tax years of the group members unless either the makeup of the affiliated group changes or the IRS consents to a revocation of the election.
- Capital and operating losses of one group member are applied against the corresponding income of the other group members even when assigning the losses to separate return years would produce a greater tax benefit. The benefit might be due, for instance, to rate discounts or changes in tax rates.
- Recognition of losses from certain intercompany transactions is deferred.
- Using consolidated amounts in computing the limitations may decrease the amounts of certain deductions and credits.
- Return elections made by the parent (e.g., to claim a credit for foreign tax payments rather than a deduction) are binding on all members of the filing group for the year.

[6]E.g., for purposes of the § 165(g)(3) ordinary deduction for losses from worthlessness of securities. For the 80% corporate control requirement of § 351, see the discussion in Chapter 4.

TAX IN THE NEWS Consolidated Return Statistics

Tax data related to 2008 consolidated Federal income tax returns show the important contribution of multinational corporations to U.S. revenues. Virtually all net corporate tax revenues are received from corporations filing consolidated returns. Essentially all foreign tax credits allowed by the Code are claimed by consolidated tax filers, probably because they are the most active and profitable of all C corporations operating in the international sector. Yet only about 43,000 consolidated returns are filed every year—a minuscule portion considering that about 1.77 million C corporations file Form 1120.

	Consolidated Returns Only	All Forms 1120
Number of returns	43,000	1,770,000
Assets ($ trillions)	55	52
Receipts ($ trillions)	18	20
Taxable income ($ billions)	886	912
Tax after credits ($ billions)	201	208
Foreign tax credits ($ billions)	99	98

- The tax basis of investments in the stock of subsidiaries is decreased when the members generate operating losses and when distributions are made from members' E & P.
- The requirement that all group members use the parent's tax year creates short tax years for the subsidiaries. As a result, a subsidiary's income may be bunched together needlessly, and one of the years of its charitable contribution and loss carryforward periods may be lost.
- Additional administrative costs may be incurred in complying with the consolidated return Regulations.

EXAMPLE 5

The following taxpayers should consider filing consolidated returns.

- Major Insurance Corporation generates billions of dollars of taxable income every year. Independent Movie Productions, Ltd., is concerned with artistic integrity, and its annual taxable loss totals $40 to $45 million per year. The accumulated losses are of no use to Independent, but Major can use them to effect an immediate tax reduction at its 35% marginal tax rate.
- Every year Parent contributes $1.2 million of its $10 million taxable income to charity. Thus, because of the 10% of taxable income limitation, Parent cannot deduct the full amount of the gift in computing taxable income. SubCo generates $3 million of taxable income every year, and it makes no charitable contributions. By filing a consolidated return with SubCo, Parent can deduct its full gift against consolidated taxable income. ■

EXAMPLE 6

The following corporations might make unattractive consolidated return partners.

- Parent sells an asset to SubCo at a $500,000 realized loss. Under the intercompany transactions rules discussed later in the chapter, this loss cannot be recognized by the consolidated group until the asset subsequently is sold to Outsider.
- ParentCo holds a large NOL carryforward, and SubCo generates a steady level of taxable income every year. Both corporations are involved in international commerce and make significant tax payments to other countries. SubCo would use these payments to compute a foreign tax credit. But if the corporations file a consolidated return, it is likely that the ParentCo group will claim the foreign tax payments as deductions against consolidated taxable income, so as to use the NOL carryforward more quickly. SubCo loses the ability to elect to claim "its" foreign tax credits. ■

8.3 Electing Consolidated Return Status

A corporation can join in a consolidated tax return if it meets three requirements, as shown in Concept Summary 8.1.

- It must be a member of an **affiliated group**.
- It cannot be ineligible to file on a consolidated basis.
- It must meet the initial and ongoing compliance requirements specified in the Code and Regulations.

Affiliated Group

An affiliated group exists when one corporation owns at least 80 percent of the voting power and stock value of another corporation.[7] This stock ownership test must be met on every day of the tax year. Multiple tiers and chains of corporations are allowed as long as the group has an identifiable parent corporation (i.e., at least 80 percent of one corporation must be owned by another).

EXAMPLE 7

Two corporate group structures are illustrated below. Both meet the 80% stock ownership test, but the structure on the right is not an affiliated group because there is no identifiable parent entity.

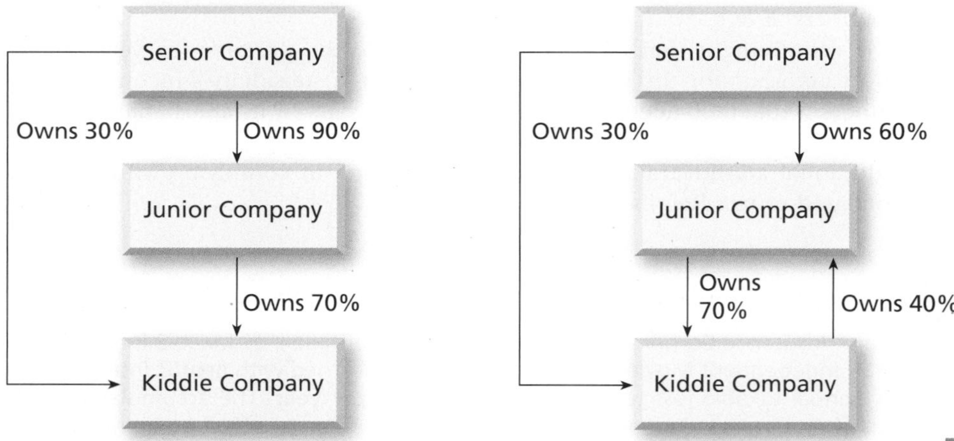

Members of an affiliated group can file tax returns in either of two ways.

- File a separate tax return for each member of the group and claim a 100 percent dividends received deduction for payments passing among them.
- Elect to file income tax returns on a consolidated basis. No 100 percent dividends received deduction is allowed for payments among group members.

Table 8.1 provides additional details as to the tax effects of making a consolidated return election.

A Federal election to form a consolidated group may not be binding for state income tax purposes. Some states allow only separate return filing, and others may define the members of an electing group or tax their income differently than the Federal rules do. See Chapter 16 for additional discussion of the multistate taxation of related corporations.

Affiliated versus Controlled Group

An affiliated group is similar but not identical to a *parent-subsidiary controlled group*, as discussed in Chapter 2. Members of a controlled group are required to share a number of tax benefits, including the following.

[7] §§ 1504(a)(1) and (2).

TABLE 8.1 Comparison of Tax Effects Available to Affiliated Group

Attribute	Treatment If Consolidated Returns Are Filed	Treatment If Separate Returns Are Filed
Tax year	All companies use the parent's tax year.	Companies use various tax years.
Change to common tax year	Required, no IRS permission needed.	Requires IRS permission.
Returns of acquired companies	Separate returns through date of consolidation, then join in consolidated return.	Continue filing for each company's tax year. No extra returns needed.
Intercompany dividend	Eliminated, not taxed.	Include in taxable income, then claim dividends received deduction.
Lower tax brackets	Share one set of rates among the group.	Share one set of rates among the group.
Accumulated earnings credit, $150,000/$250,000 floor	Share one floor among the group.	Share one floor among the group.
Liability for tax	Each company liable for the entire consolidated tax liability.	Each company liable only for its own tax.
Statute of limitations	Extension for one company applies to all in the group.	Each company retains its own statute of limitations.
Accounting methods	Need not conform to parent.	Need not conform to parent.
NOLs, capital gains/losses, § 1231 gains/losses, charitable contribution deductions, domestic production activities deduction, dividends received deductions, foreign tax credit payments and baskets, etc.	Computed on a consolidated basis.	Computed separately for each company.
Gain/loss on intercompany transactions	Deferred.	Not deferred.
Basis of parent's investment	Changes due to subsidiary operating gain/loss, taxes, and distributions.	No adjustments.

- Discounted marginal tax rates on the first $75,000 of taxable income.[8]
- The $150,000 or $250,000 accumulated earnings credit.[9]
- The $40,000 exemption in computing the alternative minimum tax liability.[10]

In addition, members of a controlled group must defer the recognition of any realized loss on intercompany sales until a sale is made at a gain to a nongroup member.[11] Similarly, any gain on the sale of depreciable property between members of a controlled group is recognized as ordinary income.[12]

A parent-subsidiary controlled group exists when one corporation owns at least 80 percent of the voting power or stock value of another corporation on the last day of the tax year.[13] Multiple tiers of subsidiaries and chains of ownership are allowed as long as the group has an identifiable parent corporation.

EXAMPLE 8

Aqua Corporation owns 80% of White Corporation. Aqua and White Corporations are members of a parent-subsidiary controlled group. Aqua is the parent corporation, and White is the subsidiary. ■

[8]§§ 11(b)(1) and 1561(a)(1).
[9]§§ 535(c)(2) and 1561(a)(2).
[10]§§ 55(d)(2) and 1561(a)(3).
[11]§§ 267(a)(1), (b)(3), and (f).
[12]§§ 1239(a) and (c).
[13]§ 1563(a)(1). For this purpose, stock attribution rules apply. In addition, all stock options are considered to be exercised by their holders. §§ 1563 (d)(1) and (e)(1) through (3).

TAX IN THE NEWS Some States Don't Allow Consolidation

Some states have been hesitant to allow a corporate conglomerate doing business within their boundaries to make a consolidation election when computing state taxable income. Perhaps these states question their constitutional ability to tax the income generated by an affiliate that is incorporated elsewhere. Another consideration may be that consolidation would permit losses generated in other states to be applied against taxable income originating in the state.

There is no real consensus among the states as to how to tax a group consolidated for Federal tax purposes. Some states require the group to make a separate election to file on a consolidated basis. Others reserve the right to force the consolidation treatment on a Federal group for state purposes. The diversity that exists is evident in the following table showing a sample of 2011 state rules applicable to consolidated returns.

State	Consolidation Allowed?
Alabama	A Federal electing group can make a separate election to file on a consolidated basis for state purposes. With no such election, all members must file separate returns.
Alaska	If the unitary group files consolidated returns for Federal purposes, it must do so for state purposes.
Arizona	A Federal electing group can elect to file on a consolidated basis in the state. The state can require a consolidated return to protect its revenues.
Arkansas	A Federal electing group can elect to file a consolidated return in the state so long as it shows some Arkansas taxable income.
Connecticut	A Federal electing group can elect to file a consolidated return in the state, but it is called a "combined return."
District of Columbia	Consolidation is allowed for a Federal electing group only with prior approval of the revenue department. All affiliates must have nexus with D.C. Special rules apply to high-tech entities.
Georgia	A Federal consolidating group can file a state consolidated return only with the revenue department's prior permission. Without such permission, all members must file separate returns.
Kansas	A Federal electing group must file a Kansas consolidated return if all of the taxable income of all of the affiliates is derived in-state. If out-of-state taxable income is present, permission must be received from the state before the group can file on a consolidated basis.
Minnesota	No consolidation allowed.
North Carolina	The taxpayer cannot elect to file a consolidated return, but the state can require one if the North Carolina income of the group is not disclosed accurately.

The parent-subsidiary relationship described in Example 8 is easy to recognize because Aqua Corporation is the direct owner of White Corporation. Real-world business organizations often are much more complex, sometimes including numerous corporations with chains of ownership connecting them. In these complex corporate structures, determining whether the controlled group classification is appropriate becomes more difficult. The ownership requirements can be met through direct ownership (as in Example 8) or through indirect ownership.

EXAMPLE 9

Red Corporation owns 80% of the voting stock of White Corporation, and White Corporation owns 80% of the voting stock of Blue Corporation. Red, White, and Blue Corporations constitute a controlled group in which Red is the common parent and White and Blue are subsidiaries. The same result would occur if Red Corporation, rather than White Corporation, owned the Blue Corporation stock.

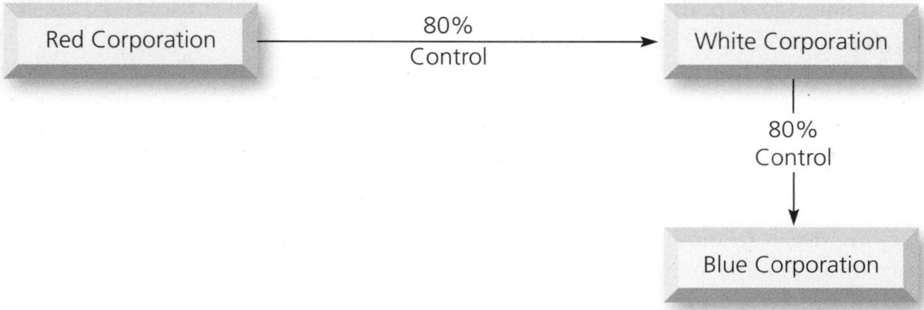

Red is the common parent of a parent-subsidiary controlled group consisting of Red, White, and Blue Corporations. ■

EXAMPLE 10

Brown Corporation owns 80% of the stock of Green Corporation, which owns 30% of Blue Corporation. Brown also owns 80% of White Corporation, which owns 50% of Blue Corporation. Brown, Green, Blue, and White Corporations constitute a parent-subsidiary controlled group in which Brown is the common parent and Green, Blue, and White are subsidiaries.

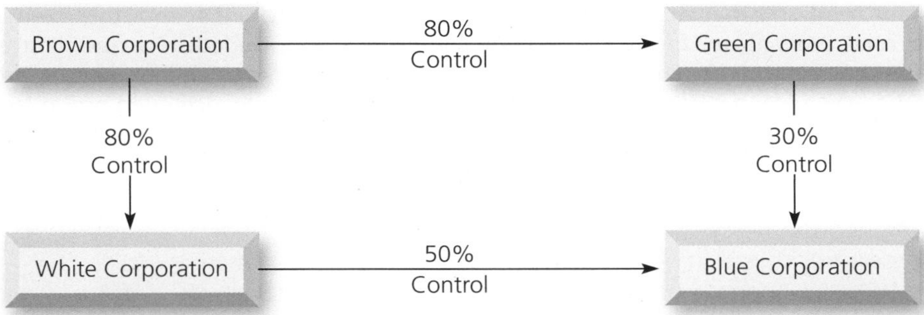

Brown is the common parent of a parent-subsidiary controlled group consisting of Brown, Green, Blue, and White Corporations. ■

The tax effects brought about by electing to file on a consolidated basis include all of the benefit-sharing effects of controlled group membership. In addition, membership in a consolidated group leads to a much more complex set of controlling tax rules, as discussed in the remainder of this chapter.

EXAMPLE 11

ParentCo owns all of the stock of SubCo, and TopCo owns all of the stock of BottomCo. Both pairs of corporations constitute affiliated groups as well as controlled groups. ParentCo and SubCo elect to file Federal income tax returns on a consolidated basis. TopCo and BottomCo do not so elect. Consequently, they file separate Federal income tax returns.

Both groups share the lower tax rates on the first $75,000 of combined taxable income—ParentCo and SubCo because they file a combined tax return, and TopCo and BottomCo because of the controlled group rules. Neither group can deduct a loss realized on an intercompany sale. But accounting for the taxable income of the consolidated group is much more complex, as indicated by the rules summarized in Table 8.1. ■

The most important differences between an affiliated group and a parent-subsidiary controlled group include the following. In each case, the affiliated group definition is more difficult to meet.

- The stock attribution rules applied in meeting the controlled group stock ownership test are not required for the affiliated group definition. In an affiliated group, the identifiable parent corporation itself must meet the stock ownership test.

- Affiliated group members must meet the stock ownership tests on *every day* of the tax year. The corresponding controlled group tests are applied only on the last day of the year.[14]

LO.4

Identify the corporations that are eligible to file on a consolidated basis.

Eligibility for the Consolidation Election

The Code lists a number of corporations that may *not* use a consolidated return to report their taxable income.[15] Thus, these corporations cannot be used to meet the stock ownership tests, and their taxable incomes cannot be included in a consolidated return. Some of the most frequently encountered entities that are ineligible for consolidated return status include the following.

- Corporations established outside the United States or in a U.S. possession.
- Tax-exempt corporations.[16]
- Insurance companies.
- Partnerships, trusts, estates, limited liability entities, and any other noncorporate entities.[17]

EXAMPLE 12

In the first ownership structure in the accompanying figure, Phillips, Rhesus, Todd, and Valiant form an affiliated group, with Phillips as the parent, under the stock ownership rules. Valiant, a life insurance company, cannot be included in a consolidated return, however, so the consolidation election is available only to Phillips, Rhesus, and Todd. In the second structure, Phillips, Rhesus, and Todd form an affiliated group, and all of them can be included in a properly executed consolidated return. Phillips is the identifiable parent of the group. Rhesus and Todd essentially form a brother-sister group below Phillips.

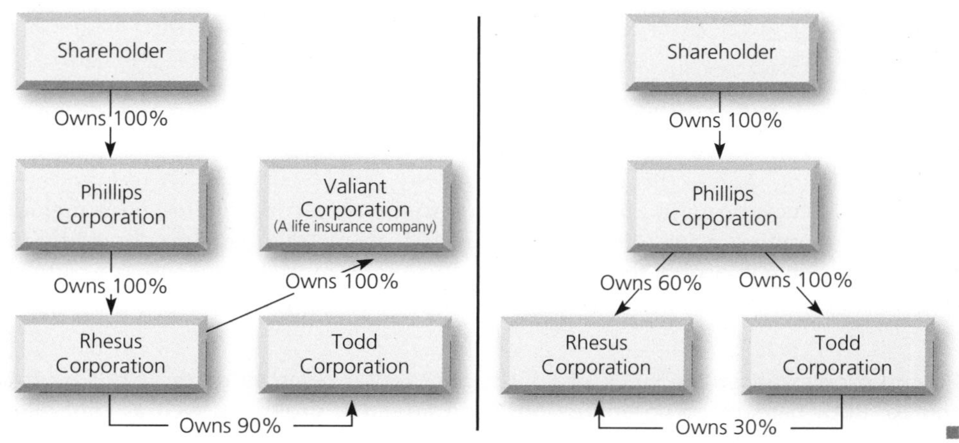

LO.5

Explain the compliance aspects of consolidated returns.

Compliance Requirements

An eligible entity that meets the stock ownership test can be included in a consolidated group if several compliance requirements are met.

The Initial Consolidated Return

The first consolidated tax return of an affiliated group must meet certain requirements.

[14] §§ 1501 and 1563(b)(1).

[15] § 1504(b).

[16] This includes any entity that is exempt from tax under § 501. See Chapter 15 for a discussion of the qualification of organizations for exempt status.

[17] Some less frequently encountered entities also are prohibited from filing on a consolidated basis. These include regulated investment companies (mutual funds) and real estate investment trusts. §§ 1504(b)(4) through (7).

- The Form 1120 for the tax year of the consolidated group should include the taxable results of the operations of all of the members of the consolidated group.[18] This return is filed in lieu of the separate returns of the group members.[19] The identified group then continues to file on a consolidated basis until an eligible group no longer exists or an election to "de-consolidate" is made.[20]
- A Form 1122 should be attached to the first consolidated tax return for each of the subsidiaries included in the group.[21] This form represents a consent by the affiliate to be included in the consolidated group.

The election must be made no later than the extended due date of the parent's return for the year. Only in the case of an inadvertent error can the election to consolidate be rescinded once this extended due date passes.

THE BIG PICTURE

EXAMPLE 13

Return to the facts of *The Big Picture* on p. 8-1. Assume that both Alexander and Hamilton use calendar tax years and that they want to file their Federal income tax returns on a consolidated basis starting with the 2012 tax year. Alexander does not elect an extended due date for its 2012 return.

If the consolidation election is to be effective, Alexander must file a Form 1120 that includes the taxable income/loss for both corporations by March 15, 2013. Hamilton must execute a Form 1122 and attach it to the consolidated Form 1120.

If Alexander and Hamilton convert their separate tax returns to the consolidated format in this manner, the election to consolidate is in force for all future tax years or until the IRS approves Alexander's application to revoke it.

An application to terminate the consolidation election must be filed at least 90 days prior to the extended due date of the consolidated return.[22] Generally, when a subsidiary leaves an ongoing consolidated group, it must wait five years before it can reenter the parent's consolidated group.[23]

Subsequent Consolidated Returns

Each consolidated tax return must include Form 851, Affiliations Schedule. This report identifies all of the corporations in the electing group, summarizes pertinent shareholdings and stock ownership changes that occurred during the tax year, and lists the estimated tax payments made by the group members for the year. Affiliates joining an existing consolidated group need not file a Form 1122, though.

Consolidated tax returns are due on the fifteenth day of the third month following the close of the group's tax year (this is March 15 for a calendar year taxpayer). A six-month extension to file the return can be obtained by executing Form 7004, but an estimated payment of the remaining tax liability for the group must accompany the extension application.

Liability for Taxes

Group members are jointly and severally liable for the entire consolidated income tax liability.[24] This rule applies to interest and penalties imposed as a result of audits as well as to tax liabilities. Furthermore, the IRS is not bound to follow internal agreements among group members in apportioning the liability.[25]

[18]A consolidation election is inferred even when specific aspects of pertinent forms are completed incorrectly, as long as the members' combined operations are reported on the Form 1120. *American Pacific Whaling Co. v. Comm.*, 35–1 USTC ¶9065, 14 AFTR 887, 74 F.2d 613 (CA–9, 1935).

[19]Reg. § 1.1502–75(a)(1).

[20]Reg. § 1.1502–75(c). The IRS permits such an election only rarely: on the parent's assertion of (1) a good-cause reason to disengage from consolidated status or (2) a substantial change in the tax law that adversely affects the consolidated tax liability.

[21]Reg. § 1.1502–75(b).

[22]Reg. § 1.1502–75(c)(1)(i).

[23]§ 1504(a)(3); Rev.Proc. 2002-32, 2002-1 C.B. 959.

[24]Reg. § 1.1502–6(a).

[25]Reg. § 1.1502–6(c).

EXAMPLE 14

Parent Corporation, a calendar year taxpayer, acquired 100% of the stock of calendar year SubCo on December 20, 2012. The group filed on a consolidated basis from that date until December 31, 2014, when all of the SubCo stock was sold to Foreign Corporation.

An IRS audit determined that Parent owed an additional $10 million in Federal income taxes relating to a sale it made on December 30, 2012. By mid-2015, however, Parent's cash-flow difficulties had brought it close to bankruptcy and forced it to cease activities.

Due to the consolidation election, the IRS can assess the delinquent taxes from SubCo (and Foreign Corporation). SubCo is liable for the full amount of any consolidated tax liability even when it is not the source of the income that led to the tax. ■

Starting with the third consolidated return year, estimated tax payments must be made on a consolidated basis.[26] Prior to that year, estimates can be computed and paid on either a separate or a consolidated basis.

Regular tax liability is computed applying the graduated tax rates to consolidated taxable income following the requirements of controlled group status. In this regard, contributions to the actual payment of the tax liability often are arranged to correspond to contributions to consolidated taxable income.

EXAMPLE 15

Parent Corporation owns 100% of the stock of SubCo, and the two corporations file a consolidated tax return beginning in year 2. Over the course of a five-year period, the corporations generate the following taxable income/loss. The low marginal rates that apply to the group's first $75,000 of taxable income might be assigned in various ways.

Year	Parent's Taxable Income	SubCo's Taxable Income	Low Brackets Assigned to Parent	Low Brackets Assigned to SubCo
1	$100,000	($10,000)	$37,500	$37,500
2	100,000	(10,000)	75,000	–0–
3	50,000	10,000	65,000	10,000
4	(15,000)	10,000	65,000	10,000
5	100,000	100,000	37,500	37,500

In year 1, the consolidated group has not yet been formed. Separate returns are filed, and the low tax brackets are apportioned equally between the two entities. Once consolidated returns begin to be filed in year 2, the indicated elections are made. For year 2, all of the low brackets are assigned to Parent, rather than wasting any on SubCo, which has a negative taxable income.

For years 3 and 4, the majority of the low brackets are assigned to Parent because the group believes that Parent's taxable income is more likely to be adjusted upward on an audit. The apportionment is made to create a cushion for Parent in the event that additional tax liability occurs after the initial return is filed. When group members' taxable incomes are close in value and/or exceed $75,000 in total, as in year 5, a simple equal apportionment of the low brackets is suggested. ■

Benefits accruing from the graduated corporate tax rates are apportioned equally among the group members unless all members consent to some other method through an annual election. The most commonly used tax-sharing agreements are the *relative taxable income* and *relative tax liability* methods. Under the relative taxable income method,[27] the consolidated tax liability is allocated among the members based on their relative amounts of separate taxable income. When the relative tax

[26] Reg. § 1.1502–5(a)(1).

[27] § 1552(a)(1); Reg. § 1.1552–1(a)(1).

liability method is used,[28] the consolidated tax liability is allocated based on the relative hypothetical separate tax liabilities of the members. IRS permission is required for the group to change from one allocation method to another.

EXAMPLE 16

The Parent consolidated group reports the following results for the tax year. Assume a 35% marginal tax rate.

	Parent	SubOne	SubTwo	SubThree	Consolidated
Ordinary income	$400	$100	$–0–	($20)	$480
Capital gain/loss	–0–	–0–	100	(25)	75
§ 1231 gain/loss	50	–0–	(50)	–0–	–0–
Separate taxable incomes	$450	$100	$ 50	($20) with a $25 capital loss carryover	
Consolidated taxable income					555
Consolidated tax liability					$194
Foreign tax credit, from SubOne					(19)
Net tax due					$175

If the group has consented to the relative taxable income method, the consolidated tax liability is allocated as follows.

	Separate Taxable Income	Allocation Ratio	Allocated Tax Due
Parent	$450	450/600	$131
SubOne	100	100/600	29
SubTwo	50	50/600	15
SubThree	–0–	–0–	–0–
Totals	$600		$175

The results are different if the relative tax liability method is in effect. Specifically, SubOne gets an immediate tax benefit for the tax credit that it brings to the group. Under neither method, though, does SubThree get any tax benefit from the losses that it brings to the consolidated group.

	Separate Taxable Income	Separate Tax Liability	Allocation Ratio	Allocated Tax Due
Parent	$450	$157.5	157.5/191	$144
SubOne	100	16.0*	16/191	15
SubTwo	50	17.5	17.5/191	16
SubThree	–0–	–0–	–0–	–0–
Totals	$600	$191.0		$175

* After applying foreign tax credit.

■

Alternative minimum tax (AMT) liability for group members is computed on the basis of consolidated AMTI. The group is allowed only one $40,000 AMT exemption, which is phased out at a rate of 25 percent of the amount by which consolidated AMTI exceeds $150,000. Similarly, the AMT adjustment for adjusted

[28] § 1552(a)(2); Reg. § 1.1552–1(a)(2).

current earnings (ACE), which is 75 percent of the excess of ACE over pre-ACE AMTI, is computed using consolidated amounts.

Tax Accounting Periods and Methods

All of the members of a consolidating group must use the parent's tax year.[29] As a result, the group may be required to file a short-year return for the first year a subsidiary is included in the consolidated return, so that the parent's year-end can be adopted.

When a mid-year acquisition occurs, both short years are used in tracking the carryforward period of unused losses and credits. Short-year income and deductions are apportioned between the pre- and postacquisition periods. At the election of the corporation being acquired, the apportionment may be done either on a daily basis or as the items are recorded for financial accounting purposes.[30]

EXAMPLE 17

All of the stock of calendar year SubCo is acquired by Parent Corporation on July 15, 2012. The corporations elect to file a consolidated return immediately upon the acquisition.

SubCo had generated a long-term capital loss in its 2009 tax year. As of January 1, 2013, only one year remains in the five-year carryforward period for the capital loss.

According to SubCo's financial accounting records, $400,000 of its $1 million accounting and taxable income for the year was generated in 2012 after the acquisition. At SubCo's election, either $400,000 (the "books" apportionment method) or $464,481 [(170 postacquisition days/366 days) × $1 million income] (the "daily" method) can be included in the first consolidated return. ■

Members of a consolidated group can continue to use the tax accounting methods that were in place prior to the consolidation election.[31] Thus, the members of a consolidated group may use different accounting methods. On the other hand, because the $5 million gross-receipts test with respect to use of the cash method of accounting is applied on a consolidated basis,[32] some of the group members may need to switch from the cash to the accrual method of tax accounting.

8.4 Stock Basis of Subsidiary

LO.6

Compute a parent's investment basis in a subsidiary.

Upon acquiring a subsidiary, the parent corporation records a stock basis on its tax balance sheet equal to the acquisition price. At the end of every consolidated return year, the parent records one or more adjustments to this stock basis, as in the financial accounting "equity" method. This treatment prevents double taxation of gain (or deduction of loss) upon the ultimate disposal of the subsidiary's shares.[33] The adjustments are recorded on the last day of the consolidated return year or on the (earlier) date of the disposal of the shares.[34]

In this regard, positive adjustments to stock basis include the following.

- An allocable share of consolidated taxable income for the year.
- An allocable share of the consolidated operating or capital loss of a subsidiary that could not utilize the loss through a carryback to a prior year.

Negative adjustments to stock basis include the following.

- An allocable share of a consolidated taxable loss for the year.
- An allocable share of any carryover operating or capital losses that are deducted on the consolidated return and have not previously reduced stock basis.
- Dividends paid by the subsidiary to the parent out of the subsidiary's E & P.

[29] Reg. § 1.1502–76(a)(1).
[30] Reg. § 1.1502–76(b)(4).
[31] Reg. § 1.1502–17(a).
[32] §§ 448(a)(1) and (c)(2).
[33] This procedure parallels the accounting for tax basis in a partnership or S corporation. See Chapters 10 and 12.
[34] Reg. § 1.1502–32(a). Basis adjustments also are allowed when necessary to determine a tax liability (e.g., when member stock is bought or sold).

THE BIG PICTURE

EXAMPLE 18

Return to the facts of *The Big Picture* on p. 8-1. Assume that Alexander acquired all of the outstanding Hamilton stock on January 1, 2011, for $1 million. The parties immediately elected to file consolidated Federal income tax returns. Hamilton reported a 2011 taxable loss of $100,000, but it generated $40,000 taxable income in 2012 and $65,000 in 2013. Hamilton paid a $10,000 dividend to Alexander in mid-2013.

Alexander holds the following stock bases in Hamilton on the last day of each of the indicated tax years.

2011	$900,000	2012	$940,000	2013	$995,000

When accumulated postacquisition negative adjustments to the stock basis of the subsidiary exceed the acquisition price plus prior positive adjustments, an **excess loss account** is created.[35] This account (1) allows the consolidated return to recognize the losses of the subsidiary in the current year and (2) enables the group to avoid the need to reflect a negative stock basis on its tax-basis balance sheet. If the subsidiary stock is redeemed or sold to a nongroup member while an excess loss account exists, the seller recognizes the balance of the account as capital gain income.[36]

EXAMPLE 19

Parent Corporation acquired all of the stock of SubCo early in year 1, for $100,000. As a result of SubCo's operations, the group records the amounts listed.

Year	Operating Gain/(Loss)	Stock Basis	Excess Loss Account
1	($40,000)	$60,000	$ -0-
2	(80,000)	-0-	20,000
3	30,000	10,000	-0-

If Parent sells the SubCo stock for $50,000 at the end of year 2, Parent recognizes a $70,000 capital gain ($50,000 amount realized − $0 adjusted basis in stock + $20,000 recovery of excess loss account). If the sale takes place at the end of year 3, the capital gain is $40,000.[37] ■

In a chain of more than one tier of subsidiaries, the computation of the stock basis amounts starts with the lowest-level subsidiary, then proceeds up the ownership structure to the parent's holdings.[38]

There is no such concept as consolidated E & P in the Federal income tax law. Rather, each entity accounts for its own share of consolidated taxable income on an annual basis, immediately recognizing within E & P any gain or loss on intercompany transactions and reducing E & P by an allocable share of the consolidated tax liability.[39]

8.5 Computing Consolidated Taxable Income

When an affiliated group computes its taxable income for the year, it does not simply add together the separate taxable income amounts of its members. Two groups of transactions are removed from the members' tax returns and receive special

[35]Reg. § 1.1502–19.

[36]Reg. §§ 1.1502–19(a)(1) and (2).

[37]The year 3 subsidiary income is used first to eliminate the excess loss account (i.e., before it creates new stock basis). Reg. § 1.1502–32(e)(3).

[38]Reg. § 1.1502–19(b)(3).

[39]Reg. § 1.1502–33(d). In the absence of an election to use some other allocation method, the consolidated tax liability is allocated to each group member according to the relative taxable income method.

FIGURE 8.1 Computing Consolidated Taxable Income

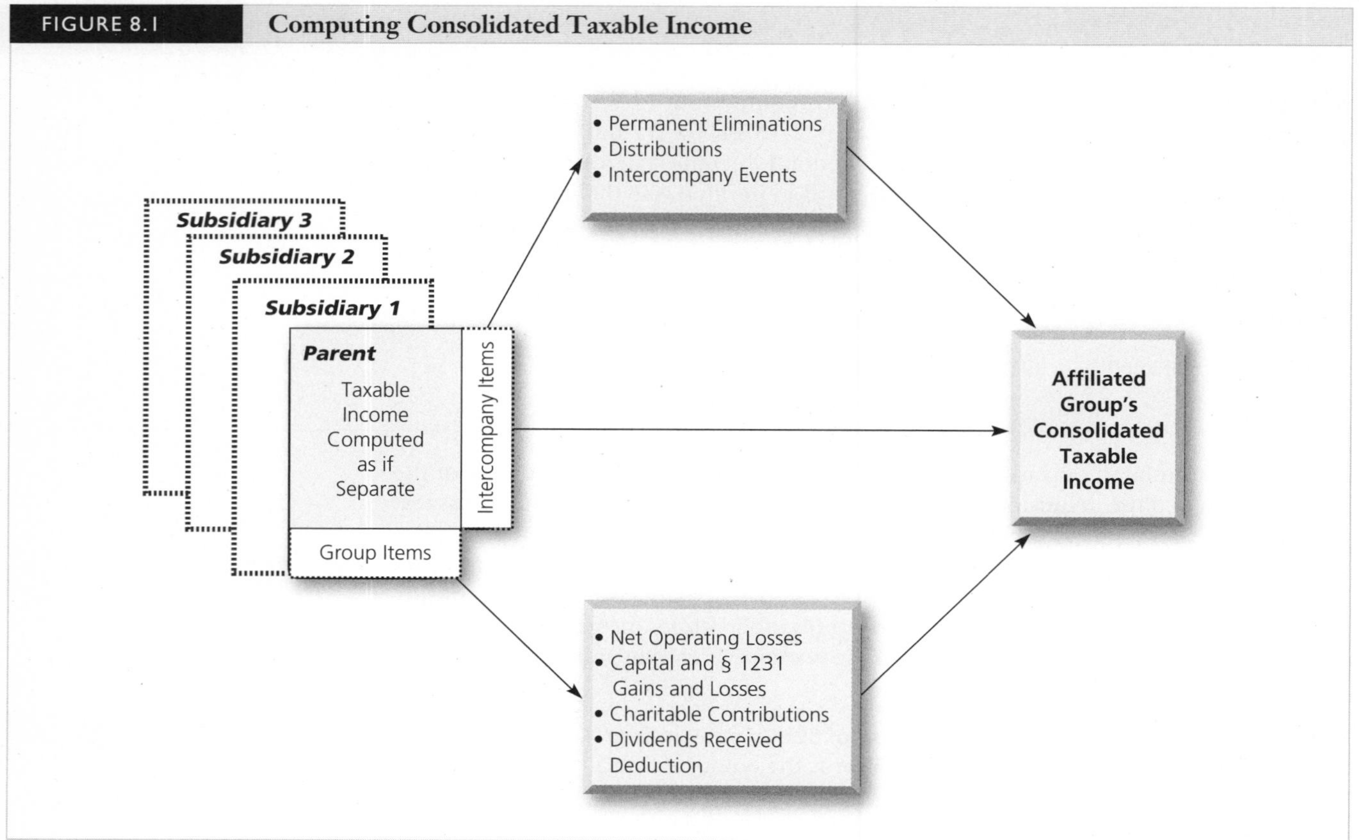

treatment. Then the special items are recombined with the remaining items of members' taxable incomes to obtain the group's consolidated taxable income for the year. Figure 8.1 illustrates how consolidated taxable income is constructed using this sequential approach.

1. Taxable income is computed for each member on a separate basis.
2. "Group items" and "intercompany items" are isolated and receive special treatment.
3. The remaining separate incomes are combined with the group and intercompany items, resulting in consolidated taxable income.

The Code requires this computational procedure to accomplish several goals.

- Certain transactions are accounted for on a consolidated basis (e.g., charitable contributions and capital gains and losses). This requires that the transactions be isolated from the separate tax returns and computed on a groupwide basis.
- Gains and losses from certain intercompany transactions are deferred until a later tax year. Consequently, they are removed from the tax returns of the members that generated them.
- A few intercompany transactions (e.g., dividend payments) are removed from the taxable income calculation altogether, never to appear in a consolidated return.

Computational Procedure

The remainder of this chapter will follow the computational procedure suggested in Figure 8.1. Figure 8.2 presents a skeleton worksheet for this computational procedure to be used in examples throughout the remainder of this chapter. More information is added to the worksheet for every additional subsidiary. In each case,

FIGURE 8.2 **Consolidated Taxable Income Worksheet**

	Separate Taxable Income	Adjustments	Post-adjustment Amounts
Parent information			
Subsidiary information			
Group-basis transactions			
Intercompany events			
Consolidated taxable income			
*Permanent eliminations.	**Group-basis transaction.		†Matching rule.

the starting point for this procedure is the separate taxable incomes of all of the group members. Adjustments then are made for group and intercompany items, as indicated in the footnotes to the worksheet.

EXAMPLE 20

Parent Corporation owns 100% of the stock of SubCo. This year Parent's taxable income amounted to $100,000, while SubCo generated a $40,000 taxable loss. There were no transactions between the two corporations, and they incurred no capital or § 1231 gains/losses, charitable contributions, dividend income, or other items that are accounted for on a group basis. Accordingly, no adjustments are required, and consolidated taxable income is $60,000.

	Separate Taxable Income	Adjustments	Post-adjustment Amounts
Parent information	$100,000		$100,000
SubCo information	(40,000)		(40,000)
Group-basis transactions			
Intercompany events			
Consolidated taxable income			$ 60,000
*Permanent eliminations.	**Group-basis transaction.		†Matching rule.

■

Typical Intercompany Transactions

LO.7

Account for intercompany transactions of a consolidated group.

General Rules

When one member of a consolidated group engages in a transaction with another member of the group, an intercompany transaction occurs. In contrast to the financial accounting treatment of most such transactions, the most commonly encountered items *remain in* the members' separate taxable incomes and therefore cancel each other out on a consolidated basis. For instance, when one group member performs services for another member during the year, the purchaser of the services incurs a deductible expenditure, while the service provider generates includible income. The net result is a zero addition to consolidated taxable income.[40]

This two-step procedure prevents the group from avoiding any related-party loss disallowances. Furthermore, when the members involved in the transaction are using different tax accounting methods, the payor's deduction for the expenditure is deferred until the year in which the recipient recognizes the related gross income.[41]

[40]Reg. §§ 1.1502–13(a)(1)(i) and (b)(1).

[41]§§ 267(a)(2) and (b)(3); Reg. § 1.1502–13(b)(2).

EXAMPLE 21

In the current year, Parent Corporation provided consulting services to its 100%-owned subsidiary, SubCo, under a contract that requires no payments to Parent until next year. Both parties use the accrual method of tax accounting. The services that Parent rendered are valued at $100,000. In addition, Parent purchased $15,000 of supplies from SubCo.

Including these transactions, Parent's taxable income for the year amounted to $500,000. SubCo reported $150,000 of separate taxable income. The group is not required to make any eliminating adjustments. The members' deductions incurred offset the income included by the other party to the intercompany transaction. The consolidated taxable income includes both Parent's $15,000 deduction for supplies and SubCo's $15,000 gross receipts from the sale, so the consolidated taxable income computation *de facto* results in an elimination similar to the kind made in financial accounting. No further adjustment is needed.

	Separate Taxable Income	Adjustments	Post-adjustment Amounts
Parent information	$500,000		$500,000
SubCo information	150,000		150,000
Group-basis transactions			
Intercompany events			
Consolidated taxable income			$650,000
*Permanent eliminations.	**Group-basis transaction.		†Matching rule.

Assume instead that Parent is a cash basis taxpayer. Because Parent will not recognize the $100,000 of service income earned in the current year until the next tax period, SubCo's related deduction also is deferred until the following year. Thus, the intercompany item—SubCo's deduction—must be eliminated from consolidated taxable income. Additional record keeping is required to keep track of this intercompany transaction (and all others like it), so that the deduction is claimed in the appropriate year.

	Separate Taxable Income	Adjustments	Post-adjustment Amounts
Parent information	$400,000		$400,000
SubCo information	150,000	+ $100,000 due to use of different tax accounting methods	250,000
Group-basis transactions			
Intercompany events			
Consolidated taxable income			$650,000
*Permanent eliminations.	**Group-basis transaction.		†Matching rule.

Several other rules also apply to intercompany transactions. Dividends received from other group members are eliminated from the recipients' separate taxable incomes, and no dividends received deduction is allowed.[42] When the distribution consists of noncash assets, the subsidiary payor realizes (but defers recognition of) any gain on the distributed property until the asset leaves the group, and the (eliminated) dividend amount equals the fair market value of the asset.[43]

[42]Reg. § 1.1502–13(f)(2). If the distribution exceeds the payor's E & P, the stock basis of the payor is reduced. When the basis reaches zero, an excess loss account is created. Reg. § 1.1502–19(a). Dividends received from nongroup members may result in a dividends received deduction; they constitute a group-basis item (discussed later in the chapter).

[43]§§ 301(b)(1) and (d); § 311(b)(1); Reg. §§ 1.1502–13(c)(7) and (f)(7).

EXAMPLE 22

Parent Corporation received a $50,000 cash dividend from 100%-owned SubCo in the current year. Including this item, Parent's separate taxable income amounted to $200,000, and SubCo reported $240,000 separate taxable income.

Parent cannot claim a dividends received deduction for this payment, but the dividend is eliminated in computing consolidated taxable income. No elimination is required for SubCo, as dividend payments are nondeductible.

	Separate Taxable Income	Adjustments	Post-adjustment Amounts
Parent information	$200,000	−$50,000 dividend received from SubCo*	$150,000
SubCo information	240,000		240,000
Group-basis transactions			
Intercompany events			
Consolidated taxable income			$390,000
*Permanent eliminations.	**Group-basis transaction.		†Matching rule.

Members' Net Operating Losses

LO.8

Identify limitations that restrict the use of losses and credits of group members derived in separate return years.

Often the election to file consolidated returns is at least partly motivated by the parent corporation's desire to use the positive tax attributes of the subsidiary corporation, especially its NOLs. A number of provisions, however, discourage corporate acquisitions that are solely tax-motivated.[44]

The usual corporate NOL computations are available for the losses of the consolidated group. Excess losses are carried back 2 years and then forward 20 years, although the parent may elect to forgo the carryback deductions for all members of the group.[45] The NOL is derived after removing any consolidated charitable contribution deduction and capital gain or loss from consolidated taxable income. These items are removed because they have their own carryover periods and rules.[46] The consolidated dividends received deduction remains a part of the consolidated NOL.[47]

EXAMPLE 23

Parent Corporation and SubCo have filed consolidated returns since both entities were incorporated in 2010. Neither group member incurred any capital gain or loss transactions during 2010–2012, nor did they make any charitable contributions. Taxable income computations for the members include the following:

Year	Parent's Taxable Income	SubCo's Taxable Income	Consolidated Taxable Income
2010	$100,000	$ 40,000	$140,000
2011	100,000	(40,000)	60,000
2012	100,000	(140,000)	?
2013	100,000	210,000	?

The 2012 consolidated loss of $40,000 can be carried back to offset 2010 consolidated taxable income. Alternatively, Parent can elect to carry the loss forward to 2013, forgoing any carryback computation. This might be appropriate given an

[44]See Chapter 7 and §§ 269, 381, 382, and 482.

[45]§ 172(b)(3).

[46]Reg. § 1.1502–24(c). No election is available that would enable the parent to forgo the net capital loss carryback.

[47]Reg. § 1.1502–21(f).

FIGURE 8.3 **SRLY and Other Limitations on Use of Net Operating Losses**

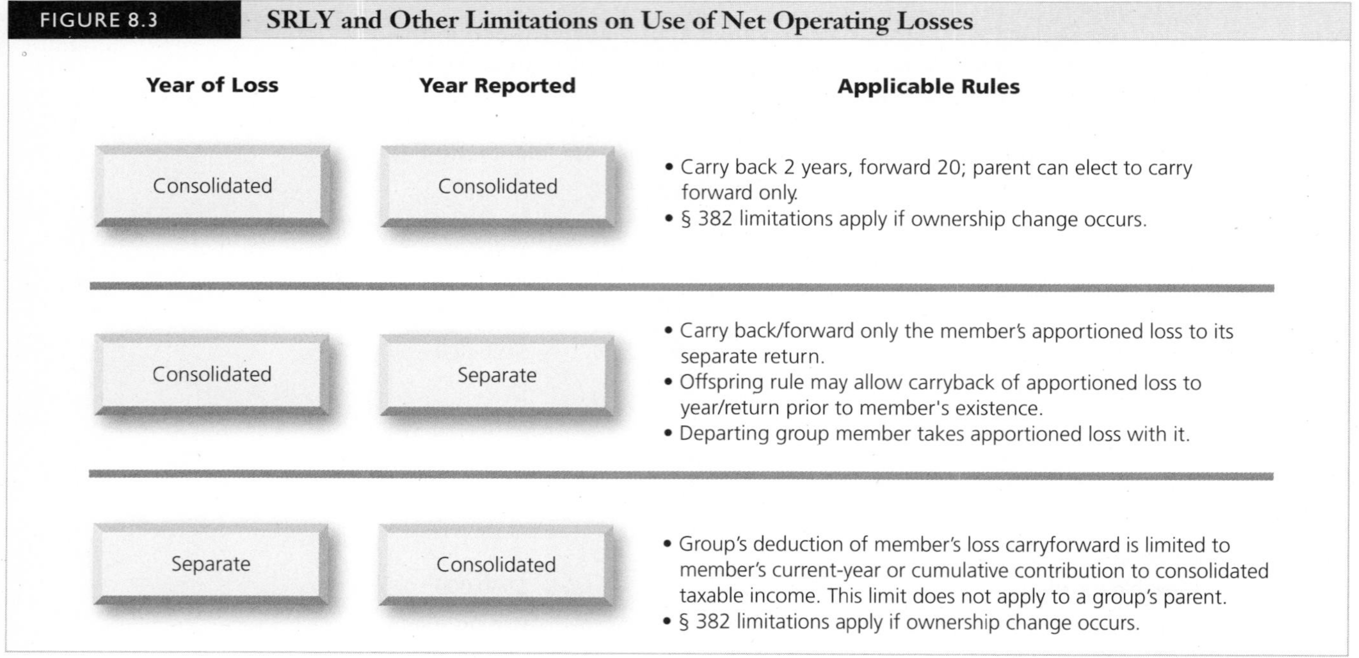

increase in statutory tax rates effective for 2013 or an application of the AMT in 2010 and 2011.

Year of Loss
Year Reported
Applicable Rules
Consolidated
Consolidated
• Carry back 2 years, forward 20; parent can elect to carry forward only.
• § 382 limitations apply if ownership change occurs.
Consolidated
Separate
• Carry back/forward only the member's apportioned loss to its separate return.
• Offspring rule may allow carryback of apportioned loss to year/return prior to member's existence.
• Departing group member takes apportioned loss with it.
Separate
Consolidated
• Group's deduction of member's loss carryforward is limited to member's current-year or cumulative contribution to consolidated taxable income. This limit does not apply to a group's parent.
• § 382 limitations apply if ownership change occurs.

Examine SubCo's 2012 NOL of $140,000. The amount resulted from the following combination of transactions for the year. Unused contributions and capital gain/loss items are subject to their own carryover periods, and they constitute group-basis items, as identified in Figure 8.1.

Operating loss	($140,000)
Net capital gain	15,000
Charitable contributions	20,000
Separate taxable income	(125,000)

■

Complications arise, however, when the corporations enter or depart from a consolidated group; members' operating losses are either incurred in a "separate return year" and deducted in a "consolidated return year" or vice versa. A variety of restrictions limit the availability of such deductions to discourage profitable corporations from acquiring unprofitable entities simply to file immediate refund claims based on loss and credit carryforwards. Figure 8.3 summarizes the applicable SRLY (separate return limitation year) limitations.

In any case where the members of a consolidated group change over time, the taxpayer must apportion the consolidated NOL among the group members. When more than one group member generates a loss for the consolidated year, the following formula is used to apportion the loss among the electing group's members.

EXAMPLE 24

Parent Corporation and SubCo have filed consolidated returns since 2011. Both entities were incorporated in 2010. Neither group member incurred any capital gain or loss transactions during 2010–2013, nor did they make any charitable contributions. Taxable income computations for the members are listed below.

Year	Parent's Taxable Income	SubCo's Taxable Income	Consolidated Taxable Income
2010*	$100,000	$ 40,000	N/A
2011**	100,000	(40,000)	$60,000
2012**	100,000	(140,000)	?
2013**	100,000	210,000	?

*Separate return year.
** Consolidated return year.

In 2012, SubCo can carry back the entire $40,000 consolidated NOL to its separate 2010 tax year, because it is solely responsible for generating the loss. SubCo files for the refund of taxes that result from the carryback, and it alone receives the refund.[48]

Alternatively, Parent could elect to forgo the carryback of the 2012 consolidated loss, thereby preserving the loss deduction for the group's subsequent years. In that case, the 2013 tax reduction from the $40,000 NOL deduction would be claimed merely by filing the 2013 consolidated tax return. Parent would receive the refund on behalf of the group. ■

In years when a group member files a separate return, only the apportioned NOL may be carried over.

EXAMPLE 25

Parent Corporation, SubOne, and SubTwo have filed consolidated returns since 2011. All of the entities were incorporated in 2010. None of the group members incurred any capital gain or loss transactions during 2010–2013, nor did they make any charitable contributions. Taxable income computations for the members are listed below.

Year	Parent's Taxable Income	SubOne's Taxable Income	SubTwo's Taxable Income	Consolidated Taxable Income
2010*	$100,000	$100,000	$ 40,000	N/A
2011**	100,000	100,000	(40,000)	$160,000
2012**	100,000	(60,000)	(120,000)	?
2013**	100,000	100,000	210,000	?

*Separate return year.
** Consolidated return year.

If Parent does not elect to forgo the carryback of the 2012 consolidated NOL of $80,000, both subsidiaries can carry losses back to their 2010 separate return years and receive separate refunds. SubOne can carry back a $26,667 loss [(SubOne's NOL $60,000/aggregate NOLs $180,000) × consolidated NOL $80,000], and SubTwo can carry back a $53,333 loss. ■

Under the so-called offspring rule, the consolidated group can use a carryback loss that is apportioned to a member of the electing group even though that member did not exist in the carryback year.[49] If the member joined the group immediately upon its incorporation but cannot use an apportioned loss in the carryback period because it was not in existence, that loss is still available to the group.[50]

EXAMPLE 26

Parent Corporation, SubOne, and SubTwo have filed consolidated returns since 2011. The first two entities were incorporated and consolidated in 2010, and SubTwo came into existence in 2011 through an asset spin-off from Parent. None of the group members incurred any capital gain or loss transactions during 2010–2013, nor did they make

[48] Reg. §§ 1.1502–78(b)(1) and (c), Example 4.
[49] Reg. § 1.1502–79(a)(2).
[50] Reg. § 1.1502–21(b)(2)(ii)(B) restricts the use of this loss to the parent if the carryback year is a separate return year for the parties.

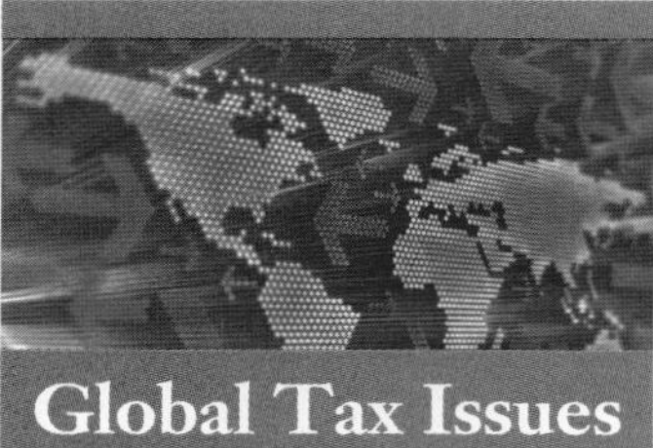

© Andrey Prokhorov, iStockphoto

Consolidated Returns and NOLs

Very few countries outside the United States allow the use of consolidated returns. In the view of most countries, tax deductions for operating losses should be used only by those who generated them, not by some sister or other related corporation. This is as much a social principle (the sanctity of the corporate entity) as a revenue-raising provision (NOL deductions mean lower tax collections).

The way European business is conducted makes this result more understandable, as the tax laws of the various countries must ensure that operating losses generated in Tedesco, for instance, are not shifted to Cadenza and converted to deductions there.

This restrictive approach to the trading of operating loss deductions is found in U.S. multistate tax law as well, where tax-oriented border incentives can be especially important. Some states (e.g., Pennsylvania) have, over a specified time period, disallowed the use of loss carryovers of any sort, whereas others (e.g., Ohio) require the taxpayer to deduct only losses assigned to the taxpayer's in-state operations. Multistate tax issues are addressed in Chapter 16.

any charitable contributions. Taxable income computations for the members are listed below.

Year	Parent's Taxable Income	SubOne's Taxable Income	SubTwo's Taxable Income	Consolidated Taxable Income
2010*	$100,000	$ 40,000	—	$140,000
2011*	100,000	100,000	($40,000)	160,000
2012*	100,000	(60,000)	(120,000)	?
2013*	100,000	100,000	210,000	?

*Consolidated return year.

If Parent does not elect to forgo the carryback of the 2012 consolidated NOL of $80,000, SubOne can carry its $26,667 loss back to 2010. SubTwo's $53,333 share of the loss can also be carried back to 2010 and used by members of the consolidated group. Under the offspring rule, SubTwo is treated as being a member of the group for the entire *group* carryback period because its existence is rooted in Parent's assets. ■

When a corporation leaves a consolidated group, it takes with it any apportioned share of any unused loss carryforwards. The losses are used on its subsequent separate returns.

EXAMPLE 27

Parent Corporation, SubOne, and SubTwo have filed consolidated returns since 2010, the year in which all of the entities were incorporated. None of the group members incurred any capital gain or loss transactions during 2010–2013, nor did they make any charitable contributions. Taxable income computations for the members are listed below.

Parent elects to forgo any loss carryback for the group's 2012 operations. On the first day of the 2013 tax year, a non-U.S. investor purchases all of the stock of SubTwo. On its 2013 separate return, SubTwo can deduct its $53,333 share of the 2012 NOL carryforward.[51]

[51] SubTwo cannot take the entire $120,000 NOL that is attributable to it. Reg. §§ 1.1502–79(a)(1)(ii) and (b)(2)(ii). Losses and carryovers first are absorbed in the current consolidated return year before any loss apportionment occurs.

Year	Parent's Taxable Income	SubOne's Taxable Income	SubTwo's Taxable Income	Consolidated Taxable Income
2010*	$100,000	$100,000	$ 40,000	$240,000
2011*	100,000	100,000	(40,000)	160,000
2012*	100,000	(60,000)	(120,000)	?
2013**	100,000	100,000	210,000	N/A

*Consolidated return year.
**Separate return year. ■

When an NOL is carried forward from a separate return year onto a consolidated return, another set of limitations, known as the **separate return limitation year (SRLY)** rules, applies.[52] The consolidated return can include an NOL carryforward from the member's SRLY period only to the extent of the lesser of its (1) current-year or (2) cumulative positive contribution to consolidated taxable income.[53]

The SRLY limitations never apply to the electing group's identifiable parent.[54]

EXAMPLE 28

Parent Corporation and SubCo have filed consolidated returns since 2011. Both entities were incorporated in 2010. Neither group member incurred any capital gain or loss transactions during 2010–2013, nor did they make any charitable contributions. Taxable income computations for the members are listed below.

Year	Parent's Taxable Income	SubCo's Taxable Income	Consolidated Taxable Income
2010*	$100,000	($40,000)	N/A
2011**	100,000	(10,000)	$90,000
2012**	100,000	15,000	?
2013**	100,000	70,000	?

*Separate return year.
**Consolidated return year.

The thrust of the SRLY rules is to limit Parent's deduction of SubCo's losses from a separate return year against consolidated income. Accordingly, none of SubCo's separate return loss from 2010 can be deducted in computing 2011 consolidated taxable income; the deduction is limited to the lesser of SubCo's current-year (zero) or cumulative (zero) contribution to consolidated taxable income.

In computing 2012 consolidated taxable income, the SubCo SRLY loss deduction is limited to $5,000, the lesser of SubCo's current-year ($15,000) or cumulative ($5,000) contribution to consolidated taxable income. The remaining SRLY deduction reduces consolidated taxable income beginning in 2013. ■

EXAMPLE 29

Parent Corporation and SubCo have filed consolidated returns since 2011. Both entities were incorporated in 2010. Neither group member incurred any capital gain or loss transactions during 2010–2013, nor did they make any charitable contributions. Taxable income computations for the members are listed below.

Year	Parent's Taxable Income	SubCo's Taxable Income	Consolidated Taxable Income
2010*	($ 40,000)	$100,000	N/A
2011**	(100,000)	(10,000)	($110,000)
2012**	20,000	165,000	?
2013**	100,000	70,000	?

*Separate return year.
**Consolidated return year.

[52] Reg. § 1.1502–21(c). The SRLY rules apply to capital loss and credit carryforwards as well.

[53] Reg. § 1.1502–21(c).

[54] Reg. § 1.1502–1(f)(2)(i), known as the "lonely parent" rule.

The 2012 consolidated return can include a deduction for Parent's entire 2010 NOL of $40,000. The deduction is not limited to the lesser of Parent's current-year ($20,000) or cumulative (zero) contribution to consolidated taxable income. SRLY rules do not apply to the group's parent. ■

When both the SRLY rules and a § 382 limitation apply because an ownership change has occurred (see Chapter 7), the § 382 provisions override the SRLY limits.[55]

EXAMPLE 30

The Parent consolidated group includes SubTwo, which was acquired as part of a § 382 ownership change. SubTwo brought with it to the group a $180,000 NOL carryforward, $125,000 of which is available this year under the SRLY rules due to SubTwo's positive contribution to the group's taxable income. The § 382 limitation with respect to SubTwo is $100,000. Accordingly, only $100,000 of the SubTwo NOL can be used to reduce consolidated taxable income this year.

If the § 382 limitation had been $200,000 instead, the full $180,000 NOL deduction would have been allowed. The § 382 rules prevail even with respect to SRLY losses that overlap with the same tax year. ■

LO.9

Derive deductions and credits on a consolidated basis.

Computation of Group Items

Several income and deduction items are derived on a consolidated-group basis. Therefore, statutory limitations and allowances are applied to the group as though it were a single corporation. This computational convention allows group members to match various types of gains and losses and to increase specific limitations, required by the Code, in a manner that optimizes the overall tax benefit.

Specifically, the following items are computed on a group basis with the usual C corporation tax effects applied to the combined group amounts (see Chapter 2).

- Net capital gain/loss.
- Section 1231 gain/loss.
- Domestic production activities deduction.
- Casualty/theft gain/loss.
- Charitable contributions.
- Dividends received deduction.
- Net operating loss.
- AMT adjustments and preferences.

Following the computational procedure of Figures 8.1 and 8.2, all of the group-basis items are removed from each member's separate taxable income. Then, using the consolidated taxable income figure to that point, statutory limitations are applied to determine group-basis gains, losses, income, and deductions.

EXAMPLE 31

Parent Corporation's current-year taxable income included $300,000 net income from operations and a $50,000 net long-term capital gain. Parent also made a $40,000 contribution to State University. Accordingly, its separate taxable income amounted to $315,000.

Income from operations	$ 300,000
Capital gain income	+50,000
Charitable contribution (maximum)	−35,000
Separate taxable income	$ 315,000

[55]Reg. §§ 1.1502–21(g) and −22(g).

SubCo generated $170,000 income from operations and incurred a $45,000 short-term capital loss. Thus, its separate taxable income was $170,000, and aggregate separate taxable income for the group amounted to $485,000.

Upon consolidation, a larger amount of Parent's charitable contribution is deductible, and its capital gain is almost fully sheltered from current-year tax.

	Separate Taxable Income	Adjustments	Post-adjustment Amounts
Parent information	$315,000	−$50,000 capital gain income** +$35,000 charitable contribution deduction**	$300,000
SubCo information	170,000	$45,000 short-term capital loss**	170,000
Group-basis transactions		+$5,000 net long-term capital gain −$40,000 charitable contribution deduction (maximum for group is $47,500)	−35,000
Intercompany events			
Consolidated taxable income			$435,000
*Permanent eliminations.	**Group-basis transaction.		†Matching rule.

Computing these items on a group basis does not always result in a reduction of aggregate group taxable income. Nevertheless, the possibility of using the group-basis computations may affect transactions by group members late in the tax year when it becomes apparent that planning opportunities may be available. It also may encourage the taxpayer to seek out fellow group members that bring complementary tax attributes to the consolidated return.

EXAMPLE 32

Parent Corporation owns 15% of the stock of Outsider Corporation throughout the year. Outsider paid a $150,000 dividend to Parent during the year. Parent also generated $400,000 of taxable operating income and sold a § 1231 asset at a $10,000 gain. Parent's separate taxable income is computed below.

Operating income	$ 400,000
Dividend income	+150,000
§ 1231 gain	+10,000
Dividends received deduction (70%)	−105,000
Separate taxable income	$ 455,000

A 10% owner of Outsider, SubCo also received a $100,000 dividend. SubCo's operations produced a $20,000 net taxable loss for the year, and it sold a § 1231 asset at a $4,000 loss. Thus, SubCo's separate taxable income is computed as follows.

Operating income	($ 20,000)
Dividend income	+100,000
§ 1231 loss	−4,000
Dividends received deduction[56]	−53,200
Separate taxable income	$ 22,800

A consolidated return increases the group's dividends received deduction,[57] but it wastes the opportunity to claim SubCo's § 1231 loss as an ordinary deduction.

	Separate Taxable Income	Adjustments	Post-adjustment Amounts
Parent information	$455,000	−$150,000 dividend received from Outsider**	$400,000
		−$10,000 § 1231 gain**	
		+$105,000 dividends received deduction**	
SubCo information	22,800	−$100,000 dividend received from Outsider**	(20,000)
		+$4,000 § 1231 loss	
		+$53,200 dividends received deduction	
Group-basis transactions		+$250,000 dividend received from Outsider	+81,000
		−$175,000 dividends received deduction (70% × $250,000)	
		+$6,000 § 1231 gain	
Intercompany events			
Consolidated taxable income			$461,000
*Permanent eliminations.	**Group-basis transaction.		†Matching rule.

■

The domestic production activities deduction, or DPAD (see Chapter 3), is allowed for an **expanded affiliated group (EAG)**.[58] If such a group files a Form 1120 as a consolidated group, the DPAD is another group item. The DPAD is computed on the basis of consolidated taxable income, not the separate taxable income amounts of the members, and the taxable income limitation is applied to this amount. The DPAD then is allocated to the group members on the basis of the qualified production activities income (QPAI) of each, regardless of whether the member has a separate taxable gain or loss for the year.[59] If the member's QPAI is negative, it is treated as zero for this purpose.

EXAMPLE 33

Except for the DPAD, the members of an electing consolidated group report the following data.

[56] Limited to 70% of taxable income before the deduction. § 246(b)(1).

[57] The group cannot apply an 80% rate for the dividends received deduction, even though aggregate group ownership in Outsider now exceeds 20%. Reg. § 1.1502–26(a)(1)(i).

[58] An expanded affiliated group includes any group of parent-subsidiary corporations in which more than 50% of each member is owned directly or indirectly by a parent corporation. An EAG can include corporations that are ineligible to elect to file a consolidated return, such as an insurance company. § 199(d)(4)(B).

[59] Intercompany sales among group members are included in qualified production activities income, but receipts from intercompany leases, rentals, and licensing are not. Reg. § 1.199–7(c).

Affiliate	Taxable Income ($ Million)	Qualified Production Activities Income (QPAI) ($ Million)	W–2 Wages ($ Million)
Brown, parent	50	80	60
Coral	(20)	40	20
Drake	10	30	–0–
Totals	40	150	80

The DPAD is computed at the group level, and then it is allocated to the affiliates based on the relative amount of each member's QPAI. Members' separate taxable incomes are recomputed for these amounts, and consolidated taxable income then is determined.

- Brown is allocated 80/150 of the group's DPAD.
- Coral is allocated 40/150 of the group's DPAD.
- Drake is allocated 30/150 of the group's DPAD.

Although Coral reported an NOL for the year, it is not separately subject to the taxable income limitation. Further, note that Drake separately would not be entitled to any DPAD because of the W–2 wage limitation. These member-level limitations are not relevant in the EAG determination of the DPAD. The DPAD is a group item on the consolidated return. ■

Items computed on a consolidated basis include the following, among others.

- All elements of AMTI and the minimum tax credit.
- All elements of the general business and research tax credits.
- The foreign tax credit.
- Recapture computations for tax credits.
- Percentage depletion amounts.

The Matching Rule

A special class of intercompany transactions receives deferral treatment under the Regulations.[60] The gain or loss realized on these transactions is removed from consolidated taxable income until the sold asset leaves the affiliated group. The purpose of this **matching rule** is to prevent group members from accelerating loss deductions that relate to sales of assets within the group. In effect, for purposes of these intercompany transactions, the group is treated as a single corporation with multiple operating divisions.

The matching rule applies to sales of assets or the performance of services among group members. The entire deferred gain or loss enters the consolidated taxable income computation when, for example, the asset is transferred outside the group through a subsequent sale. The matching rule also affects cost recovery computations when a group member purchases a business asset in an intercompany transaction.

Full gain or loss recognition also can be triggered under the *acceleration rule* when the transferor of the property leaves the group or the consolidation election is terminated.[61] The acceleration rule applies when it no longer is possible to produce a proper result under the matching rule.

Generally, the gain or loss on the sale outside the group is recognized in the same manner as it would have been on the initial transfer.[62]

[60]Reg. § 1.1502–13.

[61]Reg. § 1.1502–13(d)(1)(i).

[62]Sections 267 and 1239 may convert other types of gain into ordinary income. See especially Reg. §§ 1.267(f)–1 and 1.1239–1(a) and (b)(3).

EXAMPLE 34

Parent Corporation sold a plot of land to SubCo in the current year for $100,000. Parent had acquired the land 10 years ago for $40,000. The consolidated return also reflects the operating results of the parties: Parent generated $10,000 income, and SubCo produced a $100,000 gain.

This intercompany transaction triggers the matching rule: Parent's $60,000 realized gain is deferred through an elimination in the computation of consolidated taxable income. The $60,000 gain is recognized by the group when SubCo later sells the land to Outsider Corporation.

	Separate Taxable Income	Adjustments	Post-adjustment Amounts
Parent information	$ 70,000	________	$ 70,000
SubCo information	100,000	________	100,000
Group-basis transactions			
Intercompany events		−$60,000 gain on intercompany sale to SubCo†	−60,000
Consolidated taxable income			$110,000
*Permanent eliminations.	**Group-basis transaction.		†Matching rule.

SubCo sold the land to Outsider for $110,000 in a year in which its operating income totaled $60,000 (exclusive of the sale of the land). Parent's operating income amounted to $170,000.

	Separate Taxable Income	Adjustments	Post-adjustment Amounts
Parent information	$170,000	________	$170,000
SubCo information	70,000	________	70,000
Group-basis transactions			
Intercompany events		+$60,000 restored gain on Parent's sale to SubCo†	+60,000
Consolidated taxable income			$300,000
*Permanent eliminations.	**Group-basis transaction.		†Matching rule.

■

Generally, the matching rule is attractive to the group when intercompany sales take place at a gain. When such sales generate losses, however, the mandatory nature of the rule may become burdensome.

8.6 Tax Planning

An affiliated group's decision to file its Federal corporate income tax returns on a consolidated basis entails a complex process. Consolidation is mandatory for financial accounting purposes, but it entails an affirmative election for tax purposes. Concept Summary 8.1 is a useful decision aid for a taxpayer that is considering forming or joining a Federal consolidated group. The following discussion includes a number of additional planning opportunities for an electing group.

FINANCIAL DISCLOSURE INSIGHTS The Consolidated Group's Deferred Tax Asset Accounts

Often the GAAP balance sheet reflects deferred tax assets for several of the items discussed in this chapter. Some of the most commonly encountered of these items include the following.

- A carryover of a general business credit, research credit, foreign tax credit, or minimum tax credit.
- A net operating loss carryover traceable to current operations.
- A net operating loss that is deferred under the SRLY or §382 rules.

If there is doubt as to whether the deferred tax asset is likely to be realized in the future, a valuation allowance may be needed to offset the deferred tax asset. See Chapter 14.

Choosing Consolidated Return Partners

LO.10

Demonstrate tax planning opportunities available to consolidated groups.

Taxpayers should optimize their overall tax benefits when choosing consolidated return partners. Within the limitations of the rules discussed earlier in the chapter, attributes of potential target corporations might include some of the following.

- Loss and credit carryovers.
- Passive activity income, loss, or credits.
- Gains that can be deferred through intercompany sales.
- Contributions to consolidated ACE adjustments.
- Excess limitation amounts (e.g., with respect to charitable contributions).
- Section 1231 gains, losses, and lookback profiles.

Consolidation versus 100 Percent Dividends Received Deduction

When adequate ownership is held, a 100 percent dividends received deduction is available for payments received from subsidiaries with whom a consolidated return is *not* filed. Thus, this tax benefit is still available when the taxpayer wants to affiliate with an insurance company, a foreign entity, or other ineligible corporation. A taxpayer that cannot find potential group partners with the desired level of complementary tax attributes may also take advantage of this benefit.

Protecting the Group Members' Liability for Tax Payments

Because all group members are responsible for consolidated tax liabilities, interest, and penalties, target subsidiaries and their (present and potential) shareholders should take measures to protect their separate interests.

EXAMPLE 35

Return to the facts of Example 14. Exposure by SubCo and its successive shareholders to tax (and all other) liabilities of Parent Corporation should be minimized by including appropriate clauses in purchase contracts and related documents. For instance, (1) Foreign Corporation could alter its negotiating position so that it pays less to acquire the SubCo stock, or (2) SubCo might attempt to recover any Parent taxes that it pays through courts other than the Tax Court. ■

A short tax year may be created when a member with a nonmatching tax year joins or leaves the group. When this occurs, the group should consider measures to limit the ensuing negative tax consequences. For instance, additional income can

CONCEPT SUMMARY 8.2

The Consolidated Tax Return

1. Groups of corporations form for a variety of tax and nontax reasons. The election to file Federal income tax returns on a consolidated basis allows certain group members to use their positive tax attributes (e.g., loss or credit carryovers) to offset negative tax attributes (e.g., positive taxable income) of other members.
2. Consolidated tax returns are limited to eligible corporations that satisfy stock ownership tests and meet various compliance requirements. For instance, all group members must conform their tax years to that of the parent of the group. Group members may use different tax accounting methods, however.
3. Group members are jointly and severally liable for the overall income tax liability of the group. For the most part, computations of estimated tax liabilities must be made on a consolidated basis.
4. The stock basis of a subsidiary is derived from the acquisition price of the stock, increased by the taxable income (or decreased by the losses) of the subsidiary, and decreased by dividend distributions. An excess loss account is created when aggregate losses of the subsidiary exceed both the purchase price and ensuing income amounts. The excess loss account is recaptured as capital gain when the subsidiary stock is disposed of.
5. Under the § 382 or SRLY rules, NOL carryforwards may be deferred when they relate to subsidiaries acquired by the group. When both restrictions apply, the § 382 rules prevail.
6. In computing consolidated taxable income, certain items, such as charitable contributions and § 1231 gains and losses, are computed on a consolidated basis, while other gains and losses are deferred until later tax periods. The group is subject to severe restrictions in using any operating losses of a subsidiary that has been acquired or disposed of.

be accelerated into the short year of acquisition. This will reduce any loss carryforwards when the carryover period is effectively shortened due to the takeover. The group also should make suitable income-allocation elections in assigning income to the short year. Finally, group estimated tax payments should be computed using both consolidated and separate liability amounts to determine the more beneficial method. In this way, only the minimum quarterly tax payments are made, and the benefits of the time value of money are maximized.

In the context of a corporate takeover, the controlling intercompany documents should address the tax-sharing agreement. Members should allow for reimbursement between affiliates when a member cannot pay its allocated portion of the group's income tax liability. Another provision in the agreement should address the allocation of taxes caused by the takeover itself. For example, should some of the resulting tax liability be paid by affiliates, or should it be paid entirely by the target corporation?

Documentation Requirements

Adjustments to the basis of subsidiary stock must be fully documented, with detailed workpapers retained by the taxpayer.[63] If a tax understatement results from poor documentation of the subsidiary's stock basis, a penalty is added to the amount of tax due.[64] Because of the importance of the stock basis computations for this and other reasons, contemporaneous documentation by the parent corporation must be maintained.

[63] Reg. § 1.1502–32(q). An earlier proposed rule, not adopted, would have required the details of the basis computations to be attached to the consolidated return.

[64] The preamble to the Regulation specifies that the penalty applies to misstatements of basis due to negligence and substantial or gross misconduct by the taxpayer. TD 8560, 1994–2 C.B. 200.

REFOCUS ON THE BIG PICTURE

Should the Affiliated Group File a Consolidated Return?

If Alexander and Hamilton are restructured as an affiliated group in a qualifying reorganization and both corporations continue to exist as separate entities, the parties should consider an election to file their Federal income tax returns on a consolidated basis. Assuming that Hamilton begins to generate positive taxable income in the near future as expected, the NOLs and other attractive tax attributes that Hamilton brings to the group will be of great benefit to both corporations.

The group also may benefit from other aspects of Hamilton's tax situation, including its accumulated capital and passive losses and credits that have been carried forward due to a lack of tax liability. In all likelihood, Alexander and Hamilton are a "good match" as potential consolidated return partners.

What If?

But what if Alexander's expectations for a turnaround in Hamilton's business fortunes prove to be incorrect and the subsidiary continues to generate NOLs? The SRLY rules prevent the deductions and credits acquired from Hamilton from being of immediate use to the affiliated group. A consolidation election is beneficial only if the Hamilton subsidiary generates positive postacquisition taxable income.

KEY TERMS

Affiliated group, 8-8
Consolidated returns, 8-2
Excess loss account, 8-17
Expanded affiliated group (EAG), 8-28
Matching rule, 8-29
Separate return limitation year (SRLY), 8-25

DISCUSSION QUESTIONS

1. **LO.1** You are making a presentation to the board of directors of HugeCo about the merits of acquiring Bitty, Ltd., an important supplier. One board member knowing that you are a tax specialist, asks you to list some of the nontax reasons to make the acquisition. List at least four such motivations in a PowerPoint slide. **Communications**

2. **LO.1** Describe how a corporate entity might be restructured to enable the resulting group to qualify for a consolidation election. (Hint: Recall the corporate changes discussed in Chapter 7, such as the "Type A" reorganization.) **Decision Making**

3. **LO.2** Only a few sections in the Internal Revenue Code are devoted to the rules that control how consolidated income tax returns are filed. In contrast, the Regulations that explain and clarify those Code sections are voluminous. Given the complexity of the entities and transactions that consolidated returns involve, comment on whether this is a proper balancing of the tax-writing responsibilities in this area.

4. **LO.2** Financial accounting rules do not always match the tax treatment of transactions involving groups of U.S. corporations. List at least two areas where tax and accounting rules differ when groups of affiliated corporations are involved.

5. **LO.3** The local CPA Society is presenting its annual tax conference. Most of the attendees will be career tax professionals who work with smaller clients. You have been asked to submit an outline for your talk, "When to Use a Consolidated Tax Return: Federal Tax Law Issues." Organize an outline that lists the advantages and disadvantages of a **Communications**

consolidation election. Include at least five points in each category. Keep your points at the introductory level, as most of the members of your audience know the rest of the tax law well but do not work regularly in this area.

6. **LO.3, 4, 5** List the structural and compliance requirements under Federal income tax law that must be met before a parent and its affiliates are allowed to file on a consolidated basis. Consider only the requirements for the group to file its *first* consolidated return.

Issue ID

7. **LO.3, 10** Black, Brown, and Red Corporations are considering a corporate restructuring that would allow them to file Federal income tax returns on a consolidated basis. Black holds significant NOL carryforwards from several years ago. Brown always has been profitable and is projected to remain so. Red has been successful, but its product cycles are mature and operating losses are likely to begin three years from now and last for a decade. What tax issues should the corporations consider before electing to file on a consolidated basis?

Issue ID

8. **LO.3, 10** Continue with the facts presented in Question 7. In addition, assume that Brown Corporation has a history of making large, continuous charitable contributions in its community. In the next three years, Brown's largest investment assets will be priced such that they will be attractive candidates for sale. Modify your list of tax issues to include these considerations.

9. **LO.3, 9** Indicate whether each of the following would make good consolidated return partners in computing the affiliated group's Federal income tax.
   a. SubCo has a number of appreciated assets that it wants to sell to its parent, Huge Corporation.
   b. SubCo has a number of assets that it wants to sell to its parent, Huge. The assets have declined in market value since SubCo purchased them.
   c. ParentCo uses cost depletion in accounting for its natural resources, while SubCo wants to continue to claim percentage depletion.
   d. ParentCo uses a calendar tax year, while SubTwo has been using a September 30 tax year-end.

10. **LO.3, 5** Indicate whether each of the following would make good partners for electing to file a consolidated return for Federal income tax purposes. Explain why or why not.
    a. SubCo cannot claim its full domestic production activities deduction because of the taxable income limitation. ParentCo is highly profitable every tax year.
    b. ParentCo would like to file on a consolidated basis with SubOne because the subsidiary will be generating sizable operating losses in the next two tax years. Starting with the third tax year, though, SubOne will enter a highly profitable period.
    c. ParentCo has $2 million in suspended foreign tax credits that will expire in two more tax years. Its wholly owned subsidiary, ShortCo, generates $5 million in foreign-source income every year.
    d. This year, ParentCo generated $4 million in taxable income, and its wholly owned subsidiary, Small Corporation, reported a $3 million operating loss. Next year, though, Small is projected to start a four-year period with $20 million total taxable profits.
    e. ParentCo is highly profitable and makes a large annual gift in support of the local tax-exempt zoological gardens. SubCo reports sizable operating losses every year.

11. **LO.4** Provide the information required to complete the following chart.

	Group of Entities	Eligible to Join a Consolidated Group?	Why or Why Not Eligible?
a.	Lima City Choral Artists	________	________
b.	Columbus United Health Insurance, Ltd.	________	________
c.	Bethke Services, Inc.	________	________
d.	Tequila Teléfono, organized in El Salvador	________	________
e.	Vermont, South Carolina, and Utah Barber Shops, Inc.	________	________
f.	Capital Management Partnership	________	________
g.	Henry Pontiac Trust	________	________

12. **LO.5** The Pelican Group cannot decide whether to start to file on a consolidated basis for Federal income tax purposes, effective for its tax year beginning January 1, 2013. Its computational study of the effects of consolidation is taking longer than expected. What is the latest date by which the group must make this critical decision?

13. **LO.5** The Penguin Group cannot decide whether to cease to file on a consolidated basis for Federal income tax purposes, effective for its tax year beginning January 1, 2013. Its computational study of the effects of such a "de-consolidation" is taking longer than expected. What is the latest date by which the group must make this critical decision?

Decision Making

14. **LO.5** Lavender and Azure began to file a calendar year consolidated return for tax year 2010. The group never extends the due date of its tax returns. Lavender acquires all of the stock of Rose on January 1, 2011, and immediately joins the consolidated group. All of the Rose stock is sold to another investor at the end of 2013. Explain the significance of the following dates. Which of your answers can change if the taxpayers so elect?
    a. March 15, 2011.
    b. January 1, 2012.
    c. March 15, 2012.
    d. January 1, 2019.

15. **LO.5** The consolidated tax liability for most affiliated groups is assigned among the parent and its subsidiaries—each entity is responsible for "its share" of the tax. The Regulations allow several methods to be used to compute these allocations. Identify and describe the two most commonly used tax allocation methods.

Issue ID

16. **LO.5** Huge Corporation and its wholly owned subsidiary, Whit Corporation, file Federal tax returns on a separate basis. Huge manufactures postage meters, and Whit provides mail-order services to a cross section of clients in the state.

    Huge uses a calendar tax year, while Whit files using an April 30 year-end. Huge's gross receipts for the year total $15 million, and Whit's are $3.5 million. Identify some Federal income tax issues as to accounting periods and methods that the group would face if the corporations elected to consolidate.

Communications

17. **LO.6** Your firm has assigned you to work with Jeri Byers, the tax director of a small group of corporations. The group qualifies to file on a consolidated basis and plans to make its first election to file in that manner. In a memo for Jeri's tax file, describe some of the more important adjustments she will need to make to keep track of the parent corporation's basis in the stock of each of the subsidiaries.

18. **LO.6** An *excess loss account* is used by a parent in computing its basis in the stock it holds in a subsidiary so that the stock basis never can be less than zero. Explain.

19. **LO.6** Your client, MegaCorp, has asked for your assistance in filing the current-year consolidated Federal income tax return. MegaCorp provides you with the following items for the parent and each of the affiliates. Comment.
    - Gross income items.
    - Deductions and credit amounts.
    - Beginning and ending balance in E & P.
    - Cash distributions from the subsidiaries to the parent, MegaCorp.

20. **LO.6** Outline the process by which a consolidated group computes its Federal taxable income. Your description should match the approach taken in Figure 8.1.

Issue ID

21. **LO.7** Parent Corporation and its wholly owned subsidiary, Child Corporation, have filed Federal income tax returns on a consolidated basis since Child was incorporated many years ago. Both entities use calendar tax years. Parent uses accrual tax accounting, but Child uses the cash method.

    In December 2012, Parent renders services worth $750,000 to Child. Parent's operations for 2012 result in a $2 million loss from all other sources. Parent sends Child an invoice for the services in December 2012, and Child pays it in January 2013. What tax consequences are the parties trying to accomplish? Will this plan work? Why or why not?

Issue ID

22. **LO.7** In December 2012, Child Corporation prepays Parent Corporation $750,000 for its 2013 use of a common database system. Child is a wholly owned subsidiary of Parent, with whom Child has filed a consolidated Federal income tax return since Child was spun off from Parent many years ago. While both entities have calendar tax years, Parent uses the accrual method; Child employs the cash method of tax accounting.

    Both entities are profitable for the 2012 tax year. What tax consequences are the parties trying to accomplish? Will this plan work? Why or why not?

23. **LO.8** Tiny Corporation brought a $4 million NOL carryforward into the Mucho Group of corporations that elected to file on a consolidated basis as of the beginning of this year. Combined results for the year generated $15 million taxable income, $1.5 million of which was attributable to Tiny's activities for the year. Has Tiny been a good consolidation partner? Explain.

Decision Making

24. **LO.8** Parent and Child Corporations have filed on a consolidated basis since the mid-1970s. Junior Corporation was formed at the beginning of this year through an asset split-off from Parent. Operations this year resulted in a $2 million operating loss, one-fourth of which can be traced to Junior.

    Should Junior join the consolidated group this year? Will the group be able to carry back and claim a refund for the $500,000 NOL that is attributable to Junior? Explain.

25. **LO.8** Put owned all of the stock of Call when the two corporations were formed a decade ago. The group immediately elected to file on a consolidated basis. Now Call's management team has purchased the company from the parent and intends to carry on and expand the business into new markets.

    When Call left the Put consolidated group, the group held a $5 million NOL carryforward, $2 million of which was attributable to Call's operations under formulas used by all of the parties. Call will generate $700,000 on each of its first five years' worth of separate returns.

    Advise Call as to who "owns" the carryforwards after the corporate division.

26. **LO.8** The consolidated return Regulations employ the "SRLY" rules to limit the losses a parent can claim with respect to a newly acquired subsidiary. Explain the tax policy behind the SRLY rules. Describe how they affect the timing of loss deductions after an acquisition.

Communications

27. **LO.9** The computational method of Figure 8.1 indicates that consolidated taxable income includes a number of group items where limitations are applied on an aggregate basis. In no more than two PowerPoint slides, list as many group items as you can.

Decision Making

28. **LO.9, 10** Intercompany transactions of a consolidated group can be subject to a "matching rule" and an "acceleration rule."
    a. Define both terms.
    b. As a tax planner structuring an intercompany transaction, when would it be beneficial to use either rule?

Communications

29. **LO.9** Use a timeline to diagram the gain/loss recognition by this affiliated group.
    - Year 1: SubCo purchases a nondepreciable asset for $400.
    - Year 3: SubCo sells the asset to Parent for $575.
    - Year 4: Parent sells the asset to Stranger (not an affiliate) for $660.

Communications

30. **LO.9** Use a timeline to diagram the gain/loss recognition by this affiliated group.
    - Year 1: SubCo purchases an asset for $400.
    - Year 3: SubCo sells the asset to Parent for $300.
    - Year 4: Parent sells the asset to Stranger (not an affiliate) for $140.

Communications

31. **LO.9, 10** Junior was a member of the Rice consolidated group for many years. It left the group effective for the 2012 tax year. In 2010, Junior sold a plot of land to Parent at a $600,000 realized loss. Recognition of that loss by the group was deferred under the matching rule. As a departing group member, does Junior have any right to take the loss

with it to be used on its subsequent separate returns? Prepare two memos for the tax research file, outlining the arguments both in Junior's favor and in the remaining group's favor.

32. **LO.10** At a meeting of local tax executives last week, you heard several of the tax professionals complaining about the sizable costs that they incur in meeting and maintaining an election to file Federal consolidated income tax returns. Examine these comments in more detail. Under what circumstances might a group of affiliates decide *not* to make a consolidation election? List three or more reasons that might make a corporate group question whether it should make such an election.

33. **LO.10** Findlay Corporation was formed by three engineers. Sally brings entrepreneurial skills to the ownership group, while Patricia is the "idea person." Lois makes prototypes and works with potential manufacturers of Findlay products. Unfortunately, Findlay cannot exploit its operations due to lack of capital. **Communications**

    Huge Corporation has the needed capital and recognizes Findlay's potential. It has sent takeover overtures to the Findlay board of directors. As the chief of Findlay's tax matters, you have been asked to prepare a list of items that will be necessary should the acquisition by Huge occur. Present your list of at least three items in a PowerPoint slide.

PROBLEMS

34. **LO.2** Your client, Big Corporation, and its wholly owned subsidiary, LittleCo, file a consolidated return for Federal income tax purposes. Indicate both the financial accounting and the tax treatment of the following transactions.
    a. LittleCo pays a $1 million dividend to Big.
    b. LittleCo sells investment land to Big. LittleCo's basis in the land is $200,000. The sale price is $500,000.
    c. Six months after purchasing the land from LittleCo, Big sells the investment land to Phillips, an unrelated party, for $650,000.

35. **LO.3** Giant Corporation owns all of the stock of PebbleCo, so they constitute a Federal affiliated group and a parent-subsidiary controlled group. By completing the following chart, delineate for Giant's tax department some of the effects of an election to file Federal consolidated income tax returns.

Situation	If the Group Files a Consolidated Return	If Separate Income Tax Returns Continue to Be Filed
a. PebbleCo pays a $1 million cash dividend to Giant.	__________	__________
b. Taxable income for both group members this year is $50,000.	__________	__________
c. Giant's tax liability is $95,000, and Pebble's liability totals $75,000.	__________	__________
d. Giant uses the LIFO method for its inventories, but Pebble wants to use FIFO for its own inventories.	__________	__________

36. **LO.3** Giant Corporation owns all of the stock of PebbleCo, so they constitute a Federal affiliated group and a parent-subsidiary controlled group. By completing the following chart, delineate for Giant's tax department some of the effects of an election to file Federal consolidated income tax returns.

Situation	If the Group Files a Consolidated Return	If Separate Income Tax Returns Continue to Be Filed
a. Both Giant and PebbleCo produce taxable profits from manufacturing activities.	________	________
b. PebbleCo pays Giant an annual royalty for use of the Giant trademarks.	________	________
c. Giant uses a calendar tax year, while PebbleCo's tax year-end is March 31.	________	________
d. Giant claims a credit for its foreign tax payments, while Pebble claims a deduction for them.	________	________

37. **LO.3, 4** Apply the controlled and affiliated group rules to determine whether a parent-subsidiary controlled group or an affiliated group exists in each of the following independent situations. Circle Y for yes and N for no.

Situation	Parent-Subsidiary Controlled Group?	Affiliated Group?
a. Throughout the year, Parent owns 65% of the stock of SubCo.	Y N	Y N
b. Parent owns 70% of SubCo. The other 30% of SubCo stock is owned by Senior, a wholly owned subsidiary of Parent.	Y N	Y N
c. For 11 months, Parent owns 75% of the stock of SubCo. For the last month of the tax year, Parent owns 100% of the SubCo stock.	Y N	Y N

38. **LO.5** Grand Corporation owns all of the stock of Junior, Ltd., a corporation that has been declared bankrupt and has no net assets. Junior still owes $1 million to Wholesale, Inc., one of its suppliers, and $3.5 million to the IRS for unpaid Federal income taxes. Grand and Junior always have filed Federal income tax returns on a consolidated basis. What is Grand's exposure concerning Junior's outstanding income tax liabilities?

39. **LO.5** Parent and Sub Corporations file their Federal income tax returns on a consolidated basis. Parent, a calendar year taxpayer, owns all of the outstanding stock of Sub. The consolidation election was effective in January 2011. Both companies are profitable, and tax projections for the future appear below. How much must be remitted to the IRS for estimated payments in each year?

Tax Year	Parent's Federal Tax Estimate	Sub's Federal Tax Estimate
2011	$500,000	$150,000
2012	500,000	170,000
2013	600,000	200,000
2014	750,000	300,000

40. **LO.5** The Parent consolidated group reports the following results for the tax year. Dollar amounts are listed in millions.

	Parent	SubOne	SubTwo	SubThree	Consolidated
Ordinary income	$700	$200	$140	($90)	$ 950
Capital gain/loss	–0–	–0–	60	(25)	35
§ 1231 gain/loss	150	–0–	(50)	–0–	100
Separate taxable incomes	$850	$200	$150	($90) with a $25 capital loss carryover	
Consolidated taxable income					$1,085
Consolidated tax liability					$ 380
Energy tax credit, from SubOne					(20)
Net tax due					$ 360

Determine each member's share of the consolidated tax liability. All of the members have consented to use the relative taxable income method. Assume a 35% marginal tax rate.

41. **LO.5** Assume the same facts as in Problem 40 except that the group members have adopted the relative tax liability tax-sharing method.

42. **LO.5** ParentCo owns all of the stock of DaughterCo, and the group files its Federal income tax returns on a consolidated basis. Both taxpayers are subject to the AMT this year due to active operations in oil and gas development. No intercompany transactions were incurred this year. If the affiliates filed separate returns, they would report the following amounts.

Company	Adjusted Current Earnings (ACE)	AMT Income before the ACE Adjustment
ParentCo	$1,600,000	$1,000,000
DaughterCo	250,000	300,000
Totals	$1,850,000	$1,300,000

How does the consolidation election affect the overall AMT liability of the group?

43. **LO.6** Senior, Ltd., acquires all of the stock of JuniorCo for $30 million at the beginning of 2011. The group immediately elects to file income tax returns on a consolidated basis. Senior's operations generate a $50 million profit every year. In 2012, JuniorCo pays its parent a $9 million dividend. Operating results for JuniorCo are as follows.

2011	$ 4 million
2012	12 million
2013	15 million

a. Compute Senior's basis in the JuniorCo stock as of the end of 2011, 2012, and 2013.
b. Same as (a), except that JuniorCo's 2012 tax year produced a $6 million NOL.
c. Same as (a), except that JuniorCo's 2012 tax year produced a $40 million NOL.

44. **LO.6** WhaleCo acquired all of the common stock of MinnowCo early in year 1 for $900,000, and MinnowCo immediately elected to join WhaleCo's consolidated Federal income tax return. As part of the takeover, WhaleCo also acquired $300,000 of MinnowCo bonds. The results of MinnowCo for the first few years of the group operations were reported as follows.

Tax Year	Operating Gain/Loss	Stock Basis
1	$ 100,000	________
2	(800,000)	________
3	(600,000)	________

Determine WhaleCo's basis in its MinnowCo common stock as of the end of each tax year.

45. **LO.6** Continue with the facts of Problem 44. WhaleCo has determined that it will sell all of its MinnowCo stock at the end of year 3 for $250,000. Taking into account the rules regarding excess loss accounts, determine WhaleCo's gain/loss from its sale of the MinnowCo stock.

46. **LO.7** Compute consolidated taxable income for the calendar year Blue Group, which elected consolidated status immediately upon creation of the two member corporations in January 2011. All recognized income relates to the consulting services of the firms. No intercompany transactions were completed during the indicated years.

Year	Blue Corporation	Orange Corporation
2011	$250,000	($ 50,000)
2012	250,000	(60,000)
2013	250,000	(240,000)
2014	250,000	90,000

47. **LO.7, 8** Determine consolidated taxable income for the calendar year Yeti Group, which elected consolidated status immediately upon the creation of the two member corporations on January 1, 2011. All recognized income is ordinary in nature, and no intercompany transactions were completed during the indicated years.

Year	Yeti Corporation	Snowman Corporation
2011	$450,000	$ 70,000
2012	450,000	(310,000)
2013	450,000	(600,000)
2014	450,000	75,000

48. **LO.8** Cougar, Jaguar, and Ocelot Corporations have filed on a consolidated, calendar year basis for many years. At the beginning of the 2012 tax year, the group elects to deconsolidate. The group's $6 million NOL carryforward can be traced in the following manner: one-half to Cougar's operations and one-quarter each to Jaguar's and Ocelot's. How will Ocelot treat the NOL on its 2012 separate tax return?

49. **LO.8** The Giant consolidated group includes SubTwo, which was acquired as part of a § 382 ownership change. SubTwo brought with it to the group a large NOL carryforward, $3 million of which is available this year under the SRLY rules due to SubTwo's positive contribution to the group's taxable income. The § 382 limitation with respect to SubTwo is $500,000. How much of SubTwo's NOL can be used this year to reduce consolidated taxable income?

50. **LO.8** Child Corporation joined the Thrust consolidated group in 2011. At the time it joined the group, Child held a $2 million NOL carryforward. On a consolidated basis, the members of Thrust generated significant profits for many years.

    Child's operating results during the first few consolidated return years were as follows. The § 382 rules do not apply to the group.

2011	($ 100,000)
2012	1,600,000
2013	1,800,000

How will Child's NOLs affect consolidated taxable income for each of these years? Is any refund available with respect to the NOL that Child brought into the group? Explain.

51. **LO.9** B.I.G. Corporation sold a plot of undeveloped land to SubCo this year for $100,000. B.I.G. had acquired the land several years ago for $40,000. The consolidated return also reflects the operating results of the parties: B.I.G. generated $130,000 income from operations, and SubCo produced a $20,000 operating loss.
    a. Use the computational worksheet of Figure 8.2 to derive the group members' separate taxable incomes and the group's consolidated taxable income.
    b. Same as (a), except that SubCo sold the land to Outsider Corporation for $130,000 in a subsequent year, when its operating income totaled $20,000 (exclusive of the sale of the land), and Parent's operating income amounted to $90,000.

RESEARCH PROBLEMS

THOMSON REUTERS **CHECKPOINT**®

Note: Solutions to Research Problems can be prepared by using the **Checkpoint® Student Edition** online research product, which is available to accompany this text. It is also possible to prepare solutions to the Research Problems by using tax research materials found in a standard tax library.

Research Problem 1. Alpha and Beta have been members of an electing Federal consolidated group since the beginning of year 1. Also at the beginning of year 1, Alpha acquired and placed in service a fleet of trucks to be used in its business. The acquisition price was $1 million. Alpha used the 5-year MACRS tables to compute cost recovery deductions for the fleet; the depreciation percentages from the 5-year, mid-year convention MACRS table are listed below. Alpha did not claim any bonus depreciation for the fleet.

Year	Depreciation Rate (%)
1	20
2	32
3	19.2
4	11.52
5	11.52
6	5.26

At the beginning of year 3, Alpha sold the fleet in full to Beta for $900,000. Alpha's basis in the fleet on the date of the sale was $480,000; its realized gain on the sale totaled $420,000. Provide the following information.

a. The recognized gain of the consolidated group in year 3 from the sale.
b. The consolidated group's cost recovery deduction for the fleet in years 3 and 4.

Communications

Research Problem 2. LargeCo owns stock in Small Corporation. The voting shares and value of the Small stock owned by LargeCo are as follows.

- Common stock, 100%.
- Preferred stock, 60%.

Under Small's corporate bylaws, the board of directors manages all of the entity's operations and investments. A majority vote of the board is required before any new policy or practice is adopted.

Board members are elected in the following manner: the common shareholders elect five of the eight board members, and the preferred shareholders separately elect the other three directors.

LargeCo would like to file a consolidated tax return with Small. Is the § 1504 stock ownership test met (i.e., does LargeCo own 80% of the voting power and value of the Small stock)? Prepare a memo for your firm's tax research file that addresses this affiliated group issue.

Communications

Research Problem 3. The Cardinal Group had filed on a consolidated basis for several years. Parent Cardinal, Ltd., had a wholly owned subsidiary, Swallow, Inc. The group used a calendar tax year.

On January 25, 2012, Heron acquired all of the stock of Cardinal, including its ownership in Swallow, an important supplier for Heron's manufacturing process. All parties in the new group intended to file on a consolidated basis immediately and, indeed, used consolidated amounts in filing the 2012 Heron Group return on September 10, 2013.

During the audit of Heron Group's 2012 tax return, the IRS disallowed the use of the consolidated method because no Forms 1122 had ever been filed for the affiliates in the new group. In a memo for the tax research file, summarize the possibilities for the Heron Group to be granted an extension to elect consolidated return status.

Communications

Research Problem 4. Last year Cutlinger, Inc., acquired Donte Corporation in a state-law merger. Donte immediately joined the Cutlinger consolidated return group for state and Federal income tax purposes. Both parties use the calendar tax year.

At the time of the acquisition, Donte held some undeveloped land about 35 miles out of town known as Whispering Aspens, that it had purchased for speculation three years earlier. Donte's basis in the land was $40 million, and a recent appraisal put its value on the date of the acquisition at $4 million.

The decline in the value of Whispering Aspens reflected the generally poor operating results that Donte had been experiencing. Exclusive of the sale of the land, Donte had generated a $2 million operating loss for the two years prior to being acquired by Cutlinger, and it projected the same results for the next two years as well, now as a Cutlinger subsidiary.

The Donte board of directors had wanted to sell off Whispering Aspens for $4 million before Cutlinger made the acquisition, but Cutlinger sweetened the per-share acquisition price and convinced them to wait. Cutlinger had learned from an inside source that the tollway authority that operated a road abutting Whispering Aspens had decided to build a new interchange nearby and that Whispering Aspens now would be much more valuable in an outright sale to developers.

After the takeover, Cutlinger quickly sold off Whispering Aspens to a strip mall developer for $24 million in cash. On its consolidated tax return, the Cutlinger group reported a $16 million loss. On audit, the IRS disallowed the entire loss deduction. Mary Ellen Rogers, tax director of Cutlinger, wants your analysis of the tax results of the land sale. Write a letter to her addressing the IRS's position. Cutlinger's corporate offices are at 1101 Office Strip Lane, Suite 3, Hudson, OH 44237.

Research Problem 5. Graeter Corporation acquired all of the stock of Lesser Corporation in 2009, and the entities have filed a state and Federal consolidated income tax return ever since. In 2012, an audit notice from the state unemployment tax administration makes it clear that Lesser underpaid its 2010 state and Federal payroll taxes by $2 million. Lesser's cash flow at this time is poor, and it has insufficient funds to pay the delinquent amount plus interest and penalties. Can the state revenue agency collect the outstanding payroll tax from Graeter under the Federal "joint and several liability" rule for tax obligations of consolidated return affiliates? Explain.

Internet Activity

Use the tax resources of the Internet to address the following questions. Do not restrict your search to the Web, but include a review of newsgroups and general reference materials, practitioner sites and resources, primary sources of the tax law, chat rooms and discussion groups, and other opportunities.

Communications

Research Problem 6. Find a thread in a tax blog involving consolidated returns. Post an entry to the site concerning acceptable tax allocation formulas. Which tax-sharing methods have been most popular with the blogger's clients? Why? Have specific tax-sharing methods become more or less popular over time? What difficulties are encountered in gaining the affiliates' consent to a tax-sharing method? Has the blogger created any new and unique variations on the most common tax-sharing methods? If so, how and why did these new formulas come about? Write an e-mail to your professor summarizing the following.

a. The text of your posted message.
b. The most pertinent responses that you received in the first week after posting.
c. The professional titles of other posters to the group and the other questions that they are discussing.

Research Problem 7. Determine whether the income tax laws of your state, and those of two of its neighbors, allow Federal affiliated groups to use capital loss, passive loss, and NOL deductions. What are the NOL carryback and carryforward periods? What other limitations apply?

Research Problem 8. Find several journal articles and Web postings addressing the consolidation election. Construct a list titled "Consolidated Returns: Compliance Tips and Traps." Submit this document to your instructor. Provide citations for your research.

Communications

Research Problem 9. Identify the key details of the evolution and development of the Federal consolidated tax return rules. When were consolidated returns elective? When did they become required? What political forces were at work when the major 1966 and 1995 changes to the pertinent Federal income tax Regulations were adopted? When were NOL deduction limitations tightened or relaxed? Why? Arrange your findings using a timeline and no more than three PowerPoint slides.

Communications

Research Problem 10. Complete a review of the evolution of your state's tax laws concerning consolidated returns. Use a format similar to the one described in Research Problem 9.

Communications

CHAPTER

9 Taxation of International Transactions

LEARNING OBJECTIVES: *After completing Chapter 9, you should be able to:*

LO.1 Explain the framework underlying the U.S. taxation of cross-border transactions.

LO.2 Describe the interaction between Internal Revenue Code provisions and tax treaties.

LO.3 Apply the rules for sourcing income and deductions into U.S. and foreign categories.

LO.4 Apply foreign currency exchange rules as they affect the tax consequences of international transactions.

LO.5 Work with the U.S. tax provisions affecting U.S. persons earning foreign-source income, including the rules relating to cross-border asset transfers, antideferral provisions, and the foreign tax credit.

LO.6 Apply the U.S. tax provisions concerning nonresident alien individuals and foreign corporations.

CHAPTER OUTLINE

© kristian sekulic/istockphoto.com

THE BIG PICTURE Tax Solutions for the Real World

Going International

VoiceCo, a domestic corporation, designs, manufactures, and sells specialty microphones for use in theaters. All of its activities take place in Florida, although it ships products to customers all over the United States. When it receives inquiries about its products from foreign customers, VoiceCo decides to test the foreign market and places ads in foreign trade journals. Soon it is taking orders from foreign customers.

VoiceCo is concerned about its potential foreign income tax exposure. Although it has no assets or employees in the foreign jurisdictions, it now is involved in international commerce. Is VoiceCo subject to income taxes in foreign countries? Must it pay U.S. income taxes on the profits from its foreign sales? What if VoiceCo pays taxes to other countries? Does it receive any benefit from these payments on its U.S. tax return?

Suppose VoiceCo establishes a manufacturing plant in Ireland to meet the European demand for its products. VoiceCo incorporates the Irish operation as VoiceCo-Ireland, a foreign corporation. Ireland imposes only a 12.5 percent tax on VoiceCo-Ireland's profits. So long as VoiceCo-Ireland does not distribute profits to VoiceCo, will the profits escape U.S. taxation? What are the consequences to VoiceCo of being the owner of a so-called controlled foreign corporation? Does it have any reporting requirements with the IRS?

Read the chapter and formulate your response.

9.1 Overview of International Taxation

LO.1

Explain the framework underlying the U.S. taxation of cross-border transactions.

In today's global business environment, most large businesses are truly international in scope. Consider the most recent financial results of three "all-American" companies: Coca-Cola, Ford Motor Company, and Microsoft. Coca-Cola reported that 70 percent of its total net income is from offshore operations, Ford earned $1.2 billion in pretax profits from non-U.S. operations, and Microsoft earned 62 percent of its book net income before tax from operations outside the United States. Honda, a Japanese company, reported that 44 percent of its sales were in North America; Toyota, another Japanese company, earned 29 percent of its net revenues from automobile sales in North America.

Global trade is an integral part of the U.S. economy. In 2010, U.S. exports and imports of goods and services totaled $1.3 trillion and $1.9 trillion, respectively. This international trade creates significant U.S. tax consequences for both U.S. and foreign entities. In the most recent year for which data are available, U.S. corporations reported $350 billion in foreign-source income, paid $156 billion in income taxes to foreign governments, and claimed foreign tax credits in excess of $100 billion. U.S. corporations controlled by foreign owners reported $140 billion in U.S. taxable income.

Cross-border transactions create the need for special tax considerations for both the United States and its trading partners. From a U.S. perspective, international tax laws should promote the global competitiveness of U.S. enterprises and at the same time protect the tax revenue base of the United States. These two objectives sometimes conflict, however. The need to deal with both contributes to the complexity of the rules governing the U.S. taxation of cross-border transactions.

EXAMPLE 1

U.S. persons engage in activities outside the United States for many different reasons. Consider two U.S. corporations that have established sales subsidiaries in foreign countries. Dedalus, Inc., operates in Germany, a high-tax country, because customers demand local attention from sales agents. Mulligan, Inc., operates in the Cayman Islands, a low-tax country, simply to shift income outside the United States. U.S. tax law must fairly address both situations with the same law. ■

U.S. international tax provisions are concerned primarily with two types of potential taxpayers: U.S. persons earning foreign-source income and foreign persons earning U.S.-source income.[1] U.S. persons earning U.S.-source income are taxed under the purely domestic provisions of the Internal Revenue Code. Foreign persons earning foreign-source income are not within the taxing jurisdiction of the United States (unless this income is somehow connected to a U.S. trade or business). Figure 9.1 illustrates this categorization.

The United States taxes the worldwide income of U.S. taxpayers. Because foreign governments may also tax some of this income, these taxpayers may be subjected to double taxation. Special provisions such as the foreign tax credit can mitigate this problem. For non-U.S. taxpayers, the United States generally taxes only income earned within its borders. The U.S. taxation of cross-border transactions can be organized in terms of "outbound" and "inbound" taxation. **Outbound taxation** refers to the U.S. taxation of foreign-source income earned by U.S. taxpayers. **Inbound taxation** refers to the U.S. taxation of U.S.-source income earned by foreign taxpayers.

[1]The term *person* includes an individual, corporation, partnership, trust, estate, or association. § 7701(a)(1). The terms *domestic* and *foreign* are defined in §§ 7701(a)(4) and (5).

FIGURE 9.1 **U.S. Taxation of Cross-Border Transactions**

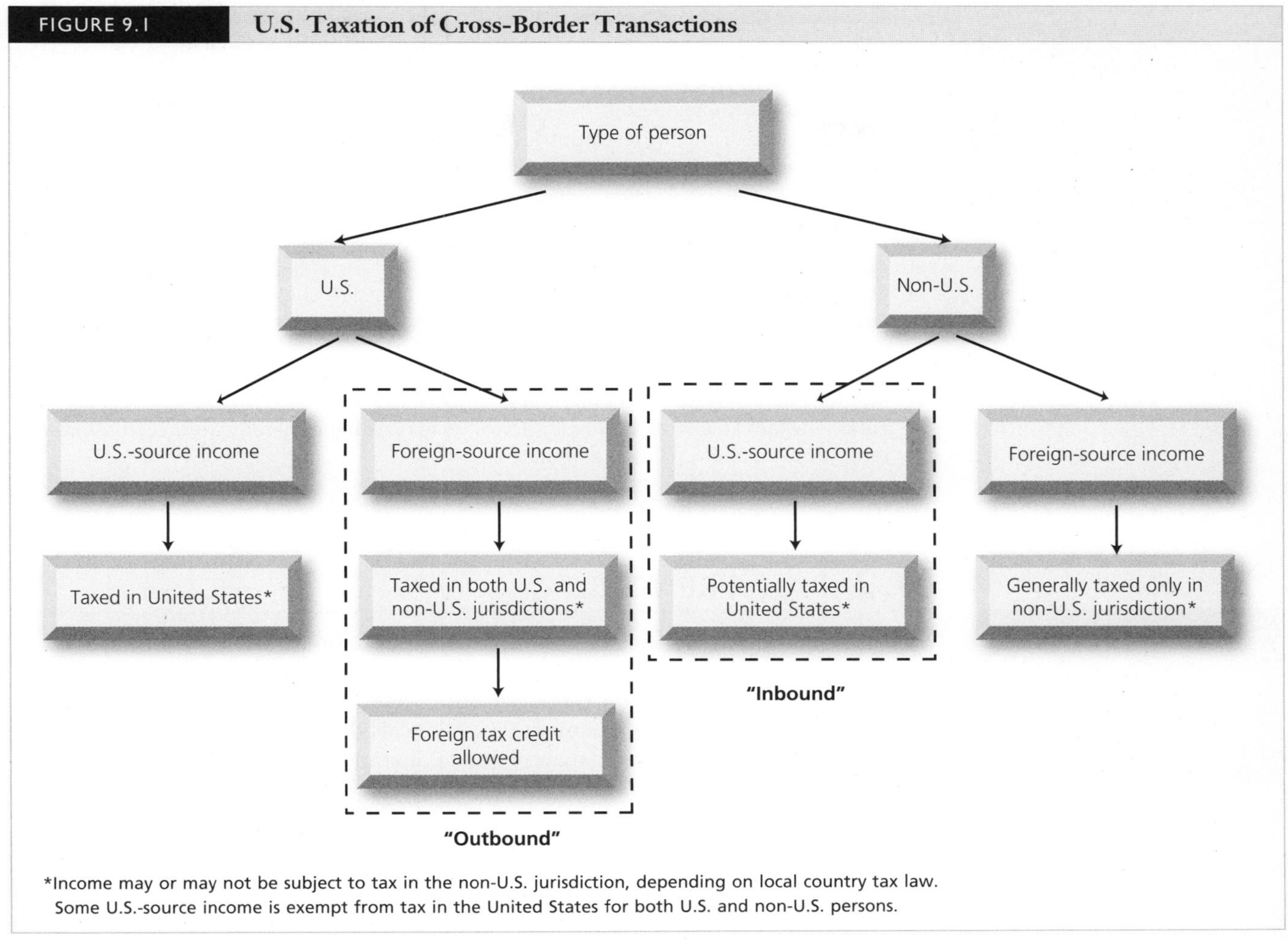

*Income may or may not be subject to tax in the non-U.S. jurisdiction, depending on local country tax law. Some U.S.-source income is exempt from tax in the United States for both U.S. and non-U.S. persons.

THE BIG PICTURE
EXAMPLE 2

Return to the facts of *The Big Picture* on p. 9-1. Assume that VoiceCo operates an unincorporated manufacturing branch in Singapore to take advantage of local materials and low labor costs. This branch income is taxed in the United States as part of VoiceCo's worldwide income, but it also is taxed in Singapore. Without the availability of a foreign tax credit to mitigate this double taxation, VoiceCo would suffer an excessive tax burden and could not compete in a global environment.

THE BIG PICTURE
EXAMPLE 3

Return to the facts of *The Big Picture* on p. 9-1. VoiceCo's major competitor is a Swiss-based foreign corporation with operations in the United States. Although not a U.S. person, the Swiss competitor is taxed in the United States on its U.S.-source business income. If the Swiss competitor could operate free of U.S. tax, VoiceCo would face a serious competitive disadvantage.

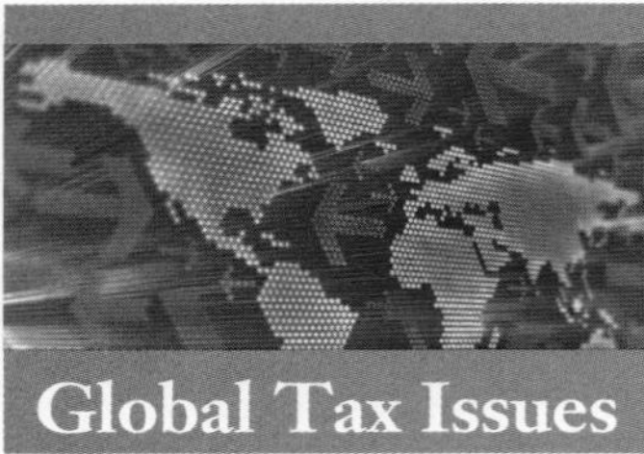

© Andrey Prokhorov, iStockphoto

Other Countries' Taxes Can Be Strange, Too

Some observers complain about the strange provisions or workings of the U.S. Federal income tax system, but other countries can be criticized in the same way. Much of Europe, for example, is less dependent on income taxes than is the United States and more dependent on transaction and wealth taxes, and these can take unusual forms. A quick survey of taxes around the globe finds the following.

- Australia: 68% tax on cigarette purchases.
- China: 80%–100% tax on purchase of autos built outside China.
- Costa Rica: 170% tax on purchase of poultry raised outside the country and 96% tax on purchase of foreign dairy products.
- Japan: 1,000% tax on purchase of rice grown outside the country.
- Sweden: 400% tax on purchase of hard liquor.
- Turkmenistan: 100% tax on luxury items, which include mineral water, cotton mittens, saws, blankets, pillows, and mattresses.

9.2 Tax Treaties

LO.2

Describe the interaction between Internal Revenue Code provisions and tax treaties.

The U.S. tax rules governing cross-border transactions are based on both the Internal Revenue Code and **tax treaties.** U.S. tax treaties are bilateral agreements between countries that provide tax relief for those persons covered by the treaties. Tax treaty provisions generally override the treatment otherwise called for under the Internal Revenue Code or foreign tax statutes. Taxpayers should attempt to resolve any conflicts between a treaty and local law. A common way of doing so is to apply the "later-in-time" rule, under which preference is given to whichever is newer, the treaty or the law.

Almost 70 income tax treaties between the United States and other countries are in effect (see Exhibit 9.1). These treaties generally provide *taxing rights* with regard to the taxable income of residents of one treaty country who have income sourced in the other treaty country. For the most part, neither country is prohibited from taxing the income of its residents. The treaties generally give one country primary taxing rights and require the other country to allow a credit for the taxes paid on the twice-taxed income.

EXAMPLE 4

ForCo, Ltd., a resident of a foreign country with which the United States has an income tax treaty, earns income attributable to a permanent establishment (e.g., place of business) in the United States. Under the treaty, the United States has primary taxing rights with regard to this income. The other country can also require that the income be included in gross income and can subject the income to its income tax, but it must allow a credit for the taxes paid to the United States on the income. ■

Which country receives primary taxing rights usually depends on the residence of the taxpayer or the presence of a permanent establishment in a treaty country to which the income is attributable. Generally, a permanent establishment is a branch, an office, a factory, a workshop, a warehouse, or another fixed place of business.

Most U.S. income tax treaties reduce the withholding tax rate on certain items of investment income, such as interest and dividends. For example, treaties with France and Sweden reduce the withholding on portfolio dividends to 15 percent and on certain interest income to zero. Many newer treaties (e.g., with the United Kingdom, Australia, and Japan) provide for no withholding on dividend payments to parent corporations. The United States has developed a Model Income Tax Convention as the starting point for negotiating income tax treaties with other countries.[2]

[2]Treasury Department Model Income Tax Convention (November 15, 2006).

FINANCIAL DISCLOSURE INSIGHTS Effective Tax Strategies Using Overseas Operations

In a global economy, publicly traded business entities can operate in many taxing jurisdictions. For instance, General Electric reports that it files current-year tax returns with more than 250 countries, amounting to over 7,000 income tax returns at the Federal and local levels worldwide. Note that this tax activity does not take into account the sales, value added, property, and other tax returns that are required by the U.S. states and localities.

The financial reports of profitable U.S. companies indicate that overseas operations can produce tax benefits of their own, not taking into account the effects of increased market share and financial stability. For instance, the trucking firm Ryder Systems recently reported current tax refunds of about $235,000 and deferred tax savings of about $500,000 on non-U.S. profits of about $11.5 million. In a recent period, Eli Lilly reduced its effective tax rate by about one-third due to overseas operations. And General Electric recently reduced its effective tax rate to a negative amount because of various income deferrals related to overseas earnings. We will address these deferral techniques later in the chapter.

9.3 Sourcing of Income and Deductions

LO.3

Apply the rules for sourcing income and deductions into U.S. and foreign categories.

The sourcing of income and deductions inside and outside the United States has a direct bearing on a number of tax provisions affecting both U.S. and foreign taxpayers. For example, foreign taxpayers generally are taxed only on income sourced inside the United States, and U.S. taxpayers receive relief from double taxation under the foreign tax credit rules based on their foreign-source income. Accordingly, an examination of sourcing rules is often the starting point in addressing international tax issues.

EXHIBIT 9.1 U.S. Income Tax Treaties in Force as of 2011

Australia	France	Lithuania	Slovenia
Austria	Germany	Luxembourg	South Africa
Bangladesh	Greece	Malta	Spain
Barbados	Hungary	Mexico	Sri Lanka
Belgium	Iceland	Morocco	Sweden
Bulgaria	India	Netherlands	Switzerland
Canada	Indonesia	New Zealand	Thailand
China	Ireland	Norway	Trinidad
Commonwealth of Independent States*	Israel	Pakistan	Tunisia
	Italy	Philippines	Turkey
Cyprus	Jamaica	Poland	United Kingdom
Czech Republic	Japan	Portugal	Venezuela
Denmark	Kazakhstan	Romania	
Egypt	Korea, Republic of	Russia	
Estonia	Latvia	Slovak Republic	
Finland			

*The income tax treaty between the United States and the former Soviet Union (USSR) applies to the countries of Armenia, Azerbaijan, Belarus, Georgia, Kyrgyzstan, Moldova, Tajikistan, Turkmenistan, Ukraine, and Uzbekistan. The Commonwealth of Independent States is an association of many of the former constituent republics of the Soviet Union.

Income Sourced inside the United States

The determination of the source of income depends on the type of income realized (e.g., income from the sale of property versus income for the use of property).[3]

Interest

Interest income received from the U.S. government, from the District of Columbia, and from noncorporate U.S. residents or domestic corporations is sourced inside the United States.

There are a few exceptions to this rule. Certain interest received from a U.S. corporation that earned 80 percent or more of its active business income from foreign sources over the prior three-year period is treated as foreign-source income. Interest received on amounts deposited with a foreign branch of a U.S. corporation also is treated as foreign-source income if the branch is engaged in the commercial banking business.

EXAMPLE 5

John holds a bond issued by Delta, a domestic corporation. For the immediately preceding three tax years, 82% of Delta's gross income has been active foreign business income. The interest income that John receives for the current tax year from Delta is foreign-source income. ■

Dividends

Dividends received from domestic corporations (other than certain U.S. possessions corporations) are sourced inside the United States. Generally, dividends paid by a foreign corporation are foreign-source income. However, if a foreign corporation earned 25 percent or more of its gross income from income effectively connected with a U.S. trade or business for the three tax years immediately preceding the year of the dividend payment, that percentage of the dividend is treated as U.S. source income.

EXAMPLE 6

Ann receives dividend income from the following corporations for the current tax year.

Amount	Corporation	Effectively Connected U.S. Income for Past Three Years	U.S.-Source Income
$500	Green, domestic	85%	$500
600	Brown, domestic	13%	600
300	Orange, foreign	92%	276

Because Green Corporation and Brown Corporation are domestic corporations, the dividends they pay are U.S.-source income. Orange Corporation is a foreign corporation that earned 92% of its business income over the prior three years from income effectively connected with a U.S. trade or business. Because Orange meets the 25% threshold, 92% of its dividend is U.S. source. ■

Personal Services Income

The source of income from personal services is determined by the location in which the services are performed (inside or outside the United States). A limited *commercial traveler* exception is available. Under this exception, personal services

[3]Rules pertaining to the sourcing of income are found in §§ 861–865.

Why the Treaty Process Stalls

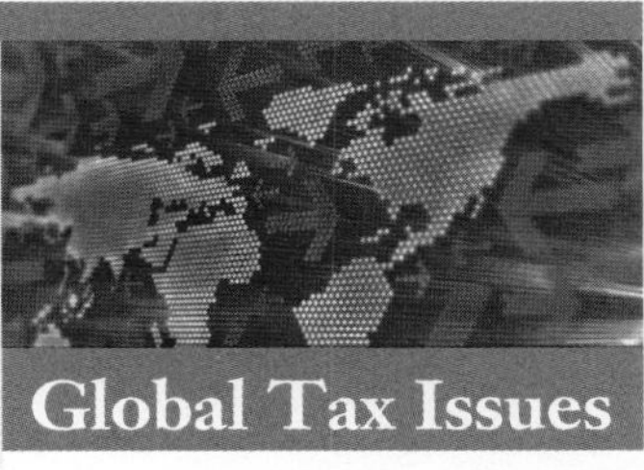

© Andrey Prokhorov, iStockphoto

The United States has negotiated several income tax treaties that have never been signed or ratified (e.g., with Argentina, Bangladesh, and Brazil). The treaty process sometimes stalls for several reasons.

Some less developed countries want a tax-sparing provision in the treaty. In other words, these countries want the United States to allow a foreign tax credit against U.S. taxes even though U.S. companies operating there actually pay no foreign taxes due to local tax holidays.

Another reason is the exchange of information provision. Some countries, for example, have anonymous bank rules that would preclude the exchange of information. Not long ago, the Parliament of Kazakhstan voted on a provision to eliminate secret bank accounts so that the United States–Kazakhstan income tax treaty could be ratified.

income must meet all the following requirements to avoid being classified as U.S.-source income.

- The services must be performed by a nonresident alien who is in the United States for 90 days or less during the taxable year.
- The compensation may not exceed $3,000 in total for the services performed in the United States.
- The services must be performed on behalf of:
  - a nonresident alien, foreign partnership, or foreign corporation that is not engaged in a U.S. trade or business or
  - an office or place of business maintained in a foreign country or possession of the United States by an individual who is a citizen or resident of the United States, a domestic partnership, or a domestic corporation.

EXAMPLE 7

Mark, a nonresident alien, is an engineer employed by a foreign oil company. He spent four weeks in the United States arranging the purchase of field equipment for his company. His salary for the four weeks was $3,500. Even though the oil company is not engaged in a U.S. trade or business and Mark was in the United States for less than 90 days during the taxable year, the income is U.S.-source income because it exceeds $3,000. ■

The issue of whether income is derived from the performance of personal services is important in determining the income's source. The courts have held that a corporation can perform personal services.[4] In addition, in the absence of capital as an income-producing factor, personal services income can arise even though there is no recipient of the services.[5] If payment is received for services performed partly inside and partly outside the United States, the income is sourced on some reasonable basis that clearly reflects income under the facts and circumstances. The number of days worked in each country generally is an acceptable measure.[6]

Rents and Royalties

Income received for the use of tangible property is sourced to the country in which the property is located. The source of income received for the use of intangible

[4]See *British Timken Limited*, 12 T.C. 880 (1949), and Rev.Rul. 60–55, 1960–1 C.B. 270.

[5]See *Robida v. Comm.*, 72–1 USTC ¶9450, 29 AFTR 2d 72–1223, 460 F.2d 1172 (CA–9, 1972). The taxpayer was employed in military PXs around the world. He generated large slot machine winnings and claimed the foreign earned income exclusion. The IRS challenged the exclusion on the grounds that the winnings were not earned income because there was no recipient of Robida's services. The court, however, found that, in the absence of capital, the winnings were earned income.

[6]Reg. § 1.861–4(b). See *Stemkowski*, 76 T.C. 252 (1981).

property (e.g., patents, copyrights, and secret processes and formulas) is the country in which the property is used.

Sale or Exchange of Property

Generally, the location of real property determines the source of any income derived from the property. Income from the disposition of U.S. real property interests is U.S.-source income.

The source of income from the sale of personal property (assets other than real property) depends on several factors, including the following:

- Whether the property was produced by the seller.
- What type of property was sold (e.g., inventory or a capital asset).
- Where the residence of the seller was.

Generally, income, gain, or profit from the sale of personal property is sourced according to the residence of the seller. Income from the sale of purchased inventory, however, is sourced in the country in which the sale takes place.[7]

When the seller has produced the inventory property, the income must be apportioned between the country of production and the country of sale. Gross income is sourced under a 50/50 allocation method unless the taxpayer elects to use the independent factory price (IFP) method or the separate books and records method. The 50/50 method assigns one-half of the inventory profits from export sales to the location of the production assets and one-half to the place of title passage. The IFP method may be elected only where an IFP exists.[8] If the manufacturer or producer regularly sells to wholly independent distributors, this can establish an *independent* factory or production price.

Under § 865, income from the sale of personal property other than inventory is sourced at the residence of the seller unless one of the following exceptions applies.

- Gain on the sale of depreciable personal property is sourced according to prior depreciation deductions to the extent of the deductions. Any excess gain is sourced the same as the sale of inventory.
- Gain on the sale of intangibles is sourced according to prior amortization deductions to the extent of the deductions. Contingent payments, however, are sourced as royalty income.
- Gain attributable to an office or a fixed place of business maintained outside the United States by a U.S. resident is foreign-source income.
- Income or gain attributable to an office or a fixed place of business maintained in the United States by a nonresident is U.S.-source income.

Losses are sourced depending on the nature of the property. Different rules exist for the disposition of stock versus other personal property.[9]

Transportation and Communication Income

Income from transportation beginning *and* ending in the United States is U.S.-source income. Fifty percent of the income from transportation beginning *or* ending in the United States is U.S.-source income, unless the U.S. point is only an intermediate stop. Income from space and ocean activities conducted outside the jurisdiction of any country is sourced according to the residence of the person conducting the activity.

International communication income derived by a U.S. person is sourced 50 percent in the United States when transmission is between the United States and a foreign country. International communication income derived by foreign

[7] §§ 861(a)(6) and 865. The sale is deemed to take place where title passes. See Reg. § 1.861–7(c) regarding title passage. There has been considerable conflict in this area of tax law. See, for example, *Liggett Group, Inc.*, 58 TCM 1167, T.C.Memo. 1990–18.

[8] § 863(b)(2), Reg. § 1.863–3, and Notice 89–10, 1989–1 C.B. 631.

[9] See Reg. § 1.861–8(e)(7) and Temp.Reg. § 1.865–1T(a)(1). See Reg. §§ 1.865–(2)(a)(1) and (2) regarding the source of losses on the disposition of stock.

TAX IN THE NEWS Sourcing Income in Cyberspace

The use of the Internet for more and more consumer and business transactions is posing problems for the taxing authorities. Consumers purchase books, music, clothing, and food from online retailers. Businesses negotiate with suppliers via online auctions of products and services. Consultants provide services to their clients over the Internet. Very few transactions do not have a counterpart that takes place in cyberspace. The existing income-sourcing rules were developed long before the existence of the Internet, and taxing authorities are finding it challenging to apply these rules to Internet transactions.

Where does a sale take place when the web server is in the Cayman Islands, the seller is in Singapore, and the customer is in Texas? Where is a service performed when all activities take place online? These questions and more must be answered by the United States and its trading partners as e-commerce grows in size and importance.

persons is foreign-source income unless it is attributable to an office or another fixed place of business in the United States. In that case, it is U.S.-source income.

Software Income

Income from the sale or license of software is sourced depending on how the income is classified. A transfer of software is classified as either the transfer of a copyright (e.g., the right to the computer program itself) or the transfer of a copyrighted article (the right to use a copy of the computer program).[10] If the transfer is considered a transfer of a copyright, the income is sourced using the royalty income rules. If the transfer is considered a transfer of a copyrighted article, the income is treated as resulting from a sale of the article and is sourced based on the personal property sales rules.

Income Sourced outside the United States

The provisions for sourcing income outside the United States are not as detailed and specific as those for determining U.S.-source income. Basically, § 862 provides that if interest, dividends, compensation for personal services, income from the use or sale of property, or other income is not U.S.-source income, then it is foreign-source income.

Allocation and Apportionment of Deductions

The United States levies a tax on *taxable income.* Deductions and losses, therefore, must be allocated and apportioned between U.S.- and foreign-source gross income to determine U.S.- and foreign-source taxable income. Deductions directly related to an activity or property are allocated to classes of income. This is followed by apportionment between the statutory and residual groupings (e.g., foreign versus domestic) on some reasonable basis.[11] A deduction not definitely related to any class of gross income is ratably allocated to all classes of gross income and apportioned between U.S.- and foreign-source income.

EXAMPLE 8

Ace, Inc., a domestic corporation, has $2 million gross income and a $50,000 expense, all related to real estate activities. The expense is allocated and apportioned using gross income as a basis as follows.

[10] Reg. § 1.861–18.

[11] Reg. § 1.861–8.

	Gross Income			Apportionment	
	Foreign	U.S.	Allocation	Foreign	U.S.
Sales	$1,000,000	$500,000	$37,500*	$25,000	$12,500**
Rentals	400,000	100,000	12,500	10,000	2,500***
			$50,000	$35,000	$15,000

* $50,000 × ($1,500,000/$2,000,000).
** $37,500 × ($500,000/$1,500,000).
*** $12,500 × ($100,000/$500,000).

If Ace could show that $45,000 of the expense was directly related to sales income, the $45,000 would be allocated to that class of gross income, with the remainder allocated and apportioned ratably based on gross income. ■

Interest expense is allocated and apportioned based on the theory that money is fungible. With limited exceptions, interest expense is attributable to all of the activities and property of the taxpayer, regardless of the specific purpose for incurring the debt on which interest is paid. Taxpayers allocate and apportion interest expense on the basis of assets, using either the fair market value or the tax book value of the assets.[12] Special rules apply in allocating and apportioning interest expense in an affiliated group of corporations.

THE BIG PICTURE
EXAMPLE 9

Return to the facts of *The Big Picture* on p. 9-1. Assume that VoiceCo generates U.S.-source and foreign-source gross income for the current year. VoiceCo's assets (measured at tax book value) are as follows:

Assets generating U.S.-source income	$18,000,000
Assets generating foreign-source income	5,000,000
	$23,000,000

VoiceCo incurs interest expense of $800,000 for the current year. Using the tax book value method, interest expense is apportioned to foreign-source income as follows:

$$\frac{\$5{,}000{,}000 \text{ (foreign assets)}}{\$23{,}000{,}000 \text{ (total assets)}} \times \$800{,}000 = \$173{,}913$$

Specific rules also apply to research and development (R&D) expenditures, certain stewardship expenses, legal and accounting fees and expenses, income taxes, and losses. Although U.S. companies incur about 90 percent of their R&D expenditures at U.S. facilities, several billion dollars are spent on foreign R&D each year. The Regulations provide that a portion of a U.S. company's R&D expenditures is treated as foreign-source expense if the R&D relates to foreign product sales.

Transfer Pricing

Taxpayers may be tempted to minimize taxation by manipulating the source of income and the allocation of deductions arbitrarily through **transfer pricing**. This manipulation is more easily accomplished between or among related persons. The IRS uses § 482 to counter such actions. The provision gives the IRS the power to

[12] Reg. § 1.861–9T. Reg. § 1.861–10T(b) describes circumstances in which interest expense can be directly allocated to specific debt. This exception to the fungibility concept is limited to cases in which specific property is purchased or improved with nonrecourse debt.

reallocate gross income, deductions, credits, or allowances between or among organizations, trades, or businesses owned or controlled directly or indirectly by the same interests. This can be done whenever the IRS determines that reallocation is necessary to prevent the evasion of taxes or to reflect income more clearly. Section 482 is a "one-edged sword" available only to the IRS. The taxpayer generally cannot invoke § 482 to reallocate income and expenses.[13]

ETHICS & EQUITY When Can 1 + 1 = 3?

Pharma, Inc., a U.S. pharmaceutical company, operates in the United States and in Ireland through a wholly owned Irish subsidiary corporation. Pharma manufactures certain aspects of a drug in the United States at a cost of $50 million and sells this product to its Irish subsidiary for $70 million, producing a $20 million profit in the United States. The Irish subsidiary completes the manufacturing of the drug at a cost of $10 million and sells the final product to unrelated customers in Europe for $85 million, producing a $5 million profit in Ireland [$85 million sales price − $70 million cost of goods sold (purchased inventory) − $10 million additional processing costs]. In the aggregate, Pharma and its Irish subsidiary have produced a product at a cost of $60 million and sold it for $85 million, resulting in $25 million in total profits.

What if the IRS decides that the transfer price of $70 million was too low and should have been $74 million? This would indicate that $24 million of the profit should have been in the United States and $1 million in Ireland. Should the tax authorities in Ireland automatically make the transfer pricing adjustment on their side (i.e., reduce the Irish subsidiary's income to $1 million from $5 million)? What if the IRS and the Irish tax authorities disagree and Pharma and its subsidiary end up paying tax on $29 million in profits ($24 million in the United States and $5 million in Ireland) even though only $25 million of economic profits actually exist? Is this fair to the taxpayer? What recourse should Pharma have when it is caught between two governments that disagree?

EXAMPLE 10

Consider the transaction depicted in Figure 9.2. A U.S. corporation manufactures and sells inventory to an unrelated foreign customer. The sales price for the inventory is $1,000, and the related cost of goods sold (COGS) is $600. All of the resulting profit of $400 is taxed to the U.S. corporation, resulting in a $140 U.S. income tax liability ($400 × 35%). If the U.S. corporation has no business presence in the foreign jurisdiction and is merely selling to a customer located there, the foreign government is unlikely to impose any local income tax on the U.S. corporation. Consequently, the total tax burden imposed on the inventory sale is $140.

Suppose instead that the U.S. corporation attempts to reduce its total tax expense by channeling the inventory sale through a foreign subsidiary in the same country as the foreign customer. In this case, because the U.S. corporation controls the foreign subsidiary, it chooses an intercompany sales price (the transfer price) that moves a portion of the profits from the United States to the foreign country.

By selling the inventory it manufactured to its 100%-owned foreign subsidiary for $700, the U.S. corporation reports only $100 of profits and an associated U.S. tax liability of $35. The foreign subsidiary then sells the inventory to the ultimate customer for $1,000 and, with a $700 COGS, earns a $300 profit. In this example, the foreign country imposes only a 10% tax on corporate profits, resulting in a foreign income tax of $30 ($300 × 10%). By using a related foreign entity in a lower-tax jurisdiction, the U.S. corporation has lowered its overall tax liability on the sale from $140 (all U.S.) to $65 ($35 U.S. and $30 foreign).

The critical question is whether the IRS will view $700 as the appropriate transfer price. The IRS may question why the foreign corporation deserved to earn $300 of the total $400 profit related to the manufacture and sale of the inventory. In general, the U.S.

[13]Reg. § 1.482–1(a)(3).

FIGURE 9.2 **Transfer Pricing Example**

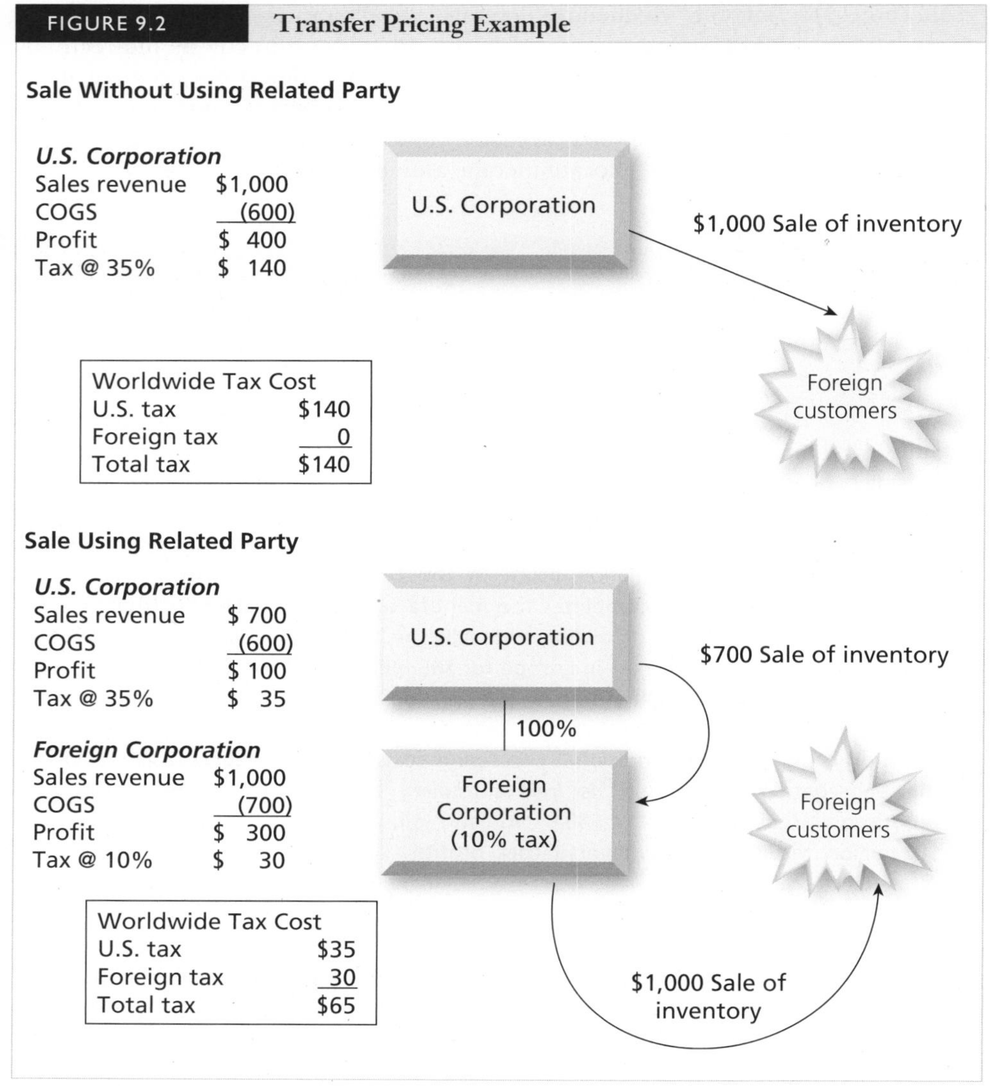

corporation must document the functions performed by the foreign corporation, the assets it owns that assist in producing the income, or the risks it takes (e.g., credit risk).

If the IRS does not consider the $300 profit earned by the foreign corporation to be appropriate, it will adjust the transfer price upward. If the IRS determines that the transfer price should have been, for example, $990, then the U.S. corporation reports a $390 profit (with $136.50 U.S. income tax) and the foreign corporation earns a $10 profit (with $1 in foreign income tax). With this change in transfer price, the U.S. corporation reduces its tax liability by only $2.50 [$140 − ($136.50 + $1)]. ■

An accuracy-related penalty of 20 percent is provided by § 6662 for net § 482 transfer price adjustments (changes in profit allocations by the IRS) for a taxable year that exceed the lesser of $5 million or 10 percent of the taxpayer's gross receipts. In addition, there is a 40 percent penalty for "gross misstatements."

As an aid to reducing pricing disputes, the IRS initiated the Advance Pricing Agreement (APA) program, whereby the taxpayer can propose a transfer pricing method for certain international transactions. The taxpayer provides relevant data, which are then evaluated by the IRS. If accepted, the APA provides a safe-harbor transfer pricing method for the taxpayer.[14]

[14]Apple Computer, Inc., accomplished the first successful APA submission in 1991.

TAX IN THE NEWS APAs Reduce Uncertainty in Transfer Pricing Disputes

An advanced pricing agreement (APA) is a contract between a taxpayer and one or more government bodies. For a set of transactions over a specified period of time, the contract specifies the methods by which transfer prices will be set by the taxpayer and allowed to stand by the taxing authority. APAs can be complex in their application, and they may take three or four years to negotiate fully.

An APA is a voluntary arrangement, and not every taxing authority approves every APA application it receives. Sometimes, the complexity of the arrangement prevents the possibility of developing an APA. A basic transfer pricing formula might adopt an arm's length price for the transaction, but that approach requires that there exist comparable transactions involving other parties.

The attraction of an APA is that the risk of an extended tax audit, with its steep associated costs, is nearly eliminated. As long as the taxpayer conducts the transaction as described in the APA application materials, the specified pricing methods should be allowed by the government bodies.

Only 10 percent of the largest taxpayers involved in international intercompany transactions have participated in the APA process. However, the volume of intercompany transactions represented by these taxpayers constitutes over 40 percent of the total dollar value of international intercompany transactions. About 10 percent of all active APA cases involve small businesses with annual gross income under $200 million.

9.4 Foreign Currency Transactions

LO.4

Apply foreign currency exchange rules as they affect the tax consequences of international transactions.

The relative value of a foreign currency and the U.S. dollar is described by the foreign exchange rate. Changes in this rate affect the dollar value of foreign property held by the taxpayer, the dollar value of foreign debts, and the dollar amount of gain or loss on a transaction denominated in a foreign currency. Almost every international tax issue requires consideration of currency exchange implications.

EXAMPLE 11

Dress, Inc., a domestic corporation, purchases merchandise for resale from Fiesta, Inc., a foreign corporation, for 50,000K (a foreign currency). On the date of purchase, 1K is equal to $1 U.S. (1K:$1). At this time, the account payable is $50,000. On the date of payment by Dress (the foreign exchange date), the exchange rate is 1.25K:$1. In other words, the foreign currency has been devalued in relation to the U.S. dollar, and Dress will pay Fiesta 50,000K, which will cost Dress only $40,000. Dress must record the purchase of the merchandise at $50,000 and recognize a foreign currency gain of $10,000 ($50,000 − $40,000). ■

In recent years, U.S. currency abroad has amounted to more than 50 percent of the U.S. currency in circulation. Taxpayers may find it necessary to translate amounts denominated in foreign currency into U.S. dollars for any of the following purposes.

- Purchase of goods, services, and property.
- Sale of goods, services, and property.
- Collection of foreign receivables.
- Payment of foreign payables.
- Foreign tax credit calculations.
- Recognition of income or loss from foreign branch activities.

The foreign currency exchange rates, however, have no effect on the transactions of a U.S. person who arranges all international transactions in U.S. dollars.

EXAMPLE 12

Sellers, Inc., a domestic corporation, purchases goods from Rose, Ltd., a foreign corporation, and pays for these goods in U.S. dollars. Rose then exchanges the U.S. dollars for the currency of the country in which it operates. Sellers has no foreign exchange

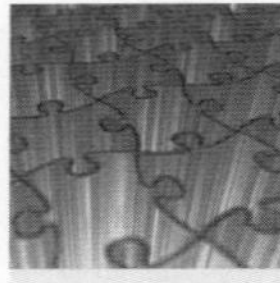

CONCEPT SUMMARY 9.1

Recognition of Foreign Exchange Gain or Loss

Transaction	Date of Recognition
Purchase or sale of inventory or business asset	Date of disposition of foreign currency
Branch profits	Remittance of branch profits
Subpart F income	Receipt of previously taxed income (accumulated E & P)
Dividend from untaxed current or accumulated E & P	No exchange gain or loss to recipient

considerations with which to contend. If instead Rose required Sellers to pay for the goods in a foreign currency, Sellers would have to exchange U.S. dollars to obtain the foreign currency to make payment. If the exchange rate changed from the date of purchase to the date of payment, Sellers would have a foreign currency gain or loss on the currency exchange. ■

The following concepts are important when dealing with the tax aspects of foreign exchange.

- Foreign currency is treated as property other than money.
- Gain or loss on the exchange of foreign currency is considered separately from the underlying transaction (e.g., the purchase or sale of goods).
- No gain or loss is recognized until a transaction is closed.

Tax Issues

The following major tax issues must be considered when dealing with foreign currency exchange.

- The date of recognition of any gain or loss (see Concept Summary 9.1).
- The source (U.S. or foreign) of the foreign currency gain or loss.
- The character of the gain or loss (ordinary or capital).

Functional Currency

The Code generally adopted the Financial Accounting Standards Board's **functional currency** approach.[15] For accounting and tax purposes, the currency of the economic environment in which the foreign entity operates generally is used as the monetary unit to measure gains and losses.

All income tax determinations are made in the taxpayer's functional currency.[16] A taxpayer's default functional currency is the U.S. dollar. In most cases, a **qualified business unit (QBU)** operating in a foreign country uses that country's currency as its functional currency. A QBU is a separate and clearly identified unit of a taxpayer's trade or business (e.g., a foreign branch).[17]

Branch Operations

When a foreign branch (QBU) uses a foreign currency as its functional currency, profit or loss is computed in the foreign currency and translated into U.S. dollars for tax purposes. The entire amount of profit or loss, not taking remittances into account, is translated using the average exchange rate for the taxable year. Exchange gain or loss is recognized upon remittances from the QBU. This

[15] ASC 830 (SFAS 52).

[16] § 985.

[17] Reg. § 1.989(a)–1(b). An individual is not a QBU; however, a trade or business conducted by an individual may be a QBU.

FINANCIAL DISCLOSURE INSIGHTS Tax Rates in Non-U.S. Jurisdictions

When Congress changes the U.S. tax law, it seldom applies tax rate changes retroactively or prospectively—the rate changes almost always are applicable on the date the tax bill is effective. Other countries do not always enact tax law changes in this way. Sometimes a country will adopt a schedule of tax rate increases or decreases to go into effect over a period of years.

Tax legislation of this sort can have an important effect on the U.S. taxpayer's effective tax rate as computed in the footnotes to the financial statements. When another country adopts prospective tax rate changes, an increase or a decrease in the effective tax rate is reported with respect to the deferred tax accounts for GAAP purposes. Specifically, the effective tax rate decreases when a tax rate cut is scheduled in a country that does business with the U.S. party, and the rate increases when a tax rate increase is adopted for future tax years. In the last three decades, most developed countries have been cutting business income tax rates.

A recent effective tax rate computation for Berkshire Hathaway showed a decrease of about one percentage point due to scheduled tax rate cuts in Germany and the United Kingdom. Allied Healthcare Products showed a similar adjustment of about two percentage points. In contrast, the effective tax rate increased by about one percentage point for American Travellers Life Insurance Company.

exchange gain or loss is ordinary, and it is sourced according to the income to which the remittance is attributable.

Distributions from Foreign Corporations

An actual distribution of E & P from a foreign corporation is included in gross income by the U.S. recipient at the exchange rate in effect on the date of distribution.[18] Thus, no exchange gain or loss is recognized.

Deemed dividend distributions under Subpart F (discussed later in the chapter) are translated at the average exchange rate for the corporation's tax year to which the deemed distribution is attributable. Exchange gain or loss can result when an actual distribution of this previously taxed income is made.

Foreign Taxes

For purposes of the foreign tax credit, foreign taxes accrued generally are translated at the average exchange rate for the tax year to which the taxes relate. Under exceptions to this rule, foreign taxes are translated at the exchange rate in effect when the foreign taxes were paid.[19]

9.5 U.S. Persons with Foreign Income

LO.5

Work with the U.S. tax provisions affecting U.S. persons earning foreign-source income, including the rules relating to cross-border asset transfers, antideferral provisions, and the foreign tax credit.

U.S. taxpayers often "internationalize" gradually over time. A U.S. business may operate on a strictly domestic basis for several years, then explore foreign markets by exporting its products abroad, and later license its products to a foreign manufacturer or enter into a joint venture with a foreign partner. If its forays into foreign markets are successful, the U.S. business may create a foreign subsidiary and move a portion of its operations abroad by establishing a sales or manufacturing facility.

A domestically controlled foreign corporation can have significant U.S. tax consequences for the U.S. owners, and any U.S. taxpayer paying foreign taxes must consider the foreign tax credit provisions. Foreign businesses likewise enter the U.S. market in stages. In either case, each step generates increasingly significant international tax consequences. Figure 9.3 shows a typical timeline for "going global."

[18] § 986(b).

[19] §§ 986(a)(1)(B) and (C).

FIGURE 9.3 **Global Activities Timeline**

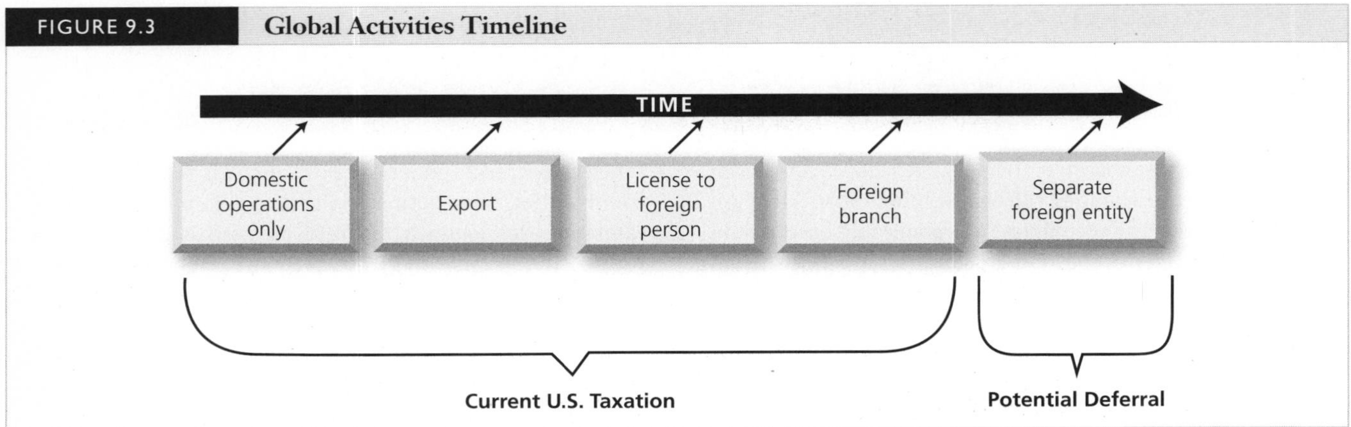

THE BIG PICTURE

EXAMPLE 13

Return to the facts of *The Big Picture* on p. 9-1. It appears that VoiceCo is moving along the Figure 9.3 Global Activities Timeline, in that it is making export sales, and it is considering a more permanent presence overseas.

Export Property

The easiest way for a U.S. enterprise to engage in global commerce is simply to sell U.S.-produced goods and services abroad. These sales can be conducted with little or no foreign presence and allow the business to explore foreign markets without making costly financial commitments to foreign operations.

The U.S. tax consequences of simple export sales are straightforward. All such income is taxed in the United States to the U.S. taxpayer. Whether foreign taxes must be paid on this export income depends on the laws of the particular foreign jurisdiction and whether the U.S. taxpayer is deemed to have a foreign business presence there (often called a "permanent establishment"). In many cases, such export income is not taxed by a foreign jurisdiction.

Cross-Border Asset Transfers

As part of "going international," a U.S. taxpayer may decide to transfer assets outside the United States so that any foreign business will be conducted outside the U.S. tax jurisdiction. To originate investment through, or transfer investment to, a foreign entity, the U.S. taxpayer must make some sort of transfer to the foreign entity. This may take the form of a cash investment or a transfer of assets of a U.S. entity.

In situations where potential taxable income is transferred to a corporation outside the U.S. taxing jurisdiction, the exchange may trigger a tax. The tax result of transferring property to a foreign corporation depends on the nature of the exchange, the assets involved, the income potential of the property, and the character of the property in the hands of the transferor or transferee. Figure 9.4 summarizes the taxation of cross-border asset transfers.

Outbound Transfers

As discussed in Chapters 6 and 7, when assets are exchanged for corporate stock in a domestic transaction, realized gain or loss may be deferred rather than recognized. Similarly, deferral treatment may be available when the following "outbound" capital

FIGURE 9.4 **Taxation of Cross-Border Asset Transfers**

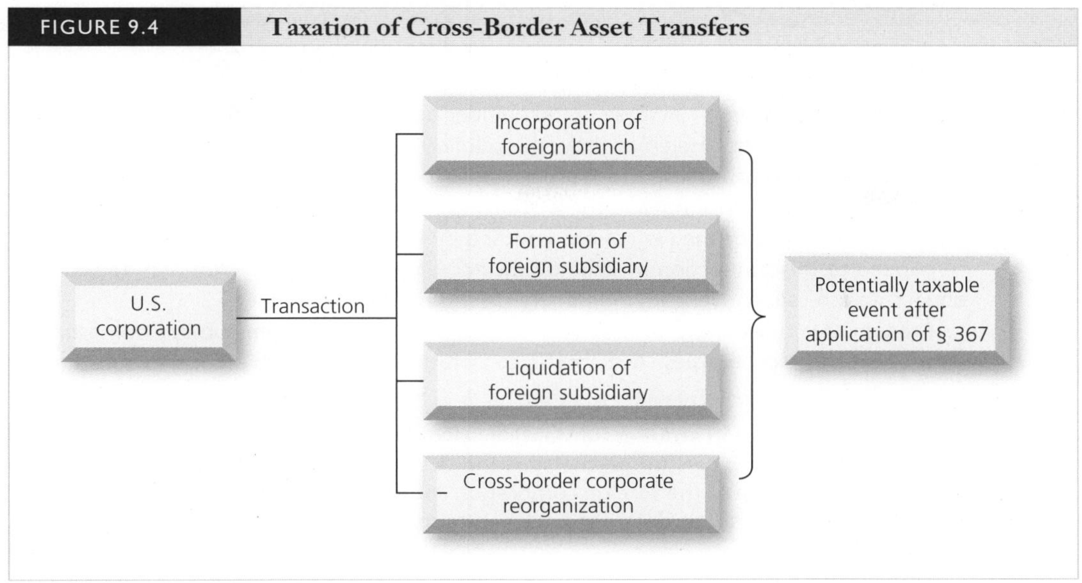

changes occur (i.e., moving corporate business across country borders and outside the United States).

- A U.S. corporation starts up a new corporation outside the U.S. (§ 351).
- A U.S. corporation liquidates a U.S. subsidiary into an existing foreign subsidiary (§ 332).
- A U.S. corporation incorporates a non-U.S. branch of a U.S. corporation, forming a new foreign corporation (§ 351).
- A foreign corporation uses a stock swap to acquire a U.S. corporation (Type "B" reorganization).
- A foreign corporation acquires substantially all of a U.S. corporation's net assets (Type "C" reorganization).

These otherwise tax-deferred transactions may trigger current taxation when foreign corporations are involved. Under § 367, the general rule is that gain deferral is not allowed when assets are leaving the U.S. taxing jurisdiction. However, a major exception allows continued tax deferral for assets transferred to a foreign corporation to be used in a trade or business carried on outside the United States.

The trade or business exception does not apply to certain "tainted" assets, and the transfer of these assets outside the United States triggers immediate gain (but not loss) recognition. The following are "tainted" assets for this purpose.

- Inventory (raw goods, work-in-progress, and finished goods).
- Installment obligations and unrealized accounts receivable.
- Foreign currency.
- Property leased by the transferor unless the transferee is the lessee.

These tainted assets are likely to turn over quickly once the asset transfer is completed, and any appreciation is likely to be recognized outside the U.S. taxing jurisdiction. Consequently, § 367 requires recognition of this gain upon transfer of the asset outside the United States.

EXAMPLE 14

Amelia, Inc., a domestic corporation, incorporates its profitable Irish manufacturing branch and creates a new wholly owned foreign corporation, St. George, Ltd., to engage in manufacturing activities in Ireland. The transfer qualifies as tax deferred

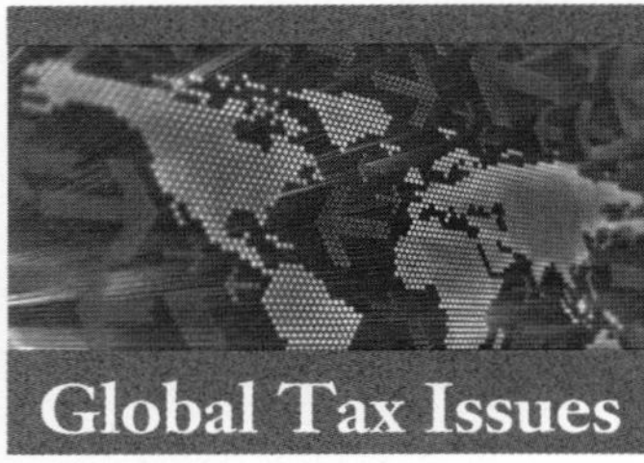

© Andrey Prokhorov, iStockphoto

Boom in Cross-Border Mergers but No Inversions

Recent years have seen an increase in the number of tax-deferred mergers taking place across national borders. Helen of Troy, the publicly traded cosmetics giant, converted itself from a U.S. corporation into a tax haven corporation without triggering any tax for its shareholders. Once outside the U.S. taxing jurisdiction, the "inverted" company was free from many of the restrictions imposed by U.S. tax law. U.S. taxing authorities responded to this transaction by issuing new Regulations [Reg. § 1.367(a)–3(c)] to shut down these so-called inversions unless very strict standards were met.

Even stricter rules apply to deter shareholders or partners from turning domestic entities into foreign entities. A domestic corporation or partnership continues to be treated as domestic if:

- A foreign corporation acquires substantially all of its properties.
- The former shareholders (or partners) of the U.S. corporation (or partnership) hold 80 percent or more of the foreign corporation's stock after the transaction.
- The foreign corporation does not have substantial business activities in its country of incorporation.

If the former shareholders or partners own at least 60 percent but less than 80 percent of the new corporation, the foreign entity remains foreign, but other restrictions may apply.

under § 351. The branch assets have always been used in Ireland. Amelia transfers the following branch assets to St. George upon its creation.

Asset	Tax Basis	Market Value	Built-in Gain/Loss
Raw materials inventory	$100	$ 400	$ 300
Accounts receivable	200	250	50
Manufacturing equipment	450	925	475
Furniture and fixtures	150	50	(100)
Total	$900	$1,625	$ 725

Although the $725 in realized gain is deferred under § 351, the gain is potentially taxable under § 367 because the assets are leaving the U.S. taxing jurisdiction. The general rule of § 367 is that all of the realized gain is recognized by Amelia. However, because St. George will use the transferred assets in the active conduct of a foreign trade or business, the realized gain remains potentially deferred. As the inventory and accounts receivable are "tainted assets," Amelia recognizes a $350 gain upon the transfer ($300 gain attributable to inventory and $50 gain from the accounts receivable). Gain is recognized on an asset-by-asset basis with no offset for losses on other assets. ■

In addition to gain on the tainted assets listed previously, any U.S. depreciation and other types of recapture potential in the assets transferred are recognized to the extent of gain realized. This provision applies only to appreciated assets for which the depreciation or other deduction has resulted in a tax benefit.

The transfer of intangibles is treated separately as a transfer pursuant to a sale for contingent payments.[20] These amounts are treated as received by the transferor over the life of the intangible; they constitute ordinary income. They are recognized by the transferor and must be commensurate with the income attributable to the intangible. A subsequent disposition by the transferee triggers income recognition to the initial transferor.

[20] § 367(d).

TAX IN THE NEWS The IRS Watches from Abroad

Taxpayers long have tried to shield information from the IRS about assets and income (e.g., in the proverbial Swiss bank account). Computing resources and cooperation among government taxing authorities make it more difficult to do so than ever before.

The IRS stations agents in Beijing, Hong Kong, Sydney, the British Virgin Islands, and other jurisdictions where it perceives that taxpayers are shifting financial resources with tax evasion motives. It often takes many years to put together a case to show the tax evasion activities of a U.S. person, but the wheels are starting to turn to accomplish just that. Typical IRS weapons include information-sharing agreements among governments and/or taxing agencies, whistleblower programs, and litigation.

The U.S. Foreign Account Tax Compliance Act (FATCA) requires that a bank (even outside the United States) provide the IRS with certain identifying information about all U.S. persons with an account at the bank. Lacking such compliance information, the bank must pay a fine if it wants to hold assets in the United States.

FATCA is an expensive rule to comply with, especially for smaller banks, and some have pulled their accounts out of the United States rather than provide the account-holder information. Should a Federal rule discourage financial investments in the United States in this manner? Aren't there other ways to crack down on U.S. tax scofflaws?

Inbound and Offshore Transfers

One objective of § 367 is to prevent E & P that has accumulated in U.S.-owned foreign corporations from escaping U.S. taxation. Section 367(b) covers the tax treatment of inbound and offshore transfers with regard to stock of a controlled foreign corporation (CFC). (CFCs are discussed in more detail in a later section.) Examples of inbound transactions include the following.

- The liquidation of a foreign corporation into a domestic parent under § 332.
- The acquisition of the assets of a foreign corporation by a domestic corporation in a Type "C" or Type "D" reorganization.

Offshore transfers include the following.

- A foreign corporation acquisition of a first- or lower-tier foreign corporation in exchange for stock of a non-CFC.
- A foreign corporate Type "B," Type "C," or Type "D" acquisition of a foreign corporation in exchange for CFC stock.
- A foreign § 351 transfer of stock or other property in a foreign corporation having a U.S. shareholder.

U.S. persons that are directly or indirectly parties to an inbound or offshore transfer involving stock of a CFC generally recognize dividend income to the extent of their pro rata share of the previously untaxed E & P of the foreign corporation.

Tax Havens

Many outbound transfers of assets to foreign corporations are to countries with tax rates higher than or equal to the U.S. rate. Thus, tax avoidance is not the motive for such transfers. Some U.S. corporations, however, make their foreign investment in (or through) a tax haven. A **tax haven** is a country where either locally sourced income or residents are subject to no or low internal taxation. A tax haven usually applies minimal rules for a taxpayer to establish residency, and it adopts little or no cooperation in international exchanges of tax and financial information. The Bahamas, Monaco, and Panama, among other countries, often are seen as tax havens.

One method of potentially avoiding taxation is to invest through a foreign corporation incorporated in a tax haven. Because the foreign corporation is a resident

FIGURE 9.5 **Use of a Tax Haven Corporation**

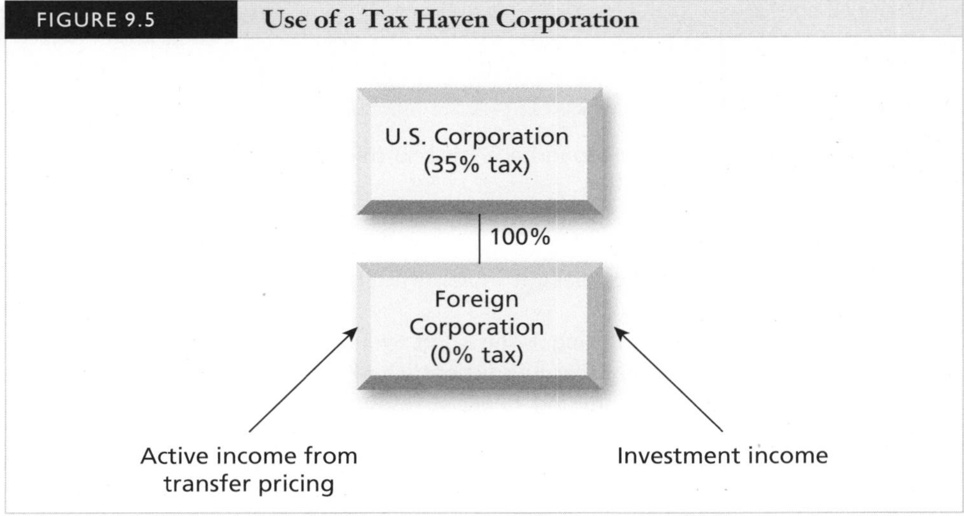

of the tax haven, the income it earns is subject to no or low internal taxes. Tax haven countries may also have provisions limiting the exchange of financial and commercial information.[21]

Figure 9.5 illustrates this use of a tax haven by a U.S. corporation. The U.S. corporation uses a foreign subsidiary corporation in a low- or no-tax country to earn either investment income or a portion of income from business activities (as illustrated previously in the transfer pricing discussion). Because the foreign subsidiary is not consolidated with the domestic parent under U.S. tax law (i.e., the foreign corporation is not a member of the U.S. corporation's affiliated group) and is not itself engaged in any U.S. trade or business, the foreign corporation is not subject to U.S. taxation. Without the application of the transfer pricing rules or the Subpart F rules (discussed later), the foreign corporation's income will escape U.S. taxation until the time that any foreign profits are repatriated back to the U.S. parent as a dividend or similar payment.

A tax haven also can, in effect, be created by an income tax treaty. For example, under an income tax treaty between Country A and Country B, residents of Country A are subject to a withholding tax of only 5 percent on dividend and interest income sourced in Country B. The United States and Country A have a similar treaty. The United States does not have a treaty with Country B, and the withholding tax is 30 percent. A U.S. corporation can create a foreign subsidiary in Country A and use that subsidiary to make investments in Country B. This practice is referred to as **treaty shopping**. If the Country B investment income had been earned directly by the U.S. corporation, it would be subject to a 30 percent withholding tax. As a result of investing through the foreign subsidiary created in Country A, the U.S. parent corporation pays only 10 percent in foreign taxes on the income earned (i.e., 5 percent to Country B and 5 percent to Country A).

Foreign Corporations Controlled by U.S. Persons

To minimize current tax liability, taxpayers often attempt to defer the recognition of taxable income. One way to do this is to shift the income-generating activity to a foreign entity that is not within the U.S. tax jurisdiction. A foreign corporation is the most suitable entity for such an endeavor because, unlike a partnership, it is not a conduit through which income is taxed directly to the owner. Because of the potential for abuse, Congress has enacted various provisions to limit the availability of deferral.

[21]Additional limitations on the use of treaty benefits are contained in § 894(c).

ETHICS & EQUITY Exporting U.S. Jobs or Improving U.S. Competitiveness?

U.S.-owned foreign corporations with exclusively overseas operations are not subject to U.S. corporate income tax on their profits. Such profits are taxed to the U.S. shareholders only upon repatriation back to the United States as dividends. In some cases, the U.S. shareholders are taxed on profits deemed to be repatriated before any actual distribution (so-called Subpart F income). When there is no Subpart F income, however, U.S. owners of foreign corporations are able to defer indefinitely any U.S. tax on all of their foreign profits. When politicians complain that companies that export jobs are receiving tax breaks, they often are referring to this deferral privilege associated with tax-savvy foreign operations.

U.S. owners of foreign corporations point out that they must compete in a global environment. Many other countries, such as the Netherlands, do not tax the offshore profits of foreign subsidiaries even if the profits are brought home. If a U.S.-owned foreign corporation cannot at least defer its U.S. taxes, it suffers a competitive disadvantage relative to a Dutch-owned subsidiary, for example. Others argue that the deferral privilege simply creates an unwarranted advantage for companies operating offshore compared with their U.S.-based counterparts.

Which argument do you find more compelling? How do you explain the incentive of tax deferral to U.S. workers whose jobs have moved offshore? How would you explain loss of tax deferral to the U.S. shareholders of a company that pays triple the corporate tax rate of its global competitors?

Controlled Foreign Corporations

Subpart F, §§ 951–964 of the Code, provides that certain types of income generated by controlled foreign corporations (CFCs) are currently included in gross income by the U.S. shareholders, without regard to actual distributions.

For Subpart F to apply, the foreign corporation must have been a CFC for an uninterrupted period of 30 days or more during the taxable year. When this is the case, U.S. shareholders include in gross income their pro rata share of Subpart F income and increase in earnings that the CFC has invested in U.S. property for the tax year. This rule applies to U.S. shareholders who own stock in the corporation on the last day of the tax year or on the last day the foreign corporation is a CFC. The gross income inclusion must be made for their taxable year in which the taxable year of the CFC ends.

EXAMPLE 15

Gray, Inc., a calendar year corporation, is a CFC for the entire tax year. Chance Company, a U.S. corporation, owns 60% of Gray's one class of stock for the entire year. Subpart F income is $100,000, and no distributions have been made during the year. Chance, a calendar year taxpayer, includes $60,000 in gross income as a constructive dividend for the tax year. ■

EXAMPLE 16

Gray, Inc., is a CFC until July 1 of the tax year (a calendar year) and earns $100,000 in Subpart F income. Terry, a U.S. citizen, owns 30% of its one class of stock for the entire year. She includes $14,877 [$100,000 × 30% × (181 days/365 days)] in gross income as a constructive dividend for the tax year. ■

A **CFC** is any foreign corporation in which more than 50 percent of the total combined voting power of all classes of stock entitled to vote or the total value of the stock of the corporation is owned by U.S. shareholders on any day during the taxable year of the foreign corporation. The foreign subsidiaries of most multinational U.S. parent corporations are CFCs. For purposes of determining whether a foreign corporation is a CFC, a **U.S. shareholder** is defined as a U.S. person who owns, or is considered to own, 10 percent or more of the total combined voting power of all classes of voting stock of the foreign corporation. Stock owned directly, indirectly, and constructively is counted.

Indirect ownership involves stock held through a foreign entity, such as a foreign corporation, foreign partnership, or foreign trust. This stock is considered to be actually owned proportionately by the shareholders, partners, or beneficiaries. Constructive ownership rules, with certain modifications, apply in determining whether a U.S. person is a U.S. shareholder, in determining whether a foreign corporation is a CFC, and for certain related-party provisions of Subpart F.[22]

EXAMPLE 17

A non-U.S. corporation has the following shareholders.

Shareholders	Voting Power	Classification
Alan	30%	U.S. person
Bill	9%	U.S. person
Carla	40%	Non-U.S. person
Dora	20%	U.S. person
Ed	1%	U.S. person

Bill is Alan's son. Alan, Bill, and Dora are U.S. shareholders. Alan owns 39%, 30% directly and 9% constructively through Bill. Bill also owns 39%, 9% directly and 30% constructively through Alan. Thus, Bill is a U.S. shareholder. Dora owns 20% directly. The corporation is a CFC because U.S. shareholders own 59% of the voting power. Ed, a U.S. person, owns 1% and is not related to any of the other shareholders. Thus, Ed is not a U.S. shareholder and would not have to include any of the Subpart F income in gross income. If Bill were not related to Alan or to any other U.S. persons who were shareholders, Bill would not be a U.S. shareholder and the corporation would not be a CFC. ■

U.S. shareholders include their pro rata share of the applicable income in their gross income only to the extent of their actual ownership.[23]

EXAMPLE 18

Bill, in Example 17, would recognize only 9% of the Subpart F income as a constructive dividend. Alan would recognize 30%, and Dora would recognize 20%. If instead Bill were a foreign corporation wholly owned by Alan, Alan would recognize 39% as a constructive dividend. ■

Subpart F Income A U.S. shareholder of a CFC does not necessarily lose the ability to defer U.S. taxation of income earned by the CFC. Only certain income earned by the CFC triggers immediate U.S. taxation as a constructive dividend. This tainted income, referred to as Subpart F income, can be characterized as income with little or no economic connection with the CFC's country of incorporation. **Subpart F** income typically includes:

- Insurance income (§ 953).
- Foreign base company income (§ 954).
- Illegal bribes.

Insurance Income Income attributable to insuring risk of loss outside the country in which the CFC is organized is Subpart F income. This rule precludes U.S. corporations from setting up offshore insurance companies in tax havens to convert expenditures for self-insurance into a deductible insurance premium.

Foreign Base Company Income Foreign base company income (FBCI) provisions target transactions whereby a CFC earns income that lacks any economic connection to its country of organization. FBCI includes:

- Foreign personal holding company income.
- Foreign base company sales income.

[22]§§ 958 and 318(a).

[23]Stock held indirectly (but not constructively) is considered actually owned for this purpose.

- Foreign base company services income.
- Foreign base company oil-related income.

Foreign personal holding company (FPHC) income commonly includes:

- Dividends, interest, royalties, rents, and annuities.
- Excess gains over losses from the sale or exchange of property (including an interest in a trust or partnership) that gives rise to FPHC income or that does not give rise to any income.
- Excess of foreign currency gains over foreign currency losses (other than any transaction directly related to the business needs of the CFC).

Foreign base company (FBC) sales income is income derived by a CFC where the CFC has very little connection with the process that generates the income and a related party is involved. If the CFC earns income from the sale of property to customers outside the CFC's country of incorporation and either the supplier or the customer is related to the CFC, such income is FBC sales income.

EXAMPLE 19

Ulysses, Ltd., is a CFC organized in the United Kingdom and owned 100% by Joyce, Inc., a U.S. corporation. Ulysses purchases finished inventory from Joyce and sells the inventory to customers in Hong Kong. This sales income constitutes FBC sales income. ■

An exception applies to property that is manufactured, produced, grown, or extracted in the country in which the CFC was organized or created and to property sold for use, consumption, or disposition within that country. In both of these situations, the CFC has participated in the economic process that generates the income.

EXAMPLE 20

If Ulysses, from Example 19, purchases raw materials from Joyce and performs substantial manufacturing activity in the United Kingdom before selling the inventory to customers in Hong Kong, the income is not FBC sales income.

Even without the manufacturing activity, sales to customers within the United Kingdom would not produce FBC sales income. ■

FBC services income is income derived from the performance of services for or on behalf of a related person and performed outside the country in which the CFC was created or organized. Income from services performed in connection with the sale of property by a CFC that has manufactured, produced, grown, or extracted such property is not FBC services income.

FBC oil-related income is income, other than extraction income, derived in a foreign country by large oil producers in connection with the sale of oil and gas products and sold by the CFC or a related person for use or consumption outside the country in which the oil or gas was extracted.

Subpart F Income Exceptions A *de minimis* rule provides that if the total amount of a foreign corporation's FBCI and gross insurance income for the taxable year is less than the lesser of 5 percent of gross income or $1 million, none of its gross income is treated as FBCI for the tax year. At the other extreme, if a foreign corporation's FBCI and gross insurance income exceed 70 percent of total gross income, all of the corporation's gross income for the tax year is treated as Subpart F income.

FBCI and insurance income subject to high foreign taxes are not included under Subpart F if the taxpayer establishes that the income was subject to an effective rate, imposed by a foreign country, of more than 90 percent of the maximum Federal corporate income tax rate. For example, the rate must be greater than 31.5 percent (90% × 35%), where 35 percent represents the highest U.S. corporate rate.

Investment in U.S. Property In addition to Subpart F income, U.S. shareholders include in gross income their pro rata share of the CFC's increase in investment in

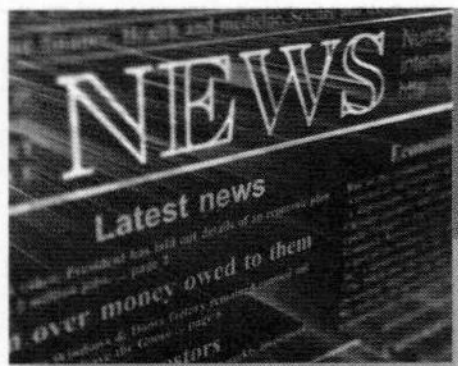

TAX IN THE NEWS Bring It Home

A one-time opportunity to bring offshore profits home to the United States was available in 2004. U.S. shareholders of foreign corporations were allowed to repatriate certain profits of their foreign subsidiaries and receive an 85 percent dividends received deduction. At a 35 percent tax rate, these recipients paid a U.S. tax of only 5.25 percent (35% × 15%).

Many U.S. corporations thought this "tax holiday" was a great idea. U.S. corporations brought home $362 billion in cash dividends eligible for this special deduction. Most of the repatriations came from technology and pharmaceutical companies. Congress had allowed the tax holiday so that the repatriated funds could create new U.S. capital investments and new U.S. jobs. But critics found that the repatriated funds tended to be used to pay dividends to shareholders and to finance stock buybacks.

Will another tax holiday be attractive in the future? Microsoft and Cisco hold $80 billion of offshore cash, totaling over 80 percent of their entire cash holdings. Microsoft acquired Luxembourg's Skype, using its offshore cash (and avoiding U.S. taxes by not having to repatriate the cash first). And others with offshore cash reserves are found to take on new U.S. debt rather than bring home their unrepatriated profits. Congress has its eye on those overseas piles of cash, but it seemingly cannot figure out the best way to bring them back to the United States.

U.S. property for the taxable year.[24] U.S. property generally includes U.S. real property, debt obligations of U.S. persons, and stock in certain related domestic corporations. The CFC must have sufficient E & P to support a deemed dividend.

EXAMPLE 21

Fleming, Ltd., a CFC, earned no Subpart F income for the taxable year. If Fleming lends $100,000 to Lynn, its sole U.S. shareholder, this debt is considered an investment in U.S. property by Fleming because it now owns a U.S. note receivable. Holding the note triggers a constructive dividend of $100,000 to Lynn, assuming that Fleming has sufficient E & P. ■

Distributions of Previously Taxed Income Distributions from a CFC are treated as being first from E & P attributable to increases in investment in U.S. property previously taxed as a constructive dividend, second from E & P attributable to previously taxed Subpart F income, and third from other E & P. Thus, distributions of previously taxed income are not taxed again as a dividend but reduce E & P. Any increase in investment in U.S. property is considered attributable first to Subpart F income and thus is not taxed twice.

EXAMPLE 22

In the current year, Jet, Inc., a U.S. shareholder, owns 100% of a CFC, from which Jet receives a $100,000 distribution. The CFC's E & P is composed of the following amounts:

- $50,000 attributable to previously taxed investment in U.S. property.
- $30,000 attributable to previously taxed Subpart F income.
- $40,000 attributable to other E & P.

Jet has a taxable dividend of only $20,000, all attributable to other E & P. The remaining $80,000 is previously taxed income. The CFC's E & P is reduced by $100,000. All of the remaining $20,000 E & P is attributable to other E & P. ■

A U.S. shareholder's basis in CFC stock is increased by constructive dividends and decreased by subsequent distributions of previously taxed income. U.S. corporate shareholders who own at least 10 percent of the voting stock of a foreign corporation are allowed an indirect foreign tax credit for foreign taxes deemed paid

[24] § 956.

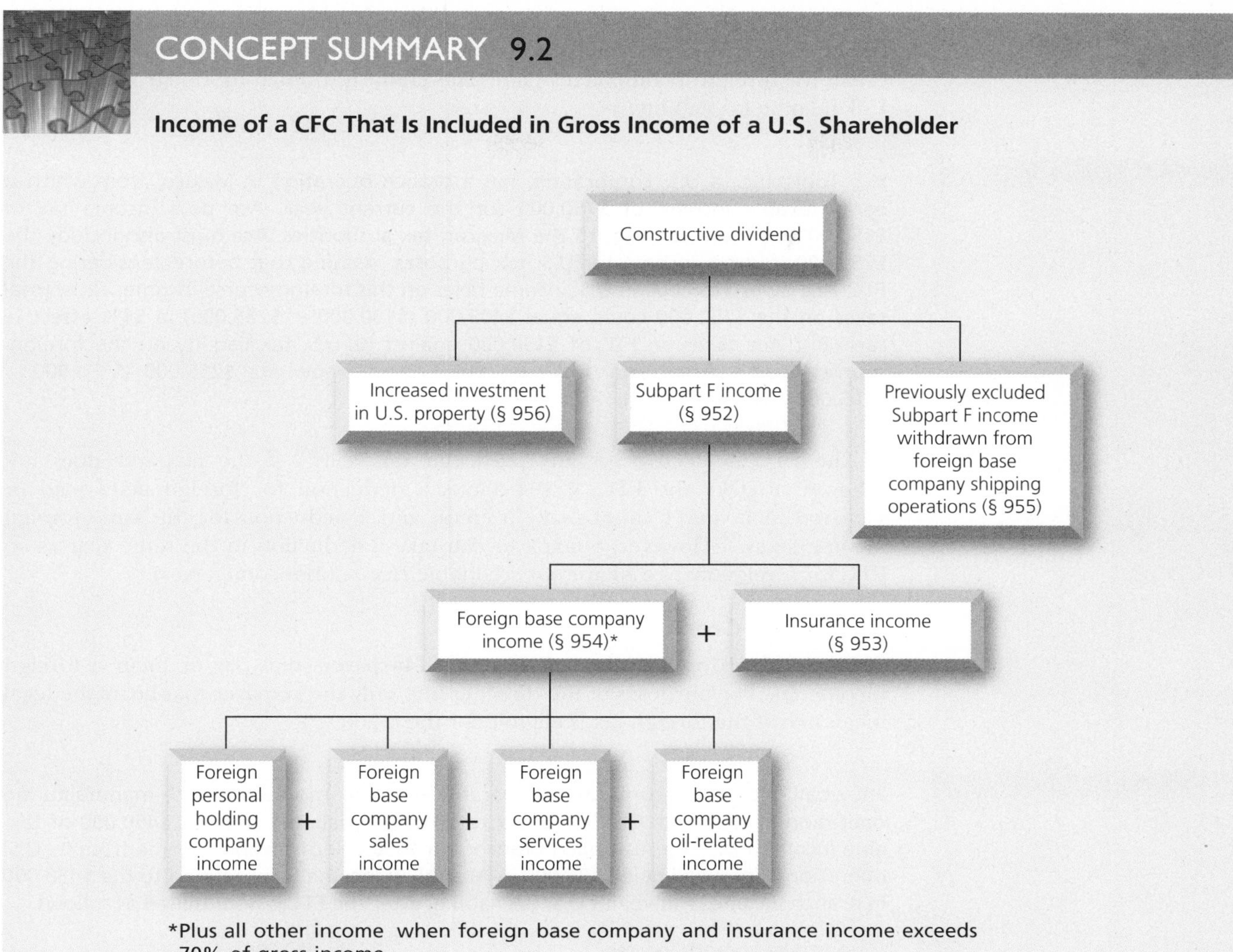

on constructive dividends included in gross income under Subpart F. The indirect credit also is available for Subpart F income attributable to certain lower-tier foreign corporations. See the foreign tax credit discussion later in this chapter. The various constructive dividend possibilities for CFC income appear in Concept Summary 9.2.

Dispositions of Stock of a CFC The Subpart F income of a CFC is currently taxed to U.S. shareholders to the extent of their pro rata share. This rule, however, does not reach the earnings of the CFC that are not included in the taxable income of the shareholders under Subpart F (e.g., active trade or business income not involving related persons). A related provision requires that gain on the sale or other disposition of stock of a CFC by a U.S. shareholder be treated as dividend income to the extent of the transferor's share of undistributed nonpreviously taxed E & P of the corporation.[25]

Foreign Tax Credit

The United States retains the right to tax its citizens and residents on their total taxable income. This approach can result in double taxation, presenting a potential problem to U.S. persons who work or invest abroad.

[25]§ 1248.

To reduce the possibility of double taxation, Congress enacted the **foreign tax credit (FTC)** provisions. Under these provisions, a qualified taxpayer is allowed a tax credit for foreign income taxes paid. The credit is a dollar-for-dollar reduction of U.S. income tax liability.

EXAMPLE 23

Ace Tools, Inc., a U.S. corporation, has a branch operation in Mexico, from which it earns taxable income of $750,000 for the current year. Ace pays income tax of $150,000 on these earnings to the Mexican tax authorities. Ace must also include the $750,000 in gross income for U.S. tax purposes. Assume that before considering the FTC, Ace owes $255,000 in U.S. income taxes on this foreign-source income. Thus, total taxes on the $750,000 could equal $405,000 ($150,000 + $255,000), a 54% effective rate. But Ace takes an FTC of $150,000 against its U.S. tax liability on the foreign-source income. Ace's total taxes on the $750,000 now are $255,000 ($150,000 + $105,000), a 34% effective rate. ■

The FTC is elective for any particular tax year.[26] If the taxpayer does not "choose" to take the FTC, § 164 allows a deduction for foreign taxes paid or incurred. A taxpayer cannot take a credit and a deduction for the same foreign income taxes.[27] However, a taxpayer can take a deduction in the same year as an FTC for foreign taxes that are not creditable (e.g., non-income taxes).

The Direct Credit

Section 901 provides a direct FTC to U.S. taxpayers that pay or incur a foreign income tax. For purposes of the direct credit, only the taxpayer that bears the legal incidence of the foreign tax is eligible for the credit.

EXAMPLE 24

Snowball, Inc., a U.S. corporation, operates an unincorporated branch manufacturing operation in Australia. On its U.S. tax return, Snowball, Inc., reports $450,000 of taxable income from the Australian branch and $650,000 of taxable income from its U.S. operations. Snowball paid $135,000 in Australian income taxes related to the $450,000 in branch income. Snowball's U.S. tax liability after the FTC is determined as follows.

Australian branch income	$ 450,000
U.S. operations income	650,000
Total taxable income	$1,100,000
U.S. tax rate	× 34%
U.S. income tax before FTC	$ 374,000
FTC	(135,000)
Net U.S. tax liability	$ 239,000

Because the effective foreign tax rate (30%) is less than the U.S. rate (34%), the $135,000 FTC is fully creditable without limitation (see the following discussion under FTC Limitations). ■

Section 903 provides U.S. taxpayers with a direct FTC for foreign taxes imposed in lieu of an income tax by the foreign government. A credit for withholding tax is the most common example of a § 903 credit. Many governments impose a withholding tax on the gross amount of certain payments of passive income to nonresidents of their countries. Even though the tax is withheld by the payor of the income, the tax is imposed directly on the recipient.

EXAMPLE 25

MettCo, Inc., a domestic corporation, receives a $5,000 dividend from DeanCo, Ltd., a foreign corporation. The foreign country imposes a 20% withholding tax on dividend payments to nonresidents. Accordingly, DeanCo withholds $1,000 ($5,000 × 20%)

[26] § 901(a).

[27] § 275.

from the dividend and remits this tax to the local country tax authorities. DeanCo pays the remaining $4,000 to MettCo.

Although MettCo did not directly pay the $1,000 in foreign tax, the entire amount is allowed as a direct tax to MettCo for FTC purposes. MettCo reports $5,000 in dividend income on its U.S. tax return (the gross amount of the dividend) but receives an FTC against any U.S. tax for the $1,000 in foreign withholding tax. ■

The Indirect Credit

If a U.S. corporation operates in a foreign country through a branch, the direct credit is available for foreign taxes paid. If, however, a U.S. corporation operates in a foreign country through a foreign subsidiary, the direct credit is not available for foreign taxes paid by the foreign corporation. An indirect credit is available to U.S. corporate taxpayers that receive actual or constructive dividends from foreign corporations that have paid foreign income taxes.[28] These foreign taxes are deemed paid by the corporate shareholders in the same proportion as the dividends actually or constructively received bear to the foreign corporation's undistributed E & P.

$$\text{Indirect FTC} = \frac{\text{Actual or constructive dividend}}{\text{Undistributed E \& P}} \times \text{Foreign taxes paid}$$

Section 78 requires a domestic corporation that chooses the FTC for deemed-paid foreign taxes to *gross up* (add to income) dividend income by the amount of deemed-paid taxes.

EXAMPLE 26

Wren, Inc., a domestic corporation, owns 50% of Finch, Inc., a foreign corporation. Wren receives a dividend of $120,000 from Finch. Finch paid foreign taxes of $500,000 on its E & P, which totals $1.2 million. Wren's deemed-paid foreign taxes for FTC purposes are $50,000.

Cash dividend from Finch	$120,000
Deemed-paid foreign taxes	
$\left(\frac{\$120{,}000}{\$1{,}200{,}000} \times \$500{,}000\right)$	50,000
Gross income to Wren	$170,000

In addition to the $120,000 cash dividend, Wren includes the $50,000 in gross income if the FTC is elected. ■

Certain ownership requirements must be met before the indirect credit is available to a domestic corporation. The domestic corporation must own 10 percent or more of the voting stock of the foreign corporation. The credit also is available for deemed-paid foreign taxes of second- and third-tier foreign corporations if the 10 percent ownership requirement is met at the second- and third-tier level. A 5 percent indirect ownership requirement must also be met. The indirect credit also is available for foreign taxes paid by fourth- through sixth-tier foreign corporations if additional requirements are met, including the requirement that these corporations be CFCs. The § 902 ownership requirements are summarized in Figure 9.6.

FTC Limitations

To prevent taxpayers from crediting foreign taxes against U.S. taxes levied on U.S.-source taxable income, the FTC is subject to a limitation. The FTC for any taxable year cannot exceed the lesser of two amounts: (1) the actual foreign taxes paid or

[28] § 902. In the formula for the indirect credit, only foreign taxes paid and E & P generated after 1986 are used.

FIGURE 9.6 **Section 902 Ownership Requirements**

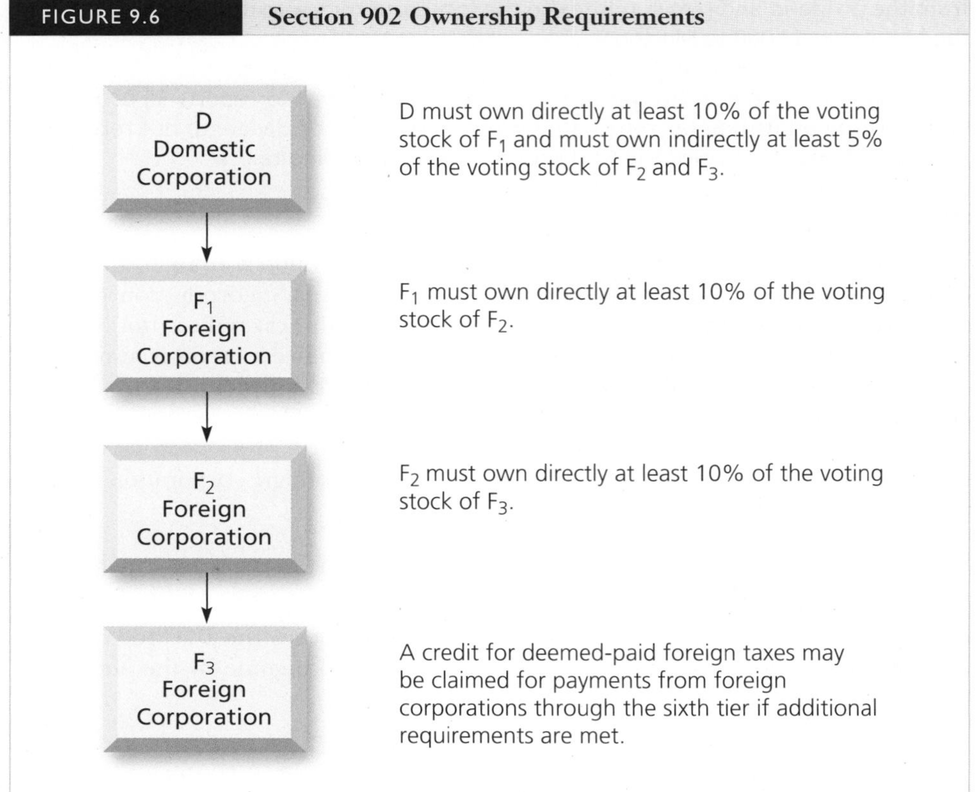
D
Domestic
Corporation
D must own directly at least 10% of the voting stock of F_1 and must own indirectly at least 5% of the voting stock of F_2 and F_3.
F_1
Foreign
Corporation
F_1 must own directly at least 10% of the voting stock of F_2.
F_2
Foreign
Corporation
F_2 must own directly at least 10% of the voting stock of F_3.
F_3
Foreign
Corporation
A credit for deemed-paid foreign taxes may be claimed for payments from foreign corporations through the sixth tier if additional requirements are met.

accrued or (2) the U.S. taxes (before the FTC) on foreign-source taxable income. The FTC limitation is derived in the following manner.

$$\text{FTC limitation} = \frac{\text{Foreign-source taxable income}}{\text{Total taxable income}^{29}} \times \text{U.S. tax before FTC}$$

EXAMPLE 27

Charlotte, Inc., a domestic corporation that invests in foreign securities, reports total taxable income for the tax year of $120,000, consisting of $100,000 in U.S.-source business profits and $20,000 of income from foreign sources. Foreign taxes of $9,500 were withheld by foreign tax authorities. Charlotte's U.S. tax before the FTC is $42,000. The company's FTC is limited to $7,000 [$42,000 × ($20,000/$120,000)]. Charlotte's net U.S. tax liability is $35,000. ■

As Example 27 illustrates, the limitation can prevent the total amount of foreign taxes paid in high-tax jurisdictions from being credited. Taxpayers could overcome this problem by generating additional foreign-source income that is subject to no or low foreign taxation.

EXAMPLE 28

Compare Domestic Corporation's FTC situations. In one, the corporation has only $500,000 of highly taxed foreign-source income. In the other, Domestic also has $100,000 of low-taxed foreign-source interest income.

[29]For FTC purposes, the taxable income of an individual, estate, or trust is computed without any deduction for personal exemptions. § 904(b)(1).

	Only Highly Taxed Income	With Low-Taxed Interest Income
Foreign-source income	$500,000	$600,000
Foreign taxes	275,000	280,000
U.S.-source income	700,000	700,000
U.S. taxes (34%)	408,000	442,000
FTC limitation	170,000*	204,000**

* $408,000 × ($500,000/$1,200,000).
** $442,000 × ($600,000/$1,300,000).

Domestic's foreign taxes increase by only $5,000 ($280,000 − $275,000), but its FTC limitation increases by $34,000 ($204,000 − $170,000). ■

Example 28 illustrates the *cross-crediting* of foreign taxes from high- and low-taxed foreign income. To prevent this practice, the FTC rules require that a separate limitation be calculated for each of certain categories (or baskets) of foreign-source taxable income and the foreign taxes attributable to that income. There are two income baskets: passive income and all other (general). Passive income generally is investment-type income; general limitation income is typically from active business sources.

EXAMPLE 29

BenCo, Inc., a U.S. corporation, has a foreign branch in France that earns taxable income of $1.5 million from manufacturing operations and $600,000 from passive activities. BenCo pays foreign taxes of $600,000 (40%) and $100,000 (16.67%), respectively, on this foreign-source income. The corporation also earns $4 million of U.S.-source taxable income, resulting in worldwide taxable income of $6.1 million. BenCo's U.S. taxes before the FTC are $2,074,000 (at 34%). The following tabulation illustrates the effect of the separate limitation baskets on cross-crediting.

Foreign Income Category	Net Taxable Amount	Foreign Taxes	U.S. Tax before FTC at 34%	FTC with Separate Limits
General	$1,500,000	$600,000	$510,000	$510,000
Passive	600,000	100,000	204,000	100,000
Total	$2,100,000	$700,000	$714,000	$610,000

Without the separate limitation provisions, the FTC would be the lesser of (1) $700,000 foreign taxes or (2) $714,000 share of U.S. tax [$2,074,000 × ($2,100,000/$6,100,000)]. The separate limitation provisions reduce the FTC by $90,000 ($700,000 − $610,000). The effect of the separate limitation rules is that the foreign-source income taxed at the foreign tax rate of 40% cannot be aggregated with foreign-source income taxed at only 16.67%. ■

A partner's distributive share of partnership income generally also is categorized in separate limitation baskets, based on the character of the partnership's income.

FTC Carryovers

The various FTC limitations can result in unused (noncredited) foreign taxes for the tax year. The carryback period is 1 year, and the carryforward period is 10 years.[30] The taxes can be credited in years when the formula limitation for that year exceeds the foreign taxes attributable to the same tax year.

The carryback and carryforward provisions are available only within a specific basket. In other words, excess foreign taxes in one basket cannot be carried over unless there is an excess limitation in the same basket for the carryover year.

[30] § 904(c).

Foreign Losses

Citizens and residents of the United States who hold foreign investments or operations directly (e.g., through a branch operation) or through a conduit entity (e.g., a partnership) can offset foreign losses against U.S.-source income, thereby reducing the U.S. income tax due on U.S.-source income. If the foreign country in which the loss is generated (sourced) taxes subsequent income from these foreign operations, the FTC could reduce or eliminate any U.S. tax on the income.

To prevent this loss of tax revenue to the United States, *overall foreign losses* are recaptured as U.S.-source income for FTC purposes.[31] This is accomplished by reducing the numerator of the FTC limitation formula. Foreign-source taxable income is reduced by the lesser of (1) the remaining unrecaptured overall foreign loss or (2) 50 percent of foreign-source taxable income for the taxable year (unless the taxpayer elects to recapture a greater percentage). Unrecaptured foreign losses are carried over indefinitely until recaptured.[32]

EXAMPLE 30

Shannon, Inc., a domestic corporation, operates a branch in Japan. The earnings record of the branch is as follows.

Year	Taxable Income (Loss)	Foreign Taxes Paid
2010	($ 15,000)	–0–
2011	(20,000)	–0–
2012	(20,000)	–0–
2013	40,000	$20,000

For 2010–2013, Shannon reports U.S.-source taxable income of $300,000 each year. Shannon's 2013 U.S. tax liability before the FTC is $115,600. Its overall foreign loss is $55,000 for 2010–2013. The FTC limitation for 2013 is $6,800 {$115,600 × [$40,000 − (50% × $40,000)]/$340,000}. ■

When a taxpayer has a loss for the tax year in one or more foreign-source categories (baskets), the loss is apportioned pro rata to foreign-source categories with income for the tax year. If there is an overall foreign loss (i.e., foreign losses exceed foreign income in all categories), the overall foreign loss then reduces U.S.-source income. A U.S. loss for the tax year is apportioned pro rata to foreign-source income in each category, but only after the apportionment of any foreign losses to those income categories.

EXAMPLE 31

During 2012, Bloom, Inc., a U.S. corporation, incurred a $10,000 loss in its manufacturing activities and had $25,000 in passive income. The loss in the general basket is apportioned to the passive basket as follows.

Foreign Income Category	Income or Loss	Foreign-Source Taxable Income
General	($10,000)	$ –0–
Passive	25,000	15,000
Total	$15,000	$15,000

In 2013, Bloom earns $25,000 in manufacturing income and $24,000 in passive income. So the previously apportioned loss is reallocated back to the affected basket as follows.

[31] § 904(f)(1).

[32] U.S.-source income also results when the entity that generated the overall foreign loss is disposed of before all of the loss is recaptured. § 904(f)(3).

FINANCIAL DISCLOSURE INSIGHTS Overseas Operations and Book-Tax Differences

Non-U.S. operations account for a large portion of the permanent book-tax differences of U.S. business entities. These differences may relate to different tax bases, different tax rate structures, or special provisions concerning tax-based financing with the other country. For instance, lower tax rates applied by Ireland, Bermuda, and the Netherlands recently reduced Cisco's current-year tax liabilities by about $1 billion per year.

Tax planning strategies using non-U.S. operations also are found in the deferred tax asset and liability accounts. Tax deferrals allowed under current U.S. tax rules and carryforwards of the foreign tax credit can be substantial for some businesses. For example, IBM recently reported a deferred tax asset relating to delays in using its FTCs amounting to about $500 million. For the operating arm of General Electric, that amount was about $2 billion.

Foreign Income Category	Income or Loss	Previously Apportioned Loss	Foreign-Source Taxable Income
General	$25,000	($10,000)	$15,000
Passive	24,000	10,000	34,000
Total	$49,000		$49,000

■

A similar treatment is used for overall domestic losses (i.e., when U.S.-source losses exceed all foreign-source income). In this case, future U.S.-source income is recharacterized as foreign source.

The Alternative Minimum Tax FTC

For purposes of the alternative minimum tax (AMT), the FTC limitation is calculated by using foreign-source alternative minimum taxable income (AMTI) in the numerator and total AMTI in the denominator of the formula and the tentative minimum tax rather than the regular tax.

$$\text{AMT FTC limitation} = \frac{\text{Foreign-source AMTI}}{\text{Total AMTI}} \times \text{Tentative minimum tax}$$

The taxpayer may elect to use regular foreign-source taxable income in the numerator if it does not exceed total AMTI. The AMT FTC limit also is determined on a basket-by-basket basis.

Other Considerations

For a foreign levy to qualify for the FTC, it must be a tax, and its predominant character must be that of an income tax in the U.S. sense.[33] A levy is a tax if it is a compulsory payment, rather than a payment for a specific economic benefit such as the right to extract oil. A tax's predominant character is that of an income tax in the U.S. sense if it reaches realized net gain and is not a *soak-up* tax (i.e., does not depend on being credited against the income tax of another country). A tax that is levied in lieu of an income tax is also creditable.[34]

EXAMPLE 32

JonesCo, a domestic corporation, generates $2 million of taxable income from operations in Larissa, a foreign country. Larissan law levies a tax on income generated in Larissa by foreign residents only in cases in which the country of residence (such as the United States) allows a tax credit for foreign taxes paid. JonesCo will not be allowed an FTC for taxes paid to Larissa, because the foreign tax is a soak-up tax. ■

[33] Reg. § 1.901–2.

[34] § 903 and Reg. § 1.903–1.

For purposes of the FTC, foreign taxes are attributable to the year in which they are paid or accrued. Taxpayers using the cash method of accounting for tax purposes may elect to take the FTC in the year in which the foreign taxes accrue.[35] The election is binding on the taxpayer for the year in which it is made and for all subsequent years.

9.6 U.S. Taxation of Nonresident Aliens and Foreign Corporations

LO.6

Apply the U.S. tax provisions concerning nonresident alien individuals and foreign corporations.

Generally, only the U.S.-source income of nonresident alien individuals and foreign corporations is subject to U.S. taxation. This reflects the reach of the U.S. tax jurisdiction. The constraint, however, does not prevent the United States from also taxing the foreign-source income of nonresident alien individuals and foreign corporations when that income is effectively connected with the conduct of a U.S. trade or business.[36] Concept Summary 9.3 at the end of this section summarizes these tax rules.

Nonresident Alien Individuals

A **nonresident alien (NRA)** individual is an individual who is not a citizen or resident of the United States. For example, Prince William is an NRA, because he is not a citizen or resident of the United States. Citizenship is determined under the immigration and naturalization laws of the United States.[37] Basically, the citizenship statutes are broken down into two categories: nationality at birth or through naturalization.

Residency

A person is a resident of the United States for income tax purposes if he or she meets either the green card test or the substantial presence test.[38] If either of these tests is met for the calendar year, the individual is deemed a U.S. resident for the year.

A foreign person issued a green card is considered a U.S. resident on the first day he or she is physically present in the United States after issuance. The green card is Immigration Form I–551. Newly issued cards are no longer green, but the form still is referred to as the "green card." Status as a U.S. resident remains in effect until the green card has been revoked or the individual has abandoned lawful permanent resident status.

The substantial presence test is applied to an alien without a green card. It is a mathematical test involving physical presence in the United States. An individual who is physically present in the United States for at least 183 days during the calendar year is a U.S. resident for income tax purposes. This 183-day requirement also can be met over a three-year period that includes the two immediately preceding years and the current year, as long as the individual is present in the United States at least 31 days during the current year.[39] For this purpose, each day of the current calendar year is counted as a full day, each day of the first preceding year as one-third day, and each day of the second preceding year as one-sixth day. A nominal presence of 10 days or less can be ignored in determining whether the substantial presence test is met.

EXAMPLE 33

Li, a foreign citizen, was present in the United States for 90 days in 2010, 180 days in 2011, and 110 days in 2012. For Federal income tax purposes, Li is a U.S. resident for 2012, because she was physically present for 185 days [(90 days × 1/6) + (180 days × 1/3) + (110 days × 1)] during the three-year period. ■

[35] § 905.

[36] §§ 871, 881, and 882.

[37] Title 8, Aliens and Nationality, *United States Code*.

[38] § 7701(b).

[39] § 7701(b)(3)(A).

The substantial presence test allows for several exceptions. Commuters from Mexico and Canada who are employed in the United States but return home each day are excepted. Also excepted are individuals who are prevented from leaving the United States by medical conditions that arose while the individuals were in the United States. Some individuals are exempt from the substantial presence test, including foreign government-related individuals (e.g., diplomats), qualified teachers, trainees and students, and certain professional athletes.

ETHICS & EQUITY Should There Be Some "Heart" in Tax Law?

In determining whether an alien is a U.S. resident for U.S. income tax purposes under the substantial presence test, days on which a medical condition prevents the person from leaving the United States are not counted as days present in the United States. The medical condition (e.g., illness or injury) must have arisen after the NRA arrived in the United States. In other words, it generally must be an unexpected illness or accident. No such exception is available, however, for a family member or another NRA who is significant to the person who becomes ill or injured. Thus, under this rule, the relative or other significant person may have to either risk being classified as a U.S. resident for the tax year or leave the ill person (or accident victim) alone in the United States. Does this limited exception ignore the human element in illness and recovery?

Nonresident Aliens Not Engaged in a U.S. Trade or Business

Certain U.S.-source income that is *not* effectively connected with the conduct of a U.S. trade or business is subject to a flat 30 percent tax. This income includes dividends; interest; rents; royalties; certain compensation; premiums; annuities; and other fixed, determinable, annual or periodic (FDAP) income. This tax generally requires the payors of the income to withhold 30 percent of gross amounts.[40] This method eliminates the problems of assuring payment by nonresidents; determining allowable deductions; and, in most instances, the filing of tax returns by nonresidents.

Interest received from certain portfolio debt investments, even though U.S. sourced, is exempt from taxation. Interest earned on deposits with banking institutions is also exempt as long as it is not effectively connected with the conduct of a U.S. trade or business.

Capital gains *not* effectively connected with the conduct of a U.S. trade or business are exempt from tax, as long as the NRA individual was not present in the United States for 183 days or more during the taxable year. If an NRA has not established a taxable year, the calendar year is used. NRAs are not permitted to carry forward capital losses.[41]

Nonresident Aliens Engaged in a U.S. Trade or Business

Two important definitions determine the U.S. tax consequences to NRAs with U.S. source income: "the conduct of a **U.S. trade or business**" and "**effectively connected income.**" Specifically, for an NRA's noninvestment income to be subject to U.S. taxation, the NRA must be considered engaged in a U.S. trade or business and must earn income effectively connected with that business.

General criteria for determining whether a U.S. trade or business exists include the location of production activities, management, distribution activities, and other business functions. Trading in commodities and securities ordinarily does not constitute a trade or business. Dealers, however, need to avoid maintaining a U.S. trading office and trading for their own accounts.

[40] §§ 871 and 1441.

[41] § 871(a)(2).

The Code does not explicitly define a U.S. trade or business, but case law looks for activities carried on in the United States that are regular, substantial, and continuous.[42] Once an NRA is considered engaged in a U.S. trade or business, all U.S.-source income other than FDAP and capital gain income is considered effectively connected to that trade or business and is therefore subject to U.S. taxation.

EXAMPLE 34

Vito, an NRA, produces wine for export. During the current year, Vito earns $500,000 from exporting wine to unrelated wholesalers in the United States. The title to the wine passes to the U.S. wholesalers in New York. Vito has no offices or employees in the United States. The income from wine sales is U.S.-source income, but because Vito is not engaged in a U.S. trade or business, the income is not subject to taxation in the United States.

Vito begins operating a hot dog cart in New York City. This activity constitutes a U. S. trade or business. Consequently, all U.S.-source income other than FDAP or capital gain income is taxed in the United States as income effectively connected with a U.S. trade or business. Thus, both the hot dog cart profits and the $500,000 in wine income will be taxed in the United States. ■

FDAP and capital gain income may be considered effectively connected income if the assets that generate this income are used in, or held for use in, the trade or business (the asset-use test) or if the activities of the trade or business are a material factor in the production of the income (the business-activities test).[43] As long as FDAP and capital gain income are not effectively connected with a U.S. trade or business, the tax treatment of these income items is the same whether NRAs are engaged in a U.S. trade or business.

EXAMPLE 35

Ingrid, an NRA, operates a U.S. business. During the year, cash funds accumulate. Ingrid invests these funds on a short-term basis so that they remain available to meet her business needs. Under the asset-use test, any income earned from these investments is effectively connected income. ■

Effectively connected income is taxed at the same rates that apply to U.S. citizens and residents, and deductions for expenses attributable to that income are allowed. NRAs with effectively connected income also are allowed a deduction for casualty and theft losses related to property located within the United States, a deduction for qualified charitable contributions, and one personal exemption. NRAs with income effectively connected with the conduct of a U.S. trade or business may also be subject to the alternative minimum tax.

Withholding Provisions

The 30 percent U.S. tax on FDAP income is generally administered by requiring the payor of the income to withhold the tax and remit it to the U.S. tax authorities. This assures the government of timely collection and relieves it of jurisdictional problems that could arise if it had to rely on recipients residing outside the United States to pay the tax. As explained earlier, income tax treaties with other countries provide for reduced withholding on certain types of FDAP income (see Exhibit 9.2 for some examples of withholding rates).

Foreign Corporations

Definition

The classification of an entity as a foreign corporation for U.S. tax purposes is an important consideration. A corporation created or organized in the United States

[42] See, for example, *Higgins v. Comm.*, 41–1 USTC ¶9233, 25 AFTR 1160, 61 S.Ct. 475 (1941), and *Continental Trading, Inc. v. Comm.*, 59–1 USTC ¶9316, 3 AFTR 2d 923, 265 F.2d 40 (CA–9, 1959).

[43] § 864(c).

EXHIBIT 9.2 **Selected Tax Treaty Withholding Rates**

	Interest	Dividends in General	Dividends Paid by U.S. Subsidiary to a Foreign Parent Corporation
Australia	10%	15%	0%
Canada	10	15	5
Ireland	0	15	5
Japan	10	15	0
Mexico	15	15	0
Philippines	15	25	20

is a domestic corporation. A foreign corporation is one that is not domestic. Thus, although McDonald's is, in reality, a global corporation, it is considered a domestic corporation for U.S. tax purposes, solely because it was organized in the United States.

Income Not Effectively Connected with a U.S. Trade or Business

U.S.-source FDAP income of foreign corporations is taxed by the United States in the same manner as that of NRA individuals—at a flat 30 percent rate. Generally, foreign corporations qualify for the same exemptions from U.S. taxation for investment income as do NRA individuals. The U.S.-source capital gains of foreign corporations are exempt from the Federal income tax if they are not effectively connected with the conduct of a U.S. trade or business.

Effectively Connected Income

Foreign corporations conducting a trade or business in the United States are subject to Federal income taxation on any U.S.-source income effectively connected with the trade or business. As with NRAs, any FDAP or capital gain income is not considered effectively connected unless the income meets the asset-use or business-activities test.[44] Foreign corporations are subject to the same tax rates on their effectively connected income as are domestic corporations.

Branch Profits Tax

The objective of the **branch profits tax** is to afford equal tax treatment to income generated by a domestic corporation controlled by a foreign corporation and to income generated by other U.S. operations controlled by foreign corporations. If the foreign corporation operates through a U.S. subsidiary (a domestic corporation), the income of the subsidiary is taxable by the United States when earned. A withholding tax applies when the branch income is repatriated (returned as dividends to the foreign parent).

In addition to the income tax imposed on effectively connected income of a foreign corporation, a tax equal to 30 percent of the **dividend equivalent amount (DEA)** for the taxable year is imposed on any foreign corporation with effectively connected income.[45] The DEA is the foreign corporation's effectively connected earnings for the taxable year, adjusted for increases and decreases in the corporation's U.S. net equity (investment in the U.S. operations).

The DEA is limited to E & P that is effectively connected, or treated as effectively connected, with the conduct of a U.S. trade or business. U.S. net equity is the sum of money and the aggregate adjusted basis of assets and liabilities directly connected to U.S. operations that generate effectively connected income.

[44] § 864(c).

[45] § 884.

EXAMPLE 36

Robin, Inc., a foreign corporation, has a U.S. branch operation with the following tax results and other information for the year.

Pretax earnings effectively connected with a U.S. trade or business	$2,000,000
U.S. corporate tax (at 34%)	680,000
Remittance to home office	1,000,000
Increase in U.S. net equity	320,000

Robin's DEA and branch profits tax are computed as follows.

E & P effectively connected with a U.S. trade or business ($2,000,000 − $680,000)	$1,320,000
Less: Increase in U.S. net equity	(320,000)
Dividend equivalent amount	$1,000,000
Branch profits tax rate	× 30%
Branch profits tax	$ 300,000

■

The 30 percent rate of the branch profits tax may be reduced or eliminated by a treaty provision. If a foreign corporation is subject to the branch profits tax, no other U.S. tax is levied on the dividend actually paid by the corporation during the taxable year.

Foreign Investment in Real Property Tax Act

Prior to 1980, NRAs and foreign corporations could avoid U.S. taxation on gains from the sale of U.S. real estate if the gains were treated as capital gains and were not effectively connected with the conduct of a U.S. trade or business. In the mid-1970s, midwestern farmers pressured Congress to eliminate what they saw as a tax advantage that would allow nonresidents to bid up the price of farmland. This and other concerns about foreign ownership of U.S. real estate led to the enactment of the Foreign Investment in Real Property Tax Act (FIRPTA) of 1980.

Under **FIRPTA**, gains and losses realized by NRAs and foreign corporations from the sale or other disposition of U.S. real property interests (USRPIs) are treated as effectively connected with the conduct of a U.S. trade or business even when those individuals or corporations are not actually so engaged. NRA individuals must pay a tax equal to the lesser of two amounts: (1) 26 (or 28) percent of their alternative minimum taxable income or (2) regular U.S. rates on the net U.S. real property gain for the taxable year.[46] For purposes of this provision, losses are taken into account only to the extent they are deductible as business losses, losses on transactions entered into for profit, or losses from casualties and thefts.

U.S. Real Property Interest

Any direct interest in real property situated in the United States and any interest in a domestic corporation (other than solely as a creditor) are U.S. real property interests.

Withholding Provisions

The FIRPTA withholding provisions require any purchaser or agent acquiring a USRPI from a foreign person to withhold 10 percent of the amount realized on the disposition.[47] A domestic partnership, trust, or estate with a foreign partner, foreign grantor treated as owner, or foreign beneficiary generally must withhold 35 percent of the gain allocable to that person on a disposition of a USRPI.

Foreign corporations also are subject to withholding provisions on certain distributions. Without this withholding, NRAs could sell USRPIs, receiving the sales proceeds outside the United States, and jurisdictional issues could make it difficult for

[46] § 897.

[47] § 1445.

FINANCIAL DISCLOSURE INSIGHTS Deferred Tax Assets Overseas

U.S. corporations are not the only entities that can have balance sheets with excessive deferred tax accounts. Restrictive regulatory rules as to how non-U.S. banks compute their capital amounts tend to create large deferred tax assets for them. These accounts attract more attention from regulators in a "down" economy, when the financial stability of the banking system is even more critical than usual.

Deferred tax assets do not affect the entity's actual cash balances, but they can affect the stock price in the short term. Even professional equity analysts can have difficulty understanding announcements of tax adjustments to the balance sheet. Regulations limit the level of deferred tax assets that banks can have in a given country, and political pressure to increase those limits is appearing, as the proportion of shareholder equity that is made up of deferred tax assets has grown significantly in the last five years.

The following are estimates from JPMorgan Chase of the magnitude of deferred tax asset balances for selected banks overseas and banks in the United States.

	Percentage of Shareholder Equity Constituted by Deferred Tax Assets
Dexia	44%
Deutsche Bank	24
Monte dei Paschi	23
UBS	21
Credit Suisse	20
U.S. banks, average	11

the U.S. tax authorities to collect any U.S. tax that might be due on gains. Certain exceptions to FIRPTA withholding are allowed.

Failure to withhold can subject the purchaser or the purchaser's agent to interest on any unpaid amount.[48] A civil penalty of 100 percent of the amount required to be withheld and a criminal penalty of up to $10,000 or five years in prison can be imposed for willful failure to withhold.[49]

Expatriation to Avoid U.S. Taxation

U.S. taxation of U.S.-source income is required of individuals who relinquished their U.S. citizenship within 10 years of deriving that income if they gave up their citizenship to avoid U.S. taxation. Furthermore, NRAs who lost U.S. citizenship within a 10-year period immediately preceding the close of the tax year must pay taxes on their U.S.-source income as though they were still U.S. citizens. This provision applies only if the expatriation had as one of its principal purposes the avoidance of U.S. taxes. Individuals are presumed to have a tax avoidance purpose if they meet either of the following criteria.[50]

- Average annual net income tax for the five taxable years ending before the date of loss of U.S. citizenship is more than $151,000 (in 2012).
- Net worth as of that date is at least $2 million.

These provisions also apply to "long-term lawful permanent residents" who cease to be taxed as U.S. residents. A long-term permanent resident is an individual (other than a citizen of the United States) who is a lawful permanent resident of the United States in at least 8 taxable years during the 15-year period ending with the taxable year in which the individual either ceases to be a lawful permanent resident of the United States or begins to be treated as a resident of another country under an income tax treaty between the United States and the other country (and does not waive the benefits of the treaty to residents of that country). An exception applies to certain individuals with dual citizenship.

The United States continues to treat individuals as U.S. citizens or residents until the taxpayers provide required information and an expatriation notice. Expatriates

[48]§§ 6601, 6621, and 6651.

[49]§§ 6672 and 7202.

[50]§ 877(a)(2). The dollar amounts are adjusted for inflation. For 2011, the net income tax threshold was $147,000.

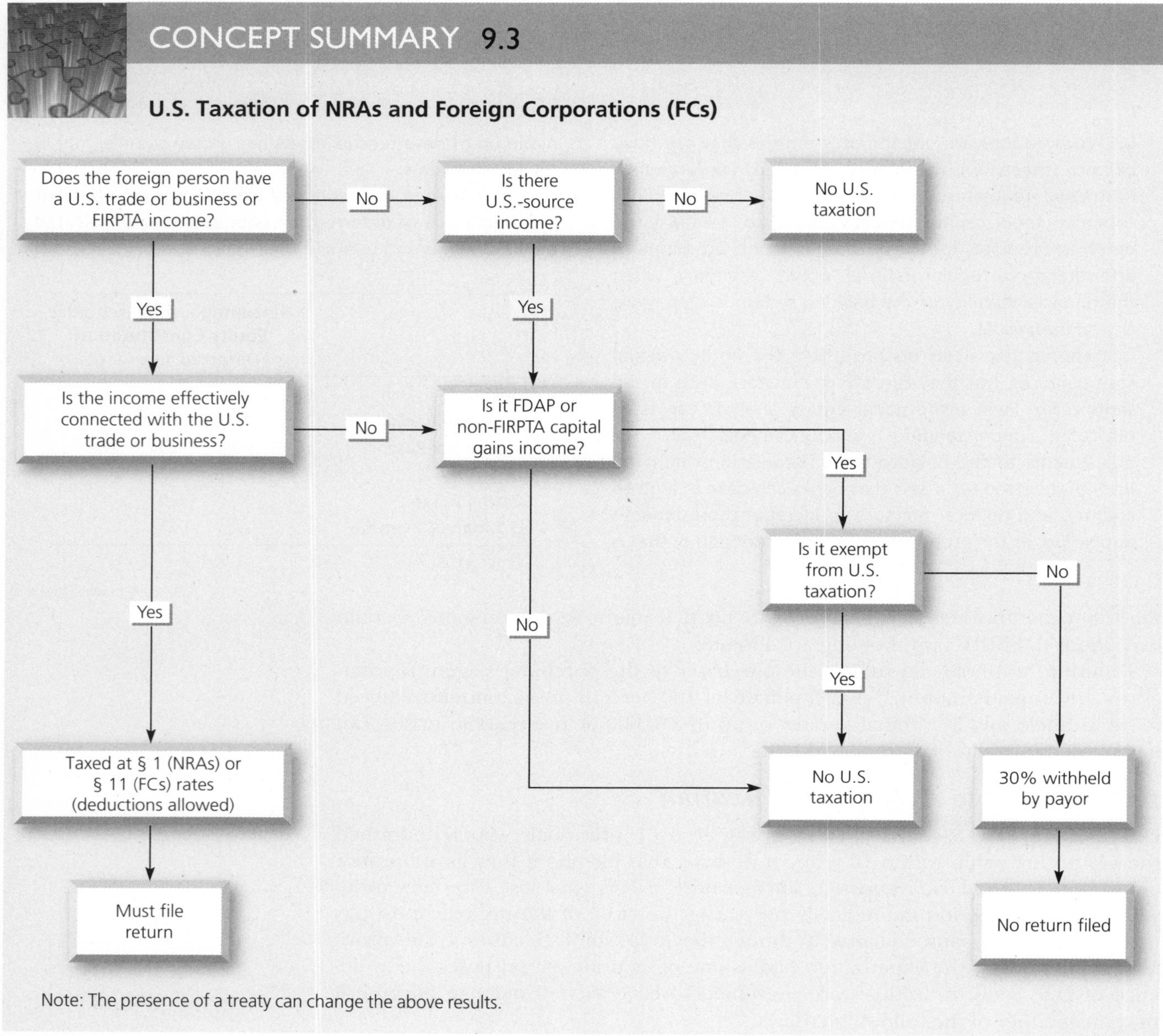

who are subject to the 10-year rule outlined previously must file an information disclosure statement annually. If an expatriate is physically present in the United States for more than 30 days during a calendar year during the 10-year period, the individual is taxed as a U.S. citizen or resident.[51] These expatriation rules, taken as a whole, make it difficult to give up U.S. citizenship or residency simply to avoid U.S. taxation.

9.7 Reporting Requirements

The U.S. tax provisions in the international area include numerous reporting requirements. Furthermore, civil and criminal penalties for noncompliance can apply.[52]

A domestic corporation that is 25 percent or more foreign-owned must file an information return and maintain certain records where they will be accessible to

[51] § 877(g)(1).

[52] See Chapter 17.

Filing Deadlines When You're Overseas

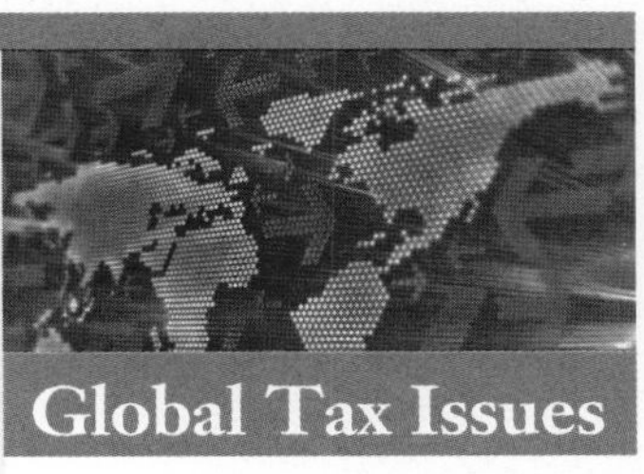

© Andrey Prokhorov, iStockphoto

What if you are situated outside the United States when you file a tax return? Working with a non-U.S. postal service can be challenging even on a good day. The established rule still seems to be that the date of the non-U.S. postmark determines whether the return is filed in a timely manner or whether a failure to file penalty will be assessed (Rev.Rul. 80–218).

The IRS seems to be having some trouble digesting this rule, though. In *Pekar*, 113 TC 158, where the non-U.S. postmark indicated that the return had been mailed before its due date, the IRS seemed to be taking a date-received position with the Tax Court. But the Service admitted its mistake in ITA 2000121085, where the reliance-on-postmark test is applied as expected.

No ruling to date has specifically addressed the application of this rule to a private express delivery service such as UPS, but neither the Code nor rulings restrict the when-delivered-to-the-carrier rule to domestic shipments either. Thus, if a U.S. taxpayer living overseas uses a private delivery service, some form of date stamping is a good idea.

the IRS.[53] In addition, any foreign corporation carrying on a trade or business in the United States must file an information return and maintain records in a similar manner.[54]

U.S. shareholders of a CFC must file a Form 5471. The U.S. partners of a controlled foreign partnership must file an information return.[55] A foreign partnership that has gross income that is either U.S.-source or effectively connected with a U.S. trade or business must file a partnership return.[56] Changes in ownership of interests in foreign partnerships (acquisitions or dispositions) must also be reported if a 10 percent or greater interest is involved.[57]

Asset transfers to foreign corporations or partnerships under certain tax-deferred transactions require information returns at the time of the transfer.[58] U.S. taxpayers that control foreign corporations or partnerships must also file annual information returns related to these entities.[59] Creation of, or a transfer to, a foreign trust by a U.S. person necessitates the filing of a Form 3520.[60]

9.8 Tax Planning

Over time, legislation has tended to reduce the ability to plan transactions and operations in a manner that minimizes tax liability. However, taxpayers who are not limited by the constraints of a particular transaction or operation can use the following suggestions to plan for maximum tax benefits.

The Foreign Tax Credit Limitation and Sourcing Provisions

The FTC limitation is partially based on the amount of foreign-source taxable income in the numerator of the limitation ratio. Consequently, the sourcing of income is extremely important. Income that is taxed by a foreign tax jurisdiction benefits from the FTC only to the extent that it is classified as foreign-source income under U.S. tax law. Thus, elements that affect the sourcing of income, such as the place of title passage, should be considered carefully before a transaction is undertaken.

[53] § 6038A.
[54] § 6038C.
[55] § 6038.
[56] § 6031(e).
[57] § 6046A.
[58] § 6038B.
[59] § 6038.
[60] § 6048.

It may be possible for a U.S. corporation to alleviate the problem of excess foreign taxes by using the following techniques.

- Generate "same basket" foreign-source income that is subject to a tax rate lower than the U.S. tax rate.
- Reduce highly taxed foreign-source income in favor of foreign-source income that is taxed at a lower rate by shifting operations or intangibles.
- Time the repatriation of foreign-source earnings to coincide with "excess limitation" years.
- Deduct foreign taxes for years when the deduction benefit would exceed the FTC benefit.
- Convert deductions related to foreign-source income so that they are related to U.S.-source income instead.

EXAMPLE 37

Della, Inc., a U.S. corporation, reports U.S.-source taxable income of $200,000, total taxable income of $300,000, and a U.S. tax liability (before the FTC) of $105,000. Della receives foreign-source taxable income, pays foreign income taxes, and computes an FTC as shown.

Basket	Amount	Foreign Taxes	FTC Limitation	Allowed FTC
Passive	$ 80,000	$ 8,000	$28,000	$ 8,000
General	20,000	8,000	7,000	7,000
	$100,000	$16,000		$15,000

If Della can shift $10,000 of passive income into the general basket, the FTC is increased by $1,000. The FTC limitation for the general basket increases to $10,500 [($30,000/$300,000) × $105,000]. This allows all $8,000 of foreign taxes related to the general basket to be credited in the current year. The allowed FTC for the passive basket remains unchanged at $8,000. ■

EXAMPLE 38

Donohoe, Inc., a U.S. corporation, reports total U.S. taxable income of $100,000, classified as follows.

	Total	U.S.-Source Income	Foreign-Source Income—General
Gross income	$150,000	$100,000	$ 50,000
Deductions	(50,000)	(40,000)	(10,000)
Taxable income	$100,000	$ 60,000	$ 40,000

U.S. income tax before the FTC is $34,000, and Donohoe's FTC limitation is $13,600 ($40,000/$100,000 × $34,000). If, through planning and analysis, Donohoe is able to convert $5,000 of the deductions related to foreign-source income to U.S. source, the total taxable income would remain the same, but the FTC limitation would increase to $15,300 ($45,000/$100,000 × $34,000). ■

The Foreign Corporation as a Tax Shelter

An NRA who is able to hold U.S. investments through a foreign corporation can accomplish much in the way of avoiding U.S. taxation. Capital gains (other than dispositions of U.S. real property interests) are not subject to U.S. taxation. This assumes that they are not effectively connected with a U.S. trade or business. The NRA can dispose of the stock of a foreign corporation that holds U.S. real property and not be subject to taxation under § 897 (FIRPTA). Furthermore, the stock of a foreign corporation is not included in the U.S. gross estate of a deceased NRA, even if all of the assets of the foreign corporation are located in the United States.

TAX IN THE NEWS So Long, It's Been Nice Knowing You

Did you ever wonder who gives up their U.S. citizenship? It is easy to find out. Section 877 requires that U.S. citizens and long-term permanent residents inform the IRS of their expatriation on Form 8854, Initial and Annual Expatriation Information Statement, in the year of expatriation and certain years thereafter.

Expatriating individuals must also give notice of an expatriating act or termination of residency to the Department of State or the Department of Homeland Security.

The government publishes the names of these individuals in the *Federal Register* each quarter. Several hundred people abandon U.S. citizenship every year.

Caution is advised when the foreign corporation may generate income effectively connected with the conduct of a U.S. trade or business. The income may be taxed at a higher rate than if the NRA individually generated the income. The tradeoff between a higher U.S. tax on this income and protection from the U.S. estate tax and § 897 must be weighed.

Planning under Subpart F

Careful timing of investment in U.S. property can reduce the potential for constructive dividend income to U.S. shareholders. The gross income of U.S. shareholders attributable to investment in U.S. property is limited to the E & P of the CFC.[61] E & P that is attributable to amounts that have been included in gross income as Subpart F income in either the current year or a prior tax year is not taxed again when invested in U.S. property.

Using the Check-the-Box Regulations

The check-the-box Regulations provide a great deal of flexibility for U.S.-based multinational corporations. Corporations can organize their branches and subsidiaries around the world in ways that optimize both local country and U.S. taxation. For example, a U.S. corporation may choose to treat its subsidiary in the United Kingdom as a partnership or unincorporated branch for U.S. tax purposes (thus taking advantage of loss flow-throughs) and a corporation under United Kingdom law (where certain tax and liability benefits may exist).

The flurry of multinational restructurings since the issuance of the check-the-box Regulations has led to some cries of foul by U.S. taxing authorities who claim that these provisions are being used in inappropriate ways.

Transferring Intangible Assets Offshore

In many industries, a company's intangible assets, such as licenses and patents, produce a relatively large share of total income. For example, the license to use a software program is much more valuable than the actual disc the customer purchases; thus, a large part of the profit from the sale of software accrues to the license holder.

Unlike manufacturing plants, intangible assets can be easily transferred to related entities outside the United States. Congress recognized this potential, and § 367 requires gain to be recognized if intangibles are transferred outside the United States. To avoid this § 367 "toll charge," companies should consider creating their intangibles offshore so that no subsequent transfer is required. Companies may choose to perform their R&D activities within subsidiaries located in tax haven countries to create and keep their valuable intangibles in low-tax jurisdictions.

[61] §§ 959(a)(1) and (2).

Transfer Pricing

U.S. multinational companies earn income across many different jurisdictions and operate through several different types of entities (e.g., subsidiary corporations, joint ventures, and partnerships). With proper planning and documentation, a U.S. corporation can organize its intercompany payments for goods and services, interest on debt, and royalties for use of intangible property in such a way as to minimize its worldwide tax burden. For example, a U.S. multinational may choose to borrow in high-tax jurisdictions (where the interest deduction will be more valuable) and earn royalty income in low-tax jurisdictions (where the income escapes heavy taxation).

Such decisions can be made within the legal framework of the tax laws of the United States and other countries. In the United States, § 482 acts to require an entity to demonstrate that it deserved to earn its profits based on the functions it performs, the assets it owns, or the risks it takes.

REFOCUS ON THE BIG PICTURE

Going International

Now you can address the questions about VoiceCo's activities that were posed at the beginning of the chapter. Simply selling into a foreign jurisdiction may not trigger any overseas income tax consequences, but such income is taxed currently to VoiceCo in the United States. When VoiceCo sets up an Irish corporation, it benefits from deferral because as a manufacturer, it can avoid deemed dividends under Subpart F. However, passive-basket income may be earned by the Irish subsidiary.

VoiceCo must file Form 5471 to report the activities of its foreign subsidiary. If VoiceCo receives dividends from its foreign subsidiary, it can claim indirect foreign tax credits. What are the foreign tax implications if VoiceCo "checks the box" on its foreign subsidiary? The U.S. tax implications?

What If?

Suppose that although VoiceCo's European sales become a substantial part of its total revenues, it decides not to create a foreign subsidiary. Instead, because shipping costs are high and customers demand quick turnaround on product orders, VoiceCo decides to license its design and manufacturing process to a local European musical instruments company for sales in Europe. The European company pays VoiceCo a royalty equal to 25 percent of the sales price on all of its sales of microphones based on VoiceCo's design. The royalty income is foreign-source income (as the underlying intangible property is exploited outside the United States).

The European country imposes a 5 percent withholding tax on all royalty payments to VoiceCo. The royalties are part of its worldwide income and so are currently taxed to VoiceCo in the United States. Will VoiceCo receive a foreign tax credit for the withholding tax?

KEY TERMS

Branch profits tax, 9-35
CFC (controlled foreign corporation), 9-21
Dividend equivalent amount (DEA), 9-35
Effectively connected income, 9-33
FIRPTA, 9-36
foreign tax credit (FTC), 9-26
Functional currency, 9-14
Inbound taxation, 9-2
Nonresident alien (NRA), 9-32
Outbound taxation, 9-2
Qualified business unit (QBU), 9-14
Subpart F, 9-22
Tax haven, 9-19
Tax treaties, 9-4
Transfer pricing, 9-10
Treaty shopping, 9-20
U.S. shareholder, 9-21
U.S. trade or business, 9-33

DISCUSSION QUESTIONS

1. **LO.1** "U.S. persons are taxed on their worldwide income." Explain.
2. **LO.1, 5** Liang, a U.S. citizen, owns 100% of ForCo, a foreign corporation not engaged in a U.S. trade or business. Is Liang subject to any U.S. income tax on her dealings with ForCo? Explain.
3. **LO.2** Kelly, a U.S. citizen, earns interest income that is sourced in Germany. How could a U.S. tax treaty with Germany reduce Kelly's taxes on the interest?
4. **LO.3** When is dividend income paid by a non-U.S. entity to a U.S. investor *not* foreign-source income? Be specific.
5. **LO.3** Write a memo outlining the issues that arise when attempting to source income that is earned from Internet-based activities. **Issue ID** **Communications**
6. **LO.3** "The IRS can use §482 to overturn all of the international tax planning that our company is doing." Explain.
7. **LO.4** Weinke is a business organized in Austria, where the local currency is the euro. Nevertheless, Weinke's U.S. branch uses the U.S. dollar as its functional currency. How can this be?
8. **LO.4** When dealing with the rules concerning gain and loss from foreign currency transactions, the taxpayer must identify its qualified business units (QBUs). What is a QBU? How many QBUs can a business operate?
9. **LO.4** Heinrik is a business organized in the United States, and its functional currency is the U.S. dollar. On a January sale to a customer in Finland, the closing price for the goods is expressed in euros, payable to Heinrik on March 1. Does Heinrik record a foreign currency gain or loss on this transaction? Be specific, and show your computations.
10. **LO.5** What are the important concepts to be considered when U.S. assets are transferred outside the country to be used in starting a new business? **Issue ID**
11. **LO.5** Write a memo to a U.S. client explaining why some of the profit generated from a non-U.S. subsidiary still is included in its U.S. taxable income. **Communications**
12. **LO.5** Summarize the ownership rules that apply in determining whether a non-U.S. entity is a controlled foreign corporation (CFC) under the U.S. Federal income tax rules.
13. **LO.5** Joanna owns 5% of Axel, a foreign corporation. Joanna's son, Fred, is considering acquiring 15% of Axel from an NRA. The remainder of Axel is owned 27% by unrelated U.S. persons and 53% by unrelated NRAs. Currently, Fred operates (as a sole proprietorship) a manufacturing business that sells goods to Axel for resale outside the United States and outside Axel's country of residence. Joanna is not concerned about the concentration of investment because she expects to sell her stock in Axel in three years at a significant capital gain. Are there tax issues that Joanna and Fred, both U.S. citizens, need to address? Explain. **Issue ID**
14. **LO.5** Linker is a corporate entity organized in France. It is owned equally by 100 U.S. shareholders. The shareholders are not related to each other; they purchased the shares from a broker. Is Linker a CFC? Explain.
15. **LO.5** QuinnCo could not claim all of the income taxes it paid to Japan as a foreign tax credit (FTC) this year. What computational limit probably kept QuinnCo from taking its full FTC?
16. **LO.5** SwitchCo, a U.S. business, paid income taxes to France relative to profitable sales it made in that country. Can it claim a deduction for these taxes in computing U.S. taxable income? A tax credit? Both? Explain.
17. **LO.5** Klein, a domestic corporation, receives a $10,000 dividend from ForCo, a wholly owned foreign corporation. The deemed-paid FTC associated with this dividend is $3,000. What is the total gross income included in Klein's tax return as a result of this dividend?

Issue ID

18. **LO.5** Molly, Inc., a domestic corporation, owns 15% of PJ, Inc., and 12% of Emma, Inc., both foreign corporations. Molly is paid gross dividends of $35,000 and $18,000 from PJ and Emma, respectively. PJ withheld and paid more than $10,500 in foreign taxes on the $35,000 dividend.

    PJ's country of residence levies a 20% tax on dividends paid to nonresident corporations. However, the tax rate is increased to 30% if the recipient is a resident of a country that provides an FTC. Taxes of $3,600 are withheld on the dividend from Emma.

    What tax issues must be considered in determining the availability and amount of the FTC allowed to Molly, Inc.?

19. **LO.5** Working with the FTC may involve "baskets" of foreign-source income and deductions. Explain this term.

20. **LO.6** In general terms, how is a non-U.S. person taxed on his or her U.S. business income? Investment income? Ignore the effects of tax treaties in your answer.

Issue ID

21. **LO.3, 6** Sloop, Inc., a foreign corporation, sells wireless devices in several countries, including the United States. In fact, currently 25% of Sloop's sales income is sourced in the United States (through branches in New York and Chicago). Sloop is considering opening additional branches in San Diego and Denver to increase U.S. sales. What tax issues must Sloop consider before making this move?

Communications

22. **LO.6** Write a memo on the difference between "inbound" and "outbound" activities in the context of U.S. taxation of international income.

Communications

23. **LO.1, 3, 5** If a U.S. taxpayer is subject to U.S. income tax on profits earned outside the United States and such profits also are subject to income tax in the foreign jurisdiction, how does the U.S. taxpayer escape double taxation? Draft a short speech that you will give to your university's Business Club.

PROBLEMS

24. **LO.4, 5** RedCo, a domestic corporation, incorporates GreenCo, a new wholly owned entity in Germany. Under both German and U.S. legal principles, this entity is a corporation. RedCo faces a 35% U.S. tax rate.

    GreenCo earns $800,000 in net profits from its German activities and makes no dividend distributions to RedCo. How much U.S. income tax will RedCo pay for the current year as a result of GreenCo's earnings, assuming no deemed dividend under Subpart F? Ignore any FTC implications.

25. **LO.3** Madison, a U.S. resident, received the following income items for the current tax year. Identify the source of each income item as either U.S. or foreign.
    a. $3,000 dividend from U.S. Flower Company, a U.S. corporation that operates solely in the eastern United States.
    b. $6,000 dividend from Stern Corporation, a U.S. corporation that had total gross income of $4 million from the active conduct of a foreign trade or business for the immediately preceding three tax years. Stern's total gross income for the same period was $5 million.
    c. $2,000 dividend from International Consolidated, Inc., a foreign corporation that had gross income of $3 million effectively connected with the conduct of a U.S. trade or business for the immediately preceding three tax years. International's total gross income for the same period was $6 million.
    d. $600 interest from a savings account at a Florida bank.
    e. $5,000 interest on Warren Corporation bonds. Warren is a U.S. corporation that derived $6 million of its gross income for the immediately preceding three tax years from operation of an active foreign business. Warren's total gross income for this same period was $7.2 million.

Communications

26. **LO.3** Gloria Wang, an NRA, is a professional golfer. She played in seven tournaments in the United States in the current year and earned $200,000 in prizes from these tournaments. She deposited the winnings in a bank account she opened in Mexico City after her first tournament win.

    Gloria played a total of 30 tournaments for the year and earned $300,000 in total prize money. She spent 40 days in the United States, 60 days in England, 20 days in

Scotland, and the rest of the time in South America. Write a letter to Gloria explaining how much U.S.-source income she will generate, if any, from her participation in these tournaments and whether any of her winnings are subject to U.S. taxation. Gloria's address is AV Rio Branco, 149-4#, Rio de Janeiro, RJ 20180, Brazil.

27. **LO.3** Determine whether the source of income for the following sales is U.S. or foreign.
    a. Suarez, an NRA, sells stock in Home Depot, a U.S. corporation, through a broker in San Antonio.
    b. Chris sells stock in IBM, a U.S. corporation, to her brother, Rich. Both Chris and Rich are NRAs, and the sale takes place outside the United States.
    c. Crows, Inc., sells inventory produced in the United States to customers in Europe. Title passes in the international waters of the Atlantic Ocean.
    d. Doubles, Inc., a U.S. corporation, manufactures equipment in Malaysia and sells the equipment to customers in the United States.

28. **LO.3, 6** Determine whether the source of income in each of the following situations is U.S. or foreign.
    a. Development, Inc., a U.S. corporation, earns $400,000 in royalty income from Far East, Ltd., a foreign corporation, for the use of several patented processes in Far East's manufacturing business located in Singapore.
    b. Marion, an NRA, is an employee of a foreign corporation. During the tax year, she spends 75 days in the United States purchasing cloth for her employer, a clothing manufacturer. Her yearly salary is $150,000 (translated to U.S. dollars). Marion spends a total of 250 days working during the year. Her employer has no other business contacts with the United States.
    c. Jacques, an NRA, sells an apartment building to Julie, a U.S. resident. The building is located in Denver. The closing takes place in Jacques's country of residence.
    d. A domestic corporation sells depreciable personal property that it has been using in its foreign branch operations. The property sells for $180,000, has a tax basis of $75,000, and has been depreciated for tax purposes to the extent of $77,000. The property is located in a foreign country but is sold to another domestic corporation. The sales transaction takes place in the United States.

29. **LO.3** Chock, a U.S. corporation, purchases inventory for resale from distributors within the United States and resells this inventory at a $1 million profit to customers outside the United States. Title to the goods passes outside the United States. What is the sourcing of Chock's inventory sales income?

30. **LO.3** Willa, a U.S. corporation, owns the rights to a patent related to a medical device. Willa licenses the rights to use the patent to IrishCo, which uses the patent in its manufacturing facility located in Ireland. What is the sourcing of the $1 million royalty income received by Willa from IrishCo for the use of the patent?

31. **LO.3** USCo incurred $100,000 in interest expense for the current year. The tax book value of USCo's assets generating foreign-source income is $5 million. The tax book value of USCo's assets generating U.S.-source income is $45 million. How much of the interest expense is allocated and apportioned to foreign-source income?

32. **LO.3** Create, Inc., produces inventory in its foreign manufacturing plants for sale in the United States. Its foreign manufacturing assets have a tax book value of $5 million and a fair market value of $15 million. Its assets related to the sales activity have a tax book value of $2 million and a fair market value of $5 million. Create's interest expense totaled $400,000 for the current year. **Decision Making**
    a. What amount of Create's interest expense is allocated and apportioned to foreign-source income using the tax book value method? Using the fair market method?
    b. If Create wants to maximize its FTC, which method should it use?

33. **LO.4** Peck, Inc., a U.S. corporation, purchases weight-lifting equipment for resale from HiDisu, a Japanese corporation, for 75 million yen. On the date of purchase, 75 yen is equal to $1 U.S. (¥75:$1). The purchase is made on December 15, 2012, with payment due in 90 days. Peck is a calendar year taxpayer. On December 31, 2012, the foreign exchange rate is ¥80:$1. What amount of foreign currency gain or loss, if any, must Peck recognize for 2012 as a result of this transaction? For 2013?

Communications

34. **LO.4** Table, Inc., a U.S. corporation, operates a manufacturing branch in Mexico and a sales branch in Canada. The Mexican branch uses the peso for all of its activities, and the Canadian branch uses the Canadian dollar for all of its activities. Write a letter to Karen Burns, Table's tax director, explaining the number of foreign qualified business units the company will have from these activities. Table's address is 840 Logan Avenue, Madison, WI 53705.

35. **LO.4** Bench, Inc., a U.S. corporation, operates a sales branch in France. Although the operations are located in France, where the euro is the local currency, all of the branch's sales are to customers in the United Kingdom. The revenue is collected in British pounds, and the sales branch's employees are paid in British pounds. What functional currency should Bench use for its France sales branch?

Issue ID

36. **LO.4** Juarez is a citizen and resident of the United States. He pays all of his living expenses in U.S. dollars. He operates an unincorporated trade or business buying and selling rare books over the Internet to customers in Mexico. All income and expenses of the rare book business are in pesos. Explain to Juarez the number of qualified business units he has, and help him determine the related functional currency of the QBUs.

Issue ID

Communications

37. **LO.4, 6** Marian Manufacturing, Inc., a calendar year domestic corporation, operates a branch in Ireland. In the current year, the branch generated 750,000 euros in net profit. On December 31 of the current year, one euro equaled $1.35. The average exchange rate for the current year between the euro and the dollar was $1.25. Write a memo to Margaret Zhang, the controller of Marian, explaining (1) how and when the Irish profits will be taxed to Marian in the United States and (2) under what conditions a foreign currency gain or loss will be recognized.

38. **LO.4, 5** Teal, Inc., a foreign corporation, pays a dividend to its shareholders on November 30. Red, Inc., a U.S. corporation and 7% shareholder in Teal, receives a dividend of 10,000K (a foreign currency). Pertinent exchange rates are as follows.

November 30	.9K:$1
Average for year	.7K:$1
December 31	2K:$1

What is the dollar amount of the dividend received by Red, Inc.? Does Red have a foreign exchange gain or loss on receipt of the dividend?

39. **LO.5** Hometown, a U.S. C corporation, makes a sale to a customer in Sustainia, a country that applies a 25% income tax to business profits. The customer found out about Hometown through an Internet search. Hometown has no facilities or employees outside the United States. Hometown's profit on the sale totals $1,000. Where is the tax levied on this $1,000 profit?

40. **LO.5** USCo incorporated its foreign branch operations in Italy by transferring the branch's assets to a foreign corporation in return solely for stock in the new corporation. All of the branch's assets are located outside the United States and are used in the active conduct of a foreign trade or business. Is this transaction automatically eligible for tax deferral under § 351? Explain.

41. **LO.5** Buckeye Corporation transferred inventory (basis of $10, fair market value of $40) and machinery used in a U.S. factory (basis of $50, fair market value of $85) to MapleLeaf, a newly formed corporation in Canada, in exchange for all of MapleLeaf's stock. Buckeye previously deducted $30 of depreciation related to the machinery on its U.S. tax return. How much gain, if any, must Buckeye recognize on the transfers of the property to MapleLeaf?

Communications

42. **LO.5** WorldCo, a domestic corporation, is planning to incorporate a branch that it has been operating in a foreign country. WorldCo's branch has a large amount of inventory. In no more than three PowerPoint slides, outline the tax results of transferring this inventory to a newly formed foreign corporation.

Issue ID

Communications

43. **LO.5** Beach, Inc., a domestic corporation, operates a branch in Mexico. Over the last 10 years, this branch has generated $50 million in losses. For the last 3 years, however, the branch has been profitable and has earned enough income to entirely offset the prior losses. Most of the assets are fully depreciated, and a net gain would be recognized if the assets were sold.

Beach's CFO believes that Beach should incorporate the branch now so that this potential gain can be transferred to a foreign corporation, thereby avoiding U.S. tax and, as an added benefit, avoiding U.S. taxes on future income. Draft a memo to Claire Quinty, the CFO, addressing the tax issues involved in the proposed transaction.

44. **LO.5** USCo owns 65% of the voting stock of LandCo, a Country X corporation. Terra, an unrelated Country Y corporation, owns the other 35% of LandCo. LandCo owns 100% of the voting stock of OceanCo, a Country Z corporation. Assuming that USCo is a U.S. shareholder, do LandCo and OceanCo meet the definition of a CFC? Explain.

45. **LO.5** Hart Enterprises, a U.S. corporation, owns 100% of OK, Ltd., an Irish corporation. OK's gross income for the year is $10 million. Determine OK's Subpart F income (before any expenses) from the transactions that it reported this year.
    a. OK received $600,000 from sales of products purchased from Hart and sold to customers outside Ireland.
    b. OK received $1 million from sales of products purchased from Hart and sold to customers in Ireland.
    c. OK received $400,000 from sales of products purchased from unrelated suppliers and sold to customers in Germany.
    d. OK purchased raw materials from Hart, used these materials to manufacture finished goods, and sold these goods to customers in Italy. OK earned $300,000 from these sales.
    e. OK received $100,000 for the performance of warranty services on behalf of Hart. These services were performed in Japan for customers located in Japan.
    f. OK received $50,000 in dividend income from investments in Canada and Mexico.

46. **LO.5** Round, Inc., a U.S. corporation, owns 80% of the only class of stock of Square, Inc., a CFC. Square is a CFC until May 1 of the current tax year (not a leap year). Round has held the stock since Square was organized and continues to hold it for the entire year. Round and Square are both calendar year taxpayers. Square's Subpart F income for the tax year is $1 million, current E & P is $2.5 million, and no distributions have been made for the tax year. What amount, if any, must Round include in gross income under Subpart F for the tax year?

47. **LO.5** Brandy, a U.S. corporation, operates a manufacturing branch in Chad, which does not have an income tax treaty with the United States. Brandy's worldwide Federal taxable income is $30 million, so it is subject to a 35% marginal tax rate. Profits and taxes in Chad for the current year are summarized as follows. Compute Brandy's foreign tax credit associated with its operations in Chad.

Income Item	Chad Income This Year	Chad Tax Rate	Chad Tax Paid
Manufacturing profits	$2,500,000	20%	$500,000
Dividend	300,000	5%	15,000

48. **LO.5** Weather, Inc., a domestic corporation, operates in both Fredonia and the United States. This year, the business generated taxable income of $600,000 from foreign sources and $900,000 from U.S. sources. All of Weather's foreign-source income is in the general limitation basket. Weather's total taxable income is $1.5 million. Weather pays Fredonia taxes of $228,000. What is Weather's FTC for the tax year? Assume a 34% U.S. income tax rate.

49. **LO.5** Blunt, Inc., a U.S. corporation, earned $600,000 in total taxable income, including $80,000 in foreign-source taxable income from its German branch's manufacturing operations and $30,000 in foreign-source taxable income from its Swiss branch's engineering services operations. Blunt paid $32,000 in German income taxes and $1,800 in Swiss income taxes. Compute Blunt's U.S. tax liability after any available FTCs. Blunt's marginal U.S. tax rate is 34%.

50. **LO.5** Dunne, Inc., a U.S. corporation, earned $400,000 in total taxable income, including $50,000 in foreign-source taxable income from its branch manufacturing operations in Brazil and $20,000 in foreign-source income from interest earned on bonds issued by

Dutch corporations. Dunne paid $25,000 in Brazilian income taxes and $3,000 in Dutch income taxes. Compute Dunne's U.S. tax liability after any available FTCs. Assume that the U.S. tax rate is 34%.

51. **LO.5** ABC, Inc., a domestic corporation, has $50 million of taxable income, including $15 million of general limitation foreign-source taxable income, on which ABC paid $5 million in foreign income taxes. The U.S. tax rate is 35%. What is ABC's foreign tax credit?

52. **LO.5** Mary, a U.S. citizen, is the sole shareholder of CanCo, a Canadian corporation. During its first year of operations, CanCo earns $14 million of foreign-source taxable income, pays $6 million of Canadian income taxes, and distributes a $2 million dividend to Mary. Can Mary claim a deemed-paid (indirect) FTC on her Form 1040 with respect to receipt of the dividend distribution from CanCo? Why or why not?

53. **LO.5** ABC, Inc., a domestic corporation, owns 100% of HighTax, a foreign corporation. HighTax has $50 million of undistributed E & P, all of which is attributable to general limitation income, and $30 million of foreign income taxes paid. HighTax distributes a $5 million dividend to ABC. The dividend, which is subject to a 5% foreign withholding tax, is ABC's only item of income during the year. ABC's marginal U.S. tax rate is 35%. What amount of FTC and carryover is produced by the dividend?

54. **LO.5** USCo, a domestic corporation, reports worldwide taxable income of $1.5 million, including a $400,000 dividend from ForCo, a wholly owned foreign corporation. ForCo holds $16 million in undistributed E & P, and it has paid $10 million of foreign income taxes attributable to these earnings. All foreign income is in the general limitation basket. What is USCo's deemed-paid FTC related to the dividend received (before consideration of any limitation)?

55. **LO.5** USCo, a domestic corporation, reports worldwide taxable income of $500,000, including a $300,000 dividend from ForCo, a wholly owned foreign corporation. ForCo holds $1 million in undistributed E & P, and it has paid $200,000 of foreign income taxes attributable to these earnings. All foreign income is in the general limitation basket. What is USCo's deemed-paid FTC related to the dividend received (before consideration of any limitation)?

56. **LO.5** Plane, Inc., a U.S. corporation, earned $600,000 in total taxable income for the current year. This total includes $750,000 in U.S.-source income, $50,000 in foreign-source income in the passive basket, and a $200,000 loss in the general limitation basket. Plane paid $5,000 in foreign income taxes related to the passive basket and incurred no taxes related to the general limitation basket. What is Plane's allowed FTC for the current year?

57. **LO.5** Elmwood, Inc., a domestic corporation, owns 15% of Correy, Ltd., a Hong Kong corporation. The remaining 85% of Correy is owned by Fortune Enterprises, a Canadian corporation. At the end of the current year, Correy has $400,000 in undistributed E & P and $200,000 in foreign taxes related to this E & P.

    On the last day of the year, Correy pays a $40,000 dividend to Elmwood. Elmwood's taxable income before the dividend is $200,000. What is Elmwood's tax liability after consideration of the dividend and any allowed FTC, assuming a 34% U.S. tax rate?

Communications

58. **LO.5** Your client Chips, Inc., is engaged in the cookie production business, with production plants in Florida and Singapore. The U.S. plant has always produced profits, but the Singapore operation has generated $100,000 in losses since inception. This year, the Singapore operation began producing net profits. Draft a letter to Sally Jackson, the CFO of Chips, explaining why a portion of the current-year foreign-source income must be recharacterized as U.S.-source for FTC limitation purposes. Chips's address is 9921 East Call Street, Starke FL 32091.

59. **LO.5** Skills, Inc., a U.S. corporation, reports current foreign-source income classified in two different FTC income baskets. It earns $50,000 in passive foreign-source income and suffers a net loss of $30,000 in the general limitation basket. What is the numerator of the FTC limitation formula for the passive basket in the current year? Explain.

60. **LO.5** Canteen, Inc., a U.S. corporation, owns 100% of NewGrass, Ltd., a foreign corporation. NewGrass earns only general limitation income. During the current year, NewGrass paid Canteen a $10,000 dividend. The deemed-paid foreign tax credit associated

with this dividend is $3,000. The foreign jurisdiction requires a withholding tax of 20%, so Canteen received only $8,000 in cash as a result of the dividend. What is Canteen's total U.S. gross income reported as a result of the $8,000 cash dividend?

61. **LO.5** For which of the following foreign income inclusions is a U.S. corporation potentially allowed an indirect FTC under § 902?
    a. Interest income from a 5% owned foreign corporation.
    b. Interest income from a 60% owned foreign corporation.
    c. Dividend income from a 5% owned foreign corporation.
    d. Dividend income from a 60% owned foreign corporation.

62. **LO.5** Night, Inc., a domestic corporation, earned $300,000 from foreign manufacturing activities on which it paid $90,000 of foreign income taxes. Night's foreign sales income is taxed at a 50% foreign tax rate. What amount of foreign sales income can Night earn without generating any excess FTCs for the current year? Assume a 34% U.S. tax rate.

Decision Making

63. **LO.4, 5** Partin, Inc., a foreign subsidiary of Jones, Inc., a U.S. corporation, has pretax income of 200,000 euros for 2012. Partin accrues 60,000 euros in foreign taxes on this income. The average exchange rate for the tax year to which the taxes relate is 1.35 €$1. None of the income is Subpart F income. If the net earnings of 140,000 euros are distributed when the exchange rate is 1.25 €$1, what are the deemed-paid taxes available to Jones? Assume that 2012 is Partin's first year of operation.

64. **LO.5** Collins, Inc., a domestic corporation, operates a manufacturing branch in Singapore. During the current year, the manufacturing branch produces a loss of $300,000. Collins also earns interest income from investments in Europe, where it earns $800,000 in passive income. Collins paid no foreign income taxes related to the Singapore branch, but it paid $64,000 in foreign income taxes related to the passive income. Collins pays U.S. income taxes at the 34% tax rate. What is Collins's allowable FTC for the current year?

65. **LO.3, 4, 5** You are the head tax accountant for the Venture Company, a U.S. corporation. The board of directors is considering expansion overseas and asks you to present a summary of the U.S. tax consequences of investing overseas through a foreign subsidiary. Prepare a detailed outline of the presentation you will make to the board.

Communications

66. **LO.5** Money, Inc., a U.S. corporation, has $500,000 to invest overseas. For U.S. tax purposes, any additional gross income earned by Money will be taxed at 34%. Two possibilities for investment are:
    a. Invest the $500,000 in common stock of Exco (a foreign corporation). Exco common stock pays a dividend of $3 per share each year. The $500,000 would purchase 10,000 shares (or 10%) of Exco's only class of stock (voting common). Exco expects to earn $10 million before taxes this year and to be taxed at a flat rate of 40%. Its current E & P before taxes is estimated to be $9.4 million. Exco's government does not withhold on dividends paid to foreign investors.
    b. Invest the $500,000 in Exco bonds that pay interest at 7% per year. Assume that the bonds will be acquired at par, or face, value. Exco's government withholds 25% on interest paid to foreign investors.

    Analyze these two investment opportunities, and determine which would give Money the better return after taxes. Make sure you consider the effect of the FTC. Write a letter to Money's CFO Jeffrey Howard, advising the corporation of your findings. Money's address is 9201 West South Street, Woodstock IL 60098.

Decision Making

Communications

67. **LO.2, 6** IrishCo, a manufacturing corporation resident in Ireland, distributes products through a U.S. office. Current-year taxable income from such sales in the United States is $12 million. IrishCo's U.S. office deposits working capital funds in short-term certificates of deposit with U.S. banks. Current-year interest income from these deposits is $150,000.

    IrishCo also invests in U.S. securities traded on the New York Stock Exchange. This investing is done by the home office. For the current year, IrishCo records realized capital gains of $300,000 and dividend income of $50,000 from these stock investments. Compute IrishCo's U.S. tax liability, assuming that the U.S.-Ireland income tax treaty reduces withholding on dividends to 15% and on interest to 5%. Assume a 34% U.S. tax rate.

68. **LO.6** Vanguard, S.A., a Peruvian corporation, manufactures inventory in Peru. The inventory is sold to independent distributors in the United States, with title passing to the purchaser in the United States. Vanguard has no employees or operations within the United States. All sales activities are conducted via telephone and Internet communication between Vanguard's home office and its U.S. customers. Explain whether Vanguard incurs any income effectively connected with a U.S. trade or business.

69. **LO.6** Clario, S.A., a Peruvian corporation, manufactures furniture in Peru. It sells the furniture to independent distributors in the United States. Because title to the furniture passes to the purchasers in the United States, Clario reports $1 million in U.S.-source income. Clario has no employees or operations in the United States related to its furniture business.

    As a separate line of business, Clario buys and sells antique toys. Clario has a single employee operating a booth on weekends at a flea market in Waldo, Florida. The antique toy business generated $9,000 in net profits from U.S. sources during the current year.

    What is Clario's effectively connected income for the current year?

70. **LO.6** Palm, Ltd., a foreign corporation, operates a sales branch in the United States that constitutes a U.S. trade or business. Rather than return the profits from the sales branch to the foreign home office, Palm invests the profits in certificates of deposit at U. S. banks. Explain whether the interest earned on these CDs is considered effectively connected with Palm's U.S. trade or business.

Communications

71. **LO.6** Trace, Ltd., a foreign corporation, operates a trade or business in the United States. Trace's U.S.-source income effectively connected with this trade or business is $800,000 for the current year. Trace's current-year E & P is $600,000. Trace's net U.S. equity was $8.2 million at the beginning of the year and $8.6 million at year-end. Trace is a resident in a country that has no income tax treaty with the United States. Prepare a letter to Tanner Martin, Trace's Tax VP, reporting Trace's branch profits tax liability for the current year, along with at least one planning idea for reducing the branch profits tax. Trace uses the following address for its U.S. affairs: 9148 Church Street, Marietta GA 30060.

72. **LO.6** Martinho is a citizen of Brazil and lives there year-round. He has invested in a plot of Illinois farmland with a tax basis to him of $1 million. Martinho has no other business or investment activities in the United States. He is not subject to the alternative minimum tax. Upon sale of the land for $1.5 million to Emma, an Illinois person, what are the Federal income tax consequences to Martinho?

73. **LO.6** Continue with the facts of Problem 72. What are the Federal income tax withholding requirements with respect to Martinho's sale? Who pays the withheld amount to the U. S. Treasury?

Issue ID

Communications

74. **LO.6** John McPherson is single, an attorney, and a U.S. citizen. He recently attended a seminar where he learned he could give up his U.S. citizenship, move to Bermuda (where he would pay no income tax), and operate his law practice long distance via the Internet with no U.S. tax consequences. Write a letter informing John of the tax consequences of his proposed actions. His address is 1005 NE 10th Street, Gainesville, GA 32612.

75. **LO.6** ForCo, a foreign corporation not engaged in a U.S. trade or business, received a $500,000 dividend from USCo, a domestic corporation. ForCo incurred $20,000 in expenses related to earning the dividend. All of USCo's income is from U.S. sources. ForCo is not eligible for any treaty benefits. What is the withholding tax on the dividend paid to ForCo?

76. **LO.6** ForCo, a foreign corporation not engaged in a U.S. trade or business, received a $200,000 dividend from USCo, a domestic corporation. ForCo incurred $5,000 in expenses related to earning the dividend. All of USCo's income is from U.S. sources. ForCo is not eligible for any treaty benefits. What is the withholding tax on the dividend paid to ForCo?

77. **LO.6** ForCo, a foreign corporation not engaged in a U.S. trade or business, received an $800,000 dividend from USCo, a domestic corporation. ForCo incurred $40,000 in expenses related to earning the dividend. All of USCo's income is from U.S. sources. ForCo is eligible for an income tax treaty that limits withholding on dividends to 10%. What is the withholding tax on the dividend paid to ForCo?

TAX RETURN PROBLEMS

1. Fleming Products, Inc., a U.S. corporation, has a branch in Canada. The branch earns taxable income of $1 million from manufacturing operations and $500,000 from passive investment. Fleming Products pays Canadian income tax of $400,000 (40%) and $100,000 (20%), respectively, on this foreign-source income. The corporation also earns U.S.-source taxable income from manufacturing operations of $4 million, resulting in worldwide taxable income of $5.5 million. The U.S. taxes before the FTC are $1.87 million (at 34%). Fleming Products (employer ID number 11–1111111) accrues taxes for purposes of the FTC. This information is summarized below.

Income Category	Gross Income	Direct Expenses	Indirect Expenses	Taxable Income	Foreign Taxes
U.S. manufacturing	$ 9,000,000	$4,460,000	$ 540,000	$4,000,000	NA
Foreign manufacturing	5,000,000	3,700,000	300,000	1,000,000	$400,000
Passive investment	1,000,000	440,000	60,000	500,000	100,000
Total	$15,000,000	$8,600,000	$ 900,000*	$5,500,000	$500,000

*This $900,000 represents expenses not definitely allocable to any of the corporation's activities. It is allocated and apportioned based on relative gross income.

Complete a Form 1118 to compute Fleming's FTC in the general limitation income and passive categories. Use the fill-in forms at **www.irs.gov**.

2. Cotton Export, Inc., a domestic corporation, has the following taxable income amounts for the current tax year and incurs foreign income taxes as shown.

Type of Income	Source	Amount	Foreign Taxes
Sales	Canada	$ 830,000	$339,000
	U.S.	300,000	–0–
Dividends*	Canada	20,000	5,100**
	U.S.†	25,000	–0–
		$1,175,000	$344,100

U.S. taxes before FTC = $399,500.

*From a portfolio of foreign stocks, all owned less than 1% by vote or value.
**Included in dividend amount (i.e., the $20,000 is before the $5,100 in withholding taxes).
† Net of dividends received deduction.

Gross foreign-source sales income is $1.2 million. Deductions allocable to foreign sales income total $320,000, and the apportioned share of deductions not definitely allocable to foreign sales income is $50,000.

Gross foreign-source dividend income is $21,000. There are no deductions definitely allocable to dividend income. The apportioned share of deductions not definitely allocable to foreign-source dividend income is $1,000.

Determine Cotton's FTC by completing the appropriate Form 1118s. Use the fill-in forms at **www.irs.gov**.

RESEARCH PROBLEMS

THOMSON REUTERS **CHECKPOINT**®

Note: Solutions to Research Problems can be prepared by using the **Checkpoint® Student Edition** online research product, which is available to accompany this text. It is also possible to prepare solutions to the Research Problems by using tax research materials found in a standard tax library.

Communications

Research Problem 1. Jerry Jeff Keen, the CFO of Boots Unlimited, a Texas corporation, has come to you regarding a potential restructuring of business operations. Boots has long manufactured its western boots in plants in Texas and Oklahoma. Recently, Boots has explored the possibility of setting up a manufacturing subsidiary in Ireland, where manufacturing profits are taxed at 10%. Jerry Jeff sees this as a great idea, given that the alternative is to continue all manufacturing in the United States, where profits are taxed at 34%. Boots plans to continue all of the cutting, sizing, and hand tooling of leather in its U.S. plants. This material will be shipped to Ireland for final assembly, with the finished product shipped to retail outlets all over Europe and Asia. Your initial concern is whether the income generated by the Irish subsidiary will be considered foreign base company income. Address this issue in a research memo, along with any planning suggestions.

Partial list of research aids:
§ 954(d).
Reg. § 1.954–3(a).
Bausch & Lomb, 71 TCM 2031, T.C.Memo. 1996–57.

Research Problem 2. List at least four forms the tax law requires when a U.S. person invests in overseas or investment business entities.

Research Problem 3. Polly Ling is a successful professional golfer. She is a resident of a country that does not have a tax treaty with the United States. Ling plays matches around the world, about one-half of which are in the United States. Ling's reputation is without blemish; in fact, she is known as being exceedingly honest and upright, and many articles discuss how she is a role model for young golfers due to her tenacious and successful playing style and her favorable character traits. Every year, she reports the most penalty strokes on herself among the participants in womens' matches, and this is seen as reinforcing her image as an honest and respectful competitor.

This combination of quality play and laudable reputation has brought many riches to Ling. She comes to you with several Federal income tax questions. She knows that, as a non-U.S. resident, any of her winnings from tournament play that occurs in the United States are subject to U.S. income taxation. But what about each of the following items? How does U.S. tax law affect Ling? Apply the sourcing rules in this regard, and determine whether the graduated U.S. Federal income tax rate schedules apply.

- Endorsement income from YourGolf, for wearing clothing during matches with its logo prominently displayed. Ling must play in at least 10 tournaments per year that are televised around the world. She also must participate in photo sessions and in blogs and tweets associated with the tournaments. Payment to Ling is structured as a flat fee, with bonuses paid if she finishes in the top five competitors for each match. This is known as an *on-court endorsement.*
- Endorsement income from GolfZone, for letting the company use her likeness in a video game that simulates golf tournaments among known golfers and other players that the (usually middle-aged men and women) gamers identify. In this way, the gamer seems to be playing against Ling on famous golf courses. Two-thirds of all dollar sales of the game licenses are to U.S. customers.
- Endorsement income from Eliteness, for appearing in print and Internet ads that feature Ling wearing the company's high-end watches. One-fifth of all dollar sales of the watches are to U.S. customers. The latter two items are known as *off-court endorsements.*

Internet Activity

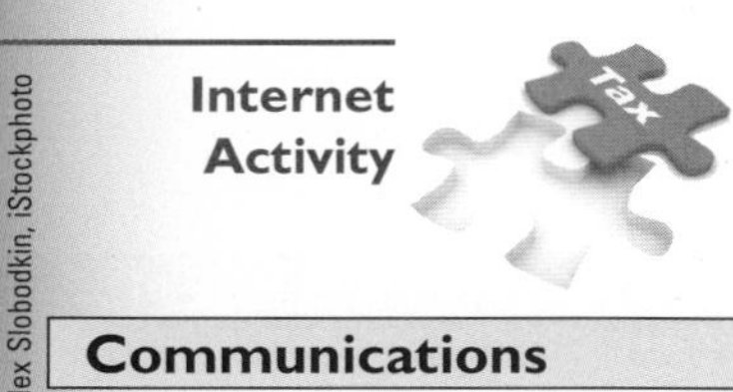

Use the tax resources of the Internet to address the following questions. Do not restrict your search to the Web, but include a review of newsgroups and general reference materials, practitioner sites and resources, primary sources of the tax law, chat rooms and discussion groups, and other opportunities.

Communications

Research Problem 4. Locate data on the size of the international economy, including data on international trade, foreign direct investment by U.S. firms, and investment in the United States by foreign firms. Useful web locations include **www.census.gov** and **www.bea.gov**. Prepare an analysis of the data for a three-year period using spreadsheet and graphing software, and e-mail the results to your instructor.

Communications

Research Problem 5. The IRS's web page at **www.irs.gov** contains many useful links to publications, tax forms and instructions, and tax revenue statistics. Locate web pages for at least three other countries' taxing authorities. In no more than three PowerPoint slides, show your classmates the web address for each of these pages and describe how these web pages compare with the IRS's page in terms of content and ease of use.

Research Problem 6. For your analysis, choose 10 countries, one of which is the United States. Create a table showing whether each country applies a worldwide or territorial approach to international income taxation. Then list the country's top income tax rate on business profits. Send a copy of your table to your instructor.

Communications

Research Problem 7. Find the text of various tax treaties currently in force in the United States. In an e-mail to your instructor, address the following items.

Communications

a. How does the U.S. income tax treaty with Germany define "business profits" for multinational businesses?
b. How does the U.S. income tax treaty with Japan treat the FIRPTA provisions?
c. List five countries with which the United States has entered into an estate tax treaty.
d. What is the effective date of the latest income tax treaty with the United Kingdom?
e. List five countries with which the United States does *not* have in force a bilateral income tax treaty.

part 3

Flow-Through Entities

Unlike C corporations, some business entities are taxed under the conduit principle. Generally, this means the tax attributes of various transactions are retained as they flow through the entity to the owners. With limited exceptions, no tax is imposed at the entity level. Part 3 discusses two types of flow-through entities—partnerships and corporations that make the Subchapter S election. Part 3 also integrates the material on corporations (Part 2) with flow-through entities in regard to the decision-making process. By comparing the tax attributes of C corporations, S corporations, and partnerships, the owners are provided with the tools needed to choose the appropriate form for conducting a business.

CHAPTER

10 Partnerships: Formation, Operation, and Basis

LEARNING OBJECTIVES: *After completing Chapter 10, you should be able to:*

LO.1 Distinguish among the various types of entities treated as partnerships for tax purposes.

LO.2 Describe the conceptual basis for partnership taxation and how partnership income is reported and taxed.

LO.3 Describe the tax effects of forming a partnership with cash and property contributions.

LO.4 Identify elections available to a partnership, and specify the tax treatment of expenditures of a newly formed partnership.

LO.5 Specify the accounting methods available to a partnership.

LO.6 List and explain the methods of determining a partnership's tax year.

LO.7 Calculate a partnership's taxable income and separately stated items, and describe how the partnership's income is reported.

LO.8 Outline and discuss the requirements for allocating income, gains, losses, deductions, and credits among the partners, and describe how that income is reported.

LO.9 Determine a partner's basis in the partnership interest.

LO.10 Explain how liabilities affect a partner's basis.

LO.11 Illustrate a partner's capital account rollforward, and explain why the year-end balance might differ from the partner's year-end basis in the partnership interest.

LO.12 List and review the limitations on deducting partnership losses.

LO.13 List and explain the special rules that govern the treatment of transactions between a partner and the partnership.

LO.14 Provide insights regarding advantageous use of a partnership.

CHAPTER OUTLINE

THE BIG PICTURE Tax Solutions for the Real World

WHY USE A PARTNERSHIP, ANYWAY?

For 15 years, Maria has owned and operated a seaside bakery and café called The Beachsider. Each morning, customers line up on the boardwalk in front of the building and enjoy fresh coffee and croissants while waiting for a table. "The building is too small," Maria commented to her landlord, Kyle. "Is there any way we can expand?" The Beachsider is one of several older buildings on 3 acres of a 10-acre parcel that Kyle's family has owned for years. The remaining 7 acres are undeveloped.

Kyle and Maria talked to Josh, a real estate developer, and he proposed an expansion to The Beachsider and upgrades to the other buildings. The improvements would preserve the character of the original shopping center, and the remaining acreage would be available for future expansion. Kyle and Maria were impressed with Josh's vision and excited about the plans to upgrade the property and expand Maria's business.

The parties agreed to form a partnership to own and operate The Beachsider and to improve and lease the other buildings. Josh summarized the plan as follows: "Kyle and Maria will each contribute one-half of the capital we need. Kyle's real estate is valued at about $2 million. Maria's bakery equipment and the café furnishings are valued at about $500,000. The improvements will cost about $1.5 million, which Maria has agreed to contribute to the partnership."

Josh continued, "You have agreed that I do not need to contribute any capital to the partnership. I will oversee the construction, and when it is complete, I will vest in a 5 percent interest in the partnership's capital. On an ongoing basis, I will oversee the partnership's operations in exchange for a fixed salary and 20 percent of the partnership's ongoing profits. The construction is estimated to be completed in June of this year, and my capital interest is estimated to be valued at $200,000 at that time."

What are the tax consequences if the trio forms Beachside Properties as a partnership to own and operate the shopping center? What issues might arise later in the life of the entity?

Read the chapter and formulate your response.

10.1 Overview of Partnership Taxation

This chapter and the next two chapters analyze two types of entities that may offer advantages over regular corporations. These entities are partnerships and S corporations, which are called *flow-through* or *pass-through* entities because the owners of the trade or business choose to avoid treating the enterprise as a separate taxable entity. Instead, the owners are taxed on a proportionate share of the entity's taxable income at the end of each of its taxable years.

As described in the *Tax in the News* feature on the next page, partnerships are used in almost every imaginable industry and use of these entities is on the rise.

This chapter addresses partnership formation and operations. Chapter 11 focuses on dispositions of partnership interests, partnership distributions, and optional basis adjustments. Chapter 12 discusses the taxation of S corporations.

LO.1

Distinguish among the various types of entities treated as partnerships for tax purposes.

What Is a Partnership?

A partnership is an association formed by two or more persons to carry on a trade or business, with each contributing money, property, labor, or skill, and with all expecting to share in profits and losses. A "person" can be an individual, trust, estate, corporation, association, or another partnership.[1] For Federal income tax purposes, a partnership includes a syndicate, a group, a pool, a joint venture, or other unincorporated organization through which any business, financial operation, or venture is carried on. The entity must not be otherwise classified as a corporation, trust, or estate.

Types of Partnerships

The types of entities that may be taxed as partnerships include general partnerships, limited partnerships, limited liability partnerships, limited liability limited partnerships, and limited liability companies. These entities are typically distinguished based on the types of business permitted to be conducted by the entity and the extent to which the partners are personally liable for the entity's debts.

- A **general partnership** (GP) consists of two or more partners who are **general partners**; there are no **limited partners**. Creditors of a general partnership can collect from both the partnership's assets and the personal assets of the owner-partners. A general partner can be subject to a malpractice judgment brought against the partnership, even though the partner was not personally involved in the malpractice. General partnerships are often used for both operating activities (e.g., product manufacturing or sales) and corporate joint ventures.
- A **limited liability company** (LLC) combines the corporate benefit of limited liability for the owners with the benefits of partnership taxation, including the single level of tax and special allocations of income, losses, and cash flows. Owners are technically considered to be "members" rather than partners. A properly structured LLC is generally treated as a partnership for all Federal tax purposes. Almost all states permit capital-intensive companies, nonprofessional service-oriented businesses, and some professional service-providing companies to operate as LLCs.
- A **limited partnership** (LP) is a partnership with at least one general partner and one or more limited partners. For liability protection, the general partners are often corporations or LLCs. These partnerships often have numerous limited partners and are used to raise capital for real estate development, oil and gas exploration, research and development, and various financial product investment vehicles. Typically, only the general partners are personally liable to creditors; each limited partner's risk of loss is restricted to that partner's equity investment in the entity.

[1]§§ 7701(a)(1) and (2).

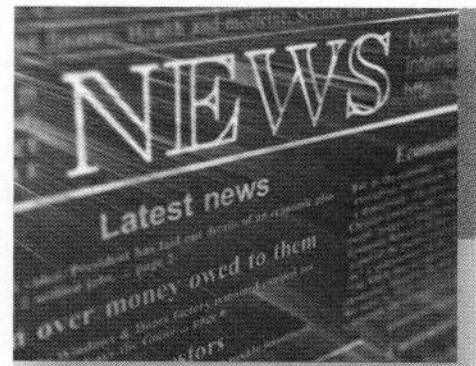

TAX IN THE NEWS The Extent of Partnership Usage

Partnerships come in all flavors and sizes! In less than a decade, the number of U.S. partnerships increased by 50 percent—from about 2 million entities in 2000 to over 3 million entities in 2009. In 2009 (the last year for which data are available), partnership entities owned assets with a combined gross book value of about $19 trillion. Over 60 percent (almost 2 million) of these entities are limited liability companies; the vast majority of the rest are either general partnerships or limited partnerships. The balance includes limited liability partnerships, limited liability limited partnerships, and entities that checked "Other" on Form 1065.

The "partner mix" is shifting. Corporations are increasingly using the partnership entity form to expand operations or to create joint ventures with other entities. From 2006–2008, for the first time, more than half of partnership income and losses was allocated to corporations; in 2009, the trend reverted to the historic norm in which most allocations were to individual partners.

Partnerships are used in almost every type of industry—from agriculture to health care to waste management. Almost half of all partnerships are engaged in some sort of real estate business, but over one-half of assets are owned by partnerships in the finance and insurance sector. Certain elements of the tax law make partnerships especially appealing for activities such as research and development, and oil and gas exploration and extraction. All kinds of service activities are operated through some sort of partnership (especially limited liability partnerships): partnerships are common in the accounting, finance, law, education, and transportation services industries.

Source: IRS, *Statistics of Income Bulletin,* Fall 2002 and Fall 2011 reports based on 2000 and 2009 filing years.

- A **limited liability partnership** (LLP) is treated similarly to a general partnership in most states. The primary difference between an LLP and a general partnership is that an LLP partner is not personally liable for any malpractice committed by other partners. The LLP is currently the organizational form of choice for the large accounting firms. LLPs are discussed in more detail in Chapter 11.
- A **limited liability limited partnership** (LLLP) is an extension of the limited partnership form in which all partners, whether general or limited, are accorded limited liability. At this writing, about half of U.S. states permit formation of LLLPs or recognize LLLPs formed in another state. Existing limited partnerships can acquire LLLP status by filing a proper request with the appropriate state jurisdiction.

A partnership is governed by a **partnership agreement**, which should explain the rights and obligations of the partners; the allocation of income, deductions, and cash flows; initial and future capital contribution requirements; conditions for terminating the partnership; and other matters. The governing agreement of an LLC has a similar structure and is known as an **operating agreement**.

THE BIG PICTURE
EXAMPLE 1

Return to the facts of *The Big Picture* on p. 10-1. When Beachside Properties is formed, Kyle, Maria, and Josh must decide which type of partnership to utilize.

With a general partnership, Kyle, Maria, and Josh would each be jointly and severally liable for all entity debts. With a limited partnership, one of the partners would be designated as a general partner and would be liable for all entity debts. Because all three partners want to have limited liability, they decide not to use a general or limited partnership.

They do not consider a limited liability partnership because that entity form is typically reserved for service-providing entities.

With a limited liability company (or, if their state permits, a limited liability limited partnership), each partner's losses will be limited to the partner's contributed capital. Therefore, Kyle, Maria, and Josh decide to form Beachside Properties as an LLC.

The "Check-the-Box" Regulations

The IRS's "check-the-box" Regulations allow most unincorporated business entities—such as general partnerships, limited partnerships, LLPs, LLLPs, and LLCs—to select their Federal tax status.[2] As discussed in Chapter 2, if an unincorporated entity has two or more owners, it generally can choose to be taxed as either a partnership or a C corporation.

Election Out of Subchapter K

A partnership generally may elect out of the partnership taxation rules if it is involved in certain activities.[3] If a proper election is made, the partnership is disregarded for Federal tax purposes and its operations are reported directly on the owners' tax returns. Such elections "out" of partnership status are not common.

LO.2

Describe the conceptual basis for partnership taxation and how partnership income is reported and taxed.

Key Concepts in Taxation of Partnership Income

A partnership is not a taxable entity.[4] Rather, the taxable income or loss of the partnership flows through to the partners at the end of the partnership's tax year.[5] The partners report their allocable share of the partnership's income or loss on their tax returns. The partnership itself pays no Federal income tax on its income; instead, the partners' individual tax liabilities are affected by the activities of the entity.

EXAMPLE 2

Adam contributes land with a basis and value of $60,000 in exchange for a 40% interest in the calendar year ABC Partnership. In 2012, the partnership generates $200,000 of ordinary taxable income. Because the partnership needs capital for expansion and debt reduction, ABC makes no cash distributions during 2012. Adam is taxed on his $80,000 allocable share of the partnership's 2012 income, even though he received no distributions from the entity during 2012.

The same result would occur if the partnership reported a loss: the partnership would allocate 40% of the loss to Adam, and he would deduct the loss, subject to the loss limitations discussed later in this chapter. ■

Conceptual Basis for Partnership Taxation

The unique tax treatment of partners and partnerships can be traced to two legal concepts: the **aggregate (or conduit) concept** and the **entity concept**. These theories influence practically every partnership tax rule.

Aggregate (or Conduit) Concept The aggregate concept treats the partnership as a channel through which income, credits, deductions, and other items flow to the partners. The partnership is regarded as a collection of taxpayers joined in an agency relationship. For example, the income tax is imposed on the partners rather than the partnership.

Entity Concept The entity concept treats partners and partnerships as separate units and gives the partnership its own tax ''personality'' by (1) requiring a partnership to file an information tax return and (2) treating partners as separate and distinct from the partnership in certain transactions between a partner and the entity.

Combined Concepts Some rules governing the formation, operation, and liquidation of a partnership contain a blend of the entity and aggregate concepts.

Separately Stated Items

In keeping with the aggregate theory, many items of partnership income, expense, gain, or loss retain their identity as they flow through to the partners. This separate flow-through of certain items is required because such **separately stated items** *might*

---

[2]Reg. §§ 301.7701–1 to –3.
[3]§ 761(a).
[4]§ 701.
[5]§ 702.

affect any two partners' tax liabilities in different ways. When preparing the tax return, the partner takes each of these items into account separately.[6] For example, charitable contributions are separately stated because partners need to compute their own deduction limitations for charitable contributions.

Typically, a partnership combines income and expenses related to the partnership's trade or business activities into a single income or loss amount that is passed through to the partners. As shown in Example 18, most other partnership items, such as investment income, gains, and losses, are separately stated.

Partners' Ownership and Allocation of Partnership Items

Another "aggregate" concept is that each partner typically owns both a **capital interest** and a **profits (loss) interest** in the partnership. A capital interest is measured by a partner's **capital sharing ratio**, which is the partner's percentage ownership of the capital of the partnership.

A profits (loss) interest is simply the partner's percentage allocation of the partnership's current operating results. **Profit and loss sharing ratios** are usually specified in the partnership agreement and are used to determine each partner's allocation of the partnership's ordinary taxable income (loss) and separately stated items.[7]

The partnership agreement may provide for a **special allocation** of various items to specified partners. It may also allocate items in a different proportion from the general profit and loss sharing ratios. As discussed later in the chapter, for a special allocation to be recognized for tax purposes, it must produce nontax economic consequences to the partners receiving the allocation.[8]

Inside and Outside Basis

In Chapters 10 and 11, there are numerous references to inside and outside basis. **Inside basis** refers to the partnership's adjusted tax basis for each asset it owns. **Outside basis** represents each partner's basis in the partnership interest. In many cases—especially upon formation of the partnership—the sum of the partnership's inside bases in its assets equals the sum of the partners' outside bases in their partnership interests.

When income or gain flows through to a partner from the partnership, the partner's outside basis in the partnership interest is increased. When a deduction or loss flows through to a partner, basis is reduced. The justification for these increases and decreases in the partner's basis is to ensure that these items are taxed only once.

EXAMPLE 3

In Example 2, Adam's outside basis in the partnership interest is $60,000 after his contribution of land in exchange for the partnership interest. The partnership's inside basis in the land is also $60,000. When Adam reports his $80,000 share of the partnership's income, his outside basis is increased to $140,000.

If Adam sells his interest at the beginning of 2013 for $140,000, he would have no gain or loss. Instead, if there were no adjustments to basis, Adam's basis would be only $60,000 and he would be taxed on an $80,000 gain in addition to paying tax on his $80,000 share of ABC's income. Without the basis adjustment, partnership income would be subject to double taxation. ■

Partnership Reporting

In keeping with the entity concept, a partnership must file an information return, Form 1065. This return accumulates information related to the partnership's operations and separately stated items. On this return, the partnership makes most elections regarding the treatment of partnership items, but no tax is calculated or paid with the return. This return is due by the fifteenth day of the fourth month following the end of the tax year. For a calendar year partnership, this deadline is April 15. An automatic five-month extension is available (to September 15 for a calendar year partnership). As part of this return, the partnership prepares a **Schedule K–1**

[6] § 703(a)(1).
[7] § 704(a).
[8] § 704(b).

for each partner that shows that partner's share of partnership items. Each partner receives a copy of Schedule K–1 for use in preparing the respective partner's tax return.

Anti-Abuse Provisions

Largely because of the interplay between the entity and aggregate concepts and their implementation in the tax law, partnership taxation is often flexible. For example, partnership operating income or losses can sometimes be shifted among partners, and partnership capital gains and losses can sometimes be shifted from one partner to another. The Code contains many provisions designed to thwart unwarranted allocations, but the IRS believes opportunities still abound for tax avoidance. As Chapter 11 notes, the IRS has adopted Regulations that allow it to recharacterize transactions that it considers to be "abusive."[9]

10.2 Formation of a Partnership: Tax Effects

LO.3

Describe the tax effects of forming a partnership with cash and property contributions.

Contributions to the Partnership

When a partnership is formed, the partners contribute cash and other property in exchange for the interest in the partnership. The property might be encumbered by debt that is assumed by the partnership. The property might be appreciated or depreciated.

Gain or Loss Recognition

In most situations, § 721 provides that neither the partner nor the partnership recognizes any realized gain or loss that results when a partner contributes property to a partnership. This applies when the property is contributed in exchange for a partnership interest upon formation of the entity or if the contribution occurs at some later date. The realized gain or loss is deferred.[10]

There are two reasons for this treatment. First, forming a partnership allows investors to combine their assets toward greater economic goals than could be achieved separately. Only the form of ownership, rather than the amount owned by each investor, has changed. Second, because the partnership interest received is typically an illiquid asset, the partner may not have sufficient cash with which to pay the tax.

EXAMPLE 4

Alicia transfers two assets to the Wren Partnership on the day the entity is created, in exchange for a 60% profit and loss interest worth $60,000. She contributes cash of $40,000 and retail display fixtures (basis to her as a sole proprietor, $8,000; fair market value, $20,000). Alicia *realizes* a $12,000 gain [$60,000 fair market value of partnership interest less $48,000 basis ($40,000 cash plus $8,000 basis in fixtures)].

Under § 721, Alicia *does not recognize* the $12,000 realized gain in the year of contribution. She received only an illiquid partnership interest; she received no cash with which to pay any resulting tax liability. ■

EXAMPLE 5

Assume the same facts as in Example 4, except that the fixtures Alicia contributes to the partnership have an adjusted basis of $25,000. She has a $5,000 *realized* loss [$60,000 − ($40,000 + $25,000)], which she cannot deduct. Section 721 applies to losses as well as gains.

Alicia could achieve the same economic result, with the added benefit of a loss deduction, if she sold the fixtures at fair market value and contributed $60,000 cash to the partnership. The partnership could then use the contribution to buy similar fixtures. ■

[9] Reg. § 1.701–2.

[10] § 721.

Basis Issues

When a partner makes a tax-deferred contribution of an asset to the capital of a partnership, any potential gain or loss recognition is postponed rather than excluded.[11] The contributed assets held by the partnership and the partnership interest held by the partner are both assigned a basis that is derived from the partner's basis in the contributed property.

Partnership's Basis in Assets The partnership's basis in the contributed assets (inside basis) equals the partner's basis in the property prior to its transfer to the partnership. This is called a *carryover basis*: the partner's basis "carries over" to the partnership.

Partner's Basis in the Partnership Interest The partner's outside basis in the new partnership interest is the same as the partner's basis in the contributed assets. This is called a *substituted basis*: the basis in assets is "substituted" for the basis in the partnership interest.

EXAMPLE 6

Luis transfers property in exchange for a one-third interest in the JKL Partnership. The property has an adjusted basis to Luis of $10,000 and a fair market value of $30,000. Luis has a $20,000 realized gain on the exchange ($30,000 – $10,000), but under § 721, he does not recognize any of the gain.

Luis's basis for his partnership interest is the amount necessary to recognize the $20,000 deferred gain if his partnership interest is subsequently sold for its $30,000 fair market value. This amount, $10,000, is the substituted basis.

The partnership's basis for the contributed property is the amount necessary to allow for the recognition of the $20,000 deferred gain if the property is subsequently sold for its $30,000 fair market value. This amount, also $10,000, is the carryover basis. ■

Holding Period

Partnership's Holding Period in Assets. The holding period for the contributed asset carries over to the partnership. Thus, the partnership's holding period for the contributed assets includes the period during which the partner owned the asset.

Partner's Holding Period in the Partnership Interest. The partner's holding period in the partnership interest depends on the type of assets contributed to the entity. If a partner contributes only capital and § 1231 assets, the partner's holding period in the partnership interest is the same as that partner's holding period for these assets. If only cash or assets that are not capital or § 1231 assets are contributed, the holding period in the partnership interest begins on the date the partnership interest is acquired. If both categories of assets are contributed, the partnership interest is apportioned and a separate holding period applies to each portion.

Exceptions to § 721

In certain situations, the nonrecognition provisions of § 721 do not apply. The most widely applicable situations are when:

- appreciated stocks are contributed to an investment partnership;
- the transaction is essentially a taxable exchange of properties;
- the transaction is a disguised sale of properties; or
- the partnership interest is received in exchange for services rendered to the partnership by the partner.

Investment Partnership

If the transfer consists of appreciated stocks and securities and the partnership is an investment partnership, it is possible that the realized gain on the stocks and

---

[11] § 723.

securities will be recognized by the contributing partner at the time of contribution.[12] This provision prevents multiple investors from using the partnership form to diversify their investment portfolios on a tax-free basis. A similar provision, § 351(e), applies to corporations (see Chapter 4).

Exchange

If a transaction is essentially a taxable exchange of properties, tax on the gain is not deferred under the nonrecognition provisions of § 721.[13]

EXAMPLE 7

Sara owns land, and Brandon owns stock. Sara would like to have Brandon's stock, and Brandon wants Sara's land. If Sara and Brandon both contribute their property to newly formed SB Partnership in exchange for interests in the partnership, the tax on the transaction appears to be deferred under § 721. The tax on a subsequent distribution by the partnership of the land to Brandon and the stock to Sara also appears to be deferred under § 731 (discussed in Chapter 11). Not so! The IRS will disregard the passage of the properties through the partnership and will hold, instead, that Sara and Brandon exchanged the land and stock directly. Thus, the transactions will be treated as any other taxable exchange. ■

Disguised Sale

A similar result occurs in a **disguised sale** of property or of a partnership interest. A disguised sale may occur when a partner contributes appreciated property to a partnership and soon thereafter receives a distribution from the partnership. This distribution may be viewed as a payment by the partnership for purchase of the property.[14]

EXAMPLE 8

Kim transfers property to the existing KLM Partnership. The property has an adjusted basis of $10,000 and a fair market value of $30,000. Two weeks later, the partnership distributes $30,000 cash to Kim. Under § 731, the distribution would not be taxable to Kim if the basis for her partnership interest prior to the distribution was greater than the $30,000 cash distributed. However, the transaction appears to be a disguised purchase-sale transaction. Therefore, Kim must recognize gain of $20,000 on transfer of the property, and the partnership is deemed to have purchased the property for $30,000. ■

Extensive Regulations under § 707 outline situations in which the IRS will presume that a disguised sale has occurred. For example, a disguised sale is presumed to exist if both of the following occur:

- A contractual agreement requires a contribution by one partner to be followed within two years by a specified distribution from the partnership.
- The distribution is to be made without regard to partnership profits. In other words, the forthcoming distribution is not subject to significant "entrepreneurial risk."

The Regulations also outline situations in which a distribution generally will *not* be deemed to be part of a disguised sale. They include a distribution that occurs more than two years after the property is contributed and a distribution that is deemed "reasonable" in relation to the capital invested by the partner and in relation to distributions made to other partners.

Services

A partner may receive an interest in partnership capital or profits in exchange for services rendered to the partnership. In certain circumstances, receipt of such an interest does not qualify for nonrecognition treatment under § 721.

[12] § 721(b).
[13] Reg. § 1.731–1(c)(3).
[14] § 707(a)(2)(B).

Capital Interest Received in Exchange for Services When a partner receives a fully vested interest in partnership capital (i.e., unrestricted liquidation rights) in exchange for services, the receipt of the interest is generally taxable to the partner. Services are not treated as "property" that can be transferred to a partnership on a tax-free basis. Instead, the partner performing the services recognizes ordinary compensation income. Generally, the partner's ordinary income equals the amount the partner would receive if the partnership was liquidated immediately following the contribution of services, less any amount the partner paid for the interest.[15] However, if the interest is subject to a "substantial risk of forfeiture" (as defined under § 83), the liquidation value would be $0; so the partner would not recognize any income.

Profits Interest Received in Exchange for Services When a partner receives an interest in the partnership's future profits in exchange for services, the partner is not typically required to recognize any income at the time the interest is received, even if the partner is fully vested in the partnership interest. The amount of the partnership's future profits cannot typically be determined, and no liquidation rights exist; so there is no current value to the interest. However, receipt of the profits interest might be currently taxable to the partner if (1) the future income of the partnership is assured, (2) the partnership interest is sold within two years of its receipt, or (3) the interest relates to a limited partnership interest in a publicly traded partnership.[16]

Effect on the Partnership and Other Partners In the case of a transfer of either an interest in partnership profits or capital, the partnership may deduct any amount included in the service partner's income if the services are of a deductible nature.[17] If the services are not deductible by the partnership, they must be capitalized. For example, the cost of architectural plans created by a partner are capitalized and included in the basis of the structure built with those plans. Alternatively, day-to-day management services performed by a partner for the partnership are usually deductible by the partnership. Further effects on the partnership and the remaining partners are discussed in regulations that are beyond the scope of this chapter.

EXAMPLE 9

Bill, Carlos, and Dave form the BCD Partnership, with each receiving a one-third interest in the capital and profits of the partnership. Dave receives his one-third interest as compensation for tax planning services he rendered prior to the formation of the partnership. The value of a one-third capital interest in the partnership (for each of the parties) is $20,000. Dave recognizes $20,000 of compensation income, and he has a $20,000 basis in his partnership interest. The same result would occur if the partnership had paid Dave $20,000 for his services and he immediately contributed that amount to the entity for a one-third ownership interest. The partnership will probably treat the $20,000 as a startup expense under § 195. ■

Other Issues Relative to Contributed Property

When property is contributed to a partnership, other issues arise, including depreciation and cost recovery of the assets, character of any subsequent gain or loss on disposition of the assets, and allocations related to the precontribution gain or loss inherent in the property.

Depreciation Method and Period

If depreciable property is contributed to the partnership, the partnership is usually required to use the same cost recovery method and life used by the partner. The partnership merely "steps into the shoes" of the partner and continues the same

[15] § 83(a) and Notice 2005–43, 2005–1 C.B. 1221, (5/20/2005).

[16] Rev.Proc. 93–27, 1993–2 C.B. 343.

[17] § 83(h).

cost recovery calculations. The partnership may not elect under § 179 to immediately expense any part of the basis of depreciable property it receives from the transferor partner.

Intangible Assets

If a partner contributes an existing "§ 197" intangible asset to the partnership, the partnership generally will "step into the shoes" of the partner in determining future amortization deductions. Section 197 intangible assets include goodwill, going-concern value, information systems, customer- or supplier-related intangible assets, patents, licenses obtained from a governmental unit, franchises, trademarks, covenants not to compete, and other items.

EXAMPLE 10

On September 1, 2010, at a cost of $120,000, James obtained a license to operate a television station from the Federal Communications Commission. The license is effective for 20 years. On January 1, 2012, he contributes the license to the JS Partnership in exchange for a 60% interest. The value of the license is still $120,000 at that time.

The license is a § 197 asset because it is a license with a term greater than 15 years. The cost is amortized over 15 years. James claims amortization for 4 months in 2010 and 12 months in 2011. Thereafter, the partnership steps into James's shoes in claiming amortization deductions. ■

Intangible assets that do not fall under the § 197 rules are amortized over their useful life, if any.[18]

Gain or Loss on Disposition of Receivables, Inventory, and Losses

To prevent ordinary income from being converted into capital gain, gain or loss is treated as ordinary when the partnership disposes of either of the following:[19]

- Contributed receivables that were unrealized in the contributing partner's hands at the contribution date. Such receivables include the right to receive payment for goods or services delivered or to be delivered.
- Contributed property that was inventory in the contributor's hands on the contribution date, if the partnership disposes of the property within *five years of the contribution.* For this purpose, inventory includes all tangible property except capital assets and real or depreciable business assets.

EXAMPLE 11

Deon operates a cash basis retail electronics store as a sole proprietor. Raul is an enterprising individual who likes to invest in small businesses. On January 2 of the current year, Deon and Raul form the DR Partnership. Their partnership contributions are as follows:

	Adjusted Basis	Fair Market Value
From Deon:		
Receivables	$ –0–	$ 20,000
Land used as parking lot*	12,000	50,000
Inventory	25,000	50,000
From Raul:		
Cash	120,000	120,000

*The parking lot had been held for nine months at the contribution date.

Within 30 days of formation, DR collects the receivables and sells the inventory for $50,000 cash. It uses the land for the next 10 months as a parking lot, then sells it

[18] Reg. § 1.167(a)–3.

[19] § 724. For this purpose, § 724(d)(2) waives the holding period requirement in defining § 1231 property.

for $35,000 cash. DR realized the following income in the current year from these transactions:

- Ordinary income of $20,000 from collecting receivables.
- Ordinary income of $25,000 from sale of inventory.
- § 1231 gain of $23,000 from sale of land.

Because the land takes a carryover holding period, it is treated as having been held 19 months at the sale date, thus meeting the one-year holding period requirement for receiving § 1231 classification. ■

A similar rule is designed to prevent a capital loss from being converted into an ordinary loss. Under the rule, if contributed property is disposed of at a loss and the property had a "built-in" capital loss on the contribution date, the loss is treated as a capital loss if the partnership disposes of the property *within five years of the contribution.* The capital loss is limited to the amount of the "built-in" loss on the date of contribution.

EXAMPLE 12

Assume the same facts as Example 11, except for the following:

- Deon held the land for investment purposes. It had a fair market value of $8,000 at the contribution date.
- DR used the land as a parking lot for 10 months and sold it for $6,500.

DR realizes the following income and loss from the land contribution and sale transactions:

- Capital loss of $4,000 from sale of the land ($12,000 − $8,000).
- § 1231 loss of $1,500 from sale of the land ($8,000 − $6,500).

Because the land was sold within five years of the contribution date, the $4,000 built-in loss is a capital loss. The postcontribution loss of $1,500 is a § 1231 loss because DR used the property in its business. ■

Allocations Related to Contributed Property

As discussed later in the chapter, special allocations must be made relative to contributed property that is appreciated or depreciated. The partnership's income and losses must be allocated under § 704(c) to ensure that the inherent gain or loss is not shifted away from the contributing partner.

THE BIG PICTURE

EXAMPLE 13

Return to the facts of *The Big Picture* on p. 10-1. Assume that Kyle has a basis of $600,000 in the $2 million of real estate he contributed and that Maria has a $0 basis in the bakery equipment and the café furnishings.

When Beachside Properties, LLC, is formed, no tax results for the LLC or for Kyle or Maria. Kyle does not recognize his $1.4 million realized gain, nor does Maria recognize her $500,000 realized gain.

Kyle takes a substituted basis of $600,000 for his interest, and Maria takes a substituted basis of $1.5 million ($1.5 million for contributed cash + $0 for contributed property). Beachside Properties assumes a carryover basis of $600,000 for the real estate contributed by Kyle and $0 for the property contributed by Maria. To the extent the buildings and other land improvements are depreciable, the LLC "steps into Kyle's shoes" in calculating depreciation deductions.

When Josh vests in his 5% capital interest in the LLC, the $200,000 value of the interest is taxable to him because it is a capital interest received in exchange for services. Beachside Properties will probably capitalize this amount because it relates to construction. Josh's 20% interest in the future profits of the partnership will be taxed to him as profits are earned by the partnership.

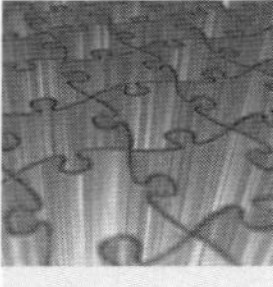

CONCEPT SUMMARY 10.1

Partnership Formation and Initial Basis Computation

1. Generally, partners or partnerships do not recognize gain or loss when property is contributed for capital interests.
2. Partners contributing property for partnership interests take the contributed property's adjusted basis for their *outside basis* in their partnership interest. The partners are said to take a substituted basis in their partnership interest.
3. The partnership will continue to use the contributing partner's basis for the *inside basis* in property it receives. The contributed property is said to take a carryover basis.
4. The holding period of a partner's interest includes that of contributed property when the property was a § 1231 asset or capital asset in the partner's hands. Otherwise, the holding period starts on the day the interest is acquired. The holding period of an interest acquired by a cash contribution starts at acquisition.
5. The partnership's holding period for contributed property includes the contributing partner's holding period.
6. The partnership "steps into the partner's shoes" in calculating depreciation and amortization of contributed property.
7. Certain provisions prevent the recharacterization of ordinary income to capital gains for inventory and accounts receivable and prevent capital losses from being converted to ordinary losses.
8. Section 721 does not apply to partnership interests received in certain transactions, including formation of certain investment partnerships, disguised property exchanges, disguised sales, and receipt of a fully vested capital interest in exchange for services.

Concept Summary 10.1 reviews the rules that apply to partnership asset contribution and basis adjustments.

LO.4

Identify elections available to a partnership, and specify the tax treatment of expenditures of a newly formed partnership.

Tax Accounting Elections

A newly formed partnership must make numerous tax accounting elections. These elections are formal decisions on how a particular transaction or tax attribute should be handled. Most of these elections must be made by the partnership rather than by the partners individually.[20] For example, the *partnership* makes the elections involving the following items:

- Taxable year and accounting method (cash, accrual, or hybrid).
- Cost recovery methods and assumptions.
- Section 179 deductions for certain tangible personal property.
- Inventory method.
- Cost or percentage depletion method, excluding oil and gas wells.
- Treatment of research and experimentation costs.
- Amortization of organizational costs and amortization period.
- Amortization of startup expenditures and amortization period.
- Determination of "qualified production activities income" (QPAI) and production-related wages for purposes of § 199 for some partnerships.
- Optional basis adjustments for property (§ 754, discussed in Chapter 11).
- Election out of partnership rules.

Each partner is bound by the decisions made by the partnership relative to the elections. If the partnership fails to make an election, a partner cannot make the election individually.

Although most elections are made by the partnership, each *partner* individually is required to make a specific election for the following relatively narrow tax issues:

- Whether to reduce the basis of depreciable property first when excluding income from discharge of indebtedness.

[20] § 703(b).

- Whether to claim cost or percentage depletion for oil and gas wells.
- Whether to take a deduction or a credit for taxes paid to foreign countries and U.S. possessions.

Initial Costs of a Partnership

In its initial stages, a partnership incurs expenses relating to some or all of the following: forming the partnership (organizational costs), admitting partners to the partnership, marketing and selling partnership units to prospective partners (syndication costs), acquiring assets, starting business operations (startup costs), negotiating contracts, and other items.

Organizational Costs

Organizational costs include expenditures that are (1) incident to the creation of the partnership; (2) chargeable to a capital account; and (3) of a character that, if incident to the creation of a partnership with an ascertainable life, would be amortized over that life. Organizational costs include accounting fees and legal fees connected with the partnership's formation. The expenditures must be incurred within a period that starts a reasonable time before the partnership begins business. The period ends with the due date (without extensions) of the tax return for the initial tax year.

The partnership may elect to deduct up to $5,000 of these costs in the year in which it begins business. This amount must be reduced, however, by the organizational costs that exceed $50,000. Any organizational costs that cannot be deducted under this provision are amortizable over 180 months beginning with the month in which the partnership begins business.[21]

In general, the partnership is deemed to have elected the $5,000 deduction and 180-month amortization treatment simply by deducting the proper amounts on the tax return.[22]

Startup Costs

Startup costs include operating costs that are incurred after the entity is formed but before it begins business. Such costs include marketing surveys prior to conducting business, pre-operating advertising expenses, costs of establishing an accounting system, costs incurred to train employees before business begins, and salaries paid to executives and employees before the start of business.

The partnership may elect to deduct up to $5,000 of startup costs in the year in which it begins business. This amount must be reduced, however, by the startup costs that exceed $50,000.[23] Costs that are not deductible under this provision are amortizable over 180 months beginning with the month in which the partnership begins business. Again, the partnership, in general, is treated as making a deemed election to deduct and/or amortize these costs simply by treating the amounts as specified in the tax return.[24]

EXAMPLE 14

The calendar year Bluejay Partnership was formed on July 1, 2012, and immediately started business. Bluejay incurred $4,000 in legal fees for drafting the partnership agreement and $2,200 in accounting fees for providing tax advice of an organizational nature. In addition, the partnership incurred $20,000 of pre-opening advertising expenses and $34,000 of salaries and training costs for new employees before opening for business. The partnership selected the accrual method of accounting and will deduct and amortize organizational and startup costs as permitted under §§ 709 and 195.

Bluejay incurred $6,200 ($4,000 + $2,200) of organizational costs in 2012. The partnership may deduct $5,040 of these costs on its 2012 tax return. This deduction is the sum of the $5,000 permitted deduction and the $40 ($1,200 × 6/180) amortization deduction for the $1,200 of organizational costs that exceed the $5,000 base amount.

---

[21] § 709(b).
[22] Reg. § 1.709–1.
[23] § 195(b)(1).
[24] Reg. § 1.195–1.

Bluejay incurred $54,000 ($20,000 + $34,000) of startup costs in 2012. The partnership may deduct $2,767 of these costs on its tax return for 2012. This deduction is the sum of the following:

- $5,000 reduced by the $4,000 ($54,000 − $50,000) amount by which the startup costs exceed $50,000.
- $1,767 ($53,000 × 6/180) amortization of the remaining $53,000 ($54,000 − $1,000) of startup costs for six months. ■

Acquisition Costs of Depreciable Assets

As mentioned earlier, the partnership typically determines its depreciation deductions by "stepping into the shoes" of the contributing partner. If additional costs are incurred, though, the additional basis is treated as a new MACRS asset, placed in service on the date the cost is incurred (e.g., the date the asset is transferred to the partnership). For example, legal fees and transfer taxes incurred in transferring assets to a partnership must be capitalized. Cost recovery for these amounts commences when the underlying property is placed in service.

Syndication Costs

Syndication costs are capitalized, but no amortization election is available.[25] Syndication costs include the following expenditures incurred for promoting and marketing partnership interests:

- Brokerage fees.
- Registration fees.
- Legal fees paid for security advice or advice on the adequacy of tax disclosures in the prospectus or placement memo for securities law purposes.
- Accounting fees related to offering materials.
- Printing costs of prospectus, placement memos, and other selling materials.

LO.5

Specify the accounting methods available to a partnership.

Method of Accounting

Like a sole proprietorship, a newly formed partnership may adopt either the cash or accrual method of accounting or a hybrid of these two methods.

However, a few special limitations on cash basis accounting apply to partnerships.[26] The cash method of accounting may not be adopted by a partnership that

- has one or more C corporation partners or
- is a tax shelter.

A C corporation partner does *not* preclude cash basis treatment if

- the partnership meets the $5 million gross receipts test described below,
- the C corporation partner(s) is a qualified personal service corporation, such as an incorporated attorney, or
- the partnership is engaged in the business of farming.

A partnership meets the $5 million gross receipts test if it has not received average annual gross receipts of more than $5 million for all tax years. "Average annual gross receipts" is the average of gross receipts for the three tax years ending with the tax period prior to the tax year in question. For new partnerships, the period of existence is used. Gross receipts are annualized for short taxable periods. A partnership must change to the accrual method the first year after the year in which its average annual gross receipts exceed $5 million and must use the accrual method thereafter.

A tax shelter is a partnership whose interests have been sold in a registered offering or a partnership in which 35 percent of the losses are allocated to limited partners.

[25] § 709(a).

[26] § 448.

FIGURE 10.1 **Deferral Benefit If Partnership Used a Fiscal Year and All Partners Were on the Calendar Year**

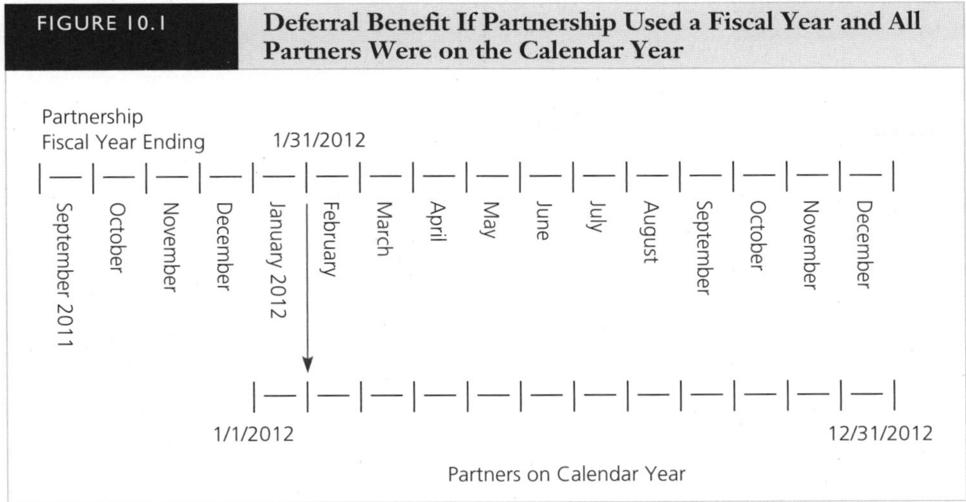

EXAMPLE 15

Jason and Julia are both attorneys. In 2009, each of them formed a professional personal service corporation to operate their separate law practices. In 2012, the two attorneys decide to form the JJ Partnership, which consists of the two professional corporations. In 2012, JJ's gross receipts are $6 million. JJ may adopt the cash method of accounting, as it is a partnership consisting of qualified personal service corporations. Because JJ has no C corporate partners that are not personal service corporations, the cash method is available even though JJ's average annual gross receipts are greater than $5 million. JJ may also adopt the accrual method of accounting or a hybrid of the cash and accrual methods. ■

Taxable Year of the Partnership

LO.6

List and explain the methods of determining a partnership's tax year.

Partnership taxable income (and any separately stated items) flows through to each partner at the end of the *partnership's* taxable year. A *partner's* taxable income, then, includes the distributive share of partnership income for any *partnership* taxable year that ends during the partner's tax year.

When all partners use the calendar year, it would be beneficial in present value terms for a profitable partnership to adopt a fiscal year ending with January 31. Why? As Figure 10.1 illustrates, when the adopted year ends on January 31, the reporting of income from the partnership and payment of related taxes can be deferred for up to 11 months. For instance, income earned by the partnership in September 2011 is not taxable to the partners until January 31, 2012. It is reported in the partner's tax return for the year ended December 31, 2012, which is not due until April 15, 2013. Even though each partner may be required to make quarterly estimated tax payments, some deferral is still possible.

Required Taxable Years

To prevent excessive deferral of taxation of partnership income, Congress and the IRS have adopted a series of rules that prescribe the *required* taxable year an entity must adopt if no alternative tax years (discussed in the next section) are selected.

Three rules are presented in Figure 10.2.[27] The partnership must consider each rule in order. The partnership's required taxable year is the taxable year determined under the first rule that applies. The partnership uses the tax year of the "majority partners" if partners owning more than 50 percent of partnership capital and profits have the same tax year. The partnership uses the tax year of the "principal partners" if all partners who own 5 percent or more of capital or profits have the same tax year.

[27] § 706(b).

FIGURE 10.2 **Required Tax Year of Partnership**

In Order, Partnership Must Use	Requirements
Majority partners' tax year	• More than 50% of capital *and* profits is owned by partners who have the same taxable year.
Principal partners' tax year	• All partners who own 5% or more of capital *or* profits are principal partners. • All principal partners must have the same tax year.
Year with smallest amount of income deferred	• "Least aggregate deferral rule" (Example 16).

If no year-end is determined under either of these tests, the partnership determines a year under the **least aggregate deferral rule**. Under this rule, the partnership tests the year-ends that are used by the various partners to determine the weighted-average deferral of partnership income. The year-end that offers the least amount of deferral is the *required tax year* under this rule.

EXAMPLE 16

Crimson, Inc., and Indigo, Inc., are equal partners in the CI Partnership. Crimson uses the calendar year, and Indigo uses a fiscal year ending August 31. Neither Crimson nor Indigo is a majority partner as neither owns more than 50%. Although Crimson and Indigo are both principal partners, they do not have the same tax year. Therefore, the general rules indicate that the partnership's required tax year must be determined by the "least aggregate deferral rule." The following computations support August 31 as CI's tax year, because the 2.0 product using that year-end is less than the 4.0 product when December 31 is used.

Test for 12/31 Year-End

Partner	Year Ends	Profit Interest		Months of Deferral		Product
Crimson, Inc.	12/31	50%	×	–0–	=	0.0
Indigo, Inc.	8/31	50%	×	8	=	4.0
Aggregate number of deferral months						4.0

Test for 8/31 Year-End

Partner	Year Ends	Profit Interest		Months of Deferral		Product
Crimson, Inc.	12/31	50%	×	4	=	2.0
Indigo, Inc.	8/31	50%	×	–0–	=	0.0
Aggregate number of deferral months						2.0

■

Alternative Tax Years

If the required tax year is undesirable to the entity, three other alternative tax years may be available:

- Establish to the IRS's satisfaction that a *business purpose* exists for a different tax year. This will typically be a "natural business year" (as defined)[28] that ends following a peak season or shortly thereafter.
- Elect a tax year so that taxes on partnership income are deferred for not more than *three months* from the *required* tax year.[29] This election is highly restrictive, can be expensive, and is not often made.

[28] Rev.Proc. 2006–46, 2006–2 C.B. 859, § 5.07.

[29] § 444.

- Elect a 52- to 53-week taxable year that ends with reference to the required taxable year or to the taxable year elected under the three-month deferral rule.

10.3 Operations of the Partnership

LO.7

Calculate a partnership's taxable income and separately stated items, and describe how the partnership's income is reported.

An individual, a corporation, a trust, an estate, or another partnership can become a partner in a partnership. Because a partnership is a tax-reporting, rather than a taxpaying, entity for purposes of its Federal (and state) income tax computations, the partnership's income, deductions, credits, and alternative minimum tax (AMT) preferences and adjustments can ultimately be reported and taxed on any of a number of income tax returns (e.g., Forms 1040 [individuals], 1041 [fiduciaries, see Chapter 20], 1120 [C corporations], and 1120S [S corporations]).

A partnership is subject to all other taxes in the same manner as any other business. Thus, the partnership files returns and pays the outstanding amount of pertinent sales taxes and property taxes. For employees (not partners), the partnership files returns and pays Social Security, unemployment, and other payroll taxes.

Measuring and Reporting Partnership Income

The partnership's Form 1065 organizes and reports the transactions of the entity for the tax year. Each of the partnership's tax items is reported on Schedule K of that return. Each partner receives a Schedule K–1 that reports the partner's allocable share of partnership income, credits, and preferences for the year. The IRS also receives a copy of each K–1.

Income Measurement

The measurement and reporting of partnership income require a two-step approach. Certain items must be netted at the partnership level, and other items must be segregated and reported separately on the partnership return and each partner's Schedule K–1.

Among the many income and deduction items passed through separately are the following:

- Net short-term and net long-term capital gains or losses.
- Section 1231 gains and losses.
- Charitable contributions.
- Portfolio income items (qualified and ordinary dividends, interest, and royalties).
- Expenses related to portfolio income.
- Immediately expensed tangible personal property (§ 179).
- Guaranteed payments, discussed later in the chapter.
- Passive activity items such as rental real estate income or loss.
- Intangible drilling and development costs.
- Taxes paid to foreign countries and U.S. possessions.[30]

The reason for separately reporting the preceding items is rooted in the aggregate or conduit concept. These items affect various exclusions, deductions, and credits at the partner level and must pass through without loss of identity so that the proper tax for each partner may be determined.[31]

[30] § 702(a).

[31] § 702(b).

A partnership is not allowed to claim the following deductions:

- Net operating losses (NOLs).
- Depletion of oil and gas interests.
- Dividends received deduction.

Items that are only allowed by legislative grace to individuals, such as standard deductions or personal exemptions, are not allowed to the partnership. If a partnership makes a payment on behalf of a partner, such as for alimony, medical expenses, or other items that constitute itemized deductions to individuals, the partnership treats the payment as a distribution or guaranteed payment (discussed later) to the partner, and the partner determines whether to claim the deduction.

THE BIG PICTURE

EXAMPLE 17

Return to the facts of *The Big Picture* on p. 10-1. In its second year of operations, Beachside Properties, LLC, reports income and expenses from operating the café as well as rent income and expenses from leasing the other buildings. Beachside's activities are summarized as follows:

Sales revenue	$600,000
Cost of sales	200,000
Salaries to employees	100,000
Cost recovery deductions	60,000
Utilities, supplies, and repairs	40,000
Taxes and licenses (including payroll taxes)	20,000
Charitable contributions	6,000
Short-term capital gain	12,000
Net income from rental real estate	300,000
Qualified dividends received	4,000
Exempt income (bond interest)	2,100
AMT adjustment (cost recovery)	5,000
Payment of medical expenses on behalf of partner Kyle	4,000

The LLC experienced a $20,000 net loss from operations last year, its first year of business.

Beachside will determine its ordinary income or loss for the year, along with its separately stated items. In addition, Beachside will report additional information the partners might need to prepare their individual income tax returns.

Beachside is not a allowed a deduction for last year's $20,000 NOL—this item was passed through to the LLC members in the previous year. The LLC is not allowed to deduct the payment for Kyle's medical expenses. This payment is probably handled as a distribution to Kyle, who may report it as a medical expense on his Schedule A in determining his itemized deductions. The AMT adjustment is not a separate component of the LLC's income, and it must be reported by Beachside's members so that they can properly calculate any AMT liability.

Partnership Reporting

Form 1065 Ordinary Income and Separately Stated Items. The partnership's income is reported on Form 1065. See Form 1065 for 2011 in Appendix B, and refer to it during the following discussion. Form 1065 contains five pages. Page 1 summarizes the partnership's ordinary income and loss from the partnership's trade or business activities. Pages 2 and 3 provide information about the partnership's activities and general information about the partners. Page 4 (Schedule K) accumulates information related to separately stated items and other information the partners need to prepare their returns. Reported on the first line of Schedule K is the partnership's ordinary trade or business income from Form 1065, page 1.

Page 5 provides several schedules, including a balance sheet (Schedule L), a reconciliation of book and "taxable" income [Schedules M–1 and the Analysis of Net Income (Loss)], and a reconciliation of partners' beginning and ending capital (Schedule M–2).

THE BIG PICTURE

EXAMPLE 18

Continue with the facts of Example 17. Beachside's ordinary income is determined and reported on the partnership return as follows:

Nonseparately Stated Items (Ordinary Income)—Form 1065, Pages 1 and 4	
Sales revenue	$ 600,000
Cost of sales	(200,000)
Salaries to employees	(100,000)
Cost recovery deductions	(60,000)
Utilities, supplies, and repairs	(40,000)
Taxes and licenses (including payroll taxes)	(20,000)
Ordinary income [Form 1065, page 1, line 22, and Form 1065, page 4 (Schedule K), line 1]	$ 180,000

Beachside's separately stated income and deduction items are:

Separately Stated Income and Deductions (Schedule K)	
Net income from rental real estate (line 2)	$300,000
Qualified dividends received (line 6)	4,000
Short-term capital gain (line 9a)	12,000
Charitable contributions (line 13a)	6,000

Other items reported on Schedule K The partnership must also report any information the partners need to prepare a complete and accurate income tax return. This information is reported on Schedule K and includes the partner's share of the following:

- Information necessary to calculate the domestic production activities deduction (DPAD) described in Chapter 3.
- AMT preferences and adjustments, for use in calculating the partner's alternative minimum tax.
- Self-employment income, for use in calculating the partner's self-employment tax.
- Foreign-source income and other information the partners need to calculate any foreign tax credit or deduction.

When pass-through entities conduct activities eligible for the DPAD, special rules apply.[32] The following rules apply in calculating the DPAD for a partnership:

- Whether an activity qualifies for the DPAD is determined at the entity level.
- The actual § 199 deduction is calculated at the partner level.

[32]See § 199(d)(1) and Reg. § 1.199–5.

- For many types of partnerships, QPAI and W–2 wages related to production can be calculated at the entity level.[33] Details of this calculation are beyond the scope of this chapter.
- On Schedule K–1, each partner is allocated a share of the amounts needed to calculate the DPAD, such as QPAI and W–2 wages related to domestic production activities.

THE BIG PICTURE

EXAMPLE 19

Continue with the information in Examples 17 and 18. In addition to the business income and separately stated items described in Example 18, the LLC also reports the following information that the partners will utilize in preparing their tax returns:

Additional Information (Schedule K)	
AMT adjustment—cost recovery (line 17a)	$5,000
Tax-exempt income—bond interest (line 18a)	2,100

In addition, to the extent Beachsider's activities are eligible for the § 199 deduction, relevant information would be reported to the LLC members.

Reconciling Taxable Income The partnership reconciles "book" income with income reported on the return. Refer again to the Form 1065 in Appendix B.

The partnership nets certain amounts from Schedule K and reports that amount on line 1 of the Analysis of Net Income (Loss) (page 5 of Form 1065) to determine the partnership's equivalent of "taxable income." This is the amount to which book income must be reconciled on either Schedule M–1 or Schedule M–3.

Schedule M–1 is found on page 5 of Form 1065. Schedule M–3 is a separate three-page form. In general, Schedule M–3 is required in lieu of Schedule M–1 if the partnership (1) has $10 million or more in assets at the end of the year, (2) has $35 million of receipts during the year, or (3) meets certain other conditions. In addition, Schedule M–3 is required if a partner owns a 50 percent or more interest in partnership profits, loss, or capital and is required to file its own Schedule M–3 (or if a 50 percent partner's assets or income are not known). If a partnership is required to file Schedule M–3, it must also answer various questions on Schedule C.

The net taxable income calculated on the Analysis of Net Income (Loss) schedule should agree with the reconciled taxable income on Schedule M–1 (line 9) or the reconciled amount from Schedule M–3, Part II.

Reconciling Partners' Capital Schedule M–2 reconciles partners' beginning and ending capital accounts. The analysis of capital accounts on Schedule M–2 reflects contributions to and distributions from the partnership as well as the partnership's income, gains, losses, and deductions. Schedule M–2 can be prepared using any of several methods, including the tax basis, generally accepted accounting principles (GAAP), or the "§ 704(b) book" method. The method used on Schedule M–2 should also be used in preparing the capital account reconciliation on the partners' Schedules K–1.

Schedule L (on page 5 of Form 1065) generally shows an accounting-basis balance sheet. If the capital reconciliation method used in Schedule M–2 differs from the method used for Schedule L, a reconciling schedule should be provided.

[33] Rev.Proc. 2007–34, 2007–1 C.B. 1345.

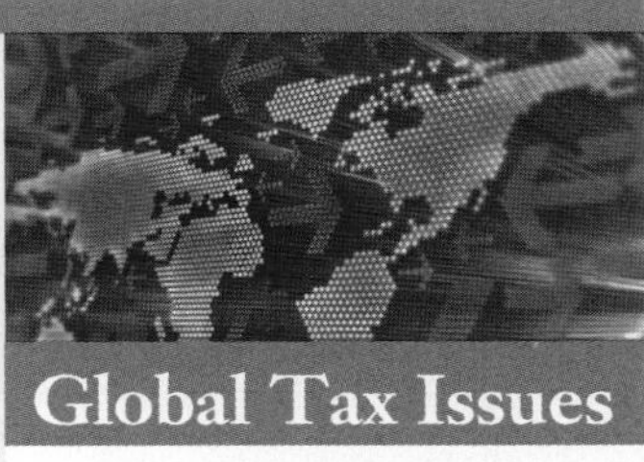

© Andrey Prokhorov, iStockphoto

Various Withholding Procedures Applicable to Foreign Partners

A U.S. partnership may have foreign partners, and these partners will be taxed on their U.S. income. Because it might be difficult for the IRS to collect the tax owed by such foreign partners, several Code sections provide for various withholding procedures. The procedures differ depending on whether the income is "effectively connected with a U.S. trade or business," derived from investment property, or related to real estate transactions.

If the partnership purchases real property from a foreign seller, for example, the partnership is required to withhold 10 percent of the purchase price. If a partnership sells a U.S. real property interest, it must typically withhold 35 percent of the gain allocated to a foreign partner. Further, if the partnership receives "fixed and determinable annual or periodic payments" (FDAP), such as dividends, interest, or rents, it is required to withhold 30 percent (or lower treaty rate) of the foreign partner's distributive share of such income.

Finally, if the partnership has U.S. business income, it must withhold and pay an amount equal to the highest U.S. tax rate applicable to the foreign taxpayer's allocable share of partnership income.

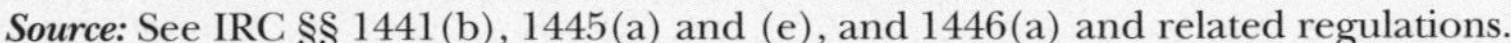

Source: See IRC §§ 1441(b), 1445(a) and (e), and 1446(a) and related regulations.

THE BIG PICTURE

EXAMPLE 20

Continue with the facts in Examples 17 and 18, but now consider the book-tax reconciliation. Beachside Properties, LLC, must prepare the Analysis of Income (Loss) and Schedule M–1 on Form 1065, page 5. In preparing these schedules, the LLC combines the ordinary income of $180,000 and the four separately stated income and deduction amounts in Example 18 to arrive at "net income" of $490,000. This amount is shown on line 1 of the Analysis of Income (Loss) and is the amount to which book income is reconciled on Schedule M–1, line 9.

Withdrawals

Capital withdrawals by partners during the year do not affect the partnership's income measuring and reporting process. These items usually are treated as distributions made on the last day of the partnership's tax year. Distributions are discussed in Chapter 11.

Penalties

A partner's share of each partnership item should be reported on the partner's tax return in the same manner as presented on the Form 1065. If a partner treats an item differently, the IRS must be notified of the inconsistent treatment.[34] If a partner fails to notify the IRS, a negligence penalty may be added to the tax due.

To encourage the filing of a partnership return, a penalty of $195 per partner per month (or fraction thereof, but not to exceed 12 months) is imposed on the partnership for failure to file a complete and timely information return without reasonable cause.[35]

[34] § 6222.

[35] § 6698.

A "small partnership" with 10 or fewer partners who are individuals (other than nonresident aliens), corporations, or an estate of a partner is exempt from these penalties.[36]

LO.8

Outline and discuss the requirements for allocating income, gains, losses, deductions, and credits among the partners, and describe how that income is reported.

Partner Allocations and Reporting

After ordinary income, separately stated items, and other related information are determined at the partnership level, those amounts must be allocated among the partners and reported on their tax returns.

Economic Effect

As shown by the example of Beachside Properties in *The Big Picture,* a partnership agreement or an LLC's operating agreement can provide that any partner may share capital, profits, and losses in the same ratios or in different ratios. For example, a partner could have a 25 percent capital sharing ratio, yet be allocated 30 percent of the profits and 20 percent of the losses of the partnership. Such special allocations have, at times, been used in an attempt to manipulate the allocation of tax benefits among partners. The Regulations[37] are designed to prevent unfair use of such manipulation. Although these rules are too complex to discuss in detail, the general outline of one of these rules—the **economic effect test**—can be easily understood.

In general, the economic effect test requires the following:

- An allocation of income or gain to a partner must increase the partner's capital account, and an allocation of deduction or loss must decrease the partner's capital account.
- When the partner's interest is liquidated, the partner must receive net assets that have a fair market value equal to the positive balance in the capital account.
- A partner with a negative capital account must restore that account upon liquidation of the interest. Restoration of a negative capital account can best be envisioned as a contribution of cash to the partnership equal to the negative balance.

These capital account maintenance requirements are designed to ensure that a partner bears the economic burden of a loss or deduction allocation and receives the economic benefit of an income or gain allocation.

EXAMPLE 21

Eli and Sanjay each contribute $20,000 cash to the newly formed ES Partnership. The partnership uses the cash to acquire a depreciable asset for $40,000. The partnership agreement provides that the depreciation is allocated 90% to Eli and 10% to Sanjay. Other items of partnership income, gain, loss, or deduction are allocated equally between the partners. Upon liquidation of the partnership, property will be distributed to the partners in accordance with their positive capital account balances. Any partner with a negative capital account must restore the capital account upon liquidation. Assume that the first-year depreciation on the equipment is $4,000. Also, assume that nothing else happens in the first year that affects the partners' capital accounts.

Eli's capital account is $16,400 ($20,000 − $3,600), and Sanjay's capital account has a balance of $19,600 ($20,000 − $400) after the first year of partnership operations. The Regulations require that a hypothetical sale of the asset for its $36,000 adjusted basis on the last day of the year and an immediate liquidation of the partnership should result in Eli and Sanjay receiving distributions equal to their capital accounts. According to the partnership agreement, Eli would receive $16,400, and Sanjay would receive $19,600 of the cash in a liquidating distribution. Eli, therefore, bears the economic burden of $3,600 depreciation because he contributed $20,000 to the partnership and would receive only $16,400 upon liquidation. Likewise, Sanjay's economic burden is $400 because he would receive only $19,600 of his original $20,000 investment. The agreement, therefore, has economic effect. ■

[36] § 6231(a)(1)(B).

[37] Reg. § 1.704–1(b).

EXAMPLE 22

Assume the same facts as in Example 21, except that the partnership agreement provides that Eli and Sanjay will receive equal amounts of cash upon liquidation of the partnership. The hypothetical sale of the asset for its $36,000 adjusted basis and the immediate liquidation of the partnership would result in each partner receiving $18,000 cash. Because each partner contributed $20,000 to the partnership and each partner would receive $18,000 upon liquidation, each partner bears the economic burden of $2,000 of depreciation. The original 90%/10% allocation of depreciation to the two partners is defective, and the IRS will require that the depreciation be reallocated equally ($2,000 each) to the two partners to reflect the economic burden borne by each partner. ■

Substantiality

Partnership allocations must also have "substantial" effect. In general, an allocation does not meet the "substantial" test unless it has economic consequences in addition to tax consequences that might benefit a subset of the partners.

EXAMPLE 23

When the Sheldon-Fowler LLC was formed, Sheldon contributed cash and Fowler contributed some municipal bonds she had held for investment purposes. The municipal bond interest income of $15,000 flows through to the partners as a separately stated item, so it retains its tax-exempt status. The partnership agreement allocates all of this income to Sheldon because he is subject to a higher marginal income tax bracket than is Fowler. The partnership also allocates $15,000 more of the partnership's ordinary business income to Fowler than to Sheldon. These offsetting allocations are not effective for income tax purposes because they have no before-tax economic purpose and only serve to reduce the partners' combined income tax liability. ■

Precontribution Gain or Loss

Certain income, gain, loss, and deductions relative to contributed property may not be allocated under the rules described above. Instead, **precontribution gain or loss** must be allocated among the partners to take into account the variation between the basis of the property and its fair market value on the date of contribution.[38] The partnership keeps track of these differences in its "§ 704(b) book" accounting records. For nondepreciable property, *built-in* gain or loss on the date of contribution must be allocated to the contributing partner when the property is eventually disposed of by the partnership in a taxable transaction. If the property is depreciable, Regulations describe allowable methods of allocating depreciation deductions.[39]

THE BIG PICTURE

EXAMPLE 24

Return to the facts of *The Big Picture* on p. 10-1. When Beachside Properties, LLC, was formed, Kyle contributed property valued at $2 million with a basis of $600,000. Maria contributed equipment and furnishings with a $0 basis and a $500,000 value. For § 704(b) book accounting purposes, Beachside records the land and other properties at their fair market values. For tax purposes, the LLC takes carryover bases in the properties. The LLC must keep track of the differences between the basis in each property and the value at the contribution date. If any of this property is sold, the gain must be allocated to the contributing partner to the extent of any previously unrecognized built-in gain.

For example, if Beachside sells the land contributed by Kyle for $2.3 million, the gain would be calculated and allocated as follows:

[38] § 704(c)(1)(A).

[39] Reg. § 1.704–3.

	§ 704 (b) Book	Tax
Amount realized	$2,300,000	$2,300,000
Less: Adjusted basis	2,000,000	600,000
Gain realized	$ 300,000	$1,700,000
Built-in gain to Kyle	–0–	1,400,000
Remaining gain (allocated proportionately)	$ 300,000	$ 300,000

For tax purposes, Kyle would recognize $1,520,000 of the gain [($300,000 × 40%) + $1,400,000], Maria would recognize $120,000 ($300,000 × 40%), and Josh would recognize $60,000 ($300,000 × 20%).

If contributed property has built-in losses at the contribution date, allocations related to the built-in loss can be made only to the contributing partner. For purposes of allocations to other partners, the partnership's basis in the loss property is treated as being the fair market value of the property at the contribution date.[40]

Schedule K–1

Once the partnership's items are calculated on Schedule K, they are allocated among the partners and reported on their Schedules K–1. Schedule K summarizes the tax-related items for the entire partnership; Schedule K–1 summarizes the tax-related items for each partner, after considering the allocation conventions outlined in the partnership agreement or required under the Code. For each partnership item, the sum of the amounts allocated to all of the partners should equal the partnership's total amount per Schedule K. If an amount is specially allocated, that allocation will be reflected in the amounts reported on Schedule K–1.

Refer to Schedule K–1 in Appendix B. Part I includes information about the partnership. Part II includes information about the partner, including the partner's profit-, loss- and capital-sharing percentages; share of partnership liabilities at the beginning and end of the year; and changes in the partner's capital account during the year.

Part III includes the information the partners use in completing their tax return. Lines 1 to 13 reflect the partner's distributive share of the partnership's income and deductions, including any amounts specially allocated to that partner. Lines 14 to 17 are used in determining other taxes or credits the partner should (or must) consider, such as self-employment tax, alternative minimum tax, foreign taxes, and various tax credits. The remaining lines are used in determining the partner's outside basis in the partnership interest.

THE BIG PICTURE

EXAMPLE 25

Consider the facts of Examples 17 and 18. Maria, a 40% owner, will receive a Schedule K–1 from Beachside Properties, on which she is allocated a 40% share of ordinary income and separately stated items. On her Form 1040, Maria includes $72,000 of ordinary income, a $2,400 charitable contribution, a $4,800 short-term capital gain, $120,000 of passive rental income, and $1,600 of qualified dividend income. On the first page of Form 1040, Maria lists her $840 share of tax-exempt interest. In determining her AMT liability (if any), Maria takes into account a $2,000 positive adjustment.

If any amounts had been specially allocated to Maria, the allocation would be reflected in the amount shown on her Schedule K–1.

[40] § 704(c)(1)(C).

In her personal tax return, Maria combines the partnership's amounts with similar items from sources other than Beachside. For example, if Maria has a $3,000 long-term capital loss from a stock transaction, the overall net short-term capital gain calculated on Schedule D of her 1040 is $1,800.

For each LLC item, the sum of the allocated amounts on Josh's, Kyle's, and Maria's K–1s will equal the totals on Beachside Properties' Schedule K.

Concept Summary 10.2 reviews the tax reporting rules for partnership items at both the partnership and the partner level.

ETHICS & EQUITY Built-in Appreciation on Contributed Property

In the "old days," one partner could contribute cash and another partner could contribute an equal value of appreciated property with no subsequent record-keeping requirements. Future depreciation deductions and gains on sale of the property could be allocated to both partners equally, thereby shifting income from one taxpayer to another. A partner in a lower tax bracket (or with expiring net operating losses and the like) could report the share of the gain on sale of the asset with a relatively low corresponding tax burden.

Section 704(c)(1)(A) was added to the Code to ensure that the partner contributing the property pays tax on any built-in gain. This prevents income shifting among taxpayers and loss of revenue to the U.S. Treasury.

There is no corresponding provision for S corporations—gains and losses and depreciation expense are allocated among the shareholders without regard to any built-in appreciation on contributed property.

What theory of partnership taxation supports this difference in treatment?

Partner's Basis

LO.9

Determine a partner's basis in the partnership interest.

Initial Basis in the Partnership Interest

A partner's basis in the partnership interest is important for determining the treatment of distributions from the partnership to the partner, establishing the deductibility of partnership losses, and calculating gain or loss on the partner's disposition of the partnership interest.

A partner's basis is not reflected anywhere on the Schedule K–1. Instead, each partner should maintain a personal record of the partner's basis in the partnership interest. A partner's adjusted basis in a newly formed partnership usually equals (1) the adjusted basis in any property contributed to the partnership plus (2) the fair market value of any services the partner performed for the partnership (i.e., the amount of ordinary income reported by the partner for services rendered to the partnership).

If a partnership interest is acquired after the partnership is formed, the method of acquisition controls how the partner's initial basis is computed. If the partnership interest is purchased from another partner, the purchasing partner's basis is the amount paid (cost basis) for the partnership interest. The basis of a partnership interest acquired by gift is the donor's basis for the interest plus, in certain cases, some or all of the transfer (gift) tax paid by the donor. The basis of a partnership interest acquired through inheritance generally is the fair market value of the interest on the date the partner dies. Exceptions may apply for decedents dying in 2010.

Basis—Effect of Partnership Operations

After the partner is admitted to the partnership, the partner's basis is adjusted for numerous items. The following operating results *increase* a partner's adjusted basis:

CONCEPT SUMMARY 10.2

Tax Reporting of Partnership Items

Item	Partnership Level	Partner Level
1. Compute partnership ordinary income or loss.	Form 1065, line 22, page 1. Schedule K, Form 1065, line 1, page 4.	Schedule K–1 (Form 1065), line 1. Each partner's share is passed through for separate reporting. Some amounts may be specially allocated to specific partners. For income: Each partner's basis is increased. For losses: Each partner's basis is decreased • The amount of a partner's loss deduction may be limited. • Losses that may not be deducted are carried forward for use in future years.
2. Separately reported income and deduction items such as portfolio income, capital gain and loss, and § 179 deductions.	Schedule K, Form 1065, various lines, page 4.	Schedule K–1 (Form 1065), various lines. Each partner's share of each item is passed through for separate reporting.
3. Net earnings from self-employment (see p. 10-36).	Schedule K, Form 1065, line 14, page 4.	Schedule K–1 (Form 1065), line 14.
4. Additional calculations that partner is required to make (e.g., AMT and foreign tax credits).	Schedule K, Form 1065, various lines, page 4.	Schedule K–1 (Form 1065), various lines. Each partner's share of each item is passed through and considered in various calculations.

- The partner's proportionate share of partnership income (including capital gains and tax-exempt income).
- The partner's proportionate share of any increase in partnership liabilities (as discussed in the next section).

The following operating results *decrease* the partner's adjusted basis in the partnership:

- The partner's proportionate share of partnership deductions and losses (including capital losses).
- The partner's proportionate share of nondeductible expenses.
- The partner's proportionate share of any reduction in partnership liabilities.[41]

Under no circumstances can the partner's adjusted basis for the partnership interest be reduced below zero.

Increasing the adjusted basis for the partner's share of partnership taxable income is logical because the partner has already been taxed on the income. By increasing the partner's basis, the partner is not taxed again on the income when he or she sells the interest or receives a distribution from the partnership.

It is also logical that the tax-exempt income should increase the partner's basis. If the income is exempt in the current period, it should not contribute to the recognition of gain when the partner either sells the interest or receives a distribution from the partnership.

EXAMPLE 26

Tyler is a one-third partner in the TUV Partnership. His proportionate share of the partnership income during the current year consists of $20,000 of ordinary taxable income and $10,000 of tax-exempt income. None of the income is distributed to Tyler. The adjusted basis of Tyler's partnership interest before adjusting for his share of income is

[41] §§ 705 and 752.

$35,000, and the fair market value of the interest before considering the income items is $50,000.

The unrealized gain inherent in Tyler's investment in the partnership is $15,000 ($50,000 − $35,000) before adjusting for his share of income. Tyler's proportionate share of the income items should increase the fair market value of the interest to $80,000 ($50,000 + $20,000 + $10,000). By increasing the adjusted basis of Tyler's partnership interest to $65,000 ($35,000 + $20,000 + $10,000), the unrealized gain inherent in Tyler's partnership investment remains at $15,000. The $20,000 of ordinary taxable income is taxed to Tyler this year and should not be taxed again when Tyler either sells his interest or receives a distribution. Similarly, the exempt income is exempt this year and should not increase Tyler's gain when he either sells his interest or receives a distribution from the partnership. ■

Decreasing the adjusted basis for the partner's share of deductible losses, deductions, and noncapitalizable, nondeductible expenditures follows this same logic. An item that is deductible currently should not contribute to creating a loss when the partnership interest is sold or when a distribution is received from the partnership. Similarly, a noncapitalizable, nondeductible expenditure should neither be deductible nor contribute to a loss upon a later sale or distribution transaction.

Basis—Effect of Partnership Liabilities

LO.10

Explain how liabilities affect a partner's basis.

A partner's adjusted basis is affected by the partner's share of partnership debt.[42] Partnership debt includes any partnership obligation that creates an asset; results in an expense to the partnership; or results in a nondeductible, noncapitalizable item at the partnership level. This definition includes certain contingent liabilities.[43] The definition also includes most debt that is considered a liability under financial accounting rules except for accounts payable of a cash basis partnership.

Under § 752, an increase in a partner's share of partnership debt is treated as a cash contribution by the partner to the partnership. A partner's share of partnership debt increases as a result of increases in the total amount of partnership debt. A decrease in a partner's share of partnership debt is treated as a cash distribution from the partnership to the partner. A partner's share of partnership debt decreases as a result of (1) decreases in the total amount of partnership debt and (2) assumption of the partner's debt by the partnership.

EXAMPLE 27

Jim and Becky contribute property to form the JB Partnership. Jim contributes cash of $30,000. Becky contributes land with an adjusted basis and fair market value of $45,000, subject to a liability of $15,000. The partnership borrows $50,000 to finance construction of a building on the contributed land. At the end of the first year, the accrual basis partnership owes $3,500 in trade accounts payable to various vendors. Assume that no other operating activities occurred. If Jim and Becky share equally in liabilities, the partners' bases in their partnership interests are determined as follows:

Jim's Basis		Becky's Basis	
Contributed cash	$30,000	Basis in contributed land	$ 45,000
Share of debt on land (assumed by partnership)	7,500	Less: Debt assumed by partnership	(15,000)
		Share of debt on land (assumed by partnership)	7,500
Initial basis	$37,500	Initial basis	$ 37,500
Share of construction loan	25,000	Share of construction loan	25,000
Share of trade accounts payable	1,750	Share of trade accounts payable	1,750
Basis, end of first year	$64,250	Basis, end of first year	$ 64,250

[42] § 752.

[43] Reg. § 1.752–1(a)(4)(ii).

In this case, it is reasonable that the parties have an equal basis, because each is a 50% owner and they contributed property with identical *net* bases and identical *net* fair market values. ■

EXAMPLE 28

Assume the same facts as in Example 27. In the second year, the partnership generates $70,000 of taxable income from operations and repays both the $50,000 construction loan and the $3,500 trade accounts payable. The taxable income is allocated equally to each partner and increases each partner's basis by $35,000. The $26,750 ($25,000 + $1,750) reduction of each partner's share of liabilities is treated as a cash distribution to each partner and reduces each partner's adjusted basis by that amount. The $72,500 adjusted basis for each partner at the end of the second year is computed as follows:

Jim's Basis		Becky's Basis	
Basis, beginning of second year	$ 64,250	Basis, beginning of second year	$ 64,250
Share of taxable income	35,000	Share of taxable income	35,000
Share of construction loan paid	(25,000)	Share of construction loan paid	(25,000)
Share of trade accounts payable paid	(1,750)	Share of trade accounts payable paid	(1,750)
Basis, end of second year	$ 72,500	Basis, end of second year	$ 72,500

■

Partnership debt is classified as either recourse or nonrecourse. **Recourse debt** is partnership debt for which the partnership or at least one of the partners is personally liable. This personal liability can exist, for example, through the operation of state law or through personal guarantees that a partner makes to the creditor. Personal liability of a party related to a partner (under attribution rules) is treated as the personal liability of the partner. **Nonrecourse debt** is debt for which no partner (or party related to a partner) is personally liable. Lenders of nonrecourse debt generally require that collateral be pledged against the loan. Upon default, the lender can claim only the collateral, not the partners' personal assets. Note that for an LLC, most debt will be treated as nonrecourse debt because the LLC members typically are not personally liable for the debt.

Recourse Debt Rules Recourse debt is allocated in a manner designed to recognize the extent to which a partner bears the "economic risk of loss." Under the Regulations, recourse debt created after January 29, 1989, is shared in accordance with a **constructive liquidation scenario.**[44]

Under this scenario, the following events are *deemed* to occur at the end of each taxable year of the partnership:

1. Most partnership assets (including cash) become worthless.
2. The worthless assets are sold at fair market value ($0), and losses on the deemed sales are determined.
3. These losses are allocated to the partners according to their loss sharing ratios. These losses reduce the partners' capital accounts.
4. Any partner with a (deemed) negative capital account balance is treated as contributing cash to the partnership to restore that negative balance to zero.
5. The cash deemed contributed by the partners with negative capital balances is used to pay the liabilities of the partnership.
6. The partnership is deemed to be liquidated immediately, and any remaining cash is distributed to partners with positive capital account balances.

A partner's share of partnership recourse liabilities equals the amount of that partner's cash contribution that would be used (in step 5 above) to pay partnership recourse liabilities.

[44] See Reg. § 1.752–2.

EXAMPLE 29

On January 1 of the current year, Hannah and Ian each contribute $20,000 cash to the newly created HI Partnership. Each partner has a 50% interest in partnership capital and profits. Losses are allocated 60% to Hannah and 40% to Ian. The first year of partnership operations resulted in the following balance sheet as of December 31:

	Basis	FMV		Basis	FMV
Cash	$12,000	$12,000	Recourse payables	$30,000	$30,000
Receivables	7,000	7,000	Hannah, capital	19,500	19,500
Land and buildings	50,000	50,000	Ian, capital	19,500	19,500
	$69,000	$69,000		$69,000	$69,000

The recourse debt is shared in accordance with the constructive liquidation scenario. All of the partnership assets (including cash) are deemed to be worthless and sold for $0. This creates a loss of $69,000 ($12,000 + $7,000 + $50,000).

The constructive liquidation scenario results in the $69,000 loss being allocated $41,400 to Hannah and $27,600 to Ian. As a consequence, Hannah's capital account has a negative balance of $21,900, and Ian's account has a negative balance of $8,100. Each partner is deemed to contribute cash equal to these negative capital accounts, and the cash would be used to pay the recourse liabilities under the liquidation scenario. Accordingly, Hannah and Ian share $21,900 and $8,100, respectively, in the recourse debt. The debt allocation percentages (73% to Hannah and 27% to Ian) are different from the partners' 60%/40% loss sharing ratios.

Note that if the partners shared losses equally, the intuitive result would arise. The $69,000 constructive liquidation loss would be allocated equally ($34,500 each) to Hannah and Ian. As a result, each partner would have a $15,000 negative capital account that would correspond to that partner's share of the partnership's recourse debt. ■

Nonrecourse Debt Rules As previously noted, most debt of an LLC will fall into the nonrecourse category. Nonrecourse debt is allocated in three stages. First, an amount of debt equal to the amount of *minimum gain* is allocated to partners who share in minimum gain per the partnership agreement. In general, minimum gain approximates the amount of nonrecourse (mortgage) liability on a property in excess of the "book" basis of the property. Generally, the "book" basis for nondepreciable contributed property is its fair market value on the contribution date. Further details of the minimum gain calculation are beyond the scope of this text.

Second, the amount of nonrecourse debt equal to the remaining *precontribution gain* under § 704(c) is allocated to the partner who contributed the property and debt to the partnership. For this purpose, the remaining precontribution gain is the excess of the current nonrecourse debt balance on the contributed property over the current tax basis of the contributed property.[45] Note that this calculation is only relevant when the "book" and "tax" bases of the contributed property are different.

Third, any remaining nonrecourse debt generally is allocated to the partners in accordance with their profit sharing ratios.

EXAMPLE 30

Ted contributes a nondepreciable asset to the TK Partnership in exchange for a one-third interest in the capital, profits, and losses of the partnership. The asset has an adjusted tax basis to Ted and the partnership of $24,000 and a fair market value and "book" basis on the contribution date of $50,000. The asset is encumbered by a nonrecourse note (created January 1, 2011) of $35,000. Because the "book" basis exceeds the nonrecourse debt, there is no minimum gain. Under § 704(c) principles, the Regulations provide that the first $11,000 of the nonrecourse debt ($35,000 debt − $24,000 basis) is allocated to Ted. The remaining $24,000 nonrecourse debt is allocated according to the profit sharing ratio, and Ted's share is $8,000. Therefore, Ted shares in $19,000 ($11,000 + $8,000) of the nonrecourse debt.

[45]Reg. § 1.704–3.

Ted's basis in his partnership interest is determined as follows:

Substituted basis of contributed property	$ 24,000
Less: Liability assumed by partnership	(35,000)
Plus: Allocation of § 704(c) debt	11,000
Basis before remaining allocation	$ -0-
Plus: Allocation of remaining nonrecourse debt	8,000
Basis in partnership interest	$ 8,000

The § 704(c) allocation of nonrecourse debt prevents Ted from receiving a deemed distribution ($35,000) in excess of his basis in property he contributed ($24,000). Without this required allocation of nonrecourse debt, in some cases, a contributing partner would be required to recognize gain on a contribution of property encumbered by nonrecourse debt. ■

Other Factors Affecting Basis Calculations

The partner's basis is also affected by (1) postacquisition contributions of cash or property to the partnership, (2) postacquisition distributions of cash or property from the partnership, and (3) special calculations that are designed to allow the full deduction of percentage depletion for oil and gas wells. Postacquisition contributions of cash or property affect basis in the same manner as contributions made upon the creation of the partnership. Postacquisition distributions of cash or property reduce basis.

THE BIG PICTURE

EXAMPLE 31

Return to the facts of *The Big Picture* in Example 17. Example 25 described how the income and deduction items of Beachside Properties, LLC, are allocated to Maria on her Schedule K–1. But how is Maria's basis affected by those items?

Assume that at the beginning of that tax year (Beachside's second year of operations), Maria's basis in her LLC interest was $1.6 million, including a $200,000 share of the LLC's $500,000 of nonrecourse debt. At the end of the year, Beachside had $600,000 of debt, which was again treated as nonrecourse to all of the LLC members.

During the year, Maria contributes to the LLC cash of $100,000 and additional property (basis of $0 and fair market value of $50,000). On December 31, the LLC distributes $20,000 cash to her. Maria's share of Beachside's income, gain, and deductions is as described in Example 25.

Maria's basis can be calculated using the ordering rules shown in Figure 10.3 on the next page. At the end of the year, Maria's basis is as follows:

Beginning basis	$1,600,000
Contributions, including increase in share of liabilities:	
Share of net increase in LLC liabilities [40% × ($600,000 − $500,000)]	40,000
Cash contribution to LLC capital	100,000
Maria's basis in noncash capital contribution	-0-
Share of LLC income items:	
Ordinary LLC income	72,000
LLC's net passive income from rental real estate	120,000
Tax-exempt income	840
Short-term capital gain	4,800
Qualified dividend income	1,600
Distributions and withdrawals:	
Capital withdrawal	(20,000)
Share of LLC deduction items:	
Charitable contribution	(2,400)
Ending basis	$1,916,840

As will be explained in Chapter 11, Maria could withdraw cash from the LLC up to the amount of her basis without paying tax on the distribution.

Maria's basis does not appear on the LLC's tax return or on her Schedule K–1. All partners are responsible for maintaining their own basis calculations.

A partner is required to compute the adjusted basis only when necessary and thus can avoid the inconvenience of making day-to-day calculations of basis. When a partnership interest is sold, exchanged, or retired, however, the partner must compute the adjusted basis as of the date the transaction occurs. Computation of gain or loss requires an accurate calculation of the partner's adjusted basis on the transaction date.

Figure 10.3 below summarizes the rules for computing a partner's basis in a partnership interest.

Partner's Capital Account

LO.11

Illustrate a partner's capital account rollforward, and explain why the year-end balance might differ from the partner's year-end basis in the partnership interest.

As mentioned earlier in the chapter, the partner's basis is not the same as the partner's capital account. Think of the capital account as an accounting calculation of the partner's ownership in the entity.

The capital account analysis (sometimes called a "rollforward" or "reconciliation") is shown on the partner's Schedule K–1 (see Appendix B). This calculation shows the change in the partner's capital account from the beginning to the end of the tax year. The partner's ending capital account balance is rarely the same amount as the partner's basis. Just as the tax and accounting bases of a specific asset may differ, a partner's capital account and basis in the partnership interest may not be equal for a variety of reasons. For example, a partner's basis includes the partner's share of partnership liabilities; these liabilities are not reported as part of the partner's capital account. The partner's share of partnership liabilities is shown separately in Part II of the Schedule K–1.

On Schedule K–1, the partner's capital account analysis can be prepared using any of several methods, including the tax basis, GAAP, or the § 704(b) book method. The method selected, which is indicated on the Schedule K–1, should be the same method that was used in preparing the partnership's Schedule M–2. In some cases, the partner's ending basis in the partnership interest will equal the

FIGURE 10.3 **Partner's Basis in Partnership Interest**

Basis is generally adjusted in the following order:

Initial basis. Amount paid for partnership interest, or gift or inherited basis (including share of partnership debt). Amount paid can be amount contributed to the partnership or amount paid to another partner or former partner.

+ Partner's subsequent contributions, including increases in the partner's share of partnership debt

+ Since interest acquired, partner's share of the partnership's
  - Taxable income items
  - Exempt income items
  - Excess of depletion deductions over adjusted basis of property subject to depletion

− Partner's distributions and withdrawals, including decreases in the partner's share of partnership debt

− Since interest acquired, partner's share of the partnership's
  - Separately stated deductions
  - Nondeductible items not chargeable to a capital account
  - Special depletion deduction for oil and gas wells

    Loss items

The basis of a partner's interest can never be negative.

sum of the partner's ending capital and the partner's share of liabilities. This could happen, for example, when the partner has been in the partnership since its inception and the capital account analysis is prepared on a tax basis.

The total of the partners' beginning and ending capital account balances on all Schedules K–1 should equal the beginning and ending balances shown on the partnership's Schedule M–2 (Analysis of Partners' Capital Accounts). These beginning and ending amounts should also equal the partners' capital accounts shown on the partnership's balance sheet (Schedule L) if Schedule L is prepared using the same method as the capital accounts.

THE BIG PICTURE

EXAMPLE 32

The last example illustrated the calculation of Maria's basis in her interest in Beachside Properties, LLC. Maria's Schedule K–1 will also show her capital account rollforward from the prior year to the current year. Assume that her capital account is calculated on a tax basis and that the beginning capital account balance was $1.4 million. The reconciliation shown on Schedule K–1 will be as follows:

Beginning capital account	$1,400,000
Capital contributed during the year	100,000
Current-year increase (decrease)	196,840
Withdrawals and distributions	(20,000)
Ending capital account	$1,676,840

Although this will not always be the case, Maria's ending capital account balance differs from her ending basis by the amount of her $240,000 share of the LLC's nonrecourse debt.

LO.12

List and review the limitations on deducting partnership losses.

Loss Limitations

Partnership losses flow through to the partners for use on their tax returns. However, the amount and nature of the losses allowed in a partner's tax computations may be limited. When limitations apply, all or a portion of the losses are held in suspension until a triggering event occurs. Only then can the losses be used to determine the partner's tax liability. No time limit is imposed on such carryforwards of losses.

Three different limitations may apply to partnership losses that are passed through to a partner:

1. The first is the overall limitation contained in § 704(d). This limitation allows the deduction of losses only to the extent the partner has adjusted basis for the partnership interest.
2. Losses that are deductible under the overall limitation may then be subject to the at-risk limitation of § 465. Losses are deductible under this provision only to the extent the partner is at risk for the partnership interest.
3. Any losses that survive this second limitation may be subject to a third limitation, the passive loss rules of § 469.

Only losses that make it through all of these applicable limitations are eligible to be deducted on the partner's tax return.

EXAMPLE 33

Megan is a partner in a partnership that does not invest in real estate. On January 1, 2012, Megan's adjusted basis for her partnership interest is $50,000, and her at-risk amount is $35,000. Her share of losses from the partnership for 2012 is $60,000, all of which is passive. She has one other passive income-producing investment that produced $25,000 of passive income during 2012.

Megan will be able to deduct $25,000 of partnership losses on her Form 1040 for 2012. Her deductible loss is calculated as follows:

Applicable Provision	Deductible Loss	Suspended Loss
§ 704(d) overall limitation	$50,000	$10,000
§ 465 at-risk limitation	35,000	15,000
§ 469 passive loss limitation	25,000	10,000

Megan can deduct only $50,000 under the overall limitation. Of this $50,000, only $35,000 is deductible under the at-risk limitation. Under the passive loss limitation, passive losses can be deducted only against passive income. Thus, Megan can deduct only $25,000 on her return in 2012. ■

Overall Limitation

A partner may deduct loss items and deductions flowing through from the partnership only to the extent of the partner's adjusted basis in the partnership. A partner's adjusted basis in the partnership is determined at the end of the partnership's taxable year. It is adjusted for any partnership income and gain items and contributions and distributions made during the year, but it is determined *before considering any loss or deduction items for the year.* (In Figure 10.3, basis would be calculated through "partner's distributions and withdrawals.")

Losses that cannot be deducted because of this rule are suspended and carried forward (never back) for use against future increases in the partner's adjusted basis. Such increases might result from additional capital contributions, from sharing in additional partnership debts, or from future partnership income.

EXAMPLE 34

Courtney and Daniel do business as the CD Partnership, sharing profits and losses equally. All parties use the calendar year. At the start of the current year, the basis of Courtney's partnership interest is $25,000. The partnership sustains an operating loss of $80,000 in the current year. For the current year, only $25,000 of Courtney's $40,000 allocable share of the partnership loss can be deducted under the overall limitation. As a result, the basis of Courtney's partnership interest is zero as of January 1 of the following year, and Courtney must carry forward the remaining $15,000 of partnership losses. ■

EXAMPLE 35

Assume the same facts as in Example 34, and assume that the partnership earns a profit of $70,000 for the next calendar year. Courtney reports net partnership income of $20,000 ($35,000 distributive share of income − the $15,000 carryforward loss). The basis of Courtney's partnership interest becomes $20,000. ■

At-Risk Limitation

Under the at-risk rules, the partnership losses from business and income-producing activities that individual partners and closely held C corporation partners [as defined in § 542(a)(2)] can deduct are limited to amounts that are economically invested in the partnership. Invested amounts include cash and the adjusted basis of property contributed by the partner and the partner's share of partnership earnings that has not been withdrawn.[46] A closely held C corporation exists when five or fewer individuals own more than 50 percent of the entity's stock under appropriate attribution and ownership rules.

When some or all of the partners are personally liable for partnership recourse debt, that debt is included in the adjusted basis of those partners. Usually, those partners also include the debt in their amount at risk.

[46] § 465(a).

No partner, however, carries any financial risk on nonrecourse debt. Therefore, as a general rule, partners cannot include nonrecourse debt in their amount at risk even though that debt is included in the adjusted basis of their partnership interest. This rule has an exception, however, that applies in many cases. Real estate nonrecourse financing provided by a bank, retirement plan, or similar party or by a Federal, state, or local government generally is deemed to be at risk.[47] Such debt is termed **qualified nonrecourse debt**. In summary, although the general rule provides that nonrecourse debt is not at risk, the overriding exception may provide that it is deemed to be at risk.

When determining a partner's loss deduction, the overall limitation rule is invoked first. That is, the deduction is limited to the partner's outside basis at the end of the partnership year. Then, the at-risk provisions are applied to see if the remaining loss is still deductible. Suspended losses are carried forward until a partner has a sufficient amount at risk in the activity to absorb them.[48]

EXAMPLE 36

Kelly invests $5,000 in the Kelly Green Limited Partnership as a 5% general partner. Shortly thereafter, the partnership acquires the master recording of a well-known vocalist for $250,000 ($50,000 from the partnership and $200,000 secured from a local bank by means of a *recourse* mortgage). Assume that Kelly's share of the recourse debt is $10,000, and her basis in her partnership interest is $15,000 ($5,000 cash investment + $10,000 debt share). Because the debt is recourse, Kelly's at-risk amount is also $15,000. Kelly's share of partnership losses in the first year of operations is $11,000. Kelly is entitled to deduct the full $11,000 of partnership losses under both the overall and the at-risk limitations because this amount is less than both her outside basis and at-risk amount.

If, instead, the bank loan had been nonrecourse, Kelly would be able to deduct only $5,000 of the flow-through loss. The amount she has at risk in the partnership does not include the nonrecourse debt. (The debt does not relate to real estate, so it is not qualified nonrecourse debt.) ■

Passive Activity Rules

A partnership loss share may be disallowed under the passive activity rules. These rules apply to partners who are individuals, estates, trusts, closely held C corporations, or personal service corporations. The rules require the partners to separate their interests in partnership activities into three groups:

- *Active.* Earned income, such as salary and wages; income or loss from a trade or business in which the partner materially participates; and guaranteed payments received by the partner for services.
- *Portfolio.* Annuity income, interest, dividends, guaranteed payments from a partnership for interest on capital, royalties not derived in the ordinary course of a trade or business, and gains and losses from disposal of investment assets.
- *Passive.* Income from a trade or business activity in which the partner does not materially participate on a regular, continuous, and substantial basis,[49] or income from many rental activities.

Material participation in an activity is determined annually. The IRS has provided a number of objective tests for determining material participation. In general, these tests require the partner to have substantial involvement in daily operations of the activity. By definition, a partner treated as a limited partner is typically considered *not* to materially participate in partnership activities.[50]

Rent income from real or personal property generally is passive income, regardless of the partner's level of participation. Exceptions are made for rent income from activities where substantial services are provided (e.g., certain developers and

[47] § 465(b)(6).
[48] § 465(a)(2).
[49] §§ 469(c)(1) and (2).
[50] § 469(h)(2).

TAX IN THE NEWS **LLC Members Not Automatically Treated as Passive**

Under § 469(h)(2), "no interest in a limited partnership as a limited partner shall be treated as an interest with respect to which a taxpayer materially participates." The IRS has taken the position that because a member of an LLC has limited liability with respect to the entity's debts, that member has an "interest in a limited partnership" and cannot, by definition, be a material participant in an LLC's activities.

In *Paul D. Garnett*, 132 T.C. 368 (2009) (and similar rulings), the Tax Court ruled that the taxpayer's mere status as a member of an LLC did not lead to a presumption that he should be treated as *not* being a material participant in the LLC's activities. The court stated that the determinative test was whether the LLC member participated in LLC activities and not whether the LLC member was protected from entity liabilities.

The effect of this ruling is that it will be much easier for an LLC member to claim a loss from the LLC. The member will not automatically be treated as a passive, nonmaterial participant, resulting in a disallowed loss.

resorts); from hotels, motels, and other transient lodging; from short-term equipment rentals; and from certain developed real estate. In addition, rental real estate is not treated as a passive activity for a person who qualifies as a real estate professional.

Usually, passive activity losses can be offset only against passive activity income.[51] In determining the net passive activity loss for a year, losses and income from all passive activities are aggregated. The amount of suspended losses carried forward from a particular activity is determined by the ratio of the net loss from that activity to the aggregate net loss from all passive activities for the year.

In any one year, individuals can offset up to $25,000 of passive losses from rental real estate against active and portfolio income.[52] The $25,000 maximum is reduced by 50 percent of the difference between the taxpayer's modified AGI and $100,000. Thus, when the taxpayer's modified AGI reaches $150,000, the offset is eliminated. The offset is available to those who actively (rather than materially) participate in rental real estate activities.

For additional information regarding loss limitations, the passive loss rules, and the rental real estate exception, refer to *Individual Income Taxes* (South-Western Federal Taxation), Chapter 11.

10.4 Transactions between Partner and Partnership

LO.13

List and explain the special rules that govern the treatment of transactions between a partner and the partnership.

Many types of transactions occur between a partnership and one of its partners. The partner may contribute property to the partnership, perform services for the partnership, or receive distributions from the partnership. The partner may borrow money from or lend money to the partnership. Property may be bought and sold between the partner and the partnership. Several of these transactions were discussed earlier in the chapter. The remaining types of partner-partnership transactions are the focus of this section.

Guaranteed Payments

If a partnership makes a payment to a partner, the payment may be a draw against the partner's share of partnership income; a return of some or all of the partner's original capital contribution; or a guaranteed payment, among other treatments. A **guaranteed payment** is a payment for services performed by the partner or for the use of the partner's capital. The payment may not be determined by reference to

[51] § 469(a)(1).

[52] § 469(i).

partnership income. Guaranteed payments are usually expressed as a fixed-dollar amount or as a percentage of capital the partner has invested in the partnership. Whether the partnership deducts or capitalizes the guaranteed payment depends on the nature of the payment.

EXAMPLE 37

David, Derek, and Danielle formed the accrual basis DDD Partnership in 2012. The partnership and each of the partners are calendar year taxpayers. According to the partnership agreement, David is to manage the partnership and receive a $21,000 distribution from the entity every year, payable in 12 monthly installments. Derek is to receive an amount that is equal to 18% of his capital account, as it is computed by the firm's accountant at the beginning of the year, payable in 12 monthly installments. Danielle is the partnership's advertising specialist. She withdraws approximately 4% of the partnership's net income for her personal use. David and Derek receive guaranteed payments from the partnership, but Danielle does not. ■

Guaranteed payments resemble the salary or interest payments of other businesses.[53] Deductible guaranteed payments, like any other deductible expenses of a partnership, can create an ordinary loss for the entity. If the partnership distributes appreciated property to pay the guaranteed payment, the partnership must recognize a gain on the transfer.[54]

A partner who receives guaranteed payments during a partnership year must include the payments in income as if they were received on the last day of the partnership year. Guaranteed payments are always taxable as ordinary income to the recipient partner. The partner's guaranteed payment is reported on Schedule K–1. The partner uses this information (in lieu of a Form W–2 or 1099) to report the income on the partner's tax return.

EXAMPLE 38

Continue with the situation introduced in Example 37. For calendar year 2012, David receives the $21,000 as provided by the partnership agreement, Derek's guaranteed payment for 2012 is $17,000, and Danielle withdraws $20,000. Before considering these amounts, the partnership's ordinary income for 2012 is $650,000.

The partnership can deduct its payments to David and Derek, so its 2012 ordinary income is $612,000 ($650,000 − $21,000 − $17,000). Thus, each of the equal partners is allocated $204,000 of ordinary partnership income for their 2012 individual income tax returns ($612,000 ÷ 3). In addition, David reports the $21,000 guaranteed payment as income on his 2012 tax return, and Derek similarly includes the $17,000 guaranteed payment in his 2012 income. Danielle's partnership draw is deemed to have come from her allocated $204,000 (or from the accumulated partnership income that was taxed in prior years) and is not taxed separately to her. Danielle's basis, though, is reduced by the $20,000 distribution.

Instead, if DDD had a natural business year that ended, for example, on March 31, the guaranteed payments to David and Derek made after DDD's year ended March 31, 2012, would be reported on David and Derek's Schedule K–1 as of March 31, 2013, and on their personal tax returns for calendar year 2013. ■

Self-Employment Tax of Partners

A partner is not treated as an employee for tax purposes. Thus, a partner is not subject to withholding on any guaranteed payments, and the partnership cannot generally deduct its payments for any fringe benefits paid to the partners.

Certain partnership income reported by a partner who is an individual taxpayer may be considered "net earnings from self-employment" and is subject to self-employment (SE) tax. Section 1402 provides that SE income includes the partner's distributive share of income from a partnership's trade or business, whether or not

[53] § 707(c).

[54] Rev.Rul. 2007–40, 2007–1 C.B. 1426.

that income is distributed. This provision applies to income allocated to a "general partner" and income earned by a "limited partner" that is in the nature of compensation for services performed for or on behalf of the partnership.[55]

For a general partner, both the partner's allocable share of income and any guaranteed payments for services are subject to the SE tax. For a limited partner, any guaranteed payment for services rendered to the partnership is subject to the SE tax. Recall that an LLC member often is treated similarly to a limited partner.

Proposed Regulations provide guidance regarding how to determine whether a partner or an LLC member should be treated as a general partner or a limited partner. These regulations provide, in general, that a partner or an LLC member will be treated as a general partner if

- the partner has personal liability for partnership debts by virtue of status as a partner,
- the partner can enter into contractual relationships on behalf of the partnership, or
- the partner works more than 500 hours in the partnership's trade or business during the tax year.

If the partner is treated as a general partner solely because of the "hours worked" limitation, the interest can still be treated as a limited interest (for purposes of classifying the partner's distributive share of income) if there is at least one other limited partner with identical rights.

Because of the proposed status of these Regulations, taxpayers are not required to comply with them or disclose any noncompliance. These Regulations are highly controversial and have existed since 1997 without being finalized. At this point, however, they are the only guidance available.

THE BIG PICTURE

EXAMPLE 39

Return to the facts of *The Big Picture* on p. 10-1. Assume that Josh was elected as managing member of Beachside Properties, LLC; he has the sole authority to contract for the LLC and works 1,000 hours per year in the business. Maria works 1,000 hours per year in the café. After surrendering his land to Beachside, Kyle has generally not been involved in the LLC's operations.

Kyle and Josh each receive a guaranteed payment of $5,000 per month from the LLC. Josh's payment is for services, and Kyle's is for use of his $2 million of land. Maria receives a guaranteed payment of $10,000 per month, of which $5,000 is for services and $5,000 is for the use of her $2 million of capital.

If Beachside follows the Proposed Regulations, the members' distributive shares and guaranteed payments will be treated as follows:

	Distributive Share (Proposed Regulations)	**Guaranteed Payments [§ 1402(a)(13)]**
Kyle	Not SE income	Not SE income (payment is for capital; not services)
Maria	Not SE income*	$5,000 SE income (services) and $5,000 not SE income (capital)
Josh	SE income	SE income (payment is for services to the LLC)

* Under the Proposed Regulations, Maria's distributive share is not SE income. She is not personally liable for the LLC's debt, and she is not authorized to contract on behalf of the LLC. Even though she works for the LLC more than 500 hours per year, another LLC member (Kyle) has the same rights as Maria; because Kyle would be classified as a limited partner, Maria is also classified as such.

[55] §§ 1402(a) and (a)(13). See also Prop.Reg. § 1.1402(a)–2(h).

Other Transactions between a Partner and a Partnership

Certain transactions between a partner and the partnership are treated as if the partner were an outsider, dealing with the partnership at arm's length.[56] Loan transactions, rental payments, and sales of property between the partner and the partnership are generally treated in this manner. In addition, payments for services are treated this way when the services are short-term technical services the partner also provides for parties other than the partnership.

EXAMPLE 40

Chad, a one-third partner in the ABC Partnership, owns a tract of land the partnership wants to purchase. The land has a fair market value of $30,000 and an adjusted basis to Chad of $17,000. If Chad sells the land to the partnership, he recognizes a $13,000 gain on the sale and the partnership takes a $30,000 cost basis in the land. If the land has a fair market value of $10,000 on the sale date, Chad recognizes a $7,000 loss. ■

The time for deducting a payment by an accrual basis partnership to a cash basis service partner depends upon whether the amount is a guaranteed payment or a payment to a partner who is treated as an outsider. A guaranteed payment is includible in the partner's income on the last day of the partnership year when it is properly accrued by the partnership, even though the payment may not be made to the partner until the next taxable year. Conversely, the *partner's* method of accounting controls the timing of the deduction if the payment is treated as made to an outsider. This is because a deduction cannot be claimed for such amounts until the recipient partner is required to include the amount in income under the partner's method of accounting.[57] Thus, a partnership cannot claim a deduction until it actually makes the payment to the cash basis partner, but it could accrue and deduct a payment due to an accrual basis partner even if payment was not yet made.

EXAMPLE 41

Rachel, a cash basis taxpayer, is a partner in the accrual basis RTC Partnership. On December 31, 2012, the partnership accrues but does not pay $10,000 for deductible services that Rachel performed for the partnership during the year. Both Rachel and the partnership are calendar year taxpayers.

If the $10,000 accrual is a guaranteed payment, the partnership deducts the $10,000 in its calendar year ended December 31, 2012, and Rachel includes the $10,000 in her income for the 2012 calendar year. The fact that Rachel is a cash basis taxpayer and does not actually receive the cash in 2012 is irrelevant.

If the payment is classified as a payment to an outsider, the partnership cannot deduct the payment until Rachel actually receives the cash. If, for example, Rachel performs janitorial services (i.e., not in her capacity as a partner) and receives the cash on March 25, 2013, the partnership deducts the payment and Rachel recognizes the income on that date. ■

Sales of Property

Certain sales of property are subject to special rules. No loss is recognized on a sale of property between a person and a partnership when the person owns, directly or indirectly, more than 50 percent of partnership capital or profits.[58] The disallowed loss may not vanish entirely, however. If the transferee eventually sells the property at a gain, the disallowed loss reduces the gain the transferee would otherwise recognize.

EXAMPLE 42

Blake sells land (adjusted basis to him, $30,000; fair market value, $45,000) to a partnership in which he controls a 60% capital interest. The partnership pays him only $20,000 for the land. Blake cannot deduct his $10,000 realized loss. Blake and the partnership are related parties, and the loss is disallowed.

[56] § 707(a).

[57] § 267(a)(2).

[58] § 707(b).

When the partnership sells the land to an outsider at a later date, it receives a sales price of $44,000. The partnership can offset the recognition of its $24,000 realized gain on the subsequent sale ($44,000 sales proceeds − $20,000 adjusted basis) by the amount of the $10,000 prior disallowed loss ($30,000 − $20,000). Thus, the partnership recognizes a $14,000 gain on its sale of the land. ■

Using a similar rationale, any gain that is realized on a sale or exchange between a partner and a partnership in which the partner controls a capital or profits interest of more than 50 percent must be recognized as ordinary income, unless the asset is a capital asset to both the seller and the purchaser.[59]

EXAMPLE 43

Kristin purchases some land (adjusted basis, $30,000; fair market value, $45,000) for $45,000 from a partnership in which she controls a 90% profits interest. The land was a capital asset to the partnership. If Kristin holds the land as a capital asset, the partnership recognizes a $15,000 capital gain. However, if Kristin is a land developer and the property is not a capital asset to her, the partnership must recognize $15,000 ordinary income from the sale, even though the property was a capital asset to the partnership. ■

10.5 Tax Planning

LO.14

Provide insights regarding advantageous use of a partnership.

Choosing Partnership Taxation

A partnership often provides tax advantages over a Subchapter C or Subchapter S corporation. A partnership is subject to only a single level of taxation. Corporate income, however, is taxed at the entity level and upon distribution to corporate owners as dividends. Partnership income may be subject to high tax rates at the partner level, but this tax will generally be lower than the combined layers of tax on corporate income.

For both C and S corporations, each income or loss allocation or distribution is required to be proportionate to the ownership interest of each shareholder. A partnership, though, may adjust its allocations of income and cash flow among the partners each year according to their needs, as long as the allocation meets the substantial economic effect and capital account maintenance rules discussed in the chapter.

Upon liquidation of a C or S corporation, any previously unrealized income, such as appreciation of corporate assets, is recognized at the entity level. As discussed in Chapter 11, a partnership generally may liquidate tax-free.

Many states impose reporting and licensing requirements on corporate entities, including S corporations. These include franchise or capital stock tax returns that may require annual assessments and costly professional preparation assistance. Partnerships, on the other hand, often have no reporting requirements beyond Federal and state informational tax returns. (Note, however, that some states impose franchise taxes and additional filing requirements on LLCs.)

For smaller business operations, a partnership enables several owners to combine their resources at low cost. It also offers simple filing requirements, the taxation of income only once, and the ability to discontinue operations relatively inexpensively.

For larger business operations, a partnership offers a unique ability to raise capital with low filing and reporting costs compared to, for example, corporate bond issuances. Special allocations of income and cash-flow items may be used by partnerships to meet the objectives of the owners.

[59] § 707(b)(2).

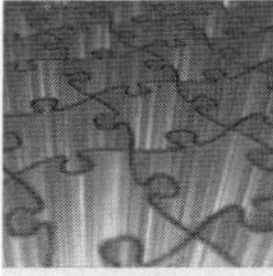

CONCEPT SUMMARY 10.3

Advantages and Disadvantages of the Partnership Form

The partnership form may be attractive when one or more of the following factors is present:

- The entity is generating net taxable losses and/or valuable tax credits, which will be of use to the owners.
- The owners want to avoid complex corporate administrative and filing requirements.
- Other means of reducing the effects of the double taxation of corporate business income (e.g., compensation to owners, interest, and rental payments) have been exhausted.
- The entity does not generate material amounts of tax preference and adjustment items, which increase the alternative minimum tax liabilities of its owners.
- The entity is generating net passive income, which its owners can use to claim immediate deductions for net passive losses that they have generated from other sources.
- The owners want to make special allocations of certain income or deduction items that are not possible under the C or S corporation forms.
- The owners anticipate liquidation of the entity within a short period of time. Liquidation of a C or S corporation would generate entity-level recognized gains on appreciated property distributed.
- The owners have adequate bases in their ownership interests to facilitate the deduction of flow-through losses and the assignment of an adequate basis to assets distributed in kind to the owners.

The partnership form may be less attractive when one or more of the following factors is present:

- The tax paid by the individual owners on the entity's income is greater than the tax the entity would pay if it were a C corporation, and the income is not expected to be distributed soon. (If distributed by a C corporation, double taxation would likely occur.)
- The entity is generating net taxable income without distributing any cash to the owners. The owners may not have sufficient cash with which to pay the tax on the entity's earnings.
- The type of income the entity is generating (e.g., business and portfolio income) is not as attractive to its owners as net passive income would be because the owners could use net passive income to offset the net passive losses they have generated on their own.
- The entity is in a high-exposure business, and the owners want protection from personal liability. An LLC, LLP, or LLLP structure may be available, however, to limit personal liability.
- The owners want to avoid Federal self-employment tax.
- The entity has already been formed as a corporation, and conversion to partnership status could result in significant taxes in the course of liquidation.
- Partnership operations are complex (indicating that Form 1065 might not be filed until near the due date for the return), but partners with the same tax year need to file their returns as early as possible for personal reasons (e.g., to meet debt requirements or to receive a tax refund).

Concept Summary 10.3 enumerates various factors that the owners of a business should consider in deciding whether to use a C corporation, an S corporation, or a partnership as a means of doing business. Refer back to this list after reading Chapters 11 (advanced partnership topics) and 12 (S corporations). Chapter 13 includes a more detailed discussion of the tax effects of various forms of conducting business.

Formation and Operation of a Partnership

Potential partners should be cautious in transferring assets to a partnership to ensure that they are not required to recognize any gain upon the creation of the entity. The nonrecognition provisions of § 721 are relatively straightforward and resemble the provisions under § 351, which permit certain tax-free property transfers to corporations. However, any partner can make a tax-deferred contribution of assets to the entity either at the inception of the partnership or later. This possibility is not available to less-than-controlling shareholders in a corporation.

The partners should anticipate the tax benefits and pitfalls that are presented in Subchapter K and should take appropriate actions to resolve any potential problems before they arise. Typically, all that is needed is an appropriate provision in the partnership agreement (e.g., with respect to differing allocation percentages for gains and losses). Recall, however, that a special allocation of income, expense, or credit items in the partnership agreement must satisfy certain requirements before it is acceptable to the IRS.

Basis Considerations and Loss Deduction Limitations

If a partnership incurs a loss for the taxable year, careful planning will help ensure that the partners can claim the deduction.

A partner can contribute capital to the partnership before the end of the tax year. Alternatively, the partnership could incur additional debt. The partner's cash contribution or share of debt increases the partner's basis in the partnership interest. If the loss also meets the "at-risk" and "passive" hurdles, the loss can be deducted.

In the following year, if the partnership is expected to report taxable income, the partner could withdraw cash or pay off debt equal to the income. The partner's cash contribution would have to be invested in the partnership for only a short time. Similarly, the partnership's additional debt would not have to be maintained for a long period of time.

Partnership Reporting Requirements

For most small (under 100 partners) partnerships, the tax return is due by the fifteenth day of the fourth month following the tax year-end (April 15 for a calendar year partnership). If all partners and the partnership have the same tax year, the partnership tax return will be due on the same date as the return for any partners who are individual taxpayers. The partnership return will be due one month *after* the due date for the return of a partner that is a Subchapter C or Subchapter S corporation. For example, suppose a partnership has an individual and a Subchapter S corporation as partners and all taxpayers use the calendar year. The individual partner's tax return will be due on April 15 (the same date as the partnership's return), but the S corporation's tax return will be due on March 15 (a month earlier).

The partners cannot file an accurate return until they receive the Schedule K–1 from the partnership. A good accountant will pay attention to the partners' status and will attempt to schedule completion of partnership tax returns to accommodate the partners' filing requirements. Still, in some situations, the partners may have to obtain extensions for filing their tax returns because they have not received their Schedule K–1 in time.

In extreme cases, a partner may need to file a return by the original due date (e.g., to meet debt financing requirements or to request a refund of overpaid taxes). In that case, the partner can estimate income from the partnership in the original return and then file an amended return when the Schedule K–1 from the partnership is received.

Transactions between Partners and Partnerships

Partners should be careful when engaging in transactions with the partnership to ensure that no negative tax results occur. A partner who owns a majority of the partnership generally should not sell property at a loss to the partnership because the loss is disallowed. Similarly, a majority partner should not sell a capital asset to the partnership at a gain if the asset is to be used by the partnership as other than a capital asset. The gain on this transaction is taxed as ordinary income to the selling partner rather than as capital gain.

As an alternative to selling property to a partnership, the partner should consider a lease arrangement. The partner recognizes rent income, and the partnership has a rent expense. A partner who needs more cash immediately can sell the property to an outside third party; then the third party can lease the property to the partnership for a fair rental.

The timing of the deduction for a payment by an accrual basis partnership to a cash basis partner varies depending on whether the payment is a guaranteed payment or is treated as a payment to an outsider. If the payment is a guaranteed payment, the deduction occurs when the partnership makes the accrual. If the payment is treated as a payment to an outsider, the actual date the payment is made controls the timing of the deduction.

Drafting the Partnership Agreement

Although a written partnership agreement (or LLC operating agreement) is not always required, many rules governing the tax consequences to partners and their partnerships refer to such an agreement. Remember that a partner's distributive share of income, gain, loss, deduction, or credit is determined in accordance with the partnership agreement. Consequently, if taxpayers operating a business in partnership form want a measure of certainty as to the tax consequences of their activities, a carefully drafted partnership agreement is crucial. An agreement that sets forth the obligations, rights, and powers of the partners should prove invaluable in settling controversies among them and provide some degree of certainty as to the tax consequences of the partners' actions.

REFOCUS ON THE BIG PICTURE

Why Use a Partnership, Anyway?

© Roderick Paul Walker/Alamy

After considering the various types of partnerships, Kyle, Maria, and Josh decide to form Beachside Properties as an LLC (see Example 1). On formation of the entity, there was no tax to the LLC or to any of its members (see Example 13). Beachside Properties computes its income as shown in Examples 17 and 18. Beachside determines additional information the partners will need (Example 19) and reconciles book and tax income (Example 20). The income is allocated to the partners (Examples 24 and 25). The LLC's income affects the members' bases and capital accounts as shown in Examples 31 and 32. An important consideration for the LLC members is whether their distributive shares and guaranteed payments will be treated as self-employment income (see Example 39).

What If?

What happens in the future when the LLC members decide to expand or renovate Beachside's facilities? At that time, the existing members can contribute additional funds, the LLC can obtain new members, or the entity can solicit third-party financing. An LLC is not subject to the 80 percent control requirement applicable to the formation of and subsequent transfers to a corporation. Therefore, new investors can contribute cash or other property in exchange for interests in the LLC—and the transaction will qualify for tax-deferred treatment under § 721.

KEY TERMS

Aggregate concept, 10-4
Capital interest, 10-5
Capital sharing ratio, 10-5
Conduit Concept, 10-4
Constructive liquidation scenario, 10-28
Disguised sale, 10-8
Economic effect test, 10-22
Entity concept, 10-4
General partners, 10-2
General partnership, 10-2
Guaranteed payment, 10-35
Inside basis, 10-5
Least aggregate deferral rule, 10-16
Limited liability company, 10-2
Limited liability limited partnership, 10-3
Limited liability partnership, 10-3
Limited partners, 10-2
Limited partnership, 10-2
Nonrecourse debt, 10-28
Operating agreement, 10-3
Outside basis, 10-5
Partnership agreement, 10-3
Precontribution gain or loss, 10-23
Profit and loss sharing ratios, 10-5
Profits (loss) interest, 10-5
Qualified nonrecourse debt, 10-34
Recourse debt, 10-28
Schedule K–1, 10-5
Separately stated items, 10-4
Special allocation, 10-5
Syndication costs, 10-14

DISCUSSION QUESTIONS

1. **LO.1** How is a partnership defined for Federal income tax purposes? What parties can own an interest in a partnership?
2. **LO.1** What is a partnership agreement? What types of provisions does it include?
3. **LO.1** Name the five types of partnerships discussed in this chapter. What factors are considered in determining the type of partnership entity to utilize?
4. **LO.2** Describe the differences and similarities between the entity concept and the aggregate or conduit concept of partnership taxation.
5. **LO.2** What are separately stated items? Why are they important?
6. **LO.2** What is "inside" basis? "Outside" basis?
7. **LO.2** Describe how a partnership reports its income for tax purposes. Who makes most elections related to partnership income and deductions? What theory underlies this treatment?
8. **LO.2, 8, 13** Orange, LLC, was formed when Green, Inc., contributed $400,000 of cash and Rose contributed nondepreciable assets valued at $200,000 with a basis of $10,000. In addition, Rose will perform significant management services for the LLC. For most items, the members intend to allocate profits, losses, and liquidating distributions equally. How can (or must) special allocations be used to compensate the members for the differences between the bases and values of contributed property and time devoted to LLC activities? **Issue ID**
9. **LO.3** Compare the provision for the nonrecognition of gain or loss on contributions to a partnership (i.e., § 721) with the similar provision related to corporate formation (i.e., § 351). What are the major differences and similarities?
10. **LO.3** When can the formation of a partnership result in a taxable gain to one or more of the new partners?
11. **LO.3** Kelsey and Christopher are forming the KC Partnership, in which Kelsey will own a 40% interest and Christopher will own a 60% interest. Kelsey will contribute appreciated land, and Christopher will contribute cash. What is the tax effect of the formation to Kelsey, Christopher, and the partnership? **Issue ID**
12. **LO.3** Jonathan owns property (basis of $200,000, value of $300,000). He plans to contribute the property to the JJG Partnership in exchange for a 25% interest. **Issue ID** **Decision Making**
    a. What issues arise if the partnership distributes $150,000 of cash to Jonathan three months after the property contribution?
    b. How can the risk of adverse tax consequences be minimized?

13. **LO.3, 4** How does a partnership calculate depreciation on property that is contributed by a partner? If the partnership incurs additional costs that must be capitalized (i.e., transfer taxes related to changing the title), how are those costs treated?

Communications

14. **LO.4** What types of expenditures might a new partnership incur? How are those costs treated for Federal tax purposes? Create a chart describing the expenditure, the treatment, and the Code section requiring this treatment.

Issue ID

15. **LO.4** Tina and Rex plan to form the TR Partnership to acquire, own, and manage a certain rental real estate property. The financial information has been accumulated into an Offering Memorandum that is currently being brokered to investors (for a 6% commission). What types of costs is the partnership likely to incur? How will those costs be treated?

16. **LO.5** When can a partnership use the cash method of accounting?

17. **LO.6** How is the taxable year of a newly formed partnership determined?

18. **LO.7** What types of information are reported on the partnership's Schedule K? How does Schedule K relate to the partnership's Schedule M–1 (or M–3) and Schedule M–2?

19. **LO.8** What is the purpose of the three rules that implement the economic effect test?

20. **LO.9, 10** Discuss the adjustments that must be made to a partner's basis in the partnership interest. When are such adjustments made?

21. **LO.10** Describe, in general terms, how a partnership's liabilities affect a partner's basis in the partnership interest.

22. **LO.11** What is a partner's capital account? Describe how a partner's ending capital account balance is determined. In addition to the material in the chapter, refer to Schedule K–1 in Appendix B.

23. **LO.12** Describe the three limitations that apply to the deductibility of a loss from a partnership. In what order are these limitations applied?

24. **LO.13** What is a guaranteed payment? When is it deducted by the partnership? When is it reported in the recipient partners' income?

25. **LO.13** When is partnership income subject to self-employment tax for an individual partner?

26. **LO.10, 12, 14** Discuss situations in which the partnership entity form might be more advantageous (or disadvantageous) than operating as a Subchapter C or S corporation.

PROBLEMS

27. **LO.3** Emma and Laine form the equal EL Partnership. Emma contributes cash of $100,000. Laine contributes property with an adjusted basis of $40,000 and a fair market value of $100,000.
    a. How much gain, if any, must Emma recognize on the transfer? Must Laine recognize any gain?
    b. What is Emma's basis in her partnership interest?
    c. What is Laine's basis in her partnership interest?
    d. What basis does the partnership take in the property transferred by Laine?

Decision Making

28. **LO.3, 14** Scott and Amber form the equal Toucan, LLC, with a cash contribution of $100,000 from Scott and a property contribution (adjusted basis of $110,000, fair market value of $100,000) from Amber.
    a. How much gain or loss, if any, does Amber realize on the transfer? Does Amber recognize any gain or loss?
    b. What is Scott's basis in his LLC interest?
    c. What is Amber's basis in her LLC interest?
    d. What basis does the LLC take in the property transferred by Amber?
    e. Are there more effective ways to structure the formation? Explain.

29. **LO.3** Liz and John formed the equal LJ Partnership on January 1 of the current year. Liz contributed $80,000 of cash and land with a fair market value of $90,000 and an

adjusted basis of $75,000. John contributed equipment with a fair market value of $170,000 and an adjusted basis of $20,000. John had previously used the equipment in his sole proprietorship.

a. How much gain or loss will Liz, John, and the partnership realize?
b. How much gain or loss will Liz, John, and the partnership recognize?
c. What bases will Liz and John take in their partnership interests?
d. What bases will LJ take in the assets it receives?
e. Are there any differences between inside and outside basis? Explain.
f. How will the partnership depreciate any assets it receives from the partners?

30. **LO.3** Jared and Chelsea form the equal JC Partnership. Jared contributes cash of $20,000 and land (fair market value of $80,000, adjusted basis of $65,000), and Chelsea contributes the assets of her sole proprietorship (value of $100,000, adjusted basis of $125,000). What are the tax consequences of the partnership formation to Jared, Chelsea, and JC Partnership?

Issue ID

31. **LO.3** Assume the same facts as in Problem 30, except that Chelsea sells her assets to a third party for $100,000 and then contributes that cash to the partnership. The partnership locates equivalent assets that it purchases for $110,000. How do these changes affect the tax result for Chelsea and the partnership? How does the economic result differ?

Issue ID
Decision Making

32. **LO.3, 9, 14** Sam and Drew are equal partners in SD, LLC, formed on June 1 of the current year. Sam contributed land that he inherited from his uncle in 2005. Sam's uncle purchased the land in 1980 for $30,000. The land was worth $100,000 when Sam's uncle died. The fair market value of the land was $200,000 at the date it was contributed to the partnership.

Drew has significant experience developing real estate. After the LLC is formed, he will prepare a plan for developing the property and secure zoning approvals for the LLC. Drew would normally bill a third party $50,000 for these efforts. Drew will also contribute $150,000 cash in exchange for his 50% interest in the LLC. The value of his 50% interest is $200,000.

a. How much gain or income will Sam recognize on his contribution of the land to the LLC? What is the character of any gain or income recognized?
b. What basis will Sam take in his LLC interest?
c. How much gain or income will Drew recognize on the formation of the LLC? What is the character of any gain or income recognized?
d. What basis will Drew take in his LLC interest?

33. **LO.3, 14** Continue with the facts presented in Problem 32.

Decision Making

a. Construct a balance sheet for SD, LLC, assuming that Drew's services are completed immediately after forming SD. The balance sheet should reflect the LLC's basis in assets and the fair market value of these assets.
b. Outline any planning opportunities that may minimize current taxation to any of the parties.

34. **LO.3, 14** Continue with the facts presented in Problem 32. At the end of the first year, the LLC distributes $100,000 cash to Sam. No distribution is made to Drew.

Decision Making

a. Under general tax rules, how would the payment to Sam be treated?
b. How much income or gain would Sam recognize as a result of the payment?
c. Under general tax rules, what basis would the LLC take in the land Sam contributed?
d. What alternative treatment might the IRS try to impose?
e. Under the alternative treatment, how much income or gain would Sam recognize?
f. Under the alternative treatment, what basis would the LLC take in the land contributed by Sam?
g. How can the transaction be restructured to minimize risk of IRS recharacterization?

35. **LO.3** The JM Partnership was formed to acquire land and subdivide it as residential housing lots. On March 1, 2012, Jessica contributed land valued at $600,000 to the partnership in exchange for a 50% interest. She had purchased the land in 2004 for $420,000 and held it for investment purposes (capital asset). The partnership holds the land as inventory.

On the same date, Matt contributed land valued at $600,000 that he had purchased in 2002 for $720,000. He became a 50% owner. Matt is a real estate developer, but he held this land personally for investment purposes. The partnership holds this land as inventory.

In 2013, the partnership sells the land contributed by Jessica for $620,000. In 2014, the partnership sells the real estate contributed by Matt for $580,000.

a. What is each partner's initial basis in his or her partnership interest?
b. What is the amount of gain or loss recognized on the sale of the land contributed by Jessica? What is the character of this gain or loss?
c. What is the amount of gain or loss recognized on the sale of the land contributed by Matt? What is the character of this gain or loss?
d. How would your answer in (c) change if the property was sold in 2019?

Issue ID

36. **LO.4** In 2012, Tim and Molly form TM Partnership, Ltd. (an LLLP), to own and operate certain real estate. Tim contributed land, and Molly contributed cash to be used for setting up the entity and creating a plan for developing the property. Once a development plan was in place, the partnership sold interests in the partnership to investors to raise funds for constructing a shopping center. The partnership incurred expenses of $12,000 for forming the entity and $52,000 for starting the business (e.g., setting up the accounting systems, locating tenants, and negotiating leases). It also paid $18,000 in transfer taxes for changing the ownership of the property to the partnership's name. The brokerage firm that sold the interests to the limited partners charged a 6% commission, which totaled $600,000. The calendar year partnership started business in September 2012. Describe how all of these initial expenses are treated by the partnership.

Issue ID

37. **LO.3, 4, 5, 6, 7** Finch, Inc., a calendar year general contractor, and Cardinal, Inc., a development corporation with a July 31 year-end, formed the equal FC, LLC, on January 1 of the current year. Both LLC members are C corporations. The LLC was formed to construct and lease shopping centers in Seattle, Washington. Finch contributed cash of $1 million, equipment (basis of $200,000, fair market value of $500,000), building permits, and architectural designs created by Finch's employees (basis of $0, fair market value of $200,000). Cardinal contributed land (basis of $500,000, fair market value of $700,000) and cash of $1 million. The cash was used as follows:

Legal fees for drafting LLC agreement	$ 20,000
Materials and labor costs for construction in progress on shopping center	1,900,000
Office expense (utilities, rent, overhead, etc.)	80,000

What issues must the LLC address in preparing its initial tax return?

38. **LO.4** On July 1 of the current year, the R & R Partnership (an LLLP) was formed to operate a bed and breakfast inn. The partnership paid $3,000 in legal fees for drafting the partnership agreement and $5,000 for accounting fees related to organizing the entity. It also paid $10,000 in syndication costs to locate and secure investments from limited partners. In addition, before opening the inn for business, the entity paid $15,500 for advertising and $36,000 in costs related to an open house just before the grand opening of the property. The partnership opened the inn for business on October 1.
a. How are these expenses classified?
b. How much may the partnership deduct in its initial year of operations?
c. How are costs treated that are not deducted currently?

Issue ID

39. **LO.5** Browne and Red, both C corporations, formed the BR Partnership on January 1, 2010. Neither Browne nor Red is a personal service corporation, and BR is not a tax shelter. BR's gross receipts were $4.6 million, $5 million, $6 million, and $7 million, respectively, for the four tax years ending in 2010, 2011, 2012, and 2013. Describe the methods of accounting available to BR in each tax year.

Issue ID

40. **LO.3, 4, 5** The Pelican Partnership was formed on August 1 of the current year and admitted Morlan and Merriman as equal partners on that date. The partners both contributed $300,000 of cash to establish a children's clothing store in a local shopping mall. The partners spent August and September buying inventory, equipment, supplies, and advertising for their "Grand Opening" on October 1. Following are some of the costs the partnership incurred during its first year of operations:

Legal fees to form partnership	$10,000
Advertising for "Grand Opening"	25,000
Advertising after opening	10,000
Consulting fees for establishing accounting system	10,000
Rent, five months at $2,000/month	10,000
Utilities at $1,000 per month	5,000
Salaries to salesclerks	50,000
Payments to Morlan and Merriman for services ($6,000/month each for three months, beginning in October)	36,000
Tax return preparation expense	12,000

In addition, the partnership purchased all of the assets of Granny Newcombs, Inc. Of the total purchase price for these assets, $200,000 was allocated to the trade name and logo.

Determine how each of these costs is treated by the partnership, and identify the period over which the costs can be deducted, if any.

41. **LO.6** AzureCo, AuburnCo, and AquamarineCo formed the AAA Partnership on January 1 of the current year. AzureCo is a 50% partner, and AuburnCo and AquamarineCo are each 25% partners. All of the partners and AAA use the cash method of accounting. For reporting purposes, AzureCo uses a fiscal year with a June 30 year-end, AuburnCo uses a fiscal year with an October 31 year-end, and AquamarineCo uses a calendar year. What is AAA's required tax year under the least aggregate deferral method?

42. **LO.3, 7, 8** Phoebe and Parker are equal members of Phoenix Investors, LLC. They are real estate investors who formed the LLC several years ago with equal cash contributions. Phoenix then purchased a piece of land.

On January 1 of the current year, to acquire a one-third interest in the entity, Reece contributed to the LLC some land she had held for investment. Reece purchased the land five years ago for $75,000; its fair market value at the contribution date was $90,000. No special allocation agreements were in effect before or after Reece was admitted to the LLC. Phoenix holds all land for investment.

Immediately before Reece's property contribution, the balance sheet of Phoenix Investors, LLC, was as follows:

	Basis	FMV		Basis	FMV
Land	$30,000	$180,000	Phoebe, capital	$15,000	$ 90,000
			Parker, capital	15,000	90,000
	$30,000	$180,000		$30,000	$180,000

a. At the contribution date, what is Reece's basis in her interest in the LLC?
b. When does the LLC's holding period begin for the contributed land?
c. On June 30 of the current year, the LLC sold the land contributed by Reece for $90,000. How much is the recognized gain or loss? How is it allocated among the LLC members?
d. Prepare a balance sheet reflecting basis and fair market value for the LLC immediately after the land sale described in (c). Assume that no other transactions occurred during the tax year.

43. **LO.7, 8** Assume the same facts as in Problem 42, with the following exceptions:

- Reece purchased the land five years ago for $120,000. Its fair market value was $90,000 when it was contributed to the LLC.
- Phoenix sold the land contributed by Reece for $84,000.

a. How much is the recognized gain or loss? How is it allocated among the LLC members?

b. Prepare a balance sheet reflecting basis and fair market value for the LLC immediately after the land sale. Also prepare schedules that support the basis and fair market value of each LLC member's capital account.

44. **LO.7, 9, 10** Andrea and Michael are equal partners in the accrual basis AM Partnership. At the beginning of the current tax year, Andrea's capital account has a balance of $200,000, and the partnership has recourse debts of $100,000 payable to unrelated parties. Assume that all partnership recourse debt is shared equally between the partners. The following information about AM's operations for the current year is obtained from the partnership's records:

Taxable income	$320,000
Tax-exempt interest income	6,000
§ 1231 gain	9,000
Short-term capital loss	2,000
Political contribution	1,000
Charitable contribution	2,000
Cash distribution to Andrea	50,000

Assume that year-end partnership debt payable to unrelated parties is $140,000. If all transactions are reflected in her beginning capital and basis in the same manner, what is Andrea's basis in the partnership interest:

a. At the beginning of the year?

b. At the end of the year?

45. **LO.7, 9, 13** The KL Partnership is owned equally by Kayla and Lisa. Kayla's basis is $20,000 at the beginning of the tax year. Lisa's basis is $16,000 at the beginning of the year. KL reported the following income and expenses for the current tax year:

Sales revenue	$150,000
Cost of sales	80,000
Distribution to Lisa	15,000
Depreciation expense	20,000
Utilities	14,000
Rent expense	18,000
Long-term capital gain	6,000
Payment to Mercy Hospital for Kayla's medical expenses	12,000

a. Determine the ordinary partnership income and separately stated items for the partnership.

b. Calculate Kayla's basis in her partnership interest at the end of the tax year. What items should Kayla report on her Federal income tax return?

c. Calculate Lisa's basis in her partnership interest at the end of the tax year. What items should Lisa report on her Federal income tax return?

46. **LO.7, 9, 12, 13** How would the answers in Problem 45 change if partnership revenues were $100,000 instead of $150,000?

47. **LO.3, 7, 9, 10** Suzy contributed business-related assets valued at $360,000 (basis of $200,000) in exchange for her 40% interest in the Suz-Anna Partnership. Anna contributed land and a building valued at $640,000 (basis of $380,000) in exchange for the remaining 60% interest. Anna's property was encumbered by a qualified nonrecourse debt of $100,000, which was assumed by the partnership. The partnership reports the following income and expenses for the current tax year:

Sales	$560,000
Utilities, salaries, and other operating expenses	360,000
Short-term capital gain	10,000
Tax-exempt interest income	4,000

Charitable contributions	$ 8,000
Distribution to Suzy	10,000
Distribution to Anna	20,000

During the current tax year, Suz-Anna refinanced the land and building. At the end of the year, Suz-Anna had recourse debt of $100,000 for partnership accounts payable and qualified nonrecourse debt of $200,000.

a. What is Suzy's basis after formation of the partnership? Anna's basis?
b. What income and separately stated items does the partnership report on Suzy's Schedule K–1? What items does Suzy report on her tax return?
c. Assume that all partnership debts are shared proportionately. At the end of the tax year, what are Suzy's basis and amount at risk in her partnership interest?

48. **LO.11** Continue with the facts in Problem 47, and assume that Suz-Anna prepares the capital account rollforward on the partners' Schedules K–1 on a tax basis.
    a. What is Suzy's capital account balance at the beginning of the tax year?
    b. What is Suzy's capital account balance at the end of the tax year?
    c. What accounts for the difference between Suzy's ending capital account and her ending tax basis in the partnership interest?

49. **LO.3, 7, 9, 10** Continue with the facts presented in Problem 47, except that Suz-Anna was formed as an LLC instead of a general partnership. **Issue ID**
    a. How would Suz-Anna's ending liabilities be treated?
    b. How would Suzy's basis and amount at risk be different?

50. **LO.3, 7, 9, 12** Bryan and Cody each contributed $120,000 to the newly formed BC Partnership in exchange for a 50% interest. The partnership used the available funds to acquire equipment costing $200,000 and to fund current operating expenses. The partnership agreement provides that depreciation will be allocated 80% to Bryan and 20% to Cody. All other items of income and loss will be allocated equally between the partners. Upon liquidation of the partnership, property will be distributed to the partners in accordance with their capital account balances. Any partner with a negative capital account must contribute cash in the amount of the negative balance to restore the capital account to $0. **Issue ID**

    In its first year, the partnership reported an ordinary loss (before depreciation) of $80,000 and depreciation expense of $36,000. In its second year, the partnership reported $40,000 of income from operations (before depreciation), and it reported depreciation expense of $57,600.
    a. Calculate the partners' bases in their partnership interests at the end of the first and second tax years. Are any losses suspended? Explain.
    b. Does the allocation provided in the partnership agreement have economic effect? Explain.

51. **LO.7, 9, 12** Continue with the facts presented in Problem 50. On the first day of the third tax year, the partnership sold the equipment for $150,000 and distributed the cash in accordance with the partnership agreement. The partnership was liquidated at this time. **Issue ID**
    a. Calculate the partners' bases in their partnership interests after reflecting any gain or loss on disposal of the equipment.
    b. How will partnership cash balances be distributed to the partners upon liquidation?
    c. What observations can you make regarding the value of a deduction to each partner?

52. **LO.7, 9** Chris and Lauren each contributed $90,000 cash to the cash basis CL Partnership. The partnership uses all $180,000 of the cash to purchase a depreciable asset. The partnership agreement provides that depreciation is allocated 60% to Chris and 40% to Lauren. All other items of partnership income, gain, loss, or deduction are allocated equally between the two partners. During the first year of operations, the partnership produces $30,000 of income before depreciation and deducts $30,000 of depreciation. At the end of the first year, the partnership sells the depreciable asset for its $150,000 book value. Following these transactions, the partnership has $180,000 of cash ($150,000 from sale of the asset and $30,000 from operations). Assume that nothing else happens

in the first year that affects the partners' capital accounts. The partnership then distributes all cash to the partners and liquidates at the end of the first year.

a. How much cash is distributed to each partner in the liquidating distribution under the economic effect test?
b. If the partnership distributes $30,000 cash to Lauren on June 30 of the current year, how much cash is distributed to each partner in the liquidating distribution under the economic effect test?

53. **LO.10** The MGP General Partnership was created on January 1 of the current year by having Melinda, Gabe, and Pat each contribute $10,000 cash to the partnership in exchange for a one-third interest in partnership income, gains, losses, deductions, and credits. On December 31 of the current year, the partnership balance sheet reads as follows:

	Basis	FMV		Basis	FMV
Assets	$60,000	$75,000	Recourse debt	$30,000	$30,000
			Melinda, capital	14,000	19,000
			Gabe, capital	14,000	19,000
			Pat, capital	2,000	7,000
				$60,000	$75,000

Pat's capital account is less than Melinda's and Gabe's capital accounts because Pat has withdrawn more cash than the other partners have.

How do the partners share the recourse debt as of December 31 of the current year?

Communications

54. **LO.3, 9, 10** Paul and Anna plan to form the PA General Partnership by the end of the current year. The partners will each contribute $80,000 cash, and in addition, the partnership will borrow $240,000 from First State Bank. The $400,000 will be used to buy an investment property. The property will serve as collateral, and both partners will be required to personally guarantee the debt.

The tentative agreement provides that 60% of operating income, gains, losses, deductions, and credits will be allocated to Paul for the first five years the partnership is in existence. The remaining 40% is allocated to Anna. Thereafter, all partnership items will be allocated equally. The agreement also provides that capital accounts will be properly maintained and that each partner must restore any deficit in the capital account upon the partnership's liquidation.

The partners would like to know, before the end of the tax year, how the $240,000 liability will be allocated for basis purposes. Using the format (1) facts, (2) issues, (3) conclusion, and (4) law and analysis, draft a memo to the tax planning file for the PA Partnership that describes how the debt will be shared between the partners for purposes of computing the adjusted basis of each partnership interest.

Issue ID

Decision Making

55. **LO.9, 10, 12, 14** The BCD Partnership plans to distribute cash of $20,000 to partner Brad at the end of the tax year. The partnership reported a loss for the year, and Brad's share of the loss is $10,000. At the beginning of the tax year, Brad's basis in his partnership interest, including his share of partnership liabilities, was $15,000. The partnership expects to report substantial income in future years.

a. What rules are used to calculate Brad's ending basis in his partnership interest?
b. How much gain or loss will Brad report for the tax year?
c. Will the deduction for the $10,000 loss be suspended? Why or why not?
d. Could any planning opportunities be used to minimize any negative tax ramifications of the distribution? Explain.

Communications

56. **LO.10, 12** Jasmine Gregory is a 20% member in Sparrow Properties, LLC, which is a lessor of residential rental property. Her share of the LLC's losses for the current year is $100,000. Immediately before considering the deductibility of this loss, Jasmine's capital account (which, in this case, corresponds to her basis excluding liabilities) reflected a balance of $50,000. Jasmine has personally guaranteed a $10,000 debt of the LLC that is allocated to her as a recourse debt. Her share of the LLC's nonrecourse debt is $30,000. This debt cannot be treated as qualified nonrecourse debt. Jasmine spends several hundred hours a year working for Sparrow Properties.

Jasmine is also a managing member of Skylark Rentals, LLC, which is engaged in long-term (more than 30 days) equipment rental activities. (This is considered a passive activity.) Jasmine's share of Skylark's income is $36,000.

Jasmine's modified adjusted gross income before considering the LLCs' activities is $300,000. The "active participation" rental real estate deduction is not available to Jasmine. Determine how much of Sparrow's $100,000 loss Jasmine can deduct on her current calendar year return. Using the format (1) facts, (2) issues, (3) conclusion, and (4) law and analysis, draft an internal office memo for the client's tax file describing the loss limitations. Identify the Code sections under which losses are suspended.

57. **LO.13** Burgundy, Inc., and Violet are equal partners in the calendar year BV, LLC. Burgundy uses a fiscal year ending April 30, and Violet uses a calendar year. Burgundy receives an annual guaranteed payment of $100,000 for use of capital contributed by Burgundy. BV's taxable income (after deducting the payment to Burgundy, Inc.) is $80,000 for 2012 and $90,000 for 2013.
    a. What is the amount of income from the LLC that Burgundy must report for its tax year ending April 30, 2013?
    b. What is the amount of income from the LLC that Violet must report for her tax year ending December 31, 2013?

58. **LO.13** Continue with the facts presented in Problem 57. Assume that Burgundy, Inc.'s annual guaranteed payment is increased to $120,000 starting on January 1, 2013, and the LLC's taxable income for 2012 and 2013 (after deducting Burgundy's guaranteed payment) is the same (i.e., $80,000 and $90,000, respectively). What is the amount of income from the LLC that Burgundy, Inc. must report for its tax year ending April 30, 2013?

59. **LO.7, 13** Nicole, a calendar year individual, owns 30% of Creole Cravings, Inc., a C corporation that was formed on February 1, 2012. She receives a $5,000 monthly salary from the corporation, and Creole Cravings generates $200,000 of taxable income (after accounting for payments to Nicole) for its tax year ending January 31, 2013.
    a. How do these activities affect Nicole's 2012 adjusted gross income?
    b. Assume instead that Creole Cravings is a partnership (January 31 year-end) and that it classifies Nicole's salary as a guaranteed payment. How do these activities affect Nicole's 2012 and 2013 adjusted gross income?

60. **LO.13** Four GRRLs Partnership is owned by four sisters. Leah holds a 70% interest; each of the others owns 10%. Leah sells investment property to the partnership for its fair market value of $100,000 (Leah's basis is $150,000).
    a. How much loss, if any, may Leah recognize?
    b. If the partnership later sells the property for $160,000, how much gain must it recognize?
    c. If Leah's basis in the investment property was $20,000 instead of $150,000, how much, if any, gain would she recognize on the sale? How would the gain be characterized?

TAX RETURN PROBLEMS

1. Ryan Ross (111–11–1111), Oscar Oleander (222–22–2222), Clark Carey (333–33–3333), and Kim Kardigan (444–44–4444) are equal members in ROCK the Ages, LLC. ROCK serves as agents and managers for prominent musicians in the Los Angeles area. The LLC's Federal ID number is 55–5555555. It uses the cash basis and the calendar year and began operations on January 1, 2000. Its current address is 6102 Wilshire Boulevard, Suite 2100, Los Angeles, CA 90036. ROCK was the force behind such music icons as Rhiannon and Ulster and has had a very profitable year. The following information was taken from the LLC's income statement for the current year:

Revenues:	
Fees and commissions	$4,800,000
Taxable interest income from bank deposits	1,600
Tax-exempt interest	3,200
Gains and losses on stock sales	4,000
Total revenues	$4,808,800

Expenses:	
Advertising and public relations	$ 420,000
Charitable contributions	8,000
Section 179 expense	20,000
Employee salaries	1,200,000
Guaranteed payment, Ryan Ross, office manager	600,000
Guaranteed payment, other members	900,000
Entertainment, subject to 50% disallowance	48,000
Travel	120,000
Legal and accounting fees	108,000
Office rentals paid	86,000
Interest expense on operating line of credit	6,000
Insurance premiums	16,000
Office expense	60,000
Payroll taxes	96,000
Utilities	12,000
Total expenses	$3,700,000

During the past couple of years, ROCK has taken advantage of bonus depreciation and § 179 deductions and fully remodeled the premises and upgraded its leasehold improvements. This year, ROCK wrapped up its remodel with the purchase of $20,000 of office furniture for which it will claim a § 179 deduction. (For simplicity, assume that ROCK uses the same cost recovery methods for both tax and financial purposes.) There is no depreciation adjustment for alternative minimum tax purposes.

ROCK invests much of its excess cash in non-dividend-paying growth stocks and tax-exempt securities. During the year, the LLC sold two securities. On June 15, 2011, ROCK purchased 1,000 shares of Tech, Inc. stock for $72,000; it sold those shares on December 15, 2011, for $60,000. On March 15, 2005, ROCK purchased 2,000 shares of BioLabs, Inc. stock for $104,000; it sold those shares for $120,000 on December 15, 2011.

Net income per books is $1,108,800. The firm's activities do not constitute "qualified production activities" for purposes of the § 199 deduction. On January 1, 2011, the members' capital accounts equaled $160,000 each. No additional capital contributions were made in 2011. In addition to their guaranteed payments, each member withdrew $240,000 cash during the year. The LLC's balance sheet as of December 31, 2011, is as follows:

	Beginning	Ending
Cash	$ 340,000	??
Tax-exempt securities	80,000	80,000
Marketable securities	420,000	600,000
Leasehold improvements, furniture, and equipment	820,000	840,000
Accumulated depreciation	(820,000)	(840,000)
Total assets	$ 840,000	$??
Operating line of credit	$ 200,000	$ 160,000
Capital, Ross	160,000	??
Capital, Oleander	160,000	??
Capital, Carey	160,000	??
Capital, Kardigan	160,000	??
Total liabilities and capital	$ 840,000	$??

Assume that all debt is shared equally by the members. Each member has personally guaranteed the debt of the LLC.

None of the members, all of whom are U.S. citizens, sold any portion of their interests in ROCK during the year. All of the entity's financial operations are concentrated in California. The LLC had no foreign bank accounts or operations and no interest in any U.S. or foreign trusts, corporations, or partnerships. The LLC is not publicly traded and is not a statutory tax shelter. The LLC is not subject to consolidated audit procedures. Ryan Ross is the tax matters partner.

The business code for "Agents and Managers for Artists, Athletes, Entertainers, and Other Public Figures" is 711410. ROCK is not a partner in any other partnership. The LLC's Form 1065 was prepared by Ryan Ross and sent to the Ogden, UT IRS Service Center. All members are active in LLC operations.

a. Prepare Form 1065, Schedule K, and relevant supporting schedules for ROCK the Ages, LLC, leaving blank any items where insufficient information has been provided. If you are using tax return preparation software, also prepare Form 4562 and Schedule D. (Note: You can assume that the answer to each "yes/no" question on Form 1065, page 3 is "no" unless otherwise discussed above.)
b. Prepare Schedule K–1 for Ryan Ross, 15520 W. Earlson Street, Pacific Palisades, CA 90272.

2. On January 1, 2005, the Branson Company (EIN 22–2222222) and Porto Engineering, Inc. (EIN 33–3333333), formed Branto, LLC (an equally owned joint venture). During its first four years, the LLC worked with the U.S. Department of Homeland Security and the National Transportation Safety Board to design and develop a specific device for airport passenger screening. Porto provides engineering expertise, and Branson provides high-tech manufacturing, selling, and distribution expertise. Early in 2010, the two governmental agencies recommended the product. In 2011, Branto's screening device is being succesfully marketed, sold, delivered, and installed in airports around the United States.

   The LLC uses the accrual method of accounting and the calendar year for reporting purposes. Its current address is 3750 Airport Boulevard, Seattle, WA, 98124. The following information was taken from the trial balance supporting the LLC's GAAP-basis (audited) financial statements for the 2011 calendar year:

Revenues:	
Sales revenues	$40,000,000
Interest income	50,000
Total revenues	$40,050,000
Amounts related to cost of goods sold:	
Beginning inventory	$ 2,000,000
Materials purchases	8,000,000
Labor	9,000,000
Additional § 263A costs	–0–
Other costs: Various items	2,700,000
Book depreciation	1,275,000
Less: Ending inventory	(3,000,000)
Total amounts work in progress	$19,975,000
Other costs *not* related to production:	
Salaries and wages	$ 1,000,000
Taxes and licenses	300,000
Charitable contributions	100,000
Interest expense	200,000
Meals and entertainment (subject to 50% disallowance)	1,200,000
Travel expenses	800,000
Employee benefit programs	300,000
Insurance (including key employee life insurance of $100,000)	300,000
Legal and professional fees	600,000
Office expenses	2,000,000
Sales and promotion expenses	2,500,000
Utilities	800,000
Warranty expense (increase to reserves; not fixed and determinable)	300,000
Total other costs disbursements	$10,400,000
Net income per books and GAAP-basis audited financial statements	$ 9,675,000

The beginning and ending GAAP-basis balance sheets for the LLC were as follows at December 31, 2011:

	Beginning	Ending
Cash	$ 975,000	$ 1,825,000
Accounts receivable	620,000	2,600,000
Inventories	2,000,000	3,000,000
U.S. government obligations	1,000,000	1,000,000
Land	600,000	600,000
Buildings and equipment	12,000,000	15,000,000
Accumulated depreciation	(6,375,000)	(7,650,000)
Total assets	$10,820,000	$16,375,000
Accounts payable	$ 420,000	$ 800,000
Other current liabilities:		
Operating line of credit (guaranteed by LLC members)	1,000,000	2,000,000
Warranty reserves (not guaranteed by members)	200,000	500,000
Mortgage notes on building	5,000,000	6,000,000
Capital, Branson Company	2,100,000	3,537,500
Capital, Porto Engineering, Inc.	2,100,000	3,537,500
Total liabilities and capital	$10,820,000	$16,375,000

The LLC uses the lower of cost or market method for valuing inventory. Branto is subject to § 263A; for simplicity, assume that § 263A costs are reflected in the same manner for book and tax purposes. Branto did not change its inventory accounting method during the year. There were no write-downs of inventory items, and Branto does not use the LIFO method.

The LLC claimed $2,499,270 of depreciation expense for tax purposes (book depreciation is $1,275,000). All tax depreciation expense should be reported on Schedule A. The LLC placed $3 million of assets in service during the current year; this exceeds the threshold for eligibility for a § 179 deduction. Tax depreciation amounts reflect bonus depreciation deductions (and these assets are not subject to AMT adjustments). Depreciation for assets placed in service in prior years creates an adjustment of ($276,900) for AMT purposes. (This is a negative amount—book depreciation for these assets is greater than tax depreciation.)

All borrowings were used exclusively for business operations; consequently, none of the interest expense is considered investment interest expense. The LLC members were required to guarantee the debt related to the operating line of credit. The accounts payable, accrued warranty claim liabilities, and mortgage were not guaranteed by the members. The mortgage relates to the real property and is considered qualified nonrecourse financing. The partners share equally in all LLC liabilities, because all initial contributions and all ongoing allocations and distributions are pro rata.

The LLC's activities are eligible for the domestic production activities deduction (DPAD). For simplicity, assume that the LLC's qualified production activities income (QPAI) is $9.5 million. The LLC's production-related W–2 wages are $10 million.

No guaranteed payments were paid to either of the LLC members. Instead, the members each withdrew $3.4 million of cash during the year. The LLC has never made a distribution to the partners of noncash property. The LLC has not made a § 754 election and had no transactions during the current year that would warrant such an election. None of the members sold any portion of their interests in the LLC during the year.

Both LLC members are U.S. Subchapter C corporations. The LLC's operations are entirely restricted to the United States, and all sales were to U.S. businesses. The LLC had no foreign operations, no foreign bank accounts, and no interest in any foreign trusts or other LLCs. None of the members contributed cash or other property to the LLC during the year.

Both members are classified as "corporations" and "LLC member-managers" on Schedule K–1. The capital account analysis on Schedule K–1 is prepared on a tax basis. On the Analysis of Income (Loss), the IRS's instructions indicate that the amounts for any LLC members should be reported on the line for limited partners.

The IRS's business code for "Other specialty trade contractors" is 238900. The LLC files its tax return in Ogden, Utah. Branson Company is located at 3750 Airport Boulevard, Seattle, WA 98124 (the same as the LLC's address). Porto Engineering, Inc., is located at 42100 Highway 980 West, Tacoma, WA 98401. The LLC member corporations are each owned by several unrelated individual taxpayers. Branson Company is the tax matters partner.

The capital account reconciliation on the partners' Schedules K–1 is prepared on a GAAP basis. The LLC is required to file Schedule M–3, Form 8916–A (Supplemental Attachment to Schedule M–3), and Schedule C with its Form 1065. Schedule L must be prepared on a financial reporting basis.

a. Prepare pages 1–5 of Form 1065 for Branto, LLC. Do not prepare Form 4562. Leave any items blank where insufficient information has been provided. Prepare supporting schedules as necessary if adequate information is provided. You may assume that the answer to each "yes/no" question on page 3 is "no" unless discussed above.
b. Prepare Schedule M–3 and Form 8916–A (page 1). Do not prepare Schedule C. Hint: You will find four book-tax differences (two temporary differences and two permanent differences).
c. Prepare Schedule K–1 for 50% LLC member Branson Company.

RESEARCH PROBLEMS

Note: Solutions to Research Problems can be prepared by using the **Checkpoint® Student Edition** online research product, which is available to accompany this text. It is also possible to prepare solutions to the Research Problems by using tax research materials found in a standard tax library.

THOMSON REUTERS
CHECKPOINT®

Research Problem 1. Barney, an individual, and Aldrin, Inc., a domestic C corporation, have decided to form BA, LLC. The new LLC will produce a product that Barney recently developed and patented. Barney and Aldrin, Inc., will each own a 50% capital and profits interest in the LLC. Barney is a calendar year taxpayer, while Aldrin, Inc., is taxed on a July 1–June 30 fiscal year. The LLC does not have a "natural business year" and elects to be taxed as a partnership.

a. Determine the taxable year of the LLC under the Code and Regulations.
b. Two years after formation of the LLC, Barney sells half of his interest (25%) to Aldrin, Inc. Can the LLC retain the taxable year determined in part a? Why or why not?

Communications

Research Problem 2. Your clients, Grayson Investments, Inc. (Ana Marks, President), and Blake Caldwell, each contributed $200,000 of cash to form the Realty Management Partnership, a limited partnership. Grayson is the general partner, and Blake is the limited partner. The partnership used the $400,000 cash to make a down payment on a building. The rest of the building's $4 million purchase price was financed with an interest-only nonrecourse loan of $3.6 million, which was obtained from an independent third-party bank.

The partnership allocates all partnership items equally between the partners except for the MACRS deductions and building maintenance, which are allocated 70% to Blake and 30% to Grayson. The partnership definitely wants to satisfy the "economic effect" requirements of Reg. §§ 1.704–1 and 1.704–2 and will reallocate MACRS, if necessary, to satisfy the requirements of the Regulations.

Under the partnership agreement, liquidation distributions will be paid in proportion to the partners' positive capital account balances. Capital accounts are maintained as required in the Regulations. Grayson Investments has an unlimited obligation to restore its capital account, while Blake is subject to a qualified income offset provision.

Assume that all partnership items, except for MACRS, will net to zero throughout the first three years of the partnership operations. Also assume that each year's MACRS deduction will be $200,000 (to simplify the calculations).

Draft a letter to the partnership evaluating the allocation of MACRS in each of the three years under Reg. §§ 1.704–1 and −2. The partnership's address is 53 East Marsh Ave., Smyrna, GA 30082. Do not address the "substantial" test.

Research Problem 3. Harrison has considerable experience as a leasing agent for residential rental properties. Alameda Properties (not a publicly traded partnership) has offered Harrison a position handling leasing activities for a new limited liability limited partnership that is being formed to construct and manage three apartment complexes. Alameda is willing to hire Harrison for a minimum of two years to lease and manage the properties, but the partnership is unable to pay the $100,000 annual salary Harrison requires without impairing its ability to pay necessary cash distributions to the limited partners.

Alameda is willing to pay Harrison a $60,000 salary for two years, increasing to a market salary thereafter. Alameda is also willing to allow Harrison to purchase a 10% interest in the partnership, but Harrison cannot afford the required $25,000 capital contribution.

The partnership expects to have income and cash flows from operations of approximately $200,000 per year. The annual cash flows will be distributed to the partners each year during the estimated seven-year holding period of the properties.

Harrison and Alameda Properties have approached you for assistance in structuring a mutually satisfactory arrangement. You are aware that a partner can be awarded an interest in the future profits of a partnership and have learned from a colleague that in 2005, the IRS issued a Notice and Proposed Regulations that outline procedures for structuring an arrangement to avoid current taxation of the expected future profits. You have suggested that in lieu of requiring Harrison to pay the $25,000 purchase price, Alameda could grant Harrison a 10% interest in Alameda's future profits.

a. Under Notice 2005–43, what actions must the partnership take to ensure that the profits interest is nontaxable? What is the tax result for receipt of a nonforfeitable future profits interest?

b. Alameda has an interest in making sure that Harrison remains with the company and wants to attach a three-year forfeiture clause to the profits interest. In other words, if Harrison leaves the company within three years, his profits interest is terminated. What additional considerations arise under Notice 2005–43 if the profits interest is not fully vested?

c. What are the advantages and disadvantages of the proposed structure to each party?

d. At this writing, one of the IRS's targeted items in its "priority guidance plan" is to issue guidelines related to a partner's receipt of a profits interest or an interest in the capital of the partnership (also called a "carried interest"). Review the current tax rules and regulations to determine whether the IRS has acted on this. If so, how would those rules affect Harrison if he had received a 10% interest in partnership capital rather than future partnership profits?

Internet Activity

Use the tax resources of the Internet to address the following questions. Do not restrict your search to the Web, but include a review of newsgroups and general reference materials, practitioner sites and resources, primary sources of the tax law, chat rooms and discussion groups, and other opportunities.

Research Problem 4. Print an article posted by a law firm that comments on pitfalls to avoid in drafting partnership agreements. Ideally, use the home page of a firm that has offices in your state.

Research Problem 5. Use the search feature on your favorite news site on the Web (e.g., CNN, ABC News, or Fox News) and search for news on partnerships, LLCs, or limited partnerships. What entities did you find that are taking advantage of the partnership entity form? (Make sure these entities are truly legal partnerships. Some entities called "partnerships" by the news media actually involve transfers of stock or formation of a corporation to manage the joint venture.)

Research Problem 6. Find the home page of a partnership that seems to be soliciting financing from new partners. Comment on the portrayal of the pertinent tax law that is included in the materials, especially with respect to the at-risk rules and the passive activity limitations.

CHAPTER

11 Partnerships: Distributions, Transfer of Interests, and Terminations

LEARNING OBJECTIVES: *After completing Chapter 11, you should be able to:*

LO.1 Determine the tax treatment of proportionate nonliquidating distributions from a partnership to a partner.

LO.2 Determine the tax treatment of proportionate distributions that liquidate a partnership.

LO.3 Describe the tax treatment that applies to distributions treated as disguised sales and distributions of marketable securities and precontribution gain property.

LO.4 Specify and explain the general concepts governing tax treatment of disproportionate distributions.

LO.5 Determine the tax treatment under § 736 of payments from a partnership to a retiring or deceased partner.

LO.6 Calculate the selling partner's amount and character of gain or loss on the sale or exchange of a partnership interest.

LO.7 Describe tax issues related to other dispositions of partnership interests.

LO.8 Calculate the optional adjustments to basis under § 754.

LO.9 Outline the methods of terminating a partnership.

LO.10 Identify the special considerations of a family partnership.

LO.11 Describe the application of partnership provisions to limited liability companies (LLCs) and limited liability partnerships (LLPs).

LO.12 List and evaluate various tax planning considerations related to partnership distributions and sales of partnership interests.

CHAPTER OUTLINE

THE BIG PICTURE Tax Solutions for the Real World

THE LIFE CYCLE OF A PARTNERSHIP

In the previous chapter, Josh, Kyle, and Maria created Beachside Properties, LLC, to own and operate the Beachsider Café and to own, manage, and lease the remaining properties in the Shorefront Center. The 10-acre center includes 3 developed acres (including the Beachsider Café) and 7 acres being held for expansion. Josh, Kyle, and Maria own, respectively, 20 percent, 40 percent, and 40 percent shares in the LLC's profits and losses and 5 percent, 47.5 percent, and 47.5 percent interests in its capital. The entity was formed as an LLC to achieve some measure of limited liability as to potential losses (see Chapter 10).

Several years have passed since the LLC was formed. The LLC interests and the net underlying assets are currently valued at approximately $10 million (including $1 million of goodwill for the Beachsider Café). During this period, the LLC has made significant distributions of cash and property to its members.

The population in the area has grown substantially, and it appears to be a good time to develop the remaining seven acres of the property. The cost of development is estimated at $10 million. Josh wants to manage the expansion, but Kyle and Maria are nearing retirement age and would prefer to dispose of their interests (valued at $9.5 million, or 95 percent of the net LLC value). Josh has been approached by a group of developers who are willing to invest the $19.5 million necessary to make the improvements and to purchase Kyle's and Maria's interests.

The transfer of Kyle's and Maria's interests and the admission of the new LLC members can be accomplished in two ways. First, the LLC could admit the new members for $19.5 million of cash and use $9.5 million to redeem the interests of Kyle and Maria. Alternatively, Kyle and Maria could sell their LLC interests directly to the new members for $9.5 million; the new members would also contribute $10 million of cash to the LLC for the expansion. Although the two alternatives have identical economic effects, the tax results could differ substantially.

How are the distributions of cash and property to the LLC members treated over the years? What are the tax consequences of admitting the new members to the LLC and redeeming the interests of Kyle and Maria? What are the results if the new members acquire the interests directly from Kyle and Maria and contribute the cash for expansion to the LLC?

Read the chapter and formulate your response.

11 Introduction

The previous chapter examined the tax effects of partnership formation and operations. Most operating transactions of a partnership present few tax problems; under the aggregate theory of partnership taxation, revenues earned and expenses paid by the partnership flow through to the tax returns of the partners. If the partners are individuals, the transactions are then handled like other individual tax matters.

However, a number of special tax provisions, many of them complex, govern the effects of the following transactions, which are discussed in this chapter:

- Nonliquidating (current) distributions, or routine distributions from the partnership to the partners. In most cases, these distributions create no recognized gain or loss to the partner receiving the distribution. This treatment contrasts with that of corporate distributions, which may result in dividend income to the shareholder.
- Liquidating distributions, after which the recipient of the distribution is no longer a partner. The general rule here is that gain or loss is not recognized by either the liquidated partner or the partnership. There are exceptions, however, that may result in gains or losses that are usually capital in nature.
- Sale of a partnership interest to a new or existing partner. This results in the selling partner receiving a return of capital and capital gain or loss. The result follows both the aggregate and the entity theories discussed in the last chapter. The general tax treatment is similar to that of a stock sale made by a shareholder in a C or S corporation; the taxpayer recognizes a gain or loss. The gain or loss is allocated between capital and ordinary amounts based on the partnership's underlying assets—an example of the aggregate theory at work.

This chapter also discusses an optional election a partnership may make concerning adjustments to basis when a partnership interest is sold. Partnership terminations and special problems associated with family partnerships are also outlined. The chapter closes with discussions of two specialized business forms, limited liability companies and limited liability partnerships.

11.1 Distributions from a Partnership

The tax treatment of distributions from a partnership to a partner was introduced in Chapter 10 in the context of routine cash withdrawals (or "draws") and cash distributions from a continuing partnership to a continuing partner. These draws and distributions reduce the partner's outside basis by the amount of the cash received. The partnership's inside basis in assets is similarly reduced.

THE BIG PICTURE

EXAMPLE 1

Return to the facts of *The Big Picture* on on p. 11-1. Assume that Josh's basis in his interest in Beachside Properties, LLC, is $300,000. The LLC distributes $50,000 cash to Josh at the end of the year. Josh does not recognize any gain on the distribution and reduces his basis by $50,000 (the amount of the distribution) to $250,000.

The result in Example 1 arises whether or not a similar distribution is made to Kyle or Maria, the other members of Beachside Properties, LLC. In a partnership or LLC, it is not critical that all partners or members receive a distribution at the same time as long as capital account balances are maintained appropriately and final distributions are in accordance with ending capital account balances (see Chapter 10). Capital account maintenance requirements ensure that each partner eventually receives the proper amount, even though current distributions are not in accordance with ownership percentages.

A payment from a partnership to a partner is not necessarily treated as a distribution. For example, as discussed in Chapter 10, a partnership may pay interest or rent to a partner for use of the partner's capital or property, make a guaranteed payment to a partner, or purchase property from a partner.

If a payment *is* treated as a distribution from the partnership to the partner, it will fall into one of two categories:

- Liquidating distributions.
- Nonliquidating distributions.

These distributions may consist of cash or partnership property. Whether a distribution is a **liquidating** or **nonliquidating distribution** depends solely on whether the partner remains a partner in the partnership after the distribution is made. A *liquidating* distribution occurs either (1) when a partnership itself liquidates and distributes all of its property to its partners or (2) when an ongoing partnership redeems the interest of one of its partners. This second type of liquidating distribution occurs, for example, when a partner retires from a partnership or when a deceased partner's interest is liquidated. The two types of liquidating distributions receive differing tax treatment, as later sections of the chapter will explain.

A *nonliquidating* distribution (often called a "current distribution") is any other distribution from a continuing partnership to a continuing partner—that is, any distribution that is not a liquidating distribution. Nonliquidating distributions are of two types: draws or partial liquidations. A *draw* is a distribution of a partner's share of current or accumulated partnership profits that have been taxed to the partner in current or prior taxable years of the partnership. A *partial liquidation* is a distribution that reduces the partner's interest in partnership capital but does not liquidate the partner's entire interest in the partnership. The distinction between the two types of nonliquidating distributions is largely semantic, as the basic tax treatment typically does not differ.

EXAMPLE 2

Kate joins the calendar year KLM Partnership on January 1, 2012, by contributing $40,000 cash to the partnership in exchange for a one-third interest in partnership capital, profits, and losses. Her distributive share of partnership income for the year is $25,000. If the partnership distributes $65,000 ($25,000 share of partnership profits + $40,000 initial capital contribution) to Kate on December 31, 2012, the distribution is a nonliquidating distribution as long as Kate continues to be a partner in the partnership. This is true even though Kate receives her share of profits plus her entire investment in the partnership. In this case, $25,000 is considered a draw, and the remaining $40,000 is a partial liquidation of Kate's interest. If, instead, the partnership is liquidated or Kate ceases to be a partner in the ongoing partnership, the $65,000 distribution is a liquidating distribution. ■

A distribution is generally tax-deferred. However, in certain circumstances, the partner may recognize capital gain (or loss) and ordinary income (or loss) when a distribution is received from the partnership.

A distribution may be either proportionate or disproportionate. In a **proportionate distribution**, a partner receives the appropriate share of certain ordinary income-producing assets of the partnership. A **disproportionate distribution** occurs when the distribution increases or decreases the distributee partner's interest in certain ordinary income-producing assets. The tax treatment of disproportionate distributions is very complex.

The initial discussion and examples in this chapter describe the treatment of proportionate current and liquidating distributions. Special rules related to property distributions are discussed next. The discussion of distributions concludes with a brief overview of the rules pertaining to disproportionate distributions.

LO.1

Determine the tax treatment of proportionate nonliquidating distributions from a partnership to a partner.

Proportionate Nonliquidating Distributions

In general, neither the partner nor the partnership recognizes gain or loss when a proportionate nonliquidating distribution occurs.[1] The partner usually takes a carryover basis for the assets distributed.[2] The distributee partner's outside basis is reduced (but not below zero) by the amount of cash and the adjusted basis of property distributed to the partner by the partnership.[3] As the following example illustrates, a distribution does not change a partner's overall economic position.

EXAMPLE 3

Steven is a one-fourth partner in the SP Partnership. On December 31 of the current tax year, his basis in his partnership interest is $40,000. The fair market value of the interest is $70,000. The partnership distributes $25,000 cash to him on that date. The distribution is not taxable to Steven or the partnership. The distribution reduces Steven's adjusted basis in the partnership to $15,000 ($40,000 − $25,000), and the fair market value of his partnership interest is, arguably, reduced to $45,000 ($70,000 − $25,000). ■

EXAMPLE 4

Assume the same facts as in Example 3, except that in addition to the $25,000 cash, the partnership distributes land with an adjusted basis to the partnership of $13,000 and a fair market value of $30,000 on the date of distribution. The distribution is not taxable to Steven or the partnership. Steven reduces his basis in the partnership to $2,000 [$40,000 − ($25,000 + $13,000)] and takes a carryover basis of $13,000 in the land. The fair market value of Steven's remaining interest in the partnership is, arguably, reduced to $15,000 [$70,000 − ($25,000 + $30,000)].

If Steven had sold his partnership interest for $70,000 rather than receiving the distributions, he would have realized and recognized gain of $30,000 ($70,000 selling price − $40,000 outside basis). Because he has not recognized any gain or loss on the distribution of cash and land, he should still have the $30,000 of deferred gain to recognize at some point in the future. This is exactly what will happen. If Steven sells the cash, land, and remaining partnership interest on January 1 of the next year (the day after the distribution), he realizes and recognizes gains of $17,000 ($30,000 − $13,000) on the land and $13,000 ($15,000 − $2,000) on the partnership interest. These gains total $30,000, which is the amount of the original deferred gain. ■

Note the difference between the tax theory governing distributions from C corporations and partnerships. In a C corporation, a distribution from current or accumulated income (earnings and profits) is taxable as a dividend to the shareholder, and the corporation does not receive a deduction for the amount distributed. This is an example of corporate income being subject to double taxation. In a partnership, a distribution from current or accumulated profits is not taxable because Congress has decided that partnership income should be subject to only a single level of taxation. Because a partner pays taxes when the share of income is earned by the partnership, this income is not taxed again when distributed.

These results make sense under the entity and aggregate concepts. The entity concept is applicable to corporate dividends, so any amount paid as a dividend is treated as a transfer by the corporate entity to the shareholder and is taxed accordingly. Under the aggregate theory, though, a partner receiving a distribution of partnership income is treated as merely receiving something already owned. Whether the partner chooses to leave the income in the partnership or receive it in a distribution makes no difference.

Cash Distributions

Gain Recognition A proportionate nonliquidating distribution of cash is taxable to the partner if the distributed cash exceeds the outside basis of the partner's interest in the partnership.[4]

[1] §§ 731(a) and (b).
[2] § 732(a)(1).
[3] § 733.
[4] § 731(a)(1).

EXAMPLE 5

Samantha is a one-third partner in the SMP Partnership. Her basis in this ownership interest is $50,000 on December 31, 2012, after accounting for the calendar year partnership's 2012 operations and for Samantha's 2012 capital contributions. On December 31, 2012, the partnership distributes $60,000 cash to Samantha. She recognizes a $10,000 gain from this distribution ($60,000 cash received − $50,000 basis in her partnership interest). Most likely, this gain is taxed as a capital gain.[5] ■

As you can see, distributions *from* current and accumulated earnings are taxed differently to shareholders and partners, but cash distributions *in excess* of accumulated profits are taxed similarly for corporate shareholders and partners in partnerships. Both shareholders and partners are allowed to recover the cumulative capital invested in the entity tax-free.

Liability Reduction Treated as Cash Distribution Recall from Chapter 10 that the reduction of a partner's share of partnership debt is treated as a distribution of cash from the partnership to the partner. A reduction of a partner's share of partnership debt, then, first reduces the partner's basis in the partnership. Any reduction of a share of debt in excess of a partner's basis in the partnership is taxable to the partner as a gain.

EXAMPLE 6

Returning to the facts of Example 5, assume that Samantha's $50,000 basis in her partnership interest included a $60,000 share of partnership liabilities. If the partnership repays all of its liabilities, Samantha is treated as receiving a $60,000 distribution from the partnership. The first $50,000 of this distribution reduces her basis to $0. The last $10,000 distributed creates a taxable gain to her of $10,000. ■

Marketable Security Distributions Treated as Cash A distribution of marketable securities can also be treated as a distribution of cash. Determining the treatment of such distributions is complicated because several exceptions may apply and the basis in the distributed stock must be calculated. Such distributions are discussed later under Property Distributions with Special Tax Treatment: Marketable Securities.

Loss Recognition The distributee partner cannot recognize a loss on a proportionate nonliquidating distribution. This loss is deferred because tax law typically does not permit losses to be recognized until the loss is certain to occur and the amount is known. After the nonliquidating distribution, the partner still owns the partnership interest, which has an indeterminate future value. Only when a final liquidating distribution is received is the loss certain and known in amount—and potentially deductible.

EXAMPLE 7

Henry has a $50,000 basis in his partnership interest. Assume that on December 31, he receives a distribution of $10,000 cash. As a result of the distribution, his basis in the partnership interest is reduced to $40,000.

Henry knows the partnership has fallen on hard times and that future distributions will probably not amount to more than a few hundred dollars. He may not recognize a loss, even though a loss probably exists. The amount of the loss is not fixed and determinable because he still owns the partnership interest. ■

Property Distributions

In general, a distributee partner does not recognize gain from a property distribution. If the basis of property distributed by a partnership exceeds the partner's basis

[5] § 731(a). If the partnership holds any "hot assets," however, Samantha will probably recognize some ordinary income. See § 751(b) and the related discussion of ordinary income ("hot") assets and disproportionate distributions later in this chapter.

in the partnership interest, the distributed asset takes a substituted basis. This ensures that the partner does not receive asset basis that is not "paid for."

EXAMPLE 8

Amanda has a $50,000 basis in her partnership interest. The partnership distributes land it owns with a basis and a fair market value of $60,000. Amanda does not recognize any gain on this distribution because it is a distribution of property. However, Amanda should not be allowed to take a carryover basis of $60,000 in the land, when her basis in her partnership interest is only $50,000. Amanda takes a substituted basis of $50,000 in the land. Her basis in her partnership interest is reduced by the basis she takes in the asset received, or $50,000. Therefore, Amanda has a $50,000 basis in the land and a $0 basis in her partnership interest, and she recognizes no gain on this distribution. ■

The rule that no gain or loss is recognized on a property distribution from a partnership has several exceptions. These situations may arise for either a current or liquidating distribution, so discussion of these exceptions is deferred until all of the general rules are discussed (see Property Distributions with Special Tax Treatment later in the chapter).

Ordering Rules

When the inside basis of the distributed assets exceeds the distributee partner's outside basis, the assets are deemed distributed in the following order:

- Cash is distributed first.
- Unrealized receivables and inventory are distributed second.
- All other assets are distributed last.

Unrealized receivables are receivables that have a value to the partnership, but for which the related income has not yet been realized or recognized under the partnership's method of accounting. The term *unrealized receivables* applies only to amounts that will ultimately be realized and recognized as ordinary income. If the partnership uses the cash method of accounting, trade receivables from services or sales are unrealized receivables. If the partnership uses the accrual method, income has already been recognized, so trade receivables are not unrealized receivables. Unrealized receivables include receivables from sales of ordinary income property and rights to payments for services. For some purposes, unrealized receivables also include depreciation recapture income that would arise if the partnership sold its depreciable assets. Installment gains are unrealized receivables if the gain will be taxed as ordinary income when realized.

Inventory, for purposes of these ordering rules, includes any partnership assets except cash, capital, or § 1231 assets. For example, all accounts receivable are considered to be inventory, although only cash basis receivables are "unrealized receivables."

Because the partner typically does not recognize a gain from a *property* distribution, the Code provides that the partner's basis for property received cannot exceed the partner's basis in the partnership interest immediately before the distribution. For each level of asset distribution, the relevant adjustments are made to the partner's basis in the interest. In other words, after a cash distribution, the partner's basis in the interest is recomputed before determining the effect of a distribution of unrealized receivables or inventory. The basis is again recomputed before determining the effect of a distribution of other assets. If the remaining outside basis at the end of any step is insufficient to cover the entire inside basis of the assets in the next step, that remaining outside basis is allocated among the assets within that class.[6]

[6] § 732.

EXAMPLE 9

Lindsey has a $48,000 basis in her partnership interest. On October 10, 2012, the partnership distributes to her cash of $12,000, cash basis receivables with an inside basis of $0 and a fair market value of $10,000, and a parcel of land with a basis and fair market value to the partnership of $60,000. Lindsey has a realized gain on the distribution of $34,000 ($12,000 + $10,000 + $60,000 − $48,000). None of that gain is recognized, however, because the $12,000 cash distribution does not exceed her $48,000 adjusted basis for her partnership interest. In determining the basis effects of the distribution, the cash is treated as being distributed first, reducing Lindsey's adjusted basis to $36,000 ($48,000 − $12,000). The receivables are distributed next, taking a $0 carryover basis to Lindsey. Her adjusted basis remains at $36,000. The land is distributed last, taking a substituted basis of $36,000 and reducing her adjusted basis for her partnership interest to $0. ■

When more than one asset in a particular class is distributed, special rules apply. Usually, if the partner's remaining adjusted basis for the partnership interest is less than the partnership's adjusted basis for the distributed assets in the particular class, the partner's adjusted basis for each distributed asset is computed by following three steps:

Step 1 Each distributed asset within the class initially takes a carryover basis.

Step 2 If necessary, this carryover basis for each of these assets is reduced in proportion to their respective amounts of unrealized depreciation (amount that carryover basis is greater than fair market value). Under no circumstances, however, can the basis of any asset be reduced below its fair market value in step 2.

Step 3 Any remaining decrease in basis is allocated among all of the distributed assets in the class in proportion to their respective adjusted bases (as determined in step 2).

EXAMPLE 10

Assume the same facts as in Example 9, except that Lindsey receives two parcels of land, rather than a single parcel. The partnership's basis for the parcels is $15,000 for Parcel 1 and $45,000 for Parcel 2. Each parcel has a fair market value of $30,000. Lindsey has a realized gain on the distribution of $34,000 ($12,000 + $10,000 + $60,000 − $48,000). None of that gain is recognized, however, because the $12,000 cash distribution does not exceed her $48,000 adjusted basis.

As in Example 9, Lindsey takes a $12,000 basis for the cash and a $0 carryover basis for the receivables and has a $36,000 adjusted basis for her partnership interest after these two items are distributed. Because two parcels of land are distributed and because Lindsey's remaining $36,000 adjusted basis for her partnership interest is less than the partnership's $60,000 total basis for the two parcels of land, Lindsey's adjusted basis for each parcel of land is computed by following these steps:

Step 1 She initially takes a carryover basis of $15,000 for Parcel 1 and $45,000 for Parcel 2.

Step 2 She reduces the basis of Parcel 2 to its lower fair market value of $30,000. The basis for Parcel 1 is not adjusted in this step because Parcel 1 has a fair market value greater than its basis.

Step 3 The remaining $9,000 difference between her $36,000 basis for the partnership interest and the $45,000 ($15,000 + $30,000) basis for the land parcels after step 2 is allocated to the two parcels in proportion to their respective bases (as computed in step 2). Therefore, the amount of the step 3 basis reduction allocated to Parcel 1 is:

$$\$9{,}000 \times \frac{\$15{,}000}{\$45{,}000} = \$3{,}000$$

Lindsey's basis for Parcel 1 is $12,000 ($15,000 − $3,000). The amount of the step 3 basis reduction allocated to Parcel 2 is:

$$\$9{,}000 \times \frac{\$30{,}000}{\$45{,}000} = \$6{,}000$$

Lindsey's basis for Parcel 2 is $24,000 ($30,000 − $6,000). ■

EXAMPLE 11

Assume the same facts as in Example 10 and that Lindsey sells both parcels of land early in 2013 for their fair market values, receiving proceeds of $60,000 ($30,000 + $30,000). She also collects $10,000 from the cash basis receivables. Now she recognizes all of the $34,000 gain that she deferred upon receiving the property from the partnership [$60,000 amount realized − $36,000 basis for the two parcels ($12,000 + $24,000) + $10,000 collected − $0 basis for the receivables]. ■

Review the tax results of Examples 9 and 10. Although Lindsey does not recognize any of the gain she realizes from the distribution, she has a zero outside basis for her partnership interest. If Lindsey expects the partnership to generate net losses in the near future, she will *not* find this zero basis attractive. She may be unable to deduct her share of these future losses when they flow through to her on the last day of the partnership's subsequent tax year.

The low basis that Lindsey has assigned to the parcels of land is of no significant detriment to her if she does not intend to sell the land in the near future. Because land does not generate cost recovery deductions, the substituted basis is used only to determine Lindsey's gain or loss upon her disposition of the land in a taxable sale or exchange.

Concept Summary 11.1 reviews the general rules that apply to proportionate nonliquidating partnership distributions.

ETHICS & EQUITY Arranging Tax-Advantaged Distributions

The Sparrow Partnership plans to distribute $200,000 cash to its partners at the end of the year. Marjorie is a 40 percent partner and would receive $80,000. Her basis in the partnership is only $10,000, however, so she would be required to recognize a $70,000 gain if she receives a cash distribution. She has asked the partnership instead to purchase a parcel of land she has found on which she will build her retirement residence. The partnership will then distribute that land to her. Under the partnership distribution rules, Marjorie would take a $10,000 basis in land worth $80,000. Her basis in the partnership would be reduced to $0, and the $70,000 gain is deferred. Do you think this is an appropriate transaction?

LO.2

Determine the tax treatment of proportionate distributions that liquidate a partnership.

Proportionate Liquidating Distributions

Proportionate liquidating distributions consist of a single distribution or a series of distributions that result in the termination of the partner's entire interest in the partnership. If the partnership continues in existence after the partner's interest is liquidated, the rules of § 736 govern the classification of the liquidating payments. These rules are discussed later in the chapter. Other rules apply, however, if the partner's interest is liquidated because the partnership is also liquidating. This section examines the latter type of liquidating distribution.

The partnership itself does not recognize either gain or loss on a proportionate liquidating distribution. The following discussion outlines rules for allocation of basis and possible gain or loss recognition by partners. These rules are summarized in Concept Summary 11.2 at the end of this section.

Gain Recognition and Ordering Rules

When a partnership liquidates, the liquidating distributions to a partner usually consist of an interest in several or all of the partnership assets. The gain recognition and ordering rules parallel those for nonliquidating distributions, except that the partner's *entire* basis in the partnership interest is allocated to the assets received in the liquidating distribution, unless the partner is required to recognize a loss. A loss may be recognized when *only* cash, unrealized receivables, or inventory is received in the distribution. As a result of the ordering rules, the basis of

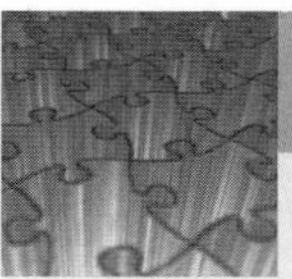

CONCEPT SUMMARY 11.1

Proportionate Nonliquidating Distributions (General Rules)

1. Neither the distributee partner nor the partnership recognizes any gain or loss on a proportionate nonliquidating distribution. However, if cash distributed exceeds the distributee partner's outside basis, gain is recognized. Property distributions generally do not result in gain recognition.
2. The distributee partner usually takes the same basis in the distributed property that the property had to the partnership (carryover basis). However, where the inside basis of distributed property exceeds the partner's outside basis, the basis assigned to the distributed property cannot exceed that outside basis (substituted basis).
3. Gain recognized by the distributee partner on a proportionate nonliquidating distribution is capital in nature.
4. Loss is never recognized on a proportionate nonliquidating distribution.

Calculations

1. Partner's outside basis.	______
2. Less: Cash distributed to partner.	______
3. Gain recognized by partner (excess of Line 2 over Line 1).	______
4. Partner's remaining outside basis (Line 1 − Line 2). If less than $0, enter $0.	______
5. Partner's basis in unrealized receivables and inventory distributed (enter lesser of Line 4 or the partnership's inside basis in the unrealized receivables and inventory).	______
6. Basis available to allocate to other property distributed (Line 4 − Line 5).	______
7. Partnership's inside basis of other property distributed.	______
8. Basis to partner of other property distributed (enter lesser of Line 6 or Line 7).	______
9. Partner's remaining outside basis (Line 6 − Line 8).	______

some assets may be adjusted upward or downward to absorb the partner's remaining outside basis. Unrealized receivables or inventory are never "stepped up," although they may be "stepped down."

The general ordering and gain recognition rules for a proportionate liquidating distribution are summarized as follows:

- Cash is distributed first and results in a capital gain if the amount distributed exceeds the partner's basis in the partnership interest. The cash distributed reduces the liquidated partner's outside basis dollar for dollar. The partner's basis cannot be reduced below zero.
- The partner's remaining outside basis is then allocated to unrealized receivables and inventory up to an amount equal to the partnership's adjusted bases in those properties. If the partnership's bases in the unrealized receivables and inventory exceed the partner's remaining outside basis, the remaining outside basis is allocated to the unrealized receivables and inventory.
- Finally, if the liquidating partner has any remaining outside basis, that basis is allocated to the other assets received.[7]

EXAMPLE 12

When Tara's basis in her partnership interest is $70,000, she receives cash of $15,000, a proportionate share of inventory, and land in a distribution that liquidates both the partnership and her entire partnership interest. The inventory has a basis to the partnership of $20,000 and a fair market value of $30,000. The land's basis is $8,000, and the fair market value is $12,000. Under these circumstances, Tara recognizes no gain or loss. After Tara's $70,000 basis is reduced by the $15,000 cash received, the remaining $55,000 is allocated first to the inventory and then to the land. The basis of the inventory in Tara's hands is $20,000, and the basis of the land is $35,000. ■

When more than one asset in a particular class is distributed in a proportionate liquidating distribution, special rules may apply. If the partner's remaining basis for

[7] §§ 731 and 732.

the partnership interest is less than the partnership's basis for the distributed assets in the particular class, the partner's basis for each distributed asset is computed as illustrated in Example 10. If, however, the partner's remaining basis for the partnership interest is greater than the partnership's basis for the distributed assets in the "other assets" class, the partner's basis for each remaining distributed asset is computed by following three steps:

Step 1 Each distributed asset within the "other assets" class initially takes a carryover basis.

Step 2 Then, this carryover basis for each of these assets is increased in proportion to their respective amounts of unrealized appreciation (amount that fair market value is greater than carryover basis). Under no circumstances, however, can the basis of any asset be increased above its fair market value in step 2.

Step 3 Any remaining increase in basis is allocated among all of the distributed assets in the "other assets" class in proportion to their respective fair market values.

EXAMPLE 13

Assume the same facts as in Example 12, except that Tara receives two parcels of land instead of one. The partnership's basis for the parcels is $2,000 for Parcel 1 and $6,000 for Parcel 2. Each parcel has a fair market value of $6,000.

Tara takes a $15,000 basis for the cash and a $20,000 carryover basis for the inventory. She has a $35,000 basis for her partnership interest after these two items are distributed. Because two parcels of land are distributed and because Tara's remaining $35,000 basis for her partnership interest exceeds the partnership's $8,000 basis for the two parcels of land, Tara's basis for each parcel of land is computed by following these steps:

Step 1 She initially takes a carryover basis of $2,000 for Parcel 1 and $6,000 for Parcel 2.

Step 2 She increases the basis of Parcel 1 by $4,000 to its fair market value of $6,000. The basis for Parcel 2 is not affected in this step because Parcel 2 has a fair market value equal to its basis.

Step 3 Tara's $23,000 ($35,000 − $6,000 − $6,000) remaining basis for her partnership interest is allocated to each land parcel in proportion to each parcel's respective $6,000 fair market value. Therefore, $11,500 [($6,000/$12,000) × $23,000] is allocated to each parcel. Tara's basis in Parcel 1 is $17,500 ($2,000 + $4,000 + $11,500). Her basis in Parcel 2 is also $17,500 ($6,000 + $11,500). ■

Loss Recognition

The distributee partner recognizes a *loss* on a liquidating distribution if both of the following are true:

1. The partner receives *only* cash, unrealized receivables, or inventory.
2. The partner's outside basis in the partnership interest exceeds the partnership's inside basis for the assets distributed. This excess amount is the loss recognized by the distributee partner.[8]

The word *only* is important. A distribution of any other property precludes recognition of the loss.

EXAMPLE 14

When Ramon's outside basis is $40,000, he receives a liquidating distribution of $7,000 cash and a proportionate share of inventory having a partnership basis of $3,000 and a fair market value of $10,000. Ramon is not allowed to "step up" the basis in the inventory, so it is allocated a $3,000 carryover basis. Ramon's unutilized outside basis is $30,000 ($40,000 − $7,000 − $3,000). Because he received a liquidating distribution of *only* cash and inventory, he recognizes a capital loss of $30,000 on the liquidation. ■

[8] § 731(a)(2).

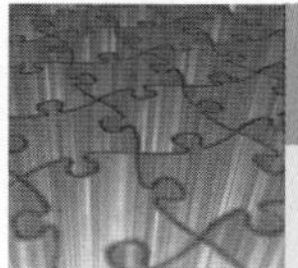

CONCEPT SUMMARY 11.2

Proportionate Liquidating Distributions When the Partnership Also Liquidates (General Rules)

1. Generally, neither the distributee partner nor the partnership recognizes gain or loss when a partnership liquidates. However, a partner recognizes gain if the cash received exceeds the partner's outside basis. A partner recognizes loss when (a) the partner receives only cash, unrealized receivables, or inventory and (b) the partner's outside basis is greater than the partnership's inside basis of the assets distributed.
2. A partner's basis in distributed assets must be determined in a certain order. Cash is distributed first, inventory and unrealized receivables second, and all other assets last. Assets in the last category take a substituted basis equal to the distributee partner's remaining outside basis.
3. Gain or loss recognized by a distributee partner in a proportionate distribution that liquidates a partnership is usually capital in nature.

Calculations

1. Partner's outside basis.	
2. Less: Cash distributed to partner.	
3. Gain recognized by partner (excess of Line 2 over Line 1).	
4. Partner's remaining outside basis (Line 1 – Line 2). If less than $0, enter $0.	
5. Partner's basis in unrealized receivables and inventory distributed (enter lesser of Line 4 or the inside basis in the unrealized receivables and inventory).	
6. Basis to partner of other property distributed (Line 4 – Line 5).	
7. Loss recognized by partner (if no other property was distributed, enter amount from Line 6).	
8. Partner's remaining outside basis.	$0

EXAMPLE 15

Assume the same facts as in Example 14, except that in addition to the cash and inventory, Ramon receives the desk he used in the partnership. (Assume that the distribution is proportionate to the partners.) The desk has an adjusted basis of $100 to the partnership. Applying the rules outlined above to this revised fact situation produces the following results:

Step 1 Cash of $7,000 is distributed to Ramon, and it reduces his outside basis to $33,000.

Step 2 Inventory is distributed to Ramon. He takes a $3,000 carryover basis in the inventory and reduces his outside basis in the partnership to $30,000.

Step 3 The desk is distributed to Ramon. Because the desk is not cash, an unrealized receivable, or inventory, he cannot recognize a loss. Therefore, Ramon's remaining basis in his partnership interest is allocated to the desk. He takes a $30,000 basis for the desk. ■

What can Ramon do with a $30,000 desk? If he continues to use it in a trade or business, he can depreciate it. Once he has established his business use of the desk, he could sell it and recognize a large § 1231 loss. If the loss is isolated in the year of the sale, it is an ordinary loss. Thus, with proper planning, no liquidated partner should be forced to recognize a capital loss instead of an ordinary loss.

Gain recognized by the withdrawing partner on the subsequent disposition of inventory is ordinary income unless the disposition occurs more than five years after the distribution.[9] The withdrawing partner's holding period for all other property received in a liquidating distribution includes the partnership's related holding period.

Concept Summary 11.2 outlines the general rules that apply to proportionate liquidating partnership distributions.

[9] § 735(a)(2).

LO.3

Describe the tax treatment that applies to distributions treated as disguised sales and distributions of marketable securities and precontribution gain property.

Property Distributions with Special Tax Treatment

Recall that a distribution from a partnership to a partner usually does not result in taxable gain. This section discusses three exceptions in which a proportionate distribution, either liquidating or nonliquidating, may result in gain to the partner.

Disguised Sales

As discussed in Chapter 10, a disguised sale is a transaction in which a partner contributes appreciated property to a partnership and soon thereafter receives a distribution of cash or property from the partnership. If the IRS determines that the payment is part of a "purchase" of the property, rather than a distribution from the partnership, the usual sale or exchange rules apply. The partner is treated as having sold the property and must report a gain on the sale. The partnership takes a cost basis in the property purchased. See Chapter 10 for additional discussion.

Marketable Securities

The fair market value of a marketable security distributed to a partner is generally treated as a cash distribution.[10] Some or all of the value of the security over the partner's outside basis prior to the distribution is a taxable gain. The partner must assign a basis to the security received in the distribution, so the distribution ordering rules must be taken into account.

The term *marketable securities* is broadly defined and includes almost any debt or equity interest that is actively traded, including options, futures contracts, and derivatives. Marketable securities are *not* treated as cash if (1) they were originally contributed by the partner to whom they are now distributed (certain exceptions apply to this provision), (2) the property was not a marketable security when acquired by the partnership, or (3) the partner is an eligible partner of an investment partnership, as defined in Chapter 10.

The primary purpose of this rule is to stop the tax avoidance that otherwise would occur if a partnership purchased marketable securities with the intent of immediately distributing them to the partner. As the "Ethics & Equity" feature earlier in this chapter indicated, a partnership can purchase property desired by a partner, distribute that property to the partner, and allow the partner to defer tax on any appreciation inherent in the partnership interest. This rule prevents a partnership from arranging such a transaction with marketable securities.

If, on the distribution date, the marketable security is appreciated, it probably was not acquired by the partnership in an effort to assist the distributee partner in reducing the tax on the distribution. The portion of the security value treated as cash is reduced by a proportionate share of the appreciation inherent in the distributed security. The amount of the reduction is the excess of (1) the partner's share of appreciation in this particular security before the distribution over (2) the partner's share of appreciation in the portion of the security retained by the partnership. If the partner's interest in the partnership is liquidated, the gain on the partner's share of the distributed security is deferred. The "reduction" is intended to take into account the partnership's intent, or lack thereof, to reduce the partner's gains.

EXAMPLE 16

Assume that the A to Z Partnership has the following balance sheet:

	Basis	FMV		Basis	FMV
ZYX Corporation security	$4,000	$10,000	Andrew, capital	$ 500	$ 2,000
Land	1,000	10,000	Other partners, capital	4,500	18,000
Total	$5,000	$20,000	Total	$5,000	$20,000

[10] § 731(c).

The partnership distributes $2,000 (value) of the ZYX stock to 10% partner Andrew in liquidation of his partnership interest. The amount of the distribution treated as cash is the $2,000 fair market value of the stock reduced by Andrew's decrease in his share of the inside appreciation in the stock. Before the distribution, Andrew's share of appreciation in this stock was $600 [10% × ($10,000 − $4,000)]. *His share* of appreciation in the stock retained by the partnership is $0, because he no longer owns an interest in the partnership. The $2,000 value of the stock is reduced by $600 ($600 appreciation before − $0 after distribution). Andrew is treated as if he received a cash distribution of $1,400.

Andrew's outside basis was $500 before the distribution. The $1,400 deemed cash distribution triggers gain recognition of $900. ■

The distributee partner's basis in the security is the sum of (1) the basis in the stock as determined under the regular distribution rules (see the previous discussion under Ordering Rules) and (2) the gain recognized on the distribution.

EXAMPLE 17

In Example 16, the stock would take a substituted basis of $500 to Andrew under the distribution ordering rules. This basis is the lesser of the partnership's inside basis in the stock of $800 (20% × $4,000) or Andrew's outside basis of $500 (see Concept Summary 11.2). The recognized gain of $900 increases Andrew's basis in the stock to $1,400 ($500 + $900).

This basis determination preserves the inherent built-in gain in Andrew's partnership interest. Before the distribution, Andrew has $1,500 of appreciation in his interest ($2,000 − $500). After considering the $900 gain on the stock distribution, he should have $600 of untaxed appreciation. The stock value is $2,000, and Andrew's basis is $1,400; so the untaxed appreciation is the expected $600 amount. ■

Unless otherwise indicated, the remaining examples in this chapter assume that the partnership is not distributing marketable securities.

Precontribution Gain

Taxable gains may arise on a distribution of property to a partner where precontribution (built-in) gains exist. Specifically, if a partner contributes appreciated property to a partnership, the contributing partner recognizes gain in two situations:

1. If the contributed appreciated property is distributed to another partner within seven years of the contribution date, the contributing partner recognizes the remaining net precontribution gain on the property.[11] The contributing partner's basis in the partnership interest is increased by the amount of gain recognized. Also, the basis of the distributed property is increased by this same amount to prevent double taxation of this precontribution gain when the distributee partner later sells the asset.

EXAMPLE 18

In 2012, Rick contributes nondepreciable property with an adjusted basis of $10,000 and a fair market value of $40,000 to the RTCO Partnership in exchange for a one-fourth interest in profits and capital. In 2013, when the property's fair market value is $50,000, the partnership distributes the property to Tom, another one-fourth partner. Because the property was contributed to the partnership within seven years of the date the property was distributed and precontribution gain of $30,000 ($40,000 − $10,000) was attributable to the property, the built-in gain on the property is taxable to Rick. Therefore, Rick must pay tax on the $30,000 built-in gain in 2013, the year the property was distributed to Tom. Rick increases his basis in his partnership interest by the $30,000 gain recognized. Tom also increases his basis in the property received by $30,000.

Note that if the partnership were to sell the property to an unrelated third party for $40,000 in 2013, the result would be the same for Rick. Under § 704(c)(1)(A),

[11] § 704(c)(1)(B).

recognized built-in gains must be allocated to the partner who contributed the property, and the partner's outside basis is increased accordingly. ■

2. The second situation occurs where the partnership distributes *any* property other than cash to a partner within seven years after *that* partner contributes appreciated property to the partnership. In this case, the partner recognizes the lesser of (a) the remaining net precontribution (built-in) gain or (b) the excess of the fair market value of the distributed property over the partner's basis in interest before the distribution.[12] The distributee partner's basis in his or her partnership interest is increased by the amount of gain recognized. To maintain a parity between inside and outside basis, the partnership is allowed to increase its basis in the precontribution gain property remaining in the partnership.

   An exception applies if the partner originally contributed the distributed property. The partnership is merely returning property to the original contributor, and the partner is not required to recognize built-in gain. The general rules that govern property distributions apply.

EXAMPLE 19

In 2010, Bill contributed land to the BMC Partnership. His basis in the land was $16,000. The fair market value at the contribution date was $40,000. In 2012, the partnership distributes other property with an adjusted basis of $16,000 and fair market value of $65,000 to Bill. Bill's basis in his partnership interest was $12,000 immediately before the distribution. Because Bill contributed precontribution gain property within seven years of receiving the distribution of other property, he recognizes gain on the distribution. The maximum he must recognize is the net precontribution gain, or $24,000 ($40,000 fair market value − $16,000 adjusted basis of property contributed). He compares this amount to the excess of the fair market value of the distributed property over his basis in his partnership interest, or $53,000 ($65,000 fair market value of property − $12,000 adjusted basis in interest prior to distribution).

Because the $24,000 precontribution gain is less than the $53,000 inherent gain, Bill recognizes gain of $24,000. His basis in his partnership interest increases by the $24,000 gain recognized to $36,000, and the partnership's basis in the "precontribution gain" property Bill originally contributed also increases by $24,000 to $40,000. ■

EXAMPLE 20

Assume the same facts as in Example 19, except that Bill's basis in his partnership interest was $60,000 before the distribution. In this case, the excess value of the distributed property is only $5,000 ($65,000 − $60,000), so Bill only recognizes gain of $5,000, with corresponding adjustments to the basis of his partnership interest and the partnership's basis in the precontribution gain property.

The remaining precontribution gain of $19,000 ($24,000 − $5,000) is charged to Bill at some point in the future if the partnership sells the precontribution gain property or distributes it to another partner within seven years of its contribution. Some or all of the remaining precontribution gain may also be recognized if other appreciated property is distributed to Bill within seven years of the original contribution. ■

If the distribution occurs more than seven years after the original contribution, Bill recognizes no gain and the distribution is handled under the general distribution rules described earlier in this section.

LO.4

Specify and explain the general concepts governing tax treatment of disproportionate distributions.

Disproportionate Distributions

An additional exception to the general gain and loss nonrecognition rule arises when a partnership makes a "disproportionate distribution" of assets. A disproportionate distribution occurs when a partnership makes a distribution of cash or property to a

[12] § 737.

partner and that distribution increases or decreases the distributee partner's proportionate interest in certain of the partnership's ordinary income-producing assets.

These ordinary income-producing assets, called **hot assets**, include substantially **appreciated inventory** and unrealized receivables. Unrealized receivables are rights to receive future amounts that will result in ordinary income when the income is recognized. Inventory, as the term is used here, has a much broader meaning than usual. It includes all assets that are not cash, capital, or § 1231 assets. Substantially appreciated inventory is inventory that has a fair market value in excess of 120 percent of the partnership's adjusted basis for the inventory.

The taxation of disproportionate distributions is based on the aggregate theory of taxation. Under this theory, each partner is deemed to own a proportionate share of the underlying assets of the partnership. In line with this concept, each partner is responsible for recognizing and reporting the proportionate share of ordinary income potential of these assets, such as would arise on the sale of substantially appreciated inventory or on the collection of cash basis receivables.

Section 751(b) maintains each partner's proportionate share of ordinary income by recasting any transaction in which a disproportionate distribution of hot assets is made. If the distributee partner receives less than a proportionate share of hot assets, the transaction is treated as if two separate events occurred: (1) the partnership made a distribution of some of the hot assets to the distributee partner, and (2) that partner immediately sold these hot assets back to the partnership. The partner recognizes ordinary income on the sale of the hot assets, and the partnership takes a cost basis for the hot assets purchased.

EXAMPLE 21

The balance sheet of the AB Partnership is as follows on December 31 of the current tax year:

	Basis	FMV		Basis	FMV
Cash	$26,000	$26,000	Abby, capital	$13,000	$26,000
Unrealized receivables	–0–	26,000	Bob, capital	13,000	26,000
Total	$26,000	$52,000	Total	$26,000	$52,000

Abby and Bob are equal partners in the partnership. The partnership makes a liquidating distribution of the unrealized receivables to Abby and the cash to Bob. Because the unrealized receivables are a hot asset, Abby has received more than her proportionate share of the hot asset and Bob has received less than his proportionate share. Section 751 recasts the transaction into two separate events. First, Bob is deemed to receive a current distribution of his 50% share of hot assets (basis = $0; fair market value = $13,000), which he then immediately sells back to the partnership for $13,000 of the cash. Bob recognizes $13,000 ordinary income on the sale, and the partnership takes a $13,000 basis in the receivables purchased. The remaining $13,000 cash received by Bob reduces his adjusted basis for his partnership interest to $0 ($13,000 cash distributed − $13,000 adjusted basis).

Abby receives both the $13,000 receivables the partnership purchased from Bob and her share of the remaining $13,000 unrealized receivables. She takes a substituted basis of $13,000 in the receivables and reduces her adjusted basis for her partnership interest to $0. When she collects all $26,000 of the receivables, she will recognize $13,000 of ordinary income ($26,000 cash collected − $13,000 basis for receivables).

Although the mechanical rules of § 751(b) are complicated, the application of the rules in this example has ensured that each partner eventually recognizes his or her $13,000 share of ordinary income. Bob recognizes his share at the time the partnership is liquidated. Abby's share is recognized when she collects the unrealized receivables. ■

Although most of the problems and examples in this text involve proportionate distributions, be aware that disproportionate distributions occur frequently in practice. The calculation of ordinary income in disproportionate distributions can become extremely complex. These more difficult calculations are not discussed in this text.

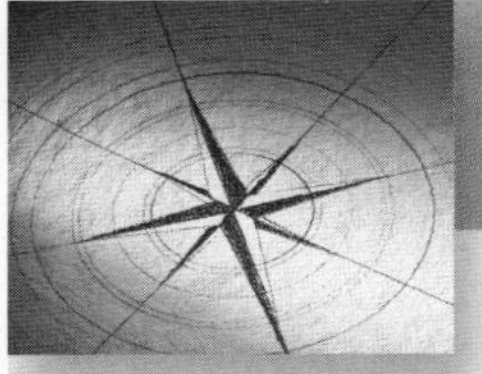

ETHICS & EQUITY Partnerships as Tax Shelters

"Tax shelter" investments offer benefits both through the economic performance potential of the investment asset or activity and through the tax savings afforded by utilizing various tax provisions. Some types of tax shelters are operated through partnerships. For example, in some industries (e.g., research and development, oil and gas, and real estate), the partnership form provides a means of efficiently raising capital, and various provisions in Subchapter K (and elsewhere in the Code) offer additional tax advantages.

In the case of certain real estate investments, the liabilities included in the partner's basis can be used to shield the partnership's losses resulting from depreciation deductions and operations of the entity. If the partnership agreement is carefully drafted, active partners may be able to claim ordinary losses greatly in excess of their capital contributions. As long as the liability provides adequate basis, the partner can continue to claim losses.

When the liabilities are repaid or forgiven, the situation changes. The partner is treated as receiving a current distribution of cash and recognizes a capital gain on the payment or forgiveness of the debt. This has been called a "phantom gain" because the partner must recognize a gain with no corresponding cash with which to pay the tax. Partnerships have been known to refinance debt over extensive periods of time simply to avoid this result.

As a tax planning strategy, these real estate ventures offer the partners an ordinary loss deduction during the earlier operating years (at up to about a 36 percent Federal savings rate), with capital gains being recognized (generally as unrecaptured § 1250 gains taxed at up to 25 percent) when the debt is repaid.

What are your thoughts on this potential for tax rate arbitrage? What do you think of the practice of using certain types of partnerships to take advantage of various provisions of the tax law?

11.2 Liquidating Distributions to Retiring or Deceased Partners

LO.5

Determine the tax treatment under § 736 of payments from a partnership to a retiring or deceased partner.

Payments made by an ongoing partnership in complete liquidation of a retiring partner's interest are classified under § 736 as either *income* or *property* payments. Payments made to a successor to the interest of a deceased partner are similarly classified by § 736.[13] It is critical to observe that § 736 only classifies the payments. Other Code Sections provide the rules for computing the tax effects of these payments. Although these payments can be made in cash, property, or both cash and property, this discussion assumes that all payments are made in cash.

From a practical standpoint, the partnership and the retiring partner negotiate a total buyout package. The retiring partner expects compensation for the partner's proportionate share of the fair market value of each partnership asset. The partner also expects to be compensated for a share of the partnership's going-concern value. *Property* payments [called § 736(b) payments] represent the former type of buyout provision, and *income* payments [§ 736(a) payments] typically represent the latter. Once the total buyout price is determined, § 736 provides rules for determining the allocation between income and property payments, but leaves some room for negotiation between the partner and the partnership over which component of the buyout represents each type of payment.

Treatment of Property/Income Payments

The following provides an overview of the tax treatment of property and income payments:

- *Property payments—in general.* In general, property payments [§ 736(b) payments] are cash distributions paid by the partnership to the partner in

[13]A successor is typically the estate of the deceased or the party who inherits the decedent's interest.

exchange for the partner's interest in partnership assets. The partnership may not deduct these amounts. If the partnership owns no hot assets, the property payment is treated under the normal proportionate distribution rules.

- *Income payments—in general.* Income payments [§ 736(a) payments] are treated as a partner's distributive share of partnership income or, alternatively, as a guaranteed payment to the retiring partner.

EXAMPLE 22

Pamela receives cash of $15,000 in liquidation of her partnership interest, in which she has a basis of $10,000. The partnership owns no hot assets. After following all of the classification requirements of § 736, $12,000 of this amount is classified as a property payment and $3,000 is classified as a guaranteed payment. The $12,000 property payment is treated as a distribution from the partnership in exchange for her partnership interest, so Pamela recognizes a $2,000 capital gain on this part of her liquidation proceeds ($12,000 property payment − $10,000 basis in interest). She recognizes $3,000 ordinary income for the guaranteed payment, and the partnership deducts the same amount. ■

Property Payments

Cash payments made for the partner's pro rata share of the fair market value of each partnership asset are classified as § 736(b) payments. The following items are not treated as § 736(b) payments, however, if (1) the partnership is primarily a service provider (i.e., "capital is *not* a material income-producing factor for the partnership") and (2) the retiring or deceased partner was a general partner in the partnership:

- Payments made for the partner's pro rata share of unrealized receivables. For purposes of this rule, unrealized receivables do *not* include potential depreciation recapture.
- Payments made for the partner's pro rata share of the partnership goodwill, unless the partnership agreement states that the payments are for goodwill. This exception applies only to payments for goodwill that exceed the partner's pro rata share of the partnership's inside basis for goodwill.
- Certain annuities and lump-sum payments made to retiring partners or a deceased partner's successors.

If such payments are made by a service-oriented partnership to a general partner, they are classified as § 736(a) payments. Conversely, if these payments are made by a capital-intensive partnership or to a limited partner or a partner treated as a limited partner (e.g., an inactive member of an LLC), they are classified as § 736(b) payments.

EXAMPLE 23

The ABC Partnership has the following balance sheet at the end of the current tax year:

	Basis	FMV		Basis	FMV
Cash	$36,000	$36,000	Anne, capital	$15,000	$27,000
Unrealized receivables	–0–	18,000	Bonnie, capital	15,000	27,000
Land	9,000	27,000	Cindy, capital	15,000	27,000
Total	$45,000	$81,000	Total	$45,000	$81,000

Partner Anne is a general partner retiring from the service-oriented partnership. She receives $36,000 cash, none of which is stated to be for goodwill. Because the fair market value of Anne's share of the three recorded assets is only $27,000 (1/3 × $81,000), the $9,000 excess payment is for unstated goodwill.

The payment Anne receives for her interest in the cash and land is a § 736(b) property payment. This payment is $21,000, consisting of $12,000 paid for the cash (1/3 × $36,000) and $9,000 paid for Anne's share of the fair market value of the land (1/3 × $27,000). The remaining cash of $15,000 is for her $6,000 interest in the unrealized receivables and for the $9,000 of unstated goodwill and is a § 736 (a) payment. ■

Section 736(b) payments for "nonhot" assets are treated first as a return of the partner's outside basis in the partnership.[14] Once the entire basis is returned, any additional amounts are taxed to the partner as capital gain. If the cash distributions are not sufficient to return the partner's entire outside basis, the shortfall is taxed to the partner as a capital loss.[15]

EXAMPLE 24

In Example 23, the property payment of $21,000 cash includes amounts for Anne's share of land and cash only, neither of which is a hot asset. If Anne's outside basis is $15,000, she recognizes capital gain of $6,000 [($12,000 + $9,000) − $15,000] on the distribution. However, if Anne's outside basis is $25,000, she recognizes a $4,000 capital loss on the distribution [($12,000 + $9,000) − $25,000]. The partnership cannot deduct any part of the $21,000 property payment. ■

If part of the property payment is for the partner's share of hot assets, the § 736(b) payment is allocated between the portion related to hot assets and the portion related to other assets. The portion of the payment *not* related to hot assets is treated as described in Example 24. The portion of the payment related to hot assets is treated as discussed earlier under Disproportionate Distributions. Distributions that are disproportionate to the partner's share of hot assets of the partnership are treated as two separate transactions:

- First, the partner's proportionate share of hot assets is deemed to be distributed. A partner cannot step up the basis in hot assets, so on the distribution, the hot assets take the lesser of the partnership's inside basis for the hot assets or the partner's outside basis in the interest.
- Second, these hot assets are deemed to be sold back to the partnership at fair market value. A portion of the § 736(b) payment is allocated to the partnership's deemed purchase of the hot assets.

EXAMPLE 25

If Anne, in Example 23, was treated as a limited partner (e.g., she was an inactive partner in an LLC or LLP) or the partnership was capital-intensive, the entire payment of $36,000 is a § 736(b) property payment. The $36,000 payment is allocated between hot assets and other assets. The payment for cash and land is a payment for Anne's other assets, as is the payment for partnership goodwill. The payment for the unrealized receivables, however, is a payment for Anne's share of the partnership's hot assets.

The partnership is treated first as distributing Anne's $6,000 proportionate share of unrealized receivables. Anne's carryover basis in the receivables is $0.

Anne then resells the unrealized receivables to the partnership for their $6,000 fair market value. She reports $6,000 of ordinary income on this sale. The partnership now has a basis of $6,000 in its $18,000 of accounts receivable.

The partnership paid Anne $36,000. Of this amount, $6,000 is to "repurchase" her share of receivables; the remaining $30,000 is in exchange for the partnership's other assets ($12,000 for cash + $9,000 for land + $9,000 for goodwill). Anne calculates and reports a $15,000 capital gain ($30,000 payment − $15,000 basis) in addition to the $6,000 ordinary income. ■

[14] §§ 736(b) and 731(a)(1).

[15] § 731(a)(2).

Income Payments

All payments that are not classified as § 736(b) property payments are categorized as § 736(a) income payments. These income payments are further classified into two categories. Payments that are *not* determined by reference to partnership income are treated as guaranteed payments. They are fully taxable as ordinary income to the distributee partner and are fully deductible by the continuing partnership.

Section 736(a) income payments that are determined by reference to partnership income are treated as distributive shares of that income (i.e., an allocation of partnership income for the year). They are taxed to the distributee partner according to their character to the partnership. Thus, for example, they may be taxed as capital gain as well as ordinary income.[16] Because this capital gain and ordinary income are allocated to the liquidated partner, the payments reduce the amount of partnership capital gain and ordinary income allocated to the remaining partners.[17]

EXAMPLE 26

Continue with the same facts as in Example 23 where the partnership is service-oriented. The $6,000 cash payment ($18,000 × 1/3) for Anne's pro rata share of the unrealized receivables is classified as a § 736(a) income payment, as is the $9,000 payment for unstated goodwill.

Because the $15,000 § 736(a) income payment ($6,000 + $9,000) is not determined by reference to partnership income, the payment is classified as a guaranteed payment. It is included as ordinary income on Anne's tax return and is deductible by the partnership. ■

The following table summarizes the taxation results of Examples 23 through 26, for a partnership where capital is not a material income-producing factor and where it is. In both cases, Anne's basis in her partnership interest was $15,000 before the distribution.

	Tax Character to Anne		Deduction to ABC
Service-oriented partnership:			
§736(b)(Example 24)	$ 6,000	capital gain	None
§736(a)(Example 26)	15,000	ordinary income	$15,000
Total gain	$21,000		
Capital-intensive partnership:			
§736(b)(Example 25)	$15,000	capital gain	None
§736(b)(Example 25)	6,000	ordinary income	None
§736(a)(Example 25)	–0–	ordinary income	None
Total gain	$21,000		

As this table illustrates, the characterization under § 736 does not change the overall gain; in both cases, Anne recognizes total gain of $21,000. This is appropriate because she receives $36,000 cash against a basis of $15,000.

The character of Anne's income differs solely as a result of the characterization of goodwill. For the service-oriented partnership with unstated goodwill, the payment for goodwill results in ordinary income to a general partner. For the capital-intensive partnership, or if the partner is a limited partner, goodwill results in capital gain.

From the partnership's point of view, it is entitled to a deduction for goodwill payments only if it is a service partnership and the retiring partner is a general partner, and then only if the goodwill payment is not stated in the partnership agreement.

The partnership's position also differs as a result of the treatment of unrealized receivables. As a service partnership, it can claim a current deduction for the amount of the distribution related to the receivables. As a capital-intensive partnership,

[16] § 702(b).

[17] Reg. § 1.736–1(a)(4).

ABC has a cost basis in the receivables when it is deemed to repurchase them from Anne. When the receivables are collected, the partnership's ordinary income is reduced.

THE BIG PICTURE

EXAMPLE 27

Return to the facts of *The Big Picture* on p. 11-1. Recall that the members of Beachside Properties, LLC, are considering two alternatives for its future expansion. Assume that they decide to admit new partners for $19.5 million and use $9.5 million of the cash to redeem the interests of Kyle and Maria.

Because the LLC itself is not liquidating, the distribution to Kyle and Maria is classified under § 736. The current balance sheet for Beachside Properties, LLC, is as follows:

	Basis	Fair Market Value
Cash	$1,000,000	$ 1,000,000
Accounts receivable and inventory	500,000	1,000,000
Land	500,000	6,000,000
Buildings and other § 1231 property	2,000,000	3,000,000
Goodwill	–0–	1,000,000
Total assets	$4,000,000	$12,000,000
Debt	$2,000,000	$ 2,000,000
Capital, Josh	300,000*	500,000
Capital, Kyle	400,000*	4,750,000
Capital, Maria	1,300,000*	4,750,000
Net assets	$4,000,000	$12,000,000

*The LLC members' capital accounts correspond to their bases, excluding their shares of the LLC's liabilities. The members' bases are not proportionate because the bases of the contributed properties were not proportionate. Also, over time, some LLC income was retained to provide operating cash flows, and some of the members have withdrawn more cash than others.

Capital is a "material income-producing factor" for Beachside Properties, LLC. Therefore, in this redemption scenario, the entire $9.5 million distribution from the LLC to Kyle and Maria is a § 736(b) payment for their interests in the partnership's property. Kyle and Maria will recognize a gain to the extent that this cash distribution (including forgiveness of their shares of the LLC's debt) exceeds their bases in the LLC interests.

Because Kyle and Maria receive cash in lieu of their shares of the LLC's unrealized receivables (including potential depreciation recapture) and inventory, this is a disproportionate distribution. They will recognize ordinary income to the extent that their gain relates to these receivables and inventory. The remaining gain will be a capital gain.

As there are no § 736(a) payments, the LLC cannot claim any deductions. Absent a § 754 election (discussed later), the basis of the LLC's property will not be affected.

Series of Payments

Frequently, the partnership and retiring partner agree that the buyout payment may be made over several years in specified installments. This minimizes the negative cash-flow impact on the partnership and allows the retiring partner to maximize the dollar amount of the buyout arrangement. In certain cases, such as where a retiring partner has been instrumental in developing a business relationship with specific clients, the parties can agree that the buyout payments will be determined by reference to the future income generated by those clients or by reference to overall partnership income, rather than being fixed in amount. If the partners deal

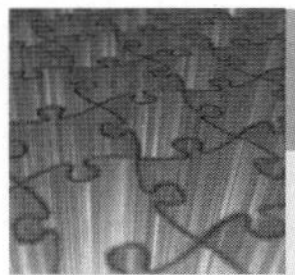

CONCEPT SUMMARY 11.3

Liquidating Distributions of Cash When the Partnership Continues

1. Payments made by an ongoing partnership to a liquidating partner are classified as § 736(a) income payments or as § 736(b) property payments.
2. Section 736(b) property payments are payments made for the liquidated partner's share of partnership assets.
3. If the partnership is a service provider and the partner is a general partner, payments made for the liquidated partner's share of certain unrealized receivables, certain goodwill that is not provided for in the partnership agreement, and certain annuity payments are classified as § 736(a) income payments.
4. Section 736(a) income payments are the payments mentioned in item 3 above and any other payments that are not classified as § 736(b) property payments.
5. To the extent the § 736(b) property payment is for the partner's share of partnership hot assets, the partner is deemed to have received and sold his or her share of such assets to the partnership. The partner reports ordinary income on this transaction, and the partnership will have a cost basis in the hot asset.
6. To the extent the § 736(b) property payments are classified as a payment for the partner's share of the partnership's "nonhot" assets, the payment is taxed as a return of the partner's outside basis. Any excess cash received over the partner's outside basis is taxed as capital gain.
7. Section 736(a) income payments are further classified as either guaranteed payments or distributive shares. Guaranteed payments are taxable as ordinary income to the partner and are deductible by the partnership. Distributive shares retain the same tax character to the partner as they had to the partnership. Distributive shares paid to the liquidated partner are excludible from the continuing partners' tax returns.

at arm's length and specifically agree to the §§ 736(a) and (b) allocation and timing of each class of payment, the agreement normally controls.[18] In the absence of an agreement classifying the payments under § 736, Regulations specify classification rules for each payment. In either situation, certain tax planning opportunities arise that are beyond the scope of this text.

Concept Summary 11.3 reviews the rules for liquidating distributions under § 736.

11.3 Sale of a Partnership Interest

LO.6

Calculate the selling partner's amount and character of gain or loss on the sale or exchange of a partnership interest.

A partner can sell or exchange a partnership interest, in whole or in part. The transaction can be between the partner and a third party; in this case, it is similar in concept to a sale of corporate stock. Or, as described in the last section, the transaction can be between the partner and the partnership, in which case it is similar in concept to a redemption of corporate stock by the entity. The transfer of a partnership interest produces different results from the transfer of corporate stock because both the entity and aggregate concepts apply to the partnership situation, whereas only the entity concept applies to a sale of stock. The effect of the different rules is that gain or loss resulting from a sale of a partnership interest may be divided into capital gain or loss and ordinary income or loss.

General Rules

Generally, the sale or exchange of a partnership interest results in gain or loss, measured by the difference between the amount realized and the selling partner's adjusted basis in the partnership interest.[19]

Liabilities

In computing the amount realized and the adjusted basis of the interest sold, the selling partner's share of partnership liabilities must be determined, as discussed in Chapter 10. The purchasing partner includes any assumed indebtedness as a part of the consideration paid for the partnership interest.[20]

[18] Reg. § 1.736–1(b)(5).
[19] § 741.
[20] § 742.

EXAMPLE 28

Cole originally contributed $50,000 in cash for a one-third interest in the CDE Partnership. During the time Cole was a partner, his share of partnership income was $90,000 and he withdrew $60,000 cash. Cole's capital account balance is now $80,000, and partnership liabilities are $45,000, of which Cole's share is $15,000. Cole's outside basis is $95,000 ($80,000 capital account + $15,000 share of partnership debts).

Cole sells his partnership interest to Stephanie for $110,000 cash, with Stephanie assuming Cole's share of partnership liabilities. The total amount realized by Cole is $125,000 ($110,000 cash received + $15,000 of partnership debts transferred to Stephanie). Cole's gain on the sale is $30,000 ($125,000 realized − adjusted basis of $95,000).

Stephanie's adjusted basis for her partnership interest is the purchase price of $125,000 ($110,000 cash paid + $15,000 assumed partnership debt). ■

Income Allocation

When a partner sells an entire interest in the partnership:

- Income for the partnership interest for the tax year is allocated between the buying partner and the selling partner, and
- The partnership's tax year "closes" with respect to the selling partner.

The closing of the tax year causes the selling partner to report the share of income on the sale date rather than at the end of the partnership's tax year.

The selling partner's basis is adjusted for the allocated income or loss before the partner calculates the gain or loss on the sale of the interest.

EXAMPLE 29

On September 30, 2012, Erica sells her 20% interest in the Evergreen Partnership to Jason for $25,000. Erica is a calendar year taxpayer. Evergreen owns no hot assets, and its tax year ends on June 30.

On July 1, 2012, Erica's basis in the partnership interest was $8,000. Her share of current partnership income is $10,000 for the period she owned the partnership interest (July 1 to September 30). Because the partnership's tax year closes with respect to Erica, she must report $10,000 of income on her 2012 tax return. Her basis in the partnership interest is increased to $18,000, and she recognizes a $7,000 capital gain on the sale.

Note that Erica will also report income from Evergreen's tax year ending on June 30, 2012, on her 2012 tax return. ■

There are several acceptable methods of determining the partner's share of income.[21] Under one method, the partnership merely prorates annual income and allocates an amount to the buying and selling partners based on the number of days (or months) in the partnership's tax year in which they were partners. Another method is called the *interim closing of the books* method. As the name implies, the partnership determines its actual income through the date the selling partner sold the interest and allocates a proportionate share of that income to the partner. If partnership earnings are seasonal, the two methods can produce vastly different results.

EXAMPLE 30

Trevor sold his 40% interest in the Owl Partnership to Megan on July 1 of the current tax year. Both Trevor and the partnership report on a calendar year basis. The partnership's income was $60,000 through June 30, and its income for the last half of the year was $2,000. Under the annual proration method, the partnership's income for the year is $62,000, of which 40%, or $24,800, is allocated to the 40% interest. Based on the number of months each was a partner, both Trevor and Megan report income of $12,400 for the current year.

Under the interim closing method, Trevor is allocated 40% of $60,000, or $24,000, and Megan is allocated 40% of $2,000, or $800 of partnership income. ■

[21] § 706(d)(1) and Regulations and 2009 Proposed Regulations thereunder.

If the partnership uses the cash method for certain items such as interest, taxes, rent, or other amounts that accrue over time, it must allocate these items to each day in the tax year over which they economically accrue and use the interim closing method for these items in determining the amount allocated to a selling partner.[22]

Tax Reporting

The partnership is not required to issue a Schedule K–1 to the selling partner until the normal filing of its tax return. The partner, though, is required to include the share of partnership income as of the sale date. Consequently, the partner may have to obtain an extension for filing his or her personal return until the partnership provides a Schedule K–1. If the partnership uses an IRS-approved fiscal year and the partner uses a calendar year, income bunching may occur, as described in Example 29.

Partners who sell or exchange a partnership interest must promptly notify the partnership of the transfers. After notification is received, the partnership may be required to file an information statement with the IRS for the calendar year in which the transfers took place. The statement lists the names and addresses of the transferors and transferees. The partnership provides all parties with a copy of the statement.

Effect of Hot Assets

A major exception to capital gain or loss treatment on the sale or exchange of a partnership interest arises when a partnership has hot assets. As noted previously, *hot assets* are *unrealized receivables* and *inventory*, assets that, when collected or disposed of by the partnership, would cause it to recognize ordinary income or loss. When a partner sells the interest in a partnership, it is as if the partnership had sold its hot assets and allocated to the selling partner the partner's proportionate share of the ordinary income or loss created by the sale. The primary purpose of this rule is to prevent a partner from converting ordinary income into capital gain through the sale of a partnership interest.[23]

Unrealized Receivables

The term *unrealized receivables* generally has the same meaning as in the earlier discussion of disproportionate distributions. As previously noted, unrealized receivables include the accounts receivable of a cash basis partnership and, for sale or exchange purposes, depreciation recapture potential.[24]

EXAMPLE 31

The cash basis Thrush Partnership owns only a $10,000 receivable for rendering health care advice. Its basis in the receivable is zero because no income has been recognized. This item is a hot asset because ordinary income is not generated until Thrush collects on the account.

Jacob, a 50% partner, sells his interest to Mark for $5,000. If Jacob's basis in his partnership interest is $0, his total gain is $5,000. The entire gain is attributable to Jacob's share of the unrealized receivable, so his gain is taxed as ordinary income. ■

Depreciation recapture represents ordinary income the partnership would recognize if it sold depreciable property. Under the aggregate theory, the selling partner's share of depreciation recapture potential is treated as an unrealized receivable and is taxed to the selling partner as ordinary income, rather than capital gain. (Recall that depreciation recapture is *not* treated as an unrealized receivable for § 736 purposes, discussed previously.)

[22] § 706(d)(2).
[23] § 751(a).
[24] § 751(a)(1).

EXAMPLE 32

Andrew sells his 40% interest in the accrual basis Wren Partnership. The partnership has a depreciable business asset that it originally purchased for $25,000. The asset now has an adjusted basis of $15,000 and a market value of $30,000. Depreciation recapture potential is $10,000 ($25,000 − $15,000). In this case, Wren holds a $10,000 unrealized receivable with a zero basis and a $20,000 ($30,000 − $10,000) nonhot asset with an adjusted basis of $15,000. If Wren sold the asset for $30,000, it would recognize $10,000 of ordinary income and $5,000 of § 1231 gain. Therefore, Andrew recognizes $4,000 ($10,000 × 40%) of ordinary income when he sells his partnership interest. ■

The effect of the hot asset rule is that a partner selling an interest in a partnership with hot assets must usually recognize both ordinary income (loss) and capital gain (loss).

EXAMPLE 33

Ahmad sells his interest in the equal ABC Partnership to Dave for $17,000 cash. On the sale date, the partnership's cash basis balance sheet reflects the following:

	Basis	FMV		Basis	FMV
Cash	$10,000	$10,000	Liabilities	$ 9,000	$ 9,000
Accounts receivable (for services)	–0–	30,000	Capital accounts		
Nonhot assets	14,000	20,000	Ahmad	5,000	17,000
			Beth	5,000	17,000
			Chris	5,000	17,000
Total	$24,000	$60,000	Total	$24,000	$60,000

The total amount realized by Ahmad is $20,000 ($17,000 cash price + $3,000 of debt assumed by Dave). Because Ahmad's basis for his partnership interest is $8,000 ($5,000 capital account + $3,000 debt share), the total gain recognized on the sale is $12,000 ($20,000 − $8,000).

Because the partnership has an unrealized receivable, the hot asset rule applies. If ABC sold the accounts receivable for $30,000, Ahmad's proportionate share of the ordinary income recognized on this sale would be $10,000 ($30,000 × 1/3). Consequently, $10,000 of the $12,000 recognized gain on the sale relates to Ahmad's interest in the unrealized receivables and is taxed to him as ordinary income. The remaining gain of $2,000 is taxed to him as a capital gain.

Note that under the hot asset rule, Ahmad still reports $12,000 of income or gain; the hot asset rule merely reclassifies part of the gain as ordinary income. The effect of the rule is that the partnership's inherent ordinary income is allocated to the partner who earned it. ■

EXAMPLE 34

Assume the same facts as in Example 33, except that Ahmad's basis in his partnership interest is $10,000. Under these circumstances, Ahmad's capital gain or loss is zero. Ahmad still has $10,000 of ordinary income because of the unrealized receivables.

If Ahmad's basis in the partnership interest is $11,000 (instead of $10,000), an unusual result occurs. Ahmad has a $9,000 overall gain ($20,000 amount realized − $11,000 basis). The receivables generate $10,000 of ordinary income, and Ahmad recognizes a capital *loss* of $1,000 on the rest of the sale. ■

Inventory

For a sale or exchange of a partnership interest, the term *inventory* includes all partnership property except money, capital assets, and § 1231 assets. Receivables of an accrual basis partnership are included in the definition of inventory, as they are neither capital assets nor § 1231 assets.[25] This definition also is broad enough to include all items considered to be unrealized receivables.

[25] § 751(d).

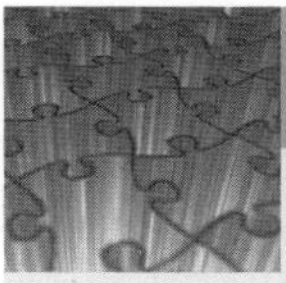

CONCEPT SUMMARY 11.4

Sale of a Partnership Interest

1. A partnership interest is a capital asset and generally results in capital gain or loss on disposal.
2. The outside bases of the selling and buying partners, as well as the pertinent selling price and purchase price, include an appropriate share of partnership debt.
3. Partnership income or loss for the interest is allocated between the selling and buying partners. The selling partner's basis is adjusted before the gain or loss on the sale is calculated.
4. The partnership's tax year closes with respect to the selling partner on the sale date; the seller reports partnership income at that time, and income "bunching" may occur.
5. When hot assets are present, the selling partner's overall gain or loss is reclassified into a capital gain or loss portion and an ordinary income or loss amount related to the partnership's underlying hot assets.
6. Hot assets consist of unrealized receivables and inventory.
7. Unrealized receivables include amounts earned by a cash basis taxpayer from services rendered. They also include depreciation recapture potential that would result if an asset were sold at a gain.
8. Inventory includes all partnership property except cash, capital assets, and § 1231 assets. Inventory also includes unrealized receivables.

EXAMPLE 35

Jan sells her one-third interest in the JKL Partnership to Matt for $20,000 cash. On the sale date, the partnership balance sheet reflects the following:

	Basis	FMV		Basis	FMV
Cash	$10,000	$10,000	Jan, capital	$15,000	$20,000
Inventory	21,000	30,000	Kelly, capital	15,000	20,000
Capital assets	14,000	20,000	Luis, capital	15,000	20,000
Total	$45,000	$60,000	Total	$45,000	$60,000

The overall gain on the sale is $5,000 ($20,000 − $15,000). Jan's share of the appreciation in the inventory is $3,000 [($30,000 − $21,000) × 1/3]. Therefore, she recognizes $3,000 of ordinary income because of the inventory and $2,000 of capital gain from the rest of the sale. ■

THE BIG PICTURE

EXAMPLE 36

Return to the facts of *The Big Picture* on p. 11-1. Recall that the second restructuring option for Beachside Properties, LLC, is for Kyle and Maria to sell their interests directly to the new members of the LLC. The new members will pay $4.75 million each to Kyle and Maria in exchange for their interests in the LLC. The new members will then contribute $10 million of cash to Beachside Properties for the expansion.

Refer back to the balance sheet in Example 27. Kyle and Maria will receive cash of $9.5 million (total) plus relief of their shares of the LLC's debt. Their bases in the LLC interests equal their capital account balances plus their shares of the LLC's liabilities. The difference must be recognized as a gain.

The gain is ordinary income to the extent that it relates to Kyle's and Maria's shares of the LLC's accounts receivable, inventory, and depreciation recapture. The remaining gain is a capital gain. Absent a § 754 election (discussed later), the basis of the LLC's property will not be affected.

Concept Summary 11.4 enumerates the rules that apply to sales of partnership interests.

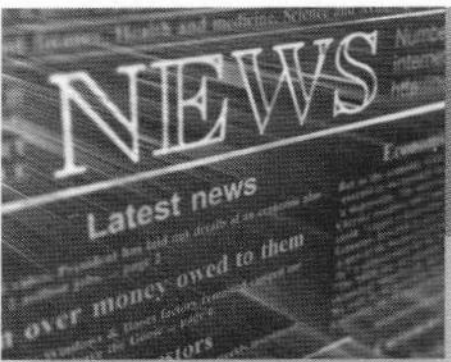

TAX IN THE NEWS Simplifying Partnership Taxation—A Losing Battle?

Partnership taxation has become increasingly complex. The tax treatment of a distribution differs depending on the type of property involved, whether it is appreciated, to whom it is distributed, and how it was originally acquired by the partnership. The "look through" provisions on sale of a partnership interest require the assets to be segregated not only into ordinary or capital gains and losses but also by the various types of capital gains (i.e., collectible gains, unrecaptured § 1250 gains, etc.). Liability-sharing rules vary depending on what type of liability it is, what type of partner (general or limited) it is, and when the liability was created. And the "substantial economic effect" rules include numerous pages of regulations on when and how to allocate income and loss among the partners.

The U.S. Treasury Department and other parties have called for simplification of the rules. For example, several proposals have been presented to repeal or simplify the "hot asset" provisions of § 751. Yet so far, none of these changes have materialized, and some of the IRS's planned Regulation projects will add even more complexity to this already challenging area.

Source: 2010–2011 Priority Guidance Plan, Department of the Treasury (Year-End Update, September 2, 2011).

11.4 Other Dispositions of Partnership Interests

LO.7

Describe tax issues related to other dispositions of partnership interests.

Partnership interests may be reduced or terminated, and partnerships liquidated, in a variety of other ways, including the following:

- Transfer of the interest to a corporation when the partners control the corporation after the transfer.
- Transfer of the interest to a corporation when the partners *do not* control the corporation after the transfer.
- Like-kind exchanges.
- Death of a partner.
- Gifts.

Transfers to a Corporation

Transfers of a partnership interest to a corporation may take place when one or all partners are ready to retire from the business; they may exchange the partnership interest for stock in an existing corporation and cease to be involved in the day-to-day operations of the business. Alternatively, many partnerships incorporate simply to obtain the protection from liability or other advantages of the corporate form and make no real changes in business operations. Incorporation may occur at a time when the business is expanding and wants to obtain equity capital from issuing shares to outsiders. The corporate form may also provide tax advantages for a successful business that prefers to retain some earnings for internal expansion without having them taxed at the high individual tax rates of the owners.

Recall from Chapter 4 the controlled corporation rules of § 351. These rules provide that gain or loss is not recognized on the transfer of property to a corporation solely in exchange for stock in that corporation if, immediately after the exchange, the stockholders are in control of the corporation.

In many cases, including most of those in which an existing partnership is incorporated and continues to operate, § 351 conditions are met, and the transfer of the partnership interest to the corporation is a nontaxable exchange. If the partners transferring the property do not satisfy the 80 percent control requirements of § 351, they recognize gain or loss on the transfer according to standard rules for sales or exchanges.

If the partnership interest transferred represents 50 percent or more of the total interest in capital or profits, the partnership is terminated. Partnership termination is discussed later in the chapter.

Incorporation Methods

Consider the situation where the partners decide to incorporate an existing partnership by creating a new corporation owned entirely by the partners. At least three alternative methods are available for structuring the incorporation transaction:

- Each partner's interest is transferred to the corporation in exchange for stock under the usual § 351 rules. As a result, the partnership terminates, and the corporation owns all partnership assets and liabilities. The corporation takes a substituted basis for the assets, and the old partners have a substituted basis for the stock.
- The partnership transfers all of its assets to the corporation in exchange for stock and the assumption of partnership liabilities. The stock then is distributed to the partners (generally in a liquidating distribution) in proportion to their partnership interests. The corporation takes a carryover basis for the assets, and the old partners have a substituted basis for the stock.
- The partnership makes a pro rata distribution of all of its assets and liabilities to its partners in complete liquidation. The partners then transfer their undivided interests in the assets and liabilities to the corporation in exchange for stock under § 351. The corporation's basis for the assets is the substituted basis of those assets to the partners. The partners have a substituted basis for the stock.

Assuming that existing partnership debt does not exceed the basis of transferred assets, none of the three incorporation methods generates a recognized gain or loss. They may, however, result in different inside and outside basis amounts. Thus, selecting the appropriate incorporation method is crucial.

Like-Kind Exchanges

The nontaxable like-kind exchange rules do not apply to the exchange of interests in different partnerships.[26] These exchanges are fully taxable under the sale or exchange rules discussed previously. However, an exchange of interests in the same partnership is generally a nontaxable event.[27]

Death of a Partner

If a partner dies, the taxable year of the partnership closes with respect to that partner on the date of death.[28] The deceased partner's share of partnership income or loss is computed to that date and is reported on the partner's final Form 1040.

In professional partnerships, local law may prohibit an estate or other successor from continuing as a partner (beyond a certain time period). Ideally, these entities will have a buy-sell agreement in place that spells out the terms under which the remaining partners can buy out or liquidate the deceased partner's interest in the partnership. The previously discussed rules pertaining to sales and liquidations of partnership interests apply to these transactions.

Gifts

Generally, the donor of a partnership interest recognizes neither gain nor loss. If the donor's entire interest is transferred, all items of partnership income, loss, deduction, or credit attributable to the interest are prorated between the donor and donee.

---

[26] § 1031(a)(2)(D).

[27] Rev.Rul. 84–52, 1984–1 C.B. 157.

[28] § 706(c)(2)(A).

The taxable year of the partnership does not close with respect to the donor, however, so the donor reports his or her share of partnership income or loss at the end of the partnership's tax year.

As the following "Ethics & Equity" feature indicates, the gift of an interest in a partnership owning unrealized receivables can be problematic.

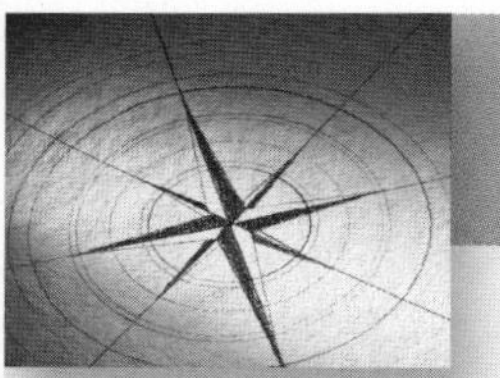

ETHICS & EQUITY Assignment of Income

Mark is a partner in a cash basis partnership that specializes in personal injury matters. Cases are accepted on a contingent fee basis. If the client wins, the firm gets 30 percent of the recovery. If the client loses, no fee results. Just before a large judgment is awarded, Mark gives half of his partnership interest to his son, an attorney. The son recognizes as income the portion of the award attributable to the partnership interest he received as a gift. What is Mark trying to accomplish? Will it work?

11.5 Optional Adjustments to Property Basis

LO.8

Calculate the optional adjustments to basis under § 754.

When a partner purchases a partnership interest, the purchase price reflects what the acquiring partner believes the interest in the partnership is worth. This price reflects, to a large extent, the value the partner places on the partnership's assets. Because the value of the assets probably differs from their inside bases, a discrepancy exists between the purchasing partner's outside basis and that partner's share of the inside basis of partnership assets.

If the partnership makes an **optional adjustment election** or **§ 754 election**, the inside basis of the partnership property can be adjusted to reflect the purchase price paid by the partner. If the election is not made, the statute produces some inequitable results.

EXAMPLE 37

A partnership owns a building with an adjusted basis of $450,000 and a fair market value of $900,000. George buys a one-third interest in the partnership for $300,000 (an amount equal to one-third of the value of the building). The partnership does not make an election under § 754. Although the price George paid for the interest was based on fair market value, the building's depreciation continues to be determined on the partnership's adjusted basis of $450,000, of which George's share is only $150,000. ■

EXAMPLE 38

In contrast, assume that the building in Example 37 had an adjusted basis of $300,000 and a fair market value of $150,000. Assume also that George purchased the one-third interest for $50,000 (an amount equal to one-third of the value of the building). Although the purchase price was based on fair market value, George obtains the benefit of *double* depreciation deductions because these deductions are calculated on the adjusted basis of the depreciable property ($300,000), which is twice the property's market value. ■

A result similar to that in Example 37 can take place when a partnership purchases a retiring partner's interest with a cash payment that is greater than that partner's outside basis for the partnership interest. Without a § 754 election, the partnership cannot increase the adjusted basis of its assets for the excess cash paid to the retiring partner.[29]

The partnership can make an optional adjustment-to-basis election for any year in which a transfer or distribution occurs by attaching a statement to a timely filed

[29] §§ 743(a) and 734(a), respectively.

partnership return (including extensions).[30] An election is binding for the year for which it is made and for all subsequent years, unless the IRS consents to its revocation. Permission to revoke is granted for business reasons, such as a substantial change in the nature of the business or a significant increase in the frequency of interest transfers. Permission is not granted if it appears the primary purpose is to avoid downward adjustments to basis otherwise required under the election.

In one type of situation, a basis adjustment must generally be made even if the partnership has not made a § 754 election. A basis adjustment is generally *required* if a sale or distribution occurs and the partnership has a substantial built-in loss. A substantial built-in loss exists when the partnership's adjusted basis for all partnership property exceeds the fair market value of the property by more than $250,000. If in Example 38, the fair market value of partnership property had been less than $50,000, a basis adjustment would have been required.

Adjustment: Sale or Exchange of an Interest

If the § 754 optional adjustment-to-basis election is in effect and a partner's interest is sold to or exchanged with a third party or a partner dies, the partnership adjusts the basis of its assets as illustrated in the following calculation:[31]

Transferee's outside basis in the partnership	$xxx
Less: Transferee's share of the inside basis of all partnership property	(xxx)
Adjustment	$xxx

If the amount calculated is positive, the partnership increases the adjusted basis of its assets. If the amount is negative, the basis of the assets is decreased. In either case, the adjustment affects the basis of partnership property with respect to the transferee partner only. When a portion of the optional adjustment results in a step-up of depreciable property, the step-up amount is depreciated as if it were a newly acquired asset. The transferee partner, therefore, shares in the depreciation taken by the partnership on the original asset and, in addition, reports all of the depreciation taken on the step-up basis created by the optional adjustment.

The partner's basis in each property item for which an optional adjustment has been made equals the partner's share of the inside basis for the property item plus or minus the partner's optional basis adjustment that is allocated to that property.

EXAMPLE 39

Keith is a member of the KLM Partnership, and all partners have equal interests in capital and profits. The partnership has made an optional adjustment-to-basis election. Keith's interest is sold to Sean for $76,000. The balance sheet of the partnership immediately before the sale shows the following:

	Basis	FMV		Basis	FMV
Cash	$ 15,000	$ 15,000	Capital accounts		
Depreciable assets	150,000	213,000	Keith	$ 55,000	$ 76,000
			Leah	55,000	76,000
			Morgan	55,000	76,000
Total	$165,000	$228,000	Total	$165,000	$228,000

The adjustment is the difference between the basis of Sean's interest in the partnership and his share of the adjusted basis of partnership property. The basis of Sean's interest is his purchase price, or $76,000. His one-third share of the adjusted basis of partnership property is $55,000 ($165,000 × 1/3). The optional adjustment that is added to the basis of partnership property is $21,000.

[30] § 754.

[31] § 743(b).

Transferee's outside basis in partnership	$ 76,000
Less: Transferee's share of inside basis of all partnership property	(55,000)
Adjustment	$ 21,000

The $21,000 basis increase is treated as a new depreciable asset. Depreciation on this asset is allocated to Sean. If the partnership later sells all of the underlying assets, Sean's share of the gain takes into account the remaining (undepreciated) balance of the $21,000 step-up. ■

Adjustment: Partnership Distributions

Optional adjustments to basis are also available to the partnership when property is distributed to a partner. If a § 754 optional adjustment-to-basis election is in effect, the basis of partnership property is *increased* by the following:[32]

- Any gain recognized by a distributee partner.
- The excess of the partnership's adjusted basis for any distributed property over the adjusted basis of that property in the hands of the distributee partner.

Conversely, the basis of partnership property is *decreased* by the following:

- Any loss recognized by a distributee partner.
- In the case of a liquidating distribution, the excess of the distributee partner's adjusted basis of any distributed property over the basis of that property to the partnership.

EXAMPLE 40

Ryan has a basis of $50,000 in his partnership interest and receives a building with an adjusted basis to the partnership of $120,000 in termination of his interest. (The partnership has no hot assets.) The building's basis in Ryan's hands is $50,000 under the proportionate liquidating distribution rules. If an optional adjustment-to-basis election is in effect, the partnership increases the basis of its remaining property by $70,000.

Partnership's adjusted basis in distributed property	$120,000
Less: Distributee's basis in distributed property	(50,000)
Increase	$ 70,000

■

EXAMPLE 41

Assume the same facts as in Example 40, except that the partnership's basis in the building was $40,000. Ryan's basis in the building is still $50,000, and the partnership reduces the basis of its remaining property by $10,000.

Distributee's basis in distributed property	$ 50,000
Less: Partnership's adjusted basis in distributed property	(40,000)
Decrease	$ 10,000

■

Although these rules may seem confusing at first reading, understanding the theory on which they are based helps to clarify the situation. Section 734(b) assumes that the inside basis for all partnership assets equals the outside basis for all of the partners' interests immediately before the distribution. When this equality exists both before and after a distribution, no adjustment to the basis of partnership property is necessary. However, when the equality does not exist after the distribution, an adjustment can bring the inside and outside bases back into equality. This is the adjustment that is made by the two increases and the two decreases described in the bulleted lists above.

EXAMPLE 42

Assume that the Cardinal Partnership has an inside basis of $12,000 for its assets, which have a fair market value of $15,000. Aaron, Bill, and Chelsea each have outside bases of $4,000 for their partnership interests. If the partnership liquidates partner Aaron's

[32] § 734(b).

interest with a $5,000 cash distribution, the resulting balance sheet is unbalanced as follows:

	Inside (Assets)		Outside (Capital)
Before	$12,000	=	$12,000
Distribution	(5,000)	≠	(4,000)
After	$ 7,000	≠	$ 8,000

This unbalanced situation can be eliminated by adding $1,000 to the inside basis of the formula. Note that this is the same amount as the gain that Aaron recognizes on the distribution ($5,000 cash − $4,000 outside basis = $1,000 gain). Therefore, by adding the amount of Aaron's gain to the inside basis of the partnership assets, the inside basis = outside basis formula is back in balance.

Inside (Assets)		Outside (Capital)
$7,000	≠	$8,000
+1,000		
$8,000	=	$8,000

Note that if the partnership liquidates Aaron's interest with a distribution of land having a $5,000 inside basis, the same unbalanced situation occurs. Although this transaction does not create any recognized gain for Aaron, the $1,000 optional adjustment is the excess of the $5,000 inside basis of the distributed property over the $4,000 substituted basis of that property to Aaron. ■

The two optional adjustment decreases are also explained by this type of analysis.

The basis adjustments created by distributions affect the bases of all remaining partnership properties. Therefore, any depreciation deductions taken on such basis adjustments are allocated to all partners remaining in the partnership after the distribution. The *partnership* also takes these basis adjustments into account in determining any gains or losses on subsequent sales of partnership properties.

THE BIG PICTURE

EXAMPLE 43

Return to the facts of *The Big Picture* on p. 11-1. Recall that the members of Beachside Properties, LLC, are considering two restructuring options. For either option, Beachside Properties could make a § 754 election and reflect an adjustment to the basis of the LLC's property.

- *Step-up related to sale of interests.* On a sale of the interests to the new LLC members, the step-up would equal the difference between the $9.5 million paid and Kyle's and Maria's share of the inside basis of the LLC's property. This step-up of approximately $7.6 million [$9.5 million − (95% × $2 million net assets)] would be allocated to the various partnership properties under the rules of § 755 (not discussed in this chapter). Deductions related to the step-up, such as depreciation, would be allocated to the new developer group.
- *Step-up related to distribution in liquidation of the partners' interests.* If the LLC redeems the interests of Kyle and Maria, the LLC can step up the bases of its remaining assets by the amount of gain recognized by Kyle and Maria. This step-up is approximately $7.8 million [$9.5 million distribution − $1.7 million total basis in partnership interests (Kyle's basis of $400,000 + Maria's basis of $1.3 million)] and benefits all of the remaining partners in the partnership.

Note that the step-up differs depending on whether there is a sale or redemption, because Kyle's and Maria's share of the basis of the assets differs from their basis in the LLC interests.

11.6 Termination of a Partnership

LO.9

Outline the methods of terminating a partnership.

When does a partnership's final tax year end? Technically, it ends when the partnership terminates, which occurs on either of the following events:

- No part of the business continues to be carried on by any of the partners in a partnership.
- Within a 12-month period, there is a sale or exchange of 50 percent or more of the partnership's capital and profits.[33]

The partnership terminates and its tax year closes when the partnership incorporates or when one partner in a two-party partnership buys out the other partner, thereby creating a sole proprietorship. A termination also occurs when the partnership ceases operations and liquidates.

The partnership taxable year usually does not close upon the death of a partner or upon the liquidation of a partner's interest, unless the liquidation of the interest of one partner in a two-partner partnership effectively terminates the partnership on the liquidation date. However, the partnership year will close in respect to the deceased or liquidated partner.[34] The deceased or liquidated partner's share of partnership income or loss is computed to the date of death or liquidation and reported on the partner's tax return for the year in which the death or liquidation occurs.

The partnership year does not close upon the entry of a new partner to the partnership. It also does not close upon the sale or exchange of an existing partnership interest unless the transaction results in 50 percent or more of the interests in the partnership capital and profits being sold within a 12-month period.

EXAMPLE 44

Partner Olaf, who held a one-third interest in the NOP Partnership, died on November 20, 2012. The partnership uses an approved fiscal year ending September 30, while Olaf used a calendar year. The executor of Olaf's estate chose an October 31 year-end for the estate.

The partnership's tax year does not close with Olaf's death; it does close, however, with respect to Olaf. Olaf's final income tax return includes his share of income from the partnership's fiscal year ending September 30, 2012, as well as income allocated to Olaf for the period from October 1, 2012, to November 20, 2012. Olaf's estate or successor in interest reports Olaf's share of income from November 21, 2012, through September 30, 2013.

■

A **technical termination of a partnership** occurs when the partnership business operations continue but the partnership terminates because there has been a sale or exchange of the requisite 50 percent capital and profits interests within 12 months. If the same interest (less than 50 percent) is sold more than once, only one sale is considered in determining whether more than 50 percent has been sold within 12 months. The terminated partnership is deemed to liquidate by transferring its assets and liabilities to a newly formed partnership, which continues its

[33] § 708(b)(1).

[34] § 706(c)(2)(A).

business operations.[35] A technical termination may have numerous consequences, such as creating a different taxable year for the new partnership or modifying the cost recovery methods to be used by the new partnership.

THE BIG PICTURE

EXAMPLE 45

Return to the facts of *The Big Picture* on p. 11-1. Before the sale or redemption, Kyle's and Maria's combined interests equal 95% of the LLC's capital and 80% of the LLC's profits interests. If they both sell their interests within a 12-month period, they will cause a technical termination of the existing LLC and a new LLC will be deemed to be formed. Although not a devastating result, it must be dealt with by redetermining the LLC's basis in its assets and reestablishing the (new) LLC as an entity. (Note: The partners could structure the sale so that the termination did not occur, for example, by having Kyle and Maria sell less than a 50% interest in the LLC in one year and the remaining interest more than 12 months later.)

If the LLC redeems the interests under § 736 (as described in Example 27), there is no sale or exchange transaction and no technical termination of the LLC.

11.7 Other Issues

LO.10

Identify the special considerations of a family partnership.

Partnership rules also generally apply to family partnerships, limited liability companies, and limited liability partnerships. This section examines the special considerations applicable to these entities.

Family Partnerships

Family partnerships are owned and controlled primarily by members of the same family. Such partnerships may be established for a variety of reasons. A daughter may have a particular expertise that, coupled with her parents' abilities, allows them to establish a successful business. Often, however, one primary reason for establishing a family partnership is the desire to save taxes. If the parents are in higher marginal tax brackets than the children, family tax dollars are saved by allocating some of the partnership income to the children.

Valid family partnerships are difficult to establish for tax purposes. A basic tenet of tax law is that income must be taxed to the person who performs the services or owns the capital that generates the income. A parent, therefore, cannot transfer only a profits interest to a child and expect the transfer to be recognized for tax purposes.

Capital versus Services

Because of the concern that family partnerships are established primarily for tax avoidance purposes, a family member is recognized as a partner only in the following cases:

- Capital is a material income-producing factor in the partnership, and the family member's capital interest is acquired in a bona fide transaction (even if by gift or purchase from another family member) in which ownership and control are received.
- Capital is not a material income-producing factor, but the family member contributes substantial or vital services.[36]

If a partnership derives a substantial portion of its gross income from the use of capital, such as inventories or investments in plant, machinery, or equipment, the capital is considered to be a material income-producing factor. Ordinarily, capital

[35] Reg. § 1.708–1(b).

[36] § 704(e).

is not a material income-producing factor if the partnership's income consists principally of fees, commissions, or other compensation for personal services performed by partners or employees.

Children as Partners

When capital is a material income-producing factor and a partnership interest is transferred by gift or sale to a child who is under age 19 (or a student under age 24), the kiddie tax may apply. Under the kiddie tax, some of the dependent child's distributive share of partnership income may be taxed at the parent's tax rate, unless the income share constitutes earned income. Regardless of age, if the child provides bona fide services to a partnership and the income share constitutes earned income, the parent-partner's tax rate is avoided.

EXAMPLE 46

Karen operates a first-floor-window-washing business in a summer lakeside resort city. Relatively small amounts of capital are required to operate the sole proprietorship (buckets, sponges, squeegees, etc.). During the summer, Karen normally hires middle and high school students to wash windows. Her 17-year-old daughter and 15-year-old son want to work in the business during the summer to earn money for spending and for college. Each obtains the necessary summer work permit. Karen creates the KDS Partnership and gives each child a 5% interest.

Karen figures that if her children were paid an hourly rate, about 5% of KDS's profits would be distributed to them as wages. Karen believes that an ownership interest will help the children learn what running a profitable business entails and prepare them for an active business life after their education is completed.

Because capital is not a material income-producing factor in the business and the children's profit percentages approximate what they would earn if they were paid an hourly rate, all of the income is classified as earned income. Thus, the kiddie tax is avoided. ■

Gift of Capital Interest

If a family member acquires a capital interest by gift in a family partnership in which capital is a material income-producing factor, only part of the income may be allocated to this interest. First, the donor of the interest is allocated an amount of partnership income that represents reasonable compensation for services to the partnership. Then, the remaining income is divided among the partners in accordance with their capital interests in the partnership. An interest purchased by one family member from another is considered to be created by gift for this purpose.[37]

EXAMPLE 47

A partnership in which a parent transferred a 50% interest by gift to a child generated a profit of $90,000. Capital is a material income-producing factor. The parent performed services valued at $20,000. The child performed no services. Under these circumstances, $20,000 is allocated to the parent as compensation. Of the remaining $70,000 of income attributable to capital, at least 50%, or $35,000, is allocated to the parent. ■

LO.11

Describe the application of partnership provisions to limited liability companies (LLCs) and limited liability partnerships (LLPs).

Limited Liability Companies

Owners of small businesses often want to combine the limited liability of a corporation with the pass-through provisions of a partnership. S corporations, described in Chapter 12, provide some of these advantages. The limited liability company is a form of entity that goes further in combining partnership taxation with limited personal liability for all owners of the entity.

[37] § 704(e)(3).

Taxation of LLCs

A properly structured LLC with two or more owners is generally taxed as a partnership. Because none of the LLC members are personally liable for any debts of the entity, the LLC is effectively treated as a limited partnership with no general partners. As described in Chapter 10, this results in unusual application of partnership taxation rules in areas such as allocation of liabilities to the LLC members, inclusion or exclusion of debt for at-risk purposes, passive or active status of a member for passive loss purposes, and determination of a member's liability for self-employment tax.

Converting to an LLC

A partnership can convert to an LLC with few, if any, tax ramifications: the old elections of the partnership continue, and the partners retain their bases and ownership interests in the new entity. However, a C or S corporation that reorganizes as an LLC is treated as having liquidated prior to forming the new entity. The transaction is taxable to both the corporation and the shareholders. See the "Tax in the News" feature on the next page for considerations related to converting a C or S corporation to partnership or LLC status.

Advantages of an LLC

An LLC offers certain advantages over a limited partnership, including the following:

- Generally, none of the owners of an LLC are personally liable for the entity's debts. General partners in a limited partnership have personal liability for partnership recourse debts.
- Limited partners cannot participate in the management of the partnership. All owners of an LLC have the legal right to participate in the entity's management.

The advantages of an LLC over an S corporation are discussed in Chapter 13.

Disadvantages of an LLC

The disadvantages of an LLC stem primarily from the entity's relative newness. There is only a limited body of case law interpreting the various state statutes, so the application of some provisions is uncertain. An additional uncertainty for LLCs that operate in more than one jurisdiction is which state's law will prevail and how it will be applied.

Among other factors, statutes differ from state to state as to the type of business an LLC can conduct—particularly as to the extent to which certain service-providing firms can operate as LLCs. A service entity may find that it can operate as an LLC in one state but not in another.

Limited Liability Partnerships

Although the name is similar, a limited liability partnership (LLP) is quite different from a limited partnership. All states permit LLPs to be formed. Also, as described in Chapter 10, about 20 states have adopted legislation authorizing a variation known as a limited liability limited partnership (LLLP). The difference between a general partnership and an LLP is small, but very significant. Recall that general partners are jointly and severally liable for all partnership debts. In some states, partners in a registered LLP are jointly and severally liable for contractual liability (i.e., they are treated as general partners for commercial debt). They are also always personally liable for their own malpractice or other torts. They are not, however, personally liable for the malpractice and torts of their partners. As a result, the exposure of their personal assets to lawsuits filed against other partners and the partnership is considerably reduced.

An LLP must have formal documents of organization and register with the state. Because the LLP is a general partnership in other respects, it does not have to pay

TAX IN THE NEWS Converting a C or S Corporation to a Partnership Entity

Shareholders may decide to convert their existing C or S corporation to a partnership for various reasons (e.g., to avoid double taxation or to pass through losses). Unfortunately, this process is not as tax neutral as the incorporation of a partnership. In general, the conversion is treated as a liquidation of the corporate entity and the formation of a partnership.

Recall from earlier chapters that the liquidation of a corporation (C or S) is a taxable event (§§ 331 and 336). The assets are distributed from the corporation, and this triggers gain at the entity level (and a corporate-level tax if the entity is a C corporation). The gain is the difference between the basis and the fair market value of the distributed assets.

The tax resulting from a conversion, however, is less burdensome when the economy is depressed and asset values are low (corporate-level gain is minimized or possibly eliminated). Also beneficial are the current relatively low tax rates—capital gains are generally taxed to individuals at only a 15 percent maximum tax rate. Thus, taxpayers may be able to take advantage of difficult economic times and lower tax rates by converting a double-taxed corporate entity to a more tax-efficient LLC or LLP.

any state franchise taxes on its operations—an important difference between LLPs and LLCs in states that impose franchise taxes on LLCs. LLPs are taxed as partnerships under Federal tax statutes.

The conversion of a general partnership into a registered LLP is a continuation of the old partnership for tax purposes if all of the general partners become LLP partners and hold the same proportionate interests in the LLP that they held in the general partnership. This means that all of the old partnership's elections continue in the LLP, including accounting methods, the taxable year-end, and the § 754 election.

Anti-Abuse Regulations

The IRS has issued Regulations that allow it to disregard the form of a partnership transaction when it believes that the transaction (or series of transactions) is abusive.[38] Under the Regulation, a transaction is abusive if it satisfies two tests. First, it must have a principal purpose of substantially reducing the present value of the partners' aggregate Federal tax liability. In addition, the potential tax reduction must be inconsistent with the intent of Subchapter K. If the IRS disregards the form of a transaction, it will recast the transaction in a manner that reflects the transaction's underlying economic arrangement.

It is often difficult to determine whether a proposed transaction will substantially reduce the present value of the partners' aggregate tax liability. Partners may not know their personal tax situations until the transaction occurs and the partner's tax return is completed. Practitioners are concerned that the IRS could try to use "perfect hindsight" to determine if a transaction should be recast. This could make it difficult to anticipate the ultimate tax treatment of many partnership transactions.

The IRS says that it will not recast transactions that are bona fide business arrangements and offers several examples in the Regulation. The IRS has also announced that a field examiner cannot invoke the Regulation without approval. Review by a partnership specialty group within the IRS is required before the IRS will challenge a taxpayer's treatment of a transaction under this Regulation.

[38]Reg. § 1.701–2.

11.8 Tax Planning

LO.12

List and evaluate various tax planning considerations related to partnership distributions and sales of partnership interests.

Planning Partnership Distributions

In planning for any partnership distributions, be alert to the following possibilities:

- When gain recognition is undesirable, ascertain that cash distributions from a partnership, including any debt assumptions or repayments, do not exceed the basis of the receiving partner's interest.
- Distributions of marketable securities may also result in gain, but the current gain can be minimized if the securities *are* appreciated.
- When a partner is to receive a liquidating distribution and the full basis of the interest will not be recovered, the partner's capital loss can be ensured by providing that the only assets received by the partner are cash, unrealized receivables, and inventory. If a capital loss is undesirable, however, the partnership should also distribute a capital or § 1231 asset that will take the partner's remaining basis in the interest. This may result in a more desirable ordinary deduction or loss in the future.
- Current and liquidating distributions may result in ordinary income recognition for either the receiving partner or the partnership if hot assets are present. When such income is undesirable, consider making a distribution of hot assets pro rata to the receiving partner.
- If precontribution gain property is contributed to a partnership, gain to the contributing partner can be further deferred if the partnership waits seven years before (1) distributing the precontribution gain property to another partner or (2) distributing other partnership property to the precontribution gain partner if the value of the other property exceeds the partner's basis in the partnership.
- When the partnership agreement initially is drafted, consider including provisions that govern liquidating distributions of partnership income and property. The specifics of the agreement generally will be followed by the IRS if these and other relevant points are addressed early in the life of the entity.

Sales and Exchanges of Partnership Interests

Delaying Ordinary Income

A partner planning to dispose of a partnership interest in a taxable transaction might consider either an installment sale or a pro rata distribution of hot assets, followed by a sale of the remaining interest in the partnership. Although the partner will have ordinary income when these hot assets are collected or sold, the partner can spread the income over more than one tax year by controlling the collection or disposal dates.

Basis Adjustment for Transferee

If a partnership interest is acquired by purchase, the purchaser may want to condition the acquisition on the partnership's promise to make an election to adjust the basis of partnership assets. Making the election under § 754 results in the basis in the partner's ratable share of partnership assets being adjusted to reflect the purchase price. Failure to do so could result in the loss of future depreciation deductions or could convert ordinary losses into capital losses.

Comparing Sales to Liquidations

When a partner disposes of an entire interest in a partnership for a certain sum, the *before-tax* result of a sale of that interest to another partner or partners is the same as the liquidation of the interest under § 736. In other words, if both transactions result in the partner receiving the same amount of pre-tax dollars, the partner

TAX IN THE NEWS Tax Treatment of "Carried Interests"

Limited partnerships are often used as vehicles for raising capital. For example, investors might purchase interests in a limited partnership created to purchase a specific rental real estate property (or properties).

This partnership might be formed by a real estate property management firm using funds loaned by a mortgage banking firm and with the partnership interests marketed by a brokerage house. The developer, lender, and promoter are often noncorporate firms that accept a "carried interest"—typically, a capital interest in the partnership—in lieu of receiving current compensation for their services. The investment is structured so that there is no value in the carried interest at the time it is awarded—therefore, receipt of the carried interest in exchange for services does not result in current taxation. When the limited partnership is eventually sold or liquidated, these parties receive a gain allocation or a liquidating distribution from the partnership.

For example, assume that Real Property Developers Group, LLC, accepts a 5 percent interest (at no current cost) in the capital of Rental Property, Ltd. The LLC performs all services entailed in acquiring, managing, and syndicating the limited partnership offering. (Assume that the LLC does not receive any allocations of the limited partnership's operating income or expenses.)

When Rental Property, Ltd., is liquidated, the LLC receives a $10 million liquidating distribution. This results in a capital gain because the LLC had no basis in the partnership interest. The arrangement is very attractive as it yields a $10 million capital gain at the end instead of ordinary income when the entity is formed and during the life of the partnership.

For several years, this type of arrangement has been under fire in the financial press. Congress has made several attempts to pass legislation that would result in ordinary income treatment for "carried interests." It may be just a matter of time before one of these bills is enacted.

The current treatment does have supporters, though. Venture capital firms accept a tremendous amount of risk and incur substantial expenses in forming such ventures, many of which are unsuccessful.

The question to be resolved is one of characterization. Should the risk-bearing developer, syndicator, and lender be forced to recognize ordinary income for the performance of services? Or should they be awarded capital gains treatment when the partnership is terminated, reflecting the risk inherent in the venture? This is not an inconsequential matter—as of 2007, the Joint Committee on Taxation estimated that, cumulatively, over $78 billion had been paid in carried interests and that an even greater value had been awarded but not yet paid.

Source: Present Law and Analysis Relating to Tax of Partnership Carried Interests, Joint Committee on Taxation, JCX-41-07, July 10, 2007.

should be ambivalent about which form the transaction takes unless one form offers tax savings that the other does not. The *after-tax* result of a sale of a partnership interest and a liquidation of a partner's interest by an ongoing partnership may differ considerably.

Payments over Time

One difference occurs when the payment for that interest is extended over several years. When a partner sells the partnership interest to another partner, the selling partner can postpone the recognition of income under the installment sale rules. These rules are very restrictive and require that gain and income be recognized at least as quickly as the proportionate share of the receivable is collected. However, in a liquidation, more flexibility may be available. Under § 736, the § 736(b) payments for partnership property can be made before the income payments under § 736(a). Furthermore, the § 736(b) payments can be treated as a return of basis first, with gain recognized only after the distributee partner has received amounts equal to the basis. This treatment results in a deferral of gain and income recognition under § 736 that is not available under the installment sale provisions.

Payments for Goodwill

The partner who purchases a partnership interest often pays an amount that can be attributed, in part, to partnership goodwill. Purchased goodwill is included in a purchasing partner's outside basis for the partnership interest. The partner cannot amortize the goodwill unless (1) the asset qualifies as a § 197 intangible, amortizable over 15 years and (2) the partnership makes an election under § 754 to adjust the basis of partnership assets to reflect the purchase price paid. In many cases, the purchasing partner will not obtain a tax benefit from the goodwill until the partnership interest is disposed of.

Under § 736, amounts paid by a service partnership for a general partner's share of partnership goodwill can be treated as a § 736(a) payment. If this payment is a guaranteed payment, it is deductible by the partnership. If it is a distributive share, it is excludible from the income stream of the remaining partners. In effect, this is also like a deduction. If (1) capital is a material income-producing factor of the partnership or (2) the distributee partner was a limited partner, payments for goodwill constitute § 736(b) property payments. These payments are not deductible by the partnership and result in increased capital gain (or decreased capital loss) to the retiring partner.

Valuation Problems

Both the IRS and the courts usually consider the value of a partner's interest or any partnership assets agreed upon by all partners to be correct. Thus, when planning the sale or liquidation of a partnership interest, the results of the bargaining process should be documented. To avoid valuation problems on liquidation, include a formula or agreed-upon valuation procedure in the partnership agreement or in a related buy-sell agreement.

Termination of Partnership

A partnership terminates if 50 percent or more of the total interest in partnership capital and profits is sold within a 12-month period. A liquidation under § 736, however, is not considered a sale or exchange under this rule. Therefore, a partnership can liquidate a partner's interest without terminating a three-partner partnership, for example, even if the liquidated partner had a 98 percent interest in partnership capital and profits immediately before the liquidating distribution.

A sale and a liquidation of a partnership interest also differ in other respects that are beyond the scope of this text. The point to remember is that differences exist that may result in considerable after-tax savings for the partners. Careful planning can result in a properly structured transaction.

Other Partnership Issues

Choice of Entity

The partnership liquidation rules demonstrate the tax advantages of the partnership form over the C corporation in the final stage of the business's life:

- A service partnership can effectively claim deductions for its payment to a retiring general partner for goodwill.
- The partnership liquidation itself is not a taxable event. Under corporate rules, however, liquidating distributions and sales in preparation for a distribution are fully taxable.
- Tax liability relative to the liquidation is generated at the partner level, but only upon a recognition event (such as receipt of cash in excess of basis or sale of an asset received in a distribution). The timing of this event is usually under the control of the (ex-)partner. In this manner, the tax obligations can be placed in the most beneficial tax year and rate bracket.

Family Partnerships

If possible, make certain that very young and elderly members of a family partnership contribute services to the entity, so as to justify their income allocations. These services can comprise the most routine facets of the business, including monitoring and operating copy machines and providing ongoing maintenance of the indoor and outdoor landscaping environments. Although no more than a market level of compensation can be assigned for this purpose, the services themselves constitute evidence of the active role the partner plays in the operations of the entity.

As there is no equivalent of the kiddie tax for elderly taxpayers, retention of the founding members of the partnership past the nominal retirement age can facilitate the income-shifting goals of a family where the founding members are not independently wealthy.

REFOCUS ON THE BIG PICTURE

THE LIFE CYCLE OF A PARTNERSHIP

Two things are happening when the new developers become members of Beachside Properties, LLC. The developers are buying out the interests of two existing LLC members, and they are providing cash with which to expand the LLC's operations.

The expansion itself raises no specific tax problems. An LLC can admit new members with no immediate tax consequences. In addition to the issues addressed earlier in the chapter, the LLC's operating agreement should be modified to ensure that there is no shift in ownership rights between Josh and the new LLC members.

What If?

Changing the facts, assume that the developers have only $5 million in cash, with good prospects for receiving an additional $5 million over the next two years and $9.5 million more in the third year. The LLC has found a bridge loan and temporary financing of $10 million to cover costs during this interim period. This loan, though, is not large enough to also completely buy out Kyle's and Maria's interests. Thus, Kyle and Maria have agreed to accept installment payments for the sale or redemption of their interests.

Now the buyout of Kyle and Maria can be treated either as an installment sale or as a redemption under § 736 requiring a series of payments. While the specific results of these arrangements are beyond the scope of this chapter, different tax consequences might arise as to the timing and character of Kyle's and Maria's gain recognition.

KEY TERMS

Appreciated inventory, 11-15
Disproportionate distribution, 11-3
Hot assets, 11-15
Liquidating distribution, 11-3
Nonliquidating distribution, 11-3
Optional adjustment election, 11-28
Proportionate distribution, 11-3
§ 754 election, 11-28
Technical termination of a partnership, 11-32
Unrealized receivables, 11-6

DISCUSSION QUESTIONS

1. **LO.1, 8** ABC Partnership distributed cash and appreciated land to partner Bell in a proportionate nonliquidating distribution. What is the effect to Bell and ABC?

2. **LO.1** How is the basis determined for land and inventory received in a proportionate nonliquidating distribution? How is the partner's basis in the partnership interest affected?

3. **LO.1** How does a proportionate nonliquidating distribution of cash from a partnership to a partner compare with one from a Subchapter C corporation to a shareholder?

4. **LO.2** Describe the tax treatment to the partner of a proportionate liquidating distribution (where the partnership also liquidates) of cash, land, and inventory. When might the partner recognize a gain or loss?

5. **LO.2** How is the partner's basis determined for land and inventory received in a proportionate liquidating distribution (where the partnership also liquidates)? How is the partner's basis in the partnership interest affected?

6. **LO.2** What is the effect on a partnership of a proportionate liquidating distribution of cash, appreciated land, and inventory where the partnership also liquidates? How does this compare to liquidating distributions from a corporation?

7. **LO.1, 2** The LizMack Partnership distributes the following assets to partner Liz: **Issue ID**

   - $20,000 cash.
   - Inventory with a $20,000 value and a $10,000 basis to the partnership.
   - A parcel of land with a $30,000 value and a $35,000 basis to the partnership.

   What issues must be considered in determining the tax treatment of the distribution?

8. **LO.1, 2** What theories of taxation underlie the rules related to proportionate liquidating and nonliquidating distributions? (In other words, what are these distribution rules trying to accomplish?) **Issue ID**

9. **LO.3** What issues arise if a partner contributes appreciated property to a partnership and that property is later distributed to another partner? **Issue ID**

10. **LO.4** What is a disproportionate distribution? What is the theory underlying the disproportionate distribution rules? What are they trying to accomplish?

11. **LO.5** Distinguish between the treatment of § 736 income and property payments. What are the tax consequences of such payments to the retiring partner, the remaining partners, and the partnership?

12. **LO.1, 4, 6** What are hot assets? How do they affect a partner's gain or loss on sale of a partnership interest?

13. **LO.6, 8** Jody sells her partnership interest to Bill for $10,000. What issues must be addressed by Jody, Bill, and the partnership? **Issue ID**

14. **LO.7** What methods can be used when a partnership incorporates? Why is it important to specify the method being used?

15. **LO.7** What tax consequences result from the death of a partner?

16. **LO.8** Why might a partner want the partnership to make a § 754 election? Why might the partnership not want to make the election?

17. **LO.8** Who makes the optional adjustment-to-basis election? How is the election made? What is its effect on future years?

18. **LO.9** Describe the various types of events that can cause a partnership termination. Which of these can cause a "technical" termination?

19. **LO.1, 2, 3, 4, 5, 6, 8, 10, 12** Comment on the validity of each of the following statements.
    a. A partner may recognize a capital gain if a proportionate nonliquidating distribution of cash exceeds the partner's basis in the partnership interest.
    b. A partner may recognize a capital loss in a proportionate liquidating distribution if the assets received include cash, a marketable security, and land.
    c. In a proportionate liquidating distribution, if a partner receives cash equal to the basis in the partnership interest, any other property received will take a $0 basis.
    d. If a partner contributes property with a precontribution gain and that property is later distributed to another partner, the contributing partner generally must recognize a capital gain in the amount of any previously unrecognized precontribution gain.
    e. In a disproportionate distribution, either the partnership or the distributee partner might be required to recognize ordinary income.

f. In a redemption of a partnership interest under § 736, a payment to a limited partner in a service partnership for goodwill that is provided for in the partnership agreement is treated as a § 736(b) property payment.
g. Under § 736, all payments to a retiring partner are either property payments [§ 736(b)] or income payments [§ 736(a)].
h. In a sale of a partnership interest, the partner will recognize capital gain to the extent that the selling price exceeds the partner's basis in the partnership interest.
i. A partnership may make a § 754 election if a partner recognizes gain on a distribution of cash from the partnership.
j. A § 754 election might be appropriate if a partner purchases a partnership interest from another partner for substantially less than the partner's share of the underlying basis in partnership assets.
k. A family member can be recognized as a partner in a partnership in which capital is *not* a material income-producing factor only if that partner provides substantial services to the partnership.
l. Both the tax and the economic consequences are the same whether a partnership redeems the partner's interest in the partnership or that interest is sold to a new partner for an equivalent amount of cash.

20. **LO.11** To what extent are the personal assets of a general partner, limited partner, or member of an LLC subject to (a) contractual liability claims such as trade accounts payable and (b) malpractice claims against the entity? Answer the question for partners or members in a general partnership, an LLP, a nonprofessional LLC, and a limited partnership.

PROBLEMS

21. **LO.1** Greg's outside basis in his interest in the GO Partnership is $360,000. In a proportionate nonliquidating distribution, the partnership distributes to him cash of $60,000, inventory (fair market value of $200,000, basis to the partnership of $160,000), and land (fair market value of $50,000, basis to the partnership of $80,000). The partnership continues in existence.
a. Does the partnership recognize any gain or loss as a result of this distribution? Explain.
b. Does Greg recognize any gain or loss as a result of this distribution? Explain.
c. Calculate Greg's basis in the land, in the inventory, and in his partnership interest immediately following the distribution.

22. **LO.1** When Melanie's outside basis in the TMF Partnership is $200,000, the partnership distributes to her $40,000 cash, an account receivable (fair market value of $80,000, inside basis to the partnership of $0), and a parcel of land (fair market value of $200,000, inside basis to the partnership of $180,000). Melanie remains a partner in the partnership, and the distribution is proportionate to the partners.
a. Determine the recognized gain or loss to the partnership as a result of this distribution.
b. Determine the recognized gain or loss to Melanie as a result of the distribution.
c. Determine Melanie's basis in the land, account receivable, and TMF Partnership after the distribution.

23. **LO.1** In each of the following independent cases in which the partnership owns no hot assets, indicate:

- Whether the partner recognizes gain or loss.
- Whether the partnership recognizes gain or loss.
- The partner's adjusted basis for the property distributed.
- The partner's outside basis in the partnership after the distribution.

a. Kim receives $20,000 cash in partial liquidation of her interest in the partnership. Kim's outside basis for her partnership interest immediately before the distribution is $3,000.
b. Kourtni receives $40,000 cash and land with an inside basis to the partnership of $30,000 (value of $50,000) in partial liquidation of her interest. Kourtni's outside basis for her partnership interest immediately before the distribution is $80,000.

c. Assume the same facts as in (b), except that Kourtni's outside basis for her partnership interest immediately before the distribution is $60,000.
d. Klois receives $50,000 cash and inventory with a basis of $30,000 and a fair market value of $50,000 in partial liquidation of her partnership interest. Her basis was $90,000 before the distribution. All partners received proportionate distributions.

24. **LO.8** Assume the facts of Problem 23. In each independent case, are additional planning opportunities available to the partnership to maximize its inside basis in its assets? If so, by how much can the basis be increased? What is the effect of any basis increase to the distributee partner or the other partners? **Decision Making**

25. **LO.1** Mark's basis in his partnership interest is $39,000. In a proportionate nonliquidating distribution, Mark receives $30,000 cash and two inventory items with bases of $10,000 each to the partnership. The values of the inventory items are $15,000 and $5,000.
a. How much gain or loss, if any, must Mark recognize on the distribution?
b. What basis will Mark take in each inventory item?

26. **LO.1** Cari Hawkins is a 50% partner in the calendar year Hawkins-Henry Partnership. On January 1, 2012, her basis in her partnership interest is $160,000. The partnership has no taxable income or loss for the current year. In a nonliquidating distribution on December 15, the partnership distributes $120,000 cash to Cari and inventory proportionately to all partners. Cari's share of the inventory has a basis of $50,000 (fair market value of $60,000). In January 2013, Cari asks your advice regarding treatment of 2012 operations and distributions. Using the format (1) facts, (2) issues, and (3) conclusion and analysis, draft a letter to Cari at the Hawkins-Henry Partnership (1622 E. Henry Street, St. Paul, MN 55118). Your letter should address the following points and provide enough information for the client to understand the applicable tax provisions but without including specific citations. **Communications**
a. How much gain or loss does the partnership recognize as a result of 2012 activities?
b. How much gain or loss must Cari recognize in 2012?
c. What is Cari's basis in inventory received?
d. What is Cari's basis in her partnership interest at the end of 2012?
e. Are there other considerations Cari and/or the partnership should address? Explain.

27. **LO.1, 2** At the beginning of the tax year, Monica's basis in the MIP LLC was $100,000, including Monica's $50,000 share of the LLC's liabilities. At the end of the year, MIP distributed to Monica cash of $20,000 and inventory (basis of $10,000, fair market value of $16,000). In addition, MIP repaid all of its liabilities by the end of the year.
a. If this is a proportionate nonliquidating distribution, what is the tax effect of the distribution to Monica and MIP? After the distribution, what is Monica's basis in the inventory and in her MIP interest?
b. Would your answers to (a) change if this had been a proportionate liquidating distribution? Explain.

28. **LO.1, 3, 4** Vincent is a 50% partner in the TAV Partnership. He became a partner three years ago when he contributed land with a value of $60,000 and a basis of $30,000 (current value is $100,000). Tyler and Anita each contributed $30,000 cash for a 25% interest. Vincent's basis in his partnership interest is currently $150,000; the other partners' bases are each $75,000. The partnership has the following assets: **Issue ID**

	Basis	FMV
Cash	$200,000	$200,000
Accounts receivable	–0–	200,000
Marketable securities	70,000	100,000
Land	30,000	100,000
Total	$300,000	$600,000

In general terms, describe the tax result if TAV distributes a $50,000 interest in the land each to Tyler and Anita and $100,000 of accounts receivable to Vincent at the end of the current year. Calculations are not required.

Issue ID

29. **LO.1, 3, 4** Assume the same facts as in Problem 28, except that TAV distributes $100,000 of cash to Vincent, $50,000 of marketable securities to Tyler, and $50,000 of accounts receivable to Anita. In general terms, describe the tax result of the distribution.

Issue ID

30. **LO.1, 3, 4** Assume the same facts as Problem 28, except that TAV distributes a $50,000 interest in the land and $50,000 of accounts receivable to Vincent and $25,000 of cash and $25,000 of accounts receivable each to Anita and Tyler. In general terms, describe the tax result of the distribution.

Issue ID

31. **LO.2, 3, 4, 12** Use the assets and partners' bases from Problem 28. Assume that the partnership distributes all of its assets in a liquidating distribution. In deciding the allocation of assets, what issues should the partnership consider to minimize each partner's taxable gains?

32. **LO.2** In each of the following independent liquidating distributions in which the partnership also liquidates, determine the amount and character of any gain or loss to be recognized by each partner and the basis of each asset (other than cash) received. In each case, assume that distributions of hot assets are proportionate to the partners.
    a. Landon has a partnership basis of $40,000 and receives a distribution of $50,000 in cash.
    b. Mark has a partnership basis of $50,000 and receives $20,000 cash and a capital asset with a basis to the partnership of $25,000 and a fair market value of $40,000.
    c. Neil has a partnership basis of $100,000 and receives $40,000 cash, inventory with a basis to the partnership of $30,000, and a capital asset with a partnership basis of $20,000. The inventory and capital asset have fair market values of $20,000 and $30,000, respectively.
    d. Oscar has a partnership basis of $40,000 and receives a distribution of $10,000 cash and an account receivable with a basis of $0 to the partnership (value is $15,000).

Decision Making

33. **LO.2, 12** The basis of Jesse's partnership interest is $90,000. Jesse receives a pro rata liquidating distribution consisting of $30,000 cash, land with a basis of $50,000 and a fair market value of $60,000, and his proportionate share of inventory with a basis of $20,000 to the partnership and a fair market value of $22,000. Assume that the partnership also liquidates.
    a. How much gain or loss, if any, must Jesse recognize as a result of the distribution?
    b. What basis will Jesse take in the inventory and land?
    c. If the land is sold two years later for $60,000, what are the tax consequences to Jesse?
    d. What are the tax consequences to the partnership as a result of the liquidating distribution?
    e. Is any planning technique available to the partnership to avoid any "lost basis" results? Explain.
    f. Would your answer to (b) change if this had been a nonliquidating distribution? Explain.

34. **LO.2** Assume the same facts as in Problem 33, except that Jesse's basis in the partnership is $120,000 instead of $90,000.
    a. How much gain or loss, if any, must Jesse recognize on the distribution?
    b. What basis will Jesse take in the inventory and land?
    c. What are the tax consequences to the partnership?
    d. Would your answer to (a) or (b) change if this had been a nonliquidating distribution? Explain.

Decision Making

35. **LO.2, 12** Paula's basis in her partnership interest is $60,000. In liquidation of her interest, the partnership distributes to Paula cash of $20,000 and inventory (basis of $5,000 and value of $7,000).
    a. How much gain or loss, if any, must Paula recognize as a result of the distribution?
    b. What basis will Paula take in the inventory?
    c. What are the tax consequences to the partnership?
    d. Can you recommend an alternative distribution? Explain.
    e. Would your answer to (a) or (b) change if this had been a nonliquidating distribution? Explain.

36. **LO.2** Julie's basis in her partnership interest is $108,000. In a proportionate distribution in liquidation of the partnership, Julie receives $50,000 cash and two parcels of land

with bases of $20,000 each to the partnership. The partnership holds both parcels of land for investment, and the parcels have fair market values of $10,000 and $30,000.

a. How much gain or loss, if any, must Julie recognize on the distribution?
b. What basis will Julie take in each parcel?
c. If the land had been held as inventory by the partnership, what effect, if any, would it have on your responses to (a) and (b)?

37. **LO.2, 12** Assume the same facts as in Problem 36, except that Julie receives $50,000 cash and a desk having a basis of $1,200 to the partnership and a fair market value of $2,000.

Decision Making

a. How much loss, if any, may Julie recognize on the distribution?
b. What basis will Julie take in the desk?
c. Suppose Julie's 15-year-old son uses the desk for his personal use for one year before Julie sells it for $1,000. How much loss may Julie recognize on the sale of the desk? What tax planning procedures could have prevented this result?

38. **LO.3** In 2009, Adrianna contributed land with a basis of $16,000 and a fair market value of $25,000 to the A&I Partnership in exchange for a 25% interest in capital and profits. In 2012, the partnership distributes this property to Isabel, also a 25% partner, in a nonliquidating distribution. The fair market value has increased to $30,000 at the time the property is distributed. Isabel's and Adrianna's bases in their partnership interests are each $40,000 at the time of the distribution.

a. How much gain or loss, if any, does Adrianna recognize on the distribution to Isabel? What is Adrianna's basis in her partnership interest following the distribution?
b. What is Isabel's basis in the land she received in the distribution?
c. How much gain or loss, if any, does Isabel recognize on the distribution? What is Isabel's basis in her partnership interest following the distribution?
d. How much gain or loss would Isabel recognize if she later sells the land for its $30,000 fair market value? Is this result equitable?
e. Would your answers to (a) and (b) change if Adrianna originally contributed the property to the partnership in 2000? Explain.

39. **LO.3** Derek contributed a tract of undeveloped land to the Nightingale Partnership in 2009. He originally paid $20,000 for the property in 1999, but its value was $70,000 at the date of the contribution. In 2012, the partnership distributes another parcel of land to Derek; the land has a basis to the partnership of $30,000. The fair market value of the distributed property is $100,000 in 2012. Derek's basis in his partnership interest is $60,000 immediately before the distribution.

a. How much gain or loss, if any, does Derek recognize on the distribution?
b. What is Derek's basis in his partnership interest following the distribution?
c. What is Derek's basis in the property he receives in the distribution?
d. After the distribution, what is the partnership's basis in the property originally contributed by Derek?
e. Would your answers to (b), (c), and (d) change if Derek originally contributed the property to the partnership in 2000? Explain.

40. **LO.3, 5** The FABB Partnership distributes a marketable security to 25% partner Fred in complete liquidation of his interest in the partnership. Use the following facts to answer the questions that follow:

- The partnership's basis in the security is $10,000, and its value is $20,000. The partnership did not own any of this particular security following the distribution.
- Fred's basis in the partnership interest is $5,000 immediately prior to the distribution.
- Fred is a general partner, and capital is a material income-producing factor to the partnership.
- The partnership owns no hot assets.

a. How is the security classified under § 736?
b. What is the amount of the security distribution that is treated as a cash distribution?
c. How much gain does Fred report on the distribution?
d. What is Fred's basis in the security he receives in the distribution?

Decision Making

41. **LO.5, 12** Damon owns a 20% interest as a general partner in the Vermillion Partnership, which provides consulting services. The partnership distributes $60,000 cash to Damon in complete liquidation of his partnership interest. Damon's share of partnership unrealized receivables immediately before the distribution is $20,000. The partnership has no other hot assets. Assume that none of the cash payment is for goodwill. Damon's basis for his partnership interest immediately before the distribution is $30,000.
    a. How is the cash payment treated under § 736?
    b. How much gain or loss must Damon recognize on the distribution? What is the character of these amounts?
    c. How does the partnership treat the distribution to Damon?
    d. What planning opportunities might the partnership want to consider?

42. **LO.6** RBP Partnership is a service-oriented partnership that has three equal general partners. One of them, Barry, sells his interest to another partner, Dale, for $90,000 cash and the assumption of Barry's share of partnership liabilities. On the sale date, the partnership's cash basis balance sheet is as follows. Assume that the capital accounts *before* the sale reflect the partners' bases in their partnership interests, excluding liabilities. The payment exceeds the stated fair market value of the assets because of goodwill that is not recorded on the books.

	Basis	FMV		Basis	FMV
Cash	$120,000	$120,000	Note payable	$ 30,000	$ 30,000
Accounts receivable	–0–	90,000	Capital accounts		
Capital assets	30,000	75,000	Barry	40,000	85,000
			David	40,000	85,000
			Dale	40,000	85,000
Total	$150,000	$285,000	Total	$150,000	$285,000

a. What is the total amount realized by Barry on the sale?
b. How much, if any, ordinary income must Barry recognize on the sale?
c. How much capital gain must Barry report?
d. What is Dale's basis in the partnership interest acquired?

43. **LO.5** Assume in Problem 42 that Barry's partnership interest is not sold to another partner. Instead, the partnership makes a liquidating distribution of $90,000 cash to Barry, and the remaining partners assume his share of the liabilities. How much gain or loss must Barry recognize? How is it characterized? Assume that Barry is a general partner, there is no provision for the payment for goodwill in the partnership agreement, and capital is not a material income-producing factor to the partnership.

44. **LO.6, 8** Diana, a partner in the cash basis HDA Partnership, has a one-third interest in partnership profits and losses. The partnership's balance sheet at the end of the current year is as follows:

	Basis	FMV		Basis	FMV
Cash	$120,000	$120,000	Hannah, capital	$ 90,000	$250,000
Receivables	–0–	240,000	Diana, capital	90,000	250,000
Land	150,000	390,000	Alexis, capital	90,000	250,000
Total	$270,000	$750,000	Total	$270,000	$750,000

Diana sells her interest in the HDA Partnership to Kenneth at the end of the current year for cash of $250,000.
a. How much income must Diana report on her tax return for the current year from the sale? What is its nature?
b. If the partnership does not make an optional adjustment-to-basis election, what are the type and amount of income that Kenneth must report in the next year when the receivables are collected?

c. If the partnership did make an optional adjustment-to-basis election, what are the type and amount of income that Kenneth must report in the next year when the receivables are collected? When the land (which is used in the HDA Partnership's business) is sold for $420,000? Assume that no other transactions occurred that year.

45. **LO.6, 7, 9** At the end of last year, June, a 30% partner in the four-person BJJM Partnership, has an outside basis of $75,000 in the partnership, including a $60,000 share of partnership debt. June's share of the partnership's § 1245 recapture potential is $40,000. All parties use the calendar year. Describe the income tax consequences to June in each of the following independent situations that take place in the current year:
   a. On the first day of the tax year, June sells her partnership interest to Marilyn for $120,000 cash and the assumption by Marilyn of the appropriate share of partnership liabilities.
   b. June dies after a lengthy illness on April 1 of the current year. June's brother immediately takes June's place in the partnership.

46. **LO.6, 7, 9** Briefly discuss how your responses in Problem 45 would change if the BJJM Partnership had $360,000 of unrealized receivables at the end of the current year, including the § 1245 recapture potential.

47. **LO.9** For each of the following independent fact patterns, indicate whether a termination of the partnership has occurred for tax purposes. Assume that no other partnership interests are sold either one year before or one year after the transactions described.
   a. Paige sells her interest in capital and profits of the PQR Partnership. She owns a 48% interest in capital and a 60% interest in the partnership's profits.
   b. Ryan and Rob are equal partners in the R & R Partnership. Ryan dies on January 15, 2012. Rob purchases Ryan's interest from his estate on March 15, 2012. Answer for January 15, 2012.
   c. Answer (b) for March 15, 2012.
   d. Joel, a 52% partner in the profitable J & D Partnership, gives his entire interest to his son on July 1, 2012.
   e. Jessica sells her 50% interest in the FJK Partnership to new partner Ashley.
   f. Carol, Cora, and Chris are equal partners in the Canary Partnership. On January 22, 2012, Cora sells her entire interest to Ted. On December 29, 2012, Carol sells a 15% interest to Earl. On January 25, 2013, Chris sells his interest to Frank.

48. **LO.10** Fred and Samuel, father and son, operate a local restaurant as an LLC. The FS, LLC earned a profit of $120,000 in the current year. Samuel's equal partnership interest was acquired by gift from Fred. Assume that capital is a material income-producing factor and that Fred manages the day-to-day operations of the restaurant without any help from Samuel. Reasonable compensation for Fred's services is $60,000.
   a. How much of the LLC's income is allocated to Fred?
   b. What is the maximum amount of the LLC's income that can be allocated to Samuel?
   c. Assuming that Samuel is 15 years old, has no other income, and is claimed as a dependent by Fred, how is Samuel's income from the LLC taxed?

RESEARCH PROBLEMS

THOMSON REUTERS
CHECKPOINT®

Note: Solutions to Research Problems can be prepared by using the **Checkpoint® Student Edition** online research product, which is available to accompany this text. It is also possible to prepare solutions to the Research Problems by using tax research materials found in a standard tax library.

Decision Making

Research Problem 1. Your client, Paul, owns a one-third interest as a managing (general) partner in the service-oriented PRE, LLP. He would like to retire from the limited liability partnership at the end of the current year and asks your help in structuring the buyout transaction.

WWW **For the latest in changes to tax legislation, visit www.cengagebrain.com**

Based on interim financial data and revenue projections for the remainder of the year, the LLP's balance sheet is expected to approximate the following at year-end:

	Basis	FMV		Basis	FMV
Cash	$ 60,000	$ 60,000	Paul, capital	$ 60,000	$150,000
Accounts receivable	–0–	180,000	Rachel, capital	60,000	150,000
Land (capital asset)	120,000	210,000	Erik, capital	60,000	150,000
Total assets	$180,000	$450,000	Total capital	$180,000	$450,000

Although the LLP has some cash, the amount is not adequate to purchase Paul's entire interest in the current year. The LLP has proposed to pay Paul, in liquidation of his interest, according to the following schedule:

December 31, 2012	$50,000
December 31, 2013	$50,000
December 31, 2014	$50,000

Paul has agreed to this payment schedule, but the parties are not sure of the tax consequences of the buyout and have temporarily halted negotiations to consult with their tax advisers. Paul has retained you to ascertain the income tax ramifications of the buyout and to make sure he secures the most advantageous result available. Using the IRS Regulations governing partnerships, answer the following questions.

a. If the buyout agreement between Paul and PRE is silent as to the treatment of each payment, how will each payment be treated by Paul and the partnership?

b. As Paul's adviser, what payment schedule should Paul negotiate to minimize his current tax liability?

c. Regarding the LLP, what payment schedule would ensure that the remaining partners receive the earliest possible deductions?

d. What additional planning opportunity might be available to the partnership?

Research Problem 2. The accrual basis Four Winds Partnership owned and operated three storage facilities in Milwaukee, Wisconsin. The partnership did not have a § 754 election in effect when partner Taylor sold her 25% interest to Patrick for $250,000. The partnership has no debt. There are no § 197 assets, and assume that there is no depreciation recapture potential on the storage facility buildings.

At the time of the transfer, the partnership's asset bases and fair market values were as follows:

	Basis	Fair Market Value
Cash	$ 50,000	$ 50,000
Accounts receivable	150,000	150,000
Storage facility #1	500,000	200,000
Storage facility #2	400,000	500,000
Storage facility #3	300,000	100,000
Total assets	$1,400,000	$1,000,000

The value of two of the properties is less than the partnership's basis because of downturns in the real estate market in the area.

Patrick's share of the inside basis of partnership assets is $350,000, and his share of the fair market value of partnership assets is $250,000.

a. What adjustment is required regarding Patrick's purchase of the partnership interest? Must a § 754 election be made? Why or why not?

b. Using the basis allocation rules of § 755 and the Regulations thereunder, calculate the amount of the total adjustment to be allocated to each of the partnership's assets.

c. Would an adjustment be required if the partnership was a venture capital firm and, instead of storage facilities, its three primary assets were equity interests owned in target firms? What requirements would have to be satisfied to avoid making a basis adjustment?

Research Problem 3. The Western States Partnership is a calendar year, cash basis general partnership. The partnership was formed in 2008 and consists of 19 individual partners. Sarah has a 10% capital and profits interest in the partnership, while each of the other partners owns a 5% interest. In October 2012, during an audit of Jason, a 5% partner, the IRS disallowed a $500 charitable contribution deduction that was claimed on his 2010 tax return. This amount was reported by Western States on the charitable deduction line of Jason's Schedule K–1. On a schedule attached to each partner's K–1 for 2010, the partnership indicated that it made a $10,000 deductible contribution to a foreign charity and reported that amount in the charitable deductible line of Western State's Schedule K. The IRS properly claims that contributions to foreign-based charities are not allowed for income tax purposes and seeks to adjust the returns of Jason and any other partner who claimed a deduction for his or her share.

a. Based on the IRS audit of Jason's return, must the IRS audit each of the other partners' returns to determine which partners claimed the incorrect deduction? Explain.
b. Assume that the partnership has not designated a tax matters partner. Which partner, if any, must fulfill the role?
c. What is the latest date the IRS may bring action against Jason on this issue? Assume that the partnership filed the 2010 Form 1065 on April 10, 2011.
d. Assume that Jason recognized that the contribution was not allowable and did not claim his share on his return. What should Jason have done when filing his 2010 tax return to indicate his disagreement with the tax treatment of the item on the Schedule K–1?

Internet Activity

Use the tax resources of the Internet to address the following questions. Do not restrict your search to the Web, but include a review of newsgroups and general reference materials, practitioner sites and resources, primary sources of the tax law, chat rooms and discussion groups, and other opportunities.

Communications

Research Problem 4. Print an article written by a tax adviser discussing the merits of the family limited partnership. Write a memo discussing one of the following issues.

a. The effects of Revenue Ruling 93–12 and subsequent case law on the use of the entity.
b. The effects of § 704(e) on income computations for the entity.
c. The accuracy of the computations made by the author in the article.

Your memo should include a summary of the findings presented in the article and a summary and discussion of your thoughts. For example, you may want to address situations in which family limited partnerships may be beneficial or pitfalls in structuring such an entity.

Research Problem 5. On what form or attachment does a partnership report that it has made a § 754 election? Prepare such a form using the facts of Example 39 in the text.

Research Problem 6. Download a copy of the legislation with which your state began to allow the formation of limited liability companies. What types of business activities can an LLC conduct in your state?

CHAPTER

12 S Corporations

LEARNING OBJECTIVES: *After completing Chapter 12, you should be able to:*

LO.1 Explain the tax effects that S corporation status has on shareholders.

LO.2 Identify corporations that qualify for the S election.

LO.3 Explain how to make an S election.

LO.4 Explain how an S election can be terminated.

LO.5 Compute nonseparately stated income and identify separately stated items.

LO.6 Allocate income, deductions, and credits to shareholders.

LO.7 Determine how distributions to S corporation shareholders are taxed.

LO.8 Calculate a shareholder's basis in S corporation stock.

LO.9 Explain the tax effects that losses have on shareholders.

LO.10 Compute the built-in gains and passive investment income penalty taxes.

LO.11 Engage in tax planning for S corporations.

CHAPTER OUTLINE

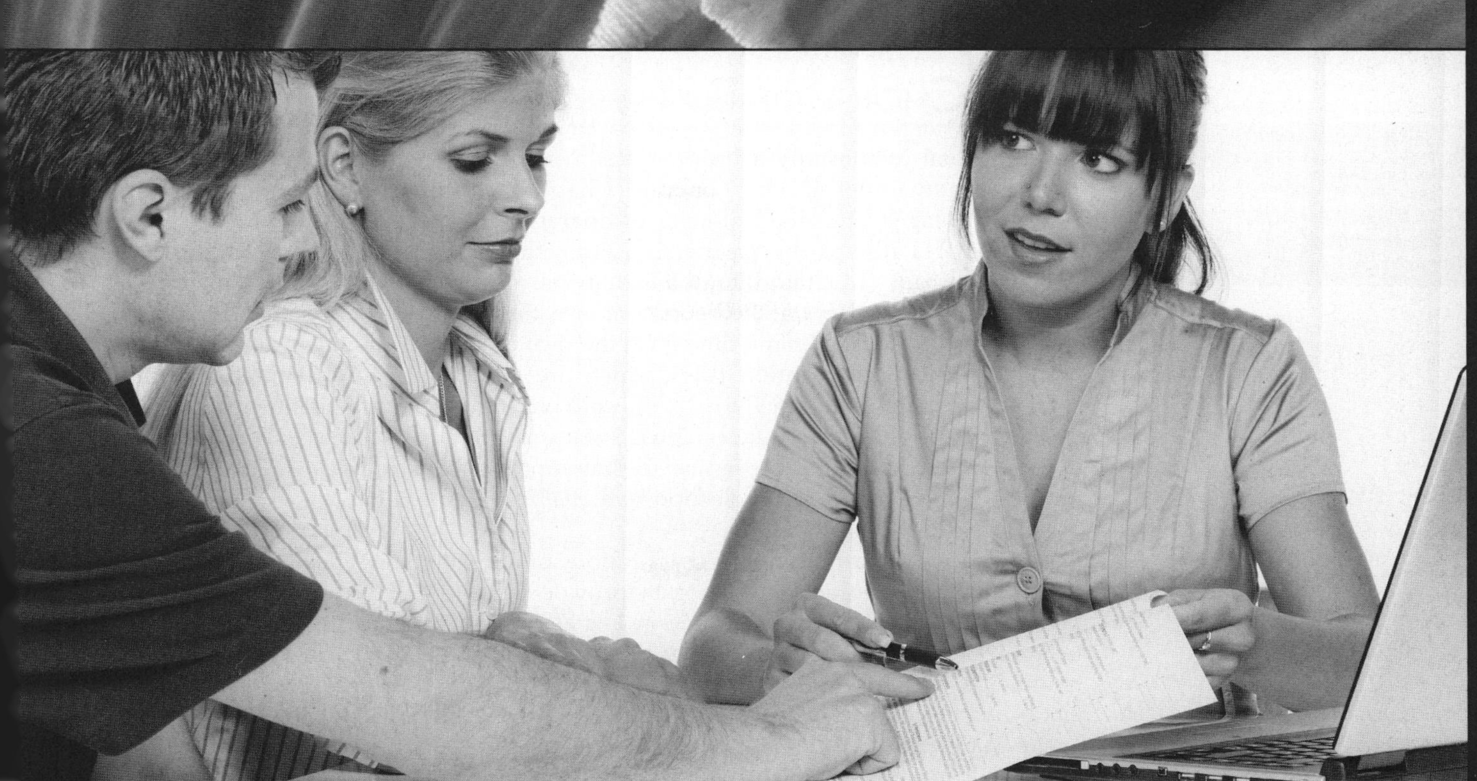

THE BIG PICTURE Tax Solutions for the Real World

© Gina Sanders/Shutterstock.com

DEDUCTIBILITY OF LOSSES AND THE CHOICE OF BUSINESS ENTITY

Cane, Inc., has been a C corporation for a number of years, earning taxable income of less than $100,000 per year. Thus, the business has been subject to the lower C corporation tax rates, but due to cheap imports from China, Cane's two owners, Smith and Jones, expect operating losses for the next two or three years. They hope to outsource some of the manufacturing to Vietnam and turn the company around. How can they deduct these anticipated future losses?

The corporation receives some tax-exempt income, generates a small domestic production activities deduction (DPAD), and holds some C corporation earnings and profits. Each owner draws a salary of $92,000. Cane has two classes of stock, voting and nonvoting common stock. Cane is located in Texarkana, Texas. Smith lives in Texas, and Jones lives in Arkansas. Both are married to nonresident aliens.

Should Smith and Jones elect so that Cane is taxed as an S corporation? Does Cane need to liquidate or go through some type of reorganization before it makes an S election?

Read the chapter and formulate your response.

12.1 Choice of Business Entity

LO.1

Explain the tax effects that S corporation status has on shareholders.

An individual establishing a business has a number of choices as to the form of business entity under which to operate. Chapters 2 through 7 outline many of the rules, advantages, and disadvantages of operating as a regular corporation. Chapters 10 and 11 discuss the partnership entity, and Chapter 11 covers the limited liability company (LLC) and limited liability partnership (LLP) forms.

Another alternative, the **S corporation**, provides many of the benefits of partnership taxation and at the same time gives the owners limited liability protection from creditors. The S corporation rules, which are contained in **Subchapter S** of the Internal Revenue Code (§§ 1361–1379), were enacted to allow flexibility in the entity choice that businesspeople face. Thus, S status combines the legal environment of C corporations with taxation similar to that applying to partnerships. S corporation status is obtained through an election by a *qualifying* corporation with the consent of its shareholders.

S corporations are treated as corporations under state law. They are recognized as separate legal entities and generally provide shareholders with the same liability protection afforded by C corporations. For Federal income tax purposes, however, taxation of S corporations resembles that of partnerships. As with partnerships, the income, deductions, and tax credits of an S corporation flow through to shareholders annually, regardless of whether distributions are made. Thus, income is taxed at the shareholder level and not at the corporate level. Payments to S shareholders by the corporation are distributed tax-free to the extent the distributed earnings were previously taxed. Further, C corporation penalty taxes such as the accumulated earnings tax, personal holding company tax, and alternative minimum tax do not apply to an S corporation.

Although the Federal tax treatment of S corporations and partnerships is similar, it is not identical. For instance, liabilities affect an owner's basis differently, and S corporations may incur a tax liability at the corporate level. Furthermore, an S corporation may not allocate income like a partnership, and distributions of appreciated property are taxable in an S corporation situation (see Concept Summary 12.2 later in this chapter). In addition, a variety of C corporation provisions apply to S corporations. For example, the liquidation of C and S corporations is taxed in the same way. As a rule, where the S corporation provisions are silent, C corporation rules apply.

Today, the choice of a flow-through entity for a closely held business often is between an S corporation (a Federal tax entity) and an LLC (a state tax entity). Although an S corporation resembles an LLC, there are differences. A two-or-more-member LLC operates under partnership tax principles, whereas, as just explained, partnership taxation rules do not always apply to an S corporation.

An Overview of S Corporations

As the following examples illustrate, S corporations can be advantageous even when the individual tax rate exceeds the corporate tax rate.

EXAMPLE 1

An S corporation earns $300,000 in 2012. The marginal individual tax rate applicable to shareholders is 35% on ordinary income and 15% on dividends. The applicable marginal corporate tax rate is 34%. All after-tax income is distributed currently.

	C Corporation	S Corporation
Earnings	$ 300,000	$ 300,000
Less: Corporate tax	(102,000)	–0–
Available for distribution	$ 198,000	$ 300,000
Less: Tax at owner level	(29,700)	(105,000)
Available after-tax earnings	$ 168,300	$ 195,000

TAX IN THE NEWS S Corporations by the Numbers

In 2008, a total of 4,049,944 S corporation returns were filed—a modest 1.5 percent increase from 2007. There were 6,930,746 S shareholders, averaging about 1.7 shareholders each. Around 69 percent of all corporations have made the S election. The wholesale/retail (651,937) and construction (570,987) industries accounted for the largest number of returns. Total S corporation receipts were more than $6.12 trillion, with $360 billion of net income and $121 billion of deficits.

The S corporation generates an extra $26,700 of after-tax earnings ($195,000 − $168,300) when compared with a similar C corporation. The C corporation might be able to reduce this disadvantage, however, by paying out its earnings as compensation, rents, or interest expense. Tax at the owner level can also be deferred or avoided by not distributing after-tax earnings. ■

EXAMPLE 2

A new corporation elects S status and incurs a net operating loss (NOL) of $300,000. The shareholders may use their proportionate shares of the NOL to offset other taxable income in the current year, providing an immediate tax savings. In contrast, a newly formed C corporation is required to carry the NOL forward for up to 20 years and does not receive any tax benefit in the current year. Hence, an S corporation can accelerate NOL deductions and thereby provide a greater present value for tax savings generated by the loss. ■

When to Elect S Corporation Status

The planner begins by determining the appropriateness of an S election. The following factors should be considered.

- If shareholders have *high marginal rates* relative to C corporation rates, it may be desirable to avoid S corporation status. Although C corporation earnings can be subject to double taxation, good tax planning mitigates this result (e.g., when the owners take profits out as salary). Likewise, profits of the corporation may be taken out by the shareholders as capital gain income through stock redemptions, liquidations, or sales of stock to others. Alternatively, C corporation profits may be paid out as dividends, subject to a 15 percent maximum tax rate. Any distribution of profits or sale of stock can be deferred to a later year, thereby reducing the present value of shareholder taxes. Finally, potential shareholder-level tax on corporate profits can be eliminated by a step-up in the basis of the stock upon the shareholder's death.
- S corporation status allows shareholders to *realize tax benefits from corporate losses immediately*—an important consideration in new business enterprises where losses are common. Thus, if corporate NOLs are anticipated and there is unlikely to be corporate income over the near term to offset with the NOLs, S corporation status is advisable. However, the deductibility of the losses to shareholders must also be considered. The *at-risk* and *passive loss limitations apply to losses* generated by an S corporation. In addition, as discussed later in this chapter, shareholders may not deduct losses in excess of the basis in their stock. Together these limits may significantly reduce the benefits of an S election in a loss setting.
- If the entity electing S status is currently a C corporation, *NOL carryovers* from prior years *cannot be used* in an S corporation year. Even worse, S corporation years reduce the 20-year carryover period. And the corporation may be subject to some corporate-level taxes if it elects S status (e.g., see the discussion of the built-in gains tax later in this chapter).

- Because S corporations are flow-through entities, separately stated deduction and income items *retain any special tax characteristics* when they are reported on shareholders' returns. Whether this consideration favors S status depends upon the character of income and deductions of the S corporation. For instance, it may be an advantage to receive the flow-through of passive income, or the qualified domestic production activities deduction, on the shareholder's tax return, making the S election more attractive. *Charitable contributions are not subject to the 10 percent limitation* at the corporate level, but an S corporation cannot take advantage of special provisions for contributions of inventory and scientific equipment.
- *State and local tax laws also should be considered* when making the S election. Although an S corporation usually escapes Federal income tax, it may not be immune from state and local taxes. State taxation of S corporations varies. Some states, including Michigan, treat them the same as C corporations, resulting in a corporate tax liability from an income or franchise tax.
- The choice of S corporation status is *affected by a variety of other factors.* For example, the corporate alternative minimum tax (see Chapter 3) may be avoided in an S corporation. An in-depth discussion of entity choice is provided in Chapter 13.

12.2 Qualifying for S Corporation Status

LO.2

Identify corporations that qualify for the S election.

Definition of a Small Business Corporation

To achieve S corporation status, a corporation *first* must qualify as a **small business corporation**. If each of the following requirements is met, then the entity can elect S corporation status.

- Is a domestic corporation (incorporated and organized in the United States).
- Is an eligible corporation (see the following section for ineligible types).
- Issues only one class of stock.
- Is limited to a theoretical maximum of 100 shareholders.
- Has only individuals, estates, and certain trusts and exempt organizations as shareholders.
- Has no nonresident alien shareholders.

Unlike other provisions in the tax law (e.g., § 1244), no maximum or minimum dollar sales or capitalization restrictions apply to small business corporations.

Ineligible Corporations

Small business corporation status is not permitted for non-U.S. corporations, nor for certain banks and insurance companies.

Any domestic corporation that is not an ineligible corporation can be a qualified Subchapter S corporation subsidiary (QSSS) if the S corporation holds 100 percent of its stock and elects to treat the subsidiary as a QSSS.[1] The QSSS is viewed as a division of the parent, so the parent S corporation can own a QSSS through another QSSS. QSSSs have a separate existence for legal purposes, but they exist only within the parent S corporation for tax purposes.

One Class of Stock

A small business corporation may have only one class of stock issued and outstanding.[2] This restriction permits differences in voting rights, but not differences in distribution or liquidation rights.[3] Thus, two classes of common stock that are identical except that one class is voting and the other is nonvoting would be treated

[1] § 1361(b)(3)(B).

[2] § 1361(b)(1)(D).

[3] § 1361(c)(4).

TAX IN THE NEWS GAO Attacks S Corporations

According to the U.S. Government Accountability Office (GAO), S corporations not only are one of the fastest-growing business types, but they also are likely to make errors on their tax returns. In a report to the Senate Finance Committee, the GAO said that 68 percent of S corporation returns filed for tax years 2003 and 2004 misreported at least one item. About 80 percent of the time, such misreporting favored the taxpayer.

A majority of S corporations used paid preparers. Nevertheless, 71 percent of those returns were noncompliant. Mistakes in calculating shareholder basis were one of the major problems. Some S corporations also failed to pay adequate wages to shareholders, underreporting roughly $23.6 billion. This underreporting resulted in billions of dollars in lost employment taxes to the government.

Source: Government Accountability Office, *Tax Gap: Actions Needed to Address Noncompliance with S Corporation Tax Rules,* December 15, 2009.

as a single class of stock for small business corporation purposes. In contrast, voting common stock and voting preferred stock (with a preference on dividends) would be treated as two classes of stock. Authorized and unissued stock or treasury stock of another class does not disqualify the corporation. Likewise, unexercised stock options, phantom stock, stock appreciation rights, warrants, and convertible debentures usually do not constitute a second class of stock.

The determination of whether stock provides identical rights as to distribution and liquidation proceeds is made based on the provisions governing the operation of the corporation. These *governing provisions* include the corporate charter, articles of incorporation, bylaws, applicable state law, and binding agreements relating to distribution and liquidation proceeds. Employment contracts, loan agreements, and other commercial contracts are *not* considered governing provisions.[4]

THE BIG PICTURE
EXAMPLE 3

Return to the facts of *The Big Picture* on p. 12-1. Cane, Inc., could elect to be an S corporation as long as the two classes of common stock are identical except that one class is voting and the other class is nonvoting.

You learn that both shareholders have binding employment contracts with Cane, Inc. The amount of compensation paid by the corporation to Jones under her employment contract is reasonable, but the amount paid to Smith under his employment contract is excessive, resulting in a constructive dividend. Smith's employment contract was not prepared to circumvent the one-class-of-stock requirement.

Because employment contracts are not considered governing provisions, Cane still is treated as though it has only one class of stock if an S election is made.

Although the one-class-of-stock requirement seems straightforward, it is possible for debt to be reclassified as stock, resulting in an unexpected loss of S corporation status.[5] To mitigate concern over possible reclassification of debt as a second class of stock, the law provides a set of *safe-harbor provisions.*

First, straight debt *issued in an S corporation year* will not be treated as a second class of stock and will not disqualify the S election.[6] The characteristics of straight debt include the following.

- The debtor is subject to a written, unconditional promise to pay on demand or on a specified date a sum certain in money.

[4]Reg. § 1.1361–1(l)(2).
[5]Refer to the discussion of debt-versus-equity classification in Chapter 4.
[6]§ 1361(c)(5)(A).

- The interest rate and payment date are not contingent on corporate profits, management discretion, or similar factors.
- The debt is not convertible to stock.
- The debt is held by a creditor who is an individual (other than a nonresident alien), an estate, or a qualified trust.
- Straight debt can be held by creditors actively and regularly engaged in the business of lending money.

In addition to straight debt under the safe-harbor rules, short-term unwritten advances from a shareholder that do not exceed $10,000 in the aggregate at any time during the corporation's taxable year generally are not treated as a second class of stock. Likewise, debt that is held by stockholders in the same proportion as their stock is not treated as a second class of stock, even if it would be reclassified as equity otherwise.[7]

Number of Shareholders

A small business corporation theoretically is limited to 100 shareholders. If shares of stock are owned jointly by two individuals, they will generally be treated as separate shareholders.

Family members may be treated as one shareholder for purposes of determining the number of shareholders. The term *members of the family* includes a "common ancestor, the lineal descendants of the common ancestor, and the spouses (or former spouses) of the lineal descendants or common ancestor."[8] An estate of a family member also may be treated as a family member for purposes of determining the number of shareholders.

EXAMPLE 4

Fred and Wilma (husband and wife) jointly own 10 shares in Marlins, Inc., an S corporation, with the remaining 290 shares outstanding owned by 99 other unrelated shareholders. Fred and Wilma get divorced; pursuant to the property settlement approved by the court, the 10 shares held by Fred and Wilma are divided between them—5 to each. Before the divorce settlement, Marlins had 100 shareholders under the small business corporation rules. After the settlement, it still has 100 shareholders and continues to qualify as a small business corporation. A former spouse is treated as being in the same family as the individual to whom he or she was married. ■

Type of Shareholder Limitation

Small business corporation shareholders may be resident individuals, estates, certain trusts, and certain tax-exempt organizations.[9] Charitable organizations, employee benefit trusts exempt from taxation, and a one-person LLC classified as a disregarded entity also can qualify as shareholders of an S corporation. This limitation prevents partnerships, corporations, limited liability partnerships, most LLCs, and most IRAs and Roth IRAs from owning S corporation stock. Partnerships and corporate shareholders could easily circumvent the 100-shareholder limitation as illustrated in the following example.

EXAMPLE 5

Saul and 105 of his close friends want to form an S corporation. Saul reasons that if he and his friends form a partnership, the partnership can then form an S corporation and act as a single shareholder, thereby avoiding the 100-shareholder rule. Saul's plan will not work because partnerships cannot own stock in a small business corporation. ■

Although partnerships and corporations cannot own small business corporation stock, small business corporations can be partners in a partnership or shareholders

[7] Reg. § 1.1361–1(l)(4).

[8] §§ 1361(c)(1)(A)(ii) and (B)(i). The need for an affirmative election to treat family members as a single shareholder was eliminated in 2005. Notice 2005–91, 2005–51 I.R.B. 1164 provides insight into the determination of who is a family member.

[9] § 1361(b)(1)(B). Foreign trusts, charitable remainder trusts, and charitable lead trusts cannot be shareholders.

in a corporation. This ability allows the 100-shareholder requirement to be bypassed in a limited sense. For example, if two small business corporations, each with 100 shareholders, form a partnership, then the shareholders of both corporations can enjoy the limited liability conferred by S corporation status and a single level of tax on partnership profits.

Nonresident Aliens

Nonresident aliens cannot own stock in a small business corporation.[10] That is, individuals who are not U.S. citizens *must live in the United States* to own S corporation stock. Therefore, shareholders with nonresident alien spouses in community property states[11] cannot own S corporation stock because the nonresident alien spouse would be treated as owning half of the community property.[12] Similarly, if a resident alien shareholder moves outside the United States, the S election will be terminated.

THE BIG PICTURE

EXAMPLE 6

Return to the facts of *The Big Picture* on p. 12-1. Because Jones lives in Arkansas, a common law property state, the fact that he is married to a nonresident alien spouse would not affect an S election. However, because Smith lives in Texas, a community property state, as it stands, his nonresident alien spouse would be treated as owning half of his community property stock, and an S election would not be allowed. To qualify for S status, Smith could move to Arkansas or his spouse could move to Texas (becoming a resident alien).

Making the Election

LO.3

Explain how to make an S election.

To become an S corporation, a *small business corporation* (defined previously) must file a valid election with the IRS. The election is made on Form 2553. For the election to be valid, it should be filed on a timely basis and all shareholders must consent.

For S corporation status to apply in the current tax year, the election must be filed either in the previous year or on or before the fifteenth day of the third month of the current year.

THE BIG PICTURE

EXAMPLE 7

Return to the facts of *The Big Picture* on p. 12-1. Suppose that, in 2012, shareholders Smith and Jones decide to become an S corporation beginning January 1, 2013. Because the C corporation uses a calendar tax year, the S election can be made at any time in 2012 or by March 15, 2013. An election after March 15, 2013, will not be effective until the 2014 calendar tax year.

There is a simplified method of requesting relief for late S elections that were intended to be effective as of the date of the election. The entity must file a properly completed Form 2553 with a Form 1120S no later than six months after the due date of the tax return (excluding extensions) of the entity for the first tax year in which the S election was intended. The Form 2553 must explain the reason for the failure to timely file the election. Sufficient reasonable cause might occur, for example, where both the corporation's accountant and its attorney failed to file

[10] § 1362(b)(1)(C).

[11] Assets acquired by a married couple are generally considered community property in these states: Arizona, California, Idaho, Louisiana, Nevada, New Mexico, Texas, Washington, Wisconsin, and (if elected by the spouses) Alaska.

[12] See *Ward v. U.S.*, 81–2 USTC ¶9674, 48 AFTR 2d 81–5942, 661 F.2d 226 (Ct.Cls., 1981), where the court found that the stock was owned as community property. Because the taxpayer-shareholder (a U.S. citizen) was married to a citizen and resident of Mexico, the nonresident alien prohibition was violated. If the taxpayer-shareholder had held the stock as separate property, the S election would have been valid.

the election because each believed the other had done so, or because there was miscommunication as to who was responsible for filing.

Even if the 2½-month deadline is met, an S election is not valid unless the corporation qualifies as a small business corporation for the *entire* tax year. Otherwise, the election will be effective for the following tax year.

A corporation that does not yet exist cannot make an S corporation election.[13] Thus, for new corporations, a premature election may not be effective. A new corporation's 2½-month election period begins at the earliest occurrence of any of the following events.

- When the corporation has shareholders.
- When it acquires assets.
- When it begins doing business.[14]

EXAMPLE 8

Several individuals acquire assets on behalf of Rock Corporation on June 29, 2012, and begin doing business on July 3, 2012. They subscribe to shares of stock, file articles of incorporation for Rock, and become shareholders on July 7, 2012. The S election must be filed no later than 2½ months after June 29, 2012 (i.e., on or before September 12) to be effective for 2012. ■

The IRS can correct errors in electing S status where a taxpayer can show that the mistake was inadvertent, the entity otherwise was qualified to be an S corporation, and it acted as if it were an S corporation. Under certain conditions, automatic relief is granted without the need for a letter ruling request and the normal user fee.

An LLC that makes a timely and valid election to be classified as an S corporation need not "check the box" on a Form 8832. The LLC must meet all of the other S corporation requirements.

Shareholder Consent

A qualifying election requires the consent of all of the corporation's shareholders.[15] Consent must be in writing, and it must generally be filed by the election deadline. A consent extension is available only if Form 2553 is filed on a timely basis, reasonable cause is given, and the interests of the government are not jeopardized.[16]

EXAMPLE 9

Vern and Yvonne decide to convert their C corporation into a calendar year S corporation for 2012. At the end of February 2012 (before the election is filed), Yvonne travels to Ukraine and forgets to sign a consent to the election. Yvonne will not return to the United States until June and cannot be reached by fax or e-mail.

Vern files the S election on Form 2553 and requests an extension of time to file Yvonne's consent to the election. Vern indicates that there is a reasonable cause for the extension: a shareholder is out of the country. Because the government's interest is not jeopardized, the IRS probably will grant Yvonne an extension of time to file the consent. Vern must file the election on Form 2553 on or before March 15, 2012, for the election to be effective for the 2012 calendar year. ■

Both husband and wife must consent if they own their stock jointly (as joint tenants, tenants in common, tenants by the entirety, or community property). This requirement has led to considerable taxpayer grief—particularly in community property states where the spouses may not realize that their stock is jointly owned as a community asset.

[13] See, for example, *T.H. Campbell & Bros., Inc.*, 34 TCM 695, T.C.Memo. 1975–149; Ltr.Rul. 8807070.

[14] Reg. § 1.1372–2(b)(1). Also see, for example, *Nick A. Artukovich*, 61 T.C. 100 (1973).

[15] § 1362(a)(2).

[16] Rev.Rul. 60–183, 1960–1 C.B. 625; *William Pestcoe*, 40 T.C. 195 (1963); Reg. § 1.1362–6(b)(3)(iii).

EXAMPLE 10

Three shareholders, Amy, Monty, and Dianne, incorporate in January and file Form 2553. Amy is married and lives in California. Monty is single, and Dianne is married; both live in South Carolina. Because Amy is married and lives in a community property state, her husband also must consent to the S election. South Carolina is not a community property state, so Dianne's husband need not consent. ■

Finally, for current-year S elections, persons who were shareholders during any part of the taxable year before the election date but were not shareholders when the election was made must also consent to the election.[17]

EXAMPLE 11

On January 15, 2012, the stock of Columbus Corporation (a calendar year C corporation) was held equally by three individual shareholders: Jim, Sally, and LuEllen. On that date, LuEllen sells her interest to Jim and Sally. On March 14, 2012, Columbus Corporation files Form 2553. Jim and Sally indicate their consent by signing the form. Columbus cannot become an S corporation until 2013 because LuEllen did not indicate consent. Had all three shareholders consented by signing Form 2553, S status would have taken effect as of January 1, 2012. ■

Loss of the Election

LO.4

Explain how an S election can be terminated.

An S election remains in force until it is revoked or lost. Election or consent forms are not required for future years. However, an S election can terminate if any of the following occurs.

- Shareholders owning a majority of shares (voting and nonvoting) voluntarily revoke the election.
- A new shareholder owning more than one-half of the stock affirmatively refuses to consent to the election.
- The corporation no longer qualifies as a small business corporation.
- The corporation does not meet the passive investment income limitation.

Voluntary Revocation

A **voluntary revocation** of the S election requires the consent of shareholders owning a majority of shares on the day the revocation is to be made.[18] A revocation filed up to and including the fifteenth day of the third month of the tax year is effective for the entire tax year, unless a later date is specified. Similarly, unless an effective date is specified, revocation made after the first 2½ months of the current tax year is effective for the following tax year.

EXAMPLE 12

The shareholders of Petunia Corporation, a calendar year S corporation, voluntarily revoke the S election on January 5, 2012. They do not specify a future effective date in the revocation. If the revocation is properly executed and timely filed, Petunia will be a C corporation for the entire 2012 calendar year. If the election is not made until June 2012, Petunia will remain an S corporation in 2012 and will become a C corporation at the beginning of 2013. ■

A corporation can revoke its S status *prospectively* by specifying a future date when the revocation is to be effective. A revocation that designates a future effective date splits the corporation's tax year into a short S corporation year and a short C corporation year. The day on which the revocation occurs is treated as the first day of the C corporation year. The corporation allocates income or loss for the entire year on a pro rata basis, using the number of days in each short year.

---

[17] § 1362(b)(2)(B)(ii).

[18] § 1362(d)(1).

EXAMPLE 13

Assume the same facts as in the preceding example, except that Petunia designates July 1, 2012, as the revocation date. Accordingly, June 30, 2012, is the last day of the S corporation's tax year. The C corporation's tax year runs from July 1, 2012, to December 31, 2012. Income or loss for the 12-month period is allocated between the two short years (i.e., 184/366 to the C corporation year). ■

Rather than allocating on a pro rata basis, the corporation can elect to compute actual income or loss attributable to the two short years. This election requires the consent of everyone who was a shareholder at any time during the S corporation's short year and everyone who owns stock on the first day of the C corporation's year.[19]

EXAMPLE 14

Assume the same facts as in the preceding example, except that all of Petunia's shareholders consent to allocate the income or loss to the two short tax years based on its actual realization. Assume further that Petunia experiences a total loss of $102,000, of which $72,000 is incurred in the first half of the year. Because $72,000 of the loss occurs before July 1, this amount is allocated to the S corporation short year, and only $30,000 is allocated to the C corporation year. ■

Loss of Small Business Corporation Status

If an S corporation fails to qualify as a small business corporation at any time after the election has become effective, its status as an S corporation ends. The termination occurs on the day the corporation ceases to be a small business corporation.[20] Thus, if the corporation ever has more than 100 shareholders, a second class of stock, or a nonqualifying shareholder, or otherwise fails to meet the definition of a small business corporation, the S election is immediately terminated.

EXAMPLE 15

Peony Corporation has been a calendar year S corporation for three years. On August 13, 2012, one of its 100 shareholders sells *some* of her stock to an outsider. Peony now has 101 shareholders, and it ceases to be a small business corporation. For 2012, Peony is an S corporation through August 12, 2012, and a C corporation from August 13 to December 31, 2012. ■

Passive Investment Income Limitation

The Code provides a **passive investment income (PII)** limitation for S corporations that were previously C corporations or for S corporations that have merged with C corporations. If an S corporation has C corporation E & P and passive income in excess of 25 percent of its gross receipts for three consecutive taxable years, the S election is terminated as of the beginning of the fourth year.[21]

EXAMPLE 16

For 2009, 2010, and 2011, Diapason Corporation, a calendar year S corporation, received passive income in excess of 25% of its gross receipts. If Diapason holds accumulated E & P from years in which it was a C corporation, its S election is terminated as of January 1, 2012. ■

PII includes dividends, interest, rents, gains and losses from sales of capital assets, and royalties net of investment deductions. Rents are not considered PII if the corporation renders significant personal services to the occupant.

EXAMPLE 17

Violet Corporation owns and operates an apartment building. The corporation provides utilities for the building, maintains the lobby, and furnishes trash collection for

[19] § 1362(e)(3).
[20] § 1362(d)(2)(B).
[21] § 1362(d)(3)(A)(ii).

tenants. These activities are not considered significant personal services, so any rent income earned by the corporation will be considered PII.

Alternatively, if Violet also furnishes maid services to its tenants (personal services beyond what normally would be expected from a landlord in an apartment building), the rent income would no longer be PII. ■

Reelection after Termination

After an S election has been terminated, the corporation must wait five years before reelecting S corporation status. The five-year waiting period is waived if:

- There is a more-than-50-percent change in ownership of the corporation after the first year for which the termination is applicable, or
- The event causing the termination was not reasonably within the control of the S corporation or its majority shareholders.

12.3 Operational Rules

S corporations are treated much like partnerships for tax purposes. With a few exceptions,[22] S corporations generally make tax accounting and other elections at the corporate level. Each year, the S corporation determines nonseparately stated income or loss and separately stated income, deductions, and credits. These items are taxed only once, at the shareholder level. All items are allocated to each shareholder based on average ownership of stock throughout the year. The *flow-through* of each item of income, deduction, and credit from the corporation to the shareholder is illustrated in Figure 12.1.

Computation of Taxable Income

LO.5

Compute nonseparately stated income and identify separately stated items.

Subchapter S taxable income or loss is determined in a manner similar to the tax rules that apply to partnerships, except that S corporations amortize organizational expenditures under the C corporation rules[23] and must recognize gains, *but not losses,* on distributions of appreciated property to shareholders.[24] Other special provisions affecting only the computation of C corporation income, such as the dividends received deduction, do not extend to S corporations.[25] Finally, as with partnerships, certain deductions of individuals are not permitted, including alimony payments, personal moving expenses, certain dependent care expenses, the personal exemption, and the standard deduction.

In general, S corporation items are divided into (1) nonseparately stated income or loss and (2) separately stated income, losses, deductions, and credits that could affect the tax liability of any shareholder in a different manner, depending on other factors in the shareholder's tax situation. In essence, nonseparate items are aggregated into an undifferentiated amount that constitutes Subchapter S ordinary income or loss. An S corporation's separately stated items are identical to those separately stated by partnerships. These items retain their tax attributes on the shareholder's return. Separately stated items are listed on Schedule K of the 1120S. They include the following.

- Tax-exempt income.
- Long-term and short-term capital gains and losses.
- Section 1231 gains and losses.
- Charitable contributions (no grace period).
- Passive gains, losses, and credits.
- Certain portfolio income.

[22]A few elections can be made at the shareholder level (e.g., the choice between a foreign tax deduction or credit).

[23]§§ 248 and 1363(b).

[24]§ 1363(b).

[25]§ 703(a)(2).

FIGURE 12.1 **Flow-Through of Separate Items of Income and Loss to S Corporation Shareholders**

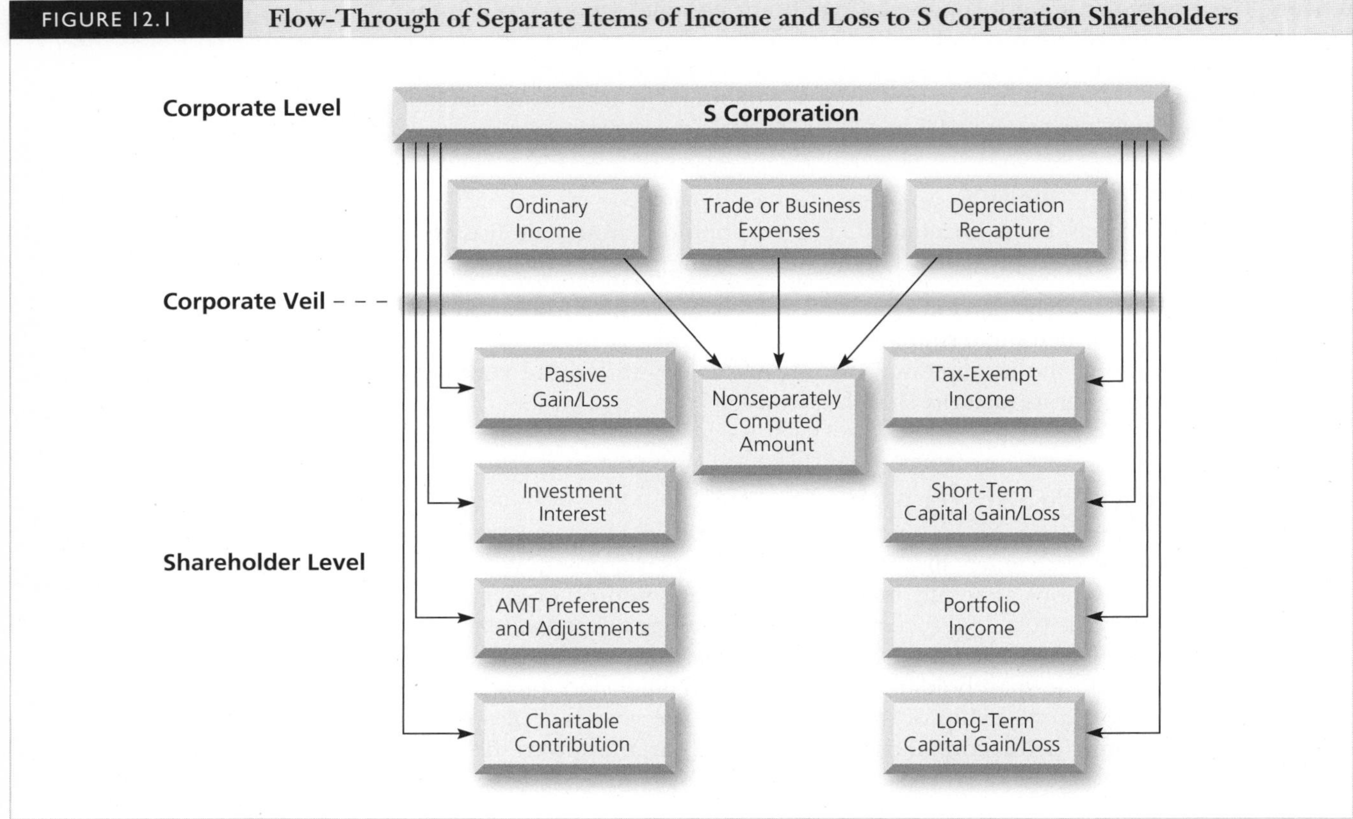

- Section 179 expense deduction.
- Domestic production gross receipts and deductions.
- Tax preferences and adjustments for the alternative minimum tax.
- Depletion.
- Foreign income or loss.
- Recoveries of tax benefit items.
- Intangible drilling costs.
- Investment interest, income, and expenses.

EXAMPLE 18

The following is the income statement for Jersey, Inc., an S corporation.

Sales		$ 40,000
Less cost of sales		(23,000)
Gross profit on sales		$ 17,000
Less: Interest expense	$1,200	
Charitable contributions	400	
Advertising expenses	1,500	
Other operating expenses	2,000	(5,100)
Book income from operations		$ 11,900
Add: Tax-exempt interest	$ 300	
Dividend income	200	
Long-term capital gain	500	1,000
Less: Short-term capital loss		(150)
Net income per books		$ 12,750

Subchapter S ordinary income for Jersey is calculated as follows, using net income for book purposes as the starting point.

Net income per books		$12,750
Separately stated items		
Deduct: Tax-exempt interest	$300	
Dividend income	200	
Long-term capital gain	500	(1,000)
Add: Charitable contributions	$400	
Short-term capital loss	150	550
Subchapter S ordinary income		$12,300

The $12,300 of Subchapter S ordinary income, as well as each of the five separately stated items, are divided among the shareholders based upon their stock ownership. ■

Allocation of Income and Loss

LO.6

Allocate income, deductions, and credits to shareholders.

Each shareholder is allocated a pro rata portion of nonseparately stated income or loss and all separately stated items. The pro rata allocation method assigns an equal amount of each of the S items to each day of the year. If a shareholder's stock holding changes during the year, this allocation assigns the shareholder a pro rata share of each item for *each* day the stock is owned. On the date of transfer, the transferor (and not the transferee) is considered to own the stock.[26]

The per-day allocation must be used, unless the shareholder disposes of his or her entire interest in the entity.[27] In case of a complete termination, a short year may result. If a shareholder dies during the year, his or her share of the pro rata items up to and including the date of death is reported on the final individual income tax return.

EXAMPLE 19

Assume in the previous example that Pat, a shareholder, owned 10% of Jersey's stock for 100 days and 12% for the remaining 265 days. Using the required per-day allocation method, Pat's share of the S corporation items is as follows.

	Schedule K Totals	Pat's Share 10%	Pat's Share 12%	Pat's Schedule K–1 Totals
Ordinary income	$12,300	$337	$1,072	$1,409
Tax-exempt interest	300	8	26	34
Dividend income	200	5	17	22
Long-term capital gain	500	14	44	58
Charitable contributions	400	11	35	46
Short-term capital loss	150	4	13	17

Pat's share of the Subchapter S ordinary income is the total of $12,300 × [0.10 × (100/365)] plus $12,300 × [0.12 × (265/365)], or $1,409. Each of the Schedule K–1 totals from the right-hand column flows through to the appropriate lines on Pat's individual income tax return (Form 1040). ■

[26] Reg. § 1.1377–1(a)(2)(ii).

[27] §§ 1366(a)(1) and 1377(a)(1).

EXAMPLE 20

If Pat in the previous example dies after owning the stock 100 days, his share of the S corporation items is reported on his final individual income tax return (Form 1040). Thus, only the items in the column labeled 10% in Example 19 are reported on Pat's final tax return. S corporation items that occur after Pat's death most likely would flow through to the income tax return of Pat's estate (Form 1041). ■

The Short-Year Election

If a shareholder's interest is completely terminated by disposition or death during the tax year, all shareholders holding stock during the year and the corporation may elect to treat the S taxable year as two taxable years. The first year ends on the date of the termination. Under this election, an interim closing of the books is undertaken, and the shareholders report their shares of the S corporation items as they occurred during the short tax year.[28]

The short-year election provides an opportunity to shift income, losses, and credits between shareholders. The election is desirable in circumstances where more loss can be allocated to taxpayers with higher marginal rates.

EXAMPLE 21

Alicia, the owner of all of the shares of an S corporation, transfers her stock to Cindy halfway through the tax year. There is a $100,000 NOL for the entire tax year, but $30,000 of the loss occurs during the first half of the year. Without a short-year election, $50,000 of the loss is allocated to Alicia, and $50,000 is allocated to Cindy. If the corporation makes the short-year election, Cindy is allocated $70,000 of the loss. Of course, the sales price of the stock would probably be increased to recognize the tax benefits being transferred from Alicia to Cindy. ■

In the case of the death of a shareholder, a short-year election prevents the income and loss allocation to a deceased shareholder from being affected by post-death events.

EXAMPLE 22

Joey and Karl equally own Rose, Inc., a calendar year S corporation. Joey dies on June 29 of a year that is not a leap year. Rose has income of $250,000 for January 1 through June 29 and $750,000 for the remainder of the year. Without a short-year election, the income is allocated by assigning an equal portion of the annual income of $1 million to each day (or $2,739.73 per day) and allocating the daily portion between the shareholders. Joey is allocated 50% of the daily income for the 180 days from January 1 to June 29, or $246,575.70 [($2,739.73/2) × 180]. Joey's *estate* is allocated 50% of the income for the 185 days from June 30 to December 31, or $253,425.02 [($2,739.73/2) × 185].

If the short-year election is made, the income of $250,000 from January 1 to June 29 is divided equally between Joey and Karl, so that each is taxed on $125,000. The income of $750,000 from June 30 to December 31 is divided equally between Joey's estate and Karl, or $375,000 to each.

Under either alternative, Karl reports income of $500,000. However, with the short-year election, $375,000 is allocated to Joey's estate versus only $253,425.02 without the election. Because the estate income tax rates are more progressive than the income tax rates on individuals, Joey's heirs would prefer that the election not be made. ■

Tax Treatment of Distributions to Shareholders

The amount of any distribution to an S corporation shareholder is equal to the cash plus the fair market value of any other property distributed. How the distribution is taxed depends upon whether the S corporation has C corporation **accumulated earnings and profits** (AEP, described in Chapter 5).

---

[28] § 1377(a)(2).

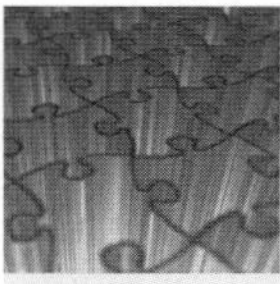

CONCEPT SUMMARY 12.1

Classification Procedures for Distributions from an S Corporation

Where No Earnings and Profits Exist	Where Earnings and Profits Exist
	1. Distributions are tax-free to the extent of the AAA.
	2. Distributions from AEP constitute dividend income.†
	3. Distributions are tax-free to the extent of the other adjustments account (OAA).
1. Distributions are nontaxable to the extent of shareholder's basis of stock.*	4. Any residual distribution amount is nontaxable to the extent of shareholder's basis of stock.*
2. Excess is treated as gain from a sale or exchange of stock (capital gain in most cases).	5. Excess is treated as gain from a sale or exchange of stock (capital gain in most cases).

* The distribution reduces the stock basis. Once stock basis reaches zero, any distribution from the AAA is treated as a gain from the sale or exchange of stock. Thus, the shareholder's stock basis is an upper limit on what a shareholder may receive tax-free.

† The AAA bypass election is available to pay out AEP before reducing the AAA [§ 1368(e)(3)].

No C Corporation AEP

If the S corporation has never been a C corporation or if it has no C corporation AEP, the distribution is a tax-free recovery of capital to the extent that it does not exceed the shareholder's adjusted basis in the stock of the S corporation. When the amount of the distribution exceeds the adjusted basis of the stock, the excess is treated as a gain from the sale or exchange of property (capital gain in most cases). The vast majority of S corporations fall into this favorable category.

EXAMPLE 23

Twirl, Inc., a calendar year S corporation, has no AEP. During the year, Juan, an individual shareholder of the corporation, receives a cash distribution of $12,200 from Twirl. Juan's basis in his stock is $9,700. Juan recognizes a capital gain of $2,500, the excess of the distribution over the stock basis ($12,200 − $9,700). The remaining $9,700 is tax-free, but it reduces Juan's basis in his stock to zero. ■

C Corporation AEP

S corporations with C corporation AEP blend the entity and conduit approaches to taxation. This blending treats distributions of pre-election (C corporation) and postelection (S corporation) earnings differently. Distributions of C corporation AEP are taxed as dividends (0/15% rate), while distributions of previously taxed S corporation earnings are tax-free to the extent of the shareholder's adjusted basis in the stock.

Concept Summary 12.1 outlines the taxation of distributions. These rules are intended to prevent two problems that result when a C corporation has been converted to an S corporation.

- Tax manipulation could result in AEP from the C corporation years being withdrawn without taxation, because S corporation shareholders are taxed on income, not on distributions.
- On the other hand, double taxation could occur. Earnings from the S corporation years might both flow to the shareholders' tax returns as income and be taxed as dividends as if the corporation were a C corporation.

A special account is required to track undistributed earnings of an S corporation that have been taxed to shareholders previously. Distributions from this account, known as the **accumulated adjustments account (AAA)**, are tax-free. The AAA begins

EXHIBIT 12.1 Adjustments to the Corporate AAA

Increase by:

1. Schedule K income items other than tax-exempt income.
2. Nonseparately computed income.
3. Depletion in excess of basis in the property.

Decrease by:

4. Negative Schedule K adjustments other than distributions (e.g., losses and deductions).
5. Any portion of a distribution that is considered to be tax-free from the AAA (but not below zero).

Note: When the combination of items 1 through 4 results in a negative number, the AAA is adjusted first for the distribution and then for the adjustments in items 1 through 4.

with a zero balance on the first day of an S corporation's first tax year. Essentially, the AAA is the cumulative total of undistributed nonseparately and separately stated items for S corporation taxable years beginning after 1982. Thus, the account parallels the calculation of C corporation AEP. Calculation of the AAA applies to all S corporations, but the AAA is most important to those that have been C corporations. The AAA provides a mechanism to ensure that the earnings of an S corporation are taxed to shareholders only once.

The AAA is computed by making adjustments in the order specified in Exhibit 12.1. Its balance is determined at the end of each year rather than at the time distributions are made. When more than one distribution occurs in the same year, a pro rata portion of each distribution is treated as having been made out of the AAA.

In calculating the amount in the AAA for purposes of determining the tax treatment of current-year distributions, the net negative adjustments (e.g., the excess of losses and deductions over income) for that tax year are ignored. Tax-exempt income and related expenses (e.g., insurance proceeds and premiums paid for life insurance) do not affect the AAA.

A shareholder has a proportionate interest in the AAA, regardless of the size of his or her stock basis.[29] However, because the AAA is a corporate account, no connection exists between the prior accumulated S corporation income and any specific shareholder.[30] Thus, the benefits of the AAA can be shifted from one shareholder to another shareholder. For example, when one S shareholder transfers stock to another shareholder, any AAA balance on the purchase date may be distributed tax free to the purchaser. Similarly, issuing additional stock to a new shareholder in an S corporation with a positive balance in the AAA dilutes the account relative to the existing shareholders.

The AAA (unlike the stock basis) can have a negative balance. All losses decrease the AAA balance, even those in excess of the shareholder's stock basis. However, *distributions* may not make the AAA negative or increase a negative balance.

Distribution Ordering Rules

A cash distribution from an S corporation with AEP comes first from the AAA (limited to stock basis).[31] Distributions from the AAA are tax-free. The remaining distribution is taxed as a dividend to the extent of AEP. After AEP is fully distributed, any residual amount is applied against the other adjustments account (OAA, discussed in the next section) and then the shareholder's remaining stock basis. The reduction in the shareholder's stock basis is a tax-free recovery of capital.[32] Any distributions once the stock basis reaches zero are taxed as capital gains.

[29] § 1368(c).

[30] § 1368(e)(1)(A).

[31] §§ 1368(c)(1) and (e)(1). Before 1983, an account similar to the AAA was in place, namely, **previously taxed income** (PTI). An S corporation in existence before 1983 might still hold some PTI.

[32] § 1368(c).

EXAMPLE 24

Short, a calendar year S corporation, distributes $1,300 cash to its only shareholder, Otis, on December 31, 2012. Otis's basis in his stock is $1,400, Short's AAA balance is $500, and Short holds $750 AEP before the distribution.

According to the distribution ordering rules, the first $500 is a tax-free recovery of basis from the AAA. The next $750 is a taxable dividend distribution from AEP. The remaining $50 of cash is a tax-free recovery of basis. Immediately after the distribution, Short holds a zero balance in its AAA and AEP. Otis's stock basis now is $850.

	Corporate AAA	Corporate AEP	Otis's Stock Basis*
Balance before the distribution	$ 500	$ 750	$1,400
Distribution ($1,300)			
From AAA	(500)		(500)
From AEP		(750)	
From stock basis			(50)
Balance after the distribution	$ –0–	$ –0–	$ 850

*Details of basis adjustments are discussed later in the chapter. ■

EXAMPLE 25

Assume the same facts as in the preceding example. During the following year, Short reports zero ordinary income and distributes $1,000 to Otis. Of the distribution, $850 is a tax-free recovery of basis, and $150 is taxed to Otis as a capital gain. ■

With the consent of all of its shareholders, an S corporation can elect to have a distribution treated as if it were made from AEP rather than from the AAA. This mechanism is known as an AAA **bypass election**. This election may be desirable as a simple means by which to eliminate a small AEP balance.

EXAMPLE 26

Collett, a calendar year S corporation, has AEP of $12,000 and a balance of $20,000 in the AAA. Collett Corporation may elect to distribute the AEP first, creating a $12,000 dividend for its shareholders, before using the AAA. ■

Schedule M-2

S corporations report changes in the AAA on Schedule M-2 of Form 1120S. Schedule M-2 contains a column labeled **other adjustments account (OAA)**. This account includes items that affect basis but not the AAA, such as tax-exempt income and any related nondeductible expenses. For example, life insurance proceeds received and insurance premiums paid are traced through the OAA. Distributions are made from the OAA after AEP and the AAA are depleted to zero. Distributions from the OAA generally are tax-free.

EXAMPLE 27

During 2012, Sparrow, an S corporation, records the following items.

AAA, beginning of the year	$ 8,500
Ordinary income	25,000
Tax-exempt interest	4,000
Key employee life insurance proceeds received	5,000
Payroll penalty expense	2,000
Charitable contributions	3,000
Unreasonable compensation	5,000
Premiums on key employee life insurance	2,100
Distributions to shareholders	16,000

Sparrow's Schedule M-2 for the current year appears as follows.

Schedule M-2 **Analysis of Accumulated Adjustments Account, Other Adjustments Account, and Shareholders' Undistributed Taxable Income Previously Taxed** (see instructions)

		(a) Accumulated adjustments account	(b) Other adjustments account	(c) Shareholders' undistributed taxable income previously taxed
1	Balance at beginning of tax year	*8,500*		*6,250*
2	Ordinary income from page 1, line 21	*25,000*		
3	Other additions		*9,000***	
4	Loss from page 1, line 21	( )		
5	Other reductions	(*10,000**)	(*2,100*)	
6	Combine lines 1 through 5	*23,500*	*6,900*	
7	Distributions other than dividend distributions	*16,000*		
8	Balance at end of tax year. Subtract line 7 from line 6	*7,500*	*6,900*	*6,250*

**$2,000 (payroll penalty) + $3,000 (charitable contributions) + $5,000 (unreasonable compensation).*
***$4,000 (tax-exempt interest) + $5,000 (life insurance proceeds).*

Schedule M-3: Net Income or Loss Reconciliation

S corporations that have total assets on Schedule L at the end of the tax year that equal or exceed $10 million must file Schedule M-3 in lieu of Schedule M-1. For purposes of measuring total assets at the end of the year, assets are not netted or offset against liabilities. Total assets are determined using the accrual method of accounting unless both (1) the tax return of the corporation is prepared using an overall cash method of accounting, and (2) no entity includible in the Federal tax return prepares or is included in financial statements prepared on an accrual basis.

The Schedule M-3 for S corporations is not identical to that for C corporations. Part I asks certain questions about the corporation's financial statements, and it reconciles book net income or loss to the income or loss for the tax year of the entity's Federal tax return. Parts II and III reconcile specific book income or loss items with corresponding amounts on the U.S. tax return.

The IRS estimates that it takes about 87 hours to complete the Schedule M-3 of an S corporation, but many practitioners believe that more time may be required. A more complete discussion of Schedule M-3 is found in Chapter 2.

ETHICS & EQUITY Avoiding Schedule M-3

Your S corporation client has read that a Schedule M-3 is now required for all S corporations with at least $10 million of assets. He says that the new schedule will reveal between 75 to 90 percent of the company's book-tax differences. Although this new schedule will help IRS agents find abusive transactions, your client is concerned that it will impose additional compliance burdens. The client's S corporation is approaching $10 million of assets, and he is thinking of either distributing some of the entity's business assets to himself or engaging in a spin-off. Are these techniques ethical?

Effect of Terminating the S Election

Normally, distributions to shareholders from a C corporation are taxed as dividends to the extent of E & P. However, any distribution of *cash* by a corporation to shareholders during a one-year period[33] following S election termination receives special treatment. Such a distribution is treated as a tax-free recovery of stock basis to the extent that it does not exceed the AAA.[34] Because *only* cash distributions reduce the AAA during this *postelection termination period*, a corporation should not make property distributions during this time. Instead, the entity should sell property and distribute the proceeds to shareholders. However, post-termination distributions that are charged against the OAA do not get tax-free treatment. To take

[33]The period is approximately one year in length. The post-termination transition period is discussed later in the chapter.

[34]§§ 1371(e) and 1377(b).

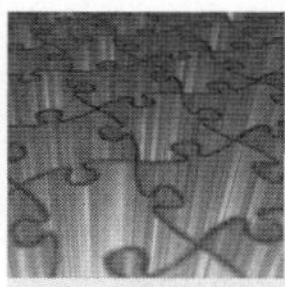

CONCEPT SUMMARY 12.2

Consequences of Noncash Distributions

	Appreciated Property	Depreciated Property
S corporation	Realized gain is recognized by the corporation, which passes it through to the shareholders. Such gain increases a shareholder's stock basis, generating a basis in the property equal to FMV. On the distribution, the shareholder's stock basis is reduced by the FMV of the property (but not below zero).	Realized loss is not recognized. The shareholder takes an FMV basis in the property.
C corporation	Realized gain is recognized under § 311(b) and increases E & P (net of tax). The shareholder reports a taxable dividend to the extent of corporate E & P equal to the property's FMV. The shareholder takes an asset basis equal its FMV.	Realized loss is not recognized. The shareholder takes an FMV basis in the property.
Partnership	No gain to the partnership or partner. The partner takes a carryover basis in the asset, but the asset basis is limited to the partner's basis in the partnership.	Realized loss is not recognized. The partner takes a carryover basis in the asset, but the asset basis is limited to the partner's basis in the partnership.

advantage of post-termination benefits, an S corporation must know the amount of both the AAA and the OAA as of the date the election terminates.

EXAMPLE 28

Quinn, the sole shareholder of Roman, Inc., a calendar year S corporation, elects during 2012 to terminate the S election, effective January 1, 2013. As of the end of 2012, Roman has an AAA of $1,300. Quinn can receive a nontaxable distribution of cash during a post-termination period of approximately one year to the extent of Roman's AAA. Although a cash distribution of $1,300 during 2013 would be nontaxable to Quinn, it would reduce the adjusted basis of his stock. ■

Tax Treatment of Noncash Property Distributions by the Corporation

LO.7

Determine how distributions to S corporation shareholders are taxed.

An S corporation recognizes a gain on any liquidating or nonliquidating distribution of appreciated property in the same manner as if the asset were sold to the shareholder at its fair market value.[35] The corporate gain is passed through to the shareholders. The character of the gain—capital gain or ordinary income—depends upon the type of asset being distributed. There is an important reason for this gain recognition rule. Without it, property might be distributed tax-free (other than for certain recapture items) and later sold without income recognition to the shareholder because the shareholder's basis equals the asset's fair market value.

The S corporation does not recognize a loss when distributing assets that are worth less than their basis. As with gain property, the shareholder's basis is equal to the asset's fair market value. Thus, the potential loss is postponed until the shareholder sells the stock of the S corporation. Because loss property receives a step-down in basis without any loss recognition by the S corporation, distributions of loss property should be avoided.

EXAMPLE 29

Turnip, Inc., an S corporation for 10 years, distributes a tract of land held as an investment to Chang, its majority shareholder. The land was purchased for $22,000 many

[35] § 311(b).

years ago and is currently worth $82,000. Turnip recognizes a capital gain of $60,000, which increases the AAA by $60,000. The gain appears on Turnip's Schedule K, and a proportionate share of it passes through to the shareholders' tax returns. Then the property dividend reduces the AAA by $82,000 (the fair market value). The tax consequences are the same for appreciated property, whether it is distributed to the shareholders and they dispose of it, or the corporation sells the property and distributes the proceeds to the shareholders.

If the land had been purchased for $82,000 and was currently worth $22,000, Chang would take a $22,000 basis in the land. The $60,000 realized loss is not recognized at the corporate level. The loss does not reduce Turnip's AAA. Only when the S corporation sells the asset does it recognize the loss and reduce AAA. ■

EXAMPLE 30

Assume the same facts as in the previous example, except that Turnip is a C corporation ($1 million E & P balance) or a partnership. The partner's basis in the partnership interest is $100,000.

	Appreciated Property		
	S Corporation	**C Corporation**	**Partnership**
Entity gain/loss	$60,000	$60,000	$ –0–
Owner's gain/loss/dividend	60,000	82,000	–0–
Owner's basis in land	82,000	82,000	22,000
	Property That Has Declined in Value		
	S Corporation	**C Corporation**	**Partnership**
Entity gain/loss	$ –0–	$ –0–	$ –0–
Owner's gain/loss/dividend	–0–	22,000	–0–
Owner's basis in land	22,000	22,000	82,000

■

LO.8

Calculate a shareholder's basis in S corporation stock.

Shareholder's Basis

The calculation of the initial tax basis of stock in an S corporation is similar to that for the basis of stock in a C corporation and depends upon the manner in which the shares are acquired (e.g., gift, inheritance, purchase, exchange under § 351, etc.). Once the initial tax basis is determined, various transactions during the life of the corporation affect the shareholder's basis in the stock. Although each shareholder is required to compute his or her own basis in the S shares, neither Form 1120S nor Schedule K–1 provides a place for deriving this amount.

A shareholder's basis is increased by stock purchases and capital contributions. Operations during the year cause the following upward adjustments to basis.[36]

- Nonseparately computed income.
- Separately stated income items (e.g., nontaxable income).
- Depletion in excess of basis in the property.

Basis then is reduced by distributions not reported as income by the shareholder (e.g., an AAA distribution). Next, the following items reduce basis (*but not below zero*).

- Nondeductible expenses of the corporation (e.g., fines, penalties, and illegal kickbacks).
- Nonseparately computed loss.
- Separately stated loss and deduction items.

As under the partnership rule, basis first is increased by income items; then it is decreased by distributions and finally by losses.[37] In most cases, this *losses last* rule is advantageous to the S shareholder.

[36]§ 1367(a).

[37]Reg. § 1.1367–1(f).

EXAMPLE 31

In its first year of operation, Iris, Inc., a calendar year S corporation in Clemson, South Carolina, earns income of $2,000. On February 2 in its second year of operation, Iris distributes $2,000 to Marty, its sole shareholder. During the remainder of the second year, the corporation incurs a $2,000 loss.

Under the S corporation ordering rules, the $2,000 distribution is tax-free AAA to Marty, and the $2,000 loss is deductible by Marty if he has a sufficient stock basis. ■

A shareholder's basis in the stock can never be reduced below zero. Once stock basis is zero, any additional basis reductions from losses or deductions, but *not* distributions, decrease (but not below zero) the shareholder's basis in loans made to the S corporation. Any excess of losses or deductions over both bases is *suspended* until there are subsequent bases. Once the basis of any debt is reduced, it is later increased (only up to the original amount) by the subsequent *net* increase resulting from *all* positive and negative basis adjustments. The debt basis is adjusted back to the original amount by any "net increase" before any increase is made in the stock basis.[38] "Net increase" for a year is computed after taking distributions (other than those from AEP) into consideration. A distribution in excess of stock basis does not reduce any debt basis. If a loss and a distribution occur in the same year, the loss reduces the stock basis last, *after* the distribution.

EXAMPLE 32

Stacey, a sole shareholder, has a $7,000 stock basis and a $2,000 basis in a loan that she made to a calendar year S corporation with no AEP. At the beginning of 2012, the corporation's AAA and OAA balances are $0. Subchapter S ordinary income for 2012 is $8,200. During 2012, the corporation received $2,000 of tax-exempt interest income.

Cash of $17,300 is distributed to Stacey on November 15, 2012. Stacey recognizes only a $100 capital gain.

	Corporate AAA	Corporate OAA	Stacey's Stock Basis	Stacey's Loan Basis
Beginning balance	$ -0-	$ -0-	$ 7,000	$2,000
Ordinary income	8,200		8,200	
Exempt income		2,000	2,000	
Subtotal	$ 8,200	$ 2,000	$17,200	$2,000
Distribution ($17,300)				
From AAA	(8,200)		(8,200)	
From OAA		(2,000)	(2,000)	
From stock basis			(7,000)	
Ending balance	$ -0-	$ -0-	$ -0-	$2,000
Distribution in excess of basis = Capital gain			$ 100	

Pass-through losses can reduce loan basis, but distributions do not. Stock basis cannot be reduced below zero, but the $100 excess distribution does not reduce Stacey's loan basis. ■

The basis rules for an S corporation are similar to the rules for determining a partner's interest basis in a partnership. However, a partner's basis in the partnership interest includes the partner's direct investment plus a *ratable share* of any partnership liabilities.[39] If a partnership borrows from a partner, the partner receives a basis increase as if the partnership had borrowed from an unrelated third party.[40] In contrast, except for loans from the shareholder to the corporation, corporate

[38] § 1367(b)(2); Reg. § 1.1367–2(e).
[39] § 752(a).
[40] Reg. § 1.752–1(e).

borrowing has no effect on S corporation shareholder basis. Loans from a shareholder to the S corporation have a tax basis only for the shareholder making the loan.

The fact that a shareholder has guaranteed a loan made to the corporation by a third party has no effect on the shareholder's loan basis, unless payments actually have been made as a result of that guarantee.[41] If the corporation defaults on indebtedness and the shareholder makes good on the guarantee, the shareholder's indebtedness basis is increased to that extent.

A flow-through deduction is available for a shareholder loan only where there is clear evidence that the S corporation is liable to the shareholder. A shareholder looking for this result should borrow the money from the bank and then loan the money to the S corporation.

If a loan's basis has been reduced and is not restored, income is recognized when the S corporation repays the shareholder. If the corporation issued a note as evidence of the debt, repayment constitutes an amount received in exchange for a capital asset and the amount that exceeds the shareholder's basis is entitled to capital gain treatment.[42] However, if the loan is made on open account, the repayment constitutes ordinary income to the extent that it exceeds the shareholder's basis in the loan.[43] Each repayment is prorated between the gain portion and the repayment of the debt.[44] Thus, a note should be given to ensure capital gain treatment for the income that results from a loan's repayment.

EXAMPLE 33

Sammy is a 57% owner of Falcon, an S corporation in Brooklyn, New York. At the beginning of the year, his stock basis is zero. Sammy's basis in a $12,000 loan made to Falcon and evidenced by Falcon's note has been reduced to $0 by prior losses. At the end of the year, he receives a $13,000 distribution. During the year, his net share of corporate taxable income is $11,000. Because there is no "net increase" (i.e., his share of income is less than the amount of the distribution), Sammy's debt basis is not restored. Instead, his share of income increases his stock basis to $11,000. Therefore, on receipt of the $13,000 distribution, $11,000 is a tax-free recovery of his stock basis, and $2,000 is a capital gain.[45] ■

EXAMPLE 34

Assume in the previous example that the distribution that Sammy receives is only $8,000. Because the "net increase" is $3,000 ($11,000 income share in excess of $8,000 distribution), the debt basis is restored by $3,000. Accordingly, the remaining income share not used to increase debt basis ($8,000) is used to increase Sammy's stock basis to $8,000. Therefore, on receipt of the $8,000 distribution, all $8,000 is tax-free, reducing the stock basis back to zero. ■

LO.9

Explain the tax effects that losses have on shareholders.

Treatment of Losses

Net Operating Loss

One major advantage of an S election is the ability to pass through any net operating loss of the corporation directly to the shareholders. A shareholder can deduct an NOL for the year in which the S corporation's tax year ends. The corporation is not entitled to any deduction for the NOL. A shareholder's basis in the stock is reduced to the extent of any pass-through of the NOL, and the shareholder's AAA is reduced by the same deductible amount.[46]

---

[41]See, for example, *Estate of Leavitt*, 90 T.C. 206 (1988), *aff'd* 89–1 USTC ¶9332, 63 AFTR 2d 89–1437, 875 F.2d 420 (CA–4, 1989); *Selfe v. U.S.*, 86–1 USTC ¶9115, 57 AFTR 2d 86–464, 778 F.2d 769 (CA–11, 1985); *James K. Calcutt*, 91 T.C. 14 (1988).

[42]*Joe M. Smith*, 48 T.C. 872 (1967), *aff'd* and *rev'd* in 70–1 USTC ¶9327, 25 AFTR 2d 70–936, 424 F.2d 219 (CA–9, 1970); Rev.Rul. 64–162, 1964–1 C.B. 304.

[43]Reg. § 1.1367–2. Open account debt is treated as if it were evidenced by a note if the shareholder's principal balance exceeds $25,000 at the end of the tax year.

[44]Rev.Rul. 68–537, 1968–2 C.B. 372.

[45]§ 1367(b)(2)(B); Reg. § 1.1367–2(e).

[46]§§ 1368(a)(1)(A) and (e)(1)(A).

THE BIG PICTURE

EXAMPLE 35

Return to the facts of *The Big Picture* on p. 12-1. If Smith and Jones make the S election for Cane, Inc., they each can pass through any NOLs to the extent of the current stock basis. If the new S corporation incurs an NOL of $84,000 during 2012, both shareholders are entitled to deduct $42,000 against other income for the tax year in which Cane's tax year ends. Any NOL incurred before the S election is in effect does not flow through to the two shareholders as long as the S election is maintained.

Deductions for an S corporation's loss pass-throughs (e.g., NOL, capital loss, and charitable contributions) cannot exceed a shareholder's adjusted basis in the stock *plus* the basis of any loans made by the shareholder to the corporation. If a taxpayer is unable to prove the tax basis, the loss pass-through can be denied.[47] As noted previously, once a shareholder's adjusted stock basis has been eliminated by a loss pass-through, any excess loss reduces the shareholder's basis for any loans made to the corporation (*but never below zero*). The basis for loans is established by the actual advances made to the corporation, and not by indirect loans.[48] If the shareholder's basis is insufficient to allow a full flow-through and there is more than one type of loss (e.g., in the same year the S corporation incurs both a passive loss and a net capital loss), the flow-through amounts are determined on a pro rata basis.

EXAMPLE 36

Ralph is a 50% owner of an S corporation for the entire year. His stock basis is $10,000, and his shares of the various corporate losses are as follows.

Ordinary loss from operations	$8,000
Capital loss	5,000
§ 1231 loss	3,000
Passive loss	2,000

Based upon a pro rata approach, the total $10,000 allocable flow-through would be split among the various losses as follows.

$$\text{Ordinary loss} = \frac{\$8,000}{\$18,000} \times \$10,000 = \$\ 4,444.44$$

$$\text{Capital loss} = \frac{\$5,000}{\$18,000} \times \$10,000 = \$\ 2,777.78$$

$$\S\ 1231\ \text{loss} = \frac{\$3,000}{\$18,000} \times \$10,000 = \$\ 1,666.67$$

$$\text{Passive loss} = \frac{\$2,000}{\$18,000} \times \$10,000 = \underline{\$\ 1,111.11}$$

$$\text{Total allocated loss} \qquad \underline{\underline{\$10,000.00}}$$

■

Distributions made by an S corporation are taken into account *before* applying the loss limitations for the year. Thus, distributions reduce the shareholder's stock basis used in determining the allowable loss for the year, but a flow-through loss does *not* reduce stock basis when accounting for distributions made during the year.

EXAMPLE 37

Pylon, Inc., a calendar year S corporation, is partly owned by Doris, who has a beginning stock basis of $10,000. During the year, Doris's share of a long-term capital gain

[47]See *Donald J. Sauvigne*, 30 TCM 123, T.C.Memo. 1971–30.

[48]*Ruth M. Prashker*, 59 T.C. 172 (1972); *Frederick G. Brown v. U.S.*, 83–1 USTC ¶9364, 52 AFTR 2d 82–5080, 706 F.2d 755 (CA–6, 1983).

(LTCG) is $2,000, and her share of an ordinary loss is $9,000. If Doris receives a $6,000 distribution, her deductible loss is calculated as follows.

Beginning stock basis	$10,000
Add: LTCG	2,000
Subtotal	$12,000
Less: Distribution	(6,000)
Basis for loss limitation purposes	$ 6,000
Deductible loss	($ 6,000)
Unused loss	($ 3,000)

Doris's stock now has a basis of zero. ■

A shareholder's share of an NOL may be greater than both stock basis and loan basis. A shareholder is entitled to carry forward a loss to the extent that the loss for the year exceeds basis. Any loss carried forward may be deducted *only* by the *same* shareholder if and when the basis in the stock or loans to the corporation is restored.[49]

EXAMPLE 38

Dana has a stock basis of $4,000 in an S corporation. He has loaned $2,000 to the corporation and has guaranteed another $4,000 loan made to the corporation by a local bank. Although his share of the S corporation's NOL for the current year is $9,500, Dana may deduct only $6,000 of the NOL on his individual tax return. Dana may carry forward $3,500 of the NOL, to be deducted when the basis in his stock or loan to the corporation is restored. Dana has a zero basis in both the stock and the loan after the flow-through of the $6,000 NOL. ■

Any loss carryover due to insufficient basis remaining at the end of an approximately one-year post-termination transition period is *lost forever.* The post-termination period includes the 120-day period beginning on the date of any determination pursuant to an audit of a taxpayer that follows the termination of the S corporation's election and that adjusts a Subchapter S item.[50] Thus, if a shareholder has a loss carryover, he or she should increase the stock or loan basis and flow through the loss before disposing of the stock.

Net operating losses from C corporation years cannot be utilized at the corporate level (except with respect to built-in gains, discussed later in this chapter), nor can they be passed through to the shareholders. Further, the carryforward period continues to run during S status.[51] Consequently, the S election may not be appropriate for a C corporation with NOL carryforwards. When a corporation is expecting losses in the future, an S election should be made *before* the loss years.

At-Risk Rules

As discussed in Chapter 11, S corporation shareholders, like partners, are limited in the amount of loss they may deduct by their "at-risk" amounts. The rules for determining at-risk amounts are similar, but not identical, to the partner at-risk rules. These rules apply to the shareholders, but not to the corporation. An amount at risk is determined separately for each shareholder. The amount of the corporate losses that are passed through and deductible by the shareholders is not affected by the amount the corporation has at risk.

EXAMPLE 39

Shareholder Ricketts has a basis of $35,000 in his S corporation stock. He takes a $15,000 nonrecourse loan from a local bank and lends the proceeds to the S corporation. Ricketts now has a stock basis of $35,000 and a debt basis of $15,000. However, due to the at-risk limitation, he can deduct only $35,000 of losses from the S corporation. ■

---

[49]§ 1366(d).

[50]§ 1377(b)(1).

[51]§ 1371(b).

Passive Losses and Credits

Section 469 provides that net passive losses and credits are not deductible when incurred and must be carried over to a year when there is passive income. Thus, one must be aware of three major classes of income, losses, and credits—active, portfolio, and passive. S corporations are not directly subject to the limits of § 469, but corporate rental activities are inherently passive, and other activities of an S corporation may be passive unless the shareholder(s) materially participate(s) in operating the business. An S corporation may engage in more than one such activity. If the corporate activity involves rentals or the shareholders do not materially participate, any loss or credit that flows through is passive. The shareholders are able to apply such losses or credits only against income from other passive activities.

A shareholder's stock basis is reduced by passive losses that flow through to the shareholder, even though the shareholder may not be entitled to a current deduction due to the passive loss limitations. The existence of material participation is determined at the shareholder level. There are seven tests for material participation, including a need to participate in the activity for more than 500 hours during the taxable year.[52]

EXAMPLE 40

Heather is a 50% owner of an S corporation engaged in a passive activity. A nonparticipating shareholder, she receives a salary of $6,000 for services as a result of the passive activity. Heather has $6,000 of earned income as a result of the salary. The $6,000 salary creates a $6,000 deduction/passive loss, which flows through to the shareholders. Heather's $3,000 share of the loss may not be deducted against the $6,000 of earned income. Under § 469(e)(3), earned income is not taken into account in computing the income or loss from a passive activity. ■

Tax on Pre-Election Built-in Gain

LO.10

Compute the built-in gains and passive investment income penalty taxes.

Normally, an S corporation does *not* pay an income tax, because all items flow through to the shareholders. But an S corporation that was previously a C corporation may be required to pay a built-in gains tax, LIFO recapture tax, general business credit recapture, or passive investment income tax.

Without the **built-in gains tax** (§ 1374), it would be possible to avoid the corporate double tax on a disposition of appreciated property by electing S corporation status.

The § 1374 tax generally applies to C corporations converting to S status after 1986. It is a *corporate-level* tax on any built-in gain recognized when the S corporation disposes of an asset in a taxable disposition within 10 calendar years after the date on which the S election took effect. The 10-year holding period is reduced to 7 years for tax years beginning in 2009 and 2010, and to 5 years for 2011.[53] The holding period begins on the date of the S election.

General Rules

The base for the § 1374 tax includes any unrealized gain on appreciated assets (e.g., real estate, cash basis receivables, and goodwill) held by a corporation on the day it elects S status. The highest corporate tax rate (currently 35 percent) is applied to the unrealized gain when any of the assets are sold. Furthermore, the gain on the sale (net of the § 1374 tax)[54] passes through as a taxable gain to shareholders.

EXAMPLE 41

Zinnia, Inc., a C corporation, owns a single asset with a basis of $100,000 and a fair market value of $500,000. Zinnia elects S corporation status. Section 1374 imposes a corporate-level tax that must be paid by Zinnia if it sells the asset after electing S status. Upon sale of the asset, the corporation owes a tax of $140,000 ($400,000 × 35%). The shareholders have a $260,000 taxable gain ($400,000 − $140,000). Hence, the built-in gains tax effectively imposes a double tax on Zinnia and its shareholders. ■

[52]Reg. § 1.469–5T(a).

[53]§ 1374(d)(7)(B).

[54]§ 1366(f)(2).

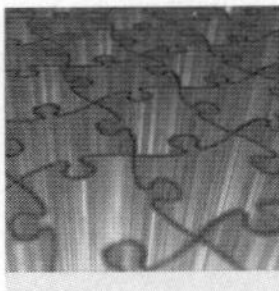

CONCEPT SUMMARY 12.3

Calculation of the Built-in Gains Tax Liability

Step 1. Select the smaller of built-in gain or taxable income (C corporation rules).*

Step 2. Deduct unexpired NOLs and capital losses from C corporation tax years.

Step 3. Multiply the tax base obtained in step 2 by the top corporate income tax rate.

Step 4. Deduct any business credit carryforwards and AMT credit carryovers arising in a C corporation tax year from the amount obtained in step 3.

Step 5. The corporation pays any tax resulting from step 4.

* Any net recognized built-in gain in excess of taxable income is carried forward to the next year, as long as the next year is within the 5-, 7-, or 10-year recognition period.

The maximum amount of gain that is recognized over the required (5-, 7-, or 10-year) holding period is limited to the *aggregate net* built-in gain of the corporation at the time it converted to S status. Thus, at the time of the S election, unrealized gains of the corporation are offset against unrealized losses. The net amount of gains and losses sets an upper limit on the tax base for the built-in gains tax. Any appreciation after the conversion to S status is subject to the regular S corporation pass-through rules.

Contributions of assets with realized losses on the date of conversion reduce the maximum built-in gain and any potential tax under § 1374.[55] In addition, built-in losses and built-in gains are netted each year to determine the annual § 1374 tax base. Thus, an incentive exists to contribute loss assets to a corporation before electing S status. However, the IRS position is that contributions of loss property within two years before the earlier of the date of conversion or the date of filing an S election are presumed to have a tax avoidance motive and will not reduce the corporation's net unrealized built-in gain.

Normally, tax attributes of a C corporation do *not* carry over to a converted S corporation. For purposes of the tax on built-in gains, however, certain carryovers are allowed. In particular, an S corporation can offset built-in gains with unexpired NOLs or capital losses from C corporation years.

THE BIG PICTURE

EXAMPLE 42

Return to the facts of *The Big Picture* on p. 12-1. If Cane, Inc., becomes an S corporation, a built-in gain may be recognized. Assuming that Cane reports a $50,000 built-in gain on conversion and that it holds a $20,000 NOL carryforward for C corporation years before the S election, the NOL carryforward is applied against the built-in gain. Cane's built-in gains tax applies only to $30,000.

Concept Summary 12.3 summarizes the calculation of the built-in gains tax.

LIFO Recapture Tax

To preclude deferral of gain recognition by a C corporation that is electing S status, any LIFO recapture amount at the time of the S election is subject to a corporate-level tax.

The taxable LIFO recapture amount equals the excess of the inventory's value under FIFO over the LIFO value. No negative adjustment is allowed if the LIFO value is higher than the FIFO value.

[55] §§ 1374(c)(2) and (d)(1).

The resulting tax is payable in four equal installments, with the first payment due on or before the due date for the corporate return for the last C corporation year (without regard to any extensions). The remaining three installments are paid on or before the due dates of the succeeding corporate returns. No interest is due if payments are made by the due dates, and no estimated taxes are due on the four tax installments. The basis of the LIFO inventory is adjusted to account for this LIFO recapture amount, but the AAA is not decreased by payment of the tax.

Passive Investment Income Penalty Tax

A tax is imposed on the excess passive income of S corporations that possess AEP from C corporation years. The tax rate is the highest corporate rate for the year (35 percent in 2012). The rate is applied to excess net passive income (ENPI), which is determined using the following formula:

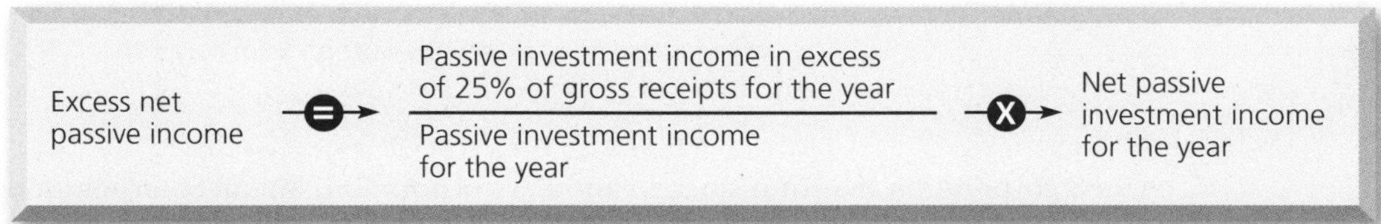

Passive investment income (PII) includes gross receipts derived from royalties, passive rents, dividends, interest, and annuities. Only the net gain from the disposition of capital assets is taken into account in computing PII gross receipts.[56] Passive investment income does not include built-in gains (or losses) recognized during the 5-, 7-, or 10-year waiting period. Net passive income is passive income reduced by any deductions directly connected with the production of that income. Any passive income tax reduces the amount the shareholders must take into income.

The excess net passive income cannot exceed the C corporate taxable income for the year before considering any NOL deduction or the special deductions allowed by §§ 241–250 (except the organizational expense deduction).[57]

EXAMPLE 43

Barnhardt Corporation, an S corporation, has gross receipts for the year totaling $264,000 (of which $110,000 is PII). Expenditures directly connected to the production of the PII total $30,000. Therefore, Barnhardt has net PII of $80,000 ($110,000 − $30,000), and its PII for the tax year exceeds 25% of its gross receipts by $44,000 [$110,000 PII − (25% × $264,000)]. Excess net passive income (ENPI) is $32,000, calculated as follows.

$$\text{ENPI} = \frac{\$44{,}000}{\$110{,}000} \times \$80{,}000 = \$32{,}000$$

Barnhardt's PII tax is $11,200 ($32,000 × 35%). ■

Other Operational Rules

Several other points may be made about the possible effects of various Code provisions on S corporations.

- An S corporation is required to make estimated tax payments with respect to tax exposure because of any recognized built-in gain and excess passive investment income.

[56] § 1362(d)(3)(B) and (C).

[57] §§ 248, 1374(d)(4), and 1375(a) and (b).

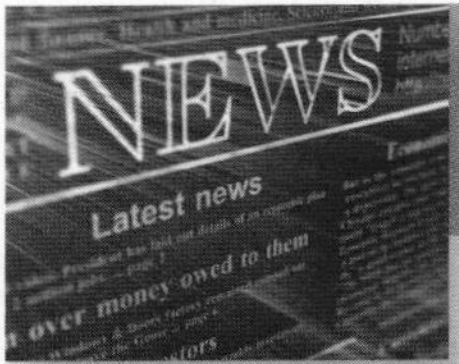

TAX IN THE NEWS The Self-Employment Income Advantage

A significant advantage of an S corporation involves the current definition of self-employment income. Although compensation for services rendered to an S corporation is subject to FICA taxes, a shareholder's share of income from an S corporation is not self-employment income. The rationale for this S corporation loophole is that the S shareholder does not personally carry on the entity's trade or business. In contrast, the earned income of a partnership or proprietorship is treated as self-employment income to the partner or proprietor.

The choice between a salary and pass-through income is not clear-cut, however.

- Although a salary is subject to payroll tax and pass-through income is not [*P.B. Ding v. Comm.*, 200 F.3d 587 (CA–9, 1999)], this nonearned income does not accrue Social Security benefits for its recipient.
- S corporation income distributions do not count as compensation for computing an employee's contribution formula for a retirement plan.
- The IRS and the courts require an S shareholder to take a reasonable salary (see footnote 68).
- If a partner or proprietor reports salary income from other sources and the aggregate salaries exceed the annual FICA ceiling, a partnership or proprietorship entity may provide tax savings over an S corporation.

- An S corporation may own stock in another corporation, but an S corporation may not have a C corporation shareholder. An S corporation is *not* eligible for a dividends received deduction.
- An S corporation is *not* subject to the 10 percent of taxable income limitation applicable to charitable contributions made by a C corporation.
- Any family member who renders services or furnishes capital to an S corporation must be paid reasonable compensation. Otherwise, the IRS can make adjustments to reflect the value of the services or capital.[58] This rule may make it more difficult for related parties to shift Subchapter S taxable income to children or other family members.
- Although § 1366(a)(1) provides for a flow-through of S items to a shareholder, it does not create self-employment income.[59] This treatment of earned income of S corporations is attractive compared to the treatment of a proprietorship or a partnership whose income is taxed as self-employment income to the owners. Compensation for services rendered to an S corporation is, however, subject to FICA taxes. Congress is considering a change to this rule.

EXAMPLE 44

Mickey and Dana each own one-third of a fast-food restaurant, and their 14-year-old son owns the other shares. Both parents work full-time in the restaurant operations, but the son works infrequently. Neither parent receives a salary this year, when the taxable income of the S corporation is $160,000. The IRS can require that reasonable compensation be paid to the parents to prevent the full one-third of the $160,000 from being taxed to the son. Otherwise, this would be an effective technique to shift earned income to a family member to reduce the total family tax burden. Furthermore, low or zero salaries can reduce FICA taxes due to the Federal government. ■

EXAMPLE 45

Dave is a professor at a southeastern university, earning a salary of $150,000. He also has consulting income of $80,000. If the consulting business is organized as an S corporation, Dave should withdraw a reasonable salary from the S corporation for his services. The S corporation pays payroll and withholding tax on the salary. Dave receives a tax credit for any overpayment of the employee share of the FICA tax, but the S corporation does not receive a similar credit.

[58] § 1366(e). In addition, beware of an IRS search for the "real owner" of the stock under Reg. § 1.1373–1(a)(2).

[59] Rev.Rul. 59–221, 1959–1 C.B. 225.

If the business is operated as a proprietorship, Dave is exempt from the Social Security portion of the self-employment tax because his university salary exceeds the annual FICA ceiling. Here, operating as a proprietorship offers a tax advantage over an S corporation. ■

- An S corporation is placed on the cash method of accounting for purposes of deducting business expenses and interest owed to a cash basis related party.[60] Thus, the timing of the shareholder's income and the corporate deduction must match.
- An S corporation may not deduct a payment to one of its shareholders (e.g., a year-end performance bonus) until the payee reports the income.
- The S election is not recognized by the District of Columbia and several states, including Connecticut, Michigan, New Hampshire, and Tennessee. Thus, some or all of the entity's income may be subject to a state-level income tax (e.g., a "sting tax" on large S corporations in Massachusetts).
- If § 1244 stock is issued to an S corporation, the S corporation and its shareholders may not treat losses on such stock as ordinary losses. However, an S corporation may issue § 1244 stock to its shareholders to obtain ordinary loss treatment.
- The § 1202 exclusion of gain on disposition of small business stock is *not* available for S stock.
- Losses may be disallowed due to a lack of a profit motive. If the activities at the corporate level are not profit-motivated, the losses may be disallowed under the hobby loss rule of § 183.[61]
- A penalty is imposed for failure to file (including extensions) timely S corporation returns. The penalty is $195 per month times the number of S corporation shareholders. The penalty is assessed against the corporation for a maximum of 12 months.[62]
- Code § 1372(a) applies partnership treatment for certain fringe benefits to more-than-2 percent shareholder-employees of S corporations. Thus, these shareholders are not entitled to exclude certain fringe benefits from gross income. A more-than-2 percent shareholder-employee is allowed an above-the-line (*for* AGI) deduction on Form 1040 for accident and health insurance premiums.[63]
- If an S corporation excludes cancellation of debt (COD) income from gross income, the excluded amount is applied to reduce S corporation tax attributes.[64]

12.4 Tax Planning

LO.11

Engage in tax planning for S corporations.

When the Election Is Advisable

Effective tax planning with S corporations begins with the determination of whether the election is appropriate. In this context, one should consider the following factors.

- Are losses from the business anticipated? If so, the S election may be highly attractive because these losses pass through to the shareholders.
- What are the tax brackets of the shareholders? If the shareholders are in high individual income tax brackets, it may be desirable to avoid S corporation status and have profits taxed to the corporation at lower C rates (e.g., 15 percent or 25 percent). However, the income still is not in the owners' hands.

---

[60] § 267(b).

[61] *Michael J. Houston*, 69 TCM 2360, T.C.Memo. 1995–159; *Mario G. De Mendoza, III*, 68 TCM 42, T.C.Memo. 1994–314.

[62] § 6699.

[63] Notice 2008–1, 2008–2 I.R.B. 251.

[64] §§ 108(a), 108(b)(2).

- When the shareholders are in low individual income tax brackets, the pass-through of corporate profits is attractive, and reducing the combined income tax becomes the paramount consideration. Under these circumstances, the S election could be an effective tax planning tool. Note, however, that although an S corporation usually escapes Federal taxes, it may not be immune from state and local taxes imposed on corporations or from several Federal penalty taxes.
- Does a C corporation have an NOL carryover from a prior year? Such a loss cannot be used in an S year (except for purposes of the built-in gains tax). Even worse, S years count in the 20-year carryover limitation. Thus, even if the S election is made, one might consider terminating the election before the carryover limitation expires. Such a termination would permit the loss to be utilized by what is now a C corporation.
- Both individuals and C corporations are subject to the alternative minimum tax. Many of the tax preference and adjustment items are the same, but some apply only to corporate taxpayers while others are limited to individuals. The alternative minimum tax adjustment relating to adjusted current earnings could create havoc with some C corporations (refer to Chapter 3). S corporations are not subject to this tax.
- S corporations and partnerships have limited flexibility in the choice of a tax accounting period.[65]

Making a Proper Election

Once the parties have decided the election is appropriate, it becomes essential to ensure that the election is made properly.

- Make sure all shareholders consent. If any doubt exists concerning the shareholder status of an individual, it would be wise to have that party issue a consent anyway.[66] Too few consents are fatal to the election; the same cannot be said for too many consents.
- Make sure the election is timely and properly filed. Either hand-carry the election to an IRS office or send it by certified or registered mail. The date used to determine timeliness is the postmark date, not the date the IRS receives the election. A copy of the election should become part of the corporation's permanent files.
- Ascertain when the timely election period begins to run for a newly formed corporation. An election made too soon (before the corporation is in existence) is worse than one made too late. If serious doubts exist as to when this period begins, filing more than one election might be considered a practical means of guaranteeing the desired result.
- It still is beneficial for an S corporation to issue § 1244 stock (refer to Chapter 4). This type of stock allows the original shareholder to obtain an ordinary deduction for a loss on the sale or worthlessness of the stock, rather than long-term capital loss treatment. Shareholders have nothing to lose by complying with § 1244.

Preserving the Election

Recall that an election can be lost intentionally or unintentionally in several ways, and that a five-year waiting period generally is imposed before another S election is available. To preserve an S election, the following points should be kept in mind.

- As a starting point, all parties concerned should be made aware of the various transactions that lead to the loss of an election.
- Watch for possible disqualification of a small business corporation. For example, the death of a shareholder could result in a nonqualifying trust becoming

[65] Entity tax-year constraints are discussed in Chapter 10.

[66] See *William B. Wilson*, 34 TCM 463, T.C.Memo. 1975–92.

a shareholder. The latter circumstance might be avoided by utilizing a buy-sell agreement or binding the deceased shareholder's estate to turn in the stock to the corporation for redemption or, as an alternative, to sell it to the surviving shareholders.[67]

Planning for the Operation of the Corporation

Operating an S corporation to achieve optimum tax savings for all parties involved requires a great deal of care and, most important, an understanding of the applicable tax rules.

Accumulated Adjustments Account

Although the corporate-level accumulated adjustments account (AAA) is used primarily by an S corporation with accumulated earnings and profits (AEP) from a Subchapter C year, all S corporations should maintain an accurate record of the AAA. Because there is a grace period for distributing the AAA after termination of the S election, the parties must be in a position to determine the balance of the account.

EXAMPLE 46

Nobles, Inc., an S corporation, has no C corporation AEP. Over the years, Nobles made no attempt to maintain an accurate accounting for the AAA. Now the S election has been terminated, and Nobles has a grace period for distributing the AAA tax-free to its shareholders. A great deal of time and expense may be necessary to reconstruct the AAA balance. ■

When AEP is present, a negative AAA may cause double taxation of S corporation income. With a negative AAA, the recognition of current income restores the negative AAA balance to zero, but a subsequent distribution then is considered to be in excess of AAA and is taxable as a dividend to the extent of AEP. Distributions during the year reduce the stock basis for determining the allowable loss for the year, but the loss does *not* reduce the stock basis for determining the tax status of distributions made during the year. In determining the tax treatment of distributions by an S corporation having AEP, any net adjustments (e.g., excess of losses and deductions over income) for the tax year are ignored.

The AAA bypass election may be used to reduce exposure to the accumulated earnings tax or personal holding company tax in post-S years. This bypass election allows AEP to be distributed instead.

EXAMPLE 47

Zebra, Inc., an S corporation during 2011, has a significant amount in its AEP account. The shareholders expect to terminate the election in 2012, when Zebra will be subject to the lower corporate income tax rates. Because Zebra as a C corporation may be subject to the accumulated earnings penalty tax in 2012, the shareholders may want to use the AAA bypass election to distribute some or all of the AEP. Of course, any distributions of the AEP account in 2011 would be taxable to the shareholders. ■

Salary Structure

The amount of salary paid to a shareholder-employee of an S corporation can have varying tax consequences and should be considered carefully. Larger amounts might be advantageous if the maximum contribution allowed for the shareholder-employee under the corporation's retirement plan has not been reached. Smaller amounts may be beneficial if the parties are trying to shift taxable income to lower-bracket

[67]See Chapter 19 for a discussion of buy-sell agreements. Most such agreements do not create a second class of S stock. Rev.Rul. 85–161, 1985–2 C.B. 191; *Portage Plastics Co. v. U.S.*, 72–2 USTC ¶9567, 30 AFTR 2d 72–5229, 470 F.2d 308 (CA–7, 1973).

© Andrey Prokhorov, iStockphoto

TAX IN THE NEWS Some Guidelines for Compensating S Shareholder-Employees

The IRS issued a fact sheet in 2008 providing taxpayers with these factors to use to determine reasonable compensation for an S shareholder.

- Training, education, and experience.
- Duties and responsibilities.
- Time and effort devoted to business.
- Dividend history.
- Payments to nonshareholders-employees.
- Timing and manner of paying bonuses to key employees.
- What comparable businesses pay for similar services.
- Compensation agreements.
- Use of formula to determine compensation.

Sources: FS-2008-25, Wage Compensation for S Corporation Officers, August 2008; Tony Nitti, "S Corporation Shareholder Compensation: How Much Is Enough?" *The Tax Adviser*, August 2011, pp. 534–539.

shareholders, reduce payroll taxes, curtail a reduction of Social Security benefits, or restrict losses that do not pass through because of the basis limitation.

A strategy of decreasing compensation and correspondingly increasing distributions to shareholder-employees often results in substantial savings in employment taxes. However, a shareholder of an S corporation cannot always perform substantial services and arrange to receive distributions rather than compensation so that the corporation may avoid paying employment taxes. The IRS may deem the shareholder to be an employee, with any distributions recharacterized as wages subject to FICA and FUTA taxes.[68] In effect, the IRS requires that reasonable compensation be paid to shareholder-employees. For planning purposes, some level of compensation should be paid to all shareholder-employees to avoid any recharacterization of nonpassive distributions as deductible salaries—especially in personal service corporations.

A District Court decision[69] provided the methodology that the IRS and the courts are using to determine reasonable compensation. Where profits are generated primarily by the personal efforts of a shareholder, a significant portion of the profits should be paid in the form of compensation rather than distributions. The greater the responsibility, experience, and effort of the employee-shareholder, the higher the appropriate salary. Tax advisers should use financial ratios from the Risk Management Association, data from Robert Half and the Bureau of Labor Statistics, and the AICPA's Management of an Accounting Practice Survey to determine appropriate compensation for shareholder-employees.

THE BIG PICTURE

EXAMPLE 48

Return to the facts of *The Big Picture* on p. 12-1. The two shareholders should consider reducing their $92,000 salary and instead receiving a larger undistributed share of the S corporation income. A shareholder's share of pass-through S corporation income is not treated as self-employment income, whereas compensation is subject to a 12.4% Social Security tax and 2.9% Medicare tax. By receiving the $92,000 as a distribution rather than salary, each shareholder saves $14,076 ($92,000 × 15.3%). But *Watson* might lead Cane to allow each shareholder a mix of pass-through income and salary.

[68] Rev.Rul. 74–44, 1974–1 C.B. 287; *Spicer Accounting, Inc. v. U.S.*, 91–1 USTC ¶50,103, 66 AFTR 2d 90–5806, 918 F.2d 90 (CA–9, 1990); *Radtke v. U.S.*, 90–1 USTC ¶50,113, 65 AFTR 2d 90–1155, 895 F.2d 1196 (CA–7, 1990); *Joseph M. Grey Public Accountant, P.C.*, 119 T.C. 121 (2002).

[69] *David E. Watson, P.C. v. U.S.*, 2010–1 USTC ¶50,444, 105 AFTR 2d 2010–2624, 714 F.Supp.2d 954 (S.D. Iowa, 2010).

The IRS can require that reasonable compensation be paid to family members who render services or provide capital to the S corporation. The IRS also can adjust the items taken into account by family-member shareholders to reflect the value of services or capital they provided (refer to Example 44).

Unreasonable compensation traditionally has not been a problem for S corporations, but deductible compensation under § 162 reduces an S corporation's taxable income, which is relevant to the built-in gains tax. Compensation may be one of the larger items an S corporation can use to reduce taxable income to minimize any built-in gains penalty tax. Thus, IRS agents may attempt to classify compensation as unreasonable to increase the § 1374 tax.

Deductions for various tax-free fringe benefits are denied to a more-than-2 percent shareholder-employee of an S corporation. Such benefits include group term life insurance, medical insurance, and meals and lodging furnished for the convenience of the employer. These items are treated as wages and are subject to most payroll taxes. The employee can deduct medical insurance premiums on his or her tax return.

Loss Considerations

A net loss in excess of tax basis may be carried forward and deducted only by the same shareholder in succeeding years. Thus, before disposing of the stock, a shareholder should increase the basis of such stock/loan to flow through the loss. The next shareholder does not obtain the loss carryover.

Any unused loss carryover in existence upon the termination of the S election may be deducted only in the next tax year and is limited to the individual's *stock* basis (not loan basis) in the post-termination year.[70] The shareholder may want to purchase more stock to increase the tax basis to absorb the loss.

The NOL provisions create a need for sound tax planning during the last election year and the post-termination transition period. If it appears that the S corporation is going to sustain an NOL or use up any loss carryover, each shareholder's basis should be analyzed to determine whether it can absorb the share of the loss. If basis is insufficient to absorb the loss, further investments should be considered before the end of the post-termination transition year. Such investments can be accomplished through additional stock purchases from the corporation or from other shareholders to increase basis. This action ensures the full benefit from the NOL carryover.

EXAMPLE 49

A calendar year C corporation has an NOL of $20,000 in 2011. The corporation makes a valid S election in 2012 and has another $20,000 NOL in that year. At all times during 2012, the stock of the corporation was owned by the same 10 shareholders, each of whom owned 10% of the stock. Tim, one of the 10 shareholders, has a stock basis of $1,800 at the beginning of 2012. None of the 2011 NOL may be carried forward into the S year. Although Tim's share of the 2012 NOL is $2,000, the deduction for the loss is limited to $1,800 in 2012 with a $200 carryover. ■

Avoiding the Passive Investment Income Tax

Too much passive investment income (PII) may cause an S corporation to incur a § 1375 penalty tax and/or terminate the S election. Several planning techniques can be used to avoid both of these unfavorable events. Where a small amount of AEP exists, an AAA bypass election may be appropriate to purge the AEP, thereby avoiding the passive income tax altogether. Alternatively, the corporation might reduce taxable income below the excess net passive income; similarly, PII might be accelerated into years in which there is an offsetting NOL. In addition, the tax can be avoided if the corporation manufactures needed gross receipts. By increasing gross receipts without increasing PII, the amount of PII in excess of 25 percent of

[70] § 1366(d)(3)

gross receipts is reduced. Finally, performing significant services or incurring significant costs with respect to rental real estate activities can elevate the rent income to nonpassive.

If the corporation does not have sufficient cash, the distributions can be restructured so that the corporation's notes are issued to the shareholders. Or the S corporation can make a deemed dividend election, using shareholder consents to treat the dividends as paid, with the deemed distributions then presumed to come back to the corporation on the last day of the tax year.[71]

EXAMPLE 50

An S corporation has paid a passive investment income penalty tax for two consecutive years. In the next year, the corporation has a large amount of AAA. If the AEP account is small, a bypass election may be appropriate to purge the corporation of the AEP. Without any AEP, no passive investment income tax applies, and the S election is not terminated. Any distribution of AEP to the shareholders constitutes taxable dividends, however.

Another alternative is to manufacture a large amount of gross receipts without increasing PII through an action such as a merger with a grocery store. If the gross receipts from the grocery store are substantial, the amount of the PII in excess of 25% of gross receipts is reduced. ■

Figure 12.2 shows four alternatives that a C corporation intending to elect S treatment may use to reduce its tax liability.

Managing the Built-in Gains Tax

The taxable income limitation encourages an S corporation to create deductions or accelerate deductions in the years that built-in gains are recognized. Although the postponed built-in gain is carried forward to future years, the time value of money makes the postponement beneficial. For example, payment of compensation, rather than a distribution, creates a deduction that reduces taxable income and postpones the built-in gains tax.

EXAMPLE 51

Mundy, Inc., an S corporation converted from a C corporation, has built-in gain of $110,000 and taxable income of $120,000 before payment of salaries to its two shareholders. If Mundy pays at least $120,000 in salaries to the shareholders (rather than a distribution), its taxable income drops to zero and the built-in gains tax is postponed. Thus, Mundy needs to keep the salaries as high as possible to postpone the built-in gains tax in future years and reap a benefit from the time value of money. Of course, paying the salaries may increase the payroll tax burden if the salaries are below FICA and FUTA limits. ■

Controlling Adjustments and Preference Items

The individual alternative minimum tax (AMT) affects more taxpayers than ever before because the tax base has expanded and the difference between regular tax rates and the individual AMT rate has been narrowed. In an S corporation setting, tax preferences flow through proportionately to the shareholders, who, in computing the individual AMT, treat the preferences as if they were directly realized. Thus, the S corporation may not take advantage of the AMT exemption available to a small corporation, but there is no ACE adjustment. Further, if an S corporation has a built-in gain under § 1374, the entity does not pay an AMT on the transaction.

Domestic Production Activities Deduction

Domestic production gross receipts (DPGR), attributable cost of goods sold (CGS), and allocable deductions earned by the S corporation are passed through to the shareholders. These corporate-level DPGR, CGS, and allocable deductions are combined with any DPGR, CGS, and allocable deductions that the shareholder has from other sources. The DPAD has no effect on a shareholder's stock basis.

[71]Reg. § 1.1368–1(f)(3).

FIGURE 12.2 **Four Alternatives to Reduce Tax Liabilities for Passive-Type C Corporations Electing S Treatment**

Alternative 1: Eliminate AEP before the S election by paying dividends, taxed at the 0/15% rate.

Alternative 2: Liquidate the C corporation and reincorporate as an S corporation. Exposure to the AEP is eliminated.

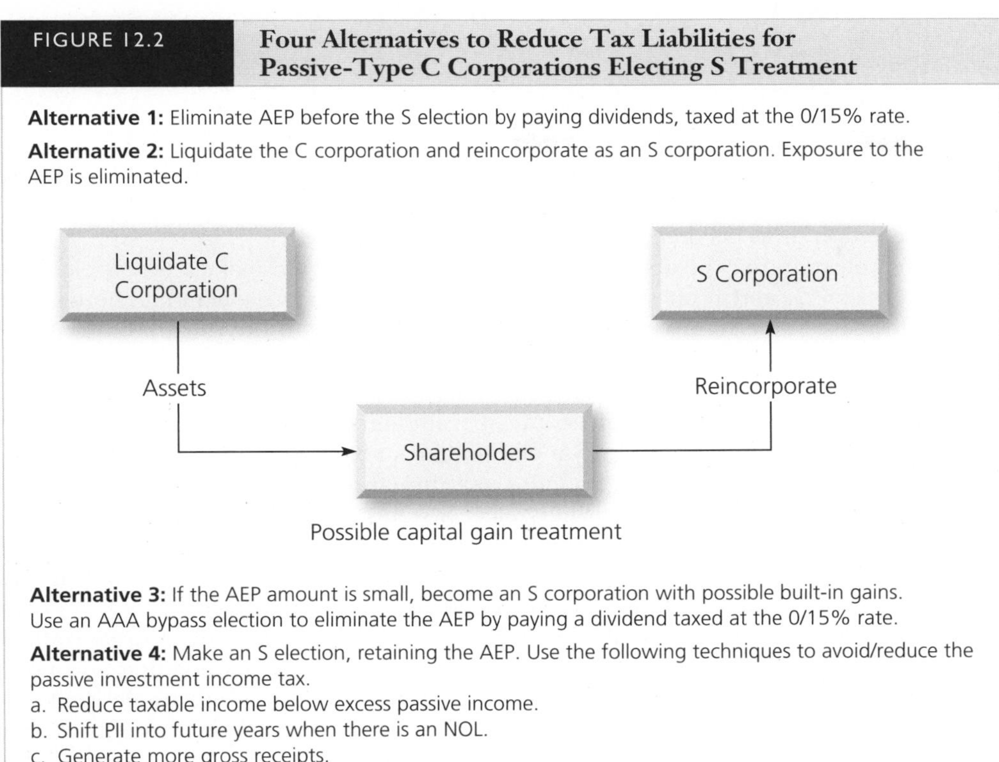

Alternative 3: If the AEP amount is small, become an S corporation with possible built-in gains. Use an AAA bypass election to eliminate the AEP by paying a dividend taxed at the 0/15% rate.

Alternative 4: Make an S election, retaining the AEP. Use the following techniques to avoid/reduce the passive investment income tax.

a. Reduce taxable income below excess passive income.
b. Shift PII into future years when there is an NOL.
c. Generate more gross receipts.
d. Perform significant services or incur significant costs if a rental type of business.

An allocable portion of the S corporation's W–2 wages is passed through to the shareholder, but only those wages that are properly allocable to DPGR. See Chapter 3 for the calculation of the qualified domestic production activities deduction (DPAD).

EXAMPLE 52

An S corporation reports $100,000 DPGR and $75,000 of wages, and its qualified production activities income (QPAI) is $25,000. Shareholder Kirby has a 50% interest in the S corporation. All expenses that reduce DPGR constitute wages, and all wages paid relate to DPGR.

Kirby is allocated $12,500 of QPAI and $37,500 of wages. ■

Liquidation of an S Corporation

S corporations are subject to many of the same liquidation rules applicable to C corporations (refer to Chapter 6). In general, the distribution of appreciated property to S shareholders in complete liquidation is treated as if the property were sold to the shareholders in a taxable transaction. Unlike a C corporation, however, the S corporation itself incurs no incremental tax on the liquidation gains, because such gains flow through to the shareholders subject only to the built-in gains tax of § 1374.

Any corporate gain increases the shareholder's stock basis by a like amount and reduces any gain realized by the shareholder when he or she receives the liquidation proceeds. Thus, an S corporation usually avoids the double tax that is imposed on C corporations. However, when an S corporation liquidates, all of its special tax attributes disappear (e.g., AAA, AEP, C corporation NOLs, and suspended losses).

REFOCUS ON THE BIG PICTURE

Using a Flow-Through Entity to Achieve Deductibility of Losses

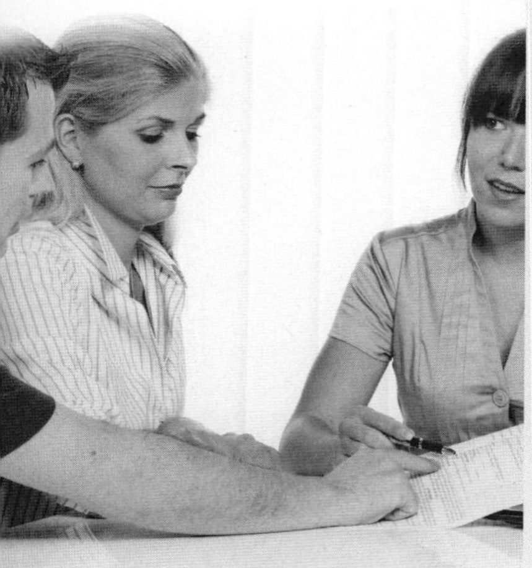

© Gina Sanders/Shutterstock.com

As long as Smith and Jones, the owners of Cane, Inc., maintain C corporation status, they cannot deduct on their individual tax returns any NOLs the business incurs. For the owners to deduct any future NOLs on their Forms 1040, Cane needs to be operated as a flow-through entity. The most logical alternatives are to make an S election or to become a limited liability company.

An S election may be appropriate for Cane. Cane should make a timely election on Form 2553, and both shareholders must consent to the election. The owners should make the election on or before the fifteenth day of the third month of the current year.

Normally, an S corporation does not pay any income tax because all items (including NOLs) flow through to the shareholders. A C corporation making an S election may be required to pay a built-in gains tax or a LIFO recapture tax. The base for the built-in gains tax includes any unrealized gain on appreciated assets held by Cane on the day the owners elect S status. The highest corporate rate is applied to the unrealized gain when any of the built-in gain assets are sold. If the corporation uses the LIFO inventory method, any LIFO recapture amount at the time of the S election is subject to a corporate-level tax.

Cane does not need to liquidate or engage in a tax-deferred reorganization when converting to an S corporation. An S corporation can have voting and nonvoting common stock, provided that all shares have the same economic rights to corporate income or loss. Data used to compute a DPAD flows through to the shareholders.

Cane might get rid of the tax-exempt income, which will not be reflected in the AAA. Although it is reflected in stock basis, tax-exempt income (as part of the OAA) is distributed to the shareholders only after the S corporation has distributed all of its C corporation earnings and profits.

KEY TERMS

Accumulated adjustments account (AAA), 12-15

Accumulated earnings and profits, 12-14

Built-in gains tax, 12-25

Bypass election, 12-17

Other adjustments account (OAA), 12-17

Passive investment income (PII), 12-10

Previously taxed income, 12-16

S corporation, 12-2

Small business corporation, 12-4

Subchapter S, 12-2

Voluntary revocation, 12-9

DISCUSSION QUESTIONS

1. **LO.1** Which of these characteristics are found with an S corporation?
   a. Limited liability to shareholder.
   b. Personal holding company.
   c. Liabilities affect the owner's basis.
   d. Distributions of appreciated property are taxable at the corporate level.
   e. Treated as a corporation under state laws.

2. **LO.1** The alternative minimum tax applies to an S corporation. Discuss the validity of this statement.

3. **LO.1** Explain how the net operating loss rules apply to a new S corporation. To a new C corporation?

4. **LO.1** How can a C corporation mitigate its double taxation potential?

5. **LO.2** Which of the following are requirements to be an S corporation?
   a. Only one class of stock.
   b. Cannot have an estate as a shareholder.
   c. Cannot use a phantom stock plan.
   d. Cannot be a foreign corporation.
   e. Cannot have a resident alien.

6. **LO.2** What is a qualified S corporation subsidiary (QSSS)? Elaborate.

7. **LO.2** What requirements must an entity meet to elect S corporation status?

8. **LO.2** Would any of these items be considered a second class of stock for an S corporation?
   a. Voting preferred stock (with a preference on dividends).
   b. Treasury stock of another class.
   c. Phantom stock.
   d. Unexercised stock options.
   e. Warrants.
   f. Stock appreciation rights.
   g. Convertible debentures.

9. **LO.2** Outline the characteristics of an S corporation's *straight debt*.

10. **LO.2** Would any of these items be considered a second class of stock for an S corporation?
    a. Short-term unwritten advances from a shareholder that do not exceed $10,000 in the aggregate at any time during the corporation's taxable year.
    b. Debt that is held by shareholders in the same proportion as their stock holdings.
    c. Section 1244 stock.

11. **LO.2** Which of the following can be a shareholder of an S corporation?
    a. Resident alien.
    b. Partnership.
    c. Charitable remainder trust.
    d. IRA.
    e. Estate.
    f. One-person LLC (disregarded entity).

12. **LO.1** Bob Roman, the major owner of an S corporation, approaches you for some tax planning help. He would like to exchange some real estate in a like-kind transaction under § 1031 for real estate that may have some environmental liabilities. Prepare a letter to Bob outlining your suggestion. Bob's address is 8411 Huron Boulevard, West Chester, PA 19382.

    Issue ID
    Communications

13. **LO.2, 3** On March 2, 2012, the two 50% shareholders of a calendar year corporation decide to elect S status. One of the shareholders, Terry, purchased her stock from a previous shareholder (a nonresident alien) on January 18, 2012. Identify any potential problems for Terry or the corporation.

    Issue ID

14. **LO.4** Caleb Samford calls you and says that his two-person S corporation was involuntarily terminated in February 2011. He asks you if they can make a new S election now, in November 2012. Draft a memo for the file, outlining what you told Caleb.

    Communications

15. **LO.5** Indicate whether each of the following items is available to an S corporation.
    a. Amortization of organizational expenditures.
    b. Dividends received deduction.
    c. Standard deduction.
    d. Personal exemption.
    e. Section 179 expense deduction.

16. **LO.6** Using the categories in the following legend, classify each transaction as a plus (+) or minus (−) on Schedule M-2 of Form 1120S. An answer might look like one of these: "+AAA" or "−OAA."

Legend
AAA = Accumulated adjustments account
OAA = Other adjustments account
NA = No direct effect on Schedule M-2

a. Receipt of tax-exempt interest income.
b. Unreasonable compensation determined.
c. Depreciation recapture income.
d. Nontaxable life insurance proceeds.
e. Expenses related to tax-exempt securities.
f. Charitable contributions.
g. Business gifts in excess of $25.
h. Nondeductible fines and penalties.
i. Administrative expenses.

Issue ID

17. **LO.6, 11** Collette's S corporation has a small amount of accumulated earnings and profits (AEP), requiring the use of the more complex distribution rules. Collette's accountant tells her that this AEP forces the maintenance of the AAA figure each year. Identify relevant tax issues facing Collette.

Communications

18. **LO.6, 8** Scott Tyrney owns 21% of an S corporation. He is confused with respect to the amounts of the corporate AAA and his stock basis. Write a brief memo to Scott identifying the key differences between AAA and an S shareholder's stock basis.

19. **LO.8** For each of the following independent statements, indicate whether the transaction will increase (+), decrease (−), or have no effect (*NE*) on the adjusted basis of a shareholder's stock in an S corporation.
a. Expenses related to tax-exempt income.
b. Short-term capital gain.
c. Nonseparately computed loss.
d. Section 1231 gain.
e. Depletion *not* in excess of basis.
f. Separately computed income.
g. Nontaxable return-of-capital distribution by the corporation.
h. Advertising expenses.
i. Business gifts in excess of $25.
j. Depreciation recapture income.
k. Dividends received by the S corporation.
l. LIFO recapture tax computed at the date of the S election.
m. Recovery of a bad debt previously deducted.
n. Long-term capital loss.
o. Corporate distribution out of AAA.

Issue ID

20. **LO.9** Sheila Jackson is a 50% shareholder in Washington, Inc., an S corporation. This year, Jackson's share of the Washington loss is $100,000. Jackson has income from several other sources. Identify at least four tax issues related to the effects of the S corporation loss on Jackson's tax return.

Decision Making

21. **LO.1, 11** One of your clients is considering electing S status. Texas, Inc., is a six-year-old company with two equal shareholders, both of whom paid $30,000 for their stock. Going into 2012, Texas has a $110,000 NOL carryforward from prior years. Estimated income is $40,000 for 2012 and $25,000 for each of the next three years. Should Texas make an S election for 2012? Why or why not?

22. **LO.11** How can an S corporation avoid the passive investment income tax?

23. **LO.11** How does the alternative minimum tax affect an S corporation? Its shareholders?

PROBLEMS

24. **LO.5, 6** A calendar year S corporation's profit and loss statement shows net profits of $90,000 (book income). The corporation is owned equally by three shareholders. From

supplemental data, you obtain the following information about items included in the book income.

Tax-exempt interest income	$ 2,000
Dividends received	9,000
§ 1231 gain	6,000
Depreciation recapture income	12,000
Recovery of bad debts	4,000
Short-term capital loss	(6,000)
Salary to owners (each)	(10,000)
Cost of goods sold	(95,000)
Administrative expenses	(4,500)
Selling expenses	(21,200)
Distribution to shareholders	(6,000)

a. Compute the entity's nonseparately computed income or loss.
b. What would be the portion of taxable income or loss for Chang, one of the shareholders?

25. **LO.5, 6** Saul, Inc., a calendar year S corporation, incurred the following items.

Tax-exempt interest income	$ 7,000
Sales	130,000
Depreciation recapture income	12,000
Short-term capital gain	30,000
§1231 gain	12,000
Cost of goods sold	(42,000)
Administrative expenses	(15,000)
Depreciation expense	(17,000)
Charitable contributions	(14,000)

a. Calculate Saul's nonseparately computed income or loss.
b. If Maynor is a 40% owner, what is his share of the short-term capital gain?

26. **LO.5, 6** Who, Inc., is a calendar year S corporation. Who's book income this year totals $172,000. Who is owned equally by four shareholders. From supplemental data, you obtain the following information about items included in book income.

Tax-exempt interest income	$ 3,200
Dividends received	9,000
§ 1231 gain	6,000
Depreciation recapture income	13,270
Recovery of bad debts	4,000
Short-term capital loss	(8,000)
Salary to owners (each)	(11,000)
Cost of goods sold	(110,000)
Selling expenses	(26,100)
Distribution to shareholders	(12,600)

a. Compute Who's nonseparately computed income or loss.
b. How much ordinary income or loss is reported by Sally, one of Who's shareholders?
c. How much dividend income is reported on Sally's Schedule K–1?

27. **LO.6, 8, 9** Betty is a shareholder in a calendar year S corporation. At the beginning of the year, her stock basis is $10,000, her share of the AAA is $2,000, and her share of corporate AEP is $6,000. She receives a $6,000 distribution, and her share of S corporation items includes a $2,000 long-term capital gain and a $9,000 ordinary loss. Determine the effects of these events on the AAA, stock basis, and AEP.

28. **LO.6** Noon, Inc., a calendar year S corporation, is equally owned by Ralph and Thomas. Thomas dies on April 1 (not a leap year), and his estate selects a March 31 fiscal year. Noon has $400,000 of income for January 1 through March 31 and $600,000 for the remainder of the year.
   a. Determine how income is allocated to Ralph and Thomas under the pro rata approach.
   b. Determine how income is allocated to Ralph and Thomas under the per-books method.

Decision Making

29. **LO.5, 6** McLin, Inc., is a calendar year S corporation. Its AAA balance is zero.
   a. McLin holds $90,000 of AEP. Tobias, the sole shareholder, has an adjusted basis of $80,000 in his stock. Determine the tax aspects if a $90,000 salary is paid to Tobias.
   b. Same as part (a), except that McLin pays Tobias a $90,000 dividend from AEP.

30. **LO.6, 7, 8** Tiger, Inc., a calendar year S corporation, is owned equally by four shareholders: Ann, Becky, Chris, and David. Tiger owns a piece of investment land that was purchased for $160,000 four years ago. On September 14, 2012, when the land is worth $240,000, it is distributed to David. Assuming that David's basis in his S corporation stock is $270,000 on the distribution date, discuss any tax ramifications.

31. **LO.6, 11** During the year, Wheel, a calendar year S corporation in Stillwater, Oklahoma, generates the following AMT items: a positive adjustment of $66,000 for mining exploration costs, an excess depletion tax preference of $96,000, and a positive certified pollution control facility adjustment of $36,000. The firm's positive ACE adjustment is $102,000. If Pam Epstein is a one-third Wheel shareholder, what effect do these items have on her individual tax return?

Communications

32. **LO.6, 8, 9, 11** In 2012, Spence, Inc., a calendar year S corporation, generates an ordinary loss of $110,000 and makes a distribution of $140,000 to its sole shareholder, Storm Nelson. Nelson's stock basis at the beginning of the year is $200,000. Write a memo to your senior manager, Aaron McMullin, discussing the tax treatment of Spence's activities.

33. **LO.6** Lonergan, Inc., a calendar year S corporation in Athens, Georgia, had a balance in AAA of $200,000 and AEP of $110,000 on December 31, 2012. During 2013, Lonergan, Inc., distributes $140,000 to its shareholders, while sustaining an ordinary loss of $120,000. Calculate the balance in Lonergan's AAA and AEP accounts at the end of 2013.

34. **LO.6** If the beginning balance in Strauder, Inc.'s OAA is $5,700 and the following transactions occur, what is Strauder's ending OAA balance?

Depreciation recapture income	$22,700
Payroll tax penalty	(4,200)
Tax-exempt interest income	4,995
Nontaxable life insurance proceeds	50,000
Life insurance premiums paid (nondeductible)	(3,333)

35. **LO.6** Peres, Inc., a calendar year S corporation, holds an AAA balance of $767,050 at the beginning of 2012. During the year, the following items are recorded. Calculate Peres's ending AAA balance.

Sales income	$206,000
Loss from real estate operation	(5,000)
Officers' life insurance proceeds	100,000
Premiums paid for officers' life insurance	(3,600)
Dividend income	17,000
Interest income	3,000
Charitable contributions	(19,000)
§179 depreciation expenses	(2,500)
Administrative expenses	(42,000)
Cash distribution to shareholders	(71,300)

36. **LO.6, 7, 8** Money, Inc., a calendar year S corporation in Denton, Texas, has two unrelated shareholders, each owning 50% of the stock. Both shareholders have a $400,000 stock basis as of January 1, 2012. At the beginning of 2012, Money has an AAA of $300,000 and AEP of $600,000. During 2012, Money has operating income of $100,000. At the end of the year, Money distributes securities worth $1 million, with an adjusted basis of $800,000. Determine the tax effects of these transactions.

37. **LO.6, 7, 8** Assume the same facts as in Problem 36, except that the two shareholders consent to an AAA bypass election.

38. **LO.8, 9** At the beginning of 2011, Christine Wheat has a basis of $5,000 in her stock of a calendar year S corporation, Zhou, Inc. She holds no debt of the S corporation. During 2011, Wheat's total share of Zhou's losses and deductions is $16,000, consisting of $10,000 of ordinary loss and $6,000 of nondeductible, noncapital expenses. For 2012, Wheat's share of Zhou's ordinary income is $12,000. Assuming no Reg. § 1.1367–1(g) election, how are these facts treated by Christine Wheat?

39. **LO.8, 9** Assume the same facts as in Problem 38, except that a Reg. § 1.1367–1(g) election is made. How does your answer change?

40. **LO.8** Jeff, a 52% owner of an S corporation, has a stock basis of zero at the beginning of the year. Jeff's basis in a $10,000 loan made to the corporation and evidenced by a corporate note has been reduced to zero by pass-through losses. During the year, his net share of the corporate taxable income is $11,000. At the end of the year, Jeff receives a $15,000 distribution. Discuss the tax effects of the distribution.

41. **LO.8** Assume the same facts as in Problem 40, except that there is no $15,000 distribution, but the corporation repays the loan principal to Jeff. Discuss the tax effects.

42. **LO.8** Assume the same facts as in Problem 40, except that Jeff's share of corporate taxable income is only $8,000, and there is no distribution. However, the corporation repays the $10,000 loan principal to Jeff. Discuss the tax effects. Assume that there was no corporate note (i.e., only an account payable). Does this change your answer? Explain.

43. **LO.5, 6, 11** Red Lion, Inc., is an S corporation with a sizable amount of AEP from a C corporation year. The S corporation has $400,000 investment income and $400,000 investment expense in 2012. The company makes cash distributions to enable its sole shareholder to pay her taxes. What are the tax aspects to consider? **Issue ID**

44. **LO.6, 9** At the beginning of the year, Ann and Becky own equally all of the stock of Whitman, Inc., an S corporation. Whitman generates a $120,000 loss for the year (not a leap year). On the 189th day of the year, Ann sells her half of the Whitman stock to her son, Scott. How much of the $120,000 loss, if any, belongs to Scott?

45. **LO.6, 9** In Problem 44, how much of the Whitman loss belongs to Ann and Becky? Becky's stock basis is $41,300.

46. **LO.5, 6, 8, 9** A calendar year S corporation has an ordinary loss of $80,000 and a capital loss of $20,000. Ms. Freiberg owns 30% of the corporate stock and has a $24,000 basis in her stock. Determine the amounts of the ordinary loss and capital loss, if any, that flow through to Ms. Freiberg. Prepare a tax memo for the files. **Communications**

47. **LO.5, 6, 8** Emeline, Inc., of Auburn, Alabama, is an accrual basis S corporation with three equal shareholders. The three cash basis shareholders have the following stock basis at the beginning of the year: Andre, $12,000; Crum, $22,000; and Barbara, $31,000. Emeline reports the following income and expense items.

Operating loss	($30,000)
Short-term capital gain	37,500
Long-term capital loss	(6,000)
Nondeductible fees and penalties	(3,000)

Emeline distributes $6,000 cash to each of the shareholders during the tax year. Calculate each of the shareholders' stock bases at the end of the year.

48. **LO.10** Rodeo, Inc., a cash basis S corporation in College Station, Texas, formerly was a C corporation. Rodeo records the following assets and liabilities on January 1, 2012, the date its S election is made.

	Adjusted Basis	Fair Market Value
Cash	$ 200,000	$ 200,000
Accounts receivable	–0–	105,000
Equipment	110,000	100,000
Land	1,800,000	2,500,000
Accounts payable	–0–	110,000

During 2012, Rodeo collects the accounts receivable and pays the accounts payable. The land is sold for $3 million, and taxable income for the year is $590,000. What is Rodeo's built-in gains tax?

49. **LO.4, 10, 11** Sweetwater, Inc., is an S corporation in Sour Lake, Texas.
   a. In 2012, Sweetwater's excess net passive income is $42,000. Sweetwater holds $31,000 of accumulated earnings and profits from a C corporation year. It reports $58,000 of taxable income and AMT adjustments of $17,000 for the year. Calculate any passive investment income penalty tax.
   b. In part (a), what if taxable income were $39,000?
   c. If this will be the third consecutive year the company may be subject to the penalty tax on excessive passive investment income, what could Sweetwater do before the end of the year to avoid the tax?

Issue ID

50. **LO.5, 6, 11** Bonnie and Clyde each own one-third of a fast-food restaurant, and their 13-year-old daughter owns the other shares. Both parents work full-time in the restaurant, but the daughter works infrequently. Neither Bonnie nor Clyde receives a salary during the year, when the ordinary income of the S corporation is $180,000. An IRS agent estimates that reasonable salaries for Bonnie, Clyde, and the daughter are $30,000, $35,000, and $10,000, respectively. What adjustments would you expect the IRS to impose upon these taxpayers?

Communications

51. **LO.11** Friedman, Inc., an S corporation, holds some highly appreciated land and inventory and some marketable securities that have declined in value. It anticipates a sale of these assets and a complete liquidation of the company over the next two years. Arnold Schwartz, the CFO, calls you, asking how to treat these transactions. Prepare a tax memo indicating what you told Arnold in the phone conversation.

52. **LO.6, 10** Ray Crockett sold 1,000 shares of his stock in Yellow, Inc., an S corporation. He sold the stock for $13,240, after he had owned it for five years. Ray had paid $137,400 for the stock, which was issued under § 1244. Ray is married and is the original owner of the 1,000 shares. Determine the appropriate tax treatment of any gain or loss on the stock sale.

Decision Making

53. **LO.11** Ruby is the owner of all of the shares of an S corporation. Ruby is considering receiving a salary of $80,000 from the business. She will pay 7.65% FICA taxes on the salary, and the S corporation will pay the same amount of FICA tax. If Ruby reduces her salary to $40,000 and takes an additional $40,000 as a distribution, how much total tax could be saved?

54. **LO.10** Blue Corporation elects S status effective for calendar year 2011. As of January 1, 2011, Blue holds two assets.

	Adjusted Basis	Fair Market Value
Land	$50,000	$110,000
IBM Stock	55,000	40,000

Blue sells the land in 2012 for $120,000. Calculate Blue's 2012 recognized built-in gain, if any.

Issue ID

55. **LO.1, 6, 8, 9, 11** Orange, Inc., a calendar year corporation in Clemson, South Carolina, elects S corporation status for 2012. The company generated a $74,000 NOL in 2011 and another NOL of $43,000 in 2012. Orange recorded no other transactions for the year.

At all times in 2011 and 2012, the stock of the corporation is owned by the same four shareholders, each owning 25% of the stock. Pete, one of the shareholders, holds a $6,020 basis in the Orange stock at the beginning of 2012. Identify the Federal income tax issues that Pete faces.

TAX RETURN PROBLEMS

1. Dane Henderson (123–45–6781) and Jace McClean (123–45–6782) are 70% and 30% owners, respectively, of Chocolat, Inc. (11–1111111), a candy company located at 45 Avenue A, Dime Box, TX 77853.

   The following information was taken from the Chocolat income statement for 2011.

Tax-exempt interest income	$ 10,000
Interest income, corporate bonds	100,000
Gross sales receipts	2,400,000
Beginning inventory	9,607
Direct labor	203,102
Direct materials purchased	278,143
Direct other costs	249,356
Ending inventory	3,467
Salaries and wages	442,103
Officers' salaries	150,000
Repairs	216,106
Depreciation	15,254
Interest expense	25,222
Rent expense (operating)	40,000
Taxes	65,101
Charitable contributions (cash)	20,000
Advertising expense	30,000
Payroll penalties	15,000
Other deductions	49,899
Net income	704,574

A comparative balance sheet appears below.

	January 1, 2011	December 31, 2011
Cash	$ 47,840	$?
Accounts receivable	93,100	123,104
Inventories	9,607	3,467
Prepaid expenses	8,333	17,582
Building and equipment	138,203	185,348
Accumulated depreciation	(84,235)	?
Land	2,000	2,000
Total assets	$214,848	$844,422
Accounts payable	$ 42,500	$ 72,300
Notes payable (less than 1 year)	4,500	2,100
Notes payable (more than 1 year)	26,700	24,300
Capital stock	30,000	30,000
Retained earnings	111,148	?
Total liabilities and capital	$214,848	$844,422

Chocolat's accounting firm provided the following additional information.

- Distributions to shareholders total $100,000.
- The company's S corporation election was made on January 15, 2007.

Using the above information, prepare a complete Form 1120S and a Schedule K–1 for Dane Henderson, 545 Avenue C, Dime Box, TX 77853. If any information is missing, make realistic assumptions and list them.

2. John Jacobs (111–11–1111), Sam Franklin (123–45–6789), and Sandra Moore (987–65–4321) are, respectively, 55%, 35%, and 10% owners of Textiles, Inc. (12–3456789), a textile manufacturing company located at 4044 Main Street, Kannapolis, NC 28083. The company's first S election was made on January 1, 1992. The following information was taken from the financial income statement for 2011.

Business income	$ 38,000
Interest income	230,000
Tax-exempt interest income	37,000
Distributive partnership income	9,000,000
Gross sales	111,831,710
Beginning inventory	500,000
Direct labor	41,200,000
Direct materials purchased	24,800,000
Ending inventory	1,100,000
Taxes (payroll)	3,923,500
Contributions to United Fund (public charity)	44,500
Meals and entertainment (before 50% limitation)	79,000
Fines on illegal activities	34,000
Life insurance premiums (Textiles is the beneficiary)	98,000
Compensation to shareholder-officers (proportionate to ownership)	2,820,910
Salaries and wages	7,500,000
Interest expense	1,722,200
Bad debt expense	820,000
Repairs	1,500,000
Depreciation (same amount for book and Federal income taxes)	1,615,400
Advertising	425,000
Pension plan contributions	600,000
Employee benefit programs	287,500
Amortization expenses	820,000
Other deductions	63,700
Book income	$ 39,383,000

A comparative book-basis balance sheet appears below.

	January 1, 2011	December 31, 2011
Cash	$ 4,784,000	$?
Accounts receivable	9,310,000	15,313,600
Inventories	500,000	1,100,000
Prepaid expenses	1,033,300	758,200
Loans to shareholders	31,300	72,700
Building and trucks	13,820,300	24,434,800
Accumulated depreciation	(8,423,500)	?
Land	180,900	1,651,300
Life insurance	1,156,600	1,834,400
Total assets	$22,392,900	$41,451,800

	January 1, 2011	December 31, 2011
Accounts payable	$ 4,979,700	$ 8,296,500
Notes payable (less than one year)	512,200	898,900
Loans from shareholders	15,575,100	19,196,700
Notes payable (more than one year)	2,182,100	3,383,500
Loan on life insurance	531,200	1,620,600
Capital stock	100,300	100,300
Paid-in capital	955,900	955,900
Retained earnings	(831,400)	?
Treasury stock	(1,612,200)	(1,612,200)
Total liabilities and capital	$22,392,900	$41,451,800

You must determine whether a Schedule M–3 is to be prepared by the entity. If a Schedule M-3 is required, omit Form 8916–A.

Textiles's accounting firm and the corporate books and records provide the following additional information.

Distributions to shareholders	$18,900,000
Income from U.S. partnership	
Distributive share	9,000,000
Ordinary income	4,800,000
Charitable contributions	3,000,000
Accumulated adjustments account (AAA), beginning balance	(831,400)
Other adjustments account (OAA), beginning balance	–0–

- A Canadian subsidiary shows net income of $6 million, assets of $44 million, and liabilities of $12 million on Textiles's financial statement. The subsidiary is not an includible corporation.
- Salaries and wages include $1.2 million of deferred compensation.
- Of the amortization amount, only $90,000 is deductible currently.
- Of the bad debt expense, $230,000 is not deductible this year.
- Of other expenses, $3,700 is permanently not deductible.

Using the above information, prepare a complete Form 1120S and a Schedule K–1 for John Jacobs (1245 Brantley Road, Kannapolis, NC 28083). If any information is missing, make realistic assumptions and list them.

RESEARCH PROBLEMS

THOMSON REUTERS **CHECKPOINT**®

Note: Solutions to Research Problems can be prepared by using the **Checkpoint® Student Edition** online research product, which is available to accompany this text. It is also possible to prepare solutions to the Research Problems by using tax research materials found in a standard tax library.

Research Problem 1. The tax treatment of fringe benefits for more-than-2% shareholder-employees of S corporations is less favorable than that for nonowners or employees of some other entities. What fringe benefits are subject to this limitation? What fringe benefits escape this limitation?

Communications

Research Problem 2. Locate and summarize in an e-mail to your instructor the holdings reported in these items involving S corporations.

a. Ltr.Rul. 9803023.

b. *Jerome R. Vainisi*, 132 T.C. 1 (2008).

c. TAM 200247002.

d. Rev.Proc. 97–48, 1997–2 C.B. 521.

Research Problem 3. Bushong, Inc., a calendar year S corporation, has a "tax cash-flow" provision in its shareholder agreement. Bushong must make annual distributions by the December 31 following a tax year in which there is an income pass-through. Each distribution must be in an amount sufficient to enable shareholders to pay their state and Federal income taxes on the pass-through.

The agreement also provides that if an audit adjustment is made to items reported on the Schedule K–1, Bushong can make a discretionary distribution to handle the increased taxes resulting from the adjustment.

The shareholders want to change the agreement. Under the proposal, if an audit adjustment is made and Bushong makes a discretionary payment, the payment would be in accordance with the shareholders' ownership shares during the tax year of the adjustment, rather than as of the distribution date.

Would the proposal create a second class of stock and terminate Bushong's S election? Explain.

Communications

Research Problem 4. Sam is selling his S corporation, Superbody Fitness, Inc. He will receive 80% cash and 20% of another S corporation fitness center. As part of this transaction, should Sam liquidate Superbody Fitness? Outline your analysis in an e-mail to your instructor.

Use the tax resources of the Internet to address the following questions. Do not restrict your search to the Web, but include a review of newsgroups and general reference materials, practitioner sites and resources, primary sources of the tax law, chat rooms and discussion groups, and other opportunities.

Research Problem 5. Develop a list of the pros and cons for a proposal by Congress to restructure the Federal income tax law for flow-through entities and to integrate Subchapters K and S.

Communications

Research Problem 6. Go to the website of a newspaper or business magazine. Find a case study of how to start a small business and choose the best tax entity (e.g., C corporation or S corporation). Summarize your findings in an e-mail to your instructor.

Communications

Research Problem 7. Outline the Treasury Department's tax reform proposal to treat pass-through entities as corporations. Summarize your findings in an e-mail to your instructor.

Communications

Research Problem 8. Summarize in no more than five PowerPoint slides what a tax adviser can learn from the *David E. Watson, P.C.*, 714 F.Supp.2d 95 (S.D. Iowa, 2010) decision.

CHAPTER

13 Comparative Forms of Doing Business

LEARNING OBJECTIVES: *After completing Chapter 13, you should be able to:*

LO.1 Identify the principal legal and tax forms for conducting a business.

LO.2 Explain the relative importance of nontax factors in making business decisions.

LO.3 Distinguish between the forms for conducting a business according to whether they are subject to single taxation or double taxation.

LO.4 Identify techniques for avoiding double taxation and for controlling the entity tax.

LO.5 Review and illustrate the applicability and the effect of the conduit and entity concepts on contributions to the entity, operations of the entity, entity distributions, passive activity loss and at-risk rules, and special allocations.

LO.6 Analyze the effect of the disposition of a business on the owners and the entity for each of the forms for conducting a business.

LO.7 Compare the tax consequences of the various forms of doing business.

CHAPTER OUTLINE

THE BIG PICTURE Tax Solutions for the Real World

Selection of a Tax Entity Form

Milly and Doug are going to start a dot-com business in which they both will participate on an active basis. They have an adequate amount in savings to finance the business. Limited liability is a significant factor for the business, but equally important is the minimization of income taxes. They have narrowed the choice of business forms to a C corporation or a general partnership. Annual earnings of the business before taxes are expected to be $200,000, and any after-tax profit will be distributed to Milly and Doug. Assume that both Milly and Doug are single and that their marginal tax rate is 28 percent. Advise Milly and Doug on the choice of business form.

Read the chapter and formulate your response.

13 Introduction

A variety of factors, both tax and nontax, affect the choice of the form of business entity. The form that is appropriate at one point in the life of an entity and its owners may not be appropriate at a different time.

EXAMPLE 1

Matte Enterprises is formed in the current year to operate an upscale bakery. Losses are expected in the first two years, with profits thereafter as Matte expands into neighboring communities. To finance this expansion, investments by outsiders will be required.

In the first two years, a flow-through entity such as an S corporation may be beneficial rather than organizing as a C corporation. However, as expansion is financed through investments by outsiders, it may not be possible to maintain S corporation status. On the other hand, depending on the distribution policy of Matte, C corporation status may be desirable. ■

This chapter provides the basis for comparatively analyzing the tax consequences of business decisions for five types of tax entities (sole proprietorship, partnership, corporation, S corporation, and limited liability company). Understanding the comparative tax consequences for the different types of entities and being able to apply them effectively to specific fact patterns can lead to effective tax planning.

13.1 Forms of Doing Business

LO.1

Identify the principal legal and tax forms for conducting a business.

The principal *legal* forms for conducting a business entity are a sole proprietorship, partnership, limited liability company, and corporation.[1] From a *Federal income tax* perspective, these same forms are available with the corporate form being divided into two types (S corporation and C or regular corporation). In most instances, the legal form and the tax form are the same. In some cases, however, the IRS may attempt to tax a business entity as a form different from its legal form. This reclassification normally takes one of two possible approaches:

- The IRS ignores the corporate form and taxes the owners directly (the corporate entity lacks substance).
- The IRS ignores the partnership form and taxes the partnership as if it were a corporation.

The IRS may try to reclassify a corporation for several reasons. One reason is to prevent taxpayers from taking advantage of the potential disparity between the corporate and individual tax rates. Although the highest corporate statutory rate and the highest individual statutory rate are now the same (35 percent), the specific corporate and individual rates applicable to a particular taxpayer may differ. For example, an individual may be in the 35 percent bracket, and the corporation may be in the 15 percent, 25 percent, or 34 percent bracket. Another reason for taxing the owners directly is to make them ineligible for favorable taxation of certain fringe benefits (see the subsequent discussion in Favorable Treatment of Certain Fringe Benefits).

[1]A business entity can also be conducted in the form of a trust or an estate. These two forms are not discussed in this chapter. See the discussion of the income taxation of trusts and estates in Chapter 20.

TAX IN THE NEWS When Is a Tax Cut for Some a Tax Increase for Others?

The Federal income tax liability is comprised of two components: a tax base and a tax rate. Federal tax revenues can be increased by raising either component or by raising both components.

A major benefit of a flow-through entity (a partnership, an LLC, and an S corporation) and the sole proprietorship is an absence of double taxation (taxation at both the entity level and the owner level).

Both the Obama administration and Congress are considering ways to lower the corporate tax rate and yet not increase the deficit. One proposal would increase the tax base by curtailing deductions. Another would be to "tax certain large businesses that presently are taxed as small businesses." Under this approach, certain entities would be denied the flow-through approach and would be subject to double taxation (at the entity level and at the owner level).

As expected, both large and small businesses that are organized as C corporations would support a tax rate cut. However, both large and small businesses that presently are subject to single taxation would oppose being subject to double taxation. In addition, businesses that would not benefit from the corporate rate cut oppose seeing their tax liability increase as a result of increasing the tax base.

Senator Max Baucus, the chair of the Senate Finance Committee, and Congressman Dave Camp, the chair of the House Ways and Means Committee, have stated a preference for achieving corporate tax rate reduction as part of comprehensive tax reform.

Source: Adapted from John D. McKinnon, "Plans for Slashing Corporate Taxes Worry Some Firms," *Wall Street Journal*, May 7, 2011, page A4.

In the case of a partnership, reclassification of a partnership as if it were a corporation can subject the business entity to double taxation. In addition, the resultant loss of conduit status prevents partnership losses from being passed through to the tax returns of the partners.

The taxpayer generally is bound for tax purposes by the legal form that is selected. A major statutory exception to this is the ability of an S corporation to receive tax treatment similar to that of a partnership.[2] In addition, taxpayers sometimes can control which set of tax rules will apply to their business operations. The "check-the-box" Regulations provide an elective procedure that enables certain entities to be classified as partnerships for Federal income tax purposes even though they have corporate characteristics.[3] These Regulations have greatly simplified the determination of entity classification.

A **limited liability company (LLC)** is a hybrid business form that combines the corporate characteristic of limited liability for the owners with the tax characteristics of a partnership.[4] All of the states now permit this legal form for conducting a business.

The most frequently cited benefit of an LLC is the limited liability of the owners. Compared to the other forms of ownership, LLCs offer additional benefits but also certain disadvantages. Refer to the coverage of the advantages and disadvantages of an LLC in Chapter 11 on p. 11-35.

An individual conducting a sole proprietorship files Schedule C of Form 1040. If more than one trade or business is conducted, a separate Schedule C is filed for each trade or business. A partnership files Form 1065. A corporation files Form 1120, and an S corporation files Form 1120S. An LLC that has elected to be taxed as a partnership files Form 1065.

[2]§§ 1361 and 1362.

[3]Reg. §§ 301.7701–1 through −4, and −6. Note that if the business has only one owner, the elective procedure enables the entity to be classified as a sole proprietorship.

[4]Depending on state law, an LLC may be organized as a limited liability corporation or a limited liability partnership.

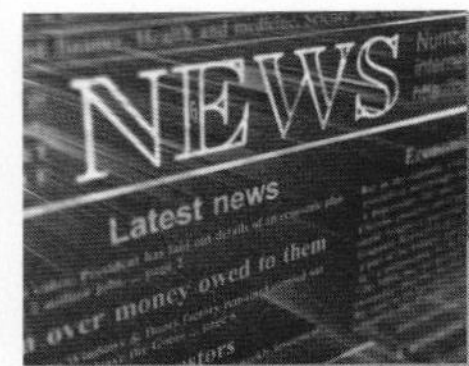

TAX IN THE NEWS Professional Service Firms and Organizational Form

Many professional service firms (e.g., accountants, architects, and lawyers) have chosen to become limited liability partnerships (LLPs). In the accounting profession, this includes all of the Big 4 (i.e., Deloitte, Ernst & Young, KPMG, and PricewaterhouseCoopers) and most regional and local accounting firms.

An LLP helps to provide protection for the purely personal assets of the partners. Under the LLP organizational structure, the only partners whose personal assets are at risk to pay a judgment are those actually involved in the negligence or wrongdoing at issue. Note, however, that the entity is still responsible for the full judgment. Thus, the capital of the entity is still at risk.

LO.2

Explain the relative importance of nontax factors in making business decisions.

13.2 Nontax Factors

Taxes are only one of many factors to consider in making any business decision. Above all, any business decision should make economic sense.

EXAMPLE 2

Albert is considering investing $10,000 in a limited partnership. He projects that he will be able to deduct the $10,000 within the next two years (his share of partnership losses). Because Albert's marginal tax rate is 35%, the deductions will produce a positive cash-flow effect of $3,500 ($10,000 × 35%). However, there is a substantial risk that he will not recover any of his original investment. If this occurs, his negative cash flow from the investment in the limited partnership is $6,500 ($10,000 − $3,500). Albert must decide if the investment makes economic sense. ■

Capital Formation

The ability of an entity to raise capital is a factor that must be considered. A sole proprietorship is subject to obvious limitations. Compared to the sole proprietorship, the partnership has a greater opportunity to raise funds through the pooling of owner resources.

EXAMPLE 3

Adam and Beth decide to form a partnership, AB. Adam contributes cash of $200,000, and Beth contributes land with an adjusted basis of $60,000 and a fair market value of $200,000. The partnership is going to construct an apartment building at a cost of $800,000. AB pledges the land and the building to secure a loan of $700,000. ■

The limited partnership offers even greater potential than the general partnership form because a limited partnership can secure funds from investors (limited partners).

EXAMPLE 4

Carol and Dave form a limited partnership, CD. Carol contributes cash of $200,000, and Dave contributes land with an adjusted basis of $60,000 and a fair market value of $200,000. The partnership is going to construct a shopping center at a cost of $5 million. Included in this cost is the purchase price of $800,000 for land adjacent to that contributed by Dave. Thirty limited partnership interests are sold for $100,000 each to raise $3 million. CD also pledges the shopping center (including the land) and obtains nonrecourse creditor financing of $2 million. ■

Both the § 465 at-risk provision and the § 469 passive activity loss provision have reduced the tax attractiveness of investments in real estate, particularly in the limited partnership form. In effect, the tax consequences have a critical effect on the economic consequences.[5]

Of the different forms of business entities, the corporate form offers the greatest ease and potential for obtaining owner financing because it can issue additional shares of stock. The ultimate examples of this form are the large public companies that are listed on the stock exchanges.

Limited Liability

A corporation offers its owners limited liability under state law. This absence of personal liability on the part of the owners is the most frequently cited advantage of the corporate form.

EXAMPLE 5

Ed, Fran, and Gabriella each invest $25,000 for all the shares of stock of Brown Corporation. Brown obtains creditor financing of $100,000. Brown is the defendant in a personal injury suit resulting from an accident involving one of its delivery trucks. The court awards a judgment of $2.5 million to the plaintiff. The award exceeds Brown's insurance coverage by $1.5 million. Even though the judgment will probably result in Brown's bankruptcy, the shareholders will have no personal liability for the unpaid corporate debts. ■

Limited liability is not available to all corporations. For many years, state laws did not permit professional individuals (e.g., accountants, attorneys, architects, and physicians) to incorporate. Even though professionals are now allowed to incorporate, the statutes do not provide limited liability for the performance of professional services.

Even if state law provides for limited liability, the shareholders of small corporations may have to forgo this benefit. Quite often, such a corporation may be unable to obtain external financing (e.g., a bank loan) unless the shareholders guarantee the loan.

The limited partnership form provides limited liability to the limited partners. Their liability is limited to the amount invested plus any additional amount they agreed to invest. However, the general partner (or partners) has unlimited liability.

EXAMPLE 6

Hazel, the general partner, invests $250,000 in HIJ, a limited partnership. Iris and Jane, the limited partners, each invest $50,000. While the potential loss for Iris and Jane is limited to $50,000 each, Hazel's liability is unlimited. ■

Indirectly, it may be possible to provide the general partner with limited liability by having a corporation as the general partner (see Figure 13.1). When the entity is structured this way, the general partner (the corporation) has limited its liability under the corporate statutes. Therefore, individual A is protected from personal liability by being merely the shareholder of Corporation A. Prior to the issuance of the check-the-box Regulations, it was necessary to structure the entity very carefully to avoid the limited partnership being classified as an association and taxed as a corporation. With the check-the-box Regulations, the limited partnership depicted in Figure 13.1 can be taxed as a partnership.[6]

Other Factors

Other nontax factors may be significant in selecting an organization form, including the following:

- Estimated life of the business.
- Number of owners and their roles in the management of the business.
- Freedom of choice in transferring ownership interests.
- Organizational formality, including the related cost and extent of government regulation.

[5]See the related discussions in Chapters 10 and 11. For a comprehensive discussion of these provisions, see Chapter 11 in *South-Western Federal Taxation: Individual Income Taxes.*

[6]See the discussions of limited partnerships in Chapter 11. Also see Rev. Proc. 89–12, 1989–1 C.B. 798 and Rev.Rul. 88–76, 1988–2 C.B. 360.

FIGURE 13.1 Limited Partnership with a Corporate General Partner

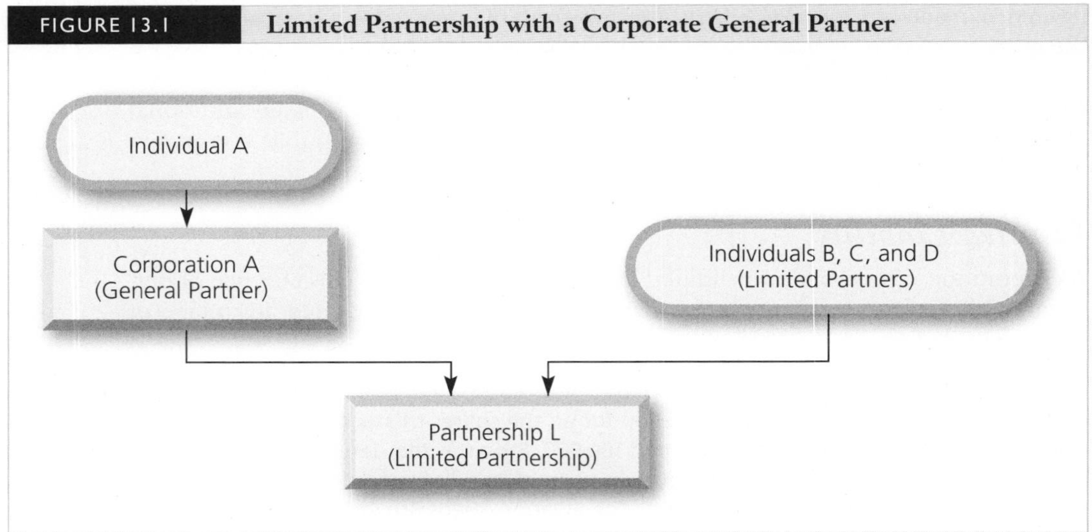

13.3 Single versus Double Taxation

LO.3

Distinguish between the forms for conducting a business according to whether they are subject to single taxation or double taxation.

Overall Impact on Entity and Owners

The sole proprietorship, partnership, and LLC are subject to *single* taxation. This result occurs because the owner(s) and the entity generally are not considered separate for tax purposes. Thus, the tax liability is levied at the owner level rather than at the entity level.

On the other hand, the corporate form is subject to *double* taxation. This is frequently cited as the major tax disadvantage of the corporate form. Under double taxation, the entity is taxed on the earnings of the corporation, and the owners are taxed on distributions to the extent they are made from corporate earnings. If the corporation is a personal service corporation (see Chapter 2), the corporation is subject to a flat tax rate of 35 percent.

The S corporation provides a way to attempt to avoid double taxation and to subject the earnings to a lower tax rate (the actual individual tax rate may be lower than the actual corporate tax rate). However, the ownership structure of an S corporation is restricted in both the number and type of shareholders. In addition, statutory exceptions subject the entity to taxation in certain circumstances. To the extent these exceptions apply, double taxation may result. Finally, the distribution policy of the S corporation may encounter difficulties with the *wherewithal to pay* concept.

EXAMPLE 7

Hawk Corporation has been operating as an S corporation since it began its business two years ago. For both of the prior years, Hawk incurred a tax loss. Hawk has taxable income of $75,000 for 2012 and expects that its earnings will increase each year in the foreseeable future. Part of this earnings increase will result from Hawk's expansion into other communities in the state. Because most of this expansion will be financed internally, no dividend distributions will be made to the shareholders.

Assuming that all of Hawk's shareholders are in the 33% tax bracket, their tax liability for 2012 will be $24,750 ($75,000 × 33%). Although the S corporation election will avoid double taxation, the shareholders will have a wherewithal to pay problem. In addition, the actual tax liability for 2012 would have been less if Hawk had not been an S corporation [(15% × $50,000) + (25% × $25,000) = $13,750]. ■

The data in Example 7 can be used to illustrate two additional tax concepts. First, the current wherewithal to pay problem could be resolved by terminating the

Tax Rates and Economic Activity

Global Tax Issues

© Andrey Prokhorov, iStockphoto

Tax rates affect economic activity. The maximum corporate income tax rates for selected countries are as follows:

Country	Tax Rate
France	33.33%
Germany	33%*
Hong Kong	16.5%
Japan	30%
Republic of Ireland	12.5%
Russia	20%
Singapore	18%
United States	35%**
Vietnam	25%
Industrial nations' average	27%

*Standard rate of 15% is increased to 33% by the trade tax and the solidarity tax.
**Plus state average of 4.3%.

Most of these countries except the United States have recently reduced their corporate tax rates. The primary motivation for doing so was to increase the country's attractiveness as a location for foreign investment.

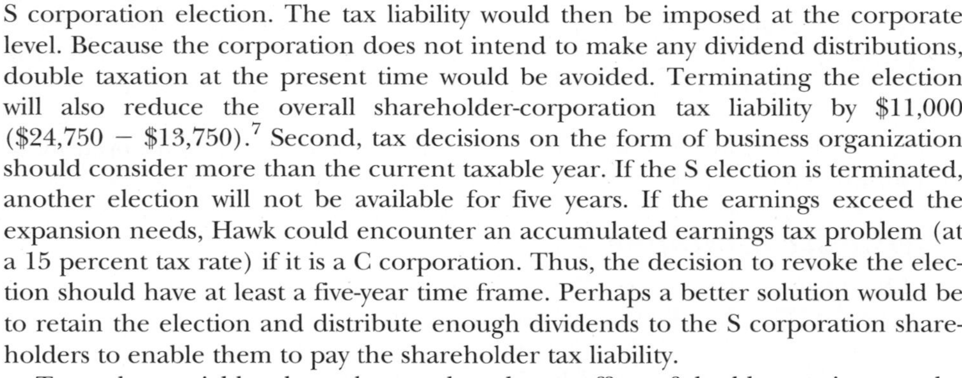

S corporation election. The tax liability would then be imposed at the corporate level. Because the corporation does not intend to make any dividend distributions, double taxation at the present time would be avoided. Terminating the election will also reduce the overall shareholder-corporation tax liability by $11,000 ($24,750 − $13,750).[7] Second, tax decisions on the form of business organization should consider more than the current taxable year. If the S election is terminated, another election will not be available for five years. If the earnings exceed the expansion needs, Hawk could encounter an accumulated earnings tax problem (at a 15 percent tax rate) if it is a C corporation. Thus, the decision to revoke the election should have at least a five-year time frame. Perhaps a better solution would be to retain the election and distribute enough dividends to the S corporation shareholders to enable them to pay the shareholder tax liability.

Two other variables that relate to the adverse effect of double taxation are the timing and form of corporate distributions. If no distributions are made in the short run, then only single taxation occurs in the short run.[8] To the extent double taxation does occur in the future, the cash-flow effect should be discounted to the present. Second, when the distribution is made, is it in the form of a dividend or a return of capital (a stock redemption or a complete liquidation)?[9]

EXAMPLE 8

Gray Corporation has taxable income of $100,000 for 2012. Gray's tax liability is $22,250. All of Gray's shareholders are in the 33% bracket. If dividends of $77,750 are distributed in 2012, the shareholders will have a tax liability of $11,663 ($77,750 × 15%), assuming the dividends are qualified dividends. The combined corporation-shareholder tax liability is $33,913 ($22,250 + $11,663) for a combined effective tax rate of 33.9%. ■

[7] The absence of distributions to shareholders could create an accumulated earnings tax problem under § 531. However, as long as earnings are used to finance expansion, the "reasonable needs" provision will be satisfied and the corporation will avoid any accumulated earnings tax.

[8] This assumes that there is no accumulated earnings tax problem. See the subsequent discussion of distributions in Minimizing Double Taxation.

[9] See the coverage of dividends in Chapter 5 and the coverage of stock redemptions and complete liquidations in Chapter 6.

FIGURE 13.2 **Bar Graph Illustration of Dividend versus Stock Redemption**

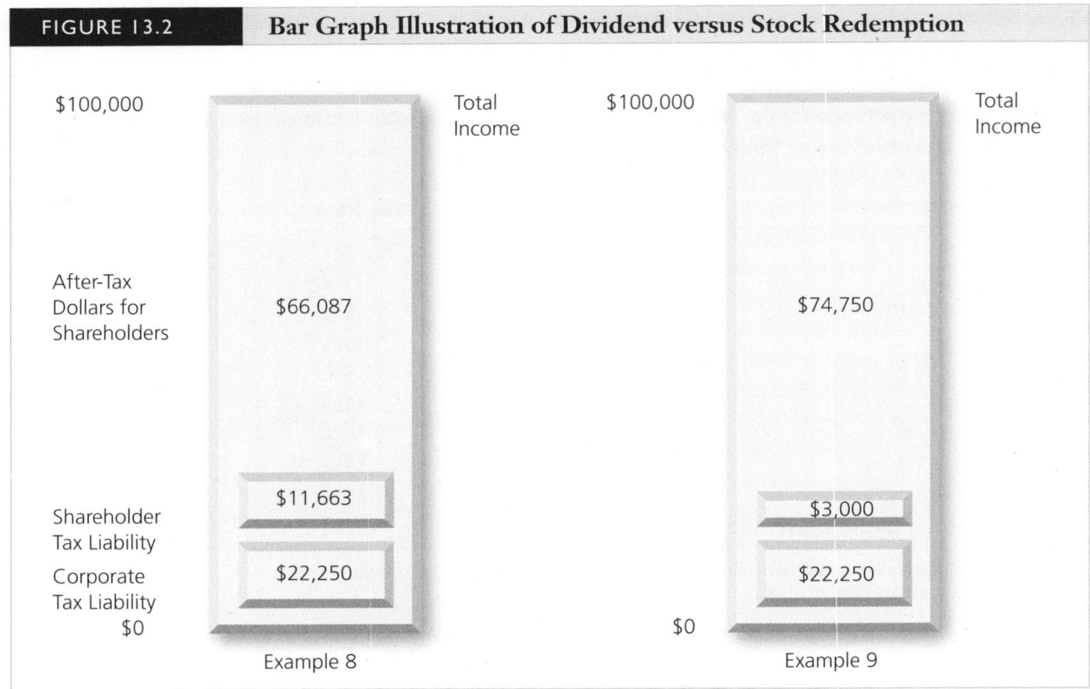

EXAMPLE 9

Assume the same facts as in Example 8, except that the form of the distribution is a stock redemption and the basis for the redeemed shares is $57,750. The shareholders have a recognized gain of $20,000 and a tax liability of $3,000 ($20,000 × 15% beneficial capital gain rate). The combined corporation-shareholder tax liability is $25,250 ($22,250 + $3,000) for a total effective tax rate of 25.25%. ■

The differences in the tax consequences in Examples 8 and 9 are even more obvious when illustrated in bar graph form (see Figure 13.2).

Alternative Minimum Tax

All of the forms of business are directly or indirectly subject to the alternative minimum tax (AMT).[10] For the sole proprietorship and the C corporation, the effect is direct (the AMT liability calculation is attached to the tax form that reports the entity's taxable income—Form 1040 or Form 1120). For the partnership, LLC, and S corporation, the effect is indirect (the tax preferences and adjustments are passed through from the entity to the owners, and the AMT liability calculation is not attached to the tax form that reports the entity's taxable income—Form 1065 or Form 1120S).

When compared with the other forms of business, the C corporation appears to have a slight advantage. The corporate AMT rate of 20 percent is less than the individual AMT rates of 26 and 28 percent. An even better perspective is provided by comparing the maximum AMT rate with the maximum regular rate for both the individual and the corporation. For the individual, the AMT rate is 80 percent (28%/35%) of the maximum regular rate. The AMT rate for the corporation is 57 percent (20%/35%) of the maximum regular rate. Therefore, on the basis of comparative rates, the C corporation does have an advantage. In addition, as discussed next, under certain circumstances, a C corporation is exempt from the AMT.

The apparent corporate AMT rate advantage may be more than offset by the AMT adjustment that applies only to the C corporation. This is the adjustment for adjusted current earnings (ACE). The amount of the adjustment is 75 percent of

[10] § 55.

the excess of ACE over unadjusted alternative minimum taxable income (AMTI). If unadjusted AMTI exceeds ACE for the tax year, the adjustment is negative.[11]

If the ACE adjustment continually causes the C corporation to be subject to the AMT, the owners should consider electing S corporation status if the eligibility requirements can be satisfied. Because the S corporation does not have this item as an adjustment, it may be possible to reduce the tax liability.

The AMT does not apply to small corporations for tax years beginning after December 31, 1997. For this purpose, a C corporation is classified as a small corporation if both of the following apply:

- It was treated as a small corporation exempt from the AMT for all prior years beginning after 1997.
- Its annual average gross receipts for the three-year period (or portion thereof during which the corporation was in existence) ending before its current tax year did not exceed $7.5 million ($5 million if the corporation had only one prior tax year).

However, if a corporation ever fails the gross receipts test, it is ineligible for small corporation classification in future years.

Tax legislation enacted in 1998 provided an additional opportunity for a C corporation to be classified as a small corporation. A C corporation automatically is classified as a small corporation in its first year of existence.

If the AMT is going to apply for the taxable year, the entity should consider accelerating income into the current taxable year and delaying deductions so that the resultant increased taxable income will be taxed at the lower AMT rate. For the C corporation, the potential rate differential is 15 percentage points (20 percent AMT rate versus 35 percent regular rate). For the individual taxpayer (i.e., as a sole proprietor, as a partner, or as an S corporation shareholder), the potential tax rate differential is 7 percentage points (28 percent highest AMT rate versus 35 percent regular rate). A present value analysis should be used to ensure that the acceleration of income and delaying of deductions do not increase actual tax liabilities.

State Taxation

In selecting a form for doing business, the determination of the tax consequences should not be limited to Federal income taxes. Consideration should also be given to state income taxes and, if applicable, local income taxes.[12]

The S corporation provides a good illustration of this point. Suppose the forms of business being considered are a limited partnership and a corporation. An operating loss is projected for the next several years. The owners decide to operate the business in the corporate form. The principal nontax criterion for the decision is the limited liability attribute of the corporation. The owners consent to an S corporation election so that the corporate losses can be passed through to the shareholders to deduct on their individual tax returns. However, assume that state law does not permit the S corporation election on the state income tax return. Thus, the owners will not receive the tax benefits of the loss deductions that would have been available on their state income tax returns if they had chosen the limited partnership form. As a result of providing limited liability to the owner who would have been the general partner for the limited partnership, the loss deduction at the state level is forgone.

13.4 Controlling the Entity Tax

LO.4

Identify techniques for avoiding double taxation and for controlling the entity tax.

Of the five forms of business entities, it appears at first glance that only the corporation needs to be concerned with controlling the entity tax. If control is defined in the narrow sense of double taxation, then this issue is restricted to the corporate

[11]§§ 56(c)(1) and (f). See the discussion of the corporate AMT in Chapter 3.

[12]See the discussion of multistate corporate taxation in Chapter 16.

form. However, from the broader perspective of controlling the tax liability related to the business entity's profits, whether that tax is imposed at the entity or the owner level, all five business forms are encompassed.

Techniques that can be used to minimize the current-period tax liability include the following:

1. Distribution policy.
2. Recognition of the interaction between the regular tax liability and the AMT liability.
3. Utilization of special allocations.
4. Favorable treatment of certain fringe benefits.
5. Minimization of double taxation.

Some of the techniques apply to all five forms of business entities. Others apply to only one of the five forms. Even those that apply to all do not minimize taxes equally for all forms. Because the first three techniques are discussed elsewhere in this chapter, only the last two are discussed here.

Favorable Treatment of Certain Fringe Benefits

Ideally, a fringe benefit produces the following tax consequences:

- Deductible by the entity (employer) that provides the fringe benefit.
- Excludible from the gross income of the taxpayer (employee) who receives the fringe benefit.

From the perspective of the owner or owners of an entity, when the entity provides such favorably taxed fringe benefits to an owner, the benefits are paid for with *before-tax* dollars.

EXAMPLE 10

Rocky, the owner of Rocky's Ranch, a C corporation in the 34% tax bracket, is provided with meals and lodging that qualify for exclusion treatment under § 119. The annual cost of the meals and lodging to Rocky's Ranch is $10,000. Because the cost is deductible in calculating the taxable income of Rocky's Ranch on Form 1120, the after-tax cost to the corporation is only $6,600 [$10,000 − (34% × $10,000)]. Because the $10,000 is excluded in calculating Rocky's gross income, there is no additional tax cost at the owner level. If Rocky had paid for the meals and lodging himself, no deduction would have been permitted because these expenditures are nondeductible personal expenditures. Thus, from Rocky's perspective, the receipt of excludible meals and lodging of $10,000 is equivalent to receiving a distribution from the corporation of $15,385 [$10,000/(100% − 35%)], assuming that he is in the 35% tax bracket. ■

Not all favorably taxed fringe benefits receive exclusion treatment. Although not as attractive to the recipient, another approach provided in the Code is deferral treatment (e.g., pension plans and profit sharing plans).

Example 10 illustrates how certain fringe benefits can be used to benefit the owner of an entity and at the same time have a beneficial impact on the combined tax liability of the entity and the owner. In recognition of this, Congress has enacted various nondiscrimination provisions that generally negate favorable tax treatment if the fringe benefit program is discriminatory. In addition, the Code includes several statutory provisions that make the favorably taxed fringe benefit treatment available only to *employees* (e.g., group term life insurance and meal and lodging exclusion).[13]

The IRS defines the term *employee* restrictively. For the owner of a business entity to be treated as an employee, the entity must be a corporation.[14] For this purpose,

[13]§§ 79 and 119.

[14]Reg. § 1.79–0(b). The IRS has not been completely successful with respect to this position.

an S corporation is treated as a partnership, and a greater-than-2 percent shareholder is treated as a partner.[15]

Classification of an owner as a nonemployee produces two negative results. First, the deduction for the cost of the fringe benefit to the entity is disallowed at the entity level. Second, the owner whose fringe benefit has been paid for by the entity must include the cost of the fringe benefit in gross income.

Minimizing Double Taxation

Only the corporate form is potentially subject to double taxation. Several techniques are available for eliminating or at least reducing the second layer of taxation:

- Making distributions to the shareholders that are deductible to the corporation.
- Not making distributions to the shareholders.
- Making distributions that qualify for return of capital treatment at the shareholder level.
- Making the S corporation election.

Note that for distributions made in 2003 and after the availability of the beneficial rate (15%/0% in 2008–2012 and 15%/5% before 2008) for qualified dividends reduces the potential negative impact of double taxation (see Chapter 5).

Making Deductible Distributions

Use of the first technique requires careful advance planning. Typical distribution forms that will result in a deduction to the corporation are (1) salary payments to shareholder-employees, (2) lease rental payments to shareholder-lessors, and (3) interest payments to shareholder-creditors.

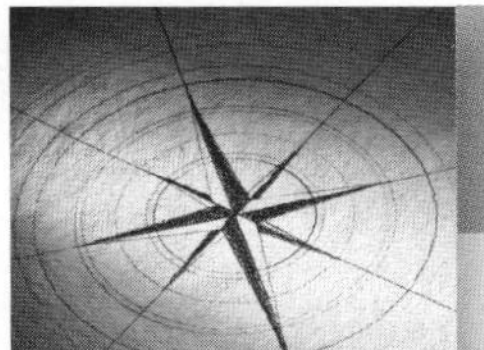

ETHICS & EQUITY A Technique for Getting a Bonus

Luis is the chief operating officer of an S corporation that has about $40 million in annual sales. During the five years he has been in his position, profits have increased between 15 and 20 percent each year. Luis owns 10 percent of the stock of the corporation, and Jay owns 90 percent. Although Luis's salary has increased each year, he has not received any bonuses.

Luis suggests that Jay establish a performance-based system that would enable Luis to receive a bonus based on the growth in the corporation's profitability. Jay believes that Luis is adequately compensated and that a bonus plan is unnecessary.

To demonstrate his displeasure with Jay's response, Luis is considering selling half of his stock to Marco, a cousin who is a citizen of Spain and a longtime resident of Madrid. Marco has expressed an interest in investing in the corporation. Luis believes that this proposed sale of stock to Marco may motivate Jay to change his mind regarding the bonus plan.

Comment on whether Luis's plan will work and on the ethics of such a plan.

Recognizing the tax benefit of this technique, the IRS scrutinizes these types of transactions carefully. All three types are evaluated in terms of *reasonableness.*[16] In addition, the interest payments may result in the IRS raising the **thin capitalization** issue and reclassifying some or all of the debt as equity.[17] IRS success with either approach raises the specter of double taxation.

---

[15] § 1372(a).

[16] § 162(a)(1). *Mayson Manufacturing Co. v. Comm.*, 49–2 USTC ¶9467, 38 AFTR 1028, 178 F.2d 115 (CA–6, 1949); *Harolds Club v. Comm.*, 65–1 USTC ¶9198, 15 AFTR 2d 241, 340 F.2d 861 (CA–9, 1965).

[17] § 385; Rev.Rul. 83–98, 1983–2 C.B. 40; *Bauer v. Comm.*, 84–2 USTC ¶9996, 55 AFTR 2d 85–433, 748 F.2d 1365 (CA–9, 1984).

EXAMPLE 11

Donna owns all of the stock of Green and is the chief executive officer. Green's taxable income before salary payments to Donna is as follows:

2010	$ 80,000
2011	50,000
2012	250,000

During the year, Donna receives a monthly salary of $3,000. In December of each year, she reviews the operations for the year and determines the year-end bonus to be paid to the key officers (only Donna for bonus purposes). Donna's yearly bonuses are as follows:

2010	$ 44,000
2011	14,000
2012	214,000

The obvious purpose of Green's bonus program is to reduce the corporate taxable income to zero and thereby avoid double taxation. The examination of Green's tax return by the IRS would likely result in a deduction disallowance for unreasonable compensation. ■

EXAMPLE 12

Tom and Vicki each contribute $20,000 to TV Corporation for all of the stock of TV. In addition, they each lend $80,000 to TV. The loan is documented by formal notes, the interest rate is 7%, and the maturity date is 10 years from the date of the loan.

The notes provide the opportunity for the corporation to make payments of $5,600 each year to both Tom and Vicki and for the payments not to be subject to double taxation. That is, the interest payments are includible in the gross income of Tom and Vicki, but are deductible by TV in calculating its taxable income. At the time of repayment in 10 years, neither Tom nor Vicki will have any gross income from the repayment because the $80,000 amount realized is equal to the basis for the note of $80,000 (return of capital concept).

If the IRS succeeded in reclassifying the notes as equity, Tom and Vicki's includible gross income of $5,600 each would remain the same (interest income would be reclassified as dividend income that may be taxed at the 15% rate). However, because the dividend payments are not deductible by TV, the corporation's taxable income would increase by $11,200 ($5,600 × 2). To make matters worse, the repayment of the notes in 10 years would not qualify for return of capital treatment and would likely result in dividend income treatment for Tom and Vicki. ■

Not Making Distributions

Double taxation will not occur unless the corporation makes (actual or deemed) distributions to the shareholders. A closely held corporation that does not make distributions will eventually encounter an accumulated earnings tax problem unless the reasonable needs requirement is satisfied. When making distribution policy decisions each year, the board of directors should be apprised of any potential accumulated earnings tax problem and take the appropriate steps to eliminate it. The accumulated earnings tax rate of 15 percent in 2012 is the same as the 15 percent rate for qualified dividends for individual taxpayers.[18]

EXAMPLE 13

According to an internal calculation made by Dolphin Corporation, its accumulated taxable income is $400,000. The board of directors would prefer not to declare any dividends, but is considering a dividend declaration of $400,000 to avoid the accumulated earnings tax. All of the shareholders are in the 35% bracket.

If a dividend of $400,000 is declared, the tax cost to the shareholders is $60,000 ($400,000 × 15%), assuming that the dividends are qualified dividends. If a dividend is

[18] § 531. See the discussion of the accumulated earnings tax in Chapter 3.

not declared and the IRS assesses the accumulated earnings tax, the tax cost to the corporation for the accumulated earnings tax also would be $60,000 ($400,000 × 15%).

To make matters worse, Dolphin will have incurred the accumulated earnings tax cost without getting any funds out of the corporation to the shareholders. If the unwise decision were now made to distribute the remaining $340,000 ($400,000 − $60,000) to the shareholders, the additional tax cost at the shareholder level would be $51,000 ($340,000 × 15%). Therefore, the combined shareholder-corporation tax cost would be $111,000 ($60,000 + $51,000). This is 185% ($111,000/$60,000) of the tax cost that would have resulted from an initial dividend distribution of $400,000. ■

The legislation that created the special tax rate of 15 percent for qualified dividends also lowered the accumulated earnings tax rate from 35 percent to 15 percent. This tax rate reduction has substantially lowered the impact of the accumulated earnings tax. In Example 13, the penalty tax at the corporate level prior to the legislative change would have been $140,000 ($400,000 × 35%). Assuming that the remaining $260,000 was distributed to the shareholders, the additional tax cost at the shareholder level would have been $91,000 ($260,000 × 35%). Therefore, the combined shareholder-corporation tax cost would have been $231,000 ($140,000 + $91,000) rather than the current $111,000. Thus, by reducing both the tax rate for the accumulated earnings tax and the tax rate on qualified dividends, this legislative change has substantially lowered the tax burden of the accumulated earnings tax.

Assuming that the accumulated earnings tax can be avoided (e.g., a growth company whose reasonable needs justify its no dividend policy), a policy of no distributions to shareholders can avoid the second layer of taxation forever. This will occur if the shares of stock are bequeathed to the taxpayer's beneficiaries. As a result of the step-up in basis rules for inherited property, the basis of the stock for the beneficiaries will be the fair market value at the date of the decedent's death rather than the decedent's basis.

Return of Capital Distributions

The magnitude of the effect of double taxation can be reduced if the corporate distributions to the shareholders can qualify for return of capital rather than dividend treatment. For an ongoing corporation, the stock redemption provisions offer an opportunity to reduce the includible gross income at the shareholder level. The corporate liquidation provisions can be used if the business entity will cease to operate in corporate form. Under redemption and liquidation rules, the distribution may be treated as a sale of some or all of the shareholder's stock resulting in a tax-free recovery of basis and capital gain.

EXAMPLE 14

Copper Corporation makes a distribution of $60,000 to its shareholders. Mark and Kate, two of the shareholders, receive $25,000 and $10,000, respectively. The form of the distribution permits the shareholders to surrender a certain number of shares of stock. The potential exists that the distribution can qualify for stock redemption treatment at the shareholder level. Mark satisfies the requirements for a substantially disproportionate distribution under § 302. Kate does not because she is in control of the corporation after the distribution (she owns 60% of the stock). Assuming that Mark's basis for the shares redeemed is $20,000, he has a capital gain of $5,000 ($25,000 − $20,000). Kate has dividend income of $10,000. She must allocate her stock basis among her remaining shares. ■

Electing S Corporation Status

Electing S corporation status generally eliminates double taxation by making the corporation a tax reporter rather than a taxpayer. Therefore, the only tax levy is at the shareholder level. Factors to consider in making this election include the following:

TAX IN THE NEWS C Corporations versus S Corporations

Are there more C corporations than S corporations? If you answered yes, you are right, but not by much. According to IRS data, 47 percent of all corporations are S corporations. Most S corporations (81 percent) have only one or two shareholders.

When it comes to share of corporate net income, C corporations win hands down. C corporations report 82 percent of net income.

- Are all of the shareholders willing to consent to the election?
- Can the qualification requirements under § 1361 be satisfied at the time of the election?
- Because the qualification requirements become maintenance requirements, can these requirements continue to be satisfied?
- For what period will the conditions that make the election beneficial continue to prevail?
- Will the corporate distribution policy create wherewithal to pay problems at the shareholder level?

EXAMPLE 15

Emerald Corporation commenced business in January 2012. The two shareholders, Diego and Jaime, are both in the 28% tax bracket. The following operating results are projected for the first five years of operations:

2012	($ 50,000)
2013	400,000
2014	600,000
2015	800,000
2016	1,000,000

The corporation plans to expand rapidly. Therefore, no distributions will be made to shareholders. In addition, beginning in 2013, preferred stock will be offered to a substantial number of investors to help finance the expansion.

If the S corporation election is made for 2012, the $50,000 loss can be passed through to Diego's and Jaime's tax returns. Therefore, the cash-flow effect would be $14,000 ($50,000 × 28%). Assume that the election is either revoked or involuntarily terminated at the beginning of 2013 as a result of the issuance of the preferred stock. The corporate tax liability for 2013 would be $136,000 ($400,000 × 34%).

If the S corporation election is not made for 2012, the $50,000 loss will be a net operating loss. The amount can be carried forward to reduce the 2013 corporate taxable income to $350,000 ($400,000 − $50,000). The resultant tax liability is $119,000 ($350,000 × 34%).

Should the S corporation election be made for just the one-year period? The answer is unclear. With an assumed after-tax rate of return to Diego and Jaime of 10%, the value of the $14,000 one year hence is $15,400 ($14,000 × 110%). Even considering the time value of money, the combined corporation-shareholder negative cash-flow effect of $120,600 ($136,000 − $15,400) in the case of an S election is not significantly different from the $119,000 corporate tax liability that would result for a regular corporation. The differential is even less when related accounting and/or legal fees are considered. ■

Another benefit of electing S corporation status is that the corporation is not subject to the accumulated earnings or personal holding company taxes.

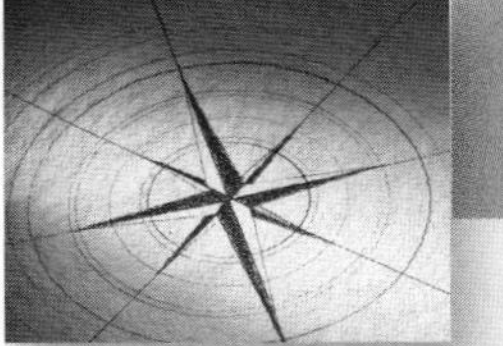

ETHICS & EQUITY Divorce and the S Election

Palm, Inc., is a calendar year S corporation. Counting married couples as one shareholder, Palm has 100 shareholders (none of whom are related). Palm's taxable income is about $2 million, and it normally distributes 80 percent of its earnings to shareholders. Valeria and Gus Sanders each own 10 percent of the stock of Palm.

After considerable marital discord and lengthy legal proceedings, Valeria and Gus's divorce was finalized on November 22, 2012. On Thanksgiving, however, they began a reconciliation that led to their remarriage on December 31, 2012. Even though the divorce meant that there were 101 shareholders for a little over one month in 2012, Palm files as an S corporation for 2012. According to Palm's accountant, the continued S status is justified because the remarriage "fixed the tax problem." She concludes that obtaining the IRS's approval not to terminate the S election is unnecessary because, in substance, Gus and Valeria were always husband and wife.

Evaluate the accountant's conclusion.

13.5 Conduit versus Entity Treatment

LO.5

Review and illustrate the applicability and the effect of the conduit and entity concepts on contributions to the entity, operations of the entity, entity distributions, passive activity loss and at-risk rules, and special allocations.

Under the **conduit concept**, the entity is viewed as merely an extension of the owners. Under the **entity concept**, the entity is regarded as being separate and distinct from its owners. The effects that these different approaches have in the following areas are examined for the partnership (and LLC), C corporation, and S corporation:

- Recognition at time of contribution to the entity.
- Basis of ownership interest.
- Results of operations.
- Recognition at time of distribution.
- Passive activity losses.
- At-risk rules.
- Special allocations.

The sole proprietorship is not analyzed separately because the owner and the business are in essence the same. In one circumstance, however, a tax difference does occur. Recognition does not occur when an owner contributes an asset to a sole proprietorship. Thus, the basis generally is a carryover basis. However, if the asset is a personal use asset, the sole proprietorship's basis is the *lower of* the adjusted basis or the fair market value at the date of contribution. Also note that if a personal use asset is contributed to a partnership or corporation, this *lower of* rule applies.

Effect on Recognition at Time of Contribution to the Entity

Because the conduit approach applies for the partnership and LLC, § 721 provides for no recognition on the contribution of property to the partnership or LLC in exchange for an ownership interest. Section 721 protects both a contribution associated with the formation of the partnership or LLC and later contributions. The partnership or LLC has a carryover basis for the contributed property, and the owners have a carryover basis for their ownership interests.[19]

Because the entity approach applies for the corporation, the transfer of property to a corporation in exchange for its stock is a taxable event. However, if the § 351 control requirement (80 percent) is satisfied, no gain or loss is recognized. In this case, both the corporate property and the shareholders' stock will have a carryover basis.[20] This control requirement makes it more likely that shareholders who contribute appreciated property to the corporation *after* the formation of the corporation will recognize gain.

[19]See the pertinent discussion in Chapter 10.

[20]See the pertinent discussion in Chapter 4.

TAX IN THE NEWS State Governments Paying for Jobs Development

State and local governments continue to offer direct and indirect subsidies (e.g., cash payments, infrastructure development, and tax holidays) in an effort to woo companies that will generate jobs for the area. Providing such incentives in light of the current economic situation makes good sense.

For example, Virginia, under Governor Robert McDonnell, has increased its spending on such economic-incentive deals by 56 percent in the last year. McDonnell believes that job creation is the best way to raise additional tax revenue to pay for government services. The Virginia unemployment rate has been declining and was down to 6.3 percent in March 2011.

However, two new features are appearing in many of these economic-incentive deals. First, states are being more specific as to the job growth they expect from the new business. Second, if the jobs do not materialize as projected, more and more states are inserting clawback provisions in their agreements. Clawback provisions require companies to return some or all of the funds provided by the state government if the promised jobs are not created. In 2010, for example, Massachusetts revoked tax breaks or other economic development perks for 74 companies for failure to create the promised jobs. This compares with 18 such revocations in 2007.

Source: Adapted from Jennifer Levitz, "States to Business: Give Our Cash Back," *Wall Street Journal*, April 22, 2011, p. A1.

To the extent the fair market value of property contributed to the entity at the time of formation is not equal to the property's adjusted basis, it may be desirable to make a special allocation associated with the subsequent sale of the contributed property by the entity. With a special allocation, the owner contributing the property receives the tax benefit or detriment for any recognized gain or loss that subsequently results because of the initial difference between the adjusted basis and the fair market value. For the partnership or LLC, this special allocation treatment is mandatory. No such allocation is available for the C corporation form because the gain or loss is recognized at the corporation level rather than at the shareholder level. For the S corporation, no such allocation is available. The recognized gain or loss will be reported on the shareholders' tax returns based on their stock ownership.

EXAMPLE 16

Khalid contributes land with an adjusted basis of $10,000 and a fair market value of $50,000 for a 50% ownership interest. At the same time, Tracy contributes cash of $50,000 for the remaining 50% ownership interest. Because the entity is unable to obtain the desired zoning, it subsequently sells the land for $50,000.

If the entity is a C corporation, Khalid has a realized gain of $40,000 ($50,000 − $10,000) and a recognized gain of $0 resulting from the contribution. His basis for his stock is $10,000, and the corporation has a basis for the land of $10,000. The corporation has a realized and recognized gain of $40,000 ($50,000 − $10,000) when it sells the land. Thus, what should have been Khalid's recognized gain becomes the corporation's taxable gain. There is no way the corporation can directly allocate the recognized gain to Khalid. The corporation could distribute the land to Khalid and let him sell the land, but the distribution may be taxable to Khalid as a dividend, and gain may be recognized at the corporate level on the distribution.

If the entity is a partnership or an LLC, the tax consequences are the same as in the C corporation illustration except for the $40,000 recognized gain on the sale of the land. The partnership or LLC has a realized and recognized gain of $40,000 ($50,000 − $10,000). However, even though Khalid's share of profits and losses is only 50%, all of the $40,000 recognized gain is allocated to him. If the entity is an S corporation, the tax consequences are the same as in the C corporation illustration except that Khalid reports $20,000 of the recognized gain on his tax return and Tracy reports $20,000 also. ■

Note that not all contributions of assets to corporations are made by shareholders. States and local governments continue to lure businesses to locate in a particular state or locality with promises of tax breaks and grants. See the additional discussion of this topic in the "Tax in the News" feature on the previous page.

Effect on Basis of Ownership Interest

In the case of a partnership or an LLC, the contribution of property to the entity in exchange for an ownership interest is not a taxable event under § 721. Therefore, the owner's basis for the ownership interest is a carryover basis. For C and S corporations, the nontaxable and related carryover basis results are appropriate only if the 80 percent control requirement of § 351 is satisfied. If the control requirement is not satisfied, any realized gain or loss on the transaction is recognized and the stock basis is equal to the fair market value of the contributed property.

In a partnership or an LLC, because the owner is the taxpayer, profits and losses of the entity affect the owner's basis in the entity interest. Likewise, the owner's basis is increased by the share of entity liability increases and is decreased by the share of entity liability decreases. This liability effect enables the owner to potentially benefit from the leverage concept. Accordingly, the owner's basis changes frequently.[21]

For the C corporation, the corporation is the taxpayer. Therefore, the shareholder's basis for the stock is not affected by corporate profits and losses or corporate liability increases or decreases.

The treatment of an S corporation shareholder falls between that of the owner of a partnership or LLC interest and the C corporation shareholder. The S corporation shareholder's stock basis is increased by the share of profits and decreased by the share of losses, but it is not affected by corporate liability increases or decreases. Thus, unlike the owner of a partnership or LLC interest, the S corporation shareholder does not potentially benefit from the leverage concept.

THE BIG PICTURE
EXAMPLE 17

Return to the facts of *The Big Picture* on p. 13-1. In the third year of operations, the entity chosen by Milly and Doug (either a partnership or a C corporation) needs additional working capital. Consequently, they agree to admit Peggy as an owner. Peggy contributes cash of $100,000 to the entity for a 30% ownership interest. The entity borrows $50,000 and repays $20,000 of this amount by the end of the taxable year. The profits for the year are $90,000.

If the entity is a partnership, Peggy's basis at the end of the period is $136,000 ($100,000 investment + $9,000 share of net liability increase + $27,000 share of profits). (Note that Peggy's basis would be the same if the entity was an LLC—an entity form that Milly and Doug should have considered.) If Peggy is a C corporation shareholder instead, her stock basis is $100,000 ($100,000 original investment). If the corporation is an S corporation (another entity form that Milly and Doug should have considered), Peggy's stock basis is $127,000 ($100,000 + $27,000).

Effect on Results of Operations

The entity concept is responsible for producing potential double taxation for the C corporation form (the corporation is taxed on its earnings, and the shareholders are taxed on the distribution of earnings). Thus, from the perspective of taxing the results of operations, the entity concept appears to be a disadvantage for the corporation. However, whether the entity concept actually produces disadvantageous results depends on the following:

- Whether the corporation generates positive taxable income.
- The tax rates that apply for the corporation and for the shareholders.
- The distribution policy of the corporation.

[21] §§ 705 and 752.

As discussed previously, techniques exist for getting cash out of the corporation to the shareholders without incurring double taxation (e.g., compensation payments to shareholder-employees, lease rental payments to shareholder-lessors, and interest payments to shareholder-creditors). Because these payments are deductible to the corporation, they reduce corporate taxable income. If the payments can be used to reduce corporate taxable income to zero, the corporation will have no tax liability.

The maximum individual tax bracket is the same as the maximum corporate tax bracket (35 percent). However, in a specific situation, the corporate tax rates that apply may be greater than or less than the applicable individual rates. This opportunity for the corporation to be subject to a lower tax rate is less likely to be available for personal service corporations. There, the only rate available is 35 percent.[22]

Double taxation can occur only if distributions (actual or constructive) are made to the shareholders. Thus, if no distributions (actual or constructive) are made and if the entity can avoid the accumulated earnings tax (e.g., based on the statutory credit or the reasonable needs adjustment) and the personal holding company tax (e.g., the corporation primarily generates active income), only one current level of taxation will occur. If distributions do occur in the future with respect to current earnings, the resultant tax liability should be discounted for the interim period. If the distribution can qualify for return of capital treatment (stock redemption or liquidation) rather than dividend treatment, the shareholder tax liability is decreased. Ideally, taxation of the earnings at the shareholder level can be avoided permanently if the stock passes through the decedent shareholder's estate.

Application of the entity concept does result in the earnings components losing their identity when they are passed through to shareholders in the form of dividends. This may produce a negative result for capital gains. Because capital gains lose their identity when passed through in the form of dividends, they cannot be used to offset capital losses at the shareholder level. An even more negative result is produced when dividends are paid out of tax-exempt income. Tax-exempt income is excludible in calculating corporate taxable income, but is included in calculating current earnings and profits. Thus, what should not be subject to taxation (an exclusion) is taxed because of the entity concept.

The partnership, the LLC, and the S corporation use the conduit concept in reporting the results of operations. Any item that is subject to special treatment on the taxpayer-owners' tax return is reported separately to the owners. Other items are netted and reported as taxable income. Thus, taxable income merely represents those income and deduction items that are not subject to special treatment.[23]

Many of the problems the entity concept may produce for the C corporation form are not present for the partnership, LLC, or S corporation. Included in this category are double taxation, problems with the reasonableness requirement, and loss of identity of the income or expense item at the owner level.

Only the partnership and LLC completely apply the conduit concept in reporting the results of operations. In several circumstances, the S corporation is subject to taxation at the corporate level, including the tax on built-in gains and the tax on certain passive investment income.[24] This limited application of the entity concept necessitates additional planning to attempt to avoid taxation at the corporate level.

Effect on Recognition at Time of Distribution

The application of the conduit concept results in distributions not being taxed to the owners. The application of the entity concept produces the opposite result. Therefore, distributions can be made to partners, to LLC owners, or to S corporation shareholders tax-free, whereas the same distribution would produce dividend income treatment for C corporation shareholders.

In this regard, a distinction must be made between distributions of earnings and other distributions for the S corporation. The S corporation generally is treated as

[22] § 11(b)(2).

[23] §§ 701, 702, 1363, and 1366.

[24] §§ 1374 and 1375.

TAX IN THE NEWS **Certain Partnership Distributions of Appreciated Property**

Section 311(b) of the Internal Revenue Code, which is applicable to C corporations and S corporations, provides that realized gain on the distribution of appreciated property to a shareholder results in recognized gain to the corporation. There is no similar statutory provision for the distribution of appreciated property made by a partnership to a partner.

However, the IRS has held that in one limited circumstance, a distribution of appreciated property made by a partnership to a partner results in recognized gain to the partnership. If the appreciated property is distributed to the partner in satisfaction of a guaranteed payment under § 707(c), the distribution is treated as a sale or exchange under § 1001 rather than a distribution under § 731.

a conduit with respect to its operations. However, as previously discussed, in several cases, the entity concept is applied and the S corporation becomes a taxpayer rather than merely a tax reporter. In effect, the conduit concept applies to S corporation operations unless otherwise specified in Subchapter S of the Code. Because distributions of earnings are included in the operations category, they are subject to conduit treatment through the application of the accumulated adjustments account (AAA).[25] Distributions in excess of earnings qualify for return of capital treatment.

A combination entity/conduit concept applies to property distributions to S corporation shareholders. As discussed above, the conduit concept applies with respect to the shareholder. However, if the property distributed is appreciated property, § 311(b) provides that the realized gain is recognized at the corporate level (same treatment as a C corporation). This corporate-level gain recognition is an application of the entity concept. Then, however, the conduit concept is applied to the pass-through of the gain to the shareholders.

THE BIG PICTURE

EXAMPLE 18

Return to the facts of *The Big Picture* on p. 13-1. Tan is an S corporation that is equally owned by Milly and Doug. Tan distributes two parcels of land to Milly and Doug. Tan has a basis of $10,000 for each parcel. Each parcel has a fair market value of $15,000. The distribution results in a $10,000 ($30,000 − $20,000) recognized gain for Tan. Milly and Doug each report $5,000 of the gain on their individual income tax returns.

Stock redemptions and complete liquidations are not covered by the provisions of Subchapter S. Therefore, the tax consequences of an S corporation stock redemption are determined under the C corporation provisions in § 302, while those for a complete liquidation are determined under the C corporation provisions in §§ 331 and 336.

Effect on Passive Activity Losses

The passive loss rules apply to the partnership, LLC, and S corporation, but apply to the C corporation only for personal service corporations and closely held corporations. A *closely held corporation* is defined as a corporation that meets the stock ownership requirement under the personal holding company provisions. That is, more than 50 percent of the value of the outstanding stock at any time during the last half of the taxable year is owned by or for not more than five individuals. The definition of a personal service corporation is modified slightly from the standard definition under § 269A. A corporation is classified as a § 469 *personal service corporation* only if the following requirements are satisfied:

[25] § 1368.

TAX IN THE NEWS When Rent Is Active Rather Than Passive

A major shareholder of a closely held S corporation leased an airplane to the corporation at a fair rental. As part of the lease agreement, the owner provided a pilot and crew. The lease also required that a replacement airplane be made available when repairs were needed for the leased aircraft. If the deductions associated with the airplane exceed the rent income, is any such loss active or passive? According to a recent Revenue Ruling, significant services are being provided. Thus, the lease activity is classified as active rather than passive, and the loss is not subject to the § 469 passive activity limits.

- The principal activity of the corporation is the performance of personal services.
- The services are substantially performed by owner-employees.
- Owner-employees own more than 10 percent in value of the stock of the corporation.

The general passive loss rules apply to the personal service corporation. Therefore, passive losses cannot be offset against either active income or portfolio income. For the closely held corporation, the application of the passive loss rules is less harsh. Although passive losses cannot be offset against portfolio income, they can be offset against active income.

The statutory language of § 469(a)(2), which describes the taxpayers subject to the passive loss rules, does not mention the partnership, LLC, or S corporation. Instead, it mentions the individual taxpayer. Because the conduit concept applies, the passive activity results are separately stated at the partnership, LLC, or S corporation level and are passed through to the owners with the identity maintained.

Effect of At-Risk Rules

The at-risk rules of § 465 apply to the partnership, LLC, and S corporation. Although the statutory language of § 465(a) mentions none of these, the conduit concept that applies to these entities results in the application of § 465. Section 465 also applies to closely held C corporations (defined the same as under the passive loss rules). However, exceptions are available for closely held corporations that are actively engaged in equipment leasing or are defined as qualified C corporations.

The application of the at-risk rules produces a harsher result for the partnership and the LLC than for the S corporation. This occurs because the partnership and the LLC, in the absence of § 465, would have a greater opportunity to use the leveraging concept.

EXAMPLE 19

Walt is the general partner, and Ira and Vera are the limited partners in the WIV limited partnership. Walt contributes land with an adjusted basis of $40,000 and a fair market value of $50,000 for his partnership interest, and Ira and Vera each contribute cash of $100,000 for their partnership interests. They agree to share profits and losses equally. To finance construction of an apartment building, the partnership obtains $600,000 of nonrecourse financing [not qualified nonrecourse financing under § 465(b)(6)] using the land and the building as the pledged assets. Each partner's basis for the partnership interest is as follows:

	Walt	Ira	Vera
Contribution	$ 40,000	$100,000	$100,000
Share of nonrecourse debt	200,000	200,000	200,000
Basis	$240,000	$300,000	$300,000

Without the at-risk rules, Ira and Vera could pass through losses up to $300,000 each even though they invested only $100,000 and have no personal liability for the nonrecourse debt. However, the at-risk rules limit the loss pass-through to the at-risk basis, which is $100,000 for Ira and $100,000 for Vera. Note that the at-risk rules can also affect the general partner. Because Walt is not at risk for the nonrecourse debt, his at-risk basis is $40,000. If the mortgage were recourse debt, his at-risk basis would be $640,000 ($40,000 + $600,000). Thus, as a result of the at-risk rules, leveraging is available only for recourse debt for partners who have potential personal liability. ■

EXAMPLE 20

Assume the same facts as in Example 19, except that the entity is an S corporation and Walt receives 20% of the stock and Ira and Vera each receive 40%. The basis for their stock is as follows:

Walt	$ 40,000
Ira	100,000
Vera	100,000

The nonrecourse debt does not affect the calculation of stock basis. The stock basis for each shareholder would remain the same even if the debt were recourse debt. Only direct loans by the shareholders increase the ceiling on loss pass-through (basis for stock plus basis for loans by shareholders). ■

Effect of Special Allocations

An advantage of the conduit concept over the entity concept is the ability to make special allocations. Special allocations are not permitted for the C corporation form. Indirectly, however, the corporate form may be able to achieve results similar to those produced by special allocations through payments to owners (e.g., salary payments, lease rental payments, and interest payments) and through different classes of stock (e.g., preferred and common). However, even in these cases, the breadth of the treatment and the related flexibility are less than that achievable under the conduit concept.

Although the S corporation is a conduit, it is treated more like a C corporation than a partnership or an LLC with respect to special allocations. This treatment results from the application of the per-share and per-day rule in § 1377(a). Although the S corporation is limited to one class of stock, it can still use the payments to owners procedure. However, the IRS has the authority to reallocate income among members of a family if fair returns are not provided for services rendered or capital invested.[26]

EXAMPLE 21

The stock of an S corporation is owned by Debra (50%), Helen (25%), and Joyce (25%). Helen and Joyce are Debra's adult children. Debra is in the 35% bracket, and Helen and Joyce are in the 15% bracket. Only Debra is an employee of the corporation. She is paid an annual salary of $20,000, whereas employees with similar responsibilities in other corporations earn $100,000. The corporation generates earnings of approximately $200,000 each year.

It appears that the reason Debra is paid a low salary is to enable more of the earnings of the S corporation to be taxed to Helen and Joyce, who are in lower tax brackets. Thus, the IRS could use its statutory authority to allocate a larger salary to Debra. ■

The partnership and LLC have many opportunities to use special allocations, including the following:

- The ability to share profits and losses differently from the share in capital.
- The ability to share profits and losses differently.
- The special allocation required under § 704(c) for the difference between the adjusted basis and the fair market value of contributed property.
- The special allocation of any item permitted under § 704(a) if the substantial economic effect rule of § 704(b) is satisfied.

[26] § 1366(e).

- The optional adjustment to basis permitted under § 754 and calculated under § 734 that results from distributions.
- The optional adjustment to basis permitted under § 754 and calculated under § 743 that results from an acquisition by purchase, taxable exchange, or inheritance.

13.6 FICA and Self-Employment Taxes

Payroll (employment) taxes can be a significant cost for a business and its owners, with a combined tax rate of 15.3 percent. Such costs can be classified into two categories.

- FICA taxes (Social Security and Medicare).
- Self-employment tax.

FICA

FICA (Federal Insurance Contribution Act) taxes are imposed on the wages of employees using the following rates:[27]

Social Security	6.2%
Medicare	1.45%

Such amounts are withheld by the employer from the employees' wages.

FICA withholding ceases for the Social Security portion once the employee has earned wages subject to the Social Security taxes of $110,100 in 2012 (indexed for inflation). All of the wages of an employee are subject to Medicare taxes. In addition, the employer must pay to the IRS an amount equal to the FICA tax normally withheld from employee wages (i.e., a matching 6.2% + 1.45%).[28]

Self-Employment Tax

The purpose of the self-employment tax is to provide Social Security and Medicare benefits for self-employed individuals. The self-employment tax is 15.3 percent (13.3 percent for 2011 and 2012) of self-employment income up to $110,100 (indexed for inflation) and 2.9 percent of self-employment income in excess of $110,100 (indexed for inflation).[29] In other words, for 2012 the self-employment tax is 10.4 percent of self-employment earnings up to $110,100 (for the Social Security portion) plus 2.9 percent of the total amount of self-employment earnings (for the Medicare portion).

Impact on the Entity and Its Owners

Depending on the type of tax entity, FICA taxes and self-employment taxes have different impacts on the entity and its owners as follows:

- *Sole proprietorship.* The wages of employees of the sole proprietorship are subject to FICA taxes, which must be matched by the sole proprietorship. The Schedule C income of the sole proprietorship is subject to the self-employment tax.
- *Partnership.* The wages of employees of the partnership are subject to FICA taxes, which must be matched by the partnership. A partner is not considered to be an employee. However, guaranteed payments (i.e., compensation for services rendered) made by the partnership to a partner are treated as self-employment income subject to the self-employment tax.[30] The partner's

[27] § 3101. The Tax Relief Act of 2010 reduced the employee's Social Security rate for 2011 from 6.2 percent to 4.2 percent. Subsequent legislation extended the 4.2 percent rate to 2012.

[28] § 3111. The employer's Social Security rate for 2011 and 2012 remains at 6.2%.

[29] § 1401.

[30] §§ 707(c) and 1402.

distributive share of the net earnings of the partnership is subject to self-employment tax.

- *Limited partnership.* The wages of employees of the limited partnership are subject to FICA taxes, which must be matched by the limited partnership. A limited partner is not considered to be an employee. However, guaranteed payments (i.e., compensation for services rendered) made by the limited partnership to a partner are treated as self-employment income subject to the self-employment tax.[31] A limited partner's distributive share of the net earnings of the limited partnership is not subject to self-employment tax.
- *C corporation.* The wages of employees of the corporation are subject to FICA taxes, which must be matched by the corporation. A shareholder who works for the corporation is an employee of the corporation and is subject to FICA taxes as an employee. The net earnings of the corporation have no effect on such a shareholder's self-employment income.
- *S corporation.* The wages of employees of the corporation are subject to FICA taxes, which must be matched by the corporation. A shareholder who works for the corporation is an employee of the corporation and is subject to FICA taxes as an employee. A shareholder's share of the net earnings of the corporation is not self-employment income, although the shareholder is subject to income tax on such earnings. In this respect, the shareholder of an S corporation receives more beneficial treatment than a sole proprietor or a partner whose share of the entity's net earnings is subject to self-employment tax.
- *LLC.* The wages of employees of an LLC are subject to FICA taxes, which must be matched by the LLC. If an LLC owner is treated as a limited partner, the LLC owner's distributive share of the net earnings of the LLC is not subject to the self-employment tax. Conversely, if an LLC owner is not treated as a limited partner, the LLC owner's distributive share of the net earnings of the LLC is subject to the self-employment tax.

13.7 Disposition of a Business or an Ownership Interest

LO.6

Analyze the effect of the disposition of a business on the owners and the entity for each of the forms for conducting a business.

A key factor in evaluating the tax consequences of disposing of a business is whether the disposition is viewed as the sale of an ownership interest or as a sale of assets. Generally, the tax consequences are more favorable if the transaction is treated as a sale of the ownership interest.

Sole Proprietorship

Regardless of the form of the transaction, the sale of a sole proprietorship is treated as the sale of individual assets. Thus, gains and losses must be calculated separately. Classification as capital gain or ordinary income depends on the nature and holding period of the individual assets. Ordinary income property such as inventory will result in ordinary gains and losses. Section 1231 property such as land, buildings, and machinery used in the business will produce § 1231 gains and losses (subject to depreciation recapture under §§ 1245 and 1250). Capital assets such as investment land and stocks qualify for capital gain or loss treatment.

If the amount realized exceeds the fair market value of the identifiable assets, the excess is attributed to goodwill, which produces capital gain for the seller. If instead, the excess payment is attributed to a covenant not to compete, the related gain is classified as ordinary income rather than capital gain. Thus, the seller prefers the excess to be attributed to goodwill.

[31] §§ 707(c) and 1402(a)(13).

Unless the legal protection provided by a covenant not to compete is needed, the buyer is neutral as to whether the excess is attributed to goodwill or a covenant. Both goodwill and a covenant are § 197 intangibles and are amortized over a 15-year statutory period.

EXAMPLE 22

Seth, who is in the 35% tax bracket, sells his sole proprietorship to Wilma for $600,000. The identifiable assets are as follows:

	Adjusted Basis	Fair Market Value
Inventory	$ 20,000	$ 25,000
Accounts receivable	40,000	40,000
Machinery and equipment*	125,000	150,000
Buildings**	175,000	250,000
Land	40,000	100,000
	$400,000	$565,000

* Potential § 1245 recapture of $50,000.
** Potential § 1250 recapture of $20,000.

The sale produces the following results for Seth:

	Gain (Loss)	Ordinary Income	§ 1231 Gain	Capital Gain
Inventory	$ 5,000	$ 5,000		
Accounts receivable	–0–			
Machinery and equipment	25,000	25,000		
Buildings	75,000	20,000	$ 55,000	
Land	60,000		60,000	
Goodwill	35,000			$35,000
	$200,000	$50,000	$115,000	$35,000

If the sale is structured this way, Wilma can deduct the $35,000 paid for goodwill over a 15-year period. If instead, Wilma paid the $35,000 to Seth for a covenant not to compete for a period of seven years, she still would amortize the $35,000 over a 15-year period. However, this would result in Seth's $35,000 capital gain being reclassified as ordinary income. If the covenant has no legal relevance to Wilma, in exchange for treating the payment as a goodwill payment, she should negotiate for a price reduction that reflects the benefit of the tax on capital gains to Seth. ■

Partnership and Limited Liability Company

The sale of a partnership or an LLC can be structured as the sale of assets or as the sale of an ownership interest. If the transaction takes the form of an asset sale, it is treated the same as for a sole proprietorship (described previously). The sale of an ownership interest is treated as the sale of a capital asset under § 741 (subject to ordinary income potential under § 751 for unrealized receivables and substantially appreciated inventory). Thus, if capital gain treatment can produce beneficial results for the taxpayer, the sale of an ownership interest is preferable.

From the buyers' perspective, the form does not produce different tax consequences. If the transaction is an asset purchase, the basis for the assets is the amount paid for them. Assuming that the buyers intend to continue to operate in the partnership or LLC form, the assets can be contributed to the entity under § 721. Therefore, the owners' basis for their entity interest is equal to the purchase price for the assets. Likewise, if ownership interests are purchased, the owners' basis is the purchase price and the entity's basis for the assets is the purchase price because the original entity will have terminated.[32]

A problem may arise if an individual purchases an entity interest from another partner or limited liability entity owner and the amount paid exceeds the new owner's pro rata share of the entity's basis for the assets. If the new owner does not acquire at least a 50 percent capital and profits interest, the old entity may not terminate.[33]

EXAMPLE 23

Paul purchases Sandra's partnership interest for $100,000. He acquires both a 20% capital interest and a 20% interest in profits and losses. At the purchase date, the assets of the partnership are as follows:

	Adjusted Basis	Fair Market Value
Cash	$ 10,000	$ 10,000
Inventory	30,000	35,000
Accounts receivable	15,000	15,000
Machinery and equipment	70,000	90,000
Buildings	100,000	150,000
Land	175,000	200,000
	$400,000	$500,000

In effect, Paul paid $100,000 for his 20% share of partnership assets ($500,000 × 20%). His basis for his partnership interest reflects the purchase price of $100,000. However, Paul's proportionate share of the partnership assets is based on the partnership's adjusted basis for the assets of $400,000 (i.e., $400,000 × 20% = $80,000). Because Paul's acquisition of his ownership interest from Sandra did not result in a termination of the partnership, the partnership's adjusted basis for the assets does not change. Therefore, if the partnership were to liquidate all of its assets immediately for $500,000, Paul's share of the recognized gain of $100,000 ($500,000 − $400,000) would be $20,000 ($100,000 × 20%). This result occurs even though Paul paid fair market value for his partnership interest.

The Code does provide an opportunity to rectify this inequity to Paul. If the partnership elects the optional adjustment to basis under § 754, the operational provisions of § 743 will result in Paul having a special additional basis for each of the appreciated partnership assets.

The amount is the excess of the amount Paul effectively paid for each of the assets over his pro rata share of the partnership's basis for the assets.

	Amount Paid (20% Share)	Pro Rata Share of Adjusted Basis	Special Basis Adjustment
Cash	$ 2,000	$ 2,000	$ –0–
Inventory	7,000	6,000	1,000
Accounts receivable	3,000	3,000	–0–
Machinery and equipment	18,000	14,000	4,000
Buildings	30,000	20,000	10,000
Land	40,000	35,000	5,000
	$100,000	$80,000	$20,000

Therefore, if the partnership sells the inventory, Paul's share of the ordinary income is $1,000 ($5,000 × 20%). He then reduces this amount by his special additional basis of $1,000. Thus, the net effect, as it equitably should be, is $0 ($1,000 − $1,000). ■

As Example 23 illustrates, the optional adjustment-to-basis election under § 754 provides a way to avoid the aforementioned problem. However, four additional factors need to be considered. First, the election must be made by the partnership (or

[32] § 708(b)(1)(B).

[33] §§ 708(b)(1)(A) and (B).

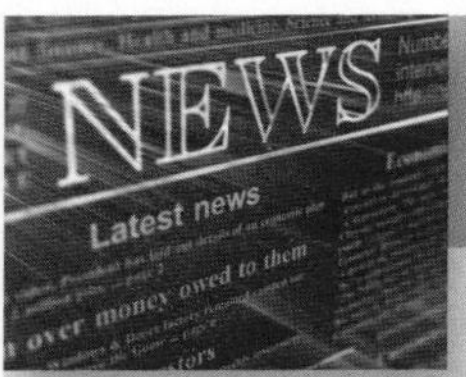

TAX IN THE NEWS A One-Way Street for Partners

Janel paid $800,000 for Waldo's partnership interest in the DWT Partnership. Waldo's outside basis was $600,000, which equaled his share of the partnership's inside basis for the partnership assets. Unless the partnership makes a § 754 election, Janel will eventually pay income taxes on the $200,000 difference between her outside basis of $800,000 and her share of the inside basis of $600,000. However, a § 754 election will activate § 743 and provide her with a special basis adjustment of $200,000. But does she recognize the need for making the § 754 election, and will the other partners cooperate?

Suppose the amounts are reversed (i.e., Janel paid $600,000 for an inside basis of $800,000). In this situation, Janel would prefer to avoid making the § 754 election. Congress has limited the ability to make this choice. The statutory language of § 743 was modified to require an automatic downward basis adjustment if the partnership has a "substantial built-in loss" at the time of the transfer.

Note that this § 743 treatment applies only to losses. For built-in gains, an affirmative § 754 election still is necessary to receive a § 743 upward basis adjustment.

LLC), not just by the acquiring partner. Therefore, the acquiring partner should obtain a written agreement from the other partners indicating that they will consent to the § 754 election. Second, the election is a continuing election. Thus, while the election benefits an acquiring partner if the partnership assets are appreciated at the date of acquisition, it produces detrimental consequences (i.e., a negative special basis adjustment) if the adjusted basis exceeds the fair market value of the assets at the acquisition date. Third, the election activates not only the operational provisions of § 743 but also the operational provisions of § 734 with respect to partnership distributions. Fourth, if the members of the partnership change frequently, record keeping can become complex.

C Corporation

The sale of the business held by a C corporation can be structured as either an asset sale or a stock sale. The stock sale has the dual advantage to the seller of being less complex both as a legal transaction and as a tax transaction. It also has the advantage of providing a way to avoid double taxation. Finally, the gain or loss on the sale of the stock is a capital gain or loss to the shareholder.

THE BIG PICTURE

EXAMPLE 24

Return to the facts of *The Big Picture* on p. 13-1. Milly and Doug each own 50% of the stock of Tan Corporation. They now have owned the business for 10 years. Milly's basis for her stock is $40,000, and Doug's basis for his stock is $60,000. They agree to sell the stock to Rex for $300,000. Milly has a long-term capital gain of $110,000 ($150,000 − $40,000), and Doug has a long-term capital gain of $90,000 ($150,000 − $60,000). Rex has a basis for his stock of $300,000. Tan's basis for its assets does not change as a result of the stock sale.

Structuring the sale of the business as a stock sale may produce detrimental tax results for the purchaser. As Example 24 illustrates, the basis of the corporation's assets is not affected by the stock sale. If the fair market value of the stock exceeds the corporation's adjusted basis for its assets, the purchaser is denied the opportunity to step up the basis of the assets to reflect the amount in effect paid for them through the stock acquisition. Note that this is similar to the problem at the partnership (or LLC) level if the § 754 election is not made.

For an asset sale, the seller of the business can be either the corporation or the shareholders. If the seller is the corporation, the corporation sells the business (the assets), pays any debts not transferred, and makes a liquidating distribution to the shareholders. If the sellers are the shareholders, the corporation pays any debts that will not be transferred and makes a liquidating distribution to the shareholders; then the shareholders sell the business.

Regardless of the approach used for an asset sale, double taxation will occur. The corporation is taxed on the actual sale of the assets and is taxed as if it had sold the assets when it makes the liquidating distribution of the assets to the shareholders who then sell the assets. The shareholders are taxed when they receive cash or assets distributed in kind by the corporation.

The asset sale resolves the purchaser's problem of not being able to step up the basis of the assets to their fair market value. The basis for each asset is the amount paid for it. To operate in corporate form (assuming that the purchaser is not a corporation), the purchaser needs to transfer the property to a corporation in a § 351 transaction.

From the perspective of the seller, the ideal form of the transaction is a stock sale. Conversely, from the purchaser's perspective, the ideal form is an asset purchase. Thus, a conflict exists between the buyer's and the seller's objectives regarding the form of the transaction. Therefore, the bargaining ability of the seller and the purchaser to structure the sale as a stock sale or an asset sale, respectively, has become more critical.

Rather than sell the entire business, an owner may sell his or her ownership interest. Because the form of the transaction is a stock sale, the results for the selling shareholder will be the same as if all of the shareholders had sold their stock (i.e., capital gain or capital loss to the shareholder).

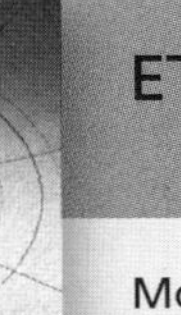

ETHICS & EQUITY Selling Stock versus Selling Corporate Assets: Relevance of Double Taxation

Molly owns all of the stock of Peach, Inc., a C corporation that she wants to sell. Since she started the business, the fair market value of the corporate assets and the value of her stock investment have appreciated by about $7 million. The C corporation's marginal tax rate is 34 percent. Unfortunately, the buyer of the corporation is only interested in purchasing its assets and does not want to buy the stock.

Molly's objective is to avoid double taxation, and she is considering the following alternatives:

1. Sell the C corporation stock for its fair market value to her wholly owned S corporation. The S corporation will then liquidate the C corporation. As the value of the assets received will equal the purchase price of the stock, no gain will result and only the C corporation will be subject to tax.
2. Have the C corporation elect S corporation status and then liquidate.
3. Liquidate the C corporation (i.e., sell the assets). Because the sale of the assets produces the same results as a sale of the stock, she will account for the liquidation as a stock sale.
4. Offer the buyer a $500,000 reduction in the purchase price if he will agree to purchase the stock rather than the corporate assets.

Evaluate these four alternatives in terms of achieving Molly's objective and from an ethical perspective.

S Corporation

Because the S corporation is a corporation, it is subject to the provisions for a C corporation discussed previously. Either an asset sale at the corporate level or a liquidating distribution of assets produces recognition at the corporate level. However, under the conduit concept applicable to the S corporation, the recognized amount is taxed at the shareholder level. Therefore, double taxation is avoided directly (only the shareholder is involved) for a stock sale and indirectly (the conduit concept ignores the involvement of the corporation) for an asset sale.

See Concept Summary 13.1 for a summary of the tax consequences of the disposition of a business.

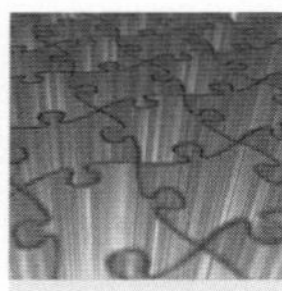

CONCEPT SUMMARY 13.1

Tax Treatment of Disposition of a Business

Form of Entity	Form of Transaction	Tax Consequences	
		Seller	**Buyer**
Sole proprietorship	Sale of individual assets.	Gain or loss is calculated separately for the individual assets. Classification as capital or ordinary depends on the nature and holding period of the individual assets. If amount realized exceeds the fair market value of the identifiable assets, the excess is allocated to goodwill (except to the extent identified with a covenant not to compete), which is a capital asset.	Basis for individual assets is the allocated cost. Prefers that any excess of purchase price over the fair market value of identifiable assets be identified with a covenant not to compete if the covenant has legal utility. Otherwise, the buyer is neutral because both goodwill and covenants are amortized over a 15-year statutory period.
	Sale of the business.	Treated as if a sale of the individual assets (as above).	Treated as if a purchase of the individual assets (as above).
Partnership and limited liability company	Sale of individual assets.	Treatment is the same as for the sole proprietorship.	Treatment is the same as for the sole proprietorship. If the intent is to operate in partnership or LLC form, the assets can be contributed to a partnership or LLC under § 721.
	Sale of ownership interest.	Entity interest is treated as the sale of a capital asset under § 741 (subject to ordinary income potential under § 751 for unrealized receivables and substantially appreciated inventory).	Basis for new owner's ownership interest is the cost. The new entity's basis for the assets is also the pertinent cost (i.e., contributed to the entity under § 721), because the original entity will have terminated.
C corporation	Sale of corporate assets by corporation (i.e., corporation sells assets, pays debts, and makes liquidating distribution to the shareholders).	Double taxation occurs. Corporation is taxed on the sale of the assets with the gain or loss determination and the classification as capital or ordinary treated the same as for the sole proprietorship. Shareholders calculate gain or loss as the difference between the stock basis and the amount received from the corporation in the liquidating distribution. Capital gain or loss usually results, because stock typically is a capital asset.	Basis for individual assets is the allocated cost. If the intent is to operate in corporate form, the assets can be contributed to a corporation under § 351.
	Sale of corporate assets by the shareholders (i.e., corporation pays debts and makes liquidating distribution to the shareholders).	Double taxation occurs. At the time of the liquidating distribution to the shareholders, the corporation is taxed as if it had sold the assets. Shareholders calculate gain or loss as the difference between the stock basis and the fair market value of the assets received from the corporation in the liquidating distribution. Capital gain or loss usually results, because stock typically is a capital asset.	Same as above.

Tax Treatment of Disposition of a Business—Continued

Form of Entity	Form of Transaction	Tax Consequences	
		Seller	**Buyer**
	Sale of corporate stock.	Enables double taxation to be avoided. Because the corporation is not a party to the transaction, there are no tax consequences at the corporate level. Shareholders calculate gain or loss as the difference between the stock basis and the amount received for the stock. Capital gain or loss usually results, because stock typically is a capital asset.	Basis for the stock is its cost. The basis for the corporate assets is not affected by the stock purchase.
S corporation	Sale of corporate assets by corporation.	Recognition occurs at the corporate level on the sale of the assets with the gain or loss determination and the classification as capital or ordinary treated the same as for the sole proprietorship. Conduit concept applicable to the S corporation results in the recognized amount being taxed at the shareholder level. Double taxation associated with the asset sale is avoided, because the shareholder's stock basis is increased by the amount of gain recognition and decreased by the amount of loss recognition. Shareholders calculate gain or loss as the difference between the stock basis and the amount received from the corporation in the liquidating distribution. Capital gain or loss usually results, because stock typically is a capital asset.	Basis for individual assets is the allocated cost. If the intent is to operate in corporate form (i.e., as an S corporation), the assets can be contributed to a corporation under § 351.
	Sale of corporate assets by the shareholders.	At the time of the liquidating distribution to the shareholders, recognition occurs at the corporation level as if the corporation had sold the assets. The resultant tax consequences for the shareholders and the corporation are the same as for the sale of corporate assets by the S corporation.	Same as above.
	Sale of corporate stock.	Same as the treatment for the sale of stock of a C corporation.	Same as the treatment for the purchase of stock of a C corporation.

13.8 Converting to Other Entity Types

Rather than disposing of a business, the owners may decide to convert the tax entity form to a different tax entity form. This raises three primary issues.

- Does the conversion result in the recognition of gain or loss?
- What is the basis for the ownership interest in the new entity form?
- What is the basis of the assets of the new entity form?

Sole Proprietorship

The conversion of a sole proprietorship into another entity form can be achieved without any recognition of gain or loss at the entity level or at the owner level. This applies regardless of the new entity form. If the proprietorship is converted into a partnership or an LLC, nonrecognition can be achieved under the provisions of the Code. If it is converted into a corporation (either an S corporation or a C corporation), nonrecognition can also be achieved.[34]

In transfers to a partnership, the basis of an ownership interest (partner or LLC owner) will be a carryover basis. In transfers to a corporation, a shareholder's basis for stock will be a carryover basis.[35]

As to the entity, the partnership's or LLC's basis for its assets also is a carryover basis, and the corporation's basis for its assets is likewise a carryover basis.[36]

C Corporation

A C corporation can convert to any of the following entity forms, which permit having multiple owners.

- Partnership or LLC.
- S corporation.

Converting to the S corporation tax entity form merely requires the election of S status. As discussed in Chapter 12, the S election can be made only if all shareholders consent to the election and if the qualification requirements are satisfied.[37] Note that the qualification requirements become maintenance requirements that must be met to retain the S election.

Therefore, the election of S status produces the following tax consequences:

- No recognition of gain or loss.
- Carryover basis for the shareholders' stock.
- Carryover basis for the assets of the corporation.

A corporation can also convert to a partnership or LLC form. Unfortunately, to make this conversion, the corporation must be liquidated. This produces the following tax consequences.

- Recognition of gain or loss at the corporate level.[38]
- Recognition of gain or loss at the shareholder level.[39]
- Fair market value basis for the assets distributed in liquidation.[40]

After liquidation, it is necessary to contribute the assets to the new entity (i.e., the partnership or the LLC). The tax consequences to the owners and to the entity would be the same as those for a sole proprietorship that converts to a partnership or an LLC.

Partnership

A partnership can convert to either of the following entity forms, which permit having multiple owners:

- C corporation.
- S corporation.

The partners can transfer their partnership interests to a corporation (either a C corporation or an S corporation) in exchange for the stock of the corporation. Because this will satisfy the § 351 requirements, any realized gain or loss is not recognized.[41] If, however, the 80 percent control requirement is not satisfied, the realized gain or loss is recognized to the partners.[42]

[34] §§ 721(a) and 351(a).
[35] §§ 722 and 358(a).
[36] §§ 723 and 362(a).
[37] §§ 1361(a), 1361(b), 1362(a), and 1362(a)(1).
[38] § 336(a).
[39] § 331(a).
[40] § 334(a).
[41] § 351(a).
[42] § 368(c).

Assuming that the § 351 requirements for nonrecognition are satisfied, the following occur:[43]

- The basis of the stock to the shareholders is a carryover basis.
- The basis of the assets to the corporation is a carryover basis.

13.9 Overall Comparison of Forms of Doing Business

LO.7

Compare the tax consequences of the various forms of doing business.

See Concept Summary 13.2 for a detailed comparison of the tax consequences of the following forms of doing business: sole proprietorship, partnership, limited liability company, S corporation, and C corporation.

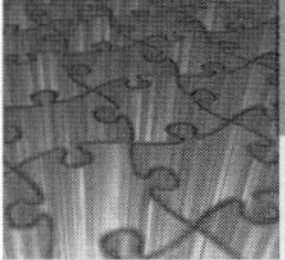

CONCEPT SUMMARY 13.2

Tax Attributes of Different Forms of Business (Assume that Partners and Shareholders Are All Individuals)

	Sole Proprietorship	Partnership/Limited Liability Company*	S Corporation**	Regular (C) Corporation***
Restrictions on type or number of owners	One owner. The owner must be an individual.	Must have at least 2 owners.	Only individuals, estates, certain trusts, and certain tax-exempt entities can be owners. Maximum number of shareholders limited to 100.****	None, except that some states require a minimum of 2 shareholders.
Incidence of tax	Sole proprietorship's income and deductions are reported on Schedule C of the individual's Form 1040. A separate Schedule C is prepared for each business.	Entity not subject to tax. Owners in their separate capacity subject to tax on their distributive share of income. Entity files Form 1065.	Except for certain built-in gains and passive investment income when earnings and profits are present from C corporation tax years, entity not subject to Federal income tax. S corporation files Form 1120S. Shareholders are subject to tax on income attributable to their stock ownership.	Income subject to double taxation. Entity subject to tax, and shareholder subject to tax on any corporate dividends received. Corporation files Form 1120.
Highest tax rate	35% at individual level.	35% at owner level.	35% at shareholder level.	35% at corporate level plus 15%/0% on any corporate dividends at shareholder level (if qualified dividends; otherwise 35%).

[43] §§ 358(a) and 362(a).

Tax Attributes of Different Forms of Business—Continued

	Sole Proprietorship	Partnership/Limited Liability Company*	S Corporation**	Regular (C) Corporation***
Choice of tax year	Same tax year as owner.	Selection generally restricted to coincide with tax year of majority owners or principal owners or to tax year determined under the least aggregate deferral method.	Restricted to a calendar year unless IRS approves a different year for business purposes or other exceptions apply.	Unrestricted selection allowed at time of filing first tax return.
Timing of taxation	Based on owner's tax year.	Owners report their share of income in their tax year with or within which the entity's tax year ends. Owners in their separate capacities are subject to payment of estimated taxes.	Shareholders report their shares of income in their tax year with or within which the corporation's tax year ends. Generally, the corporation uses a calendar year, but see "Choice of tax year" above. Shareholders may be subject to payment of estimated taxes. Corporation may be subject to payment of estimated taxes for the taxes imposed at the corporate level.	Corporation subject to tax at close of its tax year. May be subject to payment of estimated taxes. Dividends will be subject to tax at the shareholder level in the tax year received.
Basis for allocating income to owners	Not applicable (only one owner).	Profit and loss sharing agreement. Cash basis items of cash basis entities are allocated on a daily basis. Other entity items are allocated after considering varying interests of owners.	Pro rata share based on stock ownership. Shareholder's pro rata share is determined on a daily basis, according to the number of shares of stock held on each day of the corporation's tax year.	Not applicable.
Contribution of property to the entity	Not a taxable transaction.	Generally not a taxable transaction.	Is a taxable transaction unless the § 351 requirements are satisfied.	Is a taxable transaction unless the § 351 requirements are satisfied.
Character of income taxed to owners	Retains source characteristics.	Conduit—retains source characteristics.	Conduit—retains source characteristics.	All source characteristics are lost when income is distributed to owners.
Basis for allocating a net operating loss to owners	Not applicable (only one owner).	Profit and loss sharing agreement. Cash basis items of cash basis entities are allocated on a daily basis. Other entity items are allocated after considering varying interests of owners.	Prorated among shareholders on a daily basis.	Not applicable.
Limitation on losses deductible by owners	Investment plus liabilities.	Owner's investment plus share of liabilities.	Shareholder's investment plus loans made by shareholder to corporation.	Not applicable.

Tax Attributes of Different Forms of Business—Continued

	Sole Proprietorship	Partnership/Limited Liability Company*	S Corporation**	Regular (C) Corporation***
Subject to at-risk rules	Yes, at the owner level. Indefinite carryover of excess loss.	Yes, at the owner level. Indefinite carryover of excess loss.	Yes, at the shareholder level. Indefinite carryover of excess loss.	Yes, for closely held corporations. Indefinite carryover of excess loss.
Subject to passive activity loss rules	Yes, at the owner level. Indefinite carryover of excess loss.	Yes, at the owner level. Indefinite carryover of excess loss.	Yes, at the shareholder level. Indefinite carryover of excess loss.	Yes, for closely held corporations and personal service corporations. Indefinite carryover of excess loss.
Tax consequences of earnings retained by entity	Taxed to owner when earned and increases his or her investment in the sole proprietorship.	Taxed to owners when earned and increases their respective interests in the entity.	Taxed to shareholders when earned and increases their respective bases in stock.	Taxed to corporation as earned and may be subject to penalty tax if accumulated unreasonably.
Nonliquidating distributions to owners	Not taxable.	Not taxable unless money received exceeds recipient owner's basis in entity interest. Existence of § 751 assets may cause recognition of ordinary income.	Generally not taxable unless the distribution exceeds the shareholder's AAA or stock basis. Existence of accumulated earnings and profits could cause some distributions to be dividends.	Taxable in year of receipt to extent of earnings and profits or if exceeds basis in stock.
Capital gains	Taxed at owner level with opportunity to use alternative tax rate.	Conduit—owners must account for their respective shares.	Conduit, with certain exceptions (a possible penalty tax)—shareholders must account for their respective shares.	Taxed at corporate level with a maximum 35% rate. No other benefits.
Capital losses	Only $3,000 of capital losses can be offset each tax year against ordinary income. Indefinite carryover.	Conduit—owners must account for their respective shares.	Conduit—shareholders must account for their respective shares.	Carried back three years and carried forward five years. Deductible only to the extent of capital gains.
§ 1231 gains and losses	Taxable or deductible at owner level. Five-year lookback rule for § 1231 losses.	Conduit—owners must account for their respective shares.	Conduit—shareholders must account for their respective shares.	Taxable or deductible at corporate level only. Five-year lookback rule for § 1231 losses.
Foreign tax credits	Available at owner level.	Conduit—passed through to owners.	Generally conduit—passed through to shareholders.	Available at corporate level only.
§ 1244 treatment of loss on sale of interest	Not applicable.	Not applicable.	Available.	Available.
Basis treatment of entity liabilities	Includible in interest basis.	Includible in interest basis.	Not includible in stock basis.	Not includible in stock basis.
Built-in gains	Not applicable.	Not applicable.	Possible corporate tax.	Not applicable.

Tax Attributes of Different Forms of Business—Continued

	Sole Proprietorship	Partnership/Limited Liability Company*	S Corporation**	Regular (C) Corporation***
Special allocations to owners	Not applicable (only one owner).	Available if supported by substantial economic effect.	Not available.	Not applicable.
Availability of fringe benefits to owners	None.	None.	None unless a 2%-or-less shareholder.	Available within antidiscrimination rules.
Effect of liquidation/ redemption/ reorganization on basis of entity assets	Not applicable.	Usually carried over from entity to owner unless a § 754 election is made, excessive cash is distributed, or more than 50% of the capital interests are transferred within 12 months.	Taxable step-up to fair market value.	Taxable step-up to fair market value.
Sale of ownership interest	Treated as the sale of individual assets. Classification of recognized gain or loss depends on the nature of the individual assets.	Treated as the sale of an entity interest. Recognized gain or loss is classified as capital under § 741, subject to ordinary income treatment under § 751.	Treated as the sale of corporate stock. Recognized gain is classified as capital gain. Recognized loss is classified as capital loss, subject to ordinary loss treatment under § 1244.	Treated as the sale of corporate stock. Recognized gain is classified as capital gain. Recognized loss is classified as capital loss, subject to ordinary loss treatment under § 1244.
Distribution of appreciated property	Not taxable.	No recognition at the entity level.	Recognition at the corporate level to the extent of the appreciation. Conduit—amount of recognized gain is passed through to shareholders.	Taxable at the corporate level to the extent of the appreciation.
Splitting of income among family members	Not applicable (only one owner).	Difficult—IRS will not recognize a family member as an owner unless certain requirements are met.	Rather easy—gift of stock will transfer tax on a pro rata share of income to the donee. However, IRS can make adjustments to reflect adequate compensation for services.	Same as an S corporation, except that donees will be subject to tax only on earnings actually or constructively distributed to them. Other than unreasonable compensation, IRS generally cannot make adjustments to reflect adequate compensation for services and capital.
Organizational costs	Startup expenditures are eligible for $5,000 limited expensing (subject to phaseout) and amortizing balance over 180 months.	Organizational costs are eligible for $5,000 limited expensing (subject to phaseout) and amortizing balance over 180 months.	Same as partnership.	Same as partnership.

Tax Attributes of Different Forms of Business—Continued

	Sole Proprietorship	Partnership/Limited Liability Company*	S Corporation**	Regular (C) Corporation***
Charitable contributions	Limitations apply at owner level.	Conduit—owners are subject to deduction limitations in their own capacities.	Conduit—shareholders are subject to deduction limitations in their own capacities.	Limited to 10% of taxable income before certain deductions.
Alternative minimum tax	Applies at owner level. AMT rates are 26% and 28%.	Applies at the owner level rather than at the entity level. AMT preferences and adjustments are passed through from the entity to the owners.	Applies at the shareholder level rather than at the corporate level. AMT preferences and adjustments are passed through from the S corporation to the shareholders.	Applies at the corporate level. AMT rate is 20%. Exception for small corporations.
ACE adjustment	Does not apply.	Does not apply.	Does not apply.	The adjustment is made in calculating AMTI. The adjustment is 75% of the excess of adjusted current earnings over unadjusted AMTI. If the unadjusted AMTI exceeds adjusted current earnings, the adjustment is negative.
Tax preference items	Apply at owner level in determining AMT.	Conduit—passed through to owners who must account for such items in their separate capacities.	Conduit—passed through to shareholders who must account for such items in their separate capacities.	Subject to AMT at corporate level.

* Refer to Chapters 10 and 11 for additional details on partnerships and limited liability companies.
** Refer to Chapter 12 for additional details on S corporations.
*** Refer to Chapters 2 through 9 for additional details on regular (C) corporations.
**** Spouses and family members are treated as one shareholder.

13.10 Tax Planning

EXAMPLE 25

Eva is a tax practitioner in Kentwood, the Dairy Center of the South. Many of her clients are dairy farmers. She recently had tax planning discussions with two of her clients, Jesse, a Line Creek dairy farmer, and Larry, a Spring Creek dairy farmer.

Jesse recently purchased his dairy farm. He is 52 years old and just retired after 30 years of service as a chemical engineer at an oil refinery in Baton Rouge. Eva recommended that he incorporate his dairy farm and elect S corporation status for Federal income tax purposes.

Larry has owned his dairy farm since 2006. He inherited it from his father. At that time, Larry retired after 20 years of service in the U.S. Air Force. He has a master's degree in Agricultural Economics from LSU. His farm is incorporated, and shortly after the date of incorporation, Eva had advised him to elect S corporation status. She now advises him to revoke the S election. ■

Example 25 raises a number of interesting questions. Does Eva advise all of her dairy farmer clients to initially elect S corporation status? Why has she advised Larry to revoke his S election? Will she advise Jesse to revoke his S election at some time in the future? Will she advise Larry to make another S election at some time in the future? Why did she not advise Larry to terminate his corporate status? Could Larry and Jesse have achieved the same tax consequences for their dairy farms if they had operated the farms as partnerships instead of incorporating? Does the way the farm is acquired (e.g., purchase versus inheritance) affect the choice of business entity for tax purposes?

Example 25 illustrates the relationship between tax planning and the choice of business form; it also raised a variety of questions about the advice given by the tax practitioner. By this time, the student should be able to develop various scenarios supporting the tax advice given. The actual fact situations that produced the tax adviser's recommendations were as follows:

- Jesse's experience in the dairy industry consists of raising a few heifers during the last five years he was employed. Eva anticipates that Jesse will have tax losses for the indeterminate future. In choosing between the partnership and the S corporation forms, Jesse indicated that he and his wife must have limited liability associated with the dairy farm.
- Larry was born and raised on his father's dairy farm. Both his education and his Air Force managerial experience provide him with useful tools for managing his business. However, Larry inherited his farm when milk prices were at a low for the modern era. Because none of her dairy farm clients were generating tax profits at that time, Eva anticipated that Larry would operate his dairy farm at a loss. Larry, like Jesse, thought that limited liability was imperative. Thus, he incorporated the dairy farm and made the S corporation election.
- For the first two years, Larry's dairy farm produced tax losses. Since then, the dairy farm has produced tax profits large enough to absorb the losses. Larry anticipates that his profits will remain relatively stable in the $50,000 to $75,000 range. Because he is in the 28 percent marginal tax bracket and anticipates no dividend distributions to him from the corporation, his tax liability associated with the dairy farm will be less if he terminates the S corporation election.

As Jesse and Larry's example illustrates, selection of the proper business form can result in both nontax and tax advantages. Both of these factors should be considered in making the selection decision. Furthermore, this choice should be reviewed periodically, because a proper business form at one point in time may not be the proper form at a different time. Note that another business form Eva could have considered for Jesse is the LLC.

In selecting the right entity for conducting any business, tax consequences are important. In looking at the attributes, consideration should be given to the tax consequences of the following:

- Contribution of assets to the entity by the owners at the time the entity is created and at later dates.
- Taxation of the results of operations.
- Distributions to owners.
- Disposition of an ownership interest.
- Termination of the entity.

REFOCUS ON THE BIG PICTURE

SELECTION OF A TAX ENTITY FORM

Although Milly and Doug have narrowed their choice of tax entity to either a C corporation or a general partnership, the tax adviser should not be so limited in suggesting which of the various entities achieve the clients' objectives. As the tax expert, the adviser has a much clearer perspective and may point out factors the clients have overlooked.

Because Milly and Doug want limited liability so that their other assets will not be at risk, this eliminates the use of a general partnership. Likewise, the limited partnership option (which does provide limited liability for the limited partner) is not feasible because both Milly and Doug intend to be active in operating the business.

Thus, the remaining choices to be reviewed are the following:

- C corporation.
- S corporation.
- LLC.

C Corporation

The C corporation satisfies the clients' limited liability objective. However, the C corporation is subject to the Federal income tax at the entity level. In addition, the shareholders are taxed (likely at a 15 percent rate) on the distributions of the after-tax earnings. Presuming taxable income of $200,000, the following takes place:

Tax at corporate level	$ 61,250
Tax at shareholder level	
Milly ($69,375 × 15%)	10,406
Doug ($69,375 × 15%)	10,406
Combined entity/owner tax liability	$ 82,062
After-tax cash flow ($200,000 – $82,062)	$117,938

S Corporation

The S corporation also satisfies the limited liability objective. Because the S corporation is not subject to Federal income taxation at the entity level, only the shareholders are taxed on the earnings of the corporation. The following occurs:

Tax at corporate level	$ –0–
Tax at shareholder level	
Milly ($100,000 × 28%)	28,000
Doug ($100,000 × 28%)	28,000
Combined entity/owner tax liability	$ 56,000
After-tax cash flow ($200,000 – $56,000)	$ 144,000

LLC

The LLC also generally satisfies the limited liability objective. Under the check-the-box Regulations, the owners can elect to have the LLC taxed as a partnership. Because the LLC is not subject to Federal income taxation at the entity level, only the owners are taxed on the earnings of the LLC. The following occurs:

Tax at the LLC level	$ –0–
Tax at the owner level	
Milly ($100,000 × 28%)	28,000
Doug ($100,000 × 28%)	28,000
Combined entity/owner tax liability	$ 56,000
After-tax cash flow ($200,000 – $56,000)	$ 144,000

It appears that either the S corporation or the LLC meets Milly and Doug's objectives of having limited liability and minimizing their tax liability. The LLC offers an additional advantage in that an LLC does not have to satisfy the numerous statutory qualification requirements that must be met to elect and maintain S status. Based on the facts in this situation, however, it is unlikely that satisfying these requirements would create any difficulty for Milly and Doug.

© Simon Potter/Cultura /Jupiter Images

KEY TERMS

Conduit concept, 13-15
Entity concept, 13-15
Limited liability company (LLC), 13-3
Thin capitalization, 13-11

DISCUSSION QUESTIONS

1. **LO.1** What are the principal legal forms for conducting a business entity? What are the principal Federal income tax forms for doing so?

2. **LO.1, 3** Compare C and S corporations as to the taxation of the entity and its owners.

3. **LO.1** What are the advantages of a limited liability company compared to an S corporation?

4. **LO.3** The maximum corporate tax rate of 35% is the same as the maximum rate applicable to individuals. Consequently, for any additional taxable income, the corporate tax liability will be the same as the individual tax liability. Do you agree? Why or why not?

5. **LO.2, 3** All of the Big 4 accounting firms changed their ownership form from a general partnership to a limited liability partnership. Discuss the legal and tax ramifications of this modification of ownership form.

6. **LO.2** Several taxpayers would like to conduct a business in partnership form with all of the owners having limited liability. Can a partnership, other than a limited liability partnership, be structured so that this objective is accomplished? If so, what, if any, tax pitfalls exist?

Decision Making

7. **LO.2** Samuel is considering opening a lawn-servicing business.
   a. What nontax factors should Samuel consider in choosing a business entity?
   b. Are nontax factors more important than tax factors to Samuel? Explain.

Decision Making

8. **LO.1, 2, 3** Abe is an entrepreneur who likes to be actively involved in his business ventures. He is going to invest $500,000 in a business that he projects will produce a tax loss of approximately $100,000 per year in the short run. However, once consumers become aware of the new product being sold by the business and the quality of the service it provides, he is confident the business will generate a profit of at least $125,000 per year. Abe has substantial other income (from both business ventures and investment activities) each year. Advise Abe on the business form he should select for the short run. He will be the sole owner.

Decision Making

9. **LO.3, 4, 7** Sam is trying to decide whether he should operate his business as a C corporation or as an S corporation. Due to potential environmental hazard problems, it is imperative that the business have limited liability. Sam is leaning toward the S corporation form because it avoids double taxation. However, he is concerned that he may encounter difficulty several years in the future when he may want to issue some preferred stock to his son as a way of motivating him to remain active in the business. Sue, Sam's friend, says that he can maintain maximum flexibility by operating as a C corporation. According to her, Sam can avoid double taxation by paying himself a salary equal to the before-tax earnings. As Sam's tax adviser, what is your advice to him?

10. **LO.3** Paul, who is in the 33% tax bracket, is the sole shareholder of a corporation and receives a salary of $60,000 each year. To avoid double taxation, he makes an S election for the corporation. The corporation currently is earning $100,000, and he expects earnings to grow at a rate between 15% and 20% per year. The earnings are reinvested in the growth of the corporation, and no plans exist for distributions to Paul. What problem may Paul have created by making the S election?

11. **LO.3** Is an S corporation subject to the ACE adjustment in calculating the AMT? If so, how is the ACE adjustment calculated for an S corporation? How does it affect the shareholders?

12. **LO.3** Violet Corporation, a C corporation in the 34% tax bracket, will be subject to the AMT this year. Armen, Violet's president, has heard that it can be advantageous to accelerate income and defer deductions to a tax year in which the taxpayer is subject to the

AMT. He wonders about the logic of doing this because it would increase Violet's total Federal income tax liability. Violet does not expect to be subject to the AMT next year, but will remain in the 34% bracket. Clarify this planning approach for Armen.

13. **LO.3** Mary and Richerd plan to establish a retail business that will have outlets in six cities in a southeastern state. Because the business probably will generate losses in at least the first three years, they want to use an entity that will pass the losses through to them for both Federal and state income tax purposes. They have narrowed their choices to an S corporation and a limited liability company. Advise Mary and Richerd on selecting an entity form. **Decision Making**

14. **LO.4** "A favorably taxed fringe benefit is deductible by the employer and is excludible from the gross income of the employee." To what extent is this statement correct?

15. **LO.4** Tan, Inc., a C corporation, has been in existence for five years and has accumulated E & P of $990,000. It projects future earnings to continue at about $200,000 per year. David, Tan's sole shareholder and CEO, receives an annual salary of $400,000. **Issue ID**
    a. What issues do David and Tan need to consider if their objective is to avoid double taxation?
    b. Should avoiding double taxation be a goal of David and Tan? Why or why not?

16. **LO.4** What techniques can the shareholders of a C corporation use to reduce its taxable income and thereby minimize or avoid double taxation? How can the IRS challenge these techniques?

17. **LO.4** Teresa is considering contributing $900,000 to the capital of Beige, Inc., a C corporation. A business acquaintance suggests that, instead, she should invest only $600,000 in capital and lend the $300,000 balance to the corporation. The interest rate on the loan would be the Federal rate of 5.5%. Are there any tax benefits to this advice? Any tax pitfalls? Explain. **Decision Making**

18. **LO.4** Is it possible to permanently avoid double taxation of a C corporation by never making distributions to shareholders (because the stock will appreciate in value and the heirs will receive a step-up in basis on the death of the shareholder)? Explain.

19. **LO.4** Orange and Rust have both been in business for approximately nine years. Each corporation has 14 shareholders and taxable income of about $350,000 per year. Neither corporation has made any dividend distributions nor plans to do so in the near future. Explain why Orange may have an accumulated earnings tax problem, while Rust does not.

20. **LO.4, 5** Arnold is going to conduct his business in corporate form. What factors should he consider in deciding whether to operate as a C corporation or as an S corporation? **Decision Making**

21. **LO.4** Tammy and Willy own 40% of the stock of Roadrunner, an S corporation. The other 60% is owned by 99 other shareholders (all are single and unrelated). Tammy and Willy have agreed to a divorce and are in the process of negotiating a property settlement. **Issue ID**
    a. Identify the relevant tax issues for Tammy and Willy.
    b. The divorce resulted in the Roadrunner stock being distributed equally to Tammy and Willy. What could either party do to change the tax status of Roadrunner?

22. **LO.5** Sabrina is going to contribute an SUV to her wholly owned business. She purchased the SUV three years ago for $58,000 and used it exclusively for personal purposes during this period. The fair market value of the SUV is $40,000. Are the tax consequences different if Sabrina contributes the SUV to an S corporation in which she is a 100% shareholder rather than a C corporation in which she is a 100% shareholder? If the business is a sole proprietorship? Explain.

23. **LO.5** Answer the following questions:
    a. How are the nonrecognition rules for contributions of property to a partnership by a partner similar to those for contributions of property to a corporation by a shareholder?
    b. How, if at all, do the nonrecognition rules differ?

24. **LO.5** Why are special allocations either permitted or required for the partners in a partnership, yet are not permitted for the shareholders in a C corporation or an S corporation?

25. **LO.5** Entity liabilities have an effect on a partner's basis in the partnership interest. Yet entity liabilities do not have any effect on a corporate shareholder's stock basis (for either a C corporation or an S corporation). What is the reason for this difference?

26. **LO.5** Identify the effect of each of the following on a partner's basis for a partnership interest and a shareholder's (both C corporation and S corporation) basis for stock:
    - Profits.
    - Losses.
    - Liability increase.
    - Liability decrease.
    - Contribution of assets.
    - Distribution of assets.

27. **LO.5** The conduit concept applies to an S corporation. Are there any circumstances in which an S corporation is a taxpayer rather than merely a tax reporter? Explain.

28. **LO.5** Dexter, a partner in the Warbler Partnership, uses the cash method of accounting.
    a. Are the distributions of earnings by the partnership to Dexter taxed to him? Explain.
    b. Would the answer in (a) change if Dexter was a shareholder and Warbler, Inc., was an S corporation? Explain.

29. **LO.5** A partner's ability to pass through and deduct his or her share of the partnership loss is limited by the partnership interest basis.
    a. Does the Code further limit the loss pass-through and deduction with the § 465 at-risk rules? Explain.
    b. In this regard, what effect do the § 469 passive activity loss rules have?
    c. Which potentially are more restrictive: the § 465 at-risk rules or the § 469 passive activity loss rules?

30. **LO.6** Boswell wants to sell his sole proprietorship, a hair salon, to Eleanor for $450,000.
    a. Does it matter to Boswell whether the form of the transaction is a sale of the business or a sale of the individual assets? Explain.
    b. Is the answer in (a) affected by whether the assets of the sole proprietorship have appreciated in value or declined in value?

Issue ID

31. **LO.6** Vladimir owns all of the stock of Rose, Inc., a C corporation. The fair market value of the stock (and Rose's assets) is about five times Vladimir's adjusted basis for the stock. He is negotiating with an investor group for the sale of the corporation. Identify the relevant tax issues for Vladimir.

32. **LO.2, 3, 4, 5, 6** Using the legend provided, indicate which form of business entity each of the following characteristics describes. Some of the characteristics may apply to more than one form of business entity.

Legend		
SP	=	Applies to sole proprietorship
P	=	Applies to partnership
S	=	Applies to S corporation
C	=	Applies to C corporation
N	=	Applies to none

    a. Has limited liability.
    b. Greatest ability to raise capital.
    c. Subject to double taxation.
    d. Not subject to double taxation.
    e. Could be subject to accumulated earnings tax.
    f. Limit on types and number of shareholders.

g. Has unlimited liability.
h. Sale of the business can be subject to double taxation.
i. Profits and losses affect the basis for an ownership interest.
j. Entity liabilities affect the basis for an ownership interest.
k. Distributions of earnings are taxed as dividend income to the owners.
l. Total invested capital cannot exceed $1 million.
m. AAA is an account that relates to this entity.

33. **LO.5** Using the legend provided, indicate which form of business entity each of the following characteristics describes. Some of the characteristics may apply to more than one form of business entity.

Legend
P = Applies to partnership
S = Applies to S corporation
C = Applies to C corporation

The basis for an ownership interest is:
a. Increased by an investment by the owner.
b. Decreased by a distribution to the owner.
c. Increased by entity profits.
d. Decreased by entity losses.
e. Increased as the entity's liabilities increase.
f. Decreased as the entity's liabilities decrease.

34. **LO.5, 6** Green Partnership, a general partnership, has many opportunities to use special allocations. One of the special allocations available to Green is the optional adjustment-to-basis election under §§ 754 and 743 when a new partner acquires a partnership interest from an existing partner. Discuss the relevant factors that should be considered before making this election.

PROBLEMS

35. **LO.2** Sea Green Enterprises has the following assets and liabilities on its balance sheet:

	Net Book Value	Fair Market Value
Assets	$600,000	$925,000
Liabilities	200,000	200,000

Sea Green has just lost a product liability suit with damages of $10 million being awarded to the plaintiff. Although Sea Green will appeal the judgment, legal counsel indicates the judgment is highly unlikely to be overturned by the appellate court. The product liability insurance carried by Sea Green has a policy ceiling of $6 million. What is the amount of liability of Sea Green Enterprises and its owners if the form of the business entity is:
a. A sole proprietorship?
b. A partnership?
c. A C corporation?
d. An S corporation?

36. **LO.3** Red, White, Blue, and Magenta have taxable income as follows:

Corporation	Taxable Income
Blue	$ 91,000
White	320,000
Red	800,000
Magenta	50,000,000

a. Calculate the marginal tax rate and the effective tax rate for each of the C corporations.
b. Explain why the marginal tax rate for a C corporation can exceed 35%, but the effective tax rate cannot.

Decision Making
Communications

37. **LO.1, 2, 3** Amy and Jeff Barnes are going to operate their florist shop as a partnership or as an S corporation. After paying salaries of $45,000 to each of the owners, the shop's earnings are projected to be about $60,000. The earnings are to be invested in the growth of the business. Write a letter to Amy and Jeff Barnes (5700 Redmont Highway, Washington, D.C. 20024) advising them as to which of the two entity forms they should select.

Decision Making

38. **LO.2, 3** Jack, a married taxpayer, is going to establish a manufacturing business. He anticipates that the business will be profitable immediately due to a patent he holds. He anticipates that profits for the first year will be about $250,000 and will increase at a rate of about 25% per year for the foreseeable future. He will be the sole owner of the business. Advise Jack on the form of business entity he should select. Assume that Jack and his spouse will be in the 35% tax bracket.

Decision Making

39. **LO.3** Sand Corporation will begin operations on January 1. Earnings for the next five years are projected to be relatively stable at about $95,000 per year. The shareholders of Sand are in the 33% tax bracket.
    a. Assume that Sand will reinvest its after-tax earnings in the growth of the company. Should Sand operate as a C corporation or as an S corporation?
    b. Assume that Sand will distribute its after-tax earnings each year to its shareholders. Should Sand operate as a C corporation or as an S corporation?

40. **LO.3** Mabel and Alan, who are in the 35% tax bracket, recently acquired a fast-food franchise. Each of them will work in the business and receive a salary of $175,000. They anticipate that the annual profits of the business, after deducting salaries, will be approximately $450,000. The entity will distribute enough cash each year to Mabel and Alan to cover their Federal income taxes associated with the franchise.
    a. What amount will the entity distribute if the franchise operates as a C corporation?
    b. What amount will the entity distribute if the franchise operates as an S corporation?
    c. What will be the amount of the combined entity/owner tax liability in (a) and (b)?

41. **LO.3** Owl is a closely held corporation owned by eight shareholders (each has 12.5% of the stock). Selected financial information provided by Owl follows:

Taxable income	$6,250,000
Positive AMT adjustments (excluding ACE adjustment)	600,000
Negative AMT adjustments	(30,000)
Tax preferences	5,000,000
Retained earnings	900,000
Accumulated E & P	2,000,000
ACE adjustment	750,000

    a. Calculate Owl's tax liability if Owl is a C corporation.
    b. Calculate Owl's tax liability if Owl is an S corporation.
    c. How would your answers in (a) and (b) change if Owl was not closely held (e.g., 5,000 shareholders with no shareholder owning more than 2% of the stock)?

Decision Making

42. **LO.3** Falcon Corporation, a calendar year taxpayer, is a deepwater offshore drilling company that is planning to sell drilling equipment that it no longer needs. The drilling equipment has an adjusted basis of $400,000 ($700,000 − $300,000 depreciation) and a fair market value of $500,000. The AMT adjusted basis is $425,000. The buyer of the drilling equipment would like to close the transaction prior to the end of the calendar year. Falcon is uncertain whether the tax consequences would be better if the sale took place this year or next year and is considering the following options:

    - $500,000 in cash payable on December 31, 2012.
    - The sale is closed on December 31, 2012, with the consideration being a $500,000 note issued by the buyer. The maturity date of the note is January 2, 2013, with the equipment being pledged as security.

Falcon projects that its taxable income for 2012 and 2013 will be $400,000 (gross receipts of about $9.5 million) without the sale. Falcon has other AMT adjustments and tax preferences of $425,000 in 2012, which will not recur in 2013. Determine the tax consequences to Falcon under both options and recommend the option that is preferable.

43. **LO.4** Three sisters and their brother, all unmarried, own and operate a dairy farm. They live on the farm and take their meals on the farm for the "convenience of the employer." The fair market value of their lodging is $60,000, and the fair market value of their meals is $26,000. The meals are prepared by the farm cook who prepares their meals along with those of the ten other farm employees. Determine the tax consequences of the meals and lodging to the sisters and their brother if the farm is:
   a. Incorporated.
   b. Not incorporated.

44. **LO.4** A business entity's taxable income before the cost of certain fringe benefits paid to owners and other employees is $400,000. The amounts paid for these fringe benefits are as follows:

	Owners	Other Employees
Group term life insurance	$20,000	$40,000
Meals and lodging incurred for the convenience of the employer	50,000	75,000
Pension plan	30,000*	90,000

* H.R. 10 (Keogh) plan for partnership and S corporation.

The business entity is equally owned by four owners.
   a. Calculate the taxable income of the business entity if the entity is a partnership, a C corporation, and an S corporation.
   b. Determine the effect on the owners for each of the three business forms.

45. **LO.4** Turtle, a C corporation, has taxable income of $600,000 before paying salaries to the three equal shareholder-employees, Britney, Shania, and Alan. Turtle follows a policy of distributing all after-tax earnings to the shareholders.
   a. Determine the tax consequences for Turtle, Britney, Shania, and Alan if the corporation pays salaries to Britney, Shania, and Alan as follows:

Option 1		Option 2	
Britney	$270,000	Britney	$135,000
Shania	180,000	Shania	90,000
Alan	150,000	Alan	75,000

   b. Is Turtle likely to encounter any tax problems associated with either option? Explain.

46. **LO.4** Parrott, Inc., a C corporation, is owned by Abner (60%) and Deanna (40%). Abner is the president, and Deanna is the vice president for sales. All three are cash basis taxpayers. Late in 2011, Parrott encounters working capital difficulties. Therefore, Abner loans the corporation $810,000, and Deanna loans the corporation $540,000. Each loan is on a 5% note that is due in five years with interest payable annually. Determine the tax consequences to Parrott, Abner, and Deanna for 2012 if:
   a. The notes are classified as debt.
   b. The notes are classified as equity.

47. **LO.4** Marci and Jennifer each own 50% of the stock of Lavender, a C corporation. After each of them is paid a "reasonable" salary of $125,000, the taxable income of Lavender is normally around $600,000. The corporation is about to purchase a $2 million shopping mall ($1.5 million allocated to the building and $500,000 allocated to the land). The mall will be rented to tenants at a net rent income (i.e., includes rental commissions, depreciation, etc.) of $500,000 annually. Marci and Jennifer will contribute $1 million each to the corporation to provide the cash required for the acquisition. Their CPA has suggested that Marci and Jennifer purchase the shopping mall as individuals and lease it to Lavender for a fair rental of $300,000. Both Marci and Jennifer are in the 35% tax bracket. The

Decision Making

acquisition will occur on January 2, 2012. Determine whether the shopping mall should be acquired by Lavender or by Marci and Jennifer in accordance with their CPA's recommendation. Assume that the depreciation on the shopping mall in 2012 is $37,000.

48. **LO.3, 4** Flower, Inc., a C corporation, has taxable income of $800,000 for 2012. It has used up the accumulated earnings credit and has no additional "reasonable needs of the business" for the current tax year. Determine the total potential tax liability for Flower:
    a. If it declares no dividends.
    b. If it declares and pays dividends equal to the after-tax earnings.
    c. In (a) and (b) if Flower is an S corporation.

Decision Making

49. **LO.4** Since Garnet Corporation was formed five years ago, its stock has been held as follows: 525 shares by Frank and 175 shares by Grace. Their basis in the stock is $350,000 for Frank and $150,000 for Grace. As part of a stock redemption, Garnet redeems 125 of Frank's shares for $175,000 and 125 of Grace's shares for $175,000.
    a. What are the tax consequences of the stock redemption to Frank and Grace?
    b. How would the tax consequences to Frank and Grace be different if, instead of the redemption, they each sell 125 shares to Chuck (an unrelated party)?
    c. What factors should influence their decision on whether to redeem or sell the 250 shares of stock?

Decision Making

50. **LO.4** Clay Corporation has been an electing S corporation since its incorporation 10 years ago. During the first three years of operations, it incurred total losses of $250,000. Since then, Clay has generated earnings of approximately $180,000 each year. None of the earnings have been distributed to the three equal shareholders, Claire, Lynn, and Todd, because the corporation has been in an expansion mode. At the beginning of 2012, Claire sells her stock to Nell for $400,000. Nell has reservations about the utility of the S election. Therefore, Lynn, Todd, and Nell are discussing whether the election should be continued. They expect the earnings to remain at approximately $180,000 each year. However, because they perceive that the expansion period is over and Clay has adequate working capital, they may start distributing the earnings to the shareholders. All of the shareholders are in the 33% tax bracket. Advise the three shareholders on whether the S election should be maintained.

Decision Making

51. **LO.5** Andrew and Evans form a business entity with each contributing the following property:

	Andrew	Evans
Cash	$400,000	
Land		$400,000*

*Fair market value. Adjusted basis is $125,000.

Three months later, the land is sold for $465,000 because of unexpected zoning problems. The proceeds are to be applied toward the purchase of another parcel of land to be used for real estate development. Determine the tax consequences to the entity and to the owners upon formation and the later sale of the land if the entity is:
    a. A partnership.
    b. An S corporation.
    c. A C corporation.
    d. Is it possible to structure the disposition of the land so as to defer any recognition of tax consequences? Explain.

52. **LO.5** Agnes, Becky, and Carol form a business entity with each contributing the following:

	Adjusted Basis	Fair Market Value	Ownership Percentage
Agnes: Cash	$100,000	$100,000	40%
Becky: Land	60,000	120,000	40%
Carol: Services		50,000	20%

Becky's land has a $20,000 mortgage that is assumed by the entity. Carol, an attorney, receives her ownership interest in exchange for legal services. Determine the recognized gain to the owners, the basis for their ownership interests, and the entity's basis for its assets if the entity is:

a. A partnership.
b. A C corporation.
c. An S corporation.

53. **LO.5** Melinda has a 30% ownership interest in an entity for which she initially contributed $180,000. She is one of the original owners of the business. None of the owners are related. During the life of the business, the following have occurred:

- Cumulative losses of $250,000 during the first three years.
- Profits of $200,000 in the next year.
- Distributions to owners of $90,000 at the end of year 3.
- Distribution to Melinda of $50,000 that redeems 25% of her ownership interest at the end of year 4. No other owners redeem any of their ownership interest.

Determine the tax consequences to Melinda if the entity is:

a. A partnership.
b. An S corporation.
c. A C corporation.

54. **LO.5** An entity engages in the following transactions during the taxable year:

- Sells stock held for four years as an investment for $50,000 (adjusted basis of $28,000).
- Sells land used in the business for $70,000. The land has been used as a parking lot and originally cost $50,000.
- Receives tax-exempt interest on municipal bonds of $9,000.
- Receives dividends on IBM stock of $75,000.

Describe the effect of these transactions on the entity and its owners if the entity is:

a. A partnership.
b. A C corporation.
c. An S corporation.

55. **LO.5** Swift Corporation distributes land (basis of $55,000 and fair market value of $120,000) to Sam and cash ($240,000) to Allison in exchange for part of their stock. Other shareholders do not redeem any of their stock. Sam surrenders shares of stock that have a basis of $25,000. Prior to the stock redemption, Sam owned 20% of the Swift stock, and after the redemption, he owns 15%. At the same time, Swift distributes cash to Allison, and she surrenders shares of stock with a basis of $40,000. Prior to the stock redemption, Allison owned 70% of the Swift stock, and after the redemption, she owns 60%. Determine the tax consequences to Swift, Sam, and Allison if Swift is:

a. A C corporation.
b. An S corporation.

56. **LO.5** Indigo, Inc., a personal service corporation, has the following types of income and losses for 2012:

Active income	$325,000
Portfolio income	49,000
Passive loss	333,000

a. Calculate Indigo's taxable income for 2012.
b. Assume that instead of being a personal service corporation, Indigo is a closely held corporation. Calculate Indigo's taxable income for 2012.
c. Would the answer in (b) change if the passive loss is only $320,000 rather than $333,000? Explain.

57. **LO.5** Jo and Velma are equal owners of the JV Partnership, with Jo investing $500,000 and Velma contributing land and a building (adjusted basis of $125,000; fair market value of $500,000). In addition, the entity borrows $250,000 using recourse financing and $100,000 using nonrecourse financing.

a. What are Jo's and Velma's bases for their partnership interests (i.e., outside bases)?
b. What are Jo's and Velma's at-risk bases?

58. **LO.5** Megan owns 55% and Vern owns 45% of a business entity. The owners would like to share profits with 55% for Megan and 45% for Vern and to share losses with 80% for Vern and 20% for Megan. Determine the tax consequences for 2012 if the entity has a tax loss of $160,000 and is:
   a. A partnership.
   b. A C corporation.
   c. An S corporation.

59. **LO.6** Emily and Freda are negotiating with George to purchase the business he operates in corporate form (Pelican, Inc.). The assets of Pelican, Inc., a C corporation, are as follows:

Asset	Basis	FMV
Cash	$ 20,000	$ 20,000
Accounts receivable	50,000	50,000
Inventory	100,000	110,000
Furniture and fixtures*	150,000	170,000
Building**	200,000	250,000
Land	40,000	150,000

*Potential depreciation recapture under § 1245 is $45,000.
**The straight-line method was used to depreciate the building. The balance in the accumulated depreciation account is $340,000.

George's basis for the stock of Pelican, Inc., is $560,000. George is in the 35% tax bracket, and Pelican, Inc., is in the 34% tax bracket.
   a. Assume that Emily and Freda purchase the stock of Pelican from George and that the purchase price is $908,000. Determine the tax consequences to Emily and Freda, Pelican, and George.
   b. Assume that Emily and Freda purchase the assets from Pelican and that the purchase price is $908,000. Determine the tax consequences to Emily and Freda, Pelican, and George.
   c. Assume that the purchase price is $550,000 because the fair market value of the building is $150,000 and the fair market value of the land is $50,000. Also assume that no amount is assigned to goodwill. Emily and Freda purchase the stock of Pelican from George. Determine the tax consequences to Emily and Freda, Pelican, and George.

Decision Making

60. **LO.6** Hector and Walt are purchasing the Copper Partnership from Jan and Gail for $700,000, with Hector and Walt being equal partners. Based on the negotiations, Jan and Gail have succeeded in having the transaction structured as the purchase of the partnership rather than the purchase of the individual assets. The adjusted basis of the individual assets of the Copper Partnership is $580,000.
   a. What are Hector's and Walt's bases for their partnership interests (i.e., outside bases)?
   b. What is Copper's adjusted basis for its assets after the transaction? Would a § 754 optional adjustment-to-basis election be helpful? Why or why not?

Decision Making

61. **LO.6** Gail and Harry own the GH Partnership, which has conducted business for 10 years. The bases for their partnership interests are $100,000 for Gail and $150,000 for Harry. GH Partnership has the following assets:

Asset	Basis	FMV
Cash	$ 10,000	$ 10,000
Accounts receivable	30,000	28,000
Inventory	25,000	26,000
Building*	100,000	150,000
Land	250,000	400,000

*The straight-line method has been used to depreciate the building. Accumulated depreciation is $70,000.

Gail and Harry sell their partnership interests to Keith and Liz for $307,000 each.
   a. Determine the tax consequences of the sale to Gail, Harry, and GH Partnership.
   b. From a tax perspective, would it matter to Keith and Liz whether they purchase Gail's and Harry's partnership interests or the partnership assets from GH Partnership?

62. **LO.6** Damon Allred is going to purchase either the stock or the assets of Platinum Corporation. All of the Platinum stock is owned by Charley. Damon and Charley agree that Platinum is worth $900,000. The tax basis for Platinum's assets is $750,000. Write a letter to Damon advising him on whether he should negotiate to purchase the stock or the assets. Also prepare a memo for the files. Damon's address is 100 Village Green, Chattanooga, TN 37403.

Decision Making

Communications

RESEARCH PROBLEMS

Note: Solutions to Research Problems can be prepared by using the **Checkpoint® Student Edition** online research product, which is available to accompany this text. It is also possible to prepare solutions to the Research Problems by using tax research materials found in a standard tax library.

THOMSON REUTERS **CHECKPOINT®**

Research Problem 1. The stock of Ebony, Inc., is owned as follows:

	Percent Ownership	Basis	FMV
Alma	30	$2,700	$270,000
Ben	30	2,700	270,000
Debbie	20	1,800	180,000
Clyde	20	1,800	180,000

Alma and Ben are the parents of Debbie and Clyde. Managerial positions in Ebony are as follows: Alma is the chief executive officer (CEO), Ben is the chief operating officer (COO), Debbie is the chief financial officer (CFO), and Clyde is the vice president for human resources. Alma and Ben have owned their stock for 30 years, and Debbie and Clyde have owned their stock for 10 years. Alma and Ben are considering disposing of their stock and would like to use the funds to acquire a more lucrative investment. Their initial plan was to have Ebony redeem their stock. However, their accountant has indicated that because they intend to retain their positions as officers, the redemption will not qualify under § 302(b)(3). The accountant suggests that they sell their stock to several outsiders who want to acquire an interest in Ebony. As Debbie and Clyde expect to move into the CEO and COO positions in a few years, they oppose a sale to outsiders. They are concerned about the loss of family control that would result.

How can this family dilemma be resolved?

Research Problem 2. Dr. Sanders is a veterinarian who is the sole shareholder of Vet, Inc., an S corporation. The corporation offers consulting and surgical services to other veterinarians that Dr. Sanders provides. Dr. Sanders does not receive regular payments from the corporation, but withdraws funds as the need arises. During the current year, he withdraws $118,000, and the net income of the corporation is $225,000. The corporation does not deduct the $118,000, nor does Dr. Sanders include it in his gross income. Dr. Sanders does, however, report the $225,000 in his gross income. Because Dr. Sanders has recognized all of the corporation's income, he sees no need to pay himself a salary. He justifies the treatment by arguing that he is not an employee (i.e., he is the owner) of the corporation and that the Federal income tax consequences are the same. Evaluate the approach taken by Dr. Sanders and Vet, Inc.

Research Problem 3. Amanda and Paul are equal owners in Talon, Inc., an S corporation, and each has an adjusted basis in the stock of $80,000. In the current year, Talon has a loss of $200,000, and its Schedule K–1s allocate $100,000 to each shareholder.

Amanda and Paul are also equal partners in a partnership. Two years ago, to provide additional working capital to Talon, the partnership loaned it $100,000. The loan bore all of the usual attributes of a bona fide loan (i.e., a formal note, market interest rate, and payment schedule). The loan was recorded as a note receivable by the partnership and as a note payable on the S corporation accounting records. Formal minutes authorizing the loan stated that the partnership was acting as an agent for Amanda and Paul.

Amanda and Paul each deducted their share (i.e., $100,000) of the S corporation loss. They contend that their combined stock basis and debt basis for § 1366(d) purposes is $130,000 ($80,000 + $50,000). The IRS maintains that the basis of each shareholder is only $80,000 (the basis in the stock). The loan cannot count as part of the shareholder's debt basis as it was not made directly to the S corporation. Evaluate the positions of the taxpayers and the IRS.

Research Problem 4. Crane is a partner in the Cardinal Partnership. A dispute arose with the partnership regarding his share of current earnings. The partnership contends that the amount is $75,000, while Crane believes his share is $100,000.

Crane ceased being a partner on November 1, 2012. As a result of the dispute, the partnership distributed only $75,000 and placed the disputed $25,000 in escrow. However, Crane's Schedule K–1 from the partnership included the full $100,000. Crane believes that the K–1 should include only the $75,000 that is not in dispute. Is Crane correct? Explain.

Internet Activity

Use the tax resources of the Internet to address the following questions. Do not restrict your search to the Web, but include a review of newsgroups and general reference materials, practitioner sites and resources, primary sources of the tax law, chat rooms and discussion groups, and other opportunities.

Research Problem 5. Find a newspaper article about a state that contributed assets to an auto company as a location inducement and later recovered some or all of the assets under a "clawback" provision. What are the tax consequences to the auto company when it returns these assets to the state?

Research Problem 6. Find an article describing how a specific business put together its employee fringe benefit package in light of the limitations presented by the tax law and the business's form of operation.

Communications

Research Problem 7. Find a newspaper article that discusses the increasing regulation of "corporate America." Outline the pros and cons of such regulation from your viewpoint and that of the author. In this regard, does it matter whether S or C corporations are involved?

Research Problem 8. Determine whether your state income tax permits an S corporation election and whether it permits an LLC to be taxed as an S corporation.

part 4

Advanced Tax Practice Considerations

The tax professional interacts with a number of different groups and must abide by the rules of various agencies and governmental authorities when servicing clients. For publicly traded entities, additional reporting to shareholders is required as to tax consequences, requiring a reconciliation of tax and book income amounts. When the taxpayer is exempt from Federal income taxation, disclosure and operating requirements often differ from those applicable to the corporate tax model. Many businesses operate in more than one U.S. state and must account for the taxable activities in each. Lastly, the conduct of a tax professional's practice is bound by ethical and operational constraints, exposing both the taxpayer and the tax advisor to penalties, interest, and other sanctions. In this Part of the text, we examine in more detail these aspects of tax practice.

CHAPTER

14 Taxes on the Financial Statements

LEARNING OBJECTIVES: *After completing Chapter 14, you should be able to:*

LO.1 Determine the differences between book and tax methods of computing income tax expense.

LO.2 Compute a corporation's book income tax expense.

LO.3 Describe the purpose of the valuation allowance.

LO.4 Interpret the disclosure information contained in the financial statements.

LO.5 Identify the GAAP treatment concerning tax uncertainties and unrepatriated foreign earnings.

LO.6 Use financial statement income tax information to benchmark a company's tax position.

CHAPTER OUTLINE

© Pukhov Konstantin/Shutterstock.com

THE BIG PICTURE Tax Solutions for the Real World

Taxes on the Financial Statements

Raymond Jones, the CEO of Arctic Corporation, would like some help in reconciling the amount of income tax expense on Arctic's financial statements with the amount of income tax reported on the company's corporate income tax return for its first year of operations. Mr. Jones does not understand why he can't simply multiply the financial statement income by the company's 35 percent marginal tax rate to get the financial tax expense. While the financial statements show book income before tax of $25 million, the reported Federal tax expense is only $7.7 million. In addition, the corporate tax return reports taxable income of $19 million and Federal income taxes payable of only $6.65 million.

Without knowing the specifics of the company's financial statements, does Arctic's situation look reasonable? Why is Arctic's financial tax expense not equal to $8.75 million ($25 million × 35%)? What causes the $1.05 million difference between the taxes shown on the financial statements and the taxes due on the tax return?

Read the chapter and formulate your response.

14 Introduction

GlobalCo is a U.S. corporation with operations in 40 different states and 27 different countries. It pays income taxes in virtually all of these jurisdictions. GlobalCo's investors and competitors are interested in understanding GlobalCo's effective tax rate. An examination of its financial statements indicates that GlobalCo has a 28 percent effective tax rate. How much of GlobalCo's tax expense is related to U.S. Federal tax, state and local tax or taxes in foreign countries? What portion of its tax cost is currently paid versus deferred to some future period? Has GlobalCo recorded any deferred tax assets, representing future tax savings, or deferred tax liabilities, representing future tax costs? How does GlobalCo's effective tax rate for the current year compare to prior years or to other companies in the same industry? Why is GlobalCo's effective tax rate not simply 35 percent, the statutory corporate rate for large U.S. corporations?

The bottom line result of the many tax planning ideas, advice, and compliance efforts provided by tax professionals to their clients is captured in a simple summary number—income tax expense. A U.S. corporation's tax expense is reported in its annual Federal tax return, its financial statements, and other regulatory filings and is often the starting point for state and local tax returns. As it turns out, however, deriving a corporation's income tax expense is not so simple.

A corporation may report millions of dollars in tax expense in its financial statements and yet pay virtually nothing to the U.S., state, or foreign governments. Alternatively, a corporation may pay substantial amounts to the U.S., state, and foreign governments and report very little income tax expense in its financial statements. Why do such differences exist? Which income tax expense is the "correct" number? How can data regarding a corporation's income tax expense provide valuable information for the corporation, its competitors, and tax professionals assisting in the planning function? This chapter addresses these questions.

14.1 Book-Tax Differences

LO.1

Determine the differences between book and tax methods of computing income tax expense.

A significant difference may exist between a corporation's Federal income tax liability as reported on its Form 1120 (tax) and the corporation's income tax expense as reported on its financial statements (book) prepared using **generally accepted accounting principles (GAAP)**. This book-tax difference is caused by any or all of the following.

- Differences in reporting entities included in the calculation.
- Different definition of taxes included in the income tax expense amount.
- Different accounting methods.

A corporation's activities are captured in its accounting records, producing general ledger results. At the end of the year, these records are summarized to produce a trial balance. Adjustments to these accounting data may be necessary to produce both the corporation's financial statements and its corporate income tax return. These book and tax adjustments rarely match. As discussed below, different entities may be included in the reports, and the book and tax rules can be quite different. On a tax return, Schedule M–1 or M–3 reconciles the difference between a corporation's book income and its taxable income. See Figure 14.1.

Different Reporting Entities

A corporate group must consolidate all U.S. and foreign subsidiaries within a single financial statement for book purposes when the parent corporation controls more than 50 percent of the voting power of those subsidiaries.[1] In cases where the

[1] *Consolidation*, ASC Topic 810 (formerly *Consolidation of All Majority Owned Subsidiaries*, Statement of Financial Accounting Standards No. 94). Certain adjustments are made to reduce book income for the after-tax income related to minority shareholders.

TAX IN THE NEWS The Watchdog Is Watching

A recent report by the SEC listed the watchdog agency's areas of focus with respect to the financial statements of publicly traded corporations as they pertain to issues in accounting for income taxes. Inquiries and comment letters from the SEC can be anticipated in these areas. The most important of the focus areas include the following.

- Realizability of deferred tax assets—how positive and negative evidence supporting the deferrals is assessed by the taxpayer.
- Uncertain tax positions—whether ASC 740-10 (FIN 48) disclosures are comprehensive and complete.
- Foreign earnings—whether sufficient information is provided concerning the reinvestments of overseas earnings and their effects on the effective tax rate.
- Intraperiod allocation—how the tax accounts reflect transactions involving continuing operations and income from other sources.

The Edgar database is a good place to follow trends in the agency's information requests and the taxpayer's responses.

parent corporation owns between 20 and 50 percent of another corporation, the parent uses the **equity method** to account for the earnings of the subsidiary. Under the equity method, the parent currently records its share of the subsidiary's income or loss for the year.[2] Corporations that own less than 20 percent of other corporations typically use the *cost method* to account for income from these investments and include income only when actual dividends are received.

FIGURE 14.1 **Flow of Accounting Data**

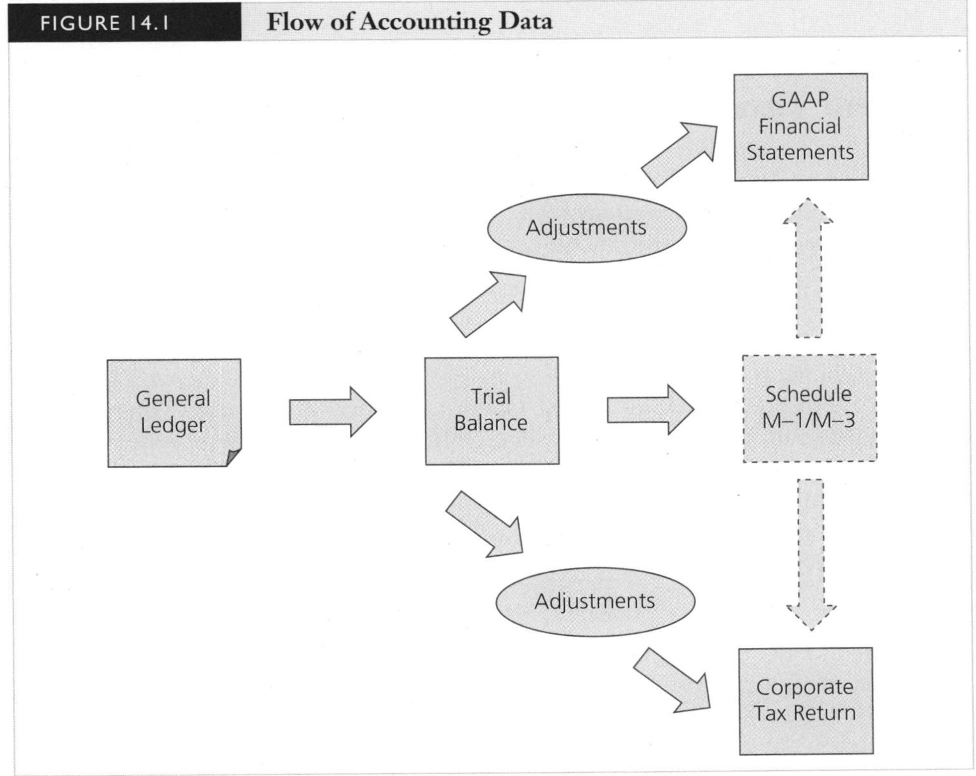

[2] *Investments—Equity Method and Joint Ventures*, ASC Topic 323 (formerly *The Equity Method of Accounting for Investments in Common Stock*, Accounting Principles Board Opinion No. 18).

THE BIG PICTURE

EXAMPLE 1

Return to the facts of *The Big Picture* on p. 14-1. Arctic Corporation owns 100% of Gator, Inc., a domestic corporation; 100% of Hurricane, Ltd., a foreign corporation; and 40% of Beach, Inc., a domestic corporation. Arctic's combined financial statement includes its own net income and the net income of both Gator and Hurricane. In addition, Arctic's financial statement includes its 40% share of Beach's net income. Arctic's financial statement includes the income of these subsidiaries regardless of whether Arctic receives any actual profit distributions from its subsidiaries.

For Federal tax purposes, a U.S. corporation may elect to include any *domestic* subsidiaries that are 80 percent or more owned in its consolidated U.S. tax return.[3] The income of foreign subsidiaries and less than 80 percent owned domestic subsidiaries is not included in the consolidated tax return.

THE BIG PICTURE

EXAMPLE 2

Return to the facts of *The Big Picture* on p. 14-1. Also assume the facts presented in Example 1. If Arctic elects to include Gator as part of its consolidated Federal income tax return, Arctic's return includes its own taxable income and the taxable income generated by Gator. Hurricane's taxable income is not included in the consolidated return because it is a non-U.S. corporation. Beach, although a domestic corporation, cannot be consolidated with Arctic because Arctic owns only 40% of the stock. Income from Hurricane and Beach will be included in Arctic's U.S. taxable income only when Arctic receives actual or constructive dividends.

Different Taxes

The income tax expense reported on a corporation's financial statement is the combination of the entity's Federal, state, local, and foreign income taxes. This number includes both current and deferred tax expense amounts. The distinction between current and deferred income taxes is discussed later in this chapter.

THE BIG PICTURE

EXAMPLE 3

Return to the facts of *The Big Picture* on p. 14-1. Also assume the facts presented in Example 1. For book purposes, Arctic, Gator, and Hurricane combine their income and expenses into a single financial statement. The book tax expense for the year includes all Federal, state, local, and foreign income taxes paid or accrued by these three corporations. In addition, the tax expense amount includes any future Federal, state, local, or foreign income tax expenses (or tax savings) on income reported in the current income statement.

The income tax expense computed on the Federal income tax return is the U.S. *Federal* income tax expense. This amount is based on the U.S. corporation's taxable income. State income taxes are reported on the Federal tax return, but as deductions in arriving at taxable income.

[3] §§ 1501–1504. An election to consolidate an 80% or more owned subsidiary generally can be changed only with the permission of the IRS.

TAX IN THE NEWS Stock Options—GAAP v. Tax

In March 2004, the Financial Accounting Standards Board proposed that companies be required to report the value of options they provide to their employees as an expense on their financial statements beginning in 2005. The International Accounting Standards Board adopted a similar rule effective in 2004. Some companies feared the effect this rule might have on their share prices, with the lower net income that stock option expensing would produce. High-tech companies were particularly concerned about this proposal because they are heavy users of stock options to attract employees.

Ultimately, the FASB issued *Compensation—Stock Compensation*, ASC Topic 718-10 (formerly *Share-Based Payment*, Statement of Financial Accounting Standards No. 123R). The standard requires that the compensation cost relating to share-based payments be recognized as an expense in the income statement. The standard applies to many types of stock-based compensation, including stock options, performance-based awards, and employee share purchase plans.

The issue came up again with respect to nonqualified stock options that were issued when the stock market bottomed out in 2008 and 2009. The employer's tax deductions for option-based compensation are allowed only when the shares acquired by option are sold (i.e., when the executive recognizes gross income on the Form 1040). But the compensation deduction is allowed at the stock price on the sale date (say, $100), and not at its price on the date that the option was issued (say, $2).

The related GAAP compensation expense is computed on the option issuance date (here, $2). A large book-tax difference is created, and in the year in which the option is exercised, the employer's Federal income tax can be greatly reduced or eliminated by the deduction.

THE BIG PICTURE

EXAMPLE 4

Return to the facts of *The Big Picture* on p. 14-1. Also assume the facts presented in Example 1. Arctic and Gator file a consolidated Federal tax return. The tax expense reported on the Form 1120 is only the U.S. Federal income tax expense for the consolidated taxable income of Arctic and Gator. This tax expense does not include the income taxes that Arctic and its subsidiaries paid to state, local, or foreign governments.

Different Methods

Many differences exist between book and tax accounting methods. Some are simply **temporary differences**, with income and expenses appearing in both the financial statement and the tax return, but in different periods (i.e., a timing difference). Others are **permanent differences**, with items appearing in the financial statement or the tax return, but not both.

Examples of temporary differences include the following.

- *Depreciation on fixed assets.* Taxpayers may use an accelerated depreciation method under the modified accelerated cost recovery system (MACRS) rules but a straight-line method for book purposes. Even if identical methods are used, the period over which the asset is depreciated may differ between book and tax.
- *Compensation-related expenses.* Several differences exist in this category. For example, under GAAP, corporations accrue the future expenses related to providing postretirement benefits other than pensions (e.g., health insurance coverage). However, these expenses are deductible for tax purposes only when paid.
- *Accrued income and expenses.* Although most income and expense items are recognized for tax and book purposes in the same period, a number of items potentially appear in different periods. For example, warranty expenses are accrued for book purposes but are not deductible for tax purposes until

incurred. Inventory write-offs are accrued for book but are not deductible for tax until incurred. On the income side, different methods regarding the timing of income recognition may create temporary differences. For instance, GAAP recognizes income and loss when the *fair value* of most investment assets changes during the year, while tax rules recognize such realized gain or loss only upon a sale or other taxable disposition of the asset.

- *Net operating losses.* Operating losses from one tax year may be used to offset taxable income in another tax year. Thus, the losses incurred in one year for book purposes may be used as a deduction for tax purposes in a different year.
- *Intangible assets.* Goodwill and some other intangibles are not amortizable for book purposes. However, GAAP requires an annual determination of whether the intangible has suffered a reduction in value (i.e., impairment).[4] If an intangible has suffered an impairment, a current expense is required to reduce the intangible's book value to the lower level. For tax purposes, certain intangibles can be amortized over 15 years.[5]

Examples of permanent differences include the following.

- *Nontaxable income.* A common example is municipal bond interest, which is income for book purposes but is not taxable.
- *Nondeductible expenses.* For example, the disallowed portion of meals and entertainment expense and certain penalties are not deductible for tax purposes but are expensed in arriving at book income.[6]
- *Tax credits.* Credits such as the research activities credit reduce Federal income tax liability but have no corresponding book treatment.

EXAMPLE 5

Wise, Inc., reported the following results for the current year.

Book income (before tax)	$ 685,000
Tax depreciation in excess of book	(125,000)
Nondeductible warranty expense	65,000
Municipal bond interest income	(35,000)
Taxable income (Form 1120)	$ 590,000

Wise reports net income before tax of $685,000 on its financial statement but must adjust this amount for differences between book and tax income. Tax depreciation in excess of book is a tax deduction not deducted for book purposes, and warranty expense is deductible for book purposes but not yet deductible for tax. Both of these items are temporary differences because they will eventually reverse (with book depreciation eventually exceeding tax depreciation and the warranty expense ultimately deducted for tax when incurred). The municipal bond interest is a permanent difference because this income will never be subject to tax. ■

Tax Return Disclosures

Book-tax differences are reported in the Federal income tax returns of most business entities. Some of this material was discussed in Chapter 2.

Figure 14.2 contains the **Schedule M–1** from Form 1120, the corporate income tax return. The purpose of Schedule M–1 is to reconcile book income to the taxable income reported on the tax return. Line 1 is the net income or loss per books,

[4] *Intangibles—Goodwill and Other,* ASC Topic 350 (formerly *Goodwill and Other Intangible Assets,* Statement of Financial Accounting Standards No. 142).

[5] § 197. Prior to 1994, goodwill and similar intangibles were not amortizable for tax purposes but were amortizable for book purposes over a maximum period of 40 years. Thus, goodwill acquired during this period triggered a permanent difference (amortizable for book but not for tax).

[6] Federal income taxes are another example of this type of permanent book-tax difference.

FIGURE 14.2 **Schedule M–1**

Schedule M-1 **Reconciliation of Income (Loss) per Books With Income per Return**
Note: Schedule M-3 required instead of Schedule M-1 if total assets are $10 million or more—see instructions

1	Net income (loss) per books		7	Income recorded on books this year not included on this return (itemize): Tax-exempt interest $	
2	Federal income tax per books				
3	Excess of capital losses over capital gains				
4	Income subject to tax not recorded on books this year (itemize):				
5	Expenses recorded on books this year not deducted on this return (itemize):		8	Deductions on this return not charged against book income this year (itemize):	
a	Depreciation $		a	Depreciation $	
b	Charitable contributions $		b	Charitable contributions $	
c	Travel and entertainment $				
			9	Add lines 7 and 8	
6	Add lines 1 through 5		10	Income (page 1, line 28)—line 6 less line 9	

and line 2 adds back the book tax expense to get back to book income before tax.[7] The remainder of Schedule M–1 contains positive and negative adjustments for both temporary and permanent differences until arriving at taxable income on line 10. **Schedule M–3** is required for a consolidated tax group with total year-end assets of $10 million or more. Other corporations may file a Schedule M–3 voluntarily. Appendix B of this text includes a copy of the Schedule M–3.

The Schedule M–3 provides the IRS with more detailed information than is provided in the Schedule M–1. A more specific "book income" starting point is used, with the taxpayer identifying the source of the book net income amount by answering a series of questions in Part I. Detail then is provided on differences due to the income or loss from foreign entities, along with data about eliminated intercompany transactions. The list of potential book-tax differences is significantly more comprehensive than that in the Schedule M–1, with income items reported in Part II and deduction items reported in Part III. And unlike the Schedule M–1, Schedule M–3 requires identification of whether a book-tax difference is temporary or permanent.

Schedule M–1 or M–3 typically is used as the starting point for IRS audits of corporations. Identifying large differences between book and taxable income may offer the IRS auditor insights into tax saving strategies (some perhaps questionable) employed by the taxpayer. Concept Summary 14.1 summarizes the book-tax differences in arriving at income tax expense.

The income tax note of the financial statements also contains a tax reconciliation, but as discussed later, the purpose and content of this reconciliation are quite different. The book-tax differences reported on Schedule M–1 and M–3 relate to *current-year* differences in book income and taxable income. These items are related to the temporary and permanent differences that occur in determining a corporation's book tax expense. However, for book purposes, the temporary differences are the result of the *cumulative* changes in deferred tax assets and liabilities (as discussed later).

Uncertain Tax Positions

The IRS requires that large corporations list the tax return positions they have taken that may not be fully supported by the law. Schedule UTP ("uncertain tax

[7]Line 1, "Net income (loss) per books," is not defined in the instructions to the form, and corporations seem to use various starting points in the Schedule M–1 (e.g., only the book income from U.S. members of the group). The Schedule M–3 is more specific in defining book income.

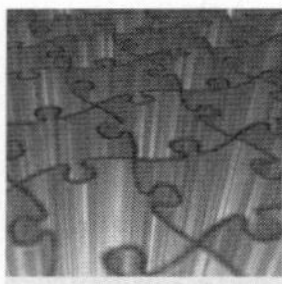

CONCEPT SUMMARY 14.1

Income Amounts—Book versus Tax

Financial Statement	U.S. Federal Income Tax Return
Reporting entities • 50% or more owned domestic and foreign subsidiaries *must* be consolidated. • Share of income from 20%–50% owned domestic and foreign corporations included in current income.	**Reporting entities** • 80% or more owned domestic subsidiaries *may* be consolidated. • Share of income from other corporations reported only when actual or constructive dividends are received.
Income tax expense • Federal income taxes. • State income taxes. • Local income taxes. • Foreign income taxes. • Current and deferred.	**Income tax expense** • Federal income taxes. • Current only.
Methods • Temporary differences. • Permanent differences. • Income tax note reconciliation.	**Methods** • Temporary differences. • Permanent differences. • Schedule M–1 or M–3 reconciliation.

positions") is added to the Form 1120 for all corporations with assets of at least $10 million in 2014 ($50 million for 2012 and 2013). Tax professionals worry that they will be alerting the IRS to specific items that will be most vulnerable to audit adjustments. Because tax returns are confidential documents, though, the public does not have access to a corporation's Schedule UTP.

Disclosures on the Schedule UTP include an enumeration of tax return positions for the current and prior tax years where:

- the taxpayer or a related party recorded a reserve against the Federal income tax expense on its audited financial statements, and
- the taxpayer did not record a tax reserve based on its analysis of expected litigation. This means that in the taxpayer's view, the probability of settling the item with the IRS is less than 50 percent and the taxpayer determines that it is more likely than not (a greater than 50 percent likelihood) to prevail on the merits of the issue in litigation.

Disclosures are not required for items that are immaterial under GAAP rules, or for which the filing position is sufficiently certain that no financial accounting reserve is required.

The IRS maintains that it will limit releases of the Schedule UTP to other taxing jurisdictions, and that it will not use Schedule UTP data to usurp the attorney-client and tax practitioner privileges of confidentiality or the work-product doctrine. Taxpayers are not required to disclose the amounts of any reserves or the precise nature of the tax planning technique that led to the reserve for the filing position.

The Schedule UTP represents a new level of information exchange between the IRS and the taxpayer, focusing on filing-year disclosures rather than audit-year items. The IRS admits that it is directing its audit efforts toward large business entities, and it says that its compliance activities will be both more efficient and more effective as a result.

FINANCIAL DISCLOSURE INSIGHTS The Book-Tax Income Gap

The corporate financial scandals of Enron, WorldCom, and others heightened interest in whether corporations are making appropriate disclosures (i.e., transparency) and in whether they are shouldering their fair share of the tax burden. Adding fuel to the fire is the fact that the gap between book income and taxable income seems to be growing.

According to one study, over the last five years, 115 companies in the Standard and Poor's stock index incurred a Federal and state income tax rate of less than 20 percent. In fact, the rate for 39 of those companies was less than 10 percent.

At least 30 of the Fortune 500 companies paid zero or negative Federal corporate income taxes over a recent three-year period. These companies included General Electric, American Electric Power, Boeing, and PG&E. Pepco Holdings reported an effective Federal income tax rate of *negative* 57.6 percent!

The firms maintained that they had paid all of their required tax liabilities, and that a poor economy and effective income tax planning had resulted in their zero or negative effective tax rates. General Electric, with an in-house tax staff of almost 1,000, claimed a $3.2 billion tax refund while it reported worldwide profits of $14 billion and U.S. profits of $5 billion.

The company came under fire for reducing the number of its U.S. employees while generating profits and refusing to bring them back to the United States. GE responded that the income tax rates in other countries where it operates are lower than those of the United States, and that it made economic sense for the company to manage its tax liabilities on a worldwide basis. GE is in large part today a credit and financial services company, and many of its tax incentives relate to accounting for interest and lease transactions.

Congress and the U.S. Treasury are concerned about the increased efforts by corporations to reduce U.S. income tax obligations and have issued regulations that require disclosure of certain "tax shelter" transactions. Corporations counter that the large differences in book and tax income are a function of the different rules and objectives of GAAP for financial statements and the Internal Revenue Code for tax returns. Actually, low effective tax rates often are traceable to one or more of the following.

- Use of NOL carryovers.
- Large investments in depreciable assets.
- Use of tax incentives (e.g., to encourage new companies and targeted industries such as high-tech and domestic manufacturing).
- Negotiations and settlements with revenue agencies.[9]
- The application of tax planning techniques.

14.2 INCOME TAXES IN THE FINANCIAL STATEMENTS

LO.2

Compute a corporation's book income tax expense.

GAAP Principles

As pointed out earlier, a corporation's financial statements are prepared in accordance with GAAP. The purpose and objectives of these statements are quite different from the objective of the corporation's income tax return.

The **ASC 740 (SFAS 109)** approach produces a total income tax expense (also called the **income tax provision**) for the income currently reported on a corporation's combined financial statement.[8] This approach follows the matching principle, where all of the expenses related to earning income are reported in the same period as the income without regard to when the expenses are actually paid.

[8] *Income Taxes,* ASC Topic 740 (formerly *Accounting for Income Taxes,* Statement of Financial Accounting Standards No. 109).

[9] For instance, AstraZeneca recently reduced its effective tax rate after settling an audit with U.S. and U.K. tax authorities about its transfer pricing policies (see Chapter 9). Its liability after the settlement was less than the tax reserve it had set aside on its GAAP statements with respect to the audit.

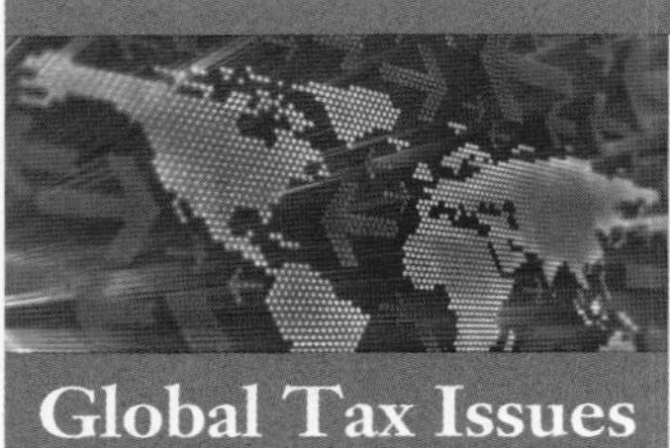

© Andrey Prokhorov, iStockphoto

Accounting for Income Taxes in International Standards

The FASB and the International Accounting Standards Board (IASB) have worked to move the GAAP and IFRS treatment of income taxes closer together in light of the proposed convergence of GAAP and IFRS. Both ASC 740 (SFAS 109) and IAS 12 (the IFRS guidance for income taxes) are based on a balance sheet approach.

Nevertheless, several significant differences exist between the two standards. These include the thresholds for recognition and approach to valuation allowances, the treatment of foreign subsidiaries and undistributed earnings, and the measurement of uncertain tax positions.[10]

EXAMPLE 6

PanCo, Inc., earns $100,000 in book income before tax and is subject to a 35% marginal Federal income tax rate. PanCo records a single temporary difference. Tax depreciation exceeds book depreciation by $20,000. Accordingly, PanCo's taxable income is $80,000 ($100,000 − $20,000 additional tax deduction). On its income tax return, PanCo reports total Federal tax expense of $28,000 ($80,000 × 35%). On its financial statement, PanCo reports a total tax expense of $35,000 ($100,000 × 35%). This $7,000 book-tax difference is the difference between the book and tax basis of the depreciable asset times the current corporate tax rate ($7,000 = $20,000 × 35%).

Although PanCo did not actually pay the $7,000 this year, in future years when the book-tax depreciation difference reverses, the $7,000 eventually is paid. Hence, the *future* income tax expense related to the current book income is reported in the current year. ■

The total book tax expense under ASC 740 (SFAS 109) is made up of both current and deferred components. The **current tax expense** theoretically represents the taxes actually payable to (or refund receivable from) the governmental authorities for the current period. Although an oversimplification, think of this amount as the actual check the taxpayer writes to the government (or refund received) for the current year. Keep in mind, though, that the current portion of the book income tax expense rarely matches the taxpayer's actual tax liability. Numerous items may lead to differences between actual current tax payments and the reported current tax expense. Figure 14.3 summarizes the computation of a corporation's current tax expense.

The deferred component of the book tax expense is called the **deferred tax expense** or **deferred tax benefit**. This component represents the future tax cost (or savings) connected with income reported in the current-period financial statement. Deferred tax expense or benefit is created as a result of temporary differences. More technically, ASC 740 (SFAS 109) adopts a **balance sheet approach** to measuring deferred taxes. Under this approach, the deferred tax expense or benefit is the change from one year to the next in the net **deferred tax liability** or **deferred tax asset**.

A deferred tax liability is the expected future tax liability related to current income (measured using enacted tax rates and rules).[11] A deferred tax liability is created in the following situations.

- An item is deductible for tax in the current period but is not expensed for book until some future period.

[10]One can keep up with the FASB and the IASB's work on the "Income Tax Project" by visiting the FASB website at **www.fasb.org** and searching for the "Technical Plan and Project Updates" section under "Projects."

[11]If the tax rate will be different in future years, the *enacted* future tax rate should be used in the computation.

FIGURE 14.3 Current Tax Expense*

	Pretax book income
±	Schedule M–1/M–3 adjustment
	Taxable income before NOLs
−	NOL carryforwards
	Taxable income
×	Applicable tax rate
	Current tax expense (provision) before tax credits
−	Tax credits
	Current tax expense (tax provision)

*Simplified calculation.

- Income is includible currently for book purposes but is not includible in taxable income until a future period.

In essence, a deferred tax liability is created when the book basis of an asset exceeds its tax basis (the opposite results in a deferred tax asset).

EXAMPLE 7

PJ Enterprises earns net income before depreciation of $500,000 in 2012 and $600,000 in 2013. PJ has a single depreciable asset acquired in 2012 for $80,000. For tax purposes, PJ may deduct $60,000 in depreciation expense for the first year and $20,000 in depreciation expense for the second year (i.e., it uses an accelerated method). For book purposes, assume that PJ depreciates the asset on a straight-line basis over two years ($40,000 depreciation expense per year).

2012

	Book		Tax
Income before depreciation	$500,000		$500,000
Depreciation	(40,000)		(60,000)
Income after depreciation	$460,000		$440,000
Corporate tax rate	× 35%		× 35%
Income tax expense/payable	$161,000		$154,000
Current tax expense	$154,000		
Deferred tax expense	$ 7,000		
Starting adjusted basis in depreciable asset	$ 80,000		$ 80,000
Ending adjusted basis in depreciable asset	(40,000)		(20,000)
Change in adjusted basis	$ 40,000		$ 60,000
Book-tax balance sheet difference		$20,000	
Corporate tax rate		× 35%	
Deferred tax liability		$ 7,000	

In this example, it is easy to "back into" the deferred tax expense amount of $7,000 by simply taking the difference between the tax payable per the tax return ($154,000) and the book tax expense ($161,000). This is referred to as the "APB 11" approach, as it applies to the method used before ASC 740 (SFAS 109). This may provide a quick check on the calculation in simple cases, but will not always be correct. The correct computation of the deferred tax expense is based on the difference between the book and tax asset basis numbers ($20,000) at the enacted corporate tax rate (35%).

2013

	Book		Tax
Income before depreciation	$600,000		$600,000
Depreciation	(40,000)		(20,000)
Income after depreciation	$560,000		$580,000
Corporate tax rate	× 35%		× 35%
Income tax expense/payable	$196,000		$203,000
Current tax expense	$203,000		
Deferred tax expense	($ 7,000)		
Starting adjusted basis in depreciable asset	$ 40,000		$ 20,000
Ending adjusted basis in depreciable asset	(−0−)		(−0−)
Change in adjusted basis	$ 40,000		$ 20,000
Book-tax balance sheet difference	↘	($20,000)	↙
Corporate tax rate		× 35%	
Deferred tax liability		($ 7,000)	

In 2013, the book-tax difference in the asset basis reverses, with a resulting reverse in the deferred tax liability account. ■

EXAMPLE 8

Continue with the facts in Example 7. The following journal entries record the book tax expense (provision) for each year. Notice that the book total tax expense combines the current amount (income tax payable) and the future amount (deferred tax liability).

2012 journal entry		
Income tax expense (provision)	$161,000	
Income tax payable		$154,000
Deferred tax liability		7,000
2013 journal entry		
Income tax expense (provision)	$196,000	
Deferred tax liability	7,000	
Income tax payable		$203,000

At the end of 2012, the balance sheet reflects a net deferred tax liability of $7,000. At the end of 2013, the balance sheet contains no deferred tax liability because the temporary difference that created the deferred tax liability has reversed itself. ■

A deferred tax asset is the expected future tax benefit related to current book income (measured using enacted tax rates and rules). A deferred tax asset is created in the following situations.

- An expense is deductible for book in the current period but is not deductible for tax until some future period.
- Income is includible in taxable income currently but is not includible in book income until a future period.

EXAMPLE 9

MollCo, Inc., earns net income before warranty expense of $400,000 in 2012 and $450,000 in 2013. In 2012, MollCo deducts $30,000 in warranty expense for book purposes related to expected warranty repairs. This warranty expense is not deductible for tax purposes until actually incurred. Assume that the $30,000 warranty expense is paid in 2013 and that this is MollCo's only temporary difference.

2012			
	Book		**Tax**
Income before warranty expense	$400,000		$400,000
Warranty expense	(30,000)		—
Income after warranty expense	$370,000		$400,000
Corporate tax rate	× 35%		× 35%
Income tax expense/payable	$129,500		$140,000
Current tax expense	$140,000		
Deferred tax expense	($ 10,500)		
Basis in warranty expense payable	$ 30,000		$ -0-
Book-tax balance sheet difference	↘	($30,000)	↙
Corporate tax rate		× 35%	
Deferred tax asset		($10,500)	

Once again, it is easy to "back into" the deferred tax expense amount of $10,500 simply by taking the difference between the tax expense per the tax return ($140,000) and the book tax expense ($129,500). However, the correct computation of the deferred tax expense is based on the difference between the book and tax basis in the warranty expense payable ($30,000) at the corporate tax rate (35%).

2013			
	Book		**Tax**
Income before warranty expense	$450,000		$450,000
Warranty expense	—		(30,000)
Income after depreciation	$450,000		$420,000
Corporate tax rate	× 35%		× 35%
Income tax expense/payable	$157,500		$147,000
Current tax expense	$147,000		
Deferred tax expense	$ 10,500		
Basis in warranty expense payable	$ -0-		$ 30,000
Book-tax balance sheet difference	↘	$30,000	↙
Corporate tax rate		× 35%	
Deferred tax asset		$10,500	

In 2013, the book-tax difference in warranty expense payable reverses, with a resulting elimination of the deferred tax asset account. ■

EXAMPLE 10

Continue with the facts in Example 9. The following journal entries record the book tax expense (provision) for each year. Notice that the book total tax expense combines the current amount (income tax payable) and the future amount (deferred tax asset).

2012 journal entry		
Income tax expense (provision)	$129,500	
Deferred tax asset	10,500	
Income tax payable		$140,000
2013 journal entry		
Income tax expense (provision)	$157,500	
Deferred tax asset		$ 10,500
Income tax payable		147,000

At the end of 2012, the balance sheet reflects a net deferred tax asset of $10,500. At the end of 2013, the balance sheet contains no deferred tax asset because the temporary difference that created the deferred tax asset has reversed. ■

FINANCIAL DISCLOSURE INSIGHTS Tax Losses and the Deferred Tax Asset

Although a current-year net operating loss (NOL) represents a failure of an entity's business model to some, others see it as an immediate tax refund. But when an NOL hits the balance sheet as a deferred tax asset, the story is not over. The NOL creates or increases a deferred tax asset that may or may not be used in future financial accounting reporting periods: the key question for a financial analyst is whether the entity will generate enough net revenue in future years to create a positive tax liability that can be offset by the NOL carryover amount.

For every reporting period, the managers of a business entity holding a loss carryforward must assess whether the loss is likely to be used to create cash flow in the future, as it offsets operating or other profits from future years. When it is more likely than not that a loss carryforward *will not be realized*, GAAP requires that a valuation allowance be created to reduce the deferred tax asset to a lower amount that is expected to be realized in the future. The valuation allowance is a contra-asset account (like accumulated depreciation on a fixed asset) against the deferred tax asset.

A valuation allowance against an NOL carryforward might be created when there is doubt as to the level of the entity's future net profits. The valuation allowance is reduced or eliminated, though, when it appears that the NOL will be fully realized due to any of the following.

- Future years' net income from operations or other activities.
- New product orders or contracts for business.
- The reversal of other temporary book-tax differences.
- An effective use of tax planning strategies.

Evidence that a loss carryforward might not be realized in the future includes the following.

- A series of operating losses in previous years for the reporting entity.
- A history of the entity's tax losses expiring unused.
- Open transactions, such as lawsuits and regulatory challenges, that might reduce future profits of the business.

The current version of IFRS does not allow for a valuation allowance. Under IAS 12, a deferred tax asset is recorded only when it is "probable" (a higher standard than GAAP's "more likely than not") that the deferred tax amount will be realized, and then only to the extent of that probable amount. Thus, no offsetting valuation allowance is needed.

Deferred tax assets and liabilities are reported on the balance sheet just as any other asset or liability would be. However, the interpretation of these assets and liabilities is quite different. Typically, an asset is "good" because it represents a claim on something of value, and a liability is "bad" because it represents a future claim against the corporation's assets. In the case of deferred tax assets and liabilities, the interpretation is reversed. Deferred tax liabilities are "good" because they represent an amount that may be paid to the government in the future. In essence, deferred tax liabilities are like an interest-free loan from the government with a due date perhaps many years in the future. Deferred tax assets, on the other hand, are future tax benefits and thus are similar to a receivable from the government that may not be received until many years in the future.

LO.3

Describe the purpose of the valuation allowance.

Valuation Allowance

Much of GAAP is based on the **conservatism principle**. That is, accounting rules are designed to provide assurance that assets are not overstated and liabilities are not understated. Current recognition of deferred tax liabilities does not require significant professional judgment because future tax liabilities always are expected to be settled. However, under ASC 740 (SFAS 109), deferred tax assets are recognized only when it is probable that the future tax benefits will be realized.

EXAMPLE 11

Warren, Inc., reported book income before tax of $2 million in 2012. Warren's taxable income is also $2 million (no temporary or permanent differences). Warren has a current U.S. income tax liability for 2012 of $700,000 before tax credits ($2 million × 35%).

During 2012, Warren paid $100,000 in foreign income taxes that it is not able to use as a credit on its 2012 tax return because of the foreign tax credit (FTC) limitation (see Chapter 9). Warren's auditors believe it is more likely than not that Warren will be able to use the $100,000 in FTCs within the next 10 years before they expire. Consequently, the future tax benefit of the FTCs is accounted for in the current-year book tax expense as a $100,000 future tax benefit.

The current and deferred tax expense are calculated as follows.

	Book	Tax
Income tax expense/payable	$600,000	$700,000
Current tax expense	$700,000	
Deferred tax expense (benefit)	($100,000)	

Warren makes the following journal entry to record the book income tax expense and deferred tax asset related to the expected use of the FTCs.

Income tax expense (provision)	$600,000	
Deferred tax asset	100,000	
Income tax payable		$700,000

Because Warren is able to record the benefit of the future FTCs, its effective tax rate is 30% ($600,000 tax expense/$2 million book income before tax). ■

When a deferred tax asset does not meet the *more likely than not* threshold for recognition, ASC 740 (SFAS 109) requires that a **valuation allowance** be created. The valuation allowance is a contra-asset account that offsets all or a portion of the deferred tax asset.

EXAMPLE 12

Assume that the auditors in Example 11 believe that Warren will be able to use only $40,000 of the FTCs, with the remaining $60,000 expiring. In this case, the future tax benefit recognized currently should be only $40,000 rather than the full $100,000. To implement this reduction in the deferred tax asset, Warren must record a valuation allowance of $60,000, resulting in a book tax expense of $660,000.

	Book	Tax
Income tax expense/payable	$660,000	$700,000
Current tax expense	$700,000	
Deferred tax expense (benefit)	($ 40,000)	

Warren makes the following journal entry to record the book income tax expense and deferred tax asset related to the expected use of the FTCs.

Income tax expense (provision)	$660,000	
Deferred tax asset	100,000	
Valuation allowance		$ 60,000
Income tax payable		700,000

Warren must reduce the deferred tax asset by $60,000, which increases its effective tax rate to 33% ($660,000 tax expense/$2 million book income before tax), compared with the 30% effective tax rate in Example 11. ■

To determine whether a valuation allowance is required, both positive and negative evidence must be evaluated. Negative evidence (i.e., evidence suggesting that the deferred tax asset will not be realized) includes the following.

- History of losses.
- Expected future losses.

- Short carryback/carryforward periods.
- History of tax credits expiring unused.

Positive evidence (i.e., support for realizing the current benefit of future tax savings) includes the following.

- Strong earnings history.
- Existing contracts.
- Unrealized appreciation in assets.
- Sales backlog of profitable orders.

The valuation allowance is examined for appropriateness each year. The allowance may be increased or decreased if facts and circumstances change in the future.

LO.4

Interpret the disclosure information contained in the financial statements.

Tax Disclosures in the Financial Statements

As illustrated earlier, any temporary differences create deferred tax liabilities or deferred tax assets and these amounts appear in the corporation's balance sheet.

The Balance Sheet

As with any asset or liability, these accounts are classified as either current or noncurrent, based on the assets or liabilities that created the temporary difference. If the deferred tax liability or asset is not related to any asset, then the classification is based on the expected reversal period.

EXAMPLE 13

JenCo, Inc., has a deferred tax liability generated because tax depreciation exceeds book depreciation on manufacturing equipment. Because the equipment is classified as a noncurrent asset, the deferred tax liability is classified as noncurrent. JenCo also reports a deferred tax asset related to bad debt expenses deductible for book purposes but not yet deductible for tax purposes. Because the bad debt expense is related to accounts receivable, a current asset, the associated deferred tax asset is classified as current.

If JenCo incurs an NOL, a deferred tax asset is created, because of the future tax benefit provided by the NOL deduction. The NOL is not related to any specific asset or liability. Accordingly, the deferred tax asset is classified based on when the corporation expects to use the NOL. If the expected use is more than one year in the future, the deferred tax asset is classified as noncurrent. ■

A corporation may have both deferred tax assets and liabilities, current and noncurrent. The corporation reports the *net* current deferred tax assets or liabilities and the *net* noncurrent deferred tax assets or liabilities.

THE BIG PICTURE

EXAMPLE 14

Return to the facts of *The Big Picture* on p. 14-1. Arctic Corporation holds the following deferred tax asset and liability accounts for the current year.

Current deferred tax assets	$50,000
Current deferred tax liabilities	72,000
Noncurrent deferred tax assets	93,000
Noncurrent deferred tax liabilities	28,000

On its balance sheet, Arctic reports a $22,000 current net deferred tax liability ($72,000 − $50,000) and a $65,000 noncurrent net deferred tax asset ($93,000 − $28,000).

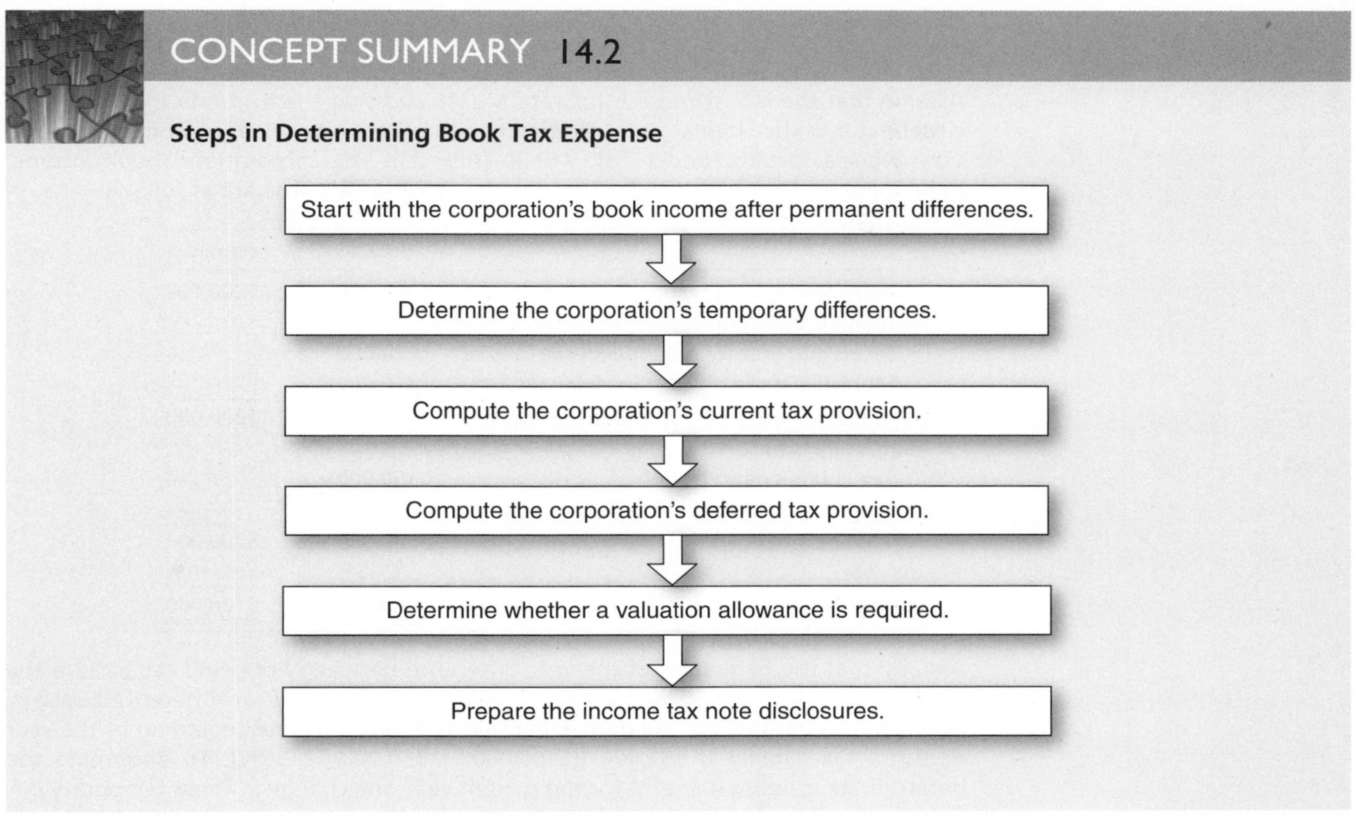

CONCEPT SUMMARY 14.2
Steps in Determining Book Tax Expense
Start with the corporation's book income after permanent differences.
Determine the corporation's temporary differences.
Compute the corporation's current tax provision.
Compute the corporation's deferred tax provision.
Determine whether a valuation allowance is required.
Prepare the income tax note disclosures.

© Andrey Prokhorov, iStockphoto

The Income Statement

In its income statement, a corporation reports a total income tax expense that consists of both the current tax expense (or benefit) and the deferred tax expense (or benefit). The tax expense must be allocated to income from continuing operations, discontinued operations, extraordinary items, prior-period adjustments, and the cumulative effect of accounting changes. Additional disclosures are required for the tax expense allocated to income from continuing operations (e.g., current versus deferred, benefits of NOL deductions, and changes in valuation allowances).

Financial Statement Footnotes

The income tax note contains a wealth of information, including the following.

- Breakdown of income between domestic and foreign.
- Detailed analysis of the provision for income tax expense.
- Detailed analysis of deferred tax assets and liabilities.
- Effective tax **rate reconciliation** (dollar amount or percentage).
- Information on use of ASC 740-30 (APB 23) for the earnings of foreign subsidiaries.
- Discussion of significant tax matters.

Rate Reconciliation

The purpose of the rate reconciliation is to demonstrate how a corporation's actual book effective tax rate relates to its "hypothetical tax rate" as if the book income were taxed at the U.S. corporate rate of 35 percent. Although similar to Schedule M–1 or M–3, the tax note rate reconciliation generally reports only differences triggered by permanent differences. As discussed in the benchmarking section later in this chapter, an analysis of the rate reconciliation can provide substantial clues as to the tax planning strategies adopted (or not adopted) by a company.

The steps in determining a corporation's income tax expense for book purposes are summarized in Concept Summary 14.2.

Illustrations

EXAMPLE 15

BoxCo, Inc., a domestic corporation, owns 100% of PaperCo, Ltd., an Irish corporation. Assume that the U.S. corporate tax rate is 35% and that the Irish rate is 10%. As discussed later in the chapter, BoxCo reports neither book nor taxable income for PaperCo's overseas profits, under ASC 740-30 (APB 23). The corporations' book income, permanent and temporary differences, and current tax expense are as follows.

	BoxCo	PaperCo
Book income before tax	$300,000	$200,000
Permanent differences		
Meals and entertainment expense	20,000	—
Municipal bond interest income	(50,000)	—
Book income after permanent differences	$270,000	$200,000
Temporary differences		
Tax > book depreciation	(50,000)	—
Book > tax bad debt expense	10,000	—
Taxable income	$230,000	$200,000
Tax rate	× 35%	× 10%
Current tax expense	$ 80,500	$ 20,000

Assume that the beginning-of-the-year difference between book and tax basis in the depreciable assets is $150,000 and that the beginning-of-the-year difference between book and tax basis in the bad debt expense is $50,000. Thus, the beginning-of-the-year deferred tax liability is $35,000 [($150,000 − $50,000) × 35%]. To determine the deferred tax expense (benefit) for the current year, the change in these temporary differences from the beginning to the end of the year must be determined and then multiplied by the appropriate tax rate.

Temporary Differences	Beginning of Year	Change	End of Year
Depreciation	$150,000	$ 50,000	$200,000
Bad debts	(50,000)	(10,000)	(60,000)
Total temporary differences	$100,000	$ 40,000	$140,000
Tax rate	× 35%	× 35%	× 35%
	$ 35,000	$ 14,000	$ 49,000

The deferred tax liability increased by $14,000 for the year. Consequently, BoxCo's total tax expense for book purposes is $114,500.

Current tax expense	
Domestic	$ 80,500
Foreign	20,000
Deferred tax expense	
Domestic	14,000
Foreign	—
Total tax expense	$114,500

The journal entry to record the book income tax expense is constructed as follows.

Income tax expense (provision)	$114,500	
Income tax payable		$100,500
Deferred tax liability		14,000

BoxCo's book income is $500,000 (the combined book income of both BoxCo and PaperCo). The effective tax rate reconciliation is based on this book income, with the dollar amounts in the table representing the tax expense (benefit) related to the item and the percentage representing the tax expense (benefit) as a percentage of book income.

For example, the municipal bond interest of $50,000 reduces tax liability by $17,500 ($50,000 × 35%). This $17,500 as a percentage of the $500,000 book income is 3.5%.

	Effective Tax Rate Reconciliation	
	$	**%**
Hypothetical tax at U.S. rate	$175,000	35.0
Disallowed meals and entertainment expense	7,000	1.4
Municipal bond interest	(17,500)	(3.5)
Foreign income taxed at less than U.S. rate	(50,000)	(10.0)
Income tax expense (provision)	$114,500	22.9

Only permanent differences appear in the rate reconciliation. Temporary differences do not affect the *total* book income tax expense; they simply affect the amount of the tax expense that is current versus deferred. ■

EXAMPLE 16

Assume the same facts as Example 15, except that a new Federal income tax law is enacted before the end of the current year that will increase the corporate tax rate to 40% beginning next year. In this case, multiply the year-end total temporary differences of $140,000 by 40% rather than 35%. This results in an increase in the deferred tax liability of $21,000.

Temporary Differences	Beginning of Year	End of Year	Effect
Depreciation	$150,000	$200,000	
Bad debts	(50,000)	(60,000)	
Total temporary differences	$100,000	$140,000	
Tax rate	× 35%	× 40%	
Deferred tax liability	$ 35,000	$ 56,000	$21,000

The current-year deferred tax liability amount is a function of both the change in temporary differences at the enacted rate ($40,000 × 40%) and the additional 5% tax on the beginning temporary differences [$100,000 × (40% − 35%)]. This example illustrates the need for the "balance sheet" approach of ASC 740 (SFAS 109). Use of the APB 11 shortcut method would have produced the wrong answer with these facts. ■

EXAMPLE 17

LibbyCo, Inc., is a U.S. corporation that operates retail outlets selling eyeglasses. During the current year, LibbyCo reported pretax book income of $1,800. LibbyCo's U.S. corporate tax rate is 34%; it has no NOLs, credits, or foreign or state income taxes; and it is not subject to the alternative minimum tax.

LibbyCo's tax and book balance sheet is summarized below, along with book-tax basis differences for all assets and liabilities.

	Tax Debit/ (Credit)	Book Debit/ (Credit)	Difference
Assets			
Cash	$ 2,000	$ 2,000	$ –0–
Accounts receivable	5,400	5,400	–0–
Buildings	400,000	400,000	–0–
Accumulated depreciation	(315,000)	(330,000)	15,000
Furniture & fixtures	100,000	100,000	–0–
Accumulated depreciation	(70,000)	(45,000)	(25,000)
Total assets	$122,400	$132,400	($ 10,000)

	Tax Debit/ (Credit)	Book Debit/ (Credit)	Difference
Liabilities			
Accrued vacation pay	$ –0–	($ 25,000)	$25,000
Note payable	(16,400)	(16,400)	–0–
Total liabilities	($ 16,400)	($ 41,400)	$25,000
Stockholders' Equity			
Paid-in capital	($ 6,000)	($ 6,000)	
Retained earnings	(100,000)	(85,000)	
Total liabilities and stockholders' equity	($ 122,400)	($132,400)	

The difference between the book and tax basis of these assets and liabilities is the cumulative difference from all prior years. These differences are *not* the Schedule M–1 or M–3 differences. To determine the temporary differences for the current year and any associated deferred tax liability or deferred tax asset, these differences are compared to the basis differences at the beginning of the year.

Assume the following beginning-of-the-year book-tax differences. The end-of-the-year differences are calculated above. The differences are classified based on whether they produce a future tax benefit (*deductible temporary differences*) or a future tax cost (*taxable temporary differences*).

	Beginning of Year	Current-Year Difference	End of Year
Deductible Temporary Differences			
Buildings—accumulated depreciation	$10,000	$ 5,000	$ 15,000
Accrued vacation pay	17,000	8,000	25,000
Subtotal	$27,000	$13,000	$ 40,000
Applicable tax rate	× 34%		× 34%
Gross deferred tax asset	$ 9,180		$ 13,600
	↘		↙
Change in deferred tax asset		$ 4,420	
Taxable Temporary Differences			
Furniture & fixtures—accumulated depreciation	($22,000)	($ 3,000)	($ 25,000)
Subtotal	($22,000)	($ 3,000)	($ 25,000)
Applicable tax rate	× 34%		× 34%
Gross deferred tax liability	($ 7,480)		($ 8,500)
	↘		↙
Change in deferred tax liability		($ 1,020)	
Net deferred tax asset / (deferred tax liability)	$ 1,700	$ 3,400	$ 5,100

The journal entry to record the deferred tax asset is constructed as follows.

Deferred tax asset	$3,400	
Income tax expense		$3,400

In addition to the temporary differences identified above, LibbyCo also reported two permanent differences between book and taxable income. It earned $1,400 in tax-exempt municipal bond interest, and it incurred $2,000 in nondeductible meals and entertainment expense. With this information, the current tax expense is determined as follows.

Pretax book income	$ 1,800
Book-tax adjustments	
Permanent items	
Tax-exempt income	(1,400)
Nondeductible meals and entertainment	2,000
Temporary differences	
Building depreciation	5,000
Accrued vacation pay	8,000
Furniture & fixtures depreciation	(3,000)
Taxable income	$12,400
Current tax expense (34%)	$ 4,216

The building depreciation for book purposes exceeds tax depreciation, the furniture and fixtures depreciation for tax purposes exceeds book depreciation, and the accrued vacation pay is deductible for book purposes but is not yet deductible for tax. These current-year temporary differences, combined with the two permanent items, also constitute the Schedule M–3 differences.

The journal entry to record the current tax expense is constructed as follows.

Income tax expense	$4,216	
Current income tax payable		$4,216

Assuming that no valuation allowance is required, the effect of these entries on the income statement is as follows. The current-year change in the deferred tax asset allows the book tax expense to be reduced by $3,400, producing a total book tax expense of $816 ($4,216 − $3,400).

Net income before tax	$1,800
Provision for income tax expense	(816)
Net income after tax	$ 984

The income tax footnote rate reconciliation is presented as follows.

Tax on book income at statutory rate	$612	34.00%
Tax-exempt income	(476)	(26.44)%
Nondeductible meals and entertainment	680	37.77%
Provision for income tax expense	$816	45.33%

With these facts, the short-cut APB 11 method below produces the same results as the ASC 740 (SFAS 109) method. Note that this would not be true had there been changes to LibbyCo's applicable tax rate from the prior year, or if a valuation allowance had been required.

Pretax book income	$ 1,800
Permanent items	
Tax-exempt income	(1,400)
Nondeductible meals and entertainment	2,000
Book equivalent to taxable income	$ 2,400
Statutory tax rate	× 34%
Total book tax expense	$ 816

Special Issues

Financial Accounting for Tax Uncertainties

LO.5

Identify the GAAP treatment concerning tax uncertainties and unrepatriated foreign earnings.

Companies take positions in their tax returns that may not ultimately survive the scrutiny of the IRS or other tax authorities. If a taxpayer loses the benefit of a favorable tax position after a future audit, the loss of this tax benefit may unfavorably affect the company's financial statement tax expense in that future year. The additional tax cost will become part of the current tax expense, yet the income this tax is related to would have been reported in the initial year. This result wreaks havoc with a company's effective tax rate.

To avoid this increase in effective tax rate, companies may book a reserve (or "cushion") for the uncertain tax position in the initial year. That is, rather than book the entire tax benefit (and thus reduce tax expense in the current year), the company may book only a portion (or none) of the tax benefit. If the company later loses the actual tax benefit upon audit, to the extent the additional tax imposed is charged against the reserve (or "cushion"), the additional tax does not affect the future-year tax expense. If the company's tax position is not challenged in the future (or the company successfully defends any challenge), the reserve can be released. This release reduces the current tax expense in the future (release) year and lowers the company's effective tax rate in that year.

Prior to 2006, SFAS 5, "Accounting for Contingencies," addressed the accounting for uncertain events in the financial statements. Some of the SFAS 5 rules addressed the use of a required reserve related to taxes. Even with SFAS 5, the FASB was concerned that companies too freely used the tax reserve as a "cookie jar" to shift earnings from one period to another. To add more structure to the accounting for tax reserves, in July 2006, the FASB released Financial Interpretation No. 48 (FIN 48), "Accounting for Uncertainty in Income Taxes." The approach required under ASC 740-10 (FIN 48) results in significantly more disclosure about uncertain tax positions by companies.

Application of ASC 740-10 (FIN 48) essentially is a two-step process—recognition and measurement. First, a tax benefit from an uncertain tax position may be *recognized* in the financial statements only if it is more likely than not (a greater than 50 percent likelihood) that the position would be sustained on its technical merits. That is, audit or detection risk cannot be considered. This first step determines whether any of the tax benefit is recognized. If the uncertain tax position meets the more likely than not threshold, the second step is to determine the amount of the tax benefit to report.

Measurement is based on the probabilities associated with the position not being challenged or being challenged with a negotiated settlement or litigation. All of the relevant facts and circumstances as of the financial statement reporting date should be used in determining the probability of the ultimate outcome.

The recognition and measurement of uncertain tax positions must be reassessed at each reporting date. ASC 740-10 (FIN 48) requires a reconciliation of the beginning and ending balances of the unrecognized tax benefits and a discussion of potential changes in these unrecognized tax benefits that might occur over the next 12 months.

Earnings of Foreign Subsidiaries

As discussed earlier, a corporate group's financial statements include both domestic and foreign controlled subsidiaries. However, foreign corporations, even those controlled by U.S. shareholders, are not part of a U.S. consolidated tax return. Consequently, U.S. taxpayers can achieve deferral of current U.S. taxes on foreign income if they operate their foreign activities through foreign subsidiary corporations in jurisdictions with lower tax rates than the United States (see Chapter 9). Although the *actual* U.S. taxes on foreign corporations' profits are deferred, the reported effective tax rate for financial statement purposes may not reflect this deferral, because ASC 740 (SFAS 109) requires that a corporate group report both current and deferred income tax expense.

EXAMPLE 18

USCo, a domestic corporation, operates a manufacturing facility in Singapore through a Singapore corporation. Assume that the U.S. tax rate is 35% and that the Singapore tax rate is 6%. For the current year, USCo earns $600,000 in taxable income. The Singapore corporation earns $400,000 in taxable income from its operations, pays $24,000 in taxes to Singapore, and makes no distributions to its U.S. parent. The Singapore corporation is not taxed in the United States because it is not a U.S. person and has no activities in the United States. USCo is not taxed on the Singapore profits because it has not received any distributions of these profits. Accordingly, USCo has achieved deferral and reduced its worldwide cash tax costs.

However, for financial statement purposes, the USCo group includes the $400,000 in Singapore profits in its net income. It reports both the Singapore tax and any *potential* U.S. tax (after allowable FTCs) as its total tax expense.

U.S. Tax Return		**Potential U.S. Tax on Non-U.S. Income**	
Income	$600,000	Income	$400,000
Tax rate	× 35%	Tax rate	× 35%
U.S. tax	$210,000	Total tax	$140,000
		Foreign tax credit	(24,000)
		Net U.S. tax	$116,000

Consequently, the total tax expense for financial statement purposes is $350,000. Keep in mind that the actual deferred tax liability is determined by multiplying the difference in the book and tax basis of the foreign subsidiary by the U.S. tax rate. There is a book-tax difference because the tax basis in the subsidiary is the original cost and the book basis has increased under the equity method of accounting by the equity in the subsidiary's earnings.

Current U.S. tax	$210,000
Current foreign tax	24,000
Deferred U.S. tax	116,000
Total tax expense	$350,000

The financial statement effective tax rate on global income is 35% ($350,000 total tax expense/$1,000,000 net income). Thus, although USCo paid only $234,000 in taxes, its after-tax book income does not reflect the savings generated from operating in Singapore, a low-tax country. ■

ASC 740-30 (APB 23) provides an exception to ASC 740 (SFAS 109) for income from foreign subsidiaries.[12] If a corporation documents that it is **permanently reinvesting** the earnings of its foreign subsidiaries outside the United States, the corporation does not record as an expense any future U.S. income tax the corporation may pay on such earnings.

EXAMPLE 19

Assume that USCo, in Example 18, uses ASC 740-30 (APB 23) to avoid reporting the $116,000 in deferred taxes. Because USCo plans to reinvest its Singapore earnings indefinitely outside the United States, it is not required to include the deferred U.S. taxes as part of its total tax expense. Thus, USCo's total financial statement income remains $1 million, but its total tax expense is only $234,000 (the taxes currently paid to the United States and Singapore). The resulting financial statement effective tax rate is 23.4% ($234,000/$1,000,000), and the USCo group's after-tax book income reflects the Singapore tax savings. ■

Using ASC 740-30 (APB 23) is not an "all or nothing" decision. It can be adopted in some years and not others. Even within a year it may be used for only a portion of foreign subsidiary earnings.

THE BIG PICTURE

EXAMPLE 20

Return to the facts of *The Big Picture* on p. 14-1. Recall from Example 1 that Arctic Corporation has a wholly owned foreign subsidiary, Hurricane, Ltd. Assume that Arctic also owns 100% of another foreign corporation, Typhoon, Ltd. Arctic can choose to apply ASC 740-30 (APB 23) to both of its foreign subsidiaries in 2011 and to only Hurricane in 2012. In 2013, Arctic can choose to use ASC 740-30 (APB 23) for 40% of Hurricane's earnings and 80% of Typhoon's earnings.

[12]Formerly *Opinion No. 23—Accounting for Income Taxes—Special Areas,* Accounting Principles Board.

ASC 740-30 (APB 23) is a major issue only when the foreign subsidiary is taxed at rates below the applicable U.S. tax rate. Otherwise, there is no deferral potential. However, using ASC 740-30 (APB 23) may limit the availability of creating deferred tax assets when foreign subsidiaries pay taxes at greater than the U.S. rate. Then the multinational group potentially could use its excess foreign taxes as credits on the U.S. tax return (see Chapter 9).

EXAMPLE 21

AmeriCo, a domestic corporation, operates a manufacturing facility in the Netherlands through Vander, a Dutch corporation. Assume that the U.S. tax rate is 35% and that the Netherlands tax rate also is 35%. For the current year, AmeriCo earns $400,000 in taxable income. Vander earns $300,000 in taxable income from its operations, pays $105,000 in taxes to the Netherlands, and makes no distributions to its U.S. parent.

Vander is not taxed in the United States because it is not a U.S. person and has no activities in the United States. AmeriCo is not taxed on the Netherlands profits because it has not received any distributions of these profits.

For financial statement purposes, the AmeriCo group includes the $300,000 of Vander's profits in its net income. It reports both the Dutch tax and any *potential* U.S. tax (after allowable FTCs) as its total tax expense.

U.S. Tax Return		Potential U.S. Tax on Foreign Income	
Income	$400,000	Income	$ 300,000
Tax rate	× 35%	Tax rate	× 35%
U.S. tax	$140,000	Total tax	$ 105,000
		FTC	(105,000)
		Net U.S. tax	$ –0–

Consequently, the total tax expense for financial statement purposes is $245,000.

Current U.S. tax	$140,000
Current foreign tax	105,000
Total tax expense	$245,000

The financial statement effective tax rate on global income is 35% ($245,000 total tax expense/$700,000 book net income). Even without ASC 740-30 (APB 23), there is no deferred U.S. tax on the Dutch income, because AmeriCo would pay no additional U.S. tax upon the repatriation of Vander's earnings after its use of the available FTC.

Note that application of a valuation allowance against the deferred tax asset created by the FTC would affect the book effective tax rate. ■

ETHICS & EQUITY Disclosing Aggressive Tax Positions

In 2012, Dickinson, Inc., reports an effective tax rate of 36 percent, and Badger, Inc., reports an effective tax rate of 21 percent. Both companies are domestic and operate in the same industry. Your initial examination of the financial statements of the two companies indicates that Badger apparently is doing a better job with its tax planning, explaining the difference in effective tax rates. Consequently, all else being equal, you decide to invest in Badger.

In a subsequent year, it comes to light that Badger had used some very aggressive tax planning techniques to reduce its reported tax expense. After examination by the IRS, Badger loses the tax benefits and reports a very large tax expense in that year. Over this multiple-year period, it turns out that Dickinson had the lower effective tax rate after all.

Do you believe Badger was ethical in not fully disclosing the aggressiveness of its tax positions in its 2012 financial statement? How does ASC 740 (FIN 48) affect Badger's disclosure requirement? Does ASC 740 (FIN 48) still leave room for ethical decision making by management in determining how to report uncertain tax positions?

14.3 Benchmarking

LO.6

Use financial statement income tax information to benchmark a company's tax position.

As the *outcome* of the taxpayer's activities combined with the tax professional's advice, the income tax expense amount may appear to be of little interest to anyone beyond the taxpayer that makes the payment and the government agencies that collect it. The tax year is over, the transactions completed, and the final costs tallied. Still, this historical tax information may prove very valuable. A company's income tax expense is one of the single largest expense items on its income statement, and understanding the components of this expense is a critical activity for the tax professional.

Consider a typical baseball game. Two teams meet, interact following a specific set of rules, and ultimately complete the game generating a final score. Of course, the final score is of immediate interest to the teams and the fans, but once the game is over, the score and associated statistics (runs, hits, and errors) are relegated to the history books. Yet these statistics still are quite useful. A team coach may use the game statistics to evaluate the strengths and weaknesses of the players to assist in improving performance. Other teams in the league may use the statistics to develop strategies for upcoming games. Players can use the statistics to benchmark themselves against their performance in prior games or against players in other teams. In short, there is a wealth of information in these historical data.

A taxpayer's reported income tax expense likewise is a valuable source of information for the company, its tax advisers, and its competitors. The reported information provides clues about a company's operational and tax planning strategies.

Companies may benchmark their tax situation to other years' results or to other companies in the same industry. The starting point for a **benchmarking** exercise usually is the data from the income tax note rate reconciliation.

Dynamic Benchmarking

Figure 14.4 contains the tax rate reconciliation information from the income tax notes for two recent years of Sears Holding Corporation (Sears) and Wal-Mart Stores, Inc. (Wal-Mart). Both companies are listed on the New York Stock Exchange, are in the same industry, and operate both inside and outside the United States. Although the income and tax expense amounts of both companies are quite different in magnitude, the tax amounts are converted to percentage of income numbers for comparability purposes. In year 1, Sears reported an effective tax rate that was 12 percentage points higher than Wal-Mart's rate. In year 2, Sears's effective tax rate was 4.9 points below Wal-Mart's rate. What factors created these differences? Rate reconciliation information can provide clues.

Sears reported a higher effective tax rate in year 1 because its state and local income tax burden is higher and because it suffered a goodwill impairment (the goodwill write-off is not tax deductible). These increase items were offset by reductions caused by certain basis differences in a domestic subsidiary, larger benefits from tax credits, and a larger benefit from a favorable resolution of tax matters.

When comparing effective tax rates, it is important to consider which components of the effective tax rate produce one-time effects. For example, for year 2, the effective tax rates of both companies were much more similar (Sears was about 5 percentage points lower than Wal-Mart). In particular, without the large effects of nondeductible goodwill and the domestic subsidiary basis difference, Sears approached the effective tax rate of Wal-Mart. Consequently, it appears that there are no long-term structural differences in the tax burdens faced by the two companies. This is not surprising given that both companies are incorporated in the United States, are in the same industry, and operate in many of the same jurisdictions.

However, items such as the nondeductible goodwill difference do indicate that there may be potential fundamental differences in how Sears's management deals with growth via expansion rather than acquisitions. It is acquired goodwill rather than the home-grown sort that faces potential impairment. The Sears example

FIGURE 14.4 **Tax Rate Reconciliation for Sears and Wal-Mart**

	Sears		Wal-Mart	
	Year 2	Year 1	Year 2	Year 1
Hypothetical tax (benefit) at U.S. Federal rate	35.0%	35.0%	35.0%	35.0%
State and local income taxes, net of Federal benefit	6.0	7.2	1.9	1.7
Tax credits	(3.0)	(6.3)		
Resolution of income tax matters	(6.2)	(6.8)		
Basis difference in domestic subsidiary	—	(30.2)		
Non-U.S. income taxed at different rates	(0.9)	(2.3)	(1.7)	(1.6)
Nondeductible goodwill	—	50.0		
Other	(1.6)	(0.4)	(1.0)	(1.0)
	29.3%	46.2%	34.2%	34.1%
Book income before tax (in millions)	$420.0	$184.0	$20,898.0	$20,158.0

shows that the results of past and current strategic decisions eventually may show up in the income tax footnote.

Refining the Analysis

In addition to comparing effective tax rates, companies can compare levels of deferred tax assets and liabilities.

EXAMPLE 22

Akiko Enterprises reports a net deferred tax liability of $280,000. Asare, Inc., a company in the same industry, reports a net deferred tax liability of $860,000. Seeing deferred tax liabilities on the balance sheet indicates that both companies are benefiting from deferring actual tax payments (essentially, an interest-free loan from the government). At first glance, it may appear that Asare is doing better in this regard. However, what if Akiko holds total assets of $2.6 million and Asare's assets total $19.2 million? This information indicates that Akiko has 10.8% ($280,000/$2.6 million) of its total assets "financed" with an interest-free loan from the government, while Asare has only 4.5% ($860,000/$19.2 million) of its assets "financed" with its deferred tax liabilities. ■

A company may do a more refined benchmarking analysis by examining each component of its deferred tax assets and liabilities as a percentage of total assets. For example, a company can examine how the deferred tax assets or liabilities related to property, plant, and equipment compare with those of its competitors. The nature of the components of deferred tax liabilities and deferred tax assets becomes quite important in a benchmarking analysis.

EXAMPLE 23

LinCo reports total book income before taxes of $10 million and a total tax expense of $3.2 million, producing a 32% effective tax rate. TuckCo also reports book income before taxes of $10 million. TuckCo's total tax expense is $3.1 million, producing an effective tax rate of 31%. At first glance, it appears that both companies are similar with regard to effective tax rates. The total tax expense divided between current and deferred is as follows (in millions).

	LinCo	TuckCo
Current tax expense	$ 4.1	$ 4.2
Deferred tax benefit	(0.9)	(1.1)
Total tax expense	$ 3.2	$ 3.1

Again, it appears that both companies have created deferred tax assets in the current year that are expected to produce tax savings in the future. Knowing the nature of the underlying deferred tax assets will add greatly to one's interpretation of the effective tax rates.

The deferred tax asset generating LinCo's $900,000 expected future tax savings is the use of an NOL carryover. The deferred tax asset generating TuckCo's expected future tax savings is generated by different book and tax methods in accounting for warranty expense. This additional information reveals that LinCo has previously incurred losses, and it is critical that it earn future income so as to use the NOL.

This is quite different from TuckCo's situation, which reveals only that common differences in accounting methods exist. Although the tax positions of LinCo and TuckCo seem very similar on the surface, a closer look reveals a striking difference. ■

EXAMPLE 24

WageCo and SalaryCo are both in the same industry, and both report a 38% effective tax rate. Their book income and current, deferred, and total tax expense were reported as follows.

	WageCo	SalaryCo
Book income before tax	$1,500,000	$2,300,000
Current tax expense	$ 980,000	$ 24,000
Deferred tax expense (benefit)	(410,000)	850,000
Total tax expense	$ 570,000	$ 874,000
Effective tax rate	38%	38%

WageCo's total tax expense is highly dependent on the current recognition of future tax savings of $410,000. SalaryCo appears to be deferring a substantial portion of its tax expense to future years. Although both companies report a 38% effective tax rate, the details indicate that the two companies face very different tax situations. ■

Sustaining the Tax Rate

It is important in benchmarking exercises to remove the effect of one-time items in comparing sustainable effective tax rates across time or companies. Examples of one-time items include restructuring costs, legal settlements, and IRS or other tax liability settlements. A one-time item may seem beneficial or detrimental to a company's effective tax rate. But the very nature of such an item implies that it has little to do with the company's long-term sustainable tax costs.

EXAMPLE 25

MetalCo and IronCo are both in the same industry and report the following tax rate reconciliations in their tax footnotes.

	MetalCo	IronCo
Hypothetical tax at U.S. rate	35.0%	35.0%
State and local taxes	2.2	2.1
Foreign income taxed at less than U.S. rate	(6.2)	(6.1)
Tax Court settlement on disputed tax issue	(18.6)	—
Effective tax rate	12.4%	31.0%

Although it appears that MetalCo has a significantly lower effective tax rate (12.4%) than IronCo's 31%, removing MetalCo's one-time item related to the court settlement indicates that both companies have a 31% effective tax rate (12.4% + 18.6% = 31%). ■

Uses of Benchmarking Analysis

Benchmarking is part science and part art. A useful analysis requires both an accountant's knowledge of how the underlying financial statements are constructed, including arriving at the appropriate tax expense, and a detective's sense of where to look and what questions to ask.

In addition to benchmarking, financial analysts perform an important function for the capital markets in their detailed analyses of companies. The analyst combs through both the financial reports and other information about a company to produce an informed opinion on how a company is performing. Analysts' earnings forecasts often are an important metric to examine when making decisions about investing in companies.

An experienced financial analyst typically will have a good handle on interpreting financial statement information. However, even experienced analysts will often "punt" when it comes to interpreting the tax information contained in a financial statement, preferring to look at net income before taxes (or even EBITDA, earnings before interest, taxes, depreciation, and amortization). A great deal of useful information about a company is contained in its tax footnote, and analysts might have an edge if they work at understanding the mysteries of taxes in the financial statements.

14.4 Tax Planning

Releasing Valuation Allowances

When a corporation records a valuation allowance, it loses the ability to recognize the benefit of future tax savings in the current period. However, all is not lost if the taxpayer can demonstrate that facts and circumstances have changed. For example, if a taxpayer generates an NOL, it records a deferred tax asset for the future tax savings related to using the NOL. However, if the evidence suggests that it is more likely than not that the NOL will expire unused, a valuation allowance must be recorded.

To reduce this valuation allowance, the taxpayer must demonstrate that there will be future taxable income sufficient to absorb the NOL within the carryforward period. Sources of future taxable income include reversals of temporary differences that will produce future taxable income and other sources of future profits. Taxpayers also may demonstrate that the adoption of new tax planning strategies will allow the use of deferred tax assets.

THE BIG PICTURE

EXAMPLE 26

Return to the facts of *The Big Picture* on p. 14-1. Arctic Corporation's $3 million deferred tax asset for an NOL carryforward has been offset by a $1 million valuation allowance, due to doubts over the levels of future sales and profitability. But this year, Arctic completed improvements to its inventory management system that are likely to increase the contribution margin of every product that Arctic sells. In addition, two of Arctic's largest customers have secured financing that will relieve the financial difficulties that have restricted them. In fact, Arctic just received purchase orders from those customers that will increase unit sales by 20% over the next 18 months. As a result, Arctic's auditors now support a release of $200,000 of the valuation allowance in the current quarter.

EXAMPLE 27

Assume that Warren, Inc., from Example 12, adopts new planning strategies in 2013 that will allow it ultimately to use all $100,000 of its FTC carryforward. Warren earns $2.3 million in book income before tax and reports $2.3 million in taxable income in 2013 (i.e., no permanent or temporary differences). The current tax expense is $805,000 ($2.3 million × 35%).

Based on new evidence (implementation of tax planning strategies), the auditors determine that the entire $100,000 in FTCs will be used in the future before expiration. Accordingly, the $60,000 valuation allowance from 2012 is "released," and the tax benefit of this release affects the 2013 financial results as follows.

	Book	Tax
Income tax expense/payable	$745,000	$805,000
Current tax expense	$805,000	
Deferred tax expense	($ 60,000)	

Warren makes the following journal entry to record the book income tax expense and valuation allowance release related to the expected use of the FTCs.

Income tax expense (provision)	$745,000	
Valuation allowance	60,000	
Income tax payable		$805,000

Warren's effective tax rate for 2013 is 32.4% ($745,000/$2.3 million). Without the valuation allowance release, Warren's effective tax rate would have been 35% ($805,000/$2.3 million). This tax rate benefit is realized even though the $100,000 in FTC carryforwards have yet actually to be used in Warren's tax return. ■

Reducing Effective Tax Rates with ASC 740-30 (APB 23)

Because ASC 740-30 (APB 23) allows for higher reported book earnings (no deferred U.S. tax expense is recorded), its use may be reflected in higher stock prices and increased shareholder wealth. Although academic studies find mixed evidence on this effect, many U.S. multinationals with foreign subsidiaries do in fact use ASC 740-30 (APB 23) to avoid reporting U.S. deferred taxes on foreign earnings.

The "permanent reinvestment" exception should not be employed unless the corporation truly expects to keep its foreign earnings outside the United States. Using ASC 740-30 (APB 23) and then repatriating foreign profits after all can cause extreme spikes in a corporation's effective tax rate.

EXAMPLE 28

USCo, a domestic corporation, owns 100% of Shamrock, Ltd., an Irish corporation. Assume that the U.S. tax rate is 35% and that the Irish tax rate is 10%. In 2012, USCo earns $100,000 in taxable income and pays $35,000 to the United States. Shamrock earns $400,000 in taxable income and pays $40,000 in taxes to Ireland. Shamrock makes no distributions to its U.S. parent and is not taxed in the United States because it is not a U.S. person and has no activities in the United States.

USCo is not taxed on the Irish profits because it has not received any distributions of these profits. Furthermore, USCo uses ASC 740-30 (APB 23) to avoid recording any deferred U.S. income tax expense on its financial statements. Accordingly, USCo has achieved deferral and reduced its worldwide cash tax costs and book income tax expense.

USCo's total tax expense for financial statement purposes is $75,000.

Current U.S. tax	$35,000
Current foreign tax	40,000
Total tax expense	$75,000

The financial statement effective tax rate on USCo's global income is 15% ($75,000 total tax expense/$500,000 net income). Thus, the USCo group has achieved higher after-tax book income and earnings per share.

In 2013, USCo earns $200,000 in taxable income and pays $70,000 to the United States. Shamrock breaks even for the year and pays no taxes to Ireland. In 2013, USCo decides to have Shamrock pay it a dividend of $360,000.

FINANCIAL DISCLOSURE INSIGHTS Valuation Allowances for NOLs

Financial analysts use the valuation allowance system to help them determine an entity's expected future cash flows. Some critics of the GAAP rules for valuation allowances maintain that the process allows management to manipulate profits and earnings per share in an arbitrary fashion.

Only a few of the largest business entities, supported by going-concern assumptions and access to worldwide debt and equity capital, need to record a sizable valuation allowance. But valuation allowances also often are found in the financial reports of smaller entities and those in volatile industries, whose future profitability is likely to present questions.

In a recent reporting year, for instance, the following telecommunications businesses reported a valuation allowance related to expectations that their NOLs (for Federal and/or state taxing jurisdictions) would expire unused.

	Deferred Tax Assets ($000)	Valuation Allowance ($000)
Verizon	10,750	2,700
Bell South	2,100	1,100
AT&T	11,400	1,050
SBC Communications	3,900	150

Establishing a valuation allowance does not affect the entity's internal cash balances, but it might have an effect on the stock price. Valuation allowances can be "released" by management when evidence develops that the carryforwards are more likely to be used in the future, for example, if profitability improves and appears to be sustainable. For instance, the homebuilder Toll Brothers created a large valuation allowance when the real estate market collapsed, but it will release the allowance when housing prices stabilize and increase.

Several corporations estimated that the 2010 health care reform legislation would force them to create a sizable valuation allowance, because the mandated expenditures would reduce future profitability. The following are examples of these estimates.

	Reduction in Deferred Tax Assets Due to Health Care Reform ($ million)
AT&T	1,000
John Deere	150
Caterpillar	100
3M	90

U.S. Tax Return	
U.S. income	$200,000
Foreign dividend*	400,000
Taxable income	$600,000
Tax rate	× 35%
	$210,000
FTC	(40,000)
Net U.S. tax	$170,000

*The total gross income is the $360,000 cash dividend grossed up by the $40,000 potential FTC (see Chapter 9).

For book purposes, USCo reports only $200,000 in net income (the $400,000 in Irish income was included in book income in 2012 and is not included again). The 2013 total tax expense for financial statement purposes is $170,000.

Current U.S. tax	$170,000
Current foreign tax	–0–
Total tax expense	$170,000

The financial statement effective tax rate on USCo's global income is 85% ($170,000 total tax expense/$200,000 net income). This extremely high effective rate is caused by the mismatching of the Irish income (reported in 2012) and the U.S. taxes on the Irish income (reported in 2013). ■

Comparing Tax Savings

Many different types of tax planning strategies can produce tax savings. Yet even when planning ideas produce identical current cash-flow effects, some ideas may have an edge. CEOs and CFOs of public companies are focused on the bottom line—the company's net income after tax and related earnings per share. A CFO is likely to be just as interested in an idea's effect on the company's bottom line income as on the cash tax savings.

For example, consider two tax planning ideas that each produce $700,000 of current tax savings. The first idea generates its $700,000 in tax savings by increasing tax depreciation relative to book depreciation by $2 million ($700,000 = $2 million × 35%). The second idea produces research activities tax credits of $700,000, thus reducing current-year tax by $700,000.

Idea 1 produces its current tax savings via a temporary difference. Accordingly, the book tax expense will not reflect the $700,000 in tax savings. Instead, this $700,000 simply moves from the current tax category into the deferred tax category. Even if the book-tax difference is not expected to reverse in the next 30 years (effectively generating "permanent" savings), the book-tax expense does not reflect this savings.

In contrast, idea 2 produces its current tax savings via a permanent difference. Thus, the book-tax expense also declines by $700,000. This item is a reconciling item in the income tax note rate reconciliation.

REFOCUS ON THE BIG PICTURE

TAXES ON THE FINANCIAL STATEMENTS

Raymond Jones should understand that the tax expense reported on the company's financial statements and the tax payable on the company's income tax returns often differ as a result of differences in the reporting entities used in the calculation and the different accounting methods used for book purposes and tax purposes. The use of different accounting methods may result in both temporary and permanent differences in financial statement income and taxable income. Examples of permanent differences include nontaxable income such as municipal bond interest and tax credits. Temporary differences include depreciation differences and other amounts that are affected by the timing of a deduction or inclusion, but they ultimately result in the same amount being reflected in the financial statements and income tax returns.

Permanent differences such as municipal bond interest cause Arctic's book income to be greater than its taxable income. In calculating the tax expense shown on the financial statements, Arctic's book income must be adjusted for these permanent differences. This results in an effective tax rate for financial statement purposes (30.8 percent) that is below the top U.S. statutory corporate income tax rate of 35 percent.

In this case, Arctic's income tax expense of $7.7 million is higher than the current Federal income tax payable. This results from timing differences and creates a $1.05 million deferred tax liability that is reported on the company's balance sheet. Unlike other liabilities, deferred tax liabilities are "good" in the sense that they represent an amount that may be paid to the government in the future rather than today.

What If?

Mr. Jones is concerned about a newspaper article that said that companies reporting less tax on their tax returns than on their financial statements were cheating the IRS. Is this an accurate assessment?

While differences in income taxes payable to the IRS and financial tax expense can result from aggressive and illegal tax shelters, differences also result from different methods of accounting that are required for financial statement reporting using GAAP and tax laws as enacted by Congress.

KEY TERMS

ASC 740 (SFAS 109), 14-9
ASC 740-30 (APB 23), 14-23
Balance sheet approach, 14-10
Benchmarking, 14-25
Conservatism principle, 14-14
Current tax expense, 14-10
Deferred tax asset, 14-10
Deferred tax benefit, 14-10
Deferred tax expense, 14-10
Deferred tax liability, 14-10
Equity method, 14-3
Generally accepted accounting principles (GAAP), 14-2
Income tax provision, 14-9
Permanent differences, 14-5
Permanently reinvesting, 14-23
Rate reconciliation, 14-17
Schedule M–1, 14-6
Schedule M–3, 14-7
Temporary differences, 14-5
Valuation allowance, 14-15

DISCUSSION QUESTIONS

1. **LO.1** Evaluate the following statement: For most business entities, book income differs from taxable income because "income" has different meanings for the users of the data in the income computation.

2. **LO.1** Parent, a domestic corporation, owns 100% of Block, a foreign corporation, and Chip, a domestic corporation. Parent also owns 45% of Trial, a domestic corporation. Parent receives no distributions from any of these corporations. Which of these entities' net income is included in Parent's income statement for current-year financial reporting purposes?

3. **LO.1** Parent, a domestic corporation, owns 100% of Block, a foreign corporation, and Chip, a domestic corporation. Parent also owns 45% of Trial, a domestic corporation. Parent receives no distributions from any of these corporations. Which of these entities' taxable income is included in Parent's current-year Form 1120, U.S. income tax return? Parent consolidates all eligible subsidiaries.

Communications

4. **LO.1** Marcellus Jackson, the CFO of Mac, Inc., notices that the tax liability reported on Mac's tax return is less than the tax expense reported on Mac's financial statements. Provide a letter to Jackson outlining why these two tax expense numbers differ. Mac's address is 482 Linden Road, Paris, KY 40362.

Issue ID

5. **LO.1** Define the terms *temporary difference* and *permanent difference* as they pertain to the financial reporting of income tax expenses. Describe how these two book-tax differences affect the gap between book and taxable income.

Communications

6. **LO.1** In no more than three PowerPoint slides, list several commonly encountered temporary and permanent book-tax differences. The slides will be used in your presentation next week to your school's Future CPAs Club.

7. **LO.1** Indicate whether the following items create temporary or permanent differences.
   a. Book depreciation in excess of tax depreciation.
   b. Tax depreciation in excess of book depreciation.
   c. Municipal bond interest income.
   d. Disallowed meals and entertainment expense for tax purposes.
   e. Increase in the allowance for doubtful accounts.
   f. Increase in the reserve for warranty settlements.

8. **LO.2** Indicate whether the following temporary differences produce deferred tax assets or deferred tax liabilities (considered independently).
   a. Book depreciation in excess of tax depreciation.
   b. Tax depreciation in excess of book depreciation.
   c. Increase in the allowance for doubtful accounts.
   d. Increase in the reserve for warranty settlements.
   e. Foreign tax credits that are not allowed in the current year because of the FTC limitation.
   f. A current-year NOL.

9. **LO.5** Indicate whether the following temporary differences produce current or noncurrent deferred tax assets or deferred tax liabilities (considered independently).
   a. Book depreciation in excess of tax depreciation.
   b. Tax depreciation in excess of book depreciation.

c. Increase in the allowance for doubtful accounts.
d. Increase in the reserve for warranty settlements.
e. Write-down for impairment of book goodwill.
f. A current-year NOL.

10. **LO.1** Evaluate the following statement: The primary purpose of the Schedule M–1 and Schedule M–3 is to help the IRS craft its audits of the taxpayer. (Hint: Focus on the primary reason the IRS wants to see this information.)

11. **LO.2** Cramer, a stock analyst, wants to understand how the income tax expense reported in financial statements will affect stock prices. Briefly describe the objective of ASC 740 (SFAS 109) with regard to reporting income tax expense.

12. **LO.2** Skipper, Inc., earns pretax book net income of $500,000 in 2012. Skipper acquires a depreciable asset in 2012, and first-year tax depreciation exceeds book depreciation by $80,000. Skipper has no other temporary or permanent differences. Assuming that the U.S. tax rate is 35%, compute Skipper's total income tax expense, current income tax expense, and deferred income tax expense.

13. **LO.2** Using the facts of Problem 12, determine the 2012 end-of-year balance in Skipper's deferred tax asset and deferred tax liability balance sheet accounts.

14. **LO.2** Skipper, in Problem 12, reports $600,000 of pretax book net income in 2013. Skipper's book depreciation exceeds tax depreciation in this year by $50,000. Skipper has no other temporary or permanent differences. Assuming that the U.S. tax rate is 35%, compute Skipper's total income tax expense, current income tax expense, and deferred income tax expense.

15. **LO.2** Using the facts of Problem 14, determine the 2013 end-of-year balance in Skipper's deferred tax asset and deferred tax liability balance sheet accounts.

16. **LO.2** Mini, Inc., earns pretax book net income of $750,000 in 2013. Mini deducted $20,000 in bad debt expense for book purposes. This expense is not yet deductible for tax purposes. Mini has no other temporary or permanent differences. Assuming that the applicable U.S. tax rate is 35%, compute Mini's total income tax expense, current income tax expense, and deferred income tax expense.

17. **LO.2** Using the facts of Problem 16, determine the 2013 end-of-year balance in Mini's deferred tax asset and deferred tax liability balance sheet accounts.

18. **LO.2** Mini, in Problem 16, reports $800,000 of pretax book net income in 2014. Mini did not deduct any bad debt expense for book purposes but did deduct $15,000 in bad debt expense for tax purposes. Mini has no other temporary or permanent differences. Assuming that the U.S. tax rate is 35%, compute Mini's total income tax expense, current income tax expense, and deferred income tax expense.

19. **LO.2** Using the facts of Problem 18, determine the 2014 end-of-year balance in Mini's deferred tax asset and deferred tax liability balance sheet accounts.

20. **LO.3** What is a valuation allowance? Why is such a book account created? Be specific.

21. **LO.3** Timber, Inc., hopes to report a total book-tax expense of $50,000 in the current year. This $50,000 expense consists of $80,000 in current tax expense and a $30,000 tax benefit related to the expected future use of an NOL by Timber. If the auditors determine that a valuation allowance of $10,000 must be placed against Timber's deferred tax assets, what is Timber's total book-tax expense?

22. **LO.3** You saw on the online Business News Channel that YoungCo has "released one-third of its valuation allowances because of an upbeat forecast for sales of its tablet computers over the next 30 months." What effect does such a release likely have on YoungCo's current-year book effective tax rate? Be specific.

23. **LO.1** Lily Enterprises acquires another corporation. This acquisition created $30 million of goodwill for both book and tax purposes. The $30 million in goodwill is amortized over 15 years for tax purposes but is not deductible for book purposes unless impaired. Will this book-tax difference create a permanent or temporary book-tax difference for Lily?

Decision Making

24. **LO.6** Lydia is the CFO of FarmTime, Inc. FarmTime's tax advisers have recommended two tax planning ideas that will each provide $8 million of current-year cash tax savings. One idea is based on a timing difference and is expected to reverse 20 years in the future. The other idea creates a permanent difference that never will reverse. Determine whether these ideas will allow FarmTime to reduce its reported book income tax expense for the current year. Illustrate in a spreadsheet your preference for one planning strategy over the other. Which idea will you recommend to Lydia?

Communications

25. **LO.1, 5** Sam Taggart, the CEO of Skate, Inc., has reviewed Skate's tax return and its financial statement. He notices that both the Schedule M–3 and the rate reconciliation in the income tax note provide a reconciliation of tax information. However, he sees very little correspondence between the two schedules. Outline the differences between these two schedules in a letter to Sam. Skate's address is 499 Lucerne Avenue, Ocala, FL 34482.

Decision Making

26. **LO.4** RadioCo, a domestic corporation, owns 100% of TVCo, a manufacturing facility in Ireland. TVCo has no operations or activities in the United States. The U.S. tax rate is 35%, and the Irish tax rate is 15%. For the current year, RadioCo earns $400,000 in taxable income. TVCo earns $800,000 in taxable income from its operations, pays $120,000 in taxes to Ireland, and makes no distributions to RadioCo.
    a. Determine RadioCo's effective tax rate for book purposes with and without the permanent reinvestment assumption of ASC 740-30 (APB 23).
    b. Under what conditions should RadioCo adopt ASC 740-30 (APB 23) for TVCo's earnings?

Issue ID

27. **LO.4** Zhang, the CFO of TechCo, Inc., has used ASC 740-30 (APB 23) to avoid reporting any U.S. deferred tax expense on $30 million of the earnings of TechCo's foreign subsidiaries. All of these subsidiaries operate in countries with lower tax rates than the United States. Zhang wants to bring home $20 million in profits from these foreign subsidiaries in the form of dividends. How will this profit repatriation affect TechCo's book effective tax rate?

Issue ID

28. **LO.4** Jaime, the CFO of BuildCo, Inc., has used ASC 740-30 (APB 23) to avoid reporting any U.S. deferred tax expense on $100 million of the earnings of BuildCo's foreign subsidiaries. All of these subsidiaries operate in countries with higher tax rates than the ones that apply under U.S. law. Jaime wants to bring home $30 million in profits from these foreign subsidiaries in the form of dividends. How will this profit repatriation affect BuildCo's book effective tax rate?

29. **LO.6** RoofCo reports total book income before taxes of $20 million and a total tax expense of $8 million. FloorCo reports book income before taxes of $30 million and a total tax expense of $12 million. The companies' breakdown between current and deferred tax expense (benefit) is as follows:

	RoofCo	FloorCo
Current tax expense	$10.0	$13.0
Deferred tax benefit	(2.0)	(1.0)
Total tax expense	$ 8.0	$12.0

RoofCo's deferred tax benefit is from a deferred tax asset created because of differences in book and tax depreciation methods for equipment. FloorCo's deferred tax benefit is created by the expected future use of an NOL. Compare and contrast these two companies' effective tax rates. How are they similar? How are they different?

Communications

30. **LO.6** LawnCo and TreeCo operate in the same industry, and both report a 30% effective tax rate. Their book income and current, deferred, and total tax expense are reported below.

	LawnCo	TreeCo
Book income before tax	$500,000	$650,000
Current tax expense	$200,000	$ 20,000
Deferred tax expense (benefit)	(50,000)	175,000
Total tax expense	$150,000	$195,000
Effective tax rate	30%	30%

ShrubCo is a competitor of both these companies. Prepare a letter to Laura Collins, VP-Taxation of ShrubCo, outlining your analysis of the other two companies' effective tax rates, using only the information above. ShrubCo's address is 9979 West Third Street, Peru IN 46970.

31. **LO.6** HippCo and HoppCo operate in the same industry and report the following tax rate reconciliations in their tax footnotes.

	HippCo	HoppCo
Hypothetical tax at U.S. rate	35.0%	35.0%
State and local taxes	2.7	3.9
Foreign income taxed at less than U.S. rate	(12.5)	(7.8)
Tax Court settlement on disputed tax issue	6.0	—
Effective tax rate	31.2%	31.1%

Compare and contrast the effective tax rates of these two companies.

32. **LO.6** Comment on this statement: Benchmarking book-tax differences among entities requires more than just financial accounting skills.

PROBLEMS

33. **LO.2** Phillips, Inc., a cash basis C corporation, completes $100,000 in sales for year 1, but only $75,000 of this amount is collected during year 1. The remaining $25,000 from these sales is collected promptly during the first quarter of year 2. The applicable income tax rate for year 1 and thereafter is 30%. Compute Phillips's year 1 current and deferred income tax expense.

34. **LO.2** Continue with the results of Problem 33. Prepare the GAAP journal entries for Phillips's year 1 income tax expense.

35. **LO.2** Sing-Li, Inc., an accrual basis C corporation, sells widgets on credit. Its book and taxable income for year 1 totals $42,000, before accounting for bad debts. Sing-Li's book allowance for uncollectible accounts increased for year 1 by $12,000, but none of the entity's bad debts received a specific write-off for tax purposes. The applicable income tax rate for year 1 and thereafter is 30%. Compute Sing-Li's year 1 current and deferred income tax expense.

36. **LO.2** Continue with the results of Problem 35. Prepare the GAAP journal entries for Sing-Li's year 1 income tax expense.

37. **LO.2** Rubio, Inc., an accrual basis C corporation, reports the following amounts for the tax year. The applicable income tax rate is 30%. Compute Rubio's taxable income.

Book and taxable income including the items below	$80,000
Increase in book allowance for anticipated warranty costs	5,000
Interest income from City of Westerville bonds	10,000
Bribes paid to Federal inspectors	17,000

38. **LO.2** Continue with the results of Problem 37. Determine Rubio's income tax expense and GAAP income for the year.

39. **LO.2** Willingham, Inc., an accrual basis C corporation, reports year 1 book and taxable income of $2 million, before accounting for its investment activities. The applicable tax rate is 35% for year 1 and thereafter. Compute Willingham's year 1 current and deferred income tax expense.

The entity owns one investment asset, which it purchased many years ago for $1 million. At the end of year 1, the asset's fair value is $1.8 million. Willingham reports no other year 1 book-tax differences.

40. **LO.2** Continue with the results of Problem 39. Prepare the GAAP journal entries for Willingham's year 1 income tax expense.

41. **LO.2** Relix, Inc., is a domestic corporation with the following balance sheet for book and tax purposes at the end of the year. Based on this information, determine Relix's net deferred tax asset or net deferred tax liability at year-end. Assume a 34% corporate tax rate and no valuation allowance.

	Tax Debit/(Credit)	Book Debit/(Credit)
Assets		
Cash	$ 500	$ 500
Accounts receivable	8,000	8,000
Buildings	750,000	750,000
Accumulated depreciation	(450,000)	(380,000)
Furniture & fixtures	70,000	70,000
Accumulated depreciation	(46,000)	(38,000)
Total assets	$ 332,500	$ 410,500
Liabilities		
Accrued litigation expense	$ –0–	($ 50,000)
Note payable	(78,000)	(78,000)
Total liabilities	($ 78,000)	($ 128,000)
Stockholders' Equity		
Paid-in capital	($ 10,000)	($ 10,000)
Retained earnings	(244,500)	(272,500)
Total liabilities and stockholders' equity	($ 332,500)	($ 410,500)

42. **LO.2** Based on the facts and results of Problem 41 and the beginning-of-the-year book-tax basis differences listed below, determine the change in Relix's deferred tax assets for the current year.

	Beginning of Year
Accrued litigation expense	$34,000
Subtotal	$34,000
Applicable tax rate	× 34%
Gross deferred tax asset	$11,560

43. **LO.2** Based on the facts and results of Problem 41 and the beginning-of-the-year book-tax basis differences listed below, determine the change in Relix's deferred tax liabilities for the current year.

	Beginning of Year
Building—accumulated depreciation	($57,000)
Furniture & fixtures—accumulated depreciation	(4,200)
Subtotal	($61,200)
Applicable tax rate	× 34%
Gross deferred tax liability	($20,808)

44. **LO.2** Based on the facts and results of Problems 41–43, determine Relix's change in net deferred tax asset or net deferred tax liability for the current year. Provide the journal entry to record this amount.

45. **LO.2** In addition to the temporary differences identified in Problems 41–44, Relix, Inc., reported two permanent differences between book and taxable income. It earned $2,375 in tax-exempt municipal bond interest, and it incurred $780 in nondeductible meals and entertainment expense. Relix's book income before tax is $4,800. With this additional information, calculate Relix's current tax expense.

46. **LO.2** Provide the journal entry to record Relix's current tax expense as determined in Problem 45.

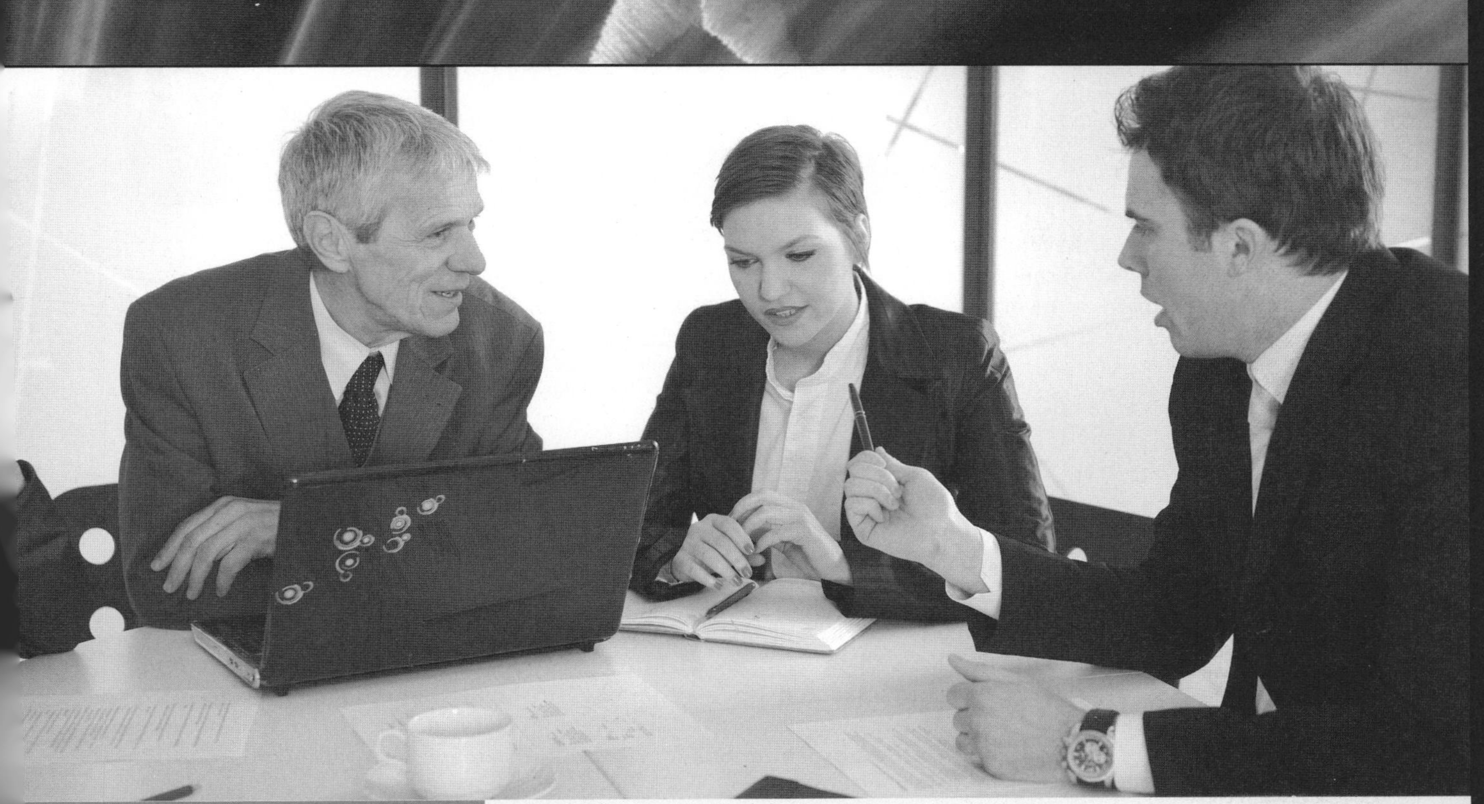

© Zurijeta/Shutterstock.com

THE BIG PICTURE Tax Solutions for the Real World

Effect of a For-Profit Business on a Tax-Exempt Entity

For an entity to be tax-exempt, it must serve the common good. This common good can include a mission as broad as that of a public charity such as the Red Cross or as narrow as that of a private foundation that operates a historic museum that depicts life in the eighteenth century. Most exempt organizations are exempt under § 501(c)(3).

Hopeful, Inc., is a § 501(c)(3) organization that provides temporary lodging and psychological services for abused women. Its annual operating budget is $12 million. More than two decades ago, Betty Jones was a recipient of the services provided by Hopeful. Now Hopeful's administrator has been notified by the attorney for Betty's estate that her will transfers to Hopeful the legal ownership (100 percent of the outstanding stock) of Taste Good Ice Cream, a chain of 40 gourmet ice cream shops located in Virginia, North Carolina, and South Carolina. The business has been in existence for eight years and has produced substantially higher profits each year.

Hopeful's board is considering the following options regarding the inheritance from Betty and has hired you to provide an analysis of the tax consequences of each option.

- Sell the stock of Taste Good Ice Cream and contribute the net proceeds to Hopeful's endowment.
- Continue to conduct the Taste Good Ice Cream business as a division of Hopeful.
- Continue to conduct the business as a wholly owned subsidiary of Hopeful.

With the second and the third options, the existing management team will remain in place. After-tax profits not needed to expand the ice cream shop chain will be used by Hopeful in carrying out its exempt mission.

Read the chapter and formulate your response.

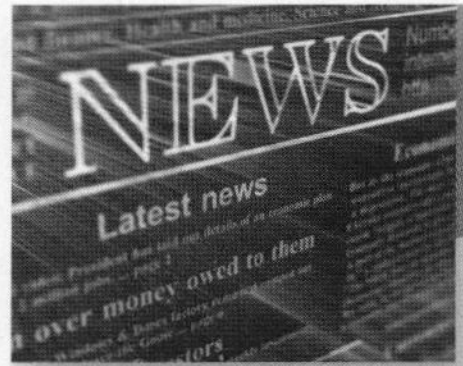

TAX IN THE NEWS Giving to Churches

For the past several years, there has been a significant variance in the percentage of churches that say giving has increased when compared with the previous year.

2008	46%
2009	35%
2010	43%

Source: "State of the Plate" survey, Evangelical Council for Financial Accountability.

15 Introduction

Ideally, any entity that generates profit would prefer not to be subject to the Federal income tax. All of the types of entities discussed in Chapter 13 are subject to the Federal income tax at one level (e.g., sole proprietorships, partnerships, S corporations, and LLCs generally are subject only to single taxation) or more (e.g., C corporations are subject to double taxation). In contrast, entities classified as **exempt organizations** may be able to escape Federal income taxation altogether.

The tax-exempt sector is an important component of the U.S. economy. More than 2 million tax-exempt entities file tax returns with the IRS. These entities employ almost 12 million workers, representing about 10 percent of the total U.S. workforce. They control about $3.5 trillion in assets. The IRS audits about 8,000 of these entities every tax year.

Churches are among the types of organizations that are exempt from Federal income tax. Nevertheless, one must be careful not to conclude that anything labeled a church will qualify for exempt status.

During the 1970s and 1980s, a popular technique for attempting to avoid Federal income tax was the establishment of so-called mail-order churches. For example, in one scheme, a nurse obtained a certificate of ordination and a church charter from an organization that sold such documents.[1] The articles of incorporation stated that the church was organized exclusively for religious and charitable purposes, including a religious mission of healing the spirit, mind, emotions, and body. The nurse was the church's minister, director, and principal officer. Taking a vow of poverty, she transferred all of her assets, including a house and car, to the church. The church assumed all of the nurse's liabilities, including the mortgage on her house and her credit card bills. The nurse continued to work at a hospital and deposited her salary in the church's bank account. The church provided her with a living allowance sufficient to maintain or improve her previous standard of living. She was also permitted to use the house and car for personal purposes.

The IRS declared that such organizations were shams and not bona fide churches. For a church to be tax-exempt under § 501(c)(3), none of its net earnings may be used to the benefit of any private shareholder or individual. In essence, the organization should serve a public rather than a private interest. Although the courts have consistently upheld the IRS position, numerous avoidance schemes such as this one have been attempted.

Another technique being marketed as a way to avoid Federal income taxes is to set up shop as a credit counselor. Credit counselors have an opportunity to qualify for tax-exempt status under § 501(c)(3). Supposedly, such tax-exempt organizations exist to help debt-laden consumers learn to practice sound financial management and become debt-free. Unfortunately, in reality, some credit

[1] Rev.Rul. 81–94, 1981–1 C.B. 330.

TAX IN THE NEWS Who Are the Donors?

Gifts are a major source of funds for many charities. Charitable giving by Americans in 2010 totaled $291 billion, about 2.1 percent of GDP. This represents an increase of 3.8 percent over 2009. The bulk of charitable gifts are made by individuals and their estates.

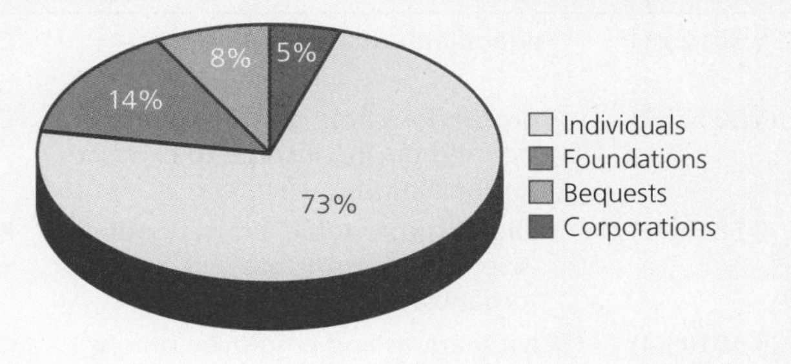

Source: Giving USA, 2010.

counseling organizations push consumers into debt repayment schedules with high, poorly disclosed fees that leave the debtor in worse financial shape than before the "counseling." Apparently, the primary motive of such techniques is to earn profits. These unsavory practices have caused Congress to call for greater IRS scrutiny. The IRS has revoked or is in the process of revoking the tax-exempt status of the 41 credit counselors it has audited. Such credit counselors have earned more than 40 percent of the industry's $1 billion in annual revenues.

As discussed in Chapter 1, the major objective of the Federal tax law is to raise revenue. If revenue raising were the only objective, however, the Code would not contain provisions that permit certain organizations to be either partially or completely exempt from Federal income tax. Social considerations also may affect the tax law. This objective bears directly on the decision by Congress to provide for exempt organization tax status. The House Report on the Revenue Act of 1938 explains:

> The exemption from taxation of money or property devoted to charitable and other purposes is based upon the theory that the Government is compensated for the loss of revenue by its relief from the financial burden which would otherwise have to be met by appropriations from public funds, and by the benefits resulting from the promotion of the general welfare.[2]

Recognizing this social consideration objective, Subchapter F (Exempt Organizations) of the Code (§§ 501–530) provides the authority under which certain organizations are exempt from Federal income tax. Exempt status is not open-ended in that two general limitations exist. First, the nature or scope of the organization may result in it being only partially exempt from tax.[3] Second, the organization may engage in activities that are subject to special taxation.[4]

15.1 Types of Exempt Organizations

LO.1

Identify the different types of exempt organizations.

An organization qualifies for exempt status *only* if it fits into one of the categories provided in the Code. Examples of qualifying exempt organizations and the specific statutory authority for their exempt status are listed in Exhibit 15.1.[5]

[2]See 1939–1 (Part 2) C.B. 742 for a reprint of H.R. No. 1860, 75th Congress, 3rd Session.

[3]See the subsequent discussion of Unrelated Business Income Tax.

[4]See the subsequent discussions of Prohibited Transactions and Taxes Imposed on Private Foundations.

[5]Section 501(a) provides for exempt status for organizations described in §§ 401 and 501. The orientation of this chapter is toward organizations that conduct business activities. Therefore, the exempt organizations described in § 401 (qualified pension, profit sharing, and stock bonus trusts) are outside the scope of the chapter and are not discussed.

EXHIBIT 15.1 **Types of Exempt Organizations**

Statutory Authority	Brief Description	Examples or Comments
§ 501(c)(1)	Federal and related agencies.	Commodity Credit Corporation, Federal Deposit Insurance Corporation, Federal Land Bank.
§ 501(c)(2)	Corporations holding title to property for and paying income to exempt organizations.	Corporation holding title to college fraternity house.
§ 501(c)(3)	Religious, charitable, educational, scientific, literary, etc., organizations.	Boy Scouts of America, Red Cross, Salvation Army, Episcopal Church, PTA, United Fund, University of Richmond.
§ 501(c)(4)	Civic leagues and employee unions.	Garden club, tenants' association promoting tenants' legal rights in entire community, League of Women Voters.
§ 501(c)(5)	Labor, agricultural, and horticultural organizations.	Teachers' association, organization formed to promote effective agricultural pest control, organization formed to test soil and to educate community members in soil treatment, garden club.
§ 501(c)(6)	Business leagues, chambers of commerce, real estate boards, etc.	Chambers of Commerce, American Plywood Association, National Football League (NFL), Professional Golfers Association (PGA) Tour, medical association peer review board, organization promoting acceptance of women in business and professions.
§ 501(c)(7)	Social clubs.	Country club, rodeo and riding club, press club, bowling club, college fraternities.
§ 501(c)(8)	Fraternal beneficiary societies.	Lodges. Must provide for the payment of life, sickness, accident, or other benefits to members or their dependents.
§ 501(c)(9)	Voluntary employees' beneficiary associations.	Provide for the payment of life, sickness, accident, or other benefits to members, their dependents, or their designated beneficiaries.
§ 501(c)(10)	Domestic fraternal societies.	Lodges. Must not provide for the payment of life, sickness, accident, or other benefits and must devote the net earnings exclusively to religious, charitable, scientific, literary, educational, and fraternal purposes.
§ 501(c)(11)	Local teachers' retirement fund associations.	Only permitted sources of income are amounts received from (1) public taxation, (2) assessments on teaching salaries of members, and (3) income from investments.
§ 501(c)(12)	Local benevolent life insurance associations, mutual or cooperative telephone companies, etc.	Local cooperative telephone company, local mutual water company, local mutual electric company.
§ 501(c)(13)	Cemetery companies.	Must be operated exclusively for the benefit of lot owners who hold the lots for burial purposes.
§ 501(c)(14)	Credit unions.	Other than credit unions exempt under § 501(c)(1).
§ 501(c)(15)	Mutual insurance companies.	Mutual fire insurance company, mutual automobile insurance company.
§ 501(c)(16)	Corporations organized by farmers' cooperatives for financing crop operations.	Related farmers' cooperative must be exempt from tax under § 521.
§ 501(c)(19)	Armed forces members' posts or organizations.	Veterans of Foreign Wars (VFW), Reserve Officers Association.
§ 501(c)(20)	Group legal service plans.	Provided by a corporation for its employees.
§ 501(d)	Religious and apostolic organizations.	Communal organization. Members must include pro rata share of the net income of the organization in their gross income as dividends.
§ 501(e)	Cooperative hospital service organizations.	Centralized purchasing organization for exempt hospitals.
§ 501(f)	Cooperative service organization of educational institutions.	Organization formed to manage universities' endowment funds.
§ 529	Qualified tuition programs.	Prepaid tuition and educational savings programs.
§ 530	Coverdell Education Savings Accounts.	Qualified education savings accounts.

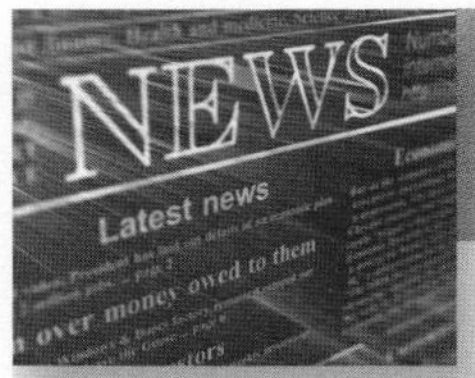

TAX IN THE NEWS **Who Are the Donees?**

The recipients of charitable gifts can be classified as shown in the chart. Religious and educational organizations and foundations account for 60 percent of the donees. Religious organizations alone receive over one-third of all charitable gifts.

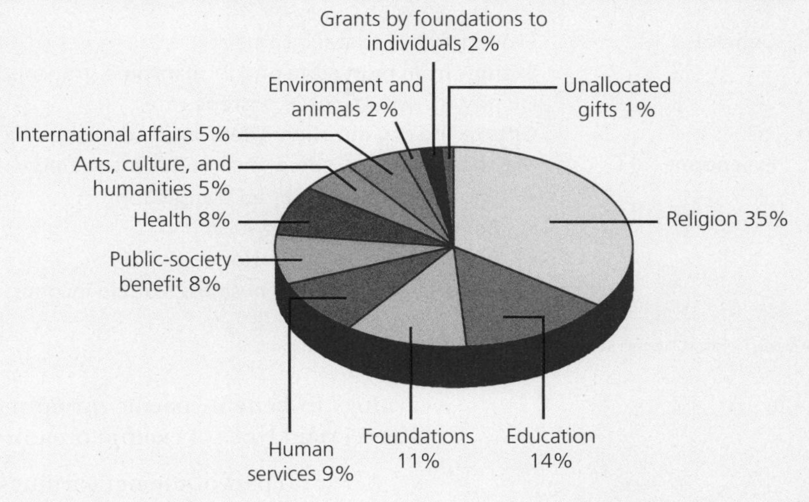

Source: Giving USA, 2010.

15.2 Requirements for Exempt Status

LO.2

Enumerate the requirements for exempt status.

Exempt status frequently requires more than mere classification in one of the categories of exempt organizations. Many of the organizations that qualify for exempt status share the following characteristics.

- The organization serves some type of *common good.*[6]
- The organization is *not* a *for-profit* entity.[7]
- *Net earnings* do not benefit the members of the organization.[8]
- The organization does not exert *political influence.*[9]

Serving the Common Good

The underlying rationale for all exempt organizations is that they serve some type of *common good.* However, depending on the type of the exempt organization, the term *common good* may be interpreted broadly or narrowly. If the test is interpreted broadly, the group being served is the general public or some large subgroup thereof. If it is interpreted narrowly, the group is the specific group referred to in the statutory language. One of the factors in classifying an exempt organization as a private foundation is the size of the group it serves.

Not-for-Profit Entity

The organization may not be organized or operated for the purpose of making a profit. For some types of exempt organizations, the *for-profit prohibition* appears in the statutory language. For other types, the prohibition is implied.

Net Earnings and Members of the Organization

What uses are appropriate for the net earnings of a tax-exempt organization? The logical answer would seem to be that the earnings should be used for the exempt purpose of the organization. However, where the organization exists for the good of a specific group of members, such an open-ended interpretation could permit net

[6]See, for example, §§ 501(c)(3) and (4).
[7]See, for example, §§ 501(c)(3), (4), (6), (13), and (14).
[8]See, for example, §§ 501(c)(3), (6), (7), (9), (10), (11), and (19).
[9]See, for example, § 501(c)(3).

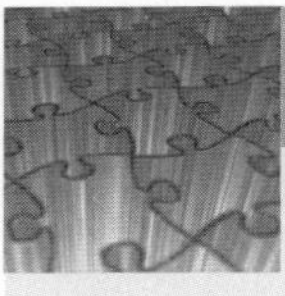

CONCEPT SUMMARY 15.1

Consequences of Exempt Status

General	Exempt from Federal income tax. Exempt from most state and local income, franchise, sales, and property taxes. Qualify for reductions in postage rates. Gifts to the organization often can be deducted by donor.
Exceptions	May be subject to Federal income tax associated with the following. • Engaging in a prohibited transaction. • Being a feeder organization. • Being a private foundation. • Generating unrelated business taxable income.

earnings to benefit specific group members. Therefore, the Code specifically prohibits certain types of exempt organizations from using their earnings in this way.

> . . . no part of the net earnings . . . inures to the benefit of any private shareholder or individual.[10]

In other instances, a statutory prohibition is unnecessary because the definition of the exempt organization in the Code effectively prevents such use.

> . . . the net earnings of which are devoted exclusively to religious, charitable, scientific, literary, educational, and fraternal purposes.[11]

Political Influence

Religious, charitable, educational, etc., organizations are generally prohibited from attempting to influence legislation or participate in political campaigns. Participation in political campaigns includes participation both *on behalf of* a candidate and *in opposition to* a candidate.

Only in limited circumstances are such exempt organizations permitted to attempt to influence legislation. See the subsequent discussion under Prohibited Transactions.

FINANCIAL DISCLOSURE INSIGHTS Effects of Sarbanes-Oxley on Nonprofit Entities

The rules of the Sarbanes-Oxley Act do not apply to nonprofit entities. Nevertheless, some nonprofits voluntarily comply with its provisions. For example, New York's Julliard School and the International Swimming Hall of Fame in Fort Lauderdale have adopted the governance practices, code of ethics, and increased transparency required by Sarbanes-Oxley. Factors contributing to such adoption by nonprofits include the following.

- Accounting firms that audit nonprofits want to see the same financial controls now in place at for-profits.
- Nonprofit trustees are demanding more transparency.
- Nonprofit trustees are concerned that their professional reputations could be hurt if money is misused or the nonprofit falters.

[10] § 501(c)(6).

[11] § 501(c)(10).

ETHICS & EQUITY For the Good of the People

Matthew Ayres is the founder, and the man behind the throne, of the Church for Today television ministry. Ministry broadcasts originate from church services in California and New York and are transmitted via cable throughout the United States. Although the membership of the Church for Today is small (approximately 5,000 members), the typical member is quite wealthy. In addition to receiving contributions from its members, the church solicits and receives donations from viewers of the TV broadcasts. The church is tax-exempt under § 501(c)(3).

The stated mission of the church is religious in nature. However, Matthew firmly believes, as do the members of the board of deacons of the church, that certain societal goals must be accomplished for the prophecies of the church to come true (i.e., their divine being expects them to be active missionaries). Among its basic beliefs, the church advocates government control and possession of all guns, the legalization of drugs, abortion on demand once approved by the appropriate government agency, the withdrawal of all U.S. troops from foreign soil and the termination of all military alliances, the abolition of capital punishment, and the availability of tuition-free university education to all U.S. citizens.

The ministers of the Church for Today are expected to include these basic beliefs, at the subliminal level, in their sermons. Some do so more effectively and more frequently than others, but all are required to do so. Matthew and the board of deacons are dismayed that American society has not adopted many of their beliefs.

Accordingly, Matthew proposes to the board of deacons that the church take a more proactive role. The employment contract of the ministers now will require them to include the basic beliefs in their sermons in an active manner. No longer can the church's positions just be incorporated subliminally. All of the beliefs must be covered quarterly, and every sermon must present at least one of the basic doctrines. The ministers will encourage the church members and TV viewers actively to support these positions at both the state and Federal levels.

As a new member of the board of deacons, you wholeheartedly support Matthew's position. However, you are concerned about the effects of this open advocacy of positions on the tax-exempt status of the church. Matthew responds that the "church has friends in high places" and assures you that the tax-exempt status will not be endangered. What should you do?

15.3 Tax Consequences of Exempt Status: General

LO.3

Apply the tax consequences of exempt status, including the different consequences for public charities and private foundations.

An organization that is appropriately classified as one of the types of exempt organizations is generally exempt from Federal income tax. Four exceptions to this general statement exist, however. An exempt organization that engages in a *prohibited transaction* or is a so-called *feeder organization* is subject to tax. If the organization is classified as a *private foundation*, it may be partially subject to tax. Finally, an exempt organization is subject to tax on its *unrelated business taxable income.*

In addition to being exempt from Federal income tax, an exempt organization may be eligible for other benefits, including the following.

- The organization may be exempt from state income tax, state franchise tax, sales tax, or property tax.
- The organization may receive discounts on postage rates.
- Donors of property to the exempt organization may qualify for charitable contribution deductions on their Federal and state income tax returns. However, *not* all exempt organizations are qualified charitable contribution recipients (e.g., gifts to the National Football League, PGA Tour, and Underwriters Laboratories are not deductible).

Prohibited Transactions

Engaging in a § 503 prohibited transaction can produce three negative results. First, part or all of the organization's income may be subject to Federal income tax. Second and even worse, the organization may forfeit its exempt status. Finally, intermediate sanctions may be imposed on certain exempt organization insiders.

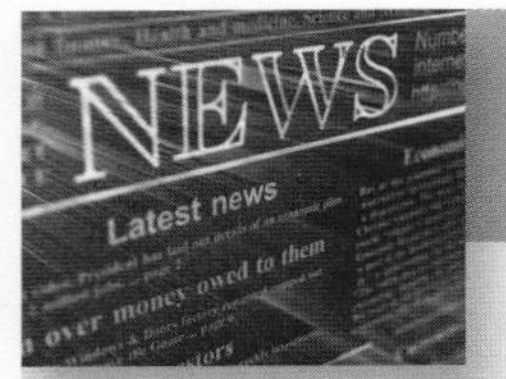

TAX IN THE NEWS The Effect of the Recession on Charitable Contributions

Tax-exempt entities have two key causes for concern associated with the contributions they receive. One is immediate, and the other is in the future.

The first concern is the economy and its effect on contributions. In 2008, the amount of charitable contributions declined by 2 percent—the first time since 1987 (the year of the "Black Monday" stock market collapse) that contributions had declined. In 2009, contributions fell again, marking the first time in half a century that they had declined two years in a row. The obvious explanation was the recession. Logically, if people are earning less income, they may be inclined to give less. Fortunately, in 2010, giving increased by 3.8 percent.

Source: Giving USA, 2010.

Failure to Continue to Qualify

Organizations initially qualify for exempt status only if they are organized as indicated in Exhibit 15.1. The initial qualification requirements then effectively become maintenance requirements. Failure to continue to meet the qualification requirements results in the loss of the entity's exempt status.

New Faith, Inc., is an excellent example of an exempt organization that failed to continue to qualify for tax exemption.[12] The stated purposes of the organization were to feed and shelter the poor. In its application for exempt status, New Faith indicated that it would derive its financial support from donations, bingo games, and raffles. The IRS approved the exempt status.

New Faith's only source of income was the operation of several lunch trucks, which provided food to the general public in exchange for scheduled "donations." Evidence provided by the organization to the Tax Court did not show that the food from the lunch trucks was provided free of charge or at reduced prices. In addition, no evidence was presented to show that the people who received food for free or at below-cost prices were impoverished or needy. The court concluded that the primary purpose of the activity was the conduct of a trade or business. It upheld the IRS's revocation of New Faith's exempt status.

Election Not to Forfeit Exempt Status for Lobbying

Organizations exempt under § 501(c)(3) (religious, charitable, educational, etc., organizations) are subject to limits on their attempts to influence legislation (lobbying activities) and participate in political campaigns.[13] Substantial lobbying or political activity can result in the forfeiture of exempt status.

Certain exempt organizations are permitted to engage in lobbying (but not political) activities that are greater than an insubstantial part of their activities, by making a § 501(h) election.[14] Eligible for the election are most § 501(c)(3) organizations (educational institutions, hospitals, and medical research organizations; organizations supporting government schools; organizations publicly supported by charitable contributions; certain organizations that are publicly supported by various sources including admissions, sales, gifts, grants, contributions, or membership fees; and certain organizations that support certain types of public charities).

An eligible § 501(c)(3) organization must make an affirmative election to participate in lobbying activities on a limited basis. The lobbying expenditures of electing organizations are subject to a ceiling. Exceeding the ceiling can lead to the forfeiture of exempt status. Even when the ceiling is not exceeded, a tax may be imposed on some of the lobbying expenditures (as discussed subsequently).

[12] *New Faith, Inc.*, 64 TCM 1050, T.C.Memo. 1992–601.

[13] § 501(c)(3). Even a single Internet link to a partisan political site can taint the exempt entity.

[14] Religious organizations and private foundations cannot make this election.

FIGURE 15.1 **Calculation of Lobbying Nontaxable Amount**

Exempt Purpose Expenditures	Lobbying Nontaxable Amount Is
Not over $500,000	20% of exempt purpose expenditures*
Over $500,000 but not over $1 million	$100,000 + 15% of the excess of exempt purpose expenditures over $500,000
Over $1 million but not over $1.5 million	$175,000 + 10% of the excess of exempt purpose expenditures over $1 million
Over $1.5 million	$225,000 + 5% of the excess of exempt purpose expenditures over $1.5 million

* Exempt purpose expenditures generally are the amounts paid or incurred for the taxable year to accomplish the following purposes: religious, charitable, scientific, literary, educational, fostering of national or international amateur sports competition, or the prevention of cruelty to children or animals.

Two terms are key to the calculation of the ceiling amount: **lobbying expenditures** and **grass roots expenditures.** Lobbying expenditures are made for the purpose of influencing legislation through either of the following.

- Attempting to affect the opinions of the general public or any segment thereof.
- Communicating with any legislator or staff member or with any government official or staff member who may participate in the formulation of legislation.

Grass roots expenditures are made for the purpose of influencing legislation by attempting to affect the opinions of the general public or any segment thereof.

The statutory ceiling is imposed on both lobbying expenditures and grass roots expenditures and is computed as follows.

- 150% × Lobbying nontaxable amount = Lobbying expenditures ceiling.
- 150% × Grass roots nontaxable amount = Grass roots expenditures ceiling.

The *lobbying nontaxable amount* is the lesser of (1) $1 million or (2) the amount determined in Figure 15.1.[15] The *grass roots nontaxable amount* is 25 percent of the lobbying nontaxable amount.[16]

An electing exempt organization is assessed a tax on **excess lobbying expenditures** as follows.[17]

- 25% × Excess lobbying expenditures = Tax liability.

Excess lobbying expenditures are the greater of the following.[18]

- Excess of the lobbying expenditures for the taxable year over the lobbying nontaxable amount.
- Excess of the grass roots expenditures for the taxable year over the grass roots nontaxable amount.

EXAMPLE 1

Tan, Inc., a qualifying § 501(c)(3) organization, incurs lobbying expenditures of $500,000 for the taxable year and grass roots expenditures of $0. Exempt purpose expenditures for the taxable year are $5 million. Tan elects to be eligible to make lobbying expenditures on a limited basis.

Applying the data in Figure 15.1, the lobbying nontaxable amount is $400,000 [$225,000 + 5%($5,000,000 − $1,500,000)]. The ceiling on lobbying expenditures is $600,000 (150% × $400,000). Therefore, the $500,000 of lobbying expenditures are under the permitted $600,000. However, the election results in the imposition of tax on the excess lobbying expenditures of $100,000 ($500,000 lobbying expenditures − $400,000 lobbying nontaxable amount). The resulting tax liability is $25,000 ($100,000 × 25%). ■

[15] § 4911(c)(2).
[16] § 4911(c)(4).
[17] § 4911(a)(1).
[18] § 4911(b).

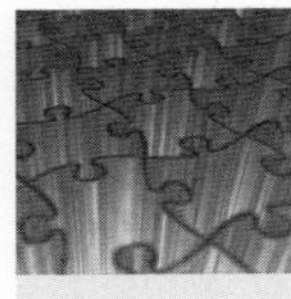

CONCEPT SUMMARY 15.2

Exempt Organizations and Influencing Legislation

Factor	Tax Result
Entity subject to rule	§ 501(c)(3) organization.
Effect of influencing legislation	Subject to tax on lobbying expenditures under § 4912. Forfeit exempt status under § 501(c)(3). Not eligible for exempt status under § 501(c)(4).
Effect of electing to make lobbying expenditures	Permitted to make limited lobbying expenditures. Subject to tax under § 4911.

A § 501(c)(3) organization that makes disqualifying lobbying expenditures is subject to a 5 percent tax on the lobbying expenditures for the taxable year. A 5 percent tax may also be levied on the organization's management. The tax is imposed on management only if the managers knew that making the expenditures was likely to result in the organization no longer qualifying under § 501(c)(3) and if the managers' actions were willful and not due to reasonable cause. The tax does not apply to private foundations (see the subsequent discussion).[19] Concept Summary 15.2 capsulizes the rules on influencing legislation.

Intermediate Sanctions

Prior to 1996, the IRS had only two options available for dealing with exempt organizations (other than private foundations) engaging in prohibited transactions. First, it could attempt to subject part or all of the organization's income to Federal income tax. Second, it could revoke the exempt status of the organization. For private foundations, an additional option was available. The IRS could impose certain taxes on private foundations for engaging in so-called prohibited transactions (see Concept Summary 15.3 later in the chapter).

Tax legislation enacted in 1996 added another option to the IRS toolbox—**intermediate sanctions**—for so-called public charities.[20] The intermediate sanctions take the form of excise taxes imposed on disqualified persons (any individuals who are in a position to exercise substantial influence over the affairs of the organization) who engage in *excess benefit transactions* and on exempt organization managers who participate in such a transaction knowing that it is improper. Such excess benefit transactions include transactions in which a disqualified person engages in a non-fair-market-value transaction with the exempt organization or receives unreasonable compensation.

The excise tax on the disqualified person is imposed at a rate of 25 percent of the excess benefit. For the exempt organization management, the excise tax is imposed at a rate of 10 percent of the excess benefit (unless such participation is not willful and is due to reasonable cause) with a statutory ceiling of $20,000 for any excess benefit transaction. These excise taxes are referred to as first-level taxes.

A second-level tax is imposed on the disqualified person if the excess benefit transaction is not corrected within the taxable period. This excise tax is imposed at a rate of 200 percent of the excess benefit.

Feeder Organizations

A **feeder organization** carries on a trade or business for the benefit of an exempt organization and remits its profits to the exempt organization. Such organizations are not

[19] § 4912.

[20] § 4958.

exempt from Federal income tax. This provision is intended to prevent an entity whose primary purpose is to conduct a trade or business for profit from escaping taxation merely because all of its profits are payable to one or more exempt organizations.[21]

Some income and activities are *not* subject to the feeder organization rules.[22]

- Rent income that would be excluded from the definition of the term *rent* for purposes of the unrelated business income tax (discussed subsequently).
- A trade or business where substantially all of the work is performed by volunteers.
- The trade or business of selling merchandise where substantially all of the merchandise has been received as contributions or gifts.

THE BIG PICTURE

EXAMPLE 2

Return to the facts of *The Big Picture* on p. 15-1. Recall that Hopeful, Inc., an exempt organization under § 501 (c) (3) that provides temporary lodging and psychological services to abused women, is trying to decide what it should do with Taste Good Ice Cream, a chain of gourmet ice cream shops that it has received as a bequest. Assume that Hopeful has decided to operate Taste Good as a subsidiary, with the profits going to Hopeful to support its tax-exempt mission. The subsidiary will be a taxable entity (a feeder organization) subject to the Federal income tax using the corporate tax rates.

15.4 Private Foundations

LO.4

Determine which exempt organizations are classified as private foundations.

Tax Consequences of Private Foundation Status

Certain exempt organizations are classified as **private foundations**. This classification produces two negative consequences. First, the classification may have an adverse impact on the contributions received by the donee exempt organization. Contributions may decline because the tax consequences for donors may not be as favorable as if the entity were not a private foundation.[23] Second, the classification may result in taxation at the exempt organization level. The reason for this less beneficial tax treatment is that private foundations define common good more narrowly and therefore are seen as not being supported by, and operated for the good of, the public.

Definition of a Private Foundation

All § 501(c)(3) organizations are private foundations by default, unless one of the statutory exceptions applies. The following § 501(c)(3) organizations are *not* private foundations.[24]

1. Churches; educational institutions; hospitals and medical research organizations; charitable organizations receiving a major portion of their support from the general public or the United States, a state, or a political subdivision thereof that is operated for the benefit of a college or university; and governmental units (favored activities category).
2. Organizations that are broadly supported by the general public (excluding disqualified persons), by governmental units, or by organizations described in (1) above.
3. Entities organized and operated exclusively for the benefit of organizations described in (1) or (2) [a supporting organization].
4. Entities organized and operated exclusively for testing for public safety.

[21] § 502(a).
[22] § 502(b).
[23] § 170(e)(1)(B)(ii).
[24] § 509(a).

To meet the broadly supported requirement in (2) above, both of the following tests must be satisfied.

- External support test.
- Internal support test.

Under the *external support test,* more than one-third of the organization's support each taxable year *normally* must come from the three groups listed in (2) above, in the following forms.

- Gifts, grants, contributions, and membership fees.
- Gross receipts from admissions, sales of merchandise, performance of services, or the furnishing of facilities in an activity that is not an unrelated trade or business for purposes of the unrelated business income tax (discussed subsequently). However, such gross receipts from any person or governmental agency in excess of the greater of $5,000 or 1 percent of the organization's support for the taxable year are not counted in the numerator of the support fraction.
- Amounts received from disqualified persons are not included in the numerator of the support fraction. Disqualified persons include:
  - Substantial contributors whose cumulative gifts and bequests to the exempt entity exceed both 2 percent of aggregate contributions received by the entity and $5,000.
  - Members of the governing body of the exempt entity including officers, directors, trustees, and their families.
  - Generally, corporations, partnerships, trusts, and estates that are affiliated with a disqualified person, using a 35 percent ownership/beneficiary control test.

The *internal support test* limits the amount of support *normally* received from the following sources to one-third of the organization's support for the taxable year.[25]

- Gross investment income (gross income from interest, dividends, rents, and royalties).
- Unrelated business taxable income (discussed subsequently) minus the related tax.

EXAMPLE 3

Lion, Inc., a § 501(c)(3) organization, received the following support during the taxable year.

Governmental unit A for services rendered	$ 30,000
Governmental unit B for services rendered	20,000
General public for services rendered	20,000
Gross investment income	15,000
Contributions from individual substantial contributors (disqualified persons)	15,000
Total support	$100,000

For purposes of the *external support test,* the support from A is counted only to the extent of $5,000 (greater of $5,000 or 1% of $100,000 support). Likewise, for B, only $5,000 is counted as support. Thus, the total countable support is $30,000 ($20,000 from the general public + $5,000 + $5,000), and Lion fails the test for the taxable year ($30,000/$100,000 = 30%; need > 33.3%). The $15,000 received from disqualified persons is excluded from the numerator but is included in the denominator.

External Support Test	
Governmental unit A for services rendered	$ 5,000
Governmental unit B for services rendered	5,000
General public for services rendered	20,000
Total countable support	$30,000

$\frac{\$30{,}000}{\$100{,}000} = 30\%$ Fails external support test

[25]The external and internal support tests generally must be met in each of the four preceding tax years. When these tests are met, public charity status is granted for the current year and for the subsequent year. Reg. §§ 1.509(a)–3(c) and 1.170A–9(e)(4)(i).

TAX IN THE NEWS Donor-Advised Funds: A Hot Topic

Suppose a wealthy taxpayer would like to make a substantial charitable contribution and qualify for the charitable contribution deduction this year. However, he has not yet identified the recipient of the contribution. Or the taxpayer has identified the recipient, but wants the charity to disburse the funds over a number of years. Or the taxpayer wants to make the contribution this year, but be permitted to advise the charitable organization in future years as to the possible use of the donated funds. Can the taxpayer achieve any of these goals and still be eligible for the charitable contribution deduction this year?

There is a way to meet the wealthy taxpayer's objectives. He can make his contribution to a "donor-advised fund." Such funds are components of a qualified charitable organization.

To receive this favorable treatment, however, certain statutory and administrative requirements must be met. Even though the donor may advise as to how the funds are to be used, the charitable organization must have ultimate control over their distribution. For any contributions to donor-advised funds made after February 13, 2007, the donor must obtain written acknowledgment from the charitable organization that it has exclusive legal control over the contributed assets.

Recognizing the potential for abuse in this area, both the Senate Finance Committee and the House Ways and Means Committee have identified donor-advised funds as a potential topic for additional legislation.

In calculating the *internal support test*, only the gross investment income of $15,000 is included in the numerator. Thus, the test is satisfied ($15,000/$100,000 = 15%; cannot > 33%) for the taxable year.

Internal Support Test	
Gross investment income	$15,000
Unrelated business taxable income	–0–
Total countable support	$15,000

$\frac{\$15,000}{\$100,000} = 15\%$ Passes internal support test

Because Lion did not satisfy both tests, it does not qualify as an organization that is broadly supported. ■

The intent of the two tests is to exclude from private foundation status those § 501(c)(3) organizations that are responsive to the general public rather than to the private interests of a limited number of donors or other persons.

Examples of § 501(c)(3) organizations that would be classified as private foundations, except that they receive broad public support, include the United Fund, the Girl Scouts, university alumni associations, and symphony orchestras.

Taxes Imposed on Private Foundations

LO.5

Recognize the taxes imposed on private foundations and calculate the related initial tax and additional tax amounts.

In general, a private foundation is exempt from Federal income tax. However, because a private foundation is usually not a broadly, publicly supported organization, it may be subject to the following taxes.[26]

- Tax based on investment income.
- Tax on self-dealing.
- Tax on failure to distribute income.
- Tax on excess business holdings.
- Tax on investments that jeopardize charitable purposes.
- Tax on taxable expenditures.

[26] §§ 4940–4945.

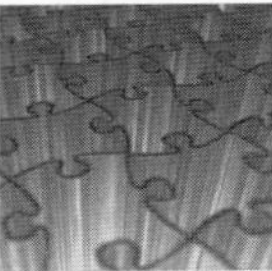

CONCEPT SUMMARY 15.3

Taxes Imposed on Private Foundations

			Private Foundation		Foundation Manager	
Type of Tax	**Code Section**	**Purpose**	**Initial Tax**	**Additional Tax**	**Initial Tax**	**Additional Tax**
On investment income	§ 4940	Audit fee to defray IRS expenses.	2%*			
On self-dealing	§ 4941	Engaging in transactions with disqualified persons.	5%**	200%**	2.5%†	50%†
On failure to distribute income	§ 4942	Failing to distribute adequate amount of income for exempt purposes.	15%	100%		
On excess business holdings	§ 4943	Investments that enable the private foundation to control unrelated businesses (usually by owning >35% of outstanding shares).	5%	200%		
On jeopardizing investments	§ 4944	Speculative investments that put the private foundation's assets at risk.	5%	25%	5%‡	5%†
On taxable expenditures	§ 4945	Expenditures that should not be made by private foundations.	10%	100%	2.5%‡	50%†

* May be possible to reduce the tax rate to 1%. In addition, an exempt operating foundation [see §§ 4940(d)(2) and 4942(j)(3)] is not subject to the tax.
** Imposed on the disqualified person rather than the foundation.
† Subject to a statutory ceiling of $10,000.
‡ Subject to a statutory ceiling of $5,000.

These taxes restrict the permitted activities of private foundations. Two levels of tax may be imposed on the private foundation and the foundation manager: an initial tax and an additional tax. The initial taxes (first-level), with the exception of the tax based on investment income, are imposed because the private foundation engages in so-called *prohibited transactions.* The additional taxes (second-level) are imposed only if the prohibited transactions are not corrected within a statutory time period.[27] See Concept Summary 15.3 for additional details.

The tax on a failure to distribute income will be used to illustrate how expensive these taxes can be and the related importance of avoiding their imposition. Both an initial (first-level) tax and an additional (second-level) tax may be imposed on a private nonoperating foundation for failure to distribute a sufficient portion of its income. The initial tax is imposed at a rate of 15 percent on the undistributed income for the taxable year that is not distributed by the end of the following taxable year. The initial tax is imposed on such undistributed income for each year until the IRS assesses the tax.

[27] § 4961.

The additional tax is imposed at a rate of 100 percent on the amount of the inadequate distribution that is not distributed by the assessment date. The additional tax is effectively waived if the undistributed income is distributed within 90 days after the mailing of the deficiency notice for the additional tax. Extensions of this period may be obtained.

Undistributed income is the excess of the distributable amount (in effect, the amount that should have been distributed) over qualifying distributions made by the entity. The distributable amount is the excess of the minimum investment return over the sum of (1) the unrelated business income tax and (2) the excise tax based on net investment income.[28] The minimum investment return is 5 percent of the excess of the fair market value of the foundation's assets over the unpaid debt associated with acquiring or improving these assets. The foundation's assets employed directly in carrying on the foundation's exempt purpose are not used in making this calculation.

EXAMPLE 4

Gold, Inc., a private foundation, has undistributed income of $80,000 for the taxable year 2009. It distributes $15,000 of this amount during 2010 and an additional $45,000 during 2011. An IRS deficiency notice is mailed to Gold on August 5, 2012. The initial tax is $12,750 [($65,000 × 15%) + ($20,000 × 15%)].

At the date of the deficiency notice, no additional distributions have been made from the 2009 undistributed income. Therefore, because the remaining undistributed income of $20,000 has not been distributed by August 5, 2012, an additional tax of $20,000 ($20,000 × 100%) is imposed.

If Gold distributes the $20,000 of undistributed income for 2009 within 90 days of the deficiency notice, the additional tax is waived. Without this distribution, however, the foundation will owe $32,750 in taxes. ■

Exhibit 15.2 shows the classifications of exempt organizations and indicates the potential negative consequences of classification as a private foundation.

15.5 Unrelated Business Income Tax

LO.6

Determine when an exempt organization is subject to the unrelated business income tax and calculate the amount of the tax.

As explained in the previous section, private foundations are subject to excise taxes for certain actions. One of these excise taxes penalizes the private foundation for using the foundation to gain control of unrelated businesses (tax on excess business holdings). However, *unrelated business* has different meanings for purposes of that excise tax and for the unrelated business income tax.

The **unrelated business income tax (UBIT)** is designed to treat the entity as if it were subject to the corporate income tax. Thus, the rates that are used are those applicable to a corporate taxpayer.[29]

In general, **unrelated business income (UBI)** is derived from activities not related to the exempt purpose of the exempt organization. The tax is levied because the organization is engaging in substantial commercial activities.[30] Without such a tax, nonexempt organizations (regular taxable business entities) would be at a substantial disadvantage when trying to compete with the exempt organization. Thus, the UBIT is intended to neutralize the exempt entity's tax advantage.[31]

It is the source of the business profits that triggers the UBIT, and not their use. UBI that is employed for the entity's exempt purpose still is subject to the tax.

[28] § 4940.

[29] § 511(a)(1).

[30] § 512(a)(1).

[31] Reg. § 1.513–1(b).

EXHIBIT 15.2 **Exempt Organizations: Classification**

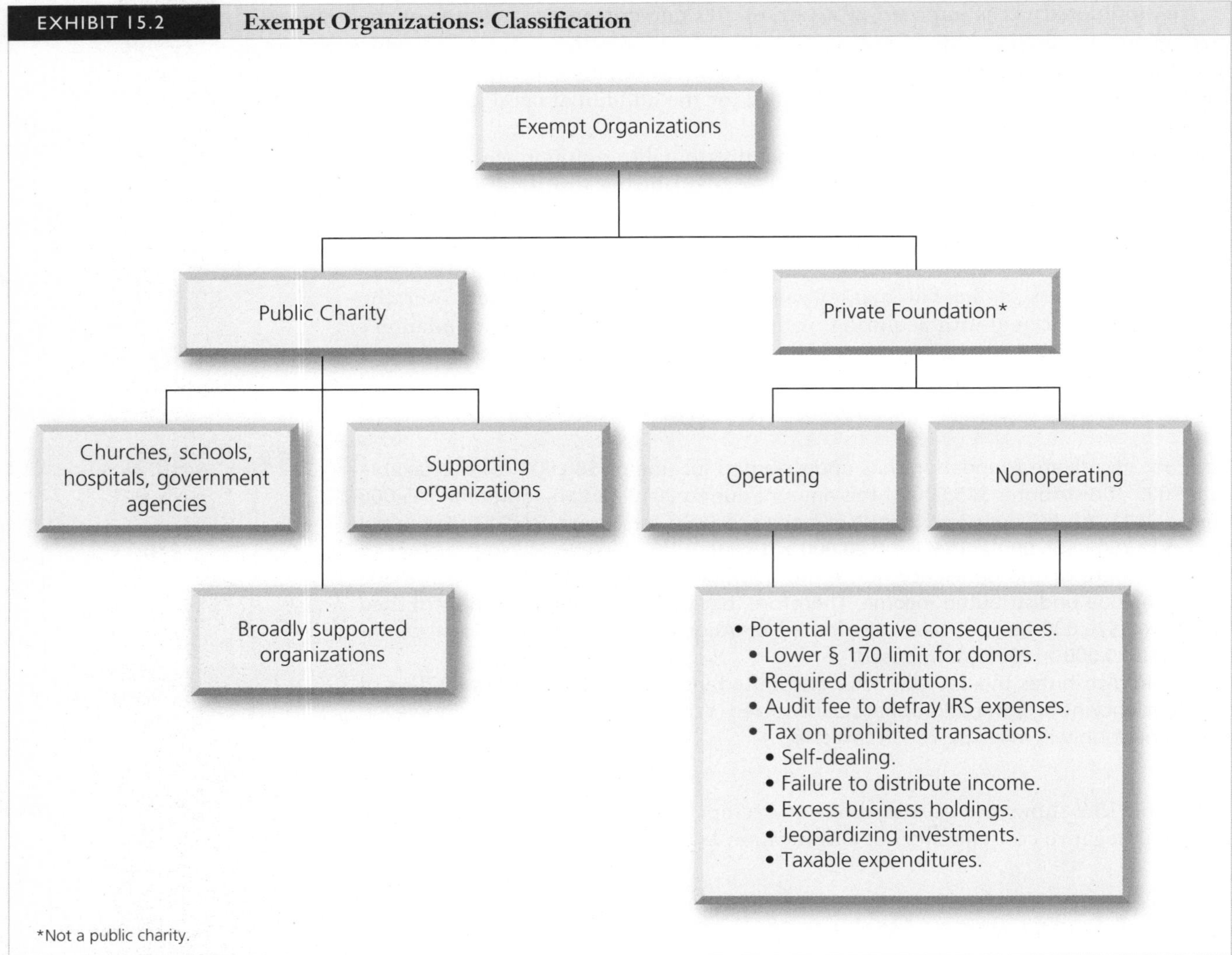

*Not a public charity.

THE BIG PICTURE

EXAMPLE 5

Return to the facts of *The Big Picture* on p. 15-1. Recall that Hopeful, Inc., an exempt organization under § 501 (c) (3), has received Taste Good Ice Cream, a chain of gourmet ice cream shops, as a bequest. Assume that Hopeful has decided to operate Taste Good as a division. Although the income from Taste Good's shops will be used to support Hopeful's exempt purpose of providing temporary lodging and psychological services to abused women, the net revenue constitutes unrelated business income; therefore, it is subject to the UBIT.

The UBIT applies to all organizations that are exempt from Federal income tax under § 501(c), except Federal agencies. In addition, the tax applies to state colleges and universities.[32]

A materiality exception generally exempts an entity from being subject to the UBIT if such income is insignificant. See the later discussion of the $1,000 statutory deduction generally available to all exempt organizations.

[32] § 511(a)(2) and Reg. § 1.511–2(a)(2).

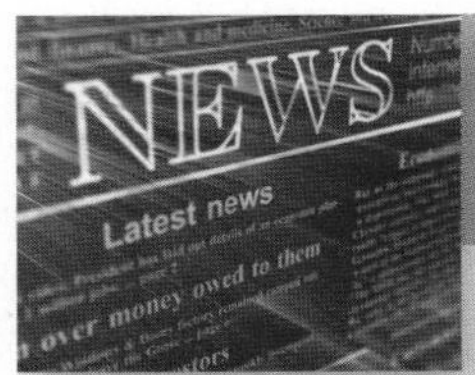

TAX IN THE NEWS **Getting Back More Than a Charitable Foundation Gives**

Charitable foundations typically give away money in carrying out their tax-exempt mission. Unless they are educational institutions, private foundations must distribute 5 percent of their investment assets every year for charitable purposes. Generally, private foundations meet this requirement by making grants.

However, there is another way that private foundations can satisfy this 5 percent requirement and at the same time create the potential for receiving back more from the recipient than the amount initially disbursed. This opportunity is called "program-related investing" (PRI), which can take several forms.

In one type of PRI, rather than making a grant to the recipient, a private foundation loans money to what would otherwise be the recipient and then collects interest (usually at a below-market interest rate) on the loan. In other forms of PRI, a private foundation makes an equity investment in the recipient or guarantees a loan that the recipient obtains from a conventional source.

PRI provides a way for a private foundation to conserve its assets, leverage its asset utilization (i.e., money potentially can be recycled to multiple recipients), and at the same time carry out its tax-exempt mission (i.e., a key requirement for PRI under the tax law). In addition, many of those involved in private foundations believe that expecting investment returns from the PRI recipient results in a greater buy-in, more accountability, and greater effort on the part of the recipient.

Unrelated Trade or Business

An exempt organization may be subject to the UBIT in the following circumstances.[33]

- The organization conducts a trade or business.
- The trade or business is not substantially related to the exempt purpose of the organization.
- The trade or business is regularly carried on by the organization.

The Code specifically exempts the following activities from classification as an unrelated trade or business. Thus, even if all of the above factors are present, the activity is not classified as an unrelated trade or business.

- The individuals performing substantially all of the work of the trade or business do so without compensation (e.g., an orphanage operates a retail store for sales to the general public, and all of the work is done by volunteers).
- The trade or business consists of selling merchandise, and substantially all of the merchandise has been received as gifts or contributions (e.g., thrift shops).
- For § 501(c)(3) organizations and for state colleges or universities, the trade or business is conducted primarily for the convenience of the organization's members, students, patients, officers, or employees (e.g., a laundry operated by the college for laundering dormitory linens and students' clothing and a college bookstore).
- For most employee unions, the trade or business consists of selling to members, at their usual place of employment, work-related clothing and equipment and items normally sold through vending machines, snack bars, or food-dispensing facilities.

Definition of Trade or Business

Trade or business, for this purpose, is broadly defined. It includes any activity conducted for the production of income through the sale of merchandise or the performance of services. An activity need not generate a profit to be treated as a trade or business. The activity may be part of a larger set of activities conducted by the

[33] § 513(a) and Reg. § 1.513–2(a).

organization, some of which may be related to the exempt purpose. Being included in a larger set does not cause the activity to lose its identity as an unrelated trade or business.[34]

EXAMPLE 6

Health, Inc., is an exempt hospital that operates a pharmacy. The pharmacy provides medicines and supplies to the patients in the hospital (i.e., it contributes to the conduct of the hospital's exempt purpose). In addition, the pharmacy sells medicines and supplies to the general public. The activity of selling to the general public constitutes a trade or business for purposes of the UBIT. ■

Not Substantially Related to the Exempt Purpose

Exempt organizations frequently conduct unrelated trades or businesses to provide income to help defray the costs of conducting the exempt purpose (like the ice cream shops in Example 5). Providing financial support for the exempt purpose will not prevent an activity from being classified as an unrelated trade or business and thereby being subject to the UBIT.

To be related to the accomplishment of the exempt purpose, the conduct of the business activities must be causally related and contribute importantly to the exempt purpose. Whether a causal relationship exists and the degree of its importance are determined by examining the facts and circumstances. One must consider the size and extent of the activities in relation to the nature and extent of the exempt function that the activities serve.[35]

EXAMPLE 7

Art, Inc., an exempt organization, operates a school for training children in the performing arts. As an essential part of that training, the children perform for the general public. The children are paid at the minimum wage for the performances, and Art derives gross income by charging admission to the performances.

The income from admissions is not income from an unrelated trade or business, because the performances by the children contribute importantly to the accomplishment of the exempt purpose of providing training in the performing arts. ■

EXAMPLE 8

Assume that the facts are the same as in Example 7, except that four performances are conducted each weekend of the year. Assume that this number of performances far exceeds that required for training the children. Thus, the part of the income derived from admissions for these excess performances is income from an unrelated trade or business. ■

The trade or business may sell merchandise that has been produced as part of the accomplishment of the exempt purpose. The sale of such merchandise is normally treated as related to the exempt purpose. However, if the merchandise is not sold in substantially the same state it was in at the completion of the exempt purpose, the gross income subsequently derived from the sale of the merchandise is income from an unrelated trade or business.[36]

EXAMPLE 9

Help-Self, Inc., an exempt organization, conducts programs for the rehabilitation of the handicapped. One of the programs includes training in radio and television repair. Help-Self derives gross income by selling the repaired items. The income is substantially related to the accomplishment of the exempt purpose. ■

An asset or a facility used in the exempt purpose may also be used in a nonexempt purpose. Income derived from use for a nonexempt purpose is income from an unrelated trade or business.[37]

[34]Reg. § 1.513–1(b).
[35]Reg. § 1.513–1(d).
[36]Reg. § 1.513–1(d)(4)(ii).
[37]Reg. § 1.513–1(d)(4)(iii) addresses the allocation of expenses to exempt and nonexempt activities.

EXAMPLE 10

Civil, Inc., an exempt organization, operates a museum. As part of the exempt purpose of the museum, educational lectures are given in the museum's theater during the operating hours of the museum. In the evening, when the museum is closed, the theater is leased to an individual who operates a movie theater. The lease income received from the individual who operates the movie theater is income from an unrelated trade or business. ■

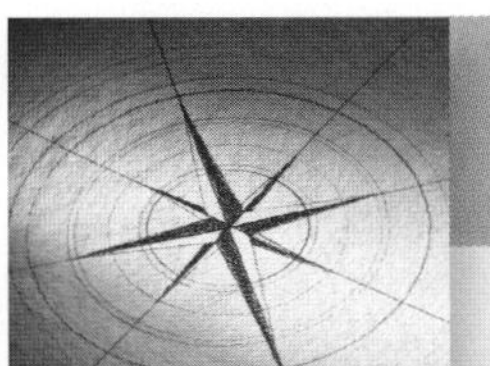

ETHICS & EQUITY Unrelated Business Income Tax: Substantially Related

Mops and More, a § 501(c)(3) organization, makes mops and brooms that it sells to the general public. The exempt organization's mission is to provide short-term employment opportunities and temporary housing for recovering drug addicts during the two-month period they are at a halfway house. Profits from the sales of the mops and brooms are used to support the halfway house. The laborers are paid the minimum wage, with half of this amount going toward their room and board at the halfway house. In prior years, approximately 90 percent of the laborers involved in the production of the mops and brooms were recovering addicts staying at the halfway house. The remaining 10 percent were permanent employees who trained and supervised the recovering addicts.

In prior years, Mops and More has not filed a Form 990–T (Exempt Organization Business Income Tax Return). The treasurer of Mops and More believes that the sale of the mops and brooms does not constitute unrelated business income, because the production of the items is substantially related to the mission of the exempt organization.

For the current tax year, there is a substantial drop in the number of recovering addicts who stay at the halfway house. To meet production quotas, the organization hires foreign workers who are legally in this country on temporary visas. They account for 70 percent of the labor force in the current year.

The treasurer believes that this shift from recovering addicts to foreign workers is temporary in nature. So she does not believe it is necessary to file a Form 990–T. Has she acted appropriately?

Special Rule for Corporate Sponsorship Payments

The term *unrelated trade or business* does not include the soliciting and receiving of qualified sponsorship payments.[38]

A payment qualifies as a qualified sponsorship payment if it meets the following requirements.

- There is no arrangement or expectation that the trade or business making the payment will receive any substantial benefit other than the use or acknowledgment of its name, logo, or product lines in connection with the activities of the exempt organization.
- Such use or acknowledgment does not include advertising the payor's products or services.
- The payment does not include any payment for which the amount is contingent upon the level of attendance at one or more events, broadcast ratings, or other factors indicating the degree of public exposure to one or more events.

EXAMPLE 11

Pets, Inc., a manufacturer of cat food, contributes $25,000 to Feline Care, Inc., an exempt organization that cares for abandoned cats. In return for the contribution, Feline agrees to put Pets' corporate logo in its monthly newsletter to donors. Under these circumstances, the $25,000 payment is a qualified sponsorship payment and is not subject to the UBIT. ■

EXAMPLE 12

Assume the same facts as in Example 11, except that Feline agrees to endorse Pets' cat food in its monthly newsletter by stating that it feeds only Pets' cat food to its cats. The $25,000 is not a qualified sponsorship payment and is subject to the UBIT. ■

[38] § 513(i).

Special Rule for Bingo Games

A special provision applies in determining whether income from bingo games is from an unrelated trade or business. Under this provision, a *qualified bingo game* is not an unrelated trade or business if both of the following requirements are satisfied.[39]

- The bingo game is legal under both state and local law.
- Commercial bingo games (conducted for a profit motive) ordinarily are not permitted in the jurisdiction.

EXAMPLE 13

Play, Inc., an exempt organization, conducts weekly bingo games. The laws of the state and municipality in which Play conducts the games expressly provide that exempt organizations may conduct bingo games, but do not permit profit-oriented entities to do so. Because both of the requirements for bingo games are satisfied, the bingo games conducted by Play are not an unrelated trade or business. ■

EXAMPLE 14

Game, Inc., an exempt organization, conducts weekly bingo games in City X and City Y. State law expressly permits exempt organizations to conduct bingo games. State law also provides that profit-oriented entities may conduct bingo games in X, which is a resort community. Several businesses regularly conduct bingo games there.

The bingo games conducted by Game in Y are not an unrelated trade or business. However, the bingo games that Game conducts in X are an unrelated trade or business, because commercial bingo games are regularly permitted to be conducted there. ■

Special Rule for Distribution of Low-Cost Articles

If an exempt organization distributes low-cost items as an incidental part of its solicitation for charitable contributions, the distributions may not be considered an unrelated trade or business. A low-cost article is an item that costs $9.90 (indexed annually) or less for 2012. Examples of such items are pens, stamps, stickers, stationery, and address labels. If more than one item is distributed to a person during the calendar year, the costs of the items are combined.[40]

Special Rule for Rental or Exchange of Membership Lists

If an exempt organization conducts a trade or business that consists of either exchanging with or renting to other exempt organizations the organization's donor or membership list (mailing lists), the activity is not an unrelated trade or business.[41]

Other Special Rules

Other special rules are used in determining whether each of the following activities is an unrelated trade or business.[42]

- Qualified public entertainment activities (e.g., a state fair).
- Qualified convention and trade show activities.
- Certain services provided at cost or less by a hospital to other small hospitals.
- Certain pole rentals by telephone or electric companies.

Unrelated Business Income

Even when an exempt organization conducts an unrelated trade or business, a tax is assessed only if the exempt organization regularly conducts the activity and the business produces unrelated business income.

Regularly Carried on by the Organization

An activity is classified as unrelated business income only if it is regularly carried on by the exempt organization. This provision ensures that only activities that are actually

[39] § 513(f).
[40] § 513(h)(1)(A).
[41] § 513(h)(1)(B).
[42] §§ 513(d), (e), and (g).

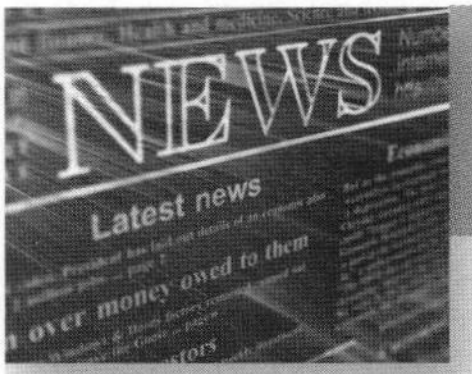

TAX IN THE NEWS Should the NCAA Be Tax-Exempt?

The National Collegiate Athletic Association (NCAA) is a tax-exempt organization. Although donors cannot deduct contributions to the NCAA as charitable contributions, the NCAA itself does not pay taxes on its revenues.

Several members of Congress have questioned whether the NCAA should be tax-exempt. Among them is former Congressman Bill Thomas (served as chairman of the House Ways and Means Committee), who suggested that the NCAA's tax-exempt status amounts to a government subsidy from the taxpayers. Another concern is that the NCAA's member educational institutions may be using their tax-exempt status to help pay for escalating athletic program costs, including coaches' multimillion-dollar salaries, chartered travel, and state-of-the-art athletic facilities.

competing with taxable organizations are subject to the UBIT. Accordingly, factors to be considered in applying the *regularly carried on* test include the frequency of the activity, the continuity of the activity, and the manner in which the activity is pursued.[43]

EXAMPLE 15

Silver, Inc., an exempt organization, owns land that is located next to the state fairgrounds. During the 10 days of the state fair, Silver uses the land as a parking lot and charges individuals attending the state fair for parking there. The activity is not regularly carried on. ■

EXAMPLE 16

Black, Inc., an exempt organization, has its offices in the downtown area. It owns a parking lot adjacent to its offices on which its employees park during the week. On Saturdays, it rents the spaces in the parking lot to individuals shopping or working in the downtown area. Black is conducting a business activity on a year-round basis, even though it is only for one day per week. Thus, an activity is regularly being carried on. ■

Unrelated Business Income Defined

Unrelated business income is generally that derived from the unrelated trade or business, reduced by the deductions directly connected with the conduct of the unrelated trade or business.[44]

Unrelated Business Taxable Income

General Tax Model

The model for unrelated business taxable income (UBTI) appears in Figure 15.2.

Positive adjustments[45]

1. A charitable contribution deduction is permitted without regard to whether the gift is associated with the unrelated trade or business. However, to the extent the charitable contributions deducted in calculating net unrelated business income (see Figure 15.2) exceed 10 percent of UBTI (without regard to the charitable contribution deduction), the excess amount is disallowed (i.e., a positive adjustment results).

EXAMPLE 17

Brown, Inc., an exempt organization, has UBTI of $100,000 (excluding any modifications associated with charitable contributions). Total charitable contributions (all associated with the unrelated trade or business) are $13,000. Assuming that the $13,000 is deducted in calculating net unrelated business income, the excess of $3,000 [$13,000 − 10%($100,000)] is a positive adjustment in calculating UBTI. ■

[43] § 512(a)(1) and Reg. § 1.513–1(c).

[44] § 512(a)(1).

[45] §§ 512(a)(1) and (b) and Reg. § 1.512(b)–1.

FIGURE 15.2 Tax Formula for Unrelated Business Taxable Income

Gross unrelated business income
– Deductions
= Net unrelated business income
± Modifications
= Unrelated business taxable income

2. Unrelated debt-financed income net of the unrelated debt-financed deductions (see the subsequent discussion of Unrelated Debt-Financed Income).
3. Certain net interest, annuity, royalty, and rent income received by the exempt organization from an organization it controls (80 percent test). This provision overrides the modifications for these types of income (negative adjustment 3).

Negative adjustments

1. Income from dividends, interest, and annuities, net of all deductions directly related to producing such income.
2. Royalty income, regardless of whether it is measured by production, gross income, or taxable income from the property, net of all deductions directly related to producing such income.
3. Rent income from real property and from certain personal property net of all deductions directly related to producing such income. Personal property rents are included in the negative adjustment only if the personal property is leased with the real property. In addition, the personal property rent income must be incidental (does not exceed 10 percent of the gross rent income under the lease) to be used in computing the negative adjustment. In both of the following cases, however, none of the rent income is treated as a negative adjustment.

   - More than 50 percent of the rent income under the lease is from personal property.
   - Rent income is calculated using the tenant's profits.

EXAMPLE 18

Beaver, Inc., an exempt organization, leases land and a building (realty) and computers (personalty) housed in the building. Under the lease, $46,000 of the rent is for the land and building, and $4,000 is for the computers. Expenses incurred for the land and building are $10,000. The net rent income from the land and building of $36,000 ($46,000 − $10,000) and the income from the computers of $4,000 are negative adjustments. ■

EXAMPLE 19

Assume the same facts as in Example 18, except that the rent income is $35,000 from the land and building and $15,000 from the computers. Because the rent income from the computers exceeds $5,000 (10% × $50,000) and is not incidental, it is not a negative adjustment. ■

EXAMPLE 20

Assume the same facts as in Example 18, except that the rent income is $20,000 from the land and building and $30,000 from the computers. Because more than 50% of the rent income under the lease is from the computers, neither the rent income from the land and building nor that from the computers is a negative adjustment. ■

If the lessor of real property provides significant services to the lessee, such income, for this purpose, is not rent income.

4. Gains and losses from the sale, exchange, or other disposition of property *except for* inventory.

EXAMPLE 21

Beaver, the owner of the land, building, and computers in Example 18, sells these assets for $450,000. Their adjusted basis is $300,000. Beaver's recognized gain of $150,000 is a negative adjustment. ■

5. Certain research income net of all deductions directly related to producing that income.
6. The charitable contribution deduction is permitted without regard to whether the gift is associated with the unrelated trade or business. Therefore, to the extent the charitable contributions exceed those deducted in calculating net unrelated business income (see Figure 15.2), the excess is a negative adjustment in calculating UBTI. In making this calculation, though, the 10 percent of UBTI (without regard to the charitable contribution deduction) limit still applies (see positive adjustment 1).

EXAMPLE 22

Canine, Inc., an exempt organization, has UBTI of $100,000 (excluding any modifications associated with charitable contributions). The total charitable contributions are $9,000, of which $7,000 (those associated with the unrelated trade or business) has been deducted in calculating net unrelated business income. Therefore, the remaining $2,000 of charitable contributions make up a negative adjustment in calculating UBTI. ■

7. A "standard deduction" of $1,000 is allowed.

EXAMPLE 23

Petit Care, Inc., an exempt organization, reports net unrelated business income of $800. Because Petit claims a $1,000 statutory deduction, its UBTI is $0. Therefore, its income tax liability is $0. ■

After UBTI is determined, that amount is subject to tax using the regular corporate tax rates.

EXAMPLE 24

Patient, Inc., an exempt organization, has UBTI of $500,000. Patient's income tax liability is $170,000 ($500,000 UBTI × 34% corporate tax rate). ■

Unrelated Debt-Financed Income

In the formula for calculating UBTI (see Figure 15.2), unrelated debt-financed income is one of the positive adjustments. Examples of income from debt-financed property include rent income from real estate or tangible personal property, dividends from corporate stock, and gains from the disposition of debt-financed property. Gains from unrelated business income property are also included to the extent the gains are not otherwise treated as unrelated business income.

In terms of the UBIT, the positive adjustment for unrelated debt-financed income is a significant one. Without this provision, a tax-exempt organization could use borrowed funds to acquire unrelated business or investment property and use the untaxed (i.e., exempt) earnings from the acquisition to pay for the property.

Definition of Debt-Financed Income

Debt-financed income is the gross income generated from debt-financed property. *Debt-financed property* is all property of the exempt organization that is held to produce income and on which there is acquisition indebtedness, *except* for the following.[46]

- Property where substantially all (at least 85 percent) of the use is for the achievement of the exempt purpose of the exempt organization.[47]
- Property whose gross income is otherwise treated as unrelated business income.

[46] § 514(b).

[47] Reg. § 1.514(b)–1(b)(1)(ii).

- Property whose gross income is from the following sources and is not otherwise treated as unrelated business income.
  - Income from research performed for the United States or a Federal governmental agency, or a state or a political subdivision thereof.
  - For a college, university, or hospital, income from research.
  - For an organization that performs fundamental (i.e., not applied) research for the benefit of the general public, income from research.
- Property used in an activity that is not an unrelated trade or business.

If the 85 percent test is not satisfied, only the portion of the property that is *not* used for the exempt purpose is debt-financed property.

EXAMPLE 25

Deer, Inc., an exempt organization, owns a five-story office building on which there is acquisition indebtedness. Three of the floors are used for Deer's exempt purpose. The two other floors are leased to Purple Corporation. In this case, the *substantially all* test is not satisfied. Therefore, 40% of the office building is debt-financed property, and 60% is not. ■

Certain land that is acquired by an exempt organization for later exempt use is excluded from debt-financed property if the following requirements are satisfied.[48]

- The principal purpose of acquiring the land is for use (substantially all) in achieving the organization's exempt purpose.
- This use will begin within 10 years of the acquisition date.
- At the date when the land is acquired, it is located in the *neighborhood* of other property of the organization for which substantially all of the use is for achieving the organization's exempt purpose.

Even if the third requirement is not satisfied, the land still is excluded from debt-financed property if it is converted to use for achieving the organization's exempt purpose within the 10-year period. Qualification under this provision will result in a refund of taxes previously paid. If the exempt organization is a church, the 10-year period becomes a 15-year period and the neighborhood requirement is waived.

Definition of Acquisition Indebtedness

Acquisition indebtedness is debt sustained by the exempt organization in association with the acquisition of property. More precisely, *acquisition indebtedness* consists of the unpaid amounts of the following for debt-financed property.[49]

- Debt incurred in acquiring or improving the property.
- Debt incurred before the property was acquired or improved, but which would not have been incurred without the acquisition or improvement.
- Debt incurred after the property was acquired or improved, but which would not have been incurred without the acquisition or improvement.

EXAMPLE 26

Red, Inc., an exempt organization, acquires land for $100,000. To finance the acquisition, Red mortgages the land and receives loan proceeds of $80,000. Red leases the land to Duck Corporation. The mortgage is acquisition indebtedness. ■

EXAMPLE 27

Rose, Inc., an exempt organization, makes improvements to an office building that it rents to Bird Corporation. Excess working capital funds are used to finance the improvements. Rose is later required to mortgage its laboratory building, which it uses for its exempt purpose, to replenish working capital. The mortgage is acquisition indebtedness. ■

[48] § 514(b)(3).

[49] § 514(c)(1). Educational organizations can exclude certain debt incurred for real property acquisitions from classification as acquisition indebtedness.

Exempt Organizations	Statutory Authority
Girl Scouts	§ 501(c)(1)
Catholic Church	§ 501(c)(2)
National Football League (NFL)	§ 501(c)(3)
American Red Cross	§ 501(c)(4)
Salvation Army	§ 501(c)(5)
United Fund	§ 501(c)(6)
Bill and Melinda Gates Foundation	§ 501(c)(7)
University of Richmond	§ 501(c)(8)
Underwriters Laboratories (UL)	§ 501(c)(9)
PGA Tour	§ 501(c)(10)
Veterans of Foreign Wars (VFW)	§ 501(c)(11)
Dallas Rodeo Club	§ 501(c)(12)
PTA	§ 501(c)(13)
Toano Cemetery Association	§ 501(c)(14)
Alpha Chi Omega Sorority	§ 501(c)(15)
Green, Inc., Legal Services Plan	§ 501(c)(16)
National Press Club	§ 501(c)(19)
Federal Deposit Insurance Corporation (FDIC)	§ 501(c)(20)
League of Women Voters	§ 501(d)

37. **LO.2, 3** Innovation, Inc., a § 501(c)(3) medical research organization, makes lobbying expenditures of $1.1 million. Innovation incurs exempt purpose expenditures of $15 million in carrying out its medical research mission. **Decision Making**
    a. Determine the tax consequences for Innovation if it does not elect to be eligible to participate in lobbying activities on a limited basis.
    b. Determine the tax consequences for Innovation if it does elect to be eligible to participate in lobbying activities on a limited basis.
    c. In light of pending health care legislation, Innovation is considering increasing its lobbying expenditures by 50% annually. Advise Innovation whether this is a wise thing to do from an after-tax perspective.

38. **LO.3** Wish, Inc., a § 501(c)(3) organization, pays unreasonable compensation to Molly, the treasurer of Wish. Molly's compensation is $600,000. Assume that reasonable compensation would be $500,000.
    a. Determine any adverse tax consequences for Wish, Inc.
    b. Determine any adverse tax consequences for Molly.

39. **LO.3, 6, 8** Roadrunner, Inc., is an exempt medical organization. Quail, Inc., a sporting goods retailer, is a wholly owned subsidiary of Roadrunner. Roadrunner inherited the Quail stock last year from a major benefactor of the medical organization. Quail's taxable income is $550,000. Quail will remit all of its earnings, net of any taxes, to Roadrunner to support the exempt purpose of the parent. **Decision Making** **Communications**
    a. Is Quail subject to Federal income tax? If so, calculate the liability.
    b. Arthur Morgan, the treasurer of Roadrunner, has contacted you regarding minimizing or eliminating Quail's tax liability. He would like to know if the tax consequences would be better if Quail were liquidated into Roadrunner. Write a letter to Morgan that contains your advice. Roadrunner's address is 500 Rouse Tower, Rochester, NY 14627.
    c. Would your answer in (a) change if Roadrunner had acquired the Quail stock by purchase or gift rather than by inheritance? Discuss.
    d. How would the tax consequences change if Quail's taxable income was only $100,000 and it remitted only 75% of its earnings, net of taxes, to Roadrunner?

40. **LO.3** Respond, Inc., a § 501(c)(3) organization, receives the following revenues and incurs the following expenses.

Grant from Gates Foundation	$ 60,000
Charitable contributions received	700,000
Expenses in carrying out its exempt mission	740,000
Net income before taxes of Landscaping, Inc., a wholly owned for-profit subsidiary	425,000

Landscaping, Inc., remits all of its after-tax profits each year to Respond. Calculate the amount of the Federal income tax, if any, for Respond and for Landscaping.

Communications

41. **LO.4** Pigeon, Inc., a § 501(c)(3) organization, received support from the following sources.

Governmental unit A for services rendered	$ 6,300
Governmental unit B for services rendered	4,500
Fees from the general public for services rendered (Each payment was of $100)	75,000
Gross investment income	39,000
Contributions from disqualified persons	26,000
Contributions from other than disqualified persons (Each gift was of $50)	160,000
Total support	$310,800

a. Does Pigeon satisfy the test for receiving broad public support? Why or why not?
b. Is Pigeon a private foundation? Be specific in your answer.
c. Arnold Horn, Pigeon's treasurer, has asked you to advise him on whether Pigeon is a private foundation. Write a letter to him in which you address the issue. His address is 250 Bristol Road, Charlottesville, VA 22903.

42. **LO.5** Gray, Inc., a private foundation, reports the following items of income and deductions. Gray is not an exempt operating foundation, and it is not eligible for the 1% tax rate.

Interest income	$ 29,000
Rent income	61,000
Dividend income	15,000
Royalty income	22,000
Unrelated business income	80,000
Rent expenses	(26,000)
Unrelated business expenses	(12,000)

a. Calculate the net investment income.
b. Calculate the tax on net investment income.
c. What is the purpose of the tax on net investment income?

43. **LO.5** Egret, Inc., a private foundation, has been in existence for 10 years. During this period, Egret has been unable to satisfy the requirements for classification as a private operating foundation. At the end of 2011, it had undistributed income of $320,000. Of this amount, $170,000 was distributed in 2012, and $150,000 was distributed during the first quarter of 2013. The IRS deficiency notice was mailed on August 1, 2014.
a. Calculate the initial tax for 2011, 2012, and 2013.
b. Calculate the additional tax for 2014.

Decision Making

44. **LO.5, 8** Otis is the CEO of Rectify, Inc., a private foundation. Otis invests $500,000 (80%) of the foundation's investment portfolio in derivatives. Previously, the $500,000 had been invested in corporate bonds with an AA rating that earned 7% per annum. If the derivatives investment works as Otis's investment adviser claims, the annual earnings could be as high as 20%.
a. Determine whether Rectify is subject to any of the taxes imposed on private foundations.
b. If so, calculate the amount of the initial tax.
c. If so, calculate the amount of the additional tax if the act causing the imposition of the tax is not addressed within the correction period.
d. Are Otis and the foundation better off financially if the prohibited transaction, if any, is addressed within the correction period? Explain.

45. **LO.5** The board of directors of White Pearl, Inc., a private foundation, consists of Charlyne, Beth, and Carlos. They vote unanimously to provide a $325,000 grant to Marcus, their business associate. The grant is to be used for travel and education and does not qualify as a permitted grant to individuals (i.e., it is a taxable expenditure under § 4945). Each director knows that Marcus was selected for the grant because he is a friend of the organization and that the grant is a taxable expenditure.
    a. Calculate the initial tax imposed on White Pearl.
    b. Calculate the initial tax imposed on the foundation manager (i.e., board of directors).

46. **LO.6** The Open Museum is an exempt organization that operates a gift shop. The museum's annual operations budget is $3.2 million. Gift shop sales generate a profit of $900,000. Another $600,000 of endowment income is generated. Both the income from the gift shop and the endowment income are used to support the exempt purpose of the museum. The balance of $1.7 million required for annual operations is provided through admission fees. **Communications**

    Wayne Davis, a new board member, does not understand why the museum is subject to tax at all, particularly because the profits are used in carrying out the mission of the museum. The museum's address is 250 Oak Avenue, Peoria, IL 61625.
    a. Calculate the amount of unrelated business income.
    b. Assume that the endowment income is reinvested in the endowment fund, rather than being used to support annual operations. Calculate the amount of unrelated business income.
    c. As the museum treasurer, write a letter to Wayne explaining the reason for the tax consequences. Mr. Davis's address is 45 Pine Avenue, Peoria, IL 61625.

47. **LO.6** Upward and Onward, Inc., a § 501(c)(3) organization that provides training programs for welfare recipients, reports the following income and expenses from the sale of products associated with the training program. Calculate Upward and Onward's UBIT.

Gross income from sales	$850,000
Cost of goods sold	212,000
Advertising and selling expenses	52,000
Administrative expenses	225,000

    a. Assume that the sale of the training program products is substantially related to Upward and Onward's exempt purpose.
    b. Assume that the sale of the training program products is not substantially related to Upward and Onward's exempt purpose.

48. **LO.6** Perch, Inc., an exempt organization, has unrelated business taxable income of $4 million. **Communications**
    a. Calculate Perch's UBIT.
    b. Prepare an outline of a presentation you are going to give to the new members of Perch's board on why Perch is subject to the UBIT even though it is an exempt organization.

49. **LO.6** For each of the following organizations, determine its UBTI and any related UBIT.
    a. AIDS, Inc., an exempt charitable organization that provides support for individuals with AIDS, operates a retail medical supply store open to the general public. The net income of the store, before any Federal income taxes, is $305,000.
    b. The local Episcopal Church operates a retail gift shop. The inventory consists of the typical items sold by commercial gift shops in the city. The director of the gift shop estimates that 80% of the gift shop sales are to tourists and 20% are to church members. The net income of the gift shop, before the salaries of the three gift shop employees and any Federal income taxes, is $300,000. The salaries of the employees total $80,000.
    c. Education, Inc., a private university, has vending machines in the student dormitories and academic buildings on campus. In recognition of recent tuition increases, the university has adopted a policy of merely trying to recover its costs associated with the vending machine activity. For the current year, however, the net income of the activity, before any Federal income taxes, is $75,000.

50. **LO.6** For each of the following organizations, determine its UBTI and any related UBIT.
   a. Worn, Inc., an exempt organization, provides food for the homeless. It operates a thrift store that sells used clothing to the general public. The thrift shop is staffed solely by four salaried employees. All of the clothes it sells are received as contributions. The $100,000 profit generated for the year by the thrift shop is used in Worn's mission of providing food to the homeless.
   b. Small, Inc., an exempt organization, recorded gross unrelated business income of $900 and unrelated business expenses of $400.
   c. In Care, Inc., is a §501(c)(3) exempt organization. It owns a convenience store and gas pumps, which it received as a bequest from a patron. The store/gas pumps entity is organized as StopBy, a C corporation. Because StopBy is profitable, In Care hires a manager and several employees to run the entity. For the current year, StopBy's profit is $640,000. All of this amount is distributed by StopBy to In Care to use in carrying out its exempt mission.

51. **LO.6** Ongoing Forward, Inc., an exempt organization, reports gross unrelated business income of $22,000 and unrelated business expenses of $15,000. Calculate the amount of any UBIT.

Communications

52. **LO.6** Falcon Basketball League, an exempt organization, is a youth basketball league for children ages 12 through 14. The league has been in existence for 30 years. In the past, revenue for operations has been provided through community fund-raising and the sale of snacks at the games by the parents. Due to a projected revenue shortfall of approximately $5,000, the governing board has decided to charge admission to the basketball games of $1.00 for adults and $0.50 for children.
   a. Will the admission charge affect Falcon's exempt status? Explain.
   b. What are the tax consequences to Falcon of the net income from snack sales and the new admission fee?
   c. As the volunteer treasurer of the Falcon League, prepare a memo for the board in which you explain the effect, if any, of the admission fee policy on Falcon's exempt status.

53. **LO.6** Onward, Inc., is an exempt organization that assists disabled individuals by training them in digital TV repair. Used digital TVs are donated to Onward, Inc., by both organizations and individuals. Some of the donated digital TVs are operational, but others are not. After being used in the training program, the digital TVs, all of which are now operational, are sold to the general public. Onward's revenues and expenses for the current period are as follows.

Contributions	$ 700,000
Revenues from digital TV sales	3,600,000
Administrative expenses	500,000
Materials and supplies for digital TV repairs	800,000
Utilities	25,000
Wages paid to disabled individuals in the training program (at minimum-wage rate)	1,200,000
Rent for building and equipment	250,000

   Any revenues not expended during the current period are deposited in a reserve fund to finance future activities.
   a. Is the digital TV repair and sales activity an unrelated trade or business?
   b. Calculate the net income of Onward, Inc., and the related Federal income tax liability, if any.

54. **LO.6** Save the Squirrels, Inc., a § 501(c)(3) organization that feeds the squirrels in municipal parks, receives a $250,000 contribution from Animal Feed, Inc., a corporation that sells animal feed. In exchange for the contribution, Save the Squirrels will identify Animal Feed as a major supporter in its monthly newsletter. Determine Save the Squirrels's UBTI and any related UBIT under the following independent assumptions:
   a. Save the Squirrels receives no other similar payments.
   b. Save the Squirrels agrees to identify Animal Feed as a major supporter and to include a half-page advertisement for Animal Feed products in its monthly newsletter as a result of the contribution.

55. **LO.6** Faith Church is exempt from Federal income taxation under § 501(c)(3). To supplement its contribution revenue, it holds bingo games on Saturday nights. It has the licenses and permits required to do so. The net income from the bingo games is $90,000. Of these funds, $60,000 are used to support the ministry of the church. The balance of $30,000 is invested in Faith's endowment fund for church music. Faith Church is located in a resort city where bingo games can be conducted by churches, charities, and for-profit entities.
   a. Will conducting the bingo games affect the exempt status of Faith Church? Explain.
   b. Calculate the Federal tax liability, if any, associated with the bingo games.

56. **LO.6** Fish, Inc., an exempt organization, reports unrelated business taxable income of $500,000 (excluding the deduction for charitable contributions). During the year, Fish makes charitable contributions of $54,000, of which $38,000 are associated with the unrelated trade or business.
   a. Calculate Fish's unrelated business taxable income (UBTI).
   b. Assume that the charitable contributions are $41,000, of which $38,000 are associated with the unrelated trade or business. Calculate the UBTI.

57. **LO.3, 6** Comfort, Inc., an exempt hospital, is going to operate a pharmacy that will be classified as an unrelated trade or business. Comfort establishes the pharmacy as a wholly owned subsidiary. During the current year, the subsidiary generates taxable income of $280,000 and pays dividends of $200,000 to Comfort.
   a. What are the tax consequences to the subsidiary?
   b. What are the tax consequences to Comfort?

58. **LO.6** Tranquility, Inc., an exempt organization, leases factory equipment to Blouses, Inc. Blouses is a taxable entity that manufactures women's clothing for distribution through upscale department stores. Blouses owns the land and building where it conducts its manufacturing operations. The original cost of the building to Blouses was $900,000, and the cost recovery deduction for the current year is $23,076. Rent income to Tranquility for the factory's equipment is $320,000, and the related expenses are $170,000. Calculate the effect of the equipment lease on Tranquility's unrelated business taxable income.

59. **LO.6** Kind, Inc., an exempt organization, leases land, a building, and factory equipment to Shirts, Inc. Shirts is a taxable entity that manufactures shirts for distribution through its factory outlet stores. The rent income and the related expenses for Kind are as follows.

	Rent Income	Rent Expenses
Land and building	$100,000	$40,000
Factory equipment	125,000	25,000

   a. Calculate the amount of Kind's unrelated business taxable income.
   b. Assume instead that Kind's rent income and expenses are as follows. Compute UBTI.

	Rent Income	Rent Expenses
Land and building	$100,000	$20,000
Factory equipment	125,000	50,000

60. **LO.6** Assistance, Inc., an exempt organization, sells the following assets during the tax year. Determine the effect of these transactions on Assistance's unrelated business taxable income.

Asset	Gain (Loss)	Use
Land and building	$ 80,000	In exempt purpose
Land	50,000	Leased to a taxable entity
Equipment	(20,000)	Leased to a taxable entity
Automobile	(5,000)	In exempt purpose

61. **LO.6** Medical, Inc., an exempt organization, has unrelated business taxable income of $450,000 (excluding any modifications associated with charitable contributions). Of total charitable contributions of $44,000 made by Medical, $40,000 are associated with its unrelated trade or business. Determine the effect of the charitable contributions on Medical's unrelated business taxable income.

62. **LO.6** Crow, Inc., an exempt organization, owns a building that cost $800,000. Depreciation of $300,000 has been deducted. The building is mortgaged for $600,000. The mortgage was incurred at the acquisition date. The building contains 10,000 square feet of floor space. Crow uses 8,000 square feet of the building in carrying on its exempt purpose and leases the remaining 2,000 square feet to Uranium Corporation. Is the building debt-financed property? Why or why not?

63. **LO.6** Benevolent, Inc., an exempt organization, owns the following properties. Calculate the adjusted basis to Benevolent of its debt-financed property.

Property	Basis	Acquisition Indebtedness	% Used in Exempt Purpose
Building A	$400,000	$300,000	100%
Building B	450,000	–0–	90
Building C	600,000	200,000	85
Building D	900,000	500,000	70

64. **LO.7** Seagull, Inc., a § 501(c)(3) exempt organization, uses a tax year that ends on October 31. Seagull's gross receipts are $600,000, and related expenses are $580,000.
    a. Is Seagull required to file an annual Form 990?
    b. If so, what is the due date?

65. **LO.7** Education, Inc., a § 501(c)(3) organization, is a private foundation with a tax year that ends on May 31. Gross receipts for the fiscal year are $180,000, and the related expenses are $160,000.
    a. Is Education required to file an annual information return?
    b. If so, what form is used?
    c. If so, what is the due date?
    d. How would your answers in (a), (b), and (c) change if Education was an exempt organization that was not a private foundation?

66. **LO.8** Historic Burg is an exempt organization that operates a museum depicting eighteenth-century life. Sally gives the museum an eighteenth-century chest that she has owned for 10 years. Her adjusted basis is $55,000, and the chest's appraised value is $100,000. Sally's adjusted gross income is $300,000. Calculate Sally's charitable contribution deduction if Historic Burg is:
    a. A private operating foundation (deduct FMV, 30% AGI limit).
    b. A private nonoperating foundation (deduct basis, 50% AGI limit).

RESEARCH PROBLEMS

THOMSON REUTERS
CHECKPOINT®

Note: Solutions to Research Problems can be prepared by using the **Checkpoint® Student Edition** online research product, which is available to accompany this text. It is also possible to prepare solutions to the Research Problems by using tax research materials found in a standard tax library.

Research Problem 1. Allied Fund, a charitable organization exempt under § 501(c)(3), has branches located in each of the 50 states. Allied is not a private foundation. Rather than having each of the state units file an annual return with the IRS, Allied would like to file a single return that reports the activities of all of its branches. Is this permissible? What is the due date of the return?

Partial list of research aids:
§ 6033.
§ 6072.
Reg. § 1.6033–2(d).

Research Problem 2. Heal, Inc., a tax-exempt hospital, was sold to its shareholders for $6.6 million. The IRS determined that the fair market value of the hospital was $7.8 million. An IRS agent is proposing that the tax-exempt status of the hospital be revoked because the sale of the hospital to the shareholders for less than the fair market value resulted in "private inurement" to them. Evaluate the IRS's proposal in a memo to the research file.

Communications

Research Problem 3. A Native American tribal government issued $10 million of bonds, paying interest at 5%. The disclosure document associated with the bonds stated that the bonds were tax-exempt. Is this correct? If so, provide documentation for such classification. Are there any exceptions? If so, what are they?

Research Problem 4. City Hospital, a tax-exempt hospital, has purchased a sports and fitness center located about three miles from the hospital. It is a state-of-the-art fitness center that includes an open fitness room with cardiovascular and strength equipment, an indoor track, exercise rooms, racquetball and tennis courts, an aquatic area with two pools, and a nutrition center/juice bar. The hospital's overall goals for the center are to enhance cardiovascular, physical, and psychosocial function; reduce morbidity and mortality; improve quality of life; and promote compliance with a lifelong prevention program.

Communications

The membership of the center will consist of three segments of the community: the general public, employees, and former rehabilitation patients. Each group will be charged a monthly fee and an initiation fee with a reduced fee provided for employees. Within each category, the fees vary depending on the member's age and restrictions on availability of the facilities during specific hours. The hospital hired a professional consulting firm to conduct a survey of the community to ensure that the fee structure would achieve its goal of making the center facilities available to an economic cross section of the community.

You have been contacted by Anne Dexter, the chief financial officer for the hospital. She is concerned that some or perhaps all of the revenue from the sports and fitness center will be classified as unrelated business income and therefore be subject to the UBIT. Write a letter to Ms. Dexter that contains your findings, and prepare a memo for the tax files. City Hospital's address is 1000 Board Street, Billings, MT 59101.

Research Problem 5. The American Accounting Association holds its regional meetings at seven locations in the spring and its national meeting in August of each year. The meetings include the formal presentation of papers, panel discussions, business sessions, and various committee meetings. In addition, textbook publishers are permitted to display their wares in a publisher's exhibit hall. The book exhibitors must pay a fee to the AAA for the right to do so. Are these fees unrelated business income?

Research Problem 6. A volunteer fire department located in Green County holds tax-exempt status. As a way of raising funds to support its firefighting activities, the department obtained the permission of the owners of three taverns located in Green County to place "tip jars" in the taverns. A tip jar is a gambling device from which patrons purchase sealed pieces of paper containing numbers, series of numbers, or symbols that may entitle the patron to cash or other prizes. The tip jars are legal under state law and under the county ordinance for tax-exempt organizations.

Under the county ordinance, the tax-exempt organization must receive at least 70% of the net proceeds after the winnings are paid, and the business where the tip jar is located must receive no more than 30%. Under the arrangement with the three taverns, the volunteer fire department received 80%.

The three taverns included the 20% they received in their gross income in calculating their taxable income. Because the volunteer fire department is tax-exempt, it did not pay Federal income taxes on the 80% it received.

The IRS determines that the tip jar income received by the volunteer fire department is unrelated business income and issues a deficiency notice. Evaluate the position of the IRS.

Research Problem 7. Roger is the pastor at the Third Ecumenical Church in Atlanta. Over lunch with Priscilla, the pastor at another church with whom Roger went to seminary, Roger learns that another friend's church recently had its tax-exempt status revoked for

Communications

engaging in political activities. From time to time, certain political figures "give testimony" at Roger's church. Being concerned about his own church's tax-exempt status, he asks you to provide him with the types of activities his church should not engage in or permit.

Locate a recent Revenue Ruling that you can use to provide Roger with the desired information. Summarize the ruling with two PowerPoint slides.

Internet Activity

Use the tax resources of the Internet to address the following questions. Do not restrict your search to the Web, but include a review of newsgroups and general reference materials, practitioner sites and resources, primary sources of the tax law, chat rooms and discussion groups, and other opportunities.

Communications

Research Problem 8. Download an application for tax-exempt status that would be filed with the IRS. Write a one-page letter to an organization that is contemplating the filing of such an application. The letter should walk through the application and highlight the information that must be provided and the estimated time required to comply with the directives of the form.

Research Problem 9. Determine whether the Kellogg Foundation is a private foundation. Print a copy of its Form 990 or Form 990–PF.

Communications

Research Problem 10. Verify the exempt status of the symphony orchestra that performs closest to your home. Who are its three highest-paid associates? Send an e-mail to your instructor explaining how you found this information.

Research Problem 11. Use **www2.guidestar.org** to obtain the following information on the Jamestown Yorktown Foundation, Inc., which is located in Williamsburg, Virginia.

- Locate the foundation's website.
- Under what paragraph of § 501(c) is the organization exempt from Federal income tax?
- Use the Form 990 to determine the amount of compensation paid to officers and directors.

CHAPTER

16 Multistate Corporate Taxation

LEARNING OBJECTIVES: *After completing Chapter 16, you should be able to:*

LO.1 Illustrate the computation of a multistate corporation's state tax liability.

LO.2 Define nexus and explain its role in state income taxation.

LO.3 Distinguish between allocation and apportionment of a multistate corporation's taxable income.

LO.4 Describe the nature and treatment of business and nonbusiness income.

LO.5 Discuss the sales, payroll, and property apportionment factors.

LO.6 Apply the unitary method of state income taxation.

LO.7 Discuss the states' income tax treatment of S corporations, partnerships, and LLCs.

LO.8 Describe other commonly encountered state and local taxes on businesses.

LO.9 Recognize tax planning opportunities available to minimize a corporation's state and local tax liability.

CHAPTER OUTLINE

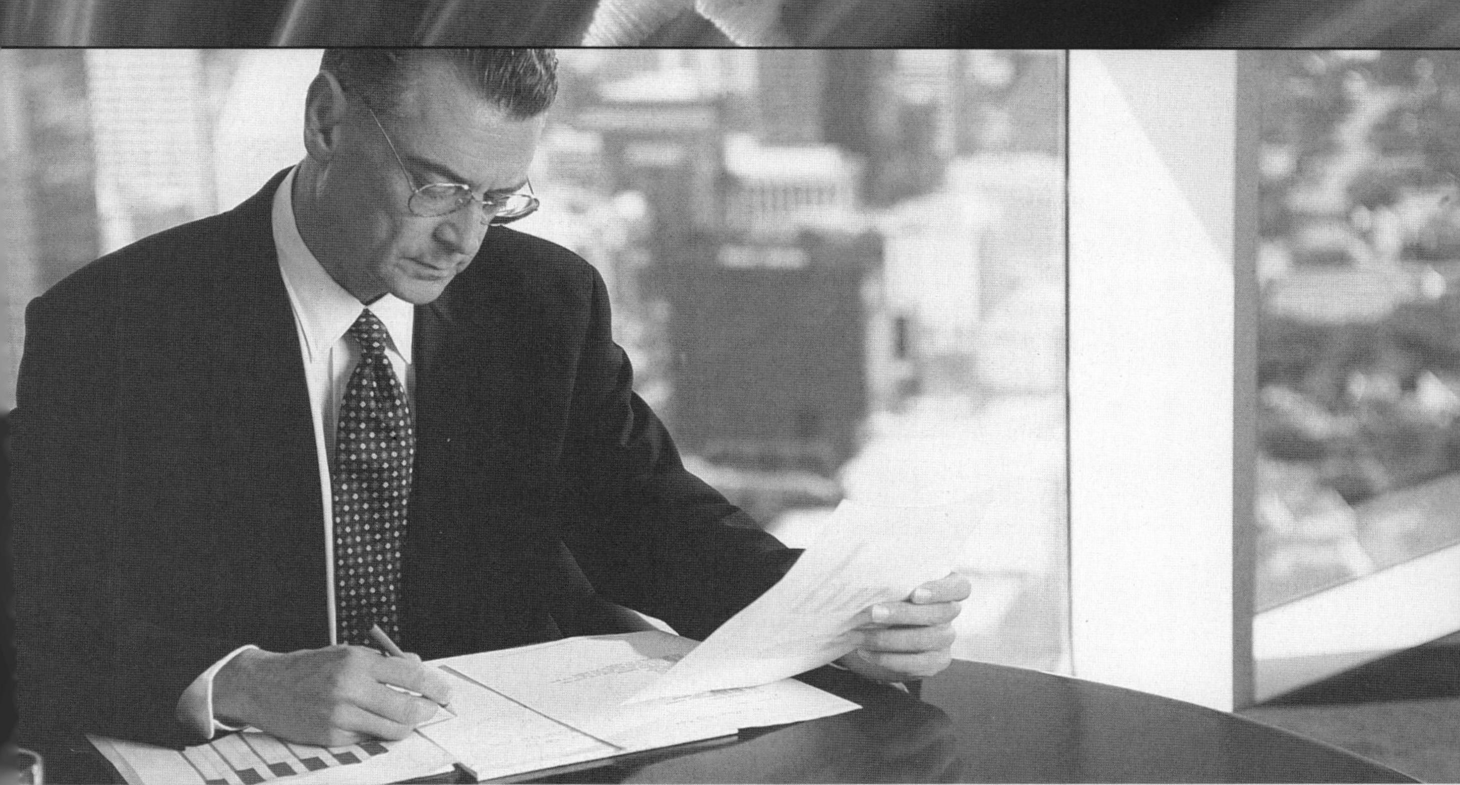

THE BIG PICTURE Tax Solutions for the Real World

© Stockbyte/Jupiter Images

Making a Location Decision in a Multistate Tax Environment

LocalCo has customers in most U.S. states. It does not employ a traditional sales force. Instead, it sells its products exclusively through Internet solicitations and its elaborate website.

LocalCo has two product lines: cell phone accessories, which it manufactures in Alabama, and various sports-themed apparel items, all of which are produced in California. LocalCo has been quite profitable in the past, and it holds a sizable investment portfolio, made up chiefly of U.S. Treasury securities. Banking, payroll, and other administrative operations are located in rural New York State, where the entity is incorporated. LocalCo's rank and file employees receive compensation packages that are below the national median, but its top 10 executives are very highly paid.

In an effort to "go green," LocalCo wants to hold down its costs for shipping raw materials to its manufacturing facilities and for sending its sold goods to customers. Thus, it is considering the construction of a sizable new multifunction building. Ideally, the new facility would have access to both interstate highways and a reliable airport with excess capacity for freight operations.

How will LocalCo's expansion decision be affected by state and local tax considerations?

Read the chapter and formulate your response.

16 INTRODUCTION

Although most of this text concentrates on the effects of the Federal income tax law upon the computation of a taxpayer's annual tax liability, a variety of tax bases apply to most business taxpayers. For instance, a multinational corporation may be subject to tax in a number of different countries (see Chapter 9). Similarly, the taxpayer may be subject to a county-level wheel tax on its business vehicles, a state sales or use tax on many of its asset purchases, and state and local income or franchise taxes on its net income or on the privilege of doing business in the taxing jurisdiction. Indeed, estimates are that about 40 percent of the tax dollars paid by business taxpayers go to state and local authorities.

Businesses operate in a multistate environment for a variety of reasons. For the most part, nontax motivations drive such location decisions as where to build new plants or distribution centers or whether to move communications and data processing facilities and corporate headquarters. For instance, a business typically wants to be close to its largest markets and to operate in a positive private- and public-sector business climate, where it has access to well-trained and reasonably priced labor, suppliers and support operations, sources of natural resources, communication facilities, and transportation networks.

Many location decisions, though, are motivated by multistate tax considerations.

- The taxpayer's manufacturing, wholesaling, sales, retailing, and credit operations each may be centered in a different state to take advantage of various economic development incentives created by politicians. Several states are making highly visible efforts to attract movie and television projects by granting a refundable credit (often at 25 to 35 percent of in-state expenditures) to film production companies. Such credits are offered by New York and California to retain film production work and by Mississippi and Illinois to attract it.
- In addition to flying over virtually the entire country, the major airlines depart from and land in the majority of the states. Which state's income tax should apply to the ticket income? Should sales or income tax apply to sales of movies or liquor while the plane is airborne?
- Local political concerns lead to a multiplicity of tax rules as politicians attempt to serve their constituents by introducing a variety of special tax incentives. This variety can be confusing, however. Taxpayers may have difficulty determining whether they qualify for energy or enterprise zone credits, S corporation status, exemptions from sales tax liability or income tax withholding, or gasoline tax relief at the local level.
- Politicians have a strong incentive to impose new tax burdens on visitors and others who have no direct say in their reelection. Thus, it is increasingly common to see tourist and hotel-bed taxes on convention delegates, often approaching a rate of 20 percent; city payroll taxes on commuters; and the use of obscure tax formulas that otherwise discriminate against those with limited contact in the area.
- Each jurisdiction in which the entity is subject to tax represents a geometrical increase in compliance responsibilities. For instance, how many tax returns must be filed by a three-shareholder S corporation operating in 15 states?
- Various states and localities have adopted revenue-raising statutes that vary in sophistication and operate on different time schedules. For instance, only a few states have adopted an alternative minimum tax, and states that impose the tax have tended to select different bases. In addition, the aggressiveness with which departments of revenue enforce their tax statutes varies greatly from state to state, even in a context of ongoing pressure to enhance revenues. Accordingly, the taxpayer must deal with a patchwork of germane taxing and enforcement provisions in an environment that is often uncertain.

This chapter reviews the basic tax concepts that are predominant among most states that impose a tax based on net income, and it discusses the major areas in which tax planning can reduce a corporation's overall state tax burden.

Most of this chapter is devoted to a discussion of state taxes that are based on income. Each state is free to identify its corporate tax by a different term. Not all

TAX IN THE NEWS **Paying the States' Bills**

The states collect more than $700 billion in taxes annually (i.e., more than $2,000 per person). The corporate income tax accounts for only a small portion of the states' revenues—5 percent. This percentage is even less than the contribution of the Federal corporate tax to the U.S. government's revenues. Most of the states' property tax collections (2 percent of the total) are received by counties and smaller taxing jurisdictions.

The States' Tax Revenue Sources, 2010

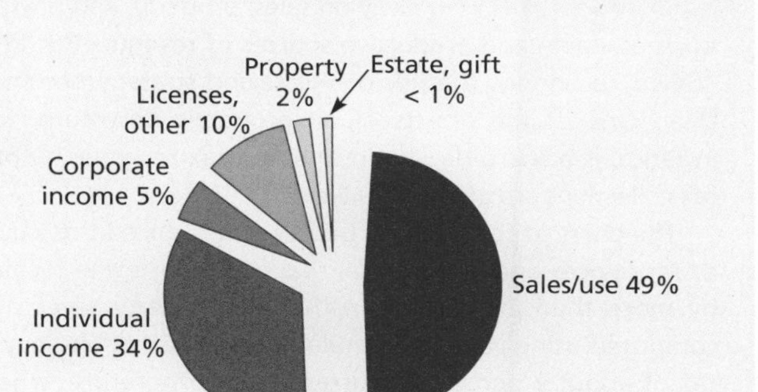

Source: U.S. Census.

of the states that impose a tax on corporate income call the tax an "income tax." Rather, some states refer to their tax on corporate income as a franchise tax,[1] a business tax, a license tax, or a business profits tax.

16.1 Overview of Corporate State Income Taxation

Forty-six states and the District of Columbia impose a tax based on a corporation's taxable income. Because each state is free to create its own tax provisions, the tax practitioner could be faced with 47 entirely different state tax provisions.[2] Fortunately, however, to simplify the filing of tax returns and increase compliance with state tax laws, the majority of states "piggyback" onto the Federal income tax base. This means that they have adopted *en masse* part or all of the Federal provisions governing the definition of income and the allowance of various exemptions, exclusions, and deductions. None of the states, however, has piggybacked its tax collections with the IRS.

Computing State Income Tax

LO.1

Illustrate the computation of a multistate corporation's state tax liability.

In more than 40 of the states that impose a corporate income tax, the starting point in computing the tax base is taxable income as reflected on the Federal corporate income tax return (Form 1120). Those states whose computation of state taxable income is not coupled to the Federal tax return have their own state-specific definitions of gross and taxable income. Nonetheless, even these states typically adopt most Federal income and deduction provisions.

Although Federal tax law plays a significant role in the computation of state taxable income, there is a wide disparity in both the methods used to determine a state's taxable income and the tax rates imposed on that income. As only a few states apply more than one or two tax rates to taxable income, there is little progressivity to these tax systems. State tax credits typically are designed to encourage increased hiring and investment in local facilities. Cities and states often use targeted tax credits to entice businesses to expand within their borders. For instance,

[1]Although a franchise tax in some states is a business privilege tax based on a corporation's capital stock or net worth, several states use that term for the tax they impose on a corporation's net income.

[2]The District of Columbia operates in much the same manner as a state and imposes a tax based on income. Four states impose no corporate income tax at all: Nevada, South Dakota, Washington, and Wyoming. Corporations, however, are subject to a business and occupation tax in Washington. Several states base the tax on the entity's gross receipts.

TAX IN THE NEWS As the Economy Goes, So Go Local Tax Collections

City and county governments depend heavily on sales, property, and payroll taxes as stable and productive sources of revenue. But in a "down" economy, the risk of this taxing strategy becomes clear. One of the effects of an economic downturn, for instance, is a sharp decline in sales/use tax revenues. Other tax collections are affected as well.

The burst of the housing bubble has reduced the value of residences and commercial real estate, in some locales by more than 20 percent. Although property taxes are computed using various formulas, most jurisdictions levy a tax of about 2 percent of current value. Therefore, when property values fall, a proportionate reduction in tax collections occurs.

Several large cities levy taxes of 1 to 3 percent on the wages of those who work in the city. These taxes are justified as a way to recoup the costs of the police and transportation services that commuters enjoy. When unemployment increases and pay raises are few and far between, these payroll tax collections drop significantly.

Some jurisdictions have tried to make up for their revenue shortfalls by creating new fees, raising the amounts charged for traffic tickets and garbage collection, and increasing tax audits and other enforcement measures.

Many states use the U.S. Treasury Offset Program (TOP) to seize funds from the taxpayer's Federal income tax refund and pay obligations to the state. For instance, a Federal Form 1120 refund could be diverted to pay an income tax due at the state level or a balance due to the taxpayer's unemployment compensation account. An individual taxpayer's Federal refund could be used to pay off a prior year's obligation due to a claim made by an injured spouse. However, TOP funds first are applied to higher-priority obligations (e.g., delinquent child support payments) before a state income tax offset is made.

As the majority of state and local government expenditures go toward the salaries and benefits of their employees, a revenue pinch can create further problems. Expected results are cuts in government services and personnel layoffs.

a state might offer a $10,000 credit for each new job created by the taxpayer or a 15 percent credit for taxpayers who purchase automobiles that were assembled in the state.

The formula used by a multistate corporation to determine its tax liability in a typical state is illustrated in Figure 16.1.

Operational Implications

Generally, the accounting period and methods used by a corporation for state tax purposes must be consistent with those used on the Federal return. States often apply different rules, however, in identifying the members of a group filing a consolidated return and the income of each group member that is subject to tax.

As the starting point for computing state taxable income often is directly related to the Federal taxable income amount, most states also piggyback onto the IRS's audit process. Consequently, virtually all of the states that levy an income tax require notification of the final settlement of a Federal income tax audit. State authorities then adjust the originally calculated state tax liability appropriately.

State Modifications

Federal taxable income generally is used as the starting point in computing the state's income tax base, but state adjustments or modifications often are made to Federal taxable income to:

- Reflect differences between state and Federal tax statutes.
- Remove income that a state is constitutionally prohibited from taxing.

The required modifications to Federal taxable income vary significantly among the states. Accordingly, this discussion is limited to the most common additions and subtractions that the states require. Exhibit 16.1 lists the most frequently encountered modifications. In computing the taxable income for a given state, only a selected number of these modifications may be applicable.

FIGURE 16.1 **Computing Corporate State Income Tax Liability**

	Starting point in computing taxable income*
±	State modification items
	State tax base
±	Total net allocable income/(loss) *(nonbusiness income)*
	Total apportionable income/(loss) *(business income)*
×	State's apportionment percentage
	Income apportioned to the state
±	Income/(loss) allocated to the state
	State taxable income/(loss)
×	State tax rate
	Gross income tax liability for state
−	State's tax credits
	Net income tax liability for the state

*Most states use either line 28 or line 30 of the Federal corporate income tax return (Form 1120). In other states, the corporation is required to identify and report each element of income and deduction on the state return.

EXAMPLE 1

Blue Corporation is subject to tax only in State A. The starting point in computing A taxable income is Federal taxable income. Modifications then are made to reflect, among other provisions, the exempt status of interest on A obligations, all dividends received from other U.S. corporations, and the disallowance of a deduction for state income taxes. Blue generated the following income and deductions this year.

Sales	$1,500,000
Interest on Federal obligations	50,000
Interest on municipal obligations of State B	100,000
Dividends received from 50% owned U.S. corporations	200,000
Total income	$1,850,000
Expenses related to Federal obligations	$ 1,000
Expenses related to municipal obligations	5,000
State income tax expense	50,000
Depreciation allowed for Federal tax purposes (the deduction allowed for state purposes is $300,000)	400,000
Other allowable deductions	1,000,000
Total deductions	$1,456,000

Blue's taxable income for Federal and state purposes is $139,000 and $295,000, respectively.

Federal Taxable Income	
Sales	$1,500,000
Interest on Federal obligations	50,000
Dividends received from U.S. corporations	200,000
Total income	$1,750,000
Expenses related to Federal obligations	$ 1,000
State income tax expense	50,000
Depreciation	400,000
Other allowable deductions	1,000,000
Total deductions	$1,451,000
Taxable income before special deductions	$ 299,000
Less: Dividends received deduction (80% × $200,000)	160,000
Federal taxable income	$ 139,000

EXHIBIT 16.1 Common State Modifications

Addition Modifications

* Interest income received on state and municipal obligations and any other interest income that is exempt from Federal income tax. For this purpose, some states exempt interest earned on their own obligations.
* Expenses deducted in computing Federal taxable income that are directly or indirectly related to U.S. obligations.
* Income-based franchise and income taxes imposed by any state and the District of Columbia that were deducted in computing Federal taxable income.
* The amount by which the Federal deductions for depreciation, amortization, or depletion exceed those permitted by the state.
* The amount by which the state gain or loss from the disposal of assets differs from the Federal gain or loss. Due to the difference in permitted depreciation methods and other adjustments, a corporation's assets may have different Federal and state tax bases. This adjustment is not necessary if the state and Federal basis provisions are identical.

Adjustments required as a result of different elections being made for state and Federal purposes. Examples of such elections include the methods under which income from installment sales or long-term contracts is determined.

Federal net operating loss deduction, if the starting point in the computation of taxable income is Federal taxable income after special deductions.

Subtraction Modifications

* Interest on U.S. obligations or obligations of Federal agencies to the extent included in Federal taxable income but exempt from state income taxes under U.S. law.
* Expenses that are directly or indirectly related to the state and municipal interest that is taxable for state purposes.
* Refunds of franchise and income taxes imposed by any state and the District of Columbia, to the extent included in Federal taxable income.
* The amount by which the state deductions for depreciation, amortization, or depletion exceed the deductions permitted for Federal tax purposes.

Adjustments required as a result of different elections being made for state and Federal purposes, as above.

Dividends received from other U.S. corporations, to the extent included in Federal taxable income.

Net operating loss deduction as determined for state tax purposes.

Federal income tax paid.

*Required by most states.

State A Taxable Income	
Federal taxable income	$139,000
Addition Modifications	
Interest on State B obligations	100,000
State income tax expense	50,000
Excess depreciation deduction allowed for Federal purposes ($400,000 − $300,000)	100,000
Expenses related to Federal obligations	1,000
Subtraction Modifications	
Expenses related to State B obligations	(5,000)
Dividends from other corporations, to extent included in Federal taxable income ($200,000 − $160,000)	(40,000)
Interest on Federal obligations	(50,000)
State A taxable income	$295,000

FINANCIAL DISCLOSURE INSIGHTS State/Local Taxes and the Tax Expense

In applying GAAP principles for a business entity, state and local tax expenses are found in several places in the taxpayer's financial reports. In the tax footnote, the state/local tax costs often are reported in dollar and/or percentage terms, in both current and deferred components. The following are examples of state/local tax expenses that were reported in a recent year.

	Current State/ Local Tax Expenses ($ million)	Deferred State/ Local Tax Expenses ($ million)
Eli Lilly	49	(1)
ExxonMobil	340	221
Ryder Systems	6	3
Ford Motor	7	(59)

Corporations also report permanent book/tax differences in determining the effective tax rate for the reporting period. In a recent year, Berkshire Hathaway reported that state/local permanent book/tax differences reduced its effective income tax rate by about 1.5 percentage points. Ford Motor reported a similar rate reduction, but Ryder Systems' effective tax rate increased by about 6 percentage points for the year due to such permanent book/tax differences.

EXAMPLE 2

Continue with the facts of Example 1, except that the $100,000 of municipal bond interest was generated from State A obligations. The computation of Federal taxable income is unaffected by this change. Because A exempts interest on its own obligations from taxation, Blue's A taxable income is $200,000.

State A Taxable Income	
Federal taxable income	$139,000
Addition Modifications	
State income tax expense	50,000
Excess depreciation deduction allowed for Federal purposes ($400,000 − $300,000)	100,000
Expenses related to Federal obligations	1,000
Subtraction Modifications	
Dividends from other U.S. corporations, to extent included in Federal taxable income ($200,000 − $160,000)	(40,000)
Interest on Federal obligations	(50,000)
State A taxable income	$200,000

■

The UDITPA and the Multistate Tax Commission

The Uniform Division of Income for Tax Purposes Act (**UDITPA**) is a model law relating to the assignment of income among the states for corporations that maintain operations in more than one state (multistate corporations). Many states have adopted the provisions of the UDITPA, either by joining the Multistate Tax Compact or by modeling their laws after the provisions of the UDITPA.

The **Multistate Tax Commission (MTC)** writes regulations and other rules that interpret the UDITPA. When a new MTC rule or regulation is created, the member states propose its adoption to their respective legislatures. The majority of member states adopt the regulations with no exceptions or only minor changes.[3]

[3] Many of the states that are not members of the Multistate Tax Compact also model their laws after the UDITPA and the MTC regulations.

LO.2

Define nexus and explain its role in state income taxation.

Jurisdiction to Impose Tax: Nexus and Public Law 86–272

The state in which a business is incorporated has the jurisdiction to tax the corporation, regardless of the volume of its business activity within the state. Whether a state can tax the income of a business that is incorporated in another state usually depends on the relationship between the state and the corporation.

Nexus describes the degree of business activity that must be present before a taxing jurisdiction has the right to impose a tax on an out-of-state entity's income. State law defines the measure of the relationship that is necessary to create nexus. Typically, sufficient nexus is present when a corporation derives income from sources within the state, owns or leases property in the state, employs personnel in the state, or has physical or financial capital there. **Public Law 86–272** limits the states' right to impose an income tax on certain interstate activities.[4] This Federal law prohibits a state from taxing a business whose only connection with the state is to solicit orders for sales of tangible personal property that is sent outside the state for approval or rejection. If approved, the orders must be filled and shipped by the business from a point outside the state.

Only the sales of tangible personal property are immune from taxation under the law, however. Leases, rentals, and other dispositions of tangible personal property are not protected activities. Moreover, dispositions of real property and intangible property, as well as sales of services, are not protected by Public Law 86–272. In this regard, each state constructs its own definition of tangible and intangible property. Thus, because property ownership is not a protected activity, providing company-owned communications, document processing, or computer equipment to an out-of-state salesperson may create nexus with a state, even though the salesperson merely solicits sales orders there.

An activity that consists merely of solicitation is immune from taxation. The statute does not define the term *solicitation*, but the Supreme Court has held that *solicitation of orders* includes any explicit verbal request for orders and any speech or conduct that implicitly invites an order.[5] The Court also created a *de minimis* rule, allowing immunity from nexus where a limited amount of solicitation occurs.

Exhibit 16.2 summarizes the activities the MTC has identified as being directly related to solicitation (protected activities) and activities unrelated to solicitation (which establish income tax nexus for the entity).

Independent Contractors

Public Law 86–272 extends immunity to certain in-state activities conducted by an independent contractor that would not be permitted if performed directly by the taxpayer. Generally, an independent contractor may engage in the following limited activities without establishing income tax nexus for the principal: (1) soliciting sales, (2) making sales, and (3) maintaining a sales office.

16.2 Allocation and Apportionment of Income

LO.3

Distinguish between allocation and apportionment of a multistate corporation's taxable income.

A corporation that conducts business activities in more than one state must determine the portion of its net income that is subject to tax by each state. A corporation that has established sufficient nexus with another state generally must both **allocate** and **apportion** its income.

Apportionment is a means by which a corporation's business income is divided among the states in which it conducts business. Under an apportionment procedure, a corporation determines allowable income and deductions for the company as a whole and then apportions some of its net income to a given state, according to an approved formula.

[4] 15 U.S.C. 381–385.

[5] *Wisconsin Department of Revenue v. William Wrigley, Jr., Co.*, 112 S.Ct. 2447 (1992).

EXHIBIT 16.2 Common Nexus Definitions under Public Law 86–272

General rule: P.L. 86–272 immunity from nexus applies where the sales representative's activities are ancillary to the order-solicitation process.

Activities That Usually Do Not Create Nexus

- Advertising campaigns.
- Carrying free samples only for display or distribution.
- Owning or furnishing automobiles to salespersons.
- Passing inquiries or complaints on to the home office.
- Checking customers' inventories for reorder.
- Maintaining a sample or display room for two weeks or less during the year.
- Maintaining an office for an employee, including an office in the home.

Activities Usually Sufficient to Establish Nexus

- Making repairs or providing maintenance.
- Collecting delinquent accounts; investigating creditworthiness.
- Conducting installation or supervising installation.
- Conducting training classes, seminars, or lectures for persons other than sales personnel.
- Approving or accepting orders.
- Picking up or replacing damaged or returned property.
- Hiring, training, or supervising personnel other than sales employees.
- Providing shipping information and coordinating deliveries.
- Carrying samples for sale, exchange, or distribution in any manner for consideration or other value.
- Owning, leasing, maintaining, or otherwise using any of the following facilities or property in the state.
  - Real estate
  - Repair shop
  - Parts department
  - Employment office
  - Meeting place for directors, officers, or employees
  - Purchasing office
  - Warehouse
  - Stock of goods
  - Call center
  - Mobile retailing (e.g., trucks with driver-salespersons)

Factor Presence Nexus

A few states, following an MTC model statute, automatically assign nexus to a taxpayer that exceeds at least one of the following bright-line thresholds for the tax year. The factor presence nexus standard ties more closely the nexus rules with the apportionment formula of the jurisdiction, and it may provide additional uniformity among the states as to measuring the taxpayer's business activities.

- $50,000 of property
- $50,000 of payroll
- $500,000 of sales
- 25% of total property
- 25% of total payroll
- 25% of total sales

Allocation is a method under which specific components of a corporation's income, net of related expenses, are directly assigned to a certain state. Allocation differs from apportionment in that allocable income is assigned to one state, whereas apportionable income is divided among several states. Nonapportionable (nonbusiness) income generally includes:

- Income or losses derived from the sale of nonbusiness real or tangible property, or
- Income or losses derived from rentals and royalties from nonbusiness real or tangible personal property.

This income is allocated to the state where the property that generated the income or loss is located.

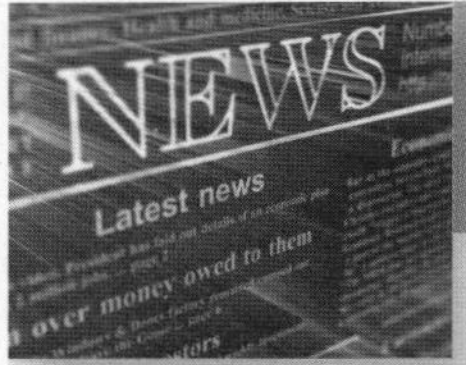

TAX IN THE NEWS So Where Did You Work Today?

It is the dream of many intellectual-property employees to work at home with the employer's computer and communications equipment. Not only is the dress code based on the worker's comfort, but the employee can avoid the time and cost of commuting. The employer saves by not having to provide office space.

But what are the tax effects when the employee or independent contractor submits work to an employer located in a different state? The general rule has been that state income taxes fall in full in the state where the work is done. Is this still the rule, or must the employee apportion the hours of the day among the various states that receive the work product? If so, on what basis should such apportionment be made? Furthermore, how will the worker avoid potential taxation of the same income by more than one state?

A few states and cities, most notably in New York, are aggressively trying to impose income taxes on the work of telecommuters that enters the state. In these situations, enough nexus purportedly exists to permit the levying of income taxes on telecommuters based in other states. The finding of nexus with New York (both the city and the state) can be an expensive proposition for the worker and employer.

For now, it will be up to the states considering this form of taxation to decide if the additional revenue is worth the risk of angering the desirable high-tech information workers who play a large role in our economy.

As Figure 16.1 indicated, total allocable (nonapportionable) income or loss typically is removed from corporate net income before the state's apportionment percentage is applied. The nonapportionable income or loss assigned to a state then is combined with the income apportionable to that state to arrive at total income subject to tax in the state.

EXAMPLE 3

Green Corporation conducts business in States N, O, P, and Q. Green's $900,000 taxable income consists of $800,000 apportionable income and $100,000 allocable income generated from transactions conducted in State Q. Green's sales, property, and payroll are evenly divided among the four states, and the states all employ an identical apportionment formula. Accordingly, $200,000 of Green's income is taxable in each of States N, O, and P. Green is subject to income tax on $300,000 of income in State Q.

Apportionable income	$800,000
Apportionment percentage (apportionable income is divided equally among the four states)	× 25%
Income apportioned to each state	$200,000

	State N	State O	State P	State Q
Income apportioned	$200,000	$200,000	$200,000	$200,000
Income allocated	–0–	–0–	–0–	100,000
Taxable income	$200,000	$200,000	$200,000	$300,000

■

The Apportionment Procedure

Apportionment assumes that the production of business income is linked to business activity, and the laws of each state define a number of factors believed to indicate the amount of corporate activity conducted within the state. However, apportionment often does not provide a uniform division of an organization's income based on its business activity, because each state is free to choose the type and number of factors it believes are indicative of the business activity conducted within its borders. Therefore, a corporation may be subject to state income tax on more or less than 100 percent of its income.

An equally incongruous consequence of apportionment may occur when the operations in a state result in a loss.

EXAMPLE 4

Red Corporation's operations include two manufacturing facilities, located in States A and B, respectively. The plant located in A generated $500,000 of income, and the plant located in B generated a loss of $200,000. Therefore, Red's total taxable income is $300,000.

By applying the statutes of each state, Red determines that its apportionment factors for A and B are .65 and .35, respectively. Accordingly, Red's income is apportioned to the states as follows.

Income apportioned to State A: $.65 \times \$300{,}000 = \$195{,}000$
Income apportioned to State B: $.35 \times \$300{,}000 = \$105{,}000$

Red is subject to tax in B on $105,000 of income, even though the operations conducted in that state resulted in a loss. ■

Business and Nonbusiness Income

LO.4

Describe the nature and treatment of business and nonbusiness income.

Business income is assigned among the states by using an apportionment formula. In contrast, *nonbusiness income* is either apportioned or allocated to the state in which the income-producing asset is located. For instance, income derived from the rental of nonbusiness real property generally is allocated to the state in which the property is located.

EXAMPLE 5

TNT Corporation, a manufacturer of explosive devices, is a multistate taxpayer that has nexus with States P and Q. During the taxable year, TNT's net sales of explosive devices were $900,000; $600,000 of these sales were made in P, and $300,000 were made in Q. The corporation also received $90,000 from the rental of nonbusiness real property located in P.

Both states employ a three-factor apportionment formula under which sales, property, and payroll are equally weighted. However, the states do not agree on the definition of apportionable income. Under P's tax provisions, nonbusiness rent income is allocable and business income is apportionable, while Q requires a corporation to apportion all of its (business and nonbusiness) income. The sales factor (the ratio of in-state sales to total sales) for each of the states is computed as follows.

$$\text{State P: } \frac{\$600{,}000 \text{ (sales in State P)}}{\$900{,}000 \text{ (total sales)}} = 66.67\%$$

$$\text{State Q: } \frac{\$300{,}000 \text{ (sales in State Q)}}{\$990{,}000 \text{ (total sales)}^{*}} = 30.30\%$$

*Because rent income is treated as business income, rents are included in the denominator of the sales factor. ■

EXAMPLE 6

Continue with the facts of Example 5, except that the rent income was generated from property located in Q, rather than from property located in P. Although the sales factor for P remains the same, the sales factor for Q changes.

$$\text{State P: } \frac{\$600{,}000 \text{ (sales in State P)}}{\$900{,}000 \text{ (total sales)}} = 66.67\%$$

$$\text{State Q: } \frac{\$390{,}000 \text{ (sales in State Q)}}{\$990{,}000 \text{ (total sales)}} = 39.39\%$$

Due to the composition of the sales factor in the two states, TNT's income never is perfectly apportioned: the aggregate of the sales factors is either more or less than 100%. ■

Business income arises from the taxpayer's regular course of business or constitutes an integral part of the taxpayer's regular business.[6] In determining whether an item of income is (apportionable) business income, state courts have developed a variety of approaches to determine what constitutes a taxpayer's "regular course of business."[7]

[6] MTC Reg. IV.1.(a).

[7] *Atlantic Richfield Co. v. State of Colorado and Joseph F. Dolan*, 601 P.2d 628 (Colo.S.Ct., 1979); *Appeal of A. Epstein and Sons, Inc.* (Cal.State Bd. of Equalization, 1984).

A few states, including Connecticut and Rhode Island, fail to distinguish between business and nonbusiness income. In these states, all of a corporation's income is deemed to be business income and subject to apportionment.

EXAMPLE 7

Scarlet Corporation is subject to income tax in several states. Scarlet earned $2.5 million from the sales of its products and $1 million from the sale of assets that were unrelated to its regular business operations.

In the states that distinguish between business and nonbusiness income, $2.5 million of Scarlet's income is apportioned to the state according to the state's apportionment formula. The gain on the sale of the nonbusiness assets is allocated to the state in which the assets were located. In the states that subject a corporation's entire income to apportionment, $3.5 million ($2,500,000 + $1,000,000) is apportioned to the states in which the taxpayer conducts business. ■

Nonbusiness income is "all income other than business income."[8] Usually, nonbusiness income comprises passive and portfolio income, such as dividends, interest, rents, royalties, and certain capital gains. However, passive or portfolio income may be classified as business income when the acquisition, management, and disposition of the underlying property constitute an integral part of the taxpayer's regular business operation.

EXAMPLE 8

Gray Corporation owns and operates two manufacturing facilities, one in State A and the other in State B. Due to a temporary decline in sales, Gray has rented 10% of its A facility to an unaffiliated corporation. Gray generated $100,000 net rent income and $900,000 income from manufacturing.

Both A and B classify such rent income as allocable nonbusiness income. By applying the statutes of each state, as discussed in the next section, Gray determines that its apportionment factors are 0.40 for A and 0.60 for B.

Income Subject to Tax in State A	
Taxable income	$1,000,000
Less: Allocable income	(100,000)
Apportionable income	$ 900,000
Times: Apportionment factor	× 40%
Income apportioned to State A	$ 360,000
Plus: Income allocated to State A	100,000
Income subject to tax in State A	$ 460,000

Income Subject to Tax in State B	
Taxable income	$1,000,000
Less: Allocable income	(100,000)
Apportionable income	$ 900,000
Times: Apportionment factor	× 60%
Income apportioned to State B	$ 540,000
Plus: Income allocated to State B	–0–
Income subject to tax in State B	$ 540,000

■

EXAMPLE 9

Continue with the facts of Example 8, but assume that B does not distinguish between business and nonbusiness income. Thus, all of Gray's income is apportionable.

Gray properly determines that its apportionment factors are 0.40 for A and 0.58 for B. Because the apportionment factors used by the two states are derived differently, Gray's income that is subject to tax does not equal 100%.

[8] UDITPA § 1(e).

Income Subject to Tax in State A	**$ 460,000**
Income Subject to Tax in State B	
Apportionable income	$1,000,000
Times: Apportionment factor	× 58%
Income apportioned to State B	$ 580,000

Due to differences in the states' definitions of apportionable and allocable income, $1.04 million of Gray's $1 million Federal taxable income is subject to state income taxation. ■

Apportionment Factors: Elements and Planning

LO.5

Discuss the sales, payroll, and property apportionment factors.

Business income is apportioned among the states by determining the appropriate apportionment percentage for each state that has a right to tax the entity. To determine the apportionment percentage for each state, a ratio is established for each of the factors included in the state's apportionment formula. Each ratio is calculated by comparing the level of a specific business activity within a state to the total corporate activity of that type. The ratios then are summed, averaged, and appropriately weighted (if required) to determine the corporation's apportionment percentage for a specific state.

Although apportionment formulas vary among jurisdictions, the traditional three-factor formula equally weights sales, property, and payroll.[9] However, most of the states now use a modified three-factor formula, where the sales factor receives more than a one-third weight. The use of a higher-weighted sales factor tends to pull a larger percentage of an out-of-state corporation's income into the taxing jurisdiction of the state, because the corporation's major activity within the state—the sales of its products—is weighted more heavily than are its payroll and property activities. Overweighting the sales factor, however, provides tax relief for corporations that are domiciled in the state. Those corporations generally own significantly more property and incur more payroll costs (factors that are given less weight in the apportionment formula) within the state than do out-of-state corporations.

EXAMPLE 10

Musk Corporation realized $500,000 of taxable income from the sales of its products in States A and B. Musk's activities in both states establish nexus for income tax purposes. Musk's sales, payroll, and property in the states include the following.

	State A	State B	Total
Sales	$1,250,000	$750,000	$2,000,000
Property	2,500,000	-0-	2,500,000
Payroll	1,500,000	-0-	1,500,000

If State B uses an equally weighted three-factor apportionment formula, $62,500 of Musk's taxable income is apportioned to B.

Sales ($750,000/$2,000,000)	=	37.5%
Property ($0/$2,500,000)	=	-0-
Payroll ($0/$1,500,000)	=	-0-
Sum of apportionment factors		37.5%
Average	÷	3
Apportionment factor for State B		12.5%
Taxable income	×	$500,000
Income apportioned to State B		$ 62,500

[9]Certain industries, such as financial services institutions, insurance companies, air and motor carriers, pipeline companies, and communications providers, typically are required to use special apportionment formulas.

If State B uses a double-weighted sales factor in its three-factor apportionment formula, $93,750 of Musk's taxable income is apportioned to B.

Sales ($750,000/$2,000,000)	=	37.5% × 2	=	75%
Property ($0/$2,500,000)	=			–0–
Payroll ($0/$1,500,000)	=			–0–
Sum of apportionment factors				75%
Average			÷	4
Apportionment factor for State B				18.75%
Taxable income			×	$500,000
Income apportioned to State B				$ 93,750

When a state uses a double-weighted sales factor, typically a larger percentage of an out-of-state corporation's income is subject to tax in the state. Here, an additional $31,250 ($93,750 − $62,500) of Musk's income is subject to tax in B. ■

A single-factor apportionment formula consisting solely of a sales factor is even more detrimental to an out-of-state corporation than an apportionment factor that double-weights the sales factor.[10]

EXAMPLE 11

PPR Corporation, a retailer of paper products, owns retail stores in States A, B, and C. A uses a three-factor apportionment formula under which the sales, property, and payroll factors are equally weighted. B uses a three-factor apportionment formula under which sales are double-weighted. C employs a single-factor apportionment factor, based solely on sales.

PPR's operations generated $800,000 of apportionable income, and its sales, payroll activity, and average property owned in each of the three states are as follows.

	State A	State B	State C	Total
Sales	$500,000	$400,000	$300,000	$1,200,000
Payroll	100,000	125,000	75,000	300,000
Property	150,000	250,000	100,000	500,000

$280,000 of PPR's apportionable income is assigned to A.

Sales ($500,000/$1,200,000)	=	41.67%
Payroll ($100,000/$300,000)	=	33.33%
Property ($150,000/$500,000)	=	30.00%
Sum of apportionment factors		105.00%
Average	÷	3
Apportionment factor for State A		35.00%
Apportionable income	×	$800,000
Income apportioned to State A		$280,000

$316,640 of PPR's apportionable income is assigned to B.

Sales ($400,000/$1,200,000)	=	33.33% × 2	=	66.66%
Payroll ($125,000/$300,000)			=	41.67%
Property ($250,000/$500,000)			=	50.00%
Sum of apportionment factors				158.33%
Average			÷	4
Apportionment factor for State B				39.58%
Apportionable income			×	$800,000
Income apportioned to State B				$316,640

[10]Currently, Colorado, Georgia, Illinois, Indiana, Iowa, Maine, Michigan, Nebraska, New York, Oregon, South Carolina, Texas, and Wisconsin require the use of a single-factor apportionment formula for all taxpayers.

$200,000 of PPR's apportionable income is assigned to C.

Sales ($300,000/$1,200,000)	=	25.00%
Sum of apportionment factors		25.00%
Average	÷	1
Apportionment factor for State C		25.00%
Apportionable income	×	$800,000
Income apportioned to State C		$200,000

Summary	
Income apportioned to State A	$280,000
Income apportioned to State B	316,640
Income apportioned to State C	200,000
Total income apportioned	$796,640

Due to the variations in the apportionment formulas employed by the various states, only 99.58% ($796,640/$800,000) of PPR's income is apportioned to the states in which it is subject to tax. ■

The Sales Factor

The **sales factor** is a fraction whose numerator is the corporation's total sales in the state during the tax period. The denominator is the corporation's total sales everywhere during the tax period. Gross sales for this purpose generally are net of returns, allowances, and discounts. Moreover, interest income, service charges, and carrying charges are included in the sales factor. Federal and state excise taxes and state sales taxes are included in the factor if these taxes are either passed on to the buyer or included in the selling price of the goods.

Because the sales factor is a component in the formula used to apportion a corporation's business income to a state, only sales that generate business income are includible in the fraction. The "sales" factor actually resembles a "receipts" factor in most states, because it also generally includes business income from the sale of inventory or services, interest, dividends, rentals, royalties, sales of assets, and other business income. Income on Federal obligations, however, is not included in the sales factor.

When the sale involves capital assets, some states require that the gross proceeds, rather than the net gain or loss, be included in the fraction. Most states allow incidental or occasional asset sales and sales of certain intangible assets to be excluded from gross receipts.[11]

In determining the numerator of the sales factor, most states follow the UDITPA's "ultimate destination concept," under which tangible asset sales are assumed to take place at the point of delivery, not at the location at which the shipment originates.

EXAMPLE 12

Olive Corporation, whose only manufacturing plant is located in State A, sells its products to residents of A through its local retail store. Olive also ships its products to customers in States B and C. The products that are sold to residents of A are assigned to A, while the products that are delivered to B and C are assigned to B and C, respectively. ■

Dock Sales

Dock sales occur where a purchaser uses its owned or rented vehicles, or a common carrier with which it has made arrangements, to take delivery of the product at the seller's shipping dock. Most states apply the destination test to dock sales in the same manner as it is applied to other sales. Thus, if the seller makes dock sales to a purchaser that has an out-of-state location to which it returns with the product, the sale is assigned to the purchaser's state.

[11] MTC Reg. IV.18.(c).

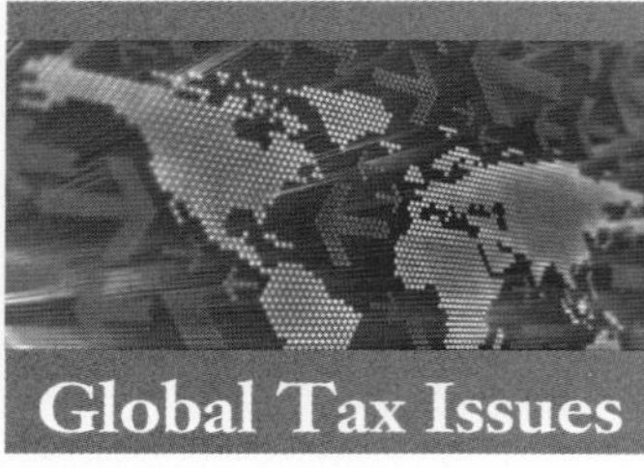

© Andrey Prokhorov, iStockphoto

Throwback Rule Involving Other Countries

A throwback rule seems inappropriate when the sale is made to a purchaser in another country, where the transaction is subject to a value-added or gross receipts tax (but no income tax). In these cases, the taxpayer truly is subject to double taxation, as state taxes increase but no Federal foreign tax credit is available. Nonetheless, most of the throwback states fail to distinguish between U.S. and overseas throwback sales.

Throwback Rule

Out-of-state sales that are not subject to tax in the destination state are pulled back into the origination state if that state has adopted a **throwback rule**. About half of the states apply this exception to the destination test.

The throwback rule provides that when a corporation is not subject to tax in the destination state or the purchaser is the U.S. government, the sales are treated as in-state sales of the origination state and the actual destination of the product is disregarded. Consequently, when the seller is immune from tax in the destination state under Public Law 86–272, the sales are considered to be in-state sales of the origination state if that state has a throwback provision.

EXAMPLE 13

Braun Corporation's entire operations are located in State A. Seventy percent ($700,000) of Braun's sales are made in A, and the remaining 30% ($300,000) are made in State B. Braun's solicitation of sales in B is limited to mailing a monthly catalog to its customers in that state. However, Braun employees do pick up and replace damaged merchandise in State B.

The pickup and replacement of damaged goods establish nexus with A. Braun's activities in B are sufficient (as determined by A's law) to subject Braun to a positive tax, based on its income. Therefore, Braun is permitted to apportion its income between A and B. However, B's definition of activities necessary to create nexus is less strict than that imposed by A; in B, the mere pickup and replacement of damaged goods do not subject a corporation's income to tax.

Braun's taxable income is $900,000. Both A and B impose a 10% corporate income tax and include only the sales factor in their apportionment formulas. If A has not adopted a throwback rule, Braun's effective state income tax rate is 7%.

	Apportionment Factors	Net Income	Tax Rate	Tax
State A	70%	$900,000	10%	$63,000
State B	*	900,000	10%	–0–
Total tax liability				$63,000
Effective state income tax rate: $63,000/$900,000 =				7%

* As determined under B's laws, Braun's income is not apportionable to State B, because of insufficient nexus.

If A has adopted a throwback rule, Braun does not benefit from its lack of nexus with B, because the sales in B are considered to be in-state sales of A. Thus, Braun's effective tax rate is 10%.

	Apportionment Factors	Net Income	Tax Rate	Tax
State A	100%	$900,000	10%	$90,000
State B	–0–	900,000	10%	–0–
Total tax liability				$90,000
Effective state income tax rate: $90,000/$900,000 =				10%
Tax increase due to throwback provision ($90,000 – $63,000)				$27,000

■

The Payroll Factor

The **payroll factor** is determined by comparing the compensation paid for services rendered within a state to the total compensation paid by the corporation. Generally, the payroll factor is a fraction whose numerator is the total amount a corporation paid or accrued for compensation in a state during the tax period. The denominator is the total amount paid or accrued by the corporation for compensation during the tax period. For purposes of the payroll factor, compensation includes wages, salaries, commissions, and any other form of remuneration paid or accrued to employees for personal services. Compensation may also include the value of board, rent, housing, lodging, and other benefits or services furnished to employees by the taxpayer in return for personal services, if these amounts constitute Federal gross income.

Payments made to an independent contractor or any other person who is not properly classifiable as an employee generally are excluded from the numerator and denominator of the payroll factor. Some states, including Delaware and North Carolina, exclude from the payroll factor the compensation paid to corporate officers.

More than half of the states provide that earnings paid to a cash or deferred compensation plan, excluded from Federal gross income under § 401(k), are to be included in the numerator and the denominator of the payroll factor. Accordingly, the total compensation that is included in the denominator of a corporation's payroll factor may vary among the states in which the corporation's income is apportioned.

EXAMPLE 14

Mice Corporation's sales office and manufacturing plant are located in State A. Mice also maintains a manufacturing plant and sales office in State C. For purposes of apportionment, A defines payroll as all compensation paid to employees, including contributions to § 401(k) deferred compensation plans. Under the statutes of C, neither compensation paid to officers nor contributions to § 401(k) plans are included in the payroll factor. Mice incurred the following personnel costs.

	State A	State C	Total
Wages and salaries for employees other than officers	$350,000	$250,000	$600,000
Salaries for officers	150,000	100,000	250,000
Contributions to § 401(k) plans	30,000	20,000	50,000
Total	$530,000	$370,000	$900,000

The payroll factor for State A is computed as follows.

$$\frac{\$530{,}000}{\$900{,}000} = 58.89\%$$

Because C excludes from the payroll factor any compensation paid to officers and contributions to § 401(k) plans, C's factor is computed as follows.

$$\frac{\$250{,}000}{\$600{,}000} = 41.67\%$$

The aggregate of Mice's payroll factors is 100.56% (58.89% + 41.67%). In certain cases, the sum of a corporation's payroll factors may be significantly more or less than 100%. ■

The compensation of an employee normally is not split between two or more states during the year, unless he or she is transferred or changes positions during the year. Instead, each employee's compensation is allocated to only one state. Under the UDITPA, compensation is treated as being paid in the state (it is included in the numerator of the payroll factor) in which the services primarily are performed.

When an employee's services are performed in more than one state, his or her compensation is attributed to the employee's base of operations or, if there is no base of operations in any state in which some part of the service is performed, to the place from which the services are directed or controlled. When no services are performed in the state that serves as the base of operations or the place from which the services are directed, the employee's compensation is attributed to his or her state of residency.[12]

EXAMPLE 15

Geese Corporation has its headquarters and a manufacturing plant in State A. Reggie, a resident of State Y, works at the A manufacturing plant. His compensation is included in the numerator of A's payroll factor, as the service is performed entirely in A. ■

Only compensation that is related to the production of apportionable income is included in the payroll factor. Accordingly, in those states that distinguish between business and nonbusiness income, compensation related to the operation, maintenance, protection, or supervision of nonbusiness income is not includible in the payroll factor.

EXAMPLE 16

Dog Corporation, a manufacturer of automobile parts, is subject to tax in States X and Y. Dog incurred the following payroll costs.

	State X	State Y	Total
Wages and salaries for officers and personnel of manufacturing facilities	$450,000	$350,000	$800,000
Wages and salaries for personnel involved in nonbusiness rental activities	50,000	–0–	50,000

If both states distinguish between business and nonbusiness income in determining apportionable income and include officers' compensation in the payroll factor, Dog's payroll factors are computed as follows:

Payroll factor for State X: $450,000/$800,000 = 56.25%
Payroll factor for State Y: $350,000/$800,000 = 43.75% ■

EXAMPLE 17

Continue with the facts of Example 16, but assume that Y defines apportionable income as the corporation's total income (business and nonbusiness income). Dog's payroll factor for X remains unchanged, but its payroll factor for Y is reduced.

Payroll factor for State X: $450,000/$800,000 = 56.25%

Payroll factor for State Y: $350,000/$850,000* = 41.18%

*$800,000 (compensation related to business income) + $50,000 (compensation related to nonbusiness income). ■

In deriving the payroll factors, compensation is prorated between business and nonbusiness sources.

EXAMPLE 18

Tall Corporation, a manufacturer of paper products, operates paper mills in States A and B. In addition, the corporation owns nonbusiness rental real property in A. Tall incurred the following compensation expenses:

	State A	State B	Total
Wages and salaries for mill employees	$1,200,000	$1,500,000	$2,700,000
Wages and salaries for administrative staff	600,000	500,000	1,100,000
Compensation of officers	800,000	400,000	1,200,000

[12]UDITPA § 14.

Ten percent of the time spent by the administrative staff located in A and 5% of the time spent by officers located in A are devoted to the operation, maintenance, and supervision of the nonbusiness rental property. Both states exclude such rent income from the definition of apportionable income.

Payroll factor for State A

$$\frac{[\$1{,}200{,}000 + 90\%(\$600{,}000) + 95\%(\$800{,}000)]}{[\$2{,}700{,}000 + 90\%(\$600{,}000) + \$500{,}000 + 95\%(\$800{,}000) + \$400{,}000]} = \frac{\$2{,}500{,}000}{\$4{,}900{,}000} = 51.02\%$$

Payroll factor for State B

$$\frac{(\$1{,}500{,}000 + \$500{,}000 + \$400{,}000)}{[\$2{,}700{,}000 + 90\%(\$600{,}000) + \$500{,}000 + 95\%(\$800{,}000) + \$400{,}000]} = \frac{\$2{,}400{,}000}{\$4{,}900{,}000} = 48.98\%$$

■

The Property Factor

The **property factor** generally is a fraction whose numerator is the average value of the corporation's real property and its tangible personal property owned and used or rented and used in the state during the taxable year. The denominator is the average value of all of the corporation's real property and its tangible personal property owned or rented and used during the taxable year, wherever it is located. In this manner, a state's property factor reflects the extent of total property usage by the taxpayer in the state.

For this purpose, property includes land, buildings, machinery, inventory, equipment, and other real and tangible personal property, other than coins or currency.[13] Other types of property that may be included in the factor are offshore property, outer space property (satellites), and partnership property.

In the case of property that is in transit between locations of the taxpayer or between a buyer and seller, the assets are included in the numerator of the destination state. With respect to mobile or movable property such as construction equipment, trucks, and leased equipment, which is both in- and outside the state during the tax period, the numerator of a state's property factor generally is determined on the basis of the total time the property was within the state.

Property owned by the corporation typically is valued at its average original or historical cost plus the cost of additions and improvements, but without adjusting for depreciation. Some states allow property to be included at net book value or adjusted tax basis. The value of the property usually is determined by averaging the values at the beginning and end of the tax period. Alternatively, some states allow or require the amount to be calculated on a monthly basis if annual computation results in or requires substantial distortions.

EXAMPLE 19

Blond Corporation, a calendar year taxpayer, owns property in States A and B. Both A and B require that the average value of assets be included in the property factor. A requires that the property be valued at its historical cost, and B requires that the property be included in the property factor at its net book value.

Account Balances at January 1

	State A	State B	Total
Inventories	$ 150,000	$100,000	$ 250,000
Building and machinery (cost)	200,000	400,000	600,000
Accumulated depreciation for building and machinery	(150,000)	(50,000)	(200,000)
Land	50,000	100,000	150,000
Total	$ 250,000	$550,000	$ 800,000

[13]MTC Reg. IV.10.(a).

Account Balances at December 31			
	State A	**State B**	**Total**
Inventories	$ 250,000	$ 200,000	$ 450,000
Building and machinery (cost)	200,000	400,000	600,000
Accumulated depreciation for building and machinery	(175,000)	(100,000)	(275,000)
Land	50,000	100,000	150,000
Total	$ 325,000	$ 600,000	$ 925,000

State A Property Factor

Historical Cost	**January 1**	**December 31**	**Average**
Property in State A	$ 400,000*	$ 500,000**	$ 450,000
Total property	1,000,000†	1,200,000‡	1,100,000

* $150,000 + $200,000 + $50,000.
** $250,000 + $200,000 + $50,000.
† $250,000 + $600,000 + $150,000.
‡ $450,000 + $600,000 + $150,000.

$$\text{Property factor for State A: } \frac{\$450,000}{\$1,100,000} = 40.91\%$$

State B Property Factor

Net Book Value	**January 1**	**December 31**	**Average**
Property in State B	$550,000	$600,000	$575,000
Total property	800,000	925,000	862,500

$$\text{Property factor for State B: } \frac{\$575,000}{\$862,500} = 66.67\%$$

Due to the variations in the property factors, the aggregate of Blond's property factors equals 107.58%. ■

Leased property, when included in the property factor, is valued at eight times its annual rental. Annual rentals may include payments such as real estate taxes and insurance made by the lessee in lieu of rent.

EXAMPLE 20

Jasper Corporation is subject to tax in States D and G. Both states require that leased or rented property be included in the property factor at eight times the annual rental costs and that the average historical cost be used for other assets. Information regarding Jasper's property and rental expenses follows.

Average Historical Cost	
Property located in State D	$ 750,000
Property located in State G	450,000
Total property	$1,200,000

Lease and Rental Expenses	
State D	$ 50,000
State G	150,000
Total	$200,000

Property factor for State D

$$\frac{[\$750,000 + 8(\$50,000)]}{[\$1,200,000 + 8(\$200,000)]} = \frac{\$1,150,000}{\$2,800,000} = 41.07\%$$

Property factor for State G

$$\frac{[\$450{,}000 + 8(\$150{,}000)]}{[\$1{,}200{,}000 + 8(\$200{,}000)]} = \frac{\$1{,}650{,}000}{\$2{,}800{,}000} = 58.93\%$$ ■

Only property that is used in the production of apportionable income is includible in the numerator and denominator of the property factor. In this regard, idle property and property that is used in producing nonapportionable income generally are excluded. However, property that is temporarily idle or unused generally remains in the property factor.

16.3 The Unitary Theory

LO.6

Apply the unitary method of state income taxation.

The **unitary theory** developed in response to the early problems that states faced in attributing the income of a multistate business among the states in which the business was conducted. Originally, this theory was applied to justify apportionment of the income of multiple operating divisions within a single company. Over the years, however, the concept has been extended to require the combined reporting of certain affiliated corporations, including those outside the United States.

When two affiliated corporations are subject to tax in different states, each entity must file a return and report its income in the state in which it conducts business. Each entity reports its income separately from that of its affiliated corporations. In an effort to minimize overall state income tax, multistate entities have attempted to separate the parts of the business that are carried on in the various states.

EXAMPLE 21

Arts Corporation owns a chain of retail stores located in several states. To enable each store to file and report the income earned only in that state, each store was organized as a separate subsidiary in the state in which it did business. In this manner, each store is separately subject to tax only in the state in which it is located. ■

Most states attempt to assign as much of an entity's income to in-state sources as possible, so the *unitary* approach to computing state taxable income is attractive to them. Under this method, a corporation is required to file a **combined return** that includes the results from all of the operations of the related corporations, not just from those that transacted business in the state. In this manner, the unitary method allows a state to apply the apportionment formula to a firm's nationwide or worldwide unitary income. To include the activities of the corporation's subsidiaries in the apportionment formula, the state must determine that the subsidiaries' activities are an integral part of a unitary business and, as a result, are subject to apportionment.

What Is a Unitary Business?

A unitary business operates as a unit and cannot be segregated into independently operating divisions. The operations are integrated, and each division depends on or contributes to the operation of the business as a whole. It is not necessary that each unit operating within a state contribute to the activities of all divisions outside the state.

The unitary theory ignores the separate legal existence of the entities and focuses instead on practical business realities. Accordingly, the separate entities are treated as a single business for state income tax purposes, and the apportionment formula is applied to the combined income of the unitary business.

EXAMPLE 22

Continue with the facts of Example 21. Arts manufactured no goods, but conducted central management, purchasing, distribution, advertising, and administrative departments. The subsidiaries carried on a purely intrastate business, and they paid for the goods and services received at the parent company's cost, plus overhead. Arts and the subsidiaries constitute a unitary business due to their unitary operations (purchasing, distribution, advertising, and administrative functions). Accordingly, in states that have adopted the unitary method, the income and apportionment factors of the entire unitary group are combined and apportioned to the states in which at least one member of the group has nexus. ■

EXAMPLE 23

Crafts Corporation organized its departments as separate corporations on the basis of function: mining copper ore, refining the ore, and fabricating the refined copper into consumer products. Even though the various steps in the process are operated substantially independently of each other with only general supervision from Crafts' executive offices, Crafts is engaged in a single unitary business. Its various divisions are part of a large, vertically structured enterprise in which each business segment needs the products or raw materials provided by another. The flow of products among the affiliates also provides evidence of functional integration, which generally requires some form of central decision or policy making, another characteristic of a unitary business. ■

Notice that the application of the unitary theory is based on a series of subjective observations about the organization and operation of the taxpayer's businesses, whereas the availability of Federal controlled and affiliated group status (see Chapter 8) is based on objective, mechanical ownership tests. More than half of the states require or allow unitary reporting.

Tax Effects of the Unitary Theory

Use of the unitary approach by a state eliminates several of the planning techniques that could be used to shift income between corporate segments to avoid or minimize state taxes. In addition, the unitary approach usually results in a larger portion of the corporation's income being taxable in states where the compensation, property values, and sales prices are high relative to other states. This occurs because the larger in-state costs (numerators in the apportionment formula) include in the tax base a larger portion of the taxable income within the state's taxing jurisdiction. This has an adverse effect on the corporation's overall state tax burden if the states in which the larger portions are allocated impose a high tax rate relative to the other states in which the business is conducted.

The presence of a unitary business is favorable when losses of unprofitable affiliates may be offset against the earnings of profitable affiliates. It also is favorable when income earned in a high-tax state may be shifted to low-tax states due to the use of combined apportionment factors.

EXAMPLE 24

Rita Corporation owns two subsidiaries, Arts and Crafts. Arts, located in State K, generated taxable income of $700,000. During this same period, Crafts, located in State M, generated a loss of $400,000. If the subsidiaries are independent corporations, Arts is required to pay K tax on $700,000 of income. However, if the corporations constitute a unitary business, the incomes, as well as the apportionment factors, of the two entities are combined. As a result, the combined income of $300,000 ($700,000 − $400,000) is apportioned to unitary states K and M. ■

EXAMPLE 25

Eve Corporation, a wholly owned subsidiary of Dan Corporation, generated $1 million taxable income. Eve's activities and sales are restricted to State P, which imposes a 10% income tax. Dan's income for the taxable period is $1.5 million. Dan's activities and sales are restricted to State Q, which imposes a 5% income tax. Both states use a three-factor apportionment formula that equally weights sales, payroll, and property. Sales, payroll, and average property for each of the corporations are as follows.

	Eve Corporation	Dan Corporation	Total
Sales	$3,000,000	$7,000,000	$10,000,000
Payroll	2,000,000	3,500,000	5,500,000
Property	2,500,000	4,500,000	7,000,000

Water's Edge Is Not a Day at the Beach

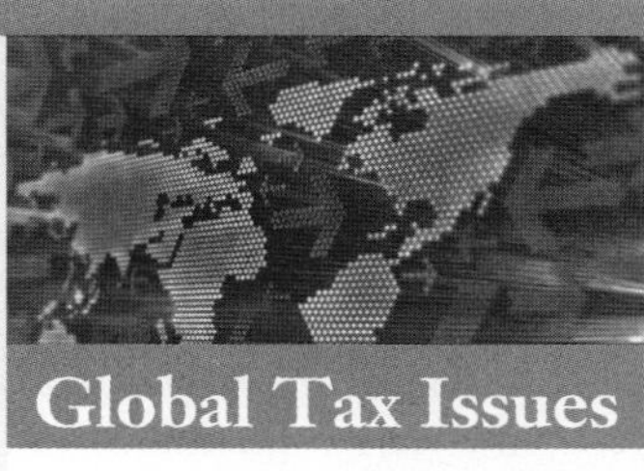

As a result of pressure from the business community, the Federal government, and foreign countries, most of the states that impose an income tax on a unitary business's worldwide operations permit a multinational business to elect **water's edge** unitary reporting as an alternative to worldwide unitary filing.

The water's edge provision permits a multinational corporation to elect to limit the reach of the state's taxing jurisdiction over out-of-state affiliates to activities occurring within the boundaries of the United States. The decision to make a water's edge election may have a substantial effect on the tax liability of a multinational corporation. For instance, a water's edge election usually cannot be revoked for a number of years without permission from the appropriate tax authority.

Moreover, corporations making this election may be assessed an additional tax or fee for the privilege of excluding out-of-state entities from the combined report.

If the corporations are independent entities, the overall state income tax liability is $175,000.

State P (10% × $1,000,000)	=	$100,000
State Q (5% × $1,500,000)	=	75,000
Total state income tax		$175,000

If the corporations are members of a unitary business, the income and apportionment factors are combined in determining the income tax liability in unitary states P and Q. As a result of the combined reporting, the overall state income tax liability is reduced.

State P Income Tax				
Total apportionable income			$2,500,000	
Apportionment formula				
Sales ($3,000,000/$10,000,000)	=	30.00%		
Payroll ($2,000,000/$5,500,000)	=	36.36%		
Property ($2,500,000/$7,000,000)	=	35.71%		
Total		102.07%		
Average (102.07% ÷ 3)			× 34.02%	
State P taxable income			$ 850,500	
Tax rate			× 10%	
State P tax liability				$85,050

State Q Income Tax				
Total apportionable income			$2,500,000	
Apportionment formula				
Sales ($7,000,000/$10,000,000)	=	70.00%		
Payroll ($3,500,000/$5,500,000)	=	63.64%		
Property ($4,500,000/$7,000,000)	=	64.29%		
Total		197.93%		
Average (197.93% ÷ 3)			× 65.98%	
State Q taxable income			$1,649,500	
Tax rate			× 5%	
State Q tax liability				$ 82,475
Total state income tax, if unitary				$167,525
Total state income tax, if nonunitary				175,000
Tax reduction from unitary combined reporting				$ 7,475

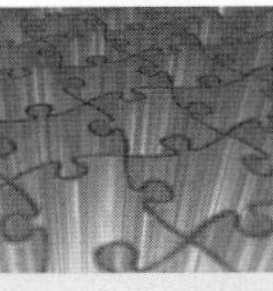

CONCEPT SUMMARY 16.1

Principles of Multistate Corporate Income Taxation

1. Taxability of an organization's income in a state other than the one in which it is incorporated depends on the laws, regulations, and judicial interpretations of the other state; the nature and level of the corporation's activity in, or contacts with, that state; and, to a limited extent, the application of P.L. 86–272.
2. Each state has adopted its own multistate income tax laws, regulations, methods, and judicial interpretations; consequently, the nonuniformity of state income taxing provisions provides a multitude of planning techniques that allow a multistate corporation to reduce its overall state tax liability legally.
3. The apportionment procedure is used to assign the income of a multistate taxpayer to the various states in which business is conducted. Generally, nonbusiness income is allocated, rather than apportioned, directly to the state in which the nonbusiness income-generating assets are located.
4. The various state apportionment factors and formulas offer planning opportunities in that more or less than 100% of the taxpayer's income may be subjected to state income tax.
5. Most states employ an equally weighted three-factor apportionment formula. In some states, the sales factor is doubled, and in a few states, only the sales factor is used in apportioning multistate taxable income. Generally, the greater the relative weight assigned to the sales factor, the greater the tax burden on out-of-state taxpayers.
6. The sales factor is based upon the destination concept except where a throwback rule applies. The payroll factor generally includes compensation that is included in Federal gross income, but some states include excludible fringe benefits. An employee's compensation usually is not divided among states. The property factor is derived using the average undepreciated historical costs for the assets and eight times the rental value of the assets.
7. The unitary theory may require the taxpayer to include worldwide activities and holdings in the apportionment factors. A water's edge election can limit these amounts to U.S. transactions.

The results of unitary reporting would have been detrimental if Q had imposed a higher rate of tax than P, because a larger percentage of the corporation's income is attributable to Q when the apportionment factors are combined. ■

The principles of multistate corporate income tax are set forth in Concept Summary 16.1.

Consolidated and Combined Returns

As discussed in Chapter 8, an affiliated group of corporations may file a consolidated return if all members of the group consent. Once such a return has been filed, the group must continue to file on a consolidated basis as long as it remains in existence, or until permission to file separate returns has been obtained. The consolidated return essentially treats the controlled corporations as a single taxable entity. Thus, the affiliated group pays only one tax, based upon the combined income of its members after certain adjustments (e.g., net operating losses) and eliminations (e.g., intercompany dividends and inventory profits).

Several states permit affiliated corporations to file a consolidated return if such a return has been filed for Federal purposes. The filing of a consolidated return is mandatory in only a few states.

Usually, only corporations that are subject to tax in the state can be included in a consolidated return unless specific requirements are met or the state permits the inclusion of corporations without nexus.

Do not confuse elective consolidated returns with required combined returns in unitary states. A combined return is filed in every unitary state in which one or more unitary members have nexus. The computations reflect apportioned and allocated income of the unitary members, resulting in a summary of the taxable income of the entities in each state. The combined method chiefly permits the unitary taxpayer to develop the summary of assigned taxable incomes, which is accepted by (and disclosed to) all of the states.

16.4 Taxation of S Corporations

LO.7

Discuss the states' income tax treatment of S corporations, partnerships, and LLCs.

The majority of the states that impose a corporate income tax have special provisions, similar to the Federal law, that govern the taxation of S corporations. Only a few states—including Tennessee and Texas—and the District of Columbia do not provide special (no corporate-level tax) treatment for Federal S corporations. In addition, Massachusetts imposes a corporate-level tax on S corporations that have gross receipts in excess of $6 million. Some states, including Illinois, Texas, and California, apply a corporate-level tax, at special rates, on an S corporation.

In the non-S election states, a Federal S corporation generally is subject to tax in the same manner as a regular C corporation. Accordingly, if a multistate S corporation operates in any of these states, it is subject to state income tax and does not realize one of the primary benefits of S status—the avoidance of double taxation. Other potential tax-related benefits of the S election, including the pass-through of net operating losses and the reduction in the rate of tax imposed on individual and corporate taxpayers, may be curtailed.

EXAMPLE 26

Bryan, an S corporation, has established nexus in States A and B. A recognizes S status, while B does not. Bryan generated $600,000 of ordinary business income and $100,000 of dividends that were received from corporations in which Bryan owns 50% of the stock. Bryan's State B apportionment percentage is 50%.

For B tax purposes, Bryan first computes its income as though it were a C corporation. It then apportions the resulting income to B. Assuming that B has adopted the Federal provisions governing the dividends received deduction, Bryan's income, determined as though it were a C corporation, is $620,000 [$600,000 + (100% − 80%) × $100,000]. Accordingly, Bryan may be subject to B corporate income tax on $310,000 ($620,000 × 50% apportionment percentage) of taxable income. ■

Eligibility

All of the states that recognize S status permit a corporation to be treated as an S corporation for state purposes only if the corporation has a valid Federal S election in place. Generally, the filing of a Federal S election is sufficient to render the corporation an S corporation for state tax purposes. In most states, an entity that is an S corporation for Federal tax purposes automatically is treated as an S corporation for state tax purposes. Wisconsin allows the entity to *elect out* of its S status for state purposes.

Corporate-Level Tax

Although S corporations generally are not taxable entities, Federal income tax liability may arise if the corporation has excess passive investment income or recognized built-in gains (see Chapter 12). Several states have adopted similar provisions; therefore, an S corporation is exempt from the related state income tax only to the extent it is exempt from corresponding Federal income taxes. In the majority of these states, the imposition of Federal income taxes generates a corporate-level tax for state purposes to the extent corporate income is allocated or apportioned to the state.

EXAMPLE 27

Amp, an S corporation, has nexus with States X and Y, both of which recognize S status. X imposes a corporate-level tax on S corporations to the extent the corresponding Federal tax applies. Amp is subject to the § 1374 tax. This year, its Federal excessive passive income is $60,000. The amount of income subject to tax in X depends on Amp's apportionment percentage for X.

If Amp's State X apportionment percentage is 50%, Amp is subject to a corporate-level tax in X on $30,000 of passive income ($60,000 × 50%). ■

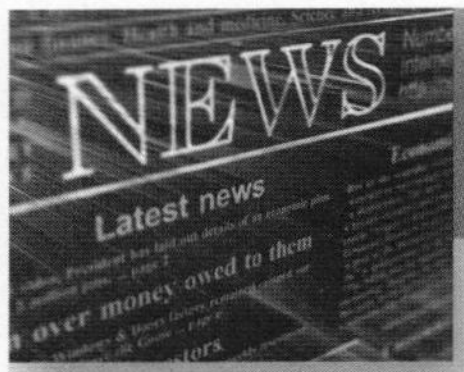

TAX IN THE NEWS What Are You Taxing?

Taxware.com, an observer of the state and local tax scene, has identified several of the most unusual sales and use tax laws that remain on the books of various states.

- Kentucky horse breeders pay sales tax on "stud fees" related to the breeding of Thoroughbred horses.
- North Carolina is a "tax-free zone" for motor sport racing teams. This includes a refund for the sales tax allocated to the fuel used by the aircraft that transport team members to the state.
- Cloth diapers are exempt from sales tax in Wisconsin, but disposables are taxable.
- Ohioans receive a tax break when they die. Makeup applications are exempt from sales tax when they are applied in a mortuary, but not when they occur in a beauty salon.
- Pennsylvania taxes air, in the form of a fee for the vacuum cleaner used at a car wash. No tax applies, though, for air used to inflate tires by a similar machine.

A few states deviate from the Federal S corporation provisions and provide that an S corporation is entirely exempt from state income tax only if all of its shareholders are residents of the state. In these states, an S corporation is taxed on the portion of its income that is attributable to nonresident shareholders. Some of these states permit the S corporation to escape corporate-level tax on this income if its nonresident shareholders sign a form, agreeing to pay state tax on their share of the corporation's income. Moreover, about half of the states require the corporation to withhold taxes on the nonresident shareholders' portions of the entity's income.

EXAMPLE 28

ARGO, an S corporation, is subject to income tax only in Vermont. On the last day of its taxable year, 40% of ARGO's stock is held by nonresident shareholders. To the extent ARGO's stock is held by resident shareholders, the corporation is not subject to income tax. Accordingly, ARGO is not subject to tax on 60% of its income.

The corporation *is* subject to tax on the remaining 40% of its income. ARGO may be able to avoid this corporate-level tax by withholding Vermont income tax for its nonresident shareholders. ■

In an effort to decrease compliance burdens and simplify the filing process for nonresident shareholders of S corporations, several states allow an S corporation to file a single income tax return and pay the resulting tax on behalf of some or all of its nonresident shareholders. State requirements for the filing of a "block" or **composite return** vary substantially.

16.5 Taxation of Partnerships and LLCs

Most states apply income tax provisions to partnerships, limited liability companies (LLCs), and limited liability partnerships (LLPs) in a manner that parallels Federal treatment. The entity is a tax-reporting, not a taxpaying, entity. Income, loss, and credit items are allocated and apportioned among the partners according to the terms of the partnership agreement and state income tax law.

Some states require that the entity make estimated tax payments on behalf of out-of-state partners. This approach helps to ensure that nonresident partners file appropriate forms and pay any resulting tax to the state. A few states, including Michigan for partnerships and Texas for LLCs, apply an entity-level tax on operating income. As is the case with S corporations, some states allow composite returns to be filed relative to out-of-state partners.

Generally, an in-state partner computes the income tax resulting from all of the flow-through income from the entity. The partner then is allowed a credit for income taxes paid to other states on this income.

Key issues facing partnerships doing business in multiple states include those listed here. Applicable law varies from state to state, and more complex transactions may not yet be addressed by existing law.

- Whether the partnership automatically has nexus with every state in which a partner resides.
- Whether a partner is deemed to have nexus with every state in which the partnership does business.
- How to assign the income/loss of a partner upon retirement or when a liquidating distribution is received.

16.6 Other State and Local Taxes

LO.8

Describe other commonly encountered state and local taxes on businesses.

State and Local Sales and Use Taxes

Forty-five states and the District of Columbia impose a consumers' sales tax on retail sales of tangible personal property for use or consumption. In many of these states, in-state localities, including cities, towns, school districts, and counties, also have the power to levy a sales tax. A consumers' sales tax is a tax imposed directly on the purchaser who acquires the asset at retail; the tax is measured by the price of the sale. The vendor or retailer merely acts as a collection agent for the state.

A use tax is designed to complement the sales tax. The use tax has two purposes: to prevent consumers from evading sales tax by purchasing goods outside the state for in-state use and to provide an equitable sales environment between in-state and out-of-state retailers.

Generally, sales of tangible personal property are subject to tax. In several states, selected services are subject to tax.

Each jurisdiction that applies a sales/use tax defines its own tax base (i.e., which items are taxable and to whom). For a multistate business, complying with the thousands of sets of sales/use tax statutes and regulations can be a difficult burden. In an effort to ease this confusion, state and local government officials and the MTC developed the Streamlined Sales Tax Project (SSTP). Members working in conjunction with the SSTP write model laws for taxing jurisdictions to adopt, thereby allowing for a more uniform application of the rules and for a more efficient exchange of information among revenue agencies.

To date, the most popular SSTP rules are those defining which products and services are subject to sales/use tax. For instance, SSTP rules set out the items of clothing that would be subject to tax, but each jurisdiction decides on its own whether to include clothing in the tax base and whether to allow "back-to-school" clothing amnesties during specific weeks of the year. However, little interest has been shown in having identical sales/use tax rates among the jurisdictions.

Almost all of the states that have adopted a sales/use tax are members of the SSTP, but only about half of them automatically adopt model SSTP laws.

Sales/Use Tax Exemptions

A majority of the states exempt sales of certain items from the sales/use tax base. The most common exemptions and exclusions include the following.

- *Sales for resale* are exempt because the purchaser is not the ultimate user of the sold property. For instance, meat purchased by a grocer and a garment purchased by a retailer are not subject to sales/use tax under the resale rule.
- *Casual or occasional sales* that occur infrequently are exempt from the sales/use tax base chiefly for administrative convenience. Most states exclude rummage sales, the transfer of an entire business, sales of used autos, and the like under this rule.
- Most *purchases by exempt organizations* are excluded from taxable sales. Charities, governments and their agencies, and other organizations qualifying for

Federal income tax exemption are relieved of sales/use tax liabilities in all of the states.

- *Sales of targeted items* can be exempt to improve the equity of the sales/use tax system. Sales of groceries, medical prescriptions and equipment, and school clothes can fall into this category and become nontaxable. Special exemptions for sales of farm, industrial, and computing equipment might also qualify under this type of exclusion.
- Certain *sales to manufacturers, producers, and processors* may also be exempt. Exemptions usually include one or more of the following.
  - Containers and other packing, packaging, and shipping materials actually used to transfer merchandise to customers of the purchaser.
  - Machines and specific processing equipment and repair parts or replacements exclusively and directly used in manufacturing tangible personal property.

ETHICS & EQUITY Taxing Clicks and Bricks

The states' enforcement efforts tend to be lax concerning sales/use tax collections for sales conducted on the Internet. But does this audit-deployment decision give Internet retailers an unfair advantage over bricks-and-mortar businesses that must collect sales tax on the sales they make? Local retailers have invested in physical stores and merchandise and make up most downtown and shopping mall areas. Why should the law effectively allow a tax holiday for clicks-and-mortar Internet sellers, which have invested in just-in-time inventories and intangible assets such as e-commerce web software? Do Internet retailers carry more political clout than those with stores or other physical presence in the state?

Comment on the equity of the current situation regarding Internet sales and the sales/use tax.

Sales/Use Tax Nexus

A separate set of nexus rules applies in determining whether a seller must collect a sales/use tax from a customer. Strictly, the tax must be collected only if the seller has a *physical presence* (e.g., a store building but not a web page) in the state.

The regular solicitation of sales by independent brokers establishes sufficient nexus to require a nonresident seller to register and collect the use tax, even though the seller does not have regular employees, agents, and an office or other place of business in the state.[14] As a result, a corporation may be required to collect sales and use taxes in a state even though it is immune from the imposition of an income tax.

Sales/Use Tax on Services

Most sales/use tax laws were developed 50 or more years ago, when the U.S. economy was based on manufacturing and merchandising. Today, with perhaps two-thirds of all retail transactions in the United States consisting at some level of the rendering of services, the sales/use tax may be considered inadequate at generating revenues for the taxing jurisdictions. Consequently, some states have been adding specific service transactions to the sales/use tax base.

The services most commonly being subjected to tax include transactions involving hotels and restaurants, hair and beauty salons, entertainment events, cable and satellite television subscriptions, and lawn care. To date, taxation of legal/accounting, medical, education, and advertising services has been blocked by the professional associations of the providers of these services. Revenue shortfalls at the state and local level, however, may force legislatures to expand the sales/use tax base to include a broader array of services in the future.

[14] *Quill Corp. v. North Dakota*, 112 S.Ct. 1904 (1992); *Scripto, Inc. v. Carson*, 80 S.Ct. 619 (1960).

TAX IN THE NEWS How Do You Tax a Cloud?

The trend in the tech world toward *cloud computing* has reached the point where state legislatures must issue rulings concerning the sales/use taxation of this procedure.

Cloud computing has become feasible now that the Internet is supported by a great deal of high-speed bandwidth, allowing users to access files and programs quickly and accurately from almost any location. Under a cloud computing model, both software programs and specific user data files are stored on remote server computers, often rather than on the hard drives of the user's various workstations.

Under a cloud-based system, both a text document and the word processing program that modifies it are located on the server computer. A user can access and modify the file from a desktop at the office, from a laptop at home, and from a tablet or smartphone on the road. The edited file is saved and can be accessed later from any of the user's locations or by another team member with whom the user is collaborating.

But how do sales/use tax laws address this new computing model? Assume that a piece of software is purchased or updated and that a sales/use tax applies. Where should the user remit the tax?

- To State A, where the server computer is housed?
- To State B, where the software manufacturer is based?
- To States C, D, or E, where the purchaser uses the files in a business or personal setting?

Only a few states have issued rulings on these matters to date, and even this small number of interpretations often is self-contradictory. It is likely that Congress will need to "act as the referee" and craft laws that will both allow states to enact sales/use tax laws that are appropriate to their revenue needs and to apply those laws so that it is clear which single state should receive the tax. Until Congress acts, therefore, the evolution of laws adopted by the states is certain to create uncertainty.

Local Property Taxes

Property taxes, a major source of revenue at the city and county level, often are designated as *ad valorem* taxes because they are based on the value of property that is located in the state on a specific date. Generally, that date fixes taxable ownership, situs (location), and the valuation of the property. Nonetheless, to avoid tax evasion, personal property that is temporarily outside the state may be taxed at the domicile of the owner.

Property taxes can take the form of either real property taxes or personal property taxes. States apply different tax rates and means of assessment to the two classes of property. The methods of assessing the value of the real and tangible property also vary in different taxing jurisdictions.

Although a personal property tax may be imposed on both intangible and tangible property, most states limit the tax to tangible property. The distinction between the various items of personal property is important because special rates, computations, or exemptions apply to certain types of property. For instance, inventory constitutes tangible personal property, but is exempt from taxation in most states.

Other Taxes

States may impose a variety of other state and local taxes on corporations, including incorporation or entrance fees or taxes, gross receipt taxes, stock transfer taxes, realty transfer and mortgage recording taxes, license taxes, and franchise taxes based on net worth or capital stock outstanding.

Administrative Taxes

An *incorporation tax* is an excise tax for the corporate privilege conferred on the business. At the time the business is incorporated, the state generally imposes a fee or tax for the privilege of conducting business as a corporation within the state. Similarly, an out-of-state corporation usually must pay an entrance fee or tax before it can transact business in a state other than its state of incorporation.

TAX IN THE NEWS The Amazon Tax

Amazon long has enjoyed its no-nexus status as a strictly virtual seller, collecting sales/use taxes only in its headquarters state of Washington and in the three states with Amazon distribution centers. But pressure is building for Amazon to collect sales/use tax on all of its sales. Not only do states need additional revenues, but Amazon's competitors want a "level playing field."

Amazon has built a strong business with its broad catalog, easy-to-use user interface, free shipping, and easy returns policy. But the sales-tax-free advantage that Amazon enjoys in most states also has been critical to its profitability. Various estimates show that were Amazon to start collecting sales/use tax on all of its sales, it would lose about $650 million in annual sales. The states would collect about $11 billion in new taxes every year if all e-tailers would remit sales/use tax for all e-sales.

Charges of nexus from California have been met by Amazon in an interesting way. Amazon's physical presence in the state seemed hard to deny, given the fact that the Kindle was designed there and that several Amazon search companies are based in Silicon Valley. But the state granted a relaxed approach to nexus enforcement for one year, in exchange for Amazon locating in the state several new, large facilities and the jobs that come with them. This compromise gives Amazon one year in which to lobby for more friendly sales/use tax collection rules.

To counter the loss of significant sales/use tax revenues on Internet transactions due to inadequate collection methods, New York and about a dozen other states have found nexus through a vendor's use of sales, distribution, and marketing affiliates. For instance, suppose a consumer clicks on a link on an Amazon.com page to Overstock.com, Target.com, or some other retailer and then purchases goods from the vendor. These states contend that Amazon has sales/use tax nexus because of the physical presence established in-state *by use of the affiliate*, even though Amazon itself has no such presence.

This so-called Amazon tax has been supported by most lower-level courts that have reviewed the issue. The taxpayers are appealing those holdings—not surprisingly, given that most of Amazon's affiliates (e.g., Target) have outlets in nearly every U.S. state and that considerable sales/use tax revenue is at stake.

Some states base the incorporation tax on the par value of the authorized stock. To prevent tax evasion, a few of these states impose a similar fee or tax on subsequent increases in the corporation's authorized stock. Where the incorporation fee or tax is based on the amount of authorized stock, the tax may be based on the total amount of the stock, even though the corporation conducts business in several states.

A *license tax* is an excise tax on the privilege of engaging in a certain business, occupation, or profession. A jurisdiction may impose business, occupational, or professional license taxes as a means of generating revenue or regulating the activities of the business, occupation, or profession for the public welfare.

Stock and realty transfer and mortgage recording taxes are nonrecurring taxes that are imposed at the time of recording or transfer. *Stock transfer taxes* are imposed on the transfer of shares or certificates of stock of domestic and foreign corporations. The tax typically is based on the number of shares transferred and the par or market value of the stock. Generally, the following stock transfers are exempt from the transfer tax: original issues, deposits of stock as security for a loan, and transfers to a broker for sale or purchase.

The base of the *realty transfer tax* usually is measured by the consideration paid or to be paid for the realty. The *mortgage recording tax* may be based on the actual consideration given, the value of the property, or the debt to be secured by the instrument.

Collections of Unclaimed Property

All of the U.S. states enforce rules that allow them to take possession of certain unclaimed property. In operation, this procedure acts like a tax on business with large consumer operations.

Unclaimed property might take the form of an unused gift card or a paycheck the employee has not yet cashed. On the balance sheet, these amounts are reported as payables by the business. After a stated period of time passes (usually 7 to 15 years) and an effort is made to contact the holder of the business's obligation, the value of the property reverts to the state. These rights of the states often are referred to as *escheat* laws.

Because unclaimed property rules are not enacted as a taxing statute, the usual nexus and apportionment tests do not apply. Instead, the property is taken by the state in which the business is incorporated.[15]

Capital Stock and Franchise Taxes

Typically, a *capital stock tax* is an excise tax imposed on a domestic corporation for the privilege of existing as a corporation or imposed on an out-of-state corporation, either for the privilege of doing business or for the actual transaction of business within the state. This annual tax usually is based on the book value of the corporation's net worth, including capital, surplus, and retained earnings. In a few states, a corporation is subject to a *franchise tax* only to the extent the tax exceeds the corporate income tax, but in the majority of states, the entity is subject to both taxes.

The majority of capital stock taxes are apportioned if the corporation does business or maintains an office in another state. In some states, however, the tax is levied on the entire authorized or issued capital stock of a domestic corporation, even though the corporation may be engaged in business in other states. For corporations based in other states, the tax is imposed only on the capital that is employed in the state as determined by an apportionment formula.

EXAMPLE 29

The balance sheet of Bull, a domestic corporation of State A, at the end of its taxable year is as follows.

Cash	$100,000
Equipment (net of $50,000 accumulated depreciation)	150,000
Building (net of $75,000 accumulated depreciation)	225,000
Land	125,000
Total assets	$600,000
Accounts payable and other short-term liabilities	$100,000
Long-term liabilities	200,000
Capital stock	50,000
Paid-in capital in excess of par value	50,000
Retained earnings	200,000
Total liabilities and equity	$600,000

A imposes a 2% franchise tax based on the entire net worth of a domestic corporation. Bull is subject to a franchise tax in A of $6,000 ($600,000 assets − $300,000 liabilities = $300,000 net worth × 2% rate). ■

EXAMPLE 30

Continue with the facts of Example 29, except that A subjects a domestic corporation to tax only on the capital that is employed in the state. Bull properly determines that its A apportionment percentage is 20%. In this case, Bull's A franchise tax liability is $1,200 ($300,000 net worth × 20% apportionment percentage = $60,000 capital employed in A × 2% rate). ■

[15] *Texas v. New Jersey*, 379 U.S. 674 (1965).

ETHICS & EQUITY Encouraging Economic Development through Tax Concessions

The tax professional occasionally is in a position to negotiate with a state or city taxing jurisdiction to garner tax relief for a client as an incentive to locate a plant or distribution center in that geographic area. In times when construction budgets are high and interstate competition is fierce to attract or retain businesses that are making location decisions, such tax concessions can be significant.

For instance, to encourage a business to build a large distribution center in the area, community leaders might be agreeable to (1) paying for roads, sewer, water, and other improvements through taxpayer bonds; (2) reducing property taxes by 50 percent for the first 10 years of the center's operations; and (3) permanently excluding any distribution-related vehicles and equipment from the personal property tax.

An incentive-granting community provides the concessions even though the influx of new workers will place a great strain on public school facilities and likely necessitate improvements in traffic patterns and other infrastructure. Local residents, even those who obtain jobs at the new facility, and the tax adviser may wonder whether tax concessions, such as the $22,500 per new or retained job that Illinois gave to the trucker Navistar, are supportable in light of these changes in the community's quality of life.

Consider the position of a large employer that has been located in the area for more than 50 years. By how much should it be willing to absorb the tax increases that result when economic development concessions are used to attract new, perhaps temporary, businesses to the area? Should the employer challenge the constitutionality of the grant of such sizable tax breaks to some, but not all, business taxpayers in the jurisdiction?

Should higher "impact fees" be assessed on new developments? Does your analysis change if the new business competes with the longtime resident for sales? For employees? For political power?

16.7 Tax Planning

LO.9

Recognize tax planning opportunities available to minimize a corporation's state and local tax liability.

The inconsistencies in the tax laws and rates among the states not only complicate state tax planning but also provide the nucleus of pertinent planning opportunities. Although several tax planning devices are available to a corporation that does business in only one state, most planning techniques are directed toward corporations that do business or maintain property in more than one state. All suggested tax planning strategies should be reviewed in light of practical business considerations and the additional administrative and other costs that may be incurred, because simply minimizing state taxes may not be prudent from a business perspective.

Selecting the Optimal State in Which to Operate

Because the states employ different definitions of the amount and type of activity necessary to establish nexus, a company has some latitude in selecting the states by which it will be taxed. When a corporation has only a limited connection with a high-tax state, it may abandon that activity by electing an alternative means of accomplishing the same result. For example, if providing a sales representative with a company-owned BlackBerry constitutes nexus in an undesired state, the company could eliminate its connection with that state by reimbursing sales personnel for equipment expenses, instead of providing a company communications device. Similarly, when nexus is caused by conducting customer training sessions or seminars in the state, the corporation could bypass this connection. This can be done by sending the personnel to a nearby state in which nexus clearly has been established or in which the activity would not constitute nexus.

In addition, when sufficient activity originates from the repair and maintenance of the corporation's products or the activities performed by the sales representatives within the state, the organization could incorporate the service or sales divisions. This would invalidate a nonunitary state's right to tax the parent corporation's income; only the income of the service or sales divisions would be subject to tax. However, this technique is successful only if the incorporated division is a *bona fide* business operation. Therefore, the pricing of any sales or services between the new subsidiary and the parent corporation must be at arm's length, and the operations of the new corporation preferably should result in a profit.

Although planning techniques often are employed to disconnect a corporation's activities from an undesirable state, they can also be utilized to create nexus in a desirable state. For example, when the presence of a company-owned computer creates nexus in a desirable state, the corporation could provide its sales representatives in that state with company-owned equipment, rather than reimbursing or providing increased compensation for equipment costs.

Establishing nexus in a state is advantageous, for instance, when that state has a lower tax rate than the state in which the income currently is taxed or when losses or credits become available to reduce tax liabilities in the state.

EXAMPLE 31

Bird Corporation generates $500,000 of taxable income from selling goods; specifically, 40% of its product is sold in State A and 60% in State B. Both states levy a corporate income tax and include only the sales factor in their apportionment formulas. The tax rate in A is 10%; B's rate is only 3%. Bird's manufacturing operation is located in A; therefore, the corporation's income is subject to tax in that state. Currently, Bird is immune from tax under Public Law 86–272 in B. Because A has adopted a throwback provision, Bird incurs $50,000 of state income taxes.

	Apportionment Formula	Net Income	Tax Rate	Tax
State A	100/100	$500,000	10%	$50,000
State B	0/100	500,000	3%	–0–
Total tax liability				$50,000

Because B imposes a lower tax rate than A, Bird substantially reduces its state tax liability if sufficient nexus is created with B.

	Apportionment Formula	Net Income	Tax Rate	Tax
State A	40/100	$500,000	10%	$20,000
State B	60/100	500,000	3%	9,000
Total tax liability				$29,000

■

A corporation may benefit by storing inventory in a low- or no-tax state because the average property value in the state in which the manufacturing operation is located is reduced significantly. When the manufacturing operation is located in a high-tax state, the establishment of a distribution center in a low- or no-tax state may reduce the overall state tax liability.

EXAMPLE 32

Trill Corporation realized $200,000 of taxable income from selling its product in States A and B. Trill's manufacturing plant, product distribution center, and warehouses are located in A. The corporation's activities within the two states are as follows.

	State A	State B	Total
Sales	$500,000	$200,000	$700,000
Property	300,000	50,000	350,000
Payroll	100,000	10,000	110,000

Trill is subject to tax in A and B. Both states utilize a three-factor apportionment formula that equally weights sales, property, and payroll; however, A imposes a 10% corporate income tax, while B levies a 3% tax. Trill incurs a total income tax liability of $17,575.

Apportionment Formulas						
	State A			State B		
Sales	$500,000/$700,000	=	71.43%	$200,000/$700,000	=	28.57%
Property	$300,000/$350,000	=	85.71%	$50,000/$350,000	=	14.29%
Payroll	$100,000/$110,000	=	90.91%	$10,000/$110,000	=	9.09%
Total			248.05%			51.95%
Apportionment factor (totals/3)			82.68%			17.32%
Income apportioned to the state ($200,000 × apportionment factor)			$165,360			$34,640
Tax rate			× 10%			× 3%
Tax liability			$ 16,536			$ 1,039
Total tax liability				$17,575		

EXAMPLE 33

Continue with the facts of Example 32, and further assume that Trill's product distribution center and warehouse operations were acquired for $200,000 and the payroll of these operations is $20,000. Ignoring all nontax considerations, Trill could reduce its tax liability by $3,514 (a 20% reduction) by moving its distribution center, warehouses, and applicable personnel to B.

	State A	State B	Total
Sales	$500,000	$200,000	$700,000
Property	100,000	250,000	350,000
Payroll	80,000	30,000	110,000

Apportionment Formulas						
	State A			State B		
Sales	$500,000/$700,000	=	71.43%	$200,000/$700,000	=	28.57%
Property	$100,000/$350,000	=	28.57%	$250,000/$350,000	=	71.43%
Payroll	$80,000/$110,000	=	72.73%	$30,000/$110,000	=	27.27%
Total			172.73%			127.27%
Apportionment factor (totals/3)			57.58%			42.42%
Income apportioned to the state ($200,000 × apportionment factor)			$115,160			$ 84,840
Tax rate			× 10%			× 3%
Tax liability			$ 11,516			$ 2,545
Total tax liability				$14,061		
Tax imposed before move to State B				17,575		
Tax reduction due to move				$ 3,514		

Restructuring Corporate Entities

One of the major objectives of state tax planning is to design the proper mix of corporate entities. An optimal mix of entities often generates the lowest combined state income tax for the corporation. Ideally, the income from all of the entities will be subject to a low tax rate or no tax at all. However, this generally is not possible. Consequently, the goal of designing a good corporate combination often is to situate the highly profitable entities in states that impose a low (or no) income tax.

Matching Tax Rates and Corporate Income

When the corporation must operate in a high-tax state, divisions that generate losses also should be located there. Alternatively, unprofitable or less profitable operations can be merged into profitable operations to reduce the overall income subject to tax in the state. An ideal candidate for this type of merger may be a research and development subsidiary that is only marginally profitable but is vital to the parent corporation's strategic goals. By using computer simulation models, a variety of different combinations can be tested to determine the optimal corporate structure.

Unitary Operations

By identifying the states that have adopted the unitary method and the criteria under which a particular state defines a unitary business, a taxpayer may reduce its overall state tax by restructuring its corporate relationships to create or guard against a unitary relationship. For instance, an independent business enterprise can be made unitary by exercising day-to-day operational control and by centralizing functions such as marketing, financing, accounting, and legal services.

THE BIG PICTURE

EXAMPLE 34

Return to the facts of *The Big Picture* on p. 16-1. LocalCo already operates in both unitary and nonunitary states. Application of unitary corporate income tax rules can make tax planning more difficult. Subjecting certain LocalCo activities to the unitary theory could either increase or decrease the combined corporate income tax liability of the affiliates, depending especially on the apportionment formulas applied in the unitary states.

LocalCo needs to make projections of the profitability of its operations in the new multifunction building. Then LocalCo should determine the income tax effects of expanding its operations into several target states, including both unitary and nonunitary jurisdictions, and compare how the unitary rules (and all associated compliance costs) affect its after-tax profits.

Passive Investment Companies

The creation of a **passive investment company** is another restructuring technique utilized to minimize a corporation's state tax burden. Nonbusiness or passive income generally is allocated to the state in which the income-producing asset is located, rather than apportioned among the states in which the corporation does business. Therefore, significant tax savings may be realized when nonbusiness assets are located in a state that either does not levy an income tax or provides favorable tax treatment for passive income. The corporation need not be domiciled in the state to benefit from these favorable provisions. Instead, the tax savings can be realized by forming a passive investment subsidiary to hold the intangible assets and handle the corporation's investment activities. The passive investment subsidiary technique usually produces the desired result in any no-tax state. Delaware, however, often is selected for this purpose due to its other corporate statutory provisions and favorable political, business, and legal climate.

Delaware does not impose an income tax upon a corporation whose only activity within the state is the maintenance and management of intangible investments and the collection and distribution of income from such investments or from tangible property physically located in another state. Consequently, trademarks, patents, stock, and other intangible property can be transferred to a Delaware corporation whose activity is limited to collecting passive income. The assets can be transferred to the subsidiary without incurring a Federal income tax under § 351 (see Chapter 4).

However, to receive the desired preferential state tax treatment, the holding company's activities within the state must be sufficient to establish income tax nexus in the state. The passive investment company should avoid performing any activity outside the state that may result in establishing nexus with another state. In addition, the formation of the subsidiary must be properly implemented to ensure the legal substance of the operation. The passive investment company must have a physical office, and it must function as an independent operation. Ensuring nexus and proper formation is not difficult because numerous consulting organizations are available to furnish new passive investment companies with all of the elements necessary to fulfill these requirements.

Because the subsidiary's activities are confined to Delaware (or some other no- or low-tax state) and its operations generate only passive income, its income will not be taxed in any nonunitary state. Moreover, most states exclude dividends from taxation or otherwise treat them favorably; therefore, the earnings of a passive investment subsidiary can be distributed as a dividend to the parent at a minimal tax cost. If the state in which the parent is located does not levy the full income tax on dividends received, the entire measure of passive income may escape taxation.

Formation of a passive investment subsidiary also may favorably affect the parent corporation's apportionment formula in nonunitary states because the passive income earned by the subsidiary is excluded from the numerator of its sales factor.

EXAMPLE 35

Purple Corporation generates $800,000 of taxable income; $600,000 is income from its manufacturing operations, and $200,000 is dividend income from passive investments. All of Purple's sales are made and assets are kept in State A, which imposes a 10% corporate income tax and permits a 100% deduction for dividends received from subsidiaries. The corporation is not subject to tax in any other state. Consequently, Purple incurs $80,000 of income tax (tax base $800,000 × tax rate 10%).

If Purple creates a passive investment subsidiary in State B, which does not impose an income tax upon a corporation whose only activity within the state is the maintenance and management of passive investments, Purple's tax liability is reduced by $20,000 (a 25% decrease). Because passive income is nonbusiness income (which is allocated for state tax purposes to the state in which it is located), the income earned from its passive investments is not subject to tax in A.

	State A (Purple Corporation)	State B (Passive Investment Company)
Taxable income	$600,000	$200,000
Tax rate	× 10%	× –0–*
Tax liability	$ 60,000	$ –0–
Total tax liability		$ 60,000
Tax imposed without restructuring		80,000
Tax reduction due to use of subsidiary		$ 20,000

* B does not impose an income tax on a passive investment corporation.

The income earned by the subsidiary from its passive investments can be distributed to Purple as a dividend without incurring a tax liability because A allows a 100% deduction for dividends that are received from subsidiary corporations. ■

These desired results, however, will not be fully available in states that view the entire corporate operation as being unitary. Because those states require combined reporting, the income earned by the passive investment subsidiary is included in the corporation's apportionable or allocable income.

Subjecting the Corporation's Income to Apportionment

When a multistate organization is domiciled in a high-tax state, some of its apportionable income is eliminated from the tax base in that state. In light of the high tax rate, this may result in significant tax savings. Apportioning income will be especially effective where the income that is attributed to the other states is not subject to income tax.

TAX IN THE NEWS Leave That Giraffe at Home!

Passive investment subsidiaries make some states very angry. Revenue departments complain that millions of dollars of taxable income are fleeing to Delaware or Nevada. Industrial states such as Ohio and Michigan regard the device as a means of creating a tax haven within the United States, in much the same way as the Cayman Islands serve as a haven from the Federal income tax. Somewhat ironically, even the revenue authorities of Switzerland have criticized the United States for allowing such a technique to flourish, and some countries characterize the United States as a tax haven when the device is used.

One of the means by which the states have attacked the use of passive investment subsidiaries is the *Geoffrey* rule. The device is named after Geoffrey the Giraffe, the mascot of Toys 'R Us. Over a decade ago, the Supreme Court of South Carolina held that the presence of intangible assets, including corporate logos and mascots such as Geoffrey, created nexus with the state. Thus, some taxable income could be apportioned to a state where the intangible asset is used. The *Geoffrey* decision came as a surprise to many tax advisers, and the rule now limits some of the planning opportunities formerly available to those operating in nonunitary jurisdictions.

About one-half of the states have attempted, usually through administrative rules, to adopt the *Geoffrey* approach. Other states either have not addressed the issue or purposely have ignored the rule to avoid the appearance of a hostile tax climate that could impede the recruitment of new businesses. Many states want to close this loophole but without seeming unfriendly to business.

The other popular approach used by the states to attack passive investment subsidiaries is to require combined reporting under the unitary theory. Almost a dozen states have adopted required combined reporting, or are considering legislation to do so, in the last few years. These states include New York, Pennsylvania, and Maryland. The unitary tax movement no longer is only a western states phenomenon.

Because the taxes of some taxpayers go up under combined reporting while the taxes of others decrease, there often is no political force to block the adoption of unitary taxation. In fact, pressure for states to "go unitary" may be fueled by media reports of how well multistate tax planning can work (e.g., how Wal-Mart saves billions in taxes by paying rent for the use of property owned by its affiliates).

Some now are touting unitary tax theories on the basis of fairness. They say that the corporate income tax may be assessed more equitably in today's economy by using the broadest tax base and apportionment data possible.

The income removed from the taxing jurisdiction of the domicile state entirely escapes state income taxation when the state to which the income is attributed (1) does not levy a corporate income tax, (2) requires a higher level of activity necessary to subject an out-of-state company to taxation than that adopted by the state of domicile, or (3) is prohibited under Public Law 86–272 from taxing the income (assuming that the domicile state has not adopted a throwback provision). Thus, the right to apportion income may provide substantial benefits because the out-of-state sales are excluded from the numerator of the sales factor and may not be taxed in another state.

However, to acquire the right to apportion its income, the organization must have sufficient activities in or contacts with one or more other states. Whether the type and amount of activities and/or contacts are considered adequate is determined by the other state's nexus rules. Therefore, a corporation should analyze its current activities in and contacts with other states to determine which, if any, activities or contacts could be redirected so that the corporation gains the right to apportion its income.

THE BIG PICTURE
EXAMPLE 36

Return to the facts of *The Big Picture* on p. 16-1. Most corporate taxpayers consist of a parent corporation and perhaps one or more existing subsidiaries. Given its expansion plans, LocalCo has the opportunity to determine "from scratch" in which states it wants to create nexus for the operations in the multifunction building.

The tax professional needs to offer advice to LocalCo's board of directors as to where the building might be situated and how the operations of any related sales and administrative personnel might be structured in an effort to provide optimal tax consequences. Nexus issues to be considered include the following.

- Is income tax nexus created with the target state?
- Is sales/use tax nexus created with the target state?
- How are the income tax apportionment factors affected by the expansion plans (e.g., whether the target state uses a property factor in the apportionment formula and, if so, how it is weighted)?
- Would a building such as that planned by LocalCo receive any special computational treatment for the target state's property factor (e.g., in averaging the building's costs or applying accumulated depreciation)?

ETHICS & EQUITY Can You Be a Nowhere Adviser?

The intent of much of today's multistate income tax planning is to create so-called *nowhere sales*, such that the income from the transaction is not subject to tax in any state. Suppose, for instance, that a sale is made from Georgia (a state with no throwback rule) into Nevada (the place of ultimate destination, but a state with no income tax). No state-level income tax liability is generated.

Is it ethical for a tax adviser to suggest such a strategy? Could you ethically propose the establishment of a sales office in a nonthrowback state, thereby avoiding state income tax on a transaction that is fully taxable under Federal rules?

Planning with Apportionment Factors

Sales Factor

The sales factor often yields the greatest planning opportunities for a multistate corporation. In-state sales include those to purchasers with a destination point in that state; sales delivered to out-of-state purchasers are included in the numerator of the sales factor of the destination state. However, to be permitted to exclude out-of-state sales from the sales factor of the origination state, the seller generally must substantiate the shipment of goods to an out-of-state location. Therefore, the destinations of sales that a corporation makes and the means by which the goods are shipped must be carefully reviewed. The corporation's overall state tax possibly can be reduced by establishing a better record-keeping system or by manipulating the numerator of the sales factor by changing the delivery location or method.

For example, a corporation may substantially reduce its state tax if the delivery location of its sales is changed from a state in which the company is taxed to one in which it is not. This technique may not benefit the corporation if the state in which the sales originate has adopted the throwback rule.

Property Factor

Because most fixed assets are physically stationary in nature, the property factor is not so easily manipulated. Nonetheless, significant tax savings can be realized by establishing a leasing subsidiary in a low- or no-tax state. If the property is located in a state that does not include leased assets in the property factor, the establishment of a subsidiary from which to lease the property eliminates the assets from the property factor in the parent's state.

Permanently idle property generally is excluded from the property factor. Accordingly, a corporation should identify and remove such assets from the property factor to ensure that the factor is not distorted. It is equally important to identify and remove nonbusiness assets from the property factor in states that distinguish between business and nonbusiness income.

EXAMPLE 37

The property factor valuations of Quake Corporation's holdings are as follows.

	State A	Total
Equipment (average historical cost)	$1,200,000	$2,000,000
Accumulated depreciation (average)	800,000	1,000,000

Twenty percent of the equipment in State A is fully depreciated and is idle. Assuming that A includes property in the factor at historical cost, Quake's property factor is 54.55% [($1,200,000 − $240,000 idle property)/($2,000,000 − $240,000)]. If the idle property is not removed from the property factor, Quake's property factor in A is incorrectly computed as 60% ($1,200,000/$2,000,000). ■

Payroll Factor

The payroll factor provides planning potential where several corporate employees spend substantial periods of time outside their state of employment or the corporation is able to relocate highly paid employees to low- or no-tax states.

Use of an independent contractor who works for more than one principal can be beneficial under certain circumstances. Because the commissions paid to independent contractors are excluded from the payroll factor, the taxpayer may reduce its payroll factor in a high-tax state.

EXAMPLE 38

Yellow Corporation's total payroll costs are $1.4 million. Of this amount, $1 million was attributable to State A, a high-tax state. Yellow's payroll factor in A is 71.43% ($1,000,000/$1,400,000).

Assuming that $200,000 of the A compensation had been paid to sales representatives and that Yellow replaced its sales force with independent contractors, Yellow's payroll factor in A would be reduced to 66.67% [($1,000,000 − $200,000)/($1,400,000 − $200,000)]. ■

Sales/Use Tax Compliance

Today, state and local tax administrators face a major problem: how can governments get their sales/use tax revenues from mail-order, phone, and Internet sales? The problem is that the governments must rely on the seller to collect sales and use taxes, rather than collecting them directly from the purchaser. Consequently, a seller conceivably must deal with thousands of different sales/use taxing jurisdictions, each with its own forms and filing deadlines, rates of applicable tax, and definitions of what is taxable or exempt. Examples of issues on which jurisdictions may disagree include the following.

- Are snack foods exempt groceries or taxable candy?
- Are therapeutic stockings exempt medical supplies or taxable clothing?
- Which types of software are subject to tax?

Large retailers such as Wal-Mart, Amazon, and Radio Shack can develop software to handle these problems, but smaller businesses cannot afford to create their own software or to purchase someone else's. The result has been a very low level of compliance by sellers with respect to out-of-state sales transactions.

Governments meanwhile have limited resources to enforce tax rules that have long been on the books. Many states ask individuals and businesses to include the unpaid use taxes for Internet, phone, and mail-order purchases on their annual income tax returns, but the number of taxpayers complying is insignificant. This is not a matter of "increasing the taxes on the Internet economy," but rather of collecting revenues that already are due and are desperately needed to balance state budgets.

Sales/Use Taxes on Capital Changes

The tax adviser must be aware of the effects that sales and use taxes may have on a transaction that might otherwise be free from income tax. For example, although the transfer of property to a controlled corporation in exchange for its stock generally is not subject to corporate income taxes, several states provide that such transfers constitute taxable sales for sales and use tax purposes. Similarly, a corporate reorganization may be structured to avoid the imposition of income taxes, but under the statutes of several states, such transfers are considered to be taxable sales and, accordingly, are subject to sales and use taxes.

Capital Stock Taxation

Capital stock tax liabilities can be significant for capital-intensive taxpayers to the extent they reinvest a large portion of retained earnings (the tax base) in productive assets. If all nontax factors are equal, a taxpayer with sizable exposure to a capital stock tax should consider the following techniques.

- Funding expansion with debt, rather than retained earnings.
- Funding subsidiary operations with debt, rather than direct capital contributions.
- Regularly paying dividends to parent companies that are domiciled in tax-favored states such as Delaware and Nevada.

REFOCUS ON THE BIG PICTURE

MAKING A LOCATION DECISION IN A MULTISTATE TAX ENVIRONMENT

LocalCo holds a competitive advantage with the states and localities in negotiating where its new facility should be located. Politicians like to attract new facilities to their jurisdictions as a way to create construction jobs and to expand the income and sales/use tax base. LocalCo's top management should work with the governors and development executives of the states that are final candidates for the location of the proposed new building.

LocalCo's agenda for these negotiations should include the following items.

- Many states offer targeted tax incentives to attract and retain "clean" businesses like LocalCo. Such incentives might include property tax abatements, research and investment credits, and tax waivers for the state and local income and payroll taxes on new jobs. The company should determine whether it qualifies for any existing incentives. If a state does not currently offer incentives, perhaps its tax law could be amended to provide them.
- LocalCo should also ascertain how the potential locations apply income and sales/use taxes to Internet sales. How aggressive are these tax laws at the present time (e.g., as to the application of P.L. 86–272 and other nexus rules)? What is the level of projected state budget deficits and cash-flow needs, and what are the chances that the laws of the target states will be modified in the near future?
- Currently, LocalCo's manufacturing operations are split between a very low-tax state (Alabama) and a very high-tax state (California). Under a relocation plan that makes good business sense, nexus might be eliminated with California and shifted to a low-tax jurisdiction. Nevada is a good candidate, given its proximity to the current sportswear location.
- California applies the unitary theory of income taxation. LocalCo should determine whether unitary rules increase or decrease its total tax burden.

- Corporate headquarters currently are located in New York, another high-tax jurisdiction. If the new facility is located in a corporation-favorable, low-tax state, the company should consider moving its headquarters there.
- Relocating the corporate headquarters would also benefit the entity's highly paid executives. The individual income and sales/use tax burden of employees should be a factor in LocalCo's decision.
- In any event, shifting the entity's investment income to a low-tax jurisdiction appears advisable. Use of a passive investment company will carry out this tax planning objective.
- States often assess special taxes on trucking and airport functions and might even apply different income tax apportionment formulas to these operations. LocalCo's tax department and its outside advisers should research these features of the various relevant tax systems to avoid any unexpected surprises.

What If?

If LocalCo did not have a history of strong profitability, some of these state and local tax recommendations might be different. In that case, the company would consider issues such as how a state applies loss and credit carryovers. In addition, if there is no state income tax liability to pay, income tax credits and deductions would be less attractive, so the negotiations might focus on property and payroll taxes instead.

KEY TERMS

Allocate, 16-8
Apportion, 16-8
Combined return, 16-21
Composite return, 16-26
Dock sales, 16-15
Multistate Tax Commission (MTC), 16-7
Nexus, 16-8
Passive investment company, 16-35
Payroll factor, 16-17
Property factor, 16-19
Public Law 86–272, 16-8
Sales factor, 16-15
Throwback rule, 16-16
UDITPA, 16-7
Unclaimed property, 16-31
Unitary theory, 16-21
Water's edge, 16-23

DISCUSSION QUESTIONS

1. **LO.1** You are working with the top management of one of your clients in selecting the U.S. location for a new manufacturing operation. Craft a plan for the CEO to use in discussions with the economic development representatives of several candidate states. In no more than two PowerPoint slides, list some of the tax incentives the CEO should request from a particular state during the negotiations. Be both creative and aggressive in the requests. **Issue ID** **Communications**

2. **LO.1** Complete the following chart by indicating whether each item is true or false. Explain your answers by reference to the overlap of rules appearing in Federal and most state income tax laws.

	Item	True or False
a.	Some states use Federal taxable income as their income tax base, while others modify this amount or create their own state taxable income.	___
b.	Federal tax accounting methods such as LIFO inventory and specific write-off of bad debts are followed for state income tax purposes.	___
c.	State rules as to which entities can join in a consolidated return match those of Federal law.	___
d.	The corporate income tax systems of most states can be described as having progressive rate structures.	___
e.	A typical state income tax credit would equal 10% of the costs incurred to purchase and install solar energy panels for an existing factory.	___

3. **LO.1** In designing and drafting corporate income tax statutes and regulations, is each of the U.S. states "on its own"? (*Hint*: Use the terms *Multistate Tax Commission, MTC*, and *UDITPA* in your answer.)

4. **LO.1** Many states "outsource" their responsibility to write income tax rules to the MTC. Evaluate this statement.

Communications

5. **LO.2** In no more than three PowerPoint slides, list some general guidelines that a taxpayer can use to determine if it has an obligation to file an income tax return with a particular state. (*Hint*: Correctly use the terms *nexus* and *domicile* in your answer.)

6. **LO.2** Josie is a sales representative for Talk2Me, a communications retailer based in Fort Smith, Arkansas. Josie's sales territory is Oklahoma, and she regularly takes day trips to Tulsa to meet with customers. During a typical sales call, Josie takes the customers' current orders and, using her wireless phone, sends the orders to headquarters in Fort Smith for immediate action. Approved orders are shipped from the Little Rock warehouse. Are Josie's sales subject to the Oklahoma corporate income tax? Explain.

7. **LO.2** Continue with the facts of Question 6. CheapPhones, one of Josie's customers who is facing tight cash flow problems, wants to return about 100 defective cell phones. Talk2Me tells Josie to bring the phones back to headquarters. Fearing that she will lose CheapPhones as a customer if she does not comply with the request, Josie says, "Let me save you the time and cost of packing and shipping the defective phones. Put them in the trunk of my car, and I'll take them back." Does Josie's action change the answer to Question 6? Why or why not?

8. **LO.3** Albro, a C corporation, makes profitable sales in about a dozen U.S. states. It owns a headquarters building in one of those states and a fulfillment center in a different state. How does Albro determine the amounts of gross and taxable income that are subject to tax in each of the states in which it operates. (*Hint*: Correctly use the terms *allocate* and *apportion* in your answer.)

9. **LO.3** Indicate whether each of the following items should be *allocated* or *apportioned* by the taxpayer in computing state corporate taxable income. Assume that the state follows the general rules of UDITPA.
   a. Profits from sales activities.
   b. Gain on the sale of a plot of land held by a real estate developer.
   c. Gain on the sale of a plot of land held by a manufacturer, on which it may expand its factory.
   d. Rent income received by a manufacturer from the leasing of space to a supplier.
   e. Profits from consulting and other service activities.

10. **LO.3** Regarding the apportionment formula used to compute state taxable income, does each of the following independent characterizations describe a taxpayer that is based in-state or out-of-state? Explain.
   a. The sales factor is positively correlated with the payroll, but not the property, factor.
   b. The sales factor is much higher than the property and payroll factors.

c. The property and payroll factors are much higher than those for other nexus states.
d. The sales and payroll factors are low, but the property factor is very high.
e. The sales factor is remaining constant, but the payroll factor is decreasing.

11. **LO.3** The trend in state income taxation is to move from an equal three-factor apportionment formula to a formula that places extra weight on the sales factor. Several states now use sales-factor-only apportionment. Explain why this development is attractive to the taxing states. **Issue ID**

12. **LO.5** In computing the corporate income taxes for Iowa-based SpillCo, should a single large sale in August, in which merchandise was shipped to a customer in Kentucky, be included in the Iowa sales factor?

13. **LO.5** Continue with the facts of Question 12. Another large shipment was made in May to a customer in South Dakota, a state that does not impose any corporate income tax. Is this sale to be included in SpillCo's Iowa sales factor? Explain.

14. **LO.5** Megan is a telecommuter and works most days from her home in Tennessee. Twice a month, she travels to Georgia for a staff meeting at the Atlanta headquarters. In which state's payroll factor should Megan's compensation be included if:
    a. Megan is an employee and is covered by the qualified retirement plan of her Atlanta employer?
    b. Megan works as an independent contractor for several clients, including the Atlanta-based firm?

15. **LO.5** Keystone, your tax consulting client, is considering an expansion program that would entail the construction of a new logistics center in State Q. List at least five questions you should ask in determining whether an asset that is owned by Keystone is to be included in State Q's property factor numerator. **Issue ID**

16. **LO.6** The trend in state income taxation is for states to adopt a version of the unitary theory of multijurisdictional taxation in their statutes and regulations.
    a. Explain why some states are attracted to the unitary theory and a combined reporting scheme of multistate income taxation.
    b. Is the application of the unitary theory a help or a detriment to the taxpayer? Why?

17. **LO.6** State A enjoys a prosperous economy, with high real estate values and compensation levels. State B's economy has seen better days—property values are depressed, and unemployment is higher than in other states. Most consumer goods are priced at about 10% less in B than in A. Both A and B apply unitary income taxation to businesses that operate within the state. Does unitary taxation distort the assignment of taxable income between A and B? Explain. **Issue ID**

18. **LO.6** Your client makes the comment, "Unitary corporate income taxation is a bad idea for the business community." Is her characterization correct? Elaborate.

19. **LO.6** Carmina operates a multinational business from Colorado, a state that applies the unitary theory and requires combined state income tax reporting. Most of her offshore customers are located in the United Kingdom and Germany, where sales prices and property valuations are relatively high. Make a recommendation as to how Carmina might reduce her Colorado income tax liabilities. (*Hint*: There is an attractive unitary tax election that Carmina should consider.)

20. **LO.7** Chip and Dale are the only shareholders of VisitTime, a medical transportation firm that is organized as an S corporation. VisitTime makes quarterly estimated income tax payments, related to Chip's stock ownership, to State Q, its headquarters state. Explain.

21. **LO.7** Evaluate this statement: An S corporation can facilitate the meeting of its state income tax filing obligations by developing a common spreadsheet that allocates and apportions income among the states with which it has nexus. This spreadsheet is attached to each of the state returns to be filed. (*Hint*: Use the term *composite return* in your answer.)

22. **LO.7** The Quail LLC operates solely in State W. As a pass-through entity, Quail does not pay any W taxes. Evaluate this statement.

Issue ID

23. **LO.8** HernandezCo wants to avoid the creation of sales/use tax nexus with State G. The HernandezCo sales representatives believe that they will lose customers because of an increase in their products' prices due to the new tax obligations. Are the sales representatives correct to be concerned about their employer's sales/use tax issue? Why or why not?

Communications

24. **LO.8** Create a PowerPoint outline describing the major exemptions and exclusions from the sales/use tax base of most states. Use your slides to discuss this topic with your accounting students' club.

25. **LO.8** What is the Streamlined Sales Tax Project? What tax problems does it address?

26. **LO.8** List three or more taxes, other than the income and sales/use tax, that a state or local jurisdiction might levy.

27. **LO.9** Your client, HillTop, is a retailer of women's clothing. It has increased sales during the holiday season by advertising gift cards for in-store and online use. HillTop has found that gift card holders who come into the store tend to purchase goods that total more than the amount of the gift card. Further, about one-third of the gift cards never are redeemed, thereby yielding cash to the company without a reduction of inventory. What are the tax issues related to the gift cards confronting HillTop?

Communications

28. **LO.2, 9** Your client, Ecru Limited, is considering an expansion of its sales operations, but it fears adverse resulting tax consequences. Write a memo for the tax research file identifying the planning opportunities presented by the ability of a corporation to terminate or create income tax nexus. Make certain that you discuss the *Wrigley* case in your analysis.

Communications

29. **LO.9** Your client, Royal Corporation, generates significant interest income from its working capital liquid investments. Write a memo for the tax research file discussing the planning opportunities presented by establishing a passive investment company. Support your memo with a diagram of the resulting flow of assets and income.

30. **LO.9** Sherri has acquired a franchise to operate a QuickClip hair salon in her home state Y. QuickClip's corporate offices are located in State Z, and all financial transactions of the franchisees use QuickClip's Z banks exclusively. The franchise agreement allows Sherri to purchase and use QuickClip branded supplies and to join in national advertising campaigns, as they are crafted and carried out from Z. QuickClip (not Sherri personally) is the tenant on all of Sherri's leased salon space and other property.

    A Y tax auditor maintains that Sherri's profits are subject to that state's tax on business income. Explain to Sherri whether she has income tax nexus with Y. (*Hint*: Include the *Geoffrey* case in your explanation).

Communications

31. **LO.9** As the director of the multistate tax planning department of a consulting firm, you are developing a brochure to highlight the services it can provide. Part of the brochure is a list of five or so key techniques that clients can use to reduce state income tax liabilities. Develop this list for the brochure.

PROBLEMS

32. **LO.1** Use Figure 16.1 to compute Balboa Corporation's State F taxable income for the year.

Addition modifications	$29,000
Allocated income (total)	$25,000
Allocated income (State F)	$3,000
Allocated income (State G)	$22,000
Apportionment percentage	40%
Credits	$800
Federal taxable income	$90,000
Subtraction modifications	$15,000
Tax rate	5%

33. **LO.1** Use Figure 16.1 to provide the required information for Warbler Corporation, whose Federal taxable income totals $10 million.

    Warbler apportions 60% of its business income to State C. Warbler generates $3 million of nonbusiness income each year, and 20% of that income is allocated to C. Applying the state income tax modifications, Warbler's total business income this year is $9 million.

    a. How much of Warbler's business income does State C tax?
    b. How much of Warbler's nonbusiness income does State C tax?
    c. Explain your results.

34. **LO.1** For each of the following independent cases, indicate whether the circumstances call for an addition modification (*A*), a subtraction modification (*S*), or no modification (*N*) in computing state taxable income. Then indicate the amount of any modification. The starting point in computing State Q taxable income is the year's Federal taxable income, before any deduction for net operating losses.

    a. Federal cost recovery = $10,000, and Q cost recovery = $15,000.
    b. Federal cost recovery = $15,000, and Q cost recovery = $10,000.
    c. Federal income taxes paid = $30,000.
    d. Refund received from last year's Q income taxes = $3,000.
    e. Local property taxes, deducted on the Federal return as a business expense = $7,000.
    f. Interest income from holding U.S. Treasury bonds = $20,000.
    g. Interest income from holding Q revenue anticipation bonds = $3,000.
    h. An asset was sold for $18,000; its purchase price was $20,000. Accumulated Federal cost recovery = $11,000, and accumulated Q cost recovery = $8,000.
    i. Dividend income received from State R corporation = $10,000, subject to a Federal dividends received deduction of 70%.

35. **LO.1** Perk Corporation is subject to tax only in State A. Perk generated the following income and deductions.

Federal taxable income	$300,000
State A income tax expense	15,000
Refund of State A income tax	3,000
Depreciation allowed for Federal tax purposes	200,000
Depreciation allowed for state tax purposes	120,000

    Federal taxable income is the starting point in computing A taxable income. State income taxes are not deductible for A tax purposes. Determine Perk's A taxable income.

36. **LO.1** Flip Corporation is subject to tax only in State X. Flip generated the following income and deductions. State income taxes are not deductible for X income tax purposes.

Sales	$4,000,000
Cost of sales	2,800,000
State X income tax expense	200,000
Depreciation allowed for Federal tax purposes	400,000
Depreciation allowed for state tax purposes	300,000
Interest income on Federal obligations	50,000
Interest income on X obligations	30,000
Expenses related to carrying X obligations	10,000

    a. The starting point in computing the X income tax base is Federal taxable income. Derive this amount.
    b. Determine Flip's X taxable income assuming that interest on X obligations is exempt from X income tax.
    c. Determine Flip's X taxable income assuming that interest on X obligations is subject to X income tax.

37. **LO.4, 5** Jest Corporation owns and operates two facilities that manufacture paper products. One of the facilities is located in State D, and the other is located in State E.

Jest generated $2.8 million of taxable income, consisting of $2 million of income from its manufacturing facilities and an $800,000 gain from the sale of nonbusiness property, located in E. E does not distinguish between business and nonbusiness income, but D apportions only business income. Jest's activities within the two states are outlined below.

	State D	State E	Total
Sales of paper products	$3,000,000	$7,000,000	$10,000,000
Property	600,000	1,500,000	2,100,000
Payroll	1,200,000	1,800,000	3,000,000

Both D and E utilize a three-factor apportionment formula, under which sales, property, and payroll are equally weighted. Determine the amount of Jest's income that is subject to income tax by each state.

38. **LO.4, 5** Assume the same facts as in Problem 37, except that under the statutes of both D and E, only business income is subject to apportionment.

39. **LO.5** Dillman Corporation has nexus in States A and B. Dillman's activities for the year are summarized below.

	State A	State B	Total
Sales	$1,200,000	$ 400,000	$1,600,000
Property			
Average cost	500,000	300,000	800,000
Average accumulated depreciation	(300,000)	(100,000)	(400,000)
Payroll	2,500,000	500,000	3,000,000
Rent expense	–0–	35,000	35,000

Determine the apportionment factors for A and B assuming that A uses a three-factor apportionment formula under which sales, property (net depreciated basis), and payroll are equally weighted and B employs a single-factor formula that consists solely of sales. State A has adopted the UDITPA with respect to the inclusion of rent payments in the property factor.

40. **LO.5** Assume the same facts as in Problem 39, except that A uses a single-factor apportionment formula that consists solely of sales and B uses a three-factor apportionment formula that equally weights sales, property (at historical cost), and payroll. State B does not include rent payments in the property factor.

41. **LO.5** Assume the same facts as in Problem 39, except that both states employ a three-factor formula, under which sales are double-weighted. The basis of the property factor in A is historical cost, while the basis of this factor in B is the net depreciated basis. Neither A nor B includes rent payments in the property factor.

42. **LO.5** McKay Corporation operates in two states, as indicated below. This year's operations generated $300,000 of apportionable income.

	State A	State B	Total
Sales	$600,000	$400,000	$1,000,000
Property	300,000	300,000	600,000
Payroll	200,000	50,000	250,000

Compute McKay's State A taxable income assuming that State A apportions income based on a:

a. Three-factor formula, equally weighted.
b. Double-weighted sales factor.
c. Sales factor only.

43. **LO.5** Tootie Corporation operates in two states, as indicated below. All goods are manufactured in State A. Determine the sales to be assigned to both states in computing Tootie's sales factor for the year. Both states follow the UDITPA and the MTC regulations in this regard.

Sales shipped to A locations	$300,000
Sales shipped to B locations	500,000
Interest income from Tootie's B business checking accounts	5,000
Rent income from excess space in A warehouse	40,000
Interest income from Treasury bills in Tootie's B brokerage account, holding only idle cash from operations	65,000
One-time sale of display equipment to B purchaser (tax basis $90,000)	75,000
Royalty received from holding patent, licensed to B user	90,000

44. **LO.5, 9** State E applies a throwback rule to sales, while State F does not. State G has not adopted an income tax to date. Orange Corporation, headquartered in E, reported the following sales for the year. All of the goods were shipped from Orange's E manufacturing facilities. Determine its sales factor in those states. Comment on Orange's location strategy using only your tax computations.

Decision Making

Customer	Customer's Location	This Year's Sales
ShellTell, Inc.	E	$ 75,000,000
Tourists, Ltd.	F	40,000,000
PageToo Corp.	G	100,000,000
U.S. Department of Interior	All 50 states	35,000,000
Total		$250,000,000

45. **LO.5, 9** Quinn Corporation is subject to tax in States G, H, and I. Quinn's compensation expense includes the following.

Decision Making

	State G	State H	State I	Total
Salaries and wages for nonofficers	$200,000	$400,000	$400,000	$1,000,000
Officers' salaries	–0–	–0–	500,000	500,000
Total				$1,500,000

Officers' salaries are included in the payroll factor for G and I, but not for H. Compute Quinn's payroll factors for G, H, and I. Comment on your results.

46. **LO.5** Judy, a regional sales manager, has her office in State U. Her region includes several states, as indicated in the sales report below. Judy is compensated through straight commissions on the sales in her region and a fully excludible cafeteria plan conveying various fringe benefits to her. Determine how much of Judy's $650,000 commissions and $75,000 fringe benefit package is assigned to the payroll factor of State U.

State	Sales Generated	Judy's Time Spent There
U	$3,000,000	30%
V	4,000,000	50%
X	5,000,000	20%

47. **LO.5** Justine Corporation operates manufacturing facilities in State G and State H. In addition, the corporation owns nonbusiness rental property in H. Justine incurred the following compensation expenses.

	State G	State H	Total
Manufacturing wages	$500,000	$200,000	$700,000
Administrative wages	200,000	70,000	270,000
Officers' salaries	200,000	50,000	250,000

Thirty percent of the time spent by the administrative staff located in H and 20% of the time spent by officers located in H are devoted to the operation, maintenance, and supervision of the rental property. G includes all income in the definition of apportionable income, while H excludes nonbusiness income from apportionable income. Only G includes officers' compensation in the payroll factor numerator.

Determine Justine's payroll factors for G and H.

48. **LO.5** Kim Corporation, a calendar year taxpayer, has manufacturing facilities in States A and B. A summary of Kim's property holdings follows.

	Beginning of Year		
	State A	**State B**	**Total**
Inventory	$ 300,000	$ 200,000	$ 500,000
Plant and equipment	2,500,000	1,500,000	4,000,000
Accumulated depreciation: plant and equipment	(1,000,000)	(600,000)	(1,600,000)
Land	600,000	1,000,000	1,600,000
Rental property*	900,000	300,000	1,200,000
Accumulated depreciation: rental property	(200,000)	(90,000)	(290,000)

	End of Year		
	State A	**State B**	**Total**
Inventory	$ 400,000	$ 200,000	$ 600,000
Plant and equipment	2,800,000	1,200,000	4,000,000
Accumulated depreciation: plant and equipment	(1,200,000)	(650,000)	(1,850,000)
Land	600,000	1,200,000	1,800,000
Rental property*	1,000,000	300,000	1,300,000
Accumulated depreciation: rental property	(250,000)	(100,000)	(350,000)

* Unrelated to regular business operations.

Determine Kim's property factors for the two states assuming that the statutes of both A and B provide that average historical cost of business property is to be included in the property factor.

49. **LO.5** Assume the same facts as in Problem 48, except that nonbusiness income is apportionable in B.

Decision Making

50. **LO.5, 9** Crate Corporation, a calendar year taxpayer, has established nexus with numerous states. On December 3, Crate sold one of its two facilities in State X. The cost of this facility was $800,000.

On January 1, Crate owned property with a cost of $3 million, $1.5 million of which was located in X. On December 31, Crate owned property with a cost of $2.5 million, $700,000 of which was located in X.

X law allows the use of average annual or monthly cost amounts in determining the property factor. If Crate wants to minimize the property factor in X, which method should be used to determine the property factor there?

Decision Making

Communications

51. **LO.6, 9** True Corporation, a wholly owned subsidiary of Trumaine Corporation, generated a $400,000 taxable loss in its first year of operations. True's activities and sales are restricted to State A, which imposes an 8% income tax. In the same year, Trumaine's taxable income is $1 million. Trumaine's activities and sales are restricted to State B, which imposes an 11% income tax. Both states use a three-factor apportionment formula that equally weights sales, payroll, and property, and both require a unitary group to file on a combined basis. Sales, payroll, and average property for each corporation are as follows.

	True Corporation	Trumaine Corporation	Total
Sales	$2,500,000	$4,000,000	$6,500,000
Property	1,000,000	2,500,000	3,500,000
Payroll	500,000	1,500,000	2,000,000

True and Trumaine have been found to be members of a unitary business.

a. Determine the overall state income tax for the unitary group.
b. Determine aggregate state income tax for the entities if they were nonunitary.
c. Incorporate this analysis in a letter to Trumaine's board of directors. Corporate offices are located at 1234 Mulberry Lane, Birmingham, AL 35298.

52. **LO.6** Chang Corporation is part of a three-corporation unitary business. The group has a water's edge election in effect with respect to unitary State Q. State B does not apply the unitary concept with respect to its corporate income tax laws. Nor does Despina, a European country to which Saldez paid a $7 million value added tax this year.

Saldez was organized in Despina and conducts all of its business there. Given the summary of operations that follows, determine Chang's and Elena's sales factors in B and Q.

Corporation	Customer's Location	Sales
Chang	B	$20,000,000
	Q	60,000,000
Elena	Q	70,000,000
Saldez	Despina	50,000,000

53. **LO.7** Hernandez, which has been an S corporation since inception, is subject to tax in States Y and Z. On Schedule K of its Federal Form 1120S, Hernandez reported ordinary income of $500,000 from its business, taxable interest income of $10,000, capital loss of $30,000, and $40,000 of dividend income from a corporation in which it owns 30%. **Communications**

Both states apportion income by use of a three-factor formula that equally weights sales, payroll, and the average cost of property; both states treat interest and dividends as business income. In addition, both Y and Z follow Federal provisions with respect to the determination of taxable income for a corporation. Y recognizes S status, but Z does not. Based on the following information, write a memo to the shareholders of Hernandez, detailing the amount of taxable income on which Hernandez will pay tax in Y and Z. Hernandez corporate offices are located at 5678 Alabaster Circle, Bowling Green, KY 42103.

	State Y	State Z
Sales	$1,000,000	$800,000
Property (average cost)	500,000	100,000
Payroll	800,000	200,000

54. **LO.8** Using the following information from the books and records of Grande Corporation, determine Grande's total sales that are subject to State C's sales tax. Grande operates a retail hardware store.

Sales to C consumers, general merchandise	$1,100,000
Sales to C consumers, crutches and other medical supplies	245,000
Sales to consumers in State D, via mail order	80,000
Purchases from suppliers	55,000

55. **LO.8** As a retailer, Granite Corporation sells software programs manufactured and packaged by other parties. Granite also purchases computer parts, assembles them as specified by a customer in a purchase order, and sells them as operating stand-alone computers. All of Granite's operations take place in State F, which levies a 9% sales tax. Results for the current year are as follows.

Sales of software	$2,500,000
Purchases of computer parts	1,300,000
Sales of computer systems	8,500,000
Purchases of office supplies	60,000
Purchases of packaging materials for the computer systems	30,000
Purchases of tools used by computer assemblers	50,000

a. What is Granite's own sales tax expense for the year?
b. How much F sales tax must Granite collect and pay over to the state on behalf of other taxpayers subject to the tax?

56. **LO.8** Indicate for each transaction whether a sales (*S*) or use (*U*) tax applies or whether the transaction is nontaxable (*N*). Where the laws vary among states, assume that the most common rules apply. All taxpayers are individuals.
    a. A resident of State A purchases an automobile in A.
    b. A resident of State A purchases groceries in A.
    c. A resident of State B purchases an automobile in A.
    d. A charity purchases office supplies in A.
    e. An A resident purchases in B an item that will be in the inventory of her business.

57. **LO.8** Wayne Corporation is subject to State A's franchise tax. The tax is imposed at a rate of 1.2% of the corporation's net worth that is apportioned to the state by use of a two-factor formula (sales and property factors, equally weighted). The property factor includes real and tangible personal property, valued at historical cost as of the end of the taxable year.

    Forty percent of Wayne's sales are attributable to A, and $600,000 of the cost of Wayne's tangible personal property is located in A.

    Determine the A franchise tax payable by Wayne this year, given the following end-of-the-year balance sheet.

Cash		$ 200,000
Equipment	$1,000,000	
Accumulated depreciation	(300,000)	700,000
Furniture and fixtures	$ 800,000	
Accumulated depreciation	(50,000)	750,000
Intangible assets		450,000
Total assets		$2,100,000
Accounts and taxes payable		$ 600,000
Long-term debt		750,000
Common stock		1,000
Additional paid-in capital		249,000
Retained earnings		500,000
Total liabilities and equity		$2,100,000

Decision Making

58. **LO.5, 9** Dread Corporation operates in a high-tax state. The firm asks you for advice on a plan to outsource administrative work done in its home state to independent contractors. This work now costs the company $750,000 in wages and benefits. Dread's total payroll for the year is $8 million, of which $6 million is for work currently done in the home state.

Issue ID

Communications

59. **LO.9** Prepare a PowerPoint presentation (maximum of six slides) entitled "Planning Principles for Our Multistate Clients." The slides will be used to lead a 20-minute discussion with colleagues in the corporate tax department. Keep the outline general, but assume that your colleagues have clients operating in at least 15 states. Address only income tax issues.

RESEARCH PROBLEMS

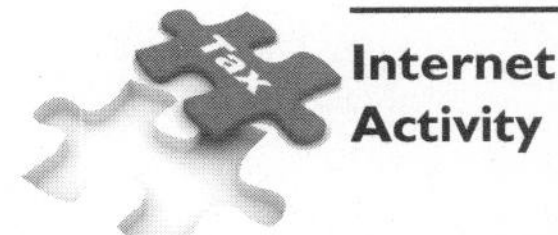

Use the tax resources of the Internet to address the following questions. Do not restrict your search to the Web, but include a review of newsgroups and general reference materials, practitioner sites and resources, primary sources of the tax law, chat rooms and discussion groups, and other opportunities.

Communications

Research Problem 1. Send an e-mail to the secretary of revenue for your home state proposing adoption of at least two of the following provisions that do not currently exist in your state.

a. Increase the apportionment weight for the sales factor.
b. Exempt computer and communications technology from the apportionment weight for the property factor.
c. Adopt a throwback rule for the sales factor.
d. Subject advertising expenditures to the sales/use tax.
e. Allow an income tax credit for 20% of the cost of in-state construction projects that are substantially completed within the next 18 months.
f. Tax the income of vendors who do not have a physical presence in your state but sell to in-state customers online.
g. Add a "nexus team" to find the taxpayers operating in your state, but based in Ohio, Illinois, or Arizona.
h. Adopt the definitions and other rules of the Streamlined Sales Tax Project.
i. Allow an income tax credit for film and television producers equal to 30% of in-state expenditures.
j. Apply a tax on S corporations operating in the state equal to 2% of the entity's hypothetical Subchapter C taxable income.
k. Convert the corporate income tax to a tax on gross receipts, in an effort to tax the profits of passive investment companies owned by in-state parent entities.

Communications

Research Problem 2. For your state and one of its neighbors, determine the following. Place your data in a chart and e-mail your findings to your professor.

a. To what extent does each state follow the rulings of the Multistate Tax Commission?
b. What is each state's apportionment formula, with factors and weightings?
c. Does the state adopt pertinent changes to the Internal Revenue Code? As of what date?
d. Has the state joined the Streamlined Sales Tax Project? Which of the project's rules has the state adopted? What is the effective date?
e. Is the tax-effectiveness of a passive investment company limited in some way? Has the state adopted the *Geoffrey* approach to the taxation of income from intangibles? Explain.
f. Does the state apply entity-level income taxes for S corporations, partnerships, and LLCs? If so, what are the terms of those taxes?
g. What are the requirements for the occasional-sale rule as an exception to the sales/use tax? Who can use this rule?
h. Describe any exemptions from the sales/use tax base that are allowed for transactions involving groceries, school clothing and supplies, religious goods, and legal services.
i. What is the discount allowed, if any, when a vendor remits sales/use tax to the state in a timely manner?
j. Does the state levy a "minimum tax" or "alternative minimum tax"? If so, what are the terms and rates for the tax?

Research Problem 3. Does Walmart.com collect use tax when it ships an order into your state? Does Dell.com? Gateway.com? Amazon.com? Crateandbarrel.com? SamGoody.com? (If your state does not have a sales tax law, answer for a neighboring state.)

Communications

Research Problem 4. Read the "tax footnote" of five publicly traded U.S. corporations. Find the effective state/local income tax rates of each. Create a PowerPoint presentation (maximum of five slides) for your instructor, summarizing the search and reporting the findings.

Communications

Research Problem 5. Find a state/local tax policy organization (e.g., the Committee on State Taxation). Read its current newsletter. In an e-mail to your instructor, summarize a major article in the newsletter. Look especially for articles on one of these topics.

- Judicial and legislative developments concerning the income taxation of intangible income (e.g., trademark royalties).
- Legislation applying a physical-presence test as the exclusive definition of nexus at the Federal level or for your state's sales/use tax.
- Responses by the states to the economic downturn (e.g., more aggressive enforcement, new taxes and fees, and installment options for the late payment of taxes and penalties).
- Development of nexus rules that apply to cloud computing services.
- The positive or negative "business tax climate" of your state and its neighbors, as measured by two or more policy centers or think tanks, and any measurable trends in the climate over the last 20 years.
- Attempts by the legislatures of your state and its neighbors to add advertising services to the sales/use tax base.
- Limitations on the taxpayer's ability to carry back net operating losses in computing your state's corporate taxable income.

Communications

Research Problem 6. Many states offer a tax credit for expenditures made in-state for new computing and energy-saving equipment. For your state and one of its neighbors, summarize in a table three of the tax incentives offered through the income, sales, or property tax structure. In your table, list at least the following. E-mail your table to the other students in your course.

- Name of the credit, deduction, exemption, etc.
- Who qualifies for the incentive (e.g., corporations, individuals, or partnerships).
- Computational base for the incentive (e.g., dollars spent).
- Rate of the credit or deduction.
- Minimums, maximums, and other limitations that apply to the incentive amount.

CHAPTER

17 Tax Practice and Ethics

LEARNING OBJECTIVES: *After completing Chapter 17, you should be able to:*

LO.1 Illustrate the organization and structure of the IRS.

LO.2 Identify the various administrative pronouncements issued by the IRS, and explain how they can be used in tax practice.

LO.3 Describe the audit process, including how tax returns are selected for audit and the various types of audits.

LO.4 Explain the taxpayer appeal process, including various settlement options available.

LO.5 Determine the amount of interest on a deficiency or a refund and when it is due.

LO.6 List and explain the various penalties that can be imposed on acts of noncompliance by taxpayers and return preparers.

LO.7 Recognize and apply the rules governing the statute of limitations on assessments and on refunds.

LO.8 Summarize the legal and ethical guidelines that apply to those engaged in tax practice.

CHAPTER OUTLINE

THE BIG PICTURE Tax Solutions for the Real World

© ID 1974/Shutterstock.com

A Tax Adviser's Dilemma

Campbell Corporation is preparing its Form 1120 for the tax year. The entity develops and manufactures a number of electronic products, including a line of GPS applications that are downloaded onto tablets and smartphones. Campbell's research department needs to work with the U.S. government on this line of software because of the potential for security breaches when the software is used in sensitive parts of the world. Other efforts of the research department include traditional software architecture and development. Projections show that the GPS products will be highly profitable, with sales concentrated among various commercial and governmental communications providers around the world.

Some of the research department's work on the GPS products clearly qualifies for the Federal income tax credit for incremental research expenditures, but for some other items, the availability of the credit is not so certain. Either the language of the pertinent Regulations is unclear in Campbell's setting or because of the innovative aspects of the products under development, the law is silent as to whether Campbell can claim the credit.

You are Campbell's tax adviser. This situation presents you with several levels of difficulty. How aggressive should you advise Campbell to be in reporting items on the Form 1120 that qualify for the incremental research credit? Will Campbell's taking an overly aggressive position on the credit trigger a tax preparer penalty for your tax consulting firm? What level of diligence should you exercise in advising Campbell as to whether specific expenditures qualify for the credit, given that your expertise with GPS software is limited to using the unit in your personal auto?

Read the chapter and formulate your response.

17 INTRODUCTION

Few events arouse so much fear in the typical individual or corporation as the receipt of a letter from the Internal Revenue Service (IRS), notifying the taxpayer that prior years' tax returns are to be the subject of an audit. Almost immediately, calls are made to the tax adviser. Advice is sought as to what to reveal (or not reveal) in the course of the audit, how to delay or avoid the audit, and how friendly one should be with the auditor when he or she ultimately arrives.

Indeed, many tax practitioners' reputations with their clients have been made or broken by the way they are observed to behave under the pressure of an audit situation. The strategy and tactics of audits—including such seemingly unimportant issues as whether the tax adviser brings doughnuts or other refreshments to the audit session, the color of his or her clothes, and the most effective negotiation techniques—are the subject of both cocktail party banter and scholarly review.

In actuality, the tax professional can render valuable services to the taxpayer in an audit context, thereby ensuring that tax payments for the disputed years are neither under- nor overreported, as part of an ongoing tax practice. In this regard, the adviser must appreciate the following.

- The elements of the Treasury's tax administration process and opportunities for appeal within the structure of the IRS.
- The extent of the negative sanctions that can be brought to bear against taxpayers whose returns are found to have been inaccurate.
- The ethical and professional constraints on the advice tax advisers can give and the actions they can take on behalf of their clients, within the context of an adversarial relationship with the IRS.

17.1 TAX ADMINISTRATION

The Treasury has delegated the administration and enforcement of the tax laws to its subsidiary agency, the IRS. In this process, the Service is responsible for providing adequate information, in the form of publications and forms with instructions, to taxpayers so that they can comply with the laws in an appropriate manner. The IRS also identifies delinquent tax payments and carries out assessment and collection procedures under the restrictions of due process and other constitutional guarantees.

The IRS is one of the largest Federal agencies. It employs about 100,000 staff members, and the total agency budget exceeds $12 billion. In meeting its responsibilities, the Service conducts audits of selected tax returns. About 1 percent of all individual tax returns are subjected to audit in a given tax year. However, certain types of both taxpayers and income—including, for instance, high-income individuals (about 4 percent for those with income exceeding $100,000, and over 12 percent for those with income exceeding $1 million), cash-oriented businesses, real estate transactions, and estate- and gift-taxable transfers (as high as 20 percent)—are subject to much higher probabilities of audit.

The audit rate for corporations with at least $250 million in assets is about 27.5 percent, but the rate drops to about 2 percent for businesses with less than $10 million in assets. In the past few years, the IRS has stepped up its audit and enforcement activities and is targeting narrower issues that are projected to produce more revenue for the time spent. Thus, audit rates for large corporations have decreased, although the dollars collected from such audits continue to increase.

Recently, much of the IRS's effort has been devoted to developing statutory and administrative requirements relative to information reporting and document matching. For instance, when a taxpayer engages in a like-kind exchange or sells a personal residence, various parties to the transaction are required to report the

TAX IN THE NEWS **How Big Is the Tax Gap?**

As directed by Congress, the IRS estimates the size of the Federal income "tax gap"—the difference between how much tax *is* collected and how much *should be* collected. The tax gap reflects the taxes not paid by nonfilers; tax cheats; delinquents; and those who interpret or apply the tax laws incorrectly, whether deliberately or innocently.

According to the most recent analysis, the tax gap is a net amount of almost $385 billion in income and employment taxes annually. More specifically, the underpayments total about $450 billion per year but are offset by $65 billion obtained through IRS enforcement efforts (audits, collection procedures, etc.).

The IRS maintains that only 85 percent of taxpayers report the "correct" amount of tax under the existing system of voluntary compliance, after accounting for audits. The main sources of the tax gap are:

- Underreporting net taxable income (84 percent of the tax gap).
- Underpayment of tax (10 percent of the tax gap).
- Nonfiling (6 percent of the tax gap).

If, by some miracle, the entire tax gap were collected each year, the current Federal budget deficit would be cut significantly. A complete elimination of the tax gap is unlikely to occur, however, for several reasons.

- Citizens are not likely to tolerate the increased audit activity and data collection necessary for the Treasury to collect all of the tax owed.
- Citizens who are so inclined will continue to commit tax fraud, even if statutory and administrative changes are made to the system to identify them. Tax cheats are always "one step ahead" of the government in this regard.
- Congress is not likely to adopt the sweeping simplification of the tax law needed to alleviate its complexity, which many see as the underlying cause of the tax gap. Taxpayers who have difficulty understanding the tax law cannot be expected to comply fully with its provisions.

nature and magnitude of the transaction to the IRS. Later, the Treasury's computers determine whether the transaction has been reported properly by comparing the information reported by the third parties with the events included on the relevant taxpayers' returns for the year.

In addition, the IRS has been placing increasing pressure on the community of tax advisers. Severe penalties may be assessed on those who have prepared the appropriate return when the Service's interpretation of applicable law conflicts with that of the preparer.

The IRS processes about 145 million individual income tax returns every year, almost 100 million of which are filed electronically (i.e., known as **e-filing**). It collects about $2.5 trillion in annual tax revenues and pays refunds to about 100 million individual taxpayers every year. The average refund exceeds $3,000.

Organizational Structure of the IRS

LO.1

Illustrate the organization and structure of the IRS.

The structure of the IRS is moving toward that illustrated in Figure 17.1. The IRS Commissioner, a presidential appointee, has organized the day-to-day operations of the agency into four divisions, based on the type of tax returns to be processed. Administrative functions, such as those relating to personnel and computer issues, are organized on a shared-services model, managed from the national office. Broader functions, such as litigation, investigations, and taxpayer relations, are managed at the national level as well.

The Chief Counsel, another presidential appointee, is the head legal officer of the IRS. The Chief Counsel's office provides legal advice to the IRS and guidance to the public on matters pertaining to the administration and enforcement of the tax laws. For instance, the Chief Counsel's duties include establishing uniform nationwide interpretive positions on the law, drafting tax guide material for taxpayers and IRS personnel, issuing technical rulings to taxpayers, and providing advice and technical assistance to IRS personnel. The Chief Counsel represents the IRS in all litigation before the Tax Court.

FIGURE 17.1 IRS National Office Organization

LO.2

Identify the various administrative pronouncements issued by the IRS, and explain how they can be used in tax practice.

IRS Procedure—Letter Rulings

When a tax issue is controversial or a transaction involves considerable tax dollars, the taxpayer often wants to obtain either assurance or direction from the IRS as to the treatment of the event. The **letter ruling** process is an effective means of dealing directly with the IRS while in the planning stages of a large or otherwise important transaction.

Rulings issued by the National Office provide a written statement of the position of the IRS concerning the tax consequences of a course of action contemplated by the taxpayer. Letter rulings do not have the force and effect of law, but they do provide guidance and support for taxpayers in similar transactions. The IRS issues rulings only on uncompleted, actual (rather than hypothetical) transactions or on transactions that have been completed before the filing of the tax return for the year in question.

In certain circumstances, the IRS will not issue a ruling. It ordinarily will not rule in cases that essentially involve a question of fact.[1] For example, no ruling will be issued to determine whether compensation paid to employees is reasonable in amount and therefore allowable as a deduction.[2]

A letter ruling represents the current opinion of the IRS on the tax consequences of a transaction with a given set of facts. IRS rulings are not unchangeable. They can be declared obsolete or superseded by new rulings in response to tax law changes. However, revocation or modification of a ruling usually is not applied retroactively to the taxpayer who received the ruling if it was relied on in good faith and if the facts in the ruling request were in agreement with the completed transaction. The IRS may revoke any ruling if, upon subsequent audit, the agent finds a misstatement or omission of facts or substantial discrepancies between the facts in the ruling request and the actual situation.

A ruling may be relied upon only by the taxpayer who requested and received it. It must be attached to the tax return for the year in question.

[1]Rev.Proc. 2012–1, I.R.B. No. 1, 15.

[2]Rev.Proc. 2012–3, I.R.B. No. 1, 115.

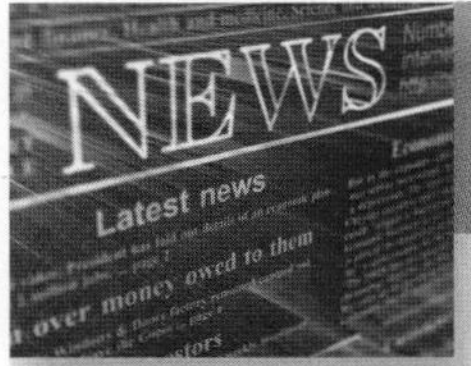

TAX IN THE NEWS IRS Audit Initiatives

The IRS's current audit initiatives seem to be aimed at chronic and high-risk noncompliance. In an age of shrinking real budget dollars for the Service, this "biggest bang for the buck" strategy may be appropriate. The Service seems to be hunting for annuities of tax dollars, rather than just maximizing current collections. For example, permanently adding a noncompliant taxpayer to the tax rolls can optimize the present value of revenue collections tied to the IRS's efforts.

Announced priority areas for the IRS audit staff include the following. The agency has stated that it is revising its training materials and case studies to reflect the revised priorities.

- Offshore credit card users.
- High-risk, high-income taxpayers.
- Tax shelters, abusive schemes, and their promoters.
- High-income nonfilers.
- Unreported income.
- Transfer pricing involving transactions between U.S. companies and their foreign affiliates.
- Employment taxes.
- Transfers of intangible assets to offshore affiliated companies.
- Executive compensation (particularly stock option transactions).
- Claims of the research credit.
- Abuse of the rules for tax-exempt entities.
- Further research as to audit initiatives.

Letter rulings benefit both the IRS and the taxpayer. They not only help promote a uniform application of the tax laws but also may reduce the potential for litigation or disputes with IRS agents. In addition, they make the IRS aware of significant transactions being consummated by taxpayers. A fee of $11,500 is charged for processing a ruling request; the fee is reduced to $625 if the taxpayer's income is less than $250,000.

IRS Procedure—Other Issuances

In addition to issuing unpublished letter rulings and published rulings and procedures, the IRS issues determination letters and technical advice memoranda.

A **determination letter** relates to a completed transaction when the issue involved is covered by judicial or statutory authority, Regulations, or rulings. Determination letters are issued for various estate, gift, income, excise, and employment tax matters.

EXAMPLE 1

True Corporation recently opened an auto care clinic and has employed numerous mechanics. The corporation is not certain whether its educational reimbursement plan is nondiscriminatory. True may request a determination letter. ■

EXAMPLE 2

Assume the same facts as in Example 1. True would like to establish a pension plan that qualifies for the tax advantages of § 401(k). To determine whether the plan qualifies, True should request and obtain a determination letter from the IRS. ■

EXAMPLE 3

A group of physicians plans to form an association to construct and operate a hospital. The determination letter procedure is appropriate to ascertain whether the group is subject to the Federal income tax or is tax-exempt. ■

A **technical advice memorandum (TAM)** is issued by the National Office to IRS personnel in response to a specific request by an agent, Appellate Conferee, or IRS executive. The taxpayer may request a TAM if an issue in dispute is not treated by the law or precedent and/or published rulings or Regulations. TAMs also are appropriate when there is reason to believe the IRS is not administering the tax law consistently. For example, a taxpayer may inquire why an agent proposes to disallow a certain expenditure when agents in other parts of the country permit the

TAX IN THE NEWS Tax Preparation by the Numbers

The community of taxpayers and their tax preparers is extensive and increasingly is using electronic means to meet current filing requirements. The following summary is based on recent estimates.

Number of individuals who prepare Federal tax returns for a fee	**1 million**
Percentage of all Federal tax returns that were filed using computer software and/or a paid tax preparer	**80%**
Number of Federal tax returns filed by paid preparers using tax filing software	**62 million**
Number of self-prepared Federal tax returns filed by taxpayers using tax filing software	**32 million**
Number of unpaid volunteers who registered with the IRS to assist taxpayers with filing requirements	**80,000**

By one estimate, the cost of compliance with Federal tax laws exceeds $425 billion per year. Roughly, this means that compliance costs act as an additional tax of about 30 cents for every tax dollar collected. This amount exceeds the annual costs of compensation for all of the workers at Walmart, UPS, IBM, McDonald's and Citigroup combined.

For this study, the following items were counted as costs of tax compliance.

- The value of taxpayers' time spent record keeping, filing, planning, and otherwise complying with the tax laws.
- Tax collection costs (chiefly wages and benefits) of IRS employees.
- Expenditures made to professional tax preparers, consultants, and other preparers.

deduction. Technical advice requests arise from the audit process, whereas ruling requests are issued before any IRS audit.

Administrative Powers of the IRS

Examination of Records

The IRS can examine the taxpayer's books and records as part of the process of determining the correct amount of tax due. The IRS can also require the persons responsible for the return to appear and to produce any necessary books and records.[3] Taxpayers are required to maintain certain record-keeping procedures and retain the records necessary to facilitate the audit.

Burden of Proof

If the taxpayer meets the record-keeping requirement and substantiates income and deductions properly, the IRS bears the burden of proof in establishing a tax deficiency during litigation. The taxpayer must have cooperated with the IRS regarding reasonable requests for information, documents, meetings, and interviews. For individual taxpayers, the IRS's burden of proof extends to penalties and interest amounts that it assesses in a court proceeding with the taxpayer.[4]

Assessment and Demand

The Code permits the IRS to assess a deficiency and to demand payment for the tax. However, no assessment or effort to collect the tax may be made until 90 days after a statutory notice of a deficiency (a *90-day letter*) is issued. The taxpayer therefore has 90 days to file a petition to the U.S. Tax Court, effectively preventing the deficiency from being assessed or collected pending the outcome of the case.[5]

Following assessment of the tax, the IRS issues a notice and demand for payment. The taxpayer can be given as little as 10 days to pay the tax after the demand for payment is issued.

[3] § 7602.

[4] §§ 7491(a)(1), (a)(2)(B), and (c).

[5] §§ 6212 and 6213.

If the IRS believes the assessment or collection of a deficiency is in jeopardy, it may assess the deficiency and demand immediate payment.[6] The taxpayer can avoid (*stay*) the collection of the jeopardy assessment by filing a bond for the amount of the tax and interest. This action prevents the IRS from selling any property it has seized.

Collection

If the taxpayer neglects or refuses to pay the tax after receiving the demand for payment, a lien in favor of the IRS is placed on all property (realty and personalty, tangible and intangible) belonging to the taxpayer.

The levy power of the IRS is very broad. It allows the IRS to garnish (*attach*) wages and salary and to seize and sell all nonexempt property by any means. After a notice period, the IRS can make successive seizures on any property owned by the taxpayer until the levy is satisfied.[7] A taxpayer's principal residence is exempt from the levy process, unless the disputed tax, interest, and penalty exceed $5,000 and a U.S. District Court judge approves of the seizure.[8]

The Audit Process

LO.3

Describe the audit process, including how tax returns are selected for audit and the various types of audits.

Selection of Returns for Audit

The IRS utilizes mathematical formulas to select tax returns that are most likely to contain errors and yield substantial amounts of additional tax revenues upon audit. The IRS does not disclose all of its audit selection techniques. However, some observations can be made regarding the probability of a return's selection for audit.

- Certain groups of taxpayers are subject to audit more frequently than others. These groups include individuals with gross income in excess of $100,000, self-employed individuals with substantial business income and deductions, and cash businesses where the potential for tax evasion is high.

EXAMPLE 4

Tracey owns and operates a liquor store. As nearly all of her sales are for cash, Tracey might be a prime candidate for an audit by the IRS. Cash transactions are easier to conceal than those made on credit. ■

- If a taxpayer has been audited in a past year and the audit led to the assessment of a substantial deficiency, the IRS often makes a return visit.
- An audit might materialize if information returns (e.g., Form W–2 and Form 1099) are not in substantial agreement with the income reported on the taxpayer's return. Obvious discrepancies do not necessitate formal audits and usually can be handled by correspondence with the taxpayer.

EXAMPLE 5

The IRS audits Phil's Form 1040 and finds that his dividend income increased sharply. The auditor wonders how Phil financed this stock purchase, as there were no corresponding stock sales on his return that would create cash with which to make the acquisition.

Upon further inquiry, the auditor learns that the dividend yielding stock was a gift to Phil from his mother, Julie. Accordingly, the IRS investigates whether Julie filed a Federal gift tax return for the year of the stock transfer. ■

- If an individual's itemized deductions are in excess of norms established for various income levels, the probability of an audit increases. Certain deductions (e.g., casualty and theft losses, business use of the home, and tax-sheltered investments) are sensitive areas, as the IRS realizes that many taxpayers

[6] § 6861. A jeopardy assessment is appropriate, for instance, when the IRS fears that the taxpayer will flee the country or destroy valuable property.

[7] The taxpayer can keep certain personal and business property and a minimal amount of his or her income as a subsistence allowance, even if a lien is outstanding. § 6334.

[8] §§ 6334(a)(13)(A) and (e)(1).

determine the amount of the deduction incorrectly or may not be entitled to the deduction at all.

- The filing of a refund claim by the taxpayer may prompt an audit of the return.
- Some returns are selected because the IRS has targeted a specific industry or type of tax return for in-depth review. This enables examiners to develop special skills and interests applicable to those returns. In the Industry Specialization Program (ISP), returns might be selected from retailers, energy developers, or health care operations for special review. In the Market Segment Specialization Program (MSSP), specialized auditors focus on returns that show passive losses, involve construction activities, or include legal or consulting income.
- Information often is obtained from outside sources, including other government agencies, news items, and informants.

EXAMPLE 6

After 15 years, Betty is discharged by her employer, Dr. Franklin. Shortly thereafter, the IRS receives a letter from Betty stating that Franklin keeps two sets of books, one of which substantially understates his cash receipts. ■

The statistical models used by the IRS to select individual tax returns for audit come from random audits of a small number of taxpayers, who are required to document every entry they made on the Form 1040. The latest round of these National Research Program (NRP) audits resulted in the construction of new Discriminant Function (DIF) scores that project the amount of revenue the IRS will gain from pursuing tax returns with various statistical profiles. The higher the DIF score, the better the return to the IRS from pursuing the audit, and the higher the probability of selection for an examination.

These data-seeking audits are controversial and have led to taxpayer complaints to Congress about the stress they create.[9] But the data from older DIF models no longer reflected the U.S. service-based, information-powered economy. Consequently, the underlying models require more frequent updating for effective enforcement of the tax laws. The IRS believes that by constantly updating the NRP data through a diligent review of randomly selected tax returns, changes in tax avoidance behaviors will be detected and fewer routine audits will be required.

ETHICS & EQUITY Can the IRS Pretend to Be Your Friend?

Should IRS agents be allowed to identify audit subjects by reading the society page of the newspaper, looking for indicators of wealth? What if the agency subscribes to Facebook and seeks comments from its "friends" as to income windfalls and stock market dealings? In the past, some state and local taxing agencies have used social networking sites for audit selection purposes. State and local revenue agents have used the sites to find self-employed individuals who advertise their business and report about upcoming income-producing events. The sites also have been used to determine whether a taxpayer who has requested an extension of time to pay a delinquent tax actually is strapped for cash.

Some state tax officials claim that looking for a taxpayer's self-declarations on a website is a much more efficient way to find income understatements than searching through most other sources of nonstatistical data. Should taxing agencies be using Google, Facebook, and other public-domain online sources of taxpayer information to help identify tax returns for audit?

[9] On average, the total annual NRP audit sample consists of 13,000 returns. Some of these returns are analyzed without contacting the taxpayer, and other taxpayers are contacted only by mail with queries about one or two items. Only a few returns are subjected to "line-by-line" review. Most of the returns are reviewed for a period of three tax years.

Many individual taxpayers mistakenly assume that if they do not hear from the IRS within a few weeks after filing their return or if they receive a refund check, no audit will be forthcoming. As a practical matter, most individual returns are examined about two years from the date of filing. If not, they generally remain unaudited. All large corporations, however, are subject to annual audits.

Role of Informants

The IRS can pay rewards to persons who provide information that leads to the detection and punishment of those who violate the tax laws. The rewards are paid at the discretion of the IRS. Such a payment usually cannot exceed 15 percent of the taxes, fines, and penalties recovered as a result of such information.[10]

About 500 informant rewards are paid in the typical year. The average reward paid is about $4,500. In a recent year, the IRS collected about $475 million from the informants' program, and it paid rewards of about $19 million (i.e., at approximately a 4 percent rate).

Another IRS office, through the so-called **Whistleblower Program**, offers special rewards to informants who provide information concerning businesses or high-income (gross income exceeds $200,000) individuals when more than $2 million of tax, penalty, and interest is at stake. Some informants claim that hundreds of millions of dollars of tax, penalty, and interest are due from allegedly noncompliant taxpayers.

A whistleblower reward can reach 30 percent of the amount collected by the Treasury and traceable to the whistleblower's information. The reward can be reduced if the whistleblower participated in the original understatement of tax. About 500 cases are initiated every year as a result of tips from whistleblowers.

The whistleblower rewards are paid out of the taxes recovered under the informant and whistleblower programs. To claim a reward of this sort, an informant files Form 211 with the IRS. Federal income taxes are withheld from the whistleblower reward, usually at a 28 percent rate. A whistleblower has 30 days to appeal to the IRS if his or her claim is denied or reduced from the original amount requested.

Verification and Audit Procedures

The filed tax return immediately is reviewed for mathematical accuracy. A check is also made for deductions, exclusions, etc., that are clearly erroneous. One obvious error would be the failure to comply with the 7.5 percent limitation on the deduction for medical expenses.

About 2 percent of all paper-filed individual returns show a math error. The math error rate for e-filed returns is only 0.1 percent. When a math or clerical error occurs, the Service Center merely sends the taxpayer revised computations and a bill or refund as appropriate.

Taxpayers usually are able to settle routine tax disputes (e.g., queries involving the documentation of deductions) through a by-mail-only *correspondence audit* with the IRS, without the necessity of a formal meeting.

Office audits are conducted in an office of the IRS. Individual returns with few or no items of business income are usually handled through the office audit procedure. In most instances, the taxpayer is required merely to substantiate a deduction, a credit, or an item of income that appears on the return. The taxpayer presents documentation in the form of canceled checks, invoices, etc., for the items in question.

The *field audit* procedure commonly is used for corporate returns and for returns of individuals engaged in business or professional activities. This type of audit generally involves a more complete examination of a taxpayer's transactions.

A field audit is conducted by IRS agents at the office or home of the taxpayer or at the office of the taxpayer's representative. The agent's work may be facilitated by

[10] § 7623 and Reg. § 301.7623–1.

TABLE 17.1 IRS Audit Information by Type

	Conducted (Number)	Conducted (Percent)
Correspondence audit	1,125,000	78%
Office audit	50,000	3%
Field audit	450,000	19%

a review of certain tax workpapers and discussions with the taxpayer's representative about items appearing on the tax return. Table 17.1 summarizes key information about the various tax audits.

Prior to or at the initial interview, the IRS must provide the taxpayer with an explanation of the audit process that is the subject of the interview and describe the taxpayer's rights under that process. If the taxpayer clearly states at any time during the interview the desire to consult with an attorney, a CPA, or an enrolled agent or any other person permitted to represent the taxpayer before the IRS, then the IRS representative must suspend the interview.[11]

Any officer or employee of the IRS must, upon advance request, allow a taxpayer to make an audio recording of any in-person interview with the officer or employee concerning the determination and collection of any tax.[12]

Settlement with the Revenue Agent

Following an audit, the IRS agent may either accept the return as filed or recommend certain adjustments. The **Revenue Agent's Report (RAR)** is reviewed within the IRS. In most instances, the agent's proposed adjustments are approved.

Agents must adhere strictly to IRS policy as reflected in published rulings, Regulations, and other releases. The agent cannot settle an unresolved issue based upon the probability of winning the case in court. Usually, issues involving factual questions can be settled at the agent level, and it may be advantageous for both the taxpayer and the IRS to reach agreement at the earliest point in the settlement process. For example, it may be to the taxpayer's advantage to reach agreement at the agent level and avoid any further opportunity for the IRS to raise new issues.

If agreement is reached upon the proposed deficiency, the taxpayer signs Form 870 (Waiver of Restrictions on Assessment and Collection of Deficiency in Tax). One advantage to the taxpayer of signing Form 870 at this point is that interest stops accumulating on the deficiency 30 days after the form is filed.[13] When this form is signed, the taxpayer effectively waives the right to receive a statutory notice of deficiency (90-day letter) and to subsequently petition the Tax Court. In addition, it is no longer possible for the taxpayer later to go to the IRS Appeals Division. The signing of Form 870 at the agent level generally closes the case. However, the IRS is not restricted by Form 870 and may assess additional deficiencies if deemed necessary.

LO.4

Explain the taxpayer appeal process, including various settlement options available.

The Taxpayer Appeal Process

If agreement cannot be reached at the agent level, the taxpayer receives a copy of the Revenue Agent's Report and a **30-day letter**. The taxpayer has 30 days to request an administrative appeal. If an appeal is not requested, a **90-day letter** is

[11] § 7521(b).
[12] § 7521(a).
[13] § 6601(c).

FIGURE 17.2 **Income Tax Appeal Procedure**

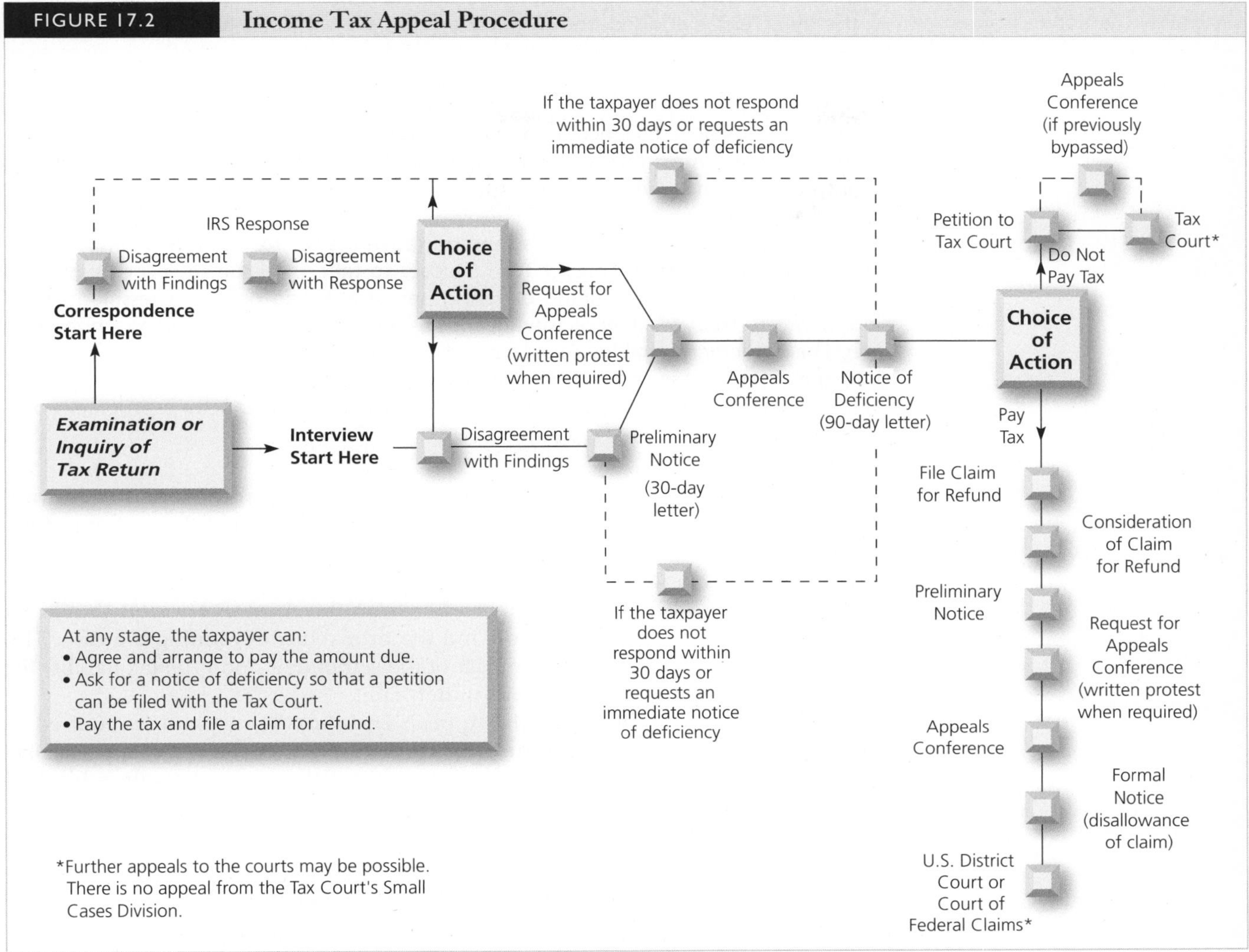

issued. Figure 17.2 illustrates the taxpayer's alternatives when a disagreement with the IRS persists.

A taxpayer who wants to appeal must make an appropriate request to the Appeals Division. The request must be accompanied by a written protest except in the following cases.

- The proposed tax deficiency does not exceed $10,000 for any of the tax periods involved in the audit.
- The deficiency resulted from a correspondence or office audit (i.e., not as a result of a field audit).

The Appeals Division is authorized to settle all tax disputes based on the hazards of litigation (the chances of winning in court). Because the Appeals Division has final settlement authority until a 90-day letter has been issued, the taxpayer may be able to negotiate a settlement. In addition, an overall favorable settlement may be reached by "trading" disputed issues. The Appeals Division occasionally may raise new issues if the grounds are substantial and of significant tax impact.

Both the Appeals Division and the taxpayer have the right to request technical advice memoranda from the National Office of the IRS. A TAM that is favorable to the taxpayer is binding on the Appeals Division. Even if the TAM is favorable to the IRS, the Appeals Division nevertheless may settle the case based on the hazards of litigation.

EXAMPLE 7

At the time Terri is audited, the corporation that she controls had advances outstanding to her in the amount of $80,000. The IRS field agent held that these advances were constructive dividends to her (refer to the discussion in Chapter 5). Some facts point toward this result (e.g., the corporation is closely held, Terri has made no repayments, and the loan balance has increased over several years). Other facts, however, appear to indicate that these advances are bona fide loans (e.g., a written instrument provides for interest, Terri has the independent means of repayment, and the corporation has a good dividend-paying record).

The Appeals Division and Terri's representative assess the hazards of litigation as being 50% for each side. Thus, if Terri chooses to take the issue to court, she would have an even chance of winning or losing her case. Based on this assessment, both sides agree to treat $40,000 of the advance as a dividend and $40,000 as a bona fide loan. The agreement enables Terri to avoid $40,000 of dividend income (the loan portion) and saves her the cost of litigating the issue.

Thus, by going to the Appeals Division, Terri obtained a satisfactory settlement otherwise unobtainable from the agent. ■

Taxpayers who file a petition with the U.S. Tax Court have the option of having the case heard before the more informal Small Cases Division if the amount of tax in dispute does not exceed $50,000.[14] If the Small Cases Division is used, neither party may appeal the case.

The economic costs of a settlement offer from the Appeals Division should be weighed against the costs of litigation and the probability of winning the case. The taxpayer also should consider the impact of the settlement upon the tax liability for future periods in addition to the years under audit.

If a settlement is reached with the Appeals Division, the taxpayer is required to sign Form 870–AD. Interest stops running on the deficiency when the Appeals Division accepts the Form 870–AD. According to the IRS, this settlement is binding upon both parties unless fraud, malfeasance, concealment, or misrepresentation of material fact has occurred.

Offers in Compromise and Closing Agreements

The IRS can negotiate a compromise if the taxpayer's ability to pay the tax is doubtful. If the taxpayer is financially unable to pay the total amount of the tax, a Form 656 (Offer in Compromise) is filed. An **offer in compromise** is appropriate in the following circumstances.[15]

- There is doubt as to the taxpayer's liability for the tax (i.e., disputed issues still exist).
- There is doubt as to the collectibility of the tax (i.e., the taxpayer's net worth and earnings capacity are low).
- Payment of the disputed amount would constitute an economic hardship for the taxpayer. For instance, the taxpayer is incapable of earning a living because of a long-term illness or disability, or liquidation of the taxpayer's assets to pay the amount due would leave the taxpayer unable to meet basic living expenses.

The IRS investigates the offer by evaluating the taxpayer's financial ability to pay the tax. In some instances, the compromise settlement includes an agreement for final settlement of the tax through payments of a specified percentage of the taxpayer's future earnings. This settlement procedure usually entails lengthy negotiations with the IRS, but the presumption is that the agency will find terms upon which to enter into a compromise with the taxpayer. A 20 percent nonrefundable current payment is required to set up the compromise offer, and a $150 filing fee

[14] § 7463(a).

[15] § 7122 and Reg. § 301.7122–1(b).

ETHICS & EQUITY Our Taxing System of Self-Assessment

The United States is a large country of diverse taxpayers and businesses. Perhaps the only way the massive dollar amounts of Federal income taxes can be collected on a timely basis is through a *self-assessment* process, whereby the taxpayer is charged with disclosing a full picture of the tax year's results and the corresponding computation of taxable income. But a system of self-assessment depends heavily on the honesty and integrity of the taxpayers and their ability to know and comply with the pertinent tax rules.

A recent survey of taxpayer attitudes by the IRS Oversight Board revealed the following results.

Given the results of this survey, do you think the current self-assessment system is satisfactory? If not, should Congress create additional enforcement procedures to ensure taxpayer compliance? What sort of new reporting rules might be useful?

Why Do You Report and Pay Your Taxes Honestly? (more than one answer allowed)

Taxpayer Responses	Taxpayers Mentioning This Reason (Percent)
My own personal integrity	80%
A third party reported my information to the IRS (e.g., through a Form W–2 or 1099), so I must match that amount in my tax form	39%
Fear of an audit	35%
My neighbors report and pay their taxes honestly, so I will too	21%

What Is an Acceptable Amount by Which to Cheat on Your Income Taxes?

	Taxpayers Responding (Percent)
Not at all	89%
A little here and a little there	6%
As much as possible	3%
Other answers	3%

Source: *2010 Taxpayer Attitude Survey* at **www.ustreas.gov/irsob/reports/2010**.

is required. Low-income individuals can apply for a waiver of the fee and of the 20 percent down payment.[16]

The IRS can agree to allow taxes to be paid on an installment basis if that arrangement facilitates the tax collection. An individual who has filed timely tax returns for five years is guaranteed the right to use an installment agreement when the amount in dispute does not exceed $10,000. The taxpayer uses Form 9465 to initiate an installment plan.

The IRS provides an annual statement accounting for the status of the agreement. The agreement may later be modified or terminated because of (1) inadequate information, (2) subsequent change in financial condition, or (3) failure to pay an installment when due or to provide requested information.[17]

Every year, the IRS accepts about 10,000 offers in compromise, involving about $150 million in unpaid taxes, interest, and penalties.

A **closing agreement** is binding on both the taxpayer and the IRS except upon a subsequent showing of fraud, malfeasance, or misrepresentation of a material fact.[18] The closing agreement may be used when disputed issues carry over to future years. It may also be employed to dispose of a dispute involving a specific

[16]Reg. § 300.3(b)(1)(ii). "Low-income" is defined as less than 250% of the Federal poverty level.

[17]§ 6159.

[18]§ 7121(b).

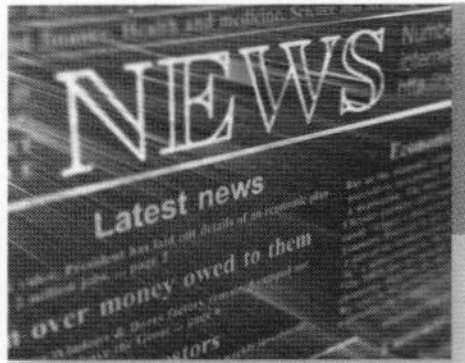

TAX IN THE NEWS Late-Night Tax Advice

What are those people on late-night TV commercials talking about when they offer to handle your back taxes with the IRS or reduce your tax bill by half?

Most of these commercials that are trying to grab your attention are promoting tax resolution firms that will put together an offer in compromise for submission to the IRS. For a sometimes sizable up-front fee, a firm will carry out the filing process for an offer in compromise and suggest terms that may be acceptable to the IRS. Because the firm has experience with these arrangements, it can likely reach an agreement on the offer in a shorter time than a typical individual would require. Although tax resolution firms may be helpful in certain situations, the IRS has warned that some firms engage in poor business practices.

Rather than pursue an offer in compromise, a taxpayer might request an installment payment schedule from the IRS. The installment approach does not avoid taxes and interest, but it does buy time for the taxpayer by allowing affordable payments over an agreed-on period of time. Moreover, it avoids the sizable up-front fees that a tax resolution firm would charge for often unsatisfactory service.

issue for a prior year or a proposed transaction involving future years. If, for example, the IRS is willing to make substantial concessions in the valuation of assets for death tax purposes, it may require a closing agreement from the recipient of the property to establish the income tax basis of the assets.

LO.5

Determine the amount of interest on a deficiency or a refund and when it is due.

Interest

Determination of the Interest Rate

Congress sets the interest rates applicable to Federal tax underpayments (deficiencies) and overpayments (refunds) close to the rates available in financial markets. The Code provides for the rates to be determined quarterly.[19] Thus, the rates that are determined during March are effective for the following April through June.

IRS interest is based on the Federal short-term rates published periodically by the IRS in Revenue Rulings. They are based on the average market yield on outstanding marketable obligations of the United States with remaining maturity of three years or less.

For noncorporate taxpayers, the interest rate applicable to *both* overpayments and underpayments is 3 percent for the first quarter of 2012. For most corporate taxpayers, the rate is 2 percent for overpayments and 3 percent for underpayments. Corporations with large overpayments or underpayments are subject to different rates.

Computation of the Amount of Interest

Interest is compounded daily.[20] Depending on the applicable interest rate, daily compounding can double the payable amount over a period of five to eight years.

Tables for determining the daily compounded amount are available from the IRS and on the Internet. The tables ease the burden of those who prepare late returns where additional taxes are due.[21]

IRS Deficiency Assessments

Interest usually accrues from the unextended due date of the return until 30 days after the taxpayer agrees to the deficiency by signing Form 870. If the taxpayer does not pay the amount shown on the IRS's notice and demand (tax bill) within 30 days, interest again accrues on the deficiency.

[19] § 6621.

[20] § 6622.

[21] Rev.Proc. 95–17, 1995–1 C.B. 556.

Refund of Taxpayer's Overpayments

If an overpayment is refunded to the taxpayer within 45 days after the date the return is filed or is due, no interest is allowed. When the taxpayer files an amended return or makes a claim for refund of a prior year's tax (e.g., when net operating loss carrybacks result in refunds of a prior year's tax payments), however, interest is authorized from the original due date of the return through the date when the amended return is filed. In general, taxpayers applying for refunds receive interest as follows.

- When a return is filed after the due date, interest on any overpayment accrues from the date of filing. However, no interest is due if the IRS makes the refund within 45 days of the date of filing.

EXAMPLE 8

Naomi, a calendar year taxpayer, files her 2011 return on December 1, 2012. The return reflects an overwithholding of $2,500. On June 8, 2013, Naomi receives a refund of her 2011 overpayment. Interest on the refund began to accrue on December 1, 2012 (not April 15, 2012). ■

EXAMPLE 9

Assume the same facts as in Example 8, except that the refund is paid to Naomi on January 5, 2013 (rather than June 8, 2013). No interest is payable by the IRS, because the refund was made within 45 days of the filing of the return. ■

- In no event will interest accrue on an overpayment unless the return that is filed is in "processible form." Generally, this means that the return must contain enough information in a readable format to enable the IRS to identify the taxpayer and to determine the tax (and overpayment) involved.
- In the case of a carryback (e.g., net operating loss, capital loss, or tax credit), interest on any refund begins to accrue on the due date of the return (disregarding extensions) for the year in which the carryback arises. Even then, however, no interest accrues until a return is filed or, if the return has been filed, if the IRS pays the refund within 45 days.

EXAMPLE 10

Top Corporation, a calendar year taxpayer, incurs a net operating loss during 2011 that it can carry back to tax year 2009 and obtain a refund. On December 28, 2012, Top files a claim for refund. The earliest that interest can begin to accrue in this situation is March 16, 2012, but because the return was not filed until December 28, 2012, the later date controls. If, however, the IRS pays the refund within 45 days of December 28, 2012, no interest need be paid. ■

Taxpayer Penalties

LO.6

List and explain the various penalties that can be imposed on acts of noncompliance by taxpayers and return preparers.

To promote and enforce taxpayer compliance with the U.S. voluntary self-assessment system of taxation, Congress has enacted a comprehensive array of penalties.

Tax penalties may involve both criminal and civil offenses. Criminal tax penalties are imposed only after the usual criminal process in which the taxpayer is entitled to the same constitutional guarantees as nontax criminal defendants. Normally, a criminal penalty provides for imprisonment. Civil tax penalties are collected in the same manner as other taxes and usually provide only for monetary fines. Criminal and civil penalties are not mutually exclusive; therefore, both types of sanctions may be imposed on a taxpayer.

The Code characterizes tax penalties as additions to tax; thus, the taxpayer cannot subsequently deduct them.

Ad valorem penalties are additions to tax that are based upon a percentage of the owed tax. *Assessable penalties,* on the other hand, typically include a flat dollar amount. Assessable penalties are not subject to review by the Tax Court, but ad valorem penalties are subject to the same deficiency procedures that apply to the underlying tax.

Failure to File and Failure to Pay

For a failure to file a tax return by the due date (including extensions), a penalty of 5 percent per month (up to a maximum of 25 percent) is imposed on the amount of tax shown as due on the return, with a minimum penalty amount of $135.[22] If the failure to file is attributable to fraud, the penalty becomes 15 percent per month, to a maximum of 75 percent of the tax.[23]

For a failure to pay the tax due as shown on the return, a penalty of .5 percent per month (up to a maximum of 25 percent) is imposed on the amount of the tax. The penalty is doubled if the taxpayer fails to pay the tax after receiving a deficiency assessment.

In all of these cases, a fraction of a month counts as a full month. These penalties relate to the net amount of the tax due.

Obtaining an extension for filing a tax return does not by itself extend the date by which the taxes due must be paid. Thus, an application for an extended due date for a tax return almost always is accompanied by a payment by the taxpayer of a good faith estimate of the taxes that will be owed with the return when it is filed by the extended due date. If the taxpayer does not make such a good faith estimate and payment, the extension itself may be voided by the IRS (e.g., when the return is filed by the extended due date with a much larger amount due than had been estimated).

EXAMPLE 11

Conchita uses an automatic six-month extension for the filing of her 2012 tax return. Thus, the return is due on October 15, 2013, not on April 15. Conchita's application for the extension includes a $5,000 check, the amount that she estimates her 2012 return will show as owing for the year when she files it in October. ■

During any month in which both the failure to file penalty and the failure to pay penalty apply, the failure to file penalty is reduced by the amount of the failure to pay penalty.

EXAMPLE 12

Jason files his tax return 10 days after the due date. Along with the return, he remits a check for $4,000, which is the balance of the tax he owes. Disregarding any interest liabilities, Jason's total penalties are as follows.

Failure to pay penalty (.5% × $4,000)		$ 20
Failure to file penalty (5% × $4,000)	$200	
Less: Failure to pay penalty for the same period	20	
Failure to file penalty		180
Total penalties		$200

The penalties for one full month are imposed even though Jason was delinquent by only 10 days. Unlike the method used to compute interest, any part of a month is treated as a whole month. ■

These penalties can be avoided if the taxpayer shows that the failure to file and/or failure to pay was due to reasonable cause and not due to willful neglect. The Code is silent as to what constitutes reasonable cause, and the Regulations do little to clarify this important concept.[24] Reasonable cause for failure to pay is presumed under the automatic six-month extension (Form 4868) when the additional tax due is not more than 10 percent of the tax liability shown on the return. In addition, the courts have ruled on some aspects of **reasonable cause**.

[22] § 6651(a). The minimum penalty cannot exceed the amount of tax due on the return.

[23] § 6651(f).

[24] Reg. § 301.6651–1(c)(1) likens reasonable cause to the exercise of "ordinary business care and prudence" on the part of the taxpayer.

TAX IN THE NEWS Relying on "Really Good" Tax Advice

The Tax Court recently addressed the application of the reasonable cause exception to the negligence penalty. It appears that highly educated and experienced taxpayers have a difficult time avoiding the penalty by claiming that they relied on the advice of a professional tax adviser.

In *Stephen G. Woodsum*, 136 T.C. __, No. 29 (2011), the director of a private equity investment firm filed a tax return of over 100 pages with gross income of about $29 million, mainly from investment transactions such as swaps and derivatives. One of the Forms 1099, reporting a $3 million gain on a swap transaction, was omitted from the return. The Court classified this as a clerical error on the part of the tax preparer, and not as a piece of tax advice upon which the taxpayer relied. Thus, the taxpayer's negligence penalty still applied. The Court found that the taxpayer did not review the tax return with reasonable rigor before signing it; had the financially savvy taxpayer performed more than a casual review of the transactions on the return, the missing gain would not have "slipped through the cracks."

The tax adviser in *Tony L. Robucci*, 100 TCM 1060, T.C. Memo 2011–19, restructured his medical clinic to eliminate its exposure to Federal employment taxes. The restructuring entailed setting up a "shell" LLC. But the new entity did not trigger any meaningful change in the day-to-day operations of the clinic, and the taxpayer never participated in legal transfers of tangible or intangible assets. The Court stated that this highly educated taxpayer should have sought a "second opinion" after getting tax advice about the restructuring that was "too good to be true." Citing *Neonatology Associates v. Comm.*, 2002–2 USTC ¶50,550, 90 AFTR 2d 2002–5442, 299 F.3d 221 (CA–3, 2002), the court charged that when "a taxpayer is presented with what would appear to be a fabulous opportunity to avoid tax obligations, he should recognize that he proceeds at his own peril." Again, lacking a reasonable cause exception, the negligence penalty was allowed to stand.

- Reasonable cause was found where the taxpayer relied on the advice of a competent tax adviser given in good faith, the facts were fully disclosed to the adviser, and he or she considered that the specific question represented reasonable cause.[25] No reasonable cause was found, however, where the taxpayer delegated the filing task to another, even when that person was an accountant or an attorney.[26]
- Among the reasons not qualifying as reasonable cause were lack of information on the due date of the return,[27] illness that did not incapacitate a taxpayer from completing a return,[28] refusal of the taxpayer's spouse to cooperate for a joint return,[29] and ignorance or misunderstanding of the tax law.[30]

Accuracy-Related Penalties

Major civil penalties relating to the accuracy of tax return data, including misstatements stemming from taxpayer negligence and improper valuation of income and deductions, are coordinated under the umbrella term **accuracy-related penalties**.[31] This consolidation of related penalties into a single levy eliminates the possibility that multiple penalties will apply to a single understatement of tax.

[25] *Estate of Norma S. Bradley*, 33 TCM 70, T.C.Memo. 1974–17.

[26] *U.S. v. Boyle*, 85–1 USTC ¶13,602, 55 AFTR 2d 85–1535, 105 S.Ct. 687 (USSC, 1985). This rule appears to apply to electronic as well as paper-based return filings, to employment as well as income taxes, and to returns where the tax preparer himself or herself commits a fraudulent act. *Brandon R. Ballantyne*, 99 TCM 1523, T.C.Memo. 2010–125; *McNair Eye Center, Inc.*, 99 TCM 1345, T.C.Memo. 2010–81. Knowledgeable taxpayers such as a tax attorney are held to a higher standard in determining negligence. *Pelton & Gunther P.C.*, 78 TCM 578, T.C.Memo. 1999–339. A taxpayer might be negligent if, when a complicated tax issue is involved, a tax expert is *not* consulted. *Zmuda v. Comm.*, 84-1 USTC ¶9,442, 53 AFTR 2d 84–1269, 731 F.2d 1417 (CA–9, 1984).

[27] *Beck Chemical Equipment Co.*, 27 T.C. 840 (1957).

[28] *Alex and Tonya Oria*, 94 TCM 170, T.C.Memo. 2007–276, and *Babetta Schmidt*, 28 T.C. 367 (1957). Compare *Estate of Kirchner*, 46 B.T.A. 578 (1942).

[29] *Electric and Neon, Inc.*, 56 T.C. 1324 (1971).

[30] *Stevens Brothers Foundation, Inc.*, 39 T.C. 93 (1965).

[31] § 6662.

The accuracy-related penalties each amount to 20 percent of the portion of the tax underpayment that is attributable to one or more of the following infractions.

- Negligence or disregard of rules and regulations.
- Substantial understatement of tax liability.
- Substantial valuation overstatement.
- Substantial valuation understatement.

The penalties apply only where the taxpayer fails to show a *reasonable basis* for the position taken on the return.[32]

Negligence

For purposes of this accuracy-related penalty, **negligence** includes any failure to make a reasonable attempt to comply with the provisions of the tax law. The penalty also applies to any disregard (whether careless, reckless, or intentional) of rules and regulations.[33] The penalty can be avoided upon a showing of reasonable cause and the fact that the taxpayer acted in good faith.[34]

The negligence penalty applies to *all* taxes, except when fraud is involved. A negligence penalty may be assessed when the taxpayer fails to report gross income, overstates deductions, or fails to keep adequate records. When the taxpayer takes a nonnegligent position on the return that is contrary to a judicial precedent or published pronouncement of the IRS, the penalty is waived if the taxpayer has a reasonable basis for the interpretation and has disclosed the disputed position on Form 8275.

Substantial Understatement of Tax Liability

The understatement penalty is designed to strike at middle- and high-income taxpayers who are tempted to play the so-called audit lottery.[35] Some taxpayers take questionable and undisclosed positions on their tax returns in the hope the return will not be selected for audit. Disclosing the positions would have called attention to the return and increased the probability of audit.

A substantial understatement of a tax liability transpires when the understatement exceeds the larger of 10 percent of the tax due or $5,000. For a C corporation, a substantial understatement is the lesser of the following.[36]

- 10 percent of the tax due, but at least $10,000.
- $10 million.

The understatement to which the penalty applies is the difference between the amount of tax required to be shown on the return and the amount of tax actually shown on the return.

The penalty is avoided under any of the following circumstances.[37]

- The taxpayer has **substantial authority** for the treatment.
- There is a *reasonable basis* for the tax return position, which is adequately disclosed in the return by attaching Form 8275.

Penalty for Overvaluation

The objective of the overvaluation penalty is to deter taxpayers from inflating values (or basis), usually of charitable contributions of property, to reduce income taxes.[38]

---

[32] Reg. § 1.6662–3(b)(3). Most tax professionals measure this standard as a 20% probability of prevailing in court.

[33] § 6662(c). There can be no intentional disregard of the rules where the underlying law is unclear, complex, or subject to disagreement. *James J. Freeland*, 51 TCM 253, T.C.Memo. 1986–10, and *Lansdown v. Comm.*, 96–1 USTC ¶50,025, 77 AFTR 2d 96–491, 73 F.3d 373 (CA–10, 1996).

[34] § 6664(c)(1).

[35] § 6662(b)(2).

[36] § 6662(d)(1).

[37] § 6662(d)(2)(B). Substantial authority is measured as of either the last day of the tax year to which the return relates or the date the return was filed. Reg. § 1.6662–4(d)(3)(iv)(C).

[38] §§ 6662(b)(3), (e), and (h).

- The penalty is 20 percent of the additional tax that would have been paid had the correct valuation been used.
- The penalty applies only when the valuation used by the taxpayer is 150 percent or more of the correct valuation. The penalty is doubled if the valuation error is *gross* (overstated by 200 percent or more).
- The penalty applies only when the resulting income tax underpayment exceeds $5,000 ($10,000 for C corporations).

EXAMPLE 13

Gretchen (a calendar year taxpayer) purchased a painting for $10,000. When the painting is worth $18,000 (as later determined by the IRS), Gretchen donates the painting to an art museum. Based on the appraisal of a cousin who is an amateur artist, she deducts $40,000 for the donation. Because Gretchen was in the 30% tax bracket, overstating the deduction by $22,000 results in a tax underpayment of $6,600.

Gretchen's penalty for overvaluation is $2,640, or *double* the regular penalty of $1,320 (20% × $6,600 underpayment). ■

The substantial valuation overstatement penalty is avoided if the taxpayer can show reasonable cause and good faith. However, when the overvaluation involves *charitable deduction property*, the taxpayer must substantiate both of the following.

- The claimed value of the property is based on a qualified appraisal made by a qualified appraiser.
- The taxpayer made a good faith investigation of the value of the contributed property.[39]

Based on these criteria, Gretchen in Example 13 would find it difficult to avoid the penalty. A cousin who is an amateur artist does not meet the definition of a qualified appraiser. Likewise, Gretchen apparently has not made her own good faith investigation of the value of the contributed property.

Penalty for Undervaluation

When attempting to minimize the income tax, it is to the benefit of taxpayers to *overvalue* deductions. When attempting to minimize transfer taxes (estate and gift taxes), however, executors and donors may be inclined to *undervalue* the assets transferred. A lower valuation reduces estate and gift taxes. An accuracy-related penalty is imposed for substantial estate or gift tax valuation understatements.[40] As with other accuracy-related penalties, reasonable cause and good faith on the part of the taxpayer are a defense.

- The penalty is 20 percent of the additional transfer tax that would have been due had the correct valuation been used on Form 706 (estate tax return) or Form 709 (gift and generation-skipping tax return).
- The penalty applies only if the value of the property claimed on the return is 65 percent or less than the amount determined to be correct. The penalty is doubled if the reported valuation error is *gross* (reported value is 40 percent or less than the correct determination).
- The penalty applies only to an additional transfer tax liability in excess of $5,000.

Appraiser's Penalty

When a valuation penalty arises because of the taxpayer's reliance on an appraisal, a further penalty can apply.[41] If the appraiser knew or reasonably should have

[39] §§ 6664(c)(2) and (3).
[40] §§ 6662(b)(5), (g), and (h).
[41] § 6695A.

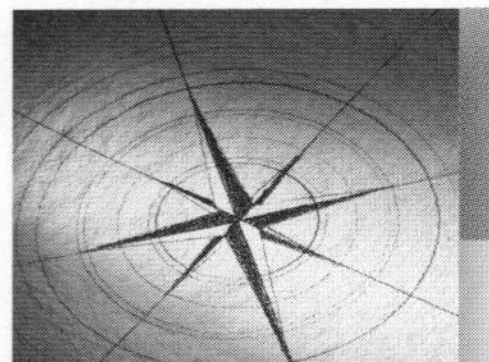

ETHICS & EQUITY Good Faith Valuations

When dealing with the undervaluation penalty, the tax adviser may shift from being in adversarial alliance with the taxpayer to being a mediator for the court. Good faith value estimates, especially for family-owned businesses, can easily vary by as much as the 65 percentage points specified for the penalty. Even a gross undervaluation can occur when someone in the business other than the donor or decedent is a particularly talented entrepreneur, an effective sales representative, and/or the founder of the company; similarly, a business may be substantially undervalued when a minority equity interest is involved or when an intangible asset conveys a sizable nominal amount of goodwill to the valuation.

Because most taxpayers are highly averse to incurring any nondeductible penalties, the client may be tempted to compromise on the business valuation "too soon" (i.e., when the return is filed), eliminating any possibility of a more favorable valuation being presented before the Appeals Division or a court. Keeping in mind all of the potential taxpayer and preparer penalties that might apply, the tax professional should stick with a good faith appraisal of the business value, no matter what its nominal amount.

How would you react if your client, a composer, wanted to deduct $100,000 for the contribution of an obscure manuscript to the Symphony Society? What if your (first) appraiser placed the value of the manuscript at $15,000? What course of action would you propose to the client concerning the deduction? Any consequent penalties?

known that the appraisal would be used as part of a tax or refund computation and that the appraised value more likely than not was improper, then the appraiser pays a penalty equal to the lesser of:

- 10 percent of the tax understatement, but at least $1,000, or
- 125 percent of the gross income received by the appraiser from the engagement (e.g., the appraisal fee collected).

This amount is in addition to the taxpayer's valuation penalty as discussed above.

Penalty for Improper Refund Claim

Whenever a taxpayer files a claim for a tax refund and the refund claim later is found to exceed the final amount allowed by the IRS or a court, a penalty of 20 percent of the disallowed refund results.[42] The penalty is waived if the taxpayer can show a *reasonable basis* for the refund claim (i.e., probably a 20 percent chance that a court would allow the refund). This penalty is meant to discourage the taxpayer from overstating the amount of the refund requested from the IRS. It does not apply to claims for the earned income tax credit.

Civil Fraud Penalty

A 75 percent civil penalty is imposed on any underpayment resulting from **fraud** by the taxpayer who has filed a return.[43] For this penalty, the burden of proof *is on the IRS* to show by a preponderance of the evidence that the taxpayer had a specific intent to evade a tax.

Once the IRS initially has established that fraud occurred, the taxpayer then bears the burden of proof to show by a preponderance of the evidence the portion of the underpayment that is not attributable to fraud.

Although the Code and Regulations do not provide any assistance in ascertaining what constitutes civil fraud, it is clear that mere negligence on the part of the

[42] § 6676.

[43] § 6663. As noted later in the chapter, underpayments traceable to fraudulent acts are not subject to a statute of limitations.

taxpayer (however great) will not suffice. Fraud has been found in cases of manipulations of the books, substantial omissions from income, and erroneous deductions.[44]

EXAMPLE 14

Frank underpaid his income tax by $90,000. The IRS can prove that $60,000 of the underpayment was due to fraud. Frank responds by a preponderance of the evidence that $30,000 of the underpayment was not due to fraud. The civil fraud penalty is $45,000 (75% × $60,000). ■

If the underpayment of tax is partially attributable to negligence and partially attributable to fraud, the fraud penalty is applied first.

Failure to Pay Estimated Taxes

A penalty is imposed for a failure to pay estimated income taxes. The penalty applies to individuals and corporations and is based on the rate of interest in effect for deficiency assessments.[45] The penalty also applies to trusts and certain estates that are required to make estimated tax payments. The penalty is not imposed if the tax due for the year (less amounts withheld and credits) is less than $500 for corporations, $1,000 for all others. For employees, an equal part of withholding is deemed paid on each due date.

Quarterly payments are to be made on or before the fifteenth day of the fourth month (April 15 for a calendar year taxpayer), sixth month, ninth month, and the first month of the following year. Corporations must make the last quarterly payment by the twelfth month of the same year.

An individual's underpayment of estimated tax is the difference between the estimates that were paid and the least of:

- 90 percent of the current-year tax,
- 100 percent of the prior-year tax (the tax year must have been a full 12 months, and a return must have been filed), and
- 90 percent of the tax that would be due on an annualized income computation for the period running through the end of the quarter.

If the taxpayer's prior-year AGI exceeds $150,000, the 100 percent requirement becomes 110 percent.

A corporation's underpayment of estimated tax is the difference between the estimates that were paid and the least of (1) the current-year tax, (2) the prior-year tax, and (3) the tax on an annualized income computation using one of three methods of computation sanctioned by the Code. For the prior-year alternative, (1) the prior tax year must have been a full 12 months, (2) a nonzero tax amount must have been generated for that year, and (3) large corporations (taxable income of $1 million or more in any of the three immediately preceding tax years) can use the alternative only for the first installment of a year.

In computing the penalty, Form 2210 (Underpayment of Estimated Tax by Individuals) or Form 2220 (Underpayment of Estimated Tax by Corporations) is used.

False Information with Respect to Withholding

Withholding from wages is an important element of the Federal income tax system, which is based on a pay-as-you-go approach. One way employees might hope to avoid this withholding would be to falsify the information provided to the employer on Form W–4 (Employee Withholding Allowance Certificate). For example, by

[44] *Dogget v. Comm.*, 60–1 USTC ¶9342, 5 AFTR 2d 1034, 275 F.2d 823 (CA–4, 1960); *Harvey Brodsky*, 21 TCM 578, T.C.Memo. 1962–105; and *Lash v. Comm.*, 57–2 USTC ¶9725, 51 AFTR 492, 245 F.2d 20 (CA–1, 1957).

[45] §§ 6655 (corporations) and 6654 (other taxpayers). Other computations can avoid the penalty. See §§ 6654(d)(2) and (k), 6655(e) and (i).

overstating the number of exemptions, income tax withholdings could be reduced or completely eliminated.

To encourage compliance, a civil penalty of $500 applies when a taxpayer claims withholding allowances based on false information. The criminal penalty for willfully failing to supply information or for willfully supplying false or fraudulent information in connection with wage withholding is an additional fine of up to $1,000 and/or up to one year of imprisonment.[46]

Failure to Make Deposits of Taxes and Overstatements of Deposits

When a business is not doing well or cash-flow problems develop, employers have a great temptation to "borrow" from Uncle Sam. One way this can be done is to fail to pay to the IRS the amounts that have been withheld from the wages of employees for FICA and income tax purposes. The IRS does not appreciate being denied the use of these funds and has a number of weapons at its disposal to discourage the practice.

- A penalty of up to 15 percent of any underdeposited amount not paid, unless the employer can show that the failure is due to reasonable cause and not to willful neglect.[47]
- Various criminal penalties.[48]
- A 100 percent penalty if the employer's actions are willful.[49] The penalty is based on the amount of the tax evaded (i.e., not collected or not accounted for or paid over). Because the penalty is assessable against the "responsible person" of the business, more than one party may be vulnerable (e.g., the president and treasurer of a corporation, and the third-party payroll service of the entity). Although the IRS may assess the penalty against several persons, it cannot collect more than the 100 percent due.
- In addition to these penalties, the actual tax due must be remitted. For instance, an employer remains liable for the employees' income and payroll taxes that should have been paid.

Failure to Provide Information Regarding Tax Shelters

The IRS has identified over two dozen transactions that it regards as "tax shelters." These arrangements, often involving leveraged financing and accelerated interest and cost recovery deductions, allegedly are motivated solely by the desire to reduce taxes and have no business or profit-seeking goals. Over the last two decades, the IRS has struggled with numerous means of identifying taxpayers who use such tax shelters.

A tax shelter organizer must register the shelter with the IRS before any sales are made to investors.[50] A penalty of up to $10,000 is assessed if the required information is not filed with the Service. This includes a description of the shelter and the tax benefits that are being used to attract investors. The shelter organizer must maintain a list of identifying information of all of its investors. Failure to fully and truthfully maintain the list can result in a penalty of up to $100,000 per investment.

Criminal Penalties

In addition to civil fraud penalties, the Code contains numerous criminal sanctions that carry various monetary fines and/or imprisonment. The difference between civil and criminal fraud is often one of degree. Thus, § 7201, dealing with attempts to evade or defeat a tax, contains the following language.

> Any person who *willfully* attempts in any manner to evade or defeat any tax imposed by this title or the payment thereof shall, in addition to other penalties provided by law, be guilty of a felony and, upon

[46] §§ 6682 and 7205.
[47] § 6656.
[48] See, for example, § 7202 (willful failure to collect or pay over a tax).
[49] § 6672.
[50] § 6111.

conviction thereof, shall be fined not more than $100,000 ($500,000 in the case of a corporation), or imprisoned not more than five years, or both, together with the costs of prosecution. [Emphasis added.]

As to the burden of proof, the IRS must show that the taxpayer was guilty of willful evasion "beyond the shadow of any reasonable doubt." Thus, to avoid a criminal tax penalty, the taxpayer needs to create a degree of reasonable doubt as to guilt. To do so, the taxpayer might assert that he or she was confused or ignorant about the application of the tax law or relied on the erroneous advice of a competent tax adviser. Another defense against a criminal tax penalty is the lack of capacity to plan and carry out tax evasion (e.g., mental disease or other medical disorder).

Violations of the Federal criminal code in the context of filing tax returns also may arise from other crimes that are not provided for in the Internal Revenue Code. Examples include:

- Making a false claim against the Federal government.
- Participating in a conspiracy to evade Federal taxes (i.e., in addition to the tax understatement).
- Making a false statement to the Federal government or filing a false document (i.e., perjury).

Statutes of Limitations

LO.7

Recognize and apply the rules governing the statute of limitations on assessments and on refunds.

A **statute of limitations** defines the period of time during which one party may pursue against another party a cause of action or other suit allowed under the governing law. Failure to satisfy any requirement provides the other party with an absolute defense should the statute be invoked. Inequity would result if no limits were placed on such suits. Permitting an extended period of time to elapse between the initiation of a claim and its pursuit could place the defense at a serious disadvantage. Witnesses may have died or disappeared; records or other evidence may have been discarded or destroyed.

Assessment and the Statute of Limitations

In general, any tax that is imposed must be assessed within three years of the filing of the return (or, if later, the unextended due date of the return).[51] Some exceptions to this three-year limitation exist.

- If no return is filed or a fraudulent return is filed, assessments can be made at any time. There is, in effect, no statute of limitations in these cases.
- If a taxpayer omits an amount of gross income in excess of 25 percent of the gross income stated on the return, the statute of limitations is increased to six years. The courts have interpreted this rule as including only items affecting income and not the omission of items affecting deductions, operating losses, or cost of sales.[52] *Gross income* here includes capital gains, but not reduced by capital losses.

EXAMPLE 15

During 2007, Jerry had the following income transactions (all of which were duly reported on his timely filed return).

Gross receipts		$ 480,000
Cost of sales		(400,000)
Net business income		$ 80,000
Capital gains and losses		
Capital gain	$ 36,000	
Capital loss	(12,000)	24,000
Total income		$ 104,000

[51] §§ 6501(a) and (b)(1).

[52] *The Colony, Inc. v. Comm.*, 58–2 USTC ¶9593, 1 AFTR 2d 1894, 78 S.Ct. 1033 (USSC, 1958).

Jerry retains your services in 2012 as a tax consultant. It seems that he inadvertently omitted some income on his 2007 return, and he wants to know if he is "safe" under the statute of limitations. The six-year statute of limitations would apply, putting Jerry in a vulnerable position only if he omitted more than $129,000 on his 2007 return [($480,000 + $36,000) × 25%]. ■

- The statute of limitations may be extended for a fixed period of time by mutual consent of the IRS and the taxpayer. This extension covers a definite period and is made by signing Form 872 (Consent to Extend the Time to Assess Tax). The extension is frequently requested by the IRS when the lapse of the statutory period is imminent and the audit has not been completed. This practice often is applied to audits of corporate taxpayers and explains why many corporations have more than three "open years."

Special rules relating to assessment are applicable in the following situations.

- Taxpayers may request a prompt assessment of the tax, forcing the IRS to examine a return.
- The assessment period for capital loss and net operating loss carrybacks generally relates to the determination of tax in the year of the loss or unused credit rather than in the carryback years.

If the IRS issues a statutory notice of deficiency to the taxpayer, who then files a Tax Court petition, the statute is suspended on both the deficiency assessment and the period of collection until 60 days after the decision of the Tax Court becomes final. The statute also is suspended when the taxpayer is "financially disabled"; that is, the taxpayer has been rendered unable to manage his or her financial affairs by a physical or mental impairment that is likely to last for a year or more or to cause the taxpayer's death. The statute continues to run if another party is authorized to act for the taxpayer in financial matters.[53]

Refund Claims and the Statute of Limitations

To receive a tax refund, the taxpayer is required to file a valid refund claim. The official form for filing a claim is Form 1040X for individuals and Form 1120X for corporations. If the refund claim does not meet certain procedural requirements, the IRS may reject the claim with no consideration of its merit.

- A separate claim must be filed for each taxable period.
- The grounds for the claim must be stated in sufficient detail.
- The statement of facts must be sufficient to permit the IRS to evaluate the merits of the claim.

The refund claim must be filed within three years of the filing of the tax return or within two years following the payment of the tax if this period expires on a later date.[54]

EXAMPLE 16

On March 10, 2010, Louise filed her 2009 income tax return reflecting a tax of $10,500. On July 11, 2011, she filed an amended 2009 return showing an additional $3,000 of tax that was then paid. On May 19, 2013, she filed a claim for refund of $4,500.

Assuming that Louise is correct in claiming a refund, how much tax can she recover? The answer is only $3,000. Because the claim was not filed within the three-year statute of limitations period, Louise is limited to the amount she actually paid during the last two years. ■

[53] Suspension of the statute of limitations has been allowed by some courts when attributable to a taxpayer disability or IRS misconduct. See *Brockamp v. Comm.*, 97–1 USTC ¶50,216, 79 AFTR 2d 97–986, 117 S.Ct. 849 (USSC, 1997). §§ 6501(c)(4) and 6511(h).

[54] §§ 6511(a) and 6513(a).

Special rules are available for claims relating to bad debts and worthless securities. A seven-year period of limitations applies in lieu of the normal three-year rule.[55] The extended period is provided in recognition of the inherent difficulty of identifying the exact year in which a bad debt or security becomes worthless.

17.2 The Tax Profession and Tax Ethics

LO.8

Summarize the legal and ethical guidelines that apply to those engaged in tax practice.

Society and its governments expect taxpayers to comply with the letter and the spirit of the tax laws. Tax audits and penalties encourage a high degree of technical tax conformity, but the proper functioning of a voluntary tax compliance system also depends on the ethics of the taxpayer and the tax adviser.

The Treasury and various professional organizations have issued ethical guidelines that are relevant to the tax profession. Professional licensing agencies also are likely to require tax professionals to receive training in ethics to obtain initial certification and to remain in good standing over time.

The Tax Professional

Who is a tax practitioner? What services does the practitioner perform? A number of different groups apply constraints on the way a tax professional conducts his or her practice.

To begin defining the term *tax practitioner*, one should consider whether the individual is qualified to practice before the IRS. Generally, practice before the IRS is limited to CPAs, attorneys, and persons who have been enrolled to practice before the IRS [**enrolled agents (EAs)**]. In most cases, EAs are admitted to practice only if they pass an examination administered by the IRS. CPAs and attorneys are not required to take this examination and are automatically admitted to practice if they are in good standing with the appropriate licensing board regulating their profession.

Persons other than CPAs, attorneys, and EAs may be allowed to practice before the IRS in limited situations. **Circular 230** ("Regulations Governing Practice before the Internal Revenue Service") issued by the Treasury Department permits certain notable exceptions.

- A taxpayer may always represent himself or herself. A person may also represent a member of the immediate family if no compensation is received for such services.
- Regular full-time employees may represent their employers.
- Corporations may be represented by any of their bona fide officers.
- Partnerships may be represented by any of the partners.
- Trusts, receiverships, guardianships, or estates may be represented by their trustees, receivers, guardians, or administrators or executors, respectively.
- A taxpayer may be represented by the registered tax return preparer who prepared the return for the year in question. See the following discussion.

EXAMPLE 17

Joel is currently undergoing an audit by the IRS for tax years 2011 and 2012. He prepared the 2011 return himself but paid AddCo, a registered tax return preparer who is not a CPA or an attorney, to prepare the 2012 return. AddCo may represent Joel only in matters concerning 2012. Joel could, of course, represent himself, or he could retain a CPA, an attorney, or an EA to represent him in matters concerning both years under examination. ■

All nonattorney tax practitioners should avoid becoming engaged in activities that constitute the *unauthorized practice of law*. If they engage in this practice (e.g., by drafting legal documents for a third party), action could be instituted against

[55] § 6511(d)(1).

them in the appropriate state court by the local or state bar association. What actions constitute the unauthorized practice of law is largely undefined, though, and such charges are filed only rarely today.

Licensing Tax Preparers

There are no minimum education or experience requirements for those who file Federal tax returns for others. But the IRS does require that all paid tax return preparers, including CPAs and attorneys, obtain a Preparer Tax Identification Number (PTIN) before they assist taxpayers with returns for a new filing season.

For most preparers, the fee to obtain PTINs is about $65 per year. This amount is in addition to any other professional, certification, or licensing fee the preparer might be required to pay (e.g., annual dues to maintain a CPA certificate).

Preparers (other than CPAs, attorneys, and enrolled agents) must pass an annual qualifying exam, designed to evaluate their familiarity with new tax laws and filing requirements that will apply for the filing season.

Efforts to "register" or "certify" tax preparers have been advocated for at least three decades, but to no avail. Increased regulation developed to govern other aspects of financial and consumer affairs led to the PTIN system effective for the 2011 filing season. The year's PTIN usually is obtained online, and confirmation of the preparer's identity, prior registrations, and testing status is needed before the PTIN is issued or renewed.

Upon receiving a PTIN, the tax professional can refer to himself or herself as a "registered tax return preparer." All of the provisions of Circular 230 (discussed below) apply to the registered preparer, including those regarding advertising and solicitation of clients. The PTIN holder can neither use the term *certified* in describing this designation nor assert that the IRS endorses his or her practice in any way.

Holding a PTIN does not by itself authorize the tax preparer to carry out tax planning services. This means that communications between the PTIN holder and his or her client are not privileged and confidential (as discussed later in the chapter).

A registered tax return preparer (who is not also a CPA or an attorney) may represent the taxpayer for whom a signed return was prepared before IRS revenue agents, but not before appeals officers, revenue officers, or IRS counsel.

The IRS may use PTIN data to identify preparers who commit a pattern of errors or who participate in fraudulent actions. With more than 1 million paid preparers at work in any filing season, the IRS must use an outside consultant to manage the registration and testing functions.

ETHICS & EQUITY Who Cheats and Why?

Tax compliance for business income of the Form 1040, Schedules C, E, and F, tends to be much lower than that for the rest of individuals' taxable income. Because of the use of Forms W-2 and 1099, the reporting of taxable transactions by wage earners and many investors is fairly thorough and tax compliance rates are high. But business income often entails the use of cash, or it is not reported to the IRS under current disclosure rules; so tax cheating may be more common on that part of the tax return.

A recent analysis of Schedule C data brings up another motivation for high or low compliance with the tax laws. Occupations (reported by industry codes) in which "integrity" is of higher value might be expected to show higher tax compliance rates. Integrity may be defined as an activity involving a public or professional reputation or one exposed to professional sanctions such as a loss of license to practice.

Assume that the importance (or lack thereof) of one's business integrity affects the taxpayer's willingness to comply with the tax law. List three occupations where this criterion might lead to high tax compliance. To low tax compliance.

IRS Rules Governing Tax Practice

Circular 230 prescribes the rules governing practice before the IRS. Following are some of the most important rules imposed on CPAs, attorneys, EAs, and all others who prepare tax returns for compensation.

- A prohibition against taking an undisclosed position on a tax return unless there is a *reasonable basis* that the position will be sustained on its merits. Generally, this standard is met when a person knowledgeable in the tax law would conclude that the position has a greater than 20 percent probability of prevailing in the court of final jurisdiction.
- A requirement that nonfrivolous tax return positions that fail the reasonable basis standard be disclosed in the return (i.e., using Form 8275).
- A prohibition against taking frivolous tax return positions. A **frivolous return** is a return with a less than 5 percent chance of being sustained by the court of final jurisdiction.

THE BIG PICTURE

EXAMPLE 18

Return to the facts of *The Big Picture* on p. 17-1. Campbell wants to claim the research credit for a testing program that it has developed, to be used by its in-house engineers before a new GPS app is released to the public. Based on their tax research on this issue, the members of your firm's tax department have severe doubts about taking the credit for this program. Your firm's position is that there is a one-in-four chance the courts would allow Campbell's credit.

Claiming the credit fails the reasonable basis standard of Circular 230. Therefore, if Campbell claims the credit, you must insist that its Form 1120 include a separate disclosure on the return, probably using Form 8275.

- A requirement to inform clients of penalties likely to apply to return positions and of ways such penalties can be avoided.
- A requirement to make known to a client any error or omission the client may have made on any return or other document submitted to the IRS.
- A duty to submit, in a timely fashion, records or information lawfully requested by the IRS.
- An obligation to exercise *due diligence* and to use the *best practices* of the tax profession in preparing, reviewing, and filing tax returns accurately. Best practices include, for instance, the tax professional's use of appropriate software, a thorough office procedure for receiving and processing client tax returns, and the execution of a plan for continuing education in technical tax matters.
- A restriction against unreasonably delaying the prompt disposition of any matter before the IRS.
- A restriction against charging the client a contingent fee for preparing an original return, although such a fee can be charged when the tax professional deals with an audited or amended return.
- A restriction against charging the client "an unconscionable fee" for representation before the IRS.
- A restriction against representing clients with conflicting interests.

Nothing prevents the "unlicensed" tax practitioner from advertising his or her specialty, directly soliciting clients, or engaging in other actions that are regulated by the standards of conduct controlling CPAs, attorneys, and EAs. Nevertheless, some constraints do govern all parties engaged in rendering tax returns for the general public.

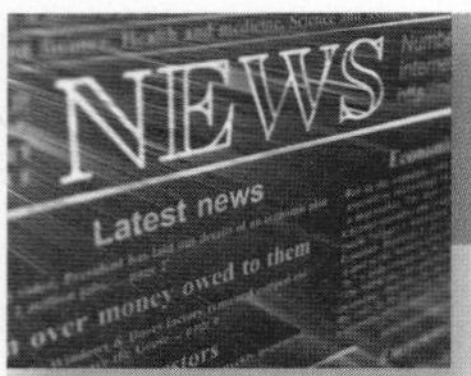

TAX IN THE NEWS Have You Been Drafted by the IRS?

With the accumulation of tax preparer penalties over the years, many tax professionals now believe that they have been "deputized" by the IRS and that, as a consequence, their ability to advise and represent their clients in an aggressive manner is limited. Has the potential for providing effective tax planning diminished as a result of the increased regulation of the tax and accounting profession, the additional disclosures the tax practitioner must make to the client and to the government, and the severity of preparer penalties?

Not so, according to the IRS. Its objective is to "ensure that attorneys, accountants, and other tax practitioners adhere to professional standards and follow the law." Here are some specific items from the IRS's plan to raise the level of tax ethics found in tax practice today.

- Strengthen ties with practitioners to achieve the highest level of professional integrity and improve tax compliance.
- Establish and communicate clear, robust, current, and meaningful standards of conduct for tax practitioners.
- Establish and maintain a vigorous, targeted, and effective system of practitioner oversight.
- Establish and administer a fair, diligent, and effective system of sanctions for practitioners who fail to observe standards of conduct.

- A person who holds himself or herself out to the general public as possessing tax expertise could be liable to the client if services are performed in a negligent manner. At a minimum, the practitioner is liable for any interest and penalties the client incurs because of the practitioner's failure to exercise due professional care.
- If a practitioner agrees to perform a service (e.g., prepare a tax return) and subsequently fails to do so, the aggrieved party may be in a position to obtain damages for breach of contract.
- All persons who prepare tax returns or refund claims for a fee must sign as preparer of the return.[56] Failure to comply with this requirement could result in a penalty assessment against the preparer.
- The Code prescribes various penalties for the deliberate filing of false or fraudulent returns. These felonies apply to a tax practitioner who either was aware of the situation or actually perpetrated the false information or the fraud.[57]
- Penalties are prescribed for tax practitioners who disclose to third parties information they have received from clients in connection with the preparation of tax returns or the rendering of tax advice.[58]

EXAMPLE 19

Sarah operates a tax return preparation service. Her brother-in-law, Butch, has just taken a job as a life insurance salesperson. To help Butch find contacts, Sarah furnishes him with a list of the names and addresses of all of her clients who report AGI of $50,000 or more. Sarah is subject to the disclosure penalty. ■

Circular 230 is administered by the IRS Office of Professional Responsibility (OPR). Among other duties, the OPR carries out disciplinary hearings and issues penalties, such as fines and licensing restrictions and retractions, relative to tax preparers. The accountancy board of most states includes a member of the OPR, so a Circular 230 violation could lead to the loss or suspension of a CPA's license at the state level as well.

[56] Reg. § 1.6065–1(b)(1). Rev.Rul. 84–3, 1984–1 C.B. 264, contains a series of examples illustrating when a person is deemed to be a preparer of the return.

[57] § 7206.

[58] § 7216.

Preparer Penalties

The Code provides penalties to discourage improper actions by tax practitioners. **Tax preparer** penalties are assessed on any person who prepares for compensation, or engages employees to prepare, a substantial portion of any Federal tax return or refund claim. The following individuals are exempt from the preparer penalties.

- An IRS employee.
- A volunteer who prepares tax returns in a government assistance effort such as Tax Counseling for the Elderly (TCE) or the Volunteer Income Tax Assistance (VITA) program.
- An employee preparing a return for the employer.
- A fiduciary preparing a return for a trust or an estate.
- An individual who provides only data processing, typing, reproduction, or other assistance in preparing a return.

The preparer penalties are applied on a "one preparer per firm, per filing position" basis, so penalty dollars can compound quickly within the tax practice. Some of the most important tax preparer penalties include the following.

1. A penalty for understatements due to taking an **unreasonable position** on a tax return.[59] The penalty is imposed if the tax position:

   - Is not disclosed on the return and there was no *substantial authority* (i.e., a greater than 40 percent chance) that the tax position would be sustained by its merits on a final court review; or
   - Is disclosed on the return and there was not a *reasonable basis* (i.e., probably a 20 percent chance) for the position.

   The penalty is computed as the greater of $1,000 or one-half of the income of the practitioner that is attributable to the return or claim that violated the conduct standard. The penalty can be avoided by showing reasonable cause and by showing that the preparer acted in good faith.

EXAMPLE 20

Josie is the tax return preparer for Hal's Form 1040. The return includes a deduction that has a 60% chance of being sustained on its merits because it is contrary to an applicable tax Regulation. If a court denies the deduction, Josie is not assessed a § 6694 penalty.

Now assume that Hal's deduction has a 30% chance of being sustained on its merits. If a court denies the deduction, Josie is assessed a § 6694 penalty (unless the disputed position was disclosed on the return with a Form 8275–R). The amount of the penalty is the greater of $1,000 or one-half of Josie's fees for preparing Hal's Form 1040.

What if Hal's deduction has a 15% chance of being sustained on its merits? If a court denies the deduction, Josie is assessed a § 6694 penalty (even if the disputed position was disclosed on the return with a Form 8275–R). The amount of the penalty is the greater of $1,000 or one-half of Josie's fees for preparing Hal's Form 1040. ■

2. A penalty for willful and reckless conduct.[60] The penalty applies if any part of the understatement of a taxpayer's liability on a return or claim for refund is due to:

   - The preparer's willful attempt to understate the taxpayer's tax liability in any manner.
   - Any reckless or intentional disregard of IRS rules or regulations by the preparer.

   The penalty is computed as the greater of $5,000 or one-half of the income of the practitioner that is attributable to the return or claim that violated the

[59] § 6694(a). For the most part, these standards match those that apply to the taxpayer penalties of § 6662(d). Stricter disclosure standards apply for tax shelter items and reportable transactions. § 6662A.

[60] § 6694(b).

conduct standard. Adequate disclosure can avoid the penalty. If both this penalty and the unreasonable position penalty (see item 1) apply to the same return, the reckless conduct penalty is reduced by the amount of the penalty for unreasonable positions.

3. A $1,000 ($10,000 for the tax returns of corporations) penalty per return or document is imposed against persons who aid in the preparation of returns or other documents they know (or have reason to believe) would result in an understatement of the tax liability of another person.[61] Thus, this penalty also applies to those other than the preparer of the actual tax return (e.g., unpaid advisers, attorneys, corporate officers and executives, and tax shelter promoters). Clerical assistance in the return preparation process does not incur the penalty.

   If this penalty applies, neither the unreasonable position penalty (item 1) nor the willful and reckless conduct penalty (item 2) is assessed.
4. A $50 penalty is assessed against the preparer for failure to sign a return or furnish the preparer's PTIN.[62]
5. A $50 penalty is assessed if the preparer fails to furnish a copy of the return or claim for refund to the taxpayer.
6. A $500 penalty may be assessed if a preparer endorses or otherwise negotiates a check for refund of tax issued to the taxpayer.

Privileged Communications

Communications between an attorney and client have long been protected from disclosure to other parties (such as the IRS and the tax courts). A similar privilege of confidentiality extends to tax advice between a taxpayer and tax practitioner, as we used that term previously. The privilege is not available for matters involving criminal charges or questions brought by other agencies, such as the Securities and Exchange Commission.[63] Nor is it allowed in matters involving promoting or participating in tax shelters.

A taxpayer likely will want to protect documents such as the tax adviser's research memo detailing the strengths and weaknesses of a tax return position or a conversation about an appeals strategy. The confidentiality privilege should be interpreted in the following manner.

- The privilege often is available when an attorney or a CPA completes a tax return for the taxpayer. But some courts have restricted the attorney's privilege in this context on the grounds that the tax professional is conducting accounting work, not offering legal advice. Others assert that the confidentiality privilege is waived when the taxpayer discloses financial data on the tax return. To the contrary, if the tax professional is providing traditional legal advice to help the client decide what to disclose on a tax return, the privilege should be available.
- The privilege for CPAs applies only to tax advice. Attorneys still can exercise the privilege concerning advice rendered as a business consultant, an estate/financial planner, etc.
- About a third of the states offer a similar confidentiality privilege for CPAs, but outside the Federal tax appeals process, protection is not yet the norm.
- The privilege is not available for tax accrual workpapers prepared as part of an independent financial audit.

AICPA Statements on Standards for Tax Services

Tax practitioners who are CPAs, attorneys, or EAs must abide by the codes or canons of professional ethics applicable to their respective professions. The various codes and canons have much in common with and parallel the standards of conduct set forth in Circular 230.[64]

[61] § 6701.
[62] § 6695.
[63] § 7525(a)(1).

[64] For an additional discussion of tax ethics, see Raabe, Whittenburg, Sanders, and Sawyers, *Federal Tax Research*, 9th ed. (Cengage Learning/South-Western, 2012), especially Chapters 1 and 14.

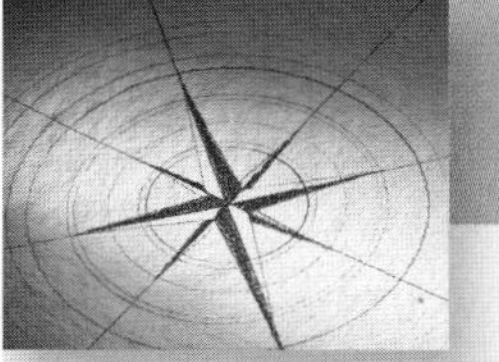

ETHICS & EQUITY Where Does My Cost Saving Go?

As is the case in many other U.S. industries, tax return preparers have been outsourcing some of their operations to lower-cost locations overseas. By some estimates, over 2 million state and Federal tax returns are completed in India alone, and such estimates are probably understated because of a lack of disclosure by tax practitioners. Tax and consulting firms defend the practice as a cost-saving measure and contend that the confidentiality of taxpayer data is not compromised.

AICPA ethics rules (applying both to tax return preparation and other work) require:

- Notice to the taxpayer before any data are shared with a third-party service provider.
- Acceptance by the practitioner of full responsibility for the third party's work (i.e., as to quality and security).

Should any cost saving that outsourcing provides be passed on to the client in the form of lower fees? Do you expect that this will occur?

The AICPA has issued a series of Statements on Standards for Tax Services (SSTSs). The Statements are enforceable standards of professional practice for AICPA members working in state or Federal tax practice. The SSTSs comprise part of the AICPA's Code of Professional Conduct. Together with the provisions of Circular 230 and the penalty provisions of the Code, the SSTSs make up a set of guidelines for the conduct of the tax practitioner who is also a CPA. Other sources of professional ethics are issued by state bar associations and CPA societies, the American Bar Association, and the associations of enrolled agents.

Key provisions of some of the SSTSs are presented next.

Statement No. 1: Tax Return Positions

Under certain circumstances, a CPA may take a position that is contrary to that taken by the IRS. To do so, however, the CPA must have a good faith belief that the position has a realistic possibility (i.e., probably a one-in-three chance) of being sustained administratively or judicially on its merits if challenged. If the taxing authority (e.g., a state revenue statute) uses a lower standard than that of a *realistic possibility*, this higher standard still applies.

The client should be fully advised of the risks involved and the penalties that may result if the position taken on the tax return is not successful. The client should also be informed that disclosure on the return may avoid some or all of these penalties.

In no case, though, should the CPA exploit the audit lottery. That is, the CPA should not take a questionable position based on the probabilities that the client's return will not be chosen by the IRS for audit. Furthermore, the CPA should not "load" the return with questionable items in the hope that they might aid the client in a later settlement negotiation with the IRS.

THE BIG PICTURE

EXAMPLE 21

Return to the facts of *The Big Picture* on p. 17-1. Campbell's new marketing program solicits the opinions of a virtual focus group to test ideas for new products. Based on your tax research, you believe that because the program relies on innovative algorithms that use online contacts to carry out the focus group activities, the program might qualify for the Federal income tax research credit even though it involves marketing research that is excluded from the credit under § 41(d)(4). Still, you believe that there is only a 30% chance the courts would allow the credit.

You meet with Shelly Watkins, Campbell's tax director, to convey the results of your research. Watkins agrees that the research credit would be turned down by an IRS auditor, but she says that Campbell never has been audited and that it is not likely to be audited as long as its legal structure and income levels do not significantly change. Watkins believes that Campbell's corporate officers will sign off on the credit, given both the firm's weak cash position and the low chances that the item will be discovered.

As a CPA, you must inform Campbell that claiming the credit for this activity does not have a realistic possibility of being sustained on its merits and that certain penalties will be assessed if the credit is claimed and not further disclosed on the return.

Whether the credit is claimed is the decision of your client, the taxpayer. But if Campbell wants to claim the credit without the required additional disclosures, you must terminate your engagement with Campbell, under the SSTS and other AICPA provisions.

Statement No. 2: Questions on Returns

A CPA should make a reasonable effort to obtain from the client, and provide, appropriate answers to all questions on a tax return before signing as preparer. Reasonable grounds may exist for omitting an answer.

- The information is not readily available, and the answer is not significant in amount in computing the tax.
- The meaning of the question as it applies to a particular situation is genuinely uncertain.
- The answer to the question is voluminous.

The fact that an answer to a question could prove disadvantageous to the client does not justify omitting the answer.

Statement No. 3: Procedural Aspects of Preparing Returns

In preparing a return, a CPA may in good faith rely without verification on information furnished by the client or by third parties. However, the CPA should make reasonable inquiries if the information appears to be incorrect, incomplete, or inconsistent. In this regard, the CPA should refer to the client's returns for prior years whenever appropriate.

EXAMPLE 22

A CPA normally can take a client's word for the validity of dependency exemptions. But suppose a recently divorced client wants to claim his three children as dependents when he does not have custody. You must act in accordance with § 152(e)(2) in preparing the return, and this will require evidence of a waiver by the custodial parent. Without this waiver, you should not claim the dependency exemptions on your client's tax return. ■

EXAMPLE 23

While preparing Sunni's income tax return for 2012, you review her income tax return for 2011. In comparing the dividend income reported on the 2011 Schedule B with that received in 2012, you note a significant decrease. Further investigation reveals the variation is due to a stock sale in 2012 that was unknown to you until now. Thus, the review of the 2011 return has unearthed a transaction that should be reported on the 2012 return. ■

If the Code or Regulations require certain types of verification (as is the case with travel and entertainment expenditures), the CPA must advise the client of these rules. Further, inquiry must be made to ascertain whether the client has complied with the verification requirements.

Statement No. 4: Estimates

A CPA may prepare a tax return using estimates received from a taxpayer if it is impracticable to obtain exact data. The estimates must be reasonable under the facts and circumstances as known to the CPA. When estimates are used, they should be presented in such a manner as to avoid the implication of greater accuracy than exists.

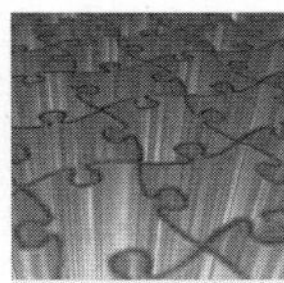

CONCEPT SUMMARY 17.1

Tax Profession and Ethics

1. The Internal Revenue Service (IRS) enforces the tax laws of the United States. Its size and form of organization reflect its various responsibilities relative to taxpayer interaction, litigation, and collection, as well as its internal functions.
2. The IRS issues various pronouncements in communicating its position on certain tax issues. These pronouncements promote the uniform enforcement of the tax law among taxpayers and among the internal divisions of the IRS. Taxpayers should seek such rulings and memoranda when the nature or magnitude of a pending transaction requires a high degree of certainty in the planning process.
3. IRS audits can take several forms. Taxpayers are selected for audit based on the probable net dollar return to the Treasury from the process. Offers in compromise and closing agreements can be a useful means of completing an audit without resorting to litigation.
4. Certain IRS personnel are empowered to consider the hazards of litigation in developing a settlement with the taxpayer during the audit process.
5. The IRS pays interest to taxpayers on overpaid taxes, starting essentially 45 days after the due date of the return, in amounts tied to the Federal short-term rate. Interest paid to the IRS on underpayments is similarly based on the Federal rate, starting essentially on the due date of the return. Interest for both purposes is compounded daily.
6. The Treasury assesses penalties when the taxpayer fails to file a required tax return or pay a tax. Penalties also are assessed when an inaccurate return is filed due to negligence or other disregard of IRS rules. Tax preparers are subject to penalties for assisting a taxpayer in filing an inaccurate return, failing to follow IRS rules in an appropriate manner, or mishandling taxpayer data or funds.
7. Statutes of limitations place outer boundaries on the timing and amounts of proposed amendments to completed tax returns that can be made by the taxpayer or the IRS.
8. Tax practitioners must operate under constraints imposed on them by codes of ethics or pertinent professional societies and by Treasury Circular 230. These rules also define the parties who can represent others in an IRS proceeding.
9. A limited privilege of confidentiality exists between the taxpayer and tax preparer.

Statement No. 5: Recognition of Administrative Proceeding or Court Decision

As facts may vary from year to year, so may the position taken by a CPA. In these types of situations, the CPA is not bound by an administrative or judicial proceeding involving a prior year.

EXAMPLE 24

Upon audit of Ramon Corporation's income tax return for 2010, the IRS disallowed $78,000 of the $600,000 salary paid to its president and sole shareholder on the grounds that it is unreasonable. You are the CPA who has been engaged to prepare Ramon's income tax return for 2012. Again, the corporation paid its president a salary of $600,000 and chose to deduct this amount. Because you are not bound for 2012 by what the IRS deemed reasonable for 2010, the full $600,000 can be claimed as a salary deduction, assuming that you and Ramon both believe that the entire salary represents reasonable compensation. ■

Statement No. 6: Knowledge of Error

A CPA should promptly advise a client upon learning of an error in a previously filed return or upon learning of a client's failure to file a required return. The advice can be oral or written and should include a recommendation of the corrective measures, if any, to be taken. The error or other omission should not be disclosed to the IRS without the client's consent.

If the past error is material and is not corrected by the client, the CPA may be unable to prepare the current year's tax return. This situation might occur if the error has a carryover effect that prevents the CPA from determining the correct tax liability for the current year.

EXAMPLE 25

In preparing a client's 2012 income tax return, you discover that final inventory for 2011 was materially understated. First, you should advise the client to file an amended return for 2011 reflecting the correct amount in final inventory. Second, if the client refuses to make this adjustment, you should consider whether the error will preclude you from preparing a substantially correct return for 2012. Because this will probably be the case (the final inventory for 2011 becomes the beginning inventory for 2012), you should withdraw from the engagement.

If the client corrects the error, you may proceed with the preparation of the tax return for 2012. You must assure yourself that the error is not repeated on the return that you are preparing. ■

Statement No. 7: Advice to Clients

In providing tax advice to a client, the CPA must use judgment to ensure that the advice reflects professional competence and appropriately serves the client's needs. No standard format or guidelines can be established to cover all situations and circumstances involving written or oral advice by the CPA.

The CPA may communicate with the client when subsequent developments affect previous advice on significant matters. However, the CPA cannot be expected to assume responsibility for initiating the communication, unless he or she is assisting a client in implementing procedures or plans associated with the advice. The CPA may undertake this obligation by specific agreement with the client.

The ethical considerations involved in tax practice are set forth in Concept Summary 17.1 on the preceding page.

17.3 Tax Planning

Strategies in Seeking an Administrative Ruling

Determination Letters

In many instances, the request for an advance ruling or a determination letter from the IRS is a necessary or desirable planning strategy. The receipt of a favorable ruling or determination reduces the risk associated with a transaction when the tax results are in doubt. For example, the initiation or amendment of a qualified pension or profit sharing plan should be accompanied by a determination letter. Otherwise, upon subsequent IRS review, the plan may not qualify, and the tax deductibility of contributions to the plan will be disallowed. In some instances, the potential tax effects of a transaction are so numerous and of such consequence that proceeding without a ruling is unwise.

Letter Rulings

In some cases, it may not be necessary or desirable to request an advance ruling. For example, it generally is not desirable to request a ruling if the tax results are doubtful and the company is committed to complete the transaction in any event. If a ruling is requested and negotiations with the IRS indicate that an adverse determination will be forthcoming, it is usually possible to have the ruling request withdrawn. However, the National Office of the IRS may forward its findings, along with a copy of the ruling request, to local IRS personnel. In determining the advisability of a ruling request, the taxpayer should consider the potential exposure of other items in the tax returns of all "open years."

A ruling request may delay the consummation of a transaction if the issues are novel or complex. Frequently, a ruling can be processed within six months, although in some instances a delay of a year or more may be encountered.

Technical Advice Memoranda

A taxpayer in the process of contesting a proposed deficiency with the Appeals Division should consider requesting a technical advice memorandum from the IRS. If the memorandum is favorable to the taxpayer, it is binding on the Appeals Division. The request may be particularly appropriate when the practitioner believes that the agent or Appeals Division has been too literal in interpreting an IRS ruling.

Considerations in Handling an IRS Audit

As a general rule, a taxpayer should attempt to settle disputes at the earliest possible stage of the administrative appeal process. It usually is possible to limit the scope of the examination by furnishing pertinent information requested by the agent. Extraneous information or fortuitous comments may result in the opening of new issues and should be avoided. Agents usually appreciate prompt and efficient responses to inquiries, because their performance may in part be judged by their ability to close or settle assigned cases.

To the extent possible, it is advisable to conduct the investigation of field audits in the practitioner's office, rather than the client's office. This procedure permits greater control over the audit investigation and facilitates the agent's review and prompt closure of the case.

Many practitioners believe that it is generally not advisable to have clients present at the scheduled conferences with the agent, because the client may give emotional or gratuitous comments that impair prompt settlement. If the client is not present, however, he or she should be advised of the status of negotiations. The client makes the final decision on any proposed settlement.

ETHICS & EQUITY Should the Client Attend an Audit?

Whether the client should be present during an audit is a matter of some debate. Certainly, the client's absence tends to slow down the negotiating process because the taxpayer must make all final decisions on settlement terms and is the best source of information for open questions of fact. Nevertheless, most practitioners discourage their clients from attending audits or conferences with the Appeals Division involving an income tax dispute. Ignorance of the law and of the conventions of the audit process can make the taxpayer a "loose cannon" that can do more harm than good if unchecked. All too often, a client will "say too much" in the presence of a government official.

In reality, though, by discouraging clients from attending the audit, practitioners may be interfering with the IRS's function of gathering evidence, depending on what precisely the taxpayer is being prevented from saying. To many practitioners, a "wrong" answer is one that increases taxes, not one that misrepresents the truth. A popular saying among tax advisers is "Don't tell me more than I want to know." Although this philosophy is supportable under various professional codes of conduct, it is hardly defensible in the larger scheme of things.

In your opinion, under what circumstances should the client attend such a session? To what degree should the tax professional "coach" the client as to how to behave in that setting? Or do a taxpayer's rights include the right to increase his or her own tax liability?

Preparing for the Audit

The tax professional must prepare thoroughly for the audit or Appeals proceeding. Practitioners often cite the following steps as critical to such preparations. Carrying out a level of due diligence in preparing for the proceeding is part of the tax professional's responsibility in representing the client.

- Make certain that both sides agree on the issues to be resolved in the audit. The goal here is to limit the agent's list of open issues.

- Identify all of the facts underlying the issues in dispute, including those favorable to the IRS. Gather evidence to support the taxpayer's position, and evaluate the evidence supporting the other side.
- Research current tax law authorities as they bear on the facts and open issues. Remember that the IRS agent is bound only by Supreme Court cases and IRS pronouncements. Determine the degree of discretion that the IRS is likely to have in disposing of the case.
- Prepare a list of points supporting and contradicting the taxpayer's case. Include both minor points bearing little weight and core principles. Short research memos also will be useful in the discussion with the agent. Points favoring the taxpayer should be mentioned during the discussion and "entered into the record."
- Prepare tax and interest computations showing the effects of points that are in dispute so that the consequences of closing or compromising an issue can be readily determined.
- Determine a "litigation point" (i.e., at which the taxpayer will withdraw from further audit negotiation and pursue the case in the courts). This position should be based on the dollars of tax, interest, and penalty involved; the chances of prevailing in various trial-level courts; and other strategies discussed with the taxpayer. One must have an "end game" strategy for the audit, and thorough tax research is critical in developing that position in this context.

Offers in Compromise

Both parties to a tax dispute may find a compromise offer useful because it conclusively settles all of the issues covered by the agreement and may include a favorable payment schedule for the taxpayer.

On the other hand, several attributes of an offer in compromise may work to the detriment of the taxpayer. Just as the IRS no longer can raise new issues as part of the audit proceedings against the taxpayer, he or she cannot contest or appeal any such agreement. As part of the offer process, the taxpayer must disclose all relevant finances and resources, including details he or she might not want the government to know, and an up-front down payment will be due. Furthermore, both parties are bound to the filing positions established by the compromise for five tax years, a level of inflexibility that may work against a taxpayer whose circumstances change over time.

Documentation Issues

The tax practitioner's workpapers should include all research memoranda, and a list of resolved and unresolved issues should be continually updated during the course of the IRS audit. Occasionally, agents request access to excessive amounts of accounting data to engage in a so-called fishing expedition. Providing blanket access to working papers should be avoided. Workpapers should be reviewed carefully to minimize opportunities for the agent to raise new issues not otherwise apparent. It is generally advisable to provide the agent with copies of specific workpapers upon request.

In unusual situations, a Special Agent may appear to gather evidence in the investigation of possible criminal fraud. When this occurs, the taxpayer should be advised to seek legal counsel to determine the extent of his or her cooperation in providing information to the agent. Further, it is frequently desirable for the tax adviser to consult his or her own personal legal counsel in such situations. If the taxpayer receives a Revenue Agent's Report, it generally indicates that the IRS has decided not to initiate criminal proceedings. The IRS usually does not take any action on a tax deficiency until the criminal matter has been resolved. If, for whatever reasons, the criminal action is dropped, the 75 percent civil fraud penalty still can be assessed.

Statute of Limitations

Extending the Statute

The IRS requests an extension of the statute of limitations when it finds that there is insufficient time to complete an audit or appellate review. The taxpayer is not compelled to agree to the extension request and may be averse to giving the IRS more time. But adverse consequences can result if the taxpayer denies the IRS request.

EXAMPLE 26

Although the statute of limitations governing Thornton's tax return is scheduled to expire in 15 days, the IRS has requested an extension for another 60 days. It wants to complete a more thorough investigation into a disputed $50,000 deduction. If Thornton refuses to agree to the extension, the IRS likely will disallow the entire deduction. However, if Thornton agrees to the extension, all or part of the deduction may be salvaged. ■

A disadvantage of extending the statute is that the IRS sometimes can raise new issues during the extension period. However, the taxpayer can take the following protective measures as a condition to agreeing to the extension.

- Shorten the extension period requested before signing the Form 872. This will reduce the chance that the IRS will find and investigate new issues.
- Restrict the scope of the issues covered by the extension (e.g., extend the period only as to the computation of cost of goods sold).
- Instead of Form 872, use a Form 872–A. This allows for an open-ended termination date of the extension. Consequently, when the examination of a disputed issue is completed, the taxpayer can request that the IRS close off the extension. This reduces the chances that the IRS will find and pursue any new issues.

Prompt Assessment

The "prompt assessment" approach forces the IRS to conduct some sort of an examination of a return. Although most taxpayers are unlikely to volunteer for an audit, the procedure is attractive in several circumstances.

- An estate or a trust (Chapters 18–20) is being terminated, and the executor or trustee needs some assurance that the entity's tax affairs are in order.
- A corporation is being liquidated, and the trustee of the liquidating trust wants to protect itself from unanticipated future income tax assessments by the IRS on years open under the statute of limitations.

A request for a prompt assessment is made by filing Form 4810. The IRS has 18 months to complete its review once the taxpayer files the request.[65]

Litigation Considerations

During the process of settlement with the IRS, the taxpayer must assess the economic consequences of possible litigation. Specifically, the probability of winning in court should be weighed against the costs of litigating the dispute (legal, support, and court costs). In some instances, taxpayers become overly emotional and do not adequately consider the economic and psychological costs of litigation.

Signing Form 870 or Form 870–AD precludes the use of the Tax Court as a forum for future litigation. In that event, the taxpayer's only recourse is to pay the taxes and sue for a refund in a different court. The Tax Court was established to provide taxpayers an opportunity to litigate issues without first paying the tax on the deficiency. Some taxpayers, however, prefer to litigate the case in a Federal

[65] § 6501(d).

District Court or the Court of Federal Claims, because the payment of tax effectively stops the running of interest on the deficiency. See Chapter 1.

In selecting a proper tax forum, consideration should be given to the decisions of the various courts in related cases. The Tax Court follows the decisions of U.S. Courts of Appeals if the court is one to which the taxpayer may appeal.[66] For example, if an individual is in the jurisdiction of the Fifth Circuit Court of Appeals and that court has issued a favorable opinion on the same issue that currently confronts the taxpayer, the Tax Court will follow this opinion in deciding the taxpayer's case, even if previous Tax Court decisions have been adverse.

If the issue involves a question in which equity is needed, strategy may dictate the choice of the Court of Federal Claims, which has frequently given greater weight to equity considerations than to strict legal precedent, or of a Federal District Court, where a jury trial is available.

Penalties

Penalties are imposed upon a taxpayer's failure to file a return or pay a tax when due. These penalties can be avoided if the failure is due to reasonable cause and not due to willful neglect. Reasonable cause, however, has not been liberally interpreted by the courts and should not be relied upon in the routine situation.[67] A safer way to avoid the failure to file penalty is to obtain from the IRS an extension of time for filing the return.

The penalty for failure to pay estimated taxes can become quite severe. Often trapped by the provision are employed taxpayers with outside income. They may forget about the outside income and assume that the amount withheld from wages and salaries is adequate to cover their liability. Not only does April 15 provide a real shock (in terms of the additional tax owed) for these persons, but a penalty situation may have evolved. One way for an employee to mitigate this problem (presuming that the employer is willing to cooperate) is described in the following example.

EXAMPLE 27

Patty, a calendar year taxpayer, is employed by Finn Corporation and earns (after withholding) a monthly salary of $4,000 payable at the end of each month. Patty also receives income from outside sources (interest, dividends, and consulting fees). After some quick calculations in early October, Patty determines that she has underestimated her tax liability by $7,500 and will be subject to the penalty for the first two quarters of the year and part of the third quarter. Patty, therefore, completes a new Form W–4 in which she arbitrarily raises her income tax withholding by $2,500 a month. Finn accepts the Form W–4, and as a result, an extra $7,500 is paid to the IRS on Patty's account for the payroll period from October through December.

Patty avoids penalties for the underpayment for the first three quarters because withholding of taxes is allocated pro rata over the year involved. Thus, a portion of the additional $7,500 withheld in October–December is assigned to the January 1–April 15 period, the April 16–June 15 period, etc. Had Patty merely paid the IRS an additional $7,500 in October, the penalty would still have been assessed for the earlier quarters. ■

To avoid tax preparer penalties, the tax professional must carry out a number of quality control measures within the context of his or her firm.

- Adopt a "tone at the top" that stresses ethical tax practice, emphasizing at all times the importance of integrity and objectivity in the context of client advocacy.
- Establish and follow ethical guidelines with respect to all forms of client communication and documentation, including tax returns and written, spoken, and electronic tax advice.

[66] *Jack E. Golsen*, 54 T.C. 742 (1970).

[67] *Dustin v. Comm.*, 72–2 USTC ¶9610, 30 AFTR 2d 72–5313, 467 F.2d 47 (CA–9, 1972), *aff'g* 53 T.C. 491 (1969).

- Apply ethical standards even before an engagement letter is prepared for a potential client. The client should be aware of, and participate in, this dedication to ethical behavior.
- Stay current on changes to penalties, ethical guidelines, and Circular 230 provisions through an ongoing educational effort that communicates rule changes and the firm's best practices to all who handle tax return data.
- Monitor the compliance of all members of the firm with the established ethical guidelines. Use a peer review process periodically to confirm that the system is working as designed and to bring third-party suggestions into the process.

Privileged Communications

The CPA needs to exercise care to ensure that the privilege of confidentiality will apply to his or her tax work. Taking the following steps can help.

- Segregate the time spent and documents produced in rendering services for tax compliance from the time and documents devoted to tax advice. Doing this will protect the privilege from being waived as to the tax advice.
- Explain the extent of the privilege to the client—specify what will and will not be protected from the IRS in a dispute.
- Do not inadvertently waive the privilege, for example, by telling "too much" to the IRS or to a third party who is not protected by the privilege.
- Indemnify the CPA for time spent protecting and enforcing the privilege once it is challenged.

REFOCUS ON THE BIG PICTURE

A Tax Adviser's Dilemma

Your work with Campbell Corporation and its incremental research credit may prove troublesome. To avoid the taxpayer and tax preparer penalties, substantial authority must exist for claiming the credit, but the tax cases and Regulations do not appear to provide much guidance with respect to research expenditures of this sort. How does one craft a tax return position when the tax law largely is silent as to the particulars of the facts of the taxpayer's situation? How much risk of incurring a tax penalty are the taxpayer and your firm willing to assume in deciding how and whether to report these expenditures?

Beyond the monetary effects of claiming the credit, you and the client must consider the publicity aspects of taking this issue to court: Does Campbell want to be the "test case" in the Tax Court on this matter? What would be the effects on your consulting firm if a preparer penalty or even loss of professional certification were to result? If the credit is to be claimed, what degree of "disclosure" does the law require?

At a minimum, your firm and Campbell's tax department must conduct thorough research of analogous situations in the law in which the incremental research credit was and was not allowed for the taxpayer. Due diligence in this regard would require that you examine how other software applications and similar technological innovations, probably having nothing to do with GPS software and national security concerns, were treated for tax credit purposes. Constrained only by the budget dollars that Campbell is willing to dedicate to this task, your research is likely to be both interesting and frustrating, as no "on point" resolution is likely to be found prior to a later audit of the Form 1120 and its disclosures.

CONTINUED

What If?

The risk profiles of the tax adviser and a client seldom are identical. What position should your firm take if Campbell's tax department decides to claim the full incremental research credit for an item on which the tax law is silent or unclear, but your firm recommends that a special disclosure be made on the return concerning the item? A disclosure of this sort would protect the parties from later assessment of tax penalties, but Campbell believes that drawing attention to the credit item would increase the likelihood of a targeted audit of the expenditures by the IRS.

Although you are certain that tax fraud is not a problem on the Campbell return, you are concerned about the ramifications of Campbell's desire to omit the recommended disclosure. Your firm might decide to leave the Campbell engagement altogether if it is especially sensitive to exposure to penalties or if it is not certain that adequate research has been done to support the tax return position. Charges of a lack of due diligence by your firm might be brought by the IRS, the firm's professional ethics or certification bodies, or the issuer of its malpractice insurance. Clearly, none of these results is attractive to your firm.

KEY TERMS

Accuracy-related penalties, 17-17
Circular 230, 17-25
Closing agreement, 17-13
Determination letter, 17-5
E-filing, 17-3
Enrolled agents (EAs), 17-25
Fraud, 17-20
Frivolous return, 17-27
Letter ruling, 17-4
Negligence, 17-18
Ninety-day letter, 17-10
Offer in compromise, 17-12
Reasonable cause, 17-16
Revenue Agent's Report (RAR), 17-10
Statute of limitations, 17-23
Substantial authority, 17-18
Tax preparer, 17-29
Technical advice memorandum (TAM), 17-5
Thirty-day letter, 17-10
Unreasonable position, 17-29
Whistleblower Program, 17-9

DISCUSSION QUESTIONS

1. **LO.1** Tax professionals should show an interest in the organizational structure of the IRS and in the various processes that are necessary to work with the agency. What is the payback to the tax professional and his or her clients for this investment of time in discerning how the IRS works?

2. **LO.1** Where does the IRS "fit" in the operations of the Federal government? Summarize its responsibilities to the government and to the taxpayers.

3. **LO.1** An article in *USA TODAY* refers to the "audit lottery" and how one's chances of being audited are higher under the current IRS leadership. What is the audit lottery? How should a tax professional view the statistics about a taxpayer's audit likelihood?

Issue ID

4. **LO.1** Recently, a politician was interviewed about fiscal policy, and she mentioned reducing the "tax gap." Explain what this term means. What are some of the pertinent political and economic issues relative to the tax gap?

5. **LO.1** Review Figure 17.1, and identify the following.
   a. The title of the IRS's chief executive officer.
   b. The title of the "IRS's attorney."
   c. The names of the four major operating divisions of the IRS.
   d. The placement in the IRS organization of the Appeals and Criminal Investigation functions.

6. **LO.1** Identify three or more of the duties of the IRS's Chief Counsel.

7. **LO.2** Your tax research has located a Tax Court case that supports the claiming of a deduction by a client, while an IRS letter ruling holds to the contrary. The pertinent facts of both the case and the ruling match those of the client. Which holding should be followed in preparing the client's tax return? Summarize your findings in a memo for the tax research file.

Communications

8. **LO.2** Your client is litigating in the Tax Court concerning a tax credit that she claimed and the IRS has denied. Who bears the burden of proof regarding the litigation?

9. **LO.2** Describe the process the IRS uses to collect the tax that is found to be due after an audit is completed. Assume that the IRS findings are not appealed but that the taxpayer does not pay the amount due as determined by the audit. Illustrate the process with no more than four PowerPoint slides. *Hint*: Use the following terms in your report—*assess, seize,* and *lien.*

Communications

10. **LO.3** Gloria and Maria work together in an insurance office. Gloria's Form 1040 seems to be audited two out of every three years, while Maria never has been audited. How does the IRS select tax returns for audit? List some of the factors that might result in the different treatment of Gloria's and Maria's returns.

11. **LO.3** When can an individual taxpayer feel certain that his or her tax return will not be audited by the IRS? One year after it is filed? Two years? Five years? Explain.

12. **LO.3, 4** Lori wants to establish that her niece Suzette actually qualifies for a dependency exemption. After the issue is raised by the IRS on audit, Lori could argue the matter with the agent, an IRS Appeals officer, or the Tax Court. Give Lori advice about how to handle her tax dispute.

13. **LO.3** Describe the three broad types of IRS audits. Give an example of an issue that each type of audit might address, and indicate how frequently such audits are conducted by the IRS.

Issue ID

14. **LO.4** Your client Raphael is in the midst of a dispute with the IRS, and it does not look like he will reach a settlement using the agency's internal channels. He would consider litigating the issue, but he cannot afford the expense of a lengthy legal battle. Explain to Raphael the advantages of using the Small Cases Division of the U.S. Tax Court. What is the precedential value of a Small Cases decision?

15. **LO.4** Describe the conditions under which your client Lee Anne might approach the IRS with an offer in compromise.

16. **LO.5** For about 15 months, Ian has been negotiating a settlement with the IRS concerning a disputed tax deduction. The IRS and Ian have agreed to the amount of prior-year taxes he must pay. Ian asks you whether he also is liable now for interest charges on his underpayment and, if so, how that interest amount is computed. As to Ian's tax payable amount, when does interest begin to accrue?

17. **LO.6** Define the following terms in the context of tax law enforcement.
    a. Civil penalty.
    b. Criminal penalty.
    c. *Ad valorem* penalty.
    d. *Assessable* penalty.
    e. Deductible penalty.

18. **LO.6** Which of the valuation penalties is likely to arise when an aggressive taxpayer reports:
    a. A charitable contribution?
    b. A business deduction?
    c. A decedent's taxable estate?

19. **LO.6** The IRS assesses special penalties when a taxpayer misreports the value of property that was the subject of a deduction or that was subject to a gift/estate tax. How are these penalties computed? *Hint*: Include the term *gross misstatement* in your answer.

20. **LO.6** Yonkers Corporation recomputes its research credit for the prior tax year and, as a result, claims a $100,000 refund. The IRS reviews the claim and allows only $20,000 of

the requested refund. If Yonkers does not appeal, is this matter finished? Is Yonkers certain to receive the full $20,000 refund allowed? Explain.

Issue ID

21. **LO.6** On October 30, Cameron determines that his tax for the year will total $10,000. If his employer is scheduled to withhold only $6,500 in Federal income taxes, what can Cameron do to avoid any underpayment penalty?

22. **LO.4, 5, 7** Indicate whether each of the following statements is true or false.
    a. The government never pays a taxpayer interest on an overpayment of tax.
    b. The IRS can compromise on the amount of tax liability if there is doubt as to the taxpayer's ability to pay.
    c. The statute of limitations for assessing a tax can extend beyond three years from the filing of a return.
    d. For a tax return that has not been filed, the statute of limitations is extended to five years from the original due date of the return.

23. **LO.4, 6** In each of the following cases, distinguish between the terms.
    a. Offer in compromise and closing agreement.
    b. Failure to file and failure to pay.
    c. 90-day letter and 30-day letter.
    d. Negligence and fraud.
    e. Criminal and civil tax fraud.

Communications

24. **LO.6** While working on the Federal income tax return for your client Best Wishes LLC, you discover that the payroll office was lax in its procedures. You found that the office allowed some employees to reduce their withholding taxes by overstating the number of exemptions to which they were entitled, and that the withholding amounts for the last two months of the tax year were not remitted to the Treasury. In no more than three PowerPoint slides, summarize the various tax penalties to which Best Wishes now is exposed. Be specific.

Issue ID

25. **LO.7** Why should the taxpayer be "let off the hook" and no longer be subject to audit exposure once the applicable statute of limitations has expired? Do statutes of limitations protect the government? Other taxpayers?

Issue ID

26. **LO.8** Consider the ethical standards under which the tax profession operates. Who regulates the behavior of tax return preparers? What documents provide the major constraints on the conduct of the tax profession?

Communications

27. **LO.8** In no more than five PowerPoint slides, prepare a presentation to your school's Accounting Alumni Club titled "How the IRS Keeps Track of Tax Preparers." Include the application of the PTIN and of Circular 230 in your remarks.

28. **LO.8** Give the Circular 230 position concerning each of the following situations sometimes encountered in the tax profession.
    a. Taking an aggressive pro-taxpayer position on a tax return.
    b. Not having a quality review process for a return completed by a partner of the tax firm.
    c. Purposely delaying compliance with a document request received from the IRS.
    d. Not keeping up with changes in the tax law.
    e. Charging $1,500 to complete a Form 1040–EZ.
    f. When representing a taxpayer in a Federal income tax audit, charging a fee equal to one-third of the reduction of the tax proposed by the IRS agent.
    g. Representing both the husband and wife as to tax matters when negotiating their divorce.
    h. Advertising on the Web for new tax clients and including *Se habla español* in the text of the ads.

29. **LO.8** Indicate whether each of the following parties could be subject to the tax preparer penalties.
    a. Tom prepared Sally's return for $250.
    b. Theresa prepared her grandmother's return for no charge.
    c. Georgia prepared her church's return for $500 (she would have charged an unrelated party $3,000 for the same work).
    d. Geoff prepared returns for low-income taxpayers under his college's VITA program.
    e. Hildy prepared the return of her corporate employer.
    f. Heejeo, an administrative assistant for an accounting firm, processed a client's return through TurboTax.

30. **LO.6, 8** In no more than three PowerPoint slides, list at least four of the Code's penalties that could be assessed against paid preparers of tax returns. Name the violation that triggers the penalty, and explain how the dollar amount of the penalty is determined.

Communications

PROBLEMS

31. **LO.5** Gordon paid the $10,000 balance of his Federal income tax three months late. Ignore daily compounding of interest. Determine the interest rate that applies relative to this amount, assuming that:
   a. Gordon is an individual.
   b. Gordon is a C corporation.
   c. The $10,000 is not a tax that is due, but is a refund payable by the IRS to Gordon (an individual).
   d. The $10,000 is not a tax that is due, but is a refund payable by the IRS to Gordon (a C corporation).

32. **LO.6** Rita forgot to pay her Federal income tax on time. When she actually filed, she reported a balance due. Compute Rita's failure to file penalty in each of the following cases.
   a. Two months late, $1,000 additional tax due.
   b. Five months late, $3,000 additional tax due.
   c. Eight months late, $4,000 additional tax due.
   d. Two and a half months late, $3,000 additional tax due.
   e. Five months late due to fraud by Rita, $4,000 additional tax due.
   f. Ten months late due to fraud by Rita, $15,000 additional tax due.

33. **LO.6** Wade filed his Federal income tax return on time but did not remit the balance due. Compute Wade's failure to pay penalty in each of the following cases. The IRS has not issued a deficiency notice.
   a. Four months late, $3,000 additional tax due.
   b. Ten months late, $4,000 additional tax due.
   c. Five years late, $5,000 additional tax due.

34. **LO.6** Compute the failure to pay and failure to file penalties for John, who filed his 2011 income tax return on December 20, 2012, paying the $10,000 amount due at that time. On April 1, 2012, John received a six-month extension of time in which to file his return. He has no reasonable cause for failing to file his return by October 15 or for failing to pay the tax that was due on April 15, 2012. John's failure to comply with the tax laws was not fraudulent.

35. **LO.6** Olivia, a calendar year taxpayer, does not file her 2011 return until December 12, 2012. At this point, she pays the $40,000 balance due on her 2011 tax liability of $70,000. Olivia did not apply for and obtain any extension of time for filing the 2011 return. When questioned by the IRS on her delinquency, Olivia asserts: "If I was too busy to file my regular tax return, I was too busy to request an extension."
   a. Is Olivia liable for any penalties for failure to file and for failure to pay?
   b. If so, compute the penalty amounts.

36. **LO.6** Orville, a cash basis, calendar year taxpayer, filed his income tax return 70 days after the due date. Orville never extended his return, and he paid the taxes that were due when he filed the return. What penalty will Orville incur, and how much will he have to pay if his additional tax is $6,000? Disregard any interest he must pay.

37. **LO.6** Maureen, a calendar year individual taxpayer, files her 2011 return on November 4, 2013. She did not obtain an extension for filing her return, and the return reflects additional income tax due of $15,000.
   a. What are Maureen's penalties for failure to file and to pay?
   b. Would your answer to (a) change if Maureen, before the due date of the return, had retained a CPA to prepare the return and it was the CPA's negligence that caused the delay? Explain.

38. **LO.6** LaVonn underpaid her taxes by $250,000. A portion of the underpayment was shown to be attributable to LaVonn's negligence ($200,000). A court found that a

portion of that deficiency constituted civil fraud ($50,000). Compute the total fraud and negligence penalties incurred.

39. **LO.6** Compute the overvaluation penalty for each of the following independent cases involving the fair market value of charitable contribution property. In each case, assume a marginal income tax rate of 35%.

	Taxpayer	Corrected IRS Value	Reported Valuation
a.	Individual	$ 40,000	$ 50,000
b.	C corporation	30,000	50,000
c.	S corporation	40,000	50,000
d.	Individual	150,000	200,000
e.	Individual	150,000	250,000
f.	C corporation	150,000	750,000

40. **LO.6** Compute the undervaluation penalty for each of the following independent cases involving the value of a closely held business in the decedent's gross estate. In each case, assume a marginal estate tax rate of 35%.

	Reported Value	Corrected IRS Valuation
a.	$ 20,000	$ 25,000
b.	100,000	150,000
c.	150,000	250,000
d.	150,000	500,000

41. **LO.6** Singh, a qualified appraiser of fine art and other collectibles, was advising Colleen when she was determining the amount of the charitable contribution deduction for a gift of sculpture to a museum. Singh sanctioned a $900,000 appraisal, even though he knew the market value of the piece was only $300,000. Colleen assured Singh that she had never been audited by the IRS and that the risk of the government questioning his appraisal was negligible.

    But Colleen was wrong, and her return was audited. The IRS used its own appraisers to set the value of the sculpture at $400,000. Colleen is in the 30% Federal income tax bracket, while Singh's fee for preparing the appraisal was $20,000.

    a. Compute the penalty the IRS can assess against Singh. (Do not consider the valuation penalty as to Colleen's return.)
    b. What is the penalty if Singh's appraisal fee was $7,500 (not $20,000)?

42. **LO.6** The Eggers Corporation filed an amended Form 1120, claiming an additional $400,000 deduction for payments to a contractor for a prior tax year. The amended return was based on the entity's interpretation of a Regulation that defined deductible advance payment expenditures. The nature of Eggers's activity with the contractor did not exactly fit the language of the Regulation. Nevertheless, because so much tax was at stake, Eggers's tax department decided to broaden its interpretation and claim the deduction.

    Eggers's tax department estimated that there was only a 15% chance that Eggers's interpretation would stand up to a Tax Court review.

    a. What is the amount of tax penalty that Eggers is risking by taking this position?
    b. What would be the result if there was a 45% chance that Eggers's interpretation of the Regulation was correct?

43. **LO.6** Moose, a former professional athlete, now supplements his income by signing autographs at collectors' shows. Unfortunately, Moose has not been conscientious about reporting all of this income on his tax return. Now the IRS has charged him with additional taxes of $100,000 due to negligence in his record keeping and $20,000 due to an intent to defraud the U.S. government of income taxes. No criminal fraud charges are brought against Moose. The District Court finds by a preponderance of the evidence that only half of the $20,000 underpayment was due to Moose's fraudulent action; the remainder was due to mere negligence. Compute the accuracy-related and civil fraud penalties in this matter.

44. **LO.6** Trudy's AGI last year was $200,000. Her Federal income tax came to $65,000, which she paid through a combination of withholding and estimated payments. This year, her AGI will be $300,000, with a projected tax liability of $45,000, all to be paid through estimates.
    a. Ignore the annualized income method. Compute Trudy's quarterly estimated tax payment schedule for this year.
    b. Assume instead that Trudy's AGI last year was $100,000 and resulted in a Federal income tax of $20,000. Determine her quarterly estimated tax payment schedule for this year.

45. **LO.6** Kold Services Corporation estimates that its 2013 taxable income will be $500,000. Thus, it is subject to a flat 34% income tax rate and incurs a $170,000 liability. For each of the following independent cases, compute Kold's 2013 minimum quarterly estimated tax payments that will avoid an underpayment penalty.
    a. For 2012, taxable income was ($200,000). Kold carried back all of this loss to prior years and exhausted the entire net operating loss in creating a zero 2012 liability.
    b. For 2012, taxable income was $450,000, and tax liability was $153,000.
    c. For 2011, taxable income was $2 million, and tax liability was $680,000. For 2012, taxable income was $400,000, and tax liability was $136,000.

46. **LO.6** The Leake Company, owned equally by Jacquie (chair of the board of directors) and Jeff (company president), is in very difficult financial straits. Last month, Jeff used the $300,000 withheld from employee paychecks for Federal payroll and income taxes to pay a creditor who threatened to cut off all supplies. To keep the company afloat, Jeff used these government funds willfully for the operations of the business, but even that effort was not enough. The company missed the next two payrolls, and today other creditors took action to shut down Leake altogether.

    How much will the IRS assess in taxes and penalties in this matter and from whom? How can you as a tax professional best offer service to Jacquie, Jeff, and Leake? Address these matters in a memo for the tax research file.

Decision Making

Communications

47. **LO.7** What is the applicable statute of limitations in each of the following independent situations?
    a. No return was filed by the taxpayer.
    b. The taxpayer incurred a bad debt loss that she failed to claim.
    c. A taxpayer inadvertently omitted a large amount of gross income.
    d. Same as (c), except that the omission was deliberate.
    e. A taxpayer innocently overstated her deductions by a large amount.

48. **LO.7** Loraine (a calendar year taxpayer) reported the following transactions, all of which were properly included in a timely filed return.

Gross receipts		$ 975,000
Cost of sales		(850,000)
Gross profit		$ 125,000
Capital gain	$ 40,000	
Capital loss	(25,000)	15,000
Total income		$ 140,000

    a. Presuming the absence of fraud, how much of an omission from gross income is required before the six-year statute of limitations applies?
    b. Would it matter if cost of sales had been inadvertently overstated by $150,000?
    c. How does the situation change in the context of fraud by Loraine?

49. **LO.5, 7** On April 3, 2009, Mark filed his 2008 income tax return, which showed a tax due of $80,000. On June 1, 2011, he filed an amended return for 2008 that showed an additional tax of $10,000. Mark paid the additional amount. On May 18, 2012, Mark filed a claim for a 2008 refund of $45,000.
    a. If Mark's claim for a refund is correct in amount, how much tax will he recover?
    b. What is the period that government-paid interest runs with respect to Mark's claim for a refund?
    c. How would you have advised him differently?

Decision Making

Communications

50. **LO.7** Chee owed $4,000 in Federal income tax when she filed her Form 1040 for 2012. She attached a sticky note to the 1040 that read, "My inventory computations on last year's (2011) return were wrong, so I paid $1,000 too much in tax." Chee then included a check for $3,000 with the Form 1040 for 2012. Write a memo for the tax research file commenting on Chee's actions.

51. **LO.8** Rod's Federal income tax returns (Form 1040) for the indicated three years were prepared by the following persons.

Year	Preparer
2011	Rod
2012	Ann
2013	Cheryl

Ann is Rod's next-door neighbor and owns and operates a pharmacy. Cheryl is a licensed CPA and is engaged in private practice. In the event Rod is audited and all three returns are examined, who may represent him before the IRS at the agent level? Who may represent Rod before the Appeals Division?

52. **LO.8** Christie is the preparer of the Form 1120 for Yostern Corporation. On the return, Yostern claimed a deduction that the IRS later disallowed on audit. Compute the tax preparer penalty that could be assessed against Christie in each of the following independent situations.

	Form 8275 Disclosure on the Return of the Disputed Deduction?	Tax Reduction Resulting from the Deduction	Probability That the Courts Would Approve the Deduction	Christie's Fee to Complete Yostern's Return
a.	No	$40,000	65%	$7,000
b.	No	40,000	35	7,000
c.	No	40,000	35	1,500
d.	Yes	40,000	35	7,000
e.	Yes	40,000	15	4,000

53. **LO.8** Discuss which penalties, if any, might be imposed on the tax adviser in each of the following independent circumstances. In this regard, assume that the tax adviser:
    a. Suggested to the client various means by which to acquire excludible income.
    b. Suggested to the client various means by which to conceal cash receipts from gross income.
    c. Suggested to the client means by which to improve her cash flow by delaying for six months or more the deposit of the employees' share of Federal employment taxes.
    d. Failed, because of pressing time conflicts, to conduct the usual review of the client's tax return. The IRS later discovered that the return included fraudulent data.
    e. Failed, because of pressing time conflicts, to conduct the usual review of the client's tax return. The IRS later discovered a mathematical error in the computation of the personal exemption.

54. **LO.8** Compute the preparer penalty the IRS could assess on Gerry in each of the following independent cases.
    a. On March 21, the copy machine was not working, so Gerry gave original returns to her 20 clients that day without providing any duplicates for them. Copies for Gerry's files and for use in preparing state tax returns had been made on March 20.
    b. Because Gerry extended her vacation a few days, she missed the Annual Tax Update seminar that she usually attends. As a result, she was unaware that Congress had changed a law affecting limited partnerships. The change affected the transactions of 25 of Gerry's clients, all of whom understated their tax as a result.
    c. Gerry heard that the IRS was increasing its audits of corporations that hold assets in a foreign trust. As a result, Gerry instructed the intern who prepared the initial drafts of the returns for five corporate clients to leave blank the question about such trusts. Not wanting to lose his position, the intern, a senior accounting major at State University, complied with Gerry's instructions.

55. **LO.8** You are the chair of the Ethics Committee of your state's CPA Licensing Commission. Interpret controlling AICPA authority in addressing the following assertions by your membership.

Decision Making

a. When a CPA has reasonable grounds for not answering an applicable question on a client's return, a brief explanation of the reason for the omission should not be provided, because it would flag the return for audit by the IRS.
b. If a CPA discovers during an IRS audit that the client has a material error in the return under examination, he should immediately withdraw from the engagement.
c. If the client tells you that she paid $500 for office supplies, but has lost the receipts, you should deduct an odd amount on her return (e.g., $499), because an even amount ($500) would indicate to the IRS that her deduction was based on an estimate.
d. If a CPA knows that the client has a material error in a prior year's return, he should not, without the client's consent, disclose the error to the IRS.
e. If a CPA's client will not correct a material error in a prior year's return, the CPA should not prepare the current year's return for the client.

RESEARCH PROBLEMS

Note: Solutions to Research Problems can be prepared by using the **Checkpoint® Student Edition** online research product, which is available to accompany this text. It is also possible to prepare solutions to the Research Problems by using tax research materials found in a standard tax library.

THOMSON REUTERS
CHECKPOINT®

Research Problem 1. Lopez always had taken his Form 1040 data to the franchise tax preparers in a local mall, but this year, his friend Cheryl asked to prepare his return. Cheryl quoted a reasonable fee, and Lopez reasoned that, with finances especially tight in Cheryl's household, she could use the money.

Communications

Lopez delivered his Forms W–2, 1099, and other documentation and said, "I'll pick up the finished return from you on Monday." Cheryl completed the return by that deadline, and without signing and reviewing the forms, Lopez allowed Cheryl to e-file it that day. The arrangement was that Cheryl would receive the refund through a special bank account and write Lopez a check for that amount, less her fee. When the refund came through about three weeks later, Cheryl wrote Lopez a check for $2,400, and all parties were satisfied. Lopez gladly used Cheryl to e-file the next year's return using the same procedures.

To his surprise, Lopez received a letter from the IRS about 18 months later. The auditor had found that the return Cheryl had e-filed vastly overstated deductions, created false dependency exemptions (using Social Security numbers that did not exist), and wrongly calculated the earned income tax credit. According to the audit report, the refund issued was $4,500—Cheryl had pocketed the difference. Thus, the corrected tax liability meant that Lopez now owed $7,000 in tax, before considering interest and penalties.

Lopez contends that he relied on Cheryl's expertise in the tax law and e-filing procedures. Consequently, there was reasonable cause for the underpayment of tax, and the IRS should waive the understatement and negligence penalties. The IRS has expressed sympathy for Lopez's position, but it maintains that the penalty should stand. What do you think? Summarize your findings in a memo for the tax research file.

Research Problem 2. In 2008, Gupta sold some shares of Wingo, a private U.S. corporation, for $40 million. On his Form 1040 Schedule D for 2008, Gupta showed the basis of the stock as $11 million, thereby reporting a $29 million capital gain. Gupta filed his return on October 1, 2009, after properly receiving an extension of the filing due date. Other income and deductions on the 2008 return netted to zero.

On March 1, 2013, while auditing the tax return of one of the purchasers of Gupta's Wingo shares, the IRS found that the basis for the shares actually was $3 million. Thus, Gupta's capital gain should have been $37 million and not $29 million.

After auditing Gupta's 2008 return, the IRS maintains that it can collect the underpaid taxes, plus interest and penalties, because the six-year statute of limitations applies (i.e., Gupta's return showed a substantial understatement of gross income). Gupta has asked you for tax advice on this matter. Did the statute of limitations expire on October 1, 2012, so that the IRS no longer can pursue the matter? Explain.

Communications

Research Problem 3. Blanche Creek (111 Elm Avenue, Plymouth, IN 46563) has engaged your firm because she has been charged with failure to file her 2010 Federal Form 1040. Blanche maintains that the "reasonable cause" exception should apply. During the entire tax filing season in 2011, she was under a great deal of stress at work and in her personal life. As a result, Blanche developed a sleep disorder, which was treated through a combination of pills and counseling.

Your firm ultimately prepared the 2010 tax return for Blanche, but it was filed far beyond the due date. Blanche is willing to pay the delinquent tax and related interest. However, she believes that the failure to pay penalty is unfair, as she was ill. Consequently, she could not be expected to keep to the usual deadlines for filing.

Write a letter to Blanche concerning these matters.

Communications

Research Problem 4. Your firm is preparing the Form 1040 of Norah McGinty, a resident, like you, of Oklahoma. You have contracted for the last three filing seasons with a firm in India, Tax Express Bangalore, to prepare initial drafts of tax returns using tax software that you provide to Tax Express. You find that the use of Tax Express Bangalore's services significantly increases the profits of your Form 1040 practice.

Your firm uses Tax Express annually to help prepare Forms 1040 for about 500 of your clients. Three of your tax managers, JaJuan, Max, and Emma, spend several weeks in the autumn every year in India, training the Bangalore staff in Federal tax law changes and in the operations of your tax software packages.

Phil, a tax associate in your Norman office, is handling Norah's return this year. Phil works with Norah to complete the online tax questionnaire that summarizes Norah's taxable events and the related dollar amounts. The questionnaire includes the Social Security numbers of Norah and her two dependent children. The children are young, and their income levels do not require them to complete income tax returns.

Phil sends the completed questionnaire and electronic files of supporting documents to the Bangalore staff at the end of the work day on Monday, using a secure file transfer site. Upon arriving at work Thursday morning, Phil finds that Tax Express has completed the Form 1040, including a payment voucher. Phil reviews the return, makes a few minor changes to it, and then meets with Norah on Saturday to convey to her the finalized documents. Norah reviews the form, and she signs it and writes a check for the amount due, mailing the return to the IRS Service Center from her home on the following Monday.

In a memo for the tax research file, discuss any special rules from the Code and Regulations that might affect your firm's use of Tax Express Bangalore for your client Norah McGinty.

Internet Activity

Use the tax resources of the Internet to address the following questions. Do not restrict your search to the Web, but include a review of newsgroups and general reference materials, practitioner sites and resources, primary sources of the tax law, chat rooms and discussion groups, and other opportunities.

Communications

Research Problem 5. Taxpayers generally "go to jail" on tax charges only when criminal activities have been involved. Find information about the criminal tax prosecutions the Treasury undertakes. How many criminal tax charges are initiated in a year? How much time does a criminal tax case take from filing charges to disposition by the IRS or a court? What issues tend to be the focus of a criminal tax prosecution? How much additional tax, interest, and penalty revenue does the Treasury collect due to its criminal prosecutions? Summarize your findings for your classmates in no more than four PowerPoint slides.

Communications

Research Problem 6. Find an article in which a tax professional describes the confidentiality privilege available under the Code for a CPA tax adviser. Then construct a list of "Confidentiality Dos and Don'ts for the CPA." Summarize the article in an e-mail to your professor.

Research Problem 7. Corporations with large estimated tax overpayments and underpayments are subject to special interest rates.

a. Find in the Code how these rates are determined.
b. List the rates that have been in effect for the last six calendar quarters.
c. Find and subscribe to a feed that will alert you automatically when the interest rate changes.

Research Problem 8. Prepare a graph illustrating the trends in IRS audit activity over the past decade, and submit it to your instructor. First, decide whether you are measuring audited returns, tax dollars recovered by audit, or budget resources dedicated to audit activities. Next, decide which types of taxpayers and returns you will be graphing. Then find your data at **www.irs.gov**.

Communications

Research Problem 9. In a PowerPoint presentation for your classmates, describe how the IRS targets certain tax issues, taxpayers, and transactions in the audit process. Give examples of high- and low-priority audit issues for the current year. (*Hint*: Search using terms such as *Tier I* and *Tier II*.)

Communications

Research Problem 10. Every year toward the end of the Form 1040 filing season, suggestions are offered to taxpayers about how to pay their taxes if they lack the funds to do so. The discussions address filing extensions, installment plans, and credit card payments. Find two online videos of this sort. Summarize the videoclips, and develop a speech outline and no more than four PowerPoint slides for a presentation you will make to your town's Young Executives Club.

Communications

Research Problem 11. Find a website that lists suggestions on how to deal with an IRS auditor during the first meeting with him or her. You might start at **www.irs.gov** by reading Publication 556. Then find at least three sites offered by tax professionals with different credentials and certifications. Summarize and evaluate each of the key points in an e-mail to your instructor.

Communications

Research Problem 12. You have been assigned the task of preparing a letter ruling request on behalf of one of the firm's clients. As the firm has not prepared a ruling request before, you are to outline the IRS's procedure for receiving and processing such a request. Summarize the more significant points in a memo for the tax file. Provide Code and other citations as needed.

Communications

part 5

Family Tax Planning

Family tax planning has as its objective the minimization of all taxes imposed on the family unit. Carrying out this objective requires familiarity with the rules applicable to transfers by gift and by death. These rules must then be applied to reduce the transfer tax burden. Also to be considered are the income tax consequences of the transfers made. Specifically, entities created as a result of these transfers (trusts and estates) are subject to unique income tax rules.

CHAPTER

18 The Federal Gift and Estate Taxes

LEARNING OBJECTIVES: *After completing Chapter 18, you should be able to:*

LO.1 Explain the nature of the Federal gift and estate taxes.

LO.2 List and analyze the Federal gift tax formula.

LO.3 List and analyze the Federal estate tax formula.

LO.4 Illustrate the operation of the Federal gift tax.

LO.5 Calculate the Federal gift tax.

LO.6 Identify the components of the gross estate.

LO.7 Describe the components of the taxable estate.

LO.8 Calculate the Federal estate tax liability.

LO.9 Review and demonstrate the role of the generation-skipping transfer tax.

CHAPTER OUTLINE

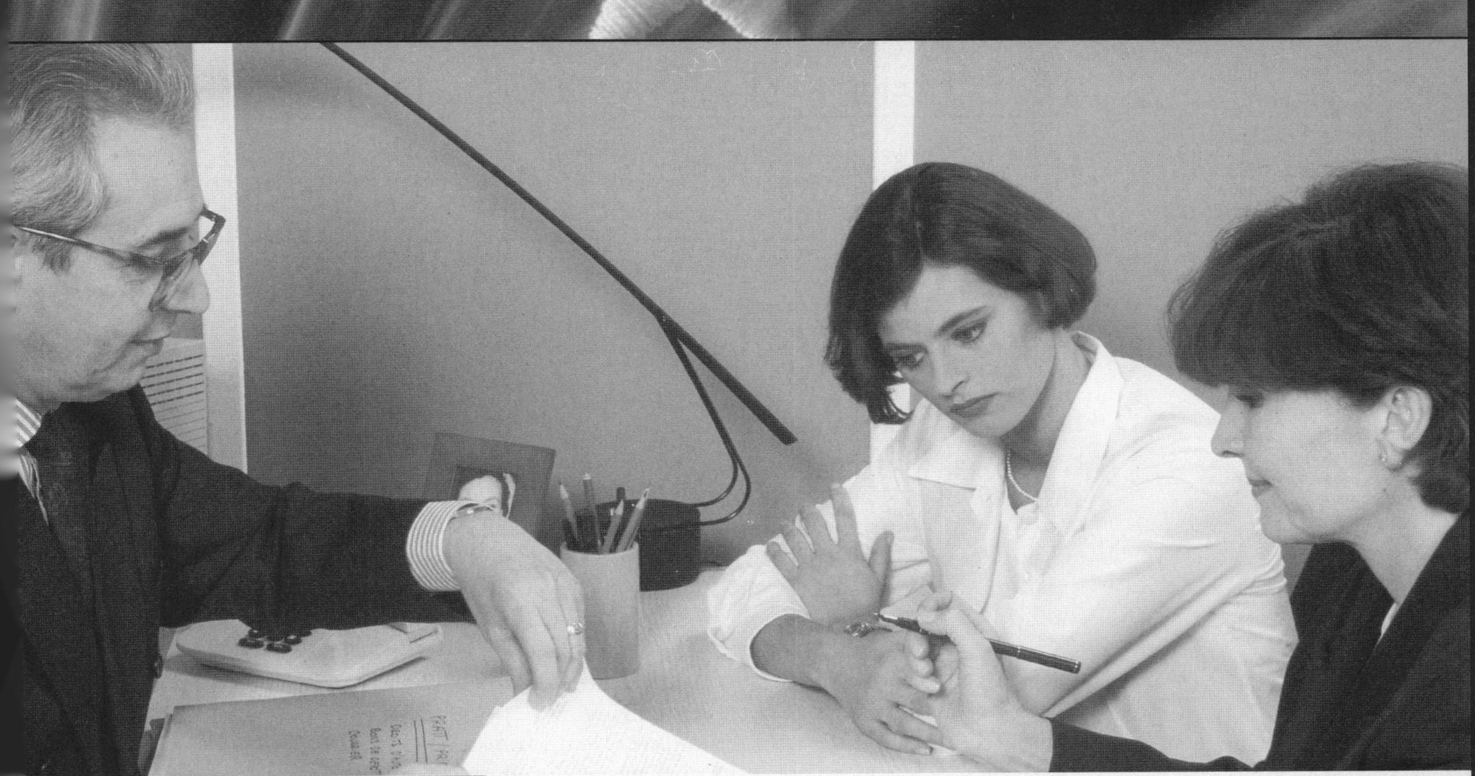

THE BIG PICTURE Tax Solutions for the Real World

©Hervé Gyssels/Photononstop/Glow Images, Inc.

An Eventful and Final Year

Over his lifetime, Peter Hood started and purchased numerous automobile dealerships that he eventually transferred to a newly formed entity, Hood Corporation. Upon his death in 2000, the stock in Hood Corporation passed in equal shares to Peter's surviving spouse, Martha, and their adult children, John and Helen.

For John Hood, 2012 proved to be an eventful and final tax year. Among the major happenings were the following.

- In January, John's divorce from his first wife, Hannah, became final.
- In February, he married Ashley, the manager of one of the Hood car dealerships.
- He made various gifts to family members.
- In July, his mother died of a heart condition, and John served as executor of her estate.
- In late November, he was seriously injured in a car accident (caused by another motorist).
- In early December, he carried out some predeath planning.
- John died of his injuries in mid-December.

What are some of the tax problems (i.e., income, gift, and estate taxes) that might be encountered as a result of these events?

Read the chapter and formulate your response.

18.1 Transfer Taxes—In General

Until now, this text has dealt primarily with the various applications of the Federal income tax. Also important in the Federal tax structure are various excise taxes that cover transfers of property. Sometimes called transaction taxes, excise taxes are based on the value of the property transferred, not on the income derived from the property. Two such taxes—the Federal gift tax and the Federal estate tax—are the central focus of Chapters 18 and 19.

LO.1

Explain the nature of the Federal gift and estate taxes.

Nature of the Taxes

Historical Background

Federal tax law imposes a tax on the gratuitous transfer of property in one of two ways. If the transfer occurs during the owner's life, it is subject to the Federal gift tax. If the property passes by virtue of the death of the owner, the Federal estate tax applies. Originally, the two taxes were governed by different rules, including separate sets of tax rates. As Congress believed that lifetime transfers of wealth should be encouraged, the gift tax rates were 25 percent lower than the estate tax rates.[1]

The Tax Reform Act of 1976 significantly changed the approach taken by the Federal gift and estate taxes. Recognizing that prior rules had not significantly stimulated a preference for lifetime over death transfers, Congress decided that all transfers should be taxed the same way. Consequently, much of the distinction between life and death transfers was eliminated. Instead of subjecting these transfers to two separate tax rate schedules, the Act substituted a **unified transfer tax** that covered all gratuitous transfers. Thus, gifts were subject to a gift tax at the same rates as those applicable to transfers at death.

The Economic Growth and Tax Relief Reconciliation Act of 2001 (EGTRRA) made further changes. Reacting to general public sentiment, Congress concluded that the Federal estate tax was objectionable because it leads to the breakup of family farms and other closely held businesses. Thus, by scheduled increases in the unified tax credit applicable to estates, the estate tax would be eliminated by 2010, but the gift tax would be retained. For budget reasons, under "sunset provisions," all changes made by EGTRRA were to expire after 2010. At the last minute, however, Congress enacted the Tax Relief Act of 2010 (TRA). Under TRA, the sunset provisions are postponed (until after 2012), and the legislation added some generous estate and gift tax provisions (maximum rate of 35 percent and a credit of $5 million). TRA is effective for 2011 and 2012. If the sunset provisions come into play after 2012, the rates will increase to a maximum of 55 percent, and the credit will decrease to $1 million.

Clearly, Congress has not been consistent in its treatment of lifetime (i.e., gift tax) and death (i.e., estate tax) transfers.

Persons Subject to the Tax

The Federal gift tax is imposed on the right to transfer property by one person (the donor) to another (the donee) for less than full and adequate consideration. The tax is payable by the donor.[2] If the donor fails to pay the tax when due, the donee may be held liable for the tax to the extent of the value of the property received.[3]

A gift by a corporation is considered a gift by the individual shareholders. A gift to a corporation is generally considered a gift to the individual shareholders.

[1]The estate tax was enacted in 1916. Because the estate tax could be avoided by making transfers just prior to dying (i.e., "deathbed gifts"), a gift tax was added in 1932.

[2]§ 2502(c).

[3]§ 6324(b). Known as the doctrine of transferee liability, this rule also operates to enable the IRS to enforce the collection of other taxes (e.g., income tax and estate tax).

U.S. Transfer Taxes and NRAs

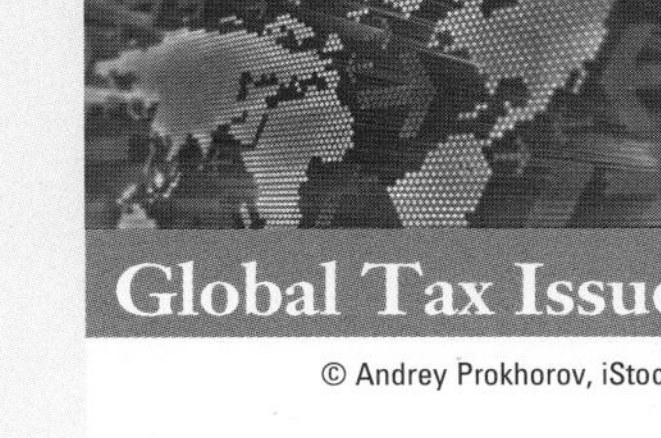

© Andrey Prokhorov, iStockphoto

For individuals who are neither residents nor citizens of the United States (i.e., nonresident aliens or NRAs), the Federal gift tax applies only to gifts of property situated within the United States. Exempted, however, are gifts of intangibles, such as stocks and bonds.

For decedents who are NRAs, the Federal estate tax is imposed on the value of property located within the United States. Unlike the gift tax, however, the estate tax applies to stock in U.S. corporations. Special reporting procedures apply to the estate taxation of NRAs—see the instructions to Form 706–NA, United States Estate (and Generation-Skipping Transfer) Tax Return, Estate of nonresident not a citizen of the United States.

Source: Code §§ 2101(a), 2501(a)(2), and 2511(a).

In certain cases, however, a gift to a charitable, public, political, or similar organization may be regarded as a gift to the organization as a single entity.[4]

Upon the death of an individual, the Federal estate tax is imposed on the entire estate.[5] The executor (or administrator) of the estate has the obligation to pay any estate tax that may be due.

If the transferor is a resident or citizen of the United States, then the location of the property transferred is immaterial. Thus, a gift by a U.S. resident of property located in Honduras is subject to the Federal gift tax. For a U.S. citizen, the place of residence at the time of the transfer is not relevant. For these purposes, "United States" includes only the 50 states and the District of Columbia and does not include U.S. possessions or territories.[6]

Types of Tax at Death

Taxes payable by virtue of a person's death fall into two categories: estate and inheritance. The U.S. government, some states, and several foreign countries impose estate taxes. Inheritance taxes are imposed by some states and other countries. Some states and countries use both types of taxes.

The Federal estate tax differs in several respects from the typical *inheritance tax.* First, the Federal estate tax is levied on the decedent's entire estate. It is a tax on the right to pass property at death. Inheritance taxes apply to the right to receive property at death and are therefore levied on the heirs. Second, the relationship of the heirs to the decedent usually has a direct bearing on the amount of the inheritance tax. In general, the more closely related the parties, the larger the exemptions and the lower the applicable rates.[7] Except for transfers to surviving spouses that may result in a marital deduction, the relationship of the heirs to the decedent has no effect on the Federal estate tax.

Formula for the Gift Tax

LO.2

List and analyze the Federal gift tax formula.

Like the income tax, which uses taxable income (not gross income) as a tax base, the gift tax usually does not apply to the full amount of the gift. Deductions and the annual exclusion may be allowed to arrive at an amount called the **taxable gift.**[8] However, unlike the income tax, which does not consider taxable income from

[4]Reg. §§ 25.0–1(b) and 25.2511–1(h)(1). But note the exemption from the Federal gift tax for certain transfers to political organizations discussed later.

[5]§ 2001(a). Subchapter A (§§ 2001 through 2058) covers the estate tax treatment of those who are either residents or citizens. Subchapter B (§§ 2101 through 2108) covers the estate tax applicable to NRAs.

[6]§ 7701(a)(9).

[7]For example, one state's inheritance tax provides an unlimited exemption for a surviving spouse and charities, $100,000 for Class A heirs (lineal descendants and ascendants), $500 for Class B heirs (collateral heirs), and $100 for Class C (other relatives and strangers). Beginning tax rates applicable to the nonexempt portion range from 2% to 10%, with the top rate applicable to Class C heirs reaching 20%.

[8]§ 2503(a).

prior years, *prior taxable gifts* must be added in arriving at the tax base to which the unified transfer tax rate is applied. Otherwise, the donor could start over again each year with a new set of progressive rates.

EXAMPLE 1

Don makes taxable gifts of $1 million in 1986 and $1 million in 2009. Presuming no other taxable gifts and *before applying the unified tax credit,* Don must pay a tax of $345,800 (see Appendix A, p. A-4) on the 1986 transfer and a tax of $780,800 (see Appendix A, p. A-7) on the 2009 transfer (using a tax base of $2 million). If the 1986 taxable gift had not been included in the tax base for the 2009 gift, the tax would have been $345,800. The correct tax liability of $780,800 is more than twice $345,800! ■

Because the gift tax is cumulative in effect, a credit is allowed against the gift taxes paid (or deemed paid) on prior taxable gifts included in the tax base. The deemed paid credit is explained later in the chapter.

EXAMPLE 2

Assume the same facts as in Example 1. Don will be allowed a credit of $345,800 against the gift tax of $780,800. Thus, his gift tax liability for 2009 becomes $435,000 ($780,800 − $345,800). ■

Because Congress did not intend for the gift tax to apply to smaller transfers, it provided for an annual exclusion. Originally set at $3,000, the amount allowed is periodically adjusted for *significant* inflation. For 2009 through 2012, the amount allowed is $13,000 (for the period 2006–2008, the exclusion was $12,000).[9]

The formula for the gift tax is summarized in Figure 18.1.

LO.3

List and analyze the Federal estate tax formula.

Formula for the Federal Estate Tax

The Federal unified transfer tax at death, commonly known as the Federal estate tax, is summarized in Figure 18.2.

The gross estate includes all of the property a decedent owns at the time of death. The inclusion may even extend to property the decedent no longer owns—see the later discussion of gifts made within three years of death[10] and certain incomplete transfers.[11] Moreover, the gross estate is to be distinguished from the probate estate, which is property that is subject to administration by the executor. (The probate estate is discussed further later in the chapter.)

Deductions from the gross estate to arrive at the taxable estate are quite extensive. In addition to the debts of the decedent (e.g., mortgages, credit card accounts, and unpaid medical bills), they even include current and past income taxes (both Federal and state). As in the case of the Federal gift tax, transfers to charity and to a spouse are deductible.

Note that the taxable estate must be adjusted further to arrive at a tax base before a tentative estate tax can be determined. The further adjustment requires the consideration of prior taxable gifts. The reason post-1976 taxable gifts are added to the taxable estate to arrive at the tax base goes back to the scheme of the unified transfer tax. Starting in 1977, all transfers, whether lifetime or by death, were to be treated the same. Consequently, taxable gifts made after 1976 must be accounted for upon the death of the donor. Any possible double tax effect of including these gifts is mitigated by allowing a credit against the estate tax for the gift taxes previously paid or deemed paid.

Role of the Unified Tax Credit

The purpose of the **unified tax credit** is to allow donors and decedents to transfer specified amounts of wealth without being subject to the gift and estate taxes.

[9] § 2503(b)(2).

[10] § 2035.

[11] §§ 2036–2038.

FIGURE 18.1 **Formula for the Federal Gift Tax**

Determine whether the transfers are considered gifts by referring to §§ 2511 through 2519; list the fair market value of only the covered transfers		$xxx,xxx
Claim the annual exclusion (per donee) as available	$13,000 each	
Determine the charitable and marital deductions	xx,xxx	xx,xxx
Taxable gifts [as defined by § 2503(a)] for the current period		$ xx,xxx
Add: Taxable gifts from prior years		xx,xxx
Total of current and past taxable gifts		$ xx,xxx
Compute the gift tax on the total of current and past taxable gifts by using the rates in Appendix A		$ x,xxx
Subtract: Gift tax paid or deemed paid on past taxable gifts and the unified tax credit		xxx
Gift tax due on transfers during the current period		$ xxx

Table 18.1 shows the unified tax credit applicable to transfers by gift and by death from 2000 through 2013.[12]

The **exclusion amount** (also termed the **exemption equivalent** and the **bypass amount**) is the amount of the transfer that will pass free of the gift or estate tax by virtue of the credit.

EXAMPLE 3

In 2012, Janet makes a taxable gift of $5.12 million. Presuming that she has made no prior taxable gifts, Janet will not owe any gift tax. Under the tax rate schedules (see Appendix A, p. A-8), the tax on $5.12 million is $1,772,800, which is the exact amount of the credit allowed.[13] ■

FIGURE 18.2 **Formula for the Federal Estate Tax**

Gross estate (§§ 2031–2046)		$xxx,xxx
Subtract:		
Expenses, indebtedness, and taxes (§ 2053)	$xx	
Losses (§ 2054)	xx	
Charitable bequests (§ 2055)	xx	
Marital deduction (§§ 2056 and 2056A)	xx	
State death taxes (§ 2058)	xx	x,xxx
Taxable estate (§ 2051)		$ xx,xxx
Add: Post-1976 taxable gifts [§ 2001(b)]		x,xxx
Tax base		$xxx,xxx
Tentative tax on tax base [§ 2001(c)]		$ xx,xxx
Subtract:		
Unified transfer tax on post-1976 taxable gifts (gift taxes paid or deemed paid)	$xx	
Tax credits (including the unified tax credit) (§§ 2010–2016)	xx	x,xxx
Estate tax due		$ xxx

[12]The unified tax credits prior to 2000 can be found in §§ 2010 and 2505.

[13]The rate schedules are contained in § 2001(c), and *some* are reproduced in Appendix A of this text. The credits are subject to indexation for inflation for 2012, but the rate schedules are not.

TABLE 18.1 **Partial List of Unified Tax Credits**

	Gift Tax		Estate Tax	
Year of Transfer	**Credit**	**Exclusion Amount**	**Credit**	**Exclusion Amount**
2000 and 2001	$ 220,550	$ 675,000	$ 220,550	$ 675,000
2002 and 2003	345,800	1,000,000	345,800	1,000,000
2004 and 2005	345,800	1,000,000	555,800	1,500,000
2006, 2007, and 2008	345,800	1,000,000	780,800	2,000,000
2009	345,800	1,000,000	1,455,800	3,500,000
2010	330,800*	1,000,000	–0–	–0–
2011	1,730,800	5,000,000	1,730,800	5,000,000
2012	1,772,800	5,120,000	1,772,800	5,120,000
2013	345,800	1,000,000	345,800	1,000,000

*Maximum gift tax rate drops to 35%.

Valuation for Estate and Gift Tax Purposes (§ 2032)

The value of the property on the date of its transfer generally determines the amount that is subject to the gift tax or the estate tax. Under certain conditions, however, an executor can elect to value estate assets on the **alternate valuation date**. The election is made by the executor of the estate and is irrevocable.

The alternate valuation date election was designed as a relief provision to ease the economic hardship that could result when estate assets decline in value over the six months after the date of death. If the election is made, all assets of the estate are valued six months after death *or* on the date of disposition if this occurs earlier.[14] The election covers *all* assets in the gross estate and cannot be applied to only a portion of the property.

EXAMPLE 4

In 2012, Robert's gross estate consists of the following property.

	Value on Date of Death	Value Six Months Later
Land	$4,800,000	$4,840,000
Stock in Brown Corporation	900,000	700,000
Stock in Green Corporation	500,000	460,000
Total	$6,200,000	$6,000,000

If Robert's executor elects the alternate valuation date, the estate must be valued at $6 million. It is not permissible to value the land at its date of death value ($4.8 million) and choose the alternate valuation date for the rest of the gross estate. ■

EXAMPLE 5

Assume the same facts as in Example 4, except that the executor sells the stock in Green Corporation for $480,000 four months after Robert's death. If the alternate valuation date is elected, the estate must be valued at $6,020,000 ($4,840,000 + $700,000 + $480,000). As to the Green stock, the value on its date of disposition controls because that date occurred prior to the six months' alternate valuation date. ■

The alternate valuation date election is not available unless the estate must file a Form 706 (Estate Tax Return). When an estate is required to file a Form 706 is discussed later in this chapter.

[14] § 2032(a)(1). For this purpose, the term *disposition* is broadly defined. It includes the transfer of property to an heir to satisfy a bequest and the use of property to fund a testamentary trust. Reg. § 20.2032–1(c).

TAX IN THE NEWS Estate Planning in Perspective

The future of the Federal estate and gift taxes is uncertain. For example, the generous provisions of TRA of 2010 (i.e., maximum rate of 35 percent and a credit of $5 million) are unlikely to be made permanent. It is also unlikely that the sunset provisions (i.e., maximum rate of 55 percent and a credit of $1 million) will be allowed to take effect in 2013—see Table 18.1. All of this uncertainty is unfortunate as one of the keys to effective tax planning is the ability to rely on the stability of the tax law.

Wealth transfers entail long-term projections that are dependent on assumptions that the relevant tax law will remain largely constant. Once an estate plan is established, practitioners and their clients generally do not anticipate the need for frequent modifications.

The somewhat drastic changes in the estate and gift tax provisions have made this traditional long-term approach impossible. Consequently, the validity of an estate plan may need to be reevaluated every time Congress meets! This legislative instability adds to compliance costs and places an unnecessary burden on both taxpayers and their practitioners.

The election of the alternate valuation date must decrease the value of the gross estate *and* decrease the estate tax liability. The reason for this last requirement is that the income tax basis of property acquired from a decedent will be the value used for estate tax purposes (discussed further in Chapter 19). Without a special limitation, the alternate valuation date could be elected solely to add to income tax basis.

EXAMPLE 6

Al's gross estate consists of assets with a date of death value of $6 million and an alternate valuation date value of $6.1 million. Under Al's will, all of his property passes outright to Jean (Al's wife). Because of the marital deduction, no estate tax results regardless of which value is used. But if the alternate valuation date could be elected, Jean would have an income tax basis of $6.1 million in the property acquired from Al. ■

The alternate valuation date cannot be elected in Example 6 for two reasons, either of which would suffice. First, the alternate valuation date will not decrease Al's gross estate. Second, the election will not decrease Al's estate tax liability. Thus, his estate must use the date of death valuation of $6 million. As a result, Jean's income tax basis in the property received from Al is $6 million.

The election of the alternate valuation date does not take into account any postdeath income earned by the property. Any accrued income, therefore, is limited to that existing as of the date of death.

EXAMPLE 7

At the time of her death, Emma owned, *among other assets*, an apartment building with a value of $800,000 on which $40,000 of rents had accrued. On the alternate valuation date, the property had a value of $780,000, and accrued rents were $30,000. If the § 2032 election is made, $820,000 ($780,000 + $40,000) as to this property is included in Emma's gross estate. The $30,000 of postdeath income is not part of her gross estate. ■

Another valuation option available for estate tax purposes is the special use valuation method. Election of this method is limited to certain situations involving interests in closely held businesses (usually farms). Special use valuation is discussed in Chapter 19.

Key Property Concepts

When property is transferred either by gift or by death, the form of ownership can have a direct bearing on any transfer tax consequences. Understanding the different forms of ownership is necessary for working with Federal gift and estate taxes.

Undivided Ownership

Assume that Dan and Vicky own an undivided but equal interest in a tract of land. Such ownership can fall into any of four categories: joint tenancy, tenancy by the entirety, tenancy in common, or community property.

If Dan and Vicky hold ownership as **joint tenants** or **tenants by the entirety**, the right of survivorship exists. This means that the last tenant to survive receives full ownership of the property. Thus, if Dan predeceases Vicky, the land belongs entirely to Vicky. None of the land will pass to Dan's heirs or will be subject to administration by Dan's executor. A tenancy by the entirety is a joint tenancy between husband and wife.

If Dan and Vicky hold ownership as **tenants in common** or as community property, death does not defeat an owner's interest. Thus, if Dan predeceases Vicky, Dan's one-half interest in the land will pass to his estate or heirs.

Community property interests arise from the marital relationship. Normally, all property acquired after marriage, except by gift or inheritance, by husband and wife residing in a community property state becomes part of the community. The following states have the community property system in effect: Louisiana, Texas, New Mexico, Arizona, California, Washington, Idaho, Nevada, Wisconsin, and (by election of the spouses) Alaska. All other states follow the common law system of ascertaining a spouse's rights to property acquired after marriage.

Partial Interests

Interests in assets can be divided in terms of rights to income and principal. Particularly when property is placed in trust, it is not uncommon to carve out various income interests that must be accounted for separately from the ultimate disposition of the property itself.

EXAMPLE 8

Under Bill's will, a ranch is to be placed in trust, life estate to Sam, Bill's son, with remainder to Sam's children (Bill's grandchildren). Under this arrangement, Sam is the life tenant and, as such, is entitled to the use of the ranch (including any income) during his life. Upon Sam's death, the trust terminates, and its principal passes to his children. Thus, Sam's children receive outright ownership in the ranch when Sam dies. ■

18.2 The Federal Gift Tax

LO.4

Illustrate the operation of the Federal gift tax.

General Considerations

In working with the gift tax, it is first necessary to determine whether a gift has in fact taken place. In addition, some transfers are excluded from the gift tax.

Requirements for a Gift

For a gift to be complete under state law, the following elements must be present.

- A donor competent to make the gift.
- A donee capable of receiving and possessing the property.
- Donative intent on behalf of the donor.
- Actual or constructive delivery of the property to the donee or the donee's representative.
- Acceptance of the gift by the donee.

Incomplete Transfers

The Federal gift tax does not apply to transfers that are incomplete. Thus, if the transferor retains the right to reclaim the property or has not really parted with the possession of the property, a taxable event has not taken place.

EXAMPLE 9

Lesly creates a trust, income payable to Mary for life, remainder to Paul. Under the terms of the trust instrument, Lesly can revoke the trust at any time and repossess the trust principal and the income earned. No gift takes place on the creation of the trust; Lesly has not ceased to have dominion and control over the property. ■

EXAMPLE 10

Assume the same facts as in Example 9, except that one year after the transfer, Lesly relinquishes his right to terminate the trust. At this point, the transfer becomes complete, and the Federal gift tax applies. ■

Business versus Personal Setting

In a business setting, full and adequate consideration is apt to exist. If the parties are acting in a personal setting, however, a gift usually is the result.

EXAMPLE 11

Grace loans money to Debby in connection with a business venture. About a year later, Grace forgives part of the loan. Grace probably has not made a gift to Debby if she and Debby are unrelated parties.[15] ■

EXAMPLE 12

Assume the same facts as in Example 11, except that Grace and Debby are mother and daughter and no business venture is involved. If the loan itself was not actually a disguised gift, the later forgiveness is probably a gift. ■

It is the position of the IRS that valuable consideration (such as would preclude a gift result) does not include a payment or transfer based on "love and affection ... promise of marriage, etc."[16] Consequently, property settlements in consideration of marriage (i.e., pre- or antenuptial agreements) are regarded as gifts.

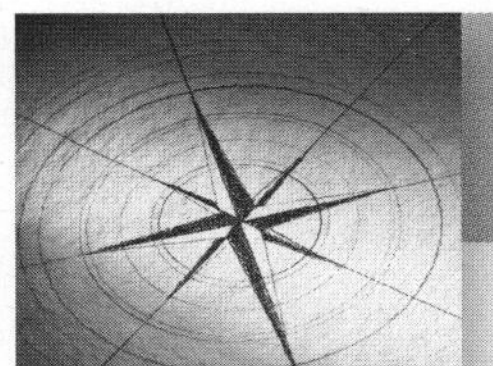

ETHICS & EQUITY It's the Thought That Counts

Joe (age 86) and Nicole (age 22) are married. Two days later, they exchange wedding gifts. Joe's gift to Nicole is stock in IBM (valued at $2 million), while Nicole's gift to Joe is a bottle of cologne (value of $32). What tax goals are they trying to accomplish? Will their plan work?

Do not conclude that the presence of *some* consideration is enough to preclude Federal gift tax consequences. Again, the answer may rest on whether the transfer occurred in a business setting.

EXAMPLE 13

Peter sells Bob some real estate for $40,000. Unknown to Peter, the property contains valuable mineral deposits and is really worth $200,000. Peter may have made a bad business deal, but he has not made a gift of $160,000 to Bob. ■

EXAMPLE 14

Assume the same facts as in Example 13, except that Peter and Bob are father and son. In addition, Peter is very much aware that the property is worth $200,000. Peter has made a gift of $160,000 to Bob. ■

---

[15] The forgiveness could result in taxable income to Debby under § 61(a)(12).

[16] Reg. § 25.2512–8.

Certain Excluded Transfers

Transfers to political organizations are exempt from the application of the Federal gift tax.[17] This provision in the Code made unnecessary the previous practice whereby candidates for public office established multiple campaign committees to maximize the number of annual exclusions available to their contributors. As noted later, an annual exclusion of $13,000 for each donee passes free of the Federal gift tax.

The Federal gift tax does not apply to tuition payments made to an educational organization (e.g., a college) on another's behalf. Nor does it apply to amounts paid on another's behalf for medical care.[18] In this regard, the law is realistic because it is unlikely that most donors would recognize these items as transfers subject to the gift tax. The payments, however, must be made directly to the provider (e.g., physician, hospital, or college). There is no requirement that the beneficiary of the service (e.g., patient or student) qualify as a dependent of the person making the payment.

THE BIG PICTURE

EXAMPLE 15

Return to the facts of *The Big Picture* on p. 18-1. After Peter died in 2000, his widow, Martha, continued to live in the family home and refused to move in with either of her children (John or Helen). As Martha's health and mental condition deteriorated, her children did everything possible to keep the family housekeeper from quitting. In fact, Helen paid for the housekeeper's gallbladder operation, and John paid the college tuition of her oldest son.

Neither Helen nor John has made gifts to the housekeeper or her son that are subject to taxation. Gifts would have occurred, however, if Helen and John had reimbursed the housekeeper for the amounts involved, instead of paying the providers (i.e., physician, hospital, and college) directly.

Satisfying an obligation of support is not subject to the gift tax. Thus, no gift takes place when parents pay for their children's education because one of the obligations of parents is to educate their children. What constitutes an obligation of support is determined by applicable state law. In many states, for example, adult children may have an obligation of support with respect to providing for indigent parents.

ETHICS & EQUITY What Constitutes Support?

When Earl's daughter, Clara, turns 40, he gives her a Mercedes convertible as a birthday present. Clara is married and has a family of her own. She is a licensed orthopedic surgeon and maintains a successful practice in the field of sports medicine.

Earl does not regard the transfer as being subject to the gift tax. As a parent, he is merely satisfying his obligation of support. Such obligation includes providing your child with transportation. Is Earl's reasoning sound?

Lifetime versus Death Transfers

Be careful to distinguish between lifetime *(inter vivos)* and death (testamentary) transfers.

[17] § 2501(a)(5).

[18] § 2503(e).

EXAMPLE 16

Dudley buys a 12-month certificate of deposit (CD) from State Bank and lists ownership as follows: "Dudley, payable on proof of death to Faye." Nine months later, Dudley dies. When the CD matures, Faye collects the proceeds from State Bank. No gift takes place when Dudley invests in the CD; Faye has received a mere expectancy (i.e., to obtain ownership of the CD upon Dudley's death). At any time before his death, Dudley may withdraw the funds or delete Faye's name from the account, thereby cutting off her expectancy. Furthermore, no gift occurs upon Dudley's death as the CD passes to Faye by testamentary disposition. As noted later, the CD will be included in Dudley's gross estate as property in which the decedent had an interest (§ 2033). ■

The payable on death (POD) designation used in Example 16 is a form of ownership frequently used in a family setting when investments are involved (e.g., stocks and bonds and savings accounts). It is very similar in effect to a revocable trust (see Example 9). Both carry the advantage of avoiding the probate estate (see Chapter 19). The POD designation, however, is simpler to use in the case of bank accounts and securities, and it avoids the need of having to create a formal trust.

Transfers Subject to the Gift Tax

Whether a transfer is subject to the Federal gift tax depends upon the application of §§ 2511 through 2519 and the applicable Regulations.

Gift Loans

Loans between related parties are quite common. Such loans are frequently made to help pay for a college education or to finance a new business owned by a family member. Presuming that the advance is a bona fide loan at the outset (i.e., a gift is not intended), the absence of a provision for adequate interest can generate a multitude of tax consequences.

EXAMPLE 17

Harold lends his daughter Venetia $400,000 to start a dental practice. The loan is payable on demand, and no interest is provided for. Assuming a Federal interest rate of 10%, *each year* the loan is outstanding, the following tax consequences ensue.

- *Gift tax*. Harold makes a gift to Venetia of $40,000 (10% × $400,000). The annual exclusion is available to offset part of this transfer.
- *Income tax*. Harold has interest income of $40,000, and Venetia has an interest deduction of a like amount.[19] Because it relates to her trade or business, Venetia has a deduction *for* adjusted gross income. ■

The Code defines a gift loan as "any below-market loan where the foregoing [sic] of interest is in the nature of a gift."[20] Unless tax avoidance was one of the principal purposes of the loan, special limitations apply if the gift loan does not exceed $100,000. In such a case, the interest element may not exceed the borrower's net investment income.[21] Furthermore, if the net investment income does not exceed $1,000, it is treated as zero. Under a $1,000 *de minimis* rule, the interest element is disregarded.

Certain Property Settlements (§ 2516)

Normally, the settlement of certain marital rights is not regarded as being for consideration and is subject to the Federal gift tax.[22] As a special exception to this general approach, Congress enacted § 2516. By this provision, transfers of property interests made under the terms of a written agreement between spouses in settlement of their marital or property rights are deemed to be for adequate

[19]Example 20 in Chapter 1 deals with a similar situation and covers any nonbusiness bad debt deduction the creditor might have if the loan is not repaid.

[20]§ 7872(f)(3).

[21]Net investment income has the same meaning given to the term by § 163(d). Generally, net investment income is investment income (e.g., interest and dividends) less related expenses.

[22]Reg. § 25.2512–8.

consideration. These transfers are exempt from the Federal gift tax if a final decree of divorce is obtained within the three-year period beginning on the date one year before the parties entered into the agreement. Likewise excluded are transfers to provide a reasonable allowance for the support of minor children (including legally adopted children) of a marriage. The agreement need not be approved by the divorce decree.

THE BIG PICTURE

EXAMPLE 18

Return to the facts of *The Big Picture* on p. 18-1. Recall that John and Hannah's divorce became final in January 2012. After extended but amicable negotiations, in September 2010, John and Hannah agreed on a property settlement. In return for the receipt of $200,000 and title to their home, Hannah released all of her marital rights. Shortly thereafter, John made the transfer. Under § 2516, the property settlement resulted in no gift tax consequences to John.

Disclaimers (§ 2518)

A **disclaimer** is a refusal by a person to accept property that is designated to pass to him or her. The effect of the disclaimer is to pass the property to someone else.

THE BIG PICTURE

EXAMPLE 19

Return to the facts of *The Big Picture* on p. 18-1. Recall that Martha died of a heart condition in July. Under her will, her estate passes in equal parts to her son and daughter or, if they disclaim, to their children. (Under a buy-sell agreement—see Chapter 19—Martha's stock in Hood Corporation is redeemed by the corporation with the insurance proceeds from a policy it took out on her life.) Helen disclaims her share of the inheritance, and the assets pass to her children.

Why might Helen disclaim her inheritance and have the property pass directly from Martha to the children? By doing so, an extra transfer tax may be avoided. If the disclaimer does not take place (i.e., Helen accepts the inheritance) and the property eventually passes to the children (either by gift or by death), the later transfer is subject to the application of either the gift tax or the estate tax.

The Federal gift tax can also be avoided in cases of a partial disclaimer of an undivided interest.

THE BIG PICTURE

EXAMPLE 20

Assume the same facts as in Example 19. John's share of his inheritance from Martha also includes the family hunting lodge. Except for the hunting lodge, John disclaims his share of the inheritance, and the remaining assets pass to his children.

To be effective, the disclaimer must be in writing and timely made. Generally, this means no later than nine months after the right to the property arose. Furthermore, the person making the disclaimer must not have accepted any benefits or interest in the property.

Other Transfers Subject to Gift Tax

Other transfers that may carry gift tax consequences (e.g., the exercise of a power of appointment and the creation of joint ownership) are discussed and illustrated in connection with the Federal estate tax.

Income Tax Considerations

Generally, a donor has no income tax consequences on making a gift.[23] A donee recognizes no income on the receipt of a gift.[24] A donee's income tax basis in the property received depends on a number of factors (e.g., donor's basis, year of gift, and gift tax incurred by donor) and is discussed elsewhere in this text.[25]

Annual Exclusion

In General

The first $13,000 of gifts made to any one person during any calendar year (except gifts of future interests in property) is excluded in determining the total amount of gifts for the year.[26] The **annual exclusion** applies to all gifts of a present interest made during the calendar year in the order in which they are made until the $13,000 exclusion per donee is exhausted. For a gift in trust, each beneficiary of the trust is treated as a separate person for purposes of the exclusion.

A **future interest** is defined as an interest that will come into being (as to use, possession, or enjoyment) at some future date. Examples of future interests include rights such as remainder interests that are commonly encountered when property is transferred to a trust. A *present interest* is an unrestricted right to the immediate use, possession, or enjoyment of property or of the income.

EXAMPLE 21

During 2012, Laura makes the following cash gifts: $8,000 to Rita and $14,000 to Maureen. Laura may claim an annual exclusion of $8,000 with respect to Rita and $13,000 with respect to Maureen. ■

EXAMPLE 22

By a lifetime gift, Ron transfers property to a trust with a life estate (with income payable annually) to June and remainder upon June's death to Albert. Ron has made two gifts: one to June of a life estate and one to Albert of a remainder interest. (The valuation of each of these gifts is discussed in Chapter 19.) The life estate is a present interest and qualifies for the annual exclusion. The remainder interest granted to Albert is a future interest and does not qualify for the exclusion. Note that Albert's interest does not come into being until some future date (upon the death of June). ■

Although Example 22 indicates that the gift of an income interest is a present interest, this is not always the case. If a possibility exists that the income beneficiary may not receive the immediate enjoyment of the property, the transfer is of a future interest.

EXAMPLE 23

Assume the same facts as in Example 22, except that the income from the trust need not be payable annually to June. It may, at the trustee's discretion, be accumulated and added to the principal. Because June's right to receive the income from the trust is conditioned on the trustee's discretion, it is not a present interest. No annual exclusion is allowed. The mere possibility of diversion is enough. It would not matter if the trustee never exercised the discretion to accumulate and did, in fact, distribute the trust income to June annually. ■

Trust for Minors

Section 2503(c) offers an important exception to the future interest rules just discussed. Under this provision, a transfer for the benefit of a person who has not attained the age of 21 on the date of the gift may be considered a gift of a present interest. This is true even though the minor is not given the unrestricted right to

[23]For situations where recognition can occur, see Chapter 19, Example 34.
[24]Both gifts and inheritances are excluded from income under § 103.
[25]Section 1015 is discussed and illustrated in Chapter 19, Examples 17 and 18.
[26]§ 2503(b).

the immediate use, possession, or enjoyment of the property. For the exception to apply, the following conditions must be satisfied.

- Both the property and its income may be expended by or for the benefit of the minor before the minor attains the age of 21.
- Any portion of the property or its income not expended by the time the minor reaches the age of 21 shall pass to the minor at that time.
- If the minor dies before attaining the age of 21, the property and its income will be payable either to the minor's estate or as the minor may designate under a general power of appointment (discussed later in the chapter).

The exception allows a trustee to accumulate income on behalf of a minor beneficiary without converting the income interest to a future interest.

Contributions to Qualified Tuition Programs

For income tax purposes, § 529 plans possess attributes that reflect the best of all possible worlds. Although no up-front deduction is allowed,[27] income earned by the fund accumulates free of income tax and distributions are not taxed if they are used for higher education purposes. A special provision allows a donor to enjoy a gift tax advantage by using five years of annual exclusions.[28]

EXAMPLE 24

Trevor and Audrey would like to start building a college education fund for their 10-year-old granddaughter Loni. In 2012, Trevor contributes $130,000 to the designated carrier of their state's § 529 plan. By electing to split the gift and using five annual exclusions [2 (number of donors) × $13,000 (annual exclusion) × 5 years = $130,000], no taxable gift results. (The gift-splitting election is discussed in detail later in this chapter.) Making the five-year election precludes Trevor and Audrey from using any annual exclusion on gifts to Loni for the next four years.[29] ■

Section 529(c)(4) provides that these college plans are not to be included in the gross estate of the transferor. This preferential treatment is needed because § 529 plans are incomplete transfers (some or all of the funds may be returned if college is not attended). As noted later, incomplete transfers are invariably subject to the estate tax.

Deductions

In arriving at taxable gifts, a deduction is allowed for transfers to certain qualified charitable organizations. On transfers between spouses, a marital deduction may be available. Because both the charitable and marital deductions apply in determining the Federal estate tax, these deductions are discussed later in the chapter.

LO.5

Calculate the Federal gift tax.

Computing the Federal Gift Tax

The Unified Transfer Tax Rate Schedule

The top rates of the unified transfer tax rate schedule originally reached as high as 70 percent. Over the years, these top rates were reduced to 55 percent and then to 45 percent for 2007.[30] Effective for 2011 and 2012, the top rate is 35 percent for both the gift tax and the estate tax. (The 35 percent rate is the lowest since the Hoover administration.) Keep in mind that the unified transfer tax rate schedule applies to all transfers (by gift or death) after 1976. Different rate schedules apply for pre-1977 gifts and pre-1977 deaths.

[27]Depending on the taxpayer's home state, some (or all) of the deduction may be allowed for *state* income tax purposes.

[28]Section 529(c)(2)(A) protects against future interest treatment.

[29]Trevor and Audrey could resort to § 2503(e)(2)(A) to avoid any gift at all. As mentioned earlier, a *direct* payment of tuition to certain educational institutions is exempt from the gift tax. But this rule does not help build an education fund for future use, as § 529 does. Recall that Loni, the granddaughter, is 10 years old.

[30]§ 2001(c)(2)(B). Note the drop in the top rate from 50% to 45% in the rate schedules for 2002 through 2007, reproduced in Appendix A. The rates for 2011 and 2012 are on p. A-8 and on the inside back cover of the text.

TAX IN THE NEWS Uncovering Unreported Gifts

How does the IRS discover that transfers between family members have been made but not reported as gifts? At least in the case of real estate, the use of state land transfer records may provide leads as to giftlike transactions that have occurred. If the values involved are large enough, further investigation by the IRS can reveal noncompliance on the part of donors in not reporting and paying any gift tax that was due.

Source: Adapted from Arden Dale, "IRS Scrutinizes Gifts of Real Estate," *Wall Street Journal*, May 26, 2011, p. C-13.

The Deemed Paid Adjustment

As noted earlier, the gift tax is cumulative in effect (see Example 1). Because this means that prior transfers will again be subject to tax, a credit is allowed for the taxes previously incurred (see Example 2). However, the amount of the credit allowed is based on the rates currently in effect. Called the *deemed paid* credit, it could be the same as, less than, or more than the tax actually paid. The difference between the deemed paid taxes and those actually paid is attributable to the change in the tax rate schedule that has taken place over the years. For example, see the variation in rates in Appendix A, pp. A-4 through A-7).

The Election to Split Gifts by Married Persons

To understand the reason for the gift-splitting election of § 2513, consider the following situations.

EXAMPLE 25

Dick and Margaret are husband and wife who reside in Michigan, a common law state. Dick has been the only breadwinner in the family, and Margaret has no significant property of her own. Neither has made any prior taxable gifts. In 2012, Dick makes a gift to Leslie of $6,026,000. Presuming that the election to split gifts did not exist, Dick's gift tax is as follows.

Amount of gift	$ 6,026,000
Subtract: Annual exclusion	(13,000)
Taxable gift	$ 6,013,000
Gift tax on $6,013,000 per Appendix A, p. A-8 [$155,800 + 35% ($6,013,000 − $500,000)]	$ 2,085,350
Subtract: Unified transfer tax credit for 2012	(1,772,800)
Gift tax due on the 2012 taxable gift	$ 312,550

■

EXAMPLE 26

Assume the same facts as in Example 25, except that Dick and Margaret always have resided in California (a community property state). Even though Dick is the sole breadwinner, income from personal services generally is community property. Consequently, the gift to Leslie probably involves community property. If this is the case, the gift tax is as follows.

	Dick	Margaret
Amount of gift	$ 3,013,000	$ 3,013,000
Subtract: Annual exclusion	(13,000)	(13,000)
Taxable gift	$ 3,000,000	$ 3,000,000
Gift tax on $3,000,000 per Appendix A, p. A-8	$ 1,030,800	$ 1,030,800
Subtract: Unified transfer tax credit for 2012	(1,772,800)	(1,772,800)
Gift tax due on the 2012 taxable gift	$ –0–	$ –0–

■

As the results of Examples 25 and 26 indicate, married donors residing in community property jurisdictions possessed a significant gift tax advantage over those residing in common law states. To rectify this inequity, the Revenue Act of 1948 incorporated into the Code the predecessor to § 2513. Under this provision, a gift made by a person to someone other than his or her spouse may be considered, for Federal gift tax purposes, as having been made one-half by each spouse. Returning to Example 25, Dick and Margaret could treat the gift passing to Leslie as being made one-half by each of them. They may do this even though the cash belonged to Dick. As a result, the parties are able to achieve the same tax consequence as in Example 26. As is the case with the owner spouse, any past taxable gifts of the nonowner spouse must be taken into account in determining the current gift tax.

To split gifts, the spouses must be legally married to each other at the time of the gift. If they are divorced later in the calendar year, they may still split the gift if neither marries anyone else during that year. They both must indicate on their separate gift tax returns their consent to have all gifts made in that calendar year split between them. In addition, both must be citizens or residents of the United States on the date of the gift. A gift from one spouse to the other spouse cannot be split. Such a gift might, however, be eligible for the marital deduction.

The election to split gifts is not necessary when husband and wife transfer jointly owned or community property to a third party. It is available, however, if the gift consists of the separate property of one of the spouses. Community property rules generally define separate property as property acquired before marriage and property acquired after marriage by gift or inheritance. The election, then, is not limited to residents of common law states.

Special Rule for Gifts Made in 2010

In addition to eliminating the estate tax for 2010, EGTRRA of 2001 provided special rules for gifts made in 2010.

- The maximum tax rate was reduced to 35 percent—see Appendix A, p. A-7.
- Although the exclusion amount remains at $1 million, the credit allowed drops to $330,800—see Table 18.1.

As previously noted, after 2010 the exclusion amounts for both the gift tax and the estate tax are the same (i.e., unified) and rise to $5 million.

Procedural Matters

Having determined which transfers are subject to the Federal gift tax and the various deductions and exclusions available to the donor, the procedural aspects of the tax should be considered. The following section discusses the return itself, the due dates for filing and paying the tax, and other related matters.

The Federal Gift Tax Return

For transfers by gift, a Form 709 (U.S. Gift Tax Return) must be filed whenever the gifts for any one calendar year exceed the annual exclusion or involve a gift of a future interest. A Form 709 need not be filed, however, for transfers between spouses that are offset by the unlimited marital deduction regardless of the amount of the transfer.[31]

EXAMPLE 27

In 2012, Larry makes five gifts, each in the amount of $13,000, to his five children. If the gifts do not involve future interests, a Form 709 need not be filed to report the transfers. ■

[31] § 6019(a)(2).

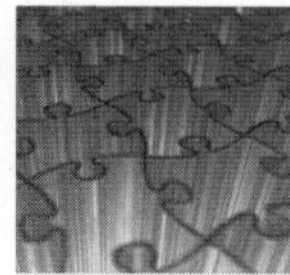

CONCEPT SUMMARY 18.1

Federal Gift Tax Provisions

1. The Federal gift tax applies to all gratuitous transfers of property made by U.S. citizens or residents. In this regard, it does not matter where the property is located.
2. In the eyes of the IRS, a gratuitous transfer is one not supported by full and adequate consideration. If the parties are acting in a business setting, such consideration usually exists. If, however, purported sales are between family members, a gift element may be suspected.
3. If one party lends money to another and intends some or all of the interest element to be a gift, the arrangement is categorized as a gift loan. To the extent the interest provided for is less than the market rate, three tax consequences result. First, a gift has taken place between the lender and the borrower as to the interest element. Second, income may result to the lender. Third, an income tax deduction may be available to the borrower.
4. Property settlements can escape the gift tax if a divorce occurs within a prescribed period of time.
5. A disclaimer is a refusal by a person to accept property designated to pass to that person. The effect of a disclaimer is to pass the property to someone else. If certain conditions are satisfied, the issuance of a disclaimer will not be subject to the Federal gift tax.
6. Except for gifts of future interests, a donor is allowed an annual exclusion of $13,000. The future interest limitation does not apply to certain trusts created for minors.
7. The election to split a gift enables a married couple to be treated as two donors. The election doubles the annual exclusion and makes the nonowner spouse's unified tax credit available to the owner spouse.
8. The election to split gifts is not necessary if the property is jointly owned by the spouses. That is the case when the property is part of the couple's community.
9. In determining the tax base for computing the gift tax, all prior taxable gifts must be added to current taxable gifts. Thus, the gift tax is cumulative in nature.
10. Gifts are reported on Form 709. The return is due on April 15 following the year of the gift.

EXAMPLE 28

During 2012, Esther makes a gift of $26,000 cash of her separate property to her daughter. To double the amount of the annual exclusion allowed, Jerry (Esther's husband) is willing to split the gift. Because the § 2513 election can be made only on a gift tax return, a Form 709 must be filed even though no gift tax will be due as a result of the transfer. ■

In Example 28, no gift tax return would be necessary if the transfer consisted of community property. Because two donors are now involved, the cap for filing becomes more than $26,000, rather than more than $13,000.

Presuming that a gift tax return is due, it must be filed on or before the fifteenth day of April following the year of the gift.[32] As is the case with other Federal taxes, when the due date falls on Saturday, Sunday, or a legal holiday, the date for filing the return is the next business day. Note that the filing requirements for Form 709 have no correlation to the accounting year used by a donor for Federal income tax purposes. Thus, a fiscal year taxpayer must follow the April 15 rule for any reportable gifts. If sufficient reason is shown, the IRS is authorized to grant reasonable extensions of time for filing the return.[33]

Key gift tax provisions are reviewed in Concept Summary 18.1.

18.3 The Federal Estate Tax

The following discussion of the estate tax coincides with the formula that appeared earlier in the chapter in Figure 18.2. The key components in the formula are the

[32] § 6075(b)(1).

[33] § 6081. Under § 6075(b)(2), an extension of time granted to a calendar year taxpayer for filing an income tax return automatically extends the due date of a gift tax return.

gross estate, the taxable estate, the tax base, and the credits allowed against the tentative tax. This formula can be summarized as follows:

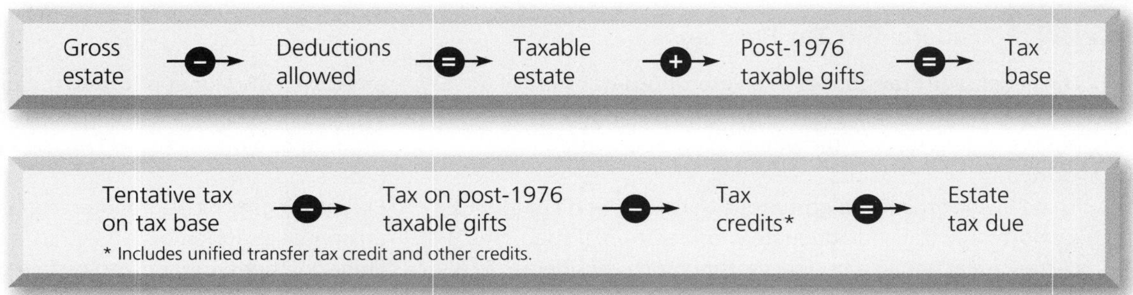

LO.6

Identify the components of the gross estate.

Gross Estate

Simply stated, the **gross estate** includes all property subject to the Federal estate tax. This depends on the provisions of the Internal Revenue Code as supplemented by IRS pronouncements and the judicial interpretations of Federal courts.

In contrast to the gross estate, the **probate estate** is controlled by state (rather than Federal) law. The probate estate consists of all of a decedent's property subject to administration by the executor or administrator of the estate. The administration is supervised by a local court of appropriate jurisdiction (usually designated as a probate court). An executor is the decedent's personal representative appointed under the decedent's will. When a decedent dies without a will or fails to name an executor in the will (or that person refuses to serve), the local probate court appoints an administrator.

The probate estate is frequently smaller than the gross estate. It contains only property owned by the decedent at the time of death and passing to heirs under a will or under the law of intestacy (the order of distribution for those dying without a will). As noted later, such items as the proceeds of many life insurance policies and distributions from retirement plans become part of the gross estate but are not included in the probate estate.

All states provide for an order of distribution in the event someone dies *intestate* (i.e., without a will). After the surviving spouse, who receives some or all of the estate, the preference is usually in the following order: down to lineal descendants (e.g., children and grandchildren), up to lineal ascendants (e.g., parents and grandparents), and out to collateral relations (e.g., brothers, sisters, aunts, and uncles).

Property Owned by the Decedent (§ 2033)

Property owned by the decedent at the time of death is included in the gross estate. The nature of the property or the use to which it was put during the decedent-owner's lifetime has no significance as far as the estate tax is concerned. Thus, personal effects (such as clothing), stocks, bonds, mutual funds, furniture, jewelry, bank accounts, and certificates of deposit are all included in the deceased owner's gross estate. No distinction is made between tangible and intangible, depreciable and nondepreciable, or business and personal assets. However, a deceased spouse's gross estate does not include the surviving spouse's share of the community property.

The application of § 2033 is illustrated as follows:

EXAMPLE 29

Irma dies owning some City of Denver bonds. The fair market value of the bonds plus any interest accrued to the date of Irma's death is included in her gross estate. Although interest on municipals normally is not taxable under the Federal income tax, it is property owned by Irma at the time of death. However, any interest accrued after death is not part of Irma's gross estate. ■

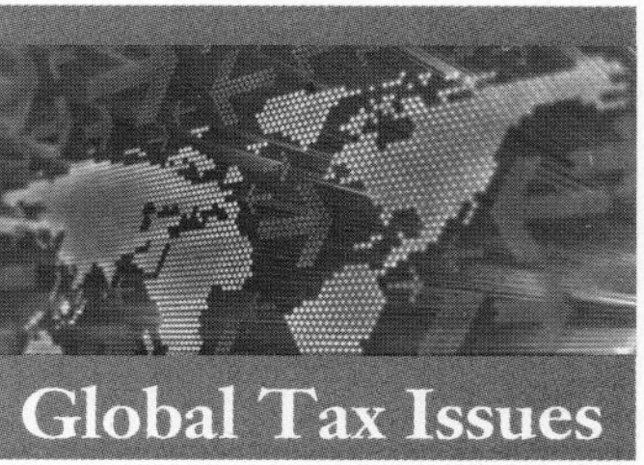

© Andrey Prokhorov, iStockphoto

Foreign Transfer Taxes—A Mixed Bag

Of the 30 countries that are members of the Organization for Economic Cooperation and Development (OECD), only the United States and the United Kingdom assess gift and estate taxes that apply to transfers during life *and* at death. The majority of OECD countries impose inheritance taxes. Six countries—Australia, Canada, Mexico, New Zealand, the Slovak Republic, and Sweden—impose neither inheritance nor estate taxes. In Canada, however, the transfer of a capital asset at death is treated as a sale, and any gain must be recognized even though no sale occurs. In Australia and Mexico, the decedent's income tax basis carries over to the heir. New Zealand does not have an estate tax, but it imposes a form of gift tax for annual lifetime transfers beyond a certain amount.

Source: Adapted from Joint Committee on Taxation, "Description and Analysis of Alternative Wealth Transfer Tax Systems," March 10, 2008, p. 3.

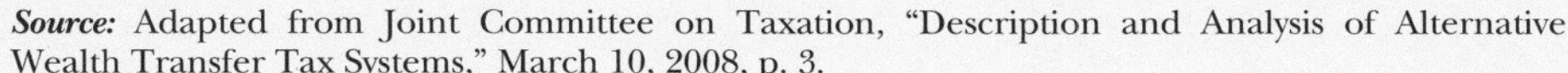

EXAMPLE 30

Sharon dies on April 7, 2012, at a time when she owns stock in Robin Corporation and Wren Corporation. On March 2 of this year, both corporations authorized a cash dividend payable on May 4. Robin's dividend is payable to shareholders of record as of April 2. Wren's date of record is April 9. Sharon's gross estate includes the following: the stock in Robin Corporation, the stock in Wren Corporation, and the dividend on the Robin stock. It does not include the dividend on the Wren stock. ■

EXAMPLE 31

Ray dies holding some promissory notes issued to him by his son. In his will, Ray forgives these notes, relieving the son of the obligation to make any payments. The fair market value of these notes is included in Ray's gross estate. ■

THE BIG PICTURE

EXAMPLE 32

Return to the facts of *The Big Picture* on p. 18-1. At the time of his death, John was the president of Hood Corporation. John's estate receives a distribution from Hood's qualified pension plan of $1.1 million consisting of the following:

Hood's contributions	$450,000
John's after-tax contributions	350,000
Income earned by the plan	300,000

John's estate also receives $150,000 from Hawk Insurance Company. The payment represents the maturity value of term life insurance from a group plan that Hood maintains for its employees. As to these amounts, John's gross estate includes $1,250,000 ($1,100,000 + $150,000). For income tax purposes, however, $750,000 ($450,000 + $300,000) is subject to tax, while $500,000 ($350,000 + $150,000) is not.

Regarding the result reached in Example 32, retirement plan benefits are invariably subject to estate tax. Besides the conventional qualified pension and profit-sharing plans involved in Example 32, retirement plans include those under § 401(k), § 403(b) for teachers, § 457 for government employees, Keogh (H.R. 10) for self-employed persons, and IRAs—both traditional and Roth. Inclusion in the gross estate occurs irrespective of income tax consequences. Thus, a benefit paid under a Roth IRA is fully subject to the estate tax even though it may not be taxable as income to the beneficiary. The possibility of an income tax deduction for estate taxes paid is covered in Chapter 20 in connection with the discussion of income in respect of a decedent.

In addition to the items noted above, § 2033 operates to include in the gross estate many assets that can be of significant value. Examples include:

- Real estate holdings (but see § 2040 for jointly owned property).
- Present value of future royalty rights (e.g., patents, copyrights, and mineral interests).
- Interests in a business (i.e., sole proprietorship and partnership).
- Collectibles (e.g., works of art and coin collections).
- Renewal value of leasehold interests.
- Terminable interests (e.g., life estates in realty or trusts) held by a surviving spouse as to which a deceased spouse's estate has made a QTIP election (discussed later in this chapter).
- Unmatured insurance policies on the lives of others.
- Proceeds from casualty and life insurance policies payable to the estate.
- Present value of pending and potential lawsuits or past judgments rendered.

THE BIG PICTURE

EXAMPLE 33

Return to the facts of *The Big Picture* on p. 18-1. Recall that John's death ultimately resulted from injuries suffered in a car accident caused by another motorist. In addition, John's auto was destroyed in the accident. Presuming that the other driver is solvent or carries casualty insurance, John's gross estate should include the present value of any expected settlement that could result from possible legal action. At the least, his estate must include the recovery expected from his own casualty policy.

Dower and Curtesy Interests (§ 2034)

In its common law (nonstatutory) form, dower generally gave a surviving widow a life estate in a portion of her husband's estate (usually the real estate he owned) with the remainder passing to their children. Most states have modified and codified these common law rules, and the resulting statutes often vary between jurisdictions. Curtesy is a similar right held by the husband in his wife's property that takes effect in the event he survives her.

Dower and curtesy rights are incomplete interests and may never materialize. Thus, if a wife predeceases her husband, the dower interest in her husband's property is lost.

EXAMPLE 34

Martin dies without a will, leaving an estate of $6.9 million. Under state law, Belinda (Martin's widow) is entitled to one-third of his property. The $2.3 million that Belinda receives is included in Martin's gross estate. Depending on the nature of the interest Belinda receives in the $2.3 million, this amount could qualify Martin's estate for a marital deduction. (This possibility is discussed at greater length later in the chapter. For the time being, however, the focus is on what is or is not included as part of the decedent's gross estate.) ■

Adjustments for Gifts Made within Three Years of Death (§ 2035)

At one time, all taxable gifts made within three years of death were included in the donor's gross estate unless it could be shown that the gifts were not made in contemplation of death. The special three-year rule for "deathbed gifts" was needed because the gift and estate taxes had not yet been merged into a unified tax. Making such gifts prior to death was advantageous then, as the lower tax rates of the separate gift tax applied.

With the adoption of the unified transfer tax system, post-1976 taxable gifts are added to the taxable estate in arriving at the tax base for determining the estate tax liability—see Figure 18.2 earlier in the chapter. Nevertheless, the three-year rule for inclusion in the gross estate has been retained for the following items.

- Inclusion in the gross estate of any gift tax paid on gifts made within three years of death. Called the *gross-up* procedure, it prevents the gift tax amount from escaping the estate tax.
- Any property interests transferred by gift within three years of death that would have been included in the gross estate and consist of transfers with a retained life estate (§ 2036), transfers taking effect at death (§ 2037), revocable transfers (§ 2038), and proceeds of life insurance (§ 2042). All except transfers taking effect at death (§ 2037) are discussed later in the chapter.

EXAMPLE 35

Before her death in 2012, Jennifer made the following taxable gifts.

Year of Gift	Nature of the Asset	Fair Market Value: Date of Gift	Fair Market Value: Date of Death	Gift Tax Paid
1992	Hawk Corporation stock	$200,000	$1,300,000	$ –0–
2010	Policy on Jennifer's life	80,000 (cash value)	1,000,000 (face value)	–0–
2010	Land	800,000	810,000	16,000

Jennifer's *gross estate* includes $1,016,000 [$1,000,000 (life insurance proceeds) + $16,000 (gross-up for the gift tax on the 2010 taxable gift)] as to these transfers. Referring to the formula for the estate tax (see Figure 18.2), the other post-1976 taxable gifts are added to the *taxable estate* (at the fair market value on the date of the gift) in arriving at the tax base. In the case of the Hawk stock, notice the substantial saving in transfer taxes that will occur. The gift tax (although none resulted) is based on $200,000, whereas an estate tax would have applied to $1.3 million. Thus, the appreciation of $1.1 million has escaped any transfer tax. Jennifer's estate is allowed a credit for the gift tax paid (or deemed paid) on the 2010 transfer. ■

The three-year rule also applies in testing for qualification under § 303 (stock redemptions to pay death taxes and administration expenses), § 2032A (special valuation procedures), and § 6166 (extensions of time to pay Federal estate taxes).[34] These provisions are discussed in Chapters 6 and 19.

Transfers with a Retained Life Estate (§ 2036)

Code §§ 2036 through 2038 were enacted on the premise that the estate tax can be avoided on lifetime transfers only if the decedent does not retain control over the property. The logic of this approach is somewhat difficult to dispute. One should not be able to escape the tax consequences of property transfers at death while remaining in a position to enjoy some or all of the fruits of ownership during life.

Under § 2036, the value of any property transferred by the deceased during lifetime for less than adequate consideration must be included if either of the following was retained:

- The possession or enjoyment of, or the right to the income from, the property.
- The right, either alone or in conjunction with any person, to designate the persons who shall possess or enjoy the property or the income.

The decedent is considered to have retained the right to the income from the property to the extent that such income is to be applied toward the discharge of his or her legal obligations.[35]

[34] §§ 2035(c)(1) and (2).

[35] § 2036(a)(1).

THE BIG PICTURE

EXAMPLE 36

Return to the facts of *The Big Picture* on p. 18-1. Before Peter Hood died in 2000, he established several trusts. One trust grants John an income interest for life (i.e., a life estate), and upon his death, the trust passes to his children (i.e., remainder interest). Upon John's death, none of the trust property is included in his gross estate. Although he held a life estate, he was not the transferor (Peter was) of the property placed in trust.

THE BIG PICTURE

EXAMPLE 37

Return to the facts of *The Big Picture* on p. 18-1. Immediately after inheriting the family hunting lodge from his mother (see Example 20), John transfers it to a newly created trust. Under the terms of the trust instrument, he retains a life estate, remainder to his children and Helen (John's sister). Upon John's death, the property in the trust will be included in his gross estate under § 2036.

In both of the preceding examples, a gift occurred when the trusts were created. In Example 36, Peter made a gift of the entire amount placed in trust. In Example 37, John made a gift of only the remainder interest—see Chapter 19 for how the value of a remainder interest is determined.

Revocable Transfers (§ 2038)

Another type of lifetime transfer that is drawn into a decedent's gross estate is covered by § 2038. The gross estate includes the value of property interests transferred by the decedent (except to the extent that the transfer was made for full consideration) if the enjoyment of the property transferred was subject, at the date of the decedent's death, to any power of the decedent to *alter, amend, revoke, or terminate* the transfer. This includes the power to change the beneficiaries or the power to accelerate or increase any beneficiary's enjoyment of the property.

The Code and the Regulations make it clear that one cannot avoid inclusion in the gross estate under § 2038 by relinquishing a power within three years of death.[36] Recall that § 2038 is one of several types of situations listed as exceptions to the usual rule excluding gifts made within three years of death from the gross estate.

The classic § 2038 situation results from the use of a revocable trust. Example 9 (earlier in this chapter) illustrates the use of a revocable trust. Example 10 shows what happens when the right of revocation is relinquished during the life of the creator of the trust. When the right of revocation is relinquished within three years of death, the trust is included in the creator's gross estate.

Annuities (§ 2039)

Annuities can be divided by their origin into commercial and noncommercial contracts. Noncommercial annuities are issued by private parties and, in some cases, by charitable organizations that do not regularly issue annuities. The two varieties have much in common, but noncommercial annuities present special income tax problems and are not discussed further.

An annuity is one or more payments extending over any period of time. The payments may be equal or unequal, conditional or unconditional, or periodic or sporadic. Annuity contracts that terminate upon the death of the person covered (i.e., annuitant) are designated as straight-life annuities. Other contracts provide for a survivorship feature (e.g., reduced payments to a surviving spouse).

[36] § 2038(a)(1) and Reg. § 20.2038–1(e)(1).

In the case of a straight-life annuity, nothing is included in the gross estate of the annuitant at death. Section 2033 (property in which the decedent had an interest) does not apply because the annuitant's interest in the contract is terminated by death. Section 2036 (transfers with a retained life estate) does not cover the situation; a transfer made for full consideration is specifically excluded from § 2036 treatment. A commercial annuity is presumed to have been purchased for full consideration unless some evidence exists to indicate that the parties were not acting at arm's length.

EXAMPLE 38

Arnold purchases a straight-life annuity that will pay him $24,000 a month when he reaches age 65. Arnold dies at age 70. Except for the payments he received before his death, nothing relating to this annuity affects Arnold's gross estate. ■

In the case of a survivorship annuity, the estate tax consequences under § 2039(a) are usually triggered by the death of the first annuitant. The amount included in the gross estate is the cost from the same company of a comparable annuity covering the survivor at his or her attained age on the date of the deceased annuitant's death.

EXAMPLE 39

Assume the same facts as in Example 38, except that the annuity contract provides for Veronica to be paid $12,000 a month for life as a survivorship feature. Veronica is 62 years of age when Arnold dies. Under these circumstances, Arnold's gross estate includes the cost of a comparable contract that provides an annuity of $12,000 per month for the life of a female, age 62. ■

Full inclusion of the survivorship element in the gross estate is subject to an exception under § 2039(b). The amount includible is to be based on the proportion of the deceased annuitant's contribution to the total cost of the contract. This is expressed by the following formula:

$$\frac{\text{Decedent's contribution to purchase price}}{\text{Total purchase price of the annuity}} \times \text{Value of the annuity (or refund) at decedent's death} = \text{Amount includible in the deceased annuitant's gross estate}$$

EXAMPLE 40

Assume the same facts as in Example 39, except that Arnold and Veronica are husband and wife and have always lived in a community property state. The premiums on the contract were paid with community funds. Because Veronica contributed half of the cost of the contract, only half of the amount determined under Example 39 is included in Arnold's gross estate. ■

The result reached in Example 40 is not unique to community property jurisdictions. The outcome would have been the same in a noncommunity property state if Veronica had furnished half of the consideration from her own funds.

In determining a decedent's contribution to an annuity contract, a special rule applies to employment-related retirement plans. In these cases, the employer's contribution to the plan is treated as having been made by the employee.

EXAMPLE 41

Under a noncontributory qualified retirement plan funded by his employer, Jim is entitled to an annuity for life. The plan also provides for a survivorship annuity for Jim's wife, Ellen, in the event he predeceases her. Upon Jim's prior death, the value of the survivorship annuity is included in his gross estate. Jim did not actually contribute to the cost of the annuity, but his employer's contributions are attributed to him. ■

Joint Interests (§§ 2040 and 2511)

Recall that joint tenancies and tenancies by the entirety are characterized by the right of survivorship. Thus, upon the death of a joint tenant, title to the property passes to the surviving tenant. None of the property is included in the *probate* estate of the deceased tenant. In the case of tenancies in common and community property, death does not defeat an ownership interest. Further, the deceased owner's interest is part of the probate estate.

The Federal *estate tax treatment* of tenancies in common or of community property follows the logical approach of taxing only the portion of the property included in the deceased owner's probate estate.

EXAMPLE 42

Homer, Wilma, and Thelma acquire a tract of land, ownership listed as tenants in common, each party furnishing $200,000 of the $600,000 purchase price. When the property is worth $900,000, Homer dies. If Homer's undivided interest in the property is 33⅓%, the gross estate *and* probate estate each include $300,000. This one-third interest is also the same amount that passes to Homer's heirs. ■

Unless the parties have provided otherwise, each tenant is deemed to own an interest equal to the portion of the original consideration he or she furnished. The parties in Example 42 could have provided that Homer would receive an undivided half interest in the property although he contributed only one-third of the purchase price. In that case, Wilma and Thelma have made a gift to Homer when the tenancy was created, and Homer's gross estate and probate estate each include $450,000.

For certain joint tenancies, the tax consequences are different. All of the property is included in the deceased co-owner's gross estate unless it can be proved that the surviving co-owners contributed to the cost of the property.[37] If a contribution can be shown, the amount to be *excluded* is calculated by the following formula:

$$\frac{\text{Surviving co-owner's contribution}}{\text{Total cost of the property}} \times \text{Fair market value of the property}$$

In computing a survivor's contribution, any funds received as a gift *from the deceased co-owner* and applied to the cost of the property cannot be counted. However, income or gain from gift assets can be counted.

EXAMPLE 43

Keith and Steve (father and son) acquire a tract of land, ownership listed as joint tenancy with right of survivorship. Keith furnished $400,000 and Steve $200,000 of the $600,000 purchase price. Of the $200,000 provided by Steve, $100,000 had previously been received as a gift from Keith. When the property is worth $900,000, Keith dies. Because only $100,000 of Steve's contribution can be counted (the other $100,000 was received as a gift from Keith), Steve has furnished only one-sixth ($100,000/$600,000) of the cost. Thus, Keith's gross estate must include five-sixths of $900,000, or $750,000. This presumes that Steve can prove that he did in fact make the $100,000 contribution. In the absence of such proof, the full value of the property is included in Keith's gross estate. Keith's death makes Steve the immediate owner of the property by virtue of the right of survivorship. None of the property is part of Keith's probate estate. ■

If the co-owners receive the property as a gift or bequest *from another*, each owner is deemed to have contributed to the cost (or value on date of death) of his or her own interest.

[37] § 2040(a).

THE BIG PICTURE

EXAMPLE 44

Return to the facts of *The Big Picture* on p. 18-1. During his lifetime, Peter Hood purchased timberland listing title as follows: "John and Helen Hood as equal tenants in common." John's basis in the property is one-half of Peter's cost. Upon John's death, one-half of the value of the timberland is included in his gross estate.

THE BIG PICTURE

EXAMPLE 45

Return to the facts of *The Big Picture* on p. 18-1. In her will, Martha leaves the Hood family residence to her children (John and Helen) as joint tenants with right of survivorship. John's income tax basis is one-half of the value on Martha's death. On John's later death, one-half of the value at that time will be included in his gross estate. Keep in mind that under the right of survivorship, outright ownership goes to Helen and none of the property passes to John's heirs.

To simplify the joint ownership rules for *married persons,* § 2040(b) provides for an automatic inclusion rule upon the death of the first joint-owner spouse to die. Regardless of the amount contributed by each spouse, one-half of the value of the property is included in the gross estate of the spouse who dies first. The special rule eliminates the need to trace the source of contributions and recognizes that any inclusion in the gross estate is neutralized by the marital deduction.

THE BIG PICTURE

EXAMPLE 46

Return to the facts of *The Big Picture* on p. 18-1. Recall that after his divorce from Hannah, John married Ashley. Because Hannah kept John's prior home as part of the property settlement (see Example 18), he purchased a new residence. He listed title to the property as "John and Ashley Hood, tenancy by the entirety with right of survivorship." Upon John's death, only one-half of the value of the property is included in his gross estate.

If Ashley had died first, one-half of the value of the residence would have been included in her gross estate even though she made no contribution to its cost.

In Example 46, inclusion in the gross estate of the first spouse to die is neutralized by the unlimited marital deduction allowed for estate tax purposes (see the discussion of § 2056 later in the chapter). Under the right of survivorship, the surviving joint tenant obtains full ownership of the property. The marital deduction generally is allowed for property passing from one spouse to another.

Whether a *gift* results when property is transferred into some form of joint ownership depends on the consideration furnished by each of the contributing parties for the ownership interest acquired.

EXAMPLE 47

Brenda and Sarah purchase real estate as tenants in common. Of the $800,000 purchase price, Brenda furnishes $600,000, and Sarah furnishes only $200,000. If each is an equal owner in the property, Brenda has made a gift to Sarah of $200,000. ■

EXAMPLE 48

Martha purchases real estate for $900,000, the title to the property being listed as follows: "Martha, Sylvia, and Dan as joint tenants with the right of survivorship." If under state law the mother (Martha), the daughter (Sylvia), and the son (Dan) are deemed to be equal owners in the property, Martha is treated as having made gifts of $300,000 to Sylvia and $300,000 to Dan. ■

Several important *exceptions* exist to the general rule that gift treatment is triggered by the creation of a joint ownership with disproportionate interests resulting from unequal consideration. First, if the transfer involves a joint bank account, there is no gift at the time of the contribution. If a gift occurs, it is when the noncontributing party withdraws the funds provided by the other joint tenant. Second, the same rule applies to the purchase of U.S. savings bonds.[38] Again, any gift tax consequences are postponed until the noncontributing party appropriates some or all of the proceeds for his or her individual use.

EXAMPLE 49

Cynthia deposits $400,000 in a bank account under the names of Cynthia and Carla as joint tenants. Both Cynthia and Carla have the right to withdraw funds from the account without the other's consent. Cynthia has not made a gift to Carla when the account is established. ■

EXAMPLE 50

Assume the same facts as in Example 49. At some later date, Carla withdraws $100,000 from the account for her own use. At this point, Cynthia has made a gift to Carla of $100,000. ■

EXAMPLE 51

Wesley purchases a U.S. savings bond that he registers in the names of Wesley and Harriet. After Wesley dies, Harriet redeems the bond. No gift takes place when Wesley buys the bond. In addition, Harriet's redemption is not treated as a gift because the bond passed to her by testamentary disposition (Harriet acquired the bond by virtue of surviving Wesley) and not through a lifetime transfer. However, the fair market value of the bond is included in Wesley's gross estate under § 2040. ■

Powers of Appointment (§§ 2041 and 2514)

A **power of appointment** is a power to determine who shall own or enjoy, at the present or in the future, the property subject to the power. It must be created by another and does not include a power created or retained by the decedent when he or she transferred his or her own property.

Powers of appointment fall into one of two classifications: *general* and *special*. A general power of appointment is one in which the decedent could have appointed himself, his creditors, his estate, or the creditors of his estate. In contrast, a special power enables the holder to appoint to others but *not* to herself, her creditors, her estate, or the creditors of her estate. Assume, for example, that Don has the power to designate how the principal of the trust will be distributed among Edie, Frank, and Georgia. At this point, Don's power is only a special power of appointment. If Don is given the further right to appoint the principal to himself, what was a special power of appointment becomes a general power.

Three things can happen to a power of appointment: exercise, lapse, and release. Exercising the power involves appointing the property to one or all of the parties designated. A lapse occurs upon failure to exercise a power. Thus, if Don fails to indicate how the principal of a trust will be distributed among Edie, Frank, and Georgia, Don's power of appointment will lapse, and the principal will pass in accordance with the terms of the trust instrument. A release occurs if the holder relinquishes a power of appointment.

Powers of appointment have the following transfer tax consequences.

1. No tax implications result from the exercise, lapse, or release of a special power of appointment.
2. A gift or an inclusion in the gross estate results from the exercise, lapse, or release of a general power of appointment.

[38] Reg. § 25.2511–1(h)(4).

TAX IN THE NEWS What Did That Decedent Own?

The following is an analysis of the asset distribution of taxable estate tax returns filed in a recent year. For those decedents who must file a Form 706, investment assets form a significant share of the total assets held.

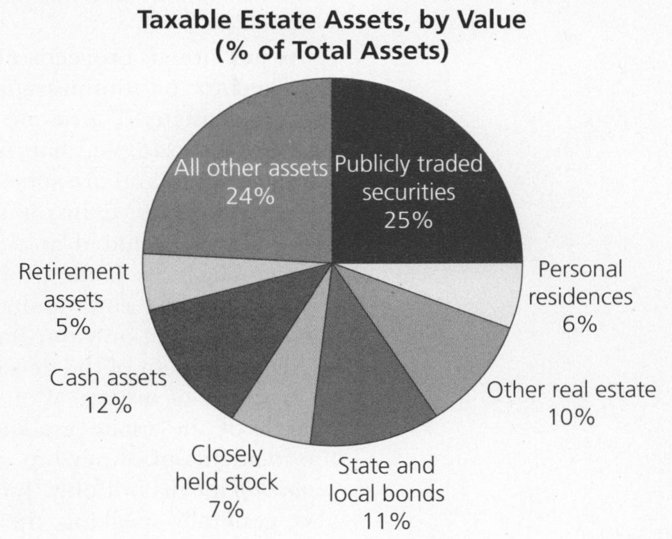

Source: Internal Revenue Service, Statistics of Income Division, *Estate Tax Returns Filed in 2009*, September 2010.

EXAMPLE 52

Justin, Monica's father, leaves his property in trust, life estate to Monica and remainder to whichever of Monica's children she decides to appoint in her will. Monica's power is not a general power of appointment because she cannot exercise it in favor of herself. Thus, regardless of whether Monica exercises the power, none of the trust property subject to the power is included in her gross estate. ■

Life Insurance (§ 2042)

Under § 2042, the gross estate includes the proceeds of life insurance on the decedent's life if (1) they are receivable by the estate, (2) they are receivable by another for the benefit of the estate, or (3) the decedent possessed any of the incidents of ownership in the policy.

Life insurance on the life of another owned by a decedent at the time of death is included in the gross estate under § 2033 (property in which the decedent had an interest) and not under § 2042. The amount includible is the replacement value of the policy.[39] Under these circumstances, inclusion of the face amount of the policy is inappropriate as the policy has not yet matured.

EXAMPLE 53

At the time of his death, Luigi owned a life insurance policy on the life of Benito, face amount of $500,000 and replacement value of $50,000, with Sofia as the designated beneficiary. Because the policy has not matured at Luigi's death, § 2042 is inapplicable. However, § 2033 (property in which the decedent had an interest) compels the inclusion of $50,000 (the replacement value) in Luigi's gross estate. If Luigi and Sofia owned the policy as community property, only $25,000 is included in Luigi's gross estate. ■

In the frequent situation where the beneficiary of the insurance is neither the insured nor the owner of the policy, no tax consequences ensue upon the beneficiary's death. Thus, in Example 53, if Sofia predeceases Benito, no transfer takes

[39]Reg. § 20.2031–8(a)(1).

place because the policy has not matured. Sofia's interest as a beneficiary is a mere expectancy and not a property interest possessing any value.

The term *life insurance* includes whole life policies, term insurance, group life insurance, travel and accident insurance, endowment contracts (before being paid up), and death benefits paid by fraternal societies operating under the lodge system.[40]

As just noted, proceeds of insurance on the life of the decedent receivable by the executor or administrator or payable to the decedent's estate are included in the gross estate. The estate need not be specifically named as the beneficiary. Assume, for example, that the proceeds of the policy are receivable by an individual beneficiary and are subject to an obligation, legally binding upon the beneficiary, to pay taxes, debts, and other charges enforceable against the estate. The proceeds are included in the decedent's gross estate to the extent of the beneficiary's obligation. If the proceeds of an insurance policy made payable to a decedent's estate are community assets and, under state law, one-half belongs to the surviving spouse, only one-half of the proceeds will be considered as receivable by or for the benefit of the decedent's estate.

Proceeds of insurance on the life of the decedent not receivable by or for the benefit of the estate are includible if the decedent at death possessed any of the incidents of ownership in the policy. In this connection, the term *incidents of ownership* means not only the ownership of the policy in a technical legal sense but also, generally speaking, the right of the insured or his or her estate to the economic benefits of the policy. Thus, it also includes the power to change beneficiaries, revoke an assignment, pledge the policy for a loan, or surrender or cancel the policy.[41]

EXAMPLE 54

At the time of death, Broderick was the insured under a policy (face amount of $1 million) owned by Gregory with Demi as the designated beneficiary. Broderick took out the policy five years ago and immediately transferred it as a gift to Gregory. Under the assignment, Broderick transferred all rights in the policy except the right to change beneficiaries. Broderick died without having exercised this right, and the policy proceeds are paid to Demi. Under § 2042(2), Broderick's retention of an incident of ownership in the policy (i.e., the right to change beneficiaries) causes $1 million to be included in his gross estate. ■

Assuming that the deceased-insured holds the incidents of ownership in a policy, how much is included in the gross estate if the insurance policy is a community asset? Only one-half of the proceeds becomes part of the deceased spouse's gross estate.

Merely purchasing a life insurance contract with someone else designated as the beneficiary does not constitute a *gift*. As long as the purchaser still owns the policy, nothing has really passed to the beneficiary. Even on the death of the insured-owner, no gift takes place. The proceeds paid to the beneficiary constitute a testamentary and not a lifetime transfer. But consider the following possibility.

EXAMPLE 55

Kurt purchases an insurance policy on his own life that he transfers to Olga. Kurt retains no interest in the policy (such as the power to change beneficiaries). In these circumstances, Kurt has made a gift to Olga. Furthermore, if Kurt continues to pay the premiums on the transferred policy, each payment constitutes a separate gift. ■

Under certain conditions, the death of the insured may constitute a gift to the beneficiary of part or all of the proceeds. This occurs when the owner of the policy is not the insured.

---

[40] Reg. § 20.2042–1(a)(1). As to travel and accident insurance, see *Comm. v. Estate of Noel*, 65–1 USTC ¶12,311, 15 AFTR 2d 1397, 85 S.Ct. 1238 (USSC, 1965). As to employer-sponsored group term life insurance, see Example 32 earlier in this chapter.

[41] Reg. § 20.2042–1(c)(2).

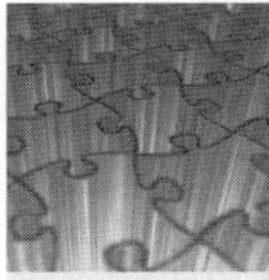

CONCEPT SUMMARY 18.2

Federal Estate Tax Provisions—Gross Estate

1. The starting point for applying the Federal estate tax is to determine which assets are subject to tax. Such assets comprise a decedent's gross estate.
2. The gross estate generally will not include any gifts made by the decedent within three years of death. It does include any gift tax paid on these transfers.
3. Based on the premise that one should not continue to enjoy or control property and not have it subject to the estate tax, certain incomplete transfers are included in the gross estate.
4. Upon the death of a joint tenant, the full value of the property is included in the gross estate unless the survivor(s) made a contribution toward the cost of the property. Spouses are subject to a special rule that calls for automatic inclusion of half of the value of the property in the gross estate of the first tenant to die. The creation of joint ownership is subject to the gift tax when a tenant receives a lesser interest in the property than is warranted by the consideration furnished.
5. A power of appointment is the right to determine who shall own or enjoy, at the present or in the future, the property subject to the power. The exercise, lapse, or release of a general power of appointment during the life of the holder is subject to the gift tax. If the exercise, lapse, or release occurs at death, the property subject to the power is included in the holder's gross estate. If, however, a special power of appointment is involved, no gift or estate tax consequences result.
6. If the decedent is the insured, life insurance proceeds are included in the gross estate if either of two conditions is satisfied. First, the proceeds are paid to the estate or for the benefit of the estate. Second, the decedent possessed incidents of ownership (e.g., the right to change beneficiaries) over the policy.

EXAMPLE 56

Randolph owns an insurance policy on the life of Frank, with Tracy as the designated beneficiary. Up until the time of Frank's death, Randolph retained the right to change the beneficiary of the policy. The proceeds paid to Tracy by the insurance company by reason of Frank's death constitute a gift from Randolph to Tracy.[42] ■

EXAMPLE 57

Hubert and Carrie live in a community property state. With community funds, Hubert purchases an insurance policy with a face amount of $1 million on his own life and designates Ann as the revocable beneficiary. Upon Hubert's death, the proceeds of the policy are paid to Ann. If under state law Hubert's death makes the transfer by Carrie complete, Carrie has made a gift to Ann of $500,000. Because the policy is community property, Carrie is the owner of only one-half of the policy. Furthermore, one-half of the proceeds of the policy ($500,000) is included in Hubert's gross estate under § 2042. ■

See Concept Summary 18.2 for a review of the components of the gross estate.

Taxable Estate

LO.7

Describe the components of the taxable estate.

After the gross estate has been determined, the next step is to compute the taxable estate. By virtue of § 2051, the **taxable estate** is the gross estate less the following: expenses, indebtedness, and taxes (§ 2053); losses (§ 2054); charitable transfers (§ 2055); the marital deduction (§§ 2056 and 2056A); and the deduction for state death taxes (§ 2058). As previously noted, the charitable and marital deductions also have gift tax ramifications (§§ 2522 and 2523).

Expenses, Indebtedness, and Taxes (§ 2053)

A deduction is allowed for funeral expenses; expenses incurred in administering property; claims against the estate; and unpaid mortgages and other charges

[42] *Goodman v. Comm.*, 46–1 USTC ¶10,275, 34 AFTR 1534, 156 F.2d 218 (CA–2, 1946).

against property, whose value is included in the gross estate (without reduction for the mortgage or other indebtedness).

Expenses incurred in administering community property are deductible only in proportion to the deceased spouse's interest in the community.[43]

Administration expenses include commissions of the executor or administrator, attorney's fees of the estate, accountant's fees, court costs, and certain selling expenses for disposition of estate property.

Claims against the estate include property taxes accrued before the decedent's death, unpaid income taxes on income received by the decedent before he or she died, and unpaid gift taxes on gifts made by the decedent before death.

Amounts that may be deducted as claims against the estate are only for enforceable personal obligations of the decedent at the time of death. Deductions for claims founded on promises or agreements are limited to the extent the liabilities were contracted in good faith and for adequate and full consideration. However, a pledge or subscription in favor of a public, charitable, religious, or educational organization is deductible to the extent that it would have constituted an allowable deduction had it been a bequest.[44]

Deductible funeral expenses include the cost of interment, the burial plot or vault, a gravestone, perpetual care of the grave site, and the transportation expense of the person bringing the body to the place of burial. No deduction is allowed for cemetery lots the decedent acquired before death for himself or herself and family, but the lots are not included in the decedent's gross estate under § 2033 (property in which the decedent had an interest).

Losses (§ 2054)

Section 2054 permits an estate tax deduction for losses from casualty or theft incurred during the period when the estate is being settled. As is true with casualty or theft losses for income tax purposes, any anticipated insurance recovery must be taken into account in arriving at the amount of the deductible loss. Unlike the income tax, however, the deduction is not limited by a floor ($100) or a percentage amount (the excess of 10 percent of adjusted gross income). If the casualty occurs to property after it has been distributed to an heir, the loss belongs to the heir and not to the estate. If the casualty occurs before the decedent's death, it should be claimed on the appropriate Form 1040. The fair market value of the property (if any) on the date of death plus any insurance recovery is included in the gross estate.

As is true of certain administration expenses, a casualty or theft loss of estate property can be claimed as an income tax deduction on the fiduciary return of the estate (Form 1041). But a double deduction prohibition applies, and claiming the income tax deduction requires a waiver of the estate tax deduction.[45]

Transfers to Charity (§§ 2055 and 2522)

A deduction is allowed for the value of property in the decedent's gross estate that is transferred by the decedent through testamentary disposition to (or for the use of) any of the following.

- The United States or any of its political subdivisions.
- Any corporation or association organized and operated exclusively for religious, charitable, scientific, literary, or educational purposes.
- Various veterans' organizations.

The organizations just described are identical to those that qualify for the Federal gift tax deduction under § 2522. With the following exceptions, they are also the same organizations that qualify a donor for an income tax deduction under § 170.

[43] *U.S. v. Stapf,* 63–2 USTC ¶12,192, 12 AFTR 2d 6326, 84 S.Ct. 248 (USSC, 1963).

[44] § 2053(c)(1)(A) and Reg. § 20.2053–5.

[45] § 642(g).

- Certain nonprofit cemetery associations qualify for income tax but not estate and gift tax purposes.
- Foreign charities may qualify under the estate and gift tax but not under the income tax.

No deduction is allowed unless the charitable bequest is specified by a provision in the decedent's will or the transfer was made before death and the property is subsequently included in the gross estate. Generally speaking, a deduction does not materialize when an individual dies intestate (without a will). The amount of the bequest to charity must be mandatory and cannot be left to someone else's discretion. It is, however, permissible to allow another person—such as the executor of the estate—to choose which charity will receive the specified donation. Likewise, a bequest may be expressed as an alternative and still be effective if the noncharitable beneficiary disclaims (refuses) the intervening interest before the due date for the filing of the estate tax return (nine months after the decedent's death plus any extensions of time granted for filing).

THE BIG PICTURE

EXAMPLE 58

Return to the facts of *The Big Picture* on p. 18-1. After John's accident, he was in the intensive care unit at a local hospital. Although physically incapacitated, he was mentally alert. In early December, he reviewed his financial affairs with his attorney and CPA and executed a new will. His prior will, drawn up several years ago, contained a bequest to the Hood Scholarship Foundation (HSF), an organization created by Peter (John's father) to provide financial assistance to community college students. As HSF's qualified status had never been evaluated by the IRS, the attorney agreed to apply for a determination letter.

John's new will kept the bequest, but only if the IRS approved HSF's qualified status. John's CPA arranged to have all of John's medical expenses (e.g., hospital and physicians) paid as incurred. He also advised John to make a substantial payment on his property taxes and state income taxes.

Marital Deduction (§§ 2056, 2056A, and 2523)

The **marital deduction** originated with the Revenue Act of 1948 as part of the same legislation that permitted married persons to secure the income-splitting advantages of filing joint income tax returns. The purpose of these statutory changes was to eliminate the major tax variations that existed between taxpayers residing in community property and common law states. The marital deduction was designed to provide equity in the estate and gift tax areas.

In a community property state, for example, no marital deduction generally was allowed, because the surviving spouse already owned one-half of the community and that portion was not included in the deceased spouse's gross estate. In a common law state, however, most if not all of the assets often belonged to the breadwinner of the family. When that spouse died first, all of these assets were included in the gross estate. Recall that a dower or curtesy interest (regarding a surviving spouse's right to some of the deceased spouse's property) does not reduce the gross estate. To equalize the situation, therefore, a marital deduction, usually equal to one-half of all separate assets, was allowed upon the death of the first spouse.

Ultimately, Congress decided to dispense with these historical justifications and recognize husband and wife as a single economic unit. Consistent with the approach taken under the income tax, spouses are considered as one for transfer tax purposes. By making the marital deduction unlimited in amount, neither the gift tax nor the estate tax is imposed on outright interspousal transfers of property. The unlimited marital deduction even includes one spouse's share of the community property transferred to the other spouse.

Passing Requirement Under § 2056, the marital deduction is allowed only for property that is included in the deceased spouse's gross estate *and* that passes or has passed to the surviving spouse. In determining whether the parties are legally married, look to state law. In this regard, some foreign divorces may raise doubts as to the validity of a subsequent remarriage. Having an ex-spouse does not qualify the decedent for a marital deduction if, in fact, the divorce is valid and final.

THE BIG PICTURE

EXAMPLE 59

Return to the facts of *The Big Picture* on p. 18-1 and Example 58. In reviewing John's prior will, the parties discovered that one of the main beneficiaries was Hannah, John's first wife. The new will substituted Ashley (John's present wife) for Hannah, thereby salvaging a marital deduction.

Property that *passes* from the decedent to the surviving spouse includes any interest received as (1) the decedent's heir or donee, (2) the decedent's surviving tenant by the entirety or joint tenant, (3) the appointee under the decedent's exercise (or lapse or release) of a general power of appointment, or (4) the beneficiary of insurance on the life of the decedent.

EXAMPLE 60

At the time of his death in the current year, Matthew owned an insurance policy on his own life (face amount of $500,000) with Minerva (his wife) as the designated beneficiary. Matthew and Minerva also owned real estate (worth $600,000) as tenants by the entirety (Matthew had furnished all of the purchase price). As to these transfers, $800,000 ($500,000 + $300,000) is included in Matthew's gross estate, and this amount represents the property that passes to Minerva for purposes of the marital deduction.[46] ■

Disclaimers can affect the amount passing to the surviving spouse. If, for example, the surviving spouse is the remainderperson under the will of the deceased spouse, a disclaimer by another heir increases the amount passing to the surviving spouse. This, in turn, will increase the amount of the marital deduction allowed to the estate of the deceased spouse.

A problem arises when a property interest passing to the surviving spouse is subject to a mortgage or other encumbrance. In this case, only the net value of the interest after reduction by the amount of the mortgage or other encumbrance qualifies for the marital deduction. To allow otherwise results in a double deduction because a decedent's liabilities are separately deductible under § 2053.

EXAMPLE 61

In his will, Oscar leaves real estate (fair market value of $500,000) to his wife. If the real estate is subject to a mortgage of $100,000 (upon which Oscar was personally liable), the marital deduction is limited to $400,000 ($500,000 − $100,000). The $100,000 mortgage is deductible under § 2053 as an obligation of the decedent (Oscar). ■

However, if the executor is required under the terms of the decedent's will or under local law to discharge the mortgage out of other assets of the estate or to reimburse the surviving spouse, the payment or reimbursement is an additional interest passing to the surviving spouse.

[46] Inclusion in the gross estate falls under § 2042 (proceeds of life insurance) and § 2040 (joint interests). Although Matthew provided the full purchase price for the real estate, § 2040(b) requires inclusion of only one-half of the value of the property when one spouse predeceases the other.

EXAMPLE 62

Assume the same facts as in Example 61, except that Oscar's will directs that the real estate is to pass to his wife free of any liabilities. Accordingly, Oscar's executor pays off the mortgage by using other estate assets and distributes the real estate to Oscar's wife. The marital deduction now becomes $500,000. ■

Federal estate taxes or other death taxes paid out of the surviving spouse's share of the gross estate are not included in the value of property passing to the surviving spouse. Therefore, it is usually preferable for the deceased spouse's will to provide that death taxes be paid out of the portion of the estate that does not qualify for the marital deduction.

Terminable Interest Limitation Certain interests in property passing from the deceased spouse to the surviving spouse are referred to as **terminable interests**. Such an interest will terminate or fail after the passage of time, upon the happening of some contingency, or upon the failure of some event to occur. Examples are life estates, annuities, estates for terms of years, and patents. A terminable interest will not qualify for the marital deduction if another interest in the same property passed from the deceased spouse to some other person. By reason of the passing, that other person or his or her heirs may enjoy part of the property after the termination of the surviving spouse's interest.[47]

EXAMPLE 63

Vicky's will places her property in trust, life estate to her husband, Brett, remainder to Andrew or his heirs. The interest passing from Vicky to Brett does not qualify for the marital deduction. It will terminate upon Brett's death, and Andrew or his heirs will then possess or enjoy the property. ■

EXAMPLE 64

Assume the same facts as in Example 63, except that Vicky created the trust during her life. No marital deduction is available for gift tax purposes for the same reason as in Example 63.[48] ■

The justification for the terminable interest rule can be illustrated by examining the possible results of Examples 63 and 64. Without the rule, Vicky could have passed property to Brett at no cost because of the marital deduction. Yet, on Brett's death, none of the property would have been included in his gross estate. Section 2036 (transfers with a retained life estate) would not apply to Brett because he was not the original transferor of the property. The marital deduction should not be available in situations where the surviving spouse can enjoy the property and still pass it to another without tax consequences. The marital deduction merely postpones the transfer tax upon the death of the first spouse and operates to shift any such tax to the surviving spouse.

The terminable interest rule can be avoided by use of a *power of appointment.*[49] Under this approach, a property interest passing from the deceased spouse to the surviving spouse qualifies for the marital deduction (and is not considered a terminable interest) if the surviving spouse is granted a general power of appointment over the property. Thus, the exercise, release, or lapse of the power during the survivor's life or at death will be subject to either the gift or the estate tax.[50] If Examples 63 and 64 are modified to satisfy this condition, the life estate passing from Vicky to Brett is not a terminable interest and will qualify for the marital deduction.

Consistent with the objective of the terminable interest rule, another approach offers an alternative means for obtaining the marital deduction. Under this provision, the marital deduction is allowed for transfers of **qualified terminable interest property** (commonly referred to as **QTIP**). This is defined as property that passes

[47] §§ 2056(b)(1) and 2523(b)(1).

[48] Examples 63 and 64 contain the potential for a qualified terminable interest property (QTIP) election discussed later in this section.

[49] For the estate tax, see § 2056(b)(5). The gift tax counterpart is in § 2523(e).

[50] §§ 2514 and 2041.

from one spouse to another by gift or at death and for which the transferee-spouse has a qualifying income interest for life.

For a donee or a surviving spouse, a qualifying income interest for life exists under the following conditions:

- The person is entitled for life to all of the income from the property (or a specific portion of it), payable at annual or more frequent intervals.
- No person (including the spouse) has a power to appoint any part of the property to any person other than the surviving spouse during his or her life.[51]

If these conditions are met, an election can be made to claim a marital deduction as to the QTIP. For estate tax purposes, the executor of the estate makes the election on Form 706 (the Federal estate tax return). For gift tax purposes, the donor spouse makes the election on Form 709 (the Federal gift tax return). The election is irrevocable.

If the election is made, a transfer tax is imposed on the QTIP when the transferee-spouse disposes of it by gift or upon death. If the disposition occurs during life, the gift tax applies, measured by the fair market value of the property as of that time.[52] If no lifetime disposition takes place, the fair market value of the property on the date of death (or alternate valuation date if applicable) is included in the gross estate of the transferee-spouse.[53]

EXAMPLE 65

In 1990, Clyde dies and provides in his will that certain assets (fair market value of $2.1 million) are to be transferred to a trust under which Gertrude (Clyde's wife) is granted a life estate with the remainder passing to their children upon Gertrude's death. Presuming that all of the preceding requirements are satisfied and Clyde's executor so elects, his estate receives a marital deduction of $2.1 million. ■

EXAMPLE 66

Assume the same facts as in Example 65, with the further stipulation that Gertrude dies in 2012 when the trust assets are worth $6.4 million. This amount is included in her gross estate. ■

Because the estate tax is imposed on assets not physically included in the probate estate, the law allows the liability for those assets to be shifted to the heirs. The amount to be shifted is determined by comparing the estate tax liability both with and without the inclusion of the QTIP. This right of recovery can be canceled by a provision in the deceased spouse's will.[54]

The major difference between the power of appointment and the QTIP exceptions to the terminable interest rules relates to the control the surviving spouse has over the principal of the trust. In the power of appointment situation, the surviving spouse can appoint the principal to himself or herself (or to his or her estate). Only if this power is not exercised will the property pass as specified in the deceased spouse's will. In the QTIP situation, however, the surviving spouse has no such control. If the QTIP election is made, the principal must pass as prescribed by the transferor (the donor in the case of a lifetime transfer or the decedent in the case of a death transfer).

Citizenship and Residency of Spouses In the case of a nonresident alien whose spouse is a U.S. citizen, the marital deduction is allowed for estate and gift tax purposes. Property passing to a surviving spouse who is not a U.S. citizen is not eligible for the estate tax marital deduction.[55] Similarly, no gift tax marital deduction is allowed where the spouse is not a U.S. citizen. However, the annual exclusion for these gift transfers is $139,000 for 2012 ($136,000 in 2011).[56]

[51] §§ 2523(f) and 2056(b)(7).
[52] § 2519.
[53] § 2044.
[54] § 2207A(a).
[55] § 2056(d)(1).
[56] § 2523(i).

For the estate tax, an exception exists for certain transfers to a surviving spouse who is not a U.S. citizen.[57] If the transfer is to a *qualified domestic trust,* the marital deduction is allowed.[58]

The requirements of a qualified domestic trust guarantee that the marital deduction property will not escape estate taxes upon the death of the surviving spouse. This would be possible if the property and spouse are outside the jurisdiction of the U.S. tax laws.

State Death Taxes (§ 2058)

The purpose of the § 2058 deduction is to mitigate the effect of subjecting property to multiple death taxes (i.e., both Federal and state). In this regard, however, it provides less relief than was available with the § 2011 credit it replaced. A credit results in a dollar-for-dollar reduction in tax, whereas the benefit of a deduction is limited by the effective tax bracket of the estate.

Computing the Federal Estate Tax

LO.8

Calculate the Federal estate tax liability.

Once the taxable estate has been determined, post-1976 taxable gifts are added to arrive at the tax base and the estate tax can be computed.

EXAMPLE 67

Horton dies in 2012, leaving a taxable estate of $5.7 million. In 2002, he made a taxable gift of $100,000 upon which he paid no tax due to the availability of the unified tax credit. Horton's estate tax is $238,000, as determined below (see Figure 18.2).

Taxable estate	$ 5,700,000
Add: Post-1976 taxable gift	100,000
Tax base	$ 5,800,000
Tentative tax on tax base from tax rate schedule (Appendix A, p. A-8) [$155,800 + 35%($5,800,000 − $500,000)]	$ 2,010,800
Less: Unified tax credit for 2012	(1,772,800)
Estate tax due	$ 238,000

■

ETHICS & EQUITY **Water Under the Bridge**

Amy, a recently deceased client, has named you as the executor of her estate. Upon examining some of her past financial affairs, you discover that she made taxable gifts in recent years. None of these gifts was reported on a Form 709. As far as you can tell without further investigation, none of these gifts resulted in a gift tax liability. When you suggest to Amy's heirs that gift tax returns should be filed reporting these transfers, they tell you not to bother as Amy's past actions are "water under the bridge" and irrelevant to your duties as executor. What should you do?

Estate Tax Credits

Unified Tax Credit (§ 2010)

The role of the unified tax credit was discussed in connection with Example 3, and its application was illustrated in Example 67. The amount of the credit depends on the year the transfer occurred, and this information is contained in Table 18.1.

Credit for State Death Taxes (§ 2011)

The Code allowed a limited credit for the amount of any death tax actually paid to any state (or to the District of Columbia) attributable to any property included in

[57] § 2056(d)(2).

[58] § 2056A.

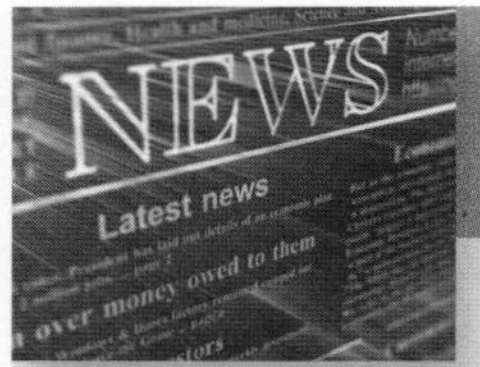

TAX IN THE NEWS Choosing the Right Year to Die

Assume three separate decedents—Tom, Jim, and Dave. Each is single and has a taxable estate of $6 million. Tom dies in 2009; Jim, in 2010; and Dave, in 2012. Assuming no prior taxable gifts and using the estate tax law in effect for the year of death, what is the result?

	Decedent		
	Tom	Jim	Dave
Estate tax due*	$1,125,000	$-0-	$308,000

*The estate tax was determined through the use of the credits in Table 18.1 and the tax rates in Appendix A (pp. A-7 and A-8) in the text.

Because no estate tax was imposed in 2010, Jim is the "lucky one"—if dying can ever be termed "lucky"! Besides Jim, such magnates as Dan Duncan (estate of $9 billion) and George Steinbrenner (estate of $1.15 billion) can also be considered lucky, as they died in 2010. Thus, it pays to die in the right year!

the gross estate. Like the credit for foreign death taxes paid, this provision mitigated the harshness of subjecting the same property to multiple death taxes.

The credit allowed was limited to the lesser of the amount of tax actually paid or the amount provided for in a table contained in § 2011(b). About a dozen states still use the procedure and table set forth in § 2011 as a means of determining the *state* estate tax that each imposes.

The § 2011 credit was phased out completely by 2005. As previously noted, the *credit* for state death taxes paid has been replaced by a *deduction* under § 2058.[59]

Credit for Tax on Prior Transfers (§ 2013)

Suppose Nancy owns some property that she passes at death to Lisa. Shortly thereafter, Lisa dies and passes the property to Rita. Assuming that both estates are subject to the Federal estate tax, the successive deaths result in a multiple effect. To mitigate the possible multiple taxation that might result, § 2013 provides relief in the form of a credit for Federal estate tax paid on prior transfers. In the preceding hypothetical case, Lisa's estate may be able to claim as an estate tax credit some of the taxes paid by Nancy's estate.

The credit is limited to the lesser of the following amounts:

1. The amount of the Federal estate tax attributable to the transferred property in the transferor's estate.
2. The amount of the Federal estate tax attributable to the transferred property in the decedent's estate.

To apply the limitations, certain adjustments must be made that are not covered in this text.[60] However, it is not necessary for the transferred property to be identified in the present decedent's estate or for it to be in existence at the time of the present decedent's death. It is sufficient that the transfer of property was subjected to the Federal estate tax in the estate of the transferor and that the transferor died within the prescribed period of time. Table 18.2 shows the correlation between the credit allowed and the time interval between the two deaths.

EXAMPLE 68

Under Nancy's will, Lisa inherits property. One year later, Lisa dies. Assume that the estate tax attributable to the inclusion of the property in Nancy's gross estate was $150,000 and that the estate tax attributable to the inclusion of the property in Lisa's gross estate is $120,000. Under these circumstances, Lisa's estate claims a credit against the estate tax of $120,000 (refer to limitation 2). ■

[59]Section 2011 is to be reinstated as to decedents dying after 2012.

[60]See the instructions to Form 706 and Reg. §§ 20.2013–2 and –3.

TABLE 18.2 Credit for Tax on Prior Transfers

Interval between Deaths	Credit Allowed
Within 2 years	100%
Within 3 to 4 years	80%
Within 5 to 6 years	60%
Within 7 to 8 years	40%
Within 9 to 10 years	20%

EXAMPLE 69

Assume the same facts as in Example 68, except that Lisa dies three years after Nancy. The applicable credit is now 80% of $120,000, or $96,000 (see Table 18.2). ■

Credit for Foreign Death Taxes (§ 2014)

A credit is allowed against the estate tax for any estate, inheritance, legacy, or succession tax actually paid to a foreign country. For purposes of this provision, the term *foreign country* means not only states in the international sense but also possessions or political subdivisions of foreign states and possessions of the United States.

The credit is allowed for death taxes paid with respect to (1) property situated in the foreign country to which the tax is paid, (2) property included in the decedent's gross estate, and (3) the decedent's taxable estate. No credit is allowed for interest or penalties paid in connection with foreign death taxes.

The credit is limited to the lesser of the following amounts:

1. The amount of the foreign death tax attributable to the property situated in the country imposing the tax and included in the decedent's gross estate for Federal estate tax purposes.
2. The amount of the Federal estate tax attributable to particular property situated in a foreign country, subject to death tax in that country, and included in the decedent's gross estate for Federal estate tax purposes.

Both of these limitations may require certain adjustments to arrive at the amount of the allowable credit. These adjustments are illustrated in the Regulations and are not discussed in this text.[61] In addition to the credit for foreign death taxes under the provisions of Federal estate tax law, similar credits are allowable under death tax conventions with a number of foreign countries. If a credit is allowed under either the provisions of law or the provisions of a convention, the credit that is most beneficial to the estate should be claimed.[62]

Procedural Matters

A Federal estate tax return, if required, is due nine months after the date of the decedent's death.[63] The time limit applies to all estates regardless of the nationality or residence of the decedent. Not infrequently, an executor will request and obtain from the IRS an extension of time for filing Form 706 (estate tax return).[64] Also available is an *automatic* six-month extension of time to file the estate tax return. To receive the extension, the executor must file Form 4768 [Application for Extension of Time to File a Return and/or Pay U.S. Estate (and Generation-Skipping Transfer) Taxes].

[61]Reg. § 20.2014–2 illustrates the foreign death tax limitation, and Reg. § 20.2014–3 covers that applicable to the U.S. estate tax. Also see the instructions to Schedule P of Form 706.

[62]Reg. § 20.2014–4 illustrates the selection process when both the § 2014 credit and an estate tax convention are involved.

[63]§ 6075(a).

[64]§ 6081.

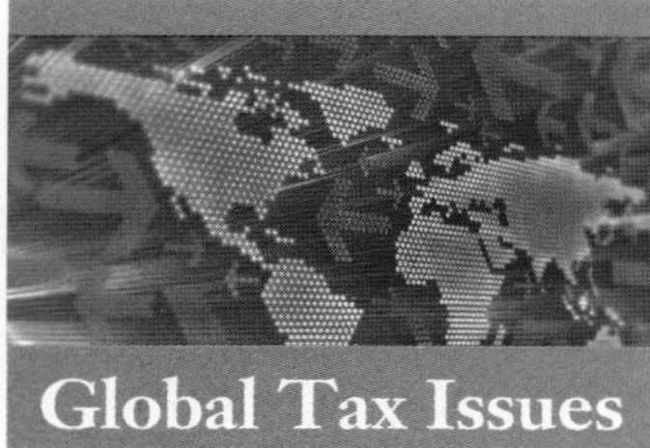

© Andrey Prokhorov, iStockphoto

Treaty Relief Is Not Abundant!

One means of mitigating double taxation at the international level is to take advantage of treaty provisions. A treaty will determine which country has primary taxing rights, and this may depend on such factors as the domicile of the decedent or the nature of the property involved (e.g., personalty or realty). Unfortunately, the United States has estate tax conventions with only 16 countries: Australia*, Austria*, Canada, Denmark*, Finland, France*, Germany*, Greece, Ireland, Italy, Japan*, the Netherlands, Norway, the Republic of South Africa, Switzerland, and the United Kingdom*. In contrast, almost 70 countries have income tax treaties with the United States (see Exhibit 9.1 in Chapter 9). Thus, treaty relief in the estate tax area is not as widespread as with income tax situations.

*Indicates the existence of a gift tax treaty as well.

The filing requirements parallel the exclusion amounts of the unified tax credit available for each year (refer to Table 18.1). The filing requirements may be lower when the decedent has made taxable gifts after 1976.[65]

EXAMPLE 70

Carlos dies in 2012, leaving a gross estate of $5,120,000. If Carlos did not make any post-1976 taxable gifts, his estate need not file Form 706. But assume that Carlos made a taxable gift of $120,000 in 2002. Because the filing requirement now becomes $5 million [$5,120,000 (the regular filing requirement for 2012) − $120,000 (the post-1976 taxable gift)], Carlos's estate must file Form 706. ■

Concept Summary 18.3 highlights the major components in arriving at the taxable estate and the mechanics of determining the estate tax liability.

18.4 The Generation-Skipping Transfer Tax

LO.9

Review and demonstrate the role of the generation-skipping transfer tax.

To prevent partial avoidance of Federal gift and estate taxes on large transfers, the tax law imposes an additional generation-skipping transfer tax.

The Problem

Previously, by structuring the transaction carefully, it was possible to bypass a generation of transfer taxes.

EXAMPLE 71

Under his will, Edward creates a trust, life estate to Stephen (Edward's son) and remainder to Ava (Edward's granddaughter) upon Stephen's death. Edward is subject to the Federal estate tax, but no tax results upon Stephen's death. Stephen held a life estate, but § 2036 does not apply because he was not the grantor of the trust. Nor does § 2033 (property owned by the decedent) come into play because Stephen's interest disappeared upon his death. The ultimate result is that the property in trust skips a generation of transfer taxes. ■

EXAMPLE 72

Joshua dies at age 89 and leaves all of his property to a trust. Under the terms of the trust instrument, trust income and corpus are to be distributed equally over a 10-year period to Amber and Ethan. Amber is Joshua's 22-year-old third wife, and Ethan is his 30-year-old grandson. As a result of this arrangement, the following tax consequences ensue: the estate tax applies on Joshua's death; income earned by the trust will be subject to income tax (see Chapter 20); and normally no transfer tax results when distributions of trust income and corpus occur. ■

[65] § 6018(a)(3).

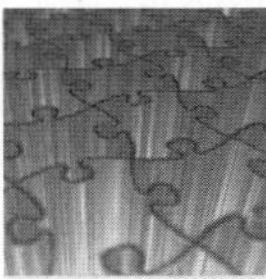

CONCEPT SUMMARY 18.3

Federal Estate Tax Provisions—Taxable Estate and Procedural Matters

1. In moving from the gross estate to the taxable estate, certain deductions are allowed.
2. Under § 2053, deductions are permitted for various administration expenses (e.g., executor's commissions), professional fees (appraisal, accounting, and legal), debts of the decedent, certain unpaid taxes, and funeral expenses.
3. Casualty and theft losses occurring during the settlement of the estate and not compensated for by insurance can be deducted (§ 2054).
4. Charitable transfers are deductible if the designated organization holds qualified status with the IRS at the time of death (§ 2055).
5. Transfers to a surviving spouse yield a marital deduction if they do not violate the terminable interest rule (§ 2056). The terminable interest rule can be avoided by the use of a general power of appointment or by making a QTIP election.
6. A deduction is allowed for certain state and local death taxes paid (§ 2058).
7. The tax base for determining the estate tax is the taxable estate plus all post-1976 taxable gifts.
8. Using the unified transfer tax rates appearing in Appendix A, determine the tax on the tax base.
9. From the tax determined under item 8, subtract the credits allowed under §§ 2010–2016.
10. If required, a Federal estate tax return (Form 706) must be filed within nine months of the date of the decedent's death.

EXAMPLE 73

Amy gives assets to Eric (her grandson). Called a direct skip, the gift would circumvent any transfer taxes that would have resulted had the assets been channeled through Eric's parents. ■

The Solution

The generation-skipping transfer tax (GSTT) is designed to preclude the avoidance of either the estate tax or the gift tax by making transfers that bypass the next lower generation. In the typical family setting, this involves transfers from grandparents to grandchildren. Such transfers, in effect, would skip any transfer tax that would result if the property were channeled through the children.

The GSTT is triggered by any of these three events: a taxable *termination* occurs, a taxable *distribution* takes place, or a *direct skip* is made.[66] Example 71 illustrates a termination event. Upon Stephen's death, the fair market value of the trust property that passes to Ava is subject to the GSTT (imposed on the trust). The GSTT will have the effect of reducing the amount Ava receives from the trust.

Example 72 illustrates a distribution event. When the trust makes a distribution to Ethan, the GSTT applies (imposed on Ethan). Any distribution to Amber is not subject to the GSTT because the spouse of the transferor (Joshua in this case) is deemed to be of the same generation.[67] The results reached in Example 72 show how ludicrous the application of the GSTT rules can be. Amber (age 22) is treated as being in the same generation as Joshua (age 89), while Ethan (age 30) is two generations removed!

Example 73 illustrates a lifetime version of the direct skip event.[68] In this situation, the GSTT is imposed upon Amy when the gift is made to Eric. Not only will Amy be subject to the GSTT but the amount of the tax represents an additional gift to Eric.[69]

The GSTT rate is the highest rate under the gift and estate tax schedule. Pursuant to transitional rules, these top rates are as follows: 35 percent (2011–2012), 45 percent (2007–2009), and 46 percent (2006). (The rates were 47 percent in 2005, 48 percent in 2004, and 49 percent in 2003.) To ameliorate the extra tax burden of the GSTT, an exemption is allowed equal to the exclusion amount applicable to the Federal estate tax (see Table 18.1).[70] For a donor who is married, the election to split the gift (under § 2513) will double the amount of the exemption.[71]

[66] § 2611.

[67] § 2651(c)(1).

[68] § 2612(c)(1). A direct skip can also take place in a testamentary transfer.

[69] § 2515.

[70] § 2631(c).

[71] § 2652(a)(2).

TAX IN THE NEWS Gift or Political Contribution?

Ms. M, an admirer of Mr. E (a former senator and a candidate for President of the United States), sends him $725,000. Because no restrictions are placed on the gift, Mr. E uses the funds to cover up an affair he was having with his pregnant mistress. When these transactions become public—Ms. M is the 100-year-old widow of Paul Mellon and an heiress to the Warner-Lambert fortune, and Mr. E is Senator John Edwards of North Carolina, who was a front-runner in the 2007–2008 presidential campaign—a troubling question arises. Was the $725,000 a gift or a campaign contribution?

If the money was a gift, Ms. M owes a gift tax on the $725,000 plus a generation-skipping tax (there is more than 37 1/2 years difference in their ages), for an approximate total of $799,000. If it was not a gift but a campaign contribution, Ms. M owes no gift tax. Under the campaign contribution scenario, however, Mr. E is in violation of campaign finance laws. In June 2011, a North Carolina grand jury indicted Mr. E on such charges.

Source: Adapted from Laura Saunders, "Surprising Tax Lesson from John Edwards' Indictment," *Wall Street Journal*, July 9–10, 2011, p. B9.

For 2011, for example, the amount of the exemption could be $10 million ($5 million × 2). The exemption can be applied to whichever transfers the grantor (or personal representative of the grantor) chooses. Any appreciation attributable to the exempted portion of the transfer is not later subject to the GSTT.

Along with the estate tax, the GSTT was not applicable for 2010.

18.5 Tax Planning

Tax planning for the Federal gift and estate tax is discussed in Chapter 19 in connection with family tax planning.

REFOCUS ON THE BIG PICTURE

An Eventful and Final Year

By making use of § 2516, John was able to carry out a property settlement with Hannah without incurring any gift tax consequences (see Example 18). Both Helen and John acted wisely when they chose to disclaim most of their inheritance from their mother. By making the disclaimers, they were able to pass the property to their children without a transfer tax being imposed (see Examples 19 and 20).

Section 2033 operates to include in the gross estate not only John's retirement plan benefits but also any settlement from a potential lawsuit (see Examples 32 and 33). Section 2036 did not apply to the trust that John's father (Peter) created, but it did apply to the one John set up (see Examples 36 and 37). The difference in treatment occurs when it is the owner who retains an interest in the property, thereby making the transfer incomplete.

John's pre-death planning was highly advantageous in several respects.

- By drawing up a new will, the loss of the charitable and marital deductions was avoided (see Examples 58 and 59).
- By prepaying state and local property and income taxes and staying current on medical expenses, John improved his Federal income tax position (see Example 58). He also avoided any estate taxes on the amounts used to pay these expenses.

KEY TERMS

Alternate valuation date, 18-6
Annual exclusion, 18-13
Bypass amount, 18-5
Disclaimer, 18-12
Exclusion amount, 18-5
Exemption equivalent, 18-5
Future interest, 18-13
Gross estate, 18-18
Joint tenants, 18-8
Marital deduction, 18-31
Power of appointment, 18-26
Probate estate, 18-18
Qualified terminable interest property, 18-33
Taxable estate, 18-29
Taxable gift, 18-3
Tenants by the entirety, 18-8
Tenants in common, 18-8
Terminable interests, 18-33
Unified tax credit, 18-4
Unified transfer tax, 18-2

DISCUSSION QUESTIONS

1. **LO.1** Why can the unified transfer tax be categorized as an excise tax? In this regard, how does it differ from an income tax?

2. **LO.1** Over the years, the tax treatment of transfers by gift and by death has not been consistent. In this regard, what were the policy considerations supporting the original rules and the changes made?

3. **LO.1** Eight years ago, Alex made gifts of all of his assets to family and friends. Although the transfers would have generated gift taxes, none were paid and no gift tax returns were filed. At present, no one knows where Alex is or even if he is still alive. The IRS has discovered that the gifts were made and is pursuing the donees for the gift tax due. Comment on the validity of the following defenses posed by the donees.
   a. The donor, not the donee, is responsible for the payment of any gift tax due.
   b. The assessment of any gift tax is barred by the statute of limitations.

4. **LO.1** Kim, a wealthy Korean national, is advised by his physicians to have an operation performed at the Mayo Clinic. Kim is hesitant to come to the United States because of the possible tax consequences. If the procedure is not successful, Kim does not want his wealth to be subject to the Federal estate tax. Are Kim's concerns justified? Explain. **Issue ID**

5. **LO.1** Carlos, a citizen and resident of Chile, would like to buy stock in General Electric and make gifts of the shares to his children. Will the Federal gift tax pose a problem for him? Explain.

6. **LO.1** To avoid both state and Federal transfer taxes (i.e., estate, inheritance, and gift), Gary (a U.S. citizen) has moved to Costa Rica. Furthermore, he plans to limit his investments to non-U.S. assets (e.g., foreign stocks and bonds and real estate). Will Gary accomplish his objective? Explain.

7. **LO.1** In what manner does an inheritance tax differ from an estate tax?

8. **LO.2** A new out-of-state client, Robert Ball, has asked you to prepare a Form 709 for a large gift he made in 2011. When you request copies of any prior gift tax returns he may have filed, he responds, "What do gifts in prior years have to do with 2011?" Send a letter to Robert at 4560 Walton Lane, Benton, AR 72015, clarifying this matter. **Communications**

9. **LO.2, 4, 5** Regarding the formula for the Federal gift tax (see Figure 18.1 in the text), comment on the following observations.
   a. Only post-1976 taxable gifts must be considered in determining the tax on a current gift.
   b. A credit is allowed for the gift taxes actually paid on prior gifts.
   c. A deduction for an annual exclusion always is available.
   d. Some gratuitous transfers might not be subject to the gift tax.

10. **LO.3** Regarding the formula for the Federal estate tax (see Figure 18.2 in the text), comment on the following.
    a. The gross estate may include property interests not owned by the decedent at the time of death.

b. The gross estate may include assets that are not part of the probate estate (i.e., subject to administration by the executor of the estate).
c. To arrive at the taxable estate, certain adjustments must be made to the gross estate.
d. In arriving at the estate tax that is due, apply the appropriate rate from the unified transfer tax rate schedule to the taxable estate.

11. **LO.3** As to the alternate valuation date of § 2032, comment on the following.
 a. The justification for the election.
 b. The main heir prefers the date of death value.
 c. An estate asset is distributed to an heir three months after the decedent's death.
 d. Effect of the election on income tax basis.

Issue ID

12. **LO.3** Hugo dies in 2012, leaving a large estate. Among other provisions in his will are charitable and marital bequests. When Hugo's executor elects the alternate valuation date, it has the effect of *decreasing* the marital deduction and *increasing* the charitable deduction of the estate. How can this be possible?

13. **LO.3** What type of ownership interest is appropriate in each of the following?
 a. A father wants to provide for his daughter during her life but wants to ensure that her younger husband (i.e., the son-in-law) does not inherit the property if he survives her.
 b. A married couple buys a home and wants to make sure that whoever survives obtains sole ownership of the property.
 c. Grandparents want to ensure that the family vacation home will be available for use by all of their children and grandchildren during their lifetimes.

14. **LO.4** Corinne wants to sell some valuable real estate to her son on an installment arrangement. Because related parties are involved, she fears that the IRS may question the selling price and contend that a portion of the transfer is a gift.
 a. Are Corinne's concerns realistic? Explain.
 b. How can Corinne protect herself from this contingency?

Issue ID

15. **LO.4** Gus (age 84) and Belle (age 18) are married in early 2012. Late in 2012, Belle confronts Gus about his failure to transfer to her the considerable amount of property he previously promised. Gus reassures Belle that she will receive the property when he dies. Because the transfer occurs at death, the estate tax marital deduction will avoid any taxes. Comment on the issues involved and any misconceptions Gus may have.

16. **LO.4** Addison provides all of the support of her dependent father, Walter, who lives with her. Because Walter is very proud and wants to appear independent, Addison gives him the money to pay his medical bills. Is Addison subject to the Federal gift tax as a result of these transfers? Explain.

Issue ID

17. **LO.4, 6** At a local bank, Jack purchases for $100,000 a five-year CD listing title as follows: "Meredith, payable on death to Briana." Four years later, Meredith dies. Briana, Meredith's daughter, then redeems the CD when it matures. Discuss the transfer tax consequences if Meredith is:
 a. Jack's wife.
 b. Jack's ex-wife.
 c. Jack's girlfriend.

Issue ID

18. **LO.4** Derek dies intestate (i.e., without a will) and is survived by a daughter, Ruth, and a grandson, Ted (Ruth's son). Derek's assets include a large portfolio of stocks and bonds and a beach house. Ruth has considerable wealth of her own, while Ted has just finished college and is unemployed. Under applicable state law, the order of priority as to heirship favors children followed by grandchildren.
 a. To minimize future transfer taxes, what action might Ruth take?
 b. What if Ruth wants only the beach house?

Issue ID

19. **LO.4** The Randalls have a married son and four grandchildren (ages 15, 17, 18, and 19). They establish a trust under which the income is to be paid annually to the grandchildren until the youngest reaches age 25. At that point, the trust terminates and the principal (corpus) is distributed to the son. What annual gift tax exclusions are allowed, if any, on the creation of the trust?

20. **LO.4** Qualified tuition programs under § 529 enjoy significant tax advantages. Describe these advantages with regard to the Federal:
    a. Income tax.
    b. Gift tax.
    c. Estate tax.

21. **LO.5** Regarding the gift-splitting provision of § 2513, comment on the following.
    a. What it was designed to accomplish.
    b. The treatment of any taxable gifts previously made by the nonowner spouse.
    c. The utility of the election in a community property jurisdiction.

22. **LO.5** In connection with the filing of a Federal gift tax return, comment on the following.
    a. No Federal gift tax is due.
    b. The gift is between spouses.
    c. The § 2513 election to split gifts is to be used.
    d. The donor uses a fiscal year for Federal income tax purposes.
    e. The donor obtained from the IRS an extension of time for filing his or her Federal income tax return.

23. **LO.4** In each of the following independent situations, indicate whether the transfer is subject to the Federal gift tax.
    a. Asa contributes to his mayor's reelection campaign fund. The mayor has promised to try to get some of Asa's property rezoned from residential to commercial use.
    b. Mary Ann inherits her father's collection of guns and mounted animals. Five months later, she disclaims any interest in the mounted animals.
    c. Same as (b). Ten months later, Mary Ann disclaims any interest in the guns.
    d. Haydon pays an orthodontist for the dental work performed on Michele, his dependent cousin.
    e. Same as (d), except that Michele is not Haydon's dependent.
    f. Floyd creates a revocable trust with his children as the beneficiaries.
    g. Florence purchases a U.S. savings bond listing herself and Taylor (her daughter) as joint owners.
    h. Same as (g). One year later, Taylor predeceases Florence.
    i. Same as (g). One year later, Florence predeceases Taylor.

24. **LO.3, 6, 8** Distinguish between the following.
    a. The gross estate and the taxable estate.
    b. The taxable estate and the tax base.
    c. The gross estate and the probate estate.

25. **LO.6** Discuss the estate tax treatment of each of the following. In all cases, assume that Mike is the decedent and that he died on July 5, 2012.
    a. Interest on State of South Dakota bonds paid on August 1, 2012.
    b. Cash dividend on Puce Corporation stock paid on August 10, 2012. Date of record was July 6, 2012.
    c. Same as (b). Declaration date was July 2, 2012.
    d. Distributions from traditional and Roth IRAs payable to Kirby (Mike's surviving spouse).
    e. Same as (d), except that Kirby is Mike's surviving daughter (not his spouse).
    f. Same as (d), except that the beneficiary is Mike's estate.

26. **LO.6** Discuss the estate tax treatment of each of the following. In all cases, assume that Rachel is the decedent and that she died on July 5, 2012.
    a. State income tax refund for 2011 received on July 6, 2012. Rachel claimed the standard deduction on her 2011 Federal income tax return.
    b. Federal income tax due for year 2011.
    c. Rachel held a life estate in a trust created by her husband. No QTIP election was made when the trust was created.
    d. Same as (c), except that a QTIP election was made.
    e. In 2011, Rachel gave an insurance policy on her life to her son, Jim, who was the beneficiary.
    f. Same as (e), except that the policy was on Jim's life (not Rachel's life).

27. **LO.6** At the time of Emile's death, he was a joint tenant with Colette in a parcel of real estate. With regard to the inclusion in Emile's gross estate under § 2040, comment on the following independent assumptions:
    a. Emile and Colette received the property as a gift from Douglas.
    b. Colette provided the entire purchase price of the property.
    c. Colette's contribution was received as a gift from Emile.
    d. Emile's contribution was derived from income generated by property he received as a gift from Colette.

28. **LO.6** With regard to "life insurance," comment on the following.
    a. What the term includes (i.e., types of policies).
    b. The meaning of "incidents of ownership."
    c. When a gift occurs upon maturity of the policy.
    d. The tax consequences when the owner of the policy predeceases the insured and the beneficiary.
    e. The tax consequences when the beneficiary of the policy predeceases the insured.

Issue ID

29. **LO.6, 7** Due to the negligence of the other driver, Adam's car is completely destroyed, and he is seriously injured. Two days later, Adam dies from injuries suffered in the accident.
    a. What, if any, are the estate tax consequences of these events?
    b. Are there any income tax consequences to Adam or his estate? Explain.

30. **LO.7** Troy predeceases his wife, Nell. Under his will, his estate is placed in trust, life estate to Nell, remainder to his children. Regarding any marital deduction allowed to Troy's estate, comment on the effect of the following independent cases.
    a. Nell is granted a power of appointment over the trust assets.
    b. Troy's executor makes a QTIP election.
    c. Nell issues a timely disclaimer that rejects her life estate.
    d. Nell elects to take against Troy's will and claim her dower interest. Under applicable state law, Nell's dower interest is outright ownership of one-third of Troy's property.

31. **LO.7** Steve and Pam are husband and wife. Steve predeceases Pam. Under Steve's will, all of his uncommitted estate passes to the children of his first marriage. Comment on any marital deduction allowed to Steve's estate in each of the following situations.
    a. Steve and Pam own real estate as tenants by the entirety.
    b. Steve and Pam own real estate as tenants in common.
    c. Steve owns an insurance policy on his life with Pam as the designated beneficiary.
    d. Pam owns an insurance policy on Steve's life with herself as the designated beneficiary.
    e. Steve owns an annuity on his life. Upon Steve's prior death, the annuity pays Pam a reduced amount for her life.
    f. Pam is the designated beneficiary of Steve's IRA.

32. **LO.7** Bernice dies and, under a will, passes real estate to her surviving husband. The real estate is subject to a mortgage. For estate tax purposes, how will any marital deduction be determined? Can Bernice's estate deduct the mortgage under § 2053? Explain.

33. **LO.7** Louis and Sonya are husband and wife. Louis dies first and leaves all of his property to Sonya. Comment on the availability of the marital deduction for estate tax purposes under the following circumstances.
    a. Louis was a nonresident alien, and Sonya is a U.S. citizen.
    b. Louis was a resident and citizen of the United States, and Sonya is a citizen of Sweden.
    c. How can the result in part (b) be changed to benefit the estate?

Issue ID

34. **LO.8** Three unmarried and childless sisters live together. All are of advanced age and in poor health, and each owns a significant amount of wealth. Each has a will that passes her property to her surviving sister(s) or, if no survivor, to their church. Within a period of two years and on different dates, all three sisters die. Discuss the Federal estate tax consequences of these deaths.

35. **LO.4, 6** Using the legend provided, classify each of the following transactions.

Legend
NT = No transfer tax imposed
GT = Subject to the Federal gift tax
ET = Subject to the Federal estate tax

a. Hal establishes a bank checking account listing ownership as "Hal and Darlene, joint tenants with right of survivorship."
b. Same as (a). Six months later, Darlene withdraws all of the funds from the account.
c. Dana purchases a certificate of deposit listing ownership as "Dana, payable upon death to Ann." Dana and Ann are sisters.
d. Same as (c). Six months later, Dana predeceases Ann.
e. Same as (c) and (d), except that Dana and Ann are not sisters but husband and wife.
f. Tim sends money to Robin College to pay for his daughter's room and board.
g. Nick pays the doctor and hospital for his niece's reconstructive (i.e., plastic) surgery. The niece is Nick's dependent.
h. Same as (g), except that the niece is not Nick's dependent.
i. Jonathan purchased land listing title as "Jonathan and Ava as joint tenants with the right of survivorship." Jonathan and Ava are brother and sister.
j. Same as (i). Two years later, Jonathan predeceases Ava.

36. **LO.8** Abby dies in the current year. In determining her Federal estate tax liability, comment on the relevance of each of the following.
a. Abby made taxable gifts in 1975 and 2008.
b. Abby held a life estate in a trust created by her late husband.
c. State death taxes paid by Abby's estate.
d. Abby's estate includes some assets inherited from a wealthy aunt several years ago.
e. Abby's estate includes some assets located in foreign countries.
f. At the time of her death, Abby was receiving payments from a straight-life annuity she purchased from an insurance company several years ago.
g. Abby was the insured on a life insurance policy taken out and owned by her son, Jackson. Upon Abby's death, Jackson collects the proceeds as the beneficiary of the policy.
h. Abby was a cotenant with her two sisters in a tenancy in common created by her parents.

37. **LO.9** In terms of the generation-skipping transfer tax, comment on the following.
a. A GSTT termination event and a GSTT distribution event look very similar.
b. A direct skip can occur only in gift situations, not in testamentary situations.
c. Spouses may be of different generations if there is enough disparity in their ages.
d. How the election to split a gift by a married donor can help avoid the tax.

PROBLEMS

38. **LO.1, 3, 6, 7** Arlene's estate includes the following assets.

	Fair Market Value	
	Date of Death	Six Months Later
Apartment building	$4,400,000	$4,380,000
Stock in Red Corporation	1,200,000	1,300,000
Stock in Tan Corporation	900,000	700,000

Accrued rents on the apartment building are as follows: $70,000 (date of death) and $60,000 (six months later). To pay expenses, the executor of Arlene's estate sells the Tan stock for $600,000 five months after her death.
a. If the § 2032 election is made, how much is included in Arlene's gross estate?
b. As to part (a), assume that the Tan stock is sold for $600,000 eight months (rather than five months) after Arlene's death. How does this change your answer, if at all?
c. How much is included in the gross estate if the § 2032 election is not made?

39. **LO.3** In each of the following independent situations, indicate whether the alternate valuation date can be elected. Explain why or why not. Assume that all deaths occur in 2012.

	Value of Gross Estate		Estate Tax Liability	
Decedent	**Date of Death**	**Six Months Later**	**Date of Death**	**Six Months Later**
Jayden	$6,000,000	$5,900,000	$240,000	$239,000
Isabella	6,100,000	6,000,000	265,000	260,000
Liam	6,100,000	6,000,000	200,000	210,000
Lily	6,500,000	6,400,000	205,000	204,000

40. **LO.4** Carl made the following transfers during 2012.

- Transferred $900,000 in cash and securities to a revocable trust, life estate to himself and remainder interest to his three adult children by a former wife.
- In consideration of their upcoming marriage, gave Lindsey (age 21) a $90,000 convertible.
- Purchased a $100,000 certificate of deposit listing title as "Carl, payable on proof of death to Lindsey."
- Purchased for $80,000 a paid-up insurance policy on his life (maturity value of $500,000). Carl designated Lindsey as the beneficiary.
- Paid a college $13,400 for his niece's tuition and $6,000 for her room and board. The niece is not Carl's dependent.
- Gave his aunt $22,000 for her gallbladder operation. The aunt is not Carl's dependent.

What are Carl's taxable gifts for 2012?

Issue ID

41. **LO.4, 7** In May 2011, Dudley and Eva enter into a property settlement preparatory to the dissolution of their marriage. Under the agreement, Dudley is to pay Eva $6 million in satisfaction of her marital rights. Of this amount, Dudley pays $2.5 million immediately, and the balance is due one year later. The parties are divorced in July. Dudley dies in December, and his estate pays Eva the remaining $3.5 million in May 2012. Discuss the tax ramifications of these transactions to the parties involved.

Issue ID

42. **LO.4** Jesse dies intestate (i.e., without a will) in May 2011. Jesse's major asset is a tract of land. Under applicable state law, Jesse's property will pass to Lorena, who is his only child. In December 2011, Lorena disclaims one-half of the property. In June 2012, Lorena disclaims the other half interest. Under state law, Lorena's disclaimer results in the property passing to Arnold (Lorena's only child). The value of the land (in its entirety) is as follows: $2 million in May 2011, $2.1 million in December 2011, and $2.2 million in June 2012. Discuss the transfer tax ramifications of these transactions.

43. **LO.5** Using property she inherited, Myrna makes a gift of $6.2 million to her adult daughter, Doris. The gift takes place in 2012. Neither Myrna nor her husband, Greg, have made any prior taxable gifts. Determine the gift tax liability if:
a. The § 2513 election to split gifts is not made.
b. The § 2513 election to split gifts is made.
c. What are the tax savings from making the election?

44. **LO.6, 7** At the time of his death on September 2, 2012, Kenneth owned the following assets.

	Fair Market Value
City of Boston bonds	$2,500,000
Stock in Brown Corporation	900,000
Promissory note issued by Brad (Kenneth's son)	300,000

In October 2012, the executor of Kenneth's estate received the following: $120,000 interest on the City of Boston bonds ($10,000 accrued since September 2) and a $7,000 cash dividend on the Brown stock (date of record was September 3). The declaration date on the dividend was August 12. The $300,000 loan was made to Brad in late 2007, and he used the money to create a very successful business. The note was forgiven by Kenneth in his will. What are the estate tax consequences of these transactions?

45. **LO.6** At the time of her death on September 4, 2012, Alicia held the following assets.

	Fair Market Value
Bonds of Emerald Tool Corporation	$ 900,000
Stock in Drab Corporation	1,100,000
Insurance policy (face amount of $400,000) on the life of her father, Mitch	80,000*
Traditional IRAs	300,000

* Cash surrender value.

Alicia was also the life tenant of a trust (fair market value of $2 million) created by her late husband Bert. (The executor of Bert's estate had made a QTIP election.) In October, Alicia's estate received an interest payment of $11,500 ($6,000 accrued before September 4, 2012) paid by Emerald and a cash dividend of $9,000 from Drab. The Drab dividend was declared on August 19 and was payable to date of record shareholders on September 3, 2012. Although Mitch survives Alicia, she is the designated beneficiary of the policy. The IRAs are distributed to Alicia's children. What is the amount included in Alicia's gross estate?

46. **LO.6** Assume the same facts as in Problem 45 with the following modifications.

- Mitch is killed by a rock slide while mountain climbing in November 2012, and the insurer pays Alicia's estate $400,000.
- Bert's executor did not make a QTIP election.
- Alicia's IRAs were the Roth type (not traditional).

What is the amount included in Alicia's gross estate?

47. **LO.6, 7** At the time of Matthew's death, he was involved in the transactions described below.

- Matthew was a participant in his employer's contributory qualified pension plan. The plan balance of $2 million is paid to Olivia, Matthew's daughter and beneficiary. The distribution consists of the following.

Employer contributions	$900,000
Matthew's after-tax contributions	600,000
Income earned by the plan	500,000

- Matthew was covered by his employer's group term life insurance plan for employees. The $200,000 proceeds are paid to Olivia, the designated beneficiary.

a. What are the estate tax consequences?
b. The income tax consequences?
c. Would the answer to part (a) change if Olivia was Matthew's surviving spouse (not his daughter)? Explain.

48. **LO.4, 6** Before her death in early 2012, Katie made the following transfers.

- In 2008, purchased stock in Green Corporation for $200,000 listing title as follows: "Katie, payable on proof of death to my son Travis." Travis survives Katie, and the stock is worth $300,000 when Katie dies.
- In 2010, purchased an insurance policy on her life for $200,000 listing Paul, another of Katie's sons, as the designated beneficiary. The policy has a maturity value of $1 million and was immediately transferred to Paul as a gift.
- In 2010, made a gift of land (basis of $300,000; fair market value of $1.3 million) to Adriana, Katie's only daughter. As a result of the transfer, Katie paid a gift tax of $150,000. The value of the land is still $1.3 million at Katie's death.
- In 2010, established a savings account with $100,000 listing title as "Katie and Wilma, joint tenants with right of survivorship." Wilma, Katie's mother, died in 2011 when the account's balance was $102,000. At Katie's death, the balance was $104,000.

As to these transfers, how much is included in Katie's gross estate?

Issue ID

49. **LO.4, 6, 7** In 2005, using $2.5 million in community property, Quinn creates a trust, life estate to his wife, Eve, and remainder to their children. Quinn dies in 2009 when the trust is worth $3.6 million, and Eve dies in 2012 when the trust is worth $5.6 million.
    a. Did Quinn make a gift in 2005? Explain.
    b. How much, if any, of the trust is included in Quinn's gross estate in 2009?
    c. How much, if any, of the trust is included in Eve's gross estate in 2012?

50. **LO.6, 9** At the time of his death, Garth was involved in the following arrangements.

    - He held a life estate in the Myrtle Trust with the remainder passing to Garth's adult children. The trust was created by Myrtle (Garth's mother) in 1984 with securities worth $900,000. The Myrtle Trust had a value of $4.7 million when Garth died.
    - Under the terms of the Myrtle Trust, Garth was given the power to provide for a disproportionate distribution of the remainder interest among his children. As Garth failed to exercise this power, the remainder interest is divided equally among the children.

    Discuss the estate tax ramifications of these arrangements as to Garth.

51. **LO.6** In 2007, Peggy, a widow, places $3 million in trust, life estate to her children, remainder to her grandchildren, but retains the right to revoke the trust. In 2011, when the trust is worth $3.1 million, Peggy rescinds her right to revoke the trust. Peggy dies in 2012 when the trust is worth $3.2 million. What are Peggy's transfer tax consequences in:
    a. 2007?
    b. 2011?
    c. 2012?

52. **LO.6, 7** In 2000, Alan purchases a commercial single premium annuity. Under the terms of the policy, Alan is to receive $120,000 annually for life. If Alan predeceases his wife, Katelyn, she is to receive $60,000 annually for life. Alan dies first at a time when the value of the survivorship feature is $900,000.
    a. How much, if any, of the annuity is included in Alan's gross estate? Taxable estate?
    b. Would the answers to part (a) change if the money Alan used to purchase the annuity was community property? Explain.
    c. Would the answer to (a) change if one-half of the annuity purchase price had been furnished by Alan's employer?

53. **LO.6** At the time of his death on July 9, 2012, Aiden was involved in the following real estate.

	Fair Market Value (on July 9, 2012)
Apartment building	$2,100,000
Tree farm	1,500,000
Pastureland	750,000
Residence	900,000

The apartment building was purchased by Chloe, Aiden's mother, and is owned in a joint tenancy with her. The tree farm and pastureland were gifts from Chloe to Aiden and his two sisters. The tree farm is held in joint tenancy, and the pastureland is owned as tenants in common. Aiden purchased the residence and owns it with his wife as tenants by the entirety. How much is included in Aiden's gross estate based on the following assumptions?
a. Aiden dies first and is survived by Chloe, his sisters, and his wife.
b. Aiden dies after Chloe, but before his sisters and his wife.
c. Aiden dies after Chloe and his sisters, but before his wife.
d. Aiden dies last (i.e., he survives Chloe, his sisters, and his wife).

54. **LO.4, 6, 7** In 2002, Gordon purchased real estate for $900,000 and listed title to the property as "Gordon and Fawn, joint tenants with right of survivorship." Gordon predeceases Fawn in 2012 when the real estate is worth $2.9 million. Gordon and Fawn are brother and sister.
    a. Did a gift occur in 2002? Explain.
    b. What, if any, are the estate tax consequences in 2012?
    c. Under part (b), would your answer change if it was Fawn (not Gordon) who died in 2012? Explain.

55. **LO.4, 6, 7** Assume the same facts as in Problem 54, except that Gordon and Fawn are husband and wife (not brother and sister).
    a. What are the gift tax consequences in 2002?
    b. What are the estate tax consequences in 2012?
    c. Under part (b), would your answer change if it was Fawn (not Gordon) who died in 2012? Explain.

56. **LO.6** In 2009, Jessica placed $250,000 in a savings account listing ownership as follows: "Jessica, Keri, and Jason, joint tenancy with the right of survivorship." Keri and Jason are Jessica's adult children. In 2010, Jason withdrew $50,000 from the account. In 2012, when the account had a balance of $210,000, Jessica predeceases her children. What are the transfer tax consequences of these transactions in:
    a. 2009?
    b. 2010?
    c. 2012?

57. **LO.5, 6, 7** In each of the independent situations below, determine the transfer tax (i.e., estate and gift) consequences of what has occurred. (In all cases, assume that Gene and Mary are married and that Ashley is their daughter.)
    a. Mary purchases an insurance policy on Gene's life and designates Ashley as the beneficiary. Mary dies first, and under her will, the policy passes to Gene.
    b. Gene purchases an insurance policy on his life and designates Ashley as the beneficiary. Gene gives the policy to Mary and continues to pay the premiums thereon. Two years after the gift, Gene dies first, and the policy proceeds are paid to Ashley.
    c. Gene purchases an insurance policy on Mary's life and designates Ashley as the beneficiary. Ashley dies first one year later.
    d. Assume the same facts as in part (c). Two years later, Mary dies. Because Gene has not designated a new beneficiary, the insurance proceeds are paid to him.
    e. Gene purchases an insurance policy on his life and designates Mary as the beneficiary. Gene dies first, and the policy proceeds are paid to Mary.

58. **LO.7** While vacationing in Florida in November 2012, Sally was seriously injured in an automobile accident (she died several days later). How are the following transactions handled for tax purposes?
    a. Bruce, Sally's son and executor, incurred $6,200 in travel expenses in flying to Florida, retrieving the body, and returning it to Frankfort, Kentucky, for burial.
    b. Early in 2012, Sally had pledged $50,000 to the building fund of her church. Bruce paid this pledge from the assets of the estate.
    c. Prior to her death, Sally had promised to give her nephew, Gary, $20,000 when he passed the bar exam. Gary passed the exam in late 2012, and Bruce kept Sally's promise by paying him $20,000 from estate assets.
    d. At the scene of the accident and before the ambulance arrived, someone took Sally's jewelry (i.e., Rolex watch and wedding ring) and money. The property (valued at $33,000) was not insured and was never recovered.
    e. As a result of the accident, Sally's auto was totally destroyed. The auto had a basis of $52,000 and a fair market value of $28,000. In January 2013, the insurance company pays Sally's estate $27,000.

59. **LO.7** In 2012, Roy dies and is survived by his wife, Marge. Under Roy's will, all of his otherwise uncommitted assets pass to Marge. Based on the property interests listed below, determine the marital deduction allowed to Roy's estate.
    a. Timberland worth $1.2 million owned by Roy, Marge, and Amber (Marge's sister) as equal tenants in common. Amber furnished the original purchase price.
    b. Residence of Roy and Marge worth $900,000 owned by them as tenants by the entirety with right of survivorship. Roy provided the original purchase price.
    c. Insurance policy on Roy's life (maturity value of $1 million) owned by Marge and payable to her as the beneficiary.
    d. Insurance policy on Roy's life (maturity value of $500,000) owned by Roy with Marge as the designated beneficiary.
    e. Distribution from a qualified pension plan of $1.6 million (Roy matched his employer's contribution of $500,000) with Marge as the designated beneficiary.

60. **LO.8** Under Rowena's will, Mandy (Rowena's sister) inherits her property. One year later, Mandy dies. Based on the following independent assumptions, what is Mandy's credit for the tax on prior transfers?
    a. The estate tax attributable to the inclusion of the property in Rowena's gross estate is $700,000, and the estate tax attributable to the inclusion of the property in Mandy's gross estate is $800,000.
    b. The estate tax attributable to the inclusion of the property in Rowena's gross estate is $1.2 million, and the estate tax attributable to the inclusion of the property in Mandy's gross estate is $1.1 million.
    c. Would your answers to parts (a) and (b) change if Mandy died seven years (rather than one year) after Rowena?

61. **LO.9** In 2012, Loretta makes a taxable gift of $2 million to her granddaughter, Bertha. Presuming that Loretta used up both her unified transfer tax credit and her generation-skipping transfer tax credit, how much tax does Loretta owe as a result of the transfer?

62. **LO.9** In 2011, Marsha died, and her after-tax estate of $6 million passed to a trust. Under the terms of the trust, Wilma (Marsha's daughter) is granted a life estate with the remainder passing to Karl (Marsha's grandson) upon Wilma's death. The trustee elects to use $3 million of the generation-skipping transfer tax exemption. Wilma dies in 2012 when the trust is worth $9 million.
    a. Presuming that the GSTT applies, is it caused by a termination event, a distribution event, or a direct skip?
    b. How much of the trust is subject to the GSTT?
    c. Who pays the tax?
    d. What is the GSTT rate that applies?

63. **LO.5, 8** In each of the following independent situations, determine the gift tax that was due and the decedent's final estate tax liability (net of any unified tax credit).

	Decedent		
	Joseph	**Brandi**	**Caden**
Year of death	2002	2005	2012
Taxable estate	$1,000,000	$1,800,000	$1,500,000
Post-1976 taxable gifts—			
Made in 2001	800,000	—	—
Made in 2002	—	900,000	—
Made in 2011	—	—	5,300,000

TAX RETURN PROBLEMS

1. Daniel L. and Lisa R. Ward live at 420 Devon Drive, Clearwater, Florida, 33758. For many years, the Wards were successful real estate developers. They retired just prior to the downturn in the market but still own several tracts of land suitable as housing projects. Their financial adviser has suggested that they make gifts of some of these investments for several reasons. First, the value of real estate is depressed, so the amount subject to a gift tax will be lower than usual. Second, the current $5 million exclusion amount may not be permanent and should be used while still available.

   Based on this advice, the Wards are not hesitant in making large gifts to their adult children: Andrew Ward, Travis Ward, and Amanda Roland. These and other gifts made by the Wards in 2011 are summarized as follows.

Transfer	Donor	
	Daniel	Lisa
Tract of land in Pinellas County (FL) to be held as tenants in common by Andrew and Travis Ward (acquired in 1990 at a cost of $900,000).	$3,000,000	$3,000,000
Tract of land in Lee County (FL) to Amanda Roland (acquired in 1991 at a cost of $600,000).	1,500,000	1,500,000
Ward Ranch, Teton County (WY), to Andrew Ward, Travis Ward, and Amanda Roland as joint tenants (inherited from father in 1988 when worth $800,000).	2,000,000	–0–
Gift to Ava and Jack Roberts, an RV, on their 50th wedding anniversary. (Ava is Lisa's older sister.)	–0–	110,000

Prepare 2011 gift tax returns (Form 709) for the Wards assuming that the § 2513 election to split gifts is made. The Wards have made no prior taxable gifts. Relevant Social Security numbers are 123-45-6789 (Daniel) and 123-45-6788 (Lisa).

2. Rachel B. Keating, a long-time widow, lives at 2410 Calhoun Boulevard, Charleston, South Carolina, 29402. In 2011, Rachel decides to make use of the generous $5 million exclusion amount, making gifts of several real estate investments to her two adult children.

   - To Valarie Cooper, daughter, a tract of undeveloped land in Richland County (SC) worth $2.6 million. The land was acquired by Rachel in 1980 for $900,000.
   - To Henry Keating, son, a tract of undeveloped land in Lexington County (SC) worth $2.5 million. The land was inherited by Rachel from her grandmother in 1970 when it was worth $300,000.

   Prepare a 2011 gift tax return (Form 709) for Rachel (Social Security number 123-45-6787). She has made no prior taxable gifts.

3. Pamela (Pam) K. Butler, age 86, died on June 6, 2011, as a result of an automobile accident. At the time of her death, Pam lived at 10318 Taylorcrest Boulevard, Houston, Texas, 77024. She is survived by three adult children: Alexis Gordon (age 55), Noah Butler (age 54), and Spencer Butler (age 52) and was predeceased by her husband, Joshua, who died in 2001. Information regarding Pam's estate is summarized as follows.

   - Pam held a life estate in the Butler Trust. The trust was created upon Joshua's death with his separate property worth $1.5 million. The executor of his estate made a QTIP election as to Pam's life estate. The trust has a value of $2.5 million on June 6, 2011.
   - In 1990 using separate funds, Joshua purchased several tracts of timber in Angelina County (TX) for $400,000 and listed title as follows: "Joshua, Pamela, and Amy Butler, joint tenants with right of survivorship." Amy is Joshua's older sister who died in 2009. As of June 6, 2011, the timber tracts are worth $1 million.
   - In 2002, Pam purchased a large ranch in Bandera County (TX) for $900,000. The ranch is in "the hill country"—a popular vacation and retirement area—and is suitable for real estate development. To help finance the purchase, Pam obtained mortgage funds through Travis Trust Company. As of June 6, 2011, the Bandera ranch is valued at $1.5 million and the balance due on the mortgage is $500,000.
   - Before his death, Joshua purchased four insurance policies on Pam's life. The policies are issued by Stilt Mutual, and each has a maturity value of $100,000. Beneficiaries under the policies are Pam's estate and each of the three Butler children. Pam inherited the policies from Joshua and owned them at the time of her death. In July 2011, Stilt pays $100,000 to Pam's estate and to each of the Butler children.
   - Pam was killed while riding as a passenger in one of her son's automobiles. While waiting for a red light, the car was rear-ended by a UDF (a national package delivery service) van. As the driver was charged with DUI and was clearly at fault, UDF offered to settle with Pam's estate and avoid the publicity of a lawsuit. In return for a cash payment of $500,000, the executor of Pam's estate accepted the offer and signed a release from further legal action. UDF paid $500,000 to the estate on September 9, 2011.

- In 2006, Pam purchased two adjoining residential lots in Alamo Heights (a suburb of San Antonio) for $400,000. Title to the property was listed in the names of Pam and her children as joint tenants with the right of survivorship. On June 6, 2011, the lots are valued at $600,000.
- Pam's other assets include:

Checking account (Progress Bank)	$ 18,000
CD at Ally Bank*	102,000
City of Waco general purpose bonds*	51,000
Personal and household effects	48,000

*Includes accrued interest to June 6, 2011.

- Liabilities and expenses in connection with estate administration are summarized as follows.

Pam's credit card debt and unpaid household bills	$26,700
Federal income tax (January 1, 2011 to June 6, 2011)	41,200
Funeral expenses	11,000
Attorney's fees	39,000
Accounting fees	19,000
Appraisal fees and court costs	23,000

- Under Pam's will, her residence (June 6, 2011 value of $900,000) passes to the Salvation Army. All of her other assets are to be distributed to her three children.

Because Alexis Gordon had so much experience in the probate of her father's estate, she is designated by Pam as executor of her estate. Probating of the estate of Pamela K. Butler was concluded on December 7, 2011.

Prepare an estate tax return (Form 706) for Pam. In this regard, make the following assumptions.

- No § 2032 election is made, and §§ 2032A and 6166 (see Chapter 19) are inappropriate.
- Disregard any request for information that is not available.
- Some deductions require a choice (Form 706 or Form 1041) and cannot be deducted twice (see Chapters 19 and 20). Resolve all choices in favor of Form 706.
- Pamela and Joshua have made no prior taxable gifts.
- Relevant Social Security numbers:

Name	Social Security Number
Joshua Butler	123-45-6786
Pamela Butler	123-45-6785
Alexis Gordon	123-45-6784
Noah Butler	123-45-6783
Spencer Butler	123-45-6782

RESEARCH PROBLEMS

THOMSON REUTERS CHECKPOINT®

Note: Solutions to Research Problems can be prepared by using the **Checkpoint® Student Edition** online research product, which is available to accompany this text. It is also possible to prepare solutions to the Research Problems by using tax research materials found in a standard tax library.

Research Problem 1. In 2000, June, a 75-year-old widow, creates an irrevocable trust naming her five adult grandchildren as the beneficiaries. The assets transferred in trust consist of marketable securities (worth $800,000) and June's personal residence (worth $400,000). Bob, June's younger brother and a practicing attorney, is designated as the trustee. Other provisions of the trust are as follows:

- Bob is given the discretion to distribute the income to the beneficiaries based on their need or add it to corpus. He is also given the power to change trust investments and to terminate the trust.
- The trust is to last for June's lifetime or, if sooner, until termination by Bob.

- Upon termination of the trust, the principal and any accumulated income are to be distributed to the beneficiaries (June's grandchildren).

For 2000, June files a Form 709 to report the transfer in trust and pays a gift tax based on value of $1.2 million ($800,000 + $400,000).

After the transfer in trust and up to the time of her death, June continues to occupy the residence. Although she pays no rent, she maintains the property and pays the yearly property taxes. June never discussed the matter of her continued occupancy of the residence with either Bob or the beneficiaries of the trust.

Upon June's death in 2008, the value of the trust is $2.3 million, broken down as follows: marketable securities and cash ($1.6 million) and residence ($700,000). Shortly thereafter, Bob sells the residence, liquidates the trust, and distributes the proceeds to the beneficiaries.

What are the estate tax consequences of these transactions to June?

Partial list of research aids:
§ 2036.
Guynn v. U.S., 71–1 USTC ¶12,742, 27 AFTR 2d 71–1653, 437 F.2d 1148 (CA–4, 1971).
Estate of Eleanor T. R. Trotter, 82 TCM 633, T.C.Memo. 2001–250.
Estate of Lorraine C. Disbrow, 91 TCM 794, T.C.Memo. 2006–34.

Research Problem 2. Grace Tipton, a widow of considerable means, dies in February 2004. One month later, her designated executor is appointed by the probate court of appropriate jurisdiction, and the administration of the Tipton estate is initiated. Among the bequests in Grace's will is one that passes $10 million to the Christian Assisted Living Foundation (CALF), but only if it is a qualified charity for purposes of § 2055. Because the status of CALF has never been evaluated by the IRS, the executor feels compelled to postpone the satisfaction of the bequest. Instead, he files the Form 706 and pays the estate tax based on the charitable deduction being allowed. Further, he requests a "closing letter" from the IRS on the Form 706 that is filed. Because the issuance of a closing letter means acceptance of the deduction, it forces the IRS to investigate the charitable nature of CALF.

After investigating the activities of CALF, the IRS finds it to be a qualified charity. Consequently, in October 2006, the IRS issues a closing letter approving the charitable deduction claimed and accepting the Form 706 as filed. Shortly thereafter, the executor transfers $11 million to CALF. The amount transferred represents $10 million for the satisfaction of the bequest and $1 million for statutory interest accrued. Under state law, interest must be paid on any bequest that is not satisfied within a one-year period after the initiation of administration. The probate court sanctions the determination and payment of the $1 million interest amount.

Subsequent to the $11 million CALF distribution, the executor files an amended Form 706. The amended return claims a refund for the estate taxes attributable to the additional $1 million paid as interest. On the amended return, the interest is classified as an administration expense under § 2053, thereby reducing the taxable estate and resulting estate tax liability. The IRS denies the claim for refund on the grounds that the interest incurred was not necessary to the administration of the estate. If the executor had satisfied the CALF bequest earlier, the accrual of interest would have been avoided. The executor counters that the delay was necessary to maintain fiduciary integrity in complying with the terms of the decedent's will. Who should prevail?

Partial list of research aids:
§ 2053(a)(2).
Reg. § 20.2053–3(a).
Pitner v. U.S., 68–1 USTC ¶12,499, 21 AFTR 2d 1571, 388 F.2d 651 (CA–5, 1967).
Turner v. U.S., 2004–1 USTC ¶60,478, 93 AFTR 2d 2004–686, 306 F.Supp.2d 668 (D.Ct.N. Tex., 2004).

Research Problem 3. Ralph Heard dies in 2008 leaving a large estate. After providing for specific bequests to friends and distant relatives, his will states, "I leave the residue of my estate to be divided between my wife and two children." Ralph's will also states, "Any estate tax is to be paid from the residue of my estate." Applicable state law contains an apportionment provision that precludes the allocation of estate taxes to assets that did not create or generate such taxes unless the decedent provided otherwise.

On the Form 706 that Ralph's executor filed for the estate, the estate taxes were deducted solely from the children's portion of the residue. After audit by the IRS, the estate taxes were charged against the entire residue of the estate.

a. What difference does it make?
b. Is the IRS's position correct? Explain.

Partial list of research aids:
§ 2056(b)(4)(A).
John David McCoy, 97 TCM 1312, T.C.Memo. 2009–61.

Research Problem 4. Before her death in 2009, Lucy entered into the following transactions.

a. In 2000, Lucy borrowed $600,000 from her brother, Irwin, so that Lucy could start a business. The loan was on open account, and no interest or due date was provided for. Under applicable state law, collection on the loan was barred by the statute of limitations before Lucy died. Because the family thought that Irwin should recover his funds, the executor of the estate paid him $600,000.
b. In 2007, she borrowed $300,000 from a bank and promptly loaned that sum to her controlled corporation. The executor of Lucy's estate prepaid the bank loan, but never attempted to collect the amount due Lucy from the corporation.
c. In 2008, Lucy promised her sister, Ida, a bequest of $500,000 if Ida would move in with her and care for her during an illness (which eventually proved to be terminal). Lucy never kept her promise, as her will was silent on any bequest to Ida. After Lucy's death, Ida sued the estate and eventually recovered $600,000 for breach of contract.
d. One of the assets in Lucy's estate was a palatial residence that passed to George under a specific provision of the will. George did not want the residence, preferring cash instead. Per George's instructions, the residence was sold. Expenses incurred in connection with the sale were claimed as § 2053 expenses on Form 706 filed by Lucy's estate.
e. Before her death, Lucy incurred and paid certain medical expenses but did not have the opportunity to file a claim for partial reimbursement from her insurance company. After her death, the claim was filed by Lucy's executor, and the reimbursement was paid to the estate.

Discuss the estate and income tax ramifications of each of these transactions.

Partial list of research aids:
§§ 61(a)(1) and (12), 111, 213, 691, 2033, and 2053.
Reg. §§ 20.2053–4(d)(4) and (7), Example (7).
Estate of Allie W. Pittard, 69 T.C. 391 (1977).
Joseph F. Kenefic, 36 TCM 1226, T.C.Memo. 1977–310.
Hibernia Bank v. U.S., 78–2 USTC ¶13,261, 42 AFTR 2d 78–6510, 581 F.2d 741 (CA–9, 1978).
Rev.Rul. 78–292, 1978–2 C.B. 233.

Internet Activity

Use the tax resources of the Internet to address the following questions. Do not restrict your search to the Web, but include a review of newsgroups and general reference materials, practitioner sites and resources, primary sources of the tax law, chat rooms and discussion groups, and other opportunities.

Research Problem 5. What type of transfer tax, if any, does your home state impose? What about the state(s) contiguous to your home state? (For Alaska, use Washington; for Hawaii, use California.)

Communications

Research Problem 6. A considerable amount of material (e.g., magazine and newspaper commentaries, journal articles, and books) is available on why the Federal estate tax should be repealed. Identify three recent sources. Summarize them in an e-mail to your instructor, and include a list of citations.

Research Problem 7. Based on the most recent IRS data available, determine the following.

a. The number of estate tax returns (Form 706) filed in a year. What percentage of these returns did the IRS audit?
b. The number of estate tax returns filed that also included GSTT situations.
c. The number of gift tax returns (Form 709) filed in a year. What percentage of these returns did the IRS audit?

Research Problem 8. Find the IRS forms noted below. List the title of each, prepare a short comment as to its purpose or use, and e-mail this information to your instructor.

Communications

a. Schedule U of Form 706.
b. Form 706–CE.
c. Form 712.
d. Form 4808.

Research Problem 9. The IRS makes available several publications that can prove useful to those involved in the administration of estates. Retrieve and summarize the following documents.

a. Publication 559.
b. Publication 510.
c. Publication 950.

Research Problem 10. Based on the most recent IRS data available, determine the following.

Communications

a. On how many Forms 706 was a charitable contribution claimed?
b. What was the total dollar amount of the charitable contribution deductions that were claimed? What percentage of the adjusted gross estate does this represent?
c. Were deductible charitable contributions made proportionately by all decedents? Were wealthier decedents more or less generous to charity? Illustrate your findings on this point in a graph, and send your report to your instructor.

CHAPTER

19 Family Tax Planning

LEARNING OBJECTIVES: *After completing Chapter 19, you should be able to:*

LO.1 Describe various established concepts used in carrying out the valuation process.

LO.2 Apply the special use valuation method in appropriate situations.

LO.3 Identify problems involved in valuing an interest in a closely held business.

LO.4 Compare the income tax basis rules applying to property received by gift and by death.

LO.5 Explain how gifts can minimize gift taxes and avoid estate taxes.

LO.6 Recognize when gifts trigger income taxes for the donor.

LO.7 Illustrate how to reduce probate costs in the administration of an estate.

LO.8 Apply procedures that reduce estate tax consequences.

LO.9 List and review procedures to obtain liquidity for an estate.

CHAPTER OUTLINE

THE BIG PICTURE Tax Solutions for the Real World

© BananaStock/Jupiterimages

Lifetime Giving—The Good and the Bad

Martin, age 75, is a wealthy widower who is considering making a lifetime gift of $500,000 to his only daughter, Francine. Among the assets Martin can choose from, *each* worth $500,000, are the following.

- Farmland (current use value of $100,000).
- Partial interest in a closely held partnership.
- Insurance policy on Martin's life with a maturity value of $3 million.
- Marketable securities (adjusted basis to Martin of $900,000).
- Unimproved residential city lot (adjusted basis to Martin of $100,000).
- Ten annual installment notes from the sale of land (basis of $200,000) with a maturity value of $700,000.

In terms of present and future tax consequences, evaluate each choice.

Read the chapter and formulate your response.

19 Introduction

Broadly speaking, *family tax planning* involves the use of various procedures that minimize the effect of taxation on transfers within the family unit. As such, planning involves a consideration not only of transfer taxes (i.e., gift and estate) but also of the income tax ramifications to both the transferor (i.e., donor or decedent) and the transferees (i.e., donees or heirs).

The valuation of the transferred property also is an essential element of family tax planning. The gift tax is based on the fair market value of the property on the date of the transfer. For the Federal estate tax, the fair market value on the date of the owner's death or the alternate valuation date (if available and elected) controls.

19.1 Valuation Concepts

LO.1

Describe various established concepts used in carrying out the valuation process.

A major emphasis of this chapter concerns the valuation of property involved in transfers by gift and by death.

Valuation in General

The Internal Revenue Code refers to "value" and "fair market value," but does not discuss these terms at length.[1] Section 2031(b) comes closest to a definition when it treats the problem of stocks and securities for which no sales price information (the usual case with closely held corporations) is available. In such situations, "the value thereof shall be determined by taking into consideration, in addition to all other factors, the value of stock or securities of corporations engaged in the same or similar line of business which are listed on an exchange."

Regulation § 20.2031–1(b) is more specific in defining fair market value as "the price at which property would change hands between a willing buyer and a willing seller, neither being under any compulsion to buy or to sell and both having reasonable knowledge of relevant facts." The same Regulation makes clear that the fair market value of an item of property is not determined by a forced sale price. Nor is the fair market value determined by the sale price of the item in a market other than that in which the item is most commonly sold to the public. Sentiment should not play a part in the determination of value. Suppose, for example, the decedent's daughter is willing to pay $500 for a portrait of her mother. If the painting is really worth $200 (i.e., what the general public would pay), then that should be its value.

The item's location must also be considered. Thus, the fair market value of property that generally is obtained by the public in a retail market is the price at which the property (or comparable items) would be sold at retail.

EXAMPLE 1

At the time of his death, Don owned three automobiles. The automobiles are included in Don's gross estate at their fair market value on the date of his death or on the alternate valuation date (if elected). The fair market value of the automobiles is determined by looking at the price a member of the general public would pay for automobiles of approximately the same description, make, model, age, condition, etc. The price a dealer in used cars would pay for these automobiles is inappropriate, because an automobile is an item obtainable by the public in a retail market. ■

[1]See, for example, §§ 1001(b), 2031(a), and 2512(a). Sections 2032A(e)(7) and (8) set forth certain procedures for valuing farms and interests in closely held businesses.

If tangible personalty is sold as a result of an advertisement in the classified section of a newspaper and the property is of a type often sold in this manner or if the property is sold at a public auction, the price for which it is sold is presumed to be the retail sales price of the item at the time of the sale. The retail sales price is also used if the sale is made within a reasonable period following the valuation date and market conditions affecting the value of similar items have not changed substantially.[2] Tangible personalty includes all property except real estate and intangible property.

Valuation of Specific Assets

Stocks and Bonds

If there is a market for stocks and bonds on a stock exchange, in an over-the-counter market, or otherwise, the mean between the highest and lowest quoted selling prices on the valuation date is the fair market value per unit. A special rule applies if no sales occurred on the valuation date but did occur on dates within a reasonable period before and after the valuation date. The fair market value is the weighted average of the means between the highest and lowest sales prices on the nearest date before and the nearest date after the valuation date. The average is weighted *inversely* by the respective number of trading days between the selling dates and the valuation date.[3]

EXAMPLE 2

Carla makes a gift to Antonio of shares of stock in Green Corporation. The transactions involving this stock that occurred closest to the date of the gift took place two trading days before the date of the gift at a mean selling price of \$10 and three trading days after the gift at a mean selling price of \$15. The \$12 fair market value of each share of Green stock is determined as follows.

$$\frac{(3 \times \$10) + (2 \times \$15)}{5} = \$12$$

■

If no transactions occurred within a reasonable period before and after the valuation date, the fair market value is determined by taking a weighted average of the means between the bona fide bid and asked prices on the nearest trading dates before and after the valuation date. However, both dates must be within a reasonable period of time.

If no actual sales prices or bona fide bid and asked prices are available for dates within a reasonable period relative to the valuation date, the mean between the highest and lowest available sales prices or bid and asked prices on that date may be taken as the value.

In many instances, there are no established market prices for securities. This lack of information is typically the case with stock in closely held corporations. Problems unique to valuing interests in closely held businesses are discussed later in this chapter.

Notes Receivable

The fair market value of notes, secured or unsecured, is the amount of unpaid principal plus interest accrued to the valuation date, unless the parties (e.g., executor or donor) establish a lower value or prove the notes are worthless. Factors such as a low interest rate and a distant maturity date are relevant in showing that a note is worth less than its face amount. Crucial elements in proving that a note is entirely or partially worthless are the financial condition of the borrower and the absence of any value for the property pledged or mortgaged as security for the obligation.[4]

[2] Rev.Proc. 65–19, 1965–2 C.B. 1002.

[3] Reg. §§ 20.2031–2(b) and 25.2512–2(b).

[4] Reg. §§ 20.2031–4 and 25.2512–4.

EXAMPLE 3

At the time of his death, Ira held a note (face amount of $50,000) issued by his son, Kevin. Although Kevin is solvent, he is relieved of the obligation because Ira forgives the note in his will. Presuming that the note is payable on demand, it is included in Ira's gross estate at $50,000 plus accrued interest. If the note is not due immediately and/or the interest provided for is under the current rate, a discount may be in order and the fair market value of the note would be less than $50,000. The burden of proof in supporting a discount for the note is on the executor. ■

ETHICS & EQUITY One Way to Handle Loans to Troublesome In-Laws

At the time of his death in 2012, Tim Landry held a note, payable on demand, in the amount of $40,000. The note had been issued by Roy Briggs, Tim's former brother-in-law, 10 years earlier. Roy used the funds to help pay the wedding and honeymoon expenses when he married Colleen Landry, Tim's sister. The couple have since separated, and Roy disappeared for parts unknown in 2006.

The executor of Tim's estate handled this matter as follows.

- Filed an amended income tax return for 2006 claiming a bad debt deduction. This set off a chain reaction, and several other amended returns had to be filed for years after 2006.
- Made no mention of the note on the Form 706 filed for Tim Landry's estate.

What, if any, could be the justification for the executor's actions? What caused the chain reaction? If an audit results, what position(s) might the IRS take?

Insurance Policies and Annuity Contracts

The value of a life insurance policy on the life of a person other than the decedent, or the value of an annuity contract issued by a company regularly engaged in selling annuities, is the cost of a comparable contract.[5]

EXAMPLE 4

Paul purchased a joint and survivor annuity contract from an insurance company (i.e., a commercial contract). Under the contract's terms, Paul is to receive payments of $120,000 per year for his life. Upon Paul's death, his wife (Kate) is to receive $90,000 annually for her life. Ten years after purchasing the annuity, when Kate is 40 years old, Paul dies. The value of the annuity contract on the date of Paul's death [and the amount includible in Paul's gross estate under § 2039(a)] is the amount the insurance company would charge in the year of Paul's death for an annuity that would pay $90,000 annually for the life of a female 40 years of age. ■

EXAMPLE 5

At the time of her death, Lana owns an insurance policy (face amount of $500,000) on the life of her son, Sam. No further payments need be made on the policy (e.g., it is a single premium policy or a paid-up policy). The value of the policy on the date of Lana's death (and the amount includible in her gross estate under § 2033 as property owned by the decedent) is the amount the insurance company would charge in the year of her death for a single premium contract (face amount of $500,000) on the life of someone Sam's age. ■

Determining the value of an insurance policy by using the amount charged for a comparable policy is more difficult when, on the date of valuation, the contract has been in force for some time and further premium payments are to be made. In such a case, the value may be approximated by adding to the interpolated terminal

[5] Reg. §§ 20.2031–8(a)(1) and 25.2512–6(a).

reserve the proportionate part of the gross premium last paid before the valuation date that covers the period extending beyond that date.[6]

The valuation of annuities issued by parties *not regularly engaged in the sale of annuities* (i.e., noncommercial contracts) requires the use of special tables issued by the IRS.

Life Estates, Terms for Years, Reversions, and Remainders

As with noncommercial annuities, the valuation of life estates, income interests for a term of years, reversions, and remainders involves the use of tables.

Because life expectancies change, the IRS is required to issue new tables at least every 10 years.[7] The current tables were issued in 2009 and are effective for transfers beginning in May of that year.[8] The tables contain 50 different possible rates (ranging from 0.2 percent to 14 percent), but *only a portion of the tables is reproduced* in Appendix A.

The tables provide only the remainder factor. If the income interest (life estate) has also been transferred, the factor to be used is one minus the remainder factor.

EXAMPLE 6

Matt transfers $1 million in trust, specifying a life estate to Rita, remainder to Rick on Rita's death. The gift took place when Rita was age 35. Assume that the appropriate rate for the month of the gift is 4.4%. Using the table extract in Appendix A (Table S on p. A–10) for a person age 35 under the 4.4% column, the value of the remainder interest is $184,230 (.18423 × $1,000,000). The life estate factor is .81577 (1.00000 − .18423). Thus, Matt has made a gift to Rita of $815,770 and a gift to Rick of $184,230. ■

In computing the value of an income interest for a term of years, a different table is used. Again, the table furnishes the remainder factor. To compute the factor for the income interest, subtract the remainder factor from one. *Only a portion of the tables is reproduced* in Appendix A.

EXAMPLE 7

Julia transfers $400,000 by gift to a trust. Under the terms of the trust, income is payable to Paul for eight years. After the eight-year period, the trust terminates, and the trust principal passes to Sara. For the month in which the trust was created, the appropriate rate was 4.6%. The present worth of $1 due at the end of eight years is .697825 (Table B on p. A–12). Thus, Julia has made a gift to Sara of $279,130 (.697825 × $400,000). The factor for the income interest becomes .302175 (1.000000 − .697825), so the gift to Paul is $120,870 (.302175 × $400,000). ■

What is the significance of dividing a gift into several distinct parts? This is important in determining the applicability of the annual exclusion and the marital deduction. Under the facts of Example 6, an annual exclusion probably would be allowed for the gift to Rita but not for the interest passing to Rick (because of the future interest limitation). If Rita is Matt's wife, no marital deduction is allowed because the life estate is a terminable interest. As noted in Chapter 18, however, this problem could be cured with a qualified terminable interest property (QTIP) election.

Why might a trust be arranged so that the income interest is limited to a term of years rather than the life of a beneficiary (compare Example 7 with Example 6)? Suppose in Example 7 that Paul is the 13-year-old son of Sara, a single parent. Julia, the grandmother, establishes the trust to ensure that Paul's support needs (e.g., medical and educational) will be provided for until he reaches the age of majority. Thereafter, the trust income will help maintain Sara. In this type of situation, however, caution is in order to avoid the possible application of the kiddie tax. Now applicable to children under the age of 19 (or under age 24 if the child

[6]The terminal reserve value of a life insurance policy generally approximates the policy's cash surrender value. For an illustration on how to arrive at the interpolated terminal reserve value, see Reg. § 20.2031–8(a)(3) (Ex. 3).

[7]§ 7520.

[8]The valuation factors in the tables represent 120% of whatever the Federal midterm rate is for the month of the valuation date.

is a full-time student, unless the child's earned income provides more than half of his or her support), the kiddie tax has the effect of taxing a child's net unearned income (i.e., unearned income in excess of $1,900) at the parents' income tax rate.

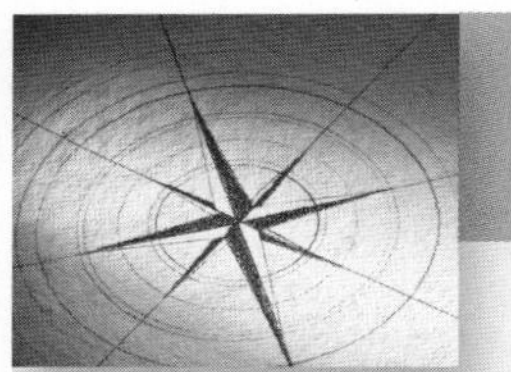

ETHICS & EQUITY Can IRS Valuation Tables Be Disregarded?

Ted Lucas (age 50) is killed in an automobile accident. One of the provisions of Ted's will establishes a trust with $3 million in assets. Under the terms of the trust, a life estate is granted to Mel (age 75) with the remainder interest passing to Faye (age 45) upon Mel's death. Mel is Ted's widower father, who is suffering from cancer of the prostate. Faye is Ted's wife, who is in good health. Under the applicable valuation tables, the life estate value in $3 million for a person age 75 is $1,031,640 (based on an interest rate of 4.2 percent).

If the Lucas estate valued Mel's estate in accordance with the IRS tables, this would reduce the marital deduction allowed for Faye's remainder interest to $1,968,360 ($3,000,000 − $1,031,640). Because Mel has cancer, however, his life estate is disregarded, and the full $3 million is claimed as a marital deduction. Is the estate correct in disregarding the valuation factor for a life estate in light of Mel's medical condition?

LO.2

Apply the special use valuation method in appropriate situations.

Real Estate and the Special Use Valuation Method

Proper valuation principles usually require that real estate be valued at its most suitable (i.e., "best" or "highest") use. Section 2032A, however, permits an executor to elect to value certain classes of real estate used in farming or in connection with a closely held business at its "current" use, rather than the most suitable use. The major objective of the **special use value** election is to provide a form of limited relief to protect the heirs against the possibility of having to sell a portion of the family farm to pay estate taxes.

EXAMPLE 8

At the time of his death, Rex owned a dairy farm on the outskirts of a large city. For farming purposes, the property's value is $1.5 million (the current use value).[9] As a potential site for a shopping center, however, the property is worth $2.2 million (the most suitable use value). The executor of Rex's estate can elect to include only $1.5 million in the gross estate. ■

The special use valuation procedure permits a reduction of no more than $1,040,000 in estate tax valuation in 2012 ($1,020,000 in 2011). This amount is subject to indexation.

EXAMPLE 9

At the time of her death in 2012, Wanda owned a farm with a most suitable use value of $3.5 million but a current use value of $2.3 million. Assuming that the property qualifies under § 2032A and the special use valuation election is made, Wanda's gross estate must include $2,460,000. Only $1,040,000 can be excluded under § 2032A. ■

The special use valuation election is available if *all* of the following conditions are satisfied.

- At least 50 percent of the adjusted value of the gross estate consists of *real* or *personal* property devoted to a qualifying use (used for farming or in a closely held business) at the time of the owner's death.[10]

[9]Sections 2032A(e)(7) and (8) set forth various methods of valuation to be applied in arriving at current use value.

[10]§§ 2032A(b)(1)(A) and (b)(2). For a definition of *farm* and *farming*, see §§ 2032A(e)(4) and (5).

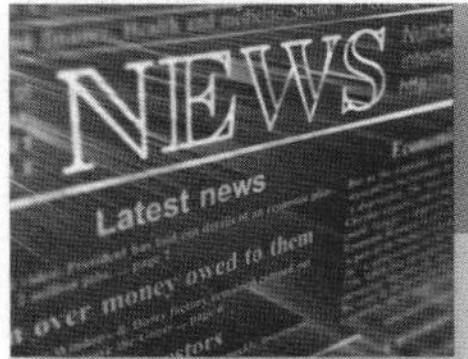

TAX IN THE NEWS Pitfalls With Special Use Valuation

The continuing increase in the value of farmland and the depressed development of commercial property (e.g., shopping centers and housing developments) means that there is less disparity between valuations under "current" and "best" use for the family farm. This diminishes the utility of § 2032A under current conditions.

Furthermore, the election of § 2032A carries a number of tax-related pitfalls.

- Planning to qualify for the election requires considerable follow-up effort, as asset values of a future estate fluctuate over time (see Examples 28 through 30 in the text).
- Making the election can have adverse income tax implications (e.g., reduced asset basis will lead to reduced amounts of allowable depreciation).
- Recapture of estate tax savings is not limited to a sale or other disposition of the property but can occur inadvertently by merely stopping qualified use (e.g., not farming).
- The recapture consequences fall on the qualified heir and do not affect other heirs of the estate. Thus, the burden caused by recapture is concentrated and not shared.
- The existence of an IRS lien on the property may discourage third-party lenders from extending credit to the qualifying heir. The result could cause a shortage of funds to meet the operating needs of the farming business.

- The *real* property devoted to a qualifying use comprises at least 25 percent of the adjusted value of the gross estate.

  For purposes of satisfying both the 50 percent test (above) and the 25 percent test, the qualifying property is considered at its most suitable use value. Thus, in Example 8, the property would be treated as if it had a value of $2.2 million (not $1.5 million). The adjusted value of the gross estate is the gross estate less certain unpaid mortgages and other indebtedness.
- The qualifying property passes to a qualifying heir of the decedent. Qualifying heirs are certain family members as set forth in § 2032A(e)(2).
- The *real* property has been owned by the decedent or the decedent's family for five out of the eight years ending on the date of the decedent's death and was devoted to a qualifying use during that period.
- The decedent or a member of the decedent's family participated materially in the operation of the farm or business during the five-year period specified above.[11]

Any estate tax savings derived from the special use valuation method are recaptured from the heir if he or she disposes of the property or ceases to use it as qualifying use property within a period of 10 years from the date of the decedent's death.

EXAMPLE 10

Assume the same facts as in Example 9. Further assume that by electing § 2032A, Wanda's estate tax liability was reduced by $245,000. Three years after Wanda's death, Otis (the qualifying heir) leases the farm to an unrelated party. At this point, Otis must pay the $245,000 additional estate tax liability that would have been imposed had § 2032A not been utilized. ■

In the event recapture occurs, the qualifying heir may *elect* to increase the income tax basis of the property by the amount of the recapture. If the election is made, however, interest on the additional estate tax due must be paid.[12]

In this regard, the Code gives the IRS security for compliance with the terms of § 2032A by placing a special lien on the qualifying property.[13]

[11] § 2032A(b)(1)(C)(ii). *Material participation* is defined in § 2032A(e)(6).

[12] § 1016(c).

[13] § 6324B.

LO.3

Identify problems involved in valuing an interest in a closely held business.

Valuation Problems with a Closely Held Business

General Guidelines

Revenue Ruling 59–60 sets forth the approach, methods, and factors to be considered in valuing the shares of closely held corporations for gift and estate tax purposes.[14] The following factors, although not all-inclusive, are fundamental and require careful analysis in each case.

- The nature of the business and the history of the enterprise from its inception.
- The economic outlook in general and the condition and outlook of the specific industry in particular.
- The book value of the stock and the financial condition of the business.
- The earning capacity of the company.
- The company's dividend-paying capacity.
- Whether the enterprise has goodwill or other intangible value.
- The prices and number of shares of the stock sold previously and the size of the block of stock to be valued.
- The market price of stocks issued by corporations in the same or a similar line of business and actively traded in a free and open market, either on an exchange or over the counter.

Some of these factors are discussed in depth in the pages to follow.

Goodwill Aspects

If a closely held corporation's record of past earnings is higher than usual for the industry, the IRS is apt to claim the presence of goodwill as a corporate asset.

EXAMPLE 11

Adam owned 70% of the stock of White Corporation, with the remaining 30% held by various family members. Over the past five years, White Corporation has generated average net profits of $200,000, and on the date of Adam's death, the book value of the corporation's stock was $500,000. If the IRS identifies 8% as an appropriate rate of return, one approach to the valuation of White stock would yield the following result.

Average net profit for the past five years	$ 200,000
8% of the $500,000 book value	40,000
Excess earnings over 8%	$ 160,000
Value of goodwill (5 × $160,000)	$ 800,000
Book value	500,000
Total value of the White stock	$1,300,000

■

Thus, the IRS might contend that the stock should be included in Adam's gross estate at 70 percent of $1,300,000, or $910,000. If the estate wants to argue for a lower valuation, relevant factors might include any of the following.

- The average net profit figure for the past five years ($200,000) may not be representative. Perhaps it includes some extraordinary gains that normally do not occur or are extraneous to the business conducted by the corporation. An example might be a windfall profit for a specific year because of an unusual market situation. The corporation may have recognized a large gain from an appreciated investment held for many years. The figure may fail to take into account certain expenses that normally would be incurred but for some justifiable reason have been deferred. In a family business during periods of expansion and development, it is not uncommon to find an unusually low salary structure. Profits might be considerably less if the owner-employees of the business were being paid the true worth of their services.

[14]1959–1 C.B. 237. See also Reg. § 20.2031–2(f).

- The appropriate rate of return for this type of business may not be 8 percent. If it is higher, there would be less goodwill because the business is not as profitable as it seems.
- If Adam was a key person in the operation of White Corporation, could some or all of any goodwill developed by the business be attributed to his efforts? If so, is it not reasonable to assume that the goodwill might be seriously impaired by Adam's death?

Other Factors

Aside from the issue of goodwill, the valuation of closely held stock must take other factors into account. For example, consider the percentage of ownership involved. If the percentage represents a *minority interest* and the corporation has a poor dividend-paying record, a substantial discount is in order.[15] The justification for the discount is the general inability of the holder of the minority interest to affect corporate policy, particularly with respect to the distribution of dividends. At the other extreme is an interest large enough to represent control, either actual or effective. Considered alone, a controlling interest calls for valuation at a premium.[16]

A controlling interest may be so large, however, that the disposition of the stock within a reasonable period of time after the valuation date could have a negative effect on the market for such shares. The **blockage rule** recognizes what may happen to per-unit value when a large block of shares is marketed at one time.[17] Most often, the rule is applied to stock that has a recognized market. The rule permits a discount from the amount at which smaller lots are selling on or about the valuation date.[18] Although the blockage rule may have a bearing on the valuation of other assets, it is more frequently applied to stocks and securities.[19]

Because most stock in closely held corporations does not trade in a recognized market, a discount for *lack of marketability* may be in order. The discount recognizes the costs that would be incurred in creating a market for such shares to effect their orderly disposition.[20] The discount could be significant considering typical underwriting expenses and other costs involved in going public.

Closely related to the reasons that an asset's marketability might be impaired is the possibility of built-in income tax consequences. In one case, the value of stock in a holding company was significantly discounted because of the income tax that would ensue if the holding company distributed its major asset to its shareholders.[21]

Resolving the Valuation Problem for Stock in Closely Held Corporations

Because the valuation of closely held stock is subject to so many variables, planning should be directed toward bringing about some measure of certainty.

EXAMPLE 12

Polly wants to transfer some of her stock in Brown Corporation to a trust formed for her children. She would also like to make a substantial contribution to her alma mater, State University. At present, the Brown stock is owned entirely by Polly and has never been traded on any market or otherwise sold or exchanged. Brown's past operations have proved profitable, and Brown has established a respectable record of dividend distributions. Based on the best available information and taking into account various adjustments (e.g., discount for lack of marketability), Polly believes each share of Brown stock possesses a fair market value of $120. ■

[15] See, for example, *Jack D. Carr*, 49 TCM 507, T.C.Memo. 1985–19.

[16] *Helvering v. Safe Deposit and Trust Co. of Baltimore, Exr. (Estate of H. Walters)*, 38–1 USTC ¶9240, 21 AFTR 12, 95 F.2d 806 (CA–4, 1938), *aff'g* 35 B.T.A. 259 (1937).

[17] Reg. § 20.2031–2(e).

[18] See, for example, *Estate of Robert Damon*, 49 T.C. 108 (1967).

[19] In *Estate of David Smith*, 57 T.C. 650 (1972), the estate of a now-famous sculptor successfully argued for the application of the blockage rule to 425 sculptures included in the gross estate. See also *Estate of Georgia T. O'Keeffe*, 63 TCM 2699, T.C.Memo. 1992–210.

[20] See, for example, *Estate of Mark S. Gallo*, 50 TCM 470, T.C.Memo. 1985–363. In this case, the taxpayer also argued that a bad product image (i.e., the Thunderbird, Ripple, and Boone's Farm brands) would depress the value of the stock. Because the trend was toward better wines, association with cheaper products had a negative consumer impact. Not emphasized were the enormous profits that the sale of the cheap wines generated.

[21] *Estate of Artemus D. Davis*, 110 T.C. 530 (1998). The major asset held by the holding company was a considerable block of substantially appreciated stock in the Winn-Dixie supermarket chain.

If Polly makes a gift of some of the stock to the trust set up for the children and uses the $120 per share valuation, what assurance is there that the IRS will accept this figure? If the IRS is successful in increasing the fair market value per share, Polly could end up with additional gift tax liability.

Polly could hedge against any further gift tax liability. Concurrently with the gift of stock to the trust formed for the children, Polly could make an outright transfer of some of the shares to State University, thereby generating an income tax deduction. Polly would base the income tax deduction on the value used for gift tax purposes. If the IRS later raises the value and assesses more gift tax, Polly can file an amended income tax return, claim a larger charitable contribution deduction, and obtain an offsetting income tax refund. To carry out this hedge, Polly would derive the amount of her gift of Brown stock by comparing her prevailing gift tax and income tax brackets for the year of the transfers. By virtue of the charitable deduction allowed for gift tax purposes by § 2522 (discussed in Chapter 18), no gift tax liability is incurred for the stock transferred to State University.

The Buy-Sell Agreement and Valuation

The main objective of a **buy-sell agreement** is to effect the orderly disposition of a business interest without the risk of the interest falling into the hands of outsiders. Moreover, a buy-sell agreement can ease the problems of estate liquidity and valuation.

Two types of buy-sell agreements exist: **entity** and **cross-purchase** arrangements. Under the entity type, the business itself (partnership or corporation) agrees to buy out the interest of the withdrawing owner (partner or shareholder). For a corporation, this normally takes the form of a stock redemption plan set up to qualify for income tax purposes under either § 302(b) or § 303. By making use of these provisions, corporate distributions can qualify for sale or exchange treatment rather than being treated as dividends (see Chapter 6). Under a cross-purchase agreement, the surviving owners (partners or shareholders) agree to buy out the withdrawing owner. The structures of the most typical buy-sell agreements are illustrated in Figure 19.1.

EXAMPLE 13

Iris, Ned, and Hal are equal and unrelated shareholders in Blue Corporation, and all three share in Blue's management. All agree to turn in their stock to the corporation for redemption at $100 per share if any one of them withdraws (by death or otherwise) from the business. Shortly thereafter, Hal dies, and the estate redeems the Blue stock at the agreed-upon price of $100 per share. ■

EXAMPLE 14

Assume the same facts as in Example 13, except that the agreement is the cross-purchase type under which each shareholder promises to buy a portion of the withdrawing shareholder's interest. When Hal dies, the estate sells the Blue stock to Iris and Ned for $100 per share. ■

Will the $100 per share paid to Hal's estate determine the amount to be included in his gross estate? The answer is *yes*, subject to the following conditions.

- The price is the result of a bona fide business agreement.
- The agreement is not a device to transfer property to family members.
- The agreement is comparable to other arrangements entered into by persons dealing at arm's length.[22]

Life insurance often is used to provide some or all of the financing needed to carry out buy-sell agreements. Such financing can be particularly necessary in the early life of a business when cash-flow problems are critical. If insurance is used in the entity type of agreement, the corporation (or partnership) takes out a policy on the life of each owner. With the cross-purchase type, however, each owner must

[22] § 2703.

FIGURE 19.1 **Structures of Typical Buy-Sell Agreements**

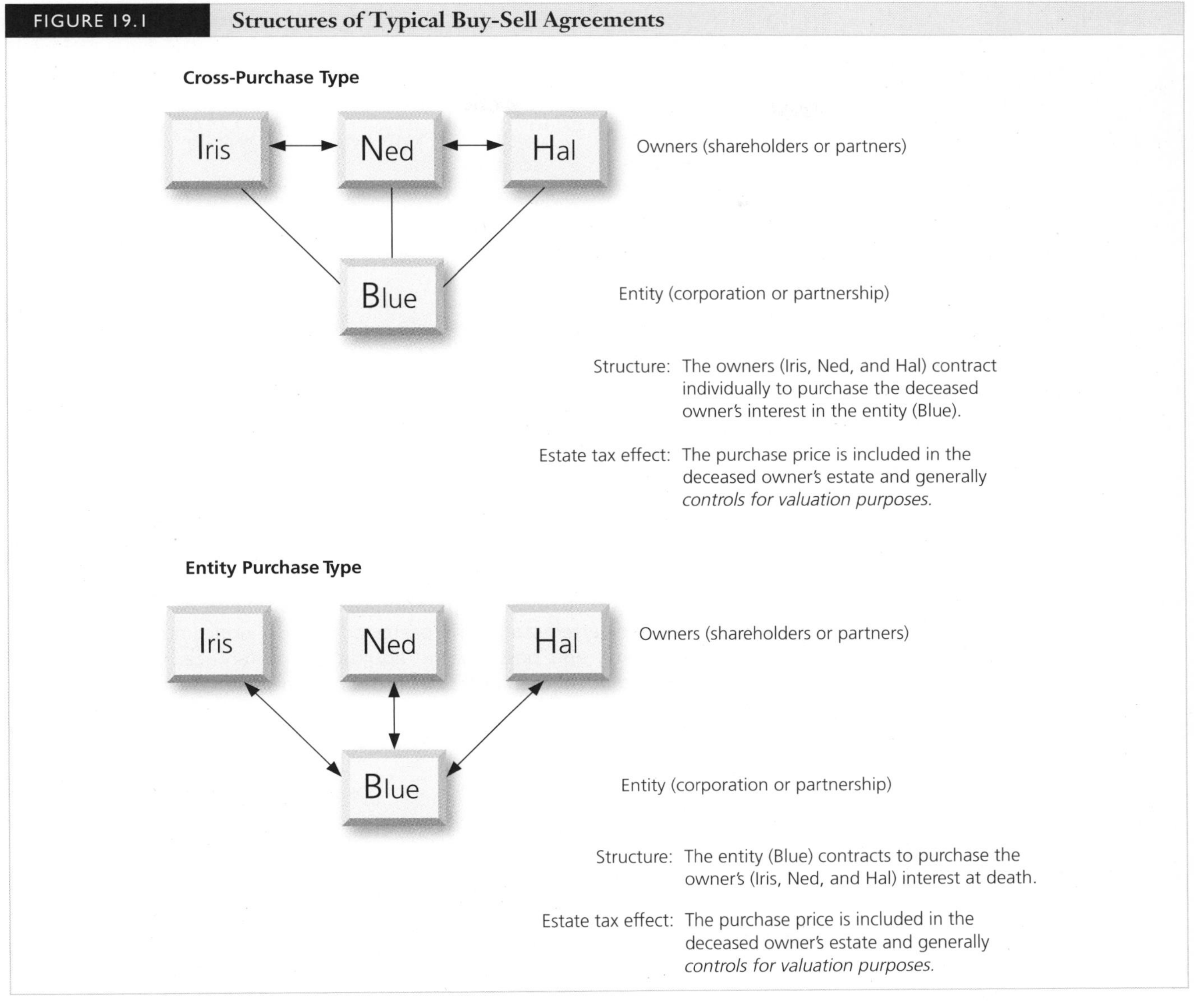
Cross-Purchase Type
Iris
Ned
Hal
Owners (shareholders or partners)
Blue
Entity (corporation or partnership)
Structure: The owners (Iris, Ned, and Hal) contract individually to purchase the deceased owner's interest in the entity (Blue).
Estate tax effect: The purchase price is included in the deceased owner's estate and generally controls for valuation purposes.
Entity Purchase Type
Iris
Ned
Hal
Owners (shareholders or partners)
Blue
Entity (corporation or partnership)
Structure: The entity (Blue) contracts to purchase the owner's (Iris, Ned, and Hal) interest at death.
Estate tax effect: The purchase price is included in the deceased owner's estate and generally controls for valuation purposes.

insure the life of every other owner, so more policies will be needed. In Example 14, full funding with insurance would require *nine* policies. By contrast, Example 13 requires only *three* policies.

Estate Freezes—Corporations

Over the years, owners of closely held businesses have searched for ways to transfer the major value of the business to their heirs while retaining some security interest. The typical approach with corporations has been for the owner to retain preferred stock and make gifts of common stock to the family. The approach freezes the amount that will be included in the owner's gross estate to the value of the preferred stock. Any post-gift appreciation in the business is attributed to the common stock and is *not* part of the owner's gross estate.

Under current law, some degree of the **estate freeze** is permitted.[23] Unfortunately, current law is designed to maximize the amount of the gift made by the donor upon the creation of the freeze. Generally, the retained interest is valued at zero, thereby resulting in the transfer of the *full* value of the business.

[23]§ 2701.

TAX IN THE NEWS Use of FLPs Requires Caution

An estate planner must exercise care when using a family limited partnership (FLP). Considering the decidedly negative attitude of the IRS, the planner must be prepared to take a defensive posture in the event of challenge. The following guidelines may be helpful.

- Avoid the appearance that tax avoidance is the only motivation for using the FLP. For example, more efficient management of the property involved is a proper business justification.
- Depending on the nature of the assets involved, temper the amount of the discount claimed. For example, taking a discount of more than 30 percent for a partnership with marketable securities is inviting IRS scrutiny.
- Be able to support the claimed discount with an appraisal.
- Avoid creating the FLP arrangement in a "deathbed" setting.
- Allow some time to elapse between the creation of the partnership and the gifts of the limited interests.
- Try to avoid funding the partnership with personal use assets (e.g., personal residence).
- Recognize the existence of the arrangement. For example, do not continue to exercise unrestricted control over the transferred property and to enjoy the benefits of ownership.

EXAMPLE 15

Quinn owns all of the stock in Robin Corporation valued as follows: $4 million common stock and $1 million preferred stock. The preferred stock is noncumulative, does not have a redemption date, and possesses no liquidation preference. Quinn gives the common stock to his adult children and retains the preferred stock. Quinn has made a gift to the children of $5 million. The $1 million worth of preferred stock Quinn retained is treated as having no value. ■

The estate freeze does, however, allow any post-transfer appreciation that develops to escape later estate taxation.

EXAMPLE 16

Assume the same facts as in Example 15. Quinn dies 10 years after the gift, when the Robin Corporation common and preferred stock are worth $10 million and $1 million, respectively. Quinn's estate includes only $1 million for the preferred stock. The $6 million appreciation on the common stock ($10 million − $4 million) has escaped a transfer tax. ■

Estate Freezes—Partnerships

Due to the statutory limitations imposed on estate freezes using corporations, the adoption of a family limited partnership (FLP) to carry out an estate freeze has become popular. A common scenario is for grandparents to form an FLP to hold a closely held business or other assets that can be expected to appreciate (e.g., real estate). The grandparents make themselves general partners and, over a period of years, make gifts of limited partnership interests to their children and grandchildren.

In valuing gifts of limited partnership interests, generous discounts (from 25 to 60 percent) are made for lack of marketability and a minority interest. As the grandparents are the general partners, they remain in control of the business (i.e., the FLP).

The overall expectation underlying the FLP approach is that a lesser value of the business can be transferred by gift than would be the case if everything were passed by death. The key to success, however, is the acceptability of the discounts used to value the gifts. Overly generous discount percentages could result in vulnerability to the penalty for undervaluation.[24]

[24] § 6662(b)(5). See the discussion of accuracy-related penalties in Chapter 17.

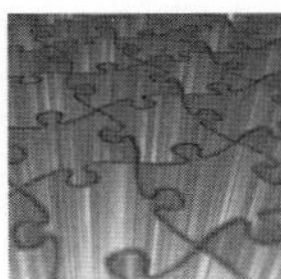

CONCEPT SUMMARY 19.1

Valuation Concepts

1. Fair market value is "the price at which property would change hands between a willing buyer and a willing seller, neither being under any compulsion to buy or to sell and both having reasonable knowledge of relevant facts."
2. Special rules govern the valuation of life insurance policies and annuity contracts. In the case of unmatured life insurance policies, value depends on whether the policies are paid up. Use of the IRS valuation tables is necessary when the annuities are issued by parties not regularly engaged in selling annuities.
3. The IRS valuation tables must be used to value multiple interests in property. Such interests include income for a term of years, life estates, and remainders.
4. Section 2032A provides valuation relief for the estates of persons who hold real estate used in farming or in connection with a closely held business. If the requirements of the provision are met and if the executor elects, the property can be valued at its *current use* rather than its *most suitable use*.
5. Determining the value of the stock in a closely held corporation presents unique problems. The presence or absence of *goodwill* at the corporate level has a direct bearing on the stock being valued. A discount may be in order for any of the following: a minority interest, lack of marketability, and the application of the blockage rule. The IRS will contend that a premium attaches to an interest that represents control of the corporation.
6. A properly structured buy-sell agreement will control the value to be assigned a deceased owner's interest in a partnership or a corporation.
7. An estate tax freeze is useful in avoiding post-transfer appreciation that develops on the partnership or corporate interest involved. However, the donor must consider the gift tax consequences that result when the freeze is created.

In light of what happened to the estate freeze of corporate stock previously discussed, it is not unlikely that Congress will enact statutory limitations on the use of FLPs.[25]

Valuation concepts are reviewed in Concept Summary 19.1.

19.2 Income Tax Concepts

LO.4

Compare the income tax basis rules applying to property received by gift and by death.

Family tax planning also involves an assessment of the income tax positions of the transferor (the donor or decedent) and the transferee (the donee or heir).

Basis of Property Acquired by Gift

The income tax basis of property acquired by gift depends on whether the donee sells the property for a gain or for a loss.

- The donee's basis for gain is the donor's adjusted basis plus only the gift tax attributable to the appreciation of the property to the point of the gift (but not to exceed the fair market value on the date of the gift). For this purpose, use the *taxable gift* amount (i.e., gift less annual exclusion).[26]

EXAMPLE 17

In 2012, Norm receives stock as a gift from Lana. The stock cost Lana $20,000 and was worth $100,000 on the date of the gift. As a result of the transfer, Lana paid a gift tax of $10,000. In arriving at Norm's basis for gain, first compute the gift tax adjustment. Only the portion of the gift tax that is attributable to the appreciation is considered. This portion is determined as follows.

[25] The current administration plans to seek legislation that will curtail the use of various discount procedures that reduce the value of businesses for transfer tax purposes. Department of the Treasury, *General Explanation of the Administration's Fiscal Year 2010 Revenue Proposals* (May 2009).

[26] §§ 1015(a) and (d). For gifts after 1920 and before 1977, the *full amount* of the gift tax is added (but not to exceed the fair market value on the date of the gift).

$$\frac{\$80{,}000\text{ (appreciation)}}{\$87{,}000\text{ (taxable gift)}} = 92\%\text{ (rounded)}$$

Consequently, Norm's income tax basis for gain is $29,200.

Lana's basis	$20,000
Allowable gift tax adjustment (92% × $10,000)	9,200
Basis for gain	$29,200

■

- The donee's basis for loss is the *lesser of* the basis for gain or the fair market value of the property on the date of the gift.

EXAMPLE 18

Connie receives stock as a gift from Trevor. The stock cost Trevor $100,000 and had a value of $20,000 on the date of the gift. No gift tax resulted from the transfer. Connie's basis for loss is $20,000—the lesser of $100,000 or $20,000. (Her basis for gain is $100,000—see Example 17.)[27] ■

Because the donee usually assumes the donor's basis in the property, transfers by gifts are considered carryover situations. Consistent with this approach, the donee's holding period includes that of the donor.

ETHICS & EQUITY Preventive Measures—Avoiding Future Misery

In preparing the income tax return of Karen, a key client, you note a significant increase in her Schedule B income. Upon your inquiry as to the source of dividends and interest, Karen tells you that her grandfather has made substantial gifts of his investments to various family members.

Other than the income received, she has no other information (e.g., original cost or dates purchased) about these investments. It is Karen's understanding that her grandfather has not filed a gift tax return (Form 709) regarding any of these gifts. What advice would you give?

Basis of Property Acquired by Death

General Rule

Except as otherwise noted in the following sections, the income tax basis of property acquired from a decedent is the fair market value on the date of death or, if elected, on the alternate valuation date. When property has appreciated in value between acquisition and date of death, the estate or heirs receive a **step-up in basis** for income tax purposes. In other words, the appreciation existing on the date of death escapes the Federal income tax. If, however, the property has declined in value, a **step-down in basis** occurs and built-in losses disappear.

THE BIG PICTURE

EXAMPLE 19

Return to the facts of *The Big Picture* on p. 19–1. Suppose Martin is considering only the city lot and the marketable securities. A gift of either asset would make $500,000 subject to the Federal gift tax. Under § 1015, her income tax basis would be $100,000 for the city lot. For the securities, however, she would have a dual basis of $900,000 for gain and $500,000 for loss purposes.

If, instead, these assets pass to Francine by Martin's death, under § 1014, she would receive a step-up in basis in the city lot (i.e., from $100,000 to $500,000) but a step-down in basis as to the marketable securities (from $900,000 to $500,000). Hence, Martin should sell the securities while he is alive, so as to benefit from the $400,000 built-in loss.

[27] If the donee later sells the gift property for less than the donee's basis and for more than its fair market value on date of gift, no gain or loss is recognized. Thus, if Connie in Example 18 sells the gift for less than $100,000 and more than $20,000, there is no recognized gain or loss.

The holding period to the estate or heir of property acquired from a decedent is automatically treated as long-term.[28]

If the property does not pass through a decedent's estate, there is no step-up (or step-down) in income tax basis.

EXAMPLE 20

In 1980, Aaron and Sandra (brother and sister) purchased land for $200,000, listing title as "joint tenants with the right of survivorship." Each furnished one-half of the purchase price. In 2012, when the land is worth $600,000, Aaron dies. Under § 2040 (see Chapter 18), Aaron's estate includes $300,000 as to the land. Sandra's income tax basis in the land is $400,000, determined as follows: $100,000 (Sandra's original cost basis) + $300,000 (amount passing through Aaron's estate). ■

Community Property

Although there is usually no change in basis for property that is not part of a decedent's gross estate (see Example 20 above), a special exception applies to community property. In such situations, the surviving spouse's half of the community takes the same basis as the half included in the deceased spouse's gross estate.[29] The following examples illustrate the reason for and the effect of this special rule.

EXAMPLE 21

Leif and Rosa were husband and wife and lived in a common law state. At the time of Leif's death, he owned assets (worth $1.6 million with a basis to him of $200,000), which he bequeathed to Rosa. Presuming that the transfer qualifies under § 2056, Leif's estate is allowed a marital deduction of approximately $1.6 million. As the property passes through Leif's estate, Rosa receives a step-up in basis to $1.6 million. ■

EXAMPLE 22

Assume the same facts as in Example 21, except that Leif and Rosa had always lived in California (a community property state). If the $1.6 million of assets are community property, only one-half of this value is included in Leif's gross estate. Because the other half does not pass through Leif's estate (it already belongs to Rosa), is it fair to deny Rosa a new basis in it? Therefore, allowing the surviving spouse's share of the community to take on a basis equal to the half included in the deceased spouse's gross estate equalizes the income tax result generally achieved in common law states through the use of the marital deduction. By giving Rosa an income tax basis of $1.6 million ($800,000 for Leif's half passing to her plus $800,000 for her half) and including only $800,000 in Leif's gross estate, the tax outcome is the same as in Example 21. ■

Effect of Valuation Elections

The election of the special use valuation method under § 2032A (discussed earlier in the chapter) and the alternate valuation date under § 2032 (see Chapter 18) will have a direct impact on income tax basis. Because the election of either of these provisions reduces the value of the property for estate tax purposes, a lower income tax basis results. Thus, any estate tax saving should be contrasted with the income tax consequences (i.e., higher gain or lower loss) when the property is sold. Either of these elections (i.e., §§ 2032 or 2032A) can alter the amount of marital or charitable deduction allowed to an estate. This possibility presumes that some of the property affected by the election passes to a surviving spouse or a qualified charity (in the case of § 2032).

When community property is involved, the election of special valuation provisions can carry a double income tax penalty. This double impact comes about because the surviving spouse's half of the community property takes on the same basis as the half included in the deceased spouse's gross estate (see Example 22).

[28]The holding period rules for gift tax purposes are in § 1223(2), while those addressing property acquired by death are in § 1223(11).

[29]§ 1014(b)(6).

EXAMPLE 23

Christopher and Samantha are married and always have lived in Arizona, a community property state. Samantha dies before Christopher. At the time of her death, their community includes stock worth $6.4 million that declined in value to $6.2 million six months later. Under Samantha's will, her share of the stock passes to her children. ■

In Example 23, the election of § 2032 means that Samantha's estate includes only $3.1 million (50% of $6.2 million) as to the stock. But the estate tax saving on $100,000 [$3.2 million (date of death value) − $3.1 million (alternate valuation date)] must be compared with the $200,000 ($100,000 for the children + $100,000 for Christopher's share of the stock) loss in income tax basis.

ETHICS & EQUITY An Executor's Revenge

In 2012, Lindsey dies and is survived by Norman (Lindsey's second husband) and Brenda (Lindsey's daughter from her first marriage). Under Lindsey's will, her property, largely made up of marketable securities, is divided equally between Norman and Brenda, with all estate expenses and taxes assigned to Brenda's portion. The will designates Norman as the executor of the estate.

Lindsay's gross estate has a date of death value of $8 million and an alternate valuation date of $7.8 million. Although the use of the alternate valuation date would save $45,000 in estate taxes, the election is not made. Why did the executor not make the election? Was the failure to make the election improper?

Step-Up in Basis and the One-Year Rule

To understand the need for § 1014(e), consider the following situation.

EXAMPLE 24

Gary and Hazel are husband and wife who reside in a common law state. When the couple learns that Hazel has a terminal illness, Gary transfers property (basis of $100,000 and fair market value of $900,000) to her as a gift. Hazel dies shortly thereafter, and under the provisions of her will, the property returns to Gary. ■

If it were not for § 1014(e), what have the parties accomplished? No gift tax occurs on the transfer from Gary to Hazel because of the application of the marital deduction. Upon Hazel's death, her bequest to Gary does not generate any estate tax because the inclusion of the property in her gross estate is offset by the marital deduction. Through the application of the general rule of § 1014, Gary ends up with the same property, with its basis stepped up to $900,000. Thus, the procedure enables Gary to get a "free" increase in income tax basis of $800,000.

When applicable, § 1014(e) forces Gary (the original donor) to assume the property with the same basis it had to Hazel immediately before her death. Hazel's basis would have been determined under § 1015 (basis of property acquired by gift). The basis would have been $100,000 (donor's adjusted basis) plus any gift tax adjustment (none in this case) and any capital additions made by the donee (none in this case), or $100,000. If § 1014(e) applies to Example 24, Gary ends up where he started (with $100,000) in terms of income tax basis.

For § 1014(e) to be operative, the following conditions must be satisfied.

- The decedent must have received appreciated property as a gift during the one-year period ending with his or her death.
- The property is acquired from the decedent by the donor (or the donor's spouse).

Even if the hazards of § 1014(e) can be avoided, channeling property through the estate of a donee can carry other pitfalls. Unless a donee spouse is involved and the gift is neutralized by the marital deduction, a gift tax could be generated by the transfer. Also, shifting property to another's estate can add to or cause probate costs to be incurred. Finally and despite assurances to the contrary, what is to prevent the donee from changing the testamentary arrangement (i.e., drawing up a new and different will) and designating someone else as the heir?

Special Rules for Deaths in 2010

Under legislation enacted in 2001, the estate tax was eliminated for 2010. With the disappearance of the estate tax, Congress deemed a full step-up in income tax basis at death to be unnecessary. Therefore, the income tax basis of the decedent carries over in the noncash assets. The carryover basis rule, however, is modified by allowing a $1.3 million (plus an extra $3 million for a surviving spouse) addition to basis for asset appreciation. Except for the possibility noted below, TRA of 2010 repealed the carryover basis at death rules.

For a person dying in 2010, the estate had a choice of two options: (1) pay *no* estate tax and use the carryover basis rules of § 1022, or (2) pay an estate tax (using the rules in effect for 2011–2012) and use the regular step-up (step-down) in basis rules (see Example 19). The IRS is to provide the details and necessary forms for making the election.

In making the choice, an executor should consider the following.

- The resulting estate tax versus potential income tax consequences.
- The timing of income tax recognition—future sales of low-basis property are less troublesome than immediate sales.
- The nature of the income that will be recognized (i.e., capital gains or ordinary income).
- Potential discord that may be created among the heirs depending on how the executor allocates the allowable appreciation (i.e., $1.3 million) among qualifying estate assets.

Income in Respect of a Decedent

Income in respect of a decedent (IRD) is income earned by a decedent to the point of his or her death but not reportable on the final income tax return under the method of accounting used. IRD is most frequently applicable to decedents using the cash basis of accounting. IRD also occurs, for example, when a taxpayer at the time of death held installment notes receivable on which the gain has been deferred. For both cash and accrual taxpayers, IRD is increasingly including post-death distributions from retirement plans [e.g., traditional IRA, § 401(k), H.R. 10 (Keogh), § 403(b)(1), and other qualified plans]. With the exception of Roth IRAs, distributions from retirement plans invariably contain an income component that has not yet been subject to income tax.

IRD is included in the gross estate at its fair market value on the appropriate valuation date. However, the income tax basis of the decedent transfers to the estate or heirs. Neither a step-up nor a step-down in basis is possible as is true of property received by death.[30] Furthermore, the recipient of IRD must classify it in the same manner (e.g., ordinary income or capital gain) as the decedent would have.[31]

How Conclusive Is the Value Used for Estate Tax Purposes?

Suppose a value is used for estate tax purposes and reflected on the estate tax return. At some future date, an heir to the property included in the gross estate believes the value used for estate tax purposes was incorrect. An heir might want a change in value for countless reasons, including the following.

[30]§ 1014(c).

[31]§ 691(a)(3). See Chapter 20 for a further discussion of IRD. Example 11 in Chapter 20 specifically deals with the IRD classification of distributions from retirement plans.

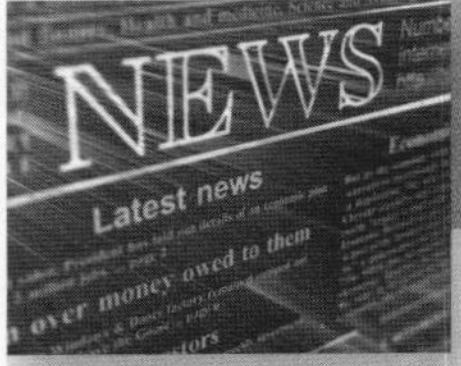

TAX IN THE NEWS Keeping an IRA Alive after the Owner's Death

One sizable asset of interest to the tax planner is the traditional IRA. Plan accumulations are characterized as income in respect of a decedent (IRD) and are subject to income tax when distributed to the beneficiary. But does the beneficiary have any flexibility as to when the distributions occur?

Taking an immediate payout, the choice most frequently made, yields the worst result. Not only is the distribution fully taxable, but the bunching effect pushes the beneficiary into the top brackets. This horrendous tax result may occur because the parties involved are not aware that a more attractive tax alternative is available.

The deferral aspects of traditional IRAs need not terminate upon the owner's death. By following certain prescribed procedures, the distributions (and income recognition) can be "stretched" over the actuarial life expectancy of the beneficiary. The following rules apply to "inherited IRAs."

- Distributions through beneficiaries should be avoided. Any transfers between plans should be direct (i.e., from trustee to trustee) and not indirect (i.e., through beneficiaries).
- The IRA must be clearly designated as an inherited IRA. Records should indicate who the decedent was, who the beneficiary is, and that the IRA is to continue in effect.
- The beneficiary usually must begin taking annual distributions from the IRA based on the beneficiary's life expectancy. In the case of a surviving spouse, the distributions need not start until the survivor reaches age 70½.
- Except in the case of a surviving spouse, the inherited IRA cannot be rolled over, added to, or combined with others—it must be kept separate.
- An income tax deduction is available to the beneficiary for any estate tax attributable to the IRA distribution. [See the discussion of § 691(c) in Chapter 20.]

Although the income tax rules dealing with lifetime IRA distributions are fairly well known, those relating to inherited situations are not. Needless to say, the tax planner needs to be aware of the "inherited IRA" and its role in postdeath distributions.

Source: *Individual Retirement Arrangements (IRAs),* IRS Publication 590.

- The property is sold. Higher value leads to higher basis and less income tax gain.
- The property is depreciable. More basis means larger depreciation deductions.
- A home equity loan is obtained. With a higher value, a larger loan is allowed.
- If the heir is a charitable organization, higher value could improve its fundraising potential.

Is there any chance of success in arguing for a different value and thereby changing the income tax basis? The answer is yes, but with definite reservations.

If the statute of limitations has not lapsed for the estate tax return, the heir may try for a higher income tax basis by having the estate tax valuation raised. Any new valuation, however, requires both cooperation from the decedent's executor and acceptance by the IRS.

If the statute of limitations has lapsed for the estate tax return, the success of the heir's challenge depends on the following factors.

- The value reflected on the estate tax return and accepted by the IRS is presumed to be correct.[32] The heir must rebut the presumption.
- To rebut the presumption of correctness, it is important to determine by what means the property was originally valued. Did the valuation result from a unilateral determination by the IRS, or was it the result of a carefully considered compromise between the estate and the IRS? The presumption is more difficult for the heir to overcome in the latter instance.
- Did the heir have a hand in setting the original value? If so, allowing the value to be changed now would seem to give the heir an unfair advantage. The heir used or influenced the use of a lower value for estate tax purposes (thereby

[32] Rev.Rul. 54–97, 1954–1 C.B. 113; *H. B. Levy*, 17 T.C. 728 (1951); and *Malcolm C. Davenport*, 6 T.C. 62 (1946).

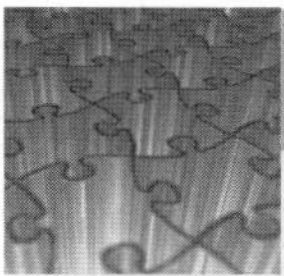

CONCEPT SUMMARY 19.2

Income Tax Concepts

1. The income tax basis of property acquired by gift is the donor's basis with appropriate adjustment for any gift tax paid. With built-in loss situations, the income tax basis is the fair market value of the property on the date of the gift.
2. The income tax basis of property acquired through the death of the owner is its fair market value on the appropriate estate tax valuation date.
3. No step-up in basis is allowed if the property returns to the donor or donor's spouse within one year.
4. Items of income in respect of a decedent do not undergo a step-up or step-down in basis.
5. The value used for estate tax purposes is presumed to establish basis for income tax purposes. This presumption can be rebutted, but only with great difficulty.

eliminating estate taxes) and now wants a higher value for income tax purposes (thereby reducing a recognized gain).[33]

- Even if no questions of fairness are raised because the heir was not involved in setting the original value, justification for a new value must be produced.

The various income tax ramifications of property transferred by gift and by death are reviewed in Concept Summary 19.2.

19.3 GIFT PLANNING

One of the ways to carry out family tax planning is to start a program of lifetime giving. The objectives of such a program are to minimize transfer taxes while keeping income tax consequences in mind.

LO.5

Explain how gifts can minimize gift taxes and avoid estate taxes.

Minimizing Gift Taxes

The Federal gift tax can be avoided through proper use of the annual exclusion. Because a new annual exclusion is available each year, spacing gifts over multiple years increases the amount that can be transferred free of gift tax.

EXAMPLE 25

Starting in 2002, Cora makes gifts in the amount of the annual exclusion to each of her five grandchildren. Taking into account the changes in the amount of the annual exclusion allowed, Cora will have transferred $660,000 through 2012 with no gift tax consequences.

Years		Amount of Exclusion
2002–2005	$11,000 (annual exclusion) × 5 (number of donees) × 4 (number of years)	$220,000
2006–2008	$12,000 (annual exclusion) × 5 (number of donees) × 3 (number of years)	180,000
2009–2012	$13,000 (annual exclusion) × 5 (number of donees) × 4 (number of years)	260,000

For married donors, the § 2513 election to split gifts can double the amount of a tax-free transfer. Referring to Example 25, if Cora is married and her husband makes the § 2513 election, $1,320,000 [$660,000 (amount allowed Cora) × 2 (number of donors)] can be transferred with no gift tax consequences.

From a practical standpoint, many donors who want to take advantage of the annual exclusion do not want to give cash or near-cash assets (e.g., marketable securities). Where

[33]In *William A. Beltzer*, 74–1 USTC ¶9373, 33 AFTR 2d 74–1173, 495 F.2d 211 (CA–8, 1974), *aff'g* 73–2 USTC ¶9512, 32 AFTR 2d 73–5250 (D.Ct. Neb., 1973), the concept of fairness was *invoked against the taxpayer* because, as the executor of the estate, he had been instrumental in setting the original value reported on the death tax return.

the value of the gift property substantially exceeds the amount of the annual exclusion, as is often the case with real estate, gifts of a partial interest are an attractive option.

EXAMPLE 26

Seth and Kate want to give a parcel of unimproved land to their three adult children and five grandchildren as equal owners. The land has an adjusted basis of $100,000, is held by Seth and Kate as community property, and has an appraised value of $416,000 as of December 19, 2011. On December 22, 2011, Seth and Kate convey a one-half undivided interest in the land to their children and grandchildren as tenants in common. This is followed by a transfer of the remaining one-half interest on January 5, 2012. Neither transfer causes gift tax because each is fully offset by annual exclusions of $208,000 [$26,000 (annual exclusion for two donors) × 8 (number of donees)]. Thus, in a period of two weeks, Seth and Kate transfer $416,000 in value free of any Federal tax consequences. ■

Further examination of Example 26 leads to the following observations.

- No income tax consequences ensue from the gift. However, had Seth and Kate first sold the land and made a gift of the cash proceeds, recognized gain of $316,000 [$416,000 (selling price) − $100,000 (adjusted basis)] would have resulted.
- The § 2513 election to split gifts is not necessary because the land was community property. If the land had been held by one of the spouses as separate property, the election would have been necessary to generate the same $416,000 of exclusions. The annual exclusion for 2012 is $13,000.
- Good tax planning generally dictates that sizable gifts of property be supported by reliable appraisals. In the case of successive gifts of partial interests in the same property, multiple appraisals should be obtained to cover each gift. This advice was not followed in Example 26 due to the short interval between gifts. Barring exceptional circumstances, the value of real estate will not change over a period of two weeks.

Minimizing Estate Taxes

Future estate taxes are reduced by the making of gifts to the extent that annual exclusions are applied in the current year. Any gift tax paid on the transfer also is removed from the estate—presuming that the three-year hazard of § 2035 is avoided.

Aside from the annual exclusion and any gift taxes paid, do lifetime gifts offer any tax advantages over transfers at death? Someone familiar with the tax law applicable to asset transfers would answer "no" to this question. Under the unified transfer tax scheme, the tax rates are the same. However, as the following discussion shows, lifetime transfers may be preferable to those at death.

Avoiding a Transfer Tax on Future Appreciation

If property is expected to appreciate in value, a gift removes the appreciation from the donor's gross estate.

THE BIG PICTURE

EXAMPLE 27

Return to the facts of *The Big Picture* on p. 19–1. One of the assets Martin is considering giving to Francine is an insurance policy on his life. Although the policy has a current value of only $500,000, it has a maturity value of $3 million. Therefore, by making a gift of $500,000, Martin would save a future inclusion in his gross estate of $3 million.

Besides life insurance, other assets that often appreciate in value include real estate, art objects, and special collections (e.g., rare books, coins, and stamps).

In making these gifts, consider the financial status of the donee. Will the gift create an economic hardship for him or her? The recipient of the family vacation home will have upkeep expenses and property taxes to pay. The donee of an art collection can anticipate maintenance costs such as storage fees and provision for security of the property (e.g., insurance against fire and theft).

Unfortunately, the properties most likely to appreciate, and thus the subject of gifts to save on estate taxes, often are "dry assets" (i.e., those that do not generate income). It may be necessary, therefore, for a donor to plan to make follow-up gifts of cash to mitigate any financial strain placed on the donee by the original gift. Returning to the facts of Example 27, if Martin decides to give Francine the insurance policy, he may need to make annual gifts to her to enable her to pay the premiums required to keep the policy from lapsing.

Providing for the Education of Family Members

Several different approaches can be taken to meet the educational needs of loved ones and still avoid any transfer taxes. One possibility is to pay tuition directly to an educational institution. As noted in Chapter 18, such payments are treated as excluded transfers under § 2503(e) and are not subject to the gift tax. In a private letter ruling, the IRS has indicated that the same treatment is available when the payment involves multiple years. Thus, grandparents can make tuition payments to a private school on behalf of their grandchildren for not only the current year but future years as well. Besides avoiding any gift tax, such payments are not subject to the estate tax on the later death of the donor.

Another approach to meeting family educational needs involves contributions to qualified tuition programs (i.e., "§ 529 plans"). Although usually touted for their income tax advantages, these plans can be structured to avoid transfer taxes. Like direct tuition payments, the contributions are not included in the gross estate on the later death of the contributor. Unlike direct tuition payments, however, the gift tax can apply and must be circumvented. This is done by judicious use of the annual exclusion. Extending contributions over several years and making the § 2513 election to split gifts are just two ways to maximize the availability of the annual exclusion. Moreover, for impatient donors, it is even possible to accelerate five years of annual exclusions into the current year (see Example 24 in Chapter 18).

Preparing for the Special Use Valuation Method

The § 2032A election is not available for valuing transfers by gift. Yet, if its use is planned in estate tax situations, gifts of nonqualifying property may aid in meeting the requirements of § 2032A. Recall that one of the requirements of § 2032A is that qualified use property must constitute at least 50 percent of the adjusted value of the gross estate.

EXAMPLE 28

In 2007, Floyd's estate includes the following.

	Fair Market Value
Farm operated by Floyd with current use value of $500,000	$3,500,000
Stock in a local bank	2,400,000
Marketable securities and cash	1,700,000

At this point, Floyd's estate does not qualify for the § 2032A election. The qualifying property [$3,500,000 (farm)] does not equal or exceed 50% of the adjusted gross estate [$3,500,000 (farm) + $2,400,000 (bank stock) + $1,700,000 (marketable securities and cash)]. ■

EXAMPLE 29

Continuing with the facts of Example 28, Floyd makes a gift of one-half of the bank stock in 2007. He dies in 2012 with no change in asset values. Floyd's estate now qualifies for § 2032A treatment because $3.5 million (farm) is 50% or more of $6.4 million

[$3,500,000 (farm) + $1,200,000 (bank stock) + $1,700,000 (marketable securities and cash)]. The election enables the estate to value the farm at current use. As a result, the estate tax on $1,040,000 in value is saved. ■

Care must be taken to avoid gifts of property within three years of death. Although such gifts usually are not included in the gross estate of the donor for estate tax purposes, they are counted when testing for the percentage requirements of § 303 (stock redemptions to pay estate taxes and administration expenses—refer to Chapter 6), § 2032A, and § 6166 (extension of time to pay estate taxes in installments—discussed later in this chapter).[34]

EXAMPLE 30

Assume the same facts as in Example 29, except that the gift occurs in 2010 (not 2007). Although only $1,200,000 of the bank stock is included in Floyd's gross estate for estate tax purposes, $2.4 million is used for the percentage requirements of the special use valuation provisions. As a result, the estate fails to qualify for the election. ■

Besides the unavailability of § 2032A for gift tax purposes, other reasons may exist for retaining special use property until death.

THE BIG PICTURE

EXAMPLE 31

Return to the facts of *The Big Picture* on p. 19–1. Making a gift of the farmland is probably unwise for two reasons. First, without further information on the other assets Martin owns (or is likely to acquire), it is impossible to ascertain how close he might be to meeting the percentage requirements of § 2032A. Second, even if the special use valuation election is not available, consider the substantial step-up in basis that occurs (i.e., $100,000 to $500,000) if the farmland is passed at death.

LO.6

Recognize when gifts trigger income taxes for the donor.

Income Tax Considerations

Income Shifting

One way to lower the overall tax burden on the family unit is to shift capital gain income from high-bracket taxpayers to lower-bracket family members. The maximum rates on dividends and net capital gain provide an excellent opportunity to take advantage of the 0 percent rate that normally would apply to certain younger donees. The maximum rate is 15%/0%, with the 0 percent rate being applicable to taxpayers below the 25 percent bracket (i.e., those in the 10 percent and 15 percent brackets).

The shifting is accomplished by giving capital assets (frequently securities) to others who make the sale and recognize the gain. If the donees are children, however, care must be taken to avoid the hazard of the kiddie tax. Under the kiddie tax, which currently applies to a child under age 19 (or to a full-time student under age 24 whose earned income is not more than 50 percent of his or her support), any gain is taxed at the parents' higher rate.[35]

EXAMPLE 32

The Millers have four daughters who are in graduate school. As each child reaches age 24, they give her enough appreciated stock to yield a gain of $30,000. The daughter sells the stock and uses the proceeds to pay for education loans. The daughter pays no tax on the recognized gain of $30,000 (0% × $30,000). Had the Millers sold the stock on their own instead of giving it, the tax would have been $4,500 (15% × $30,000). Thus, the Millers have saved $4,500 in capital gains taxes by making the transfer. If the same procedure is followed with the other three daughters, the total savings become $18,000 ($4,500 × 4). ■

[34] §§ 2035(c)(1) and (2).

[35] § 1(g)(2)(A). Children who are married and file a joint return are exempted.

In Example 32, note that the amount of the built-in gain transferred was controlled so as to keep the donee below the 25 percent income tax bracket (approximately $34,500 taxable income). Furthermore, no gift tax resulted from the transfer as the Millers are merely satisfying their obligation of support (providing an education for their child).

The procedure followed in Example 32 can be repeated with the same daughter in a later year with the same tax effect. It can also be used to shift capital gains to other family members. Furthermore, when the donees are not children, the kiddie tax problem will not be a hurdle.

If a gift of property is to shift income to the donee, the transfer must be *complete.*

EXAMPLE 33

Gloria, subject to a 35% marginal income tax rate, owns all of the stock in Orange, an S corporation. Gloria transfers by gift 60% of the Orange stock to her three married children. The children range in age from 24 to 28 and are all in the 10% income tax bracket. After the transfer, Gloria continues to operate the business. No shareholder meetings are held. Except for reporting 60% of the pass-through of Orange's profits, Gloria's children have no contact with the business. Aside from the salary paid to Gloria, Orange makes no cash distributions to its shareholders. ■

The situation posed in Example 33 occurs frequently and is fraught with danger. If the purported gift by Gloria lacks economic reality and Gloria is the true economic owner of all of Orange's stock, the pass-through to the children is disregarded.[36] The profits are taxed to Gloria at her 35 percent rate rather than to the children at their 10 percent rates. Consequently, the transfer has not accomplished the intended shifting of income.

What can be done to make the transfer in Example 33 tax-effective? First, a distribution of dividends would provide some economic benefit to the children. As the transfer is currently constituted, all that the children have received as a result of the gift is an economic detriment, because they must pay income taxes on their share of Orange's pass-through of profits. Second, some steps should be taken to recognize and protect the interests of the children as donees. Shareholder meetings should be held and attendance encouraged. That the children do not actively participate in the business of Orange is of no consequence, as long as they are given the opportunity to do so.

Income Tax Consequences to the Donor

Generally, a gift of property results in no income tax consequences to the donor. Two important exceptions, however, involve installment notes receivable and U.S. savings bonds.

A gift of an installment note receivable is a taxable disposition, and the donor is treated as if the note had been sold for its fair market value.[37] As a result, the donor recognizes the deferred profit.

THE BIG PICTURE

EXAMPLE 34

Return to the facts of *The Big Picture* on p. 19–1. Recall that another asset that Martin is considering giving Francine is installment notes receivable. Although the notes have a face amount of $700,000, due to the extended payout period and possibly other factors (e.g., a low interest rate), their current value is only $500,000. Unfortunately, Martin's basis in the notes is $200,000. Thus, because the gift is treated as a sale, Martin would have a taxable gain of $300,000 ($500,000 − $200,000).

[36] *Donald O. Kirkpatrick,* 36 TCM 1122, T.C.Memo. 1977–281; *Michael F. Beirne,* 52 T.C. 210 (1969) and 61 T.C. 268 (1973).

[37] § 453B(a).

A gift of U.S. savings bonds is not effective unless the bonds are re-registered in the donee's name.[38] This forces the donor to recognize any deferred income accrued on the bonds. The result may surprise donors who expect to postpone the recognition of interest income until the bonds are redeemed. Thus, the donor who wants to avoid income tax consequences should avoid gifts of installment notes receivable and U.S. savings bonds.

For purposes of contrasting tax results, what happens if these properties are passed by death?

- Installment notes receivable are taxed to whoever collects the notes (the estate or heirs).[39] If the notes are forgiven or canceled by the decedent's will, the income is taxed to the estate.
- Deferred interest income on U.S. savings bonds is taxed to whoever redeems the bonds (the estate or heirs).
- Recapture potential disappears at death.[40] The estate or heirs take the property free of any recapture potential existing at the time of the owner's death.

Carryover Basis Situations

When considering the income tax effect of a transfer on the donee or heir, the basis rules of §§ 1014 and 1015 warrant close examination. When appreciated property is involved, receiving the property from a decedent is preferred to a lifetime transfer.

The situation may be different, however, when the property to be transferred has depreciated in value. Presuming that the transferor cannot take advantage of the built-in loss (e.g., no existing or potential offsetting gains), should the transfer be made by gift or at death?

THE BIG PICTURE

EXAMPLE 35

Return to the facts of *The Big Picture* on p. 19–1. Assume that Martin is terminally ill and cannot take advantage of any more capital losses (e.g., he has excess capital loss carryovers from prior years). Is it preferable for Martin to give the marketable securities to Francine or for them to pass to her at his death?

If the property passes by a gift, she takes the securities with a basis for gain of $900,000 and a basis for loss of $500,000. If the property passes on account of a death, however, Francine's basis for *both* gain and loss steps down to $500,000. Thus, the gift result might protect Francine from later gain on the disposition of the securities.

19.4 Estate Planning

Estate planning considers the nontax and tax aspects of death. In the nontax area are the various steps that can be taken to reduce the costs of probating an estate. In the tax area, the focus is on controlling the amount of the gross estate and maximizing estate tax deductions.

LO.7

Illustrate how to reduce probate costs in the administration of an estate.

Probate Costs

The probate estate consists of all properties subject to administration by an executor. The administration is conducted under the supervision of a local court, usually

[38]Reg. § 25.2511–1(h)(4).

[39]The deferred gain element of an installment note is income in respect of a decedent (see the discussion earlier in this chapter and in Chapter 20) and does not receive a step-up in basis at death. § 453B(c).

[40]Contrast this result with what happens when § 1245 or § 1250 property is transferred by gift. Here, the recapture potential carries over to the donee. §§ 1245(b)(1) and 1250(d)(1).

TAX IN THE NEWS The Cost of Uncertainty

Uncertainty has become a permanent feature of the tax law. Every year, Congress decides which tax provisions will be extended for another year—or sometimes two years. In some cases, provisions are added and others are dropped. Some sunset provisions are allowed to take effect (e.g., no estate tax in 2010), but others are revoked (e.g., a $1 million exemption and a 55 percent estate tax rate for 2011). Consequently, forecasting future tax consequences has become a matter of chance.

In this atmosphere of uncertainty, estate planning has evolved into an annual and expensive event. Estate planning involves professionals (i.e., attorneys, CPAs, and appraisers) whose services can be costly. But many clients must either pay the price or risk losing the family business due to a change in the tax law that was enacted after their last visit to the estate planning team.

Source: Adapted from Emily Maltry, "For Family-Run Small Businesses, Estate-Tax Uncertainty Adds Cost," *Wall Street Journal*, December 16, 2010, p. B7.

called a probate court. In certain states, probate functions are performed by county courts, surrogate courts, or orphan's courts.

Probate costs include attorney fees, accountant fees, appraisal and inventory fees, court costs, expenses incident to the disposition of assets and satisfaction of liabilities, litigation costs needed to resolve will contests, and charges for the preparation of tax returns. The total amount of probate costs cannot be accurately predicted because so many variables are involved. A conservative range might be from 5 to 15 percent of the amount of the probate estate.

Many procedures can be used to reduce the probate estate and thereby save probate costs, including the following.

- Owning property as joint tenants (or tenants by the entirety) with right of survivorship. Upon death, the property passes to the surviving tenant and generally is not subject to probate.
- Making life insurance payable to a beneficiary other than the estate.
- Utilizing a revocable trust. Upon the death of the creator, the trust becomes irrevocable and is not subject to probate. A revocable trust is often popularly referred to as a **living trust**.
- Listing bank accounts and title to securities by use of the payable on death arrangement. As noted in Chapter 18, the designation "payable on proof of death" passes title to the property if the listed beneficiary survives the owner. A payable on death arrangement has the same effect as a revocable trust but avoids the need to create a formal trust.

In some situations, the probate estate is increased because the parties have been careless.

EXAMPLE 36

When John dies, all of the primary and secondary beneficiaries named on his life insurance policies and pension plans have predeceased him. Therefore, under the terms of the policies and pension plans, the distributions are paid to his estate. John's failure to name new beneficiaries results in an unintended increase in the probate estate. ■

Another advantage of bypassing the probate estate is that the beneficiary can obtain immediate possession and enjoyment of the property. The probate process can become prolonged, and the heir may have to await the final settlement of the estate before getting the property.

In terms of probate costs, the ownership of out-of-state real estate can cause horrendous problems. Out-of-state ownership is not uncommon with decedents who have relocated after retirement or who maintain vacation homes.

EXAMPLE 37

After retirement and five years before his death, Ted moved from Nebraska to Arizona. At death, Ted still owns a rental house in Nebraska and a vacation home in Idaho. To clear title to these properties, Ted's executor must institute ancillary probate proceedings in Nebraska and Idaho. This will result in additional attorney fees and court costs. ■

The solution to the dilemma posed in Example 37 is to dispose of these properties before death. Although this may generate some legal fees, they will be far less than the cost of ancillary probate proceedings.

LO.8

Apply procedures that reduce estate tax consequences.

Controlling the Amount of the Gross Estate

Unlike the probate estate, the gross estate determines what property is subject to the Federal estate tax. In fact, many of the steps taken to reduce the probate estate will not have a similar effect on the gross estate—see the discussion of §§ 2036 and 2038 in Chapter 18.

Valuation procedures sometimes can be applied to control the amount of the gross estate. The special use valuation method of § 2032A can be elected when the estate consists of real estate used in farming or in connection with a closely held business. When the estate comprises assets that have declined in value shortly after death, the use of the alternate valuation date of § 2032 (see Chapter 18) is advised.

Proper Handling of Estate Tax Deductions

Estate taxes can be reduced either by decreasing the size of the gross estate or by increasing the total allowable deductions. The lower the taxable estate, the less estate tax generated. Planning with deductions involves the following considerations.

- Making proper use of the marital deduction.
- Working effectively with the charitable deduction.
- Taking advantage of the bypass amount.
- Optimizing other deductions and losses allowed under §§ 2053 and 2054.

Approaches to the Marital Deduction

When planning for the estate tax marital deduction, both tax and nontax factors are taken into account. Two major tax goals guide the planning. They are the *equalization* and *deferral* approaches.

- Attempt to equalize the estates of both spouses. Clearly, for example, the estate tax on $6 million is more than the estate tax on $5 million ($350,000 versus $0).
- Based on the time value of taxes deferred, try to postpone estate taxation as long as possible.

Barring certain circumstances, the deferral approach generally is preferable. By maximizing the marital deduction on the death of the first spouse to die, taxes are saved and the surviving spouse can trim his or her future estate by entering into a program of lifetime giving. By making optimum use of the annual exclusion, considerable amounts can be shifted without incurring *any* transfer tax.

Tax planning must remain flexible and be tailored to the individual circumstances of the parties involved. The equalization approach may be most attractive in the following situations.

- Both spouses are of advanced age and/or in poor health, and neither is expected to survive the other for a prolonged period of time.
- The spouse who is expected to survive has considerable assets of his or her own. Keep in mind that the transfer tax rate schedules are progressive in nature.
- Because of appreciation, property worth $5 million today when it passes to the surviving spouse may be worth $8 million five years later when the survivor dies.

TAX IN THE NEWS How to Save Taxes and Protect the Environment

What do Ted Turner, Robert Redford, Clint Eastwood, and James Baker (former secretary of state) have in common? Besides being celebrities and financially well-to-do, all have issued **conservation easements** in some or all of the real estate they own. By this means, any "scenic view" that currently exists is preserved. The owner is precluded from obstructing the view by further development of the property. Allegedly, the transfer of the easement is motivated by the owner's desire to "conserve the environment." Realistically, the transfer is largely tax-motivated.

The steps involved in creating a conservation easement and the tax consequences that ensue are as follows.

- After the easement is drafted, the owner transfers it to a conservation trust. Usually, the trust is already in existence, having been created by an environmental group, and operates under the auspices of a local government agency.
- The owner obtains a generous appraisal as to the value of the easement transferred.
- The owner claims the value of the easement as an income tax deduction.
- The value of the property retained (e.g., residence or vacation home) is accordingly reduced by the value of the easement for ad valorem property tax purposes.
- Upon the owner's death, the gross estate includes the property at a discounted value due to the restrictions contained in the easement.

In summary, the conservation easement saves income, property, and estate taxes. The donor receives all of this in addition to the aura of being hailed as an environmentalist.[41]

Effejctively Working with the Charitable Deduction

As a general guide to obtaining overall tax savings, lifetime charitable transfers are preferred over testamentary dispositions. For example, an individual who gives $20,000 to a qualified charity during his or her life secures an income tax deduction, avoids any gift tax, and reduces the gross estate by the amount of the gift. By way of contrast, if the $20,000 is willed to charity, no income tax deduction is available, and the amount of the gift is includible in the decedent's gross estate (although later deducted for estate tax purposes). In short, the lifetime transfer provides a double tax benefit (income tax deduction plus reduced estate taxes) at no gift tax cost (§ 2522). The testamentary transfer merely neutralizes the effect of the inclusion of the property in the gross estate (inclusion under § 2033 and then deduction under § 2055).

A lifetime transfer to charity, however, can have income tax implications when a bargain sale arrangement is involved. In a bargain sale, the taxpayer wants to make a charitable contribution as to the appreciation while maintaining his or her investment in the property. The tax law treats these transactions as being part sale and part contribution.[42] Consequently, only a portion of the basis of the property can be utilized in determining the gain on the sale portion. This is calculated by applying the percentage resulting from dividing the sale price by the fair market value of the property.[43] Presuming that the transfer involves long-term capital gain property, the charitable deduction is the difference between its fair market value and the selling price.

EXAMPLE 38

Arthur transfers a tract of land to his church on which it will build a sanctuary. He acquired the land 20 years ago as an investment for $100,000, and it is currently worth $1 million. Because Arthur wants to recover his original investment, he sells the land to the church for $100,000. Arthur has a long-term capital gain of $90,000 [$100,000 (selling price) − $10,000 (allocated basis)] and a charitable contribution deduction of $900,000 [$1,000,000 (fair market value) − $100,000 (consideration received)]. ■

[41] If the contribution of the conservation easement occurs postmortem (i.e., after the death of the owner), the estate can claim a § 2055(f) charitable contribution. It then can elect, under § 2031(c), to *exclude* up to 40% of the value of the land subject to the easement. In computing the amount of the exclusion, the value of the land must be reduced by the charitable contribution allowed.

[42] § 1011(b).

[43] Reg. § 1.170(A)–4(c)(2)(i).

To ensure that an estate tax deduction is allowed for a charitable contribution, the designated recipient must fall within the classifications set forth in § 2055 (or § 2522). For estate tax purposes, this is the status of the organization on the date the transfer becomes effective and not the status on the date the will authorizing the transfer was executed.

EXAMPLE 39

In 2000, Lisa drew up and executed a will in which she provided for $500,000 to pass to the Rose Academy, a nonprofit educational organization described in § 2055(a)(2) and, at that time, approved by the IRS as a qualified recipient. In 2004, the qualified status of the academy was revoked for practicing racial discrimination in the enrollment of its student body.[44] Lisa dies in 2012, and the executor of her estate, being compelled to satisfy the provisions of the will, transfers $500,000 to the academy. ■

Even though Lisa may have been unaware of the action taken by the IRS in 2004, her estate is not allowed a charitable deduction. The recipient was no longer qualified on the date of Lisa's death. It may be that Lisa, even if she had known about the probable loss of the charitable deduction, would still have wanted the bequest carried out as originally conceived. If not, it is easy to see that the error was of Lisa's own making because of her failure to review her estate planning situation.

One way to circumvent the quandary posed by Example 39 (other than changing Lisa's will before her death) is to express the charitable bequest in more flexible terms. The transfer to the academy could have been conditioned on the organization's continued status as a qualified recipient at the time of Lisa's death. Alternatively, Lisa's will may grant her executor the authority to substitute a different, but comparable, charitable organization *that is qualified* in the event of the disqualification of the named group.

On occasion, a charitable bequest depends on the issuance of a disclaimer by a noncharitable heir.[45] Such a situation frequently arises with special types of property or collections, which the decedent may believe a noncharitable heir should have a choice of receiving.

EXAMPLE 40

Megan specified in her will that her valuable art collection is to pass to her son Teddy. If Teddy refuses the gift, the collection passes to the local art museum. At the time the will was drawn, Megan knew that Teddy was not interested in owning the collection. If, after Megan's death, though, Teddy issues a timely disclaimer, the collection passes to the museum, and Megan's estate takes a charitable deduction for its estate tax value. ■

EXAMPLE 41

Dick's will specifies that one-half of his disposable estate is to pass to his wife Amanda. The remainder of his property passes to a specified qualified charitable organization. If Amanda issues a timely disclaimer after Dick's death, all of the property passes to the charity and qualifies for the § 2055 charitable deduction. ■

Has Teddy in Example 40 acted wisely if he issues the disclaimer in favor of the museum? Although such a disclaimer will provide Megan's estate with a deduction for the value of the art collection, consider the income tax deduction alternative. If Teddy accepts the bequest, he still can dispose of the collection (and fulfill his mother's philanthropic objectives) through a lifetime donation to the museum. As a result, he obtains an income tax deduction of his own. Whether this plan reduces taxes for the family depends on a comparison of the mother's estate tax bracket with the estimated income tax bracket of the son. If the value of the collection

[44]Most of the organizations that are qualified recipients (which will permit the donor a charitable deduction) are listed in IRS Publication 78. This compilation, revised and supplemented from time to time, addresses § 170 (income tax deduction) transfers. Publication 78, with the exceptions noted in Chapter 18, also applies to § 2055 (estate tax deduction) and § 2522 (gift tax deduction) transfers.

[45]As noted in Chapter 18, a disclaimer is a refusal to accept the property. If the disclaimer is timely made, the property is not treated as having passed through the person issuing the disclaimer, and a gift tax is avoided.

exceeds Teddy's AGI percentage limitations, the donation could be spread over more than one year. Then, to protect against the contingency of Teddy's death before the entire collection is donated, Teddy can provide in his will that any undonated balance will pass to the museum.

The use of a disclaimer in Example 41 would be sheer folly. It would not reduce Dick's estate tax; it would merely substitute a charitable deduction for the marital deduction. Whether or not Amanda issues a disclaimer, no estate taxes will be due. Amanda should accept her bequest and, if she is so inclined, make lifetime gifts of it to a qualified charity. In so doing, she generates an income tax deduction for herself.

A special provision permits, under very limited circumstances, a tax-free distribution from an IRA to a qualified charity. The provision does not generate a charitable deduction but allows the donor to avoid the recognition of income that normally results when a distribution occurs. An estate tax saving also takes place because the donor no longer owns the amount donated upon his or her later death.[46] For the provision to apply, the donor must be age 70½ or older. The exclusion is limited to $100,000 per year and is available for distributions made in 2006 through 2011 (or later, if extended).

Taking Advantage of the Bypass Amount

The bypass amount, also known as the exclusion amount or the exemption equivalent, is the amount that can pass free of a transfer tax due to the unified credit. For a credit of $1,730,800, which is available for estate tax purposes for 2011, the bypass amount is $5 million. The bypass amount is indexed for inflation; for 2012, it is $5.12 million.

Spousal Transfers In the past, a bypass amount often was wasted upon the death of the first spouse. Human nature often compels a spouse to leave all of his or her assets to the survivor.

EXAMPLE 42

Ethan and Hope are married, and each has a net worth of $5 million. Upon Ethan's prior death, his will passes his $5 million to Hope. Although Ethan has avoided any estate tax due to the marital deduction, he has wasted his bypass amount and concentrated $10 million in Hope's potential estate. ■

For 2011 and 2012, the result reached in Example 42 is different; the bypass amount (also known as the exclusion amount) is "portable," meaning that a deceased spouse's unused exclusion amount (DSUEA) can be transferred to the surviving spouse.[47] Portability is not allowed for the exemption in computing the tax on generation-skipping transfers.

EXAMPLE 43

Assume the same facts as in Example 42. If Ethan died in 2011 and a proper election was made on his return, his DSUEA becomes available. As a result, Hope now has an exclusion amount of $10 million [$5 million (DSUEA) + $5 million (her own basic exclusion amount)]. ■

If the election is not made by the executor of the deceased spouse's estate by the regular filing date (plus extensions), then any DSUEA is lost. The election requirement could be a real trap for the unwary in cases involving a "poor spouse" where no Form 706 is due.

EXAMPLE 44

In 2011, Rowena dies leaving a gross estate of $3 million, all of which she passes to Christopher, her surviving spouse. The executor of Rowena's estate does not file a Form 706, as none is due. Because no election was made, Christopher cannot use any of Rowena's $5 million as a DSUEA. Rowena's executor needed to file a Form 706 to create the DSUEA for Christopher. ■

[46] § 408(d)(8).

[47] § 2010(c) as amended by TRA of 2010.

If a surviving spouse is predeceased by more than one spouse, the DSUEA that is available for such a surviving spouse is limited to the *lesser of* \$5 million or the unused exclusion of the last surviving spouse.

ETHICS & EQUITY Be Careful When You Remarry

Frank's wife, Kitty, died in January 2011, leaving him all of her sizable estate. In November of the same year and after a brief courtship, Frank married Ellen, also recently widowed. Before her remarriage, Ellen had made taxable gifts to her adult children, using up \$3 million of her \$5 million exclusion amount. Ellen dies in October 2012 and passes all of her remaining assets to Frank.

After Ellen's death, Frank is told by his tax adviser that he has an estate tax exclusion of \$12 million—\$5 million for himself + \$5 million from Kitty + \$2 million from Ellen. Is this tax advice correct?

Suppose that Frank and Ellen had not married but merely lived together. Would Frank be better off in terms of estate taxes? Do you see a problem of equity in these results?

Use of Disclaimers to Maximize the Benefits of the Bypass Amount In some cases, it may be possible to control the bypass amount by the judicious use of disclaimers.

EXAMPLE 45

Dylan dies in 2011 leaving an estate of \$8 million. He is survived by his wife, Emma, and two adult children. His will passes \$4 million to Emma and the remainder to the children. Emma disclaims \$1 million of her inheritance. ■

EXAMPLE 46

Assume the same facts as in Example 45, except that Dylan's will passes \$6 million to the children and the remainder to Emma. The children disclaim \$1 million of their inheritance. ■

Both examples reflect the wise use of disclaimers. In Example 45, Emma's disclaimer has the effect of increasing the children's inheritance to \$5 million, thereby optimizing the allowable bypass amount. In Example 46, the children avoid any estate tax on \$1 million (the excess over the \$5 million bypass amount) by shifting it to the remainderperson. Because the remainderperson is the surviving spouse, the \$1 million is sheltered from estate tax by the marital deduction.

Proper Handling of Other Deductions and Losses under §§ 2053 and 2054

Many § 2053 and § 2054 deductions and losses may be claimed either as estate tax deductions or as income tax deductions by the estate on the fiduciary return (Form 1041), but not both.[48] The income tax deduction is not allowed unless the estate tax deduction is waived. It is possible for these deductions to be apportioned between the two returns.

In situations where the taxpayer is terminal (i.e., death is imminent), it may be possible to shift the upcoming § 2053 expenses to obtain a lifetime income tax benefit. Thus, such items as accrued medical expenses, property taxes, and interest on home equity loans can be paid prior to death if they will be deductible on the decedent's final income tax return. Although this forgoes the § 2053 deduction that would have been available if the expenses had been paid by the estate, the estate tax saving still exists. As the funds that were used to pay these expenses are not part of the gross estate, the taxable estate is correspondingly reduced. The net result is the same estate tax saving, but with the added advantage of an income tax deduction.

[48] § 642(g) and Reg. § 20.2053–1(d).

Providing Estate Liquidity

LO.9

List and review procedures to obtain liquidity for an estate.

Recognizing the Problem

Even with effective predeath family tax planning directed toward a minimization of transfer taxes, the smooth administration of an estate necessitates a certain degree of liquidity. After all, probate costs will be incurred, and most important of all, estate taxes must be satisfied. In the meantime, the surviving spouse and dependent beneficiaries may need financial support. Without funds to satisfy these claims, estate assets may have to be sold at sacrifice prices, and most likely, the decedent's scheme of testamentary disposition will be defeated.

EXAMPLE 47

At the time of Myrtle's death, her estate was made up almost entirely of a large ranch currently being operated by Jim, one of Myrtle's two sons. Because the ranch had been in the family for several generations and was a successful economic unit, Myrtle hoped that Jim would continue its operation and share the profits with Bob, her other son. Unfortunately, Bob, upon learning that his mother had died without a will, demanded and obtained a partition and sale of his share of the property. Additional land was sold to pay for administration expenses and estate taxes. After all of the sales had taken place, the portion remaining for Jim could not be operated profitably, and he was forced to give up the family ranch activity. ■

What type of predeath planning might have avoided the result reached in Example 47? Certainly, Myrtle should have recognized and provided for the cash needs of the estate. Life insurance payable to her estate, although it adds to the estate tax liability, could have eased or solved the problem. This presumes that Myrtle was insurable or that the cost of the insurance would not be prohibitive. Furthermore, Myrtle made a serious error in dying without a will. A carefully drawn will could have precluded Bob's later course of action and perhaps kept more of the ranch property intact. The ranch could have been placed in trust, life estate to Jim and Bob, remainder to their children. With such an arrangement, Bob would have been unable to sell the principal (the ranch).

Being able to defer the payment of estate taxes may be an invaluable option for an estate that lacks cash or near-cash assets (e.g., marketable securities). In this connection, two major possibilities exist.

- The discretionary extension of time (§ 6161).
- The extension of time when the estate consists largely of an interest in a closely held business (§ 6166).

Discretionary Extension of Time to Pay Estate Taxes—§ 6161

Currently, an executor or administrator may request an extension of time for paying the estate tax for a period not to exceed 10 years from the date fixed for the payment. The IRS grants such requests whenever there is "reasonable cause." Reasonable cause is not limited to a showing of undue hardship. It includes cases in which the executor or administrator is unable to marshal liquid assets readily because they are located in several jurisdictions. It also includes situations where the estate is largely made up of assets in the form of payments to be received in the future (e.g., annuities, copyright royalties, contingent fees, or accounts receivable), or where the assets that must be liquidated to pay the estate tax must be sold at a sacrifice or in a depressed market.

Extension of Time When the Estate Consists Largely of an Interest in a Closely Held Business—§ 6166

Congress always has been sympathetic to the plight of an estate that consists of an interest in a closely held business. The immediate imposition of the estate tax in such a situation may force the liquidation of the business at distress prices or cause the interest to be sold to outside parties.

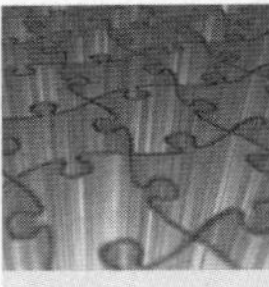

CONCEPT SUMMARY 19.3

Estate and Gift Planning

1. In reducing (or eliminating) gift taxes, take advantage of the annual exclusion and the election to split gifts. In the case of a single asset with high value (e.g., land), annual gifts of partial interests should be considered.
2. Gifts can reduce later estate taxes. This is accomplished by giving away assets that will appreciate in value (e.g., life insurance policies, art works, and rare collections).
3. Timely gifts can help an estate qualify for § 2032A (special use valuation method), § 6166 (15-year payout of estate taxes), and § 303 (stock redemptions to pay estate taxes). To be effective, the gift must avoid the three-year rule of § 2035.
4. Gifts can relieve the income tax burden on the family unit. This objective is accomplished by shifting the income from the gift property to family members who are in a lower income tax bracket. In this regard, make sure the gift is *complete* and circumvents kiddie tax treatment.
5. Avoid gifts of property that result in income tax consequences to the donor.
6. Potential *probate costs* can be an important consideration in meaningful estate planning. Some procedures that reduce these costs include joint tenancies with the right of survivorship, living trusts, and predeath dispositions of out-of-state real estate. Keep in mind that most of these procedures *do not reduce* estate taxes.
7. A program of lifetime gifts and proper use of valuation techniques will reduce a decedent's *gross* estate. Further planning can reduce the *taxable* estate by proper handling of estate tax deductions.
8. For a married decedent, the most important deduction is the *marital deduction*. The two major approaches to the marital deduction are the *equalization* and *deferral* approaches.
9. Whether the equalization approach or the deferral approach is emphasized, make use of the *bypass amount*.
10. Lifetime charitable contributions are preferable to transfers by death. The lifetime contributions provide the donor with an income tax deduction, and the amount donated is not included in the gross estate.
11. The *disclaimer* procedure can be used to control (either lower or raise) the amount of the marital deduction and to increase the amount of the charitable deduction. Disclaimers can also be effective in taking full advantage of the available bypass amount.
12. Portability provisions allow both spouses to make full use of their bypass (exclusion) amounts. After the death of one spouse, for example, the surviving spouse can add to the basic exclusion amount the deceased spouse's unused exclusion amount (DSUEA).
13. Gift planning can help ease potential *estate liquidity* problems (see item 3 above). After death, § 6166 can be useful if the estate qualifies. The provision allows installment payments of deferred estate taxes over an extended period of time.

A possible resolution of the problem is to use § 6166, which requires the IRS to accept a 15-payment procedure (5 interest-only payments, followed by 10 installment payments of the estate tax). This delay can enable the business to generate enough income to buy out the deceased owner's interest without disruption of operations or other financial sacrifice.

To meet the requirements of § 6166, the decedent's interest in a farm or other closely held business must exceed 35 percent of the decedent's adjusted gross estate.[49] The adjusted gross estate is the gross estate less the sum allowable as deductions under § 2053 (expenses, indebtedness, and taxes) and § 2054 (casualty and theft losses during the administration of an estate).

An interest in a closely held business includes the following.[50]

- Any sole proprietorship.
- An interest in a partnership carrying on a trade or business, if 20 percent of the capital interest in the partnership is included in the gross estate *or* the partnership has 45 or fewer partners.

[49] § 6166(a)(1).

[50] § 6166(b)(1).

- Stock in a corporation carrying on a trade or business, if 20 percent or more of the value of the voting stock of the corporation is included in the gross estate *or* the corporation has 45 or fewer shareholders.

In meeting the preceding requirements, a decedent and his or her surviving spouse are treated as one owner (shareholder or partner) if the interest is held as community property, tenants in common, joint tenants, or tenants by the entirety. Attribution from family members is allowed.[51]

EXAMPLE 48

Decedent Bonnie held a 15% capital interest in the Wren Partnership. Her son holds another 10%. Wren had 46 partners including Bonnie and her son. Because the son's interest is attributed to Bonnie, the estate is deemed to hold a 25% interest, and Wren (for purposes of § 6166) has only 45 partners. ■

In satisfying the more-than-35 percent test for qualification under § 6166, interests in more than one closely held business are aggregated when the decedent's gross estate includes 20 percent or more of the value of each such business.[52]

EXAMPLE 49

Henry's estate includes stock in Green Corporation and Brown Corporation, each of which qualifies as a closely held business. If the stock held in each entity represents 20% or more of the total value outstanding, the stocks can be combined for purposes of the more-than-35% test. ■

If the conditions of § 6166 are satisfied and the provision is elected, the following results transpire.

- No payments on the estate tax attributable to the inclusion of the interest in a closely held business in the gross estate need be made with the first five payments. Then, annual installments are made over a period not longer than 10 years.
- From the outset, interest at the rate of 2 percent is paid.[53] Originally, the 2 percent rate of interest applied only to the first $1 million of estate tax value. Because the estate tax value amount has been indexed for inflation, for 2012 it is $1.39 million.
- Acceleration of deferred payments may be triggered upon the disposition of the interest or failure to make scheduled principal or interest payments.[54]

ETHICS & EQUITY Is It Too Late?

Donald, who is suffering from a terminal illness, is advised by his CPA that his current estate needs an additional $180,000 in stock of Hawk Corporation to qualify for § 6166. Immediately thereafter, Donald purchases the stock. Upon Donald's death two months later, his executor elects to come under the provisions of § 6166. Presuming that the percentage requirements are satisfied, is the election proper?

In qualifying for § 6166, one should prune the potential estate of assets that may cause the 35 percent test to fail. In this regard, lifetime gifts of such assets as marketable securities and life insurance should be considered.[55]

Some of the estate planning procedures covered in the last part of this chapter appear in Concept Summary 19.3 on the previous page.

[51] As described in § 267(c)(4).

[52] § 6166(c).

[53] § 6601(j)(1).

[54] § 6166(g).

[55] A gift within three years of death is not effective for this purpose. § 2035(c)(2).

REFOCUS ON THE BIG PICTURE

LIFETIME GIVING—THE GOOD AND THE BAD

Is Martin's potential estate a possible candidate for a § 2032A election (i.e., special use valuation method)? If so, a gift of the farmland could make it hard to meet the percentage qualification requirements of § 2032A. Barring certain limitations, qualifying under § 2032A would allow the farmland to be valued at $100,000 (rather than $500,000) for estate tax purposes (see Example 31).

Is it possible that Martin's potential estate would use the deferred payment procedure of § 6166? If so, the gift of the partnership interest could impair the closely held business qualification requirement for the § 6166 election.

The gift of the life insurance policy is very attractive. By making a gift of $500,000, Martin avoids $3 million being subject to the estate tax (see Example 27). (This assumes that Martin's estate avoids the three-year trap of § 2035.)

The marketable securities might better be sold to enable Martin to recognize an income tax loss of $400,000. However, a gift could preserve some of the built-in loss for the donee (see Example 35). Otherwise, there will be a step-down in income tax basis if Martin dies with these securities.

Under the circumstances, the gift of the city lot shifts to the donee a built-in gain of $400,000. Moreover, if this property passes by death, it receives a step-up in basis (see Example 19), and the gain component disappears. In either case (i.e., gift or inheritance), the amount subject to a transfer tax is $500,000.

The installment notes receivable present a "no win" situation. If Martin transfers them by gift, he must recognize income on the transfer (see Example 34). If they pass by death, however, either the estate or the heirs will recognize the deferred gain. As the gain is income in respect of a decedent, there is no step-up in basis due to Martin's death.

KEY TERMS

Blockage rule, 19-9
Buy-sell agreement, 19-10
Conservation easements, 19-27
Cross-purchase buy-sell agreement, 19-10
Entity buy-sell agreement, 19-10
Estate freeze, 19-11
Living trust, 19-25
Probate costs, 19-25
Special use value, 19-6
Step-down in basis, 19-14
Step-up in basis, 19-14

DISCUSSION QUESTIONS

1. **LO.1** Discuss the relevance of the following in defining "fair market value" for Federal gift and estate tax purposes.
   a. § 2031(b).
   b. The definition contained in Reg. § 20.2031–1(b).
   c. The sentimental value of the property being valued.
   d. Tangible personalty sold as a result of an advertisement in the classified section of a newspaper.
   e. Sporadic sales (occuring on other than the valuation date) of stocks traded in an over-the-counter stock exchange.

2. **LO.1** At the time of his death from a terminal illness, Hugo owned the following major assets.

   - A 3,400-square-foot condominium located in Kansas City, Kansas.
   - An antique car collection.

In terms of valuing these assets for estate tax purposes, comment on these additional factors.

a. A similar condominium (same architect, same builder, and same square footage) recently sold in midtown Manhattan (NYC) for $20 million.
b. To avoid bankruptcy and to provide immediate cash for the estate, Hugo's executor sold the antique car collection to the first wholesale dealer who made an offer.

3. **LO.1** Marvin's daughter Carol was a student at an exclusive private women's college. Each year that she attended, Marvin had Carol sign a note for $40,000 to cover books, tuition, and room and board. Ten years after Carol graduated, Marvin dies without a will. The notes are found in his safe deposit box. Although Carol has become a successful business executive, Marvin never discussed the notes with her or made any attempts at collection. What are the pertinent tax issues? (Note: In answering this question, a review of the earlier part of Chapter 18 might prove useful.)

Issue ID

4. **LO.1** Six years ago, Alvin loaned his prospective brother-in-law, Bruno, $20,000. The money was used to help Bruno pay for the wedding to Alvin's sister. Shortly after the wedding, it was discovered that Bruno already was married to someone else. Before Bruno could be indicted for bigamy, he disappeared and has not been heard from since. In 2012, Alvin dies still holding Bruno's note. For tax purposes, what do you suggest as to the handling of Bruno's note?

Issue ID

5. **LO.1** Comment on the valuation for transfer tax purposes of:
   a. An annuity contract.
   b. A life insurance policy.

6. **LO.1** Brian creates a trust, life estate to Freda, remainder on Freda's death to Daniel.
   a. Presuming that the trust is irrevocable, how is the value of each gift determined?
   b. Which gift, if any, qualifies for the annual exclusion?
   c. If Freda is Brian's wife, does this transfer qualify Brian for a marital deduction? Why or why not?

7. **LO.1** Sophie creates an irrevocable trust, income interest to her granddaughter, Brandi, for six years. After six years, the remainder interest in the trust is to go to Hailey, Sophie's divorced daughter (Brandi's mother).
   a. How is the value of this transfer by gift determined?
   b. Is the annual exclusion available?
   c. What might be the justification for such an arrangement?

8. **LO.2** In connection with § 2032A, comment on the following.
   a. The reason for the provision.
   b. Who makes the election.
   c. Current utility of the election.
   d. Planning to meet the requirements for making the election.
   e. Hazards involved in the recapture provisions.
   f. Pitfalls resulting from the election.

9. **LO.3** In determining the value of goodwill attributable to stock in a closely held corporation, comment on the following factors.
   a. The corporation's average profit figure includes large gains from the sale of assets not related to the business conducted.
   b. The operations of the corporation are largely financed with loans from its shareholders (rather than from outsiders).
   c. The rate of return used by the IRS for this type of business is too low.
   d. The deceased owner was active in the operation of the business.

10. **LO.3** What effect, if any, will each of the following factors have on the valuation of stock in a closely held corporation?
   a. A minority interest is involved.
   b. A majority interest is involved.
   c. The "blockage rule."
   d. The cost the corporation would incur in going public.

Issue ID

11. **LO.3** One of the major assets in John's estate is stock in Falcon Corporation, a closely held investment company. Falcon has a large portfolio of ExxonMobil stock, acquired when crude oil was selling for under $20 a barrel. In valuing the Falcon stock for estate tax purposes, what would be an important consideration?

Issue ID

12. **LO.3** During the same year, a donor gives stock in a closely held corporation to family members and to a qualified charitable organization. In terms of tax planning, what might such a procedure accomplish?

13. **LO.3** The Sullivan family has developed a profitable business in which all adult members participate. They would like to make sure that the business stays in the family in the event of any future disruption (e.g., death, divorce, or other discord).
    a. What do you suggest?
    b. Does it matter whether the business is conducted as a corporation or a partnership? Explain.

14. **LO.3** Buy-sell agreements for a closely held business are sometimes funded with life insurance policies. Explain how such an arrangement would be set up for:
    a. A cross-purchase type.
    b. An entity type.

Issue ID

15. **LO.4** Katelyn receives stock in Kite Corporation as a gift from her father, which she sells four months later. Although Katelyn sold the stock for more than it was worth when she received it as a gift, her accountant tells her that no recognized gain results. How can this be?

Issue ID

16. **LO.4** Joshua inherited stock in Garnet Corporation from his aunt when it had a date of death value of $20,000. Four months later, Joshua sells the stock for $15,000, expecting a short-term capital loss of $5,000 to result. Are Joshua's expectations correct? What could go wrong?

17. **LO.4** When Scott discovers that his illness is terminal, his family estate planner tells him to "prune the community of loss assets." Explain what the planner means and how it could affect Scott's surviving spouse.

18. **LO.4** Before electing certain valuation provisions such as § 2032 (alternate valuation date) and § 2032A (special use valuation), income tax consequences should be taken into account. Explain this statement.

19. **LO.4** When Brent learns that his mother, Della, is terminally ill, he gives her a valuable art collection. In her will, Della leaves the collection to Melody, Brent's wife.
    a. For income tax purposes, what was Brent trying to accomplish? Will it work? Why or why not?
    b. What are some of the nontax pitfalls of this procedure?

Issue ID

20. **LO.4** Christopher has told the beneficiaries of his Roth and traditional IRAs that they will receive the distributions from these plans free of any tax. Christopher bases his advice on the "step-up" in basis that takes place when appreciated property is passed by death. Comment on the accuracy of this advice.

Communications

21. **LO.4** Jonathan Rand is distressed about the basis of some land he inherited five years ago and recently sold for a large gain. He thinks that the value placed on the property is too low. Consequently, he requests your advice as to whether he is bound by this value.
    a. Write a letter to Jonathan regarding this matter. Jonathan's address is 326 Wisteria Avenue, Charlotte, NC 28223.
    b. Include in the letter a list of further information you will need before you can assess the probability of success in challenging the value used by the estate.

Communications

22. **LO.6** Cynthia and Norton Enright own all of the stock in Ibis Company, an S corporation. The Enrights are considering making gifts of some of the stock to their children (Addison, Tracy, Jordan, and Kirby) to shift income to them. Addison (age 20) is a high school graduate and does not intend to go to college. Tracy (age 21) is married and files a joint return with her husband. Jordan (age 23) and Kirby (age 24) are full-time college students. The Enrights request your advice on how to make these gifts effectively for tax purposes.
    a. Write a letter to the Enrights on this matter. Their address is 1486 Garden Park, Elizabeth, NJ 07207.
    b. Prepare a memo for your firm's tax research files.

23. **LO.5** Making gifts can save on estate taxes. Comment on the relevance of this statement to each of the following.
    a. The amount of the annual exclusion utilized.
    b. Subsequent appreciation of the property given.
    c. Contributions to § 529 plans on behalf of family members.
    d. The amount of gift tax actually paid.

24. **LO.5** April is considering making gifts to her granddaughter, Paige, who just graduated from college. Among the assets April has in mind are an insurance policy on her own life and the family beach house. Could gifts of these items create a problem for Paige? Explain.

25. **LO.2, 5** A program of lifetime giving can help an estate qualify for the special use election of § 2032A.
    a. Explain how this objective can be achieved.
    b. What could go wrong?

26. **LO.4, 6** For income tax purposes, what difference does it make to the parties (i.e., transferor and transferee) whether the following assets are transferred by gift or by death?
    a. Installment notes receivable.
    b. U.S. savings bonds.
    c. Property with depreciation recapture potential.

27. **LO.6** Charles Horn wants his daughter Sharon to get stock that he owns in Crimson Corporation. He acquired the stock two years ago at a cost of $800,000, and it currently has a fair market value of $650,000. Charles has made prior taxable gifts and is in poor health. He seeks your advice as to whether he should gift the stock to Sharon or pass it to her under his will. Charles has a large capital loss carryover and has no prospect for any capital gains. **Decision Making** **Communications**
    a. Write a letter to Charles regarding the tax implications of the alternatives he has suggested. His address is 648 Scenic Drive, Chattanooga, TN 37403.
    b. Prepare a memo for your firm's files on this matter.

28. **LO.7** Two years ago, after his wife Esther died, Frank took early retirement. He moved from New York to New Mexico to be near his only daughter, Pamela, and her family. Although he still owns his personal residence in New York—it has been converted to rental property—he plans to buy a condo in New Mexico. Other information regarding Frank's affairs is summarized below.

    - Several policies on his life list Esther as the beneficiary.
    - His § 401(k) plans and traditional IRAs do not name secondary beneficiaries.
    - Ownership of numerous, sizable CDs is listed as joint tenancy with Esther.
    - Frank and Esther executed New York wills naming the survivor as the sole heir.
    - Title to the family hunting lodge in Idaho is in Frank's name.

    a. In terms of reducing Frank's future *probate* estate, what changes can be made? (Assume that Frank wants all of his property to pass to Pamela.)
    b. Suppose Frank wants to retain the income stream from the New York rental property (i.e., his former residence). What do you suggest?

29. **LO.8** In terms of Federal tax consequences, why are lifetime transfers to charity preferable to testamentary transfers?

30. **LO.8** What is the *bypass amount*? How can it be utilized effectively through the use of disclaimers in the case of:
    a. A surviving spouse?
    b. Nonspousal heirs?

31. **LO.9** The estate of Janet, who currently is still alive, almost meets the computational requirements for an election under § 6166. Janet is not concerned about these tests, however, because she plans to give away her life insurance policy before her death. Thus, she believes, her estate then will meet the requirements of § 6166. Any comment? **Issue ID**

PROBLEMS

32. **LO.1** When Abigail died in 2012, she owned 2,000 shares of Finch Corporation. The stock is traded in an over-the-counter market. The nearest trades before and after the date of Abigail's death are as follows.

	Per Share Mean Selling Price
Five days before Abigail's death	$300
Eight days after Abigail's death	360

Assuming that the alternate valuation date is not elected, at what value should the Finch stock be included in Abigail's gross estate?

33. **LO.1** Barry creates a trust with property valued at $6 million. Under the terms of the trust instrument, Michelle (age 50) receives a life estate, while Terry (age 25) receives the remainder interest. In the month the trust is created, the interest rate is 4.2%. Determine the value of Barry's gifts.

34. **LO.1** Arlene creates a trust with assets worth $1 million. Under the terms of the trust, Tracy (age 16) receives the income for seven years, remainder to Dawn (age 35). In the month the trust is created, the interest rate is 4.4%. Determine the value of Arlene's gifts.

35. **LO.1** In 2012, Dale (age 72) creates a trust with assets worth $6 million. Under the terms of the trust, Dale retains a life estate with the remainder passing to Nicole (age 33) upon his death. In the month the trust is created, the interest rate is 4.6%.
    a. Determine the amount of Dale's gift. Of his taxable gift.
    b. Does the answer in part (a) change if Nicole is Dale's wife? (Refer to Chapter 18, if necessary.)

36. **LO.1** Assume the same facts as in Problem 35. Dale dies four year later when the trust is worth $6.7 million. Nicole is 37, and the applicable interest rate is 4.8%.
    a. How much as to the trust is included in Dale's gross estate?
    b. Does the answer change in part (a) if Nicole is Dale's wife? (Refer to Chapter 18, if necessary.)

37. **LO.2** In each of the following independent situations occurring in 2012, determine the valuation to be used for estate tax purposes if § 2032A is elected.

Decedent	Most Suitable Use Value	Special Use Value
Perry	$3,000,000	$3,500,000
Hopkins	3,000,000	1,500,000
Morris	5,000,000	2,000,000
Allen	5,000,000	4,200,000

38. **LO.3** At her death, Inez owned 60% of the stock in Taupe Corporation, with the balance held by family members. In the past five years, Taupe has earned average net profits of $1.5 million, and on the date of Inez's death, the book value of its stock is $3.9 million. An appropriate rate of return for the type of business Taupe is in is 8%.
    a. Assuming that goodwill exists, what is the value of the Taupe stock?
    b. What factors could be present to reduce the value of such goodwill?

39. **LO.3** Kyle owns all of the stock of Blanco Corporation. The stock has a value of $3 million for the common and $800,000 for the preferred. The preferred is noncumulative, has no redemption value, and carries no preference as to liquidation. Kyle gives the common stock to his children and retains the preferred stock. What are the tax consequences?

40. **LO.3** Assume the same facts as in Problem 39. Eight years after the gift, Kyle dies. At that time, the Blanco stock is worth $4 million for the common and $1.1 million for the preferred. What are Kyle's tax consequences?

41. **LO.4** Olivia gives real estate (basis of $800,000 and fair market value of $3 million) to Ray. Determine Ray's income tax basis if the gift occurred in 2012 and Olivia paid a gift tax of $100,000.

42. **LO.4** Jacob gives stock (basis of $900,000 and fair market value of $2.2 million) to Mandy. As a result of the transfer in 2012, Jacob paid a gift tax of $90,000. Determine Mandy's gain or loss if she later sells the stock for $2.3 million.

43. **LO.4** Clinton gives stock (basis of $600,000 and fair market value of $500,000) to Morgan in 2012. As a result of the transfer, Clinton paid a gift tax of $40,000. Compute Morgan's gain or loss if she later sells the stock for:
    a. $650,000.
    b. $550,000.
    c. $480,000.

44. **LO.4, 5, 6** Ted and Marge Dean are married and have always lived in a community property state. Ted (age 92) suffers from numerous disorders and is frequently ill, while Marge (age 70) is in good health. The Deans currently need $500,000 to meet living expenses, make debt payments, and pay Ted's backlog of medical expenses. They are willing to sell any one of the following assets:

Decision Making

Communications

	Adjusted Basis	Fair Market Value
Wren Corporation stock	$200,000	$500,000
Gull Corporation stock	600,000	500,000
Unimproved land	650,000	500,000

The stock investments are part of the Deans' community property, while the land is Ted's separate property that he inherited from his mother. If the land is not sold, Ted is considering making a gift of it to Marge.
    a. Write a letter to the Deans advising them on these matters. Their address is 290 Cedar Road, Carson, CA 90747.
    b. Prepare a memo on this matter for your firm's client files.

45. **LO.4** In June 2011, Reba gives Julius a house (basis of $150,000; fair market value of $450,000) to be used as his personal residence. Before his death in May 2012, Julius installs a tennis court in the backyard at a cost of $25,000. The residence has a value of $465,000 when Julius dies. Determine the income tax basis of the property to the heir based on the following independent assumptions.
    a. The residence passes to Reba.
    b. The residence passes to Burl (Reba's husband).
    c. The residence passes to Tina (Reba's daughter).

46. **LO.5** Bill and Ellen are husband and wife with five married children and eight grandchildren. Commencing in December 2011, they would like to transfer a tract of land (worth $936,000) equally to their children (including spouses) and grandchildren as quickly as possible without making a taxable gift. What do you suggest?

Decision Making

47. **LO.2, 5** At the time of her death in 2012, Wanda has an adjusted gross estate of $6.5 million. Her estate includes the family farm, with a most suitable use value of $3.3 million and a current use value of $2.3 million. The farm is inherited by Jim, Wanda's son, who has worked it for her since 1985. Jim plans to continue farming indefinitely.
    a. Based on the information given, is the § 2032A election available to Wanda's estate?
    b. If so, what value must be used for the farm?
    c. Suppose Wanda had made a gift of securities (fair market value of $500,000) to her cousin six months before her death. Does this fact affect your analysis? Explain.

48. **LO.6** Last year, Henry sold real estate (basis of $450,000) to Bill (an unrelated party) for $1.8 million, receiving $300,000 in cash and notes for the balance. The notes carry an 8.5% rate of interest and mature annually at $500,000 each over three years. Henry did not elect out of the installment method of reporting the gain. Before any of the notes mature and when they have a fair market value of $1.3 million, Henry gives them to Jean.
    a. Disregarding the interest element, what are the tax consequences of the gift?
    b. Suppose that instead of making the gift, Henry died. The notes passed to his estate and were later sold by the executor. What is the tax result?

49. **LO.7** At the time of her death in 2012, Monica held the following assets.

	Fair Market Value
Personal residence (title listed as "Monica and Peter, tenants by the entirety with right of survivorship")	$900,000
Savings account (listed as "Monica and Rex, joint tenants with right of survivorship") with funds provided by Rex	40,000
Certificate of deposit (listed as "Monica, payable on proof of death to Rex") with funds provided by Monica	100,000
Unimproved real estate (title listed as "Monica and Rex, equal tenants in common")	500,000
Insurance policy on Monica's life, issued by Lavender Company (Monica's estate is the designated beneficiary)	300,000
Insurance policy on Monica's life, issued by Crimson Company (Rex is the designated beneficiary)	400,000
Living trust created by Monica five years ago (life estate to Peter, remainder to Rex)	800,000

Assuming that Peter and Rex survive Monica, how much is included in Monica's *probate estate?* Monica's *gross estate?* (Refer to Chapter 18 if needed.)

Decision Making

50. **LO.8** Corey, a widower, is 80 years of age and in poor health. He would like to donate unimproved land to his church. The land cost Corey $40,000 and is currently worth $200,000. In carrying out the donation, Corey wants to regain his original capital investment of $40,000. In this regard, evaluate the following options.

- An immediate donation of an 80% undivided interest in the land to the church.
- A sale of *all* of the land to the church for $40,000.
- A provision in his will passing an 80% undivided interest in the land to the church.

51. **LO.8** In terms of tax ramifications, comment on what is accomplished in the following disclaimer situations occurring in 2011.
    a. Lester dies intestate and is survived by a daughter, Nora, and a grandson, Nick. The major asset in Lester's estate is stock worth $3.5 million. Under the applicable state law of descent and distribution, children precede grandchildren in order of inheritance. As Nora is already well-off and in ill health, she disclaims Lester's property.
    b. Under her will, Audrey's estate is to pass $6 million to her son, Raymond, and the $3 million remainder to her husband, George. Raymond disclaims $1 million of his inheritance.
    c. Under Isaac's will, $4 million is to pass to his wife, Brenda, and the $4.5 million remainder to his daughter, Sybil. Brenda disclaims $500,000 of her inheritance.
    d. Under Tricia's will, her $3 million cubist art collection is to pass to her husband, Leroy. If Leroy declines, the collection is to pass to the San Francisco Museum of Modern Art. Leroy neither understands nor admires this type of art.

52. **LO.8** In each of the following *independent situations*, what bypass (exclusion) amount is available to Ava's estate when she dies in 2012? Assume that any appropriate procedures are followed, and that elections are made to transfer to Ava any DSUEA of Al, the deceased husband.
    a. Al died in 2009 and never used any of his bypass amount.
    b. Al died in early 2011 and did not use any of his bypass amount.
    c. Same as part (b). Ava remarried in 2011, and Andy, her second husband, had used $1 million of his bypass amount in making past taxable gifts. Andy predeceases Ava in late 2011.

53. **LO.9** At the time of his death in 2012, Clint had an adjusted gross estate of $6.2 million. Included in the estate is a 15% capital interest in a partnership valued at $2.6 million. Except for Clint's daughter Phoebe, none of the other 48 partners are related to him. Phoebe holds a 10% capital interest.
    a. Does Clint's estate qualify for the § 6166 election?
    b. Suppose that one year prior to his death, Clint gave $1.5 million in cash and securities to Phoebe. Does this change your analysis? Explain.

54. **LO.9** At the time of her death in 2012, June had an adjusted gross estate of $6 million. Included in the estate were the following business interests.

	Fair Market Value
A 30% capital interest in the JZ Partnership	$700,000
A 25% interest (i.e., 250 shares out of 1,000) in Silver Corporation	500,000
A catering service operated as a sole proprietorship	950,000

The JZ Partnership has 32 partners, while Silver Corporation has a total of 30 shareholders. None of the other partners or shareholders are related to June. Can June's estate qualify for an election under § 6166? Explain.

RESEARCH PROBLEMS

THOMSON REUTERS
CHECKPOINT®

Note: Solutions to Research Problems can be prepared by using the **Checkpoint® Student Edition** online research product, which is available to accompany this text. It is also possible to prepare solutions to the Research Problems by using tax research materials found in a standard tax library.

Research Problem 1. On June 1, 2009, Mario entered into a contract to sell real estate for $1 million (adjusted basis $200,000). The sale was conditioned on a rezoning of the property for commercial use. A $50,000 deposit placed in escrow by the purchaser was refundable in the event the rezoning was not accomplished.

After considerable controversy, the application was approved on November 10, and two days later, the sum of $950,000 was paid to Mario's estate in full satisfaction of the purchase price. Mario had died unexpectedly on November 1. Discuss the estate and income tax consequences of this set of facts if it is assumed that the sale of the real estate occurred:

a. After Mario's death.
b. Before Mario's death.

When do you think the sale occurred? Why?

Partial list of research aids:
§§ 691 and 1014.
George W. Keck, 49 T.C. 313 (1968), *rev'd* 69–2 USTC ¶9626, 24 AFTR 2d 69–5554, 415 F.2d 531 (CA–6, 1969).
Trust Company of Georgia v. Ross, 68–1 USTC ¶9133, 21 AFTR 2d 311, 392 F.2d 694 (CA–5, 1967).

Research Problem 2. In 2007, Troy wins the Connecticut LOTTO grand prize of $15 million. The LOTTO contest is governed by the following rules.

- The prize money is to be paid in 20 equal annual installments (in this case, $750,000 per year) with no interest provided for.
- The rights to the prize award are not assignable. If a winner dies during the payout period, however, the remaining installment payments are to be made to the winner's duly appointed executor.
- The prize award is not specifically funded or guaranteed by any state agency. It constitutes a general obligation of the state of Connecticut.

Troy dies in 2009 after having received two payments of $750,000 each. Troy's estate includes the present value of the remaining $13.5 million prize award in the estate at $4.86 million. This is determined by using the IRS table amount of $6.75 million and discounting it for absence of security (i.e., no separate funding or guarantee of payment by a state agency) and lack of marketability (i.e., the award cannot be assigned). The table used is that issued by the IRS in Reg. § 20.2031–7 under the authority of § 7520. The table is to be used in valuing, among other income interests, private (i.e., noncommercial) annuity contracts.

Upon audit of the estate tax return, the IRS disputes the deviation from the table amount. The IRS argues that the absence-of-security discount is inappropriate because the state of Connecticut has never defaulted on any of its LOTTO obligations. Furthermore, the lack-of-marketability discount is inappropriately applied to annuity-type situations. Unlike stocks and bonds and other ownership interests, private annuities are not subject to marketplace valuation procedures.

Who should prevail—the taxpayer or the IRS?

Partial list of research aids:
§§ 2039 and 7520.
Reg. § 20.7520–3(b).
O'Reilly v. Comm., 92–2 USTC ¶60,111, 70 AFTR 2d 92–6211, 973 F.2d 1403 (CA–8, 1992).
Shackleford v. U.S., 99–2 USTC ¶60,356, 84 AFTR 2d 99–5902 (D.Ct.Cal., 1999), *aff'd* in 88 AFTR 2d 2001–5658, 262 F.3d 1028 (CA–9, 2001).
Estate of Gribauskas, 116 T.C. 142 (2001), *rev'd* in 2003–2 USTC ¶60,466, 92 AFTR 2d 2003–5914, 342 F.3d 85 (CA–2, 2003).
Estate of Donovan v. U.S., 2005–1 USTC ¶50,322, 95 AFTR 2d 2005–2131 (D.Ct.Mass., 2005).

Research Problem 3. Just prior to his death, Jameson, a prominent attorney, was sued by a former client. The suit alleged malpractice on the part of Jameson and requested damages of $90 million. On filing the Form 706, the executor of Jameson's estate claimed a § 2053 deduction of $30 million as to the lawsuit. The $30 million amount was based on one of the many appraisals rendered by experts regarding the probable liability of the estate on the date of Jameson's death. Other appraisals varied by as much as $11 million. Upon audit of the Form 706 by the IRS, a deduction of $1 was allowed. After prolonged litigation and during appeal, the malpractice lawsuit was settled for $289,000. What should be the estate tax result in this case?

Partial list of research aids:
Reg. §§ 20.2053–1(b)(4) and –4(a)(2) and (b)(2).
Estate of Gertrude H. Saunders, 136 T.C. 406 (2011).

Research Problem 4. Garth dies in 2009 and is survived by his wife, Daisy, and four adult children. Among the items included in his gross estate are the following.

	Fair Market Value
Apartment building	$2,900,000
Marketable securities	600,000
Insurance policy on Daisy's life (maturity value of $600,000)	60,000
Lake cottage	300,000
Cabin cruiser	240,000

Garth's will grants Daisy a life estate in the apartment building with the remainder passing to the children. Under the IRS valuation tables, the life estate is worth $1.8 million, and the remainder is worth $1.1 million. Garth's executor does not make a QTIP election as to the life estate. Under Garth's will, the rest of his property goes to Daisy. By applicable state law, whatever Daisy disclaims passes to the children. Daisy has considerable assets of her own, and the children are self-supporting.

a. What needs to be done to maximize the bypass amount?
b. How can Daisy's potential estate tax consequences be minimized?

Use the tax resources of the Internet to address the following questions. Do not restrict your search to the Web, but include a review of newsgroups and general reference materials, practitioner sites and resources, primary sources of the tax law, chat rooms and discussion groups, and other opportunities.

Communications

Research Problem 5. Identify the following forms issued by the IRS: Forms 706–NA, 706–CE, 712, 4768, and 4808. What purpose does each serve? Summarize your comments in an e-mail to your professor.

Communications

Research Problem 6. In your state, what is the designation of the court that handles the administration of an estate? What are the statutory guidelines on fees that an executor is allowed for probating an estate? Summarize your findings in a short PowerPoint presentation.

Research Problem 7. What procedures has the IRS recommended that a surviving spouse use to take advantage of a DSUEA?

Research Problem 8. Cecil inherits a farm from his father and, as executor of the estate, makes a § 2032A special use valuation election. Five years later, the farm is disposed of.

a. How is the disposition reported to the IRS?
b. Suppose the disposition occurred due to condemnation by a public authority (i.e., an involuntary conversion took place) and Cecil reinvested some of the award in other farmland. How would your answer to part (a) change?

Research Problem 9. Review IRS Publication 4895 and Form 8939.

a. How are the two items related to each other?
b. What purpose does each serve?

Research Problem 10. IRS Notice 2011–82 relates to the portability of the estate and gift tax exemptions. What aspect of this procedure is discussed?

CHAPTER

20 Income Taxation of Trusts and Estates

LEARNING OBJECTIVES: *After completing Chapter 20, you should be able to:*

LO.1 Use working definitions with respect to trusts, estates, beneficiaries, and other parties.

LO.2 Identify the steps in determining the accounting and taxable income of a trust or an estate and the related taxable income of the beneficiaries.

LO.3 Illustrate the uses and implications of distributable net income.

LO.4 Use the special rules that apply to trusts where the creator (grantor) of the trust retains certain rights.

LO.5 Apply the Subchapter J rules in a manner that minimizes the income taxation of trusts and estates and still accomplishes the intended objectives of the grantor or decedent.

CHAPTER OUTLINE

THE BIG PICTURE Tax Solutions for the Real World

Setting Up a Trust to Protect a Family

Anna Jiang is the main breadwinner in her family, which includes her husband Tom, a social worker, and two children, Bobby, age 8, and Sally, age 13. Anna has accumulated about $2 million in after-tax investment accounts, largely made up of growth stocks that do not regularly pay dividends. Anna has addressed the problem of probate costs through joint property ownership, life insurance policies, and beneficiary arrangements for her retirement plans. She and Tom update their wills every five years or so.

Because there is a history of Alzheimer's disease in her family, Anna Jiang wants to make certain that if she becomes unable to work and cannot manage her financial assets, Tom and the children will have adequate cash flow from the $2 million of investment assets. One of Anna's colleagues at the office suggests that Anna should set up a trust to take care of her family in case a medical problem ever arises.

Read the chapter and formulate your response.

20.1 An Overview of Subchapter J

Taxpayers create trusts for a variety of reasons. Some trusts are established primarily for tax purposes, but most are designed to accomplish a specific financial goal or to provide for the orderly management of assets in case of emergency.

Because a trust is a separate tax entity, its gross income and deductions must be measured and an annual tax return must be filed. Similarly, when an individual dies, a legal entity is created in the form of his or her estate. This chapter examines the rules related to the income taxation of trusts and estates.

Table 20.1 lists some of the more common reasons for creating a trust, and Figure 20.1 illustrates the structure of a typical trust and estate.

The income taxation of trusts and estates is governed by Subchapter J of the Internal Revenue Code, §§ 641 through 692. Certain similarities are apparent between Subchapter J and the income taxation of individuals (e.g., the definitions of gross income and deductible expenditures), partnerships and limited liability entities (e.g., the pass-through principle), and S corporations (e.g., the pass-through principle and the trust or estate as a separate taxable entity). Trusts also involve several important new concepts, however, including the determination of *distributable net income* and the *tier system* of distributions to beneficiaries.

LO.1

Use working definitions with respect to trusts, estates, beneficiaries, and other parties.

What Is a Trust?

The Code does not contain a definition of a trust. However, the term usually refers to an arrangement created by a will or by an *inter vivos* (lifetime) declaration through which trustees take title to property for the purpose of protecting or conserving it for the beneficiaries.[1] Usually, trust operations are controlled by the trust document and by the fiduciary laws of the state in which the trust documents are executed.

TABLE 20.1 **Common Motivations for Creating a Trust**

Type of Trust	Financial and Other Goals
Life insurance trust	Holds life insurance policies on the insured, removes the proceeds of the policies from the gross estate (if an irrevocable trust), and safeguards against receipt of the proceeds by a young or inexperienced beneficiary.
"Living" (revocable) trust	Manages assets, reduces probate costs, provides privacy for asset disposition, protects against medical or other emergencies, and provides relief from the necessity of day-to-day management of the underlying assets.
Trust for minors	Provides funds for a college education or other needs of the minor, shifts income to other taxpayers, and transfers accumulated income without permanently parting with the underlying assets.
"Blind" trust	Holds and manages the assets of the grantor without his or her input or influence (e.g., while the grantor holds political office or some other sensitive position).
Retirement trust	Manages asset contributions as dictated by the terms of a qualified retirement plan.
Divorce trust	Manages the assets of an ex-spouse and ensures that they are distributed in a timely fashion to specified beneficiaries (e.g., as alimony or child support).
Liquidation trust	Collects and distributes the remaining assets of a corporation that is undergoing a complete liquidation.

[1] Reg. § 301.7701–4(a).

FIGURE 20.1 **Structure of a Typical Trust and Estate**

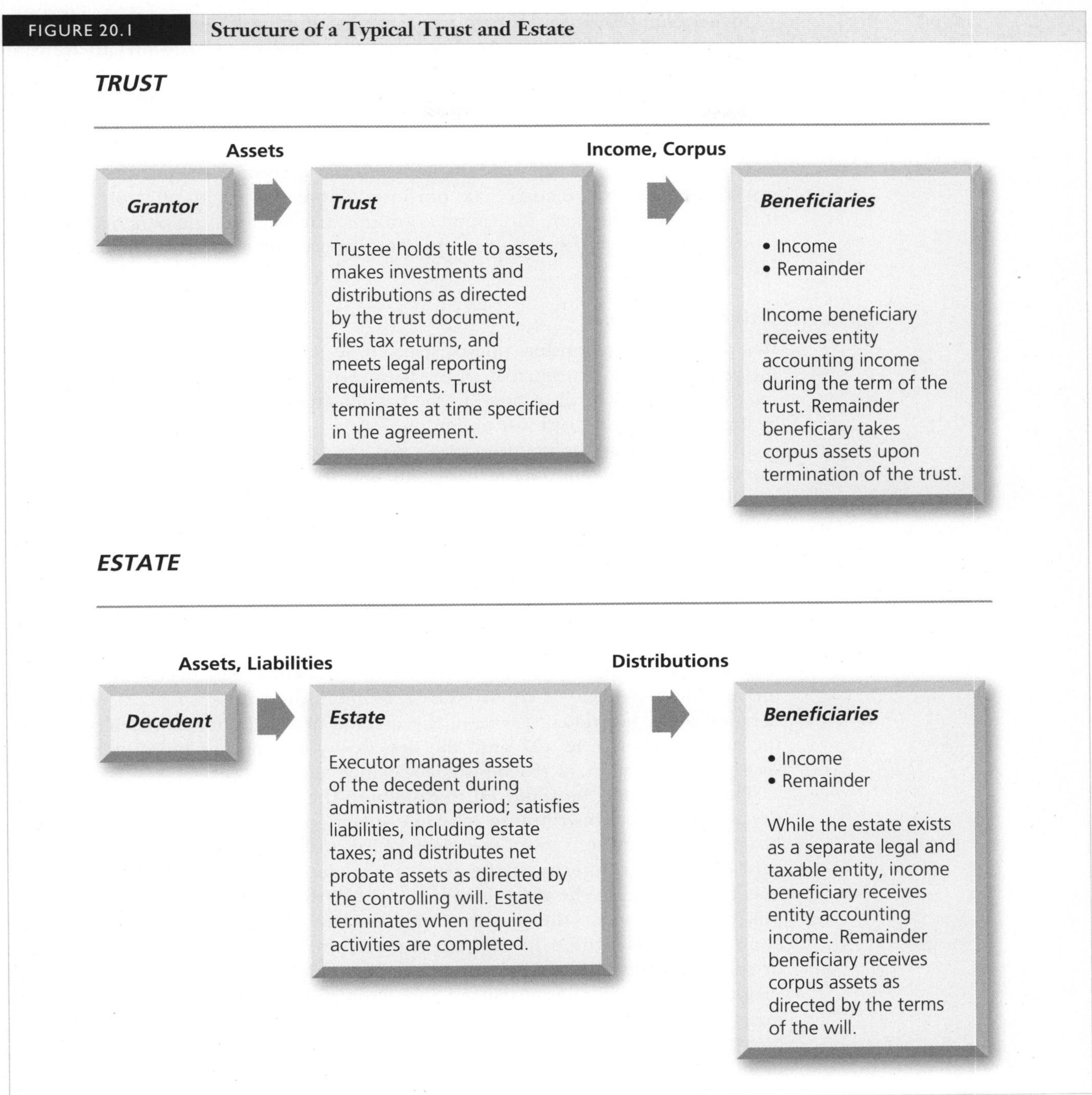

TRUST
Assets
Income, Corpus
Grantor
Trust
Trustee holds title to assets, makes investments and distributions as directed by the trust document, files tax returns, and meets legal reporting requirements. Trust terminates at time specified in the agreement.
Beneficiaries
• Income
• Remainder
Income beneficiary receives entity accounting income during the term of the trust. Remainder beneficiary takes corpus assets upon termination of the trust.
ESTATE
Assets, Liabilities
Distributions
Decedent
Estate
Executor manages assets of the decedent during administration period; satisfies liabilities, including estate taxes; and distributes net probate assets as directed by the controlling will. Estate terminates when required activities are completed.
Beneficiaries
• Income
• Remainder
While the estate exists as a separate legal and taxable entity, income beneficiary receives entity accounting income. Remainder beneficiary receives corpus assets as directed by the terms of the will.

Typically, the creation of a trust involves at least three parties: (1) The **grantor** (sometimes referred to as the settlor or donor) transfers selected assets to the trust entity. (2) The trustee, who usually is either an individual or a corporation, is charged with the fiduciary duties associated with the trust. (3) The beneficiary is designated to receive income or property from the trust.

In some situations, fewer than three persons may be involved, as specified by the trust agreement. For instance, an elderly individual who no longer can manage his or her own property (e.g., because of ill health) may create a trust under which he or she is both the grantor and the beneficiary. In this case, a family member or corporate trustee is charged with the management of the grantor's assets.

In another situation, the grantor might designate himself or herself as the trustee of the trust assets. For example, someone who wants to transfer selected assets to a minor child or elderly parent could use a trust entity to ensure that the beneficiary does not waste the property. By naming himself or herself as the trustee, the grantor retains virtual control over the property that is transferred.

Under the general rules of Subchapter J, the **grantor trusts** just described are not recognized for income tax purposes. Similarly, when only one party is involved (when the same individual is grantor, trustee, and sole beneficiary of the trust), Subchapter J rules do not apply and the entity is ignored for income tax purposes.

Other Definitions

When the grantor transfers title of selected assets to a trust, those assets become the **corpus** (body), or principal, of the trust. Trust corpus, in most situations, earns *income*, which may be distributed to the beneficiaries or accumulated for the future by the trustee, as the trust instrument directs.

In a typical trust, the grantor creates two types of beneficiaries: one who receives the accounting income of the trust and one who receives the trust corpus that remains at the termination of the trust entity. Beneficiaries in the former category hold an *income interest* in the trust, and those in the latter category hold a *remainder interest* in the trust's assets. If the grantor retains the remainder interest, the interest is known as a **reversionary interest** (corpus reverts to the grantor when the trust entity terminates).

The trust document establishes the term of the trust. The term may be for a specific number of years (*term certain*) or until the occurrence of a specified event. For instance, a trust might exist (1) for the life of the income beneficiary, in which case the income beneficiary is known as a *life tenant* in the trust corpus; (2) for the life of some other individual; (3) until the income or remainder beneficiary reaches the age of majority; or (4) until the beneficiary, or another individual, marries, receives a promotion, or reaches some specified age.

The trustee may be required to distribute the accounting income of the entity according to a distribution schedule specified in the agreement. Sometimes, however, the trustee is given more discretion with respect to the timing and nature of the distributions. If the trustee can determine, within guidelines that may be included in the trust document, either the timing of the income or corpus distributions or the specific beneficiaries who will receive them (from among those identified in the agreement), the trust is called a discretionary or **sprinkling trust**. Here, the trustee can "sprinkle" the distributions among the various beneficiaries. As discussed in Chapters 18 and 19, family-wide income taxes can be reduced by directing income to those who are subject to lower marginal tax rates. Thus, by giving the trustee a sprinkling power, the income tax liability of the family unit can be manipulated by applying the terms of the trust agreement.

For purposes of certain provisions of Subchapter J, a trust must be classified as either a **simple trust** or a **complex trust**. A simple trust (1) is required to distribute its entire accounting income to designated beneficiaries every year, (2) has no beneficiaries that are qualifying charitable organizations, and (3) makes no distributions of trust corpus during the year. A complex trust is any trust that is not a simple trust.[2] These criteria are applied to the trust every year. Thus, every trust is classified as a complex trust in the year in which it terminates (because it distributes all of its corpus during that year).

[2]Reg. § 1.651(a)–1.

TAX IN THE NEWS Must a Trust Beneficiary Even Be Human?

Humane societies encourage the general public to care for their pets and to adopt those who need owners. But sometimes people carry this compassion even further. It is not uncommon to find provisions in a will to establish endowments to care for pets that the deceased leaves behind. Two prominent, eccentric investors recently established trusts dedicating significant funds to provide for a favorite dog, and the surviving (human) family did not take well to the idea.

- Leona Helmsley was an investor who favored building and decorating luxury hotels. When Helmsley died, her will left very little of her multibillion-dollar estate to her friends and family, perhaps not surprising for someone whose temperament had earned her the nickname "The Queen of Mean." But Helmsley's dog Trouble made out very well. The will established a $12 million trust, with income distributions to be used for Trouble's five-star kennels, dog sitters and manicurists, and other general care. With an annual income allowance averaging $600,000, Trouble could afford accommodations rivaling those available for guests at Helmsley's opulent hotels. After challenges from Helmsley's family, a judge reduced the endowment to benefit Trouble to $2 million and directed the trustee to contribute the rest of trust corpus to charity.
- Gail Posner's will created a $3 million trust to support her chihuahua Conchita and two other dogs. The dogs received the right to continue to live in Posner's $8 million Miami Beach mansion. Posner's caretakers (e.g., bodyguards and housekeepers) inherited about $26 million in cash, and some of them were directed to live rent-free in the mansion to continue to care for the pets. Conchita owns a $15,000 diamond necklace and took over Posner's Cadillac Escalade when Posner acquired a new car. Posner's family is challenging the terms of the will, claiming that Posner was unduly influenced by the caretakers and that Conchita's needs should not prevail over those of the relatives.

What Is an Estate?

An estate is created upon the death of every individual. The entity is charged with collecting and conserving all of the individual's assets, satisfying all liabilities, and distributing the remaining assets to the heirs identified by state law or the will.

Typically, the creation of an estate involves at least three parties: the decedent, all of whose probate assets are transferred to the estate for disposition; the executor, who is appointed under the decedent's valid will (or the administrator, if no valid will exists); and the beneficiaries of the estate, who are to receive assets or income from the entity, as the decedent has indicated in the will. An estate's operations are controlled by the probate laws of the decedent's state of residence and by the terms of the will as interpreted by the probate court.

Recall that the assets that make up the probate estate are not identical to those that constitute the gross estate for transfer tax purposes (refer to Chapter 19). Many gross estate assets are not a part of the probate estate and thus are not subject to disposition by the executor or administrator. For instance, property held by the decedent as a joint tenant passes to the survivor(s) by operation of the applicable state's property law rather than through the probate estate. Proceeds of insurance policies on the life of the decedent, over which the decedent held the incidents of ownership, are not under the control of the executor or administrator. The designated beneficiaries of the policy receive the proceeds outright under the insurance contract.

An estate is a separate legal and taxable entity. The termination date of the estate is somewhat discretionary, as it occurs when all of the assets and income of the decedent have been distributed, all estate and decedent liabilities have been satisfied, and all other business of the entity is completed. Thus, there may be an incentive to use the estate as part of an income-shifting strategy (e.g., where the income beneficiaries are subject to low marginal tax rates).

EXAMPLE 1

Maria dies, and her estate holds a high-yield investment portfolio. Paulo, the income beneficiary, is subject to a 15% marginal state and Federal income tax rate, while Julia, the remainder beneficiary, is subject to a 30% marginal rate. The tax adviser might suggest that Maria's estate delay its final distribution of assets by a year or more to take advantage of the income tax reduction that is available before the entity terminates. ■

If an estate's existence is unduly prolonged, however, the IRS can terminate it for Federal income tax purposes after the expiration of a reasonable period for completing the duties of administration.[3]

20.2 Nature of Trust and Estate Taxation

In general, the taxable income of a trust or an estate is taxed to the entity or to its beneficiaries to the extent that each has received the accounting income of the entity. Thus, Subchapter J creates a modified pass-through principle relative to the income taxation of trusts, estates, and their beneficiaries. Whoever receives the accounting income of the entity, or some portion of it, is liable for the income tax that results.

Subchapter J produces a significant amount of income tax revenue. About 3 million Forms 1041 are filed every year, and these returns reflect the following approximate amounts.

- Gross income of $100 billion.
- Taxable income of $40 billion.
- Tax liability of $10 billion.

EXAMPLE 2

Adam receives 80% of the accounting income of the Zero Trust. The trustee accumulated the other 20% of the income at her discretion under the trust agreement and added it to trust corpus. Adam is liable for income tax only on the amount of the distribution, while Zero is liable for the income tax on the accumulated portion of the income. ■

Table 20.2 summarizes the major similarities and differences between the taxation of trusts and estates and that of other pass-through entities—partnerships, limited liability entities, and S corporations.

Tax Accounting Periods and Methods

An estate or a trust may use many of the tax accounting methods available to individuals. The method of accounting used by the grantor of a trust or the decedent of an estate need not carry over to the entity.

An estate has the same options for choosing a tax year as any new taxpayer. Thus, the estate of a calendar year decedent dying on March 3 can select any fiscal year or report on a calendar year basis. If the latter is selected, the estate's first taxable year will include the period from March 3 to December 31. If the first or last tax years are short years (less than one calendar year), income for those years need not be annualized.

To eliminate the possibility of deferring the taxation of fiduciary-source income simply by using a fiscal tax year, virtually all trusts (other than tax-exempt trusts) are required to use a calendar tax year.[4]

[3]Reg. § 1.641(b)–3(a).

[4]§ 645.

TABLE 20.2 **Tax Characteristics of Major Pass-Through Entities**

Tax Treatment	Subchapter K (Partnerships, LLCs)	Subchapter S (S Corporations)	Subchapter J (Trusts, Estates)
Taxing structure	Pure pass-through, only one level of Federal income tax.	Chiefly pass-through, usually one level of Federal income tax.	Modified pass-through, Federal income tax falls on the recipient(s) of entity accounting income.
Entity-level Federal income tax?	Never.	Rarely. See Chapter 12.	Yes, if the entity retains any accounting income amounts.
Form for reporting income and expense pass-through	Schedules K and K–1, Form 1065.	Schedules K and K–1, Form 1120S.	Schedules K and K–1, Form 1041.
Subject to entity-level AMT?	No, but preferences and adjustments pass through to owners.	No, but preferences and adjustments pass through to owners.	Yes, if the entity retains any AMT-related accounting income amounts.
Controlling documents	Partnership agreement, LLC charter.	Corporate charter and bylaws.	Trust document or will, state fiduciary or probate law.

Tax Rates and Personal Exemption

Congress's desire to stop trusts from being used as income-shifting devices has made the fiduciary entity the highest-taxed taxpayer in the Code. The entity reaches the 35 percent marginal rate with only $11,650 of 2012 taxable income, so the grantor's ability to shift income in a tax-effective manner is nearly eliminated. Table 20.3, which lists the 2012 taxes paid by various entities on taxable income of $50,000, shows how expensive the taxes on an accumulation of income within an estate or a trust can be. Proper income shifting might move assets *out of* the estate or trust and into the hands of the grantor or beneficiary.

A fiduciary's dividend income and net long-term capital gain usually is taxed at a nominal rate of no more than 15 percent. In addition to the regular income tax, an estate or a trust may be subject to the alternative minimum tax, as discussed in the next section.[5]

Both trusts and estates are allowed a personal exemption in computing the fiduciary tax liability. All estates are allowed a personal exemption of $600. The exemption available to a trust depends upon the type of trust involved. A trust that is required to distribute all of its income currently is allowed an exemption of $300. All other trusts are allowed an exemption of $100 per year.[6]

The classification of trusts as to the appropriate personal exemption is similar but not identical to the distinction between simple and complex trusts. The classification as a simple trust is more stringent.

EXAMPLE 3

Three trusts appear to operate in a similar fashion, but they are subject to different Subchapter J classifications and exemptions.

Trust Alpha is required to distribute all of its current accounting income to Susan. Thus, it is allowed a $300 personal exemption. No corpus distributions or charitable contributions are made during the year. Accordingly, Alpha is a simple trust.

Trust Beta is required to distribute all of its current accounting income; it is allowed a $300 personal exemption. The beneficiaries of these distributions are specified in the

[5] § 55.

[6] § 642(b).

TABLE 20.3 Comparative Tax Liabilities

Filing Status/Entity	Taxable Income	Marginal Income Tax Rate (%)	2012 Tax Liability
Single	$50,000	25	$ 8,530
Married, filing jointly	50,000	15	6,630
C corporation	50,000	15	7,500
Trust or estate	50,000	35	16,434

trust instrument: one-half of accounting income is to be distributed to Tyrone, and one-half is to be distributed to State University, a qualifying charitable organization. Because Beta has made a charitable distribution for the tax year, it is a complex trust.

The trustee of Trust Gamma can, at her discretion, distribute the current-year accounting income or corpus of the trust to Dr. Chapman. As the trustee is not required to distribute current accounting income, only a $100 personal exemption is allowed. During the current year, the trustee distributed all of the accounting income of the entity to Dr. Chapman, but made no corpus or charitable distributions. Nonetheless, because it lacks the current-year income distribution requirement, Gamma is a complex trust. ■

Alternative Minimum Tax

The alternative minimum tax (AMT) may apply to a trust or an estate in any tax year. Given the nature and magnitude of the tax preferences, adjustments, and exemptions that determine alternative minimum taxable income (AMTI), however, most trusts and estates are unlikely to incur the tax. Nevertheless, they could be vulnerable, for example, if they are actively engaged in cashing out the stock options of a donor/decedent who was a corporate executive.

In general, derivation of AMTI for the entity follows the rules that apply to individual taxpayers. Thus, the corporate ACE adjustment does not apply to fiduciary entities, but AMTI may be created through the application of most of the other AMT preference and adjustment items discussed in Chapter 3.

The fiduciary's AMT is computed using Schedule I of Form 1041. Two full pages of the Form 1041 are dedicated to the computation of taxable income and other items when the AMT applies to the trust or estate. A minimum tax credit might be available in future years through these computations.

The entity has a $22,500 annual AMT exemption. The exemption phases out at a rate of one-fourth of the amount by which AMTI exceeds $75,000.

A 26 percent AMT rate is applied to AMTI, increasing to 28 percent when AMTI in excess of the exemption reaches $175,000. In addition, estimated tax payments for the entity must include any applicable AMT liability.

LO.2

Identify the steps in determining the accounting and taxable income of a trust or an estate and the related taxable income of the beneficiaries.

20.3 Taxable Income of Trusts and Estates

Generally, the taxable income of an estate or a trust is computed similarly to that for an individual. Subchapter J does, however, include several important exceptions and provisions that make it necessary to use a systematic approach to calculating the taxable income of these entities. Figure 20.2 illustrates the procedure implied by the Code, and Figure 20.3 presents a systematic computation method to be followed in this chapter.

FIGURE 20.2 **Accounting Income, Distributable Net Income, and Taxable Income of the Entity and Its Beneficiaries—The Five-Step Procedure**

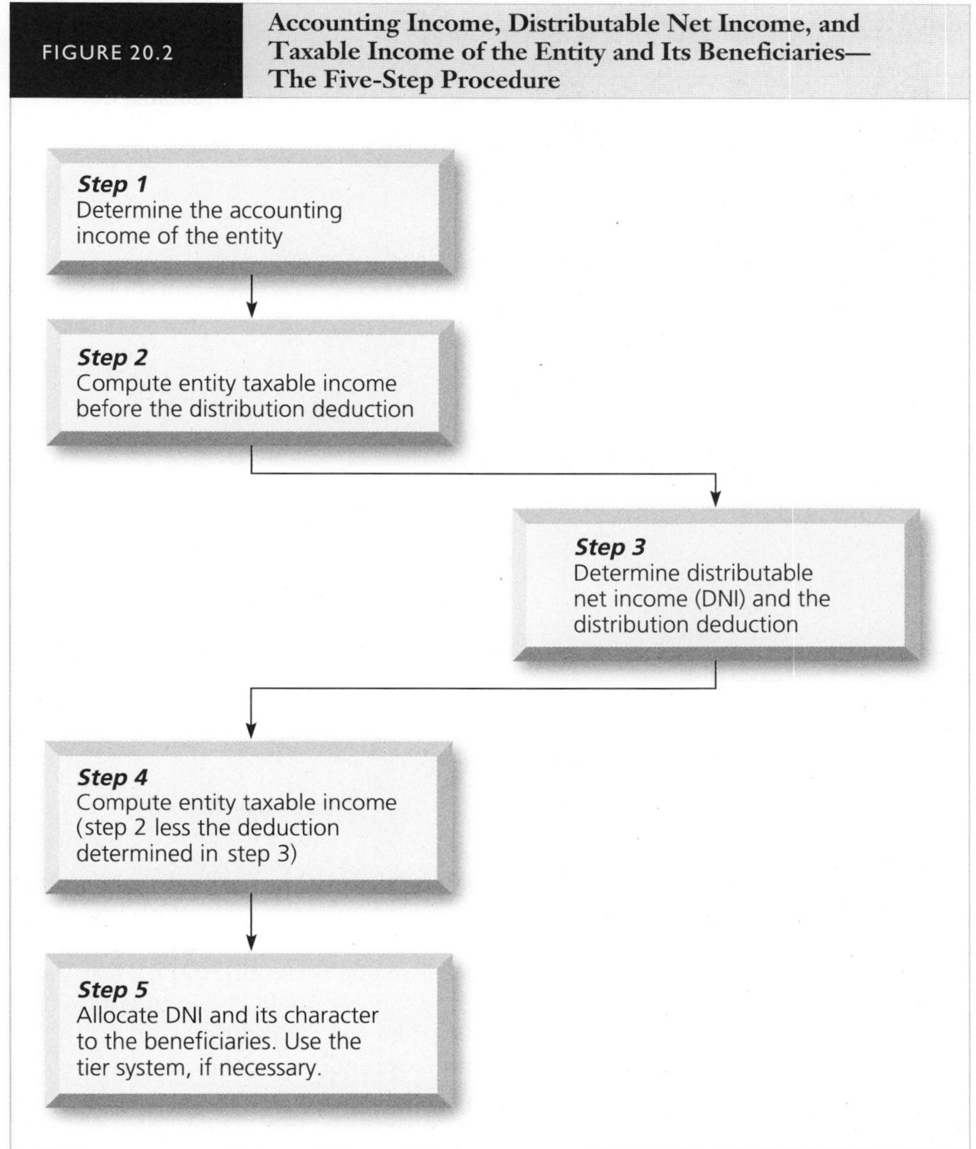

Entity Accounting Income

The first step in determining the taxable income of a trust or an estate is to compute the entity's accounting income for the period. Although this prerequisite is not apparent from a cursory reading of Subchapter J, a closer look at the Code reveals a number of references to the *income* of the entity.[7] Wherever the term *income* is used in Subchapter J without some modifier (e.g., *gross* income or *taxable* income), the statute is referring to the accounting income of the trust or estate for the tax year.

A definition of entity accounting income is critical to understanding the Subchapter J computation of fiduciary taxable income. Under state law, entity accounting income is the amount the income beneficiary of the trust or estate is eligible to receive from the entity. More importantly, the calculation of accounting income is virtually under the control of the grantor or decedent (through a properly drafted trust agreement or will). If the document has been drafted at arm's length, a court

[7]For example, see §§ 651(a)(1), 652(a), and 661(a)(1).

FIGURE 20.3 **Computational Template Applying the Five-Step Procedure**

Item	Totals	Accounting Income	Taxable Income		Distributable Net Income/Distribution Deduction
Income	______	______	______		
Income	______	______	______		
Expense	______	______	______		
Expense	______	______	______		
Personal exemption			______		
Accounting income/taxable income before the distribution deduction		______	______		
		Step 1	***Step 2***		
Exemption					______
Corpus capital gain/loss					______
Net exempt income					______
Distributable net income					______
Distribution deduction			______	***Step 3***	
Entity taxable income			______	***Step 4***	

Beneficiary taxable income is addressed in ***Step 5***.

will enforce a fiduciary's good faith efforts to carry out the specified computation of accounting income.

Entity accounting income generally is defined by state laws that are derived from the Uniform Principal and Income Act (latest major revision, 1997). Most states have adopted some form of the Uniform Act, which essentially constitutes generally accepted accounting principles (GAAP) in the fiduciary tax setting.

By allocating specific items of income and expenditure either to the income beneficiaries or to corpus, the desires of the grantor or decedent are put into effect. Table 20.4 shows typical assignments of revenue and expenditure items to fiduciary income or corpus.

Where the controlling document is silent as to whether an item should be assigned to income or corpus, state fiduciary law prevails. These allocations are an important determinant of the benefits received from the entity by its beneficiaries and the timing of those benefits.

EXAMPLE 4

The Arnold Trust is a simple trust. Mrs. Bennett is its sole beneficiary. In the current year, the trust earns $20,000 in taxable interest and $15,000 in tax-exempt interest. In addition, the trust recognizes an $8,000 long-term capital gain. The trustee assesses a fee of $11,000 for the year. If the trust agreement allocates fees and capital gains to corpus, trust accounting income is $35,000 and Mrs. Bennett receives that amount. Thus, the income beneficiary receives no immediate benefit from the trust's capital gain, and she bears none of the financial burden of the fiduciary's fees.

Interest income	$35,000
Long-term capital gain	± −0−*
Fiduciary's fees	± −0−*
Trust accounting income	$35,000

* Allocable to corpus. ■

TABLE 20.4 **Common Allocations of Items to Income or Corpus**

Allocable to Income	Allocable to Corpus
Ordinary and operating net income from trust assets	Depreciation on business assets
Interest, dividend, rent, and royalty income	Casualty gain/loss on income-producing assets
Stock dividends	Insurance recoveries on income-producing assets
One-half of fiduciary fees/commissions	Capital gain/loss on investment assets
	Stock splits
	One-half of fiduciary fees/commissions

EXAMPLE 5

Assume the same facts as in Example 4, except that the trust agreement allocates the fiduciary's fees to income. The trust accounting income is $24,000, and Mrs. Bennett receives that amount.

Interest income	$35,000
Long-term capital gain	± −0−*
Fiduciary's fees	−11,000
Trust accounting income	$24,000

* Allocable to corpus.

EXAMPLE 6

Assume the same facts as in Example 4, except that the trust agreement allocates to income all capital gains and losses and one-half of the trustee's commissions. The trust accounting income is $37,500, and Mrs. Bennett receives that amount.

Interest income	$ 35,000
Long-term capital gain	+8,000
Fiduciary's fees	−5,500*
Trust accounting income	$ 37,500

* One-half allocable to corpus.

Gross Income

The gross income of an estate or a trust is similar to that of an individual. In determining the gain or loss to be recognized by an estate or a trust upon the sale or other taxable disposition of assets, the rules for basis determination are similar to those applicable to other taxpayers. Thus, an estate's basis for property received from a decedent is stepped up or stepped down to the gross estate valuation (refer to Chapter 19 for a more detailed discussion). Property received as a gift (the usual case in trust arrangements) usually takes the donor's basis. Property purchased by the trust from a third party is assigned a basis equal to the purchase price.

Property Distributions

In general, the entity does not recognize gain or loss upon its distribution of property to a beneficiary under the provisions of the will or trust document. The distributed property has the same basis to the beneficiary of the distribution as it did to the estate or trust. Moreover, the distribution absorbs distributable net income (DNI) and qualifies for a distribution deduction (both of which are explained later in this chapter) to the extent of the lesser of the distributed asset's basis to the beneficiary or the asset's fair market value as of the distribution date.[8]

[8]§ 643(e).

THE BIG PICTURE

EXAMPLE 7

Return to the facts of *The Big Picture* on p. 20-1. Assume that Anna has established the Jiang Family Trust. The trust distributes a painting (basis of $40,000 and fair market value of $90,000) to beneficiary Sally. Sally's basis in the painting is $40,000. The distribution absorbs $40,000 of the Jiang Trust's DNI, and the trust claims a $40,000 distribution deduction relative to the transaction.

THE BIG PICTURE

EXAMPLE 8

Assume the same facts as in Example 7, except that the Jiang Trust's basis in the painting is $100,000. Sally's basis in the painting is $100,000. The distribution absorbs $90,000 of the Jiang Trust's DNI, and the trust claims a $90,000 distribution deduction.

A trustee or an executor can elect to recognize gain or loss with respect to all of its in-kind property distributions for the year. If the election is made, the beneficiary's basis in the asset is equal to the asset's fair market value as of the distribution date. The distribution absorbs DNI and qualifies for a distribution deduction to the extent of the asset's fair market value. However, the related-party rules can restrict an estate's or a trust's deduction for such losses. Generally, related parties include a trust, its trustee, its grantor, and its beneficiaries, as well as an estate, its executor, and its beneficiaries.

EXAMPLE 9

The Green Estate distributes an antique piano, basis to Green of $10,000 and fair market value of $15,000, to beneficiary Kyle. The executor elects that Green recognize the related $5,000 gain on the distribution. Accordingly, Kyle's basis in the piano is $15,000 ($10,000 basis to Green + $5,000 gain recognized). Without the election, Green would not recognize any gain, and Kyle's basis in the piano would be $10,000. ■

EXAMPLE 10

Assume the same facts as in Example 9, except that Green's basis in the piano is $18,000. The executor elects that Green recognize the related $3,000 loss on the distribution. Accordingly, Kyle's basis in the piano is $15,000 ($18,000 − $3,000). Without the election, Green would not recognize any loss, and Kyle's basis in the piano would be $18,000.

The estate cannot deduct this loss, however. Because an estate and its beneficiaries are related parties, realized losses cannot be recognized immediately.[9] The loss can be recognized if Kyle later sells the piano to a stranger. ■

Income in Respect of a Decedent

The gross income of a trust or an estate includes **income in respect of a decedent (IRD)** that the entity received.[10] For a cash basis decedent, IRD includes accrued salary, interest, rent, and other income items that were not constructively received before death. For both cash and accrual basis decedents, IRD includes, for instance, death benefits from qualified retirement plans and deferred compensation contracts.

[9] § 267(b)(13).

[10] § 691 and the Regulations thereunder. The concept of IRD was introduced in Chapter 19.

TAX IN THE NEWS A Trend Toward Dynasty Trusts

In a continuing attempt to discourage tax-motivated income shifting among family members, steep income tax rates on estates and trusts are also being seen at the state level. Although a few states (e.g., Alaska, Nevada, Texas, and Washington) do not impose any income tax on fiduciary entities, those that do are tending to increase their rates as part of their efforts to solve budget deficit woes.

Other states, however, have relaxed some of the rules that affect trusts. In such cases the objectives are to attract dollars to the state and to expand opportunities for attorneys, tax advisers, and other professionals who create and administer the entities.

One current development might be traced to the existence of the generation-skipping tax (GST), discussed in Chapter 18. After that tax was enacted, wealthy individuals and their advisers convinced about half of the states to allow a trust to survive for hundreds of years or indefinitely by modifying the time-honored limitation of the "rule against perpetuities" (i.e., a life in being plus 21 years).

If a trust can survive for a long period of time, without making distributions or terminations that cause the GST, trust corpus can grow in a steady and tax-free manner. Wealthy individuals use these "dynasty trusts" as a form of inheritance, and many states also allow the trust assets to be protected from claims of the grantor's creditors.

Dynasty trusts operate like growth stocks. They minimize income distributions by investing profits and new capital in the family businesses, artwork, and multiple homes for the beneficiaries. The trust holds the title to these hard assets so that there is no income, gift, generation-skipping, or estate tax when younger generations take possession.

Almost half of the states allow dynasty trusts, and they are available to all parties, wherever the trust grantor is located. Thus, a nonresident transferor can establish such a trust, and local laws will control.

The Obama administration sees dynasty trusts as a threat to revenues from Federal transfer taxes. A budget proposal would allow the trusts to exist indefinitely, but the exemption from Federal transfer taxation would be limited to the first 90 years after the trust is created. The proposed limitation would apply only to new trusts but cover asset additions to existing dynasty trusts.

Within 90 years, a donor might have produced over 100 descendants. And then there are the in-laws! Good tax planning using the dynasty trust can produce tax savings for many people for many years to come.

The tax consequences of IRD can be summarized as follows.

- The fair market value of the right to IRD on the appropriate valuation date is included in the decedent's gross estate. Thus, it is subject to the Federal estate tax.[11]
- The decedent's basis in the property carries over to the recipient (the estate or heirs). There is no step-up or step-down in the basis of IRD items.
- The recipient of the income recognizes gain or loss, measured by the difference between the amount realized and the adjusted basis of the IRD in the hands of the decedent. The character of the gain or loss depends upon the treatment that it would have received had it been realized by the decedent before death. Thus, if the decedent would have realized capital gain, the recipient must do likewise.
- Expenses related to the IRD (such as interest, taxes, and depletion) that were not reported properly on the final income tax return of the decedent may be claimed by the recipient. These items are known as **expenses in respect of a decedent.** Typically, such expenses also include fiduciary fees, commissions paid to dispose of estate assets, and state income taxes payable. They are deductible for both Federal estate and income tax purposes, *for* or *from* adjusted gross income (AGI) as would have been the case for the decedent.

[11]To mitigate the effect of double taxation (imposition of both the estate tax and the income tax), § 691(c) allows the recipient an income tax deduction for the incremental estate tax attributable to the net IRD. For individual recipients, this is an itemized deduction, not subject to the 2%-of-AGI floor.

TAX IN THE NEWS Coordinate Your Deductions

The deduction under § 691(c) may be one of the more obscure provisions of the tax law, but its benefits can add up fast. The deduction is allowed on the tax return of the recipient of income in respect of a decedent (IRD). IRD often is received by the estate of the decedent or a trust that he or she created under the will or during lifetime. The deduction is for the Federal estate tax attributable to the IRD item. For an individual, it is a miscellaneous itemized deduction *not* subject to the 2 percent-of-AGI floor.

Because IRD often includes the value of the survivorship feature on pensions and other retirement plans and assets, the amount subject to the estate tax can be quite high. Thus, when computing the current-year income tax for the IRD recipient, the § 691(c) deduction can be extremely valuable in offsetting the IRD received.

For instance, suppose a decedent's IRA balance generates $450,000 in attributable estate tax. If the recipient of the IRA takes the net-of-tax distribution in one year, the § 691(c) deduction shelters $450,000 in gross income and may be worth over $150,000 in Federal income taxes saved.

But taking the § 691(c) deduction is more complex than it looks. Because different tax advisers often prepare the Form 706 for the estate and the Form 1040 or 1041 for the IRD recipient, the § 691(c) deduction can get lost altogether or at least be miscomputed. When the IRD is paid out over several years, computing the § 691(c) deduction can become complex. And some tax professionals do not know the law well enough to track down the deduction, while tax software and IRS forms and publications say relatively little about it.

- If the IRD item would have created an AMT preference or adjustment for the decedent (e.g., with respect to the collection of certain tax-exempt interest by the entity), an identical AMT item is created for the recipient.

EXAMPLE 11

Amanda died on July 13 of the current year. On August 2, the estate received a check (before deductions) for $1,200 from Amanda's former employer; this was Amanda's compensation for the last pay period of her life. On November 23, the estate received a $45,000 distribution from the qualified profit sharing plan of Amanda's employer, the full amount to which Amanda was entitled under the plan. Both Amanda and the estate are calendar year, cash basis taxpayers.

The last salary payment and the profit sharing plan distribution constitute IRD to the estate. Amanda had earned these items during her lifetime, and the estate had an enforceable right to receive each of them after Amanda's death. Consequently, the gross estate includes $46,200 with respect to these two items. However, the income tax basis to the estate for these items is not stepped up (from zero to $1,200 and $45,000, respectively) upon distribution to the estate.

The estate must report gross income of $46,200 for the current tax year with respect to the IRD items. The gain recognized upon the receipt of the IRD is $46,200 [$1,200 + $45,000 (amounts realized) − $0 (adjusted bases)]. ■

Including the IRD in both the taxpayer's gross estate and the gross income of the estate may seem harsh. Nevertheless, the tax consequences of IRD are similar to the treatment that applies to all of a taxpayer's earned income. The item is subject to income tax upon receipt, and to the extent it is not consumed by the taxpayer before death, it is included in the gross estate.

EXAMPLE 12

Assume the same facts as in Example 11, except that Amanda is an accrual basis taxpayer. IRD now includes only the $45,000 distribution from the qualified retirement plan. Amanda's last paycheck is included in the gross income of her own last return (January 1 through date of death). The $1,200 salary is already properly recognized under Amanda's usual method of tax accounting. It does not constitute IRD and is not gross income when received by the executor. ■

EXAMPLE 13

Assume the same facts as in Example 11. Amanda's last paycheck was reduced by $165 for state income taxes that were withheld by the employer. The $165 tax payment is an expense in respect of a decedent and is allowed as a deduction on *both* Amanda's estate tax return *and* the estate's income tax return. ■

Ordinary Deductions

As a general rule, the taxable income of an estate or a trust is similar to that of an individual.[12] Deductions are allowed for ordinary and necessary expenses paid or incurred in carrying on a trade or business; for the production or collection of income; for the management, conservation, or maintenance of property; and in connection with the determination, collection, or refund of any tax.[13] Reasonable administration expenses, including fiduciary fees and litigation costs in connection with the duties of administration, also can be deductible.

Expenses attributable to the production or collection of tax-exempt income are not deductible.[14] The amount of the disallowed deduction is found by using a formula based upon the composition of the income elements of entity accounting income for the year of the deduction. The § 212 deduction is apportioned without regard to the accounting income allocation of such expenses to income or to corpus. The deductibility of the fees is determined strictly by the Code (under §§ 212 and 265), and the allocation of expenditures to income and to corpus is controlled by the trust agreement or will or by state law.

EXAMPLE 14

The Silver Trust operates a business and invests idle cash in marketable securities. Its sales proceeds for the current year are $180,000. Expenses for wages, cost of sales, and office administration are $80,000. Interest income recognized is $20,000 from taxable bonds and $50,000 from tax-exempt bonds. The trustee claims a $35,000 fee for its activities. According to the trust agreement, $30,000 of this amount is allocated to the income beneficiaries and $5,000 is allocated to corpus.

Sales income	$180,000
Cost of sales	−80,000
Interest income ($50,000 is exempt)	+70,000
Fiduciary's fees, as allocated	−30,000
Trust accounting income	$140,000

The sales proceeds are included in the gross income of the trust under § 61. The costs associated with the business are deductible in full under § 162. The taxable income is included in Silver's gross income under § 61, but the tax-exempt income is excluded under § 103. The fiduciary's fees are deductible by Silver under § 212, but a portion of the deduction is lost because § 265 prohibits deductions for expenses incurred in the generation of tax-exempt income.

Specifically, 50/250 of the fees of $35,000 can be traced to tax-exempt income, so $7,000 of the fees is nondeductible. For purposes of the computation, only the income elements of the year's trust accounting income are included in the denominator. Moreover, the allocation of portions of the fees to income and to corpus is irrelevant in the calculation. The disallowed deduction for fiduciary's fees is computed in the following manner.

$$\$35{,}000^{*}\text{(total fees paid)} \times \frac{\$50{,}000^{**}\ (\textit{exempt}\text{ income elements of trust accounting income})}{\$250{,}000^{**}\ (\textit{all}\text{ income elements of trust accounting income})}$$

$$= \$7{,}000\ \text{(amount disallowed)}$$

*All of the fees, and not just those that are allocated to income, are deductible by the trust under § 212.

The numerator and denominator of this fraction are ***not* reduced by expense items allocable to income (e.g., cost of sales). ■

[12] § 641(b).

[13] §§ 162 and 212.

[14] § 265.

Under § 642(g), amounts deductible as administration expenses or losses for estate tax purposes (under §§ 2053 and 2054) cannot be claimed by the estate for income tax purposes, unless the estate files a waiver of the estate tax deduction. Although these expenses cannot be deducted twice, they may be allocated as the fiduciary sees fit between Forms 706 and 1041; they need not be claimed in their entirety on either return.[15] As discussed earlier, the prohibition against double deductions does not extend to expenses in respect of a decedent.

Trusts and estates are allowed cost recovery deductions. However, such deductions are assigned proportionately among the recipients of the entity accounting income.[16]

EXAMPLE 15

Lisa and Martin are the equal income beneficiaries of the Needle Trust. Under the terms of the trust agreement, the trustee has complete discretion as to the timing of the distributions from Needle's current accounting income. The trust agreement allocates all depreciation expense to income. In the current year, the trustee distributes 40% of the current trust accounting income to Lisa and 40% to Martin; thus, 20% of the income is accumulated. The depreciation deduction allowable to Needle is $100,000. This deduction is allocated among the trust and its beneficiaries on the basis of the distribution of current accounting income: Lisa and Martin each can claim a $40,000 deduction, and the trust can deduct $20,000. ■

EXAMPLE 16

Assume the same facts as in Example 15, except that the trust agreement allocates all depreciation expense to corpus. Lisa and Martin both still claim a $40,000 depreciation deduction, and Needle retains its $20,000 deduction. The Code assigns the depreciation deduction proportionately to the recipients of entity accounting income. Allocation of depreciation to income or to corpus is irrelevant in determining which party can properly claim the deduction. ■

When a trust sells property received by transfer from the grantor, the amount of depreciation subject to recapture includes the depreciation claimed by the grantor before the transfer of the property to the trust. However, depreciation recapture potential disappears at death.

EXAMPLE 17

Jaime transferred an asset to the Shoulder Trust via a lifetime gift. The asset's total depreciation recapture potential was $40,000. If Shoulder sells the asset at a gain, ordinary income not to exceed $40,000 is recognized by the trust. Had Jaime transferred the asset after his death to his estate through a bequest, the $40,000 recapture potential would have disappeared. ■

If a trust or an estate operates a trade or business, the entity may be eligible for the domestic production activities deduction (DPAD).[17] Computation of qualified production activities income (QPAI) is made at the entity level. Each beneficiary receives, as a pass-through from the entity, his or her share of QPAI and the W–2 wages paid, based on the proportion of entity accounting income received. The DPAD then can be claimed at the beneficiary level. In the case of an individual beneficiary, the DPAD is subject to the modified AGI limitation. See Chapter 3 for further discussion of the DPAD.

Deductions for Losses

An estate or a trust is allowed a deduction for casualty or theft losses that are not covered by insurance or other arrangements. Such losses may also be deductible by an estate for Federal tax purposes under § 2054. As a result, an estate is not allowed an income tax deduction unless the estate tax deduction is waived.[18]

[15] Reg. § 1.642(g)–2.

[16] §§ 167(h) and 611(b)(3) and (4).

[17] § 199(d)(1).

[18] See Reg. § 1.642(g)–1 for requirements as to the statement waiving the estate tax deduction. In addition, see Reg. §§ 1.165–7(c) and 1.165–8(b), requiring that a statement be filed to allow an income tax deduction for such losses.

The net operating loss (NOL) deduction is available for estates and trusts (i.e., where trade or business income is generated). The carryback of an NOL may reduce the distributable net income of the trust or estate for the carryback year and therefore affect the amount taxed to the beneficiaries for that year.

Except for the possibility of unused losses in the year of termination (discussed later in the chapter), the net capital losses of an estate or a trust are used only on the fiduciary income tax return. The tax treatment of these losses is the same as for individual taxpayers.

Charitable Contributions

An estate or a complex trust is allowed a deduction for contributions to charitable organizations under certain conditions.

- The contribution is made pursuant to the will or trust instrument, and its amount is determinable using the language of that document.
- The recipient is a qualified organization. For this purpose, qualified organizations include the same charities for which individual and corporate donors are allowed deductions, except that estates and trusts are permitted a deduction for contributions to certain foreign charitable organizations.
- Generally, the contribution is claimed in the tax year it is paid, but a fiduciary can treat amounts paid in the year immediately following as a deduction for the preceding year.[19] Under this rule, estates and complex trusts receive more favorable treatment than do individuals or C corporations.

Unlike the charitable contribution deductions of individuals and corporations, the deductions of estates and complex trusts are not limited in amount (e.g., to a percentage of taxable or adjusted gross income). Nonetheless, an entity's charitable contribution may not be fully deductible. Specifically, the deduction is limited to amounts that have been included in the gross income of the entity.[20]

A contribution is deemed to have been made proportionately from each of the income elements of entity accounting income. However, if the will or trust agreement requires that the contribution be made from a specific type of income or from the current income from a specified asset, the allocation of the contribution to taxable and tax-exempt income will not be required.

THE BIG PICTURE

EXAMPLE 18

Return to the facts of *The Big Picture* on p. 20-1. Again assume that Anna has established the Jiang Family Trust. The trust has 2012 gross rent income of $80,000, expenses attributable to the rents of $60,000, and tax-exempt interest from state bonds of $20,000. Under the trust agreement, the trustee is to pay 30% of the annual trust accounting income to the United Way, a qualifying organization. Accordingly, the trustee pays $12,000 to the charity in 2013 (i.e., 30% × $40,000). The charitable contribution deduction allowed for 2012 is $9,600 [($80,000/$100,000) × $12,000].

THE BIG PICTURE

EXAMPLE 19

Assume the same facts as in Example 18, except that the trust instrument also requires that the contribution be paid from the net rent income. The agreement controls, and the allocation formula need not be applied. The entire $12,000 is allowed as a charitable deduction.

[19] § 642(c)(1) and Reg. § 1.642(c)–1(b).

[20] Reg. §§ 1.642(c)–3(b) and (c).

LO.3

Illustrate the uses and implications of distributable net income.

Deduction for Distributions to Beneficiaries

The modified pass-through approach of Subchapter J is embodied in the deduction allowed to trusts and estates for the distributions made to beneficiaries during the year. Some portion of any distribution that a beneficiary receives from a trust may be subject to income tax on the beneficiary's own return. At the same time, the distributing entity is allowed a deduction for some or all of the distribution. Consequently, the modified pass-through principle of Subchapter J is implemented. A good analogy is to the taxability of corporate profits distributed to employees as taxable wages. The corporation is allowed a deduction for the payment, but the employee receives gross income in the form of compensation.

A critical value that is used in computing the amount of the entity's distribution deduction is **distributable net income (DNI)**. As it is defined in Subchapter J, DNI serves several functions.

- DNI is the maximum amount of the distribution on which the beneficiaries can be taxed.[21]
- DNI is the maximum amount the entity can use as a distribution deduction for the year.[22]
- The makeup of DNI carries over to the beneficiaries (the items of income and expenses retain their DNI character in the hands of the distributees).[23]

Subchapter J defines DNI in a circular manner, however. The DNI value is necessary to determine the entity's distribution deduction and therefore its taxable income for the year. Nonetheless, the Code defines DNI as a modification of the entity's taxable income itself. Using the systematic approach to determining the taxable income of the entity and its beneficiaries, as shown earlier in Figure 20.2, first compute *taxable income before the distribution deduction*, modify that amount to determine DNI and the distribution deduction, return to the calculation of *taxable income*, and apply the deduction that has resulted.

Taxable income before the distribution deduction includes all of the entity's items of gross income, deductions, gains, losses, and exemptions for the year. Therefore, to compute this amount, (1) determine the appropriate personal exemption for the year and (2) account for all of the other gross income and deductions of the entity.

The next step in Figure 20.2 is the determination of *distributable net income*, computed by making the following adjustments to the entity's *taxable income before the distribution deduction*.[24]

- Add back the personal exemption.
- Add back *net* tax-exempt interest. To arrive at this amount, reduce the total tax-exempt interest by charitable contributions and by related expenses not deductible under § 265.
- Add back the entity's net capital losses.
- Subtract any net capital gains allocable to corpus. In other words, the only net capital gains included in DNI are those attributable to income beneficiaries or to charitable contributions.

Because taxable income before the distribution deduction is computed by deducting all of the expenses of the entity (whether they were allocated to income or to corpus), DNI is reduced by expenses that are allocated to corpus. The effect is to reduce the taxable income of the income beneficiaries. The actual distributions to the beneficiaries exceed DNI because the distributions are not reduced by expenses allocated to corpus. Aside from this shortcoming of Subchapter J, DNI offers a good approximation of the current-year economic income available for distribution to the entity's income beneficiaries.

DNI includes the net tax-exempt interest income of the entity, so that amount must be removed from DNI in computing the distribution deduction. Moreover, for estates and complex trusts, the amount actually distributed during the year may include discretionary distributions of income and distributions of corpus

[21] §§ 652(a) and 662(a).

[22] §§ 651(b) and 661(c).

[23] §§ 652(b) and 662(b).

[24] These and other (less common) adjustments are detailed in § 643.

permissible under the will or trust instrument. Thus, the distribution deduction for estates and complex trusts is computed as the lesser of (1) the deductible portion of DNI or (2) the taxable amount actually distributed to the beneficiaries during the year. For a simple trust, however, full distribution is always assumed, relative to both the entity and its beneficiaries, in a manner similar to the pass-through entities.

EXAMPLE 20

The Zinc Trust is a simple trust. Because of severe liquidity problems, its 2012 accounting income is not distributed to its sole beneficiary, Mark, until early in 2013. Zinc still is allowed a full distribution deduction for, and Mark still is taxable upon, the entity's 2012 income in 2012. ■

EXAMPLE 21

The Pork Trust is required to distribute its current accounting income annually to its sole income beneficiary, Barbara. Capital gains and losses and all other expenses are allocable to corpus. In the current year, Pork incurs the following items.

Dividend income	$25,000
Taxable interest income	15,000
Tax-exempt interest income	20,000
Net long-term capital gains	10,000
Fiduciary's fees	6,000

Item	Totals	Accounting Income		Taxable Income	Distributable Net Income/ Distribution Deduction
Dividend income	$25,000	$25,000		$ 25,000	
Taxable interest income	15,000	15,000		15,000	
Exempt interest income	20,000	20,000			
Net long-term capital gain	10,000			10,000	
Fiduciary fees	6,000			(4,000)	
Personal exemption				(300)	
Accounting income/ taxable income before the distribution deduction		$60,000		$ 45,700	$ 45,700
		Step 1		*Step 2*	
Exemption					300
Corpus capital gain/loss					(10,000)
Net exempt income					18,000
Distributable net income					$ 54,000
Distribution deduction			*Step 3*	(36,000)	
Entity taxable income			*Step 4*	$ 9,700	

Step 1. Trust accounting income is $60,000; this includes the tax-exempt interest income, but not the fees or the capital gains, pursuant to the trust document. Barbara receives $60,000 from the trust for the current year.

Step 2. Taxable income before the distribution deduction is computed as directed by the Code. The tax-exempt interest is excluded under § 103. Only a portion of the fees is deductible because some of the fees are traceable to the tax-exempt income. The trust claims a $300 personal exemption as it is required to distribute its annual trust accounting income.

Step 3. DNI and the distribution deduction reflect the required adjustments. The distribution deduction is the lesser of the distributed amount ($60,000) or the deductible portion of DNI ($54,000 − $18,000 net exempt income).

Step 4. Finally, return to the computation of the taxable income of the Pork Trust. A simple test should be applied at this point to ensure that the proper figure for the trust's taxable income has been determined. On what is Pork to be taxed? Pork has distributed to Barbara all of its gross income except the $10,000 net long-term capital gains. The $300 personal exemption reduces taxable income to $9,700. ■

EXAMPLE 22

The Quick Trust is required to distribute all of its current accounting income equally to its two beneficiaries, Faith and the Universal Church, a qualifying charitable organization. Capital gains and losses and depreciation expenses are allocable to income. Fiduciary fees are allocable to corpus. In the current year, Quick incurs various items as indicated.

Item	Totals	Accounting Income		Taxable Income	Distributable Net Income/ Distribution Deduction
Rent income	$100,000	$100,000		$100,000	
Expenses—rent income	30,000	(30,000)		(30,000)	
Depreciation—rent income	15,000	(15,000)			
Net long-term capital gain	20,000	20,000		20,000	
Charitable contribution				(37,500)	
Fiduciary fees	18,000			(18,000)	
Personal exemption				(300)	
Accounting income/taxable income before the distribution deduction		$ 75,000		$ 34,200	$34,200
		Step 1		*Step 2*	
Exemption					300
Corpus capital gain/loss					
Net exempt income					
Distributable net income					$34,500
Distribution deduction			*Step 3*	(34,500)	
Entity taxable income			*Step 4*	($ 300)	

Step 1. Trust accounting income of $75,000 reflects the indicated allocations of items to income and to corpus. Each income beneficiary receives $37,500.

Step 2. In the absence of tax-exempt income, a deduction is allowed for the full amount of the fiduciary's fees. Quick is a complex trust, but because it is required to distribute its full accounting income annually, a $300 exemption is allowed. The trust properly does not deduct any depreciation for the rental property. The depreciation deduction is available only to the recipients of the entity's accounting income for the period. Thus, the deduction is split equally between Faith and the church. The deduction probably is of no direct value to the church, a tax-exempt organization. The trust's charitable contribution deduction is based upon the $37,500 the charity actually received (one-half of trust accounting income).

Step 3. As there is no tax-exempt income, the only adjustment needed to compute DNI is to add back the trust's personal exemption. Subchapter J requires no adjustment for the charitable contribution. DNI is computed only from the perspective of Faith, who also received $37,500 from the trust.

Step 4. Perform the simple test (referred to above) to ensure that the proper taxable income for the Quick Trust has been computed. All of the trust's gross income has been distributed to Faith and the charity. As is the case with most trusts that distribute all of their accounting income, the Quick Trust "wastes" the personal exemption. ■

Tax Credits

An estate or a trust may claim the foreign tax credit to the extent that it is not passed through to the beneficiaries.[25] Similarly, other credits are apportioned between the estate or trust and the beneficiaries on the basis of the entity accounting income allocable to each.

[25] §§ 642(a)(1) and 901.

20.4 Taxation of Beneficiaries

The beneficiaries of an estate or a trust receive taxable income from the entity under the modified pass-through principle of Subchapter J. Distributable net income determines the maximum amount that can be taxed to the beneficiaries for any tax year. The constitution of DNI also carries over to the beneficiaries (e.g., net long-term capital gains and dividends retain their character when they are distributed from the entity to the beneficiary).

The timing of any tax consequences to the beneficiary of a trust or an estate presents a problem only when the parties involved use different tax years. A beneficiary includes in gross income an amount based upon the DNI of the trust for any taxable year or years of the entity ending with or within his or her taxable year.[26]

EXAMPLE 23

An estate uses a fiscal year ending on March 31 for tax purposes. Its sole income beneficiary is a calendar year taxpayer. For calendar year 2012, the beneficiary reports the income assignable to her for the entity's fiscal year April 1, 2011, to March 31, 2012. If the estate is terminated by December 31, 2012, the beneficiary also includes any trust income assignable to her for the short year. This could result in a bunching of income in 2012. ■

Distributions by Simple Trusts

The amount taxable to the beneficiaries of a simple trust is limited by the trust's DNI. However, because DNI includes net tax-exempt income, the amount included in the gross income of the beneficiaries could be less than DNI. When there is more than one income beneficiary, the elements of DNI are apportioned ratably according to the amount required to be distributed currently to each.

EXAMPLE 24

A simple trust has ordinary income of $40,000, a long-term capital gain of $15,000 (allocable to corpus), and a trustee commission expense of $4,000 (payable from corpus). The two income beneficiaries, Allie and Bart, are entitled to the trust's annual accounting income, based on shares of 75% and 25%, respectively.

Although Allie receives $30,000 as her share (75% × trust accounting income of $40,000), she is allocated DNI of only $27,000 (75% × $36,000). Likewise, Bart is entitled to receive $10,000 (25% × $40,000), but he is allocated DNI of only $9,000 (25% × $36,000). The $15,000 capital gain is taxed to the trust. ■

Distributions by Estates and Complex Trusts

Typically, an estate or a complex trust makes only discretionary distributions. In those cases, the DNI is apportioned ratably according to the distributed amounts.

A computational problem arises with estates and complex trusts when more than one beneficiary receives a distribution from the entity and the controlling document does not require a distribution of the entire accounting income of the entity.

EXAMPLE 25

The trustee of the Wilson Trust has the discretion to distribute the income or corpus of the trust in any proportion between the two beneficiaries of the trust, Wong and Washington. Under the trust instrument, Wong must receive $15,000 from the trust every year. In the current year, the trust's accounting income is $50,000, and its DNI is $40,000. The trustee pays $15,000 to Wong and $25,000 to Washington. ■

How is Wilson's DNI to be divided between Wong and Washington? Several arbitrary methods of allocating DNI between the beneficiaries could be devised. Subchapter J resolves the problem by creating a two-tier system to govern the taxation of beneficiaries in such situations.[27] The tier system determines which distributions

[26] §§ 652(c) and 662(c).

[27] §§ 662(a)(1) and (2).

will be included in the gross income of the beneficiaries in full, which will be included in part, and which will not be included at all.

Income that is required to be distributed currently, whether it is distributed, is categorized as a *first-tier distribution.* All other amounts properly paid, credited, or required to be distributed are *second-tier distributions.*[28] A formula is used to allocate DNI among the appropriate beneficiaries when only first-tier distributions are made and those amounts exceed DNI.

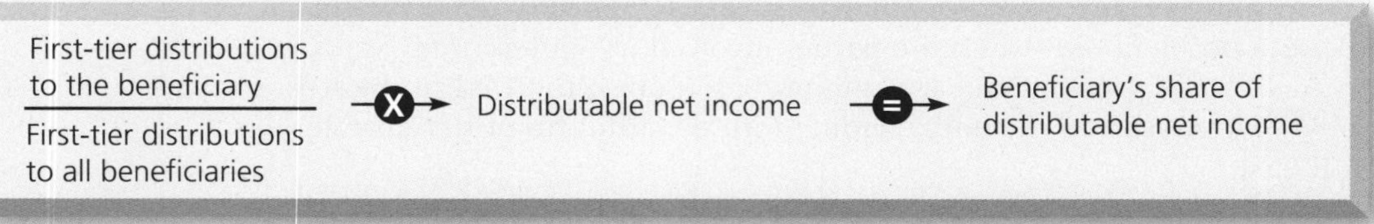

When both first-tier and second-tier distributions are made and the first-tier distributions exceed DNI, the above formula is applied to the first-tier distributions. In this case, none of the second-tier distributions are taxed, because all of the DNI has been allocated to the first-tier beneficiaries.

If both first-tier and second-tier distributions are made and the first-tier distributions do not exceed DNI, but the total of both first-tier and second-tier distributions does exceed DNI, the second-tier beneficiaries recognize income as shown below.

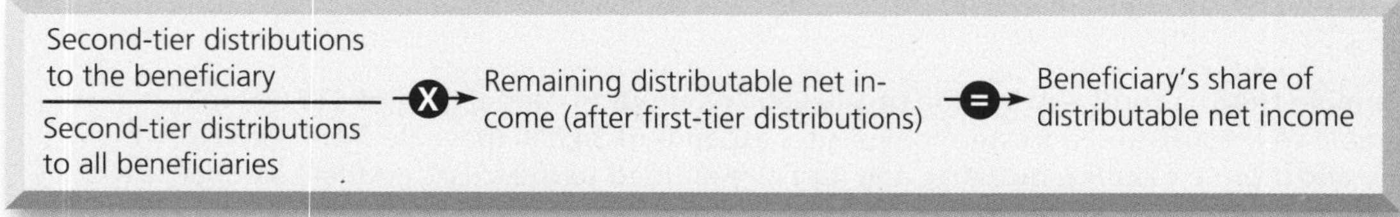

EXAMPLE 26

The trustee of the Gray Trust is required to distribute $10,000 per year to both Harriet and Wally, the two beneficiaries of the entity. In addition, he is empowered to distribute other amounts of trust income or corpus at his sole discretion. In the current year, the trust reports accounting income of $60,000 and DNI of $50,000. However, the trustee distributes only the required $10,000 each to Harriet and to Wally. The balance of the income is accumulated and added to trust corpus.

In this case, only first-tier distributions have been made, but the total amount of the distributions does not exceed DNI for the year. Although DNI is the maximum amount included by the beneficiaries for the year, they can include no more in gross income than is distributed by the entity. Thus, both Harriet and Wally may be subject to tax on $10,000 as their proportionate shares of DNI. ■

EXAMPLE 27

Assume the same facts as in Example 26, except that DNI is $12,000. Harriet and Wally each receive $10,000, but they cannot be taxed in total on more than DNI. Each is taxed on $6,000 [DNI $12,000 × ($10,000/$20,000 of the first-tier distributions)]. ■

EXAMPLE 28

Return to the facts in Example 25. Wong receives a first-tier distribution of $15,000. Second-tier distributions include $20,000 to Wong and $25,000 to Washington. Wilson's DNI is $40,000. The DNI is allocated between Wong and Washington as follows.

[28]Reg. §§ 1.662(a)−2 and −3.

(1)	**First-tier distributions**	
	To Wong	$15,000 DNI
	To Washington	–0–
	Remaining DNI = $25,000	
(2)	**Second-tier distributions**	
	To Wong	$11,111 DNI [(20/45) × $25,000]
	To Washington	$13,889 DNI [(25/45) × $25,000] ■

EXAMPLE 29

Assume the same facts as in Example 28, except that accounting income is $80,000 and DNI is $70,000. DNI is allocated between Wong and Washington as follows.

(1)	**First-tier distributions**	
	To Wong	$15,000 DNI
	To Washington	–0–
	Remaining DNI = $55,000	
(2)	**Second-tier distributions**	
	To Wong	$20,000 DNI
	To Washington	$25,000 DNI ■

Separate Share Rule

For the sole purpose of determining the amount of DNI for a complex trust or an estate with more than one beneficiary, the substantially separate and independent shares of different beneficiaries in the trust or estate are treated as *separate* trusts or estates.[29]

The separate share rule is designed to prevent the inequity that results if the corpus payments are treated under the regular rules applicable to second-tier beneficiaries. The rule also results in the availability of extra entity personal exemptions and in a greater use of lower entity tax brackets.

EXAMPLE 30

A trustee has the discretion to distribute or accumulate income on behalf of Greg and Hannah (in equal shares). The trustee also has the power to invade corpus for the benefit of either beneficiary to the extent of that beneficiary's one-half interest in the trust. For the current year, DNI is $10,000. Of this amount, $5,000 is distributed to Greg, and $5,000 is accumulated on behalf of Hannah. In addition, the trustee pays $20,000 from corpus to Greg.

Without the separate share rule, Greg is taxed on $10,000 (the full amount of the DNI). With the separate share rule, Greg is taxed on only $5,000 (his share of the DNI) and receives the $20,000 corpus distribution tax-free. The trust is taxed on Hannah's $5,000 share of the DNI that is accumulated. ■

Character of Income

Consistent with the modified pass-through principle of Subchapter J, various classes of income (e.g., dividends, passive or portfolio gain and loss, AMT preferences, and tax-exempt interest) retain the same character for the beneficiaries that they had when they were received by the entity. If there are multiple beneficiaries *and* if all of the DNI is distributed, a problem arises in allocating the various classes of income among the beneficiaries.

Distributions are treated as consisting of the same proportion as the items that enter into the computation of DNI. This allocation does not apply, however, if local

[29] § 663(c); Reg. § 1.663(c)–1(a).

law or the governing instrument specifically allocates different classes of income to different beneficiaries.[30]

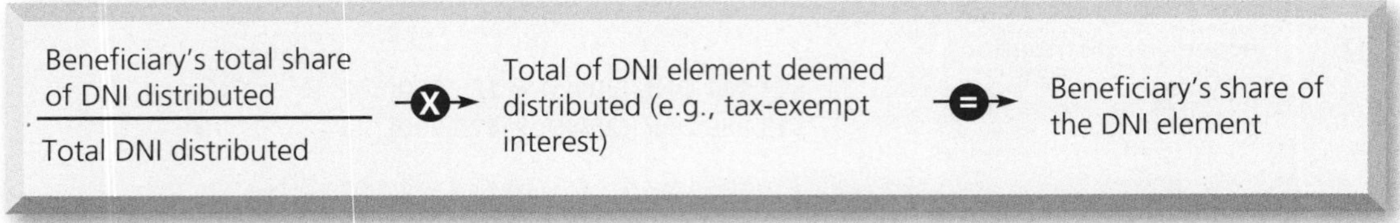

If the entity distributes only a part of its DNI, the amount of a specific class of DNI that is deemed distributed must first be determined.

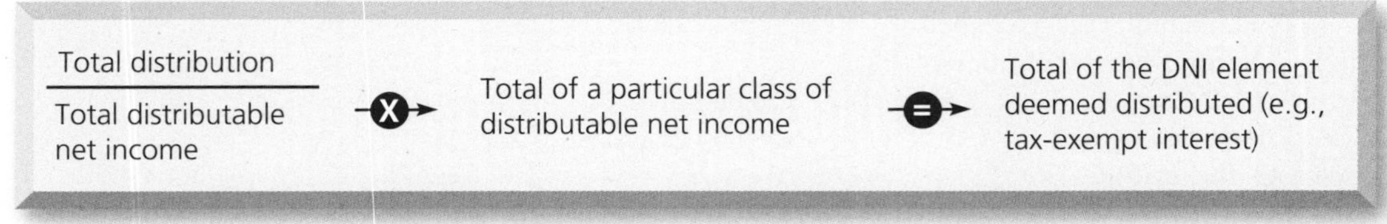

EXAMPLE 31

The Baron Trust has DNI of $40,000, including the following: $10,000 of taxable interest, $10,000 of tax-exempt interest, and $20,000 of passive activity income. The trustee distributes, at her discretion, $8,000 to Mike and $12,000 to Nancy.

Beneficiary	Amount Received	Income Type: Taxable Interest	Exempt Interest	Passive Income
Mike	$ 8,000	$2,000*	$2,000	$4,000
Nancy	12,000	3,000	3,000	6,000

* $8,000 distribution/$40,000 total DNI × $10,000 taxable interest in DNI. ■

EXAMPLE 32

Continue with the facts of Example 31. The character of the income that flows through to Mike and Nancy is effective for all other tax purposes. For instance, the $2,000 exempt interest allocated to Mike is used in computing the taxable portion of any Social Security benefits Mike receives. If this exempt interest relates to bonds issued to fund nonessential activities of the issuing agency (and not issued during 2009 and 2010), Mike includes a $2,000 AMT preference on his current-year return.

The $4,000 passive activity income that is allocated to Mike is available for offset against passive losses that he incurred from limited partnerships and rental activities for the year. Similarly, the $3,000 taxable interest income allocated to Nancy can be used to increase the amount of investment interest expense deductible by her in the year of the flow-through. The interest is treated as portfolio income to the same extent as that received directly by the taxpayer. ■

Special Allocations

Under limited circumstances, the parties may modify the character-of-income allocation method set forth above. A modification is permitted only to the extent the allocation is required in the trust instrument and only to the extent it has an

[30]Reg. § 1.662(b)–1 seems to allow special allocations, but see *Harkness v. U.S.*, 72–2 USTC ¶9740, 30 AFTR 2d 72–5754, 469 F.2d 310 (Ct.Cls., 1972).

economic effect independent of the cash-flow and income tax consequences of the allocation.[31]

EXAMPLE 33

Return to the facts in Example 31. Assume that the beneficiaries are elderly individuals who have pooled their investment portfolios to avail themselves of the trustee's professional asset management skills. Suppose the trustee has the discretion to allocate different classes of income to different beneficiaries and she designates $10,000 of Nancy's $12,000 distribution as being from the tax-exempt income. Such a designation *would not be recognized* for tax purposes, and the allocation method of Example 31 must be used.

Suppose, however, the trust instrument stipulated that Nancy was to receive all of the income from the tax-exempt securities because she alone contributed the exempt securities to trust corpus. Under this provision, the $10,000 of the nontaxable interest is paid to Nancy. This allocation *is recognized*, and $10,000 of Nancy's distribution is tax-exempt. ■

Losses in the Termination Year

The ordinary net operating and capital losses of a trust or an estate do not flow through to the entity's beneficiaries, as would such losses from a partnership or an S corporation. However, in the year in which an entity terminates its existence, the beneficiaries do receive a direct benefit from the loss carryovers of the trust or estate.[32]

Net operating losses and net capital losses are subject to the same carryover rules that otherwise apply to an individual. Consequently, NOLs can be carried back 2 years and then carried forward 20 years, while net capital losses can be carried forward only and for an indefinite period of time.

If the entity incurs a negative taxable income in the last year of its existence, the excess of deductions over the entity's gross income flows through directly to the beneficiaries. The net loss is available as a deduction *from* AGI in the beneficiary's tax year with or within which the entity's tax year ends. The amount allowed is in proportion to the relative amount of corpus assets that each beneficiary receives upon the termination of the entity, and it is subject to the 2-percent-of-AGI floor.

Any carryovers of the entity's other losses flow through to the beneficiaries in the year of termination in proportion to the relative amount of corpus assets that each beneficiary receives. The character of the loss carryover is retained by the beneficiary, except that a carryover of a net capital loss to a corporate beneficiary is always treated as short term. Beneficiaries who are individuals use these carryovers as deductions *for* AGI.

EXAMPLE 34

The Edgar Estate terminates on December 31, 2012. It had used a fiscal year ending July 31. For the termination year, the estate incurred a $15,000 negative taxable income. In addition, the estate had an unused NOL carryover of $23,000 from the year ending July 31, 2007, and an unused net long-term capital loss carryover of $10,000 from the year ending July 31, 2010. Dawn receives $60,000 of corpus upon termination, and Blue Corporation receives the remaining $40,000. Dawn and Blue are calendar year taxpayers.

Dawn can claim an itemized deduction of $9,000 [($60,000/$100,000) × $15,000] for the entity's negative taxable income in the year of termination. This deduction is subject to the 2%-of-AGI floor on her miscellaneous itemized deductions. In addition, Dawn can claim a $13,800 deduction *for* AGI in 2012 (60% × $23,000) for Edgar's NOL carryover, and she can use $6,000 of the estate's net long-term capital loss carryover with her other 2012 capital transactions.

Blue receives ordinary business deductions in 2012 for Edgar's NOLs: $6,000 for the loss in the year of termination and $9,200 for the carryover from fiscal 2007. Moreover, Blue can use the $4,000 carryover of Edgar's net capital losses to offset against its other 2012 capital transactions, although the loss must be treated as short-term. ■

[31]Reg. § 1.652(b)–2(b). This is similar to the § 704(b)(2) requirement for partnerships.

[32]Reg. §§ 1.642(h)−1 and −2.

The Sixty-Five-Day Rule

Amounts paid or credited to the beneficiaries in the first 65 days of the estate or trust's tax year may be treated as paid on the last day of the preceding taxable year.[33] This provision offers the trustee some flexibility in timing distributions so that entity-level accumulations can be avoided.

20.5 Grantor Trusts

LO.4

Use the special rules that apply to trusts where the creator (grantor) of the trust retains certain rights.

A series of special provisions applies when the grantor of the trust retains beneficial enjoyment or substantial control over the trust property or income.[34] In that event, the grantor is taxed on the trust income, and the trust is disregarded for income tax purposes. The person who is taxed on the income is allowed to claim, on his or her own return, any deductions or credits attributable to the income. Such taxes restrict the grantor's ability to redirect the income recognized from trust corpus to the trust or its beneficiaries. The trustee still files a Form 1041, but no dollar amounts are included on the mostly "blank" return. All income and deduction items are reported on the grantor's Form 1040.

Reversionary Trusts

Creation of virtually any new reversionary trust is subject to the Federal gift tax. If the grantor dies before the income interest expires, the present value of the reversionary interest is included in his or her gross estate; thus, a Federal estate tax could also result.

Powers Retained by the Grantor

Other restrictions apply concerning the extent of the powers over the trust the grantor can retain without incurring grantor trust status.[35] If any of these provisions is violated, the income of the trust is taxed to the grantor and the usual Subchapter J rules do not apply to the trust.

The grantor is taxed on the income if he or she retains (1) the beneficial enjoyment of corpus or (2) the power to dispose of the trust income without the approval or consent of any adverse party. An *adverse party* is any person having a substantial beneficial interest in the trust who could be affected adversely by the power the grantor possesses over the trust assets.[36]

A number of important powers, including the following, will *not* cause such income to be taxed to the grantor.[37]

- To apply the income toward the support of the grantor's dependents (except to the extent it actually is applied for this purpose).[38]
- To allocate trust income or corpus among charitable beneficiaries.
- To invade corpus on behalf of a designated beneficiary.
- To withhold income from a beneficiary during his or her minority or disability.
- To allocate receipts and disbursements between income and corpus.

The retention by the grantor or a nonadverse party of certain administrative powers over the trust causes the income to be taxed to the grantor. Such powers include those to deal with trust income or corpus for less than full and adequate consideration and to borrow from the trust without providing adequate interest or security.[39]

[33]See Reg. § 1.663(b)–2 for the manner and timing of the election.

[34]§§ 671–679.

[35]§§ 674–677.

[36]§§ 672(a), (b), and 674. See Reg. § 1.672(a)–1 for examples of adverse party situations.

[37]§ 674(b).

[38]§ 677(b).

[39]See Reg. § 1.675–1(b) for a further discussion of this matter.

TAX IN THE NEWS Don't Trust Your Dictionary

Today, the middle and upper classes are often including trusts in their estate plans. Usually, the purpose of the trust is to spare the survivors the time and effort required to work through a state's probate proceedings.

But planning for death can sometimes lead to confusion about terminology, especially between a living trust and a living will. A "living trust" is typically created to hold the assets of the decedent-to-be, including investments, homestead, and household goods. Assets are retitled in the name of the trustee, who periodically files a Form 1041 for the new entity. The idea underlying the living trust is to reduce the probate estate. This, in turn, lowers the fees for carrying out the probate process. Such fees often total 5 percent or so of the date of death value of the probate assets.

The living trust accomplishes virtually no Federal tax savings. The trust assets are included in the decedent's gross estate, as the living trust is an incomplete transfer (see Chapter 18). For the most part, the entity is treated as a grantor trust. Because of the retained investment and distribution powers, the donor is still liable for taxes on the taxable income of the fiduciary.

A "living will," on the other hand, is a document that conveys powers to relatives and third parties to make medical and financial decisions when the decedent-to-be can no longer do so. More appropriately referred to as a "medical power of attorney," the document expresses the person's wishes as to how and when to reduce specified medical treatments (including directives for removing life support systems).

The proper use of these documents can become tricky under controlling state law when same-sex couples are involved. The adviser must assist the clients in determining whether a same-sex partner or spouse can qualify as the holder of a medical power of attorney and whether special issues arise when a same-sex partner or spouse is named a trustee of a living trust.

The grantor of a trust is taxed on the trust's income if he or she (or a nonadverse party) possesses the power to revoke the trust.[40] In addition, a grantor is taxed on all or part of the income of a trust when, without the consent of any adverse party, the income is or, at the discretion of the grantor or a nonadverse party (or both), may be:

- Distributed to the grantor or the grantor's spouse.
- Held or accumulated for future distribution to the grantor or the grantor's spouse.
- Applied to the payment of premiums on insurance policies on the life of the grantor or the grantor's spouse.[41]

EXAMPLE 35

Frank creates an irrevocable trust for his children with a transfer of income-producing property and an insurance policy on the life of Marion, his wife. During the year, the trustee uses $3,000 of the trust income to pay the premiums on the policy covering Marion's life. Frank is taxed on $3,000 of the trust's income. ■

Moreover, trust income accumulated for the benefit of someone whom the grantor is *legally obligated* to support is taxed to the grantor, but only to the extent it is actually applied for that purpose.[42]

EXAMPLE 36

Melanie creates an irrevocable accumulation trust. Her son, Sean, is the life beneficiary, and the remainder goes to any grandchildren. During the year, the trust income of $8,000 is applied as follows: $5,000 toward Sean's college tuition and other related educational expenses and $3,000 accumulated on Sean's behalf. If, under state law, Melanie has an obligation to support Sean and if this obligation includes providing a college education, Melanie is taxed on the $5,000 that is so applied. ■

[40] § 676.

[41] § 677(a).

[42] § 677(b). The taxpayer's legal obligations vary according to state law, financial resources, and family expectations. See *Frederick C. Braun, Jr.*, 48 TCM 210, T.C.Memo. 1984–285, and *Cristopher Stone*, 54 TCM 462, T.C.Memo. 1987–454.

20.6 Procedural Matters

The fiduciary is required to file a Form 1041 (U.S. Income Tax Return for Estates and Trusts) in the following situations.[43]

- For an estate that has gross income of $600 or more for the year.
- For a trust that either has any taxable income or, if there is no taxable income, has gross income of $600 or more.

The fiduciary return (and any related tax liability) is due, before extensions, no later than the fifteenth day of the fourth month following the close of the entity's taxable year. The IRS encourages electronic filing of the Form 1041 and schedules. A paper return is filed with the Internal Revenue Service in Cincinnati, Ohio, or Ogden, Utah, depending on the location of the fiduciary's principal place of business.

Many fiduciary entities recognize capital gains during the year, through sales of assets that are part of corpus. In that event, a Schedule D is filed with the Form 1041, and the fiduciary entity or its beneficiaries can qualify for the favorable 15 percent (or lower) tax rate on long-term capital gains.

The pass-through of income and deduction items to the beneficiary is accomplished through Schedule K-1 to Form 1041. This form is similar in format and function to the Schedule K–1 for partners and S corporation shareholders (see Chapters 10 and 12). Because the typical fiduciary entity records only a few transactions during the year, the Schedule K–1 for Form 1041 is less detailed than those for Forms 1065 and 1120S. See the specimen Form 1041 and schedules in Appendix B to this text.

Trusts and estates are required to make estimated Federal income tax payments using the same quarterly schedule that applies to individual taxpayers. This requirement applies to estates and grantor trusts only for tax years that end two or more years after the date of the decedent's death. Charitable trusts and private foundations are exempt from estimated payment requirements altogether.[44]

The two-year estimated tax exception for estates recognizes the liquidity problems that an executor often faces during the early months of administering the estate. The exception does not ensure, however, that an estate in existence less than 24 months will never be required to make an estimated tax payment.

EXAMPLE 37

Juanita died on March 15, 2012. Her executor elected a fiscal year ending on July 31 for the estate. Estimated tax payments will be required from the estate starting with the tax year that begins on August 1, 2013. ■

20.7 Tax Planning

LO.5

Apply the Subchapter J rules in a manner that minimizes the income taxation of trusts and estates and still accomplishes the intended objectives of the grantor or decedent.

Many of the tax planning possibilities for estates and trusts were discussed in Chapter 19. However, several specific tax planning possibilities are available to help minimize the income tax effects on estates and trusts and their beneficiaries.

A Trust or an Estate as an Income-Shifting Device

The compressed tax rate schedule applicable to Subchapter J entities may have reversed the traditional techniques by which families set aside funds for long-term activities such as business startups, college education, and home purchases. When the tax rate schedules for trusts and estates were more accommodating, high-income individuals would shift income-producing assets to trusts to take advantage of the lower effective tax rate that would fall on the income accumulated within

[43]§§ 6012(a)(3) and (4).

[44]§ 6654(l).

CONCEPT SUMMARY 20.1

Principles of Fiduciary Taxation

1. Estates and trusts are temporary entities created to locate, maintain, and distribute assets and to satisfy liabilities according to the wishes of the decedent or grantor as expressed in the will or trust document.
2. Generally, the estate or trust acts as a conduit of the taxable income that it receives. To the extent the income is distributed by the entity, it is taxed to the beneficiary. Taxable income retained by the entity is taxed to the entity itself.
3. The entity's accounting income must first be determined. Accounting conventions that are stated in the controlling document or, lacking such provisions, in state law allocate specific items of receipt and expenditure either to income or to corpus. Income beneficiaries typically receive payments from the entity that are equal to the accounting income.
4. The taxable income of the entity is computed using the scheme in Figure 20.2. The entity usually recognizes income in respect of a decedent. Deductions for fiduciary's fees and for charitable contributions may be reduced if the entity received any tax-exempt income during the year. Cost recovery deductions are assigned proportionately to the recipients of accounting income. Upon election, realized gain or loss on assets that are properly distributed in kind can be recognized by the entity.
5. A distribution deduction, computationally derived from distributable net income (DNI), is allowed to the entity. DNI is the maximum amount on which entity beneficiaries can be taxed. Moreover, the constitution of DNI is preserved for the recipients of the distributions.
6. Additional taxes are levied under Subchapter J to discourage the retention of excessive administrative powers by the grantor of a trust when the gross income is taxed to a lower-bracket beneficiary.

the trust. The target of the plan, usually a child, would receive the accumulated income (and, perhaps, trust corpus) at a designated age, and more funds would be available because a lower tax rate had been applied over the life of the investment in the trust.

Today, such an income shift would *deplete*, rather than shelter, the family's assets, as the rates falling on individuals are much more graduated than are those applicable to fiduciaries, and the kiddie tax also penalizes attempts to shift taxable income to children. Assuming that the objectives of the plan remain unchanged, possible strategies in view of these rate changes include the following.

- Trust corpus should be invested in growth assets that are low on yield but high on appreciation, so that the trustee can determine the timing of the gain and somewhat control the effective tax rate that applies.
- Trust corpus should be invested in tax-exempt securities such as municipal bonds and mutual funds that invest in them to eliminate the tax costs associated with the investment. If this approach is taken, a trust might be unnecessary—the parent should simply retain full control over the assets and invest in the exempt securities in his or her own account.
- The grantor should retain high-yield assets, so that control over the assets is not surrendered when the tax cost is too high.
- Use of trust vehicles should be reserved for cases where professional management of the assets is necessary for portfolio growth and the additional tax costs can be justified.

Income Tax Planning for Estates

As a separate taxable entity, an estate can select its own tax year and accounting methods. The executor of an estate should consider selecting a fiscal year because this will determine when beneficiaries must include income distributions from the estate in their own tax returns. Beneficiaries must include the income for their tax year with or within which the estate's tax year ends. Proper selection of the estate's tax year can result in a smoothing out of income and a reduction of the income taxes for all parties involved.

TAX IN THE NEWS Trusts Can Hide Assets and Income

Some persons are inclined toward privacy and want to hide some or all of their assets, income, and other financial information from others. The reasons for such concealment could involve family (e.g., spouses); business partners; governmental authorities; and, most often, general creditors. Offshore trusts and business entities have served this purpose for many years, but now these persons might want to consider the use of a domestic asset protection trust (APT) for the same purpose.

States such as Delaware, Nevada, and South Dakota have been most aggressive in attracting investment assets by relaxing their laws about how trusts can conceal financial information. An APT does not reduce Federal tax liabilities—they are revocable grantor trusts, and the grantor continues to receive the pass-through of income and expenses from the trust's operations.

But, often, creditors have no access to the APT's assets or income once a notice period of perhaps two years has passed from the date the entity was established. A bankruptcy proceeding can reach the assets and income of the APT, but ex-spouses and general creditors cannot.

Not all states have the same rules governing APTs. An interested taxpayer should determine whether a particular state's APT protects assets for an out-of-state grantor. Moreover, an APT can be an expensive proposition—perhaps $15,000 to set up and $5,000 per year in annual fees to keep the simplest APT operational.

Would not an LLC or some umbrella liability insurance coverage accomplish the same asset protection and privacy objectives? Or are there other less ethical motivations for the grantor's interest in an APT? "Know your client" is good advice for a tax adviser when an APT becomes the topic of conversation.

Caution should be taken in determining when the estate is to be terminated. Selecting a fiscal year for the estate can result in a bunching of income to the beneficiaries in the year in which the estate is closed. Prolonging the termination of an estate can be effective income tax planning, but the IRS carefully examines the purpose of keeping the estate open. Because the unused losses of an estate pass through to the beneficiaries only in the termination year, the estate should be closed when the beneficiaries can enjoy the maximum tax benefit of the losses.

The timing and amounts of income distributions to the beneficiaries also present important tax planning opportunities. If the executor can make discretionary income distributions, he or she should evaluate the relative marginal income tax rates of the estate and its beneficiaries. By timing the distributions properly, the overall income tax liability can be minimized. Care should be taken, however, to time the distributions in light of the estate's DNI.

EXAMPLE 38

For several years before his death on March 7, Don had entered into annual deferred compensation agreements with his employer. These agreements collectively called for the payment of $200,000 six months after Don's retirement or death. To provide a maximum 12-month period within which to generate deductions to offset this large item of income in respect of a decedent, the executor or administrator of the estate should elect a fiscal year ending August 31. The election is made simply by filing the estate's first tax return for the short period of March 7 to August 31. ■

EXAMPLE 39

Carol, the sole beneficiary of an estate, is a calendar year, cash basis taxpayer. If the estate elects a fiscal year ending January 31, all distributions during the period of February 1 to December 31, 2012, are reported on Carol's tax return for calendar year 2013 (due April 15, 2014). Thus, assuming estimated tax requirements have otherwise been met, any income taxes that result from a $50,000 distribution made by the estate on February 20, 2012, may be deferred until April 15, 2014. ■

EXAMPLE 40

Assume the same facts as in Example 39. If the estate is closed on December 15, 2013, the DNI for both the fiscal year ending January 31, 2013, and the final tax year ending December 15, 2013, is included in Carol's tax return for the same calendar year. To avoid the effect of this bunching of income, the estate should not be closed until early in calendar year 2014. ■

EXAMPLE 41

Review Examples 28 and 29 carefully. Note, for instance, the flexibility that is available to the executor or administrator in timing the second-tier distributions of income and corpus of the estate. To illustrate, if Washington is subject to a high tax rate, distributions to him should be minimized except in years when DNI is low. In this manner, Washington's exposure to gross income from the distributions can be controlled so that most of the distributions he receives will be free of income tax. ■

In general, those beneficiaries who are subject to high income tax rates should be made beneficiaries of second-tier (but not IRD) distributions of the estate. Most likely, these individuals will have less need for an additional steady stream of (taxable) income while their income tax savings can be relatively large. Moreover, a special allocation of tax-favored types of income and expenses should be considered. For example, tax-exempt income can be directed more easily to beneficiaries in higher income tax brackets.

Income Tax Planning with Trusts

The great variety of trusts provides the grantor, trustee, and beneficiaries with excellent opportunities for tax planning. Many of the same tax planning opportunities available to the executor of an estate are available to the trustee. For instance, the distributions from a trust are taxable to the trust's beneficiaries to the extent of the trust's DNI. If income distributions are discretionary, the trustee can time the distributions to minimize the income tax consequences to all parties.

ETHICS & EQUITY Who Should Be a Trustee?

For decades, grantors have chosen a family member to be the trustee of the family savings, the children's education fund, or whatever other assets are placed into management by the trust. The relative chosen is often the most trusted but not always the one with the business sense. Now, however, as the financial work has become more complex, with wild stock market fluctuations, increased fiduciary standards, and potential conflicts of interest, some are questioning the wisdom of using a family member as the trustee.

Using a trust company or other financial institution as a trustee usually results in more stable investment returns, eliminating both the highs and the lows of the stock market cycle. Institutions can also bring other advantages.

- They do not die, run away, become mentally or physically incapacitated, or otherwise unexpectedly become unqualified for the position.
- They are not easily swayed by emotional appeals; nor do they react to family jealousies.
- They are prohibited by law from acting under a conflict of interest, such as might exist between family members when the related trustee is also a trust beneficiary.

On the negative side, human trustees often waive or discount their fiduciary fee, while institutions do not. Especially for trusts with a small corpus, institutional trustees can be prohibitively expensive. And the trust company most often is oriented toward expanding its customer base, rather than offering individual attention to existing clients.

How would you advise a client to address this delicate issue? Compromise solutions might be to:

- Appoint co-trustees. Aunt Grace or Uncle Roberto can provide the personal touch and ensure that trust decisions recognize family needs, while the trust company maximizes investment returns and furnishes professional management.
- Keep the family trustee, but hire professionals to provide advice only when needed, at an hourly rate. This approach avoids the fees based on asset values that trust companies usually charge.
- Use the advisory services of the mutual funds in which trust assets are invested, to manage and distribute the corpus and income.

Distributions of In-Kind Property

The ability of the trustee or executor to elect to recognize the realized gain or loss relative to a distributed noncash asset allows the gain or loss to be allocated to the optimal taxpayer.

EXAMPLE 42

The Yorba Linda Estate distributed some inventory, basis of $40,000 and fair market value of $41,500, to beneficiary Larry. Yorba Linda is subject to a 15% marginal income tax rate, and Larry is subject to a 33% marginal rate. The executor of Yorba Linda should elect that the entity recognize the related $1,500 realized gain, thereby subjecting the gain to the estate's lower marginal tax rate.

Tax without election, at Larry's 33% rate	$495
Tax with election, at trust's 15% rate	225

■

Deductibility of Fiduciary Expenses

Some deductions and losses may be claimed either on the estate tax return or as income tax deductions of the estate on the fiduciary return, at the taxpayer's choice.[45] In such a case, the deduction for income tax purposes is not allowed unless the estate tax deduction is waived. These deductions can be apportioned between the two returns.

EXAMPLE 43

Don's will named his surviving spouse, Donna, as the executor of his estate. The estate's assets total $10 million. The will includes bequests to pay various debts, make gifts to certain charities, and provide for the grandchildren through trusts. The will also allows for the payment of an executor's fee equal to 5% of the assets ($500,000).

Should Donna pay herself an executor's fee? If Donna is the estate's remainder beneficiary, a common occurrence, payment of the fee would result in the following.

- A deduction by the estate on the Form 706 (e.g., at the 35% marginal rate) or the estate's Form 1041 (at the 35% marginal rate).
- Gross income for services to Donna (e.g., at her individual 35% marginal tax rate).

If Donna waives the executor's fee, she will receive the $500,000 as the remainder beneficiary of the estate. Then the results would be:

- An increased marital deduction on the Form 706 (deductible at the 35% tax rate).
- No gross income to Donna, as the receipt of a bequest is nontaxable.

Almost certainly, a remainder beneficiary who is a surviving spouse would waive the fee.

If Donna is not the remainder beneficiary of the estate, the analysis becomes more difficult. Claiming the $500,000 as a fee will change the amounts the charities and grandchildren receive, because the estate assets will have been reduced.

A surviving spouse, now perhaps the head of the family, will find this a difficult choice to make while fulfilling her executor duties. ■

An expense deductible for estate tax purposes may not qualify as an income tax deduction. Interest expense incurred to carry tax-exempt bonds is disallowed for income tax purposes. If this expense is not claimed for estate tax purposes, it is completely lost.

EXAMPLE 44

The executor of Dana's estate pays $5,000 in burial expenses (authorized under local law and approved by the probate court) from estate assets. The $5,000 expense should be claimed on the estate tax return, as it is not deductible at all for income tax purposes. ■

Duties of an Executor

One of the duties of an estate's executor is to file the last income tax return of the decedent.[46] That Form 1040 is due on April 15 of the year following the date of

[45] § 642(g) and Reg. § 20.2053-1(d).

[46] § 6012(b)(1).

death, regardless of when during the year death occurs.[47] The decedent's tax year ends on the date of death, but any personal and dependency exemptions, and standard deduction, are not reduced even though a short tax year results.

The final Form 1040 may be filed simply to claim a refund of the decedent's estimated tax payments or withholdings. However, it includes gross income and deductions to the point of death and can result in income tax being due. If the decedent was married on the date of death, a joint return can be filed, with signatures of both the executor and the surviving spouse.[48]

Medical expenses incurred by the decedent but unpaid at the time of the decedent's death are treated with a special rule. If paid by the estate during a one-year period beginning with the day after death, the expenses may be claimed as an income tax deduction in the year incurred or as an estate tax deduction, but not both.[49] The expenses may be divided in any way between the decedent's Form 1040 and his or her estate tax return.

REFOCUS ON THE BIG PICTURE

Setting Up a Trust to Protect a Family

Anna Jiang and her family should consider the creation of one or more trusts to provide security in case Anna is incapacitated by medical problems and unable to manage the family's finances. One suggestion for the family might be:

1. Anna transfers some or all of the $2 million assets to the Jiang Family Trust, with quarterly income payable to Tom and the children. Recipients would be designated by the trustee, but all of the entity's accounting income must be distributed. In this way, the income could be directed to the beneficiary most in need (e.g., to pay for education expenses or to start a new business). The children could be named first-tier beneficiaries, with Tom as a second-tier income beneficiary.
2. While Anna is still healthy and earning a regular salary, the trustee could accumulate the accounting income and allow the corpus to build up. Alternatively, the trustee could make gifts to charity or fund education plans for Bobby and Sally.
3. Anna should provide clear instructions to the trustee as to her preferences on how the trust corpus should be invested and specify which of Tom's and the children's expenses should and should not be covered.
4. The children should be named as remainder beneficiaries of the Jiang Family Trust. In case the trust corpus exceeds the estate tax bypass amount, other remainder beneficiaries could be named to avoid any generation-skipping tax (see Chapters 18 and 19).
5. Amendments to the trust document should be considered whenever Tom and Anna update their wills.

What If?

If Anna remains healthy, the Jiang Family Trust might be terminated when the children reach the age of majority, as the need for financial support will have diminished. However, if Tom is unable or unwilling to take over management of the assets, the trust should continue. In this event, the trustee might shift the focus to funding long-term care for the couple, making charitable gifts, or financing the education needs of grandchildren.

The controlling trust document should be worded to provide flexibility as to the purposes and termination date of the trust. The trustee should be chosen from family members or business associates who know Anna and Tom well and are familiar with the couple's objectives.

[47] Reg. § 1.6072–1(b).

[48] § 6013(a). If an executor has not yet been appointed by the due date of a Form 1040, the surviving spouse signs for both taxpayers on a joint return. This also might occur for the prior year (when the spouse was alive) if the return for that year has not yet been filed.

[49] § 213(c).

KEY TERMS

Complex trust, 20-4
Corpus, 20-4
Distributable net income (DNI), 20-18
Expenses in respect of a decedent, 20-13
Grantor, 20-3
Grantor trusts, 20-4
Income in respect of a decedent (IRD), 20-12
Reversionary interest, 20-4
Simple trust, 20-4
Sprinkling trust, 20-4

DISCUSSION QUESTIONS

Communications

1. **LO.1** A local bank has asked you to speak at its Building Personal Wealth Conference on the topic of "What Should Your Trust Do for You?" Develop at least four PowerPoint slides, each one listing a function that a trust might be able to accomplish for an individual who has more than a modest level of financial resources.

2. **LO.1** Trusts and estates are known as *fiduciary* entities, in that a legal structure is formed to accomplish the financial and other goals of one or more individuals. List the parties who must be identified when a trust is created, and describe the responsibilities of each. Do the same for an estate.

3. **LO.1** Define the following terms.
   a. Income interest.
   b. Remainder interest.
   c. Reversionary interest.
   d. Life tenant.
   e. Term certain.

4. **LO.1** Some fiduciary entities are known as *simple trusts*, while others are *complex trusts*. How does the tax professional know whether a trust is simple or complex? When is this determination made?

5. **LO.1** In general terms, describe how the following entities are subject to the Federal income tax. (Answer only for the entity, not for its owners, beneficiaries, etc.)
   a. C corporations (Subchapter C).
   b. Partnerships (Subchapter K).
   c. S corporations (Subchapter S).
   d. Trusts and estates (Subchapter J).

Communications

6. **LO.1** Your college's accounting group has asked you to give a 10-minute speech titled "Trusts, Estates, and the AMT." The audience will be students who have completed at least one course concerning Federal income taxation. Develop a brief outline for your remarks.

7. **LO.1** Create a fact pattern that illustrates each of the following tax situations. Be specific.
   a. A simple trust.
   b. A complex trust with a $300 personal exemption.
   c. A complex trust with a $100 personal exemption.

8. **LO.2** Using Figure 20.2 as a guide, describe the computation of a fiduciary entity's accounting income, taxable income, and distributable net income.

9. **LO.2** The Liu Trust is short of cash. It is required to distribute $100,000 to Yang every year, and that payment is due in six weeks. In its asset corpus, Liu holds a number of investments that are valued at $100,000. One of them is a plot of land with a tax basis to the trust of $80,000. Assuming that the trust agreement allows, what are the Federal income tax consequences if Liu distributes this land to Yang?

Decision Making

10. **LO.2** In its first tax year, the Vasquez Estate generated $50,000 of taxable interest income and $30,000 of tax-exempt interest income. It paid fiduciary fees of $8,000. The estate is subject to a 35% marginal estate tax rate and a 40% marginal income tax rate. How should the executor assign the deductions for the payment of the fees?

11. **LO.2** The Sterling Trust owns a business and generated $100,000 in depreciation deductions for the tax year. Mona is one of the income beneficiaries of the entity. Given the following information, can Mona deduct any of the Sterling depreciation on her Form 1040? If so, how much is her deduction?

Sterling's taxable income from the business	$ 800,000
Sterling's gross income from the business	4,000,000
Mona's share of trust accounting income	500,000
Total trust accounting income	2,500,000
Mona's share of distributable net income	1,200,000
Total distributable net income	1,600,000

12. **LO.2** In 2012, the Helpful Trust agreed to make a $90,000 contribution to Local Soup Kitchen, a charitable organization. Helpful's board agreed to the gift at a November 2012 meeting, but the check was not issued until February 20, 2013 (i.e., during the next tax year). Can the trust claim a charitable contribution deduction? If so, describe how Helpful should treat its gift.

13. **LO.3** One of the key concepts in fiduciary income taxation is that of *distributable net income* (DNI). List the major functions of DNI on one PowerPoint slide, with no more than five bullets, to present to your classmates as part of the discussion of this chapter of the text. Just review the uses of DNI in Subchapter J, and do not discuss its computation. **Communications**

14. **LO.3** Use the following chart to indicate whether each of the indicated items is included in distributable net income (DNI).

Fiduciary Entity Item	Included in DNI?
Taxable interest income	?
Tax-exempt interest income	?
Capital gain allocable to corpus	?

15. **LO.2, 3, 5** The Flan Trust is scheduled to terminate in two years, when Amy Flan reaches age 30. Several years ago, the trust operated a business that generated a sizable NOL carryforward that the trust has not been able to use. In addition, due to a bearish stock market, the value of the entity's investment portfolio has declined 15% from its purchase price. What issues must you consider in advising Amy and the corporate trustee? **Issue ID**

16. **LO.4** Jada wants to transfer some assets to a trust this year; the income beneficiaries will be her two grandchildren. The trust income and assets will be used to pay the grandchildren's tuition to private high schools and universities. Upon the younger grandchild's graduation, the trust assets will return to Jada's ownership. Identify tax issues related to Jada's plan to use a temporary fiduciary entity. **Issue ID**

17. **LO.4** Carol has been promoted several times, and she may be named a partner next year. Thus, she will be subject to higher marginal income tax rates than in the past. Carol's colleague Isaiah has told her about a "college education trust" from which he pays tuition and fees for his children. He has implied that there are sizable tax advantages to setting up a trust for this purpose. **Decision Making** **Communications**

    Carol is considering establishing a similar trust to pay tuition for her own children. She believes that the trust will be able to deduct the tuition payments, something that she cannot currently do on her Form 1040. Write a memo for the tax research file addressing Carol's ideas.

18. **LO.1, 4** The Strauss Trust must file a Form 1041 for the first time, because it has recognized about $18,000 of gross income. Corpus assets are transferred to the trust on August 30. Considering only the Federal income tax effects of the creation of Strauss:
    a. What tax year should the trust select?
    b. Where should the completed Form 1041 be sent?

19. **LO.5** For tax planning purposes, should an estate adopt a calendar or a fiscal tax year? Why?

Decision Making

20. **LO.5** Comment on the following items relative to tax planning strategies of a fiduciary entity.
   a. To reduce taxes for a typical family, should income be shifted *to* a trust or *from* a trust? Why?
   b. From a tax planning standpoint, who should invest in tax-exempt bonds, the trust or its beneficiaries?
   c. To reduce overall taxes, should a high-income, wealthy beneficiary be assigned to the first or second tier of trust distributions? Why?
   d. To minimize taxes, how should a trust treat the distribution of an in-kind asset? Why?

PROBLEMS

21. **LO.1** Complete the following chart, indicating the comparative attributes of the typical simple trust and complex trust by answering yes/no or explaining the differences between the entities where appropriate.

Attribute	Simple Trust	Complex Trust
Trust could incur its own tax liability for the year	________	________
Trust generally distributes all of the DNI	________	________
Trust can deduct its charitable contributions in the year of, or the year after, payment	________	________
Trust could claim a foreign tax credit	________	________
Maximum tax rate on net long-term capital gains = 15%	________	________
AMT preferences and adjustments flow through to beneficiaries ratably	________	________
Trust can adopt the FIFO method for its inventory assets; the grantor had been using lower of cost or market	________	________
Trust can use a tax year other than the calendar year	________	________
Amount of personal exemption	________	________

22. **LO.1** Compute the Federal income tax liability for the Valerio Trust. The entity reports the following transactions for the 2012 tax year. The trustee accumulates all accounting income for the year.

Operating income from a business	$ 400,000
Dividend income, all from U.S. corporations	30,000
Interest income, City of San Antonio bonds	40,000
Fiduciary fees, deductible portion	(10,000)
Net rental losses, passive activity	(100,000)

23. **LO.1** The Purple Trust incurred the following items this year.

Taxable interest income	$75,000
Tax-exempt interest income, not on private activity bonds	60,000
Tax-exempt interest income, on private activity bonds (not issued during 2009 or 2010)	25,000

Compute Purple's tentative minimum tax for the year. Purple does not have any credits available to reduce the AMT liability.

Decision Making

24. **LO.2** The Polozzi Trust will incur the following items in the next tax year, its first year of existence.

Interest income	$ 25,000
Rent income	100,000

Cost recovery deductions for the rental activity	$ 35,000
Capital gain income	40,000
Fiduciary and tax preparation fees	7,000

Betty, the grantor of the trust, is working with you on the language in the trust instrument relative to the derivation of annual accounting income for the entity. She will name Shirley as the sole income beneficiary and Benny as the remainder beneficiary.

a. Suggest language to Betty that will maximize the annual income distribution to Shirley.

b. Suggest language to Betty that will minimize the annual distribution to Shirley and maximize the accumulation on Benny's behalf.

25. **LO.2** Complete the chart below, indicating the Calvet Trust's entity accounting income for each of the alternatives. For this purpose, use the following information.

Interest income, taxable	$300,000
Interest income, tax-exempt	30,000
Interest income, tax-exempt but AMT preference item	20,000
Long-term capital gain	25,000
Trustee fee	5,000

Trust Agreement Provisions	Trust Accounting Income
Fees and capital gains allocable to corpus	______
Capital gains allocable to corpus, one-half of fees allocable to income	______
Capital gains allocable to income, silent concerning allocation of fees	______
Fees and exempt income allocable to corpus, silent concerning allocation of capital gain/loss	______

26. **LO.1, 2, 3** Complete the following chart, indicating the comparative attributes of the typical trust and estate by answering yes/no or explaining the differences between the entities where appropriate.

Attribute	Estate	Trust
Separate income tax entity	______	______
Controlling document	______	______
Can have both income and remainder beneficiaries	______	______
Computes entity accounting income before determining entity taxable income	______	______
Termination date is determinable from controlling document	______	______
Legal owner of assets under fiduciary's control	______	______
Document identifies both income and remainder beneficiaries	______	______
Separate share rules apply	______	______
Generally must use calendar tax year	______	______

27. **LO.2** Roberto is one of the income beneficiaries of the Carol LeMans Estate. This year, as directed by the will, Roberto received all of the sales commissions that were earned and payable to Carol (cash basis) at her death, as well as one of three remaining installment payments. Compute Roberto's gross income attributable to Carol's activities for the current year, given the following financial data.

Sales commissions receivable	$60,000
Total ordinary gain on installment sale, two payments remaining after this year	50,000

28. **LO.2** Sanchez incurred the following items.

Business income	$80,000
Tax-exempt interest income	40,000
Payment to charity from 2012 income, paid 3/1/2013	20,000

Complete the following chart, indicating the charitable contributions deduction under the various assumptions.

Assumption	2012 Deduction for Contribution
Sanchez is a cash basis individual.	__________
Sanchez is an accrual basis corporation.	__________
Sanchez is a trust.	__________

29. **LO.2** The Twist Trust has generated $60,000 in depreciation deductions for the year. Its accounting income is $75,000. In computing this amount, pursuant to the trust document, depreciation was allocated to corpus. Accounting income was distributed at the trustee's discretion: $25,000 to Hernandez and $50,000 to Jackson.
    a. Compute the depreciation deductions that Hernandez, Jackson, and Twist may claim.
    b. Same as (a), except that depreciation was allocated to income.
    c. Same as (a), except that the trustee distributed $15,000 each to Hernandez and to Jackson and retained the remaining accounting income.
    d. Same as (a), except that Twist is an estate (and not a trust).

30. **LO.2, 3** The Ricardo Trust is a simple trust that correctly uses the calendar year for tax purposes. Its income beneficiaries (Lucy and Ethel) are entitled to the trust's annual accounting income in shares of one-half each. For the current calendar year, the trust generates ordinary income of $50,000, a long-term capital gain of $25,000 (allocable to corpus), and a trustee commission expense of $10,000 (allocable to corpus). Use the format of Figure 20.3 to address the following items.
    a. How much income is each beneficiary entitled to receive?
    b. What is the trust's DNI?
    c. What is the trust's taxable income?
    d. How much gross income is reported by each of the beneficiaries?

31. **LO.2, 3** Assume the same facts as in Problem 30, except that the trust instrument allocates the capital gain to income.
    a. How much income is each beneficiary entitled to receive?
    b. What is the trust's DNI?
    c. What is the trust's taxable income?
    d. How much gross income is reported by each of the beneficiaries?

32. **LO.3** Under the terms of the Lagos Trust instrument, the trustee has discretion to distribute or accumulate income on behalf of Willie, Sylvia, and Doris in equal shares. The trustee also can invade corpus for the benefit of any of the beneficiaries to the extent of each person's respective one-third interest in the trust.

    In the current year, the trust has DNI of $120,000. Distribution and accumulation amounts were as follows:

    - To Willie: $40,000 from DNI and $10,000 from corpus.
    - To Sylvia: $25,000. The remaining $15,000 DNI is accumulated.
    - To Doris: $0. The $40,000 DNI is accumulated.

    a. How much income is taxed to Willie? (*Hint*: Apply the separate share rule.)
    b. To Sylvia?
    c. To Doris?
    d. To Lagos?

33. **LO.3** The Lane Sisters Trust is required to distribute $60,000 annually equally to its two income beneficiaries, Clare and Renee. If trust income is not sufficient to pay these amounts, the trustee can invade corpus to the extent necessary. During the current year, the trust generates only taxable interest income and has DNI of $150,000; the trustee distributes $30,000 to Clare and $130,000 to Renee.
    a. How much of the $130,000 distributed to Renee is included in her gross income?
    b. How much of the $30,000 distributed to Clare is included in her gross income?
    c. Are these distributions first-tier or second-tier distributions?

34. **LO.3** The Dailey Estate has $100,000 of DNI, composed of $40,000 in dividends, $20,000 in taxable interest, $15,000 of passive activity income, and $25,000 in tax-exempt interest. The entity's two noncharitable income beneficiaries, Brenda and Del, receive cash distributions of $20,000 each. How much of each class of income is deemed to have been distributed to Brenda? To Del?

35. **LO.2, 3** The trustee of the Pieper Trust can distribute any amount of accounting income and corpus to the trust's beneficiaries, Lydia and Kent. This year, the trust incurred the following.

Taxable interest income	$40,000
Tax-exempt interest income	20,000
Long-term capital gains—allocable to corpus	80,000
Fiduciary's fees—allocable to corpus	9,000

The trustee distributed $26,000 to Lydia and $13,000 to Kent.
    a. What is Pieper's trust accounting income?
    b. What is Pieper's DNI?
    c. What is Pieper's taxable income?
    d. What amounts are taxed to each of the beneficiaries?

36. **LO.2** Each of the following items was incurred by José, the cash basis, calendar year decedent. Under the terms of the will, Dora took immediate ownership in all of José's assets, except the dividend-paying stock. The estate received José's final paycheck.

Decision Making

Applying the rules for income and deductions in respect of a decedent, indicate on which return each item should be reported: Dora's income tax return (Form 1040), the estate's first income tax return (Form 1041), or the estate's estate tax return (Form 706). More than one alternative may apply in some cases.

Item Incurred	Form(s) Reported on
a. Wages, last paycheck	________
b. State income tax withheld on last paycheck	________
c. Capital gain portion of installment payment received	________
d. Ordinary income portion of installment payment received	________
e. Dividend income, record date was two days prior to José's death	________
f. Unrealized appreciation on a mutual fund investment	________
g. Depreciation recapture accrued as of date of death	________
h. Medical expenses of last illness	________
i. Apartment building, rents accrued but not collected as of death	________
j. Apartment building, property tax accrued and assessed but not paid as of death	________

37. **LO.4** In each of the following independent cases, write a memo for the tax research file in preparation for a meeting with Gary. In each memo, explain whether the proposed plan meets his objective of shifting income and avoiding the grantor trust rules.

Decision Making
Communications

a. Gary transfers property in trust, income payable to Winnie (his wife) for life, remainder to his grandson. Gary's son is designated as the trustee.
b. Gary transfers income-producing assets and a life insurance policy to a trust, life estate to his children, remainder to his grandchildren. The policy is on Winnie's life, and the trustee (an independent trust company) is instructed to pay the premiums with income from the income-producing assets. The trust is designated as the beneficiary of the policy.
c. Gary transfers property in trust. The trust income is payable to Gary's grandchildren, as Winnie sees fit. Winnie and an independent trust company are designated as trustees.
d. Gary transfers property in trust, income payable to Winnie (Gary's ex-wife), remainder to Gary or his estate upon Winnie's death. The transfer was made in satisfaction of Gary's alimony obligation to Winnie. An independent trust company is designated as the trustee.

38. **LO.3** Determine the tax effects of the indicated losses for the Yellow Estate for both tax years. The estate holds a variety of investment assets, which it received from the decedent, Mrs. Yellow. The estate's sole income and remainder beneficiary is Yellow, Jr. All taxpayers use a calendar tax year.

Tax Year	Loss Generated
2012 (first tax year)	Taxable income ($300) Capital loss ($12,000)
2013 (final tax year)	Taxable income, all classified as ordinary ($20,000)

Decision Making

39. **LO.4** Woody wants to transfer some of the income from his investment portfolio to his daughter Wendy, age 10. Woody wants the trust to be able to accumulate income on Wendy's behalf and to meet any excessive expenses associated with her chronic medical conditions. Furthermore, Woody wants the trust to protect Wendy against his premature death without increasing his Federal gross estate. Thus, Woody provides the trustee with the powers to purchase insurance on his life and to meet any medical expenses that Wendy incurs.

    The trust is created in 2005. A whole life insurance policy with five annual premium payments is purchased during that year. The trustee spends $30,000 for Wendy's medical expenses in 2012 (but in no other year). Woody dies in 2014. Has the trust been tax-effective? Explain.

Decision Making

Communications

40. **LO.2, 3** Your client, Annie O'Toole (22 Beneficiary Lane, Bowling Green, KY 42101), has come to you for some advice regarding gifts of property. She has just learned that she must undergo major surgery, and she would like to make certain gifts before entering the hospital. On your earlier advice, she had established a plan of lifetime giving for four prior years.

    Build a spreadsheet, supplemented by a list of your assumptions, and write a cover letter to Annie, discussing each of the following assets that she is considering using as gifts to family and friends. In doing so, evaluate the income tax consequences of having such property pass through her estate to the designated heir.

    a. Annie plans to give a cottage to her son to fulfill a promise made many years ago. She has owned the cottage for the past 15 years and has a basis in it of $30,000 (fair market value of $20,000).
    b. Annie has $100,000 of long-term capital losses that she has been carrying forward for the past few years. Now she is considering making a gift of $200,000 in installment notes to her daughter. Her basis in the notes is $100,000, and the notes' current fair market value is $190,000.
    c. Annie has promised to make a special cash bequest of $25,000 to her grandson in her will. However, she does not anticipate having that much cash immediately available after her death. Annie requests your advice concerning the income tax consequences to the estate if the cash bequest is settled with some other property.

TAX RETURN PROBLEMS

1. Prepare the 2011 fiduciary income tax return (Form 1041) for the Blue Trust. In addition, determine the amount and character of the income and expense items that each beneficiary must report for 2011 and prepare a Schedule K–1 for Betty Blue. Omit all alternative minimum tax computations. The 2011 activities of the trust include the following.

Dividend income, all U.S. stocks	$50,000
Taxable interest income	30,000
Tax-exempt interest income	10,000
Fiduciary's fees	6,000

The trust and Betty both use the calendar tax year. Under the terms of the trust instrument, fiduciary's fees are allocated to income. The trustee must distribute all of the entity's accounting income to Betty Blue by February 15 of the following year. The trustee followed this charge and made no other distributions during the year. Fiduciary's fees properly were assigned as an offset to taxable interest income.

The trust was created on July 8, 1990. There are no tax credits for the year, and none of the entity's income was derived from a personal services contract. The trust has no economic interest in any foreign trust. Its Federal identification number is 11–1111111.

The trustee, Hoover State Federal Bank, is located at 4959 Cold Harbor Boulevard, Mountain Brook, AL 35223. Its employer identification number is 98–7654321. Betty lives at 67671 Crestline Road, Birmingham, AL 35212. Her Social Security number is 123–45–6789.

2. Prepare the 2011 fiduciary income tax return (Form 1041) for the Green Trust. In addition, determine the amount and character of the income and expense items that each beneficiary must report for 2011, and prepare a Schedule K–1 for Marcus White. Omit all alternative minimum tax computations. The 2011 activities of the trust include the following.

Dividend income, all qualified U.S. stocks	$10,000
Taxable interest income	50,000
Tax-exempt interest income	20,000
Net long-term capital gain, incurred 11/1/11	25,000
Fiduciary's fees	6,000

Under the terms of the trust instrument, cost recovery, net capital gains and losses, and fiduciary fees are allocable to corpus. The trustee is required to distribute $25,000 to Marcus every year. For 2011, the trustee distributed $40,000 to Marcus and $40,000 to Marcus's sister, Ellen Hayes. No other distributions were made.

In computing DNI, the trustee properly assigned all of the deductible fiduciary's fees to the taxable interest income.

The trustee paid $3,500 in estimated taxes for the year on behalf of the trust. Any 2011 refund is to be credited to 2012 estimates. The exempt income was not derived from private activity bonds.

The trust was created on December 14, 1953. It is not subject to any recapture taxes, nor does it have any tax credits. None of its income was derived under a personal services contract. The trust has no economic interest in any foreign trust. Its Federal identification number is 11–1111111.

The trustee, Wisconsin State National Bank, is located at 3100 East Wisconsin Avenue, Milwaukee, WI 53201. Its employer identification number is 11–1111111. Marcus lives at 9880 East North Avenue, Shorewood, WI 53211. His Social Security number is 123–45–6789. Ellen lives at 6772 East Oklahoma Avenue, Milwaukee, WI 53204. Her Social Security number is 987–65–4321.

RESEARCH PROBLEMS

THOMSON REUTERS
CHECKPOINT®

Note: Solutions to Research Problems can be prepared by using the **Checkpoint® Student Edition** online research product, which is available to accompany this text. It is also possible to prepare solutions to the Research Problems by using tax research materials found in a standard tax library.

Communications

Research Problem 1. The trustee of the Thornton Trust was approached by the development director of the Orrfield Symphony Orchestra (OSO) for a gift of $1 million toward the OSO building campaign. The parties agreed that, because of the size of the gift, the trust would need to obtain the funds by accumulating the income from its investment portfolio over a three-year period.

The trust's gift would be made at the end of year 3, and it would represent three years' worth of trust income from its taxable investments, plus the investment earnings on the accumulation during the three-year period. Specifically, the gift would consist of the following amounts.

Investment earnings, accumulated from year 1	$300,000
Investment earnings, accumulated from year 2	300,000
Investment earnings from year 3	300,000
Additional earnings realized from the prior years' accumulations	100,000

All of the investment earnings of the trust consisted of taxable interest, dividends, and capital gains.

Tiffany Thornton, the tax adviser to the trust, asks you whether the Federal income tax law would allow for a year 3 charitable deduction for the whole $1 million, or would the deduction be limited to only the $300,000 current-year gross income? Also, would a deduction be allowed for the $100,000 earnings on the accumulations that were realized during the three-year period? Address Tiffany's concerns in a memo for the tax research file.

Communications

Research Problem 2. Siri's revocable trust held title to a plot of investment land that she had acquired in 2003. On October 20, 2011, the trust entered into a sales contract with Hilltop Developers. A closing date of March 20, 2012, was set by the terms of the contract.

On February 3, 2012, Siri's engineers discovered a natural gas pipeline under the land, a fact that was not previously known by the parties. To allow for changes in the terms of the contract that were needed because of this discovery, the closing date for the sale was delayed until June 1, 2012.

The trust's basis in the land is $1 million. The original sales price was set at $1.1 million, reflecting difficulties in finding a purchaser in a "down" real estate market. But after the terms of the sale were adjusted, on May 20, 2012, a new $1.5 million sales price was agreed to. The closing and title transfer occurred on June 1 of that year.

Siri died on May 3, 2012. Under § 2036, the land is included in Siri's gross estate. Is the $500,000 capital gain on the sale treated as income in respect of a decedent (IRD) to her as well? Remember that, because neither party canceled the original deal, the sale was certain to occur under the contract. But Hilltop and the trust were renegotiating the terms of the contract when Siri died.

Identify the administrative and judicial precedents that are most pertinent for the parties. Cite and summarize your findings in an outline for a talk that you will deliver next week to your school's Accounting Club.

Research Problem 3. For three generations, the Dexter family has sent its children to Private University, preparing them for successful professional careers. The Edna Dexter Trust was established in the 1950s by LaKeisha's late grandmother and has accumulated a sizable corpus. It makes distributions to Edna's descendants rarely, and then only when they need large capital amounts. For example, two years ago, the trust distributed $500,000 to DuJuan Dexter to aid him in starting a practice in retirement and elder law. In most years, the trust's income is donated to a single charity.

Under the terms of the trust, Bigby Dexter, LaKeisha's uncle and legal guardian, can specify the trust beneficiaries and the amounts to be distributed to them. He can also replace the trustee and designate the charity that will receive the year's contribution.

Accordingly, the trust falls under the grantor trust rules of § 678, and Bigby reports the trust's transactions on his own Form 1040.

LaKeisha wants to attend the prestigious local Academy High School, which will require a four-year expenditure for tuition and fees of $100,000, payable in advance. She approaches the Edna Dexter trustee and requests a current-year distribution of this amount, payable directly to the Academy. Under the laws of the state, the parent or guardian has the responsibility to provide a child with a public school education (no tuition charge) until age 16.

If the payment to the Academy is made, how is it treated under the Subchapter J rules: as a charitable contribution to the Academy, as a corpus distribution to LaKeisha, or in some other manner?

Internet Activity

Use the tax resources of the Internet to address the following questions. Do not restrict your search to the Web, but include a review of newsgroups and general reference materials, practitioner sites and resources, primary sources of the tax law, chat rooms and discussion groups, and other opportunities.

Communications

Research Problem 4. How many estates filed a Form 1041 last year? Simple trusts? Complex trusts? Grantor trusts? How much Federal income tax has been collected on Forms 1041 over the last three tax years? Summarize your findings in a series of graphs to share with your classmates.

Communications

Research Problem 5. Under the income tax laws of your state applicable to fiduciaries, how are the following items allocated among the entity and the beneficiaries? Put your findings in a PowerPoint presentation for your classmates.

- Capital gain.
- Cost recovery.
- Fiduciary fees.
- Exempt interest income.
- AMT adjustments.
- § 199 manufacturers' deduction.
- General business credits.

Communications

Research Problem 6. The IRS's list of abusive tax shelters includes a "family residence trust," which attempts to create deductions for personal items such as utilities, furniture purchases, and swimming pool maintenance. Search the Web for current definitions of these trusts and descriptions of how they operate. Summarize your findings, as well as the litigation strategy of the government to curtail the use of these trusts, in an e-mail to your instructor.

Communications

Research Problem 7. Create no more than three PowerPoint slides, summarizing your state's definitions of and rules for using the following terms. *Hint*: Your state might not use these terms at all, or it might use a term that differs slightly; so make sure your Internet research is broad enough to find the equivalent terminology.

- Living will.
- Living trust.
- Medical power of attorney.

Communications

Research Problem 8. Find the language in the budget proposal of the Obama administration that would limit to 90 years the transfer tax exemptions for dynasty trusts. In no more than four PowerPoint slides, summarize the scope of the limitations, and show the tax revenues the administration believes the proposal would produce. Make certain you address the estate, gift, and generation-skipping taxes.

Communications

Research Problem 9. Find the website of a law firm that seems to specialize in fiduciary entities, preferably a firm located in your state. Ask the firm to quote you a fee for (1) establishing a simple trust and (2) filing the annual Form 1041. Summarize your findings, and your communications with the firm, in an e-mail to your instructor.

© Pali Rao, iStockphoto

Appendix A

Tax Rate Schedules and Tables

2011 Tax Rate Schedules

Single—Schedule X

If taxable income is: Over—	But not over—	The tax is:	of the amount over—
$ 0	$ 8,500	.........10%	$ 0
8,500	34,500	$ 850.00 + 15%	8,500
34,500	83,600	4,750.00 + 25%	34,500
83,600	174,400	17,025.00 + 28%	83,600
174,400	379,150	42,449.00 + 33%	174,400
379,150	....	110,016.50 + 35%	379,150

Head of household—Schedule Z

If taxable income is: Over—	But not over—	The tax is:	of the amount over—
$ 0	$ 12,150	.........10%	$ 0
12,150	46,250	$ 1,215.00 + 15%	12,150
46,250	119,400	6,330.00 + 25%	46,250
119,400	193,350	24,617.50 + 28%	119,400
193,350	379,150	45,323.50 + 33%	193,350
379,150	....	106,637.50 + 35%	379,150

Married filing jointly or Qualifying widow(er)—Schedule Y–1

If taxable income is: Over—	But not over—	The tax is:	of the amount over—
$ 0	$ 17,000	.........10%	$ 0
17,000	69,000	$ 1,700.00 + 15%	17,000
69,000	139,350	9,500.00 + 25%	69,000
139,350	212,300	27,087.50 + 28%	139,350
212,300	379,150	47,513.50 + 33%	212,300
379,150	....	102,574.00 + 35%	379,150

Married filing separately—Schedule Y–2

If taxable income is: Over—	But not over—	The tax is:	of the amount over—
$ 0	$ 8,500	.........10%	$ 0
8,500	34,500	$ 850.00 + 15%	8,500
34,500	69,675	4,750.00 + 25%	34,500
69,675	106,150	13,543.75 + 28%	69,675
106,150	189,575	23,756.75 + 33%	106,150
189,575	....	51,287.00 + 35%	189,575

2012 Tax Rate Schedules

Single—Schedule X

If taxable income is: Over—	But not over—	The tax is:	of the amount over—
$ 0	$ 8,700	.........10%	$ 0
8,700	35,350	$ 870.00 + 15%	8,700
35,350	85,650	4,687.50 + 25%	35,350
85,650	178,650	17,442.50 + 28%	85,650
178,650	388,350	43,482.50 + 33%	178,650
388,350	....	112,683.50 + 35%	388,350

Head of household—Schedule Z

If taxable income is: Over—	But not over—	The tax is:	of the amount over—
$ 0	$ 12,400	.........10%	$ 0
12,400	47,350	$ 1,240.00 + 15%	12,400
47,350	122,300	6,482.50 + 25%	47,350
122,300	198,050	25,220.00 + 28%	122,300
198,050	388,350	46,430.00 + 33%	198,050
388,350	....	109,229.00 + 35%	388,350

Married filing jointly or Qualifying widow(er)—Schedule Y–1

If taxable income is: Over—	But not over—	The tax is:	of the amount over—
$ 0	$ 17,400	.........10%	$ 0
17,400	70,700	$ 1,740.00 + 15%	17,400
70,700	142,700	9,735.00 + 25%	70,700
142,700	217,450	27,735.00 + 28%	142,700
217,450	388,350	48,665.00 + 33%	217,450
388,350	....	105,062.00 + 35%	388,350

Married filing separately—Schedule Y–2

If taxable income is: Over—	But not over—	The tax is:	of the amount over—
$ 0	$ 8,700	.........10%	$ 0
8,700	35,350	$ 870.00 + 15%	8,700
35,350	71,350	4,867.50 + 25%	35,350
71,350	108,725	13,867.50 + 28%	71,350
108,725	194,175	24,332.50 + 33%	108,725
194,175	....	52,531.00 + 35%	194,175

Income Tax Rates—Estates and Trusts

Tax Year 2011

Taxable Income		The Tax Is:	
Over—	But not Over—		Of the Amount Over—
$ 0	$ 2,300	15%	$ 0
2,300	5,450	$ 345.00 + 25%	2,300
5,450	8,300	1,132.50 + 28%	5,450
8,300	11,350	1,930.50 + 33%	8,300
11,350	....	2,937.00 + 35%	11,350

Tax Year 2012

Taxable Income		The Tax Is:	
Over—	But not Over—		Of the Amount Over—
$ 0	$ 2,400	15%	$ 0
2,400	5,600	$ 360.00 + 25%	2,400
5,600	8,500	1,160.00 + 28%	5,600
8,500	11,650	1,972.00 + 33%	8,500
11,650	....	3,011.50 + 35%	11,650

Income Tax Rates—Corporations

Taxable Income		The Tax Is:	
Over—	But not Over—		Of the Amount Over—
$ 0	$ 50,000	15%	$ 0
50,000	75,000	$ 7,500 + 25%	50,000
75,000	100,000	13,750 + 34%	75,000
100,000	335,000	22,250 + 39%	100,000
335,000	10,000,000	113,900 + 34%	335,000
10,000,000	15,000,000	3,400,000 + 35%	10,000,000
15,000,000	18,333,333	5,150,000 + 38%	15,000,000
18,333,333	....	35%	0

Unified Transfer Tax Rates

For Gifts Made and for Deaths After 1983 and Before 2002

If the Amount with Respect to Which the Tentative Tax to Be Computed Is:	The Tentative Tax Is:
Not over $10,000	18 percent of such amount.
Over $10,000 but not over $20,000	$1,800, plus 20 percent of the excess of such amount over $10,000.
Over $20,000 but not over $40,000	$3,800, plus 22 percent of the excess of such amount over $20,000.
Over $40,000 but not over $60,000	$8,200, plus 24 percent of the excess of such amount over $40,000.
Over $60,000 but not over $80,000	$13,000, plus 26 percent of the excess of such amount over $60,000.
Over $80,000 but not over $100,000	$18,200, plus 28 percent of the excess of such amount over $80,000.
Over $100,000 but not over $150,000	$23,800, plus 30 percent of the excess of such amount over $100,000.
Over $150,000 but not over $250,000	$38,800, plus 32 percent of the excess of such amount over $150,000.
Over $250,000 but not over $500,000	$70,800, plus 34 percent of the excess of such amount over $250,000.
Over $500,000 but not over $750,000	$155,800, plus 37 percent of the excess of such amount over $500,000.
Over $750,000 but not over $1,000,000	$248,300, plus 39 percent of the excess of such amount over $750,000.
Over $1,000,000 but not over $1,250,000	$345,800, plus 41 percent of the excess of such amount over $1,000,000.
Over $1,250,000 but not over $1,500,000	$448,300, plus 43 percent of the excess of such amount over $1,250,000.
Over $1,500,000 but not over $2,000,000	$555,800, plus 45 percent of the excess of such amount over $1,500,000.
Over $2,000,000 but not over $2,500,000	$780,800, plus 49 percent of the excess of such amount over $2,000,000.
Over $2,500,000 but not over $3,000,000	$1,025,800, plus 53 percent of the excess of such amount over $2,500,000.
Over $3,000,000*	$1,290,800, plus 55 percent of the excess of such amount over $3,000,000.

*For large taxable transfers (generally in excess of $10 million) there is a phaseout of the graduated rates and the unified tax credit.

Unified Transfer Tax Rates

For Gifts Made and for Deaths in 2002

If the Amount with Respect to Which the Tentative Tax to Be Computed Is:	The Tentative Tax Is:
Not over $10,000	18 percent of such amount.
Over $10,000 but not over $20,000	$1,800, plus 20 percent of the excess of such amount over $10,000.
Over $20,000 but not over $40,000	$3,800, plus 22 percent of the excess of such amount over $20,000.
Over $40,000 but not over $60,000	$8,200, plus 24 percent of the excess of such amount over $40,000.
Over $60,000 but not over $80,000	$13,000, plus 26 percent of the excess of such amount over $60,000.
Over $80,000 but not over $100,000	$18,200, plus 28 percent of the excess of such amount over $80,000.
Over $100,000 but not over $150,000	$23,800, plus 30 percent of the excess of such amount over $100,000.
Over $150,000 but not over $250,000	$38,800, plus 32 percent of the excess of such amount over $150,000.
Over $250,000 but not over $500,000	$70,800, plus 34 percent of the excess of such amount over $250,000.
Over $500,000 but not over $750,000	$155,800, plus 37 percent of the excess of such amount over $500,000.
Over $750,000 but not over $1,000,000	$248,300, plus 39 percent of the excess of such amount over $750,000.
Over $1,000,000 but not over $1,250,000	$345,800, plus 41 percent of the excess of such amount over $1,000,000.
Over $1,250,000 but not over $1,500,000	$448,300, plus 43 percent of the excess of such amount over $1,250,000.
Over $1,500,000 but not over $2,000,000	$555,800, plus 45 percent of the excess of such amount over $1,500,000.
Over $2,000,000 but not over $2,500,000	$780,800, plus 49 percent of the excess of such amount over $2,000,000.
Over $2,500,000	$1,025,800, plus 50 percent of the excess of such amount over $2,500,000.

Unified Transfer Tax Rates

For Gifts Made and for Deaths in 2003

If the Amount with Respect to Which the Tentative Tax to Be Computed Is:	The Tentative Tax Is:
Not over $10,000	18 percent of such amount.
Over $10,000 but not over $20,000	$1,800, plus 20 percent of the excess of such amount over $10,000.
Over $20,000 but not over $40,000	$3,800, plus 22 percent of the excess of such amount over $20,000.
Over $40,000 but not over $60,000	$8,200, plus 24 percent of the excess of such amount over $40,000.
Over $60,000 but not over $80,000	$13,000, plus 26 percent of the excess of such amount over $60,000.
Over $80,000 but not over $100,000	$18,200, plus 28 percent of the excess of such amount over $80,000.
Over $100,000 but not over $150,000	$23,800, plus 30 percent of the excess of such amount over $100,000.
Over $150,000 but not over $250,000	$38,800, plus 32 percent of the excess of such amount over $150,000.
Over $250,000 but not over $500,000	$70,800, plus 34 percent of the excess of such amount over $250,000.
Over $500,000 but not over $750,000	$155,800, plus 37 percent of the excess of such amount over $500,000.
Over $750,000 but not over $1,000,000	$248,300, plus 39 percent of the excess of such amount over $750,000.
Over $1,000,000 but not over $1,250,000	$345,800, plus 41 percent of the excess of such amount over $1,000,000.
Over $1,250,000 but not over $1,500,000	$448,300, plus 43 percent of the excess of such amount over $1,250,000.
Over $1,500,000 but not over $2,000,000	$555,800, plus 45 percent of the excess of such amount over $1,500,000.
Over $2,000,000	$780,800, plus 49 percent of the excess of such amount over $2,000,000.

For Gifts Made and for Deaths in 2004

(For amounts not over $2,000,000, see rates for 2003 above)	
Over $2,000,000	$780,800, plus 48 percent of the excess of such amount over $2,000,000.

For Gifts Made and for Deaths in 2005

(For amounts not over $2,000,000, see rates for 2003 above)	
Over $2,000,000	$780,800, plus 47 percent of the excess of such amount over $2,000,000.

For Gifts Made and for Deaths in 2006

(For amounts not over $2,000,000, see rates for 2003 above)	
Over $2,000,000	$780,800, plus 46 percent of the excess of such amount over $2,000,000.

Unified Transfer Tax Rates

For Gifts Made and for Deaths in 2007–2009

If the Amount with Respect to Which the Tentative Tax to Be Computed Is:	The Tentative Tax Is:
Not over $10,000	18 percent of such amount.
Over $10,000 but not over $20,000	$1,800, plus 20 percent of the excess of such amount over $10,000.
Over $20,000 but not over $40,000	$3,800, plus 22 percent of the excess of such amount over $20,000.
Over $40,000 but not over $60,000	$8,200, plus 24 percent of the excess of such amount over $40,000.
Over $60,000 but not over $80,000	$13,000, plus 26 percent of the excess of such amount over $60,000.
Over $80,000 but not over $100,000	$18,200, plus 28 percent of the excess of such amount over $80,000.
Over $100,000 but not over $150,000	$23,800, plus 30 percent of the excess of such amount over $100,000.
Over $150,000 but not over $250,000	$38,800, plus 32 percent of the excess of such amount over $150,000.
Over $250,000 but not over $500,000	$70,800, plus 34 percent of the excess of such amount over $250,000.
Over $500,000 but not over $750,000	$155,800, plus 37 percent of the excess of such amount over $500,000.
Over $750,000 but not over $1,000,000	$248,300, plus 39 percent of the excess of such amount over $750,000.
Over $1,000,000 but not over $1,250,000	$345,800, plus 41 percent of the excess of such amount over $1,000,000.
Over $1,250,000 but not over $1,500,000	$448,300, plus 43 percent of the excess of such amount over $1,250,000.
Over $1,500,000	$555,800, plus 45 percent of the excess of such amount over $1,500,000.

Gift Tax Rates

For Gifts Made Only in 2010

If the Amount with Respect to Which the Tentative Tax to Be Computed Is:	The Tentative Tax Is:
Not over $10,000	18 percent of such amount.
Over $10,000 but not over $20,000	$1,800, plus 20 percent of the excess of such amount over $10,000.
Over $20,000 but not over $40,000	$3,800, plus 22 percent of the excess of such amount over $20,000.
Over $40,000 but not over $60,000	$8,200, plus 24 percent of the excess of such amount over $40,000.
Over $60,000 but not over $80,000	$13,000, plus 26 percent of the excess of such amount over $60,000.
Over $80,000 but not over $100,000	$18,200, plus 28 percent of the excess of such amount over $80,000.
Over $100,000 but not over $150,000	$23,800, plus 30 percent of the excess of such amount over $100,000.
Over $150,000 but not over $250,000	$38,800, plus 32 percent of the excess of such amount over $150,000.
Over $250,000 but not over $500,000	$70,800, plus 34 percent of the excess of such amount over $250,000.
Over $500,000	$155,800, plus 35 percent of the excess of such amount over $500,000.

Unified Transfer Tax Rates

For Gifts Made and for Deaths in 2011–2012

If the Amount with Respect to Which the Tentative Tax to Be Computed Is:	The Tentative Tax Is:
Not over $10,000	18 percent of such amount.
Over $10,000 but not over $20,000	$1,800, plus 20 percent of the excess of such amount over $10,000.
Over $20,000 but not over $40,000	$3,800, plus 22 percent of the excess of such amount over $20,000.
Over $40,000 but not over $60,000	$8,200, plus 24 percent of the excess of such amount over $40,000.
Over $60,000 but not over $80,000	$13,000, plus 26 percent of the excess of such amount over $60,000.
Over $80,000 but not over $100,000	$18,200, plus 28 percent of the excess of such amount over $80,000.
Over $100,000 but not over $150,000	$23,800, plus 30 percent of the excess of such amount over $100,000.
Over $150,000 but not over $250,000	$38,800, plus 32 percent of the excess of such amount over $150,000.
Over $250,000 but not over $500,000	$70,800, plus 34 percent of the excess of such amount over $250,000.
Over $500,000	$155,800, plus 35 percent of the excess of such amount over $500,000.

Valuation Tables (On or After May 1, 2009)

Table S Single Life Remainder Factors Interest Rate

AGE	4.2%	4.4%	4.6%	4.8%	5.0%	5.2%	5.4%	5.6%
0	.06083	.05483	.04959	.04501	.04101	.03749	.03441	.03170
1	.05668	.05049	.04507	.04034	.03618	.03254	.02934	.02652
2	.05858	.05222	.04665	.04178	.03750	.03373	.03042	.02750
3	.06072	.05420	.04848	.04346	.03904	.03516	.03173	.02871
4	.06303	.05634	.05046	.04530	.04075	.03674	.03319	.03006
5	.06547	.05861	.05258	.04726	.04258	.03844	.03478	.03153
6	.06805	.06102	.05482	.04935	.04453	.04026	.03647	.03312
7	.07074	.06353	.05717	.05155	.04658	.04217	.03826	.03479
8	.07356	.06617	.05964	.05386	.04875	.04421	.04017	.03658
9	.07651	.06895	.06225	.05631	.05105	.04637	.04220	.03849
10	.07960	.07185	.06499	.05889	.05347	.04865	.04435	.04052
11	.08283	.07490	.06786	.06160	.05603	.05106	.04663	.04267
12	.08620	.07808	.07087	.06444	.05871	.05360	.04903	.04494
13	.08967	.08137	.07397	.06738	.06149	.05623	.05152	.04729
14	.09321	.08472	.07715	.07038	.06433	.05892	.05406	.04971
15	.09680	.08812	.08036	.07342	.06721	.06164	.05664	.05214
16	.10041	.09154	.08360	.07649	.07011	.06438	.05923	.05459
17	.10409	.09502	.08689	.07960	.07305	.06716	.06185	.05707
18	.10782	.09855	.09024	.08276	.07604	.06998	.06452	.05959
19	.11164	.10217	.09366	.08600	.07910	.07288	.06726	.06218
20	.11559	.10592	.09721	.08937	.08228	.07589	.07010	.06487
21	.11965	.10977	.10087	.09283	.08557	.07900	.07305	.06765
22	.12383	.11376	.10465	.09642	.08897	.08223	.07610	.07055
23	.12817	.11789	.10859	.10016	.09252	.08559	.07930	.07358
24	.13270	.12221	.11270	.10408	.09625	.08914	.08267	.07678
25	.13744	.12674	.11703	.10821	.10019	.09289	.08625	.08018
26	.14239	.13149	.12158	.11256	.10435	.09686	.09003	.08380
27	.14758	.13647	.12636	.11714	.10873	.10106	.09405	.08764
28	.15300	.14169	.13137	.12195	.11335	.10549	.09829	.09171
29	.15864	.14712	.13660	.12698	.11819	.11013	.10275	.09598
30	.16448	.15275	.14203	.13222	.12323	.11498	.10742	.10047
31	.17053	.15861	.14769	.13768	.12849	.12006	.11230	.10517
32	.17680	.16468	.15357	.14336	.13398	.12535	.11741	.11009
33	.18330	.17099	.15968	.14927	.13970	.13088	.12275	.11525
34	.19000	.17750	.16599	.15539	.14562	.13661	.12829	.12061

Valuation Tables (On or After May 1, 2009, *continued*)

Table S Single Life Remainder Factors Interest Rate

AGE	4.2%	4.4%	4.6%	4.8%	5.0%	5.2%	5.4%	5.6%
35	.19692	.18423	.17253	.16174	.15178	.14258	.13408	.12621
36	.20407	.19119	.17931	.16833	.15818	.14879	.14009	.13204
37	.21144	.19838	.18631	.17515	.16481	.15523	.14635	.13811
38	.21904	.20582	.19357	.18222	.17170	.16193	.15287	.14444
39	.22687	.21348	.20105	.18952	.17882	.16887	.15962	.15102
40	.23493	.22137	.20878	.19707	.18619	.17606	.16663	.15784
41	.24322	.22950	.21674	.20487	.19381	.18350	.17390	.16493
42	.25173	.23786	.22494	.21290	.20168	.19120	.18141	.17227
43	.26049	.24648	.23342	.22122	.20982	.19918	.18922	.17990
44	.26950	.25535	.24214	.22979	.21824	.20742	.19730	.18781
45	.27874	.26447	.25112	.23862	.22692	.21595	.20566	.19600
46	.28824	.27385	.26038	.24774	.23589	.22476	.21431	.20450
47	.29798	.28349	.26989	.25712	.24513	.23386	.22326	.21328
48	.30797	.29338	.27967	.26678	.25466	.24325	.23250	.22238
49	.31822	.30355	.28974	.27674	.26449	.25294	.24206	.23179
50	.32876	.31401	.30011	.28701	.27465	.26298	.25196	.24156
51	.33958	.32477	.31079	.29759	.28513	.27335	.26221	.25168
52	.35068	.33582	.32178	.30851	.29595	.28407	.27282	.26216
53	.36206	.34717	.33308	.31974	.30710	.29513	.28378	.27301
54	.37371	.35880	.34467	.33127	.31857	.30651	.29507	.28420
55	.38559	.37067	.35652	.34308	.33032	.31820	.30668	.29572
56	.39765	.38275	.36859	.35512	.34232	.33014	.31855	.30751
57	.40990	.39502	.38086	.36739	.35455	.34233	.33068	.31957
58	.42231	.40747	.39333	.37985	.36700	.35474	.34304	.33188
59	.43490	.42011	.40600	.39253	.37968	.36740	.35567	.34446
60	.44768	.43296	.41890	.40546	.39261	.38033	.36858	.35733
61	.46064	.44600	.43200	.41860	.40578	.39351	.38175	.37048
62	.47373	.45920	.44527	.43194	.41915	.40690	.39514	.38387
63	.48696	.47253	.45870	.44544	.43271	.42049	.40876	.39749
64	.50030	.48601	.47229	.45911	.44645	.43428	.42258	.41133
65	.51377	.49963	.48603	.47295	.46037	.44827	.43662	.42540
66	.52750	.51352	.50007	.48711	.47464	.46262	.45103	.43987
67	.54144	.52765	.51436	.50154	.48919	.47727	.46578	.45468
68	.55554	.54196	.52885	.51619	.50398	.49218	.48079	.46978
69	.56976	.55640	.54349	.53102	.51896	.50731	.49603	.48513

Valuation Tables (On or After May 1, 2009, *continued*)

Table S Single Life Remainder Factors Interest Rate

AGE	4.2%	4.4%	4.6%	4.8%	5.0%	5.2%	5.4%	5.6%
70	.58407	.57095	.55826	.54598	.53410	.52260	.51147	.50069
71	.59848	.58561	.57316	.56109	.54940	.53808	.52710	.51646
72	.61294	.60035	.58815	.57632	.56484	.55371	.54291	.53243
73	.62741	.61512	.60318	.59160	.58035	.56943	.55882	.54851
74	.64183	.62983	.61818	.60686	.59586	.58516	.57476	.56464
75	.65612	.64444	.63309	.62204	.61129	.60083	.59065	.58074
76	.67026	.65891	.64786	.63710	.62661	.61640	.60646	.59676
77	.68423	.67321	.66248	.65201	.64181	.63186	.62215	.61269
78	.69800	.68733	.67692	.66676	.65684	.64717	.63772	.62849
79	.71156	.70124	.69116	.68132	.67170	.66230	.65312	.64414
80	.72487	.71490	.70516	.69563	.68632	.67721	.66830	.65959
81	.73791	.72830	.71890	.70970	.70069	.69188	.68325	.67481
82	.75065	.74140	.73235	.72348	.71479	.70628	.69794	.68977
83	.76308	.75419	.74548	.73695	.72858	.72037	.71232	.70443
84	.77516	.76664	.75828	.75008	.74203	.73413	.72638	.71877
85	.78689	.77873	.77072	.76285	.75512	.74753	.74008	.73275
86	.79825	.79044	.78278	.77524	.76783	.76055	.75340	.74636
87	.80921	.80176	.79443	.78722	.78014	.77316	.76630	.75956
88	.81978	.81268	.80569	.79880	.79203	.78536	.77880	.77234
89	.82994	.82317	.81651	.80995	.80349	.79712	.79085	.78467
90	.83967	.83324	.82690	.82065	.81450	.80843	.80244	.79655
91	.84898	.84288	.83685	.83091	.82505	.81928	.81358	.80795
92	.85787	.85208	.84636	.84072	.83515	.82966	.82423	.81888
93	.86632	.86083	.85541	.85006	.84477	.83955	.83440	.82931
94	.87435	.86915	.86402	.85894	.85393	.84898	.84409	.83925
95	.88197	.87705	.87219	.86739	.86265	.85795	.85331	.84872
96	.88915	.88451	.87991	.87537	.87088	.86643	.86203	.85768
97	.89593	.89154	.88720	.88290	.87865	.87444	.87028	.86616
98	.90232	.89818	.89408	.89002	.88600	.88202	.87808	.87418
99	.90835	.90444	.90057	.89674	.89294	.88918	.88546	.88177
100	.91397	.91028	.90663	.90301	.89942	.89587	.89234	.88885
101	.91930	.91583	.91238	.90897	.90558	.90223	.89890	.89560
102	.92424	.92096	.91771	.91448	.91128	.90811	.90496	.90184
103	.92914	.92605	.92300	.91996	.91695	.91397	.91100	.90806
104	.93364	.93074	.92786	.92501	.92217	.91935	.91656	.91379
105	.93809	.93537	.93266	.92998	.92731	.92467	.92204	.91943
106	.94365	.94115	.93867	.93621	.93376	.93133	.92892	.92651
107	.94994	.94771	.94549	.94328	.94108	.93890	.93673	.93457
108	.96010	.95830	.95651	.95472	.95295	.95118	.94942	.94767
109	.97985	.97893	.97801	.97710	.97619	.97529	.97438	.97348

Valuation Tables (On or After May 1, 2009)

Table B Term Certain Remainder Factors Interest Rate

YEARS	4.2%	4.4%	4.6%	4.8%	5.0%	5.2%	5.4%	5.6%
1	.959693	.957854	.956023	.954198	.952381	.950570	.948767	.946970
2	.921010	.917485	.913980	.910495	.907029	.903584	.900158	.896752
3	.883887	.878817	.873786	.868793	.863838	.858920	.854040	.849197
4	.848260	.841779	.835359	.829001	.822702	.816464	.810285	.804163
5	.814069	.806302	.798623	.791031	.783526	.776106	.768771	.761518
6	.781257	.772320	.763501	.754801	.746215	.737744	.729384	.721135
7	.749766	.739770	.729925	.720230	.710681	.701277	.692015	.682893
8	.719545	.708592	.697825	.687242	.676839	.666613	.656561	.646679
9	.690543	.678728	.667137	.655765	.644609	.633663	.622923	.612385
10	.662709	.650122	.637798	.625730	.613913	.602341	.591009	.579910
11	.635997	.622722	.609750	.597071	.584679	.572568	.560729	.549157
12	.610362	.596477	.582935	.569724	.556837	.544266	.532001	.520035
13	.585760	.571339	.557299	.543630	.530321	.517363	.504745	.492458
14	.562150	.547259	.532790	.518731	.505068	.491790	.478885	.466343
15	.539491	.524195	.509360	.494972	.481017	.467481	.454350	.441612
16	.517746	.502102	.486960	.472302	.458112	.444374	.431072	.418194
17	.496877	.480941	.465545	.450670	.436297	.422408	.408987	.396017
18	.476849	.460671	.445071	.430028	.415521	.401529	.388033	.375016
19	.457629	.441256	.425498	.410332	.395734	.381681	.368153	.355129
20	.439183	.422659	.406786	.391538	.376889	.362815	.349291	.336296
21	.421481	.404846	.388897	.373605	.358942	.344881	.331396	.318462
22	.404492	.387783	.371794	.356494	.341850	.327834	.314417	.301574
23	.388188	.371440	.355444	.340166	.325571	.311629	.298309	.285581
24	.372542	.355785	.339813	.324586	.310068	.296225	.283025	.270437
25	.357526	.340791	.324869	.309719	.295303	.281583	.268525	.256096
26	.343115	.326428	.310582	.295533	.281241	.267664	.254768	.242515
27	.329285	.312670	.296923	.281998	.267848	.254434	.241715	.229654
28	.316012	.299493	.283866	.269082	.255094	.241857	.229331	.217475
29	.303275	.286870	.271382	.256757	.242946	.229902	.217582	.205943
30	.291051	.274780	.259447	.244997	.231377	.218538	.206434	.195021
31	.279319	.263199	.248038	.233776	.220359	.207736	.195858	.184679
32	.268061	.252106	.237130	.223069	.209866	.197468	.185823	.174886
33	.257256	.241481	.226702	.212852	.199873	.187707	.176303	.165612
34	.246887	.231304	.216732	.203103	.190355	.178429	.167270	.156829
35	.236935	.221556	.207201	.193801	.181290	.169609	.158701	.148512

Valuation Tables (On or After May 1, 2009, *continued*)

Table B Term Certain Remainder Factors Interest Rate

YEARS	4.2%	4.4%	4.6%	4.8%	5.0%	5.2%	5.4%	5.6%
36	.227385	.212218	.198089	.184924	.172657	.161225	.150570	.140637
37	.218220	.203274	.189377	.176454	.164436	.153256	.142856	.133179
38	.209424	.194707	.181049	.168373	.156605	.145681	.135537	.126116
39	.200983	.186501	.173087	.160661	.149148	.138480	.128593	.119428
40	.192882	.178641	.165475	.153302	.142046	.131635	.122004	.113095
41	.185107	.171112	.158198	.146281	.135282	.125128	.115754	.107098
42	.177646	.163900	.151241	.139581	.128840	.118943	.109823	.101418
43	.170486	.156992	.144590	.133188	.122704	.113064	.104197	.096040
44	.163614	.150376	.138231	.127088	.116861	.107475	.098858	.090947
45	.157019	.144038	.132152	.121267	.111297	.102163	.093793	.086124
46	.150690	.137968	.126340	.115713	.105997	.097113	.088988	.081557
47	.144616	.132153	.120784	.110413	.100949	.092312	.084429	.077232
48	.138787	.126583	.115473	.105356	.096142	.087749	.080103	.073136
49	.133193	.121248	.110395	.100530	.091564	.083412	.075999	.069258
50	.127824	.116138	.105540	.095926	.087204	.079289	.072106	.065585
51	.122672	.111243	.100898	.091532	.083051	.075370	.068411	.062107
52	.117728	.106555	.096461	.087340	.079096	.071644	.064907	.058813
53	.112982	.102064	.092219	.083340	.075330	.068103	.061581	.055695
54	.108428	.097763	.088164	.079523	.071743	.064737	.058426	.052741
55	.104058	.093642	.084286	.075880	.068326	.061537	.055433	.049944
56	.099864	.089696	.080580	.072405	.065073	.058495	.052593	.047296
57	.095839	.085916	.077036	.069089	.061974	.055604	.049898	.044787
58	.091976	.082295	.073648	.065924	.059023	.052855	.047342	.042412
59	.088268	.078826	.070409	.062905	.056212	.050243	.044916	.040163
60	.084710	.075504	.067313	.060024	.053536	.047759	.042615	.038033

Appendix B

Tax Forms

(Tax forms can be obtained from the IRS website: **http://www.irs.gov**)

Form **709**

Department of the Treasury
Internal Revenue Service

United States Gift (and Generation-Skipping Transfer) Tax Return

(For gifts made during calendar year 2011)
▶ **See instructions.**

OMB No. 1545-0020

2011

Part 1—General Information

1 Donor's first name and middle initial	2 Donor's last name	**3 Donor's social security number**
4 Address (number, street, and apartment number)		5 Legal residence (domicile)
6 City, state, and ZIP code		7 Citizenship (see instructions)

		Yes	No
8	If the donor died during the year, check here ▶ ☐ and enter date of death ______________ , ________.		
9	If you extended the time to file this Form 709, check here ▶ ☐		
10	Enter the total number of donees listed on Schedule A. Count each person only once. ▶		
11a	Have you (the donor) previously filed a Form 709 (or 709-A) for any other year? If "No," skip line 11b		
b	If the answer to line 11a is "Yes," has your address changed since you last filed Form 709 (or 709-A)?		
12	**Gifts by husband or wife to third parties.** Do you consent to have the gifts (including generation-skipping transfers) made by you and by your spouse to third parties during the calendar year considered as made one-half by each of you? (See instructions.) (If the answer is "Yes," the following information must be furnished and your spouse must sign the consent shown below. **If the answer is "No," skip lines 13–18 and go to Schedule A.**)		
13	Name of consenting spouse — **14** SSN		
15	Were you married to one another during the entire calendar year? (see instructions)		
16	If 15 is "No," check whether ☐ married ☐ divorced or ☐ widowed/deceased, and give date (see instructions) ▶		
17	Will a gift tax return for this year be filed by your spouse? (If "Yes," mail both returns in the same envelope.)		
18	**Consent of Spouse.** I consent to have the gifts (and generation-skipping transfers) made by me and by my spouse to third parties during the calendar year considered as made one-half by each of us. We are both aware of the joint and several liability for tax created by the execution of this consent.		

Consenting spouse's signature ▶ **Date** ▶

Part 2—Tax Computation

1	Enter the amount from Schedule A, Part 4, line 11	1	
2	Enter the amount from Schedule B, line 3	2	
3	Total taxable gifts. Add lines 1 and 2	3	
4	Tax computed on amount on line 3 (see *Table for Computing Gift Tax* in instructions)	4	
5	Tax computed on amount on line 2 (see *Table for Computing Gift Tax* in instructions)	5	
6	Balance. Subtract line 5 from line 4	6	
7	Maximum unified credit (see instructions)	7	
8	Enter the unified credit against tax allowable for all prior periods (from Sch. B, line 1, col. C) . .	8	
9	Balance. Subtract line 8 from line 7. Do not enter less than zero	9	
10	Enter 20% (.20) of the amount allowed as a specific exemption for gifts made after September 8, 1976, and before January 1, 1977 (see instructions)	10	
11	Balance. Subtract line 10 from line 9. Do not enter less than zero	11	
12	Unified credit. Enter the smaller of line 6 or line 11	12	
13	Credit for foreign gift taxes (see instructions)	13	
14	Total credits. Add lines 12 and 13	14	
15	Balance. Subtract line 14 from line 6. Do not enter less than zero	15	
16	Generation-skipping transfer taxes (from Schedule C, Part 3, col. H, Total)	16	
17	Total tax. Add lines 15 and 16	17	
18	Gift and generation-skipping transfer taxes prepaid with extension of time to file	18	
19	If line 18 is less than line 17, enter **balance due** (see instructions)	19	
20	If line 18 is greater than line 17, enter **amount to be refunded**	20	

Attach check or money order here.

Sign Here

Under penalties of perjury, I declare that I have examined this return, including any accompanying schedules and statements, and to the best of my knowledge and belief, it is true, correct, and complete. Declaration of preparer (other than donor) is based on all information of which preparer has any knowledge.

May the IRS discuss this return with the preparer shown below (see instructions)? ☐ **Yes** ☐ **No**

▶ Signature of donor — Date

Paid Preparer Use Only

Print/Type preparer's name	Preparer's signature	Date	Check ☐ if self-employed	PTIN
Firm's name ▶			Firm's EIN ▶	
Firm's address ▶			Phone no.	

Form 709 (2011) Page **2**

SCHEDULE A Computation of Taxable Gifts (Including transfers in trust) (see instructions)

A Does the value of any item listed on Schedule A reflect any valuation discount? If "Yes," attach explanation . . . . Yes ☐ No ☐

B ☐ ◄ Check here if you elect under section 529(c)(2)(B) to treat any transfers made this year to a qualified tuition program as made ratably over a 5-year period beginning this year. See instructions. Attach explanation.

Part 1—Gifts Subject Only to Gift Tax. Gifts less political organization, medical, and educational exclusions. (see instructions)

A Item number	B • Donee's name and address • Relationship to donor (if any) • Description of gift • If the gift was of securities, give CUSIP no. • If closely held entity, give EIN	C	D Donor's adjusted basis of gift	E Date of gift	F Value at date of gift	G For split gifts, enter ½ of column F	H Net transfer (subtract col. G from col. F)
Gifts made by spouse —*complete **only** if you are splitting gifts with your spouse and he/she also made gifts.*							

Total of Part 1. Add amounts from Part 1, column H . . . . ▶

Part 2—Direct Skips. Gifts that are direct skips and are subject to both gift tax and generation-skipping transfer tax. You must list the gifts in chronological order.

A Item number	B • Donee's name and address • Relationship to donor (if any) • Description of gift • If the gift was of securities, give CUSIP no. • If closely held entity, give EIN	C 2632(b) election out	D Donor's adjusted basis of gift	E Date of gift	F Value at date of gift	G For split gifts, enter ½ of column F	H Net transfer (subtract col. G from col. F)
Gifts made by spouse —*complete **only** if you are splitting gifts with your spouse and he/she also made gifts.*							

Total of Part 2. Add amounts from Part 2, column H . . . . ▶

Part 3—Indirect Skips. Gifts to trusts that are currently subject to gift tax and may later be subject to generation-skipping transfer tax. You must list these gifts in chronological order.

A Item number	B • Donee's name and address • Relationship to donor (if any) • Description of gift • If the gift was of securities, give CUSIP no. • If closely held entity, give EIN	C 2632(c) election	D Donor's adjusted basis of gift	E Date of gift	F Value at date of gift	G For split gifts, enter ½ of column F	H Net transfer (subtract col. G from col. F)
Gifts made by spouse —*complete **only** if you are splitting gifts with your spouse and he/she also made gifts.*							

Total of Part 3. Add amounts from Part 3, column H . . . . ▶

(If more space is needed, attach additional sheets of same size.) Form **709** (2011)

Form 709 (2011) Page 3

Part 4—Taxable Gift Reconciliation

1	Total value of gifts of donor. Add totals from column H of Parts 1, 2, and 3	1	
2	Total annual exclusions for gifts listed on line 1 (see instructions)	2	
3	Total included amount of gifts. Subtract line 2 from line 1	3	
	Deductions (see instructions)		
4	Gifts of interests to spouse for which a marital deduction will be claimed, based on item numbers ________ of Schedule A — 4		
5	Exclusions attributable to gifts on line 4 — 5		
6	Marital deduction. Subtract line 5 from line 4 — 6		
7	Charitable deduction, based on item nos. ________ less exclusions — 7		
8	Total deductions. Add lines 6 and 7	8	
9	Subtract line 8 from line 3	9	
10	Generation-skipping transfer taxes payable with this Form 709 (from Schedule C, Part 3, col. H, Total)	10	
11	**Taxable gifts.** Add lines 9 and 10. Enter here and on page 1, Part 2—Tax Computation, line 1	11	

Terminable Interest (QTIP) Marital Deduction. (See instructions for Schedule A, Part 4, line 4.)

If a trust (or other property) meets the requirements of qualified terminable interest property under section 2523(f), and:

a. The trust (or other property) is listed on Schedule A, and

b. The value of the trust (or other property) is entered in whole or in part as a deduction on Schedule A, Part 4, line 4,

then the donor shall be deemed to have made an election to have such trust (or other property) treated as qualified terminable interest property under section 2523(f).

If less than the entire value of the trust (or other property) that the donor has included in Parts 1 and 3 of Schedule A is entered as a deduction on line 4, the donor shall be considered to have made an election only as to a fraction of the trust (or other property). The numerator of this fraction is equal to the amount of the trust (or other property) deducted on Schedule A, Part 4, line 6. The denominator is equal to the total value of the trust (or other property) listed in Parts 1 and 3 of Schedule A.

If you make the QTIP election, the terminable interest property involved will be included in your spouse's gross estate upon his or her death (section 2044). See instructions for line 4 of Schedule A. If your spouse disposes (by gift or otherwise) of all or part of the qualifying life income interest, he or she will be considered to have made a transfer of the entire property that is subject to the gift tax. See *Transfer of Certain Life Estates Received From Spouse* in the instructions.

12 Election Out of QTIP Treatment of Annuities

☐ ◀ Check here if you elect under section 2523(f)(6) **not** to treat as qualified terminable interest property any joint and survivor annuities that are reported on Schedule A and would otherwise be treated as qualified terminable interest property under section 2523(f). See instructions. Enter the item numbers from Schedule A for the annuities for which you are making this election ▶ ________

SCHEDULE B Gifts From Prior Periods

If you answered "Yes" on line 11a of page 1, Part 1, see the instructions for completing Schedule B. If you answered "No," skip to the Tax Computation on page 1 (or Schedule C, if applicable). See instructions for recalculation of the column C amounts. Attach calculations.

A Calendar year or calendar quarter (see instructions)	B Internal Revenue office where prior return was filed	C Amount of unified credit against gift tax for periods after December 31, 1976	D Amount of specific exemption for prior periods ending before January 1, 1977	E Amount of taxable gifts
1 Totals for prior periods	1			

2	Amount, if any, by which total specific exemption, line 1, column D is more than $30,000	2	
3	Total amount of taxable gifts for prior periods. Add amount on line 1, column E and amount, if any, on line 2. Enter here and on page 1, Part 2—Tax Computation, line 2	3	

(If more space is needed, attach additional sheets of same size.)

Form 709 (2011)

Form 709 (2011) Page **4**

SCHEDULE C Computation of Generation-Skipping Transfer Tax

Note. Inter vivos direct skips that are completely excluded by the GST exemption must still be fully reported (including value and exemptions claimed) on Schedule C.

Part 1—Generation-Skipping Transfers

A Item No. (from Schedule A, Part 2, col. A)	B Value (from Schedule A, Part 2, col. H)	C Nontaxable portion of transfer	D Net Transfer (subtract col. C from col. B)
Gifts made by spouse (for gift splitting only)			

Part 2—GST Exemption Reconciliation (Section 2631) and Section 2652(a)(3) Election

Check here ▶ ☐ if you are making a section 2652(a)(3) (special QTIP) election (see instructions)

Enter the item numbers from Schedule A of the gifts for which you are making this election ▶ ____________

1	Maximum allowable exemption (see instructions)	1	
2	Total exemption used for periods before filing this return	2	
3	Exemption available for this return. Subtract line 2 from line 1	3	
4	Exemption claimed on this return from Part 3, column C total, below	4	
5	Automatic allocation of exemption to transfers reported on Schedule A, Part 3 (see instructions)	5	
6	Exemption allocated to transfers not shown on line 4 or 5, above. **You must attach a "Notice of Allocation."** (see instructions)	6	
7	Add lines 4, 5, and 6	7	
8	Exemption available for future transfers. Subtract line 7 from line 3	8	

Part 3—Tax Computation

A Item No. (from Schedule C, Part 1)	B Net transfer (from Schedule C, Part 1, col. D)	C GST Exemption Allocated	D Divide col. C by col. B	E Inclusion Ratio (Subtract col. D from 1.000)	F Maximum Estate Tax Rate	G Applicable Rate (multiply col. E by col. F)	H Generation-Skipping Transfer Tax (multiply col. B by col. G)
					35% (.35)	0	0
					35% (.35)	0	0
					35% (.35)	0	0
					35% (.35)	0	0
					35% (.35)	0	0
					35% (.35)	0	0
Gifts made by spouse (for gift splitting only)							
					35% (.35)	0	0
					35% (.35)	0	0
					35% (.35)	0	0
					35% (.35)	0	0
					35% (.35)	0	0
					35% (.35)	0	0
Total exemption claimed. Enter here and on Part 2, line 4, above. May not exceed Part 2, line 3, above			**Total generation-skipping transfer tax.** Enter here; on page 3, Schedule A, Part 4, line 10; and on page 1, Part 2—Tax Computation, line 16				

(If more space is needed, attach additional sheets of same size.)

Form **990-EZ**

Department of the Treasury
Internal Revenue Service

Short Form
Return of Organization Exempt From Income Tax

Under section 501(c), 527, or 4947(a)(1) of the Internal Revenue Code
(except black lung benefit trust or private foundation)

▶ Sponsoring organizations of donor advised funds, organizations that operate one or more hospital facilities, and certain controlling organizations as defined in section 512(b)(13) must file Form 990 (see instructions). All other organizations with gross receipts less than $200,000 and total assets less than $500,000 at the end of the year may use this form.

▶ *The organization may have to use a copy of this return to satisfy state reporting requirements.*

OMB No. 1545-1150

2011

Open to Public Inspection

A For the 2011 calendar year, or tax year beginning , 2011, and ending , 20

B Check if applicable:
- ☐ Address change
- ☐ Name change
- ☐ Initial return
- ☐ Terminated
- ☐ Amended return
- ☐ Application pending

C Name of organization

Number and street (or P.O. box, if mail is not delivered to street address) | Room/suite

City or town, state or country, and ZIP + 4

D Employer identification number

E Telephone number

F Group Exemption Number ▶

G Accounting Method: ☐ Cash ☐ Accrual Other (specify) ▶

H Check ▶ ☐ if the organization is **not** required to attach Schedule B (Form 990, 990-EZ, or 990-PF).

I Website: ▶

J Tax-exempt status (check only one) – ☐ 501(c)(3) ☐ 501(c) ( ) ◀ (insert no.) ☐ 4947(a)(1) or ☐ 527

K Check ▶ ☐ if the organization is not a section 509(a)(3) supporting organization or a section 527 organization **and** its gross receipts are normally **not** more than $50,000. A Form 990-EZ or Form 990 return is not required though Form 990-N (e-postcard) may be required (see instructions). But if the organization chooses to file a return, be sure to file a complete return.

L Add lines 5b, 6c, and 7b, to line 9 to determine gross receipts. If gross receipts are $200,000 or more, or if total assets (Part II, line 25, column (B) below) are $500,000 or more, file Form 990 instead of Form 990-EZ . . . . ▶ $

Part I Revenue, Expenses, and Changes in Net Assets or Fund Balances (see the instructions for Part I.)

Check if the organization used Schedule O to respond to any question in this Part I . . . . ☐

Revenue	1	Contributions, gifts, grants, and similar amounts received		1	
	2	Program service revenue including government fees and contracts		2	
	3	Membership dues and assessments		3	
	4	Investment income		4	
	5a	Gross amount from sale of assets other than inventory	5a		
	b	Less: cost or other basis and sales expenses	5b		
	c	Gain or (loss) from sale of assets other than inventory (Subtract line 5b from line 5a)		5c	
	6	Gaming and fundraising events			
	a	Gross income from gaming (attach Schedule G if greater than $15,000)	6a		
	b	Gross income from fundraising events (not including $ ____ of contributions from fundraising events reported on line 1) (attach Schedule G if the sum of such gross income and contributions exceeds $15,000) . .	6b		
	c	Less: direct expenses from gaming and fundraising events . . .	6c		
	d	Net income or (loss) from gaming and fundraising events (add lines 6a and 6b and subtract line 6c)		6d	
	7a	Gross sales of inventory, less returns and allowances	7a		
	b	Less: cost of goods sold	7b		
	c	Gross profit or (loss) from sales of inventory (Subtract line 7b from line 7a)		7c	
	8	Other revenue (describe in Schedule O)		8	
	9	**Total revenue.** Add lines 1, 2, 3, 4, 5c, 6d, 7c, and 8 . . . . ▶		9	
Expenses	10	Grants and similar amounts paid (list in Schedule O)		10	
	11	Benefits paid to or for members		11	
	12	Salaries, other compensation, and employee benefits		12	
	13	Professional fees and other payments to independent contractors		13	
	14	Occupancy, rent, utilities, and maintenance		14	
	15	Printing, publications, postage, and shipping		15	
	16	Other expenses (describe in Schedule O)		16	
	17	**Total expenses.** Add lines 10 through 16 . . . . ▶		17	
Net Assets	18	Excess or (deficit) for the year (Subtract line 17 from line 9)		18	
	19	Net assets or fund balances at beginning of year (from line 27, column (A)) (must agree with end-of-year figure reported on prior year's return)		19	
	20	Other changes in net assets or fund balances (explain in Schedule O)		20	
	21	Net assets or fund balances at end of year. Combine lines 18 through 20 . . . . ▶		21	

For Paperwork Reduction Act Notice, see the separate instructions. Cat. No. 10642I Form **990-EZ** (2011)

Form 990-EZ (2011) Page **2**

Part II **Balance Sheets.** (see the instructions for Part II.)

Check if the organization used Schedule O to respond to any question in this Part II . . . . ☐

		(A) Beginning of year		(B) End of year
22	Cash, savings, and investments		22	
23	Land and buildings		23	
24	Other assets (describe in Schedule O)		24	
25	**Total assets**		25	
26	**Total liabilities** (describe in Schedule O)		26	
27	**Net assets or fund balances** (line 27 of column (B) **must** agree with line 21)		27	

Part III **Statement of Program Service Accomplishments** (see the instructions for Part III.)

Check if the organization used Schedule O to respond to any question in this Part III . . ☐

Expenses (Required for section 501(c)(3) and 501(c)(4) organizations and section 4947(a)(1) trusts; optional for others.)

What is the organization's primary exempt purpose?

Describe the organization's program service accomplishments for each of its three largest program services, as measured by expenses. In a clear and concise manner, describe the services provided, the number of persons benefited, and other relevant information for each program title.

28	(Grants $) If this amount includes foreign grants, check here . . . . ▶ ☐	28a	
29	(Grants $) If this amount includes foreign grants, check here . . . . ▶ ☐	29a	
30	(Grants $) If this amount includes foreign grants, check here . . . . ▶ ☐	30a	
31	Other program services (describe in Schedule O) (Grants $) If this amount includes foreign grants, check here . . . . ▶ ☐	31a	
32	**Total program service expenses** (add lines 28a through 31a) . . . . ▶	32	

Part IV **List of Officers, Directors, Trustees, and Key Employees.** List each one even if not compensated. (see the instructions for Part IV.)

Check if the organization used Schedule O to respond to any question in this Part IV . . . . ☐

(a) Name and address	**(b)** Title and average hours per week devoted to position	**(c)** Reportable compensation (Forms W-2/1099-MISC) **(if not paid, enter -0-)**	**(d)** Health benefits, contributions to employee benefit plans, and deferred compensation	**(e)** Estimated amount of other compensation

Form 990-EZ (2011) Page **3**

Part V **Other Information** (Note the Schedule A and personal benefit contract statement requirements in the instructions for Part V.) Check if the organization used Schedule O to respond to any question in this Part V ☐

			Yes	No
33	Did the organization engage in any significant activity not previously reported to the IRS? If "Yes," provide a detailed description of each activity in Schedule O	33		
34	Were any significant changes made to the organizing or governing documents? If "Yes," attach a conformed copy of the amended documents if they reflect a change to the organization's name. Otherwise, explain the change on Schedule O (see instructions)	34		
35a	Did the organization have unrelated business gross income of $1,000 or more during the year from business activities (such as those reported on lines 2, 6a, and 7a, among others)?	35a		
b	If "Yes," to line 35a, has the organization filed a Form 990-T for the year? If "No," provide an explanation in Schedule O	35b		
c	Was the organization a section 501(c)(4), 501(c)(5), or 501(c)(6) organization subject to section 6033(e) notice, reporting, and proxy tax requirements during the year? If "Yes," complete Schedule C, Part III	35c		
36	Did the organization undergo a liquidation, dissolution, termination, or significant disposition of net assets during the year? If "Yes," complete applicable parts of Schedule N	36		
37a	Enter amount of political expenditures, direct or indirect, as described in the instructions. ▶ 37a			
b	Did the organization file **Form 1120-POL** for this year?	37b		
38a	Did the organization borrow from, or make any loans to, any officer, director, trustee, or key employee **or** were any such loans made in a prior year and still outstanding at the end of the tax year covered by this return?	38a		
b	If "Yes," complete Schedule L, Part II and enter the total amount involved 38b			
39	Section 501(c)(7) organizations. Enter:			
a	Initiation fees and capital contributions included on line 9 39a			
b	Gross receipts, included on line 9, for public use of club facilities 39b			
40a	Section 501(c)(3) organizations. Enter amount of tax imposed on the organization during the year under: section 4911 ▶ ______ ; section 4912 ▶ ______ ; section 4955 ▶ ______			
b	Section 501(c)(3) and 501(c)(4) organizations. Did the organization engage in any section 4958 excess benefit transaction during the year, or did it engage in an excess benefit transaction in a prior year that has not been reported on any of its prior Forms 990 or 990-EZ? If "Yes," complete Schedule L, Part I	40b		
c	Section 501(c)(3) and 501(c)(4) organizations. Enter amount of tax imposed on organization managers or disqualified persons during the year under sections 4912, 4955, and 4958 ▶ ______			
d	Section 501(c)(3) and 501(c)(4) organizations. Enter amount of tax on line 40c reimbursed by the organization ▶ ______			
e	All organizations. At any time during the tax year, was the organization a party to a prohibited tax shelter transaction? If "Yes," complete Form 8886-T.	40e		
41	List the states with which a copy of this return is filed. ▶ ______			
42a	The organization's books are in care of ▶ ______ Telephone no. ▶ ______ Located at ▶ ______ ZIP + 4 ▶ ______			
			Yes	No
b	At any time during the calendar year, did the organization have an interest in or a signature or other authority over a financial account in a foreign country (such as a bank account, securities account, or other financial account)?	42b		
	If "Yes," enter the name of the foreign country: ▶ ______ See the instructions for exceptions and filing requirements for **Form TD F 90-22.1, Report of Foreign Bank and Financial Accounts.**			
c	At any time during the calendar year, did the organization maintain an office outside the U.S.?	42c		
	If "Yes," enter the name of the foreign country: ▶ ______			
43	Section 4947(a)(1) nonexempt charitable trusts filing Form 990-EZ in lieu of **Form 1041**—Check here ▶ ☐ and enter the amount of tax-exempt interest received or accrued during the tax year ▶ 43			
			Yes	No
44a	Did the organization maintain any donor advised funds during the year? If "Yes," Form 990 must be completed instead of Form 990-EZ	44a		
b	Did the organization operate one or more hospital facilities during the year? If "Yes," Form 990 must be completed instead of Form 990-EZ	44b		
c	Did the organization receive any payments for indoor tanning services during the year?	44c		
d	If "Yes" to line 44c, has the organization filed a Form 720 to report these payments? *If "No," provide an explanation in Schedule O*	44d		
45a	Did the organization have a controlled entity within the meaning of section 512(b)(13)?	45a		
45b	Did the organization receive any payment from or engage in any transaction with a controlled entity within the meaning of section 512(b)(13)? If "Yes," Form 990 and Schedule R may need to be completed instead of Form 990-EZ (see instructions)	45b		

Form **990-EZ** (2011)

Form 990-EZ (2011) Page **4**

			Yes	No
46	Did the organization engage, directly or indirectly, in political campaign activities on behalf of or in opposition to candidates for public office? If "Yes," complete Schedule C, Part I	46		

Part VI **Section 501(c)(3) organizations and section 4947(a)(1) nonexempt charitable trusts only.** All section 501(c)(3) organizations and section 4947(a)(1) nonexempt charitable trusts must answer questions 47–49b and 52, and complete the tables for lines 50 and 51.

Check if the organization used Schedule O to respond to any question in this Part VI . . . . ☐

			Yes	No
47	Did the organization engage in lobbying activities or have a section 501(h) election in effect during the tax year? If "Yes," complete Schedule C, Part II	47		
48	Is the organization a school as described in section 170(b)(1)(A)(ii)? If "Yes," complete Schedule E	48		
49a	Did the organization make any transfers to an exempt non-charitable related organization?	49a		
b	If "Yes," was the related organization a section 527 organization?	49b		

50 Complete this table for the organization's five highest compensated employees (other than officers, directors, trustees and key employees) who each received more than $100,000 of compensation from the organization. If there is none, enter "None."

(a) Name and address of each employee paid more than $100,000	**(b)** Title and average hours per week devoted to position	**(c)** Reportable compensation (Forms W-2/1099-MISC)	**(d)** Health benefits, contributions to employee benefit plans, and deferred compensation	**(e)** Estimated amount of other compensation

f Total number of other employees paid over $100,000 . . . . ▶ ____________

51 Complete this table for the organization's five highest compensated independent contractors who each received more than $100,000 of compensation from the organization. If there is none, enter "None."

(a) Name and address of each independent contractor paid more than $100,000	**(b)** Type of service	**(c)** Compensation

d Total number of other independent contractors each receiving over $100,000 . . ▶ ____________

52 Did the organization complete Schedule A? **Note**: All section 501(c)(3) organizations and 4947(a)(1) nonexempt charitable trusts must attach a completed Schedule A . . . . ▶ ☐ **Yes** ☐ **No**

Under penalties of perjury, I declare that I have examined this return, including accompanying schedules and statements, and to the best of my knowledge and belief, it is true, correct, and complete. Declaration of preparer (other than officer) is based on all information of which preparer has any knowledge.

Sign Here	▶ Signature of officer			Date	
	▶ Type or print name and title				
Paid Preparer Use Only	Print/Type preparer's name	Preparer's signature	Date	Check ☐ if self-employed	PTIN
	Firm's name ▶			Firm's EIN ▶	
	Firm's address ▶			Phone no.	

May the IRS discuss this return with the preparer shown above? See instructions . . . . ▶ ☐ **Yes** ☐ **No**

Form **990-EZ** (2011)

Form **990-T**

Department of the Treasury
Internal Revenue Service

Exempt Organization Business Income Tax Return
(and proxy tax under section 6033(e))

For calendar year 2011 or other tax year beginning ____________, 2011, and ending ________, 20 ___. ▶ See separate instructions.

OMB No. 1545-0687

2011

Open to Public Inspection for 501(c)(3) Organizations Only

A ☐ Check box if address changed

B Exempt under section
☐ 501( )( )
☐ 408(e) ☐ 220(e)
☐ 408A ☐ 530(a)
☐ 529(a)

C Book value of all assets at end of year

Print or Type

Name of organization (☐ Check box if name changed and see instructions.)

Number, street, and room or suite no. If a P.O. box, see instructions.

City or town, state, and ZIP code

D Employer identification number (Employees' trust, see instructions.)

E Unrelated business activity codes (See instructions.)

F Group exemption number (See instructions.) ▶

G Check organization type ▶ ☐ 501(c) corporation ☐ 501(c) trust ☐ 401(a) trust ☐ Other trust

H Describe the organization's primary unrelated business activity. ▶

I During the tax year, was the corporation a subsidiary in an affiliated group or a parent-subsidiary controlled group? . . ▶ ☐ Yes ☐ No
If "Yes," enter the name and identifying number of the parent corporation. ▶

J The books are in care of ▶ Telephone number ▶

Part I Unrelated Trade or Business Income

			(A) Income	(B) Expenses	(C) Net
1a	Gross receipts or sales				
b	Less returns and allowances	c Balance ▶ 1c			
2	Cost of goods sold (Schedule A, line 7)	2			
3	Gross profit. Subtract line 2 from line 1c	3			
4a	Capital gain net income (attach Schedule D)	4a			
b	Net gain (loss) (Form 4797, Part II, line 17) (attach Form 4797)	4b			
c	Capital loss deduction for trusts	4c			
5	Income (loss) from partnerships and S corporations (attach statement)	5			
6	Rent income (Schedule C)	6			
7	Unrelated debt-financed income (Schedule E)	7			
8	Interest, annuities, royalties, and rents from controlled organizations (Schedule F)	8			
9	Investment income of a section 501(c)(7), (9), or (17) organization (Schedule G)	9			
10	Exploited exempt activity income (Schedule I)	10			
11	Advertising income (Schedule J)	11			
12	Other income (See instructions; attach schedule.)	12			
13	**Total.** Combine lines 3 through 12	13			

Part II Deductions Not Taken Elsewhere (See instructions for limitations on deductions.) (Except for contributions, deductions must be directly connected with the unrelated business income.)

14	Compensation of officers, directors, and trustees (Schedule K)	14	
15	Salaries and wages	15	
16	Repairs and maintenance	16	
17	Bad debts	17	
18	Interest (attach schedule)	18	
19	Taxes and licenses	19	
20	Charitable contributions (See instructions for limitation rules.)	20	
21	Depreciation (attach Form 4562) — 21		
22	Less depreciation claimed on Schedule A and elsewhere on return — 22a	22b	
23	Depletion	23	
24	Contributions to deferred compensation plans	24	
25	Employee benefit programs	25	
26	Excess exempt expenses (Schedule I)	26	
27	Excess readership costs (Schedule J)	27	
28	Other deductions (attach schedule)	28	
29	**Total deductions.** Add lines 14 through 28	29	
30	Unrelated business taxable income before net operating loss deduction. Subtract line 29 from line 13	30	
31	Net operating loss deduction (limited to the amount on line 30)	31	
32	Unrelated business taxable income before specific deduction. Subtract line 31 from line 30	32	
33	Specific deduction (Generally $1,000, but see line 33 instructions for exceptions.)	33	
34	**Unrelated business taxable income.** Subtract line 33 from line 32. If line 33 is greater than line 32, enter the smaller of zero or line 32	34	

For Paperwork Reduction Act Notice, see instructions. Cat. No. 11291J Form **990-T** (2011)

Form 990-T (2011) Page **2**

Part III Tax Computation

35 **Organizations Taxable as Corporations.** See instructions for tax computation. Controlled group members (sections 1561 and 1563) check here ▶ ☐ **See instructions** and:

a Enter your share of the $50,000, $25,000, and $9,925,000 taxable income brackets (in that order):
(1) $ **(2)** $ **(3)** $

b Enter organization's share of: **(1)** Additional 5% tax (not more than $11,750) $
(2) Additional 3% tax (not more than $100,000) $

c	Income tax on the amount on line 34 ▶	35c	
36	**Trusts Taxable at Trust Rates.** See instructions for tax computation. Income tax on the amount on line 34 from: ☐ Tax rate schedule or ☐ Schedule D (Form 1041) ▶	36	
37	**Proxy tax.** See instructions ▶	37	
38	Alternative minimum tax	38	
39	**Total.** Add lines 37 and 38 to line 35c or 36, whichever applies	39	

Part IV Tax and Payments

40a	Foreign tax credit (corporations attach Form 1118; trusts attach Form 1116)	40a			
b	Other credits (see instructions)	40b			
c	General business credit. Attach Form 3800 (see instructions)	40c			
d	Credit for prior year minimum tax (attach Form 8801 or 8827)	40d			
e	**Total credits.** Add lines 40a through 40d			40e	
41	Subtract line 40e from line 39			41	
42	Other taxes. Check if from: ☐ Form 4255 ☐ Form 8611 ☐ Form 8697 ☐ Form 8866 ☐ Other (attach schedule)			42	
43	**Total tax.** Add lines 41 and 42			43	
44a	Payments: A 2010 overpayment credited to 2011	44a			
b	2011 estimated tax payments	44b			
c	Tax deposited with Form 8868	44c			
d	Foreign organizations: Tax paid or withheld at source (see instructions)	44d			
e	Backup withholding (see instructions)	44e			
f	Credit for small employer health insurance premiums (Attach Form 8941)	44f			
g	Other credits and payments: ☐ Form 2439 ______ ☐ Form 4136 ______ ☐ Other ______ Total ▶	44g			
45	**Total payments.** Add lines 44a through 44g			45	
46	Estimated tax penalty (see instructions). Check if Form 2220 is attached ▶ ☐			46	
47	**Tax due.** If line 45 is less than the total of lines 43 and 46, enter amount owed ▶			47	
48	**Overpayment.** If line 45 is larger than the total of lines 43 and 46, enter amount overpaid ▶			48	
49	Enter the amount of line 48 you want: **Credited to 2012 estimated tax ▶** **Refunded ▶**			49	

Part V Statements Regarding Certain Activities and Other Information (see instructions)

		Yes	No
1	At any time during the 2011 calendar year, did the organization have an interest in or a signature or other authority over a financial account (bank, securities, or other) in a foreign country? If YES, the organization may have to file Form TD F 90-22.1, Report of Foreign Bank and Financial Accounts. If YES, enter the name of the foreign country here ▶		
2	During the tax year, did the organization receive a distribution from, or was it the grantor of, or transferor to, a foreign trust? If YES, see instructions for other forms the organization may have to file.		
3	Enter the amount of tax-exempt interest received or accrued during the tax year ▶ $		

Schedule A—Cost of Goods Sold. Enter method of inventory valuation ▶

1	Inventory at beginning of year	1		6	Inventory at end of year	6	
2	Purchases	2		7	**Cost of goods sold.** Subtract line 6 from line 5. Enter here and in Part I, line 2	7	
3	Cost of labor	3					
4a	Additional section 263A costs (attach schedule)	4a		8	Do the rules of section 263A (with respect to property produced or acquired for resale) apply to the organization?	Yes	No
b	Other costs (attach schedule)	4b					
5	**Total.** Add lines 1 through 4b	5					

Sign Here

Under penalties of perjury, I declare that I have examined this return, including accompanying schedules and statements, and to the best of my knowledge and belief, it is true, correct, and complete. Declaration of preparer (other than taxpayer) is based on all information of which preparer has any knowledge.

▶ Signature of officer | Date | ▶ Title

May the IRS discuss this return with the preparer shown below (see instructions)? ☐**Yes** ☐**No**

Paid Preparer Use Only

Print/Type preparer's name	Preparer's signature	Date	Check ☐ if self-employed	PTIN
Firm's name ▶			Firm's EIN ▶	
Firm's address ▶			Phone no.	

Form **990-T** (2011)

Schedule C—Rent Income (From Real Property and Personal Property Leased With Real Property)
(see instructions)

1. Description of property
(1)
(2)
(3)
(4)

2. Rent received or accrued		**3(a)** Deductions directly connected with the income in columns 2(a) and 2(b) (attach schedule)
(a) From personal property (if the percentage of rent for personal property is more than 10% but not more than 50%)	**(b)** From real and personal property (if the percentage of rent for personal property exceeds 50% or if the rent is based on profit or income)	
(1)		
(2)		
(3)		
(4)		
Total	Total	**(b) Total deductions.** Enter here and on page 1, Part I, line 6, column (B) ▶
(c) Total income. Add totals of columns 2(a) and 2(b). Enter here and on page 1, Part I, line 6, column (A) . . . ▶		

Schedule E—Unrelated Debt-Financed Income (see instructions)

1. Description of debt-financed property	**2.** Gross income from or allocable to debt-financed property	**3.** Deductions directly connected with or allocable to debt-financed property: **(a)** Straight line depreciation (attach schedule)	**(b)** Other deductions (attach schedule)
(1)			
(2)			
(3)			
(4)			

4. Amount of average acquisition debt on or allocable to debt-financed property (attach schedule)	**5.** Average adjusted basis of or allocable to debt-financed property (attach schedule)	**6.** Column 4 divided by column 5	**7.** Gross income reportable (column 2 × column 6)	**8.** Allocable deductions (column 6 × total of columns 3(a) and 3(b))
(1)		%		
(2)		%		
(3)		%		
(4)		%		
			Enter here and on page 1, Part I, line 7, column (A).	Enter here and on page 1, Part I, line 7, column (B).
Totals . . . . ▶				
Total dividends-received deductions included in column 8 . . . . ▶				

Schedule F—Interest, Annuities, Royalties, and Rents From Controlled Organizations (see instructions)

1. Name of controlled organization	**2.** Employer identification number	Exempt Controlled Organizations: **3.** Net unrelated income (loss) (see instructions)	**4.** Total of specified payments made	**5.** Part of column 4 that is included in the controlling organization's gross income	**6.** Deductions directly connected with income in column 5
(1)					
(2)					
(3)					
(4)					

Nonexempt Controlled Organizations

7. Taxable Income	**8.** Net unrelated income (loss) (see instructions)	**9.** Total of specified payments made	**10.** Part of column 9 that is included in the controlling organization's gross income	**11.** Deductions directly connected with income in column 10
(1)				
(2)				
(3)				
(4)				
			Add columns 5 and 10. Enter here and on page 1, Part I, line 8, column (A).	Add columns 6 and 11. Enter here and on page 1, Part I, line 8, column (B).
Totals . . . . ▶				

Form **1041** Department of the Treasury—Internal Revenue Service

U.S. Income Tax Return for Estates and Trusts 2011

OMB No. 1545-0092

A Check all that apply:
- ☐ Decedent's estate
- ☐ Simple trust
- ☐ Complex trust
- ☐ Qualified disability trust
- ☐ ESBT (S portion only)
- ☐ Grantor type trust
- ☐ Bankruptcy estate-Ch. 7
- ☐ Bankruptcy estate-Ch. 11
- ☐ Pooled income fund

B Number of Schedules K-1 attached (see instructions) ▶

For calendar year 2011 or fiscal year beginning , 2011, and ending , 20

Name of estate or trust (If a grantor type trust, see the instructions.)

Name and title of fiduciary

Number, street, and room or suite no. (If a P.O. box, see the instructions.)

City or town, state, and ZIP code

C Employer identification number

D Date entity created

E Nonexempt charitable and split-interest trusts, check applicable box(es), see instructions.
- ☐ Described in sec. 4947(a)(1). Check here if not a private foundation . . . ▶ ☐
- ☐ Described in sec. 4947(a)(2)

F Check applicable boxes: ☐ Initial return ☐ Final return ☐ Amended return ☐ Change in trust's name ☐ Change in fiduciary ☐ Change in fiduciary's name ☐ Change in fiduciary's address

G Check here if the estate or filing trust made a section 645 election . . . . . . ▶☐

Income	1	Interest income	1	
	2a	Total ordinary dividends	2a	
	b	Qualified dividends allocable to: **(1)** Beneficiaries ______ **(2)** Estate or trust ______		
	3	Business income or (loss). Attach Schedule C or C-EZ (Form 1040)	3	
	4	Capital gain or (loss). Attach Schedule D (Form 1041)	4	
	5	Rents, royalties, partnerships, other estates and trusts, etc. Attach Schedule E (Form 1040)	5	
	6	Farm income or (loss). Attach Schedule F (Form 1040)	6	
	7	Ordinary gain or (loss). Attach Form 4797	7	
	8	Other income. List type and amount ______	8	
	9	**Total income.** Combine lines 1, 2a, and 3 through 8 ▶	9	
Deductions	10	Interest. Check if Form 4952 is attached ▶ ☐	10	
	11	Taxes	11	
	12	Fiduciary fees	12	
	13	Charitable deduction (from Schedule A, line 7)	13	
	14	Attorney, accountant, and return preparer fees	14	
	15a	Other deductions **not** subject to the 2% floor (attach schedule)	15a	
	b	Allowable miscellaneous itemized deductions subject to the 2% floor	15b	
	16	Add lines 10 through 15b ▶	16	
	17	Adjusted total income or (loss). Subtract line 16 from line 9 . . . 17		
	18	Income distribution deduction (from Schedule B, line 15). Attach Schedules K-1 (Form 1041)	18	
	19	Estate tax deduction including certain generation-skipping taxes (attach computation)	19	
	20	Exemption	20	
	21	Add lines 18 through 20 ▶	21	
Tax and Payments	22	Taxable income. Subtract line 21 from line 17. If a loss, see instructions	22	
	23	**Total tax** (from Schedule G, line 7)	23	
	24	**Payments: a** 2011 estimated tax payments and amount applied from 2010 return	24a	
	b	Estimated tax payments allocated to beneficiaries (from Form 1041-T)	24b	
	c	Subtract line 24b from line 24a	24c	
	d	Tax paid with Form 7004 (see instructions)	24d	
	e	Federal income tax withheld. If any is from Form(s) 1099, check ▶ ☐	24e	
		Other payments: **f** Form 2439 ______ ; **g** Form 4136 ______ ; Total ▶	24h	
	25	**Total payments.** Add lines 24c through 24e, and 24h ▶	25	
	26	Estimated tax penalty (see instructions)	26	
	27	**Tax due.** If line 25 is smaller than the total of lines 23 and 26, enter amount owed	27	
	28	**Overpayment.** If line 25 is larger than the total of lines 23 and 26, enter amount overpaid	28	
	29	Amount of line 28 to be: **a Credited to 2012 estimated tax ▶** ; **b Refunded ▶**	29	

Sign Here

Under penalties of perjury, I declare that I have examined this return, including accompanying schedules and statements, and to the best of my knowledge and belief, it is true, correct, and complete. Declaration of preparer (other than taxpayer) is based on all information of which preparer has any knowledge.

▶ Signature of fiduciary or officer representing fiduciary | Date | ▶ EIN of fiduciary if a financial institution

May the IRS discuss this return with the preparer shown below (see instr.)? ☐ **Yes** ☐ **No**

Paid Preparer Use Only

Print/Type preparer's name	Preparer's signature	Date	Check ☐ if self-employed	PTIN
Firm's name ▶			Firm's EIN ▶	
Firm's address ▶			Phone no.	

For Paperwork Reduction Act Notice, see the separate instructions. Cat. No. 11370H Form **1041** (2011)

Form 1041 (2011) Page **2**

Schedule A **Charitable Deduction.** Do not complete for a simple trust or a pooled income fund.

1	Amounts paid or permanently set aside for charitable purposes from gross income (see instructions)	1	
2	Tax-exempt income allocable to charitable contributions (see instructions)	2	
3	Subtract line 2 from line 1	3	
4	Capital gains for the tax year allocated to corpus and paid or permanently set aside for charitable purposes	4	
5	Add lines 3 and 4	5	
6	Section 1202 exclusion allocable to capital gains paid or permanently set aside for charitable purposes (see instructions)	6	
7	**Charitable deduction.** Subtract line 6 from line 5. Enter here and on page 1, line 13	7	

Schedule B **Income Distribution Deduction**

1	Adjusted total income (see instructions)	1	
2	Adjusted tax-exempt interest	2	
3	Total net gain from Schedule D (Form 1041), line 15, column (1) (see instructions)	3	
4	Enter amount from Schedule A, line 4 (minus any allocable section 1202 exclusion)	4	
5	Capital gains for the tax year included on Schedule A, line 1 (see instructions)	5	
6	Enter any gain from page 1, line 4, as a negative number. If page 1, line 4, is a loss, enter the loss as a positive number	6	
7	**Distributable net income.** Combine lines 1 through 6. If zero or less, enter -0-	7	
8	If a complex trust, enter accounting income for the tax year as determined under the governing instrument and applicable local law . 8		
9	Income required to be distributed currently	9	
10	Other amounts paid, credited, or otherwise required to be distributed	10	
11	Total distributions. Add lines 9 and 10. If greater than line 8, see instructions	11	
12	Enter the amount of tax-exempt income included on line 11	12	
13	Tentative income distribution deduction. Subtract line 12 from line 11	13	
14	Tentative income distribution deduction. Subtract line 2 from line 7. If zero or less, enter -0-	14	
15	**Income distribution deduction.** Enter the smaller of line 13 or line 14 here and on page 1, line 18	15	

Schedule G **Tax Computation** (see instructions)

1	**Tax: a** Tax on taxable income (see instructions)	1a			
	b Tax on lump-sum distributions. Attach Form 4972	1b			
	c Alternative minimum tax (from Schedule I (Form 1041), line 56)	1c			
	d **Total.** Add lines 1a through 1c ▶			1d	
2a	Foreign tax credit. Attach Form 1116	2a			
b	General business credit. Attach Form 3800	2b			
c	Credit for prior year minimum tax. Attach Form 8801	2c			
d	Bond credits. Attach Form 8912	2d			
3	**Total credits.** Add lines 2a through 2d ▶			3	
4	Subtract line 3 from line 1d. If zero or less, enter -0-			4	
5	Recapture taxes. Check if from: ☐ Form 4255 ☐ Form 8611			5	
6	Household employment taxes. Attach Schedule H (Form 1040)			6	
7	**Total tax.** Add lines 4 through 6. Enter here and on page 1, line 23 ▶			7	

	Other Information	Yes	No
1	Did the estate or trust receive tax-exempt income? If "Yes," attach a computation of the allocation of expenses Enter the amount of tax-exempt interest income and exempt-interest dividends ▶ $		
2	Did the estate or trust receive all or any part of the earnings (salary, wages, and other compensation) of any individual by reason of a contract assignment or similar arrangement?		
3	At any time during calendar year 2011, did the estate or trust have an interest in or a signature or other authority over a bank, securities, or other financial account in a foreign country?		
	See the instructions for exceptions and filing requirements for Form TD F 90-22.1. If "Yes," enter the name of the foreign country ▶		
4	During the tax year, did the estate or trust receive a distribution from, or was it the grantor of, or transferor to, a foreign trust? If "Yes," the estate or trust may have to file Form 3520. See instructions		
5	Did the estate or trust receive, or pay, any qualified residence interest on seller-provided financing? If "Yes," see the instructions for required attachment		
6	If this is an estate or a complex trust making the section 663(b) election, check here (see instructions) ▶ ☐		
7	To make a section 643(e)(3) election, attach Schedule D (Form 1041), and check here (see instructions) ▶ ☐		
8	If the decedent's estate has been open for more than 2 years, attach an explanation for the delay in closing the estate, and check here ▶ ☐		
9	Are any present or future trust beneficiaries skip persons? See instructions		

661111

☐ Final K-1 ☐ Amended K-1 OMB No. 1545-0092

Schedule K-1 (Form 1041)
Department of the Treasury
Internal Revenue Service

2011

For calendar year 2011, or tax year beginning ________, 2011, and ending ________, 20 ____

Beneficiary's Share of Income, Deductions, Credits, etc.

▶ See back of form and instructions.

Part I Information About the Estate or Trust

A Estate's or trust's employer identification number

B Estate's or trust's name

C Fiduciary's name, address, city, state, and ZIP code

D ☐ Check if Form 1041-T was filed and enter the date it was filed ________

E ☐ Check if this is the final Form 1041 for the estate or trust

Part II Information About the Beneficiary

F Beneficiary's identifying number

G Beneficiary's name, address, city, state, and ZIP code

H ☐ Domestic beneficiary ☐ Foreign beneficiary

Part III Beneficiary's Share of Current Year Income, Deductions, Credits, and Other Items

1	Interest income	11	Final year deductions
2a	Ordinary dividends		
2b	Qualified dividends		
3	Net short-term capital gain		
4a	Net long-term capital gain		
4b	28% rate gain	12	Alternative minimum tax adjustment
4c	Unrecaptured section 1250 gain		
5	Other portfolio and nonbusiness income		
6	Ordinary business income		
7	Net rental real estate income	13	Credits and credit recapture
8	Other rental income		
9	Directly apportioned deductions		
		14	Other information
10	Estate tax deduction		

*See attached statement for additional information.

Note. A statement must be attached showing the beneficiary's share of income and directly apportioned deductions from each business, rental real estate, and other rental activity.

For IRS Use Only

For Paperwork Reduction Act Notice, see the Instructions for Form 1041. Cat. No. 11380D **Schedule K-1 (Form 1041) 2011**

Form **1065**
Department of the Treasury
Internal Revenue Service

U.S. Return of Partnership Income

For calendar year 2011, or tax year beginning ______, 2011, ending ______, 20____.
▶ See separate instructions.

OMB No. 1545-0099
2011

A Principal business activity	Print or type.	Name of partnership	**D Employer identification number**
B Principal product or service		Number, street, and room or suite no. If a P.O. box, see the instructions.	E Date business started
C Business code number		City or town, state, and ZIP code	F Total assets (see the instructions) $

G Check applicable boxes: **(1)** ☐ Initial return **(2)** ☐ Final return **(3)** ☐ Name change **(4)** ☐ Address change **(5)** ☐ Amended return
(6) ☐ Technical termination - also check (1) or (2)
H Check accounting method: **(1)** ☐ Cash **(2)** ☐ Accrual **(3)** ☐ Other (specify) ▶
I Number of Schedules K-1. Attach one for each person who was a partner at any time during the tax year ▶
J Check if Schedules C and M-3 are attached . . . ☐

Caution. *Include **only** trade or business income and expenses on lines 1a through 22 below. See the instructions for more information.*

Income	1a	Merchant card and third-party payments (including amounts reported on Form(s) 1099-K). For 2011, enter -0-	1a		
	b	Gross receipts or sales not reported on line 1a (see instructions)	1b		
	c	Total. Add lines 1a and 1b	1c		
	d	Returns and allowances plus any other adjustments to line 1a (see instructions)	1d		
	e	Subtract line 1d from line 1c	1e		
	2	Cost of goods sold (attach Form 1125-A)	2		
	3	Gross profit. Subtract line 2 from line 1e		3	
	4	Ordinary income (loss) from other partnerships, estates, and trusts (attach statement)		4	
	5	Net farm profit (loss) (attach Schedule F (Form 1040))		5	
	6	Net gain (loss) from Form 4797, Part II, line 17 (attach Form 4797)		6	
	7	Other income (loss) (attach statement)		7	
	8	**Total income (loss).** Combine lines 3 through 7		8	
Deductions (see the instructions for limitations)	9	Salaries and wages (other than to partners) (less employment credits)		9	
	10	Guaranteed payments to partners		10	
	11	Repairs and maintenance		11	
	12	Bad debts		12	
	13	Rent		13	
	14	Taxes and licenses		14	
	15	Interest		15	
	16a	Depreciation (if required, attach Form 4562)	16a		
	b	Less depreciation reported on Form 1125-A and elsewhere on return	16b	16c	
	17	Depletion **(Do not deduct oil and gas depletion.)**		17	
	18	Retirement plans, etc.		18	
	19	Employee benefit programs		19	
	20	Other deductions (attach statement)		20	
	21	**Total deductions.** Add the amounts shown in the far right column for lines 9 through 20.		21	
	22	**Ordinary business income (loss).** Subtract line 21 from line 8		22	

Sign Here

Under penalties of perjury, I declare that I have examined this return, including accompanying schedules and statements, and to the best of my knowledge and belief, it is true, correct, and complete. Declaration of preparer (other than general partner or limited liability company member manager) is based on all information of which preparer has any knowledge.

▶ Signature of general partner or limited liability company member manager ▶ Date

May the IRS discuss this return with the preparer shown below (see instructions)? ☐ **Yes** ☐ **No**

Paid Preparer Use Only

Print/Type preparer's name	Preparer's signature	Date	Check ☐ if self- employed	PTIN
Firm's name ▶			Firm's EIN ▶	
Firm's address ▶			Phone no.	

For Paperwork Reduction Act Notice, see separate instructions. Cat. No. 11390Z Form **1065** (2011)

Form 1065 (2011) Page **2**

Schedule B Other Information

		Yes	No
1	What type of entity is filing this return? Check the applicable box:		
a	☐ Domestic general partnership **b** ☐ Domestic limited partnership		
c	☐ Domestic limited liability company **d** ☐ Domestic limited liability partnership		
e	☐ Foreign partnership **f** ☐ Other ▶		
2	At any time during the tax year, was any partner in the partnership a disregarded entity, a partnership (including an entity treated as a partnership), a trust, an S corporation, an estate (other than an estate of a deceased partner), or a nominee or similar person?		
3	At the end of the tax year:		
a	Did any foreign or domestic corporation, partnership (including any entity treated as a partnership), trust, or tax-exempt organization, or any foreign government own, directly or indirectly, an interest of 50% or more in the profit, loss, or capital of the partnership? For rules of constructive ownership, see instructions. If "Yes," attach Schedule B-1, Information on Partners Owning 50% or More of the Partnership		
b	Did any individual or estate own, directly or indirectly, an interest of 50% or more in the profit, loss, or capital of the partnership? For rules of constructive ownership, see instructions. If "Yes," attach Schedule B-1, Information on Partners Owning 50% or More of the Partnership		
4	At the end of the tax year, did the partnership:		
a	Own directly 20% or more, or own, directly or indirectly, 50% or more of the total voting power of all classes of stock entitled to vote of any foreign or domestic corporation? For rules of constructive ownership, see instructions. If "Yes," complete (i) through (iv) below		

(i) Name of Corporation	**(ii)** Employer Identification Number (if any)	**(iii)** Country of Incorporation	**(iv)** Percentage Owned in Voting Stock

		Yes	No
b	Own directly an interest of 20% or more, or own, directly or indirectly, an interest of 50% or more in the profit, loss, or capital in any foreign or domestic partnership (including an entity treated as a partnership) or in the beneficial interest of a trust? For rules of constructive ownership, see instructions. If "Yes," complete (i) through (v) below		

(i) Name of Entity	**(ii)** Employer Identification Number (if any)	**(iii)** Type of Entity	**(iv)** Country of Organization	**(v)** Maximum Percentage Owned in Profit, Loss, or Capital

Form **1065** (2011)

Form 1065 (2011) Page **3**

		Yes	No
5	Did the partnership file Form 8893, Election of Partnership Level Tax Treatment, or an election statement under section 6231(a)(1)(B)(ii) for partnership-level tax treatment, that is in effect for this tax year? See Form 8893 for more details . . .		
6	Does the partnership satisfy **all four** of the following conditions?		
a	The partnership's total receipts for the tax year were less than $250,000.		
b	The partnership's total assets at the end of the tax year were less than $1 million.		
c	Schedules K-1 are filed with the return and furnished to the partners on or before the due date (including extensions) for the partnership return.		
d	The partnership is not filing and is not required to file Schedule M-3 . . .		
	If "Yes," the partnership is not required to complete Schedules L, M-1, and M-2; Item F on page 1 of Form 1065; or Item L on Schedule K-1.		
7	Is this partnership a publicly traded partnership as defined in section 469(k)(2)? . . .		
8	During the tax year, did the partnership have any debt that was cancelled, was forgiven, or had the terms modified so as to reduce the principal amount of the debt? . . .		
9	Has this partnership filed, or is it required to file, Form 8918, Material Advisor Disclosure Statement, to provide information on any reportable transaction? . . .		
10	At any time during calendar year 2011, did the partnership have an interest in or a signature or other authority over a financial account in a foreign country (such as a bank account, securities account, or other financial account)? See the instructions for exceptions and filing requirements for Form TD F 90-22.1, Report of Foreign Bank and Financial Accounts. If "Yes," enter the name of the foreign country. ▶		
11	At any time during the tax year, did the partnership receive a distribution from, or was it the grantor of, or transferor to, a foreign trust? If "Yes," the partnership may have to file Form 3520, Annual Return To Report Transactions With Foreign Trusts and Receipt of Certain Foreign Gifts. See instructions . . .		
12a	Is the partnership making, or had it previously made (and not revoked), a section 754 election? . . .		
	See instructions for details regarding a section 754 election.		
b	Did the partnership make for this tax year an optional basis adjustment under section 743(b) or 734(b)? If "Yes," attach a statement showing the computation and allocation of the basis adjustment. See instructions . . .		
c	Is the partnership required to adjust the basis of partnership assets under section 743(b) or 734(b) because of a substantial built-in loss (as defined under section 743(d)) or substantial basis reduction (as defined under section 734(d))? If "Yes," attach a statement showing the computation and allocation of the basis adjustment. See instructions.		
13	Check this box if, during the current or prior tax year, the partnership distributed any property received in a like-kind exchange or contributed such property to another entity (other than disregarded entities wholly-owned by the partnership throughout the tax year) . . . ▶ ☐		
14	At any time during the tax year, did the partnership distribute to any partner a tenancy-in-common or other undivided interest in partnership property? . . .		
15	If the partnership is required to file Form 8858, Information Return of U.S. Persons With Respect To Foreign Disregarded Entities, enter the number of Forms 8858 attached. See instructions ▶		
16	Does the partnership have any foreign partners? If "Yes," enter the number of Forms 8805, Foreign Partner's Information Statement of Section 1446 Withholding Tax, filed for this partnership. ▶		
17	Enter the number of Forms 8865, Return of U.S. Persons With Respect to Certain Foreign Partnerships, attached to this return. ▶		
18a	Did you make any payments in 2011 that would require you to file Form(s) 1099? See instructions . . .		
b	If "Yes," did you or will you file all required Form(s) 1099? . . .		
19	Enter the number of Form(s) 5471, Information Return of U.S. Persons With Respect To Certain Foreign Corporations, attached to this return. ▶		

Designation of Tax Matters Partner (see instructions)

Enter below the general partner designated as the tax matters partner (TMP) for the tax year of this return:

Name of designated TMP ▶		Identifying number of TMP ▶	
If the TMP is an entity, name of TMP representative ▶		Phone number of TMP ▶	
Address of designated TMP ▶			

Form **1065** (2011)

Form 1065 (2011) Page **4**

Schedule K		Partners' Distributive Share Items			Total amount
Income (Loss)	1	Ordinary business income (loss) (page 1, line 22)		1	
	2	Net rental real estate income (loss) (attach Form 8825)		2	
	3a	Other gross rental income (loss)	3a		
	b	Expenses from other rental activities (attach statement)	3b		
	c	Other net rental income (loss). Subtract line 3b from line 3a		3c	
	4	Guaranteed payments		4	
	5	Interest income		5	
	6	Dividends: a Ordinary dividends		6a	
		b Qualified dividends	6b		
	7	Royalties		7	
	8	Net short-term capital gain (loss) (attach Schedule D (Form 1065))		8	
	9a	Net long-term capital gain (loss) (attach Schedule D (Form 1065))		9a	
	b	Collectibles (28%) gain (loss)	9b		
	c	Unrecaptured section 1250 gain (attach statement)	9c		
	10	Net section 1231 gain (loss) (attach Form 4797)		10	
	11	Other income (loss) (see instructions) Type ▶		11	
Deductions	12	Section 179 deduction (attach Form 4562)		12	
	13a	Contributions		13a	
	b	Investment interest expense		13b	
	c	Section 59(e)(2) expenditures: **(1)** Type ▶ ______ **(2)** Amount ▶		13c(2)	
	d	Other deductions (see instructions) Type ▶		13d	
Self-Employ-ment	14a	Net earnings (loss) from self-employment		14a	
	b	Gross farming or fishing income		14b	
	c	Gross nonfarm income		14c	
Credits	15a	Low-income housing credit (section 42(j)(5))		15a	
	b	Low-income housing credit (other)		15b	
	c	Qualified rehabilitation expenditures (rental real estate) (attach Form 3468)		15c	
	d	Other rental real estate credits (see instructions) Type ▶ ______		15d	
	e	Other rental credits (see instructions) Type ▶ ______		15e	
	f	Other credits (see instructions) Type ▶		15f	
Foreign Transactions	16a	Name of country or U.S. possession ▶ ______			
	b	Gross income from all sources		16b	
	c	Gross income sourced at partner level		16c	
		Foreign gross income sourced at partnership level			
	d	Passive category ▶ ______ **e** General category ▶ ______ **f** Other ▶		16f	
		Deductions allocated and apportioned at partner level			
	g	Interest expense ▶ ______ **h** Other ▶		16h	
		Deductions allocated and apportioned at partnership level to foreign source income			
	i	Passive category ▶ ______ **j** General category ▶ ______ **k** Other ▶		16k	
	l	Total foreign taxes (check one): ▶ Paid ☐ Accrued ☐		16l	
	m	Reduction in taxes available for credit (attach statement)		16m	
	n	Other foreign tax information (attach statement)			
Alternative Minimum Tax (AMT) Items	17a	Post-1986 depreciation adjustment		17a	
	b	Adjusted gain or loss		17b	
	c	Depletion (other than oil and gas)		17c	
	d	Oil, gas, and geothermal properties—gross income		17d	
	e	Oil, gas, and geothermal properties—deductions		17e	
	f	Other AMT items (attach statement)		17f	
Other Information	18a	Tax-exempt interest income		18a	
	b	Other tax-exempt income		18b	
	c	Nondeductible expenses		18c	
	19a	Distributions of cash and marketable securities		19a	
	b	Distributions of other property		19b	
	20a	Investment income		20a	
	b	Investment expenses		20b	
	c	Other items and amounts (attach statement)			

Form **1065** (2011)

Form 1065 (2011) Page **5**

Analysis of Net Income (Loss)

1	Net income (loss). Combine Schedule K, lines 1 through 11. From the result, subtract the sum of Schedule K, lines 12 through 13d, and 16l . . .	1	

2 Analysis by partner type:	**(i)** Corporate	**(ii)** Individual (active)	**(iii)** Individual (passive)	**(iv)** Partnership	**(v)** Exempt organization	**(vi)** Nominee/Other
a General partners						
b Limited partners						

Schedule L **Balance Sheets per Books**

Assets	Beginning of tax year		End of tax year	
	(a)	(b)	(c)	(d)
1 Cash				
2a Trade notes and accounts receivable				
b Less allowance for bad debts				
3 Inventories				
4 U.S. government obligations				
5 Tax-exempt securities				
6 Other current assets (attach statement)				
7a Loans to partners (or persons related to partners)				
b Mortgage and real estate loans				
8 Other investments (attach statement)				
9a Buildings and other depreciable assets				
b Less accumulated depreciation				
10a Depletable assets				
b Less accumulated depletion				
11 Land (net of any amortization)				
12a Intangible assets (amortizable only)				
b Less accumulated amortization				
13 Other assets (attach statement)				
14 Total assets				
Liabilities and Capital				
15 Accounts payable				
16 Mortgages, notes, bonds payable in less than 1 year				
17 Other current liabilities (attach statement)				
18 All nonrecourse loans				
19a Loans from partners (or persons related to partners)				
b Mortgages, notes, bonds payable in 1 year or more				
20 Other liabilities (attach statement)				
21 Partners' capital accounts				
22 Total liabilities and capital				

Schedule M-1 **Reconciliation of Income (Loss) per Books With Income (Loss) per Return**
Note. Schedule M-3 may be required instead of Schedule M-1 (see instructions).

1 Net income (loss) per books		**6** Income recorded on books this year not included on Schedule K, lines 1 through 11 (itemize):	
2 Income included on Schedule K, lines 1, 2, 3c, 5, 6a, 7, 8, 9a, 10, and 11, not recorded on books this year (itemize):		**a** Tax-exempt interest $	
3 Guaranteed payments (other than health insurance)		**7** Deductions included on Schedule K, lines 1 through 13d, and 16l, not charged against book income this year (itemize):	
4 Expenses recorded on books this year not included on Schedule K, lines 1 through 13d, and 16l (itemize):		**a** Depreciation $	
a Depreciation $		**8** Add lines 6 and 7	
b Travel and entertainment $		**9** Income (loss) (Analysis of Net Income (Loss), line 1). Subtract line 8 from line 5	
5 Add lines 1 through 4			

Schedule M-2 **Analysis of Partners' Capital Accounts**

1 Balance at beginning of year		**6** Distributions: **a** Cash	
2 Capital contributed: **a** Cash		**b** Property	
b Property		**7** Other decreases (itemize):	
3 Net income (loss) per books			
4 Other increases (itemize):		**8** Add lines 6 and 7	
5 Add lines 1 through 4		**9** Balance at end of year. Subtract line 8 from line 5	

651111

☐ Final K-1 ☐ Amended K-1 OMB No. 1545-0099

Schedule K-1 (Form 1065)

2011

Department of the Treasury
Internal Revenue Service

For calendar year 2011, or tax year beginning ________, 2011 ending ________, 20____

Partner's Share of Income, Deductions, Credits, etc.

▶ See back of form and separate instructions.

Part I Information About the Partnership

A Partnership's employer identification number

B Partnership's name, address, city, state, and ZIP code

C IRS Center where partnership filed return

D ☐ Check if this is a publicly traded partnership (PTP)

Part II Information About the Partner

E Partner's identifying number

F Partner's name, address, city, state, and ZIP code

G ☐ General partner or LLC member-manager ☐ Limited partner or other LLC member

H ☐ Domestic partner ☐ Foreign partner

I What type of entity is this partner? ________

J Partner's share of profit, loss, and capital (see instructions):

	Beginning	Ending
Profit	%	%
Loss	%	%
Capital	%	%

K Partner's share of liabilities at year end:

Nonrecourse . . . . $ ________

Qualified nonrecourse financing . $ ________

Recourse . . . . $ ________

L Partner's capital account analysis:

Beginning capital account . . . $ ________

Capital contributed during the year $ ________

Current year increase (decrease) . $ ________

Withdrawals & distributions . . . $ (________)

Ending capital account . . . . $ ________

☐ Tax basis ☐ GAAP ☐ Section 704(b) book

☐ Other (explain)

M Did the partner contribute property with a built-in gain or loss?

☐ **Yes** ☐ **No**

If "Yes," attach statement (see instructions)

Part III Partner's Share of Current Year Income, Deductions, Credits, and Other Items

1	Ordinary business income (loss)	15	Credits
2	Net rental real estate income (loss)		
3	Other net rental income (loss)	16	Foreign transactions
4	Guaranteed payments		
5	Interest income		
6a	Ordinary dividends		
6b	Qualified dividends		
7	Royalties		
8	Net short-term capital gain (loss)		
9a	Net long-term capital gain (loss)	17	Alternative minimum tax (AMT) items
9b	Collectibles (28%) gain (loss)		
9c	Unrecaptured section 1250 gain		
10	Net section 1231 gain (loss)	18	Tax-exempt income and nondeductible expenses
11	Other income (loss)		
		19	Distributions
12	Section 179 deduction		
13	Other deductions	20	Other information
14	Self-employment earnings (loss)		

*See attached statement for additional information.

For IRS Use Only

For Paperwork Reduction Act Notice, see Instructions for Form 1065. Cat. No. 11394R **Schedule K-1 (Form 1065) 2011**

SCHEDULE M-3 (Form 1065)

Department of the Treasury
Internal Revenue Service

Net Income (Loss) Reconciliation for Certain Partnerships

▶ Attach to Form 1065 or Form 1065-B.
▶ See separate instructions.

OMB No. 1545-0099

2011

Name of partnership | **Employer identification number**

This Schedule M-3 is being filed because (check all that apply):

A ☐ The amount of the partnership's total assets at the end of the tax year is equal to $10 million or more.

B ☐ The amount of the partnership's adjusted total assets for the tax year is equal to $10 million or more. If box B is checked, enter the amount of adjusted total assets for the tax year __________ .

C ☐ The amount of total receipts for the tax year is equal to $35 million or more. If box C is checked, enter the total receipts for the tax year __________ .

D ☐ An entity that is a reportable entity partner with respect to the partnership owns or is deemed to own an interest of 50 percent or more in the partnership's capital, profit, or loss, on any day during the tax year of the partnership.

Name of Reportable Entity Partner	Identifying Number	Maximum Percentage Owned or Deemed Owned

E ☐ Voluntary Filer.

Part I Financial Information and Net Income (Loss) Reconciliation

1a Did the partnership file SEC Form 10-K for its income statement period ending with or within this tax year?
☐ **Yes.** Skip lines 1b and 1c and complete lines 2 through 11 with respect to that SEC Form 10-K.
☐ **No.** Go to line 1b. See instructions if multiple non-tax-basis income statements are prepared.

b Did the partnership prepare a certified audited non-tax-basis income statement for that period?
☐ **Yes.** Skip line 1c and complete lines 2 through 11 with respect to that income statement.
☐ **No.** Go to line 1c.

c Did the partnership prepare a non-tax-basis income statement for that period?
☐ **Yes.** Complete lines 2 through 11 with respect to that income statement.
☐ **No.** Skip lines 2 through 3b and enter the partnership's net income (loss) per its books and records on line 4a.

2 Enter the income statement period: Beginning ____/____/____ Ending ____/____/____

3a Has the partnership's income statement been restated for the income statement period on line 2?
☐ **Yes.** (If "Yes," attach an explanation and the amount of each item restated.)
☐ **No.**

b Has the partnership's income statement been restated for any of the five income statement periods preceding the period on line 2?
☐ **Yes.** (If "Yes," attach an explanation and the amount of each item restated.)
☐ **No.**

4a	Worldwide consolidated net income (loss) from income statement source identified in Part I, line 1	4a	
b	Indicate accounting standard used for line 4a (see instructions): 1 ☐ GAAP 2 ☐ IFRS 3 ☐ 704(b) 4 ☐ Tax-basis 5 ☐ Other: (Specify) ▶ ________		
5a	Net income from nonincludible foreign entities (attach schedule)	5a	( )
b	Net loss from nonincludible foreign entities (attach schedule and enter as a positive amount)	5b	
6a	Net income from nonincludible U.S. entities (attach schedule)	6a	( )
b	Net loss from nonincludible U.S. entities (attach schedule and enter as a positive amount)	6b	
7a	Net income (loss) of other foreign disregarded entities (attach schedule)	7a	
b	Net income (loss) of other U.S. disregarded entities (attach schedule)	7b	
8	Adjustment to eliminations of transactions between includible entities and nonincludible entities (attach schedule)	8	
9	Adjustment to reconcile income statement period to tax year (attach schedule)	9	
10	Other adjustments to reconcile to amount on line 11 (attach schedule)	10	
11	**Net income (loss) per income statement of the partnership.** Combine lines 4a through 10	11	

Note. Part I, line 11, must equal the amount on Part II, line 26, column (a).

12 Enter the total amount (not just the partnership's share) of the assets and liabilities of all entities included or removed on the following lines:

	Total Assets	Total Liabilities
a Included on Part I, line 4		
b Removed on Part I, line 5		
c Removed on Part I, line 6		
d Included on Part I, line 7		

Schedule M-3 (Form 1065) 2011 Page **2**

Name of partnership	**Employer identification number**

Part II **Reconciliation of Net Income (Loss) per Income Statement of Partnership with Income (Loss) per Return**

	Income (Loss) Items	**(a)** Income (Loss) per Income Statement	**(b)** Temporary Difference	**(c)** Permanent Difference	**(d)** Income (Loss) per Tax Return
	(Attach schedules for lines 1 through 9)				
1	Income (loss) from equity method foreign corporations				
2	Gross foreign dividends not previously taxed . . .				
3	Subpart F, QEF, and similar income inclusions . .				
4	Gross foreign distributions previously taxed . . .				
5	Income (loss) from equity method U.S. corporations				
6	U.S. dividends				
7	Income (loss) from U.S. partnerships				
8	Income (loss) from foreign partnerships				
9	Income (loss) from other pass-through entities . .				
10	Items relating to reportable transactions (attach details)				
11	Interest income (attach Form 8916-A)				
12	Total accrual to cash adjustment				
13	Hedging transactions				
14	Mark-to-market income (loss)				
15	Cost of goods sold (attach Form 8916-A)	( )			( )
16	Sale versus lease (for sellers and/or lessors) . . .				
17	Section 481(a) adjustments				
18	Unearned/deferred revenue				
19	Income recognition from long-term contracts . . .				
20	Original issue discount and other imputed interest .				
21a	Income statement gain/loss on sale, exchange, abandonment, worthlessness, or other disposition of assets other than inventory and pass-through entities .				
b	Gross capital gains from Schedule D, excluding amounts from pass-through entities				
c	Gross capital losses from Schedule D, excluding amounts from pass-through entities, abandonment losses, and worthless stock losses				
d	Net gain/loss reported on Form 4797, line 17, excluding amounts from pass-through entities, abandonment losses, and worthless stock losses .				
e	Abandonment losses				
f	Worthless stock losses (attach details)				
g	Other gain/loss on disposition of assets other than inventory				
22	Other income (loss) items with differences (attach schedule)				
23	**Total income (loss) items.** Combine lines 1 through 22				
24	**Total expense/deduction items.** (from Part III, line 31) (see instructions)				
25	Other items with no differences				
26	**Reconciliation totals.** Combine lines 23 through 25				

Note. Line 26, column (a), must equal the amount on Part I, line 11, and column (d) must equal Form 1065, Analysis of Net Income (Loss), line 1.

Name of partnership	**Employer identification number**

Part III Reconciliation of Net Income (Loss) per Income Statement of Partnership With Income (Loss) per Return—Expense/Deduction Items

Expense/Deduction Items	**(a)** Expense per Income Statement	**(b)** Temporary Difference	**(c)** Permanent Difference	**(d)** Deduction per Tax Return
1 State and local current income tax expense				
2 State and local deferred income tax expense				
3 Foreign current income tax expense (other than foreign withholding taxes)				
4 Foreign deferred income tax expense				
5 Equity-based compensation				
6 Meals and entertainment				
7 Fines and penalties				
8 Judgments, damages, awards, and similar costs				
9 Guaranteed payments				
10 Pension and profit-sharing				
11 Other post-retirement benefits				
12 Deferred compensation				
13 Charitable contribution of cash and tangible property				
14 Charitable contribution of intangible property				
15 Organizational expenses as per Regulations section 1.709-2(a)				
16 Syndication expenses as per Regulations section 1.709-2(b)				
17 Current year acquisition/reorganization investment banking fees				
18 Current year acquisition/reorganization legal and accounting fees				
19 Amortization/impairment of goodwill				
20 Amortization of acquisition, reorganization, and start-up costs				
21 Other amortization or impairment write-offs				
22 Section 198 environmental remediation costs				
23a Depletion—Oil & Gas				
b Depletion—Other than Oil & Gas				
24 Intangible drilling & development costs				
25 Depreciation				
26 Bad debt expense				
27 Interest expense (attach Form 8916-A)				
28 Purchase versus lease (for purchasers and/or lessees)				
29 Research and development costs				
30 Other expense/deduction items with differences (attach schedule)				
31 **Total expense/deduction items.** Combine lines 1 through 30. Enter here and on Part II, line 24, reporting positive amounts as negative and negative amounts as positive				

SCHEDULE C (Form 1065)
(Rev. December 2011)
Department of the Treasury
Internal Revenue Service

Additional Information for Schedule M-3 Filers

▶ **Attach to Form 1065. See separate instructions.**

OMB No. 1545-0099

Name of partnership	**Employer identification number**

		Yes	No
1	At any time during the tax year, were there any transfers between the partnership and its partners subject to the disclosure requirements of Regulations section 1.707-8?		
2	Do the amounts reported on Schedule M-3, Part II, lines 7 or 8, column (d), reflect allocations to this partnership from another partnership of income, gain, loss, deduction, or credit that are disproportionate to this partnership's share of capital in such partnership or its ratio for sharing other items of such partnership?		
3	At any time during the tax year, did the partnership sell, exchange, or transfer any interest in an intangible asset to a related person as defined in sections 267(b) and 707(b)(1)?		
4	At any time during the tax year, did the partnership acquire any interest in an intangible asset from a related person as defined in sections 267(b) and 707(b)(1)?		
5	At any time during the tax year, did the partnership make any change in accounting principle for financial accounting purposes? See instructions for a definition of change in accounting principle		
6	At any time during the tax year, did the partnership make any change in a method of accounting for U.S. income tax purposes?		

For Paperwork Reduction Act Notice, see the Instructions for Form 1065. Cat. No. 49945S **Schedule C (Form 1065) (Rev. 12-2011)**

Form **1118**
(Rev. December 2011)
Department of the Treasury
Internal Revenue Service

Foreign Tax Credit—Corporations

▶ See separate instructions.
▶ Attach to the corporation's tax return.

OMB No. 1545-0122

For calendar year 20 , or other tax year beginning , 20 , and ending , 20

Name of corporation | **Employer identification number**

Use a **separate** Form 1118 for each applicable category of income listed below. See **Categories of Income** in the instructions. Also, see **Specific Instructions**. Check only one box on each form.

☐ Passive Category Income ☐ Section 901(j) Income: Name of Sanctioned Country ▶ ____________

☐ General Category Income ☐ Income Re-sourced by Treaty: Name of Country ▶ ____________

Schedule A Income or (Loss) Before Adjustments *(Report all amounts in U.S. dollars. See **Specific Instructions**.)*

	1. Foreign Country or U.S. Possession (Enter two-letter code; see instructions. Use a separate line for each.) *	Gross Income or (Loss) From Sources Outside the United States (*INCLUDE* Foreign Branch Gross Income here *and* on Schedule F)								
		2. Deemed Dividends (see instructions)		**3.** Other Dividends		**4.** Interest	**5.** Gross Rents, Royalties, and License Fees	**6.** Gross Income From Performance of Services	**7.** Other (attach schedule)	**8.** Total (add columns 2(a) through 7)
		(a) Exclude gross-up	**(b)** Gross-up (sec. 78)	**(a)** Exclude gross-up	**(b)** Gross-up (sec. 78)					
A										
B										
C										
D										
E										
F										
Totals (add lines A through F)										

* For section 863(b) income, NOLs, income from RICs, and high-taxed income, use a single line (see instructions).

	Deductions (*INCLUDE* Foreign Branch Deductions here *and* on Schedule F)								**13.** Total Income or (Loss) Before Adjustments (subtract column 12 from column 8)
	9. Definitely Allocable Deductions					**10.** Apportioned Share of Deductions Not Definitely Allocable (enter amount from applicable line of Schedule H, Part II, column (d))	**11.** Net Operating Loss Deduction	**12.** Total Deductions (add columns 9(e) through 11)	
	Rental, Royalty, and Licensing Expenses		**(c)** Expenses Related to Gross Income From Performance of Services	**(d)** Other Definitely Allocable Deductions	**(e)** Total Definitely Allocable Deductions (add columns 9(a) through 9(d))				
	(a) Depreciation, Depletion, and Amortization	**(b)** Other Expenses							
A									
B									
C									
D									
E									
F									
Totals									

Form 1118 (Rev. 12-2011) Page 2

Schedule B Foreign Tax Credit *(Report all foreign tax amounts in U.S. dollars.)*

Part I—Foreign Taxes Paid, Accrued, and Deemed Paid *(see instructions)*

	1. Credit is Claimed for Taxes: ☐ Paid ☐ Accrued		**2.** Foreign Taxes Paid or Accrued (attach schedule showing amounts in foreign currency and conversion rate(s) used)								**3.** Tax Deemed Paid (from Schedule C—Part I, column 10, Part II, column 8(b), and Part III, column 8)
			Tax Withheld at Source on:			Other Foreign Taxes Paid or Accrued on:					
	Date Paid	Date Accrued	**(a)** Dividends	**(b)** Interest	**(c)** Rents, Royalties, and License Fees	**(d)** Section 863(b) Income	**(e)** Foreign Branch Income	**(f)** Services Income	**(g)** Other	**(h)** Total Foreign Taxes Paid or Accrued (add columns 2(a) through 2(g))	
A											
B											
C											
D											
E											
F											
Totals (add lines A through F)											

Part II—Separate Foreign Tax Credit *(Complete a **separate** Part II for **each** applicable category of income.)*

1 Total foreign taxes paid or accrued (total from Part I, column 2(h))

2 Total taxes deemed paid (total from Part I, column 3)

3 Reductions of taxes paid, accrued, or deemed paid (enter total from Schedule G) ( )

4 Taxes reclassified under high-tax kickout

5 Enter the sum of any carryover of foreign taxes (from Schedule K, line 3, column (xiv)) plus any carrybacks to the current tax year

6 Total foreign taxes (combine lines 1 through 5)

7 Enter the amount from the applicable column of Schedule J, Part I, line 11 (see instructions). If Schedule J is **not** required to be completed, enter the result from the "Totals" line of column 13 of the applicable Schedule A

8a Total taxable income from all sources (enter taxable income from the corporation's tax return)

b Adjustments to line 8a (see instructions)

c Subtract line 8b from line 8a

9 Divide line 7 by line 8c. Enter the resulting fraction as a decimal (see instructions). If line 7 is greater than line 8c, enter 1

10 Total U.S. income tax against which credit is allowed (regular tax liability (see section 26(b)) minus American Samoa economic development credit)

11 Credit limitation (multiply line 9 by line 10) (see instructions)

12 **Separate foreign tax credit** (enter the smaller of line 6 or line 11 here and on the appropriate line of Part III)

Part III—Summary of Separate Credits (Enter amounts from Part II, line 12 for **each** applicable category of income. **Do not** include taxes paid to sanctioned countries.)

1 Credit for taxes on passive category income

2 Credit for taxes on general category income

3 Credit for taxes on income re-sourced by treaty (combine all such credits on this line)

4 Total (add lines 1 through 3)

5 Reduction in credit for international boycott operations (see instructions)

6 **Total foreign tax credit** (subtract line 5 from line 4). Enter here and on the appropriate line of the corporation's tax return

Form **1118** (Rev. 12-2011)

Form **1120**
Department of the Treasury
Internal Revenue Service

U.S. Corporation Income Tax Return

For calendar year 2011 or tax year beginning ________, 2011, ending ________, 20 ____
▶ See separate instructions.

OMB No. 1545-0123
2011

A Check if:			
1a Consolidated return (attach Form 851) ☐	TYPE OR PRINT	Name	**B Employer identification number**
b Life/nonlife consolidated return ☐		Number, street, and room or suite no. If a P.O. box, see instructions.	C Date incorporated
2 Personal holding co. (attach Sch. PH) ☐		City or town, state, and ZIP code	D Total assets (see instructions) $
3 Personal service corp. (see instructions) ☐			
4 Schedule M-3 attached ☐	**E** Check if: **(1)** ☐ Initial return **(2)** ☐ Final return	**(3)** ☐ Name change	**(4)** ☐ Address change

Income

1a	Merchant card and third-party payments. For 2011, enter -0-	1a			
b	Gross receipts or sales not reported on line 1a (see instructions)	1b			
c	Total. Add lines 1a and 1b	1c			
d	Returns and allowances plus any other adjustments (see instructions)	1d			
e	Subtract line 1d from line 1c			1e	
2	Cost of goods sold from Form 1125-A, line 8 (attach Form 1125-A)			2	
3	Gross profit. Subtract line 2 from line 1e			3	
4	Dividends (Schedule C, line 19)			4	
5	Interest			5	
6	Gross rents			6	
7	Gross royalties			7	
8	Capital gain net income (attach Schedule D (Form 1120))			8	
9	Net gain or (loss) from Form 4797, Part II, line 17 (attach Form 4797)			9	
10	Other income (see instructions—attach schedule)			10	
11	**Total income.** Add lines 3 through 10 ▶			11	

Deductions (See instructions for limitations on deductions.)

12	Compensation of officers from Form 1125-E, line 4 (attach Form 1125-E) ▶			12	
13	Salaries and wages (less employment credits)			13	
14	Repairs and maintenance			14	
15	Bad debts			15	
16	Rents			16	
17	Taxes and licenses			17	
18	Interest			18	
19	Charitable contributions			19	
20	Depreciation from Form 4562 not claimed on Form 1125-A or elsewhere on return (attach Form 4562)			20	
21	Depletion			21	
22	Advertising			22	
23	Pension, profit-sharing, etc., plans			23	
24	Employee benefit programs			24	
25	Domestic production activities deduction (attach Form 8903)			25	
26	Other deductions (attach schedule)			26	
27	**Total deductions.** Add lines 12 through 26 ▶			27	
28	Taxable income before net operating loss deduction and special deductions. Subtract line 27 from line 11.			28	
29a	Net operating loss deduction (see instructions)	29a			
b	Special deductions (Schedule C, line 20)	29b			
c	Add lines 29a and 29b			29c	

Tax, Refundable Credits, and Payments

30	**Taxable income.** Subtract line 29c from line 28 (see instructions)	30	
31	Total tax (Schedule J, Part I, line 11)	31	
32	Total payments and refundable credits (Schedule J, Part II, line 21)	32	
33	Estimated tax penalty (see instructions). Check if Form 2220 is attached ▶ ☐	33	
34	**Amount owed.** If line 32 is smaller than the total of lines 31 and 33, enter amount owed	34	
35	**Overpayment.** If line 32 is larger than the total of lines 31 and 33, enter amount overpaid	35	
36	Enter amount from line 35 you want: **Credited to 2012 estimated tax ▶** **Refunded ▶**	36	

Sign Here

Under penalties of perjury, I declare that I have examined this return, including accompanying schedules and statements, and to the best of my knowledge and belief, it is true, correct, and complete. Declaration of preparer (other than taxpayer) is based on all information of which preparer has any knowledge.

▶ Signature of officer | Date | ▶ Title

May the IRS discuss this return with the preparer shown below (see instructions)? ☐ **Yes** ☐ **No**

Paid Preparer Use Only

Print/Type preparer's name	Preparer's signature	Date	Check ☐ if self-employed	PTIN
Firm's name ▶			Firm's EIN ▶	
Firm's address ▶			Phone no.	

Form 1120 (2011) Page **2**

Schedule C	**Dividends and Special Deductions** (see instructions)	**(a)** Dividends received	**(b)** %	**(c)** Special deductions **(a)** × **(b)**
1	Dividends from less-than-20%-owned domestic corporations (other than debt-financed stock)		70	
2	Dividends from 20%-or-more-owned domestic corporations (other than debt-financed stock)		80	
3	Dividends on debt-financed stock of domestic and foreign corporations		see structions	
4	Dividends on certain preferred stock of less-than-20%-owned public utilities		42	
5	Dividends on certain preferred stock of 20%-or-more-owned public utilities		48	
6	Dividends from less-than-20%-owned foreign corporations and certain FSCs		70	
7	Dividends from 20%-or-more-owned foreign corporations and certain FSCs		80	
8	Dividends from wholly owned foreign subsidiaries		100	
9	**Total.** Add lines 1 through 8. See instructions for limitation			
10	Dividends from domestic corporations received by a small business investment company operating under the Small Business Investment Act of 1958		100	
11	Dividends from affiliated group members		100	
12	Dividends from certain FSCs		100	
13	Dividends from foreign corporations not included on lines 3, 6, 7, 8, 11, or 12			
14	Income from controlled foreign corporations under subpart F (attach Form(s) 5471)			
15	Foreign dividend gross-up			
16	IC-DISC and former DISC dividends not included on lines 1, 2, or 3			
17	Other dividends			
18	Deduction for dividends paid on certain preferred stock of public utilities			
19	**Total dividends.** Add lines 1 through 17. Enter here and on page 1, line 4 ▶			
20	**Total special deductions.** Add lines 9, 10, 11, 12, and 18. Enter here and on page 1, line 29b ▶			

Form **1120** (2011)

Form 1120 (2011) Page 3

Schedule J Tax Computation and Payment (see instructions)

Part I–Tax Computation

1	Check if the corporation is a member of a controlled group (attach Schedule O (Form 1120)) . . . . ▶ ☐				
2	Income tax. Check if a qualified personal service corporation (see instructions) . . . . ▶ ☐			2	
3	Alternative minimum tax (attach Form 4626)			3	
4	Add lines 2 and 3			4	
5a	Foreign tax credit (attach Form 1118)	5a			
b	Credit from Form 8834, line 30 (attach Form 8834)	5b			
c	General business credit (attach Form 3800)	5c			
d	Credit for prior year minimum tax (attach Form 8827)	5d			
e	Bond credits from Form 8912	5e			
6	**Total credits.** Add lines 5a through 5e			6	
7	Subtract line 6 from line 4			7	
8	Personal holding company tax (attach Schedule PH (Form 1120))			8	
9a	Recapture of investment credit (attach Form 4255)	9a			
b	Recapture of low-income housing credit (attach Form 8611)	9b			
c	Interest due under the look-back method—completed long-term contracts (attach Form 8697)	9c			
d	Interest due under the look-back method—income forecast method (attach Form 8866)	9d			
e	Alternative tax on qualifying shipping activities (attach Form 8902)	9e			
f	Other (see instructions—attach schedule)	9f			
10	**Total.** Add lines 9a through 9f			10	
11	**Total tax.** Add lines 7, 8, and 10. Enter here and on page 1, line 31			11	

Part II–Payments and Refundable Credits

12	2010 overpayment credited to 2011			12	
13	2011 estimated tax payments			13	
14	2011 refund applied for on Form 4466			14	( )
15	Combine lines 12, 13, and 14			15	
16	Tax deposited with Form 7004			16	
17	Withholding (see instructions)			17	
18	**Total payments.** Add lines 15, 16, and 17			18	
19	Refundable credits from:				
a	Form 2439	19a			
b	Form 4136	19b			
c	Form 3800, line 17c and Form 8827, line 8c	19c			
d	Other (attach schedule—see instructions)	19d			
20	**Total credits.** Add lines 19a through 19d			20	
21	**Total payments and credits.** Add lines 18 and 20. Enter here and on page 1, line 32			21	

Schedule K Other Information (see instructions)

		Yes	No
1	Check accounting method: **a** ☐ Cash **b** ☐ Accrual **c** ☐ Other (specify) ▶ ______		
2	See the instructions and enter the:		
a	Business activity code no. ▶ ______		
b	Business activity ▶ ______		
c	Product or service ▶ ______		
3	Is the corporation a subsidiary in an affiliated group or a parent-subsidiary controlled group? . . . . If "Yes," enter name and EIN of the parent corporation ▶ ______		
4	At the end of the tax year:		
a	Did any foreign or domestic corporation, partnership (including any entity treated as a partnership), trust, or tax-exempt organization own directly 20% or more, or own, directly or indirectly, 50% or more of the total voting power of all classes of the corporation's stock entitled to vote? If "Yes," complete Part I of Schedule G (Form 1120) (attach Schedule G)		
b	Did any individual or estate own directly 20% or more, or own, directly or indirectly, 50% or more of the total voting power of all classes of the corporation's stock entitled to vote? If "Yes," complete Part II of Schedule G (Form 1120) (attach Schedule G) .		

Form 1120 (2011) Page **4**

Schedule K Other Information *continued* (see instructions)

		Yes	No
5	At the end of the tax year, did the corporation:		
a	Own directly 20% or more, or own, directly or indirectly, 50% or more of the total voting power of all classes of stock entitled to vote of any foreign or domestic corporation not included on **Form 851,** Affiliations Schedule? For rules of constructive ownership, see instructions. If "Yes," complete (i) through (iv) below.		

(i) Name of Corporation	**(ii)** Employer Identification Number (if any)	**(iii)** Country of Incorporation	**(iv)** Percentage Owned in Voting Stock

		Yes	No
b	Own directly an interest of 20% or more, or own, directly or indirectly, an interest of 50% or more in any foreign or domestic partnership (including an entity treated as a partnership) or in the beneficial interest of a trust? For rules of constructive ownership, see instructions. If "Yes," complete (i) through (iv) below.		

(i) Name of Entity	**(ii)** Employer Identification Number (if any)	**(iii)** Country of Organization	**(iv)** Maximum Percentage Owned in Profit, Loss, or Capital

		Yes	No
6	During this tax year, did the corporation pay dividends (other than stock dividends and distributions in exchange for stock) in excess of the corporation's current and accumulated earnings and profits? (See sections 301 and 316.)		
	If "Yes," file **Form 5452,** Corporate Report of Nondividend Distributions.		
	If this is a consolidated return, answer here for the parent corporation and on Form 851 for each subsidiary.		
7	At any time during the tax year, did one foreign person own, directly or indirectly, at least 25% of **(a)** the total voting power of all classes of the corporation's stock entitled to vote or **(b)** the total value of all classes of the corporation's stock?		
	For rules of attribution, see section 318. If "Yes," enter: **(i)** Percentage owned ▶ ________ and **(ii)** Owner's country ▶ ________		
	(c) The corporation may have to file **Form 5472,** Information Return of a 25% Foreign-Owned U.S. Corporation or a Foreign Corporation Engaged in a U.S. Trade or Business. Enter the number of Forms 5472 attached ▶ ________		
8	Check this box if the corporation issued publicly offered debt instruments with original issue discount . . . . ▶ ☐		
	If checked, the corporation may have to file **Form 8281,** Information Return for Publicly Offered Original Issue Discount Instruments.		
9	Enter the amount of tax-exempt interest received or accrued during the tax year ▶ $ ________		
10	Enter the number of shareholders at the end of the tax year (if 100 or fewer) ▶ ________		
11	If the corporation has an NOL for the tax year and is electing to forego the carryback period, check here . . . . . . ▶ ☐		
	If the corporation is filing a consolidated return, the statement required by Regulations section 1.1502-21(b)(3) must be attached or the election will not be valid.		
12	Enter the available NOL carryover from prior tax years (do not reduce it by any deduction on line 29a.) ▶ $ ________		
13	Are the corporation's total receipts (line 1c plus lines 4 through 10 on page 1) for the tax year **and** its total assets at the end of the tax year less than $250,000?		
	If "Yes," the corporation is not required to complete Schedules L, M-1, and M-2 on page 5. Instead, enter the total amount of cash distributions and the book value of property distributions (other than cash) made during the tax year. ▶ $ ________		
14	Is the corporation required to file Schedule UTP (Form 1120), Uncertain Tax Position Statement (see instructions)?		
	If "Yes," complete and attach Schedule UTP.		
15a	Did the corporation make any payments in 2011 that would require it to file Form(s) 1099 (see instructions)?		
b	If "Yes," did or will the corporation file all required Forms 1099?		

Form 1120 (2011) Page **5**

Schedule L Balance Sheets per Books

Assets	Beginning of tax year (a)	(b)	End of tax year (c)	(d)
1 Cash				
2a Trade notes and accounts receivable				
b Less allowance for bad debts	( )		( )	
3 Inventories				
4 U.S. government obligations				
5 Tax-exempt securities (see instructions)				
6 Other current assets (attach schedule)				
7 Loans to shareholders				
8 Mortgage and real estate loans				
9 Other investments (attach schedule)				
10a Buildings and other depreciable assets				
b Less accumulated depreciation	( )		( )	
11a Depletable assets				
b Less accumulated depletion	( )		( )	
12 Land (net of any amortization)				
13a Intangible assets (amortizable only)				
b Less accumulated amortization	( )		( )	
14 Other assets (attach schedule)				
15 Total assets				
Liabilities and Shareholders' Equity				
16 Accounts payable				
17 Mortgages, notes, bonds payable in less than 1 year				
18 Other current liabilities (attach schedule)				
19 Loans from shareholders				
20 Mortgages, notes, bonds payable in 1 year or more				
21 Other liabilities (attach schedule)				
22 Capital stock: a Preferred stock				
b Common stock				
23 Additional paid-in capital				
24 Retained earnings—Appropriated (attach schedule)				
25 Retained earnings—Unappropriated				
26 Adjustments to shareholders' equity (attach schedule)				
27 Less cost of treasury stock		( )		( )
28 Total liabilities and shareholders' equity				

Schedule M-1 Reconciliation of Income (Loss) per Books With Income per Return

Note: Schedule M-3 required instead of Schedule M-1 if total assets are $10 million or more—see instructions

1 Net income (loss) per books		7 Income recorded on books this year not included on this return (itemize): Tax-exempt interest $	
2 Federal income tax per books			
3 Excess of capital losses over capital gains			
4 Income subject to tax not recorded on books this year (itemize):		8 Deductions on this return not charged against book income this year (itemize):	
5 Expenses recorded on books this year not deducted on this return (itemize):		a Depreciation $	
a Depreciation $		b Charitable contributions $	
b Charitable contributions $			
c Travel and entertainment $		9 Add lines 7 and 8	
6 Add lines 1 through 5		10 Income (page 1, line 28)—line 6 less line 9	

Schedule M-2 Analysis of Unappropriated Retained Earnings per Books (Line 25, Schedule L)

1 Balance at beginning of year		5 Distributions: a Cash	
2 Net income (loss) per books		b Stock	
3 Other increases (itemize):		c Property	
		6 Other decreases (itemize):	
		7 Add lines 5 and 6	
4 Add lines 1, 2, and 3		8 Balance at end of year (line 4 less line 7)	

SCHEDULE M-3 (Form 1120)

Department of the Treasury
Internal Revenue Service

Net Income (Loss) Reconciliation for Corporations With Total Assets of $10 Million or More

▶ Attach to Form 1120 or 1120-C.
▶ See separate instructions.

OMB No. 1545-0123

2011

Name of corporation (common parent, if consolidated return) | **Employer identification number**

Check applicable box(es): (1) ☐ Non-consolidated return (2) ☐ Consolidated return (Form 1120 only)

(3) ☐ Mixed 1120/L/PC group (4) ☐ Dormant subsidiaries schedule attached

Part I Financial Information and Net Income (Loss) Reconciliation (see instructions)

1a Did the corporation file SEC Form 10-K for its income statement period ending with or within this tax year?
☐ **Yes.** Skip lines 1b and 1c and complete lines 2a through 11 with respect to that SEC Form 10-K.
☐ **No.** Go to line 1b. See instructions if multiple non-tax-basis income statements are prepared.

b Did the corporation prepare a certified audited non-tax-basis income statement for that period?
☐ **Yes.** Skip line 1c and complete lines 2a through 11 with respect to that income statement.
☐ **No.** Go to line 1c.

c Did the corporation prepare a non-tax-basis income statement for that period?
☐ **Yes.** Complete lines 2a through 11 with respect to that income statement.
☐ **No.** Skip lines 2a through 3c and enter the corporation's net income (loss) per its books and records on line 4a.

2a Enter the income statement period: Beginning MM/DD/YYYY Ending MM/DD/YYYY

b Has the corporation's income statement been restated for the income statement period on line 2a?
☐ **Yes.** (If "Yes," attach an explanation and the amount of each item restated.)
☐ **No.**

c Has the corporation's income statement been restated for any of the five income statement periods preceding the period on line 2a?
☐ **Yes.** (If "Yes," attach an explanation and the amount of each item restated.)
☐ **No.**

3a Is any of the corporation's voting common stock publicly traded?
☐ **Yes.**
☐ **No.** If "No," go to line 4a.

b Enter the symbol of the corporation's primary U.S. publicly traded voting common stock . . . . ☐

c Enter the nine-digit CUSIP number of the corporation's primary publicly traded voting common stock . . . . ☐

4a	Worldwide consolidated net income (loss) from income statement source identified in Part I, line 1 .	**4a**	
b	Indicate accounting standard used for line 4a (see instructions): (1) ☐ GAAP (2) ☐ IFRS (3) ☐ Statutory (4) ☐ Tax-basis (5) ☐ Other (specify) ______		
5a	Net income from nonincludible foreign entities (attach schedule)	**5a**	( )
b	Net loss from nonincludible foreign entities (attach schedule and enter as a positive amount) . . .	**5b**	
6a	Net income from nonincludible U.S. entities (attach schedule)	**6a**	( )
b	Net loss from nonincludible U.S. entities (attach schedule and enter as a positive amount)	**6b**	
7a	Net income (loss) of other includible foreign disregarded entities (attach schedule)	**7a**	
b	Net income (loss) of other includible U.S. disregarded entities (attach schedule)	**7b**	
c	Net income (loss) of other includible entities (attach schedule)	**7c**	
8	Adjustment to eliminations of transactions between includible entities and nonincludible entities (attach schedule)	**8**	
9	Adjustment to reconcile income statement period to tax year (attach schedule)	**9**	
10a	Intercompany dividend adjustments to reconcile to line 11 (attach schedule)	**10a**	
b	Other statutory accounting adjustments to reconcile to line 11 (attach schedule)	**10b**	
c	Other adjustments to reconcile to amount on line 11 (attach schedule)	**10c**	
11	**Net income (loss) per income statement of includible corporations.** Combine lines 4 through 10 . .	**11**	

Note. Part I, line 11, must equal the amount on Part II, line 30, column (a), and Schedule M-2, line 2.

12 Enter the total amount (not just the corporation's share) of the assets and liabilities of all entities included or removed on the following lines.

	Total Assets	Total Liabilities
a Included on Part I, line 4 . . . . ▶		
b Removed on Part I, line 5 . . . . ▶		
c Removed on Part I, line 6 . . . . ▶		
d Included on Part I, line 7 . . . . ▶		

Schedule M-3 (Form 1120) 2011 Page **2**

Name of corporation (common parent, if consolidated return)	**Employer identification number**

Check applicable box(es): **(1)** ☐ Consolidated group **(2)** ☐ Parent corp **(3)** ☐ Consolidated eliminations **(4)** ☐ Subsidiary corp **(5)** ☐ Mixed 1120/L/PC group

Check if a sub-consolidated: **(6)** ☐ 1120 group **(7)** ☐ 1120 eliminations

Name of subsidiary (if consolidated return)	**Employer identification number**

Part II Reconciliation of Net Income (Loss) per Income Statement of Includible Corporations With Taxable Income per Return (see instructions)

Income (Loss) Items (Attach schedules for lines 1 through 11)	(a) Income (Loss) per Income Statement	(b) Temporary Difference	(c) Permanent Difference	(d) Income (Loss) per Tax Return
1 Income (loss) from equity method foreign corporations				
2 Gross foreign dividends not previously taxed . . .				
3 Subpart F, QEF, and similar income inclusions . .				
4 Section 78 gross-up				
5 Gross foreign distributions previously taxed . . .				
6 Income (loss) from equity method U.S. corporations				
7 U.S. dividends not eliminated in tax consolidation				
8 Minority interest for includible corporations . . .				
9 Income (loss) from U.S. partnerships				
10 Income (loss) from foreign partnerships				
11 Income (loss) from other pass-through entities . .				
12 Items relating to reportable transactions (attach details)				
13 Interest income (attach Form 8916-A)				
14 Total accrual to cash adjustment				
15 Hedging transactions				
16 Mark-to-market income (loss)				
17 Cost of goods sold (attach Form 8916-A)	( )			( )
18 Sale versus lease (for sellers and/or lessors) . . .				
19 Section 481(a) adjustments				
20 Unearned/deferred revenue				
21 Income recognition from long-term contracts . .				
22 Original issue discount and other imputed interest .				
23a Income statement gain/loss on sale, exchange, abandonment, worthlessness, or other disposition of assets other than inventory and pass-through entities				
b Gross capital gains from Schedule D, excluding amounts from pass-through entities				
c Gross capital losses from Schedule D, excluding amounts from pass-through entities, abandonment losses, and worthless stock losses				
d Net gain/loss reported on Form 4797, line 17, excluding amounts from pass-through entities, abandonment losses, and worthless stock losses				
e Abandonment losses				
f Worthless stock losses (attach details)				
g Other gain/loss on disposition of assets other than inventory				
24 Capital loss limitation and carryforward used . . .				
25 Other income (loss) items with differences (attach schedule)				
26 **Total income (loss) items.** Combine lines 1 through 25				
27 **Total expense/deduction items** (from Part III, line 38)				
28 Other items with no differences				
29a Mixed groups, see instructions. All others, combine lines 26 through 28				
b PC insurance subgroup reconciliation totals . . .				
c Life insurance subgroup reconciliation totals . . .				
30 **Reconciliation totals.** Combine lines 29a through 29c				

Note. Line 30, column (a), must equal the amount on Part I, line 11, and column (d) must equal Form 1120, page 1, line 28.

Schedule M-3 (Form 1120) 2011

Schedule M-3 (Form 1120) 2011 Page **3**

Name of corporation (common parent, if consolidated return)	**Employer identification number**

Check applicable box(es): **(1)** ☐ Consolidated group **(2)** ☐ Parent corp **(3)** ☐ Consolidated eliminations **(4)** ☐ Subsidiary corp **(5)** ☐ Mixed 1120/L/PC group

Check if a sub-consolidated: **(6)** ☐ 1120 group **(7)** ☐ 1120 eliminations

Name of subsidiary (if consolidated return)	**Employer identification number**

Part III Reconciliation of Net Income (Loss) per Income Statement of Includible Corporations With Taxable Income per Return—Expense/Deduction Items (see instructions)

Expense/Deduction Items	**(a)** Expense per Income Statement	**(b)** Temporary Difference	**(c)** Permanent Difference	**(d)** Deduction per Tax Return
1 U.S. current income tax expense				
2 U.S. deferred income tax expense				
3 State and local current income tax expense				
4 State and local deferred income tax expense				
5 Foreign current income tax expense (other than foreign withholding taxes)				
6 Foreign deferred income tax expense				
7 Foreign withholding taxes				
8 Interest expense (attach Form 8916-A)				
9 Stock option expense				
10 Other equity-based compensation				
11 Meals and entertainment				
12 Fines and penalties				
13 Judgments, damages, awards, and similar costs				
14 Parachute payments				
15 Compensation with section 162(m) limitation				
16 Pension and profit-sharing				
17 Other post-retirement benefits				
18 Deferred compensation				
19 Charitable contribution of cash and tangible property				
20 Charitable contribution of intangible property				
21 Charitable contribution limitation/carryforward				
22 Domestic production activities deduction				
23 Current year acquisition or reorganization investment banking fees				
24 Current year acquisition or reorganization legal and accounting fees				
25 Current year acquisition/reorganization other costs				
26 Amortization/impairment of goodwill				
27 Amortization of acquisition, reorganization, and start-up costs				
28 Other amortization or impairment write-offs				
29 Section 198 environmental remediation costs				
30 Depletion				
31 Depreciation				
32 Bad debt expense				
33 Corporate owned life insurance premiums				
34 Purchase versus lease (for purchasers and/or lessees)				
35 Research and development costs				
36 Section 118 exclusion (attach schedule)				
37 Other expense/deduction items with differences (attach schedule)				
38 **Total expense/deduction items.** Combine lines 1 through 37. Enter here and on Part II, line 27, reporting positive amounts as negative and negative amounts as positive				

Form **1120S** — Department of the Treasury, Internal Revenue Service

U.S. Income Tax Return for an S Corporation

▶ **Do not file this form unless the corporation has filed or is attaching Form 2553 to elect to be an S corporation.**
▶ **See separate instructions.**

OMB No. 1545-0130 — **2011**

For calendar year 2011 or tax year beginning , 2011, ending , 20

	TYPE OR PRINT	
A S election effective date	Name	**D Employer identification number**
B Business activity code number *(see instructions)*	Number, street, and room or suite no. If a P.O. box, see instructions.	**E** Date incorporated
C Check if Sch. M-3 attached ☐	City or town, state, and ZIP code	**F** Total assets *(see instructions)* $

G Is the corporation electing to be an S corporation beginning with this tax year? ☐ Yes ☐ No If "Yes," attach Form 2553 if not already filed

H Check if: **(1)** ☐ Final return **(2)** ☐ Name change **(3)** ☐ Address change **(4)** ☐ Amended return **(5)** ☐ S election termination or revocation

I Enter the number of shareholders who were shareholders during any part of the tax year . . . . ▶

Caution. *Include **only** trade or business income and expenses on lines 1a through 21. See the instructions for more information.*

Income	1 a	Merchant card and third-party payments. For 2011, enter -0- . . .	1a	
	b	Gross receipts or sales not reported on line 1a (see instructions) . .	1b	
	c	Total. Add lines 1a and 1b	1c	
	d	Returns and allowances plus any other adjustments (see instructions)	1d	
	e	Subtract line 1d from line 1c		1e
	2	Cost of goods sold (attach Form 1125-A)		2
	3	Gross profit. Subtract line 2 from line 1e		3
	4	Net gain (loss) from Form 4797, Part II, line 17 *(attach Form 4797)* . . .		4
	5	Other income (loss) *(see instructions—attach statement)*		5
	6	**Total income (loss).** Add lines 3 through 5 . . . . ▶		6
Deductions (see instructions for limitations)	7	Compensation of officers		7
	8	Salaries and wages (less employment credits)		8
	9	Repairs and maintenance		9
	10	Bad debts		10
	11	Rents		11
	12	Taxes and licenses		12
	13	Interest		13
	14	Depreciation not claimed on Form 1125-A or elsewhere on return (*attach Form 4562*)		14
	15	Depletion **(Do not deduct oil and gas depletion.)**		15
	16	Advertising		16
	17	Pension, profit-sharing, etc., plans		17
	18	Employee benefit programs		18
	19	Other deductions (*attach statement*)		19
	20	**Total deductions.** Add lines 7 through 19 . . . . ▶		20
	21	**Ordinary business income (loss).** Subtract line 20 from line 6		21
Tax and Payments	22 a	Excess net passive income or LIFO recapture tax (*see instructions*) . .	22a	
	b	Tax from Schedule D (Form 1120S)	22b	
	c	Add lines 22a and 22b (*see instructions for additional taxes*)		22c
	23 a	2011 estimated tax payments and 2010 overpayment credited to 2011	23a	
	b	Tax deposited with Form 7004	23b	
	c	Credit for federal tax paid on fuels (*attach Form 4136*)	23c	
	d	Add lines 23a through 23c		23d
	24	Estimated tax penalty (*see instructions*). Check if Form 2220 is attached . . . . . . ▶ ☐		24
	25	**Amount owed.** If line 23d is smaller than the total of lines 22c and 24, enter amount owed . .		25
	26	**Overpayment.** If line 23d is larger than the total of lines 22c and 24, enter amount overpaid . .		26
	27	Enter amount from line 26 **Credited to 2012 estimated tax ▶**	**Refunded ▶**	27

Sign Here

Under penalties of perjury, I declare that I have examined this return, including accompanying schedules and statements, and to the best of my knowledge and belief, it is true, correct, and complete. Declaration of preparer (other than taxpayer) is based on all information of which preparer has any knowledge.

▶ Signature of officer | Date | ▶ Title

May the IRS discuss this return with the preparer shown below (see instructions)? ☐ Yes ☐ No

Paid Preparer Use Only

Print/Type preparer's name	Preparer's signature	Date	Check ☐ if self-employed	PTIN
Firm's name ▶			Firm's EIN ▶	
Firm's address ▶			Phone no.	

Form 1120S (2011) Page **2**

Schedule B **Other Information** (see instructions)	Yes	No
1 Check accounting method: **a** ☐ Cash **b** ☐ Accrual **c** ☐ Other (specify) ▶		
2 See the instructions and enter the: **a** Business activity ▶ **b** Product or service ▶		
3 At the end of the tax year, did the corporation own, directly or indirectly, 50% or more of the voting stock of a domestic corporation? (For rules of attribution, see section 267(c).) If "Yes," attach a statement showing: **(a)** name and employer identification number (EIN), **(b)** percentage owned, and **(c)** if 100% owned, was a qualified subchapter S subsidiary election made?		
4 Has this corporation filed, or is it required to file, **Form 8918,** Material Advisor Disclosure Statement, to provide information on any reportable transaction?		
5 Check this box if the corporation issued publicly offered debt instruments with original issue discount ▶ ☐ If checked, the corporation may have to file **Form 8281,** Information Return for Publicly Offered Original Issue Discount Instruments.		
6 If the corporation: **(a)** was a C corporation before it elected to be an S corporation **or** the corporation acquired an asset with a basis determined by reference to the basis of the asset (or the basis of any other property) in the hands of a C corporation **and (b)** has net unrealized built-in gain in excess of the net recognized built-in gain from prior years, enter the net unrealized built-in gain reduced by net recognized built-in gain from prior years *(see instructions)* ▶ $		
7 Enter the accumulated earnings and profits of the corporation at the end of the tax year. $		
8 Are the corporation's total receipts (*see instructions*) for the tax year **and** its total assets at the end of the tax year less than $250,000? If "Yes," the corporation is not required to complete Schedules L and M-1		
9 During the tax year, was a qualified subchapter S subsidiary election terminated or revoked? If "Yes," see instructions		
10a Did the corporation make any payments in 2011 that would require it to file Form(s) 1099 (see instructions)?		
b If "Yes," did the corporation file or will it file all required Forms 1099?		

Schedule K		**Shareholders' Pro Rata Share Items**				**Total amount**
Income (Loss)	1	Ordinary business income (loss) (page 1, line 21)			1	
	2	Net rental real estate income (loss) (*attach Form 8825*)			2	
	3a	Other gross rental income (loss)	3a			
	b	Expenses from other rental activities (*attach statement*)	3b			
	c	Other net rental income (loss). Subtract line 3b from line 3a			3c	
	4	Interest income			4	
	5	Dividends: **a** Ordinary dividends			5a	
		b Qualified dividends	5b			
	6	Royalties			6	
	7	Net short-term capital gain (loss) (*attach Schedule D (Form 1120S)*)			7	
	8a	Net long-term capital gain (loss) (*attach Schedule D (Form 1120S)*)			8a	
	b	Collectibles (28%) gain (loss)	8b			
	c	Unrecaptured section 1250 gain (*attach statement*)	8c			
	9	Net section 1231 gain (loss) (*attach Form 4797*)			9	
	10	Other income (loss) (*see instructions*) Type ▶			10	

Form **1120S** (2011)

Form 1120S (2011) Page **3**

		Shareholders' Pro Rata Share Items (continued)		**Total amount**
Deductions	11	Section 179 deduction (*attach Form 4562*)	11	
	12a	Contributions	12a	
	b	Investment interest expense	12b	
	c	Section 59(e)(2) expenditures **(1)** Type ▶ (2) Amount ▶	12c(2)	
	d	Other deductions *(see instructions)* Type ▶	12d	
Credits	13a	Low-income housing credit (section 42(j)(5))	13a	
	b	Low-income housing credit (other)	13b	
	c	Qualified rehabilitation expenditures (rental real estate) (*attach Form 3468*)	13c	
	d	Other rental real estate credits (*see instructions*) Type ▶	13d	
	e	Other rental credits (*see instructions*) Type ▶	13e	
	f	Alcohol and cellulosic biofuel fuels credit (*attach Form 6478*)	13f	
	g	Other credits (*see instructions*) Type ▶	13g	
Foreign Transactions	14a	Name of country or U.S. possession ▶		
	b	Gross income from all sources	14b	
	c	Gross income sourced at shareholder level	14c	
		Foreign gross income sourced at corporate level		
	d	Passive category	14d	
	e	General category	14e	
	f	Other (*attach statement*)	14f	
		Deductions allocated and apportioned at shareholder level		
	g	Interest expense	14g	
	h	Other	14h	
		Deductions allocated and apportioned at corporate level to foreign source income		
	i	Passive category	14i	
	j	General category	14j	
	k	Other (*attach statement*)	14k	
		Other information		
	l	Total foreign taxes (check one): ▶ ☐ Paid ☐ Accrued	14l	
	m	Reduction in taxes available for credit (*attach statement*)	14m	
	n	Other foreign tax information (*attach statement*)		
Alternative Minimum Tax (AMT) Items	15a	Post-1986 depreciation adjustment	15a	
	b	Adjusted gain or loss	15b	
	c	Depletion (other than oil and gas)	15c	
	d	Oil, gas, and geothermal properties—gross income	15d	
	e	Oil, gas, and geothermal properties—deductions	15e	
	f	Other AMT items (*attach statement*)	15f	
Items Affecting Shareholder Basis	16a	Tax-exempt interest income	16a	
	b	Other tax-exempt income	16b	
	c	Nondeductible expenses	16c	
	d	Distributions *(attach statement if required) (see instructions)*	16d	
	e	Repayment of loans from shareholders	16e	
Other Information	17a	Investment income	17a	
	b	Investment expenses	17b	
	c	Dividend distributions paid from accumulated earnings and profits	17c	
	d	Other items and amounts (*attach statement*)		
Reconciliation	18	**Income/loss reconciliation.** Combine the amounts on lines 1 through 10 in the far right column. From the result, subtract the sum of the amounts on lines 11 through 12d and 14l	18	

Form **1120S** (2011)

Form 1120S (2011) Page **4**

Schedule L **Balance Sheets per Books**

Assets	Beginning of tax year		End of tax year	
	(a)	(b)	(c)	(d)
1 Cash				
2a Trade notes and accounts receivable				
b Less allowance for bad debts	( )		( )	
3 Inventories				
4 U.S. government obligations				
5 Tax-exempt securities (*see instructions*)				
6 Other current assets (*attach statement*)				
7 Loans to shareholders				
8 Mortgage and real estate loans				
9 Other investments (*attach statement*)				
10a Buildings and other depreciable assets				
b Less accumulated depreciation	( )		( )	
11a Depletable assets				
b Less accumulated depletion	( )		( )	
12 Land (net of any amortization)				
13a Intangible assets (amortizable only)				
b Less accumulated amortization	( )		( )	
14 Other assets (*attach statement*)				
15 Total assets				
Liabilities and Shareholders' Equity				
16 Accounts payable				
17 Mortgages, notes, bonds payable in less than 1 year				
18 Other current liabilities (*attach statement*)				
19 Loans from shareholders				
20 Mortgages, notes, bonds payable in 1 year or more				
21 Other liabilities (*attach statement*)				
22 Capital stock				
23 Additional paid-in capital				
24 Retained earnings				
25 Adjustments to shareholders' equity (*attach statement*)				
26 Less cost of treasury stock		( )		( )
27 Total liabilities and shareholders' equity				

Schedule M-1 **Reconciliation of Income (Loss) per Books With Income (Loss) per Return**

Note. Schedule M-3 required instead of Schedule M-1 if total assets are $10 million or more—see instructions

1 Net income (loss) per books		5 Income recorded on books this year not included on Schedule K, lines 1 through 10 (itemize): a Tax-exempt interest $	
2 Income included on Schedule K, lines 1, 2, 3c, 4, 5a, 6, 7, 8a, 9, and 10, not recorded on books this year (itemize)			
3 Expenses recorded on books this year not included on Schedule K, lines 1 through 12 and 14l (itemize): a Depreciation $ b Travel and entertainment $		6 Deductions included on Schedule K, lines 1 through 12 and 14l, not charged against book income this year (itemize): a Depreciation $	
		7 Add lines 5 and 6	
4 Add lines 1 through 3		8 Income (loss) (Schedule K, line 18). Line 4 less line 7	

Schedule M-2 **Analysis of Accumulated Adjustments Account, Other Adjustments Account, and Shareholders' Undistributed Taxable Income Previously Taxed** (see instructions)

	(a) Accumulated adjustments account	**(b)** Other adjustments account	**(c)** Shareholders' undistributed taxable income previously taxed
1 Balance at beginning of tax year			
2 Ordinary income from page 1, line 21			
3 Other additions			
4 Loss from page 1, line 21	( )		
5 Other reductions	( )	( )	
6 Combine lines 1 through 5			
7 Distributions other than dividend distributions			
8 Balance at end of tax year. Subtract line 7 from line 6			

671111

☐ Final K-1 ☐ Amended K-1 OMB No. 1545-0130

Schedule K-1 (Form 1120S)
Department of the Treasury
Internal Revenue Service

2011

For calendar year 2011, or tax year beginning ____________, 2011 ending ____________, 20____

Shareholder's Share of Income, Deductions, Credits, etc.

▶ **See back of form and separate instructions.**

Part I Information About the Corporation

A Corporation's employer identification number

B Corporation's name, address, city, state, and ZIP code

C IRS Center where corporation filed return

Part II Information About the Shareholder

D Shareholder's identifying number

E Shareholder's name, address, city, state, and ZIP code

F Shareholder's percentage of stock ownership for tax year . . . . ______________ %

For IRS Use Only

Part III Shareholder's Share of Current Year Income, Deductions, Credits, and Other Items

1	Ordinary business income (loss)	**13**	Credits
2	Net rental real estate income (loss)		
3	Other net rental income (loss)		
4	Interest income		
5a	Ordinary dividends		
5b	Qualified dividends	**14**	Foreign transactions
6	Royalties		
7	Net short-term capital gain (loss)		
8a	Net long-term capital gain (loss)		
8b	Collectibles (28%) gain (loss)		
8c	Unrecaptured section 1250 gain		
9	Net section 1231 gain (loss)		
10	Other income (loss)	**15**	Alternative minimum tax (AMT) items
11	Section 179 deduction	**16**	Items affecting shareholder basis
12	Other deductions		
		17	Other information

* See attached statement for additional information.

SCHEDULE M-3 (Form 1120S)

Department of the Treasury Internal Revenue Service

Net Income (Loss) Reconciliation for S Corporations With Total Assets of $10 Million or More

▶ Attach to Form 1120S.
▶ See separate instructions.

OMB No. 1545-0130

2011

Name of corporation | **Employer identification number**

Part I **Financial Information and Net Income (Loss) Reconciliation** (see instructions)

1a Did the corporation prepare a certified audited non-tax-basis income statement for the period ending with or within this tax year? (See instructions if multiple non-tax-basis income statements are prepared.)

☐ **Yes.** Skip line 1b and complete lines 2 through 11 with respect to that income statement.
☐ **No.** Go to line 1b.

b Did the corporation prepare a non-tax-basis income statement for that period?

☐ **Yes.** Complete lines 2 through 11 with respect to that income statement.
☐ **No.** Skip lines 2 through 3b and enter the corporation's net income (loss) per its books and records on line 4a.

2 Enter the income statement period: Beginning ____/____/____ Ending ____/____/____

3a Has the corporation's income statement been restated for the income statement period on line 2?

☐ **Yes.** (If "Yes," attach an explanation and the amount of each item restated.)
☐ **No.**

b Has the corporation's income statement been restated for any of the five income statement periods preceding the period on line 2?

☐ **Yes.** (If "Yes," attach an explanation and the amount of each item restated.)
☐ **No.**

4a	Worldwide consolidated net income (loss) from income statement source identified in Part I, line 1 .	**4a**	
b	Indicate accounting standard used for line 4a (see instructions): (1) ☐ GAAP (2) ☐ IFRS (3) ☐ Tax-basis (4) ☐ Other (specify) ____________		
5a	Net income from nonincludible foreign entities (attach schedule)	**5a**	( )
b	Net loss from nonincludible foreign entities (attach schedule and enter as a positive amount) . . .	**5b**	
6a	Net income from nonincludible U.S. entities (attach schedule)	**6a**	( )
b	Net loss from nonincludible U.S. entities (attach schedule and enter as a positive amount)	**6b**	
7a	Net income (loss) of other foreign disregarded entities (attach schedule)	**7a**	
b	Net income (loss) of other U.S. disregarded entities (except qualified subchapter S subsidiaries) (attach schedule)	**7b**	
c	Net income (loss) of other qualified subchapter S subsidiaries (QSubs) (attach schedule)	**7c**	
8	Adjustment to eliminations of transactions between includible entities and nonincludible entities (attach schedule)	**8**	
9	Adjustment to reconcile income statement period to tax year (attach schedule)	**9**	
10	Other adjustments to reconcile to amount on line 11 (attach schedule)	**10**	
11	**Net income (loss) per income statement of the corporation.** Combine lines 4 through 10 . . . **Note.** Part I, line 11, must equal Part II, line 26, column (a).	**11**	

12 Enter the total amount (not just the corporation's share) of the assets and liabilities of all entities included or removed on the following lines:

		Total Assets	Total Liabilities
a	Included on Part I, line 4		
b	Removed on Part I, line 5		
c	Removed on Part I, line 6		
d	Included on Part I, line 7		

Schedule M-3 (Form 1120S) 2011 Page **2**

Name of corporation	**Employer identification number**

Part II **Reconciliation of Net Income (Loss) per Income Statement of the Corporation With Total Income (Loss) per Return** (see instructions)

Income (Loss) Items	**(a)** Income (Loss) per Income Statement	**(b)** Temporary Difference	**(c)** Permanent Difference	**(d)** Income (Loss) per Tax Return
1 Income (loss) from equity method foreign corporations (attach schedule)				
2 Gross foreign dividends not previously taxed				
3 Subpart F, QEF, and similar income inclusions (attach schedule)				
4 Gross foreign distributions previously taxed (attach schedule)				
5 Income (loss) from equity method U.S. corporations (attach schedule)				
6 U.S. dividends not eliminated in tax consolidation				
7 Income (loss) from U.S. partnerships (attach schedule)				
8 Income (loss) from foreign partnerships (attach schedule)				
9 Income (loss) from other pass-through entities (attach schedule)				
10 Items relating to reportable transactions (attach details)				
11 Interest income (attach Form 8916-A)				
12 Total accrual to cash adjustment				
13 Hedging transactions				
14 Mark-to-market income (loss)				
15 Cost of goods sold (attach Form 8916-A)	( )			( )
16 Sale versus lease (for sellers and/or lessors)				
17 Section 481(a) adjustments				
18 Unearned/deferred revenue				
19 Income recognition from long-term contracts				
20 Original issue discount and other imputed interest				
21a Income statement gain/loss on sale, exchange, abandonment, worthlessness, or other disposition of assets other than inventory and pass-through entities				
b Gross capital gains from Schedule D, excluding amounts from pass-through entities				
c Gross capital losses from Schedule D, excluding amounts from pass-through entities, abandonment losses, and worthless stock losses				
d Net gain/loss reported on Form 4797, line 17, excluding amounts from pass-through entities, abandonment losses, and worthless stock losses				
e Abandonment losses				
f Worthless stock losses (attach details)				
g Other gain/loss on disposition of assets other than inventory				
22 Other income (loss) items with differences (attach schedule)				
23 **Total income (loss) items.** Combine lines 1 through 22				
24 **Total expense/deduction items** (from Part III, line 32)				
25 Other items with no differences				
26 **Reconciliation totals.** Combine lines 23 through 25				

Note. Line 26, column (a), must equal the amount on Part I, line 11, and column (d) must equal Form 1120S, Schedule K, line 18.

Schedule M-3 (Form 1120S) 2011

Schedule M-3 (Form 1120S) 2011 Page **3**

Name of corporation	**Employer identification number**

Part III **Reconciliation of Net Income (Loss) per Income Statement of the Corporation With Total Income (Loss) per Return—Expense/Deduction Items** (see instructions)

	Expense/Deduction Items	(a) Expense per Income Statement	(b) Temporary Difference	(c) Permanent Difference	(d) Deduction per Tax Return
1	U.S. current income tax expense				
2	U.S. deferred income tax expense				
3	State and local current income tax expense				
4	State and local deferred income tax expense				
5	Foreign current income tax expense (other than foreign withholding taxes)				
6	Foreign deferred income tax expense				
7	Equity-based compensation				
8	Meals and entertainment				
9	Fines and penalties				
10	Judgments, damages, awards, and similar costs				
11	Pension and profit-sharing				
12	Other post-retirement benefits				
13	Deferred compensation				
14	Charitable contribution of cash and tangible property				
15	Charitable contribution of intangible property				
16	Current year acquisition or reorganization investment banking fees				
17	Current year acquisition or reorganization legal and accounting fees				
18	Current year acquisition/reorganization other costs				
19	Amortization/impairment of goodwill				
20	Amortization of acquisition, reorganization, and start-up costs				
21	Other amortization or impairment write-offs				
22	Section 198 environmental remediation costs				
23a	Depletion—Oil & Gas				
b	Depletion—Other than Oil & Gas				
24	Depreciation				
25	Bad debt expense				
26	Interest expense (attach Form 8916-A)				
27	Corporate owned life insurance premiums				
28	Purchase versus lease (for purchasers and/or lessees)				
29	Research and development costs				
30	Section 118 exclusion (attach schedule)				
31	Other expense/deduction items with differences (attach schedule)				
32	**Total expense/deduction items.** Combine lines 1 through 31. Enter here and on Part II, line 24, reporting positive amounts as negative and negative amounts as positive				

Form **1125-A**
(December 2011)
Department of the Treasury
Internal Revenue Service

Cost of Goods Sold

▶ **Attach to Form 1120, 1120-C, 1120-F, 1120S, 1065, and 1065-B.**

OMB No. 1545-2225

Name	Employer identification number

1	Inventory at beginning of year	1	
2	Purchases	2	
3	Cost of labor	3	
4	Additional section 263A costs (attach schedule)	4	
5	Other costs (attach schedule)	5	
6	**Total.** Add lines 1 through 5	6	
7	Inventory at end of year	7	
8	**Cost of goods sold.** Subtract line 7 from line 6. Enter here and on Form 1120, page 1, line 2 or the appropriate line of your tax return (see instructions)	8	

9a Check all methods used for valuing closing inventory:

(i) ☐ Cost

(ii) ☐ Lower of cost or market

(iii) ☐ Other (Specify method used and attach explanation.) ▶ ____________

b Check if there was a writedown of subnormal goods ▶ ☐

c Check if the LIFO inventory method was adopted this tax year for any goods (if checked, attach Form 970) ▶ ☐

d If the LIFO inventory method was used for this tax year, enter amount of closing inventory computed under LIFO . . . **9d** ____

e If property is produced or acquired for resale, do the rules of section 263A apply to the corporation? ☐ Yes ☐ No

f Was there any change in determining quantities, cost, or valuations between opening and closing inventory? If "Yes," attach explanation ☐ Yes ☐ No

Section references are to the Internal Revenue Code unless otherwise noted.

General Instructions

Future Developments. The IRS has created a page on IRS.gov for information about Form 1125-A and its instructions at *www.irs.gov/form1125a*. Information about any future developments affecting Form 1125-A (such as legislation enacted after we release it) will be posted on that page.

Purpose of Form

Use Form 1125-A to calculate and deduct cost of goods sold for certain entities.

Who Must File

Filers of Form 1120, 1120-C, 1120-F, 1120S, 1065, or 1065-B, must complete and attach Form 1125-A if the applicable entity reports a deduction for cost of goods sold.

Inventories

Generally, inventories are required at the beginning and end of each tax year if the production, purchase, or sale of merchandise is an income-producing factor. See Regulations section 1.471-1. If inventories are required, you generally must use an accrual method of accounting for sales and purchases of inventory items.

Exception for certain taxpayers. If you are a qualifying taxpayer or a qualifying small business taxpayer (defined below), you can adopt or change your accounting method to account for inventoriable items in the same manner as materials and supplies that are not incidental.

Under this accounting method inventory costs for raw materials purchased for use in producing finished goods and merchandise purchased for resale are deductible in the year the finished goods or merchandise are sold (but not before the year you paid for the raw materials or merchandise, if you are also using the cash method). For additional guidance on this method of accounting, see Pub. 538, Accounting Periods and Methods. For guidance on adopting or changing to this method of accounting, see Form 3115, Application for Change in Accounting Method, and its instructions

If you account for inventoriable items in the same manner as materials and supplies that are not incidental, you can currently deduct expenditures for direct labor and all indirect costs that would otherwise be included in inventory costs.

Qualifying taxpayer. A qualifying taxpayer is a taxpayer that, (a) for each prior tax year ending after December 16, 1998, has average annual gross receipts of $1 million or less for the 3 prior tax years and (b) its business is not a tax shelter (as defined in section 448(d)(3)). See Rev. Proc. 2001-10, 2001-2 I.R.B. 272.

Qualifying small business taxpayer. A qualifying small business taxpayer is a taxpayer that, (a) for each prior tax year ending on or after December 31, 2000, has average annual gross receipts of $10 million or less for the 3 prior tax years, (b) whose principal business activity is not an ineligible activity, and (c) whose business is not a tax shelter (as defined in section 448 (d)(3)). See Rev. Proc. 2002-28, 2002-18, I. R.B. 815.

Uniform capitalization rules. The uniform capitalization rules of section 263A generally require you to capitalize, or include in inventory, certain costs incurred in connection with the following.

- The production of real property and tangible personal property held in inventory or held for sale in the ordinary course of business.
- Real property or personal property (tangible and intangible) acquired for resale.
- The production of real property and tangible personal property by a corporation for use in its trade or business or in an activity engaged in for property.

See the discussion on section 263A uniform capitalization rules in the instructions for your tax return before completing Form 1125-A. Also see Regulations sections 1.263A-1 through 1.263A-3. See Regulations section 1.263A-4 for rules for property produced in a farming business.

Form **8916-A**

Department of the Treasury
Internal Revenue Service

Supplemental Attachment to Schedule M-3

▶ Attach to Schedule M-3 for Form 1065, 1120, 1120-L, 1120-PC, or 1120S.

OMB No. 1545-2061

2011

Name of common parent	**Employer identification number**
Name of subsidiary	**Employer identification number**

Part I Cost of Goods Sold

Cost of Goods Sold Items	(a) Expense per Income Statement	(b) Temporary Difference	(c) Permanent Difference	(d) Deduction per Tax Return
1 Amounts attributable to cost flow assumptions .				
2 Amounts attributable to:				
a Stock option expense				
b Other equity based compensation				
c Meals and entertainment				
d Parachute payments				
e Compensation with section 162(m) limitation . .				
f Pension and profit sharing				
g Other post-retirement benefits				
h Deferred compensation				
i Section 198 environmental remediation costs . .				
j Amortization				
k Depletion				
l Depreciation				
m Corporate owned life insurance premiums . . .				
n Other section 263A costs				
3 Inventory shrinkage accruals.				
4 Excess inventory and obsolescence reserves . .				
5 Lower of cost or market write-downs				
6 Other items with differences (attach schedule) . .				
7 Other items with no differences				
8 **Total cost of goods sold.** Add lines 1 through 7, in columns a, b, c, and d				

For Paperwork Reduction Act Notice, see page 4. Cat. No. 48657X Form **8916-A** (2011)

Appendix C

Glossary

The words and phrases in this glossary have been defined to reflect their conventional use in the field of taxation. The definitions may therefore be incomplete for other purposes.

A

Accelerated cost recovery system (ACRS). A method in which the cost of tangible property is recovered over a prescribed period of time. The approach disregards salvage value, imposes a period of cost recovery that depends upon the classification of the asset into one of various recovery periods, and prescribes the applicable percentage of cost that can be deducted each year. The modified system is referred to as MACRS. § 168.

Accelerated depreciation. Various methods of *depreciation* that yield larger deductions in the earlier years of the life of an asset than the straight-line method. Examples include the double declining-balance and the sum-of-the-years' digits methods of depreciation.

Acceleration rule. Treatment of an intercompany transaction on a *consolidated return,* when a sold asset leaves the group.

Accounting method. The method under which income and expenses are determined for tax purposes. Important accounting methods include the *cash basis* and the *accrual basis.* Special methods are available for the reporting of gain on installment sales, recognition of income on construction projects (the *completed contract* and *percentage of completion* methods), and the valuation of inventories (last-in, first-out and first-in, first-out). §§ 446–474.

Accounting period. The period of time, usually a year, used by a taxpayer for the determination of tax liability. Unless a *fiscal year* is chosen, taxpayers must determine and pay their income tax liability by using the calendar year (January 1 through December 31) as the period of measurement. An example of a fiscal year is July 1 through June 30. A change in accounting periods (e.g., from a calendar year to a fiscal year) generally requires the consent of the IRS. Usually, taxpayers are free to select either an initial calendar or a fiscal year without the consent of the IRS. §§ 441–443. See also *annual accounting period concept.*

Accrual basis. A method of accounting that reflects expenses incurred and income earned for any one tax year. In contrast to the *cash basis* of accounting, expenses need not be paid to be deductible, nor need income be received to be taxable. *Unearned income* (e.g., prepaid interest and rent) generally is taxed in the year of receipt regardless of the method of accounting used by the taxpayer. § 446(c)(2). See also *accounting method.*

Accumulated adjustments account (AAA). An account that aggregates an *S corporation's* post-1982 income, loss, and deductions for the tax year (including nontaxable income and nondeductible losses and expenses). After the year-end income and expense adjustments are made, the account is reduced by distributions made during the tax year.

Accumulated earnings and profits. Net undistributed tax-basis earnings of a corporation aggregated from March 1, 1913, to the end of the prior tax year. Used to determine the amount of dividend income associated with a distribution to shareholders. See also *current earnings and profits* and *earnings and profits.* § 316 and Reg. § 1.316–2.

Accumulated earnings credit. A reduction allowed in arriving at *accumulated taxable income,* in determining the *accumulated earnings tax.*

Accumulated earnings tax. A special tax imposed on C corporations that accumulate (rather than distribute) their earnings beyond the *reasonable needs of the business.* The accumulated earnings tax and related interest are imposed on *accumulated taxable income* in addition to the corporate income tax. §§ 531–537.

Accumulated taxable income. The base upon which the *accumulated earnings tax* is imposed. Generally, it is the taxable income of the corporation as adjusted for certain items (e.g., the Federal income tax, excess charitable contributions, the *dividends received deduction*) less the *dividends paid deduction* and the *accumulated earnings credit.* § 535.

Accumulating trust. See *discretionary trust.*

Accuracy-related penalty. Major civil taxpayer penalties relating to the accuracy of tax return data, including misstatements stemming from taxpayer *negligence* and improper valuation of income and deductions, are coordinated under this umbrella term. The penalty usually equals 20 percent of the understated tax liability.

ACE adjustment. In calculating *alternative minimum taxable income (AMTI)*, certain adjustments are added to or subtracted from *taxable income*. A *C corporation* subject to the *alternative minimum tax* computes the ACE adjustment as 75 percent of the excess of *adjusted current earnings (ACE)* over AMTI. The ACE adjustment can be negative in certain circumstances. ACE restricts/defers certain deductions and includes/accelerates certain income items, compared with AMTI.

Acquiescence. Agreement by the IRS on the results reached in some of the more significant decisions involving tax issues; sometimes abbreviated *Acq.* or *A.* See also *nonacquiescence*.

Acquisition. See *corporate acquisition*.

ACRS. See *accelerated cost recovery system*.

Ad valorem tax. A tax imposed on the value of property. The most common ad valorem tax is that imposed by states, counties, and cities on real estate. Ad valorem taxes can be imposed on personal property as well.

Adjusted basis. The cost or other basis of property reduced by *depreciation* allowed or allowable and increased by capital improvements. Other special adjustments are provided in § 1016 and the related Regulations. See also *basis*.

Adjusted current earnings (ACE). Used to determine an adjustment in computing corporate *alternative minimum taxable income* (AMTI). ACE reflects restrictions on the timing of certain recognition events. Exempt interest, *life insurance* proceeds, and other receipts that are included in *earnings and profits* but not in *taxable income* also increase ACE.

Adjusted gross estate. The *gross estate* of a *decedent* reduced by § 2053 expenses (e.g., administration, funeral) and § 2054 losses (e.g., casualty). Necessary in testing for the extension of time for installment payment of estate taxes under § 6166. See also *gross estate*.

Adjusted gross income (AGI). A tax determination peculiar to individual taxpayers. Generally, it represents the *gross income* of an individual, less business expenses and less any appropriate capital gain or loss adjustment.

Adjusted ordinary gross income (AOGI). A determination peculiar to the *personal holding company tax*. In ascertaining whether a corporation is a *personal holding company*, *personal holding company income* divided by adjusted ordinary gross income must equal 60 percent or more. Adjusted ordinary gross income is the corporation's *gross income* less net *capital gains*, *§ 1231 gains*, and certain expenses. §§ 541 and 543(b)(2).

Administration. The supervision and winding up of an *estate*. The administration of an estate runs from the date of an individual's death until all assets have been distributed and liabilities paid.

Administrator. A person appointed by the court to administer (manage or take charge of) the assets and liabilities of a *decedent* (the deceased). See also *executor*.

Affiliate. A member of an *affiliated group*. See also *consolidated return*.

Affiliated group. A parent-subsidiary group of corporations that is eligible to elect to file on a consolidated basis. Eighty percent ownership of the voting power and value of all of the corporations must be achieved on every day of the tax year, and an identifiable parent corporation must exist (i.e., it must own at least 80 percent of another group member without applying *attribution* rules).

AFTR. *American Federal Tax Reports* contain Federal tax decisions issued by the U.S. *District Courts*, U.S. *Court of Federal Claims*, U.S. *Courts of Appeals*, and the *U.S. Supreme Court*.

AFTR 2d. The second series of the *American Federal Tax Reports*, dealing with 1954 and 1986 Code case law.

Aggregate (conduit) concept. The theory of *partnership* taxation under which, in certain cases, a partnership is treated as a mere collection of the activities of each partner. See also *entity concept*.

Alimony. Alimony deductions result from the payment of a legal obligation arising from the termination of a marital relationship. Payments designated as alimony generally are included in the *gross income* of the recipient and are deductible *for* AGI by the payor.

Allocable share of income. Certain entities receive conduit treatment under the Federal income tax law. This means the *earned income* or loss is not taxed to the entity, but is allocated to the owners or beneficiaries, regardless of the magnitude or timing of corresponding distributions. The portion of the entity's income that is taxed to the owner or *beneficiary* is the allocable share of the entity's income or loss for the period. The allocations are determined by (1) the *partnership agreement* for partners, (2) a weighted-average stock ownership computation for shareholders of an *S corporation*, and (3) the controlling will or trust instrument for the beneficiaries of an *estate* or *trust*.

Allocate. The assignment of income for various tax purposes. A *multistate corporation*'s nonbusiness income usually is allocated to the state where the nonbusiness assets are located; it is not *apportioned* with the rest of the entity's income. The income and expense items of an *estate* or *trust* are allocated between income and *corpus* components. Specific items of income, expense, gain, loss, and credit can be allocated to specific partners, if a substantial economic nontax purpose for the allocation is established. See also *apportion* and *substantial economic effect*.

Alternate valuation date. Property passing from a *decedent* by death may be valued for *estate tax* purposes as of the date of death or the alternate valuation date. The alternate valuation date is six months from the date of death or the date the property is disposed of by the estate, whichever comes first. To use the alternate valuation date, the *executor* or *administrator* of the estate must make an affirmative election. Election of the alternate valuation date is not available unless it decreases the amount of the *gross estate* *and* reduces the estate tax liability.

Alternative minimum tax (AMT). AMT is a fixed percentage of *alternative minimum taxable income* (AMTI). AMTI generally starts with the taxpayer's *adjusted gross income* (for individuals) or *taxable income* (for other taxpayers). To this amount, the taxpayer (1) adds designated preference items (e.g., interest income on private activity bonds), (2) makes other specified adjustments (e.g., to reflect a longer, straight-line *cost recovery* deduction), (3) subtracts certain AMT itemized deductions for individuals (e.g., interest incurred on housing but not taxes paid), and (4) subtracts an exemption amount (e.g., $40,000 on a C corporation's return). The taxpayer must pay the greater of the resulting AMT (reduced for larger corporations by only the foreign tax credit) or the regular income tax (reduced by all allowable tax credits). The AMT does not apply at all to certain small *C corporations. AMT preferences* and *adjustments* are assigned to partners, LLC members, and *S corporation* shareholders.

Alternative minimum taxable income (AMTI). The base for computing a taxpayer's *alternative minimum tax.* Generally, the taxable income for the year, modified for AMT adjustments, preferences, and exemptions.

Amortization. The tax deduction for the cost or other basis of an *intangible asset* over the asset's *estimated useful life.* Examples of amortizable intangibles include patents, copyrights, and leasehold interests. Most intangible assets are amortized over 15 years. § 195. For tangible assets, see *depreciation.* For natural resources, see *depletion.* See also *goodwill.*

Amount realized. The amount received by a taxpayer upon the sale or exchange of property. Amount realized is the sum of the cash and the *fair market value* of any property or services received by the taxpayer, plus any related debt assumed by the buyer. Determining the amount realized is the starting point for arriving at realized gain or loss. § 1001(b). See also *realized gain or loss* and *recognized gain or loss.*

AMT adjustments. In calculating *alternative minimum taxable income (AMTI),* certain adjustments are added to or subtracted from *taxable income.* AMT adjustments generally reflect timing differences, such as the use of slower *depreciation* deductions for the *alternative minimum tax (AMT).* A *C corporation* might be subject to the *ACE adjustment.*

AMT preferences. In calculating *alternative minimum taxable income (AMTI),* certain preference items are added to *taxable income.* AMT preferences generally reflect differences between the regular tax and the *alternative minimum tax (AMT)* computational bases. For instance, interest income from certain state and local bonds may be an AMT preference item.

Annual accounting period concept. In determining a taxpayer's income tax liability, only transactions taking place during a specified tax year are taken into consideration. For reporting and payment purposes, therefore, the tax life of taxpayers is divided into equal annual *accounting periods.* See also *mitigation of the annual accounting period concept.*

Annual exclusion. In computing the *taxable gifts* for the year, each *donor* excludes the first $13,000 of a gift to each *donee.* Usually, the annual exclusion is not available for gifts of *future interests.* § 2503(b). See also *gift splitting.*

Annuitant. The party entitled to receive payments from an *annuity* contract.

Annuity. A fixed sum of money payable to a person at specified times for a specified period of time or for life. If the party making the payment (i.e., the obligor) is regularly engaged in this type of business (e.g., an insurance company), the arrangement is classified as a commercial annuity. A so-called private annuity involves an *obligor* that is not regularly engaged in selling annuities (e.g., a charity or family member).

Anticipatory assignment of income. See *assignment of income.*

Appellate court. For Federal tax purposes, appellate courts include the U.S. *Courts of Appeals* and the U.S. *Supreme Court.* If the party losing in the *trial* (or lower) *court* is dissatisfied with the result, the dispute may be carried to the appropriate appellate court.

Apportion. The assignment of the business income of a *multistate corporation* to specific states for income taxation. Usually, the apportionment procedure accounts for the property, payroll, and sales activity levels of the various states, and a proportionate assignment of the entity's total income is made, using a three-factor apportionment formula. These activities indicate the commercial *domicile* of the corporation, relative to that income. Some states exclude *nonbusiness income* from the apportionment procedure; they *allocate* nonbusiness income to the states where the nonbusiness assets are located. See also *payroll factor, property factor,* and *sales factor.*

Appreciated inventory. In *partnership* taxation, appreciated inventory is a *hot asset,* and a *partner's* share of its ordinary income potential must be allocated. If a partner sells an interest in the partnership, ordinary income is recognized to the extent of the partner's share in the partnership's inventory and *unrealized receivables.* The definition of "inventory" here is broad enough to include any accounts receivable, including unrealized receivables.

Arm's length concept. The standard under which unrelated parties would carry out a transaction. Suppose Bint Corporation sells property to its sole shareholder for $10,000. In determining whether $10,000 is an arm's length price, one would ascertain the amount for which the corporation could have sold the property to a disinterested third party.

Articles of incorporation. The legal document specifying a corporation's name, period of existence, purpose and powers, authorized number of shares, classes of stock, and other conditions for operation. The organizers of the corporation file the articles with the state of incorporation. If the articles are satisfactory and other conditions of the law are satisfied, the state will issue a charter recognizing the organization's status as a corporation.

ASC 450 (SFAS 5). Under *Generally Accepted Accounting Principles,* the rules for the financial reporting of contingent liabilities, including deferred taxes.

ASC 740 (SFAS 109). Under *Generally Accepted Accounting Principles,* the rules for the financial reporting of the tax expense of an enterprise. *Permanent differences* affect the enterprise's effective tax rate. *Temporary differences* create a *deferred tax asset* or a *deferred tax liability* on the balance sheet.

ASC 740-10 (FIN 48). Under *Generally Accepted Accounting Principles,* an interpretation of *ASC 740 (SFAS 109)* relating to when a tax benefit should be reported in an enterprise's financial statements. A tax benefit should be recorded for book purposes only if it is more likely than not that the taxpayer's filing position will be sustained after an audit, administrative appeal, and the highest applicable judicial review.

ASC 740-30 (APB 23). Under *Generally Accepted Accounting Principles,* the rules for the financial reporting of the tax expense relative to a U.S. corporation's non-U.S. subsidiary. If the parent documents that it is *permanently reinvesting* the non-U.S. earnings of a non-U.S. subsidiary, the parent does not record as an expense any U.S. income tax that the parent might pay on such earnings, i.e., the book tax expense is deferred until such earnings are (if ever) repatriated to the United States.

Assessment. The process whereby the IRS imposes a tax liability. If, for example, the IRS audits a taxpayer's income tax return and finds *gross income* understated or deductions overstated, it will assess a *deficiency* in the amount of the tax that should have been paid in light of the adjustments made.

Asset-use test. In a *corporate reorganization,* a means by which to determine if the *continuity of business enterprise* requirement is met. The acquiring corporation must continue to use the target entity's assets in the acquiror's business going forward; if this is not the case, the requirement is failed.

Assignment of income. A taxpayer attempts to avoid the recognition of income by assigning to another the property that generates the income. Such a procedure will not avoid the recognition of income by the taxpayer making the assignment if the income was earned at the point of the transfer. In this case, the income is taxed to the person who earns it.

Assumption of liabilities. In a corporate formation, corporate takeover, or asset purchase, the new owner often takes assets and agrees to assume preexisting debt. Such actions do not create *boot* received on the transaction for the new shareholder, unless there is no *bona fide* business purpose for the exchange, or the principal purpose of the debt assumption is the avoidance of tax liabilities. Gain is recognized to the extent that liabilities assumed exceed the aggregated bases of the transferred assets. § 357. See also *liabilities in excess of basis.*

At-risk amount. The taxpayer has an amount at risk in a business or investment venture to the extent that personal assets have been subjected to the risks of the business. Typically, the taxpayer's at-risk amount includes (1) the amount of money or other property that the investor contributed to the venture for the investment, (2) the amount of any of the entity's liabilities for which the taxpayer personally is liable and that relate to the investment, and (3) an allocable share of *nonrecourse debts* incurred by the venture from third parties in arm's length transactions for real estate investments.

At-risk limitation. Generally, a taxpayer can deduct losses related to a trade or business, *S corporation, partnership,* or investment asset only to the extent of the *at-risk amount.*

Attribution. Under certain circumstances, the tax law applies attribution rules to assign to one taxpayer the ownership interest of another taxpayer. If, for example, the stock of Tree Corporation is held 60 percent by Mary and 40 percent by Sam, Mary may be deemed to own 100 percent of Tree if Sam is her son. In that case, the stock owned by Sam is attributed to Mary. Stated differently, Mary has a 60 percent direct and a 40 percent indirect interest in Tree. It can also be said that Mary is the constructive owner of Sam's interest.

Audit. Inspection and verification of a taxpayer's return or other transactions possessing tax consequences. See also *correspondence audit, field audit,* and *office audit.*

Automobile expenses. Automobile expenses generally are deductible only to the extent the automobile is used in business or for the production of income. Personal commuting expenses are not deductible. The taxpayer may deduct actual out-of-pocket expenses (including depreciation and insurance), or a standard mileage rate for the tax year. For 2012, per-mile deduction amounts are 55 cents for business use of the auto, 14 cents if in support of charity, 23 cents for medical purposes, and 23 cents for a job-related move.

Avoidance. See *tax avoidance.*

B

Bailout. Various procedures whereby the owners of an entity can obtain the entity's profits with favorable tax consequences. With corporations, for example, the bailout of corporate profits might be accomplished by using fringe benefit plans, or by paying salaries or interest. The alternative of distributing the profits to the shareholders as dividends generally is less attractive, because *dividend* payments are not deductible. See also *preferred stock bailout.*

Balance sheet approach. The process under *ASC 740 (SFAS 109)* by which an entity's *deferred tax expense* or *deferred tax benefit* is determined as a result of the reporting period's changes in the balance sheet's *deferred tax asset* and *deferred tax liability* accounts.

***Bardahl* formula.** A formula approved in a *Tax Court* memorandum decision, used in the context of the *accumulated earnings tax* to compute the reasonable business needs of the corporation for working capital. Most appropriate where the corporation holds inventory.

Bargain sale or purchase. A sale or purchase of property for less than fair market value. The difference between the sale or purchase price and the fair market value of the property may have tax consequences. If, for example, a corporation sells property worth $1,000 to one of its shareholders for $700, the $300 difference probably represents a *constructive dividend* to the shareholder. Suppose, instead, the shareholder sells the property (worth $1,000) to his or her corporation for $700. The $300 difference probably represents a contribution by the shareholder to the corporation's capital. Bargain sales and purchases among members of the same family may lead to *gift tax* consequences.

Basis. The acquisition cost assigned to an asset for income tax purposes. For assets acquired by purchase, basis is cost (§ 1012). Special rules govern the basis of property received by virtue of another's death (§ 1014) or by *gift* (§ 1015), the basis of stock received on a transfer of property to a controlled corporation (§ 358), the basis of the property transferred to the corporation (§ 362), and the basis of property received upon the *liquidation* of a corporation (§ 334). See also *adjusted basis.*

Basis in partnership interest. The acquisition cost of the partner's ownership interest in the *partnership.* Includes purchase price and associated debt acquired from other *partners* and in the course of the entity's trade or business.

Benchmarking. The tax professional's use of two or more entities' effective tax rates and deferred tax balance sheet accounts. Used chiefly to compare the effectiveness of the entities' tax planning techniques, and to suggest future tax-motivated courses of action.

Beneficiary. A party who will benefit from a transfer of property or other arrangement. Examples include the beneficiary of a *trust,* the beneficiary of a life insurance policy, and the beneficiary of an *estate.*

Bequest. A transfer of *personal property* by will. To bequeath is to leave such property by will. See also *devise.*

Blockage rule. A factor to be considered in valuing a large block of stock. Application of this rule generally justifies a discount in the fair market value, because the disposition of a large amount of stock at any one time may depress the value of the shares in the marketplace.

Bona fide. In good faith, or real. In tax law, this term often is used in connection with a *business purpose* for carrying out a transaction. Thus, was there a bona fide business purpose for a shareholder's transfer of a liability to a controlled corporation? § 357(b)(1)(B). See also *business purpose.*

Book value. The net amount of an asset after reduction by a related reserve. The book value of machinery, for example, is the amount of the machinery less the reserve for *depreciation.*

Boot. Cash or property of a type not included in the definition of a nontaxable exchange. The receipt of boot causes an otherwise nontaxable transfer to become taxable to the extent of the lesser of the fair market value of the boot or the realized gain on the transfer. For example, see transfers to controlled corporations under § 351(b) and *like-kind exchanges* under § 1031(b). See also *realized gain or loss.*

Branch profits tax. A tax on the *effectively connected earnings* and profits of the U.S. branch of a *foreign corporation.* The tax is levied in addition to the usual § 11 tax, in an amount equal to 30 percent of the *dividend equivalent amount.* Treaties can override the tax or reduce the withholding percentage. Earnings reinvested in the U.S. operations of the entity are not subject to the tax until repatriation.

Bribes and illegal payments. Section 162 denies a deduction for bribes or kickbacks, fines, and penalties paid to a government official or employee for violation of law, and two-thirds of the treble damage payments made to claimants for violation of the antitrust law. Denial of a deduction for bribes and illegal payments is based upon the judicially established principle that allowing such payments would be contrary to public policy.

Brother-sister controlled group. More than one corporation owned by the same shareholders. If, for example, Clara and Dan each own one-half of the stock in Top Corporation and Bottom Corporation, then Top and Bottom form a brother-sister controlled group.

B.T.A. The Board of Tax Appeals was a trial court that considered Federal tax matters. This court is now the U.S. *Tax Court.*

Built-in gains tax. A penalty tax designed to discourage a shift of the incidence of taxation on unrealized gains from a *C corporation* to its shareholders, via an S election. Under this provision, any recognized gain during the first (5, 7, or) 10 years of S status generates a corporate-level tax on a base not to exceed the aggregate untaxed built-in gains brought into the *S corporation* upon its election from C corporation taxable years.

Built-in loss property. Property contributed to a corporation under § 351 or as a contribution to capital that has a basis in excess of its fair market value. An adjustment is necessary to step down the basis of the property to its fair market value. The adjustment prevents the corporation and the contributing shareholder from obtaining a double tax benefit. The corporation allocates the adjustment proportionately among the assets with the built-in loss. As an alternative to the corporate adjustment, the shareholder may elect to reduce the basis in the stock.

Burden of proof. The requirement in a lawsuit to show the weight of evidence and thereby gain a favorable decision. In cases of tax *fraud,* the burden of proof in a tax case is on the IRS.

Business bad debts. A tax deduction allowed for obligations obtained in connection with a *trade or business* that have become either partially or completely worthless. In contrast to *nonbusiness bad debts,* business bad debts are deductible as business expenses. § 166.

Business purpose. A justifiable business reason for carrying out a transaction. Mere tax avoidance is not an acceptable business purpose. The presence of a business purpose is crucial in the area of *corporate reorganizations* and certain *liquidations.* See also *bona fide.*

Buy-sell agreement. An arrangement, particularly appropriate in the case of a closely held corporation or a *partnership,* whereby the surviving owners (shareholders or *partners*) or the entity agrees to purchase the interest of a withdrawing owner. The buy-sell agreement provides for an orderly disposition of an interest in a business and may aid in setting the value of the interest for *estate tax* purposes. See also *cross-purchase buy-sell agreement* and *entity buy-sell agreement.*

Bypass amount. The amount that can be transferred by gift or death free of any unified transfer tax. For 2012, the bypass amount is $5.12 million for *estate tax* and $5.12 million for *gift tax.* See also *exemption equivalent amount.*

Bypass election. In the context of a distribution by an *S corporation,* an election made by the entity to designate that the distribution is first from *accumulated earnings and profits,* and only then from the *accumulated adjustments account (AAA).*

C

C corporation. A separate taxable entity, subject to the rules of Subchapter C of the Code. This business form may create a double taxation effect relative to its shareholders. The entity is subject to the regular corporate tax and a number of penalty taxes at the Federal level.

Calendar year. See *accounting period.*

Capital account. The financial accounting analog of a partner's tax *basis* in the entity.

Capital asset. Broadly speaking, all assets are capital except those specifically excluded from that definition by the Code. Major categories of noncapital assets include property held for resale in the normal course of business (inventory), trade accounts and notes receivable, and depreciable property and real estate used in a *trade or business* (§ 1231 assets). § 1221. See also *capital gain* and *capital loss.*

Capital contribution. Various means by which a shareholder makes additional funds available to the corporation (placed at the risk of the business), sometimes without the receipt of additional stock. If no stock is received, the contributions are added to the *basis* of the shareholder's existing stock investment and do not generate *gross income* to the corporation. § 118.

Capital expenditure. An expenditure added to the *basis* of the property improved. For income tax purposes, this generally precludes a full deduction for the expenditure in the year paid or incurred. Cost recovery in the form of a tax deduction later comes in the form of *depreciation*, *depletion*, or *amortization*. § 263.

Capital gain. The gain from the sale or exchange of a *capital asset*.

Capital interest. Usually, the percentage of the entity's net assets that a *partner* would receive on liquidation. Typically determined by the partner's capital sharing ratio.

Capital loss. The loss from the sale or exchange of a *capital asset*.

Capital sharing ratio. A *partner's* percentage ownership of the entity's capital.

Capital stock tax. A state-level tax, usually imposed on out-of-state corporations for the privilege of doing business in the state. The tax may be based on the entity's apportionable income or payroll, or on its *apportioned* net worth as of a specified date.

Carryover basis. When a taxpayer exchanges one asset for another, many provisions in the tax law allow the basis assigned to the received asset to be precisely that of the traded asset. Thus, no step-up or -down of *basis* occurs as a result of the exchange. For instance, when an investor contributes an asset to a corporation or *partnership*, the entity generally takes a carryover basis in the property. § 723.

Cash basis. A method of accounting that reflects deductions as paid and income as received in any one tax year. However, deductions for prepaid expenses that benefit more than one tax year (e.g., prepaid rent and prepaid interest) usually are spread over the period benefited rather than deducted in the year paid. § 446(c)(1). See also *constructive receipt of income*.

Cash surrender value. The amount of money that an insurance policy would yield if cashed in with the insurance company that issued the policy.

CCH. Commerce Clearing House (CCH) is the publisher of a tax service and of Federal tax decisions (*USTC* series).

Cert. den. By denying the Writ of Certiorari, the U.S. *Supreme Court* refuses to accept an appeal from a U.S. *Court of Appeals*. The denial of *certiorari* does not, however, mean that the U.S. Supreme Court agrees with the result reached by the lower court.

Certiorari. Appeal from a U.S. *Court of Appeals* to the U.S. *Supreme Court* is by Writ of Certiorari. The Supreme Court need not accept the appeal, and it usually does not do so (*cert. den.*) unless a conflict exists among the lower courts that must be resolved or a constitutional issue is involved. See also *cert. den.*

Cf. Compare.

Charitable contributions. Contributions are deductible (subject to various restrictions and ceiling limitations) if made to qualified nonprofit charitable organizations. A *cash basis* taxpayer is entitled to a deduction solely in the year of payment. *Accrual basis* corporations may accrue contributions at year-end if payment is properly authorized before the end of the year and payment is made within two and one-half months after the end of the year. § 170.

Check-the-box Regulations. A business entity can elect to be taxed as a *partnership*, *S corporation*, or *C corporation* by indicating its preference on the tax return. Legal structure and operations are irrelevant in this regard. Thus, by using the check-the-box rules prudently, an entity can select the most attractive tax results offered by the Code, without being bound by legal forms. Not available if the entity is incorporated under state law.

Circular 230. A portion of the Federal tax *Regulations* that describes the levels of conduct at which a *tax preparer* must operate. Circular 230 dictates, for instance, that a tax preparer may not charge an unconscionable fee or delay the execution of a tax audit with inappropriate delays. Circular 230 requires that there be a reasonable basis for a tax return position, and that no *frivolous returns* be filed.

Civil fraud. See *fraud*.

Closely held corporation. A corporation where stock ownership is not widely dispersed. Rather, a few shareholders are in control of corporate policy and are in a position to benefit personally from that policy.

Closing agreement. In a tax dispute, the parties sign a closing agreement to spell out the terms under which the matters are settled. The agreement is binding on both the IRS and the taxpayer.

Collapsing. To disregard a transaction or one of a series of steps leading to a result. See also *step transaction, substance vs. form concept*, and *telescoping*.

Combined return. In multistate taxation, a group of unitary corporations may elect or be required to file an income tax return that includes operating results for all of the *affiliates*, not just those with *nexus* in the state. Thus, apportionment data is reported for the group's worldwide or water's edge operations.

Commissioner of the IRS. The head of IRS operations, a presidential appointee.

Common law state. See *community property*.

Community property. Louisiana, Texas, New Mexico, Arizona, California, Washington, Idaho, Nevada, and Wisconsin have community property systems. The rest of the states are common law property jurisdictions. Alaska residents can elect community property status for assets. The difference between common law and community property systems centers around the property rights possessed by married persons. In a common law system, each spouse owns whatever he or she earns. Under a community property system, one-half of the earnings of each spouse is considered owned by the other spouse. Assume, for example, Hal and Wanda are husband and wife and their only income is the $50,000 annual salary Hal receives. If they live in New York (a common law state), the $50,000 salary belongs to Hal. If, however, they live in Texas (a community property state), the $50,000 salary is owned one-half each by Hal and Wanda. See also *separate property*.

Complete termination redemption. See *redemption (complete termination)*.

Completed contract method. A method of reporting gain or loss on certain long-term contracts. Under this method of accounting, all *gross income* and expenses are recognized in the tax year in which the contract is completed. Reg. § 1.451–3. See also *percentage of completion method*.

Complex trust. Not a *simple trust.* Such trusts may have charitable beneficiaries, accumulate income, and distribute corpus. §§ 661–663.

Composite return. In multistate taxation, an *S corporation* may be allowed to file a single income tax return that assigns pass-through items to resident and nonresident shareholders. The composite or "block" return allows the entity to remit any tax that is attributable to the nonresident shareholders.

Concur. To agree with the result reached by another, but not necessarily with the reasoning or the logic used in reaching the result. For example, Judge Ross agrees with Judges Smith and Tanaka (all being members of the same court) that the income is taxable but for a different reason. Judge Ross would issue a concurring opinion to the majority opinion issued by Judges Smith and Tanaka.

Condemnation. The taking of property by a public authority. The taking is by legal action, and the owner of the property is compensated by the public authority.

Conduit concept. An approach assumed by the tax law in the treatment of certain entities and their owners. Permits specified tax characteristics to pass through the entity without losing their identity. For example, long-term capital losses realized by a *limited liability company* are passed through as such to the individual members of the entity. Varying forms of the conduit concept apply for *partnerships, trusts, estates,* and *S corporations.* See also *aggregate concept.*

Consent dividend. For purposes of avoiding or reducing the penalty tax on the unreasonable accumulation of earnings or the *personal holding company tax,* a corporation may declare a consent dividend. No cash or property is distributed to the shareholders, although the corporation obtains a *dividends paid deduction.* The consent dividend is taxed to the shareholders and increases the *basis* in their stock investment. § 565.

Conservation easement. An interest in real property that maintains its natural or pristine condition. Most often it restricts the development of the property. Properly structured, the grant of such an easement can generate an income tax deduction for the donor. If the grant takes place after the owner's death, a § 2055 *charitable contribution deduction* results, and a portion of the property's value is excluded from the *gross estate.* § 2031(c).

Conservatism principle. The theory behind much of *Generally Accepted Accounting Principles,* under which assurance is provided that an entity's balance sheet assets are not overstated, nor liabilities understated. For instance, under *ASC 740 (SFAS 109),* a *deferred tax asset* is not recorded until it is more likely than not that the future tax benefit will be realized.

Consolidated return. A procedure whereby certain affiliated corporations may file a single return, combine the tax transactions of each corporation, and arrive at a single income tax liability for the group. The election to file a consolidated return usually is binding on future years. §§ 1501–1505 and related Regulations.

Consolidation. The combination of two or more corporations into a newly created corporation. Thus, Apt Corporation and Bye Corporation combine to form Cart Corporation. A consolidation may qualify as a nontaxable *reorganization* if certain conditions are satisfied. §§ 354 and 368(a)(1)(A).

Constructive dividend. A taxable benefit derived by a shareholder from his or her corporation that is not actually initiated by the board of directors as a *dividend.* Examples include *unreasonable compensation,* excessive rent payments, bargain purchases of corporate property, and shareholder use of corporate property. Constructive dividends generally are found in *closely held corporations.* See also *bargain sale or purchase.*

Constructive liquidation scenario. The means by which *recourse debt* is shared among *partners* in *basis* determination.

Constructive ownership. See *attribution.*

Constructive receipt of income. If income is unqualifiedly available although not physically in the taxpayer's possession, it still is subject to the income tax. An example is accrued interest on a savings account. Under the constructive receipt concept, the interest is taxed to a depositor in the year available, rather than the year actually withdrawn. The fact that the depositor uses the *cash basis* of accounting for tax purposes is irrelevant. See Reg. § 1.451–2.

Continuity of business enterprise. In a tax-favored *reorganization,* a shareholder or corporation that has substantially the same investment after an exchange as before should not be taxed on the transaction. Specifically, the transferee corporation must continue the historic business of the transferor or use a significant portion of the transferor's assets in the new business. See also *asset-use test* and *historic business test.*

Continuity of interest test. In a tax-favored *reorganization,* a shareholder or corporation that has substantially the same investment after an exchange as before should not be taxed on the transaction. Specifically, the seller must acquire an equity interest in the acquiring corporation equal in value to at least 50 percent of all formerly outstanding stock of the acquired entity.

Continuity of life or existence. The death or other withdrawal of an owner of an entity does not terminate the existence of the entity. This is a characteristic of a corporation, as the death or withdrawal of a shareholder does not affect the corporation's existence.

Contributions to the capital of a corporation. See *capital contribution.*

Contributory qualified pension or profit sharing plan. A plan funded with both employer and employee contributions. Since the employee's contributions to the plan are subject to income tax, a later distribution of the contributions to the employee generally is tax-free. See also *qualified pension or profit sharing plan.*

Control. Holding a specified level of stock ownership in a corporation. For § 351, the new shareholder(s) must hold at least 80 percent of the total combined voting power of all voting classes of stock. Other tax provisions require different levels of control to bring about desired effects, such as 50 or 100 percent.

Controlled foreign corporation (CFC). A non-U.S. corporation in which more than 50 percent of the total combined voting power of all classes of stock entitled to vote or the total value of the stock of the corporation is owned by *U.S. shareholders* on any day during the taxable year of the foreign corporation. For purposes of this definition, a U.S. shareholder is any U.S. person who owns, or is considered to own, 10 percent or more of the total combined voting power of all classes of voting stock of the foreign corporation. Stock owned directly, indirectly, and constructively is used in this measure.

Controlled group. A controlled group of corporations is required to share the lower-level corporate tax rates and various other tax benefits among the members of the group. A controlled group may be either a *brother-sister* or a *parent-subsidiary group.*

Corporate acquisition. The takeover of one corporation by another if both parties retain their legal existence after the transaction. An acquisition can be effected via a stock purchase or through a tax-free exchange of stock. See also *corporate reorganization* and *merger.*

Corporate liquidation. Occurs when a corporation distributes its net assets to its shareholders and ceases its legal existence. Generally, a shareholder recognizes capital gain or loss upon the liquidation of the entity, regardless of the corporation's balance in its *earnings and profits* account. The liquidating corporation recognizes gain and loss on assets that it sells during the liquidation period, and on assets that it distributes to shareholders in kind.

Corporate reorganization. Occurs, among other instances, when one corporation acquires another in a *merger* or acquisition, a single corporation divides into two or more entities, a corporation makes a substantial change in its capital structure, or a corporation undertakes a change in its legal name or domicile. The exchange of stock and other securities in a corporate reorganization can be effected favorably for tax purposes if certain statutory requirements are followed strictly. Tax consequences include the nonrecognition of any gain that is realized by the shareholders except to the extent of *boot* received. See also *corporate acquisition.*

Corpus. The body or principal of a *trust.* Suppose, for example, George transfers an apartment building into a trust, income payable to Wanda for life, remainder to Sam upon Wanda's death. Corpus of the trust is the apartment building.

Correspondence audit. An *audit* conducted by the IRS by the U.S. mail. Typically, the IRS writes to the taxpayer requesting the verification of a particular deduction or exemption. The completion of a special form or the remittance of copies of records or other support is requested of the taxpayer. See also *field audit* and *office audit.*

Court of Appeals. Any of 13 Federal courts that consider tax matters appealed from the U.S. *Tax Court,* a U.S. *District Court,* or the U.S. *Court of Federal Claims.* Appeal from a U.S. Court of Appeals is to the *U.S. Supreme Court* by *Certiorari.* See also *appellate court* and *trial court.*

Court of Federal Claims. A *trial court* (court of original jurisdiction) that decides litigation involving Federal tax matters. Appeal is to the *Court of Appeals* for the Federal Circuit.

Credit for prior transfers. The *estate tax* credit for prior transfers applies when property is taxed in the estates of different *decedents* within a 10-year period. The credit is determined using a decreasing statutory percentage, with the magnitude of the credit decreasing as the length of time between the multiple deaths increases. § 2013.

Criminal fraud. See *fraud.*

Cross-purchase buy-sell agreement. Under this type of arrangement, the surviving owners of the business agree to buy out the withdrawing owner. Assume, for example, Ron and Sara are equal shareholders in Tip Corporation. Under a cross-purchase buy-sell agreement, Ron and Sara would contract to purchase the other's interest, should that person decide to withdraw from the business. See also *buy-sell agreement* and *entity buy-sell agreement.*

Current earnings and profits. Net tax-basis earnings of a corporation aggregated during the current tax year. A corporate distribution is deemed to be first from the entity's current earnings and profits and then from accumulated earnings and profits. Shareholders recognize dividend income to the extent of the *earnings and profits* of the corporation. A *dividend* results to the extent of current earnings and profits, even if there is a larger negative balance in *accumulated earnings and profits.* § 316 and Reg. § 1.316–2.

Current tax expense. Under *ASC 740 (SFAS 109),* the book tax expense that relates to the current reporting period's net income and is actually payable (or creditable) to the appropriate governmental agencies for the current period. Also known as "cash tax" or "tax payable."

Current use valuation. See *special use value.*

Curtesy. A husband's right under state law to all or part of his wife's property upon her death. See also *dower.*

D

Death benefit. A payment made by an employer to the *beneficiary* or beneficiaries of a deceased employee on account of the death of the employee.

Debt-financed income. Included in computations of the *unrelated business income* of an *exempt organization,* the *gross income* generated from debt-financed property.

Decedent. An individual who has died.

Deduction. The Federal income tax is not imposed upon *gross income.* Rather, it is imposed upon *taxable income.* Congressionally identified deductions are subtracted from gross income to arrive at the tax base, taxable income.

Deductions in respect of a decedent. Deductions accrued at the moment of death but not recognizable on the final income tax return of a *decedent* because of the method of accounting used. Such items are allowed as deductions on the *estate tax* return and on the income tax return of the estate (Form 1041) or the *heir* (Form 1040). An example of a deduction in respect of a decedent is interest expense accrued to the date of death by a *cash basis* debtor.

Deferred compensation. Compensation that will be taxed when received and not when earned. An example is a contribution by an employer to a *qualified pension or profit sharing plan* on behalf of an employee. The contributions are not taxed to the employee until they are distributed (e.g., upon retirement).

Deferred tax asset. Under *ASC 740 (SFAS 109),* an item created on an enterprise's balance sheet by a temporary book-tax difference, such that a tax benefit is not recognized until a later date, although it already has been reported in the financial statements, e.g., the carryforward of a disallowed *deduction.*

Deferred tax benefit. Under *ASC 740 (SFAS 109)*, a reduction in the book tax expense that relates to the current reporting period's net income but will not be realized until a future reporting period. Creates or adds to the entity's *deferred tax asset* balance sheet account. For instance, the carryforward of a *net operating loss* is a deferred tax benefit.

Deferred tax expense. Under *ASC 740 (SFAS 109)*, a book tax expense that relates to the current reporting period's net income but will not be realized until a future reporting period. Creates or adds to the entity's *deferred tax liability* balance sheet account. For instance, a deferred tax expense is created when tax *depreciation* deductions for the period are "accelerated" and exceed the corresponding book depreciation expense.

Deferred tax liability. As determined under the rules of *ASC 740 (SFAS 109)*, an item created on an enterprise's balance sheet by a *temporary book-tax difference*, such that a tax benefit is recognized earlier for tax purposes than it is in the financial accounting records, e.g., the use of an accelerated cost recovery deduction.

Deficiency. Additional tax liability owed by a taxpayer and assessed by the IRS. See also *assessment* and *statutory notice of deficiency*.

Deficiency dividend. Once the IRS has established a corporation's liability for the *personal holding company tax* in a prior year, the tax may be reduced or avoided by the issuance of a deficiency dividend under § 547. The deficiency dividend procedure does not avoid the usual penalties and interest applicable for failure to file a return or pay a tax.

Deficit. A negative balance, say, in the earnings and profits account.

Demand loan. A loan payable upon request by the creditor, rather than on a specific date.

Depletion. The process by which the cost or other *basis* of a natural resource (e.g., an oil or gas interest) is recovered upon extraction and sale of the resource. The two ways to determine the depletion allowance are the cost and percentage (or statutory) methods. Under cost depletion, each unit of production sold is assigned a portion of the cost or other basis of the interest. This is determined by dividing the cost or other basis by the total units expected to be recovered. Under percentage (or statutory) depletion, the tax law provides a special percentage factor for different types of minerals and other natural resources. This percentage is multiplied by the *gross income* from the interest to arrive at the depletion allowance. §§ 613 and 613A.

Depreciation. The deduction for the cost or other *basis* of a tangible asset over the asset's *estimated useful life*. Certain favorable Code provisions may allow the taxpayer to accelerate the depreciation deductions into earlier tax years. For intangible assets, see *amortization*. For natural resources, see *depletion*.

Depreciation recapture. Upon the disposition of depreciable property used in a *trade or business*, gain or loss is measured by the difference between the consideration received (the *amount realized*) and the *adjusted basis* of the property. The gain recognized could be *§ 1231 gain* and qualify for long-term capital gain treatment. The recapture provisions of the Code (e.g., §§ 291 and 1245) may operate to convert some or all of the previous § 1231 gain into ordinary income. The justification for depreciation recapture is that it prevents a taxpayer from converting a dollar of ordinary deduction (in the form of *depreciation*) into deferred tax-favored income (§ 1231 or long-term *capital gain*). The depreciation recapture rules do not apply when the property is disposed of at a loss or via a *gift*.

Determination letter. Upon the request of a taxpayer, the IRS will comment on the tax status of a completed transaction. Determination letters frequently are used to clarify employee status, determine whether a retirement or profit sharing plan qualifies under the Code, and determine the tax-exempt status of certain nonprofit organizations.

Devise. A transfer of real estate by will. See also *bequest*.

Disclaimers. Rejections, refusals, or renunciations of claims, powers, or property. Section 2518 sets forth the conditions required to avoid *gift tax* consequences as the result of a disclaimer.

Discretionary trust. A trust under which the *trustee* or another party has the right to accumulate (rather than distribute) the income for each year. Depending on the terms of the trust instrument, the income may be accumulated for future distributions to the *income beneficiaries* or added to *corpus* for the benefit of the remainder *beneficiary*.

Disguised sale. When a partner contributes property to the entity and soon thereafter receives a distribution from the partnership, the transactions are collapsed, and the distribution is seen as a purchase of the asset by the *partnership*. § 707(a)(2)(B).

Disproportionate. Not pro rata or ratable. Suppose, for example, Fin Corporation has two shareholders, Cal and Dot, each of whom owns 50 percent of its stock. If Fin distributes a cash *dividend* of $2,000 to Cal and only $1,000 to Dot, the distribution is disproportionate. The distribution would have been proportionate if Cal and Dot had received $1,500 each.

Disproportionate distribution. A distribution from a *partnership* to one or more of its partners in which at least one partner's interest in partnership *hot assets* is increased or decreased. For example, a distribution of cash to one *partner* and hot assets to another changes both partners' interest in hot assets and is *disproportionate*. The intent of rules for taxation of disproportionate distributions is to ensure each partner eventually recognizes his or her proportionate share of partnership ordinary income.

Disproportionate redemption. See *redemption (disproportionate)*.

Dissent. To disagree with the majority. If, for example, Judge Bird disagrees with the result reached by Judges Crown and Dove (all of whom are members of the same court), Judge Bird could issue a dissenting opinion.

Distributable net income (DNI). The measure that determines the nature and amount of the distributions from *estates* and *trusts* that the *beneficiaries* must include in income. DNI also limits the amount that estates and trusts can claim as a deduction for such distributions. § 643(a).

Distribution deduction. Used to compute an *estate* or *trust's* taxable income for the year. The lesser of the amount distributed to *beneficiaries* from income, or the deductible portion of *distributable net income* for the period.

Distributions in kind. Transfers of property "as is." If, for example, a corporation distributes land to its shareholders, a distribution in kind has taken place. A sale of land followed by a distribution of the cash proceeds would not be a distribution in kind of the land.

District Court. A Federal District Court is a *trial court* for purposes of litigating Federal tax matters. It is the only trial court in which a jury trial can be obtained.

Dividend. A nondeductible distribution to the shareholders of a corporation. A dividend constitutes *gross income* to the recipient if it is paid from the *current* or *accumulated earnings and profits* of the corporation.

Dividend equivalent amount (DEA). The amount subject to the *branch profits tax,* it is equal to the *effectively connected earnings and profits* of the U.S. branch of a *foreign corporation,* reduced/(increased) by an increase/(reduction) in U.S. net equity.

Dividends paid deduction. Relative to the *accumulated earnings* and *personal holding company taxes,* reductions in the tax base are allowed to the extent that the corporation made *dividend* payments during the year. Thus, this adjustment reduces *accumulated taxable income* and *personal holding company income.*

Dividends received deduction. A deduction allowed a corporate shareholder for *dividends* received from a domestic corporation. The deduction usually is 70 percent of the dividends received, but it could be 80 or 100 percent depending upon the ownership percentage held by the payee corporation. §§ 243–246.

Divisive reorganization. A corporate division: some of the assets of one corporation are transferred to another corporation in exchange for control of the transferee. Then, in a *spinoff* or *split-off,* stock of the transferee is distributed to the transferor's shareholders.

Dock sale. A purchaser uses its owned or rented vehicles to take possession of the product at the seller's shipping dock. In most states, the sale is apportioned to the operating state of the purchaser, rather than the seller. See also *apportion* and *sales factor.*

Domestic corporation. A corporation created or organized in the United States or under the law of the United States or any state. § 7701(a)(4). Only *dividends* received from domestic corporations qualify for the *dividends received deduction* (§ 243). See also *foreign corporation.*

Domestic production activities deduction (DPAD). A deduction allowed to sole proprietors, *C corporations, partnerships, S corporations,* cooperatives, *estates,* and *trusts* for certain production activities. The deduction rate is 9 percent of *qualified production activities income.* The deduction cannot exceed 50 percent of *W–2 wages.* § 199.

Domestic production gross receipts (DPGR). A key component in computing the *domestic production activities deduction (DPAD).* Includes receipts from the sale and other disposition of qualified production property produced in significant part within the United States. § 199(c)(4).

Domicile. A person's legal home.

Donee. The recipient of a gift.

Donor. The maker of a gift.

Double-weighted apportionment formula. A means by which the total taxable income of a *multistate corporation* is assigned to a specific state. Usually, the payroll, property, and sales factors are equally treated, and the weighted average of these factors is used in the apportionment procedure. In some states, however, the sales factor may receive a double weight, or it may be the only factor considered. These latter formulas place a greater tax burden on the income of out-of-state corporations. See also *apportion, payroll factor, property factor, sales factor,* and *UDITPA.*

Dower. A wife's right to all or part of her deceased husband's property; unique to *common law* states as opposed to *community property* jurisdictions. See also *curtesy.*

E

Earned income. Income from personal services. Distinguished from passive, portfolio, and other *unearned income* (and sometimes referred to as "active" income). See §§ 469, 911, and the related Regulations.

Earnings and profits (E & P). Measures the economic capacity of a corporation to make a distribution to shareholders that is not a return of capital. Such a distribution results in *dividend* income to the shareholders to the extent of the corporation's current and accumulated *earnings and profits.*

Economic effect test. Requirements that must be met before a *special allocation* may be used by a *partnership.* The premise behind the test is that each *partner* who receives an allocation of income or loss from a partnership bears the economic benefit or burden of the allocation.

Effective tax rate. The financial statements for an entity include several footnotes, one of which reconciles the expected (statutory) income tax rate (e.g., 35 percent for a *C corporation*) with the effective tax rate, i.e., total tax expense as a percentage of book income. The reconciliation often is done in dollar and/or percentage terms.

Effectively connected income. Income of a *nonresident alien* or *foreign corporation* that is attributable to the operations of a U.S. *trade or business* under either the asset-use or the business-activities test.

E-filing. The process of submitting tax returns and other documents by the taxpayer to the IRS using a computer or other electronic equipment. Large businesses are required to file their income tax returns electronically, and the IRS has targeted that 80 percent of Forms 1040 use an e-filing option.

Employee stock ownership plan (ESOP). A type of *qualified profit sharing plan* that invests in *securities* of the employer. In a noncontributory ESOP, the employer usually contributes its shares to a *trust* and receives a *deduction* for the fair market value of the stock. Generally, the employee does not recognize income until the stock is sold after its distribution to him or her upon retirement or other separation from service.

En banc. The case was considered by the whole court. Typically, for example, only one of the judges of the U.S. *Tax Court* will hear and decide on a tax controversy. However, when the issues involved are unusually novel or of wide impact, the case will be heard and decided by the full court sitting *en banc.*

Energy tax credit–business property. Various tax credits are available to those who invest in certain energy property. The purpose of the credit is to create incentives for conservation and to develop alternative energy sources.

Enrolled agent (EA). A tax practitioner who has gained admission to practice before the IRS by passing an IRS examination and maintaining a required level of continuing professional education.

Entity. An organization or being that possesses separate existence for tax purposes. Examples are *corporations, partnerships, estates,* and *trusts.*

Entity accounting income. Entity accounting income is not identical to the *taxable income* of a *trust* or *estate*, nor is it determined in the same manner as the entity's financial accounting income would be. The trust document or will determines whether certain income, expenses, gains, or losses are allocated to the corpus of the entity or to the entity's income *beneficiaries.* Only the items that are allocated to the income beneficiaries are included in entity accounting income.

Entity buy-sell agreement. An arrangement whereby the entity is to purchase a withdrawing owner's interest. When the entity is a corporation, the agreement generally involves a *stock redemption* on the part of the withdrawing shareholder. See also *buy-sell agreement* and *cross-purchase buy-sell agreement.*

Entity concept. Even in so-called flow-through entities, tax accounting elections are made (e.g., a tax year is adopted) and conventions are adopted (e.g., with respect to cost recovery methods) at the entity level. This may seem to violate the *conduit concept,* but such exceptions tend to ease the administration of such conduit taxpayers, especially in the context of a large number of shareholders/partners/members/beneficiaries.

Equity method. Under *Generally Accepted Accounting Principles,* the method of financial reporting for the operations of a subsidiary when the parent corporation owns between 20 and 50 percent of the subsidiary's stock. Creates a book-tax difference, as the two entities' operating results are combined for book purposes, but a Federal income tax *consolidated return* cannot be filed.

Equity structure shift. A tax-free reorganization other than a *divisive reorganization* or *recapitalization.* If there is a more than 50 percent change in the ownership of a loss corporation in an equity structure shift, § 382 limits the use of *net operating loss* carryovers of the loss corporation. Specifically, the annual net operating loss carryover deduction is limited to the value of the loss corporation immediately before the equity structure shift times the *long-term tax-exempt rate.*

Escrow. Money or other property placed with a third party as security for an existing or proposed obligation. Cyd, for example, agrees to purchase Don's stock in Rip Corporation but needs time to raise the necessary funds. Don places the stock with Ernie (the escrow agent), with instructions to deliver it to Cyd when the purchase price is paid.

Estate. An entity that locates, collects, distributes, and discharges the assets and liabilities of a *decedent.*

Estate freeze. Procedures directed toward fixing and stabilizing the value of an interest retained in a business, while transferring the growth portion to family members. In the case of a *closely held corporation,* the estate freeze usually involves keeping the preferred stock and giving away the common stock. The ultimate objective is to reduce estate value when the original owner-donor dies.

Estate tax. A tax imposed on the right to transfer property by death. Thus, an estate tax is levied on the *decedent's* estate and not on the *heir* receiving the property. See also *inheritance tax.*

Estimated useful life. The period over which an asset will be used by the taxpayer. Assets such as collectible artwork do not have an estimated useful life. The amount can be used in measuring the annual tax deduction for *depreciation* and *amortization.*

Estoppel. The process of being stopped from proving something (even if true) in court due to a prior inconsistent action. Estoppel usually is invoked as a matter of fairness to prevent one party (either the taxpayer or the IRS) from taking advantage of a prior error.

Evasion. See *tax evasion.*

Excess lobbying expenditure. An excise tax is applied on otherwise tax-*exempt organizations* with respect to the excess of total *lobbying expenditures* over *grass roots expenditures* for the year.

Excess loss account. When a subsidiary has generated more historical losses than its parent has invested in the entity, the parent's *basis* in the subsidiary is zero, and the parent records additional losses in an excess loss account. This treatment allows the parent to continue to deduct losses of the subsidiary, even where no basis reduction is possible, while avoiding the need to show a negative stock basis on various financial records. If the subsidiary stock is sold while an excess loss account exists, *capital gain* income usually is recognized to the extent of the balance in the account.

Excise tax. A tax on the manufacture, sale, or use of goods; on the carrying on of an occupation or activity; or on the transfer of property. Thus, the Federal estate and gift taxes are, theoretically, excise taxes.

Exclusion amount. The value of assets that is exempt from transfer tax, due to the credit allowed for gifts or transfers by death. For gifts and deaths in 2012, the exclusion amount is $5.12 million. An exclusion amount unused by a deceased spouse may be used by the surviving spouse. Often called the *exemption equivalent amount.* See also *bypass amount.*

Executor. A person designated by a will to administer (manage or take charge of) the assets and liabilities of a *decedent.* See also *administrator.*

Exempt organization. An organization that is either partially or completely exempt from Federal income taxation. § 501.

Exemption. An amount by which the tax base is reduced for all qualifying taxpayers. Individuals can receive personal and dependency exemptions, and taxpayers apply an exemption in computing their alternative minimum taxable income. Often, the exemption amount is phased out as the tax base becomes sizable.

Exemption equivalent. The maximum value of assets that can be transferred to another party without incurring any Federal *gift* or *estate tax* because of the application of the *unified tax credit.*

Exemption equivalent amount. The taxable amount (currently $5.12 million for *gift tax* and *estate tax*) that is the equivalent of the *unified transfer tax credit* allowed. See also *bypass amount.*

Expanded affiliated group (EAG). For purposes of the *domestic production activities deduction (DPAD),* all members of an expanded affiliated group (EAG) are treated as a single corporation. Thus, the activities of any member of the group are attributed to the other members. An EAG must meet the requirements for filing a *consolidated return* with ownership levels lowered to 50 percent. § 199(d)(4)(B).

Expenses in respect of a decedent. See *deductions in respect of a decedent.*

F

Fair market value. The amount at which property would change hands between a willing buyer and a willing seller, neither being under any compulsion to buy or to sell, and both having reasonable knowledge of the relevant facts. Reg. § 20.2031–1(b).

FAS 109. See *ASC 740 (SFAS 109).*

FASB. See *Generally accepted accounting principles (GAAP).*

Federal Register. The first place that the rules and regulations of U.S. administrative agencies (e.g., the U.S. Treasury Department) are published.

F.3d. An abbreviation for the third series of the *Federal Reporter,* the official series in which decisions of the U.S. *Court of Federal Claims* and the U.S. *Court of Appeals* are published. The second series is denoted F.2d.

F.Supp. The abbreviation for *Federal Supplement,* the official series in which the reported decisions of the U.S. Federal *District Courts* are published.

Feeder organization. An entity that carries on a trade or business for the benefit of an *exempt organization.* However, such a relationship does not result in the feeder organization itself being tax-exempt. § 502.

Fiduciary. A person who manages money or property for another and who must exercise a standard of care in the management activity imposed by law or contract. A *trustee,* for example, possesses a fiduciary responsibility to the *beneficiaries* of the *trust* to follow the terms of the trust and the requirements of applicable state law. A breach of fiduciary responsibility would make the trustee liable to the beneficiaries for any damage caused by the breach.

Field audit. An *audit* conducted by the IRS on the business premises of the taxpayer or in the office of the tax practitioner representing the taxpayer. See also *correspondence audit* and *office audit.*

FIN 48. See *ASC 740–10 (FIN 48).*

Financial Accounting Standards Board. See *Generally accepted accounting principles (GAAP).*

FIRPTA. Under the Foreign Investment in Real Property Tax Act, gains or losses realized by *nonresident aliens* and non-U.S. corporations on the disposition of U.S. real estate create *U.S.-source income* and are subject to U.S. income tax.

First-in, first-out (FIFO). An *accounting method* for determining the cost of inventories. Under this method, the inventory on hand is deemed to be the sum of the cost of the most recently acquired units. See also *last-in, first-out (LIFO).*

Fiscal year. See *accounting period.*

Flat tax. In its pure form, a flat tax would eliminate all exclusions, *deductions,* and credits and impose a one-rate tax on *gross income.*

Foreign corporation. A corporation that is not created in the United States or organized under the laws of one of the states of the United States. § 7701(a)(5). See also *domestic corporation.*

Foreign currency transaction. An exchange that could generate a foreign currency gain or loss for a U.S. taxpayer. For instance, if Avery contracts to purchase foreign goods, payable in a currency other than U.S. dollars, at a specified date in the future, any change in the exchange rate between the dollar and that currency generates a foreign currency gain or loss upon completion of the contract. This gain or loss is treated as separate from the underlying transaction; it may create ordinary or *capital gain* or loss.

Foreign earned income exclusion. The Code allows exclusions for *earned income* generated outside the United States to alleviate any tax base and rate disparities among countries. In addition, the exclusion is allowed for housing expenditures incurred by the taxpayer's employer with respect to the non-U.S. assignment, and self-employed individuals can deduct foreign housing expenses incurred in a trade or business.

Foreign sales corporation (FSC). An entity that qualified for a partial exemption of its gross export receipts from U.S. tax.

Foreign-source income. Income that is not sourced within the United States. Examples include earnings from the performance of a personal services contract outside the United States, interest received from a non-U.S. corporation, and income from the use of property outside the United States.

Foreign tax credit or deduction. A U.S. citizen or resident who incurs or pays income taxes to a foreign country on income subject to U.S. tax may be able to claim some of these taxes as a deduction or a credit against the U.S. income tax. §§ 27, 164, and 901–905.

Form 706. The U.S. Estate Tax Return. In certain cases, this form must be filed for a *decedent* who was a resident or citizen of the United States.

Form 709. The U.S. Gift Tax Return.

Form 870. The signing of Form 870 (Waiver of Restriction on Assessment and Collection of Deficiency in Tax and Acceptance of Overassessments) by a taxpayer permits the IRS to assess a proposed deficiency without issuing a *statutory notice of deficiency* (90-day letter). This means the taxpayer must pay the *deficiency* and cannot file a petition to the U.S. Tax Court. § 6213(d).

Form 872. The signing of this form by a taxpayer extends the applicable *statute of limitations.* § 6501(c)(4).

Form 1041. The U.S. Fiduciary Income Tax Return, required to be filed by *estates* and *trusts.* See Appendix B for a specimen form.

Form 1065. The U.S. Partnership Return of Income. See Appendix B for a specimen form.

Form 1120. The U.S. Corporation Income Tax Return. See Appendix B for a specimen form.

Form 1120–A. The U.S. Short-Form Corporation Income Tax Return.

Form 1120S. The U.S. Small Business Corporation Income Tax Return, required to be filed by *S corporations.* See Appendix B for a specimen form.

Fraud. Tax fraud falls into two categories: civil and criminal. Under civil fraud, the IRS may impose as a penalty an amount equal to as much as 75 percent of the underpayment [§ 6651(f)]. Fines and/or imprisonment are prescribed for conviction of various types of criminal tax fraud (§§ 7201–7207). Both civil and criminal fraud involve a specific intent on the part of the taxpayer to evade the tax; mere *negligence* is not enough. Criminal fraud requires the additional element of willfulness (i.e., done deliberately and with evil purpose). In practice, it becomes difficult to distinguish between the degree of intent necessary to support criminal, rather than civil, fraud. In either situation, the IRS has the burden of proving fraud. See also *burden of proof.*

Free transferability of interests. A corporation's shareholder usually can freely transfer the stock to others without the approval of the existing shareholders.

Fringe benefits. Compensation or other benefits received by an employee that are not in the form of cash. Some fringe benefits (e.g., accident and health plans, group term life insurance) may be excluded from the employee's *gross income* and thus are not subject to the Federal income tax.

Frivolous return. A tax return that included a position that has no more than a 5 percent chance of being sustained upon review. Taxpayer and *tax preparer* penalties are assessed if a frivolous position is included in a filed tax return.

Functional currency. The currency of the economic environment in which the taxpayer carries on most of its activities and transacts most of its business.

Future interest. An interest that will come into being at some future time. Distinguished from a *present interest,* which already exists. Assume that Dora transfers securities to a newly created *trust.* Under the terms of the trust instrument, income from the securities is to be paid each year to Nan for her life, with the securities passing to Steve upon Nan's death. Nan has a present interest in the trust since she is entitled to current income distributions. Steve has a future interest since he must wait for Nan's death to benefit from the trust. The *annual exclusion* of $13,000 is not allowed for a gift of a future interest. § 2503(b). See also *gift splitting.*

G

General business credit. The summation of various nonrefundable business credits, including the *energy credit,* alcohol fuels credit, and research activities credit. The amount of general business credit that can be used to reduce the tax liability is limited to the taxpayer's net income tax reduced by the greater of (1) the *tentative minimum tax* or (2) 25 percent of the net regular tax liability that exceeds $25,000. Unused general business credits can be carried back 1 year and forward 20 years. §§ 38 and 39.

General partner. A *partner* who is fully liable in an individual capacity for the debts of the *partnership* to third parties. A general partner's liability is not limited to the investment in the partnership. See also *limited partner.*

General partnership. A *partnership* that is owned by one or more *general partners.* Creditors of a general partnership can collect amounts owed them from both the partnership assets and the assets of the *partners* individually.

General power of appointment. See *power of appointment.*

Generally accepted accounting principles (GAAP). Guidelines relating to how to construct the financial statements of enterprises doing business in the United States. Promulgated chiefly by the Financial Accounting Standards Board (FASB).

Gift. A transfer of property for less than adequate consideration. Gifts usually occur in a personal setting (such as between members of the same family). They are excluded from the income tax base but may be subject to a *transfer tax.*

Gift splitting. A special election for Federal *gift tax* purposes under which husband and wife can treat a gift by one of them to a third party as being made one-half by each. If, for example, Hal (the husband) makes a gift of $26,000 to Sharon, Winnie (the wife) may elect to treat $13,000 of the gift as coming from her. The major advantage of the election is that it enables the parties to take advantage of the nonowner spouse's (Winnie in this case) *annual exclusion* and unified credit. § 2513.

Gift tax. A tax imposed on the transfer of property by *gift.* The tax is imposed upon the *donor* of a gift and is based on the *fair market value* of the property on the date of the gift.

Gifts within three years of death. Some *taxable gifts* automatically are included in the *gross estate* of the *donor* if death occurs within three years of the gift. § 2035.

Goodwill. The reputation and built-up business of a company. For accounting purposes, goodwill has no *basis* unless it is purchased. In the purchase of a business, goodwill generally is the difference between the purchase price and the value of the assets acquired. The intangible asset goodwill is amortized over 15 years. § 195. See also *amortization.*

Grantor. A transferor of property. The creator of a *trust* usually is referred to as the grantor of the entity.

Grantor trust. A *trust* under which the *grantor* retains control over the income or *corpus* (or both) to such an extent that he or she is treated as the owner of the property and its income for income tax purposes. Income from a grantor trust is taxable to the grantor, and not to the *beneficiary* who receives it. §§ 671–679. See also *reversionary interest.*

Grass roots expenditure. *Exempt organizations* are prohibited from engaging in political activities, but spending incurred to influence the opinions of the general public relative to specific legislation is permitted by the law. See also *excess lobbying expenditure.*

Green card test. Form I-551, received from a U.S. consul as a receipt showing that the holder has immigration status in the United States, and used to refute alien status for tax purposes.

Gross estate. The property owned or previously transferred by a *decedent* that is subject to the Federal *estate tax.* Distinguished from the *probate estate,* which is property actually subject to administration by the *administrator* or *executor* of an estate. §§ 2031–2046. See also *adjusted gross estate* and *taxable estate.*

Gross income. Income subject to the Federal income tax. Gross income does not include all economic income. That is, certain exclusions are allowed (e.g., interest on municipal bonds). For a manufacturing or merchandising business, gross income usually means gross profit (gross sales or gross receipts less cost of goods sold). § 61 and Reg. § 1.61– 3(a). See also *adjusted gross income* and *taxable income.*

Gross up. To add back to the value of the property or income received the amount of the tax that has been paid. For *gifts* made within three years of death, any *gift tax* paid on the transfer is added to the *gross estate.* § 2035.

Group term life insurance. Life insurance coverage provided by an employer for a group of employees. Such insurance is renewable on a year-to-year basis, and typically no *cash surrender value* is built up.

Guaranteed payment. Made by a *partnership* to a *partner* for services rendered or for the use of capital, to the extent that the payments are determined without regard to the income of the partnership. The payments are treated as though they were made to a nonpartner and thus are deducted by the entity.

Guardianship. A legal arrangement under which one person (a guardian) has the legal right and duty to care for another (the ward) and his or her property. A guardianship is established because the ward is unable to act legally on his or her own behalf (e.g., because of *minority* [he or she is not of age] or mental or physical incapacity).

H

Head of household. An unmarried individual who maintains a household for another and satisfies certain conditions set forth in § 2(b). This status enables the taxpayer to use a set of income tax rates that are lower than those applicable to other unmarried individuals but higher than those applicable to surviving spouses and married persons filing a joint return.

Heir. A person who inherits property from a *decedent.*

Historic business test. In a *corporate reorganization,* a means by which to determine if the *continuity of business enterprise* requirement is met. The acquiring corporation must continue to operate the target entity's existing business(es) going forward; if this is not the case, the requirement is failed.

Hobby. An activity not engaged in for profit. The Code restricts the amount of losses that an individual can deduct for hobby activities so that these transactions cannot be used to offset income from other sources. § 183.

Holding period. The period of time during which property has been held for income tax purposes. The holding period is significant in determining whether gain or loss from the sale or exchange of a *capital asset* is long term or short term. § 1223.

Hot assets. *Unrealized receivables* and substantially appreciated inventory under § 751. When hot assets are present, the sale of a *partnership* interest or the *disproportionate distribution* of the assets can cause ordinary income to be recognized.

H.R. 10 plans. See *Keogh plans.*

I

Imputed interest. For certain long-term sales of property, the IRS can convert some of the gain from the sale into interest income if the contract does not provide for a minimum rate of interest to be paid by the purchaser. The seller recognizes less long-term *capital gain* and more ordinary income (interest income). § 483 and the related Regulations.

In kind. See *distributions in kind.*

Inbound taxation. U.S. tax effects when a non-U.S. person begins an investment or business activity in the United States.

Incident of ownership. An element of ownership or degree of control over a life insurance policy. The retention by an *insured* of an incident of ownership in a life insurance policy places the policy proceeds in the insured's *gross estate* upon death. § 2042(2) and Reg. § 20.2042–1(c).

Income beneficiary. The party entitled to income from property. In a typical *trust* situation, Art is to receive the income for life with *corpus* or principal passing to Bev upon Art's death. In this case, Art is the income beneficiary of the trust.

Income in respect of a decedent (IRD). Income earned by a *decedent* at the time of death but not reportable on the final income tax return because of the method of accounting that appropriately is utilized. Such income is included in the *gross estate* and is taxed to the eventual recipient (either the estate or *heirs*). The recipient is, however, allowed an income tax deduction for the *estate tax* attributable to the income. § 691.

Income interest. The right of a *beneficiary* to receive distributions from the fiduciary income of a *trust* or *estate.*

Income shifting. Occurs when an individual transfers some of his or her *gross income* to a taxpayer who is subject to a lower tax rate, thereby reducing the total income tax liability of the group. Income shifting produces a successful *assignment of income.* It can be accomplished by transferring income-producing property to the lower-bracket taxpayer or to an effective *trust* for his or her benefit, or by transferring ownership interests in a family *partnership* or in a *closely held corporation.*

Income tax provision. Under *ASC 740 (SFAS 109),* a synonym for the book tax expense of an entity for the financial reporting period. Following the "matching principle," all book tax expense that relates to the net income for the reporting period is reported on that period's financial statements, including not only the *current tax expense,* but also any *deferred tax expense* and *deferred tax benefit.*

Incomplete transfer. A transfer made by a *decedent* during lifetime that, because of certain control or enjoyment retained by the transferor, is not considered complete for Federal *estate tax* purposes. Thus, some or all of the *fair market value* of the property transferred is included in the transferor's *gross estate.* §§ 2036–2038. See also *revocable transfer.*

Indexation. Various components of the tax formula are adjusted periodically for the effects of inflation, so that the effects of the formula are not eroded by price level changes. Tax rate schedules, exemption amounts, and the standard deduction, among other items, are indexed in this manner.

Individual retirement account (IRA). Individuals with *earned income* are permitted to set aside up to 100 percent of that income per year (usually not to exceed $5,000) for a retirement account. The amount so set aside can be deducted by the taxpayer and is subject to income tax only upon withdrawal. The Code limits the amount of this contribution that can be deducted *for* AGI depending upon the magnitude of the taxpayer's AGI before the IRA contribution is considered. No deduction is allowed for a contribution to a Roth IRA, but most Roth withdrawals are completely tax-free. § 219.

Inheritance tax. A tax imposed on the right to receive property from a *decedent.* Thus, theoretically, an inheritance tax is imposed on the *heir.* The Federal *estate tax* is imposed on the estate.

Inside basis. A *partnership's* basis in each of the assets it owns.

Installment method. A method of accounting enabling certain taxpayers to spread the recognition of gain on the sale of property over the collection period. Under this procedure, the seller arrives at the gain to be recognized by computing the gross profit percentage from the sale (the gain divided by the contract price) and applying it to each payment received. § 453.

Insured. A person whose life is the subject of an insurance policy. Upon the death of the insured, the *life insurance* policy matures, and the proceeds become payable to the designated *beneficiary*.

Intangible asset. Property that is a "right" rather than a physical object. Examples are patents, stocks and bonds, *goodwill*, trademarks, franchises, and copyrights. See also *amortization* and *tangible property*.

Inter vivos transfer. A transfer of property during the life of the owner. Distinguished from testamentary transfers, where the property passes at death.

Interest-free loans. Bona fide loans that charge no interest (or a below-market rate). If made in a nonbusiness setting, the *imputed interest* element is treated as a gift from the lender to the borrower. If made by a corporation to a shareholder, a *constructive dividend* could result. In either event, the lender may recognize interest income. § 7872.

Intermediate sanctions. The IRS can assess excise taxes on disqualified persons and organization managers associated with so-called public charities engaging in excess benefit transactions. An excess benefit transaction is one in which a disqualified person engages in a non-fair market value transaction with the *exempt organization* or receives *unreasonable compensation*. Prior to the idea of intermediate sanctions, the only option available to the IRS was to revoke the organization's exempt status.

Internal Revenue Code. The collected statutes that govern the taxation of income, property transfers, and other transactions in the United States and the enforcement of those provisions. Enacted by Congress, the Code is amended frequently, but it has not been reorganized since 1954. However, because of the extensive revisions to the statutes that occurred with the Tax Reform Act of 1986, Title 26 of the U.S. Code is known as the Internal Revenue Code of 1986.

Internal Revenue Service (IRS). The Federal agency, a division of the Department of the Treasury, charged with administering the U.S. revenue enforcement and collection provisions.

International Accounting Standards Board (IASB). The body that promulgates *International Financial Reporting Standards* (IFRS). Based in London, representing accounting standard setting bodies in over 100 countries, the IASB develops accounting standards that can serve as the basis for harmonizing conflicting reporting standards among nations.

International Financial Reporting Standards (IFRS). Produced by the *International Accounting Standards Board* (IASB), guidelines developed since 2001 as to revenue recognition, accounting for business combinations, and a conceptual framework for financial reporting. IFRS provisions are designed so that they can be used by all entities, regardless of where they are based or conduct business. IFRS have gained widespread acceptance throughout the world, and the SEC is considering how to require U.S. entities to use IFRS in addition to, or in lieu of, the accounting rules of the *Financial Accounting Standards Board*.

Interpolated terminal reserve. The measure used in valuing insurance policies for *gift* and *estate tax* purposes when the policies are not paid up at the time of their transfer. Reg. § 20.2031–8(a)(3), Ex. (3).

Intestate. The condition when no will exists at the time of death. In such cases, state law prescribes who will receive the *decedent's* property. The laws of intestate succession generally favor the surviving spouse, children, and grandchildren, and then parents and grandparents and brothers and sisters.

Investment income. Consisting of virtually the same elements as *portfolio income*, a measure by which to justify a deduction for interest on *investment indebtedness*.

Investment indebtedness. Debt incurred to carry or incur investments by the taxpayer in assets that will produce *portfolio income*. Limitations are placed upon interest deductions that are incurred in connection with the debt (generally to the corresponding amount of *investment income*).

Investor losses. Losses on stock and *securities*. If stocks and bonds are capital assets in the hands of the holder, a *capital loss* materializes as of the last day of the taxable year in which the stocks or bonds become worthless. Under certain circumstances involving stocks and bonds of affiliated corporations, an ordinary loss is permitted upon worthlessness.

Involuntary conversion. The loss or destruction of property through theft, casualty, or *condemnation*. Any gain realized on an involuntary conversion can, at the taxpayer's election, be deferred for Federal income tax purposes if the owner reinvests the proceeds within a prescribed period of time in property that is similar or related in service or use. § 1033.

IRA. See *individual retirement account*.

Itemized deductions. Personal and employee expenditures allowed by the Code as deductions from *adjusted gross income*. Examples include certain medical expenses, interest on home mortgages, and *charitable contributions*. Itemized deductions are reported on Schedule A of Form 1040. Certain miscellaneous itemized deductions are reduced by 2 percent of the taxpayer's adjusted gross income.

J

Jeopardy assessment. If the collection of a tax appears in question, the IRS may assess and collect the tax immediately without the usual formalities. The IRS can terminate a taxpayer's *tax year* before the usual date if it feels that the collection of the tax may be in peril because the taxpayer plans to leave the country. §§ 6851 and 6861–6864.

Joint and several liability. Permits the IRS to collect a tax from one or all of several taxpayers. A husband and wife who file a joint income tax return usually are collectively or individually liable for the full amount of the tax liability. The same rule applies to *consolidated return* partners. § 6013(d)(3).

Joint tenants. Two or more persons having undivided ownership of property with the right of survivorship. Right of survivorship gives the surviving owner full ownership of the property. Suppose Betty and Cheryl are joint tenants of a tract of land. Upon Betty's death, Cheryl becomes the sole owner of the property. For the *estate tax* consequences upon the death of a joint tenant, see § 2040. See also *tenants by the entirety* and *tenants in common.*

Joint venture. A one-time grouping of two or more persons in a business undertaking. Unlike a *partnership,* a joint venture does not entail a continuing relationship among the parties. A joint venture is treated like a partnership for Federal income tax purposes. § 7701(a)(2).

K

Keogh plans. Retirement plans available to self-employed taxpayers. They are also referred to as H.R. 10 plans. Under such plans, a taxpayer may deduct each year up to either 20 percent of net earnings from self-employment or $50,000 for 2012, whichever is less.

Kiddie tax. See *tax on unearned income of a child under age 19/24.*

L

Lapse. The expiration of a right either by the death of the holder or upon the expiration of a period of time. Thus, a *power of appointment* lapses upon the death of the holder if he or she has not exercised the power during life or at death (through a will).

Last-in, first-out (LIFO). An *accounting method* for valuing inventories for tax purposes. Under this method, it is assumed that the inventory on hand is valued at the cost of the earliest acquired units. § 472. See also *first-in, first-out (FIFO).*

Leaseback. The transferor of property later leases it back. In a sale-leaseback situation, for example, Ron sells property to Sal and subsequently leases the property from Sal. Thus, Ron becomes the *lessee* and Sal the *lessor.*

Least aggregate deferral rule. A test applied to determine the allowable fiscal year of a *partnership* or *S corporation.* Possible tax year-ends are tested, and the fiscal year allowed by the IRS is the one that offers the least amount of income deferral to the owners on an individual basis.

Legacy. A transfer of cash or other property by will.

Legal age. The age at which a person may enter into binding contracts or commit other legal acts. In most states, a minor reaches legal age or majority (comes of age) at age 18.

Legal representative. A person who oversees the legal affairs of another; for example, the *executor* or *administrator* of an *estate* or a court-appointed *guardian* of a minor or incompetent person.

Legatee. The recipient of property that is transferred under a will by the death of the owner.

Lessee. One who rents property from another. In the case of real estate, the lessee also is known as the tenant.

Lessor. One who rents property to another. In the case of real estate, the lessor also is known as the landlord.

Letter ruling. The written response of the IRS to a taxpayer's request for interpretation of the revenue laws with respect to a proposed transaction (e.g., concerning the tax-free status of a reorganization). Not to be relied on as precedent by other than the party who requested the ruling.

LEXIS. An online database system through which a tax researcher can obtain access to the Internal Revenue Code, Regulations, administrative rulings, and court case opinions.

Liabilities in excess of basis. On the contribution of capital to a corporation, an investor recognizes gain on the exchange to the extent that contributed assets carry liabilities with a face amount in excess of the tax basis of the contributed assets. This rule keeps the investor from holding the investment asset received with a negative basis. § 357(c).

Life estate. A legal arrangement under which the *beneficiary* (the life tenant) is entitled to the income from the property for his or her life. Upon the death of the life tenant, the property is transferred to the holder of the *remainder interest.* See also *income beneficiary.*

Life insurance. A contract between the holder of a policy and an insurance company (the carrier) under which the company agrees, in return for premium payments, to pay a specified sum (the face value or maturity value of the policy) to the designated *beneficiary* upon the death of the *insured.*

Like-kind exchange. An exchange of property held for productive use in a *trade or business* or for investment (except inventory and stocks and bonds) for other investment or trade or business property. Unless non-like-kind property (*boot*) is received, the exchange is fully tax-deferred. § 1031.

Limited liability. The liability of an entity and its owners to third parties is limited to the investment in the entity. This is a characteristic of a corporation, as shareholders generally are not responsible for the debts of the corporation and, at most, may lose the amount paid for the stock issued.

Limited liability company (LLC). A form of entity allowed by all of the states. The entity is subject to Federal income tax treatment as though it were a *partnership* in which all owners of the LLC are treated much like *limited partners.* There are no restrictions on ownership, all partners may participate in management, and none of the owners has personal liability for the entity's debts.

Limited liability limited partnership (LLLP). A *limited partnership* for which the *general partners* are also protected from entity liabilities. An LLLP—or "triple LP"—can be formed in about 20 states. In those states, a limited partnership files with the state to adopt LLLP status.

Limited liability partnership (LLP). A form of entity allowed by many of the states, where a general partnership registers with the state as an LLP. Owners are *general partners,* but a *partner* is not liable for any malpractice committed by other partners. The personal assets of the partners are at risk for the entity's contractual liabilities, such as accounts payable. The personal assets of a specific partner are at risk for his or her own professional *malpractice* and tort liability, and for malpractice and torts committed by those whom he or she supervises.

Limited partner. A *partner* whose liability to third-party creditors of the *partnership* is limited to the amounts invested in the partnership. See also *general partner* and *limited partnership.*

Limited partnership. A *partnership* in which some of the partners are *limited partners.* At least one of the *partners* in a limited partnership must be a *general partner.*

Liquidating distribution. A distribution by a *partnership* or corporation that is in complete liquidation of the entity's trade or business activities. Typically, such distributions generate capital gain or loss to the investors without regard, for instance, to the *earnings and profits* of the corporation or to the partnership's *basis* in the distributed property. They can, however, lead to recognized gain or loss at the corporate level.

Liquidation. See *corporate liquidation.*

Living trust. A revocable trust. Often touted as a means of avoiding some *probate costs.*

Lobbying expenditure. An expenditure made for the purpose of influencing legislation. Such payments can result in the loss of the exempt status and the imposition of Federal income tax on an *exempt organization.*

Long-term capital gain or loss. Results from the sale or other taxable exchange of a *capital asset* that had been held by the seller for more than one year or from other transactions involving statutorily designated assets, including § 1231 property and patents.

Long-term tax-exempt rate. Used in deriving *net operating loss* limitations in the context of an *equity structure shift.* The highest of the Federal long-term interest rates in effect for any of the last three months. § 382.

Low-income housing credit. Beneficial treatment to owners of low-income housing is provided in the form of a tax credit. The calculated credit is claimed in the year the building is placed in service and in the following nine years. § 42. See also *general business credit.*

Lump-sum distribution. Payment of the entire amount due at one time rather than in installments. Such distributions often occur from *qualified pension or profit sharing plans* upon the retirement or death of a covered employee.

M

MACRS. See *accelerated cost recovery system (ACRS).*

Majority. See *legal age.*

Malpractice. Professional misconduct; an unreasonable lack of due diligence in rendering a professional skill.

Marital deduction. A deduction allowed against the *taxable estate* or *taxable gifts* upon the transfer of property from one spouse to another.

Market value. See *fair market value.*

Matching rule. Treatment of an intercompany transaction on a *consolidated return,* when a sold asset remains within the group.

Meaningful reduction test. A decrease in the shareholder's voting control. Used to determine whether a *stock redemption* qualifies for sale or exchange treatment.

Merger. The absorption of one corporation by another with the corporation being absorbed losing its legal identity. Flow Corporation is merged into Jobs Corporation, and the shareholders of Flow receive stock in Jobs in exchange for their stock in Flow. After the merger, Flow ceases to exist as a separate legal entity. If a merger meets certain conditions, it is not currently taxable to the parties involved. § 368(a)(1)(A). See also *corporate acquisition* and *corporate reorganization.*

Minimum credit (AET). A fixed amount, $150,000 for personal service firms and $250,000 for all others, below which the *accumulated earnings credit* cannot be derived. Assures that small and start-up corporations can generate a minimum amount of earnings before being subject to the *accumulated earnings tax* (AET).

Minimum tax. See *alternative minimum tax.*

Minimum tax credit (AMT). When a corporation pays an *alternative minimum tax* (AMT), a minimum tax credit is created on a dollar-for-dollar basis, to be applied against regular tax liabilities incurred in future years. The credit is carried forward indefinitely, but it is not carried back. The effect of the credit for corporate taxpayers alternating between the AMT and regular tax models is to make the AMT liabilities a prepayment of regular taxes. Noncorporate AMT taxpayers are allowed the credit, but only with respect to the elements of the AMT that reflect timing differences between the two tax models.

Minority. See *legal age.*

Mitigate. To make less severe. See also *mitigation of the annual accounting period concept.*

Mitigation of the annual accounting period concept. Various tax provisions that provide relief from the effect of the finality of the *annual accounting period concept.* For example, the *net operating loss* carryover provisions allow the taxpayer to apply the negative taxable income of one year against a corresponding positive amount in another tax accounting period. See also *annual accounting period concept.*

Mortgagee. The party who holds the mortgage; the creditor.

Mortgagor. The party who mortgages the property; the debtor.

Most suitable use value. For *gift* and *estate tax* purposes, property that is transferred normally is valued in accordance with its most suitable or optimal use. Thus, if a farm is worth more as a potential shopping center, the value as a shopping center is used, even though the transferee (the donee or heir) continues to use the property as a farm. For an exception to this rule concerning the valuation of certain kinds of real estate transferred by death, see *special use value.*

Multistate corporation. A corporation that has operations in more than one of the states of the United States. Issues arise relative to the assignment of appropriate amounts of the entity's taxable income to the states in which it has a presence. See also *allocate, apportion, nexus,* and *UDITPA.*

Multistate Tax Commission (MTC). A regulatory body of the states that develops operating rules and regulations for the implementation of the *UDITPA* and other provisions that assign the total taxable income of a *multistate corporation* to specific states.

Multitiered partnerships. See *tiered partnerships.*

N

Necessary. Appropriate and helpful in furthering the taxpayer's business or income-producing activity. §§ 162(a) and 212. See also *ordinary.*

Negligence. Failure to exercise the reasonable or ordinary degree of care of a prudent person in a situation that results in harm or damage to another. Code § 6651 imposes a penalty on taxpayers who show negligence or intentional disregard of rules and Regulations with respect to the underpayment of certain taxes. See also *accuracy-related penalty.*

Net operating loss. To mitigate the effect of the annual accounting period concept, § 172 allows taxpayers to use an excess loss of one year as a deduction for certain past or future years. In this regard, a carryback period of 2 (or more) years and a carryforward period of 20 years currently are allowed. See also *mitigation of the annual accounting period concept.*

Net worth method. An approach used by the IRS to reconstruct the income of a taxpayer who fails to maintain adequate records. The IRS estimates *gross income* for the year as the increase in net worth of the taxpayer (assets in excess of liabilities), with appropriate adjustment for nontaxable receipts and nondeductible expenditures. The net worth method often is used when tax *fraud* is suspected.

Nexus. A *multistate corporation*'s taxable income can be *apportioned* to a specific state only if the entity has established a sufficient presence, or *nexus,* with that state. State law, which often follows the *UDITPA,* specifies various activities that lead to nexus in various states.

Ninety-day letter. See *statutory notice of deficiency.*

Nonacquiescence. Disagreement by the IRS on the result reached by selected tax decisions. Sometimes abbreviated *Nonacq.* or *NA.* See also *acquiescence.*

Nonbusiness bad debt. A bad debt loss that is not incurred in connection with a creditor's *trade or business.* The loss is classified as a *short-term capital loss* and is allowed only in the year the debt becomes entirely worthless. In addition to family loans, many *investor losses* are nonbusiness bad debts. § 166(d). See also *business bad debts.*

Nonbusiness income. Income generated from investment assets or from the taxable disposition thereof. In some states, the nonbusiness income of a *multistate corporation* is held out of the apportionment procedure and allocated to the state in which the nonbusiness asset is located. See also *allocate* and *apportion.*

Noncontributory qualified pension or profit sharing plan. A plan funded entirely by the employer with no contributions from the covered employees. See also *qualified pension or profit sharing plan.*

Nonliquidating distribution. A payment made by a *partnership* or corporation to the entity's owner is a nonliquidating distribution when the entity's legal existence does not cease thereafter. If the payor is a corporation, such a distribution can result in *dividend* income to the shareholders. If the payor is a partnership, the *partner* usually assigns a *basis* in the distributed property that is equal to the lesser of the partner's basis in the partnership interest or the basis of the distributed asset to the partnership. In this regard, the partner first assigns basis to any cash that is received in the distribution. The partner's remaining basis, if any, is assigned to the noncash assets according to their relative bases to the partnership.

Nonrecourse debt. Debt secured by the property that it is used to purchase. The purchaser of the property is not personally liable for the debt upon default. Rather, the creditor's recourse is to repossess the related property. Nonrecourse debt generally does not increase the purchaser's *at-risk amount.*

Nonresident alien. An individual who is neither a citizen nor a resident of the United States. Citizenship is determined under the immigration and naturalization laws of the United States. Residency is determined under § 7701(b) of the Internal Revenue Code.

Nonseparately stated income. The net income of an *S corporation* that is combined and allocated to the shareholders. Other items, such as *capital gains* and *charitable contributions,* that could be treated differently on the individual tax returns of the shareholders are not included in this amount but are allocated to the shareholders separately.

Not essentially equivalent redemption. See *redemption (not equivalent to a dividend).*

Obligee. The party to whom someone else is obligated under a contract. Thus, if Coop loans money to Dawn, Coop is the obligee and Dawn is the obligor under the loan.

Obligor. See *obligee.*

Offer in compromise. A settlement agreement offered by the IRS in a tax dispute, especially where there is doubt as to the collectibility of the full *deficiency.* Offers in compromise can include installment payment schedules, as well as reductions in the tax and penalties owed by the taxpayer.

Office audit. An *audit* conducted by the IRS in the agent's office. See also *correspondence audit* and *field audit.*

On all fours. A judicial decision exactly in point with another as to result, facts, or both.

Operating agreement. The governing document of a *limited liability company.* This document is similar in structure, function, and purpose to a *partnership agreement.*

Optimal use value. Synonym for *most suitable use value.*

Optional adjustment election. See *Section 754 election.*

Ordinary. Common and accepted in the general industry or type of activity in which the taxpayer is engaged. It comprises one of the tests for the deductibility of expenses incurred or paid in connection with a *trade or business;* for the production or collection of income; for the management, conservation, or maintenance of property held for the production of income; or in connection with the determination, collection, or refund of any tax. §§ 162(a) and 212. See also *necessary.*

Ordinary and necessary. See *necessary* and *ordinary.*

Ordinary gross income (OGI). A concept peculiar to *personal holding companies* and defined in § 543(b)(1). See also *adjusted ordinary gross income.*

Organizational expenditures. Items incurred early in the life of a corporate entity. Can be an immediate $5,000 amortization deduction, otherwise claimed over 180 months. Amortizable expenditures exclude those incurred to obtain capital (underwriting fees) or assets (subject to cost recovery). Typically, eligible expenditures include legal and accounting fees and state incorporation payments. Such items must be incurred by the end of the entity's first tax year. § 248.

Other adjustments account (OAA). Used in the context of a distribution from an *S corporation.* The net accumulation of the entity's exempt income (e.g., municipal bond interest).

Other property. In a *corporate reorganization,* any property in the exchange that is not stock or *securities,* such as cash or inventory. This amount usually constitutes *boot.* This result is similar to that in a *like-kind exchange.*

Outbound taxation. U.S. tax effects when a U.S. person begins an investment or business activity outside the United States.

Outside basis. A partner's *basis* in his or her *partnership* interest.

Owner shift. Any change in the respective ownership of stock by a 5 percent-or-more shareholder. Change is determined relative to a testing period of the prior three years. If there is a more-than-50 percent change in the ownership of a loss corporation, § 382 limitations apply to the use of *net operating loss* carryovers of the loss corporation.

Ownership change. An event that triggers a *§ 382 limitation* for the acquiring corporation.

P

Parent-subsidiary controlled group. A *controlled* or *affiliated group* of corporations, where at least one corporation is at least 80 percent owned by one or more of the others. The *affiliated group* definition is more difficult to meet.

Partial liquidation. A *stock redemption* where noncorporate shareholders are permitted sale or exchange treatment. In certain cases, an active business must have existed for at least five years. Only a portion of the outstanding stock in the entity is retired.

Partner. See *general partner* and *limited partner.*

Partnership. For income tax purposes, a partnership includes a syndicate, group, pool, or *joint venture,* as well as ordinary partnerships. In an ordinary partnership, two or more parties combine capital and/or services to carry on a business for profit as co-owners. § 7701(a)(2). See also *limited partnership* and *tiered partnerships.*

Partnership agreement. The governing document of a *partnership.* A partnership agreement should describe the rights and obligations of the *partners*; the allocation of entity income, deductions, and cash flows; initial and future capital contribution requirements; conditions for terminating the partnership; and other matters.

Passive foreign investment company (PFIC). A non-U.S. corporation that generates a substantial amount of *personal holding company income.* Upon receipt of an excess distribution from the entity or the sale of its shares, its *U.S. shareholders* are taxable on their pro rata shares of the tax that has been deferred with respect to the corporation's taxable income, plus an applicable interest charge.

Passive investment company. A means by which a *multistate corporation* can reduce the overall effective tax rate by isolating investment income in a low- or no-tax state.

Passive investment income (PII). Gross receipts from royalties, certain rents, dividends, interest, annuities, and gains from the sale or exchange of stock and securities. When *earnings and profits* (E & P) also exist, if the passive investment income of an *S corporation* exceeds 25 percent of the corporation's gross receipts for three consecutive years, an S election is lost.

Passive loss. Any loss from (1) activities in which the taxpayer does not materially participate and (2) rental activities. Net passive losses of most taxpayers other than corporations cannot be used to offset income from nonpassive sources. Rather, they are suspended until the taxpayer either generates net passive income (and a deduction of such losses is allowed) or disposes of the underlying property (at which time the loss deductions are allowed in full). Landlords who actively participate in the rental activities can deduct up to $25,000 of passive losses annually. However, this amount is phased out when the landlord's AGI exceeds $100,000. Another exception applies to real estate professionals. See also *portfolio income.*

Payroll factor. The proportion of a *multistate corporation*'s total payroll that is traceable to a specific state. Used in determining the taxable income that is to be apportioned to that state. See also *apportion.*

Pecuniary bequest. A bequest of money to an *heir* by a *decedent.* See also *bequest.*

Percentage depletion. See *depletion.*

Percentage of completion method. A method of reporting gain or loss on certain long-term contracts. Under this method of accounting, the gross contract price is included in income as the contract is completed. Reg. § 1.451–3. See also *completed contract method.*

Permanent (book-tax) differences. Under *ASC 740 (SFAS 109),* tax-related items that appear in the entity's financial statements or its tax return, but not both. For instance, interest income from a municipal bond is a permanent book-tax difference.

Permanently reinvesting. Under *ASC 740-30 (APB 23)* of *Generally Accepted Accounting Principles,* a special rule that relates to the book tax expense of non-U.S. subsidiaries. If a parent corporation documents that it is permanently reinvesting the non-U.S. earning of a non-U.S. subsidiary, the parent does not record as an expense any U.S. income tax that the parent might pay on such earnings, i.e., the book tax expense is deferred until such earnings are (if ever) repatriated to the United States.

Personal and household effects. Items owned by a *decedent* at the time of death. Examples include clothing, furniture, sporting goods, jewelry, stamp and coin collections, silverware, china, crystal, cooking utensils, books, cars, televisions, radios, and sound equipment.

Personal holding company (PHC). A corporation that satisfies the requirements of § 542. Qualification as a personal holding company means a penalty tax may be imposed on the corporation's undistributed *personal holding company income* for the year.

Personal holding company income. Income as defined by § 543. It includes interest, *dividends,* certain rents and royalties, income from the use of corporate property by certain shareholders, income from certain personal service contracts, and distributions from *estates* and *trusts.* Such income is relevant in determining whether a corporation is a *personal holding company* and is therefore subject to the penalty tax on personal holding companies. See also *adjusted ordinary gross income.*

Personal holding company tax. A penalty tax imposed on certain closely held corporations with excessive investment income. Assessed at the top individual tax rate on *personal holding company income,* reduced by *dividends* paid and other adjustments. § 541.

Personal property. Generally, all property other than real estate. It is sometimes referred to as personalty when real estate is termed realty. Personal property also refers to property not used in a taxpayer's trade or business or held for the production or collection of income. When used in this sense, personal property can include both *realty* (e.g., a personal residence) and *personalty* (e.g., personal effects such as clothing and furniture). See also *bequest.*

Personal service corporation (PSC). An entity whose principal activity is the providing of services by owner-employees. Subject to a flat 35 percent tax rate and limited to a calendar tax year.

Personalty. All property that is not attached to real estate (realty) and is movable. Examples of personalty are machinery, automobiles, clothing, household furnishings, inventory, and personal effects. See also *ad valorem tax* and *realty*.

Portfolio income. Income from interest, *dividends*, rentals, royalties, *capital gains*, or other investment sources. Net *passive losses* cannot be used to offset net portfolio income. See also *passive loss* and *investment income*.

Power of appointment. A legal right granted to someone by a will or other document that gives the holder the power to dispose of property or the income from property. When the holder may appoint the property to his or her own benefit, the power usually is called a general power of appointment. If the holder cannot benefit himself or herself but may only appoint to certain other persons, the power is a special power of appointment. Assume Gary places $500,000 worth of securities in *trust* granting Donna the right to determine each year how the trustee is to divide the income between Ann and Babs. Under these circumstances, Donna has a special power of appointment. If Donna had the further right to appoint the income to herself, she probably possesses a general power of appointment. For the *estate tax* and *gift tax* effects of powers of appointment, see §§ 2041 and 2514.

Precontribution gain or loss. *Partnerships* allow for a variety of *special allocations* of gain or loss among the *partners*, but gain or loss that is "built in" on an asset contributed to the partnership is assigned specifically to the contributing *partner*. § 704(c)(1)(A).

Preferences (AMT). See *alternative minimum tax (AMT)* and *tax preference items*.

Preferred stock bailout. A process where a shareholder used the issuance and sale, or later redemption, of a preferred stock dividend to obtain *long-term capital gains*, without any loss of voting control over the corporation. In effect, the shareholder received corporate profits without suffering the consequences of *dividend* income treatment. This procedure led Congress to enact § 306, which, if applicable, converts the prior long-term capital gain on the sale or redemption of the tainted stock to dividend income. See also *bailout*.

Present interest. See *future interest*.

Presumption. An inference in favor of a particular fact. If, for example, the IRS issues a notice of *deficiency* against a taxpayer, under certain conditions a presumption of correctness attaches to the assessment. Thus, the taxpayer has the *burden of proof* to show that he or she does not owe the tax listed in the deficiency notice. See also *rebuttable presumption*.

Previously taxed income (PTI). Under prior law, the undistributed taxable income of an *S corporation* was taxed to the shareholders as of the last day of the corporation's tax year and usually could be withdrawn by the shareholders without tax consequences at some later point in time. The role of PTI has been taken over by the *accumulated adjustments account*.

Principal. Property as opposed to income. The term often is used as a synonym for the *corpus* of a *trust*. If, for example, Gil places real estate in trust with income payable to Ann for life and the remainder to Barb upon Ann's death, the real estate is the principal, or corpus, of the trust.

Private foundation. An *exempt organization* subject to additional statutory restrictions on its activities and on contributions made to it. *Excise taxes* may be levied on certain prohibited transactions, and the Code places more stringent restrictions on the deductibility of contributions to private foundations. § 509.

Pro rata. Proportionately. Assume, for example, a corporation has 10 shareholders, each of whom owns 10 percent of the stock. A pro rata *dividend* distribution of $1,000 means that each shareholder receives $100.

Pro se. The taxpayer represents himself or herself before the court without the benefit of counsel.

Probate. The legal process by which the estate of a *decedent* is administered. Generally, the probate process involves collecting a decedent's assets, liquidating liabilities, paying necessary taxes, and distributing property to heirs.

Probate costs. The costs incurred in administering a *decedent's estate*. See also *probate estate*.

Probate court. The usual designation for the state or local court that supervises the administration (*probate*) of a *decedent's estate*.

Probate estate. The property of a *decedent* that is subject to administration by the *executor* or *administrator* of an estate. See also *administration*.

Profit and loss sharing ratios. Specified in the *partnership* agreement and used to determine each *partner*'s allocation of ordinary taxable income and separately stated items. Profits and losses can be shared in different ratios. The ratios can be changed by amending the *partnership agreement*. § 704(a).

Profits (loss) interest. A *partner's* percentage allocation of *partnership* operating results, determined by the *profit and loss sharing ratios*.

Property. Assets defined in the broadest legal sense. Property includes the *unrealized receivables* of a *cash basis* taxpayer, but not services rendered. § 351.

Property dividend. A *dividend* consisting of in-kind (noncash) assets of the payor, measured by the *fair market value* of the property on the date of distribution. Distribution of in-kind property causes the distributing *C* or *S corporation* to recognize any underlying realized gain, but not loss.

Property factor. The proportion of a *multistate corporation*'s total property that is traceable to a specific state. Used in determining the *taxable income* that is to be apportioned to that state. See also *apportion*.

Property tax. An *ad valorem tax*, usually levied by a city or county government, on the value of real or personal property that the taxpayer owns on a specified date. Most states exclude from the tax base intangible property and assets owned by *exempt organizations*, and some exclude inventory, pollution control or manufacturing equipment, and other items to provide relocation or retention incentives for the taxpayer.

Proportionate distribution. A distribution in which each *partner* in a *partnership* receives a *pro rata* share of *hot assets* being distributed. For example, a distribution of $10,000 of *hot assets* equally to two 50 percent partners is a proportionate distribution.

Proposed Regulation. A *Regulation* may first be issued in proposed form to give interested parties the opportunity for comment. When and if a Proposed Regulation is finalized, it becomes a *Regulation.*

PTI. See *previously taxed income.*

Public Law 86–272. A congressional limit on the ability of the state to force a *multistate corporation* to assign income to that state. Under P.L. 86–272, where orders for tangible personal property are both filled and delivered outside the state, the entity must establish more than the mere solicitation of such orders before any income can be *apportioned* to the state.

Public policy limitation. A concept precluding an income tax deduction for certain expenses related to activities deemed to be contrary to the public welfare. In this connection, the Code includes specific disallowance provisions covering such items as illegal bribes, kickbacks, and fines and penalties. §§ 162(c) and (f).

Q

Qualified business unit (QBU). A subsidiary, branch, or other business entity that conducts business using a currency other than the U.S. dollar.

Qualified dividends. Distributions made by domestic (and certain non-U.S.) corporations to noncorporate shareholders that are subject to tax at the same rates as those applicable to net long-term *capital gains.* The *dividend* must be paid out of *earnings and profits,* and the shareholders must meet certain holding period requirements as to the stock. Qualified dividend treatment applies to distributions made after 2002 and before 2013. §§ 1(h)(1) and (11).

Qualified nonrecourse debt. Debt issued on realty by a bank, retirement plan, or governmental agency. Included in the *at-risk amount* by the investor. § 465(b)(6).

Qualified pension or profit sharing plan. An employer-sponsored plan that meets the requirements of § 401. If these requirements are met, none of the employer's contributions to the plan are taxed to the employee until distributed (§ 402). The employer is allowed a deduction in the year the contributions are made (§ 404). See also *contributory qualified pension or profit sharing plan, deferred compensation,* and *noncontributory qualified pension or profit sharing plan.*

Qualified production activities income. The base for computing the *domestic production activities deduction.* It comprises qualified production receipts less allocable cost of goods sold and other deductions. § 199.

Qualified small business corporation. A *C corporation* that has aggregate gross assets not exceeding $50 million and that is conducting an active *trade or business.* § 1202.

Qualified small business stock. The shareholder may exclude from gross income 50 percent of the realized gain on the sale of the stock, if he or she held the stock for more than five years. If the stock was acquired from January 1, 2009, through September 27, 2010, the exclusion rate is 75 percent. If the stock was acquired from September 28, 2010, through December 31, 2011, the exclusion rate is 100 percent. Some of the excluded amount may constitute an *AMT preference* item. § 1202.

Qualified terminable interest property (QTIP). Generally, the *marital deduction* (for gift and *estate tax* purposes) is not available if the interest transferred will terminate upon the death of the transferee spouse and pass to someone else. Thus, if Hannah places property in trust, life estate to Will, and remainder to their children upon Will's death, this is a *terminable interest* that will not provide Hannah (or her estate) with a marital deduction. If, however, the transfer in *trust* is treated as qualified terminable interest property (the QTIP election is made), the terminable interest restriction is waived and the marital deduction becomes available. In exchange for this deduction, the surviving spouse's *gross estate* must include the value of the QTIP election assets, even though he or she has no control over the ultimate disposition of the asset. Terminable interest property qualifies for this election if the *donee* (or *heir*) is the only *beneficiary* of the asset during his or her lifetime and receives income distributions relative to the property at least annually. For gifts, the donor spouse is the one who makes the QTIP election. As to property transferred by death, the *executor* of the estate of the deceased spouse has the right to make the election. §§ 2056(b)(7) and 2523(f).

R

RAR. A Revenue Agent's Report, which reflects any adjustments made by the agent as a result of an *audit* of the taxpayer. The RAR is mailed to the taxpayer along with the *30-day letter,* which outlines the appellate procedures available to the taxpayer.

Rate reconciliation. Under *Generally Accepted Accounting Principles,* a footnote to the financial statements often includes a table that accounts for differences in the statutory income tax rate that applies to the entity (say, 35 percent) and the higher or lower *effective tax rate* that the entity realized for the reporting period. The rate reconciliation includes only *permanent differences* between the book tax expense and the entity's *income tax provision.* The rate reconciliation table often is expressed in dollar and/or percentage terms.

Realistic possibility. A preparer penalty is assessed where a tax return includes a position that has no realistic possibility of being sustained by a court.

Realized gain or loss. The difference between the amount realized upon the sale or other disposition of property and the adjusted basis of such property. § 1001. See also *adjusted basis, amount realized, basis,* and *recognized gain or loss.*

Realty. Real estate. See also *personalty.*

Reasonable cause. Relief from taxpayer and preparer penalties often is allowed where there is reasonable cause for the taxpayer's actions. For instance, reasonable cause for the late filing of a tax return might be a flood that damaged the taxpayer's record-keeping systems and made difficult a timely completion of the return.

Reasonable needs of the business. A means of avoiding the penalty tax on an unreasonable accumulation of earnings. In determining base for this tax (*accumulated taxable* *income*), § 535 allows a deduction for "such part of *earnings and profits* for the taxable year as are retained for the reasonable needs of the business." § 537.

Rebuttable presumption. A presumption that can be overturned upon the showing of sufficient proof. See also *presumption.*

Recapitalization. An "E" reorganization, constituting a major change in the character and amount of outstanding equity of a corporation. For instance, common stock exchanged for preferred stock can qualify for tax-free "E" reorganization treatment.

Recapture. To recover the tax benefit of a deduction or a credit previously taken. See also *depreciation recapture.*

Recapture potential. A measure with respect to property that, if disposed of in a taxable transaction, would result in the recapture of depreciation (e.g., § 1245), deferred LIFO gain, or deferred *installment method* gain.

Recognized gain or loss. The portion of realized gain or loss subject to income taxation. See also *realized gain or loss.*

Recourse debt. Debt for which the lender may both foreclose on the property and assess a guarantor for any payments due under the loan, even from personal assets. A lender may also make a claim against the assets of any *general partner* in a *partnership* to which debt is issued, without regard to whether that partner has guaranteed the debt.

Redemption. See *stock redemption.*

Redemption (complete termination). Sale or exchange treatment is available relative to this type of *stock redemption.* The shareholder must retire all of his or her outstanding shares in the corporation (ignoring family *attribution* rules) and cannot hold an interest, other than that of a creditor, for the 10 years following the redemption. § 302(b)(3).

Redemption (disproportionate). Sale or exchange treatment is available relative to this type of *stock redemption.* After the exchange, the shareholder owns less than 80 percent of his or her pre-redemption interest in the corporation and only a minority interest in the entity. § 302(b)(2).

Redemption (not equivalent to a dividend). Sale or exchange treatment is given to this type of *stock redemption.* Although various safe-harbor tests are failed, the nature of the redemption is such that *dividend* treatment is avoided, because it represents a meaningful reduction in the shareholder's interest in the corporation. § 302(b)(1).

Redemption to pay death taxes. Sale or exchange treatment is available relative to this type of *stock redemption,* to the extent of the proceeds up to the total amount paid by the estate or heir for estate/inheritance taxes and *administration* expenses. The stock value must exceed 35 percent of the value of the decedent's *adjusted gross estate.* In meeting this test, one can combine shareholdings in corporations where the *decedent* held at least 20 percent of the outstanding shares.

Regular corporation. See *C corporation.*

Regulations. The U.S. Treasury Department Regulations (abbreviated Reg.) represent the position of the IRS as to how the *Internal Revenue Code* is to be interpreted. Their purpose is to provide taxpayers and IRS personnel with rules of general and specific application to the various provisions of the tax law. Regulations are published in the *Federal Register* and in all tax services.

Related corporations. See *controlled group.*

Related parties. Various Code Sections define related parties and often include a variety of persons within this (usually detrimental) category. Generally, related parties are accorded different tax treatment from that applicable to other taxpayers who enter into similar transactions. For instance, realized losses that are generated between related parties are not recognized in the year of the loss. However, these deferred losses can be used to offset recognized gains that occur upon the subsequent sale of the asset to a nonrelated party. Other uses of a related-party definition include the conversion of gain upon the sale of a depreciable asset into all ordinary income (§ 1239) and the identification of *constructive ownership* of stock relative to corporate distributions, *redemptions,* liquidations, *reorganizations,* and compensation.

Remainder interest. The property that passes to a *beneficiary* after the expiration of an intervening *income interest.* If, for example, Greg places real estate in trust with income to Ann for life and remainder to Bill upon Ann's death, Bill has a remainder interest. See also *life estate* and *reversionary interest.*

Remand. To send back. An appellate court may remand a case to a lower court, usually for additional fact finding. In other words, the *appellate court* is not in a position to decide the appeal based on the facts determined by the lower court. Remanding is abbreviated *"rem'g."*

Reorganization. See *corporate reorganization.*

Research activities credit. A tax credit whose purpose is to encourage research and development. It consists of three components: the incremental research activities credit, the energy research credit, and the basic research credit. The incremental research activities credit is equal to 20 percent of the excess qualified research expenditures over the base amount. The basic research credit is equal to 20 percent of the excess of basic research payments over the base amount. § 41. The energy research credit is 20 percent of payments to an energy research consortium. See also *general business credit.*

Residential rental property. Buildings for which at least 80 percent of the gross rents are from dwelling units (e.g., an apartment building). This type of building is distinguished from nonresidential (commercial or industrial) buildings in applying the *recapture* of *depreciation* provisions. The term also is relevant in distinguishing between buildings that are eligible for a 27.5-year life versus a 31.5- or 39-year life for *MACRS* purposes.

Residual method. Used to allocate the new stepped-up *basis* of a subsidiary's assets among its property when a § 338 election is in effect. The purchase price that exceeds the aggregate *fair market values* of the tangible and identifiable *intangible assets* is allocated to *goodwill* or going-concern value. § 1060.

Return of capital. When a taxpayer reacquires financial resources that he or she previously had invested in an entity or venture, the return of his or her capital investment itself does not increase *gross income* for the recovery year. A return of capital may result from an *annuity* or insurance contract, the sale or exchange of any asset, or a distribution from a *partnership* or corporation.

Revenue Agent's Report. See *RAR.*

Revenue neutrality. A change in the tax system that results in the same amount of net aggregate revenue collected by the taxing jurisdiction. Revenue neutral, however, does not mean that any one taxpayer pays the same amount of tax as before. Thus, as a result of a tax law change, corporations could pay more taxes, but the excess revenue will be offset by lower taxes on individuals.

Revenue Procedure. A matter of procedural importance to both taxpayers and the IRS concerning the administration of the tax laws is issued as a Revenue Procedure (abbreviated Rev.Proc.). A Revenue Procedure is published in an *Internal Revenue Bulletin* (I.R.B.).

Revenue Ruling. A Revenue Ruling (abbreviated Rev.Rul.) is issued by the National Office of the IRS to express an official interpretation of the tax law as applied to specific transactions. It is more limited in application than a *Regulation.* A Revenue Ruling is published in an *Internal Revenue Bulletin* (I.R.B.).

Reversed (Rev'd.). An indication that a decision of one court has been reversed by a higher court in the same case.

Reversing (Rev'g.). An indication that the decision of a higher court is reversing the result reached by a lower court in the same case.

Reversionary interest. The *trust* property that reverts to the *grantor* after the expiration of an intervening *income interest.* Assume Gail places real estate in trust with income to Art for 11 years, and upon the expiration of this term, the property returns to Gail. Under these circumstances, she holds a reversionary interest in the property. A reversionary interest is the same as a *remainder interest,* except that, in the latter case, the property passes to someone other than the original owner (e.g., the *grantor* of a trust) upon the expiration of the intervening interest. See also *grantor trust.*

Revocable transfer. A transfer of property where the transferor retains the right to recover the property. The creation of a revocable *trust* is an example of a revocable transfer. § 2038. See also *incomplete transfer.*

Rev.Proc. Abbreviation for an IRS *Revenue Procedure.*

Rev.Rul. Abbreviation for an IRS *Revenue Ruling.*

Right of survivorship. See *joint tenants.*

S

S corporation. The designation for a small business corporation. See also *Subchapter S.*

Sales factor. The proportion of a *multistate corporation*'s total sales that is traceable to a specific state. Used in determining the *taxable income* that is to be apportioned to that state. See also *apportion.*

Sales tax. A state- or local-level tax on the retail sale of specified property. Generally, the purchaser pays the tax, but the seller collects it, as an agent for the government. Various taxing jurisdictions allow exemptions for purchases of specific items, including certain food, services, and manufacturing equipment. If the purchaser and seller are in different states, a *use tax* usually applies.

Schedule K-1. A tax information form prepared for each *partner* in a *partnership,* each shareholder of an *S corporation,* and some *beneficiaries* of certain *trusts.* The Schedule K-1 reports the owner's share of the entity's ordinary income or loss from operations, as well as the owner's share of *separately stated items.*

Schedule M-1. On the *Form 1120,* a reconciliation of book net income with Federal *taxable income.* Accounts for *temporary* and *permanent differences* in the two computations, such as *depreciation* differences, exempt income, and nondeductible items. On *Forms 1120S* and *1065,* the Schedule M-1 reconciles book income with the owners' aggregate ordinary taxable income.

Schedule M-3. An *expanded* reconciliation of book net income with Federal *taxable income* (see *Schedule M-1*). Required of *C* and *S corporations* and *partnerships*/LLCs, with total assets of $10 million or more.

Schedule PH. A tax form required to be filed by *personal holding companies.* The form is filed in addition to *Form 1120* (U.S. Corporation Income Tax Return).

Section 306 stock. Preferred stock issued as a nontaxable *stock dividend* that, if sold or redeemed, would result in ordinary income recognition. § 306(c). See also *preferred stock bailout.*

Section 306 taint. The ordinary income that would result upon the sale or other taxable disposition of *§ 306 stock.*

Section 338 election. When a corporation acquires at least 80 percent of a subsidiary in a 12-month period, it can elect to treat the acquisition of such stock as an asset purchase. The acquiring corporation's *basis* in the subsidiary's assets then is the cost of the stock. The subsidiary is deemed to have sold its assets for an amount equal to the grossed-up basis in its stock.

Section 382 limitation. When one corporation acquires another, the acquiror's ability to use the loss and credit carryovers of the target may be limited, in an anti-abuse provision specified in the Code. Generally, for instance, the maximum deduction available to the acquiror is the takeover-date value of the target times the tax-exempt interest rate on that date.

Section 754 election. An election that may be made by a *partnership* to adjust the *basis* of partnership assets to reflect a purchasing *partner's* outside basis in interest or to reflect a gain, loss, or basis adjustment of a partner receiving a distribution from a partnership. The intent of the election is to maintain the equivalence between *outside* and *inside basis.* Once the election is made, the partnership must make basis adjustments for all future transactions, unless the IRS consents to revoke the election.

Section 1231 assets. Depreciable assets and real estate used in a *trade or business* and held for the appropriate (long-term) *holding period.* Under certain circumstances, the classification also includes timber, coal, domestic iron ore, livestock (held for draft, breeding, dairy, or sporting purposes), and unharvested crops. § 1231(b). See also *Section 1231 gains and losses.*

Section 1231 gains and losses. If the combined gains and losses from the taxable dispositions of *§ 1231 assets* plus the net gain from business *involuntary conversions* (of both § 1231 assets and long-term *capital assets*) is a gain, such gains and losses are treated as *long-term capital gains* and losses. In arriving at § 1231 gains, however, the *depreciation recapture* provisions (e.g., § 1245) are applied first, to produce ordinary income. If the net result of the combination is a loss, the gains and losses from § 1231 assets are treated as ordinary gains and losses. § 1231(a).

Section 1244 stock. Stock issued under § 1244 by qualifying *small business corporations.* If § 1244 stock becomes worthless, the shareholders may claim an ordinary loss rather than the usual capital loss, within statutory limitations.

Section 1245 recapture. Upon a taxable disposition of § 1245 property, all *depreciation* claimed on such property is recaptured as ordinary income (but not to exceed any *recognized gain* from the disposition).

Section 1250 recapture. Upon a taxable disposition of § 1250 property, accelerated *depreciation* or *cost recovery* claimed on the property may be recaptured as ordinary income.

Securities. Generally, stock, debt, and other financial assets. To the extent securities other than the stock of the transferee corporation are received in a § 351 exchange, the new shareholder realizes a gain.

Separate property. In a *community property* jurisdiction, property that belongs entirely to one of the spouses is separate property. Generally, this includes property acquired before marriage or acquired after marriage by *gift* or inheritance.

Separate return limitation year (SRLY). A series of rules limits the amount of an acquired corporation's *net operating loss* carryforwards that can be used by the acquiror. Generally, a *consolidated return* can include the acquiree's *net operating loss* carryforward only to the extent of the lesser of the subsidiary's (1) current-year or (2) cumulative positive contribution to consolidated taxable income.

Separately stated item. Any item of a *partnership* or *S corporation* that might be taxed differently to any two owners of the entity. These amounts are not included in ordinary income of the entity, but instead are reported separately to the owners; tax consequences are determined at the owner level.

Sham. A transaction without substance that is disregarded for tax purposes.

Short-term capital gain or loss. Results from the sale or other taxable exchange of a *capital asset* that had been held by the seller for one year or less or from other transactions involving statutorily designated assets, including *nonbusiness bad debts.*

Simple trust. Simple trusts are those that are not complex trusts. Such *trusts* may not have a charitable beneficiary, accumulate income, or distribute corpus. See also *complex trust.*

Small business corporation. A corporation that satisfies the definition of § 1361(b), § 1244(c), or both. Satisfaction of § 1361(b) permits an S election, and satisfaction of § 1244(c) enables the shareholders of the corporation to claim an ordinary loss on the worthlessness of stock.

Small Cases Division of the U.S. Tax Court. Jurisdiction is limited to claims of $50,000 or less. There is no appeal from this court.

Special allocation. Any amount for which an agreement exists among the partners of a *partnership* outlining the method used for assigning the item among the *partners.*

Special power of appointment. See *power of appointment.*

Special use value. Permits the *executor* of an *estate* to value, for *estate tax* purposes, real estate used in a farming activity or in connection with a closely held business at its *current use value* rather than at its most suitable or *optimal use value.* Under this option, a farm is valued for farming purposes even though, for example, the property might have a higher potential value as a shopping center. For the executor of an estate to elect special use valuation, the conditions of § 2032A must be satisfied. See also *most suitable use value.*

Spin-off. A type of *reorganization* where, for example, Ace Corporation transfers some assets to Bow Corporation in exchange for enough Bow stock to represent control. Ace then distributes the Bow stock to its shareholders.

Split-off. A type of *reorganization* where, for example, Arc Corporation transfers some assets to Bond Corporation in exchange for enough Bond stock to represent control. Arc then distributes the Bond stock to its shareholders in exchange for some of their Arc stock.

Split-up. A type of *reorganization* where, for example, Ally Corporation transfers some assets to Bar Corporation and the remainder to Zip Corporation. In return, Ally receives enough Bar and Zip stock to represent control of each corporation. Ally then distributes the Bar and Zip stock to its shareholders in return for all of their Ally stock. The result of the split-up is that Ally is liquidated, and its shareholders now have control of Bar and Zip.

Sprinkling trust. When a *trustee* has the discretion to either distribute or accumulate the *entity accounting income* of the *trust* and to distribute it among the trust's income *beneficiaries* in varying magnitudes, a sprinkling trust exists. The trustee can "sprinkle" the income of the trust.

Statute of limitations. Provisions of the law that specify the maximum period of time in which action may be taken on a past event. Code §§ 6501–6504 contain the limitation periods applicable to the IRS for additional assessments, and §§ 6511–6515 relate to refund claims by taxpayers.

Statutory depletion. See *depletion.*

Statutory notice of deficiency. Commonly referred to as the 90-day letter, this notice is sent to a taxpayer upon request, upon the expiration of the *30-day letter,* or upon exhaustion by the taxpayer of his or her administrative remedies before the IRS. The notice gives the taxpayer 90 days in which to file a petition with the U.S. *Tax Court.* If such a petition is not filed, the IRS will demand payment of the assessed *deficiency.* §§ 6211–6216.

Step transaction. Disregarding one or more transactions to arrive at the final result. Assume, for example, that the shareholders of Clue Corporation liquidate the corporation and receive cash and operating assets. Immediately after the liquidation, the shareholders transfer the operating assets to newly formed Blue Corporation. Under these circumstances, the IRS may contend that the liquidation of Clue should be disregarded (thereby depriving the shareholders of capital gain treatment). What may really have happened is a *reorganization* of Clue with a distribution of boot (ordinary income) to Clue's shareholders. If so, there will be a carryover of *basis* in the assets transferred from Clue to Blue.

Step-down in basis. A reduction in the tax *basis* of property. See also *step-up in basis.*

Step-up in basis. An increase in the income tax *basis* of property. A step-up in basis occurs when a decedent dies owning appreciated property. Since the *estate* or *heir* acquires a basis in the property equal to the property's *fair market value* on the date of death (or *alternate valuation date* if available and elected), any appreciation is not subject to the income tax. Thus, a step-up in basis is the result, with no income tax consequences.

Stock attribution. See *attribution.*

Stock dividend. A *dividend* consisting of stock of the payor. Not taxable if a *pro rata* distribution of stock or stock rights on common stock. However, some stock dividends are taxable. § 305.

Stock redemption. A corporation buys back its own stock from a specified shareholder. Typically, the corporation recognizes any realized gain on the noncash assets that it uses to effect a redemption, and the shareholder obtains a *capital gain* or loss upon receipt of the purchase price.

Stock rights. Assets that convey to the holder the power to purchase corporate stock at a specified price, often for a limited period of time. Stock rights received may be taxed as a distribution of *earnings and profits.* After the right is exercised, the *basis* of the acquired share includes the investor's purchase price or *gross income,* if any, to obtain the right. Disposition of the right also can be a taxable event.

Subchapter S. Sections 1361–1379 of the Internal Revenue Code. An elective provision permitting certain *small business corporations* (§ 1361) and their shareholders (§ 1362) to elect to be treated for income tax purposes in accordance with the operating rules of §§ 1363–1379. *S corporations* usually avoid the corporate income tax, and corporate losses can be claimed by the shareholders.

Subpart F. The subpart of the Code that identifies the current tax treatment of income earned by a *controlled foreign corporation.* Certain types of income are included in U.S. *gross income* by *U.S. shareholders* of such an entity as the income is generated, not when it is repatriated.

Substance vs. form concept. A standard used when one must ascertain the true reality of what has occurred. Suppose, for example, a father sells stock to his daughter for $1,000. If the stock is really worth $50,000 at the time of the transfer, the substance of the transaction is probably a *gift* to her of $49,000.

Substantial authority. Taxpayer and *tax preparer* understatement penalties are waived where substantial authority existed for the disputed position taken on the return.

Substantial economic effect. *Partnerships* are allowed to *allocate* items of income, expense, gain, loss, and credit in any manner that is authorized in the *partnership agreement,* provided that the allocation has an economic effect aside from the corresponding tax results. The necessary substantial economic effect is present, for instance, if the post-contribution appreciation in the value of an asset that was contributed to the partnership by a *partner* was allocated to that partner for cost recovery purposes.

Substituted basis. When a taxpayer exchanges one asset for another, many provisions in the tax law allow an assignment of *basis* in the received asset to be that of the traded asset(s) in the hands of its former owner. Thus, no *step-up* or *-down of basis* occurs as a result of the exchange. For instance, when an investor contributes an asset to a corporation or *partnership,* the *partner* generally takes a substituted basis in the partnership interest (i.e., the interest has a basis equal to the aggregated bases of the assets contributed by that partner). § 723.

Survivorship. See *joint tenants.*

Syndication costs. Incurred in promoting and marketing *partnership* interests for sale to investors. Examples include legal and accounting fees, printing costs for prospectus and placement documents, and state registration fees. These items are capitalized by the partnership as incurred, with no *amortization* thereof allowed.

T

Tangible property. All property that has form or substance and is not intangible. See also *intangible asset.*

Tax avoidance. A synonym for *tax planning.* Tax minimization through legal means. Tax planning techniques include income deferral, deduction acceleration, and shifting of income to low-tax-rate jurisdictions and/or taxpayers. For example, a *cash basis* taxpayer increases his *charitable contribution* deduction by prepaying next year's church pledge. See also *tax evasion.*

Tax benefit rule. Limits the recognition of income from the recovery of an expense or loss properly deducted in a prior tax year to the amount of the deduction that generated a tax saving. Assume that last year Tom had medical expenses of $3,000 and *adjusted gross income* of $30,000. Because of the 7.5 percent limitation, he could deduct only $750 of these expenses [$3,000 − (7.5% × $30,000)]. If, this year, Tom is reimbursed by his insurance company for the $3,000 of expenses, the tax benefit rule limits the amount of income from the reimbursement to $750 (the amount previously deducted with a tax saving).

Tax Court. The U.S. Tax Court is one of four *trial courts* of original jurisdiction that decide litigation involving Federal income, *estate,* or *gift taxes.* It is the only trial court where the taxpayer must not first pay the *deficiency* assessed by the IRS. The Tax Court does not have jurisdiction over a case unless a *statutory notice of deficiency* (90-day letter) has been issued by the IRS and the taxpayer files the petition for hearing within the time prescribed.

Tax evasion. The reduction of taxes by the use of subterfuge or fraud or other nonlegal means. For example, a *cash basis* taxpayer tries to increase her *charitable contribution* deduction by prepaying next year's church pledge with a pre-dated check issued in the following year. See also *tax avoidance.*

Tax haven. A country in which either locally sourced income or residents of the country are subject to a low rate of taxation.

Tax on unearned income of a child under age 19/24. *Portfolio income,* such as interest and *dividends,* that is recognized by such a child is taxed *to him or her* at the rates that would have applied had the income been incurred by the child's parents, generally to the extent that the income exceeds $1,900. The additional tax is assessed regardless of the source of the income or the income's underlying property. If the child's parents are divorced, the custodial parent's rates are used. The parents' rates reflect any applicable *alternative minimum tax* and the phaseouts of lower tax brackets and other deductions. A special rule applies if the child is a full-time student. § 1(g).

Tax planning. See *tax avoidance.*

Tax preference items. Various items that may result in the imposition of the *alternative minimum tax.* §§ 55–58.

Tax preparer. One who prepares tax returns for compensation. A tax preparer must register with the IRS and receive a special ID number to practice before the IRS and represent taxpayers before the agency in tax *audit* actions. The conduct of a tax preparer is regulated under *Circular 230.* Tax preparers also are subject to penalties for inappropriate conduct when working in the tax profession.

Tax treaty. An agreement between the U.S. State Department and another country, designed to alleviate double taxation of income and asset transfers and to share administrative information useful to tax agencies in both countries. The United States has income tax treaties with almost 70 countries and transfer tax treaties with about 20.

Tax year. See *accounting period.*

Taxable estate. The *gross estate* of a *decedent* reduced by the deductions allowed by §§ 2053–2057 (e.g., *administration* expenses and marital and charitable deductions). The taxable estate is subject to the *unified transfer tax* at death. See also *adjusted taxable estate* and *gross estate.* § 2051.

Taxable gift. Amount of a *gift* that is subject to the *unified transfer tax.* Thus, a *taxable gift* has been adjusted by the *annual exclusion* and other appropriate deductions (e.g., marital and charitable). § 2503.

Taxable income. The tax base with respect to the prevailing Federal income tax. Taxable income is defined by the *Internal Revenue Code,* Treasury *Regulations,* and pertinent court cases. Currently, taxable income includes *gross income* from all sources except those specifically excluded by the statute. In addition, taxable income is reduced for certain allowable *deductions.* Deductions for business taxpayers must be related to a *trade or business.* Individuals can also deduct certain personal expenses in determining their taxable incomes.

Tax-free exchange. Transfers of property specifically exempted from income tax consequences by the tax law. Examples are a transfer of property to a controlled corporation under § 351(a) and a *like-kind exchange* under § 1031(a).

T.C. An abbreviation for the U.S. *Tax Court* used in citing a Regular Decision of the U.S. Tax Court.

T.C.Memo. An abbreviation used to refer to a Memorandum Decision of the U.S. *Tax Court.*

Technical advice memorandum. An interpretation of the tax law with respect to a disputed item, issued by the IRS, in response to a request from an agent, appellate conferee, or IRS executive. Often used to reconcile perceived differences in the application of the law among taxpayers or to identify an IRS position where no pertinent *Regulations* or rulings exist.

Technical termination of partnership. The entity is treated for tax purposes as though it has terminated, even though it continues in its activities. When there has been a sale or exchange of more than 50 percent of the capital interests of the *partnership* within 12 months, the partnership is deemed to have terminated when the 50 percent threshold is crossed. A new partnership immediately is formed through asset contributions by the *partners.* These activities can affect the entity's *tax year* and its bases in the assets it holds.

Telescoping. To look through one or more transactions to arrive at the final result. It is also referred to as the *step transaction* approach or the *substance vs. form concept.*

Temporary (book-tax) differences. Under *ASC 740 (SFAS 109),* tax-related items that appear in the entity's financial statements and its tax return, but in different time periods. For instance, doubtful accounts receivable often create a temporary book-tax difference, as a bad debt reserve is used to compute an expense for financial reporting purposes, but a bad debt often is deductible only under the specific write-off rule for tax purposes. The differing amounts observed for the current period create a temporary difference.

Temporary Regulation. The Treasury often issues Temporary Regulations to offer immediate guidance as to elections and other compliance matters after a change in the statute or a court ruling has been issued. Temporary Regulations carry the same precedential value as a final *Regulation,* and they should be followed as such for three years after issuance, after which they expire. Often a Temporary Regulation also is issued as a *Proposed Regulation.*

Tenants by the entirety. Essentially, a joint tenancy between husband and wife. See also *joint tenants* and *tenants in common.*

Tenants in common. A form of ownership where each tenant (owner) holds an undivided interest in property. Unlike a *joint tenancy* or a *tenancy by the entirety,* the interest of a tenant in common does not terminate upon that individual's death (there is no right of survivorship). Assume Brad and Connie acquire real estate as equal tenants in common, each having furnished one-half of the purchase price. Upon Brad's death, his one-half interest in the property passes to his *estate* or heirs, not to Connie.

Tentative minimum tax (TMT). In calculating a taxpayer's *alternative minimum tax (AMT),* the TMT is a subtotal representing the gross amount of tax liability. AMT equals the difference between the TMT and the regular tax liability. If this difference is positive, an AMT is due; if it is zero or negative, the AMT liability is zero. Only a positive AMT creates a *minimum tax credit.*

Term certain. A fixed period of years used to determine the length of an *income interest* (i.e., prior to the termination of a *trust* or *estate*).

Terminable interest. An interest in property that terminates upon the death of the holder or upon the occurrence of some other specified event. The transfer of a terminable interest by one spouse to the other may not qualify for the *marital deduction.* §§ 2056(b) and 2523(b).

Testamentary disposition. The passing of property to another upon the death of the owner.

Thin capitalization. When debt owed by a corporation to the shareholders becomes too large in relation to the corporation's capital structure (i.e., stock and shareholder equity), the IRS may contend that the corporation is thinly capitalized. In effect, some or all of the debt is reclassified as equity. The immediate result is to disallow any interest deduction to the corporation on the reclassified debt. To the extent of the corporation's *earnings and profits,* interest payments and loan repayments are treated as *dividends* to the shareholders.

Thirty-day letter. A letter that accompanies an *RAR* (Revenue Agent's Report) issued as a result of an IRS *audit* of a taxpayer (or the rejection of a taxpayer's claim for refund). The letter outlines the taxpayer's appeal procedure before the IRS. If the taxpayer does not request any such procedure within the 30-day period, the IRS issues a *statutory notice of deficiency.*

Three-factor apportionment formula. A means by which the total taxable income of a *multistate corporation* is assigned to a specific state. Usually, the payroll, property, and sales factors are treated equally, and the average of these factors is used in the apportionment procedure. In some states, however, the *sales factor* may receive a double weight, or it may be the only factor considered. These latter formulas place a greater tax burden on the income of out-of-state corporations. See also *apportion, payroll factor, property factor,* and *UDITPA.*

Throwback rule. If there is no income tax in the state to which a sale otherwise would be *apportioned,* the sale essentially is exempt from state income tax, even though the seller is *domiciled* in a state that levies an income tax. Nonetheless, if the seller's state has adopted a throwback rule, the sale is attributed to the *seller's* state, and the transaction is subjected to a state-level tax.

Tiered partnerships. An ownership arrangement wherein one *partnership* (the parent or first tier) is a partner in one or more partnerships (the subsidiary/subsidiaries or second tier). Frequently, the first tier is a holding partnership, and the second tier is an operating partnership.

Trade or business. Any business or professional activity conducted by a taxpayer. The mere ownership of rental or other investment assets does not constitute a trade or business. Generally, a trade or business generates relatively little *portfolio income.*

Transfer pricing. The process of setting internal prices for transfers of goods and services among related taxpayers. For instance, what price should be used when Subsidiary purchases management services from Parent? Section 482 allows the IRS to adjust transfer prices when it can show that the taxpayers were attempting to avoid tax by, say, shifting losses, *deductions,* or credits from low-tax to high-tax entities or jurisdictions.

Transfer tax. A tax imposed upon the transfer of property. See also *unified transfer tax.*

Transferee liability. Under certain conditions, if the IRS is unable to collect taxes owed by a transferor of *property,* it may pursue its claim against the transferee of the property. The transferee's liability for taxes is limited to the extent of the value of the assets transferred. For example, the IRS can force a *donee* to pay the *gift tax* when such tax cannot be paid by the *donor* making the transfer. §§ 6901–6905.

Treasury Regulations. See *Regulations.*

Treaty shopping. An international investor attempts to use the favorable aspects of a *tax treaty* to his or her advantage, often elevating the form of the transaction over its substance (e.g., by establishing only a nominal presence in the country offering the favorable treaty terms).

Trial court. The court of original jurisdiction; the first court to consider litigation. In Federal tax controversies, trial courts include U.S. *District Courts,* the U.S. *Tax Court,* the U.S. *Court of Federal Claims,* and the *Small Cases Division of the U.S. Tax Court.* See also *appellate court.*

Trust. A legal entity created by a *grantor* for the benefit of designated *beneficiaries* under the laws of the state and the valid trust instrument. The trustee holds a *fiduciary* responsibility to manage the trust's *corpus* assets and income for the economic benefit of all of the beneficiaries.

Trustee. An individual or corporation that assumes the *fiduciary* responsibilities under a *trust* agreement.

U

UDITPA. The Uniform Division of Income for Tax Purposes Act has been adopted in some form by many of the states. The Act develops criteria by which the total taxable income of a *multistate corporation* can be assigned to specific states. See also *allocate, apportion, Multistate Tax Commission (MTC),* and *nexus.*

Unclaimed property. A U.S. state may have the right to acquire property that has been made available to an individual or legal entity for a fixed period of time, where the claimant has not taken possession of the property after a notice period. Examples of such property that a state could acquire is an uncashed payroll check, or an unused gift card.

Undistributed personal holding company income. The tax base for the *personal holding company tax.* § 545.

Unearned income. Income received but not yet earned. Normally, such income is taxed when received, even for *accrual basis* taxpayers.

Unified transfer tax. Rates applicable to transfers by *gift* and death made after 1976. § 2001(c).

Unified transfer tax credit. A credit allowed against any *unified transfer tax.* §§ 2010 and 2505.

Uniform Gift to Minors Act. A means of transferring property (usually stocks and bonds) to a minor. The designated custodian of the property can act on behalf of the minor without requiring a *guardianship.* Generally, the custodian possesses the right to change investments (e.g., sell one type of stock and buy another), apply the income from the custodial property to the minor's support, and even terminate the custodianship. During the period of the custodianship, the income from the property is taxed to the minor, although perhaps subject to *kiddie tax* rates. The custodianship terminates when the minor reaches *legal age.*

Unitary state. A state that has adopted the *unitary theory* in its apportionment of the total *taxable income* of a *multistate corporation* to the state.

Unitary theory. Sales, property, and payroll of related corporations are combined for *nexus* and apportionment purposes, and the worldwide income of the unitary entity is *apportioned* to the state. Subsidiaries and other affiliated corporations found to be part of the corporation's unitary business (because they are subject to overlapping ownership, operation, or management) are included in the apportionment procedure. This approach can be limited if a *water's edge election* is in effect.

Unrealized receivables. Amounts earned by a *cash basis* taxpayer but not yet received. Because of the method of accounting used by the taxpayer, these amounts have a zero income tax *basis.* When unrealized receivables are distributed to a *partner,* they generally convert a transaction from nontaxable to taxable or an otherwise *capital gain* to ordinary income.

Unreasonable compensation. A deduction is allowed for "reasonable" salaries or other compensation for personal services actually rendered. To the extent compensation is "excessive" ("unreasonable"), no deduction is allowed. Unreasonable compensation usually is found in *closely held* *corporations,* where the motivation is to pay out profits in some form that is deductible to the corporation.

Unreasonable position. A *tax preparer* penalty is assessed regarding the understatement of a client's tax liability due to a tax return position that is found to be too aggressive. The penalty is avoided if there is *substantial authority* for the position, or if the position is disclosed adequately on the tax return. The penalty equals the greater of $1,000 or one-half of the tax preparer's fee that is traceable to the aggressive position.

Unrelated business income. Income recognized by an *exempt organization* that is generated from activities not related to the exempt purpose of the entity. For instance, the pharmacy located in a hospital may generate unrelated business income. § 511.

Unrelated business income tax. Levied on the *unrelated business income* of an *exempt organization.*

U.S.-owned foreign corporation. A *foreign corporation* in which 50 percent or more of the total combined voting power or total value of the stock of the corporation is held directly or indirectly by U.S. persons. A U.S. corporation is treated as a U.S.-owned foreign corporation if the *dividend* or interest income it pays is classified as foreign source under § 861.

U.S. real property interest. Any direct interest in real property situated in the United States and any interest in a *domestic corporation* (other than solely as a creditor) unless the taxpayer can establish that a domestic corporation was not a U.S. real property holding corporation during the five-year period ending on the date of disposition of such interest (the base period). See *FIRPTA.*

U.S. shareholder. For purposes of classification of an entity as a *controlled foreign corporation,* a U.S. person who owns, or is considered to own, 10 percent or more of the total combined voting power of all classes of voting stock of a foreign corporation. Stock owned directly, indirectly, and constructively is counted for this purpose.

U.S.-source income. Generally, income taxed by the United States, regardless of the citizenship or residence of its creator. Examples include income from sales of U.S. real estate and *dividends* from U.S. corporations.

U.S. Tax Court. See *Tax Court.*

U.S. trade or business. A set of activities that is carried on in a regular, continuous, and substantial manner. A non-U.S. taxpayer is subject to U.S. tax on the *taxable income* that is *effectively connected* with a U.S. trade or business.

Use tax. A *sales tax* that is collectible by the seller where the purchaser is domiciled in a different state.

USSC. An abbreviation for the U.S. *Supreme Court,* used in citing court opinions.

USTC. Published by Commerce Clearing House (*CCH*), *U.S. Tax Cases* contain all of the Federal tax decisions issued by the U.S. *District Courts,* U.S. *Court of Federal Claims,* U.S. *Courts of Appeals,* and the U.S. *Supreme Court.*

V

Valuation allowance. Under *ASC 740 (SFAS 109),* a tax-related item is reported for book purposes only when it is more likely than not that the item actually will be realized. When the "more likely than not" test is failed, a contra-asset account is created to offset some or all of the related *deferred tax asset.* For instance, if the entity projects that it will not be able to use all of its *net operating loss* carryforward due to a lack of future taxable income, a valuation allowance is created to reduce the net *deferred tax asset* that corresponds to the carryforward. If income projections later change and it appears that the carryforward will be used, the valuation allowance is reversed or "released." Creation of a valuation allowance usually increases the *current tax expense* and thereby reduces current book income, and its release often increases book income in the later reporting period.

Value. See *fair market value.*

Vested. Absolute and complete. If, for example, a person holds a vested interest in property, such interest cannot be taken away or otherwise defeated.

Voluntary revocation. The owners of a majority of shares in an *S corporation* elect to terminate the S status of the entity, as of a specified date. The day on which the revocation is effective is the first day of the corporation's C tax year.

Voting trust. A *trust* that holds the voting rights to stock in a corporation. It is a useful device when a majority of the shareholders in a corporation cannot agree on corporate policy.

W

W–2 wages. The *domestic production activities deduction (DPAD)* cannot exceed 50 percent of the manufacturer's W–2 wages paid for the year. Several methods can be used to calculate the W–2 wages. The employee's work must be involved in the production process. § 199(b)(2).

Wash sale. A loss from the sale of stock or *securities* that is disallowed because the taxpayer has, within 30 days before or after the sale, acquired stock or securities substantially identical to those sold. § 1091.

Water's edge election. A limitation on the worldwide scope of the *unitary theory.* If a corporate water's edge election is in effect, the state can consider in the *apportionment* procedure only the activities that occur within the boundaries of the United States.

WESTLAW. An online database system, produced by the West Group, through which a tax researcher can obtain access to the *Internal Revenue Code, Regulations,* administrative rulings, and court case opinions.

Wherewithal to pay. A concept of tax equity that delays the recognition of gain on a transaction until the taxpayer has received means by which to pay the tax. The *installment method,* whereunder gain is taxed proportionately as installment proceeds are received, embodies the wherewithal to pay concept. See also *involuntary conversion* and *like-kind exchange.*

Whistleblower program. An IRS initiative that offers special rewards to informants who provide evidence regarding tax evasion activities of businesses or high-income individuals. More than $2 million of tax, interest, and penalty must be at stake. The reward can reach 30 percent of the tax recovery that is attributable to the whistleblower's information.

Writ of Certiorari. See *certiorari.*

Appendix D-1

Table of Code Sections Cited

[See Title 26 U.S.C.A.]

Appendix D-2

Table of Regulations Cited

Temporary Treasury Regulations

Treasury Regulations

Treasury Regulations

Treasury Regulations

Treasury Regulations

Appendix D-3

Table of Revenue Procedures and Revenue Rulings Cited

Appendix E

Table of Cases Cited

H

I

J

K

L

M

N

O

P

Q

R

S

T

U

V

W

Z

Index

A

B

C

D

E

G

H

I

J

K

L

M

N

O

P

Q

R

S

T

U

V

W

sur

le

DONNEES sur le QUEBEC

R. BOILY
A. DUBUC
F.M. GAGNON
M. RIOUX

et la collaboration de
j.l. trudeau

1974
LES PRESSES DE L'UNIVERSITÉ DE MONTRÉAL
C.P. 6128, Montréal 101, Canada

ISBN 0 8405 0278 8
DÉPÔT LÉGAL, 4e TRIMESTRE 1974 — BIBLIOTHÈQUE NATIONALE DU QUÉBEC

Tous droits de reproduction, d'adaptation ou de traduction réservés

AVANT-PROPOS DE LA DEUXIEME EDITION

QUEBEC, HIER ET AUJOURD'HUI était un ensemble de documents sonores et écrits relativement bien intégrés les uns aux autres. Le document écrit s'est rapidement épuisé alors même que la demande pour l'ensemble continue à s'exprimer. Sur les entrefaits, les résultats du recensement de 1971 commencèrent à sortir, de même que de nombreuses autres données. Notre bibliographie devenait de mois en mois davantage périmée avec la parution d'ouvrages importants. Il nous était impossible de consentir à une simple ré-impression car il était indispensable de mettre à date plusieurs des données et de corriger quelques erreurs qui s'étaient glissées dans la première parution. A la lecture du premier document, il nous était apparu qu'une présentation graphique plus élaborée pourrait permettre, davantage que des tableaux statistiques brutalement étalés, une lecture plus percutante de certains phénomènes.

DONNEES SUR LE QUEBEC est une publication en bonne et due forme, davantage soignée, profitant de l'expérience de la première parution. On y trouvera davantage d'illustrations graphiques, moins de tableaux statistiques. La plupart des tableaux que nous avons conservés ont été mis à jour. Par contre, certaines données ont été soustraites, ou bien parce qu'elles étaient périmées ou bien parce que leur représentation, particulièrement par des cartes géographiques, n'avaient pas une qualité satisfaisante.

Cette mise à jour et cette présentation nouvelle ont entraîné des modifications nombreuses; la plus importante est sans doute l'élimination du chapitre cinq qui a entraîné la numérotation nouvelle de tous les chapitres subséquents. Ces modifications ont détruit la concordance qui rattachait la première parution au document sonore; celui-ci, en effet, réfère constamment à celle-là. Poussés par les besoins des étudiants qui, partout au Québec et ailleurs au Canada, voire même à l'étranger, se procuraient le document sonore, nous n'avions pas le temps de reprendre les enregistrements pour rétablir cette correspondance.

Toutefois, nous avons présenté une double table des matières qui permet, à celui qui cherche une référence mentionnée au document sonore, de retrouver immédiatement le lieu de sa présentation dans Données sur le Québec.

Les auteurs

DONNEES SUR LE QUEBEC

IDEE: Service d'éducation permanente

RESPONSABILITE PEDAGOGIQUE: Service d'éducation permanente
Odette Leroux
Anne Bélanger-Archambault

PRODUCTION DU CAHIER: Service d'éducation permanente

CONCEPTION GRAPHIQUE: Jacques Léonard

MONTAGE: Serge Marin et Michel Varin

QUEBEC: HIER ET AUJOURD'HUI

Données sur le Québec fait partie d'un ensemble comprenant, en outre, 24 documents sonores produits par le Centre audio-visuel de l'Université de Montréal, sous le titre "Québec: hier et aujourd'hui". Ces documents sonores ont fait l'objet d'une diffusion sur les ondes FM de Radio-Canada à l'hiver 1973. Ils sont produits en cassettes pour l'usage de l'enseignement, disponibles au Centre audio-visuel.

DOCUMENTS SONORES

PRODUCTION: Centre audio-visuel

REALISATION: Jean-Claude Thouin
Thérèse Thouin

REGIE TECHNIQUE: Claude Gareau

AVERTISSEMENT AU LECTEUR

1- Explication des symboles :

• •	: donnée non disponible
—	: donnée négligeable ou nulle
Ⓖ	: référence au glossaire, par ordre alphabétique
(N)	: note expliquée au bas du tableau
■	: signifie généralement des données sur le Québec
▨	: signifie généralement des données sur l'Ontario
▒	: signifie généralement des données sur le Canada

2- Pourcentage

La somme des pourcentages ne donne pas nécessairement un total de cent car les chiffres sont arrondis.

DONNEES SUR LE QUEBEC

En présentant ces données sur le Québec, le Service d'éducation permanente veut poursuivre sous une nouvelle forme des activités déjà anciennes d'enseignement interdisciplinaire.

En 1964 déjà, le Service d'éducation permanente offrait des cours d'abord, puis bientôt des cycles de cours et des programmes sur les civilisations. L'enseignement des civilisations française, africaine, latino-américaine fournit à des équipes d'universitaires l'occasion d'expérimenter une méthodologie qui vise à éviter la pure juxtaposition des disciplines et à dégager l'interaction des dimensions économique, politique, sociale et culturelle d'une société à un moment particulier de son développement.

En 1968, le Service d'éducation permanente voulut procéder de la même manière à l'étude de la société québécoise, des origines à nos jours. C'est d'un cycle de cours offert pendant quatre ans que devait naître le Certificat d'études québécoises.

Le cours CIVQ 330-AV nous permet aujourd'hui d'utiliser un ensemble multi-media dans cette recherche et cet enseignement interdisciplinaire. Nous espérons atteindre ainsi un public plus nombreux et l'aider à mieux saisir la diversité et la complexité de la réalité québécoise.

Le directeur du Service d'éducation permanente,

Gaëtan Daoust
Montréal, avril 1974

ENSEIGNEMENT INDIVIDUALISE

La difficulté de l'enseignement individualisé consiste en l'intégration des media utilisés. Ainsi, ce cours de civilisation québécoise : Québec, hier et aujourd'hui - CIVQ 330-AV, est la cinquième expérience menée par le Centre audio-visuel pour le compte de divers départements désireux de rejoindre aussi bien des étudiants externes que des étudiants réguliers.

Les quatre professeurs de ce cours multidisciplinaire expliquent plus loin le rôle des documents audio et de ce document scripto dans la présentation de la matière. A chaque exploitation pédagogique à venir, les responsables de l'Education permanente ou des organismes qui utilisent cette entité pédagogique compléteront éventuellement l'information de base par des séminaires, conférences ou des visionnements et suivront le travail de chaque étudiant par des travaux dirigés ou des consultations ad hoc.

La formule de ce type d'enseignement individualisé se précise et de plus en plus on dissocie la production des documents fondamentaux conçus en fonction des exigences de la matière elle-même de l'exploitation pédagogique élaborée en fonction des besoins particuliers de groupes d'étudiants bien identifiés.

Plus encore que les autres, ce cours est une oeuvre d'équipe qui groupe des professeurs de divers départements, de nombreux invités, des spécialistes de l'Education permanente, de la Liste externe de la Faculté des arts et sciences, du Bureau de l'information et du Centre audio-visuel.

Le directeur du Centre audio-visuel,

Jean Cloutier
Montréal, avril 1974

NOTES BIOGRAPHIQUES DES PROFESSEURS

Robert BOILY

Licencié en droit de la Faculté de droit de l'Université de Montréal, diplômes de l'Institut d'études politiques de Paris et de la Faculté de droit de l'Université de Paris.

Professeur au Département de science politique de l'Université de Montréal depuis 1962, dont il est aujourd'hui le directeur.

Domaine d'enseignement et de recherches : l'analyse comparée des systèmes politiques, les partis et le phénomène électoral. Depuis plusieurs années a consacré une majeure partie de son intérêt en ces domaines à l'étude du Québec. Quelques publications portant sur les élites politiques du Québec, la réforme électorale, la sociologie électorale de la région de Montréal sont nées de ces recherches sur le Québec.

A participé aussi depuis plusieurs années à de nombreuses expériences dans l'enseignement des adultes ou d'introduction à la politique en milieu syndical.

Membre de la direction de la revue "Maintenant".

Alfred DUBUC

Né à Chicoutimi le 7 février 1929. A fait ses études secondaires au Collège Jean-de-Brébeuf de Montréal. Licencié en droit de l'Université de Montréal en 1953, en sciences politique et sociale de l'Universitéde Louvain (Belgique) en 1957, docteur ès lettres de la Sorbonne (Université de Paris), en 1969.

A enseigné l'histoire économique et sociale au Département de sciences économiques de l'Université de Montréal de 1959 à 1969 et au Département d'histoire de l'Université du Québec à Montréal depuis 1969, dont il a été directeur de 1970 à 1972.

Ses recherches et ses publications portent principalement sur les problèmes de développement économique et social et, plus particulièrement, sur l'histoire industrielle, sur la méthodologie et l'enseignement de l'histoire.

François-Marc GAGNON

Né le 18 juin 1935, détient une maîtrise en philosophie (Université de Montréal) et un doctorat en histoire de l'art (Sòrbonne). Il a dirigé la Section d'histoire de l'art du Département d'histoire de l'Université de Montréal et enseigne en histoire de l'art canadien et contemporain. Son mémoire de doctorat a été publié sous le titre : "Jean Dubuffet - aux sources de la figuration humaine", P.U.M., 1972. Il est l'auteur de quelques monographies sur des peintres et des sculpteurs québécois. Il dirige une recherche subventionnée par le Ministère de l'éducation du Québec et le Conseil des Arts du Canada sur la vie et l'oeuvre du peintre Paul-Emile Borduas.

Marcel RIOUX

Né à Amqui (Québec) le 22 janvier 1919; a fait ses études secondaires au Séminaire de Rimouski et au Collège de Philosophie d'Ottawa; ses études supérieures aux universités de Montréal et de Paris. Il a été attaché au Musée National du Canada (1947-1959) et a enseigné à l'Université Carleton d'Ottawa (1959-1961) et à l'Université de Montréal depuis 1961. Il a mérité la médaille de l'Association Canadienne-française pour l'avancement des sciences en 1956.

Publications :

Livres - La culture de l'Ile verte, 1955, Musée National.
- Belle-Anse, 1958, Musée National.
- La société canadienne-française, 1964.
- La question du Québec, 1969.
- Rapport de la Commission d'Enquête sur l'Enseignement des Arts, (3 vols), 1969.
- Les Québécois, Paris, Seuil, 1974.

Articles : une cinquantaine d'articles au Canada, France, Etats-Unis, Belgique, etc ...

INTRODUCTION GENERALE

Le document que nous présentons est un outil que l'on devra utiliser dans le cadre d'une entreprise d'éducation qui se veut interdisciplinaire et multiforme; le thème général en est : le Québec d'aujourd'hui.

Les signataires de cette introduction ont consacré une bonne partie de leur carrière à des recherches sur le Québec, soit en histoire économique, en science politique, en histoire de l'art ou en sociologie. Ensemble, ils se sont engagés dans une expérience dans laquelle ces disciplines variées se confrontent les unes aux autres à l'occasion des réponses qu'ils tentent d'apporter aux questions que se posent les Québécois sur leur propre société et sur la société contemporaine en général.

A cette fin, ils ont élaboré deux instruments principaux : des documents sonores et le document écrit que voici. Bien que ne remplissant pas les mêmes fonctions et se situant à des niveaux différents de réalité, ces deux outils sont complémentaires et devront être tous deux utilisés si l'on veut connaître et interpréter des aspects essentiels du Québec d'aujourd'hui.

Documents sonores

Les vingt-quatre documents sonores que comprend notre entreprise ont été conçus, non en fonction des questions auxquelles s'attachent ordinairement nos disciplines universitaires, mais pour cerner les problèmes que se posent quotidiennement les Québécois au sujet de leur société, de leur culture et d'eux-mêmes. Bien que chacune de ces questions soit vaste et mette en cause des phénomènes multiples, la tradition universitaire les a séparées les unes des autres dans ses programmes d'études et ses recherches. Nous avons tenté, au contraire,de projeter sur ces interrogations un éclairage multidisciplinaire. Au lieu de vouloir simplifier les questions et les réponses, nous avons voulu, au contraire, essayer de montrer que rien n'est aussi simple que certains hommes politiques et certains spécialistes veulent le faire croire. Aussi, chaque question que les Québécois se posent, nous avons essayé de la replacer dans un contexte plus global - économique - politique - socio-culturel - pour montrer comment elle pourra être éventuellement résolue.

L'intention de l'interdisciplinarité ne doit cependant pas être confondue avec un confusionnisme qui se contenterait de décréter que tout est dans tout et inversement. L'orientation théorique qui nous est commune nous commande de considérer qu'en dernière instance ce sont les phénomènes économiques entre les individus et les groupes qui, à leur tour, vont influer sur la production symbolique de la société, c'est-à-dire sur les valeurs et les systèmes d'interprétation du monde. Il va sans dire que ces sous-systèmes - économique , politique et culturel - s'interinfluencent et agissent l'un sur l'autre. Dans les documents sonores nous avons voulu poser les questions dans l'ordre que sous-tend notre orientation théorique.

Nous commençons à nous poser les mêmes questions que le grand public se pose au sujet de l'économie du Québec. Est-ce une région sous-développée de l'Amérique du Nord? Le problème du chômage est-il plus grave qu'ailleurs? Comment interpréter le fait que le Québec se pose des questions au sujet de son économie alors qu'aux Etats-Unis, par exemple, on parle de plus en plus de la qualité de la vie, des malaises socio-culturels?

Ce qui nous amène à parler du problème de la crise de l'autorité dans les sociétés modernes et au Québec, plus particulièrement. Quel est le rôle de l'Etat dans cette conjoncture? Pourquoi tant de contestations et de violence? La participation des citoyens aux prises de décisions est-elle la solution à tous ces problèmes? Et les jeunes, que veulent-ils?

Dans une dernière série de documents sonores, nous discutons ensuite de culture québécoise, de ses valeurs et de ses finalités. Est-elle encore viable? Et le joual? Et l'art populaire? Notre système d'éducation est-il bien adapté à une société en transition?

En conclusion à toutes ces interrogations sur l'économie, la politique et le culturel, nous nous posons des questions sur l'identité québécoise, la minorité anglophone du Québec et l'avenir de l'homme québécois.

Documents écrits

Les documents sonores partent des interrogations des Québécois eux-mêmes; ils tentent d'y répondre en les éclairant de diverses considérations et en insistant sur le fait que,dans un monde en mutation profonde, il ne saurait y avoir de réponse simple et catégorique. Tout au plus des avenues de recherches et de réflexions.

Les documents écrits qui accompagnent ces discussions veulent fournir un certain nombre de faits dont on doit tenir compte si l'on veut cerner la réalité québécoise. Nous avons organisé ces données et ces statistiques en trois grandes catégories.

1- Quelles sont les ressources naturelles et humaines du Québec? Sur quoi peut-il compter pour se développer? Ses citoyens sont-ils en possession des techniques acquises dans les processus d'éducation et qui sont nécessaires à toute vie industrielle et économique.

2- Quel est l'état de l'économie québécoise? Sa production et son revenu? Son épargne et ses investissements? Présente-t-elle des faiblesses? Dans quels secteurs et pourquoi?

3- Enfin, une dernière catégorie de documents fournit des renseignements sur l'Etat québécois, son fonctionnement, ses priorités et la place qu'il occupe dans les structures de pouvoir. Quelle répartition fait-il des taxes qu'il recueille de ses citoyens et des entreprises? Vers l'éducation? La sécurité sociale? Comment la transmission de l'information se fait-elle?

Nous avons essayé de relier les deux séries de documents afin d'en permettre une utilisation plus efficace. On trouvera dans les pages qui suivent une analyse de contenu des documents écrits, d'autre part, les documents sonores renvoient, autant que faire se peut, aux documents colligés ici.

Nous aurons atteint notre but si nous avons réussi à sensibiliser les usagers de ces documents à la complexité des situations auxquelles doit faire face le Québécois, comme tout homme contemporain, du fait que nos problèmes sont en grande partie ceux des autres sociétés et à la certitude que nous avons que, si des solutions doivent être élaborées, ce devra être par la participation du plus grand nombre à l'information et à la prise de décision. La vie publique doit devenir l'affaire de tout le monde.

Robert Boily
Alfred Dubuc
François-Marc Gagnon
Marcel Rioux

avril 1974

SOMMAIRE

INTRODUCTION

Dans cette première partie, le lecteur trouvera un premier visage du Québec, le moins sujet à interprétation pourrait-on dire, son visage physique tel que la géographie nous le révèle et sa population, objet des études du démographe : donc des cartes géographiques, des statistiques sur l'évolution de la population, des pyramides d'âge ... Mais qu'il s'arrête un peu plus au choix de statistiques et de tableaux que nous lui proposons, il lui apparaîtra aussitôt que c'est d'une terre habitée donc transformée que nous voulons lui parler. Si près de ses sources que nous la prenions, à ras de terre pour ainsi dire, et dans les données brutes des chiffres de sa population, la nature québécoise au double sens de son paysage et du tempérament de ses habitants - nous paraît déjà marquée par une culture québécoise, comme à un niveau différent de son économie reflète une politique québécoise, entendue au sens le plus large.

Ainsi, ce n'est donc pas seulement la géographie physique du Québec qui va vous retenir ici, mais une géographie marquée par la présence de l'homme : le Québec déjà singulièrement marqué par une histoire dont les traces partout visibles déterminent son visage dans un sens déjà irréversible.

A ce visage géographique du Québec vient se superposer un visage économique et administratif qui, relevant des décisions de l'homme, achève de lui donner sa forme et donc sa culture entendue au sens d'une prise en charge de son environnement et du conditionnement de son esprit.

Des remarques analogues s'appliquent à sa population. La population que nous étudions est une population répartie, distribuée sur le territoire. Après avoir été longtemps à majorité rurale, la population du Québec est maintenant surtout urbaine. Même ses taux de natalité, de mortalité et d'accroissement naturel reflètent une tentative de s'adapter aux conditions économiques vécues. Cette population est également répartie selon l'origine ethnique et la langue maternelle et se définit enfin par strates sociales. Une fois de plus donc, nous retrouvons la nature étroitement mêlée à la culture, la donnée brute déjà déterminée.

1.1 Divisions géographiques des données statistiques

1.1.a LE TERRITOIRE DU QUEBEC ET LA REPARTITION DE SA POPULATION

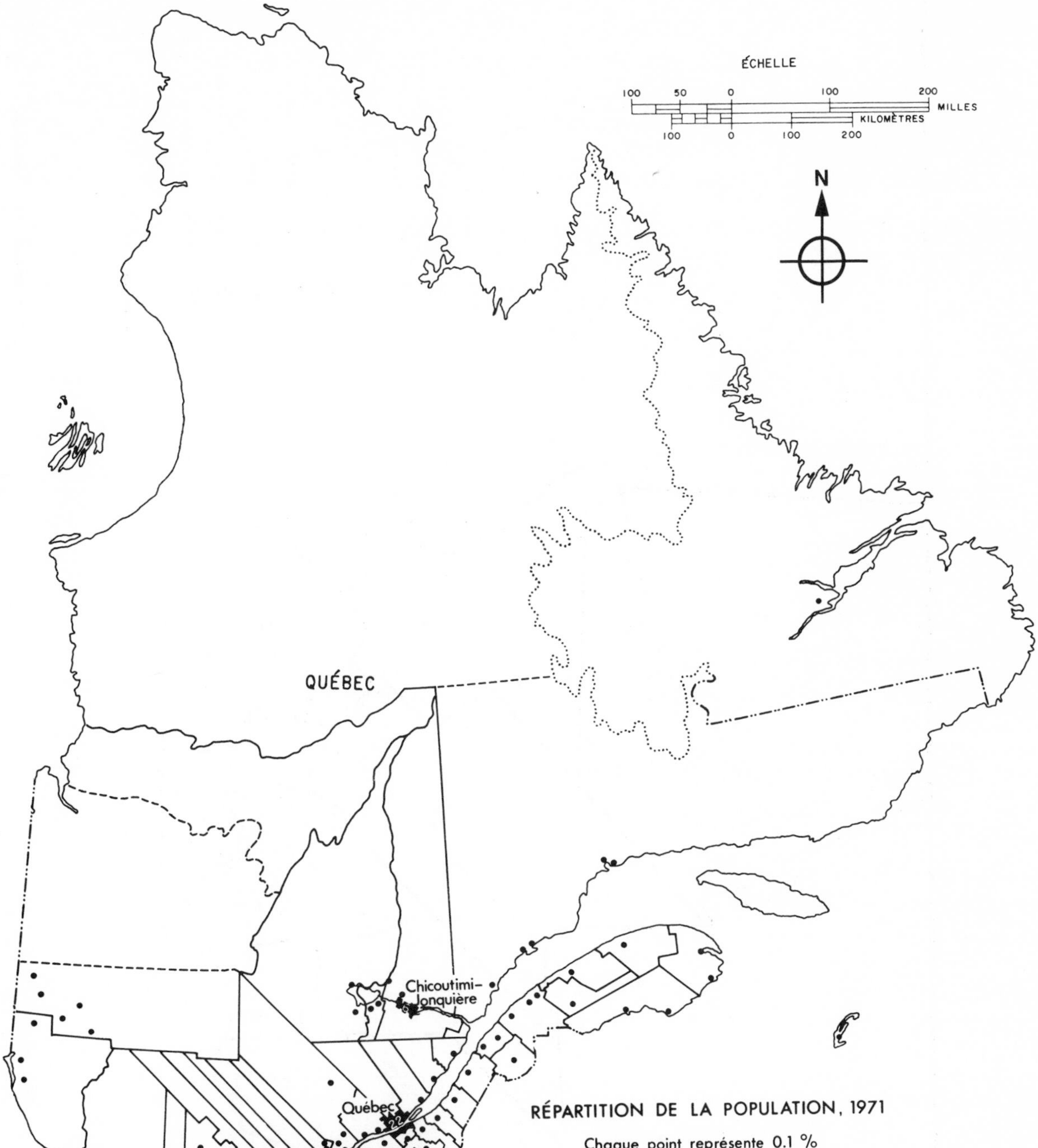

ÉCHELLE

100 50 0 100 200 MILLES

KILOMÈTRES 100 0 100 200

N

QUÉBEC

Chicoutimi-Jonquière

Québec

22

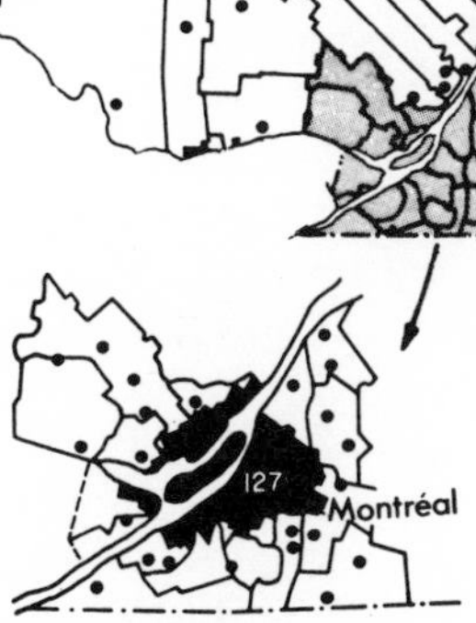

127

Montréal

RÉPARTITION DE LA POPULATION, 1971

Chaque point représente 0.1 % de la population totale du Canada.

EXPLICATION

La population est représentée sur la présente carte par des points dont chacun équivaut à 21,568 personnes. Les divisions territoriales de la carte sont les divisions de recensement et les régions métropolitaines de recensement; dans ce dernier cas la population est indiquée par un chiffre correspondant au nombre de points. La somme des points et des chiffres dans un territoire donné représente le pourcentage de la population du Canada pour ce territoire.

La population des divisions de recensement a été extrapolée de telle façon qu'un point placé sur une limite de division de recensement signifie que les 21,568 personnes sont en partie dans les deux divisions. Là où la densité de la population est faible, un point peut représenter le centre de population répartie sur une grande étendue. Ainsi, la carte donne une représentation exacte de la population, mais la répartition est plus généralisée dans les régions où la population est clairsemée.

RECENSEMENT DU CANADA, 1971

1.1 Divisions géographiques des données statistiques

1.1.b REGIONS ECONOMIQUES, QUEBEC

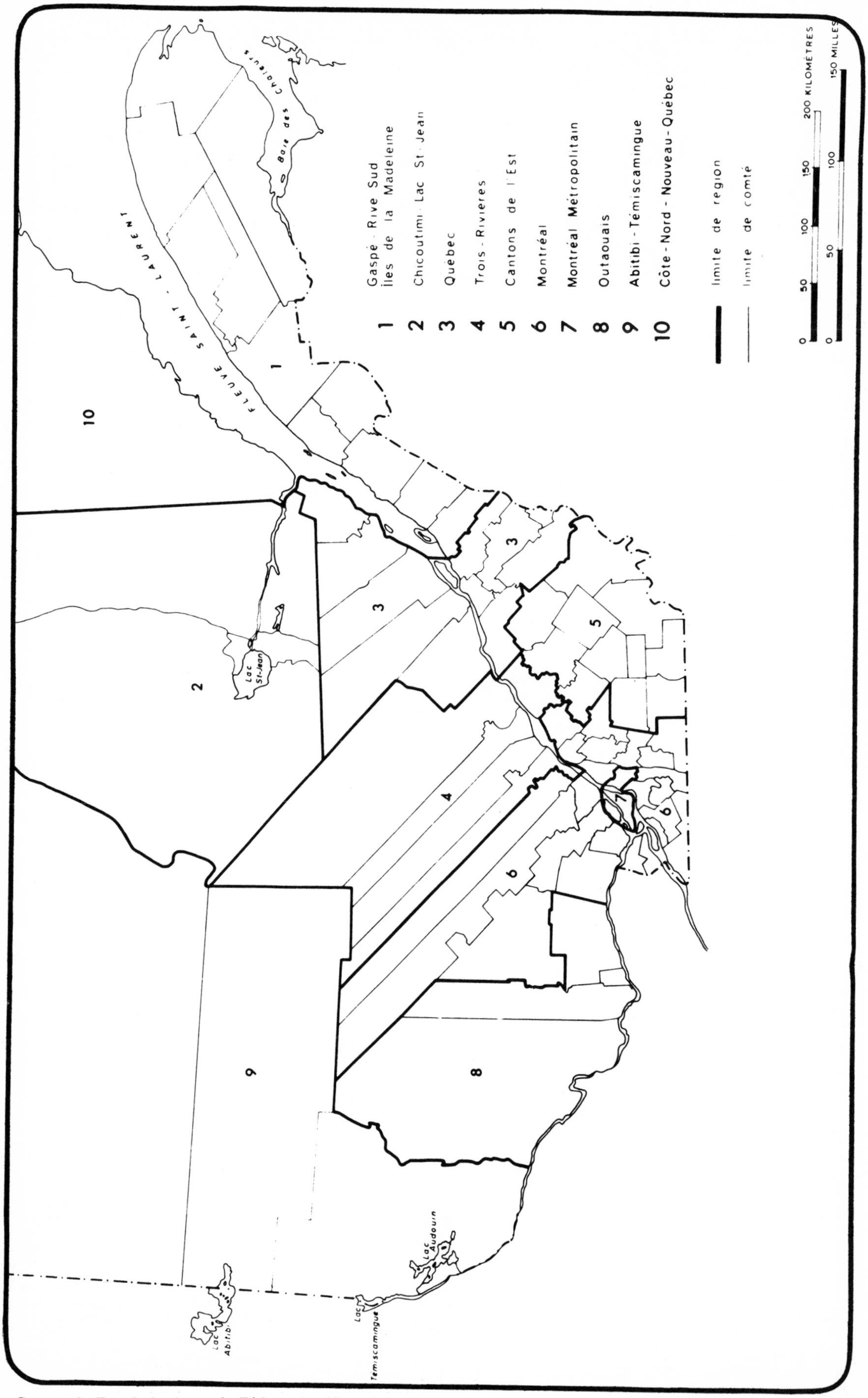

1 Gaspé - Rive Sud Îles de la Madeleine
2 Chicoutimi - Lac St-Jean
3 Québec
4 Trois-Rivières
5 Cantons de l'Est
6 Montréal
7 Montréal Métropolitain
8 Outaouais
9 Abitibi - Témiscamingue
10 Côte-Nord - Nouveau-Québec

limite de région
limite de comté

Source: *Centre de Psychologie et de Pédagogie,* Montréal, 1969.

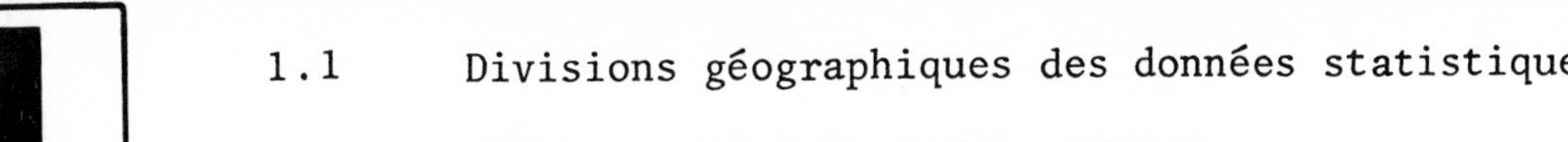

1.1 Divisions géographiques des données statistiques

1.1.c REGIONS ADMINISTRATIVES, QUEBEC

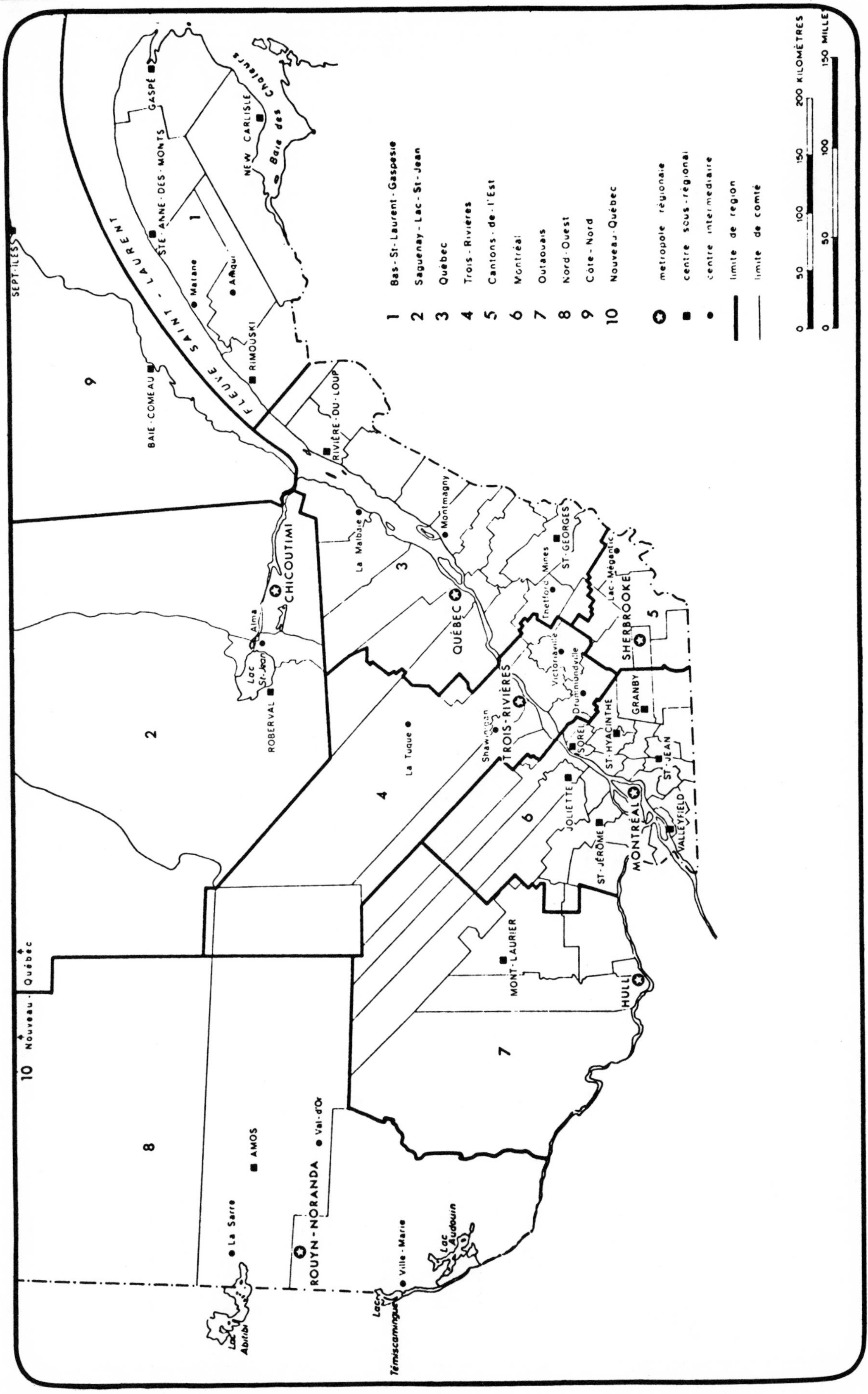

1 Bas-St-Laurent-Gaspésie
2 Saguenay-Lac-St-Jean
3 Québec
4 Trois-Rivières
5 Cantons-de-l'Est
6 Montréal
7 Outaouais
8 Nord-Ouest
9 Côte-Nord
10 Nouveau-Québec

métropole régionale
centre sous-régional
centre intermédiaire
limite de région
limite de comté

Source: *Centre de Psychologie et de Pédagogie*, Montréal, 1969.

1.2 Géographie régionale

1.2.a RESSOURCES NATURELLES, PAR REGIONS ADMINISTRATIVES, QUEBEC, ANNEES CHOISIES

Région	Ventes agricoles 1965		Pêche commerciale 1970		Forêt 1968-1969		Mines 1969			Energie 1969	
	valeur en $	% province	valeur en $ au débarquement	% province	volume de coupe en pi.³	% province	principaux gisements	expéditions valeur en $	employés	équipement	production Kilowatts ou barils/jour
Bas-St-Laurent-Gaspésie	13,732,090	3.6	9,570,641	86.0	71,954,373	12.0	calcaire cuivre sable tourbe total	. . . . . . 829,215 40,155,000	1,083	2 centrales hydroélectriques 3 centrales thermiques	10,650 KWH 47,797 KWH
Saguenay-Lac-St-Jean	25,847,983	4.1	–	–	124,601,152	20.0	calcaire cuivre granit or sable tourbe total	466,202 81,872,975 1,366,202 . . 365,536 . . 85,162,615	2,307	18 centrales hydroélectriques	2,870,247 KWH
Québec	94,774,570	24.6	–	..	121,139,800	12.3	amiante calcaire granit grès sable talc tourbe total	86,924,994 4,117,166 2,305,209 515,247 873,877 . . 3,144,074 98,016,795	5,567	–	–
Trois-Rivières	58,630,540	15.2	–	–	64,194,803 terres publiques	10.4	amiante calcaire granit grès sable tourbe total	. . 967,986 785,316 . . 774,919 . . 3,601,576	232	12 centrales hydroélectriques 3 centrales thermiques 1 centrale nucléaire	1,572,825 KWH 13,200 KWH 250,000 KWH
Cantons-de-l'Est	29,336,860	7.6	–	–	27,017,470	–	amiante calcaire cuivre feldspath et quartz granit sable tourbe total	. . . . 2,676,763 150,722 . . 82,959,536	2,574	12 centrales hydroélectriques 1 centrale thermique	34,140 KWH 4,000 KWH

Montréal	151,427,530	39.4	152,640	1.7	57,336,850		magnésite columbium brucite et autres calcaire feldspath et quartz granit sable total	 5,573,564 25,735,152 4,045,315 1,641,585 2,028,849 39,024,465	1,870	10 centrales hydroélectriques 1 centrale thermique 4 aléoducs 6 raffineries 2 gazoducs	 2,450,980 KWH 600,000 KWH 676,000 b/j (N) 460,600 b/j 242,000,000 pieds3/jour
Outaouais	11,814,850	3.1	–	–	92,399,563		calcaire cuivre et nickel feldspath et quartz fer granit sable total	1,726,846 – 602,445 . . 463,984 399,083 19,556,090	626	14 centrales hydroélectriques 1 gazoduc 1 pipeline	 1,034,905 KWH – 54,000 b/j
Nord-Ouest	8,601,960	2.2	103,411	1.1	123,772,705	. .	cuivre granit molybdène or sable zinc total	87,723,323 . . 6,459,094 23,663,046 – 53,426,222 171,305,725	6,103	5 centrales hydroélectriques 1 gazoduc	 524,640 . .
Côte-Nord	–	–	2,100,000	9.2	1,017,059	. .	fer granit silice total	416,193,438 582,335	. .	9 centrales hydroélectriques La centrale de Churchill fournira à elle seule 5,225,000 KWH	 7,070,000 KWH
Nouveau-Québec	–	–	–	–	–	. .	Le potentiel minier du Nouveau-Québec est énorme mais inexploité. On y trouve entre autres de l'amiante, du cuivre et du nickel.			On compte développer le potentiel hydroélectrique de la Baie James.	

Note: b/j: barils par jour.

Source: *Traits généraux de la région administrative no 1, 2, 3, 4, 5, 6, 7, 8, 9 et 10* (9 publications), Ministère de l'Industrie et du Commerce, Québec, 1972.

1.2 Géographie régionale

1.2.b METROPOLES ET SUPERFICIES, REGIONS ADMINISTRATIVES, QUEBEC 1970

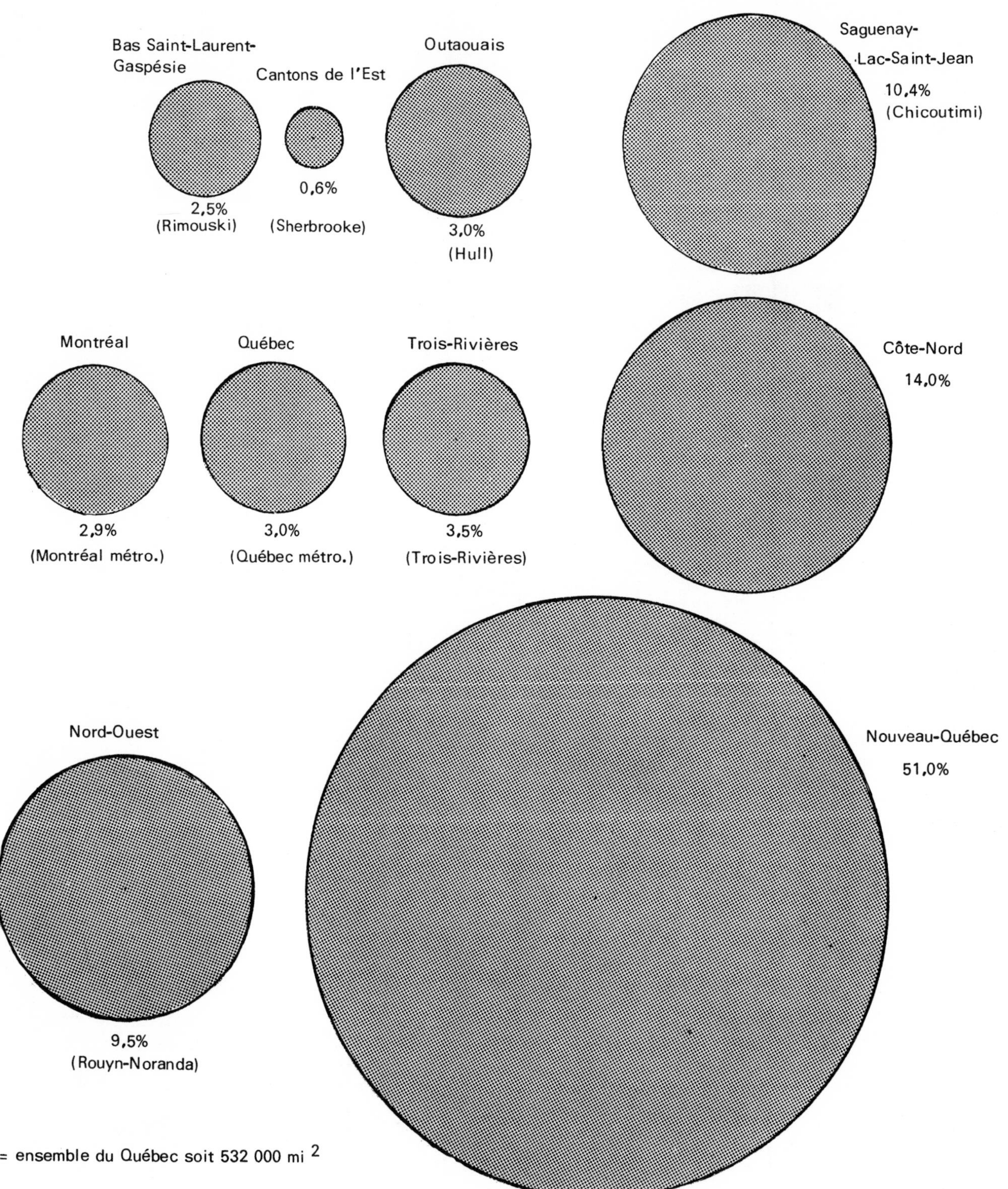

Source: *Traits généraux de la région administrative no 1, 2, 3, 4, 5, 6, 7, 8, 9, 10, (9 publications)*, Ministère de l'Industrie et du Commerce, Québec, 1972.

2.1 Répartition de la population

2.1.a QUEBEC, ONTARIO, CANADA, 1851-1971, ANNEES DE RECENSEMENT

	QUEBEC	ONTARIO	CANADA
	population	population	population
1851	890,261	952,004	2,436,297
1861	1,111,566	1,396,091	3,229,633
1871	1,191,516	1,620,851	3,689,257
1881	1,359,027	1,926,922	4,324,810
1891	1,488,535	2,114,321	4,833,239
1901	1,648,898	2,182,947	5,371,315
1911	2,005,776	2,527,292	7,206,643
1921	2,360,510	2,933,662	8,787,949
1931	2,874,662	3,431,683	10,376,786
1941	3,331,822	3,787,655	11,506,655
1951	4,055,681	4,597,542	14,009,429
1961	5,259,211	6,236,092	18,238,247
1971	6,027,764	7,703,106	21,568,311

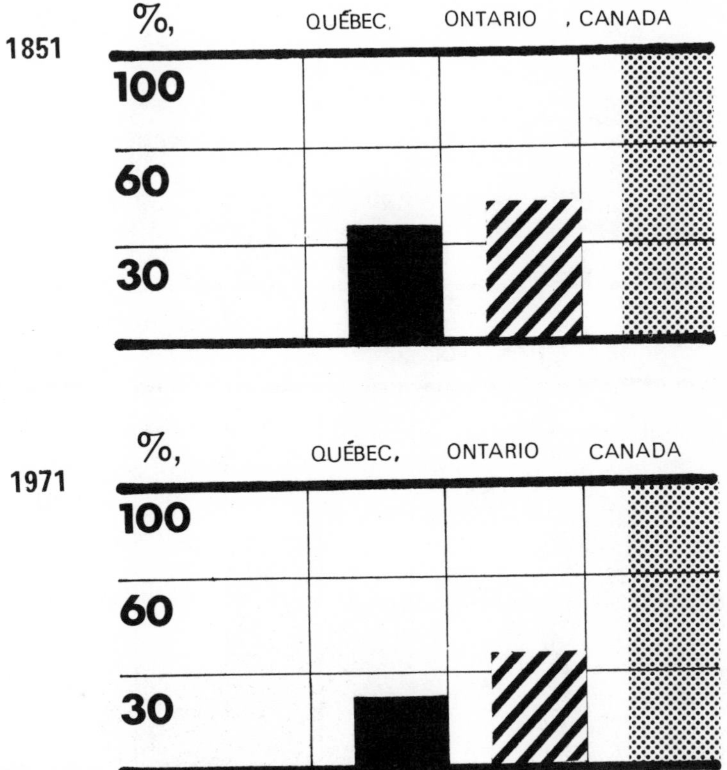

Sources: Urquhart et Buckley, *Historical Statistics of Canada,* Cambridge University Press, Cambridge, 1965.

Statistique Canada, Division du Recensement C. D. et S., Ottawa, 1972.

2.1 Répartition de la population

2.1.b PAR REGIONS ADMINISTRATIVES, QUEBEC, 1961-1966-1970

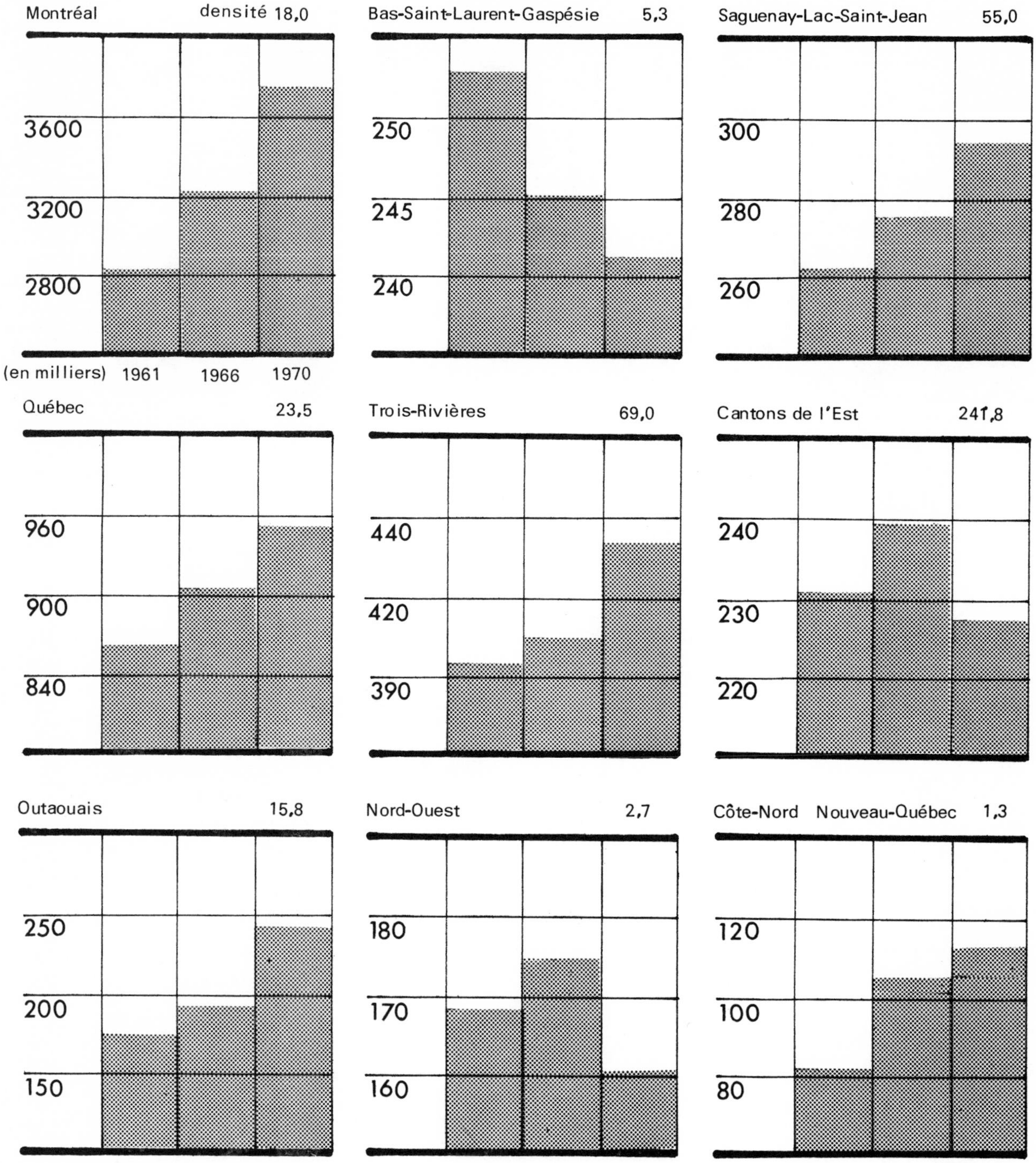

Montréal densité 18,0
3600
3200
2800
(en milliers) 1961 1966 1970

Bas-Saint-Laurent-Gaspésie 5,3
250
245
240

Saguenay-Lac-Saint-Jean 55,0
300
280
260

Québec 23,5
960
900
840

Trois-Rivières 69,0
440
420
390

Cantons de l'Est 241,8
240
230
220

Outaouais 15,8
250
200
150

Nord-Ouest 2,7
180
170
160

Côte-Nord Nouveau-Québec 1,3
120
100
80

ensemble du Québec: 5 259 211 - 5 780 845 - 6 371 032 10,0

Sources: Document préparé par Action Sociale Jeunesse, Montréal, 1968.

Traits généraux de la région administrative no 1, 2, 3, 4, 5, 6, 7, 8, 9 et 10, (9 publications), Ministère de l'Industrie et du Commerce, Québec, 1972.

2.1 Répartition de la population

2.1.c VILLES DE 5 000 HABITANTS ET PLUS PAR REGIONS ADMINISTRATIVES, QUEBEC, 1er JUIN 1971

REGION ADMINISTRATIVE
villes par importance:population

Bas-St-Laurent-Gaspésie	
Rimouski	26,887
Gaspé	17,211
Matane	11,841
Mont-Joli	6,698
Ste-Anne-des-Monts	5,546
Percé	5,617
Saguenay-lac-St-Jean	
Chicoutimi	33,893
Jonquières	28,430
Alma	22,622
Arvida	18,448
Chicoutimi-Nord	14,086
Kenogami	10,970
Port-Alfred	9,228
Chibougamau	9,701
Roberval	8,330
Dolbeau	7,633
Bagotville	6,041
Québec	
Québec	186,088
Ste-Foy	68,385
Charlesbourg	33,443
Thetford-Mines	22,003
Lévis	16,597
Beauport	14,681
Sillery	13,932
Giffard	13,135
Lauzon	12,809
Rivière-du-Loup	12,760
Orsainville	12,520
Montmagny	12,432
Loretteville	11,644
Vanier	9,717
St-Romuald d'Etchemin	8,394
Ancienne-Lorette	8,304
St-Georges	7,554
Courville	6,222
St-Georges-Ouest	6,000
Donnaconna	5,940
Charny	5,175
Trois-Rivières	
Trois-Rivières	55,869
Drummondville	31,813
Cap-de-la-Madeleine	31,463
Shawinigan	27,792
Victoriaville	22,047
Grand-Mère	17,137
La Tuque	13,099
Drummondville-Sud	8,989
Bécancour	8,182
Trois-Rivières-Ouest	8,057
Plessisville	7,204
Cantons-de-l'Est	
Sherbrooke	80,711
Magog	13,281
Asbestos	9,749
Lac Mégantic	6,770
Coaticook	6,569
Windsor	6,023
Montréal	
Montréal	1,214,352
Laval	228,010
Longueuil	97,590
Montréal-Nord	89,139
Verdun	74,718
La Salle	72,912
St-Laurent	62,955
St-Léonard	52,040
Lachine	44,423
Pointe-aux-Trembles	35,567
Granby	34,385
Anjou	33,886
Pierrefonds	33,010
Valleyfield	30,173
Outremont	28,552
Pointe-Claire	27,303
St-Jérôme	26,524
Dollard-des-Ormeaux	25,217
St-Hyacinthe	24,562
Côte-St-Luc	24,375
Westmount	23,606
Brossard	23,452
St-Hubert	21,741
Mont-Royal	21,561
Dorval	20,469
Joliette	20,127
Boucherville	19,997
Repentigny	19,520
Beaconsfield	19,389
Sorel	19,347
St-Lambert	18,616
Chateauguay-Centre	17,942
Ste-Thérèse	17,175
Chateauguay	15,797
Greenfield Park	15,348
Laflèche	15,113
Ste-Scholastique	14,787
Beloeil	12,274
Cowansville	11,920
Tracy	11,842
Lachute	11,813
Chambly	11,469
Blainville	9,630
St-Eustache	9,479
Iberville	9,331
Terrebonne	9,212
Mascouche	8,812
Deux-Montagnes	8,631
La Prairie	8,309
Le Moyne	8,194
Beauharnois	8,121
Ste-Thérèse-Ouest	7,278
Hampstead	7,033
St-Pierre	6,801
Farnham	6,496
Montréal-Ouest	6,368
Dorion	6,209
Pincourt	5,899
St-Antoine	5,831
Mont-St-Hilaire	5,758
Ste-Agathe-des-Monts	5,532
Candiac	5,185
Montréal-Est	5,076
Outaouais	
Hull	63,580
Gatineau	22,321
Pointe-Gatineau	15,640
Mont-Laurier	8,240
Buckingham	7,304
Aylmer	7,198
Maniwaki	6,689
Nord-Ouest	
Rouyn	17,821
Val-d'Or	17,421
Noranda	10,741
Amos	6,984
Malartic	5,347
La Sarre	5,185
Côte-Nord	
Sept-Iles	24,320
Hauterive	13,181
Baie-Comeau	12,109
Nouveau-Québec	
Aucune ville n'a 5,000 habitants et plus	
Schefferville	3,450

Source: Statistique Canada, *Recensement du Canada 1971,* Bulletin provisoire, Ottawa, 1972.

2.1 Répartition de la population

2.1.d PAR COMTES ELECTORAUX, QUEBEC, 1965-1971, TOUTES LES ANNEES

Comté	1965	1966	1967	1968	1969	1970	1971
Abitibi	116 056	114 725	112 084	111 125	111 805	109 277	113 636
Argenteuil	31 404	31 200	30 062	29 929	29 981	29 301	30 980
Arthabaska	46 565	49 567	47 985	48 704	49 782	49 996	51 561
Bagot	20 734	22 968	21 579	21 326	21 909	21 907	23 718
Beauce	58 974	64 275	58 053	57 195	57 305	57 546	64 189
Beauharnois	49 366	51 942	49 920	50 706	51 454	51 346	51 968
Bellechasse	24 686	24 045	23 403	23 306	24 007	23 512	23 766
Berthier	26 327	27 035	25 837	25 902	26 104	25 982	27 325
Bonaventure	40 266	43 624	43 280	42 197	43 179	41 315	42 670
Brome	14 916	14 190	14 914	15 055	14 766	14 680	15 395
Chambly	171 756	190 464	186 517	199 667	218 284	221 592	232 499
Champlain	110 704	112 341	108 099	107 666	108 147	109 158	112 632
Charlevoix	29 623	31 049	30 898	30 056	29 903	29 878	30 454
Châteauguay	42 944	46 698	45 147	46 656	47 848	49 222	53 907
Chicoutimi	159 324	161 773	162 954	162 334	162 542	162 228	162 625
Compton	19 460	22 459	18 732	18 306	18 038	17 704	21 435
Deux-Montagnes	36 790	39 125	37 825	38 652	40 162	46 526	52 793
Dorchester	36 671	33 669	37 100	36 510	36 433	36 233	32 587
Drummond	58 738	63 281	59 563	58 675	58 799	58 627	63 366
Frontenac	30 895	28 848	28 026	27 639	27 503	26 915	27 406
Gaspé et Iles de la Madeleine	71 732	72 955	71 137	69 860	70 062	69 887	73 773
Hull et Gatineau	137 334	146 394	142 829	145 873	149 940	153 540	165 521
Huntingdon	13 835	16 421	15 209	15 032	14 846	13 731	16 058
Iberville	17 869	19 538	18 777	18 492	18 959	18 743	20 396
(G) Iles de Montréal et Jésus	2 167 344	2 119 266	2 287 873	2 313 461	2 307 695	2 333 265	2 180 179
Joliette	46 321	48 920	46 859	47 577	48 350	48 602	51 645
Kamouraska	26 991	26 593	25 961	25 660	25 688	25 246	26 371
Labelle	30 054	30 167	30 587	31 192	31 031	30 979	30 709
Lac-St-Jean	101 616	105 909	102 092	101 102	101 196	99 365	102 778
Laprairie	35 990	44 980	46 436	49 633	53 169	50 453	62 247
L'Assomption	47 074	49 839	50 250	51 172	53 257	57 426	62 427
Lévis	53 728	58 375	56 549	57 161	57 978	58 784	63 126
L'Islet	23 603	24 382	23 489	23 022	22 884	22 605	23 360

Comté	1965	1966	1967	1968	1969	1970	1971
Lotbinière	28 342	28 765	27 732	27 459	26 948	26 886	27 527
Maskinongé	19 833	21 466	20 873	20 932	20 831	20 357	21 139
Matane et Matapédia	66 943	63 227	61 781	60 915	59 840	58 857	57 300
Mégantic	55 293	57 504	56 059	54 616	54 612	55 297	57 919
Missisquoi	30 422	32 600	31 599	31 445	31 998	32 116	34 025
Montcalm	22 261	19 260	18 698	18 645	19 479	19 688	21 155
Montmagny	25 444	26 751	24 906	24 935	25 666	25 380	26 309
Montmorency	24 663	25 948	24 516	24 141	24 938	24 544	25 546
Napierville	11 798	11 822	11 539	11 636	11 940	12 034	12 145
Nicolet	30 186	30 829	30 292	29 683	30 176	29 918	30 152
Papineau	31 996	31 952	31 920	31 410	31 297	31 238	31 859
Pontiac	23 000	20 113	19 348	19 580	19 988	19 531	20 323
Portneuf	47 950	51 749	49 353	49 069	48 879	48 947	51 207
Québec	365 413	383 092	377 993	390 401	399 613	406 503	421 198
Richelieu	41 759	44 835	43 969	45 348	45 412	45 344	47 400
Richmond	40 541	41 426	40 739	40 468	40 182	39 946	41 231
Rimouski	69 178	65 629	63 966	63 836	62 761	62 588	64 487
Rouville	26 747	29 171	28 428	29 263	30 007	29 918	32 062
Saguenay	94 266	107 663	104 225	105 199	104 593	97 694	113 076
St-Hyacinthe	46 587	48 842	46 702	47 038	46 885	46 973	50 379
St-Jean	38 630	41 621	42 420	42 807	44 351	45 689	45 698
St-Maurice	112 839	112 695	108 475	112 609	114 155	112 551	108 054
Shefford	55 567	60 161	56 959	56 701	58 471	58 801	62 296
Sherbrooke	85 912	93 199	94 261	93 342	95 960	98 846	101 726
Soulanges	11 007	10 757	10 947	10 779	11 271	11 220	11 482
Stanstead	36 971	37 247	36 994	36 891	36 759	36 264	36 401
Témiscamingue	58 638	60 312	58 114	57 956	57 866	55 507	55 823
Témiscouata et Rivière-du-Loup	68 054	66 136	67 564	64 015	63 864	63 298	62 840
Terrebonne	120 084	122 781	121 981	127 636	133 581	132 710	140 000
Vaudreuil	32 523	34 053	33 446	35 183	36 042	36 053	36 766
Verchères	29 848	30 885	30 398	30 907	32 027	32 641	35 416
Wolfe	17 469	16 793	16 677	16 477	15 742	15 609	16 281
Yamaska	15 058	15 535	15 099	14 832	14 861	14 481	15 277
Province	5 685 000	5 780 845	5 868 000	5 927 000	5 984 000	6 013 000	6 028 000

Source: *Tableaux-types de comptes économiques du Québec: Revenus et dépenses, 1946-1970*. Ministère de l'Industrie et du Commerce, Québec, 1972.

2.1 Répartition de la population

2.1.e POPULATION Ⓖ URBAINE, RURALE AGRICOLE ET RURALE NON AGRICOLE, QUEBEC, ONTARIO, CANADA, 1891-1971, ANNEES DE RECENSEMENT

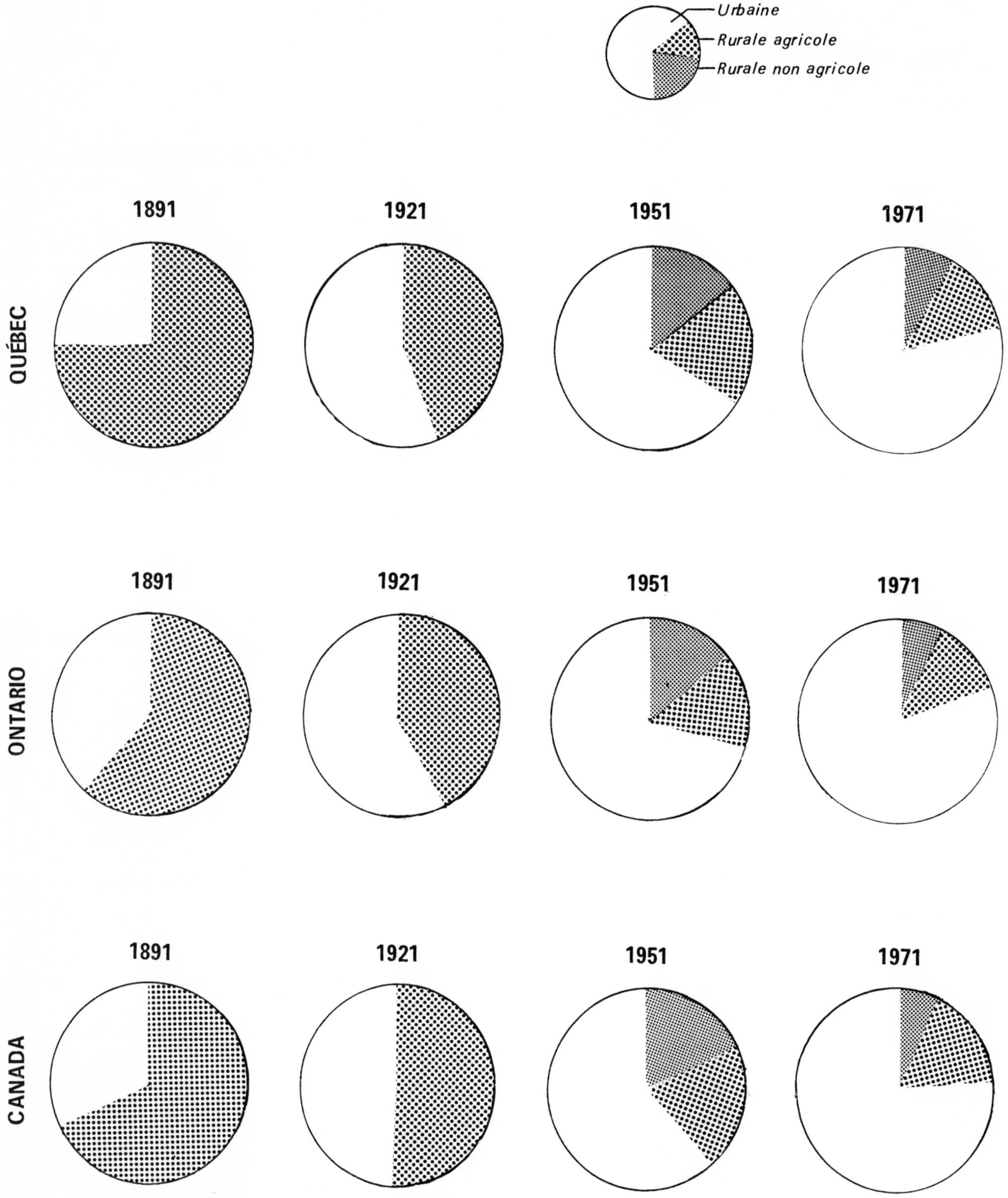

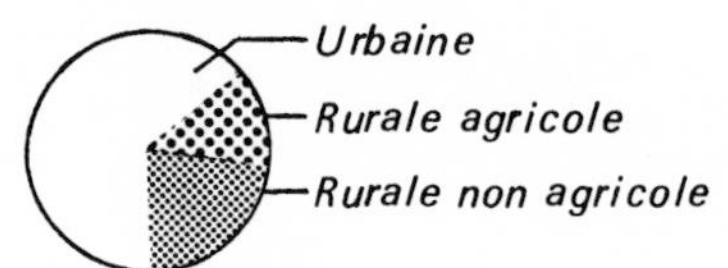

QUÉBEC

1891 1921 1951 1971

ONTARIO

1891 1921 1951 1971

CANADA

1891 1921 1951 1971

Source: Statistique Canada, *Recensements du Canada 1891, 1901, 1911, 1921, 1931, 1941, 1951, 1961, 1966,* Ottawa.

2.1 Répartition de la population

2.1.f SELON L'ORIGINE Ⓖ ETHNIQUE ET LA LANGUE Ⓖ MATERNELLE, QUEBEC, 1961

Origine ethnique	population	Langue maternelle (langue française / langue anglaise / autre langue)	%
Français	4,241,354	4,164,880	98.2
		68,339	1.6
		8,135	0.2
Britanniques	567,057	53,383	9.4
		511,293	90.2
		2,381	0.4
Allemands	39,457	5,988	15.2
		10,179	25.8
		23,290	59.0
Italiens	108,552	14,762	13.6
		6,387	5.9
		87,403	80.5
Juifs	74,677	1,773	2.4
		40,904	54.8
		32,000	42.8
Néerlandais	10,442	685	6.6
		4,149	39.7
		5,608	53.7
Polonais	30,790	1,945	6.3
		7,555	24.5
		21,290	69.2
Scandinaves	11,295	1,728	15.3
		6,425	56.9
		3,142	27.8
Ukrainiens	16,588	939	5.7
		3,527	21.3
		12,122	73.0
Indiens et Esquimaux	21,343	2,632	12.3
		2,388	11.2
		16,323	76.5
Russes	13,694	554	4.0
		6,725	49.1
		6,415	46.9
Autres Européens	96,112	15,168	15.8
		16,194	16.8
		64,750	67.4
Asiatiques	14,801	2,413	16.3
		3,621	24.5
		8,767	59.2
Autres non-déclarés	13,049	2,839	21.8
		9,716	74.5
		494	3.7
toutes origines **QUEBEC**	**5,259,211**	**4,269,689**	**81.2**
		697,402	**13.3**
		292,120	**5.5**

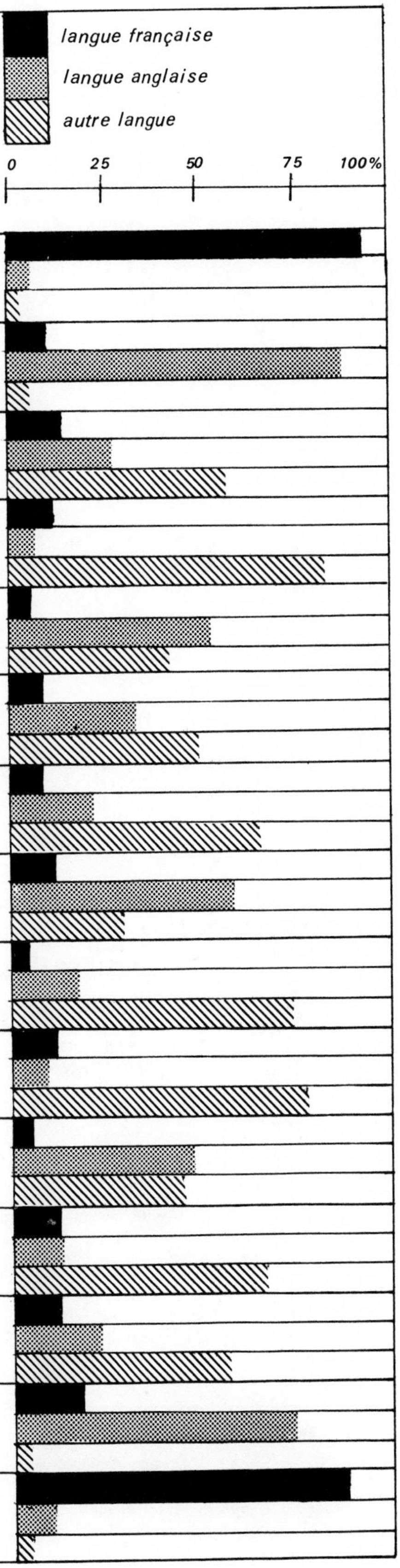

Source: *Rapport de la Commission Royale d'Enquête sur le bilinguisme et le biculturalisme*, Ottawa, 1969.

2.1 Répartition de la population

2.1.g SELON L'ORIGINE ETHNIQUE, LA LANGUE Ⓖ MATERNELLE ET LA LANGUE Ⓖ OFFICIELLE PARLEE, CANADA, PROVINCES ET MONTREAL, 1931-1971, ANNEES DE RECENSEMENT

CANADA

	Origine ethnique			Langue maternelle			Langue(s) officielle(s) parlée(s)			
	% française	% britannique	% autre	% français	% anglais	% autre	% français seulement	% anglais seulement	% français anglais	% ni anglais ni français
1931	28.2	51.8	19.9	27.3	57.0	15.7	13.6	69.6	15.1	1.8
1941	30.3	49.7	20.0	29.2	56.4	14.4	19.0	67.2	12.8	1.0
1951	30.8	47.9	21.3	29.0	59.1	11.9	19.6	67.0	12.3	1.1
1961	30.4	43.8	25.8	28.1	58.4	13.5	19.1	67.4	12.2	1.3
1971	..	..	..	26.9	60.1	13.0	..	..	..	..

COLOMBIE-BRITANNIQUE

	Origine ethnique			Langue maternelle			Langue(s) officielle(s) parlée(s)			
	% française	% britannique	% autre	% français	% anglais	% autre	% français seulement	% anglais seulement	% français anglais	% ni anglais ni français
1931	2.2	70.6	27.3	..	..	..	..	91.6	3.0	5.3
1941	2.7	69.9	27.4	1.4	78.4	20.2	..	95.1	2.9	2.0
1951	3.6	63.4	33.0	1.6	82.7	15.7	..	95.5	3.4	1.0
1961	4.1	59.3	36.6	1.6	80.9	17.5	0.1	95.3	3.5	1.0
1971	..	..	..	1.7	82.7	15.5	..	..	..	..

ALBERTA

	Origine ethnique			Langue maternelle			Langue(s) officielle(s) parlée(s)			
	% française	% britannique	% autre	% français	% anglais	% autre	% français seulement	% anglais seulement	% français anglais	% ni anglais ni français
1931	5.2	53.2	41.5	..	..	..	0.8	88.4	4.5	6.3
1941	5.4	50.2	44.4	4.0	62.9	33.1	0.4	92.8	4.6	2.2
1951	6.0	48.1	45.9	3.6	69.0	27.4	0.6	92.5	4.3	2.6
1961	6.2	45.2	48.6	3.2	72.2	24.6	0.4	94.1	4.3	1.2
1971	..	..	..	2.8	77.6	5.6	..	..	..	..

SASKATCHEWAN

	Origine ethnique			Langue maternelle			Langue(s) officielle(s) parlée(s)			
	% française	% britannique	% autre	% français	% anglais	% autre	% français seulement	% anglais seulement	% français anglais	% ni anglais ni français
1931	5.5	47.5	47.0	..	..	..	0.8	87.7	4.8	6.7
1941	5.6	44.4	50.0	4.9	55.8	39.3	0.5	91.8	5.2	2.5
1951	6.2	42.3	51.5	4.4	62.0	33.6	0.5	92.2	4.9	2.3
1961	6.5	40.4	53.1	3.9	69.0	27.1	0.4	93.6	4.5	1.4
1971	..	..	..	3.4	74.0	22.5	..	..	..	..

MANITOBA

	Origine ethnique			Langue maternelle			Langue(s) officielle(s) parlée(s)			
	% française	% britannique	% autre	% français	% anglais	% autre	% français seulement	% anglais seulement	% français anglais	% ni anglais ni français
1931	6.7	52.6	40.7	..	..	..	1.3	85.7	6.2	6.7
1941	7.3	49.4	43.3	7.1	56.0	36.9	0.8	88.7	7.5	3.0
1951	8.5	46.7	44.8	7.0	60.2	32.8	1.0	88.3	7.5	3.1
1961	9.1	43.0	47.9	6.6	63.4	30.0	0.9	89.6	7.4	2.1
1971	..	..	..	6.1	67.1	26.8	..	..	..	..

ONTARIO

	Origine ethnique			Langue maternelle			Langue(s) officielle(s) parlée(s)			
	% française	% britannique	% autre	% français	% anglais	% autre	% français seulement	% anglais seulement	% français anglais	% ni anglais ni français
1931	8.7	74.0	17.2	..	..	..	1.9	90.2	6.4	1.5
1941	9.9	72.2	17.9	7.6	81.1	11.3	1.6	90.4	7.5	0.5
1951	10.4	67.0	22.6	7.4	81.7	10.9	1.7	89.5	7.8	0.9
1961	11.0	59.5	29.5	6.8	77.5	15.7	1.5	89.0	7.9	1.6
1971	..	..	..	6.2	77.5	16.2	..	..	..	..

NOUVEAU-BRUNSWICK

	Origine ethnique			Langue maternelle			Langue(s) officielle(s) parlée(s)			
	% française	% britanique	% autre	% français	% anglais	% autre	% français seulement	% anglais seulement	% français anglais	% ni anglais ni français
1931	33.6	62.6	3.8	..	..	..	16.2	65.5	18.1	0.1
1941	35.8	60.5	3.7	34.5	64.1	1.4	18.0	63.6	18.3	0.1
1951	38.3	57.1	4.6	35.9	63.1	1.0	19.5	61.8	18.6	—
1961	38.8	55.2	6.0	35.2	63.3	1.5	18.7	62.0	19.0	0.2
1971	..	..	..	34.0	64.7	1.3	..	..	..	..

NOUVELLE-ECOSSE

	Origine ethnique			Langue maternelle			Langue(s) officielle(s) parlée(s)			
	% française	% britanique	% autre	% français	% anglais	% autre	% français seulement	% anglais seulement	% français anglais	% ni anglais ni français
1931	11.0	76.4	12.5	..	..	..	1.8	91.1	6.6	0.3
1941	11.5	77.0	11.5	7.2	88.9	3.9	1.2	91.8	6.9	0.1
1951	11.5	75.1	13.4	6.1	91.6	2.3	1.2	92.6	6.1	—
1961	11.9	71.3	16.8	5.4	92.3	2.3	0.8	92.9	6.1	0.2
1971	..	..	..	5.0	93.0	2.0	..	..	..	..

ILE-DU-PRINCE-EDOUARD

	Origine ethnique			Langue maternelle			Langue(s) officielle(s) parlée(s)			
	% française	% britanique	% autre	% français	% anglais	% autre	% français seulement	% anglais seulement	% français anglais	% ni anglais ni français
1931	14.7	83.8	1.5	..	..	..	1.5	87.6	10.8	—
1941	15.6	82.8	1.6	11.2	87.6	1.2	1.0	88.2	10.8	—
1951	15.7	81.9	2.4	8.6	90.7	0.7	1.0	90.1	8.9	—
1961	16.6	79.8	3.6	7.6	91.3	1.1	1.2	91.1	7.6	0.2
1971	..	..	..	6.6	92.3	1.0	..	..	..	..

TERRE-NEUVE

	Origine ethnique			Langue maternelle			Langue(s) officielle(s) parlée(s)			
	% française	% britanique	% autre	% français	% anglais	% autre	% français seulement	% anglais seulement	% français anglais	% ni anglais ni français
1931	..	..	..	..	..	..	..	..	..	..
1941	..	..	..	..	..	..	..	..	..	..
1951	2.7	93.5	3.8	0.6	98.9	0.5	..	98.6	1.1	0.2
1961	3.7	93.7	2.6	0.7	98.6	0.7	0.1	98.5	1.1	0.2
1971	..	..	..	0.7	98.6	0.7	..	..	..	..

QUEBEC

	Origine ethnique			Langue maternelle			Langue(s) officielle(s) parlée(s)			
	% française	% britanique	% autre	% français	% anglais	% autre	% français seulement	% anglais seulement	% français anglais	% ni anglais ni français
1931	79.0	15.0	6.0	..	..	..	47.7	14.7	37.1	0.5
1941	80.9	13.6	5.5	81.6	14.1	4.3	60.5	12.3	26.8	0.4
1951	82.0	12.1	5.9	82.5	13.8	3.7	62.5	11.4	25.6	0.5
1961	80.6	10.8	8.6	81.2	13.3	5.5	61.9	11.6	25.5	1.1
1971	..	..	..	80.7	13.1	6.2	..	..	..	..

ILES DE MONTREAL ET JESUS

	Origine ethnique			Langue maternelle			Langue(s) officielle(s) parlée(s)			
	% française	% britanique	% autre	% français	% anglais	% autre	% français seulement	% anglais seulement	% français anglais	% ni anglais ni français
1931	..	..	..	..	..	..	..	..	..	..
1941	..	..	..	..	..	..	..	..	..	..
1951	64.0	21.9	14.1	64.9	26.3	8.8	35.9	23.2	40.0	0.9
1961	61.2	17.5	21.3	63.9	23.3	12.8	38.2	22.1	37.4	2.3
1971	..	..	..	64.2	21.4	14.4	..	..	..	..

Sources: Statistique Canada, *Recensements du Canada 1931, 1941, 1951, 1961*, Ottawa.

Statistique Canada, Division du Recensement C.D. et S., Ottawa, 1972.

2

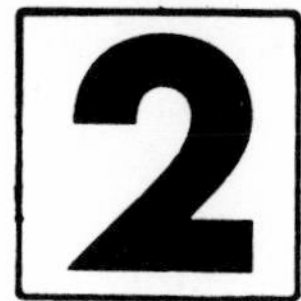

2.2 Mouvements de population

2.2.a IMMIGRANTS INSCRITS, QUEBEC, ONTARIO, CANADA, 1958-1970, ANNEES CHOISIES

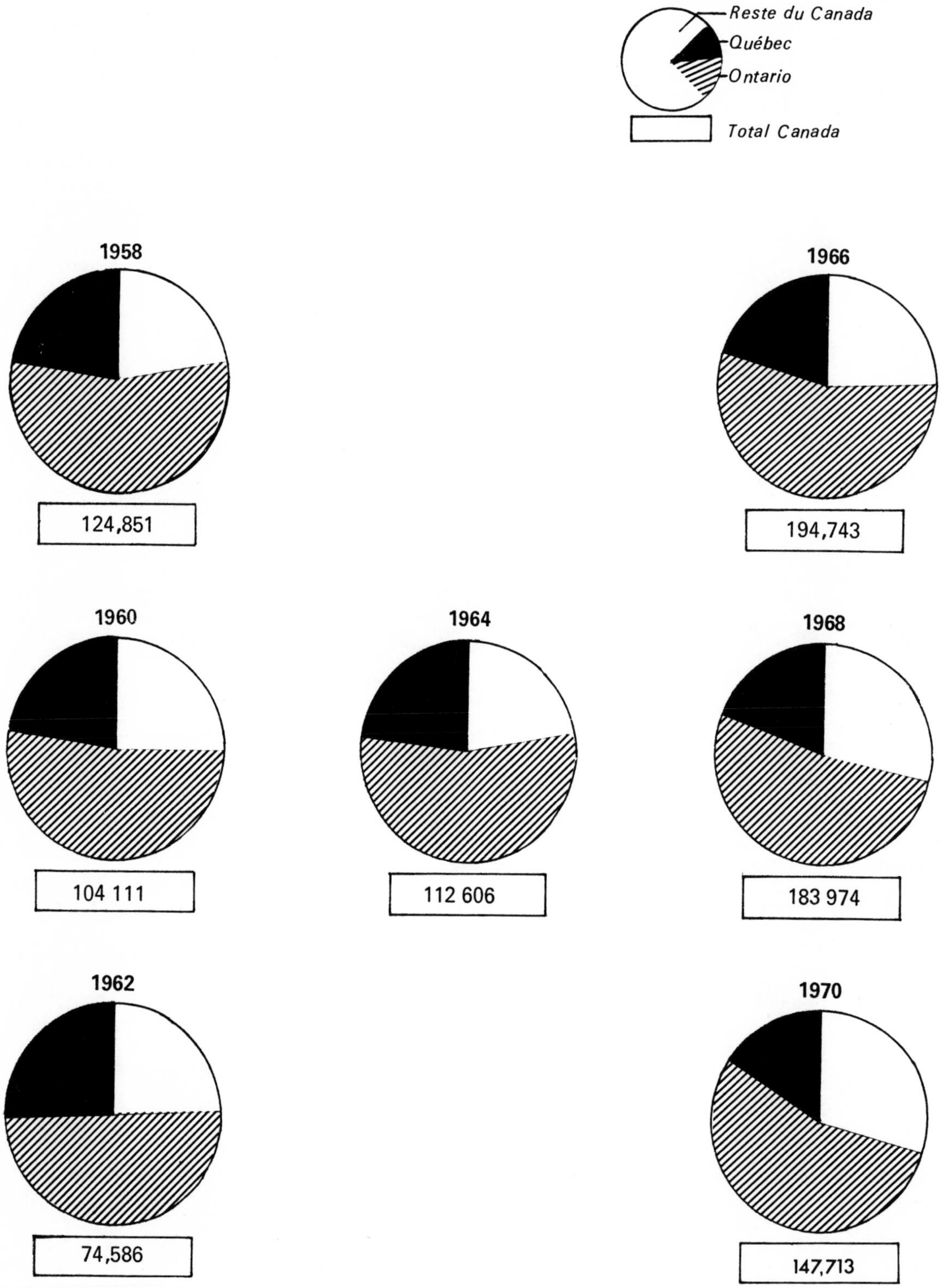

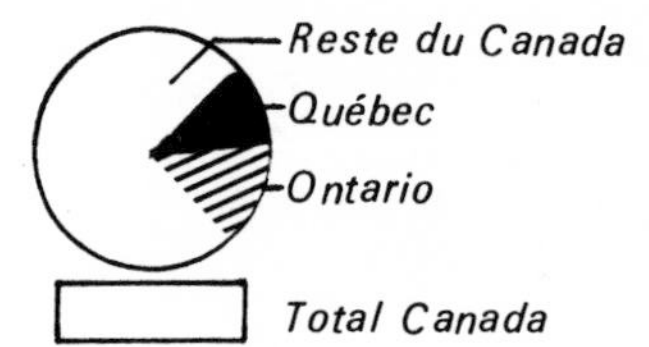

Reste du Canada
Québec
Ontario
Total Canada
1958
124,851
1966
194,743
1960
104 111
1964
112 606
1968
183 974
1962
74,586
1970
147,713

Sources: *Annuaires du Québec 1971 et 1972.*

2.2 Mouvements de population.

2.2.b MIGRATION Ⓖ NETTE, PAR REGIONS ADMINISTRATIVES, QUEBEC, 1951-1961.

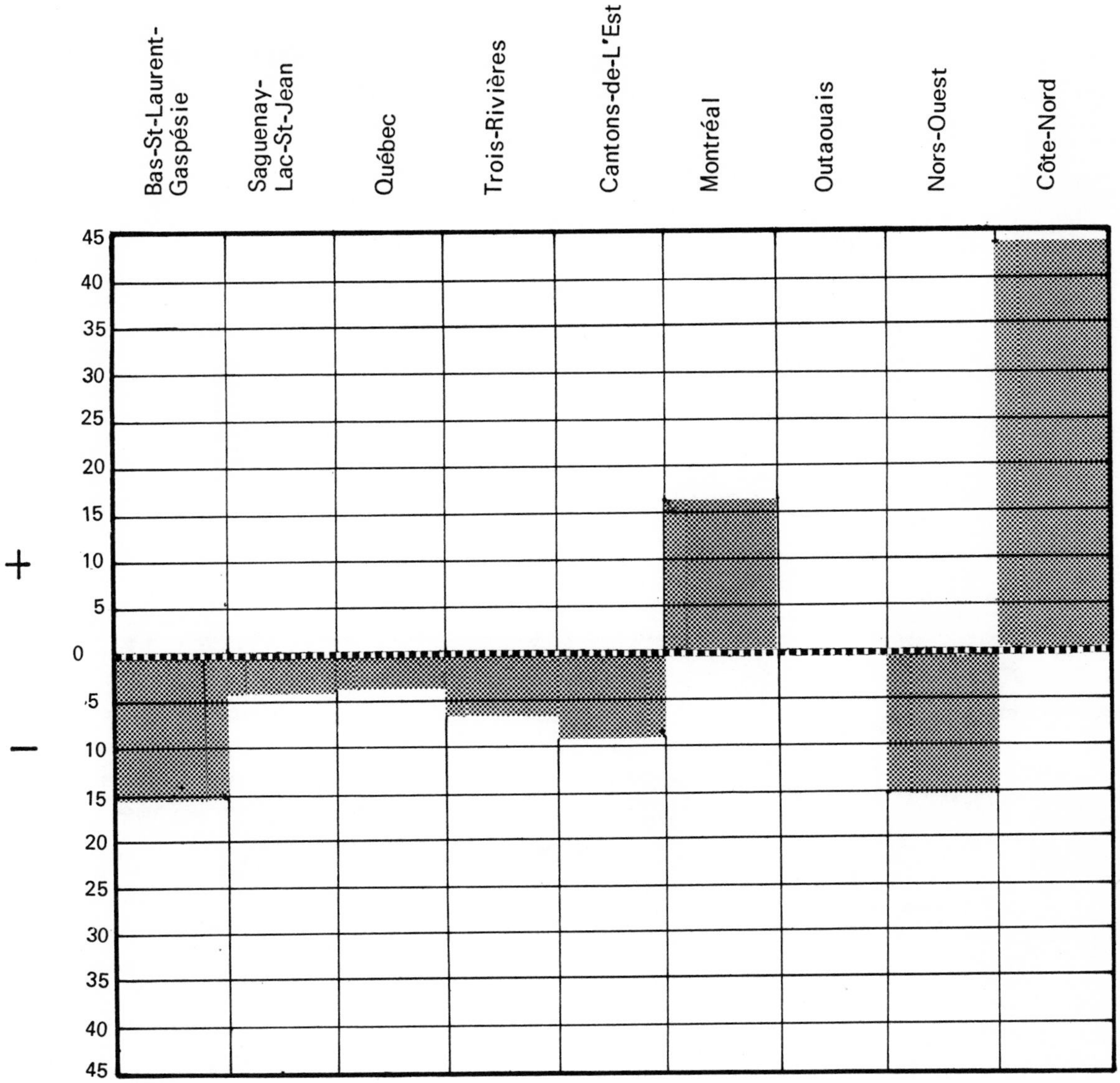

Bas-St-Laurent-Gaspésie
Saguenay-Lac-St-Jean
Québec
Trois-Rivières
Cantons-de-L'Est
Montréal
Outaouais
Nors-Ouest
Côte-Nord

+ 45 40 35 30 25 20 15 10 5 0
− 5 10 15 20 25 30 35 40 45

Source: Document préparé par Action Sociale Jeunesse, Montréal 1968.

2.3 Démographie

2.3.a TAUX DE NATALITE Ⓖ, DE MORTALITE Ⓖ ET D'ACCROISSEMENT Ⓖ NATUREL, QUEBEC, ONTARIO, CANADA, 1951-1970, ANNEES CHOISIES

	Taux de natalité			**Taux de mortalité**			**Taux d'accroissement naturel**		
	Québec	Ontario	Canada	**Québec**	Ontario	Canada	**Québec**	Ontario	Canada
1951	29.8	25.0	27.2	8.6	9.6	9.0	21.2	15.4	18.2
1956	29.4	26.6	28.0	7.6	8.7	8.2	21.8	17.9	19.8
1961	26.1	25.3	26.1	7.0	8.2	7.7	19.1	17.1	18.4
1966	19.0	19.0	19.4	6.7	7.8	7.5	12.3	11.2	11.9
1967	17.3	17.8	18.2	6.6	7.7	7.4	10.7	10.1	10.8
1968	16.3	17.3	17.6	6.7	7.6	7.4	9.6	9.7	10.2
1969	16.0	17.5	17.6	6.7	7.5	7.3	9.3	10.0	10.3
1970	15.3	17.6	17.4	6.7	7.4	7.3	8.6	10.2	10.1

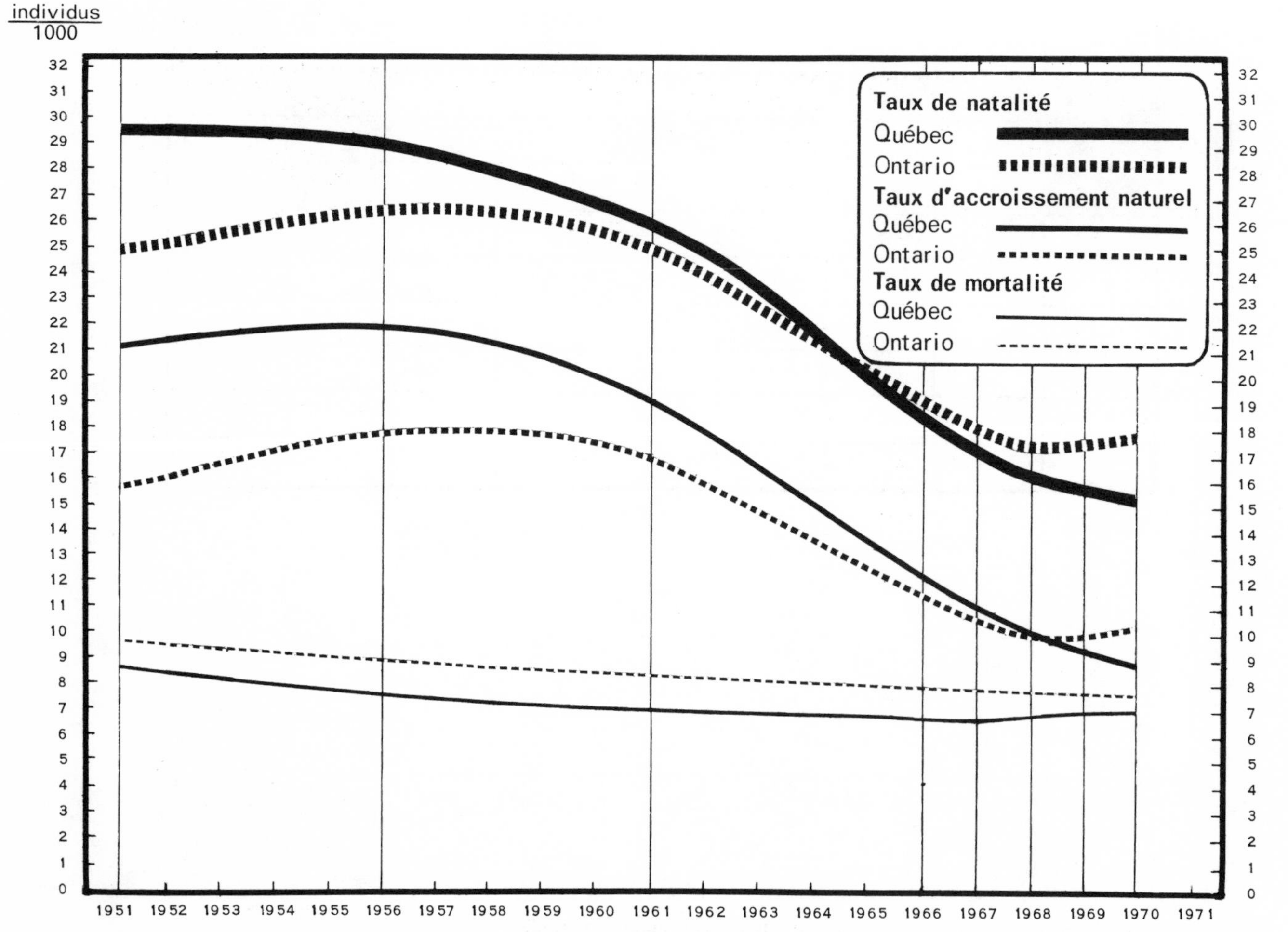

Source: Statistique Canada No 84-202, *Statistique de l'Etat Civil 1969,* Ottawa, 1971.

2.3 Démographie

2.3.b TAUX COMPARATIFS DE MORTALITE Ⓖ, QUEBEC, ONTARIO, CANADA, 1926-1969, ANNEES CHOISIES

	Québec	Ontario	Canada
1926	16.8	13.0	13.9
1931	14.6	11.7	12.2
1936	12.6	11.2	11.5
1941	12.9	10.4	11.2
1946	11.2	9.3	9.9
1951	10.2	8.7	9.0
1956	9.1	8.1	8.2
1961	8.4	7.6	7.6
1966	7.8	7.2	7.2
1967	7.6	7.1	7.1
1968	7.6	7.0	7.1
1969	7.6	6.9	7.0
1970			
1971			

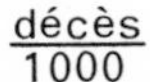

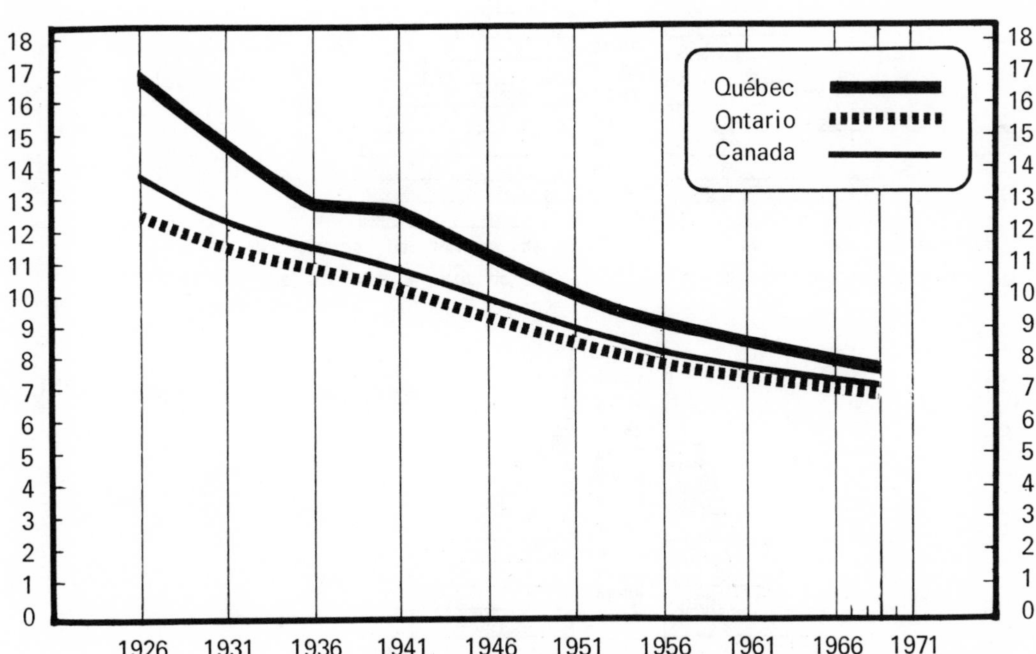

Source: Statistique Canada No 84-202, *Statistique de l'Etat Civil 1969,* Ottawa, 1971.

2

2.3 Démographie

2.3.c PYRAMIDES Ⓖ D'AGE, QUEBEC, 1931-1971, ONTARIO, 1971, ANNEES DE RECENSEMENT

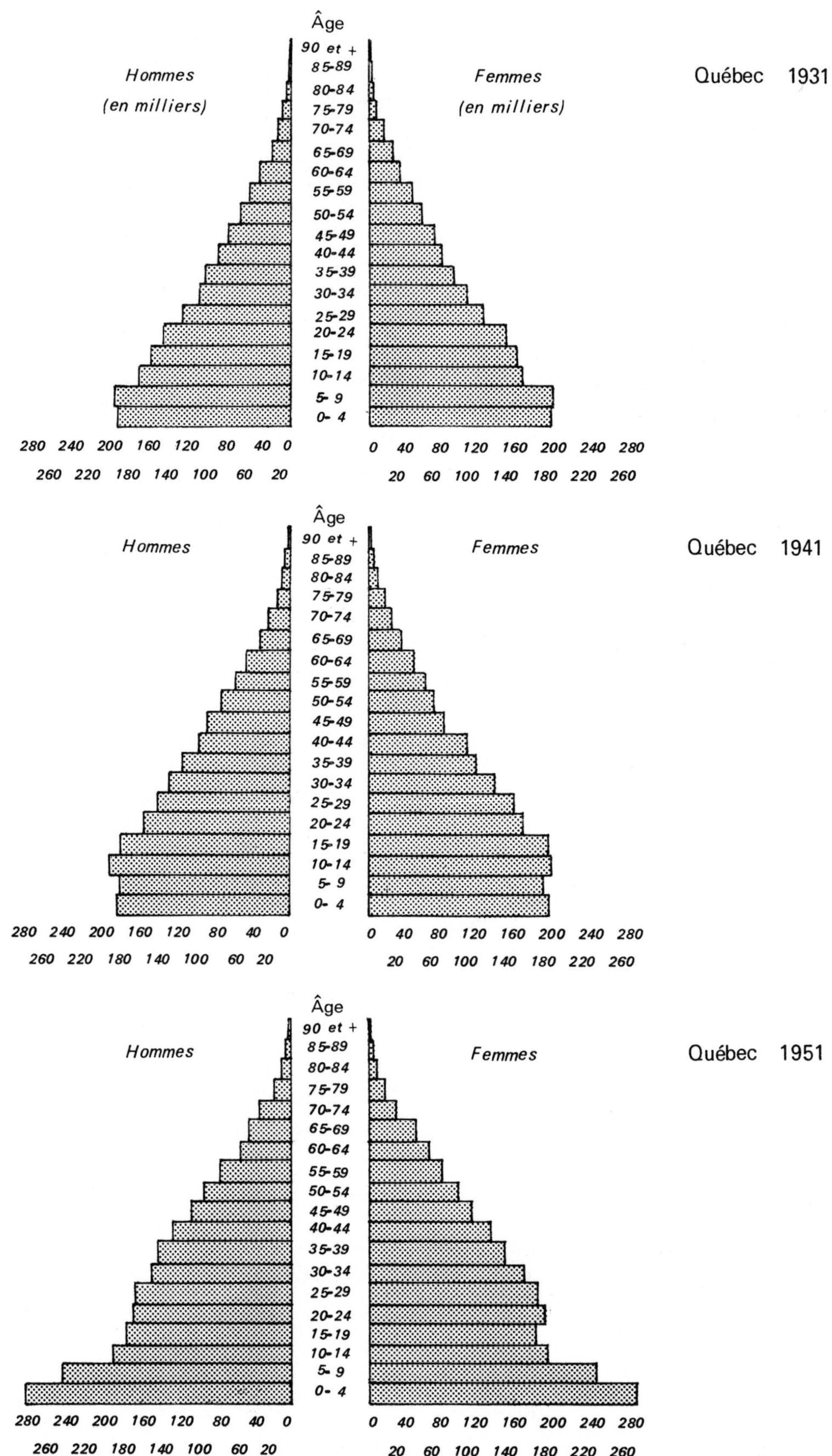

Source: Statistique Canada, *Recensements du Canada 1931, 1941, 1951, 1961,* Ottawa.
Statistique Canada, division du Recensement, C.D. et S., Ottawa, 1972.

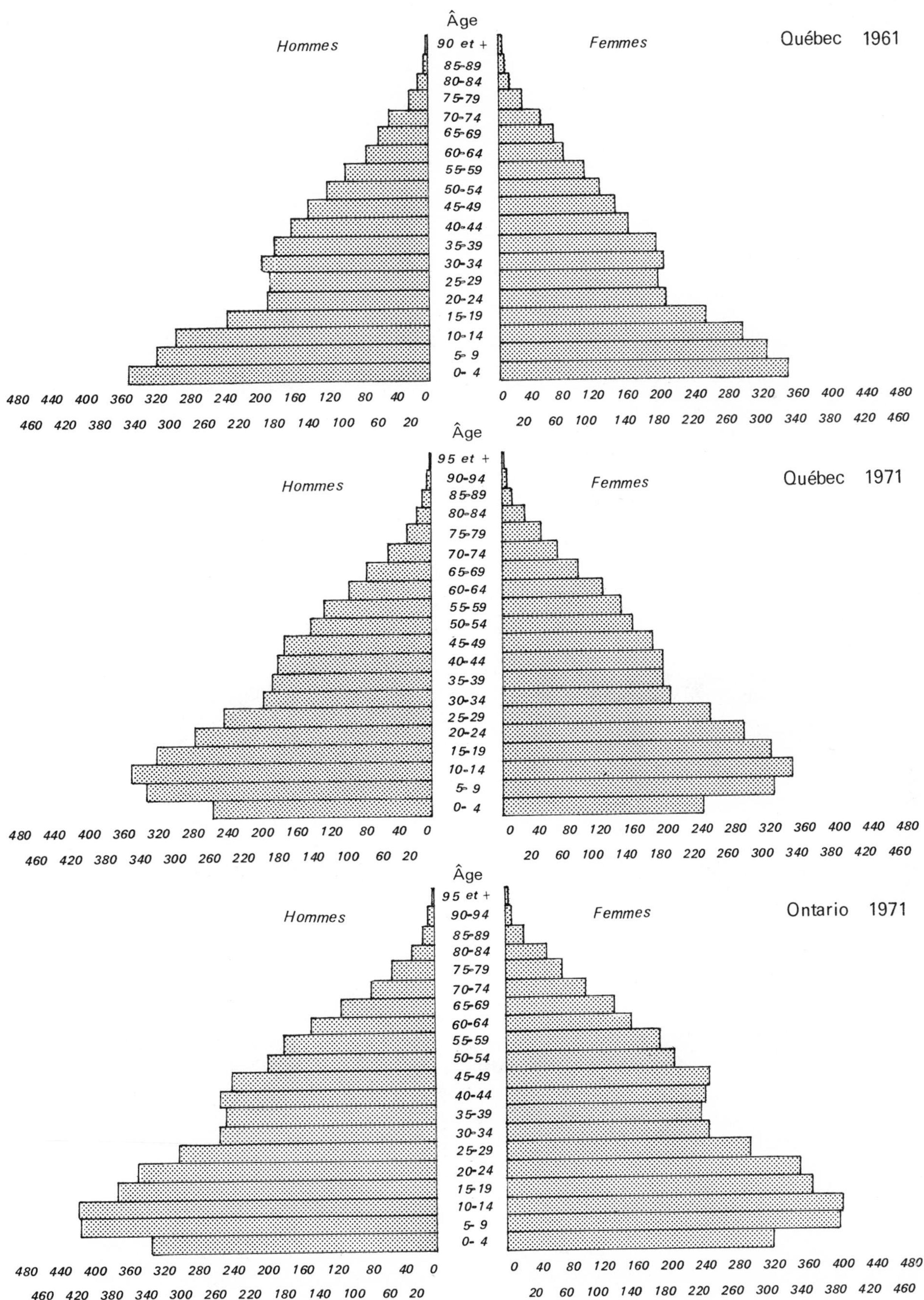

Source: Statistique Canada, Division du Recensement, C.D. et S., Ottawa, 1972.

2

2.3 Démographie

2.3.d ESPERANCE Ⓖ DE VIE, SELON LE SEXE ET L'AGE, QUEBEC, ONTARIO, CANADA, 1931-1966, ANNEES DE RECENSEMENT

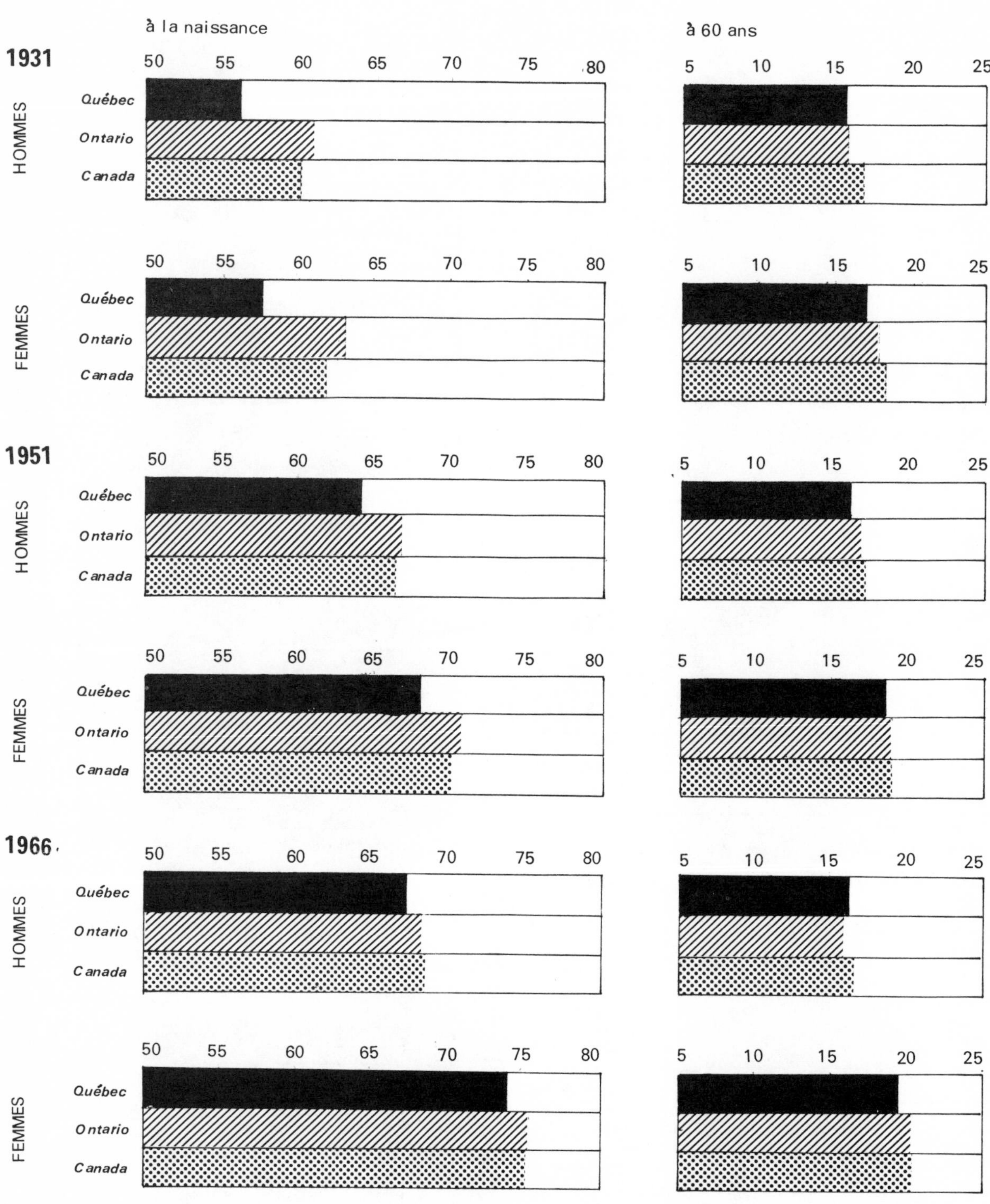

Source: Statistique Canada No 84-202, *Statistiques de l'Etat civil 1969*, Ottawa, 1971.

2.3 Démographie

2.3.e TAUX DE FECONDITE Ⓖ SELON L'AGE, QUEBEC, ONTARIO, CANADA, 1956-1969, ANNEES CHOISIES

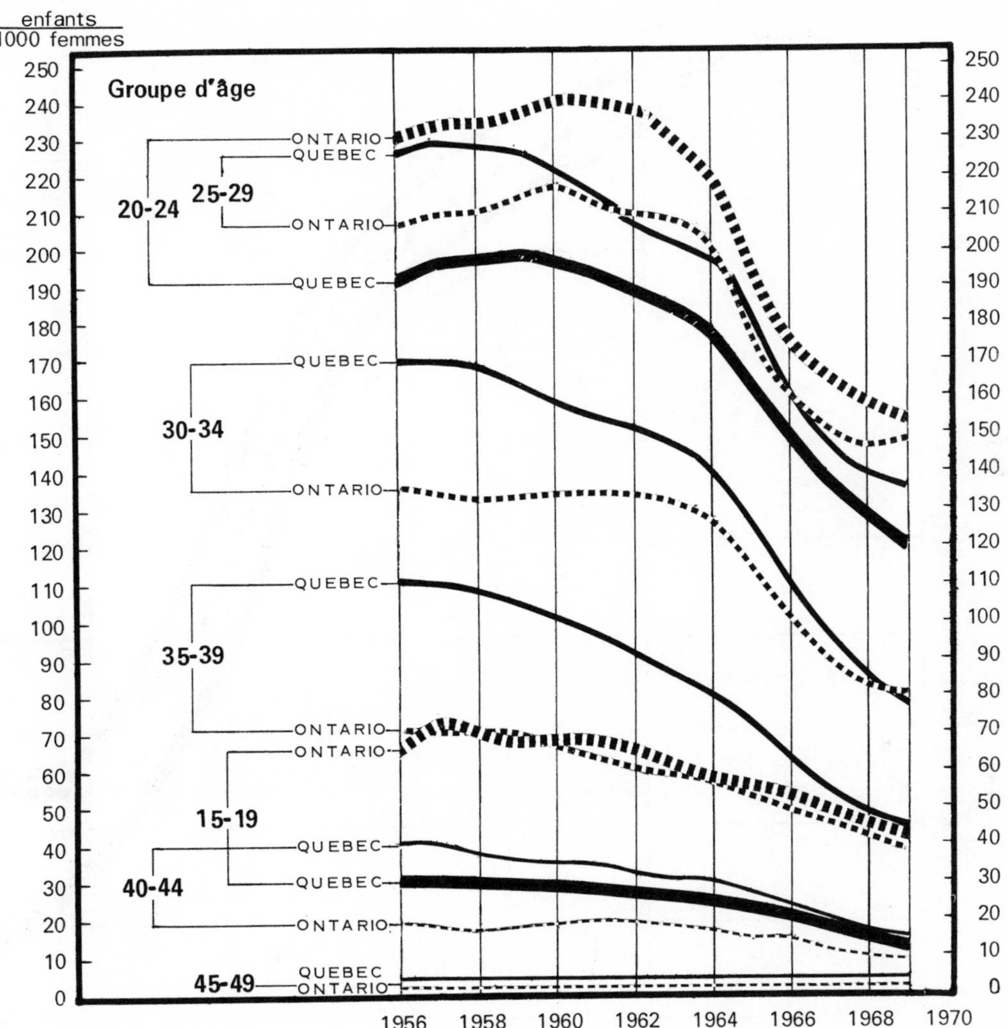

Sources: Statistique Canada No 84-202, *Statistique de l'Etat Civil 1969,* Ottawa, 1971.

Statistique Canada No 84-201, *Statistique de l'Etat Civil, Rapport préliminaire 1970,* Ottawa, 1972.

2

2.3 Démographie

2.3.f TAUX DE REPRODUCTION (G) BRUTE, QUEBEC, ONTARIO, CANADA, 1956-1970, ANNEES CHOISIES

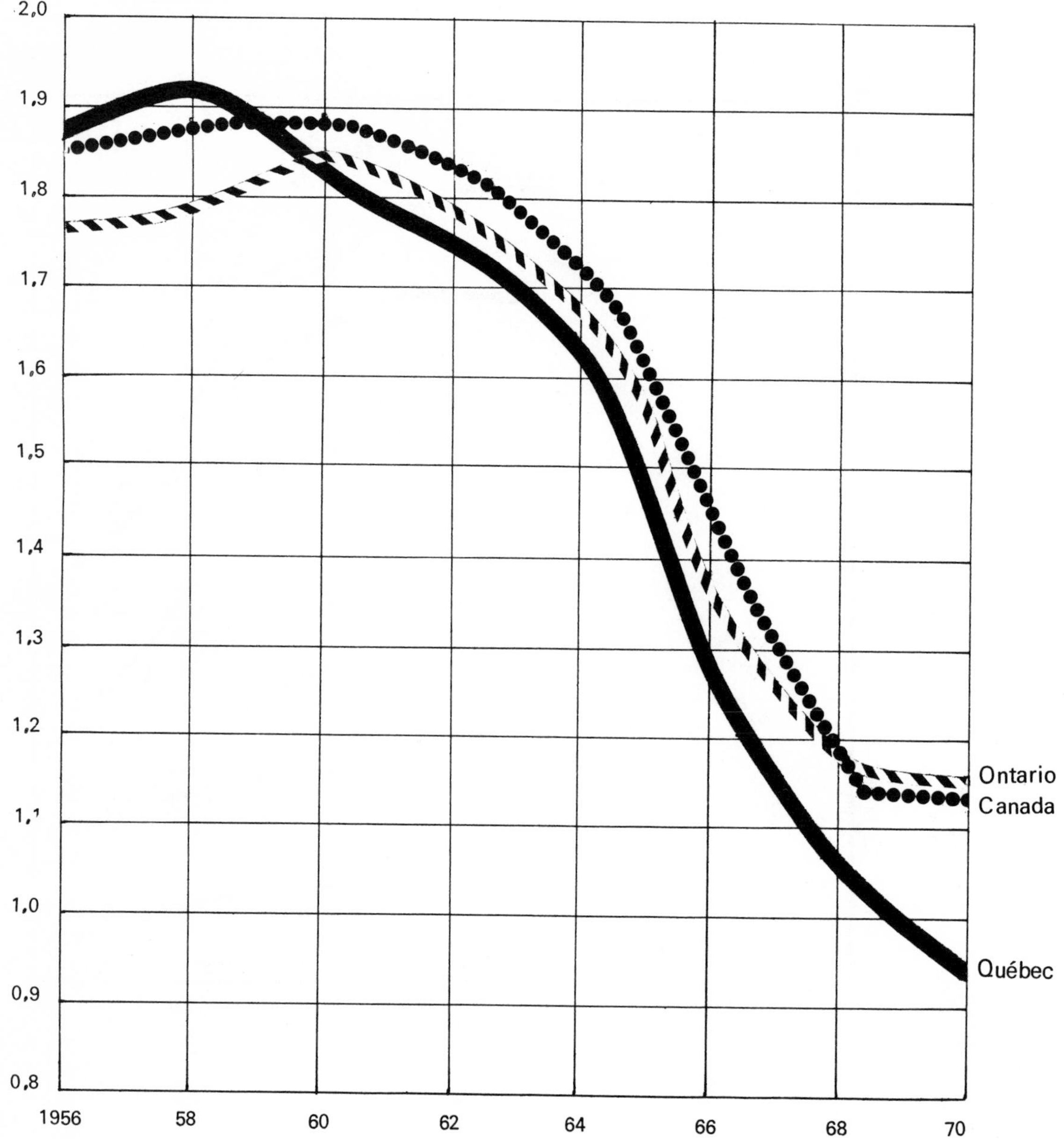

Sources: Statistique Canada No 84-201, *Statistique de l'Etat Civil, Rapport préliminaire 1970*, Ottawa, 1972.

3

3.1 Education

3.1.a FREQUENTATION SCOLAIRE, SELON LES NIVEAUX, QUEBEC, 1920-1971, ANNEES CHOISIES, EN MILLIERS

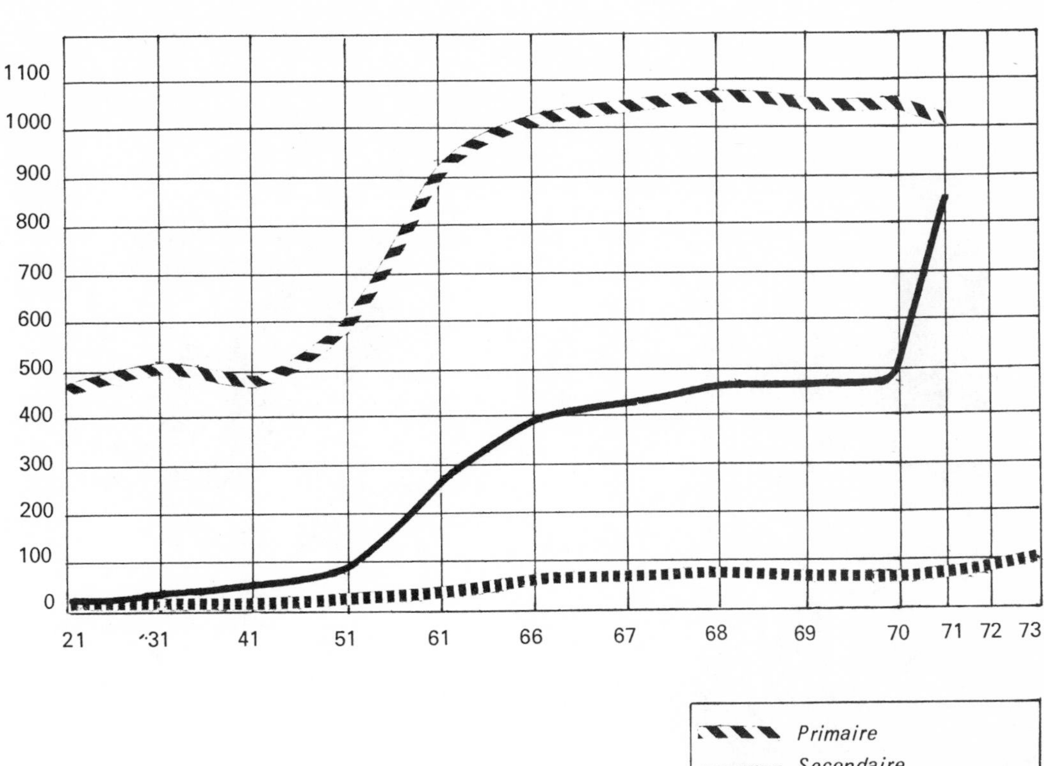

Années	Nombre de C.E.G.E.P.	Collège I	Collège II	Collège III	Total de la fréquentation
1967-1968	**12**	6,625	–	–	**6,625**
1968-1969	**23**	20,663	12,119	2,768	**35,550**
1969-1970	**30**	26,130	17,297	3,875	**47,302**
1970-1971	**38**	36,143	23,527	4,252	**63,922**

Sources: *Annuaires du Québec* 1966 et 1971.

Rapports du Ministère de l'Education, 1967 à 1971, Québec.

Rapports du Surintendant de l'Instruction Publique 1958-1962, Québec

Statistique Canada No 81-201, *Statistique provisoire de l'enseignement,* Ottawa.

Urquhuart & Buckley, *Historical Statistics of Canada,* Cambridge University Press, 1965.

3

3.1 Education

3.1.b FREQUENTATION UNIVERSITAIRE A TEMPS PLEIN DANS LES DIFFERENTES UNIVERSITES DU QUEBEC, 1961-1966-1971

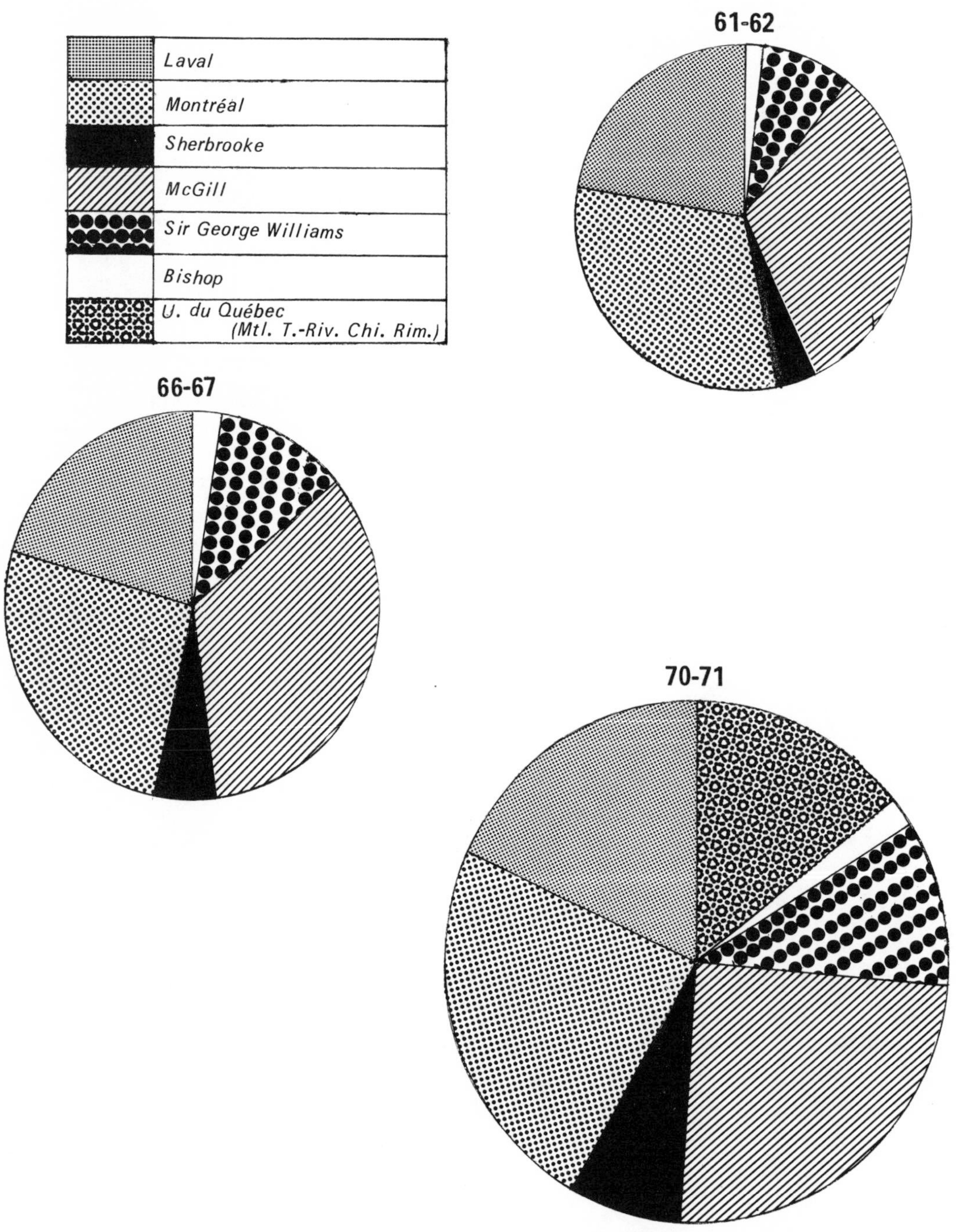

Sources: *Annuaire du Québec 1972.*

Rapports du Ministère de l'Education 1961 à 1969, Québec.

3

3.1 Education

3.1.c ETUDIANTS A PLEIN TEMPS PAR GROUPES D'AGE ET PAR SEXES, QUEBEC, 1921-1941-1961

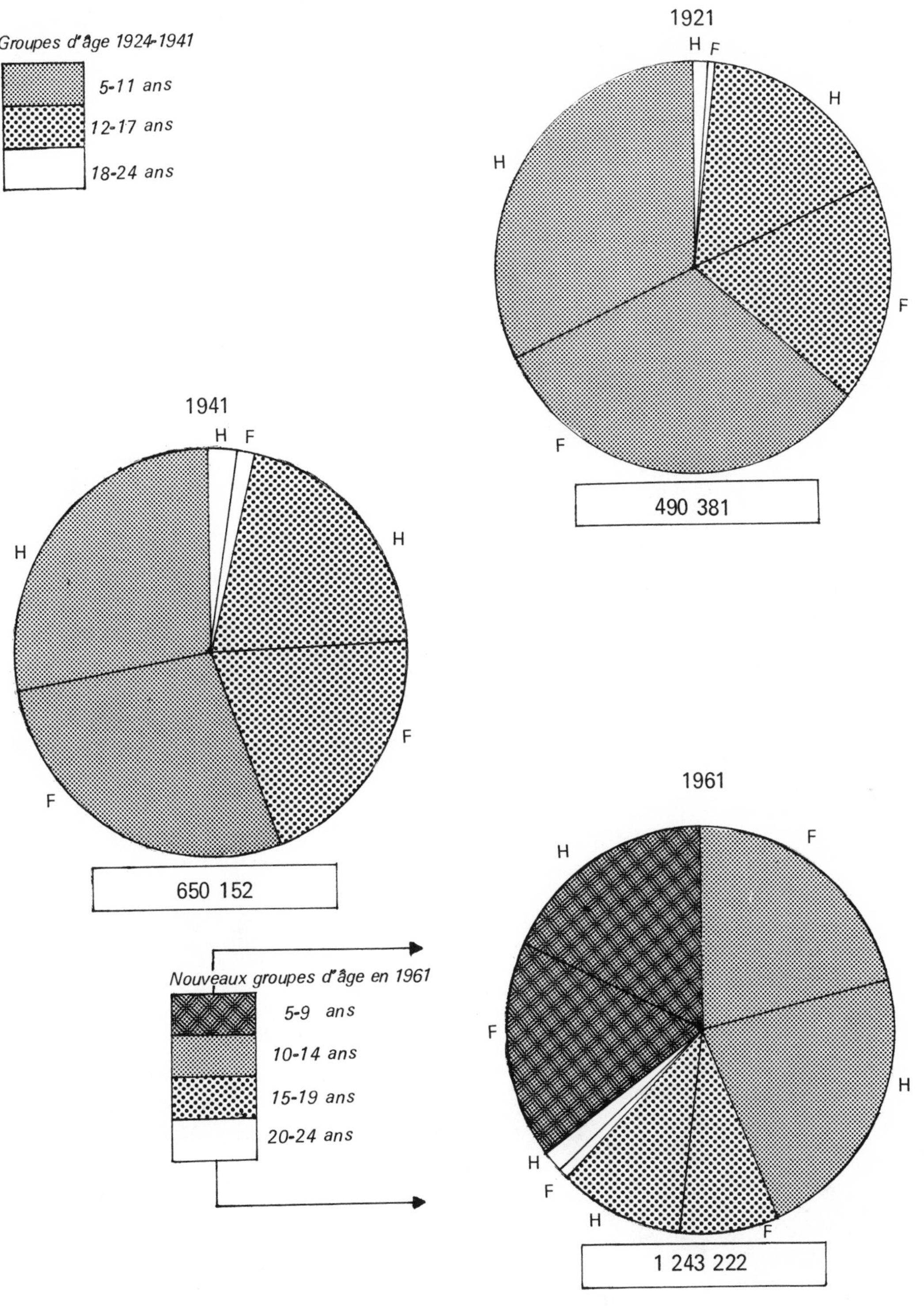

Sources: Urquhuart & Buckley, *Historical Statistics of Canada*, Cambridge University Press, 1965.

Statistique Canada No 92-550, *Fréquentation scolaire et années de scolarité*, Ottawa.

3

3.1 Education

3.1.d EDUCATION DES ADULTES SELON LE GENRE DE FORMATION, QUEBEC, 1958-1965 (N)

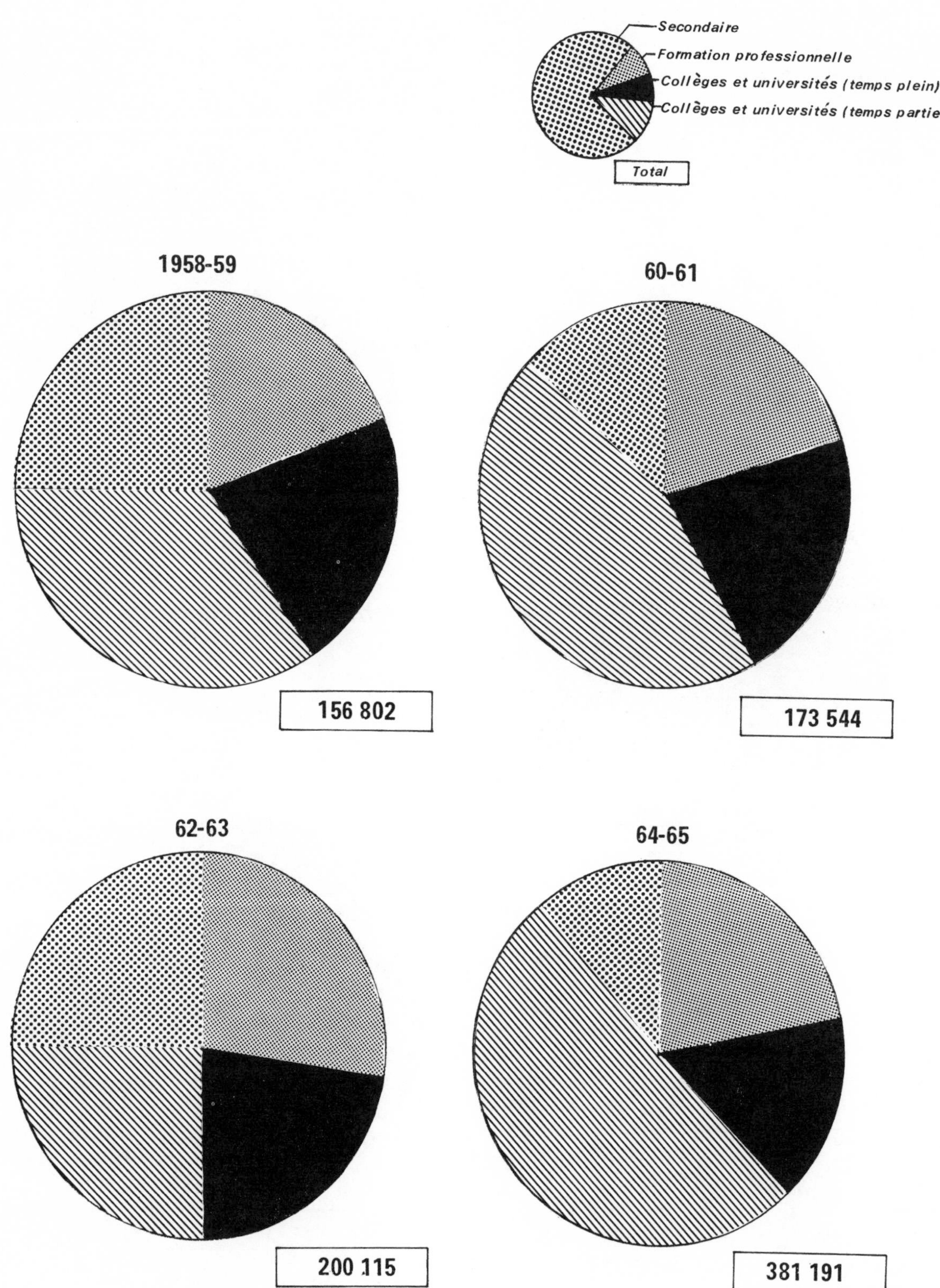

Source: Statistique Canada No 81-207, *Education populaire*, Ottawa.

Note: Statistique Canada a cesse de publier ces statistiques en 1965.

3

3.1 Education

3.1.e NIVEAU SCOLAIRE ATTEINT PAR LA MAIN-D'OEUVRE MASCULINE NON AGRICOLE SELON L'ORIGINE Ⓖ ETHNIQUE, CERTAINES PROVINCES ET ZONES Ⓖ METROPOLITAINES, 1961

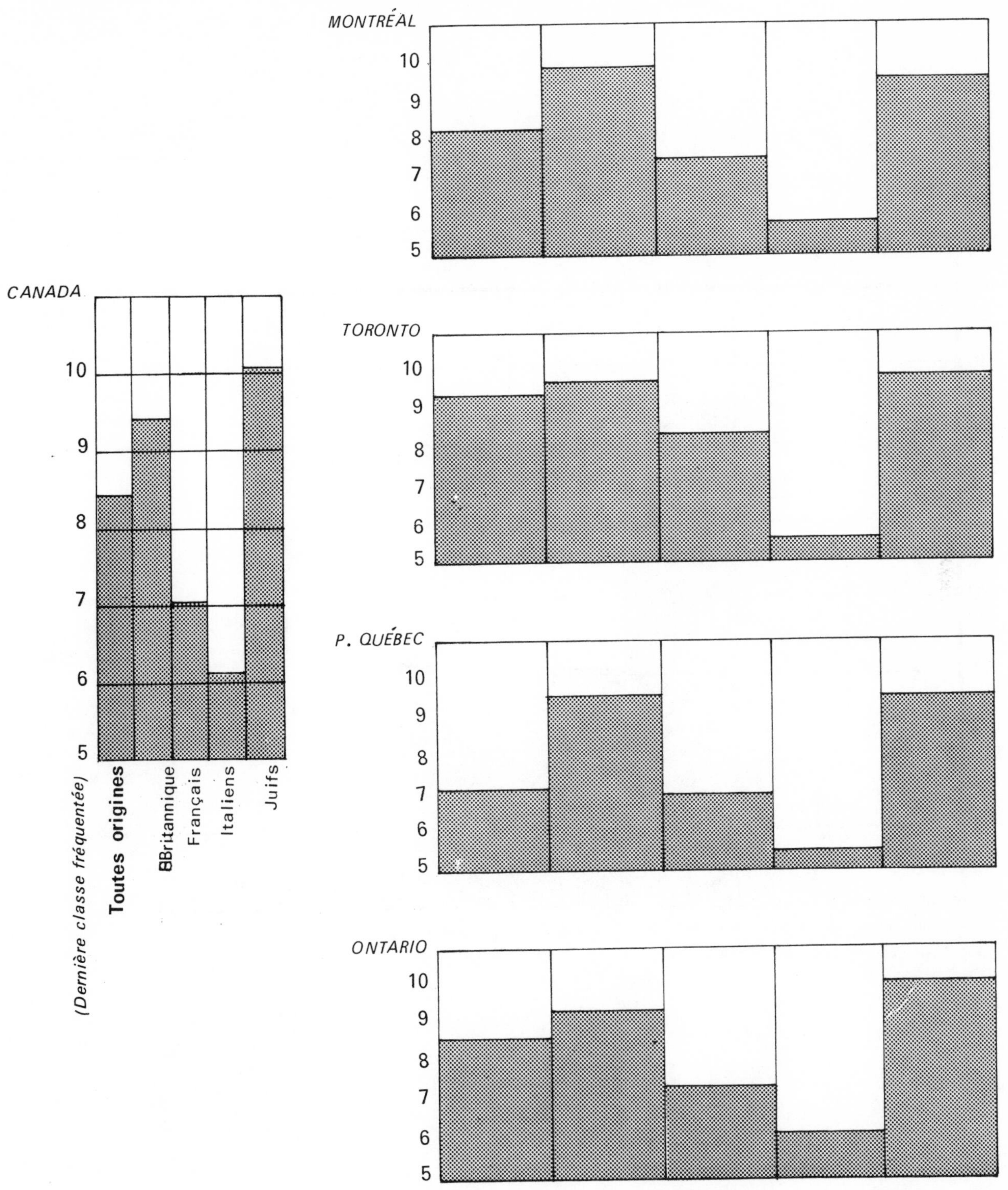

Source: *Rapport de la Commission Royale d'Enquête sur le Bilinguisme et le Biculturalisme*, Ottawa, 1969.

3.1 Education

3.1.f TAUX DE SCOLARISATION DE LA POPULATION NE FREQUENTANT PLUS L'ECOLE, PAR GROUPES D'AGE, QUEBEC, 1961

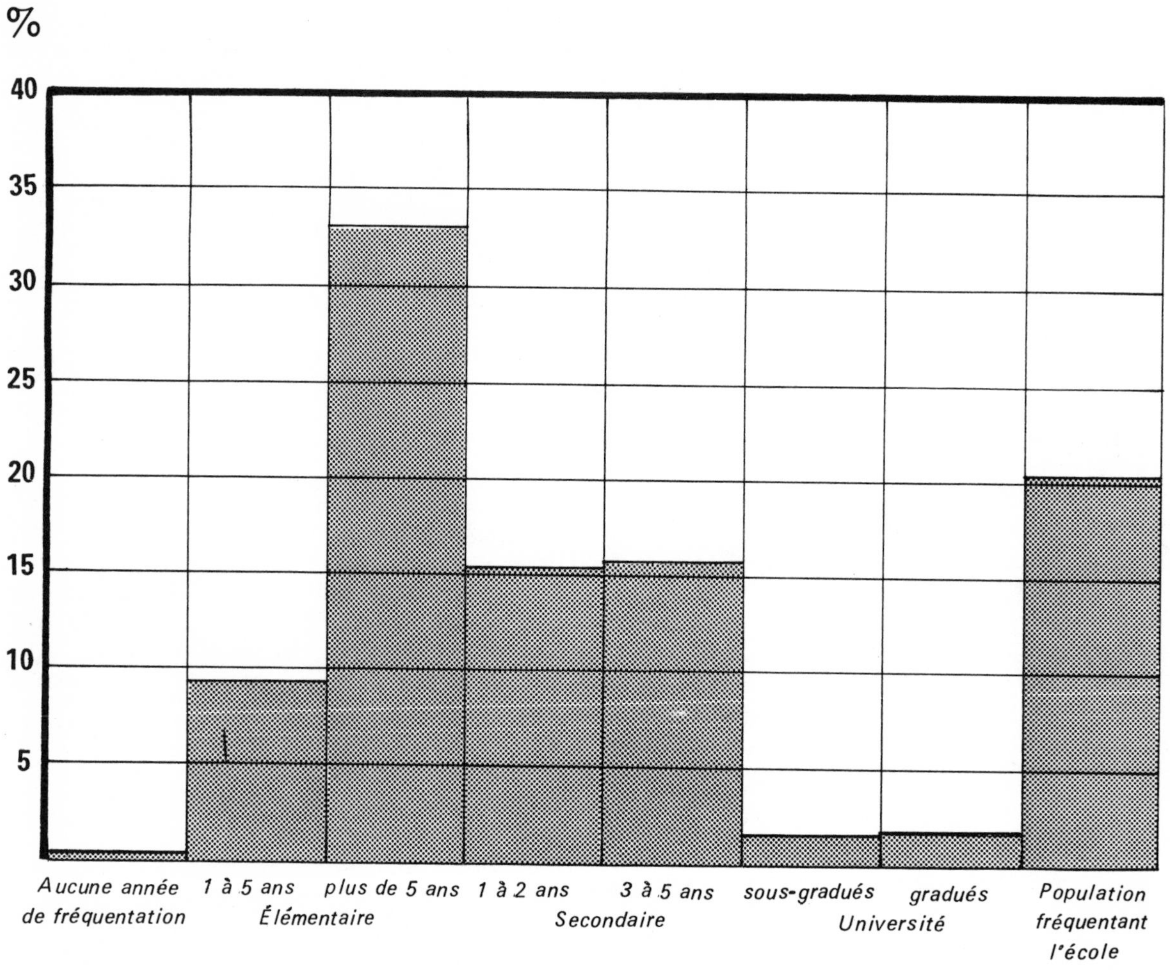

Source: Statistique Canada No 92-550, *Recensement du Canada 1961*, Ottawa.

4

4.1 Répartition de la main-d'oeuvre

4.1.a QUEBEC, ONTARIO, CANADA, 1951-1961-1971

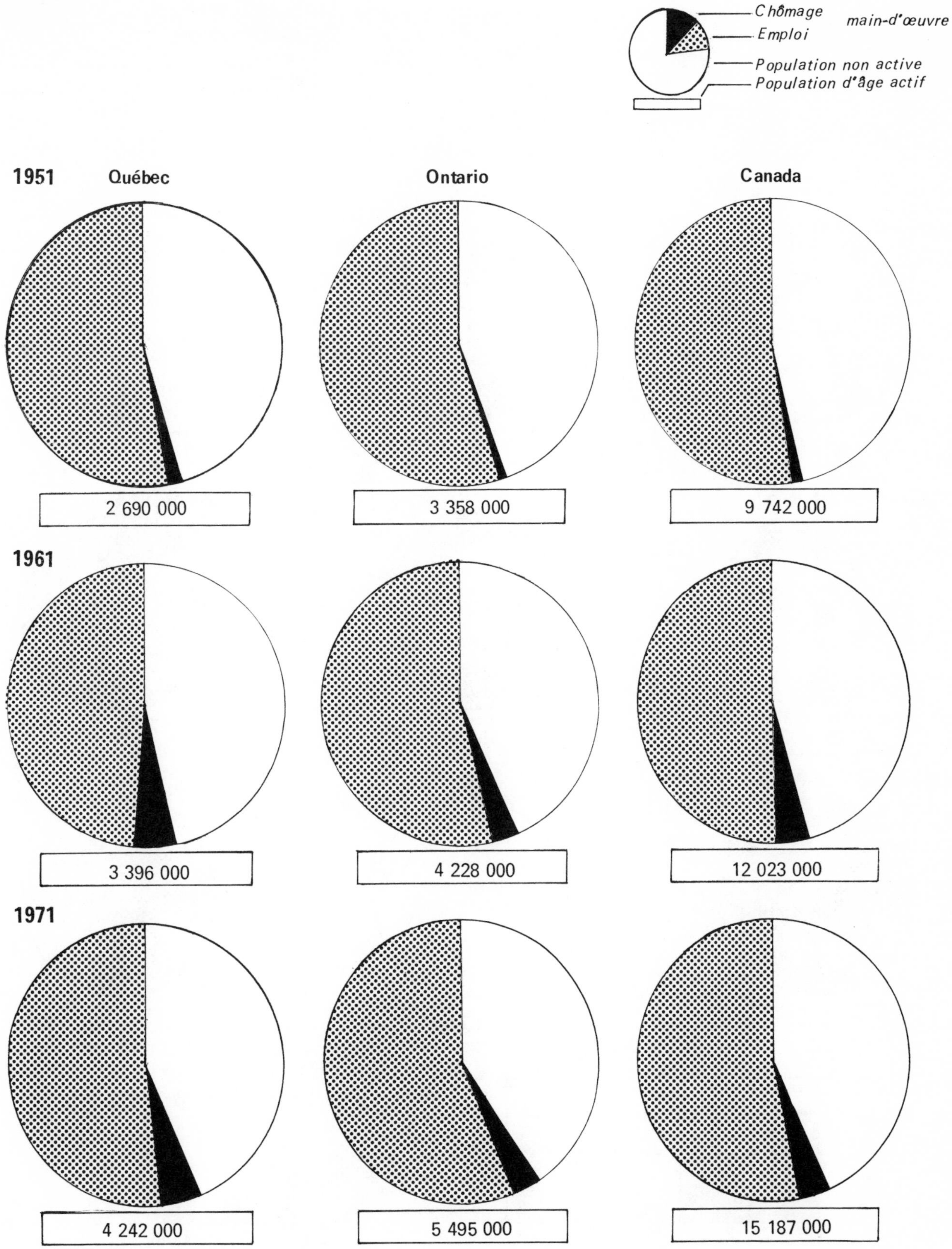

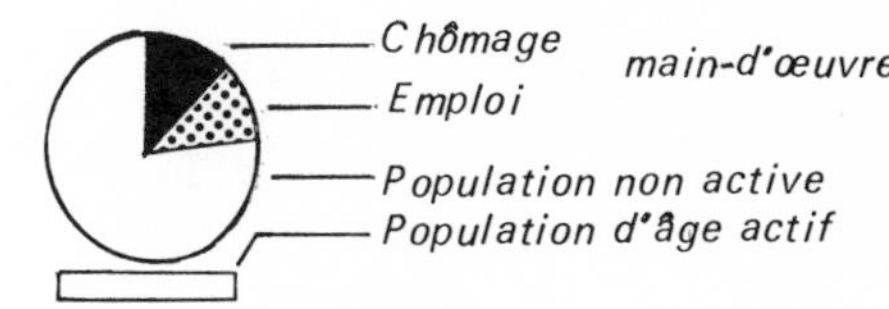

Chômage
Emploi
main-d'œuvre
Population non active
Population d'âge actif
1951
Québec
Ontario
Canada
2 690 000
3 358 000
9 742 000
1961
3 396 000
4 228 000
12 023 000
1971
4 242 000
5 495 000
15 187 000

Sources: *Annuaires du Québec* 1963 à 1972.

Statistique Canada, *Recensements du Canada 1921, 1931, 1941*, Ottawa.

4

4.1 Répartition de la main-d'oeuvre

4.1.b PAR REGIONS ADMINISTRATIVES, QUEBEC, 1968

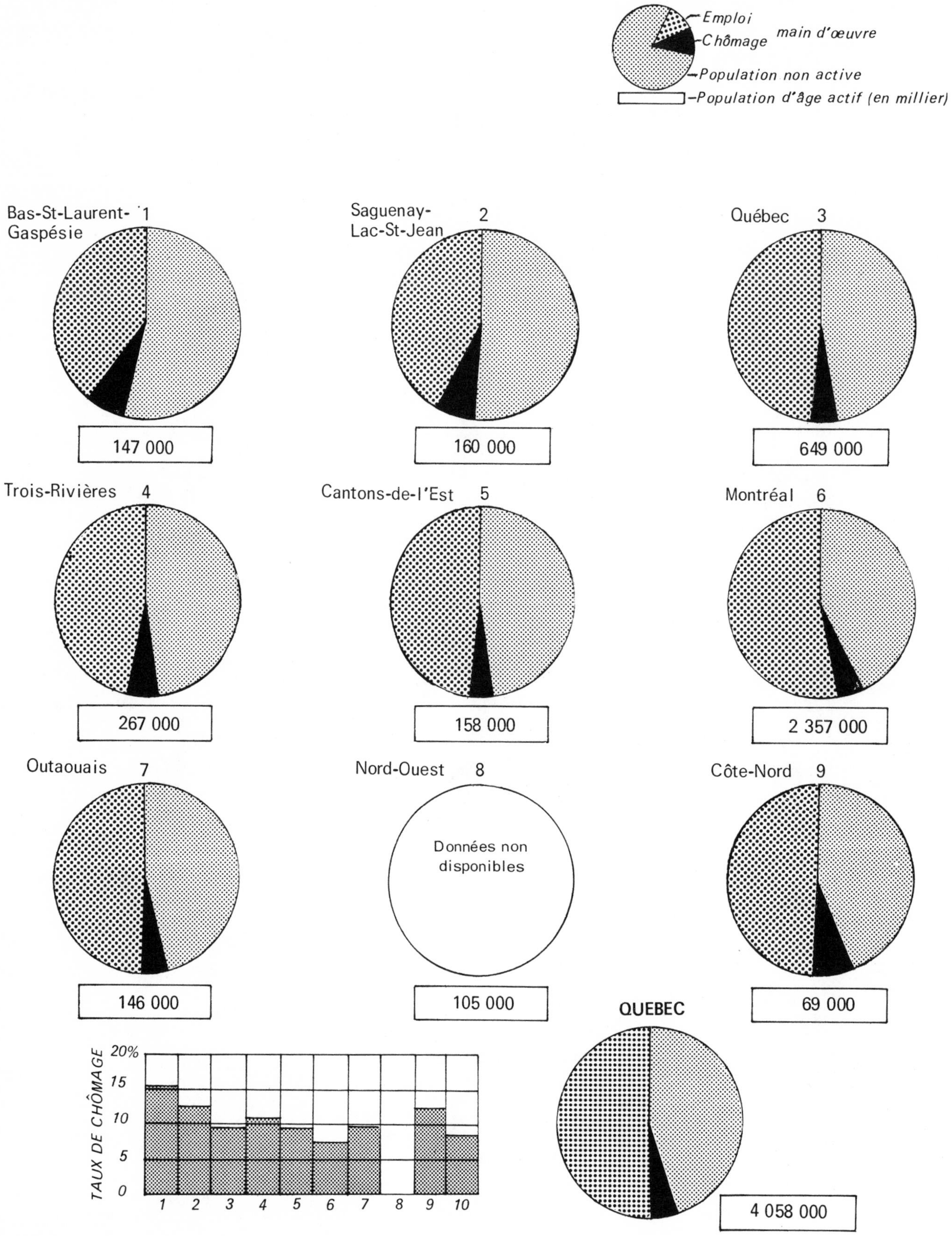

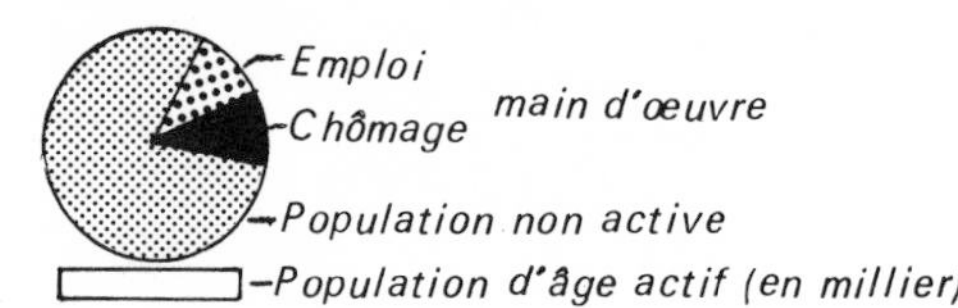

Emploi
Chômage
main d'œuvre
Population non active
Population d'âge actif (en millier)
Bas-St-Laurent- Gaspésie 1
147 000
Saguenay-Lac-St-Jean 2
160 000
Québec 3
649 000
Trois-Rivières 4
267 000
Cantons-de-l'Est 5
158 000
Montréal 6
2 357 000
Outaouais 7
146 000
Nord-Ouest 8
Données non disponibles
105 000
Côte-Nord 9
69 000
QUEBEC
4 058 000
TAUX DE CHÔMAGE
20%
15
10
5
0
1 2 3 4 5 6 7 8 9 10

Source: *Traits généraux de la région administrative no 1, 2, 3, 4, 5, 6, 7, 8, 9 et 10,* (9 publications), Ministère de l'Industrie et du Commerce, Québec, 1972.

4.1 Répartition de la main-d'oeuvre

4.1.c SELON L'AGE, QUEBEC, 1946-1970, ANNEES CHOISIES

Groupes d'âge	
(ligne hachurée)	14-19 ans
(ligne fine)	20-24 ans
(ligne épaisse)	25-44 ans
(ligne pointillée)	45-64 ans
(ligne pointillée épaisse)	65 ans et plus

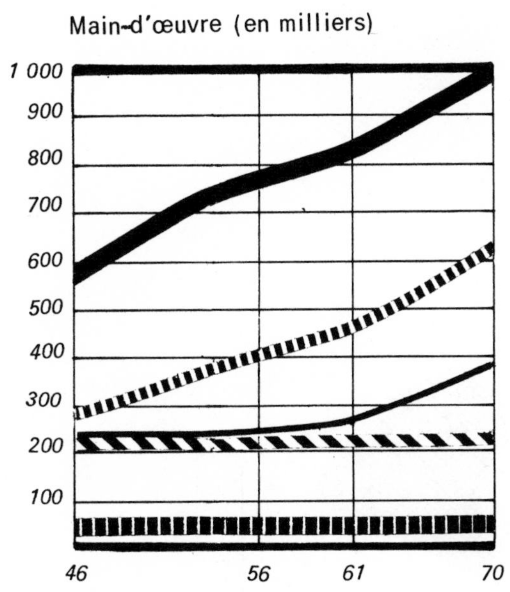

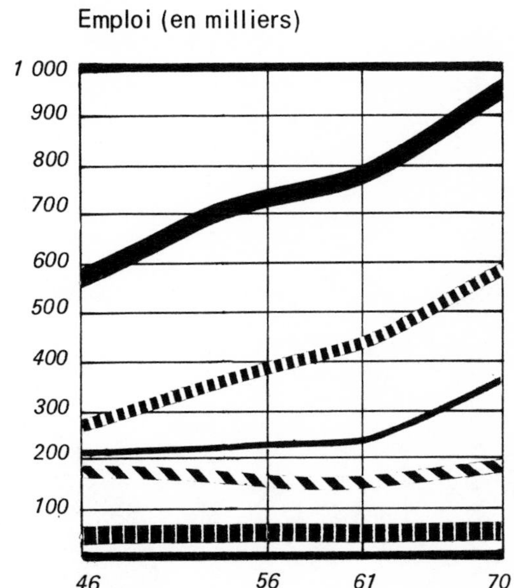

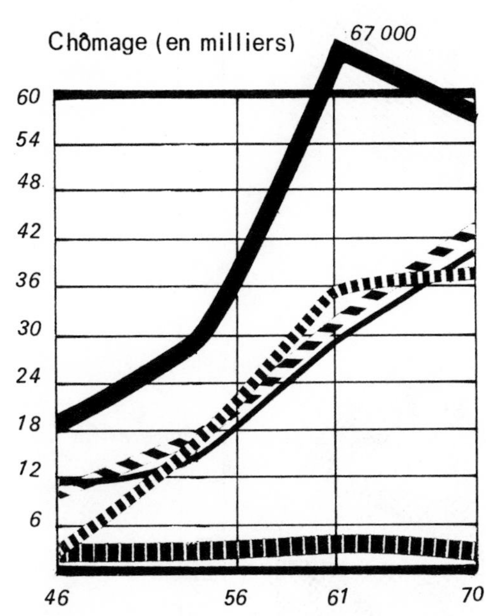

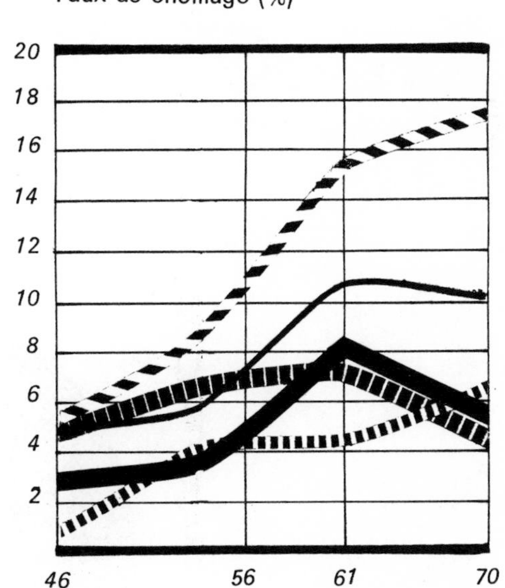

Source: *Annuaires du Québec* 1963 et 1972.

4

4.1 Répartition de la main-d'oeuvre

4.1.d PAR GRANDS SECTEURS Ⓖ ECONOMIQUES, QUEBEC, ONTARIO, CANADA, 1921-1941-1961

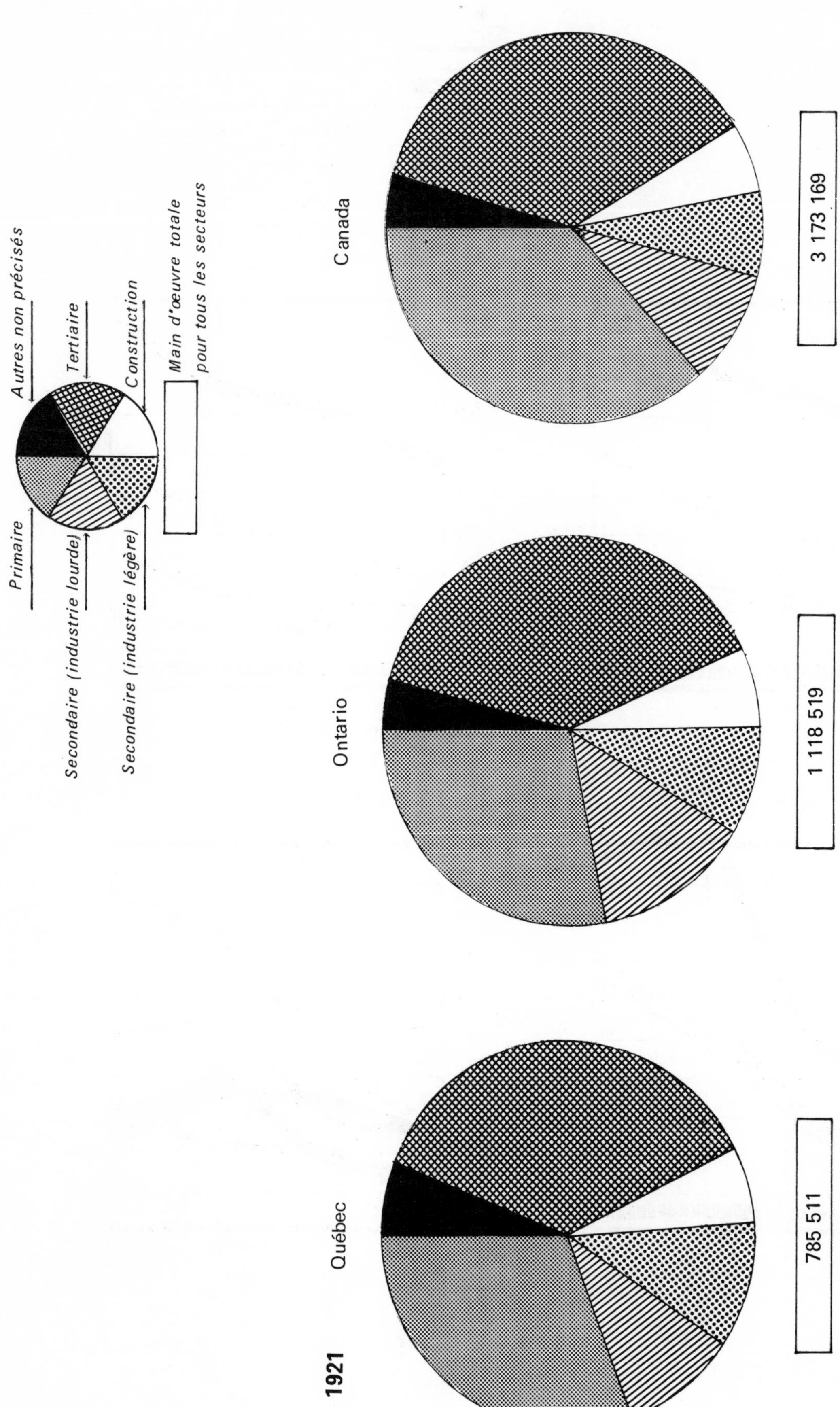

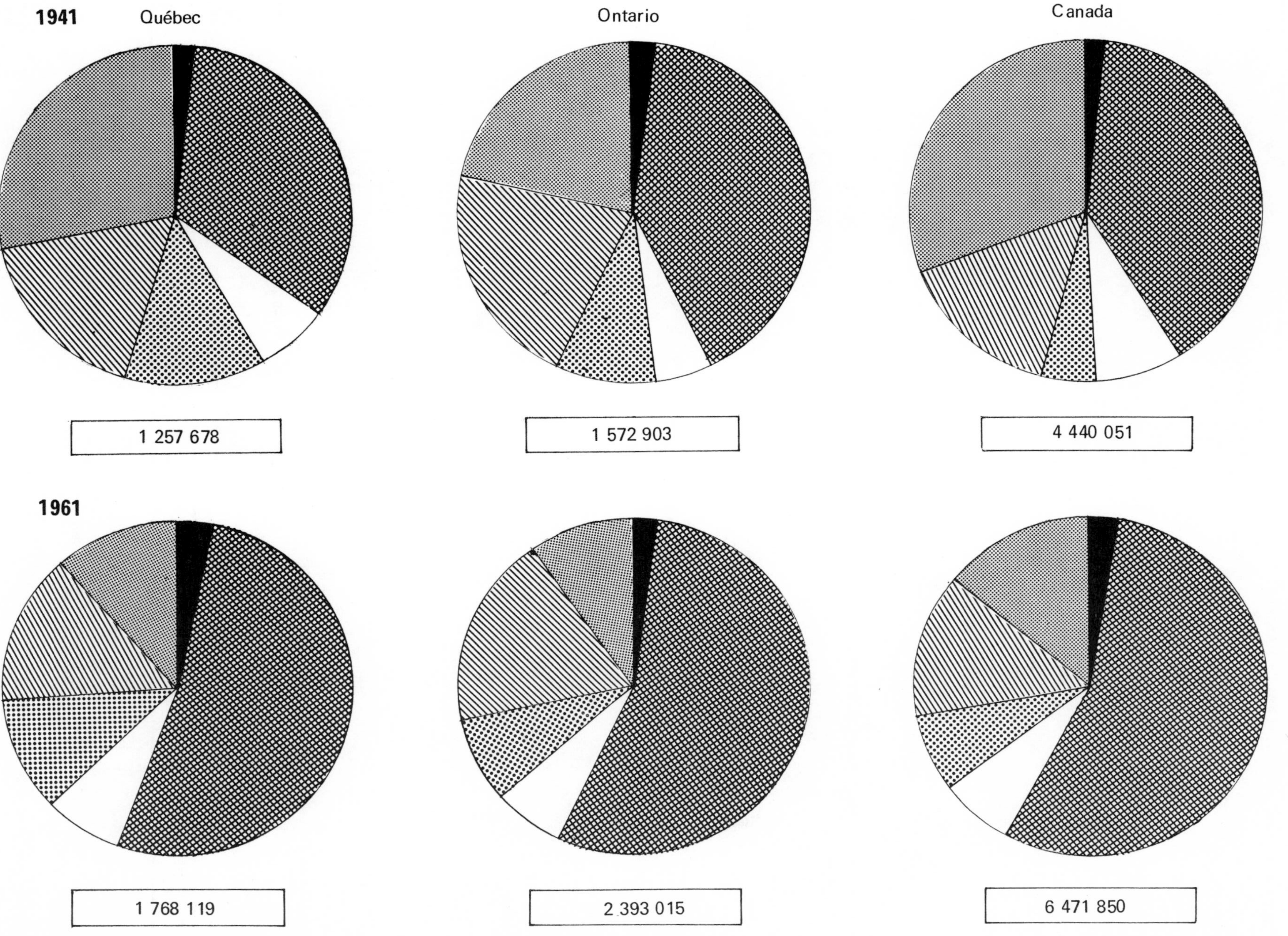

Source: Statistique Canada, *Recensements du Canada 1921, 1941, 1961*, Ottawa.

Note: Voir au glossaire: "Industries selon les secteurs".

4.1 Répartition de la main-d'oeuvre

4.1.e SELON L'INDUSTRIE (G) ET LE SEXE, QUEBEC, ONTARIO, CANADA, 1961 (N)

Industrie	QUEBEC			ONTARIO			CANADA		
	hommes	femmes	Main-d'oeuvre totale	hommes	femmes	Main-d'oeuvre totale	hommes	femmes	Main-d'oeuvre totale
Agriculture	115,638	15,559	131,197	144,664	24,111	168,775	562,075	78,711	640,786
Forêt	41,894	547	42,441	17,282	653	17,935	106,387	2,193	108,580
Pêche	2,948	81	3,029	2,087	98	2,185	35,748	515	36,263
Mines, carrières et puits de pétrole	25,080	774	25,854	41,652	1,008	42,660	116,852	4,850	121,702
Aliments et boissons	48,005	10,725	58,730	64,038	20,520	84,558	169,569	49,616	219,185
Tabac	3,226	3,627	6,853	1,218	707	1,925	4,490	4,343	8,833
Caoutchouc	3,978	1,611	5,589	10,304	2,435	12,739	14,754	4,090	18,844
Cuir	9,767	7,532	17,299	8,177	6,208	14,385	18,839	14,327	33,166
Textiles	25,900	10,488	36,388	14,420	8,249	22,669	41,935	20,317	62,252
Habillement	19,710	38,224	57,940	9,776	13,986	23,762	32,708	59,220	91,928
Bois	21,351	1,090	22,441	18,045	1,922	19,967	93,207	5,664	98,871
Meubles et articles d'ameublement	12,106	1,307	13,413	13,693	2,458	16,151	31,049	4,647	35,696
Papier et produits connexes	33,634	4,331	37,965	31,840	5,883	37,723	88,938	12,702	101,640
Imprimerie, édition et industries connexes	16,498	4,977	21,475	30,741	11,765	42,506	62,649	21,616	84,265
Bonnetterie	4,140	5,946	10,086	2,707	5,276	7,983	7,307	12,439	19,746
Industries métalliques primaires	22,550	1,628	24,178	47,316	2,710	50,026	85,161	4,995	90,156
Produits métalliques	24,208	2,377	26,585	50,400	7,693	58,093	91,841	11,375	103,216
Machinerie	7,895	984	8,879	31,902	4,544	36,446	43,909	5,912	49,821
Matériel de transport	30,759	2,023	32,782	58,604	6,699	65,303	108,430	9,591	118,021
Appareils électriques	19,884	6,461	26,345	39,452	14,951	54,403	62,674	22,250	84,924
Minéraux non-métalliques	13,522	1,293	14,815	19,767	2,482	22,249	42,485	4,534	47,019
Produits du pétrole et de la houille	4,363	538	4,901	4,649	436	5,085	15,249	1,710	16,959
Industries chimiques produits connexes	19,285	6,213	25,498	26,807	8,960	35,767	52,661	16,849	69,510
Industries manufacturières diverses	10,254	4,027	19,281	20,768	10,776	31,544	35,019	15,794	50,813
Construction	123,900	2,461	126,361	149,293	4,573	153,866	420,317	10,776	431,093
Electricité, gaz, eau	16,043	1,483	17,526	24,964	4,148	29,112	62,140	8,364	70,504
Transports et communications	123,839	19,903	143,742	140,650	25,461	166,111	458,052	74,730	532,782
Commerce	185,266	62,772	248,038	249,951	120,589	370,540	690,028	301,462	991,490
Finances	36,482	25,681	62,163	51,303	47,151	98,454	124,310	104,545	228,855
Services	148,531	202,333	350,864	192,337	274,790	467,127	513,917	749,445	1,263,362
Administration publique et défense	82,397	16,797	99,194	142,091	39,172	181,263	396,239	86,686	482,925
Autres	36,366	14,901	51,267	39,769	11,934	51,703	116,579	42,014	158,593
Total pour toutes les industries	**1,289,425**	**478,644**	**1,768,119**	**1,700,567**	**692,448**	**2,393,015**	**4,705,518**	**1,766,332**	**6,471,850**

Note: Voir au glossaire: "Industries selon les secteurs".

Source: Statistique Canada No 94-518, *Recensement du Canada 1961*, Ottawa.

4.1 Répartition de la main-d'oeuvre

4.1.f SELON LA PROFESSION(G) ET L'ORIGINE(G) ETHNIQUE, QUEBEC, 1961

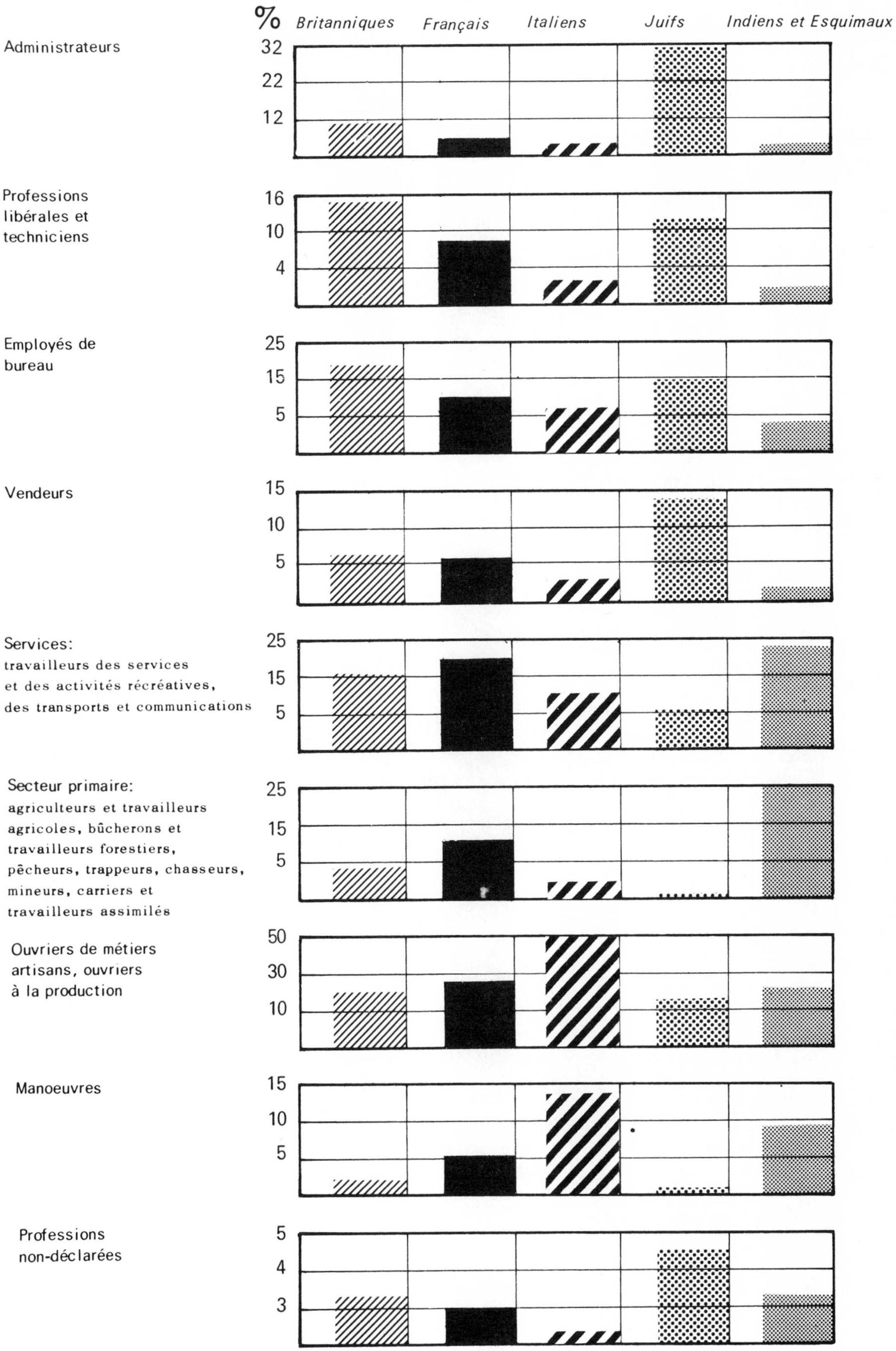

Source: Statistique Canada No 94-515, *Recensement du Canada, 1961,* Ottawa.

MOBILITE SOCIALE (1)

Cet article porte sur l'étude de la stratification et de la mobilité des deux groupes ethniques majoritaires au Québec.

La mobilité que cette étude a tenté de mesurer s'effectue entre deux points bien précis de la vie de l'individu : la naissance et le mariage. La question principale qui est posée est celle-ci : avec quelle intensité le statut transmis à la naissance (à sa naissance le statut d'un individu est déterminé par le statut de sa famille) marque-t-il celui que l'individu occupera à l'âge adulte? C'est ce que nos auteurs définissent comme l'héritage professionnel Ⓖ. La variation de distribution des occupations par rapport à l'origine ethnique et au statut social est analysée dans la période 1954-1964.

L'échantillonnage a été fait par le tirage d'un dossier sur 15 de la population des registres de mariage. Ces dossiers contenaient les données suivantes : date et lieu de naissance, lieu de résidence projetée après le mariage, religion, occupation et origine ethnique.

(1) Tiré de Jacques DOFNY et Muriel GARON-AUDY, "Mobilités professionnelles au Québec", Sociologie et Société, 1,2 (nov. 1969).

4.2 Mobilité sociale

4.2.a HERITAGE PROFESSIONNEL

	1954	1964
professions libérales et haute administration	47,50	23,53
semi-professionnels et cadres moyens	19,05	29,11
cols-blancs	33,77	28,09
ouvriers spécialisés et semi-spécialisés	40,51	35,45
manœuvres	43,48	26,74
services personnels et publics	5,50	12,64
fermiers	26,58	9,44

4.2.b REPARTITION EN POURCENTAGES DES PROFESSIONS DES FILS SELON LEUR ORIGINE SOCIALE, POPULATION FRANCOPHONE, QUEBEC, 1964

profession du fils	profession du père							fils	
	1	2	3	4	5	6	7	totaux	%
1. professions libérales et haute administration	23,53	7,59	14,61	7,20	1,87	3,45	2,04	73	4,71
2. semi-professionnels et cadres moyens	50,00	29,11	24,72	14,99	11,50	16,09	11,85	235	15,16
3. cols-blancs	11,76	16,46	28,09	21,90	16,84	22,99	8,15	245	15,80
4. ouvriers spécialisés et semi-spécialisés	2,94	24,05	14,98	35,45	32,09	28,74	36,48	501	32,32
5. manœuvres	8,82	13,92	8,99	10,66	26,74	16,09	25,74	312	20,13
6. services	2,94	8,86	5,62	8,36	9,89	12,64	6,30	124	8,00
7. fermiers	0,00	0,00	0,00	1,44	1,07	0,00	9,44	60	3,87
totaux	(34)	(79)	(89)	(347)	(374)	(87)	(540)	(1550)	
distribution des pères en %	2,19	5,10	5,74	22,39	24,13	5,61	34,84		

4.2 Mobilité sociale

4.2.c OCCUPATION DES FILS, POPULATION URBAINE FRANCOPHONE ET ANGLOPHONE, QUEBEC, 1954, 1964

	CF		CA	
	1954	1964	1954	1964
non manuels	27,60	42,83	50,00	66,07
ouvriers spécialisés et semi-spécialisés	34,23	34,81	23,64	21,43
manœuvres	25,99	13,63	7,27	8,04
services	10,21	8,26	18,18	3,57

4.2.d ECARTS DE DISTANCIATION PROFESSIONNELLE ENTRE FRANCOPHONES ET ANGLOPHONES, POPULATION URBAINE, QUEBEC, 1954, 1964

		1954		1964	
		pères CF moins pères CA	fils CF moins fils CA	pères CF moins pères CA	fils CF moins fils CA
non manuels	1. professions libérales et hautes administration	- 8,60	-10,46	- 5,82	- 4,44
non manuels	2. semi-professionnels et cadres moyens	0,10	- 4,80	- 5,56	-10,87
non manuels	3. cols-blancs	- 0,13	- 7,14	- 8,30	- 7,95
	4. ouvriers spécialisés et semi-spécialisés	1,06	10,59	- 0,84	13,38
	5. manœuvres	13,20	18,72	12,56	5,59
	6. services publics	- 7,69	- 8,43	- 2,36	0,50
	7. services personnels	2,50	0,46	- 1,72	4,19
	8. fermiers	- 0,44	1,06	12,02	- 0,41

4.2 Mobilité sociale

4.2.e TAUX DE CHOMAGE ET TAUX DE LA MAIN-D'OEUVRE EN FORMATION, QUEBEC, ANNEE SCOLAIRE 1969-1970

4.3 L'INDUSTRIE DE LA CONSTRUCTION DOMICILIAIRE ET LES BESOINS DE LOGEMENTS AU QUEBEC (1)

Ces graphiques mettent en évidence l'interaction entre l'économie globale du Québec et le développement de l'industrie de la construction domiciliaire.

Il transparaît de cet ensemble que l'incidence de l'industrie de la construction sur l'économie globale est capitale, car elle englobe tout aussi bien la construction d'édifices industriels, commerciaux et gouvernementaux. Ces investissements représentent une part importante du produit national brut québécois.

Une des principales propositions de L. Daneau est d'évaluer le volume de construction domiciliaire nécessaire pour satisfaire les besoins du Québec, ce volume étant surtout fonction du facteur démographique. Il est donc fait état de l'accroissement des familles et des ménages et de l'étendue de l'évolution des besoins de logement au Québec pour la décennie 1970-1980.

Le principal problème qui semble ressortir de cette analyse de la situation de l'industrie de la construction domiciliaire, c'est celui qui concerne l'urgence d'une politique de conciliation entre les besoins de logement grandissants et les coûts de construction croissants.

(1) Tiré de Marcel DANEAU, "L'industrie de la construction domiciliaire au Québec", Recherches sociographiques, 9,3 (déc. 1968), 225 et ss.

4.3 Besoins de logements

4.3.a INVESTISSEMENTS PUBLICS ET PRIVES DANS LA CONSTRUCTION EN GENERAL ET DANS LE SECTEUR DE L'HABITATION, QUEBEC, 1950-1965

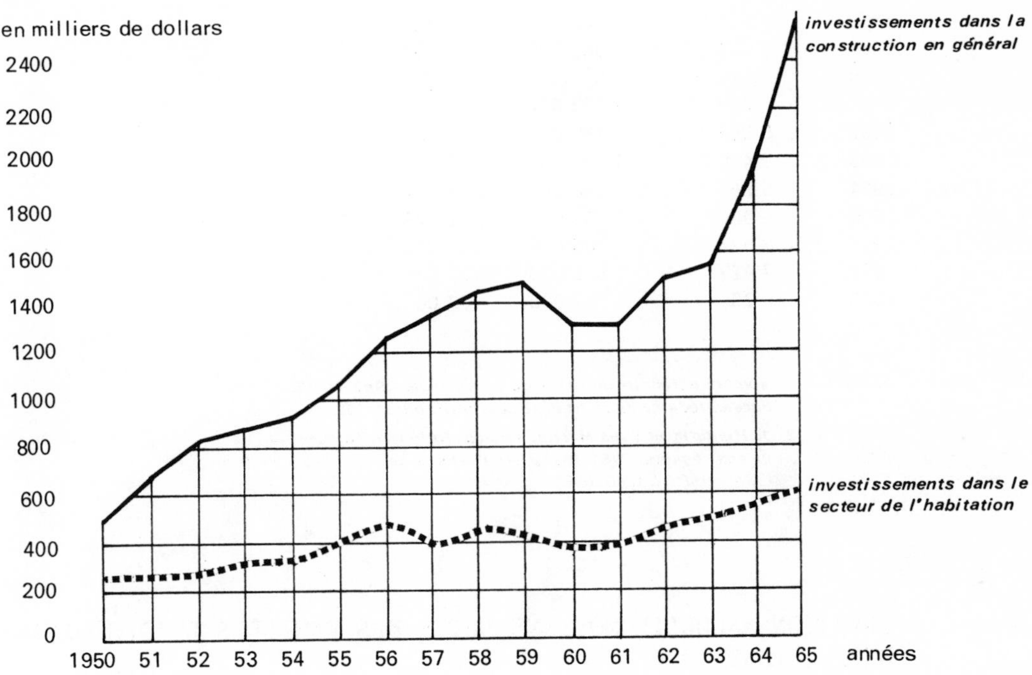

4.3 Besoins de logements

4.3.b NOMBRE DE FAMILLES, QUEBEC, 1951-1981

Année	Population (en milliers)	Nombre estimatif (G) de familles	Nombre estimatif net, (G) de familles formées
1951	4 056	856 041	24 311
1952	4 174	890 000	23 407
1953	4 269	901 000	23 696
1954	4 388	935 000	22 347
1955	4 517	971 000	19 614
1956	4 628	970 414	23 096
1957	4 769	1 012 000	31 676
1958	4 904	1 040 000	20 180
1959	5 024	1 053 000	19 481
1960	5 142	1 078 000	20 374
1961	5 259	1 103 822	15 564
1962	5 366	1 135 000	14 982
1963	5 468	1 157 000	15 967
1964	5 562	1 190 268	24 234
1966	5 907	1 252 000	26 798
1971	6 627	1 405 000	30 065
1976	7 427	1 575 000	33 695
1981	8 288	1 757 000	37 001

Sources : 1. Nombre estimatif de familles au Canada, 1952 à 1963. Bureau fédéral de la statistique, Bulletin 91-204.

2. J. Henripin et Yves Martin, La population du Québec et ses régions, 1961-1981, Les Presses de l'Université Laval, 1964.

4.3.c FORMATION ANNUELLE MOYENNE NETTE DES FAMILLES ET DES MENAGES, QUEBEC, 1951-1976

(en milliers)

Années	Familles (G)	Ménages (G) familiaux	Ménages non familiaux (G)	Total des ménages (G)
1951-56	21,9	23,7	3,2	26,9
1956-61	22,6	24,6	7,4	32,0
1961-66	18,7	20,2	9,0	29,2
1966-71	28,1	29,4	8,2	37,6
1971-76	32,8	34,8	7,9	42,7

Source : Calculs basés sur des données du Conseil économique du Canada, Étude no 4-W.M. Itling, Demande d'habitations pour 1970, p. 14.

4.3 Besoins de logements

4.3.d CHANGEMENTS ANNUELS MOYENS DU STOCK D'HABITATIONS, QUEBEC, 1951-1976

(en milliers d'unités)

	1951-56	1956-61	1961-66	1966-71	1971-76
Formation nette de ménages	26,9	32,0	29,2	37,6	42,7
Ménages familiaux	23,7	24,6	20,2	29,4	34,8
Ménages non familiaux	3,2	7,4	9,0	8,2	7,9
- Hausse du nombre de logements inoccupés	2,0	3,0	3,3	2,0	2,4
- Augmentation nette totale du stock d'habitations	28,9	35,0	32,5	39,6	45,1

Source : *Calculs basés sur des données du Conseil économique du Canada. Etude no 4-W.M. Itling. Demande d'habitations pour 1970. p. 20.*

4.3.e BESOINS DE NOUVEAUX LOGEMENTS, QUEBEC, 1961, 1976.

(en milliers d'unités)

	Augmentation nette du stock immobilier (total de 5 ans)	Remplacements nets (total de 5 ans)	Nouveaux logements (total de 5 ans)	Nouveaux logements (chiffres annuels)
1961-66 ...	162,5	30,2	192,7	38,5
1966-71 ...	·198,0	34,8	232,8	46,6
1971-76 ...	225,5	45,3	270,8	54,1

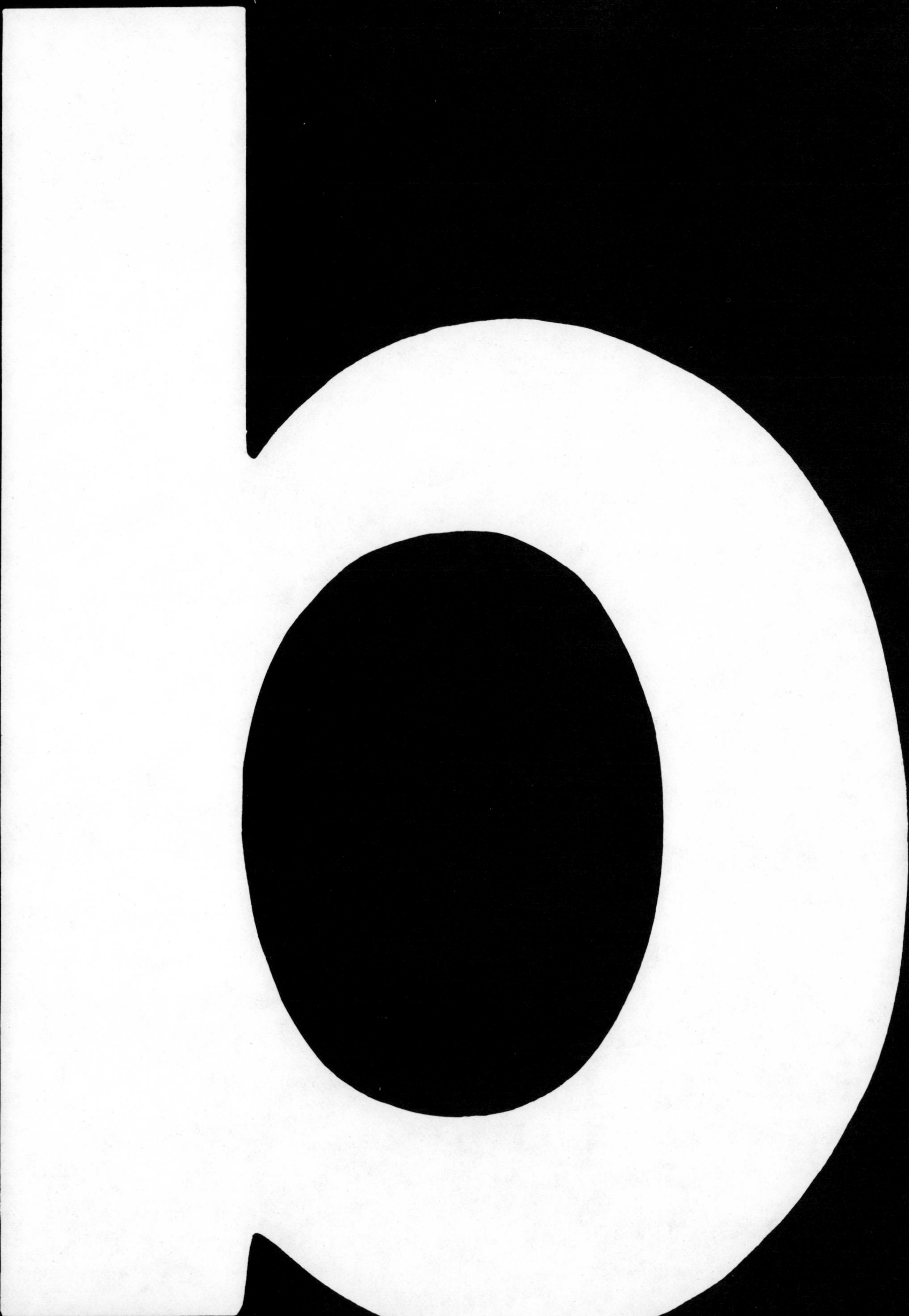

INTRODUCTION

Cette deuxième partie de notre document répond à deux objectifs principaux : elle a pour but premier de fournir les matériaux nécessaires, indispensables même, à la compréhension du document sonore,en deuxième lieu, elle vise à fournir un ensemble de données complémentaires sur des éléments de la société et de l'économie québécoise qu'il était impossible d'aborder à cause des limites de temps et, plus particulièrement, à cause de la pédagogie particulière imposée par la performance audio à laquelle nous étions astreints.

En ce qui concerne le contenu, le titre "Economie" donné à cette partie ne doit pas induire à confusion. En effet, notre approche étant fondamentalement interdisciplinaire et notre conception théorique reconnaissant la base économique première de la société, de la politique et de la culture québécoise, les matériaux ici réunis serviront, non seulement à l'ensemble des présentations sonores de l'économie québécoise, mais encore seront un support aux présentations des autres aspects, politiques et culturels, de la société québécoise.

Voilà pourquoi nous n'avons pas suivi dans l'exposition de ces données "économiques" l'ordre des sept documents sonores traitant de l'économie québécoise. La science économique, telle que nous la concevons, n'a pas cette prétention de vouloir imposer aux autres sciences sociales l'ordonnancement de ses préoccupations. D'ailleurs, l'ordre donné aux sept documents sonores appelés "économiques" ne répond lui-même à aucune prétention théorique; les sept documents sonores veulent être tout simplement l'illustration de sept problèmes, choisis subjectivement parmi tant d'autres, que rencontre aujourd'hui l'économie québécoise.

Nul ne contestera que les problèmes que nous avons choisis d'illustrer ne soient réels et ne s'imposent aujourd'hui à la conscience que le Québécois prend de lui-même et de sa société: le contraste de la richesse et de la pauvreté; la formation d'une épargne relativement importante, sans que les Québécois puissent toujours décider d'eux-mêmes de son orientation et des canaux d'investissement; le contrôle étranger de son économie; le paradoxe d'une économie de consommation et de faible développement du secteur secondaire de sa production; les problèmes du travail; ceux du non-travail et des loisirs; la dispersion et l'inégalité de l'activité économique sur le territoire du Québec. Nous aurions pu traiter d'autres aspects, certes; mais ceux-ci nous sont apparus particulièrement significatifs. Nous les avons choisis pour cela, sans plus.

Pour présenter les données de base de l'économie québécoise, nous avons préféré un ordre qui s'impose par sa simplicité et permet une consultation aisée quelle que soit la nature des préoccupations que l'on poursuit. Le chapitre 5 présente l'infrastructure socio-culturelle: l'équipement scolaire (5.1) et hospitalier (5.2) l'équipement en musées, cinémas et bibliothèques (5.3) et celui des mass-média (5.4).

Le chapitre le plus important - et le plus considérable - est le sixième: il traite d'un ensemble de réalités que nous avons appelées "activités économiques". On y trouvera toutes les données sur la production de tous les secteurs de l'économie (6.1), sur la consommation (6.2), sur le commerce extérieur (6.3). Apparaît ensuite la comptabilité globale du Québec: les données du revenu et du produit national (6.4). Les statistiques de la production par le compte de la valeur ajoutée méritent une attention particulière (6.5). Les fluctuations de la conjoncture, par leur amplitude relativement considérable, caractérisent certains aspects de l'économie québécoise (6.6). Nous présentons, finalement, quelques données sur le contrôle étranger de notre économie (6.7).

L'économie québécoise n'est pas refermée sur elle-même et, par son intégration à des marchés voisins, se développe sous l'effet de mécanismes qui, le plus souvent, prennent racine à l'extérieur d'elle-même. C'est pourquoi nous avons mis les données québécoises en parallèle avec les données canadiennes et ontariennes chaque fois que cela nous était possible. Certes, d'autres marchés, de dimensions plus vastes, exercent-ils une influence tout aussi efficace sur elle. Mais celle-ci ne s'exerce pas aussi directement que les deux autres, ne serait-ce que par l'hétérogénéité des politiques fiscales et monétaires. Cependant nous en avons tenu compte en présentant certaines données du contrôle étranger.

Cette partie, intitulée "économie" n'est pas une description de l'économie québécoise. Elle ne contient même pas toutes les données économiques fondamentales. On trouvera ailleurs celles qui concernent la population et le marché du travail.

Elle ne présente pas de données qui, quoique non immédiatement économiques, peuvent avoir une influence considérable sur la production et la répartition des richesses. Elle ne vaut que par son voisinage avec les autres parties.

Elle n'est pas non plus une explication de l'économie québécoise. On en trouvera quelques fragments dans le document sonore.

5.1 Equipement scolaire

5.1.a ECOLES ET AUTRES INSTITUTIONS D'ENSEIGNEMENT, QUEBEC, 1950-1968, ANNEES CHOISIES

Ecoles et institutions d'enseignement	1950-1951	1955-1956	1960-1961	1965-1966	1966-1967	1967-1968
Ecoles dans les commissions scolaires	8,646	8,420	6,770	5,347	4,835	4,398
Collèges classiques	126	176	181	167	172	158
Autres institutions indépendantes d'enseignement élémentaire et secondaire	484	663	691	330	310	341
Instituts familiaux	38	44	47	40	33	25
Ecoles normales	95	108	114	75	68	51
Ecoles d'enseignement agricole	17	17	15	13	11	11
Ecoles de métiers et institutions techniques	38	41	55	73	70	69
Autres institutions	. .	. .	5	396	364	370

Sources: *Annuaire du Québec* 1972.

Statistique Canada No 81-220, *Statistiques de l'enseignement-estimations,* Ottawa.

Rapports du Ministère de l'Education, 1966-1967 et 1968, Québec.

5.1 Equipement scolaire

5.1.b INSTITUTIONS SECONDAIRES, COLLEGIALES ET UNIVERSITAIRES, PAR REGIONS ADMINISTRATIVES, QUEBEC, 1972

Région	Secondaire	Collégial	Universitaire
Bas-St-Laurent Gaspésie	6 commissions scolaires régionales catholiques 1 commission scolaire protestante	2 C.E.G.E.P. français (Rimouski et Matane) 1 C.E.G.E.P. bilingue (Gaspé)	Université du Québec à Rimouski
Saguenay-Lac-St-Jean	5 régionales catholiques	1 C.E.G.E.P. régional du Saguenay-Lac-St-Jean 4 campus (Chicoutimi, Jonquières, Alma et St-Félicien)	Université du Québec à Chicoutimi
Québec	11 commissions scolaires régionales catholiques 5 commissions scolaires catholiques non affiliées 20 commissions scolaires protestantes non affiliées	7 C.E.G.E.P. français (François-Xavier Garneau, La Pocatière, Lévis-Lauzon, Limoilou, Rivière-du-Loup, Ste-Foy et Thetford) 1 C.E.G.E.P. anglais (St-Lawrence) 15 institutions privées: collèges, écoles normales et séminaires	Université Laval, Ecole nationale d'administration publique, Institut national de la recherche scientifique
Trois-Rivières	7 commissions scolaires catholiques régionales 1 commission scolaire catholique non affiliée 3 commissions scolaires protestantes non affiliées	3 C.E.G.E.P. (Shawinigan, Trois-Rivières et Victoriaville) 2 institutions privées	Université du Québec à Trois-Rivières
Cantons-de-L'Est	2 commissions scolaires régionales catholiques 1 commission scolaire protestante 1 commission scolaire française non affiliée 15 institutions privées	1 C.E.G.E.P. français (Sherbrooke) 1 C.E.G.E.P. anglais (Champlain)	Université de Sherbrooke (française) Université Bishop's (anglaise)

Source: *Traits généraux de la région administrative No 1, 2, 3, 4, 5, 6, 7, 8, 9 et 10,* Ministère de l'Industrie et du Commerce, Québec, 1972.

Région	Secondaire	Collégial	Universitaire
Montréal	19 commissions scolaires régionales catholiques 7 commissions scolaires régionales protestantes 15 commissions scolaires catholiques non affiliées 6 commissions scolaires protestantes non affiliées 78 institutions privées françaises 14 institutions privées anglaises 6 institutions privées bilingues	15 C.E.G.E.P. français (Ahuntsic, André-Laurendeau, Bois de Boulogne, Edouard-Montpetit, Granby, Joliette, Lionel-Groulx, Maisonneuve, Montmorency, St-Hyacinthe, St-Jean, St-Jérôme, St-Laurent, Valleyfield, Vieux-Montréal) 4 C.E.G.E.P. anglais (Champlain, Dawson, John Abbott, Vanier) 16 institutions privées françaises 1 institution privée anglaise 1 institution privée bilingue	Université de Montréal (française) Université du Québec à Montréal (française) Université McGill (anglaise) Université Sir George Williams (anglaise)
Outaouais	4 commissions scolaires régionales catholiques 1 commission scolaire protestante 3 commissions scolaires catholiques non affiliées 1 commission scolaire protestante non affiliée 3 institutions privées	1 C.E.G.E.P. français (Hull)	Université du Québec (direction des études universitaires) à Hull (français) Université d'Ottawa à Ottawa (bilingue) Université St-Paul à Ottawa (bilingue) Université Carleton à Ottawa (anglaise) Université Algonquin à Ottawa (bilingue)
Nord-Ouest	4 commissions scolaires régionales catholiques 2 commissions scolaires catholiques non affiliées 10 commissions scolaires protestantes non affiliées 1 institution privée française	1 C.E.G.E.P. français (Rouyn Noranda)	Université du Québec à Trois-Rivières, campus de Rouyn-Noranda
Côte-Nord	2 commissions scolaires régionales catholiques 2 commissions scolaires catholiques non affiliées 4 commissions scolaires protestantes non affiliées	1 C.E.G.E.P. régional 2 campus (Baie-Comeau, Hauterive)	–
Nouveau-Québec	1 commission scolaire Ministère des Affaires Indiennes et du Nord Canadien	–	–

5.1 Equipement scolaire

5.1.c ECOLES ET PROFESSEURS, PAR CATEGORIES D'ECOLES, QUEBEC, 1965-1972

Années	Nombre d'écoles / Nombre de professeurs	Catégorie d'écoles: Publiques	Privées	Indiennes	Esquimaudes
1965-1966	Nombre d'écoles	**4,550**	**810**	**26**	**11**
	Nombre de professeurs	62,200	6,300	151	37
1966-1967	Nombre d'écoles	**4,570**	**780**	**26**	**11**
	Nombre de professeurs	68,200	6,300	155	35
1967-1968	Nombre d'écoles	**4,100**	**780**	**26**	**11**
	Nombre de professeurs	73,000	6,350	155	34
1968-1969	Nombre d'écoles	**4,100**	**700**	**25**	**10**
	Nombre de professeurs	67,000	6,800	149	37
1969-1970	Nombre d'écoles	**3,500**	**650**	**25**	**10**
	Nombre de professeurs	70,700	4,400	148	40
1970-1971	Nombre d'écoles	**3,300**	**600**	**25**	..
	Nombre de professeurs	73,000	4,100	170	..
1971-1972 (N)	Nombre d'écoles	**3,170**	**540**	**24**	..
	Nombre de professeurs	74,400	3,700	165	..

Note: Estimations.

Sources: *Annuaire du Québec,* 1972.

Rapports du Ministère de l'éducation, 1966, 1967 et 1968, Québec.

Statistique Canada, No 81-220, *Statistiques de l'enseignements-estimations,* Ottawa.

5.2 Equipement hospitalier

NOMBRE D'HOPITAUX ET DE LITS, QUEBEC, ONTARIO, CANADA, 1969

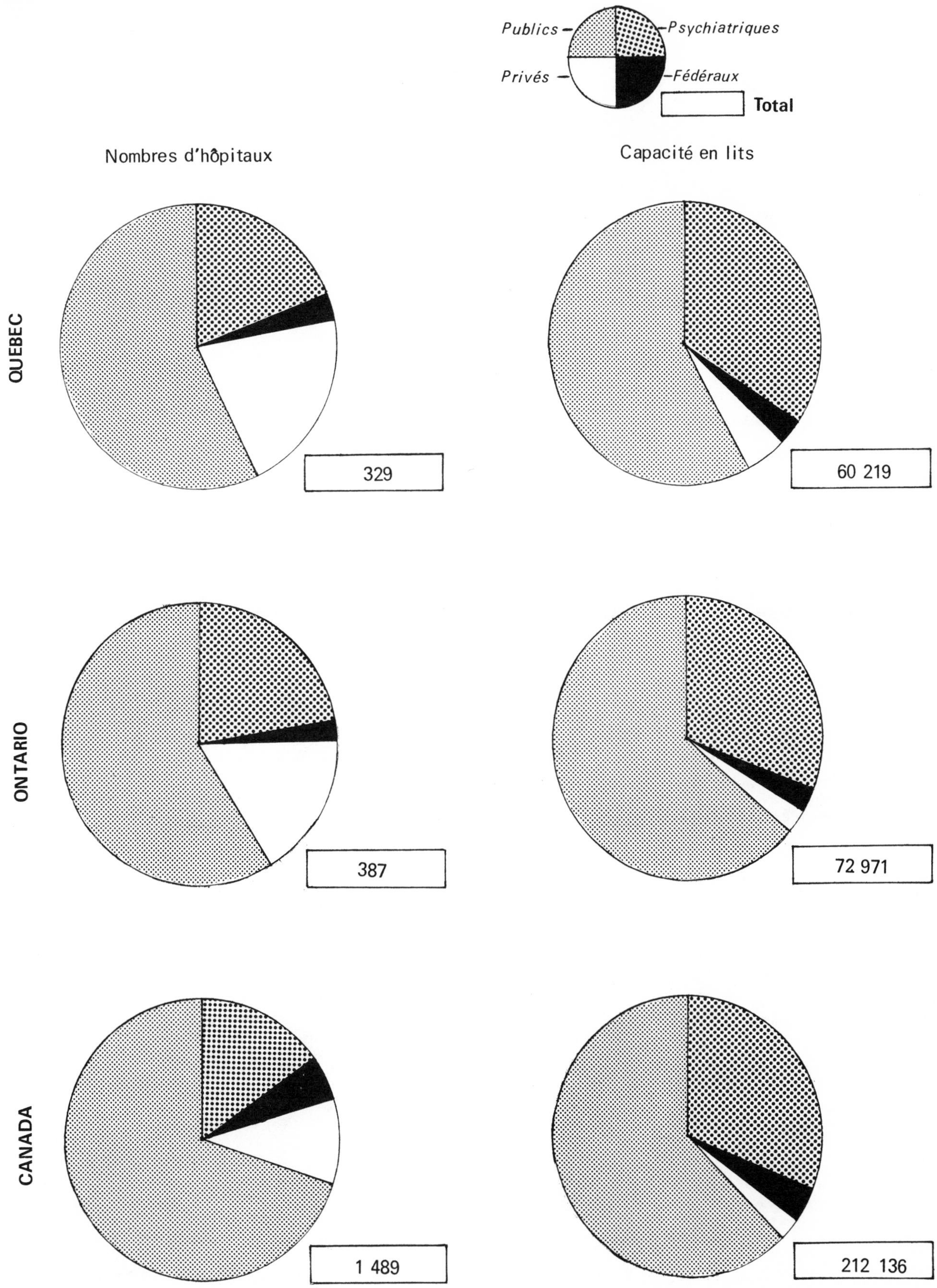

Sources: Statistique Canada, No 83-205, *La statistique de l'hygiène mentale, volume 3,* Ottawa.

Statistique Canada, No 83-216, *La statistique hospitalière, volume 7, indicateurs hospitaliers,* Ottawa.

5.3 Equipement culturel

5.3.a LES MUSEES DU QUEBEC, LOCALISATIONS ET CARACTERISTIQUES, 1964

Endroit no.	nom du musée	année de fondation	autorité dirigeante	période d'ouverture	langue(s) d'usage	spécialités
Arthabaska						
1.	Musée Laurier	1928	province	été (tous les jours)	français	beaux-arts histoire provinciale et locale
Carillon						
2.	Musée Carillon	1938	indépendant	été	français anglais	histoire locale
Caughnawaga						
3.	Catherine Tekakwita	1717	indépendant	toute l année	français anglais indien espagnol italien	histoire canadienne provinciale, locale (Indien)
Chambly						
4.	Fort Chambly	1921	gouvernement fédéral	été (tous les jours)	français anglais	histoire locale et provinciale
Chicoutimi						
5.	Le Musée Saguenayen	1954	indépendant	toute l'année (6 jours par semaine)	français	artisanat peinture moderne et canadienne histoire locale et régionale archéologie géologie minéralogie
Coaticook						
6.	Centre Culturel	1961	municipalité	toute l'année (tous les jours)	français anglais	beaux-arts canadiens
Drummondville						
7.	Galerie D'Exposition Caisse Populaire St-Frédéric	1963	indépendant	toute l'année (tous les jours)	français anglais	beaux-arts
Granby						
8.	Société Zoologique de Granby Inc.	1952	indépendant	été (tous les jours)	français anglais	zoologie
Ile-Aux-Noix						
9.	Fort Lennox	1921	gouvernement fédéral	été (tous les jours)	français anglais	histoire provinciale et locale
Joliette						
10.	Musée du Séminaire	1960	institution d'éducation	sur demande	français	beaux-arts, anciens, modernes, canadiens
Kamouraska						
11.	Institut de Technologie Agricole	1859	institution d'éducation provinciale	toute l'année (6 jours par semaine)	français anglais	industrie agricole histoire naturelle
Knowlton						
12.	Brome County Historical Society Museum	1897	indépendant	été (tous les jours)	français anglais	art canadien histoire locale artisanat indien

Source: Statistique Canada No 81-529, *Musées et Galeries d'art, 1964,* Ottawa.

Endroit no.	nom du musée	année de fondation	autorité dirigeante	période d'ouverture	langue(s) d'usage	spécialités
Lachine						
13.	Musée Sainte-Anne	1918	institution d'éducation	année scolaire	français anglais latin	anthropologie botanique géologie paléontologie zoologie numismatique philathélie
Longueuil						
14.	Collège de Longueuil	1867	institution d'éducation	toute l'année (tous les jours)	français	zoologie
15.	Musée Historique Charles Le Moyne	1963	indépendant	toute l'année (5 jours par semaine)	français anglais	histoire canadienne et locale
Montréal						
16.	Musée de la Banque de Montréal	1963	indépendant	toute l'année (5 jours par semaine)	. .	histoire canadienne et locale numismatique
17.	Canadian Handicrafts Guild Permanent Collection		indépendant	toute l'année (5 jours par semaine)	français anglais	arts décoratifs artisanat (indien et esquimau)
18.	Canadian Railway Museum	1958	indépendant	été	français anglais	histoire du chemin de fer et du tramway excursions
19.	Centre d'Art du Mont-Royal	1963	municipalité	toute l'année (tous les jours)	français anglais	beaux-arts, anciens, modernes, canadiens
20.	Château de Ramezay	1890	indépendant	toute l'année (tous les jours)	français anglais	art canadien histoire canadienne
21.	Galerie Nova et Vetera	1962	institution d'éducation	année scolaire (2 jours par semaine)	français	sculptures meubles anciens du Québec
22.	Musée McCord	1919	institution d'éducation	sur demande	anglais	archéologie canadienne arts artisanat histoire
23.	Jardin Botanique	1931	municipalité	toute l'année (tous les jours)	français anglais	botanique
24.	Musée des Beaux-Arts	1860	indépendant	toute l'année (tous les jours)	français anglais	oriental occidental arts décoratifs beaux-arts archéologie

Endroit no.	nom du musée	année de fondation	autorité dirigeante	période d'ouverture	langue(s) d'usage	spécialités
25.	Musée des Soeurs de Ste-Croix	1889	indépendant	toute l'année (tous les jours)	français anglais	botanique géologie minéralogie paléontologie zoologie
26.	Musée des Sourds-Muets	1880	institution d'éducation	sur demande	français anglais	industrie et technologie histoire et sciences naturelles
27.	Exposition sur St-Joseph et Musée du Fr. André	1945	indépendant	toute l'année (tous les jours)	français anglais	oriental et occidental arts et artisanat religieux beaux-arts histoire canadienne provinciale, locale
28.	Musée Historique Canadien Limitée	1934	indépendant	toute l'année (tous les jours)	français anglais	personnages de cire
29.	Musée Notre-Dame	1937	indépendant	toute l'année (tous les jours)	français anglais	arts décoratifs artisanat et peintures arts anciens et canadiens histoire provinciale et locale
30.	Notre-Dame de Bon-Secours Church	1952	indépendant	toute l'année (tous les jours)	. .	histoire locale (vieilles églises de Montréal)
31.	Musée Redpath	1882	institution d'éducation	toute l'année (tous les jours)	français anglais	archéologie canadienne anthropologie géologie minéralogie paléontologie zoologie
32.	Telephone Historical Collection and Panorama of Telephone Progress	1930	indépendant	toute l'année (5 jours par semaine)	français anglais	histoire des communications
Murray-Bay						
33.	Manoir Richelieu Hôtel	. .	indépendant	été	anglais	art canadien histoire canadienne
Nicolet						
34.	Séminaire de Nicolet	. .	institution d'éducation	toute l'année (tous les jours)	français	histoire locale zoologie
Percé						
35.	Le Centre d'Art de Percé	1957	indépendant	été (tous les jours)	français	peinture moderne géologie minéralogie
Pointe-Claire						
36.	Stewart Hall, City of Pte-Claire Cultural Centre	1962	municipalité	toute l'année (6 jours par semaine)	français anglais	centre d'exposition
Québec						
37.	Archives du Québec	1934	province	toute l'année (tous les jours)	français anglais	arts décoratifs artisanat histoire provinciale monnaies et médailles du Canada et de l'étranger
38.	Centre de Biologie, Aquarium	1959	province	toute l'année	. .	zoologie
39.	Les Voûtes Jean-Talon	1957	indépendant	été (5 jours par semaine)	français anglais	histoire locale
40.	Maison Maillou	1958	municipalité	toute l'année (5 jours par semaine)	français anglais	arts décoratifs artisanat meubles histoire locale
41.	Musée de Minéralogie et de Géologie de l'Université Laval	1852	institution d'éducation	toute l'année (5 jours par semaine)	français	histoire naturelle

Endroit no.	nom du musée	année de fondation	autorité dirigeante	période d'ouverture	langue(s) d'usage	spécialités
Québec						
42.	Musée du Québec	1922	province	toute l'année (tous les jours)	. .	beaux-arts
43.	Musée du Séminaire de Québec	. .	institution d'éducation	toute l'année (tous les jours)	français	arts décoratifs et beaux-arts orientaux et occidentaux histoire canadienne anthropologie botanique zoologie
44.	Musée Historique Inc.	. .	indépendant	toute l'année (tous les jours)	. .	histoire locale
45.	Musée historique de l'Hôtel-Dieu du Québec	1958	indépendant	sur demande	français	artisanat peinture française histoire locale
46.	Musée Royal 22e Régiment	1948	gouvernement fédéral indépendant	toute l'année (tous les jours)	français anglais	histoire militaire
Rawdon						
47.	Earle Moore's Canadiana Settlement	1959	indépendant	été	anglais	histoire locale et provinciale
Rigaud						
48.	Musée du Collège Bourget	1880	institution d'éducation	année scolaire (sur demande)	français	histoire canadienne provinciale, locale histoire naturelle
Rimouski						
49.	Musée du Séminaire	1925	institution d'éducation	toute l'année (sur demande)	français anglais	anthropologie botanique géologie minéralogie zoologie
Ste-Anne-De-Beaupré						
50.	Musée historique	. .	indépendant	toute l'année (tous les jours)	français anglais	peintures anciennes modernes canadiennes
St-Félicien						
51.	Bibliothèque Municipale	1962	municipalité	toute l'année	français	arts décoratifs peinture canadienne histoire canadienne provinciale, locale histoire et sciences naturelles
St-Lin-des-Laurentides						
52.	Sir Wilfred Laurier's Birthplace	. .	gouvernement fédéral	toute l'année (tous les jours)	français anglais	histoire locale et provinciale
Sherbrooke						
53.	La Galerie d'Art	1964	institution d'éducation	année scolaire (tous les jours)	français anglais	beaux-arts
Stanbridge East						
54.	Cornell Mill Museum	1961	indépendant	été (tous les jours)	français anglais	histoire locale et provinciale
Tadoussac						
55.	Chauvin House	. .	indépendant	été	français anglais	histoire locale
Trois-Rivières						
56.	Musée Pierre Boucher	1934	institution d'éducation	sur demande	français	arts décoratifs artisanat peinture canadienne histoire locale et provinciale
Vaudreuil						
57.	Musée historique de Vaudreuil	1954	indépendant	toute l'année (tous les jours)	français anglais	peintures et sculptures anciennes, modernes et canadiennes histoire canadienne, provinciale, locale

5.3 Equipement culturel

5.3.b REVENUS DES MUSEES, SELON LE GENRE DE MUSEES, QUEBEC, ONTARIO, CANADA, 1964

Revenus Ⓖ courants de fonctionnement ($'000)

Québec, Ontario Canada et genre de musée	Institutions répondantes	Subventions fédérales	Subventions provinciales	Subventions du gouvernement local	Droits d'entrée	Droits des membres	Dons	Dotations	Ventes de publications	Autres et non répartis	Total
QUEBEC											
Art	**12**	–	67	24	58	68	109	42	25	78	**471**
Histoire	**15**	49	1	5	219	3	–	–	5	200	**483**
Science	**3**	–	35	–	150	–	1	–	–	85	**271**
Total	30	**49**	**103**	**29**	**428**	**71**	**111**	**42**	**29**	**363**	**1,225**
ONTARIO											
Art	**20**	832	13	216	17	78	65	–	3	100	**1,325**
Histoire	**61**	277	27	357	555	6	2	11	150	197	**1,582**
Science	**6**	–	1,246	15	33	8	–	–	–	773	**2,075**
Total	87	**1,109**	**1,286**	**589**	**605**	**92**	**67**	**11**	**153**	**1,069**	**4,981**
CANADA											
Art	**49**	848	223	373	93	251	206	66	30	274	**2,365**
Histoire	**140**	1,654	328	576	808	10	9	11	160	460	**4,018**
Science	**25**	6	1,696	37	357	8	24	–	25	929	**3,083**
Total	214	**2,510**	**2,248**	**987**	**1,258**	**269**	**239**	**77**	**215**	**1,663**	**9,466**

Source: Statistique Canada No 81-529, *Musées et Galeries d'art, 1964,* Ottawa.

5.3 Equipement culturel

5.3.c DEPENSES DES MUSEES, SELON LE GENRE DE MUSEES, QUEBEC, ONTARIO, CANADA, 1964

Dépenses Ⓖ courantes de fonctionnement ($'000)

Québec, Ontario Canada et genre de musée	Institutions répondantes	Administration			Recherche		Entretien		Publications	Autres et non répartis	Total
		Traitements	Matières et fournitures d'étalage	Autres	Traitements	Autres	Traitements	Autres			
QUEBEC											
Art	**12**	191	–	96	–	–	114	70	4	71	**548**
Histoire	**15**	138	24	130	57	2	10	59	13	22	**455**
Science	**3**	39	2	12	38	4	24	–	–	–	**119**
Total	30	**369**	**27**	**238**	**95**	**6**	**149**	**129**	**17**	**93**	**1,122**
ONTARIO											
Art	**20**	712	132	111	–	12	85	29	59	118	**1,258**
Histoire	**61**	375	39	54	45	2	253	176	13	490	**1,447**
Science	**6**	435	63	18	360	18	267	15	14	884	**2,075**
Total	87	**1,521**	**234**	**183**	**405**	**32**	**605**	**219**	**87**	**1,492**	**4,779**
CANADA											
Art	**49**	1,125	139	248	42	25	216	109	70	342	**2,315**
Histoire	**140**	758	81	252	104	4	359	283	30	1,968	**3,839**
Science	**25**	716	111	78	433	34	351	35	23	1,013	**2,794**
Total	214	**2,600**	**330**	**578**	**580**	**63**	**927**	**426**	**123**	**3,322**	**8,949**

Source: Statistique Canada No 81-529, *Musées et Galeries d'art, 1964,* Ottawa.

5.3 Equipement culturel

5.3.d REPARTITION DES MUSEES (G), SELON LE GENRE D'INSTITUTIONS, QUEBEC, ONTARIO, CANADA, 1964

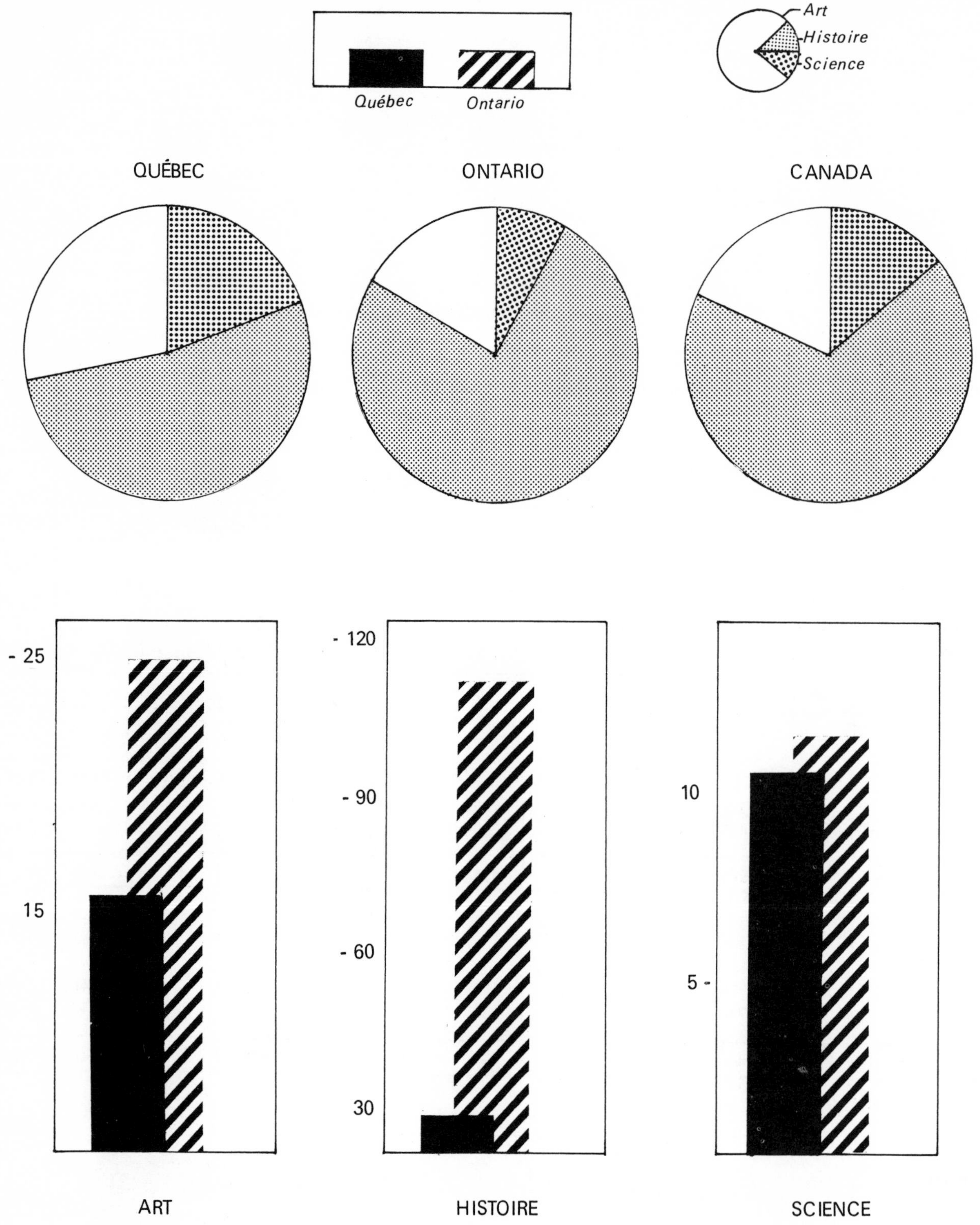

Source: Statistique Canada No 81-529, *Musées et Galeries d'art, 1964,* Ottawa.

5.3.e CARACTERISTIQUES DES MUSEES, SELON L'AUTORITE DIRIGEANTE, QUEBEC, ONTARIO, CANADA, 1964

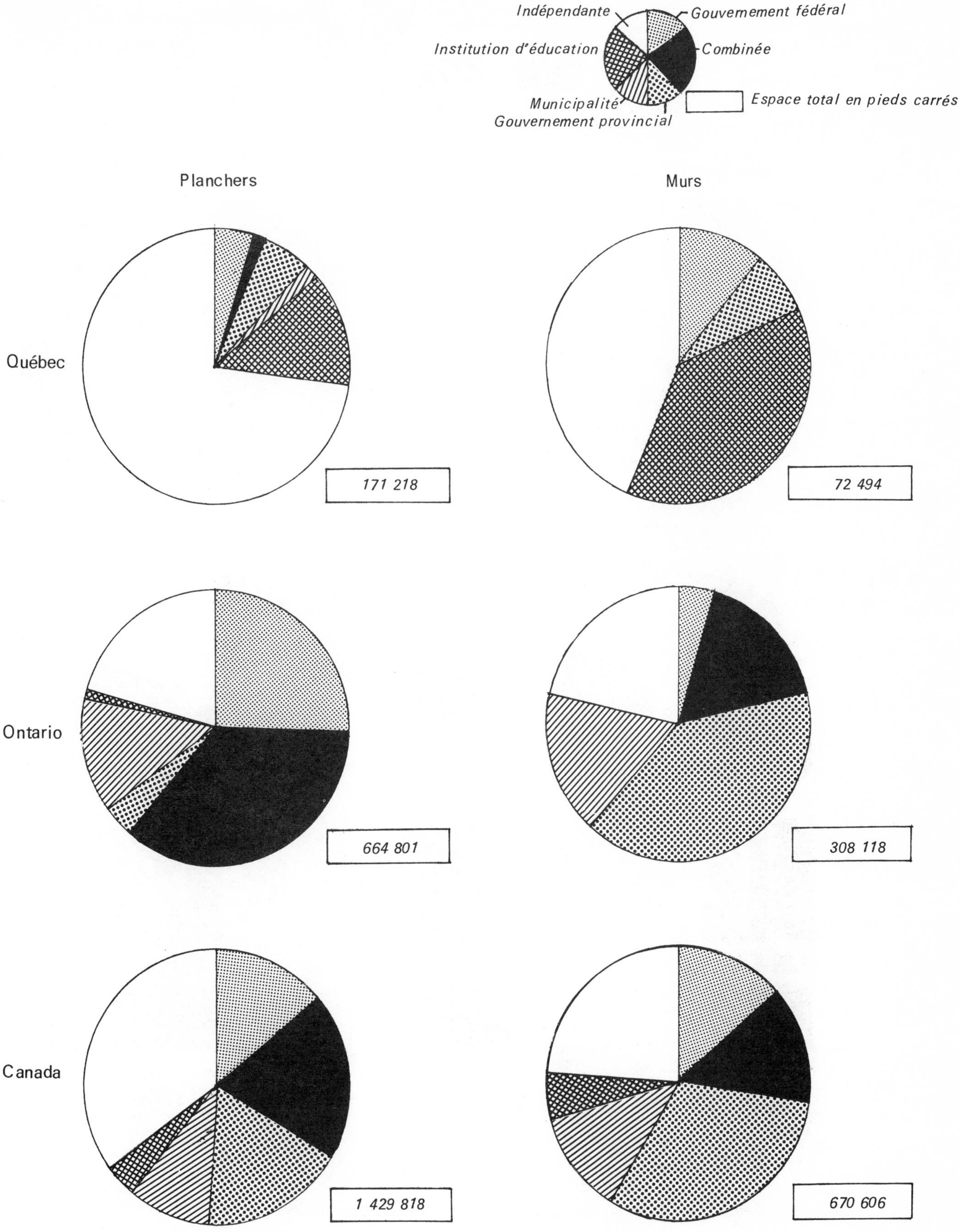

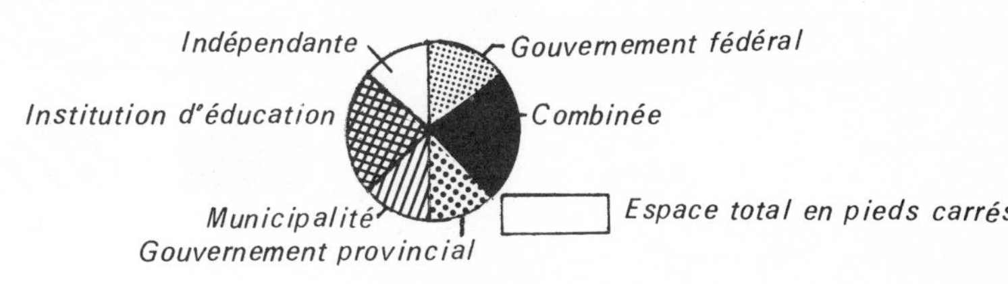

Planchers

Murs

Québec

171 218

72 494

Ontario

664 801

308 118

Canada

1 429 818

670 606

Source: Statistique Canada No 81-529, *Musées et Galeries d'Art 1964,* Ottawa.

5.3 Equipement culturel

5.3.f BIBLIOTHEQUES URBAINES ET REGIONALES, POPULATIONS DESSERVIES, QUEBEC, ONTARIO, CANADA, 1968

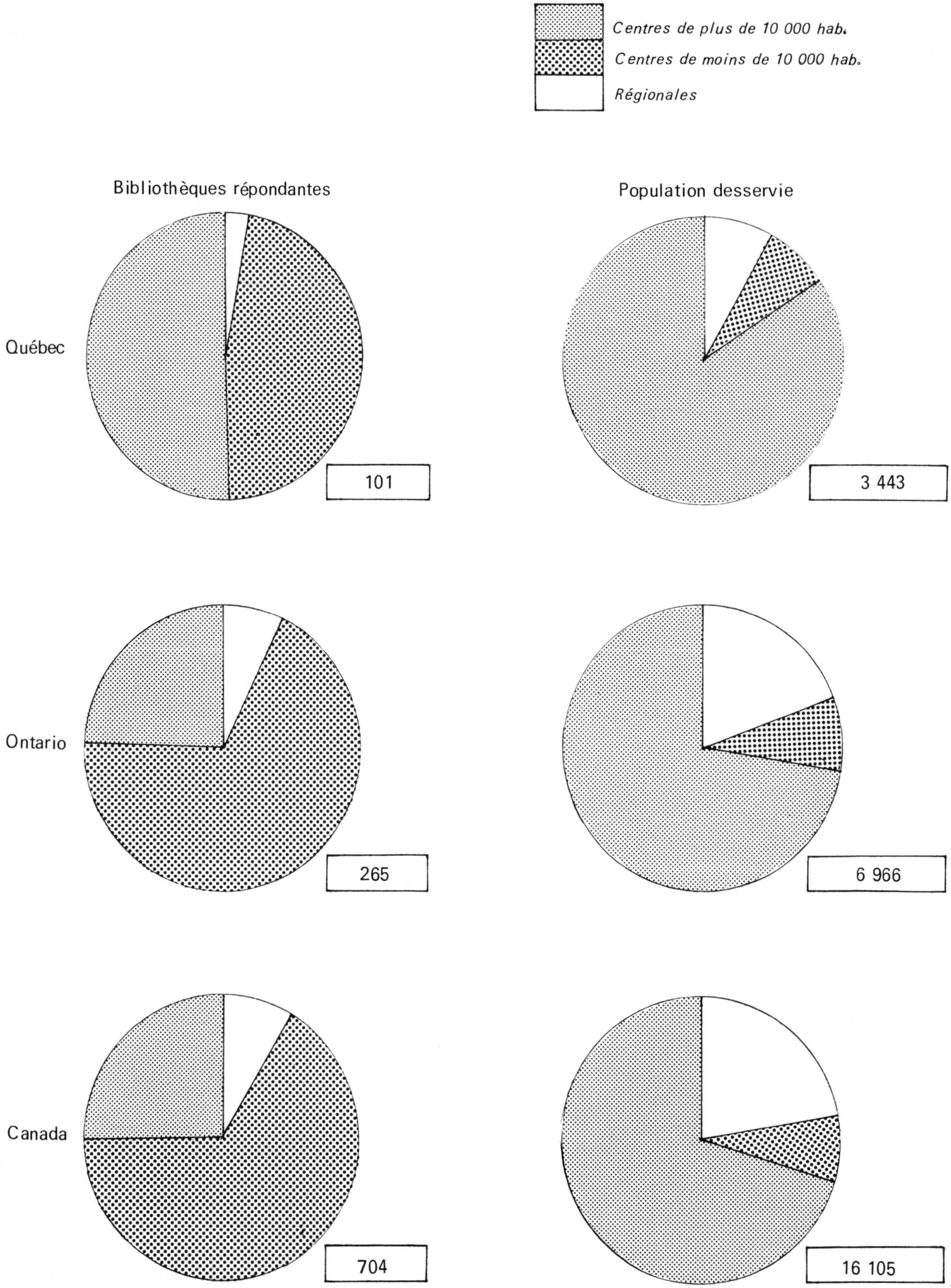

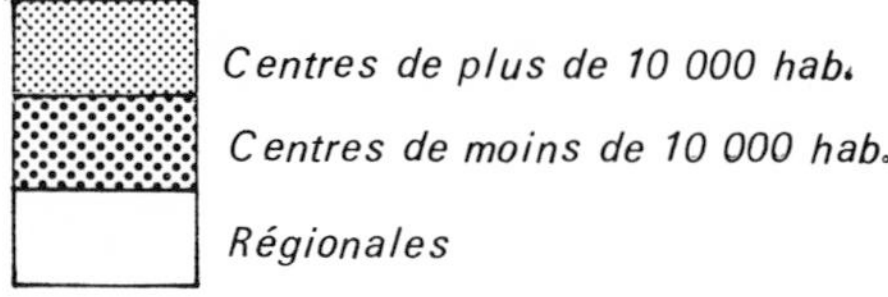

Bibliothèques répondantes

Population desservie

Québec

101

3 443

Ontario

265

6 966

Canada

704

16 105

Source: Statistique Canada, No 81-206, *Relevé des bibliothèques partie 2*, Ottawa, 1968.

5.3 Equipement culturel

5.3.g CINEMAS, QUEBEC, ONTARIO, CANADA ET VILLE DE MONTREAL, 1960, 1965 ET 1970

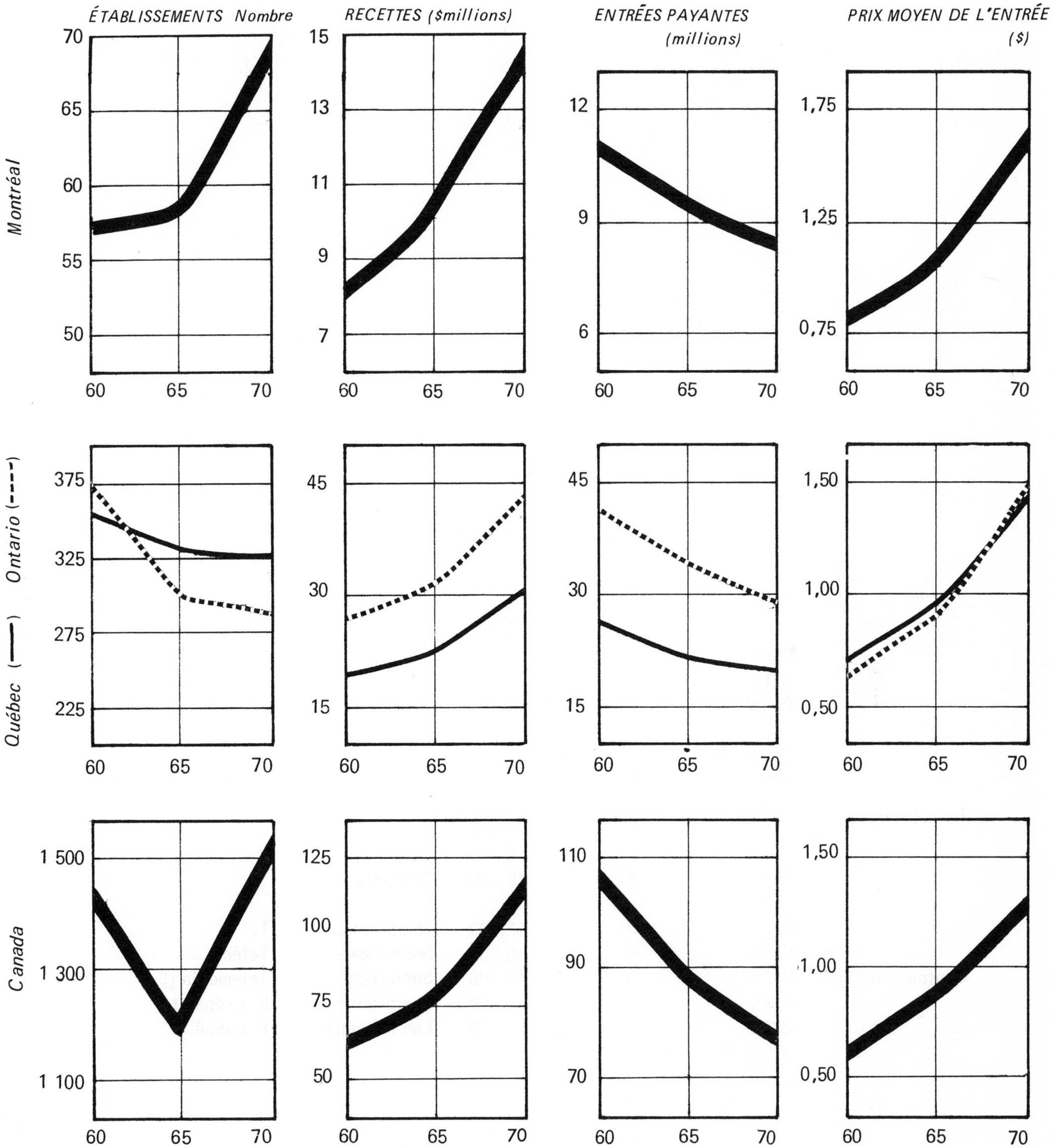

Source: Statistique Canada No 63-207, *Cinémas et distributeurs de films,* 1965, 1966 et 1969, Ottawa.

5

5.4 Mass-media

5.4.a POSTES DE RADIO, PAR REGIONS ADMINISTRATIVES, QUEBEC, 1970

Région	Nom Poste	Langue F (Française) A (Anglaise)	Puissance maximum en watts	Centre d'émission	Principaux actionnaires Ⓖ
Bas-St-Laurent-Gaspésie	CJBR	F	10,000	Rimouski	Télémédia Limitée (Beaubien)
	CJBR-FM	F	20,000	Rimouski	Télémédia (Beaubien)
	CKBL	F	10,000	Matane	R. Lapointe
	CHNC	F	10,000	New-Carlisle	Divers (Dr. Houde)
Saguenay-Lac-St-Jean	CFGT	F	1,000	Alma	Divers
	CJMD	F	. .	Chibougamau	J.M. Duchaine
	CBJ	F	10,000	Chicoutimi	Radio-Canada
	CJMT	F	1,000	Chicoutimi	Tremblay-Laroche
	CHVD	F	. .	Dolbeau	J.M. Duchaine
	CHRL	F	1,000	Roberval	Benoit Lévesque
Québec	CHRC-FM	F	81,000	Québec	Baribeau, Pratte, Lepage
	CHRC	F	50,000	Québec	Baribeau, Pratte, Lepage
	CJRD	F	10,000	Québec	R. Crépault
	CKCV	F	10,000	Québec	Baribeau, Pratte, Lepage
	CJFP	F	10,000	Rivière-du-Loup	Divers (Simard)
	CKRB	F	10,000	St-Georges	Y. Thibodeau
	CBV	F	5,000	Québec	Radio-Canada
	CKBM	F	1,000	Montmagny	A. Mercier
	CFLS	F	250	Lévis	Bégin, Coté, Ruel
	CFOM	A	250	Québec	Baribeau, Pratte, Lepage
Trois-Rivières	CFDM-FM	F	100,000	Drummondville	Divers
	CHRD	F	10,000	Drummondville	Divers
	CFLM	F	. .	La Tuque	J. Trépanier (33%)
	CKSM	F	10,000	Shawinigan	Pratte, Desmarais, Brillant
	CJTR	F	10,000	Trois-Rivières	R. Crépault
	CHLN	F	10,000	Trois-Rivières	Télémédia (Beaubien)
Cantons-de-L'Est	CHLT-FM	F	62,000	Sherbrooke	Télémédia (Beaubien)
	CHLT	F	10,000	Sherbrooke	Télémédia (Beaubien)
	CKTS	A	10,000	Sherbrooke	Télémédia (Beaubien)
	CJRS	F	10,000	Sherbrooke	R. Crépault
	CKFL	F	1,000	Lac Mégantic	F. Labbé

Sources: *Traits généraux de la région administrative No 1, 2, 3, 4, 5, 6, 7, 8, 9 et 10,* (9 publications), Ministère de l'Industrie et du Commerce, Québec, 1972.

Rapport de la Commission Davis, *Les Mots, la Musique et les Sous,* Ottawa, 1970.

Région	Nom	Langue	Puissance	Centre d'émission	Principaux actionnaires
	Poste	F (Française) A (Anglaise)	maximum en watts		
	CKVL-FM	F-A	307,000	Montréal	J. Tietolman
	CFGL-FM	F	100,000	Laval	J.P. Coallier - R. Saucier
	CBF	F	50,000	Montréal	Radio-Canada
	CJMS	F	50,000	Montréal	R. Crépault
	CKAC	F	50,000	Montréal	Télémédia (Beaubien)
	CKLM	F	50,000	Montréal	Divers (Baribeau & Fils 20%)
	CKVL	F	50,000	Montréal	J. Tietolman
	CBM	A	50,000	Montréal	Radio-Canada
	CJAD	A	50,000	Montréal	Standard Broadcasting Corp. Ltd.
	CJFM	A	41,200	Montréal	Standard Broadcasting Corp. Ltd.
Montréal	CFQR-FM	A	41,400	Montréal	Bushwell Communications Ltd.
	CKGM-FM	F-A	41,200	Montréal	G.W. Stirling
	CKMF	F	40,000	Montréal	, .
	CHEF	F	10,000	Granby	Desmarais, Parisien, Francoeur
	CHRS	F	10,000	St-Jean	J.P. Auclair
	CJSO	F	10,000	Sorel	H. Olivier
	CFOX	A	10,000	Montréal	Gordon Sinclair Jr.
	CKGM	A	10,000	Montréal	G.W. Stirling
	CFMB	F-A	10,000	Montréal	Stanczykowski
	CFCF	A	5,000	Montréal	Bushwell Communications Ltd.
	CKJL	F	1,000	St-Jérôme	J. Lalonde
	CKBS	F	250	St-Hyacinthe	Divers (J.M. Lorange)
	CKCH-FM	F	74,000	Ottawa-Hull	Télémédia (Beaubien)
Outaouais	CKCH	F	5,000	Hull	Télémédia (Beaubien)
	CKML	F	1,000	Mt-Laurier-Maniwaki	Divers
	CKVD	F	10,000	Val-d'Or	J.Y. Gourd
	CHAD	F	1,000	Amos	J.Y. Gourd
Nord-Ouest	CKLS	F	1,000	La Sarre	J.Y. Gourd
	CKRN	F	1,000	Rouyn	J.Y. Gourd
	CKVT	F	1,000	Rouyn-Noranda	J.Y. Gourd
	CKVM	F	275	Ville-Marie	Divers (900 actionnaires égaux)
Côte-Nord	CKCN	F-A	10,000	Sept-Iles	R. Lapointe
	CHLC	F	5,000	Hauterive	Divers (Martel-Desjardins)
Nouveau-Québec			(ondes courtes)		Radio-Canada

5

5.4 Mass-media

5.4.b JOURNAUX, PAR REGIONS ADMINISTRATIVES, QUEBEC, 1970

Région	Nom du journal	Langue F(Française) A(Anglaise)	Tirage nombre	Lieu	Type H(Hebdo) Q(Quotidien)
Bas-St-Laurent Gaspésie	Le Progrès et l'Echo	F	10,037	Rimouski	H
	Le Rimouskois	F	10,000	Rimouski	H
	Le Péninsulaire	F	5,049	Mont-Joli	H
	La Voix Gaspésienne	F	3,608	Matane	H
	L'Avant-Poste Gaspésien	F	2,999	Amqui	H
	Nouvelles	F	2,750	Mont-Joli	H
	Gaspé peninsula voyageur	F-A	. .	Murdochville	H
	Le Madelinot	F	. .	Cap-aux-Meules	H
Saguenay-Lac-St-Jean	**Le Soleil du Saguenay-Lac-St-Jean** (Famille Gilbert)	**F**	. .	**Chicoutimi**	**Q**
	Progrès-Dimanche	F	36,000	Chicoutimi	H
	Progrès Régional	F	35,750	Chicoutimi	H
	Le Lac-St-Jean	F	5,683	Alma	H
	Le Réveil au Saguenay	F	5,075	Jonquières	H
	L'Etoile-du-Lac	F	4,800	Roberval	H
	La Sentinelle	F	2,533	Chibougamau	H
Québec	**Le Soleil** (Famille Gilbert)	**F**	**158,645**	**Québec**	**Q**
	L'Action (divers)	**F**	**25,234**	**Québec**	**Q**
	Le journal de Québec (Péladeau)	**F**	**14,141**	**Vanier**	**Q**
	Rond-Point	F	18,000	Ste-Foy	H
	Nouvelles	F	15,500	St-George	H
	L'Appel	F	10,500	Ste-Foy	H
	L'Eclaireur-Progrès	F	8,174	St-George	H
	Le Progrès	F	7,850	Thetford	H
	La Tribune	F	7,500	Lévis	H
	Le Peuple	F	7,379	Montmagny	H
	La Voix du Sud	F	6,843	Lac Etchemin	H
	Le St-Laurent	F	6,818	Rivière-du-Loup	H
	L'Elan de la Rive-Sud	F	5,500	Lévis	H
	Le Guide	F	3,800	Ste-Marie de Beauce	H
	Chronicle Telegraph	A	3,797	Québec	H
	Le Courrier de Montmagny	F	3,792	Montmagny	H
Trois-Rivières	**Le Nouvelliste** (Desmarais, Parisien, Francoeur)	**F**	**49,251**	**Trois-Rivières**	**Q**
	L'Echo du St-Maurice	F	20,000	Shawinigan	H
	La Voix de Shawinigan Grand'Mère	F	18,750	Shawinigan	H
	La Nouvelle	F	12,000	Victoriaville	H
	Le Journal du Cap	F	11,500	Cap-de-la-Madeleine	H
	La Parole	F	11,091	Drummondville	H
	Courrier-Sud	F	10,000	Nicolet	H
	L'Union	F	8,413	Victoriaville	H
	Le Courrier de Laviolette	F	8,260	Grand-Mère	H
	La Feuille d'Erable	F	3,960	Plessisville	H
	L'Echo de Louiseville	F	3,755	Louiseville	H
	L'Echo	F	3,300	La Tuque	H
Cantons-de-L'Est	**La Tribune** (Desmarais, Parisien, Francoeur)	**F**	**42,690**	**Sherbrooke**	**Q**
	Sherbrooke Daily Record (Black, Radler, White)	**A**	**7,240**	**Sherbrooke**	**Q**
	Le Citoyen	F	6,650	Asbestos	H
	L'Echo de Frontenac	F	3,530	Lac Mégantic	H
	Le Journal de Compton	F-A	2,778	East Angus	H
	Le Progrès	F	2,600	Coaticook	H
	Le Progrès	F-A	2,550	Magog	H
	Stanstead Journal	A	2,340	Rock Island	H
	The Campus	A	1,750	Lennoxville	H

Sources: *Traits généraux de la région administrative No 1, 2, 3, 4, 5, 6, 8, 9 et 10*, (9 publications), Ministère de l'Industrie et du Commerce, Québec 1972.

Rapport de la Commission Davis, *Les Mots, la Musique et les Sous*, Ottawa, 1970.

Région	Nom du journal	Langue F(Française) A(Anglaise)	Tirage nombre	Lieu	Type H(Hebdo) Q(Quotidien)
Montréal	**La Presse** (Desmarais, Parisien, Francoeur)	**F**	**218,570**	**Montréal**	**Q**
	The Star (Famille Mc Connell)	**A**	**181,713**	**Montréal**	**Q**
	Montréal-Matin (Faribeault, Lagarde, Doucet et Cloutier)	**F**	**147,713**	**Montréal**	**Q**
	The Gazette (Southam)	**A**	**134,713**	**Montréal**	**Q**
	Le Journal de Montréal (Péladeau)	**F**	**48,345**	**Montréal**	**Q**
	Le Devoir (Société coopérative)	**F**	**40,000**	**Montréal**	**Q**
	Dimanche-Matin	F	280,000	Montréal	H
	Le Petit-Journal	F	182,000	Montréal	H
	Allô-Police	F	147,807	Montréal	H
	Echos-Vedette	F	127,716	Montréal	H
	Photo-Journal	F	109,743	Montréal	H
	La Patrie	F	108,244	Montréal	H
	50 journaux	F	moins de 100,000 chacun	Région de Montréal	H
	11 journaux	A	moins de 100,000 chacun	Région de Montréal	H
Outaouais	**Le Droit** (Missionnaires Oblats de Marie-Immaculée)	**F**	**38,220**	**Ottawa-Hull**	**Q**
	La Revue de Gatineau	F	5,800	Gatineau	H
	L'Echo de la Lièvre	F	5,000	Mont-Laurier	H
	La Gatineau	F	3,780	Maniwaki	H
	La Vallée de la Petite-Nation	F	3,100	Buckingham	H
	Shawville Equity	A	2,859	Shawville	H
	Le Bulletin de Buckingham	F	2,800	Buckingham	H
	The Sunday Reporter	A	2,450	Aylmer	H
	Le Progrès de Hull	F	2,200	Hull	H
	Buckingham Post	A	1,000	Buckingham	H
Nord-Ouest	La Frontière	F	10,000	Rouyn-Noranda	H
	L'Echo Abitibien	F	5,900	Val-d'Or	H
	Press	A	4,500	Rouyn-Noranda	H
	L'Echo d'Amos	F	2,500	Amos	H
	L'Echo d'Abitibi-Ouest	F	2,200	La Sarre	H
	Monitor	A	1,990	Rouyn-Noranda	H
	The Star	A	1,350	Val-d'Or	H
	L'Echo de Malartic	F	1,000	Malartic	H
Côte-Nord	L'Elan Sept-Ilien	F	9,800	Sept-Iles, Port-Cartier, Havre St-Pierre, Schefferdville	H
	Le Nordic	F	8,500	Baie-Comeau, Hauterive	H
	Le Meilleur Journal-Le Nordic	F-A	8,500	Port-Cartier, Sept-Iles	H
	L'Avenir and Sept-Iles Journal	F-A	4,800	Port-Cartier, Sept-Iles	H
	La Côte-Nord	F-A	4,400	Baie-Comeau, Hauterive, Forestville	H
	Le Nordic	F-A	2,500	Gagnon, Schefferdville	H

5.4.c POSTES DE TELEVISION, PAR REGIONS ADMINISTRATIVES, QUEBEC, 1971

Région	Nom Poste	Langue F (Française) A (Anglaise)	Puissance Ⓖ video en watts	audio en watts	Centre d'émission	Principaux actionnaires
Bas-St-Laurent-Gaspésie	CKBL-TV	F	303,000	182,000	Matane	R. Lapointe
	CJBR-TV	F	100,000	56,000	Rimouski	Télémédia (Beaubien)
	CHAU-TV	F-A	100,000	52,000	Carleton	Desmarais, Brillant Pratte
	CKCW-TV	A	25,000	15,000	Moncton	Moncton Broadcasting Company
Saguenay-Lac-St-Jean	CJPM-TV	F	52,000	100,000	Chicoutimi	Divers (Succession De Sève)
	CKRS-TV	F	21,000	42,000	Jonquières	Divers (Lepage et Baribeau)
Québec	CBVT	F	173,000	. .	Québec	Radio-Canada
	CFCM-TV	F	100,000	. .	Québec	Famous Players (Pratte, Baribeau, Lepage)
	CKMI-TV	A	13,830	. .	Québec	Famous Players (Pratte, Baribeau, Lepage)
	CKRT-TV	F	49,500	. .	Rivière-du-Loup	Divers (L. Simard)
Trois-Rivières	CKTM-TV	F	325,000	. .	Trois-Rivières	H. Audet
Cantons-de-L'Est	CHLT-TV	F	316,000	186,000	Sherbrooke	Télémédia (Beaubien)
Montréal	CFCF-TV	A	325,000	160,000	Montréal	Bushnell Communications Limited
	CFTM-TV	F	100,000	50,000	Montréal	Succession J.A. De Sève
	CBMT	A	100,000	15,000	Montréal	Radio-Canada
	CBFT	F	100,000	10,000	Montréal	Radio-Canada
Outaouais	CBOFT	F	125,000	25,600	Ottawa-Hull	Radio-Canada
Nord-Ouest	CKRN-TV	F	115,000	23,500	Rouyn-Noranda	Northern Radio (J.Y. Gourd)

Sources: *Traits généraux de la région administrative No 1, 2, 3, 4, 5, 6, 7, 8, 9 et 10,* (9 publications), Ministère de l'Industrie et du Commerce, Québec, 1972.

Rapport de la Commission Davis, *Les Mots, la Musique et les Sous,* Ottawa, 1970.

6.1 Production

6.1.a ACTIVITES MANUFACTURIERES, PAR REGIONS ADMINISTRATIVES, QUEBEC, 1967

Région	Etablissements Ⓖ nombre	Etablissements % province	Employés nombre	Employés % province	Expéditions valeur ($000)	Expéditions % province	Principaux produits fabriqués	
Bas-St-Laurent Gaspésie	275	2.5	5,360	1.0	104,497	0.9	bois d'oeuvre, papier-journal, carton ondulé,	papier de doublure, cuivre, poissons,
Saguenay-Lac-St-Jean	255	2.4	16,791	3.2	486,646	4.4	aluminium, papier et carton bois d'oeuvre,	sulfite, machinerie, abattage, aliments.
Québec	1,496	13.9	41,223	7.8	836,041	7.6	pâtes et papiers, construction navale, vêtements, machinerie, sport,	imprimerie, et édition motoneige, explosifs, tabac, pain.
Trois-Rivières	803	7.5	40,815	7.7	888,625	8.0	pâtes et papiers, aluminium papier-journal, textile,	produits chimiques, vêtements, matériel électrique.
Cantons-de-l'Est	338	3.2	19,737	4.0	436,994	3.5	caoutchouc, cuir, tissu synthétique, machinerie,	amiante, textiles, pâtes et papiers, bonnetterie, confiserie.
Montréal	**7,082**	**65.7**	**348,817**	**66.5**	**7,726,619**	**75.5**	aéronautique, automobile, machinerie, communications, tabac.	navires, verrerie, fonte et affinage, matériel électrique.
Outaouais	178	1.7	9,622	2.0	237,782	1.9	pâtes et papiers, viandes, masonite,	meubles, produits chimiques industriels.
Nord-Ouest	158	1.5	4,782	1.0	285,611	2.3	pâtes, fonderie, sciage.	déroulage, cuivre, or, zinc.
Côte-Nord	44	0.4	2,411	0.5	55,758	0.4	pâtes et papiers, aluminium, imprimerie et édition, produits laitiers, boulangerie, eaux gazeuses,	portes et châssis, produits chimiques, béton, explosifs, préparation du poisson, fonderie de fer, pièces mécaniques.
Nouveau-Québec	–	–	–	–	–	–	scieries, canots.	production artisanale esquimaude

Source: *Traits généraux de la région administrative* No *1, 2, 3, 4, 5, 6, 7, 8, 9 et 10,* (9 publications), Ministère de l'Industrie et du Commerce, Québec, 1972.

6.2 Consommation

6.2.a DEPENSES SELON LES POSTES DU BUDGET, SELON LE REVENU Ⓖ DISPONIBLE, QUEBEC, 1959 (N)

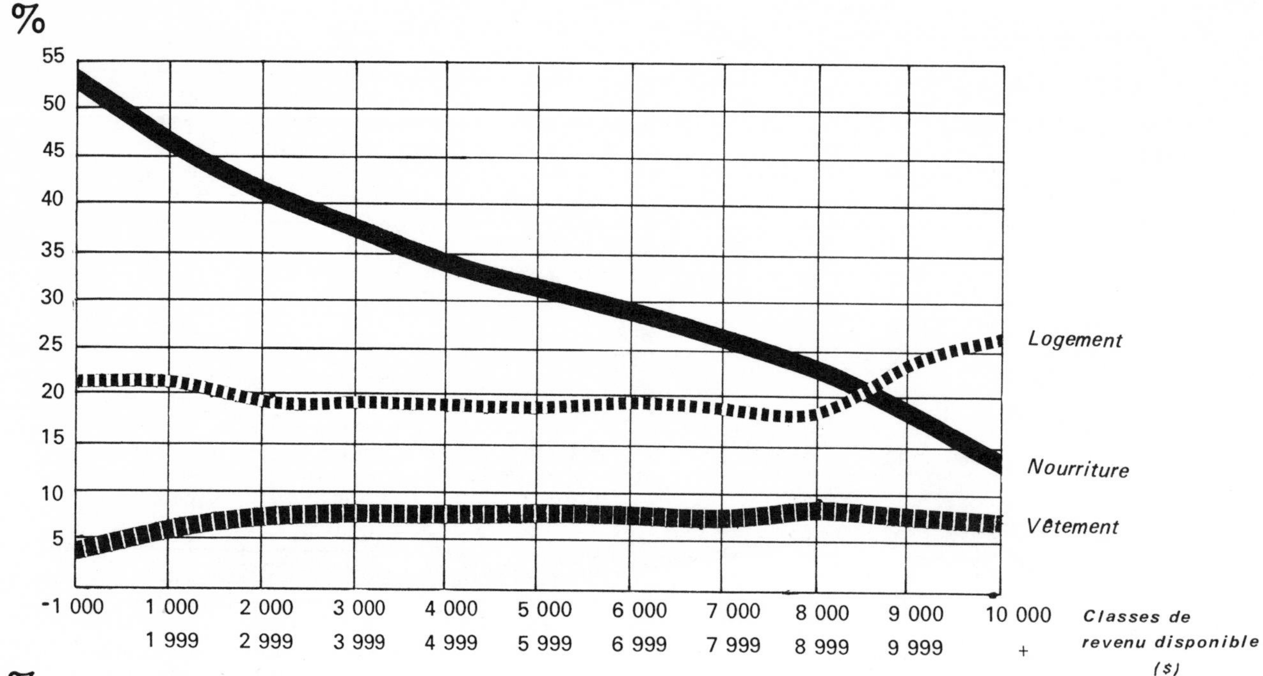

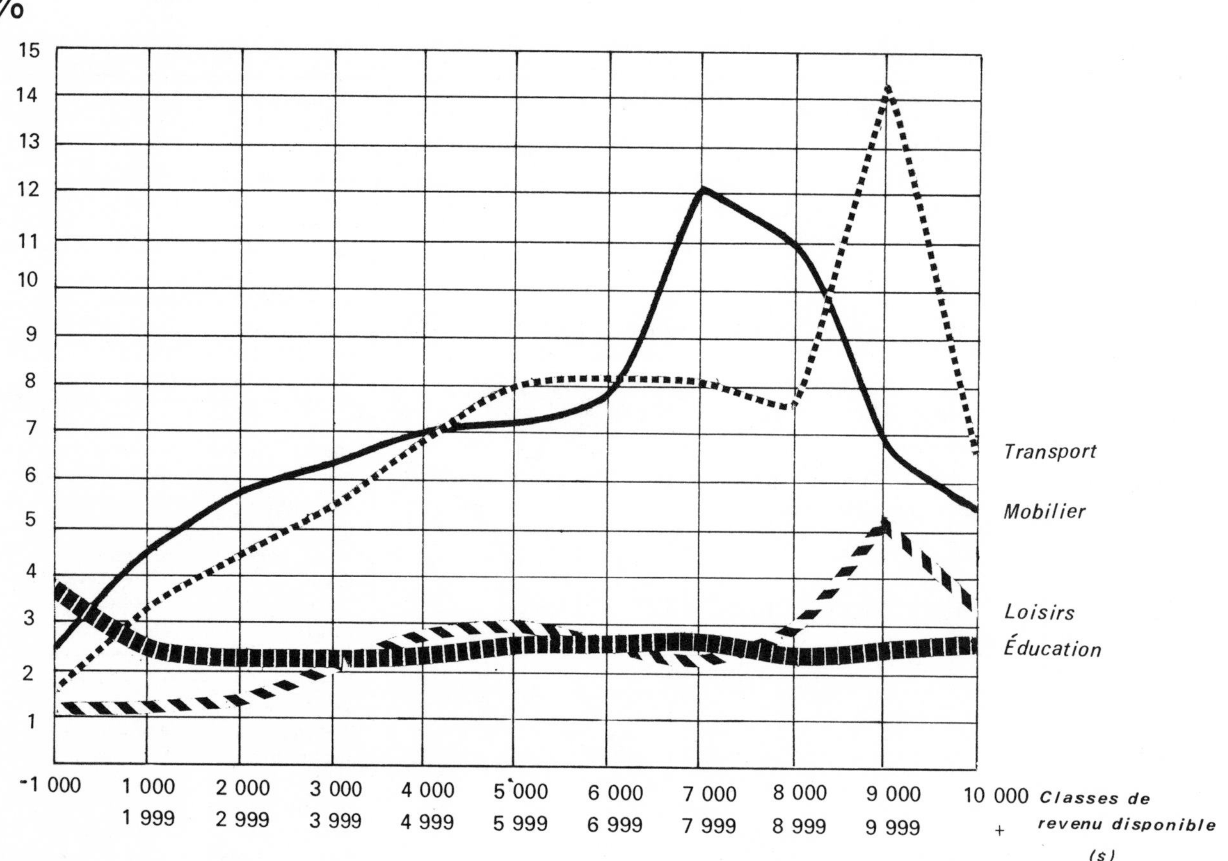

Source: Tremblay et Fortin, *Comportements économiques de la famille salariée du Québec*, P.U.L., Québec, 1964.

Note: L'échantillon comportait 1,500 ménages répartis à travers le Québec et les classes de revenus; l'erreur d'échantillon est inférieure à 10%.

6.2.a DEPENSES SELON LES POSTES DU BUDGET, SELON LE REVENU (G) DISPONIBLE, QUEBEC, 1959 (suite)

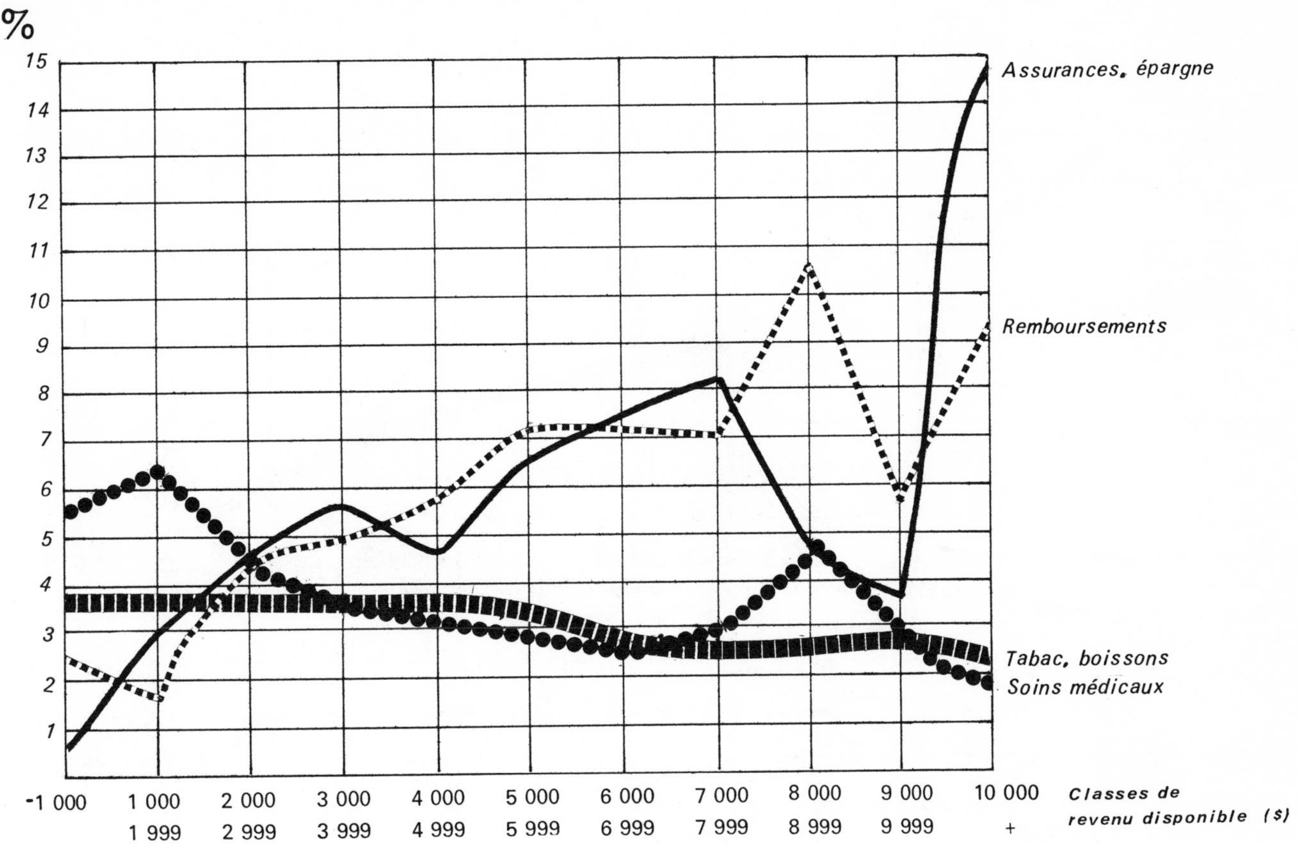

6.2.b DETTE TOTALE A LA FIN DE L'ANNEE SELON LES PRINCIPAUX PRETEURS, CANADA, 1938-1969, ANNEES CHOISIES.

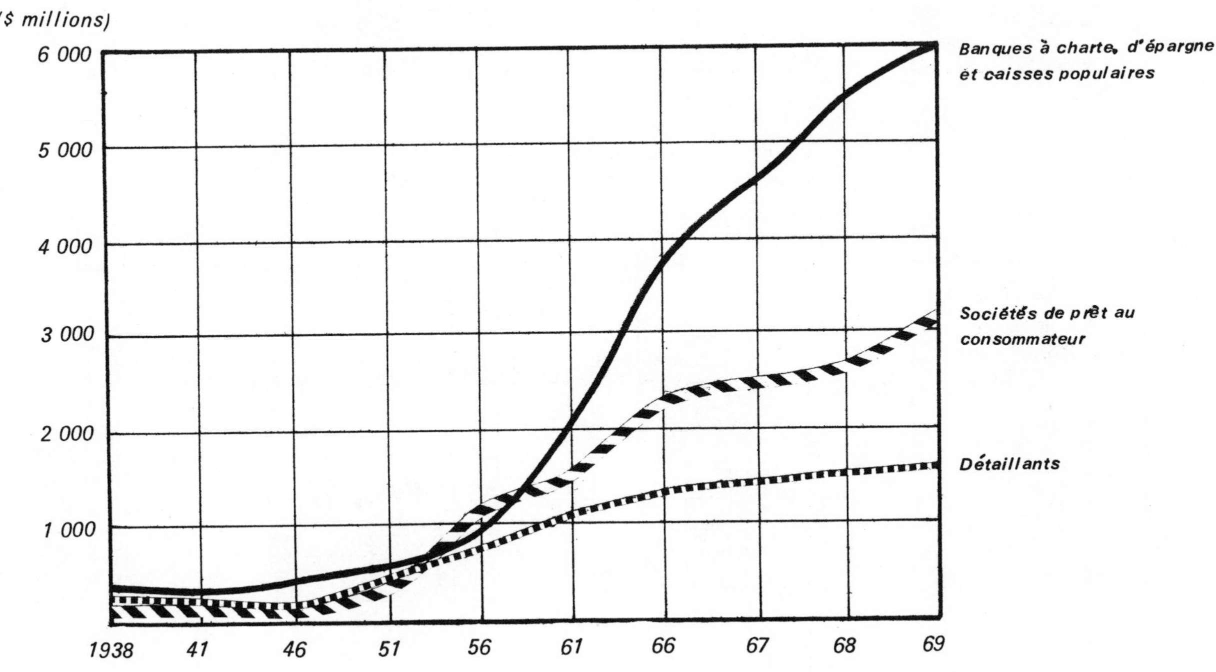

Source: Statistique Canada, *Revue statistique du Canada*, mars et juin 1965, avril 1970, Ottawa.

6

6.2 Consommation

6.2.c DEPENSES SELON LES POSTES DU BUDGET, SELON L'OCCUPATION DU CHEF DU MENAGE, QUEBEC, 1959

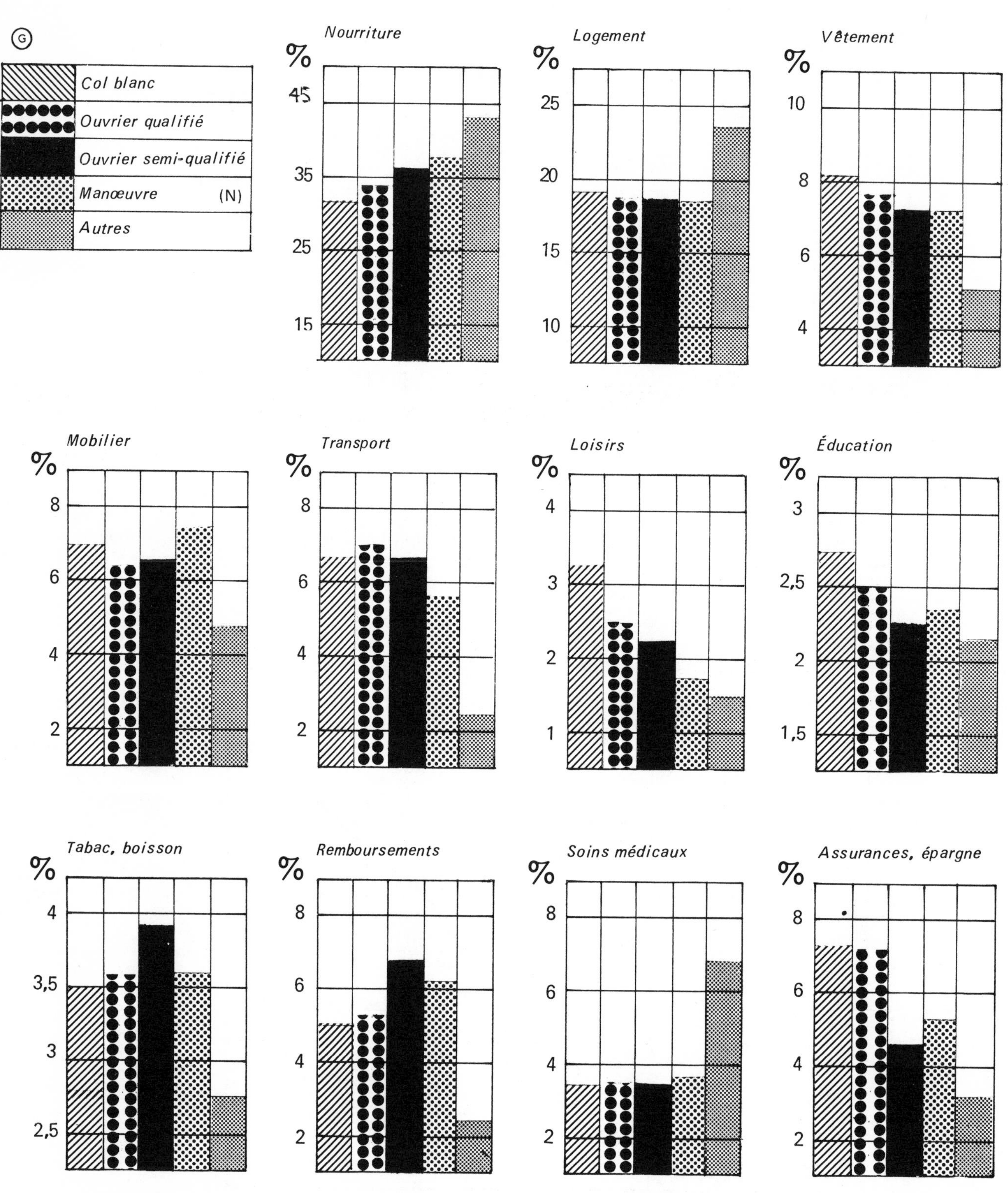

Note: Voir "Professions", au glossaire.

Source: Tremblay et Fortin, *Comportements économiques de la famille salariée du Québec*, P.U.L., Québec, 1964.

6.3 Commerce extérieur

6.3.a EXPORTATIONS, IMPORTATIONS, SOMMES QUINQUENNALES, QUEBEC, CANADA, 1925-1969

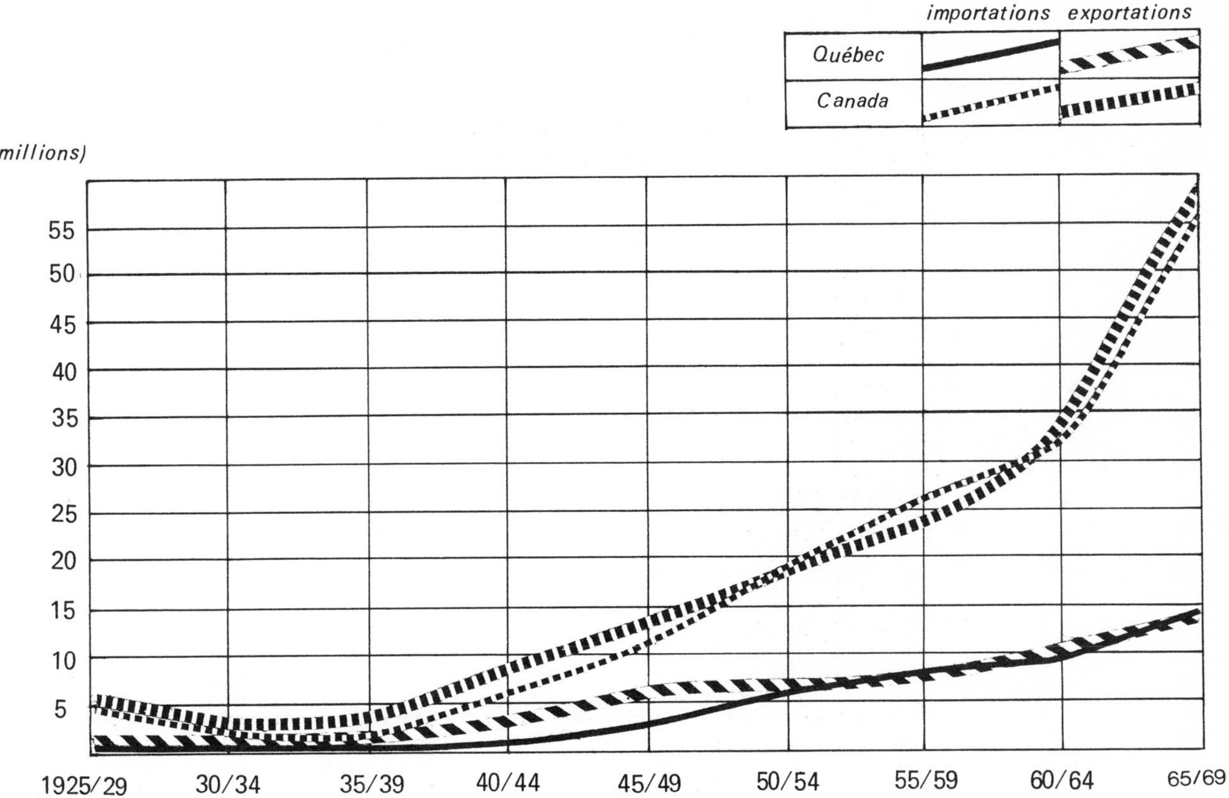

6.3.b BALANCE (G) COMMERCIALE, SOMMES QUINQUENNALES, CANADA (N), 1925-1969.

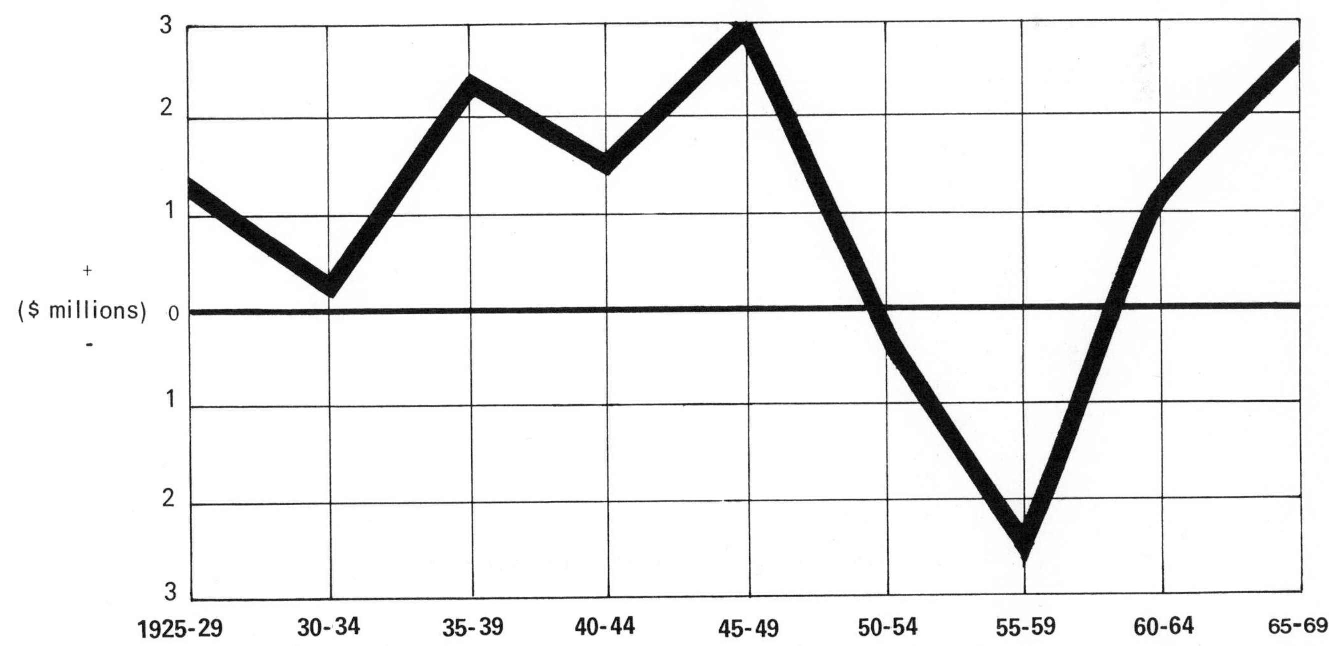

Note: On ne peut calculer la balance commerciale pour le Québec car ce dernier n'a pas de frontières politiques avec les autres provinces.

Source: *Annuaires du Québec*, 1944, 1966 et 1972.

6

6.3 Commerce extérieur

6.3.c VALEUR DES EXPORTATIONS Ⓖ DU QUEBEC HORS DU CANADA, PAR REGIONS GEOGRAPHIQUES ET PAR PAYS, QUEBEC, MOYENNE 1966-1970

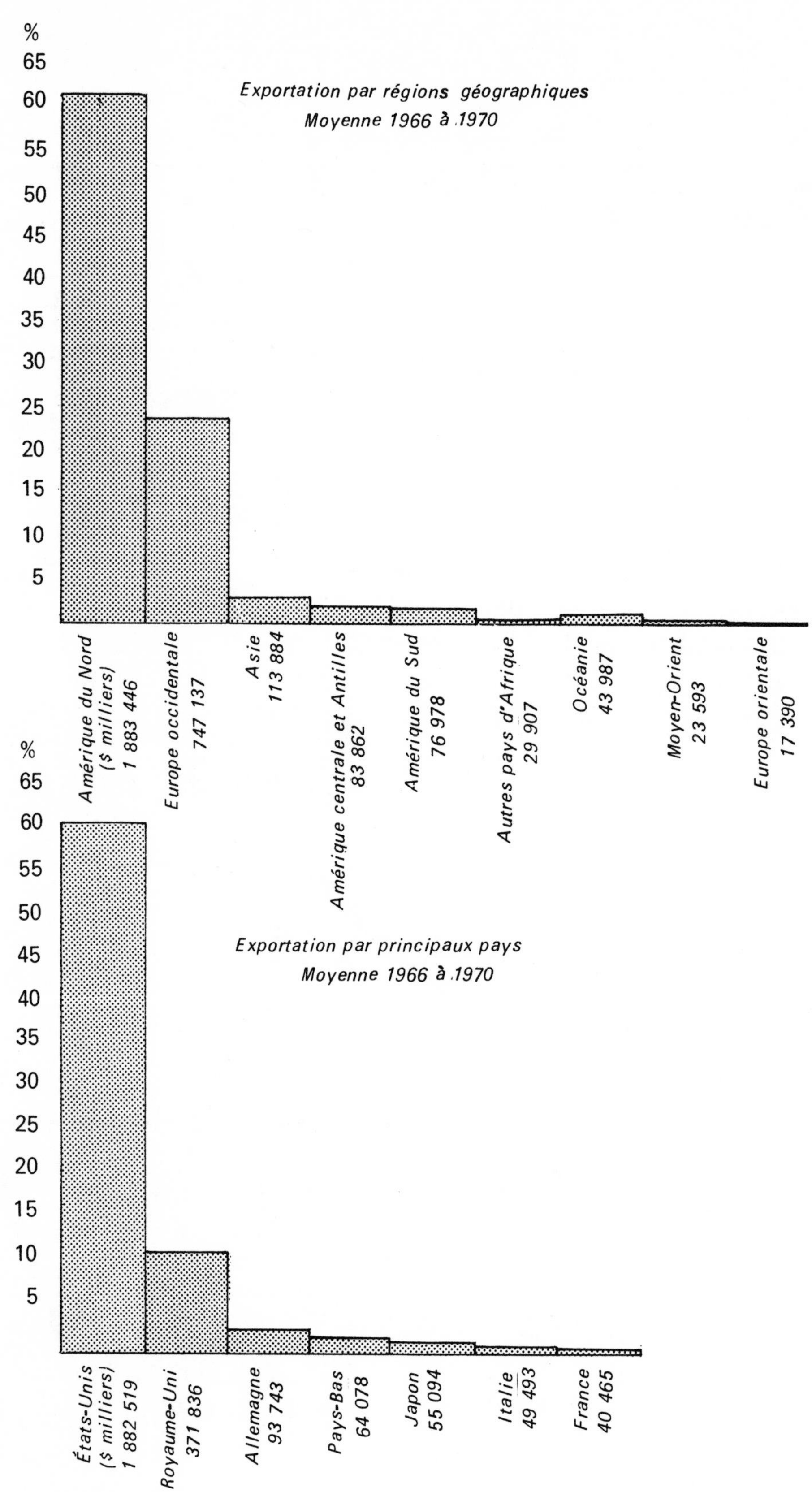

Source: *Annuaire du Québec*, 1972.

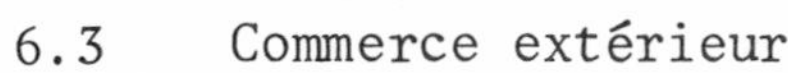

6.3 Commerce extérieur

6.3.d VALEUR DES IMPORTATIONS Ⓖ PASSANT PAR LES PORTS DE DOUANE DU QUEBEC ET DES EXPORTATIONS Ⓖ DU QUEBEC HORS DU CANADA, SELON LES 11 PRINCIPAUX PRODUITS, QUEBEC, MOYENNE 1966-1970

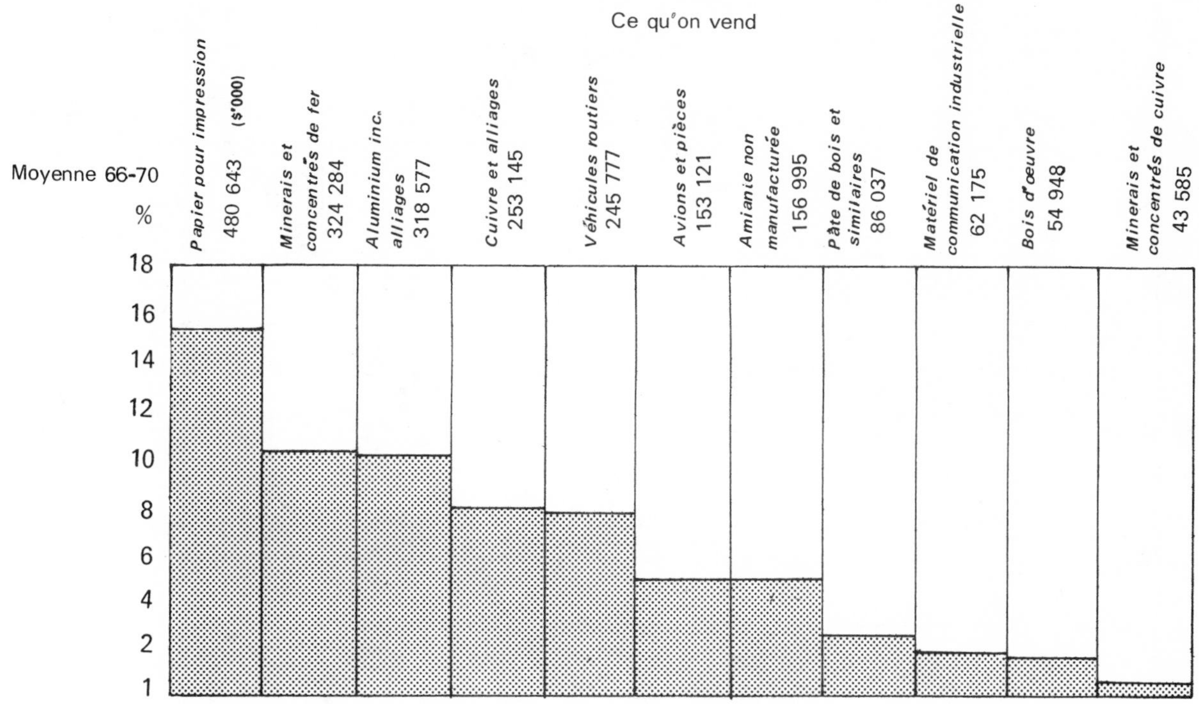

Ce qu'on vend

	Moyenne 66-70 ($'000)
Papier pour impression	480 643
Minerais et concentrés de fer	324 284
Aluminium inc. alliages	318 577
Cuivre et alliages	253 145
Véhicules routiers	245 777
Avions et pièces	153 121
Amianie non manufacturée	156 995
Pâte de bois et similaires	86 037
Matériel de communication industrielle	62 175
Bois d'œuvre	54 948
Minerais et concentrés de cuivre	43 585

%: 18, 16, 14, 12, 10, 8, 6, 4, 2, 1

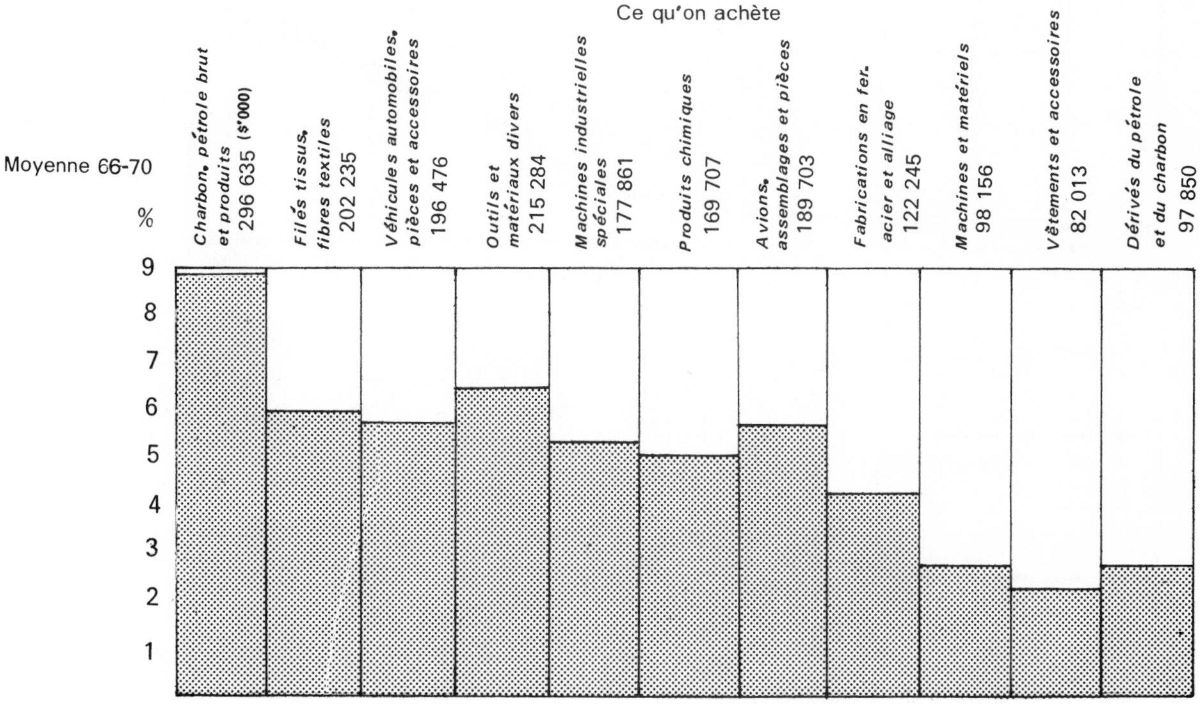

Ce qu'on achète

	Moyenne 66-70 ($'000)
Charbon, pétrole brut et produits	296 635
Filés tissus, fibres textiles	202 235
Véhicules automobiles, pièces et accessoires	196 476
Outils et matériaux divers	215 284
Machines industrielles spéciales	177 861
Produits chimiques	169 707
Avions, assemblages et pièces	189 703
Fabrications en fer, acier et alliage	122 245
Machines et matériels	98 156
Vêtements et accessoires	82 013
Dérivés du pétrole et du charbon	97 850

%: 9, 8, 7, 6, 5, 4, 3, 2, 1

Source: *Annuaire du Québec*, 1972.

6.4 Comptes économiques du Québec

6.4.a REMUNERATION DES SALARIES (N), QUEBEC, ONTARIO, CANADA, 1926-1971, ANNEES CHOISIES

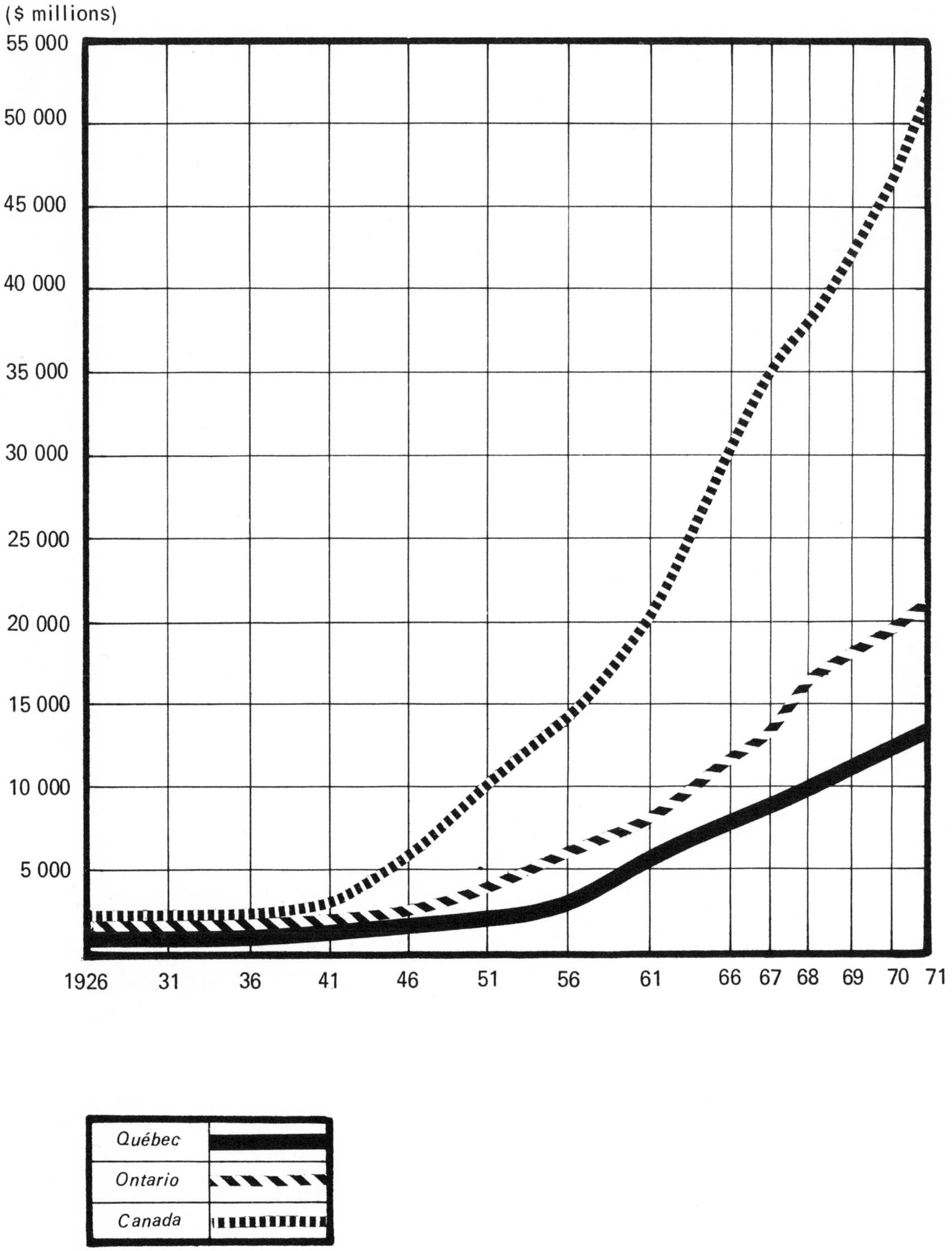

Note: Voir "Revenu personnel", au glossaire.

Sources: Statistique Canada No 13-201, *Comptes nationaux: Revenus et dépenses, 1956-1970*, Ottawa.

Statistique Canada No 13-502, *Comptes nationaux: Revenus et dépenses, 1926-1956*, Ottawa.

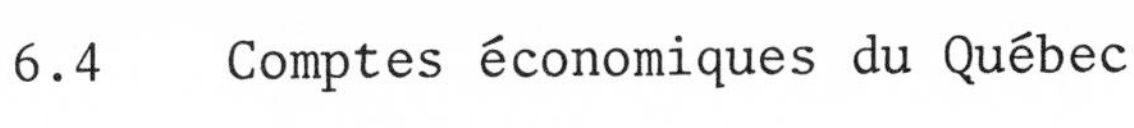

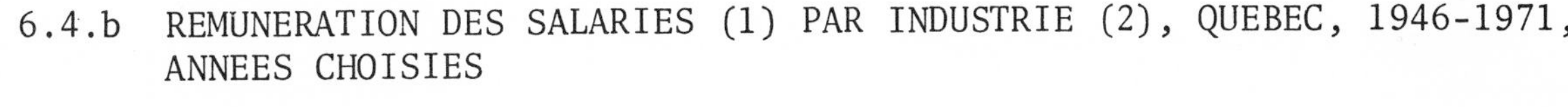

6.4.b REMUNERATION DES SALARIES (1) PAR INDUSTRIE (2), QUEBEC, 1946-1971, ANNEES CHOISIES

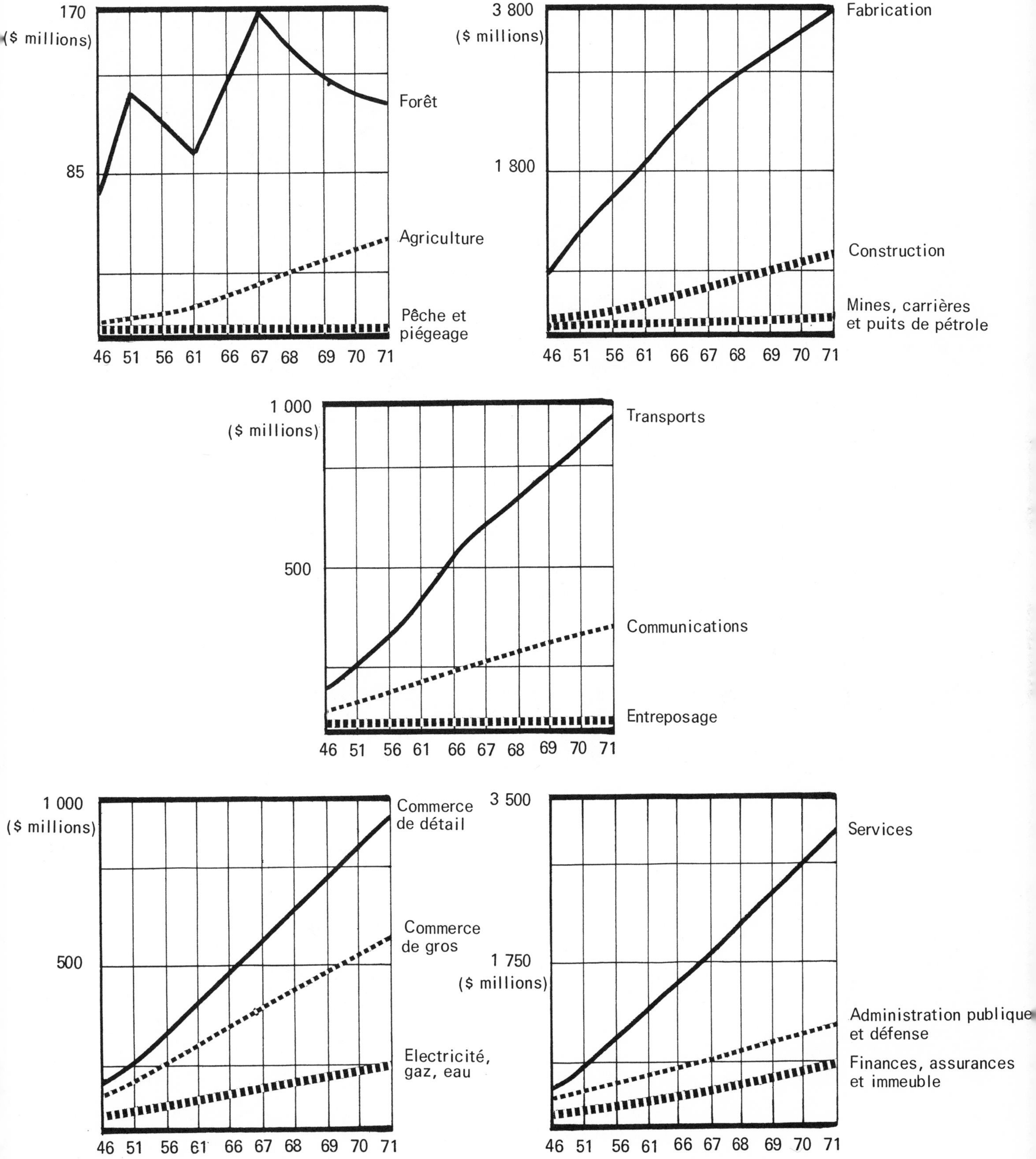

170
($ millions)
85
Forêt
Agriculture
Pêche et piégeage
46 51 56 61 66 67 68 69 70 71

3 800
($ millions)
1 800
Fabrication
Construction
Mines, carrières et puits de pétrole
46 51 56 61 66 67 68 69 70 71

1 000
($ millions)
500
Transports
Communications
Entreposage
46 51 56 61 66 67 68 69 70 71

1 000
($ millions)
500
Commerce de détail
Commerce de gros
Electricité, gaz, eau
46 51 56 61 66 67 68 69 70 71

3 500
1 750
($ millions)
Services
Administration publique et défense
Finances, assurances et immeuble
46 51 56 61 66 67 68 69 70 71

Note (1): Voir "Revenu personnel", au glossaire.
Note (2): Voir "Industries selon les secteurs", au glossaire.

Source: *Tableaux-types des comptes économiques du Québec, Revenus et dépenses, 1946-1970*, Ministère de l'Industrie et du Commerce, Québec, 1970

6.4. Comptes économiques du Québec

6.4.c REVENU Ⓖ DU TRAVAIL PAR ORIGINE Ⓖ ETHNIQUE, QUEBEC, 1961

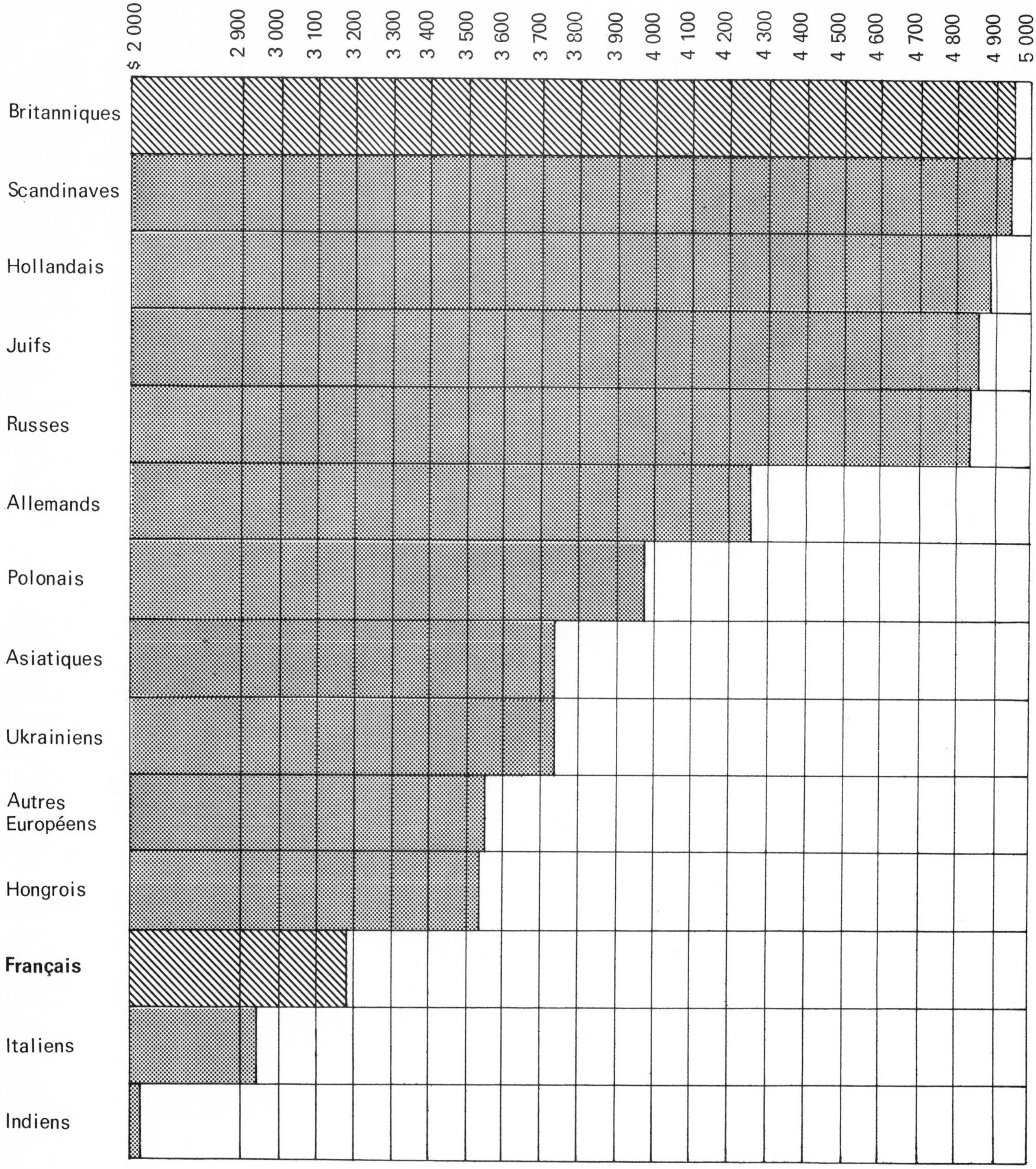

Source: *Rapport de la Commission royale d'Enquête sur le Bilinguisme et le Biculturalisme*, Ottawa, 1969.

6.4 Comptes économiques du Québec

6.4.d REVENU MOYEN SELON L'ORIGINE (G) ETHNIQUE, CANADA ET PROVINCES, 1961

Province	**Toute origine** $	indice	Britanniques indice	Français indice	**Origine ethnique** Allemands indice	Italiens indice	Juifs indice	Ukrainiens indice	Autres indice
Terre-Neuve	2,972	100	99.5	93.4	–	–	. .	. .	–
Ile-du-Prince-Edouard	2,933	100	105.4	87.1	–	. .	. .	. .	–
Nouvelle-Ecosse	3,634	100	102.6	87.1	83.6	–	–	–	101.4
Nouveau-Brunswick	3,499	100	106.1	85.8	118.4	–	–	–	101.8
Québec	**4,227**	**100**	**140.0**	**91.7**	**111.6**	**82.6**	**178.0**	**102.1**	**104.4**
Ontario	**4,706**	**100**	**105.9**	**87.0**	**94.7**	**77.4**	**136.8**	**91.3**	**91.5**
Manitoba	4,434	100	108.4	82.4	94.1	–	174.6	84.1	87.9
Saskatchewan	4,086	100	109.3	84.9	90.8	–	–	93.4	89.2
Alberta	4,595	100	112.6	93.1	89.4	80.9	–	94.3	84.3
Colombie-Britannique Yukon et Territoires du Nord-Ouest	4,772	100	106.9	95.2	87.8	76.6	–	88.6	87.6
CANADA revenu moyen ($)	**4,414**		**4,852**	**3,872**	**4,207**	**3,621**	**7,426**	**4,128**	**4,153**
indice	**100**		**109.9**	**87.7**	**95.3**	**82.0**	**168.2**	**93.5**	**94.0**

Source: *Rapport de la Commission royale d'Enquête sur le Bilinguisme et le Biculturalisme,* Ottawa, 1969.

6.4 Comptes économiques du Québec

6.4.e REVENU GLOBAL MOYEN SELON L'ORIGINE (G) ETHNIQUE ET LA LANGUE (G) OFFICIELLE, QUEBEC, CANADA, 1961

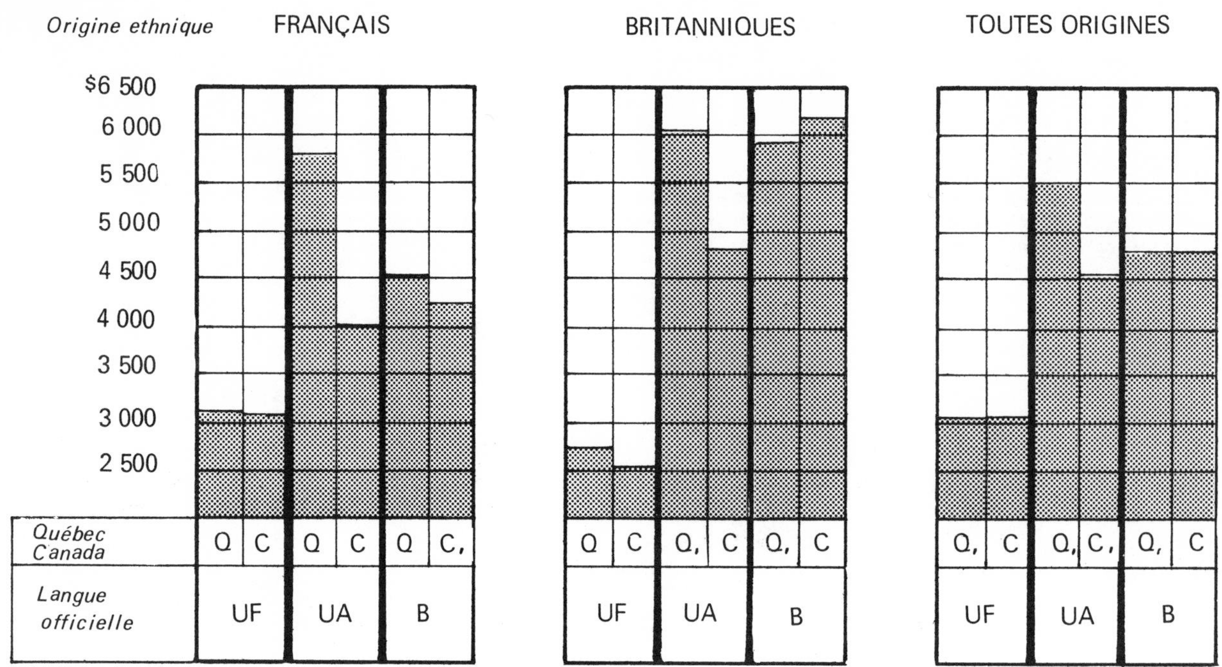

UF : unilingue français UA : unilingue anglais B : bilingue

Source: *Rapport de la Commission royale d'Enquête sur le Bilinguisme et le Biculturalisme*, Ottawa, 1969.

6.4.f COMPOSANTES DU REVENU PERSONNEL, QUEBEC, 1971.

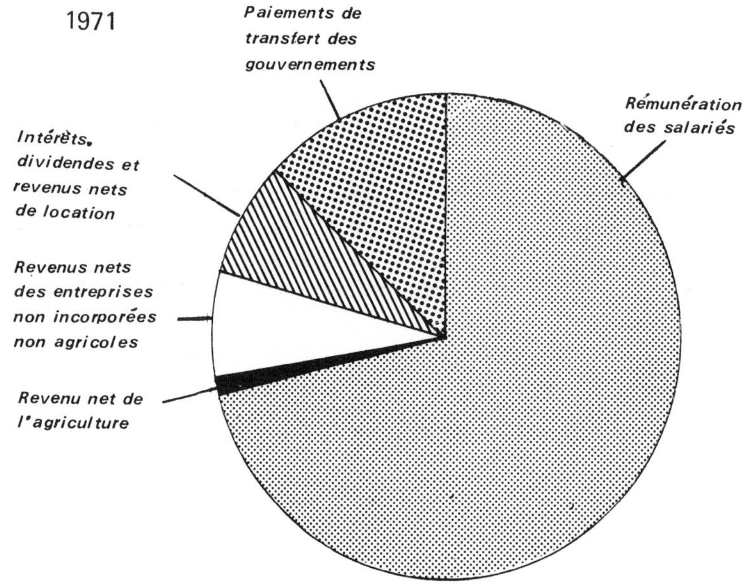

Sources: *Tableaux-types des comptes économiques du Québec, Revenus et dépenses, 1946-1970*, Ministère de l'Industrie et du Commerce, Québec, 1970.

Statistique Canada, No 13-502, *Comptes nationaux, revenus et dépenses, 1926-1956*, Ottawa.

6.4.g LES COMPOSANTES DU REVENU Ⓖ PERSONNEL, QUEBEC, 1926-1970, ANNEES CHOISIES

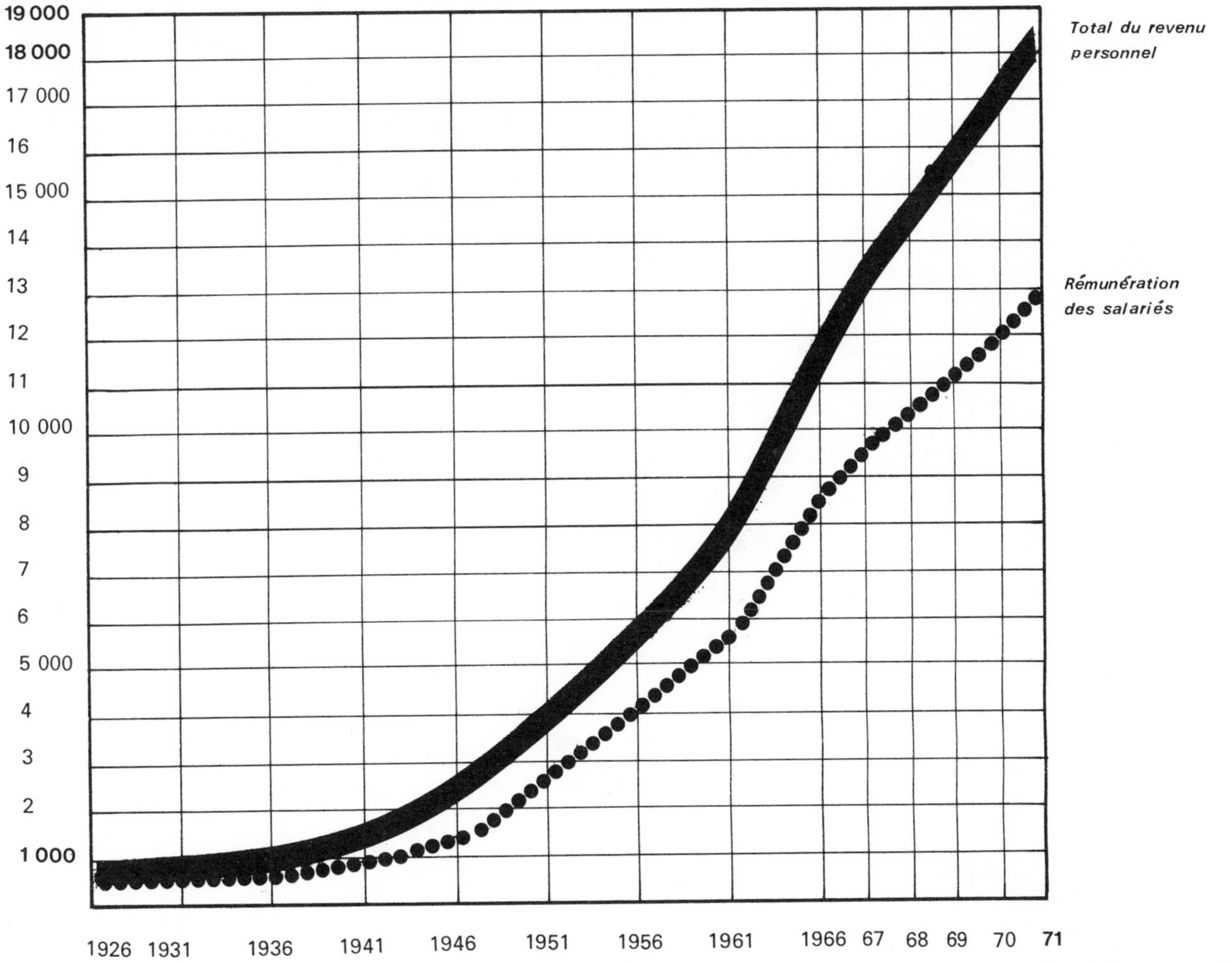

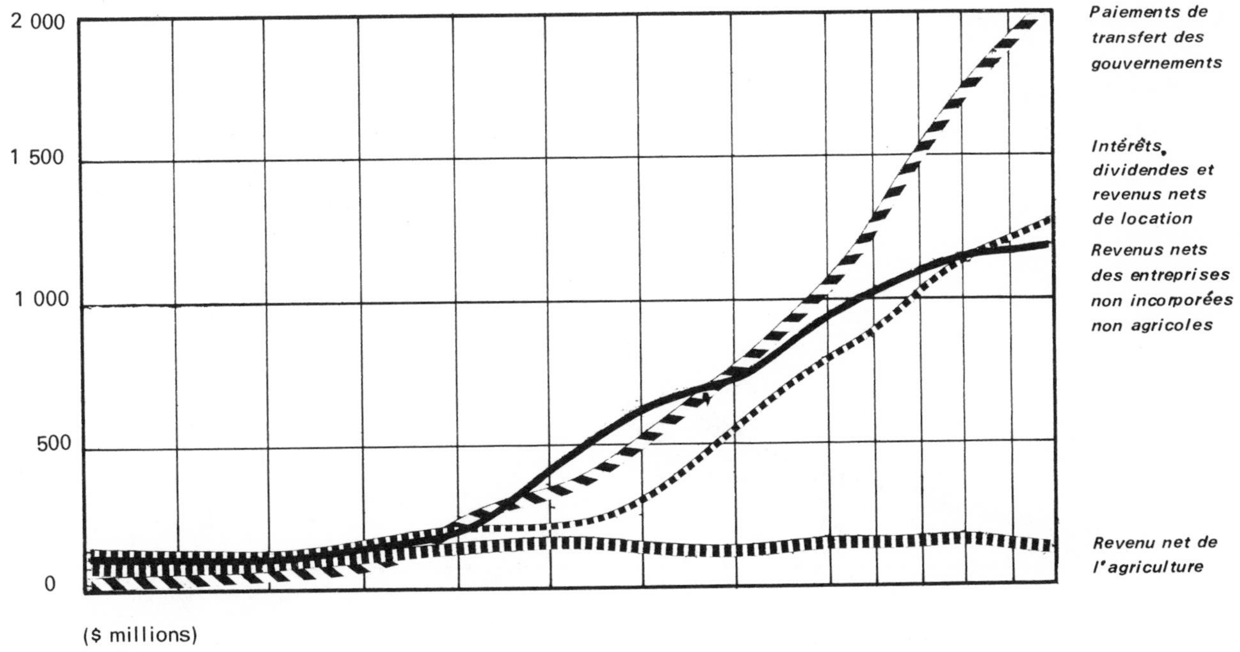

Sources: *Tableaux-types des comptes économiques du Québec, Revenus et dépenses, 1946-1970*, Ministère de l'Industrie et du Commerce, Québec, 1970.

Statistique Canada, No 13-502, *Comptes nationaux, revenus et dépenses, 1926-1956*, Ottawa.

6.4 Comptes économiques du Québec

6.4.h REVENU PERSONNEL, QUEBEC, ONTARIO, CANADA, 1926-1970, ANNEES CHOISIES

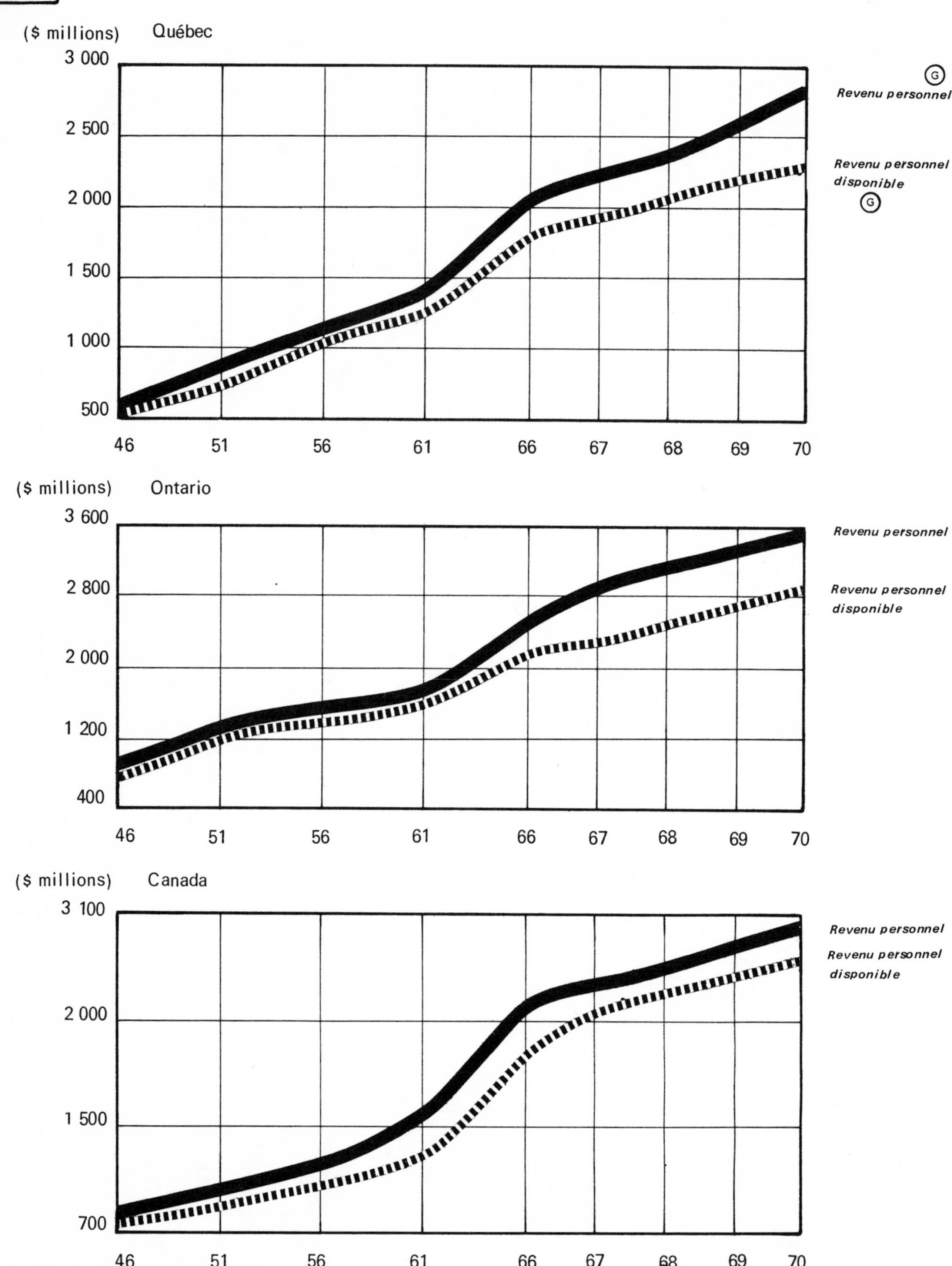

Sources: *Tableaux-types des comptes économiques du Québec, Revenus et dépenses, 1946-1970,* Ministère de l'Industrie et du Commerce, Québec, 1970.

Statistique Canada No 13-502, *Comptes nationaux, Revenus et dépenses, 1926-1970,* Ottawa.

Annuaire du Québec, 1972.

6.4 Comptes économiques du Québec

6.4.i UTILISATION DU REVENU Ⓖ PERSONNEL, QUEBEC, 1946-1970, ANNEES CHOISIES

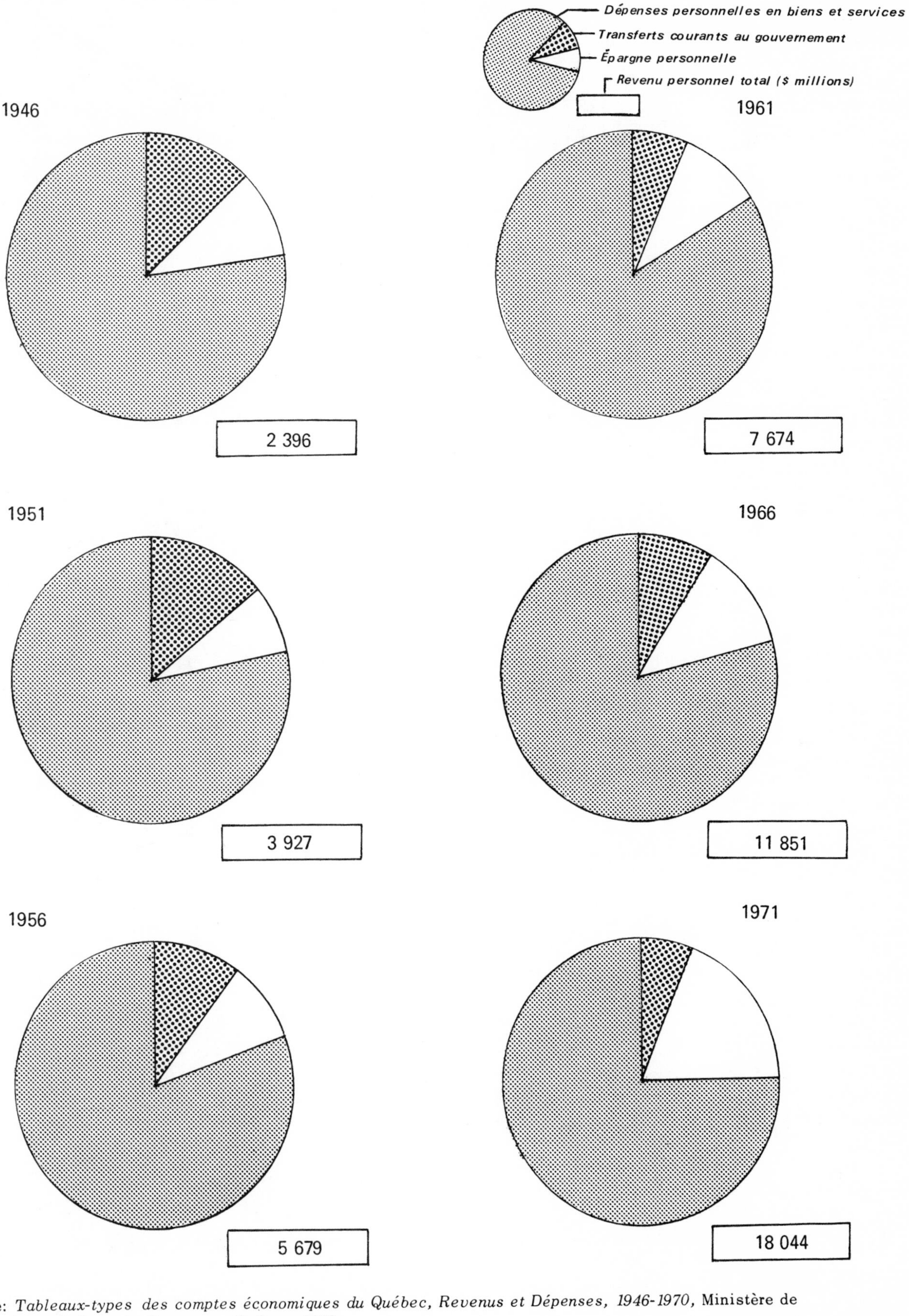

Source: *Tableaux-types des comptes économiques du Québec, Revenus et Dépenses, 1946-1970*, Ministère de l'Industrie et du Commerce, Québec, 1970.

6.4 Comptes économiques du Québec

6.4.j REVENU (G) PERSONNEL PER CAPITA PAR COMTES, QUEBEC, 1965-1970, TOUTES LES ANNEES

Comté	1965	1966	1967	1968	1969	1970
Abitibi	1,171	1,386	1,768	1,772	2,030	2,141
Argenteuil	1,528	1,571	1,831	1,971	2,301	2,048
Arthabaska	1,331	1,493	1,731	1,971	2,229	2,400
Bagot	1,206	1,176	1,577	1,547	1,917	1,963
Beauce	882	1,042	1,276	1,381	1,710	1,981
Beauharnois	1,783	1,983	2,165	2,268	2,332	2,746
Bellechasse	729	915	1,026	1,287	1,208	1,446
Berthier	1,102	1,738	2,363	2,779	2,222	2,502
Bonaventure	869	848	1,272	1,256	1,227	1,525
Brome	1,408	1,268	1,409	1,461	1,964	2,044
Chambly	2,020	2,205	2,634	2,589	2,826	3,186
Champlain	1,102	1,656	1,944	2,043	2,542	2,354
Charlevoix	1,013	1,353	1,522	1,464	1,739	1,874
Châteauguay	1,909	2,056	2,349	2,443	2,779	3,027
Chicoutimi	1,337	1,601	1,750	1,860	2,024	2,379
Compton	1,079	1,158	1,549	1,475	1,885	2,203
Deux-Montagnes	1,223	1,738	2,037	2,406	2,465	2,343
Dorchester	573	861	890	876	1,070	1,159
Drummond	1,549	1,564	1,949	2,045	2,330	2,456
Frontenac	680	971	1,000	1,085	1,345	1,523
Gaspé et Iles de la Madeleine	781	918	971	1,217	1,284	1,631
Hull et Gatineau	1,842	1,892	2,214	2,447	2,647	2,937
Huntingdon	1,156	1,427	1,184	1,463	1,482	2,185
Iberville	1,287	1,075	1,705	1,946	2,373	1,707
Iles de Montréal et Jésus	2,535	2,813	2,829	2,980	3,194	3,295
Joliette	1,360	1,676	1,644	1,723	1,965	2,387
Kamouraska	667	1,053	1,118	1,481	1,479	1,743
Labelle	665	862	1,145	1,218	1,482	1,356
Lac St-Jean	1,053	1,218	1,460	1,474	1,640	1,801
Laprairie	1,806	1,823	2,414	2,357	2,501	4,004
L'Assomption	1,530	1,665	1,713	2,247	2,534	2,299
Lévis	1,805	1,730	2,106	2,501	2,690	2,705
L'Islet	763	656	724	1,129	1,005	1,416
Lotbinière	812	973	1,046	1,056	1,262	1,599
Maskinongé	756	1,118	1,294	1,337	1,728	1,670
Matane et Matapédia	687	917	1,037	1,165	1,303	1,376
Mégantic	1,320	1,426	1,660	1,886	2,252	2,423
Missisquoi	1,545	1,656	2,058	2,099	2,219	2,335
Montcalm	764	1,038	963	1,287	1,437	1,676
Montmagny	1,061	1,308	1,406	1,724	1,558	2,009
Montmorency	1,135	1,233	1,388	1,946	1,844	2,037
Napierreville	1,187	1,184	1,821	1,117	1,340	1,745

Source: *Tableaux-types des comptes économiques du Québec; Revenus et dépenses, 1946-1970,* Québec, 1970.

Comté	1965	1966	1967	1968	1969	1970
Nicolet	762	973	1,288	1,314	1,590	1,772
Papineau	1,156	1,408	1,599	1,910	1,981	2,145
Pontiac	1,000	1,193	1,655	1,481	1,451	1,587
Portneuf	1,418	1,217	1,359	1,569	2,066	1,859
Québec	2,137	2,261	2,512	2,694	2,922	3,218
Richelieu	1,964	2,052	2,367	2,381	2,598	2,801
Richmond	1,406	1,593	1,572	1,902	2,165	2,303
Rimouski	1,026	1,265	1,517	1,488	1,832	2,061
Rouville	1,570	1,406	2,112	1,879	2,232	2,540
Saguenay	2,153	1,802	2,189	2,176	2,304	2,866
St-Hyacinthe	1,567	1,699	1,928	2,126	2,218	2,123
St-Jean	1,838	1,706	1,958	1,892	2,367	2,123
St-Maurice	2,189	1,952	2,168	2,300	2,339	2,692
Shefford	1,728	1,646	2,038	2,310	2,428	2,534
Sherbrooke	1,909	1,974	2,208	2,453	2,772	2,914
Soulanges	1,454	2,045	1,371	1,762	2,040	1,783
Stanstead	1,542	1,477	1,785	1,897	2,203	2,344
Témiscamingue	1,569	1,708	1,791	2,001	2,022	2,270
Témiscouata et Rivière-du-Loup	691	847	1,037	1,218	1,252	1,438
Terrebonne	1,690	1,800	2,149	2,272	2,320	2,713
Vaudreuil	1,845	1,968	2,543	2,586	2,830	2,968
Verchères	1,474	2,007	2,107	2,717	2,935	3,002
Wolfe	859	1,191	1,260	1,335	1,842	1,730
Yamaska	930	901	1,060	1,348	1,480	1,865
PROVINCE	1,880	2,055	2,247	2,394	2,599	2,783

6.4 Comptes économiques du Québec

6.4.k PRODUIT Ⓖ INTERIEUR BRUT AU COUT DES FACTEURS PAR INDUSTRIES Ⓖ, QUEBEC, 1946-1969, ANNEES CHOISIES

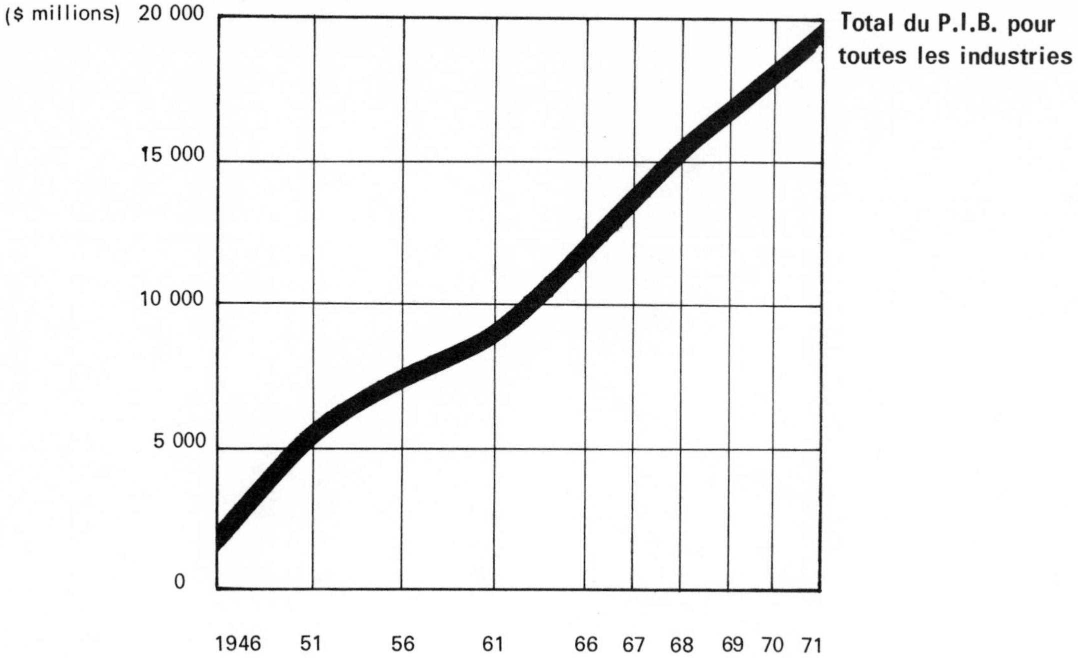

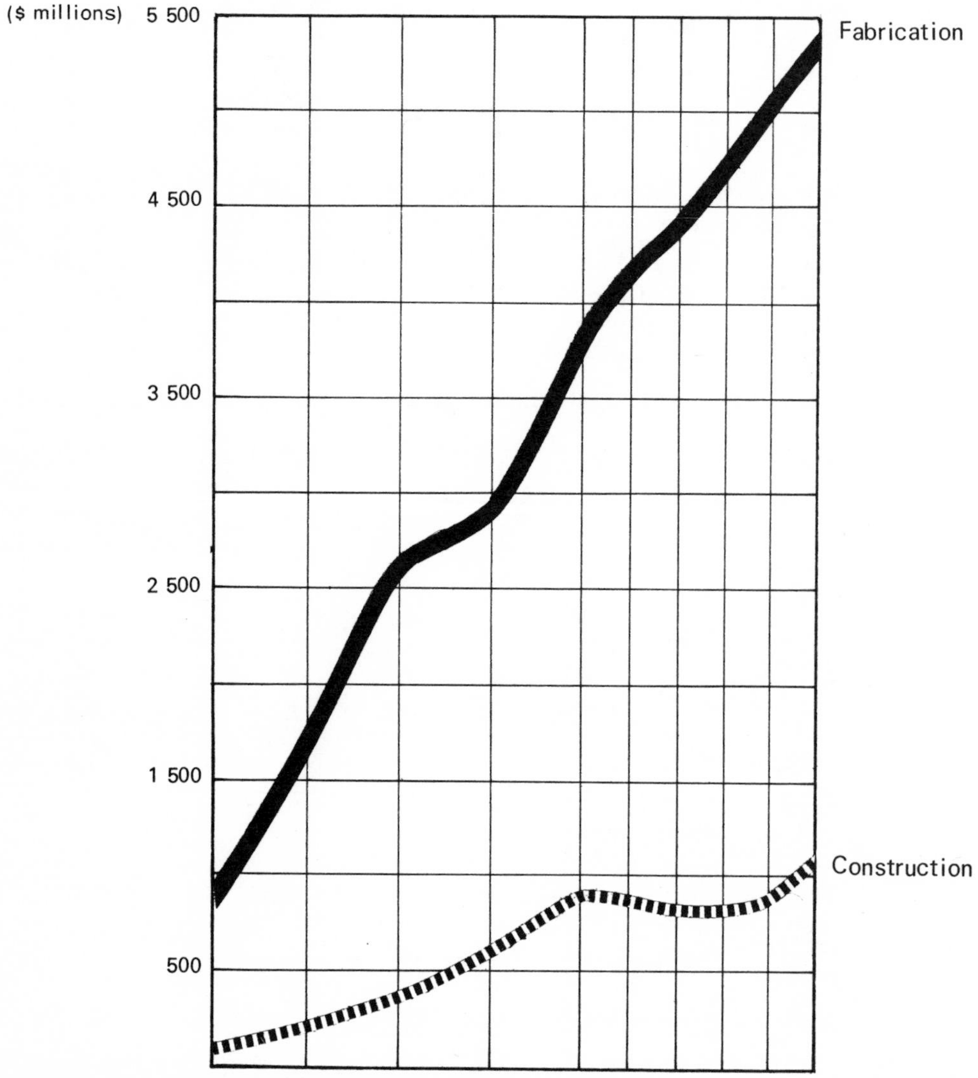

Source: *Tableaux-types des comptes économiques du Québec, Revènus et dépenses, 1946-1970,* Ministère de l'Industrie et du Commerce, Québec, 1970.

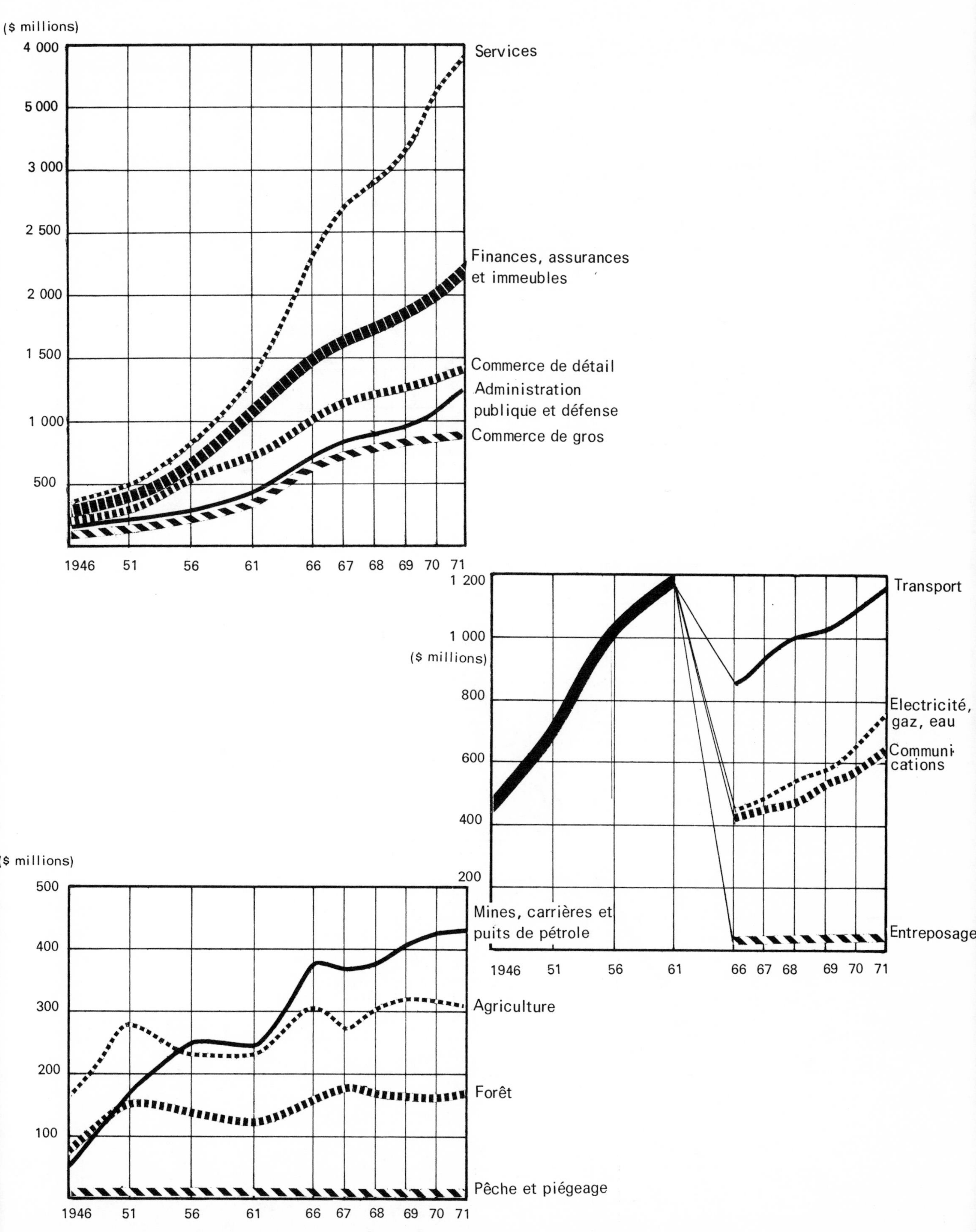
($ millions)
4 000
5 000
3 000
2 500
2 000
1 500
1 000
500
Services
Finances, assurances et immeubles
Commerce de détail
Administration publique et défense
Commerce de gros
1946
51
56
61
66
67
68
69
70
71
1 200
1 000
($ millions)
800
600
400
200
Transport
Electricité, gaz, eau
Communi- cations
Entreposage
($ millions)
500
400
300
200
100
Mines, carrières et puits de pétrole
Agriculture
Forêt
Pêche et piégeage

6.4 Comptes économiques du Québec

6.4.1 STRUCTURE DE REPARTITION DES REVENUS, 1970, QUEBEC, ONTARIO, CANADA

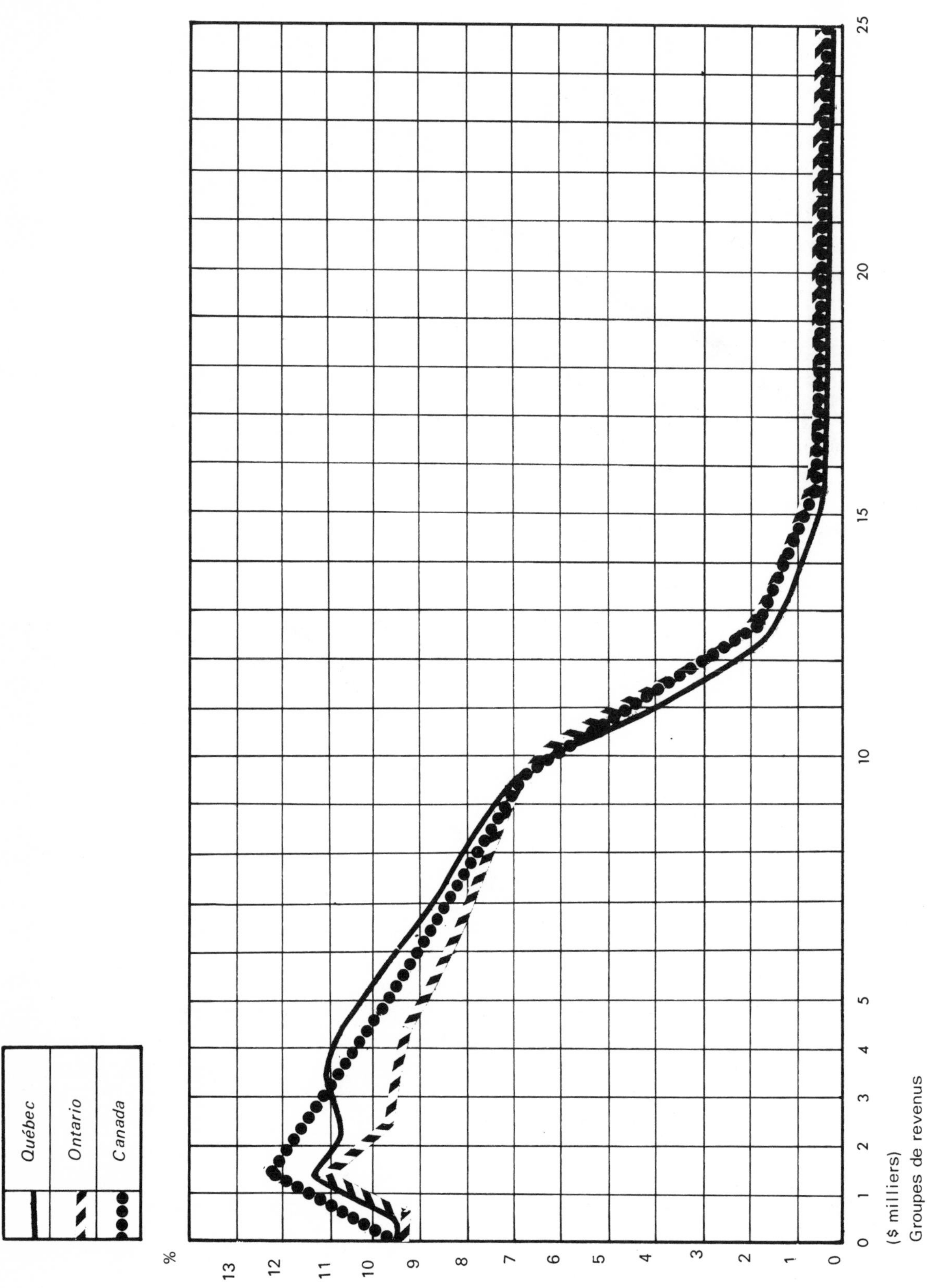

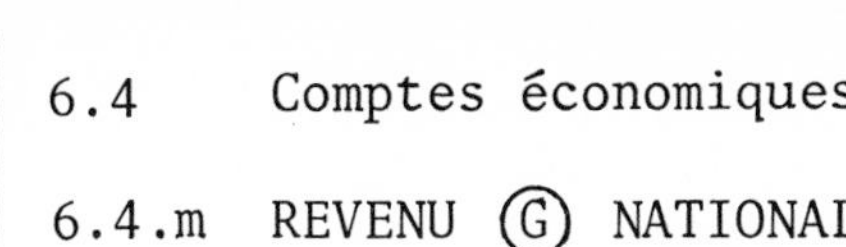

6.4 Comptes économiques du Québec

6.4.m REVENU Ⓖ NATIONAL NET ET PRODUIT Ⓖ NATIONAL BRUT, QUEBEC, 1946-1970, ANNEES CHOISIES

		1946	1951	1956	1961	1966	1971
1	Rémunération des salariés (N)	1 493	2 807	4 091	5 474	8 688	12 956
2	Solde et indemnités militaires (N)	29	31	69	74	83	135
3	Bénéfices des sociétés avant impôts	483	1 003	1 204	1 097	1 681	2 128
4	Moins: dividendes versés à l'étranger	-67	-121	-138	-168	-213	-231
5	Intérêts et revenus divers de placements (N)	41	116	211	333	520	953
6	Revenu net revenant aux agriculteurs au titre de la production agricole (N)	143	240	165	147	209	169
7	Revenu net des entreprises individuelles non agricoles y compris les loyers (N)	307	440	661	759	976	1 288
8	Ajustement de la valeur Ⓖ des stocks	-83	-205	-75	-11	-84	-149
total des 8 chiffres précédants							
9	**Revenu national net au coût des facteurs**	2 346	4 311	6 188	7 705	11 860	17 749
10	Impôts indirects moins Ⓖ subventions	366	647	937	1 311	2 239	3 377
11	Provisions pour Ⓖ consommation de capital et réévaluations diverses	268	489	910	1 201	1 168	2 153
12	Erreur statistique Ⓖ d'estimation	20	-51	33	37	47	-107
total des 4 chiffres précédants							
13	**Produit national brut au prix du marché**	3 000	5 396	8 068	10 254	15 814	22 672

Note: Voir "Revenu personnel", au glossaire.

Source: *Tableaux-types des comptes économiques du Québec, Revenus et dépenses, 1946-1970,* Ministère de l'Industrie et du Commerce, Québec, 1970.

6.4 Comptes économiques du Québec

6.4.n DEPENSES D'INVESTISSEMENT Ⓖ, QUEBEC, ONTARIO, CANADA, 1960-1972, TOUTES LES ANNEES

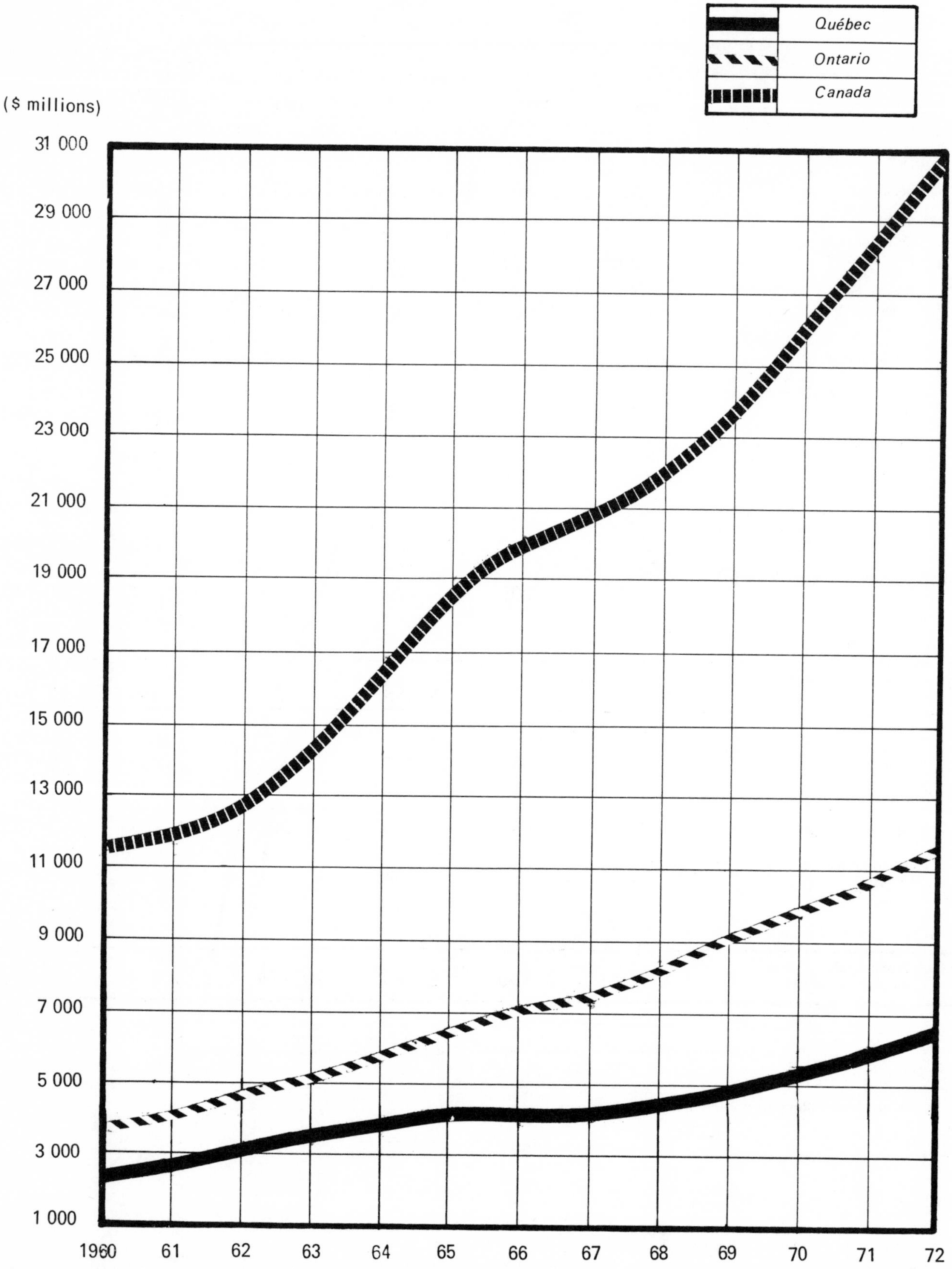

Source: Statistique Canada No 61-205 F, *Investissements privés et publics au Canada,* Ottawa.

6.5 Valeur ajoutée

6.5.a VALEUR AJOUTEE, QUEBEC, ONTARIO, 1936-1969, ANNEES CHOISIES

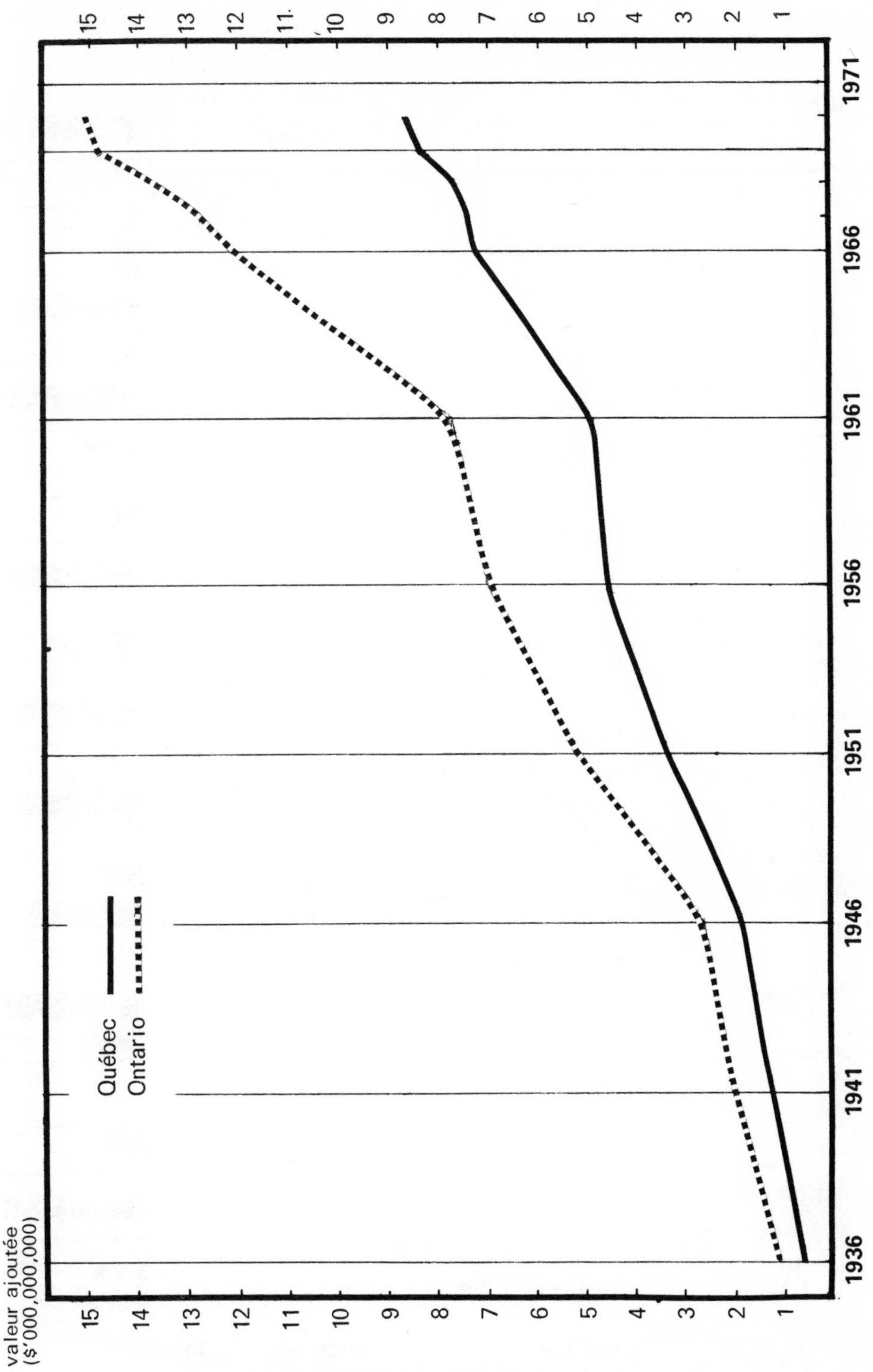

valeur ajoutée
($'000,000,000)

15 14 13 12 11 10 9 8 7 6 5 4 3 2 1

Québec
Ontario

1936 1941 1946 1951 1956 1961 1966 1971

6

6.5 Valeur ajoutée

6.5.b REPARTITION DE LA VALEUR Ⓖ AJOUTEE SELON LES INDUSTRIES Ⓖ MANUFACTURIERES, QUEBEC, ONTARIO, 1961-1968, MOYENNE POUR LES HUIT ANNEES

Industrie (manufacturière)	QUEBEC valeur ajoutée ($'000)		ONTARIO valeur ajoutée ($'000)	
Aliments et boissons	627,648	16.4	1,000,976	12.5
Produits du tabac	98,020	2.6	54,674	0.7
Caoutchouc	49,929	1.3	187,183	2.3
Cuir	84,751	2.2	78,697	1.0
Textiles	304,995	8.0	217,988	2.7
Bonnetterie	74,446	1.9	47,327	0.6
Habillement	324,900	8.5	127,828	1.6
Bois	121,156	3.2	117,534	1.5
Meubles et articles d'ameublement	98,214	2.6	129,840	1.6
Papier et produits connexes	483,713	12.6	460,062	5.8
Imprimerie, édition et industries connexes	208,713	5.4	390,222	5.0
Produits métalliques primaires	297,275	7.8	745,583	9.3
Produits métalliques (sauf machines et matériel de transport)	298,645	7.8	705,009	8.8
Machinerie (sauf matériel électrique)	106,351	2.8	533,802	6.7
Matériel de transport	268,924	7.0	1,123,144	14.1
Appareils et matériel électriques	275,714	7.2	618,678	7.7
Produits minéraux non-métalliques	162,177	4.2	272,500	3.4
Produits du pétrole et de la houille	80,184	2.1	93,498	1.2
Produits chimiques et connexes	310,588	8.1	627,628	7.9
Produits manufacturiers divers	126,435	3.3	356,746	4.5
Total (industries)	**4 402 778**	**100**	**7 888 919**	**100**

Comparaison des %

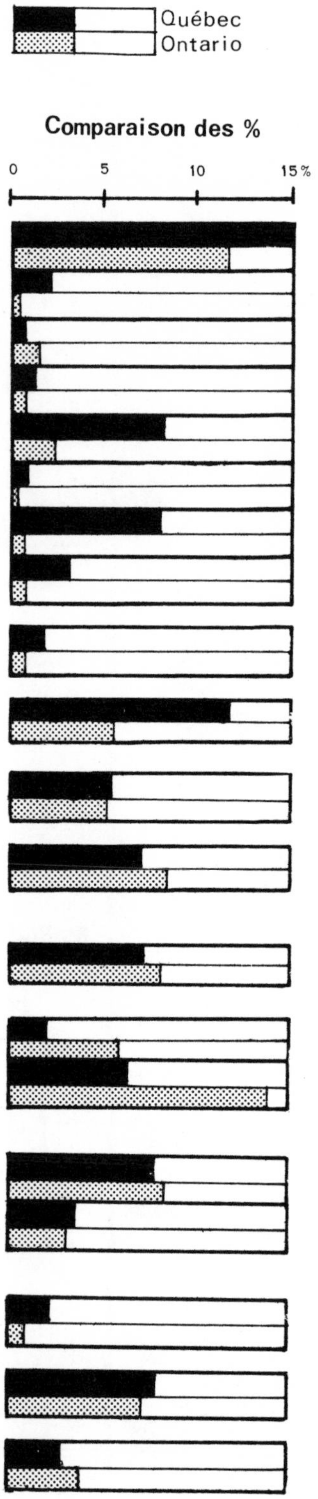

Sources: Statistique Canada No 31-205, *Industries manufacturières du Canada, Section C, Québec,* Ottawa.

Statistique Canada No 31-206, *Industries manufacturières du Canada, Section D, Ontario,* Ottawa.

6.5 Valeur ajoutée

6.5.c VALEUR Ⓖ AJOUTEE SELON LES INDUSTRIES Ⓖ PRODUCTRICES DE BIENS, QUEBEC, ONTARIO, 1926-1970, ANNEES CHOISIES

Année	Québec / Ontario	Agriculture ($'000)	%	Forêts ($'000)	%	Pêche ($'000)	%	Piégeage ($'000)	%	Mines ($'000)	%	Electricité ($'000)	%	Industrie manufacturière ($'000)	%	Construction ($'000)	%	Valeur ajoutée (toutes les industries) ($'000) 100%
1926	**Québec**	**116,416**	. .	. .	. .	**2,470**	. .	**2,150**	. .	**17,427**	. .	**25,855**	. .	**399,991**	. .	. .	. .	. .
	Ontario	220,746	. .	. .	. .	2,522	. .	3,429	. .	53,289	. .	39,552	. .	667,059	. .	. .	. .	. .
1931	**Québec**	**79,674**	. .	. .	. .	**1,636**	. .	**1,415**	. .	**19,512**	. .	**41,976**	. .	**404,034**	. .	. .	. .	. .
	Ontario	147,431	. .	. .	. .	2,041	. .	1,789	. .	64,912	. .	46,415	. .	624,809	. .	. .	. .	. .
1936	**Québec**	**88,223**	**13.5**	**27,674**	**4.2**	**1,877**	**0.3**	**1,449**	**0.2**	**26,651**	**4.1**	**45,913**	**7.0**	**377,515**	**57.8**	**84,000**	**12.9**	**653,302**
	Ontario	145,835	12.9	18,307	1.6	1,714	0.2	1,796	0.2	97,474	8.6	51,984	4.6	681,471	60.4	124,000	11.0	1,128,581
1941	**Québec**	**128,670**	**10.1**	**56,696**	**4.5**	**2,080**	**0.2**	**1,391**	**0.1**	**64,570**	**5.1**	**69,461**	**5.5**	**815,687**	**64.2**	**132,000**	**10.4**	**1,269,955**
	Ontario	208,960	10.4	32,696	1.6	3,031	0.1	2,775	0.1	158,461	7.9	65,316	3.3	1,360,056	67.8	174,000	8.7	2,005,295
1946	**Québec**	**185,394**	**9.9**	**137,673**	**7.4**	**4,475**	**0.2**	**5,308**	**0.3**	**55,974**	**3.0**	**84,822**	**4.5**	**1,125,992**	**60.2**	**181,000**	**9.7**	**1,870,638**
	Ontario	336,670	13.3	73,149	2.9	5,597	0.2	7,793	0.3	106,809	4.2	73,547	2.9	1,659,284	65.4	272,600	10.7	2,535,449
1951	**Québec**	**296,209**	**8.8**	**220,059**	**6.6**	**3,376**	**0.1**	**2,350**	**0.1**	**164,881**	**4.9**	**129,474**	**3.9**	**2,083,934**	**62.1**	**452,700**	**13.5**	**3,352,983**
	Ontario	582,660	11.0	118,526	2.2	7.035	0.1	5,214	0.1	178,554	3.4	127,319	2.4	3,569,400	67.7	684,300	13.0	5,273,008
1956	**Québec**	**231,681**	**5.1**	**224,899**	**5.0**	**4,440**	**0.1**	**1,162**	**0.0**	**243,074**	**5.4**	**171,088**	**3.8**	**2,888,149**	**63.8**	**759,200**	**16.8**	**4,523,692**
	Ontario	424,170	6.0	125,917	1.8	7.927	0.1	2,990	0.0	246,454	3.5	231,411	3.3	4,868,570	69.3	1,116,300	15.9	7,023,740
1961	**Québec**	**263,039**	**5.5**	**174,283**	**3.6**	**4,710**	**0.1**	**1,888**	**0.0**	**255,675**	**5.3**	**242,067**	**5.0**	**3,207,856**	**66.9**	**663,235**	**13.8**	**4,792,955**
	Ontario	536,631	7.0	115,324	1.5	5,746	0.1	2,470	0.0	414,013	5.4	311,511	4.0	5,429,853	70.4	1,217,448	15.8	7,713,594
1966	**Québec**	**351,092**	**4.9**	**172,864**	**2.4**	**7,536**	**0.1**	**2,066**	**0.0**	**458,974**	**6.4**	**336,386**	**4.7**	**4,704,799**	**65.9**	**1,102,560**	**15.4**	**7,136,277**
	Ontario	793,752	6.5	116,407	1.0	5,995	0.0	3,983	0.0	499,935	4.1	401,325	3.3	8,648,180	71.3	1,655,543	13.6	12,125,120
1967	**Québec**	**350,694**	**4.8**	**180,445**	**2.5**	**7,882**	**0.1**	**1,520**	**0.0**	**448,999**	**6.2**	**373,290**	**5.1**	**4,855,896**	**66.8**	**1,049,508**	**14.4**	**7,268,234**
	Ontario	744,421	5.8	115,872	1.0	5,988	0.0	2,598	0.0	642,512	5.0	426,656	3.3	9,032,055	70.9	1,761,999	13.8	12,732,101
1968	**Québec**	**372,232**	**4.8**	**166,327**	**2.2**	**8,648**	**0.1**	**1,932**	**0.0**	**438,275**	**5.7**	**417,286**	**5.4**	**5,215,464**	**67.8**	**1,070,735**	**13.9**	**7,691,899**
	Ontario	771,617	5.6	111,414	0.8	5,968	0.0	3,354	0.0	722,997	5.3	470,507	3.4	9,714,889	71.2	1,845,569	13.5	13,646,316
1969	**Québec**	**398,678**	**4.8**	**181,810**	**2.2**	**9,221**	**0.1**	**2,714**	**0.0**	**488,216**	**5.8**	**447,844**	**5.4**	**5,672,740**	**67.9**	**1,156,943**	**13.8**	**8,358,166**
	Ontario	825,584	5.6	125,697	0.8	7,389	0.0	4,906	0.0	651,482	4.4	524,928	3.5	10,635,970	71.9	2,020,345	13.6	14,796,301
1970	**Québec**	*338 329*	*4,5*	*157 742*	*1,8*	*11 273*	*0,1*	*1 828*	*0,0*	*494 767*	*5,8*	*524 614*	*6,1*	*5 797 861*	*67,4*	*1 224 533*	*14,3*	*8 600 947*
	Ontario	816 522	5,4	110 454	0,7	6 535	0,0	3 476	0,0	840 958	5,6	583 083	3,9	10 524 756	69,6	2 237 754	14,8	15 123 538

Source: Statistique Canada No 61-202, *Survey of Production, System of National Account. Domestic Product by industry*, Ottawa, 1971.

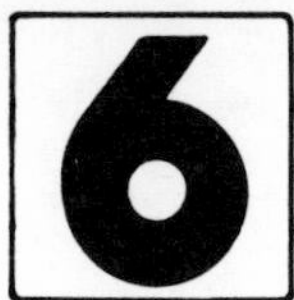

6

6.6 Conjoncture (G)

QUEBEC, 1946-1970

(G) **Revenu personnel par habitant**

(G) **Prix à la consommation**

Population, Main-d'oeuvre et Emploi (G) (G)

Taux de chômage (G)

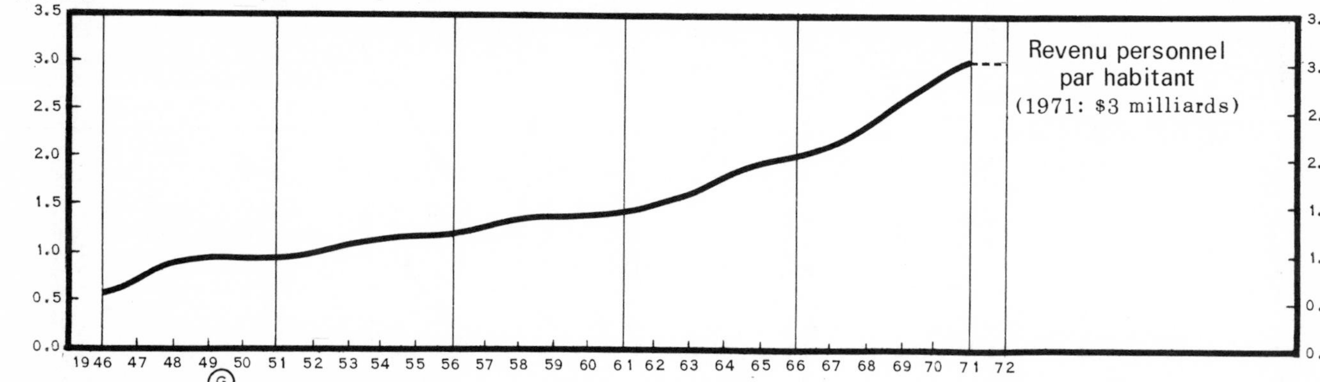

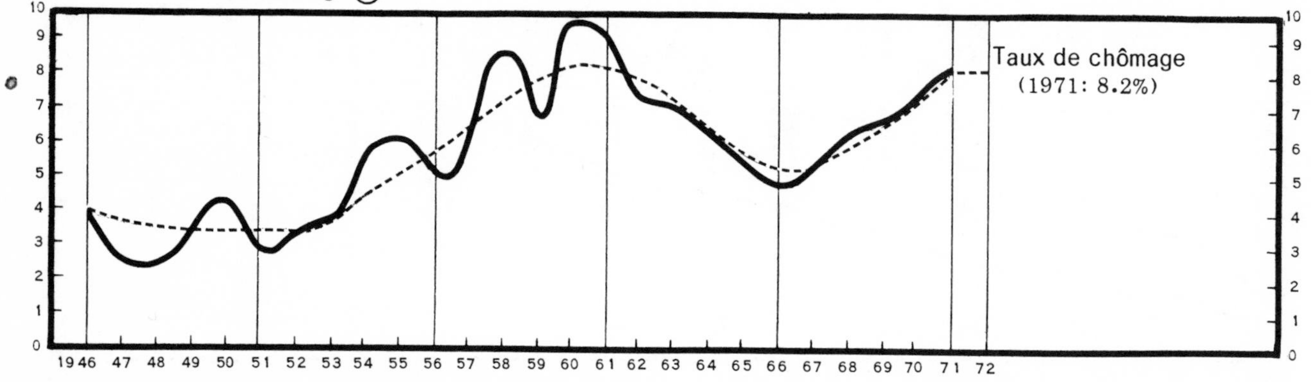

Sources: *Annuaire du Québec*, 1946-1972.

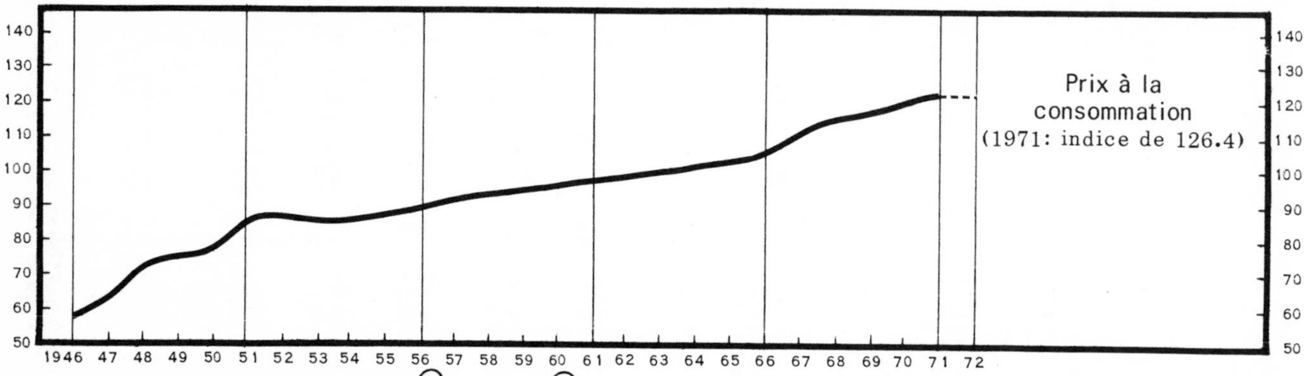

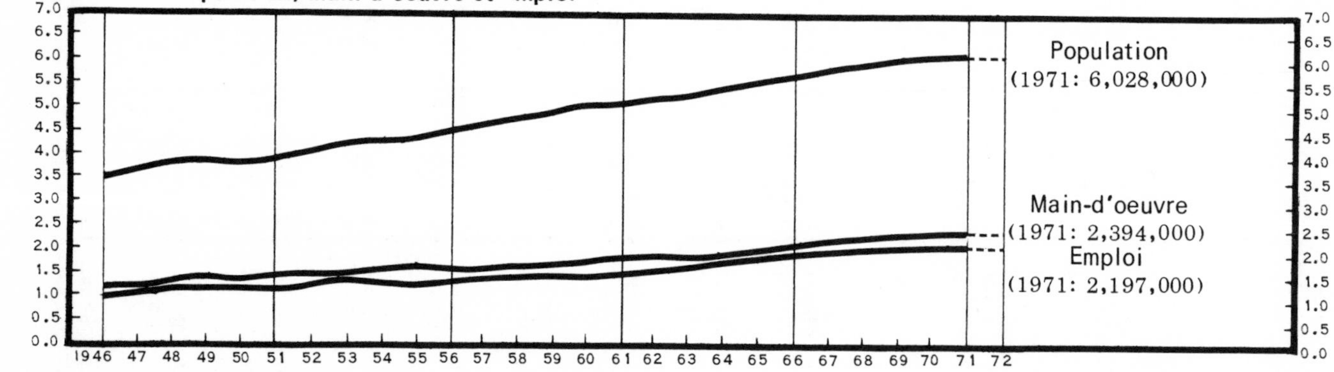

Annuaire du Canada, 1946-1972.

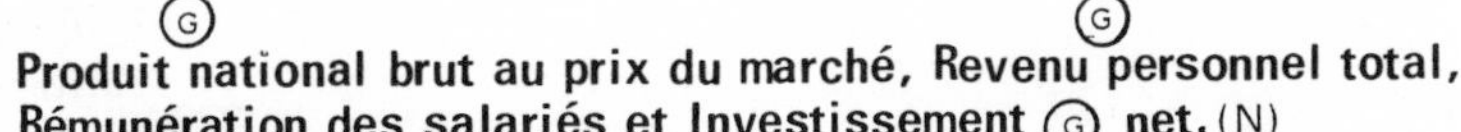

Produit national brut au prix du marché, Revenu personnel total, Rémunération des salariés et Investissement net. (N)

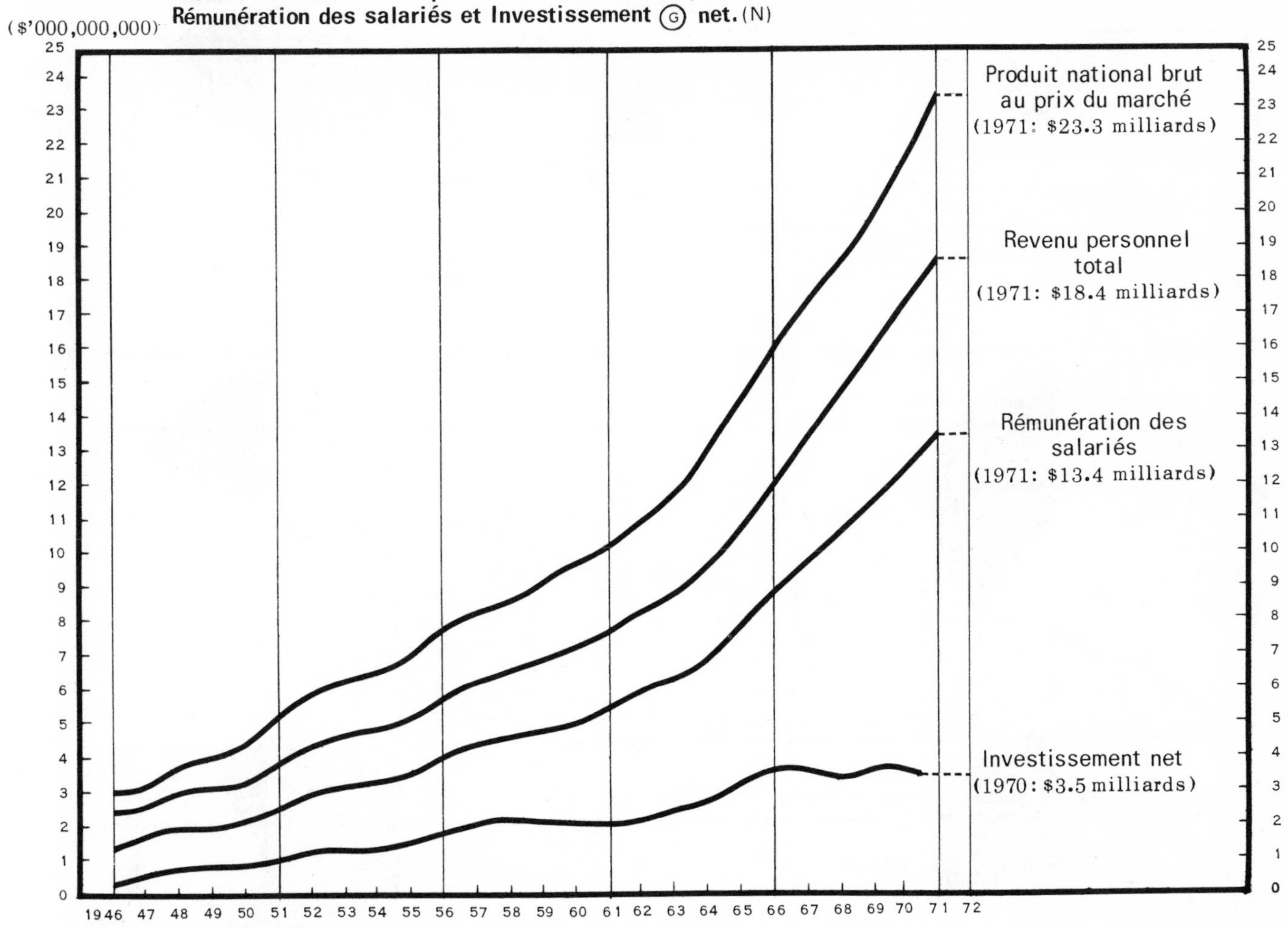

($'000,000,000)

Produit national brut au prix du marché (1971: $23.3 milliards)

Revenu personnel total (1971: $18.4 milliards)

Rémunération des salariés (1971: $13.4 milliards)

Investissement net (1970: $3.5 milliards)

0 1 2 3 4 5 6 7 8 9 10 11 12 13 14 15 16 17 18 19 20 21 22 23 24 25

1946 47 48 49 50 51 52 53 54 55 56 57 58 59 60 61 62 63 64 65 66 67 68 69 70 71 72

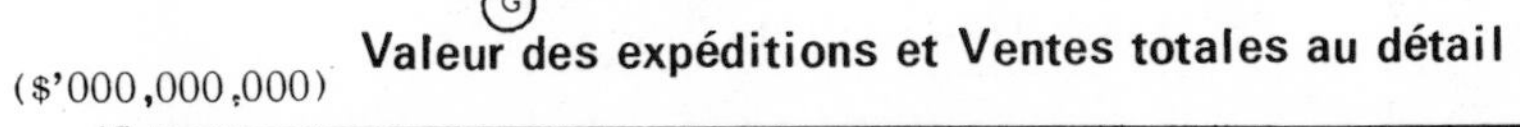

Valeur des expéditions et Ventes totales au détail

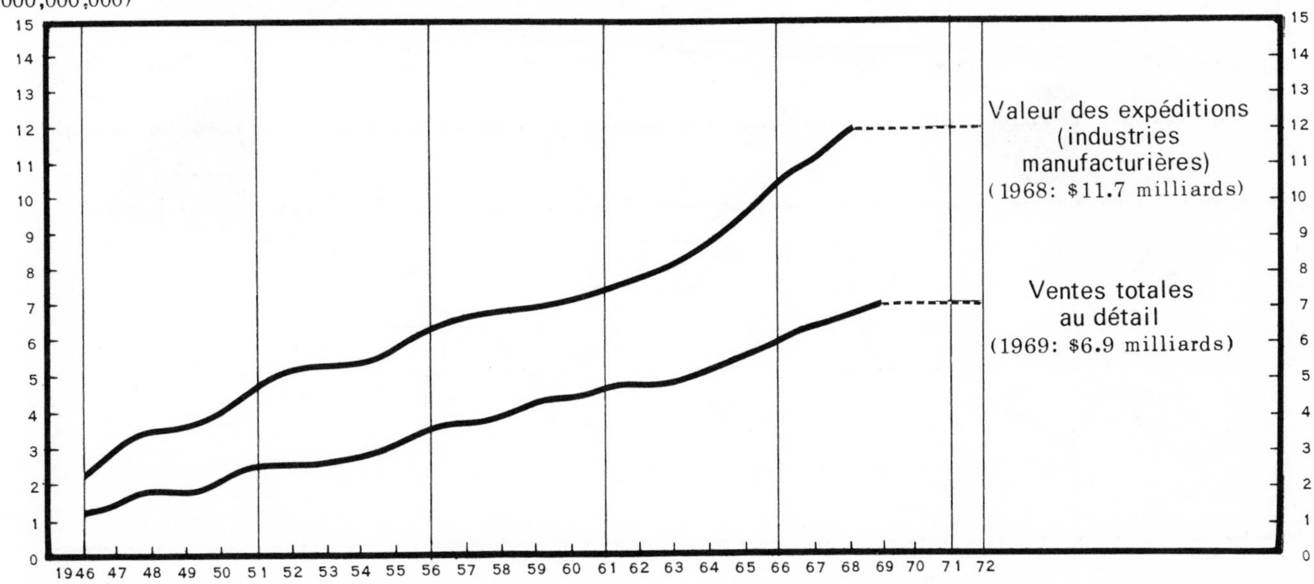

6.7 Contrôle de l'économie

6.7.a IMPORTANCE DES ETABLISSEMENTS (G) SELON L'ORIGINE ETHNIQUE DE LA MAIN-D'OEUVRE (G) EMPLOYEE, QUEBEC, 1961

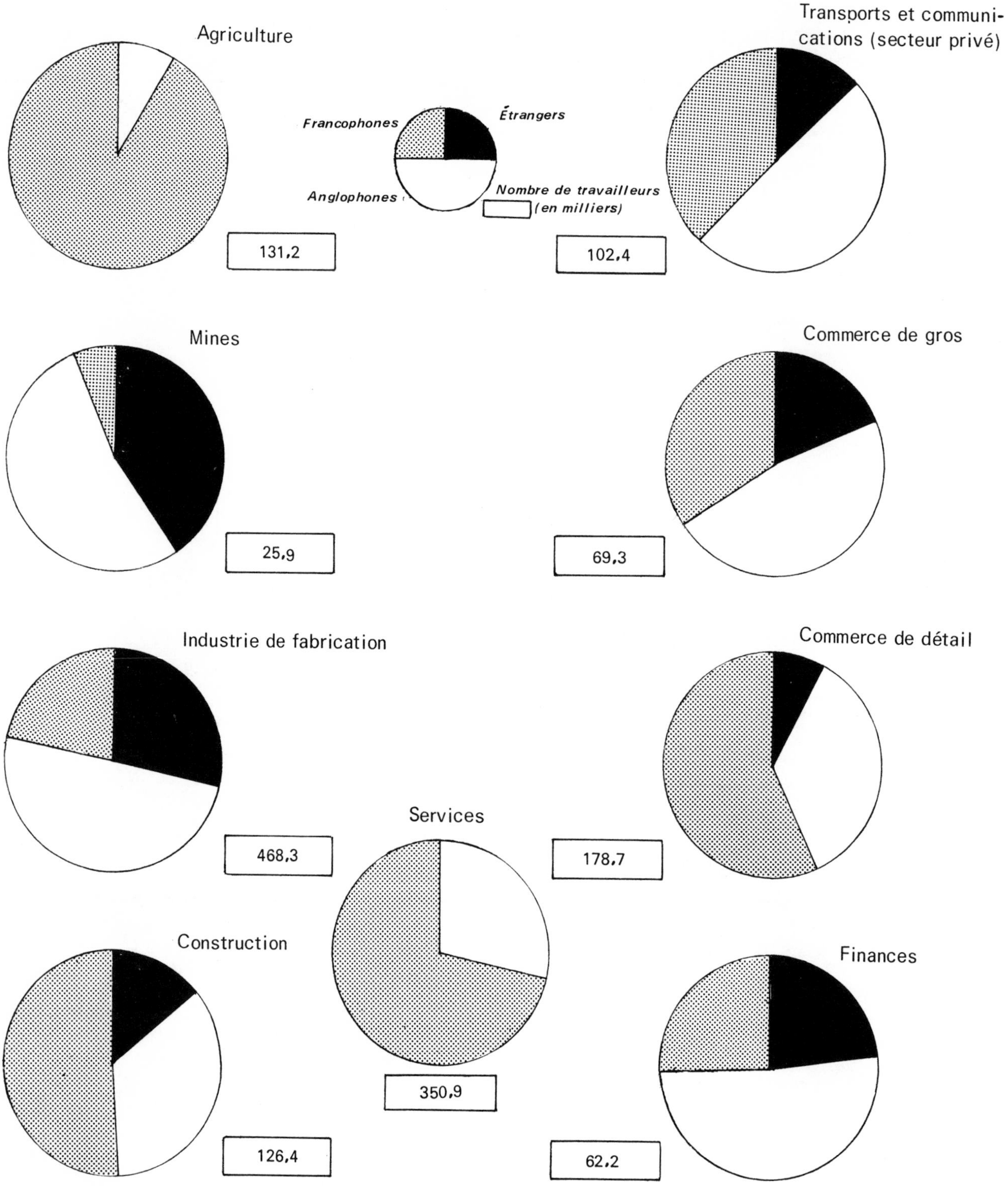

Note: Voir "Industries selon les secteurs", au glossaire.

Source: *Rapport de la Commission royale d'Enquête sur le Bilinguisme et le Biculturalisme*, Ottawa, 1969.

6.7 Contrôle de l'économie

6.7.b CONTROLE ETRANGER ET AMERICAIN DE CERTAINES INDUSTRIES Ⓖ CANADIENNES, 1926-1963, ANNEES CHOISIES

Industrie — % contrôle étranger / — % **contrôle américain**		1926	1939	1948	1956	1961	1962	1963
Industrie manufacturière	% contrôle étranger	35	38	43	52	59	60	60
	% contrôle américain	**30**	**32**	**39**	**41**	**45**	**45**	**46**
Mines et affinage	% contrôle étranger	38	42	40	58	59	58	59
	% contrôle américain	**32**	**38**	**37**	**52**	**52**	**52**	**52**
Pétrole et gaz naturel	% contrôle étranger	–	–	–	80	72	74	74
	% contrôle américain	**–**	**–**	**–**	**73**	**63**	**63**	**62**
Chemins de fer	% contrôle étranger	3	3	3	2	2	2	2
	% contrôle américain	**3**	**3**	**3**	**2**	**2**	**2**	**2**
Autres services publics	% contrôle étranger	20	26	24	4	5	4	4
	% contrôle américain	**20**	**26**	**24**	**4**	**4**	**4**	**4**
Total y compris le commerce	% contrôle étranger	17	21	25	31	33	34	34
	% contrôle américain	**15**	**19**	**22**	**26**	**26**	**27**	**27**

Source: Bernard Bonin, *Investissements étrangers à long terme au Canada,* Montréal, Les Presses de l'Ecole des H.E.C., 1967.

6.7 Contrôle de l'économie

6.7.c CONCENTRATION Ⓖ DES INVESTISSEMENTS Ⓖ DIRECTS ETRANGERS SELON LES SECTEURS INDUSTRIELS, CANADA, 1954 ET 1963

Secteur industriel industrie	Total du capital des entreprises canadiennes ($'000,000) 100%	Partie du capital contrôlée par ... Canada ($'000,000)	%	Etats-Unis ($'000,000)	%	Autres pays ($'000,000)	%	Total du contrôle étranger en 1954 %	1963 %
Secteur manufacturier									
Automobiles et pièces	**573**	15	**3**	558	97	–	–	95	**97**
Caoutchouc	**216**	6	**3**	195	90	15	7	93	**97**
Produits chimiques	**367**	45	**22**	295	54	27	24	75	**78**
Appareils électriques	**641**	22	**23**	161	66	458	11	77	**77**
Aéronautique	**253**	55	**22**	85	33	113	45	36	**78**
Instruments aratoires	**207**	104	**50**	103	50	–	–	35	**50**
Pâtes et papiers	**2,313**	1,217	**53**	817	35	279	12	56	**47**
Textiles	**713**	568	**80**	96	13	49	7	18	**20**
Boissons	**589**	488	**83**	101	17	–	–	20	**17**
Fer et acier	**874**	752	**86**	14	2	108	12	6	**14**
Autres	**5,888**	1,790	**30**	3,154	54	944	16	–	**70**
Total du secteur manufacturier	**13,654**	5,451	**40**	6,308	46	1,895	14	51	**60**
Pétrole et gaz naturel	**7,295**	1,841	**26**	4,609	62	845	12	69	**74**
Secteur minier									
Fonte et raffinerie des métaux non-ferreux	**1,066**	521	**49**	545	51	–	–	–	**51**
Autres minerais	**2,743**	1,038	**38**	1,435	52	270	10	–	**62**
Total du secteur minier	**3,809**	1,559	**41**	1,980	52	270	7	51	**59**
TOTAL DES SECTEURS INDUSTRIELS	**24,758**	8,851	**36**	12,897	52	3,010	12	–	**60**

Source: Kari Levitt, La Capitulation tranquille, Montréal, Réédition Québec, 1972.

6.7 Contrôle de l'économie

6.7.d INVESTISSEMENTS (G) DIRECTS ETRANGERS AU CANADA SELON CERTAINES INDUSTRIES (G), 1945 ET 1965

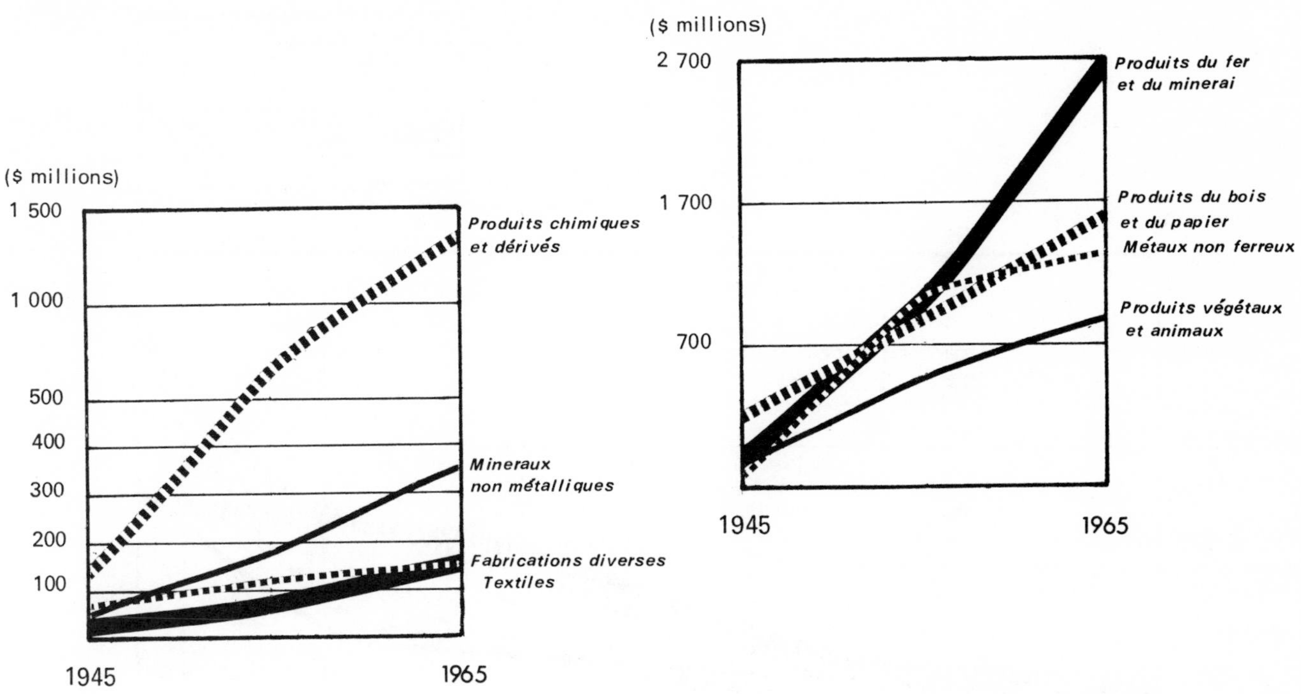

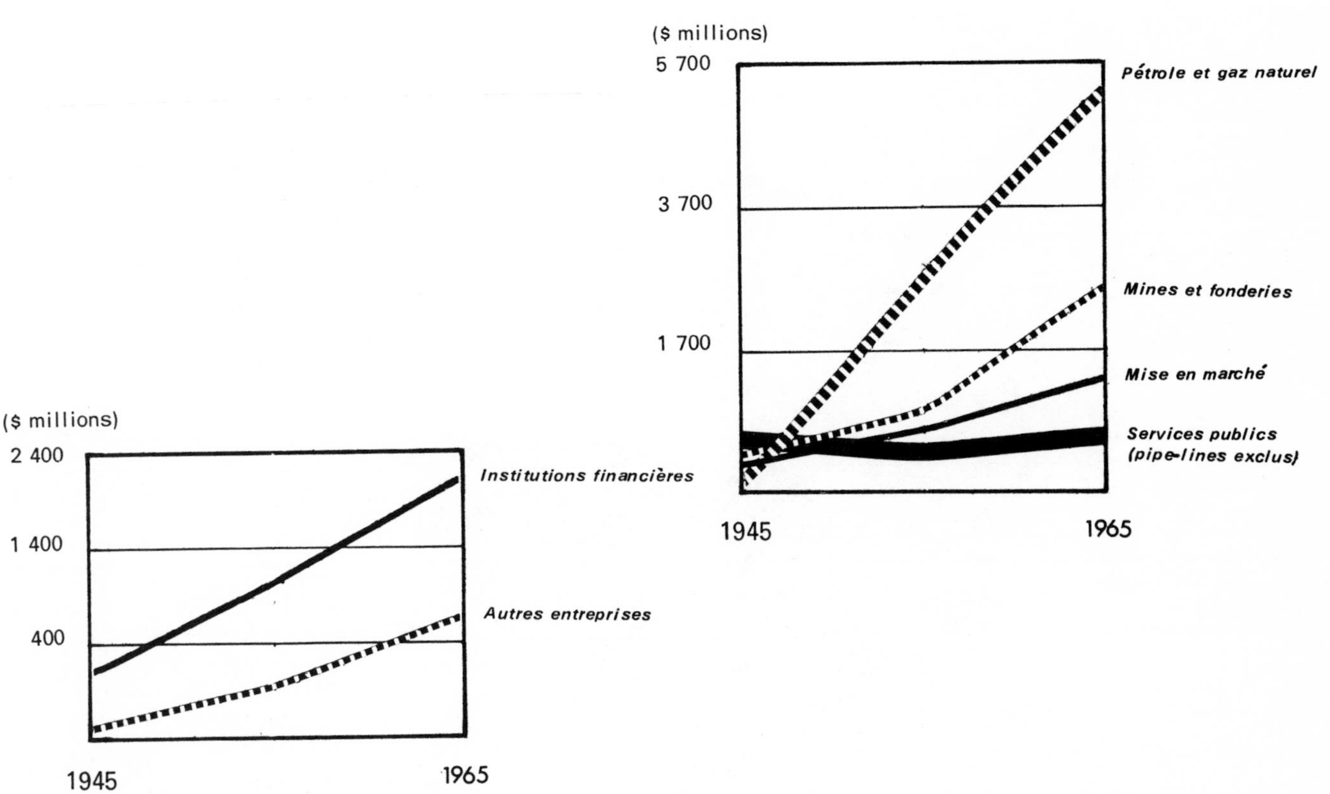

Source: Kari Levitt, La Capitulation tranquille, Montréal, Réédition Québec, 1972.

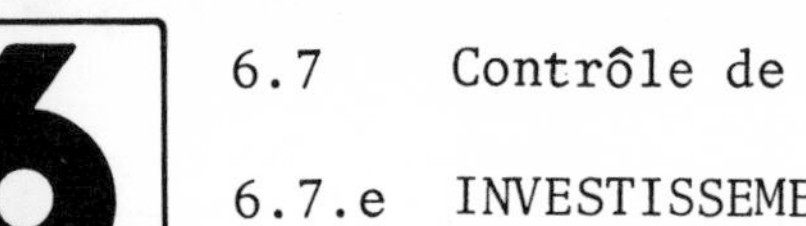

6.7 Contrôle de l'économie

6.7.e INVESTISSEMENTS DIRECTS AMERICAINS A TRAVERS LE MONDE, 1924-1966, ANNEES CHOISIES

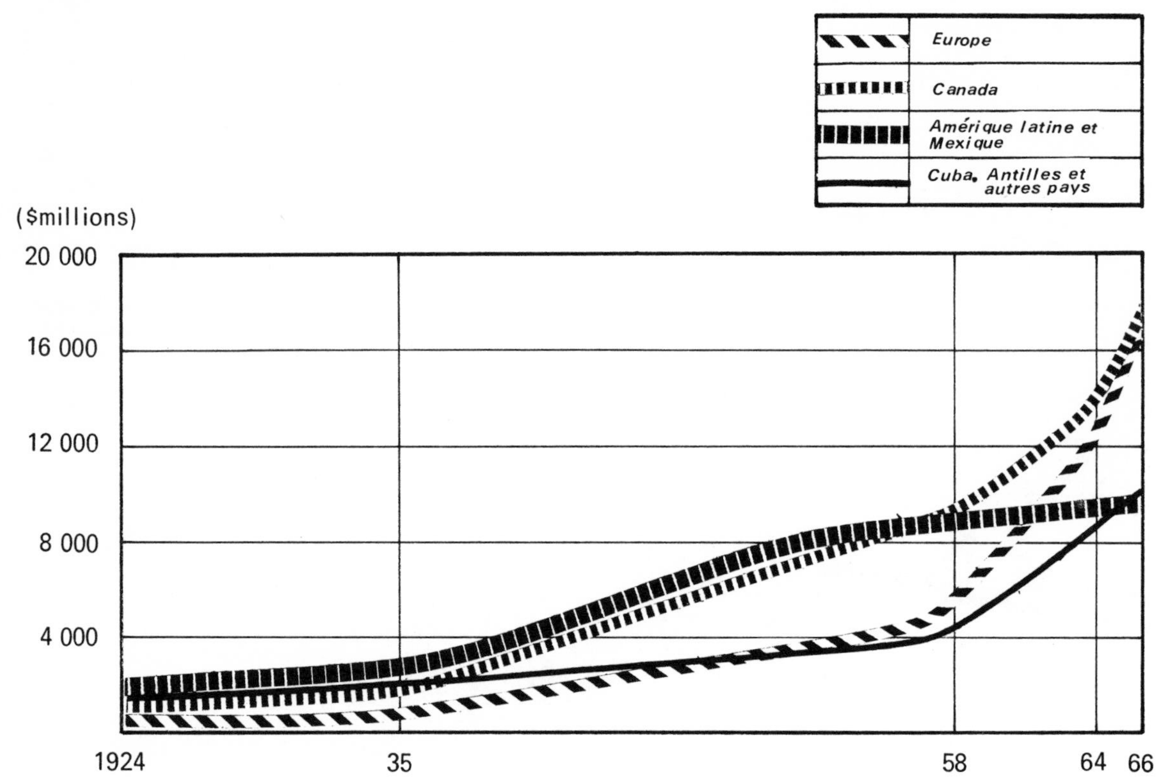

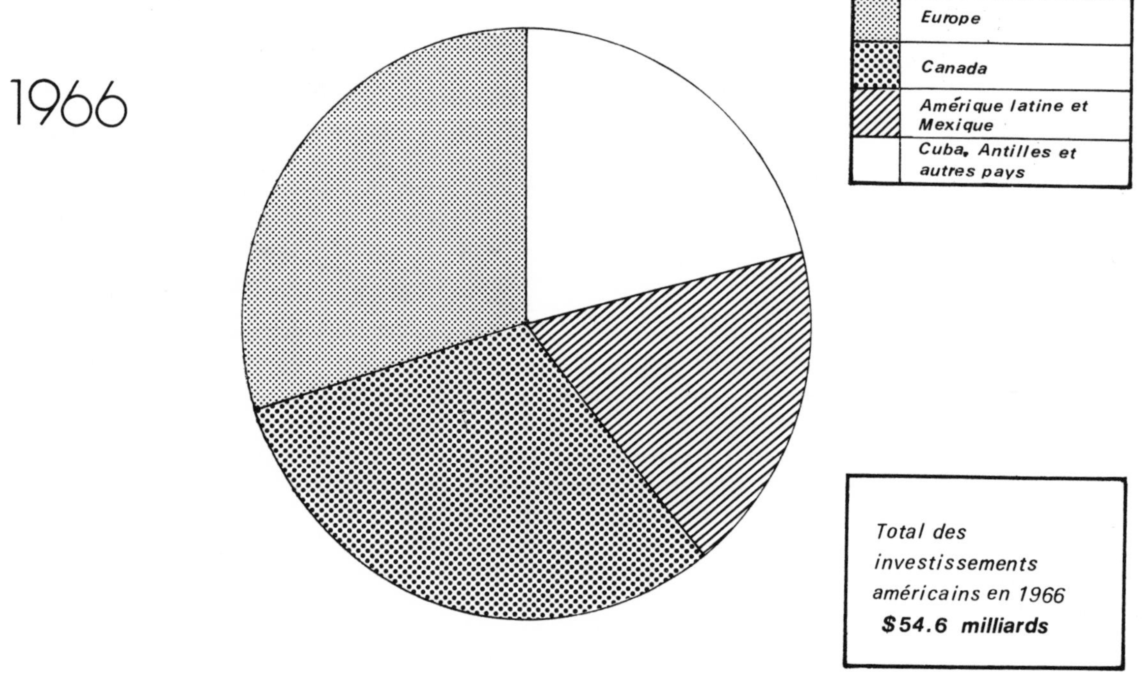

Source: Kari Levitt, La Capitulation tranquille, Montréal, Réédition Québec, 1972.

6.7.f SOURCES DE FINANCEMENT DES SOCIETES AMERICAINES A L'ETRANGER, MOYENNE POUR TROIS ANS, 1963-1965

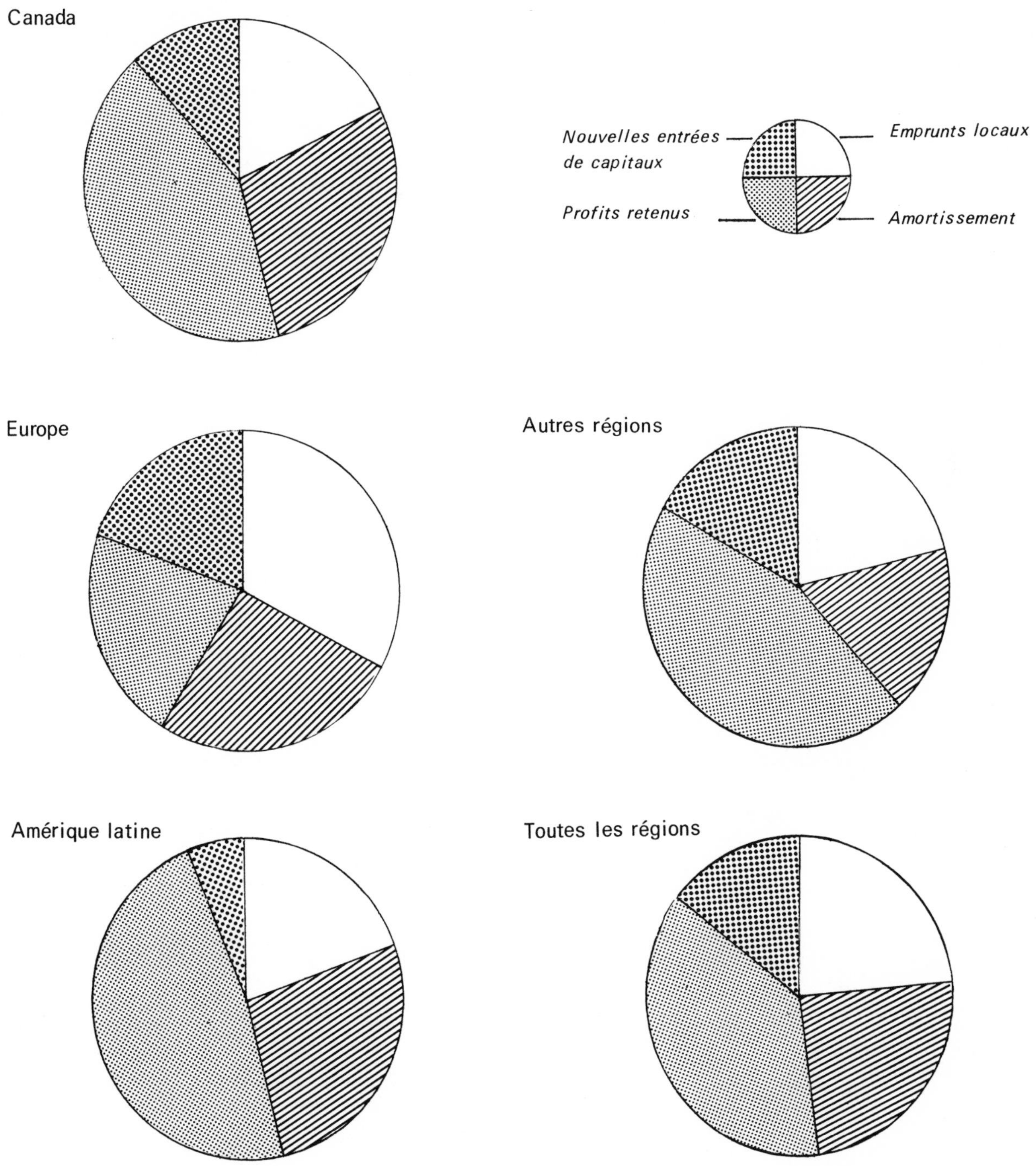

Source: Kari Levitt, La Capitulation tranquille, Montréal, Réédition Québec, 1972.

INTRODUCTION

Certains pourront s'étonner de retrouver ici, dans cette troisième partie consacrée à la politique, autant d'organigrammes, de tableaux, de statistiques. Certes, pas plus que pour l'économique ou le social, tout le politique ne peut être compris dans de telles données. Pourtant cette approche est indispensable à celui qui veut acquérir certaines connaissances de base. Aussi, c'est le réseau complexe des institutions politiques et administratives du système politique québécois que dessinent ces organigrammes et ces statistiques. C'est quelques-unes des nombreuses activités importantes de l'Etat québécois en matière sociale, éducative, économique, etc... qu'ils évoquent, de même que quelques traits de certains des acteurs politiques les plus au coeur de la vie politique québécoise. Tout comme pour l'économique, nous verrons ici les structures, les activités et les acteurs. Les structures représentent les instruments que cette société possède pour résoudre les problèmes, les défis qui sont les siens. Comme telles, elles représentent aussi des choix. Les activités, ce sont les choix actualisés dans la vie politique concrète.

Quant aux acteurs, il faut en distinguer deux sortes. Les officiels, ceux qui possèdent formellement le droit de décider politiquement et qui dans notre système proviennent des partis politiques. Ils ont pour les aider les fonctionnaires de tous niveaux et de tous services, administrations ou régies. Il y a aussi tous ceux qui, dans les divers domaines d'activités, représentent les pouvoirs sociaux, économiques, religieux, etc... que l'on nomme souvent les groupes de pression. Désigner ainsi les divers acteurs ne résout pas le problème fondamental de savoir où se trouve le véritable pouvoir politique dans notre système politique et c'est là la limite voulue de ce type de données.

Evoquer de cette manière les structures, les activités et les hommes ne nous permet pas non plus de rejoindre directement la dimension, pourtant fondamentale dans la vie politique, des idées, des doctrines et des idéologies politiques. C'est pourtant elle qui se retrouve derrière les structures adoptées, les priorités établies, les origines sociales des hommes politiques et les liens qu'ils ont avec tel ou tel groupe social ou économique; elle explique les changements survenus dans le rôle de l'Etat québécois tout comme les résistances à ces changements ou les aspirations aux dépassements des objectifs de la révolution tranquille. Il ne nous était pas possible d'illustrer valablement ces divers courants de pensées par des organigrammes ou des statistiques. Le lecteur devra pourtant apprendre à les connaître par les textes et il trouvera dans les éléments bibliographiques fournis des indications précieuses pour ses recherches.

Nous avons réparti ces diverses données en deux grands chapitres. Un premier décrit les structures, c'est-à-dire les institutions politiques et administratives et leurs pouvoirs et responsabilités. La juxtaposition de ces renseignements et leur étalement sur quelques décennies permettent de saisir l'ampleur des transformations survenues au Québec dans la machine politique par suite du changement de l'idée même que les Québécois se font de l'Etat. L'expansion qu'a connue le budget du Québec dans le domaine de l'éducation, de la santé et des affaires sociales illustre bien ces transformations et explique les tensions qui se sont développées entre le fédéral et le provincial en matières fiscale et constitutionnelle.

Un deuxième chapitre est consacré aux éléments moteurs de la vie politique, c'est-à-dire aux partis et aux groupes qui, par la pression et l'influence, cherchent à obtenir de l'Etat des interventions qui leur permettent de rencontrer leurs objectifs propres. Si parmi ces divers groupes nous avons en quelque sorte prévilégié les syndicats c'est en partie à cause du rôle de plus en plus important qu'on leur voit jouer dans la vie politique du Québec depuis quelques années. Il faut cependant se souvenir que les grandes compagnies et les groupes financiers sont aussi des forces politiques déterminantes, tout comme l'Eglise l'a été dans le passé et le demeure encore partiellement.

Nous ne pouvions illustrer tous les éléments essentiels des partis et des groupes qui animent la vie politique québécoise. Seuls quelques-uns ont été retenus et le lecteur devra compléter, par ses recherches, son observation et ses connaissances. Dans certains cas il trouvera ailleurs dans ce document écrit des données de base sur quelques-uns de ces acteurs; c'est notamment le cas pour certains groupes économiques ou, encore, pour un des acteurs principaux, le simple citoyen. C'est en effet celui-ci que nous trouvons décrit sous de nombreux aspects dans les divers chapitres de ce texte. Dans d'autres cas, c'est dans les documents sonores que de précieux renseignements seront fournis: ainsi pour l'Eglise, les syndicats ou les mass-média.

Il est donc important de ne pas perdre de vue que les données de cette partie ne forment pas un ensemble exhaustif. D'ailleurs, nous l'aurions voulu que les connaissances accumulées jusqu'à ce jour sur le Québec ne nous le permettraient pas. Il nous semble toutefois que, à partir de celles qui ont été retenues, le lecteur pourra se faire une idée des principales caractéristiques de notre système parlementaire, de ses composantes, des pouvoirs de celles-ci, de leurs rôles, de quelques-uns des principaux acteurs, le tout replacé dans une perspective historique chaque fois que cela était possible. C'est aussi la complexité atteinte par notre système qu'il lui est possible de percevoir, tout comme la variété très grande des champs d'intervention de l'Etat québécois. C'est l'ampleur des changements vécus au Québec, surtout depuis la révolution tranquille, qui se retrouve ici décrite dans le développement inouï de l'organigramme politique et administratif, tout comme parfois dans le boulversement des nombreuses statistiques. Ce sont aussi les insuffisances et les goulots d'étranglement qui sont tantôt évoqués, tantôt mis en évidence. Bref, derrière le caractère froid et rigide de ces données, c'est le Québec vivant, bouillonnant des dix dernières années qui est ainsi évoqué et qu'il faut tenter de retrouver.

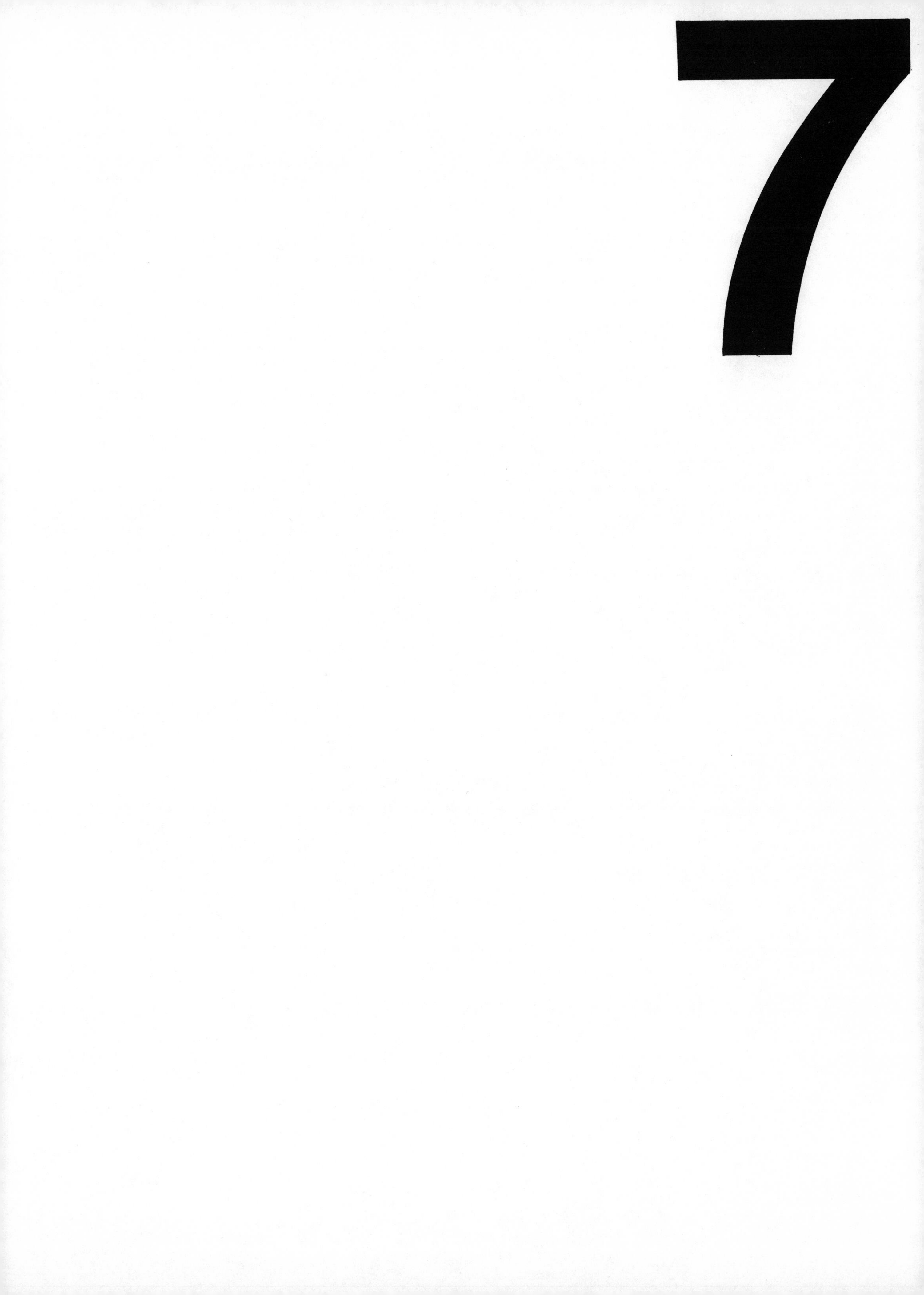
7

DIVISION 1: LES INSTITUTIONS POLITIQUES, ADMINISTRATIVES ET JUDICIAIRES DU QUÉBEC*

Le Québec est théoriquement une des dix parties qui, sous l'appellation de « provinces », dans un sens particulier au Canada, constituent l'État fédératif canadien, mais par suite de son histoire et du caractère français de la majorité de sa population, il possède des institutions politiques, administratives et juridiques qui témoignent d'une certaine originalité. Au sein du fédéralisme, il a sa propre constitution comme les autres provinces et comme les états aux États-Unis, en Australie et les cantons en Suisse. S'identifiant avec la Nouvelle-France d'autrefois qui s'était perpétuée dans le Bas-Canada, sans que celui-ci ne puisse vraiment disparaître malgré l'Union de 1840, le Québec est cependant né officiellement, le 1er juillet 1867, comme entité politique par l'effet de l'Acte de l'Amérique du Nord britannique. Sa constitution formelle, c'est-à-dire un texte écrit, est prévue dans un certain nombre d'articles de cette loi qui s'appliquent plus particulièrement au Québec, les articles 71 à 81 et les articles qui visent en même temps l'Ontario et le Québec, les articles 81 à 88. Cette constitution, comme c'est l'usage dans les pays dont les institutions politiques ont subi l'influence de la Grande-Bretagne, est complétée par des textes de loi, des interprétations judiciaires et surtout par des conventions qui forment la constitution au sens matériel, c'est-à-dire l'ensemble des dispositions prévoyant l'organisation et le fonctionnement des organes de l'état.

Il faut souligner l'importance des conventions car la vie politique du Québec, comme celle de tout le Canada, est baignée par ces accords tacites entre ceux qui se livrent au jeu politique, accords qui peuvent n'être pas écrits, qui sont dépourvus de sanctions légales, qu'on ne plaide pas devant les tribunaux, mais qui n'en sont pas moins compris et observés par les intéressés en vertu d'un sentiment commun de leur nécessité. On respecte les conventions comme des règles de jeu parce qu'on sait qu'en s'y soumettant même lorsqu'elles sont désavantageuses, on pourra éventuellement en profiter. C'est ainsi qu'aucun texte de loi n'exige qu'un gouvernement mis en minorité à l'Assemblée nationale démissionne, mais il le fait parce qu'il sait qu'un gouvernement formé du parti opposé l'imitera lorsqu'il sera placé dans la même situation. Les conventions peuvent se transformer lentement. Elles naissent, se développent, se modifient au gré des événements et le temps seul peut les établir. On a même déjà soutenu avec une pointe d'humour qu'à proprement parler, une convention n'était jamais violée parce que l'acte qui la contredit prouve par lui-même qu'on ne considère pas la règle que la convention consacre comme définitive. Un système politique qui repose sur des conventions ne satisfait pas toujours des esprits avides de clarté et de certitude, mais il a l'avantage d'être souple et d'évoluer facilement. Ajoutons que certaines conventions peuvent se transformer en lois constitutionnelles.

Le Québec est maître de sa constitution en vertu du paragraphe 1 de l'article 92 de l'Acte de l'Amérique du Nord britannique qui dit que dans chaque province la législature a le droit exclusif d'adopter des lois concernant la constitution de cette province, sauf, ajoute-t-on, « en ce qui concerne la fonction de lieutenant-gouverneur ». Cette fonction ne pourrait être abolie ou modifiée par une loi provinciale. C'est ainsi qu'en 1919, le Comité judiciaire du Conseil privé a décidé dans « In re The Initiative and Referendum Act » [1] que la législature du Manitoba ne pouvait décréter qu'une loi naissait de l'approbation populaire à la suite d'un référendum, parce que c'était toucher à la fonction du lieutenant-gouverneur dont la sanction est la procédure finale dans l'adoption d'une loi. Le Québec a, à plusieurs reprises, amendé sa constitution par de simples lois. C'est ainsi qu'en 1886, on a porté de quatre à cinq ans la durée des fonctions maximum des députés et qu'en 1968, on a aboli le Conseil législatif. [2]

L'État du Québec ?

Depuis quelques années, sans qu'il y ait eu de décisions officielles, on a tendance à remplacer la désignation « Province de Québec », qu'on corrige d'ailleurs par « Province du Québec » par celle d'« État du Québec ». C'est ce que l'Office provincial de la langue française du Québec a demandé aux journalistes au début de 1963. On a prétendu qu'un tel

---

* *Cette division a été préparée par Me Jean-Charles Bonenfant, professeur à l'Université Laval de Québec, qui a également revisé les données contenues dans ce chapitre, mises à jour à la date du 30 juin 1971.*

1 *Appeal Cases*, 1919, p. 935.

2 49-50 Vict., ch. 97, et 19 Eliz. II, ch. 9.

Source: *Annuaire du Québec* 1972.

changement violait la constitution du Canada parce que l'Acte de l'Amérique du Nord britannique de 1867 consacre la désignation de « Province de Québec ». Il semble bien que même si c'est une dérogation à la lettre, ce ne soit pas une violation de l'esprit de la constitution. Il est vrai que les textes ne parlent pas de l'État du Québec, mais l'absence du mot n'entraîne pas nécessairement l'absence de la chose. Si par état on entend simplement une forme du gouvernement, un régime politique, la consécration du pouvoir, personne ne peut nier qu'il y a un état québécois, qu'on appelle provincial par opposition à l'état fédéral, mais « état » a, dans les dictionnaires, un sens plus essentiel, celui de « groupement humain fixé sur un territoire déterminé, soumis à une même autorité (souveraine au regard du droit constitutionnel) et pouvant être considéré comme une personne morale ». C'est en ce sens qu'on se demande s'il y a un état du Québec et ceux qui répondent affirmativement soulignent que le Québec est souverain dans la sphère assignée aux « provinces ». Ce qui lui manque, c'est la souveraineté extérieure qui entraînerait une existence pleine et entière en regard du droit international. On peut donc parler dans un sens restreint de l'État du Québec sans mettre en danger le fédéralisme, mais par ailleurs pour éviter des polémiques inutiles il semble bien que l'usage s'établit de dire le Québec, tout court, comme au niveau fédéral l'appellation « Dominion du Canada » disparait pour faire place uniquement au mot Canada.

On retrouve dans le Québec la division classique des trois pouvoirs, l'exécutif, le législatif et le judiciaire mais, comme dans bien d'autres états, il n'est pas toujours facile d'en tracer les frontières précises.

Section 1: Le pouvoir exécutif

Dans le Québec, comme dans les autres provinces du Canada, le lieutenant-gouverneur incarne la Couronne au même titre que le gouverneur général dans le Canada tout entier. L'article 58 de l'Acte de l'Amérique du Nord de 1867 décrète qu'il y aura, pour chaque province, un fonctionnaire appelé lieutenant-gouverneur, que le Gouverneur général nommera par instrument sous le Grand Sceau du Canada. Au moment de la naissance de la Confédération, quelques-uns de ses adversaires exprimèrent la crainte que le lieutenant-gouverneur ne soit qu'un agent du gouvernement fédéral dans la politique provinciale. À l'époque, ces craintes étaient justifiées car on avait donné au lieutenant-gouverneur le droit de réserver les projets de loi de la législature provinciale à la sanction du gouvernement fédéral. Soixante-douze projets furent ainsi réservés, de 1867 à nos jours, la dernière fois en Saskatchewan, en 1961, mais à cette occasion le gouvernement de M. Diefenbaker accorda immédiatement la sanction, et la convention semble bien établie aujourd'hui que la réserve ne se pratique plus. On a vu aussi naguère dans l'histoire du Québec un lieutenant-gouverneur destituer un premier ministre et se voir, à son tour, destitué par le gouvernement fédéral. Ce fut le cas de Luc Letellier de Saint-Just, lieutenant-gouverneur d'origine libérale, qui, en 1878, démit Charles Boucher de Boucherville, premier ministre conservateur, qui jouissait pourtant de la confiance de l'Assemblée législative. L'année suivante, le gouvernement conservateur de John A. Macdonald démettait, à son tour, Letellier de Saint-Just.

Aujourd'hui, dans ce domaine, les passions politiques se sont apaisées, les conventions constitutionnelles se sont précisées et sans que rien n'ait été changé dans les textes, le lieutenant-gouverneur d'une province participe à l'indépendance, à l'impartialité, à la quiétude et au caractère symbolique de la Couronne dans les pays d'institutions politiques d'origine britannique. Le lieutenant-gouverneur est nommé, généralement pour cinq ans, et il est payé par le gouvernement fédéral, mais la jurisprudence a reconnu qu'il représente directement la Reine pour les fins provinciales. La Couronne ne fait que traduire la volonté populaire, car maintenant elle agit toujours selon les recommandations des représentants du peuple faisant partie du Conseil exécutif. En effet, on se demande s'il est encore quelque domaine où la Reine, le Gouverneur général et le Lieutenant-gouverneur peuvent agir seuls ! Peut-être pour choisir un premier ministre ou pour empêcher celui-ci de violer un important principe de droit constitutionnel, mais alors ils essaient de prévoir le sentiment de la majorité des représentants du peuple qui, éventuellement, devront ratifier leur décision. L'exécutif provincial est donc bicéphale puisqu'il a une tête apparente, le lieutenant-gouverneur, et une tête réelle le premier ministre. C'est une différence essentielle de nos institutions avec celles des États-Unis où le président incarne seul l'exécutif.

L'article 63 de l'Acte de l'Amérique du Nord britannique de 1867 prévoyait que « dans l'Ontario et le Québec, le Conseil exécutif se composera des personnes que le lieutenant-gouverneur jugera, de temps à autre, à propos de nommer, et tout d'abord des fonctionnaires suivants : un procureur général, un secrétaire et régistraire de la Province, un trésorier de la Province, un commissaire des terres de la Couronne, un commissaire de l'Agriculture, avec en plus dans le Québec, le président du Conseil législatif et un solliciteur général ». La législature du Québec a depuis transformé considérablement la structure du Conseil exécutif. Au 30 juin 1971, il se composait [3] de ceux que la loi appelle « les fonctionnaires suivants » :

Un premier ministre qui de droit est président du Conseil ;
Un ministre de la justice qui, autrefois, dans le Québec, s'appelait procureur général, nom qu'il porte dans d'autres provinces ;
Un ministre des affaires intergouvernementales ;
Un ministre des affaires culturelles ;
Un ministre des finances qui, autrefois, dans le Québec s'appelait trésorier provincial, nom qu'il porte encore dans d'autres provinces ;
Un ministre du revenu ;
Un ministre des richesses naturelles ;
Un ministre des terres et forêts ;
Un ministre de l'agriculture et de la colonisation ;
Un ministre de la voirie ;
Un ministre des travaux publics ;
Un ministre du travail ;
Un ministre des affaires sociales ;
Un ministre des affaires municipales ;
Un ministre du tourisme, de la chasse et de la pêche ;
Un ministre de l'industrie et du commerce ;
Un ministre des transports ;
Un ministre de l'éducation ;
Un ministre des institutions financières, compagnies et coopératives ;
Un ministre de l'immigration ;
Un ministre de la fonction publique ;
Un ministre des communications.

La loi de l'exécutif prévoit que le lieutenant-gouverneur en conseil peut définir les devoirs qui doivent être remplis par tout membre du Conseil exécutif, transférer un ou plusieurs services d'un ministère du contrôle d'un membre du Conseil exécutif au contrôle d'un autre membre et modifier le nom sous lequel un membre du Conseil exécutif ou un ministère est désigné. Il faut cependant que l'arrêté en conseil pris à cet effet soit publié dans la *Gazette officielle du Québec*.

On prévoit encore, comme en 1867, l'existence dans le Conseil exécutif d'un solliciteur général qui remplit généralement aux côtés du ministre de la justice les « fonctions et devoirs de nature légale ou juridique que lui assigne le lieutenant-gouverneur du conseil. » Le conseil exécutif peut aussi comprendre des ministres auxquels on n'a pas confié la responsabilité d'une section de l'administration. On les appelait autrefois ministres sans portefeuille et on les désigne aujourd'hui sous l'appellation de ministres d'état. On leur attribue parfois des tâches administratives auprès d'un ministre titulaire. Un membre du Conseil exécutif peut être nommé par arrêté en conseil vice-président du Conseil et il est chargé, à ce titre, d'exercer les fonctions et pouvoirs du président lorsque ce dernier est absent de la capitale. Les membres du Conseil doivent devenir membres de l'Assemblée nationale, mais la loi ne fixe aucun délai pour leurs élections. Un ministre peut détenir plus d'un portefeuille ministériel, mais il ne peut toucher que le traitement attaché à une seule de ses fonctions. Il est interdit aux membres du Conseil exécutif d'assumer les fonctions de directeur ou d'administrateur d'une société à caractère commercial, industriel ou financier qui transige directement ou indirectement avec le gouvernement du Québec.

Les textes de loi parlent du Conseil exécutif du Québec, mais par imitation de ce qui existe à Londres et à Ottawa, on emploie aussi pour désigner les hommes qui le forment les mots « ministère » et « cabinet ». Lorsqu'on utilise le mot ministère, on souligne la qualité de chefs de sections de l'administration que possèdent la majorité des membres du Conseil exécutif ; par ailleurs, comme le cabinet proprement dit est un comité du Conseil privé et que, contrairement à Londres et à Ottawa, un tel organisme n'existe pas à Québec, on peut affirmer que lorsqu'on emploie le mot c'est par analogie pour appuyer sur le rôle de conseillers que jouent ses membres, rôle qui est plus politique qu'administratif. Rappelons qu'en Grande-Bretagne, on distingue entre le ministère et le cabinet, le premier comprenant

[3] S.R.Q. 1964, ch. 9, complété par les amendements.

tous les ministres à la tête des diverses parties de l'administration et le second ne désignant que les plus importants d'entre eux.

Le premier ministre

Au sommet de l'exécutif, il y a le premier ministre. Peu de textes prévoient son existence et ses formes d'activité qui se sont développées de la fin du dix-huitième siècle jusqu'à nos jours. Chef du parti majoritaire à moins qu'il soit à la tête d'une coalition, il est appelé par le lieutenant-gouverneur à former le cabinet ; il choisit ses ministres qui dépendent à ce point de lui qu'ils cessent d'occuper leurs fonctions s'il meurt ou s'il démissionne, mais il ne peut continuer à exercer son autorité que pour autant qu'il jouit de la confiance de ses collègues et en définitive de la majorité des députés de l'Assemblée nationale. C'est le chef du gouvernement. On lui reconnait comme prérogatives le pouvoir de recommander au lieutenant-gouverneur la convocation, la prorogation et la dissolution de la législature, le pouvoir de choisir les membres du Conseil exécutif et de les faire destituer et de nommer les sous-ministres et quelques hauts fonctionnaires de même rang. Ce n'est tout de même pas un dictateur et on a souvent dit qu'il était « primus inter pares », le premier parmi des égaux, c'est-à-dire parmi des collègues qui acceptent librement sa direction.

Avec ses collègues, il est soumis au jeu de deux principes qui ne sont pas prévus dans des textes de loi, mais qui reposent sur des conventions constitutionnelles édifiées au cours des siècles : la responsabilité ministérielle et la solidarité ministérielle.

La première est une règle en vertu de laquelle le pouvoir exécutif est soumis au contrôle de la Chambre basse avec comme conséquence pour le premier ministre d'être obligé de démissionner si le gouvernement ne possède plus la confiance des représentants du peuple, ce qui se produit lorsqu'il est mis en minorité par un vote parlementaire sur une question importante ou lorsqu'il est défait aux élections. Toutefois, dans le premier cas, au lieu de démissionner, le premier ministre peut demander la tenue d'élections générales. Autrefois, jusqu'au milieu du dix-neuvième siècle, en Grande-Bretagne, un premier ministre défait aux élections attendait la réunion des Chambres pour démissionner mais maintenant à Québec, comme à Londres ou à Ottawa, un gouvernement défait aux urnes ne pourrait pour rester au pouvoir qu'invoquer le caractère indécis des résultats. La responsabilité ministérielle exige que le premier ministre et ses collègues soient membres de l'Assemblée nationale ou s'ils ne le sont pas, qu'ils fassent diligence pour y entrer. La responsabilité ministérielle veut aussi que les ministres soient responsables de leurs actes et de ceux de leurs subordonnés devant la Chambre.

Les membres du Conseil exécutif sont en outre soumis au principe de la solidarité ministérielle qu'il ne faut pas confondre avec la solidarité parlementaire. Celle-ci veut qu'un député vote habituellement avec son parti, mais il peut parfois s'en séparer sans inconvénient grave. La solidarité ministérielle est beaucoup plus rigoureuse. Comme les mots l'indiquent, elle existe entre les ministres ; elle n'exige pas qu'ils soient toujours du même avis et qu'ils ne discutent pas entre eux, mais elle signifie que lorsqu'une décision importante est prise par le Conseil exécutif tous les ministres doivent l'appuyer publiquement. Lorsque l'un d'entre eux est en désaccord, il ne lui reste qu'à démissionner.

Le Conseil exécutif siège à huis-clos et ses délibérations sont tenues secrètes. Son quorum, qu'il fixe lui-même, n'est actuellement que de quatre membres. Il s'exprime par la voix du premier ministre ou de son représentant, par des arrêtés en conseil et par des minutes. Le lieutenant-gouverneur, qui ne siège pas au Conseil, décrète ce que ce dernier lui a recommandé à la suite d'une proposition formulée par un membre du Conseil : d'où l'appellation d'arrêté du lieutenant-gouverneur en conseil. Les minutes sont des résumés qu'on fait des délibérations mais parfois, pour formuler une opinion plutôt qu'une décision formelle, on en stylise et publie un extrait. Le Conseil exécutif n'a de pouvoirs que pour autant qu'il en a reçu du législateur ou en vertu de prérogatives, subsistance plutôt rare des pouvoirs royaux d'autrefois que le parlement n'a pas fait disparaître.

Le Conseil exécutif moralement sûr de l'appui de l'Assemblée nationale est en fait sinon en théorie l'institution politique la plus importante de l'état. Il suggère les lois et il les applique. Il désigne les titulaires des fonctions publiques les plus importantes. Aux moments de crise, il prend les grandes décisions qui s'imposent ; il oriente les événements ; bref, il gouverne.

La fonction législative de l'exécutif

Si paradoxal que cela puisse paraître, le Conseil exécutif du Québec, à l'exemple d'organismes analogues dans le monde, remplit de plus en plus une double fonction législative.

Presque tous les projets de lois publiques sont proposés par le gouvernement après avoir été étudiés et approuvés par le Conseil exécutif ; la plupart des députés qui appuient le parti au pouvoir n'osent y apporter des modifications et par ailleurs, l'opposition minoritaire en est presque toujours incapable. C'est dire que si la loi naît formellement dans les institutions législatives proprement dites, elle tire ses véritables origines dans le pouvoir exécutif. Ce dernier légifère aussi par voie de délégation. En effet, la plupart des lois prévoient que le lieutenant-gouverneur en conseil peut adopter des règlements pour des fins précises et souvent même, d'une façon générale, pour mettre en application les dispositions de la loi. Ces règlements sont habituellement en vigueur lors de leur publication dans la *Gazette officielle du Québec*. Ils se sont multipliés ces dernières années ; ils ont pris une grande importance et c'est pourquoi, on songe à les codifier comme les lois.

Prolongements de l'exécutif

L'exécutif se prolonge jusqu'à un certain point par l'administration dont il est question plus loin et les commissions d'enquête. La plupart des fonctionnaires, sauf ceux qui sont attachés plus particulièrement au corps législatif, sont à des degrés divers des représentants de l'exécutif. Les commissions d'enquête qu'on dit « royales », parce que la Reine est le symbole de l'exécutif, sont des organismes auxquels le gouvernement confie l'étude d'un problème. Le système fonctionne dans plusieurs pays, mais il est particulièrement lié aux institutions britanniques. Il a connu, ces dernières années, au Canada, et plus particulièrement dans le Québec, une grande popularité. La loi[4] prévoit que lorsque le lieutenant-gouverneur en conseil juge à propos de faire tenir une enquête sur « quelqu'objet qui a trait au bon gouvernement de la province, sur la gestion de quelque partie des affaires publiques, sur l'administration de la justice ou sur quelque matière importante se rattachant à la santé publique ou au bien-être de la population, il peut, par une commission émise à cette fin, nommer un ou plusieurs commissaires pour conduire cette enquête. » On peut aussi créer une commission par une loi spéciale. Ce fut l'origine d'une des plus importantes commissions du Québec, la Commission royale d'enquête sur les problèmes constitutionnels, qui, mieux connue sous l'appellation de Commission Tremblay, du nom de son président, le juge Thomas Tremblay, a présenté son rapport en 1956. Parmi les autres commissions des dernières années qui sont restées célèbres, signalons la Commission royale d'enquête sur l'enseignement, qui, dans ses recommandations publiées de 1963 à 1966, a suggéré une transformation fondamentale du système d'éducation du Québec, la Commission royale d'enquête sur la fiscalité qui, en 1965, a proposé un nouveau système fiscal pour le Québec et la Commission d'enquête sur l'administration de la justice en matière criminelle et pénale au Québec qui, au milieu de 1970, avait déjà publié une douzaine de tomes. Toutes les recommandations des commissions ne sont pas mises en vigueur ; le gouvernement est libre de les accepter ou de les refuser, mais il est sûr que ces enquêtes créent un climat de recherche et de réflexion et constituent un phénomène important et parfois original de nos institutions politiques.

Section 2: Le pouvoir législatif

L'article 71 de l'Acte de l'Amérique du Nord britannique de 1867 disait qu'il y aura, pour le Québec, « une législature composée du lieutenant-gouverneur et de deux chambres, appelées Conseil législatif du Québec et Assemblée législative du Québec ». Théoriquement le représentant de la Reine fait donc partie du pouvoir législatif et un projet, après avoi été voté, a besoin de son approbation, qu'on appelle sanction, pour devenir une loi. La sanction est maintenant automatique et depuis quelques années, à Québec, elle se fait san apparat dans le bureau du lieutenant-gouverneur.

Québec a été la dernière province du Canada à posséder une chambre haute. So Conseil législatif, créé, en 1867, par l'Acte de l'Amérique du Nord britannique, possédai 24 membres qui, pendant longtemps, furent nommés à vie à la discrétion du gouvernement Ses pouvoirs, comme ceux du Sénat canadien, étaient absolus et il pouvait même faire éche à une mesure de nature financière. Cette Chambre haute non élective a consenti, en 196 à voter la loi qui l'abolissait le 31 décembre de l'année en cours.

L'Assemblée nationale

Le pouvoir législatif véritable n'appartient donc maintenant qu'à une seule Chamb appelée autrefois « Assemblée législative » et désignée, depuis 1968, sous l'appellati d'« Assemblée nationale ». En vertu d'une loi adoptée en 1971, les députés ont droit au tit

4 S.R.Q. 1964, ch. 11.

de membres de l'Assemblée nationale, avec le sigle MAN, qui a remplacé le titre de membre du Parlement du Québec, MPQ.[5] Au début de la Confédération, le Québec était divisé en soixante-cinq circonscriptions électorales ayant chacune le droit d'élire un député à l'Assemblée législative. Le nombre de circonscriptions a augmenté avec les années et il est, depuis 1965, de 108. La législature du Québec peut, par une simple loi, modifier les bases de la représentation à l'Assemblée nationale, où on constate présentement une inégalité considérable entre les petites et les grandes circonscriptions. Jusqu'en 1970 il existait en vertu de l'article 80 de l'Acte de l'Amérique du Nord britannique, dix-sept circonscriptions, dites « privilégiées » parce qu'on ne pouvait toucher à leurs frontières sans le consentement de la majorité absolue de leurs représentants. La disposition avait été adoptée en 1867 pour protéger des circonscriptions habitées alors par une population en grande majorité anglo-saxonne et protestante : Pontiac, Ottawa, Argenteuil, Huntingdon, Missisquoi, Brome, Shefford, Stanstead, Compton, Wolfe et Richmond et la ville de Sherbrooke. Les circonscriptions primitives se sont transformées ; elles en ont engendré d'autres auxquelles elles ont transmis leur privilège si bien qu'en général on regardait maintenant comme « privilégiées » : Pontiac, Compton, Brome, Argenteuil, Mégantic, Stanstead, Sherbrooke, Missisquoi, Wolfe, Richmond, Shefford, Huntingdon, Frontenac, Hull, Papineau, Témiscamingue et Labelle. Les exigences de l'article 80 rendaient difficiles non seulement les changements de frontières des circonscriptions « privilégiées » mais aussi les changements concernant les circonscriptions qui leur étaient limitrophes. Par ailleurs, ces circonscriptions n'étaient plus habitées par une majorité anglo-saxonne et protestante. Aussi, souhaitait-on en plusieurs milieux la disparition d'une protection qui ne correspondait plus à la réalité démographique et qui rendait difficile un remaniement équitable de la carte électorale. En décembre 1970, la Législature a adopté une loi qui abrogeait la disposition.[6]

En juillet 1971, elle a adopté le projet de loi N° 80 créant une Commission de la réforme des districts électoraux. Elle relèvera de l'Assemblée nationale qui en nomme les membres et à laquelle elle fait rapport. Elle est formée de trois membres dont le président général des élections qui la préside. Elle est permanente et après les élections générales, elle doit soumettre des avis et des rapports si elle le juge nécessaire. Elle doit cependant présenter un premier rapport avant le 1er mars 1972. Elle devra s'assurer que chaque district électoral comprend 32,000 électeurs en admettant toutefois un écart de 25 pour cent en plus ou en moins lorsque cela paraîtra nécessaire. Elle pourra cependant s'écarter exceptionnellement de ces critères pour des considérations spéciales d'ordre géographique ou démographique.

La dissolution des Chambres qui entraîne la tenue des élections est ordonnée à la discrétion du gouvernement, mais celles-ci doivent avoir lieu au moins tous les cinq ans. Des élections partielles ont aussi lieu lorsqu'un siège est vacant, mais rien n'oblige le gouvernement à les tenir dans un certain délai. La tenue des élections est placée sous la haute surveillance du président général des élections qui est nommé par l'Assemblée nationale. Dans chaque circonscription, la loi est appliquée par un président d'élection. Les circonscriptions sont divisées en sections de trois cents électeurs et dont la superficie ne dépasse pas huit milles de longueur par huit milles de largeur. Il y a un bureau de votation par section avec un scrutateur, accompagné d'un greffier de scrutin, le premier recommandé par le candidat du parti ministériel et le second par le candidat de l'opposition officielle. Le suffrage est vraiment universel, les femmes ayant obtenu le droit de vote en 1941 et l'âge des votants ayant été abaissé, en 1963, à 18 ans. Pour se présenter comme candidat, il faut également avoir 18 ans. Pour être électeur, il faut cependant être de citoyenneté canadienne et être domicilié dans le Québec au moins un an avant la date fixée pour le recensement qui se fait avant chaque élection, des listes permanentes n'existant pas.

La loi électorale de 1963[7] a limité les dépenses électorales, mais elle a en même temps innové en décrétant que l'état en assumait une partie. Selon cette loi, seul un agent officiel, désigné par un parti ou un candidat peut faire des dépenses électorales pendant les élections. On entend par dépenses électorales tous les frais encourus pendant une élection pour favoriser directement ou indirectement, l'élection d'un candidat ou celle des candidats d'un parti. L'agent officiel d'un candidat doit, dans les soixante jours qui suivent la proclamation de l'élection d'un candidat, remettre au président général des élections un état des dépenses électorales. L'agent officiel d'un parti doit faire de même dans un délai prévu. Sont reconnus par le président général des élections le parti du premier ministre ou du chef de l'opposition officielle et un parti qui, aux dernières élections générales avait dix candidats officiels ou qui, aux élections générales en cours, démontre qu'il aura ce nombre.

[5] 1971, Bill N° 58.
[6] 1970, Bill N° 65.
[7] S.R.Q., 1964, ch. 7.

Les députés sont élus au scrutin majoritaire à un tour, c'est-à-dire, que, comme le stipule la loi électorale « le candidat qui, après l'addition des votes, a reçu le plus grand nombre de suffrages, doit être déclaré élu ». Le système a bien fonctionné tant que deux grands partis seulement rivalisaient pour se succéder au pouvoir, mais on se demande s'il convient maintenant que plusieurs partis se font la lutte.

L'Assemblée nationale fonctionne d'après des règlements et des coutumes qui ont été considérablement modernisés ces dernières années. Son quorum est de trente députés mais la présence de vingt d'entre eux suffit lorsqu'une commission de l'Assemblée siège en même temps qu'elle. Convoquée théoriquement par une proclamation du lieutenant-gouverneur, la première session d'une législature débute par l'élection d'un président qu'on appelait autrefois l'Orateur parce qu'il parlait au nom des élus du peuple. Le Président reste en fonction, à moins qu'il démissionne, jusqu'aux prochaines élections. Il est le maître des délibérations et il est appelé à voter au cas d'égalité des voix.

À Québec, le représentant de la Reine ne fait plus maintenant qu'un bref discours, survivance de l'ancien discours du trône dans lequel le souverain disait pourquoi il avait convoqué les députés, donnait un aperçu de l'état du pays et l'indication plus ou moins précise des mesures dont seraient saisis les législateurs. La brève intervention plutôt symbolique du lieutenant-gouverneur est suivie d'une sorte de discours inaugural du premier ministre auquel répondent le chef de l'opposition et les chefs des autres partis. Les premiers jours de la session donnent encore lieu à un débat général qui, théoriquement, est le débat sur l'adresse en réponse au discours du trône. Dès le dix-septième siècle, en Grande-Bretagne, la Chambre des communes et la Chambre des Lords prirent l'habitude de répondre par une adresse au discours que le souverain avait prononcé à l'ouverture de la session. Ce n'est plus maintenant qu'un acte de courtoisie sans signification profonde qui permet aux députés de disserter sur tous les sujets et au gouvernement d'obtenir un vote d'approbation. À Québec, comme partout ailleurs, on a établi des limites à ce débat général qui se répète d'ailleurs d'une façon analogue à l'occasion du budget.

L'Assemblée nationale siège comme telle et elle se transforme aussi en commissions plénières qui sont au nombre de trois, la commission des subsides, la commission des voies et moyens et la commission plénière en général. La première étudie les crédits demandés par le gouvernement, la seconde, les impôts, et la troisième scrute le détail des lois adoptées en seconde lecture. Il y a en second lieu des commissions élues composées de quelques membres seulement de l'Assemblée. On les dit permanentes ou spéciales selon qu'elles sont constituées d'avance pour s'occuper de tous les sujets d'une certaine catégorie mis à l'étude au cours de la session ou qu'elles sont constituées spécialement en vue d'examiner un sujet particulier.

Un changement important dans la marche du travail parlementaire à Québec, ces dernières années, a été engendré par une utilisation plus considérable et plus méthodique des commissions élues permanentes ou spéciales. Les commissions permanentes existent maintenant en fonction de chaque section de l'administration ayant à sa tête un ministre. On y a joint quelques autres commissions comme celle de la présidence et celle des comptes publics. De plus en plus les crédits et les lois sont discutés dans la commission dont ils relèvent. Les commissions siègent aussi pendant les vacances de l'Assemblée nationale, ce qui donne à celle-ci une activité plus continue.

Par suite du jeu de la majorité parlementaire, l'Assemblée nationale est dominée par le premier ministre et ses collègues du Conseil exécutif, mais la coutume et quelques dispositions législatives reconnaissent un statut spécial à celui qui est à la tête du parti qui compte le plus de députés en Chambre après le parti gouvernemental et qu'on appelle chef de l'opposition. À la première session, de la vingt-neuvième législature, en juillet 1970, le bill 1, Loi modifiant la Loi de la Législature, a accordé une indemnité additionnelle et une allocation supplémentaire à chaque député qui dirige, à l'Assemblée nationale, un parti de l'opposition dont l'effectif reconnu comprend au moins douze députés ou qui y dirige un parti de l'opposition dont l'effectif comprend moins de douze députés mais qui a obtenu vingt pour cent des votes dans l'ensemble du Québec aux élections générales. Le premier ministre a pris l'habitude de déléguer une partie de ses tâches parlementaires à un autre ministre. De même, le chef de l'opposition peut aussi confier à un autre député de son parti la direction du travail parlementaire.

Parmi les autres députés qui sont appelés à jouer un rôle particulier, il faut mentionner les adjoints parlementaires et les whips. En vertu de la Loi de la Législature, le lieutenant-gouverneur en conseil peut, parmi les députés, nommer des adjoints parlementaires dont le nombre n'excède pas 12. L'adjoint parlementaire est chargé d'assister le ministre auquel il est adjoint en la manière que celui-ci détermine et, en l'absence du ministre, de représenter à l'Assemblée nationale le ministère dont il a la direction. Le « whip », appellation qui vient de l'opération qui à la chasse consistait à rassembler les chiens, existe en vertu de la tradition parlementaire et, pour chaque parti, il est à la fois un animateur et un surveillant qui voit à la présence et à l'efficacité de ses collègues en Chambre.

On peut affirmer que l'Assemblée nationale connaît quatre formes principales d'activité : c'est un centre de renseignements pour les représentants du peuple ; c'est la source des crédits ; c'est le forum du peuple et c'est surtout un corps législatif.

À la fin du dix-huitième siècle, les questions posées par les députés aux ministres du gouvernement sont devenues une partie importante de la procédure de la Chambre des communes britanniques. Le système a été imité par tous les parlements et il est pratiqué au Québec depuis longtemps. Au début de chaque séance, selon une procédure établie, un député peut poser une question se rapportant à quelque matière d'intérêt public. On peut aussi demander la production de documents. Le système des questions ainsi que celui de la production de documents est un puissant instrument de surveillance des représentants du peuple sur le pouvoir exécutif. Une tâche importante des députés est le vote des crédits annuels car, en vertu de la vieille règle décrétant qu'il n'y a pas d'impôt sans représentation, toutes les dépenses doivent avoir été prévues dans le budget qui couvre la période du 1er avril au 31 mars. Des budgets supplémentaires sont aussi adoptés soit pour des dépenses de l'exercice financier en cours, soit pour compléter le budget de l'année suivante. L'Assemblée nationale, à l'occasion du débat sur l'adresse en réponse au discours du trône, du débat sur le budget ainsi qu'à la faveur de motions spéciales est aussi témoin d'expression d'opinions sur les problèmes qui passionnent l'opinion publique. Enfin, elle est avant tout un corps législatif.

Il existe deux sortes de lois : les lois publiques et les lois privées. Les premières concernent l'intérêt public et elles sont généralement proposées par leur membre du conseil exécutif quoiqu'un simple député puisse le faire. Les secondes concernent des intérêts particuliers ou locaux et elles sont fondées sur la pétition des intéressés. Un projet de loi, que par suite de la tradition anglaise on appelle bill, est soumis à une procédure élaborée dont les principales étapes sont les suivantes. La première lecture se résume à l'annonce de l'objet du projet et elle ne provoque aucun débat. À la seconde lecture, le projet, qui est imprimé en français et en anglais, est étudié dans son principe. S'il est voté par la majorité, il est alors étudié en détail soit en commission plénière générale ou dans une commission spéciale. C'est à cette phase qu'il subit, si cela est nécessaire, des amendements. Il franchit finalement l'étape de la troisième lecture et il devient loi par la sanction du lieutenant-gouverneur. La loi peut être mise en vigueur immédiatement, mais elle peut aussi ne le devenir que sur proclamation, c'est-à-dire lorsque le gouvernement le jugera à propos.

Section 3: Le système judiciaire

Le système judiciaire québécois se situe à l'intérieur du fédéralisme canadien qui a prévu un partage assez complexe des compétences en matière de droit. En vertu du par. 14 de l'article 92 de l'Acte de l'Amérique du nord britannique, les provinces ont juridiction dans l'administration de la justice y compris la constitution, le coût et l'organisation des tribunaux provinciaux de juridiction tant civile que criminelle, mais par ailleurs, en vertu de l'article 96, le gouvernement fédéral nomme et paie les juges de plusieurs de ces tribunaux.

Les cours d'institution provinciale

Les tribunaux qui relèvent de l'autorité législative du Québec, ont une juridiction en matières civiles, criminelles ou mixtes. Ce sont : la Cour du banc de la reine, la Cour supérieure, la Cour provinciale, la Cour des sessions de la paix, la Cour du bien-être social et les cours municipales. Les juridictions de la Cour du banc de la reine, de la Cour supérieure, de la Cour provinciale et de la Cour des sessions de la paix sont générales et s'étendent à toute la province ; celles des cours de bien-être social et des cours municipales sont restreintes à des districts judiciaires, à des districts électoraux ou à des localités.

Cour du banc de la reine — La Cour du banc de la reine est composée de 12 juges nommés par le gouvernement fédéral, dont le juge en chef se trouve le juge en chef du Québec. La Cour du banc de la reine siégeant en appel et les juges qui la composent, ont une juridiction civile d'appel dans toute l'étendue du Québec, avec compétence sur toutes les causes en matières et choses susceptibles d'appel, venant de tous les tribunaux dont, suivant la loi, il y a appel, à moins que cet appel ne soit affecté à la compétence des autres tribunaux. Cette juridiction est définie aux articles 25 à 30 du Code de procédure civile. La Cour du banc de la reine a aussi juridiction pour entendre les appels d'un jugement ou d'un verdict d'acquittement ou de culpabilité prononcé sur une accusation imputant un acte criminel, ou d'une sentence. Présidée par un juge de la Cour supérieure et composée d'un jury, où, depuis 1971, les femmes peuvent siéger, la Cour du banc de la reine exerce une juridiction en première instance en matière criminelle, lorsque l'inculpé est condamné à subir son procès à la suite d'un acte d'accusation.

Cour supérieure — La Cour supérieure est composée de 92 juges nommés par le gouvernement fédéral. C'est le tribunal de droit commun qui connaît en première instance de toute demande qu'une disposition formelle de la loi n'a pas attribuée exclusivement à un autre tribunal. Elle connaît aussi en première instance par voie d'évocation, des demandes portées devant la Cour provinciale et se rapportant à un honoraire d'office, à un droit de la couronne, à un titre à des terres ou héritages, ou à quelque autre droit immobilier mis en question par la contestation, à une rente ou autre matière pouvant affecter les droits contre les parties, pourvu que la valeur de ces droits, s'ils sont patrimoniaux, excède le taux de compétence de la Cour provinciale. Enfin, à l'exception de la Cour d'appel, les tribunaux relevant de la compétence de la Législature du Québec ainsi que les corps politiques et les corporations de la province sont soumis au droit de surveillance et de réforme de la Cour supérieure, en la manière et dans la forme prescrites par la loi.

Cour provinciale — La Cour provinciale est composée de 110 juges nommés par le lieutenant-gouverneur en conseil, dont un juge en chef et un juge en chef adjoint. Elle connaît, à l'exclusion de la Cour supérieure, de toute demande : 1° dans laquelle la somme demandée ou la valeur de la chose réclamée est inférieure à $3,000., sauf les demandes de pension alimentaire et celle réservée à la Cour de l'échiquier du Canada ; 2° en exécution, annulation, résolution ou en résiliation de contrat, lorsque l'intérêt du demandeur dans l'objet du litige est d'une valeur inférieure à $3,000. ; 3° en résiliation de bail, lorsque le montant réclamé pour loyer ou dommage n'atteint pas $3,000.

La cour provinciale connaît aussi de toute demande tant personnelle qu'hypothécaire formée : 1° en recouvrement des taxes dues à une corporation municipale ou scolaire ; 2° en recouvrement de cotisations pour la construction ou la réparation d'immeubles servant à des fins paroissiales ; 3° en annulation ou en cassation de rôle d'évaluation. Elle possède aussi une juridiction exclusive pour connaître en dernier ressort de toute demande ou action relativement à l'usurpation ou l'exercice illégal d'une charge dans une corporation municipale ou scolaire.

Cour des sessions de la paix — La Cour des sessions de la paix est composée de 53 juges, nommés par le lieutenant-gouverneur en conseil, qui exercent en matières criminelles et pénales tous les pouvoirs qui lui sont attribués par les lois fédérales et provinciales.

Cour de bien-être social — Composée de 35 juges nommés par le Conseil exécutif, cette cour est autorisée à connaître des cas de jeunes délinquants au sens de la loi sur les jeunes délinquants (S.R.Q. 52, chap. 160). En outre, sa juridiction s'étend à l'admission des enfants dans les écoles de protection de la jeunesse, à l'adoption des enfants et aux contraventions aux règlements municipaux commises par des enfants âgés de moins de 18 ans.

Cour municipale — Le conseil d'une cité ou d'une ville peut, par règlement, établir une Cour municipale qui doit être présidée par un juge municipal nommé par le lieutenant-gouverneur en conseil. Le juge municipal doit être un avocat ayant au moins cinq années d'exercice, sauf dans les cités et villes de moins de 10,000 âmes où il peut être nommé après trois ans d'exercice. L'acceptation de cette charge ne rend pas le juge inhabile à exercer sa profession devant une cour de justice autre que cette Cour municipale. Le conseil d'une municipalité peut adopter un règlement pour soumettre son territoire à la juridiction de la Cour municipale d'une autre municipalité située en totalité ou en partie dans un rayon de 10 milles de la première. Le conseil d'une municipalité où une telle Cour municipale existe, s'il y concourt, adopte un règlement à cet effet, le tout devant être approuvé par le lieutenant-gouverneur en conseil. Cette cour a juridiction pour entendre sommairement toute action intentée en vertu d'un règlement municipal.

Les cours d'institution fédérale

Cour suprême du Canada — La Cour suprême du Canada a été instituée en 1875 et sa nature et son fonctionnement aujourd'hui sont prévus au ch. S-19, S.R.C. Elle se compose d'un juge en chef et de huit juges puînés tous nommés par le gouvernement fédéral ; ceux-ci ne peuvent être démis de leurs fonctions que sur une adresse conjointe des deux Chambres fédérales, et cessent d'occuper leur charge à l'âge de 75 ans. La Cour suprême a une juridiction générale d'appel partout au Canada, tant en matière civile que criminelle ; elle peut aussi donner avis sur la constitutionnalité d'une loi ou d'une initiative fédérale à la demande du Conseil privé, de la Chambre des communes et du Sénat, et se prononcer en dernière instance sur toute cause qui implique une interprétation des dispositions de la constitution fédérale. On peut en appeler du jugement de la Cour d'appel d'une province dans toute cause où l'objet du litige est d'une valeur d'au moins $10,000. et de tout autre jugement final d'une Cour d'appel provinciale, avec la permission de celle-ci ; en outre, la Cour suprême peut agréer en appel tout jugement rendu au Canada, qu'il soit final ou non. Les appels en matière criminelle sont régis par la loi constituante de chacune de ses cours. Le jugement de la Cour suprême du Canada est sans appel.

Cour fédérale du Canada — Le 1er juin 1971, en vertu du bill c-172 adopté en 1970 par le Parlement canadien, la Cour fédérale du Canada a remplacé la Cour d'échiquier qui existait depuis 1875. La Cour fédérale est formée de deux divisions appelées, la première, Division d'appel de la Cour fédérale, et, la seconde, Division de première instance de la Cour fédérale. La Cour est composée d'un juge-en-chef qui est président de la Cour et président de la division d'appel, d'un juge-en-chef adjoint qui est président de la division de première instance et d'au plus dix autres juges. Elle entend les poursuites contre le gouvernement fédéral, elle sert de tribunal d'appel dans ces poursuites et elle est en même temps un organisme de surveillance et à l'occasion de redressement des organismes administratifs fédéraux. À la Cour fédérale est liée la Cour d'amirauté qui a juridiction dans le domaine maritime.

7.1 Pouvoirs exécutif, législatif et judiciaire.

7.1.b ORGANIGRAMME DU SYSTEME POLITIQUE QUEBECOIS.

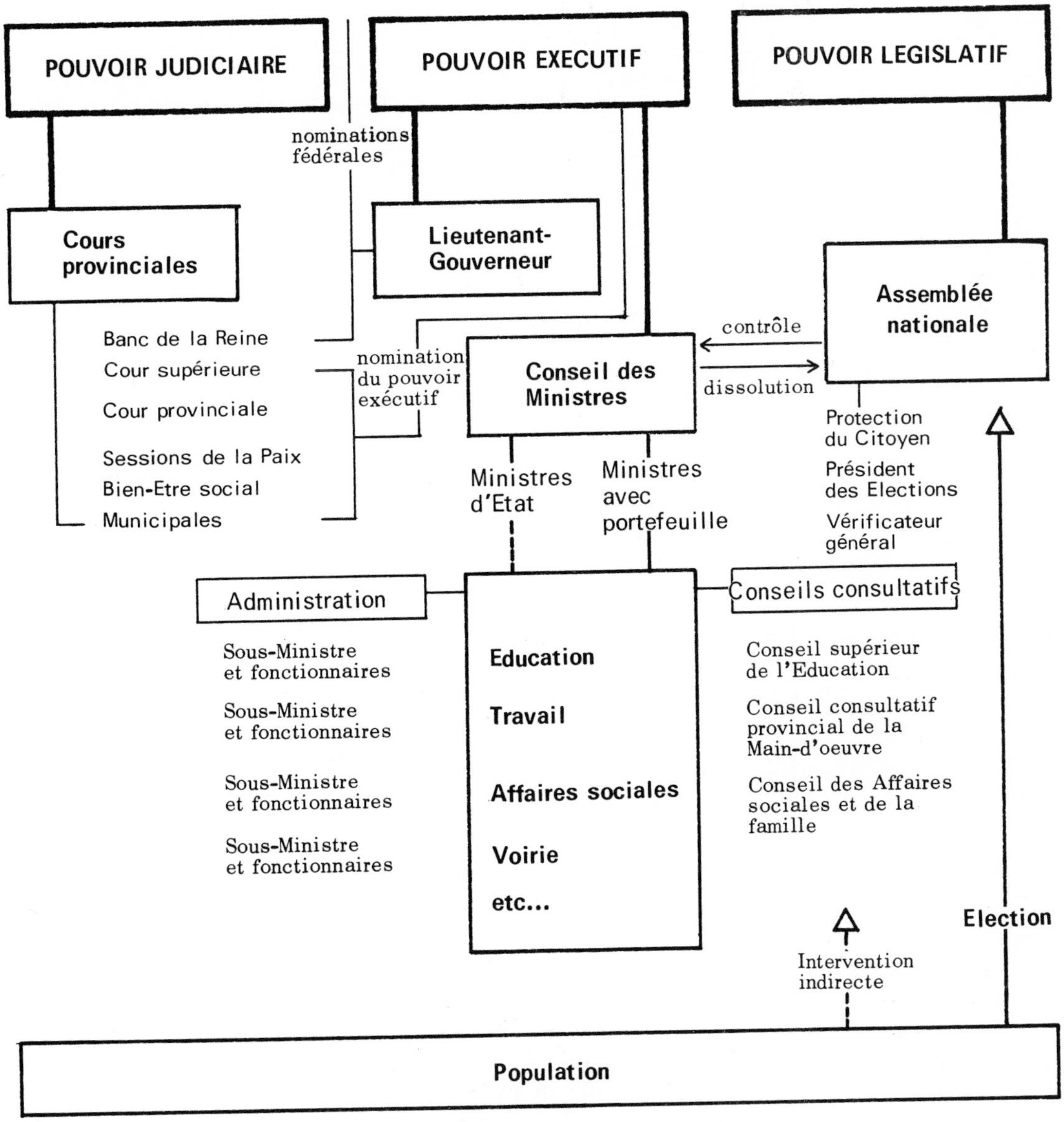

Source: Document fourni par M. Robert Boily

7.1 Pouvoirs exécutif, législatif et judiciaire

7.1.c LES POUVOIRS LEGISLATIFS DU QUEBEC

Type de pouvoir	Description sommaire
LES POUVOIRS PROPRES Ceux que l'A.A.B.N. accordait au Québec d'une manière exclusive.	**Ceux de l'article 92** En matière de revenus: pouvoir de taxation directe (revenus, héritages, consommation d'essence, alcool, etc...), pouvoir d'emprunt sur son crédit, allocations de permis aux établissements commerciaux. Pouvoir d'amender sa constitution (sauf le poste de Lieutenant-gouverneur) Administration et vente des terres publiques. Propriété et gestion des richesses naturelles. Aménagement du territoire et travaux publics de nature locale. Constitution des compagnies pour fins provinciales (banques). Propriété et droits civils. Etablissement, entretien et administration des hôpitaux, asiles etc... (domaine de la santé). Administration de la justice. Contrôle des institutions municipales. **Ceux de l'article 93** Pouvoirs en matière d'éducation (pouvoirs limités par les droits des minorités religieuses).
LES POUVOIRS CONCURRENTS Ceux que l'on retrouve au fédéral et au provincial avec priorité de l'un ou l'autre niveau.	**Ceux de l'article 94A (1951-1968)** Pensions de vieillesse (priorité provinciale) **Ceux de l'article 95** Agriculture, immigration (priorité fédérale)
LES POUVOIRS RESIDUELS Ceux que l'interprétation judiciaire a reconnu aux provinces en s'appuyant sur le contrôle qu'exercent les provinces en matière de propriété privée et de droit civil (pour le Québec).	Production et distribution des biens: réglementation de la production, commerce, mise en marché. Assurance chômage (abandonné au fédéral en 1940). Domaine de la législation du travail: heures de travail, salaires, allocations-retraites conflits ouvriers syndicalisme Santé publique Assurances

Source: Document fourni par M. Robert Boily.

7.2 Pouvoir exécutif: éléments descriptifs

7.2.a ORGANIGRAMME DU CONSEIL DES MINISTRES ET DES ORGANISMES AUXILIAIRES

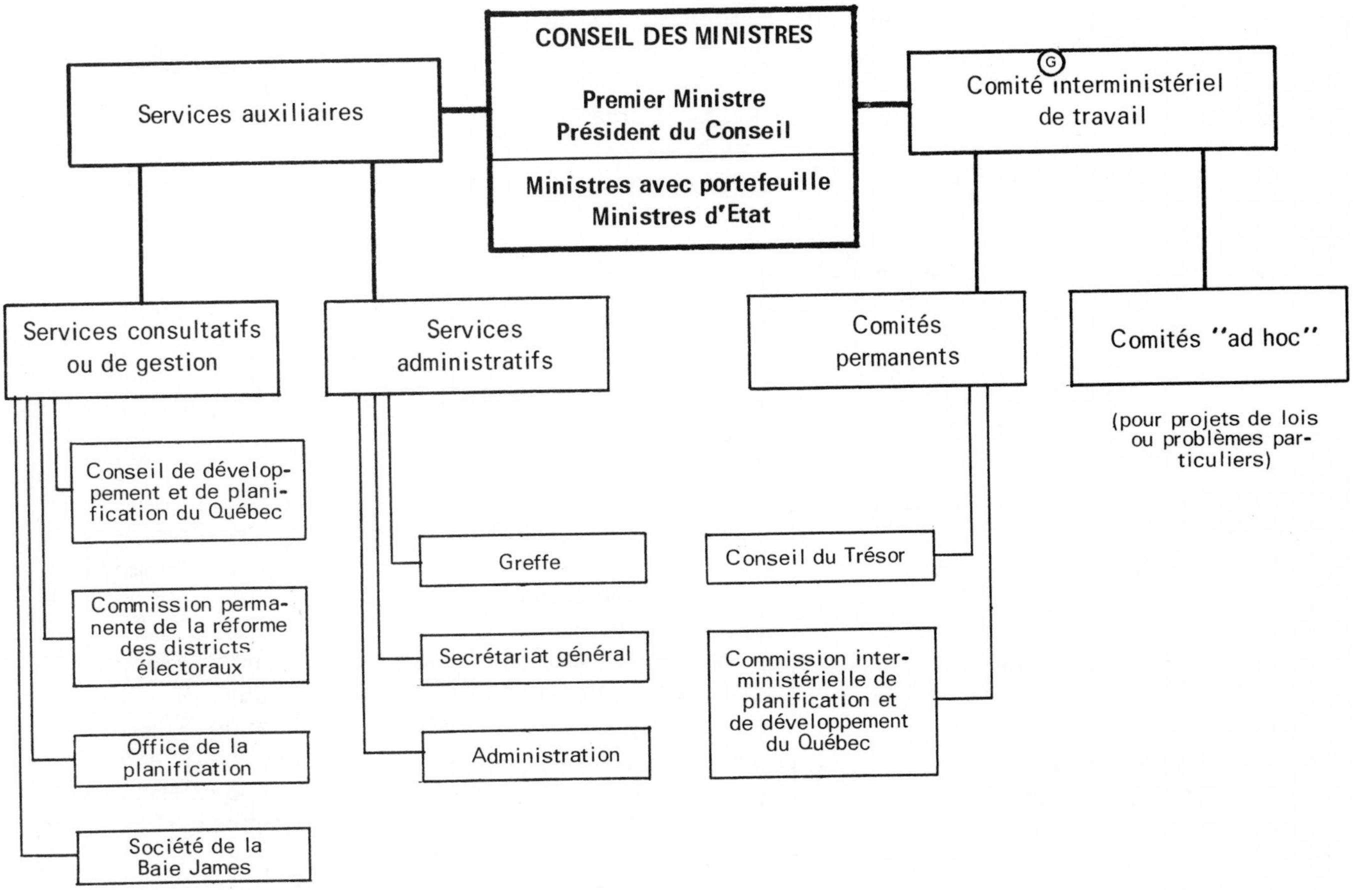

Source: Document fourni par M. Robert Boily

7.2 Pouvoir exécutif: éléments descriptifs

7.2.b COMPOSITION DU CONSEIL DES MINISTRES, 1867 ET 1974

1867 Poste du conseil exécutif		(janvier 1974) Poste du conseil exécutif	
Président du Conseil législatif	devenu	Premier ministre (président du Conseil)	Robert Bourassa
Procureur général	devenu	Justice	Jérôme Choquette
Trésorier	devenu	Finances	Raymond Garneau
Commissaire de l'Agriculture	devenu	Agriculture	Normand Toupin
Solliciteur général	demeuré	Solliciteur général	Roy Fournier
Commissaire des Terres de la Couronne	disparu		
Secrétaire et Régistraire	disparu		
		Revenu	Gérald Harvey
		Affaires intergouvernementales	Gérard D. Lévesque
		Affaires culturelles	Denis Hardy
		Richesses naturelles	Gilles Masse
		Terres et Forêts	Kevin Drummond
		Travaux publics et Approvisionnement	Raymond Mailloux
		Travail et Main d'oeuvre	Jean Cournoyer
		Affaires sociales	Claude E. Forget
		Tourisme, Chasse et Pêche	Claude Simard
		Industrie et Commerce	Guy St-Pierre
		Transports	Raymond Mailloux
		Education	François Cloutier
		Institutions financières, compagnies et coopératives	William Tetley
		Immigration	Jean Bienvenue
		Fonction publique	Oswald Parent
		Communications	Jean-Paul l'Allier
		Affaires municipales et environnement	Victor C. Goldbloom
		Haut-Commissariat à la jeunesse, aux loisirs et aux sports	Paul Phaneuf

MINISTRES D'ETAT (1974)

•Affaires municipales et environnement	Georges Vaillancourt
•Affaires sociales	Lise Bacon
•Assemblée nationale, président	Jean-Noël Lavoie
•Conseil exécutif	Fernand Lalonde
•Transports	Raymond Mailloux
•Office de développement de l'Est du Québec	Robert Quenneville
•Office de planification et de développement du Québec	Bernard Lachapelle

7.2 Pouvoir exécutif: éléments descriptifs.

7.2.c LES MINISTERES: DATES DE FONDATION ET FONCTIONS ACTUELLES

Nom du ministère	Année de fondation	Principales fonctions
Agriculture et Colonisation	1867	Promotion et bien-être des cultivateurs par l'amélioration de l'agriculture (production et consommation).
Finances	1868	Elaboration des budgets et saine administration.
Terres et Forêts	1868	Surveille, contrôle et gère les terres publiques, protection contre les incendies.
Travaux publics	1888	Administration des biens immobiliers de l'Etat, construction et entretien des ponts.
Voirie	1914	Entretien d'un réseau routier d'environ 45,000 milles: l'améliorer et l'étendre au besoin.
Affaires municipales	1918	S'occupe des problèmes municipaux, de pollution, d'hygiène, de planification urbaine, de lutte aux incendies, d'évaluation, etc...
Travail et Main-d'Oeuvre	1931	Favorise les relations de travail entre employeurs et salariés. Fait respecter les droits de tous dans le contexte de la "libre entreprise".
Industrie et Commerce	1943	Favorise le développement industriel et commercial. Recensement des activités économiques.
Transports	1952	Gère le transport routier, ferroviaire, fluvial er aérien.
Revenu	1961	Administration des lois fiscales et conseiller du gouvernement sur les questions relatives aux revenus.
Affaires culturelles	1961	Vise à l'épanouissement des arts et lettres et au rayonnement de la culture française.
Richesses naturelles	1961	Favorise l'exploitation des richesses naturelles.
Tourisme, Chasse et Pêche	1963	Favorise le développement du tourisme: parcs, campings, etc...; gère les réserves de chasse, de pêche et d'oiseaux.
Education	1964	Se consacre à l'éducation, assiste la jeunesse dans la préparation de son avenir, développe les institutions d'enseignement.
Justice	1965	Préparation et application de la loi.
Affaires intergouvernementales	1967	Coordonne les activités du gouvernement et des ministères et organismes à l'extérieur du Québec. Relations avec les autres provinces et le fédéral.
Fonction publique	1968	Etablit les fonctions et postes du personnel, négocie la convention collective.
Immigration	1968	Favorise l'établissement d'immigrants au Québec, veille à leur adaptation au milieu et à la conservation de leurs coutumes ethniques.
Institutions financières, compagnies et coopératives	1968	Protège l'épargnant et le consommateur, anime le développement économique par le biais des institutions.
Affaires sociales	1970	Conception et application des politiques de bien-être et de santé.

Source: *Annuaire du Québec* 1972

7.2 Pouvoir exécutif: éléments descriptifs

7.2.d ORGANISMES DEPENDANT DE LA RESPONSABILITE DES MINISTERES

Nom du ministère	Principaux organismes
Premier ministre ou ministre délégué	Commission interministérielle de planification et de développement du Québec, Conseil de planification et de développement du Québec, Office de planification et de développement du Québec, Société de développement de la Baie James, Commission permanente de la réforme des districts électoraux.
Affaires culturelles	Bureau de surveillance du cinéma, Commission des bibliothèques publiques du Québec, Commission de l'enseignement de la musique et d'art dramatique de la province de Québec, Commission des monuments historiques du Québec, Conservatoire de musique et d'art dramatique de la province de Québec, Comité consultatif de l'assurance-édition, Comité consultatif du livre, Comité consultatif de Place Royale, Comité d'études dramatiques du Conservatoire, Comité d'études musicales du Conservatoire, Office du film du Québec, Office de la langue française, Régie du Grand Théâtre de Québec.
Affaires municipales	Bureau d'assainissement des eaux du Québec Métropolitain, Bureau des commissaires pour le rachat des rentes seigneuriales, Commission d'aménagement de la Communauté urbaine de Québec, Commission municipale de Québec, Commission de transport de la Communauté urbaine de Montréal, Commission de transport de la Communauté régionale de l'Outaouais, Conseil de sécurité publique de la Communauté urbaine de Montréal, Régie des eaux du Québec, Société d'aménagement de l'Outaouais, Société d'habitation du Québec, Syndicat national du rachat des rentes seigneuriales.
Affaires sociales	Commission d'appel de l'aide et des allocations sociales, Conseil des affaires sociales et de la famille, Conseil consultatif de pharmacologie, Conseil de l'Optat, Conseil supérieur de la famille, Office de prévention et de traitement de l'alcoolisme et des autres taxicomanies (Optat), Régie de l'assurance-maladie du Québec, Régie des rentes du Québec.
Agriculture et Colonisation	Comité consultatif de l'assurance-récolte, Comité consultatif de l'Office du crédit agricole du Québec, Comité consultatif de la Régie des marchés agricoles, Raffinerie de sucre du Québec, Office du crédit agricole du Québec, Régie de l'assurance-récolte du Québec, Régie des marchés agricoles du Québec.
Communications	Office d'information et de publicité du Québec, Office de radio-télédiffusion du Québec, Régie des services publics.
Education	Commission de l'éducation des adultes, Commission de l'enseignement élémentaire, Commission de l'enseignement secondaire, Commission de l'enseignement collégial, Commission consultative de l'enseignement privé, Commission de l'enseignement supérieur du conseil, Commission de planification de l'université du Québec, Commission de la recherche universitaire, Comité catholique de l'éducation, Comité protestant de l'éducation, Conseil supérieur de l'éducation, Conseil des études de l'université du Québec, Conseil des universités, Conseil consultatif du régime de retraite des enseignants, Université du Québec.

Source: *Annuaire du Québec* 1972

Nom du ministère	Principaux organismes
Finances	Caisse de dépôt et de placement du Québec, Fonds d'indemnisation des victimes d'accidents d'automobiles, Régie de la Place des Arts, Société générale de financement du Québec, Société d'exploitation des loteries et courses du Québec, Société des alcools du Québec, Sidbec.
Fonction publique	Commission de la fonction publique du Québec.
Industrie et Commerce	Centre de recherche industrielle du Québec, Société du développement industriel du Québec, Société du parc industriel du centre du Québec.
Immigration	Commission interministérielle des affaires des immigrants, Comité consultatif de l'immigration.
Institutions financières	Commission des valeurs mobilières du Québec, Conseil de la protection du consommateur, Office de la protection du consommateur, Comité consultatif concernant les agents de réclamations, Régie de l'assurance-dépôt du Québec.
Justice	Commission de contrôle des permis d'alcool du Québec, Commission des loyers, Commission de police du Québec, Institut de police du Québec, Régie des loteries et courses du Québec, Conseil consultatif de la justice.
Richesses naturelles	Commission hydroélectrique de Québec (Hydro-Québec), Office de l'électrification rurale du Québec, Régie de l'électricité et du gaz, Société québécoise d'exploration minière (Soquem), Société québécoise d'initiatives pétrolières (Soquip).
Terres et Forêts	Commission de géographie, Société de cartographie du Québec, Société de récupération et d'exploitation forestière du Québec (Rexfor).
Tourisme, Chasse et Pêche	Conseil de la faune, Conseil d'artisanat du Québec, Conseil du tourisme de la province de Québec, Centrale d'artisanat du Québec.
Transports	Bureau des expropriations de Montréal, Régie des transports,Société des traversiers Québec-Lévis.
Travail et Main-d'Oeuvre	Bureau de conciliation concernant le salaire minimum, Commission des accidents du travail de Québec, Commission du salaire minimum, Conseil consultatif du travail et de la main-d'oeuvre, Comité consultatif provincial de la main-d'oeuvre, Comité des avantages sociaux de l'industrie de la construction, Commission de l'industrie de la construction.
Travaux publics	Société de développement immobilier du Québec.
Voirie	Office des autoroutes du Québec.

7

7.2 Pouvoir exécutif: éléments descriptifs

7.2.e STRUCTURE-TYPE D'UN MINISTERE

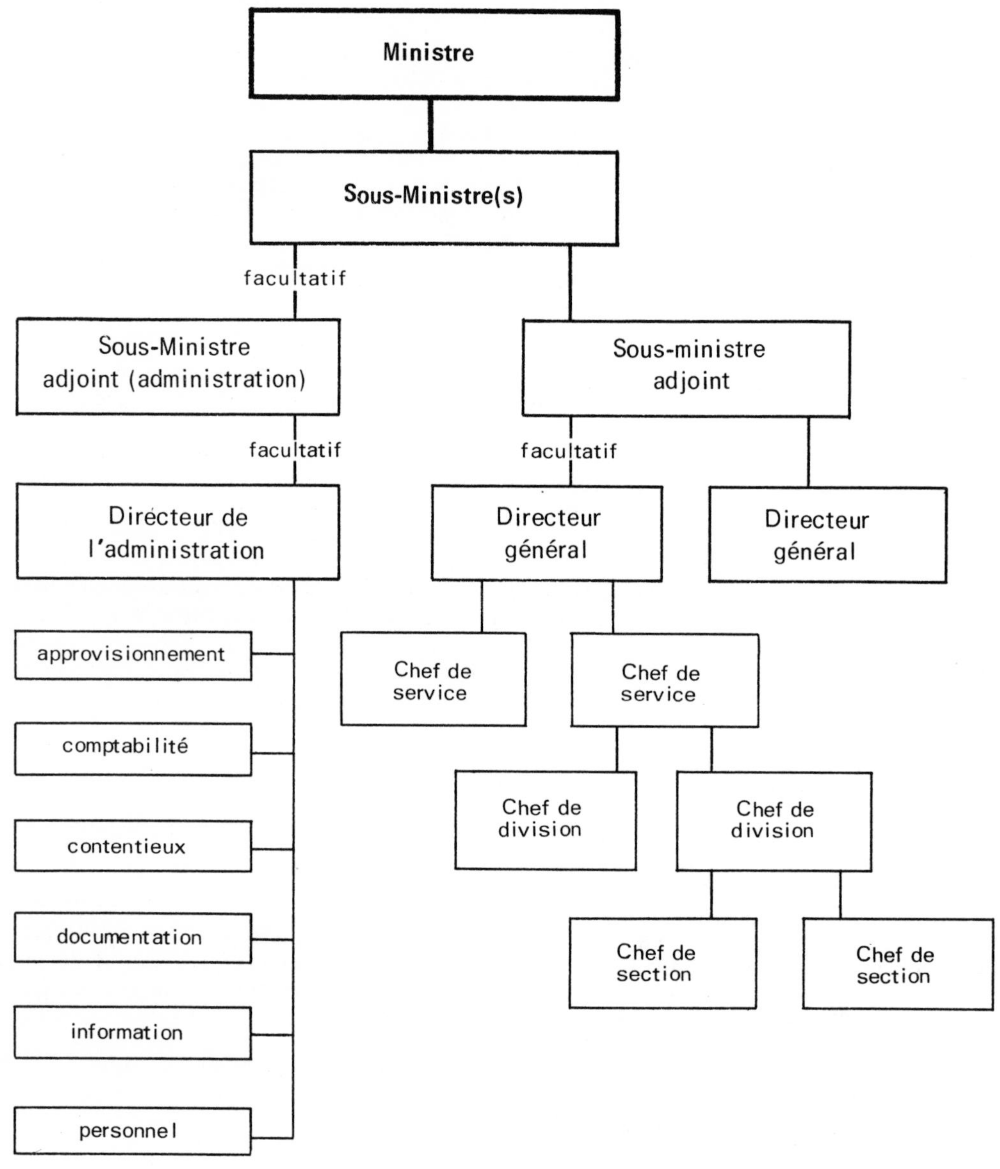

Source: *Annuaire du Québec* 1972

7.2 Pouvoir exécutif: éléments descriptifs

7.2.f EFFECTIFS DE L'ADMINISTRATION QUEBECOISE 1933-1970, ANNEES CHOISIES

Employés du gouvernement

Année	Administrations Ⓖ et régies Ⓖ	Entreprises Ⓖ publiques	**Total des employés**
	nombre d'employés		
1933	6,770	1,302	**8,072**
1944	12,852	3,346	**16,198**
1956	24,708	6,436	**31,141**
1961	29,413	7,800	**37,213**
1966	43,916	14,356	**58,272**
1967	47,848	17,675	**65,523**
1968	52,140	20,056	**72,196**
1969	53,301	18,569	**71,870**
1970	53,700	16,366	**70,066**

Nombre d'employés par 1,000 habitants

7.2.g REMUNERATION DES FONCTIONNAIRES, QUEBEC, ONTARIO, CANADA, 1970.

	QUEBEC	**ONTARIO**	**CANADA** pour les 10 provinces, Territoires du Nord-Ouest et Yukon
Fonctionnaires provinciaux (1 janvier 1970)	73,331	116,634	337,851
Fonctionnaires provinciaux (31 décembre 1970)	75,751	124,028	357,284
Rémunération totale (en 1970) ($'000)	516,199	963,470	2,428,740
Rémunération annuelle moyenne par employé (1970)	$6,925	$8,006	$6,987

Source: *Annuaire du Québec* 1972

7.3 Pouvoir exécutif: budget et priorités gouvernementales

7.3.a PRINCIPALES SOURCES DE REVENU DU GOUVERNEMENT DU QUEBEC, EN POURCENTAGE, ANNEES FISCALE 1973-1974

Principales sources de revenus, 1973-1974

Source	%	Répartition
Ⓖ Impôts sur les revenus et sur les biens	40%	80% Particuliers
		13% Sociétés
		7% Autres
Ⓖ Taxes à la consommation	28%	58% Vente en détail
		28% Carburants
		14% Autres
Gouvernement fédéral	22%	
Ⓖ Droits et permis	5%	
Sociétés d'Etat et divers	5%	

Source: *Discours du budget,* Ministère des Finances, Québec

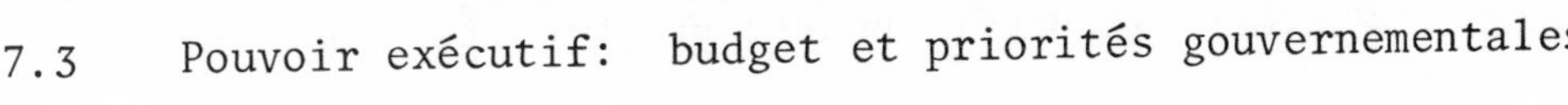

7.3 Pouvoir exécutif: budget et priorités gouvernementales

7.3.b REPARTITION DES DEPENSES DU GOUVERNEMENT DU QUEBEC, SELON LES GRANDES FONCTIONS ECONOMIQUES, EN POURCENTAGE, ANNEE FISCALE 1972-1973

Budget des dépenses, 1972-1973

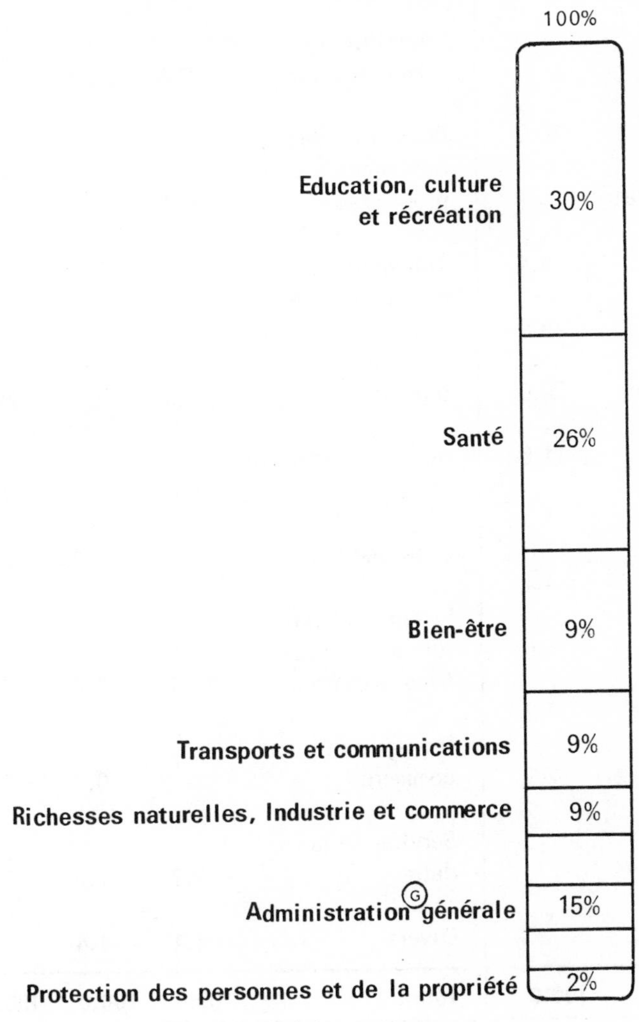

Source: *Discours sur le budget,* Ministère des Finances, Québec.

7.3 Pouvoir exécutif: budget et priorités gouvernementales.

7.3.c EVOLUTION DES PRIORITES BUDGETAIRES DU GOUVERNEMENT DU QUEBEC, EN POURCENTAGE, 1869-1968, ANNEES CHOISIES.

Catégorie	**1869** %
Législation	10.0
Service de la dette Ⓖ	—
Service civil	9.4
Justice	24.9
Education et culture	20.6
Santé et Bien-être	11.6
Travaux publics	4.3
Agriculture	4.1
Colonisation	5.0
Terres et forêts	7.2
Autres	2.9
Total	**100.0**

Catégorie	**1952** %	**1959** %	**1963** %	**1965** %	**1968** %
Législation et administration	5.4	3.5	3.7	3.0	2.8
Protection des personnes et des propriétés	4.1	4.3	4.9	3.9	3.8
Transports et communications	31.6	25.4	17.7	17.3	11.6
Santé et bien-être	20.0	25.0	29.5	28.2	37.3
Services récréatifs et culturels	0.4	0.4	0.5	0.4	0.7
Enseignement	16.3	22.1	28.8	27.4	26.2
Ressources naturelles et Industries primaires	11.4	9.6	6.7	5.5	5.2
Industrie et commerce	–	0.7	0.6	1.1	0.5
Service de la dette	9.7	7.6	5.2	5.3	3.5
Divers	1.1	1.4	2.4	7.9	7.4
Total:	**100.0**	**100.0**	**100.0**	**100.0**	**100.0**

Source: *Discours sur le budget*, Ministère des Finances, Québec.

Ministères	1971-1972		1972-73		1973-74	
	($'000)	%	($'000)	%	($'000)	%
Affaires culturelles	18,422	0.4	18 052	0,4	21 089,5	0,4
Affaires intergouvernementales	7,125	0.2	7 127	0,1	8 415,7	0,2
Affaires municipales	64,090	1,5	68 839	1,5	94 506,0	1,8
Affaires sociales	1,492,360	35.0	1 754 394	37,5	1 862 860,2	36,4
Agriculture et colonisation	84,265	2.2	88 214	1,9	101 024,0	2,1
Assemblée nationale	11,079	0.3	12 027	0,3	13 158,7	0,3
Communications	21,654	0.5	25 027	0,5	28 368,1	0,5
Conseil exécutif	33,520	0.8	38 094	0,8	54 506,4	1,1
Conseil du Trésor	710		868		1 643,1	
Education	1,279,400	30.0	1 349 309	28,9	1 445 712,0	28,2
Finances	39,137	1.0	41 571	0,9	49 104,6	0,9
Fonction publique	4,126	0.1	5 170	0,1	4 910,3	0,1
Immigration	1,650		1 258		2 089,8	
Industrie et commerce	49,450	1.1	35 568	0,8	42 221,6	0,8
Institutions financières, compagnies et coopératives	4,513	0.1	4 545	0,1	6 161,6	0,1
Justice	112,763	2.7	138 829	3,0	153 711,7	3,0
Revenu	172,522	4.1	212 974	4,6	229 172,2	4,5
Richesses naturelles	19,542	0.4	21 606	0,5	24 538,8	0,5
Terres et forêts	37,648	0.9	37 307	0,8	39 780,1	0,8
Tourisme, chasse et pêche	24,011	0.5	29 114	0,6	34 760,3	0,7
Transports	20,534	0.4	470 548	10,1	567 576,2	11,1
Travail et main-d'oeuvre	19,858	0.4	18 234	0,4	26 102,4	0,5
Travaux publics	79,506	1.9	80 710	1,7	78 580,5	1,5
Voirie	383,727	9.2	404 264	9,6	228 825,0	4,5
Service de la dette	169,602	4.3	203 923	4,4		
Tous les ministères	**4,151,214**	**100.0**	4 673 386	100,0	5 118 818,8	100,0

7.3 Pouvoir exécutif: budget et priorités gouvernementales

7.3.d EVOLUTION DES SOURCES DE REVENU DU GOUVERNEMENT DU QUEBEC, EN POURCENTAGE, 1951-1973, ANNEES CHOISIES

Sources de revenus

Année ($'000) / %	Impôts sur les revenus et sur les biens (G)	Taxes à la consommation (G)	Gouvernement fédéral	Droits et permis (G)	Sociétés d'Etat et divers	**Total des revenus**
1951	84,762	79,480	2,739	24,285	46,404	237,670
	35.6	**33.4**	**1.1**	**10.2**	**19.5**	**100.0**
1956	117,430	116,325	3,173	77,552	59,786	374,276
	31.4	**31.1**	**0.8**	**20.7**	**16.0**	**100.0**
1961	249,515	210,195	71,773	101,886	53,092	686,461
	36.3	**30.6**	**10.4**	**14.8**	**7.7**	**100.0**
1966	601,632	577,050	219,973	142,408	76,537	1,617,600
	37.2	**35.7**	**13.6**	**8.8**	**4.7**	**100.0**
1967	780,900	681,800	424,065	159,125	97,875	2,143,765
	36.4	**31.8**	**19.8**	**7.4**	**4.6**	**100.0**
1968	1,017,200	888,400	470,700	201,408	112,275	2,689,983
	37.8	**33.0**	**17.5**	**7.5**	**4.2**	**100.0**
1969	1,142,000	906,000	584,669	208,400	116,500	2,957,569
	38.6	**30.6**	**19.8**	**7.0**	**3.9**	**100.0**
1970	1,247,200	978,900	886,352	214,100	142,600	3,469,152
	35.9	**28.2**	**25.5**	**6.2**	**4.1**	**100.0**
1971	1,426,000	1,033,000	1,032,900	235,300	153,300	3,880,500
	36.7	**26.6**	**26.6**	**6.1**	**3.0**	**100.0**
1972	1 682 000	1 242 000	956 500	242 000	204 500	4 327 000
	39,0	**28,0**	**22,0**	**6.0**	**5,0**	**100,0**
1973	1 940 300	1 331 000	1 095 400	230 200	244 100	4 841 000
	40,0	**28,0**	**22,0**	**5,0**	**5,0**	**100,0**

Source: *Discours sur le budget,* Ministère des Finances, Québec.

7.4 Pouvoir législatif

7.4.a COMPOSITION DE L'ASSEMBLEE NATIONALE: LA REPRESENTATION DES PARTIS, 1867-1973

Année	Nombre de comtés électoraux		Libéral (parti libéral)			Conservateurs (Union Nationale)			Autres
			députés élus	sièges obtenus	suffrages obtenus	députés élus	sièges obtenus	suffrages obtenus	députés élus
	#	%	#	%	%	#	%	%	#
1867	65	100.0	14	20.0	45.0	50	80.0	55.0	1
1871	65	100.0	20	29.3	35.0	45	70.7	65.0	–
1875	65	100.0	19	31.0	44.0	43	69.0	56.0	3
1878	65	100.0	31	44.6	49.0	32	55.4	51.0	2
1881	65	100.0	15	21.6	42.0	49	78.4	56.0	1
1886	65	100.0	31	55.4	51.0	28	44.6	49.0	6
1890	73	100.0	42	64.3	53.0	24	34.2	47.0	7
1892	73	100.0	21	28.7	45.0	51	71.3	55.0	1
1897	74	100.0	51	69.0	54.3	23	31.0	45.7	–
1900	74	100.0	67	90.5	56.3	7	9.5	43.8	–
1904	74	100.0	68	92.0	67.7	6	8.0	25.4	–
1908	74	100.0	58	78.3	55.3	13	17.5	39.9	3
1912	81	100.0	64	80.0	54.3	15	18.6	45.1	2
1916	81	100.0	75	92.5	64.6	6	7.5	35.1	–
1919	81	100.0	74	91.2	70.0	5	6.0	23.7	2
1923	85	100.0	64	75.3	55.3	19	23.5	44.4	2
1927	85	100.0	75	88.2	62.7	9	11.8	36.6	1
1931	90	100.0	79	87.7	55.6	11	12.3	44.2	–
1935	90	100.0	48	53.3	50.2	42	46.7	48.7	–
1936	90	100.0	14	15.6	41.8	76	84.4	57.5	–
1939	86	100.0	70	81.4	54.2	15	17.4	39.2	1
1944	91	100.0	37	40.3	39.5	48	52.8	35.8	6
1948	92	100.0	8	8.7	38.3	82	89.1	51.0	2
1952	92	100.0	23	25.0	46.0	68	73.8	51.5	1
1956	93	100.0	20	21.5	44.5	72	77.4	52.0	1
1960	95	100.0	52	53.7	51.3	42	45.2	46.6	1
1962	95	100.0	63	64.1	56.4	31	32.6	42.1	1
1966	108	100.0	50	46.3	47.2	56	51.9	40.9	2

	Nombre de comtés électoraux		Libéraux (parti libéral)			Conservateurs (Union Nationale)			Ralliement créditiste			Parti Québécois			Autres
			députés élus	sièges obtenus	suffrages obtenus	députés élus	sièges obtenus	suffrages obtenus	députés élus	sièges obtenus	suffrages obtenus	députés élus	sièges obtenus	suffrages obtenus	députés élus
	#	%	#	%	%	#	%	%	#	%	%	#	%	%	#
1970	108	100.0	72	66.6	45.4	17	15.5	19.65	12	11.1	11.19	7	6.5	23.1	0
1973 *	110	*100,0*	102	*92,7*	*54,5*		0	*5,1*	2	*1,8*	*10,0*	6	*5,5*	*30,1*	

** données provisoires*

Source: *Annuaire du Québec* 1972

7.4 Pouvoir législatif

7.4.b COMPOSITION DE L'ASSEMBLEE NATIONALE: ELECTION DE 1973 (1)

Comté électoral	Allégance Politique	Député élu PROVINCE (sans l'Ile de Montréal)	Majorité
Abitibi - Est	Lib.	Roger Houde	6,657
Abitibi - Ouest	"	Jean-Hughes Boutin	2,712
Argenteuil	"	Zoël Saindon	8,811
Arthabaska	"	Gilles Masse	9,500
Beauce - Nord	"	Denis Sylvain	14,198
Beauce - Sud	Créd.	Fabien Roy	907
Beauharnois	Lib.	Gérard Cadieux	3,549
Bellechasse	"	Pierre Mercier	1,048
Berthier	"	Denis Michel	6,570
Bonaventure	"	Gérard D. Lévesque	9,483
Brome - Missisquoi	"	Glen Brown	9,504
Chambly	"	Guy Saint-Pierre	6,911
Champlain	"	Normand Toupin	8,821
Charlesbourg	"	André Harvey	8,822
Charlevoix	"	Raymond Mailloux	10,010
Châteauguay	"	George Kennedy	8,095
Chauveau	"	Bernard Lachapelle	8,642
Chicoutimi	P.Q.	Marc-André Bédard	1,259
Deux-Montagnes	Lib.	Jean-Paul L'Allier	7,979
Drummond	"	Robert Malouin	6,798
Dubuc	"	Ghislain Harvey	4,270
Duplessis	"	Donald Galienne	2,497
Frontenac	"	Henri Lecours	4,184
Gaspé	"	Guy Fortier	6,949
Gatineau	"	Michel Gratton	11,638

(1) Données provisoires

Comté électoral	Allégance Politique	Député élu PROVINCE (sans l'Ile de Montréal)	Majorité
Hull	Lib.	Oswald Parent	7,414
Huntingdon	"	Kenneth Fraser	8,086
Iberville	"	Jacques Tremblay	2,429
Iles-de-la-Madeleine	"	Louis-Philippe Lacroix	1,813
Jean-Talon	"	Raymond Garneau	10,196
Johnson	"	Jean-Claude Boutin	3,947
Joliette - Montcalm	"	Robert Quenneville	6,077
Jonquière	"	Gérald Harvey	4,245
Kamouraska - Témiscouata	"	J.M. Pelletier	5,393
Lac-St-Jean	"	Roger Pilote	3,331
Laporte	"	André Déom	407
L'Assomption	"	Jean Perreault	1,713
Laurentide - Labelle	"	Roger Lapointe	2,388
Laviolette	"	Prudent Carpentier	4,824
Lévis	"	Vincent Gagnon	7,596
Limoilou	"	Fernand Houde	5,697
Lotbinière	"	Georges Massicotte	3,080
Louis-Hébert	"	Gaston Desjardins	777
Maskinongé	"	Yvon Picotte	5,276
Matane	"	Marc-Yvan Côté	2,675
Matapédia	"	Bona Arsenault	2,459
Mégantic - Compton	"	Omer Dionne	4,505
Montmagny - L'Islet	"	Julien Giasson	5,451
Montmorency	"	Marcel Bédard	5,973
Napierville - Laprairie	"	Paul Berthiaume	12,294
Nicolet - Yamaska	"	Benjamin Faucher	4,789
Orford	"	G. Vaillancourt	10,274
Papineau	"	Marc Assard	10,254
Pontiac - Témiscamingue	"	Jean-Guy Larivière	6,543

Comté électoral	Allégance Politique	Député élu PROVINCE (sans l'Ile de Montréal)	Majorité
Portneuf	Lib.	Michel Pagé	7,555
Prévost	"	Bernard Parent	3,938
Richelieu	"	Claude Simard	5,734
Richmond	"	Yvon Vallières	355
Rimouski	"	Claude St-Hilaire	4,518
Rivière-du-Loup	"	Paul Lafrance	6,008
Roberval	"	Robert Lamontagne	7,681
Rouyn - Noranda	Créd.	Camille Samson	1,006
Saguenay	P.Q.	Lucien Lessard	2,293
Saint-François	Lib.	Gérard Déziel	5,679
St-Hyacinthe	"	F. Cornellier	7,790
Saint-Jean	"	Jacques Veilleux	4,678
St-Maurice	"	Marcel Bédard	1,453
Shefford	"	Richard Verreault	3,529
Sherbrooke	"	Jean-Paul Pépin	6,608
Tachereau	"	Irenée Bonnier	4,750
Taillon	"	Guy Leduc	577
Terrebonne	"	Denis Hardy	3,984
Trois-Rivières	"	Guy Bacon	8,007
Vanier	"	Armand Dufour	5,981
Vaudreuil - Soulanges	"	Paul Phaneuf	7,551
Verchères	"	Marcel Ostiguy	5,416

Comté électoral	Allégance Politique	Député élu ILE DE MONTREAL	Majorité
Anjou	Lib.	Yves Tardif	828
Bourassa	"	Lise Bacon	3,889
Bourget	"	Jean Boudreault	299
Crémazie	"	Jean Bienvenue	1,396
D'Arcy-McGee	"	Victor Goldbloom	25,525
Dorion	"	Alfred Bossé	13,484
Fabre	"	Gilles Houde	2,672
Gouin	"	Jean Beauregard	636
Jacques-Cartier	"	Noël St-Germain	12,657
Jeanne-Mance	"	Aimé Brisson	5,835
L'Acadie	"	François Cloutier	10,352
Lafontaine	P.Q.	Marcel Léger	1,972
Laurier	Lib.	André Marchand	9,519
Laval	"	Jean-Noël Lavoie	11,673
Maisonneuve	P.Q.	Robert Burns	2,276
Marguerite-Bourgeois	Lib.	Fernand Lalonde	13,695
Mercier	"	Robert Bourassa	2,882
Milles-Iles	"	Bernard Lachance	2,151
Mont-Royal	"	John Ciacia	19,813
Notre-Dame-de-Grâce	"	William Tetley	23,301
Outremont	"	Jérôme Choquette	8,325
Pointe-Claire	"	Arthur Séguin	23,548
Robert-Baldwin	"	Jean Cournoyer	20,332
Rosemont	"	Gilles Bellemare	2,026
Saint-Anne	"	George Springate	4,414
Saint-Henri	"	Gérard Shanks	3,548
Saint-Jacques	P.Q.	Claude Charron	2,306

Comté électoral	Allégance Politique	Député élu ILE DE MONTREAL	Majorité
Saint-Laurent	Lib.	Claude Forget	13,416
Saint-Louis	"	Harry Blanks	7,960
Sainte-Marie	"	Jean-Claude Malépart	77
Sauvé	P.Q.	Jacques-Yvan Morin	2,760
Verdun	Lib.	Lucien Caron	11,200
Viau	"	Fernand Picard	5,063
Westmount	"	Kevin Drummond	17,752

7.4.c ECART ENTRE LE POURCENTAGE DE VOIX ET LE POURCENTAGE DE SIEGES SELON LES PARTIS RECONNUS, ELECTIONS DE 1956 A 1973, QUEBEC

Année	Partis	% de sièges	— % de voix	= Ecart
1956	P.L.Q.	*21,5*	*44,5*	-23,0
	U.N.	*77,4*	*52,0*	+25,4
1960	P.L.Q.	*53,7*	*51,3*	+2,4
	U.N.	*45,2*	*46,6*	-1,4
1962	P.L.Q.	*69,1*	*56,9*	+7,7
	U.N.	*32,6*	*42,1*	-9,5
1966	P.L.Q.	*46,3*	*47,2*	- 0,9
	U.N.	*51,9*	*40,9*	+11,0
	R.I.N.	—	*5,6*	- 5,6
	R.N.	—	*3,2*	- 3,2
1970	P.L.Q.	*67,0*	*45,5*	+21,5
	U.N.	*16,0*	*20,0*	- 4,0
	P.Q.	*6,0*	*23,5*	-17,5
	R.C.	*11,0*	*11,0*	—
1973	P.L.Q.	*92,7*	*54,5*	+38,2
	U.N.	*0,0*	*5,1*	- 5,1
	P.Q.	*5,5*	*30,1*	-24,6
	R.C.	*1,8*	*10,0*	- 8,2

7.4.d COMTES SUR-REPRESENTES ET COMTES SOUS-REPRESENTES PAR RAPPORT A LA MOYENNE PROVINCIALE DE 1970, QUEBEC.

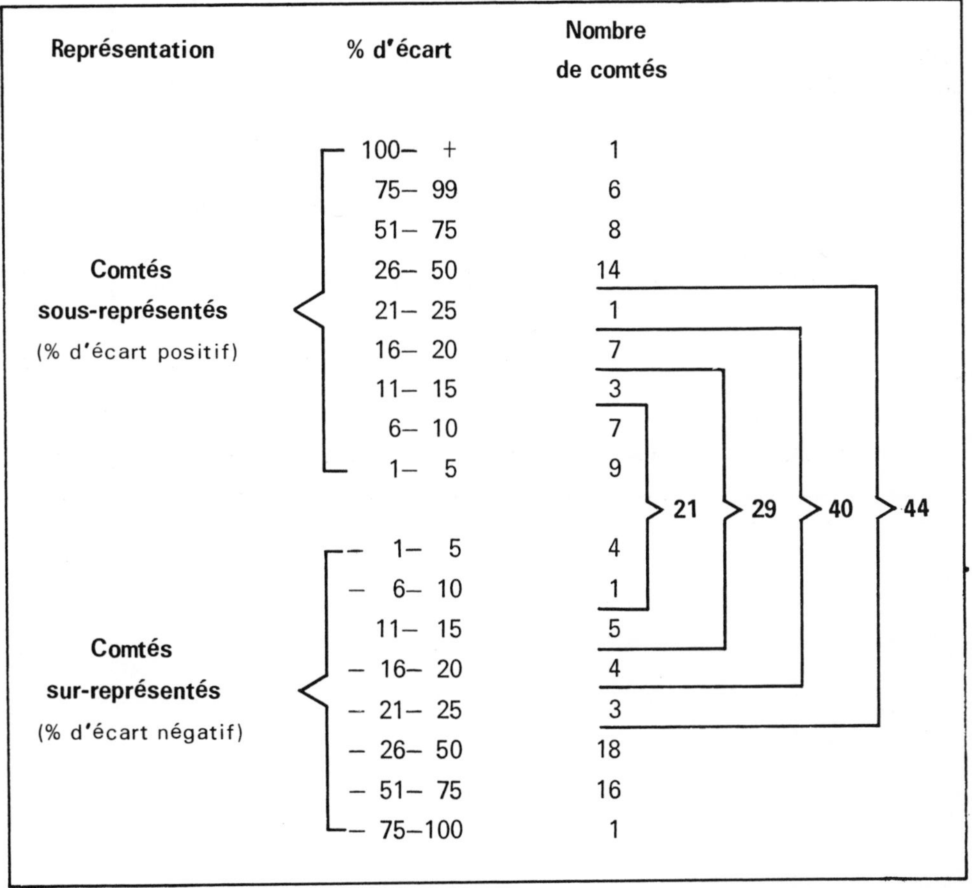

Représentation	% d'écart	Nombre de comtés
Comtés sous-représentés (% d'écart positif)	100– +	1
	75– 99	6
	51– 75	8
	26– 50	14
	21– 25	1
	16– 20	7
	11– 15	3
	6– 10	7
	1– 5	9
Comtés sur-représentés (% d'écart négatif)	– 1– 5	4
	– 6– 10	1
	11– 15	5
	– 16– 20	4
	– 21– 25	3
	– 26– 50	18
	– 51– 75	16
	– 75–100	1

Source: Boily, Robert, *La réforme électorale*, Montréal, Editions du Jour, 1971.

7.4 Pouvoir législatif

7.4.e DEPENSES ELECTORALES AUX ELECTIONS DE 1970, SELON LES DIFFERENTS PARTIS

Type de dépenses	Libéral	Nouveau Parti démocratique du Québec	Parti Québécois	Ralliement créditiste	Union Nationale	Total des dépenses des partis reconnus	Total des dépenses (tous les candidats)
	Partis reconnus						Candidats
	$	$	$	$	$	$	$
Dépenses permises	**849,527**	**150,850**	**849,527**	**765,624**	**849,527**	**3,465,057**	**7,457,131**
Location de bureaux	340	–	7,369	3,905	13,949	25,564	263,270
Services	102,846	99	17,815	40,412	102,566	263,739	1,650,727
Frais de voyage et louage de voitures	58,230	21	26,817	22,890	21,569	129,529	246,901
Articles fournis	38,866	991	37,394	206	63,168	140,627	455,455
Publicité	627,048	2,281	174,337	20,414	577,292	1,401,375	1,745,289
Créances contestées	7	–	2,258	397	–	2,664	3,764
Toutes les dépenses	**827,340**	**3,394**	**265,994**	**88,226**	**778,545**	**1,963,501**	**4,402,173**

Source: *Annuaire du Québec 1972*.

7.4.f LE CYCLE LEGISLATIF

Genèse de la loi créant un ministère de l'éducation (Bill 1960)

Faisant suite aux critiques adressées au système d'enseignement du Québec, le gouvernement Lesage propose un projet de loi créant une Commission royale d'enquête; loi votée par l'Assemblée le 28 février 1961.

A la suite d'une proposition faite par le ministre de la Jeunesse, Jean Gérin-Lajoie, au Cabinet, adoption par celui-ci d'un arrêté en Conseil (21 avril 1961) constituant la Commission royale d'enquête. ("Commission Parent")

Le 23 avril 1963 publication de la 1ère tranche du rapport: on y recommande la création d'un ministère de l'Education et d'un Conseil Supérieur de l'Education.

Sur réception de cette 1ère tranche du rapport, le ministre crée au sein de son ministère un comité pour étudier le document (le ministre, le sous-ministre et principaux adjoints). Parallèlement à cette étude, le ministre consulte des personnes du monde de l'enseignement et de l'épiscopat.

A la suite de cette étude et de ces consultations,présentation au Cabinet par le ministre d'un mémoire dans lequel il est recommandé de former un ministère et un Conseil supérieur de l'Education.

Acceptation du mémoire par le Cabinet et instruction est donnée aux conseillers juridiques de préparer le texte d'un projet de loi à partir des recommandations du mémoire.

Soumission du texte préparé par les conseillers juridiques au comité de législation.

Acceptation du texte par le Cabinet et dépôt du projet de loi à l'Assemblée législative où il subit sa 1ère lecture (le 26 juin 1963).

Nombreuses critiques publiques et privées auprès du Premier ministre et du ministre de la Jeunesse. Le 8 juillet 1963, le Premier ministre retire du feuilleton de la Chambre le Bill 60. Annonce est faite que les personnes et les groupes ont jusqu'au 19 septembre pour transmettre leurs suggestions et leurs mémoires.

Le 15 janvier 1964 le Bill 60 revient devant la Chambre et subit à nouveau sa 1ère lecture. Quelques modifications mineures avaient été apportées. C'est dans le préambule du projet que les modifications les plus importantes avaient été apportées touchant surtout le respect de la confessionnalité.

Adoption en 2ème et 3ème lecture sans modification, après étude en commission et Assemblée plénière.

Présentation du texte voté par l'Assemblée législative au Conseil législatif. Un amendement important est apporté: ce qui était dans le préambule est placé à l'intérieur même de la loi l'incorpore définitivement à la loi.

Renvoi du texte voté par le Conseil à l'Assemblée législative. Celle-ci le ratifie sans modification.

Sanction par le Lieutenant-gouverneur.

Source: Document fourni par M. Robert Boily.

7.4.g RESULTATS DES ELECTIONS FEDERALES AU QUEBEC SELON LES DEUX PRINCIPAUX PARTIS, 1867-1972

Année	Libéraux			Conservateurs			Autres		
	Nombre de votes	votes %	députés #	Nombre de votes	votes %	députés #	Nombre de votes	votes %	députés #
1867	–	–	20	–	–	45	–	–	–
1872	–	–	27	–	–	38	–	–	–
1874	–	–	33	–	–	32	–	–	–
1878	–	–	20	–	–	45	–	–	–
1882	–	–	17	–	–	48	–	–	–
1887	–	–	32	–	–	33	–	–	–
1891	–	–	35	–	–	30	–	–	–
1896	120,321	53.5	49	102,884	45.8	16	1,485	0.7	–
1900	133,566	56.3	56	103,253	43.5	7	501	0.2	–
1904	144,992	56.4	54	111,550	43.4	11	522	0.2	–
1908	162,176	57.3	53	115,569	40.8	11	5,377	1.9	1
1911	164,281	50.7	27	159,299	49.2	37	469	0.1	1
1917	243,431	72.7	62	76,014	25.1	3	–	–	–
1921	558,056	71.6	65	163,743	21.0	–	–	–	–
1925	469,475	58.3	60	273,818	34.0	4	60,273	7.4	1
1926	507,775	62.7	60	266,824	33.0	4	8,787	1.0	1
1930	542,135	52.6	40	456,037	44.3	24	22,089	2.1	1
1935	623,579	53.6	55	323,177	27.8	5	199,765	17.2	5
1940	868,663	73.0	61	231,851	19.5	3	70,983	5.9	1
1945	722,707	50.4	54	138,344	9.6	1	553,118	39.0	10
1949	984,131	61.1	66	397,803	24.7	2	211,366	13.1	5
1953	1,001,655	64.0	66	455,688	29.1	4	89,430	5.7	5
1957	1,116,028	61.5	63	562,133	31.0	9	111,899	6.1	3
1958	1,005,120	49.2	25	935,881	45.8	50	83,248	4.2	–
1962	830,250	39.2	35	620,475	29.3	14	639,198	30.2	26
1963	966,172	45.1	47	413,562	19.3	8	738,311	34.4	20
1965	928,530	44.8	55	432,901	20.9	9	675,881	32.6	11
1968	1,170,417	52.5	56	466,492	20.9	4	547,383	24.5	14
1972	1 215 359	49,7	56	428 099	17,5	2	803 133	32,8	16

7.4.h RESULTATS DES ELECTIONS FEDERALES AU QUEBEC SELON LES QUATRE PRINCIPAUX PARTIS, 1962-1972

Année	Parti Libéral	Parti Conservateur	Nouveau Parti Démocratique	Crédit Social	Autres
1962	830,250	620,475	91,795	542,433	4,970
1963	966,172	413,562	151,061	578,347	8,903
1965	928,125	432,941	244,423	356,962	74,429
1968	1,170,417	466,492	163,827	358,966	24,590
1972	1 215 359	428 099	160 908	572 467	69 758

Source: *Annuaire du Québec 1972*.

7.5 Sécurité sociale et éducation.

7.5.a REGIME Ⓖ DES RENTES DU QUEBEC, STATISTIQUES REGIONALES, 1967-1970, TOUTES LES ANNEES

Région	1967		1968		1969		1970	
	($'000)	%	($'000)	%	($'000)	%	($'000)	%
Bas-St-Laurent Gaspésie	4.1	1.8	105.8	3.0	327.0	2.6	620.5	2.4
Saguenay-Lac-St-Jean	6.4	2.8	202.0	5.7	641.9	5.1	1,229.8	4.7
Québec	36.6	16.4	527.2	14.9	1,970.2	15.7	3,935.2	15.1
Trois-Rivières	12.0	5.3	238.3	6.7	883.3	7.0	1,743.2	6.7
Cantons-de-l'Est	8.7	3.9	138.5	3.9	504.0	4.0	956.3	3.7
Montréal	144.5	64.6	2,077.3	58.7	7,157.0	57.0	5,402.3	59.1
Outaouais	3.7	1.6	76.4	2.2	318.1	2.5	689.9	2.6
Nord-Ouest	3.5	1.5	81.1	2.3	314.1	2.5	591.4	2.3
Côte-Nord	0.6	0.3	27.8	0.8	134.9	1.1	296.8	1.1
Nouveau-Québec	3.7	1.6	62.3	1.8	293.8	2.3	579.9	2.2
QUEBEC	**223.7**	**100.0**	**3,536.7**	**100.0**	**12,544.2**	**100.0**	**26,045.5**	**100.0**

Source: *Annuaire du Québec* 1972

7.5.b PROFESSIONNELS DE LA SANTE PAYES PAR LE REGIME D'ASSURANCE-MALADIE DU QUEBEC, 1971

coût moyen ($) par visite chez un professionnel de la santé

Région	Catégories de médecins et groupes de spécialités						
	Ensemble des médecins	Médecins omnipraticiens	Médecins spécialistes	Spécialités chirurgicales	Spécialités médicales	Spécialités de laboratoire	Radiologie
Bas-St-Laurent Gaspésie	8,50	6,75	12,71	16,08	8,66	14,47	14,47
Saguenay-Lac-St-Jean	7,77	5,55	11,34	18,69	7,61	9,23	9,23
Québec	8,61	5,92	12,20	18,23	8,70	11,92	9,53
Trois-Rivières	8,31	5,70	13,47	19,96	9,12	10,43	10,43
Cantons-de-l'Est	8,94	5,99	11,88	15,54	8,77	10,24	12,63
Montréal	8,82	5,87	11,60	16,29	8,47	17,10	13,33
Outaouais	7,51	6,03	11,08	15,97	6,16	–	13,58
Nord-Ouest	7,66	6,41	11,02	10,44	8,38	–	8,38
Côte-Nord Nouveau-Québec	7,48	6,20	16,67	19,95	8,00	–	8,00
QUEBEC	**8,64**	**5,91**	**11,78**	**16,64**	**8,47**	**12,03**	**13,11**

nombre de professionnels de la santé par 1 000 000 habitants

Région	Catégories de professionnels						
	Médecins omnipraticiens	Médecins spécialistes	Ensemble des médecins	Chirurgiens dentistes	Spécialistes chirurgie buccale	Optométristes	Ensemble des professionnels
Bas-St-Laurent-Gaspésie	41	29	69	8	–	9	86
Saguenay-Lac-St-Jean	39	41	80	8	–	7	96
Québec	60	73	133	7	–	6	146
Trois-Rivières	43	44	86	15	–	9	110
Cantons-de-l'Est	53	92	146	8	1	10	165
Montréal	61	85	146	4	1	10	160
Outaouais	43	21	64	8	–	7	79
Nord-Ouest	30	18	48	11	–	10	69
Côte-Nord	39	12	50	11	–	6	67
Nouveau-Québec	9	9	17	–	–	–	17
QUEBEC	**55**	**71**	**126**	**6**	**–**	**9**	**141**

Source: *Statistiques annuelles 1971*, Régie de l'Assurance-maladie du Québec, Québec.

7.5.c REPARTITION DES MEDECINS SELON LA CLASSE DE PAIEMENT ET LA REGION ADMINISTRATIVE, QUEBEC, 1972

Classe de paiements ($ milliers)

Région (Nombre de médecins / Pourcentage par région)	0-4	4-9.9	10-19.9	20-29.9	30-39.9	40-49.9	50-59.9	60-69.9	70-79.9	80-89.9	90-99.9	100-199.9	200-+	Total des médecins 100% par région
Bas-St-Laurent-Gaspésie	14	6	17	25	8	24	19	16	14	6	5	8	—	162
	8,7	3,7	10,5	15,4	4,9	14,8	11,7	9,9	8,7	3,7	3,1	4,9		100
Saguenay-Lac-St-Jean	25	15	13	11	14	27	24	30	32	15	4	15	—	225
	11,1	6,7	5,8	4,9	6,2	12,0	10,7	13,3	14,2	6,7	1,8	6,6		100
Québec	249	108	131	89	121	165	150	98	65	37	19	39	—	1 271
	19,6	8,5	10,3	7,0	9,5	13,0	11,8	7,7	5,1	2,9	1,5	3,1		100
Trois-Rivières	28	18	29	34	42	60	51	48	21	17	8	10	—	366
	7,7	4,9	7,9	9,3	11,5	16,4	13,9	13,1	5,7	4,7	2,2	2,7		100
Cantons-de-l'Est	49	33	29	34	49	42	33	19	12	11	10	7	—	328
	14,9	10,1	8,8	10,4	14,9	12,8	10,1	5,8	3,7	3,4	3,0	2,1		100
Montréal	876	445	583	484	525	597	533	329	232	170	92	209	13	5 088
	17,2	8,8	11,5	9,5	10,3	11,7	10,5	6,5	4,6	3,3	1,8	4,0	0,3	100
Outaouais	13	22	14	8	10	20	18	22	14	6	4	7	—	158
	8,2	13,9	8,9	5,1	6,3	12,7	11,4	14,0	8,9	3,8	2,5	4,3		100
Nord-Ouest	4	3	5	6	8	5	13	4	7	6	2	8	—	71
	5,6	4,2	7,1	8,5	11,3	7,1	18,2	5,6	9,9	8,5	2,8	11,2		100
Côte-Nord Nouveau-Québec	3	1	4	3	5	9	4	8	6	5	2	2	—	52
	5,8	1,9	7,7	5,8	9,6	17,3	7,7	15,4	11,5	9,6	3,9	3,8		100
Total par classe de paiements — Nombre de médecins	1 261	651	825	694	782	949	845	574	403	273	146	305	13	7 721
Pourcentage	16,3	8,4	10,7	9,0	10,1	12,3	10,9	7,5	5,2	3,5	1,9	4,0	0,2	100

(1) Nouveau-Québec : nombre total : 2
classe : $60 000-$69 999 .

Source : *Statistiques annuelles*, 1972, Régie de l'Assurance-maladie du Québec, Québec.

7.5.d ASSISTANCE SOCIALE PAR REGIONS ADMINISTRATIVES, QUEBEC, 1968

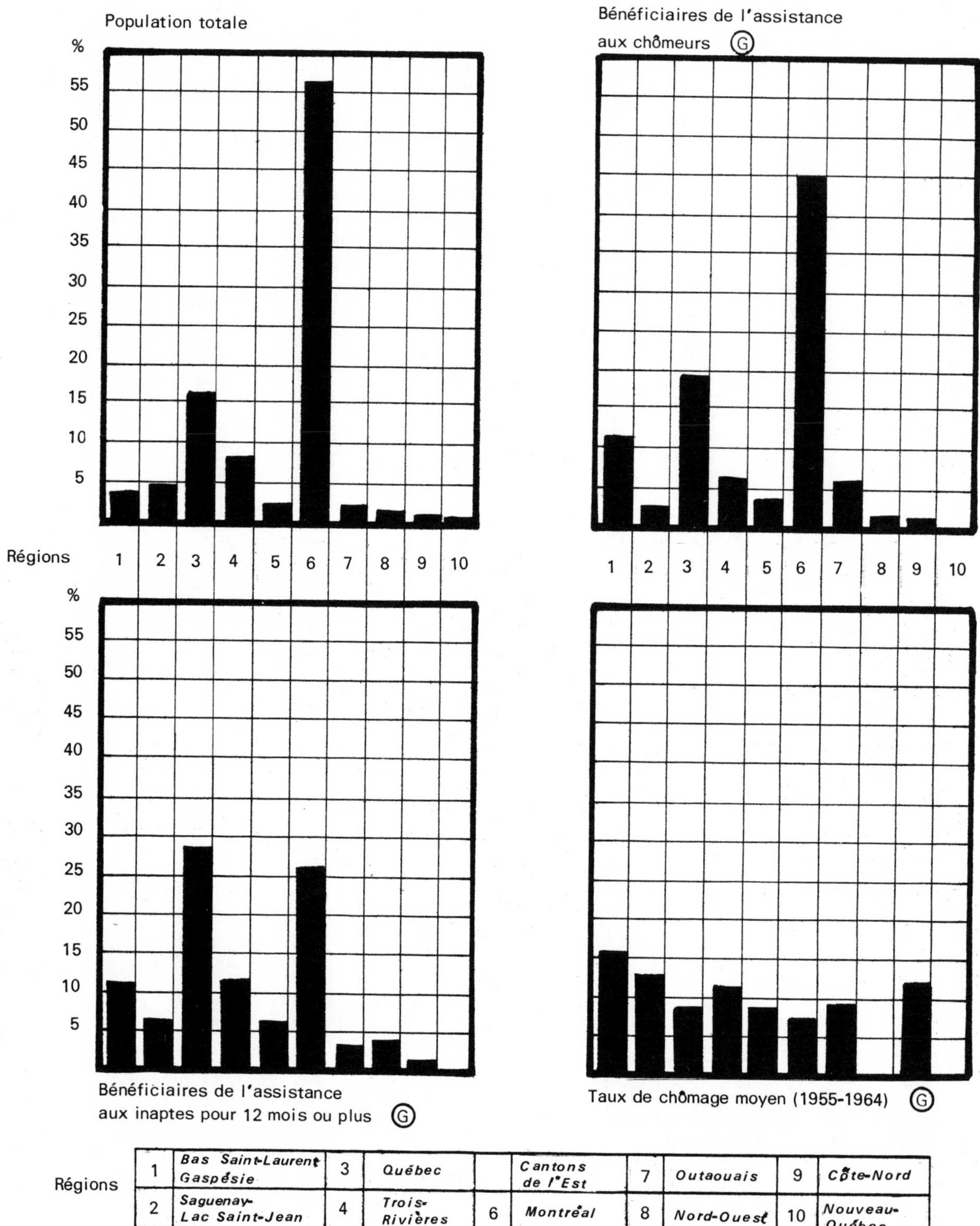

Source: *Ne comptons que sur nos propres moyens*, C.S.N., Montréal, 1971.

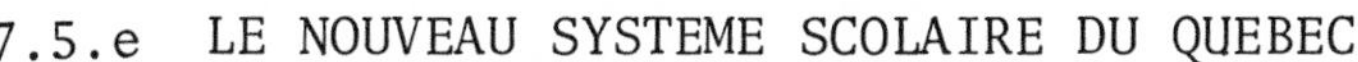

7.5.e LE NOUVEAU SYSTEME SCOLAIRE DU QUEBEC

Le nouveau système scolaire

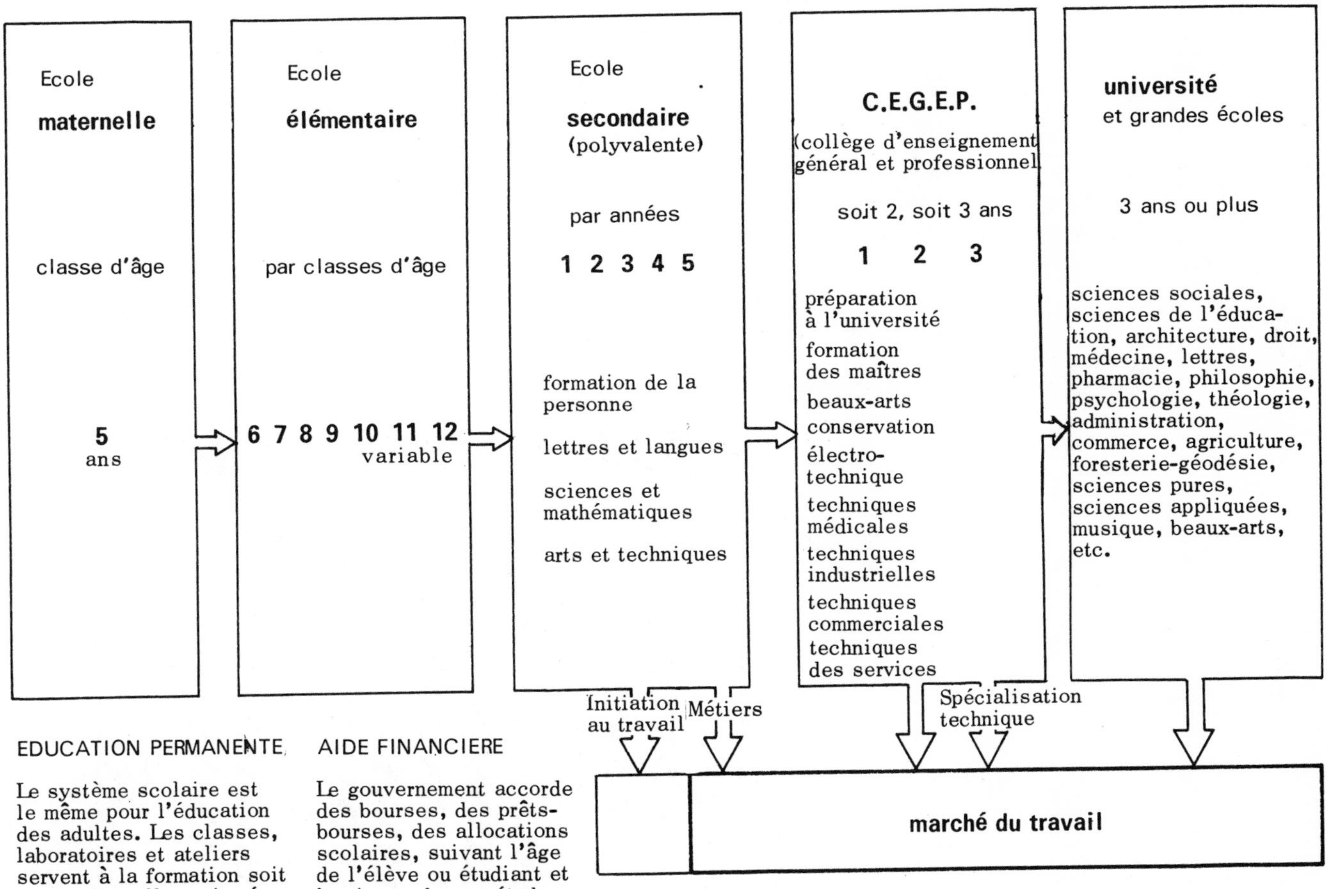

Ecole maternelle
classe d'âge
5 ans

Ecole élémentaire
par classes d'âge
6 7 8 9 10 11 12
variable

Ecole secondaire (polyvalente)
par années
1 2 3 4 5
formation de la personne
lettres et langues
sciences et mathématiques
arts et techniques

C.E.G.E.P.
(collège d'enseignement général et professionnel)
soit 2, soit 3 ans
1 2 3
préparation à l'université
formation des maîtres
beaux-arts
conservation
électro-technique
techniques médicales
techniques industrielles
techniques commerciales
techniques des services

université et grandes écoles
3 ans ou plus
sciences sociales, sciences de l'éducation, architecture, droit, médecine, lettres, pharmacie, philosophie, psychologie, théologie, administration, commerce, agriculture, foresterie-géodésie, sciences pures, sciences appliquées, musique, beaux-arts, etc.

Initiation au travail — Métiers — Spécialisation technique

marché du travail

EDUCATION PERMANENTE

Le système scolaire est le même pour l'éducation des adultes. Les classes, laboratoires et ateliers servent à la formation soit professionnelle, soit générale des adultes.

AIDE FINANCIERE

Le gouvernement accorde des bourses, des prêts-bourses, des allocations scolaires, suivant l'âge de l'élève ou étudiant et le niveau de ses études.

Source: *Annuaire du Québec* 1971

7.5 Sécurité sociale et éducation

7.5.f REPARTITION DES NEO-CANADIENS INSCRITS A LA C.E.C.M., SELON LA LANGUE D'ENSEIGNEMENT, 1931-1963, ANNEES CHOISIES

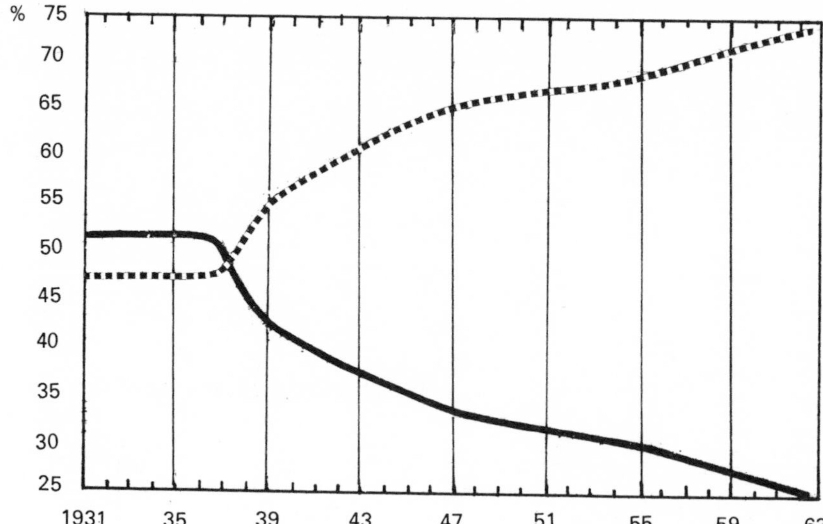

7.5.g REPARTITION DES NEO-CANADIENS INSCRITS A LA C.E.C.M., SELON LA LANGUE D'ENSEIGNEMENT ET L'ORIGINE Ⓖ ETHNIQUE, 1955-56 ET 1962-63

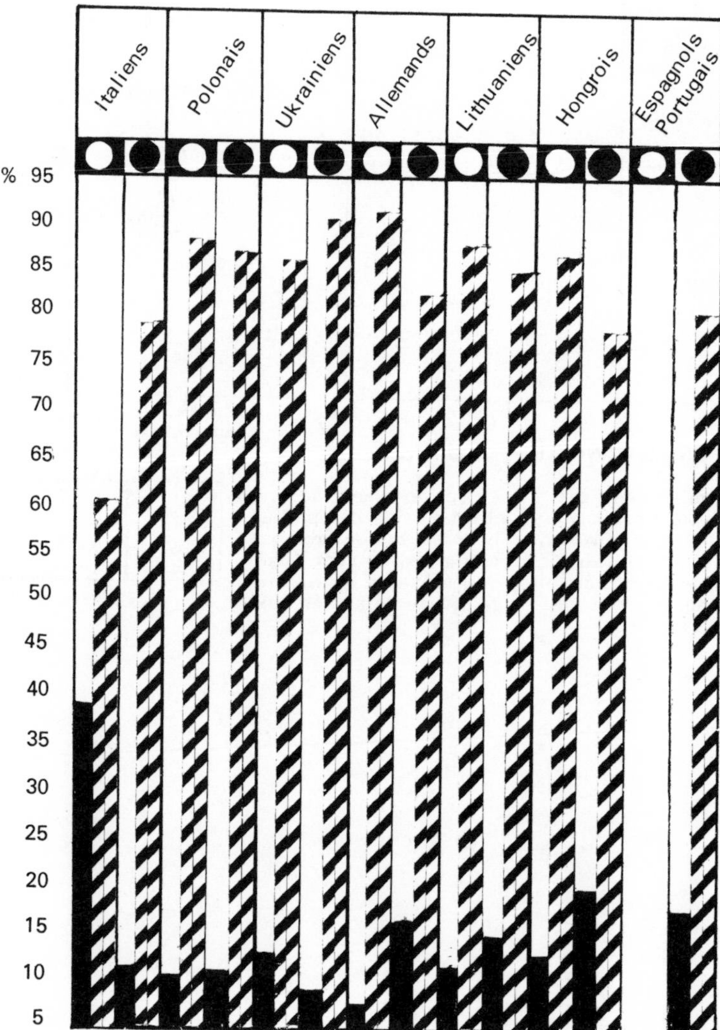

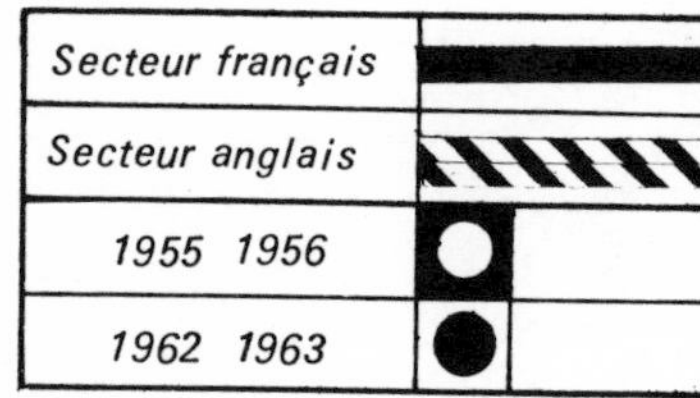

Source: Filières de la C.E.C.M.

8.1 La structure des partis politiques québécois: 3 exemples

8.1.a ORGANIGRAMME DU PARTI LIBERAL DU QUEBEC.

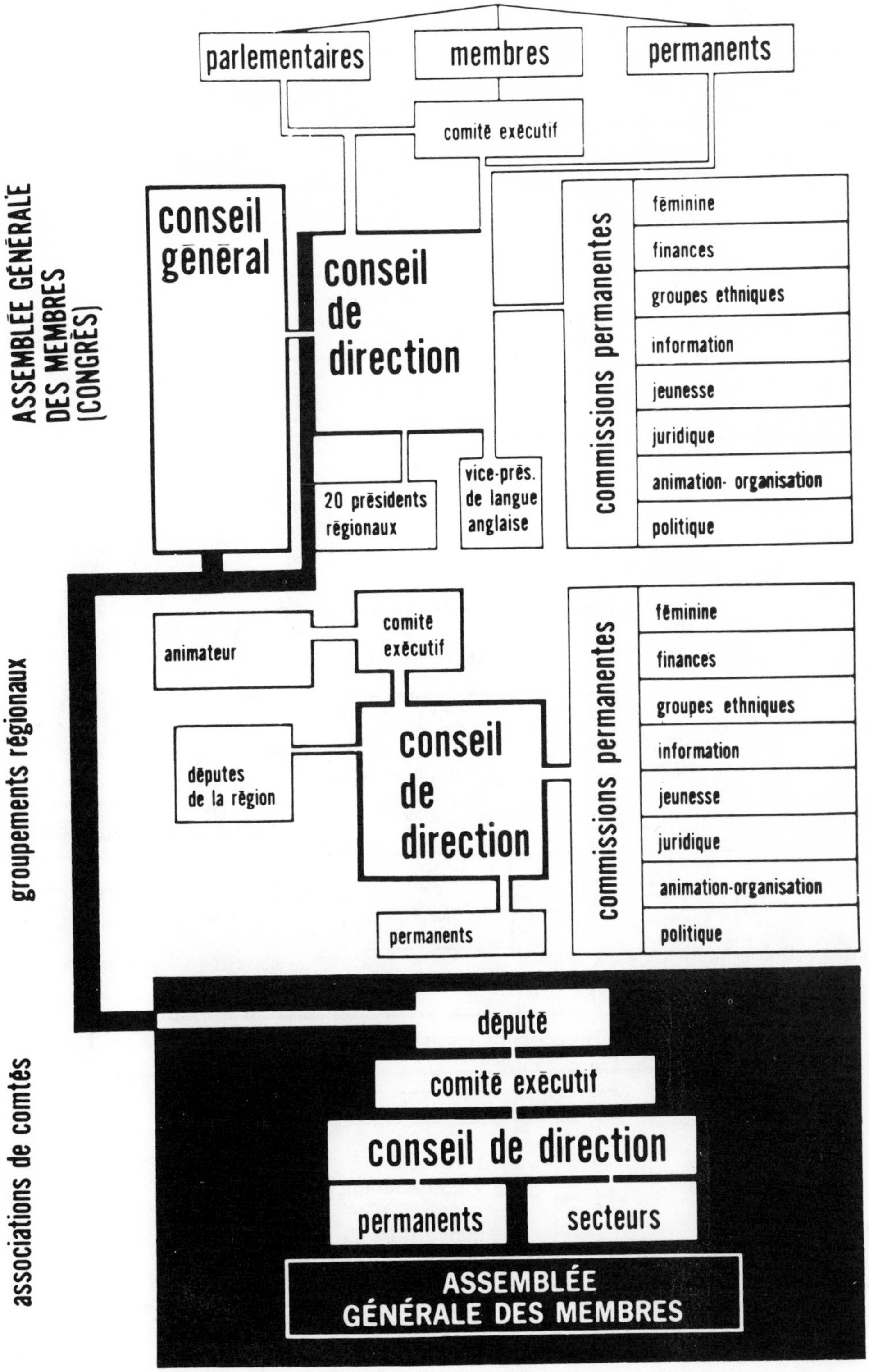

ASSEMBLÉE GÉNÉRALE DES MEMBRES (CONGRÈS)

parlementaires
membres
permanents
comité exécutif
conseil général
conseil de direction
20 présidents régionaux
vice-prés. de langue anglaise
commissions permanentes
féminine
finances
groupes ethniques
information
jeunesse
juridique
animation- organisation
politique

groupements régionaux

animateur
comité exécutif
députés de la région
conseil de direction
permanents
commissions permanentes
féminine
finances
groupes ethniques
information
jeunesse
juridique
animation-organisation
politique

associations de comtés

député
comité exécutif
conseil de direction
permanents
secteurs
ASSEMBLÉE GÉNÉRALE DES MEMBRES

Source: *Constitution,* Parti libéral du Québec, Congrès tenu en novembre 1971.

8.1 La structure des partis politiques québécois: 3 exemples

8.1.b ORGANIGRAMME DU PARTI QUEBECOIS

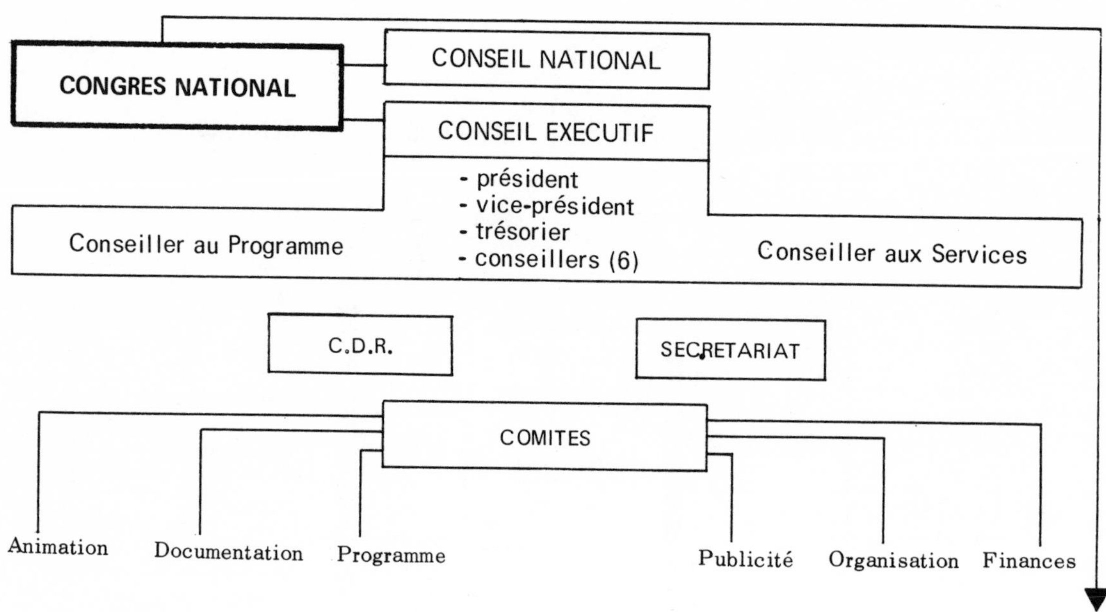

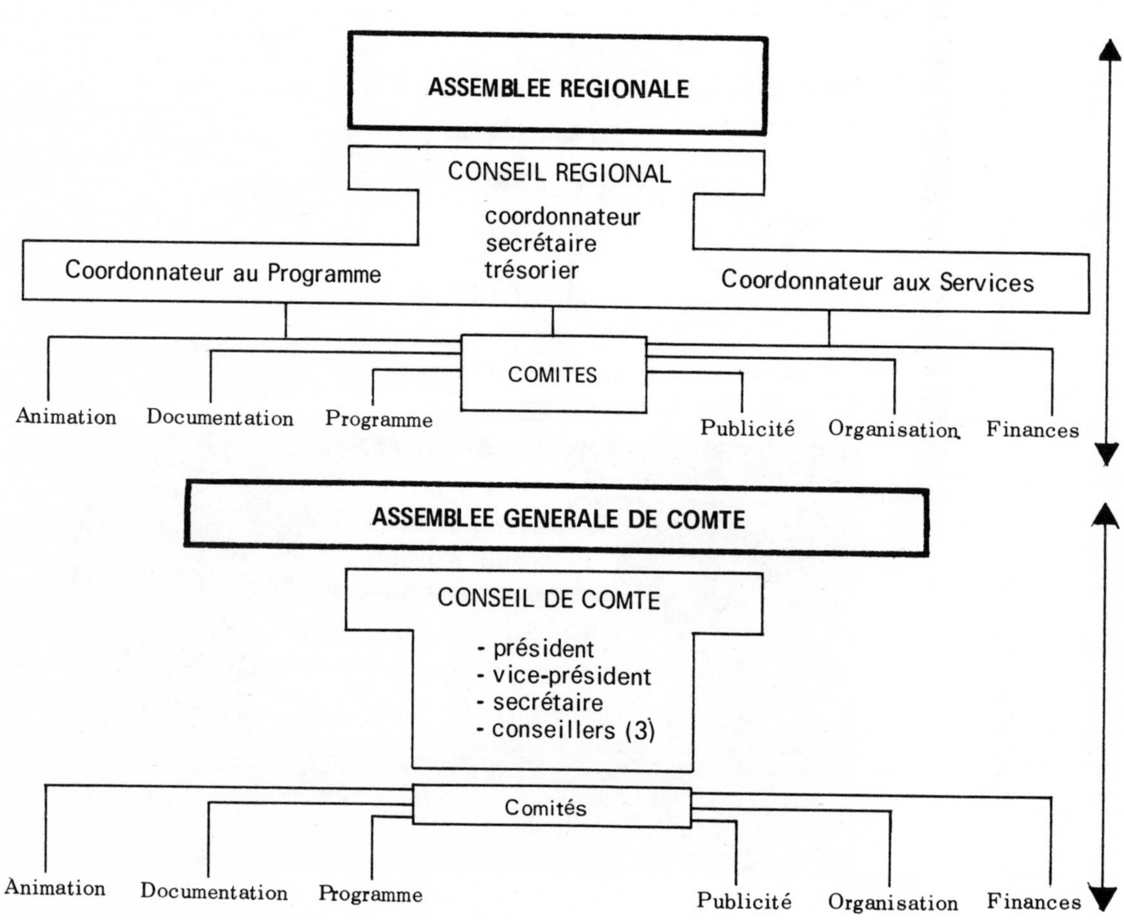

Source: Larocque, André, *Défis au Parti québécois*, Montréal, Editions du Jour, 1970.

8.1 La structure des partis politiques québécois: 3 exemples

8.1.c ORGANIGRAMME DE L'UNION NATIONALE

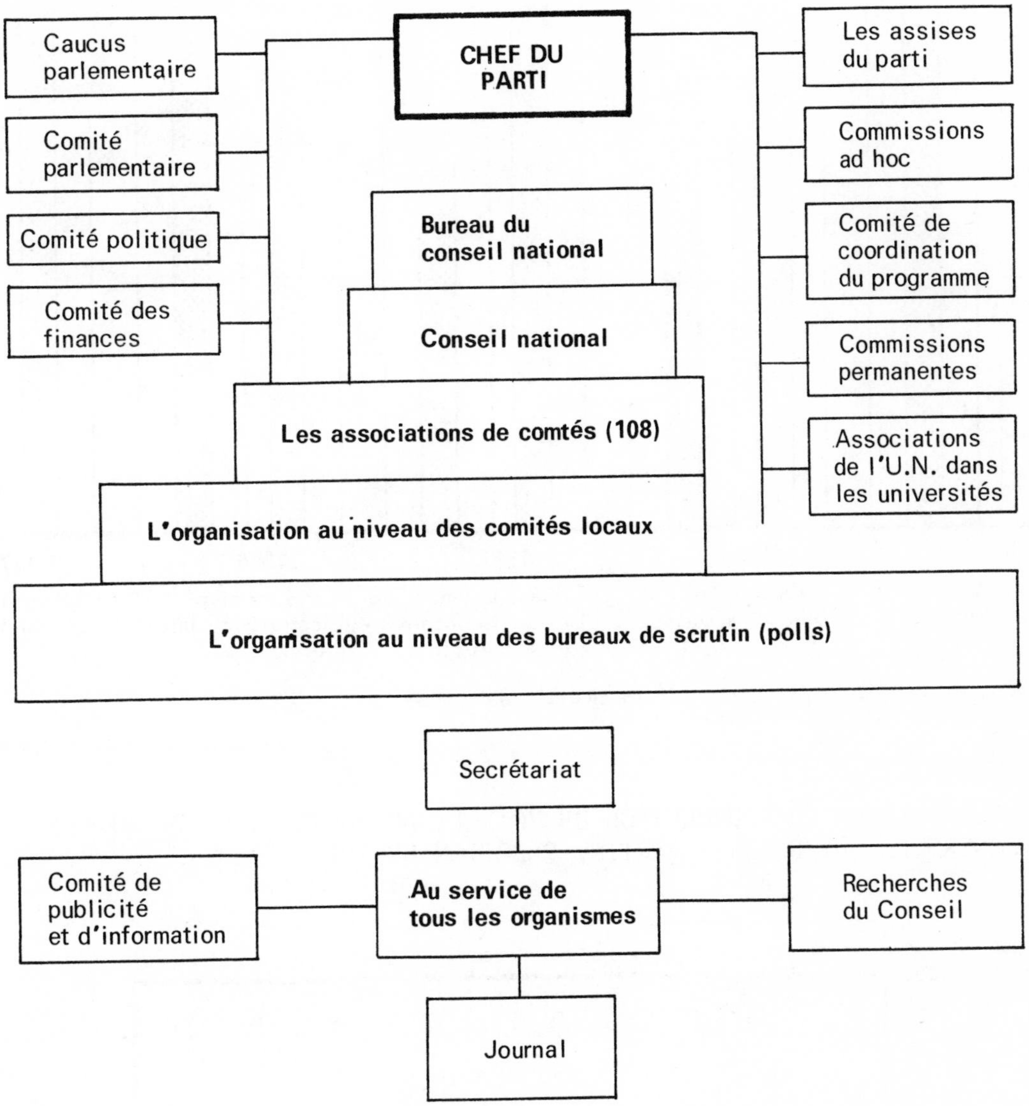

Source: Larocque, André, *Défis au Parti québécois,* Montréal, Editions du Jour, 1970.

8

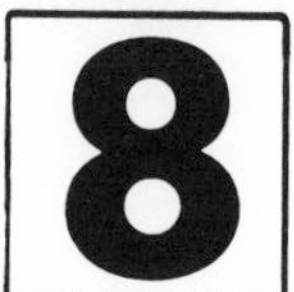

8.2 La force électorale des partis

8.2.a REPARTITION DU POURCENTAGE DE VOIX ET DU POURCENTAGE DE SIEGES ENTRE LES DEUX PRINCIPAUX PARTIS, ELECTIONS DE 1956 A 1970

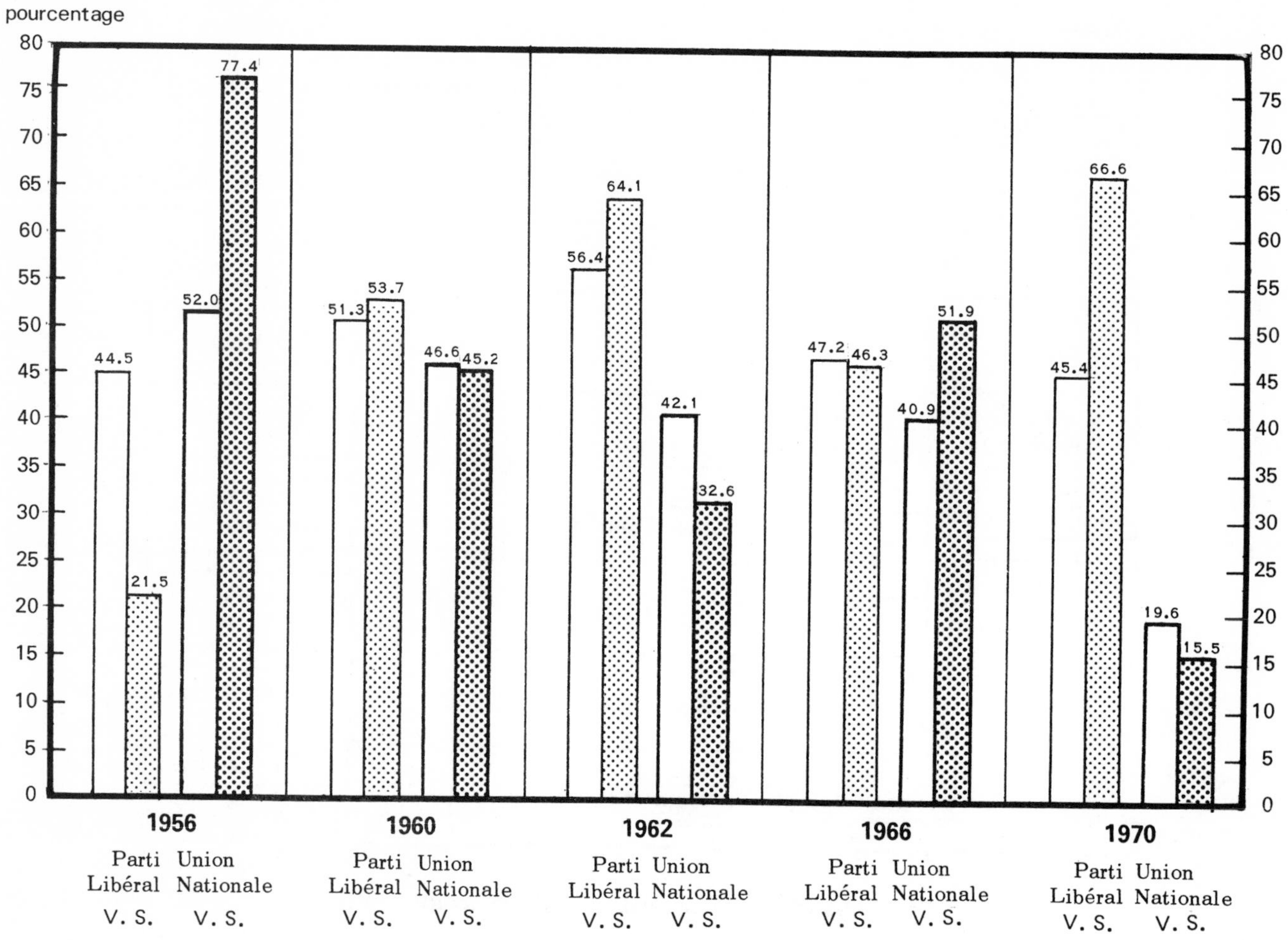

pourcentage
80 75 70 65 60 55 50 45 40 35 30 25 20 15 10 5 0
44.5
21.5
52.0
77.4
51.3
53.7
46.6
45.2
56.4
64.1
42.1
32.6
47.2
46.3
40.9
51.9
45.4
66.6
19.6
15.5
1956
Parti Libéral V. S.
Union Nationale V. S.
1960
Parti Libéral V. S.
Union Nationale V. S.
1962
Parti Libéral V. S.
Union Nationale V. S.
1966
Parti Libéral V. S.
Union Nationale V. S.
1970
Parti Libéral V. S.
Union Nationale V. S.

V. (% des voix ou suffrages obtenus), S. (% des sièges obtenus)

8.2.b REPARTITION DU POURCENTAGE DE VOIX ET DU POURCENTAGE DE SIEGES ENTRE LES DIFFERENTS PARTIS, ELECTION DE 1973.

pourcentage
100 90 80 70 60 50 40 30 20 10 0
54,5
92,7
30,1
5,5
5,1
0
10,0
1,8
Parti Libéral V. S.
Parti Québécois V. S.
Union Nationale V. S.
Ralliement Créditiste V. S.

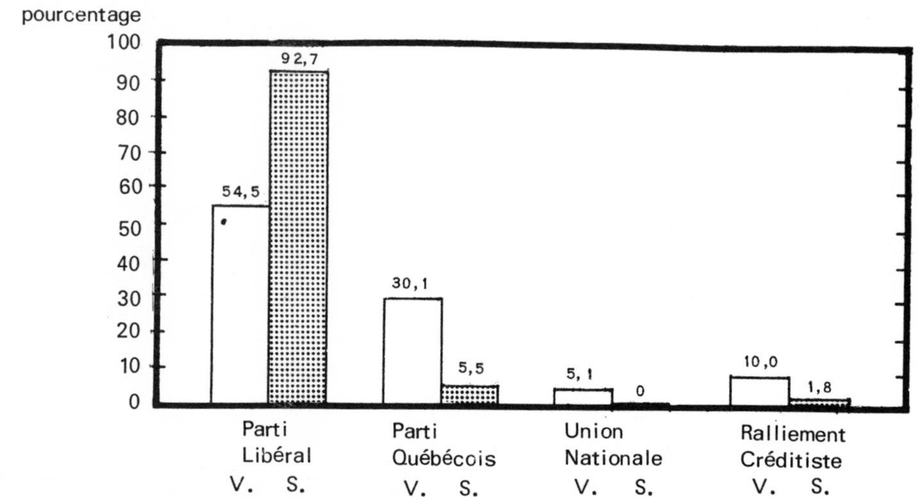

Source: *Boily Robert,* La réforme électorale, *Montréal,Editions du Jour, 1970.*

8.2 La force électorale des partis

8.2.c REPARTITION DES VOIX EXPRIMEES POUR LES DIFFERENTS PARTIS, ELECTIONS DE 1956 A 1966, PROVINCES ET MONTREAL

Année	région métropolitaine / ensemble du Québec	Parti Libéral %	Union Nationale %	Tiers-partis et indépendants %	**Total des voix** %
1956	Montréal	48.6	43.5	7.9	100
	Province	**44.4**	**51.5**	**3.7**	**100**
1960	Montréal	52.6	42.7	4.7	100
	Province	**51.4**	**46.6**	**2.0**	**100**
1962	Montréal	64.6	32.7	3.1	100
	Province	**56.4**	**42.1**	**1.5**	**100**
1966	Montréal	53.1	30.1	16.1	100
	Province	**47.2**	**40.9**	**11.9**	**100**
1970	Montréal				
	Province				

8.2.d REPARTITION DES VOIX EXPRIMEES POUR LES DIFFERENTS PARTIS, ELECTION DE 1970, PROVINCE ET MONTREAL.

Endroit (nombre / %)	Electeurs inscrits	Votes valides	**Parti Libéral**	**Union Nationale**	**Parti Québécois**	**Ralliement Créditiste**	**Autres**
Ensemble de la Province	3,478,891	2,872,970	1,304,341	564,544	662,404	321,370	20,311
	100.00	**82.58**	**45.40**	**19.65**	**23.06**	**11.19**	**0.70**
Ile de Montréal et ville Laval	1,254,893	1,005,100	568,522	103,354	297,007	22,427	13,790
	36.07	**80.09**	**56.57**	**10.29**	**29.55**	**2.23**	**1.36**
Province sans l'île de Montréal et ville Laval	2,223,998	1,867,870	735,819	461,190	365,397	298,943	6,521
	63.93	**83.98**	**39.39**	**24.69**	**19.56**	**16.01**	**0.35**

Source: *Annuaire du Québec 1972*.

8.3 Les assises sociales des partis: personnel parlementaire

8.3.a CARACTERISTIQUES DU PERSONNEL PARLEMENTAIRE, 1936-1970, QUEBEC.

Principaux caractères	1936 candidats élus	1936 %	1939 candidats élus	1939 %	1944 candidats élus	1944 %	1948 candidats élus	1948 %
Niveaux d'instruction								
primaire	19	21.8	13	15.1	19	20.8	21	22.8
secondaire	19	21.8	23	26.7	21	23.1	22	23.8
supérieur	40	46.1	40	46.6	44	48.2	38	41.4
inconnus	9	10.3	10	11.6	7	7.7	11	12.0
Total des élus (échantillon)	**87**	**100**	**85**	**100**	**91**	**100**	**92**	**100**
Types d'occupations								
Professions libérales	40	46.1	41	47.6	45	49.5	38	41.4
Semi-professionnels	1	1.1	2	2.3	1	1.1	–	–
Industriels	10	11.6	9	10.5	10	11.0	10	10.8
Commerçants	21	24.1	24	28.0	19	20.8	26	28.1
Employés et ouvriers	3	3.4	3	3.5	6	6.6	6	6.6
Cultivateurs	12	13.7	6	7.0	10	11.0	11	12.0
Inconnus	–	–	1	1.1	–	–	1	1.1
Total des élus (échantillon)	**87**	**100**	**85**	**100**	**91**	**100**	**92**	**100**
Ⓖ **Classes sociales**								
Classe moyenne supérieure	51	58.7	51	59.3	52	57.1	48	52.1
Classe moyenne inférieure	21	24.1	27	31.4	23	25.3	29	31.4
Classe ouvrière	3	3.4	2	2.3	5	5.5	4	4.5
Classe paysanne	11	12.7	–	–	10	11.0	11	12.0
Inconnus	1	1.1	–	–	1	1.1	–	–
Total des élus (échantillon)	**87**	**100**	**85**	**100**	**91**	**100**	**92**	**100**

Sources: Documents fournis par M. Robert Boily.

Lemieux, Vincent (sous la direction de), *Quatre élections provinciales au Québec: 1956-1966*, Québec, P.U.L., 1969

Principaux caractères	1952 candidats élus	1952 %	1956-66 candidats élus	1956-66 %	1966 candidats élus	1966 %	1970 candidats élus	1970 %
Niveaux d'instruction								
primaire	15	16.8	8	4.1	2	1.9	1	0.9
secondaire	20	22.5	63	31.6	29	27.8	31	28.5
supérieur	44	49.5	115	57.8	69	66.5	72	66.6
inconnus	10	11.2	13	6.5	4	3.8	4	3.7
Total des élus (échantillon)	**89**	**100**	**199**	**100**	**104**	**100**	**108**	**100**
Types d'occupations								
Professions libérales	44	49.5	105	52.7	64	61.6	50	46.3
Semi-professionnels	–	–	14	7.1	10	7.7	18	16.1
Industriels	7	7.8	26	13.1	8	9.7	10	9.2
Commerçants	23	25.9	34	17.1	15	14.4	11	10.1
Employés et ouvriers	5	5.6	5	2.5	1	0.9	12*	10.3
Cultivateurs	9	10.1	12	6.0	5	0.9	6	5.5
Inconnus	1	1.1	3	1.5	1	4.8	1	0.9
Total des élus (échantillon)	**89**	**100**	**199**	**100**	**104**	**100**	**108**	**100**
Classes sociales Ⓖ								
Classe moyenne supérieure	52	58.4	120	60.3	68	65.5	57	52.7
Classe moyenne inférieure	24	27.0	59	29.6	29	27.8	42	38.8
Classe ouvrière	3	3.4	5	2.5	6	5.8	2	1.8
Classe paysanne	9	10.1	12	6.1	–	–	6	5.5
Inconnus	1	1.1	3	1.5	1	0.9	1	0.9
Total des élus (échantillon)	**89**	**100**	**199**	**100**	**104**	**100**	**108**	**100**

* (cols bleus: 10)

8.3 Les assises sociales des partis: personnel parlementaire

8.3.b CARACTERISTIQUES DES DEPUTES LIBERAUX, 1956-1970

Principaux caractères	1956 candidats élus	%	1960 candidats élus	%	1962 candidats élus	%	1966 candidats élus	%	1970 candidats élus	%
Niveaux d'instruction										
primaire	1	5.9	–	–	1	1.6	–	–	–	–
secondaire	3	17.6	13	26.0	19	29.7	10	20.0	20	27.7
supérieur	12	70.6	32	64.0	38	59.3	38	76.0	52	72.3
inconnus	1	5.9	5	10.0	6	9.4	2	4.0	–	–
Total des élus (échantillon)	**17**	**100**	**50**	**100**	**69**	**100**	**50**	**100**	**72**	**100**
Types d'occupations										
Professions libérales	10	58.9	31	62.0	38	59.4	36	72.0	39	54.1
Semi-professionnels	2	11.8	3	6.0	2	3.1	5	10.0	12	16.6
Industriels	4	23.5	6	12.0	8	12.5	2	4.0	7	9.7
Commerçants	–	–	6	12.0	9	14.1	3	6.0	10	13.9
Employés et ouvriers	–	–	1	2.0	2	3.1	–	–	–	–
Cultivateurs	–	–	2	4.0	4	6.2	3	6.0	4	5.5
Inconnus	1	5.9	1	2.0	1	1.6	1	2.0	–	–
Total des élus (échantillon)	**17**	**100**	**50**	**100**	**69**	**100**	**50**	**100**	**72**	**100**
Classes sociales (G)										
Classe moyenne supérieure	13	76.5	39	78.0	46	71.9	39	78.0	44	61.1
Classe moyenne inférieure	3	17.6	7	14.0	12	18.7	7	14.0	23	31.9
Classe ouvrière	–	–	1	2.0	1	1.6	–	–	1	1.4
Classe paysanne	–	–	2	4.0	4	6.2	3	6.0	4	5.5
Inconnus	1	5.9	1	2.0	1	1.6	1	2.0	–	–
Total des élus (échantillon)	**17**	**100**	**50**	**100**	**69**	**100**	**50**	**100**	**72**	**100**

Sources: Documents fournis par M. Robert Boily.

Lemieux, Vincent (sous la direction de), *Quatre élections provinciales au Québec: 1956-1966,* Québec P.U.L., 1969.

8.3 Les assises sociales des partis: personnel parlemantaire

8.3.c CARACTERISTIQUES DES DEPUTES DE L'UNION NATIONALE, 1956-1970

Principaux caractères	1956 candidats élus	%	1960 candidats élus	%	1962 candidats élus	%	1966 candidats élus	%	1970 candidats élus	%
Niveaux d'instruction										
primaire	5	7.6	1	2.4	–	–	2	3.7	–	–
secondaire	23	34.8	18	43.9	12	40.0	19	35.2	3	17.6
supérieur	32	48.5	21	51.3	18	60.0	31	57.4	13	76.5
inconnus	6	9.1	1	2.4	–	–	2	3.7	1	5.9
Total des élus (échantillon)	**66**	**100**	**41**	**100**	**30**	**100**	**54**	**100**	**17**	**100**
Types d'occupations										
Professions libérales	27	40.9	17	41.5	16	53.3	28	51.9	9	52.9
Semi-professionnels	4	6.1	3	7.3	2	6.7	5	9.3	1	5.9
Industriels	9	13.6	6	14.6	3	10.0	6	11.1	1	5.9
Commerçants	13	19.7	8	19.5	6	20.0	12	22.2	3	17.6
Employés et ouvriers	3	4.6	2	4.9	1	3.3	1	1.8	1	5.9
Cultivateurs	7	10.6	5	12.2	2	6.7	2	3.7	1	5.9
Inconnus	3	4.5	–	–	–	–	–	–	1	5.9
Total des élus (échantillon)	**66**	**100**	**41**	**100**	**30**	**100**	**54**	**100**	**17**	**100**
Classes sociales Ⓖ										
Classe moyenne supérieure	30	45.4	20	48.8	18	60.0	29	53.7	10	58.8
Classe moyenne inférieure	22	33.3	14	34.1	9	30.0	22	40.7	5	29.4
Classe ouvrière	4	6.1	2	4.9	1	3:3	1	1.9	–	–
Classe paysanne	7	10.6	5	12.2	2	6.7	2	3.7	1	5.9
Inconnus	3	4.6	–	–	–	–	–	–	1	5.9
Total des élus (échantillon)	**66**	**100**	**41**	**100**	**30**	**100**	**54**	**100**	**17**	**100**

Sources: Documents fournis par M. Robert Boily.
Lemieux, Vincent (sous la direction de), *Quatre élections provinciales au Québec 1956-1966*, Québec, P.U.L., 1969.

8.4 Clientèle électorale

8.4.a INTENTION DE VOTE SELON LA LANGUE MATERNELLE AVANT L'ELECTION DE 1970, TROIS SONDAGES

Langue Ⓖ maternelle	Sondages	Parti Libéral %	Parti Québécois %	Ralliement Créditiste %	Union Nationale %
Francophones	CROP	29	36	16	18
	LE SOLEIL	35	34	14	17
	REGENSTREIF	34	30	14	20
Anglophones	CROP	64	5	13	10
	LE SOLEIL	72	16	3	10
	REGENSTREIF	76	3	3	17
Toutes catégories	**CROP**	**33**	**30**	**17**	**18**
	LE SOLEIL	**38**	**32**	**13**	**16**
	REGENSTREIF	**39**	**28**	**11**	**20**

8.4.b INTENTION DE VOTE SELON LE GROUPE D'AGE AVANT L'ELECTION DE 1970, TROIS SONDAGES

Groupe d'âge	Sondages	Parti Libéral %	Parti Québécois %	Ralliement Créditiste %	Union Nationale %
18-24 ans	CROP	34	39	11	12
	LE SOLEIL	30	49	11	10
	REGENSTREIF	30	44	9	16
25-34 ans	CROP	28	38	19	12
	LE SOLEIL	42	34	13	10
	REGENSTREIF	45	30	9	16
35-44 ans	CROP	35	24	11	25
	LE SOLEIL	39	26	13	21
35-49 ans	REGENSTREIF	41	24	14	20
45-64 ans	CROP	34	31	16	16
50-64 ans	REGENSTREIF	44	15	12	28
45-54 ans	LE SOLEIL	38	28	12	20
55-64 ans	LE SOLEIL	40	20	15	28
65 ans et plus	CROP	35	13	27	25
	LE SOLEIL	54	12	15	20
	REGENSTREIF	38	10	13	36
Toutes catégories	**CROP**	**33**	**30**	**17**	**18**
	LE SOLEIL	**38**	**32**	**13**	**16**
	REGENSTREIF	**39**	**28**	**11**	**20**

Source: Vincent Lemieux, Marcel Gilbert et André Blais, *Une élection de réalignement* Montréal, Editions du Jour, 1970.

8.4 Clientèle électorale

8.4.c INTENTION DE VOTE SELON L'OCCUPATION AVANT L'ELECTION DE 1970, DEUX SONDAGES

Sondage: LE SOLEIL

Occupation	P.L.Q.	P.Q.	R.C.	U.N.
Professionnels, cadres	47	30	3	20
cols blancs	31	46	8	13
cultivateurs, artisans, commerçants	42	4	9	35
Ouvriers spécialisés	35	30	21	14
Ouvriers non spécialisés	25	28	29	19
Ménagères	44	30	12	14
Etudiants	36	44	7	13
Chômeurs, retraités et autres	56	17	17	17
Toutes catégories	**38**	**32**	**13**	**16**

Sondage: REGENSTREIF

Occupation	P.L.Q.	P.Q.	R.C.	U.N.
Professions libérales	51	33	–	16
Cols blancs	44	38	8	8
Vendeurs	56	18	7	18
Propriétaires, gérants	38	12	15	35
Ouvriers spécialisés	36	31	18	15
Manoeuvres, journaliers	28	44	10	18
Ménagères	42	20	12	24
Autres, dont étudiants	33	40	6	20
Retraités	40	–	13	47
Cultivateurs	36	18	16	30
Toutes catégories	**39**	**28**	**11**	**20**

8.4.d INTENTION DE VOTE SELON LA SCOLARITE AVANT L'ELECTION DE 1970, TROIS SONDAGES

Sondage: CROP

Scolarité	P.L.Q.	P.Q.	R.C.	U.N.
0 - 7	36	20	27	17
8 - 12	30	35	14	17
13 et plus	37	42	4	15
Toutes catégories	**33**	**30**	**17**	**18**

Sondage: LE SOLEIL

Scolarité	P.L.Q.	P.Q.	R.C.	U.N.
0 - 7	42	24	18	16
8 - 12	41	29	13	16
13 - 15	28	48	10	14
16 et plus	35	35	8	22
Toutes catégories	**38**	**32**	**13**	**16**

Sondage: REGENSTREIF

Scolarité	P.L.Q.	P.Q.	R.C.	U.N.
Elémentaire (non complet)	34	12	19	30
Elémentaire (complet)	40	19	15	26
Secondaire (non complet)	28	34	12	25
Secondaire (complet)	50	25	8	16
Ecole Technique	38	52	1	7
Université	54	26	3	16
Toutes catégories	**39**	**28**	**11**	**20**

Source: Vincent Lemieux, Marcel Gilbert et André Blais, *Une élection de réalignement*, Montréal, Editions du Jour, 1970.

8.5 Organisation et effectifs des syndicats

8.5.a STRUCTURES DE LA CONFEDERATION DES SYNDICATS NATIONAUX (CSN)

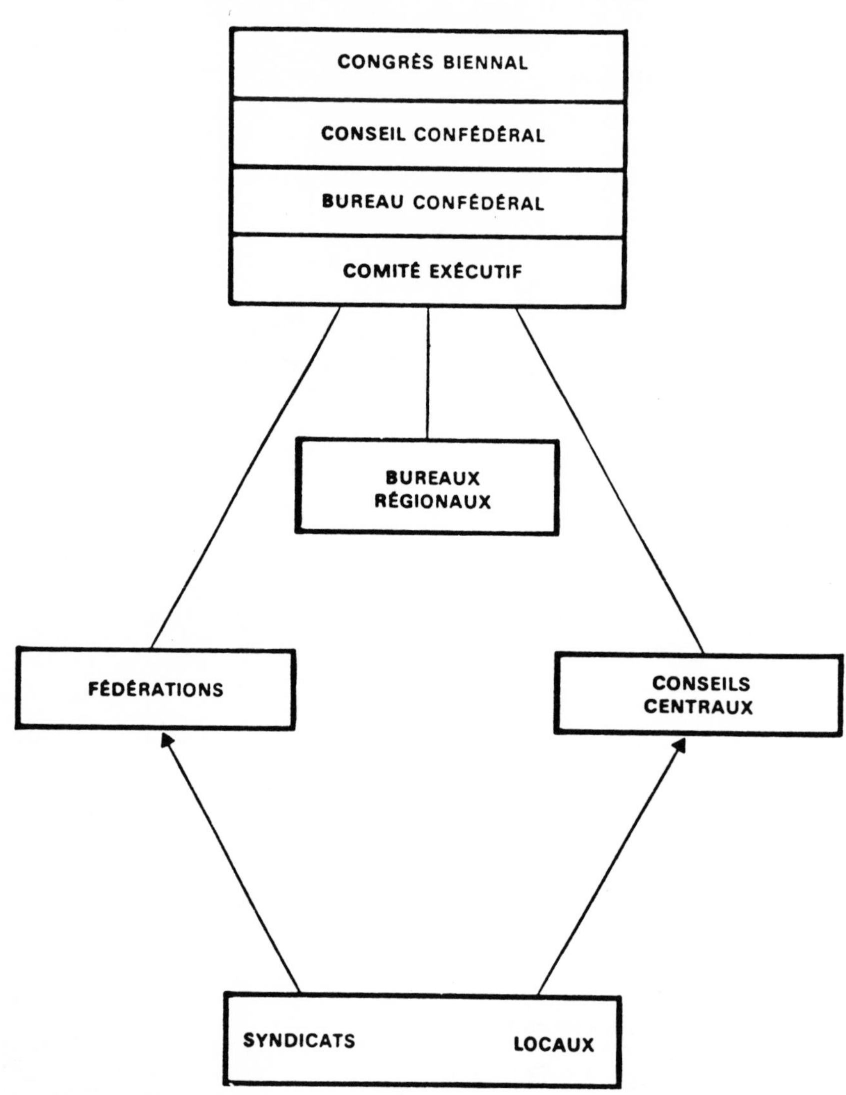

Source: Document fourni par M. Léo Roback

8.5 Organisation et effectifs des syndicats

8.5.b STRUCTURES DU SYNDICALISME (G) INTERNATIONAL AU CANADA

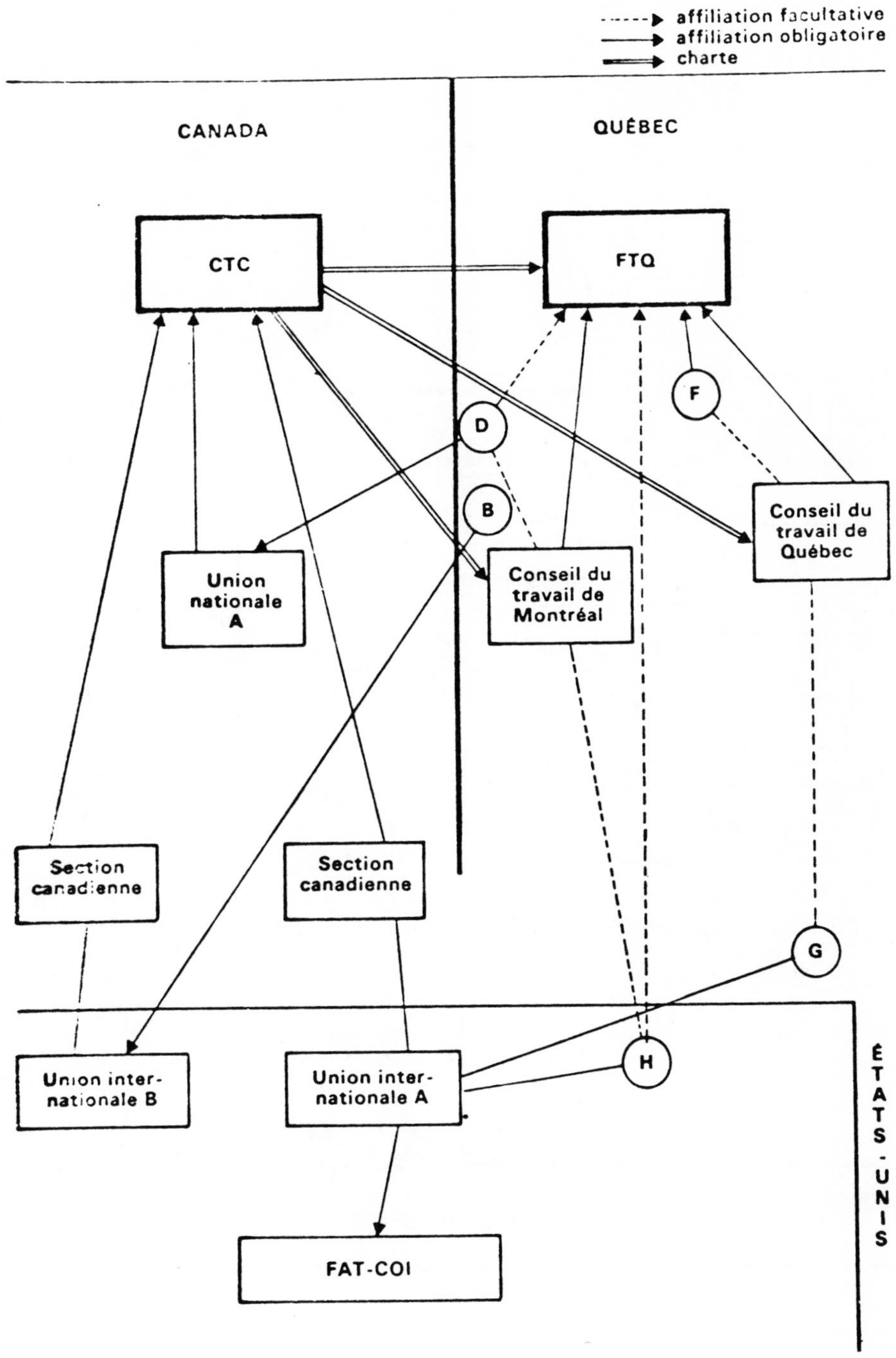

Source: Document fourni par M. Léo Roback

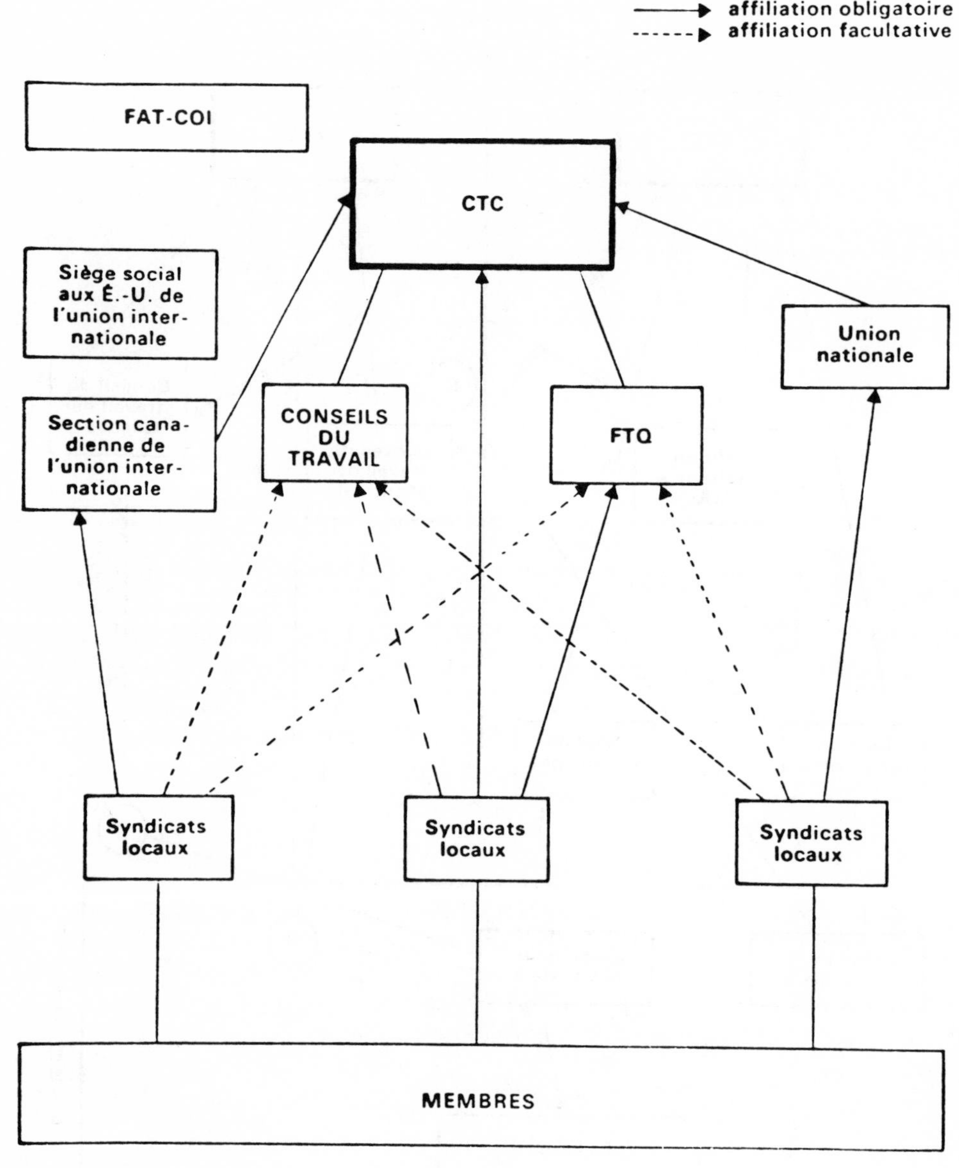

affiliation obligatoire
affiliation facultative
FAT-COI
CTC
Siège social aux É.-U. de l'union internationale
Section canadienne de l'union internationale
CONSEILS DU TRAVAIL
FTQ
Union nationale
Syndicats locaux
Syndicats locaux
Syndicats locaux
MEMBRES

8.5 Organisation et effectifs des syndicats

8.5.c STRUCTURES DE LA FEDERATION DES TRAVAILLEURS DU QUEBEC (FTQ)

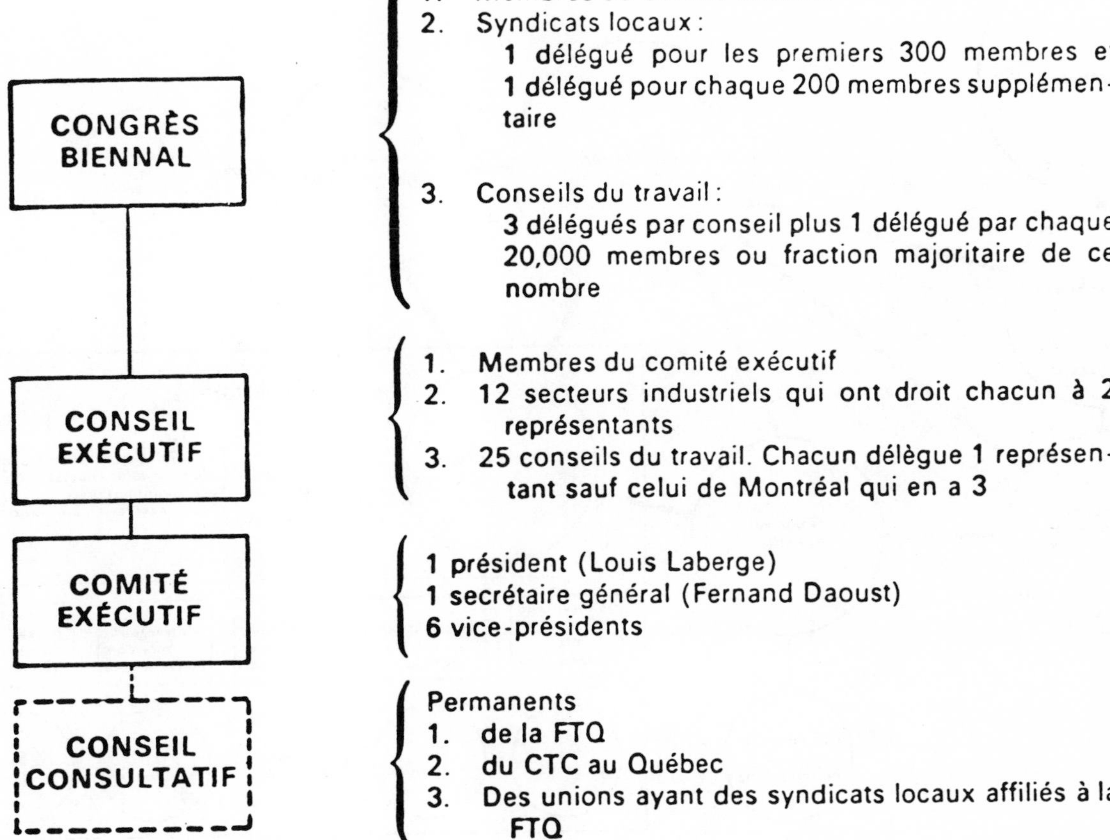

Source: Document fourni par M. Léo Roback

8.5.d STRUCTURES DE LA CORPORATION DES ENSEIGNANTS DU QUEBEC (CEQ)

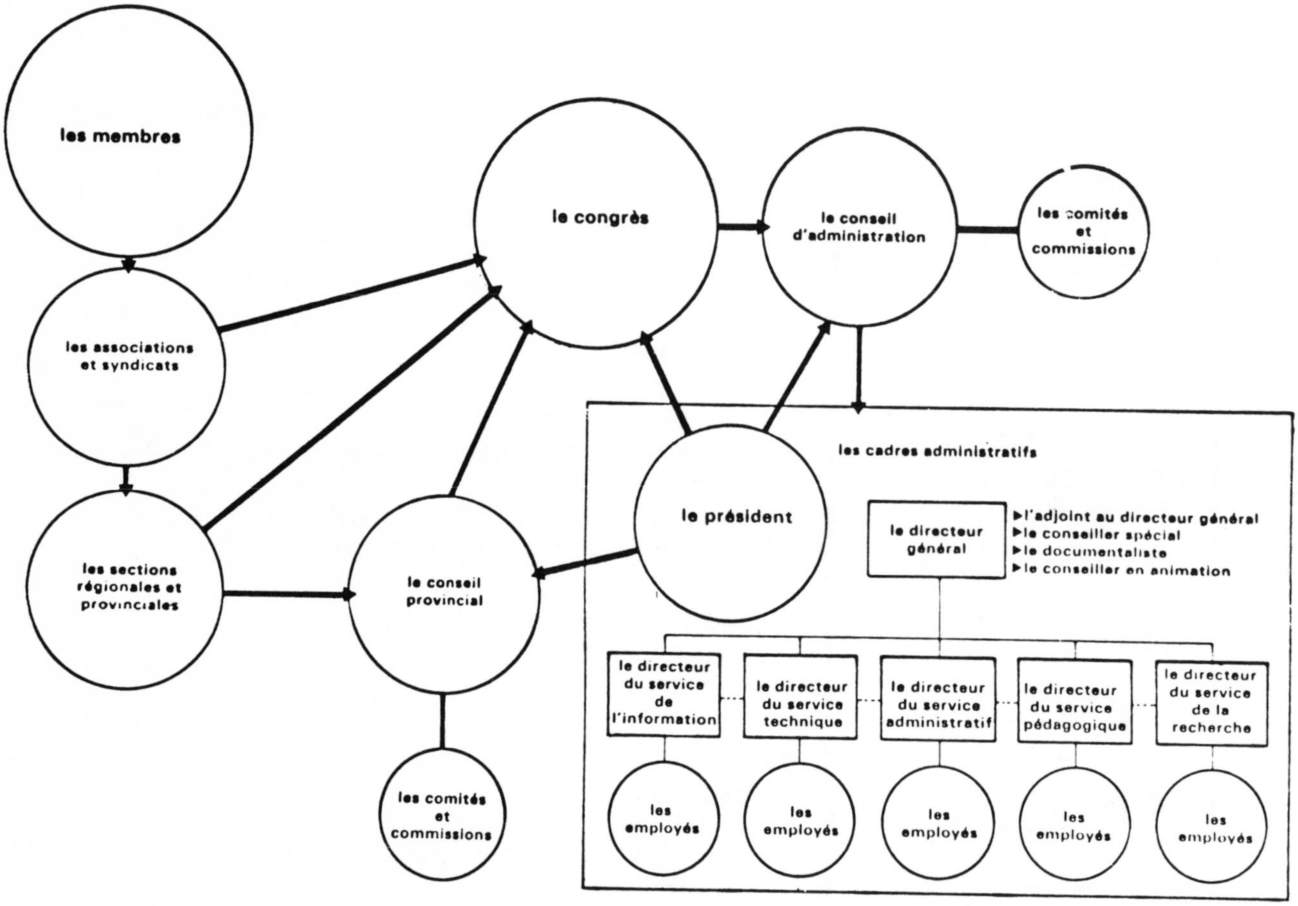

les membres

le congrès

le conseil d'administration

les comités et commissions

les associations et syndicats

les cadres administratifs

le président

le directeur général

▶l'adjoint au directeur général
▶le conseiller spécial
▶le documentaliste
▶le conseiller en animation

les sections régionales et provinciales

le conseil provincial

le directeur du service de l'information

le directeur du service technique

le directeur du service administratif

le directeur du service pédagogique

le directeur du service de la recherche

les comités et commissions

les employés

les employés

les employés

les employés

les employés

Source: Document fourni par M. Léo Roback

8.5 Organisation et effectifs des syndicats

8.5.e CROISSANCE DES EFFECTIFS SYNDICAUX Ⓖ, QUEBEC, ONTARIO, CANADA, 1921-1972

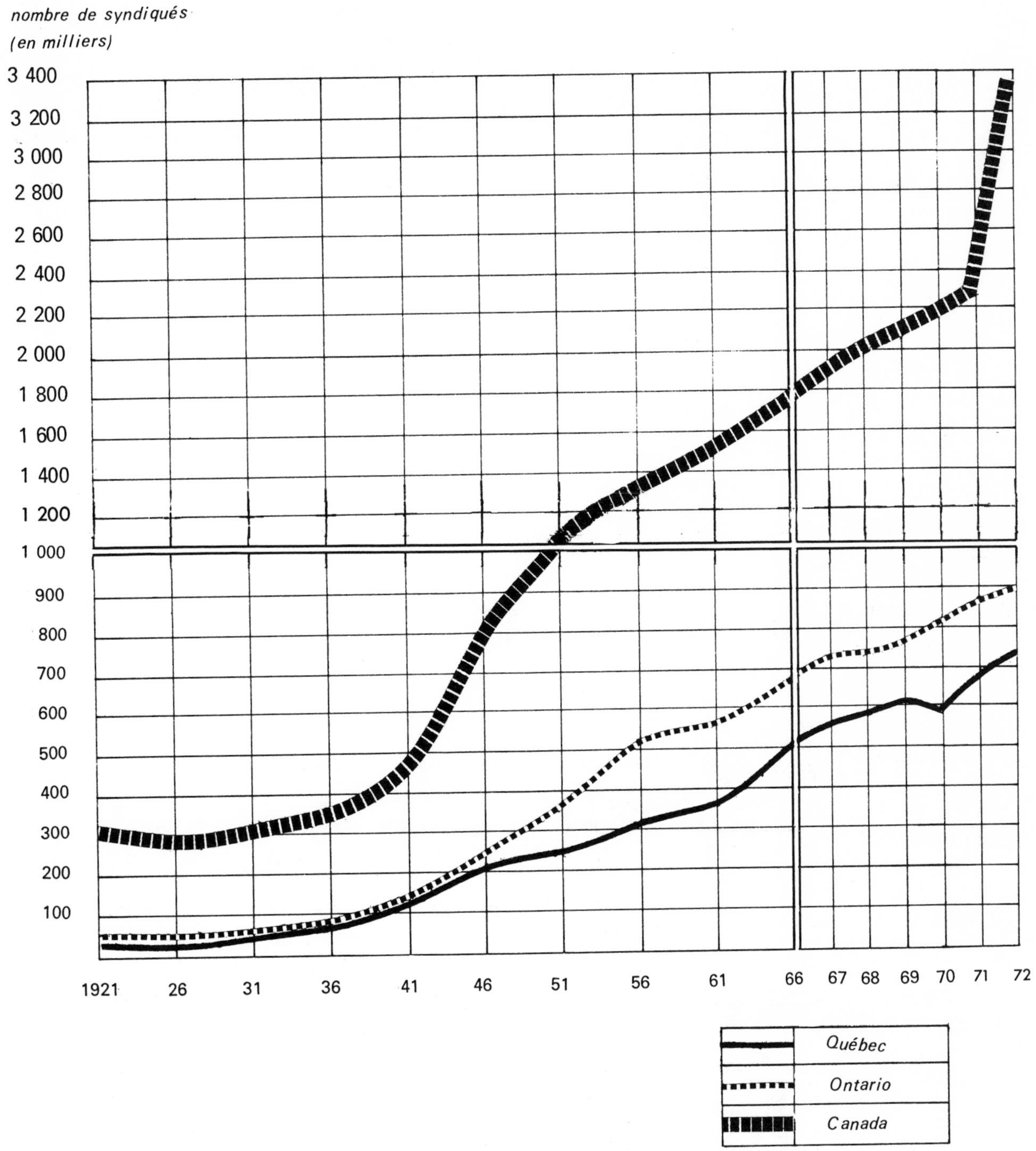

Sources: Statistique-Canada, Rapport de 1971, CALURA partie II (Corporation and Labours Act), Canada.

Labour organizations in Canada, Ministère de la Main-d'oeuvre et de l'Immigration, Ottawa.

8.5 Organisation et effectifs des syndicats

8.5.f TAUX DE SYNDICALISATION Ⓖ, QUEBEC, 1961-1968

Année	Taux de syndicalisation (syndiqués / main-d'oeuvre) %
1961	25.6
1962	24.9
1963	27.3
1964	29.0
1965	31.2
1966	32.4
1967	32.1
1968	39.1

8.5.g EFFECTIFS SYNDICAUX Ⓖ SELON LE SECTEUR Ⓖ ECONOMIQUE ET LA CENTRALE D'AFFILIATION, QUEBEC, 1968.

Centrale	# syndiqués / **pourcentage**	Primaire	Secondaire	Construction	Tertiaire
C.T.C.	# syndiqués	928	26,954	6,387	70,451
	pourcentage	**1.5**	**5.2**	**7.8**	**6.5**
F.T.Q.	# syndiqués	12,607	122,622	20,388	59,409
	pourcentage	**19.7**	**23.5**	**24.8**	**5.4**
C.S.N.	# syndiqués	4,081	66,116	20,082	128,105
	pourcentage	**6.4**	**12.7**	**24.4**	**11.9**
T.A.T.	# syndiqués	881	4,350	–	5,790
	pourcentage	**1.4**	**.8**	–	**1.5**
I N D.	# syndiqués	9,601	24,675	–	118,734
	pourcentage	**15.0**	**4.7**	–	**11.0**
Total	# syndiqués	28,098	244,717	46,857	382,489
	pourcentage	**44.0**	**47.0**	**56.9**	**35.3**

Source: *Québec-Travail*, Ministère du Travail, Québec, 1972.

8.5.h TAUX DE SYNDICALISATION Ⓖ SELON L'INDUSTRIE Ⓖ ET LE SECTEUR Ⓖ ECONOMIQUE, QUEBEC, 1968

Secteur (industrie)	**Taux de syndicalisation** $\left(\frac{\text{syndiqués}}{\text{main-d'oeuvre}}\right)$ %
Primaire	
Agriculture	.8
Forêt	78.5
Mines et carrières	47.9
Primaire	**44.0**
Secondaire	
Aliments et boissons	35.2
Tabac	78.2
Cuir	47.0
Caoutchouc	60.0
Textiles	53.0
Bonneterie	12.8
Vêtements	56.3
Bois	30.0
Meubles	31.9
Pâtes et papiers	72.9
Imprimerie	33.4
Prod. métalliques primaires	68.0
Prod. du métal	32.9
Machinerie	45.0
Equipement de transport	53.6
Prod. électriques	64.3
Prod. minéraux non métalliques	56.9
Pétrole	37.8
Produits chimiques	28.2
Manufactures diverses	19.1
Secondaire	**47.0**
Construction	**56.9**
Tertiaire	
Services commerciaux	0.5
Commerce de détail	19.9
Commerce de gros	1.7
Services personnels	3.9
Finances	2.4
Administration publique	61.4
Education	96.8
Communications	70.1
Services récréatifs	50.9
Transports	47.9
Santé	40.7
Services divers	
Tertiaire	**35.3**

Source: *Québec-Travail,* Ministère du Travail, Québec, 1972.

8.5 Organisation et effectifs des syndicats

8.5.i EFFECTIFS SYNDICAUX Ⓖ SELON LES SECTEURS Ⓖ ET CERTAINES INDUSTRIES Ⓖ, QUEBEC, 1968

Secteurs	Industries	Nombre de salariés	Effectifs syndicaux	Effectifs syndicaux — Nombre de salariés	Taux de syndicalisation du secteur
				%	%
Primaire	Forêts	20,100	16,864	83.9	
	Mines, carrières et puits de pétrole	25,400	12,237	48.1	63.9
Secondaire	Fabrication (manufacture)	515,500	229,755	44.5	
Construction	Construction	82,400	48,064	58.3	46.4
Tertiaire	Transports, communications et services d'utilité publique	175,800	95,680	54.4	
	Commerce	244,700	47,673	19.4	
	Finances, assurances et immeuble	79,100	1,707	2.1	
	Services communautaires, commerciaux et personnels	451,700	170,577 (1)	37.7	
	Administration publique (fédérale, provinciale et municipale)	131,898	73,181	55.4	35.8
Total		1,726,598	695,738	40	

(1) Le chiffre d'« Effectif des syndicats par industrie au Québec » correspondant à cette catégorie est de 80,577. Cependant il ne comprenait pas le secteur de l'enseignement. Nous évaluons à environ 90,000 les effectifs de la CEQ, la PAPT, la PACT, le SPE et les syndicats des CEGEP.

Source: Document fourni par M. Léo Roback

8.5 Organisation et effectifs des syndicats

8.5.j EMPLOYES COUVERTS PAR CONVENTION COLLECTIVE, SELON L'OCCUPATION ET CERTAINES INDUSTRIES Ⓖ, QUEBEC, 1968

		Cols blancs			Cols bleus			Total		
Secteurs	Industries	Nombre d'employés	Employés couverts par conv. coll.	%	Nombre d'employés	Employés couverts par conv. coll.	%	Nombre d'employés	Employés couverts par conv. coll.	%
Primaire	Mines, carrières et puits de pétrole	4,716	283	6	17,968	15,452	86	22,684	15,735	69.3
Secondaire	Fabrication	95,800	12,454	13	289,282	202,497	70	385,082	214,951	55.8
Tertiaire	Transports et communications	35,513	13,495	38	42,244	38,864	92	77,757	52,359	67.3
	Commerce	28,898	1,156	4	37,535	9,383	25	66,433	10,539	15.8
	Finances, assurances et immeuble	48,292	966	2	3,954	356	9	52,246	1,322	2.5
	Services sociaux, commerciaux, industriels et personnels	81,439	33,390	41	135,198	70,303	52	216,637	103,693	47.8
	Administration publique	54,873	43,898	80	35,354	24,747	70	90,227	68,645	76.0
Total		349,531	105,642	30.3	561,535	361,602	64.3	911,066	467,244	51.2

Source: Document fourni par M. Léo Roback

8.5 Organisation et effectifs des syndicats

8.5.k EFFECTIFS SYNDICAUX (G) SELON LE TYPE D'UNION ET LA NATURE DE L'AFFILIATION, CANADA, 1968

Type d'unions	Nature de l'affiliation	Nombre d'unions	Nombre de syndicats locaux	Effectifs	%
Unions inter-nationales	FAT-COI/CTC	85	4,321	1,110,921	51.1
	CTC seulement	6	254	143,781	6.6
	FAT-COI seulement	5	9	549	
	Non affiliées	6	304	104,095	4.8
Unions nationales	CTC	19	2,679	362,592	16.7
	CSN	12	1,003	207,083	9.5
	Non affiliées	33	755	182,698	8.4
Syndicats locaux directement affiliés	au CTC		133	14,949	0.7
	à la CSN		4	289	
Syndicats locaux indépendants			131	46,140	2.1
Total		166	9,593	2,173,107	100.0

Source: Document fourni par M. Léo Roback

8.5 Organisation et effectifs des syndicats

8.5.1 EFFECTIFS DE LA CONFEDERATION DES SYNDICATS NATIONAUX (CSN), 1968

Fédération	Syndicats locaux	Effectifs
Bâtiment et bois	122	39,532
Commerce	127	16,469
Enseignants	25	3,371
Fonctionnaires provinciaux	1	31,740
Imprimerie et information	25	3,503
Ingénieurs et cadres	18	3,777
Métallurgie, mines et produits chimiques	140	34,637
Pâtes et papiers, forêts	55	10,839
Services (Hôpitaux)	210	55,625
Services publics	207	26,306
Textile	41	8,982
Vêtement	45	8,635
Syndicats affiliés directement à la CSN	5	949
Total	1,021	244,365

Source: Document fourni par M. Léo Roback

8.5 Organisation et effectifs des syndicats

8.5.m EFFECTIFS DE LA CORPORATION DES ENSEIGNANTS DU QUEBEC (CEQ), 1968

Sections ou fédérations	Associations	Effectifs
Fédération des Enseignants Gaspésiens – Madelinots	3	1,505
Fédération des Enseignants du Saguenay – Lac St-Jean	4	4,856
Fédération des Enseignants de Québec	11	10,999
Ass. des Inst. et Inst. de la banlieue de Québec	1	1,700
Section Mauricie – Nicolet	6	6,307
Section de l'Estrie	1	2,810
Fédération des Enseignants de Champlain	9	9,117
Fédération des Enseignants de l'Île de Montréal	7	4,388
Alliance des Professeurs de Montréal	1	10,290
Fédération des Enseignants de Laval	9	6,004
Fédération Laurentienne des Enseignants	3	3,206
Fédération des Enseignants de l'Ouest du Québec	5	2,978
Fédération des Enseignants du Nord-Ouest du Québec	1	2,888
Fédération des Enseignants du Golfe – Côte-Nord	3	1,342
Fédération des Enseignants de la Mitis	3	2,154
Fédération provinciale des CEGEP		1,077
Fédération des services personnels aux étudiants		150
Association Professionnelle des cadres scolaires		275
Association des enseignants retraités		1,100
Total	67	73,137

Source: Document fourni par M. Léo Roback

8.6 Organisation et effectifs des syndicats

8.6.a EVOLUTION HISTORIQUE DU SYNDICALISME

Les débuts du syndicalisme au Québec remontent assez loin. On considère que la première organisation proprement syndicale fut celle des imprimeurs à Québec, fondée en 1827. À partir de cette date, plusieurs syndicats se sont formés parmi les métiers reconnus de l'époque, notamment chez les typographes, les charpentiers-menuisiers, les tailleurs, les maçons-briqueteurs et autres. Il s'agit, bien entendu, de groupements locaux, sans affiliation, et le plus souvent de courte vie. Les activités de ces premiers syndicats étaient centrées surtout sur la réglementation des salaires et des heures de travail et sur les services dits de « mutualité » (prestations de maladie et de décès).

C'est à partir des années 1850 que le syndicalisme commença à se donner des assises plus durables, même si le statut juridique des syndicats devait demeurer fort ambigu jusqu'en 1872, lorsque le Parlement du Canada légiféra pour expliciter qu'une association ouvrière ne pourrait plus être considérée comme une « coalition illégale ». Ce « certificat de citoyenneté » donna une forte impulsion aux activités déjà en cours pour créer des organisations syndicales solides, permanentes, structurées. Un certain nombre des syndicats était déjà affilié aux jeunes unions internationales fondées aux États-Unis. Vers les années 1880 de nombreux syndicats locaux existaient déjà dans les principales villes du pays, regroupant les métiers classiques. À ces organisations de travailleurs professionnels s'ajoutaient les Chevaliers du Travail, mouvement né aux États-Unis après la Guerre Civile et qui connut un essor rapide durant les années '80 et un déclin aussi subit. À la différence des syndicats de métier (qui devaient fonder la Fédération américaine du travail au début des années '80) les Chevaliers du Travail recrutèrent les travailleurs non qualifiés (« le travail ») aussi bien que les professionnels (« les métiers ») et les deux catégories se retrouvaient dans la même structure territoriale (l'assemblée locale).

Bien qu'étant en concurrence, les deux types d'organisations syndicales collaborèrent ensemble pour créer des structures « horizontales », soit des conseils des métiers et du travail au niveau des villes, et surtout le Congrès des métiers et du travail du Canada.

Les différences structurelles entre les syndicats de métier et les assemblées des Chevaliers du Travail reflétaient, en effet, une divergence fondamentale entre les deux sur le plan des objectifs et les modes d'action. Les syndicats de métier, dès leurs débuts, étaient préoccupés par la défense et la promotion des intérêts économico-professionnels (salaires, conditions de travail, sécurité de l'emploi) de leurs membres — les travailleurs professionnels étant considérés comme les seuls « syndicables » — *à l'intérieur du système socio-économique existant*. Il s'agissait « de contrôler l'offre de travail en même temps que de transiger avec les employeurs en utilisant la pression économique ».[1] D'où la préférence accordée à l'action économique (négociation collective et grève) plutôt qu'à l'action politique. D'où aussi la nécessité de construire des organisations fortement structurées, dotées de ressources financières adéquates, à même des cotisations élevées.

L'Ordre des Chevaliers du Travail, par contre, était *réformiste* dans ses objectifs, s'inspirant d'une idéologie à la fois plus « radicale » et « conservatrice » que celle des syndicats de métier. Les Chevaliers du Travail, loin de vouloir insérer les travailleurs de plain-pied dans le système industriel capitaliste, afin d'en profiter au maximum, refusaient le système, préconisant l'abolition du salariat et une économie fondée sur l'artisanat, la petite entreprise, et les coopératives de production et de consommation. Ces objectifs, qui impliquaient une communauté d'intérêts entre employeurs et travailleurs, privilégiaient l'éducation et l'action politique, plus que l'action économique centrée autour de la négociation collective et la mise sur place de relations du travail durables pour réglementer les conditions de travail.

---

(1) L.-M. Tremblay, œuvre citée, p. 93.

Source: Document fourni par M. Léo Roback

L'orientation globale des Chevaliers du Travail envers le système socio-économique n'est pas sans rappeler sur certains aspects, celle des premiers syndicats catholiques au Québec, bien que d'inspiration doctrinale très différente et provenant du contexte des États-Unis du XIXe siècle. Ce n'est pas, peut-être, par pur hasard que les premiers syndicats catholiques québécois (parmi les travailleurs de la chaussure à Québec en 1901) avaient fait partie auparavant, de l'assemblée locale des Chevaliers du Travail.

Au cours de son évolution depuis le début du siècle, le syndicalisme catholique au Québec (CTCC de 1921 à 1960, CSN depuis 1960) a traversé diverses étapes. À ses débuts, la CTCC était un mouvement réformiste, se donnant pour objectif d'« épurer » les institutions syndicales au Québec de la neutralité confessionnelle et du matérialisme des unions internationales. Le syndicalisme catholique à l'époque se définissait comme un élément intégrant et important de l'« apostolat social » visant à instaurer une société chrétienne, contre les vices du libéralisme économique et des valeurs matérialistes. Dans cette première phase (jusqu'aux années '30) le syndicalisme catholique affichait surtout un caractère *para-syndical*. Se remettant sur pied après le creux de la « Crise », la CTCC entra lentement dans la deuxième phase de son évolution, soit celle d'une expansion des effectifs, notamment dans les secteurs industriels en dehors de Montréal (pâtes et papiers, textile, amiante, bâtiment, chaussure, métallurgie). Cette expansion s'accompagnait d'un nouvel accent sur l'action économico-professionnelle, y compris un certain nombre de grèves d'envergure, comme celles de Sorel en 1936 et de la Dominion Textile en 1937. C'est dans cette période que la *fédération* (structure verticale axée sur l'action économique) supplante le *conseil central* (structure horizontale ayant comme fonction primordiale l'éducation et autres activités para-professionnelles, voire même para-syndicales) comme la structure principale.

Avec l'adoption de la Loi des relations ouvrières du Québec, en 1944 et la montée au pouvoir d'un nouveau type de leadership en 1946, la CTCC devait évoluer encore plus rapidement dans le sens de la « maturité syndicale », pour devenir plus aggressive sur le plan de l'action revendicative, même au prix d'un affrontement croissant avec le pouvoir politique.

Le processus de déconfessionnalisation fut amorcé en 1943 et achevé, à toutes fins pratiques en 1960 avec l'adoption du nouveau nom (confédération des syndicats nationaux). À la fin de la « révolution tranquille », la CSN ressemblait au syndicalisme nord-américain en ce qui concerne la nature des objectifs professionnels, la priorité accordée à ceux-ci et les méthodes pour les atteindre. La CSN se distinguait des autres syndicats aux États-Unis et au Canada principalement par son engagement idéologique chrétien qui informait, inspirait et justifiait sa stratégie.

Depuis 1967, la CSN semble entrer dans une autre phase de son évolution. D'abord, l'expansion spectaculaire des effectifs s'arrête. Si la CSN a plus que doublé ses effectifs entre 1960 et 1966-1967 (augmentation de 110% entre 1960 et 1966, et de 140% de 1960 et 1967), les années qui suivirent, accusent un bilan peu dynamique (une hausse de 8% entre 1967 et 1970).(1)

Deuxièmement, la croissance si rapide de 1960-1966 eut lieu largement dans le secteur public, notamment dans les hôpitaux, la fonction publique provinciale et les services municipaux et éducatifs. Or, c'est précisément dans ce secteur, où le syndicat doit transiger avec un employeur qui est en même temps législateur et administrateur de la chose publique. Les tactiques traditionnelles de la négociation collective s'avèrent moins efficaces, voire même non-utilisables. La négociation collective *décentralisée* du secteur privé qui permet aux syndicats de faire valoir une force économique ou conjonctive favorable dans une entreprise donnée est supplantée par un système *centralisé*, du côté patronal, caractérisé par une grande uniformité des positions patronales devant les différents syndicats représentant les salariés des divers sous-secteurs publics.

Quoi qu'il en soit, la CSN de 1971 semble se diriger vers une nouvelle prise de conscience et une remise en question de ses stratégies. Il ne s'agit pas, bien entendu, d'un « tout ou rien », d'un choix net entre les objectifs professionnels et para-professionnels et ceux visant la société globale. L'enjeu du débat porte plutôt sur les priorités à accorder aux divers ordres d'objectifs, et portant sur l'affectation des ressources.

---

(1) R. Parent, Rapport du secrétaire général au 44e Congrès de la CSN, Montréal 1970.

8.7 Activités des syndicats: les conflits de travail

8.7.a DUREE Ⓖ EN JOURS-HOMMES DES GREVES ET LOCK-OUTS PAR JURIDICTION Ⓖ

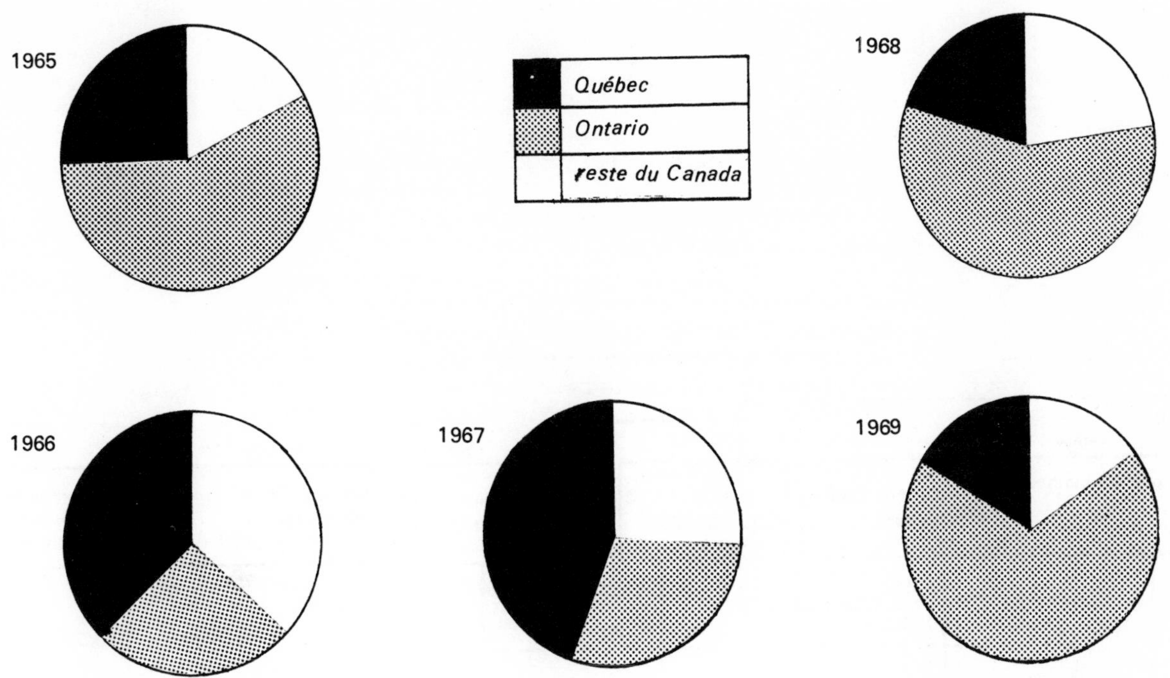

8.7.b GREVES ET LOCK-OUTS PAR INDUSTRIE Ⓖ, QUEBEC, 1970

Industrie	Grèves et lock-outs déclarés dans l'année	Grèves et lock-outs en cours durant l'année		
		Grèves et lock-outs	Travailleurs en cause	Durée en jours-homme
Agriculture	–	–	–	–
Exploitation forestière	1	1	103	5 970
Pêche et piégeage	–	–	–	–
Mines	6	6	3 859	20 090
Industrie manufacturière	73	73	13 951	327 820
Construction	8	8	2 176	35 650
Transport et services publics	9	9	7 877	31 160
Commerce	11	12	948	19,860
Finance	1	1	227	1 140
Services	15	15	12 816	107 300
Administration publique	9	9	6 790	54 130
Total	133	134	48 747	603 120

Source: Strikes and Lockouts in Canada 1971, Ministère du Travail, Canada,

8.8 Les mass-media

8.8.a ORGANIGRAMME DES ENTREPRISES PRATTE, BARIBEAU ET LEPAGE

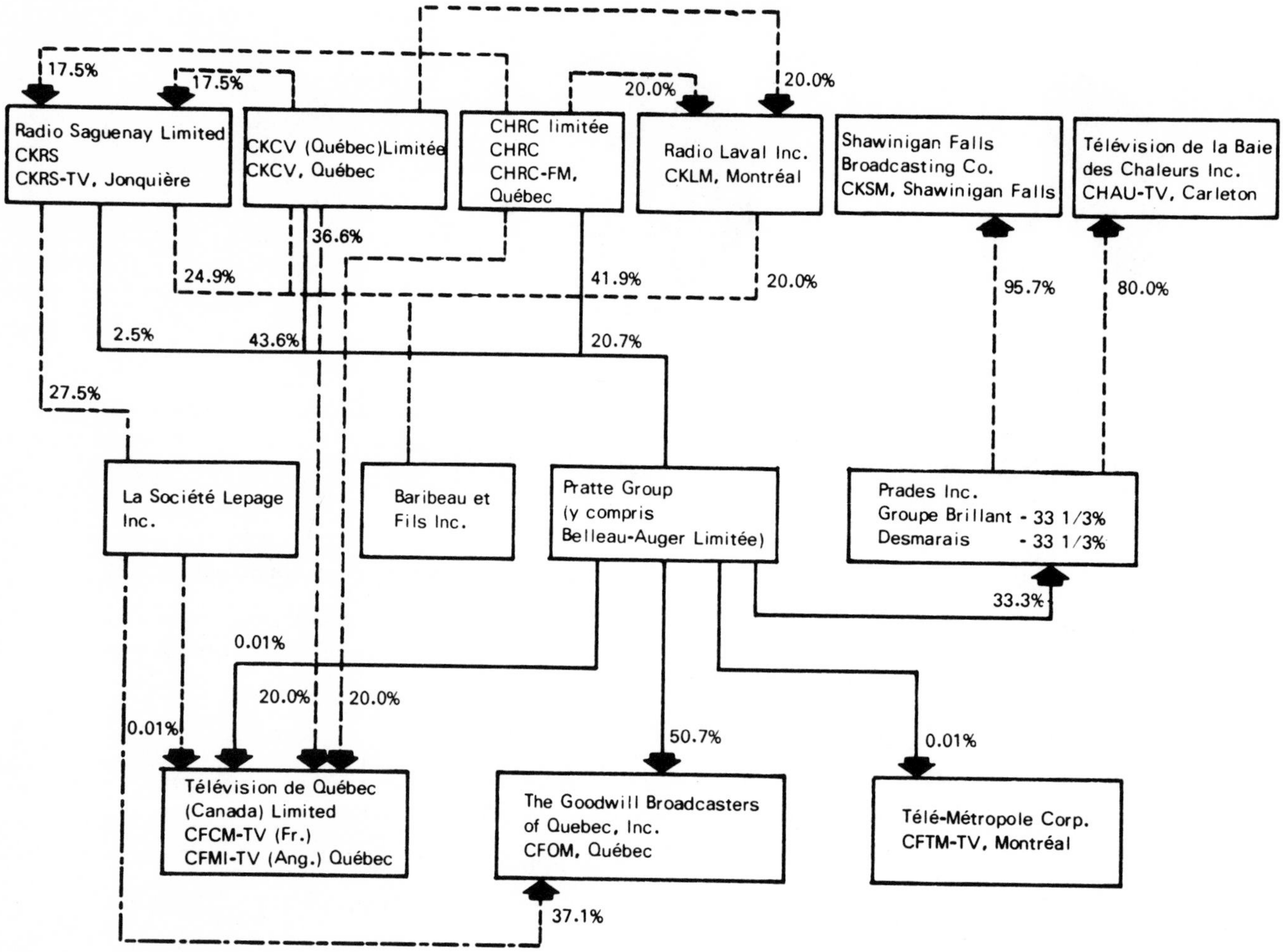

Source: Rapport de la Commission Davis, *Les mots, la musique et les sous*, Ottawa, 1970.

8.8 Les mass-media

8.8.b ORGANIGRAMME DES ENTREPRISES DESMARAIS, PARISIEN ET FRANCOEUR

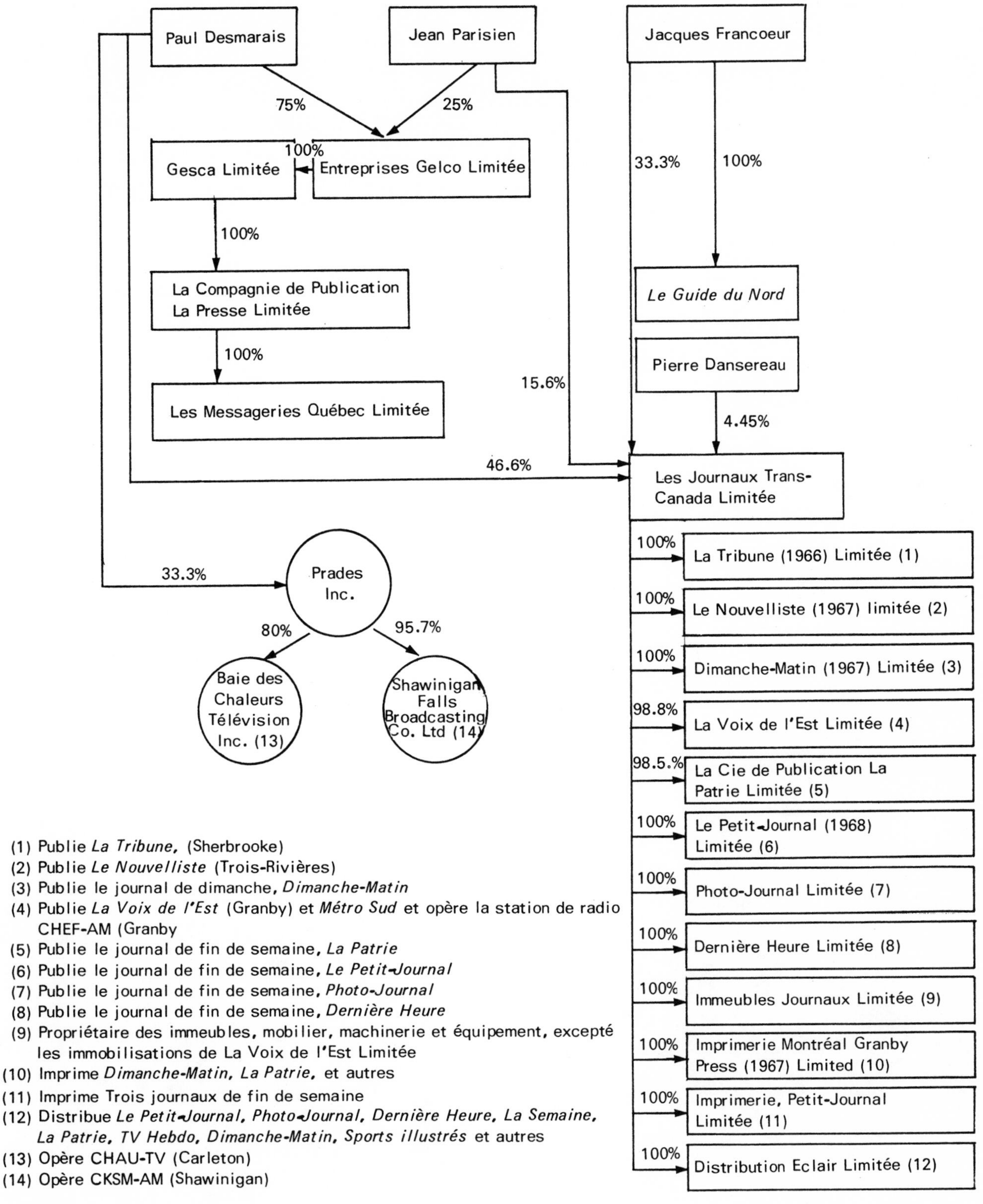

Source: Rapport de la Commission Davis, *Les mots, la musique et les sous,* Ottawa, 1970.

GLOSSAIRE

ABSTENTIONNISME : comportement qui consiste à refuser soit occasionnellement, soit systématiquement de participer à la vie politique en particulier au moment des élections. Le calcul des abstentions exclut les voix exprimées pour l'un ou l'autre des partis et les bulletins rejetés.

ACCROISSEMENT NATUREL (TAUX D' __) : accroissement naturel (naissances moins décès) pour 1,000 habitants. Aussi, taux de natalité moins taux de mortalité.

ACTIONNAIRES (PRINCIPAUX __) : actionnaires qui détiennent des quantités importantes d'actions et peuvent exercer une influence prépondérante sur les décisions de la société.

ADMINISTRATION : ensemble des personnes intégrées dans une structure fonctionnelle qui, sous la direction d'un ministre ou d'une autre personne mandatée par la législature, sont chargées de l'exécution ou de l'application selon le cas, de lois édictées par celle-ci dans un domaine particulier. L'administration se distingue de la régie et de l'entreprise publique (société d'Etat) par sa dépendance de l'exécutif et par sa polyvalence. On parlera d'administration générale chaque fois que l'organisme administratif a un rôle polyvalent et relativement large. C'est le cas des ministères. On parlera d'administration spécialisée chaque fois que l'organisme administratif a un rôle plus restreint que l'on peut difficilement intégrer à un ministère. Exemple : la Sécurité du Québec, la Protection civile, les Régies ...

AJUSTEMENT DE LA VALEUR DES STOCKS : au cours d'une année, les prix des biens peuvent varier. Lors de l'enquête des statisticiens, les livres comptables des compagnies peuvent évaluer les ventes ou les stocks à des prix différents de ceux du marché. On corrige ces erreurs au titre de l'ajustement de la valeur des stocks. Le mot "inventaire", anglicisme (inventory), est souvent utilisé pour désigner stock.

AMORTISSEMENT : somme qu'on met de côté chaque année pour remplacer l'équipement usé durant l'année. Cette somme représente la dépréciation, c'est-à-dire la valeur qu'un équipement (machine, immeuble, etc ...) perd pendant l'année.

ASSISTANCE AUX CHOMEURS : programme provincial dont le but est de venir en aide aux chômeurs lorsque l'assurance-chômage (programme fédéral) n'est pas suffisante ou disponible.

ASSISTANCE AUX INAPTES : programme provincial d'assistance aux personnes incapables de travailler.

BALANCE COMMERCIALE : différence entre la valeur des exportations et celle des importations. Elle est dite "favorable" quand les exportations dominent et "défavorable" quand les importations dépassent les exportations.

BANQUE A CHARTE : banque commerciale dont les conditions de création et de fonctionnement sont fixées dans un document émis par le gouvernement fédéral appelé charte. Elle est caractéristique du système bancaire canadien. Seules quelques banques qui ont un acte d'incorporation provincial (La Banque d'Economie du Québec et la Banque d'Epargne de la Cité et du District de Montréal), les Caisses populaires et les Caisses d'Economie échappent à la réglementation fédérale.

BIENS CULTURELS : en plus de biens physiques, une société se donne des biens symboliques (oeuvres littéraires et artistiques, environnement...) par lesquels elle s'exprime comme collectivité et exprime ses aspirations. A leur tour, ces biens symboliques conditionnent la pensée d'une société et le décor de sa vie d'une manière qui permet de la distinguer des autres sociétés.

BUDGET : prévision des revenus et dépenses au début de l'exercice financier.

BUREAUCRATIE : système d'organisation où les statuts et les rôles, les droits et les devoirs, les conditions d'accès à un poste, les contrôles et les fonctions sont définis par leur situation dans une ligne hiérarchique et donc par une certaine délégation d'autorité.

CHOMAGE (TAUX DE __) : partie de la main-d'oeuvre (en pourcentage) qui est sans travail : $\frac{\text{Nombre de chômeurs X 100}}{\text{Main-d'oeuvre}}$

CHOMEURS : aux termes de la loi, comprend toutes les personnes qui durant la semaine pendant laquelle les données statistiques ont été recueillies, étaient sans travail et cherchaient du travail ou en auraient cherché si elles n'avaient pas été malades, en congédiement indéterminé ou prolongé, ou persuadées qu'il n'y avait pas de travail approprié dans leur localité.

CIRCONSCRIPTION SOUS-REPRESENTEE : partant du principe que le droit de vote de chaque citoyen doit être légal (avoir le même poids), la population de chaque district électoral ne doit pas s'éloigner de la population électorale moyenne du Québec (nombre d'électeurs divisé par le nombre de sièges). Quand la population d'une circonscription est de beaucoup supérieure à la moyenne provinciale on dit que cette circonscription est sous-représentée.

CIRCONSCRIPTION SUR-REPRESENTEE : se dit d'une circonscription dont la population électorale est passablement inférieure à la moyenne provinciale (un écart de 25% et plus).

CLASSE SOCIALE : Il y a plusieurs définitions de la notion de classe, certaines fort différentes, voire, même, parfois contradictoires les unes par rapport aux autres. Cette notion tient à la conception générale que l'on se fait de l'histoire des sociétés et, plus profondément, aux intérêts que l'on défend dans la vie économique et la vie politique; c'est donc une notion idéologique. La notion de classe est liée à la notion de propriété.

Pour certains, selon que l'on participe à la propriété des moyens de production ou que l'on en est exclu, on est de la classe dominante ou de la classe dominée; la notion de classe permet d'établir la relation étroite entre la vie politique et la vie économique; pour eux, l'histoire s'explique par la lutte des classes.

Pour d'autres, en réaction contre les premiers, cette notion est périmée et ne s'applique pas aux sociétés industrialisées du 20e siècle, dans lesquelles les revenus sont plus équitablement distribués et la propriété plus largement répartie; on retient de la notion les caractéristiques de revenu et d'occupation, mais on en exclu celle de la participation effective au pouvoir.

Des auteurs très nombreux ont introduit la notion de classe moyenne; cette notion tout aussi idéologique que les premières, cherche à démontrer que la plus grande partie de la population a un niveau de vie relativement élevé et qu'il n'y a plus d'opposition entre possédants et non-possédants; ces auteurs refusent de prendre en considération la réalité du pouvoir politique; cependant, pour tenir compte davantage de la réalité socio-économique, certains de ces auteurs reconnaissent qu'il faille introduire des distinctions fondamentales parmi les membres de cette large classe moyenne; le Classe moyenne supérieure (industriels, financiers, haute administration, professions libérales); 2e Classe moyenne inférieure (commerçants, petits administrateurs, semi-professionnels; on distingue en outre deux autres groupes à qui on donne des définitions particulières : 3e classe ouvrière; 4e classe paysanne.

Ces distinctions selon les occupations ne procurent pas toute la clarté qu'elles voudraient introduire, car les lignes de démarcation ne reposent ni sur des critères précis, ni sur des fondements théoriques rigoureux.

COL-BLANC : comprend : employés de bureau, gérants, contremaîtres, etc ...

COLLEGES ELECTORAUX : ensemble de personnes qui possèdent le droit d'élire quelqu'un à un poste. Au Québec, l'ensemble des électeurs de chaque district électoral forme un collège électoral. Aux Etats-Unis, on parle aussi de collège électoral pour désigner le groupe restreint constitué par les grands électeurs, soit ceux qui ont le droit d'élire le Président et le Vice-Président des Etats-Unis.

COMITES INTERMINISTERIELS : regroupement de ministres concernés par une question et souvent de quelques hauts fonctionnaires soit pour étudier un rapport, soit pour faire un rapport.

COMMISSION ROYALE D'ENQUETE : organisme créé par une loi de l'Assemblée législative avec précision de mandat, et dont les membres sont nommés par le Conseil des ministres . La Commission Royale d'Enquête est formée de personnes extérieures au Parlement à qui on demande de faire l'étude d'une question donnée pour en faire ensuite rapport à l'Assemblée. Le gouvernement demeure toujours libre d'adopter ou d'ignorer les recommandations d'une Commission Royale d'Enquête.

COMMISSIONS PARLEMENTAIRES : regroupement de députés pour l'étude de projets de loi ou de problèmes. Certaines Commissions sont permanentes (Commission de l'Education); d'autres sont temporaires et ad hoc. Au Québec, on a utilisé longtemps et on continue d'utiliser parfois l'expression "Comité" pour désigner les Commissions parlementaires. (ex.: Comité des délits publics ...).

COMMISSION SCOLAIRE LOCALE : Commission scolaire administrant les effectifs scolaires d'une communauté restreinte. On a entrepris de les regrouper depuis quelques années.

COMMISSION SCOLAIRE REGIONALE : regroupement des commissions scolaires locales au niveau d'une région.

CONCENTRATION DES INVESTISSEMENTS : activité des institutions financières ayant pour objet de regrouper l'épargne de plusieurs et de l'orienter vers des investissements dans un même secteur afin d'en prendre le contrôle.

CONJONCTURE : mouvement de l'activité économique globale comportant des moments de hausse et de baisse se succédant sans cesse. On parle de "conjoncture cyclique", de "fluctuations conjonctuelles", etc... Situation qui résulte d'une rencontre de circonstances et qui est considérée comme le point de départ d'une évolution.

CONSEIL EXECUTIF : organe gouvernemental formé du premier ministre et de l'ensemble des ministres (avec portefeuille ou d'Etat). Au Québec, on parle indifféremment du Conseil exécutif, du Conseil des Ministres ou du Cabinet. L'expression Conseil des Ministres semble être aujourd'hui la plus fréquente.

CREDIT A LA CONSOMMATION : tout emprunt contracté auprès d'un établissement ou d'un individu prêteur en vue de l'achat d'un bien de consommation.

DEPENSES COURANTES DE FONCTIONNEMENT : dépenses d'opération.

DEPENSES DE CAPITAL : dépenses en achat de terrain, de bâtiment et d'équipement, etc ...

DEPENSES PERSONNELLES EN BIENS ET SERVICES : tout déboursé d'un individu pour obtenir un bien durable, non-durable, ou un service. Les dépenses des sociétés et des gouvernements sont exclues.

DEPENSES PROJETEES : montants que les sociétés et les gouvernements ont l'intention d'investir au moment où les données statistiques sont recueillies.

DEPENSES REELLES PROVISOIRES : premières estimations (non-définitives) des dépenses d'investissement.

DROITS ET PERMIS: partie des revenus de l'Etat provenant de la vente de droit et de permis. (Ex.: permis de vente d'alcool, permis de conduire, etc ...).

DUREE DES GREVES ET LOCK-OUT : dans chaque grève ou lock-out, on multiplie le nombre de personnes touchées par le nombre de jours du conflit. En additionnant les résultats de tous les conflits de travail pour la province ou pour le pays durant une période de temps donnée, on évalue l'ampleur des conflits.

EMPLOYES : comprend toutes les personnes qui, au moment de l'enquête, on fait un travail quelconque moyennant rémunération ou bénéfice, ou avaient un emploi mais n'ont pas travaillé à cause de mauvais temps, maladie, différends industriels, vacances ou autre.

EMPRUNTS LOCAUX : emprunts contractés par les firmes multinationales dans le pays d'adoption afin de financer leurs investissements. Un investissement étranger est financé en partie avec l'épargne du pays qui reçoit la firme multinationale.

ENTREPRISE : firme ou groupe de firmes ayant même propriétaire et même direction financière.

ENTREPRISES PUBLIQUES : par opposition à la Régie, l'entreprise publique désigne une entreprise nationalisée, mais dont la gestion jouit d'une assez grande autonomie. Il s'agit d'une société d'Etat. Ex.: l'Hydro-Québec.

EPARGNE PERSONNELLE : comprend : l'épargne des individus, les intérêts sur les dettes des consommateurs et les remises personnelles des non-résidents.

EQUIPEMENT CULTUREL : ensemble de réseaux de communication qu'une société se donne pour s'exprimer et diffuser l'image qu'elle se donne d'elle-même à l'intérieur de ses frontières. V.g. les musées, galeries d'art, salles de cinéma, maisons d'édition, théâtres, salles de concert ... font partie de l'équipement culturel d'une société contemporaine.

ERREUR STATISTIQUE D'ESTIMATION : il existe deux méthodes pour estimer le produit national brut :

a) la somme des dépenses des consommateurs, des entreprises et des gouvernements.
b) la valeur de la production de toutes les entreprises.

Les deux résultats ne sont jamais identiques à cause des imperfections dans la cueillette des données ou dans le traitement statistique. Pour égaliser ces deux résultats, on procède conventionnellement de la façon suivante : on trouve d'abord la différence entre les deux estimations et on la divise par deux. Cette moitié s'appelle "l'erreur statistique d'estimation". On retranche ce montant de l'estimation la plus haute et on l'ajoute à la plus basse. On obtient ainsi une seule donnée pour un même phénomène.

ESPERANCE DE VIE : l'espérance de vie est le nombre d'années qu'une personne peut espérer vivre encore étant donné son âge, son sexe et son lieu de résidence. Elle tend à augmenter au fur et à mesure qu'un pays se développe et qu'il améliore les conditions de santé et d'hygiène de sa population. Aussi est-elle la donnée communément utilisée pour mesurer l'amélioration dans le temps des conditions de vie d'une population. Elle sert en outre aux compagnies d'assurance-vie pour fixer le montant des primes qu'elles demandent à leurs assurés.

ETABLISSEMENT : la plus petite unité ou entité exploitante distincte pouvant déclarer tous les éléments de la statistique industrielle de base. La majorité des établissements sont des firmes, mais plusieurs firmes comptent plus d'un établissement ... Théoriquement, l'établissement n'exerce qu'un genre d'activité et en un seul lieu, mais, dans la pratique, cet établissement idéal se rencontre rarement ... L'établissement possède un système comptable autonome et détaillé ... S'il exerce plusieurs activités, c'est l'activité dominante qui est inscrite.

ETABLISSEMENT HOTELIER : comprend : hôtels, motels, maisons de chambres et autres maisons de logement où le voyageur peut trouver à se loger seulement ou à se loger et manger.

EXPORTATIONS DU QUEBEC ET HORS DU CANADA : le Québec n'ayant pas de frontières nationales, les seules exportations qu'on peut calculer sont celles qui traversent les frontières canadiennes. Ainsi, les ventes d'un établissement québécois à un établissement ontarien ne comptent pas comme exportation. Cependant, un camion chargé à Montréal et qui sort du Canada par Windsor ou Halifax, compte comme exportation du Québec.

FECONDITE PAR AGE (TAUX DE __) : nombre d'enfants nés durant l'année pour 1,000 femmes d'un groupe d'âge donné. La somme des taux de fécondité par âge donne le nombre d'enfants que 1,000 femmes auraient durant leur vie féconde (15 à 49 ans) si les taux de fécondité étaient maintenus.

FERME : exploitation d'un acre ou plus, qui a vendu au cours des 12 mois antérieurs au recensement pour $50.00 ou plus de produits agricoles.

FERME COMMERCIALE : au recencement de 1966 : ferme procurant un revenu de $2,500.00 ou plus. Au recensement de 1971, cette catégorie particulière fut abolie et intégrée dans la catégorie générale de "ferme économique".

FIRME : (notion de nature juridique) consiste en un propriétaire unique, une association de personnes, une société ou une coopérative. La firme peut consister en un ou plusieurs établissements et elle peut s'adonner à une ou plusieurs activités économiques.

FORMATION BRUTE DE CAPITAL FIXE : dépenses en biens capitaux sans aucune déduction pour l'amortissement.

GRADUE : anglicisme désignant un étudiant du 2e cycle (maîtrise) ou du 3e cycle (doctorat).

HERITAGE PROFESSIONNEL : détermination du statut professionnel du fils par celui du père.

IDEOLOGIE : ensemble à cohérence relative de représentations, de valeurs et de croyance qui caractérise une classe sociale.

ILES DE MONTREAL ET JESUS : Ahuntsic, Bourget, Bourassa, D'Arcy Mc Gee, Dorion, Fabre, Gouin, Jacques-Cartier, Jeanne-Mance, Lafontaine, Laurier, Laval, Maisonneuve, Marguerite-Bourgeois, Mercier, Notre-Dame-de-Grâce, Olier, Outremont, Robert-Baldwin, Ste-Anne, St-Henri, St-Jacques, St-Laurent, St-Louis, Ste-Marie, Verdun, Westmount.

IMMOBILISATIONS : Actifs d'une société investis dans des biens durables : immeubles, machines, etc ...

IMPLANTATION ELECTORALE : étalement géographique du vote traduisant les zones de force et de faiblesse des partis.

IMPORTATIONS PASSANT PAR LES PORTS DE DOUANE DU QUEBEC : importations entrant au Canada par les douanes canadiennes situées sur le territoire du Québec. Comme ces produits peuvent se diriger vers d'autres provinces, on ne peut pas connaître les importations du Québec de façon précise.

IMPOTS DIRECTS : impôts levés directement sur le revenu net des individus ou des sociétés.

IMPOTS INDIRECTS : impôts versés par un individu (commerçant, propriétaire, etc ...) mais chargé à un autre (consommateur, locataire, etc ...) comprend : taxes de vente, taxes de propriétaire, taxes de douane, licences et droits. Ces taxes sont toujours comprises dans le prix de vente d'un bien ou d'un service.

IMPOTS INDIRECTS MOINS SUBVENTIONS : (cette notion apparaît dans la comptabilité nationale au chapitre du Produit national brut au prix du marché). Les subventions sont des sommes que les gouvernements versent à des entreprises, des organismes ou des individus pour encourager la hausse de leurs investissements ou de leur production. On soustrait ces montants des impôts indirects pour connaître la recette nette des gouvernements.

IMPOTS SUR LES REVENUS ET SUR LES BIENS : impôt prélevé sur les revenus et les biens d'une personne.

INDICATEURS ECONOMIQUES : phénomènes économiques permettant d'analyser la conjoncture; chômage, prix, etc ...

INDICE : traitement statistique permettant de comparer des séries de chiffres et de calculer des taux de croissance. On porte un chiffre à la base 100 et,par une règle de trois, on calcule les autres chiffres en fonction de la base.

INDUSTRIE : ensemble d'établissements qui exercent une activité économique identique ou semblable.

INDUSTRIES PRODUCTRICES DE BIENS : comprend agriculture, forêts, pêche, piégeage, mines, électricité, industries manufacturières et construction.

INDUSTRIES SELON LES SECTEURS

A- SECTEUR PRIMAIRE : ensemble des industries dont l'activité principale consiste à extraire et à exploiter les ressources naturelles ...
Comprend les industries suivantes :

1- AGRICULTURE : comprend : toutes les exploitations agricoles qui se livrent principalement à la production agricole : fermes expérimentales et d'institutions, petites exploitations agricoles (ventes de moins de $1,200.00 par année), fermes commerciales, services annexes de l'agriculture.

2- FORET : comprend : les établissements dont l'activité économique est l'abattage des arbres et les services forestiers.

3- PECHE : comprend toute personne, famille ou établissement s'adonnant principalement à la pêche commerciale en mer ou dans les eaux intérieures. Comprend aussi les services de pêche.

4- CHASSE ET PIEGEAGE OU TRAPPE : comprend : établissements (y compris individus) s'occupant principalement de chasse et piégeage des animaux sauvages pour fins commerciales.

5- MINES, CARRIERES ET PUITS DE PETROLE : comprend : l'extraction et (dans la plupart des cas) le traitement des mines métalliques, combustibles minéraux, autres mines non-métalliques les carrières et sablières, les services miniers.

B- SECTEUR SECONDAIRE : le secteur secondaire est l'ensemble des industries dont la tâche principale est de transformer des matières premières en un produit fini. Comprend les industries 6 à 25.

INDUSTRIES MANUFACTURIERES : établissements qui transforment des matières premières afin de produire une marchandise. On compte 20 industries manufacturières principales. C'est aussi ce qu'on appelle le secteur secondaire ou le secteur de la fabrication.

INDUSTRIE LEGERE : ensemble des industries manufacturières dont l'activité principale consiste à produire des biens non-durables. Elle se distingue particulièrement par l'utilisation d'une grande quantité de main-d'oeuvre et d'une quantité faible de capital. Comprend les industries 6 à 14.

6- ALIMENTS ET BOISSONS : comprend : industrie de la viande, industrie laitière, du poisson, conserves et préparation de fruits et légumes, grains, boulangeries et pâtisseries, autres fabrications d'aliments, et industrie des boissons.

7- TABAC : comprend : le traitement du tabac en feuilles et les manufacturiers de produits du tabac.

8- CUIR : comprend : tanneries, fabriques de chaussures, de gants, de valises, sacs à mains et menus articles en cuir.

9- CAOUTCHOUC : comprend principalement : manufacturiers de chaussures en caoutchouc, de chambres à air et de pneus et autres industries du caoutchouc.

10- TEXTILES : comprend : les établissements dont l'activité principale consiste en la filature et le tissage du coton, de la laine; comprend aussi l'industrie des textiles synthétiques et les autres industries textiles.

11- BONNETERIE : industries des bas, chausettes et tricots.

12- VETEMENT : comprend : les industries des vêtements sur mesure, des vêtements d'hommes, des vêtements de femmes, des vêtements d'enfants, des article de fourrure, des chapeaux et casquettes, des corsets et soutiens-gorge et les autres industries du vêtement.

13- BOIS : comprend : scieries, fabriques de placage et contre-plaqués, industrie des portes et châssis et du rabotage, fabriques de boîtes en bois, industrie de cercueils et industries diverses du bois, sauf l'abattage des arbres.

14- MEUBLE ET ARTICLES D'AMEUBLEMENT : comprend les industries de meubles de maison, de bureau, les autres industries du meuble et l'industrie des lampes électriques et des abat-jour.

INDUSTRIE LOURDE : ensemble des industries manufacturières dont l'activité principale consiste à produire des biens durables. Elle se distingue particulièrement par l'utilisation d'un fort volume de capital et d'une quantité relativement faible de main-d'oeuvre. Comprend les industries 15 à 25.

15- PAPIER ET PRODUITS CONNEXES : comprend l'industrie des pâtes et papiers, les manufacturiers de papier-toiture asphalté, de boîtes et sacs en papier et des autres transformations du papier.

16- IMPRIMERIE, EDITION ET PRODUITS CONNEXES : comprend : imprimerie commerciale, gravure, stéréotypie et industries connexes, l'édution seulement, l'imprimerie et édition.

17- METALLIQUES PRIMAIRES : comprend : industries du fer et de l'acier, fabriques de tubes et tuyaux d'acier, fonderies de fer, fonte et affinage; laminage,moulage et refoulage de l'aluminium, du cuivre et alliages et des autres métaux.

18- PRODUITS METALLIQUES (SAUF LES MACHINES ET LE MATERIEL DE TRANSPORT) : comprend : industrie des chaudières et des plaques; de la fabrication des éléments de charpentes métalliques; des produits métalliques d'architecture et d'ornements; de l'estampage, du matriçage et du revêtement des métaux, du fil métallique et ses produits manufacturiers de quincaillerie, d'outils et de coutellerie, d'appareils de chauffage et ateliers d'usinage; industrie des produits métalliques divers.

19- MACHINERIE (SAUF LE MATERIEL ELECTRIQUE) : comprend : manufacturiers de matériel agricole, manufacturiers de machines et matériel divers, manufacturiers de matériel frigorifique et de conditionnement de l'air, manufacturiers de machines de bureaux et de magasin.

20- MATERIEL DE TRANSPORT : comprend : manufacturiers d'avions et d'éléments; manufacturiers de véhicules automobiles; manufacturiers de carosseries de camions et remorques; manufacturiers de pièces et accessoires d'automobiles; manufacturiers de matériel roulant de chemin de fer; construction et réparation d'embarcation, manufacturiers de véhicules divers.

21- APPAREILS ET MATERIEL ELECTRIQUES : comprend : manufacturiers de petits appareils électriques; manufacturiers de gros appareils (électriques ou non); manufacturiers d'appareils électro-ménagers, de radio et de télévision; manufacturiers d'appareils de télécommunication; manufacturiers de matériel électrique industriel; manufacturiers de batteries; manufacturiers de fils et câbles électriques; manufacturiers d'appareils électriques divers.

22- MINERAUX NON-METALLIQUES : comprend : manufacturiers de chaux, de ciment, de produits du gypse, de produits en béton, industrie du béton préparé, manufacturiers de produits d'argile, de produits réfractaires, de produits en pierre, de laine minérale, de produits en amiante, de verre et d'articles en verre, d'abrasifs et d'autres produits minéraux non-métalliques.

23- PRODUITS DU PETROLE, DU CHARBON ET DE LEURS DERIVES : comprend : les raffineries de pétrole et les manufacturiers d'autres dérivés du pétrole et du charbon.

24- CHIMIQUES ET CONNEXES : comprend principalement : manufacturiers d'explosifs et de munitions, d'engrais mélangés, de matière plastique et de résine synthétique, de produits médicinaux et pharmaceutiques, de peinture et de vernis, de savons et de composés de nettoyage, de produits de toilette, de produits chimiques industriels.

25- DIVERSES : comprend manufacturiers d'instruments scientifiques et professionnels; de bijouterie et d'orfèverie; de stores vénitiens; d'articles en matières plastiques; industrie des balais, brosses et vadrouilles; des articles de sports et des jouets; d'apprêt et teinture de la fourrure; des enseignes et étalages; industries manufacturières diverses non classées ailleurs.

C- SECTEUR DE LA CONSTRUCTION :

26- INDUSTRIE DE LA CONSTRUCTION : comprend : entreprises générales qui s'adonnent principalement à la construction, la rénovation et la réparation des bâtiments, des routes, des ponts et des rues et autres. Comprend aussi les entreprises spécialisées (sous-contractants ou sous-traitants).

D- SECTEUR TERTIAIRE : ensemble des industries dont l'activité principale consiste à fournir des services aux individus ou à faciliter l'échange et la circulation des biens et de l'argent. Comprend les industries de 27 à 32.

27- SERVICES SOCIAUX, COMMERCIAUX, INDUSTRIELS ET PERSONNELS : comprend : enseignement et services connexes; santé et oeuvres sociales; organismes religieux; cinématographie et services récréatifs, services extérieurs des entreprises; services personnels; services divers (professions libérales).

28- TRANSPORTS, COMMUNICATIONS ET AUTRES SERVICES D'UTILITE PUBLIQUE : comprend : tous les établissements dont l'activité principale concerne les transports de toutes sortes, l'entreposage, les communications et la production et distribution de l'eau, du gaz et de l'électricité.
Exemples : taxis, autobus, entretien des routes et ponts, élévateurs à grains, radiodiffusion et télévision, services téléphoniques, postes, électricité, etc ...

29- COMMERCE DE DETAIL : revente des marchandises au grand public pour consommation personnelle ou ménagère.

30- COMMERCE DE GROS : intermédiaire entre la production et le commerce de détail : la revente des marchandises à des détaillants, des industries, des commerçants, des institutions, des professionnels, d'autres grossistes, ou encore il sert d'agent dans ces transactions.

31- FINANCES, ASSURANCES ET IMMEUBLES : comprend : établissements d'épargne et de crédit ; sociétés de placement et agents de change; assureurs; agences d'assurances et d'immeuble; exploitants immobiliers.

32- ADMINISTRATION PUBLIQUE ET DEFENSE NATIONALE : comprend : administration fédérale, défense et autres; administration provinciale; administration municipale; bureaux des gouvernements étrangers.

INFIDELITE DANS LA REPRESENTATION DES OPINIONS : distorsion entre le pourcentage de voix exprimées pour les divers partis et la représentation de ces partis en nombre de sièges à l'Assemblée Nationale.

INTENTION DE VOTE : choix d'un électeur tel qu'exprimé dans un sondage pré-électoral.

INVESTISSEMENT (DEPENSES D' __) : dépenses ayant pour but la création et la réparation de biens capitaux, c'est-à-dire d'immeubles de toutes sortes, d'équipements, de machineries, etc ... Dans la comptabilité nationale, on compte à ce titre les dépenses de capital des entreprises et des gouvernements.

INVESTISSEMENTS DIRECTS : investissement effectué dans le but de créer sous une forme ou une autre une organisation permanente à l'étranger qui fabriquera, façonnera et commercialisera des produits destinés à la consommation locale ou, dans certains cas, à la vente dans de tierces régions. L'investissement direct s'effectue généralement par la création d'une succursale ou par l'achat d'une entreprise. Cette forme d'investissement, générale au XXe siècle, se distingue de l'investissement indirect qui consiste en un prêt à l'étranger.

JURIDICTION : droit d'intervention dans un domaine. L'étendue et les limites de ce droit sont généralement définies dans une constitution.

LANGUE MATERNELLE : première langue qu'une personne a parlée et qu'elle comprend encore. Pour les enfants en bas âge, c'est la langue ordinairement parlée au foyer.
N.B.: La langue maternelle n'est pas nécessairement l'anglais ou le français.

LANGUE OFFICIELLE PARLEE : la ou les langue(s) que la personne recensée déclare pouvoir parler. Les réponses recensées au Canada se divisent en 4 catégories : unilingues anglais, unilingues français, bilingues (français et anglais) et ni français ni anglais.

MAIN-D'OEUVRE : partie de la population civile (militaires exclus) en âge de travail (14 ans et plus) ne vivant pas dans des institutions, qui se trouve sur le marché du travail, c'est-à-dire ou bien employée ou bien en chômage, durant la semaine pendant laquelle les données statistiques ont été recueillies. Il est bon de souligner qu'une partie importante de la population d'âge actif ne fait pas partie de la main-d'oeuvre : tous ceux qui ne se présentent pas ou qui ne se présentent plus sur le marché du travail: ainsi, une partie importante des femmes et tous ceux qui, dans certaines régions où l'activité économique est ralentie, ne demandent pas d'emploi et vivent d'assistance sociale. De même, aujourd'hui, un certain nombre de jeunes.

MENAGES NON-FAMILIAUX : comprenant les personnes occupant des logements distincts, comme les célibataires, les veufs ou veuves, les étudiants ou toute autre personne vivant seule ou en groupe.

METROPOLE REGIONALE : arrondissement vers lequel convergent la plupart des activités administratives de la région.

MIGRATION NETTE : nombre de personnes qui s'installent dans une région, une province ou un pays moins ceux qui quittent.

MIGRATION NETTE (RAPPORT DE __) : migration nette divisée par la population au début de la décennie en pourcentage.

MORTALITE (TAUX COMPARATIFS DE __) : le taux de mortalité peut varier beaucoup suivant les changements dans la structure par âge (une population qui a beaucoup de vieillards compte plus de décès, même si l'état de santé général y est meilleur). On contourne cette difficulté en normalisant les taux, c'est-à-dire en ajustant les taux annuels de mortalité de chaque groupe d'âge à une population type (habituellement, la population réelle d'une année donnée). Ainsi, on peut calculer ce qu'aurait été, chaque année, le taux de mortalité générale si la structure par âge et sexe de la population s'était maintenue constante durant toute la période.

MORTALITE (TAUX DE __) : nombre de décès enregistrés pour 1,000 habitants pendant une période donnée.

MUSEE D'ART : établissement dans lequel sont rassemblées et classées des collections d'objets présentant un intérêt artistique, en vue de leur conservation et de leur présentation au public. Forme une part importante de l'équipement culturel d'une société contemporaine. Les musées ont des services de conservation et d'éducation.

MUSEE D'HISTOIRE : comme le musée d'art, le musée historique est un établissement de conservation et de diffusion de collection d'objets mais à caractère plus spécifiquement historique qu'artistiques. La ligne de démarcation entre les deux domaines n'est pas toujours facile à faire.

MUSEE DE SCIENCE : établissement qui rassemble et classe des collections d'objets présentant un intérêt scientifique en vue de leur conservation et leur présentation au public.

NATALITE (TAUX DE __) : nombre d'enfants nés vivants pour 1,000 habitants pendant une période donnée.

ORIGINE ETHNIQUE : se détermine par l'ethnie de l'ancêtre paternel. Au recensement de 1971, on a posé à chaque personne la question : "A quel groupe ethnique ou culturel appartenait votre ancêtre paternel (ou vous-même) à son arrivée sur le continent?".

OUVRIER QUALIFIE : personne qui possède un métier, une connaissance spécialisé.

OUVRIER SEMI-QUALIFIE : ouvrier qui exerce une fonction parcellaire, l'intérieur d'une chaîne, par exemple.

PAIEMENTS DE TRANSFERT DES GOUVERNEMENTS ET DES SOCIETES : transaction dans laquelle les biens, les services ou l'argent sont donnés sans aucune contrepartie. Il peut s'agir de dons de charité, du paiement de l'assurance-chômage, etc.

PARCS INDUSTRIELS : arrondissement où sont concentrées plusieurs industries (surtout manufacturières). La ville qui établit le parc industriel accorde des services et des exemptions d'impôts aux usines qui acceptent de s'y installer.

PARTICIPATION (TAUX DE __) : proportion de la population de 14 ans et plus qui participe à la main-d'oeuvre. En général, les personnes qui ne participent pas à la main-d'oeuvre sont les étudiants, les ménagères, les invalides, les retraités, etc ...
Taux de participation : $\frac{\text{Main-d'oeuvre X 100}}{\text{Population d'âge actif}}$
Dans certaines régions de faible activité économique, ce taux peut être relativement bas; les individus sachant qu'il n'y a pas d'emploi, ne se présentent même pas sur le marché du travail et vivent d'assistance sociale.

POPULATION (ACCROISSEMENT DE LA __) : augmentation de la population : accroissement naturel plus migration nette, c'est-à-dire la différence entre l'immigration et l'émigration; si l' émigration dépasse l'immigration, la migration nette sera négative.

POPULATION (ACCROISSEMENT NATUREL DE LA __) : accroissement naturel (naissances moins décès) pour 1,000 habitants. Aussi, taux de natalité moins taux de mortalité.

POPULATION D'AGE ACTIF : se compose de la partie de la population civile âgée de 14 ans et plus.

POPULATION (DENSITE DE LA __) : Il s'agit du nombre de personnes qui demeurent dans une même unité de surface, c'est-à-dire le mille carré.

POPULATION RURALE AGRICOLE : la définition de la population rurale agricole a varié selon les époques. Pour la période de 1891 à 1941, il s'agit de toute personne non-urbaine ayant un emploi dans l'agriculture ... En 1951, 1961 et   , il s'agit de toute personne vivant dans des fermes situées dans des régions rurales, indépendamment de leur emploi.

La population agricole comprend toutes les personnes vivant dans un logement situé dans une ferme de recensement* selon la définition du recensement quelle que soit leur profession. Le chiffre de cette population englobe les populations agricoles rurales aussi bien qu'urbaines. Les personnes vivant dans une ferme de recensement située dans une cité , ville ou village font partie de la population agricole des subdivisions voisines. Dans les bulletins de recensement de la population (Recensement 1971, bulletin 92-709 : "Répartition selon la catégorie d'habitat"), la population rurale agricole comprend toutes les personnes vivant dans une exploitation située dans une région rurale, quelle que soit leur profession. La population des fermes de recensement* comprend donc certaines personnes qui n'ont rien à voir avec l'exploitation agricole et qui tirent leurs revenus de l'exercice d'activités non agricoles. En contrepartie, les exploitants agricoles et leur famille qui n'habitent pas leur exploitation agricole - par exemple, ceux qui habitent une localité voisine - ne sont pas pris en compte.

* Ferme de recensement : ferme, ranch ou autre exploitation agricole de un acre ou plus dont les ventes de produits agricoles, au cours des douze mois précédant la date du recensement, se sont élevées à $50.00 ou plus.

POPULATION RURALE NON AGRICOLE : de 1891 à 1941 : personne vivant hors des centres constitués et ayant un emploi non-agricole. A partir de 1951, c'est toute personne vivant en région rurale, mais pas sur une ferme.

POPULATION URBAINE : de 1891 à 1941, toute personne habitant un centre constitué (quelle que soit la population de ce centre) était classée urbaine. En 1951, on a défini comme urbaine toute personne vivant dans les cités, villes et villages de 1,000 habitants et plus, constitués on non. De 1956 à 1961, on ajoute à ces derniers, les personnes habitant les secteurs périphériques des agglomérations urbaines quand l'ensemble comprend 10,000 habitants et plus.

PRIX A LA CONSOMMATION (INDICE DES __) : pour pouvoir évaluer l'amplitude des mouvements des prix à la consommation, on calcule le taux de leur variation par rapport au niveau des prix d'une année de base considéré comme 100. Aujourd'hui, au Canada, l'année de base est 1961. Auparavant, l'année de base était 1949. On rapproche ainsi l'année de base après un certain nombre d'années pour pouvoir tenir compte des changements dans les habitudes de consommation des citoyens et modifier l'importance relative de chaque bien dans l'indice en fonction des nouvelles préférences. C'est pourquoi on appelle cet indice : le coût de la vie.

PRIX DE GROS (INDICE DES __) : indice des prix courants dans le commerce de gros.

PRODUIT INTERIEUR BRUT AU COUT DES FACTEURS : production totale des résidents du Québec. On prend le produit national brut et on enlève la contribution des non-résidents après avoir ajouté la contribution des résidents au produit national brut de toute autre entité politique. L'expression "au coût des facteurs" signifie que le calcul est basé sur les données des producteurs sur les divers éléments de leur coût de production.

PRODUIT NATIONAL BRUT AU PRIX DU MARCHE : quantité de biens et services qui sont produits par une économie pendant une période donnée avec ses ressources. L'expression "biens et services produits" est entendue dans son sens le plus large : transformation de matière première, soins de santé, transport, même pièces de théâtre font partie de la production et du produit national brut. Pour le calculer, on additionne la valeur aux prix du marché des biens et services produits dans une période donnée (dans notre cas, un an) par les résidents québécois à l'intérieur des frontières. L'expression "au prix du marché" signifie que le calcul statistique est basé sur les dépenses déclarées des gouvernements, des entreprises et des individus, en soustrayant ou en additionnant, selon le cas, les variations des stocks. Le mot "brut" indique qu'on a calculé et inclus la valeur de l'amortissement.

PROFESSION : nature du travail des personnes faisant partie de la main-d'oeuvre. Il ne s'agit pas de la formation de la personne mais de la nature de son emploi actuel ou de son dernier emploi dans le cas des chômeurs.

1- ADMINISTRATEURS : actionnaires élus par l'assemblée des actionnaires pour voir aux décisions importantes de l'entreprise. Ils font rapport à l'assemblée annuelle des actionnaires. Ils forment le Conseil d'Administration.

2- PROFESSIONS LIBERALES ET TECHNICIENS : comprend : ingénieurs professionnels, spécialistes des sciences physiques, biologistes et spécialistes des sciences agricoles, personnel enseignant, spécialistes de la santé, juristes, clergé et ministres du culte, artistes, écrivains et musiciens, autres professions libérales.

3- EMPLOYES DE BUREAU : comprend : teneurs de livres et caissiers, mécanographes, commis, agents de transport, sténos et dactylos, assistants et autres. Correspondent à ceux que l'on appelle les collets blancs par opposition aux collets bleus (ouvriers).

4- VENDEURS : comprend : contremaîtres de commerce; vendeurs à l'enchère et à domicile; colporteurs et camelots; pompistes; publicitaires; agent d'assurance et d'immeuble; courtiers et autres.

5- TRAVAILLEURS DES SERVICES ET DES ACTIVITES RECREATIVES : comprend : travailleurs des services de la protection; intendants, garçons de table, cuisiniers et travailleurs assimilés; athlètes, comédiens et travailleurs assimilés; autres travailleurs des services.

6- TRAVAILLEURS DES TRANSPORTS ET DES COMMUNICATIONS : comprend : inspecteurs et contremaîtres de transport; pilotes, navigateurs et mécaniciens navigants; conducteurs de chemins de fer; conducteurs de transport routier; autres travailleurs des transports; inspecteurs et contremaîtres des communications; autres travailleurs des communications.

7- AGRICULTEURS ET TRAVAILLEURS AGRICOLES : comprend : cultivateurs et éleveurs, gérants de ferme, ouvriers agricoles, jardiniers et autres.

8- BUCHERONS ET TRAVAILLEURS FORESTIERS : comprend : contremaîtres, gardes-forestiers, bûcherons.

9- PECHEURS, TRAPPEURS ET CHASSEURS : comprend : les personnes dont l'activité principale consiste à pêcher, trapper ou chasser.

10- MINEURS, CARRIERS ET TRAVAILLEURS ASSIMILES : comprend : contremaîtres dans les mines, carrières et puits de pétrole; prospecteurs, boiseurs, mineurs, bocardeurs, foreurs de puits, manoeuvres de mines, carriers.

11- OUVRIERS DE METIER, ARTISANS, OUVRIERS A LA PRODUCTION ET TRAVAILLEURS ASSIMILES : ouvriers ayant une formation technique adaptée à leur occupation. Comprend : travailleurs de la production d'aliments; du caoutchouc; du cuir; fileurs, tisseurs; tailleurs et fourreurs; menuisiers; travailleurs de l'industrie chimique; imprimeurs et relieurs; travailleurs des métaux; bijoutiers et horlogers; machinistes; plombiers et tôliers; mécaniciens et réparateurs; électriciens et électroniciens; peintres, tapissiers et vitriers; ouvriers de la construction; travailleurs de l'argile, du verre et de la pierre; conducteurs de machines fixes; débardeurs; cantonniers et poseurs de rail; autres ouvriers à la production et travailleurs assimilés.

12- MANOEUVRE : ouvriers sans aucune formation technique appropriée à leur travail et sans aucune spécialisation. Comprend les manoeuvres dans les industries manufacturières, de la construction et des services.

13- PROFESSIONS NON DECLAREES : comprend : les personnes qui n'ont pas déclaré de profession au recensement.

PROFITS RETENUS : partie des profits qui n'est pas distribuée aux actionnaires sous forme de dividendes. On l'utilise pour investir ou pour renforcer la position financière de la compagnie. Cette retenue permet aux actionnaires de payer moins d'impôts sur le revenu et de voir se hausser la valeur de leurs actions.

PROVISIONS POUR CONSOMMATION DE CAPITAL ET REEVALUATIONS DIVERSES : à la fin d'une année de production, l'équipement (capital) de la société a subi une certaine usure. Une partie de la valeur créée pendant l'année doit servir à remplacer le capital usé. Cette partie constitue en gros le poste "Provisions pour consommation de capital et réévaluations diverses". C'est une partie du produit national brut mais pas du revenu national net puisque personne ne touche de revenus dans ce cas.

PUISSANCE AUDIO : puissance d'émission du son d'un poste émetteur de télévision.

PUISSANCE VIDEO : puissance de l'émetteur pour l'image à la télévision (en watts).

PYRAMIDE D'AGE : représentation géométrique de la structure des âges d'une population à un moment précis. Les âges des hommes sont inscrits à gauche, ceux des femmes, à droite. Les effectifs de population par tranches d'âge sont superposées sur le plan horizontal. Une pyramide parfaite serait symétrique. Selon la forme de pyramide, on peut voir d'un coup d'oeil si la population est relativement jeune (base de la pyramide évasée) ou relativement vieille (sommet de la pyramide élargi).

RECENSEMENT : relevé périodique d'un ensemble de données touchant la population, le revenu, etc ... Au Canada, le recensement complet a lieu tous les 10 ans (années finissant par 1) et un recensement partiel a lieu entre les recensements complets (années finissant par 6).

REGIE : entreprises publiques dont l'administration est entièrement confiée à des fonctionnaires. Se distingue de la Société d'Etat par le degré moindre d'autonomie de gestion. Exemples de régies : La Régie des Rentes du Québec, La Régie des Alcools. La régie peut, soit effectuer elle-même l'administration directe d'une activité économique (Ex.: Régie des Alcools), soit exercer un rôle de surveillance et de contrôle (Ex.: Régie de l'Electricité et du Gaz).

REGIME DES RENTES DU QUEBEC : caisse à laquelle souscrivent tous les travailleurs du Québec et qui donne droit à plusieurs avantages comme la pension, les rentes aux inaptes et aux nécessiteux, etc ...

REMBOURSEMENTS : part du budget qui sert à rembourser l'intérêt et le capital sur les emprunts.

REPRODUCTION BRUTE (TAUX DE __) : ce taux constitue la moyenne d'enfants qu'aurait eus chaque femme qui atteint cinquante ans, si les taux de fécondité de l'année de base s'étaient maintenus. Quand le taux de reproduction brut descend au-dessous de un, les femmes, durant la période fertile de leur vie, n'ont pas assez d'enfants pour renouveler la population, même si ces enfants vivent jusqu'à maturité. C'est le cas, actuellement, au Québec.

REVENU DE CAPITAL : appréciation de la valeur d'un bien (immeuble , action de corporation, etc.) provenant de la hausse de son prix sur le marché; se distingue du revenu courant (loyers, dividendes, intérêts, etc.).

REVENU COURANT DE FONCTIONNEMENT : revenus d'opération.

REVENU GLOBAL : ensemble des revenus d'un individu : salaires, intérêts, dividendes, rentes et loyers ...

REVENU MOYEN DU TRAVAIL : comprend : les salaires et les revenus des cultivateurs. Exclut les revenus de placements comme dividendes, intérêts, loyers, etc ...

REVENU NATIONAL NET AU COUT DES FACTEURS : l'ensemble des revenus que les Québécois ont gagné pendant un an. En effet, toute personne ou société qui produit des biens ou des services crée de la valeur. Cette nouvelle valeur, exprimée en dollars, sert à payer les facteurs de production : salaires, profits, intérêts, etc ... Le mot "net" indique qu'on a soustrait la valeur de l'amortissement.

REVENU PERSONNEL TOTAL : mesure tout revenu gagné par des résidents québécois. Il s'agit du revenu avant impôts. Comprend les revenus suivants :

1- REMUNERATION DES SALARIES : tous les paiements faits aux Québécois au titre de salaires. Exclut les revenus des personnes à leur propre compte.

2- SOLDES ET INDEMNITES MILITAIRES : rémunération des membres des forces armées au Canada et outre-mer, y compris les paiements en nature et en service (logement, nourriture, vêtements, etc ...).

3- REVENU NET REVENANT AUX AGRICULTEURS AU TITRE DE LA PRODUCTION AGRICOLE : comprend : ventes de produits agricoles, valeur des produits agricoles consommés sur la ferme, changements dans la valeur de la ferme, moins dépenses d'opération et dépenses de capital sur la ferme. Tous les autres revenus des fermiers sont exclus, étant comptabilisés sous d'autres titres.

4- REVENU NET DES ENTREPRISES NON-INCORPOREES NON-AGRICOLES : comprend : le revenu net de toute entreprise non-incorporée non-agricole dans presque toutes les industries, y compris le revenu net des professionnels indépendants (médecins, avocats ...).

5- INTERETS ET REVENUS DIVERS DE PLACEMENT ; intérêt et revenu net de location des personnes; revenus de placement des gouvernements ... Tous les revenus qui résultent d'un placement.

6- PAIEMENTS DE TRANSFERT DES GOUVERNEMENTS : paiements effectués par les gouvernements en versements de sécurité sociale et en intérêts sur la dette publique.

7- DIVIDENDES : profits d'une entreprise distribués aux actionnaires. Ils varient d'une année à l'autre selon les résultats de l'activité de l'entreprise et selon la décision des administrateurs d'en retenir une partie dans les réserves pour dépenses futures de capital.

REVENU PERSONNEL PER CAPITA : revenu personnel divisé par le nombre d'habitants (tenant compte de ceux qui n'ont aucun revenu).

REVENU PERSONNEL DISPONIBLE : revenu personnel moins impôts directs ... Il s'agit ici de l'impôt sur le revenu qui est touché sur le salaire. Les autres taxes indirectes (taxes de vente, etc ...) ne sont pas incluses.

REVENU PERSONNEL DISPONIBLE PER CAPITA : revenu personnel disponible divisé par le nombre d'habitants.

SCOLARISATION (TAUX DE __) : nombre d'années qu'une population passe à l'école en moyenne.

SECTEUR ECONOMIQUE : les 4 grands secteurs économiques sont les secteurs primaire (extraction et exploitation du sol), secondaire (transformation) construction et tertiaire (service). Cf. Industries selon les secteurs.

SERVICE DE LA DETTE : intérêts payés par un organisme (Etat, ...).

SOCIETES DE PRET AU CONSOMMATEUR (MAISON DE FINANCE) : sociétés dont l'activité principale consiste à prêter de l'argent et à tirer des revenus d'intérêt. On les appele couramment les "compagnies de finance".

SOUS-GRADUE : étudiant postulant un diplôme de 1er cycle (baccalauréat ou licence).

SYNDICATS

CENTRALE OU CONFEDERATION DE __ : Organismes regroupant des syndicats locaux dans une organisation plus large.

CONSEIL REGIONAUX DE __ : regroupement de syndicats locaux à l'échelle d'une région.

SYNDICATS (EFFECTIFS __) : nombre de salariés qui sont syndiqués dans les divers secteurs de l'économie.

FEDERATION DE __ : regroupement de syndicats locaux sur la base d'un travail semblable ... Exemple : les Métallos ...

LOCAUX : unités syndicales dont la base est ordinairement l'établissement.

UNION INTERNATIONALE DE __ : groupement de syndicats locaux sur la base de plusieurs pays.

SYNDICALISATION (TAUX DE __) : nombre de personnes inscrites à un syndicat par rapport au nombre de personnes dans la main-d'oeuvre non-agricole.

TAXE A LA CONSOMMATION : taxe imposée sur le prix de vente des biens de consommation et payée par le consommateur.

TECHNOCRATIE : ensemble du haut personnel de l'Etat et des entreprises (privées ou publiques) qui occupe des postes dirigeants, en raison de sa compétence technique, sans devoir son rôle dominant à l'élection ou à un titre de propriété.

TRANSFERTS COURANTS AU GOUVERNEMENT : comprend : impôts sur le revenu, droits de succession et contributions aux caisses publiques de pension, de sécurité sociale et autres.

VALEUR AJOUTEE : ce qui est ajouté à la valeur du produit depuis la forme de matière première jusqu'à celle du produit qui sort de l'établissement. En langage comptable, c'est la valeur brute des livraisons ou des recettes comptables d'exploitation moins le coût des matières intermédiaires, des fournitures, du combustible et de l'électricité utilisés. C'est la valeur qui a été ajoutée par l'établissement.

VALEUR DES EXPEDITIONS : produits expédiés par un établissement en valeur monétaire, qu'ils aient été payés ou non.

BIBLIOGRAPHIE SOMMAIRE

(Cette bibliographie ne mentionne que des ouvrages fondamentaux et de nature générale; on trouvera dans chacun de ces volumes des références à des travaux plus approfondis.)

1. OUVRAGES DE BIBLIOGRAPHIE

BOILY, Robert, Québec 1940-1969; bibliographie: le système politique québécois et son environnement, Montréal, P.U.M., 1971.

DUROCHER, René et P.A. LINTEAU, Histoire du Québec: bibliographie sélective (1867-1970), (édition préliminaire), Trois-Rivières, Boréal Express, 1970.

GARIGUE, P., A Bibliographical Introduction to the Study of French Canada, Montréal, McGill University Press, 1956.

GARIGUE, P., Bibliographie du Québec (1955-1965), Montréal, P.U.M., 1957.

LEBLANC, A.E. et G.D. THWAITES, Le monde ouvrier au Québec; bibliographie rétrospective, Montréal, P.U.Q., 1973.

SOUTHAM, Peter. Bibliographie des bibliographies sur l'économie, la société et la culture du Québec - 1940-1971. Québec, Institut supérieur des sciences humaines, Université Laval, 1972.

2. HISTOIRE DU QUEBEC.

2.1. HISTOIRE GENERALE.

BERGERON, Léandre, Petit manuel d'histoire du Québec, Montréal, Editions québécoises, 1971.

BILODEAU, R., R. COMEAU, A. GOSSELIN et D. JULIEN, Histoire des Canadas, Montréal, Hurtubise H.M.H., 1971.

RUMILLY, Robert, Histoire de la Province de Québec, 41 volumes, Montréal, divers éditeurs, 1940-1969.

RYERSON, Stanley B., Capitalisme et confédération, Montréal, Parti-Pris, 1972.

VAUGEOIS, D. et J. LACOURSIERE, Canada-Québec, synthèse historique, Nouvelle édition, Montréal, Renouveau pédagogique, 1969.

2.2. HISTOIRE ECONOMIQUE

COMEAU, R. (sous la direction de), Economie québécoise, Montréal, P.U.Q., 1969.

FAUCHER, Albert, Histoire économique et unité canadienne, Montréal, Fides, 1970.

FAUCHER, Albert, Québec en Amérique au 19e siècle, Montréal, Fides, 1973.

HAMELIN, J. et Y. ROBY, Histoire économique du Québec, 1851-1896, Montréal, Fides, 1971.

LETARTE, Jacques, Atlas d'histoire économique et sociale du Québec, 1851-1901, Montréal, Fides, 1971.

OUELLET, F., Histoire économique et sociale du Québec, 1760-1850, structure et conjoncture, 2 vol., Montréal, Fides, 1971.

2.3. HISTOIRE SOCIO-POLITIQUE

BERNARD, J.P., Les Rouges: libéralisme, nationalisme et anti-cléricalisme au milieu du XIXe siècle, Montréal, P.U.Q., 1971.

BOURQUE, Gilles, Question nationale et classes sociales au Québec, 1760-1840, Montréal, Parti-Pris, 1970.

BRUNET, Michel, Québec, Canada anglais; deux itinéraires, un affrontement, Montréal, H.M.H., 1969.

CHARBONNEAU, H. (sous la direction de), La Population du Québec: études rétrospectives, Trois-Rivières, Boréal Express, 1973.

DUBUC, A., "Les classes sociales au Canada". Annales. Economies, Sociétés, Civilisations, juil.-août 1968, vol. 22, 829-844.

LAJEUNESSE, Marcel. L'Education au Québec XIX-XXe siècles, Trois-Rivières, Boréal-Express, 1971.

OUELLET, F., Eléments d'histoire sociale du Bas-Canada, Montréal, H.M.H., 1972.

ROY, Jean-Louis, Les Programmes électoraux du Québec, 2 vol., Montréal, Leméac, 1970 et 1971.

SEGUIN, Maurice, L'Idée d'Indépendance au Québec, Trois-Rivières, Boréal Express, 1968.

SEGUIN, M., La "Nation canadienne" et l'agriculture (1760-1850), Trois-Rivières, Boréal Express, 1970.

VOISINE, N., Histoire de l'Eglise catholique au Québec (1608-1970), Commission d'étude sur les laïcs et l'Eglise, Montréal, Fides, 1971.

WALLOT, J.P., Un Québec qui bougeait, Trois-Rivières, Boréal Express, 1973.

2.4. LA REVOLUTION TRANQUILLE.

BERGERON, Gérard, Du duplessisme à Trudeau et Bourassa 1956-1971, Montréal, Parti-Pris, 1971.

HARVEY, F. et P. SOUTHAM, Chronologie du Québec, 1940-1971, Québec, Institut Supérieur des sciences humaines, Université Laval, 1972.

LAPALME, V. et N. BERNARD, Travailleurs québécois et question nationale, Dossiers Mobilisation, 2e édition, Montréal, Librairie Progressiste, 1974.

MILNER, S.H. et Henry, The Decolonization of Quebec, Toronto, Mc Clelland and Stewart, 1973.

REID, Malcolm, The Shouting Signpainters: A litterary and political account of Quebec revolutionary nationalism, Toronto, Mc Clelland and Stewart, 1972.

2.5. OCTOBRE 1970

CHODOS, R. et N. AUF DER MAUR (sous la direction de), Quebec, A Chronicle 1968-1972, Toronto, James Lewis and Samuel, 1972.

DUFRESNE, J.V. (sous la direction de), Octobre 70, un an ... après, traduit et adapté de HAGGART, R. et GOLDEN, A.E., Rumours of War, Montreal, H.M.H., 1971.

DUMONT, Fernand, La vigile du Québec. Octobre 1970: l'impasse?, Montréal, H.M.H., 1971.

PELLETIER, Gérard, La crise d'octobre, Montréal, Editions du Jour, 1971.

"Québec 70, la réaction tranquille", Socialisme québécois, no. 21-22, Montréal, 1971.

ROTSTEIN, A. (sous la direction de), Power Corrupted, the October Crisis and the Repression of Quebec, Toronto, New Press, 1971.

3. ECONOMIE QUEBECOISE

BLANCHARD, Raoul, L'Est du Canada français: province de Québec, 2 vol., Montréal, Beauchemin, 1960.

FORTIN, Gérald, La Fin d'un règne, Montréal, H.M.H., 1971.

GIRARD, J., Géographie de l'industrie manufacturière du Québec, 2 vol., Québec, Ministère de l'Industrie et du Commerce, 1970.

JAUVIN, P., Sous-développement au Québec et dans le monde, Montréal, Centre d'animation de culture ouvrière, 1971.

LEBEL, G., Horizon 1980: une étude sur l'évolution de l'économie du Québec de 1946 à 1968 et sur ses perspectives d'avenir, Québec, Ministère de l'Industrie et du Commerce, 1970.

LEVITT, Kari, La Capitulation tranquille: la main-mise américaine sur le Canada, Montréal, Réédition Québec, 1972.

ST-GERMAIN, Maurice, Une économie à libérer, Montréal, P.U.M., 1973.

4. POLITIQUE QUEBECOISE

BERGERON, Gérard, Le Canada français après deux siècles de patience, Paris, Seuil, 1967.

BOILY, Robert, La Réforme électorale au Québec, Montréal, Editions du Jour, 1971.

DESROSIERS, Richard (sous la direction de), Le personnel politique québécois, Trois-Rivières, Boréal Express, 1972.

LEMIEUX, Vincent (sous la direction de), Quatre élections provinciales au Québec, 1956-1966, Québec, P.U.L., 1969.

MORIN, Claude, Le Pouvoir québécois ... en négociation, Trois-Rivières, Boréal Express, 1972.

5. SOCIETE QUEBECOISE

BELANGER, W. Pierre et Guy ROCHER, Ecole et société au Québec; éléments d'une sociologie de l'éducation, Montréal, H.M.H., 1970.

HUGHES, E.C., Rencontre de deux mondes, Montréal, Parizeau, 1945.

MAHEU, Robert, Les Francophones du Canada, 1941-1991, Montréal, Parti-Pris, 1970.

MIGUE, L. (sous la direction de), Le Québec d'aujourd'hui, regards d'universitaires, Montréal, H.M.H., 1971.

PARTI-PRIS, Les Québécois, Préface de Jacques Berque, Cahiers Libres, 99-100, Paris, Maspéro, 1967.

RIOUX, M. et Y. MARTIN, La Société canadienne-française, Montréal, H.M.H., 1971.

RYAN, Claude (sous la direction de), Le Québec qui se fait, Montréal, H.M.H., 1971.

6. SYNDICALISME QUEBECOIS

DION, Gérard, et autres, Le Syndicalisme canadien, une réévaluation, Québec, P.U.L., 1968.

LIPTON, Charles, The Trade Union Movement of Canada 1827-1959, Canadian Social Publications, 1966.

TRUDEAU, P.E., La Grève de l'amiante, Montréal, Cité Libre, 1956. Nouvelle édition: Montréal, Editions du Jour, 1970.

TREMBLAY, L.M., Le Syndicalisme québécois, Montréal, P.U.M., 1972.

Documents des centrales syndicales:

C.E.Q., L'Ecole au service de la classe dominante, 20e Congrès de la C.E.Q., juin 1972.

C.S.N., Ne comptons que sur nos propres moyens, Montréal, octobre 1971.

F.T.Q., L'Etat, rouage de notre exploitation, Montréal, décembre 1971.

7. L'ART AU QUEBEC

BORDUAS, P.E., Refus Global, Shawinigan, Mythra-Mythe, 1948. Réédition: Montréal, Brochu, 1972.

HARPER, J.R., La Peinture au Canada, des origines à nos jours, Québec, P.U.L., 1966.

JASMIN, A., F. GAGNON, G. MOLINARI et C. TOUSIGNANT, Peinture canadienne-française, (débats, Conférence de Sève), Montréal, P.U.M., 1971.

"Les automatistes", (collection), Montréal, La barre du jour, 1969.

ROBERT, Guy, Borduas, Montréal, P.U.Q., 1972.

8. ESSAIS SUR LE QUEBEC

RIOUX, Marcel, La Question du Québec, Paris, Seghers, 1969.

RIOUX, Marcel, Les Québécois, Paris, Seuil, 1974.

ROCHER, Guy, Le Québec en mutation, Montréal, H.M.H., 1973.

9. LES COMMISSIONS D'ENQUETE

(Nos gouvernements procèdent, à intervales irréguliers, à de grandes enquêtes sur des aspects particuliers de politique et de vie nationale. En général, les enquêtes comprennent des recherches approfondies par des scientifiques. Il ne faut donc pas se contenter des rapports de ces commissions, mais rechercher aussi les travaux qu'elles ont publiés.)

9.1. GOUVERNEMENT DU QUEBEC

Commission Bélanger, Commission royale d'enquête sur la fiscalité, Québec, Imprimeur de la Reine, 1965.

Commission Parent, Commission royale d'enquête sur l'enseignement dans la Province de Québec, Québec, Editeur officiel du Québec, 1966.

Commission Castonguay-Neveu, Commission d'enquête sur la santé et le bien-être social, Québec, Editeur officiel du Québec, 1967.

Commission Prévost, Commission d'enquête sur l'administration de la justice en matière criminelle et pénale au Québec, Québec, Editeur officiel du Québec 1968.

Commission Rioux, Commission d'enquête sur l'enseignement des arts au Québec, Québec, Editeur officiel du Québec, 1969.

Commission Gendron, Commission d'enquête sur la situation de la langue française et sur les droits linguistiques au Québec, Québec, Editeur officiel du Québec, 1972.

9.2. GOUVERNEMENT DU CANADA

Commission Porter, Commission royale d'enquête sur le système bancaire et financier, Ottawa, Imprimeur de la Reine, 1964.

Commission Hall, Commission royale d'enquête sur les services de santé Ottawa, Imprimeur de la Reine, 1964.

Commission Carter, Commission royale d'enquête sur la fiscalité, Ottawa, Imprimeur de la Reine, 1966.

Commission Laurendeau-Dunton, Commission royale d'enquête sur le bilinguisme et le biculturalisme, Ottawa, Imprimeur de la Reine, 1969.

10. ANNUAIRES ET RECENSEMENTS.

10.1. ANNUAIRES

(Chaque année, les gouvernements du Canada et du Québec publient chacun un annuaire qui, en plus des nombreuses statistiques de l'année, publient des études, parfois rétrospectives, sur des domaines variés de la vie nationale.)

QUEBEC

Annuaire statistique, de 1914 à 1961.

Annuaire du Québec, depuis 1962.

CANADA

Annuaire du Canada, depuis 1867.

10.2. RECENSEMENTS DU CANADA

Recensements décennaux: depuis 1851, le gouvernement du Canada procède à un recensement à l'année 1 de chaque décennie. Avant 1851, on procédait à intervales irréguliers. Tous les recensements antérieurs à 1871 ont été publiés dans celui de 1871.

Recensements interdécennaux: depuis 1956, on procède, à l'année 6 de chaque décennie, à un recensement additionnel, moins complet que le recensement décennal.

Ces recensements sont publiés, depuis 1971 par Statistique-Canada, auparavant par le Bureau fédéral de la statistique.

11. PERIODIQUES

Actualité économique, Montréal, trimestriel, 1925.

Artscan.

Cahiers des Dix, Montréal, annuel, 1936.

Liberté.

MacLean's (édition française), Montréal, mensuel.

Maintenant, Montréal, mensuel. (autrefois La Revue Dominicaine)

Parti-Pris, Montréal.

Presqu'Amérique.

Recherches sociographiques, Québec, trois fois l'an, 1960.

Relations, Montréal, mensuel.

Revue d'histoire de l'Amérique française, Montréal, trimestriel, 1947.

Socialisme 64 ... 70, devenu _Socialisme québécois_, 1964.

Sociologie et société, Montréal, P.U.M., 1968.

Vie des arts

TABLE DES MATIERES

*Voir l'avant-propos, page 5.